DATE DUE

GAYLORD			PRINTED IN U.S.A.

Congressional Quarterly's

GUIDE
TO THE
CONGRESS
OF THE UNITED STATES

ORIGINS, HISTORY and PROCEDURE

PUBLISHED BY

Congressional Quarterly Service

1735 K Street, N.W.   Washington, D.C., 20006

INTRODUCTION

THE Congress of the United States, like most other institutions in our contentious time, is under determined attack for a host of real and imagined ills. The indictment makes unhappy reading. Our highest legislative forum stands accused of irrelevance, irresponsibility and irresolution. Public disenchantment with the way Congress does things—or fails to do them—mounted in intensity as the decade of the 1970s unfolded. It was a period of undeclared war abroad and declared war between the generations at home. In both these trials, the Congress was found wanting.

Critics yielded to despair over the sight of a seemingly impotent and interminable 91st Congress, which adjourned on Jan. 2, 1971, less than 24 hours before the constitutional deadline. A Republican President and a Democratic-controlled Congress had been unable to agree on the sure course of national and international goals. President Richard M. Nixon voiced especially strong criticism of the Senate. "In the final month and weeks of 1970," he said in a statement, "the nation was presented with the spectacle of a legislative body that had seemingly lost the capacity to decide and the will to act."

While Mr. Nixon's comments might be attributed to political exigencies, there seemed little doubt that the reputation of the whole Congress had been slipping for some time. The erosion of its powers—especially those in the gray areas of war and foreign policy—rendered it pusillanimous in the eyes of some Americans. In addition, Congress in many cases not only had conceded the initiative in originating legislation but also had lost the dominant influence it once held in shaping the final content of legislation. Was the U.S. Congress about to repeat the sad history of other national legislatures in this century which became quaint chambers full of rhetoric but empty of power?

BEFORE we conclude that the lawmaking machinery is headed for a final breakdown, the counter-arguments should be heard. This volume, Congressional Quarterly's *Guide to the Congress of the United States*, contains much material that could be used as an exhibit for the defense. The complexity of the lawmaking institution—plus the dilemmas posed by the legislative issues themselves—have combined on many occasions to create the appearance of Congressional ineffectiveness. Much of the public impatience with Congress is based on a simple misunderstanding of and ignorance about the workings of the legislative process. This book aims to contribute to a more complete understanding of the role assigned to the Congress by the Founding Fathers and amplified by later generations.

The debate over the matter of Congressional versus Presidential power is hardly a new one. Indeed, the confrontations in the late 1960s and early 1970s are modest eruptions when compared with those of the 19th century. It is only necessary to recall the Jacksonian Revolution that in the 1830s pitted President Andrew Jackson against the Whigs in Congress. "We are in the midst of a revolution," complained Henry Clay in 1833, "rapidly tending toward a total change of the pure republican character of our government, and to the concentration of all power in the hands of one man."

Abraham Lincoln's Administration reached the high-water mark in the exercise of executive power in the United States. Lincoln pushed the boundaries of executive power far into the legislative sphere through his Emancipation Proclamation, his Reconstruction plan, and his spending of millions of dollars of public money without Congressional appropriation. But the subordination of the Congress was destined to pass. When Andrew Johnson tried to continue the Lincoln tradition without the emergency of a war and without Lincoln's personal prestige, he became the object of a strong public reaction. In the Congressional elections of 1866 the verdict of the electorate was so overwhelmingly against Johnson that the next House of Representatives would stand almost three to one against him. The balance in the Federal system envisaged by the Constitution has a way of being restored.

IN A DAY of the hydrogen bomb and the intercontinental ballistic missile, the Presidency has become so weighted with significance in the popular mind that Congress frequently seems to operate in the shadows of real power. But even today executive power cannot easily circumvent Capitol Hill—unless the Congress is willing to be bypassed. Powers previously relinquished or neglected are retrievable at the instant an aroused Congress, backed by the public, musters the energy and will to demand a coordinate voice. It is well to remember that for all its fits and starts, all its cumbersome and vexing ways, the Congress has on a number of occasions since the end of World War II displayed surprising energy and perseverance in disposing of the American people's business.

With the perspective of history we can see that the current contretemps in Congress may be but a phase and that, given time, the pendulum is capable of swinging back to the side of representative government. Even now there are intimations that Congress is conscious of the dangers inherent in public disapproval of its record in conducting the public business. The impasses which so tortured relations between the White House and Capitol Hill involve fundamental issues; far from demonstrating Congressional indifference or impotence, they could be read as signs of an assertion of constitutional rights.

Encouraging as these latent signs of reawakening may be to defenders of Congress, they do come late in the day. The nation is moving toward its 200th anniversary celebration in 1976 under the cloud of difficult domestic and foreign problems that will require close cooperation between all branches of Government if political, social and economic calamity is to be averted. An image of ineptitude, indifference, selfish interest and lack of order in the national legislature undermines public respect for all government. The temptation is great to see each struggle between the Executive and Legislative Branches as a constitutional Armageddon. But it is fairer to suppose that the continuing struggle for power was contemplated by the Founding Fathers and that it will remain a part of the American system so long as the Constitution remains in force.

WILLIAM B. DICKINSON, JR.
Supervisory Editor

About This Book

Congressional Quarterly's *Guide to the Congress of the United States* presents in one definitive volume the origins and development of the U.S. Congress. The *Guide* explains how Congress works, its powers, the pressures upon it, and prospects for change—even its housekeeping. For the first time, a single volume provides this information in a complete, well-organized way, and indexed for quick reference.

The CQ *Guide* is intended for the use of reporters and editors, scholars in political science, history and government, students, librarians, politicians and citizens interested in their Federal Government. At the end of every subchapter the reader will find a thorough bibliography of sources to permit further research.

The *Guide* is a product of the same CQ research system that for a quarter-century has provided researchers and scholars with a number of elements essential to the understanding of the national political process. Regular subscribers to the CQ Service are familiar with the *Weekly Report*, which follows the activities of the Congress on a week-to-week basis, and with the CQ *Almanac*, a hard-cover book that constitutes the full historical record of a particular session, issued on an annual basis.

In addition, CQ also has published *Congress and the Nation* in two volumes. The first volume provides a comprehensive summary of legislation and politics from 1945 through 1964; the second performs the same service for the years 1965-68, the Johnson years. The *Congress and the Nation* series and the *Guide* are not offered as part of the regular subscription but must be purchased separately.

How to Use This Book

Briefly study the *Summary* of the *Table of Contents* which follows this introduction. It indicates the organization of the CQ *Guide to the Congress of the United States*. A detailed Table of Contents follows the Summary, showing the outline and content of each chapter.

Note the organization of each subject area. The Powers of Congress chapter, for example, is broken down into a number of subchapters enumerating the various powers. This method eliminates the need to look in a number of different places in the book for material on a specific subject. Nevertheless, a detailed *Index* begins at the second thumb tab to further isolate a particular fact or incident and make it easy to find under deadline.

The *Appendix*, which can be reached at the first thumb tab, contains material which will be used with most of the chapters of the book—thumbnail biographies of every member of the House and Senate since 1789; the Declaration of Independence, Articles of Confederation, Constitution of the United States, etc. Pages in the Appendix are number: 1a, 2a, 3a, etc.

An added feature at the end of each subchapter is a detailed *Bibliography* that will point the way to sources used in the preparation of the material and permit the reader to pursue additional research on his own.

The Writers

The work of many people went into the writing, editing and production of the CQ *Guide*. Principal writers and the subchapters for which they were responsible:

Chapter I, Origins and Development
  Constitutional Beginnings: William Korns
  History of the House: William Korns
  History of the Senate: Mary Wilson Cohn
Chapter II, Congress at Work
  The Legislative Process: Mary Wilson Cohn, with Prentice Bowsher
  Leadership: James Phillips
  Committees: Mary Wilson Cohn, with Stanley Wellborn
  Seniority: Prentice Bowsher
Chapter III, Powers
  Fiscal: David Tarr
  Foreign Affairs: Prentice Bowsher
  Nominations: Mary Wilson Cohn
  Investigations: Prentice Bowsher
  Impeachment: Prentice Bowsher
  Commerce: Mary Wilson Cohn
  Amending: Park Teter
  Seating of Members: William Gerber
  Election of Presidents: Mary Wilson Cohn
  Private Bills: William Gerber
  Seat of Government: William Gerber
Chapter IV, Housing and Support
  Capitol, Office Buildings: Prentice Bowsher
  Library of Congress: William Gerber
  Pay and Perquisites: Prentice Bowsher, with Alan Ehrenhalt, Jack McWethy and Esther Safran
  General Accounting Office: Jack McWethy
Chapter V, Congress and the Electorate
  Who Elects: James Phillips
  Who Gets Elected: James Phillips
  Campaign Financing: William Gerber
  Reapportionment: Warden Moxley
Chapter VI, Pressures
  Constituency: Park Teter
  Lobbies: James Phillips
  Executive Branch: James Phillips
  Court: James Phillips
  Internal: James Phillips
  The Press: James Phillips
Chapter VII, Ethics
  Ethics: Georgiana Rathbun
Appendix: Jackie Westcott
Index: William Gerber

The following persons were responsible for the editing and production of the *Guide:*
Supervisory Editor: William B. Dickinson, Jr.
Chief Copy Editor: Buel W. Patch
Production Supervisor: Richard C. Young
Proofers: Diane Huffman, Elizabeth Parker, Margaret O'Brien. Clearance: Mary Costello.
Dust Jacket and Cover Design: Howard Chapman

Special acknowledgement is due the entire staff of Congressional Quarterly Service, whose week-by-week coverage of the Congress provided the base of information necessary for this volume. We also are indebted to Nelson Poynter, editor and president of Congressional Quarterly Inc., and Richard N. Billings, executive editor of Congressional Quarterly Inc., for their faithful support and encouragement of this ambitious project.

GLOSSARY OF CONGRESSIONAL TERMS

Act—The term for legislation which has passed both houses of Congress and has been signed by the President or passed over his veto, thus becoming law.

Also used technically for a bill that has been passed by one house and engrossed.

Adjournment sine die—Adjournment without definitely fixing a day for reconvening; literally "adjournment without a day." A session can continue until noon, Jan. 3, of the following year, when a new session usually begins.

Adjournment to a Day Certain—Adjournment under a motion or resolution which fixes the next time of meeting. Neither house can adjourn for more than three days without the concurrence of the other. A session of Congress is not ended by adjournment to a day certain.

Amendment—Proposal of a Congressman to alter the language or stipulations in a bill or act. It is usually printed, debated, and voted upon in the same manner as a bill.

Appeal—A Congressman's challenge of a ruling or decision made by the presiding officer of the Senate or House. The Congressman appeals to Members of the chamber to override the decision. If carried by a majority vote, the appeal nullifies the chair's ruling.

Appropriation Bill—Grants the actual monies approved by authorization bills, but not necessarily to the total permissible under the authorization bill. Normally an appropriation bill originates in the House, and is not acted on until its authorization measure is enacted. Regular appropriations are supposed to be passed before the start of the fiscal year to which they apply, but in recent years this has rarely happened. *(See Continuing Appropriations.)* In addition to general appropriation bills, there are two specialized types. *(See Deficiency and Supplemental.)*

Authorization Bill—Authorizes a program, specifies its general aim and conduct, and unless "open-ended," puts a ceiling on monies that can be used to finance it. Usually enacted before appropriation bill is passed. *(See Contract Authorization.)*

Bills—Most legislative proposals before Congress are in the form of bills, and are designated as HR (House of Representatives) or S (Senate) according to the house in which they originate and by a number assigned in the order in which they were introduced, from the beginning of each two-year Congressional term. "Public bills" deal with general questions, and become Public Laws if approved by Congress and signed by the President. "Private bills" deal with individual matters such as claims against the Government, immigration and naturalization cases, land titles, etc., and become Private Laws if approved and signed.

The introduction of a bill, and its referral to an appropriate committee for action, follows the process given in "How A Bill Is Passed." *(See also Concurrent Resolution, Joint Resolution, Resolution, in this Glossary.)*

Bills Introduced—In the Senate, any number of Senators may join in introducing a single bill. In the House, until 1967, only one Member's name could appear on a single bill. But the House April 25, 1967, voted to allow cosponsorship of bills, setting a limit of 25 cosponsors on any one bill.

Many bills in reality are committee bills and are introduced under the name of the chairman of the committee or subcommittee as a formality. All appropriation bills fall into this category, as do many other bills, particularly those dealing with complicated, technical subjects. A committee frequently holds hearings on a number of related bills, and may agree on one of them or on an entirely new bill. *(See Clean Bill and By Request.)*

Bills Referred—When introduced, a bill referred to the committee which has jurisdiction over the subject with which the bill is concerned. The appropriate reference for bills is spelled out in the Legislative Reorganization Act of 1946. Bills are referred by the Speaker in the House and the Presiding Officer in the Senate. Appeals may be made from their decisions.

Budget—The document sent to Congress by the President in January of each year estimating Government revenue and expenditures for the ensuing fiscal year and recommending appropriations to detail. The President's Budget Message forms the basis for Congressional hearings and legislation on the year's appropriations.

By Request—A phrase used when a Senator or Representative introduces a bill at the request of an executive agency or private organization but does not necessarily endorse the legislation.

Calendar—An agenda or list of pending business before committees or either chamber. The House uses five legislative calendars. *(See Consent, Discharge, House, Private and Union Calendar.)*

In the Senate, all legislative matters reported from committee go on a single calendar. They are listed there in order, but may be called up irregularly by the Majority Leader either by a motion to do so, or by obtaining the unanimous consent of the Senate. Frequently the Minority Leader is consulted to assure unanimous consent. Only cloture can limit debate on bills thus called up. *(See Call of the Calendar.)*

The Senate also uses one non-legislative calendar, for treaties, etc. *(See Executive Calendar.)*

Calendar Wednesday—In the House on Wednesdays, committees may be called in the order in which they appear in Rule X of the House Manual, for the purpose of bringing up any of their bills from the House or the Union Calendars, except bills which are privileged. General debate is limited to two hours. Bills called up from the Union Calendar are considered in Committee of the Whole. Calendar Wednesday is not observed during the last two weeks of a session, and may be dispensed with at other times -- by a two-thirds vote. It usually is dispensed with.

Call of the Calendar—Senate bills which are not brought up for debate by a motion or a unanimous consent agreement are brought before the Senate for action when the calendar listing them in order is "called." Bills considered in this fashion are usually noncontroversial, and debate is limited to five minutes for each Senator on a bill or on amendments to it.

Chamber—Meeting place for the total membership of either the House or the Senate, as distinguished from the respective committee rooms.

Clean Bill—Frequently after a committee has finished a major revision of a bill, one of the committee members, usually the chairman, will assemble the changes plus what is left of the original bill into a new measure and introduce it as a "clean bill." The new measure, which carries a new number, is then sent to the floor for consideration. This often is a timesaver, as committee-recommended changes do not have to be considered one at a time by the chamber.

Clerk of the House—Chief administrative officer of the House of Representatives with duties corresponding to those of the Secretary of the Senate. *(See Secretary of the Senate.)*

Cloture—The process by which debate can be limited in the Senate, other than by unanimous consent. A motion for cloture can apply to any measure before the Senate, including a proposal to change the chamber's rules. It requires 16 Senators' signatures for introduction and the votes of two-thirds of the Senators present and voting. It is put to a roll-call vote one hour after the Senate meets on the second day following introduction of the motion. If voted, cloture limits each Senator to one hour of debate.

Committee—A subdivision of the House or Senate which prepares legislation for action by the parent chamber, or makes investigations as directed by the parent chamber. There are several types of committees. *(See Standing, and Select or Special.)* Most standing committees are divided into subcommittees, which study legislation, hold hearings, and report their recommendations to the full committee. Only the full committee can report legislation for action by the House or Senate.

Committee of the Whole—The working title of what is formally "The Committee of the Whole House (of Representatives) on the State of the Union." Unlike other committees, it has no fixed membership. It is comprised of any 100 or more House Members who participate —on the floor of the chamber—in debating or altering legislation before the body. Such measures, however, must first have passed through the regular committees and be on the calendar.

Technically, the Committee of the Whole considers only bills directly or indirectly appropriating money, authorizing appropriations, or involving taxes or charges on the public. Actually, the Committee of the Whole often considers other types of legislation. Because the Committee of the Whole need number only 100 Representatives, a quorum is more readily attained, and business is expedited. None of the group's votes can be

the time-consuming roll calls which require yeas and nays for the record.

When the full House resolves itself into the Committee of the Whole, it supplants the Speaker with a "chairman." The measure is debated or amended, with non-roll-call votes as needed. When the Committee completes its action on the measure, it dissolves itself by "rising." The Speaker returns, and the full House hears the erstwhile chairman of the Committee report that group's recommendations. The full House then acts upon them.

At this time Members may demand a roll-call vote on any amendment *adopted* in the Committee of the Whole.

Concurrent Resolution—A concurrent resolution, designated H Con Res or S Con Res, must be passed by both houses but does not require the signature of the President and does not have the force of law. Concurrent resolutions generally are used to make or amend rules applicable to both houses or to express the sentiment of the two houses. A concurrent resolution, for example, is used to fix the time for adjournment of a Congress. It might also be used to convey the congratulations of Congress to another country on the anniversary of its independence.

Conference—A meeting between the representatives of the House and Senate to reconcile differences between the two houses over provisions of a bill. Members of the conference committee are appointed by the Speaker and the President of the Senate and are called "managers" for their respective chambers. A majority of the managers for each house must reach agreement on the provisions of the bill (often a compromise between the versions of the two chambers) before it can be sent up for floor action in the form of a "conference report." There it cannot be amended, and if not approved by both chambers, the bill goes back to conference. Elaborate rules govern the conduct of the conferences. All bills which are passed by House and Senate in slightly different form need not be sent to conference; either chamber may "concur" in the other's amendments. *(See Custody of the Papers.)*

Congressional Record—The daily, printed account of proceedings in both House and Senate chambers, with debate, statements, and the like reported verbatim. Committee activities are not covered, excepting their reports to the parent body. Highlights of legislative and committee action are embodied in a Digest section of the Record, and Congressmen are entitled to have their extraneous remarks printed in an appendix. They may edit and revise remarks made on the floor, and frequently do, so that quotations reported by the press are not always found in the Record.

Congressional Terms of Office—Begin on Jan. 3 of the year following the general election.

Consent Calendar—Members of the House may place on this calendar any bill on the Union or House Calendar which is considered to be noncontroversial. Bills on the Consent Calendar are normally called on the first and third Mondays of each month. On the first occasion when a bill is called in this manner, consideration may be blocked by the objection of any Member. On the second time, if there are three objections, the bill is stricken from the Consent Calendar; if less than three Members object, the bill is given immediate consideration.

A bill on the Consent Calendar may be postponed in another way. A Member may ask that the measure be passed over "without prejudice." In that case, no objection is recorded against the bill, and its status on the Consent Calendar remains unchanged.

A bill stricken from the Consent Calendar remains on the Union or House Calendar.

Continuing Appropriations—When a fiscal year begins and Congress has not yet enacted all the regular appropriation bills for that year, it passes a joint resolution "continuing appropriations" for Government agencies at rates generally based on their previous year's appropriations.

Contract Authorizations—Found in both authorization and appropriation bills, these authorizations are stop-gap provisions which permit the Federal Government to let contracts or obligate itself for future payments from funds not yet appropriated. The assumption is that funds will be available for payment when contracted debts come due.

Correcting the Record—Rules prohibit Members from changing their votes after the result has been announced. But frequently, hours, days, or months after a vote has been taken, a Member announces that he was "incorrectly recorded" and requests -- and almost always receives -- unanimous consent to have the vote corrected in the permanent edition of the Congressional Record. This occurs more frequently in the House than in the Senate. Errors in the text of the Record may be corrected in the same manner.

Custody of the Papers—To reconcile differences on a bill between the House and Senate, a conference may be arranged. The chamber with "custody of the papers" -- the engrossed bill, engrossed amendments, messages of transmittal -- is the only body empowered to request the conference. That body then has the advantage of acting last on the conference report when it is submitted.

Deficiency Appropriation—An appropriation to cover the difference between an agency's regular appropriation and the amount deemed necessary for it to operate for the full fiscal year. In recent years deficiency bills have usually been called supplemental appropriations.

Dilatory Motion—A motion, usually made upon a technical point, for the purpose of killing time and preventing action on a bill. The rules outlaw dilatory motions, but enforcement is largely within the discretion of the presiding officer.

Discharge a Committee—Relieve a committee from jurisdiction over a measure before it. This is rarely a successful procedure, attempted more often in the House than in the Senate.

In the House, if a committee does not report a bill within 30 days after the bill was referred to it, any Member may file a discharge motion. This motion, treated as a petition, needs the signatures of 218 Members (a majority of the House). After the required signatures have been obtained, there is a delay of seven days. Then, on the second and fourth Monday of each month, except during the last six days of a session, any Member who has signed the petition may be recognized to move that the committee be discharged. Debate on the motion to discharge is limited to 20 minutes, and, if the motion is carried, consideration of the bill becomes a matter of high privilege.

If a resolution to consider a bill (*See Rule*) is held up in the Rules Committee for more than seven legislative days, any Member may enter a motion to discharge the Committee. The motion is handled like any other discharge petition in the House.

Occasionally, to expedite noncontroversial legislative business, a committee is discharged upon unanimous consent of the House, and a petition is not required. *(For Senate procedure, see Discharge Resolution.)*

Discharge Calendar—The House calendar to which motions to discharge committees are referred when they have the necessary 218 signatures and are awaiting action.

Discharge Petition—In the House, a motion to discharge a committee from considering a bill. The motion or petition, requires signatures of 218 House Members.

Discharge Resolution—In the Senate, a special motion any Senator may introduce to relieve a committee from consideration of a bill before it. The resolution can be called up on motion for approval or disapproval, in the same manner as other matters of Senate business. *(For House procedure, see Discharge a Committee.)*

Division Vote—Same as Standing Vote. *(See below.)*

Enacting Clause—Key phrase in bills saying, "Be if enacted by the Senate and House of Representatives...." A successful motion to strike it from legislation kills the measure.

Engrossed Bill—The final copy of a bill as passed by one chamber, with the text as amended by floor action and certified to by the Clerk of the House or the Secretary of the Senate.

Enrolled Bill—The final copy of a bill which has been passed in identical form by both chambers. It is certified to by an officer of the house of origin (House Clerk or Senate Secretary) and then sent on for signatures of the House Speaker, the Senate President, and the U.S. President. An enrolled bill is printed on parchment.

Executive Calendar—This is an additional, nonlegislative calendar, in the Senate, on which Presidential documents such as treaties and nominations are listed.

Executive Document—A document, usually a treaty, sent to the Senate by the President for consideration or ratification. These are identified for each session of Congress as Executive A, 90th Congress, 1st Session; Executive B, etc. They are referred to committee in the same manner as other measures. Unlike legislative documents, however, treaties do not die at the end of a Congress, but remain "live" proposals until acted on by the Senate or withdrawn by the President.

Executive Session—Meeting of a Senate or a House committee (or, very rarely, of the entire chamber) which only the group's members are privileged to attend. Frequently witnesses appear before committees meeting in executive session, and other Congressmen may be invited, but the public and press are not allowed.

Expenditures—The actual spending of money as distinguished from the appropriation of it. Expenditures are made by the disbursing officers of the Administration; appropriations are made only by Congress. The two are rarely identical in any fiscal year; expenditures may represent money appropriated one, two or more years previously.

Filibuster—A time-delaying tactic used by a minority in an effort to prevent a vote on a bill which probably would pass if brought to a vote. The most common method is to take advantage of the Senate's rules permitting unlimited debate, but other forms of parliamentary maneuvering may be used. The stricter rules in the House make filibusters more difficult, but they are attempted from time to time through devices such as repeated demands for quorum calls.

Fiscal Year—Financial operations of the Government are carried out in a 12-month fiscal year, beginning on July 1 and ending on June 30. The fiscal year carries the date of the calendar year in which it ends.

Floor Manager—A Member, usually representing sponsors of a bill, who attempts to steer it through debate and revision to a final vote in the chamber. Floor managers are frequently chairmen or ranking members of the committee that reported the bill. Managers are responsible for apportioning the time granted supporters of the bill for debating it. The Minority Leader or the ranking minority member of the committee often apportions time for the opposition.

Frank—A Congressman's facsimile signature on envelopes, used in lieu of stamps for his official outgoing mail, thus postage-free. Also the privilege of sending mail postage-free.

Germane—Pertaining to the subject matter of the measure at hand. All House amendments must be germane to the bill. The Senate requires that amendments be germane only when they are proposed to general appropriation bills, bills being considered under cloture, or often when proceeding under an agreement to limit debate.

Grants-in-Aid—Payments by the Federal Government which aid the recipient state, local government or individual in administering specified programs, services or activities.

Hearings—Committee sessions for hearing witnesses. At hearings on legislation, witnesses usually include specialists, government officials and spokesmen for persons affected by the bills under study. Hearings related to special investigations bring forth a variety of witnesses. Committees sometimes use their subpena power to summon reluctant witnesses. The public and press may attend "open" hearings, but are barred from "closed" or "executive" hearings.

The committee announces its hearings, from one day to many weeks in advance, and may invite certain persons to testify. Persons who request time to testify may be turned down by the committee but most requests are honored.

Hopper—Box on House Clerk's desk where bills are deposited on introduction.

House—The House of Representatives, as distinct from the Senate, although each body is a "house" of Congress.

House Calendar—Listing for action by the House of Representatives of public bills which do not directly or indirectly appropriate money or raise revenue.

Immunity—Constitutional privilege of Congressmen to make verbal statements on the floor and in committee for which they cannot be sued or arrested for slander or libel. Also, freedom from arrest while traveling to or from sessions of Congress or on official business. Congressmen in this status may be arrested only for treason, felonies or a breach of the peace, as defined by Congressional manuals.

Joint Committee—A committee composed of a specified number of Members of both House and Senate. Usually a joint committee is investigative in nature. There are a few standing joint committees, such as the Joint Committee on Atomic Energy and the Joint Economic Committee.

Joint Resolution—A joint resolution, designated H J Res or S J Res, requires the approval of both houses and the signature of the President, just as a bill does, and has the force of law if approved. There is no real difference between a bill and a joint resolution. The latter is generally used in dealing with limited matters, such as a single appropriation for a specific purpose.

Joint resolutions also are used to propose amendments to the Constitution. These do not require Presidential signature, but become a part of the Constitution when three-fourths of the states have ratified them.

Journal—The official record of the proceedings of the House and Senate. The Journal records the actions taken in each chamber, but unlike the Congressional Record, it does not include the verbatim report of speeches, debate, etc.

Law—An Act of Congress which has been signed by the President, or passed over his veto by the Congress. Laws are listed numerically by Congress; for example, the Civil Rights Act of 1964 (HR 7152) became Public Law 88-352 during the 88th Congress.

Legislative Day—The "day" extending from the time either house meets after an adjournment until the time it next adjourns. Because the House normally adjourns from day to day, legislative days and calendar days usually coincide. But in the Senate, a legislative day may, and frequently does, extend over several calendar days. *(See Recess.)*

Lobby—A group seeking to influence the passage or defeat of legislation. Originally the term referred to persons frequenting the lobbies or corridors of legislative chambers in order to speak to lawmakers.

The exact definition of a lobby and the activity of lobbying is a matter of opinion. By some definitions, lobbying is limited to attempts at direct influence by personal interview and persuasion. Under other definitions, lobbying includes attempts at indirect influence, such as stirring members of a group to write or visit Congressmen, or attempting to create a climate of opinion favorable to a desired legislative action.

The right to attempt to influence legislation is based on the 1st Amendment to the Constitution, which says Congress shall make no law abridging the right of the people "to petition the Government for a redress of grievances."

Majority Leader—Chief strategist and floor spokesman for the party in nominal control in either chamber. He is elected by his party colleagues and is virtually program director for his chamber, since he usually speaks for its majority.

Majority Whip—In effect, the assistant majority leader, in House or Senate. His job is to help marshal majority forces in support of party strategy.

Manual—The official handbook in each house prescribing its organization, procedures and operations in detail. The Senate Manual contains standing rules, orders, laws and resolutions affecting Senate business; the House Manual is the equivalent for that chamber. Both volumes contain previous codes under which Congress functioned and from which it continues to derive precedents. Committee powers are outlined. The rules set forth in the Manuals may be changed by elaborate chamber actions also specified by the Manuals.

Marking Up a Bill—Going through a measure, usually in committee, taking it section by section, revising language, penciling in new phrases, etc. If the bill is extensively revised, the new version may be introduced as a separate bill, with a new number. *(See Clean Bill.)*

Memorial—A request for Congressional opposition or an objection from an organization or citizens' group to particular legislation or government practice under the purview of Congress. All communications, both supporting and opposing legislation, from state legislatures are embodied in memorials. They are referred to appropriate committees unless the legislation dealt with in the memorial has been reported to the Senate, in which case the memorial is placed on the table. It can be called up for consideration at the time the bill is read for amendments. *(See Petition.)*

Minority Leader—Floor leader for the minority party. *(See Majority Leader.)*

Minority Whip—Performs duties of whip for the minority party. *(See Majority Whip.)*

Morning Hour—The time set aside at the beginning of each legislative day for the consideration of regular routine business. The "hour" is of indefinite duration in the House, where it is rarely used. In the Senate it is the first two hours of a session following an adjournment, as distinguished from a recess. The morning hour can be terminated earlier if the morning business has been completed. This business includes such matters as messages from the President, communications from the heads of departments, messages from the House, the presentation of petitions and memorials, reports of standing and select committees, and the introduction of bills and resolutions.

During the first hour of the morning hour in the Senate, no motion to proceed to the consideration of any bill on the calendar is in order except by unanimous consent. During the second hour, motions can be made but must be decided without debate. Senate committees may meet while the Senate is in the morning hour.

Motion—Request by a Congressman for any one of a wide array of parliamentary actions. He "moves" for a certain procedure, or the consideration of a measure or a vote, etc. The precedence of motions, and whether they are debatable, is set forth in the House and Senate Manuals.

Nominations—Appointments to office by the Executive Branch of the Government, subject to Senate confirmation. Although most nominations win quick Senate approval, some are controversial and become the topic of hearings and debate. Sometimes Senators object to appointees for patronage reasons—for example, when a nomination to a local federal job is made without consulting the Senators of the state concerned. Then a Senator may use the stock objection that the nominee is "personally obnoxious" to him. Usually other Senators join in blocking such an appointment out of courtesy to their colleague.

One Minute Speeches—Addresses by House Members at the beginning of a legislative day. The speeches may cover any subject, but are limited strictly to one minute's duration.

Override a Veto—If the President disapproves a bill and sends it back to Congress with his objections, Congress may override his veto by a two-thirds vote in each chamber. The Constitution requires a yea-and-nay roll call. The question put to each house is: "Shall the bill pass, the objections of the President to the contrary notwithstanding?" *(See also Pocket Veto and Veto.)*

Pair—A "gentlemen's agreement" between two lawmakers on opposite sides to withhold their votes on roll calls so their absence from Congress will not affect the outcome of record voting. If passage of the measure requires a two-thirds majority, a pair would require two Members favoring the action to one opposed to it.

Two kinds of pairs—special and general—are used; neither is counted in vote totals. The names of lawmakers pairing on a given vote and their stands, if known, are printed in the Congressional Record.

The special pair applies to one or a series of roll-call votes on the same subject. On special pairs, lawmakers usually specify how they would have voted.

A general pair in the Senate, now rarely used in the chamber, applies to all votes on which the Members pairing are on opposite sides, and it lasts for the length of time pairing Senators agree on. It usually does not specify a Senator's stand on a given vote.

The general pair in the House differs from the other pairs. No agreement is involved and the pair does not tie up votes. A Representative expecting to be absent may notify the House Clerk he wishes to make a "general" pair. His name then is paired arbitrarily with that of another Member desiring a general pair, and the list is printed in the Congressional Record. He may or may not be paired with a Member taking the opposite position. General pairs in the House give no indication of how a Congressman would have voted. *(See Record Vote and Stand.)*

Petition—A request or plea sent to one or both chambers from an organization or private-citizens group asking support of particular legislation or favorable consideration of a matter not yet receiving Congressional attention. They are referred to appropriate committees and considered or not, according to committee decision. *(See Memorial.)*

Pocket Veto—The act of the President in withholding his approval of a bill after Congress has adjourned—either for the year or for a specified period. When Congress is in session, a bill becomes law without the President's signature if he does not act upon it within 10 days, excluding Sundays, from the time he gets it. But if Congress adjourns within that 10-day period, the bill is killed without the President's formal veto.

Point of Order—An objection raised by a Congressman that the chamber is departing from rules governing its conduct of business. The objector cites the rule violated, the chair sustaining his objection if correctly made. Order is restored by the chair's suspending proceedings of the chamber until it conforms to the prescribed "order of business." Members sometimes raise a "point of no order"—when there is noise and disorderly conduct in the chamber.

President of the Senate—Presiding officer of the upper chamber, normally the Vice President of the United States. In his absence, a President pro tempore (President for the time being) presides.

President pro tempore—The chief officer of the Senate in the absence of the Vice President. He is elected by his fellow Senators. The recent practice has been to elect to the office the Senator of the majority party with longest continuous service.

Previous Question—In this sense, a "question" is an "issue" before the House for a vote and the issue is "previous" when some other topic has superseded it in the attention of the chamber. A motion for the previous question, when carried, has the effect of cutting off all debate and forcing a vote on the subject originally at hand. If, however, the previous question is moved and carried before there has been any debate on the subject at hand and the subject is debatable, then 40 minutes of debate is allowed before the vote. The previous question is sometimes moved in order to prevent amendments. The motion for the previous question is a debate-limiting device and is not in order in the Senate.

Private Calendar—Private House bills dealing with individual matters such as claims against the Government, immigration, land titles, etc., are put on this calendar. When it is before the chamber, two Members may block a private bill, which then is recommitted to committee.

Backers of a private bill thus recommitted have another recourse. The measure can be put into an "omnibus claims bill"—several private bills rolled into one. As with any bill, no part of an omnibus claims bill may be deleted without a vote. When a private bill goes back to the floor in this form, it can be defeated only by a majority of those present. The Private Calendar can be called on the first and third Tuesdays of each month.

Privilege—Privilege relates to the rights of Congressmen and to the relative priority of the motions and actions they may make in their respective chambers. The two are distinct. "Privileged questions" concern legislative business. "Questions of privilege" concern legislators themselves. *(See below.)*

Privileged Questions—The order in which bills, motions and other legislative measures may be considered by Congress is governed by strict priorities. A motion to table, for instance, is more privileged than a motion to recommit. Thus, a motion to recommit can be superseded by a motion to table, and a vote would be forced on the latter motion only. A motion to adjourn, however, would take precedence over this one, and is thus considered of the "highest privilege."

Pro Forma Amendment—See Strike Out the Last Word.

Questions of Privilege—These are matters affecting Members of Congress individually or collectively.

Questions affecting the rights, safety, dignity and integrity of proceedings of the House or Senate as a whole are questions of privilege of the House or Senate, as the case may be.

Congressmen singly involve questions of "personal privilege." A Member's rising to a question of personal privilege is given precedence over almost all other proceedings. An annotation in the House Rules points out that the privilege of the Member rests primarily on the Constitution, which gives him a conditional immunity from arrest and an unconditional freedom to speak in the House.

Quorum—The number of Members whose presence is necessary for the transaction of business. In the Senate and House, it is a majority of the membership (when there are no vacancies, this is 51 in the Senate and 218 in the House). A quorum is 100 in the Committee of the Whole House. If a point of order is made that a quorum is not present, the only business in order is either a motion to adjourn or a motion to direct the Sergeant-at-Arms to request the attendance of absentees.

Readings of Bills—Traditional parliamentary law required bills to be read three times before they were passed. This custom is of little modern significance except in rare instances. Normally the bill is considered to have its first reading when it is introduced and printed, by title, in the Congressional Record. Its second reading comes when floor consideration begins. (This is the most likely point at which there is an actual reading of the bill, if there is any.) The third reading (usually by title) takes place when action has been completed on amendments.

Recess—Distinguished from adjournment in that a recess does not end a legislative day and therefore does not interfere with unfinished business. The rules in each house set forth certain matters to be taken up and disposed of at the beginning of each legislative day. The House, which operates under much stricter rules than the Senate, usually adjourns from day to day. The Senate often recesses.

Recommit to Committee—A simple motion, made on the floor after deliberation on a bill, to return it to the committee which reported it. If approved, recommittal usually is considered a death blow to the bill. In the House a motion to recommit can be made only by a Member opposed to the bill, and in recognizing a Member to make the motion, the Speaker gives the minority party preference over the majority.

A motion to recommit may include instructions to the committee to report the bill again with specific amendments or by a certain date. Or the instructions may be to make a particular study, with no definite deadline for final action.

Reconsider a Vote—A motion to reconsider the vote by which an action was taken has, until it is disposed of, the effect of suspending the action. In the Senate the motion can be made only by a Member who voted on the prevailing side of the original question, or by a Member who did not vote at all. In the House it can be made only by a Member on the prevailing side.

A common practice after close votes in the Senate is a motion to reconsider, followed by a motion to table the motion to reconsider. On this motion to table, Senators vote as they voted on the original question, to enable the motion to table to prevail. The matter is then finally closed and further motions to reconsider are not entertained. In the House, as a routine precaution, a motion to reconsider usually is made every time a measure is passed. Such a motion almost always is tabled immediately, thus shutting off the possibility of future reconsideration except by unanimous consent.

Motions to reconsider must be entered in the Senate within the next two days of actual session after the original vote has been taken. In the House they must be entered either on the same day or on the next succeeding day the House is in session.

Record Vote—This is a roll call of the entire chamber membership, to which each Member on the floor must answer "yea," "nay," or, if he does not wish to vote, "present." The Constitution requires yea-and-nay votes on the question of overriding a veto. In other cases, they can be obtained by the demand of one-fifth of the Members present. In the House, the yeas and nays are required automatically whenever a Member objects to a non-record vote taken when a quorum was not present, if the question is one which requires a quorum. The yeas and nays are not taken in the Committee of the Whole.

Report—Both a verb and a noun, as a Congressional term. A committee which has been examining a bill referred to it by the parent chamber "reports" its finding and recommendations to the chamber when the committee returns the measure. The process is called "reporting" a bill.

A "report" is the document setting forth the committee's explanation of its action. House and Senate reports are numbered separately and are designated S Rept or H Rept. Conference reports are numbered and designated in the same way as regular House reports.

Most reports favor a bill's passage. Adverse reports are occasionally submitted, but more often, when a committee disapproves a bill, it simply fails to report it at all. When a committee report is not unanimous, the dissenting committeemen may file a statement of their views, called Minority Views and referred to as a Minority Report. Sometimes a bill is reported without recommendation.

Recision—An item in an appropriation bill rescinding, or cancelling, funds previously appropriated but not spent.

Resolution—A simple resolution, designated H Res or S Res, deals with matters entirely within the prerogatives of one house or the other. It requires neither passage by the other chamber nor approval by the President, and does not have the force of law. Most resolutions deal with the rules of one house. They also are used to express the sentiments of a single house, as condolences to the family of a deceased Member or to give "advice" on foreign policy or other executive business. (*Also see Concurrent and Joint Resolutions.*)

Rider—A provision, usually not germane, tacked on to a bill which its sponsor hopes to get through more easily by including in other legislation. Riders become law if the bills embodying them do. Riders providing for legislation in appropriations bills are outstanding examples, though technically they are banned.

Rule—The term has two specific Congressional meanings. A rule may be a standing order governing the conduct of House or Senate business and listed in the chamber's book of rules. The rules deal with duties of officers, order of business, admission to the floor, voting procedures, etc.

In the House, a rule also may be a decision made by its Rules Committee about the handling of a particular bill on the floor. The Committee may determine under which standing rule a bill shall be considered, or it may provide a "special rule" in the form of a resolution. If the resolution is adopted by the House, the temporary rule becomes as valid as any standing rule, and lapses only after action has been completed on the measure to which it pertains.

A special rule sets the time limit on general debate. It may also waive points of order against provisions of the bill in question or against specified amendments intended to be proposed to the bill. It may even forbid all amendments or all amendments except, in some cases, those proposed by the legislative committee which handled the bill. In this instance it is known as a "closed" or "gag" rule as opposed to an "open" rule which puts no limitation on floor action, thus leaving the bill open to alteration. *(See Suspend the Rules.)*

Secretary of the Senate—Chief administrative officer of the Senate, responsible for direction of duties of Senate employees, education of pages, administration of oaths, receipt of registration of lobbyists and other activities necessary for the continuing operation of the Senate.

Select or Special Committee—A committee set up for a special purpose and a limited time by resolution of either House or Senate. Most special committees are investigative in nature.

Senatorial Courtesy—Sometimes referred to as "the courtesy of the Senate," it is a general practice without written rule applied to consideration of executive nominations. In practice, generally it means nominations from a state are not to be confirmed unless they have been approved by the Senators of the President's party of that state, with other Senators following their lead in the attitude they take toward such nominations.

Sine Die—See Adjournment sine die.

Slip Laws—The first official publication of a bill that has been enacted into law. Each is published separately in unbound single-sheet or pamphlet form. It usually takes two to three days from the date of Presidential approval to the time when slip laws become available.

Speaker—The presiding officer of the House of Representatives, elected by its Members.

Special Session—A session of Congress after it has adjourned sine die, completing its regular session. Special sessions are convened by the President of the United States under his constitutional powers.

Stand—A lawmaker's position, for or against, on a given issue or vote. He can make known his stand on a roll-call vote by answering "yea" or "nay," by "pairing" for or against, or by "announcing" his position to the House or Senate. Members also may go on record by answering the Congressional Quarterly Poll of unrecorded Congressmen on roll calls. *(See Pair, and Record Vote, above.)*

Standing Committee—A group permanently provided for by House or Senate rules. The standing committees at present are specified by the Legislative Reorganization Act of 1946, which broadly defines their respective jurisdictions.

Standing Vote—A non-record vote used in both House and Senate. A standing vote, also called a division vote, is taken as follows: Members in favor of a proposal stand and are counted by the presiding officer; then Members opposed stand and are counted. There is no record of how individual Members voted. In the House, the presiding officer announces the number of and against. In the Senate, usually only the result is announced.

Statutes-at-Large—A chronological arrangement of the laws enacted in each session of Congress. Though indexed, the laws are not arranged by subject matter nor is there an indication of how they affect previous law. *(See U.S. Code.)*

Strike from the Record—Remarks made on the House floor may offend some Member, who moves that the offending words be "taken down" for the Speaker's cognizance, and then expunged from the verbatim report to be carried in the Congressional Record.

Strike Out the Last Word—A move whereby House Members are entitled to speak for a fixed time on a measure then being debated by the chamber. A Member gains recognition from the chair by moving to strike out the last word of the amendment or section of the bill then under consideration. The motion is pro forma, and customarily requires no vote.

Substitute—A motion, an amendment, or an entire bill introduced in place of pending business. Passage of a substitute measure kills the original measure by supplanting it. A substitute may be amended.

Supplemental Appropriations—Normally are passed after the regular appropriation, but supposedly before the fiscal year to which they apply. Deficiencies are passed in the same fiscal year to which they apply but in recent practice have been called supplementals.

Suspend the Rules—Often a time-saving procedure for passing bills in the House. The wording of the motion, which may be made by any Member recognized by the Speaker, is: "I move to suspend the rules and pass the bill...." A favorable vote by two-thirds of those present is required for passage. Debate is limited to 40 minutes and no amendments from the floor are permitted. If a two-thirds favorable vote is not attained, the bill may be considered later under regular procedures.

Table a Bill—The motion to "lay on the table" is not debatable in either house, and is usually a method of making a final, adverse disposition of a matter. In the Senate, however, different language is sometimes used. The motion is worded to let a bill "lie on the table," perhaps for subsequent "picking up." This motion is more flexible, merely keeping the bill pending for later action, if desired.

Teller Vote—In the House, Members file past tellers and are counted as for or against a measure, but they are not recorded individually. The teller vote is not used in the Senate. In the House, tellers are ordered upon demand of one-fifth of a quorum. This is 44 in the House, 20 in Committee of the Whole.

Treaties—Executive proposals which must be submitted to the Senate for approval by two-thirds of the Senators present. Before they act on such foreign policy matters, Senators usually send them to committee for scrutiny. Treaties are read three times and debated in the chamber much as are legislative proposals, but are rarely amended. After approval by the Senate, they are ratified by the President.

Twenty-One-Day Rule—Permits the Speaker to recognize a committee member to call up for House consideration any bill reported by the committee that has been before the Rules Committee for 21 days without having received a rule for floor debate. Repealed in 1967.

Unanimous Consent—Synonymous with Without Objection. *(See below.)*

Union Calendar—Bills which directly or indirectly appropriate money or raise revenue are placed on this House calendar according to the date reported from committee.

U.S. Code—A consolidation and codification of the general and permanent laws of the United States arranged by subject under 50 Titles, the first six dealing with general or political subjects, and the other 44 alphabetically arranged from Agriculture to War and National Defense. The Code is now revised every six years and a supplement is published after each session of Congress.

Veto—Disapproval by the President of a bill or joint resolution, other than one proposing an amendment to the Constitution. When Congress is in session, the President must veto a bill within 10 days, excluding Sundays, after he has received it; otherwise it becomes law with or without his signature. When the President vetoes a bill, he returns it to the house of its origin with a message stating his objections. The veto then becomes a question of high privilege. *(See Override a Veto.)*

When Congress has adjourned, the President may pocket veto a bill by failing to sign it. *(See Pocket Veto.)*

Voice Vote—In either House or Senate, Members answer "aye" or "no" in chorus and the presiding officer decides the result. The term also is used loosely to indicate action by unanimous consent or without objection.

Whip—See Majority Whip.

Without Objection—Used in lieu of a vote on noncontroversial motions, amendments or bills, which may be passed in either the House or the Senate if no Member voices an objection.

Summary of Table of Contents

TABLE OF CONTENTS

Introduction

Chapter 1—The Origins and Development of Congress

Subchapter 2

History of the House of Representatives 33

Subchapter 3

History of the Senate 59

Tables, Charts and Summaries

Chapter 2—Congress at Work

Subchapter 1

The Legislative Process 103

Subchapter 2

Leadership in House and Senate 129

Subchapter 3

Subchapter 4

Tables, Charts and Summaries

Chapter 3—The Powers of Congress

Subchapter 1

Subchapter 2

The Power of Congress in Foreign Affairs 197

Subchapter 3

Senate Confirmation of Nominations 227

Subchapter 9

Power to Elect the President 319

Subchapter 10

The Function of Private Bills 329

Subchapter 11

Control of the Seat
of Government 353

Tables, Charts
and Summaries

Chapter 4—Housing and Support of Congress

Subchapter 1

The Capitol and Office Buildings 369

Chapter 5—Congress and the Electorate

Chapter 6—Pressures on Congress

Subchapter 1

Subchapter 2

Tables, Charts and Summaries

Chapter 7—Ethics in Congress

Tables, Charts and Summaries

Appendix

GUIDE TO THE U.S. CONGRESS

Chapter 1—The Origins and Development of Congress

The Origins and Development of Congress

THE 55 delegates who gathered in Philadelphia in the summer of 1787 faced a challenge of no mean proportions: how were they to devise a system of government that would bind 13 sovereign and rival states into one firm union without threatening the traditional freedoms for which the American colonists so recently had fought?

Americans, with their predominantly English heritage, were wedded to the principles of representative government and personal freedom that had developed in England from the time of Magna Carta. They had gone to war against the mother country to preserve their freedoms from the encroachments of centralized power.

But independence had brought new problems. Men's allegiance still was directed toward the state, and most were reluctant to yield state sovereignty to any superior governmental power. The Articles of Confederation, the first basic law of the new nation, reflected this widespread distrust of centralized power. Under the Articles the United States was little more than a league of sovereign states, bickering and feuding among themselves. The states retained control over most essential governmental functions, and Congress—in which each state had one vote—was the sole organ of central government. So limited were its powers that it could not levy taxes or regulate trade, and it had no sanction to enforce any of its decisions.

The inadequacies of the Articles of Confederation, brought into sharp focus by Shays's Rebellion in 1786, gave impetus to a growing movement for governmental reform that culminated in the Philadelphia convention the following year. There the delegates addressed themselves to the task of forming "a more perfect Union."

In the Constitution that emerged from these deliberations, the concept of government by consent of the governed formed the basic principle; accountability was the watchword. The rights of the people were to be protected by diffusing power among "opposite and rival interests."

The Constitution strengthened central authority, but national powers were carefully enumerated and other powers were reserved to the states and the people. The Constitution provided for a President, to be chosen by electors in each state, a national judiciary and a legislature of two chambers. The House of Representatives was to be popularly elected, while the Senate, which shared certain executive powers with the President, was to be chosen by the state legislatures. Under the terms of the "Great Compromise," each state was to have two votes in the Senate, but representation in the House was to be proportional to population in the various states. Restraints

The Federalist View

"The fabric of American empire ought to rest on the solid basis of THE CONSENT OF THE PEOPLE. The streams of national power ought to flow immediately from that pure, original fountain of all legitimate authority."

Alexander Hamilton, *The Federalist*, No. 22

"If men were angels, no government would be necessary. If angels were to govern men, neither external nor internal controls on government would be necessary. In framing a government which is to be administered by men over men, the great difficulty lies in this: you must first enable the government to control the governed; and in the next place oblige it to control itself. A dependence on the people is, no doubt, the primary control on the government; but experience has taught mankind the necessity of auxiliary precautions."

James Madison, *The Federalist*, No. 51

"In the extended republic of the United States, and among the great variety of interests, parties, and sects which it embraces, a coalition of a majority of the whole society could seldom take place on any other principles than those of justice and the general good...."

Ibid.

on power were provided not only by the Federal plan, but by the separation of powers within the national Government coupled with an elaborate system of checks and balances. "In the compound republic of America," wrote Madison in *The Federalist*, "the power surrendered by the people is first divided between two distinct governments, and then the portion allotted to each subdivided among distinct and separate departments. Hence a double security arises to the rights of the people. The different governments will control each other, at the same time that each will be controlled by itself."

The Convention had heeded Randolph's advice "to insert essential principles only," and the final draft of the Constitution provided only a broad framework for the new Government. Thus for nearly 200 years the document has proved flexible enough to meet the nation's changing needs without extensive formal revision. Although many modern governmental practices would seem alien to the constitutional framers, the basic structure continues to operate in much the way they planned it. Through continuous contests for power the "constituent parts" of the Government have pursued Madison's goal of "keeping each other in their proper places," while the ballot box has remained the ultimate guardian of the popular will.

Separate Roles of House and Senate

The House—"the grand depository of the democratic principles of the Government"—was expected by Hamilton to be "a full match, if not an overmatch, for every other member of the Government." The Senate, it was hoped, would serve as a check on the "democratic licentiousness" of the popularly elected lower chamber, but whether it would be more "responsible" or more "aristocratic" than the House depended on one's point of view. The Senate's special authority over appointments and treaties was counterbalanced by the right of the House to originate all revenue bills.

At first the House, under the leadership of Madison and Clay, was the preeminent chamber of Congress, but the Senate quickly emerged as a powerful legislative force. In the years preceding the Civil War it was the chief forum for the discussion of national issues, and in the post-Reconstruction era it became the dominant arm of the Government. The House, as its membership increased, was compelled to adopt a variety of procedures that diminished the power of individual Representatives but assured its ability to act when action was desired. The Senate remained a comparatively small body which found elaborate institutional structures unnecessary for the deliberation that it saw as its paramount function.

"It is indispensable," wrote Woodrow Wilson in 1885, "that besides the House of Representatives which runs on all fours with popular sentiment, we should have a body like the Senate which may refuse to run with it at all when it seems to be wrong—a body which has time and security enough to keep its head, if only now and then and but for a little while, till other people have had time to think. The Senate is fitted to do deliberately and well the revising which is its properest function, because its position as a representative of state sovereignty is one of eminent dignity, securing for it ready and sincere respect, and because popular demands, ere they reach it with definite and authoritative suggestion, are diluted by passage through the feelings and conclusions of the state legislatures, which are the Senate's only immediate constituents. The Senate commonly feels with the House, but it does not, so to say, feel so fast. It at least has a chance to be the express image of those judgments of the nation which are slower and more temperate than its feelings."

Wilson's concept of the Senate might have been satisfactory to the framers of the Constitution, but in the 20th century it would no longer serve. As the Progressive era advanced, an increasingly restive public demanded more genuinely popular government, and in 1912 the Senate reluctantly agreed to a constitutional amendment providing for the direct election of Senators. The House, too, felt the pressures of the times: the power of the

Speaker which "Czar" Reed had established in the name of party responsibility in 1890 was dismantled under the banner of popular rule in 1910.

The 17th Amendment, by taking Senatorial elections out of the hands of the state governments, blurred the constitutional distinction between the Senate and House, and from the time of its adoption in 1913 the Senate came more and more to resemble the lower chamber. At times it, rather than the House, would appear to be the more representative legislative body. Both chambers, however, were subject to continuing charges that they failed to represent the will of the electorate. Although Members of Congress ran for office as Republicans or Democrats, the absence of unity within the national parties precluded party responsibility in legislative action. Moreover, the institutional characteristics of Congress itself often prevented a legislative majority from working its will. Campaigns against the seniority system, under which Senators and Representatives rose to power within their respective chambers, the Senate filibuster and secrecy in Congressional activities all represented attempts to make Congress more accountable to the people. The same goal prompted demands for reapportionment of the House to make Congressional districts more nearly equal in population.

Congress and Presidential Power

Meanwhile, the rapid growth of Presidential power in the 20th century, spurred by a major economic depression and two world wars, posed a threat to the viability of Congress as a coequal branch of Government. As the volume and complexity of Government business increased, legislative initiative shifted from the Capitol to the White House, and Congress with its antiquated procedures often found that it was no match for the tremendous resources of the Executive Branch. In two major reorganization acts of the post-World War II era, Congress tried to strengthen its position vis-a-vis the Presidency. Repeated clashes with the President over the spending, war and treaty powers marked the legislators' determination to resist executive usurpation of the powers assigned to them by the Constitution.

As the 1960s drew to a close, the entire constitutional system was subjected to new strains, the result of an unpopular war in Southeast Asia and massive civil disorders at home. Ghetto riots signaled the despair of the blacks, campus unrest the disillusionment of the young, and antiwar demonstrations the determination of mounting thousands of Americans to force a speedy withdrawal from Vietnam. As faith in political solutions to the nation's problems declined, defiance of law became a commonplace expression of citizen frustration. Even those who believed in traditional governmental processes were dismayed by the apparent impotence of those processes. By 1971, it appeared that the nation's Government would have to renew its compact with the people if the constitutional system was to fulfill its promise. The doctrine of government by consent of the governed seemed to require no less.

The Constitutional Beginnings

WHEN the Federal Convention met in Philadelphia in 1787 to consider revising the Articles of Confederation, the reasons for seeking a more effective form of national government for the newly independent United States of America seemed manifest and pressing. The exact form that government should take was by no means clear, however, and substantial compromise was required before agreement could be reached.

What finally emerged as the Constitution of the United States nevertheless reflected in good measure the shared experience of men who had grown up in a colonial America that was predominantly English in origin, and who had finally rebelled against English sovereignty when that seemed the only way to preserve the freedom they had come to expect as a part of their English heritage.

America's Colonial Background

Almost a century passed between Columbus' voyage of discovery in 1492 and Sir Walter Raleigh's attempt in 1587 to plant the first English settlement in the New World—the ill-fated "Lost Colony" on Roanoke Island in what is now North Carolina. By then, Spain had seized the Caribbean and much of South and Central America (with its gold and silver) and had placed outposts in Florida. But at the beginning of the 17th century, most of North America was still unexplored, Spain's power was on the wane, and England was primed for colonial venture.

English Dominance

Private initiative was the prime mover behind settlement of America by the English during the 17th century, when all of the 13 colonies except one were founded. Several were started by promoters with an eye to profits or the creation of new feudal domains. Religious strife underlay the "Great Migration" of Puritans to New England (and the West Indies) during the repressive reign of Charles I (1625-49). Poverty drove many others to take a chance on America. Whatever the motive for settlement, though, it was entirely a civilian undertaking, receiving little more help from the state than a charter to the land to be settled.

The English achieved their dominant position along the Atlantic seaboard in two waves of colonization. Virginia, Maryland and the New England colonies were founded before 1642, when the outbreak of civil war in England absorbed English energies. After restoration of the monarchy in 1660, the English added New York, New Jersey, Pennsylvania, Delaware and the Carolinas. Georgia, the 13th colony, was founded in 1733. By 1700, the colonies had a population of 200,000—largely of English origin—stretched along a thousand miles of coast from Maine to the Carolinas.

Roots of Self-Government

By the time Jamestown was founded in 1607, Englishmen had already attained significant rights and privileges. English justice was grounded on a solid body of common law that included the right to trial by jury, and no Englishman could be deprived of life, liberty or property without due process in the courts. The first colonists brought with them "all Liberties, Franchises, and Immunities" of Englishmen at home, along with the models of English courts and other organs of local government.

The long English struggle for the right of self-government was also well-advanced by the beginning of the 17th century. The Crown was still supreme, and it would take the beheading of Charles I in 1649 and the dethroning of James II in 1688 to assure Parliament ascendancy over the King. Already, though, the two houses of Parliament —the Lords and the Commons—symbolized the principle of government by law and representative assembly, and this principle too was soon transplanted to America. In 1619, the Virginians (then about 1,000 in number) elected 22 "burgesses" to a General Assembly.

After Virginia became a royal colony, the Governor and Council were appointed by the King, but popular representation in the Assembly was retained. And the charter of Maryland, issued in 1632, made explicit provision for law-making "with the Advice, Assent and Approbation of the Free-Men of the same Province, or of the greater Part of them, or of their Delegates or Deputies, whom We will shall be called together for the framing of Laws when and as often as Need shall require...."

The organizers of the Massachusetts Bay Company carried matters considerably further when they voted to transfer the entire enterprise and its charter as "one Body corporate and politique" to New England. On their arrival in 1630, the officers promptly established themselves as the government of the Bay Colony, subject only to annual election thereafter by the stockholder-colonists. The founders of Massachusetts thereby asserted a right to full

---

Reference

See Appendix table of contents (first thumb tab) for texts of the Declaration of Independence, the Articles of Confederation, the Constitution and other documents relating to the origins of Congress.

Colonial Beginnings

Virginia. The Virginia Company of London, a joint stock company with a charter from James I, founded the first permanent English settlement in America at Jamestown in 1607. After severe setbacks, the company found tobacco to be a thriving crop and profitable export and began to attract new settlers with "head rights" to 50 acres of land. The company was dissolved in 1624, when Virginia became a royal colony whose population reached 15,000 in 1648.

Maryland. In 1632 Charles I gave a proprietary charter to Maryland (originally a part of Virginia) to Sir George Calvert, who wanted a feudal domain for his family that would serve also as a refuge for English Catholics. Settlement began at St. Mary's in 1634. Protestants soon outnumbered Catholics, leading to continuing friction between settlers and proprietor. Maryland became a royal colony in 1692 but was restored to the Calvert family in 1715.

Massachusetts. A small band of Pilgrims founded Plymouth in 1620. Few others came until 1630, when John Winthrop and other Puritan organizers of the Massachusetts Bay Company arrived with 1,000 colonists to settle Boston and nearby towns. The Bay Colony (which attained a population of 16,000 by 1643) remained a self-governing Puritan commonwealth until its charter was annulled in 1684. In 1691 Massachusetts became a royal colony, incorporating Plymouth and Maine as well.

Connecticut. Thomas Hooker led a group of Puritans from the Bay Colony to found Hartford in 1636. About the same time other groups of Puritans settled Saybrook and New Haven. Modeled along the theocratic lines of Massachusetts, these and other settlements were joined when Connecticut in 1662 obtained from Charles II its own charter as a self-governing colony. The colony retained this status until 1776.

Rhode Island. Providence was founded in 1636 by Roger Williams, a strong believer in religious freedom who had been banished from the Bay Colony for opposing the intolerant and conformist rule of Governor Winthrop and the Puritans. The area drew other free thinkers and nonconformists, and in 1644 the settlements federated as Rhode Island and Providence Plantations. They obtained a royal charter of their own in 1663 and remained a self-governing colony until the Revolution.

New Hampshire. Various groups of Antinomians, Puritans and Anglicans began a number of settlements between 1623 and 1640 on land granted to John Mason by Charles I. Massachusetts annexed these settlements briefly, and border disputes between the two continued even after New Hampshire became a royal colony in 1679. The Governor of Massachusetts served also as Governor of New Hampshire from 1699 to 1741.

New York. The Dutch West Indies Company founded New Netherland with posts at Albany (1624) and on the island of Manhattan (1626). Confined largely to the Hudson River Valley, the Dutch colony had a population of about 10,000 when it was seized by the English in 1664 and renamed New York as part of a grant by Charles II to his brother, the Duke of York, of all land between the Connecticut and Delaware Rivers. The Duke attempted to run the colony without an assembly until 1683; as James II, he made it a royal colony in 1685.

New Jersey. In 1665, the Duke of York gave the land between the Hudson and Delaware Rivers to Lord John Berkeley and Sir George Carteret (former Governor of the Isle of Jersey), who named the area New Jersey. The two proprietors later sold East and West Jersey separately, and although the two were reunited as a royal colony in 1702, confusion of land titles continued to plague New Jersey. The colony had the same Governor as New York until 1738.

Pennsylvania. William Penn, a Quaker convert, received proprietary title to Pennsylvania from the Duke of York in 1681. Penn attracted settlers from the Continent as well as England with promises of political and religious liberty and the offer of land on generous terms. German Mennonites were among the first to come, settling Germantown in 1683. Pennsylvania prospered under Penn's tolerant rule, and it remained a proprietary colony until the Revolution.

Delaware. Lewes on Delaware Bay was settled by the Dutch in 1631. They were followed by Swedes, who held forth as New Sweden until overcome by Dutch forces in 1655. The area was conquered by the English in 1664 and was included in the grant to the Duke of York, who sold it to William Penn in 1682. Known as the "Lower Counties," Delaware had its own assembly after 1704 but had the same proprietary Governor as Pennsylvania until 1776.

Carolinas. In 1663 Charles II gave proprietary title to all land between Virginia and Florida to the Carolina Proprietors, a group of promoters led by Sir John Colleton and the Earl of Shaftesbury. Charleston, the first settlement, was founded in 1670 by settlers from England and Barbados; later, French Huguenots and Scots came to settle. After rice and indigo were introduced, South Carolina became a plantation colony like Virginia. North Carolina, first settled by people from Virginia and New England, became an area of small farms. The two halves became royal colonies in 1729.

Georgia. Gen. James Oglethorpe and other English philanthropists envisioned Georgia as a refuge for debtors. They founded Savannah in 1733, and in the next eight years brought over about 1,800 charity colonists. Many of these colonists moved on to South Carolina, however, and Georgia had a population of little more than 2,000 when it became a royal colony in 1752.

self-government that neither the King nor Parliament had contemplated or would be prepared to challenge for another 50 years.

The great distance that separated England from America was itself a major factor in promoting a spirit of independence and self-reliance among the early colonists. Many of those drawn to America were predisposed to resist authority in any event, and this attitude was reinforced by the free availability of land and the harshness of frontier living. In New England, where entire congregations of Puritans would often emigrate and settle together in a town of their own, the town meeting became a unique instrument of self-government that was exceptionally democratic for the times.

Origins of Conflict With England

England left the colonies pretty much to themselves initially, but it was not for lack of a concept of the role they would be expected to play. Under the prevailing economic doctrine of the times—mercantilism—the central goal of any nation-state was self-sufficiency, and it was taken for granted that all profits of empire should accrue to the benefit of the mother country. Thus the English were quick to try to monopolize the trade in Virginia tobacco, the first American product to find a wide market. And in 1660 they began systematic efforts to exploit colonial trade, with the first of a series of Acts of Trade and Navigation.

These laws were designed to maximize English profits on the transport of colonial imports and exports and the marketing of major colonial products. They required all trade between England and the colonies to be carried by English or colonial-built ships manned by English subjects; stipulated that colonial imports from other countries in Europe first be landed and reloaded at English ports; and prohibited exports of specified colonial products to countries other than England. Tobacco was the first of these "enumerated" items, and eventually every important American export except salt fish was added to the list.

The trade acts were not without some benefit to the colonies. But in exchanging their raw products for English manufactures, the colonists rarely found the terms of trade to their advantage. When tobacco prices collapsed in the 1660s, for example, Virginians had no recourse against the English merchants who raised the prices of goods sent in exchange. This situation was aggravated by England's continuing refusal to permit its coins to circulate in the colonies. To get specie (gold or silver), the colonists had to sell their products in the West Indies or other markets.

The trade acts were met with widespread evasion in the colonies; smuggling, bribery and the use of false documents were commonplace. New Englanders, who ran a chronic deficit in their balance of trade with England, were especially resourceful in evading the trade acts. Massachusetts went so far as to refuse to obey them, asserting that the laws of England "do not reach America" because the colonies were unrepresented in Parliament. For this and similar acts of defiance against English authority, the Bay Colony's charter was annulled in 1684.

When James II came to the throne in 1685, England moved to strengthen colonial administration by consolidating the New England colonies, New York and the Jerseys into one Dominion of New England; for three years these colonies were ruled by Sir Edmund Andros as Governor-general with the aid of an appointed council but no representative assembly. The colonists bridled at being taxed without their consent and were quick to overthrow Andros and other dominion officials as soon as they received word of the "Glorious Revolution" of 1688 and the expulsion of James from England. The concept of the Dominion was promptly abandoned.

The accession of William and Mary in 1689 marked the beginning of a transfer of power from the Crown to Parliament and of a series of colonial wars that ended in 1763 with the English in control of all of America east of the Mississippi. Mercantilist aims continued to dominate English colonial policy throughout this period, and new restrictions were placed on colonial trade. But the American colonists went on growing in numbers, economic strength and political assertiveness.

Growth of the Colonies

Between 1700 and 1760, large families and new immigrants boosted the colonial population from 200,000 to about 1,700,000. Persons of English stock were in the majority over-all and among colonial leaders; the first Adams came in 1636, the first Washington in 1656, the first Franklin in 1685. Other major ethnic groups in 1760 were the Scotch-Irish (estimated to number 280,000) and the Germans (170,000), whose forebears had started coming to America toward the end of the 17th century. Finding the best land along the seaboard already taken, most had moved on to settle the back country between tidewater and the Appalachians.

Even more numerous in the American population of 1760 were an estimated 310,000 Negro slaves. The Spaniards brought the first African slaves to the New World in the 16th century; a Dutch ship brought the first 20 to Virginia in 1619. The English saw nothing wrong in slavery, and the Puritans regularly took Indians as slaves and sold them in the West Indies. But they made poor slaves compared to the Africans, and by 1690 there were some 10,000 Negroes in America.

Slaves helped to meet a chronic shortage of labor in colonial America at a time when most colonists wanted and could easily get their own land. Slavery eventually declined in the North, where it became unprofitable, but it flourished in the plantation economy of the South; the number of slaves in Virginia, the Carolinas and Georgia grew rapidly during the 18th century. Americans vied with the English slave traders in meeting the demand. Yankee slavers were especially successful in trading New England rum for Africans, who were then sold in the West Indies for sugar and molasses with which to make more rum.

Profits from slave labor and the slave trade thus added to a prosperity that was sustained by a rise in prices for colonial produce in England and the rest of Europe. In 1731 exports leaving Charleston included 42,000 barrels of rice, 14,000 barrels of pitch, tar and turpentine, and 250,000 deerskins. Virginia and Maryland shipped more tobacco, while Pennsylvania found a growing market for its wheat and flour. The fur trade was centered in New York. The New England colonies exported large quantities of ship timber and lumber of all types along with salt fish and meat.

Most of the colonial products were not competitive with those of England, but when competition did appear, restrictions followed. The Woolens Act of 1699 barred sale of colonial cloth outside the place where it was woven. Parliament in 1732 banned the export of hats from one colony to another. To protect English exports of iron and steel products, the colonies in 1750 were ordered to stop building various kinds of mills. After the British West Indies complained that the Americans were buying cheaper sugar and molasses from the French, Parliament passed the Molasses Act of 1733, placing a stiff duty on imports from the French islands. For the most part, however, these restrictions were poorly enforced and easily evaded by the Americans.

Governors vs. Assemblies

As the American population and economy grew, so did the problems of English colonial administration. All of the colonies were permitted to elect their own assemblies after the Dominion of New England collapsed in 1689, but only Connecticut and Rhode Island kept the right to elect their governors as well. The governors of the royal colonies (which eight became) were appointed by the King and those of the proprietary colonies with the King's approval. And it was these royal and proprietary governors who had primary responsibility for enforcing English laws and regulations in America.

The governors were armed with great legal authority. They had the right of absolute veto over colonial legislation, the authority to prorogue (or terminate) and dissolve assemblies, and the power to dismiss judges and create courts, long after the Crown had been stripped of these prerogatives in England. But the real power of the governors was effectively limited by their dependence on the colonial assemblies (in almost all cases) for their salaries and operating revenues. As one wrote of his troubles, "I have to steer between Scylla and Charybdis, to please the King's ministers at home and a touchy people here, to luff for one and bear away for another."

By contrast, the powers of the assemblies, though nowhere carefully defined by charter or statute, grew steadily. In time they claimed and exercised the right to lay taxes, raise troops, incur debts, issue currency, and otherwise initiate all legislation. They commonly passed only short-term revenue bills, stipulated in detail how appropriations were to be spent, tacked riders on essential money bills, and vied with the governors for control of patronage.

Claiming prerogatives similar to those of the House of Commons, the assemblies made the most of their power of the purse to extract concessions from the governors. When one governor asked for a fixed revenue for five years, the assembly demanded the right to appoint every official to be paid from the grant. The New York Assembly was reported in 1754 to "have wrested from Your Majesty's governor the nomination of all offices of government, the custody and direction of the public military stores, the mustering and direction of troops raised for Your Majesty's service, and in short almost every other part of executive government."

If the governors found it impolitic to veto some colonial legislation, it could still be killed by the royal disallowance. Acts so vetoed included ones that discriminated against religious minorities, assessed duties on the products of neighboring colonies, authorized unbacked issues of paper currency, and restricted the slave trade. But preventing the assemblies from taking unwanted action was not the same as winning their support for imperial projects, as the English found out during their wars with the French. *(See box.)*

At such times English requisitions on the colonies for men, money and supplies were honored by the assemblies slowly, in part or not at all, especially in those colonies that were not under fire. The "bread colonies"

of New York and Pennsylvania were notorious for continuing to trade with the French in time of war. But all of the colonies resisted imperial direction in some degree and cherished their independence one from another. Not one of the assemblies ratified the Albany Plan of Union of 1754, although it had been drafted with the approval of representatives from 7 of the 13 colonies. *(See box.)*

Growth of Colonial Indignation

The Seven Years War doubled the national debt of England (to 130 million pounds), quadrupled the prospective costs of administering the greatly enlarged empire in America (to 300,000 pounds a year), and helped thereby to put the government of George III, crowned in 1760, on a collision course with the colonists. To the mercantilists in Parliament, it now seemed logical to plug the loopholes in trade controls and to make the colonies pay a share of the costs of imperial overhead. The shift in English colonial policy began in 1763 when George Grenville became prime minister.

Grenville's first step was to set aside the claims of Virginia and other colonies to portions of the vast lands taken from the French. By the Proclamation of 1763, the entire region between the Appalachians and the Mississippi south of Quebec and north of Florida was reserved for the Indians. And the English adhered to this policy despite strong pressures from highly placed speculators (including Benjamin Franklin) who promoted the settlement of such proposed inland colonies as Vandalia, Charlotiana and Transylvania.

At the same time, Parliament began to strengthen enforcement of trade controls. Admiralty courts, which tried smuggling cases without juries, could now move such trials to Halifax in Nova Scotia at considerable cost to those whose goods and ships were detained. Colonial issues of paper money, which had been permitted during the war, were banned by the Currency Act of 1764. And to lighten the British tax load, Grenville pushed three other laws through Parliament.

• The Revenue Act of 1764, for "defraying the expenses of defending, protecting and securing" the colonies, cut in half the widely evaded duty laid on foreign molasses in 1733 but placed new duties on such colonial imports as wine, silk and linen. It also "enumerated" more colonial products, including hides and skins, that could be exported only to England.

• The Quartering Act of 1765 required the colonies to contribute to the upkeep of the 10,000 troops England planned to station in America. The colonies were to supply them with barracks or other quarters and with some of their provisions and were to pay a part of the money costs.

• The Stamp Act of 1765 required that revenue stamps costing up to 20 shillings in specie be affixed to all licenses, legal documents, leases, notes and bonds, newspapers, pamphlets, almanacs, advertisements and other documents issued in the colonies. Passed on March 22, the law was to take effect Nov. 1 and was expected to yield 60,000 pounds a year.

None of these measures sat well with the Americans, but opposition focused on the Stamp Act as the first direct tax ever laid on the colonies by Parliament. Americans believed they could be taxed only by their own assemblies and that the Stamp Act, which was taxation without

Colonial Wars

Between 1689 and 1763, the American colonies were involved in four wars born of European conflicts and the imperial rivalries of England, France and Spain. At the outset French Canada was only sparsely settled and Spanish Florida not at all, but the French had built a lucrative fur trade with Indians throughout the Great Lakes region while La Salle had sailed down the Mississippi in 1682 and claimed Louisiana. Most of the fighting that ensued, however, involved New England and New York.

King William's War: 1689-97 (called War of the League of Augsburg in Europe). When William of Orange became King of England, the English joined a continental alliance against Louis XIV of France. In America, French and Indians raided English settlements in New York, New Hampshire and Maine. New Englanders captured the French base at Port Royal, Nova Scotia, but an English attempt to take Quebec failed. The Treaty of Ryswick restored Port Royal to the French.

Queen Anne's War: 1702-13 (War of the Spanish Succession). In America, French and Indians burned Deerfield and raided most of the frontier settlements of Massachusetts and New Hampshire. The French captured the English post of St. John's, Newfoundland, while the English and colonials retook Port Royal. But expeditions against Quebec and Montreal again failed. By the Treaty of Utrecht the French accepted British sovereignty over Nova Scotia and Hudson's Bay and the English inherited Spain's monopoly over the slave trade with its colonies.

King George's War: 1745-48 (War of the Austrian Succession). The major military event in America was the capture of Louisbourg, a French fortress on Cape Breton Island, by an army of 4,000 colonial militiamen led by William Pepperell, a Maine merchant. By the Treaty of Aachen, England restored Louisbourg to France in exchange for Madras in India but paid the cost of the colonial campaign.

French and Indian War: 1754-63 (the Seven Years War). In America, this world-wide conflict focused on upper New York and western Pennsylvania where the French built several forts. The English fared badly until William Pitt came to power in 1758 and reorganized the war effort under new and younger generals. The French were dislodged from Fort Duquesne (renamed Pittsburgh), Fort Niagara and Fort Ticonderoga, and in 1759 the English took Quebec, then Montreal the next year. The English also defeated the French in India and the West Indies and, after Spain entered the war in 1762, took Havana and Manila.

The Peace of Paris (1763) left England dominant in North America. France ceded Canada and all claims east of the Mississippi to England and gave Louisiana to Spain. England also got Spanish Florida in exchange for Havana, and Manila reverted to Spain.

---

representation, was unconstitutional. The Virginia House of Burgesses so resolved at the urging of Patrick Henry, while the Massachusetts House of Representatives called for an intercolonial meeting to be held in New York in October.

The Stamp Act Congress was attended by 28 delegates from nine colonies. They affirmed their allegiance to the Crown, asserted their right as Englishmen not to be taxed without their consent, noted that the colonists were not represented in the House of Commons, and concluded that "no taxes ever have been or can be constitutionally imposed on them, but by their respective legislatures." The delegates urged Parliament to repeal the Stamp Act and other recent laws that had "a manifest tendency to subvert the rights and liberties of the colonists." *(See Appendix for text of resolutions.)*

The English insisted that Parliament represented and acted in behalf of all Englishmen. But they could not ignore the sharp drop in exports that followed a colonial boycott of English goods or the attacks on royal officials by colonial mobs calling themselves "Sons of Liberty." When it became clear in 1766 that the Stamp Act could not be enforced, it was repealed. But Parliament, through a Declaratory Act, asserted its authority to legislate for the colonies "in all cases whatsoever" and declared colonial resolves to the contrary to be "utterly null and void."

The Intolerable Acts

Following repeal of the Stamp Act, Chancellor of the Exchequer Charles Townshend proposed an increase of customs receipts to get the needed revenue. Parliament passed laws in 1767 laying new duties on imports by the colonies of paper, lead, glass, paint and tea; reorganizing the customs service in America; and authorizing broad use of general search warrants known as Writs of Assistance to ferret out violations. The Townshend Acts were greeted by a new outbreak of protests, colonial merchants revived their nonimportation agreements, and the adverse effects on English business again persuaded Parliament to retreat. When Lord North came to power in 1770, all of the Townshend duties except the one on tea were repealed. Most of the colonists were appeased, trade revived, and for three "quiet years" England and the colonies lived in relative harmony.

To American radicals like Samuel Adams of Massachusetts, this period of calm foreshadowed a further attack on colonial liberties, for the English had begun to pay the salaries of the royal governors and other officials from their increased customs receipts, thus freeing them from the hold of the assemblies. Adams, Henry, Thomas Jefferson and others, who now questioned the right of Parliament to legislate for the colonies in any respect, formed committees of correspondence that became the underground of the resistance movement.

The "quiet years" ended abruptly in 1773 when the faltering East India Company was authorized to "dump" a surplus of tea on the American colonies by undercutting the price of tea smuggled in from Holland. Colonial merchants, foreseeing ruinous competition, joined the radicals in protesting the Tea Act, and everywhere the colonists prepared to boycott the first shipments. In Boston, however, Adams and John Hancock urged direct action, and

Albany Plan of Union

The Albany Congress of 1754 was initiated by the British in an effort to nail down the "wavering friendship" of their long-time allies, the six Indian nations of the Iroquois Confederacy, which had come under increasing French pressure on the western frontier. The Americans who represented the seven colonies that took part—Massachusetts, New Hampshire, Connecticut, Rhode Island, New York, Pennsylvania and Maryland—were more ambitious and adopted a Plan of Union drafted largely by Benjamin Franklin of Pennsylvania. *(See Appendix for text.)*

JOIN, or DIE.

Wood engraving in the "Pennsylvania Gazette," 1754

The Plan called on Parliament to create "one general government" in America to be administered by a President-General appointed by the Crown and a Grand Council of representatives from all of the colonies (in proportion to their financial contributions) elected by the assemblies. This government would have sole authority to regulate Indian affairs and the purchase and sale of new lands, as well as the power to raise troops for the common defense and to levy "such general duties, imposts or taxes...as may be collected with the least inconvenience to the people."

Both the British government and the colonial assemblies opposed the Albany Plan as involving too large a grant of power. The English were not prepared to give the colonies so much autonomy, while the assemblies were not ready to share their power to tax. "The different and contrary reasons of dislike to my plan made me suspect that it was really the true medium," Franklin later wrote, "and I am still of the opinion it would have been happy for both sides of the water if it had been adopted."

As it was, the Albany Plan reflected a growing awareness of the need for a common approach to administration of the far-flung and expanding American colonies. Rejection of the Plan was a major landmark on the road that led to the Constitutional Convention of 1787.

on Dec. 16, 1773, a mob disguised as Indians boarded three tea ships and dumped their cargoes into the harbor.

The Boston Tea Party alarmed many Americans who opposed British policy (Franklin called it "an act of violent injustice"), but it also provoked the English government into a series of coercive acts that drove the colonists together. On March 25, 1774, the House of Commons ordered the Port of Boston closed until the city paid for the tea thrown into the harbor. That order was followed by laws revising the Massachusetts charter to strengthen royal control and transferring to England the trials of colonists charged with murder.

To these "Intolerable Acts" Parliament added one that alienated most of Protestant America by giving to the French-Canadian—and Catholic—royal province of Quebec all of the land west of the Appalachians lying north of the Ohio River and east of the Mississippi. The Quebec Act of June 22 was regarded as another punitive measure by most colonists ("No Popery," proclaimed a Puritan banner) and helped to muster broad support for a "general congress of all the colonies" proposed by the Virginia and Massachusetts assemblies.

First Continental Congress

Every colony except Georgia (whose Governor blocked the selection of delegates) was represented at the First Continental Congress, which met in Philadelphia on Sept. 5, 1774. The fifty-five men who attended were described by John Adams as "one-third Whig; one-third Tory; the rest mongrel." Conservatives like Joseph Galloway of Pennsylvania hoped to conciliate the English, while radicals like the Adams cousins wanted to defy all British controls. These "Loyalist" and "Republican" forces were evenly balanced at the outset, according to Galloway's later account, but the latter got the upper hand by "calling to their assistance the aid of their factions" in agitating for strong measures, news of which was "dispatched by express to Congress."

The turning point came when Paul Revere arrived with the Suffolk Resolves, adopted by a convention of towns around Boston, which called on Massachusetts to arm itself against efforts to "enslave America" and urged Congress to adopt economic sanctions against England. To Galloway, these "inflammatory resolves...contained a complete declaration of war against Great Britain," and many others agreed. But most delegates felt compelled to register their support of Massachusetts. By a vote of six colonies to five they set aside Galloway's plan (based on the Albany Plan of Union of 1754) to give Parliament and a colonial legislature joint control over American affairs, and endorsed the Suffolk Resolves.

The Congress then adopted a Declaration of Rights and Grievances against all British acts to which "Americans cannot submit" *(see Appendix for text)* and approved a wide-ranging nonimportation, nonconsumption and nonexportation agreement or "Association" as "the most speedy, effectual and peaceable" means of swaying England. Locally elected committees were directed to enforce this commercial boycott by publicizing violations so that "all such foes to the rights of British-America may be publicly known and universally condemned as the enemies of American liberty." On Oct. 22, 1774, the Continental Congress adjourned, after agreeing to meet again the following May if necessary.

George III believed that "the colonies must either submit or triumph" and Lord North's Parliamentary majority agreed. The Earl of Chatham, Edmund Burke and others urged conciliation, while English merchants, hit by the American boycott, petitioned for "healing remedies," but to no avail. In the colonies patriot forces began to gather arms and supplies and to train militia, and in Massachusetts they soon controlled all of the colony outside of Boston where the Governor, Gen. Gage, was installed with 5,000 British troops.

On April 19, 1775, Gage sent 1,000 of these men to destroy patriot stores in Lexington and Concord. They were met by minutemen, firing broke out, and the British lost 247 in dead and wounded before getting back to Boston. These turned out to be the opening shots of the Revolutionary War, although more than a year was to pass before the Americans were sufficiently united to declare their independence.

Revolution and Confederation

When the Second Continental Congress met on May 10, 1775, in Philadelphia, most of the delegates still hoped to avoid both war and independence. Faced with pleas for help from Massachusetts, the delegates agreed in mid-June to raise a Continental Army of 20,000 men, to ask the colonies for $2 million (in proportion to their population) for the army's support, and to make George Washington (a delegate from Virginia) the army's commander-in-chief.

Soon afterward, however, the Congress approved a petition to George III (drafted by John Dickinson) asking for "a happy and permanent reconciliation" between the colonies and England. The delegates also adopted a Declaration of the Causes and Necessity of Taking up Arms (drafted by Dickinson and Jefferson) in which they disavowed any desire for independence but resolved "to die free men rather than live slaves."

The King's response, on Aug. 23, was to proclaim a state of rebellion in America. The British began to hire mercenaries in Germany and to incite the Iroquois against the colonials, while Congress authorized an expedition against Canada and efforts to contact "our friends abroad" for aid. Yet the legislatures of five colonies took positions against independence that autumn. Pennsylvania's delegation to the Congress was told to "utterly reject any proposition...that may cause or lead to a separation from our mother country or a change in the form of this government."

The British gave no signs of retreating, however, and the appearance in January 1776 of Thomas Paine's pamphlet "Common Sense" marked the beginning of what was to be a rising demand for independence. Paine argued that it was time for Americans to stand on their own feet, for there was "something absurd in supposing a continent to be perpetually governed by an island" and "it is evident that they belong to different systems: England to Europe, America to itself." Paine also put the onus for the colonies' troubles on the King rather than Parliament.

Declaration of Independence

Pressure on the Congress to act reached a climax when, on June 7, 1776, Richard Henry Lee of Virginia introduced a resolution stating that "these United Colonies are, and of right ought to be, free and independent States." Jefferson, John Adams, Franklin, Roger Sherman and Robert Livingston were named to draw up a declaration, but it was largely Jefferson's draft that was presented on June 28. Lee's resolution was adopted July 2; Jefferson's Declaration was then debated and slightly amended (to strike out an indictment of the British slave trade, for example) before it was approved July 4 by all of the delegations except New York's, which later voted for it after receiving new instructions. *(See Appendix for text.)*

The greater part of the Declaration—and the most important to Americans at that time—consisted of a recitation of every grievance against English colonial policy that had emerged since 1763. The grievances were presented as "facts" to prove that George III was seeking "the establishment of an absolute Tyranny over these States" and to justify their decision to dissolve "all political connection" with Britain. But it was the preamble that was to exert the greatest influence on others as a statement of political philosophy with universal appeal. Rooted in the concept of natural rights as developed by such philosophers as Hooker, Hobbes and Locke, the preamble made these assertions:

"We hold these truths to be self-evident, that all men are created equal, that they are endowed by their Creator with certain unalienable Rights, that among these are Life, Liberty and the pursuit of Happiness. That to secure these rights, Governments are instituted among Men, deriving their just powers from the consent of the governed. That whenever any Form of Government becomes destructive of these ends it is the Right of the People to alter or to abolish it, and to institute new Government, laying its foundation on such principles and organizing its powers in such form, as to them shall seem most likely to effect their Safety and Happiness."

In conclusion, the signers, who styled themselves "the Representatives of the united States of America, in General Congress, Assembled," declared that "these United Colonies are, and of Right ought to be Free and Independent States," that as such "they have full Power to levy War, conclude Peace, contract Alliances, establish Commerce, and to do all other Acts and Things which Independent States may of right do," and that in support of this stand "we mutually pledge to each other our Lives, our Fortunes and our Sacred Honor."

Formation of State Governments

The Declaration of Independence committed the colonies to wage a war that was already under way and that would drag on for more than five years before England gave up the struggle. The Declaration also put an end to "equal time" for the many Americans who remained loyal to the King; Tories who refused to sign an oath of allegiance to the United States suffered imprisonment and confiscation of property; as many as 80,000 fled to Canada and England. At home, the Declaration put to immediate test the capacity of the patriots to govern.

As early as the fall of 1774, Massachusetts had set up a provisional government in response to the Coercive Acts. As revolutionary sentiment grew, patriots took control of provincial assemblies and conventions, and the royal governors and judges began to leave. New Hampshire adopted a constitution in January 1776, South

The Revolutionary War

Those Americans who waged and won the Revolutionary War did so under severe handicaps. Many others (one-third, said Patriot John Adams; four-fifths, said Loyalist Joseph Galloway) were opposed to the cause of independence to the end, and more than a few collaborated openly with the British. Apathy was widespread and parochialism common; as in earlier times of trouble, those who were not in the direct line of fire were often unwilling either to fight the war or to help pay for it.

As commander-in-chief, George Washington was plagued by problems of raising and maintaining effective military forces. At no time did he have many more than 30,000 men under arms, less than half of whom were regulars enlisted for three years. The balance were militia, signed up for as little as three months, who (complained Washington) "come in, you cannot tell how; go, you cannot tell when, and act, you cannot tell where, consume your provisions, exhaust your stores and leave you at last at a critical moment."

The Continental Congress assumed responsibility for prosecuting the war, but it had no power to tax or to compel actions by the states, and its requisitions for money and supplies were no better honored than those of the British had been. The war was largely financed by paper money—some $240 million in national bills and $210 million in state bills—which depreciated to the point of being "not worth a Continental." Without subsidies and loans of about $8 million from France, and that country's military intervention in 1778, the war might have been lost.

However, England also was sharply divided by the war, and the opposition increased in Parliament as time went on. For lack of recruits at home, the government was forced to hire 30,000 mercenaries in Germany to supplement the 15,000 regulars sent to America. The transport, supply and direction of those forces over a distance of 3,000 miles was even more difficult after France entered the war as America's ally.

Major developments in the war were as follows:

1775. Washington took command after Battle of Bunker Hill (June 17), and British were holed up in Boston until they evacuated the city March 17, 1776. Meanwhile, Americans under Ethan Allen and Benedict Arnold had marched on Canada, taken Montreal (Nov. 13), been badly beaten at Quebec (Dec. 31) and had withdrawn.

1776. After buildup of forces at Halifax and in Quebec, the British launched three campaigns. Clinton sailed for the Carolinas, was beaten off at Charleston June 28 and withdrew. Carleton and Burgoyne marched for Albany, but were stopped at Ticonderoga in October. Howe sailed for New York, inflicted heavy losses on Washington in several battles, and occupied the city Sept. 15 (until the end of the war). Washington retreated into New Jersey and across the Delaware, then recrossed it the night of Dec. 25 to surprise and capture 1,000 Hessians at Trenton. He then went into winter quarters at Morristown with fewer than 5,000 men.

1777. In August Howe sailed up Chesapeake Bay with 15,000 men, defeated Washington at Brandywine Creek, and occupied Philadelphia Sept. 25. Washington set up winter quarters at Valley Forge. Meanwhile, Burgoyne launched two-pronged attack on Albany, suffered a series of reverses in August and September in battles with Arnold and others, and surrendered Oct. 17 at Saratoga with 5,000 men. Burgoyne's defeat led to French-American treaty of alliance, signed Feb. 6, 1778.

1778. The British offered wide concessions to end the war short of independence, but Congress rejected the offer June 17. Clinton (Howe's successor) evacuated Philadelphia, moving back to New York. The British raided coastal towns, while George Rogers Clark seized British posts north of the Ohio, but no decisive battles were fought.

1779. The British captured Savannah Dec. 29, 1778, and took control of Georgia, but Americans under Benjamin Lincoln successfully defended Charleston. However, Lincoln's attempt to retake Savannah (with help of French fleet) failed Oct. 9. Spain joined the war against England June 21 but did not enter alliance with Americans.

1780. The war went badly for the Americans. Long unpaid and underfed, troops in Morristown mutinied. On May 12 the British captured Charleston and 5,000 troops—the worst American defeat of the war. Benedict Arnold defected to the British in September.

1781. The South was the major fighting arena. Americans under Nathaniel Greene beat Cornwallis at Cowpens, South Carolina (Jan. 17). In July Cornwallis moved north with 7,000 men to fortify Yorktown, Virginia. More than 15,000 American and French troops converged there in September; surrounded on land and sea, Cornwallis surrendered his army Oct. 17.

1782. The House of Commons resolved, March 4, to give up the struggle, Lord North resigned, and a new government asked for peace talks. Congress named John Adams (envoy to the Netherlands), John Jay (envoy to Spain), Benjamin Franklin (envoy to Paris) and Henry Laurens to negotiate jointly with the French. Jay, suspicious of the French (who supported Spanish claims in America), persuaded the others to enter separate negotiations with the British in September. A preliminary treaty was signed Nov. 30 pending Anglo-French accord.

1783. The Treaty of Paris, signed Sept. 3 (ratified by Congress Jan. 14, 1784), was a triumph for Americans. It validated independence and claims to the West, fixing the boundary with Canada along the St. Lawrence and the Great Lakes, and retained American fishing rights around Newfoundland. It also validated American private debts to England and stated that Congress would "earnestly recommend" to the states that they restore property confiscated from the Tories. At the same time, England gave West and East Florida back to Spain. The last British troops left New York Nov. 25. Washington resigned Dec. 23 to take "leave of all the employments of public life."

Carolina followed suit in March, and on May 10 the Continental Congress advised all of the colonies to form new governments. All except Massachusetts and the self-governing charter colonies of Connecticut and Rhode Island had done so by July 4, 1777, first anniversary of the signing of the Declaration of Independence. Four days later, Vermont, not previously a separate colony, declared its independence and adopted a constitution. Connecticut and Rhode Island did not get around to replacing their colonial charters by state constitutions until 1818 and 1842, respectively.

The new state constitutions of the Revolutionary period emerged in various ways. Those of South Carolina, Virginia and New Jersey were drafted by legislative bodies without explicit authorization and put into effect without popular consent. Those of New Hampshire, Georgia, Delaware, New York and Vermont were authorized but were not submitted to the voters for approval. In Maryland, Pennsylvania and North Carolina the constitutions were authorized and ratified by the voters. Only Massachusetts and New Hampshire (which wrote a new constitution in 1784 to replace the one adopted in 1776) employed what was to become the standard method of electing a constitutional convention and putting the product to a vote of the people.

Although they varied in detail, the new constitutions reflected a number of concepts held in common by Americans of the period. All were written, because the unwritten British constitution had been a source of such contention between the colonists and England. All included or were accompanied by some kind of "Bill of Rights" to secure those English liberties that George III had violated, such as freedom of speech, press and petition and the rights of habeas corpus and trial by jury. All paid tribute to the doctrine of separation of powers between the legislative, executive and judiciary, as it had been developed in England after the revolution of 1688 and expounded by Montesquieu's "Spirit of Laws" published in 1748.

Separation did not mean balance, however, and most of the constitutions betrayed the colonists' great fear of executive authority, born of their many conflicts with the Crown and the royal governors. Executive power was weakened in every state except New York, Massachusetts and New Hampshire, and the governors of only two states were given the power of veto. In most cases the state legislature appointed the judiciary, although efforts were made to protect the independence of judges by preventing their arbitrary removal.

Power under most state constitutions was lodged in the legislatures. Ten of these were bicameral (Pennsylvania, Georgia and Vermont had one house), but the lower house was predominant. Virginia's constitution provided, for example, that: "All laws shall originate in the House of Delegates, to be approved of or rejected by the Senate, or to be amended, with consent of the House of Delegates; except money bills, which in no instance shall be altered by the Senate, but wholly approved or rejected."

All of the constitutions recognized the people as sovereign, but few entrusted them with much power. The Pennsylvania constitution (copied by Vermont), written by radicals who came to power early in 1776 after a major reapportionment of the colonial assembly, was the most democratic. It replaced governor and upper chamber with an executive council from whose ranks a president was chosen. Its members could serve no more

First State Constitutions

	Date Adopted
New Hampshire (1st)	Jan. 6, 1776
South Carolina (1st)	March 26, 1776
Virginia	June 29, 1776
New Jersey	July 2, 1776
Delaware	Aug. 22, 1776
Pennsylvania	Sept. 28, 1776
Maryland	Nov. 11, 1776
North Carolina	Dec. 18, 1776
Georgia	Feb. 5, 1777
New York	April 20, 1777
Vermont*	July 8, 1777
South Carolina (2nd)	March 19, 1778
Massachusetts	June 15, 1780
New Hampshire (2nd)	June 13, 1784

* Vermont became a state in 1791.

than three years in seven while Assemblymen were limited to four years in seven, all to guard against "the danger of establishing an inconvenient aristocracy." There were no property qualifications for voting or for holding office.

Most other states adhered to prerevolutionary limits on suffrage. Ownership of some amount of property was generally required as a qualification to vote, and more was required to hold office. The property qualification for state senator in New Jersey and Maryland was 1,000 pounds, in South Carolina 2,000 pounds. Most states also imposed religious qualifications for public office.

Articles of Confederation

When Richard Henry Lee called for a declaration of independence on June 7, 1776, he proposed also that "a plan of confederation be prepared and transmitted to the respective Colonies for their consideration and approbation." On June 11 Congress agreed and named a committee of 13 (one from each colony) to undertake the task. The plan recommended, based on a draft by John Dickinson, was presented July 12, but it was not until Nov. 15, 1777, that Congress, after much debate and some revision, adopted the Articles of Confederation and Perpetual Union. *(See Appendix for text.)*

The Articles reflected the dominant motive of Americans who were rebelling against British rule—to preserve their freedoms from the encroachments of centralized power. Even as Congress was struggling with tenuous authority to prosecute the war (and it gave Washington dictatorial powers over the army in December 1776), few of the delegates or other American leaders were prepared to entrust a national government with any power that would diminish the sovereignty and independence of the states. Thus the scope of Federal authority was not a central issue in the design of the confederation.

What was at issue was the relative standing of 13 rival and jealous states. Would they be represented equally in the national legislature (as they were in the Continental Congress and as the smaller states desired) or in proportion to their population (as the larger states wished)? Cost of a national government would have to be shared, but on what basis—wealth, population or (as the southerners insisted) the white population only? States without claims to lands west of the Appalachians thought Congress should control the area; those with claims were reluctant to give them up.

As finally adopted, the Articles conferred less authority on the national government than had been proposed in the Albany Plan of Union of 1754. They did little more than legalize what Congress was already doing by sufferance of the states. Congress remained the sole organ of government; the states retained their equality in Congress, having one vote each; and of the specific powers delegated to Congress the most important could not be exercised without the assent of nine of the 13 states.

The delegated authority included the power to declare war, enter treaties and alliances, raise an army and a navy, regulate coinage and borrow money. Congress was empowered also to regulate Indian affairs, establish a postal service, and adjudicate disputes between the states. But it had no power to tax (other than to charge postage); the costs of government would be allocated to the states in proportion to the value of their land and improvements as determined by Congress. The states were also to be assigned quotas for troops "in proportion to the number of white inhabitants." But in no case did Congress have any power to compel the states to comply.

The Articles provided that Congress be composed of from two to seven delegates from each state (and from Canada if it chose to join). The delegates were to be selected annually and paid by the states, and they could serve no more than three years in any six. Members of Congress were barred from holding any Federal post for pay and were immune from arrest while in attendance and from action for anything said in debate—provisions that were later incorporated in the Constitution. A Committee of the States (with one delegate from each) was authorized to act for Congress during a recess on such matters as did not require the assent of nine states.

Congress was authorized to appoint "such other committees and civil officers as may be necessary for managing the general affairs of the United States." Following ratification, Robert Livingston was named as Secretary of Foreign Affairs, Robert Morris as Superintendent of Finance, and Gen. Benjamin Lincoln as Secretary of War. But the Articles made no provision for a Federal executive or judiciary, gave Congress no sanction by which to enforce any of its decisions, left control of taxation and tariffs with the states, and required the unanimous consent of the states to adopt any amendment.

Final ratification was delayed by the reluctance of Maryland, New Jersey and Delaware to act until the states with western claims agreed to cede them to the national government. Cession of state claims did not actually begin until 1784, but it was clear by the start of 1781 that the states would cede, and Maryland, the last holdout, ratified the Articles March 1, 1781. Congress proclaimed them to be in effect the same day.

Trials of the Confederation

Adoption of the Articles of Confederation did nothing to relieve the chaotic state of Federal finances. Of $10 million requisitioned by Congress in the first two years, the states paid in less than $1.5 million. From 1781 to 1786, Federal collections averaged half a million a year, which was barely enough to meet current expenses. After

two years as Superintendent of Finance, Robert Morris resigned in 1783, saying "our public credit is gone." The foreign debt of the United States increased from less than $8 million in 1783 to more than $10 million in 1789, plus almost $1.8 million in unpaid interest.

Congress recognized the need for some independent financial authority even before the Articles took effect. A month earlier, it had asked the states for authority to levy a duty of 5 percent on all imports. But it took unanimous agreement to amend the Articles, and the proposal died in 1782 when Rhode Island rejected it. In 1783 Congress again asked for the power to levy import duties, and this time New York refused approval.

Peace put an end to the destruction and drain of war, but it also underscored the weakness and disunity of the now sovereign and independent American states. As agreed in the peace treaty with England, Congress in 1783 "earnestly recommended" that the states restore property confiscated from the Loyalists, but few of them took any steps to do so. And instead of helping British merchants to recover their prewar debts (as the treaty obligated them to do), many of the states enacted laws to make recovery more difficult. The British, in turn, refused to evacuate several posts on the American side of the border with Canada.

The inability of Congress to force the states to comply with terms of the peace treaty contributed to the refusal of England, France and Spain to enter commercial treaties with the Confederation. Lacking any authority over trade, Congress was unable to retaliate when the British in 1783 closed Canada and the British West Indies to American shipping, and the attempts of the states to retaliate individually failed completely. The weakness of the Confederation also encouraged Spain to close the Mississippi to American ships in 1784 and to intrigue for the secession of frontier areas north of the Floridas.

Congress was equally powerless to help resolve a postwar conflict between debtors and creditors that was aggravated by a depression and a shortage of currency. Most of the states stopped issuing paper money and set out to pay off their war debts by raising taxes. At the same time, merchants and other creditors began to press for the collection of private debts. Squeezed on all sides, debtors (who were mostly farmers) clamored for relief through state laws to put off the collection of debts and to provide cheap money.

In response to this pressure, seven of the states resorted to paper money issues in 1786 during the worst of the depression. Debtors put over their entire program in Rhode Island where creditors, compelled by law to accept repayment in highly depreciated paper money, fled the state to avoid doing so. But in Massachusetts, where the commercial class was in power, the state government refused to issue paper money and pressed forward with a deflationary program of high taxes; cattle and land were seized for debts, debtors crowded the jails, and all petitions for relief were ignored.

Out of this turmoil came Shays's Rebellion of 1786, an uprising of distressed farmers in central Massachusetts led by Daniel Shays. Although the rebellion was put down by state militia in fairly short order, there was a good deal of sympathy for the rebels. Their leaders were treated leniently, and a newly elected legislature acted to meet some of their demands. But the rebellion aroused the fears of many Americans for the future, pointed up another weakness of the Confederation (for Congress had been unable to give Massachusetts any help), and gave a strong push to the gathering movement for governmental reform.

The Movement for Reform

The state of the union under the Articles of Confederation had become a source of growing concern to leading Americans well before Shays's Rebellion shook the confidence of a wider public. In voluminous correspondence beginning as early as 1780, George Washington, John Jay, Thomas Jefferson, James Madison, James Monroe and many others expressed their fear that the union forged in blood could not survive the strains of internal dissension and external weakness without some strengthening of central authority.

To Washington, writing in 1783, it was clear "that the honor, power and true interest of this country must be measured by a Continental scale, and that every departure therefrom weakens the Union, and may ultimately break the band which holds us together. To avert these evils, to form a Constitution that will give consistency, stability, and dignity to the Union and sufficient powers to the great Council of the Nation for general purposes" was a challenge to every patriot.

How to form such a Constitution was not yet clear. Opinions varied widely as to what would be "sufficient powers...for general purposes." Alexander Hamilton, in 1780 (when he was only 23), thought Congress should be given "complete sovereignty" over all but a few matters. But Congress had ignored proposals of its own committees in 1781 that it seek authority to use troops "to compel any delinquent State to fulfill its Federal engagement" and to seize "the property of a State delinquent in its assigned proportion of men and money." And when there was wide agreement on giving Congress authority to levy a Federal import duty, the effort to amend the Articles foundered on the rule of unanimity.

At Hamilton's urging, the New York assembly asked Congress in 1782 to call a general convention of the states to revise the Articles. The Massachusetts Legislature seconded the request in 1785. Congress studied the proposal but was unable to reach agreement. Then, in 1785, Virginia and Maryland worked out a plan to resolve conflicts of those two states over navigation and commercial regulations. This gave Madison the idea of calling a general meeting on commercial problems. In January 1786 the Virginia Assembly issued the call for a meeting in Annapolis the following September.

Nine states named delegates to the Annapolis Convention, but the dozen who assembled represented only five states—New York, New Jersey, Pennsylvania, Delaware and Virginia. Rather than seek a commercial agreement from so small a group, Madison and Hamilton persuaded the delegates to adopt a report, Sept. 14, that described the state of the Union as "delicate and critical." The report recommended that the states appoint commissioners to meet the next May in Philadelphia "to devise such further provisions as shall appear to them necessary to render the constitution of the Federal Government adequate to the exigencies of the Union."

The proposal was deliberately vague. Madison and Hamilton knew that many others would oppose giving the central government much more power. And some, they knew, preferred the alternative of dividing the union into two or more confederations of states with closer economic and political ties. Southerners were convinced that this was the ultimate objective of John Jay's offer to Spain to give up free navigation of the Mississippi in return for trading concessions of interest to New England. Monroe (a Virginia delegate to Congress) saw it as part of a scheme "for dismembering the Confederacy and throwing the states eastward of the Hudson into one government."

The Virginia Assembly, prodded by Madison and Washington, agreed on Oct. 16, 1786, to send delegates to Philadelphia, and six other states took similar action before Congress, on Feb. 21, 1787, moved to retain control of the situation. Its resolution endorsed the proposed convention for the "sole and express purpose of revising the Articles of Confederation and reporting to Congress and the several Legislatures" its recommendations. Officially, therefore, the convention was to be no more than advisory to Congress.

The Convention of 1787

Soon after the Philadelphia Convention opened on May 25, 1787, the delegates were asked to decide whether to try to patch up the Articles of Confederation or to ignore them and draw up a new plan of government. Congress, the state legislatures and many of the delegates expected no more than a revision of the Articles that would somehow strengthen the Confederation without altering the system of state sovereignty. But Madison and others who had worked to bring about a convention were convinced of the need for fundamental reform and for a new constitution as the only means of achieving it.

The Virginia Plan

These "nationalists" had come prepared, and on May 29 they seized the initiative. Edmund Randolph, acting for the Virginians, introduced 15 resolutions that added up to a plan for a new "National Government" of broad powers *(see Appendix for text)*. The Virginia Plan called for a "National Legislature" of two houses, one to be elected by the people and the other by members of the first; a "National Executive" to be chosen by the Legislature; and a "National Judiciary." The legislature would have power to legislate in all cases where the states were "incompetent" or would interrupt "the harmony of the United States," and to "negative" state laws contrary to the articles of union. And the states would be represented in both chambers in proportion to their wealth or white population.

The Convention moved at once into Committee of the Whole to consider the Randolph resolutions. They clearly envisaged a central government that, unlike that of the Confederation, would operate directly upon the people and independently of the states. It was to be a "national government" in contrast to the "merely Federal" system that had been tried and found wanting. What the Virginians had in mind, though, was a system in which national and state governments would exercise dual sovereignty over the people within separate and prescribed fields. Randolph said that his plan "only means to give the national government power to defend and protect itself—to take, therefore, from the respective

Details of the Convention

All of the 13 states except Rhode Island (whose upper house balked) were represented at the Federal Convention of 1787. They appointed 74 delegates in all, but only 55 attended. On May 14, when the Convention was scheduled to open at the State House in Philadelphia, only the Virginia and Pennsylvania delegates were on hand. It was May 25 before delegates from a majority of the states (seven) had arrived and the 29 present could organize. From then until the Convention finished its work on Sept. 17, the comings and goings of delegates held the average attendance to little more than 30.

Delegates. The 55 delegates who took part included many of the most distinguished men in America. Eight had signed the Declaration of Independence, seven had been governors of their states, 39 had served in Congress. More than half were college graduates, and at least 33 had been lawyers. Most of them had held prominent posts in the Revolution, and all were men of position and substance in their states. A majority were under 50 (five were under 30), and only four were over 60 years of age.

George Washington (then 55) and Benjamin Franklin (the oldest at 81) were the most influential Americans of the time. Washington, who had not wanted to be a delegate but had yielded for fear that his absence might be taken for indifference to the outcome, was the unanimous choice on May 25 to preside over the Convention, in which role he took limited but effective part in the deliberations.

Those credited with influencing most the decisions of the Convention were Gouverneur Morris and James Wilson of Pennsylvania, James Madison of Virginia and Roger Sherman of Connecticut, each of whom spoke well over 100 times. Others who took leading roles were George Mason and Edmund Randolph of Virginia, Oliver Ellsworth of Connecticut, Rufus King and Elbridge Gerry of Massachusetts, John Rutledge and Charles Pinckney of South Carolina, Alexander Hamilton of New York, John Dickinson of Delaware and William Peterson of New Jersey.

Not among the delegates were John Jay, busy as Secretary of Foreign Affairs, and America's envoys to France and England—Thomas Jefferson and John Adams. Also missing were such Revolutionary leaders as Samuel Adams, Patrick Henry (who "smelled a rat"), John Hancock, Christopher Gadsden, and Richard Henry Lee, who later wrote that "probably not one man in ten thousand in the United States had an idea that the old ship was to be destroyed."

Rules. The Convention adopted rules May 28 and 29. There was some talk of the larger states getting more votes than the smaller, but the Convention followed the Articles of Confederation in giving one vote to each state. The rule provided that seven states would constitute a quorum and that "all questions should be decided by a majority of the states which shall be fully represented." This rule was amended to permit reconsideration of any vote—a step taken many times during the Convention.

Reconsideration was made easier by a rule of secrecy providing that "nothing spoken in the House be printed, or otherwise published or communicated without leave." Most delegates agreed with Madison that secrecy was needed "to secure unbiased discussion within doors and to prevent misconceptions and misconstructions without." The press was critical, but the delegates abided by the rule. The official journal, limited to a report of formal motions and votes, was closed until 1819. Madison's shorthand notes, withheld until 1840, provided the fullest account.

Procedure. The Convention began by moving into committee of the whole to debate the Virginia resolutions, which called for a new national government composed of a bicameral legislature, an executive and a judiciary. The smaller states then rallied behind a New Jersey Plan for a modest revision of the Articles of Confederation. After that plan was defeated June 19, the members reverted to convention, and a threatened deadlock was broken by the "Great Compromise" of July 16 giving to each state an equal vote in the Senate.

On July 24 a committee of detail (Gorham of Massachusetts, Ellsworth, Wilson, Randolph and Rutledge) was appointed to draft a constitution based on agreements already reached. The Convention took a ten-day recess during which Washington went fishing near Valley Forge. The draft presented Aug. 6 included changes and additions which were discussed and refined through the following month. On Sept. 8 another committee (Johnson of Connecticut, Hamilton, Gouverneur Morris, Madison and King) was named "to revise the stile and arrange the articles which had been agreed to by the House." The final document (polished by Morris) was put before the Convention on Sept. 17.

The Signing. At this point Dr. Franklin said: "There are several parts of this Constitution which I do not at present approve, but I am not sure I shall never approve them." He would accept the Constitution, however, "because I expect no better and because I am not sure that it is not the best." And he hoped that "every member of the Convention who may still have objections to it, would, with me, on this occasion doubt a little of his own infallibility, and to make manifest our unanimity, put his name to this instrument."

Franklin then moved that the Constitution be signed as having been "Done in Convention by the unanimous consent of the States present." The motion was approved as was one final change to increase representation in the House from one member for every 40,000 inhabitants to one for every 30,000—a change supported by Washington, in his only speech of the Convention, as in the "interests of the people." The Constitution was then signed by all except three of the 42 delegates present—Mason and Randolph of Virginia and Gerry of Massachusetts. After resolving that it should be submitted to special conventions of the states "for their assent and ratification," the Convention adjourned.

Legislatures of States no more sovereignty than is competent to this end."

Such a dual system was unknown in 1787. To many delegates the term "national government" implied a unitary or consolidated regime of potentially unlimited powers that would extinguish the independence of the states. However, on May 30, with only Connecticut opposed and New York divided, they adopted Randolph's proposition "that a National Government ought to be established consisting of a supreme Legislative, Executive and Judiciary." This opening commitment by most of the delegates then present reflected the air of crisis in which they met.

The next step of the Committee of the Whole was to take up and approve several of the specific proposals of the Virginia Plan. As the debate proceeded, some members from smaller states became alarmed by the insistence of the larger states on proportional representation in both houses of the proposed Legislature. Under one formula, this would have given Virginia, Pennsylvania and Massachusetts—the three most populous states—13 of 28 seats in the Senate as well as a similar share of seats in the House. This spelled domination to those accustomed to the equality of states which prevailed in the Congress of the Confederation, and in the Convention as well.

To Luther Martin of Maryland, such a plan meant "a system of slavery which bound hand and foot ten states of the Union and placed them at the mercy of the other three." John Dickinson of Delaware declared that "we would rather submit to a foreign power than submit to be deprived of an equality of suffrage in both branches of the Legislature, and thereby be thrown under the domination of the large states." New Jersey would "never confederate" on such a basis, said William Paterson, for "she would be swallowed up" and he would "rather submit to a monarch, to a despot, than to such a fate."

The New Jersey Plan

On June 11 the Committee voted, six states to five, to constitute the Senate on the same proportional basis as the House. That decision led Paterson and others to draft a "purely Federal" alternative to the Virginia Plan. The New Jersey Plan, presented June 15 *(see Appendix for text)*, proposed amending the Articles of Confederation to give Congress authority to levy import duties and to regulate trade. It would have provided also for a plural executive to be chosen by Congress and for a Federal judiciary. It proposed that treaties and acts of Congress "shall be the supreme law," and that the executive be authorized to "call forth the power of the Confederated States" to enforce the laws if necessary. But the plan would have left each state with an equal voice in Congress and most of the attributes of sovereignty.

Paterson argued that his plan "accorded first with the powers of the Convention, and second with the sentiments of the people.... Our object is not such a Government as may be best in itself, but such a one as our constituents have authorized us to prepare and as they will approve." The nationalists rejected this concept of their responsibility; as Hamilton put it, the Union was in peril, and "to rely on and propose any plan not adequate to these exigencies, merely because it was not clearly within our powers, would be to sacrifice the means to the end."

Madison was the last to speak against the New Jersey Plan, pointing up serious problems of the Confederation for which it offered no solution. On June 19 the delegates were asked to decide whether the Randolph resolutions "should be adhered to as preferable to those of Mr. Paterson." Seven states voted yes and only three states no. That settled the issue of partial versus total reform; a clear majority of the delegates were now committed to abandoning the Articles and to drafting a new constitution.

Drafting of the Constitution

The task was to take three months. There were few points of unanimity among the 55 men participating. Delegates from the same state were frequently divided and, as a result, occasionally unable to vote. The records of the Convention also reveal that, although the nationalists won over a majority to their cause at an early stage, the original Virginia Plan was unacceptable in many of its details. The Constitution could not have been written without some degree of willingness on all sides to compromise in the interests of designing a workable and acceptable plan.

This became evident soon after defeat of the New Jersey Plan when the small states continued to demand and the large states to oppose equal representation in the Senate. On July 2 the Convention split five to five on this issue, with Georgia divided. Faced with a deadlock, the Convention named a committee to seek a compromise. It proposed on July 5 that, in return for equality of state representation in the Senate, the House be given sole power to originate money bills, which the Senate could accept or reject but not modify. This formula was finally approved July 16, five states to four, with Massachusetts divided and New York not voting because two of its three delegates had departed never to return.

Without this "Great Compromise" the Convention would have collapsed. As Madison pointed out, however, "the great division of interests" in America was not between the large and small but between the northern and southern states, partly because of climate but "principally from the effects of having or not having slaves." Although the southerners were for the most part supporters of a strong central government, they were determined to limit its power to discriminate against the South's special interests in slavery, agricultural exports and western expansion. This stand necessitated other compromises that accounted for some of the key provisions of the new plan of government.

What finally emerged Sept. 17 as the Constitution of the United States was a unique blend of national and Federal systems based on republican principles of representative and limited government. It met the basic objective of the nationalists by providing for a central government of ample powers that could function independently of the states. It also met the concerns of states' rights supporters by surrounding that government with checks and balances to prevent the tyranny of any one branch or the whole over the people or the states. And it retained the flexibility embodied in Randolph's advice "to insert essential principles only, lest the operation of government should be clogged by rendering those provisions permanent and unalterable which ought to be accommodated to times and events."

Legislative Nomenclature, 1787

The Constitutional Convention continued to speak of the "Legislature of the United States" and its "first branch" and "second branch" until these terms were changed, in the Aug. 6 report of the committee of detail, to "Congress of the United States," "House of Representatives," and "Senate." The term "Congress" was taken from the Articles of Confederation. "House of Representatives" was the name of the first branch in five states (others being called Assembly, House of Delegates and House of Commons), while the second branch was called "Senate" in all but two states.

Provisions of the Constitution relating to both House and Senate referred to "each House" in keepin with English usage. But the terms "upper house" and "lower house," also taken from English usage to denote the Senate and the House, were not included in the Constitution.

The text of the Constitution *(see Appendix)* does not follow the order in which the separate provisions were developed. The Convention moved generally from decisions on broad principles to questions of detail and precision. But the interdependent nature of the various parts of the plan made for frequent reconsideration of decisions in one area to take account of subsequent decisions in another but related area. As a result, many of the provisions were altered or added in the final weeks of the Convention. How the major provisions were developed is described in the following sections.

The Structure of Congress

The Convention's early decision that a national government, if formed, should consist of three Branches—Legislative, Executive and Judicial—was undisputed. This division of governmental functions had been recognized from early colonial times and was reflected in most of the state constitutions. The failure of the Articles of Confederation to separate the functions was generally recognized as a serious mistake. The decision as to three branches also implied broad acceptance of the principle of separation of powers, although most of the provisions of the Constitution that gave effect to the principle were adopted on practical rather than theoretical grounds.

A Bicameral Legislature. The Virginia Plan called for a legislature of two houses, according to a practice initiated by Parliament, followed by most of the colonial governments and retained by 10 of the 13 states. The Continental Congress and the Congress of the Confederation were unicameral, but once the Convention had decided to abandon the Articles there was little question that the new Congress should be bicameral. *(See box for origin of terms.)* As George Mason saw it, the minds of Americans were settled on two points—"an attachment to republican government (and) an attachment to more than one branch in the Legislature." Only Pennsylvania dissented when the Committee of the Whole voted for two houses, and the Convention confirmed the Committee's decision, June 21, by a vote of seven states to three.

Election of the House. The nationalists insisted that the new Government rest on the consent of the people rather than the state legislatures. So they held it essential that at least "the first branch" or House be elected "by the people immediately," as Madison put it. The Government "ought to possess...the mind or sense of the people at large," said James Wilson, and for that reason "the Legislature ought to be the most exact transcript of the whole society." The House "was to be the grand depository of the democratic principles of the government," said Mason.

Those who were suspicious of a national government preferred election of the House by the state legislatures. "The people immediately should have as little to do" with electing the government as possible, said Roger Sherman, because "they want information and are constantly liable to be misled." Elbridge Gerry was convinced that "the evils we experience flow from the excess of democracy," while Charles Pinckney thought "the people were less fit judges" than the legislatures to choose members of the House. Election by the legislatures was twice defeated, however, and popular election of the House was confirmed June 21 by a vote of nine states to one.

Election of the Senate. The Virginia Plan proposed that the House elect the "second branch" or Senate from persons nominated by the state legislatures. There was little support for this plan because it would have made the Senate subservient to the House. Most delegates agreed with Gouverneur Morris that it was to be the Senate's role "to check the precipitation, changeableness and excesses of the first branch." (The role of representing the states emerged later, after the decision for equal representation.) Neither was there any support for the view of Madison and Wilson that the people should elect the Senate as well as the House. Election of the Senate by the state legislatures was carried unanimously in Committee of the Whole, June 7, and confirmed June 25 by a Convention vote of nine states to two.

Basis of Representation. The Virginia Plan called for representation of the states in both House and Senate in proportion to their wealth or free population. This proposal led to the revolt of the small states, which was ended by the vote of July 16 for equal representation of the states in the Senate. But while the principle of proportional representation in the House was never seriously challenged, the idea of basing it on wealth or the free population raised questions that led to adoption of important qualifications.

To retain southern support for proportional representation in the Senate, Wilson had proposed on June 11 that the House be apportioned according to a count of the whole number of free citizens and three-fifths of all others (meaning slaves) except Indians not paying taxes. This formula (first proposed in Congress in 1783) was adopted with only New Jersey and Delaware opposed. Then on July 9 the Convention decided in another connection *(see below)* that the new Congress should have power "to regulate the number of Representatives upon the principles of wealth and number of inhabitants." Since southerners regarded slaves as property, this led northerners who wanted representation to be based on population alone to ask why slaves should be counted at all.

As a result, on July 11 the Convention voted, six states to four, to exclude blacks from the formula of June 11. At this point Gouverneur Morris proposed that the power of Congress to apportion the House according to wealth and numbers be subject to a proviso "that direct taxation shall be in proportion to representation," and the proviso was adopted without debate. The slave issue now appeared in a different light, for it seemed that the South must pay for any increases in representation it would gain by counting slaves. So the northerners dropped the opposition to the three-fifths count demanded by the southerners, and on July 13 the Convention restored that provision.

Because it was now agreed that representation was to be based solely on population (counting all whites and three-fifths of blacks), the word "wealth" was deleted from the provision adopted July 9. This resolution of the question gave five free voters in a slave state a voice in the House equivalent to that of seven free voters in a non-slave state, according to Rufus King, but it was "a necessary sacrifice to the establishment of the Constitution."

Size of Congress. The committee that recommended equal representation in the Senate on July 5 also proposed that each state have one vote in the House for every 40,000 inhabitants. This proposal precipitated the debate on representation discussed above, during which it was decided to let Congress regulate the future size of the House to allow for population changes and the admission of new states. Upon reflection, however, it was seen that under this arrangement a majority in Congress would be able to block a reapportionment and even to change the basis of representation for slaves. Northerners and southerners now agreed that "the periods and rules of revising the representation ought to be fixed by the Constitution."

Randolph was the first to propose a regular census, and on July 13 the Convention adopted the plan, finally incorporated in Article I, Section 2, linking the apportionment of Representatives to an "enumeration" every 10 years of the "whole number of free persons...and three fifths of all others." On Aug. 8 it was decided that the number of Representatives "shall not exceed one for every 40,000," a figure that was lowered to 30,000 on the last day of the Convention. Until the first census should be taken, the size of the House was fixed at 65 Representatives allotted as set forth in Article I.

The size of the Senate was fixed on July 23 when the Convention considered and adopted (with Maryland alone voting against it) a proposal that the body should "consist of two members from each state, who shall vote per capita." A proposal to allow each state three Senators had been turned down on the ground that it would penalize poorer and more distant states, and that "a small number was most convenient for deciding on peace and war," as Gorham put it. The idea that Senators should vote individually rather than as a delegation came from Gerry, who wanted to "prevent the delays and inconveniences" that had occurred in Congress under the unit rule for voting. Although this provision was at odds with the decision that the states should be equally represented in the Senate, it was accepted with little objection and included in Article I, Section 3.

Terms of Office. There was strong attachment in the Convention to the tradition of annual elections—"the only defense of the people against tyranny," according to Gerry. But Madison argued that Representatives would

need more than one year to become informed about the interests of other states, and his proposal of a three-year term for the House was adopted June 12. Many delegates still wanted more frequent elections. "The Representatives ought to return home and mix with the people," said Sherman, for "by remaining at the seat of Government they would acquire the habits of the place which might differ from those of their constituents." On reconsideration June 21, the Convention compromised on biennial elections and a two-year term for Representatives.

The delegates also changed their minds about the Senate, agreeing first to a term of seven years although the terms of state senators varied from two to a maximum of five. When this decision was reviewed, alternatives of four, six and nine years were considered. Charles Pinckney opposed six years because Senators would be "too long separated from their constituents, and will imbibe attachments different from that of the state." But having decided on biennial elections for the House, the Convention voted June 26 to make it a six-year term in the Senate with one-third of the members to be elected every two years.

Qualifications of Voters. The report of the committee of detail, Aug. 6, provided that the qualifications of electors for the House should be the same as those required by the states for "the most numerous branch" of their own legislatures. Because property and other voting qualifications varied widely from state to state, no uniform standard seemed feasible. When Gouverneur Morris proposed giving Congress power to alter the qualifications, Ellsworth replied: "The clause is safe as it is—the states have staked their liberties on the qualifications which we have proposed to confirm." A proposal by Morris and others to limit the franchise to those who owned land was rejected, and on Aug. 8 the Convention adopted the committee proposal without dissent.

Regulation of Elections. The committee of detail also proposed that the states regulate the times and places of electing Senators and Representatives, but that Congress retain the power to change the regulations. The states should not have the last word in this regard, said Madison, since "it was impossible to foresee all the abuses that might be made of the discretionary power." The Convention adopted this provision Aug. 9 but amended it Sept. 14 by adding "except as to the places of choosing Senators," who were to be elected by the state legislatures. The purpose of the change was to "exempt the seats of Government in the States from the power of Congress."

Qualifications of Members. The Convention decided in June on a minimum age of 30 for Senators and 25 for Representatives. The committee of detail added two more qualifications: United States citizenship (three years for the House, four for the Senate) and residence within the state to be represented. Fearful of making it too easy for foreigners to be elected, the Convention lengthened the citizenship requirement to seven years for Representatives and nine years for Senators, after voting down 14 years as likely (in Ellsworth's view) to discourage "meritorious aliens from emigrating to this country."

Some delegates wanted to require residence in a state for a minimum time, from one to seven years. Mason feared that "rich men of neighboring states may employ with success the means of corruption in some particular district and thereby get into the public councils after having failed in their own state." But these proposals were voted down, and it was left that "no person shall be a Representative (or Senator) who shall not, when elected, be an inhabitant of that state in which he shall be chosen."

The Convention debated the desirability of a property qualification. Most of the state constitutions required members of their legislatures to own certain amounts of property. Dickinson doubted "the policy of interweaving into a Republican Constitution a veneration of wealth," but on July 26, by a vote of eight states to three, the Convention instructed the committee of detail to draft a property qualification. As reported, this would have given Congress authority to establish "uniform qualifications...with regard to property." But when the provision was debated on Aug. 10, it was rejected and there was no further effort to include a property qualification.

There was even less disposition to include a religious qualification, although all of the states except New York and Virginia imposed such a qualification on state representatives. The Convention's outlook on this point was made clear when, in debating an oath of office on Aug. 30, the delegates adopted without dissent Charles Pinckney's proviso (which became a part of Article VI) that "no religious test shall ever be required as a qualification to any office or public trust under the United States." The only qualifications established by the Constitution for election to Congress, therefore, related to age, citizenship and residence.

Pay of Members. The Virginia Plan wanted members of the National Legislature to be paid "liberal stipends" without saying who should pay them. To the nationalists, however, one of the weaknesses of the Confederation was that Members of Congress were paid by their states. So on June 12, after substituting "fixt" for "liberal," the Committee of the Whole agreed that in the case of Representatives "the wages should be paid out of the National Treasury." But on June 22 Ellsworth moved that the states pay. Randolph opposed the change, saying it would create a dependence that "would vitiate the whole system." Hamilton agreed, saying "those who pay are the masters of those who are paid." The motion was rejected, four states to five.

When the pay of Senators was discussed on June 26, Ellsworth again moved that the states pay. Madison argued that this would make Senators "the mere agents and advocates of state interests and views, instead of being the impartial umpires and guardians of justice and general good." Ellsworth's motion was again defeated, five states to six. Despite this, the Aug. 6 report of the committee of detail provided that the pay of Senators and Representatives should be "ascertained and paid" by the states. But Ellsworth and others had now changed their minds, and on Aug. 14 the Convention voted, nine to two, to pay Members out of the National Treasury.

Whether the amount of pay should be fixed in the Constitution was another matter. To let Congress set its own wages, said Madison, "was an indecent thing and might, in time, prove a dangerous one." Ellsworth proposed five dollars a day. Others thought the decision should be left to Congress, although Sherman was afraid the Members would pay themselves too little rather than too much, "so that men ever so fit could not serve unless they were at the same time rich." On Aug. 14, however, the Convention voted to give Congress full authority to fix its own pay by law.

Eligibility to Office. Because of the attachment of several states to the theory of rotation in office, the Articles of Confederation had provided that "no person shall be capable of being a delegate for more than three years in any term of six years." This rule had forced out of Congress some of its better members and was widely criticized. The Virginia Plan proposed, nevertheless, that Members ought "to be incapable of re-election for the space of...after the expiration of their term of service, and to be subject to recall." But this provision was eliminated in Committee of the Whole, without debate or dissent, and no further effort was made to qualify the eligibility of Representatives or Senators for re-election.

Whether Members of Congress should be eligible to hold other office was debated at much greater length. Under the Articles, a delegate was not "capable of holding any office under the United States for which he, or another for his benefit, receives any salary, fees or emolument of any kind." But the Congress had appointed many delegates to diplomatic and other jobs, and the practice had created much resentment. There was also a general concern over the office-seeking propensities of state legislators. So the Virginia Plan proposed making any Member of Congress "ineligible to any office established by a particular state, or under the authority of the United States...during the term of service and for the space of...after its expiration."

Although this provision—with the time of "one year" inserted in the blank—was adopted in Committee of the Whole, June 12, the Convention reconsidered and modified it several times before the final form was approved on Sept. 3. Delegates who wanted to shut the door on appointments saw them as a source of corruption. "What led to the appointment of this Convention?" asked Mercer, and answered: "The corruption and mutability of the Legislative Councils of the States." Those opposed to too many strictures feared they would discourage good men from running for Congress. "The Legislature would cease to be a magnet to the first talents and abilities," said Charles Pinckney.

The compromise that emerged was a twofold disqualification. Members could not be appointed during their terms to Federal offices created during those terms or for which the pay was increased, and no one holding Federal office could be a Member at the same time. The provision, incorporated in Section 6 of Article I, made no reference to state office or to ineligibility following expiration of a Member's term.

Regulation of Congress. Section 5 of Article I included four provisions for the regulation of House and Senate that originated with the committee of detail and were only slightly modified in Convention.

• The provision that "Each House shall be the Judge of the Elections, Returns and Qualifications of its own Members..." was found in the constitutions of eight states and was agreed to without debate.

• The provision that "Each House may determine the Rules of its Proceedings, punish its Members for disorderly Behaviour, and, with the Concurrence of two-thirds, expel a Member" was amended to require a two-thirds vote for expulsion. The change, proposed by Madison because "the right of expulsion was too important to be exercised by a bare majority of a quorum," was approved by a unanimous vote.

• The provision that "Each House shall keep a Journal, and from time to time publish the same..." stemmed from a similar provision in the Articles. When Madison proposed giving the Senate some discretion in the matter, Wilson objected that "the people have a right to know what their agents are doing or have done, and it should not be in the option of the Legislature to conceal their proceedings." The Convention voted to require publication of the Journals of each House, but with the proviso "excepting such parts as may in their judgment require secrecy." The clause also provided for recording the "yea" and "nay" votes of Members, although some delegates objected that "the reasons governing the votes never appear along with them."

• The provision that "Neither House, during the Session of Congress, shall, without the Consent of the other, adjourn for more than three days, nor to any other Place than that in which the two Houses shall be sitting," was agreed to after brief debate. Most of the state constitutions had similar provisions, reflecting a common commitment to legislative independence born of colonial experience with the right of royal governors to suspend and dissolve the assemblies.

The Powers of Congress

The Virginia resolutions proposed that the National Legislature be empowered—

"to enjoy the Legislative Rights vested in Congress by the Confederation and moreover to legislate in all cases to which the separate States are incompetent, or in which the harmony of the United States may be interrupted by the exercise of individual Legislation;

"to negative all laws passed by the several States, contravening in the opinion of the National Legislature the articles of Union; and

"to call forth the force of the Union against any member of the Union failing in its duty under the articles thereof."

These proposals reflected the great concern of the nationalists with the powerlessness of Congress under the Confederation to protect the interests of the United States at large against the "prejudices, passions and improper views of the State Legislatures," in the words of Dickinson. Madison deplored "a constant tendency in the States to encroach on the Federal authority, to violate National treaties, to infringe the rights and interests of each other, to oppress the weaker party within their respective jurisdiction." So it seemed essential that, in addition to adequate authority to legislate for the general interests of the Union, the new national government should possess the power to restrain the states and to compel their obedience.

When these proposals were first discussed May 31, some delegates wanted an "exact enumeration" of powers before voting, but the first of the Virginia resolutions was approved after brief debate without dissent. The second, granting a power to negate state laws akin to the royal disallowance of colonial laws, was also approved "without debate or dissent." When the third resolution was called up, however, Madison moved to set it aside because he feared that "the use of force against a State would look more like a declaration of war than an infliction of punishment." Although the New Jersey Plan contained a similar provision, there was no further consideration of this power by the Convention.

On June 8, Charles Pinckney proposed that the power to nullify state laws be extended to all such laws Congress "should judge to be improper." Such an expansion would "enslave the states," said Gerry, and the motion was rejected, seven states to three. Strong opposition now developed to any power to negate state laws. Madison continued to defend it as "the most mild and certain means of preserving the harmony of the system," but Gouverneur Morris concluded that it would "disgust all the States." On July 17 the Convention reversed its earlier action by voting seven to three against the power to "negative." The problem of securing conformity of states to national law was finally resolved by adoption of a "supremacy" clause and the specific prohibition of certain state laws. *(See Judiciary below.)*

The Convention on July 17 also reconsidered the first of the Virginia resolutions. Sherman proposed as a substitute that Congress be empowered "to make laws binding on the people of the United States in all cases which may concern the common interests of the Union; but not to interfere with the Government of the individual States in any matters of internal police which respect the Government of such States only, and wherein the general welfare of the United States is not concerned." This formulation (in which the term "general welfare" made its first appearance in the Convention) seemed too restrictive to most delegates and it was rejected, eight to two. Then, by a vote of six states to four, the Convention inserted in the resolution approved May 31 the additional power to legislate "in all cases for the general interests of the Union."

When this broad grant of legislative authority was examined by the committee of detail, named "to report a Constitution conformable to the Resolutions passed by the Convention," it seemed so vague and unlimited that the committee decided to replace it with an enumeration of specified powers. Eighteen of these powers were listed in the report of Aug. 6, which also contained, for the first time, lists of powers to be denied to Congress and to the states. The various lists formed the basis for the powers and prohibitions that were finally incorporated in Sections 8, 9 and 10 of Article I of the Constitution, of which the major provisions were developed as explained in the following pages.

The Power to Tax

The committee's first proposal—that Congress "shall have the power to lay and collect taxes, duties, imposts and excises"—was adopted Aug. 16 without dissent. The Convention then became embroiled in the issue of paying off the public debt and soon amended the tax clause to provide that Congress "shall fulfill the engagements and discharge the debts of the United States and shall have the power to lay and collect taxes," etc. Butler and others objected that this provision would require Congress to redeem at face value all Government paper, including that held by "bloodsuckers who had speculated on the distresses of others and bought up securities at heavy discounts." They thought Congress should be free to buy up such holdings at less than full value.

As a result, the Convention dropped the language added to the tax clause and adopted in its place the declaration found in Article VI that "All debts contracted and engagements entered into before the adoption of this Constitution shall be as valid against the United States under this Constitution as under the Confederation." This declaration left open the question of full or partial redemption, which was to become a major issue in the First Congress.

But some delegates now thought that the power to tax should be linked explicitly to the purpose of paying the debt. Their position led to further amendment of the tax clause on Sept. 4 to provide that Congress "shall have power to lay and collect taxes, duties, imposts and excises, to pay the debts and provide for the common defense and general welfare of the United States." The further proviso in the first clause of Section 8 that "all duties, imposts and excises shall be uniform throughout the United States" had been approved earlier as a part of the effort to prevent Congress from discriminating against the commerce of any one state.

It was to be argued later that inclusion of the words "general welfare" was intended to confer an additional and unlimited power on Congress. The records of the Convention indicate, however, that when it was decided to qualify the power to tax "to pay the debts," it became necessary to make it clear that this was not the only purpose for which taxes could be levied. "To provide for the common defense and general welfare" was taken from the Articles of Confederation and used to encompass all of the other specific and limited powers vested by the Constitution in Congress.

Direct Taxes. As already noted, in settling the basis for representation in the House, the Convention had linked the apportionment of "direct taxes" as well as Representatives to a count of all whites and three-fifths of blacks. When this provision was reconsidered Aug. 20, King asked "what was the precise meaning of direct taxation" but, according to Madison, "no one answered." The only direct taxes in use at that time were land taxes and capitation or poll taxes. Because southerners feared that Congress might seek to levy a special tax on slaves, the committee of detail recommended and the Convention later adopted a further provision, incorporated in Section 9, that "No Capitation, or other direct, Tax shall be laid, unless in Proportion" to the count required by Section 2. Another limitation on the power to tax—also adopted as a concession to the South—prohibited levies on exports.

Power to Regulate Commerce

Trade among the states and with other countries was severely handicapped under the Confederation by a lack of uniformity in duties and commercial regulations. The states commonly discriminated against the products of neighboring states, incurring retaliation in kind that added to the divisiveness and suspicions of the times. To Madison and many others, it was as essential to the new plan of government that Congress have the power to regulate commerce as it was that it have the power to tax. It soon became clear, however, that the southern states would not accept a Constitution that failed to protect their vested interest in slave labor and agricultural exports from the burdensome restrictions that a Congress controlled by northerners might seek to impose.

As a result, the committee of detail proposed that Congress have the power "to regulate commerce with foreign nations and among the several states" subject to two limitations—a ban on export taxes and a prohibition against any effort to tax or outlaw the slave trade. The general power to regulate commerce was approved on Aug. 16 without dissent. (The words "and with the Indian Tribes" were added Sept. 4.) But the proposed limitations met with considerable opposition.

In keeping with mercantilist doctrines, it was common practice at that time for governments to tax exports; the idea of prohibiting such action was novel. "To deny this power is to take from the Common Government half the regulation of trade," said Wilson. It was also to deny Congress the power to menace the livelihood of the South by taxing the exports of rice, tobacco and indigo on which its economy was largely dependent. Other northerners considered this concession to the South as wise as it was necessary; Gerry said the Convention had already given Congress "more power than we know how will be exercised." On Aug. 21, by a vote of seven states to four, the Convention agreed that "No Tax or Duty shall be laid on Articles exported from any State." This provision was placed in Section 9 of Article I in the final draft.

The second limitation on the power to regulate commerce provided that no tax or duty was to be laid "on the migration or importation of such persons as the several States shall think proper to admit; nor shall such migration or importation be prohibited." The limitation was designed to meet the South's objection to any interference with the slave trade, although those words were carefully avoided. Luther Martin thought it was "inconsistent with the principles of the Revolution and dishonorable to the American character to have such a feature in the Constitution." But most other delegates, including those opposed to slavery, argued that it was a political rather than a moral issue.

Some northerners, as well as southerners, agreed with Ellsworth that "the morality or wisdom of slavery" should be left to the states to determine. "Let us not intermeddle," he said, predicting that "slavery, in time, will not be a speck in our country." Many others agreed with Mason that the "infernal traffic" in slaves was holding back the economic development of the country, and that for this reason the national government "should have power to prevent the increase of slavery." Since the provision reported by the committee of detail was clearly unacceptable to many delegates, a committee was named to seek a compromise.

It now proposed that Congress be barred from prohibiting the slave trade until 1800, but that it have power to levy a duty on slaves as on other imports. Both provisions were approved Aug. 25, the first by a vote of seven states to four after the year 1800 had been changed to 1808, and the second after limiting the duty to $10. So the power of Congress to regulate commerce was further limited by these provisions respecting slaves, which became the first clause of Section 9 of Article I.

Still another limit on the commerce power, sought by the South and recommended by the committee of detail, would have required a two-thirds vote of both House and Senate to pass a navigation act. England had used such laws to channel colonial imports and exports into British ships and ports, and southerners now feared that the North, where shipping was a major interest, might try to monopolize the transport of their exports (then largely confined to English vessels) by a law requiring them to be carried aboard American ships.

Northern delegates were strongly opposed to the two-thirds proposal, and in working out the compromise on the slave trade succeeded in having it dropped. As a result, Charles Pinckney moved to require a two-thirds vote of both houses to enact any commercial regulation. This motion was rejected Aug. 29, seven states to four, and the Convention confirmed the decision to drop the proposed two-thirds rule for navigation acts. Mason (one of three who refused to sign the Constitution) later argued that a bare majority of Congress should not have the power to "enable a few rich merchants in Philadelphia, New York and Boston to monopolize the staples of the Southern States."

A relatively minor limitation on the power to regulate commerce was adopted to allay the fear of Maryland that Congress might require ships traversing Chesapeake Bay to enter or clear at Norfolk or another Virginia port in order to simplify the collection of duties. As approved Aug. 31 and added to Section 9, it provided that "No Preference shall be given by any Regulation of Commerce or Revenue to the Ports of one State over those of another; nor shall Vessels bound to or from one State be obliged to enter, clear or pay Duties in another."

War and Related Powers

The Articles of Confederation had given Congress the "sole and exclusive right and power of determining on peace and war." The committee of detail proposed giving to the new Congress as a whole the power to "make war" and to the Senate alone the power to make treaties. The treaty power was later divided between the President and the Senate. But in discussing the war power, Aug. 17, Charles Pinckney was for giving it to the Senate since "it would be singular for one authority to make war, and another peace." On the other hand, Butler thought the war power should rest with the President, "who will have all the requisite qualities and will not make war but when the Nation will support it." Neither view drew any support, and the Convention voted to give Congress the power "to declare war." The word "declare" had been substituted for "make" to leave the President free to repel a sudden attack. As Sherman put it, "The Executive should be able to repel, and not commence, war."

On Aug. 18, the Convention agreed to give Congress the power "to raise and support Armies," "to provide and maintain a Navy," and "to make Rules for the Government and Regulation of the land and naval Forces." All were taken from the Articles of Confederation. Gerry, voicing the old colonial fears of a standing army, wanted a proviso that "in time of peace" the army should consist of no more than two or three thousand men, but his motion was unanimously rejected. On Sept. 5, however, the Convention added to the power to "raise and support Armies" the proviso "but no Appropriation of Money to that Use shall be for a longer Term than two Years." This was intended to quiet fears similar to those that had led the British to require annual appropriations for the army.

The Convention approved without dissent the power, proposed by the committee of detail and included in Section 8, "to provide for calling forth the Militia to execute the Laws of the Union, suppress Insurrections and repel Invasions." But a further proposal by Mason that Congress have power to regulate the militia alarmed the defenders of state sovereignty. To Gerry, this was "the last point remaining to be surrendered." Others argued that the states would never agree "to give the militia out of their hands."

The shortcomings of the militia during the Revolutionary War were a bitter memory to most of the delegates, however, and they shared the practical view of Madison that "as the greatest danger to liberty is from large standing armies, it is best to prevent them by an effectual provision for a good militia." So on Aug. 23 the Convention adopted the provision, as later incorporated in Section 8, giving Congress power "to provide for organizing, arming, and disciplining the Militia, and for governing such Part of them as may be employed in the Service of the United States...."

Miscellaneous Powers

The committee of detail proposed that Congress retain the power granted in the Articles "to borrow money and emit bills on the credit of the United States." But state emissions of paper money in 1786 had contributed greatly to the alarms that had led to the calling of the Convention, and most delegates agreed with Ellsworth that this was a "favorable moment to shut and bar the door against paper money." So the words "and emit bills" were struck out, with only two states dissenting, before this provision was approved Aug. 16.

Most of the other powers of Congress specified in Section 8 of Article I were derived from the Articles of Confederation or included as appropriate to the new plan of government, and were approved with little debate or dissent. This was true of provisions respecting naturalization and bankruptcy, coinage, counterfeiting, post offices, copyrights, inferior tribunals, piracies, and the seat of government. It was true also of the final provision of Section 8—proposed by the committee of detail and adopted Aug. 20 without debate—which was to be dubbed the "sweeping clause" of the Constitution.

That clause authorized Congress "to make all Laws which shall be necessary and proper for carrying into Execution the foregoing Powers, and all other Powers vested by this Constitution in the Government of the United States, or in any Department or Officer thereof." The intent of this grant was simply to enable Congress to enact legislation giving effect to the specified powers. No member of the Convention suggested that it was meant to confer some power in addition to those previously specified. But the meaning of the clause and of the words "necessary and proper" was to become the focus of the continuing controversy between broad and strict constructionists of the Constitution that began with passage by the First Congress of a law to create a national bank.

Special Case of Money Bills

The committee named to resolve the issue of equal vs. proportional representation in the Senate proposed as a compromise that each state have one vote in the Senate, but that the House originate all bills for raising and appropriating money and paying government salaries, and that the Senate be denied the right to amend such bills. Included in the proposal was the phrase that "No money shall be drawn from the public Treasury, but in pursuance of appropriations to be originated in the first branch." Seven states at this time required that money bills originate in the lower house, but only four of those states forbade amendment by the upper house. Some delegates objected that such a provision would be "degrading" to the Senate, but it was approved July 6, five states to three.

The committee of detail phrased the provision as follows: "All bills for raising or appropriating money, and for fixing the salaries of the officers of Government, shall originate in the House of Representatives, and shall not be altered or amended by the Senate." Madison was for striking the entire provision as likely to promote "injurious altercations" between House and Senate; others insisted that it was necessary because the people "will not agree that any but their immediate representatives shall meddle with their purse." The Convention's division on the question reflected contrasting concepts of the Senate as likely to be the most responsible branch or the most aristocratic one, to be strengthened or checked accordingly.

On Aug. 8 the Convention reversed itself, voting seven states to four to drop the provision. Further debate, however, underscored the importance of reaching a compromise, and the one finally proposed was adopted Sept. 8, nine to two. It provided that "All bills for raising revenue shall originate in the House of Representatives, and shall be subject to alterations and amendments by the Senate; no money shall be drawn from the Treasury but in consequence of appropriations made by law." The first sentence, slightly revised, was incorporated in the final draft as the first clause of Section 7, while the second sentence was made one of the limitations on the powers of Congress listed in Section 9 of Article I.

The Constitution thus gave the House exclusive power to originate any bill involving taxes or tariffs of any kind, but it did not extend that power to appropriation bills. However, the House assumed the additional power, on the basis of the consideration it had received in the Convention, and it became the recognized prerogative of the House to originate spending as well as revenue bills.

Admission of New States

As early as 1780, the Continental Congress had resolved that lands ceded to the United States "shall be disposed of for the common benefit of the United States, and be settled and formed into distinct republican States, which shall become members of the Federal Union, and have the same rights of sovereignty, freedom and independence as the other States." By 1786 the Congress of the Confederation was in possession of all land south of Canada, north of the Ohio, west of the Alleghenies and east of the Mississippi. Provisions for governing this great territory were laid down by Congress in the Northwest Ordinance of July 13, 1787.

The Ordinance provided that, upon attaining a population of 5,000 free male inhabitants of voting age, the territory would be entitled to elect a legislature and send a nonvoting delegate to Congress. It provided also that no less than three nor more than five states were to be formed out of the territory. Each state was to have at least 60,000 free inhabitants to qualify for admission to

the Union "on an equal footing with the original States in all respects whatever." And the Ordinance declared that "there shall be neither slavery nor involuntary servitude in the said territory...."

As this far-sighted plan was being approved in New York by the Congress of the Confederation, Gouverneur Morris and other eastern delegates to the Constitutional Convention in Philadelphia were arguing strongly against equality for the new states. "The busy haunts of men, not the remote wilderness, are the proper school of political talents," said Morris. "If the western people get the power into their hands, they will ruin the Atlantic interests. The back members are always most adverse to the best measures." Morris agreed with Gerry that the number of new states to be admitted should be limited "in such a manner that they would never be able to outnumber the Atlantic States."

Among those of an opposing view were the delegates of Virginia and North Carolina, whose western lands were to become Kentucky and Tennessee. Mason argued that the western territories "will either not unite with or will speedily revolt from the Union, if they are not in all respects placed on an equal footing." In time, he thought, they might well be "both more numerous and more wealthy" than the seaboard states. Madison was certain that "no unfavorable distinctions were admissible, either in point of justice or policy."

In the light of this debate, the committee of detail proposed on Aug. 6 that Congress have the power to admit new states "with the consent of two-thirds of the members present in each House" (the Articles of Confederation required the consent of nine states) and, in the case of a state formed from an existing state, the consent of the legislature of that state. New states were to be admitted, moreover, "on the same terms with the original States." But when this proposal was considered Aug. 29, the Convention adopted a motion by Morris to strike out the provision for equality.

Morris and Dickinson then offered a new draft, eliminating the condition of a two-thirds vote, which was adopted and became the first clause of Section 3 of Article IV. It provided simply that new states "may be admitted" by Congress, subject to the consent of the state legislatures where concerned. Although this provision of the Constitution was silent as to the status of new states, Congress was to adhere in practice to the principle of equality in admitting them.

The Convention then adopted the provision governing territories set out in the second clause of Section 3 of Article IV. Madison had first proposed adding such a provision to the Constitution to give a legal foundation to the Northwest Ordinance, since the Articles of Confederation had given Congress no explicit power to legislate for territories. A proviso ruling out prejudice to "any claims of the United States or of any particular state" was added because some delegates feared that, without it, the terms on which new states were admitted might favor the claims of some state to vacant lands ceded by Britain.

Power of Impeachment

It was decided early in the Convention that the Executive should be "removable on impeachment and conviction of malpractice or neglect of duty." Who should impeach and try him, however, depended on how he was to be chosen. So long as Congress was to elect the President—and that decision stood until Sept. 4—few delegates were willing to give Congress the additional power to remove him. The final decision to have the President chosen by Presidential electors helped to resolve the problem.

The Virginia Plan called for the National Judiciary to try "impeachments of any National officers," without specifying who would impeach. Because all of the state constitutions vested that power in the lower house of the assembly, the committee of detail proposed removal of the President on impeachment by the House and conviction by the Supreme Court "of treason, bribery or corruption." No action was taken on this proposal until the special committee, in advancing the plan for Presidential electors, suggested that the Senate try all impeachments and that conviction require the concurrence of two-thirds of the Members present.

When this plan was debated Sept. 8, Charles Pinckney opposed trial by the Senate on the ground that if the President "opposes a favorite law, the two Houses will combine against him, and under the influence of heat and faction throw him out of office." But the Convention adopted the formula for impeachment by the House, trial by the Senate, and conviction by a two-thirds vote. It also extended the grounds for impeachment from treason and bribery to "other high crimes and misdemeanors" and made the Vice President and other civil officers similarly impeachable and removable. These provisions were incorporated in Sections 2 and 3 of Article I and in Section 4 of Article II.

Limits on Powers of Congress

Section 9 of Article I as finally adopted imposed eight specific limitations on the powers of Congress. Five of the limitations—those relating to the slave trade, capitation taxes, export taxes, preference among ports, and appropriations—have been discussed in connection with the powers to tax, to regulate commerce and to originate money bills. The others were adopted as follows:

• On Aug. 28, Charles Pinckney moved to adopt a provision of the Massachusetts Constitution that barred suspension of the writ of habeas corpus except "on the most urgent occasions" and then for a period not to exceed one year. This was amended and adopted to provide that "the Privilege of the Writ of Habeas Corpus shall not be suspended, unless when in Cases of Rebellion or Invasion the public Safety may require it."

• On Aug. 22, Gerry proposed a prohibition on the passage of bills of attainder and ex post facto laws. Some delegates objected that such a provision would imply "an improper suspicion" of Congress and was "an unnecessary guard." The Convention agreed, however, that "No Bill of Attainder or ex post facto Law shall be passed." A later motion by Mason to strike out ex post facto laws (on the ground that the ban might prevent Congress from redeeming the debt at less than face value) was unanimously rejected.

• On Aug. 23 the Convention adopted the two provisions that make up the final clause of Section 9, both of which were taken from the Articles of Confederation. The bar to titles of nobility was proposed by the committee of detail. The bar to acceptance of "emolument, office or title" from foreign governments without the consent of

Congress was urged by Pinckney to help keep American officials "independent of external influence."

Pinckney and others proposed adding to the Constitution a number of provisions similar to those contained in the Bills of Rights of the various states. On Sept. 12, Gerry moved to appoint a committee to draft a Bill of Rights, but 10 states voted no. Anxious to complete their work and return home, the delegates were in no mood to spend additional time on something most of them believed to be unnecessary, since none of the powers to be vested in Congress seemed to countenance legislation that might violate individual rights. However, omission of a Bill of Rights became a major issue in seeking ratification of the Constitution and led to assurances that it would be amended promptly to include the missing guarantees.

The Executive

No question troubled the Convention more than the place to give the Executive in the new plan of government. The office did not exist under the Articles of Confederation, which placed the executive function in Congress. A long-standing fear of executive authority had led Americans "to throw all power into the Legislative vortex," as Madison put it, and under most of the state constitutions the Executives were indeed "little more than cyphers, the Legislatures omnipotent." How much more authority and independence to give the National Executive remained in dispute until the very end of the Convention.

The Virginia Plan had in view a National Executive chosen by the National Legislature for a fixed term, ineligible for reappointment, and empowered with "a general authority to execute the National laws" as well as "the Executive rights vested in Congress by the Confederation." Debate on these proposals disclosed a spectrum of views ranging from that of Sherman, who thought the Executive should be "nothing more than an institution for carrying the will of the Legislative into effect," to that of Gouverneur Morris, who felt the Executive should be "the guardian of the people" against legislative tyranny.

Until September, the Convention favored a single executive chosen by Congress for one term of seven years, whose powers would be limited by the fact that Congress would appoint judges and ambassadors and make treaties. This plan for legislative supremacy was then abandoned for the more balanced one that was finally adopted and incorporated in Article II of the Constitution. The President would be chosen by electors for a four-year term without limit as to re-election, and he would have the power to make all appointments subject to confirmation by the Senate and to make treaties subject to approval by two-thirds of the Senate. Major provisions of Article II were developed as related below.

A Single Executive. Randolph, who presented the Virginia Plan, opposed a single Executive as "the foetus of monarchy" and proposed three persons, who, Mason thought, should be chosen from the northern, middle and southern states. But Wilson foresaw "nothing but uncontrolled, continued and violent animosities" among three persons; a single executive, he said, would give "most energy, dispatch and responsibility to the office." On June 4, the delegates voted for a single executive, seven states to four, and the Convention confirmed the decision July 17 without dissent.

The committee of detail then proposed that "the Executive Power of the United States shall be vested in a single person" to be called the President and to have the title of "His Excellency." These provisions were adopted Aug. 24 without debate, but in drafting the final document the committee of style dropped the title and provided simply that "the Executive Power shall be vested in a President of the United States of America." The omission from the Constitution of any title other than President helped to defeat a proposal in the First Congress that he be addressed as "His Highness."

Method of Election, Term of Office. These questions were closely related. If Congress were to choose the President, most delegates thought he should have a fairly long term and be ineligible for reappointment. For as Randolph put it, "if he should be reappointable by the Legislature, he will be no check on it." But if the President was to be chosen in some other manner, a shorter term with re-eligibility was generally acceptable. Thus the method of election was the key question.

The Convention first decided that Congress should choose the President for a single seven-year term. On reflection, however, some delegates thought this would not leave him sufficiently independent. Wilson proposed election by electors chosen by the people, but Gerry considered the people "too little informed of personal characters" to choose electors, and the proposal was rejected, eight to two. Gerry himself proposed that the Governors of the states pick the President to avoid the corruption he foresaw in having Congress choose him, but this plan also was rejected.

Several other methods were proposed, and at one point the delegates agreed on choice by electors chosen by the state legislatures. But this decision was soon reversed. However, when Morris on Aug. 24 renewed Wilson's original proposal for electors chosen by the people, only six states were opposed and five were in favor. Three of the latter were smaller states that had opposed an earlier decision to have the Senate and the House ballot jointly when electing a President, thereby giving the large states a bigger voice in making the selection.

All of the questions concerning the President were then reconsidered by a special committee on postponed matters, whose report of Sept. 4 recommended most of the provisions that were finally adopted. According to Morris, the committee rejected choice of the President by Congress because of "the danger of intrigue and faction" and "the opportunity for cabal." Instead, it proposed that he be chosen by electors equal in number to the Senators and Representatives from each state, who would be chosen as each state decided. They would vote by ballot for two persons, at least one of whom could not be an inhabitant of their state. The one receiving a majority of the electoral votes would become President, the one with the next largest vote would become Vice President. In the event of a tie, or if no one received a majority, the Senate would decide.

The plan provided for a four-year term with no restriction as to re-election; shifted from the Senate to the President the power to appoint ambassadors and judges and to make treaties subject to Senate approval (see below), and gave the Senate instead of the Supreme Court the power to try impeachments. This realignment of powers between the President and the Senate appealed to the small states because it was generally assumed that the Senate (in which each state was to be represented equally) would have the final say in choosing the President in most cases.

For the same reason, however, some delegates now feared that the combination of powers to be vested in the Senate would (in Randolph's words) "convert that body into a real and dangerous aristocracy." Sherman thereupon proposed moving the final election of the President from the Senate to the House, with the proviso that each state have one vote. The change, which preserved the influence of the small states while easing the fears expressed about the Senate, was quickly adopted, as was the rest of the electoral plan and the four-year term without limit as to re-eligibility.

Qualifications. The committee of detail first proposed that a President be at least 35 years of age, a citizen, and an inhabitant of the United States for 21 years, just as age, citizenship and minimum period of residence were the only qualifications stipulated for Senators and Representatives. The special committee added the qualification that the President must be "a natural born citizen or a citizen at the time of the adoption of this Constitution," and it reduced the time of residence within the United States to at least 14 years "in the whole." The phrase "in the whole" was dropped by the committee of style in drafting the final provision in Section 1 of Article II, which was also adjusted to make it clear that the qualifications for President applied equally to the Vice President.

The Vice President. No such office was contemplated by the Convention until Sept. 4, when the special committee proposed that a Vice President, chosen for the same term as the President, serve as ex officio President of the Senate. (A vice president or lieutenant governor served in a similar capacity in four of the 13 states.) The proposal was designed to provide a position for the runner-up in the electoral vote, and to give the Senate an impartial presiding officer without depriving any state of one of its two votes.

When this proposal was debated Sept. 7, Mason objected that "it mixed too much the Legislative and the Executive." Gerry thought it tantamount to putting the President himself at the head of the Senate because of "the close intimacy that must subsist between the President and the Vice President." But Sherman noted that "if the Vice President were not to be President of the Senate, he would be without employment." The Convention then adopted the proposal with only Massachusetts opposed. The provision that the Vice President "shall be President of the Senate, but shall have no Vote unless they be equally divided" was placed in Section 3 of Article I.

The Convention never discussed the role of the Vice President as successor to the President in the event of the latter's removal by death or otherwise. It seems to have contemplated that he would merely perform the duties of President until another was elected. Thus the special committee proposed that in case of the President's removal (by impeachment), "death, absence, resignation or inability to discharge the powers or duties of his office, the Vice President shall exercise those powers and duties until another President be chosen, or until the inability of the President be removed."

This language was revised by the committee of style to provide that "in case of the removal of the President from office, or of his death, resignation, or inability to discharge the powers and duties of the said office, the same shall devolve on the Vice President." The revised wording, incorporated in Article II, left it unclear as to whether it was the "said office" or the "powers and duties" that were to "devolve" on the Vice President. The right of the Vice President to assume the office of President was first asserted by John Tyler in 1841 and became the established practice.

There remained the question of providing for the office in the event both men were removed. Randolph proposed that Congress designate an officer to "act accordingly until the time of electing a President shall arrive." Madison objected that this would prevent an earlier election, so it was agreed to substitute "until such disability be removed, or a President shall be elected." The committee of style ignored this change, so the Convention voted on Sept. 15 to restore it. The final provision, authorizing Congress to designate by law an officer to "act as President" until "a President shall be elected," was joined to the earlier provision concerning the Vice President in Article II.

The President's Powers

Initially, the Convention conferred only three powers on the President—"to carry into effect the National laws," "to appoint to offices in cases not otherwise provided for," and to veto bills. The committee of detail proposed a number of additional powers drawn from the state constitutions, most of which were adopted with little discussion or change. This was true of provisions (placed in Section 3 of Article II) for informing Congress "of the State of the Union" and recommending legislation, for convening and adjourning Congress, for receiving ambassadors, and for seeing "that the Laws be faithfully executed."

The Convention also agreed without debate that "the President shall be Commander in Chief of the Army and Navy" and of the militia when called into national service; almost all of the state constitutions vested a similar power in the state executives. The power of the President "to grant reprieves and pardons except in cases of impeachment" was likewise approved, although Mason argued that Congress should have this power while Randolph wanted to bar pardons for treason as "too great a trust" to place in the President. These two provisions were included in Section 2 of Article II.

Power to Appoint. The appointive powers of the President were limited until September to "cases not otherwise provided for." The Virginia Plan had proposed that judges be appointed by the legislature (a practice followed in all except three states), but the Convention voted to give the power to the Senate alone as the "less numerous and more select body." In July the delegates considered and rejected alternative proposals that judges be appointed by the President alone, by the President with the advice and consent of the Senate, and by the President unless two-thirds of the Senate should disagree.

All this was changed when, on Sept. 7, the Convention adopted the proposal of the special committee that the President appoint ambassadors and other public ministers, justices of the Supreme Court and all other officers of the United States "by and with the Advice and Consent of the Senate." This power (incorporated in Section 2) was further qualified Sept. 15 by requiring that

---

The Cabinet

In 1787 eight states had a Privy Council to advise the Governor, and the idea of providing for a similar body to advise the President was discussed at length in the Convention. Gerry and others thought it would "give weight and inspire confidence" in the Executive. To Franklin, "a Council would not only be a check on a bad President, but be a relief to a good one." But Gouverneur Morris saw it in a different light: "Give him an able Council and it will thwart him; a weak one, and he will shelter himself under their sanction." On Aug. 22 the committee of detail submitted the following proposal (first offered by Morris and Charles Pinckney) to the Convention:

"The President of the United States shall have a Privy Council which shall consist of the President of the Senate, the Speaker of the House of Representatives, the Chief Justice of the Supreme Court, and the principal officer in the respective departments of Foreign Affairs, Domestic Affairs, War, Marine, and Finance, as such departments of office shall from time to time be established, whose duty it shall be to advise him in matters respecting the execution of his office, which he shall think proper to lay before them; but their advice shall not conclude him, nor affect his responsibility for the measures which he shall adopt."

The Convention did not vote on the foregoing proposal. The Sept. 4 report of the special committee proposed only that the President "may require the Opinion in writing of the principal Officer in each of the executive Departments, upon any Subject relating to the Duties of their respective Offices." This provision, adopted Sept. 7 (after the Convention had rejected, eight states to three, a proposal by Mason for an Executive Council to be appointed by Congress), was included among the powers of the President set out in Section 2 of Article II.

The word "Cabinet" was not used in the Convention or the Constitution. But as that institution developed under Washington and later Presidents, it conformed to the limited role that had been envisioned in the Morris-Pinckney proposal for a Privy Council.

---

offices not otherwise provided for "be established by law" and by authorizing Congress to vest appointment of inferior officers in the President, the courts or the heads of departments. Nothing was said of a power of removal from office—a power that was to become a much-argued issue.

Treaty Power. The proposal that the Senate alone have the power to make treaties (first put forward by the committee of detail) drew considerable opposition. Mason said it would enable the Senate to "sell the whole country by means of treaties." Madison thought the President, representing the whole people, should have the power. Morris argued for a provision that "no treaty shall be binding...which is not ratified by a law." Southern delegates were especially concerned to prevent abandonment by treaty of free navigation of the Mississippi.

The issue was referred to the special committee on postponed matters, which recommended vesting the President with the power to make treaties subject to the advice

The Two-Thirds Rule

To the men who drafted the Constitution, a major weakness of the Articles of Confederation was the rule that nine (or two-thirds) of the 13 states must concur in all important decisions. So there was broad agreement on the general principle (embodied in Article I, Section 5) that in the two Houses of Congress "a Majority of each shall constitute a Quorum to do Business." With respect to certain powers, however, a requirement for something greater than a majority seemed essential to a balanced design of government.

As finally approved, the Constitution imposed a two-thirds requirement in six instances. No one was to be convicted on impeachment nor could a treaty be made without the concurrence of two-thirds of the Senators "present." Neither House could expel a Member without "the concurrence of two-thirds." If vetoed, a bill could be enacted by the votes of two-thirds of both Houses. Congress could propose amendments to the Constitution "whenever two-thirds of both Houses shall deem it necessary." And if the House was called on to ballot for President, a quorum was to "consist of a Member or Members from two-thirds of the States...."

The Convention also considered but rejected proposals to require the consent of two-thirds of both Houses to the admission of new states and to the enactment of laws to regulate foreign commerce (leaving these matters to be decided by majority vote), and to permit export taxes to be levied by a two-thirds vote of both Houses (leaving a flat prohibition on such taxes).

Of the provisions included in the Constitution, only those relating to the Senate's role in trying impeachments and approving treaties made it clear that the decision rested with two-thirds of the Members "present," not with two-thirds of the entire membership. There is persuasive evidence that the latter interpretation was intended by the delegates for the provisions relating to vetoes, expulsion of Members, and constitutional amendments. However, in the absence of an explicit requirement to that effect, Congress assumed that two-thirds of Members "present" was likewise sufficient for a decision in those cases—an assumption sustained by the Supreme Court in 1919 (248 U.S. 276) and 1920 (253 U.S. 380).

and consent of two-thirds of the Senators present. The latter provision provoked extended debate. Motions were made and rejected to strike out the two-thirds requirement, to require consent of two-thirds of all Members of the Senate, to require a majority of the whole number of Senators, to provide that "no treaty should be made without previous notice to the Members and reasonable time for their attending."

On Sept. 7 the Convention voted to except peace treaties from the two-thirds rule. Madison then moved to authorize two-thirds of the Senate alone to make a peace treaty, arguing that the President "would necessarily derive so much power and importance from a state of war

that he might be tempted, if authorized, to impede a treaty of peace." The motion was rejected, but after further debate on the advantages and disadvantages of permitting a majority of the Senate to approve a peace treaty, the Convention reversed itself and made all treaties subject to the concurrence of two-thirds of the Senators present.

Veto Power. The Virginia Plan had proposed joining the Judiciary with the Executive in exercising the power to veto acts of the Legislature, subject to repassage. Because it was expected that the Judiciary might have to pass on the constitutionality of legislation, most delegates thought it improper to give the Judiciary a share of the veto power, and the proposal was rejected. Wilson and Hamilton favored giving the Executive an absolute veto, but on June 4 the delegates voted, eight states to two, for Gerry's motion (based on the Massachusetts constitution) for an Executive veto that could be overridden if two-thirds of each branch of the Legislature so voted.

When this provision was reconsidered on Aug. 15, it was in the context of a plan to lodge in Congress the power to elect the President, to impeach him, and to appoint judges. Many delegates now agreed with Wilson that such an arrangement would not give "a sufficient self-defensive power either to the Executive or Judiciary Department," and the Convention voted to require a vote of three-fourths of each House to override a veto. But on Sept. 12, after having adopted the Presidential elector plan and other changes proposed by the special committee, the Convention restored the two-thirds provision.

The veto power was incorporated in Section 7 of Article I, setting out the procedure for the enactment of a bill with or without the President's signature. This section also made provision for the "pocket veto" of a bill when "the Congress by their Adjournment prevent its return, in which Case it shall not become Law." Although some delegates indicated a belief that the two-thirds provision was intended to apply to the entire membership of the House and Senate, a two-thirds vote of those present came to be accepted in practice.

The Judiciary

Article III of the Constitution, relating to "the judicial Power of the United States," was developed in the Convention with relative ease. The Virginia Plan called for "one or more supreme tribunals" and inferior tribunals to be appointed by the National Legislature and to try all cases involving crimes at sea, foreigners and citizens of different states, "collection of the National revenue," impeachments, and "questions which may involve the national peace and harmony." The Convention went on to spell out the jurisdiction of these courts in greater detail, but the only basic changes made in the plan were to vest the Senate and finally the President with the power to appoint judges, and to transfer the trial of impeachments from the Supreme Court to the Senate.

"Inferior Tribunals." The delegates agreed to one Supreme Court without debate, but some objected to establishing any lower courts. Rutledge thought that the state courts should hear all cases in the first instance, "the right of appeal to the Supreme National Tribunal being sufficient to secure the National rights and uniformity of judgments." Sherman deplored the expense.

But Madison argued that without lower courts "dispersed throughout the Republic, with final jurisdiction in many cases, appeals would be multiplied to an oppressive degree." Randolph said the state courts "cannot be trusted with the administration of the National laws." As a compromise, the Convention agreed to permit Congress to decide whether to "ordain and establish" inferior courts.

Appointment of Judges. The proposal that the National Legislature appoint the judiciary was based on similar provisions in most of the state constitutions. Wilson, arguing that "intrigue, partiality and concealment" would result from such a method, proposed appointment by the President. Madison urged appointment by the Senate as "a less numerous and more select body," and this plan was approved June 13. A proposal that the President appoint judges "by and with the advice and consent of the Senate" was defeated by a tie vote July 18, but that was the method finally adopted in September as a part of the compromise that also moved the trial of impeachments from the Supreme Court to the Senate.

Tenure of Judges. Both the Virginia Plan and the New Jersey Plan provided that judges would hold office "during good behaviour"—a rule long considered essential to maintaining the independence of the Judiciary. When this provision was considered Aug. 27, Dickinson proposed that judges "may be removed by the Executive on the application by the Senate and the House of Representatives." Others objected strongly, Wilson contending that "the Judges would be in a bad situation, if made to depend on every gust of faction which might prevail in two branches of our Government." Only Connecticut voted for the proposal, and the Convention agreed to tenure during good behavior.

Jurisdiction. Most of the provisions embodied in Section 2 of Article III, specifying the cases to which "the judicial Power shall extend," and in which cases the Supreme Court would have original and in which cases appellate jurisdiction, were set out in the Aug. 6 report of the committee of detail and adopted by the Convention on Aug. 27 with little change or debate. The most important change was made in the committee's first provision, extending jurisdiction to "all cases arising under the laws" of the United States, when the Convention voted to insert the words "the Constitution and" before "the laws." This made it clear that the Supreme Court was ultimately to decide all questions of constitutionality, whether arising in state or Federal courts.

Article III did not explicitly authorize the Court to pass on the constitutionality of Acts of Congress, but the Convention clearly anticipated the exercise of that power as one of the acknowledged functions of the courts. Several delegates noted that state courts had "set aside" laws in conflict with the state constitutions. The Convention debated at great length (and rejected four times) a proposal to join the Court with the President in the veto power; Wilson favored it because "laws may be unjust, may be unwise, may be dangerous, may be destructive, and yet may not be so unconstitutional as to justify the Judges in refusing to give them effect." Mason agreed that the Court "could declare an unconstitutional law void." No delegate denied the power, and only two disapproved of it.

In that connection, the Convention never acted on a proposal by Charles Pinckney (taken from the Massachusetts constitution) that the President, the Senate and the House each "shall have authority to require the opinions of the Supreme Judicial Court upon important questions of law and upon solemn occasions." Such a provision might have forestalled the enactment of many laws that later were held by the Court to be unconstitutional.

Supremacy Clause. The role of the Judiciary in determining the constitutionality of laws was also implicit in the provision, incorporated in Article VI, which asserted that the Constitution, the laws and the treaties of the United States "shall be the supreme Law of the Land." This provision first appeared on July 17 after the Convention had reversed itself and voted to deny Congress the proposed power to negative or veto state laws "contravening in its opinion the Articles of Union." Anxious to place some restraint on the free-wheeling state legislatures, the Convention adopted instead and without dissent a substitute offered by Luther Martin and drawn directly from the New Jersey Plan of June 14.

The substitute provided that the laws and treaties of the United States "shall be the supreme law of the respective States, as far as those acts or treaties shall relate to the said States, or their citizens and inhabitants—and that the Judiciaries of the several States shall be bound thereby in their decisions, anything in the respective laws of the individual States to the contrary notwithstanding." In its report of Aug. 6, the committee of detail dropped the qualifying phrase "as far as those acts or treaties shall relate to the said States," substituted the word "Judges" for "Judiciaries" in the next clause and the words "Constitutions or laws" for "laws" in the final proviso, and made a few other word changes.

The Convention agreed to these changes Aug. 23 and to another prefacing the entire provision with "This Constitution." Further revision by the committee of style changed "supreme law of the several States" to "supreme law of the land," in what became the final phrasing of the provision in Article VI. The effect of the various changes was to make it clear that all judges, state and Federal, were bound to uphold the supremacy of the Constitution over all other acts.

The "supremacy" clause was reinforced by the further provision in Article VI that all Members of Congress and of the state legislatures, as well as all executive and judicial officers of the national and state governments "shall be bound by Oath or Affirmation to support this Constitution."

Limits on Powers of the States. The "supremacy" clause was designed to prevent the states from passing laws contrary to the Constitution. Since the Constitution was also to specify the powers granted to Congress, those powers were denied by implication to the states. By the same reasoning, however, any powers not granted to Congress remained with the states. To eliminate any doubt of their intention to put an end to irresponsible acts of the individual states, the delegates decided to specify what the states could not or must do. Acts prohibited to the states were placed in Section 10 of Article I, while those required of them were placed in Sections 1 and 2 of Article IV.

Most of these provisions (many of which were taken from the Articles of Confederation) were proposed by the committee of detail and adopted by the Convention Aug. 28 with little debate or change. The committee had proposed that no state be allowed to make anything but gold or silver legal tender without the consent of Congress, but the Convention voted for an absolute prohibition on such laws, Sherman saying this was "a favorable crisis for crushing paper money." The Convention also added a provision, drawn from the Northwest Ordinance, aimed at the welter of state laws favoring debtors over creditors: no state was to pass any ex post facto law or law impairing the obligation of contracts.

The provisions of Article IV requiring each state to give "full faith and credit" to the acts of other states, to respect "all Privileges and Immunities" of all citizens, and to deliver up fugitives from justice were derived from the Articles. To these the Convention added the provision, requested by southerners, that became known as the "fugitive slave" clause, requiring such persons to be "delivered up on Claim of the Party to whom such Service or Labour may be due." As with the rest of the Constitution, the enforcement of these provisions was assigned, by the "supremacy" clause, to the Courts.

Amendment and Ratification

Amendment. A major reason for calling the Convention of 1787 had been the impossibility of obtaining the unanimous approval of the states that was required to amend the Articles of Confederation. So there was general agreement that it was better to provide for amending the Constitution "in an easy, regular and constitutional way, than to trust to chance and violence," as Mason put it. But the method for doing so received little consideration until the final days of the Convention.

The committee of detail was the first to propose that the legislatures of two-thirds of the states have the sole power to initiate amendments by petitioning Congress to call a convention for that purpose. This provision was adopted Aug. 30 after a brief debate during which no one supported the argument of Gouverneur Morris that Congress also should have the power to call a convention on its own. But, on reconsideration Sept. 10, Hamilton asserted that Congress "will be the first to perceive and will be the most sensible to the necessity of amendments," and he proposed that two-thirds of the Senate and House also have the power to call a convention.

Wilson moved that amendments be adopted when ratified by two-thirds of the states. When that proposal was defeated, six states to five, Wilson moved to substitute ratification by three-fourths of the states, which was approved without dissent. The Convention then adopted a new formula, providing that Congress "shall" propose amendments "whenever two-thirds of both Houses shall deem necessary or on the application of two-thirds" of the state legislatures, and that such amendments would become valid when ratified by the legislatures or conventions of three-fourths of the states as Congress might direct.

Under this formula, any amendment requested by two-thirds of the states would be submitted directly to the states for ratification. As modified Sept. 15, on the motion of Morris, the formula provided instead that, on the application of two-thirds of the states, Congress "shall call a Convention for proposing Amendments."

Thus, as finally drafted, Article V provided that, in proposing amendments to the Constitution, Congress would act directly while the states would act indirectly. In either case, however, amendments would take effect when approved by three-fourths of the states.

While working out these terms, the Convention also adopted two restrictions on the amending power. As a concession to the southern states, the Convention had already agreed (in Section 9 of Article I) to prohibit Congress from outlawing the slave trade before 1808 or levying any direct tax unless in proportion to a count of all whites and three-fifths of blacks. On Sept. 10, Rutledge noted that unless a similar limit were placed on the amending power, the provisions "relating to slaves might be altered by the States not interested in that property and prejudiced against them." So it was agreed, without debate, to add the proviso that no amendment adopted before 1808 "shall in any manner affect" those two provisions of Article I.

Sherman now worried that "three fourths of the States might be brought to do things fatal to particular States, as abolishing them altogether or depriving them of their equality in the Senate." He proposed, as a further proviso to the amending power, that "No state shall without its consent be affected in its internal police, or deprived of its equal suffrage in the Senate." The term "internal police" covered much more than most delegates were prepared to exclude, and only three states supported Sherman. But the more limited proviso that "no State, without its Consent, shall be deprived of its equal suffrage in the Senate" was accepted without debate and added to Article V.

Ratification. According to the resolution of Congress, the Philadelphia Convention was to meet for the "sole and express purpose of revising the Articles of Confederation and reporting to Congress and the several Legislatures" its recommendations. But the nationalists who organized the Convention and persuaded it to ignore these narrow instructions were determined that the fate of the new Constitution should not be entrusted to the state legislatures, but that the instrument should be ratified "by the supreme authority of the people themselves," as Madison put it. The legislatures, he pointed out, were in any event without power to consent to changes that "would make essential inroads on the State Constitutions."

By "the people themselves" the nationalists meant special conventions elected for the purpose. Conventions would be more representative than the legislatures, which excluded "many of the ablest men," and they would be more likely to favor the Constitution than would be legislatures that (as King said) "being to lose power will be most likely to raise objections." Opposed to this view were delegates like Ellsworth, who thought conventions were "better fitted to pull down than to build up Constitutions," and Gerry, who said the people "would never agree on anything." But the Convention rejected Ellsworth's motion for ratification by the legislatures and agreed July 23, nine states to one, that the Constitution should be submitted to popularly elected conventions.

This decision was followed, on Aug. 31, by the key decision that the Constitution should enter into force when approved by the conventions of no more than nine of the 13 states. By this time, only a few of the delegates still felt as Martin did that "unanimity was necessary to dissolve the existing Confederacy." Seven and ten were also proposed as minimums, but nine was chosen as the more familiar figure, being the number required to act on important matters under the Articles. It was also clearly impractical to require (as the committee of detail had proposed) that the Constitution be submitted to the Congress "for their approbation," so it was agreed to strike out that provision.

Randolph and Mason (two of the three delegates who finally refused to sign the Constitution) continued to argue that it should be submitted to another "General Convention," along with any amendments proposed by the state conventions, before it was finally acted on. Few others believed another such gathering could improve the product significantly, and their proposal was unanimously rejected Sept. 13. As finally drafted, Article VII provided simply that "the Ratifications of the Conventions of nine States shall be sufficient for the Establishment of this Constitution between the States so ratifying the Same."

By a separate resolution adopted Sept. 17, it was agreed that the Constitution should "be laid before the United States in Congress assembled," and that in the opinion of the Convention it should then be submitted to "a Convention of Delegates, chosen in each State by the People thereof." As soon as nine states had ratified, the resolution continued, the Congress should set a day for the election of Presidential electors, Senators and Representatives, and "the Time and Place for commencing Proceedings under this Constitution."

The Campaign for Ratification

Ten days after the Philadelphia Convention had adjourned on Sept. 17, 1787, the Congress of the Confederation submitted the Constitution to the states for their consideration and the struggle for ratification began. In that contest, ironically, those who had argued successfully in the Convention for a "national" rather than a "merely Federal" plan and who now took the lead in urging ratification, called themselves Federalists (although there was no reference to anything "federal" in the Constitution). Those who opposed the Constitution became, of necessity, Antifederalists.

These two factions, out of which the first political parties were formed, tended to reflect long-standing divisions among Americans between commercial and agrarian interests, creditors and debtors, men of great or little property, tidewater planters and the small farmers of the interior. But there were important and numerous exceptions to the tendency of Federalists and Antifederalists to divide along class, sectional and economic lines. Among the Antifederalists were some of the wealthiest and most influential men of the times, including George Mason, Patrick Henry, Richard Henry Lee, George Clinton, James Winthrop and many others.

As in drafting the Constitution, the Federalists seized the initiative in seeking speedy ratification. The ensuing campaign of political maneuver, persuasion and propaganda was intense and bitter. Both sides questioned the motives of the other and exaggerated the dire consequences of one or the other course. All Antifederalists, wrote Ellsworth, were either "men who have lucrative and influential State offices" or "tories, debtors in desperate circumstances, or insurgents." To Luther Martin, the object of the Federalists was "the total abolition of all State Governments and the erection on their ruins of one great and extreme empire."

All of the newspapers of the day published extensive correspondence on the virtues and vices of the new plan of government. The fullest and strongest case for the Constitution was put in a series of letters written by Madison, Hamilton and Jay under the name of "Publius." Seventy-seven of the letters were published in New York City newspapers between Oct. 27 and April 4, 1788, and in book form (along with eight additional letters) as "The Federalist" on May 28, 1788. These letters probably had only small influence in bringing about ratification, but "The Federalist" came to be regarded as the classic exposition of the Constitution as seen by two of its framers.

Political maneuvers were common in both camps. In Pennsylvania, Federalists moved to call a convention before Congress had officially submitted the Constitution. Nineteen Antifederalists thereupon withdrew from the Assembly, depriving it of a quorum until a mob seized two of them and dragged them back. When the Massachusetts Convention met, the Antifederalists were in the majority until John Hancock, the president, was won over to the Federalist side by promises of support for the new post of Vice President of the United States.

Among the major arguments advanced against the Constitution were the failure to include a Bill of Rights and the fear that the Presidency would tend toward monarchy through endless re-election. Federalists met the first argument by pledging the early enactment of amendments, which Massachusetts and Virginia were particularly determined should be included. The fear of monarchy was mitigated by a widespread assumption (held also in the Convention) that George Washington would become the first President. This assumption, together with the fact that most Americans knew Washington and Franklin supported the Constitution, contributed as much as anything to the success of the ratification campaign.

The Delaware Convention was the first to ratify, unanimously, on Dec. 7, 1787. Then came Pennsylvania, by a vote of 46 to 23, Dec. 12; New Jersey, unanimously, Dec. 19; Georgia, unanimously Jan. 2, 1788; Connecticut, 128 to 40, January 9; Massachusetts, 187 to 168, Feb. 6; Maryland, 63 to 11, April 26; South Carolina, 149 to 73, May 23; and New Hampshire, 57 to 46, June 21. This met the requirement for approval by nine states, but it was clear that without the approval of Virginia and New York the Constitution would stand on shaky ground.

In Virginia, according to Ellsworth, "the opposition wholly originated in two principles: the madness of Mason, and enmity of the Lee faction to Gen. Washington." But Randolph, who had refused with Mason to sign the Constitution, was brought over to its support, and on June 25 the Federalists prevailed, by a vote of 89 to 79. New York, where Governor Clinton led the Antifederalists, finally ratified on July 26 by an even narrower margin of 30 to 27, after Hamilton and Jay had threatened that otherwise New York City would secede and join the Union as a separate state. North Carolina ratified on Nov. 21, 1789, and Rhode Island (which had not taken part in the Philadelphia Convention) became the last of the 13 states to ratify, on May 29, 1790.

In accord with the request of the Philadelphia Convention, the Congress of the Confederation on Sept. 13, 1788, fixed the City of New York (where it sat) as the seat of the new government, the first Wednesday of January 1789 as the day for choosing Presidential electors, the first Wednesday of February for the meeting of electors, and the first Wednesday of March for the opening session of the new Congress.

The First Elections

The Constitution empowered the state legislatures to prescribe the method of choosing their Presidential electors as well as the time, place and manner of electing their Representatives and Senators. Virginia and Maryland put the choice of electors directly to the people; in Massachusetts, two were chosen at large while the other eight were picked by the legislature from 24 names submitted by the voters of the eight Congressional districts. Elsewhere, all electors were chosen by the legislature. But in New York, where Federalists controlled the Senate and Antifederalists dominated the Assembly, the two houses became deadlocked on the question of acting by joint or concurrent vote, and the legislature adjourned without choosing electors.

Elections to the House also involved a number of spirited contests between Federalists and Antifederalists, although the total vote cast (estimated between 75,000 and 125,000) amounted to a small fraction of the free population of 3,200,000. In Massachusetts and Connecticut, several elections were required in some districts before one candidate obtained a majority. Elbridge Gerry, who had refused to sign the Constitution, finally beat Nathaniel Gorham (also a delegate to the Philadelphia Convention) after saying he no longer opposed it. In New Jersey the law did not fix a time for closing the polls and they stayed open for three weeks; the elections of all four New Jersey Representatives were contested when the House was finally organized.

Although March 4, 1789, had been fixed as the day for "commencing proceedings" of the new Government, only 13 of the 59 Representatives and eight of the 22 Senators had arrived in New York City by then. (Seats allotted to North Carolina and Rhode Island were not filled until 1790, after those states had ratified the Constitution.) It was not until April 1 that a 30th Representative arrived to make a quorum of the House, while the Senate attained its quorum of 12 on April 6. The two houses then met jointly, for the first time, to count the electoral vote.

As everyone had assumed would happen, each of the 69 electors had cast one vote for George Washington, who thus became President by unanimous choice. (Four additional electors—two from Maryland and two from Virginia—had failed to show up on Feb. 4 to vote.) Of 11 other men among whom the electors distributed their second vote, John Adams received the highest number—34—and was declared Vice President.

Adams arrived in New York on April 21, Washington on the 23rd, and the inaugural took place on the 30th. Washington took the oath of office prescribed by the Constitution on the balcony of Federal Hall (New York's former City Hall that housed the President and both houses of Congress until all moved to Philadelphia in 1790). The President then went to the Senate chamber to deliver a brief inaugural address, in the course of which he declined to accept whatever salary Congress might confer on the office. Thus, by April 30, 1789, the long task of designing and installing a new Government for the United States had been completed; the job of making it work lay ahead.

Bibliography

Andrews, Charles M., *The Colonial Period of American History.* Yale University Press, 1934.

Beard, Charles A., *An Economic Interpretation of the Constitution of the United States.* Macmillan, 1935, 1949.

Brant, Irving, *James Madison: Father of the Constitution, 1787-1800.* Bobbs-Merrill, 1950.

Burnett, Edmund C., *The Continental Congress.* Macmillan, 1941.

Commager, Henry Steele (ed.), *Documents of American History.* Appleton-Century-Crofts, 1963 (eighth edition).

Elliot, Jonathan (ed.), *The Debates in the Several State Conventions in the Adoption of the Federal Constitution* (5 vols.). Taylor & Maury, 1854 (second edition).

Farrand, Max, *The Framing of the Constitution of the United States.* Yale University Press, 1913.

—(ed.), *The Records of the Federal Convention of 1787* (4 vols.). Yale University Press, 1911, 1937.

Jensen, Merrill, *The Articles of Confederation.* University of Wisconsin Press, 1940.

Kelly, Alfred H. and Harrison, Winfred A., *The American Constitution: Its Origin and Development.* W. W. Norton & Co., Inc., 1963 (third edition).

Lodge, Henry Cabot (ed.), *The Federalist.* G.P. Putnam's Sons, 1904.

McLaughlin, Andrew C., *The Confederation and the Constitution, 1783-1789.* Collier Books (division of Crowell-Collier Publishing Co.), 1962.

Morgan, Edmund S., *The Birth of the Republic.* University of Chicago Press, 1956.

Nevins, Allan, *The American States During and After the Revolution, 1775-1789.* Macmillan, 1924.

Rossiter, Clinton, *1787: The Grand Convention.* Macmillan, 1966.

Smith, David G., *The Convention and the Constitution: The Political Ideas of the Founding Fathers.* St. Martin's Press, Inc., 1965.

Van Doren, Carl, *The Great Rehearsal: The Story of the Making and Ratifying of the Constitution of the United States.* Viking Press, Inc., 1948.

Warren, Charles, *The Making of the Constitution.* Little, Brown, 1928.

Wright, Benjamin F., *Consensus and Continuity, 1776-1787.* Boston University Press, 1958.

History of the House of Representatives

WHEN the 30th of the 59 Representatives elected to the First Congress reached New York on April 1, 1789, the assembled quorum promptly chose as Speaker of the House a fellow Member, Frederick A. C. Muhlenberg of Pennsylvania. Next day, Muhlenberg named a committee of 11 to draw up the first rules of procedure, which the House adopted April 7. The first standing committee of the House—a seven-member Committee on Elections—was chosen April 13, and its report accepting the credentials of 49 members was approved April 18. By then, the House was already debating the first tariff bill.

By contrast, it took five years of study and negotiation to produce agreement in the 91st Congress on a limited revision of House rules. The House had long since become a highly structured institution governed by an elaborate set of rules, precedents and customs, all closely guarded by its most senior, privileged and influential Members. Since its founding, however, the House had often adapted its procedures to the needs of the times, and its continuing ability to do so seemed to be confirmed by the passage of the Legislative Reorganization Act of 1970.

From the beginning, politics and personalities have played their part in influencing the timing and direction of changes in House procedure and organization. But it was the rapid increase in the size of its membership in the 19th century and of its workload in the 20th century that compelled development of what became the major features of the legislative process in the House—strict limitations on floor debate, a heavy reliance on the committee system, and the elaboration of techniques for channeling and maintaining the flow of House business.

It was Speaker Thomas B. Reed who told the House, in 1890, that "the object of a parliamentary body is action, and not stoppage of action." But how to insure the right of a majority to "work its will" has been a perennial challenge in the House, conceived to become "the grand depository of the democratic principles of the Government." The men, parties and events that contributed to the evolution of the House as a legislative body are the focus of this account.

The Formative Years: 1789-1809

The great majority of the Representatives elected to the First Congress had served in the Continental Congress or in their state legislatures, and the procedures followed in those bodies (which were derived in large part from English parliamentary practice) formed the basis for the first rules of the House. Those rules included provisions that:

• The Speaker was to preside over the House, preserve decorum and order, put questions and decide all points or order. He was to announce the results of votes and to vote in all cases of ballot by the House.

• Committees of three or fewer members were to be appointed by the Speaker, while larger ones were to be chosen by ballot.

• Members could not introduce bills or speak more than twice to the same question without leave of the House. They were required to vote if present, unless excused, and barred from voting if not present or if they had a direct personal interest in the outcome.

The first rules also set forth legislative procedure. As in the Continental Congress, the principal forum for considering and perfecting legislation was to be the Committee of the Whole House—the House itself under another name. When sitting in Committee of the Whole, a Member other than the Speaker occupied the chair and certain motions permitted in the House—such as the previous question and the motion to adjourn—were not in order, nor were roll-call votes taken. Amendments rejected in Committee could not be offered again in the House except as part of a motion to recommit. As in the House, it took a majority of the Members to make a quorum in Committee of the Whole.

Early House Procedure

In the early years of the House, it was the practice to begin discussion of all major legislative proposals in Committee of the Whole House on the State of the Union. After broad agreement had been reached on the principles involved, a select committee was named to draft a bill. When this committee reported back to the House, the bill itself was referred to a Committee of the Whole for section-by-section debate and approval or amendment. Its work completed, the Committee "rose," the Speaker resumed the chair, and the House either accepted or rejected the amendments agreed to in Committee of the Whole. This was followed by a third and final reading of the engrossed or complete bill and passage by the House.

Since there were no time limits as yet on the right of Members to speak, even the small membership of the First and Second Congresses found this procedure cumbersome. Rep. James Madison blamed the "delays and perplexitites" of the House on "the want of precedents." But Rep. Fisher Ames of Massachusetts saw the problem as an excessive concern with detail in the "unwieldy" Committee of the Whole, for "a great, clumsy machine is applied to the slightest and most delicate operations— the hoof of an elephant to the strokes of mezzotinto."

A small time-saver was introduced in 1790, when the House amended its rules to permit the Speaker to appoint all committees "unless otherwise specially directed by the House." Similarly, in 1794, the House empowered the Speaker to name the chairman of the Committee of the Whole, who had been elected each time theretofore. But the practice of hammering out the broad terms of major legislation in Committee of the Whole before naming a select committee to draft a bill (more than 350 select committees were formed during the Third Congress) prevailed into the 1800s.

By confiding each proposal to a special committee that ceased to exist when a bill was reported, the House kept effective control over the legislation. But as its business multiplied and its membership increased (to 106 after the census of 1790 and to 142 after that of 1800), the House began to delegate increasing responsibility for initiating legislation to standing or permanent committees. Four were established by 1795; between 1802 and 1809, six were added. Among the more important were the Committees on Interstate and Foreign Commerce, created in 1795; Ways and Means, a select committee made permanent in 1802; and Public Lands, whose establishment in 1805 was prompted by the Louisiana Purchase.

The Emergence of Parties

Neither the Constitution nor the first rules of the House envisioned a role for political parties in the legislative process. The triumph of Federalists over Antifederalists in winning ratification of the Constitution, the unanimous and nonpartisan choice of Washington as the first President, and the great preponderance of nominal Federalists elected to the First Congress tended to obscure the underlying economic, sectional and philosophic differences of the times. But these differences were not long in surfacing after Alexander Hamilton took office as the first Secretary of the Treasury, armed with a charter from Congress "to digest and prepare plans for the improvement and management of the revenue and for the support of the public credit."

Hamilton, a skilled financier, administrator and political organizer at 34, quickly responded with proposals for paying off the national and state debts at par and for creating a Bank of the United States. Designed to establish confidence in the new Federal Government, these proposals also appealed to the mercantile and moneyed interests to whom Hamilton looked for support in his desire to strengthen central authority. Since most of those elected to the First Congress shared his outlook (and not a few stood to profit from his proposals), he soon emerged as the effective leader of a new Federalist party, meeting frequently with its adherents in caucus to plan legislative strategy.

Madison was the first to take issue with the substance of Hamilton's program as well as the dominance of the Executive in guiding the decisions of the House. He was joined shortly by his close friend and fellow Virginian, Thomas Jefferson, who became Secretary of State in 1790. An agrarian who extolled liberty over

order, Jefferson soon concluded that Hamilton's purpose was "to prepare the way for a change from the present republican form of government to that of monarchy." The cleavage was reinforced by the French Revolution and the wars that followed in its wake; Hamilton and the Federalists, with strong commercial and other ties to England, urged American neutrality, while Jefferson and his followers looked on the French as democratic allies to be helped.

By 1792, Madison and Jefferson were the recognized leaders of a nascent Republican party of opposition, rooted in southern fears of Federalist economic policies and rising agrarian antagonism to the "aristocratic" views of Hamilton, Vice President John Adams and other prominent Federalists. In the Third through the Sixth Congresses, spanning Washington's second term and Adams' single term as President, the House was closely divided between Republicans and Federalists. But in 1800 Jefferson's party emerged with a clear majority, and during his two terms as President the Republicans outnumbered the Federalists in the House two and three to one.

Leadership in the House

With the early emergency of two parties, choice of a Speaker soon fell to the party with a majority in the House. Thus in 1799, Theodore Sedgwick of Massachusetts was elected Speaker over Nathaniel Macon of North Carolina by a vote of 44 to 38, a margin that approximated that of Federalists over Republicans in the Sixth Congress. Two years later, Macon was elected Speaker by the heavy Republican majority in the Seventh Congress.

As party choices, the early Speakers were not unwilling to use their powers in support of party policies. In 1796, when House Republicans mounted an attack on Jay's treaty with Britain, Speaker Jonathan Dayton, a Federalist, twice voted to produce ties that resulted in the defeat of anti-treaty motions. Republicans in the Sixth Congress found the rulings of Sedgwick so partisan that they refused to join in the by-then customary vote of thanks of the Speaker at adjournment.

But these early Speakers were not the actual political or legislative leaders of the House. Until he left the Treasury in 1795, Hamilton—operating through Members of his own choice—dominated the Federalist majority—an "all-powerful" leader, according to one Republican, who "fails in nothing he attempts." And as the leader of House Republicans until he left Congress in 1797, Madison was seen in much the same light by Federalist Fisher Ames, who wrote: "Virginia moves in a solid column and the discipline of the party is as severe as the Prussian. Deserters are not spared."

As Republicans (or Democrats, as the Federalists soon took to calling them), Jefferson and Madison were opposed in principle to the concept of Executive supremacy embraced by Hamilton and the early Federalists. When he became President in 1801, Jefferson promptly discarded a favored symbol of Federalist theory—the personal appearance of the President before a joint session of Congress to read his annual State of the Union message or "speech from the throne"—and instituted the practice (followed by all Presidents until Wilson) of sending up the message to be read by a clerk. But Jefferson also took steps to assert his leadership over the new Republican majority in the House.

Jefferson's Secretary of the Treasury, Swiss-born Albert Gallatin (who had succeeded Madison as leader of House Republicans) soon became as adept as Hamilton had been in guiding Administration measures through the party caucus and the House. Moreover, Jefferson picked his own Floor Leader, who was now named Chairman of the Committee on Ways and Means at the same time. The men who held the posts of Floor Leader and Ways and Means chairman during Jefferson's tenure were known as the President's spokesmen in establishing party policy. When one of these leaders, the tempestuous John Randolph, broke with Jefferson over a plan to acquire Florida, the President had him deposed as the Committee chairman.

Randolph, meanwhile, had already affronted some Members of the House by his conduct as Ways and Means chairman. James Sloan complained in 1805 that he had tied up Committee business "by going to Baltimore or elsewhere, without leave of absence" and by keeping Treasury estimates "in his pockets or locked up in his drawer," and that he had rushed out important bills at the end of the session "when many Members are gone home." Sloan proposed that all standing committees be elected by ballot and choose their own chairmen. Committees were given the choice of selecting their own chairmen under a rule adopted in the Eighth Congress, but selection of chairmen (as well as committee members) reverted to the Speaker at the beginning of the 11th Congress.

In sum, the first 20 years of the House saw the beginnings of the standing committee system and the emergence of a Floor Leader and committee chairmen as key men in the legislative process. But that process was dominated, by and large, by the Executive Branch, and the effective decisions on legislative issues were reached behind the scenes in closed caucuses of the majority party. As Federalist Josiah Quincy lamented in 1809, the House "acts and reasons and votes, and performs all the operations of an animated being, and yet, judging from my own perceptions, I cannot refrain from concluding that all great political questions are settled somewhere else than on this floor."

Congress Takes the Lead: 1809-1829

The era of Executive supremacy over Congress came to an end under Jefferson's successor, James Madison, whose strong performance in the Constitutional Convention, in the House and as Secretary of State for eight years was not matched in the Presidency. Although he was nominally backed by Republican majorities during his two terms in office, Madison soon lost control of his party to a group of young "war hawks" (as John Randolph dubbed them) first elected to the 12th Congress, who pushed the President into the War of 1812 against England. Led in the House by Henry Clay and John C. Calhoun, these men capitalized on Madison's weakness and a rising resistance to Executive control to effect a shift of power to Congress that was not reversed until Jackson became President in 1829.

Clay as Speaker

Henry Clay first came to national attention while serving briefly as a Senator from Kentucky in 1810-11. He then spoke eloquently of the need for "a new race of heroes" to carry on the "deeds of glory and renown" of America's founders. He proposed the conquest of Canada, asserting that "the militia of Kentucky are alone competent to place Montreal and Upper Canada at your feet." It was as spokesman for a new nationalism, affronted by British interference with American trade and shipping, that Clay entered the House in 1811 and—although only 34 and a newcomer—was promptly elected Speaker by like-minded Republicans. Using to the full his power to appoint committees and their chairmen, Clay put his fellow "war hawks" in all of the key positions. Together they took control of the House.

Clay was the first to put the stamp of leadership on the office of Speaker. Earlier occupants had asserted the Speaker's claim to high public rank as "the elect of the elect of all the people" (as Macon put it), and they had used the office to forward party interests. But it was Clay who first exercised the Speaker's potential as leader of the House in fact as well as name. A forceful presiding officer, Clay was also an accomplished debater who frequently used his right to speak in the House as in Committee of the Whole. Gifted with great charm and tact, Clay remained Speaker as long as he was in the House. Although he resigned his seat twice—in 1814 (to help negotiate an end to the War of 1812) and in 1820—he was again elected Speaker as soon as he returned to the House, in 1815 and in 1823.

It was up to the Speaker, said Clay in 1823, to be prompt and impartial in deciding questions of order, to display "patience, good temper, and courtesy" to every Member, and to make "the best arrangement and distribution of the talent of the House" for the dispatch of public business. Above all, he said, the Speaker must "remain cool and unshaken amidst all the storms of debate, carefully guarding the preservation of the permanent laws and rules of the House from being sacrificed to temporary passions, prejudices or interests."

This was no easy job in Clay's time, when political passions were strong, the size of House membership continued to increase (to 186 after the census of 1810 and to 213 after that of 1820), and the right of debate was essentially unlimited. It is true that the House (after becoming exasperated with the unyielding tactics of Barent Gardenier, a New Yorker who once held the floor for 24 hours) had decided in 1811 that a majority could shut off further debate by calling for the previous question—the device which in time became the normal means of closing debate in the House. But in this period John Randolph was not alone in regarding this as a "gag" rule, and it was not easily invoked. Under the existing rules, moreover, those skilled in parliamentary tactics (as Randolph was) could and frequently did succeed in tying up House proceedings.

Clay once outwitted Randolph. It was after the House in 1820, had finally passed the hotly disputed Missouri Compromise bill to admit Missouri as a slave state but to bar slavery in any future state north of 36° 30' north latitude. When Randolph, who opposed the bill, moved the next day to reconsider the vote, the

Speaker held the motion to be out of order pending completion of the prescribed order of business. Clay then proceeded to sign the bill and send it to the Senate before Randolph could renew his motion. The Speaker's action was upheld, in effect, when the House refused, 61-71, to consider Randolph's subsequent motion to censure the Clerk for having removed the bill.

Growth of Standing Committees

Efforts to refine House procedures continued in the period 1809-1829. The first rule to establish a daily order of business was adopted in 1811. In 1812 the Committee on Enrolled Bills was given leave to report at any time—a privilege later granted to certain other committees in order to expedite consideration of important bills. A rule adopted in 1817 enabled the House to protect itself against business it did not wish to consider. In 1820 the House created by rule the first calendars of the Committee of the Whole. And in 1822 it was decided that no rule should be suspended except by a two-thirds vote.

But the chief development in House procedures during this period was the proliferation of standing committees and their emergence as the principal forums for the initial consideration of proposed legislation—a practice recognized in 1822 by a rule giving standing committees "leave to report by bill or otherwise." The number of select committees "raised" to draft bills had dropped from 350 in the Third Congress (1793-95) to 70 in the 13th Congress (1813-15). And the number of standing committees grew from 10 in 1809 to 28 in 1825.

Among the standing committees were the Committee on the Judiciary, made permanent in 1813, and the Committees on Military Affairs, Naval Affairs and Foreign Affairs, all created in 1822. Six Committees on Expenditures in as many Executive Departments were established by Clay in 1816 to check up on economy and efficiency in the Administration. Between 1816 and 1826 these and other House committees conducted at least 20 major investigations. The inquiries included such matters as the conduct of General Andrew Jackson in the Seminole War, charges against Secretary of the Treasury William Crawford, and the conduct of John Calhoun as Secretary of War.

Decline of "King Caucus"

In Clay's time as Speaker, the party caucus still afforded House Republicans an important means of reaching legislative decisions. It took Federalist Daniel Webster less than two weeks after being seated in 1813 to conclude that "the time for us to be put on the stage and moved by the wires has not yet come," since "before anything is attempted to be done here, it must be arranged elsewhere." And Webster soon noted that the caucus worked "because it was attended with a severe and efficacious discipline, by which those who went astray were to be brought to repentance." But the extent of party unity among Republicans had already started to decline under Jefferson as a result of sectional rivalries, and while the Federalists continued to lose ground as a national party, factionalism increased among the Republicans in Congress.

The change was reflected also in the rise and fall of the Congressional caucus as the agency for selecting party nominees for President and Vice President. The practice began in 1800, when both Federalist and Republican members of the House and Senate met secretly to pick running mates for Jefferson and Adams. In 1804, Jefferson was renominated unanimously and openly by a caucus of 108 Republican Senators and Representatives. Four years later, a caucus of 94 Republican Members nominated Madison over the protests of others who preferred Monroe. But only 83 of the 133 Republicans in Congress attended the caucus that renominated Madison in 1812, just before he asked Congress for the declaration of war against England that Clay and others had been urging.

The Republican caucus of 1816 drew 119 of the party's 141 Members in the House and Senate. Madison was known to favor the nomination of Monroe (his Secretary of State), but there was rising opposition to continuation of the Virginia "dynasty" in the White House, and Madison was nominated by only 65 votes to 54 for Secretary of War William Crawford of Georgia. By 1820, however, there was no real opposition in either party to Monroe, who was credited with bringing about "the era of good feelings" and had kept clear of the controversy over the Missouri Compromise. Fewer than 50 Members showed up for the caucus that found it inexpedient to make any nomination, and Monroe was reelected with every electoral vote but one.

The race to succeed Monroe began almost at once and included three members of his Cabinet—Crawford, Calhoun and John Quincy Adams—as well as Henry Clay and Andrew Jackson, hero of the Battle of New Orleans. When it appeared that Crawford would get a majority in a caucus, supporters of the other candidates began to denounce the caucus system. As a result, only 66 of the 261 Senators and Representatives then seated in Congress attended the caucus that nominated Crawford early in 1824. The election that fall gave Jackson a plurality but not a majority of the popular and electoral votes, and the choice went to the House, which picked Adams. *(See Power to Elect the President, Chapter III.)*

The Presidential contest of 1824 marked the end of the old party system and the Congressional nominating caucus. Helping to kill the caucus were changes in voting procedures and an expansion of the suffrage. Between 1800 and 1824, the number of states in which the electors were chosen by popular vote instead of by the Legislature increased from four out of 16 to 18 out of 24. Four years later, in 1828, the electors were popularly chosen in all except two of the 24 states, and the popular vote jumped from less than 400,000 in 1824 to more than 1.1 million. With the emergence of a mass electorate, aspirants for the Presidency were forced to seek a much broader base of support than the Congressional caucus.

A House Divided: 1829-1861

National politics entered a period of increasing turmoil, lasting until the Civil War, during the Presidency of Andrew Jackson. Jackson made unprecedented use of the veto and of the removal and patronage powers of his office to establish his primacy over Congress. Two new parties emerged during the two-term "reign" of "King Andrew" (1829-37): the Jacksonian Democrats, heirs to the agrarian and states' rights philosophy of the Jeffersonian Republicans, and the Whigs, spokesmen for the commercial and industrial interests once represented by the Federalists. But the Democrats now embraced the Federalist principle of Executive leadership, while the Whigs extolled the Republican doctrine of legislative supremacy and tried thereafter to weaken the Presidency.

The power and influence of the House began to decline under Jackson, when the size of the membership was increased to 242. Such former luminaries of the House as Henry Clay, Daniel Webster and John Calhoun moved to the Senate, which now became the major arena of debate on national policy. Party control of the Presidency, the House and the Senate fluctuated considerably after Jackson. Increasingly, however, both Democrats and Whigs found themselves divided by the issue of slavery and its extension to the new territories and states beyond the Mississippi. The issue was reflected in the bitter election battles for the Speakership that occurred in 1839, 1849, 1855 and 1859.

Contests to Elect the Speaker

Intra-party contests for Speaker were not new in the House. In 1805, when Republicans outnumbered Federalists almost four to one, it took four ballots to re-elect Macon, a southerner, over Joseph B. Varnum, the Northern candidate. Two years later, when there were five candidates, Varnum won on the second ballot after Macon withdrew. By 1820—the year of the Missouri Compromise—the issue of slavery was an explicit part of the sectional contest for Speaker; to replace Clay, who had resigned, the House cast 22 ballots before electing John W. Taylor of New York, the antislavery candidate, over William Lowndes of South Carolina, a compromiser.

Next year, Taylor was one of five candidates in a contest that underscored the breakup of the Republicans and foreshadowed the Presidential race of 1824. Taylor lost on the 12th ballot to Philip C. Barbour of Virginia, a Crawford supporter whom Adams called "a shallow-pated wildcat, fit for nothing but to tear the Union to rags and tatters." And in 1834, when Andrew Stevenson resigned in his fourth term as Speaker (only to see the Senate reject his nomination as Minister to Great Britain), it took 10 ballots to elect John Bell over his fellow Tennessean, James K. Polk.

Contest of 1839. Martin Van Buren, Jackson's handpicked successor, was elected President in 1836, but Democrats barely won control of the House in the 25th Congress (1837-39). When it adjourned, Whigs deplored the "most partial and unjust rulings" of Speaker Polk, who then left the House to become Governor of Tennessee. At the opening of the 26th Congress on Dec. 2, 1839, the House found itself with 120 Democrats, 118 Whigs, and five contested seats in New Jersey. Control of the House rested on the decision of these contests, but the Clerk (who presided under House practice pending election of a Speaker) refused to choose between the claimants or to put any question until the House was organized.

After four days of bitter debate, the Members elected a temporary chairman—the venerable John Quincy Adams, who had returned to the House in 1831. But it was Dec. 14 before it was decided to elect a

Speaker without the New Jersey votes. There were six candidates to start, and John W. Jones of Virginia led on the first five ballots. But Robert M. T. Hunter—also of Virginia—was elected Dec. 16 on the 11th ballot (when there were 13 candidates) because he "finally united all the Whig votes and all the malcontents of the Administration," according to Adams.

Contest of 1849. Control of the House passed to the Whigs in the 27th Congress (1841-43), then to the Democrats in the 28th and 29th, then back to the Whigs in the 30th (1847-49) during the last two years of the Polk Administration. Zachary Taylor, the Whig candidate, was elected President in 1848, but neither party had a majority in the House when the 31st Congress met on Dec. 3, 1849, because a number of "Free-Soil" Whigs and Democrats refused to support the leading candidates for Speaker—Robert C. Winthrop of Massachusetts, Whig Speaker in the previous Congress, and Howell Cobb, a Democrat from Georgia. The pending issue was what to do about slavery in the territory won in the war against Mexico, and the Free Soilers were determined to prevent the election of a Speaker who would appoint pro-slavery majorities to the Committees on Territories and the District of Columbia.

Cobb led 11 candidates on the first ballot with 103 votes. But there were five recognized factions in the House—Whigs, Democrats, Free Soilers, Native Americans and Taylor Democrats—and neither Cobb nor Winthrop, who alternated in the lead for 60 ballots, could get a majority. Finally, on Dec. 22, the House voted, 113 to 106, to elect a Speaker by a plurality, so long as it was a majority of a quorum. Cobb, the pro-slavery candidate, was elected on the 63rd ballot when he received 102 votes to 100 for Winthrop, with 20 votes spread among eight other candidates. This decision was then confirmed by a majority vote of the House.

Contest of 1855. Pro-slavery Democrats held firm control of the House in the 32nd and 33rd Congresses (1851-55), when Linn Boyd of Kentucky was Speaker. But their attempt to extend slavery into the Kansas and Nebraska Territories produced a large turnout of anti-slavery forces in the elections of 1854—the first in which a new Republican party, successor to the Whigs, participated. When the 34th Congress convened on Dec. 3, 1855, the House membership was divided among 108 Republicans or Whigs, 83 Democrats and 43 members of minor parties that sprang up in the 1850s. Although the so-called "Anti-Nebraska men" were in the majority, they were unable to unite behind any candidate for Speaker; two months passed and 133 ballots were taken before a choice was made.

The 21 candidates on the first ballot were led by William A. Richardson of Illinois with 74 votes. As in previous contests, various motions to help resolve the deadlock—including one to drop the low man on each ballot until only two remained—were made and tabled as the voting continued. After a series of votes in which Nathaniel P. Banks of Massachusetts fell only a few votes short of a majority, the House finally agreed to follow the plurality rule of 1849. On Feb. 2, 1856, Banks was declared Speaker. On the 133rd ballot he had received 103 votes to 100 for William Aiken of South Carolina. Banks, who had been elected to the 33rd Congress as a Coalition Democrat and to the 34th as a candidate of the nativist American Party of "Know Nothings," fulfilled the expectations of the anti-slavery forces by his committee appointments.

Contest of 1859. Democrats won the Presidency in 1856 with James Buchanan, last of the "northern men with southern principles." They also gained control of the House in the 35th Congress (1857-59). But the 36th opened on Dec. 5, 1859, with no party in control of the House, which was composed of 109 Republicans, 101 Democrats and 27 "Know Nothings." Pro- and anti-slavery blocs were again deadlocked over the choice of a Speaker. With passions running high and debate unchecked by a presiding Clerk who refused to decide any points of order, the struggle continued for two months.

John Sherman of Ohio, the Republican choice, led the early balloting, receiving at one point 110 votes, just six short of a majority. But Sherman had become anathema to the pro-slavery camp, and the Republicans finally concluded that he couldn't be elected. So Sherman withdrew on the 39th ballot, and the Republicans switched their support to William Pennington of New Jersey, a new Member of the House and politically unknown. Pennington received 115 votes on the 40th ballot (compared to one on the 38th) and was elected on the 44th, on Feb. 1, 1860, by a bare majority of 117 votes out of 233. Pennington's distinction (shared with Clay) of being chosen Speaker in his first term ended there, for he was defeated at the polls the next year and served only the one term in the House.

Changes in House Rules

Agitation over the issue of slavery was not confined to the contests over the choice of a Speaker. In 1836, John Quincy Adams challenged a House practice (begun in 1792) of refusing to receive petitions and memorials on the subject of slavery. Adams offered a petition from citizens of Massachusetts for the abolition of slavery in the District of Columbia. His action led to protracted debate and the adoption of a resolution (by a vote of 117 to 68) that any papers dealing with slavery "shall, without being either printed or referred, be laid upon the table and that no further action whatever shall be had thereon."

Adams, who considered adoption of the resolution to be "a direct violation of the Constitution of the United States, of the rules of this House, and of the rights of my constituents," reopened the issue in 1837 by asking the Speaker how to dispose of a petition he had received from 22 slaves. Southerners moved at once to censure Adams. The move failed, but the House agreed, 162-18, that "slaves do not possess the right of petition secured to the people of the United States by the Constitution." Further agitation led the House in 1840 to adopt (by a vote of 114-108) a rule that no papers "praying the abolition of slavery...shall be received by this House or entertained in any way whatever." Four years later, however, the rule was rescinded by a vote of 108-80.

Other rules adopted in this period were more significant to the long-range development of House procedures. In 1837, for example, precedence was given to floor consideration of revenue and appropriation bills, and the inclusion of legislation in an appropriation bill (which had led the Senate to kill a number of such bills) was barred. In 1841, the House finally agreed to limit to one hour the time allowed any Member in a debate—a proposal made first in 1820 after John Randolph had spoken for more than four hours against the Missouri Compromise. At the same time, to prevent indefinite debate in Committee of the Whole, a rule was adopted providing that the House by majority vote could discharge the Committee from consideration of a bill after pending amendments were disposed of without debate.

Objection to the latter provision led in 1847 to adoption of the "Five-Minute Rule," giving any Member that much time to explain his amendment. But this rule encouraged a practice of offering and then withdrawing scores of amendments in an effort to delay action on controversial bills. So the rule was amended in 1850 to prohibit the withdrawal of any amendment without unanimous consent. But the House was still at the mercy of a determined minority; during debate on the Kansas-Nebraska bill in 1854, according to Asher Hinds, opponents engaged in "prolonged dilatory operations, such as the alternation of the motions to lay on the table, for a call of the House, to excuse individual Members from voting, to adjourn, to reconsider votes whereby individual members were excused from voting, to adjourn, to fix the day to which the House should adjourn, and, after calls of the House had been ordered, to excuse individual absentees," all of which required 109 roll calls and consumed many days.

In 1858, the House agreed to set up a select committee to "digest and revise" the accumulation of more than 150 rules. The Committee included the Speaker—the first time that officer had served on any committee of the House. While its report was not acted on, most of its recommendations were repeated in 1860 by another committee named the day Pennington was finally chosen Speaker. As approved by the House in March, this first general revision of the rules was largely of a technical nature, although it included important changes affecting use of the previous question and the motion to strike the enacting clause. On balance, however, the revised rules of 1860 left ample opportunity for a resolute minority to keep a closely divided House tied up in parliamentary knots for days at a time.

Apart from the adoption of the first limitations on debate—the "Hour Rule" and the "Five-Minute Rule" in the 1840s—there was little significant change in House procedures in the period 1829-1860. The system of standing committees that had been established by 1825 (when there were 28) was expanded by the addition of eight more. The Committee on Ways and Means continued to handle both appropriations and revenue bills, and while its chairman was not always the designated Floor Leader of the majority party, he was always among the most influential Members. The Speaker continued to appoint Members to committees and to designate their chairmen.

But none of the Speakers who followed Clay achieved his stature or influence. Of the 14 who were elected between 1825 and 1860, only three—Stevenson, Polk and Boyd—served for more than one Congress. In only one respect was the job of leading the House made, not easier, but at least no more difficult: the size of the membership increased to 242 in 1833 and was kept about the same for the next 40 years. Otherwise, the rising passions of the country doomed the House to increasing turmoil as Americans moved toward the "irrepressible conflict" of the Civil War.

New Complexities: 1861-1890

The Civil War all but eliminated the South from national politics and representation in Congress for eight years. Most of the 66 House seats held by the 11 secessionist states in 1860 remained vacant from 1861 to 1869. The war also greatly weakened the Democratic Party outside the South; as in the War of 1812, when the Federalists were tarred for their pro-British sympathies, the Democrats suffered from their identification with the southern cause. And Democratic weakness helped the Republicans to keep control of the Presidency until 1885, of the Senate until 1879, and of the House until 1875.

At the same time, the war and its aftermath gave rise to bitter conflict between Congress and the President leading to the impeachment of Andrew Johnson in 1868 and to a prolonged period of legislative dominance thereafter. The years from 1860 to 1890 saw a further expansion of House membership, an intensification of House efforts to control Government spending, an increase in the number and power of House committees, and a continuing struggle to adapt the rules of the House to its legislative purposes.

"Congress Is Paramount"

President Lincoln assumed unprecedented powers during the Civil War, at a time when the Republican majorities in Congress were dominated by Radicals committed to the Whig doctrine of legislative supremacy. The conflict between Lincoln and Congress was sharpest over the issue of Reconstruction. Lincoln, who held that the Confederate states had never left the Union, was prepared to restore their political rights as quickly as possible. But the Radicals were determined to reshape the power structure of the South before readmitting the secessionists and insisted that the decision rested with Congress.

When Lincoln set up new governments in Louisiana and Arkansas in 1863, the Radicals passed a bill to place all Reconstruction authority under the direct control of Congress. Lincoln pocket-vetoed the bill after Congress had adjourned in 1864, whereupon the Radicals issued the Wade-David Manifesto asserting that "the authority of Congress is paramount and must be respected." If the President wanted their support, said the Radicals, "he must confine himself to his executive duties—to obey and execute, not make the laws—to suppress by arms armed rebellion, and leave political reorganization to Congress."

The Radicals proceeded to put their views into effect with a vengeance under Andrew Johnson, the Tennessee Democrat who became President when Lincoln was assassinated in 1865 and whose views were openly sympathetic to the established order in the South. Passed over Johnson's veto were numerous bills the effects of which were to give Congress full control over Reconstruction and to strip the President of much of his authority.

One of these measures was the Tenure of Office Act of 1867, passed on the suspicion that Johnson intended to fire Secretary of War Stanton. The law made it a "high misdemeanor" to remove without the Senate's approval any official whose nomination had been confirmed by the Senate. After Johnson—holding the law to be unconstitutional—had suspended Stanton from office, the House voted, 126-47, to impeach him. Tried by the Senate, Johnson was acquitted May 16, 1868, when a vote of 35 to 19 for conviction fell one short of the two-thirds required by the Constitution. *(See Power of Impeachment, Chapter III.)*

But Johnson was left powerless for the remainder of his term.

Power of the Purse

The Civil War led to renewed efforts by the House to control Federal expenditures (which climbed from $63 million in 1860 to $1.3 billion in 1865) by a more careful exercise of its power over appropriations. Until then, the Committee on Ways and Means had handled all supply as well as revenue bills, in addition to bills on monetary matters. But in 1865 the House agreed with little opposition to transfer some of these responsibilities to two new standing committees—a Committee on Appropriations and a Committee on Banking and Currency. Speaking of the former, the sponsor of the change declared that "we require of this new Committee their whole labor in the restraint of extravagant and illegal appropriations."

Congress now began to tighten controls on spending. Wartime authority to transfer funds from one account to another was repealed, agencies were required to return unexpended funds to the Treasury, and obligation of funds in excess of appropriations was prohibited. Although Congress continued to make lump-sum appropriations to the Army and the Navy, it specified in great detail the amounts and purposes for which money could be spent by the civilian departments and agencies. These efforts helped to keep Federal expenditures below $300 million in every year except one from 1871 to 1890.

The House's "power of the purse" was exercised to another end during the Administration of Rutherford B. Hayes (1877-81), the Republican successor to U.S. Grant (1869-77). Democrats were again in the majority in the House in the 45th Congress (1877-79) and won control of both chambers in the 46th, but by margins too small to be able to override a veto. So in their attempts to repeal certain Reconstruction laws, the Democrats revived the practice of adding legislative riders to supply bills in the hope of forcing the President to accept them. But Hayes vetoed a series of such bills, rejecting the tactic as an attempt at "coercive dictation" by the House.

In one veto message, Hayes attacked the principle that "the House of Representatives has the sole right to originate bills for raising revenue, and therefore has the right to withhold appropriations upon which the existence of the Government may depend unless the Senate and the President shall give their assent to any legislation which the House may see fit to attach to appropriation bills." If allowed to prevail, Hayes said, this doctrine "will result in a consolidation of unchecked and despotic power in the House." Unable to override his vetoes, the Democrats finally passed the supply bills without the riders.

Meanwhile, House members of both parties were becoming concerned over a concentration of power in the Appropriations Committee itself. In 1877, the Committee was deprived of its jurisdiction over appropriations for rivers and harbors—the "pork barrel" on which Members relied to finance projects of interest to their districts. The Agriculture appropriation was taken from the Committee in 1880, and in 1885, it was stripped of authority over six other supply bills—Army, Navy, Military Academy, Consular and Diplomatic Affairs, Post Office and Post Roads, and Indian Affairs—all of which were transferred to the appropriate legislative committees.

In taking from the Appropriations Committee control over bills comprising almost one-half of the Federal budget, the House was apparently moved by hostility to Chairman Samuel J. Randall (D Pa.) and what was considered to be the Committee's excessive concern for economy under his leadership. The feeling was widespread and bipartisan; three-fourths of the Democrats and of the Republicans joined in the vote of 227 to 70 to strip the Committee of a giant share of its jurisdiction. They were led, moreoever, by the senior members of most of the other important committees, underscoring the rivalry that had developed among House committees.

The effect of this decision in 1885 was to reinforce the decentralization of power in the House and to give added weight to the criticism of Congress voiced by Woodrow Wilson that year in a book entitled *Congressional Government*. According to Wilson, power in the House was scattered among "47 seigniories, in each of which a Standing Committee is the court-baron and its chairman lord-proprietor." Wilson noted that, "by custom, seniority in Congressional service determines the bestowal of the principal chairmanships," and that on the House floor "chairman fights against chairman for use of the time of the assembly."

Wilson attributed the lack of strong party control in the House to the fact that committees were not composed entirely of members of the majority, as he believed they should be. "The legislation of a session does not represent the policy of either (party)," he wrote; "it is simply an aggregate of the bills recommended by committees composed of members from both sides of the House, and it is known to be usually, not the work of the majority men upon the Committees, but compromise conclusions...of the committeemen of both parties."

Speakers and the Rules

If power in the House was not dispersed among the standing committees and their chairmen, it was also true (as Wilson noted) that "he who appoints those committees is an autocrat of the first magnitude." While Speakers had held that authority since the earliest days of the House, its exercise had assumed new importance with the broadening legislative interests of the country and of the House.

Schuyler Colfax, first elected to the House from Indiana in 1854, served as Republican Speaker from 1863 to 1869, when he left the House to become Vice President during the first term of President Grant. Although Colfax enjoyed as much personal popularity as

had Henry Clay, he was not a forceful Speaker and was regarded as a figurehead in a House dominated by Thaddeus Stevens (R Pa.), who became chairman of the Ways and Means Committee in 1861 and of the newly created Appropriations Committee in 1865. Stevens, who engineered the impeachment of President Johnson, was described by George Boutwell, a fellow Republican, as "a tyrant in his rule as leader of the House" who was "at once able, bold and unscrupulous." Stevens "commanded universal party obedience," according to a Democratic leader of the time.

Colfax's successor as Speaker was James G. Blaine of Maine, one of the founders of the Republican Party, who entered the House in 1863. As Speaker from 1869 to 1875, Blaine was an avowed partisan of Republican principles and successfully manipulated committee assignments to produce majorities favorable to legislation he desired. Like Clay, Blaine aspired to become President. But after losing the Republican nomination to Rutherford B. Hayes in 1876 and to James A. Garfield in 1880, he was nominated in 1884 only to lose the election to Democrat Grover Cleveland.

Democrats won control of the House in 1875. After the death in 1876 of their first choice for Speaker, Michael C. Kerr of Indiana, they elected Samuel J. Randall of Pennsylvania, who had entered the House with Blaine and Garfield in 1863. Randall, who was Speaker until 1881, initiated a thorough revision of House rules in 1880 designed "to secure accuracy in business, economy in time, order, uniformity and impartiality." The net effect of these changes was to increase to some extent the ability of floor leaders and committee chairmen to expedite legislation on the floor. The Committee on Rules, which had been a select committee since 1789 and had been chaired by the Speaker since 1858, was made a standing committee, and it soon began to make systematic use of special orders or rules which, when adopted by majority vote of the House, governed the amount of time to be allowed for debate on major bills and the extent to which Members might offer amendments.

The Democrats lost control of the House in the 47th Congress (1881-83) but regained it in the 48th Congress (1883-85). They then passed over Randall (because he had opposed the party's low-tariff policy) and elected John G. Carlisle of Kentucky as Speaker. Carlisle, a Member since 1877 who remained Speaker from 1883 to 1889, made notable use of his power of recognition to forestall motions he opposed. By the device of asking "For what purpose does the gentleman rise?," Carlisle was able to withhold recognition from any Member whose purpose he did not share. But Carlisle did not lead a united party; in 1884, for example, Democrats lost a tariff reduction bill through the defection of "Randall and the 40 thieves."

Blaine, Randall and Carlisle all contributed importantly to the body of precedents by which Speakers were guided under the House rules. But none was able or willing to prevent determined minorities from obstructing the business of the House. Under Carlisle, in particular, the House was frequently subjected to organized filibusters and such dilatory tactics as the "disappearing quorum" which was likely to result in endless roll calls to no purpose but delay. These displays, coupled with a disappointing legislative output, led to increasing public criticism of the House and to demands that the rules be modified "to permit the majority to control the business for which it is responsible," as the *New York Tribune* put it.

The Reed Rules

The opportunity for reform came when Republicans took control of the House in 1889 and elected Thomas B. Reed of Maine as Speaker. First elected to the House in 1876, Reed had been a leader of House Republicans since 1882 when he became a member of the Rules Committee and an increasingly outspoken critic of the rules. Trying to direct the work of the House under the rules, he once said, was like trying "to run Niagara through a quill." In this period, said Reed, "the only way to do business inside the rules is to suspend the rules."

When the 51st Congress convened on Dec. 2, 1889, the House was composed of 330 Members, with Republicans in a small majority. Reed was elected Speaker over Carlisle on a party-line vote, and in keeping with long-standing practice the rules of the 50th Congress were referred to the five-member Rules Committee (of which the Speaker was chairman) while the House proceeded under general parliamentary law. With several election contests pending, it was expected that the Republicans would settle them in their favor (as party majorities had always done) in order to increase their majority, before adopting new rules.

On Jan. 29, 1890, the Republicans called up the West Virginia election case of Smith vs. Jackson. Charles F. Crisp of Georgia, the Democratic leader, immediately raised the question of consideration, to be decided by majority vote. The roll call produced 161 "yeas," two "nays" and 165 not voting—mostly Democrats who, although present, were using the device of the "disappearing quorum" to block action. But when the point of "no quorum" was made (since less than one-half of the Members had voted), Speaker Reed ordered the Clerk to enter the names of those present and refusing to vote; he then ruled that a quorum was present and consideration in order.

In the ensuing uproar, Reed was denounced as a "tyrant" and a "czar" but held to his ground. An appeal from his ruling was tabled by a majority of a quorum. When next day, in order to make a quorum, he again counted non-voting Democrats who were present, he refused to allow another appeal on the ground that the House had already decided the question. Reed went on to declare that he would refuse to recognize any Member rising to make a dilatory motion, saying:

"There is no possible way by which the orderly methods of parliamentary procedure can be used to stop legislation. The object of a parliamentary body is action, and not stoppage of action. Hence, if any Member or set of Members undertakes to oppose the orderly progress of business, even by the use of the ordinarily recognized parliamentary motions, it is the right of the majority to refuse to have those motions entertained...."

Reed's rulings on dilatory motions and the counting of a quorum were incorporated in the revised rules reported by the Rules Committee, Feb. 6, 1890, and adopted by the House after four days of debate by a vote of 161 to 144. Of the rule that "no dilatory motion shall be entertained by the Speaker," the Committee report said:

"There are no words which can be framed which will limit Members to the proper use of proper motions. Any motion the most conducive to progress in the public business...may be used for purposes of unjust and oppressive delay.... Why should an assembly be kept from its work by motions made only to delay and to weary, even if the original design of the motion was salutary and sensible?"

In addition to these changes in the rules, the revision of 1890 reduced the size of the quorum required in Committee of the Whole from one-half of the membership of the House to 100 Members—a change that facilitated floor action as the size of the House continued to grow. The revised rules also took account of the fact that the House had long since abandoned its original requirement that Members obtain leave to introduce bills; the practice of introducing bills simply by filing them with the Clerk was now made a rule.

Coincidentally, the number of bills introduced, which had first passed the 1,000 mark in the 24th Congress (1835-37) and had not exceeded 2,000 until the 40th Congress (1867-69), reached a new peak of more than 19,000 in the 51st Congress (1889-91). But the fate of most of these bills continued to be as described by Woodrow Wilson in 1885: "As a rule, a bill committed (to committee) is a bill doomed. When it goes from the Clerk's desk to a committee room, it crosses a parliamentary bridge of sighs to dim dungeons of silence whence it will never return."

Under the Reed Rules of 1890, the Speaker was enabled to take effective command of the House. By his authority to name the members and chairmen of all committees, he had the power to reward or to punish his fellow Members. As chairman of the Rules Committee (which now shared with Ways and Means and Appropriations the right to report at any time and thereby get immediate access to the floor), he could control the timing and content of bills to be brought before the House. And now, with unlimited power of recognition, he could determine in large measure what was to be taken up on the floor.

Tyranny and Reaction: 1890-1919

Although the Democrats dropped the rule against the "disappearing quorum" when they took control of the House in the 52nd Congress (1891-93), they restored it in the 53rd (1893-95), and Charles F. Crisp of Georgia, the Democratic Speaker in both Congresses, made just as full use of his powers as had Reed in the 51st. Crisp (who persuaded two rivals to withdraw from the party contest for Speaker by promising them the chairmanships of Appropriations and Ways and Means) once refused to entertain an appeal by Reed from a ruling, refused to let Reed speak any further, and directed the Sergeant at Arms to see that he took his seat.

Reed, who served as Minority Leader during these four years and as Speaker again for the next two Congresses (1895-99), was able by his forceful leadership of House Republicans to restore the concept of party responsibility within the House. His chief aides in the 51st Congress included William McKinley (R Ohio), as chairman of the Ways and Means Committee, and Joseph G. Cannon (R Ill.), as chairman of the Appropriations Committee. McKinley left the House in 1891 (to become Governor, then President in 1897), and when Reed resumed the Speakership in 1895 he named Nelson Dingley

(R Maine) to head Ways and Means. Cannon again became chairman of Appropriations in 1897, when Reed also named James A. Tawney (R Minn.) as the first Republican Whip, charged with keeping party members on the floor and voting with the leadership. Under Reed, House Republicans achieved an exceptional degree of party unity during the 1890s, occasionally voting solidly for measures on which they had been sharply divided in caucus.

The centralization of power in the House during this period coincided with another, less visible change of significance. Until the Civil War, few Members had chosen—or had been enabled by the voters—to make a career of service in the House. As late as the 1870s, more than half of the 293 Representatives then elected to the House every two years were freshmen, and the mean length of service for all Members was barely two terms. Thus, although Speakers for some time had followed seniority to a degree in appointing Members to committees of their choice and in advancing them to chairmanships, it was not a matter of great importance to most Members when they failed to do so.

By 1899, however, the proportion of newcomers among the 357 Members entering the House had fallen to 30 percent, while the mean period of service had increased to more than three terms. As more Members sought to stay in the House for longer periods, it became of increasing importance to them that they have the opportunity to gain political recognition through specialization and rising influence within the committee structure. There was thus a growing demand among Members of both parties for assurance that their seniority would be respected in assigning them rank on committees of their choice. The resulting new expectations contributed to the reaction against centralization that began under Speaker Cannon.

The Revolt Against "Cannonism"

Speaker Reed resigned from the House in 1899, having broken with President McKinley over American intervention in Cuba and the annexation of Hawaii. The Republican majority in the 56th Congress (1899-1901) replaced Reed with David B. Henderson of Iowa, who served two ineffective terms as Speaker (1899-1903) before retiring from the House. In 1903, when Joseph G. Cannon was finally elected Speaker by the Republicans (having been an unsuccessful candidate in 1881, 1889 and 1899), he was the oldest Representative in point of age (67) and service (28 years) ever to have headed the House.

Like Reed, Cannon set out to rule the House and its Republican majority through his control of the Rules Committee and the key chairmen. He kept Sereno E. Payne (R N.Y.) as Majority Leader and chairman of the Ways and Means Committee (positions to which Payne was first appointed by Henderson in 1899.) He also retained Tawney as Majority Whip until 1905, when he named him chairman of Appropriations. Cannon turned over the committee assignments of Democrats to their leader, John Sharp Williams of Mississippi, subject to his veto. But Williams used his authority to build party unity among the Democrats, and Cannon took back the privilege in 1908 when Champ Clark (D Mo.) succeeded Williams as Minority Leader.

As a strong conservative, Cannon was out of sympathy with much of the progressive legislation sought by President Theodore Roosevelt (1901-1909) and by a growing number of liberal Republicans and Democrats

in the House. To maintain control, therefore, he made increasing use of his powers as Speaker to block legislation that he opposed and to thwart and punish Members who opposed him. In a period of rising public interest in political reform, "Cannonism" came to be a synonym for the arbitrary use of the Speaker's powers to obstruct the legislative will, not of the majority party, but of a new majority of House Members of both parties.

The movement to curb Cannon got under way during the last session of the 60th Congress when, just before final adjournment on March 3, 1909, the House adopted the "Calendar Wednesday" rule. This set aside Wednesday of each week for calling the roll of committees, whose chairmen or other authorized members could then call up bills that their committees had reported without getting clearance from the Rules Committee. At the time, progressives considered this a major reform because it seemed to insure the House a chance to act on measures favored in committee but opposed by the leadership. In practice, however, the procedure proved ineffective and in later years the House commonly agreed to dispense with Calendar Wednesday by unanimous consent.

When the 61st Congress first met, in special session, on March 15, 1909, the House was composed of 219 Republicans and 172 Democrats. But the Republicans included about 30 insurgents led by George W. Norris of Nebraska and John M. Nelson of Wisconsin. After helping to elect Cannon to a fourth term as Speaker, the Republican insurgents joined with the Democrats to defeat the usual motion to adopt the rules of the preceding Congress. Clark, the Democratic leader, then offered a resolution to take from the Speaker his existing authority to appoint all committees, to limit that authority to only five committees (of which the only important one would be Ways and Means), to remove the Speaker from the Rules Committee, and to enlarge that body from five to 15 members.

Although 28 Republicans joined in supporting the Clark resolution, 22 Democrats led by Rep. John J. Fitzgerald (N.Y.) voted with the majority of Republicans to defeat it. The House thereupon adopted a compromise resolution, offered by Fitzgerald, which passed over the principal abuses complained of and only slightly curtailed the Speaker's authority. The main change was to establish a Consent Calendar for minor bills of particular interest to individual Members and to set aside two days each month when bills on this Calendar could be called up without the prior approval of the Speaker and passed by unanimous consent. (Adoption of this rule led both parties to designate certain Members as official "objectors," to prevent passage of bills opposed for any reason within the party. But the Consent Calendar became a useful device for processing minor bills.)

Agitation against "Cannonism" nevertheless continued, and the coalition of Democrats and progressive Republicans finally prevailed in 1910. Taking advantage of a parliamentary opening on March 16, Rep. Norris asked for immediate consideration of a reform resolution modeled on Clark's that had been bottled up in the Rules Committee. When Cannon held the motion out of order, the House overruled him by a decisive vote. Debate then began on the Norris resolution, which stripped the Speaker of all authority to appoint committees and their chairmen, removed him from the Rules Committee, and expanded that committee to 10 members who would choose their own chairman.

Rep. Nelson expressed the feelings of the insurgents in these terms: "Have we not been punished by every means at the disposal of the powerful House organization? Members long chairmen of important committees, others holding high rank—all with records of faithful and efficient party service to their credit—have been ruthlessly removed, deposed and humiliated before their constituents and the country because, forsooth, they would not cringe or crawl before the arbitrary power of the Speaker and his House machine.... We are fighting with our Democratic brethren for the common right of equal representation in this House, and for the right of way of progressive legislation in Congress."

The House finally adopted the Norris resolution on March 19, by a vote of 191 to 156, after a continuous session of 29 hours during which Cannon had done his best to round up absentees among his supporters. Recognizing the nature of his defeat, Cannon invited a motion to declare the Chair vacant so that the House might elect a new Speaker. Rep. A.S. Burleson (D Texas) made the motion, but it was quickly tabled; Cannon, known to the House as "Uncle Joe," was personally popular with many Members, and the Republican insurgents were unwilling to help elect a Democrat. Cannon remained Speaker until the end of the 61st Congress in 1911 and a Member of the House (except in the 63rd Congress) until 1923, by which time he had completed 46 years of service.

The revolt against "Cannonism" was consolidated in 1911, when the Democrats took control of the House, elected Champ Clark as Speaker, and adopted a revised body of rules that incorporated most of the changes agreed to in 1909-10. The new rules provided that all members of the standing committees, including their chairmen, would be "elected by the House, at the commencement of each Congress." The rules of 1911 included the Calendar Wednesday and Consent Calendar innovations of 1909, as well as a discharge rule (adopted in 1910) by which a petition signed by a majority of House Members could be used to free a bill locked up in any committee. Also established at this time was a special calendar for private bills, which could be called up two days each month.

Return of the Caucus

No less important than the rules of 1911 were the procedures adopted by the Democratic majority for organizing their control of the House. At the party caucus of Jan. 19 that nominated Clark for Speaker, it was also agreed that Oscar W. Underwood of Alabama would be Majority Leader and chairman of the Ways and Means Committee. And it was decided that the Democratic members of Ways and Means would constitute the party's Committee on Committees to draw up the committee assignments of all Democrats, leaving to the Republicans (who first established their own Committee on Committees in 1917) the selection of their own committeemen. In practice, therefore, the election of committees and their chairmen now took the form of a perfunctory vote to approve the slates drawn up by key members of the majority and minority parties and endorsed by the party caucus.

Underwood rather than Speaker Clark became the recognized leader of House Democrats from 1911 to 1915 (when he moved to the Senate), and he made frequent use of the party caucus to develop unity on legislative issues. Democratic caucus rules at this time provided that "in deciding upon action in the House involving party policy or principle, a two-thirds vote of those present and voting at a caucus meeting shall bind all members of the caucus" so long as the vote represented a majority of the Democrats in the House. But no member could be bound "upon questions involving a construction of the Constitution of the United States or upon which he made contrary pledges to his constituents prior to his election or received contrary instructions by resolution or platform from his nominating authority."

A typical caucus resolution of 1911 bound Democrats to vote for certain bills reported by the Ways and Means Committee and "to vote against all amendments, except formal committee amendments, to said bills and motions to recommit, changing their text from the language agreed upon in this conference." Underwood also used the caucus to develop legislative proposals which would then be referred to committees for formal approval, to instruct committees as to which bills they might or might not report, and to instruct the Rules Committee on the terms to be included in its special orders governing floor consideration of major bills.

Thus the power once concentrated in the hands of Speaker Cannon and "his House machine" now passed to the Democratic caucus, which was dominated by Underwood as Majority Leader. As James R. Mann (R Ill.), the Minority Leader, put it in 1911: "The gentleman from Alabama, Oscar Underwood, is not only the leader of the Democratic majority in the House, but he is the Democratic majority. He is not only the chairman of the Ways and Means Committee, but he is the Ways and Means Committee. In the old days they used to honor the Speaker of the House as being the Grand Chief Mogul, the man of power. The Speaker of the House today is the servant, not the master, of the gentleman from Alabama."

Underwood and his Democratic majority were unable to accomplish much in the 62nd Congress (1911-13), when William Howard Taft was still President and Republicans controlled the Senate. But when Democrat Woodrow Wilson (who had defeated Speaker Clark for the nomination) became President in 1913, the party controlled both houses of the new Congress, and Underwood (as he later recalled) was ready to act: "When the 63rd Congress met, there was a large and thoroughly organized Democratic majority ready to do business for the nation. They were not raw recruits in legislative matters; they were veterans organized and trained in legislative work and procedure. They had not been in power long enough to become divided into cliques, or to be swayed by outside influences. They were primarily loyal to their party and its principles, and desirous of passing legislation that would be responsive to the needs of the country."

Wilson and Congress

As President, Wilson revived the custom of Washington and Adams (abandoned by Jefferson and his successors) of addressing Congress in person. He worked closely with the Democratic leaders in both houses and conferred frequently with committees and individual members to solicit support for his legislative program. With Wilson's help, Underwood and the Democrats were able to effect House passage of four major pieces of legislation in the 63rd Congress—the Underwood Tariff Act, the Federal Reserve Act, the Clayton Antitrust Act, and the Federal Trade Commission Act.

The Democrats were not so united on foreign policy, however. Both Speaker Clark and Majority Leader Underwood disagreed with Wilson over repeal of the exemption from Panama Canal tolls originally accorded to American coastwise shipping. Claude Kitchin (D N.C.), who had become second-ranking Democrat on Ways and Means in 1913 and who succeeded Underwood as chairman and Majority Leader in 1915, openly challenged the President on several issues, notably when Wilson asked for a declaration of war against Germany in 1917. Clark later denounced the President's military conscription program.

Reflecting these disagreements, the strong party unity displayed by House Democrats during Wilson's first term began to fracture in his second. When the party lost control of the House at the mid-term elections of 1918, the binding party caucus had ceased to be an effective instrument in the hands of the leadership. The Republican minority, meanwhile, had all but abandoned use of the binding caucus in 1911, erecting in its place a non-binding "conference" used for little more than to choose the party's nominee for Speaker and to ratify committee slates. By 1919, the House was no longer willing to accept the centralization of power that had developed under Speakers Reed, Crisp and Cannon and Majority Leader Underwood. Party leaders thus were faced with the task of finding new ways to build and maintain consensus.

Accompanying this change—and helping to account for it—was a hardening of the unwritten "rule" of seniority that virtually guaranteed succession to committee chairmanships by the next-ranking majority members on the committees. Democrats violated the "rule" three times in 1911 and on a few occasions thereafter, as did the Republicans. But Representatives could now fairly count on rising in the ranks of their committees (so long as they were re-elected) upon the retirement or death of the more senior members of those committees. Such assurance gave to sitting chairmen and ranking members a degree of independence from dictation that put a new premium on the persuasive skills of party leaders.

Recognition of seniority in the advancement of committee members still left the party committees on committees with the job of assigning vacancies to newcomers and to Representatives seeking to switch from one committee to another. The task of filling vacancies was complicated by keen competition among individuals and among state and regional delegations for the right to places on such choice committees as Ways and Means and Appropriations; in the inevitable bargaining, the political loyalties of the competitors weighed as much as their interests and capabilities. The filling of important committee vacancies was to remain a significant tool in the hands of party leaders.

Republican Years: 1919-1931

By the end of the First World War in 1918, a majority of American voters were already anxious for the "return to normalcy" promised to them two years later by Warren G. Harding as the Republican nominee for President. The mid-term elections of 1918 replaced Democratic with Republican majorities in both houses of the 66th Congress (1919-21), during which President Wilson lost his historic battle with the Senate over the Treaty of Versailles. With the election of Harding in 1920 began a decade of undivided Republican control of the Executive and Legislative Branches of the Federal Government, lasting until Democrats recaptured the House in 1931.

These were not years of Presidential leadership or strong party government. Harding's Administration was marked by widespread corruption, brought to light by Senate investigators after his death in 1923. As Harding's successor, Calvin Coolidge (1923-29) did little to push his legislative program through Congress. President Herbert Hoover (1929-33) was unable to deal effectively with the economic depression that began soon after he took office. Meanwhile, Republican control of the Senate was occasionally nominal, and a minority of party progressives often held the balance of power. Party conservatives were more successful in keeping control of the House during the 1920s, and legislative conflicts between the Senate and the House were common. A notable case in point involved the Senate-approved "lame duck" amendment to the Constitution, which House leaders managed to block until 1932.

There were some important changes in the organization and procedures of the House in this period. Full authority over money bills was reconcentrated in the Appropriations Committee in 1920, and some minor committees were abolished in 1927. Republican leaders introduced, then abandoned, use of a party Steering Committee to guide their legislative program. Under pressure from progressives, House rules were modified in 1924, but the Rules Committee continued to exercise tight control over the legislative options of Members. Meanwhile, the representative quality of the "first branch" declined as the House put off until 1931 the reapportionment of seats that should have followed the census of 1920.

New Budget System

Until 1920, there was no central system for drawing up the Federal Budget or for its consideration in Congress. The Secretary of the Treasury did no more than compile the estimates of the various departments, which in the House were referred to eight different committees, each of which would report an appropriation bill with no reference to total expenditures or revenues. Nor were all of the requests of a department considered by one committee and appropriated in one bill; other committees commonly reported bills that included appropriations. This process, which was repeated in the Senate, led to rising criticism; as Rep. Alvan T. Fuller (R Mass.), founder of the Packard Motor Co., put it in 1918: "The President is asking our business men to economize and become more efficient while we continue to be the most inefficient and expensive barnacle that ever attached itself to the ship of state."

To improve control over expenditures within the Executive Branch, President Wilson in 1919 proposed a new budget system. Although he vetoed the first bill passed by Congress in 1920 (because it placed the Comptroller General beyond his power of removal), a second bill, signed by President Harding, became the Budget and Accounting Act of 1921. This measure directed the President to prepare and transmit to Congress each year a budget showing Federal revenues and expenditures for the previous and current years and estimates for the ensuing year. It set up a Bureau of the Budget as his agency to do the work, and it created a General Accounting Office under the Comptroller General to assist Congress in exercising oversight of the administration of Federal funds.

Anticipating the passage of this bill, the House on June 1, 1920, voted to restore to the Committee on Appropriations the jurisdiction over all supply bills granted to it originally in 1865 *(see above)*. A sizable number of senior House Republicans and Democrats opposed the move, and the House barely agreed to the special rule bringing the resolution to the floor, which was adopted by a vote of 158 to 154. The resolution, which was then approved by a vote of 200 to 117, provided for an increase in the size of the Appropriations Committee from 21 to 35 members. At the same time, the House barred its conferees on appropriation bills from accepting Senate amendments that contravened the rules of the House unless so authorized by a separate House vote on each such amendment.

Most of the responsibility for reviewing Budget estimates was now lodged in 10 five-member subcommittees of the House Appropriations Committee, each of which passed on the requests of one or more agencies. Parallel subcommittees were set up by the Senate Appropriations Committee, and in 1922 it, like the House, was given exclusive authority over money bills. These steps toward a more systematic approach to Federal expenditures came at a time of general concern for greater economy in Government and helped to hold outgo to little more than $3 billion a year from 1922 to 1930. With revenues of close to $4 billion each year, the public debt was reduced from $25 billion in 1919 to $16 billion in 1930.

Additional House Changes

When the Republicans regained control of the House in 1919, their leading contender for Speaker was Rep. James R. Mann (R Ill.), who had been Minority Leader since 1911. But Mann had offended many of his party colleagues by objecting to passage of their private bills, while others feared that he would seek to recentralize power in the manner of his mentor and close friend, former Speaker Cannon. So the Republican conference, looking for more of a figurehead as Speaker, nominated the respected but less forceful Frederick H. Gillett (R Mass.), a Member of the House since 1893. Mann refused the title of Majority Leader, which went to Frank W. Mondell (R Wyo.), and for the first time this position was divorced from the chairmanship of the Ways and Means Committee.

In a further effort to decentralize power, the Republicans created a five-member Steering Committee chaired by the Majority Leader and barred both the Speaker and the chairman of the Rules Committee from sitting on it. Complaints about the narrow range of views and states represented on the Steering Committee led to expansion of its membership to eight in the 67th Congress (1921-23), when Mondell also took to inviting the Speaker, the chairman of Rules and others to sit with the Committee, which met almost daily and served as the major organ of party leadership from 1919 to 1925.

With a Republican majority of 300 in the 67th Congress, party leaders nevertheless came in for growing criticism for blocking action on measures with wide support in the House. Rules Committee Chairman Philip P. Campbell (R Kan.), for one, simply refused to report a number of resolutions approved by a majority of his Committee to authorize certain investigations. He once told the Committee: "You can go to hell. It makes no difference what a majority of you decide. If it meets with my disapproval, it shall not be done. I am the committee. In me repose absolute obstructive powers." And Campbell's right to

pocket a resolution was upheld by Speaker Gillett and, on appeal, by the House.

But Campbell and many other Republicans were defeated in the elections of 1922, and when the 68th Congress met in December of 1923 the House consisted of 225 Republicans and 207 Democrats. Lack of a larger majority enabled a group of about 20 reform-minded Republican progressives to hold up the election of a Speaker in an effort to bring about some liberalization of the rules. For two days and eight ballots the two party nominees— Speaker Gillett and Minority Leader Finis J. Garrett (D Tenn.)—received about 195 votes each, while the progressives cast 17 votes for Rep. Henry A. Cooper (R Wis.).

Then Nicholas Longworth (R Ohio), who had succeeded Mondell as Majority Leader, persuaded the insurgents to support the election of Gillett in return for a promise to allow full debate on revision of the rules in January; Gillett was re-elected Speaker on the ninth ballot. Democrat Henry T. Rainey (Ill.) congratulated Longworth for having steered safely "between the Scylla of progressive Republicanism...and the Charybdis of conservative Republicanism.... There is not a scratch on the ship. The paint is absolutely intact."

The promised debate consumed five days and led to a number of changes in House rules. One, designed to outlaw the "pocket veto" exercised by Chairman Campbell, required the Rules Committee to "present to the House reports concerning rules, joint rules, and order of business within three legislative days of the time when ordered reported by the Committee." The new rule provided also that if the Member making the report failed to call it up within the next nine days, any other Member designated by the Committee could do so.

The House also agreed at this time, by a vote of 253 to 114, to amend the discharge rule first adopted in 1910. The amended rule reduced from 218 (or a majority of Members) to 150 the number required to sign a motion to discharge a committee from further consideration of a bill. Once signed, however, such a motion could be called up only on the first and third Mondays of the month and was subject to other constraints. The single attempt (led by Democrats) to use the new rule in the 68th Congress was successfully thwarted by the Republican leadership.

Disciplining of Progressives

President Coolidge won an easy victory in the election of 1924, when he received almost 16 million votes to eight million for Democrat John W. Davis and less than five million for the Progressive candidate, Sen. Robert M. La Follette (R Wis.). At the same time, the Republican majority of 225 in the House was increased to 247 in the 69th Congress. This gain wiped out the leverage that party progressives had been able to exert at the beginning of the 68th Congress and opened the way for party leaders to discipline those—including most of the Wisconsin delegation—who had supported La Follette in the 1924 campaign.

By the time the new Congress met on Dec. 7, 1925, the Republican conference had agreed to nominate Majority Leader Longworth for Speaker (Gillett having been elected to the Senate), to oust progressive leaders James A. Frear and John M. Nelson of Wisconsin from their seats on the Ways and Means and Rules Committees, and to let the other insurgents know that their committee assignments would depend on how they voted for Speaker and for a new and tougher discharge rule. The insurgents responded by again nominating and voting for Rep. Cooper because, as Frear put it:

"The Wisconsin delegation in Congress today finds itself challenged by those assuming to be in control of the Republican party by threats and intimidation on the one hand and by the offer of party recognition with its favors and patronage on the other. We refuse to compromise, or to bargain with Mr. Longworth or with any other Member of the House on an issue affecting our rights as Representatives in Congress to vote our convictions....Neither flattery nor suggestions concerning committee assignments nor threats will cause the Wisconsin delegation in the House to deviate...."

Longworth was easily elected Speaker on the first ballot, receiving 229 votes to 173 for Democratic Leader Garrett and 13 for Cooper. By a vote of 210 to 192, the House then agreed to substitute for the discharge rule of 1924 a new rule described by Rep. Charles R. Crisp (D Ga. and son of the one-time Speaker) as one that "hermetically seals the door against any bill ever coming out of a committee when the Steering Committee or the majority leaders desire to kill the bill without putting the members of this House on record on the measure."

The new rule to "instruct" committees not only required that "a majority of the membership" (or 218 instead of 150) sign the motion to discharge, but also stipulated that a similar majority second its consideration by a teller vote, for which most Members would rarely show up. Moreover, the motion could be called up only on the third Monday of the month, and if it then failed to be seconded as prescribed, it could not be brought up again during the same Congress. (Not surprisingly, the rule was never invoked during its life, which ended when Democrats revived the old discharge rule in 1931.)

Ten days later, when the Republican slate of committee assignments was submitted to the House, those progressives who had voted for Cooper and against the new rule found themselves demoted to the bottom of their committees. (Senate progressives who had supported La Follette were also dropped to the foot of their committees.) Other Republicans had apparently been brought into line by threats of similar action, according to Minority Leader Garrett, who said "it was demanded that 71 gentlemen who at the beginning of the 68th Congress thought a discharge rule was proper should change their votes, demanded that they should eat the bravest words that many of them ever spoke in order to maintain their standing with the party."

These developments at the beginning of the 69th Congress reflected Longworth's determination to play the role of party leader in the House. He had already stated his belief that it was the duty of the Speaker, "standing squarely on the platform of his party, to assist in so far as he properly can the enactment of legislation in accordance with the declared principles and policies of his party and by the same token resist the enactment of legislation in violation thereof...." As Speaker, Longworth ignored the party Steering Committee and for six years (1925-31) personally took charge of the House with the aid of Majority Leader John Q. Tilson (R Conn.) and Rules Committee Chairman Bertrand H. Snell (R N.Y.). Their success in maintaining control of the House drew from Democrat Crisp in 1931 the charge that this "autocratic triumvirate" had "reduced the House to a mere cipher—an impotent legislative body."

Norris Amendment Blocked

The power of House Republican leaders during the 1920s was illustrated by their success in blocking an amendment to the Constitution designed to abolish the regular "short" session of every Congress by advancing from March to January the time when the life of the previous Congress would expire and that of the new one begin *(see box on Terms and Sessions of Congress)*. House leaders liked the short session because its automatic termination on March 3 strengthened their ability to control the legislative output of the House. Sponsored by Sen. George W. Norris (R Neb.), the progressive who had helped to curb the powers of Speaker Cannon in 1910, the proposed abolition of the short session was approved six times by the Senate before the House, in 1932, finally consented to what became the 20th Amendment.

The effort to adopt what was popularly called the "lame duck" amendment began during the short session of the 67th Congress, which met from Dec. 4, 1922, to March 3, 1923. Sen. Thaddeus H. Caraway (D Ark.) jokingly offered a resolution "that all members defeated at the recent polls abstain from voting on any but routine legislation" and asked that it be referred to the Senate Agriculture Committee, of which Sen. Norris was chairman. The Committee reported instead a joint resolution embodying the "lame-duck" amendment, and the Senate endorsed it on Feb. 13 by a vote of 63 to 6—well over the two-thirds majority required by the Constitution.

The Norris resolution was approved a week later by the House Election Committee, and a special rule for its consideration was ordered reported by majority vote of the Rules Committee. But the chairman of the Rules Committee, Rep. Philip P. Campbell, pocketed the rule, refusing to report it. Then, while sitting as Speaker for the ailing Gillett during the last few days of the session, Campbell (who was himself a "lame duck," having been defeated the previous November) refused to recognize Members who were seeking recognition for the purpose of appealing to the House to override his refusal to report the rule.

On March 18, 1924, in the first session of the 68th Congress, the Senate again adopted the Norris resolution, by a vote of 63 to 7, and three days later it was again reported to the House by the Election Committee. This time, however, it was blocked in the Rules Committee, leading Norris to accuse House leaders of "killing it, not directly but smothering it without giving the House of Representatives an opportunity to vote." Norris added that the resolution was "being held up because machine politicians can get more out of this jam (of legislation at the end of the short session) than the people's Representatives can get." The resolution died with the adjournment of the 68th Congress on March 3, 1925.

The Senate approved the proposed amendment for a third time on Feb. 15, 1926, in the first session of the 69th Congress, by a vote to 73 to 2, and on Feb. 24 it was again reported to the House by a unanimous vote of the Election Committee. Chairman Hays B. White (R Kan.) then discussed the problem he faced under the rules: "Gentlemen, realize how meager is the chance to reach the resolution under the Calendar Wednesday rule. That is the logical and proper rule under which it should be considered....I cannot get unanimous consent...nor can I hope to pass a

Terms and Sessions of Congress

Under the Constitution, Representatives were to be elected "every second year" and Congress was to meet at least once each year "on the first Monday in December, unless they shall by law appoint a different day." But the Continental Congress, which had been asked by the Federal Convention to fix "the time and place for commencing proceedings" of the new Government, told the First Congress to meet on the first Wednesday of March 1789, which happened to be the 4th. Soon afterward, Congress decided that the terms of office of the President, Senators and Representatives would begin on March 4 of the year following their election and expire, in the case of Representatives, two years later.

Out of these decisions developed the practice of long and short sessions. The Fourth Congress, for example, met for the first time on Dec. 7, 1795, and remained in session until June 1, 1796. A second session, beginning Dec. 5 of that year, lasted until March 3, 1797, when by law the terms of the Representatives elected in 1794 expired. Congresses thereafter were often called into special session by the President, or themselves fixed earlier dates for meeting. But for more than 140 years Congress stuck closely to the basic pattern of two sessions—the first a long one of six months or so that began in December more than a year after the elections, and the second a short one that met from December to March after the next elections.

The political consequences of this schedule became apparent in short order. Presidents inaugurated on March 4 were generally free to make recess appointments and take other actions without consulting Congress until the following December. The short sessions became prey to filibusters and other delaying tactics by Members determined to block legislation that would die upon the automatic adjournment of Congress on March 3. Moreover, the Congresses that met in short session always included a substantial

number of "lame-duck" Members who had been defeated at the polls, yet were able quite often to determine the legislative outcome of the session.

Dissatisfaction with the short session began to mount after 1900. During the Wilson Administration, each of four such sessions ended with a Senate filibuster and the loss of important bills including one or more appropriation bills. Sen. George W. Norris (R Neb.) became the leading advocate of a constitutional amendment to abolish the short session by starting the terms of Congress and the President in January instead of March. The Senate approved the Norris amendment five times during the 1920s, only to see it blocked in the House each time. It was finally approved by both chambers in 1932, and became the 20th Amendment upon ratification by the 36th state in 1933.

The Amendment established Jan. 3 of the year following election as the day on which the terms of Senators and Representatives would begin and end, and Jan. 20 as the day on which the President and Vice President would take office. It provided also that Congress should meet annually on Jan. 3 "unless they shall by law appoint a different day." The second session of the 73rd Congress was the first to convene on the new date, Jan. 3, 1934, while Franklin D. Roosevelt was the first President to be inaugurated on Jan. 20, at the start of his second term in 1937.

The Amendment was intended to permit Congress to extend its first session for as long as necessary and to complete the work of its second session before the next election, thereby obviating legislation by a "lame-duck" body. Congress met in almost continuous session during World War II, however, and the 81st Congress met after the elections of 1950 to deal with the Korean War. The Senate alone met after the 1954 elections to act on the censure of Sen. Jospeh R. McCarthy (R Wis.). And in 1970 the 91st Congress resumed work after the midterm elections. By then, the average Congress was in session for 16 to 20 months of its 24-month tenure, and its workload was still mounting.

measure fundamental as this under a motion to suspend the rules....The last alternative is for the Rules Committee to grant a special rule for its early consideration." But the rule was not forthcoming before the final adjournment of the 69th Congress on March 3, 1927.

On Jan. 4, 1928, in the first session of the 70th Congress, the Senate again adopted the Norris resolution, by a vote of 65 to 6, and this time its supporters in the House managed to bring it to the floor. According to Rep. Ole J. Kvale (FL Minn.), the leaders who had kept the House from voting on it for so long "did not dare block it any longer." Rules Committee Chairman Snell acknowledged that "if it had not been for the significant application of these two words, lame duck, the propaganda that has been spread throughout this country would never have been one-half as effective as it has been, and if it had not been for that propaganda I doubt whether this proposition would be on the floor at this time." The amendment was endorsed by a majority on

March 9, 1928, but the vote of 209 to 157 fell 35 short of the two-thirds required for approval.

The Senate approved the Norris resolution for a fifth time on June 7, 1929, by a vote of 64 to 9. A slightly amended version was reported in the House on April 8, 1930, but was not taken up on the floor until Feb. 24, 1931, a week before adjournment. Speaker Longworth then offered a further amendment, to provide that the second session of each Congress should expire automatically on May 4. The Longworth amendment was adopted by a vote of 230 to 148 before the resolution itself was approved, 290 to 93. But the measure was locked in conference when Congress adjourned on March 3.

When the 72nd Congress convened in December 1931, however, Democrats took control of the House, and after the Senate had adopted the resolution for the sixth time on Jan. 6, 1932, 63 to 7, the House quickly followed suit by a vote of 335 to 56 on Feb. 16. Within less than a year, the 20th Amendment had been ratified by three-fourth of the states.

Struggle Over Reapportionment

By 1920, no state had lost a seat in the House through reapportionment since Maine and New Hampshire were deprived of one each after the census of 1880. The reason was that Congress had regularly agreed to increase the total membership by a sufficient number to prevent such a loss. Thus the House was enlarged to 357 Members after the census of 1890, to 391 after that of 1900 and to 435 after that of 1910.

The 1920 census showed that unless the size of the House were again increased, 11 states would lose seats through reapportionment while eight would gain. One argument against such a shift was that voiced by Rep. John E. Rankin (D Miss.) in 1921: "The census was taken at a time when we were just emerging from the World War, and when so many thousands of people had left the farms and the small towns temporarily and gone to the large cities of the North and East that a reapportionment under that census would necessarily take from Mississippi and other agricultural states their just representation and place it to the credit of the congested centers."

Limit on Size of House. To avoid reducing the representation of any state, the House Census Committee early in 1921 reported a bill that would have increased the membership to 483, with the additional seats going to 25 states whose population relative to that of the others had grown the most. But the House proceeded to reverse the Committee, voting 267 to 76 to keep the membership at 435. Proponents of that limit argued that the great size of the membership had already resulted in serious limitations on the right to debate and an over-concentration of power in the hands of the leadership. Much was also made of the increased costs of a larger membership.

The bill passed by the House on Jan. 19, 1921, therefore provided for reapportionment on the basis of the existing membership and would have taken 12 seats from 11 states. But the Senate failed to act on the measure before the 66th Congress adjourned on March 3. When the 67th Congress was called into special session a month later, the House Census Committee, by a vote of 9 to 7, reported a new bill that would have fixed the membership at 460 and cost only two states—Maine and Missouri —one seat each. But on Oct. 14, 1921, the House voted 146 to 142 to recommit the bill to committee, and no further action was taken.

By 1925, it was clear that the wartime shift of population from rural to urban areas was not to be reversed. Such rapidly growing cities as Los Angeles and Detroit began to clamor for the increased representation in the House to which they were entitled. When the House Census Committee still refused to report a new bill, Rep. Henry E. Barbour (R Calif.) moved, April 8, 1926, to discharge the Committee from further consideration of a bill similar to that passed in 1921. Barbour argued that the bill was privileged under the Constitution, while Rules Committee Chairman Snell, raising a point of order, denied that reapportionment was mandatory under the Constitution.

Speaker Longworth found that three of his predecessors—Keifer, Reed and Henderson—had ruled, to the contrary, that Congress was required to order a new apportionment after each census. But Longworth said he doubted whether such a ruling was correct, and he put to the House this question: "Is the consideration of the bill called up by the motion of the gentleman from California in order as a question of constitutional privilege, the rule prescribing the order of business to the contrary notwithstanding?" By a vote of 87 yeas to 265 nays, the House decided the question in the negative.

Coolidge for Reapportionment. In January 1927, President Coolidge made it known for the first time that he favored enactment of a reapportionment bill. When the House Census Committee refused to act, its chairman, E. Hart Fenn (R Conn.), moved on March 2, the day before adjournment, to suspend the rules and pass his bill to authorize a reapportionment of the House by the Secretary of Commerce on the basis of the 1930 census. With only 40 minutes of debate allowed under the rule (which also required a two-thirds vote) and a filibuster under way in the Senate, the House rejected the Fenn motion by a vote of 183 to 197.

The Fenn bill was rewritten early in the 70th Congress, but on May 18, 1928, the House voted 186 to 165 to recommit it to committee. After further revision, the measure was passed by voice vote on Jan. 11, 1929. Reported to the Senate four days later, it was finally abandoned by its supporters on Feb. 27—five days before the end of the session—in the face of a threatened filibuster by Senators from states that were destined to lose seats in the House.

President Hoover called the 71st Congress into special session on April 15, 1929, and listed provision for the 1930 census and for reapportionment as "matters of emergency legislation." On June 13, 1929, the Senate passed, 48 to 37, a combined census-reapportionment bill that had been approved by voice vote of the House two days earlier.

Automatic Reapportionment. The 1929 law established a permanent system for reapportioning the 435 seats in the House following each census. It provided that immediately after the convening of the 71st Congress in December 1930, the President should transmit to Congress a statement of the apportionment of Representatives to each state according to the existing size of the House. Failing enactment of new apportionment legislation by Congress, that apportionment would go into effect for ensuing elections without further action and would remain in effect until another census had been taken. Reapportionment would be effected in the same manner after each decennial count of the population.

The reapportionment based on the 1930 census resulted in a major reshuffling of House seats in the 73rd Congress, which was elected in 1932. Twenty-one states lost a total of 27 seats; Missouri alone lost three, and Georgia, Iowa, Kentucky and Pennsylvania two each. Among the 11 states to which these seats were transferred, California alone gained nine, increasing the size of its delegation from 11 to 20. Other states to win more than one additional seat were Michigan (four), Texas (three), and New Jersey, New York and Ohio (two each).

Democratic Years: 1931-1947

The Great Depression that began in 1929 foreshadowed the end of Republican rule in Washington. The party's majority of 267 in the House of the 71st Congress (1929-31) evaporated in the mid-term elections of 1930, when the returns indicated that the next House would be composed of 218 Republicans, 216 Democrats and one independent. By the time the 72nd Congress met on Dec. 7, 1931, however, 14 Representatives-elect (including Speaker Longworth) had died, and special elections to fill the vacancies had resulted in a net gain of four seats for the Democrats, giving them control of the House.

With 12 million Americans unemployed by 1932, Democrat Franklin D. Roosevelt was elected President along with commanding Democratic majorities in both houses of Congress. A strong party leader, Roosevelt in his first term (1933-37) obtained the enactment of a broad range of "New Deal" economic and social measures. He was less successful in dealing with Congress in his second term (1937-41), when he came into conflict with a "conservative coalition" opposed to his domestic programs. Germany's attack on Poland in 1939, followed by the fall of France in 1940, helped to re-elect Roosevelt to an unprecedented third term (1941-45) that was largely devoted to waging and winning the Second World War. But Legislative-Executive relations deteriorated during the war and when Roosevelt died at the beginning of a fourth term in 1945, Congress was in open rebellion against his plans for postwar reconstruction.

The Democrats who led the House during these years worked closely with the President and did their best, by and large, to marshal support for Administration requests. But their power to shape the legislative output of the House was sharply curtailed after 1937, when a coalition of Southern Democrats and Republicans gained effective control of the Rules Committee, which had been a key arm of House leaders since 1880. The focus of reformers became much broader during the war, however, when the capacity of Congress as a whole to function effectively as a co-equal branch came under attack. This situation led to passage of the Legislative Reorganization Act of 1946.

Party Leaders

The long tenure of southern Democrats became clear when the party took control of the House in 1931. John Nance Garner of Texas, who had become Minority Leader on the retirement of Rep. Finis J. Garrett of Tennessee in 1929, was elected Speaker. A Member since 1903, Garner was then the second-ranking Democrat in the House. Third-ranking Henry T. Rainey (Ill.) was named Majority Leader. But southerners became chairmen of 28 of the 47 standing committees of the House. Among them were Edward W. Pou (N.C., since 1901), chairman of Rules; Joseph W. Byrns (Tenn., since 1909), Appropriations; James W. Collier (Miss., since 1909), Ways and Means; and Sam Rayburn (Texas, since 1913), Interstate and Foreign Commerce.

When Garner became Vice President in 1933, House Democrats elevated Rainey to Speaker and made Byrns the new Majority Leader. Rainey died in 1934, and Byrns was elected Speaker at the beginning of the

74th Congress in 1935, to be succeeded as Majority Leader by William B. Bankhead (Ala.), who had become chairman of the Rules Committee on the death of Pou in 1934. When Byrns died in 1936, Bankhead became Speaker and the Democrats chose Rayburn as Majority Leader. Bankhead remained Speaker until his death in 1940, when he was succeeded by Rayburn, and a northern Democrat—John W. McCormack of Massachusetts—became Majority Leader. Rayburn and McCormack remained in these posts until Republicans took control of the House in 1947.

While the Democrats had been in the minority during the 1920s, southerners had constituted more than one-half of their ranks and there was little occasion for complaint about an unwarranted influence in party councils. But when the party won control of the House in 1931, northern and western Democrats pressed for a larger voice in committee assignments. They proposed entrusting the assignments to a new committee on committees (in place of the one composed of Democratic members of the Ways and Means Committee) to be made up of one member from each state having Democratic representation in the House. This committee would also choose a nine-member steering committee to be in charge of the legislative program.

Steering Committee. These steps were not agreed to in 1931, although additions to the Ways and Means Committee (including Rep. McCormack) brought about a better balance of geographical representation. By 1933, however, the Democratic majority in the House had been increased to 313 Members, nearly two-thirds of whom were from states outside the South. So it was agreed to set up a Steering Committee composed of the Speaker, Majority Leader and Whip, chairmen of the Appropriations, Ways and Means and Rules Committees and of the party caucus, plus 15 Representatives from as many zones to be chosen by Democratic Members within those areas. The Steering Committee operated with some success during the 73rd Congress (1933-35), but fell into disuse thereafter.

Gag Rules. The Rules Committee itself was the major tool of House Democratic leaders during the 73rd Congress, which was called into special session by President Roosevelt on March 9, 1933, and asked to pass a series of emergency recovery measures almost sight unseen. Ten of the measures were brought to the House floor under special "closed" rules—drafted by the Rules Committee and adopted by majority vote—that barred all except committee amendments, waived points of order, and sharply limited debate. Among the laws enacted at this session of 100 days with the help of these "gag" rules were the Emergency Banking Act, the Economy Act, the Emergency Relief Act, the first Agricultural Adjustment Act, the Tennessee Valley Authority Act, and the National Industrial Recovery Act.

Faced with mounting opposition to cuts in veterans' benefits and government salaries ordered under the Economy Act, the Rules Committee at the opening of the second session on Jan. 3, 1934, brought in a rule to bar amendments to any appropriation bill for the remainder of the session that would conflict with the economy program of 1933. The purpose, said Rep. Bankhead, was to have the House "deliberately determine for today and hereafter...whether they are going to follow the President's recommendations or not."

Minority Leader Bertrand H. Snell (R N.Y.), saying that he had never been opposed to special rules so long as they were "fairly fair," called this "the most vicious, the most far-reaching special rule" ever proposed. No majority, he said, had "ever dared bring in a rule that not only hog-tied and prohibited the Members from expressing themselves on the legislation in hand but even extended through the entire session of Congress." The real purpose, said Snell, was that "you think it will be easier to hog-tie your own men today than it will after we have been in session for five months." Snell was joined by all of the Republicans, 84 Democrats and five Farmer-Labor Members in voting against the rule, which was barely adopted, 197 to 192.

The only major change in the standing rules of the House in this period involved the discharge rule. When the Democrats took control of the House in 1931, they replaced the unworkable rule of 1925 with that of 1924, which was altered slightly to reduce from 150 to 145 the number of signatures needed to place a discharge motion on the calendar. But that number was increased to 218 or a majority of the House (as it had been from 1910 to 1924) at the beginning of the 74th Congress in 1935, when Democrats in the House numbered 322 and the leadership was finding it difficult to maintain party unity.

The Conservative Coalition

Party unity was badly shaken at the beginning of the 75th Congress in 1937 when President Roosevelt submitted a plan to reorganize the Supreme Court, through the appointment of additional justices, in order to get a majority that could be counted on to uphold the constitutionality of New Deal measures, of which several had been overturned. This plan to "pack" the Court (which died in the Senate) created a furor in the country and led to a new alignment of conservative Democrats and Republicans in Congress generally and on the House Rules Committee in particular.

The "conservative coalition" first appeared in August of 1937, when the Rules Committee voted 10 to 4 against granting a special rule for floor consideration of an Administration bill that eventually became the Fair Labor Standards Act. The Committee was then chaired by Rep. John O'Connor (D N.Y.) and was composed of five northern Democrats, five southern Democrats, and four Republicans. After its refusal to grant the special rule, House leaders obtained 218 signatures on a discharge petition, but when they brought the bill to the floor in December the House voted 216 to 198 to recommit it to the Labor Committee.

When the Rules Committee in 1938 again refused to clear the wage-hour bill, House leaders once more resorted to the discharge rule to bring the bill to a vote, obtaining passage this time by a margin of 314 to 97. (Although the House had occasionally passed a bill by use of the discharge rule, the Fair Labor Standards Act of 1938 was the first such measure to become law.) Chairman O'Connor's defection in this case made him one of the targets of President Roosevelt's attempted purge of anti-New Deal Democrats in the 1938 primaries. At a press conference, Aug. 16, 1938, Mr. Roosevelt denounced the Rules chairman as "one of the most effective obstructionists in the lower house." O'Connor,

unlike other prominent targets of the purge effort, lost his bid for renomination.

O'Connor was succeeded as chairman of the Rules Committee in 1939 by Rep. Adolph J. Sabath of Illinois, the senior House Democrat by then and an ardent New Dealer. But Sabath continued to be outvoted in the Committee by a coalition of Republicans and southern Democrats led by Reps. E. E. Cox (D Ga.) and Howard W. Smith (D Va.). During the 76th Congress (1939-40), the Committee began the practice of demanding, as the price of sending Administration bills to the floor, substantive changes in these bills to accord with the views of conservatives.

Not only did the coalition use its power on the Rules Committee to block or water down Administration measures; it was also in a position to clear measures opposed by the Administration. Thus the Committee in 1939 authorized an investigation of the National Labor Relations Board; in 1943, an investigation of activities of Executive agencies "beyond the scope of their authority"; and in 1944, an investigation of the Government's seizure of properties of Montgomery Ward & Co. All were intended to embarrass the Administration. Also in 1944, the Committee reported a rule to bring to the floor a price control bill that had been rejected by the Banking and Currency Committee and never reported to the House. Speaker Rayburn took the floor to denounce the rule, saying the Rules Committee "was never set up to be a legislative committee," and the House voted it down.

At the beginning of the 79th Congress in 1945, the size of the Rules Committee was reduced from 14 to 12 members consisting of eight Democrats and four Republicans. Sabath was still chairman, but whenever Reps. Cox and Smith decided to vote with the Republicans they could produce a tie that would block Committee action. In 1945, for example, the Committee by a vote of six to six refused a direct request by President Truman for a rule that would permit the House to vote on a bill to establish a permanent Fair Employment Practices Commission. The coalition also blocked a rule to permit consideration of an Administration bill to raise the minimum wage from 40 to 65 cents an hour.

In 1946, when the Rules Committee was asked to clear an Administration-backed labor relations bill reported by the House Labor Committee, it reported instead a rule to permit substitution of a more drastic measure known as the Case (R S.D.) bill, which had just been introduced. Chairman Sabath denounced the action as "arbitrary" and "undemocratic," but in this case a majority of House members upheld the Committee majority by adopting the rule and passing the Case substitute, which was later vetoed.

The Rules Committee thus ceased to be a dependable arm of the Democratic leadership after 1937, when the coalition of conservative Democrats and Republicans took control. While the views of members of the coalition on social and economic issues were in conflict with those of most Democrats in the House, they frequently reflected the legislative preferences of a bipartisan majority, and it was the support of this broader conservative coalition that enabled those who controlled the Rules Committee to make the most effective use of its powers.

Legislative Reorganization

Talk of the need for Congressional reform mounted during World War II, when the powers of the Executive Branch were vastly enlarged. A report of the American Political Science Association asserted in 1945: "Congress must modernize its machinery and methods to fit modern conditions if it is to keep pace with a greatly enlarged and active Executive Branch. This is a better approach than that which seeks to meet the problem by reducing and hamstringing the Executive. A strong and more representative Legislature, in closer touch with and better informed about the administration, is the antidote to bureaucracy."

Responding to such criticisms, the House and Senate agreed early in 1945 to establish a Joint Committee on the Organization of Congress composed of six Members from each house equally divided among Democrats and Republicans. Sen. Robert M. La Follette Jr. (Prog Wis.) was named chairman with Rep. A. S. Mike Monroney (D Okla.) as vice chairman. From March 13 through June 29, 1945, the group took extensive testimony from more than 100 witnesses, including many Members of Congress.

Among the proposals heard were several to restrict the power of the House Rules Committee. Rep. Christian A. Herter (R Mass.) thought the Committee should be required to grant, within a specified time, requests for special orders on bills favorably reported by the legislative committees. Herter said: "The House Committee on Rules should not have the power of deciding which committee reports shall be considered by the whole House, but should be confined merely to determining the order of their consideration. The Rules Committee ought not to be permitted to prevent the submission of favorable committee reports to the whole House." Rep. Sherman Adams (R N.H.) thought a unanimous report from a legislative committee should automatically give a bill the right of way without reference to Rules.

But in its final report on March 4, 1946, the La Follette-Monroney Committee made no recommendations concerning Rules "because of a lack of agreement within the Committee as to workable changes in existing practices." Nor did the Committee recommend any of the various proposals it had received to select committee chairmen on some other basis than seniority, or proposals to make it easier to limit debate in the Senate. The report nevertheless included a broad range of proposals designed to streamline the committee structure, strengthen Congressional control over the Budget, reduce the workload of Congress, and improve staff assistance, and most of these reforms were incorporated in the Legislative Reorganization Act of 1946 that was signed by President Truman on Aug. 2. Its major provisions:

Committees. The law reduced the number of standing committees from 33 to 15 in the Senate and from 48 to 19 in the House, dropping inactive committees and merging others with related functions. The House committees were: Agriculture, Appropriations, Armed Services, Banking and Currency, District of Columbia, Education and Labor, Expenditures in the Executive Departments (name changed to Government Operations in 1952), Foreign Affairs, House Administration, Interior and Insular Affairs, Interstate and Foreign Commerce, Judiciary, Merchant Marine and Fisheries, Post Office and Civil Service, Public Works, Rules, Un-American Activities (name changed to Internal Security in 1969), Veterans' Affairs, and Ways and Means. (Un-American Activities, a select committee before and during World War II, had been made a standing committee by a 208-186 vote of the House on Jan. 3, 1945.)

All standing committees (except Appropriations) were directed to fix regular days for meeting, keep complete records of committee action including votes, and open all hearings to the public "except executive sessions for marking up bills or for voting, or where the committee by a majority vote orders an executive session." The Act made it the duty of each committee chairman "to report or cause to be reported promptly to the House any measure approved by his committee and to take or cause to be taken necessary steps to bring the matter to a vote." But no measure was to be reported from any committee unless a majority of the members were actually present.

Legislative Budget. The Act directed the House Ways and Means, the Senate Finance, and the Appropriations Committees of both houses, acting as a Joint Budget Committee, to prepare each year a Legislative Budget, including estimates of total receipts and expenditures. The Budget Committee's report was to be accompanied by a concurrent resolution for adopting the budget and fixing the amount to be appropriated. Congress was prohibited from appropriating more than estimated receipts without at the same time authorizing an increase in the public debt. *(See Fiscal Powers, Chapter III.)* The Act did not include a proposal that the President be required to reduce all appropriations by a uniform percentage if expenditures were later found to be exceeding receipts.

Workload. The Act prohibited the introduction of private bills for the payment of pensions or tort claims, the construction of bridges, or the correction of military or naval records—categories of legislation that at one time consumed much time. But Congress did not accept the Joint Committee's proposal that the District of Columbia be given home rule, a step that would have eliminated the District Committees in both houses and a considerable amount of legislative work.

Staff. The Act authorized each standing committee to appoint four professional and six clerical staff members, although no limit was placed on the number that could be hired by the Appropriations Committees. It also made the existing Legislative Reference Service which provided information for Committees and Members requesting it, a separate department of the Library of Congress. The Joint Committee had recommended the appointment of a Director of Personnel, authorized to establish the equivalent of a Civil Service for legislative employees, but this proposal was eliminated in the Senate.

Salaries. The Act increased the salaries of Senators and Representatives from $10,000 to $12,500, effective in 1947, and retained an existing $2,500 non-taxable expense allowance for all Members. The salaries of the Vice President and the Speaker were raised to $20,000. The Act also brought Members of Congress under the Civil Service Retirement Act and made them eligible for benefits at age 62 after at least six years of service.

The Legislative Reorganization Act also included, as Title III, the Federal Regulation of Lobbying Act which for the first time required lobbyists to register with and report their expenditures to the Clerk of the House. But it did not include a provision, recommended by the La Follette-Monroney Committee, that both parties establish seven-member Policy Committees in each chamber, with the majority Policy Committees to "serve as a formal council to meet regularly with the Executive, to facilitate the formulation and carrying out of national policy and to improve relationships between the Executive and Legislative Branches of government." (The Senate, but not the House, agreed later in 1946 to set up party Policy Committees.)

Despite its obvious shortcomings, the 1946 Act was regarded at the time as a major achievement. But its provisions for a legislative budget soon proved to be unworkable, while the Regulation of Lobbying Act was too weak to shed much light on the purposes and activities of pressure groups. In reducing the number of standing committees, it was hoped to limit Representatives to serving on one committee (and Senators on two) in order to make more efficient use of their time. But this practice broke down in later years with the establishment in both chambers of numerous subcommittees and several select committees. The reform of 1946 skirted the issue of the distribution of power within Congress and did not resolve the question of the balance of power between Congress and the Executive; these remained troublesome issues throughout the postwar years.

Postwar Developments: 1947-1970

The Democrats lost control of the House and Senate to the Republicans in the 80th Congress (1947-48) and the 83rd (1953-54) but won majorities in all of the other Congresses from 1949 through 1972. Meanwhile, the Presidency passed from Democrat Harry Truman (1945-52) to Republican Dwight D. Eisenhower (1953-60), who was followed by Democrats John F. Kennedy (1961-63) and Lyndon B. Johnson (1963-68) and Republican Richard M. Nixon (1969-72). Thus during two years under Truman, six under Eisenhower and (prospectively) four under Nixon the President was faced with a Congress controlled by the other party.

These periods of divided government tended to emphasize the partisan aspects of conflict between the President and Congress over public policy. But none of the postwar Presidents was in full command of his own party in Congress, whether it was in the majority or minority, and all were forced at times to seek bipartisan support to get their programs enacted. House Democrats always included 60 or more southern conservatives who were opposed to many of their party's economic and social programs, while a score of moderate to liberal Republicans were frequently at odds with the party's conservative majority.

Leadership in the House was relatively stable in this period. As after the Civil War and World War I, the control of Federal expenditures became a central issue after World War II, and attempts by Congress generally and the House Appropriations Committee in particular to exercise "the power of the purse" were matters of controversy. There was continuing agitation over the power of the House Rules Committee to block

or reshape major legislation, leading to several efforts to restrict the powers of the Committee. Talk of the need for broad-scale Congressional reform increased in the 1960s, and in 1970 the House finally agreed to a reorganization bill that had cleared the Senate in 1967.

Party Leaders

Sam Rayburn of Texas was the unrivaled leader of House Democrats from 1940 until his death in 1961, serving as Speaker in all but the Republican-controlled 80th and 83rd Congresses, when he acted as Minority Leader. Rayburn was a strong Speaker whose influence was enhanced by his veneration of the House as an institution and his high personal standing with most of his colleagues. Faced with a divided party on many issues, he relied heavily on his personal friendships with key Members on both sides of the aisle to attain his ends. And younger Democrats who followed his advice—"to get along, go along"—could expect to be rewarded with preferment of some kind, especially if they could demonstrate talent and a capacity for hard work.

Rayburn's preferences were controlling when it came to Democratic committee assignments. In 1948 he obtained the removal from the Un-American Activities Committee of three Democrats who had supported Dixiecrat Strom Thurmond in the 1948 Presidential campaign. He saw to it that Democrats named to vacancies on the Ways and Means Committee were favorable to reciprocal trade bills and opposed to reductions in the oil depletion allowance. And he turned the Education and Labor Committee from a predominantly conservative into a liberal body during the 1950s by an infusion of younger Democrats. But Rayburn resisted pressure from party liberals to restructure the Rules Committee until 1961, when he reluctantly agreed to go along *(see below)*.

When Rayburn died late that year, after 49 years in the House, Democrats chose as the new Speaker John W. McCormack of Massachusetts, who had served as Majority Leader during Rayburn's entire tenure as Speaker. Carl Albert (D Okla.) was named Majority Leader at the same time. McCormack's performance as Speaker suffered by comparison with that of Rayburn. Criticism of his weakness as a party leader culminated at the beginning of the 91st Congress in 1969, when 58 Democrats voted for Morris K. Udall (D Ariz.) for Speaker in the party caucus. Although easily re-elected Speaker, McCormack decided in 1970 to retire at the end of his term, after 42 years in the House, and Carl Albert was designated to succeed him as Speaker.

House Republicans were led from 1939 to 1959 by Joseph W. Martin Jr. (R Mass.), who also served as Speaker in the 80th and 83rd Congresses, when Charles A. Halleck (R Ind.) held the post of Majority Leader. Martin, a close friend of Rayburn's, was considered by more conservative House Republicans to be too accommodating to the Democratic leadership during the 1950s, and in 1959 he lost his post as Minority Leader to Halleck, an outspoken partisan. In time, Halleck incurred the opposition of younger Republicans seeking a more forceful and positive style of leadership, and in 1965 he was himself ousted when the Republican Conference, by a 73-67 vote, named Gerald R. Ford (R Mich.) as Minority Leader.

Efforts to Control Spending

In 1947, pursuant to the requirement of the Legislative Reorganization Act of 1946, the Republican-controlled 80th Congress formed a Joint Committee on the Legislative Budget which quickly agreed to ceilings on appropriations and expenditures that were substantially under the amounts projected in President Truman's Budget. The House approved these ceilings, but the Senate increased them and insisted that any Budget surplus be used to reduce the public debt rather than to provide a tax cut desired by House leaders. As a result, the resolution embodying the Legislative Budget died in conference.

In 1948, both chambers reached quick agreement on a Legislative Budget that projected a surplus of $10 billion (or more than twice the President's estimate) and paved the way for passage of a tax cut over the President's veto. But Republican leaders expressed doubt about the efficacy of the Legislative Budget as a device for reducing expenditures. Rep. John Taber (N.Y.), then chairman of the House Appropriations Committee, called it "a stab in the dark." His Senate counterpart, H. Styles Bridges (N.H.), said it was "a pre-game guess at the final score." In fact, the projected surplus vanished in fiscal 1949, which ended with a deficit of $1.8 billion.

When the Democrats took control of the 81st Congress, Rep. Clarence Cannon (D Mo.) again became chairman of the House Appropriations Committee. In his view, the Legislative Budget had been "singularly unsuccessful" and "any attempt to continue it would be a futile and useless gesture." Congress put off a decision by voting to postpone until May 1 the deadline for the Joint Committee's recommendations, but these were never forthcoming. The provisions of the 1946 Act for a Legislative Budget remained a part of the law, but Congress made no further effort to comply with them.

In 1950 Cannon tried another approach to expenditure control by having his Committee draft a single omnibus appropriations bill that carried almost $37 billion in spending authority as finally enacted. But this bill was quickly outdated by the Korean War and the need for large supplemental appropriations. More important, the omnibus approach had the effect of reducing the authority of the Appropriations Committee's subcommittees and their chairmen. Cannon asserted that "every predatory lobbyist, every pressure group seeking to get its hands into the U.S. Treasury, every bureaucrat seeking to extend his empire downtown is opposed to the consolidated bill." But in 1951 the Committee voted 31 to 18 to return to the traditional method of separate appropriation bills.

Cannon and his Committee were in full agreement, however, in opposing the concept of a Joint Budget Committee, to be composed of several members of the Senate and House Appropriations Committees. Bills to create such a group were passed by the Senate eight times between 1952 and 1967 but were never accepted by the House. Rep. George H. Mahon (D Texas), who succeeded Cannon as chairman of the House Committee in 1964, summed up the prevailing view of the House on this proposal in 1965 when he said that "every key provision of the bill...is, in my judgment, either unsound, unworkable, or unnecessary."

House-Senate Feud. Behind Mahon's statement lay a long history of resentment over the Senate's claim to co-equal status in the appropriations process, where the House had always asserted its primacy. The issue boiled over in 1962 when the House Appropriations Committee demanded that conference meetings (traditionally held on the Senate side) be rotated between the Senate and House sides of the Capitol. The Senate Appropriations Committee countered by proposing that it initiate one-half of all appropriation bills. The ensuing deadlock froze action on pending bills for months.

The House Committee complained at one point that "in the past 10 years the Senate conferees have been able to retain $22 billion of the $32 billion in increases which the Senate added to House appropriations—a 2 to 1 ratio in favor of the body consistently advocating larger appropriations, increased spending, and corresponding deficits." Sen. A. Willis Robertson (D Va.) called the communication in which this complaint was voiced "the most insulting document that one body has ever sent to another." When the Senate adopted a continuing resolution (to let Federal agencies keep on spending at the old rate until appropriations for the new fiscal year had been approved), the House went on record, 245-1, that the Senate action was "an infringement on the privileges" of the House. The Senate resolved, in turn, that "the acquiescence of the Senate in permitting the House to first consider appropriation bills cannot change the clear language of the Constitution nor affect the Senate's co-equal power to originate any bill not expressly 'raising revenue.' "

The feud was allowed to die without resolution. While it was true that the Senate had consistently voted for larger expenditures than the House, it was also true that Congress had managed generally to authorize less spending than was proposed by the postwar Presidents. Yet the amounts authorized grew more or less steadily after 1947, and it became increasingly apparent that the capacity of Congress to control expenditures through its "power of the purse" was quite limited.

Checking the Rules Committee

The negative power of the House Rules Committee was forcefully displayed during the Republican 80th Congress in connection with efforts to enact a major housing bill. The Committee insisted that the Banking and Currency Committee delete provisions for public housing and slum clearance before it would agree to release the bill. The Committee also refused to allow the House to vote on a universal military training bill reported by the Armed Services Committee, and it was only under strong pressure from Speaker Martin that the Committee cleared a bill to revive the lapsed Selective Service System.

Liberals dominated the Democratic majority of 263 elected to the House in 1948, but they were again faced with the prospect that the 12-member Rules Committee would be controlled by a conservative coalition of four Republicans and three southern Democrats—Reps. E.E. Cox (Ga.), Howard W. Smith (Va.) and William M. Colmer (Miss.). So with the backing of Speaker Rayburn the party caucus voted 176 to 48 for a "21-day rule" proposed by Rules Committee Chairman Adolph G. Sabath (D Ill.). The rule authorized the chairman of any legislative committee which had reported a bill favorably, and requested a special rule from the Rules Committee, to bring the matter to the House floor if the Committee failed to act within 21 calendar days of the request.

Adopted by the House on Jan. 3, 1949, by a procedural vote of 275 to 143, the 21-day rule was used eight times during the 81st Congress to obtain House passage of bills blocked in the Rules Committee, such as an anti-poll tax bill and statehood measures for Alaska and Hawaii. An effort to repeal the new rule in 1950, led by Rep. Cox, was rejected by the House by a vote of 183 to 236.

The Democrats lost 29 seats in the 1950 elections and when the 82nd Congress met on Jan. 3, 1951, Cox again moved to drop the rule. It had been adopted in 1949, he said, because the Rules Committee had "refused to stampede under the lash of the whip applied by strong unofficial minority groups." Rep. Charles A. Halleck (R Ind.) supported repeal because it was the job of the Rules Committee to screen "unwise, unsound, ill-timed, spendthrift and socialistic measures." Sabath protested that repeal would permit an "unholy alliance" of southern Democrats and Republicans to "tear down the rights of every Member of the House." But 91 Democrats joined 152 Republicans to repeal the 21-day rule by a vote of 243 to 180.

Smith's Reign. Control of the Rules Committee by a conservative coalition was virtually unchallenged for the next decade. Rep. Smith, who became chairman in 1955, made the most of his power to censor the legislative program of the House. Because the Committee had no regular meeting day and could be called together only by the chairman, it was sometimes unable to clear any bills during the final days of a session when Smith simply "disappeared" to his Virginia farm.

In 1958, 283 Democrats were elected to the House—their largest majority since 1936—and party liberals again talked of curbing the Rules Committee. They proposed changing the ratio of Democrats to Republicans on the Committee from 8-4 to 9-3 and reinstituting the 21-day rule. Speaker Rayburn was opposed to any changes, however, and the liberals called off their drive. They said the Speaker had assured them that "legislation which had been duly considered and reported by legislative committees will be brought before the House for consideration within a reasonable period of time."

Rayburn however, was unable to fulfill his pledge during the 86th Congress (1959-60). When Democrat John F. Kennedy was elected President in 1960 (along with a reduced Democratic majority of 263 in the House), if was clear that much of his program might be stymied unless Administration Democrats gained control of the Rules Committee when the 87th Congress convened in 1961. Rayburn decided to try to enlarge the Committee from 12 to 15 members to make room for the addition of two loyal Democrats and thus create an 8 to 7 majority that would act favorably on Administration bills. But his plan was stoutly opposed by Chairman Smith and Republican Leader Halleck, and it took Rayburn and his lieutenants a month of maneuvering and lobbying to round up enough votes to win.

Enlargement of Committee. The House finally adopted the rule to increase the size of the Committee from 12 to 15 on Jan. 31, 1961, by a vote of 217 to 212. Voting for the change were 195 Democrats, including 47 southerners led by Rep. Carl Vinson (Ga.), and 22

Republicans, including former Speaker Martin. Opposed were 64 Democrats—all except one of them southerners—and 148 Republicans. The new balance thus achieved on the Rules Committee proved to be precarious. A major school aid bill was effectively killed by the Committee in 1961 when James J. Delaney (D N.Y.), a Catholic from a heavily Catholic district, joined the conservative coalition in voting against it because no provision was made for aid to parochial schools. Two pro-Administration southern Democrats on the Committee helped to kill a bill to create a Department of Urban Affairs in 1962, after Robert C. Weaver, a Negro, was designated to become the new Secretary.

Terms of the resolution adopted in 1961 limited the enlargement of the Committee to the life of the 87th Congress. But the House on Jan. 9, 1963, at the beginning of the 88th Congress, agreed by a vote of 235 to 196 to make the change permanent. Although party ratios had scarcely changed, the resolution was supported this time by 207 Democrats, 59 of them southerners, and 28 Republicans, and opposed by 148 Republicans and 48 Democrats, all except three of them southerners.

New Rules. Democratic leaders nevertheless continued to have problems with the Rules Committee. But the election of President Johnson in 1964, together with a Democratic majority of 295 in the House, paved the way for three further changes in the House rules at the beginning of the 89th Congress in 1965, again over the opposition of a bipartisan coalition. The new rules were adopted Jan. 4 by voice vote after a motion for the previous question ending all debate had been approved by a roll-call vote of 224 to 202. Only 16 Republicans voted with 208 Democrats for the motion, while 79 Democrats (all except four of them southerners) and 123 Republicans were opposed.

The first of the new rules revived, with one change, the 21-day rule that had been in force during the 81st Congress. Under the 1949 rule the Speaker had been required to recognize the chairman or other member of the committee seeking to bring before the House a bill that had been denied a rule by the Rules Committee for 21 days. The 1965 rule left the question of recognition to the discretion of the Speaker, thereby ensuring that no bill opposed by the leadership could be brought up under the rule.

The second new rule permitted the Speaker to recognize a Member to offer a motion that would permit the House to send a bill to conference with the Senate by majority vote, provided that this action was approved by the committee with jurisdiction over the bill. Previously, it had been necessary to obtain unanimous consent or approval of a special rule from the Rules Committee to send a bill to conference, or to suspend the rules by a two-thirds vote.

The third change agreed to in 1965 repealed a rule dating from 1789 that had permitted any Member to demand the reading in full of the engrossed (or final) copy of a House bill. Members opposed to legislation had frequently used this privilege to delay final passage of a bill until it could be printed.

The 21-day rule was employed successfully eight times during the 89th Congress, and the threat of its use persuaded the Rules Committee to send several other controversial measures to the floor. As in 1951, however, Republican gains in the 1966 elections opened the way to repeal of the rule at the beginning of the 90th Congress; the vote on Jan. 10, 1967, was 233 to 185. The prevailing coalition included 157 Republicans and 69 southern Democrats. The two other rules adopted in 1965 were retained.

Repeal of the 21-day rule in 1967 proved to be of little consequence during the 90th Congress, largely because of two other developments affecting the Rules Committee. Chairman Smith had been defeated in a primary election in 1966, as had another Committee Democrat, and these vacancies were filled by Administration supporters. Smith's successor as chairman, Rep. Colmer of Mississippi, was no less strong a conservative, but he was now outvoted on the Committee. This became apparent on Feb. 28, 1967, when for the first time in its history the Committee adopted a set of rules to govern its procedures. These rules took from the chairman his exclusive power to set meeting dates, required the consent of a Committee majority to table a bill, and set limits on proxy voting by members. The net effect of these changes was substantial cooperation with the Democratic leadership in 1967-68 and the end of a decade of agitation for reform of the Committee. The situation remained substantially the same during the 91st Congress (1969-70).

Pressures for Reform

Efforts to modify the organization and procedures of the House after 1946 were not confined to the protracted struggle for control of the Rules Committee. Both the Senate and the House came under pressure to curb the free-wheeling activities of their investigating committees in the early 1950s. The questionable conduct of some Senators and Representatives raised new doubts about Congressional ethics in the 1960s to which both chambers were forced to respond. Mounting criticism of the methods and operations of Congress as a whole led both chambers to begin a re-examination in 1965 that finally produced a second reorganization act in 1970. These developments are discussed below.

Fair Play Code. The efforts of the House Un-American Activities Committee to expose subversion and disloyalty through public hearings became a subject of great controversy in the early 1950s. The Committee's access to television was cut off in 1952 when Speaker Rayburn effectively banned radio, television or film coverage of any House committee hearings by holding that there was no authority for such coverage in the rules of the House. But criticism increased in the Republican-controlled 83rd Congress when Chairman Harold H. Velde (R Ill.) of the Un-American Activities Committee and Sen. Joseph R. McCarthy (R Wis.), head of the Senate Permanent Investigations Subcommittee, were accused of conducting "one-man" investigations and mistreating witnesses.

McCarthy was eventually censured by the Senate in 1954 for contemptuous treatment of two Senate committees. *(See Congressional Investigations, Chapter III.)* The Rules Committees of both chambers held hearings in 1954 on proposals to reform committee procedures. On March 23, 1955, the House adopted 10 new rules respecting committee conduct which—

● Required a quorum of not less than two committee members for taking testimony and receiving evidence.

● Allowed witnesses at investigative hearings to be accompanied by counsel "for the purpose of advising them concerning their constitutional rights."

● Stipulated that if a committee found that evidence "may tend to defame, degrade, or incriminate any person," it receive such evidence in executive (or closed) session and allow such person to appear as a witness and request the subpoena of others.

● Barred the release or use in public sessions of evidence or testimony received in executive session without the consent of the committee.

The Senate Rules Committee recommended a similar set of standards in 1955, but the Senate left it to individual committees to draw up their own rules of conduct. Those adopted by the Permanent Investigations Subcommittee in 1955, when Sen. John L. McClellan (D Ark.) became chairman, incorporated provisions similar to those approved by the House. Although the investigative practices of Congressional committees continued to vary considerably thereafter, the question of the fair treatment of witnesses declined in importance as a public issue.

Congressional Ethics. Corruption has been a constant companion of Government and politics in every age, and Members of Congress were never imune to the temptations of using public office for private gain. But except for the occasional scandal of a Member convicted of a crime or disciplined by his colleagues for misconduct, the ethics of Congress as a whole did not begin to stir broad public interest until the years following World War II. Contributing to this interest were the rising costs of political campaigns and an increasing concern with conflicts of interest at all levels of Government. The fact that some Members of Congress continued to engage in private law practice or other business activities, and to hold a financial interest in such Government-regulated businesses as banks and television stations, added to the concern.

Pressure to do something about Congressional ethics was intensified in 1963 by charges that Robert G. (Bobby) Baker had used his office as Secretary to the Senate Majority to promote his outside business interests. The Senate responded by establishing in 1964 a six-member bipartisan Select Committee on Standards and Conduct empowered to investigate "allegations of improper conduct" by Senators and Senate employees, to recommend disciplinary action, and to draw up a code of ethical conduct. Its first inquiry led to the Senate's censure of Sen. Thomas J. Dodd (D Conn.) in 1967 by a vote of 92 to 5, for misuse of political campaign contributions.

In 1968 the Select Committee recommended and the Senate adopted new rules aimed at the practices disclosed in the Baker and Dodd cases. Included were provisions to regulate the outside employment of Senate employees, to require a full accounting of campaign contributions and limit the uses to which they could be put, and to require Senators and higher-ranking employees to file copies of their tax returns and some other financial data with the Comptroller General each year. But this information was to remain confidential (although accessible to the Select Committee) and the only public accounting required under the new rules was of gifts of $50 or more and honoraria of $300 or more. The

Senate, by a vote of 40 to 44, had rejected a proposal for full public disclosure of the finances of its members.

The House, meanwhile, had become embroiled in attempts to discipline Rep. Adam Clayton Powell (D N.Y.), a Member since 1945, chairman of the Education and Labor Committee since 1961, and one of the few Negroes in the House. Powell was indicted for tax evasion in 1958 and eventually paid $28,000 in back taxes and penalties. He was sued for libel in 1960 and held in contempt of court in the case on several occasions. He kept his wife on his payroll at $20,000 a year although she lived in Puerto Rico. But it was his extensive travels at public expense, his prolonged absences from Congress and his high-handed actions as a committee chairman that turned most of his colleagues against him.

At the beginning of the 90th Congress in 1967, the Democratic caucus removed Powell as chairman of the Education and Labor Committee, and the House voted 365-65 to deny him his seat pending an investigation by a special committee. Its report recommended that Powell be seated but that he be censured for "gross misconduct," stripped of his seniority and fined $40,000 for misuse of public funds. But on March 1 the House rejected these proposals and voted instead to exclude Powell from the 90th Congress and declare his seat vacant.

Powell promptly filed suit in Federal court to regain his seat on the grounds that he met the constitutional qualfications for membership and that the House had no authority to exclude him. A district court dismissed the case for lack of jurisdiction, and the Court of Appeals affirmed the finding, noting that the case involved a political question which, if decided by the courts, would constitute a violation of the separation of power. On June 16, 1969, however, the Supreme Court reversed the lower courts by a vote of 7 to 1; the opinion by Chief Justice Earl Warren held that Powell had been improperly excluded by the House.

Powell had been overwhelmingly re-elected by his Harlem constituency following his exclusion in 1967, but he had made no effort to take his seat during the remainder of the 90th Congress. Re-elected in 1968, he presented himself at the opening of the 91st Congress in 1969. By this time tempers had cooled. The House by a vote of 254-158 adopted a resolution that permitted him to take his seat but fined him $25,000 "as punishment" and stripped him of his seniority. Powell accepted the judgment, but his career in the House was ended in 1970 when he was defeated in the primary election.

The Powell case, together with the Senate's actions, helped to persuade the House in 1967 to establish its own 12-member, bipartisan Committee on Standards of Official Conduct. In 1968 the Committee recommended and the House adopted (as Rule 43) a Code of Official Conduct which included provisions that—

• Forbade a Member or employee to use his official position improperly to receive compensation.

• Prohibited the acceptance of gifts of "substantial value" from an individual or group with a direct interest in legislation before Congress.

• Prohibited acceptance of honoraria of more than "the usual and customary value" for speeches and articles.

• Required Representatives to keep campaign funds separate from personal funds and not to convert campaign funds to personal use.

• Required that, unless some other purpose was made clear in advance, all funds raised at testimonial events must be treated as campaign contributions subject to the reporting requirements and spending limits of the Corrupt Practices Act.

• Required that employees of a Member perform the work for which they were paid.

The House also adopted at the same time a new rule (Rule 44) that required Members and officers of the House, their principal assistants, and professional staff members of committees to file with the Committee on Standards of Official Conduct each year a report disclosing certain financial interests—which were to be available to the public—and a sealed report on the amount of income from those interests. As under the Senate rules, the sealed report could be opened by the Committee only if it determined that it was essential to an investigation, while the data that might be made public were extremely limited.

The new rules adopted by the Senate and House in 1968 did not put an end to the questioning of Congressional ethics. The practice of certain Senators in introducing hundreds of private immigration bills for Chinese ship-jumpers came under fire in 1969 and an aide to Speaker McCormack was indicted for influence peddling in 1970. When Supreme Court Justice Abe Fortas resigned in 1969 following disclosures of certain financial activities, Sen. Clifford P. Case (R N.J.) renewed his argument that public confidence in the Government "will not be restored until Congress makes it mandatory for Supreme Court Justices and all other members of the Federal Judiciary, as well as Members of Congress and high officials in the Executive Branch, to make full, regular and, most importantly, public reports of their income and financial activities." But when or whether a majority of Senators and Representatives would agree to make a full public disclosure or their finances remained an open question in 1971.

Reorganization Bill. The efficiency and equity of Congressional procedures also were questioned with increasing frequency in the 1960s, and in 1965 the Senate and the House agreed to set up a new Joint Committee on the Organization of the Congress modeled on the committee headed by Sen. Robert M. LaFollette Jr. (Prog. Wis.) and Rep. A. S. Mike Monroney (D Okla.) that had put through the Legislative Reorganization Act of 1946. A Senator since 1951, Monroney was named co-chairman of the new committee along with Rep. Ray J. Madden (D Ind.). After extensive hearings in 1965, the Committee in 1966 issued a long list of recommendations most of which were incorporated in a bill passed by the Senate in 1967. But the bill met with strong opposition from committee chairmen and other senior Members of the House and remained bottled up in the Rules Committee until the end of the 90th Congress.

The reform effort was renewed in the 91st Congress, and in 1970 the House was finally able to act on a bill of its own. Passed by the House on Sept. 17, the bill was accepted by the Senate on Oct. 6. As finally enacted, the Legislative Reorganization Act of 1970—like that of 1946— fell considerably short of the objectives of reformers. It contained nothing affecting the seniority system, the power of the House Rules Committee, or the two-thirds rule for limiting Senate debate. But it included a number of important provisions designed to give both chambers access to more information on Government finances, to give the minority party more staff assistance on committees, and to maintain a continuing review of legislative needs through a Joint Committee on Congressional Operations.

Among the more important provisions affecting only the House was one requiring that, upon the request of one-fifth of a quorum, a teller vote be recorded and the names of Members voting for, against, or not voting on the question be printed in the Record. Previously, it was not possible to tell how—or whether—a Member had voted on amendments accepted or rejected by teller vote in Committee of the Whole, where the final shape of legislation considered by the House was largely determined.

The 1970 law also amended the rules of the House to:

- Require all committees except Rules to file reports on bills ordered reported within seven days after a majority of the committee files a request that the report be filed.
- Extend to most bills reported to the House the 1946 requirement that reports on general appropriation bills be available for three days prior to House consideration.
- Permit any committee by majority vote to allow an open hearing to be broadcast over radio or television subject to certain ground rules for coverage. (No such coverage had been permitted since Speaker Rayburn's ruling of 1952.)
- Permit all committees to sit without special leave while the House is in session, except when a bill is being read for amendment under the five-minute rule.
- Allow the House (on the request of any Member) to vote separately on any nongermane amendment added by the Senate to a House-passed bill.
- Dispense with the reading of the daily Journal unless otherwise ordered by the Speaker or a majority of Members present.

(For complete provisions of the Legislative Reorganization Act of 1970, see Chapter II, The Legislative Process; for seniority system, see Chapter II, p. 171.)

Bibliography

Books

Alexander, De Alva S., *History and Procedure of the House of Representatives.* Houghton Mifflin Co., 1916.

Bolling, Richard, *House Out of Order.* Dutton, 1965.

—, *Power in the House.* Dutton, 1968.

Brown, George Rothwell, *The Leadership of Congress.* Bobbs-Merrill, 1922.

Burns, James MacGregor, *Congress on Trial.* Harper & Bros., 1949.

Carroll, Holbert N., *The House of Representatives and Foreign Affairs.* University of Pittsburgh Press, 1958.

Ch'iu, Ch'ang Wei, *The Speaker of the House of Representatives Since 1896.* Columbia University Press, 1928.

Clapp, Charles L., *The Congressman: His Work as He Sees It.* The Brookings Institution, 1963.

Congress and the Nation, 1945-1964 (Vol. I). Congressional Quarterly Inc., 1965.

Congress and the Nation, 1965-1968 (Vol. II). Congressional Quarterly Inc., 1969.

Fenno, Richard F., *The Power of the Purse: Appropriations Politics in Congress.* Little, Brown, 1966.

Follett, Mary P., *The Speaker of the House of Representatives.* Longmans, Green & Co., Inc., 1896.

Froman, Lewis A., *Congressmen and Their Constituencies.* Rand McNally, 1963.

Galloway, George B., *History of the House of Representatives.* Thomas Y. Crowell Company, 1961.

Griffith, Ernest S., *Congress, Its Contemporary Role.* New York University Press, 1956.

Harlow, Ralph V., *The History of Legislative Methods in the Period Before 1825.* Yale University Press, 1917.

Hasbrouck, Paul DeWitt, *Party Government in the House of Representatives.* Macmillan, 1927.

MacNeil, Neil, *Forge of Democracy: The House of Representatives.* David McKay Company, Inc., 1963.

McConachie, L.G., *Congressional Committees: A Study of the Origin and Development of Our National and Local Legislative Methods.* Thomas Y. Crowell Company, 1898.

McCown, Ada C., *The Congressional Conference Committee.* Columbia University Press, 1927.

Miller, Clem, *Member of the House.* Charles Scribner's Sons, 1962.

Riddick, Floyd M., *The United States Congress; Organization and Procedure.* National Capitol Publishers, Inc., 1949.

Ripley, Randall B., *Party Leaders in the House of Representatives.* The Brookings Institution, 1967.

Robinson, James A., *The House Rules Committee.* Bobbs-Merrill Company, Inc., 1963.

Schmeckebier, Laurence F., *Congressional Apportionment.* The Brookings Institution, 1941.

Steiner, Gilbert Y. *The Congressional Conference Committee, Seventieth to Eightieth Congress.* University of Illinois Press, 1951.

Wallace, Robert Ash, *Congressional Control of Federal Spending.* Wayne State University Press, 1960.

Wilmerding, Lucius, *The Spending Power, a History of the Efforts of Congress to Control Expenditures.* Yale University Press, 1943.

Wilson, Woodrow, *Congressional Government.* Meridian Books edition, 1956.

Young, Roland, *The American Congress.* Harper & Bros., 1958.

Government Publications

Biographical Directory of the American Congress, 1774-1961. Government Printing Office, 1961.

Hinds, Asher C. and Cannon, Clarence, *Precedents of the House of Representatives of the United States* (11 vols.). Government Printing Office, 1907 and 1936.

History of the Senate

TO GLADSTONE it was "the most remarkable of all the inventions of modern politics." To Bryce it was a "happy accident." Bagehot called it a blunder, and other critics have been even more severe. However described, the Senate of the United States clearly ranks as the most powerful second legislative chamber in the world today.

It is not, however, precisely what its creators had in mind. Edmund Randolph said its purpose was to provide a cure for the "turbulence and follies of democracy," and James Madison asserted that "the use of the Senate is to consist in its proceeding with more coolness, with more system, and with more wisdom, than the popular branch." In the Constitutional Convention, Madison maintained that the purpose of the Senate was first "to protect the people against their rulers; secondly to protect the people against the transient impressions into which they themselves might be led.... They themselves, as well as a numerous body of Representatives, were liable to err also, from fickleness and passion. A necessary fence against this danger would be to select a portion of enlightened citizens, whose limited number, and firmness might seasonably interpose against impetuous councils...." Gouverneur Morris hoped simply "that the Senate will show us the might of aristocracy." Opponents feared it might become an American House of Lords.

Compromise of 1787

Under the "Great Compromise" of 1787, the House of Representatives was to represent the "national principle," while the Senate was to be an expression of the "Federal principle." Not only would each state have two votes in the Senate, but the election of Senators by the state legislatures would serve as a means of making the states "a constituent part of the national establishment." Although the basis of representation assured each state an equal voice, Senators voted as individuals, they were paid by the Federal Government rather than the states, and the legislatures that elected them had no power to recall them. Thus it is not surprising that most Senators refused to consider themselves merely the agents of the state governments. Efforts by state legislatures to "instruct" their Senators had only mixed success, but the practice did not die out entirely until 1913, when the adoption of the 17th Amendment took the election of Senators out of legislative hands.

The framers of the Constitution left unsettled many questions concerning the relationships among the branches of Government, and it remained for the Senate —born of compromise and fashioned after no serviceable model—to seek its own place in the governmental structure. In unending competition with the other branches for a meaningful share of power, the Senate for nearly two centuries has been trying to define its role, and the history of the Senate is in large part the story of this quest.

Early Conceptions of Senate Role

It had been confidently predicted that the popularly elected House of Representatives would be the predominant chamber in the national legislature, with the Senate acting chiefly as a revisory body. At first the House did overshadow the Senate, both in power and prestige, but within a few decades the Senate—endowed with executive functions which the House did not share and blessed with a smaller and more stable membership—had achieved primacy over the lower chamber. Later the balance of power shifted from time to time, but the Senate never followed the British House of Lords into decline.

As the nation's population expanded, the size of the House mushroomed, while the Senate, in which the large and the small states were equally represented, remained a comparatively small body. Growth compelled the House to impose stringent limitations on floor debate, to rely heavily on its committee system and to develop elaborate techniques to channel the flow of business—all steps that diminished the power of individual Representatives. Such restrictions were not considered necessary in the Senate, where in any case Members tended to view themselves as ambassadors of sovereign states, and the right of unlimited debate became the most cherished tradition of the upper chamber. To the House, action was the primary object; in the Senate, deliberation was paramount.

It had also been expected that the Senate would serve as an advisory council to the President, but natural friction between the two branches, aggravated by the rise of the party system, made such a relationship impracticable. As time passed, the Senate was far more likely to try to manage the President than to advise him. In the 19th century the Senate was often the dominant force in the Government, but the rapid expansion of Presidential power in the 20th century was accompanied by a corresponding decline in the power of the Legislative Branch, and the Senate increasingly felt that its existence as a viable legislative institution was threatened.

Insulation From Popular Pressure

The framers had expressed their distrust of democracy by providing for election of Senators by the state legislatures rather than directly by the people. In "refining the popular appointment by successive filtrations," they hoped to assure excellence, guard against "mutability" and incidentally protect the interests of the propertied classes. Under this system, which Madison in *The Federalist* described as "probably the most congenial with public opinion," the Senate enjoyed its periods of greatest prestige. But as suffrage expanded and the democratization of government increased, pressure arose for direct election of Senators. At length, the Senate was forced to participate in its own reform, and in 1912 Congress approved a proposed constitutional amendment providing for direct election. The 17th Amendment, ratified in 1913, curtailed the abuses that had so frequently been associated with legislative election, but its other effects were difficult to measure. At any rate, no revolutionary change in the over-all character of the institution could be discerned.

Senate's Slowness to Act

So successful were the framers in insulating the Senate from popular pressure that the body often seemed to care more for what Bryce called its "collective self-esteem" than it did for public opinion. Sometimes it could be forced to act—as in the case of the 17th Amendment and the adoption of the cloture rule in 1917—but its resistance to impetuous action was for the most part all its creators could have wished.

Sometimes any action at all seemed beyond its capacity. In the declining days of the 91st Congress in December 1970, the Senate found itself at such an impasse. Several filibusters were in progress, others were threatened, and the public was dismayed by what President Nixon was to call "the spectacle of a legislative body that had seemingly lost the capacity to decide and the will to act."

The Senate met this situation in typical fashion. When complaints were voiced that Senate conferees had given in too often to their House counterparts, thereby thwarting the will of the Senate, Majority Leader Mike Mansfield (D Mont.) warned: "If it wishes, the Senate as an institution can reduce itself to a House of Lords." And later, in proposing an executive session to consider ways to break the legislative logjam, Mansfield remarked: "We (the leaders) are disturbed at the image which this body is showing to the American people, but we are more disturbed at the image we are showing to ourselves."

When the 92nd Congress convened a few weeks later, the Senate exhibited a characteristic determination to protect its internal structures from external attack. The biennial attempt to tighten curbs on the filibuster ended, as usual, in failure, as did a move to select committee chairmen on some basis other than seniority. Reform of the seniority system was urged as a way "to restore confidence in the legislative process," but the leading opponent of the anti-seniority proposal, Majority Whip Robert C. Byrd (D W.Va.), asserted that the proposed change would be "disruptive not only of comity among Members but destructive of the Senate itself to a considerable degree." The Senate apparently agreed: the proposal was killed by a vote of 48-26.

The Formative Years: 1789-1809

Only eight Senators had reached New York City by March 4, 1789, the date fixed for the first meeting of Congress, and a quorum of the 22-man Senate—two of the 13 states had not yet ratified the Constitution—did not appear until April 6, five days after the House had organized. Crucial questions concerning the nature of the Senate and its proper role in the new Government remained to be worked out.

Was the upper chamber to be principally a council to revise and review House measures, or a fully coequal legislative body? Should it also serve in a quasi-executive capacity as an advisory council to the President, particularly with respect to appointments and treaties? Was the Senate primarily the bastion of state sovereignty, the defender of propertied interests, a necessary check on the "democratic licentiousness" of the popularly elected House, or was it, as its opponents charged, a threat to republican principles and an incipient American House of Lords? Even the method of electing Senators was in dispute: Were they to be chosen by joint or concurrent vote of bicameral state legislatures? This issue, which was not resolved until 1866, cost New York its Senate representation during most of the first session of Congress. The terms of individual Senators were also in doubt. Under the Constitution, the first Senators were to be divided into three classes—with terms of two, four and six years respectively—so that one-third of the Senate might be chosen every second year. To avoid charges of favoritism, the Senate resorted to choice by lot in making the division.

Senate Relations With House. The first Senate, preoccupied with questions of form and precedence, was quick to claim for itself superiority over the House, but the lower chamber initially was the more important legislative body. James Madison chose to serve in the House rather than the Senate on the ground that, "being a young man and desirous of increasing his reputation as a statesman, he could not afford to accept a seat in the Senate."

In the earliest days of the first session, while the House was addressing itself to the financial problems of the infant nation, the Senate devoted three weeks to the consuming problem of an appropriate title of dignity for the President. The debate apparently was instigated by Vice President John Adams, whose penchant for ceremony earned him the mocking title of "His Rotundity."

The Senate's early insistence on form and its claim to deference from the House led to disputes over the method of transmitting communications between the two chambers, wording of the enacting clause in proposed legislation and proposals (briefly accepted) for differential pay for Senators. With a mixture of resentment and amusement, the House rebuffed most Senate efforts to enhance its own prestige, the Senate soon abandoned its "aristocratic" claims, and relations between the two chambers became generally cordial.

Although the Senate initiated bills from the very beginning, in the earliest years most laws originated in the House (78 percent from 1789 to 1809) with the Senate acting as a revisory body. During the first session of the First Congress only five bills were introduced in the Senate, of which four—including the important Judiciary Act—were passed. During the same period, the House originated and passed 26 bills; two of these were rejected by the Senate, one was lost in conference, and the Senate modified at least 20 of the remaining 23.

Relations With the President. The concept of the Senate as an advisory council to the President never was realized. President Washington took informal advice, not from the Senate as a body, but from Alexander Hamilton, Madison (a House Member) and others. The constitutional role of the Senate in the appointment process also fell short of the consultative role that some framers of the Constitution had envisioned. Washington's exercise of the appointment power carefully stressed the separate natures of the nomination and confirmation processes, a point underscored by his decision to submit nominations to the Senate in writing rather than in person. The Senate's role as an advisory council was further restricted in 1789, when the Senate narrowly accepted House-passed language vesting in the President alone the power to remove Executive officers. Under Washington's successors Members of Congress had greater influence over appointments, but the principle of Executive initiative remained firmly established.

Washington only once attempted to put into practice his avowed intention to confer in person with the Senate over the terms of proposed treaties. The disastrous failure of this effort *(see box)* was followed by a gradual decline in Senate participation in the early stages of treaty-making, a development that made possible greater freedom of action when the time came to vote on ratification.

The Jay Treaty with England was perhaps the most crucial issue to come before the Senate in these early years. The controversy over this unpopular treaty, which for a time threatened the very existence of the Senate, had important effects upon the chamber's relations with both the President and the House of Representatives. *(See Foreign Affairs, Chapter III.)*

Relations With the States. The concept of Senators as agents of state sovereignty led to repeated but largely unsuccessful efforts to make Senators accountable to their state legislatures. Some Members of Congress, Representatives as well as Senators, felt an obligation to make periodic reports on their activities to the state governments, and a continuing controversy raged over the right of state legislatures to instruct their Senators. Instruction was more general in the South than in the North, but there was no unanimity of opinion on the question. However, with the emergence of political parties, party loyalty gradually took the place of the expected state allegiance.

Early Senate Procedure

Courtesy, dignity and informality marked the proceedings of the early Senate. A body that on a chill morning might leave its seats to gather around the fireplace had no need for an elaborate system of regulation. At the first session in 1789 the Senate adopted only 20 short rules, a number deemed sufficient to control the proceedings of a Senate no larger than some modern-day Congressional committees. In 1806, the number of rules rose to 40; most of the new ones dealt with nominations and treaties.

Washington in the Senate

President Washington's early view was that "in all matters respecting treaties, oral communications (with the Senate) seem indispensably necessary." Accordingly, on Aug. 22, 1789, the President and his Secretary of War, Gen. Henry Knox, appeared in the Senate chamber to consult with the Senate about a treaty with southern Indians. Sen. William Maclay of Pennsylvania gave an account of the proceedings in his *Journal.*

A paper containing the President's proposals was hurriedly read to the Senate by the Vice President, but Members were not able to hear because of the noise of carriages passing in the street outside. The windows were closed and the proposals read again. In the silence that followed, the Vice President began to put the first question, but Maclay, fearing "that we should have these advices and consents ravished in a degree from us," rose and called for reading of the treaties and supporting documents alluded to in the President's paper. The President "wore an aspect of stern displeasure." Maclay "saw no chance of a fair investigation of subjects while the President of the United States sat there, with his Secretary of War, to support his opinions and over-awe the timid and neutral part of the Senate." Therefore, he backed a move to refer the entire subject to a committee. At this suggestion, the President "started up in a violent fret," exclaiming "This defeats every purpose of my coming here." After he had "cooled down, by degrees," the President agreed to a two-day postponement, then withdrew from the chamber "with a discontented air."

On his return to the Senate two days later, Washington was "placid and serene, and manifested a spirit of accommodation," but the atmosphere was still tense, and "a shamefacedness, or I know not what, flowing from the presence of the President, kept everybody silent." At length, the business was concluded and the President departed. The experience was not one that he ever cared to repeat.

The rules left a wide area of decision to the Senate President, particularly Rule 16 which gave him sole authority to decide points of order. Vice President Adams presided over the Senate (1789-97) with no specific guides on procedure, but his successor, Thomas Jefferson (1797-1801), felt the need to compile "some known system of rules" and precedents "by which I judge and am willing to be judged." The result was *Jefferson's Manual of Parliamentary Procedure*, which was also adopted by the House in 1837.

Closed Sessions. Following the practice of the Congress of the Confederation, the Senate originally met behind closed doors. Total secrecy was not maintained, however, since Senators often freely discussed their activities outside the chamber, and the Senate *Journal* and sketchy reports of Senate action appeared in print from time to time. The principal result of the closed-door policy was to focus public attention on the widely reported debates of the House and to encourage suspicion of the "aristocratic" Senate. Beginning in 1790, various state

Rules of the First Senate

I. The President having taken the chair, and a quorum being present, the journal of the preceding day shall be read, to the end that any mistakes may be corrected that shall have been made in the entries.

II. No member shall speak to another, or otherwise interrupt the business of the Senate, or read any printed paper while the journals or public papers are reading, or when any member is speaking in any debate.

III. Every member, when he speaks, shall address the chair, standing in his place, and when he has finished shall sit down.

IV. No member shall speak more than twice in any one debate on the same day, without leave of the Senate.

V. When two members shall rise at the same time, the President shall name the person to speak; but in all cases the person first rising shall speak first.

VI. No motion shall be debated until...seconded.

VII. When a motion shall be made and seconded, it shall be reduced to writing, if desired by the President, or any member, delivered in at the table, and read by the President before the same shall be debated.

VIII. While a question is before the Senate, no motion shall be received unless for an amendment, for the previous question, or for postponing the main question, or to commit, or to adjourn.

IX. The previous question being moved and seconded, the question for the chair shall be: "Shall the main question now be put?" and if the nays prevail, the main question shall not then be put.

X. If a question in a debate include several points, any member may have the same divided.

XI. When the yeas and nays shall be called for by one-fifth of the members present, each member called upon shall, unless for special reasons he be excused by the Senate, declare, openly and without debate, his assent or dissent to the question. In taking the yeas and nays, and upon the call of the House, the names of the members shall be taken alphabetically.

XII. One day's notice at least shall be given of an intended motion for leave to bring in a bill.

XIII. Every bill shall receive three readings previous to its being passed; and the President shall give notice at each, whether it be the first, second, or third; which readings shall be on three different days, unless the Senate unanimously direct otherwise.

XIV. No bill shall be committed or amended until it shall have been twice read, after which it may be referred to a committee.

XV. All committees shall be elected by ballot, and a plurality of votes shall make a choice.

XVI. When a member shall be called to order, he shall sit down until the President shall have determined whether he is in order or not; and every question of order shall be decided by the President, without debate; but, if there be a doubt in his mind, he may call for the sense of the Senate.

XVII. If a member be called to order for words spoken, the exceptionable words shall be immediately taken down in writing, that the President may be better enabled to judge the matter.

XVIII. When a blank is to be filled, and different sums shall be proposed, the question shall be taken on the highest sum first.

XIX. No member shall absent himself from the service of the Senate without leave of the Senate first obtained.

XX. Before any petition or memorial, addressed to the Senate, shall be received and read at the table, whether the same shall be introduced by the President or a member, a brief statement of the contents of the petition or memorial shall verbally be made by the introducer.

legislatures determined to press for open sessions of the Senate, in part as a means of enforcing accountability from their Senators.

After four defeats in four years, the Senate in 1794 finally voted to open its sessions "after the end of the present session of Congress, and, so soon as suitable galleries shall be provided for the Senate chamber." Almost two years went by before the galleries were erected and the rule put into effect, but at the beginning of the first session of the Fourth Congress, in December 1795, the Senate's doors were finally opened to the public. The immediate effects of this action were not great, since the Senate sessions were too decorous to attract widespread attention, and the more spirited House remained the center of public interest. Furthermore, there were no official reporters of debates, and no accommodation for newspaper reporters was made in the Senate until 1802, after the Government had moved to Washington.

Light Workload. The demands upon early Senators do not appear to have been unduly burdensome. Ordinarily the Senate met at 11 a.m., except near the end of the session when the press of business was great, and 3 p.m. adjournments were common. Sen. William Maclay of Pennsylvania, whose *Journal* provides a prejudiced but invaluable record of the Senate in the First Congress, frequently notes that the Senate adjourned its own tedious debates so that Members could go and listen to the livelier ones in the House. Absenteeism, a continuing problem, was only in part attributable to the difficulties of travel at this period. Accordingly, in 1798 the Senate finally added enforcement machinery to its rule prohibiting absence without leave.

Because most legislation originated in the House, the Senate had little to do early in the session; under the so-called de novo rule of 1790, all bills died at the end of each session of Congress, so the Senate did not have House-passed bills from a previous session on which to work. The House scornfully rejected Senate proposals that the two chambers jointly prepare a legislative program for an entire session; however, joint committees often were appointed near the end of sessions to determine what business had to be completed before adjournment. Much of the legislative output of each session was pushed through in the closing days. In the second session of the Sixth Congress, for example, the Senate passed 35 bills, one-third of them on the final day.

Presidential messages provided a partial agenda for each session. Washington and Adams delivered their messages in person annually, and each chamber prepared a reply which was delivered orally with great ceremony. Since these replies were carefully debated and amended, they provided a valuable opportunity for consideration of the over-all legislative situation. Jefferson abandoned his predecessors' practice and delivered his messages in writing; such messages were not thought to require a reply.

Rules on Debate. Dilatory tactics occasionally appeared in the early Senate, but apparently they did not present a serious problem. Only three of the 1789 rules had any direct bearing on limitation of debate: Rule 4, providing that no Member should speak more than twice in any one debate on the same day without leave of the Senate; Rule 6, providing that no motion should be debated until seconded; and Rule 16, providing that every question of order should be decided by the President without debate. The previous question, authorized under Rule 9, was not then used to close debate but rather to remove a question from further consideration by reverting to a previous one. The previous question was dropped when the rules were revised in 1806. At the same time, a motion to adjourn was made undebatable, and in 1807 the same restriction was applied to an amendment of the third reading of a bill.

Although bills could be introduced by individual Members with the permission of the majority after one day's notice, the more common practice was to move the appointment of a committee to report a bill. Thus only a limited number of bills were introduced and most of those introduced were passed.

Committee System. Standing committees as they are known today did not exist in the early Senate. Legislation was handled by ad hoc committees, which were appointed to consider a particular issue and disbanded once their work was finished, with the full Senate maintaining firm control over their activities. Membership was flexible, although the same Senators were frequently assigned to committees dealing with a particular field of legislation. Following British precedent, opponents of a measure were excluded from the committee that considered it, and the Federalist majority frequently excluded Republicans from committees that were to consider bills involving party issues.

Membership and Turnover

In terms of previous experience, Members of the early Senate were well qualified to serve in the national legislature. Of the 94 men in the Senate between 1789 and 1801, 18 had served in the Constitutional Convention, 42 in the Continental Congress or the Congress of the Confederation, and 84 in their state or provincial legislatures. Only one or two were without experience in some governmental capacity. A majority were men of wealth and social prominence, but they were a young "council of elders"—the average age in 1799 was only 45 years.

Experience did not bear out the warnings of those who feared that Senators would entrench themselves in office for life. Of the 94 Senators who served between 1789 and 1801, 33 resigned within that period before completing their terms, and only six did so in order to take other Federal posts. Frequent resignations continued for many years—35 in the period 1801-13—and the rate of re-election also was low.

Emergence of Parties

Political parties had no place in the constitutional framework, and early Senate voting indicated chiefly sectional or economic divisions within the chamber. But upon the presentation of Alexander Hamilton's financial measures, the Senate—like the House—began to exhibit a spirit of partisanship; supporters of a strong central Government, chiefly representatives of mercantile and financial interests, banded together as Federalists under the leadership of Hamilton, while exponents of agrarian democracy, led by Madison and Jefferson, became known as Republicans. Party alignments, still quite fluid in 1791,

---

Secret Sessions

Even after the Senate in 1795 opened its doors for regular legislative sessions, it continued to hold closed (secret) executive sessions for the consideration of treaties and nominations. Under a rule of 1800, all confidential documents from the President and all treaties laid before the Senate were to be kept secret until the injunction of secrecy was removed. In 1820 a similar restriction was adopted for nominations, and in 1844 penalties were provided for violations of these rules.

In practice, however, secrecy was difficult to maintain, and repeated efforts to abolish the secret sessions finally bore fruit. In 1888, the Senate for the first time kept its doors open during the consideration of a treaty, and thereafter treaties increasingly came to be considered in open sessions. With few exceptions, nominations were considered in secret session until 1929. The Senate then, by a vote of 69-5, amended Rule 38 to provide for open sessions for the consideration of all Senate business, including treaties and nominations, unless the Senate in closed session decided by majority vote to consider a particular matter in closed session.

Although treaties and nominations are no longer considered in secret sessions, the Senate still goes into closed session from time to time, usually for the discussion of classified information. In such sessions, the public, the press and most Senate aides are required to leave the chamber and galleries. Frequently a censored transcript of the discussion is released later.

From the end of World War II to the close of the 91st Congress in January 1971, the Senate held seven secret sessions: in 1963 to discuss classified information concerning missile defenses; in 1966 to consider establishment of a special committee to oversee the Central Intelligence Agency; in 1968 and again in 1969 to consider classified material connected with the antiballistic missile program; also in 1969 to discuss U.S. activities in Laos and Thailand; and twice in 1970 to consider the Senate's legislative schedule.

---

gradually hardened in the next two years as they were inflamed by the excesses of the French Revolution and troubled relations with Great Britain. By 1794 Sen. John Taylor of Virginia could write:

"The existence of two parties in Congress is apparent. The fact is disclosed almost upon every important question. Whether the subject be foreign or domestic—relative to war or peace—navigation or commerce—the magnetism of opposite views draws them wide as the poles asunder."

The Federalists held the Senate until 1801, but in 1794 the Republicans came close to overturning that control. The Federalists succeeded in unseating Albert Gallatin on a 14-12 party-line vote, but on six other occasions during the session they needed the casting vote of Vice President Adams to carry their program.

Approval of the Jay Treaty in 1795 united the Federalists and firmly identified the Senate in the public mind as the focus of the Federalist party. From that time on, both Federalists and Republicans voted with a high degree

---

The Early Senate

This eyewitness description of the Senate in session about 1796 was offered by William McKoy in a series of articles in Poulson's American Daily Advertiser *in 1828-29:*

Among the thirty Senators of that day there was observed constantly during the debate the most delightful silence, the most beautiful order, gravity, and personal dignity of manner. They all appeared every morning full-powdered and dressed, as age or fancy might suggest, in the richest material. The very atmosphere of the place seemed to inspire wisdom, mildness, and condescension. Should any of them so far forget for a moment as to be the cause of a protracted whisper while another was addressing the Vice-President, three gentle taps with his silver pencilcase upon the table by Mr. Adams immediately restored everything to repose and the most respectful attention, presenting in their courtesy a most striking contrast to the independent loquacity of the Representatives below stairs, some few of whom persisted in wearing, while in their seats and during the debate, their ample *cocked* hats, placed "fore and aft" upon their heads....

---

of party regularity. During the Fourth, Fifth and Sixth Congresses, the Federalists enjoyed a roughly 2-1 edge over the Republicans in the Senate, while the House was closely divided between the two parties. But the rapprochement with France engineered by President Adams deprived the Federalists of their principal issue, and this development, combined with invasion of the chamber by Members from newly admitted southern and western states, broke the power of Federalism in the Senate. In the elections of 1800, Jefferson's Republicans won the Presidency and both houses of Congress. When the Seventh Congress convened in December 1801, the Republicans held a narrow Senate majority. Federalist strength in the Senate continued to decline throughout Jefferson's term of office.

Leadership in the Senate

The Constitution solved the problem of a job for the Vice President by making him President of the Senate and it directed the Senate to choose a President pro tempore to act for him in his absence, but there were good reasons why neither of these officers could supply effective legislative leadership.

The Vice President was not chosen by the Senate but imposed upon it from outside, and there was no necessity for him to be sympathetic to its aims. Precedent was set by John Adams who, although clearly in general agreement with the majority of the Senate during his term as Vice President, conceived of his role as simply that of presiding officer and made little effort to guide Senate action. His successor, Republican leader Thomas Jefferson, could not have steered the Federalist-controlled Senate even if he had wished to do so, although he did maintain a watching brief for the Republican party in the upper chamber.

The President pro tempore was elected by the Senate from among its own Members, but he could not supply

legislative leadership because his term was too random and temporary. By custom a President pro tempore was elected only for the current absence of the Vice President, and his term ended with the reappearance of the Vice President. During the period 1789-1809, 25 Senators served as President pro tempore.

Thus the mantle of legislative leadership soon fell upon individual Senators—Oliver Ellsworth, Rufus King and others—and more importantly upon the Executive Branch. Presidents Washington and Adams shared a strong belief in the separation of powers. Neither was willing to take upon himself the role of legislative leader, but Alexander Hamilton had no such qualms. As Secretary of the Treasury until 1795—and even after his retirement to private life—Hamilton not only developed a broad legislative program but functioned, in the words of one historian, "as a sort of absentee floor leader," in almost daily contact with his friends in the Senate.

Under Jefferson and his secretary of the Treasury, Albert Gallatin, legislative leadership continued to emanate from the Executive Branch. Jefferson, wrote Sen. Timothy Pickering of Massachusetts, tried "to screen himself from all responsibility by calling upon Congress for advice and direction.... Yet with affected modesty and deference he secretly dictates every measure which is seriously proposed."

By the end of Jefferson's Administration, the Senate had established internal procedures and sampled its various functions. It had both initiated and revised proposed legislation, given its advice and consent to treaties and nominations, tried its first impeachments and conducted its first investigations. But the breadth of its powers was not yet clear; relations with the House, the Executive Branch and the state governments were still only tentatively charted and awaited further tests.

The Emerging Senate: 1809-1829

Two decades of legislative supremacy began with the Administration of Jefferson's successor, James Madison, for the "Father of the Constitution" proved himself incapable of Presidential leadership. He soon lost control of his party to the young "war hawks" of the House, who succeeded in forcing him into the War of 1812, and thereafter he suffered repeated defeats at the hands of Congress.

James Monroe was no more fortunate in his relations with Congress than Madison had been; at the time of his second inauguration Henry Clay commented that "Mr. Monroe has just been re-elected with apparent unanimity, but he had not the slightest influence on Congress."

Neither Madison nor Monroe was temperamentally fit for legislative leadership, and both were further handicapped by their obligation to the Congressional caucus that had nominated them for the Presidency. The situation of John Quincy Adams was even more difficult, since he owed his very election to the House of Representatives.

Rising Senate Influence

Under the Speakership of Henry Clay, the House took a commanding role in Government, but the influence of the Senate was on the rise. The trend toward Senate dictation of Executive appointments, which had begun late in Jefferson's term of office, continued and increased under Madison. When he sought to make Gallatin Secretary of State, the Senate blocked his choice and forced him to accept a Secretary of its own choosing.

The importance of the Senate's treaty and appointment powers, in which the House had no share, was only one factor in the Senate's rise. The rapidly expanding size of the House soon suggested the advantages of serving in a smaller body; in 1820, there were still only 46 Senators. The Senate's longer term and more stable membership also made it seem a more desirable place in which to serve. Henry Clay "moved on" from the Senate to the House in 1811, but by 1823 Martin Van Buren was able to claim that the Senate, more than any other branch, controlled all the efficient power of Government.

The Senate's legislative importance increased only gradually. In the early years, most proposed legislation originated in the House, and the great debates surrounding the War of 1812 occurred there. But the Senate took a leading role in the struggle over the Missouri Compromise of 1820 and succeeded in imposing upon the House an amendment barring slavery in any future state north of 36° 30' north latitude. Since this was the part of the country in which the population was expanding most rapidly, proponents of slavery could no longer hope to uphold the cause of states' rights in the House. The Senate—where the two sides were more evenly matched—inevitably became the forum for the great anti-slavery debates of the following decades.

Change of Party Alignments

Party alignments changed during the 1809-29 period. The withering Federalist party ceased to be a factor in national politics after the election of 1816, but Republican supremacy was marred by increasing factionalism. Suffrage expanded, and the newly enfranchised small farmers of the South and West had little in common with the landed aristocracy that was the backbone of the Republican party. Thus the democratic masses turned from slave-holding planters to the leadership of Andrew Jackson of Tennessee, an exponent of their fiercely egalitarian philosophy. When the House of Representatives made Adams President in 1825, although Jackson led in popular voting, the Republican party split, and a new Democratic party was organized by Jackson's lieutenants. In 1826, the Democrats won control of both houses of Congress, and in 1828 they placed Jackson in the Presidency of which they thought he had been defrauded four years earlier.

Growth of Standing Committees

The Senate lagged behind the House in establishing a formal committee structure. In its first quarter-century it created only four standing committees, all chiefly administrative in nature: the Joint Standing Committee on Enrolled Bills, the Senate Committee on Engrossed Bills, the Joint Standing Committee for the Library, and the Senate Committee to Audit and Control the Contingent Expenses of the Senate.

During this period most of the legislative committee work fell to ad hoc select committees, usually of three members, appointed as the occasion demanded. But eventually the need to appoint so many committees (between 90 and 100 in the session of 1815-16) exhausted the patience of the Senate, and in 1816 it added 11 standing committees to the existing four: Foreign Relations, Finance, Commerce and Manufactures, Military Affairs, the Militia, Naval Affairs, Public Lands, Claims, the Judiciary, the Post Office and Post Roads, and Pensions. Most of the new committees were parallel in function to previously created committees of the House. The usual membership was five; this number would rise to seven by mid-century and to nine by 1900.

Senate committees were chosen by ballot until 1823, but in that year the Senate adopted an amendment to its rules giving the "presiding officer" authority to name committees, unless otherwise ordered by the Senate. At first this power was exercised by the President pro tempore, an officer of the Senate's own choosing, but early in the 19th Congress (1825-27) Vice President Calhoun assumed the appointment power and used it to place Jackson supporters in key committee posts. In the face of this patent effort to embarrass the Adams Administration, the Senate quickly returned to the rule of choice by ballot. In 1828 the rule was changed again, this time to give appointment power to the President pro tempore, but in 1833 the Senate once more reverted to choice by ballot.

A general revision of the Senate rules in 1820, bringing the total number of rules to 45, was remarkable chiefly for incorporating the provisions relating to standing committees that the Senate had adopted four years earlier. No great spirit of reform was involved; as in the case of other general revisions of Senate rules, the 1820 revision represented chiefly an attempt to codify changes that had accumulated over a number of years.

"A Senate of Equals"

Daniel Webster was to describe the upper chamber in 1830 as a "Senate of equals, of men of individual honor and personal character, and of absolute independence," who knew no master and acknowledged no dictation. In such a body it is not surprising that no single leader had emerged to parallel the rise of Henry Clay in the House.

Statesmen of prominence served in the Senate during the 1809-29 period. The roster included four future Presidents—Andrew Jackson, Martin Van Buren, William Henry Harrison and John Tyler—and a number of Presidential hopefuls. By the close of the period, the great figures of the ensuing Golden Age were beginning to gather in the chamber: Thomas Hart Benton of Missouri arrived in 1821, Robert Y. Hayne of South Carolina in 1823 and Daniel Webster of Massachusetts in 1827. Henry Clay of Kentucky, after serving briefly in the Senate in 1810-11, betook himself to the House; he was to return to the Senate in 1831. John C. Calhoun would resign as John Quincy Adams' Vice President in 1832 to succeed Hayne as Senator from South Carolina.

Until Calhoun took office in 1825, the Vice Presidents of the period were not significant figures. Madison's first Vice President, George Clinton, was old and feeble and died in office, as did his successor, Elbridge Gerry. Monroe's Vice President, Daniel D. Tompkins, hardly ever entered the Senate chamber.

Senate Votes by Vice Presidents

From the beginning of the American Republic, the Executive Branch has put to good use the authority granted the Vice President under the Constitution to vote in the Senate in the event of a tie. Through 1970, Vice Presidents had cast Senate votes on 214 occasions. Some of those votes were recorded against questions that would have failed of approval even if the Vice President had not voted, because a question on which the Senate is evenly divided automatically falls by the wayside. In such cases the Vice President's negative vote was superfluous; the only purpose it served was to make known his own opposition to the proposal. Records are not available to show exactly how many of the 214 votes cast by Vice Presidents were in the affirmative and thus decisive.

The first recorded vote by a Vice President was a negative vote cast by John Adams on July 18, 1789, the effect of which was to support the President's right to remove an appointed official without consulting the chamber of Congress which had given original consent to the appointment. The House had included in a bill establishing the Department of Foreign Affairs language that implied recognition of the President's sole power of removal. When the bill reached the upper chamber, the Senate—sitting "as in Committe of the Whole"—first rejected a motion to strike out this language on a 10-10 tie vote.

This action is not recorded in the Senate *Journal*, but Sen. William Maclay's *Journal* for July 16, 1789, describes the scene: "After all the arguments were ended and the question taken, the Senate was ten to ten, and the Vice President with joy cried out, 'It is not a vote,' without giving himself time to declare the division of the House and give his vote in order." Two days later, when the bill came up for final action, a roll call was demanded on the same question. One Senator was absent and another Senator on the opposing side withheld his vote, so the Senate was divided 9-9 when the Senate Secretary called for the Vice President's vote. Adams voted nay.

The vote was one of 29 cast by Adams—a record approached only by John C. Calhoun, who cast 28 votes as Vice President. Although the Adams vote had no effect on determination of the question at issue, he considered his stand in support of the President's removal power one of his most important acts in public life.

One important vote by a Vice President was cast on July 28, 1846, when George M. Dallas broke a tie in favor of the Polk Administration's tariff reform bill. This was the last time the tariff would be revised under a Democratic President until the Wilson Administration.

Among other important Vice Presidential votes were two cast by Thomas R. Marshall on foreign policy issues. On Feb. 2, 1916, his vote carried an amendment to a Philippines bill pledging full independence to the islands by March 4, 1921. (The amendment was modified in conference to provide for independence as soon as a stable government could be established.) On April 4, 1919, Marshall cast the deciding vote to table a resolution calling for withdrawal of American troops from Russia as soon as practicable. (American and Allied troops had been dispatched to Archangel and Vladivostok in 1918 to aid Czechoslovaks under attack by Austrian and German prisoners released by the Bolsheviks. American troops were withdrawn from North Russia in July 1919 and from Siberia early in 1920.)

Two relatively recent tie-breaking Senate votes of importance were cast by Richard M. Nixon. On April 22, 1959, the then Vice President voted to table a motion to reconsider the Senate's acceptance of an amendment to a labor reform bill; the amendment aimed to protect union members from coercion and arbitrary actions by union leaders. On Feb. 3, 1960, Nixon broke a tie by voting to table a motion to reconsider the Senate's rejection of an education bill amendment to authorize annual appropriations of $1.1 billion for an indefinite period for school construction and teachers' salaries.

Following is a list of the number of votes cast by each Vice President through 1970:

Period	Vice President	Number of Votes Cast
1789-1797	John Adams	29
1797-1801	Thomas Jefferson	3
1801-1805	Aaron Burr	3
1805-1812	George Clinton	11
1813-1814	Elbridge Gerry	8
1817-1825	Daniel D. Tompkins	5
1825-1832	John C. Calhoun	28
1833-1837	Martin Van Buren	4
1837-1841	Richard M. Johnson	14
1841	John Tyler	0
1845-1849	George M. Dallas	19
1849-1850	Millard Fillmore	3
1853	William R. King	0
1857-1861	John C. Breckinridge	10
1861-1865	Hannibal Hamlin	7
1865	Andrew Johnson	0
1869-1873	Schuyler Colfax	13
1873-1875	Henry Wilson	1
1877-1881	William A. Wheeler	5
1881	Chester A. Arthur	3
1885	Thomas A. Hendricks	0
1889-1893	Levi P. Morton	4
1893-1897	Adlai E. Stevenson	2
1897-1899	Garret A. Hobart	1
1901	Theodore Roosevelt	0
1905-1909	Charles W. Fairbanks	0
1909-1912	James S. Sherman	4
1913-1921	Thomas R. Marshall	4
1921-1923	Calvin Coolidge	0
1925-1929	Charles G. Dawes	2
1929-1933	Charles Curtis	3
1933-1941	John N. Garner	3
1941-1945	Henry A. Wallace	4
1945	Harry S Truman	1
1949-1953	Alben W. Barkley	7
1953-1961	Richard M. Nixon	8
1961-1963	Lyndon B. Johnson	0
1965-1969	Hubert H. Humphrey	4
1969-	Spiro T. Agnew	1
TOTAL		214

SOURCE: Library of Congress, Congressional Research Service.

Vice President Calhoun, hostile to the Adams Administration and harboring Presidential ambitions of his own, had no desire to alienate the Senate by exercising undue authority, but he was a commanding figure and his influence was felt. Hayne generally served as his spokesman on the floor.

Calhoun took advantage of his position to make obviously biased committee appointments, but in other respects he assumed as little authority as possible. Although all of his predecessors in the chair had assumed direct authority to call Senators to order for words used in debate, Calhoun contended that his power was appellate only and refused to act unless an offending Senator was first called to order by another Senator. He would not "for ten thousand worlds look like a usurper," Calhoun declared. His refusal to act on his own initiative led the Senate in 1828 to amend its rules; henceforth the chair would have the power to call a Senator to order, but for the first time in Senate history the rule permitted an appeal from the chair's decision on a question of order.

During the 1809-29 period, greater continuity of service developed in the office of President pro tempore. John Gaillard occupied the post for most of the period between 1814 and 1825 and presided over the Senate almost continuously during five years when Tompkins was Vice President. Elected by the Senate and thus considering himself entitled to its support, Gaillard enforced the rules rigidly but did not exercise a true leadership role.

The Golden Age: 1829-1861

In the years leading up to the Civil War, the Senate became the chief forum for the discussion of national policy and a "lofty pulpit" from which to address the nation. The preeminent national issue in the period between the Missouri Compromise of 1820 and the outbreak of war in 1861 was the struggle between North and South over slavery; the Senate, where owing to the system of representation the two sides were equally matched, inevitably became the principal battleground.

Sectional interests were more important than party during these years preceding the Civil War, and party divisions were often blurred. The Jacksonian Democrats adopted the agrarian and states' rights philosophy of the Jeffersonian Republicans, but their concept of strong executive leadership was at odds with Jeffersonian views. Meanwhile, the Whig party was formed of the coalition of eastern financial and business interests that had once constituted the strength of the Federalists, but the Whigs were committed to a doctrine of legislative supremacy that was alien to Federalist thought.

The Democratic party split over the question of slavery, and many southern Democrats—fearing Jackson's vigorous Presidential leadership and resentful of his stand against nullification—allied themselves with the Whigs, hoping to find protection for states' rights and the institution of slavery under the Whig banner of legislative supremacy. However, the Whig party had no answer to the slavery question, and in the 1850s it gave way to the new Republican party, an alliance of northern interests dedicated to preventing the spread of slavery into the territories. Mounting southern defiance of northern opin-

ion led to a North-South split in the Democratic party, and secession and war soon followed.

In this age of giants three men dominated the Senate chamber. All were former House Members, and all suffered from Presidential aspirations that were to influence the shifting coalitions of a turbulent era. Daniel Webster of Massachusetts—Whig, spokesman for eastern moneyed interests, sectionalist turned nationalist, supreme orator—entered the Senate in 1827 and remained there for most of the period until 1850. Henry Clay of Kentucky—Whig, westerner, brilliant tactician and compromiser—served in the chamber between 1831 and 1842 and again in 1849-52. John C. Calhoun of South Carolina—outstanding logician, devoted son of the South and champion of the right of secession—stepped down from the Vice Presidency in 1832 to defend his nullification doctrine on the Senate floor and remained a Senator for most of the period until his death in 1850.

De Tocqueville in 1834 contrasted the "vulgarity" of the House with the nobility of the Senate, where "scarcely an individual is to be found...who does not recall the idea of an active and illustrious career." The Senate, he said, "is composed of eloquent advocates, distinguished generals, wise magistrates, and statesmen of note, whose language would, at all times, do honor to the most remarkable parliamentary debates of Europe."

Senate's Preeminence Over House

De Tocqueville could think of only one explanation for the Senate's superiority: its Members were elected by elected bodies, whereas House Members were elected by the people directly. Thomas Hart Benton disputed this analysis. Not only did the Senate enjoy advantages of smaller membership, longer term and greater age and experience on the part of its Members, he said, but it was composed of "the pick of the House of Representatives, and thereby gains doubly—by brilliant accession to itself and abstraction from the other."

Undoubtedly the Senate's greater stability of membership contributed to its preeminence over the House, where the Jacksonian concept of rotation in office led to great turnover. More significant, perhaps, was the introduction of the spoils system and the Senate's increasing domination of the appointment process. Finally, growth had strengthened the Senate by turning it from a small intimate body into one large enough for oratory and the exercise of brilliant parliamentary skills. With the addition of two Senators from every new state, the Senate increased from 48 Members at the beginning of Jackson's Administration to 66 in Buchanan's. Its roster included such luminaries as Benton of Missouri, Lewis Cass of Michigan, Sam Houston of Texas, Jefferson Davis and Henry S. Foote of Mississippi, William H. Seward of New York, Stephen A. Douglas of Illinois and Charles Sumner of Massachusetts.

Quarrel With President Jackson

The eclipse of Presidential power that had begun under Madison came to an end when Andrew Jackson became President in 1829. Backed by strong popular majorities and skilled in the uses of patronage, Jackson was able to dominate the House, but in the Senate he met vigorous opposition from the new Whig party, a
(Continued on p. 70)

Political Party Affiliations in Congress . . .

(Letter symbols for political parties: Ad—Administration; AM—Anti-Masonic; C—Coalition; D—Democratic; DR—Democratic-Republican; F—Federalist; J—Jacksonian; NR—National Republican; Op—Opposition; R—Republican; U—Unionist; W—Whig. Figures are for the beginning of the first session of each Congress.)

Year	Congress	House Majority party	Principal minority party	Other (except vacancies)	Senate Majority Party	Principal minority party	Other (except vacancies)	President
1971-1972	92nd	D-254	R-180	—	D-54	R-45	—	R (Nixon)
1969-1971	91st	D-243	R-192	—	D-57	R-43	—	R (Nixon)
1967-1968	90th	D-246	R-187	—	D-64	R-36	—	D (L. Johnson)
1965-1966	89th	D-295	R-140	—	D-68	R-32	—	D (L. Johnson)
1963-1964	88th	D-258	R-176	—	D-67	R-33	—	D (L. Johnson) D (Kennedy)
1961-1962	87th	D-263	R-174	—	D-65	R-35	—	D (Kennedy)
1959-1960	86th	D-283	R-153	—	D-64	R-34	—	R (Eisenhower)
1957-1958	85th	D-233	R-200	—	D-49	R-47	—	R (Eisenhower)
1955-1956	84th	D-232	R-203	—	D-48	R-47	1	R (Eisenhower)
1953-1954	83rd	R-221	D-211	1	R-48	D-47	1	R (Eisenhower)
1951-1952	82nd	D-234	R-199	1	D-49	R-47	—	D (Truman)
1949-1951	81st	D-263	R-171	1	D-54	R-42	—	D (Truman)
1947-1948	80th	R-245	D-188	1	R-51	D-45	—	D (Truman)
1945-1946	79th	D-242	R-190	2	D-56	R-38	1	D (Truman)
1943-1944	78th	D-218	R-208	4	D-58	R-37	1	D (F. Roosevelt)
1941-1942	77th	D-268	R-162	5	D-66	R-28	2	D (F. Roosevelt)
1939-1941	76th	D-261	R-164	4	D-69	R-23	4	D (F. Roosevelt)
1937-1938	75th	D-331	R-89	13	D-76	R-16	4	D (F. Roosevelt)
1935-1936	74th	D-319	R-103	10	D-69	R-25	2	D (F. Roosevelt)
1933-1934	73rd	D-310	R-117	5	D-60	R-35	1	D (F. Roosevelt)
1931-1933	72nd	D-220	R-214	1	R-48	D-47	1	R (Hoover)
1929-1931	71st	R-267	D-167	1	R-56	D-39	1	R (Hoover)
1927-1929	70th	R-237	D-195	3	R-49	D-46	1	R (Coolidge)
1925-1927	69th	R-247	D-183	4	R-56	D-39	1	R (Coolidge)
1923-1925	68th	R-225	D-205	5	R-51	D-43	2	R (Coolidge)
1921-1923	67th	R-301	D-131	1	R-59	D-37	—	R (Harding)
1919-1921	66th	R-240	D-190	3	R-49	D-47	—	D (Wilson)
1917-1919	65th	D-216	R-210	6	D-53	R-42	—	D (Wilson)
1915-1917	64th	D-230	R-196	9	D-56	R-40	—	D (Wilson)
1913-1915	63rd	D-291	R-127	17	D-51	R-44	1	D (Wilson)
1911-1913	62nd	D-228	R-161	1	R-51	D-41	—	R (Taft)
1909-1911	61st	R-219	D-172	—	R-61	D-32	—	R (Taft)
1907-1909	60th	R-222	D-164	—	R-61	D-31	—	R (T. Roosevelt)
1905-1907	59th	R-250	D-136	—	R-57	D-33	—	R (T. Roosevelt)
1903-1905	58th	R-208	D-178	—	R-57	D-33	—	R (T. Roosevelt)
1901-1903	57th	R-197	D-151	9	R-55	D-31	4	R (T. Roosevelt) R (McKinley)
1899-1901	56th	R-185	D-163	9	R-53	D-26	8	R (McKinley)
1897-1899	55th	R-204	D-113	40	R-47	D-34	7	R (McKinley)
1895-1897	54th	R-244	D-105	7	R-43	D-39	6	D (Cleveland)
1893-1895	53rd	D-218	R-127	11	D-44	R-38	3	D (Cleveland)
1891-1893	52nd	D-235	R-88	9	R-47	D-39	2	R (B. Harrison)
1889-1891	51st	R-166	D-159	—	R-39	D-37	—	R (B. Harrison)
1887-1889	50th	D-169	R-152	4	R-39	D-37	—	D (Cleveland)
1885-1887	49th	D-183	R-140	2	R-43	D-34	—	D (Cleveland)
1883-1885	48th	D-197	R-118	10	R-38	D-36	2	R (Arthur)
1881-1853	47th	R-147	D-135	11	R-37	D-37	1	R (Arthur) R (Garfield)
1879-1881	46th	D-149	R-130	14	D-42	R-33	1	R (Hayes)

... and the Presidency: 1789 to 1971

(Letter symbols for political parties: Ad—Administration; AM—Anti-Masonic; C—Coalition; D—Democratic; DR—Democratic-Republican; F—Federalist; J—Jacksonian; NR—National Republican; Op—Opposition; R—Republican; U—Unionist; W—Whig. Figures are for the beginning of the first session of each Congress.)

| Year | Congress | House | | | Senate | | | President |
		Majority party	Principal minority party	Other (except vacancies)	Majority party	Principal minority party	Other (except vacancies)	
1877-1879	45th	D-153	R-140	—	R-39	D-36	1	R (Hayes)
1875-1877	44th	D-169	R-109	14	R-45	D-29	2	R (Grant)
1873-1875	43rd	R-194	D-92	14	R-49	D-19	5	R (Grant)
1871-1873	42nd	R-134	D-104	5	R-52	D-17	5	R (Grant)
1869-1871	41st	R-149	D-63	—	R-56	D-11	—	R (Grant)
1867-1869	40th	R-143	D-49	—	R-42	D-11	—	R (A. Johnson)
1865-1867	39th	U-149	D-42	—	U-42	D-10	—	R (A. Johnson) R (Lincoln)
1863-1865	38th	R-102	D-75	9	R-36	D-9	5	R (Lincoln)
1861-1863	37th	R-105	D-43	30	R-31	D-10	8	R (Lincoln)
1859-1861	36th	R-114	D-92	31	D-36	R-26	4	D (Buchanan)
1857-1859	35th	D-118	R-92	26	D-36	R-20	8	D (Buchanan)
1855-1857	34th	R-108	D-83	43	D-40	R-15	5	D (Pierce)
1853-1855	33rd	D-159	W-71	4	D-38	W-22	2	D (Pierce)
1851-1853	32nd	D-140	W-88	5	D-35	W-24	3	W (Fillmore)
1849-1851	31st	D-112	W-109	9	D-35	W-25	2	W (Fillmore) W (Taylor)
1847-1849	30th	W-115	D-108	4	D-36	W-21	1	D (Polk)
1845-1847	29th	D-143	W-77	6	D-31	W-25	—	D (Polk)
1843-1845	28th	D-142	W-79	1	W-28	D-25	1	W (Tyler)
1841-1843	27th	W-133	D-102	6	W-28	D-22	2	W (Tyler) W (W. Harrison)
1839-1841	26th	D-124	W-118	—	D-28	W-22	—	D (Van Buren)
1837-1839	25th	D-108	W-107	24	D-30	W-18	4	D (Van Buren)
1835-1837	24th	D-145	W-98	—	D-27	W-25	—	D (Jackson)
1833-1835	23rd	D-147	AM-53	60	D-20	NR-20	8	D (Jackson)
1831-1833	22nd	D-141	NR-58	14	D-25	NR-21	2	D (Jackson)
1829-1831	21st	D-139	NR-74	—	D-26	NR-22	—	D (Jackson)
1827-1829	20th	J-119	Ad-94	—	J-28	Ad-20	—	C (John Q. Adams)
1825-1827	19th	Ad-105	J-97	—	Ad-26	J-20	—	C (John Q. Adams)
1823-1825	18th	DR-187	F-26	—	DR-44	F-4	—	DR (Monroe)
1821-1823	17th	DR-158	F-25	—	DR-44	F-4	—	DR (Monroe)
1819-1821	16th	DR-156	F-27	—	DR-35	F-7	—	DR (Monroe)
1817-1819	15th	DR-141	F-42	—	DR-34	F-10	—	DR (Monroe)
1815-1817	14th	DR-117	F-65	—	DR-25	F-11	—	DR (Madison)
1813-1815	13th	DR-112	F-68	—	DR-27	F-9	—	DR (Madison)
1811-1813	12th	DR-108	F-36	—	DR-30	F-6	—	DR (Madison)
1809-1811	11th	DR-94	F-48	—	DR-28	F-6	—	DR (Madison)
1807-1809	10th	DR-118	F-24	—	DR-28	F-6	—	DR (Jefferson)
1805-1807	9th	DR-116	F-25	—	DR-27	F-7	—	DR (Jefferson)
1803-1805	8th	DR-102	F-39	—	DR-25	F-9	—	DR (Jefferson)
1801-1803	7th	DR-69	F-36	—	DR-18	F-13	—	DR (Jefferson)
1799-1801	6th	F-64	DR-42	—	F-19	DR-13	—	F (John Adams)
1797-1799	5th	F-58	DR-48	—	F-20	DR-12	—	F (John Adams)
1795-1797	4th	F-54	DR-52	—	F-19	DR-13	—	F (Washington)
1793-1795	3rd	DR-57	F-48	—	F-17	DR-13	—	F (Washington)
1791-1793	2nd	F-37	DR-33	—	F-16	DR-13	—	F (Washington)
1789-1791	1st	Ad-38	Op-26	—	Ad-17	Op-9	—	F (Washington)

SOURCE: *Historical Statistics of the United States*

combination of commercial and industrial interests dedicated to the principle of legislative supremacy. The Whigs were quick to challenge Jackson on questions of policy and Executive prerogative, and his term was marked by repeated and acrimonious contests with the Senate over legislation and appointments.

These disputes reached a peak in 1834 when the Senate, outraged by Jackson's removal of deposits from the Bank of the United States and his refusal to hand over communications to his Cabinet relating to that subject, adopted a resolution censuring the President for his actions. The resolution, pushed through by Clay, charged "that the President, in the late Executive proceedings in relation to the public revenue, has assumed upon himself authority and power not conferred by the Constitution and laws and in derogation of both."

Jackson countered with a message, which the Senate refused to receive, declaring that so serious a charge as that contained in the censure resolution called for impeachment. Because impeachment could originate only in the House, he protested the Senate's action as a violation of the Constitution.

Benton, Jackson's leader in the Senate, promptly undertook a campaign to vindicate Jackson by expunging the censure resolution from the Senate *Journal*. Under pressure from the President, some state legislatures instructed their Senators to support Benton's efforts, while others forced anti-Jacksonian Senators into retirement. By the time Jackson's second term was drawing to a close in 1837, the Jacksonian Democrats had gained control of the Senate, and the expunging resolution finally was adopted by a 24-19 vote.

In one of the most dramatic scenes of Senate history the terms of the resolution were carried out: "...the Secretary of the Senate...shall bring the manuscript journal of the session of 1833-34 into the Senate, and, in the presence of the Senate, draw black lines round the said resolve, and write across the face thereof, in strong letters, the following words: 'Expunged by order of the Senate, the 16th day of January, in the year of our Lord 1837.'"

Whigs vs. President Tyler

Undeterred by their failure to dominate Jackson, the Whigs persisted in their efforts to establish the doctrine of legislative supremacy. With the election of Whig President William Henry Harrison, they thought their moment had come. Daniel Webster was named Secretary of State, Clay supporters were put in other Cabinet positions, and Harrison's inaugural address—revised by Webster—was a model statement of Whig doctrine. But Harrison died after only one month in office, to be succeeded by John Tyler, a states-rights Virginian who had been elected Vice President on the Whig ticket.

At first Clay, as the leading Whig Member of Congress, thought he could assume effective leadership of the Government, and he even introduced a set of resolutions that were designed to be the party's legislative program. But Tyler, it turned out, was determined to be President in fact as well as title, and the two men soon clashed head-on. Tyler's exercise of the veto power drove the Whigs to threats of impeachment and abortive efforts to force his resignation, but Clay was unable to push through his own legislative program. Although all Presidents had

trouble with appointments during this period, Tyler, who lacked support in either party, was more unfortunate than most. Many of his nominations, including four to the Cabinet, were rejected by the Senate.

After Tyler's Presidency the Whigs were never again able to muster a majority in the Senate that would permit them to put their doctrine of legislative supremacy to a test. Difficulties with nominations continued, for this was the height of the spoils system, but a succession of strong Presidents established a pattern of executive leadership that even the weakness of Pierce and Buchanan could not entirely destroy.

Great Debates Over Slavery

Oratory in the Senate reached its peak in the years leading up to the Civil War, and visitors often thronged the galleries to hear the great debates over slavery. Never had the Senate seemed so splendid as in this period when it served as the forum for the nation.

But the courtesy and decorum of the early Senate gradually began to crumble under the mounting pressures of the time. Although debates were for the most part still close and brief, passions sometimes ran high and legislative obstruction became increasingly common. Filibusters were now often threatened and occasionally undertaken, but they were not yet fully exploited as a means of paralyzing the Senate, and Senators seldom admitted that they were employing dilatory tactics.

The first notable Senate filibuster occurred in 1841, when dissident Senators held the floor for 10 days in opposition to a bill to remove the Senate printers. Later in the same year a Whig move to reestablish the Bank of the United States was subject to an unsuccessful two-week filibuster. Henry Clay said the tactics of the minority would "lead to the inference that embarrassment and delay were the objects aimed at," and he threatened to introduce a rule to limit debate. Unabashed, the filibusterers invited Clay to "make his arrangements at his boarding house for the winter" and warned that they would resort to "any possible extremity" to prevent restriction of debate. Unable to obtain majority support for his "gag rule," Clay never carried out his threat, and the bank bill eventually passed, only to be vetoed by President Tyler.

In 1846 a bill providing for U.S.-British joint occupancy of Oregon was filibustered for two months. The measure was finally brought to a vote through use, apparently for the first time, of the unanimous consent agreement—a device still employed to speed action in the Senate. Later in 1846 the Wilmot Proviso was talked to death in the closing hours of the session. The proviso, which the House had attached as a rider to an appropriation bill in the early months of the Mexican War, stipulated that slavery be excluded from any territory that might be acquired from Mexico.

Slavery was again the issue in the extended debates over the Compromise of 1850, Clay's valiant attempt to resolve the sectional controversies that were tearing the nation apart. In a chamber more crowded than at any time since the Webster-Hayne debates two decades earlier, the great triumvirate—Webster, Clay and Calhoun —made their last joint appearance in the Senate. The dying Calhoun dragged himself into the chamber to hear his final speech read by his colleague Mason.

Violence in the Senate. Violence threatened when Sen. Henry S. ("Hangman") Foote of Mississippi brandished a pistol at Missouri's Benton, who was well known as a deadly duelist. Only the intervention of other Senators prevented bloodshed.

Greater violence marked the 1856 debate on the Kansas statehood bill. Two South Carolina Representatives attacked Charles Sumner while he sat at his desk in the Senate chamber and bludgeoned him so severely that the Massachusetts Senator was unable to resume his seat until 1859.

In the next few years, as the nation drifted toward war, debates continued to reflect the rancor of the period. Oratory had little place in a chamber where all Members were said to carry arms, and by the time the Senate moved into its present quarters in 1859 the great epoch of Senate debate was at an end. Oratory had flourished in the intimate grandeur of the old hall; in the new chamber—vast and acoustically poor—a new style of debate emerged.

The Committee System

The most important procedural development of the 1829-61 period occurred in 1846 when the Senate transferred responsibility for making committee assignments to the party organizations in the chamber. As long as committee assignments were determined by ballot, majority party control of the committees could not be assured, and, although by 1829 the majority usually controlled the working committees, the opposition party still held important chairmanships.

When the second session of the 29th Congress met in December 1846, the Senate first rejected a proposal to let the Vice President name the committees and then, in accordance with the regular rule, began balloting for chairmen. Midway through this process the balloting rule was suspended, and the Senate proceeded to elect on one ballot a list of candidates for all of the remaining committee vacancies that had been agreed upon by the majority and minority. From that time on, the choice of committees has usually amounted to a routine acceptance by the Senate of lists agreed upon by representatives of the caucus or conference of the two major parties.

The fact that the party organizations did not become the standard instrument of committee selection until 1846 gives some indication of the limited use of party discipline in the early years of the Senate. During this period, party authority was confined to organizational questions; when it came to substantive issues, Senators voted as individuals rather than as Democrats or Whigs.

Party influence in the Senate was enhanced by the new method of committee selection, but rank within committees was thereafter increasingly determined by seniority, thus making chairmanships less subject to party control. Experience had always played a major role in making committee assignments, but as long as committees were elected by ballot, rigid adherence to seniority was impossible. However, with the introduction of party lists in 1846 strict compliance with seniority began to be enforced. The bitter sectional disputes leading up to the Civil War may well have encouraged the use of seniority to avoid fierce inter-party struggles for committee control.

The system was not, of course, impartial in distributing its favors. In 1859 a northern Democrat called the

Webster Replies to Hayne

A resolution to inquire into the expediency of limiting the sale of public lands, introduced by Sen. Samuel A. Foote of Connecticut in December 1829, touched off a great debate in which the Senate addressed itself to the problems of sectional rivalry and constitutional interpretation in which it was so deeply involved. Many Senators took part in the debate, but the two principal speakers were Robert Y. Hayne of South Carolina and Daniel Webster of Massachusetts. In his second reply to Hayne, delivered Jan. 26-27, 1830, Webster attacked the doctrine of state sovereignty and nullification advanced by Hayne and affirmed the sovereignty of the Constitution and the national Government over the states. The closing paragraphs of this speech, perhaps the most eloquent ever delivered on the Senate floor, epitomize the golden age of oratory:

I have not allowed myself, sir, to look beyond the Union, to see what might lie hidden in the dark recess behind. I have not coolly weighed the chances of preserving liberty when the bonds that unite us together shall be broken asunder. I have not accustomed myself to hang over the precipice of disunion, to see whether, with my short sight, I can fathom the depth of the abyss below; nor could I regard him as a safe counselor in the affairs in this government whose thoughts should be mainly bent on considering, not how the Union may be best preserved but how tolerable might be the condition of the people when it should be broken up and destroyed. While the Union lasts, we have high, exciting, gratifying prospects spread out before us, for us and our children. Beyond that I seek not to penetrate the veil.

God grant that in my day, at least, that curtain may not rise! God grant that on my vision never may be opened what lies behind! When my eyes shall be turned to behold for the last time the sun in heaven, may I not see him shining on the broken and dishonored fragments of a once glorious Union; on states dissevered, discordant, belligerent; on a land rent with civil feuds, or drenched, it may be, in fraternal blood! Let their last feeble and lingering glance rather behold the gorgeous ensign of the republic, now known and honored throughout the earth, still full high advanced, its arms and trophies streaming in their original luster, not a stripe erased or polluted, nor a single star obscured, bearing for its motto, no such miserable interrogatory as "What is all this worth?" nor those other words of delusion and folly, "Liberty first and Union afterwards"; but everywhere, spread all over in characters of living light, blazing on all its ample folds, as they float over the sea and over the land, and in every wind under the whole heavens, that other sentiment, dear to every true American heart—Liberty *and* Union, now and forever, one and inseparable!

seniority usage "intolerably bad" and complained that it had "operated to give to Senators from slave-holding states the chairmanship of every single committee that controls the public business of this Government. There is not one exception."

There had been one exception earlier in the same year; Stephen A. Douglas of Illinois was chairman of the Committee on Territories. But the Democratic caucus had removed him from the chairmanship, in spite of his seniority, because he refused to go along with President Buchanan and the southern wing of the party on the question of slavery in the territories.

By the time of the Civil War the committee structure of the Senate had assumed roughly its contemporary form. A loose aggregation of ad hoc committees appointed for the occasion had given way to a formal system of standing committees, whose members owed their appointments to the party organization and their advancement within committees to the seniority system.

Toward Party Government: 1861-1901

During the Civil War and Reconstruction periods, the Republicans controlled the Presidency, the Senate and the House throughout seven consecutive Congresses, ending in 1875. Not only did the Democrats lose the southern seats in Congress, most of which were vacant from 1861 to 1869, but many northern Democrats defected to the Republicans rather than remain in a party so closely tied to the southern cause.

This period of Republican hegemony was marked by a power struggle between Congress and the White House. During the war Congress sought to assert its authority through such mechanisms as the Joint Committee on the Conduct of the War, consisting of three Senators and four Representatives, which exercised a wide range of authority. Yet President Lincoln managed not only to retain his independence of Congress, but also to increase the armed forces, call for volunteers, spend money on defense, issue a code of regulations for the armed forces, suspend the writ of habeas corpus, and even emancipate the slaves in the states "in rebellion" without waiting for authority from Congress.

When the President issued a proclamation of Reconstruction in December 1863, Congress passed the Wade-Davis bill transferring Reconstruction powers to itself. In response to the President's pocket veto of this measure, the Radical Republicans in Congress issued the Wade-Davis Manifesto, which declared: "...the authority of Congress is paramount and must be respected; that the body of Union men in Congress will not submit to be impeached by him (the President) of rash and unconstitutional legislation; and if he wishes our support he must confine himself to his executive duties—to obey and execute, not to make the laws—to suppress by arms and armed rebellion, and leave political reorganization to Congress."

Era of Radical Republicans

The Republican Congress achieved its aims after Lincoln was assassinated. It passed its own Reconstruction Act, overrode President Andrew Johnson's veto of a civil rights bill and set up Gen. Ulysses S. Grant as General of the Army in Washington, requiring all army orders to be issued through him (thus bypassing the President as Commander in Chief) and forbidding the President to remove or transfer the General without prior consent of the Senate. Over Johnson's veto, Congress passed the

Tenure of Office Act which required approval by the Senate of the removal of officials appointed with its advice and consent. When Johnson dismissed his Secretary of War to test in the courts the constitutionality of the Act, the House impeached him, and the Senate came within one vote of removing him from office. Congress had broken the authority of the Executive. Under a compliant President Grant, the Republican "Directory" governed.

In this period of one-party Government, the House, led by Radical Republican Thaddeus Stevens of Pennsylvania, overshadowed the Senate. But following the failure of the effort to impeach Johnson and the death of Stevens, House prestige declined, and the Senate rapidly became the dominant arm of the national legislature. During the remainder of the 19th century, while control of the House shifted back and forth between the two parties, the Republicans managed to maintain control of the Senate in all except two Congresses, and during this period modern party government developed in the upper chamber.

Meanwhile, later Presidents were able to recoup some of the power lost under Grant. With public support, Rutherford B. Hayes refused to let the Republican Senate dictate his Cabinet and customs appointments, and Grover Cleveland's defense of the Presidential appointment power led to repeal of the Tenure of Office Act, but on the whole the Senate remained the most powerful force in the Government. When William McKinley became President in 1897, Congress and the White House entered a period of almost unprecedented harmony. "We never had a President who had more influence with Congress than McKinley," said Sen. Shelby M. Cullom (R Ill.). "I have never heard of even the slightest friction between him and the party leaders in Senate and House."

Power of Party Bosses in Senate

The character of the Senate underwent a marked change in the post-Civil War era. Its membership grew from 74 in 1871 to 90 in 1901, and, as state politics became more centralized, a new breed of Senator entered the chamber. The great constitutional orators of the prewar period were succeeded by "party bosses"—professional politicians who had risen through the ranks of their state party organizations and who came to Washington only after they had consolidated their power over the state party structure. As long as they maintained state control, they were immune from external political reprisal, but their dedication to party and their acceptance of the need for discipline made them good "party Senators," willing to compromise their differences in order to maintain harmony within the party. To these men the Senate was a career, and a striking increase in average length of Senate service occurred during this period. *(See box.)*

The public viewed the Senate's changing character with grave suspicion, and the growing power of party organizations was widely attributed to the "trusts." Ostrogorski charged in 1902 that the economic interests "equipped and kept up political organizations for their own use, and ran them as they pleased, like their trains." Other observers held that political centralization and business concentration were parallel developments, not directly related, but they agreed that the corporations contributed to the power of the party chiefs.

Average Years of Service—All Senators

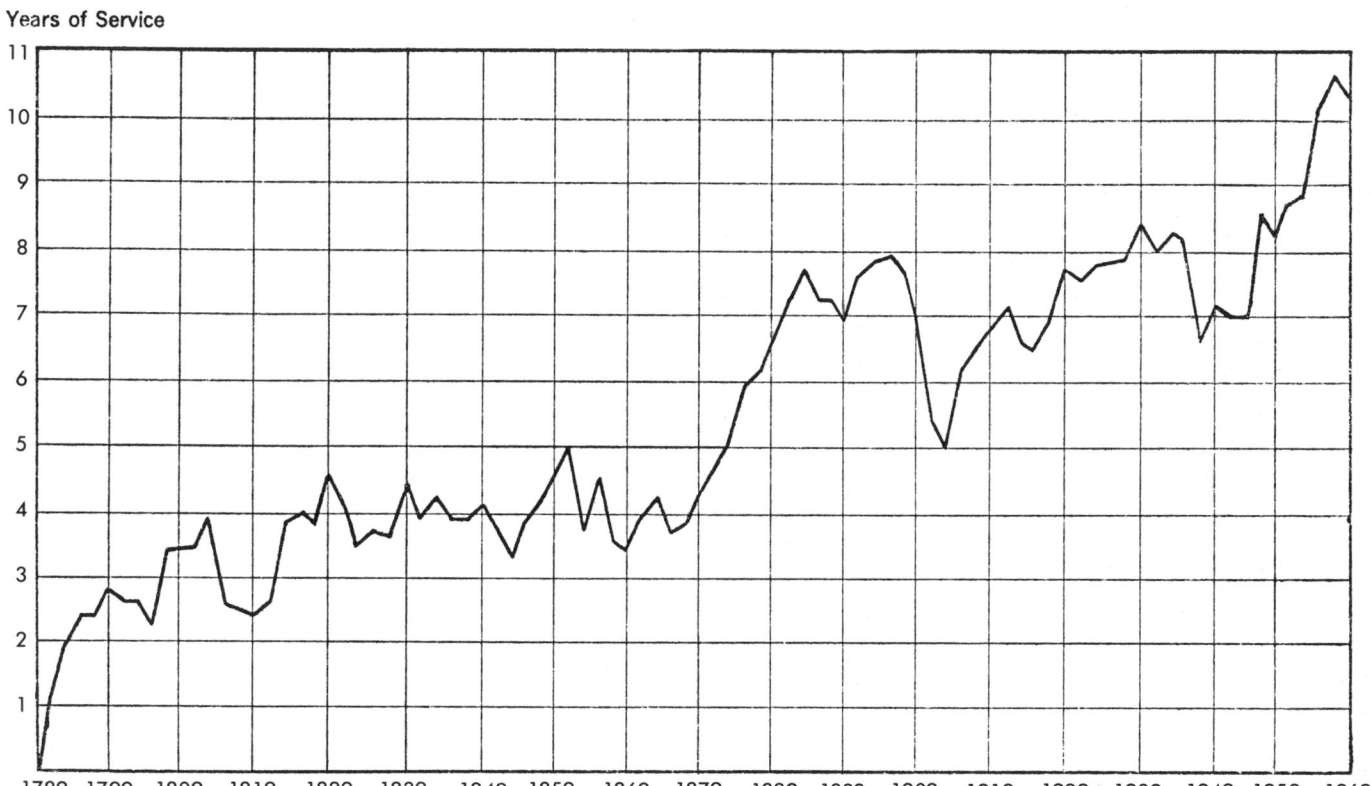

Years of Service

SOURCE: Randall B. Ripley, *Power in the Senate*. St. Martin's Press, 1969.

Loss of Public Esteem at End of Century

Lobbying by business groups became a vital element in government during the last part of the 19th century, but business itself was not unified and its efforts were too haphazard for it to attain great political control. Still, some of the lobbying practices of the period—ranging from wholesale distribution of railroad passes to loans and sales of stock at attractive prices to Members of Congress—fostered the impression of widespread Senate corruption.

The Senate's "usurpation" of Executive power, its failure to impose limitations on debate and the undoubted existence of corruption all contributed to the chamber's loss of public esteem. By the close of the 19th century, the Senate was described in derogatory, but somewhat unfair, fashion as a "Millionaires' Club," and it was without question the most unpopular branch of the national Government. Dissatisfaction with the Senate led to the movement for direct election of Senators, through which reformers hoped to curtail both the power of political parties and the political influence of the corporations. By 1900, it had become clear that a constitutional amendment providing for direct election would eventually be enacted.

Development of Party Leadership

Political parties assumed responsibility for organizational matters in the pre-Civil War Senate, and party authority was extended during the war to substantive questions as well. However, the Senate had no strong tradition of leadership and party discipline was expected to lapse after the war ended. Indeed, the Republican and Democratic parties themselves were expected to disintegrate, as other parties had done before them, once the issues that had brought them together were resolved.

Although the parties failed to dissolve, party influence in the upper chamber did decline for a time; when Grant's Administration began in 1869, political parties compelled unity only on organizational questions. Disputes over committee assignments were settled in the caucus, and pressing issues were discussed there, but caucus decisions could hardly be considered binding as long as there was no leader to enforce discipline or exact reprisals. The Republican caucus did remove Charles Sumner of Massachusetts from the chairmanship of the Foreign Relations Committee in 1871, when his differences with President Grant had become so extreme that he would communicate neither with the President nor his Secretary of State, but this was after all an organizational question.

In Defense of the Senate

In 1897, Sen. George F. Hoar (R Mass.) rose to the defense of the Senate in an article in the *Forum*. Hoar contended that the Senate "should be judged not by considering its conduct or its composition at the time when the judgment is to be expressed, but by a review of a whole century of its history." He continued:

"We have a right to show in what we have improved. We have a right to say that the evil influences of the lobby in legislation for private and not public ends, which, like the ointment of the hand, bewrayed themselves in the atmosphere of the Senate Chamber and in its corridors, are all gone to-day. We have a right to say that drunkenness, which existed when I first entered public life, is not known there to-day, and that Senators no longer bring whiskey-soaked brains to meet the high demands of the public service. We have a right to say that the use of executive patronage for personal advancement—so that each Senator who supported the Administration had a little army of followers devoted to his personal interests, supported at the public cost—has gone by. We have a right to say, also, that if important legislation, demanded for the public welfare, is often defeated by obstructive measures or prolonged and needless debate now, for the eighty years while slavery ruled, and while the strict State-rights construction prevailed, such legislation was not even introduced and its chances were not worth considering. We have a right to say that the work the Senators now give to the public service, day and night, is a constant, hard work which was unknown in either House of Congress, save to a very few persons, fifty years ago. Men who belonged to the minority were not permitted to share even in the ordinary routine business of legislation. It was considered almost an audacity in former times for one of them to move to adjourn. Levi Lincoln told me that his time, when he was a Whig member of Congress, hung heavily on his hands, and that neither he nor any of his Whig colleagues was permitted to take the slightest share in the duties of legislation.

"Talk about the degeneracy of the Senate! I am writing these lines upon the desk, I am seated in the chair, by whose side Charles Sumner was stricken down in the Senate Chamber for defending liberty—his comely and beautiful head the target for a ruffian's bludgeon. There were Senators standing by and looking on and approving. There were others standing by without interfering. The Senate neither dared to punish nor to censure the action; and the offender was fined $300 in a police court. This was forty years ago. Read Oliphant's account of the passage of the reciprocity treaty of 1854—a treaty which, as Lord Elgin described it, floated through on waves of champagne! Laurence Oliphant, the British Secretary, tells the story to his mother—a story, if it be true, as disgraceful to him and his superior as to us. But he excuses himself with the comment, 'If you have got to deal with hogs, what are you to do?'

"Talk of the degeneracy of the Senate to men who remember the time when a Vice-President was inaugurated in a state of maudlin intoxication; or the earlier days when Foote uttered in debate his threat to Hale, that he should be hung on the tallest tree in the forest if he should come to Mississippi; when the same man drew his pistol on Benton in the Senate Chamber; when Butler poured out his loose expectoration, and Mason gave exhibition of his arrogant plantation manners; or when Sumner likened Douglas to the noisome, squat, and nameless animal, who switched his tongue and filled the Senate with an offensive odor—therein quoting an epithet once applied to Lord North in the House of Commons."

Conkling's Influence. The possibilities of party leadership first became apparent in the Senate career of Roscoe Conkling of New York in the 1870s. Conkling gathered around him a loyal following, and after 1873 his faction usually controlled the Committee on Committees and thus was able to reward his supporters with valuable committee posts. But the Conkling forces stood together only on organizational questions; their influence on substantive legislation was not great. When Conkling resigned his Senate seat in 1881, following an altercation with President Garfield over appointments, the Senate reverted to its old independent ways. "No one," wrote Woodrow Wilson in 1885, "is *the* Senator. No one may speak for his party as well as for himself; no one exercises the special trust of acknowledged leadership. The Senate is merely a body of individual critics...."

Modern Party Discipline

Republican Leaders. Modern party discipline made its appearance in the Senate in the 1890s under the leadership of William B. Allison of Iowa, Nelson W. Aldrich of Rhode Island and their fellow members of the School of Philosophy Club, an informal group that met regularly for poker at the home of James McMillan of Michigan. When Allison, because he had served in the Senate longer than any other member of his party, was elected chairman of the Republican caucus in March 1897, this group assumed control of the Senate. Previous caucus chairmen had not viewed the office as a vehicle for concentrating party authority, but Allison was quick to see the possibilities of his new position. Holding that "both in the committees and in the offices, we should use the machinery for our own benefit and not let other men have it," Allison took advantage of his appointment powers to monopolize party offices.

Since the mid-1880s, a Republican Steering Committee had been appointed biennially to help schedule legislative business. Unlike previous caucus leaders, Allison determined to chair this committee himself, and he filled the committee with other members of his group. Under Allison's guidance, the Steering Committee arranged the order of business in minute detail and also managed proceedings on the floor.

Allison likewise dominated the Committee on Committees, which had responsibility for assignments to the working committees. The caucus chairman had great leeway in making appointments to this group, and Allison was able to staff it with a majority that would be receptive to his wishes; its chairman was always a member of the ruling faction. Committee chairmanships were by this time invariably filled through seniority, and Allison and Aldrich made no attempt to overturn the seniority rule, to which they owed their own committee chairmanships (Allison on Appropriations and Aldrich on Finance). But seniority did not apply to the filling of committee vacancies, and here the party leaders found an opportunity to reward their supporters and punish dissidents. Access to positions of influence soon depended on the favor and support of the party leaders. When Albert J. Beveridge of Indiana entered the Senate in 1899, he directed his appeal for committee preferment to Allison, in shrewd recognition of the existing order. "I feel that the greatest single point is gained in the possession of your friendship," Beveridge said. "I will labor very hard, strive very earnestly to deserve your consideration."

Caucus approval of the committee slates and order of business became a mere formality, but the caucus still met to consider important questions. Through the caucus mechanism divisive questions were compromised in privacy, and the party was enabled to speak with a united voice on the floor. Caucus decisions were not formally binding ("We can get along without" that, Allison remarked), but once the party leadership was capable of enforcing discipline on those who broke ranks, party solidarity became the norm. "Senators willing to abandon the opportunity to increase their authority could act freely, following their own inclinations," historian David Rothman noted. "The country might honor their names but the Senate barely felt their presence."

Democratic Leadership. Under the leadership of Arthur P. Gorman of Maryland, Senate Democrats developed a power structure similar to that devised by the Republicans. As chairman of the Democratic caucus in the 1890s, Gorman chaired not only the Steering Committee but the Committee on Committees as well, and in some ways his control over his party was greater than that of Allison and Aldrich over the Republicans. But the Democrats were in the minority most of the time, they often split on substantive issues, and Gorman never attained the power that his Republican counterpart achieved. The lack of harmony within Democratic ranks led, in 1903, to the adoption of a rule making the decisions of the Democratic caucus binding upon a two-thirds vote. Allison had considered such a rule unnecessary for the Republicans, but Gorman enthusiastically supported it.

Attitude Toward Party Control

The growth of party government was viewed with grave misgivings by the country at large and was by no means always popular in the Senate itself. As early as 1872 the Liberal Republicans were protesting efforts by "a few Members of the Senate" to use the party organization to "seek to control first a majority of the Members belonging to that organization and then of the Senate." Similar complaints came from the Mugwumps in the 1880s and the Populists in the 1890s. The Senate in 1899 took one step toward dispersing authority within the chamber when it transferred responsibility for major appropriations bills from the Appropriations Committee to various legislative committees. The change was pressed, not in caucus, but on the floor where dissidents within both parties were able to carry it over the combined opposition of the Republican and Democratic leaders.

By the end of the 19th century, political parties had assumed a decisive role in the legislative process. The parties named the committees which made the first tentative decisions on proposed legislation, and they also determined what bills would be considered on the floor. When divisive legislative questions arose, party members compromised their differences within the caucus and went forth in disciplined ranks to ratify caucus decisions on the floor, often acting without debate or the formality of a roll-call vote.

The Republicans had a plurality, but not a majority, of the Senate when the Dingley tariff bill came from the House in April 1897. Allison, with only the help of the Republican members of the Finance Committee, framed the schedules, which all but three of the Republicans agreed in advance to support. After limited debate in the caucus, the bill went to the Senate floor where united Republican support passed it over solid Democratic opposition. The Republicans, said Benjamin R. Tillman of South Carolina, "under the stress of party orders, I suppose, given by the caucus, sit by quietly and vote. They say nothing...and every schedule prepared by the party caucus is voted for by them unanimously." Tillman was wrong in only one particular; he credited the caucus with more influence than it actually had.

Election Law of 1866

For more than 75 years after the adoption of the Constitution, Congress took no advantage of its constitutional power to regulate Congressional elections, and the method of electing Senators was left to the states. At first, Senators generally were chosen by concurrent vote of the two houses of the state legislature, each sitting separately. Later, in about half the states it became common for the two houses to elect Senators by per capita voting in joint session.

The election system had serious flaws. Insistence on a majority vote in each house caused frequent deadlocks, which not only kept the legislature from handling other business but also caused the state to lose its representation in the U.S. Senate. Irregular practices abounded, and the Senate itself was forced to decide many election contests resulting from the lack of a uniform election law.

Accordingly, Congress in 1866 enacted legislation designed to correct these problems. The 1866 law provided that on the second Tuesday after the organization of a legislature when a Senator was to be elected, the two houses should meet separately and by voice vote name a person for Senator. On the following day the results of the voting were to be canvassed at a joint session of the two houses. If one candidate had won a majority of both houses, he was to be declared elected, but if this was not the case, "the joint assembly shall meet at twelve o'clock, meridian, of each succeeding day during the session of the legislature, and take at least one vote until a Senator shall be elected."

Senatorial elections were regulated by this law for almost half a century, until the adoption of the 17th Amendment in 1913, but the measure was not a success. Deadlocks continued to occur, and irregularities increased. George H. Haynes summarized the problems of legislative election that led to the direct election movement: "...not a few, but nearly half the states of the Union suffered from serious deadlocks. These contests, the outcome of which was often as much a matter of chance as would be the throw of dice, aroused men's worst passions and gave rise now to insistent charges of bribery, now to riot, to assault and to threats of bloodshed, such that legislative sessions had to be held under protection of martial law. Fourteen contests lasted throughout an entire session of the legislature without effecting an election. Four states submitted to the heavy cost and inconvenience of special sessions to elect Senators. Six states preferred to accept vacancies, thus losing their 'equal suffrage in the Senate,' while the country was deprived of a Senate constituted as the fathers had intended. At times legislative election led to positive and flagrant misrepresentation of the state in the Senate. To the individual state it brought a domination of state and local politics by the fierce fight for a single federal office, and interference with the work of lawmaking, ranging all the way from the exaction of a few hours of the legislators' time to the virtual annihilation of the legislature, which had been constituted to care for the interests of the state."

Rise of the Filibuster

The oratorical splendor that had brought renown to the Senate in the years preceding the Civil War disappeared with the settlement of the slavery question, and for the remainder of the 19th century Senate debate was not noted for its brilliance. As crucial legislative decisions came to be made in party councils, few floor speeches were delivered for the purpose of swaying votes, and attendance at formal sessions of the Senate became a tedious duty. "It would be a capital thing," wrote George F. Hoar in 1897, "to attend Unitarian conventions if there were not Unitarians there, so too it would be a delightful thing to be a United States Senator if you did not have to attend the sessions of the Senate."

Filibusters, increasingly common as the century advanced, became virtually an epidemic in the 1880s and 1890s. As a result, the Senate suffered a marked loss of public esteem for its failure to impose stringent curbs on debate. Cloture proposals were introduced from time to time, but the Senate held fast to its cherished tradition of unlimited speech.

Wartime pressures produced two notable filibusters. In 1863 the conference report on a bill to secure the President against loss in any action brought against him for having suspended the writ of habeas corpus was subject to an intense filibuster in the closing hours of the session. But the filibuster failed when the presiding officer, in the face of obvious obstruction, called for a vote and refused to entertain an appeal. The tactics of the filibusterers were described by Sen. Lyman Trumbull (R Ill.): "Motion after motion was made here last night to lay on the table, to postpone indefinitely, to adjourn, to adjourn, to adjourn and to adjourn again, and the yeas and nays called on each occasion." Similar tactics were employed by Sumner in 1865 to postpone the readmission of Louisiana. He felt so strongly on the issue that he declared himself "justified in employing all the instruments that I find in the arsenal of parliamentary warfare."

Democratic proposals to suspend or repeal statutes allowing the use of Federal troops in state elections were the subject of the next great filibusters, in 1876 and 1879. In the 1879 filibuster Republicans relied on dilatory motions, roll-call votes and refusal to answer quorum calls, whereupon the President pro tempore ruled that he could count a quorum to determine whether enough Senators were present to do business.

Famous Filibusters

In the famous filibuster of 1881, the Democratic minority prevented the Republicans from organizing the Senate until the resignations of two Senators (Conkling and Thomas C. Platt of New York) had given the Democrats numerical control. The filibuster made it impossible for the upper chamber to take action on any legislation from March 24 to May 16 of that year.

In 1890 a bill to provide Federal aid to education sponsored by Henry W. Blair (R N.H.) was filibustered from Feb. 26 to March 20 by Blair himself in an effort to get sufficient support for passage. Believing he had won the requisite strength, Blair permitted the bill to come to a vote, but two Senators at the last minute decided to vote against it. The bill was defeated, 31-37, with Blair himself voting nay in order to be eligible to move reconsideration. The measure was never revived.

A dramatic filibuster against the Lodge "Force Bill" lasted intermittently from Dec. 2, 1890, to Jan. 26, 1891. The measure would have established Federal supervision over polling places at national elections in order to prevent exclusion of Negro voters in southern states. After seven weeks of debate, the bill's supporters tried to put through a rule for majority cloture. When this failed, the Senate was held in continuous session for four days and nights in an effort to exhaust the filibusterers. Eventually, after 33 days of actual obstruction, the bill was dropped to permit the enactment of vital appropriation bills before the 51st Congress expired in March 1891. During the debate, West Virginia Democrat C. J. Faulkner nominally held the floor for 11½ hours, although for nearly eight hours of that time he was relieved of the necessity of speaking through the absence of a quorum.

In 1893, a filibuster against repeal of the silver purchase clause of the Sherman Act lasted from Aug. 29 to Oct. 24. After 46 days of actual filibuster and 13 continuous day-and-night sittings, the repealer was passed Oct. 30 and sent to the President. The minority made shameless use of every weapon in the filibuster arsenal—dilatory motions, roll-call votes and quorum calls, in addition to talk. A new record was set by Nebraska Populist William V. Allen who held the floor, with interruptions, for 14 hours.

This filibuster aroused widespread public concern over the conduct and future of the Senate. "To vote without debating is perilous, but to debate and never vote is imbecile," wrote Sen. Henry Cabot Lodge (R Mass.) shortly after the struggle ended. "As it is, there must be a change, for the delays which now take place are discrediting the Senate.... A body which cannot govern itself will not long hold the respect of the people who have chosen it to govern the country...."

In 1897, during a mild filibuster on a naval appropriation bill, the chair ruled that a quorum call could not be ordered unless business had intervened since the last quorum call. However, since there was as yet no suggestion that debate was not business, this ruling had only limited value in curbing the excesses of the filibuster.

In 1901, Montana Republican Thomas H. Carter, who was retiring from the Senate in a few hours, filibustered against a "pork-barrel" rivers and harbors bill from the night of March 3 until the Senate adjourned *sine die* at noon March 4 (legislative day of March 3). The bill was a raid on the Treasury, Carter said, and he was performing a "public service" in preventing it from becoming law. He readily yielded for other business but resumed his item-by-item denunciation of the bill whenever necessary. No determined attempt was made to stop him, and the bill died.

Early filibusters had not been notably successful, but as obstructionists gradually shifted to bolder techniques the Senate was unable to restrain them, and by the beginning of the 20th century the filibuster had assumed scandalous proportions. This was, says Franklin Burdette, "the heyday of brazen and unblushing aggressors. The power of the Senate lay not in votes but in sturdy tongues and iron wills. The premium rested not upon ability and statesmanship but upon effrontery and audacity."

Senate Rules on Debate

The House of Representatives, whose entire membership is elected anew every two years, must adopt its rules at the beginning of each new Congress. But the Senate, as a continuing body, faces no such task; its rules remain in force from Congress to Congress unless the Senate decides to change them. Several revisions of the Senate rules have occurred since the first rules were adopted in 1789, but these revisions have been chiefly codifications of changes that had accumulated over a number of years.

Two such codifications occurred in the 1861-1901 period. The first, in 1868, increased the number of rules to an all-time maximum of 53, and it reflected some wartime strains. Another codification, in 1884, brought the number of rules down to 40. Although many changes in Senate rules have been adopted since that time, no further codification has taken place.

"Rules are never observed in this body; they are only made to be broken. We are a law unto ourselves." So spoke John J. Ingalls (R Kan.) in 1876. His comment may explain why rules reform has not played as significant a role in the history of the Senate as it has in the House.

Efforts to limit Senate debate provide a notable exception. In the last half of the 19th century, many proposals were offered to curtail debate either through the use of the previous question or some other means. Most of the proposals were simply ignored, but a few minor changes affecting debate were agreed to.

In 1862, the Senate adopted a resolution stating that "in consideration in secret session of subjects relating to the rebellion, debate should be confined to the subject matter and limited to five minutes, except that five minutes be allowed any Member to explain or oppose a pertinent amendment." Adoption of this resolution was attributable to the exigencies of wartime. In later years it also became customary for the Senate, in the closing days of a session when the need for haste was great, to apply a five-minute limit on debate on appropriations bills.

Anthony Rule. In 1870, the Senate first adopted the so-called Anthony Rule, the most important limitation of debate it had yet agreed to, as a means of expediting its business. The rule was so successful in speeding action on noncontroversial bills that in 1880 it became part of the Standing Rules, where it now appears as Rule VIII:

"At the conclusion of the morning business for each day, unless upon motion the Senate shall at any time otherwise order, the Senate will proceed to the consideration of the Calendar of Bills and Resolutions, and continue such consideration until 2 o'clock; and bills and

resolutions that are not objected to shall be taken up in their order, and each Senator shall be entitled to speak once and for five minutes only upon any question; and the objection may be interposed at any stage of the proceedings, but upon motion the Senate may continue such consideration; and this order shall commence immediately after the call for 'concurrent and other resolutions,' and shall take precedence of the unfinished business and other special orders. But if the Senate shall proceed with the consideration of any matter notwithstanding an objection, the foregoing provisions touching debate shall not apply."

Sen. Henry B. Anthony (R R.I.) explained that the purpose of the rule was not to curb debate on controversial bills, but merely to hasten action on routine measures: "There are a great many bills that no Senator objects to, but they are kept back in their order by disputed cases. If we once relieve the Calendar of unobjected cases, we can go through with it in order without any limitation of debate."

The Anthony Rule greatly speeded the handling of routine measures without prejudice to the right of Senators to demand longer debate on controversial bills. Another change that helped to facilitate the business of the Senate was the decision in 1875 that an amendment to an appropriation bill might be laid on the table without prejudice to the bill itself. This rule was so successful that its application was later extended to amendments to any bill.

Still, the Senate cherished its tradition of unlimited debate—even if, under an 1872 precedent, that debate was not relevant to the subject under consideration. And in 1881 it rejected, as a form of the previous question, a proposed amendment to the Anthony Rule. Whereas under that rule a single Senator by objecting could block immediate consideration of a bill on call of the Calendar, under the proposed amendment it could not have been passed over unless at least five Senators objected. Sen. George F. Edmunds (R Vt.) said in opposition to the amendment: "I think it is of greater importance to the public interest, in the long run and in the short run, that every bill on your Calendar should fail than that any Senator should be cut off from the right of expressing his opinion and the grounds of it upon every measure that is to be voted upon here...."

The Senate apparently agreed. When the revised rules of 1884 emerged from the Senate Rules Committee at the close of 1883, they included a provision for the previous question but the provision was rejected on the Senate floor.

The Era of Reform: 1901-1921

The "Progressive Era," which had begun with movements for economic reform in the 1880s and 1890s, gathered momentum and a radical democratic character after the turn of the century and gradually faded into the background during World War I. The progressive program was foreshadowed in the platform of the Populist party, which in 1892 polled over a million votes for its Presidential candidate, James B. Weaver. Though the party, centered in the agrarian Midwest and West, soon declined, many of its programs were gradually adopted by the two major parties.

Early Progressive Legislation. Under popular pressure, Congress had enacted such early "progressive" legislation as civil service reform (1883), the Interstate Commerce Act (1887), the Sherman Antitrust Act (1890), conservation legislation (1891) and an income tax law (1894). But the income tax was invalidated by the Supreme Court, and the other measures were rendered ineffective by their vagueness and their loopholes, by court rulings and by unenthusiastic administration.

Finding themselves thus frustrated, and laying the blame on the supposed sinister influence of vested interests, reformers concluded that more democratic control of the Government was necessary to secure the laws they sought. Accordingly, the reform movement turned increasingly toward such measures as direct election of Senators, direct primaries, women's suffrage and laws against corrupt election practices. In the House, the reformers were determined to break the power of the Speaker.

The power of the Senate declined after Theodore Roosevelt became President in 1901. Roosevelt was an aggressive leader who took an active role in promoting legislation. Concentration of authority in the House Speaker had brought cohesion to the lower chamber, which was now prepared to challenge Senatorial leadership, and Roosevelt worked mainly through informal contacts with the Speaker of the House to advance his legislative program.

Insurgent Movement in Congress

Congress went along, somewhat reluctantly, with Roosevelt's progressive program, passing such measures as the Hepburn Act, which strengthened the Interstate Commerce Commission, pure food and drug laws and a workman's compensation act. But William Howard Taft, who was elected in 1908, failed to press Roosevelt's policies in the face of Old Guard opposition, and the defeat of legislation sought by progressives in both parties led to the development of an insurgent movement among western Republicans in Congress.

In the House, Republican insurgents led the revolt against Speaker Cannon, while in the Senate the "Band of Six"—La Follette of Wisconsin, Beveridge of Indiana, Dolliver and Cummins of Iowa, Bristow of Kansas and Clapp of Minnesota—unsuccessfully challenged the Aldrich machine on the Payne-Aldrich tariff bill. Enactment of this distinctly protectionist measure led to resounding Republican defeats in the Congressional elections of 1910 and the formation of the Progressive ("Bull Moose") party which nominated Roosevelt for President in 1912. The split between the Roosevelt and Taft wings of the Republican party gave an easy victory to the Democrats, and under President Woodrow Wilson the Government entered a period of progressive rule that lasted through most of Wilson's first term.

Wilson Reforms. The President's early relations with Congress were easy. He returned to the pre-Jeffersonian practice of addressing the Congress in person and frequently went to the President's room in the Capitol to confer with committees or individual Members. Under his leadership "the first caucus of Democratic Senators that anyone can remember" was proposed in 1913, to marshal party support for the Underwood tariff-cutting bill. Other legislative victories included the income tax

(made valid by a constitutional amendment submitted to the states in 1909 and belatedly ratified on the eve of Wilson's inauguration), direct election of Senators, the Clayton Antitrust Act and the Federal Reserve and Federal Trade Commission Acts.

This flow of progressive legislation ended when the United States entered World War I in 1917. During the war, Wilson assumed almost dictatorial powers, and criticism of his policies was silenced, but with the President's ill-timed appeal for election of a Democratic Congress in the fall of 1918, the opposition surfaced. In the ensuing election, Republicans captured control of both houses of Congress, and the President went off to the Paris Peace Conference a rejected hero. Wilson's health broke in his futile efforts to enlist support for the League of Nations, and the Republican Senate first emasculated, then rejected the Treaty of Versailles in which the League Covenant was embedded. With the election of a Republican Congress in 1918, a new period of Congressional hegemony was at hand.

The 17th Amendment, providing for direct election of Senators, was undoubtedly the most important development in the evolution of the Senate during the Progressive Era, but other significant changes also occurred. Political parties were beginning to assume their modern place in the legislative structure, and as party leadership roles became institutionalized during the early years of the century, formally identifiable Majority and Minority Leaders emerged. With the admission of Arizona to statehood in 1912, the membership of the Senate increased to 96; no further changes in size would occur for nearly half a century. Finally, in 1917 the Senate was driven by the excesses of filibustering to adopt its first cloture rule, permitting two-thirds of those present and voting to bring debate to a close.

Direct Election of Senators

The Constitution provided for the election of Senators by the state legislatures. But the 17th Amendment, ratified in 1913, changed the Constitution to provide for direct election of Senators. The change was part of the Progressive Era's movement toward more democratic control of government. Being less immediately dependent on popular sentiment than the House, the Senate did not seek to reform itself. Only strong pressure from the public, expressed through the House of Representatives, the state governments, pressure groups, petitions, referenda and other means, convinced the Senate that it must participate in its own reform.

It was common in the Progressive Era to attribute legislative disappointments to the dealings of vested interests operating behind the scenes. A Senate chosen by state legislatures, whose decisions were often made in closed-door party caucuses, could not easily escape suspicion. Moreover, the high-tariff views of the Senate served to link this body in the public mind with the great corporations that were widely accused of improper influence on politics. The popular image of the Senate in the Progressive Era was a far cry from the picture presented by de Tocqueville in an earlier age.

Pressures on the Senate. Andrew Johnson, who as President subsequently came within one vote of removal from office at the hands of the Senate, was an early advocate of Senate reform. Twice as a Representative, once as a Senator, and again as President in 1868, Johnson presented resolutions calling for direct election of Senators. But in the first 80 years of Congress, a total of only nine resolutions proposing a constitutional amendment to that effect were introduced in Congress. In the 1870s and 1880s the number increased, and by 1912 a total of not less than 287 such joint resolutions had been introduced. Not until 1892 was a resolution reported favorably from committee in the House. In the next decade such a resolution was carried five times in the House with only a handful in opposition. But the proposed amendment to the Constitution was not allowed to reach a vote in the Senate until 1911.

Petitions from farmers' associations and other organizations, particularly in the West, and party platforms in state elections pressed the issue until the national parties took it up. Direct election of Senators was a plank in the Populist program at every election, beginning in 1892, and in the Democratic platform in each Presidential election year from 1900 to 1912. Starting in California and Iowa in 1894, state legislatures addressed Congress in favor of a direct election amendment, until by 1905 the legislatures in 31 of the 45 states had taken this step, many of them repeatedly. Referenda held in three states showed approval of the amendment by votes of 14 to 1 in California, 8 to 1 in Nevada, and 6 to 1 in Illinois. Support was strongest in the West and North Central states, where every legislature petitioned Congress at least once, and weakest in the Northeast, where only Pennsylvania's legislature voted to address Congress in support of direct election.

In 1900, when the House voted 240-15 in favor of submitting an amendment for direct election of Senators, it was favored by a majority of the Representatives from every state except Maine and Connecticut.

Other Tactics. Still the Senate did not act. Since the Senators would not even consider a change in the method of electing them, other tactics were adopted. Between 1902 and 1911 even the House did not vote on any resolution for direct election of Senators. But the states were finding ways to achieve the same results without a constitutional amendment.

The spread of direct primaries in the 1890s led in many states to expressions of popular choice of Senator on the primary ballot. Though not legally binding on the legislatures, this choice was likely to be ratified. In the South, the primary winners were soon being "elected" by the one-party legislatures almost as a matter of course. But in states that did not have a one-party system, especially those lacking clear party lines, primaries were less effective in guaranteeing that the popular choice would be ratified by the legislature.

Oregon led the way in devising a system to guarantee popular choice of Senators in spite of the Constitution's assignment of this task to the legislatures. In 1901 an Oregon law was enacted enabling voters to express their choice for Senator in the same manner as they voted for Governor, except that the vote for Senator had no legal force. But the law specified that when the legislature assembled to elect a Senator, "it shall be the duty of each house to count the votes and announce the candidate having the highest number, and thereupon the houses shall proceed to the election of a Senator." In the first

test of this system, the man who led the field with 37 percent of the popular vote for Senator secured scant support from the legislators, who scattered their votes among 14 candidates. After a five-week deadlock, the legislature chose a man who had not received a single vote in the popular election.

Far from being discouraged at this mockery of "the people's choice," the people of Oregon in 1904 used their new initiative and referendum powers to petition for and approve a new law. Henceforth each candidate for Senator was to be nominated by petition, and allowed to include on the petition a 100-word statement of principles, and on the ballot a 12-word statement to be printed after his name. The legislators, who could not be denied their constitutional power to name Senators, were permitted to include in their nomination petitions their signatures to either "Statement No. 1" or "Statement No. 2." The former pledged the signer always to vote "for that candidate for United States Senator in Congress who has received the highest number of the people's votes...without regard to my individual preference." The second statement was a pledge to regard the popular vote "as nothing more than a recommendation, which I shall be at liberty to wholly disregard...." Meanwhile, citizen groups circulated pledges, which were widely subscribed to, that the signer would not support or vote for any candidate to the legislature who did not endorse "Statement No. 1."

The first legislature elected after enactment of this law promptly ratified the "people's choice" for Senator. And two years later, when 83 of the 90 members of the legislature were Republicans, the Democratic popular choice was elected. He received 53 votes, including all 52 who had endorsed "Statement No. 1."

The "Oregon System" was adopted in other states in modified forms. By December 1910 it was estimated that 14 of the 30 Senators about to be named by state legislatures had already been designated by popular vote.

The Issue in the Senate. Gradually the mounting external pressures began to be felt within the "citadel," as the Senate was sometimes called. Some of the Senators were themselves products of the new systems of popular election. In fact, the leader within the Senate in the fight for the 17th Amendment, Sen. William E. Borah (R Idaho), had entered the Senate through a popular mandate after an earlier defeat at the hands of the Idaho legislature.

Beginning in 1901, some of the legislatures were no longer content to request Congress to submit a constitutional amendment to the states. They called for a convention to amend the Constitution, a method as yet untried but obligatory once two-thirds of the states so petition Congress. Some Senators, though they opposed popular election, feared that such a convention, like the original Constitutional Convention, might exceed its original mandate and preferred to submit to the states a specific amendment for direct election of Senators.

When a resolution for the amendment was referred to the Senate Judiciary Committee, rather than to the more hostile Committee on Privileges and Elections that customarily considered it, a favorable report was at last obtained in 1910. A committee amendment, supported by southern Senators, would have modified Congress' power to alter state regulations of elections by making it not applicable to popular election of Senators. On the floor the committee amendment was, in effect, removed by a vote of 50-37. But Feb. 28, 1911, the resolution itself then failed, 54-33, to secure the necessary two-thirds majority.

In a special session later that year, the House passed 296-16 the direct election resolution. But the House version was the same as that reported by the Senate Committee, giving the states all control over election regulations. The Senate, on a 45-44 roll call decided by Vice President James S. Sherman's tie-breaking vote, again rejected the committee amendment, and adopted the original resolution, 64-24. A deadlock between the two houses was broken in the next session when on May 13, 1912, the House, 238-39, finally concurred in the Senate version. By May 31, 1913, three-fourths of the states had ratified.

The immediate effects of the 17th Amendment were difficult to assess. Even before its adoption, the direct primary movement had diminished the power of the legislatures, and by 1913 three-fourths of the candidates for the Senate were being nominated in direct primaries. The terms of the Senators in office at the time the Amendment was ratified ended variously in 1915, 1917 and 1919, so the 66th Congress (1919-21) was the first in which all Members of the Senate were the products of direct election. "By that time," George B. Galloway pointed out, "56 of the Senators who owed their togas originally to state legislatures had been re-elected by the people, three had died, and 37 had disappeared from the scene either voluntarily or by popular verdict. In other words, more than half of those last chosen by legislative caucus were subsequently approved by the people."

Restraining the Filibuster

In the early years of the 20th century, filibusters continued to be undertaken with frequency and a high degree of success. But mounting opposition to the practice led, in 1908, to efforts to curb obstruction through interpretation of existing rules and, in 1917, to the Senate's first cloture rule.

Meanwhile, 1903 proved to be vintage year for the filibuster. Democratic Sen. Benjamin R. ("Pitchfork Ben") Tillman of South Carolina filibustered against an appropriation bill until an item for payment of war claims to his state was restored. The item was put back in the bill after Tillman threatened to read Byron's "Childe Harold" and other poems into the record until his colleagues surrendered from boredom.

While Tillman resorted to "legislative blackmail," in Speaker Cannon's phrase, Republican Sen. Albert J. Beveridge of Indiana chose a different method. Beveridge, chairman of the Territories Committee and an opponent of statehood for Arizona and New Mexico, led a filibuster against an omnibus statehood bill. Taking advantage of a custom that no vote should be taken on a measure in the absence of the chairman of the committee that had handled it, Beveridge hid for days in the Washington home of Gifford Pinchot and finally slipped away to Atlantic City. The bill ultimately was dropped.

In 1908, a bitter two-day filibuster against the conference report on the Aldrich-Vreeland Currency bill brought the first significant steps to curb obstruction. Republican Sen. Robert M. La Follette Sr. of Wisconsin held the floor for 18 hours and 23 minutes, a record that stood until 1938, but he was interrupted by 29 quorum calls and three roll calls on questions of order. La Follette fortified himself periodically with eggnogs from the Senate restaurant. According to one account, he rejected one of these eggnogs as doped, and it later was found to contain a fatal dose of ptomaine. No charge of a deliberate poisoning attempt was made.

The filibusterers' cause finally was lost when blind Sen. Thomas P. Gore (D Okla.) yielded the floor after learning that Sen. William J. ("Gumshoe Bill") Stone (D Mo.), who was scheduled to relieve him, was in the chamber. But Stone had been called to the cloakroom, and the blind Gore surrendered the floor. The conference report was approved on a hastily demanded roll call.

First Curbs on Obstruction

Three important curbs on obstruction resulted from the 1908 filibuster. They were rulings that: (1) the chair could count a quorum if enough Senators were present, even on a vote, whether or not they answered to their names; (2) debate did not count as intervening business for the purpose of deciding if a quorum call was in order; and (3) Senators could by enforcement of existing rules be prevented from speaking more than twice on the same subject in one day.

During a 1914 Republican filibuster against a rivers and harbors bill, the chair ruled that Senators could not yield for any purpose, even for a question, without unanimous consent. The Senate tabled an appeal from this ruling, 28-24, but reversed itself the next day and the rules remained unchanged.

In 1915, a successful filibuster was organized against President Wilson's Ship Purchase bill. Republican Sen. Reed Smoot of Utah spoke for 11 hours and 35 minutes without relief and without deviating from the subject. After almost a month of obstruction, seven Democrats who thought the filibuster should give way to other important legislation joined the Republicans to move that the bill be recommitted. "Regular" Democrats then staged a five-day reverse filibuster until they regained control of the chamber. The Republican filibuster then was renewed. A Democratic motion to close the debate was blocked, and the bill finally was dropped, but as a result of the filibuster three important appropriation bills failed.

"Eleven Willful Men"

The public was disgusted by this episode, but it took one more great filibuster to force the Senate into action. The occasion came in 1917 when the Administration's Armed Neutrality bill was talked to death by an 11-man bloc in the closing days of the 64th Congress. Seventy-five Senators who signed a statement in support of the measure asked that it be entered in the Record "to establish that the Senate favors the legislation and would pass it, if a vote could be had." Let it be noted that not all of the obstruction came from the Republican side of the aisle. On the last day of the session, when it was clear that the bill was doomed, the Democrats staged their own filibuster to keep an outraged La Follette from being able to speak against the measure before crowded Senate galleries.

No sooner had the session ended than President Wilson issued an angry statement: "The Senate of the United States is the only legislative body in the world which cannot act when its majority is ready for action. A little group of willful men, representing no opinion but their own, have rendered the great government of the United States helpless and contemptible...." Wilson immediately called the Senate into special session and demanded that it amend its rules so that it could act and "save the country from disaster."

The Senate yielded, and a conference of Republican and Democratic leaders hastily drew up the Senate's first cloture rule. After only six hours of debate, Rule 22 was adopted by the chamber March 8, 1917, by a vote of 76-3.

Rule 22's Limits on Debate

The new rule provided for limitation of debate "upon any pending measure" by vote of two-thirds of the Senators present and voting, two days after a cloture motion had been submitted by 16 Senators. Thereafter, debate was limited to one hour for each Senator on the bill itself and all amendments and motions affecting it. No new amendments could be offered except by unanimous consent. Amendments that were not germane to the pending business, and amendments and motions clearly designed to delay action, were out of order.

The limited aim of the sponsors was made apparent when an amendment was offered to authorize cloture by majority instead of two-thirds vote. The amendment was attacked as a "breach of faith" and was withdrawn before a vote could be taken. And in 1918 the Senate rejected, 34-41, a proposal to allow use of the previous question to limit debate during the war period.

For a time it looked as if the Senate would never make use of its new tool against obstruction, but the interminable debates on the Treaty of Versailles in 1919 finally provided an occasion. The Senate adopted its first cloture motion Nov. 15, 1919, on a 78-16 roll call, and four days later the treaty itself was brought to a vote, after 55 days of debate.

Party Leadership

The system of party leadership that had evolved in the Senate in the closing years of the 19th century became institutionalized in the early years of the 20th with the creation of formally designated majority and minority leadership positions. *(See Leadership in House and Senate, Chapter II.)*

Both Republicans and Democrats for many years had elected chairmen of the party caucuses, but the caucus chairman was not necessarily the effective leader of his party in the Senate. Allison and Gorman served as chairmen of their respective caucuses, but the position was not essential to their control; Aldrich, the most powerful Member of the Senate until his retirement in 1911, never held any official position other than the chairmanship of the Finance Committee.

With the departure of these dynamic leaders from the chamber, power was fragmented within the parties. It became common for both Republicans and Democrats to elect a different floor leader in each session, and the floor leadership did not necessarily correspond with the caucus chairmanship. Under these conditions party unity was hard to maintain.

In 1911, the Democrats—already in control of the House and looking forward to the election of a Democratic Senate two years later—instituted the practice of electing a single, readily identifiable leader, who held the dual posts of floor leader and chairman of the party caucus. The Republicans, threatened by insurgents within their ranks, took a similar course in 1913. Subsequently party whips (assistant floor leaders) were added to the leadership structure—in 1913 by the Democrats and in 1915 by the Republicans. Since this period, the Majority and Minority Leaders have usually been the acknowledged spokesmen for their parties in the Senate.

The importance of the leadership role was underscored in 1913, when progressive Senate Democrats deposed conservative leader Thomas S. Martin (Va.) and engineered the election as Majority Leader of John W. Kern (Ind.), who had served in the Senate only two years. The Steering Committee, appointed by Kern and dominated by progressives, made committee assignments in such a way as to assure Administration control of major committees; seniority was ignored when necessary. The Steering Committee also recommended rules, later adopted by the caucus, that permitted a majority of committee members to call meetings, elect subcommittees and appoint conferees. Thus party authority was augmented and the power of committee chairmen curbed in a movement that somewhat paralleled the revolt against Cannonism in the House.

Early in the 20th century, both parties replaced the title "caucus" with "conference," in formal recognition of the non-binding nature of these party meetings. The Democratic caucus in 1903 adopted a binding caucus rule, but there is no evidence that it was ever used, and when Kern in 1913 proposed holding a binding caucus on the tariff bill, opposition was so vigorous that the idea had to be dropped. The compromise finally achieved preserved the appearance of a non-binding "conference," though Democratic Senators were under such strong pressure to support caucus decisions that the effect of a binding caucus was maintained.

Republican Stalemate: 1921-1933

After its victory over Woodrow Wilson on the League of Nations, the Senate was in no mood to submit to Presidential leadership. It expected to assume control of the Government in the Republican Administrations that followed Wilson, but after the House revamped its appropriations procedures in 1920 the lower chamber increasingly challenged Senate primacy.

Wilson's three Republican successors, faithful to the GOP doctrine of legislative independence, made little effort to direct Congress in legislative matters. When a group of Republican Senators tapped one of their own, Sen. Warren G. Harding of Ohio, for the Republican Presidential nomination in 1920, he came recommended as a man who "would, when elected, sign whatever bill the Senate sent him and not send bills for the Senate to pass." When Harding appeared before the Senate in 1921 to urge a balanced budget, the Senate berated him for interfering in its business and the House was offended that the issue had not been raised in the chamber where money bills must originate. Harding's subsequent feeble efforts to exert leadership were rebuffed by Congress, and his Administration was tarnished by scandals that were exposed by Senate investigators after his death in 1923.

The succeeding Vice President, Calvin Coolidge, was even less inclined to leadership than Harding had been. "I have never felt that it was my duty to attempt to coerce Senators or Representatives, or to make reprisals," Coolidge wrote. "The people sent them to Washington. I felt I had discharged my duty when I had done the best I could with them." The Senate rejected Coolidge's nomination of Charles Beecher Warren as Attorney General, the first rejection of a Cabinet nomination since 1868, but in other respects it largely ignored the passive President.

More aggressive leadership was expected of Herbert Hoover, but he lacked political experience and, as a recent convert to Republicanism, was distrusted by many members of his own party. Friction with the Legislative Branch thwarted his efforts to deal with the economic depression that engulfed the nation early in his single term of office.

If the Presidents of the 1920s were unable to lead the Government, Congress itself was not much more successful. Although Republicans controlled the White House from 1921 to 1933, the House from 1919 to 1931 and the Senate from 1919 to 1933, the party solidarity that had characterized the McKinley era no longer existed. Throughout the 1920s a "progressive" farm bloc dominated by western Republicans held the balance of power in Congress, and the decade was marked by persistent deadlocks on major issues.

Meanwhile, significant internal developments took place in the chamber. A major consolidation of the committee system occurred in 1921, and exclusive authority over spending was restored to the Appropriations Committee in 1922 after introduction of the new budget system. In 1932, the Senate finally succeeded in winning House concurrence to the Lame-Duck Amendment, which altered the terms and sessions of Congress. But experience did not bear out the hope of Sen. George W. Norris (R Neb.), sponsor of the amendment, that it would end the filibusters that continued to plague the Senate in the 1920s. Of the nine cloture votes taken during that decade, only three succeeded, and opponents of the filibuster continued to seek new ways to halt obstruction.

Republican Insurgency

Agriculture did not share in the prosperity of the 1920s, and efforts to relieve the farmers' plight led to a breakdown of party government and the development of legislative blocs representing sectional and economic interests. Efforts to enact agricultural relief legislation brought a split between eastern and western Republicans and the establishment of a powerful bipartisan farm bloc within Congress. Insurgent Republicans, mostly from the Great Plains and Rocky Mountain areas, usually kept their formal ties to the Republican party but cooperated with the Democrats on sectional economic legislation. In the House, Republican regulars for the most part kept the upper hand, but in the Senate Republican control was often only nominal. Insurgents frequently succeeded in blocking Administration legislation although they lacked the strength to carry their own legislative program. The

divisions of the period extended to organizational matters within the chamber.

The Congressional elections of 1922 were a disaster for the regular Republicans. Not only did the Republican majority decline from 167 to 15 in the House and from 22 to 6 in the Senate, but throughout the farm states progressive Republicans won over regulars. When the 68th Congress met in December 1923, the insurgents challenged the regulars' control.

The insurgent Republicans and the two Farmer-Labor Senators from Minnesota accepted committee assignments from the Republicans but did not attend the Republican conference. When the committee lists came to the floor, La Follette led an effort to remove Albert B. Cummins of Iowa from the chairmanship of the Interstate Commerce Committee. A month-long deadlock ensued. La Follette, as it happened, was the second-ranking Republican on the Committee, and the regular Republicans, unable to elect Cummins, had no intention of letting La Follette succeed to the chairmanship. Finally, on the thirty-second ballot, the regulars threw their support to the Committee's ranking Democrat, Ellison D. Smith of South Carolina, and Smith was elected chairman although he was of the minority party. Cummins continued as a member of the Committee and also retained his office as President pro tempore.

In 1924, La Follette ran for President under the Progressive banner, polling 16 percent of the vote but carrying only his own state of Wisconsin. The Republicans gained five seats in the Senate, and party leaders felt strong enough to retaliate against the irregulars who had supported the Progressive ticket. Thus the Republican conference adopted a resolution that the disloyal Senators "be not invited to future Republican conferences and be not named to fill any Republican vacancies on Senate committees." The irregulars were permitted to keep the committee assignments they then held, but in many instances they were placed at the bottom of the list. In the Senate reorganization two years later, however, they were welcomed back into the Republican fold.

The "progressives" continued to be a thorn in the side of the regular Republicans. In his last two years in office, Hoover had to contend with a Democratic House in which the Republican progressives regularly sided with the opposition. The situation in the Senate was not much better. Hoover himself described it thus:

"The new Senate (of the 72nd Congress) comprised 48 Republicans, 47 Democrats, and 1 Farmer-Labor. But actually we had no more than 40 real Republicans, as Senators Borah, Norris, Cutting, and others of the left wing were against us.

"Senator James Watson, Republican Senate leader, rejected my advice that the Democrats be allowed to organize the Senate and thereby convert their sabotage into responsibility. I felt that I could deal more constructively with the Democratic leaders if they held full responsibility in both houses, than with an opposition in the Senate conspiring in the cloakrooms to use every proposal of mine for demagoguery. Watson, of course, liked the extra importance of being majority leader, and the Republicans liked to hold committee chairmanships and the nicer offices in the Capitol."

Cloture in Practice

Early experience with the Senate cloture rule bore out the predictions of those who expected it to be used only sparingly. Between 1917, when the rule was adopted, and the end of the Hoover Administration in 1933, the Senate took only 11 cloture votes, of which five occurred in one two-week period in 1927.

Four of the 11 votes were successful. In addition to the 1919 vote on the Treaty of Versailles, the Senate in 1926 ended a 10-day filibuster against the World Court Protocol by adopting cloture on a 68-26 vote, and in 1927 it voted cloture twice—on a branch banking bill, 65-18, and on a prohibition reorganization measure, 55-27. The seven measures on which cloture failed included two tariff bills, a bill for development of the Lower Colorado River Basin and the Glass Banking bill against which Huey Long (D La.) staged his first filibuster early in 1933. On this occasion cloture failed by a single vote.

Some issues were too touchy for cloture even to be attempted. During the third session of the 67th Congress in 1922, a group of southern Senators mounted a filibuster against the Dyer anti-lynching bill. On behalf of the obstructionists, Oscar W. Underwood (D Ala.) said: "It is perfectly apparent that you are not going to get an agreement to vote on this bill.... I want to say right now to the Senate that if the majority party insist on this procedure, they are not going to pass the bill and they are not going to do any other business.... We are going to transact no other business until we have an understanding about this bill.... We are willing to take the responsibility, and we are going to do it." The obstructionists were as good as their word: the Senate was unable to transact any legislative business until the anti-lynching bill was formally put aside on the last day of the session, but no cloture vote was ever taken.

Similarly, in 1927 no attempt was made to invoke cloture on a filibuster against extending the life of a special campaign investigating committee headed by James A. Reed of Missouri. A small group of Senators succeeded in killing the committee, which had exposed corruption in the 1926 election victories of Frank L. Smith (R Ill.) and William S. Vare (R Pa.), although a majority of the Senate clearly favored its extension.

As it became apparent that Rule 22 in its existing form was not a completely effective weapon against the filibuster, new curbs on obstruction were proposed. During the 1922 filibuster on the Dyer anti-lynching bill, Republican Whip Charles Curtis (R Kan.) asked the chair to follow the precedent of Speaker Reed that, notwithstanding the absence of a specific rule on the question, dilatory motions could be ruled out of order under general parliamentary law. Such a precedent would have established a significant tool against obstruction, but Vice President Coolidge declined to rule.

The next Vice President, however, was made of sterner stuff. When Charles G. Dawes made his inaugural address to the Senate in 1925, he coupled a scathing denunciation of the existing Senate rules with a call for new curbs on debate. Not content with attacking the Senate on its own turf, Dawes took his campaign to the country, where he encountered the rather surprising opposition of the American Federation of Labor. The Dawes scheme, said the AFL ominously, "emanates from the secret chambers of the predatory interests." Although Dawes aroused widespread public interest in the problem, the Senate took no action on rules reform proposals.

The Lame-Duck Amendment

One Member of the Senate thought he saw a way to end the filibuster. George W. Norris (R Neb.), a progressive who earlier had participated in the House revolt against Speaker Cannon, proposed a constitutional amendment that would eliminate the "short" sessions of Congress in which so many filibusters occurred.

Under the Constitution and existing law, a Congress that was elected in November of an even-numbered year did not take office until March 4 of the following odd-numbered year and did not meet in its first regular session until December of that year, 13 months after its election. Meanwhile, the old Congress regularly met in December following the election of its successor and remained in session until the term of the new Congress began in March. This was known as the short session, in which "lame-duck" Members who had been repudiated at the polls often determined the course of legislation. The fixed adjournment date was an invitation to filibusters, because merely by talking long enough Members could block action until the old Congress expired; it was hardly surprising that the short sessions were seldom productive.

Accordingly, Norris proposed an amendment to the Constitution to abolish the short session by starting the terms of Congress and the President in January instead of March and providing that Congress should meet annually in January rather than December. The Senate approved the change six times before the House agreed to it in 1932. The 20th Amendment became part of the Constitution in 1933.

The first Senate vote on the Norris amendment came early in 1923, during the short session of the 67th Congress. Reported from the Senate Agriculture Committee, of which Norris was chairman, the resolution proposing the amendment was adopted by the Senate Feb. 13 on a 63-6 vote. In the House the amendment was reported by the Election Committee and approved by a majority of the Rules Committee, but Rules Chairman Philip P. Campbell (R Kan.), himself a lame duck, managed to keep it from the floor.

In 1924, the Norris amendment was again approved by the Senate, 63-7, and again reported by the House Election Committee, but this time it was blocked in the Rules Committee. The same thing happened in 1926, when the Senate approved the amendment by a vote of 73-2.

The Norris amendment finally reached the House floor in 1928, after the Senate had approved it for a fourth time, 65-6. However, the House vote of 209-157 fell 35 short of the two-thirds required for approval under the Constitution.

In the next Congress, the 71st, the Senate approved the Norris resolution for a fifth time, 64-9. The House adopted a different version, 290-93, and the measure died in conference.

Final action came in the following Congress, when the Democrats had won control of the House. Early in 1932, the Senate adopted the Norris resolution for a sixth time, 63-7, and the House quickly cleared it, 335-56. It became the 20th Amendment upon ratification by the 36th state early in 1933. *(Continued on p. 86)*

Filibusters and the Senate . . .

Filibustering is the practice by which a minority of a legislative body employs extended debate and dilatory tactics to delay or block action favored by the majority.

The word filibuster is derived from the Dutch word *Vrijbuiter,* meaning freebooter. Passing into Spanish as *filibustero*, it was used to describe military adventurers from the United States who in the mid-1800s fomented insurrections against various Latin American governments.

The first legislative use of the word is said to have occurred in the House in 1853, when a Representative accused his opponents of "filibustering against the United States." By 1863, filibuster had come to mean delaying action on the floor, but the term did not gain wide currency until the 1880s.

Although the word filibuster as applied to legislative obstruction is relatively new, the tactics it describes are as old as parliamentary government. What are now called filibusters occurred in the colonial assemblies, and obstructive tactics were a feature of Congress from its earliest days. A bill to establish a "permanent residence" for the national Government was subjected to a House filibuster early in the First Congress. When the same bill reached the Senate, Pennsylvania's Sen. William Maclay complained that "the design of the Virginians and the South Carolina gentlemen was to talk away the time so that we could not get the bill passed."

Obstruction in the House

Legislative obstruction was characteristic of the House long before it became common in the Senate. But the unwieldy size of the lower chamber's membership soon led to various curbs on debate. The previous-question motion, first adopted in 1789, has been used since 1811 to close debate and bring the matter under consideration to an immediate vote. Under a rule adopted in 1798, House Members are permitted to speak only once on a subject in general debate; since 1841, they have been limited to one hour. Since 1847, debate on amendments has been limited to five minutes for each side, and since 1880, a rule of relevancy has been enforced by the Speaker. These limitations on debate curbed the practice of filibustering in the House, although delaying tactics continued to be used from time to time.

Obstruction in the Senate

The Senate, with its cherished tradition of unlimited debate, offered a more favorable climate for obstruction. By the end of the 19th century the upper chamber had become notorious as the home of the filibuster.

The first notable Senate filibuster occurred in 1841, when dissident Senators held the floor for 10 days in opposition to a bill to shift the Senate's printing to new contractors. In the next 40 years filibusters were undertaken with increasing frequency and boisterousness, but they were not usually successful. In the last two decades of the 19th century, the practice assumed almost epidemic proportions, and as filibusterers used more daring techniques their rate of success increased. Efforts to curb obstruction in the 20th century had only limited effectiveness. The filibuster came to be identified with southern efforts to block civil rights legislation (although northern liberals occasionally found it a useful device as well); until 1964 the Senate was never able to invoke cloture on a civil rights filibuster.

Filibustering Techniques

The most important tool of the filibusterer is long-continued talk, for which a strong physical constitution is a prerequisite. Other techniques are dilatory motions, roll-call votes, quorum calls, points of order and appeals, and the interjection of other business. Successful use of these devices calls for deft use of parliamentary procedure; Senators with less than expert knowledge are likely to rely on talk, since a parliamentary blunder could spell defeat for their cause.

The longest speech in the history of the Senate was made by Strom Thurmond (D S.C.). During a filibuster against passage of the Civil Rights Act of 1957, Thurmond spoke for 24 hours and 18 minutes in a round-the-clock session Aug. 28-29, 1957. Second place goes to Wayne Morse (Ind. Ore.), who in April 1953 spoke for 22 hours and 26 minutes on the tidelands oil bill. The third-place record was set in 1908 by Robert M. La Follette Sr. (R Wis.), who held the floor for 18 hours and 23 minutes in a fight over the Aldrich-Vreeland currency bill. In fourth place is Huey P. Long (D La.), who in June 1935 spoke for 15 hours and 30 minutes on an amendment to a bill extending the National Industrial Recovery Act.

Since the Senate has no strict rule of relevancy, speakers do not always confine themselves to the subject under consideration. Long in 1935 entertained his colleagues with recipes for southern "pot likker," and Glen H. Taylor (D Idaho), a former tent show performer, spent eight and one-half hours in 1947 expounding on fishing, baptism, Wall Street and his children in an effort to delay a vote on overriding President Truman's veto of the Taft-Hartley Act. In this connection, special credit perhaps is due to Reed Smoot (R Utah), who during a successful 1915 filibuster against President Wilson's Ship Purchase bill spoke for 11 hours and 35 minutes without relief and without deviating from the subject.

As a rule, a filibuster is most likely to succeed near the end of a session, when comparatively brief obstruction can imperil all pending legislation. Before the adoption of the 20th ("Lame Duck") Amendment to the Constitution in 1933, Congress was required to meet annually in December. When Congress met in December of an even-numbered year, following the election of its successor, it could remain in session only until March 4 of the following year, when the term of the new Congress began. During this short, or lame-duck, session— in which Members who had been repudiated at the polls participated—filibusters were an almost routine occurrence. In mid-session, a filibuster may be successful if urgent legislation is delayed by the obstruction or

. . . Cloture Rule: A Recapitulation

if the filibuster has a large number of Senators participating and is well enough organized to continue indefinitely.

Anti-Filibuster Techniques

Several techniques can be employed against the filibuster. The most spectacular, and probably least effective, is the use of prolonged sessions to break the strength of the obstructionists. A second technique is strict observance of existing Senate rules. Widely ignored rules provide that a speaker must stand, rather than sit or walk about; permit the presiding officer to take a Senator "off his feet" for using unparliamentary language; require that business intervene between quorum calls; and prohibit the reading of speeches or other material by a clerk without Senate consent. Finally, a Senator may be refused an opportunity to speak more than twice on a subject in any one day (a legislative day may spread over several calendar days if the Senate recesses rather than adjourns) "without leave of the Senate."

Senate Cloture Rule

The Senate's ultimate check on the filibuster is the provision for cloture, or limitation of debate, contained in Rule 22 of its Standing Rules. The original Rule 22 was adopted in 1917 following a furor over the "talking to death" in the Senate of a proposal by President Wilson for arming American merchant ships before U.S. entry into World War I. The 1917 rule required only the votes of two-thirds of the Senators present and voting to invoke cloture. In 1949, during a parliamentary battle preceding scheduled consideration of a Fair Employment Practices Commission bill, the requirement was raised to two-thirds of the entire Senate membership.

The most recent revision of the rule, in 1959, provided for limitation of debate by vote of two-thirds of the Senators present and voting, two days after a cloture petition was submitted by 16 Senators. Thereafter, debate was limited to one hour for each Senator on the bill itself and on all amendments and motions affecting it. No new amendments could be offered except by unanimous consent. Amendments that were not germane to the pending business, and amendments and motions clearly designed to delay action, were out of order. The rule applied both to ordinary business and to motions to change the Senate rules.

Between 1917 and 1959, the Senate took 22 cloture votes, and only four succeeded. After 1959, cloture votes occurred more frequently but were still rarely successful. Efforts were made at the beginning of each new Congress to amend Rule 22 to reduce the number of votes required to shut off debate. The most frequently offered proposal would have made it possible for three-fifths of those present and voting to invoke cloture.

Following is a list of the 53 cloture votes taken as of March 9, 1971. Only eight of these (shown in **dark type**) were successful. In the right-hand column is

shown the vote necessary to invoke cloture under the proposed 3/5-majority vote. Seven additional cloture votes (shown in *italics*) would have been successful using the proposed change.

Issue	Date	Vote	Yea Votes Needed 2/3 Majority	3/5 Majority
Versailles Treaty	Nov. 15, 1919	78-16	63	56
Emergency tariff	Feb. 2, 1921	36-35	48	43
Tariff bill	July 7, 1922	45-35	54	48
World Court	Jan. 25, 1926	68-26	63	56
Migratory birds	June 1, 1926	46-33	53	47
Branch banking	Feb. 15, 1927	65-18	56	50
Disabled officers	Feb. 26, 1927	51-36	58	52
Colorado River	Feb. 26, 1927	32-59	61	55
D.C. buildings	Feb. 28, 1927	52-31	56	50
Prohibition Bureau	Feb. 28, 1927	55-27	55	49
Banking Act	Jan. 19, 1933	58-30	59	53
Anti-lynching	Jan. 27, 1938	37-51	59	53
Anti-lynching	Feb. 16, 1938	42-46	59	53
Anti-poll tax	Nov. 23, 1942	37-41	52	47
Anti-poll tax	May 15, 1944	36-44	54	48
Fair Employment Practices Commission	Feb. 9, 1946	48-36	56	50
British loan	May 7, 1946	41-41	55	49
Labor disputes	May 25, 1946	3-77	54	48
Anti-poll tax	July 31, 1946	39-33	48	43
FEPC	May 19, 1950	52-32	64*	58*
FEPC	July 12, 1950	55-33	64*	58*
Atomic Energy Act	July 26, 1954	44-42	64*	58*
Civil Rights Act	March 10, 1960	42-53	64	57
Amend Rule 22	Sept. 19, 1961	37-43	54	48
Literacy tests	May 9, 1962	43-53	64	58
Literacy tests	May 14, 1962	42-52	63	56
Comsat Act	Aug. 14, 1962	63-27	60	54
Amend Rule 22	Feb. 7, 1963	54-42	64	58
Civil Rights Act	June 10, 1964	71-29	67	60
Legislative reapportionment	Sept. 10, 1964	30-63	62	56
Voting Rights Act	May 25, 1965	70-30	67	60
Right-to-work repeal	Oct. 11, 1965	45-47	62	55
Right-to-work repeal	Feb. 8, 1966	51-48	66	59
Right-to-work repeal	Feb. 10, 1966	50-49	66	59
Civil Rights Act	Sept. 14, 1966	54-42	64	58
Civil Rights Act	Sept. 19, 1966	52-41	62	56
D.C. Home Rule	Oct. 10, 1966	41-37	52	47
Amend Rule 22	Jan. 24, 1967	53-46	66	59
Open Housing	Feb. 20, 1968	55-37	62	55
Open Housing	Feb. 26, 1968	56-36	62	55
Open Housing	March 1, 1968	59-35	63	56
Open Housing	March 4, 1968	65-32	65	58
Fortas Nomination	Oct. 1, 1968	45-43	59	53
Amend Rule 22	Jan. 16, 1969	51-47	66	59
Amend Rule 22	Jan. 28, 1969	50-42	62	55
Electoral College	Sept. 17, 1970	54-36	60	54
Electoral College	Sept. 29, 1970	53-34	58	53
Supersonic transport	Dec. 19, 1970	43-48	61	55
Supersonic transport	Dec. 22, 1970	42-44	58	52
Amend Rule 22	Feb. 18, 1971	48-37	57	51
Amend Rule 22	Feb. 23, 1971	50-36	58	52
Amend Rule 22	March 2, 1971	48-36	56	50
Amend Rule 22	March 9, 1971	55-39	63	57

Between 1949 and 1959 the cloture rule required the affirmative vote of two-thirds of Senate membership rather than two-thirds of Senators who voted.

The Amendment established Jan. 3 of the year following election as the day on which the terms of Senators and Representatives would begin and end, and Jan. 20 as the day on which the President and Vice President would take office. It provided also that Congress should meet annually on Jan. 3 "unless they shall by law appoint a different day."

The second session of the 73rd Congress was the first to convene on the new date, Jan. 3, 1934. And the first President to take office on Jan. 20 was Franklin D. Roosevelt at the beginning of his second term in 1937. It quickly became clear, however, that the Amendment would not eliminate the filibuster, as Norris had hoped. The final sessions of the 73rd and 74th Congresses, the first to function under it, both ended in filibusters.

(For further details on terms and sessions of Congress, as well as a complete legislative history of the Norris amendment, see History of the House of Representatives, Chapter I.)

Committee Reorganization

The Senate's standing committee system had expanded fantastically since the middle of the 19th century, and by 1921 it was ripe for pruning. The 25 standing committees of 1853 increased to 42 by 1889, and in the next quarter-century this number almost doubled. Five select committees graduated to standing-committee status in 1884, three more did so in 1896, and all of the remaining select committees were made standing committees in 1909. At the same time, nine new standing committees were created, followed by three more in 1913, bringing the total number to an all-time high of 74.

The expansion of the committee system was only in part a reflection of the increasing complexity of Senate business; committees also provided welcome clerical service and office space for their chairmen in the days before such assistance was available to all Members. Thus "sinecure committees" had a way of surviving long after any need for them was gone. (Benefits did not go only to the party in power; in 1907, the Republicans took 61 chairmanships but assigned 10 others to the minority, and several committees were established solely for the purpose of creating chairmanships.)

When the 67th Congress convened in April 1921, the Senate effected a major consolidation of its committee system by reducing the number of committees from 74 to 34 and abolishing a number of long-defunct bodies such as the Committee on Revolutionary Claims.

The revision of the committee system was initiated by the Republican Committee on Committees, which at the same time proposed to increase the Republican margin on each of the major committees to reflect Republican gains in the Senate. To Democratic protests against "steam roller" tactics, Sen. Frank B. Brandegee (R Conn.), the committee chairman, replied: "Criticisms are purely professional. The Republicans are responsible to the country for legislation and must have control of committees. That's not tyranny; that's representative government—the rule of the majority." The Republican proposal was adopted, 45-25, without substantial change.

A further modification of the committee system occurred in 1922 when the Senate, following the lead of the House, restored exclusive spending powers to the Appropriations Committee (from which they had been taken in 1899). When the eight appropriation bills previously considered by other Senate committees were taken up, three ad hoc members (one in the case of a conference) from the appropriate committee were to serve with the Appropriations Committee. At the same time, Appropriations was deprived of its power to report amendments proposing new or general legislation.

The change in appropriations procedure was part of a larger effort to develop a more systematic approach to Federal expenditures in both the Executive and Legislative Branches. The Budget and Accounting Act of 1921 set up a Bureau of the Budget to assist the President in preparing an annual budget that reconciled Federal revenues and expenditures; it also created a General Accounting Office to strengthen Congressional surveillance over Government spending. *(For more details, see Fiscal Powers, Chapter III, and General Accounting Office, Chapter IV.)*

Democratic Leadership: 1933-1947

Franklin D. Roosevelt entered the White House in 1933, in the middle of a great depression, with overwhelming popular support and commanding majorities in both houses of Congress. Asked prior to his election what authority he would seek from Congress, Roosevelt had answered, "Plenty," and he was as good as his word.

Called into special session March 9, 1933, Congress in the next "hundred days" embarked on a whirlwind legislative course dictated by the President. The House on March 9 passed an emergency banking bill, which had not then even been printed, in 38 minutes; the Senate took a little longer, two hours and 15 minutes, but the measure was ready for the President's signature before the day ended.

With time the pace slackened somewhat, but the pattern of action remained the same. The President would send a brief message to Congress, accompanied by a detailed draft of the legislation he proposed. Congress had been outraged when Lincoln dared to submit his own draft bills, but it readily accepted such action from Roosevelt and the practice soon became routine. Given the President's popularity and the prevailing economic conditions, opposition was futile and often nonexistent, and the President's proposals were promptly enacted. Congress did not long continue to be a rubber stamp, but throughout his first term (1933-37) Roosevelt was able—through negotiation, compromise and the exercise of his patronage powers—to obtain the enactment of a broad range of "New Deal" social and economic programs.

In his second term (1937-41), a conservative coalition of Republicans and southern Democrats frequently opposed Roosevelt on domestic issues. The coalition thwarted his plan to enlarge the Supreme Court and successfully opposed him on other measures. During the President's unprecedented third term (1941-45), wartime issues were paramount. As in previous wars, the Executive Branch assumed extraordinary powers, and Congress became increasingly restive under Executive domination. As the war drew to a close, opposition to Roosevelt's domestic policies mounted, and by the time the President died shortly after the start of his fourth term in 1945, Congress was in open revolt. His successor, Harry S Truman, won broad Congressional support for his foreign policy measures, but his domestic programs were largely ignored.

Growth of the Congressional Workload, 1789-1971

	First Congress (1789-91)	78th Congress (1943-45)	84th Congress (1955-57)	91st Congress (1969-71)
Measures introduced:	268	7,845	16,782	29,040
House	142	5,628	12,467	23,575
Senate	126	2,217	4,315	5,465
Laws Enacted:	118	1,157	1,921	941
Public	108	568	1,028	695
Private	10	589	893	246
Nominations Confirmed	211	21,371	82,694	133,797

Even before the war ended, Congress began to consider ways of modernizing its machinery so that it would be able to handle its mounting volume of business *(see box)* and regain some of the initiative it had lost to the Executive Branch. The resulting Legislative Reorganization Act of 1946 was only partially successful in meeting these goals. In the Senate no action was taken to strengthen the cloture rule, although filibusters were used repeatedly to defeat civil rights legislation.

President and Senate

President Roosevelt, at times assisted by Vice President Garner, was his own legislative leader in the Senate during his first term, and Senate Democratic leaders viewed themselves as the loyal lieutenants of the President. Senate rules and procedures precluded the close control exercised by party leaders in the House, but the Senate leaders were more experienced than their House counterparts and they were often more successful in advancing Administration programs.

Roosevelt in Control. When Sen. Joseph T. Robinson (D Ark.) became Majority Leader in 1933, he revived the Democratic caucus and won from Democratic Senators an agreement, adopted by a vote of 50-3, to make caucus decisions on Administration bills binding by majority vote. The rule read:

"Resolved, That until further order the chairman (Robinson) is authorized to convene Democratic Senators in caucus for the purpose of considering any measure recommended by the President; and that all Democratic Senators shall be bound by the vote of the majority of the conference; provided, that any Senator may be excused from voting for any such measure upon his expressed statement to the caucus that said measure is contrary to his conscientious judgment or that said measure is in violation of pledges made to his constituents as a candidate."

Although there is no evidence that Robinson ever made use of the binding caucus rule, non-binding caucuses frequently were held to mobilize party support. In the House the majority leadership worked through the Steering Committee and the Whip organization, but in the Senate the Steering Committee served only as a

committee on committees, while it is doubtful if the Policy Committee ever even met.

The Senate had more potential dissidents than the House, among them many southern Democrats who had risen to key committee chairmanships through the seniority system, but Roosevelt was remarkably successful at keeping them in line. Agriculture Chairman Ellison D. Smith (S.C.) was not sympathetic to the proposed Agricultural Adjustment Act of 1933, but after a conference at the White House his committee reported the measure with this comment: "This bill...was drafted by the Department of Agriculture and is practically unchanged from the bill as presented to Congress. Considerable hearings were had by the Senate Committee, but on account of the desire of the Administration that no change be made the bill is presented to the Senate in practically an unchanged form...."

As long as the Democrats maintained their tremendous margins in Congress and were able to curb the dissidents within their own party, the leadership could afford to ignore the minority—especially since many Republicans supported early New Deal proposals. But by the beginning of Roosevelt's second term in 1937, these conditions no longer prevailed, and a conservative coalition of Republicans and southern Democrats emerged in opposition to New Deal programs.

Failure of Court Packing and F.D.R. Purge

Stung by the Supreme Court's invalidation of major Administration acts, Roosevelt sent to the Senate, Feb. 5, 1937, a proposal to enlarge the Court by providing for the appointment of additional Justices, up to a total of six, to assist those who did not retire within six months after reaching the age of 70. For once, public opinion was not with the President, and Senate Republicans sat on their hands while conservative and New Deal Democrats contested the issue. A series of Court decisions favorable to New Deal programs weakened support, as did the sudden death of Sen. Robinson, the Administration floor leader, on July 13.

In the leadership contest that followed, Alben W. Barkley (D Ky.), with Roosevelt's implied support, defeated Pat Harrison (D Miss.) for the majority leadership in a fight that brought to the surface the deep split in

Democratic ranks. It also cost Roosevelt his court plan, which was rejected shortly thereafter.

Struggling to reassert his party leadership, Roosevelt decided to intervene in Democratic primaries in 1938 in an effort to block the renomination of conservative Democrats in Congress. The "purge" was notably unsuccessful; Senators on the purge list were triumphantly returned to office, and the President's only victory was in unseating Rep. John J. O'Connor (D N.Y.), chairman of the House Rules Committee. As a further embarrassment, Republicans gained eight seats in the November election.

Growing Opposition to Roosevelt

With the onset of World War II, opposition to Roosevelt was muted. Wartime supplies were freely voted, and in the Senate the Special Committee to Investigate the National Defense Program, set up in 1941 under the chairmanship of Harry S Truman (D Mo.), earned the President's gratitude for serving as a "friendly watchdog" over defense spending without embarrassing the Administration. However, as the war went on, it became apparent that opposition to the President on domestic issues was rising.

The antagonism between Roosevelt and Congress came to the surface in February 1944, when the President against the advice of party leaders vetoed a revenue bill, the first veto of such a measure by any President. The action was denounced by Barkley on the floor of the Senate, Feb. 23, as "a calculated and deliberate assault upon the legislative integrity of every Member of Congress." Barkley said: "Other Members of Congress may do as they please, but as for me I do not propose to take this unjustifiable assault lying down.... I dare say that, during the last seven years of tenure of Majority Leader, I have carried the flag over rougher territory than ever traversed by any previous Majority Leader. Sometimes I have carried it with little help from the other end of Pennsylvania Avenue." The following day Barkley's resignation as Floor Leader was accepted, but he was at once re-elected by unanimous vote of the Democratic caucus.

Roosevelt's problems with Congress increased after his election to a fourth term in 1944. His proposals for postwar economic and social legislation were ignored, and his nomination of Henry A. Wallace as Secretary of Commerce was confirmed only after the Reconstruction Finance Corporation had been removed from Commerce Department control. By the time of his death in April 1945, Congress was in open revolt.

When Truman succeeded Roosevelt, many observers predicted a renewal of the happy relationship between Congress and the Executive that had prevailed in the McKinley Administration. Like McKinley, Truman was a former Member of Congress who enjoyed the goodwill of his colleagues, but his honeymoon with Congress did not last long. Although he was markedly successful in pushing his foreign policy programs, the old conservative coalition stood ready to oppose him on domestic issues. With the election of a Republican House and Senate in 1946, the Democrats' 14-year leadership of Congress came to an end.

Reorganization Act of 1946

Even before the Second World War ended, the tremendous expansion of the size and the authority of the Government, especially the Executive Branch, led to a debate on reform of Congress. Proposals ranged from granting the President constitutional power to dissolve Congress to limiting selection of page boys to residents of the District of Columbia.

But two themes dominated the debate—the relationship between the organization of Congress and its increased workload, and the relations between Congress and the Executive Branch.

The feeling of many Members of Congress was expressed by Rep. Jerry Voorhis (D Calif.) when he urged approval of a concurrent resolution to set up the Joint Committee on the Organization of Congress. Voorhis on Jan. 18, 1945, said, "...in the midst of this war we have to grant executive power, of course we have, of the most sweeping nature." But he wanted the groundwork laid "in order that this Congress may perform its functions efficiently, effectively, and in accord with the needs of the people of this nation and so that it will become not merely an agency that says yes or no to executive proposals, but an agency capable of, and actually performing the function of bringing forth its own constructive program for the needs of the people of this nation. Thus it will take its place and keep its place as an altogether coequal branch of our Government."

The variety of complaints and suggestions aimed at Congress defied enumeration, but their general nature was partially indicated by the report of a committee on Congress of the American Political Science Association. In summary the report said Congress was handicapped by: (1) the excessive burden of local and private matters, (2) lack of adequate, independent technical advice, and of sufficient secretarial service, (3) too many committees and diffusion of responsibility, (4) inadequate communication with the Executive, (5) inadequate facilities for inspection and review of administrative action, (6) the "importunities" of special-interest groups, (7) the need of a redistribution of power, especially in the House, and (8) inadequate compensation of its personnel. The handicaps were followed by 10 recommendations designed to mitigate them. Then the report expressed the belief "that Congress must modernize its machinery and methods to fit modern conditions if it is to keep pace with a greatly enlarged and active Executive Branch. This is a better approach than that which seeks to meet the problem by reducing and hamstringing the Executive. A strong and more representative Legislature, in closer touch with and better informed about the Administration, is the antidote to bureaucracy."

In February 1945, Congress set up a Joint Committee on the Organization of Congress, with Sen. Robert M. La Follette Jr. (Prog. Wis.) as chairman, and Rep. A. S. Mike Monroney (D Okla.) as vice chairman. After extensive hearings the Committee submitted a detailed report that formed the basis of the Legislative Reorganization Act of 1946 (PL 79-601). Passed with bipartisan support in both houses, the most important provisions of the Act were:

Salary. Congressional salaries were raised from $10,000 to $12,500, retaining the existing $2,500 expense account (the Committee had recommended $15,000, dropping the expense account), the salary of the Speaker was raised to $20,000, and a Congressional pension plan was established.

Staff. Each standing committee was authorized to appoint by majority vote up to four professional staff members, with the exception of the two Appropriations Committees, which were authorized to appoint such professional staff as, by majority vote of the committee, was deemed necessary. The Act also established the Legislative Reference Service as a separate department in the Library of Congress to furnish Congress with information bearing on legislation. A committee proposal setting up a director of personnel, thus reducing patronage on staffs, was defeated in the Senate. Another committee proposal providing each Member of Congress with an administrative assistant was dropped, except for one each for the Speaker, Majority Leader and Minority Leader in the House. Later in the year a supplemental appropriations bill provided administrative assistance for Senators and Senate Policy Committees.

Workload. The Act banned introduction of private bills for payment of pensions or tort claims, construction of bridges, or correction of military records. A committee proposal for home rule for the District of Columbia, also regarded as a means of reducing the workload of Congress, was dropped.

Lobbying. Lobbyists were required to register and report their expenditures to the Clerk of the House.

Committees. The number of standing committees was reduced in the Senate from 33 to 15 and in the House from 48 to 19, and the jurisdiction of each committee was defined. All standing committees were required to fix regular meetings and keep records of all committee action. Submission in advance of written statements was to be required of all witnesses as far as practicable. A committee proposal prohibiting appointment of special committees was dropped.

Oversight. Each standing committee was directed to exercise "continuous watchfulness" over the execution by administrative agencies of laws whose subject matter fell within its jurisdiction.

Legislative Budget. The House Ways and Means, Senate Finance and both Appropriations Committees were directed to prepare each year a legislative budget, including estimated total receipts and expenditures. The report was to be accompanied by a concurrent resolution adopting the budget, and fixing the maximum amount to be appropriated. Congress was prohibited from appropriating more than estimated receipts without specifically, by concurrent resolution, authorizing an increase in the Federal debt.

Actions Not Taken. Several major recommendations of the Joint Committee were omitted in the final version of the Act. A Congressional Personnel Office was to coordinate operations of the various service and housekeeping staffs of Congress and to remove all such staff positions from patronage and place them under a "Congressional civil service." Majority and minority Policy Committees of seven Members each were to be set up in the House and Senate for the determination and expression of majority and minority policy. The majority Policy Committees of the two houses were to "serve as a formal council to meet regularly with the Executive, to facilitate the formulation and carrying out of national policy, and to improve relationships between the executive and legislative branches of the Government."

Senate Committees

The Legislative Reorganization Act of 1946 reduced the number of standing committees of the Senate from 33 to 15 by dropping inactive committees and merging others with related functions. In the following quarter-century the Senate made only minor changes in the committee system it had established in 1946.

1946 Committee Roster. Agriculture and Forestry, Appropriations, Armed Services, Banking and Currency, District of Columbia, Expenditures in the Executive Departments, Finance, Foreign Relations, Interstate and Foreign Commerce, Judiciary, Labor and Public Welfare, Post Office and Civil Service, Public Lands, Public Works and Rules and Administration.

Post-1946 Changes. Two new standing committees were created between 1946 and 1971: Aeronautical and Space Sciences in 1958 and Veterans' Affairs in 1970.

Four existing committees changed their names: Public Lands became Interior and Insular Affairs in 1948; Expenditures in the Executive Departments became Government Operations in 1952; Interstate and Foreign Commerce became Commerce in 1961; and Banking and Currency became Banking, Housing and Urban Affairs in 1970.

In addition, select and special committees were created from time to time.

(A rider to the first fiscal 1947 supplemental appropriations bill authorized establishment of the current Senate Policy Committees later in 1946.)

The Joint Committee heard evidence, but made no recommendations, with regard to proposals to select committee chairmen on some basis other than seniority, and to restrict the power of the House Rules Committee. The issue of limitation of debate in the Senate was beyond the committee's terms of reference. Thus questions directly involving the distribution of power within Congress were largely excluded from the Reorganization Act.

Effects of the Act. The Reorganization Act had mixed results. Although the reduced number of standing committees remained essentially the same after the 1946 changes, subcommittees proliferated and the number of committee staff members increased. The legislative budget, with no provision for enforcement, was abandoned after three experiments with it. The private bills eliminated in the Act reduced the Congressional workload, but the number of private immigration bills increased greatly. (*See Function of Private Bills, Chapter III.*) The lobby registration requirement, lacking teeth and subject to differing interpretation, also failed to meet its purpose. That the 1946 Act contributed to Congressional efficiency there can be little question, but its failure to resolve the greater problems of distribution of power within Congress and relations between Congress and the Executive Branch gave rise to continuing pressure for further reforms.

Filibusters and Civil Rights

Obstruction continued to plague the Senate throughout the New Deal era, but no significant new curbs on the filibuster were imposed. The Senate took no cloture votes in the 73rd and 74th Congresses, but in the years 1938-46 it took eight such votes—four in 1946 alone. None of the eight votes came within striking distance of the required two-thirds majority.

The most notorious filibuster of the early New Deal period was Huey P. Long (D La.), who was at odds with the Roosevelt Administration over patronage in Louisiana and other matters. Long staged his most famous filibuster in 1935, during debate on proposed extension of the National Industrial Recovery Act. The "Kingfish" spoke for 15½ hours, a record for the time, filling 85 pages of the *Congressional Record* with remarks that ranged from commentaries on the Constitution to recipes for southern "pot likker," turnip greens and corn bread. His avowed intent was "to save to the sovereign states their rights and prerogatives" and "to preserve the right and prerogative of the Senate as to the qualifications of important officers." Long conducted his last filibuster, against a deficiency appropriation bill, less than two weeks before his assassination in the summer of 1935.

As time went by, the filibuster increasingly came to be associated with civil rights legislation. Southern Senators might lack the votes to defeat civil rights measures outright, but they found they could accomplish the same objective through obstruction. Proponents of civil rights legislation could not muster the requisite two-thirds majority to invoke cloture on a southern filibuster even if they had the simple majority needed for action on substantive issues. Accordingly, the southerners used the filibuster to keep civil rights bills from coming to a vote.

Most of the great filibusters of the period involved civil rights. Anti-lynching bills were filibustered in 1935 and 1938, and anti-poll-tax measures were filibustered in 1942, 1944 and 1946. Fair employment practices legislation was filibustered in 1946.

It was hard to keep Senators in the chamber during these exhibitions. At one point during the 1942 debate when a quorum could not be mustered and the business of the Senate halted, the Sergeant at Arms was directed to "request the attendance" of absent Senators, and at length 44 Senators—five short of a quorum—appeared. He was then directed to "compel the attendance" of absent Members. After some delay, he reported that 43 Senators were out of town and eight others were in Washington but could not be located. The exasperated Senate finally ordered him to "execute warrants of arrest" upon absent Senators. He was saved from this embarrassing duty by the timely appearance of five Senators to complete the quorum. (The Sergeant at Arms had not always been so fortunate; during debate on the Lower Colorado River project in 1927, several infuriated Senators actually were brought into the chamber under arrest.)

Rule 22 proved totally ineffectual against these sustained and organized southern filibusters. Six of the eight unsuccessful cloture votes in the years 1938-46 dealt with civil rights issues; on four of the six votes, cloture did not win even a simple majority.

Two minor curbs on obstruction were imposed during the period. The first dealt with the quorum call, a favorite obstructionist tool. During a 1935 filibuster by Long, the chair ruled that a quorum call constitutes business and that Senators who yield for a quorum call lose the floor. Under this ruling a Senator who yields twice for a quorum call while the same question is before the Senate may be denied the right to speak again on that question during the same legislative day. The second curb, contained in the Reorganization Acts of 1939 and 1945, limited debate on Presidential reorganization plans.

The Legislative Reorganization Act of 1946 contained no provisions on debate limitation, since that subject was outside the purview of the Joint Committee on the Organization of Congress, but by 1946 many Senators were convinced that further debate curbs were needed if the Senate was to meet its postwar responsibilities.

Divided Government: 1947-1972

The election of a Republican Congress in 1946 marked the beginning of a period of divided Government that was to last through much of the postwar period. During 12 of the following 26 years Congress would be controlled, although sometimes only nominally, by the party in opposition to the President.

Democratic President Harry S Truman (1945-53) faced a Republican House and Senate in the 80th Congress (1947-49). His successor, Republican Dwight D. Eisenhower (1953-61) had a Republican Congress only in his first two years in office (1953-55). The Democrats controlled Congress throughout the terms of Democratic Presidents John F. Kennedy (1961-63) and Lyndon B. Johnson (1963-69), but when Republican Richard M. Nixon was elected in 1968, he became the first President since Zachary Taylor to fail to win control of at least one house of the new Congress in his initial election. Republican gains in the 1970 elections still left both House and Senate in Democratic hands for the duration of Nixon's first term.

In only two Congresses did Republicans organize the Senate. In the 80th Congress (1947-49) they enjoyed a 51-45 margin, but in the 83rd (1953-55) their margin was so narrow that the death of Majority Leader Robert A. Taft (R Ohio) gave temporary numerical superiority to the Democrats. In the 82nd, 84th and 85th Congresses, the Democratic margin of control was also razor-thin, but after the Democratic sweep in the 1958 elections the Democrats had comfortable majorities.

Need of Presidents for Bipartisan Support

Throughout the postwar period the parties themselves were often badly split, and both Republican and Democratic Presidents were forced to seek bipartisan support to get their programs enacted. Although Truman and the Republicans were often at loggerheads on domestic issues, Sen. Arthur H. Vandenberg (R Mich.) led his once-isolationist party colleagues into a new bipartisan foreign policy in cooperation with the Democratic Administration. President Eisenhower often received more support from Democrats than he did from members of his own party, particularly on foreign policy questions in the early years of his Administration, but partisanship increased as the 1960 elections approached, and many domestic bills failed of enactment.

President Kennedy's relations with Congress were far from ideal, although the Senate was generally more responsive to his proposals than the House, but much of Kennedy's program was enacted after Johnson succeeded him in November 1963. Early in his Administration, Johnson won spectacular legislative victories, but with the escalation of the war in Vietnam and the rise of disorder at home he lost control of Congress and was forced into retirement in 1968. During the Nixon Administration, Congress and the President were repeatedly in conflict.

Congress and the Public

Throughout the postwar period, the Senate—like Congress as a whole—was preoccupied with the problem of preserving for itself a viable role in the governmental process. The rapid expansion of the power of the Executive Branch in the 20th century had seriously weakened legislative authority, but at the same time the volume and complexity of legislative business continued to mount. Meanwhile, Congress as an institution suffered increasing public disfavor.

In an effort to reassert its eroded prerogatives and improve its legislative machinery, Congress in 1946 and 1970 enacted major legislative reorganization bills. In an effort to improve its public image, both chambers in 1968 adopted codes of ethics and rules requiring limited financial disclosure. But sensitive internal matters, such as the seniority system and limitation of Senate debate, remained vexing problems.

From Senate to White House

If the Senate as an institution lost status in the postwar era, Senators individually seemed to gain in influence. Traditionally, the Senate was considered a poor springboard for the Presidency; prior to World War II only 12 Senators including Garfield, who was elected but did not serve, had gone on to the White House. But of the five postwar Presidents, only Eisenhower had not previously served in the Senate. Truman, Johnson and Nixon all went first from the Senate to the Vice Presidency; Kennedy won Presidential election while serving in the Senate. In addition, many of the unsuccessful Presidential contenders in both parties between 1952 and 1968 were Senate men—among them Republicans Robert A. Taft Sr. (Ohio) and Barry Goldwater (Ariz.) and Democrats Estes Kefauver (Tenn.), Richard B. Russell (Ga.), Hubert H. Humphrey (Minn.), Stuart Symington (Mo.), Eugene J. McCarthy (Minn.), Robert F. Kennedy (N.Y.) and George McGovern (S.D.).

Other Senate developments of the postwar era included an increase in membership from 96 to 100, when Alaska and Hawaii became states in 1959, and the censure of two Senators—Joseph R. McCarthy (R Wis.) in 1954 and Thomas J. Dodd (D Conn.) in 1967. *(See Seating and Disciplining of Members, Chapter III.)*

Postwar Party Leadership

Senate leadership in both parties was fairly stable during the years following World War II.

Barkley. On the Democratic side, Alben W. Barkley (Ky.) retained the floor leadership until his resignation in 1949 to become Vice President. The Democrats then had two Majority Leaders in as many Congresses—Scott W. Lucas (Ill.) in the 81st and Ernest W. McFarland (Ariz.) in the 82nd, both of whom lost their Senate seats after two years in the leadership post.

Johnson. When the 83rd Congress met in January 1953, with the Republicans in control, the Democrats chose as their Minority Leader Lyndon B. Johnson (Texas), a former House Member who had served only four years in the Senate. Johnson was close to House Speaker Sam Rayburn (D Texas) and had the backing of powerful Senate conservatives, notably Robert S. Kerr (D Okla.) and Richard B. Russell (D Ga.), but he promptly built bridges to the liberal Democratic faction in the Senate in an effort to heal the deep liberal-conservative split within the party. Johnson soon became one of the most powerful leaders in Senate history, serving as Minority Leader in 1953-54 and as Majority Leader from 1955 until his resignation to become Vice President in 1961.

As a leader, Johnson was celebrated for his powers of persuasion and his manipulative skills. He revitalized the Democratic Policy Committee, saw to it that liberals won seats both on it and on the Steering Committee (committee on committees) and modified the seniority system to assure freshman Senators at least one major committee assignment (a practice later adopted by the Republicans as well). On the floor, efficiency was promoted through the use of such devices as unanimous consent agreements, aborted quorum calls and night sessions. Through an active intelligence operation headed by Robert G. (Bobby) Baker, Secretary to the Senate Majority, Johnson kept himself informed about what the Senate was really thinking, and he was adept at rounding up votes for acceptable compromises. A system of rewards and punishments supplemented the famous Johnson "treatment." An apostle of "moderation" and "consensus government," Johnson supported the Eisenhower Administration on many major questions and frequently solicited Republican support in the Senate. Such was his skill that in 1957 he was able to bring about passage of the first civil rights bill since Reconstruction without a filibuster and without splitting the Democratic party.

Mansfield. Johnson's successor as Majority Leader was Mike Mansfield (D Mont.). Mansfield had served as party whip under Johnson, but his permissive style of leadership was in sharp contrast to the Johnson methods. Mansfield held the respect of his colleagues, but he was not an aggressive leader, and under him the Johnson system gave way to a collegial leadership pattern in which the Policy Committee and the legislative committees played important roles.

Republican Leaders

On the Republican side, party authority was less concentrated than under the Democrats. Robert A. Taft Sr. (Ohio) had been the de facto Republican power in the Senate since the early 1940s and chairman of the Policy Committee from the time it was created in 1947, but he did not feel it necessary to assume the floor leadership of his party until the Eisenhower Administration took office in 1953.

After Taft's death in July 1953, the floor leadership went to William F. Knowland (Calif.), a conservative who frequently split with the Eisenhower Administration on major issues, but H. Styles Bridges (N.H.) often spoke for the Republicans as chairman of the Policy Committee. Knowland was succeeded as Minority Leader in 1959 by Everett McKinley Dirksen (Ill), one of the most colorful party leaders in recent history. His style, notes one observer, was "one of remaining vague on an issue, or taking an initial position from which he could negotiate: bargaining with the majority party, the President and his own colleagues, and eventually accepting a compromise." When Dirksen died in 1969, he was succeeded as Minority Leader by Hugh Scott (Pa.), a liberal Republican who sometimes found it difficult to serve as spokesman for the Nixon Administration in the Senate.

Use of Cloture to Pass Civil Rights Acts

As filibusters continued to block civil rights legislation in the years following World War II, liberal Senators made persistent efforts to revise the Senate cloture rule to make it easier to cut off debate. Amendments to Rule 22 in 1949 and 1959 did not bring an end to obstruction in the Senate, and during the 1960s cloture votes were taken with increasing frequency.

Four such votes were successful. In 1962 the Senate voted 63-27 for a Mansfield-Dirksen motion to invoke cloture on a liberal filibuster against the Administration's communications satellite bill. This was the first successful cloture vote since 1927 and only the fifth since the adoption of Rule 22 in 1917. In 1964, the Senate for the first time in its history invoked cloture, by a 71-29 vote, on a southern filibuster against civil rights legislation. This action was followed by successful cloture votes on two other civil rights measures—the voting rights bill of 1965 and, on the fourth try, the open housing bill of 1968.

The discovery that it was possible to impose cloture on civil rights bills under the existing rule took some of the steam out of liberal efforts to reform Rule 22. But in the closing days of the 91st Congress in 1970, the Senate became embroiled in a confusion of filibusters on a variety of major questions. Although this spectacle led to soul-searching within the Senate and to calls from President Nixon for procedural reform, when the 92nd Congress met a few weeks later the Senate once again declined to strengthen its curbs on the filibuster.

Revision of Cloture Rule in 1949

In its original form, Rule 22 required the votes of two-thirds of the Senators present and voting to invoke cloture. Over the years, however, a series of rulings and precedents rendered Rule 22 virtually inoperative by holding that it could not be applied to debate on procedural questions. By 1948 such were the precedents that President Pro Tempore Arthur H. Vandenberg (R Mich.) ruled, during a filibuster against an attempt to bring up an anti-poll tax bill, that cloture could not be used on a motion to proceed to consideration of a bill. In making his ruling, Vandenberg conceded that "in the final analysis, the Senate has no effective cloture rule at all."

In 1949, the Truman Administration, desiring to clear the way for a broad civil rights program, backed a change in the cloture rule. After a long and bitter floor fight, the Senate adopted a "compromise," backed by conservative Republicans and southern Democrats, that was actually more restrictive than the rule it replaced. The new rule required the votes of two-thirds of the entire Senate membership (instead of two-thirds of those present and voting) to invoke cloture, but allowed cloture to operate on any pending business or motion with the exception of debate on motions to change the Senate rules themselves (on which cloture previously had operated).

Because under this rule cloture could not be used to cut off a filibuster against a change in the rules, and because any attempt to change Rule 22 while operating under this rule appeared hopeless, Senate liberals devised a new approach. Senate rules had always continued from one Congress to the next in accordance with the theory that the Senate was a continuing body, but the liberals now challenged this conception, arguing that the Senate had a right to adopt new rules by general parliamentary procedure—majority vote—at the beginning of a new Congress.

Accordingly, in 1953 and 1957, at the opening of the 83rd and 85th Congresses respectively, Sen. Clinton P. Anderson (D N.M.) moved that the Senate consider the adoption of new rules. On both occasions his motion was tabled, but during the 1957 debate Vice President Richard M. Nixon offered a significant "advisory opinion" on how the Senate could proceed to change its rules. Citing the section of the Constitution which provides that "each house may determine the rules of its proceedings," Nixon said he believed the Senate could adopt new rules "under whatever procedures the majority of the Senate approves."

Although each incoming Senate had traditionally operated under existing rules, Nixon said that in his opinion the Senate could not be bound by any previous rule "which denies the membership of the Senate the power to exercise its constitutional right to make its own rules." In this light he said he regarded as unconstitutional the section of Rule 22 banning any limitation of debate on proposals to change the rules. The Vice President explained that he was stating his personal opinion and that the question of constitutionality of the rule could be decided only by the Senate itself. The Senate did not take a vote on the question.

Change in Cloture in 1959

A modest revision of Rule 22 was accomplished in 1959. Senate liberals hoped to make it possible to invoke cloture by a simple majority or by a three-fifths vote, but they were defeated in their efforts to bring about such a substantial change. Instead, a bipartisan leadership group engineered a slight revision of the rule which the southern bloc opposed but did not really fight. The changes were basically designed and put through by Johnson, who seized the initiative from the liberals, and were adopted on a 72-22 roll call.

The 1959 revision permitted cloture to be invoked by two-thirds of those present and voting (rather than two-thirds of the full membership as the 1949 rule had required) and also applied the cloture rule to debate on motions to change the Senate rules. At the same time the Senate added to Rule 32 the following language: "The rules of the Senate shall continue from one Congress to the next unless they are changed as provided in these rules." This language buttressed the position of those who maintained that the Senate was a continuing body, but liberal opponents of the filibuster never conceded the point.

Later Efforts at Revision

Further efforts to ease the filibuster rule occurred at the beginning of each of the next six Congresses, from 1961 to 1971. In 1969, liberal strategy focused on obtaining a ruling from Vice President Hubert H. Humphrey, who was about to retire as presiding officer of the Senate, that a simple majority could invoke cloture on rules debates at the start of a new Congress. After a cloture motion was filed on a liberal proposal to reduce the requirement for cloture from two-thirds to three-fifths of those present and voting, Humphrey announced, in answer to a parliamentary inquiry, that if a majority, but less than two-thirds, of those present and voting voted for cloture he would rule that the majority prevailed. He said that such a ruling, because it could be appealed by the Senate, would enable the Senate to decide the constitutional issue by a simple majority vote, without debate. Humphrey added that if he held that the cloture motion had failed because of the lack of a two-thirds vote, he would be inhibiting the Senate from deciding the constitutional question.

In explaining the ruling he proposed to make, Humphrey said: "On a par with the right of the Senate to determine its rules, though perhaps not set forth so specifically in the Constitution, is the right of the Senate, a simple majority of the Senate, to decide constitutional questions.

"If a majority—this is the view of the Chair—but less than two-thirds, of those present and voting, vote in favor of this cloture motion, the question whether the motion has been agreed to is a constitutional question. The constitutional question is the validity of the Rule 22 requirement for an affirmative vote by two-thirds of the Senate before a majority of the Senate may exercise its right to consider a proposed change in the rules. If the Chair were to announce that the motion for cloture had not been agreed to because the affirmative vote had fallen short of the two-thirds required, the Chair would not only be violating one established principle by deciding the constitutional question himself, he would be violating the other established principle by inhibiting, if not effectively preventing, the Senate from exercising its right to decide the constitutional question....

"The Chair informs the Senate that in order to give substance to the right of the Senate to determine or change its rules and to determine whether the two-thirds requirement of Rule 22 is an unconstitutional inhibition on that right at the opening of a new Congress, if a majority of the Senators present and voting but fewer than two-thirds vote in favor of the pending motion for cloture, the Chair will announce that a majority having agreed to limit debate on Senate Resolution 11, to amend Rule 22 at the opening of a new Congress, debate will proceed under the cloture provisions of that rule."

When the cloture motion came to a vote Jan. 16, 1969, a slim majority (51-47) voted for cloture, and Humphrey ruled that debate would proceed under the limitations of Rule 22. Opponents of the rules change immediately appealed his decision, and Humphrey's ruling was reversed, 45-53. The vote on the appeal meant that cloture was not invoked and left the Senate to continue the debate on the motion to consider the rules change proposal. Proponents of the change did not have enough support to limit debate under the two-thirds rule, and so ended another round in the rules reform fight.

In 1971, liberals were once again disappointed in their efforts to ease the cloture rule. After four failures to invoke cloture under the two-thirds requirement, they returned to the 1959 strategy of seeking cloture by a simple majority vote. They had hoped for favorable rulings from Vice President Spiro Agnew, but Agnew avoided the issue by being out of town and President Pro Tempore Allen J. Ellender (D La.), an opponent of rules change, was in the chair. When Ellender ruled that the fourth cloture vote of 55-39 had failed because it was less than a two-thirds majority, Jacob K. Javits (R N.Y.) challenged his ruling, but the challenge was tabled, 55-37, and the rules change proposal was put aside for another two years.

After the vote, Mansfield, who had offered the tabling motion, gave this explanation of his action: "I have said time and time and time again that I am against a mere majority vote to bring about a change in the rules, because I think to do so would alter the position of the Senate in our scheme of government. If the (Javits) appeal were upheld, then it would be only a matter of time before a majority would be able to cut off debate on any issue. That is the real issue at this time. The heart of the institution is at stake."

Other Rules Changes

Two minor changes in Senate rules were adopted in 1964. The first amended Rule 8 to provide for a three-hour period after the morning hour when debate on a pending measure, or amendments to that measure, must be germane. The period could be waived by unanimous consent or motion without debate. The intent of the proposal was to speed passage of pending bills by preventing speeches on irrelevant matters until late in each day's session, and it was adopted over proposals for more stringent germaneness rules. Senators immediately found one loophole: a nongermane amendment could be offered (and later withdrawn), and debate on that amendment would be in order. The rule was seldom applied in practice.

In the second change, the Senate amended Rule 25 to permit Senate standing committees to meet until completion of the morning hour—a period of up to two hours at the beginning of each legislative day when routine business is conducted. Previously unanimous consent had been required for committees to meet at any time when the Senate was in session.

Early in the 92nd Congress in 1971, the Senate leadership offered 10 "suggestions" to Senators that were designed to increase efficiency on the floor. Senators were asked not to seek unanimous consent to exceed the three-minute limit during the morning hour, although speeches of up to 15 minutes in length could be arranged in advance, and they were asked to make any longer speeches late in the day. Senators also were asked to observe the 1964 germaneness rule (the Pastore rule) and were put on notice that 20 minutes was the maximum time allotted for a roll-call vote.

The Integrity of the Senate

To much of the American public the Senate did not present a favorable image in the years following World War II. Not only did it often seem unable, by virtue of its antiquated procedures, to do the work the public expected it to do, but the integrity of its personnel was frequently under attack. The Senate is not a body to be stampeded by public opinion, and it approached this problem in its own way.

McCarthy. From 1950 until 1954, Sen. Joseph R. McCarthy (R Wis.) was by all odds the most controversial Member of the Senate. McCarthy's career as a Communist-hunter began with a speech in Wheeling, W.Va., in February 1950 in which he charged that 205 Communists were working in the State Department with the knowledge of the Secretary of State. From that time until his formal censure by the Senate in 1954, McCarthy and his freewheeling accusations of Communist sympathies among high- and low-placed Government officials absorbed much of the public's attention. The phenomenon of "McCarthyism" had a major impact on the psychological climate of the early 1950s. Taking over the chairmanship of the Senate Government Operations Committee in 1953, McCarthy investigated the State Department, the Voice of America, the Department of the Army and other agencies. An opinion-stifling "climate of fear" was said to be one of the results of his probes.

For several years McCarthy's colleagues showed no disposition to tangle with him, but the Army-McCarthy hearings, televised in the spring of 1954, led finally to his censure by the Senate in a special session following the mid-term election of 1954. In the end McCarthy was censured, by a vote of 67-2, not for his "habitual contempt of people" as Sen. Ralph E. Flanders (R Vt.) had originally proposed, but for contemptuous treatment of the Senate itself—for his failure to cooperate with the Subcommittee on Privileges and Elections in 1952 and for his abuse of the select committee that had considered the censure charges against him. The censure resolution asserted that McCarthy had "acted contrary to Senatorial ethics and tended to bring the Senate into dishonor and disrepute, to obstruct the constitutional processes of the Senate, and to impair its dignity. And such conduct is hereby condemned."

McCarthy remained in the Senate until his death in 1957, but he lost his committee and subcommittee chairmanships in the next, Democratic-controlled Congress, and his activities no longer attracted much attention in the Senate, the press or elsewhere.

Meanwhile, alleged excesses in treatment of witnesses by Congressional committees led in 1954 to an extensive search for a "fair-play" code to govern Congressional investigations. Most criticism was directed at the Senate Permanent Investigations Subcommittee, headed by McCarthy, and at the House Un-American Activities Committee. In 1955, the House amended its rules to provide a minimum standard of conduct for House committees. The Senate adopted no general rules on the subject, but the Permanent Investigations Subcommittee under the chairmanship of John L. McClellan (D Ark.) adopted new safeguards for the protection of witnesses.

Bobby Baker. In 1963, the Senate was shaken by charges that Robert G. (Bobby) Baker had used his position as Secretary to the Senate Majority to promote outside business interests. Baker, who served as Secretary to the Majority from 1955 until his resignation under fire in August 1963, was no ordinary Senate functionary. Exposure of his numerous "improprieties" led to criticism of the Senate as a whole and prompted a review of Congressional ethics.

A protege of Lyndon B. Johnson, to whom the case was particularly embarrassing, Baker had access to leadership councils and was known as the Senate's "most powerful employee." He headed Johnson's intelligence network in the Senate and was celebrated for his ability to forecast the outcome of close votes. Johnson once hailed "his tremendous fund of knowledge about the Senate, which is almost appalling in one so young."

In the wake of disclosures about Baker's wide-ranging business ventures, the Senate instructed its Rules and Administration Committee to investigate his activities from the standpoint of Congressional ethics. The Committee's Democratic majority, in reports issued in 1964 and 1965, accused Baker of "many gross improprieties" but cited no actual violations of law. Committee Republicans charged that the investigation was incomplete and a "whitewash." Both Republicans and Democrats called for rules requiring financial-disclosure statements by Members of Congress and their employees.

Baker ultimately was convicted in court and imprisoned for income tax evasion, theft and conspiracy to defraud the Government. Meanwhile, largely because of embarrassments caused by the Baker scandal, the Senate in 1964 created a Select Committee on Standards and Conduct to investigate "allegations of improper conduct by Senators and Senate employees," to recommend disciplinary action and to draw up a code of ethical conduct. The House established a similar committee in 1967.

Dodd. The Select Committee's first investigation began in 1966. It involved charges by syndicated columnists Drew Pearson and Jack Anderson that Sen. Thomas J. Dodd (D Conn.) had misused political campaign funds contributed to him and had committed other offenses. The Committee in April 1967 recommended that the Senate censure Dodd for misuse of political funds and for double-billing for official and private travel. The Senate on June 23 censured Dodd on the first charge by a 92-5 roll-call vote but refused, on a 51-45 vote, to censure him on the second charge. The action marked the seventh time in its history that the Senate had censured one of its Members. After the vote was taken, the issue was closed, and Dodd continued to serve in the Senate until he was defeated for re-election in 1970.

Adoption of Ethics Codes

Concern over conflicts of interest at all levels of Government had been rising since World War II, but Congress showed no inclination to adopt self-policing measures.

Pressures generated by the Baker and Dodd cases in the Senate and by investigation of the activities of Rep. Adam C. Powell (D N.Y.) in the House were largely responsible for the adoption of limited financial-disclosure rules in both chambers in 1968.

In the Senate, a code of conduct proposed by the Select Committee on Standards and Conduct was adopted without substantial change on March 22, 1968, by a 67-1 vote. Included were provisions to regulate the outside employment of Senate employees, to require a full accounting of campaign contributions and limit the uses to which they could be put, and to require Senators and top employees to file detailed financial reports each year. However, these reports were to be available only to the Select Committee, and the only public accounting required was of gifts of $50 or more and honoraria of $300 or more. The Senate rejected, 40-44, a proposal for full public disclosure of Members' finances. The proposal had been pressed by Sen. Joseph S. Clark (D Pa.), who was a persistent advocate of Congressional reform.

The code of conduct was embodied in four additions to the Senate Rules:

Rule 41. Stipulated that no officer or employee of the Senate might engage in any other employment or paid activity unless it was not inconsistent with his duties in the Senate. Directed employees to report their outside employment to specified supervisors, including Senators, who were to take such action as they considered necessary to avoid a conflict of interest by the employee.

Rule 42. Directed that a Senator or a declared candidate for the Senate might accept a contribution from a fund-raising event for his benefit only if he had given express approval before funds were raised and if he received a full accounting of the sources and amounts of each contribution. Official events of his party were exempted from these restrictions.

Permitted a Senator or candidate to accept contributions from an individual or an organization provided that a complete accounting of the sources and amounts were made by the recipient.

Specified that a Senator or candidate might use such contributions for the expenses of his nomination and election and for the following purposes: travel expenses to and from the Senator's home state; printing and other expenses of sending speeches, newsletters and reports to his constituents; expenses of radio, television and other media reports to constituents; telephone, postage and stationery expenses not covered by Senate allowances; and subscriptions to home-state newspapers.

Required disclosure of gifts, from a single, non-family source, of $50 or more under the provisions of Rule 44. (*See below.*)

Rule 43. Prohibited employees of the Senate from receiving, soliciting or distributing funds collected in connection with a campaign for the Senate or any other Federal office. Exempted from the rule Senators' assistants who were designated to engage in such activity and who earned more than $10,000 a year. Required that the Senator file the names of such designated aides with the Secretary of the Senate, as public information.

Rule 44. Required each Senator, declared candidate and Senate employee earning more than $15,000 a year to file with the U.S. Comptroller General, by May 15 each year, a sealed envelope containing the following reports:

- A copy of his U.S. income tax returns and declarations, including joint statements.
- The amount and source of each fee of $1,000 or more received from a client.
- The name and address of each corporation, business or professional enterprise in which he was an officer, director, manager, partner or employee, and the amount of compensation received.
- The identity of real or personal property worth $10,000 or more that he owned.
- The identity of each trust or fiduciary relation in which he held a beneficial interest worth $10,000 or more and the identity, if known, of any interest the trust held in real or personal property over $10,000.
- The identity of each liability of $5,000 or more owed by him or his spouse jointly.
- The source and value of all gifts worth $50 or more received from a single source.

Specified that the information filed with the Comptroller General would be kept confidential for seven years and then returned to the filer or his legal representative. If the filer died or left the Senate, his reports would be returned within a year.

Provided that the Select Committee on Standards and Conduct might, by a majority vote, examine the contents of a confidential filing and make the file available for investigation to the Committee staff. Required that due notice be given to an individual under investigation and an opportunity provided for him to be heard by the Committee in closed session.

Required each Senator, candidate and employee earning more than $15,000 a year to file with the Secretary of the Senate by May 15 each year the following information, which was to be kept for three years and made available for public inspection:

- The accounting required under Rule 42 of all contributions received in the previous year (amounts under $50 might be totaled and not itemized).
- The amount, value and source of any honorarium of $300 or more.

Senate-Executive Contests for Power

One of the principal purposes of the Legislative Reorganization Act of 1946 was to help Congress hold its own against the rapidly expanding power of the Executive Branch. In this it was only partly successful. By the end of World War II it seemed clear that legislative initiative had shifted, apparently irretrievably, from Congress to the President, and during the postwar era Congress was for the most part concerned with preserving its powers to approve, revise or reject Presidential programs.

In these years the Senate's sense of itself was frequently offended by what it viewed as Presidential encroachments on its constitutional functions. In 1954 the Senate came within one vote of approving a proposed constitutional amendment—the so-called Bricker Amendment—to restrict the President's power to negotiate treaties and other international agreements. Other conflicts arose over the spending power, the war power and, to a lesser extent, the appointment power. Frequently the Senate was in contention with the House as well as the Executive Branch.

Contests Over Spending Power

In the 1946 Act Congress tried to assert new and meaningful control over the budget process through the creation of a legislative budget. After three unsuccessful attempts to use this device, it was abandoned as an unqualified failure.

In 1947, the Joint Committee on the Legislative Budget, composed of members of the House Ways and Means and Appropriations Committees and the Senate Finance and Appropriations Committees, agreed to ceilings on appropriations and expenditures that were substantially lower than the amounts projected in President Truman's budget. The House approved the ceilings, but the Senate increased them and insisted that an expected budget surplus be applied to debt retirement rather than to reduction of taxes as House leaders proposed. As a result, the budget resolution died in conference.

In 1948, both houses adopted the same legislative budget, but Congress appropriated $6 billion more than the agreed-upon ceiling. In 1949, the process broke down entirely when the deadline for a budget was moved from Feb. 15 to May 1. By that date 11 appropriation bills had passed the House and 9 had passed the Senate; the legislative budget was never produced.

Failure of the legislative budget prompted a serious effort in Congress in 1950 to combine the numerous separate appropriation bills into one omnibus measure. The omnibus measure was approved by Congress about two months earlier than the last of the separate measures in 1949. In addition, the appropriations total was about $2.3 billion less than the President's combined budget requests. Chairman Clarence Cannon (D Mo.) of the House Appropriations Committee hailed the omnibus approach as "the most practical and efficient method of handling the annual budget," but in spite of his support the House Appropriations Committee in 1951 voted 31-18 to return to the traditional method of separate handling of appropriation bills; the omnibus approach had undercut the authority of subcommittees and their chairmen. Following the vote, Cannon charged that "every predatory lobbyist, every pressure group seeking to get its hands into the U.S. Treasury, every bureaucrat seeking to extend his empire downtown is opposed to the consolidated bill."

The Senate in 1953 voted to make another attempt at an omnibus bill and to place limitations on various forms of spending, but the proposal was not acted on in the House. Another Senate proposal, for the creation of a Joint Budget Committee to provide Congress with meaningful fiscal information, was approved by the Senate eight times between 1952 and 1967 but was never accepted by the House.

As years went by, Congress discovered that the "power of the purse," long considered one of its principal sources of power over the Executive Branch, was not the bulwark of legislative authority it had thought. Congress generally managed to authorize less spending than was proposed by postwar Presidents, but it proved unable to consider the budget as a whole and it lacked effective control over actual expenditures. This point was underscored by repeated conflicts with the White House over "backdoor spending" and the impounding by executive agencies of funds appropriated by Congress. Congressional frustration found expression in the frequent enactment of spending ceilings not to be exceeded by the Executive Branch.

Meanwhile, long-standing disagreement between the Senate and House over their respective roles in the appropriations process caused a rift between the two chambers. In 1962 this issue produced a Senate-House feud that delayed final action on appropriation bills and kept Congress in turmoil through much of the session. The feud started as a spat over the physical location of conference committee meetings and quickly moved on to the larger issues of whether the Senate could (1) initiate its own appropriation bills and (2) add to House-passed appropriation bills funds for items either not previously considered by the House or considered and rejected.

When the Senate passed a continuing resolution to provide temporary financing for Federal agencies pending final Congressional action on their regular appropriations, the House called the action an infringement on its "immemorial" right to initiate appropriation bills. In retaliation, the Senate adopted a resolution stating that "the acquiescence of the Senate in permitting the House to first consider appropriation bills cannot change the clear language of the Constitution nor affect the Senate's coequal power to originate any bill not expressly 'raising revenue.' " Although the two chambers eventually reached a truce, the basic issues were never resolved. *(See Fiscal Powers, Chapter III.)*

Exercise of the War Power

Events of the post-World War II era frequently reminded Congress that its constitutional power to declare war counted for little in the modern world. But in the late 1960s the Senate mounted a substantial challenge to the President's authority over military involvement.

Truman. Congress did not seriously challenge President Truman's war powers until 1951. At issue then was the President's authority to dispatch troops to Korea and to Western Europe. Sen. Robert A. Taft Sr. (R Ohio) opened a three-month-long "great debate" on Jan. 5, 1951, by asserting that Truman had "no authority whatever to commit American troops to Korea without consulting Congress and without Congressional approval." Moreover, he said, the President had "no power to agree to send American troops to fight in Europe in a war between members of the Atlantic Pact and Soviet Russia."

The debate revolved principally around the troops-to-Europe issue. It came to an end April 4, when the Senate adopted two resolutions approving the dispatch of four divisions to Europe. One of the resolutions stated that it was the sense of the Senate that "no ground troops in addition to such four divisions should be sent to Western Europe...without further Congressional approval." But neither resolution gained the force of law, for the House took no action.

Truman never asked Congress for a declaration of war in Korea, and he waited until Dec. 16, 1950—six months after the outbreak of hostilities—to proclaim the existence of a national emergency. In defense of this course, it was argued that the Russians or Chinese or both had violated post-World War II agreements on Korea and that emergency powers authorized during World War II could still be applied.

The Korean conflict provided two further tests of Presidential powers. In 1951, the nation was split when Truman dismissed Gen. Douglas A. MacArthur as United

Nations military commander in the Far East because of a dispute over policy. The Senate Foreign Relations and Armed Services Committees reviewed the ouster, and their joint hearings were credited with cooling the atmosphere throughout the country. So bitter was the controversy that the Committees refrained from making any formal report, but the President's right to remove MacArthur was conceded and the principle of civilian control over the military upheld. In 1952, Congress ignored Truman's request for approval of his seizure of the nation's steel mills, an action taken under his war powers, and the Supreme Court later ruled that the seizure was without statutory authority and constituted a usurpation of the powers of Congress.

Eisenhower. Presidents who followed Truman made frequent use of their war powers, sometimes in cooperation with Congress. For example, President Eisenhower asked Congress in 1955 for advance approval of the use of American armed force in the event of a Communist attack on Formosa or the Pescadores Islands. A resolution to that effect was adopted within a week. However, Eisenhower landed troops in Lebanon in July 1958 strictly on his own authority. In a special message to Congress, July 15, he said the action was designed to protect American lives and "to assist the Government of Lebanon in the preservation of Lebanon's territorial integrity and independence, which have been deemed vital to U.S. national interests and world peace."

Kennedy. President Kennedy, responding to Soviet threats to Allied rights in West Berlin, asked Congress on July 16, 1961, for authority to call up Ready Reservists and to extend the enlistments of men already on active duty. Such authority was granted in a joint resolution signed by the President Aug. 1. Kennedy could not wait for Congressional approval of his actions in the Cuban missile crisis of October 1962. Confronted with a buildup of Soviet missile bases in Cuba, he ordered an immediate naval quarantine of Cuba to prevent delivery of additional Russian missiles. More than any other crisis of the postwar period, the Cuban episode illustrated the vast sweep of Presidential power in times of great emergency.

Johnson. Congress virtually abdicated its power to declare war in Vietnam when it adopted, in August 1964, the Gulf of Tonkin resolution authorizing the President to "take all necessary measures" to stop aggression in Southeast Asia. The resolution was requested by President Johnson and adopted by a vote of 88-2 in the Senate and 414-0 in the House. The President considered the resolution adequate authority for expanding U.S. involvement in the Vietnam war, but in following years, as public support for the war deteriorated, Congress was to have second thoughts about its 1964 action; the Tonkin Gulf resolution was repealed in January 1971.

Nixon. Objections to the President's exercise of power were pressed most vigorously in the Senate. In a major effort to reassert Congressional prerogatives in foreign policy, the Senate in 1969 adopted a "national commitments" resolution designed to place the Executive Branch on notice that the Senate regarded the commitment of U.S. forces to the defense of a foreign country as requiring Congressional approval. As a sense-of-the-Senate resolution, however, the measure did not have the force of law.

In 1970, the Senate returned to the question of the war power, challenging the Nixon Administration's military involvement in Cambodia and engaging in extended debates on an amendment to set a date for U.S. withdrawal from Vietnam. Congress finally approved a modified restriction on the use of ground troops in Cambodia, but the Senate twice rejected the so-called "end-the-war" amendment. Military actions in Laos subsequently reopened Congressional debates on the war issue.

Confirmation of Appointments

The Senate in the postwar era vigorously defended its power to advise and consent to Presidential nominations. One Cabinet nomination was rejected—that of Lewis L. Strauss as Secretary of Commerce in 1959—and other high-level appointees were subjected to searching inquiry by the Senate. Conflict of interest loomed large as an issue, and nominees were frequently required to divest themselves of stock holdings and sever outside business connections as the price of confirmation.

Increasingly, judicial nominations became a center of controversy. President Johnson's nomination of Associate Justice Abe Fortas to be Chief Justice was blocked by a Senate filibuster in 1968, and two of President Nixon's Supreme Court nominees were rejected outright —Clement F. Haynsworth Jr. in 1969 and G. Harrold Carswell in 1970. In advance of the vote on Carswell, President Nixon said that rejection of the nomination would impair his constitutional responsibilities and the constitutional relationship of the President to Congress. In a letter to a Republican Senator, he asserted: "It is the duty of the President to appoint and of the Senate to advise and consent. But if the Senate attempts to substitute its judgment as to who should be appointed, the traditional constitutional balance is in jeopardy and the duty of the President under the Constitution impaired." Many Senators considered the Nixon letter a denial of the Senate's constitutional role in the appointment process, and the Senate went on to reject the Carswell nomination by a vote of 45-51. "The Senate has reasserted itself," said Sen. J. W. Fulbright (D Ark.) after the vote.

Legislative Reorganization Act of 1970

Early in the 1960s concern over the ability of Congress to meet its constitutional responsibilities led to mounting pressure for new reform legislation. In 1965, the Senate and House created a Joint Committee on the Organization of the Congress, modeled on the committee that had drafted the 1946 Reorganization Act and headed by Sen. A. S. (Mike) Monroney (D Okla.), cosponsor of the earlier law, and Rep. Ray J. Madden (D Ind.). After a comprehensive study, the Committee in 1966 reported its recommendations, most of which were incorporated in a bill passed by the Senate in 1967. That bill met stubborn opposition in the House and never reached the floor. But reform pressures persisted, and in 1970 the House finally passed a reform bill of its own. This measure was accepted by the Senate and enacted into law (PL 91-510).

The 1970 Act was designed to improve the operations of Congress, in committee and on the floor of both chambers, to provide Congress with better means of evaluating the Federal Budget and to improve Congressional resources for research and information. It did not touch on such sensitive and controversial subjects as the seniority system, the Senate cloture rule or the power of the House Rules Committee.

In provisions applicable only to the Senate, the 1970 Act amended the Senate rules to:

● Allow a majority of a committee to call a meeting when the chairman does not call a meeting on request. (The House, but not the Senate, had this procedure available.)

● Provide that the ranking majority member of the committee preside at any meeting from which the chairman is absent. (This was already the custom in most committees.)

● Require that Senate committees adopt and publish rules of committee procedure. (Under existing rules, there was no such requirement.)

● Provide that committee business meetings be open to the public except during sessions to mark up bills, to vote or when the committee by majority vote decides otherwise. (In 1970, 33 percent of all Senate committee meetings were closed to the public, a much lower percentage than in the House.)

● Provide that committee hearings be open to the public except when the committee decides that the testimony may relate to national security, may reflect adversely on an individual's character or reputation or may contain confidential information.

● Require that all roll-call votes taken in committee on a measure or amendment—and the positions of Senators voting—be announced in the committee report on that measure unless previously made public.

● Provide that committee reports on bills be filed within seven calendar days (excluding days the Senate is not in session) after a majority of the committee files a written request that the report be filed.

● Provide that no proxy vote may be cast on a motion to report a bill if committee rules forbid the use of a proxy on such a motion; prescribe that proxies only be voted on such a motion upon the affirmative request of an absent member.

● Allow committee members (who indicate this intention) three days to file supplementary, minority or additional views to be included with the committee report on a bill or other matter. (There was no similar provision in existing rules; generally, time was allowed for the filing of such views.)

● Prohibit the Senate from considering any bill or other matter reported from a standing committee unless the committee report on the measure has been available for at least three days (excluding Saturday, Sunday and legal holidays) prior to consideration. This rule did not apply to declarations of war or emergency, to legislative veto procedures or to executive reorganization plans, and could be waived by agreement of the Senate Majority and Minority Leaders. (There was no such provision in existing rules.)

● Specify procedures to govern procurement of funds for committees in excess of the annual $10,000 limit.

● Require committees (except the Senate Appropriations Committee) to announce hearings at least one week in advance unless there is good reason that they begin earlier. (There was no such provision in existing rules.)

● Provide that a majority of the minority party members of a committee (except the Senate Appropriations

Committee) are entitled to call witnesses during at least one day of hearings on a matter. (Many committees by custom allowed minority members this opportunity.)

● Allow any open hearing to be broadcast over radio or television under whatever rules the committee may adopt.

● Forbid Senate committees (except the Appropriations Committee) to sit while the Senate is in session unless special leave has been obtained from the Senate Majority and Minority Leaders.

● Require each standing committee (except the Senate Appropriations Committee) to report annually on its activities reviewing the execution of laws enacted within its jurisdiction. (Committees already possessed this review function but had not been required to make reports.)

● Require that every conference report be printed as a Senate report and be accompanied by an explanatory statement prepared jointly by House and Senate conferees. (By existing custom, only House conferees prepared such a statement and conference reports were usually only printed as House reports.)

● Divide debate on a conference report evenly between majority and minority. (By existing custom, such time was not formally divided and was controlled by the chairman of the conferees.)

● Require a quorum of the Senate Appropriations Committee to be present for a vote to report an appropriations bill from committee. (This was Committee practice but existing rules exempted the Appropriations Committee from the requirement.)

● Rename the Senate Banking and Currency Committee the Senate Banking, Housing and Urban Affairs Committee.

● Reduce the size of certain Senate committees; provide that, in the future, Senators may be members of only two major committees and one minor, select, or joint committee; that no Senator may serve on more than one of the Armed Services, Appropriations, Finance or Foreign Relations Committees; that no Senator may hold the chairmanship of more than one full committee and one subcommittee of a major committee. (This provision would not deprive any Senator of any committee position or chairmanship currently held, but would apply to all future assignments.)

● Create a Senate Committee on Veterans' Affairs.

(For complete provisions of the Legislative Reorganization Act of 1970, see Legislative Procedure, Chapter II.)

Seniority System Upheld

At the beginning of the 92nd Congress in 1971, Sens. Fred R. Harris (D Okla.) and Charles McC. Mathias (R Md.) led an unsuccessful move to scrap the seniority system in the selection of committee chairmen.

Their proposal would have amended Rule 24 to require that committee chairmen and ranking minority members be nominated individually by majority vote of the party caucuses and elected individually by majority vote of the full Senate at the beginning of each new Congress. Other committee members also would be elected individually, but a plurality would be sufficient for election. The proposal stipulated that the caucuses should not be "bound by any tradition, custom or principle of seniority."

Under existing practice, committee lists—based on seniority—were recommended by the party caucuses and usually approved by the Senate en bloc, although at the insistence of Harris and Mathias committee chairmen were individually elected in 1971.

The Harris-Mathias rules change proposal was adversely reported by the Rules and Administration Committee and tabled (killed) by the Senate March 16 on a 48-26 vote. During debate preceding the vote, Mathias said the proposed change would "restore confidence in the Government by making it clear to the American people that merit is the standard by which we are going to make the choice of our leadership." Sen. Robert C. Byrd (D W.Va.), leading the opposition, contended that the Senate had no right to regulate the proceedings of party caucuses and that "bloodletting battles" for committee chairmanships would occur if the proposal were adopted. Byrd said the proposal "as written would be disruptive not only of comity among Members but destructive of the Senate itself to a considerable degree."

Bibliography

Books

Bates, Ernest Sutherland, *The Story of Congress, 1789-1935.* Harper & Brothers, 1936.

Benton, Thomas Hart, *Thirty Years' View* (2 vols.). Greenwood Press edition, 1968.

Binkley, Wilfred E., *President and Congress.* Vintage edition, 1962.

Burdette, Franklin L., *Filibustering in the Senate.* Princeton University Press, 1940.

Clark, Joseph S., *Congress: the Sapless Branch.* Harper & Row, 1964.

Clark, Joseph S. et al., *The Senate Establishment.* Hill and Wang, 1963.

Congress and the Nation, 1945-64 (Vol. I). Congressional Quarterly Inc., 1965.

Congress and the Nation, 1965-68 (Vol. II). Congressional Quarterly Inc., 1969.

Galloway, George B., *Congress at the Crossroads.* Thomas Y. Crowell Co., 1946.

Galloway, George B., *The Legislative Process in Congress.* Thomas Y. Crowell Co., 1953.

Hamilton, Alexander et al., *The Federalist Papers.* New American Library edition, 1961.

Harris, Joseph P., *The Advice and Consent of the Senate.* Greenwood Press edition, 1968.

Haynes, George H., *The Senate of the United States: Its History and Practice* (2 vols.). Houghton Mifflin Co., 1938.

Jones, Charles O., *The Minority Party in Congress.* Little, Brown & Co., 1970.

Kerr, Clara H., *The Origin and Development of the United States Senate.* Andrus & Church, 1895.

Luce, Robert, *Legislative Procedure.* Houghton Mifflin Co., 1922.

Maclay, William, *The Journal of William Maclay, United States Senator from Pennsylvania, 1789-91.* Ungar Publishing Co., 1965 edition.

Matthews, Donald R., *U.S. Senators and Their World.* University of North Carolina Press, 1960.

McConachie, L. G., *Congressional Committees: A Study of the Origins and Development of Our National and Local Legislative Methods.* Thomas Y. Crowell Co., 1898.

Ripley, Randall B., *Majority Party Leadership in Congress.* Little, Brown & Co., 1969.

Ripley, Randall B., *Power in the Senate.* St. Martin's Press, 1969.

Rodgers, Lindsay, *The American Senate.* Alfred A. Knopf, 1926.

Rothman, David J., *Politics and Power: The United States Senate, 1869-1901.* Harvard University Press, 1966.

Silbey, Joel H., *The Shrine of Party: Congressional Voting Behavior, 1841-52.* University of Pittsburgh Press, 1967.

Tocqueville, Alexis de, *Democracy in America* (2 vols.). Vintage edition, 1945.

White, William S., *Citadel: The Story of the U.S. Senate.* Harper & Brothers, 1956, 1957.

Wilson, Woodrow, *Congressional Government.* Meridian edition, 1956.

Articles

Boeckel, Richard, "Secret Sessions of the Senate," *Editorial Research Reports*, Jan. 29, 1929, p. 87.

Wheildon, L. B., "Majority Cloture for the Senate," *Editorial Research Reports*, March 19, 1947, p. 199.

Government Publications

Biographical Directory of the American Congress, 1774-1961. Government Printing Office, 1961.

Galloway, George B. et al., *Limitation of Debate in the Congress of the United States: A Compendium, Including a Select Bibliography.* Library of Congress, Legislative Reference Service, revised July 1970.

Riddick, Floyd M., *Majority and Minority Leaders of the Senate.* Senate Document 91-20, 91st Congress, 1st session, Government Printing Office, 1969.

Swanstrom, Roy, *The United States Senate, 1787-1801.* Senate Document 64, 87th Congress, 1st session, Government Printing Office, 1962.

Watkins, Charles L., and Riddick, Floyd M., *Senate Procedure, Precedents and Practices.* Government Printing Office, 1958.

Note: Congress in 1964 (PL 88-383) authorized a program of Federal aid to public and nonprofit private organizations for the collecting, preserving, compiling, microfilming and publishing of documentary source material significant to the history of the United States. Under this program, the National Historical Publications Commission in 1971 was preparing to begin publication of an 18-volume history of the First Congress.

Chapter 2—Congress at Work

The Legislative Process

ARTICLE I of the Constitution grants all legislative powers of the Federal Government to a Congress consisting of two chambers, a Senate and a House of Representatives, and provides that proposed legislation must be passed by both chambers and submitted to the President for his approval before it can become law. The Founding Fathers, it has been said, did not expect the lawmaking function to be unduly burdensome, because they thought Congress would confine itself chiefly to external affairs and leave domestic affairs to state and local governments. Alexander Hamilton even surmised that Congress would have little to do once the central Government was established.

The First Congress, whose term ran from 1789 to 1791, consisted of 26 Senators and 65 Representatives, serving in behalf of a population of about four million in 13 states hugging the Atlantic coast. Concerns of the Congress were limited in scope and volume, and a few simple rules were sufficient to guide its deliberations. Only 268 bills were introduced in the First Congress; 108 were enacted into public law. Most dealt with the establishment of the new Government and its relations with the states, or with matters of defense or foreign relations.

Period of Congressional Supremacy

At first, Congress apparently expected to conduct most of its significant deliberations on the chamber floor. In early years the full body considered any question brought before it and indicated the line of action to be followed before appointing a select committee to work out proper legislation. But as time passed the volume and complexity of legislative business increased, and the recurrent nature of many questions led gradually to the establishment of standing committees. For a time these continuing groups functioned as advisers whose reports were carefully considered on the floor, but by 1885 they had become such a powerful force in determining the shape of legislation that Woodrow Wilson could write: "It is now, though a wide departure from the form of things, no great departure from the fact to describe ours as a government by the Standing Committees of Congress."

A succession of weak Presidents in the years following the Civil War had made possible the Congressional supremacy Wilson deplored, but Congress would not long be able to retain its commanding role. World War I marked the beginning of a dramatic expansion of Federal authority into almost every area of human activity, and strong Presidents were quick to reassert eroded Executive prerogatives. Congress, operating under antiquated procedures more in keeping with a simpler era, gradually relinquished its policy-making role, and legislative initiative shifted from the Capitol to the White House.

Strengthening of Presidential Leadership

The President's control over policy was strengthened by the Budget and Accounting Act of 1921, which enabled him for the first time to draw up a unified national budget—a detailed business and financial plan for the Government which reconciled proposed spending and estimated revenues. Prior to 1921, no system existed, either in Congress or the Executive Branch, for unified consideration or control of fiscal policy; Congress still has no machinery for comprehensive budget review.

From time to time Congress still tries to seize for itself the policy-making functions now exercised by the Executive Branch, but these ventures into Congressional Government enjoy only limited success. Congress may be able to block Presidential programs, but it does not speak with a unified voice and it has no means of developing a comprehensive program of its own.

Today the President's Budget, submitted to Congress shortly after it assembles each January, offers the framework of the President's program for the nation in the coming year. Together with the State of the Union address and various special messages, it forms the basis of legislative action to meet the expanding needs of more than 200 million Americans.

Gathered to exercise its legislative responsibilities is a Congress of 100 Senators and 435 Representatives elected from 50 states extending from Maine to Hawaii and from Florida to Alaska. Membership in Congress is no longer a part-time job: Congress meets in almost year-round sessions, and its concerns are encyclopedic. The 91st Congress (1969-71) was in session for 704 days, during which 29,040 bills were introduced and 695 were enacted into public law.

Institutional Structure of Congress

As its membership has grown and the volume and complexity of its business have multiplied, the institutional characteristics of Congress also have changed. Congress today is a very different institution from that contemplated by its creators.

Perhaps the most noteworthy characteristic of the modern Congress is its diffusion of power. The Senate and House both are marked by a disintegrated internal

Terms and Sessions of Congress

The two-year period for which a House of Representatives is elected constitutes a Congress. Under the 20th Amendment to the Constitution, adopted in 1933, this period begins at noon Jan. 3 of each odd-numbered year and ends at noon Jan. 3 of the next odd-numbered year. Congresses are numbered consecutively, and the Congress that met in January 1971 was the 92nd in a series that began in 1789.

Under the Constitution, Congress is required to "assemble" at least once each year, and the 20th Amendment provides that these annual meetings shall begin at noon on Jan. 3 unless Congress "shall by law appoint a different day." Each Congress, therefore, has two regular sessions, the first beginning in January of the odd-numbered year and the second beginning in January of the even-numbered year. In addition, the President may "on extraordinary occasions" convene one or both houses in special session.

In practice, the annual sessions may run as long as 12 months. The Legislative Reorganization Act of 1970 stipulates that "unless otherwise provided by the Congress," the Senate and House "shall adjourn sine die not later than July 31 of each year" or, in the case of a nonelection year, take a 30-day recess in August. The provision is not applicable if "a state of war exists pursuant to a declaration of war by the Congress." Sine die adjournment ends a session of Congress. Within a session, Congress may adjourn to a day certain, although neither house can adjourn for more than three days without the consent of the other.

structure coupled with a lack of strong party control. Leadership is divided between the committee chairmen and the party leaders; there is no unity of command.

The institutional structure is decentralized through the committee system. The standing committees of Congress—17 in the Senate and 21 in the House, each with a specialized jursidiction—constitute the cornerstone of the legislative process. The committee system provides a convenient division of labor for the awesome Congressional workload and makes it possible for Members, through long experience, to develop expertise in complex fields of legislation. It also creates an independent power base for its chairmen and ranking members.

The committees, their leadership determined by the Congressional seniority system, hold virtually life-or-death power over legislation. They may approve, alter, kill or ignore any measure referred to them, and by and large the committees' decisions will not be overruled by the parent chamber. When a bill reaches the floor, the committee guides it to passage; when it goes to conference, committee members are chosen to meet with their counterparts from the other chamber to hammer out its final language. At every stage the committee plays a determining role.

Seniority System vs. Party Leadership

Since committee chairmen hold power through the seniority system—that is, by tenure in office rather than election—they are not subject to direct control by the elected party leaders. Furthermore, the party leadership structure in Congress is itself so fragmented (among the House Speaker, floor leaders and the like) that real party government is impossible to achieve. This fragmentation is one of the fruits of the "revolution of 1910," which decentralized the party leadership that previously had been exercised by the Speaker of the House.

Party leadership is the more difficult in Congress because, in practice, there are no parties to be led. Members of Congress are responsible to a local electorate, independent of the national party and frequently at variance with it. Thus party unity is difficult to achieve, and attempts to bind party membership on voting are rarely made. Voting blocs in Congress represent shifting coalitions of divergent interests that frequently cross party lines. The "conservative coalition" of Republicans and southern Democrats voting against northern Democrats, for example, has been a potent legislative force in recent years.

Characteristics of Senate and House

Each chamber of Congress also has its own special characteristics. The Senate, with only 100 Members, can afford to be far more relaxed in its procedures than the 435-Member House of Representatives. Furthermore, each Senator is an ambassador from a "sovereign" state and as such is accorded more deference, even indulgence, than a Representative from a smaller district within a state.

In consequence, the House is more hierarchically organized and power is less evenly distributed than in the Senate, where even a freshman Member occupies a position of some stature. A Representative must expect to serve a long apprenticeship before he can rise to prominence in the House. Similarly, the House operates under a more rigid system of rules designed to expedite its business. Because debate is limited and the amending process frequently curtailed, the House is able to dispose of legislation with great speed.

By comparison, the Senate is a leisurely and informal institution. It usually operates in a spirit of comity where the prerogatives of all Members are respected. Much of its business is handled by unanimous consent, rather than by elaborate procedures spelled out in the rules. One of its most cherished traditions is the privilege of unlimited debate; its amending powers are broad. Given these conditions, it is not surprising that the Senate may spend weeks considering a measure that the House dispatched in one sitting.

The key steps in formulating and enacting legislation are described in the following pages. The legislative process is complex and varied. Accomplished lawmakers know how to select the methods best suited to advance their legislative goals. For, as George B. Galloway observed: "The structure and procedures of Congress can be used to facilitate or obstruct legislative action. They are not neutral elements in the process of lawmaking."

Longest Sessions of Congress

Congress	Session	Convened	Adjourned	No. of days
76th	3rd	Jan. 3, 1940 -	Jan. 3, 1941	366
77th	1st	Jan. 3, 1941 -	Jan. 2, 1942	365
81st	2nd	Jan. 3, 1950 -	Jan. 2, 1951	365[1]
80th	2nd	Jan. 6, 1948 -	Dec. 31, 1948	361[2]
88th	1st	Jan. 9, 1963 -	Dec. 30, 1963	356
91st	1st	Jan. 3, 1969 -	Dec. 23, 1969	355[3]
65th	2nd	Dec. 3, 1917 -	Nov. 21, 1918	354
79th	1st	Jan. 3, 1945 -	Dec. 21, 1945	353[4]
80th	1st	Jan. 3, 1947 -	Dec. 19, 1947	351[5]
78th	1st	Jan. 6, 1943 -	Dec. 21, 1943	350[6]
91st	2nd	Jan. 19, 1970 -	Jan. 2, 1971	349[7]
77th	2nd	Jan. 5, 1942 -	Dec. 16, 1942	346
40th	2nd	Dec. 2, 1867 -	Nov. 10, 1868	345[8]
78th	2nd	Jan. 10, 1944 -	Dec. 19, 1944	345[9]
90th	1st	Jan. 10, 1967 -	Dec. 15, 1967	340
83rd	2nd	Jan. 6, 1954 -	Dec. 2, 1954	331[10]
63rd	2nd	Dec. 1, 1913 -	Oct. 24, 1914	328
50th	1st	Dec. 5, 1887 -	Oct. 20, 1888	321
51st	1st	Dec. 2, 1889 -	Oct. 1, 1890	304
31st	1st	Dec. 3, 1849 -	Sept. 30, 1850	302
89th	1st	Jan. 4, 1965 -	Oct. 23, 1965	293
67th	2nd	Dec. 5, 1921 -	Sept. 22, 1922	292
82nd	1st	Jan. 3, 1951 -	Oct. 20, 1951	291

1 *Congress recessed from Sept. 23 to Nov. 27.*
2 *Congress recessed from June 20 to July 26 and Aug. 7 to Dec. 31.*
3 *Congress recessed from Aug. 15 to Sept. 3.*
4 *The House was in recess from July 21 to Sept. 5 and the Senate from Aug. 1 to Sept. 5.*
5 *Congress recessed from July 27 to Nov. 17.*
6 *Congress recessed from July 8 to Sept. 14.*
7 *The House was in recess from Aug. 14 to Sept. 9, and both chambers recessed from Oct. 14 to Nov. 16.*
8 *No business was transacted after July 27. Congress took three recesses between July 27 and Nov. 10.*
9 *Congress recessed from April 1-12, June 23 to Aug. 1 and Sept. 21 to Nov. 14.*
10 *The House adjourned sine die on Aug. 20. The Senate was in recess from Aug. 20 to Nov. 8 and from Nov. 18 to Nov. 29, and adjourned sine die on Dec. 2.*

Origin and Sponsorship of Legislation

Legislative proposals may originate in a number of different ways. A Member of Congress, of course, may himself develop the idea for a piece of legislation; assistance in drafting legislative language is available from the Office of Legislative Counsel in the Senate and House. Pressure groups—business, labor, farm, civil rights organizations and the like—are another fertile source of legislation; many such organizations not only provide detailed technical knowledge in specialized fields but also employ experts in the art of drafting bills. Constituents, either as individuals or groups, also may propose legislation; frequently a Member of Congress will introduce such a bill "by request" whether or not he supports its purposes.

Today the bulk of legislation considered by Congress originates in the Executive Branch (although key Members of Congress may participate in the formulation of Administration programs). Each year the President outlines his legislative program in his State of the Union and Budget messages and in special messages. Executive departments and agencies then transmit to Congress drafts of proposed legislation to carry out the President's program. These bills usually are introduced by the chairman of the committee or subcommittee having jurisdiction over the subject involved—or by the ranking minority member if the chairman is not of the President's party.

Sometimes committees consider proposals that have not been formally introduced in bill form. The committee then formulates its own bill, which is introduced by the chairman. This is the usual practice with appropriation and revenue bills.

No matter how a legislative proposal originates, it can be introduced only by a Member of Congress. In the House a Member (including the Resident Commissioner of Puerto Rico and the District of Columbia Delegate) may introduce any one of several types of bills and resolutions by handing the measure to the Clerk of the House or by placing it in a box called the hopper; he need not seek recognition for the purpose. A Senator first gains recognition of the presiding officer to announce the introduction of a bill. If objection is offered by any Senator, introduction of the bill is postponed until the following day. If there is no objection, the bill is read twice by title and referred to the appropriate committee. A House bill is considered read for the first time when it is referred to committee.

As the next step, in the House and the Senate, the bill is numbered (in order of introduction), referred to committee, labeled with the sponsor's name and sent to the Government Printing Office so that copies can be made for subsequent study and action.

There is no limit to the number of bills a Member may introduce. Senate bills may be jointly sponsored and carry several Senators' names; since 1967, the House also has permitted multiple sponsorship of bills, with a limit of 25 cosponsors on any one bill. The Constitution stipulates that "all bills for raising revenue shall originate in the House of Representatives," and this stipulation has generally been interpreted to include appropriation bills. All other bills may originate in either chamber; major legislation usually is introduced in both houses in the form of companion bills.

Although thousands of pieces of legislation are introduced in every Congress, most never receive any consideration. In the 91st Congress (1969-71), 29,040 bills were introduced in the Senate and House; of these, only 2,250 were reported by committees. Bills not disposed of die with the Congress in which they were introduced and must be reintroduced in the following Congress to be eligible for consideration.

Types of Congressional Measures

Measures considered and acted upon by the House and the Senate include not only bills but also a variety of resolutions. The nomenclature and designations follow:

Bills are prefixed with "HR" when introduced in the House and with "S" when introduced in the Senate, followed by a number assigned in the order of introduction from the beginning of each Congress. Bills are used as the form for most legislation, whether general or special, public or private. When passed by both chambers in identical form and signed by the President (or repassed over his veto), they become public or private laws.

Joint Resolutions are designated H J Res or S J Res. A joint resolution requires the approval of both houses

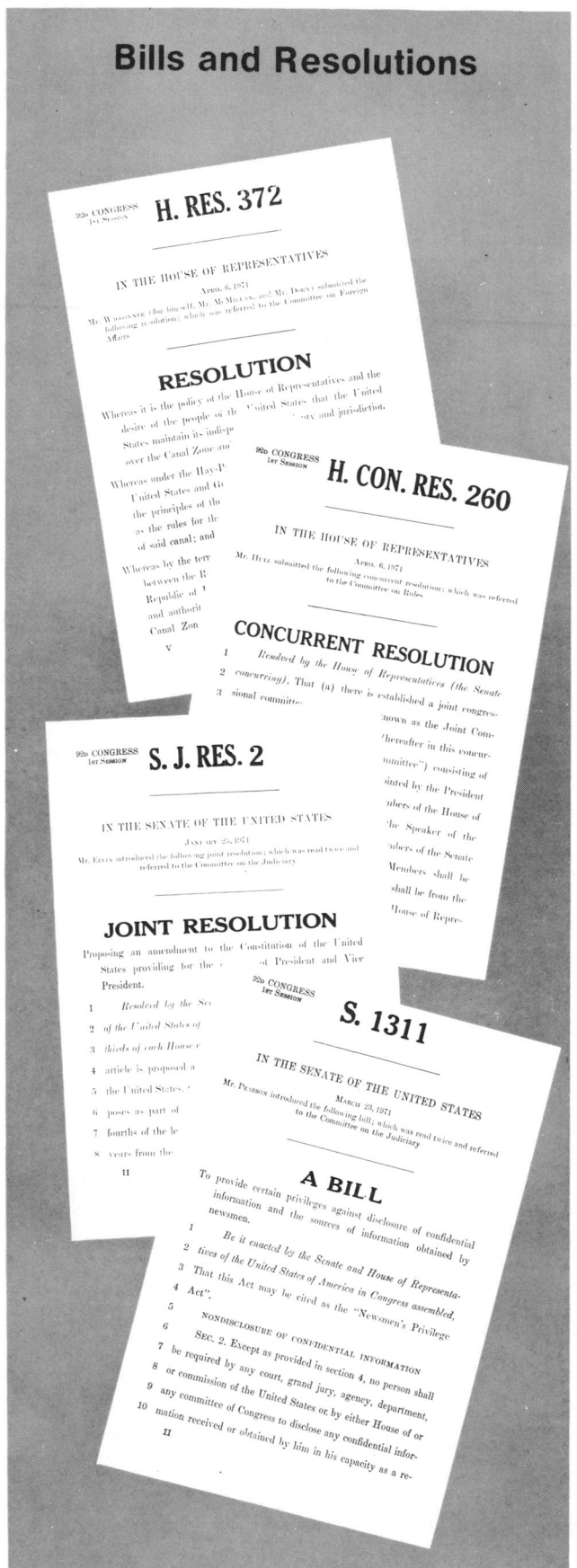

Bills and Resolutions

and the signature of the President, just as a bill does, and has the force of law if approved. There is no real difference between a bill and a joint resolution. The latter is generally used in dealing with limited matters, such as a single appropriation for a specific purpose. Joint resolutions are used also to propose amendments to the Constitution. These must be approved by two-thirds of both houses; they do not require the President's signature but become a part of the Constitution when ratified by three-fourths of the states.

Concurrent Resolutions are designated H Con Res or S Con Res. They are used for matters affecting the operations of both houses, such as fixing the time of adjournment of a Congress or expressing the "sense" of the two chambers on some question. They must be passed by both houses but do not require the signature of the President and do not have the force of law.

Resolutions are designated H Res or S Res. A simple resolution deals with matters entirely within the prerogatives of one house or the other. It requires neither passage by the other chamber nor approval by the President and does not have the force of law. Most resolutions deal with the rules of one house. They also are used to express the opinion of a single house on a current issue.

Committee Referral

Nearly all bills are referred to committees. A bill is referred to the appropriate committee by the House parliamentarian on the Speaker's order or by the Senate President, subject to the will of the chamber. In the Senate, the sponsor of a bill may indicate his preference for referral, but this is not binding.

Generally, custom and rule govern the referral of legislation to committees; the jurisdiction of the standing committees is spelled out in House Rule 10 and Senate Rule 25. *(See Appendix.)* Sometimes, however, the presiding officer has a measure of discretion—for example, in the case of new programs or bills involving overlapping jurisdictions—and bills may be drafted to take advantage of this situation. In 1963 a controversial civil rights bill was referred to the Senate Commerce Committee instead of the southern-dominated Judiciary Committee because its subject matter, public accommodations, fell within the commerce clause of the Constitution. Occasionally when problems of overlapping jurisdiction arise, bills may be referred to more than one committee.

Committee Action

The standing committees of Congress, operating as little legislatures, determine the fate of most legislative proposals. Committee members and staff frequently have a high degree of expertise in the subjects under their jurisdiction, and it is at the committee stage that a bill comes under the sharpest Congressional scrutiny.

A committee has several options with respect to a piece of legislation: it may consider and report it favorably, with or without amendments; rewrite it entirely; reject it or report it unfavorably; or simply refuse to consider it. Failure of a committee to act on a bill usually is equivalent to killing it; the measure can be withdrawn from the group's purview only by a discharge petition signed by a majority of the House membership on House bills, or by adoption of a special resolution in the Senate. Discharge attempts rarely succeed.

When a bill reaches a committee, it is placed on the group's calendar. (Most standing committees periodically publish cumulative calendars of business, detailing all action on measures referred to them.) Then the normal course of action for major bills is as follows:

Agency Views. The committee first requests comment from interested agencies of the Government. The agencies give their views on the effect of the proposed legislation and how it would accord with the President's program.

Subcommittee Assignment. A bill may be considered by the full committee in the first instance, but more often the committee chairman assigns it to a subcommittee for study and hearings. Especially in the House, where chairmen tend to exercise tight control over their committees, this power of assignment may be used to promote or impede the suggested legislation.

Hearings. The subcommittee usually schedules hearings on the bill and invites testimony from interested public and private witnesses. Other witnesses may testify at their own request. Most witnesses offer prepared statements, following which they may be questioned by subcommittee members. The hearings may be brief and perfunctory or they may go on for weeks. Because the demands on a Member's time are so great, frequently only a few subcommittee members with a special interest in the subject will participate in the hearings.

Most hearings are held in open session, but some are held in closed (executive) session, or a combination of open and closed hearings may be used. Until 1971, all hearings of the House Appropriations Committee were in closed session. Hearings on national security matters frequently are closed.

Hearings on legislation may serve a variety of purposes: to seek information on the subject under consideration; to test public opinion; to build support for the bill; or even to delay action on it. Sometimes hearings serve primarily as a safety valve for the release of group tensions.

Markup Session. After the hearings have ended, the subcommittee meets, usually in executive session, to "mark up" the bill—that is, to decide on legislative language for recommendation to the full committee. The subcommittee may approve the bill unaltered, amend it, rewrite it—or block it altogether. It then reports its recommendations to the full committee.

Full Committee Action. When the full committee receives the bill, it may repeat the subcommittee procedures, all or in part, or it may—as in the case of the Appropriations Committees—simply ratify the action of the subcommittee. When a committee votes on its recommendation to the House or Senate, it is said to "order the bill reported." Occasionally a committee may order a bill reported unfavorably; most of the time a report, submitted by the chairman of the committee to the House or Senate, calls for favorable action on the legislation, since the committee can effectively "kill" legislation by simply failing to take any action.

Frequently the committee proposes amendments to the bill. If they are substantial and the legislation is complicated, the committee may order introduction of a

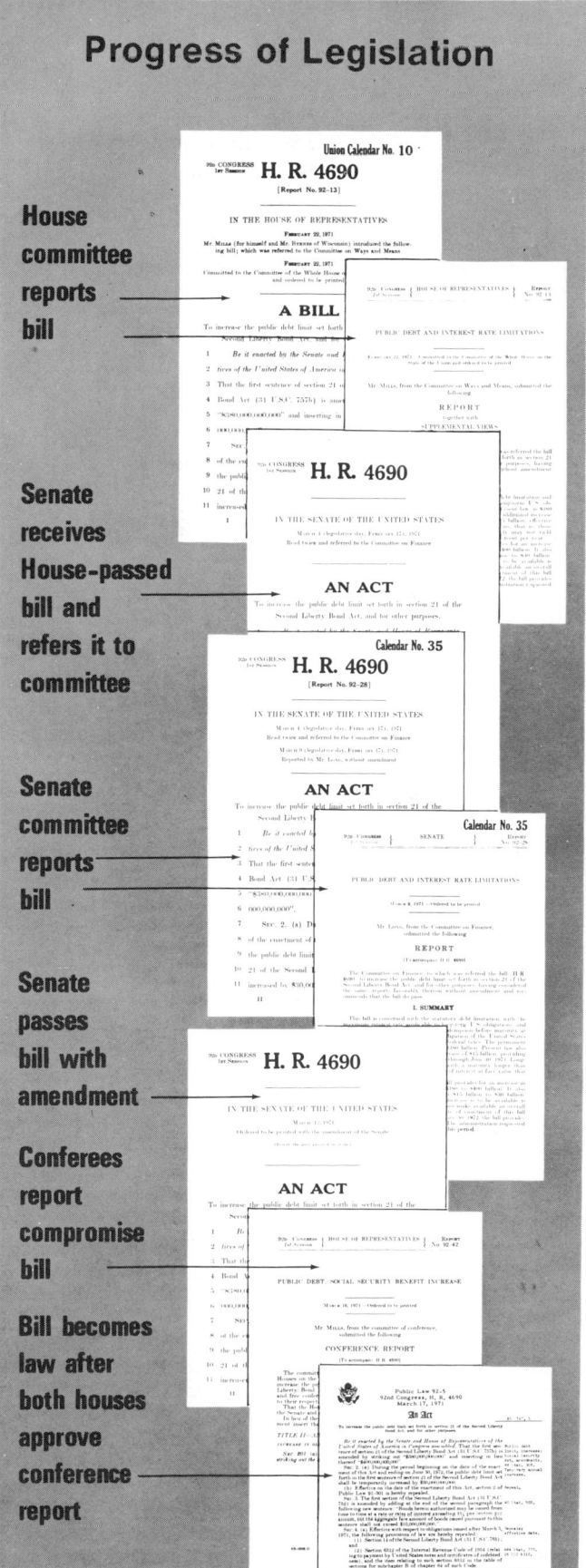

Progress of Legislation

House committee reports bill →

Senate receives House-passed bill and refers it to committee →

Senate committee reports bill →

Senate passes bill with amendment →

Conferees report compromise bill →

Bill becomes law after both houses approve conference report →

The Congressional Day

Ordinarily the Senate and House meet at noon daily, although sometimes an earlier meeting is scheduled. In each chamber the session opens with a prayer, followed by "reading" and approval of the Journal. (Actual reading usually is dispensed with but occasionally is demanded for dilatory purposes. Under the Legislative Reorganization Act of 1970, the House Journal cannot be read unless the Speaker or a majority of those present so orders.)

What happens next depends on whether the chamber recessed or adjourned at the conclusion of its last previous sitting. If it adjourned, a new "legislative day" (the period from adjournment to adjournment) now begins, and the rules set forth certain matters to be taken up and disposed of at the beginning of the session. If it recessed, the same legislative day continues, and the chamber may move on to its unfinished business without further preliminaries. The distinction is less significant in the House, which normally adjourns from day to day, than in the Senate, where a legislative day frequently extends over several calendar days.

Senate. The Senate sets aside the first two hours of a legislative day as a "morning hour" for the consideration of routine business. This business includes such matters as messages from the President, communications from department heads, messages from the House, presentations of petitions and memorials, reports of standing and select committees and the introduction of bills and resolutions. Senators are limited to brief statements, usually three minutes.

During the first hour of the morning hour, no motion to proceed to the consideration of any bill on the calendar is in order except by unanimous consent. During the second hour, motions may be made but must be decided without debate. At the conclusion of morning business or after the hour of 1 o'clock, any Senator may move to take up a bill out of its regular order on the calendar; if the bill is not disposed of by the time the morning hour ends, it is displaced by the unfinished business, if any.

Although not required under the rules, a morning hour frequently is arranged by unanimous consent following a recess.

At 2 o'clock, or earlier if the morning business has been completed, the Senate moves on to unfinished business or to the business planned by the Majority Leader for the day. Unlike the more orderly House, the Senate frequently interrupts consideration of a bill to take care of other business. The Senate may take up a bill, lay it aside temporarily to consider another, return to consideration of the first, then pause for speeches unrelated to the subject technically under consideration, etc. Generally its pace is leisurely, and it may take days or weeks to dispose of one piece of legislation.

House. The House tends to operate on a Monday-to-Thursday schedule, with Mondays reserved primarily for non-controversial legislation considered under special procedures.

Although the House rules provide for a morning hour, that procedure is rarely employed. Following approval of the Journal, the Speaker recognizes Members for one-minute speeches and submission of material to be inserted in the *Congressional Record*. Bills are introduced, reports filed and messages, petitions and memorials received. This constitutes the morning business of the House, after which the chamber turns to legislative business, sitting either as the House or in Committee of the Whole.

The House is able to dispose of most bills in one or two days. Once it takes up a bill, it generally sticks with it until action is completed, and the stringent House rules preclude undue delay.

Typically, the House sets aside a time at the close of the day's session—following the disposal of legislative business—for "special orders." At this time, Members who have requested time in advance are permitted to make speeches on various subjects for inclusion in the *Congressional Record*. Few other Members stay in the chamber to listen. The special-orders time is followed by adjournment.

Bells. Daily life on Capitol Hill is punctuated by the ringing of bells, intended to alert Members not in their seats to what is going on in Senate or House. Systems of electric bells or buzzers are installed in the Capitol and the Senate and House Office Buildings (and even in some nearby restaurants) to summon Members when their presence is required for votes or other purposes. Conveniently located wall lights show how many bells have rung. Different systems are used by the Senate and the House.

In the Senate, one bell means a roll-call vote; two, a quorum call; three, a call of absentees (live quorum); four, adjournment or recess; five, not currently used; six, morning business concluded.

In the House, one bell means a teller vote; two, a recorded teller or a roll-call vote; three, a quorum call; four, adjournment; and five, a recess.

"clean bill" embodying the proposed amendments. The original bill is then put aside and the "clean bill," with a new number, is reported to the floor. If the amendments are not extensive, the original bill is "reported with amendments." The chamber must approve, alter or reject the committee amendments before the bill itself can be put to a vote.

Report. When a committee sends a bill to the chamber floor, it justifies its actions in a written statement, called a report, which accompanies the bill. The report describes the purposes and scope of the bill, explains the committee amendments, notes proposed changes in existing law and usually includes the texts of communications from department and agency heads whose views on the legislation have been solicited. Often committee members opposing a measure submit a dissenting minority report.

Reports are numbered, by Congress and chamber, in the order in which they are filed (S Rept 91-1, H Rept 91-1, etc.) and immediately printed. The reported bill also is printed, with committee amendments indicated by showing insertions in italics and deletions in stricken-through type. The report number also is shown on the bill, and the bill and report both carry the calendar number.

House and Senate Calendars

After a bill is reported back to the house where it originated, it is placed on a calendar. Although bills are placed on the calendar in chronological order, they are not necessarily called up for floor action in that order.

House. There are five legislative calendars in the House, issued in one cumulative calendar titled *Calendars of the United States House of Representatives and History of Legislation.* This calendar, which is printed daily when Congress is in session, lists all bills on each of the five legislative calendars. It also gives a capsule legislative history of all measures reported by Senate and House committees, together with other valuable reference material. Each Monday's edition carries a subject index.

The five legislative calendars are:

The Union Calendar to which are referred "bills raising revenue, general appropriations bills and bills of a public character directly or indirectly appropriating money or property." Technically it is the Calendar of the Committee of the Whole House on the State of the Union, so called because bills listed on it are first considered in the Committee of the Whole House on the State of the Union and reported back to the House for its final approval.

The House Calendar to which are referred "all bills of a public character not raising revenue nor directly or indirectly appropriating money or property."

The Consent Calendar to which are referred bills of a noncontroversial nature which already are on either the Union or House Calendars. The Consent Calendar is called on the first and third Mondays of each month; bills are passed without objection and without debate.

The Private Calendar to which are referred bills for relief in the nature of claims against the United States or private immigration bills. The Private Calendar is called on the first and third Tuesdays of each month, and bills are passed without debate.

The Discharge Calendar to which are referred motions to discharge committees from further consideration of a bill when the necessary signatures are signed to a discharge petition.

Consent Calendar and discharge procedures are described in detail later in this subchapter; private-bill procedure is discussed in Chapter III.

Senate. The Senate has only two calendars, the *Executive Calendar,* on which treaties and nominations are listed, and the *Calendar of Business* (General Orders), to which all legislation is assigned.

A bill is brought before the Senate in one of two ways, either on call of the calendar (when bills must be considered in the order in which they were placed on the calendar) or by special action to take up a bill out of order.

The call of the calendar is used for noncontroversial legislation (similar to bills on the Consent Calendar in the House.) This procedure is described below.

Scheduling of Floor Action

House. Although a variety of methods exist for bringing up legislation on the House floor, for most major bills the route to floor action lies through the House Rules Committee. This Committee is empowered to report "rules" governing the floor consideration of legislation. *(A history of the Committee appears in Evolution of Committees, Chapter II.)*

Usually the chairman of the committee that favorably reported the bill, supported by the bill's sponsor and other committee members, appears before the Rules Committee to request a special rule. The request, considered by the Rules Committee in the same fashion that other committees consider legislative measures, is in the form of a simple resolution providing for consideration of the bill. The resolution sets the time limit on general debate and governs the amending process. It may forbid all amendments or all amendments except, in some cases, those proposed by the legislative committee that handled the bill. In this instance it is known as a "closed rule," as opposed to an "open rule," which permits amendments from the floor. The resolution also may waive points of order against provisions of the bill or against specified amendments intended to be proposed to the bill. This waiver permits the House to violate its own rules by barring any objection to such violation; a typical example might involve legislative provisions in a general appropriations bill, not permitted under the House rules.

When the Rules Committee reports a rule, ordinarily it must lie over for one day. It then is called up, debated and adopted by majority vote. (Very few rules are rejected.) This clears the way for action on the bill itself.

There are certain limitations on the Rules Committee's power. It is not allowed to report a rule that denies the minority the right to make a motion to recommit a bill. If it reports a rule to dispense with Calendar Wednesday, such a rule must be adopted by a two-thirds vote rather than the customary simple majority. When the Committee approves a rule, its report must be filed within three legislative days. If not immediately considered, the resolution goes on the calendar; if the member making the report does not call it up within seven legislative days, any member of the committee may do so. The resolution cannot be called up on the day it is reported except by two-thirds vote, although this does not apply during the last three days of the session.

The Committee does not always grant rules when it is asked to so, and frequently it has been subject to criticism on this ground. Sometimes the Committee arbitrarily blocks or delays legislation—as happened with civil rights bills in the early 1960s, when the Committee was under the chairmanship of Rep. Howard W. Smith (D Va.). At other times the Committee may require substantive changes in a bill as the price for its approval. For the most part the Committee works closely with the majority leadership, and it is probably fair to say that most bills it blocks either are opposed by the leaders or by a majority of the House.

If the Rules Committee refuses to grant a rule for a bill, it may be brought up under suspension of the rules or through the use of discharge or Calendar Wednesday procedures. These procedures, seldom successful, are described below. Another method of getting around the

Committee was the 21-day rule, adopted in 1965 but abandoned in 1967. Enlargement of the Committee from 12 to 15 members in 1961 helped to strengthen leadership control over the group's action.

Bills from certain committees have privileged status and may be considered by the House without a rule from the Rules Committee. In most cases committee reports are supposed to be available for three days prior to floor consideration. Revenue bills do not require a rule, but the Ways and Means Committee usually seeks one anyway in order to get a closed rule that precludes floor amendments. Similarly, general appropriations bills are privileged, although in this case both the printed reports and hearings must be available for three days prior to consideration, but the Appropriations Committee may nonetheless seek a rule waiving points of order against the bill. Rivers and harbors, public lands and general veterans' pension bills are among others that do not require a rule, although they, too, usually are sent to the Rules Committee.

Other bills have privileged status on special legislative days, also without a rule from the Rules Committee. These special situations are discussed below.

Senate. Unlike the House, the Senate has no elaborate rules or procedures for bringing bills to the floor, and it has no counterpart of the House Rules Committee.

Theoretically, under the rules, any Senator at almost any time may offer a motion to call up a bill; a simple majority is required for adoption. During the morning hour (before 2 p.m. at the beginning of a legislative day) such a motion is undebatable; at other times, however, it is subject to debate—or even filibuster, which can only be stopped by invoking cloture, a process that requires a two-thirds majority vote. Occasionally controversial bills meet defeat at this stage.

In practice, floor action is scheduled by the Majority Leader with the help of the majority Policy Committee and after consultation with the Minority Leader. Effort is made to accommodate the wishes of individual Senators, and important bills are seldom kept from the floor. The most common way to call up bills is by unanimous consent.

House Floor Procedures

Floor action on a major House bill ordinarily begins when the Speaker recognizes the member of the Rules Committee who has been designated to call up the rule for the bill's consideration. The rule may be debated for up to one hour, with half the time allotted to opponents of the bill. A typical open rule may provide:

"Resolved, That upon the adoption of this resolution it shall be in order to move that the House resolve itself into the Committee of the Whole House on the State of the Union for the consideration of the bill (H.R.—), entitled, etc. After general debate, which shall be confined to the bill and continue not to exceed——hours, to be equally divided and controlled by the chairman and the ranking minority member of the Committee on——, the bill shall be read for amendment under the five-minute rule. At the conclusion of the consideration of the bill for amendment, the Committee shall rise and report the bill to the House with such amendments as may have been adopted and the previous question shall be con-

sidered as ordered on the bill and amendments thereto to final passage without intervening motion except one motion to recommit with or without instructions."

After the rule has been adopted, by simple majority, the House resolves itself into the Committee of the Whole House on the State of the Union (working title: Committee of the Whole) for preliminary consideration of the bill.

Action in Committee of Whole

Although only bills on the Union Calendar must be considered in Committee of the While, other bills may be so considered on motion. In practice, most important bills are considered in Committee of the Whole. (If a bill is considered in the House proper, the amount of time for debate is determined either by special rule or is allocated with an hour for each Member if the bill is under consideration without a rule.)

The Committee of the Whole procedure goes back to a period in English history when the Speaker of the House of Commons was regarded as a friendly agent of the King; the Committee of the Whole was devised so that during periods of strained King-Commons relations members could elect a chairman of their own and proceed to discuss matters, particularly matters pertaining to the King's household expenses, without the normal restrictions of a House of Commons session.

As used in the House of Representatives, Committee of the Whole procedure differs in several ways from procedure of the House proper. The Speaker does not preside but appoints a chairman to take his place. A quorum consists of 100 Members, rather than a majority of the House (218 if there are no vacancies). No roll-call votes are taken in Committee of the Whole; action is by voice, division (standing) or teller vote, and Members' votes are not individually recorded except in the case of record teller votes, authorized under the Legislative Reorganization Act of 1970. *(For explanation of voting methods, see box.)*

The Committee debates and amends bills, subject to approval by the full House, but it cannot pass them. It cannot itself recommit a bill, although it may report to the House with a recommendation that the bill be recommitted or that the enacting clause be stricken (a means of killing the measure); these recommendations must be voted on by the full House.

Role of Floor Manager

Floor action is guided by the legislative committee that reported the bill; its members occupy seats at the tables on either side of the center aisle. Ordinarily the committee chairman (or someone designated by him) acts as floor manager for the proponents of the bill, while the ranking minority member leads the opposition. *Cannon's Procedure* describes the floor manager's role:

"A chairman directed to report a bill to the House ceases to function individually so far as that measure is concerned and becomes the representative of the committee in charge of the bill. Although he may have opposed the bill or parts of it in committee, he either steps aside and permits the next ranking member of the

Methods of Voting in House and Senate

House. The House has four different methods of voting, one or more of which may be used in deciding a single question. Occasionally the House takes several votes on the same proposition, testing first simple and then more complex voting methods, before a final decision is reached. The four methods of voting:

Voice Vote. This is the usual method of voting when a proposition is first put to the House, although other methods also are in order. The presiding officer calls for the "ayes" and "noes" in turn, Members answer in chorus, and the chair decides the result.

Division (Standing) Vote. If the result of a voice vote is in doubt or a further test is desired, a division may be demanded. In this case, Members in favor of a proposal stand and are counted by the presiding officer; then Members opposed stand and are counted. Only vote totals are announced; there is no record of how individual Members voted.

Teller Vote. A teller vote may be ordered upon demand of one-fifth of a quorum (20 in the Committee of the Whole and 44 in the House). The chair appoints two tellers from opposite sides and directs the Members to pass between them up the center aisle to be counted. The ayes pass through first, then the nays.

Prior to 1971, only vote totals were announced, but a House floor amendment to the Legislative Reorganization Act of 1970 opened the way to recorded teller votes. Under the 1970 Act, it is possible to record the votes of individual Members on a teller vote taken during consideration of a bill in Committee of the Whole at the request of one-fifth of a quorum (20). Members are permitted at least 12 minutes from the beginning of the vote to reach the floor and be counted.

Under the record-teller vote procedure, tellers must first be ordered and then a separate demand for "tellers with clerks" may be made. If one-fifth of a quorum support this demand, a recorded teller vote is ordered. Members write their names on green (for "aye") or red (for "no") cards which they hand to tally clerks in the rear of the chamber. Those voting "aye" pass up one aisle and those voting "no" pass up another. The tally clerks examine the cards and place them in red or green ballot boxes. Upon completion of the vote, the ballots are counted and the result announced. The votes of individual Members are made public just as they would be on a roll-call vote.

Roll-Call Vote. Yeas and nays are ordered by one-fifth of those present (as opposed to one-fifth of a quorum for tellers). They are not taken in Committee of the Whole. Under this procedure, the Clerk calls the roll, and each Member answers "yea" or "nay" as his name is called. If he does not wish to vote, he may answer "present." The Speaker's name is called only at his own request; he is required to vote only if his vote would be deciding, but sometimes Speakers have voted on other occasions. (The Speaker also votes, if he chooses, on record teller votes in Committee of the Whole.)

The Constitution requires yea-and-nay votes on the question of overriding a veto. Under the House rules, the yeas and nays are required automatically whenever a Member objects to a non-record vote taken when a quorum was not present, if the question is one that requires a quorum. This is known as an automatic roll call.

Roll-call votes are a time-consuming process in the 435-Member House. After the first call of the roll, the Clerk goes through the list again repeating the names of those who failed to respond before. Following the second call, Members standing in the "well" of the House may be recorded. Each yea-and-nay vote takes about half an hour. This time may be reduced in the future through the use of electronic voting equipment, authorized under the 1970 Reorganization Act.

Senate. Like the House, the Senate uses voice, division (standing) and roll-call votes. It does not employ the teller vote. Vote totals are seldom made public on division votes; usually only the result is announced.

The Senate does not follow the House practice of voting on a single proposition by several different methods; once the result of a vote has been announced in the Senate, the demand for a different kind of vote is not in order.

Roll calls are much easier to obtain and more frequently taken in the Senate than in the House. As in the House, they are available upon demand of one-fifth of those present, but in practice a Senator is seldom denied a roll-call vote on an issue if he insists on one. Roll calls usually are planned and announced in advance. They take far less time than in the House because the Senate is so much smaller. Yeas and nays are required on a vote to override a veto. The Vice President votes only in case of a tie.

Pairs. Pairs are "gentlemen's agreements" used by Members of the House and Senate to cancel out the effect of absences on roll-call votes. A Member who expects to be absent for a roll call pairs off with another Member, both of them agreeing not to vote. Pairs are not counted in vote totals, although the names of lawmakers pairing on a given vote and their stands, if known, are printed in the *Congressional Record*. If the roll call is one that requires a two-thirds majority, a pair requires two Members favoring the action to one opposed to it.

A *live pair* covers one or several specific issues. A Member who would vote "yea" pairs with a Member who would vote "nay." Thus both announce their stands. Live pairs may determine the outcome of a vote if a Member who is present withholds his vote because he has a pair with one who is absent.

A *general pair,* widely used in the House, is a more arbitrary method of matching absent Congressmen, not involving announcement of their stands. No agreement is involved and the pair does not tie up votes. A Representative expecting to be absent may notify the House Clerk that he wishes to make a general pair. His name is then paired with that of another Member desiring a general pair, and the list is printed in the *Congressional Record.* He may or may not be paired with a Member taking the opposite position.

committee to take charge of the bill on the floor or subordinates his personal views and devotes every effort to securing its consideration and passage in the form in which reported to the House. He is precluded from accepting modifications and is under the obligation of interposing points of order against vulnerable amendments although personally he may approve of them. If for exceptional reasons he deems it necessary to offer an amendment or digress from the instructions under which the bill was reported, he should yield his seat to the next ranking member and explain unequivocally that the action is taken in his individual capacity and not as a member of the committee. So binding are the obligations of a chairman in the handling of a bill reported by his committee that charges to the effect that he is not sincerely cooperating to secure its passage give rise to a question of privilege."

The rule under which the bill is considered provides for a certain number of hours of general debate to be divided equally between the chairman and ranking minority member of the committee that reported the bill. The chairman controls time for supporters of the bill, the ranking minority member for opponents. Usually each opens and closes debate for his side and yields remaining time first to other committee members, then to other Representatives who wish to speak. No amendments may be offered during general debate.

At the conclusion of general debate under an open rule, the bill is read for amendment under the five-minute rule. This constitutes the second reading of the bill. The measure may be read section by section (or line by line, title by title, etc.), with amendments in order to each section as it is read, or it may be considered as read and open to amendment at any point. Debate on an amendment is limited to five minutes for supporters and five minutes for opponents, but additional time may be obtained by offering pro forma amendments to "strike out the last word." In contrast to Senate practice, amendments must be germane, not only to the bill but also to the section to which they are offered.

Committee amendments are always taken up first but may be changed, as may all amendments, up to the second degree; an amendment to an amendment to an amendment is not in order. Although amendments in the third degree are not permitted, up to four amendments in the first and second degree may be pending at the same time: an amendment to the bill, an amendment to the amendment, a substitute for the original amendment and an amendment to the substitute. They are voted on in the following order, as diagrammed in *Cannon's Procedure:*

TEXT

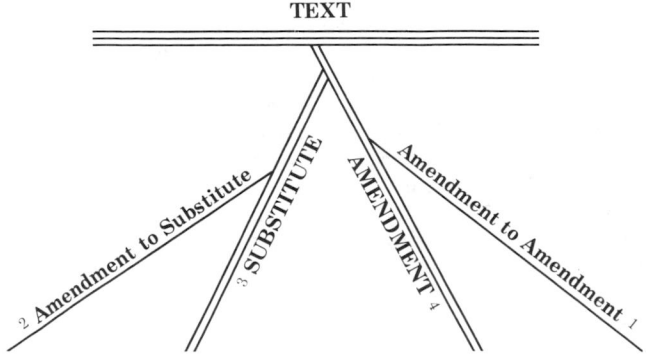

If the substitute is agreed to, the fourth vote is on the amendment as amended by the substitute.

More than one vote may be taken on a given amendment. The Committee of the Whole may first take a voice vote, then move on to standing and/or teller votes before finally deciding a question. (Amendments accepted in Committee of the Whole also are subject to roll-call votes after the bill is reported to the full House.)

The mark of an accomplished floor manager is his ability to get his bill through the House intact, and in voting on amendments Representatives are under considerable pressure to support the actions of the committee that reported the bill. Expressing the traditional view of the House hierarchy, Cannon gives the following advice to Members:

"Generally speaking, and in the absence of convictions to the contrary, Members are justified in voting with the committee. Committees are not infallible but they have had long familiarity with the subject under discussion, and have made an intimate study of the particular bill before the House and after mature deliberation have made formal recommendations and, other considerations being equal, are entitled to support on the floor. *Members should be particularly wary of proponents of amendments disapproved by the committee who station Members or employees at the doors to accost Members arriving in response to the bells and who have not heard the debate.* It is a questionable practice and should serve to put Members on their guard until they have ascertained the committee's point of view."

The Legislative Reorganization Act of 1970 provides for 10 minutes of debate on any amendment offered on the floor—even if debate has been closed on the section to which the amendment is proposed—so long as the amendment has been printed in the *Congressional Record* at least one day before consideration. Previously, an amendment received no explanation at all during consideration of a bill when a majority of the Committee of the Whole agreed to cut off debate on a section before there had been any debate on the amendment.

Action by the Full House

When the Committee of the Whole has completed action on a bill, it "rises," the Speaker returns to the chair, and the erstwhile chairman of the Committee of the Whole reports the action of the Committee and its recommendations. Only amendments *adopted* in Committee of the Whole are reported to the House.

If the previous question has been ordered, the full House votes immediately on amendments reported by the Committee. At this point Members may demand a roll call on any amendment adopted in Committee of the Whole. There is no way to obtain another vote on an amendment rejected in the Committee of the Whole unless it can be incorporated in a recommittal motion with instructions.

(The previous question motion is a device to cut off debate and force a vote on the subject under consideration. Unless it is ordered, the bill and amendments would be subject to further debate and amendment. The previous question is not used in the Senate.)

Once the amendments have been disposed of, the question is on engrossment and third reading (by title

Obstruction in the House

Although stringent House curbs on debate preclude a filibuster in the Senate fashion, Members sometimes make use of parliamentary stalling tactics with similar effect.

A dramatic example of dilatory tactics that became the equivalent of a Senate filibuster was given in 1968. The stalling maneuvers delayed adjournment a few days and at one point kept the House in continuous session for 32 hours and 17 minutes, the longest sitting in 93 years. Three bills were involved—a legislative reorganization bill, a campaign spending reform measure and a bill to permit television debates among the three major Presidential candidates. All failed of enactment.

The principal delaying effort came Oct. 8 and 9 when Republicans—saying they sought action on the reform bills—forced the House to stay in its third longest session in history before it passed the TV debate bill. When Senate Republicans—also using delaying maneuvers—succeeded in having the measure killed, a group of House Democratic liberals then used stalling tactics to hold up adjournment from Oct. 10 to Oct. 14 in an unsuccessful effort to force the Senate to act on the TV bill.

On Oct. 8 the Republican group combined full reading of the Journal, 33 quorum calls, three roll-call votes and other tactics to delay proceedings for 20 hours before the House considered the TV debate bill. Democrats asserted that Republican Presidential candidate Richard M. Nixon did not want to debate his Democratic opponent, Vice President Hubert H. Humphrey, while the Republicans responded that they were concerned with the two reform measures.

During the entire 32-hour, 17-minute Oct. 8-9 session, 45 roll calls were taken (37 quorum calls and 8 record votes). The doors of the House were closed during quorum calls for the first time since 1950 and later were locked for the first time since 1917.

According to the Congressional Research Service of the Library of Congress, the Oct. 8-9 session was surpassed in length only twice: by a 46-hour, 25-minute session in 1875 on a civil rights bill, and by a 35½-hour session in 1854 on the Kansas-Nebraska bill.

motion to reconsider, and this motion itself may be followed by a move to lay the motion on the table. Usually those voting for the bill's passage vote for the tabling motion, thus safeguarding the final passage action. With that, the bill has been formally passed by the chamber. While a motion to reconsider is pending, the bill cannot be sent to the Senate.

At this point, the bill officially becomes an "act," although it continues generally to be referred to as a bill. An engrossed copy of the bill as passed by the House, certified by the Clerk of the House, is printed on blue paper and transmitted to the Senate for its action.

Alternative House Procedures

The procedures described above indicate the usual route of a major bill through the House, but certain alternative methods, described below, are available.

Consent Calendar. Members of the House may place on this calendar any bill on the House or Union Calendar which is considered to be noncontroversial. Bills on the Consent Calendar are normally called on the first and third Mondays of each month. When a bill is called in this manner the first time, consideration may be blocked by the objection of any Member. The second time, if there are three objections, the bill is stricken from the Consent Calendar; if less than three Members object, the bill is given immediate consideration. Each party assigns official objectors to police the Consent Calendar and to act for absent Members.

A bill on the Consent Calendar may be postponed in another way. A Member may ask that the measure be passed over "without prejudice." In that case, no objection is recorded against the bill, and its status on the Consent Calendar remains unchanged.

A bill stricken from the Consent Calendar remains on the Union or House Calendar.

Suspension of the Rules. This is often a time-saving procedure for passing bills in the House. The wording of the motion, which may be made by any Member recognized by the Speaker, is: "I move to suspend the rules and pass the bill...." A favorable vote by two-thirds of those present is required for passage. Debate is limited to 40 minutes and no amendments from the floor are permitted. If a two-thirds favorable vote is not obtained, the bill may be considered later under regular procedures.

Suspension of the rules is in order on the first and third Mondays of the month and during the last six days of the session, but it may occur at other times as well. The Speaker has absolute power of recognition, but the rules direct that individuals be given preference on the first Monday and committees on the third.

Discharge Petition. The discharge petition is a little-used device designed to permit a majority of Representatives to bring to the House floor legislation blocked by a legislative committee or by the Rules Committee.

The modern discharge rule was first adopted in 1910. The present form of the rule, adopted in 1935, enables a majority of the House to bring to the House floor after a complicated series of parliamentary steps: (1) any public bill that has been before a standing committee of the House for 30 days; or (2) any committee-

only) of the bill. A Member opposed to the bill may offer a motion to recommit the measure to the committee that reported it. There are two kinds of recommittal motions: a simple motion to recommit, which defeats the bill if it is adopted; or a motion to recommit with instructions (to report the bill back with amendments, after study, by a certain date, etc.). The motion to recommit with instructions, on which 10 minutes of debate is allowed under the 1970 Act, is frequently used by the minority to present an alternative program. Although recommittal votes seldom succeed, they often provide a better test of Members' views than a vote on passage.

If the recommittal vote fails, the next question is on final passage. That vote may be followed by a pro forma

Discharge Petition

The discharge petition is a little-used device designed to enable a majority of Representatives to bring to the House floor legislation blocked by a legislative committee or the Rules Committee.

The following table shows the extent to which the discharge petition was used between its adoption in 1910 and the close of the 91st Congress in 1971. Although 24 bills were pried loose from committee by the discharge method and 20 of them ultimately passed the House, only two were finally enacted: the Fair Labor Standards Act of 1938 and the 1960 Federal pay raise bill.

Congress	Petitions Filed	Bills Discharged	Discharged Bills That Passed House
61 (1909-11)	223	figures not available	
62-67 (1911-23)	241		
68 (1923-25)	4	1	0
69 (1925-27)	4	0	0
70 (1927-29)	2	0	0
71 (1929-31)	5	0	0
72 (1931-33)	12	1	1
73 (1933-35)	31	1	1
74 (1935-37)	33	2	0
75 (1937-39)	43	3	2
76 (1939-41)	37	2	2
77 (1941-43)	15	1	1
78 (1943-45)	21	3	3
79 (1945-47)	35	1	1
80 (1947-49)	20	1	1
81 (1949-51)	34	3	3
82 (1951-53)	14	0	0
83 (1953-55)	10	1	1
84 (1955-57)	6	0	0
85 (1957-59)	7	1	1
86 (1959-61)	5	1	1
87 (1961-63)	6	0	0
88 (1963-65)	5	0	0
89 (1965-67)	6	1	1
90 (1967-69)	4	0	0
91 (1969-71)	12	1	1
TOTAL	835	24	20

approved bill that has been before the House Rules Committee for seven legislative days without receiving a special rule for floor debate. In addition, the discharge rule may be used to dislodge from the Rules Committee a special rule for debate on a bill that has been before a standing committee for 30 days—a combination of the first two procedures.

This is how the procedure works: If a bill has been before a legislative committee for 30 days (or the Rules Committee for seven days), any Member may file a discharge motion, popularly called a discharge "petition." When 218 Members, a majority of the House, have signed the petition, it is placed on the Discharge Calendar where it must remain for seven legislative days before it can be called up. This seven-day "grace

period" makes it possible for the committee, if it chooses, to act on the bill before the discharge petition is considered. On the second and fourth Mondays of each month, except during the last six days of a session, any Member who has signed the petition may be recognized to move that the committee be discharged. Debate on the motion is limited to 20 minutes, equally divided between proponents and opponents, and if the motion carries, consideration of the bill becomes a matter of high privilege. The House may consider the measure immediately or place it on one of the calendars.

Although the discharge method is seldom used successfully, the threat of such a move may be used to spur committee action. *(For actual use of the discharge petition since 1910, see box.)*

Calendar Wednesday. This is a method for bringing to the House floor a bill that has been blocked by the Rules Committee. Under the procedure, each Wednesday committees may be called in the order in which they appear in Rule 10 of the House Manual (that is, alphabetically), for the purpose of bringing up any of their bills from the House or Union Calendars, except bills that are privileged. General debate is limited to two hours. Bills called up from the Union Calendar are considered in Committee of the Whole and amendments are taken up under the five-minute rule. Since the Calendar Wednesday procedure requires action to be completed in the same legislative day, it is vulnerable to dilatory action by opponents of the bill in question.

Calendar Wednesday is not observed during the last two weeks of a session and may be dispensed with at other times by a two-thirds vote. In practice, it usually is dispensed with by unanimous consent.

Between 1950 and 1970 the procedure was used successfully only twice: Feb. 15, 1950, in connection with the Fair Employment Practices Act, and May 4, 1960, in connection with the Area Redevelopment Act.

Other Methods. Special legislative days are set aside twice each month for the consideration of private bills and District of Columbia business. These procedures are described in detail in Chapter III.

The so-called "21-day rule," a device under which legislative committees could bring to the floor bills that had been blocked by the Rules Committee, was in force in the House in the 81st (1949-51) and 89th (1965-67) Congresses. The 1965 rule permitted the chairman or any other member of a committee that had favorably reported a bill to bring a rule (authorizing House action on the bill) directly to the floor for adoption by majority vote. This was permitted on the second or fourth Monday of the month, if the Rules Committee had not granted clearance to the bill within 21 calendar days after a resolution to call up the bill had been filed by the legislative committee. Discretion remained with the Speaker to recognize the member from the committee, so that it was highly unlikely, if not impossible, for a bill to come up successfully under this procedure without leadership approval. (The 1949 rule *required* the Speaker to recognize the Member who was calling up a 21-day resolution.) The 21-day rule was employed successfully only eight times in the 89th Congress, but the threat of its use was credited with bringing about the release of other bills from the Rules Committee.

Senate Floor Procedures

Although the Senate has an elaborate framework of parliamentary machinery to guide its deliberations, in practice its procedures are far more flexible than those of the House. Almost anything can be done by unanimous consent, or the rules can be suspended by a two-thirds vote.

Bills may be brought to the Senate floor on call of the calendar (a process described below) or they may be called up through adoption, by majority vote, of a motion to consider a particular measure. A motion to consider a bill is not debatable if it is made during the morning hour (before 2 p.m.); after that hour it is subject to debate which can only be limited by invoking cloture. In practice, most major bills are taken up by unanimous consent in accord with the schedule worked out by the Majority Leader.

Unlike the House, the Senate does not consider bills in Committee of the Whole, and it does not set aside a period for general debate before the amending process begins.

Once he is recognized by the presiding officer, a Senator may speak virtually as long as he likes and on any subject he chooses unless he violates the rules of the Senate. He may yield temporarily for the consideration of other business, or he may yield to another Senator for a question, but he may not parcel out time to other Members as is the practice in the House. Under the rules, no Senator is permitted to speak more than twice on the same subject in the same legislative day; however, since each amendment is considered a different subject, this is not an effective limit on debate. Under a rule adopted in 1964, debate is required to be germane for three hours following the morning hour, but this stricture usually is ignored.

The previous question as a device for bringing debate to a close is not used in the Senate. The only bar to unlimited debate is the cloture rule (Rule 22), which requires the assent of two-thirds of those present and voting to cut off debate. This rule is discussed in detail below.

In practice, unanimous consent agreements are widely used to expedite business and schedule votes. In a typical situation the procedure is as follows: After debate on a bill (or amendment, motion, etc.) has gone on for some time, the Majority Leader will consult with the Minority Leader and other interested Senators in an effort to work out an agreement on control of remaining debate and the time of voting. Because a single objection will block a unanimous consent request, care is taken to protect the rights of all Senators and to assure that those who wish to speak will have an opportunity to do so. The Majority Leader then rises on the floor and, following a quorum call to alert absent Senators, asks for unanimous consent to end debate and vote at a particular time.

Amendment Process in Senate

When a bill is taken up, it is immediately open to virtually unlimited amendment. Committee amendments are taken up first and, like other amendments, may be amended to the second degree. Frequently the Senate by unanimous consent agrees to the committee amendments en bloc and provides that the bill as amended be considered as an original text for the pur-

---

Roll-Call Vote Records

The 91st Congress took 1,110 roll-call votes (excluding quorum calls), the highest number in at least two decades. The high for a single year was in 1970 when 688 roll calls were taken. Both chambers set individual highs in 1970.

Year	House	Senate	Total
1970*	266	422	688
1969	177	245	422
1968	233	281	514
1967	245	315	560
1966	193	235	428
1965	201	258	459
1964	113	305	418
1963	119	229	348
1962	124	224	348
1961	116	204	320
1960	93	207	300
1959	87	215	302
1958	93	200	293
1957	100	107	207
1956	73	130	203
1955	76	87	163
1954	76	171	247
1953	71	89	160
1952	72	129	201
1951	109	202	311
1950	154	229	383
1949	121	227	348
1948	79	189	268
1947	84	138	222

through Jan. 2, 1971.

---

pose of further amendment. Substitute amendments are in order, in which case both the original amendment and the substitute would be open to amendment at the same time. The text of one bill may be offered as a substitute for another.

Except in the case of general appropriations bills, amendments need not be germane. An amendment may be modified or withdrawn before some action has been taken on it; once adopted, an amendment is not subject to further amendment unless a motion to reconsider the previous action is adopted by majority vote. Occasionally a bill's floor manager will agree to inclusion of an amendment, saying he will "take it to conference"; it is likely to die there. Pro forma amendments, used in the House to gain additional speaking time, are not offered in the Senate since debate is unlimited anyway.

Voting in the Senate is by voice, division (standing) or roll-call vote. There is no teller vote, and, unlike the House, the Senate uses only one method of voting on a single question. Roll calls, required on demand of one-fifth of those present, are easily obtained and the Senate takes many more such votes than the House does. *(For description of voting methods, see box above.)*

When action on amendments is completed, the bill is ready for engrossment and third reading (usually by title only), followed by the vote on passage. A motion to reconsider may be offered by any Senator on the winning

Symbols of Authority: Mace and Gavel

Mace in the House. The most treasured possession of the House of Representatives is the mace, a traditional symbol of legislative authority. The concept, which the House borrowed from the British House of Commons, had its origin in Republican Rome, where the fasces—an axe bound in a bundle of rods—symbolized the power of the magistrates.

The mace was adopted by the House in its first session in 1789 as a symbol of office for the Sergeant at Arms, who is charged with preserving order on the House floor. The first mace was destroyed when the British burned the Capitol in 1814, and for the next 27 years a mace of painted wood was used. The present mace, in use since 1841, is a replica of the original mace of 1789. It consists of a bundle of 13 ebony rods bound in silver, terminating in a silver globe topped by a silver eagle with outstretched wings—46 inches high in all. It was made by William Adams, a New York silversmith, for the sum of $400.

The Sergeant at Arms, custodian of the mace, is charged with its use when necessary to preserve order. There have been a number of occasions in the history of the House when the Sergeant at Arms, on order of the Speaker, has lifted the mace from its pedestal and "presented" it before an unruly Member. On each such occasion order is said to have been promptly restored. At other times the Sergeant at Arms, bearing the mace, has passed up and down the aisles to quell boisterous behavior in the chamber.

The mace also serves a second purpose. When the House is in regular session, it rests on a tall green marble pedestal at the right of the Speaker's desk, but when the House is sitting in Committee of the Whole it is moved to a low white marble pedestal nearby. Thus, upon entering the chamber a Representative can tell at a glance whether the House is meeting in regular session or in Committee of the Whole.

Gavel in the Senate. The Senate has no mace, but it cherishes to an almost equal degree another symbol—a small silver-capped ivory gavel without a handle which, according to tradition, was used by Vice-President Adams in calling the first Senate to order in 1789. Evidence exists that it was in use at least as early as 1831, and it remained in use until 1954 when it began to disintegrate beyond repair.

A replica of the old gavel, a gift of the Government of India, was presented to the Senate on Nov. 17, 1954. On that occasion Vice President Richard M. Nixon offered this assurance: "For the benefit of those who have been in the galleries in the past, and those who will be there in the future, we shall place the old gavel, which no longer can be used because it is coming apart, in a box, which will be kept on the Senate rostrum while the Senate is in session. We shall use in its place the gavel of solid ivory, which has been presented to us...by the largest democracy in the world."

Accordingly, since that time a case containing both the old and the new gavels is carried into the Senate chamber and placed on the Vice President's desk just before the opening of each Senate session. The new gavel is removed from the case for use by the presiding officer; the old gavel is not used but remains on the desk in its case, a symbol of the continuity of the Senate.

---

side, or one who did not vote, within two days of that vote. If the bill passed without a record vote, any Senator may make the motion. In practice, a pro forma motion to reconsider usually is offered and in turn tabled, in order to nail down the final action.

Motions to recommit are seldom used in the Senate, perhaps because the amending process is so much more flexible than it is in the House.

Alternative Senate Procedures

Because the normal Senate procedures are so flexible, there is less need than in the House for alternative methods of bringing bills to the floor. In the Senate reported bills usually can be taken up without difficulty, and legislative obstruction is more likely to occur on the floor, in the form of a filibuster.

Reported bills may be taken up on call of the calendar, which is used for noncontroversial legislation similar to bills on the Consent Calendar in the House. Although the calendar may be called following the conclusion of morning business on any day and is privileged on Mondays, it usually is called only once or twice a month. When the calendar is called, bills that are not objected to are taken up in order and each Senator is limited to five minutes' debate on each bill. If objection is raised, the bill may either be passed over or, upon motion, considered. If the majority votes to proceed with consideration of the bill, the five-minute rule no longer applies.

Under the Discharge Rule, any Senator during the morning hour may submit a motion to discharge a committee from further consideration of proposed legislation. The motion must lie over for one legislative day; it then may be brought up and a simple majority vote is sufficient to discharge the committee. This procedure is seldom used.

A more common method of forcing action on a legislative proposal is by offering it as a floor amendment to a pending bill. Since, except in the case of general appropriations bills, there is no Senate rule requiring amendments to be germane to the bill to which they are offered, this is a simple way of bringing a bill to the floor. An outstanding example occurred in 1960 when the Senate leadership made good on a promise to act on civil rights legislation, although none had been reported by the Judiciary Committee. It did so by calling up a minor House-passed bill and inviting Senators to offer civil rights amendments to it. In 1965, Sen. Everett McKinley Dirksen (R Ill.) brought to the floor a minor baseball bill and then succeeded in substituting for its text the text of a proposed constitutional amendment, blocked by the Judiciary Committee, which dealt with state legislative apportionment.

Tax legislation is frequently subject to non-germane riders for a special reason: the Constitution requires that revenue measures originate in the House, which means in the Ways and Means Committee; the Senate is restricted to amending House-passed tax bills. The Senate does not often load a bill with unrelated amendments, but when it does the event can be spectacular. An example was the 1966 Foreign Investors Tax Act, which became known as the "Christmas Tree Bill" because of the multitude of unrelated amendments added in committee and on the floor—among them an amendment to establish a Presidential Election Campaign Fund, which was itself killed by a non-germane rider to another tax bill the following year.

Senate riders sometimes are the result of logrolling, sometimes are accepted out of courtesy to the sponsoring Senator who has a strong interest in the proposal, and sometimes are approved simply because they are popular but with the knowledge that they will be quietly dropped in conference later.

In the case of a House-passed bill, another method of bypassing committees is available: Senate rules provide that a House-passed bill may be placed directly on the Senate calendar without being referred to committee. This method was used to keep the civil rights bills of 1957 and 1964 out of the hostile Senate Judiciary Committee.

Senate Cloture Rule

The Senate's ultimate check on the filibuster is the provision for cloture, or limitation of debate, contained in Rule 22 of its Standing Rules.

As last amended in 1959, Rule 22 provides for winding up debate by a two-thirds vote of the Senators present and voting, taken two days after a cloture motion has been filed by 16 Senators. Following adoption of a cloture motion, debate is limited to one hour for each Senator on the bill itself and on all motions and amendments affecting it. No new amendments may be offered except by unanimous consent. Amendments that are not germane to the pending business and amendments and motions clearly designed to delay action are out of order. The rule applies both to ordinary business and to motions to change the Senate rules.

The original Rule 22 was adopted by the Senate in 1917 following a furor over the "talking to death" of President Woodrow Wilson's proposal, before American entry into World War I, to arm American merchant ships against the German submarine menace. In its 1917 form, Rule 22 required two-thirds of the Senators present and voting to invoke cloture. Over the years, however, a series of rulings and precedents made the rule virtually inoperative by holding that it could not be applied to debate on procedural questions, although it could be used on attempts to change Senate rules.

In 1949, when the Truman Administration was seeking enactment of a civil rights measure, the rule was changed to require two-thirds of the entire Senate membership to invoke cloture, but it allowed cloture to operate on any pending business or motions, with the exception of debate on motions to change the Senate rules themselves.

In 1959, the rule was changed again, largely at the instigation of then Majority Leader Lyndon B. Johnson (D Texas). Under the 1959 rule, once again cloture could be imposed by two-thirds of those present and voting, and it could be applied to motions to change the Senate rules. At the same time, language was added to Senate Rule 32 stating that: "The rules of the Senate shall continue from one Congress to the next unless they are changed as provided in these rules."

The language added to Rule 32 was aimed at a key question with which the Senate had wrestled for years: Was the Senate, since one-third of its membership was elected every two years, a continuing body which should operate under rules carried over from Congress to Congress, or should it adopt new rules by general parliamentary procedure—majority vote—at the beginning of each Congress? (The House, all of whose Members are elected every two years, adopts its rules at the beginning of each Congress.) If the Senate was a continuing body, rules changes could be talked to death unless two-thirds of the membership supported the proposed changes and would support cloture. If not, a filibuster could be stopped by majority vote at the beginning of a new Congress and substantive proposals for changes in the rules could be voted on. The language added to Rule 32 buttressed the position of those who maintained that the Senate was a continuing body, but liberal opponents of the filibuster never conceded the point and continued their efforts to liberalize the cloture rule at the beginning of each new Congress.

Between 1917 and final adjournment of the 91st Congress in 1971, 49 votes were taken on cloture motions; only eight were successful. (*See History of the Senate, Chapter I.*)

Action in Second House

After a bill has been passed by one house, an engrossed copy is transmitted to the other house.

When the Senate receives a House-passed bill, usually it refers the measure to the appropriate committee, which frequently already is considering a similar measure. However, on rare occasions the House-passed bill is referred directly to the Senate calendar. A bill first passed by the Senate and transmitted to the House must go to committee unless a similar House bill has already been reported from committee and placed on the calendar.

Under normal procedure, then, a bill passed by one chamber and transmitted to the other is referred to the appropriate committee, from which it must follow the same route to passage as a bill originating in that chamber. Amendments may be offered at both the committee and floor action stages, and the bill as it emerges from the second house may differ significantly from the version passed by the first. Frequently, one chamber may approve a version of a bill that is greatly at variance with the version already passed by the other house, and then substitute its text for the language of the other, retaining only the latter's bill designation.

If a bill is passed in identical form by both House and Senate, no further legislative action is required. But if the versions passed by the two chambers are not identical, all differences must be reconciled before the measure can be sent to the President.

If the second house has made changes in the bill, it may simply return it to the chamber of origin, which then has the option of accepting the other chamber's amendments, accepting with further amendments or disagreeing and requesting a conference. Or the second house itself may request a conference at the time it returns the bill to the chamber of origin. Only the chamber in possession of the "papers"—engrossed bill, engrossed amendments and messages of transmittal—can request a conference.

If the amendments are of a minor or noncontroversial nature, they usually are agreed to without a conference. Major amendments sometimes are accepted to avoid further floor action that might end in scuttling the bill.

Under the Legislative Reorganization Act of 1970 a separate House vote may be taken, upon the request of any Member, on any nongermane amendment added by the Senate to a House-passed bill.

Conference

Sen. Bennett Champ Clark of Missouri once introduced a resolution providing that "all bills and resolutions shall be read twice and, without debate, referred to conference." He was joking, of course, but his proposal highlights the crucial role of the conference committee in hammering out the final form of legislation.

A conference cannot take place until both chambers formally agree that it be held. The Senate usually requests or agrees to a conference by unanimous consent. In the House this action generally is taken either by unanimous consent or by majority adoption of a rule from the Rules Committee providing for a conference on a particular bill. Prior to 1965, the House could bypass the Rules Committee only by unanimous consent or by suspension of the rules, for which a two-thirds majority is required. Since 1965, it has been possible to send a bill to conference by simple majority vote, without recourse to the Rules Committee, if the committee with jurisdiction over the bill approves. This method is seldom employed.

Although conferees (known as "managers") theoretically are appointed by the presiding officers of the two chambers, in practice they are designated by the chairmen of the committees that considered the bill. Both majority and minority parties are represented, and seniority ordinarily governs the selection. On a major bill, the chairman usually selects himself, the ranking minority member and other senior members of the committee to staff the conference delegation. Where a subcommittee has exercised major responsibility for a bill, its senior members may be chosen. Only rarely will a conferee be appointed who is not on the appropriate committee.

The number of conferees from each chamber may vary, with from 3 to 15 or more Members in each group, depending on the length or complexity of the legislation involved. There may be five Senators and three Representatives on the conference committee, or the reverse. But a majority vote controls the action of each group so that a larger representation does not give one chamber a voting advantage over the other chamber's conferees.

The Legislative Reorganization Act of 1946 stipulates that conferees must have demonstrated support for the bill which passed their chamber, but this provision is not enforced.

All conference committee meetings are held in executive session—closed to the public and to the press. No minutes are taken and no official records of debate or voting are kept. Staff aides or other expert assistants may be permitted to attend. Traditionally, most conferences have taken place on the Senate side of the Capitol.

Authority of Conferees

The authority of the conferees theoretically is limited to matters in disagreement between the two chambers; they are not authorized to delete matter agreed to by both the Senate and the House nor to bring in entirely new provisions. When the disagreement involves numbers, conferees are limited to the range between the figure proposed by one house and the figure proposed by the other.

In practice, however, the conferees have wide latitude except where the matters in disagreement are very specific. When one house has struck out everything after the enacting clause and inserted a substitute for the bill approved by the other house, the entire subject is technically in disagreement and the conferees may report an entirely new bill if they choose to do so. In such a case, the Legislative Reorganization Act of 1946 stipulates that they may not include in their report "matter not committed to them by either house," but they may include "matter which is a germane modification of subjects in disagreement." The Legislative Reorganization Act of 1970 reinforced this provision by amending House rules to provide that any language concerning "a specific additional topic, question, issue or proposition" that neither chamber sent to conference "shall not constitute a germane modification of the matter in disagreement." It also forbade House conferees to modify any topic beyond the scope of the differing versions of the bill sent to conference.

Conference Bargaining

Some of the hardest bargaining in the entire legislative process takes place in the conference committee, and frequently the conference takes days or even weeks. Conferences on involved appropriations bills sometimes are particularly drawn out.

As a conference proceeds, conferees reconcile their differences, but generally they grant concessions only insofar as they remain sure that the chamber they represent will accept the compromises. Unwanted amendments that were hard to oppose publicly on the floor may be quietly weeded out. The threat of a Senate filibuster on the conference report may influence the conferees' deliberations. Time also may be a factor, especially at the end of a Congress when delay may cause a bill to die in conference.

If the conferees find they are unable to reach agreement, they may return to their respective chambers for instructions. (Conferees may be, but seldom are, instructed at the time of their appointment.) Or they may simply report their failure to reach agreement to the parent chamber and allow it to act as it wishes.

Under the rules, House conferees may be instructed or discharged and replaced if they fail to make a report within 20 calendar days of their appointment (or within 36 hours of their appointment during the last six days of a session). This rule was adopted in 1931 but has rarely been invoked.

The Conference Report

When the conferees have reached agreement, they prepare a conference report explaining their actions. One or more amendments may be "reported in disagreement"; these amendments are acted upon separately following floor action on the conference report.

The 1970 Reorganization Act prohibited House conferees from agreeing to a nongermane Senate amendment unless authorized to do so by a vote of the House. The House had often been forced to vote on the bill as a whole, having to defeat the bill or accept the nongermane amendment. The new rule applied the same rules to nongermane Senate amendments as were already applied to legislative amendments to appropriation bills. In practice, conferees reported such amendments in disagreement and moved for a House vote to agree to them.

The conference report must be signed in duplicate by a majority of conferees from each chamber and submitted in document form to each house for its approval. Minority reports are not permitted. Traditionally the report was printed only in the House, together with an explanation by the House conferees, but under the 1970 Act an explanatory statement must be prepared jointly by the House and Senate conferees and the conference report must be printed in the Senate as well as the House.

In both chambers consideration of conference reports is highly privileged and can interrupt most other business. The house that agreed to the conference acts first on the report, followed by the house that requested it. Approval of the report constitutes approval of the compromise bill.

Under the 1970 Act, conference reports are supposed to be available for three days before the House may consider them. The Act stipulated also that debate on a conference report was to be equally divided between the majority and minority in each chamber.

The House, though it does so infrequently, may send a completed conference report to its Rules Committee before the report reaches the floor. This has happened when the conferees inserted into a bill new material that might make the conference report subject to a point of order. The Rules Committee then may grant a rule waiving points of order against the report.

Conference reports cannot be amended; they must be accepted or rejected in their entirety, and they are very seldom rejected. They may be recommitted to the conferees, with or without instructions, but neither chamber may recommit a conference report after it has been approved by the other chamber, because approval constitutes discharge of that chamber's conferees. In such cases, a conference report can be recommitted only by concurrent resolution.

If amendments have been reported in disagreement, each chamber, after it acts on the conference report, votes separately on the disputed amendments just as if no conference had taken place on them. If agreement between the two houses is not achieved by this method, the conference procedure begins anew with respect to the amendments remaining in disagreement.

Conference Disputes

The conference machinery does not always work smoothly. In 1962 a feud between the Senate and House Appropriations Committees blocked conference action on major appropriation bills for months, and in 1970 several conference disputes marred the closing days of the 91st Congress.

The most frequently voiced complaint about the conference system is the charge—raised from time to time in both Senate and House—that conferees are not in sympathy with the position taken by their own chamber and do not sufficiently defend it against the opposition of the other chamber's conferees. This question figured in a 1970 dispute over continued provision of funds for development of the supersonic transport (SST) plane. The House had included $290 million for the plane in the fiscal 1971 Transportation Department appropriation bill; the Senate had provided no funds at all, but four of the seven Senate conferees had voted for full funding. The conferees, after only three hours of deliberation, agreed on $210 million. "If we stayed there until the cows came home, the answer would have been the same," said Senate conferee John O. Pastore (D R.I.). "The fact is that the House was adamant, but the Senate did try." The House promptly adopted the conference report, but in the Senate opponents of the SST launched a filibuster that delayed adjournment of the 91st Congress until an agreement on temporary funding was reached. Early in the 92nd Congress, both chambers voted to kill the SST program.

The SST dispute was one of several that Senate Majority Leader Mike Mansfield (D Mont.) had in mind in December 1970 when he said: "I think all too often the Senate compromises too much.... All I am asking is that Senators stand on their feet and not give in too often or too easily, as they do on occasion with the House."

Final Steps

After a bill has been passed by both the House and the Senate, all of the original papers are sent to the enrolling clerk of the chamber in which the bill originated. He then prepares an enrolled bill which is printed on parchment paper. When this bill has been certified as correct by the Secretary of the Senate or the Clerk of the House, depending on which chamber originated the bill, it is signed first (no matter whether it originated in Senate or House) by the Speaker of the House and then by the President of the Senate. It is next sent to the White House to await Presidential action.

The President has 10 days (Sundays excepted) from the time he receives the bill to act upon it. If he approves the measure, he signs it, dates it and usually writes the word "Approved" on the document. Under the Constitution, however, only his signature is required.

If the President does not want the bill to become law, he may veto it by returning it to the chamber in which it originated without his signature and with a message stating his objections. If no action on the message is taken there, the bill dies.

However, an attempt may be made to override the President's veto and enact the bill, "the objections of the President to the contrary notwithstanding." Such action requires a two-thirds vote of those present, who must number a quorum and vote by roll call. Debate may precede this vote, with motions permitted to lay the message on the table, to postpone action on it or to refer it to committee. If the vote to override the veto succeeds in the first house, the measure is sent to the second house for its action. If the veto is overridden by a two-thirds vote in both houses, the bill becomes law without the President's signature. But if either house fails to register a two-thirds vote for the bill, the veto stands, and the bill is dead.

A bill may become law without the President's signature, not only by the overriding of a veto, but also if the President fails to sign it within 10 days (Sundays excepted) from the time he receives it, provided Congress is in session. Under this provision, the President may occasionally permit the enactment of legislation that he does not care to veto but does not wish to approve affirmatively. But if Congress adjourns before the 10 days expire, a bill not signed by the President does not become law. It has been what is called pocket-vetoed.

The pocket veto was the subject of dispute in the closing days of the 91st Congress, when President Nixon took advantage of a six-day Congressional recess to pocket-veto a medical training bill. The measure had passed both houses by nearly unanimous votes, indicating that a regular veto would be overridden. Some Congressional critics of the President's action contended that he could not pocket-veto a bill during a brief recess, rather than following an adjournment, of Congress and that the bill actually had become law without his signature. The Justice Department argued that judicial precedents and the practice of other Presidents supported Nixon's exercise of the pocket-veto power in this case. The dispute was expected to be resolved in the courts.

When bills are passed finally and signed, or passed over a veto, they are given law numbers in numerical order as they become law. There are two series of numbers, one for public and one for private laws, starting at the number "1" for each two-year term of Congress. They are then identified by law number and by Congress—i.e., Private Law 21, 90th Congress; Public Law 250, 90th Congress (or PL 90-250).

Bibliography

Books

Bailey, Stephen K., *Congress Makes a Law.* Columbia University Press, 1950.

Binkley, Wilfrid E., *President and Congress.* Vintage edition, 1962.

Congressional Quarterly, *Congress and the Nation,* Vols. I and II, and annual *CQ Almanacs.*

Froman, Lewis A. Jr., *The Congressional Process.* Little, Brown, 1967.

Galloway, George B., *History of the United States House of Representatives.* Thomas Y. Crowell, 1961.

——— , *The Legislative Process in Congress.* Thomas Y. Crowell, 1953.

Gross, Bertram M., *The Legislative Struggle.* McGraw-Hill, 1953.

Luce, Robert, *Legislative Procedure.* Houghton Mifflin, 1922.

Riddick, Floyd M., *The U.S. Congress: Organization and Procedure.* National Capitol Publishers, 1949.

Wilson, Woodrow, *Congressional Government.* Meridian edition, 1956.

Government Publications

Cannon, Clarence, *Cannon's Procedure in the House of Representatives.* Government Printing Office, 1963.

Watkins, Charles L., and Riddick, Floyd M., *Senate Procedure, Precedents and Practices.* Government Printing Office, 1958.

Legislative Reorganization Act of 1970

Some significant changes in legislative procedure were approved by Congress in the Legislative Reorganization Act of 1970 (PL 91-510). The measure was designed to improve the operations of Congress, both in committee and on the floor, to provide Congress with better means of evaluating the Federal Budget and to improve Congressional research and information resources.

The product of a decade's effort by reform-minded Senators and Representatives, PL 91-510 constituted the first substantial attempt at Congressional reorganization since the Legislative Reorganization Act of 1946. That Act was never fully enforced and had proved only partially successful. Early experience with the 1970 Act suggested that it, too, might frequently be disregarded. *(See box.)*

Genesis of the Act

The 1970 Act grew out of a study by the Joint Committee on the Organization of the Congress in 1965-66. The Senate in 1967 passed a bill embodying most of the Joint Committee's recommendations, but that measure met stubborn opposition in the House and never reached the floor. Persistent pressure finally forced the House to pass a reform bill of its own in 1970; floor amendments substantially strengthened the modest reforms recommended by the House Rules Committee which reported the bill. Prospects for enactment of reform legislation in the 91st Congress seemed so poor that the Senate had decided not to consider any such measure unless the House acted first, but when the House-passed bill reached the upper chamber the Senate quickly added provisions relating to its own operations and the measure was enacted into law.

Neither the 1946 nor the 1970 Act was really a comprehensive reform measure. Questions directly involving the distribution of power within Congress were largely excluded from both Acts, and neither touched upon such sensitive and controversial subjects as the seniority system, the power of the House Rules Committee or limitation of debate in the Senate. *(For details of the 1946 Act, see Chapter I.)*

Principal Reforms

Nonetheless, the 1970 Act—like its predecessor—contained a number of provisions that promised to have a significant impact on the future actions of Congress. The most dramatic procedural reform was a provision that made it possible for House Members to be individually recorded on teller votes. Previously, many crucial questions had been decided by non-recorded teller votes while the House was sitting in Committee of the Whole; Members had voted in virtual anonymity, and often many of them did not vote at all.

In its second experience with the record teller-vote procedure, the House on March 18, 1971, voted to cut off funds for further development of the supersonic transport (SST) aircraft. In 1970, the House had voted $290 million for the plane, but the only record votes relating to the SST controversy were on procedural questions. Thus the record teller vote in 1971 marked the first occasion on which Representatives were directly recorded on the issue, and the House, reversing its earlier

---

Reforms Disregarded

The 92nd Congress, within two months after it convened in January 1971, had disregarded or suspended at least four key provisions of the Legislative Reorganization Act of 1970:

● The House agreed to disregard a provision of the 1970 Act that required one-third of each committee's investigative funds to be used to hire minority staff members.

● The Senate, in approving a resolution to create a Joint Committee on Environment, included language exempting appointments to the committee from a provision of the 1970 Act that limited Senators to one joint committee assignment.

● The House by unanimous consent waived a provision of the Act barring the House from considering a conference report until it had been printed and made available to Members for three days. The waiver, requested by Ways and Means Committee Chairman Wilbur D. Mills (D Ark.) in connection with a bill to raise the debt ceiling and increase Social Security benefits, also precluded any Member from requesting a separate House vote on the nongermane Social Security amendment, which the Senate had added to the bill. The procedure for a separate vote on nongermane Senate riders was established by the 1970 Act.

● Committees varied in their compliance with a provision specifying that the results of all record votes taken by committees to report bills to the floor must be printed in the committee reports, and that the positions of individual members on such votes must be made available to the public. Some committees complied in full with these provisions. However, the House Agriculture Committee, in reporting one bill, did not include the vote in its report, although it made it available upon request. And the Ways and Means Committee, in its report on the debt limit bill, included in its report the 20-3 vote by which its action was taken but did not make the names available, stating that no record vote was taken.

---

stand, voted 217-204 to delete the funds. "I think the teller vote made the difference," said Rep. Sidney R. Yates (D Ill.), a leader of the SST foes.

The 1970 Act opened to the public eye more of the operations of Congress and the positions of its Members by:

● Encouraging more open committee meetings and hearings.

● Requiring that all committee roll-call votes be made public.

● Allowing broadcasting and television coverage of committee hearings.

● Providing that House teller votes be recorded upon request, ending the secrecy surrounding Members' positions on important amendments.

The measure was expected to expedite House proceedings by:

- Allowing all House committees to sit without special leave while the House was in session so long as it was not reading a bill for amendment under the five-minute rule.
- Dispensing with the reading of the Journal unless the Speaker or a majority of the Members present so ordered.
- Allowing the call of the roll for a quorum to be suspended as soon as a quorum was obtained.

The law would safeguard the rights of the ideological or political minority by:
- Writing into the rules a specific time period for additional views to be added to a committee report.
- Allowing minority members of a committee to select two of the committee's six permanent professional staff.
- Stating that minority members could call witnesses of their choosing during at least one day of hearings on a measure or topic.
- Requiring that debate on a conference report be evenly divided between the majority and minority sides.

Provisions which might slow Congressional proceedings but which would give Members a better opportunity to base their votes on knowledge of a particular measure would:
- Require the committee report on a bill (and committee hearings on an appropriations bill) to be available for at least three days before the House or Senate voted on the bill.
- Allow 10 minutes debate on any amendment offered on the floor of the House which had been printed in the *Congressional Record* at least one day prior to consideration.
- Require a conference report to be available for three days before the House voted on its adoption.

The Act also provided for a modernized data processing system for Federal fiscal and budgetary information, closer scrutiny by Congress of the current and projected costs of all Federal programs, increased staff assistance for Congressional committees, and a continuing study of the operations of Congress by a joint committee.

Major Provisions of 1970 Act

Title I—The Committee System

The bill recognized the right of both the House and the Senate to change their own rules of procedure at any time. (The Constitution, Article I, Section 5, states: "Each House may determine the Rules of its Proceedings.")

HOUSE

It amended the rules of the House to:
- Provide that the ranking majority member of the committee preside at any meeting from which the chairman is absent. (This was already the custom in most committees.)
- Provide that committee business meetings and hearings be open to the public unless the committee by majority vote decides otherwise. (In 1970, 48 percent of all House committee meetings were closed to the public. The House Appropriations Committee was recorded as holding all its meetings behind closed doors; only 7 percent of the 1970 meetings of the House Education and Labor Committee were closed. *See Appendix.*)
- Require that all roll-call votes taken in committee—and each Member's vote—be made public and that committee reports on bills contain the vote by which the

committee ordered the bill reported. (Under existing rules, such votes were not necessarily made public.)
- Provide that committee reports on bills be filed within seven calendar days (excluding days the House was not in session) after a majority of the committee filed a written request that the report be submitted. This provision did not apply to the House Rules Committee with regard to House rules and House business. (Under existing rules, the chairman had the duty to report a bill and act to bring it to a vote on the floor.)
- Prohibit proxy voting in committee except when the committee's written rules permit it, when the proxy is limited to a specific matter, and is in writing, designating the person to whom it is given. (Proxy votes were not mentioned in existing House rules; different committees allowed them in different circumstances.)
- Allow committee members (who indicate this intention) three days (excluding Saturday, Sunday and legal holidays) to file supplementary, minority or additional views to be included with the committee report on a bill or other matter. This provision did not apply to the House Rules Committee. (There was no similar provision in existing rules; generally, time was allowed for the filing of such views.)
- Prohibit the House from considering any bill or other matter (except from the Appropriations, House Administration, Standards, or Rules Committees) unless the committee report on the measure has been available for at least three days (excluding Saturday, Sunday and legal holidays) prior to consideration. This rule did not apply to declarations of war or emergency, or to legislative veto procedures, or Executive reorganization plans. (There was no such provision in existing rules.)
- Prohibit the House from considering any general appropriations bill until printed committee hearings and the report on the bill have been available for at least three days (excluding Saturday, Sunday and legal holidays) prior to consideration. (A similar provision in existing House rules did not exclude Saturdays, Sundays and holidays.)
- Authorize the Speaker—if no motion is offered for House consideration of a bill within seven days after a rule for its consideration has been granted—to recognize a member of the committee that reported the bill to move for consideration, if so authorized by the committee.
- Specify procedures by which funds are provided to meet committee expenses. (Existing rules did not contain such provisions, but the procedures set forth were generally followed.)
- Require that no less than one-third of a committee's funds be used for minority staff. (There was no such provision in existing rules.)
- Require committees to announce hearings at least one week in advance unless there is good reason that they begin earlier. This provision did not apply to the House Rules Committee. (There was no such provision in existing rules.)
- Provide that a majority of the minority party members of a committee are entitled to call witnesses during at least one day of hearings on a matter. (Many committees by custom allowed minority members this opportunity.)
- Allow any open hearing to be broadcast over radio or television if a majority of the committee involved so

votes and if the broadcast is carried out in accordance with rules specifying that coverage shall be live, without commercial sponsorship; no subpoenaed witness be photographed, or the testimony broadcast, without his consent; and equipment be limited so as not to obstruct the hearings. (Broadcasting was not permitted under existing House rules.)

• Provide that all committees could sit without special leave while the House was in session except when a bill was being read for amendment under the five-minute rule. The five-minute rule limitation would not apply to the Appropriations, Government Operations, Internal Security, Rules, and Standards Committees. (Under existing rules, only the Government Operations, Rules, Standards, and Internal Security Committees could sit without special leave while the House was in session.)

• Require each standing committee (except the Appropriations, House Administration, Rules, and Standards Committees) to report annually on its review of the execution of laws enacted within its jurisdiction. (Committees already had this review function but had not been required to report on its exercise.)

• Allow 10 minutes' debate on any amendment offered on the floor—even if debate has been closed on the section to which the amendment is proposed—so long as the amendment has been printed in the *Congressional Record* at least one day before consideration. (Under existing rules, an amendment received no explanation at all during consideration of a bill when a majority of the Committee of the Whole agreed to cut off debate on a section before there had been any debate on the amendment.)

• Provide that, upon request of one-fifth of a quorum, a teller vote be recorded by clerks or electronic devices; that Members be given not less than 12 minutes to be counted; and that the record include the names of Members voting for, against and not voting on the question. (Under existing rules, only the outcome of such votes was recorded, not the positions of Members voting. All amendments were accepted or rejected in the Committee of the Whole by voice, standing, or teller votes, on which Members' positions remained unknown.)

• Provide that once a quorum is obtained, the call of the House for a quorum can be ended; that for 30 minutes from the beginning of the call Members may register their presence by signing in on tally sheets. (Under existing rules, once the call of the House for a quorum was begun, the entire roll had to be called, which took at least 30-35 minutes.)

• Provide for 10 minutes' debate on a motion to send a bill back to committee with instructions, with the time divided evenly between the person making the motion and the persons opposed. (In existing practice, a resolution issued by the Rules Committee for consideration of a bill usually specified that there would be no debate on a motion to recommit.)

• Require that every conference report be printed as a House report and be accompanied by an explanatory statement prepared jointly by House and Senate conferees. (In existing practice, the report was printed as a House report but only House conferees prepared such a statement.)

• Divide debate on a conference report evenly between majority and minority. (In existing practice, such time was not formally divided and was controlled by the chairman of the conferees.)

• Forbid conferees to include any language in a conference version of a bill which concerns a topic which neither chamber sent to conference; or to modify any topic beyond the scope of the differing versions of the bill sent to conference. (Existing rules stated that a conference report should not include matter not sent to conference by either chamber.)

• Prohibit the House from considering a conference report unless the report and accompanying statement have been printed in the *Congressional Record* three calendar days (excluding Saturday, Sunday and legal holidays) prior to consideration and copies are available on the floor. This rule would not apply during the last six days of a session. (Existing rules provided only that the House might not consider a conference report—except in the last six days of a session—until it had been printed in the *Congressional Record*, and conference reports were often brought up for a vote with little or no notice.)

• Allow a separate House vote, upon the request of any Member, on any nongermane amendment added by the Senate to a House-passed bill (requiring only a majority vote to approve the amendment); prohibit House conferees from agreeing to a nongermane Senate amendment unless authorized to do so by a vote on that amendment by the House. (In existing practice, the House had often been forced to vote on the bill as a whole, having to defeat the bill or accept the nongermane amendment. This new rule applied the same rules to nongermane Senate amendments as were already applied to legislative amendments to appropriations bills. In existing practice, conferees reported such amendments in disagreement and moved for a House vote to agree to them.)

• Direct that the Journal not be read daily unless the Speaker or a motion supported by a majority of the Members present so orders. (Such reading was routinely omitted by unanimous consent under existing practice, but the objection of one Member was enough to require that the Journal be read in full, a tactic occasionally used to delay or to force action on some measure.)

• Provide that the Resident Commissioner from Puerto Rico be elected to standing committees just as any elected Member of the House and that he be allowed to vote in committee. (Under existing rules, the Commissioner was an additional, nonvoting member of the Agriculture, Armed Services and Interior Committees.)

SENATE

Amended the Legislative Reorganization Act of 1946 to amend the rules of the Senate to:

• Allow a majority of a committee to call a meeting when the chairman does not call a meeting on request. (The House, but not the Senate, had this procedure available.)

• Provide that the ranking majority member of the committee preside at any meeting from which the chairman is absent. (This was already the custom in most committees.)

• Require that Senate committees adopt and publish rules of committee procedure. (Under existing rules, there was no such requirement.)

• Provide that committee business meetings be open to the public except during sessions to mark up bills, to vote or when the committee by majority vote decides otherwise. (In 1970, 33 percent of all Senate committee meetings were closed to the public, a much lower percentage than in the House. *See Appendix.)*

• Provide that committee hearings be open to the public except when the committee decides that the testimony may relate to national security, may reflect adversely on an individual's character or reputation or may contain confidential information.

• Require that all roll-call votes taken in committee on a measure or amendment—and the positions of Senators voting—be announced in the committee report on that measure unless previously made public.

• Provide that committee reports on bills be filed within seven calendar days (excluding days the Senate is not in session) after a majority of the committee files a written request that the report be filed.

• Provide that no proxy vote may be cast on a motion to report a bill if committee rules forbid the use of a proxy on such a motion; prescribe that proxies be voted only on such a motion upon the affirmative request of an absent member.

• Allow committee members (who indicate this intention) three days to file supplementary, minority or additional views to be included with the committee report on a bill or other matter. (There was no similar provision in existing rules; generally, time was allowed for the filing of such views.)

• Prohibit the Senate from considering any bill or other matter reported from a standing committee unless the committee report on the measure has been available for at least three days (excluding Saturday, Sunday and legal holidays) prior to consideration. This rule did not apply to declarations of war or emergency, to legislative veto procedures or to Executive reorganization plans, and could be waived by agreement of the Senate Majority and Minority Leaders. (There was no such provision in existing rules.)

• Specify procedures to govern procurement of funds for committees in excess of the annual $10,000 limit.

• Require committees (except the Senate Appropriations Committee) to announce hearings at least one week in advance unless there is good reason that they begin earlier. (There was no such provision in existing rules.)

• Provide that a majority of the minority party members of a committee (except the Senate Appropriations Committee) are entitled to call witnesses during at least one day of hearings on a matter. (Many committees by custom allowed minority members this opportunity.)

• Allow any open hearing to be broadcast over radio or television under whatever rules the committee may adopt.

• Forbid Senate committees (except the Appropriations Committee) to sit while the Senate is in session unless special leave has been obtained from the Senate Majority and Minority Leaders.

• Require each standing committee (except the Senate Appropriations Committee) to report annually on its activities reviewing the execution of laws enacted within its jurisdiction. (Committees already possessed this review function but had not been required to make reports.)

• Require that every conference report be printed as a Senate report and be accompanied by an explanatory statement prepared jointly by House and Senate conferees. (By existing custom, only House conferees prepared such a statement and conference reports were usually only printed as House reports.)

• Divide debate on a conference report evenly between majority and minority. (By existing custom, such time was not formally divided and was controlled by the chairman of the conferees.)

• Require a quorum of the Senate Appropriations Committee to be present for a vote to report an appropriations bill from committee. (This was Committee practice but existing rules exempted the Appropriations Committee from the requirement.)

• Rename the Senate Banking and Currency Committee the Senate Banking, Housing and Urban Affairs Committee.

• Reduce the size of certain Senate committees; provide that, in the future, Senators may be members of only two major committees and one minor, select, or joint committee; that no Senator may serve on more than one of the Armed Services, Appropriations, Finance or Foreign Relations Committees; that no Senator may hold the chairmanship of more than one full committee and one subcommittee of a major committee. (This provision would not deprive any Senator of any committee position or chairmanship currently held, but would apply to all future assignments.)

• Create a Senate Committee on Veterans' Affairs.

Title II—Fiscal Controls

• Directed the Secretary of the Treasury and the Director of the Office of Management and Budget to set up and maintain a standardized data processing system for Federal budgetary and fiscal data.

• Directed the Secretary and Director to furnish to Congressional committees, upon request, information on the location and nature of available data on Federal programs, activities, receipts and expenditures.

• Directed the Comptroller General to review and analyze the results of Government programs; to make cost benefit studies of the programs at the direction of Congress or on his own initiative or upon request of any Congressional committee; to assist Congressional committees in analyzing cost-benefit studies furnished by any Federal agencies or in conducting such studies.

• Required that the President send Congress—as part of the Budget—five-year forecasts of the costs of every new or expanded Federal program.

• Required that the President update the Budget for the next fiscal year and the five-year cost forecasts at midyear, beginning with 1972, and transmit to Congress a supplemental summary of those revisions by June 1 each year.

• Required the Comptroller General (or a designated employee of the General Accounting Office (GAO)) to explain to any Congressional committee so requesting any GAO report relevant to legislation, appropriations or programs within the committee's jurisdiction.

• Directed the Comptroller General to deliver copies of GAO reports to the Appropriations and Government Operations Committees and to any other committees requesting them.

• Limited to one year the period of time for which a GAO employee could be assigned fulltime to work with any Congressional committee.

• Required Federal agencies to report to the Government Operations Committees—no later than 60 days after a GAO report made recommendations concerning that agency—what action has been taken with respect to those recommendations.

• Required the House Appropriations Committee, within 30 days after the President sent the Budget to Congress, to hold hearings on the Budget and receive testimony from the Director of the Office of Management and Budget, the Secretary of the Treasury, and the chairman of the Council of Economic Advisers; and that such hearings be open except when the national security requires otherwise.

• Required that committee reports on all measures—except revenue bills—include cost estimates for the programs affected for that year and the next five years. This provision did not apply to the House Appropriations, Administration, Rules, and Standards Committees or the Senate Appropriations Committee.

Title III—Sources of Information

• Increased to six from four the number of permanent professional staff for each Congressional standing committee, two of whom, in addition to one of the six permanent clerical staff members, might be selected by a majority of the committee's minority party members. This provision did not apply to the House and Senate Appropriations Committees or to the House Standards Committee.

• Authorized standing committees—with the approval of the Senate Rules or House Administration Committee—to hire temporary consultants.

• Authorized standing committees—with the approval of the Senate Rules or House Administration Committee—to provide staff members with specialized training.

• Authorized salaries of Senate committee staff personnel comparable to those of House committee staff personnel.

• Redesignated the Legislative Reference Service the Congressional Research Service, redefining its duties to assist Congressional committees by providing research and analytical services, records, documents and other information and data, including memoranda on proposed legislation; and expanding its staff resources.

• Directed the House Parliamentarian, after the compilation of parliamentary precedents of the House

currently under way (the first since 1936) was completed, to compile such precedents every five years.

Title IV—Congress as an Institution

• Created a Joint Committee on Congressional Operations to continue the study of the operations and organization of Congress and to recommend improvements, including possible uses of automatic data processing systems.

• Abolished the Joint Committee on Immigration and Nationality Policy, which, established in 1952, had never met.

• Created a Capitol Guide Service to provide free tours of the Capitol.

• Provided that Congress take a 30-day recess in August of every nonelection year, unless it had already adjourned or a state of war existed.

• Converted the House payroll system from the base pay standard using 1945 figures to a gross pay standard reflecting the 17 pay raises since 1945 and showing the actual amounts paid to House employees.

• Provided that Senate pages be between 14 and 18 years old and that House pages be between 16 and 18; and authorized the construction of the John W. McCormack Residential Page School.

• Authorized the Speaker of the House to appoint a commission to plan and oversee the modernization of the House galleries, including the enclosure of the galleries with soundproof glass.

Title V—Office of the Legislative Counsel, House of Representatives

• Established the Office of Legislative Counsel for the House of Representatives, expanding and defining its duties.

Title VI—Effective Dates

• Provided that most of the provisions, with a few exceptions, would become effective immediately before noon Jan. 3, 1971.

The Parliamentarians of House and Senate

Two of the most influential—and publicly unnoticed—Capitol Hill officials are the Parliamentarians of the House and the Senate. Their roles extend far beyond that of mere arbiters of parliamentary practice.

Consulted by White House legislation-drafters, relied upon heavily by Congressional leaders, and sought out for advice by experienced Members of both parties, the Parliamentarians' influence is greatest in the guarded, private, behind-the-scenes procedural mechanics that transform an idea into a piece of enacted legislation.

The Parliamentarians, serving unbroken terms in Congress after Congress, become masters of the legal and technical skills which are the backbone of successful legislating. They are at home in the specialized Congressional world of bills, resolutions, amendments, rules, precedents and parliamentary maneuvering. And they are acknowledged experts in routing a bill to the right committee, preparing it for floor debate and protecting it from opposition attacks.

Long-Term Nature of the Job

Parliamentarians are appointed by the leadership of the House and Senate, but because of their highly skilled, technical functions, the Parliamentarians traditionally remain in office regardless of changes in political control of the two chambers. For example, the present House Parliamentarian, Lewis Deschler, has held the job since 1928. His counterpart in the Senate, Floyd M. Riddick, has been Parliamentarian since 1965, succeeding Charles L. Watkins, who had first become Parliamentarian in 1923.

The acquired experience of the Parliamentarians admits them to the innermost political councils. Deschler, for example, was a member of Speaker Sam Rayburn's "Board of Education." This was a group of House friends of the Speaker which would meet about sundown over drinks for political policy and strategy talks. Deschler drew key roles in preparing the 1957 civil rights bill for House action. He checked the draft bill to make sure the wording would permit consideration by a sympathetic committee. He checked committee changes in the measure to make sure the House germaneness rule still would bar unwanted floor amendments, and he cleared the rule for the bill, readying it for floor action. Because civil rights advocates and opponents both had sought parliamentary advice from Deschler, he could warn the Speaker of an upcoming floor fight and could predict the mood of the House.

Evolution of the Office

Despite the importance of the Parliamentarians, the origin of the office is uncertain. In the 19th century, presiding officers of the House and Senate either made their own parliamentary rulings or turned for advice to senior Members, or to senior clerks around the desk. Gradually it became a practice to rely on one of the clerks for advice on parliamentary matters. Finally, as sessions became longer, and legislation (and Congressional rules and precedents) became more complex, a separate

---

Congressional Parliamentarians

Listed below are persons who have performed the functions of Parliamentarian in the House and Senate. The House did not formally establish the post until 1927, the Senate not until 1937.

House

Charles R. Crisp	1891-95
Asher C. Hinds	1895-1911
Joel Bennett Clark	1911-15
Clarence Cannon	1915-21
Lehr Fess	1921-28
Lewis Deschler	1928-

Senate

Edward J. Hickey	(?)-1923
Charles L. Watkins	1923-65
Floyd M. Riddick	1965-

---

position was created with sole responsibility for parliamentary matters. The House established the post of Parliamentarian in 1927; the Senate followed suit in 1937. *(See box for list of Parliamentarians.)*

The position of Parliamentarian is an ambiguous one, with few clearly defined responsibilities. In fact, the Parliamentarians are available to perform virtually any task assigned by the leadership.

The Parliamentarians of the House and Senate, together with their assistants, do share some common functions. They advise the presiding officers on the always changing parliamentary situation and on parliamentary procedures. To do so a parliamentarian is present at all floor sessions, sitting directly in front of the presiding officer in the Senate, and just to his right in the House. The Parliamentarians are responsible for referring bills, resolutions and other communications to committees with proper jurisdiction. The Parliamentarians also prepare and maintain compilations of the precedents of each chamber.

The House Parliamentarian is appointed by the Speaker; the Senate Parliamentarian is appointed by the Secretary of the Senate.

Influence of Parliamentarians

For a number of reasons, the House Parliamentarian has emerged as a more influential figure than the Parliamentarian of the Senate.

In part, the disparity is a matter of differing personalities of the men who have held the posts. House Parliamentarian Deschler, whose long tenure has left an immense mark on the office, is an aggressive man, ready and eager to assume new functions and new responsibilities. Senate Parliamentarians Watkins and Riddick have been more self-effacing and less prone to seek additional duties.

More importantly, the disparity reflects basic differences in the power and composition of the House and Senate. In the Senate, power is diffused; there is no single overriding political post. Thus the Parliamentarian, who serves the presiding officer, may find himself working with the Vice President (the constitutional President of the Senate), the President pro tem or a Senator picked as the acting President pro tem. Furthermore, the Vice President and the Senate majority may be of different political parties. As a result, the Parliamentarian of the Senate lacks a firm base of political power from which to operate.

Quite a different situation exists in the House. The House Parliamentarian is first, last and always the Speaker's man. And the Speaker is an important political power, regardless of varying personal operating styles. With the Speaker's political weight behind him, the House Parliamentarian can afford to play off one committee chairman against another, or to upset a senior House Member. The House Parliamentarian never can thwart the Speaker, but in areas of indifference to the Speaker, such as routine bills or minor committees, the Parliamentarian can exercise some discretionary authority as the Speaker's representative.

The comparatively smaller size of the Senate, its greater stability and its less restrictive rules also contribute to the disparity. The value of an expert in procedural technicalities is measurably enhanced when his constituency is a 435-member body that includes a sizable contingent of freshman and junior Members, and the group is governed by numerous, complex and restrictive rules and precedents.

Evidence of the disparity appears concretely in comparisons of the Parliamentarians' salaries, staffs and offices. The House Parliamentarian presides over a staff of three assistants and a clerk, and a $150,000 annual budget. The staff is housed in the Speaker's Room, off the House chamber. The Parliamentarian's own office is around the corner, also off the chamber and several steps closer to the floor than even the office of the Speaker. At $42,192, the Parliamentarian's salary makes him the highest paid official in the House.

Two assistants and a secretary comprise the Senate Parliamentarian's staff. The Parliamentarian and his staff, whose combined salaries are $80,000, share a first floor Capitol office, a flight below the Senate chamber and the offices of the leadership. The Parliamentarian's $29,100 salary ranks him behind a number of other Senate officials.

Parliamentarians and Legislation

The influence wielded by Parliamentarians on the shape of legislation and the course of floor action is subtle but important. Does the White House or the leadership want a certain committee to consider a new bill? The Parliamentarians can suggest how to word the measure so it will fall under that committee's jurisdiction. Is a Senate filibuster blocking action on a measure favored by the leadership? The Senate Parliamentarian can guide the leadership in attempts to end the filibuster by invoking the cloture process. Do potential House floor amendments threaten to unravel carefully worded compromises on a controversial bill? The House

Parliamentarian can protect the agreements through skilled application of the House germaneness rule—supported by judiciously selected precedents.

The public rarely sees one of the Parliamentarians at work as adviser and tactician. These roles are carried out in private sessions, sometimes involving only the Parliamentarian and a single Member. Both sides are understandably reluctant to break this confidential relationship.

One example, drawn from the House side, shows Parliamentarian Deschler openly at work as adviser and tactician. In a 1969 dispute over seating Rep. Adam Clayton Powell (D N.Y.), the House leadership favored admitting Powell to the 91st Congress without any sanctions. Others sought to penalize the flamboyant Harlem Member, who had been excluded by the House from the 90th Congress for misusing public funds.

When Judiciary Committee Chairman Emanuel Celler (D N.Y.) offered a leadership resolution for the swearing-in of Powell, Speaker John W. McCormack (D Mass.) blocked a move by Powell opponents to add a $30,000 fine and a forfeit of seniority. In doing so, McCormack upheld a point of order by Celler against the opposition amendment for failing to meet the House rule of germaneness. Yet the Powell debate was taking place before the House had adopted its rules for the new Congress. McCormack quickly demonstrated that he had prepared himself for the obvious question of how he could invoke a House rule before it had been adopted. "The Chair anticipated that the question of germaneness would be raised and has had the precedents of the House thoroughly researched," the Speaker said. Then he sustained Celler's point of order. Citing a precedent based on a 1913 decision of Speaker Champ Clark (D Mo.), McCormack explained: "While the House is governed by general parliamentary usage prior to the adoption of rules, the Speakers have been inclined to give weight to the precedents of the House in the interpretation of that usage." Thus the leadership, through Deschler's research and advice, won its point. However, Powell's opponents won the battle when the House in a subsequent resolution agreed to seat Powell but to fine him $25,000 and to strip him of his seniority.

Codification of Precedents

Although the Parliamentarians of both chambers shun publicity and attempt to avoid controversies, they are not always successful.

House Parliamentarian Deschler became involved in a political controversy over codifying recent House precedents. The precedents were last codified in 1936. Precedents established since then were scattered through the pages of House debate in the *Congressional Record.* (There is no current codification of Senate precedents either, but the more informal atmosphere of the Senate renders precedents less important.)

Pressure to compile a new House codification, and to keep it up to date, built up among younger Representatives. They frequently found themselves at odds with the House leadership, particularly under Speaker McCormack, but often were caught off guard when forced to match precedents with Deschler. Deschler maintained a private file of post-1936 precedents, clipped from the *Record* and pasted in notebooks kept in his office.

Starting in 1965, Congress provided money annually in the Legislative Branch appropriations bill specifically for codification. Deschler hired his daughter, Mrs. Joan Deschler Eddy, as a $13,399-a-year research assistant to help with the task. The Legislative Reorganization Act of 1970 specifically directed the House Parliamentarian, following completion of the codification currently under way, to update the precedents every five years.

Bibliography

Biographical Directory of the American Congress, compiled by James L. Harrison. Government Printing Office, 1950.

Bolling, Richard, *House Out of Order.* E.P. Dutton & Co., 1966.

Cannon, Clarence, edit., *Cannon's Precedents of the House of Representatives.* Government Printing Office, 1936.

Hinds, Asher C., edit., *Hinds' Precedents of the House of Representatives.* Government Printing Office, 1907.

Leadership in House and Senate

FEW INSTITUTIONS of the Congress exert as much influence on the legislative process as do the party leaderships of the House (particularly the office of Speaker) and the Senate. In each chamber, the two major parties have set up elaborate leadership mechanisms that define the party's legislative policies and put on pressure to carry them out. Without the effective operation of these mechanisms, the two chambers might be paralyzed by factional bickering and the pace of legislative activity in all probability would slow to a crawl.

In the House, the leadership structure consists of the Speaker, who is both the chamber's presiding officer and the majority party's over-all leader; a majority and minority floor leader; assistant floor leaders (called Whips) who have numerous assistants, and a variety of supporting organizations such as special committees to assist with party strategy, legislative scheduling and the assignment of party members to the standing committees of the House.

In the Senate, there is no party official comparable to the Speaker. The Vice President is the constitutional President of the Senate and, in his absence, the President pro tempore presides, but neither office ever has been endowed with political power comparable to that of the Speakership. The remainder of the Senate leadership apparatus, however, is similar in function and power to that of the House. Today, these leadership structures are so influential that few bills sponsored by individual Members have any chance of passage without the endorsement of at least one party's leadership group.

Of all the leadership positions in Congress, the only one that has functioned continuously since 1789 is the Speakership—a post established by the Constitution. Although the post of President pro tempore of the Senate also was established by the Constitution, it was not filled on a continuing basis until 1890. Prior to that time, the Senate elected a President pro tempore only on occasions when the Vice President was absent, and in some sessions it let the office stand vacant. All the other leadership posts in both chambers were set up by party caucuses or conferences.

Speaker of the House

For the first two decades of Congress, the Speaker was largely a figurehead, but by the eve of the War of 1812, he had become the dominating leader in Congress. The power of the Speakership ebbed and flowed until the early 1900s, when the significance of the office reached its peak. By 1910, however, arbitrary use of power by a series of autocratic Speakers had culminated in drastic reform of the rules. The Speaker was stripped of most of his power, including authority to sit on the House Rules Committee (which Speakers had both sat on and chaired since 1858), authority to appoint committee members and absolute authority over recognition of Members.

Those changes have stood. All subsequent Speakers who have achieved influence in the House have done so through personal prestige and persuasion. Today, the Speaker's primary powers are presiding over the House; deciding points of order; referring bills and resolutions to the appropriate House committees; and appointing members of select committees and conference committees and chairmen of the Committee of the Whole (the parliamentary format in which most House floor action is transacted). The Speaker may participate in debate and may vote, like any other Member, although most recent Speakers have voted only to break a tie.

Most 20th-century Speakers have sought to apply their authority within parliamentary limits and yet to aid their own party whenever possible. As Floyd M. Riddick noted in his book *The U.S. Congress: Organization and Procedure,* "Tradition and unwritten law require that the Speaker apply the rules of the House consistently, yet in the twilight zone a large area exists where he may exercise great discrimination and where he has many opportunities to apply the rules to his party's advantage." One notable example of such discrimination occurred in 1941, when a ruling by House Speaker Sam Rayburn (D Texas) won him credit for having made possible the passage of a bill extending the military draft. After the measure passed by the narrow margin of 203 to 202, Rayburn employed a series of parliamentary maneuvers to prevent the bill's reconsideration despite a considerable outcry from Republicans that he was using his power arbitrarily. Historians have observed that the entire preparedness program for World War II might have been disrupted if the bill had not been passed when it was.

Although the Constitution does not specify that the Speaker must be a Member of the House, no non-Member has ever been elected to the post. Since the 19th century, only relatively senior members have been named Speaker. (Prior to 1896, the average period of House service by Members becoming Speaker was seven years; from 1896 to 1971, it was more than 22 years.) It also has become an unwritten tradition to elevate the party's floor leader to

Reference

See Appendix table of contents (first thumb tab) for list of all Speakers of the House, Presidents pro tempore of the Senate and Majority and Minority Leaders and Whips of both chambers.

the Speakership once an opening occurs, or in the case of the minority party, when it comes into the majority. Since the Civil War, neither party has ousted a sitting Speaker as long as the party remained in the majority, and only two former Speakers (J. Warren Keifer, R Ohio 1881-83 and Joseph W. Martin Jr., R Mass. 1947-49, 1953-55) have been removed from leadership positions when the party was in the minority. As Randall B. Ripley observed in his book *Party Leaders in the House of Representatives,* "In general, the Speaker retains leadership status in his party as long as he remains in the House."

Leaders of the Senate

Because of the greater manageability of the Senate, owing to its smaller size, leadership structures in that chamber developed more slowly than they did in the House. Some individual Senators created their own followings at times, but it was not until the 1890s that an effective party structure appeared. From 1890 until 1911, a Republican clique led by Senators William B. Allison (Iowa) and Nelson W. Aldrich (R.I.) was able to dominate the Senate even though neither Senator was formally designated as party floor leader.

Toward the latter part of the Allison-Aldrich era, both parties formally organized their leadership in the Senate, vesting power in appointed party leaders (but not in the President pro tem, whose function has been limited for the most part to presiding in the Vice President's absence). Since the Allison-Aldrich period, there have been only four powerful leadership organizations in the Senate—those of Majority Leaders John W. Kern (D Ind.) during the Wilson Administration, Joseph T. Robinson (D Ark.) in the New Deal era of the 1930s, Lyndon B. Johnson (D Texas) in the 1950s, and Minority Leader Everett McKinley Dirksen (R Ill.) in the 1960s. Both of the Senate floor leaders of the 92nd Congress, Mike Mansfield (D Mont.), the Majority Leader since 1961, and Hugh Scott (R Pa.), Minority Leader since late 1969, have been more reluctant than Johnson and Dirksen to use the full power of their offices and thus have achieved less striking results.

Tools of Leadership

Party leaders in both houses have relied on a variety of resources to achieve their objectives. Whenever possible, both parties take advantage of the chamber's rules, particularly with regard to filibustering by the minority party (or by a faction of the majority party) in the Senate. Leaders rely upon a whole range of tangible rewards to influence the course of legislation, including selective use of committee assignments, allocation of public works projects, award of campaign funds from the Congressional and Senatorial Campaign Committees, help in obtaining outside campaign contributions and promises to campaign for a Member's re-election.

A less tangible but equally important tool has been the leadership's expression of approval and personal friendliness toward the party faithful and coolness toward party defectors. As Randall Ripley noted in his study of the House, "The party leaders are in good position to influence the attitude of the House toward a Member early in his career by telling other Members what they think of him. There are also visible ways, such as the Speaker's selection of Members to preside over the House or over the Committee of the Whole, by which party

leaders indicate the younger Members whom they regard highly."

Most party leaders have been eager to dispense favors to Members both of their own and of the opposition party so as to create a stack of IOUs to call upon in the event of close votes on important measures. In recent years, most leaders have relied on tact and persuasion instead of threats or harsh criticism to win Members' support. *(For full discussion, including examples of use of leadership pressures, see Internal Pressures, Chapter VI.)*

What follows is a discussion of the evolution of the Speakership and the recent development of other leadership posts. Also discussed are contested elections for leadership positions, the relations of leaders with Presidents and an alleged scandal (the only one in recent years) directly involving a leadership position.

History of the Speakership

The intentions of the framers of the Constitution with respect to the Speakership were not set forth either in the Constitution itself or in the records of the Constitutional Convention. As adopted, the Constitution's only reference to the office came in Article I, Section 2, which stated that "The House of Representatives shall choose their Speaker and other officers...." There is no evidence that the provision was put to debate.

Two respected authorities on the Speakership, Mary P. Follett and Hubert Bruce Fuller, have suggested that the failure of the Founding Fathers to elaborate on the Speaker's office indicated that the role they envisioned for the post was one similar to the speakership of the colonial legislatures—a post with which the framers were intimately familiar. In most cases, the colonial Speakers were active politicians who not only presided over the legislatures but also used their positions to further their own or their faction's legislative aims. This concept of the office differed sharply from that of the Speakership of the House of Commons; the British Speaker is a strictly non-partisan presiding officer.

Miss Follett, whose 1896 book, *The Speaker of the House of Representatives,* is widely regarded as the most authoritative study of the office, contended that a proposal put before the Constitutional Convention for a Council of State—consisting of the Speaker, the President, the President of the Senate, the Chief Justice of the United States and the heads of Federal departments—further indicated that the Founding Fathers intended the Speaker's office to be a political post. The proposal for a Council of State was seriously considered but was rejected by the Convention.

Miss Follett asserted: "Surely, those who advocated this important board could not have thought of the Speaker as a non-political moderator, as a mere parliamentary officer whom it was necessary to dissociate from politics. What they intended must be inferred from that with which they were familiar: they knew a Speaker in the colonial assemblies who was at the same time a political leader; they knew a presiding officer of (the Continental) Congress who was both a political leader and the official head of the state with important administrative functions; they knew a president of the Constitutional Convention who to his power as chairman added all the influence to be expected of one acknowledged as the foremost man of the nation. Few of their number had

(Continued on p. 132)

Order of Presidential Succession

The order in which Congressional leaders and Cabinet officers succeed to the Presidency in the event of a vacancy in that office and in the office of Vice President has been acted upon by Congress three times since 1789. Each time—in 1792, 1886 and 1947—the central question has been whether the President should be succeeded by an official appointed by him or by a Member of Congress elected by the people. Congress took the latter course in 1792, switched to appointive officials in 1886, and then to elective followed by appointive officials in 1947. Although the 25th Amendment, ratified in 1967, provided for appointment by the President of a new Vice President in the event of a vacancy in that office, it did not change the order of subsequent succession.

The original succession law, passed in 1792, provided that the President pro tempore of the Senate and the Speaker of the House, in that order, would assume the Presidency in the event that both the President and Vice President died or were disabled. In 1886, Congress removed the two Congressional leaders from the line of succession and added in their place all of the members of the President's Cabinet, in the order in which their departments had been established. In 1947, the Speaker of the House and the President pro tem of the Senate were put back on the list in that order and placed ahead of the Cabinet members.

Authority for the action of Congress was contained in Article II, Section 1 of the Constitution, which states: "In case of the removal of the President from office, or of his death, resignation or inability to discharge the powers and duties of the said office, the same shall devolve on the Vice President, and the Congress may by law provide for the case of removal, death, resignation or inability, both of the President and Vice President, declaring what officer shall then act as President, and such officer shall act accordingly, until the disability be removed, or a President shall be elected."

1886 Law. The 1886 revision of the line of succession was made in recognition of the possibility that both the President and the Vice President might die between the expiration of Congress on March 3 of odd-numbered years and the first session of the new Congress, not regularly held until the first Monday of the following December. If there had been no special session in that interim, there might be no Senate President pro tem, and there definitely would be no House Speaker, because the Speaker's term expires with the Congress that elected him. Therefore, unless there happened to be a holdover President pro tem, because the Vice President had been absent from the Senate at the end of the preceding session, there would be no one in the line of succession to assume the Presidency of the United States in event of the cited emergency.

Sen. George F. Hoar (R Mass.), who proposed the 1886 revision, argued, moreover, that if either the President pro tem or the Speaker were available, he would have to combine the responsibility of the Presidency with that of the pro tem's or the Speaker's office, whichever the case might be. Hoar asserted also that it was unlikely that anyone would be tempted to assassinate the President and the Vice President if the Presidency would then devolve upon the President's chief political advisers, his Cabinet officers. The bill passed easily and was signed into law by President Cleveland.

1947 Revision. On June 19, 1945, President Truman sent Congress a message in which he asked for a re-examination of the order of Presidential succession. At that time, the office of Vice President was vacant. Criticizing the 1886 law, Truman asserted that "It now lies within my power to nominate the person (Secretary of State or other Cabinet officers) who would be my immediate successor....I do not believe that in a democracy this power should rest with the Chief Executive." Accordingly, he asked for legislation which would put an elective official in line for the Presidency and suggested for first place, after the Vice President, the Speaker of the House as being more in touch with the people than the President pro tem of the Senate. By that time, the 20th Amendment, ratified in 1933, had eliminated the gap between the expiration of one Congress and the beginning of its successor, both the life of the old ending and the life of the new starting at noon on Jan. 3 of odd-numbered years.

The Administration bill embodying President Truman's proposal was passed by the House in 1945 but was not acted upon by the Senate. In his 1946 State of the Union Message, the President renewed his request for the bill's enactment, but the Senate still took no action. In 1947, the measure finally passed when the Republican-dominated Senate of the 80th Congress looked with favor on the possibility that one of their own rank—the Speaker of the House or President pro tem of the Senate—might succeed to the Presidency. By a strict party-line vote in the Senate and by an overwhelming margin in the House, the President's 1945 proposal finally was enacted.

The Presidential Succession Act of 1947 provided the following new line of succession after the Vice President: the Speaker of the House; the President pro tempore of the Senate; the Secretaries of State, Treasury and War (changed to Secretary of Defense by the National Security Act of 1947); the Attorney General; the Postmaster General; and the Secretaries of Navy (removed from Cabinet rank and thus from the line of succession by the 1947 National Security Act), Interior, Agriculture, Commerce, and Labor. The order of Cabinet succession was the same as under the 1886 law except for addition of the Secretaries of Commerce and of Labor, whose departments had not been established when that law was enacted. The Secretaries of Health, Education and Welfare, of Housing and Urban Development, and of Transportation joined the line of succession later under new legislation providing for automatic addition of the heads of new departments as the departments are created.

ever been in England, and there is no reason for believing, as has been frequently asserted, that they provided for a Speaker similar to the presiding officer of the House of Commons."

The term "Speaker" first appeared in Commons in 1377, when Sir Thomas Hungerford assumed the post. Until the late 17th century, the Speaker was directly responsible to the Crown. The term was derived from the fact that it was the duty of the presiding officer to interpret the will of Commons to the Crown.

The First House Speakers

The House of Representatives spelled out the duties of the Speaker on April 7, 1789, when a select committee of 11 Members reported a suggested code of standing rules and orders of procedure. The code, discussed and adopted the same day by the full House, assigned the following duties to the Speaker: presiding at House sessions, preserving decorum and order, putting questions to the House, deciding points of order, announcing the results of division and teller votes, appointing committees of not more than three members and voting in cases where his vote would be decisive (a practice known as the Speaker's "casting" vote). At first, the Speaker was elected by secret ballot, but since 1839 his selection has been made on a roll-call vote.

Because political parties had not yet been formed, the first Speaker, Frederick A. C. Muhlenberg (Pa.), who served from 1789 to 1791, was nonpartisan. In the 2nd Congress, however, clearly defined party divisions began to appear, and Muhlenberg's successor, Jonathan Trumbull (Conn.), displayed definite leanings toward President Washington's legislative program. Partisanship had become pronounced by 1799, when the Federalists elected Theodore Sedgwick (Mass.) to the Speaker's post. According to Miss Follett, "Sedgwick made many enemies by decided and even partisan acts. He was Speaker during the debates on the repeal of the Alien and Sedition Acts, and gave his influence and casting votes in favor of the Bankrupt Act and the Sedition Acts (two important Federalist measures)." In addition, Sedgwick denied a request by two reporters from the *National Intelligencer,* a leading anti-Federalist newspaper, to cover House proceedings. Sedgwick later made that decision final by exercising his casting vote on the matter when the reporters applied directly to the House.

The Speakership of Henry Clay

One of the most important periods in the evolution of the Speakership was from 1811 to 1825, during which Henry Clay, a Democratic Republican and later Whig, held the post for six terms. Clay, a popular Kentuckian who had resigned a seat in the Senate in order to run for the House, was one of only two Members ever elected Speaker during a first term in the lower chamber. (The other was William Pennington (N.J.) in 1859.) Clay owed his election to the Speaker's post in 1811 to a faction of young Democratic Republicans known as the "War Hawks," who had swept 70 House seats in the election of 1810 by promising western expansion and war with England over its interference with American shipping. On these and other issues, Clay sought to assert the supremacy of Congress over the other branches of Government, and of the Speakership over affairs of the House.

In one of his first acts as Speaker, Clay stacked key House committees with proponents of his war policy. To the Foreign Relations Committee he named three War Hawks: Peter B. Porter (DR N.Y.), who was named chairman; John C. Calhoun (DR S.C.) and Felix Grundy (DR Tenn.). In other important appointments, Clay named David R. Williams (DR N.Y.) chairman of the Committee on Military Affairs and Langdon Cheves (DR S.C.) chairman of the Naval Affairs Committee. The newly organized House immediately set out to push the Government into war with England. On Nov. 29, 1811, less than four weeks after Congress had convened, the Foreign Relations Committee issued a report recommending war.

Although President Madison sought a peaceful settlement with England, continuous pressure from Clay finally resulted in a declaration of war. On March 15, 1812, Clay presented to the Administration a program calling for a 30-day embargo on British goods, followed by a declaration of war and the acceptance of 10,000 volunteers into the army on short-term enlistments. Clay noted that while the declaration of war lay within the constitutional powers of Congress, he expected the Administration to take the responsibility of recommending it. After considerable deliberation, Madison agreed to the embargo, and on June 1 sent Congress a war message. As George Rothwell Brown noted in his book *The Leadership of Congress,* "Clay had lifted the Speakership of the House to a point of new power and responsibility, the Speaker to a place in the state where, backed by the party organization behind him, he could present to the President a program determining national policy and involving a declaration of war....Mr. Clay brought to bear upon Mr. Madison...the influence of his great office in an appeal to arms, against the pacifist sentiment of the President and most of the Cabinet."

Clay, a gifted orator, was the first House Speaker to use debate extensively as a tool to achieve his party's legislative aims. In a series of heated discussions with Josiah Quincy, a powerful Federalist from Massachusetts who thought the war would endanger New England's trade interests, Clay mobilized national support for war by casting the issue in terms of patriotism. Hubert Bruce Fuller noted in his book, *The Speakers of the House:* "No subject was so well suited to Clay's native talents (as debate); he touched the keys of inspiration and the nation echoed one strain; the boundless resources of the country, the glamor of successful war, the magic of enlarged domain, the prestige of victory. This stamped Clay, not the traditional moderator of the House, but rather party leader who could control the House....In the stirring times of his first term in the Chair, with all the bitterness of party feeling, there was scarcely a day when he did not give voice to his sentiments."

Clay reinforced his control of the House by taking advantage of such rules as that governing recognition of Members desiring to speak. A notable example was afforded in debate on the declaration of war, when John Randolph, a Virginia Democrat who had long intimidated weaker House Members with his rhetoric, sought to take the floor to oppose the war policy. Clay ruled that Randolph could not speak unless he submitted a motion to the House. When the motion was submitted, Clay ruled that Randolph still could not speak until the House considered the motion. The House refused to consider it, and Randolph was denied the floor. Clay frequently resorted to similar strategy on important issues. In his six terms as Speaker, none of his rulings from the Chair was overturned, though many were sustained only by strict party-line votes.

Unlike his predecessors, Clay remained a vigorous spokesman for his Congressional district despite his position as Speaker. He was the first Speaker, and one of the few in history, to vote in instances when his vote could make no difference in the result. Clay's voting practices and his participation in debate set the precedent that Speakers forfeited none of their normal privileges as Members in accepting the Speakership.

Notwithstanding setbacks in the war, Clay's personal popularity was not diminished. He kept his influence over the House and later attained equal or even greater influence when he returned to the Senate. Just as he had forced the war policy of the House upon President Madison in 1812, Clay imposed other foreign and domestic policies upon President Monroe after the war. Among the measures he pushed through over Monroe's opposition were various internal improvements, a protective tariff, recognition of South American governments and the Missouri Compromise. In her study of the Speakership, Mary P. Follett concluded that Clay was "the most powerful man in the nation from 1811 to 1825." According to Miss Follett, his legacy to the House included three important elements: the increase of the Speaker's parliamentary power, the broadening of the Speaker's personal influence and establishment of the Speaker's prestige as a legislative leader.

Clay's Successors Up to Civil War

With few exceptions, the Members who succeeded Clay as Speaker in the pre-Civil War era attempted to follow Clay's model of the Speakership. Among the most vigorous political partisans of that period were two Democrats, Andrew Stevenson (Va.), who held the post from 1827 to 1834, and James K. Polk (Tenn.), who served from 1835 to 1839. Both were strong advocates of the programs put forth by the Democratic Presidents who served during their tenures in the Speakership. In 1832, Stevenson cast the deciding vote against a motion that a committee to investigate the Bank of the United States (an institution strongly opposed by President Jackson) be chosen by ballot of the House; defeat of the motion meant that Stevenson was free to appoint the committee himself. Polk, who was to become President in 1845, drew considerable criticism from John Quincy Adams (Whig Mass.), a former President, who accused him of appointing House committees "in favor of the Administration" and of being "partial."

The main attempt at nonpartisanship in this period was made in 1839-41, when Robert M. T. Hunter (D Va.) was in the Speaker's chair. Hunter, elected as a compromise candidate after Whigs and Democrats had deadlocked over their own candidates, was considered fair but indecisive as a presiding officer. John Quincy Adams described him as a "good-hearted, weak-headed, young man." In his closing speech, Hunter said, "It is something if I can hope I have made it easier for those who succeed me to act on some better principle than that of giving the whole power of the House to one of the parties without regard to the rights and feelings of others. Clothe this station with the authority of justice and how much may it

not do to elevate the views of parties from themselves to their country. But arm it with the mere power of numbers and administer it with an exclusive eye to the interests of a party and it may become the engine of as much fraud and oppression as can be practiced in a country as free as ours."

Post-Civil War Speakers

The political character of the Speakership became even more pronounced during and after the Civil War. Schuyler Colfax (R Ind.), who served in the post from 1863 to 1869, frequently left the chair to participate in House debates on party issues. One House Member said of Colfax that "he sometimes announces the passage of a bill as if it were the triumph of his own work, not as if he were merely reading the record of the House." In April 1864, when a Member advocated recognition of the Confederate states, Colfax took the floor to recommend the Member's expulsion. "I recognize," Colfax said, "that there is a double duty incumbent upon me: first to the House of Representatives, to administer the duties of the Chair and the rules of the House faithfully and impartially to the best of my ability and judgment. But I feel that I owe still another duty to the people of the ninth Congressional district of Indiana, who sent me here as their Representative to speak and act and vote in their stead. It is in conforming with this latter duty to those who cannot speak here for themselves, and who, I believe, would endorse the sentiment of this resolution, that I have felt my duty to rise in my place as a Member of Congress from the state of Indiana and offer this resolution."

The Speakership of Colfax's successor, James G. Blaine (R Maine), was even more political in nature. Not since the time of Clay had a Speaker attempted so consciously to frame the committees of the House in a manner favorable to his party's program. As George Rothwell Brown noted: "Blaine created the committees as he desired them to be, bearing in mind the party necessity, naming as chairmen tried and trusted men of his own selection, men of proved ability and loyalty, who owed their allegiance to him as the head of the party in the House. Through these lieutenants, occupying every strategic place in the organization, the Speaker controlled the House and made it instantly responsive to the will of the party of which, at this period, he was one of the great leaders, if, indeed, not the greatest leader." The result of this structuring of committees was a flood of legislation favorable to business (particularly railroad) interests.

Carlisle, Reed, Crisp. Dimensions of the Speaker's office were further broadened in the late 19th century under two Democratic Speakers, John G. Carlisle (Ky.) and Charles F. Crisp (Ga.), and one Republican, Thomas B. Reed (Maine), often called "Czar" Reed.

Carlisle, who held the post from 1883 to 1889, established the concept, which endured for more than two decades, that it was the duty of the Speaker not to follow the dictates of his party, but to impose his own will on the House. Carlisle achieved that objective primarily through the power of recognition, which he used arbitrarily to further his legislative ends. Miss Follett observed that Carlisle "considered it the Speaker's duty to be the leader of Congress, to have a definite legislative policy, and to take every means in his power to secure the accomplishment of that policy. He himself shirked neither the duty nor the responsibility; again and again he opposed the will of a large majority of the House by refusing recognition to Members who wished to take up important business; his committees also, while fair and able, represented Carlisle's views more closely than anyone's else. By every other means which his office afforded, he sought, entirely regardless of his position as chairman, to impose his will on the House and to be the real source of the legislation of the United States.''

Carlisle's successor, Reed, who served from 1889-91 and again from 1895-99, expanded the powers of his office more than has any other Speaker in history except Clay. In essence, Reed's rulings from the Chair, later formally incorporated into the House rules, established the absolute right of the majority to legislate regardless of attempted obstruction by a minority.

At the outset of the 51st Congress, when Reed assumed office, filibustering by the minority had grown to such lengths that it had become difficult for the majority to transact business. (Filibustering was practiced by each of the major parties when it was in the minority.) The minority was able to paralyze the House by introducing a series of dilatory motions, such as motions to recess or adjourn, and then demanding time-consuming roll-call votes on the motions. (As provided by the Constitution, one-fifth of a House quorum could demand a roll-call vote.) Another method of obstruction was a system of "constructive absences" under which Members of the minority would fail to vote on certain questions even though they were present in the House chamber. Under established procedures, only those voting were counted for purposes of establishing the presence of a quorum, which was necessary for the transaction of business; thus a minority could stall House action by simply refusing to answer to their names on roll-call votes. Reed's rulings, attacked as arbitrary by the Democratic minority, put an end to these procedures.

On Jan. 21, 1890, Reed took his first major step against obstruction by refusing to consider a Member's demand for a teller vote on a motion to adjourn. Later that month, he announced his intention to disregard all motions and appeals, however parliamentary in character, if intended simply to delay House business. On Jan. 30, 1890, Reed made a second ruling to curb obstruction. When the yeas and nays were demanded on consideration of a contested election case, the vote came to 161 yeas, 2 nays, and 165 not voting. After the result was announced, Democrats immediately claimed that the vote was invalid because a quorum had not voted. Reed then startled the House by ruling that 130 Democrats present but not voting would be counted for the purpose of establishing a quorum. The motion thus carried by a majority of those voting. An appeal from the decision was tabled by a majority of those voting (again with a quorum present but not voting).

On the following day, the Speaker declined to reconsider the ruling. Miss Follett recalled that Reed was "denounced as a tyrant, despot, czar;...never before had the House of Representatives witnessed such a scene—its presiding officer condemned, and subjected to the most violent abuse on account of a parliamentary decision. But Mr. Reed by his calmness under personal accusations, and by the firmness with which he stood his ground against

both importunity and attack, guided the House through its stormy crisis and the establishment of a more sound and salutary principle of parliamentary law.''

On Feb. 14, 1890, the House formally adopted new rules incorporating Reed's recent rulings and other new procedures. The new code, reported by the Rules Committee chaired by Reed, provided that (1) all Members must vote unless thay had a pecuniary interest in the question at issue; (2) motions to take a recess and to fix a date of adjournment would not be entertained when a question was under debate; (3) 100 Members would constitute a quorum in the Committee of the Whole; and (4) no dilatory motion should be entertained by the Speaker. In its report to the House, the Rules Committee majority stated: "The abuse has grown to such proportions that the parliamentary law which governs American assemblies has found it necessary to keep pace with the evil, and to enable the majority by the intervention of the presiding officer to meet by extraordinary means the extraordinary abuse of power on the part sometimes of a very few Members."

The "Reed Rules" were adopted by the House after bitter debate; their most controversial provision—the counting of present but nonvoting Members to make a quorum—was upheld by the U.S. Supreme Court in an 1891 test case.

Crisp, who succeeded Reed as Speaker in the Democratic-controlled House of 1891-95, contributed to the evolution of the Speakership by strengthening the Rules Committee as an element of the Speaker's power. Although the Reed Rules as such were dropped in the 52nd Congress (1891-93), essentially the same powers were lodged in the Rules Committee. Speakers had sat on and chaired the Rules Committee since 1858 and had derived much of their power from that arrangement.

The rules of the 53rd Congress (1893-95) permitted the Rules Committee to retire from the House at any time and report a motion to put an immediate stop to filibustering. Hubert Bruce Fuller has noted that the expanded role of the Rules Committee was "a radical departure from the long-established rules and principles of parliamentary law and practice." He added: "The tyranny of Reed seemed beneficence when Crisp ruled that not even 'the question of consideration could be raised against a report from the Committee on Rules.' This Committee, dominated of course by the Speaker, became the dictator of the House and the Members were forbidden even to question its wisdom or decision...."

Era of Cannonism

The peak of the Speaker's power came during the incumbency of Joseph G. Cannon (R Ill.), a staunch conservative who instituted few parliamentary changes in the House but fully exploited those made by Carlisle, Reed and Crisp. Like Reed, Cannon also was known as "Czar." Under his reign, from 1903 to 1911, recognition of Members was made entirely arbitrary. It was reported that when Members rose without first consulting Cannon, the Speaker would say "For what purpose does the gentleman rise?" If the explanation was unsatisfactory, Cannon would invariably deny the Member the floor. Fuller reported that on days set aside for enactment by unanimous consent of purely local bills of a minor character, Cannon moved arbitrarily to reward his friends and punish his enemies. "Often on the success of these bills would depend the re-election of many men to Congress. Each Member was compelled first to consult the Speaker and secure his consent to recognition. The Speaker on these days had before him a list of the Members to be recognized and this order was scrupulously followed. Thus the Speaker's power was neither to be ignored nor defied. His smile and assent made and unmade Members, accordingly as he bestowed or withheld those powerful benefices."

Under Cannon, the House Rules Committee became an even more powerful instrument of the Speakership than it had been under Crisp. Before any House committee could report to the House, the committee was required to obtain clearance from the Rules panel, and clearance was usually granted only for measures which Cannon desired passed. Terms of the Rules Committee's clearance for consideration of bills desired by Cannon usually included sharp limits on debate and foreclosure of floor amendments. The latter practice made it possible for Cannon and his associates to attach legislative "riders" in committee which might have been voted down on the floor if brought to a separate vote. Rather than kill the entire bill, the House usually accepted such riders, which most frequently were attached to appropriation bills that were virtually assured of passage.

Unlike Speaker Reed, who had ruled the House alone, Cannon established a network of trusted lieutenants. Key committee assignments went to a group of Republicans who had become associated with Cannon in evening poker games: Sereno E. Payne (N.Y.), John Dalzell (Pa.), James R. Mann (Ill.) and Nicholas Longworth (Ohio). The Speaker and his leadership group reportedly decided much of the business of the House during the after-hours poker games.

Cannon finally was shorn of much of his power in 1910 after insurgent Republicans joined with Democrats to force a liberalization of the rules. Among other changes, the new rules prohibited the Speaker from naming or serving on the Rules Committee, denied the Speaker the right to appoint standing committees, and reduced the power of recognition by instituting procedures (Calendar Wednesday and the Calendar for Unanimous Consent) under which bills could be considered without the sponsor having to get recognition by the Speaker. All standing committees, including the Rules Committee, were to be appointed by the full House, meaning in effect the Democratic and Republican Committees on Committees, whose recommendations have always been approved routinely by the party caucuses and the full House.

Rule by Caucus or Steering Committee

Democratic Caucus. The first Speaker to preside under the liberalized rules was Champ Clark (D Mo.), who served from 1911 to 1919. During this period, real power in the House was in the hands of Oscar W. Underwood (D Ala.), who was made House Majority Leader and chairman of the Ways and Means Committee (and thus chairman of the newly established Democratic Committee on Committees made up of the Democrats on Ways and Means). Democrats in 1909 had adopted caucus rules which bound all party Members to support any party position adopted by two-thirds of the caucus, unless a Member considered the position unconstitutional or had made "contrary pledges to his constituents prior to his election or received contrary instructions by resolutions or platform from his nominating authority." Democrats later adopted a resolution pledging their support to all bills presented to the House by the Ways and Means Committee. These procedures achieved considerable party unity and control of the House throughout the first term of President Woodrow Wilson, when a large body of reform legislation was enacted.

Republican Steering Committee. Clark's successor as Speaker, Frederick H. Gillett (R Mass.), who served from 1919 to 1925, attempted to diminish the partisan character of the Speakership and restore its judicial character. With Gillett declining to assert political leadership, power in the House shifted to Majority Leader Franklin W. Mondell (R Wyo.) and a five-member Republican Steering Committee. From 1919 to 1925, the Committee met almost daily to discuss party positions and to map out strategy with committee chairmen and other Republican leaders. Randall B. Ripley observed in his book *Party Leaders in the House of Representatives:* "For the most part...the Steering Committee carried out the wishes of the Republican leaders in the House, even when these were not in accord with the Republican Administration. For example, a bill in the 68th Congress to increase civil service pensions was held up for an entire Congress and thus killed by an unfavorable Steering Committee decision despite support for it from a unanimous House Civil Service Committee, the Senate and the Administration."

Leadership under this system was so diffuse that House Republicans accomplished little during the period. Republicans found it difficult to achieve party unity even on such a traditionally partisan issue as the tariff. According to Ripley, the Steering Committee was plagued with "occasional lapses in communications between the various leaders" and its "communications with the White House were even more uncertain." "The Members," he said, "including some committee chairmen, used the loose leadership structure to pursue legislative ends other than those officially sanctioned."

Speakers Longworth, Rayburn, McCormack

Longworth. The shortcomings of leadership by the Steering Committee prompted the next House Speaker, Nicholas Longworth (R Ohio), to re-centralize power in the Speaker's office. Upon assuming the post in 1925, Longworth set forth his conception of the Speaker as party leader: "I believe it to be the duty of the Speaker, standing squarely on the platform of his party, to assist in so far as he properly can the enactment of legislation in accordance with the declared principles and policies of his party and by the same token to resist the enactment of legislation in violation thereof."

Like Cannon, Longworth established a small group of trusted associates to help him run the House. This group, called the "Big Four," consisted of Longworth; John Q. Tilson (R Conn.), the Majority Leader; Bertrand H. Snell (R N.Y.), chairman of the Rules Committee, and James Begg (R Ohio), a longtime personal friend of Longworth's. Longworth, who served as Speaker until the Democrats took control of the House in 1931, was able to achieve through personal persuasion what Cannon had done by arbitrary interpretation of the House rules. *(Continued on p. 138)*

Alleged Misuse of the Speaker's Office...

In recent years, only one major scandal has directly involved the office of a top Congressional leadership official—the conviction in 1970 of Martin Sweig, a longtime aide to House Speaker John W. McCormack (D Mass.), on a perjury charge arising from Sweig's alleged misuse of the Speaker's office. Some political figures and members of the press sought in the mid-1960s to link another scandal—alleged influence-peddling by Robert G. Baker, secretary to the Senate majority in the late 1950s and early 1960s—to the office of then Senate Majority Leader Lyndon B. Johnson (D Texas). But no evidence of Johnson's involvement was ever established.

Sweig, who had been suspended by McCormack pending the final outcome of the case, was found guilty by a jury in the U.S. District Court in New York, July 9, 1970, on one count of perjury. He was acquitted on five other perjury counts and on a charge of conspiring with Nathan M. Voloshen, a New York lawyer, to misuse the office of Speaker McCormack. On Sept. 3, Sweig, 48, was sentenced to 30 months in prison and fined $2,000. He appealed the conviction and was released on a recognizance bond of $50,000. Voloshen had pleaded guilty of conspiracy June 17, and later was fined $10,000.

Following are excerpts from testimony given at the trial by Speaker McCormack in response to questions by U.S. Attorney Whitney North Seymour Jr.:

Q Mr. Speaker...do you know a man named Nathan Voloshen?

A I do.

Q I wonder if you would tell the jury the nature of your acquaintance with him and your relationship during the period you have known him?

A I have known Mr. Voloshen—it is pretty hard to say how many years, time passes so quickly, but I would say at least 20 years....

He was a friend of mine. I considered him to be a friend of mine, developed through the years a friendship, and so I just considered him a friend of mine as much as I consider a lot of people to be friends of mine. A relationship of friendship existed....

Q Do you know whether Mr. Voloshen had a Washington office?

A No, I do not.

A Do you recall whether or not it ever came to your attention that Mr. Voloshen was using your room in the (Congressional) district office extensively?

A No.

Q It never came to your attention?

A No.

Q Do you recall whether it came to your attention Mr. Voloshen was actually meeting and conferring with clients in your office, in the district office?

A No....

Q Do you recall whether it ever came to your attention that Mr. Voloshen was making extensive use of telephones in your office?

A No. I have—that was only recently I found that out.

Q I wonder, Mr. Speaker, if you would also tell us if you know or knew a man Eugene Kinally?

A Very well, Mr. Kinally was one of my dearest friends. Mr. Kinally was my secretary and then when I got to be Majority Leader and had an administrative assistant, he was my administrative assistant since the first day I was elected to Congress in 1928, and he was a friend of mine before that....

Q He died in May 1969?

A Yes, May of last year.

Q Mr. Speaker, do you know the defendant Martin Sweig?

A Yes.

Q Will you tell us about your acquaintanceship with him, please.

A Martin Sweig, Dr. Sweig, came into—I think he was associated with me about 23 or 24 years. He came into my office as a young man, very devoted, studied hard , went to school, studied....

Sweig's Duties

Q I wonder if you could tell us what Dr. Sweig's responsibilities were, particularly during the period from 1964 to 1969.

A ...When I became Speaker, I have certain positions as Speaker. One of them I think was legislative assistant so I naturally, Dr. Sweig had come up with me throughout the years as a young man, and I appointed him to the top position in the Speaker's office....

He occupied the top position, what I might have as the top position as Speaker. The title, I let him select the title he wanted. That was really immaterial as far as I am concerned, but my impression is that the position paid $28,000 a year, it is my impression, or thereabouts....

Q At the time of Mr. Kinally's death in May of 1969 did Dr. Sweig then become the administrative assistant?

A Yes. I assume also while Mr. Kinally was sick Dr. Sweig performed the duties as administrative assistant....

Q Do you recall what salary Dr. Sweig received as administrative assistant?

A I think the salary now is $36,000 a year....

Q I wonder, Mr. Speaker, if you would tell us actually what duties Dr. Sweig had during this period both when he was administrative assistant and before that when he was effectively serving as administrative assistant.

A He had many duties to perform in collaboration with Mr. Kinally when Mr. Kinally could function effectively, taking care of mail....They sift out the mail they think I should see and also letters they think that I should personally sign....

He would dictate letters, lots of letters would come in from departments and agencies in reply to other let-

...*Excerpts From McCormack's Testimony at Sweig Trial*

ters sent to them which...wouldn't require my attention....

Dealing with Federal Agencies

Q On this matter of dealing with agencies and trying to help people out, did you set any limits as to how far your staff could go in trying to help people?

A Mr. Kinally received, in talking with him I said to him many years ago, "Now Gene, if anyone comes in with certain matters, if anyone comes in I want you to send them over to see me, let me take the responsibility of the decision."

Not that I was disturbed about their decision but I felt I should take it in certain matters, the responsibility of making decisions and take the blame as well as whatever might be the other way.

Q What kind of matters are those?

A I told him if my best friend came down to Washington, and amongst my best friends I have many who have come to Washington and wanted to make an appointment say with the Department of Justice in connection with a criminal case, I would say "Send him over to me, let me handle it" because being a lawyer I could appraise it. Or in what is a sensitive agency, such as the Internal Revenue, if someone came down on a tax case, let me handle it because I am not—only one thing I do on a tax matter, if someone wants to make an appointment I sinply say "You have to prove your case." Simply a matter of courtesy to make the appointment, but I felt as though I could handle that situation better than somebody on my staff, let me make the decision and protect themselves, in the sense if I used the word protect.

Or if it was a matter that was pending before a regulatory body, where the regulatory body was hearing evidence like we are now, like in a courtroom, I would not myself contact any member of a commission that was actually conducting a trial on any application before them, like the ICC or a trial. Making appointments is different....

Making Appointments

As far as making an appointment for someone to see somebody in any agency, I have done it, I have done it for people I don't know. They come into the office, I made appointments as a matter of courtesy rather than have them wait around three or four days trying to make an appointment with somebody in the agency, as a matter of courtesy I just called up and made an appointment for them.

But I never expressed any opinion, simply say I don't know this gentleman—if somebody was a close friend of mine I would say I have known Mr. So and So a number of years and a man that I considered to be —if I did so—a responsible gentleman. But simply make an appointment and then if it was a friend, somebody I don't know I would make an appointment, I would make it for a friend, and my office had the implied authority if not express authority to do so....

Q In connection with a request made on behalf of a friend or constituent, would members of your staff be authorized to ask the agency to take specific action, to do something one way or the other?

A No, because I could not ask anyone else to do something that I couldn't do myself if I were in their position. I couldn't imagine anyone in my office would take any other position but to follow what I have already testified and the guidelines set down by the House Committee on Ethics, which I assume you are familiar with.

Q I am familiar with them.

You indicated that you had a particular discussion with Mr. Kinally about some of these matters.

A Oh years ago I did, yes, as a general proposition.

Q Would you tell us whether you know if other members of your staff were familiar with your policies on this matter?

A I would assume so. Whether I specifically talked with Dr. Sweig or not I am unable to state now, but I know years ago I talked with Mr. Kinally and said, "Gene, certain things, certain areas are sensitive."

For example, I would never inject myself into a Selective Service Act—I mean on the Selective Service Board. Compassionate transfer or compassionate case, that's a different proposition, but I would never inject myself into trying to have somebody deferred, or anything like that, because I wouldn't think of it. That's just to give you an illustration....

Q Specifically, Mr. Speaker, in around 1968 or 1969, do you recall whether or not you received a telephone call from a general in the Army who indicated from the content of the call that he believed that he had previously spoken to you?

A I received a call last year, as I remember, from one who said he was a general. I don't remember his name now. It was a report on some matter that had come in the office about some request that somebody in the office was trying to help out on, apparently. I could tell from the talk that I had with him that he thought he had spoken with me.

So I made a note of what his report was on the case and then I sent for Dr. Sweig—he was in the other office —and I told him the story.

I said, "Martin, this general thinks he talked with me on the original conversation. Did you represent yourself as me?"

Dr. Sweig said, "No, he must be mistaken, a misunderstanding."

That's one case that I can remember.

Q Did Dr. Sweig indicate that he had in fact previously called the general?

A I didn't go that far—well, I would assume, because he said he must have been mistaken—certainly someone from my office called on the matter. The call was proper except the general felt—I could tell from the talk I had with him that he thought I was the one that had called him....

Rayburn. The prestige of the Speakership increased considerably in the 1940s and 1950s during the tenure of Sam Rayburn (D Texas), another master of the art of persuasion. Faced after World War II with a party badly split over civil rights and other domestic issues, Rayburn found that he could minimize disunity by making party decisions himself and bargaining with individuals rather than with the party as a whole. During a large share of Rayburn's 18 years as Speaker, many of his party's domestic programs were emasculated by a "conservative coalition" of Republicans and Southern Democrats; still, Rayburn was able to push through considerable legislation in the field of foreign affairs as well as several important domestic bills, including two far-reaching civil rights acts (1957 and 1960). In Ripley's opinion, the Speaker's record, in view of the split in his own party, was "enough to earn for Rayburn a reputation as an incomparable legislative wizard when faced with unfavorable odds."

McCormack. The mode of leadership adopted by Rayburn's successor, John W. McCormack (D Mass.), was more like that of the Republican leadership of the 1919-25 era than of any other recent period. Lacking the persuasive ability of a Rayburn or Longworth, McCormack placed considerable reliance on his Majority Leader, Carl Albert (D Okla.) and his Whip, Hale Boggs (D La.). Ripley has noted: "Each element of the collegial leadership had its own importance, but the lack of cohesion that had troubled the Republicans in the early 1920s was not present in this arrangement. The functions were split between the various leaders, but there were numerous integrating meetings of the three principal leaders with committee chairmen and legislative liaison officials. The unity of the Democrats was still far from perfect and some major bills were lost, especially in 1962 and 1963. But the Democrats cohered well enough in 1964, 1965 and 1966 to pass many Presidential proposals."

Vice President and President Pro Tem

The Constitution's only references to leadership posts in the Senate were contained in two passages of Article I, Section 3. One passage provided that the Vice President "shall be President of the Senate, but shall have no vote, unless they be equally divided"; the other passage provided that the "Senate shall choose...a President pro tempore, in the absence of the Vice President, or when he shall exercise the office of President of the United States."

With few exceptions, the Senate has been reluctant to place real political power in these offices. It has entrusted it instead to the Majority and Minority Leadership. Thus the powers of the Vice President and of the President pro tempore consist of little more than presiding over the Senate, and neither post has equalled the significance of the Speakership. Even the authority to preside is less significant in the upper chamber than it is in the House, because the Senate's rules, such as unlimited debate, are more liberal.

Historical studies attempting to explain the Senate's attitude toward these top offices have stressed its disinclination to delegate power to a non-Member (the Vice President) or to a Member (the President pro tempore) who may preside only at times of the Vice President's absence. If the Vice President and President pro tempore

are of different political parties—as has often been the case—the Vice President is able to neutralize the pro tem's authority at any point by merely taking the chair. Accordingly, the Senate has vested the real leadership in its party floor leaders, who in turn attempt to persuade the presiding officers (depending upon their party affiliation) to use their parliamentary powers where possible in support of party goals. *(For details of Vice President's role as presiding officer, see History of the Senate, Chapter I.)*

Evolution of Pro Tempore Post

The first President pro tempore, John Langdon of New Hampshire, was elected on April 6, 1789, before the first Vice President, John Adams, had appeared in the Senate. On April 21, 1789, Adams took his seat as presiding officer, and Langdon's service in that capacity ended. Until 1890, the Senate continued to act on the theory that a President pro tem could be elected only in the Vice President's absence and that his term expired when the Vice President returned. By 1890, when the President pro tem was first chosen to serve until "the Senate otherwise ordered," the Senate had elected Presidents pro tem on 163 occasions. In the 42nd Congress alone (1871-73) 10 such elections (all of the same man) were held.

Problems that had arisen under this procedure came under scrutiny in 1876, when the Senate directed its Committee on Privileges and Elections to make a thorough study of the matter. After considerable debate on the Committee's report, the Senate adopted the report's recommendations: (1) that the term of a President pro tempore elected at one session be considered to extend into the next session in the continuing absence of the Vice President; (2) that the death of the Vice President did not automatically vacate the office of President pro tem; and (3) that the Senate had the right to replace a President pro tem at any time it pleased.

Fourteen years later, in 1890, the Senate gave the President pro tem tenure of a sort by adopting a resolution stating that "...(I)t is competent for the Senate to elect a President pro tempore, who shall hold the office during the pleasure of the Senate and until another is elected, and shall execute the duties thereof during all future absences of the Vice President until the Senate otherwise order." That resolution was still in effect in 1971. Under its terms, the President pro tem holds the office as long as he serves in the Senate, unless the Senate elects another in his place. Thus no new election is necessary at the start of each new Congress, as it is for the Speaker of the House, unless the Senate wishes to elect a different Member to the office.

Almost inevitably, the Senate has elected Members of the majority party as President pro tem, usually on straight party-line votes. In recent years, a sitting pro tem has failed of re-election only when his party has lost its majority. Since 1945, it has become customary to elect as pro tem only the most senior Member of the majority party. Of six pro tems since 1945, only one has held less than senior rank in his party—Sen. Arthur H. Vandenberg (R Mich.), who was second-ranking Republican when elected in 1947. Before 1945, however, there were some notable exceptions to this rule. For example, Sen. George H. Moses (R N.H.) ranked only 15th in party seniority when elected in 1925, and Willard Saulsbury (D Del.) was still in his first term when elected in 1916.

Salaries of Top Congressional Leaders

Six of the top leaders of Congress—the Speaker of the House, the President pro tempore of the Senate and the Majority and Minority Leaders of both chambers—receive additional pay for their leadership duties.

Speaker. Highest paid of all Members of Congress is the House Speaker, whose compensation was increased from $43,000 to $62,500 a year under a 1969 law increasing the salaries of the Vice President and Congressional leaders.

Under legislation enacted in 1949 (and still effective in 1971), the Speaker also is allowed $10,000 for expenses (with no accounting required except for income-tax purposes). In addition to his salary and expense money, the Speaker receives annual appropriations for staff and other operating costs of running the Speaker's office (as distinguished from his own Congressional office). In fiscal 1971, the latter appropriations came to $163,490.

Following is a tabulation of the changes in the Speaker's salary, together with the dates on which the authorizing legislation was enacted:

Salary	Date Authorized
$12 per day in session	Sept. 22, 1789
$3,000 per annum	March 19, 1816
$16 per day in session	Jan. 22, 1818
$6,000 per annum	Aug. 16, 1856
$8,000 per annum	Jan. 20, 1874
$12,000 per annum	Feb. 26, 1907
$15,000 per annum	March 4, 1925
$20,000 per annum	Aug. 2, 1946
$30,000 per annum	Jan. 19, 1949
$35,000 per annum	March 2, 1955
$43,000 per annum	Aug. 14, 1964
$62,500 per annum	Sept. 15, 1969

President Pro Tempore. Under the 1969 salary legislation, the salary of the President pro tem of the Senate was raised from $42,500 to $49,500 (and to $62,500 when there is no Vice President and the President pro tem becomes the sole presiding officer). Prior to enactment of the 1969 law, the pro tem received the same pay as other Members of Congress, except that his salary was made equal to the Vice President's in times when there was a vacancy in that office. In fiscal 1971, the office of the pro tem was allotted $44,165 for staff and other operating costs.

Party Floor Leaders. The pay of the Majority and Minority Leaders of both houses also was raised to the $49,500 level under the 1969 pay legislation. Prior to passage of the Legislative Branch Appropriations Act of 1965, these leaders received the same salaries as other Members. The 1965 Act increased the salary of these top floor leaders from $30,000 (the level for all Members at that time) to $35,000.

Like the Speaker and the President pro tempore, the floor leaders receive appropriations for staff and other operating expenses. House leaders get more because of their need for larger staffs. In fiscal 1971, the appropriation for the House Majority Leader was $125,050 and that for the Minority Leader was $115,560. Each of their Senate counterparts received $88,257. Appropriations for staff and operating expenses of House Whips came to $96,515 each, and of Senate Whips to $45,114 each, in fiscal 1971. Majority and Minority Leaders in both chambers were given an additional allowance of $3,000 apiece, to be used only for official purposes.

Powers of President Pro Tempore

Powers of the pro tem as presiding officer have differed little from those of the Vice President. Among the powers of both officers (applicable to the pro tem, of course, only when he is in the chair) are recognition of Members for debate and introduction of bills, amendments and motions; the authority to decide points of order (subject to appeal to the full Senate); appointment of Senators to conference committees, though it is traditional that the presiding officer appoint the Members suggested by the floor manager of the bill in question, subject to normal party ratios; enforcement of decorum; power to administer oaths and affirmations; and appointment of the members of select committees.

The main difference in the powers of the two offices is that the pro tem, but not the Vice President, may appoint a substitute to replace him in the chair. Also, the pro tem, as a Member of the Senate, may vote on all matters, while the Vice President may vote only in the case of a tie. At various times in the 19th century, the pro tem was authorized to appoint members of standing committees. According to Walter Kravitz and Walter Oleszek, authors of *The President Pro Tempore of the*

U.S. Senate, the pro tem exercised that authority in the years 1823-26, 1828-33, 1838, 1841, 1843 and 1863.

In recent years, the only President pro tem who exerted considerable political influence was Arthur H. Vandenberg (R Mich.), who held the post during the 80th Congress (1947-49). Floyd M. Riddick (later named Senate parliamentarian) said in 1949, in his book *The United States Congress: Organization and Procedure,* that Vandenberg, who was both President pro tem and chairman of the Foreign Relations Committee, "took quite an important part in the legislative program and no doubt exerted as much influence in what was done and not done as the Speaker of the House." Riddick added: "He was firm in his rulings, of which all but one or two stood as the decision of the Senate, even though several appeals were taken; he participated in discussions of the pending legislation from the chair perhaps to an unprecedented extent during any Congress of recent years...."

A more recent pro tem, the late Sen. Richard B. Russell (D Ga.), wielded power potentially equal to that of

Vandenberg through his posts as chairman of the Senate Appropriations Committee and of its Defense Appropriations Subcommittee. Russell, however, was hospitalized during much of his term as pro tem (1969-71).

Other Leadership Posts

Since the late 19th century, both political parties have developed highly centralized party organizations to formulate and carry out party programs in the House and the Senate. In each chamber, the parties have officially designated a Majority and Minority Leader (party floor leaders), party Whips (assistant floor leaders) and various advisory bodies such as committees to develop party policy, assign Members to standing committees, and formulate party strategy for the scheduling of legislation. In the House, this party apparatus has normally been directed by the Speaker, in the Senate by the Majority and Minority Leaders.

In both chambers, leadership organizations have become so important to a party's success that major bills are rarely brought to the floor without extensive study of their prospects as well as exertion of considerable pressure from the party organizations on both sides. These leadership structures are particularly important in the House, because of its greater size and consequent unwieldiness. In his study of the House, *Forge of Democracy,* Neil Mac-Neil called the chamber's leadership organizations its "priesthood." "The Speaker," MacNeil asserted, "...has never run the House of Representatives without help. The House has been from the beginning such a sprawling, discordant mass of men that the Speaker has had to depend on lieutenants to guide and oversee its multiple operations in its committees and on the floor, and to ensure the orderly flow of responsible legislation. Indeed, over the years, a hierarchy of leaders has been constructed in the House to support the Speaker, and opposing this hierarchy has been another, created by the minority party and led by the 'shadow' Speaker, the leader of the opposition party. With the hierarchy also has been built a vast array of political and party organizations to assist the Speaker and his lieutenants in the complicated task of making the House a viable, responsible legislative body."

HOUSE

Majority Leader. The first House Member to be officially designated Majority Leader was Sereno E. Payne (R N.Y.), who assumed the post in 1899. Prior to that time, the chairman of the Ways and Means Committee was normally looked upon as party floor leader, primarily because his committee handled tariff and tax measures, which were usually the most important to come up in the House. Occasionally, the Speaker designated a trusted lieutenant other than the Ways and Means Committee chairman as the party's leader. In the interest of party harmony, he sometimes named to that post his leading rival within the party.

Until 1911, Majority Leaders were designated by the Speaker; after the revolt against Speaker Cannon in 1910, however, rank-and-file House Members took it upon themselves to exercise this authority, usually through the party caucus or conference—groups made up of the full membership of the party in the House. In 1911 the House

Democratic caucus elected Oscar W. Underwood (D Ala.) Majority Leader; when the Republicans returned to power in 1919, their Committee on Committees chose Franklin W. Mondell (R Wyo.). The Democratic caucus has continued to select the party's floor leader. Since 1923, Republicans have vested the power of selection in their party conference (a body identical except in name to the Democratic caucus).

The height of power for the Majority Leader came during President Wilson's first term, when Underwood dominated the House through the party caucus and his chairmanship of the Ways and Means Committee. George B. Galloway pointed out in his *History of the House of Representatives:* "As floor leader, Underwood was supreme, the Speaker a figurehead. The main cogs in the machine were the caucus, the floor leadership, the Rules Committee, the standing committees, and special rules. Oscar Underwood became the real leader in the House. He dominated the party caucus, influenced the rules, and as chairman of Ways and Means chose the committees. Champ Clark was given the shadow, Underwood the substance of power." After 1925, the Speakership regained much of its former power and prestige, and since then the Majority Leader has been the chief lieutenant of the Speaker.

Duties of the Majority and Minority Leaders are not spelled out in the standing rules of the House, nor is official provision made for the offices. In practice, the Majority Leader's job has been to formulate the party's legislative program in cooperation with the Speaker and other party leaders, steer the program through the House, ensure that committee chairmen report bills deemed of importance to the party, and fix the legislative schedule of the House by securing unanimous consent agreements from the membership. In this latter duty, the Majority Leader has a significant parliamentary advantage in that if a Member objects to his proposal to consider a given bill, the Majority Leader can usually achieve the same result by putting the matter to a simple majority vote on the floor.

Minority Leader. The position of Minority Leader first became identifiable in 1883. Since that time, the post has always been assumed by the candidate nominated by the minority party for the Speakership. As in the case of the Majority Leader, the selection of the Minority Leader is made by the Democratic caucus or Republican conference, depending upon which party is in the minority. For the most part, the Minority Leader's principal duty has been to obstruct the legislative program of the majority. Rarely has the minority offered its own legislative program. The only major legislative successes for the minority in the 20th century were in the 75th Congress (1937-39) and in the 87th Congress (1961-62), when a number of liberal proposals put forth by the Democratic majority were rejected. In both cases, however, large-scale defections of conservative Democrats were largely responsible for the outcome.

Everyday duties for the Minority Leader correspond to those of his majority counterpart, except that the Minority Leader has no authority over scheduling; if he objects to majority proposals for scheduling, he can always be defeated by a party-line vote on the floor. The Minority Leader is spokesman for his party and its field general on the floor. It is his duty to consult ranking minority members of House committees and see that they follow adopted party positions. If his party occupies the White House, he will probably be the President's spokesman in the House.

Randall B. Ripley observed in *Party Leaders in the House of Representatives:* "One of the Minority Leader's greatest problems is the generally demoralizing condition of minority party status. Minority Members—especially those in a long-standing minority—are less likely to be informed about what the House is doing. They are on the losing side much of the time both in committee and on the floor. They have little patronage inside the Capitol. Their smaller committee staffs make it difficult to prepare legislative positions, and they usually are unable to obtain such assistance from the Executive Branch. Yet they want to be informed, to win, and to have patronage, committee staffs and Executive Branch cooperation. When they cannot gain these objectives, one target of their frustrations is the Minority Leader."

Ripley found that Minority Leaders were much more likely than Majority Leaders to retire voluntarily or to be ousted from their positions. Ripley's study, conducted in 1967, showed that of 13 Minority Leaders in the 20th century, five had stepped down voluntarily, while only two of 12 Majority Leaders had done so. No Majority Leader had been ousted by his party, while three Minority Leaders had been thrown out. Six Majority Leaders had succeeded to the Speakership, while only three Minority Leaders had become Speaker. After Ripley's study was made, another Majority Leader, Carl Albert (D Okla.), became Speaker. Albert was elected to the post in 1971 following the retirement from Congress of Speaker John W. McCormack (D Mass.).

Whips. From the outset, parties have relied on their more influential members to ensure party regularity on important issues before the House. During most of the 19th century, however, such Members were employed in that capacity only on the occasion of a particular floor fight. It was not until 1899 that one of the parties officially designated a Member as party Whip. Randall Ripley found that the term "derives from the British fox-hunting term 'whipper-in' used to describe the man responsible for keeping the hounds from leaving the pack." It was first applied to the British Parliament around 1770.

Whips help their floor leader keep track of the whereabouts of party Members, assist in exerting pressure on Members to vote the party line, induce Members to turn out for votes, compile lists on how Members are likely to vote, and arrange "pairs" between opposing Members. A Whip serves as the party's acting floor leader in the absence of the regular leader. In recent years, the Democratic Whip organization has consisted of a Chief Whip, appointed by the Democratic Floor Leader, and 15 to 18 Assistant Whips selected on a regional basis by state delegations. The Republican organization has consisted of a Chief Whip, a Deputy Whip, four regional Whips and 15 area Whips. From 1919 to 1965, the Republican Whip was selected by the party's Committee on Committees. Since 1965, the selection has been made by the party conference. Traditionally, the Chief Republican Whip has selected his own assistants.

In recent years, Whip organizations of the two parties have sometimes pooled their information in order to attain an accurate over-all picture of the mood of the House respecting important bills. Neil MacNeil said in *Forge of*

Democracy: "On some (W)hip counts, or 'nose counts' as they have been called,...each (Whip) has told the other how his party members would divide on a given bill. Between them, they have sometimes been able to forecast a House vote almost to the man as much as a week in advance. Armed with such intelligence, the Majority and Minority Leaders have mapped out their strategy on floor action. If the (W)hip's nose count has shown that the House would vote down a bill as it stood, the leaders have agreed to alter the bill with an amendment or two to woo at least some of the bill's opponents into favoring it."

Because of the liberal-conservative split that has troubled the Democratic party since the 1930s, House Democratic Whips have had more difficulty than their Republican counterparts in controlling their Members. A study by Randall Ripley of seven key roll-call votes in 1962 showed that while the average support score for all Assistant Democratic Whips was 84 percent, scores for those Whips from the following southern states were considerably lower: Tennessee, Kentucky and Arkansas, 71 percent; Alabama and Florida, 67 percent; Virginia and North Carolina, 43 percent; and Texas, 29 percent. Ripley noted, however, that one Assistant Whip who supported the Administration only rarely in 1962 did "an excellent job" of reporting accurately on the voting inclinations of Members in his zone, while his successor in 1963 achieved a high support score but did an inadequate job of reporting. "Voting loyalty," Ripley concluded, "is far less important than accuracy and thoroughness."

Party Caucus. Use of party caucuses—meetings of the party's full House membership—for organizational purposes dates back to the beginning of Congress. In the Jeffersonian period, Democratic Republicans, in conjunction with the Administration, used the caucus to formulate party legislative strategy. From 1800 to 1824, party caucuses in the House chose the party's nominees for the Presidency and the Vice Presidency. After the 1820s, caucus activity diminished and caucuses met rarely over the next 60 years except to nominate the party candidate for the Speakership at the beginning of each Congress.

Revival of the caucus as a forum for discussing legislative strategy came in the 1890s, when Speaker Reed used caucuses to a limited extent for discussing policy questions. For the most part, however, the caucus under Reed functioned only to give the party's stamp of approval to decisions Reed already had made. In the early 1900s, Speaker Cannon called caucus meetings occasionally but manipulated them in much the same manner as had Reed. It was not until Cannon's overthrow that the caucus was restored to its earlier legislative significance.

As noted previously, Democrats adopted a binding caucus rule in 1909 and used it effectively throughout President Wilson's first term. Democrats used a binding caucus again in Franklin Roosevelt's first term, but they have not employed it since 1935. In recent years, the Democratic caucus has met rarely except to nominate the party candidate for Speaker, select the floor leaders and give perfunctory ratification to leadership choices for committee assignments. The only exceptions were in 1953, when the caucus met on a Republican tax bill, and in 1959, when it met on a bill to abolish the ceiling on long-term interest rates.

Republicans, who have never adopted a binding caucus rule, nonetheless used the caucus (renamed "conference" in 1911) effectively in the 1940s and 1950s to achieve a consensus among party members with respect to important legislative proposals. The conference was normally dominated by the party leadership, who resorted to it much as Reed and Cannon had done to achieve party support for their own predetermined courses of action. The conference has rarely served as a deliberative body in the true sense; an exception was its occasional use in the period 1965-69 to develop policy positions for the consideration of party floor leaders.

Committee on Committees. After the House revolt against Speaker Cannon in 1910, power to appoint members of standing committees was taken from the Speaker and vested in the membership of the full House. In 1911, the Democratic caucus delegated the authority to choose the party's committee members to a specially constituted Committee on Committees, which was made up of the Democrats on the Ways and Means Committee. The Committee's choices were subject to ratification of the caucus and the full House, but the ratification became perfunctory. In 1917, the Republican conference established a Committee on Committees, which was not necessarily made up of the party's members on Ways and Means. Decisions of the Republican Committee on Committees were subject to the same perfunctory approval as under the Democratic procedure.

Staff aides for the Democratic caucus and the Republican conference told Congressional Quarterly early in 1971 that they did not recall a single instance in which a selection by one of the Committees on Committees was reversed by the caucus, the conference or the full House. The Democratic Committee on Committees has been named by the party caucus upon recommendation of the party leadership; its Republican counterpart in the same manner by the conference.

Despite the independent authority of both Committees on Committees, Speakers have often been able to influence committee assignments. In the late 1920s, for example, Speaker Longworth had four uncooperative members of the Rules Committee replaced with his own choices. In the 1940s and 1950s, Speaker Sam Rayburn intervened frequently to influence the makeup of the Ways and Means Committee, which he insisted be stacked with Members favorable to reciprocal trade agreements and opposed to reduction of the oil and gas depletion allowance.

Steering, Policy Committees. During the present century, both parties have established groups called "Steering Committees" to assist the leadership with legislative scheduling and the formulation of party strategy. The Republican Steering Committee, appointed in 1919, dominated the House until 1925 when power again shifted to the Speaker. Although the new Speaker, Nicholas Longworth, largely ignored the Steering Committee, it continued in existence until 1949, when it was renamed the Policy Committee and expanded from eight to 22 members. Subsequently, the size of the Committee was increased to 35. The Policy Committee was considered the chief advisory board for the Minority Leader from 1959 to 1965, but it was then replaced in that role by the party conference.

Democrats established a Steering Committee in 1933, abandoned it in 1956, and reconstituted it in 1962. Since 1962, the Committee has consisted of 18 members, appointed to represent the same regions as the Whips. Ex-officio members include the Speaker, Majority Leader, Whip, chairman of the caucus, secretary of the caucus and chairman of the Congressional Campaign Committee. The Democratic Steering panel has seldom met and has had no apparent effect on party decisions.

SENATE

Floor Leaders. Emergence of readily recognizable floor leaders in the Senate did not occur until the period 1911-13. Designation of these positions was the culmination of an increasing party influence in the chamber which began around 1890. Prior to that time, leadership in the Senate, when identifiable at all, was usually vested in powerful individuals or small factions of Senators. As late as 1885, Woodrow Wilson wrote in his graduate thesis, *Congressional Government*: "The public now and again picks out here and there a Senator who seems to act and to speak with true instinct of statesmanship and who unmistakably merits the confidence of colleagues and of people. But such a man, however eminent, is never more than *a* Senator. No one is *the* Senator. No one may speak for his party as well as for himself; no one exercises the special trust of acknowledged leadership. The Senate is merely a body of individual critics...."

Until 1846, party organization in the Senate was virutally nonexistent. Committee members were selected by ballot of the full Senate without any formal recommendation by parties, or they were appointed by the Vice President or the President pro tempore. In 1846, parties began nominating the membership of standing committees for routine ratification by the full Senate. Further steps toward party control were slow to develop until well after the Civil War. According to David J. Rothman in his book *Politics and Power*, party pressures on Senators were still negligible as late as the 1870s: "No one had the authority to keep his colleagues in line, and positions of influence were distributed without regard for personal loyalties. Democratic and Republican organizations rarely attempted to schedule legislation or enforce unity in voting. In brief, Senators were free to go about their business more or less as they pleased."

Republicans—In the 1870s, Republicans sought to strengthen party control by appointing a caucus chairman, who was assumed to be the party's floor leader. The power of the chairman, Henry Anthony (R R.I.), was overshadowed, however, by the influence of a small faction of Senators led by Roscoe Conkling (R N.Y.) which sought to develop and pursue its own policies regardless of the overall party interest. The influence of the Conkling faction, which was never great enough to control the Senate, eventually petered out as the result of a series of unsuccessful feuds with Republican Presidents over patronage matters in New York State. But it was not until the 1890s and the emergence of another Republican faction led by Senators William B. Allison (Iowa) and Nelson W. Aldrich (R.I.) that a consistently effective leadership organization was established.

Allison derived his power from the chairmanship of the Appropriations Committee. Aldrich achieved his through force of personality; he held no formal position in the Senate until he became chairman of the Finance Committee in 1899. By pooling their influence, the two Republican leaders were able to dictate committee assignments, caucus positions, decisions of standing committees and scheduling decisions. Like Speaker Cannon, who dominated the House for much of the same period, Allison and Aldrich were largely successful in imposing their own conservative political views upon the entire Senate. According to Rothman, the Allison-Aldrich clique "instituted once and for all, the prerogatives of power" in the Senate. "Would-be successors or Senate rivals would now be forced to capture and effectively utilize the party posts. Allison understood clearly that 'both in the committees and in the offices, we should use the machinery for our own benefit and not let other men have it.' His heirs had no choice but to follow his dictum."

In the opinion of Rothman and other authorities, Allison and Aldrich used the tactic of after-hours poker games to cement the loyalties of key Senators. About six or eight Republican Senators usually attended the sessions, which were held at the home of Sen. James McMillan (R Mich.) and came to be known as the "School of Philosophy Club." Eventually, two principal lieutenants emerged from the group: John C. Spooner (R Wis.) and Orville H. Platt (R Conn.). The clique then became known as "The Four." Defeats for the Allison-Aldrich group were rare until President Theodore Roosevelt was able to push through a part of his progressive legislative program in the early 1900s. The group retained much of its power after Allison's death in 1908, but it disintegrated soon after Aldrich retired in 1911.

Democrats—The evolution of a centralized Democratic organization in the Senate dates back to 1889, when Sen. Arthur P. Gorman (D Md.) was named chairman of the party's caucus. Like the Allison-Aldrich group, Gorman solidified his control by appointing his political allies to positions of influence. (Gorman further merged the real power with formal party positions by assuming all of the party's top leadership posts himself, including floor leader, chairman of the Steering Committee and chairman of the Committee on Committees.) Unlike the Allison-Aldrich appointments, however, Gorman's appointments were permanent and the responsibilities of his party lieutenants were clearly defined. In this sense, Gorman is credited with contributing more to modern party organization in the Senate than did Allison and Aldrich, even though the Republican clique attained far greater political influence at the time. (During Gorman's 10 years as caucus chairman, 1889-99, Democrats were in the minority for all except two years.) Leadership in the party was dispersed after Gorman left the Senate.

In 1911, Democrats broke new ground by formally designating a floor leader (Thomas S. Martin of Virginia). It was not until 1913 and the appointment of John W. Kern (D Ind.) to the post, however, that Democrats were able to create an organization as strong as the Allison-Aldrich group had been. Kern, who worked closely with President Wilson, mobilized solid Democratic support behind the President's tariff reform, currency reform and antitrust reform programs. As Randall B. Ripley observed, Kern's "leadership was unobtrusive and effective. He wielded his powers of influencing committee assignments, scheduling and chairing the caucus to unite Democrats behind the New Freedom legislative program."

New Deal Era—Students of government have characterized the Senate floor leaders of both parties who served from 1919-1933 as largely ineffective, with the exception of Republican Majority Leader Henry Cabot Lodge (Mass.) on the issue of ratification of the Treaty of Versailles, which embodied the Covenant of the League of Nations. Lodge managed to bring about the treaty's defeat twice, in 1919 and on a second vote in 1920, despite enormous pressure from President Wilson. The next strong leader appeared in the New Deal era, when Majority Leader Joseph T. Robinson (D Ark.) pushed President Roosevelt's far-reaching legislative program through the chamber. Robinson achieved solid party support even though he sometimes disagreed personally with specific New Deal measures. It was almost 20 years before other strong floor leaders appeared.

Johnson, Dirksen—The only two Senate leaders widely acclaimed as effective in the period since Robinson have been Lyndon B. Johnson (D Texas), who served as Minority Leader from 1953 to 1955 and as Majority Leader from 1955 to 1960, and Everett McKinley Dirksen (R Ill.), Minority Leader from 1959 until his death in 1969.

Johnson, whose entire tenure as Majority Leader was spent while President Eisenhower was in the White House, became a master of compromise and thus was able to obtain legislation satisfactory both to the Democratic majority in Congress and to the Republican President. Johnson was a highly persuasive leader. He used a whole range of techniques to win cooperation, including influence on committee assignments, logrolling and personal favors. (For examples, see *Internal Pressures*, Chapter VI.)

Dirksen, whose party amounted to a small minority throughout his tenure, was able to put a Republican imprint on many Democratically inspired bills by maintaining tight party unity. Using methods similar to Johnson's, Dirksen translated party unity into amendments and other concessions although his party was seldom able to defeat important bills.

Whip Organizations. The first Whips appeared in the Senate shortly after the positions of Majority and Minority Leader were formally established. Democrats named their first Whip in 1913, Republicans theirs in 1915. Although duties of the Senate Whips have been essentially the same as those of their House counterparts, the Senate Whip organizations have rarely achieved as much success.

Senate Whips at times have openly defied stands taken by their party leaders. Such clashes have resulted largely from the fact that the Democratic caucus and the Republican conference elect their floor leaders and Whips and have sometimes been forced into regional logrolling to get agreement on their choices. Occasionally the breach between a party leader and a Whip has become public knowledge.

The most serious breach of this sort was between Majority Leader Mike Mansfield (D Mont.) and Whip Russell B. Long (D La.) in the years 1965-69. Long and Mansfield clashed openly in 1966 over a proposal by Long for Federal subsidies in Presidential election campaigns. Long exacerbated the dispute in 1967 by publishing a newsletter for constituents in which he listed his disagreements with President Johnson (which also were disagreements with Mansfield). Mansfield sought to circumvent Long's influence by appointing four Assistant Whips. In 1969, Long was defeated by Sen. Edward M. Kennedy (D Mass.), a Mansfield supporter, in his bid for re-election to the Whip's post.

The occasional differences between party leaders and Whips, coupled with the fact that the Senate is smaller and thus easier to control than the House, have left many Senate leaders reluctant to share power with their Whips. As Ripley observed in his 1969 book *Power in the Senate,* the assistance of the Whips has been "peripheral, not central, to the impact of the floor leaders." He added that only a few Whips had "developed into major influences in the party, usually through their performance of the persuasion function."

Caucuses. Early development of party caucuses in the Senate was concurrent with that in the House. In 1846, caucuses increased in importance when they acquired power over committee assignments. During the Civil War and the Reconstruction era, Republicans used the caucus frequently to discuss and adopt party positions on legislation.

In the 1890s both the Republican organization of Allison and Aldrich and the Democratic organization of Gorman used the caucus extensively, with Republicans achieving more control than Democrats. As Rothman observed in *Politics and Power:* "The Republican caucus was not binding, and yet its decisions commanded obedience, for party leadership was capable of enforcing discipline. Senators could no longer act with impunity unless they were willing to forego favorable committee posts and control of the chamber proceedings."

In 1903, Senate Democrats officially adopted a binding caucus rule, but there is no evidence that they ever put it to use. In 1933, Democrats readopted the rule, but again did not use it. Since that time, neither party has seriously considered using a binding caucus. In recent years, both parties have employed the caucus (now called "conference" by both) to collect and distribute information to Members. The Republican conference, which meets more frequently than the Democratic conference, has served also as a forum of persuasion for the leadership; the Democratic conference has been used only rarely for that purpose.

Committee on Committees. The tradition of Committes on Committees in the Senate goes back to the Civil War era, when Republicans utilized a special panel appointed by the party caucus to make both Republican and Democratic committee assignments. After the war, Republicans took control of the committee away from the caucus as a whole and vested it in the caucus chairman. Democrats set up a similar committee in 1879, appointed and chaired by the caucus chairman. The Democratic Committee on Committees in the Senate now is known as the Steering Committee.

Republicans have made seniority the absolute rule for both initial committee assignments and promotions to chairmanships. Democrats have applied the seniority rule for promotions but not for initial assignments. As in the House, decisions of the committee on committees of both parties are subject to approval of the party conferences and the full chamber, but approval has been perfunctory. *(See Seniority, Chapter II.)*

Steering, Policy Committees. What was in effect the first committee on order of business in the Senate was established in 1874, when the Republican caucus appointed a special committee to prepare a legislative schedule. That committee was replaced in the mid-1880s by a formal Steering Committee, appointed by the caucus chairman. Democrats established a Steering Committee in 1879, but discontinued it in periods when Republicans controlled the Senate and thus the legislative schedule. In 1947, both Democrats and Republicans created new Policy Committees which were assigned the scheduling duties of the old Steering Committees. (As previously noted, the Democratic Steering Committee, while retaining its name, 'was reconstituted as a committee on committees.) In years in which the Republicans have been in the minority, the Policy Committee has studied legislation and recommended policy positions to the conference and the Minority Leader. The Democratic Policy Committee has not assumed an actual policy role.

Leadership Contests

Of the top leadership positions in Congress, only the office of House Speaker is filled by a formal vote on the floor. Other posts, not recognized in the House rules, are filled by action of a party caucus or conference. The latter bodies also make nominations for the Speakership. In most elections for Speaker, the House has merely ratified the choice of the majority party; in some instances, the majority party has been splintered by factions, however, and spirited election battles have developed on the House floor.

Pre-Civil War Era. In the years before the Civil War, regional disputes, mostly over slavery, gave rise to at least 10 heated battles for the Speakership. The first was in 1809, when none of the Democratic Republican candidates could achieve a majority on the first ballot; the election finally went to Joseph B. Varnum (Mass.) after the southern candidate, Nathaniel Macon (N.C.), withdrew for reasons of health. Other minor antebellum battles occurred in 1820, when an anti-slavery candidate, John W. Taylor (D N.Y.), won on the 22nd ballot; in 1821, when Philip P. Barbour (D Va.) won on the 12th; in 1825, when Taylor recaptured the post on the second ballot; in 1834, when John Bell (Whig Tenn.) won on the 10th vote; in 1847, when Robert C. Winthrop (Whig Mass.) won on the third; and in 1861, when Galusha A. Grow (R Pa.) won on the second. Major contests for the Speakership in which the House became deadlocked for a matter of weeks or months took place in 1839, 1849, 1855 and 1859.

1839 New Jersey Controversy—The first of the prolonged battles over the Speakership began on Dec. 2, 1839, when election of the Speaker hinged on the outcome of five contested House seats in New Jersey. Excluding the five New Jersey Members, the party lineup in the House would have been 119 Democrats and 118 Whigs. Democrats sought to organize the House (and elect the new Speaker) before the New Jersey cases were decided; Whigs, in hope of winning control of the House, wanted to await the outcome of the New Jersey contests.

Chaos reigned for several days while the Clerk of the House, according to custom, refused to put any question to the House until a quorum was present. After four days of disorder, John Quincy Adams (Whig Mass.), the most powerful Member of the House, took the floor and demanded that the body proceed with the roll call, including those Members from New Jersey who held election certificates signed by the Governor of the state. The House voted overwhelmingly that Adams should take the Chair; finally, on Dec. 14, the House consented to vote for Speaker, with both New Jersey delegations excluded from participating. Although the decision was what the

Democrats had been seeking, the party's leaders were unable to hold a sufficient number of Members in line to win on the ensuing votes. Finally, on Dec. 16, Robert M. T. Hunter (D Va.), who had declared himself an independent, was elected Speaker on the 11th ballot. As Adams concluded in his *Memoirs*, Hunter "finally united all the Whig votes, and all the malcontents of the Administration."

1849 Free-Soil Dispute—The next major contest for the Speakership developed in 1849, when neither the Whigs nor the Democrats could achieve a majority because Free-Soil factions of both parties decided to act independently. The resulting deadlock lasted for three weeks and 63 ballots.

The main issue underlying the deadlock was the makeup of the House Committee on the District of Columbia and on Territories, which Free-Soilers contended should be organized in favor of the opponents of expansion of slavery. Free-Soilers thus opposed the election of both of the leading candidates for the office, Robert C. Winthrop (Whig Mass.), who they felt had been lukewarm on the slavery issue as Speaker from 1847 to 1849, and Howell Cobb (D Ga.), a strong proponent of slavery. Each faction put up its own candidate (at one time there were 11), preventing either Cobb or Winthrop from achieving a majority. At various points in the controversy, compromise solutions were considered and rejected, including proposals that the Speaker be divested of his power to appoint committees (thus leaving that authority to the full House), that the Speaker be chosen by lottery and that Members receive no salary or mileage until a Speaker was elected.

Finally, after the 59th vote, a motion was carried that the Speaker be elected by a plurality, provided that it be a majority of a quorum. On the 60th vote, Cobb led, on the 61st, Winthrop, and on the 62nd, the vote was tied. On the 63rd ballot, the issue was finally decided when Cobb won a plurality of two votes with a quorum voting. The House then confirmed his election by adopting a resolution "That Howell Cobb, a Representative from the state of Georgia, be declared duly elected Speaker of the House of Representatives for the Thirty-First Congress."

Commenting on the significance of Cobb's election, Mary P. Follett concluded in *Speaker of the House*: "Southern suspense was now relieved. If the Whigs had elected their candidate in 1849 the Civil War might have been delayed, for the committees of this Congress affected the Compromise of 1850. It is probable that Mr. Winthrop's prestige would have carried him into the Senate and eventually have affected the makeup of the Republican party. The choice of a very pronounced pro-slavery and southern man at this crisis undoubtedly aggravated the struggles of the following decade."

1855 Kansas Controversy—Six years after the Cobb-Winthrop contest, another multi-faction battle based on the slavery issue led to a deadlock in the election of a Speaker. Like the 1849 battle, the 1855 dispute focused on the question of composition of House committees either for or against slavery. The immediate concern of both sides was the effect those committees might have on the question of admission of Kansas as a free or a slave state. The dispute, which began in December 1855, lasted through 133 ballots taken over a period of almost two months.

Although anti-slavery forces held a majority of House seats, their ranks were so split by factions (mostly the new Republican party and various Free-Soil groups), that they could not unite behind a single candidate. At the outset of the election battle, on Dec. 3, 1855, 21 candidates were nominated. After 129 ballots, the House decided that, following three more roll calls, the candidate receiving the greatest number of votes would be elected. On Feb. 2, 1856, on the 133rd ballot, Nathaniel P. Banks (American Mass.) was elected with 103 votes out of 214 cast.

As in 1849, the election was subsequently confirmed by a resolution adopted by majority vote. Miss Follett pointed out: "...Mr. Banks was elected above all because it was expected that he would constitute the committees in favor of the Free-Soilers. He justified the expectation by putting a majority of anti-slavery men on the Kansas Investigation Committee, which act practically delayed the settlement of the Kansas episode until after 1857, and this gave time for the anti-slavery forces to organize."

1859 Pennington Election—The last of the great pre-war battles over the Speakership occurred in 1859. The House took 44 ballots over a period of nearly two months to decide the question. On the first day of the session, Dec. 5, the tone for the battle was set when anti-slavery advocates proposed a resolution that any candidate who endorsed the sentiments of *The Impending Crisis of the South: How to Meet It*, a book hostile to slavery, was not fit to be Speaker of the House. The next day, a second resolution was proposed, stating that "it is the duty of every good citizen of this Union to resist all attempts at renewing in Congress or out of it the slavery agitation, under whatever shape and color the attempt may be made. And that no Member shall be elected Speaker of this House whose political opinions are not known to conform to the foregoing sentiment."

Both resolutions were directed at John Sherman (R Ohio), who had endorsed the book opposing slavery. As Miss Follett wrote, "The ball thus set rolling, the discussion of slavery began, bitter and passionate on one side, eager and vehement on the other. The state of the country was reflected in the struggle for Speaker. The House was the scene of a confusion and uproar which the Clerk could not control.... Bitter personal invectives nearly led to personal encounters.... It seemed as though the Civil War was to begin in the House of Representatives."

Sherman led in the early voting, falling only six votes short of a majority on the third ballot. By the end of January, however, Republicans saw that Sherman could not be elected and shifted their support to William Pennington (Whig N.J.), a new and unknown Member. On Feb. 1, Pennington was elected with 117 votes, the minimum required to win. According to Miss Follett, Pennington as Speaker was regarded as an "impartial" presiding officer although "notably ignorant of the practice of the House." Pennington was the only Speaker other than Henry Clay ever elected to the Speakership during his first term in the House.

Progressive Insurgency of 1923. The only deadlock over the Speakership since the Civil War was in 1923, when 20 Progressive Republicans held the balance of power in the House. (Officially, there were 225 Republicans including Progressives, 205 Democrats, 1 Independent, 1 Farmer-Laborite and 1 Socialist.) The Progressives put up their own candidate, Henry A. Cooper (R Wis.), as a "protest to rules that have grown up in this body." After eight inconclusive votes, Nicholas Longworth (R

Details of 1971 Senate Democratic Whip Contest

One of the most surprising and potentially significant upsets in a leadership election in years came at the outset of the 92nd Congress, when Robert C. Byrd (D W.Va.) defeated Edward M. Kennedy (D Mass.) in Kennedy's bid for re-election as Senate Majority Whip. Kennedy's defeat eliminated him from any party leadership position in the Senate and cast doubt on his standing as a possible Presidential contender in 1972 —a standing that previously had been considered high. The outcome also resumed a longtime pattern among Senate Democrats of electing party conservatives or moderates in direct contests with liberals for leadership positions. Kennedy had upset that pattern in 1968 when he defeated Russell B. Long (D La.) in Long's bid for re-election to the post.

Byrd's surprise win took place in the Democratic conference Jan. 21, 1971, following a covert but assiduous campaign in which Byrd was able to capture several key votes that Kennedy had counted on getting. Kennedy staff aides said the Senator had canvassed his fellow Democrats once before Christmas to seek their support and canvassed them again the day before the election. He had not actually totaled his prospective votes, they said, but he believed he had enough support to win when he went into the party conference. The actual vote, which was by secret ballot, was 31-24 in Byrd's favor.

Reporters speculated that Senate Democratic Presidential candidates might have voted against Kennedy to reduce his chances of becoming a candidate in 1972. Kennedy replied, "I prefer to think that those who felt Sen. Byrd could do the best job voted for him and those who thought I could voted for me." Kennedy credited Byrd's success to his knowledge of the details of Senate procedure—knowledge which Kennedy said had been helpful to many Senators. Byrd, the Senate Democratic Secretary, had been "extremely attentive" to floor action, Kennedy said, while he (Kennedy) had been campaigning for re-election in Massachusetts in the fall of 1970.

Russell Proxy. Byrd decided to run when he learned that Sen. Richard B. Russell (D Ga.) was still alive, although in critical condition in a Washington hospital, after a respiratory attack complicated by emphysema. According to Byrd, Russell's proxy was the decisive factor in his decision to challenge Kennedy for the post. Russell died less than five hours after the conference action.

The campaign which led to Byrd's victory was marked by extreme caution and almost total lack of publicity. In mid-November 1970, two months before the conference was to meet, Byrd announced he would confer with colleagues to decide whether to try to unseat Kennedy. "I've been doing the work all along (as Democratic Secretary)," Byrd said Nov. 14. "The only difference is, I would have the title." But Byrd made no formal announcement of his intention to seek the post, and most political observers believed Kennedy had the necessary support to remain as Whip. As late as one day before the vote, Kennedy aides said Byrd could not win.

Shortly after his election, Byrd reluctantly explained why his strategy worked. "I did not know whether I would allow my name to be placed in nomination when I walked into the (conference)," Byrd said. "But I had campaigned by talking to every Democratic Senator and I knew I had 28 firm commitments." Byrd said that one of his commitments came from Russell, who lay critically ill as the conference met. Russell's proxy vote was held by Sen. Herman E. Talmadge (D Ga.), who had been instructed to cast it in favor of Byrd. However, if Russell had died before the voting began, his vote could not have been counted. "I needed all 28 votes to win, and I had determined I would not run if Sen. Russell were not alive," Byrd said.

Byrd asked Sen. Jennings Randolph, his Democratic colleague from West Virginia, to place his name in nomination only if Byrd gave him a signal during the conference. As the nominations for Whip began, Kennedy's name was placed before the Senate Democrats. At that point, an aide to Talmadge called a member of Russell's family at Walter Reed Army Hospital in Washington and learned that Russell's condition remained unchanged. When Byrd was informed of this, he nodded to Randolph, who began Byrd's nomination speech. Sen. Mike Gravel (D Alaska) seconded Byrd's nomination, and the secret voting followed.

"I was surprised to learn that my final total was 31 votes," Byrd said. "I had received vague indications from some Senators that they might vote for me, but I had only 28 commitments that were absolutely firm—the number I needed to win." Byrd said if he had decided not to run against Kennedy, he would have tried to retain his position as Senate Democratic Secretary.

Ohio), the GOP floor leader, made an agreement with the Progressives to liberalize the rules. The next day the Progressives threw their support behind the Republican candidate, Frederick H. Gillett (R Mass.), Speaker since 1919, who was re-elected.

From 1923 to 1971, there were no other floor battles for the Speakership. Over that period, one party always held a clear majority and was able to elect its man on the first ballot.

Other Leadership Disputes. In recent years, there have been several major contests within party caucuses or conferences for leadership posts in both houses of Congress. Among the more important of the contests:

• In 1951, Senate Democrats elected Ernest W. McFarland (Ariz.), a moderate, over Joseph C. O'Mahoney (Wyo.), a strong advocate of President Truman's Fair Deal program, for the Majority Leadership. McFarland's election set a pattern for the success of Democratic moderates or conservatives in contests with liberals. In 1965, Russell B. Long (La.), a moderate conservative, defeated the more liberal John O. Pastore (R.I.) and Mike Monroney (Okla.) in a race for party Whip. In 1967, conservative Robert C. Byrd (W.Va.) won the post of Secretary of the Conference against liberal Joseph S. Clark (Pa.). The only liberal victory in these Democratic contests came in 1968, when Edward M. Kennedy (Mass.) defeated Long in his bid for re-election as Whip. In 1971, however, Kennedy was defeated in his own bid for re-election by Byrd. *(See box.)*

• In 1969, Sen. Hugh Scott (R Pa.), a moderate, defeated conservative Sen. Roman Hruska (R Neb.) for Senate Republican Whip. Following the death of Senate Minority Leader Everett McKinley Dirksen (Ill.) later in the year, Scott defeated Hruska and Howard H. Baker Jr. (Tenn.) for Dirksen's old post. Robert P. Griffin (Mich.), another moderate Republican, then defeated Baker for party Whip. These developments ran counter to the GOP's postwar practice of electing mostly conservative floor leaders in contests with moderates or liberals. In four previous contested elections for top Republican leadership posts over the 1947-68 period, conservatives had won three. In 1971, Scott again defeated Baker for the Minority Leadership; Griffin was unopposed for Whip.

• After a bitter 1959 battle, House Republicans replaced their longtime floor leader, Joseph W. Martin Jr. (Mass.), with a younger and more vigorous leader, Charles A. Halleck (Ind.). Halleck's unyielding conservatism and strong-arm leadership tactics annoyed many House Republicans, particularly moderates, and in 1965 the conference replaced him with Gerald R. Ford (Mich.), a younger and more moderately conservative leader. Through 1971, the only subsequent contest for a top leadership post in the House was at the outset of the 92nd Congress (January 1971) when House Majority Whip Hale Boggs (D La.) defeated four other candidates for the post of Majority Leader, which had been vacated when Carl Albert (D Okla.) was nominated (and later elected) to the Speakership.

Leadership vs. White House

For the most part, Congressional leaders have sought to cooperate with a President of their own political party and to defeat or amend programs put forth by a President belonging to the opposite party. Over the years, however, there have been several important instances in which Congressional leaders have resisted the program of a same-party President or have developed their own legislative program and imposed it on the White House. Cases in which a party's Congressional leadership has cooperated in a substantial way with an opposing party's President are less frequent and have been limited mainly to national defense and foreign policy issues. One notable exception occurred at the beginning of the New Deal era when House Minority Leader Bertrand H. Snell (R N.Y.) threw his support behind President Roosevelt's emergency banking bill with the statement: "The house is burning down, and the President of the United States says this is the way to put out the fire." *(For Presidential pressure techniques and discussion of the leadership's cooperation with Presidents of the same party and conflicts with those of opposing parties, see Executive Branch pressures, Chapter VI.)*

Strong Presidents. Many of the conflicts between the White House and Congresses controlled by the same party have come at times of strong Presidential leadership. Lincoln, Wilson and the two Roosevelts all had difficulties with their party's Congressional leaders, although all four Presidents were largely successful in executing their programs.

The first important conflict of this kind arose during the Civil War, when Republican extremists dominated Congress and sought to interfere with Lincoln's prosecution of the war and with his plans for postwar reconstruction. The so-called Radical Republicans, like the Whigs before them, strongly espoused the theory of Congressional domination of the Government. In application of that theory, Congress in 1861 created a Joint Committee on the Conduct of the War, which went so far as to intervene in military operations. In 1864, Congress sought to undermine President Lincoln's liberal reconstruction program by passing the Wade-Davis bill to transfer responsibility for reconstruction from the President to Congress. Lincoln pocket-vetoed the bill and, so far as possible, ignored the Congressional extremists. He managed to hold the upper hand by resort to executive orders, but Congress, after Lincoln's assassination, achieved the supremacy it was seeking and retained it for more than 30 years. *(See below.)*

The next strong President to experience difficulty with his own party's leadership in Congress was Theodore Roosevelt (R), who clashed sharply with Sen. Nelson W. Aldrich (R R.I.), the unofficial but acknowledged leader of Senate Republicans. Roosevelt was able to work successfully for the most part with the powerful House leader, Speaker Joseph G. Cannon (R Ill.), by compromising on various parts of his program. Although Speaker Cannon had agreed to support the President's bill to regulate railroad rates in exchange for Roosevelt's agreement to drop tariff reform, Aldrich refused to go along. After relying mostly on Democrats to report the rate bill from the Senate committee, Roosevelt won agreement from William B. Allison (R Iowa), another leading Republican in the Senate, to take a moderate position on judicial review of Government-administered rates. This maneuver split the opposition and led to passage of the bill by an overwhelming vote. However, Aldrich continued to oppose other Administration measures and occasionally won important concessions from the President.

Although relations between President Wilson and the Democratic Congressional leadership were generally good, party leaders sometimes deserted the President on foreign policy matters. On the eve of the opening of the Panama Canal in 1914, both Speaker Champ Clark (Mo.) and House Majority Leader Oscar W. Underwood (Ala.) opposed Wilson's request to repeal a provision of existing law that would have exempted American coastwise vessels from payment of canal tolls. The exemption, which Great Britain insisted would be in violation of an Anglo-American treaty, was nevertheless eliminated.

In 1917, when Wilson asked Congress to declare war on Germany, he was opposed by Rep. Claude Kitchin (N.C.), then the House Majority Leader. Later, he was opposed by Speaker Clark on his program for military conscription. Near the end of Wilson's second term, relations between Clark and the White House were almost severed. When House Minority Leader Franklin

W. Mondell (R Wyo.) asked Clark how to get the Administration's advice on proposed legislation, Clark told him he could not say because "they never confer with me."

President Franklin D. Roosevelt, whose over-all relations with Congress were as good as or better than Wilson's, also experienced some difficulty with his party's Congressional leaders in the latter part of his Administration. During his third (wartime) term, party leaders sometimes deserted the President on domestic measures; in 1944, Senate Majority Leader Alben W. Barkley (Ky.) resigned that post when Roosevelt vetoed a revenue bill. Barkley, however, was promptly re-elected by the party caucus, and the bill was passed over the President's veto. The most active Presidents since Roosevelt—Truman, Kennedy and Johnson, all Democrats—generally commanded the support of the party's Congressional apparatus.

Weak Presidents. To a somewhat lesser extent, Congressional leaders have clashed with less active Presidents of their own party, mostly in cases of Congressional initiative on legislation. The first and most prominent of these cases was that in which Henry Clay forced President Madison into the War of 1812 and President Monroe into a series of unwanted post-war measures, including tariff revision.

Following the Civil War, the Radical Republicans in Congress were able to push through their reconstruction policy over President Andrew Johnson's veto and almost managed to convict Johnson in impeachment proceedings. In 1871, Charles Sumner (R Mass.), chairman of the Senate Foreign Relations Committee, was deposed by the Republican caucus for opposing President Grant's foreign policy and refusing to consult with the President. The next major conflict of this sort came in 1898, also over foreign policy. Speaker Thomas B. Reed (R Maine), a strong isolationist, sought but failed to block three important parts of President McKinley's foreign policy program—war with Spain, the annexation of Hawaii and acquisition of the Philippine Islands. Reed's failure to stop these moves, which led to his retirement from Congress, was largely due to their popularity with the public, not to successful application of pressure by McKinley.

The only other instances of such intra-party conflicts occurred during the Administrations of Presidents Harding and Coolidge, who were generally regarded as among the weakest of all Presidents of the United States. The Washington Naval Conference of 1921-22 was thrust on Harding by Sen. William E. Borah (R Idaho). Congressional investigations of the Harding Administration produced examples of widespread corruption and led to prosecution of a number of Administration officials. In the Coolidge Administration, the Republican Congress passed a veterans' adjusted compensation (bonus) bill over the President's veto and drastically amended various Administration bills.

Bibliography

Books

Alexander, DeAlva Stanwood. *History and Procedure of the House of Representatives.* Houghton Mifflin Co., 1916.

Bone, Hugh A., *American Politics and the Party System* (3rd ed.). McGraw-Hill, 1965.

Bone, Hugh A., *Party Committees and National Politics*, University of Washington Press, 1958.

Brown, George Rothwell, *The Leadership of Congress.* Bobbs-Merrill Co., 1922.

Chiu, Chang-Wei, *The Speaker of the House of Representatives Since 1896.* Columbia University Press, 1928.

Clark, Champ, *My Quarter Century in American Politics.* 2 vols. Harper & Bros., 1920.

Evans, Rowland and Novak, Robert, *Lyndon B. Johnson: The Exercise of Power.* New American Library, 1966.

Follett, Mary P., *The Speaker of the House of Representatives.* Longmans, Green & Co., 1896.

Fuller, Hubert Bruce, *The Speakers of the House.* Little, Brown & Co., 1909.

Galloway, George B., *History of the House of Representatives.* Thomas Y. Crowell Co., 1961.

Hasbrouck, Paul DeWitt, *Party Government in the House of Representatives.* MacMillan Co., 1927.

Haynes, George H., *The Senate of the United States* (Vol. 1). Houghton Mifflin Co., 1938.

MacNeil, Neil, *Forge of Democracy.* David MacKay Co., 1963.

Martin, Joe, *My First Fifty Years in Politics.* McGraw-Hill, 1960.

Riddick, Floyd M., *The United States Congress; Organization and Procedures.* National Capitol Publishers, 1949.

Ripley, Randall B., *Majority Party Leadership in Congress.* Little, Brown & Co., 1969.

Ripley, Randall B., *Party Leaders in the House of Representatives.* Brookings Institution, 1967.

Ripley, Randall B., *Power in the Senate.* St. Martin's Press Inc., 1969.

Rothman, David J., *Politics and Power: The United States Senate, 1869-1901.* Harvard University Press, 1966.

White, William S., *Citadel.* Harper & Bros., 1955.

White, William S., *Home Place.* Houghton Mifflin Co., 1965.

Wilson, Woodrow, *Congressional Government.* Houghton Mifflin Co., 1885.

Government Publications

Kravitz, Walter and Oleszek, Walter, *The President Pro Tempore of the U.S. Senate.* Legislative Reference Service, 1969.

Oleszek, Walter, *Party Whips in the United States Senate.* Legislative Reference Service, 1970.

Riddick, Floyd M., *Majority and Minority Leaders of the Senate* (Senate Document 91-20), Government Printing Office, 1969.

The Evolution of Committees

ONE OF THE outstanding characteristics of the United States Congress is the dominant role committees play in its proceedings. So great is the power of these small and autonomous groups that Congress is frequently said to have abdicated its lawmaking function to its committees.

The standing committees have initial jurisdiction over legislation: a committee may approve, alter (sometimes beyond recognition), kill or ignore any measure referred to it, and it is nearly impossible for a bill to reach the Senate or House floor without first winning committee approval. The committee not only decides whether a bill shall be considered on the floor; it also controls proceedings once the bill arrives there, and its members staff the conference committee that puts the bill into final form. Thus the committee plays a determining role at every stage of the legislative process.

Although committees are created by and responsible to their respective parent bodies, in practice they function with almost total independence. The Senate and House determine the jurisdictions of their committees, appropriate funds to them and theoretically may discharge them from consideration of a bill. In practice, however, discharge is so difficult that it is seldom attempted with success. A spirit of reciprocity pervades Capitol Hill, and most Members of Congress are reluctant to challenge the authority of one committee because they fear that such action might prompt similar challenges to their own committees' powers.

Congressional committees are sometimes described as "little legislatures," but they do not necessarily reflect the character or views of their parent chambers. Many factors govern committee assignments, and committees vary in their representative nature. Furthermore, committees tend to be dominated by their chairmen, products of the seniority system who may not be sympathetic to the prevailing attitudes of Congress as a whole or of the membership of their own party. Thus committees are frequently criticized for not responding to the will of the majority.

The committee system contributes to Congressional efficiency by dividing the workload among a number of relatively small groups, each with specialized knowledge of a complex field of legislation. However, this fragmentation of responsibility makes it almost impossible for Congress to formulate consistent legislative programs.

In his 1885 treatise on *Congressional Government,* Woodrow Wilson described the standing committee chairmen as "petty barons"—"selfish and warring elements" locked in competition with each other. The chairmen, he said, "do not constitute a cooperative body like a ministry. They do not consult and concur in the adoption of homo-geneous and mutually helpful measures; there is no thought of acting in concert. Each committee goes its own way at its own pace."

The committees still go their own way at their own pace, and inter-committee coordination is a continuing problem in Congress. Party discipline is weak, and the elected party leaders cannot control the committee chairmen because they do not control their selection. In the absence of strong party control, Congress is unable to make coherent policy determinations, and the committees retain their piecemeal control over the legislative process.

The organization and structure of Congressional committees are described in the following pages. Committee procedures in handling legislation are outlined in the first section of Chapter II. Committee investigative procedures are described in Chapter III.

Historical Background

Committees have become a major organizational factor in Congress by evolution, not by constitutional design. The committee concept was borrowed from the British Parliament and transmitted to the New World by way of the colonial legislatures, most notably those of Pennsylvania and Virginia. But the committee system as it has developed in Congress has been colored by the peculiar characteristics of American life.

In the earliest days, when the nation's population was small and the duties of the central Government were carefully circumscribed, Congress had little need for the division of labor which the committee system provides. A people who viewed with grave suspicion the need to delegate authority to elected representatives were served by a Congress that only grudgingly delegated its own powers to committees. Originally, legislative proposals were considered initially on the Senate or House floor, and then a special or select committee was "raised" to work out details. Once the committee reported, it was dissolved. Approximately 350 such committees were created during the Third Congress alone.

Reference

See Appendix table of contents (first thumb tab) for list of all committees and subcommittees, and their members, in the 92nd Congress, and for the number of closed and open meetings of Senate and House committees in the 91st and previous Congresses back to 1953.

(In the House, initial consideration occurred in Committee of the Whole, followed by reference to a select committee. The Committee of the Whole is not a committee as the word is usually understood, but rather the entire House operating under special rules. During the early years, when it was used to oversee the select committees, debate was unlimited.)

Gradually the select committees evolved into permanent standing committees, and legislation came to be referred directly to committees without prior consideration by the parent body. This procedure gave the committees initial power over legislation, each in its specialized area, subject to subsequent review by the full chamber.

The House led the way in the creation of standing committees. The Committee on Elections, created in 1789, was followed by Claims in 1794 and by Interstate and Foreign Commerce and Revision of the Laws in 1795. The number had risen to 10 by 1810, and a further substantial expansion occurred under President James Monroe (1817-25). Between the War of 1812 and the Civil War the standing committee became the standard vehicle for consideration of the business of the House but was not fully exploited as a source of independent power.

The Senate in its first quarter-century established only four standing committees, and all were, on the whole, more administrative than legislative. Most of the committee work fell to select committees, usually of three members, appointed as the occasion demanded. These occasions were so frequent that by the session of 1815-16 between 90 and 100 select committees were appointed. Frequently, however, related subjects would be referred to a committee that had already been set up, and the same men were often named to committees dealing with similar subjects. In 1816, the Senate, finding inconvenient the appointment of so many committees at each session, added 11 standing committees to the existing four. By 1863 the number had grown to 19.

Methods of Appointing Committees

Different methods of making committee appointments developed in the two chambers. The first rule established by the House with respect to committee appointments in 1789 reserved to the House the choice of membership on all committees of more than three members. That rule gave way, in 1790, to a rule delegating this power to the Speaker, with the reservation that the House might direct otherwise in special cases. Finally, however, the Speaker was given the right to appoint members and chairmen of all of the standing committees, a power he retained until 1911. (The principle that the committees were to be bipartisan but weighted in favor of the majority and its policies was established early.)

Certain principles governed the choices of the Speaker in making committee appointments. The wishes of the minority leadership usually were respected. Generally, seniority, length of service on the committee and factors such as geographical distribution and party regularity were considered. But the Speaker was not bound to respect this formula, and there were cases where none of the principles outweighed the Speaker's wishes. Despite complaints and attempts to change the rule, the system remained in force until 1911, when the House again reserved the right to elect members to all standing committees.

Senate committees were chosen by ballot, with pluralities decisive, until 1823. In that year a proposal that the chairmen of the five most important committees be chosen by ballot and then granted power to choose the membership of their own and other committees was rejected. The Senate instead adopted an amendment to the rules giving the "presiding officer" authority to name committees, unless otherwise ordered by the Senate. Since Vice President Daniel E. Tompkins scarcely ever entered the chamber, the choice of committees was left to the President pro tempore, who had been chosen by and was responsible to the Senate. But when the next Vice President, John C. Calhoun, used the appointing power with obvious bias, the Senate quickly and with little dissent returned to the system of electing committees.

This time the chairmen were to be picked by majority vote, and other committee members were to be chosen on one ballot with their rank determined by the size of their pluralities. A major difficulty of this arrangement was that it failed to assure the majority party of succession to the chairmanship, in the event of a vacancy, or to assure it of a majority on the committees.

The Senate in 1828 changed the rules to provide for appointment to committees by the President pro tempore, but in 1833 it reverted to choice by ballot. Choice by ballot has remained in the Senate rules down to the present, but for a time the Senate experimented with a variety of methods. It then became customary to suspend the rule by unanimous consent and designate an officer (the Vice President, the President pro tempore or the "presiding officer") to name the committees.

The current method of selecting committee members was finally hit upon in 1846. At that time a motion to entrust the Vice President with the task was defeated, and the Senate proceeded under the regular rules to name committees by ballot. But after six chairmen had been selected, a debate ensued on the method of choosing the remaining members of the committees. At first, several committees were filled by approving lists—arranged in order of succession to the chairmanship—submitted by the Majority Leader. After a number of committees had been filled in this manner, the ballot rule was suspended and the Senate approved a list for all remaining vacancies that had been agreed upon by both the majority and minority. Since 1846 the choice of committees has usually amounted to routine acceptance by the Senate of lists agreed upon by representatives of the caucus or conference of the two major parties.

Proliferation of Standing Committees

The standing committee system, firmly established in the first half of the 19th century, continued to expand in the second half. During this period the standing committees developed into powerful and autonomous institutions, increasingly independent of chamber and party control, and the committee chairmen assumed ever greater powers over legislative action. So great was their influence that Woodrow Wilson in 1885 could write: "I know not how better to describe our form of government in a single phrase than by calling it a government by the chairmen of the Standing Committees of Congress."

The committee chairmen became even more powerful figures following the House "revolution" of 1909-10, which curtailed the powers of the Speaker and split up the House leadership. Seniority, already a leading criterion in the Speaker's choice of committee chairmen, was firmly established from that time on.

The number of standing committees has varied from one period to another. It reached a peak in 1913, when there were 61 standing committees in the House and 74 in the Senate. Naturally not all were of equal importance. Some—such as Appropriations, Ways and Means, Finance and Rules—exercised great influence, but many others were created and continued chiefly as a means of providing Members of Congress with offices and clerical staff. Until 1921 the Senate declined to abolish its Committee on Revolutionary Claims because its room belonged by custom to the minority caucus.

Consolidation of Committees

Efforts to consolidate the committee system began in 1920 when the House restored to its Appropriations Committee exclusive jurisdiction over appropriations. Prior to the creation of Appropriations Committees in the House (1865) and the Senate (1867), one committee in each chamber had handled both revenue and spending legislation. In 1885 the House dispersed the powers of its Appropriations Committee among nine committees. The Senate followed the House example, and by 1914 eight of the 14 appropriations bills were not referred to the Appropriations Committee. Although this method allowed committees most familiar with a subject to consider pertinent appropriations, it resulted in a division of responsibility that permitted no unified consideration or control of financial policy as a whole. Accordingly, the House in 1920 restored exclusive spending powers to its Appropriations Committee; the Senate took similar action in 1922.

Another reorganization designed to streamline Congress was a reduction in 1921 in the number of Senate committees from 74 to 34. In many respects this "reform" was simply the formal abandonment of long defunct bodies like the Committee on Revolutionary Claims. The House in 1927 reduced the number of its committees by merging 11 expenditures committees into a single Committee on Expenditures in the Executive Departments.

The most recent major overhaul of the committee structure was effected by the Legislative Reorganization Act of 1946. By dropping minor committees and merging those with related functions, the Act achieved a reduction from 33 to 15 committees in the Senate and from 48 to 19 in the House. The Act also carefully defined the jurisdictions of each committee and attempted to set ground rules for their operations.

The committee structure created by the Legislative Reorganization Act of 1946 has undergone only minor changes in the past quarter of a century, but its effect has been weakened by the proliferation of subcommittees within the standing committee system, as well as by the creation of numerous select, special and joint committees. As for subcommittees, a 1970 study counted 112 standing and 33 select or special subcommittees in the House, 107 standing and 16 select or special subcommittees in the Senate. In addition to the standing committees—21 in the House and 16 in the Senate—there were seven major joint committees and a growing number of select committees which had been set up to examine specific problems.

Conference Committees

The conference committee is an ad hoc joint committee appointed to reconcile the differences between Senate and House versions of proposed legislation. A conference becomes necessary when the two chambers do not pass a bill in identical form and neither is willing to yield to the other. Then a conference committee, consisting of Senators and Representatives, is appointed to determine the final shape of the legislation. Only rarely does the Senate or House reject the work of a conference committee.

Traditionally, conference committees are composed of the senior members of the committees or subcommittees that handled the bill. They are appointed by the presiding officers of the House and Senate upon the recommendation of the floor manager of the bill, usually the committee or subcommittee chairman. There need not be an equal number of conferees (or "managers" as they are styled) from each house, because a majority vote determines the position of each group. Therefore a majority of both the Senate and House delegations must agree before a provision emerges from conference as a part of the bill.

Both parties are represented on a conference committee, with the majority party having a larger number, and a majority of conferees from each house must sign the conference report. Proceedings of conference committees are secret, supposedly to protect the managers from external and internal pressures. In the past, conference committees met on the Senate side of the Capitol, with the most senior Senator presiding, but this is no longer always the case.

Conferees have broad powers over the measure before them. Theoretically, they are not permitted to write new legislation in reconciling the Senate and House versions of bills, but this prohibition is sometimes bypassed. Many bills have become acceptable only after new language was provided by the conferees. Although the Legislative Reorganization Act of 1946 says that conferees must have demonstrated support for the legislation as passed in their chamber, this provision is not enforced, and conferees are frequently attacked for "so forthrightly disregarding the wishes of the common lay member of the Senate and House," as Sen. J. W. Fulbright (D Ark.) once charged.

Once the conferees have reached agreement, they prepare a conference report for submission to their parent chambers. Conference reports cannot be amended on the floor; they must be accepted or rejected in their entirety, and they are very seldom rejected. When the report is approved by the Senate and the House, the conference committee dissolves.

The conference device, used by Congress since 1789, had developed into its modern pattern by the middle of the 19th century. (*For current conference procedures, see The Legislative Process, Chapter II.*)

The Legislative Reorganization Act of 1970 reformed some committee procedures but made only minor changes in the committee structure itself. It created a new Senate Committee on Veterans' Affairs and changed the name of the Senate Banking and Currency Committee to Banking, Housing and Urban Affairs, thus providing a more accurate reflection of the Committee's jurisdiction. The defunct Joint Committee on Immigration and Nationality Policy was abolished, and a new Joint Committee on Congressional Operations was established. *(For a full list of committees and subcommittees, including members of committees in the 92nd Congress, see Appendix.)*

The Committee Structure

Today there are three principal kinds of committees: standing committees, permanent units with broad powers over legislation; select or special committees, usually temporary and chiefly investigative in nature; and joint committees, also usually investigative, with a membership drawn from both houses of Congress. Conference committees, a special variety of joint committee, serve only on an ad hoc basis. *(See box.)*

In addition, there are more than 250 subcommittees, which are functional subdivisions of the full committees. All of these groups are composed of members of the majority and minority parties, with the majority party having a numerical advantage.

Standing Committees

The standing committees are the keystone of the legislative process since they have the power to review legislative proposals and report bills to the floor. Under the Legislative Reorganization Act of 1946, Senate and House committees are organized along similar but not precisely parallel lines.

One of the purposes of the 1946 Act was to eliminate confusing and overlapping jurisdictions by grouping related subjects. The legislative committees (as distinct from the money committees) were in general regrouped to follow the major organizational divisions of the Federal Government. Responsibility for overseeing the Executive Branch was divided roughly as follows: Appropriations Committees were to review requests for spending authority, the Expenditures Committees (now Government Operations) were to oversee administration of appropriations and the quality of administration in general, and the legislative committees were to oversee administration of policy in their respective fields.

The size of the standing committees is fixed by the rules of their parent chambers; in the 92nd Congress, House committees ranged in size from 9 (Internal Security) to 55 (Appropriations), Senate committees from 7 (District of Columbia) to 24 (Appropriations). Traditionally, party ratios on the committees have corresponded roughly with the party ratio in the full chamber, except for the House Ways and Means and Rules Committees which maintain a 2-1 majority party lead.

Select or special committees are established from time to time in the Senate or House to study special problems. Their size is fixed by the resolutions that created them. Ordinarily they are not permitted to report bills. Such committees may go on from Congress to Congress, like the Senate and House Small Business Committees, but most have only a brief lifespan.

Joint committees are created by statutes or resolutions which also fix their size. Of the 10 joint committees in existence in 1970, only one—the Joint Committee on Atomic Energy—had the authority to report bills. Others, like the Joint Economic Committee, study and spotlight public problems or review the execution of programs, but they must depend on standing committees to frame legislative proposals. The Joint Committee on Internal Revenue Taxation, made up of senior members of the House Ways and Means and Senate Finance Committees, may make policy recommendations to those committees but serves chiefly to supply them with professional staff assistance. A few joint committees never meet.

Function of Subcommittees

Subcommittees provide the ultimate division of labor within the committee system. Although they enable Members of Congress to develop technical expertise in specialized fields, they are often criticized on grounds that they fragment responsibility and increase the difficulty of over-all policy review.

Subcommittees are created by and responsible to their parent committees. Their members and chairmen are selected by the full committee chairmen, and, since seniority does not necessarily govern selection, a committee chairman may use his appointment powers to advance his own goals. Sometimes quite junior members of a full committee may be given subcommittee chairmanships which permit them to play more significant roles in the legislative process than they would otherwise be able to do. Sen. Birch Bayh (D Ind.) became chairman of the Senate Judiciary Subcommittee on Constitutional Amendments shortly after he took office in 1963; from that post he directed Senate action on the Presidential disability amendment two years later.

Subcommittees vary in importance from committee to committee. Some, notably the Appropriations subcommittees in both chambers, have well-defined jurisdictions and function with great autonomy; their actions are routinely endorsed by their parent committees. Other committees carefully review and on occasion reverse the action of their subcommittees. Some committees are so dominated by their chairmen that there is little opportunity for subcommittee initiative. Finally, a few committees—House Ways and Means and, until recently, Senate Finance and House Rules—have declined to make use of subcommittees at all.

Committee Assignments

The current method of appointing committees—through chamber approval of a list of names submitted by party leaders—was adopted by the Senate in 1846 and by the House in 1911. This procedure takes place at the beginning of each new Congress. In practice it rarely involves more than assignment of new Members to committees and filling of vacancies caused by death, retirement or transfer.

The appointment process assumed new importance at the beginning of the 92nd Congress in 1971, when it figured in an attack on the Congressional seniority system. The seniority system was not abolished, but reformers scored some success in broadening control over committee assignments. *(See Seniority, Chapter II.)*

In the Senate, the Democratic committee roster is drawn up by the Democratic Steering Committee, headed by the party leader, who also names the other Steering Committee members. In 1971, the roster was made subject to caucus approval. The Republican committee roster is drawn up by the Republican Committee on Committees, which is appointed by the chairman of the Republican Conference, but the caucus does not vote on committee nominations. On the floor, the leaders of the two parties offer resolutions, which usually are adopted virtually automatically by the full chamber, making the committee appointments suggested by the party groups and in the process formalizing party ratios agreed upon by the leaders. Although Senate rules require that each prospective chairman be voted on individually, this requirement usually has been waived by unanimous consent. In 1971, however, the Senate took separate votes on each chairman.

In the House, the Democratic members of the Ways and Means Committee, who are elected by the Democratic caucus, constitute the Democratic Committee on Committees and draw up the assignments for the other committees. In 1971, their nominations were made subject to approval by the Democratic caucus. The Republican Committee on Committees, made up of one Representative from each state having at least one Republican in its House delegation, prepares a roster of Republican committee assignments and submits them to the House Republican Policy Committee for its approval. The Republican Conference does not vote on all committee nominations but, under a 1971 innovation, it does vote on the ranking Republican member of each committee. As in the Senate, the committee rosters prepared by the two parties are incorporated in resolutions which must be adopted by the full chamber. This is usually a formality, but in 1971 a House rule requiring the election of committee chairmen served as a pretext for an unsuccessful effort to unseat Rep. John L. McMillan (D S.C.) as chairman of the District of Columbia Committee.

Factors in Choice of Members

Various factors govern selection of committee members, including seniority of service in the chamber, party loyalty, regional distribution, personal preference and the favor of the leadership. Some committees typically have a special-interest cast: the Agriculture Committees are manned largely by members from farm states, the Interior Committees by members from public land states. Others—notably the "prestige" committees such as Appropriations, Ways and Means and Rules—represent a broader, national interest.

Traditionally, new Members of Congress have had to serve an apprenticeship on minor committees before being appointed to major committees. However, since 1953 the Senate Democratic leadership has followed the so-called "Johnson rule" under which freshman Senators are given at least one major committee assignment each. Senate Republicans have followed a similar practice since 1965. Although the Legislative Reorganization Act of 1946 attempted to limit the number of committees upon which an individual Member could serve, this effort was not entirely successful.

The Legislative Reorganization Act of 1970 limited future assignment of Senators to two major committees and one minor, select or joint committee. It stipulated also that no Senator could serve on more than one of the following: Armed Services, Appropriations, Finance or Foreign Relations. These restrictions did not affect existing committee assignments. In the larger House, few Members serve on more than two committees.

Once on a congenial committee, a Member of Congress usually remains there, gradually working his way up by seniority to the position of chairman or ranking minority member. He may have an opportunity to transfer from one committee to another, where he will have to start again at the bottom of the seniority ladder. Or, if he is a very junior member, he may be bumped from his committee as a result of party realignments following an election. On rare occasions committee members have been stripped of their seniority or even denied their committee seats as a punishment for party disloyalty. Two southern Representatives—John Bell Williams (D Miss.) and Albert W. Watson (D S.C.)—lost their Democratic seniority in 1965 after they had supported the Republican Presidential candidate the preceding year. It was the first such action since 1911. In the Senate, Wayne Morse (Ore.) lost his seat on two Senate committees in 1953 after he bolted the Republican party and became an independent.

The Post of Chairman

One of the most controversial features of the Congressional committee system is the unwritten rule of seniority that confers a committee chairmanship on the member of the majority party with the longest continuous service on the committee. As long as his party retains control of Congress, he may keep this position; if control passes to the other party, he changes places with the erstwhile ranking minority member until a new election gives his party a majority once again.

Only rarely is there failure to observe the rule. Occasionally a ranking committee member who is also chairman of another committee will waive his seniority to the next ranking member, thus permitting the latter to become chairman; this is more likely to occur in the Senate where, because its membership is so much smaller than that of the House, Senators may serve on more than one major committee. Sometimes a chairman will relinquish his post for reasons of age or health, as in the case of Sen. Theodore Francis Greene (D R.I.) who gave up the chairmanship of the Senate Foreign Relations Committee in 1959 at the age of 91. On a handful of occasions committee chairmen have been demoted from their chairmanships, most recently in 1967 when Rep. Adam Clayton Powell (D N.Y.) was stripped of his chairmanship of the House Education and Labor Committee shortly before he was excluded from the House itself.

Chairmanships of joint committees offer a special situation. Although historically their chairmen tended to be drawn from the Senate, in recent years the chairmanships of the major joint committees have rotated from one chamber to another at the beginning of each new Congress. When a Senator serves as chairman, the vice chairman usually is a Representative, and vice versa.

Seniority in Choice of Chairmen

Although seniority has not always governed the selection of committee chairmen, it had become well entrenched by the beginning of the 20th century. In the earliest years, the position was honorary, and the member who was named first (usually the one who proposed the committee's creation, later the one with the most ballots) became chairman. Distinction came from serving on a great many committees rather than from being "first among equals" on one. William Maclay of Pennsylvania in 1789 proposed a Senate rule stipulating that the committee chairman "should be the Senator from the most northerly state of those from whom the committee is taken." His proposal was not adopted, but it suggests the early lack of regard for committee chairmanships.

Defenders of the seniority rule find certain positive virtues in the system: it tends to reward experience in the business of the committee; it maintains stable, continuous committees manned by legislators who become specialists in their fields; and by assuring legislators of security in their committee seats it protects them from undue pressures from major lobbies, as well as from the President and the leadership. Furthermore, supporters of the seniority system contend that choice of chairmen by election or by some other means would lead to dissension, logrolling, campaigning and other evils that would make it more difficult for Congress to transact its business.

Critics of the seniority selection system argue that it takes no account of merit (except the merit of getting re-elected periodically) or competence, and that it places in positions of power men who may not be in sympathy with the national party or the Congressional majority, thus frustrating effective party discipline in Congress. The system almost inevitably puts committee control into the hands of old men, they say, those most likely to be conservative in spirit and infirm in body. It also tends to reward Members from "safe" districts or states, since they are most likely to be re-elected term after term. This has led to a preponderance of southern chairmen when the Democrats are in power and of midwesterners when the Republicans have control.

During consideration of the Legislative Reorganization Act of 1970, both the House and the Senate rejected proposals to modify or abandon use of the seniority system in the selection of committee chairmen. In 1971 the Senate killed a resolution that would have permitted the selection of committee chairmen and ranking minority members on some basis other than seniority.

Both chambers, however, moved to broaden access to positions of responsibility. The 1970 Reorganization Act stipulated that, in the future, no Senator could hold the chairmanship of more than one full committee and one subcommittee of a major committee, but the provision did not apply to chairmanships currently held. The Senate Republican Conference in January 1971 accepted a proposal that each Senator could be ranking member on only one standing committee. In the House, the Democratic caucus agreed that no Member could be chairman of more than one legislative subcommittee, thus opening more subcommittee chairmanships to junior Members. House Republicans agreed to a proposal that would permit the post of ranking Republican on each committee to be filled by conference vote, not merely by seniority.

Powers of Committee Chairmen

Initially little more than moderators of committee deliberations, the committee chairmen rapidly developed into powerful figures with broad influence over legislation. George B. Galloway in 1953 offered the following description of the role of committee chairmen: "Just as the standing committees control legislative action, so the chairmen are masters of their committees. Selected on the basis of seniority, locally elected and locally responsible, these 'lord-proprietors' hold key positions in the power structure of Congress. They arrange the agenda of the committees, appoint the subcommittees, and refer bills to them. They decide what pending measures shall be considered and when, call committee meetings, and decide whether or not to hold hearings and when. They approve lists of scheduled witnesses, select their staffs and authorize staff studies, and preside at committee hearings. They handle reported bills on the floor and participate as principal managers in conference committees. They are in a position to expedite measures they favor and to retard or pigeonhole those they dislike. Strong chairmen can often induce in executive sessions the kind of committee action that they desire. In the House of Representatives, where debate is limited, the chairman in charge of a bill allots time to whomever he pleases during debate on the floor; he also has the right to open and close the debate on bills reported by his committee; and he may move the previous question whenever he thinks best. In short, committee chairmen exercise crucial powers over the legislative process. In his little classic on *Congressional Government,* written sixty-eight years ago, Woodrow Wilson described our form of government in a single phrase by calling it 'a government by the chairmen of the standing committees of Congress.' So far as Congress is concerned, this description is, in a large sense, still true."

The power to appoint subcommittees and to assign bills to them is of great importance, because it enables the committee chairman to influence both the course of legislation and the careers of individual committee members. A strong chairman can dominate his committee by giving important subcommittee assignments to members who share his viewpoint, for seniority is not rigidly observed in making subcommittee appointments. He can also see to it that legislation in which he has an interest goes only to sympathetic subcommittees—either by creating new subcommittees for particular bills or by maintaining a stable of subcommittees with jurisdictions defined vaguely or not at all so that he can refer bills at will. Subcommittees of the House Armed Services Committee, for example, are identified only by number; the Committee's recent chairmen—Carl Vinson (D Ga.), L. Mendel Rivers (D S.C.) and F. Edward Hebert (D La.)—have been figures of almost legendary power.

Rep. John L. McMillan (D S.C.), chairman of the House District of Columbia Committee, also used the numbered subcommittee system to channel legislation to sympathetic subcommittees. But at the opening of the 92nd Congress in 1971, dissident Committee members launched an assault on what they considered McMillan's arbitrary exercise of power. Having failed to oust him from the chairmanship, they succeeded in forcing the adoption of new Committee rules to curb the chairman's power. In addition to giving the full Committee veto power over staff hiring and firing, requiring better advance notice of meetings and opening more Committee sessions to the public, the new rules provided for the creation of subcommittees with specific jurisdictions —so as to deprive the chairman of the power to assign bills to any subcommittee he chose. "I don't think this will make any difference at all," McMillan said, and subsequent events suggested that he was right. When he appointed chairmen of the newly reorganized subcommittees, he ignored seniority to bypass his critics and appoint his own supporters. "I don't think any chairman in the Congress who has any sense would appoint subcommittee chairmen who wouldn't back him," McMillan remarked.

Another potent weapon available to the committee chairman is his right to call meetings and control the agenda. Although the Legislative Reorganization Act of 1946 required committees to establish regular meeting days, it gave the chairman authority to call other meetings. In practice, a chairman may call meetings on short notice or at times when certain members are known to be absent; or he may neglect to call meetings at all. (Although procedures exist by which a committee majority can force a meeting, they are seldom invoked.) This power was used frequently by Howard W. Smith (D Va.), longtime chairman of the House Rules Committee, to postpone or thwart action on liberal legislation.

Revolts Against Chairmen

Of course, the powers of a chairman vary from committee to committee and from chairman to chairman. Although the Legislative Reorganization Act of 1946 made some effort to democratize committee procedures, it made no real inroads on the chairman's power, and subsequent efforts to develop uniform rules for all committees have not been successful. It is difficult for committee members to stage an internal revolt against their chairman, since the chairman has it within his power to make life easy for a cooperative member and hard for a rebel. Nonetheless, some committees—notably those where a decided split has existed between the chairman and a majority of his committee—have succeeded in adopting rules that limit the chairman's powers of obstruction and retaliation.

Thus the House Education and Labor Committee in 1966 adopted a set of rules to limit the power of its chairman, Adam Clayton Powell (D N.Y.), who had angered members by delaying Committee action on some bills and by refusing to call up for floor action others that the Committee actually had reported. The rules left the initiative for action with Powell in most cases but eliminated his power to block action desired by a majority. A few months later Powell was deprived of his chairmanship, but the rules remained in force.

Similarly, a revolt in the House Banking and Currency Committee led, in 1967, to a series of rules changes that stripped Chairman Wright Patman (D Texas) of much of his authority, including control over subcommittee appointments and staff hire. Patman had acquired the reputation of running the Committee in high-handed fashion.

Proxy Voting

Proxy voting, widely used in Congressional committees, is a practice that permits one committee member to authorize another committee member to cast his votes for him in his absence. Proxy voting is not permitted on the Senate or House floor.

Proxies may be general—covering all matters before a committee for a specific time or for an indefinite period, or special—limited to a particular bill and amendments.

Proponents of Congressional reform long have argued for an outright ban on proxy voting in committee. Not only does it encourage absenteeism and irresponsibility, they contend, but it also contributes to the domination of committees by their chairmen, since the chairmen are in an ideal position to wrest proxies from committee members in return for the favors they can bestow.

Prior to 1970, the use of proxies was regulated either by custom or by the rules of individual committees, and different committees permitted them in different circumstances. In some committees they were never used. The Legislative Reorganization Act of 1970 prohibited proxy voting in House committees except when the committee's rules allowed, when the proxy was limited to a specific matter, and when it was in writing, designating the person to whom it was given. For Senate committees, the Act provided that no proxy vote was to be cast on a motion to report a bill if the committee rules barred the use of a proxy on such a motion; if proxies were not barred on a motion to report a bill, they could nevertheless be voted only upon the affirmative request of an absent member.

The House Rules Committee, following the 1966 election defeat of Chairman Smith, adopted a set of rules governing Committee procedures for the first time in its history. The new regulations took from the chairman the right to set meeting dates, required the consent of a majority to table a bill and set limits on proxy voting. It was widely reported that these rules resulted from pressure by the Democratic leadership rather than pressure from within the Committee.

Rules and Procedures

Although Congress has no comprehensive code of committee procedure, general guidelines are provided by the Senate and House rules, which incorporate reforms enacted in the Legislative Reorganization Acts of 1946 and 1970.

One of the basic goals of the 1946 Act was to regularize committee procedures in regard to regular meeting days, the keeping of committee records, reporting of approved measures, the presence of a majority of committee members as a condition of committee action and the conduct of hearings. However, the 1946 rules were not uniformly observed by all committees, and continuing dissatisfaction with committee operations led, in the 1970 Reorganization Act, to further efforts to reform com-

The House Rules Committee and Its Role:

The House Rules Committee has long stood as a strategic gateway between the legislative committees and the floor of the House for a small but important part of the chamber's legislative business. The power of the Committee lies in its role of setting the agenda and allotting time for debate on those important and usually controversial bills that are not disposed of by the more routine procedures of the House. Thus the Committee often has been able to prevent or delay bills it opposes from reaching the House floor.

The only ways of bypassing the Rules Committee are the discharge petition, which requires 218 signatures to free a bill from a committee; Calendar Wednesday, a day on which committee chairmen or members they designate may, in turn, call up bills reported by their committees that have not been granted a rule; and suspension of the rules, which requires a two-thirds majority vote. These methods, seldom used successfully, are beyond the direct control of the leadership. *(For a description of these procedures, see The Legislative Process, Chapter II.)*

There have been frequent controversies over what functions the Rules Committee should perform in its strategic position: whether it should serve merely as a clearinghouse for legislative business, as the agent of the majority leadership, or as a super-legislator editing the work of the legislative committees. A basic question has been whether the fate of important and highly controversial legislation should be decided by a small handful of men or by the majority of the entire House.

Defenders of the Rules Committee system of routing legislation argue that it promotes parliamentary efficiency in the 435-Member House, and that the committee performs a unique service in blocking expensive or ill-advised bills that most House Members would not dare to oppose openly on the floor.

The Committee on Rules was established by the First Congress in 1789. Originally it was a select committee, authorized at the beginning of each new Congress, with jurisdiction over House rules. However, since the rules of one Congress were usually readopted by the next, this function was not of great importance, and for many years the Committee never made a report.

In 1858, the Speaker was made a member of the Committee, and from that time on the group gradually increased its power in the House. Rules became a standing committee as part of the general rules revision of 1880. In 1883 it began the practice of reporting special orders for the consideration of particular legis-

lation, subject to a majority vote of the House. Previously the House could take up bills out of the regular order only by unanimous consent or by suspension of the rules, which required a two-thirds majority. Other powers acquired by the Committee over the years included the right to sit while the House was in session, to have its reports immediately considered and even to report new business that had not been reported by a legislative committee. The latter power is exercised very infrequently. The Committee used it in 1964 to grant rules for two measures, both dealing with apportionment of state legislatures, that the Judiciary Committee had refused to report. One of the measures went on to House passage; the other, a proposed constitutional amendment that required a two-thirds vote for approval, was never brought up on the floor.

Before 1910, the Rules Committee functioned as an arm of the leadership in deciding what legislation could come to the floor. But in the Progressive revolt of 1909-10 against Speaker "Uncle Joe" Cannon, the Committee was made independent of the leadership. Establishment of the Discharge Calendar, Consent Calendar and Calendar Wednesday procedures in 1909 was followed in 1910 by adoption of a resolution, promoted by a coalition of Democrats and insurgent Republicans, to enlarge the Rules Committee and exclude the Speaker from membership on it. (This ban was repealed by the Legislative Reorganization Act of 1946, but no subsequent Speakers have sat on the Committee.)

By the late 1930s the Committee had come to be dominated, not by the leadership, but by a coalition of conservative Democrats and Republicans which continued in control of the Committee for most of the next quarter-century and which was successful in blocking a number of liberal measures.

Opposition to the obstructive tactics of the Rules Committee led, at the beginning of the 81st Congress in 1949, to the adoption of the "21-day rule," a device for bypassing the Committee in bringing legislation to the floor. The rule provided that the chairman of a legislative committee which had favorably reported a bill and had requested a resolution from the Rules Committee for House consideration, might bring the resolution directly to the floor for adoption if the Committee had failed to grant a rule within 21 calendar days of the request. The rule required the Speaker to recognize the Member calling up the 21-day resolution.

mittee procedures—particularly to make them more democratic and more open to public scrutiny.

Current rules stipulate that each standing committee of the House and Senate must fix regular meeting days; they also authorize the chairman to call additional meetings, and a procedure is outlined under which a meeting may be called by the committee majority if the chairman fails to do so. Committees are required to keep complete records of their transactions and to make public

their roll-call votes—all such votes for House committees, only those on measures or amendments in the Senate. Most committee meetings are to be open unless the committee by majority vote decides otherwise. (In 1970, 41 percent of all committee meetings were closed. *For tabulation, see Appendix.*)

The rules stipulate that it is the chairman's "duty" to see to it that legislation approved by his committee is reported, and they outline steps by which a commitee

Power to Expedite or Obstruct Legislation

Two years later, after the Democrats had lost 29 seats in the mid-term elections, the House repealed the 21-day rule. Although it had been used only eight times during the 1949-51 period, the threat of its use was credited with prying other bills out of the Rules Committee. Once it was repealed, the group was again free to block legislation without effective restraint.

At the beginning of the 86th Congress in 1959, a group of House Democratic liberals sought Speaker Sam Rayburn's (D Texas) support for a change in House rules that would break the conservative grip on the Committee. Following a conference with the Speaker, the group issued a statement saying that Rayburn had assured them that bills reported from legislative committees would reach the House floor and therefore they would not press for a rules change that year. However, the record of the 86th Congress showed that Rayburn often could not deliver on his promise. After the Rules Committee had blocked or delayed several measures that were destined to become key elements in the program of the new Kennedy Administration, the Democratic leadership decided that the roadblock could not be allowed to stand.

Accordingly, at the beginning of the 87th Congress in 1961, the House by a narrow margin adopted a resolution to enlarge the Committee's membership from 12 to 15 for the 87th Congress. This gave Rayburn and the Kennedy Administration a delicate but favorable 8-7 majority on most issues that came before the Committee. The plan was chosen by Rayburn over several others proposed, including a "purge" of an anti-Administration Committee Democrat, as the least "painful." By raising the number of Democratic members from 8 to 10 (Republicans from 4 to 5), it permitted the appointment to the Committee of two pro-Administration Democrats. This enlargement of the Committee was made permanent in 1963.

Nevertheless, dissatisfaction with the Rules Committee continued, and, following the Democratic sweep in the 1964 elections, the 21-day rule was revived. The new version of the rule, adopted by the House at the opening of the 89th Congress in 1965, did not require the Speaker to recognize a Member calling up a 21-day resolution as the 1949 rule had done. Under the 1965 rule the Speaker retained discretion to recognize the Member, so that it was highly unlikely, if not impossible, for a bill to come up successfully through this procedure without leadership approval. The new rule, which also was employed successfully only eight times,

was abandoned in 1967, following the Republican resurgence in the mid-term elections.

The House retained another rule, adopted in 1965, that curbed the Committee's power to block conferences on legislation. Prior to 1965, most bills were sent to conference either by unanimous consent or by House adoption of a resolution reported by the Rules Committee. The 1965 change made it possible to send a bill to conference by majority vote of the House.

Despite repeal of the 21-day rule in 1967, the Committee continued to pursue a moderate course. Several factors contributed to the Committee's less conservative posture. First, it had lost its chairman, Howard W. Smith (D Va.), as a result of his defeat in a 1966 primary election. Smith, chairman since 1955, was a skilled parliamentarian and the acknowledged leader of the House conservative coalition—a voting alliance of Republicans and southern Democrats against northern Democrats. He was replaced as chairman by William M. Colmer (D Miss.), also a conservative southerner, but Colmer was prevented from exerting the high degree of control over legislation that had characterized Smith's 12-year tenure as chairman.

Two liberal members had been added to the Committee, thus creating a more secure liberal majority, and a set of rules had been introduced to govern Committee procedure. The rules took from the chairman the right to set meeting dates, a power Smith frequently had used to postpone or thwart action on bills backed by liberals or the Administration. They also required the consent of a majority to table a bill and set limits on proxy voting.

The Committee's latent powers of obstruction were partially obscured as long as it forebore to flaunt them, but in the closing days of the 91st Congress in 1970 the Committee reverted to its old ways by refusing to clear two major bills for House floor action. The bills —one to establish an independent consumer agency and the other to strengthen the Equal Employment Opportunity Commission—had been passed by the Senate and enjoyed broad support in the House. Acting in the absence of Richard Bolling (D Mo.), a liberal who usually voted with the majority, the Committee by 7-7 tie votes refused to grant rules for the measures. This reminder of the Committee's power over legislation gave rise to new demands for reform, but when the 92nd Congress convened a few weeks later, a coalition of Republicans and southern Democrats succeeded in killing a proposal to reinstitute a variation of the 21-day rule.

---

majority may force a bill to be reported if the chairman fails to do so. The rules prohibit a committee from reporting any measure unless a majority of its members are actually present, and they place certain limits on proxy voting. *(See box.)* Members are allowed time to file supplemental and minority views for inclusion in the committee report. Committees are encouraged to announce hearings at least one week in advance, to hold them in open session and to require witnesses to file

written statements in advance. The rules allow minority party members to call witnesses during at least one day of hearings on a subject. They also limit the right of committees to sit while the Senate and House are in session.

Under the 1970 Reorganization Act, Senate committees are required to establish and publish rules of committee procedure; although there is no similar requirement for House committees, a number of them have done so.

Power Relationships

The standing committees of Congress, wrote Stephen K. Bailey in 1966, "exist to speed the work load; to facilitate meaningful deliberations on important measures and issues; to develop a degree of expertise among committee members and committee staff; and to serve as a convenient graveyard for inept proposals. They constitute the great baronies of Congressional power. Many of them look outward in jealous competition with the President, with their opposite committee in the other house, and with the whole house of which they are a part. When internally unified and buttressed in parliamentary privilege by special rules, as in the case of the House Appropriations Committee, they can almost at will dominate the business of the parent chamber."

Basis of Committee Power

Although committees also perform important investigative and oversight functions, the basis of committee power is control over legislation.

Most of the legislative decisions of Congress actually are made in committee. Modern law-making requires understanding of many complex subjects, and the committee system provides a means by which a few Members can attain a high degree of specialization in each of many fields. A committee that has subjected a bill to expert scrutiny expects its decisions to be upheld on the floor. Committees, says *Cannon's Procedure,* "are not infallible but they have had long familiarity with the subject under discussion, and have made an intimate study of the particular bill before the House and after mature deliberation have made formal recommendations and, other considerations being equal, are entitled to support on the floor."

This attitude is more prevalent in the House than in the Senate, but in both chambers Members usually are reluctant to challenge the committee, not only because they lack expert knowledge of the subject involved, but also because they would resent such a challenge if it were offered to a bill reported by one of their own committees. Thus committee power is sustained both by the practice of specialization and by the spirit of reciprocity that figures so prominently in the operations of Congress.

Function of Subcommittees

Who makes committee decisions? The chairman may exercise great influence over his committee's actions, but he alone does not determine the fate of legislation. Congressional decision-making is fragmented not only among committees but within committees. So great is the volume of legislation before a given committee that every committee member cannot hope to master the complexities of all committee business. So the trend toward specialization continues, and bills may be referred to subcommittees for consideration in depth. The subcommittees hold hearings, take testimony and make recommendations to their parent committees. Frequently only a few subcommittee members actually participate in these deliberations; they may be more closely aligned to special interest groups or executive agencies than they are to the Congressional leadership.

Although subcommittees cannot themselves report legislation directly to the floor, they are likely to resent any failure by the full committee to ratify their decisions. In effect, this often means that Congressional decision-making rests in the hands of a few subcommittee members who have taken a special interest in a bill.

Partisanship is not usually a determining influence on decision-making within a committee. Although some issues predictably generate party splits, for the most part the majority and minority party members try to work out programs both can support. This consensus approach makes it easier to win floor approval of committee recommendations, but it also precludes the development of strong party alternatives, and the absence of party responsibility reinforces committee domination of the legislative process.

All committees are not equally influential. A minor committee like the District of Columbia Committee cannot hope to attain the preeminence of such giants as Appropriations and Ways and Means, but within these limits committees frequently compete with each other for ascendancy, and power relationships fluctuate from time to time.

Conflicts Between Committees

Jurisdictional conflicts between rival committees have been a feature of Congressional history since the inception of the standing committee system. The Legislative Reorganization Act of 1946 attempted to eliminate the problem by defining each committee's jurisdiction in detail. That this effort was not entirely successful was illustrated the very next year when a fight broke out in the Senate over referral of the armed forces unification bill. In the House the measure had been handled by the Committee on Executive Expenditures, which theoretically had jurisdiction over all proposals for Government reorganization. But in the Senate the Expenditures Committee's claim to the bill was challenged successfully by the Armed Services Committee on a floor vote.

Such tangles have continued to arise, because the complexities of modern legislative problems make it impossible to define jurisdictional boundaries precisely. Sometimes committees attempt to use jurisdictional ambiguities to expand their own powers. On other occasions the ambiguities serve as a pretext for efforts to place controversial bills in friendly (or perhaps hostile) committee hands.

The relationships between the Appropriations Committees and legislative committees frequently provide striking illustrations of inter-committee rivalries. Legislative committees handle bills authorizing funds, but only the Appropriations Committees are permitted to report actual appropriations, and the legislative committees observe this restriction. The Appropriations Committees, in turn, are barred by the rules from including legislative provisions in their appropriations bills, but they habitually do so and, despite grumbling from the legislative committees, are seldom overruled on the floor. In the Senate, some senior members of legislative committees participate in Appropriations Committee deliberations on bills in their fields of interest, thus reducing one area of conflict.

Committees are often in competition with their counterparts in the other chamber. Again, the Appropriations Committees offer a vivid example: in 1962, the decorum of Congress shattered when the two committees, each headed by an octogenarian chairman, brought their long-smoldering differences into public view. At issue were questions of whether the Senate had a right to initiate its own appropriation bills, whether it could add funds to House-passed bills, who would chair conferences between the two chambers and where the conferences would be held. The dispute blocked appropriations conferences for three months and virtually bankrupted several Government agencies. Although the deadlock finally was broken, the two committees never reached full agreement on their respective roles in the appropriations process.

Guarding of Committee Status Quo

Proposals to create new committees or to realign the jurisdictions of existing ones illustrate the determination of the committees to preserve their existing powers. For years after the House had created a separate Veterans' Affairs Committee, the Senate Finance Committee refused to relinquish jurisdiction over veterans' legislation; a Senate Committee on Veterans' Affairs was finally created under the Legislative Reorganization Act of 1970. Similarly, a proposal to split the House Education and Labor Committee into two separate committees was one of the stumbling blocks to House action on legislative reorganization in the 90th Congress; the plan was abandoned during consideration of the 1970 Reorganization Act. Reformers long have urged Congress to make greater use of joint committees to expedite business, but Congress declines to do so since such a practice would threaten the existing power structure.

One example of a successful effort to create a new standing committee was the establishment of the House Un-American Activities Committee in 1945. The Committee, set up originally as a special committee in 1938, was reconstituted in each succeeding Congress until 1945. Then on the opening day of the 79th Congress, Rep. John E. Rankin (D Miss.) offered an amendment to the House Rules to make it a permanent standing committee. Rankin's unexpected move caught opponents unprepared, and his amendment carried on a 208-186 roll-call vote.

Rankin had maneuvered his amendment so that it could not be referred to committee, where it might have been killed by the combined opposition of standing committees with jurisdiction in the same area and of liberals who objected to the Committee's activities. The Committee, operating since 1969 as the House Internal Security Committee, continues to flourish, despite persistent efforts to abolish it and transfer its functions to the Judiciary Committee. *(For a review of the Committee's career, see Congressional Investigations, Chapter III.)*

It is very difficult to abolish a committee, once established, even though it no longer serves any purpose. Congress in 1952 created a Joint Committee on Immigration and Nationality Policy; the Committee never met and never performed any function, yet it was not abolished until 1970.

Competitions for Power

A 1965 dispute involving this Committee provides an illuminating glimpse of the power relationships within Congress. The episode involved the chairman of the House Judiciary Committee, Rep. Emanuel Celler (D N.Y.), and

Rep. Michael A. Feighan (D Ohio), who was chairman of both the Joint Committee and of a Judiciary subcommittee that had jurisdiction over immigration legislation. Feighan's efforts to obtain funds to activate the Joint Committee were successfully blocked by Celler, who held that control over immigration should remain within the Judiciary Committee. Celler said he had offered Feighan $100,-000 in Judiciary Committee funds but that Feighan had preferred to seek funds on his own authority. But, Celler said, "I am going to tell you that nobody is going to ride in front of me when I ride the horse of the Judiciary Committee."

Committees compete for power not only with each other and with their parent chambers—on occasion they are willing to challenge the President himself. In 1967, the House Ways and Means Committee refused to act on President Johnson's proposal for a 10-percent income tax surcharge until the President came up with an effective plan for reducing Government expenditures. The President said Committee Chairman Wilbur D. Mills (D Ark.) would live to "rue the day" he decided to block the proposal, but in fact Mills won his point.

The President finally got his tax increase in 1968, but Congress exacted as its price mandatory reductions in spending, appropriations and Federal employment levels which Mr. Johnson said "would really bring chaos to the Government." Although Mills had maintained throughout that a tax increase without expenditure controls would not be effective in curbing inflationary pressures, some observers attributed a part of his recalcitrance to pique. "I think Mills got upset because we didn't show him more attention," a high Administration official said.

Bibliography

Bailey, Stephen K., *The New Congress.* St. Martin's Press, 1966.

Cannon, Clarence, *Cannon's Procedure in the House of Representatives.* Government Printing Office, 1963.

Galloway, George B., *History of the United States House of Representatives.* Thomas Y. Crowell Co., 1961.

——, *The Legislative Process in Congress.* Thomas Y. Crowell Co., 1953.

Gross, Bertram M., *The Legislative Struggle.* McGraw-Hill, 1953.

Haynes, George H., *The Senate of the United States* (2 vols). Houghton Mifflin, 1938.

McConachie, L. G., *Congressional Committees: A Study of the Origins and Development of Our National and Local Legislative Methods.* Thomas Y. Crowell, 1898.

Morrow, William L., *Congressional Committees.* Charles Scribner's Sons, 1969.

Ripley, Randall B., *Power in the Senate.* St. Martin's Press, 1969.

Robinson, James A., *The House Rules Committee.* Bobbs-Merrill, 1963.

Steiner, Gilbert Y., *The Congressional Conference Committee.* Univ. of Illinois, 1951.

Wilson, Woodrow, *Congressional Government.* Meridian edition, 1956.

Development of Committee Staffs

Staff members of committees in Congress have been credited with doing much of the legislative work undertaken during each Congressional session.

Dependence of committee chairmen and members on staff assistance prompted the late Sen. Everett McKinley Dirksen (R Ill., 1951-69) to remark at a hearing Aug. 6, 1969: "If it weren't for the staff people that I have on these committees by virtue of seniority, I would be in a fix."

The professional and clerical employees of committees increased in both size and quality after passage of the Legislative Reorganization Act of 1946. Total number of committee staffers rose from fewer than 400 in 1946 to more than 1,600 in 1970.

Such growth caused some Members of Congress to complain about "a Government of staffs"; others initiated moves to cut back the number of committee employees. Still other Members contended that additional staff members were needed by committees. They cited the following reasons:

• Paucity in staffing of committees has led to shifting of the initiative in policymaking from Congress to the Executive Branch.

• Understaffing of standing committees has forced a proliferation of special investigating committees and subcommittees, each with their own staffs.

• Some committee staffs are so small they cannot do effective research.

Lack of Staffs in Early Days

Senators and Representatives were reluctant during the early years of Congress to admit that they required staff assistance for committees, or for that matter in their own personal offices. William L. Morrow wrote in his book *Congressional Committees,* "Legislators were considered more erudite than most citizens and they believed any suggestion for staff assistance might be interpreted as a lack of confidence in their ability to master their jobs." Thus, most chairmen kept the records of their own committees in the early part of the 19th century, although some committees occasionally hired clerks during heavy legislative periods.

Various motions to employ permanent clerks were rejected by Congress until about 1840 when, after pleas by chairmen, some clerical assistance was allowed in emergencies on a per diem or hourly basis. Funds for the part-time assistants were made available through special appropriations.

In 1856, the House Ways and Means and the Senate Finance Committees became the first committees to obtain regular appropriations for full-time clerks. Other committees followed, but their staffing generally was limited to hiring for housekeeping duties—clerks, stenographers and receptionists. Committee activities and drafting of bills usually were handled by Members or their personal aides. By 1893, 41 House committees employed clerks on an annual basis and a large number of clerks and messengers for the duration of a session of Congress.

Increased Hiring at Turn of Century

By the turn of the century, appropriations acts were regularly carrying items specifying funds for employees of all standing committees in both houses. The first comprehensive legislative pay bill authorizing appropriations for all legislative employees, including committee clerks, was enacted in 1924. That Act appropriated $270,100 for 141 Senate committee clerks and $200,490 for 120 House committee employees.

Committee staffs and personal office staffs of Members have been separated by an ill-defined line, both in practice and by statute. Staff aides on relatively inactive committees often have been utilized to supplement Members' office forces. Under the express provisions of the Legislative Pay Act of 1929, when a Senator assumed the chairmanship of a committee, the three senior clerks on his office staff became ex officio clerk and assistant clerks of that committee. Further, the Act stipulated that the clerical employees of a Senate committee also would serve as secretarial workers for the chairman of the committee.

Changes Under 1946 and 1970 Acts

1946 Reorganization. Committee staffing underwent substantial change after passage of the Legislative Reorganization Act of 1946. The number of standing committees in the Senate was reduced from 33 to 15 and in the House from 48 to 19, and the jurisdiction of each committee was more strictly defined. Early in the 1947 session, the Republican-controlled Congress added four new select and special committees to the roster of standing committees set up by the Reorganization Act. In subsequent years, a number of other special and select committees were created, but the standing committee structure remained essentially unchanged.

Committees were allowed by the 1946 Act to hire four professional staff members and up to six clerical workers each, "without regard to political affiliations and solely on the basis of fitness to perform the duties of the office." The Appropriations Committees, however, were allowed to determine the number of their employees by a majority vote of the committee. Thus, the total number of staff employees allowed under the 1946 Act was 340, plus the additional numbers needed by the Appropriations Committees.

The size of committee staffs has fluctuated above that level during much of the time since the law was passed. Additional staff members have been acquired through the adoption of resolutions in each house authorizing an increase in personnel. Some Members have believed that use of special resolutions has given better control over the size of staffs than would have resulted from amending the 1946 Act.

The establishment of more than 125 special and select subcommittees in subsequent years also increased staff hiring. Most subcommittees were authorized for a specific time period, to investigate a legislative or national problem, and were then to pass out of existence. But many of these subcommittees have continued to receive increasing appropriations, and consequently have become more firmly established, with larger staffs.

Committee Investigators

Every committee of Congress is to some degree an investigative unit. Each professional staff member is usually part investigator in discharging his duty of keeping the members on the committee well informed. But some committee staff personnel are hired specifically for investigative work.

Many committees, whether they have regular staff investigators or not, occasionally use the research services of other agencies. The General Accounting Office (GAO) and the Federal Bureau of Investigation (FBI) are two of the agencies used by committees seeking additional investigative help.

The GAO, an agency of the Legislative Branch, had 65 staff members permanently assigned to Congressional committees during 1970 for consultation and investigative work. In addition, the GAO studied and issued reports on more than 375 topics during 1970 at the request of committees or individual Members of Congress.

A Congressional Quarterly survey of House and Senate committees showed that most committees preferred not to use Executive Branch agency investigators, but occasionally the Internal Revenue Service (IRS), FBI, General Services Administration (GSA) and other agencies were used for special case work. Committees make a written request for investigative assistance from another agency and that agency assigns men to work for the committee on a particular project.

The House Appropriations Committee makes extensive use of outside assistance. Under a practice initiated in 1943, the Committee employs three FBI agents as full-time investigators. The agents, on leave of absence from the FBI, are paid by the Committee and serve for three-year terms. They are the only full-time investigators employed by the Committee. In addition to these full-time employees, the Committee during the last half of 1970 reported assistance from 32 other FBI agents, three investigators from the National Aeronautics and Space Administration, two from the Army Audit Agency and one each from the Central Intelligence Agency, the Department of Agriculture, Commerce Department, Defense Contract Audit Agency, Transportation Department and the Veterans Administration.

1970 Reorganization. Passage of the Legislative Reorganization Act of 1970 (PL 91-510) brought significant changes in committee staffing procedures. As enacted, the law:

• Increased to six from four the number of permanent professional staff members for each standing committee. Two members of the professional staff, in addition to one of the six permanent clerical staff members, might be selected by a majority of the committee's minority party members. This provision did not apply to the House and Senate Appropriations Committees or to the House Committee on Standards of Official Conduct.

• Authorized standing committees—with the approval of the Senate Rules and Administration or House Administration Committee—to hire temporary consultants.

• Authorized standing committees—with the approval of the Senate Rules and Administration or House Administration Committee—to provide staff members with specialized training.

• Authorized salaries of Senate committee staff personnel comparable to those of House committee staff personnel.

• Redesignated the Legislative Reference Service in the Library of Congress as the Congressional Research Service, redefined its duties to assist Congressional committees by providing research and analytical services, records, documents and other information and data, including memoranda on proposed legislation, and expanded its staff resources.

• Required that no less than one-third of a House committee's funds be used for minority staff. (The House, however, voted in 1971 to disregard this provision.)

Expansion of Committee Staffs

The growth in size of committee staffs has been given a hard look by many economy-minded Senators and Representatives in recent years.

In December 1947, one year after the 1946 Reorganization Act went into effect, House committees employed 254 persons, according to a 1963 statistical study of House committee staffing prepared by the Legislative Reference Service. By December 1969, according to the *Congressional Record* of Jan. 28, 1970, a total of 917 House committee and subcommittee staff members were employed.

Senate committee employees in 1946 numbered approximately 150. But in March 1970, the total for all Senate committee and subcommittee aides stood at 728, according to figures compiled by the Senate Committee on Rules and Administration.

Recruitment and Tenure. Most committee aides and clerks are appointed by the chairman or the ranking minority member, as a perquisite of office, subject only to nominal approval of the full committee. Their tenure generally is subject to the political and mortal hazards of the Members who hired the employees. Turnover on committee staffs is great but some staffers have made working for committees a career.

Even the most partisan Members of Congress generally agree that competence has become a basic criterion for appointment to the professional staff. Practically all major staff members have college degrees; many are lawyers or have other advanced study experience.

Committee Organization. The majority of Congressional committees tend to have dual staffs, one professional and one clerical. These are generally headed by a "staff director" and a "chief clerk," respectively.

Although the distinction between professional and clerical staff is blurred on many committees, the duties of each can be roughly separated. The clerical staff is responsible for keeping the committee calendar up to date, for processing committee publications, for referring bills to the appropriate departments for comment, for preparing the bill dockets, for maintaining the files, for stenographic work, and for opening and sorting mail.

Professional staffers are primarily responsible for policy matters handled by the committee. They fill the need for legal, public relations, statistical, accounting, investigative and other technical services.

A Government of Staffs?

Floor debate in the 91st Congress on the costs of committee staffing prompted some grumbling among expenditure-wary Senators. Those opposed to additional funds for committee investigations pointed to the overlapping activities of many committees and subcommittees. Others contended that Congress was suffering from the same expansionist tendencies as the Executive Branch. At the start of the 92nd Congress, the Senate had 16 standing committees, four special and select committees and 122 subcommittees. Only seven of the 57 Democratic Senators were not committee or subcommittee chairmen.

Agriculture Committee Chairman Allen J. Ellender (D La.), himself a member of three committees, one joint committee and seven subcommittees, has long been the Senate's chief critic of rising committee funding. On Feb. 17, 1969, Ellender recalled that the Senate voted in 1946 to limit itself to 15 committees with no more than 10 employees each. At that time, there were 38 committees and few if any subcommittees. Then "we began to create these subcommittees," Ellender said. Referring to the growth of committee staffs, Ellender added: "I believe that is the trouble in a good many of the committees today. They have too many employees who pass the buck to each other, and very few who do the work."

Sen. John L. McClellan (D Ark.), a member of three committees and 20 subcommittees, also decried the burgeoning of subcommittees. "I point out in all candor, and I think the chairmen of other subcommittees recognize what I say as a fact, that with so many subcommittees holding hearings, our problem is to get enough Senators to attend subcommittee hearings. Every Senator is busy with his own subcommittee, and that makes for inefficiency of the committee."

Majority Leader Mike Mansfield (D Mont.) agreed. "There is too much emphasis on staff members instead of on Senators....I think this body is getting subcommittee happy."

In 1970, Ellender renewed his criticism of the proliferation of committee staffs: "We have all these subcommittees, who are provided all of the facts. They are staffed by competent lawyers. I do not know how many there are, but there are quite a few. Most of the work is done by those lawyers. It is my belief that we simply have too many subcommittees."

Sen. John J. Williams (R Del.) observed that "It can truly be said that there is nothing more permanent than a temporary Senate committee." Referring to the duplication of work by various committees, he went on to say: "With such overlapping we almost need a committee to determine the duties of the various committees and to find out the size of their staffs. I wonder if we have not become lost in a maze created by the building up of a series of bureaucracies over which the Senate has lost control. Perhaps any one of these subcommittees considered alone can be justified, but collectively we are becoming a Government of staffs."

Salaries. Amounts appropriated for salaries of committee staff members increased dramatically during the period from 1945 to 1970. Some top executive staffers now earn almost as much as Members themselves. In 1945, each House employee was listed under "clerk hire" with annual base pay of $2,500. But during the next 25 years, there were 17 Federal pay raises.

The 1970 Reorganization Act converted the "base pay" system of the House into a monthly salary system and raised the compensation of committee employees. Annual gross salary of professional staff members currently ranges from $18,328 to $32,712. Salaries for chief clerks range from $20,416 to $32,712 annually. Certain Appropriations Committee employees may receive as much as $35,496 a year.

Salaries of House committee employees are open for public inspection at the Disbursing Office of the Clerk of the House. Senate staff salaries are on public record in a semi-annual report of the Secretary of the Senate. The reports also include compensation for travel and other personal expenses not covered by base salary.

Description of Work

Committee aides, working within the jurisdiction of the committee and in close association with members, generate and shape much of the legislation considered by Congress. Among their activities:

● **Organizing Hearings.** Staffers set up hearings on legislation and current issues. They select witnesses, prepare questions, inform the press, brief committee members, and occasionally substitute for members or chairmen who cannot attend hearings. In many instances a member will prepare a list of questions for aides to ask witnesses if he cannot be present.

● **Investigations.** Much original research is conducted by staff members on issues which come before a committee. This usually involves looking into existing legislation, court decisions and current practices. Aides often travel to areas under consideration by the committee, and sometimes hold regional hearings to get opinions from citizens interested in certain legislation.

● **Bill and Amendment Drafting.** Although staff members occasionally may actually write bills and amendments, they usually serve as liaison between the Office of the Legislative Counsel, committee members, Government agencies and special interest groups during the drafting of measures.

● **Preparing Reports.** Committee reports to accompany bills are almost entirely staff products. Often the reports are the only reference concerning the legislative matter being considered. Staff aides consult with the chairman or the majority to decide what should be emphasized in the report, including minority views. Then the staff writes the report, usually conforming to a standard format. Reports usually include three basic ingredients—the main body, which explains the bill and gives background and interpretation; the section-by-section analysis of the provisions of the bill, and a written comparison of the bill with existing law.

● **Preparation for Floor Action.** Staff aides assist in marking up bills by explaining technical provisions, outlining policy questions, analyzing proposed changes, following committee decisions and incorporating the decisions in successive revisions of the bill. The top committee

Office of the Legislative Counsel

The Office of the Legislative Counsel was created in 1919 under the Revenue Act of 1918. Originally called the Legislative Drafting Service, the Office was established to provide professional assistance to Members in the drafting of legislation. Each chamber has its own chief counsel, appointed in one case by the Speaker of the House and in the other by the President pro tempore of the Senate. Each counsel has a legal staff of between 11 and 20 persons.

Members who want to introduce a bill on a specific subject rely on the lawyers in the Office of the Legislative Counsel to put the proposal into legislative language. The lawyers analyze and research the precedents, compare the bill with existing laws, and sometimes suggest alternatives. Title V of the Legislative Reorganization Act of 1970 reconstituted the House office, upgrading its responsibilities and making its services more readily available to individual House members.

Although the Office of the Legislative Counsel continues to perform important service in the drafting of bills, there is a growing tendency on the part of Executive Branch agencies and even of some outside pressure groups to have their own experts draft the bills introduced on their behalf by Members of Congress.

aide often will accompany a bill's sponsor in the House or Senate to assist him in managing the floor action.

- **Conference Committee Work.** Staffs of corresponding committees in each house work together on preparation of conference reports and in resolving differences in a bill passed by both the House and the Senate.

- **Lobby Liaison.** Staff aides communicate frequently with lobbyists on legislative proposals before the committee. Some Members regard this activity as the most consequential of all staff work. Rep. Bob Eckhardt (D Texas) said in September 1969: "The key point of contact is usually between a highly specialized lobbyist and the specialized staff people of a standing committee. Intimate friendships spring up there—it's the rivet point. Friendships that outlast terms. They probably have a greater influence on legislation, especially if it's technical."

Power of Staff Members

Long-time professional staff members of committees of Congress sometimes acquire considerable influence over policy and the content of legislation. Roy Cohn, chief counsel to the Permanent Investigations Subcommittee headed by Sen. Joseph R. McCarthy (R Wis., 1947-57), was a dominant figure in the 1954 Army-McCarthy hearings. John R. Blandford, chief counsel of the House Armed Services Committee, once was described by Chairman L. Mendel Rivers (D S.C., 1941-70): "I think it's safe to say that he knows more about the armed services than anyone in the Pentagon—or anywhere else around Washington."

Other influential committee staffers include Carl Marcy, staff director of the Senate Foreign Relations Committee; John M. Martin Jr., chief counsel of the House Ways and Means Committee; Paul Nelson, staff director of the House Banking and Currency Committee; and John R. Stark, executive director of the Joint Economic Committee.

Minority Staffing

A continuing controversy about committee staffing is the question of hiring employees affiliated with the minority party. Because the chairman's prerogative usually prevails in placing staff members on the committee, most employees tend to be from the majority party.

Rep. James C. Cleveland (R N.H.) said in a House Republican task force report in 1966: "I strongly believe that the minority on every committee should have the right to hire and fire its own staff personnel, set their salary scales, and locate them without prior approval of the majority."

Other minority party Members of both houses have argued that the balance of committee personnel between the two parties should more nearly approximate the division of party strength in the House or Senate, or in the individual committee. Non-partisan staffing also has been advocated, but some critics feel that a non-partisan staff would be nothing more than a funnel for the views of the departments whose operations most nearly coincide with the fields of interest of the respective committees.

Failure to grant committee minorities the staff support needed to enable them to exercise their legislative function effectively was somewhat ameliorated by the Reorganization Act of 1970. The law provided for at least three full-time staff aides for the minority on most Congressional committees.

Reform Movements

Although the quality of committee staffs remains high in most cases, recommendations for employment of more professional staff workers have come from diverse quarters. Private research groups and Members themselves have pointed to increased committee workloads, emphasized the importance of having specialists for each of the major jurisdictions of a technical committee, and complained that, in the face of the more generous staffing of Executive agencies, the Congress is frustrated in its efforts to perform properly its surveillance function.

A report entitled "Making Congress More Effective," issued in September 1970 by the Committee for Economic Development, called for expert capabilities in committee staffs. The report said in part:

"We recommend that Congress strengthen its staff resources by recruitment of highly qualified specialists —physical scientists, engineers, environmentalists, physicians, economists and other social scientists, nutritionists, mathematicians, management experts, and others as occasion may require.

"Some of these resources should be pooled—as in the Legislative Reference Service and the General Accounting Office—where every committee would have access to the best technical and analytical service. Minority staffing is essential, and could also be pooled in party policy or research committees. Serious attention should be given to professional training and development of all these staffs. Special attention to data collection problems is urgently needed."

Bibliography

Books

Galloway, George B., *Congress at the Crossroads.* Thomas Y. Crowell Co., 1946.

Gross, Bertram, *The Legislative Struggle.* McGraw-Hill Inc., 1953.

Kofmehl, Kenneth, *Professional Staffs of Congress.* Purdue Research Foundation, 1962.

McInnis, Mary, ed., *We Propose: A Modern Congress.* McGraw-Hill Inc., 1966.

Morrow, William L., *Congressional Committees.* Charles Scribner's Sons, 1969.

Ripley, Randall B., *Power in the Senate.* St. Martin's Press Inc., 1969.

Robinson, James A., *The House Rules Committee.* Bobbs-Merrill Co. Inc., 1963.

Government Publications

Joint Committee on the Organization of the Congress, *Organization of Congress.* Interim Report No. 426, 89th Congress, 1st session, 1965.

——, *Organization of Congress.* Second Interim Report No. 1218, 89th Congress, 2nd session, 1966.

Library of Congress, Legislative Reference Service, *Statistical Study on the Staffing of Committees of the House of Representatives.* November 1963.

——, *Senate Committee Staffing.* Sen. Doc. 16, 88th Congress, 1st session, 1963.

Seniority: The Rule and Exceptions

SENIORITY—status based on length of service, to which are attached certain rights and privileges—pervades nearly all social institutions. An older person customarily has been granted more respect than a younger one, for example.

In the workings of Congress, seniority has flourished and has assumed a role of major importance. Seniority affects the assignment of office space, a Member's access to Congressional patronage, the deference shown Members on the floor. Seniority even affects a Member's invitations to dinner. But seniority is most apparent (and important) in the committee system; it affects assignments to committees and subcommittees, and virtually determines chairmanships.

The importance of seniority in Congress has developed as a tradition. Despite frequent references to a "seniority rule" and a "seniority system," observance of seniority is neither a law nor a formal rule. Its origins are uncertain.

Congressional and Committee Seniority

Capitol Hill seniority is based on the length of service in Congress, referred to as Congressional seniority, or on the length of consecutive service on a committee, called committee seniority. The workings of the seniority system dictate that the Member with the most years of service—regardless of other qualifications (or limitations)—is given first choice on better office space, assignment to an important committee or election to a committee chairmanship.

Seniority inherently has been an ally of older Members and of the Congressional establishment. As such, younger Members or insurgents periodically have brought it under attack. The application of seniority in doling out perquisites has seldom been questioned. Most of the debate has centered on the role of seniority in the committee system.

Committee assignments are affected by other factors than strict seniority, such as party loyalty, regional distribution and the favor of the leadership. However, a Member high on the seniority ladder is more apt to receive the assignment he seeks than one further down. Sometimes the failure to follow seniority in assignments creates resentment. Sen. Joseph S. Clark (D Pa.) staged a three-day protest in 1963 against the Senate Democratic committee-assignment process. Clark asserted that liberals who had sought changes in Senate procedures had not received committee assignments they were entitled to by seniority.

Once on a committee, a member is not dropped except in unusual circumstances. The junior minority member of a committee may be bumped from it if elections change party ratios. Members have been purged from committees (or lost seniority in some cases) when they switched party allegiance or bolted the party during a Presidential election.

As a Member rises in rank on a committee, his chances of being heard, of asking witnesses questions, and of handling major legislation increase. So do his chances of heading a subcommittee. Appointments are made by the committee chairman; the senior member of a subcommittee is not always appointed its chairman. When he becomes the senior majority member of the committee, he is entitled to be chairman. The honor is seldom declined in the House, where most Members are restricted to one major committee assignment apiece. But it frequently is declined in the Senate, where a Senator may be senior on two or more committees but is generally restricted to one major committee chairmanship.

Traditionally, senior committee members are picked to serve on conference committees, used in ironing out differences between House and Senate versions of a bill.

Seniority and Safe Constituencies

The seniority system, by rewarding length of service, has tended to place power in the hands of Members from "safe" constituencies. Such constituencies typically have been conservative, tradition-bound areas of the nation. The Northeast was a Republican stronghold in the late 1800s. Later, the South was solidly Democratic, and Republicans had shifted their base to the Midwest. Recently, safe constituencies have usually been rural ones, but a few Members from urban constituencies have become chairmen.

In the second session of the 91st Congress, 13 House chairmen were from rural districts. Of the Republicans who filled the ranking minority slots in that Congress, 11

Reference

For additional details on operation of the seniority system in the committees of Congress, and its occasional use in the disciplining of Members, see *Evolution of Committees, Chapter II* and *Seating and Disciplining of Members, Chapter III.*

were from rural districts, four from suburban and six from urban districts. In both the House and Senate the majority of senior Democrats were from the South. The majority of senior Republicans in the House were from the Midwest. And in the Senate, the majority of senior Republicans were from the East.

History of Seniority System

The history of the seniority system in Congress has become tied inextricably to development of the committee system and to party control of assignments. Parties have relied on seniority as a widely recognized—and neutral—arbiter for settling intraparty quarrels over lucrative positions. On occasion, parties have threatened their recalcitrant members with loss of seniority. In a few cases, the threat has been carried out.

Senate. In the Senate, the standing-committee system was authorized in late 1816, and party control of assignments began to appear after 1833. With party control of assignments also appeared the principle of seniority. Seniority was applied both to committee assignments and to advancement within a committee.

In the early years of the Senate, seniority played a relatively minor role in determining committee assignments. Party lines were not clearly drawn, and there was little political control of committee assignments. The Senate experimented with a variety of methods for doling out the assignments; committee memberships and chairmanships rotated frequently. As political parties emerged and grew stronger, they began to exert power over the system of committees.

By 1846, party control had become so firm that committee assignment lists supplied by the parties were approved routinely. Reliance on seniority in the Senate traditionally has dated from that year.

The power of seniority over advancement within a committee began to appear among Democratic Senators in the last decade before the Civil War. Republican Senators disregarded seniority during the 1861-77 period, when Democrats had virtually disappeared from Congress. But seniority rapidly came to dominate committee advancement as the character of the postwar Senate changed—as Democrats regained seats and as Members, accumulating year after year of uninterrupted service, began to consider the Senate a career. By the middle of the 20th century, the power of seniority was firmly entrenched in the Senate.

House. In the House, seniority at first played a secondary role. Committee assignments, minority as well as majority, and the selection of committee chairmen were determined by the Speaker, and although a Member's seniority was a useful guide, the Speaker could violate seniority for personal or political reasons. A 1969 study of seniority in the House indicated that from 1880 to 1910, Speakers had appointed 750 chairmen, and that in doing so they had followed seniority in 429 cases and disregarded it in 321 cases.

Through the years, the House Speaker amassed vast power. Gradually, a reaction set in, which led finally to a revolt. A number of insurgent liberal Republicans joined forces with a Democratic minority in 1910 to revise the House rules and to deprive the Speaker of some of his power. The revolt swirled around Speaker Joseph G. Cannon (R Ill.). Among other things, the Speaker was stripped of his power to appoint committees and committee chairmen. That power was handed over to party committees on committees as a means of diffusing power in the House. The choices made by the committees on committees, though subject to ratification by the party caucuses and approval by the full House, were almost always final.

Following the revolt of 1910, the seniority rule became increasingly important, although it still was frequently ignored. The 1969 study of seniority in the House showed that from 1910 to the end of World War II, seniority was followed in 676 of 901 appointments of committee chairmen and violated 225 times. Since World War II, the power of seniority in the House, dating traditionally from the 1910 revolt, has become virtually absolute. In the past quarter-century, there have been only half a dozen violations of seniority in naming chairmen of House committees.

Computing Seniority. Senate rank generally is determined according to the official date of the beginning of the Member's service, which is Jan. 3 except in the case of a new Member sworn in after Congress is in session. For those elected or appointed to fill unexpired terms, the date of appointment, certification or swearing-in determines the Senator's rank.

When Members are sworn in on the same day, custom decrees that those with prior political experience take precedence. Counted as political experience, in order of importance, are Senatorial, House and gubernatorial service.

In the House, rank generally is determined according to the official date of the beginning of a Member's service, which is Jan. 3 except in cases when a Member has been elected to fill a vacancy. In such cases, the date of election determines the rank.

When Members enter the House on the same day, those with prior House service take precedence, starting with those with the longest consecutive service. Experience as a Senator or a Governor is disregarded.

Debate on Seniority

Over the years, custom and tradition have enveloped the Congressional tenet of seniority. And because Congress is a continuing body which relies on customs and traditions for guidance, the strength of seniority has steadily increased. Yet violations have been perpetrated by the leaders of both parties in both houses, and retaliation by the victim has been virtually impossible. At the same time, use of seniority has on occasion elevated a physically or mentally unfit Member to the head of a committee.

As a result, controversy frequently has surrounded the criterion of seniority. Strong—and well-worn—arguments have been marshaled by its friends and its foes. Following is a selection of major points advanced in behalf of and against the system, compiled in 1970 by the Democratic Study Group, an informal organization of House liberals:

(Continued on p. 168)

Gardner's Views on the Seniority System

On Jan. 18-19, 1971, the Senate held two days of unofficial hearings on the seniority system, drawing critical attacks on the system from most witnesses. Following are excerpts from the testimony of John W. Gardner, former president of the Carnegie Corporation, HEW Secretary from 1965 to 1968, and chairman since 1970 of Common Cause, a citizens' lobby group:

The time has come to modify a long-established custom of this great deliberative body—the so-called seniority system. I should like to discuss the principle as it relates to both houses of Congress, though I recognize that your own concern lies with Senate procedures.

Let us look at the seniority system from the standpoint of accountability and responsiveness. Most of the work of the Congress is done in committees, and the committee chairmen constitute the power structure in Congress. They determine what legislation will come before Congress, whether or not hearings will be held, how $200 billion in appropriations will be allocated and so on. The taxes we pay, the condition of the economy, the quality of our lives—all are deeply influenced by the decisions of these few powerful men.

The word "dictatorial" is not too strong to describe the power they wield. The chairman dominates his committee. By giving or withholding favors he can effectively discipline committee members. He may (and often does) defy the elected leadership of the chamber. He need not exhibit loyalty to his party.

One might suppose that men who enjoy such enormous power would be chosen with great care by their fellow Members of Congress on the basis of well-accepted criteria—wisdom, experience, intelligence, integrity or leadership. But in fact—in any real sense—they are not chosen by their peers at all; and wisdom and integrity have nothing to do with the case. They gain their chairmanship on one criterion only: length of continuous service on the committee....

The breach in the principles of accountability and responsiveness is apparent. If some committee chairmen conduct themselves with unexampled arrogance, it is because there is no mechanism by which their fellow party members can call them to account. If they are utterly unresponsive to their peers, it is because they do not owe their posts to the judgment of their peers.

We propose that the Committee on Committees nominate one candidate for the chairmanship of each legislative committee and that the majority party caucus then be allowed to vote on that name individually.

No doubt the Committee on Committees will often (perhaps usually) nominate the senior member of the committee in question. No doubt the majority party caucus will often (perhaps usually) vote "yes" on the nomination. But occasionally good reasons, e.g., the infirmities of age or misconduct in office, will lead the majority party caucus to reject the senior member. And "occasionally" will be often enough. It will revive instantly the principles of accountability and responsiveness. It will re-establish in the mind of each chairman a healthy awareness that every two years he will stand before a jury of his peers.

We think the vote in the majority party caucus on each chairmanship nomination should take place automatically and should be recorded so the public will know exactly who voted for whom.

There are two levels of accountability here. The first is the accountability of chairmen to the party caucus. The second is the accountability of all Members of Congress to the public. Not only should chairmen be accountable for their performance, but the Members who select them should have to account to their constituents for the choices. I venture to say, gentlemen, that the club-like tolerance which returns unresponsive or incompetent chairmen to their positions year after year will dissolve rather quickly when Members of Congress can be asked by the public why they have continued to vote for such men....

Defenders of the seniority principle say "Yes, it is an imperfect system—but all the alternatives are disastrous." Such debaters must explain why no other parliamentary body in the free world uses the seniority system and why no state legislature in any of our 50 states uses it. If the alternatives are so disastrous, why are many other parliamentary bodies doing perfectly well with those alternatives?

Gentlemen, I recognize that there are more colorful ways of attacking the seniority system than I have chosen to use.... I recognize...that the seniority system produces an extraordinarily high age level in the power structure of Congress. In the early 1800s, Henry Clay served brilliantly as Speaker of the House beginning at the age of 33. Contrast that with the situation in the Congress just ended, in which the Speaker retired at the age of 79 and the median age of House chairmen was 69, compared with 53 for all Members of the House. Comparable figures for the Senate were 67 for chairmen and 58 for the Senate as a whole.

A system which rewards length of continuous service is, of course, grossly partial to one-party states and districts. No Senator from my native state of California —a dynamic two-party state—has held the chairmanship of a Senate standing committee in the past 24 years.

But I want to rest my case on the issues with which I began—*accountability* and *responsiveness*. We are not dealing here with a technical detail of organization. We are dealing with the capacity of one of our greatest institutions to respond flexibly and effectively in one of the deepest crises of our history.... The American people...resent the unresponsiveness of their governmental institutions. If the Members of this great deliberative body fully grasp the depth of that popular resentment, they will hasten to correct a flaw in their procedures that has so gravely damaged their reputation.

Supporting Arguments

• There are no workable alternatives to the seniority system.

• The seniority system assures capable and experienced leadership. It guarantees that chairmanships go to the members who have had the greatest opportunity to master the complicated procedures of the House and the subject matter of their committees. This experience is particularly useful in giving a chairman the greatest perspective on programs and proposals. An experienced chairman can help the committee avoid the pitfalls of approaches which have been previously tried and found unsuccessful.

• The seniority system avoids competition among committee members for the chairmanship. It thereby fosters cooperation since members are more likely to work together effectively when they are not campaigning against each other.

• The seniority system eliminates pressure group influence in the selection of the committee chairman with jurisdiction over the area of their interest.

• The seniority system works. It assures that when one chairman leaves office, he will be succeeded by a Member who, as number two man on the committee, has been anticipating the day he would become chairman and has therefore been learning the job and its responsibilities. Thus, the system fosters stability and prevents the deleterious effects of selecting a chairman who is unprepared for the job.

• The present system guarantees that the most expert politicians will become committee chairmen. Seniority presupposes political acumen. The Member with the greatest seniority has proven skill in getting re-elected. This skill is extremely useful in evaluating proposals before the Congress to determine the sentiment of the voters and the effect of enactment upon the re-election prospects of party members.

• The seniority system as it now operates permits great independence on the part of committee chairmen since they are not held to the test of party responsibility. In the House this independence prevents the emergence of a strong and autocratic Speaker. Further, it allows a chairman to make decisions based on his own best judgment as a result of his familiarity with the circumstances. Because the present system grants a chairman wide discretion, he need not act on the basis of current political fashion but may take a long range view and better serve the needs of the country.

• While the seniority system does produce occasional bad chairmen, other proposed systems would have the same result. In addition, the other proposed systems would curb the autonomy of the chairman and would prevent a chairman from acting according to his conscience without fear of reprisal from the leadership or his party.

• Seniority helps to insulate the Congress from encroachments by the White House or other quarters. A President will not seek dismissal of a committee chairman who does not support his program since such an effort would be futile. However, non-automatic chairmanships would open the door to interference in Congressional affairs by the Chief Executive, especially where he is a member of the majority party.

• The seniority system provides the best opportunity for a member of a minority group to become a committee chairman. If a member starts out young enough and continues to be re-elected to Congress by his own constituency, he will eventually become a committee chairman automatically. If chairmen were chosen by another method, it would be more difficult for blacks, women or other minority representatives to obtain the post of chairman.

• The seniority system provides the best opportunity for flexibility and compromise in fashioning new legislation. Because, in effect, committee chairmen are not now bound to a party platform or accountable to the caucus, they are freer to compromise with the minority members of their committees. This increases the possibility of enacting legislation.

• There is no need for outside control over committee chairmen because committee members themselves can spur or veto an unresponsive or obstructionist chairman.

• Automatic selection of committee chairmen promotes peace and harmony within the ranks of the party. The seniority system thus avoids the politicking, logrolling and factionalism that would accompany any other system.

• The seniority system stabilizes committee membership by discouraging members from switching committees. This enhances the effectiveness of the committee in handling legislation since not only the chairman, but also many committee members, are familiar with the subject matter.

• A chairman's age is not a valid consideration, since age alone does not reduce mental vigor, alertness or leadership ability. Nor does it mean that a man becomes more conservative or loses touch.

Opposing Arguments

• The seniority system has fragmented and diffused power, thereby crippling effective leadership and making it impossible to present and pursue a coherent legislative program.

• The seniority system not only allows chairmen to be unresponsive to their party and the leadership; it has permitted certain chairmen to obstruct, distort and emasculate party programs and policies with impunity. Thus over the past two decades, a small handful of powerful chairmen has been allowed to prevent Congress from responding to the nation's needs until the problems became searing crises. The classic example of such obstructionism was former Rep. Howard W. Smith (D Va.) who, as chairman of the Rules Committee from 1955 to 1967, personally killed or blocked civil rights, housing, education, health, welfare and other needed social legislation for years.

• The seniority system gives the power of the Democratic party in Congress to those most opposed to Democratic programs and policies.

• The seniority system has resulted in a steady increase in age of House committee chairmen. One hundred years ago the average chairman was in his forties—today he is 70 years old. There were only three chairmen under 60 years of age in the 91st Congress; of the remainder, eight were in their sixties, seven were in their seventies, and three were in their eighties. At a time when other American institutions were turning over the reins of leadership to younger men, the leaders of Congress were getting older. Thus the system aggravates the tensions and strains in the society at large, especially when it produces

Violations of Seniority in Appointment of House Committee Chairmen—1881-1969

Congress	Year	Speaker and party	Seniority followed	Seniority violated	Total committees	Congress	Year	Speaker and party	Seniority followed	Seniority violated	Total committees
47	1881	Keifer (R)	2	37	39	70	1927	Longworth (R)	43	1	44
48	1883	Carlisle (D)	8	30	38	71	1929	do	38	7	45
49	1885	do	21	19	40	72	1931	Garner (D)	27	18	45
50	1887	do	20	21	41	73	1933	Rainey (D)	38	7	45
51	1889	Reed (R)	20	27	47	74	1935	Byrns (D)	32	13	45
52	1891	Crisp (D)	12	35	47	75	1937	Bankhead (D)	42	4	46
53	1893	do	25	24	49	76	1939	Rayburn (D)	37	9	46
54	1895	Reed (R)	13	39	52	77	1941	do	39	7	46
55	1897	do	36	16	52	78	1943	do	34	11	45
56	1899	Henderson (R)	42	15	57	79	1945	do	37	9	46
57	1901	do	49	8	57	80	1947	Martin (R)	9	4	13
58	1903	Cannon (R)	43	11	54	81	1949	Rayburn (D)	19	0	19
59	1905	do	51	8	59	82	1951	do	18	0	18
60	1907	do	45	13	58	83	1953	Martin (R)	17	1	18
61	1909	do	42	18	60	84	1955	Rayburn (D)	19	0	19
62	1911	Clark (D)	25	27	52	85	1957	do	19	0	19
63	1913	do	33	20	53	86	1959	do	19	0	19
64	1915	do	50	6	56	87	1961	Rayburn (D)	20	0	20
65	1917	do	45	10	55	88	1963	McCormack (D)	20	0	20
66	1919	Gillett (R)	35	22	57	89	1965	do	20	0	20
67	1921	do	44	15	59	90	1967	do	20	1	21
68	1923	do	40	17	57	91	1969	do	21	0	21
69	1925	Longworth (R)	37	22	59			**TOTALS**	**1,326**	**552**	**1,878**

Sources: Polsby, Nelson W., Gallaher, Miriam, and Rundquist, Barry, "The Growth of the Seniority System in the U.S. House of Representatives," *American Political Science Review*, September 1969 (1881-1963 data); Democratic Study Group (1963-69 data).

powerful chairmen who are hostile to change and dedicated to protecting and preserving the status quo.

• The seniority system maintains the same individuals in power too long. For example, eight of the House chairmen in the 91st Congress had held their chairmanships for more than 12 years and three had been chairmen for 22 years. The remaining chairmen had held their posts for less than 10 years; however, their predecessors held their chairmanships for an average of 15 years each. Thus the average chairman can expect to hold power for at least a full decade and frequently longer.

• The rule of absolute seniority results, on occasion, in the selection of mediocre, senile or otherwise incompetent chairmen and preserves them in office. Ironically, Members of Congress become committee chairmen about the time in life when most other Americans are forced to retire.

• The system permits committees to become personal fiefdoms of strong chairmen and special interests.

• The system denies competent younger men a chance to exercise their leadership talents at the time in life when they are most able to meet the rigors of the job. It is therefore wasteful and inefficient.

• The seniority system produces chairmen who are generally unrepresentative of America at large and are therefore unresponsive to its needs. Only those who get re-elected time after time can reach the top of the seniority ladder and become chairman. Thus the system favors

members from static districts or machine-dominated districts, and tends to deny power to Members who represent other sections of the country, especially those sections which are changing and are more politically competitive.

Attempts to Change System

Members on a number of occasions have tried to modify the seniority system. Most of the tampering has been aimed at the Congressional committees. Few attempts have been successful.

Senate. Two early attempts at modification were made in the Senate. In 1882, Wilkinson Call (D Fla.) proposed to prohibit a Member from occupying a seat on more than one major committee. In 1919, George W. Norris (R Neb.) proposed to limit a Member to seats on no more than two major committees. Neither move was successful.

In 1953, Lyndon B. Johnson (D Texas), acting as Minority Leader, succeeded where others had failed. Johnson proposed, in what was to become known as the "Johnson Rule," that all Democratic Senators have a seat on one major committee before any Democrat is assigned to a second major committee. The proposal was a stunning blow to seniority, but it had the backing of the powerful Richard B. Russell (D Ga.) and was approved by the Democratic Steering Committee, which makes Democratic committee assignments in the Senate.

On Jan. 12, 1953, Johnson assigned two freshman Senators to key committees. Sen. Mike Mansfield (D Mont.), who had been a member of the House Foreign Affairs Committee, was assigned to the Senate Foreign Relations Committee. Sen. Stuart Symington (D Mo.), who had been the first Secretary of the Air Force in 1947, was assigned to the Armed Services Committee.

Within four years' time Johnson had assigned four other Democrats who came to the Senate in 1953 to key committees: Price Daniel (Texas) to Judiciary and Interstate and Foreign Commerce; Albert Gore (Tenn.) to Finance and the Joint Committee on Atomic Energy; Henry M. Jackson (Wash.) to Armed Services and Atomic Energy; John F. Kennedy (Mass.) to Foreign Relations.

Speaking as one who benefited from the Democratic break from its rigid Senate seniority tradition, Mansfield asserted years later: "I don't think that the plan could have worked out better than it did. It proved to be a ten-strike on Lyndon Johnson's part. It gave us newcomers a chance to use in the Senate almost at once whatever abilities we possess. It strengthened our party in the Senate and brought about better understanding and mutual respect among both the new and old Senators." Although Johnson's assignments were represented at the time as giving the liberal element in the Senate a break, Mansfield said, "It didn't work out that way. There was no delineation along that line. We were all treated alike." It was the first time that it became the accepted practice for Senate Democrats to assure their newcomers key committee spots during their first Senate term.

Later, Senate Republicans adopted a similar practice, informally in 1959 and formally through the Republican Conference in 1965.

In 1971, under renewed pressure to modify the seniority system, Senate Democrats and Republicans agreed to further changes. Democratic Leader Mike Mansfield announced Feb. 10 that a meeting of the party caucus would be held at the request of any Senator, and that any Senator would be free to challenge any nomination of a committee chairman, and that the practice of submitting Steering Committee nominations of committee chairmen and members would be continued as a regular procedure. Republicans adopted a proposal that a Senator could be the ranking minority member of only one standing committee of the Senate.

Democrats and Republicans alike established committees to study the seniority system. The three-member Democratic committee was composed of Senators Fred R. Harris (Okla.), Hubert H. Humphrey (Minn.), and Herman E. Talmadge (Ga.). The five-member Republican committee included Senators Wallace F. Bennett (Utah), J. Caleb Boggs (Del.), Clifford P. Hansen (Wyo.), Robert W. Packwood (Ore.), and Robert A. Taft Jr. (Ohio).

On March 16, 1971, the Senate rejected a major challenge to the seniority system, when it tabled, 48-26, a resolution that would have permitted the selection of committee chairmen on some basis other than seniority. The resolution, sponsored by Harris and Charles McC. Mathias (R Md.), provided that in making committee assignments "neither (party) conference shall be bound by any tradition, custom or principle of seniority."

Alternatives to Seniority

Following is a selection of major alternatives to use of seniority in naming committee chairmen. The selection was compiled in 1970 by the Democratic Study Group, an informal organization of House liberals.

- Use the seniority system to nominate chairmen, subject to majority approval by the caucus.
- Have the caucus elect committee chairmen from among the three most senior members of each committee.
- Authorize the Speaker to nominate chairmen, subject to approval by a majority of the caucus.
- Authorize the majority members of each committee to nominate the chairman, subject to caucus approval.
- Authorize the members of each committee—both majority and minority—to select the chairmen, subject to approval of the House as a whole.
- Establish a new special committee to nominate chairmen, subject to majority approval by the caucus.
- Set an age limit, and require chairmen to give up their chairmanships when they reach that age.
- Set a limit on the number of years a Member can serve as chairman and require that, after serving as chairman, the Member leave the committee and begin service on another committee.
- Rotate the chairmanship among the top three committee members every two years.

House Seniority. A major challenge to the seniority system in the House was made during floor action on the Legislative Reorganization Act of 1970. On July 28, 1970, the House debated two amendments to modify the system. Both were rejected.

The primary amendment, offered by Henry S. Reuss (D Wis.), provided that seniority need not be the sole consideration in the selection of committee chairmen. It was defeated by a teller vote, 73-160. Explaining the effect which his amendment would have, Reuss said that "a wooden application of the seniority custom is a luxury we can no longer afford." The amendment, he said, would leave to the parties the final decision on a particular method of selecting chairmen.

The House also rejected, by a teller vote of 28-196, an amendment proposed by Fred Schwengel (R Iowa) as a substitute for the Reuss amendment. The substitute provided that the chairman of each committee should be chosen, by the majority members of the committee, from among the committee's three most senior majority members.

Opponents of the Reuss and Schwengel amendments warned that "campaigns" for chairmanships would provide the opportunity for pressure groups to "wheel and deal" in support of their candidates for chairmen of certain committees. They also said that only through the seniority system could minority group members—such as William L. Dawson (D Ill.), chairman of the House Government Operations Committee—become committee chairmen.

Ken Hechler (D W.Va.) said that "the longer I serve in the Congress, the more evils I see in the seniority system, which puts a premium on those who can survive election after election, regardless of their ability, their responsiveness to public attitudes and their philosophy as it relates to the policies of their political party."

Limited House Changes in Seniority

Also during 1970, special committees appointed by both parties prepared recommendations for changes in the seniority system when the House reorganized for the 92nd Congress in January 1971.

House Democrats voted Jan. 20, 1971, to adopt modest changes in the seniority system of selecting committee chairmen. The changes were recommended by the Committee on Organization Study and Review headed by Rep. Julia Butler Hansen (D Wash.).

The principal changes agreed upon by the Democrats were:

• The Democratic Committee on Committees would recommend to the caucus nominees for the chairmanship and membership of each committee, and such recommendations need not necessarily follow seniority.

• The Committee on Committees would make recommendations to the caucus, one committee at a time; upon the demand of 10 or more Members, nominations could be debated and voted on.

• If a nomination was rejected, the Committee on Committees would submit another nomination. (The Democratic Committee on Committees consists of the Democratic Members of the House Ways and Means Committee.)

The Democrats also agreed that no Member could be chairman of more than one legislative subcommittee. This would open up subcommittee chairmanships to younger Members.

The issue of seniority was first raised in the Democratic caucus Jan. 19 when Rep. John Conyers Jr. (Mich.) challenged the seniority rights of the all-Democratic Mississippi House delegation. Conyers pointed out that the five Mississippians had refused to run on the racially integrated Democratic ticket recognized by the national party, but had run instead on an all-white ticket. Conyers argued that if the Mississippians refused to adhere to the principles of the national Democratic party, they should be stripped of their seniority and denied the right to hold committee chairmanships as Democrats. The challenge was rejected by a standing vote of 55-111.

House Republicans on Jan. 20 agreed to allow all their Members to vote on nominations for ranking minority members of each House committee.

The Republican Conference adopted without change the recommendations of a task force on seniority headed by Rep. Barber B. Conable Jr. of New York. The major change proposed in the report would allow the ranking Republican on each committee to be selected by vote, not merely by seniority. If Republicans gained control of the House the system would apply to selection of committee chairmen.

The report set up a procedure for selection of ranking members: The Republican Committee on Committees would nominate a member to be top Republican on each committee, not necessarily on the basis of seniority. The Republican Conference would vote separately by secret ballot on each nomination; if the nomination were rejected, the Committee on Committees would submit another nomination. The Committee is comprised of one Representative from each state that has Republican Members.

Action of Liberal Democrats, 1971

When House Democrats met in caucus Feb. 3, committee assignments for the 92nd Congress proposed by the Committee on Committees encountered more opposition than usual. Rep. Herman Badillo, a freshman Member representing a poor Puerto Rican district in New York City, won a fight to have his assignment to the Agriculture Committee changed to the Committee on Education and Labor. But Rep. Donald M. Fraser (Minn.), outgoing chairman of the liberal Democratic Study Group, lost his bid to win a seat on the Ways and Means Committee. Liberals lost also, by a vote of 96-126, their fight in caucus to unseat Rep. John L. McMillan (S.C.) as chairman of the District of Columbia Committee, which he had headed for 22 years. McMillan was accused of being unresponsive to the needs of the capital city.

The Democratic liberals carried the fight against McMillan to the floor of the House on Feb. 4 but lost there by a roll-call vote of 32-258. Many of the Democratic liberals who had voted in caucus to unseat McMillan changed their votes on the floor. Rep. Hale Boggs (D La.), the new Majority Floor Leader, warned that "if a minority on the Democratic side and a majority on the minority side get together, they could take over control of the entire committee system in the House." Majority Leader Gerald R. Ford (R Mich.) said the matter was "one for the Democrats to decide and not for us."

Democrats who changed their votes recognized that submission of this party conflict to decision by the whole House might open the way for future conservative coalitions to unseat liberal chairmen or even block the majority party's choice of a Speaker. Thus the real issue was protection of the right of the two parties to make their own committee assignments. And while McMillan retained his chairmanship, the fight against him seemed to have had some effect when, a week later, the Committee by an 8-to-7 vote adopted new rules designed to correct procedural abuses of which the chairman had been accused. But McMillan soon reasserted his powers when, ignoring seniority, he bypassed his critics on the Committee and appointed his own supporters as chairmen of the newly reorganized subcommittees.

Exceptions to the Rule

As the 1969 study of House seniority demonstrated, violations do occur and exceptions are made. Party leaders can tamper with the seniority system, probably not as frequently as its critics would like, but certainly more often than some of its beneficiaries would prefer. Lyndon Johnson, as one example, violated seniority among Senate Democrats, distributing political favors as he built a base of power for his climb to domination of the Senate in the 1950s.

Stripping a Member of his seniority as a punishment for political heresy also has been resorted to, usually with widespread publicity. In the Senate of 1866, for example, three Republican committee chairmen were dropped to the bottom of their committees for failing to vote with the Radical Republicans on overriding a Presidential veto of a civil rights bill.

A selection of examples of major departures from seniority follows.

Senate. In 1859 the Democratic caucus removed Stephen A. Douglas (D Ill.) from the chairmanship of the Committee on Territories because he refused to go along with President Buchanan and the southern wing of the party on the question of slavery in the territories.

In 1871 Charles Sumner (R Mass.) was removed from the chairmanship of (and membership on) the Foreign Relations Committee because of disagreement with President Grant over Grant's project for annexation of the Dominican Republic.

In 1913 Benjamin R. Tillman (D S.C.) was denied chairmanship of the Appropriations Committee, at least in part because of his age and impaired health.

In 1924 Albert R. Cummins (R Iowa) lost his chairmanship of the Interstate Commerce Committee because he was also President pro tempore. The next-ranking Republican, Robert M. La Follette (R Wis.), was then passed over because of his unpopularity with the regulars of his own party, and the chairmanship was finally given to the ranking Democrat, Ellison D. Smith (D S.C.).

In 1952 Wayne L. Morse (R Ore.) was dropped from the Armed Services and Labor and Public Welfare Committees when he left the Republican party. Morse served in the Senate as an independent from 1952 to 1955 and as a Democrat from 1955 to 1969.

In 1965 Strom Thurmond (R S.C.) was placed third on the Republican side of the Armed Services Committee after he bolted the Democratic party to support the 1964 Presidential candidacy of Barry Goldwater. As a Democrat, Thurmond had ranked seventh during the 88th Congress of 1963-65. Thurmond also had requested a seat on the Commerce Committee equivalent in rank to the one he had held on that Committee as a Democrat. But he was assigned to the Banking and Currency Committee. Thurmond's full seniority, dating from his entry into the Senate as a Democrat in 1955, though honored by the Republicans since he switched parties, was not formally recognized by the Senate Republican Conference until 1971.

House. In 1965 the Democratic caucus censured and stripped of their seniority rights Representatives John Bell Williams (Miss.) and Albert W. Watson (S.C.). Both were to continue to be recognized as Democrats. Williams and Watson had openly supported Goldwater as Republican nominee for the Presidency in 1964. The caucus action put Williams, second-ranking Democrat on the Interstate and Foreign Commerce Committee and fifth-ranking Democrat on the District of Columbia Committee, at the bottom of both Committees. Watson, a low-ranking member of the Post Office and Civil Service Committee,

stood to lose little seniority. Watson resigned his seat and successfully sought re-election in 1965 as a Republican.

In 1967 Adam Clayton Powell (D N.Y.) was investigated by a select committee which found that he had misused Congressional funds, acted contemptuously toward the courts of New York in a libel suit and kept his wife on his Congressional payroll although she did not work either in his district or in the District of Columbia, as required by law. The House on March 1, 1967, excluded Powell from the 90th Congress. The House Democratic caucus already had removed Powell from the chairmanship of the Education and Labor Committee. In 1969 Powell was seated in the 91st Congress but was fined $25,000 and made the lowest-ranking Democrat on the same Committee that he had headed. *(See Seating and Disciplining of Members, Chapter III.)*

In 1969 the Democratic caucus stripped Rep. John R. Rarick (D La.) of his seniority on the Agriculture Committee for having supported third-party candidate George C. Wallace in the 1968 Presidential campaign. Rarick was the lowest-ranking Democrat on the Committee in the 90th Congress but would have moved ahead in the 91st Congress.

Bibliography

Books

Evans, Rowland and Novak, Robert, *Lyndon B. Johnson, The Exercise of Power.* New American Library, 1966.

Galloway, George B., *Congress at the Crossroads.* Thomas Y. Crowell Co., 1946.

Haynes, George H., *The Senate of the United States.* Houghton-Mifflin Co., 1938.

Morrow, William L., *Congressional Committees.* Charles Scribner's Sons, 1969.

Ripley, Randall B., *Power in the Senate.* St. Martin's Press, 1969.

Articles

Celler, Rep. Emanuel, "The Seniority Rule in Congress," *Western Political Quarterly*, March 1961.

Goodwin, George Jr., "The Seniority System in Congress," *American Political Science Review*, June 1959.

Huitt, Ralph K., "The Morse Committee Assignment Controversy," *American Political Science Review*, June 1957.

Polsby, Nelson W., Gallaher, Miriam, and Rundquist, Barry, "The Growth of the Seniority System in the U.S. House of Representatives," *American Political Science Review*, September 1969.

Chapter 3—The Powers of Congress

Fiscal Powers: To Tax, Spend, Borrow

OF THE NUMEROUS POWERS of Congress, the "power of the purse" is the most important. All of the other powers—to enact laws, to conduct investigations, even to declare war—are as nothing without the power to finance the business of Government.

The "power of the purse" includes both the raising of revenue through taxes, tariffs and other levies, and direction through the appropriations process of the spending of the funds raised. They are opposite sides of the same coin, although Congress rarely considers them as an entity.

The taxing and appropriating powers are granted to Congress by various provisions of the Constitution. Over the years, Congress has jealously guarded these powers with the relatively recent exception of the tariff power, the exercise of which was delegated to the Executive Branch nearly 40 years ago. Occasional proposals that Congress also delegate to the President limited authority to alter tax rates have been ignored by the legislators. While Congress has always been dedicated to preserving its authority over spending, it has had difficulty in maintaining close control over Government outlays since President Franklin D. Roosevelt launched the New Deal. In spite of an apparent desire on the part of many Members of Congress—particularly those handling appropriations bills—to hold down Government spending, it has continued to rise; in the fiscal year 1970, Federal expenditures accounted for about 20 percent of the gross national product.

Origination of Tax Bills in House

Tax legislation must, under a constitutional provision, originate in the House of Representatives. Tax bills and bills having to do with tariffs are handled there by the Ways and Means Committee, one of the most powerful in Congress. After House passage, such bills go to the Senate and are referred to that chamber's Finance Committee, where amendments may be proposed. Amendments adopted by the Senate may be far-reaching. As in the case of all legislation, Senate-House differences over tax bills or measures involving tariff matters have to be resolved in conference. The final version, when agreed to by both houses, must then be approved by the President.

The Constitution does not specifically require tariff or appropriations bills to originate in the House, but that chamber has always assumed that it has exclusive rights in that regard. The Senate disagrees and on occasion has bitterly disputed the claim of the House, but it has not been able to wrest original jurisdiction from the other body. The practical result, as far as appropriations are concerned, is that the House Appropriations Committee

is more equal than its counterpart on the Senate side. The bulk of basic appropriations decisions are made in the House Committee. The general shape of any appropriations bill is derived from House consideration of the measure; what the Senate does in effect is to review the House action and hear appeals from agencies seeking changes in the allotments accorded them by the House. The Senate is free to make alterations as it deems necessary, but important changes usually are limited to revisions in the financing for a relatively small number of significant or controversial Government programs.

Separation of Taxing and Spending

Congress does not consider the two parts of Government financing as an integrated whole. Tax bills and appropriations bills are referred to different committees and are taken up and acted upon separately even though the level of spending (without deficit financing) is dependent on the amount of revenue raised. An effort in the late 1940s to tie spending and taxing together was unsuccessful, in large part because the resulting bill—and the committee formed to handle it—proved unwieldy. The task of relating spending to revenue thus falls to the Executive Branch, which attempts to accomplish it through preparation of the Federal Budget.

A related subject over which Congress has power is the national debt. The debt total has grown enormously as a result of Government spending in excess of Government revenue in most years since the early 1930s. Congress has imposed a statutory ceiling on the amount of debt which the Government may incur, but the ceiling has been revised upward time and again as budget deficits have required more borrowing. The debt ceiling has been an unusually controversial and visible issue in Congress because it has given opponents of deficit spending an opportunity to vent their displeasure over constantly rising Government outlays. But efforts to use the debt ceiling as a lid on spending have been fruitless.

Taxes and Tariffs

Financing of the Federal Government is carried out under authority granted to Congress in the first article of the Constitution. That authority is specific with regard to raising money, somewhat vague but nevertheless sweeping with regard to spending it. Article I, Section 8, Clause 1 reads:

> The Congress shall have power to lay and collect taxes, duties, imposts and excises, to pay the debts and provide for the common defense and general welfare of the United States....

Under this basic authorization, with a monumental assist from the 16th (income tax) Amendment, Congress over the years has devised a taxing system that produced in fiscal 1970 total revenue of no less than $193.8 billion. Generally, the taxing power has been liberally construed by both Congress and the courts (the most important exception being a Supreme Court decision in 1895 that overturned an attempt by Congress to impose an income tax and which led finally to adoption of the 16th Amendment). The constitutional historian C. H. Pritchett, in his book *The American Constitution*, noted that adequate sources of funds and broad authority to use them were "essential conditions for carrying on an effective government." "Consequently," he observed, "the first rule for judicial review of tax statutes is that a heavy burden of proof lies on anyone who would challenge any Congressional exercise of fiscal power. In almost every decision touching the constitutionality of Federal taxation, the Supreme Court has stressed the breadth of Congressional power and the limits of its own reviewing powers."

The terms used in Article I, Section 8 granting the taxing power were broad enough to include all known forms of taxation. Customs levies, or tariffs, on goods imported from abroad were covered by "duties" and "imposts." "Excises" covered taxes on the manufacture, sale, use or transfer of property within the United States.

Congress and the Taxing Power

Limitations. Although the power of Congress to tax is broad, it is not unlimited. There are constitutional provisions on direct taxation, for example, that proved the undoing of early efforts to tax income. Article I, Section 2, Clause 3 stipulated that "direct taxes shall be apportioned among the several states...according to their respective numbers," and Article I, Section 9, Clause 4 stated: "No capitation, or other direct, tax shall be laid, unless in proportion to the census or enumeration hereinbefore directed to be taken." The 16th Amendment opened up a great new Federal revenue source by eliminating the impossible requirement that an income tax be apportioned among the states by population.

Another restriction was imposed by the concluding words of Article I, Section 8, Clause 1: "but all duties, imposts and excises shall be uniform throughout the United States." Because all direct taxes, prior to ratification of the 16th Amendment in 1913, had to be apportioned according to population, only indirect taxes were subject to the uniformity requirement. This requirement has come to mean geographical uniformity and has guided Congress in its passage of customs and excise levies that were the primary source of revenue for the national Government until World War I.

Implied Limitations. In addition to specific restrictions, there were implied limitations on the taxing power of Congress. A major limitation extended immunity from Federal taxation to state and local governments, their property and activities. A second limitation has exempted from Federal taxation the income from state and municipal bonds. These limitations were based on the doctrine of intergovernmental tax immunity laid down in 1819 by Chief Justice Marshall in the Supreme Court's opinion in the case of *McCulloch v. Maryland.* That doctrine rested on the theory of state sovereignty and on the belief that, because "the power to tax involves the power to destroy,"

neither the Federal nor a state government could tax the property or instrumentalities of the other without infringing its sovereignty. The doctrine was applied even to the salaries of public employees.

Taxing of Public Salaries and Federal Bonds

It was long assumed that the tax immunity thus decreed could not be terminated other than by a constitutional amendment. However, in decisions handed down in 1938 and 1939, the Supreme Court sustained, respectively, the levying of a Federal income tax on the salary of an employee of the Port of New York Authority and the levying of the New York State income tax on the salary of a Federal employee. A week after the second decision, Congress completed action on the Public Salary Tax Act of 1939, which provided for Federal taxation of state and local governmental salaries and gave the Federal Government's consent to state taxation of Federal salaries.

The Supreme Court decisions of 1938 and 1939 were widely interpreted as removing constitutional objections to intergovernmental taxation of public securities as well as public salaries. President Roosevelt in 1938 and again in 1939 advocated abolition by statute of the tax exemption on income from future issues of all public securities. Congress went part way in the Public Debt Act of 1941, which provided that interest on Federal securities issued after its enactment should have no exemption as such, thus authorizing issuance of wholly taxable obligations by the Federal Government. Congress refused, however, to act on a Treasury recommendation that interest on future issues of state and municipal securities be subjected to the Federal income tax. Subsequent proposals along that line, most recently in 1969, have made no headway. State and local officials, supported by municipal bond dealers, always have contended that they would have trouble borrowing money if those securities were deprived of their special tax status.

Regulation Through Taxation

Congress has the power, confirmed by use over the years, to impose taxes for regulatory rather than revenue purposes. The leading example is the imposition of tariffs not for revenue only but also for the protection of domestic industries against competition from imports. Although the first tariff law was enacted in 1789, the Supreme Court did not have occasion to consider (and uphold) the constitutionality of this form of taxation until 1928.

Regulation through taxation has been employed in other situations even to the extent of destroying a business enterprise. In the 1860s, Congress enacted a National Banking Act providing for the incorporation of national banks with authority to issue currency notes. In 1866, it imposed a 10-percent tax on new state bank notes with the avowed purpose of driving such notes out of existence—which it did. There were numerous laws of this kind in ensuing years. Among the best known were: a stiff excise tax on oleomargarine colored to resemble butter; a tax on the manufacture of poisonous white phosphorous matches (which virtually killed the industry); taxes on registered dealers in narcotic drugs; and a special tax (later overturned by the Supreme Court) on the profits of companies employing children under 16 years of age.

Uses of the Tariff

Tariffs for Revenue. The revenue from customs duties proved adequate to meet most of the fiscal needs of the Federal Government from its inception in 1789 to the Civil War. A wartime income tax and numerous excises were then imposed to help defray war costs. However, the pattern of substantial dependence on customs receipts, supplemented increasingly by excise taxes, continued up to World War I, when income and profits taxes became the mainstay of Federal revenue. Customs receipts accounted for more than 90 percent of total Federal revenue until the Civil War. Their importance declined gradually after that, but in 1910 they still made up 49 percent of the Federal Government's revenue. In contrast, by the late 1960s, the revenue from import duties had shrunk to little more than 1 percent of the total.

Customs receipts reached a pre-Civil War peak of $64.2 million in the fiscal year 1854, exceeded $100 million for the first time in fiscal 1864 and $200 million in fiscal 1871, and reached $300 million in fiscal 1906. Although a much-reduced fraction of Federal revenue, customs receipts passed the $1-billion mark in fiscal 1960 and the $2-billion mark in fiscal 1968. There was considerable downward as well as upward movement along the way, resulting of course from the effects of economic conditions on the volume of foreign trade and to some extent from changes in the level of duties. Although the total of customs receipts rose markedly in the long run, the greatly increased expenditure requirements of the Federal Government in the present century—brought on by war, and expansion of Federal activities, as well as by population growth—forced Congress to rely mainly on more remunerative sources of Federal revenue.

Tariffs for Protection. As long as customs receipts were sufficient to meet Government needs, the tariff in effect killed two birds with one stone. It supplied a large part of Federal revenue while in the process of carrying out its principal purpose, which was to protect domestic producers, especially of manufactured goods, from a flood of foreign imports. Many of the so-called infant industries grew strong as they matured, but few reached the point of considering themselves able to get along without tariff protection. Thus, revenue considerations aside, the duties in numerous cases did more than put domestic producers on a basis of equality with foreign producers; they gave the American producers a competitive advantage.

Conflicts of Interest Over Tariffs

During the first half of the 19th century, the tariff laws offered protection mainly to manufactured goods. Western and northern farmers supported a protectionist policy for manufacturers on the assumption that industrial development, aided by high tariffs, would create a profitable home market for their products. President Polk's Secretary of the Treasury, Robert J. Walker, a Mississippian, propounded in his annual report for 1845 the doctrine that import duties restricted foreign markets for agricultural products, while forcing farmers and planters to pay higher prices for manufactured goods. That theory, however, was widely accepted only in the South, which was vitally concerned with finding export markets for its cotton.

The Republican party, founded in the West in 1854, lined up behind the protectionist principle on the eve of the Civil War, thereby availing itself of a policy which was to ensure it the enduring adherence of northern and eastern industrial elements after settlement of the slavery issue. The Democratic party, on the other hand, generally favored a moderate- or low-tariff policy and so for years retained the solid support of the agricultural South.

William Starr Myers wrote in *The Republican Party: A History* in 1928: "The industrial and business East wants a high protective tariff and has persuaded the agricultural West that the same policy of protection would apply to them. The latter has suffered continually from 'hard times,' and yet has always seemed to be impervious to the fact that it is practically impossible, under present conditions in the United States, to protect the farming interests by a high tariff. It is the play of these two forces, often cut athwart and disturbed by other issues..., that has deferred the inevitable day of some solution or compromise beneficial to both interests."

The fact that the tariff picture was not all black or white—that high tariffs were helpful to certain interests and low tariffs helpful to others—did not lower the voices of extreme protectionists or extreme free traders. But because both sides were represented in each of the major political parties, action at the showdown was sometimes surprising. In 1894, for example, when the Democrats controlled both houses of Congress, the Senate made so many upward changes in a House-passed low-tariff bill that President Cleveland refused to sign the measure, though he let it become law without his signature.

As a Member of Congress, President McKinley had been a staunch high-protectionist, but in his last public utterance he entered a strong plea for support of tariff reciprocity. In an address at Buffalo on Sept. 5, 1901, the day before he was assassinated, he said: "Our capacity to produce has developed so enormously and our products have so multiplied that the problem of more markets requires our urgent and immediate attention....We must not repose in fancied security that we can forever sell everything and buy little or nothing....We should take from our customers such of their products as we can use without harm to our industries and labor....If perchance some of our tariffs are no longer needed for revenue or to encourage and protect our industries at home, why should they not be employed to extend and promote our markets abroad?"

President Taft negotiated a reciprocity agreement with Canada in 1911 which, though accepted by Congress over considerable opposition, was not carried through by Canada. The Democrats, originally opposed to tariff reciprocity, nevertheless included in the Underwood Tariff Act of 1913 a provision specifically authorizing the President to negotiate reciprocity agreements subject to the approval of Congress. The provision was not utilized, however, and no more was heard of the subject until the Democrats revived it 20 years later.

Tariff-Making by Congress

Tariff policy occupied a place of great prominence in American politics during the long period from shortly after the Civil War to the early years of the Great Depression of the 1930s. It was the leading issue in numerous Presidential and Congressional elections. Before World War I, a change of Administrations often meant passage of a new tariff act. The McKinley tariff of 1890 (Republican) was followed by the Wilson-Gorman tariff of 1894 (Democratic) and then by the Dingley tariff of 1897 (Republican). The last-named Act had a long life—12 years—but it gave way in 1909 to the Payne-Aldrich tariff (also Republican) and then in 1913 to the Underwood tariff (Democratic).

Congress devoted an inordinate amount of its time to tariff-making, not only because the tariff was made and remade so frequently but also because the process was complex and the subject all-embracing. Affecting, actually or potentially, the varied interests of many segments of the commercial life of the country, a general revision of the tariff inevitably involved a great amount of political pulling and hauling. Tariff bills, like tax bills, originated in the House and, when reported by the Ways and Means Committee, followed the usual legislative course through the House itself, the Senate Finance Committee and the Senate, with final reconciliation of House and Senate differences by a conference committee. At each stage, the treatment of important items was apt to provoke protracted discussion. General tariff bills were so complicated and so full of special-interest provisions that few Members, other than those on the Ways and Means or Finance Committees, understood their true effect.

Drastic revision in the Senate was the usual fate of tariff bills passed by the House. The Senate made nearly 500 amendments to the McKinley bill in 1890. Its amendments to the Payne-Aldrich bill of 1909 numbered 847. And Senate amendments to the Fordney-McCumber tariff bill of 1922 reached the unprecedented total of more than 2,400. That bill, moreover, was before Congress for 20 months prior to enactment, a longer period than any tariff bill since the Civil War.

The Fordney-McCumber bill was noteworthy also for taking the first substantial step toward reform of the tariff-making process. It empowered the President, upon recommendation of the U.S. Tariff Commission (a fact-finding body created by the Revenue Act of 1916 to advise Congress on tariff matters), to alter existing rates of duty (1) by changing the tariff classification of an article to make it dutiable under a different rate; (2) by increasing or decreasing the rate by not more than 50 percent; or (3) by substituting the American selling price for the foreign valuation as the basis for assessment of duties. The Act stated specifically that readjustments were to be made only to carry out a policy of "equalizing" foreign and American costs of production.

This was the so-called flexible tariff. By mid-May 1929, more than six and one-half years after approval of the Fordney-McCumber Act in September 1922, only 36 changes of duties had been made under the flexible-tariff provision and in only five of the 36 cases had the duties been reduced. By that time, moreover, Congress was already at work on what turned out to be another general tariff revision.

Last Made-by-Congress Tariff

Soon after President Hoover took office on March 4, 1929, he called Congress into special session. A Presidential message read at the opening of the session, April 16, assigned the lawmakers the task of redeeming "two pledges given in the last election—farm relief and limited changes in the tariff." Changes in tariff rates, Hoover said, should provide an effective tariff on agricultural products "that will compensate the farmer's higher costs and higher standards of living," and should also afford additional protection to industries suffering from "a substantial slack-

ening of activity...during the past few years and a consequent decrease in employment due to insurmountable competition from abroad."

The "limited changes" asked by President Hoover became a full-blown tariff act as Congress worked its way through more than 1,800 rate paragraphs in 15 tariff schedules from "Chemicals, Oils and Paint" to "Papers and Books" and, finally, "Sundries." The House Ways and Means Committee had opened hearings on rate schedules three months before the special session began and so was able to report its bill early in May 1929, and the House passed it on May 28. A long contest in the Senate delayed passage there until March 24, 1930. It took weeks longer to resolve in conference the wide differences between the House and Senate versions of the bill. The Hawley-Smoot tariff, finally approved by President Hoover on June 17, 1930, raised tariff duties, on average, to a new peak estimated to exceed the 1922 level by 20 percent.

In addition to raising rates, the Hawley-Smoot Act made changes in the flexible-tariff provision aimed to speed up Tariff Commission investigations of production costs. The new Act also shifted major responsibility for duty changes under that provision from the President to the commission by requiring the President to accept or reject the specific rates which the commission found necessary to equalize production costs.

Shift to Executive Tariff-Making

President Hoover, in a public statement on June 15, 1930, two days before he signed the Hawley-Smoot bill, observed that "Congressional (tariff) revisions are not only disturbing to business but, with all their necessary collateral surroundings in lobbies, logrolling and the activities of group interests, are disturbing to public confidence." He added that, "particularly after the record of the last 15 months, there is a growing and widespread realization that in this highly complicated and intricately organized and rapidly shifting modern economic world the time has come when a more scientific and businesslike method of tariff revision must be devised." It was Hoover's opinion that the revised flexible-tariff provision of the new law represented a long step toward that end and gave "great hope of taking the tariff away from politics, lobbying and logrolling."

Deepening depression and a worldwide collapse of international trade in the period immediately following passage of the Hawley-Smoot Act contributed indirectly to forwarding reform in the process of tariff-making. Results of the midterm elections of 1930 enabled the Democrats to organize the House of Representatives in the 72nd Congress and almost wiped out the Republican majority in the Senate. Early in 1932 both houses approved a bill of Democratic origin requesting the President to negotiate reciprocal trade agreements with other nations "under a policy of mutual tariff concessions." Such agreements were to be subject to Congressional approval. President Hoover vetoed the bill, May 11, 1932, on the grounds that it would undermine the system of agricultural protection, "make us large importers of food products" and "drive our farmers into the towns and factories and thus demoralize our whole national economic and social stability." In the party platforms of 1932 the Republicans commended Hoover's veto and the Democrats repeated their advocacy of "reciprocal tariff agreements with other nations."

On March 2, 1934, one year almost to the day after President Roosevelt took office, he asked Congress for authority to "enter into executive commercial agreements with foreign nations" for reciprocal reductions of tariffs. The President said: "If American agricultural and industrial interests are to retain their deserved place in this (international) trade, the American government must be in a position to bargain for that place with other governments by rapid and decisive negotiation, based upon a carefully considered program, and to grant with discernment corresponding opportunities in the American market for foreign products supplementary to our own."

Delegation of Power by 1934 Act

The Reciprocal Trade Agreements Act, one of whose principal advocates was Secretary of State Cordell Hull, became law on June 12, 1934. Enacted as an amendment to the Hawley-Smoot Act of 1930, it empowered the President, without reference to the Tariff Commission or the Congress, to lower or raise existing duties by as much as 50 percent in return for equivalent concessions by a foreign nation. Although the Hoover-vetoed Democratic tariff bill of 1932 had provided for Congressional approval of reciprocal trade agreements, a Republican-sponsored amendment to that effect offered in the Senate in 1934 was decisively rejected.

Renewals of Authority. This historic transfer of tariff-making authority from Congress to the President was almost total. The delegation of power was limited initially to three years, but it was periodically renewed for similar (or shorter or longer) periods. And the limitation on the extent of duty increases or reductions was periodically modified as additional bargaining authority was needed by American tariff negotiators. The bilateral trade agreements concluded in the early years gave way after World War II to a network of multilateral agreements under GATT, the General Agreement on Tariffs and Trade. The most recent comprehensive tariff-bargaining session was the so-called Kennedy Round of negotiations, which began in 1964 and was participated in by the United States and 52 other countries. A hard-fought agreement was finally reached on May 15, 1967, only six weeks before the additional tariff-cutting authority granted the President under the Trade Expansion Act of 1962 was due to expire.

Soon after World War II, Congress had begun to re-assert its tariff-making authority to the extent of including in renewals of the Trade Agreements Act protective devices in the form of escape clauses and so-called "peril points" which the President could not ignore, in refusing relief or in cutting tariff rates, without giving Congress the reasons. By 1967, when the latest renewal of tariff-bargaining authority lapsed, protectionist sentiment in Congress, nurtured in part by development of the European Common Market as a powerful trade competitor, had grown so strong that President Johnson delayed asking for renewal of the authority. When he did make the request in 1968, Congress took no action.

Nixon Request. In a message to Congress, Nov. 18, 1969, President Nixon asked for authority "to make modest reductions in U.S. tariffs" until July 1, 1973. A bill reported by the House Ways and Means Committee Aug. 21, 1970, and passed by the House Nov. 19 would have authorized duty reductions of 20 percent or two percentage points below the rates that will prevail when the final stage of the Kennedy Round reductions goes into effect on Jan. 1, 1972. But the Senate let the bill die, leaving it to the 92nd Congress to revive the President's tariff-cutting authority.

Components of Federal Tax System

Taxes on the income and profits of individuals and corporations have become the Federal Government's basic source of revenue. Such taxes yielded only modest amounts of revenue before American entry into World War I. Sharply increased rates then pushed up the yield from $360 million in fiscal 1917 to $2.3 billion in fiscal 1918. Since that time, income and profits taxes have annually produced more revenue than all excise and other internal revenue taxes combined except in the nine fiscal years from 1933 through 1941. During those years the depression was holding down incomes and numerous new excise taxes were levied to bolster Federal revenues.

In World War II, high rates and a broadened tax base doubled and redoubled the receipts from income and profits taxes. Following a downward movement after World War II and again after the Korean War, these receipts climbed year by year almost uninterruptedly to the huge net (minus refunds) total of $124 billion in fiscal 1969. That sum accounted for about 66 percent of the Government's net budget receipts, that year nearly $188 billion. Almost $40 billion from social insurance taxes and contributions made up the next largest share (21 percent) of net budget receipts in fiscal 1969. Net excise tax receipts of $15.2 billion supplied 8 percent; estate and gift taxes yielded $3.5 billion (2 percent); miscellaneous receipts $3 billion (1.6 percent), and customs receipts $2.3 billion (1.3 percent).

Individual Income Tax

A Federal tax on personal income was first imposed during the Civil War. Pressed by the wartime need for additional funds, Congress in 1862 levied a tax on individual incomes in excess of $600. The personal exemption was raised to $1,000 in 1867, two years after the war ended, and then to $2,000 in 1870. At one point the tax was graduated up to a rate of 10 percent. The law imposing the tax expired by limitation in 1872. The levy had been challenged as violative of the constitutional requirement that direct taxes be apportioned among the states according to population, but the Supreme Court of that day ruled that it was not a direct tax.

During the 1870s and 1880s, little interest was shown in enactment of a new income-tax law. But growth of the country and accumulation of large fortunes began in the 1890s to generate pressure for a return to income taxation. After the depression of 1893 had reduced Federal revenues, Congress yielded and in 1894 levied a tax of 2 percent on personal incomes in excess of $4,000. Before the new tax law became operative, it was challenged, and this time the Supreme Court held that an income tax was a direct tax and therefore unconstitutional without apportionment (*Pollock v. Farmers' Loan & Trust Co.*, 1895).

The decision was a major defeat for the populist movement of the times and made the Court a distinctly unpopular institution. Pritchett in *The American Constitution* notes: "This surrender of the Court to entrenched wealth, in the same year that it refused to apply the Sherman Act against the sugar trust and upheld the conviction of Eugene V. Debs for violating an injunction during the Pullman strike, revealed only too clearly the judiciary's alignment on the side of capital, and earned the Court a popular reputation as a tool of special privilege which was not dispelled for forty years."

Although the Court had blocked the road to this attempted expansion of the tax system, a solution was afforded by the power of Congress and the states to revise the Constitution. A campaign to do so was begun immediately, and on Feb. 25, 1913, the 16th Amendment was officially declared ratified. The one-sentence amendment stated tersely: "The Congress shall have power to lay and collect taxes on incomes from whatever source derived, without apportionment among the several states, and without regard to any census or enumeration."

Thus the problem of apportioning income taxes was swept away and Congress was left free to do what it had tried to do two decades earlier. The new grant of power came at a providential time, for the great expansion of Federal revenue soon required by World War I would have been difficult, if not impossible, to achieve by any other means.

Congress instituted the income tax in the year the 16th Amendment was ratified. The new levy applied to wages, salaries, interest, dividends, rents, entrepreneurial income and capital gains. The law contained certain exemptions (such as interest on Federal, state and municipal bonds and salaries of state and local government employees) and allowed deductions for personal interest and tax payments and business expenses. Taxes were collected at the source on incomes in excess of $3,000. A personal exemption of $3,000 for a single person and $4,000 for a married couple was allowed. Rates were set initially at only 1 percent for the normal tax plus 1- to 6-percent surtax on larger incomes.

In the following half-century, Congress made numerous changes in the income-tax law. Joseph A. Pechman, one of the nation's leading tax authorities, cites in his book *Federal Tax Policy* the following "most significant changes" since the original 1913 Act: allowance of a credit for dependents and a deduction for charitable contributions in 1917; elimination of collection at the source in 1916 and its reinstatement in 1943 for wages and salaries of state and local government employees and discontinuance of the sale of tax-exempt Federal securities in 1941; adoption of the standard deduction in 1944; enactment of the principle of "income-splitting" for married couples in 1948; and introduction of an averaging plan for certain taxpayers and a minimum standard deduction in 1964.

Corporation Income and Profits Taxes

Congress did not encounter with a corporation income tax the constitutional difficulty that it had experienced with the tax on individual income. A corporation income tax was levied in 1909 in the guise of "a special excise tax" at a rate of 1 percent of net income in excess of $5,000. That tax, like the 1894 individual income tax, was challenged in the courts, but the Supreme Court let it stand as an excise on the privilege of doing business as a corporation.

Following ratification of the 16th Amendment, an outright corporation income tax at the same rate was made a part of the Revenue Act of 1913 alongside the individual income tax. The two taxes together, broadened and modified through the years as circumstances required, became basic elements of the nation's revenue system.

During World War I, World War II, and the Korean War, the corporation income tax was supplemented by an excess profits tax. In most other years, revenue from taxation of corporation income has been less than that from taxation of individual income. Particularly in the past decade, the individual income tax has been far and away the greater revenue producer. In fiscal 1969 the individual tax yielded $87.2 billion after refunds, the corporation tax only $36.2 billion after refunds.

Excise and Other Taxes

Excise taxes have always been a part of the Federal tax system; they were mentioned specifically in Article I, Section 8 of the Constitution among the various levies that Congress was authorized to impose. The excises levied upon ratification of the Constitution included taxes on carriages, liquor, snuff, sugar and auction sales. These and similar taxes have been controversial throughout the Republic's history, in important part because they were considered unfair and burdensome on the poor. Over the years, excises have been imposed and repealed or lowered; during every major war, the perennial liquor and tobacco taxes were supplemented by taxes on manufactured goods, licenses, financial transactions, services, luxury articles and dozens of other items that lent themselves to this form of taxation.

Congress considerably expanded the excise-tax structure during World Wars I and II and the Korean War, but by 1965 it had been largely dismantled. Numerous excises were either reduced or eliminated in a tax bill passed that year, leaving only a few major levies of this kind for sumptuary and regulatory reasons and as user charges.

The power of Congress to tax in other areas has become well established over the years. One of the most important areas has been payroll taxes, which financially underpin the old-age insurance and unemployment compensation systems. Estate taxes were imposed originally in the Civil War period, and they have been a permanent part of the national tax structure since 1916. The gift tax, levied to check avoidance of the estate tax, has been imposed on a permanent basis since 1932.

Tax Bills in Congress

Because tax proposals are among the most complicated pieces of legislation considered by Congress, close cooperation between the Executive Branch and the Congress is always required when a tax bill is being drafted. Generally, the initiative on taxes in the post-World War II period has been taken by the Administration: it has prepared the basic proposals and Congress has acted on them. There is no legal or other requirement that this be the case. Congress itself initiated a major tax-reform bill in 1969.

Constitutional Requirement. The Constitution clearly states where the legislative tax process must begin. Article I, Section 7, Clause 1 states: "All bills for raising revenue shall originate in the House of Representatives; but the Senate may propose or concur with amendments as on other bills." Thus the Senate is relegated to a bystander status on tax matters until the House has acted. Once the Senate has a House-passed tax bill in hand, however, it has virtually unlimited authority to revise it as it wishes and to initiate by amendment tax proposals which the House has not considered. This occurred in a dramatic manner on various bills considered during the 1960s; the most important were Senate addition in 1966 of a proposal to use tax dollars to finance Presidential campaigns and in 1968 of an income tax surcharge to combat inflation.

House Action

Ways and Means Committee. This Committee, one of the most powerful and prestigious in the House, handles tax matters. It was created in 1802 with responsibility for both taxing and spending. Its authority over spending was gradually diminished over the years until an Appropriations Committee was created in 1865. Today the Ways and Means Committee has jurisdiction over revenue, debt, customs, trade and Social Security legislation. In addition, the Democratic members serve as a committee on committees: they decide committee assignments for House Democrats. (The Republican Ways and Means members do not have comparable power; the GOP has a separate committee whose only duty is to act on committee assignments.)

The Ways and Means Committee in recent years has consisted of 25 members—15 belonging to the party holding a majority in the House and 10 belonging to the minority party. Unlike most other House committees, Ways and Means does not operate through subcommittees (there have been rare exceptions in the postwar years when special subcommittees have been created to study a specific problem and then disbanded). Bills are considered from the beginning by the entire Committee. The practical effect of this operating procedure is to concentrate substantial power in the Committee's chairman and, to a lesser extent, in the ranking minority member.

The Committee has had five chairmen since 1947, three Democrats and two Republicans. Of these, one—Wilbur D. Mills (D Ark.)—has gained extraordinary authority over tax legislation. This is because of his length of service (he became chairman in 1958 and still held the post in 1970), his vast knowledge of the tax laws, his position as head of the Committee which considers all tax bills as a whole, and his renowned ability to sense the sentiment of the House and the Committee and to draft tax and other measures to suit the sentiment.

The Committee, composed largely of rather senior House Members, is generally considered to be a conservative group that moves with caution after long deliberation. It has not usually been a fiery advocate of tax reform, but this attitude is considered to reflect the feeling of the entire House as much as that of the Committee itself; indeed, when given the opportunity in 1969, Mills led the Committee on a major reform of the tax laws.

Ways and Means has prided itself on its careful and professional work on tax legislation. This has helped to earn it a favorable reputation in the House and has resulted in House passage of virtually all of the bills it has brought to the floor in the past decade.

Hearings. A bill starts on its way through Ways and Means in the normal Congressional manner: testimony is collected from interested witnesses, usually leading off with the Secretary of the Treasury as the prime Administration witness (although in 1969, when the Committee took the initiative on tax legislation, the Administration witnesses did not appear until several months after the hearings began). Hearings often are lengthy: they con-

sumed almost eight weeks on the controversial Revenue Act of 1964. Sometimes, however, the group will act without hearings on relatively noncontroversial bills or on questions that were the subject of previous hearings; there were no hearings, for example, on the Excise Tax Reduction Act of 1965.

After hearings, the Committee normally will go into executive session to draft the bill (the Treasury Department may have submitted its own bill, but preparation of legal language often is left to Congressional and Treasury experts working together after the hearings have delineated the general scope of the proposals to be put into a bill). Present at the closed sessions are—in addition to Committee members—Treasury officials and Congressional and Treasury staff experts.

Floor Action. Once a tax bill has been drafted, approved and reported by the Ways and Means Committee, it is brought to the floor for consideration by the House. However, it is taken up under special procedures which have become traditional for Ways and Means bills and all but guarantee acceptance of the Committee's work without change. Technically, under House rules, revenue legislation is "privileged" business, which means that it could be brought up for consideration on the floor ahead of other measures. In practice, the Committee does not take advantage of this privilege because its bill would then be open to amendment. Instead, the Committee obtains from the Rules Committee a "closed rule" for floor action. Under this procedure, the bill is not open to amendment in the course of House debate; essentially the House must accept or reject the bill as a whole. The minority party has one opportunity, at the end of debate, to try to make changes in the bill, but significant revisions seldom result.

There is one exception to the prohibition against floor amendments: amendments which have been approved by the Ways and Means Committee (separately from the bill) may be offered on the floor by a Committee member (usually the chairman) and voted on. This procedure is not entirely superfluous. It gives the Committee an opportunity to backtrack on any provision which appears to be in danger of drawing unusual House opposition. This occurred on two notable occasions in the 1960s.

In 1962, the Committee reported a major tax bill that included an investment tax credit intended to give business an incentive to buy new equipment. However, the amount of the credit was controversial and the Rules Committee appeared reluctant to grant a closed rule until a percentage figure acceptable to the Administration, the Ways and Means Committee and House leaders could be agreed upon. The Ways and Means Committee met (some days after the bill had been officially reported) and approved a slight reduction in the credit plus changes in certain other controversial sections. The closed rule subsequently was granted and the bill—with the later amendments—was passed.

Similar action to defuse a controversy occurred in 1969 when the Ways and Means Committee reported out a tax bill that included tax reductions for most taxpayers. However, House liberals, after studying the bill, concluded that the tax relief proposal for married persions with taxable incomes of between $7,500 and $13,000 who itemized their deductions was extraordinarily small. The liberals appeared to have enough support to cause the bill considerable trouble on the House floor—and probably to deny it a closed rule from the Rules Committee—unless changes were made. Chairman Mills agreed that the bill was deficient in the respect cited and said it was due to a "misunderstanding" between him and his tax-drafting experts. The Committee met again, approved amendments (offered as floor amendments) providing a bigger reduction for the affected taxpayers, and the bill sailed through the House, 395-39.

These examples show that the power of the Ways and Means Committee over the fate of its tax bills is not absolute. Generally, however, the closed-rule procedure prevents any tinkering with a tax bill once it reaches the floor. As a result, the Ways and Means Committee, with its original jurisdiction over revenue, trade and Social Security legislation, wields enormous influence over the fate of such matters in national politics.

Use of a closed rule is justified on the ground that tax, trade and other Ways and Means bills are too complicated to be opened to revision on the floor, particularly because many of the proposed changes probably would be special-interest provisions designed to favor a small number of persons or groups; such floor proposals, it is argued, might upset carefully drafted legislation approved by the Committee.

The closed-rule procedure generally has the effect of confining Ways and Means bills to debate, and the debate lasts only a day or two. The bill then is passed (rarely is a Ways and Means bill rejected) and sent to the Senate, where a somewhat different view of handling tax matters prevails.

Senate Action

Finance Committee. A House-passed tax bill is referred to the Senate Finance Committee. This Committee, created in 1816, in recent years has had a membership of 17 Senators. It has the same jurisdiction as the House Ways and Means Committee. The Finance Committee—like its House counterpart—does not operate through subcommittees.

Compared to Ways and Means, the Finance Committee's power and influence on revenue and related matters are limited. Moreover, the Committee, through the years, has acquired something of a reputation as a haven for special-interest tax schemes. The primary reason for this trait is found in the second part of the Constitution's Article I, Section 7 on revenue matters: "...but the Senate may propose...amendments...." Because the major work on a tax bill normally is done by the House, the Finance Committee of the Senate is left with relatively little to do (compared to Ways and Means) except to tinker with the House's work and add provisions of special interest to individual Senators. As a result of the Senate's power to amend House bills, the Committee takes on something of a review or appellate role.

The Finance Committee holds hearings on bills sent to it by the House. As a rule, the first witnesses are Administration officials led by the Secretary of the Treasury. The principal testimony of these officials and witnesses who follow after is directed to specific parts of the House bill. In addition, they may repeat much of the testimony they gave to House taxwriters. Administration witnesses of both parties who have gone through the complete tax process say that it is a grueling experience, the more so when it has to be done twice.

The Committee eventually will go into closed session and make changes it deems necessary in the House bill. It may, and sometimes does, write basic changes into the measure sent to it by the House, but its revisions often will be primarily addition of new material. The Committee, like Ways and Means, is assisted in its work by Congressional tax experts (many of the same ones who assist Ways and Means) and by Treasury Department experts. Thus, the bill reported by the Finance Committee can be expected to have the characteristics of a professionally prepared tax measure which has been written after due deliberation (even though it may differ in important respects from the House bill).

Floor Action. When the tax bill reaches the floor of the Senate for debate, there may be a radical departure from the careful consideration given the measure during the three previous steps. Unlike the House, the Senate has no applicable procedures or rules to ward off amendment of a tax bill on the floor. Considering the number of tax and other financial bills that go through Congress, the Senate does not often use its amendment prerogative to basically rewrite House bills or load them with unrelated provisions. But when it does so, the event may be spectacular.

A striking example of what can happen occurred in 1966 on a bill called the Foreign Investors Tax Act. It was one of the gems of legislative logrolling and mutual accommodation among Members of Congress. The bill started out as a measure ostensibly intended to help the United States solve its balance-of-payments problems. But after the Finance Committee and the Senate itself had finished adding amendments, the bill contained provisions to help Presidential candidates, self-employed individuals, persons in mineral ore business, big-time investors, an aluminum company and even hearse owners. These amendments, called riders because they were germane to the purpose of the bill only to the extent that they would amend the Internal Revenue Code, earned the measure the appellation of the "Christmas-tree bill" in recognition of the numerous special tax benefits it would bestow on various groups. Many of the amendments were the product of intensive lobbying by individual groups and were attached to this particular bill because it was the last measure of the session—"the last train out of the station," as one Senator put it.

One of the key provisions would have established a Presidential Election Campaign Fund in the Treasury to subsidize the costs of Presidential election campaigns; the fund was to be financed by taxpayers who voluntarily designated $1 or $2 of their income-tax payments for that purpose. President Johnson called the proposal "precedent-setting." As it turned out, however, the precedent-setting plan never got off the ground: both the Senate and the House soon had second thoughts about their hasty action and suspended the provision early in 1967.

The fund was a pet project of Finance Committee Chairman Russell B. Long (D La.), who worked diligently to get it added to the House bill. Efforts such as this, particularly by powerful senior Senators, suggest one reason why special provisions may be added by the Senate to a tax bill. Senate riders sometimes are the result of simple logrolling, sometimes are accepted simply out of courtesy to the sponsoring Senator who has a strong interest in the proposal, and sometimes are approved only because they have popular appeal and it is certain that they will be quietly dropped later in conference.

All of these reasons, especially the last-mentioned, were evident in Senate action on the tax-reform bill in 1969. The House-passed measure had emerged from the Finance Committee relatively intact, but when it reached the floor, amendments began to be proposed and accepted in considerable number. Among the more popular were: an amendment to liberalize medical deductions for elderly persons; an amendment to increase minimum Social Security payments; an amendment to allow parents a tax credit for college expenses of their children; an amendment to continue for small business the benefits of the investment tax credit (which the bill repealed); and an amendment by a Senator from Alaska to retain the investment tax credit for economically depressed areas (which included all of Alaska).

This performance represented an exercise of the time-honored practice of going on record for an amendment which has considerable constituent appeal but which, many Senators know, will be killed in conference. Few will publicly admit to such conduct. However, Sen. John J. Williams (R Del.), who was the senior GOP tax expert at the time and who had always taken a dim view of such activity, sharply criticized Senators "who can vote for (amendments) and then go home and tell their constituents how much they wanted to help them" but who knew all the time that the proposals would be scrapped in the end. Williams said he had already been approached by a number of Senators who wanted him, as a conferee on the bill, to help kill amendments they voted for on the floor. "This is nothing but sheer political hypocrisy," he said. Williams refused to serve as a conferee on the tax-reform bill because he said he could not defend the Senate bill (as expected of a conferee); as it turned out, virtually all of the foregoing and other special-interest amendments were dropped from the final bill.

The length of time the Senate may spend debating a tax bill is governed by the amount of interest in the measure and the number of amendments to be disposed of. The Senate spent more than five weeks debating a 1967 tax bill which dealt with a temporary suspension of the investment tax credit (which was repealed outright in 1969). Senate action generally runs only a few days except on tax bills of the first importance.

Conference Action

The final step in the process is a conference between senior members of the House Ways and Means Committee and of the Senate Finance Committee to resolve differences between the House- and Senate-approved versions of the bill. The conference sessions usually are held in a small room maintained in the Capitol off the House floor by the Ways and Means Committee. The Committee is presided over by the Ways and Means chairman. As a rule, there are three members from the majority and two members from the minority of the Ways and Means and the Finance Committees. The number may be enlarged for major bills, but a larger number for one side or the other makes no difference because each side votes as a unit with a majority vote controlling each group.

The conference may last from a day or two to several weeks on major or controversial bills. Congressional and Treasury tax experts are present to assist the conferees.

Once all differences are resolved, the bill is sent back to each chamber for approval of the conference agreement. The House files a conference report (for both chambers) listing the differences and their resolution; it is a rather technical document and of most use to an expert; simpler explanations of conference decisions are given by senior Committee members during floor discussion of the bill in both houses. If the conference agreement is approved by both, the bill is sent to the President to be signed into law.

Joint Internal Revenue Committee

One of the most important actions taken to improve the handling of tax matters by the Legislative Branch was the creation in 1926 of the Joint Committee on Internal Revenue Taxation. The Committee itself has only 10 members—the senior members of the Ways and Means and Finance Committees. However, this is of no importance because the Joint Committee's purpose is to maintain a staff to study tax policies and problems and make recommendations to the two tax-writing Committees. The Joint Committee does not have power to report bills. Over the years, it has developed a professional and highly competent staff, which in 1969 consisted of some 30 attorneys, economists and clerical assistants, who provide much of the expert knowledge needed by the House and Senate Committees in formulating tax legislation. The Joint Committee's staff engages in all aspects of tax work from making revenue estimates to drafting tax-bill language. Members of the staff normally are present throughout the consideration of tax bills by both Committees.

Tax Policy Since World War I

Congressional Initiative. Although in most years since World War II, the Administration has taken the initiative in setting tax policy, there were two major exceptions when Congress used its constitutional power to originate tax legislation. The first instance was in 1948 when a Republican Congress passed over President Truman's veto a bill reducing individual income-tax rates, increasing the personal exemption and allowing income-splitting for married couples. The second instance was in 1969 when a Democratic Congress seized the initiative on tax reform and reduction from the newly elected Republican Nixon Administration, which did not have tax revision at the top of its list of priorities.

As time passed, the Nixon Administration gave its support to the tax-reform bill and made recommendations of its own (many of which were adopted), but it labored under the image of being a few steps behind Congress. This was particularly true of actions in the House. The Ways and Means Committee opened tax-reform hearings at the beginning of the session, several months before the new Administration was able to prepare its own proposals. In early summer the Committee reported a bill with both revenue-raising reforms and revenue-losing tax cuts that went far beyond the Treasury Department's expectations. Later in the year, the Administration brought itself more or less in line with the action of the Congress, but when the tax bill became law, most of the credit for its enactment (and the credit due was substantial because it was the most far-reaching tax-reform bill in decades) rested with Congress and especially the Ways and Means Committee.

Revenue Priority. Except in the two foregoing cases, tax policy in the period after 1945 was largely shaped by Secretaries of the Treasury Vinson, Snyder, Humphrey, Anderson and Dillon in turn, with the emphasis on revenue considerations. It was not until around 1963 that considerations of economic growth began to take precedence.

The earlier policy of revenue priority resulted in tax proposals that tended to be conservative in orientation. The most important consideration usually was to raise enough money to meet Government expenses. This view fitted the predilections of many members of tax-writing committees, particularly Ways and Means Chairman Mills. He frequently said publicly that he favored tax reduction as a means of reducing Federal revenues and forcing the Government to economize.

But the continued growth of Federal programs and over-all Government spending made tax cuts a will-o'-the-wisp goal throughout much of the period.

Congress, as a result, could do little more than comply with the Administration's requests to extend (and sometimes hike) corporation and excise taxes. Its authority over taxes did not enable it to go much beyond tinkering with the basic Administration recommendations. However, the tinkering often was extensive and the Revenue Acts of 1945, 1950, 1951, 1954, 1962 and 1964 all varied in important respects from the initial Treasury proposals. Typically, the tax law that emerged effected either a greater reduction of revenue or less of a gain than had been recommended.

New Considerations in Tax Policy

An economic philosophy popularized during the Kennedy Administration was based on the theory that the Federal Government's fiscal powers (taxing and spending) could be deliberately used to effect changes in the country's economy. President Kennedy and his economic advisers persuaded Congress to accept this philosophy, notwithstanding the fact that employment of fiscal powers in such a way was, until then, unthinkable to most legislators and other politicians. Mr. Kennedy and his successor, Lyndon B. Johnson, prevailed upon Congress to reduce taxes, and thereby reduce Federal revenues, at a time when the Budget was already in deficit. The tax cut of $11.6 billion, carried in the Revenue Act of (Feb. 26) 1964, was designed to stimulate the economy by adding to the spending power of consumers and business.

It is widely agreed that the 1964 tax cut was an important factor in continuing the economic expansion that had begun in 1961 after the most recent recession. The other side of the coin was to use a tax increase to reduce inflationary pressures when they developed. When this was tried later, the effects were much less clear.

Congress in 1968 increased taxes by placing a 10-percent surcharge on personal and corporation income-tax liabilities. The purpose was to draw spendable income away from consumers and business and thereby dampen inflationary pressures.

The effectiveness of this tax action was blurred by several considerations. First, the action came late in the inflationary cycle; many economists agreed that Congress should have enacted a tax hike in 1966, when the budgetary impact of escalating Vietnam costs became an important influence on the economy.

President Johnson had concluded, however, that Congress would not agree to a tax increase that year,

so he did not seek one (other than a few half-hearted measures that raised no new revenue). By 1967, the stark economic fact which the Administration had been trying to ignore for two years had to be faced. Inflation was in evidence throughout the economy, and the Administration had to acknowledge that higher taxes were necessary. Mr. Johnson advanced the surtax proposal in January, but he did not push it seriously with detailed recommendations, until August. The bill got no further than hearings in the Ways and Means Committee, where Chairman Mills demanded satisfactory budget reductions before he would act on the tax request (again demonstrating the power of the Committee and its chairman).

In 1968, however, there was an interesting variation on the normal power relationships in Congress which proved the potency of the constitutional power of the Senate to amend House tax bills. The Senate unexpectedly bypassed the tax-writing Ways and Means Committee, in the early spring of 1968, by adding the surcharge and a $6-billion spending cut to a comparatively innocuous House-passed bill extending certain soon-to-expire excise taxes. This action was widely viewed as an exercise in futility because Rep. Mills was not expected to agree to so important a tax provision which had originated in the Senate. But—after much political negotiation during which spring turned into summer—Mills did accept the Senate amendment. Although the bill became law, it was some two years past the time when economists believed a tax increase was most needed. This experience again raised the question of whether Congress could exercise its taxing powers swiftly enough to have the desired impact on the economy.

A second factor contributing to confusion over the surcharge's effectiveness was the part played by monetary policy during the inflationary period. It was quite clear in 1969 that inflation had not been brought under control, by the surcharge or by any other Government action. But it was learned later that the Federal Reserve Board of Governors had expected the surcharge to have a major restraining influence; for that reason, it had somewhat eased monetary conditions to keep the economy from slipping into a decline. This action, in the opinion of the economists, wiped out some of the beneficial effects of the surcharge and sent the economy along on its inflationary spiral. The Board eventually recognized its mistake and returned to a tighter monetary policy. Its adoption of that course, in combination with the continuing surcharge, helped to produce in 1969 the first signs that the inflation induced by the Vietnam war was finally being brought under control.

Proposals for Tax Rate Changes by President

The experience Congress has had so far in use of its taxing and spending powers to influence the course of the economy has been less than satisfactory. Most observers, even many conservatives in Congress, have come to the conclusion that the fiscal powers of the Legislative Branch can be so employed as to have substantial economic impact. The difficult, and as yet unanswered, question is how to use the powers to best advantage. There have been attempts in Congress in the past to relate tax revenues to planned appropriations. These efforts have ended in dismal failure. The task of budgeting, therefore, has been left to the Executive

Branch, and its record of correlating expenditures and revenues has been uneven at best.

Joseph A. Pechman has pointed out that "The most serious drawback of the tax legislative process is that it cannot be used to provide a prompt stimulus or restraint to the economy when needed." The truth of this statement was demonstrated in the 1960s; the only exception would be in times of extreme emergency or immediate danger, as was the case at the beginning of the Korean War when Congress moved swiftly to impose new taxes (but primarily to provide the Government with war revenue).

A key to the problem is timing. President Kennedy said that the necessary precise timing could be achieved if Congress would delegate to the President standby power to change tax rates, either upward or downward. "This approach," Pechman asserted, "would emphasize changes which are neutral in their impact on the existing tax structure, as opposed to changes which would alter the distribution of the tax burden."

President Kennedy in 1962 specifically asked for standby authority to lower individual income tax rates temporarily by 5 percentage points, subject to Congressional veto, and standby authority to initiate up to $2 billion in public works spending. Kennedy asked for the power again in 1963, and President Johnson renewed the request in 1964. But the tax Committees showed no interest in the proposal.

To allay fears of Executive usurpation of Congressional tax powers, President Johnson in 1965 urged improvement of procedures to speed tax action, but he did not request standby authority. Congress again took no action. In 1966, Mr. Johnson proposed "background tax studies" to permit "quick decisions and prompt action to accommodate shortrun cyclical changes." A Joint Economic Committee subcommittee in 1966 advocated standby authority for quick changes, and once again the proposal was ignored by the tax-writing Committees.

Little more was heard of the idea except for a last-minute suggestion by President Johnson just before he left office in January 1969. In his budget message, the outgoing President asked Congress not only to extend the surcharge but also to give the new President authority to remove it entirely or in part "if warranted by developments," subject to Congressional veto. For the long term, Mr. Johnson suggested that Congress delegate to the President limited authority to raise or lower income taxes within a specified range to meet economic conditions.

Power Over Spending

Revenue raised through the taxing system is not available in the Treasury to be disbursed by the Administration to meet Governmental needs simply as agency officials deem proper. The Constitution gives to Congress the basic authority to determine how monies collected by the Government shall be expended. Control of Government spending is one of the most important powers of Congress. It is protected in the Constitution by Article I, Section 9, Clause 7, which states: "No money shall be drawn from the Treasury, but in consequence of appropriations made by law; and a regular statement and account of the receipts and expenditures of all public money shall be published from time to time."

Elsewhere in the Constitution (Article I, Section 8, Clause 12) a prohibition is laid down against appropriating money "to raise and support armies" for a period longer than two years. But this limitation and the Section 9 requirement of a "regular" accounting of public funds constitutes the specific authority for and limitations on spending. However, much more is implied. The Constitution directs the Government to do various things, such as establish post offices, roads, armed forces and courts and take a decennial census, none of which could be done without expenditures of money. But until fairly recently there was always deep disagreement about the extent of the spending power of Congress. Only in the past few decades has Congress used that power to finance a vast array of activities touching most aspects of the nation's life.

Interpretation of General Welfare Clause

The constitutional provision, Article I, Section 8, Clause 1, which grants the taxing authority, ties the "power to lay and collect taxes" to the need to "pay the debts and provide for the common defense and general welfare of the United States." From the beginning, there were differences over what spending for the general welfare meant. One view was that it was limited to spending for purposes connected with the powers specifically mentioned in the Constitution; this was the strict interpretation and was associated with Madison. "Nothing is more natural nor common," he wrote in No. 41 of *The Federalist*, "than first to use a general phrase, and then to explain and qualify it by recital of particulars." The other view, associated with loose constructionists like Hamilton, was that the general welfare clause conferred upon the Government powers separate and different from those specifically enumerated in the Constitution. Under the latter interpretation the Federal Government was potentially far more powerful than the strict constructionists intended; in fact, it was something more than a Government of delegated powers.

The broad interpretation came to be the generally accepted view, but it was not until 1936 that the Supreme Court had an opportunity to give its opinion on the meaning of the controversial wording. In a decision that year (*United States v. Butler*) the Court invalidated the Agricultural Adjustment Act of 1933, which had provided Federal payments to farmers who participated in a program of production control for the purposes of price stabilization. Although this law was held unconstitutional, the Court construed the general welfare clause to mean that the Congressional power to spend was not limited by the direct grants of legislative power found in the Constitution. Rather, an expenditure was constitutional "so long as the welfare at which it is aimed can be plausibly represented as national rather than local." The 1933 law was overturned on other grounds but later re-enacted on a different constitutional basis and sustained by the Court. Decisions in the immediately following years upheld the tax provisions of the Social Security Act, thus confirming the broad scope of the general welfare clause.

Appropriations Process Before 1921

The Constitution gives the House the power to originate tax bills, but it contains no specific provision to

Senate-House Appropriations Feud

Many Senators have disputed the exclusive right of the House to originate money bills. In 1962, the dispute produced a Senate-House stalemate that put off the enactment of such bills for months.

The controversy centered on whether the Senate could (1) originate its own appropriations bills and (2) add to House-passed appropriations bills funds for items either not previously considered by the House or considered and rejected.

The dispute, which started as a spat over the physical location of conference committee meetings, became increasingly farcical as it continued into the summer and fall with two octogenarian Members of Congress as the central antagonists: 83-year-old Rep. Clarence Cannon (D Mo.), chairman of the House Appropriations Committee, and 84-year-old Sen. Carl Hayden (D Ariz.), chairman of the Senate Appropriations Committee. The feud held up final action on appropriations bills for three months until a temporary accord, reached in July, broke the stalemate. Late in the session, however, a Senate-House disagreement over agricultural research funds resulted in a three-week deadlock on the agriculture appropriations bill. The disagreement was resolved only after a bitter exchange between the Senate and House.

Further bitterness resulted when Cannon blocked action, Oct. 12, on the first fiscal 1963 supplemental appropriations bill because the Senate had added "unwarranted sums" to the measure. The response of the Senate was to adopt a resolution, Oct. 13, asserting its "coequal power" with the House to originate appropriation bills—a resolution and assertion of power which the House quietly ignored.

Although the 1962 dispute was serious and could happen again, long-time students of Congress pointed out that the two houses had been arguing throughout their existence about which one had the right to originate appropriations bills. Considering the arguments of tradition and precedent that have been marshaled on both sides, it is doubtful that any permanent settlement of the question will be reached or that the Senate will establish the right to initiate bills. The House's argument for no change was summed up by Chairman Cannon: "The priority of the House in the initiation of appropriation bills is buttressed by the strongest and most impelling of all rules, the rule of immemorial usage."

that effect concerning appropriations. However, the House has traditionally assumed the responsibility for initiating all appropriations bills and has jealously guarded this self-assumed prerogative whenever the Senate (as it does from time to time) has attempted to encroach upon it. *(This controversy flared up most recently in 1962. See box.)*

Prior to World War I, neither the expenditures nor the revenues of the Federal Government exceeded $800 million a year. No comprehensive system of budgeting had been developed, although the methods of handling funds had undergone various shifts within Congress.

Prior to the Civil War, both taxing and spending bills were handled in the House by the Ways and Means Committee. That eventually proved too difficult a task for a single committee, and in 1865 the House Appropriations Committee was created. A similar situation existed in the Senate, where an Appropriations Committee was created in 1867.

In neither chamber did the appropriations power remain exclusively in the hands of these two Committees. Between 1877 and 1885, the House removed from the Appropriations Committee jurisdiction over 8 of 14 annual appropriations bills. These bills were placed with the substantive legislative committees. The action was taken, at least in part, to deal with what was considered an excessively independent Appropriations Committee. The Senate eventually followed the House's lead and dispersed the appropriation bills among the legislative committees. Though this division of labor allowed committees most familiar with a subject to consider the pertinent appropriations, it resulted in a division of responsibility that prevented any unified consideration or control of financial policy as a whole.

Modern Budgeting Procedure

The diffuse appropriations system that had grown up in the first 130 years of the nation's life could no longer meet the financial needs of an increasingly complex Government after World War I. Federal receipts exceeded $4 billion in all except two years in the 1920s, and expenditures dropped only to about $3 billion at the lowest point (fiscal 1927). Having seen the Government spend $18.5 billion in fiscal 1919, which included the last 4½ months of the war, and having appropriated $6.5 billion for fiscal 1920, the first full postwar year, Congress decided it must reorganize its financial machinery, both to retrench on expenditures and to tighten control over the execution of fiscal policy.

The reorganization was accomplished through enactment of the Budget and Accounting Act of 1921. First, however, the House on June 1, 1920, restored exclusive spending powers to its Appropriations Committee and enlarged the Committee from 21 to 35 members (51 in 1970). The Senate on March 6, 1922, similarly concentrated spending powers in its Appropriations Committee but left the membership at the existing total of 16 (in 1970 it was 24).

In the Budget and Accounting Act, Congress sought also to reform the financial machinery of the Executive Branch. The 1921 Act established two important offices—the Bureau of the Budget and the General Accounting Office. The former was created to centralize fiscal management of the Administration directly under the President; the latter was designed to strengthen the oversight of spending. (In 1970, the Budget Bureau was reorganized into the Office of Management and Budget with orders from the President to examine more carefully how the Government was carrying out its programs and activities.)

Congress, in setting up the GAO, was attempting to strengthen its surveillance of spending. The GAO is headed by the Comptroller General and Assistant Comptroller General, appointed by the President with the advice and consent of the Senate, for a period of 15 years.

They can be removed only by joint resolution of Congress, thus making the agency responsible to Congress rather than the Administration. The Comptroller General was granted wide powers to investigate all matters relating to the use of public funds and was required to report annually to Congress, including in his report recommendations for greater economy and efficiency in public expenditures.

Many of the auditing powers and duties of the Comptroller General had already been established by the Dockery Act of 1894, which assigned them to the new Office of the Comptroller of the Treasury. But under that Act the Comptroller and his staff remained Executive officers, and Congress lacked its own agency for independent review of Executive expenditures. In 1920, Congress considered appointing its own comptroller and assistant, but there were objections that the power of Congress to appoint Federal officers was questionable and there was also fear that succeeding Congresses might remove and replace these officers on a partisan basis. These factors led in 1921 to the Budget and Accounting Act.

Appropriations Procedures

The complex budgetary process begins in the various agencies of the Executive Branch as estimates are made of the funds needed to carry out Government programs. All of the estimates are brought together in the White House (previously by the Budget Bureau but under the 1970 reorganization by the Domestic Council and the Office of Management and Budget). At this point, the requests of the agencies are coordinated with Presidential policies and expected revenues.

The President presents his Budget to Congress in January. The estimates and requests that it contains are for the fiscal year which will begin the following July 1 (fiscal years run from July 1 to June 30).

The expenditure of money by a Government agency is the last of three main steps: Congress first authorizes a program of activity for which funds will be needed and sets a ceiling on the amount of these funds. Second, Congress provides the authority to spend money, usually through appropriations but sometimes through other means *(see box)*; the amount of money provided often is less than the maximum amount specified in the authorization for the program. Third, the agency in the Government spends the money.

Once funds have been appropriated or otherwise made available, their expenditure is under the control of the departments and agencies in the Executive Branch, although the Congressional committees—particularly the Appropriations Committees—generally keep close track of how the officials are using the funds.

Authorization Requirement

The Congressional procedure which leads to the expenditure of funds is a multi-step process. The substantive legislative committees of each chamber of Congress consider the proposed programs; this is the start of the authorizing step. Once the respective programs have been authorized by vote of the two houses and the Presi-

Budget Terminology

The Federal Budget, like any budget, is a schedule of expected receipts and expenditures. The document is prepared annually by the Administration and purports to show, as nearly as can be reliably estimated, what the Government will receive and spend in the coming fiscal year.

Congress at one time or another must approve all spending, but some spending scheduled for a given year may have been approved by Congress in a previous year. The following description applies to the Federal Budget structure put into use by President Johnson in his last two years in office. The structure was based on recommendations of a study commission and differed in various respects from that of previous years.

What Congress acts upon is not proposed expenditures—as such—but requests for new Budget authority. Government agencies are permitted to enter into obligations, requiring immediate or future payments of money (expenditures), only when they have been granted Budget authority by Congressional action.

Budget authority is divided into new obligational authority (NOA) and loan authority (LA), and it usually takes the form of appropriations, which permit obligations to be incurred and payments to be made. Some Budget authority is in the form of contract authorizations, which permit obligations but require later appropriations. There are several other less important forms of Budget authority.

Thus, in any given year the Administration in its Budget asks for specific amounts of Budget authority in the form of NOA or LA. Congress, through the appropriations process, grants all, a part, or none of the authority requested.

Once NOA or LA has been approved by Congress, agencies may enter into obligations. The obligations may be immediate obligations, such as the purchase of office supplies or payment of salaries to Federal workers. Most appropriations are for obligation within the year (one-year appropriations). Some Congressional appropriations are for specified longer periods (multi-year appropriations), while other appropriations for large projects—construction or research, for example—are made available until expended (no-year appropriations).

As a result, a change in requested NOA or LA for a particular year does not necessarily change either the obligations incurred or the actual expenditures in that year by an equal amount. A change requested in NOA or LA in one year may be reflected in obligations in subsequent years and expenditures in even later years. Obligations are eliminated, or "liquidated" as Budget officials put it, by issuing checks, by disbursement of cash or by several other methods. These are the Government's expenditures, a main part of the Budget.

dent's approval, it is up to the Appropriations Committees of each chamber to recommend appropriations for the programs. Passage of the appropriations bills follows.

Controversial Backdoor Spending

One form of spending authority was particularly controversial in the 1950s and 1960s. It went under the general name of "backdoor spending," a label applied by its opponents, but it included different types of authority.

In general, backdoor spending reduced the control of Congress over Government spending, and it virtually wiped out the authority of the Appropriations Committees over the programs which it covered. Because of the latter consideration, the Committees were strongly opposed to this method of financing and eventually were successful in bringing its use almost to an end.

During President Eisenhower's second term, backdoor spending meant for the most part the authority of certain agencies to borrow funds from the Treasury to finance their operations without going to Congress for appropriations. Beginning with the Reconstruction Finance Corp. in 1932, such authority to "expend from public debt receipts" was extended to the Commodity Credit Corp., the Export-Import Bank, and the Federal National Mortgage Assn., among others. Under this method, the legislative committee (not the Appropriations Committee) responsible for a program would sponsor legislation authorizing an agency to borrow its funds directly from the Treasury, which in turn would be authorized to sell notes to obtain the money; the programs usually provided for repayment, but in practice Congress canceled large amounts of the debt owed by various agencies.

Objections to backdoor spending came to a head in 1961. After Congress had authorized financing of this kind for the new Area Redevelopment Administration, the House Appropriations Committee managed to undo the action and require the ARA to seek appropriations for all of its activities.

A second form of backdoor spending is contract authorization. Once again the legislative committees sponsor the grants of spending authority. In this case, a bill authorizes an agency or department to enter into contracts and to incur obligations prior to approval of appropriations. Contract authorization must be followed by appropriations to meet the obligations incurred. Once an agency has contract authority and has incurred obligations for a project (such as building a subway), the Appropriations Committee and Congress have no alternative but to cough up the money to pay the bills.

Under either approach the basic issue is who will control the financing of government programs. Legis-lative committees normally only see to authorizing programs and outlining their scope; the Appropriations Committees have jurisdiction over provision of the money. Some programs—over the years—have been vulnerable to attack by a conservative majority on the House Appropriations Committee. Backdoor financing shortcircuited the appropriations process and removed the programs from the financial control of the Appropriations Committees.

Use of Backdoor Financing. As noted, backdoor financing through funds borrowed from the Treasury halted in the early 1960s. Employment of contract authorization has had its ups and downs. It has tended to increase as legislative committees of Congress and Government agencies have become frustrated with spending cuts by the Appropriations Committees.

Backdoor spending began to creep back in the mid-1960s but in a form that differed in an important respect from that formerly used. In earlier periods, the legislative committees would attempt to gain approval of backdoor spending, in the form of either Treasury loans or contract authority that would in effect insulate the program from the budget knife of the Appropriations Committees. From about 1965 on, the programs financed through backdoor spending—invariably in the form of contract authority—have allowed the Appropriations Committees the final say as to the maximum amount of spending permitted for the undertaking. And these maximum amounts have usually been written into annual appropriations bills.

However, the contracts for many of the social programs financed by this method run for 30 to 40 years. As a result, once the Appropriations Committees set maximum contract authority and Government agencies enter into the contracts, Congress (and the Appropriations Committees) are committed to provide funds for the programs for a long period of time. Thus the Appropriations Committee have regained some, but by no means all, of their former nearly absolute power over spending.

Important programs financed in this manner include rent supplements, home ownership assistance and rental assistance. All date from the 1965-68 period when President Johnson was in office. A program for Federal aid to development of urban mass transit systems, approved by Congress in 1970, carries contract authority of $3.1 billion for the first five years.

Each step, first as to authorization and then as to appropriation of funds, is an essential part of the Congressional process.

The Appropriations Committees cannot act until the authorization has been signed into law. The House has had a rule since 1837 which provides that "No appropriation shall be reported in any general appropriation bill, or be in order as an amendment thereto, for any expenditure not previously authorized by law...." The Senate has a similar rule, but because appropriations bills originate in the House, the House rule is governing. There are some exceptions, such as a portion of the annual military spending that is authorized by the Constitution, but generally appropriations must await authorizations.

This requirement has led to conflict in Congress on numerous occasions. In the 1950-1970 period, Congress required to be authorized annually more and more programs that previously had permanent or multi-year authorization. The trend to annual authorizations represented a victory for the legislative committees—such as the Committee on Education and Labor in the House for matters under its jurisdiction—which felt that they had lost effective control over their programs to the Appropriations Committees. The Appropriations Committees, particularly in the House, took a dim view of the annual authorizations, in part because they tended in some degree to diminish their power.

The annual authorization trend has contributed importantly to delaying the enactment of appropriations bills beyond the July 1 beginning of the new fiscal year. Rarely since the late 1950s has Congress completed action on more than one or two appropriations bills by July 1. This has been due in part to the prohibition against appropriations action before an authorization bill is enacted. Another factor has been the increasing number and complexity of Government programs that require more time for Congressional review.

The result has been to force the Government to go into its new financial year without most of its regular funding bills enacted into law. Congress has got around the problem by adopting continuing resolutions that allow agencies to spend at certain levels (usually that of the previous fiscal year) for a specified time, which often has to be extended. This practice pleases hardly anyone, but Congress by 1971 still was unable to improve its procedures enough to get its financing bills on the books before the fiscal year began.

Handling of Appropriations in House

Although the President's budget is sent to Congress at the beginning of each regular session in massively detailed form, it is seldom debated or considered as a whole. The detailed business of studying the budget proposals and preparing the appropriations bills is done piecemeal in subcommittees.

Consideration of the budget begins in the House, which has assumed the prerogative of originating money bills in keeping with its constitutional right to originate revenue-raising measures.

The House Appropriations Committee, like the Ways and Means Committee, is one of the most powerful and prestigious. It is composed in large part of senior Members of the House elected from safe Congressional districts. It is a conservative body which believes it has a duty to reduce the Budget requests submitted to it. This, it usually does—at least over-all.

The true power of the Committee resides in its 13 (in 1969-70) Subcommittees. When the President's Budget reaches Congress, it is divided among the Subcommittees which function largely as independent kingdoms. The Subcommittees are set up along functional lines: Agriculture, Defense, Interior, Labor-HEW and so on. Generally, the members of the Subcommittees become very knowledgeable and often expert in their assigned areas. The Subcommittees, and particularly their chairmen, consequently wield substantial power over spending.

House Appropriations Subcommittee hearings have traditionally been closed, with testimony almost always restricted to that given by agency officials. A voluminous record of the hearings, along with the parent Committee's report, has usually not been made public until shortly before House floor action on an appropriation bill. As a result, few if any Members not on the Subcommittee have been prepared to challenge the bill. The Legislative Reorganization Act of 1970 provided, as did a similar 1946 Act, that all House committee and subcommittee hearings must be open, but not if a majority determines otherwise. Leeway still was left for House Appropriations to follow its accustomed practice.

The 1970 Act provided also that the House Appropriations Committee hold hearings on the President's Budget as a whole within 30 days of its receipt; directed the setting up of a standardized data processing system for Federal budgetary and fiscal data; and directed the President to send Congress five-year forecasts of the fiscal impact of all Federal programs.

House procedure on appropriation bills permits amendments from the floor. However, the prestige of the Appropriations Committee is such that few major changes are ever made. By and large, the amounts endorsed by the Appropriations Committee during the post-World War II period have been accepted by the House; Administration efforts to win "restoration" of cuts in the budget estimates have been concentrated on the Senate.

Senate Action on Appropriations

Once an appropriations bill has passed the House, it is sent to the Senate and referred to the Appropriations Committee where a parallel system of Subcommittees exists. The Senate Subcommittees review the work of the House at hearings which are open to the public. The Senate Subcommittees do not attempt to do the same amount of work on a bill that the House has already done; the time required (often it is getting late in the year by the time the Senate receives appropriations bills) and the heavy workload of most Senators preclude the same detailed consideration that is given in the House. The Senate Subcommittees are viewed more as appellate groups which listen to Administration witnesses requesting the restoration of House-cut funds. The Subcommittee normally will restore some of the funds denied by the House, although it may make cuts in other places. The Senate itself may add or restore more when the bill reaches the floor. Most appropriations bills carry larger total amounts when they pass the Senate than when they passed the House. The differences are resolved in conference, generally by splitting the difference between the two chambers.

Congress and Expenditure Control

The "power of the purse"—defined broadly to include both receipts through taxes and outlays through appropriations—clearly is a basic power which the framers of the Constitution intended to impart to Congress. Over the years, Congress has jealously and successfully guarded its powers of taxation from encroachment by the Executive Branch; as noted, this is the basic reason why Presidents Kennedy and Johnson were unsuccessful in obtaining standby authority to alter tax rates for economic purposes.

However, Congress has been much less successful, at least since New Deal days, in retaining control over Government expenditures. And it has been totally unsuccessful in relating expenditures to revenues even though the two are intrinsically linked; this responsibility has fallen to the Administration.

Efforts have been made in Congress to exert over-all control over appropriations (and in turn, therefore, Government spending)—basically with the intention of holding appropriations to a minimal level. Attempts have been made also to use the tax system to hold down Government outlays and to tie the two together in Congress. None of these undertakings has met with great success and most have been dismal failures.

Proposals to Limit Taxing Power

As Government spending increased during the 1930s and 1940s, proposals were advanced to limit the power of Congress to disburse public funds. These proposals came primarily from conservatives, both in and out of Government, who were opposed to most Government spending and particularly to the social-welfare outlays that had begun to make up an increasing share of the Federal Budget.

The efforts were directed to limiting the Government's power to tax and thereby its power to spend. They reached a peak in the late 1940s and early 1950s but never were successful. The Eisenhower Administration's acceptance of New Deal programs and the concomitant "big government" essentially ended efforts in this direction.

The proposals were numerous. One was a simple joint resolution of Congress that would have forbidden action on any new tax legislation, except to raise revenue to meet war costs, until a special study had been made of the tax system with emphasis on simplification. A proposed constitutional amendment would have banned Federal taxes on income except in periods of grave national emergency or, at other times, for the sole purpose of obtaining revenue to pay interest on and reduce the national debt. Another proposed constitutional amendment would have limited the total of all Federal taxes to a sum equal to 14 percent of the national income for the preceding year and would have required that 5 percent of the total amount collected be set aside for retirement of the national debt. An even stricter variation on this theme would have limited annual Federal tax collections used for non-military expenditures to 5 percent of the national income.

The proposal which probably gained the most support would have limited, not the total tax take, but the rates of particular taxes, primarily individual and corporation income taxes. The limitation would have been imposed by a constitutional amendment.

Experiment with Legislative Budget

In the Legislative Reorganization Act of 1946, Congress attempted to assert new and meaningful control over the budget process through creation of a Legislative Budget. After three unsuccessful attempts to use this device, it was abandoned as an unqualified failure.

The Legislative Budget's main feature was the establishment of a maximum amount to be appropriated each year. The House Ways and Means and Appropriations Committees and the Senate Finance and Appropriations Committees were to meet as a Joint Budget Committee at the beginning of each session and prepare a Legislative Budget which would include estimated total revenue receipts and expenditures for the coming fiscal year. This was to be in addition to the President's annual Budget estimates which Congress would receive before the Legislative Budget was prepared. The Legislative Budget had to be presented by Feb. 15 of each year.

The Budget report was to be accompanied by a concurrent resolution for adoption of the Budget and fixing the maximum amount to be appropriated in the coming fiscal year. Congress was not to appropriate more than the total of estimated receipts unless it included in the concurrent resolution a provision to increase the public debt by the amount of the excess appropriations.

Attempts to implement the Legislative Budget in 1947, 1948 and 1949 failed or were ineffective. In 1947, both houses adopted a concurrent resolution but the Senate added amendments. Conferees could not agree on a proposal to divide an expected surplus between tax reduction and debt retirement. In 1948, both houses adopted the same Legislative Budget, but Congress appropriated $6 billion more than the ceiling set by the resolution. In 1949, the process broke down completely when the Budget deadline was moved from Feb. 15 to May 1. By that date 11 appropriations bills had passed the House and 9 had passed the Senate; the Legislative Budget was never produced.

One of the principal reasons the Legislative Budget failed was the inability of the Joint Budget Committee to make accurate estimates of spending so early in the session and before individual agency requests had been considered in detail. In addition, the Committee was said to be inadequately staffed and, with more than 100 members, to be much too unwieldy for effective operation. Perhaps most important was the long-standing practice in Congress of acting on appropriations bills separately (as a result of the semi-autonomous status of the Subcommittees) without effective control on total outlays.

Omnibus Appropriations Bill

Failure of the Legislative Budget prompted a serious effort in Congress in 1950 to combine the numerous separate appropriations bills into one omnibus measure.

The traditional practice of acting on the separate bills one by one made it difficult to hold total outlays in check. In 1950, the House Appropriations Committee agreed to give the omnibus-bill plan a trial. The over-all bill was passed by Congress about two months earlier than the last of the separate bills had been passed in 1949. The appropriations totaled about $2.3 billion less than the President's Budget requests. The omnibus approach was praised by many observers and organizations. It was particularly well received by persons or groups seeking reductions in Federal spending. House Appropriations Committee Chairman Cannon said the bill "offers the most practical and efficient methods of handling the annual Budget."

Nevertheless, the Committee in January 1951 voted 31 to 18 (with Cannon strongly in opposition) to return to the traditional method of handling appropriations bills separately. Following the vote, Cannon charged that "Every predatory lobbyist, every pressure group seeking to get its hands into the U.S. Treasury, every bureaucrat seeking to extend his empire...is opposed to the consolidated bill."

Two years later, in 1953, the Senate proposed a return to the omnibus plan, but the House did not respond. The plan was dead. Opponents said the omnibus bill required more time and effort than separate bills. Equally important was the opposition of the House Appropriations Subcommittee chairmen, who feared that some of their power would be eroded away under the omnibus-bill plan.

Additional Proposals for Control

Balanced Budget. Another device that has been proposed to control Federal spending is the mandatory balanced budget. The proposal has taken several forms; generally it would require the President to submit a balanced budget or to include in an unbalanced budget recommendations as to the least objectionable reductions to bring it into balance. This proposal has never won wide support.

Separate Budget Session. Still another proposal made from time to time in the postwar decades is to handle appropriations bills at a session of Congress at which no other business would be taken up. Proponents of such a plan have contended that it would enable Congress to act with greater care on money bills, while making for more orderly consideration of general business at the regular sessions.

Joint Budget Committee. A proposal which had surprising resiliency in the 1950s and 1960s called for creation of a Joint Committee on the Budget. The idea originated in the Senate and was approved by that body on seven occasions between 1952 and 1965, but the House did not act on any of the Senate bills. The opposition in the House was underpinned by the traditional role of that chamber's Appropriations Committee in setting the basic mold for the appropriations bills. The Committee and its independent-minded Subcommittees have always been wary of possible encroachment on their far-reaching influence over Federal finances. Similar obstacles probably would stand in the way of a related proposal, advanced by the Committee for Economic Development in 1970, that the taxation and appropriations committees be combined in the House and in the Senate to promote coordination of Federal spending with Federal revenue.

Restrictions in Bills. It has been the traditional practice of Congress, in its continuing effort to influence the expenditure of funds, to add to appropriations bills specific restrictions on how the money provided in the bills may be spent. The effect of these provisions is to augment Congressional control over the use to which the funds may be put by the Executive Branch.

From the time the Appropriations Committees were created, both houses of Congress have had rules forbidding the Committees to include substantive legislative provisions in their bills. These rules were intended to protect the power of the legislative committees which, it was argued, should have sole authority to initiate programs and draft new laws. It was said that if the Appropriations Committees had this power, plus the power to pass on appropriations, there would be no purpose in maintaining the legislative committees.

The Appropriations Committees thus are limited to saying what the agencies cannot do with the money. Such restrictions are numerous and usually are continued from year to year. They may substantially influence policy and in that respect are more than negative limitations; they have the effect of concentrating additional power in the Appropriations Committees.

Spending Limits. Congress made a renewed effort during President Johnson's years in office to expand its influence over the aggregate of government outlays. It was in some degree successful, but the success was achieved by extending to the Executive Branch unusual authority over the nature of expenditure reductions it might make following the appropriation of funds.

This economy effort developed between 1966 and 1968 and was continued in the following years. In 1966, House Republicans were unsuccessful in attempts to amend seven appropriations bills to limit spending in the agencies covered to 95 percent of the amounts estimated in the President's Budget. In 1967, Congress added language to a continuing resolution mandating Executive Branch agencies to hold their obligations to a figure about $9.1 billion below Budget requests. Certain "uncontrollable" expenditures were exempted.

The effect of the bill, in combination with Congressional cuts in regular appropriations bills, was to reduce spending for personnel expenses and "controllable" programs by an estimated $4.1 billion to $4.3 billion below Budget estimates. However, between January, when the Administration submitted its original Budget, and November, estimated spending on programs considered "uncontrollable" had risen by about $5 billion. As a result, spending was estimated in December at $1 billion above the total estimated in January.

Another effort was made in 1968 when Congress, in combination with the income-tax surcharge, required a $6-billion cutback in Federal spending. In 1969, Congress varied the theme by establishing a ceiling of $191.9 billion on expenditures. The effect was to order a $1-billion reduction in spending, because the ceiling was $1 billion below the Nixon Administration's projections for the year. However, the ceiling was not inflexible. Congress could indirectly raise or lower it, for example, by making increases or decreases in the appropriations bills that made up the spending totals for the President's Budget. The President was authorized, moreover, to increase by as much as $2 billion the expenditures for certain programs such as Social Security and interest on the national debt.

Advocates of the expenditure ceiling admitted that it was imperfect, but they believed that it was the most successful method so far devised for Congress to reassert its control over total Government spending.

Impounding of Funds. A reverse situation came to the fore early in 1971 when Congress complained that the Administration had failed to spend almost $13 billion appropriated for domestic programs. The Administration took the position that it was under no constitutional mandate to disburse appropriated funds and was only trying to comply with Congressional limits on over-all spending. Chairman Sam J. Ervin Jr. (D N.C.) of the Senate Judiciary Subcommittee on Separation of Powers, fired back that Executive impounding of appropriated funds "patently violates the separation-of-powers doctrine" and enables the President "to modify, reshape or nullify completely laws passed by Congress." *(See The Executive Branch, Chapter VI.)*

The National Debt

Through the years, and particularly since the New Deal days of the 1930s, the national debt and Congressional control over it have been controversial subjects. The debt has become increasingly a political issue as compensatory fiscal policies and budget deficits have gained popular acceptance. Growth of the national debt gave legislators and other public officials a convenient

Federal Receipts and Outlays

(Selected Fiscal Years, 1790-1970*)

Fiscal Year	Receipts	Outlays	Surplus or Deficit
1792	$ 3,669,960	$ 5,079,532	$ —1,409,572
1800	10,848,749	10,786,075	62,674
1810	9,384,215	8,156,510	1,227,705
1815	15,729,024	32,708,139	—16,979,115
1816	47,677,671	30,586,691	17,090,980
1820	17,880,670	18,260,627	—379,957
1830	24,844,116	15,143,066	9,701,050
1835	35,430,087	17,572,813	17,857,274
1840	19,480,115	24,317,579	—4,837,464
1850	43,603,439	39,543,492	4,059,947
1860	56,064,608	63,130,598	—7,065,990
1865	333,714,605	1,297,555,224	—963,840,619
1866	558,032,620	520,809,417	37,223,203
1870	411,255,477	309,653,561	101,601,916
1880	333,526,611	267,642,958	65,883,653
1890	403,080,984	318,040,711	85,040,273
1900	567,240,852	520,860,847	46,380,005
1910	675,511,715	693,617,065	—18,105,350
1915	683,417,319	746,093,294	—62,675,975
1917	1,100,500,109	1,953,857,065	—853,356,956
1918	3,645,239,790	12,677,359,396	—9,032,119,606
1919	5,130,042,438	18,492,665,257	—13,362,622,819
1920	6,648,898,325	6,357,676,777	291,221,548
1930	4,057,884,142	3,320,211,324	737,672,818
1932	1,923,891,824	4,659,181,532	—2,735,289,708
1940	5,137,249,771	9,055,268,931	—3,918,019,161
1943	21,947,283,157	79,367,713,522	—57,420,430,365
1945	44,362,020,944	98,302,937,069	—53,940,916,126
1946	39,649,870,986	60,326,041,595	—20,676,170,609
1950	36,421,934,577	39,544,036,935	—3,122,102,357
1955	65,468,612,716	68,509,184,178	—3,040,571,462
1960	92,492,109,550	92,223,353,625	268,755,925
1965	116,833,423,592	118,429,745,187	—1,596,321,595
1967	149,552,405,078	158,254,256,640	—8,701,851,561
1968	153,671,422,120	178,832,655,042	—25,161,232,923
1969	187,792,336,889	184,556,042,683	3,236,294,206
1970	193,743,250,789	196,587,785,632	—2,844,534,843

* Fiscal years ending Dec. 31, 1790-1842; June 30 since 1843.

SOURCE: Statistical Appendix to Report of the Secretary of the Treasury for Fiscal Year 1970.

opening to express their views on Government spending; but expansion of the debt had little effect in curbing the spending.

Constitutional Authority. The Constitution, in Article I, Section 8, Clause 2, gives Congress the power "to borrow money on the credit of the United States." This is a very broad power. William H. Young noted in Ogg and Ray's *Introduction to American Government* that the power to borrow was "one of the very few powers (in the Constitution) entirely unencumbered by restrictions—with the result that Congress may borrow from any lenders, for any purposes, in any amounts, on any terms, and with or without provision for the repayment of loans, with or without interest." Young noted also that the United States has no constitutional debt limit, whereas many state constitutions and state charters for counties and local governments impose debt ceilings. The United States has had a statutory debt ceiling for many decades (*see below*), but the ceiling can be easily altered by Congress and, in fact, has been raised repeatedly—although seldom without an intense political fight in Congress.

Deficits and Composition of the Debt

Debt has been incurred by the Federal Government when it has found it necessary to spend more than it has collected in tax and other forms of revenue. When expenditures outstrip revenues, the deficit must be made up by borrowing. Through much of the nation's history, a surplus resulting from an excess of revenues over expenditures has been used, at least in part, to reduce outstanding debt. Since the long string of Federal Budget deficits began in fiscal 1931, there have been Budget surpluses in only seven years. It is during this period that the bulk of the national debt (estimated to reach $382.5 billion by the end of fiscal 1971) has been incurred.

The debt consists of various types of obligations. David J. Ott and Attiat F. Ott in *Federal Budget Policy* gave the following definitions: "The Federal debt consists of direct obligations or debts of the U.S. Treasury and obligations of Federal Government enterprises or agencies. It is...broken down into 'public debt'—that part issued by the Treasury—and 'agency debt'—that part issued by Federal agencies. The public debt consists of issues (that is, bonds, notes and bills), which are generally sold to the public (some are held by Federal agencies and trust funds), and 'special issues,' which are held only by Government agencies and trust funds. Of the issues sold to the public, some are 'marketable,' that is, they are traded on securities markets, and some are 'nonmarketable' and cannot be traded (for example, U.S. savings bonds). The latter may, however, be redeemed in cash or converted into another issue."

Debt Philosophy Prior to 1930s

Throughout most of the nation's history, the principal concern of Government in regard to budget policy was to assure that revenues were sufficient to meet expenditure requirements. This philosophy, which in application meant an approximate balance between receipts and outlays, was generally accepted from the beginning until the early 1930s.

Lewis H. Kimmel wrote in *Federal Budget and Fiscal Policy, 1789-1958:* "From the beginning of our national history, ideas in public finance have been influenced by the unfolding of events. At the outset acceptance of the balanced budget philosophy was facilitated by the adverse financial experience during the Revolutionary War and under the Articles of Confederation. There was an awareness that the public credit is a valuable resource, especially in an emergency. The experience of the preceding fifteen years suggested to Hamilton and others that the preservation of the public credit depended on the consolidation of existing indebtedness and the provision of adequate revenues for debt service. The thought that the interests of the new nation

---

Revenue Sharing in 1837

During the 1830s Treasury accounts showed a series of exceptionally large surpluses, due chiefly to sales of public lands in connection with a boom in land speculation. After the Revolutionary War the Federal Government came into possession of an enormous domain through the cession of claims to Western lands by Eastern states. Between 1810 and 1830 the annual proceeds from the sale of these lands ranged between $1 million and $2 million, but beginning in 1830 there was a considerable increase until in 1834 the receipts were nearly $5 million. In 1835 they were $14,757,600 and in 1836, $24,877,179. In the latter year revenue from this source exceeded revenue from customs for the first and last time in the history of the country.

By 1835 virtually the entire public debt had been paid off through the purchase of Government securities in the open market at a premium, and the problem of what to do with the Treasury surpluses thereafter became acute. Thomas Jefferson had foreseen that a policy of economy, coupled with national prosperity, might lead to an overflowing Treasury. In his second inaugural address he advocated a constitutional amendment clearly authorizing the use of Government funds for internal improvements, arts, manufactures and education. It was later proposed that a part of the recurring surpluses be distributed among the states to aid in education and internal improvements.

Henry Clay offered a bill in 1835 to distribute 90 percent of the proceeds of land sales to the states. Other proposals called for reductions in customs duties to cut the Government's revenues, but this course was strongly opposed by protectionists. Finally, on June 23, 1836, Congress approved a bill which provided that all money in the Treasury on January 1, 1837, reserving the sum of $5 million, should be "deposited" with the states in proportion to their representation in the House and Senate.

The amount available for distribution on Jan. 1, 1837, was about $37 million. Of this sum more than $28 million was paid out in three quarterly installments. By May 1837, however, speculation in Western lands had collapsed and a bank panic plunged the country into deep depression. A dozen years of surpluses came to an end with a large deficit, and the fourth installment was never paid to the states.

---

would be best served if Hamilton's ideas were adopted was soon translated into policy."

Kimmel pointed out that three key ideas were generally accepted by Federal officials and economists alike during the period leading up to the Civil War: (1) a low level of public expenditures was desirable; (2) the Federal Budget should be balanced in time of peace; and (3) the Federal debt should be reduced and eventually extinguished. "These ideas," he observed "were a reflection of views that were deeply rooted in the social fabric."

Principal of the Public Debt

(Selected Fiscal Years, 1790-1970*)

Fiscal Year	Total Gross Public Debt	Fiscal Year	Total Gross Public Debt	Gross Debt Per Capita
1790	$ 75,463,477	1915	$ 1,191,264,068	$ 11.85
1800	83,038,051	1918	12,455,225,365	119.13
1810	48,005,588	1919	25,484,506,160	242.56
1815	127,334,934	1920	24,299,321,467	228.23
1820	89,987,428	1930	16,185,309,831	131.51
1830	39,123,192	1935	28,700,892,625	225.55
1835	37,513 †	1940	42,967,531,038	325.23
1840	5,250,876	1945	258,682,187,410	1,848.60
1850	63,452,774	1946	269,422,099,173	1,905.42 ‡
1860	64,843,831	1948	252,292,246,513	1,720.71
1865	2,677,929,012	1950	257,357,352,351	1,696.67
1866	2,755,763,929	1955	274,374,222,803	1,660.11
1870	2,436,453,269	1960	286,330,760,848	1,584.70
1880	2,090,908,872	1965	317,273,898,984	1,630.46
1890	1,122,396,584	1967	326,220,937,795	1,638.33
1900	1,263,416,913	1969	353,720,253,841	1,740.61
1910	1,146,939,969	1970	370,918,706,950 ‡	1,805.89

* *Fiscal years ending Dec. 31, 1790-1842; June 30 since 1843.*
† *All-time low.*
‡ *All-time high.*

SOURCE: *Statistical Appendix to Report of the Secretary of the Treasury for Fiscal Year 1970.*

The Civil War, like other major wars of modern times, resulted in a much enlarged national debt. The reported debt in 1866 amounted to almost $2.8 billion in contrast to less than $90.6 million in 1861. The debt was gradually reduced after the war to a low of $961 million in 1893. However, after the Civil War, there was less concern about eliminating the outstanding debt; increasingly, the emphasis was on servicing the debt in an orderly manner. Proposals to liquidate it became fewer and fewer.

From the post-Civil War low point in 1893, the debt increased very slowly for half a dozen years and then hovered between $1.1 billion and $1.2 billion until 1917, when the United States entered World War I. The debt jumped from just under $3 billion in fiscal 1917 to a peak of $25.5 billion at the end of fiscal 1919. In the 1920s the debt receded steadily, year by year, down to $16.2 billion at the end of fiscal 1930.

Great Rise of Debt in Past 40 Years

In 1930 and following years, the nation was faced with the problems of the Great Depression. Kimmel noted of the early years of the depression: "A concerted effort was made by the President and the leadership of both parties in Congress to adhere to the balanced-budget philosophy. Yet a balanced Federal Budget was almost impossible to attain—the annually balanced-budget dogma in effect gave way to necessity. Alternatives were soon suggested, and within a few years what came to be known as compensatory fiscal theory gained numerous adherents."

The practice of using the Federal Budget to help solve national economic problems was increasingly accepted. Budget deficits and a rapidly increasing national debt were the result. The debt rose to nearly $50 billion—almost twice the World War I peak—at the end of fiscal 1941. Then came Pearl Harbor. The debt passed the $100-billion mark in fiscal 1943 and exceeded $269 billion in fiscal 1946. No steady reduction followed World War II. The debt total fluctuated for a few years but then began a new rise which took it past the World War II peak in fiscal 1954, past $300 billion in fiscal 1963 and all the way to $370.9 billion at the end of fiscal 1970.

Congress and the National Debt

The first over-all debt ceiling was established Sept. 25, 1917, by the Second Liberty Bond Act, which fixed a limit of $11.5 billion. By 1945, Congress had amended the Act 16 times, and the ceiling had been lifted to $300 billion. In June 1946, the high World War II limit was reduced to a "permanent" $275-billion ceiling. However, as Congress continued to vote more appropriations than taxes, and the Executive Branch to spend more than it took in, Budget deficits resulted and the debt continued to rise. There followed perforce repeated ceiling increases, almost all of which were accompanied by strong partisan activity in Congress and much sermonizing on the evils of Federal expenditures and indebtedness.

Although Congress actually had little choice but to increase the statutory debt limit, the heated debates—primarily in the House—suggested that the events were milestones in public financial affairs. The controversy over rising debt ceilings flowed essentially from the broader issue of Government spending. The proponents of a statutory debt ceiling—including those who would refuse to raise it or who would lower it—saw the ceiling as a form of expenditure control. They believed that a firm commitment by Congress not to increase the limit would force a halt in spending, especially spending that exceeded tax revenues.

Officials in the Executive Branch responsible for paying the Government's bills, as well as many Members—indeed, a majority—of Congress, were convinced that a debt ceiling could not control expenditures. Throughout the postwar period, Secretaries of the Treasury expressed their opposition to use of the debt ceiling for that purpose.

A typical statement came from Treasury Secretary Douglas Dillon in a 1963 speech: "Let no one labor under the delusion that the debt ceiling is either a sane or an effective instrument for the control of Federal expenditures. No one is more conscious than I of the need to keep Government spending under firm control. But this cannot be done by trying to exert controls at the tag end of the expenditure process, when the bills are coming due. The debt limit is not and cannot be made a substitute for the control of expenditures at the decisive stage of the expenditure process—when the funds are being appropriated." Even a staunch critic of Government spending, Rep. Thomas B. Curtis (R Mo.), once said that trying to stop spending by use of the debt limit was like trying to stop an elevator from going up by grabbing the indicator arrow.

One characteristic aspect of the debt-limit debate in postwar years was that the opposition to raising the limit was led by conservatives who sought to reduce Government spending. But expenditures during these years—even during the Republican Eisenhower Administration—showed a steady increase. The increase reflected not only the adoption of new Government programs but also a buildup of political pressures on Congress that made it difficult to cut and relatively easy to add to existing levels of expenditures.

When it came down to the actual voting, Congress always raised the debt ceiling enough to enable the Government to meet its financial obligations. But the attendant Congressional debate gave Members so inclined an excellent opportunity to throw the spotlight on the public indebtedness and Government spending.

Bibliography

Books

Blough, Ray, *The Federal Taxing Process.* Prentice-Hall Inc., 1952.

Congressional Quarterly, *Congress and the Nation, Vols. I and Vol. II.* Congressional Quarterly Inc., 1965, 1969.

Fenno, Richard F. Jr., *The Power of the Purse.* Little, Brown and Co. Inc., 1966.

Horn, Stephen, *Unused Power: The Work of the Senate Committee on Appropriations.* Brookings Institution, 1970.

Kimmel, Lewis H., *Federal Budget and Fiscal Policy 1879-1958.* Brookings Institution, 1959.

Kirst, Michael W., *Government without Passing Laws.* University of North Carolina Press, 1969.

Myers, William Starr, *The Republican Party: A History.* Century Company, 1928.

Ott, David J. and Ott, Attiat F., *Federal Budget Policy, Revised Edition.* Brookings Institution, 1969.

Pechman, Joseph A., *Federal Tax Policy.* Brookings Institution, 1966.

Pressman, Jeffrey L., *House vs. Senate.* Yale University Press, 1966.

Pritchett, C. Herman, *The American Constitution.* McGraw-Hill Book Co. Inc., 1959.

Saloma, John S. III, *The Responsible Use of Power.* American Enterprise Institute, 1964.

Smithies, Arthur, *The Budgeting Process in the United States.* McGraw-Hill Book Co. Inc., 1955.

Wallace, Robert Ash, *Congressional Control of Federal Spending.* Wayne State University Press, 1960.

Weidenbaum, Murray L., *Federal Budgeting, The Choice of Government Programs.* American Enterprise Institute, 1964.

Wilmerding, Lucius Jr., *The Spending Power.* Yale University Press, 1943.

Young, William H., *Ogg and Ray's Introduction to American Government.* Appleton-Century-Crofts Inc., 1956.

Articles

Boeckel, Richard M., "The Deficit and the Public Debt," *Editorial Research Reports,* May 2, 1936, p. 317-335.

Webbink, Paul, "Deadlocks in Tariff Legislation," *Editorial Research Reports,* Nov. 1, 1929, p. 865-879.

Government Publications

President's Commission on Budget Concepts, *Report of the President's Commission on Budget Concepts.* U.S. Government Printing Office, 1967.

U.S. Senate, *The Authority of the Senate to Originate Appropriations Bills.* Senate Document No. 17, 88th Congress, 1st Session. U.S. Government Printing Office, 1963.

U.S. Senate, Committee on Government Operations, *Financial Management in the Federal Government.* Senate Document No. 11, 87th Congress, 1st Session. U.S. Government Printing Office, 1961.

The Power of Congress in Foreign Affairs

HISTORICAL practice and the rush of world developments have broadened immensely the late 18th century American attitudes which limited the compass of foreign policy to the making of treaties and, if necessary, the waging of war. Yet the division of power, between Congress and the President, in the domain of foreign relations has remained as laid down in 1787 by the framers of the Constitution.

To Congress were assigned the powers "to...provide for the common defense and general welfare of the United States;...to regulate commerce with foreign nations;...to define and punish piracies and felonies committed on the high seas and offenses against the law of nations; to declare war...and make rules concerning captures on land and water; to raise and support armies; ...to provide and maintain a navy;...to make all laws which shall be necessary and proper for carrying into execution the foregoing powers...."

"The President," directed the Constitution, "shall be Commander-in-Chief of the Army and Navy....He shall have power, by and with the advice and consent of the Senate, to make treaties, provided two-thirds of the Senators present concur; and he shall nominate and, by and with the advice and consent of the Senate, shall appoint ambassadors, other public ministers, and consuls....He shall receive ambassadors and other public ministers; he shall take care that the laws be faithfully executed...."

Legislative-Executive Antagonism

The division of power over foreign affairs has stirred up antagonism between the Legislative and Executive Branches of Government on numerous occasions. Two outstanding facts have emerged from the resulting picture of alternate tension and cooperation: first, the overwhelming importance of Presidential initiative in this area of power; and second, the ever-increasing dependence of foreign policy on Congressional cooperation and support.

Issuance of a Proclamation of Neutrality by President Washington in 1793, upon the outbreak of war between France and Great Britain, marked the start of the continuing struggle between the President and Congress for control of the nation's foreign policy. The proclamation was attacked by the pro-French Jeffersonian Republicans as a usurpation by the President of authority granted to Congress. In a series of articles published in a Philadelphia newspaper under the pseudonym "Pacificus," Alexander Hamilton defended Washington's action. He argued that the conduct of foreign relations was in its nature an Executive function and therefore, except where the Constitution provided otherwise, belonged to the President, upon whom was bestowed "the executive power." Possession by Congress of the power to declare war, as well as other powers affecting foreign relations, did not diminish the discretion of the President in the exercise of the powers constitutionally belonging to him, Hamilton said.

This view was disputed by James Madison, writing as "Helvidius." Emphasizing that the vital power to declare war was vested in Congress, Madison took the position that the powers of the Executive in foreign relations were to be strictly construed. Doubt as to the exact location of any power in this field was to be resolved in favor of the Legislature. Madison attempted to bolster his argument by pointing to the confusion likely to ensue if concurrent discretionary powers were exercised by different branches of the Government. "A concurrent authority in two independent departments, to perform the same function with respect to the same thing," he declared, "would be as awkward in practice as it is unnatural in theory." Over time, however, Hamilton's view has prevailed.

Despite the widely recognized prerogatives of the President in foreign relations, the fact is that Congress has enormous powers which are indispensable to the support of any foreign policy. Congress is the branch of Government that lays and collects taxes, that creates armies and maintains navies, that pledges the public credit, that declares war and that regulates foreign commerce. Moreover, Congressional laws made in pursuance of these powers are the "supreme law of the land," according to the Constitution, and the President is bound constitutionally to "take care that" they "be faithfully executed."

Presidential Leadership in Foreign Policy

Early Presidents—Washington, Adams, Jefferson, Madison and Monroe—exercised dominant influence in determination of the country's relations with other nations. Washington's Neutrality Proclamation and his Farewell Address, and Monroe's warning against foreign intervention in the Western Hemisphere, laid the basis for American foreign policy.

Much of the 19th century was dominated by the twin domestic issues of slavery and development of the

---

Reference

See Appendix table of contents (first thumb tab) for text of testimony by former Under Secretary of State Nicholas deB. Katzenbach before Senate Foreign Relations Committee on foreign commitments.

American West, which shifted national attention away from foreign affairs. Presidential authority in that field was somewhat less effective, and the Executive Branch suffered a number of serious setbacks. A major turn in foreign policy, strongly supported by Congress, was taken in 1898. The country dropped its traditional policy of nonintervention, went to war to rid Cuba of Spanish rule, and emerged from the conflict with overseas outposts as far distant as the Philippines in the Western Pacific.

During most of the present century, particularly in the years since World War II, the President has been the leader in foreign affairs. An important exception was the 15-year period of commanding Congressional influence following Senate rejection of the Treaty of Versailles after World War I. But on the eve of the next great conflict, the country's overseas interests as interpreted by the President began to dominate American foreign policy.

On balance, the foreign-affairs legislation enacted by Congress has operated to increase Presidential powers much more frequently than it has operated to curtail them. The classic example of this tendency was the passage of the lend-lease act in the spring of 1941. It authorized the President to "sell, transfer title to, exchange, lease, lend, or otherwise dispose of" defense articles to any country "whose defense the President deems vital to the defense of the United States."

Changes in Role of Congress

As American policies toward other nations have evolved, the role of Congress in foreign affairs has shifted. The Senate, which once claimed dominant influence because of its part in treaty making, plays no part in the making of the increasingly popular executive agreements with foreign countries; executive agreements do not require Senate approval. In addition, the power of Congress to declare war has lost significance as modern weapons have made surprise attack more and more advantageous, if not a matter of necessity, for an aggressor nation. The war power of Congress has been eroded also by actions taken under the constitutional authority of the President as Commander-in-Chief.

At the same time, Congressional power as concerns other aspects of foreign affairs has greatly expanded. Legislative authority over the massive, post-World War II foreign aid and military assistance programs is a case in point. The programs have required specific Congressional authorizations and repeated Congressional appropriations. Furthermore, foreign policy implications surround a growing body of other legislation, such as Food for Peace, regulation of immigration, shipping subsidies, space exploration, the Peace Corps and import quotas. Meanwhile, the fundamental constitutional authority for a share of the treaty-making power and the war power continues to underlie this sweeping Congressional involvement in foreign affairs.

The Treaty Power

The whole of the treaty-making power is contained in a single clause of the Constitution. Spelling out Presidential authority, Article II, Section 2, Clause 2 declares: "He shall have power, by and with the advice and consent of the Senate, to make treaties, provided two-thirds of the Senators present concur...."

For years this clause served as a cornerstone of American foreign policy. It brought peace with other nations, supported American territorial expansion, established national boundaries, protected U.S. commerce and regulated Government affairs with Indian tribes.

Ambiguities in Treaty Clause

Despite its importance, the clause was ambiguous on some points, and the ambiguities led from the beginning to conflicts between the Executive and Legislative Branches. Neither the Senate procedure for advising the President nor the stage of treaty making at which the Senate was to act in an advisory capacity was defined. And, the role of the House of Representatives in treaty making, to the extent that legislation or appropriations were needed to make a treaty effective, was ignored. The Constitution was silent on all of these points.

It is generally agreed that the main purpose of the advice-and-consent formula was to provide for democratic control of foreign policy. In the early years of the nation, the Executive Branch sought to incorporate Senate advice into the process of treaty negotiation by such means as Presidential meetings with Senators, Senate confirmation of negotiators, and special Presidential messages. But as international relations became more complicated, the early Administrations abandoned, one after the other, the various devices by which the Senate's advice had been obtained.

Deprived of opportunities to make its influence felt in treaty negotiations, the Senate resorted to advising the President through drastic amendment—or outright rejection—of completed treaties. The historically dramatic climax of Senatorial dissatisfaction came in 1919 and 1920 with the prolonged debate on, and ultimate rejection of, the Treaty of Versailles, which embodied not only the World War I treaty of peace with Germany but also the Covenant of the League of Nations.

Senate's Ratification Record

Despite the shock caused by rejection of the Versailles pact, and consequent reinforcement of the Senate's popular reputation as a graveyard of treaties, its over-all record on ratification has been overwhelmingly favorable. Since 1789, only 11 treaties have been rejected through failure to receive a two-thirds majority in the Senate. The last treaty rejected was an optional protocol to the law-of-the-sea conventions, concerning compulsory settlement of disputes (Exec N, 86th Congress, 1st Session). The May 26, 1960, vote was 49-30 for the protocol, four votes short of the two-thirds required for consent to ratification. *(See box on rejected treaties.)*

Presidential reaction to rejection of the Treaty of Versailles took two forms. On the one hand, the White House made renewed efforts to court Senate support of proposed treaties by reinstituting some of the old, and developing some new, methods of associating Senators with the treaty-making process. On the other hand, there was a growing tendency to rely on the executive agreement as a vehicle of international accords, thus eliminating altogether the need for Senate approval. There was reaction also in Congress, where various constitutional amendments were proposed to curtail the power of the Senate in the making of treaties.

New Importance of Treaty Power

In the years following World War II, the treaty-making power took on added importance. Membership in the United Nations was accomplished by Senate consent to ratification of the U.N. Charter, while membership in an expanding number of international organizations was brought about either by treaty or by both House and Senate approval of appropriate legislation. Treaties were used to conclude the widening circle of U.S. mutual security agreements designed to provide collective defense against aggression. Agreements aimed to guide the peaceful and restrict the military use of atomic energy were incorporated in treaties. And as man opened new frontiers in space and under the oceans, additional treaties were concluded or proposed to govern his behavior there.

Old conflicts over treaty making persisted in the postwar years. It was a time of strong Executive Branch leadership, producing an inevitable Congressional reaction. The reaction came to a head in 1953-54 with consideration of the Bricker Amendment, which, among other things, would have had the effect of limiting Presidential treaty power. The amendment, rejected by Congress, was named for its sponsor, Sen. John W. Bricker (R Ohio).

Ironically, in view of the Bricker Amendment controversy, the postwar development and expansion of foreign aid as an aspect of U.S. foreign policy gave the Legislative Branch an unprecedented role in international relations. Foreign aid has been the subject of more than 100 enactments since 1945. Requiring in almost every instance the assent of Congress to expenditures, foreign aid proposals afforded Senators and Representatives their most consistent opportunity to support or to oppose the conduct of foreign relations by the Executive Branch. Inevitably, aid programs and policies were modified in the process, typically through lower-than-asked-for appropriations.

Action of Constitutional Convention

At the root of the recurring conflict between the President and Congress over the treaty-making power has been the doctrine of separation of powers that is so basic to the governmental structure of the United States. Congress and the Executive are in constant competition with each other for power and prestige.

During the Constitutional Convention, the treaty power came up for discussion repeatedly. At first, it was assumed that the existing power of the Continental Congress to make treaties by a two-thirds majority would simply be transferred intact to the Legislative Branch of the new Government. Continued Legislative control of treaty making was taken for granted despite the fact that it was then the exclusive prerogative of the Executive in all other governments.

The first suggestion that the treaty power should be divided between the Legislative and Executive Branches was made in the convention on June 18, 1787. Hamilton proposed an Executive elected for life, who, along with many other powers, would have "with the advice and approbation of the Senate, the power of making all treaties." There was no discussion of Hamilton's suggestion, and it appeared dead when the Aug. 6 report of the Committee of Detail proposed that "the Senate shall have power to make treaties." Debate on the Committee's report failed to resolve the issue of who was to exercise the treaty power. The section was referred back to the Committee. On Sept. 4, the report of the Committee of Eleven recommended that "the President, by and with the advice and consent of the Senate," would have the power to make treaties, and that no treaty could be made "without the consent of two-thirds of the members present." Several attempts were made to alter the proportion of the Senate whose consent would be required, and to add House participation in treaty making, but on Sept. 8 the provision as proposed in the report was finally agreed to.

There was nearly unanimous support in the convention for some means of enabling the new Government to require the states to honor treaty provisions. Although the Articles of Confederation entrusted the treaty-making power to Congress, fulfillment of Congress' promises to other nations was dependent on the state legislatures. Inaction, or adverse action, by certain states had led to violation of some articles of the Peace Treaty of 1783 with Great Britain. A solution was provided in the declaration of Article VI, Clause 2 of the Constitution that "all treaties made, or which shall be made, under the authority of the United States shall be the supreme law of the land...."

The meaning of the declaration was explained by Chief Justice John Marshall in 1829 *(Foster v. Neilson):* "Our Constitution declares a treaty to be the supreme

Treaties Killed by Lack of Two-Thirds Majority

Date of vote	Country	Vote Yea	Nay	Subject
April 17, 1844	German Zollverein	26 :	18	Reciprocity
June 27, 1860	Spain	26 :	17	Cuban Claims Convention
June 1, 1870	Hawaii	20 :	19	Reciprocity
Jan. 5, 1883	Mexico	33 :	20	Claims Convention
April 20, 1886	Mexico	32 :	26	Claims Convention
May 5, 1897	Great Britain	43 :	26	Arbitration
March 19, 1920	Multilateral	49 :	35	Treaty of Versailles
Jan. 18, 1927	Turkey	50 :	34	Amity and Commerce
March 14, 1934	Canada	46 :	42	St. Lawrence Waterway
Jan. 29, 1935	Multilateral	52 :	36	Adherence to World Court
May 26, 1960	Multilateral	49 :	30	Sea Law Convention Protocol

law of the land. It is, consequently, to be regarded in courts of justice as equivalent to an act of the legislature, whenever it operates of itself, without the aid of any legislative provision. But when the terms of the stipulation import a contract—when neither of the parties engages to perform a particular act, the treaty addresses itself to the political, not the judicial department; and the legislature must execute the contract, before it can become a rule for the Court." Hence, although Congress may have to enact legislation to carry out acts stipulated by a treaty, any self-executing treaty or part of a treaty automatically attains the status of a statute, enforceable by the courts. Provisions of various treaties periodically have been the target of legal challenges, but the Supreme Court never has ruled unconstitutional a treaty of the United States or any provision of a treaty.

Exclusion of the House from the treaty-making process was defended by Hamilton and Jay in the Federalist. Using similar arguments, they contended that the legislative role in treaty making should be limited to the Senate because decisions on treaties would thus be placed in the hands of persons chosen by the "select assemblies" of the states instead of by the rank and file, because the longer and overlapping Senate terms would provide relatively greater continuity, because the smaller size of the Senate would aid "secrecy and dispatch," and because agreement among the President, the Senate and the House would be more difficult to obtain.

Final adoption of the two-thirds rule reflected the special concern of certain states over Newfoundland fishing rights and the right of navigation on the Mississippi River.

Form of Senate Consent. In performing its constitutional treaty-making functions, the Senate merely consents to the ratification of a treaty; ratification itself is subject to Executive action. Normally, the Senate considers a resolution of advice and consent to ratification of a pending treaty. In the case of the nuclear test-ban treaty, approved by the Senate on Sept. 24, 1963, the resolution of ratification read as follows:

"Be it resolved (two-thirds of the Senators present concurring therein), that the Senate advise and consent to the ratification of the treaty banning nuclear weapons tests in the atmosphere, in outer space, and under water, which was signed at Moscow on Aug. 5, 1963, on behalf of the United States of America, the United Kingdom of Great Britain and Northern Ireland and the Union of Soviet Socialist Republics."

Consideration of First Treaties, 1789

The first treaties to be laid before the Senate under the Constitution were submitted on May 25, 1789. They were a pair of treaties with Indian tribes negotiated and signed under the authority of the Continental Congress. It was not until June 12 that the two treaties were referred to a committee for study; in the meantime, the President had submitted another treaty, a consular convention with France, concluded under the Articles of Confederation. After a series of meetings with, and reports from John Jay, Secretary of Foreign Affairs, an office held over from the Confederation, the Senate on July 29 unanimously consented to ratification of the consular treaty. This was the first

time the Senate had given its advice and consent to ratification of a treaty.

The Committee studying the two Indian treaties finally reported on Aug. 12. Instead of recommending that the Senate advise and consent to ratification (as had been done with the consular treaty with France), the committee recommended that the President "be advised to execute and enjoin an observance" of the agreements. The Senate on Sept. 8 approved the committee recommendation for one of the treaties (that with the Wyandot, Delaware, Ottawa, Chippewa, Pattawattima and Sacs nations) but took no action on the other (that with the Six Nations, except the Mohawks).

The Senate action confused President Washington. He was not certain whether the Senate meant that he should merely see that the approved treaty went into operation or that he should proceed with a formal ratification. In a message to the Senate, Sept. 17, the President asked for a clarification. His own opinion, he said, was that treaties with Indian tribes should be ratified in the same way as treaties with European nations. The Senate disagreed. A committee that studied the President's message reported, Sept. 18, that since past Indian treaties never had been solemnly ratified, it was not "expedient or necessary" to ratify the present treaties. The committee proposed a resolution to advise the President "to enjoin a due observance" of the Wyandot treaty, passing over the treaty with the Six Nations. But on Sept. 22 the Senate substituted a resolution of advice and consent to the Wyandot treaty. No action was taken on the other agreement. Senate consent to ratification of the Wyandot treaty set a precedent that endured for more than 70 years. However, a rider to the Indian Appropriations Act of 1871 provided that in the future no American Indian nation or tribe was to be considered an independent nation with which the United States could conclude a treaty. Indian affairs were to be handled subsequently by statute.

The Advice of the Senate

The first treaties considered by the Senate had been negotiated under instructions from the Continental Congress because there was no Executive in the Confederation government. Although the new Constitution provided for an Executive and authorized him to make treaties, with advice from the Senate, it failed to explain what kind of advice was appropriate or how it was to be offered. It was clear, however, that to be effective the advice would have to be given before the conclusion of negotiations.

In practice, procedures developed by Washington and the first Senate established precedents which have exerted varying degrees of influence. After an abortive attempt at personal consultation with the Senate as an executive council, Washington's usual practice, at least up to the Jay treaty negotiations with Great Britain in 1794, was to ask for advice about opening negotiations; to transmit the full instructions to be given to the negotiators; to submit their names for confirmation; and to keep the Senate fully informed of the progress of negotiations. If matters came up which were not covered in the original instructions, Washington again would call for Senate advice. When treaties would require subsequent appropriations to carry them into effect, he reported the proceedings to the House as well as to the Senate.

Additional procedures adopted by early Administrations included requests for advance appropriations to cover the cost of negotiating, naming of Senators and Representatives to the negotiating team and consulting personally with key members of the Senate, and, after its establishment in 1816, with the Foreign Relations Committee. At times Congress took the initiative by considering resolutions to suggest or to oppose negotiations.

Consultation With the Senate

While the Senate was considering the first treaties, it named a committee, Aug. 3, 1789, to meet with the President to establish ground rules for consultation on the making of treaties. Washington favored oral communications rather than written exchanges, and, following a committee recommendation, the Senate on Aug. 21 adopted a rule providing for meetings with the President either in the Senate chamber or elsewhere. Later the same day, the Senate received a message announcing that Washington was coming to the Senate chamber the next day "at half past 11 o'clock" to discuss proposed terms for a treaty with the southern Indians.

Unfamiliar with the background of the situation or with the proposed treaty terms, the Senate sought to refer the papers to a committee for study. Washington, who had hoped for prompt action, objected strenuously. He finally agreed to defer action to Aug. 24. The second meeting went more smoothly; the Senate agreed to vote its advice on each of the points raised by the President. However, Washington never again went before the Senate to consult on treaty terms or discuss foreign policy, nor did any other President until Woodrow Wilson appeared on Jan. 22, 1917, to call for "peace without victory" and propose a League for Peace; President Truman also went to the Senate in person, July 2, 1945, to ask its early consent to ratification of the United Nations Charter.

President Washington, after his initial venture in direct consultation, relied on special messages in seeking the advice of the Senate. The story that Washington said he would be damned if he ever went to the Senate again is thought to be largely apocryphal. It was based on an account in the diary of John Quincy Adams of a story told by William H. Crawford at a Cabinet meeting of President Monroe. Crawford, Monroe's Secretary of the Treasury, was only 17 years old when Washington visited the Senate. *(See History of the Senate, Chapter I.)*

Although Washington's general position was that he considered it advisable to postpone negotiations until he has received the advice of the Senate as to the propositions to be offered, he did not follow this course in the case of the Jay treaty. He submitted Jay's name as a negotiator for confirmation by the Senate but withheld the instructions to be given him. The same procedure was adopted by Washington's immediate successors, Adams and Madison, and has been followed by some other Presidents.

Polk returned to the earlier practice when in 1846 he asked the Senate's advice as to whether negotiations should be undertaken with Great Britain on the basis of proposals submitted from London for the settlement of the Oregon boundary question. Similar requests for preliminary advice were sent to the Senate by Buchanan, Lincoln, Johnson, Grant and Cleveland. Harding, in 1922, asked advice as to revival of a patents treaty with Germany. An amendment to a 1913 appropriations bill, prohibiting participation of agents of the Executive in "any international congress or conference without authority of law to do so," was declared by President Wilson to be "utterly futile" and has been observed only occasionally.

The right of the Senate to direct treaty making by proposing negotiations has been vigorously debated on the Senate floor. Proponents have defended such initiative as "the right and duty of the Senate under the Constitution," and as helpful in showing the United States to be "a unit" in its demands. Opposition Senators have contended that for the Senate to make the first move was "officious and disrespectful," and that it tended to "shelter" the President from responsibility in treaty making. In 1902 a report by the Committee on Foreign Relations declared: "The initiative lies with the President...Whether he will negotiate a treaty, and when, and what its terms shall be are matters committed by the Constitution to the discretion of the President."

Today the right of either house of Congress to offer advice about negotiations is not questioned, but the advice of the Legislative Branch is held to be no more compelling on the President than advice proffered by any body of citizens. In its decision in the Curtiss-Wright case in 1936 the Supreme Court ruled: "The President...alone negotiates. Into the field of negotiation the Senate cannot intrude, and Congress itself is powerless to invade it."

The reaction of different administrations to Senate advice to negotiate has varied. President Jackson acted on a Senate resolution in opening negotiations with Central American governments for an interoceanic canal. Cleveland replied with some asperity to a similar Senate suggestion for negotiations to limit Chinese labor. Harding refused to recognize that the Borah resolution for agreement with Great Britain and Japan on reduction of naval expenditures was responsible for the calling of the Washington Conference on the Limitation of Armament. Sponsored by Sen. William E. Borah (R Idaho), the resolution was adopted by the Senate May 26, 1921, and by the House on June 29. Formal invitations to the conference were issued Aug. 11, 1921.

Confirmation of Negotiators

Up to the end of Madison's administration, the names of treaty negotiators were consistently referred to the Senate for confirmation. Subsequent neglect of the practice was repeatedly protested in the Senate. In 1883, the Senate attempted in ratifying a treaty with Korea to revive the earlier practice by adopting a resolution which stipulated that the consent given to ratification did not "admit or acquiesce in any right or constitutional power in the President to employ any person to negotiate treaties...unless such person shall have been appointed...with the advice and consent of the Senate." Cleveland's appointment of a special commissioner with "paramount authority" to negotiate with Hawaii was declared by the Republican members of the Foreign Relations Committee to be "an unconstitutional act in that such appointee was never nominated to the Senate." When Harding sent negotiators to Haiti in 1922 without Senate confirmation, a resolution was introduced calling for an investigation of the President's power to make such appointments.

That confirmation of negotiators gave the Senate an important power was recognized by both the Senate and the Executive Branch. Commenting on the situation when one of Adams' nominations was under attack, Jefferson wrote that, were a large opposition vote registered, even if confirmation resulted, "it is supposed the President would perhaps not act under it, on the probability that more than a third would be against ratification."

Abandonment of the practice of Senate confirmation of negotiators appears to have been due to the need for secrecy which led to employment of special agents whose appointment was recognized as the right of the Executive in carrying out his constitutional duties, and to acceptance of the principle—in Jefferson's words to Citizen Genet, envoy to the United States from the first French Republic—that the President is "the only channel of communication between this country and foreign nations."

In later years, on various occasions, the Executive sought Senate confirmation of treaty negotiators. Polk submitted the names of his appointees to negotiate a treaty with Mexico. Grant nominated to the Senate the commissioners who negotiated the Treaty of Washington with Great Britain. Harding submitted the names of his appointees to the World War Foreign Debt Commission in 1922, but such submission was required by a provision of the act creating the commission, which stipulated that its members be appointed by the President, "by and with the advice and consent of the Senate."

The United Nations Participation Act of 1945 provided for Senate confirmation of the United States Representatives to the United Nations, of members of the U.S. delegation to the General Assembly, and of delegates to various UN agencies.

Submission of Negotiators' Instructions

Submission of their instructions along with the names of negotiators, amounted, while Washington was President, to an opportunity for the Senate to advise on treaty proposals. No opportunity to consider the terms of a treaty not yet agreed upon was provided during ensuing administrations until Polk submitted the skeleton of a treaty ending the war with Mexico in 1846. Preliminary drafts of treaties were sent to the Senate in a few instances by four other executives—Buchanan, Lincoln, Johnson and Grant. In 1919, the Senate requested a copy of the Treaty of Versailles as presented to the representatives of Germany. The Secretary of State replied: "The President feels it would not be in the public interest to communicate to the Senate a text that is provisional and not definite, and finds no precedent for such a procedure."

In at least two instances, the Senate (with the concurrence of the House) has "advised" the Executive by specifying the limits within which negotiators of international agreements were to operate. In the act of February 9, 1922, creating the Foreign Debt Commission it was provided that "nothing contained in this act shall be construed to authorize...the commission to extend the time of maturity of...obligations due the United States...beyond June 15, 1947, or to fix the rate of interest at less than 4 1/4 per centum per annum." In a joint resolution making funds available to send a dele-

gation to the Opium Conference of 1924, Congress specified certain results to be obtained by the negotiators.

Members of Congress as Negotiators

The first two Members of Congress to be selected to negotiate a treaty were Sen. James A. Bayard (Federalist Del.) and House Speaker Henry Clay (Ky.). Madison named them to help negotiate a treaty of peace with Great Britain in 1814. Both resigned their places in Congress on the ground that the two offices were not compatible. On three occasions resolutions have been introduced in the Senate to prohibit Members of that body from serving as treaty negotiators. The first, in 1870, was defeated after a heated all-night debate, when it was turned into a question of confidence in President Grant. The second was occasioned by McKinley's appointment, following a series of such Congressional appointments by himself and his predecessors, of three members of the Committee on Foreign Relations on the commission to negotiate the Treaty of Paris in 1898. The Committee on Foreign Relations, to which a resolution of protest was referred, hesitated to make a report that might appear to censure its own members, but it directed its chairman to visit the President and express the Senate's strong disapproval. Theodore Roosevelt's selection of Sen. Henry Cabot Lodge (R Mass.) for the Alaskan boundary tribunal led to the third and last attempt of the Senate to prohibit such service by Senators. The resolution introduced at that time was not acted upon.

Senate resentment of Wilson's failure to include any Senators on the 1919 peace commission came as a sharp contrast to its previous position. To compensate for lack of representation on the commission, a resolution calling for the appointment of a bipartisan committee of eight Senators to visit Paris during the sittings of the Peace Conference, to "make itself familiar with all facts" and report to the Senate "as often as it deemed desirable," was introduced but not acted upon. Senate attempts to advise as to negotiations through debate on the floor and through a round-robin warning against inclusion of provisions for a League of Nations in the peace treaty proved to be without effect.

As a result of Wilson's experience, the appointment of Senators to important international conferences has since been frequent. President Harding in 1921 chose the chairman of the Senate Committee on Foreign Relations, Sen. Henry Cabot Lodge (R Mass.), and the minority leader, Sen. Oscar W. Underwood (D Ala.), as delegates to the Conference on the Limitation of Armament, and Members of both houses were appointed by Hoover on the American delegation to the London Naval Conference in 1930. President F. D. Roosevelt recognized Congress in his selection of commissioners to the World Monetary and Economic Conference, in 1933 and to the International Refugee Conference in 1943.

In 1945, the eight-member U.S. delegation to the United Nations founding conference at San Francisco included four Members of Congress: Foreign Relations Committee Chairman Tom Connally (D Texas), Sen. Arthur H. Vandenberg (R Mich.), a Committee member, and Reps. Sol Bloom (D N.Y.) and Charles A. Eaton (R N.J.), chairman and ranking minority member of the House Foreign Affairs Committee. Since organization of the United Nations, two Senators and two

Role of Congressional Committees in Foreign Affairs

In dealing with international relations, the Senate Foreign Relations Committee and the House Foreign Affairs Committee hold the key roles. The Senate Committee's exclusive responsibility for treaties and for diplomatic nominations has made it traditionally the chief Congressional voice in foreign affairs.

The tendency to move from treaties to executive agreements and the growing impact of foreign-aid and military-assistance legislation since the end of World War II have tended to draw additional Congressional committees into consideration of foreign-policy matters, but the Foreign Relations and Foreign Affairs panels have continued to exert important influence.

Foreign Relations Committee. Created Dec. 10, 1816, the Senate Foreign Relations Committee rapidly became one of the most prestigious groups on Capitol Hill, primarily because of its jurisdiction over treaties. All treaties, regardless of their subject matter, are referred to the Committee, making it the bridge between the Executive and Legislative Branches in the joint process of approval required constitutionally for formal ratification. In addition, the Committee has jurisdiction over a broad variety of legislation dealing with international affairs, and over State Department and diplomatic nominations.

The Committee has attracted as members some of the most illustrious men to serve in the Senate. Among its members have been ex-President Andrew Johnson, Daniel Webster, John C. Calhoun, Roscoe Conkling and Robert A. Taft. Among its chairmen have been Charles Sumner, Henry Cabot Lodge, William E. Borah, and Arthur H. Vandenberg.

The Committee frequently has been a center of controversy, typically over an issue that has deeply divided the nation as well. In 1871, President Grant forced Sumner's removal as chairman because of a bitter dispute involving Grant's desire to annex Santo Domingo; Sumner strongly opposed annexation. Chairman Lodge was accused later of packing the Committee with Senators opposed to the League of Nations. During the prolonged debate over the Vietnam war in the 1960s, the Committee was generally regarded as being dominated by opponents of the war.

As a rule, the Committee's recommendations on treaties have been decisive; it seldom has been overruled by the full Senate. Of 200 treaties referred to the Committee from the 80th to the 84th Congress (Jan. 3, 1947, to July 27, 1956), 152 were reported to the full Senate, each of them accompanied by a favorable recommendation. The Senate approved 150; the two others were withdrawn by the Executive Branch prior to Senate action. Of the 48 treaties not reported by the Committee, 30 were withdrawn by the Executive Branch and 18 were pending before the panel at the close of the 84th Congress.

Foreign Affairs Committee. The House Foreign Affairs Committee was created on March 13, 1822. Lacking authority over either treaties or nominations, it languished in the shadow of its Senate counterpart for more than 100 years. Membership on the House Committee was considered a routine assignment, to be avoided when possible and to be relinquished as soon as possible when unavoidable. The panel acquired a measure of prestige only when the rapid expansion of American involvement abroad after World War II frequently demanded House Committee action.

The historically secondary role of the Committee did not prevent its involvement in controversy, however. During the Civil War, it became embroiled in a classic Legislative-Executive dispute over the making of foreign policy.

As part of a Congressional attempt to force President Lincoln to adopt a more vigorous policy against French interference in Mexico, the House on April 14, 1864, adopted a resolution by Foreign Affairs Committee Chairman Henry Winter Davis of Maryland that sharply criticized the French. Secretary of State William H. Seward quickly reasserted the exclusive power of the President to speak for the country in foreign affairs and told the American minister in Paris to explain the situation to the French. When the House received a copy of Seward's message, it overwhelmingly adopted another resolution by Davis claiming "a constitutional right to an authoritative voice in declaring and prescribing the foreign policy of the United States."

Other Committees. In all, more than one-half of the committees of Congress have some impact currently on foreign policy. The requirement of vast sums for foreign aid and military assistance has given the Appropriations Committees a powerful lever. The Armed Services Committees have a controlling influence over defense policy and its impact abroad. Congressional oversight of foreign policy is maintained through hearings by the House Government Operations Subcommittee on Foreign Operations and Government Information and by the Senate Government Operations Permanent Investigations Subcommittee. Immigration policies are reviewed by the Judiciary Committees. And import quota bills are referred to the House Ways and Means and the Senate Finance Committees.

Representatives have alternated as members of the U.S. delegation.

Consent of the Senate

Over the years, Senate action on treaties has led to recurring rounds of controversy. At issue traditionally have been rival claims by the President and the Senate with respect to the treaty power.

The Senate has adopted a simple resolution of consent to ratification on a vast majority of treaties submitted to it. It has modified or rejected relatively few. But the significance of some of the rejected treaties has prompted noisy criticism of the Senate's treaty-making role, and the two-thirds rule, and has spawned a variety of proposed constitutional amendments designed to modify the Senate's power.

Treaties are transmitted to the Senate by the President under an injunction of secrecy which normally is removed shortly after the Senate receives the treaty. Once a treaty is submitted, it remains before the Senate until it is disposed of favorably, or until the President requests its return and the Senate agrees.

Senate Procedure

Senate consideration of a treaty is open to Presidential discretion at a number of points. The President may refuse to submit a treaty; he may withdraw it after submission; or he may refuse to ratify it even after the Senate has given its consent.

Within the Senate, treaties are subject to the jurisdiction of the Foreign Relations Committee whether or not they involve subjects that usually require consideration by another committee. The Foreign Relations Committee considers a treaty in much the same way that it considers proposed legislation. It may hold open or closed hearings and may recommend adoption or rejection, with or without modifications. Committee actions require a majority vote of the members present; to act, according to the Legislative Reorganization Act of 1946, a committee majority must be "actually present."

After action by the Foreign Relations Committee, treaties are considered by the full Senate. The Senate used to debate treaties in closed executive session, preserving the cloak of secrecy. Pressures later developed to make public the Senate treaty debates. A fisheries treaty with Great Britain was considered—and defeated—in the first open executive session in 1888. Other public treaty debates followed, and the Senate on June 18, 1929, amended its rules to provide that all Senate business, including action on treaties, would be conducted in open session unless a Senate majority decided in a closed session to consider a particular matter in secret.

After a brief experiment (1801 to 1803) with a rule requiring a two-thirds vote on all treaty action, the Senate limited the two-thirds rule to the final question of advice and consent and to a motion for indefinite postponement. All other questions are decided by majority vote.

A separate vote normally is taken on each treaty. But that procedure is sometimes departed from when a large number of similar treaties, or a variety of non-controversial treaties, is to be considered. It has become the practice in these cases to consider the group of treaties en bloc (taking one vote on several resolutions of consent) or to take a single vote, which by unanimous consent is shown separately in the *Congressional Record* for each resolution. Although Senate rules do not require roll-call votes on treaties, that practice has become customary. It grew out of a 1952 incident in which three noncontroversial consular conventions were approved, on June 13, when only two Senators were present in the chamber. On July 20, 1953, Acting Majority Leader William F. Knowland (R Calif.) announced that "as a matter of standard operating procedure in the future, we intend, in connection with all treaties...not only to ask for a quorum call, but to ask for a yea-and-nay vote...."

Modification of Treaties

In the Constitution, there is no provision for or against amendment of treaties by the Senate. But since the time of the Jay treaty with Great Britain, the Senate has claimed authority to modify treaties after the completion of negotiations. The Senate on June 24, 1795, by a 20-10 vote consented to ratification of the Jay treaty on condition that an additional article be negotiated to suspend portions of the treaty's 12th article that related to trade between the United States and the British West Indies. Scores of later treaties have been subjected to amendments, reservations, conditions and qualifications, some of them added at the request of the President.

The wisdom of the Senate practice of amending treaties was questioned as early as 1805 by John Quincy Adams. In a Senate debate, Adams said, "I think amendments to treaties imprudent. By making them you agree to all the treaty except the particular you amend, and at the same time you leave it optional with the other party to reject the whole." A later opinion was voiced by Secretary of State Richard Olney, after Senate rejection of an Anglo-American arbitration treaty in 1897: "...Senators have exhausted their ingenuity in devising amendments to the treaty. Before the treaty came to a final vote, the Senate brand had been put upon every part of it, and the original instrument had been mutilated and distorted beyond all possibility of recognition."

On two occasions the Supreme Court has sustained the power of the Senate to amend treaties. In 1869, in the case of *Haver v. Yaker*, the Court stated: "In this country a treaty is something more than a contract, for the Federal Constitution declared it to be the law of the land. If so, before it can become a law, the Senate in whom rests the power to ratify it, must agree to it. But the Senate are not required to adopt or reject it as a whole, but may modify or amend it." And in a 1901 opinion *(Fourteen Diamond Rings v. U.S.)* the Court said: "The Senate may refuse its ratification or make it conditional upon adoption of amendments to the treaty."

Probably the best known of recent Senate qualifications of U.S. international obligations is the Connally reservation to the compulsory jurisdiction clause of the statute of the International Court of Justice. In adhering to the UN Charter in 1945, the United States accepted membership in the Court. President Truman contended that the country should also accept compulsory jurisdiction under terms of the Court's statute, which excluded matters deemed to be within the domestic jurisdiction of any nation; and on July 31, 1946, the Senate took up a resolution to that effect.

Recalling fears which led to Senate refusal in 1935, after a decade of discussion, to approve adherence to the earlier World Court, some Senators objected to letting the International Court of Justice determine what matters might or might not be within U.S. jurisdiction. To obviate this possibility, Sen. Tom Connally (D Texas) proposed adding after a clause excluding "matters which are essentially within the domestic jurisdiction of the United States" the words "as determined by the United States." The Senate agreed to the Connally reservation on Aug. 2, 1946, by a 51-12 vote, in effect negating the U.S. commitment in principle; it then adopted the amended resolution by a 60-2 vote. Subsequent attempts to repeal the reservation have been unsuccessful.

When the Senate adopts a treaty amendment, the amendment, if it is accepted by the President and the

Legislative-Executive Coordination

Recurring claims of Congress and the Executive to dominance in foreign affairs have been reflected from time to time in uncertainty, ineffectiveness and instability in American foreign policies. In recognition of the need for more systematic collaboration between the President and Congress, various schemes for more effective coordination have been proposed.

Achievement of coordination between the two branches requres prior coordination within the Congress itself, in the view of many political scientists. With its basic division into two houses and further fragmentation of responsibility for foreign-policy matters among numerous committees, concerted action has been difficult at best.

Proposals advanced in recent years to achieve greater coordination within Congress have been aimed especially at action on national security policies and at means of facilitating a more rapid response in times of crisis. The types of proposals offered have differed with the proponent's view of the proper role of Congress in foreign-policy making. The more sweeping proposals have come from those who apparently believe that Congress at the very least should have an equal voice in execution as well as establishment of policies. Other advocates of change have been willing to leave the execution of policies to the Executive as long as Congress determines the policies. Still others simply have wanted to improve Congressional machinery so that it can respond to Presidential requests more adequately. The broader proposals all have seemed to have one element in common: they have been designed, in one way or another, to enable Congress to initiate foreign-policy proposals.

The most radical proposal for change would remove many of the obstacles to cooperation and coordination by abandoning the concept of separation of powers. Numerous political scientists at one time or another have advocated amending the Constitution to institute a parliamentary system of government like that of Great Britain. With the Executive and Legislative Branches virtually one and the same, most problems of coordination would evaporate, it is said.

Another proposal—which seems to have nearly universal appeal among political scientists—would provide for a more centralized leadership in Congress. Senate Majority Leader Lyndon B. Johnson (D Texas) went far down this road in the 1950s, but the structure he built was personal, not institutional. His successor, Mike Mansfield (D Mont.), has not followed the example.

In the House, leadership responsibilities have been largely dispersed since the revolt against Speaker "Uncle Joe" Cannon in 1910. Also, there is little likelihood that the political scientists' calls for greater reliance on party responsibility will be heeded. The kind of discipline demonstrated daily in Britain's House of Commons reflects the basic homogeneity of a small nation as well as the requirements of a parliamentary system of government.

Most of the other proposals have dealt with the way in which the Congress goes about its business. Probably the most frequent suggestion has been that committees should work together on foreign-policy decisions that cut across jurisdictional lines. Some have proposed creation of a National Security Committee that would replace the Armed Services, Foreign Relations and Appropriations Committees in each house, or take members from those Committees to serve on a non-legislative coordinating committee.

---

other parties to the treaty, changes it for all parties. A Senate reservation limits only the treaty obligation of the United States, although a reservation may be so significant that the other treaty parties may file similar reservations or refuse to ratify the treaty.

The Senate Foreign Relations Committee has identified four major forms which a treaty qualification may take.

• The Senate may consent to ratification and include its views or interpretations in a Committee report accompanying the treaty.

• Senate "understandings" or "interpretations" may be included in the resolution of consent. Such language would have no legal effect on the treaty if it did not substantially affect the treaty's terms or U.S. obligations. Under normal practice, the Executive Branch would inform the other treaty parties of the interpretations or understandings.

• The Senate may add a "reservation" to the resolution of consent, involving some change in obligations under the treaty. Again, other parties would be informed of the reservation.

• The Senate may amend the terms of the treaty itself, requiring new negotiations with the other parties.

From the point of view of the Executive Branch, Senate alteration of treaties has become an increasingly serious problem in view of a growing tendency to adjust international relations through multilateral treaties. Resubmission of an amended treaty to a number of foreign governments—any one of which may wish to alter other provisions of the treaty in view of U.S. changes—presents almost insuperable obstacles to final agreement. The substitution of reservations for amendments in recent years has not lessened the difficulty, for the Senate has demanded more and more formal recognition of such reservations.

Proposed Changes in Treaty Power

For more than 70 years attempts have been made to alter the treaty-making provisions of the Constitution. Most of the proposals have been to eliminate the two-thirds rule governing Senate action on treaties or to require consent to ratification by the House as well as the Senate. The Bricker Amendment of the 1950s, which sought to curtail the President's treaty power, was a marked exception to the pattern.

Following the War with Spain, two resolutions were introduced in the House of Representatives proposing a constitutional amendment giving the power of consent to a majority of the whole Senate. In 1920, amendments were offered in both houses stipulating that consent to ratification should be by majority vote of members present in the Senate.

Between 1919 and 1928, five resolutions were introduced in the lower house to let that body share in giving "advice and consent" in the making of treaties. As Democratic candidate for President in 1924, John W. Davis endorsed the plan to substitute a majority for a two-thirds vote. William Jennings Bryan, in a Jackson Day address in 1920, advocated associating the House with the Senate. An even more fundamental change was proposed in Congress in 1921 whereby certain treaties would have to be approved by popular vote.

During World War II, recollection of Senate rejection of the Treaty of Versailles and the League of Nations prompted a number of proposals to change the provisions for treaty ratification so as to reduce the possibility that new postwar arrangements for enforcement of world peace would be rejected. Josephus Daniels, Navy Secretary in the Cabinet of Woodrow Wilson, suggested in a 1942 speech that the Constitution be amended to provide for consent to ratification by majority vote of both chambers. Proposed amendments to carry out his suggestion were introduced the following year in the House. In the Senate in 1943 a proposed amendment was introduced to allow Senate consent by a simple majority.

In 1945, while the San Francisco conference was debating the Charter of the United Nations, destined for consideration by the Senate alone, the House took up a resolution (H J Res 60) by Hatton Sumners (D Texas) to amend the Constitution to require that "Treaties shall be made by the President by and with the advice and consent of both houses of Congress." Despite general agreement that the Senate never would agree to share its treaty power, the House on May 9 adopted the resolution by a 288-88 vote.

Long Controversy Over Bricker Amendment

During 1953 and 1954 (and briefly in 1956), Congress engaged in a heated debate on an amendment to the Constitution proposed by Sen. John W. Bricker (R Ohio) which would curb the Executive's foreign-policy powers. The Bricker amendment reflected fears that American adherence to various United Nations covenants and conventions, such as the genocide convention, would enhance Federal powers and possibly interfere with enforcement of state laws by reason of the constitutional provision making treaties the "supreme law of the land." The proposed amendment stemmed also from resentment at the tendency to substitute Executive agreements, not subject to ratification, for treaties requiring Senate consent. The controversy surrounding the amendment pitted a majority in Congress against the President and turned a highly technical legal question into a wide-ranging debate between "isolationists" and "one-worlders."

On Jan. 7, 1953, Sen. Bricker and 63 cosponsors (45 Republicans and 19 Democrats) introduced S J Res 1, the revised version of a proposed constitutional amendment introduced by Bricker and 58 cosponsors on Feb. 7, 1952. As revised, the proposed amendment read:

"1. A provision of a treaty which denies or abridges any right enumerated in this Constitution shall not be of any force or effect.

"2. No treaty shall authorize or permit any foreign power or any international organization to supervise, control, or adjudicate rights of citizens of the United States within the United States enumerated in this Constitution or any other matter essentially within the domestic jurisdiction of the United States.

"3. A treaty shall become effective as internal law in the United States only through the enactment of appropriate legislation by the Congress.

"4. All executive or other agreements between the President and any international organization, foreign power, or official thereof shall be made only in the manner and to the extent to be prescribed by law. Such agreements shall be subject to the limitations imposed on treaties or the making of treaties by this article.

"5. The Congress shall have power to enforce this article by appropriate legislation."

On Feb. 16, Sen. Arthur V. Watkins (R Utah) introduced a variation of Bricker's amendment as S J Res 43, which had been drafted by the American Bar Association. Its two sections covered all except the second of Bricker's provisions. Its text:

"1. A provision of a treaty which conflicts with any provision of this Constitution shall not be of any force or effect. A treaty shall become effective as internal law in the United States only through legislation which would be valid in the absence of a treaty. Executive agreements shall be subject to regulation by the Congress and to the limitations imposed on treaties by this article.

"2. The Congress shall have power to enforce this article by appropriate legislation."

During hearings on the two resolutions, Administration officials presented a solid front in opposition to the amendment. Secretary of State John Foster Dulles said the two resolutions "would deny to all treaties the force of law, making their enforcement depend on subsequent action of the Congress and, in the case of S J Res 43, also of the 48 states. They would subject the current day-to-day conduct of foreign affairs to impediments which might be stifling."

The crux of the case for a constitutional amendment, as put by ABA spokesmen, was that some 200 treaties proposed or in preparation by UN agencies and covering a wide range of political, social and economic matters contained provisions at variance with Federal or state law.

On June 15, the full Judiciary Committee, by a 9-5 vote, reported an amended version of S J Res 1 that, except for a slight change of wording, followed the text of S J Res 43. Its key provision still declared that "a treaty shall become effective as internal law only through legislation which would be valid in the absence of a treaty."

No further action was taken before Congress adjourned. Senate debate on S J Res 1 was resumed Jan. 27, 1954, and continued through Feb. 26. A final tally that day fell one vote short (60-31) of the two-thirds majority required for Senate approval. Before the next (84th) Congress adjourned July 27, 1956, it considered briefly the question of revising the Constitution's treaty provisions along the lines advocated by Bricker. But, faced with the absence of Administration support and the prospect of a long debate, Democratic leaders refused to call up Bricker's latest proposal (again designated S J Res 1), and it died without coming to a vote.

Treaties and the House

Deprived by the Constitutional Convention of a share in the treaty-making power, the House of Representatives appeared destined to carry out a secondary role. In fact, the revenue power of the House and its domination of the appropriation process have made the lower chamber an influential—if sometimes negative— partner in treaty making.

In the first Administration, when the Senate agreed to a treaty with the Dey of Algiers for release of American captives "provided the expense do not exceed $40,-000," President Washington announced that he would wait to conclude negotiations until the money had been appropriated by Congress. The Senate objected, urging that the money be taken from the Treasury or raised by borrowing. As reported in *Jefferson's Writings,* the Senators feared that "to consult the representatives on one occasion would give them a handle always to claim it." The House then passed a bill, in 1792, appropriating a stated sum to cover the expenses involved and the Senate consented to ratification of a treaty specifying the sum appropriated.

In considering appropriations for the Jay treaty, the House called for all documents in the case. Washington refused this request on the ground that "the assent of the House of Representatives is not necessary to the validity of a treaty." The House made the necessary appropriation in 1796 after long debate, but at the same time it adopted a resolution which said "it is the constitutional right and duty of the House of Representatives in all such cases to deliberate on the expediency or inexpediency of carrying such treaty into effect and to determine and act thereon as in their judgment may be most conducive to the public good."

Submission of commercial and reciprocity treaties has led to repeated assertions of authority by the House, frequently with support in the Senate. The reciprocity treaty with Great Britain in 1854 made its effectiveness dependent upon passage of the necessary laws. In 1883 the Senate amended a reciprocity convention with Mexico to provide that it should not come into force until the legislation called for had been passed by Congress, and this treaty never took effect for lack of action by the House. The House participated in the annexation of Texas and of Hawaii, which was accomplished by joint resolution—in the first case after a treaty of annexation had been defeated in the Senate, and in the second case when a two-thirds vote in the Senate seemed doubtful. *(See box on treaty alternatives.)*

In at least one case, House opposition prevented ratification of a treaty necessitating an appropriation. Shortly before the original treaty for the purchase of the Danish West Indies was submitted in 1867, the House resolved that "in the present financial condition of the country, any further purchases of territory are inexpedient, and this House will hold itself under no obligation to vote money for any such purpose unless there is greater necessity than now exists." In the debate it was said that this resolution was intended to serve notice on the King of Denmark that "this House will not pay for that purchase." When the treaty was sent to the Senate, no action was taken. When the islands were finally acquired 50 years later, the price had risen from $7,500,000 to $25,000,000.

Lobbying on Treaties

Treaties periodically are subject to much the same forms of lobbying as regular legislative measures. Consideration of the U.S.-Soviet Consular Convention of 1964 was marked by one of the largest mail and pressure campaigns in recent years. Despite the largely hostile lobbying, the Senate consented to ratification on March 16, 1967, by a 66-28 vote.

The intense "grassroots lobbying" campaign against the convention was led by the ultra-conservative, Washington-based Liberty Lobby, an organization set up in 1955 "for the purpose of reversing the dangerous trend toward socialization internally and to defeat the insidious effort to weaken our resistance to international Communism."

Other conservative groups working against the treaty included the Manion Forum, the Dan Smoot Report, the United Republicans of America, the National Review and the Mothers of American Servicemen of South Pasadena, Calif.

Senators complained that they were swamped by mail which was, to a large extent, generated by these organizations. Opposition to the treaty far outweighed support for it.

The Liberty Lobby used its large mailing list, claimed to include more than 170,000 names, for its campaign. Much of the Liberty Lobby support was attributed to a 16-panel comic strip entitled, "The Communist Next Door." The comic strip was described by Liberty Lobby as "a new technique to reach the voters...clear, direct, motivational." The strip included such statements as: "The most obvious danger from the treaty is provision for 'diplomatic immunity'....To give Soviet personnel complete immunity is to invite an increase in Red espionage...even sabotage...since the treaty forbids any inspection of any baggage or equipment brought in as 'diplomatic pouch.' " The strip showed a conspirator assembling a suitcase-size A-bomb and ended with the appeal: "How about it, folks? Help your two Senators by letting them know how you feel about the Soviet Consular Treaty. There isn't much time left, so write today." The appeal was so successful that even House Members, who do not vote on treaties, received numerous letters.

The Liberty Lobby also purchased advertising space in 27 newspapers around the country to reproduce the comic strip. At least 17 additional papers carried the ad placed by other individuals or groups. The Liberty Lobby ads were placed in newspapers in states where at least one Senator was already opposed to the treaty or where there was a good possibility to swing an uncommitted vote, according to a Lobby spokesman. The ads appeared for the most part in newspapers in the traditionally conservative Midwest and the South. They also appeared in states or cities with large populations that had close ties to the so-called "captive" nations of Eastern Europe.

Despite frequent assertions by the House of its right to refuse appropriations pledged in a treaty, it never has failed to make such appropriations once the treaty has been ratified by the Senate.

Alternatives to Treaties

From an early date, treaties have not been the sole means of concluding an agreement between the United States and a foreign country. International accords have been arranged through executive agreements, independently concluded by the Executive Branch. On occasion, Presidents have resorted to a joint resolution when Senate consent to ratification of a treaty has been in doubt.

Executive Agreements. The courts repeatedly have upheld the authority of the President to enter into agreements or compacts with other governments without consulting the Senate. Many executive agreements concern such routine matters as the regulation of fishing rights, private claims against another government and postal agreements. Occasionally, major U.S. diplomatic policies have been carried out by executive agreements, sometimes with controversial results as in the case of the World War II summit conference agreements at Cairo, Teheran, Yalta and Potsdam. Still other executive agreements have been concluded under specific delegations of power by Congress such as tariff agreements under the Reciprocal Trade Agreements Act of 1934 and wartime aid agreements under the Lend-Lease Act of 1941.

The first known executive agreements involved international postal arrangements made by the Postmaster General, acting under authority accorded by a 1792 Act of Congress. An early example of Executive treaty making was an 1817 agreement between President Monroe and Great Britain limiting naval armaments on the Great Lakes.

Joint Resolutions. A joint resolution, the functional equivalent of an act of Congress, has been used in place of a treaty from time to time when there was fear that a treaty would not command a two-thirds majority in the Senate. A joint resolution requires only a simply majority for approval, but it must be adopted by both houses of Congress.

After Senate rejection of a treaty for the annexation of Texas in 1844, annexation was accomplished through a joint resolution approved March 1, 1845. Hawaii was annexed as a territory by a joint resolution approved July 7, 1898. Following Senate rejection of the Treaty of Versailles, President Wilson in 1920 vetoed a joint resolution "declaring peace," but President Harding on July 2, 1921, signed a similar resolution. A separate peace treaty with Germany also was concluded in 1921.

Senate Action on Major Treaties

LEAGUE OF NATIONS

Senate opposition to ratification of the Treaty of Versailles was directed principally at the League Covenant, which formed an integral part of the treaty, although other provisions, especially the Shantung settlement which favored Japan at the expense of China, also aroused strong objections. It was upon the League issue, however, that

ratification hinged. The treaty was lost in the irreconcilable conflict that developed between a large group of Republicans led by Henry Cabot Lodge of Massachusetts, chairman of the Foreign Relations Committee, who refused to accept the treaty without drastic reservations, and a group of Democratic followers of President Wilson, who in turn would not accept the Lodge reservations.

On more than one occasion during the war Lodge had publicly advocated an international league for the maintenance of international peace, but his final position was that this proposal should be postponed, in order to give opportunity for adequate study, and that to attempt to make it a part of the treaty of peace with Germany would only lead to prolonged discussion. This viewpoint was given support by 39 Republican Senators and Senators-elect who signed a round robin, drafted by Sen. Philander C. Knox (R Pa.), which was offered by Lodge in the form of a Senate resolution on March 4, 1919, the closing day of the 65th Congress. The proposed resolution declared that "the constitution of the League of Nations in the form now proposed to the Peace Conference should not be accepted by the United States" and "that the negotiations on the part of the United States should immediately be directed to the utmost expedition of the urgent business of negotiating peace terms with Germany, . . . and that the proposal for a League of Nations to insure the permanent peace of the world should be then taken up for careful and serious consideration."

The round robin received an immediate reply from President Wilson. On the evening of March 4, the day before he sailed the second time for France, he told a large audience in the Metropolitan Opera House in New York City that when he finally returned with a completed treaty, that instrument would contain not only the League Covenant but "so many threads of the treaty tied to the Covenant that you cannot dissect the Covenant from the treaty without destroying the whole vital structure. The structure of peace will not be vital without the League of Nations, and no man is going to bring back a cadaver with him."

The Committee on Foreign Relations, composed of 10 Republicans and seven Democrats, held public hearings on the treaty from July 31 to Sept. 12, 1919. The majority report, written by Lodge, recommended ratification but proposed 45 amendments and four reservations. The minority report, signed by Sen. Gilbert M. Hitchcock of Nebraska and five other Democrats, declared against any amendments and deprecated reservations. A third report, submitted by Sen. Porter J. McCumber (R N.D.), referred to the League Covenant as "a mighty step in the right direction" and pointed out that "it still leaves to each nation the right of withdrawal, and depends to a great extent upon the moral sentiment of each nation to comply with its own obligations or the enforcement of such obligations upon a recalcitrant member."

Even before the Foreign Relations Committee submitted its reports, a division of the Senate into a number of factional groups was becoming apparent. At one extreme stood the group of "Irreconcilables" or "Bitterenders," led by Senators William E. Borah (R Idaho), Hiram W. Johnson (R Calif.) and James A. Reed (D Mo.). They were opposed to the treaty with or without reservations, Borah contending that "it really incorporates a scheme which, either directly or indirectly, greatly modifies our governmental powers." At the other extreme were the Administration Democrats led by Hitchcock, who lined up with the President in favoring unconditional ratification. Between these two extremes was the important group of "Reservationists," which included Lodge. There were also the "Mild Reservationists," including Senators Thomas J. Walsh (D Mont.), Frank B. Kellogg (R Minn.) and Mc-Cumber, who wanted the treaty accepted with slight alterations, and a small group, mostly Democrats, "who, however they voted, revealed in the Senate cloakrooms hostility to the President, to most of his policies, and to the treaty."

By the end of October the friends of the treaty, as represented by the Democrats and Mild Reservationists, had succeeded in defeating all amendments proposed by the Foreign Relations Committee. Amendments were opposed not only for their content but also because they would have required approval by all other signatories of the treaty—a virtually impossible accomplishment—whereas reservations applied only to the power which made them. It was after defeat of the amendments that the struggle for reservations was seriously begun. Inability to reach a compromise there defeated the treaty.

Article 10. Opposition to the League Covenant centered on Article 10, of which President Wilson himself was the author. This article read as follows:

"The members of the League undertake to respect and preserve as against external aggression the territorial integrity and existing political independence of all members of the League. In case of any such aggression or in case of any threat or danger of such aggression the Council shall advise upon the means by which this obligation shall be fulfilled."

The Irreconcilables feared that Article 10 would draw the United States into foreign wars at the bidding of the League of Nations, a fear likewise shared by the Reservationists, although their leader, Lodge, in an address on May 27, 1916, before the League to Enforce Peace, had said he thought "the next step . . . is to put force behind international peace." Outside the Senate, Article 10 was opposed by such eminent Republicans as Elihu Root and Charles E. Hughes. In letters written in June 1919, Root disapproved that section of the Covenant, although he did not oppose establishment of a League of Nations. In a letter of July 29 Hughes characterized Article 10 as "an illusory engagement." President Wilson, on the other hand, insisted that sacrifice of this article would be equivalent to a "knife-thrust at the heart of the Covenant."

Another fear raised by the League of Nations proposal was that it would deprive the United States of full liberty of action under the Monroe Doctrine. Both Root and Hughes felt that this country was not sufficiently protected by Article 21, which provided that "Nothing in this Covenant shall be deemed to affect the validity of international engagements, such as treaties of arbitration or maintenance of peace."

Lodge Reservations. The apprehension aroused by the League Covenant and the objections to that instrument and to other parts of the treaty were reflected in the 14 reservations finally incorporated in the Lodge resolution for consent to ratification. The resolution stipulated that ratification by the United States should not become effective until the reservations had been accepted, through an exchange of notes, by three of the four following powers: Great Britain, France, Italy and Japan. The reservations may be summarized as follows:

1. Safeguards right of withdrawal from the League by declaring that if notice is given under Article 1, the United States shall be sole judge of whether it has met the condition that a member, at time of withdrawal, must have fulfilled all its international obligations and all its obligations under the Covenant.

2. "The United States assumes no obligation to preserve the territorial integrity or political independence of any other country or to interfere in controversies between nations—whether members of the League or not—under the provisions of Article 10, or to employ the military or naval forces of the United States under any article of the treaty for any purpose, unless in any particular case the Congress...shall by act or joint resolution so provide."

3. No mandate to be accepted by the United States except by action of Congress.

4. "The United States reserves to itself exclusively the right to decide what questions are within its domestic jurisdiction and declares that all domestic and political questions relating wholly or in part to its internal affairs, including immigration, labor, coastwise traffic, the tariff, commerce, the suppression of traffic in women and children, and in opium and other dangerous drugs, and all other domestic questions, are solely within the jurisdiction of the United States and are not under this treaty to be submitted in any way either to arbitration or to the consideration of the Council or of the Assembly of the League of Nations, or any agency thereof, or to the decision or recommendation of any other power."

5. "The United States will not submit to arbitration or to inquiry by the Assembly or by the Council of the League of Nations...any questions which in the judgement of the United States depend upon or relate to its long-established policy, commonly known as the Monroe Doctrine; said doctrine is to be interpreted by the United States alone and is hereby declared to be wholly outside the jurisdiction of said League of Nations and entirely unaffected by any provision contained in the said treaty of peace with Germany."

6. Withholds assent to Shantung settlement and reserves full liberty of action in any controversy between China and Japan resulting therefrom.

7. No person shall represent the United States in the League Assembly or Council, or in any commissions or tribunals under League or treaty, until appointment has been provided for by Congress.

8. Congress must approve any regulation of or interference with German-American trade by the Reparation Commission.

9. United States shall not be obligated to contribute to League expenses until an appropriation available therefor has been made by Congress.

10. If the United States adopts any plan for limitation of armaments proposed by the Council under Article 8, "it reserves the right to increase such armaments without the consent of the Council whenever the United States is threatened with invasion or engaged in war."

11. "The United States reserves the right to permit, in its discretion, the nationals of a covenant-breaking state, as defined in Article 16 of the Covenant of the League of Nations, residing within the United States or in countries other than that violating said Article 16, to continue their commercial, financial, and personal relations with the nationals of the United States."

12. Safeguards rights of American citizens under articles of the treaty providing for settlement of private debts and property interests as between nationals of Allied and enemy states.

13. Withholds assent to articles concerning the International Labor Organization, unless Congress subsequently makes provision for representation therein.

14. "The United States assumes no obligation to be bound by any election, decision, report, or finding of the Council or Assembly in which any member of the League and its self-governing dominions, colonies, or parts of empire in the aggregate have cast more than one vote, and assumes no obligation to be bound by any decision, report, or finding of the Council or Assembly arising out of any dispute between the United States and any member of the League if such member or any self-governing dominion, colony, empire, or part of empire united with it politically has voted."

The reservations disclosed a determination on the part of their authors to prevent any encroachment on the powers of Congress, as well as any encroachment on the sovereignty of the United States. In carrying out that purpose, in the view of proponents of American membership in the League, the reservations went far beyond any necessary precautions. They were so distasteful to President Wilson that he wrote to Senator Hitchcock on Nov. 18, 1919, that in his opinion the Lodge resolution "does not provide for ratification but rather for nullification of the treaty."

Ratification Votes. The Lodge resolution was finally brought to a vote during the evening of Nov. 19, 1919, and twice defeated. On the first vote there were 39 yeas (35 Republicans and 4 Democrats) and 55 nays (13 Republicans and 42 Democrats). On a reconsidered vote ratification again failed with only 41 yeas (34 Republicans and 7 Democrats) as against 51 nays (13 Republicans and 38 Democrats). Without further debate the Senate proceeded to vote on a resolution of Sen. Oscar W. Underwood (D Ala.) for simple approval of the treaty without reservations of any kind. Consent to ratification was then withheld for the third time by a vote of 38 yeas (1 Republican and 37 Democrats) to 53 nays (46 Republicans and 7 Democrats). In this last count the 13 Republican Irreconcilables, who in the two previous votes had opposed ratification even with the Lodge reservations, were joined by the whole body of Reservationists. McCumber was the sole Republican to favor unconditional consent to ratification.

The treaty issue was revived in the second session of the 66th Congress, and another vote was taken on March 19, 1920. On this occasion there was no question of unconditional approval. The resolution before the Senate contained the original Lodge reservations, slightly revised but with no essential change. President Wilson still characterized them as amounting to a "sweeping nullification of the terms of the treaty," but shortly before the vote was taken Walsh, who had opposed the Lodge resolution in the preceding November, appealed to his colleagues to accept the reservations, since the treaty was too important to be lost. Although more than a dozen Democrats responded to this plea, consent to ratification was once more denied, this time by a vote of 49 yeas (28 Republicans and 21 Democrats) to 35 nays (12 Republicans and 23 Democrats). A majority had finally been obtained, but it lacked seven votes of the two-thirds required for treaty approval.

UNITED NATIONS

Mindful of the Senate's rejection of the League of Nations in 1919, the Roosevelt Administration had begun to court bipartisan support for the United Nations long before the Dumbarton Oaks meetings of August-October 1944 at which a draft charter was drawn up; Secretary of State Cordell Hull had assured Congressional leaders of both parties in 1943 that Congress would have the final say on U.S. participation in any world security organization. The eight-member delegation to the San Francisco conference, announced Feb. 13, 1945, was picked with an eye to the widest public support. Headed by Secretary of State Edward R. Stettinius Jr. (who had succeeded Hull Dec. 1, 1944), it included Hull; Senators Tom Connally (D Texas), chairman of the Foreign Relations Committee, and Arthur H. Vandenberg (R Mich.), a Committee member; Representatives Sol Bloom (D N.Y.) and Charles A. Eaton (R N.J.), chairman and ranking minority member of the House Foreign Affairs Committee; former Gov. Harold E. Stassen (R Minn.) and Miss Virginia Gildersleeve, Dean of Barnard College. John Foster Dulles, foreign policy adviser to Gov. Thomas E. Dewey of New York during the 1944 Presidential campaign, was named a principal adviser to the delegation.

Public discussion of the Charter was intense and widespread before and during the two-month conference, at which Vandenberg and Dulles played leading roles. In San Francisco on the day the conference ended, June 26, President Truman acclaimed the Charter as a declaration of "faith that war is not inevitable." In a personal appearance before the Senate July 2, he called for prompt ratification of the Charter and the annexed statute of the International Court of Justice. Said Truman: "The choice before the Senate is now clear. The choice is not between this Charter and something else. It is between this Charter and no Charter at all."

Following a week of hearings, the Senate Foreign Relations Committee on July 13 voted 21-1 to approve the Charter (Exec F, 79th Cong., 1st Session)—the lone dissenter being Hiram W. Johnson (R Calif.), ranking minority member. During Senate debate July 23-28, most of the discussion centered on Article 43, pledging members to "make available to the Security Council, on its call and in accordance with a special agreement or agreements, armed forces, assistance and facilities, including rights of passage, necessary for the purpose of maintaining international peace and security." Burton K. Wheeler (D Mont.) and others feared this would give the U.S. delegate "the war-making power," but the President assured the Senate on July 27 that any agreements under Article 43 would be sent to Congress for "appropriate legislation to approve them." Next day the Senate gave its two-thirds assent to the establishment of the United Nations, by the overwhelming margin of 89-2. Opposed were GOP Senators William Langer (N.D.) and Henrik Shipstead (Minn.); Hiram Johnson (who died Aug. 6) announced his opposition.

NATO

Following passage of the Vandenberg Resolution in 1948, which declared U.S. determination to exercise the right of individual or collective self-defense, President Truman directed the State Department to explore the question of regional security with Canada, Britain, France,

Belgium, the Netherlands and Luxembourg. By October, these seven countries had reached tentative agreement on a collective defense arrangement and had invited Norway, Denmark, Iceland, Italy and Portugal to join them. Negotiations were concluded April 4, 1949, when representatives of the 12 nations signed the North Atlantic Treaty in Washington "to unite their efforts for collective defense and for the preservation of peace and security."

The text reaffirmed support for the United Nations and for the peaceful settlement of disputes. It also pledged the signatories to work jointly for political, economic and social stability within the North Atlantic area, defined to extend from Alaska through the North Atlantic to the three French departments in Algeria. But its key provisions called for intensified self-help and mutual aid measures to defend the area and pledged that, in the event of an armed attack against one of the members, each of the others would come to its aid by taking "such action as it deems necessary, including the use of armed force, to restore and maintain the security of the North Atlantic area." The treaty also provided for establishment of a North Atlantic Council to draw up plans for concerted action, for the admission of other nations by unanimous invitation, and for the right of members to withdraw after 20 years.

President Truman sent the treaty (Exec L, 81st Cong., 1st Session) to the Senate April 12 and urged prompt approval. The key question that arose at once concerned the relationship between the treaty and the not-yet submitted military assistance program: would approval of the treaty commit Congress to vote for the latter? To clarify the matter, such Senators as Donnell (R Mo.), Jenner (R Ind.), Morse (R Ore.), Byrd (D Va.) and George (D Ga.) called for consideration of the two together. But the Administration refused, withholding its military aid proposals until action on the treaty had been completed.

Hearings by the Senate Foreign Relations Committee, beginning April 27, produced strong backing for the treaty by Secretary of State Dean Acheson, U.S. Representative to the UN Warren R. Austin, Secretary of Defense Louis A. Johnson, Army Chief of Staff Omar N. Bradley, former Under Secretaries of State William L. Clayton and Robert A. Lovett, and former Supreme Court Justice Owen J. Roberts. Former Vice President Wallace denounced the pact, saying it would destroy the chances for European recovery and entail costs of $20 billion for military aid. On June 6, the Committee voted unanimously to approve the treaty. Its report asserted that approval would not commit the Senate to approve the arms aid request and that the treaty did not give the President any powers "to take any action, without specific Congressional authorization," which he could not already take.

The Senate debated the treaty from July 5 to 20, with Senators Tom Connally (D Texas) and Arthur H. Vandenberg (R Mich.) carrying the burden of the defense. Sen. Robert A. Taft (R Ohio) announced that he would oppose ratification without a reservation disclaiming any obligation to arm Western Europe—a step he said would "promote war." Answering Taft was Sen. John Foster Dulles (R N.Y.), sworn in July 8 as the appointed successor to Sen. Robert F. Wagner (D N.Y.): "If the impression became prevalent that this country was turning its back on international cooperation, the results would be disastrous. Other free countries...would almost certainly fall. We would be encircled and, eventually, strangled ourselves."

On July 21, 1949, the Senate proceeded to vote, rejecting three reservations by large margins before approving the treaty. The first reservation—sponsored by Senators Kenneth S. Wherry (R Neb.), Taft, and Arthur V. Watkins (R Utah)—stated that nothing in the treaty would commit the signatories "morally or legally to furnish or supply arms" to the others. It was rejected, 21-74 (D 3-49; R 18-25). Watkins then proposed two other reservations, both of which disclaimed any intention to employ U.S. armed forces without the express approval of Congress. These were rejected, 11-84 and 8-87. The Senate then approved ratification of the North Atlantic Treaty, 82-13 (D 50-2; R 32-11). The only Senator not present was Allen J. Ellender (D La.), who supported ratification.

Ban on Nuclear Tests

The world's close brush with nuclear war in the 1962 Cuban missile crisis gave impetus to the continuing search for an agreement to stop nuclear testing. Such a step, it was generally believed, would help to stabilize the nuclear balance between the United States and the Soviet Union, discourage the proliferation of nuclear arsenals among other countries, and furnish a critical turning point in the arms race. Through four years of negotiations, however, the same stumbling block had prevented agreement: America's insistence on on-site inspection of suspected violations involving hard-to-detect underground tests, and the Soviet Union's refusal to accept such inspection on Russian soil by foreign observers. Late in 1962, however, the Soviets said they might accept two or three inspections a year, in addition to several unmanned "black-box" seismic detection stations.

The Americans, British and Soviets resumed private talks in January 1963 but soon reached an impasse regarding the number of on-site inspections to be permitted. The Soviets refused to accept more than three a year, while the United States insisted on a minimum of seven. Attention then shifted to the broader 17-nation disarmament negotiations in Geneva. There, on April 5, American and Soviet delegates agreed to establish a direct telegraphic "hot line" between the White House and the Kremlin as a precaution against the kind of accident or miscalculation that might have touched off a nuclear exchange during the Cuban missile crisis. Symbolizing a mutual concern for the prevention of nuclear war, the "hot-line" agreement was formally signed June 20.

In Washington, meanwhile, Senators Hubert H. Humphrey (D Minn.) and Thomas J. Dodd (D Conn.), together with 32 cosponsors, had introduced a resolution (S Res 148) May 27 urging the United States to seek agreement on a treaty banning atmospheric and underwater tests but not those conducted underground. Their proposal sidestepped the inspection issue, since it was generally believed that any clandestine tests in the other environments could be detected by national systems without the need for on-site verification. Two weeks later, in a June 10 speech at American University calling for re-examination of attitudes toward the Soviet Union and the Cold War, President Kennedy announced that "high-level discussions will shortly begin in Moscow looking toward early agreement on a comprehensive test ban treaty."

Under Secretary of State Averell Harriman represented the United States in the negotiations that began July 15 and led, with surprising swiftness, to the initialing on July 25 of a treaty banning all except underground tests. The text bound the signatories "to prohibit, to prevent, and not to carry out any nuclear weapon test explosion, or any other nuclear explosion at any place under its jurisdiction or control (a) in the atmosphere, beyond its limits including outer space, or under water including territorial water or high seas, or (b) in any other environment if such explosion causes radioactive debris to be present outside the territorial limits of the state under whose jurisdiction or control such explosion is conducted."

The treaty also pledged the parties "to refrain from causing, encouraging, or in any way participating in" any nuclear test anywhere else. It provided that amendments could be submitted by any signatory subject to the approval of each of the three original signatories and a majority of all parties to the treaty. It declared that the treaty would be of unlimited duration, but that any party could withdraw on three months' notice if it decided that its supreme interests were being jeopardized.

Kennedy's Message to Senate

President Kennedy sent the treaty (Exec M, 88th Cong., 1st Session) to the Senate Aug. 8, following its formal signature in Moscow Aug. 5 by the United States, Great Britain and the Soviet Union, with a message designed to answer the various arguments being voiced by certain political and military leaders against the treaty. The President asserted that it would "assure the security of the United States better than continued unlimited testing on both sides," since that would lead to the proliferation of nuclear weapons and increased danger. "The risks in clandestine violation...are far smaller than the risks in unlimited testing," he contended. The nation's nuclear might would be maintained, he promised, through continued research and development and underground tests, while "we will be ready to resume testing in the atmosphere if necessary." Mr. Kennedy concluded: "It is rarely possible to recapture missed opportunities to achieve a more secure and peaceful world. To govern is to choose; and it is my judgment that the United States should move swiftly to make the most of the present opportunity and approve the pending treaty."

Key Administration officials supported ratification before the Foreign Relations Committee Aug. 12-27. Secretary of State Dean Rusk said there were no "side arrangements, understandings or conditions of any kind" to the treaty, and he stressed that it did not affect the use of nuclear weapons in the event of war. Secretary of Defense Robert S. McNamara said the treaty would "at least retard Soviet progress and prolong the duration of our technological superiority" in nuclear weapons. Atomic Energy Commission Chairman Glenn T. Seaborg said he fully supported the treaty but hoped it would be modified eventually to permit tests above ground for peaceful purposes. Speaking for the Joint Chiefs of Staff, Chairman Maxwell D. Taylor said they had conditioned their approval on four "safeguards" agreed to by the Administration: continued underground testing, maintenance of weapon research facilities and programs, preparation for prompt resumption of atmospheric tests should the Soviets violate the treaty, and improvement of detection methods and intelligence on Sino-Soviet nuclear activities.

The burden of the case against the treaty was stated by Dr. Edward Teller, the physicist credited with development of the H-bomb. Teller called the treaty a "step away from safety and possibly...toward war." He argued that it

would retard U.S. development of an anti-ballistic missile defense; block development of high-yield bombs (where the Soviets were conceded to be ahead); inhibit checks on the vulnerability of U.S. missile systems to communications and radar "black-out" caused by atmospheric explosions; make it difficult to verify the "hardness" or invulnerability of American Minuteman missile sites; and do little to prevent the proliferation of nuclear capabilities. But several other scientists disputed Teller's views; it was impossible to develop a truly effective anti-missile defense, said Dr. Herbert F. York, formerly a research scientist in the Defense Department, because "the offense will always, and by a large margin, have the advantage over the defense."

On Sept. 3, the Foreign Relations Committee reported favorably on ratification, having found "the balance of risks weighted in favor" of the pact. But as Senate debate began Sept. 9, the Preparedness Investigating Subcommittee of the Senate Armed Services Committee issued a report based on secret hearings at which Dr. Teller and Gen. Thomas S. Power, chief of the Strategic Air Command, had persuaded the group that the treaty involved "serious—perhaps formidable—military and technical disadvantages to the United States." Two days later the President gave his "unqualified and unequivocal assurances" that cautionary steps demanded by the Joint Chiefs would be pursued and that the United States would maintain "strategic forces fully insuring that this nation will continue to be in a position to destroy any aggressor, even after absorbing a first strike by surprise attack."

Senate debate focused on a series of proposed reservations to the treaty, all of which came to a vote Sept. 23. By heavy bipartisan majorities, the Senate rejected a Barry Goldwater (R Ariz.) move to condition ratification on a complete, UN-inspected withdrawal of Soviet nuclear weapons and military personnel from Cuba, 17-75; a John G. Tower (R Texas) reservation making ratification contingent upon full payment of all Soviet arrears to the UN, 11-82; and another Tower move to delay the effective date of the treaty until it was revised to provide for on-site inspections, 16-76. An "understanding" that the treaty would not inhibit the use of nuclear weapons in armed conflicts, proposed by Tower and Russell B. Long (D La.), was tabled, 61-33 (D 46-16; R 15-17). There was little opposition, however, to adding a preamble to the resolution of approval reasserting the Senate's right to pass on any future amendments to the treaty. Proposed by Armed Services Chairman Richard B. Russell (D Ga.), the preamble was approved 79-9. On Sept. 24 the Senate consented to ratification of the Treaty of Moscow by a vote of 80-19 (D 55-11; R 25-8), or 14 more than the required two-thirds majority.

The Soviet Union ratified the pact the next day, and it went into effect Oct. 10, 1963; in short order, more than 100 additional nations signed the treaty. But two major powers refused to do so: France, which had opposed any test ban because of its determination to achieve full status as an independent nuclear power; and Communist China, which was bent on the same goal and coincidentally locked in dispute with the Soviets over Khrushchev's policy of "peaceful coexistence" with the West. On Oct. 16, 1964, the Chinese entered the nuclear "club" by setting off their first fission explosion just as Khrushchev was being ousted from power in Moscow. Although anticipated by the United States and discounted in advance, the Chinese event was viewed by President Johnson as a "sad and serious" fact that would tempt other states "to equal folly."

The War Power

The war power—like the treaty power—is divided between the Congress and the President. And, no less than the treaty power, it is the subject of recurring controversy and debate involving rival claims by the Executive and Legislative Branches.

Article II, Section 2 of the Constitution provides that "The President shall be Commander-in-Chief of the Army and Navy of the United States, and of the militia of the several states, when called into the actual service of the United States."

Article I, Section 8, provides that "The Congress shall have power....to declare war, grant letters of marque and reprisal, and make rules concerning captures on land and water; to raise and support armies...; to provide and maintain a navy; to make rules for the government and regulation of the land and naval forces; to provide for calling forth the militia to execute the laws of the Union, suppress insurrections and repel invasions"; and "to provide for organizing, arming and disciplining the militia, and for governing such part of them as may be employed in the service of the United States, reserving to the states respectively, the appointment of the officers and the authority of training the militia according to the discipline prescribed by Congress."

In the past, prior to an exercise by the Legislative Branch of its constitutional power to declare war, objections to undertaking hostilities against a foreign power have invariably been raised by some Members of Congress. After a declaration of war, Congressional opposition has generally subsided—except in the case of wars which were manifestly unpopular, at least in certain sections of the country—and Congress has done what was within its power to contribute to an early victory. During wars which enjoyed the general support of the people, the Legislative Branch has usually acquiesced in requests by the Executive Branch for action on measures deemed necessary for prosecution of the war; it has seldom shown any disposition to invade the President's domain of absolute control over actual military operations.

Declared and Undeclared Wars

From other historical precedents, a new issue arose in the years following World War II. Historians recognized as "wars" nine conflicts through 1945 which involved U.S. armed forces, but only five of the nine had been accompanied by declarations of war. Congress declared war in the War of 1812, the Mexican War, the Spanish-American War, World War I and World War II. No declaration was made or requested in the Naval War with France (1798-1800), the First Barbary War (1801-05), the Second Barbary War (1815), or the various Mexican-American clashes of 1914-17.

To protect the nation's interests or meet its far-flung world commitments, the United States on several occasions since 1945 has ordered combat troops into action abroad solely on Presidential authority. American combat troops were involved in full-scale war in Korea from 1950 to 1953, and have been similarly involved in Vietnam since 1965, without a declaration of war. In two other instances,

Lebanon in 1958 and the Dominican Republic in 1965, U.S. combat troops were used to help maintain conditions of political stability in countries threatened by or undergoing civil strife. Unlike some earlier undeclared wars, the conflicts in Korea and Vietnam were prolonged and exacted a high cost in U.S. casualties and national resources. They evoked sharp criticism from Congress and large sections of the public.

Questioning of President's War Actions

The Johnson Administration's continual escalation of U.S. involvement in the Vietnam war led various Members of Congress to conclude that the President had exceeded his constitutional powers. These Members were most

---

Congress vs. the President

Following is a recent example of a Congressional attempt to clarify the war-making powers of the Congress and the President. The text is a copy of H J Res 1355, introduced Aug. 13, 1970, by Rep. Clement J. Zablocki (D Wis.) and 15 cosponsors.

Resolved by the Senate and House of Representatives of the United States of America in Congress assembled, That the Congress reaffirms its powers under the Constitution to declare war. The Congress recognizes that the President in certain extraordinary and emergency circumstances has the authority to defend the United States and its citizens without specific prior authorization by the Congress.

Sec. 2. It is the sense of Congress that whenever feasible the President should seek appropriate consultation with the Congress before involving the Armed Forces of the United States in armed conflict, and should continue such consultation periodically during such armed conflict.

Sec. 3. In any case in which the President without specific prior authorization by the Congress—

(1) commits United States military forces to armed conflict;

(2) commits military forces equipped for combat to the territory, airspace or waters of a foreign nation, except for deployments which relate solely to supply, repair, or training of United States forces, or for humanitarian or other peaceful purposes; or

(3) substantially enlarges military forces already located in a foreign nation;

the President shall submit promptly to the Speaker of the House of Representatives and to the President of the Senate a report, in writing, setting forth—

(A) the circumstances necessitating his action,

(B) the constitutional, legislative, and treaty provisions under the authority of which he took such action, together with his reasons for not seeking specific prior congressional authorization;

(C) the estimated scope of activities; and

(D) such other information as the President may deem useful to the Congress in the fulfillment of its constitutional responsibilities with respect to committing the Nation to war and to the use of United States Armed Forces abroad.

Sec. 4. Nothing in this joint resolution is intended to alter the constitutional authority of the Congress or the President, or the provisions of existing treaties.

concerned that the President had acted almost entirely on his own with only the vaguest of Congressional authorization by the Gulf of Tonkin resolution *(see below)*; the President, on the other hand, considered the resolution entirely adequate authority.

The result of this increasing Congressional concern was the introduction in the Senate in 1967 of a resolution which came to be known as the National Commitments Resolution, declaring the sense of the Senate that no future commitment of U.S. forces to hostilities abroad should be made without "affirmative action" by Congress. The resolution was adopted by the Senate June 25, 1969, by a 70-16 vote.

The debate concerned more than U.S. involvement in the Vietnam war. The basic question was how the power of the United States as a world leader should be exercised and controlled. It was at the heart of the role of the modern Presidency and the division of authority between the Presidency and Congress. It also had a very practical side beyond the immediate question of Vietnam: the State Department said the United States was definitely committed to the defense of 42 nations as a result of treaties and agreements given approval by the Senate. Defense agreements, agreements of cooperation, policy statements, and U.S. military installations in some 30 foreign countries added an unknown number of nations to the list of those that the United States might feel obligated to defend.

In 1971, limitation of the President's war powers gained the support of Chairman John C. Stennis (D Miss.) of the Senate Armed Services Committee. Stennis on May 9 announced his sponsorship of a bill that would authorize the President to order the armed forces into combat, without a declaration of war, only to repel an attack on the United States or to protect Americans abroad, and the forces would have to be withdrawn in 30 days unless Congress approved the President's action. The proposed legislation would apply only to future conflicts.

Use of the War Power

At the time the American Constitution was framed, the war-making power in all other countries was vested in the Executive. When the Convention at Philadelphia took up this question, at the session of Aug. 17, 1787, Pierce Butler, a delegate of South Carolina, proposed that the power to make war be granted to the President, "who will have all the requisite qualities and will not make war but when the Nation will support it." Elbridge Gerry of Massachusetts thereupon objected that he "never expected to hear in a republic a motion to empower the Executive alone to declare war." George Mason of Virginia also opposed "giving the power of war to the Executive, because not safely to be trusted with it." He was "for clogging rather than facilitating war."

Charles Pinckney of South Carolina contended that the proceedings of the House of Representatives were too slow and that it would be "too numerous for such deliberations." He accordingly suggested that the war power be placed in the Senate, which would be "more acquainted with foreign affairs and most capable of proper resolutions." The Convention nevertheless conferred the power on Congress as a whole. It changed the phrase "to make war," as reported by the Committee of Detail, to "to declare war," so as to leave to the President the power to repel sudden attacks but not to commence war.

The innovation of placing the war power in the Legislative rather than the Executive Branch of the Government was hailed by Jefferson as a valuable restraint upon exercise of the power. He wrote to Madison, Sept. 6, 1789: "We have already given, in example, one effectual check to the dog of war, by transferring the power of letting him loose from the Executive to the Legislative body, from those who are to spend to those who are to pay." Madison himself wrote: "The Constitution supposes what the history of all governments demonstrates, that the Executive is the branch of power most interested in war and most prone to it. It has accordingly, with studied care, vested the question of war in the Legislature."

The early Presidents made little use of such war powers as they had received. John Adams went so far in 1798, at the time of the undeclared naval war with France, as to divest himself of the title of Commander-in-Chief and confer it upon George Washington. The Senate approved that action unanimously. Three years later, President Jefferson forbade the Navy to attack the Tripoli pirates on the ground that Congress had not declared war. Alexander Hamilton ridiculed Jefferson for inaction. He said the Constitution meant that it was "the peculiar and exclusive province of Congress, when the nation is at peace, to change that state into a state of war." But "when a foreign nation declares or openly and avowedly makes war upon the United States, they are then by the very fact already at war and any declaration on the part of Congress is nugatory; it is at least unnecessary."

First Declaration of War, 1812

During the War of 1812, the first declared war in which the United States engaged after the formation of the Federal Union, Congress made no attempt to usurp any of the functions of the President as Commander-in-Chief. On the contrary, the Legislative Branch failed so completely to carry out even its own assigned functions that the successful waging of hostilities was made almost impossible.

President Madison's annual message of 1811 listed the familiar trade grievances against Great Britain and called upon Congress to "put the United States into an armor and an attitude demanded by the crisis..." Congress agreed on a bill for raising 25,000 regular soldiers in January 1812, but debate on a militia bill, authorizing the President to accept the services of 50,000 volunteers, bogged down on constitutional issues. Under the Constitution, the President could call such men into service for any one of three purposes—to execute the laws, to put down insurrection, or to repel invasion. It was well understood, however, that the proposed volunteers were to accompany the regulars on an invasion of Canada, and most Members felt that it would be unconstitutional to use them outside the limits of the United States. The question was never settled, and the bill, as approved by Madison in February, said nothing about use of the volunteers beyond the national boundaries—which proved a disastrous mistake.

Although the intention to invade Canada was openly proclaimed—and despite the fact that 25,000 regular troops probably could not be raised in time to render service for at least a year and the 50,000 volunteers probably could not be used in Canada—legislation looking to the organization of a provisional army of 20,000 men for immediate service was voted down in the House.

The nation, as a whole, remained apathetic toward the idea of actual hostilities. By June 1, 1812, when Madison asked for a declaration of war, less than half of the hoped-for 25,000 regulars had enlisted and adequate equipment was available for only 10,000 soldiers. Nevertheless, on June 3 the House voted, 79 to 49 for war; the Senate took similar action on June 18 by a vote of 19 to 13.

In accordance with the law, the Secretary of War issued a call for the militia, but the governors of Massachusetts, Rhode Island and Connecticut refused to authorize use of their troops. On July 6, 1812, Congress adjourned. Federalist Members now openly denounced the war as being against the wishes of the people. Within a month the American army under General Hull had surrendered at Detroit, almost without firing a shot. The garrison at Fort Dearborn had been massacred by Indians. A large part of Van Rensselaer's force of New York militia had been slaughtered on the Canadian side of the Niagara River, within sight of other militiamen who remained on the United States side and refused to move into foreign territory.

The 13th Congress met in special session in May 1813, and opposition to the Administration was immediately evident in the Senate. Daniel Webster offered a series of resolutions designed to embarrass Madison; numerous appointments by the President were rejected; and Josiah Quincy reported a resolution of the Massachusetts legislature characterizing the war as one "waged without justifiable cause..."

Congress reassembled in temporary quarters in the burned city of Washington in September 1814. Little hope was held that success would attend the negotiations then being carried on by peace commissioners at London. Yet with the army still at only about half its paper strength, and with enlistments falling off, Congress failed to agree to a conscription bill proposed by James Monroe, then Secretary of War as well as Secretary of State. The welcome Treaty of Ghent was signed by the American commissioners on Dec. 24, 1814, and was consented to by a unanimous Senate on Feb. 16, 1815.

Unpopular Mexican War, 1846

The War with Mexico was distinctly unpopular among large numbers of the people, particularly in the North. Recurring expressions in Congress of opposition to the prosecution of the war were in part a reflection of that antiwar sentiment.

President Tyler had long desired annexation of Texas but was balked by the Senate until after the 1844 Presidential election in which Henry Clay, who opposed annexation without the consent of Mexico, was defeated by James Polk, an ardent expansionist. On March 1, 1845, three days before Polk was inaugurated, annexation was accomplished by adoption of a joint resolution in the 28th Congress.

In the spring of 1846, Gen. Zachary Taylor led his army into a disputed strip of territory claimed by Texas but occupied exclusively by Mexicans. A clash between Mexican soldiers and a reconnoitering party of Americans occurred on April 25, but it was uncertain whether the scene of the skirmish was on Texan or Mexican soil. A few American soldiers were killed. On May 11, two days after the news of the fighting reached Polk, he sent a war message to Congress declaring that Mexico had passed the boundary of the United States, had invaded American territory and had shed American blood upon American soil. "War exists," he said, "and notwithstanding all our efforts to avoid it, exists by the act of Mexico herself."

The House at once adopted, 173 to 14, a joint resolution declaring that war existed by the act of Mexico, appropriating $10 million, and authorizing a call for 50,000 volunteers. Some opposition, in part sincere and in part partisan, was offered by northern Whigs; Joshua Giddings of Ohio condemned the proceedings as "a war against an unoffending people, without adequate or just cause, for the purpose of conquest..." Somewhat stronger opposition was voiced in the Senate, but the resolution was adopted there, May 12, by a 40-2 vote.

In the elections of 1846, the Democrats retained control of the Senate, but the House was lost to the Whigs. Moreover, as General Taylor marched victoriously through Mexico, the war was being widely denounced in the North and was proving far from universally popular in the South. By the time Congress met in December 1846, Members had gathered new courage to question the war's justification and purpose. Polk's annual message, devoted almost wholly to a defense of the war, was deeply resented by the Whigs for in it the President charged that those opposing his policies were giving aid and comfort to the enemy. Thereafter, although the necessary military measures were passed as they came up, debate was concerned less with the merits of particular measures than with the causes, the justice, and the necessity of the war itself.

Whigs asserted that it was a "President's war." In reply they were called "Mexicans," and their position was likened to that of the Federalists during the War of 1812, but the Whigs stood firm and expressed their dislike of the war in numerous resolutions. Polk soon informed Congress that although Mexico was obviously defeated, she had refused to accept a proffered peace. It was necessary, therefore, to "persuade" Mexico by levying forced contributions upon her cities and by seizing certain lands as an indemnity. Whig newspapers now clamored for withdrawal of United States troops from Mexico and stoppage of the war, and called on Congress to withhold supplies. From the people of the Eastern, middle, and Western states came scores of petitions praying that the war be ended.

The House was especially sensitive to the growing discontent. Abraham Lincoln offered his "Spot Resolutions," all of which ignored the current status of the war and were intended to probe the original causes of the conflict. A resolution presented in the House late in 1847 stated that the war should not be further prosecuted for any purpose. Another Member moved that a committee of five from the Senate and five from the House consult with the President as to the best method of ending the war. Numerous other resolutions of similar purport were introduced, though most of them did not come to a vote. However, a resolution offered in January 1848, by George Ashmun of Massachusetts, which declared the war to have been "unnecessarily and unconstitutionally begun by the President of the United States," was adopted in the House by a margin of four votes. The House adopted also a resolution calling upon the President for information as to the objectives of the war and the exact nature of the proposed terms of peace. This request was refused by Polk. On Feb. 23, the President sent the peace treaty with Mexico to the Senate, which consented to ratification March 10, 1848, by a vote of 38 to 14.

Neither the opposition of a considerable section of the population, nor the resultant "obstructionist tactics" of certain Members of Congress hampered the war effort; all necessary war measures survived the opposition. The enemy forces were so inconsiderable that no extraordinary requests had to be made of the Legislative Branch. If the United States had suffered military reverses comparable to those in the War of 1812, and requiring the passage of drastic measures by Congress, it is possible that the Whig opposition might have forced far-reaching alterations in the war plans of the advocates of expansion.

Pressure for War with Spain, 1898

War with Spain over the independence of Cuba was forced on President McKinley in 1898 by the strong expansionist sentiment in Congress and in certain sections of the press. Two years earlier, McKinley's predecessor, Grover Cleveland, had succeeded in averting a similar result only by defying the Congress. Early in 1896, a concurrent resolution according belligerent rights to the Cuban insurgents had been adopted in both houses by large majorities. After the Presidential election in November, won by McKinley on a platform calling for the independence of Cuba, a resolution granting recognition was offered in Congress. Secretary of State Olney at once declared to the press that the resolution, if adopted, "can probably be regarded only as an expression of opinion by the eminent gentlemen who vote for it." He added:

"The power to recognize the so-called Republic of Cuba as an independent state rests exclusively with the Executive. A resolution on the subject...is inoperative as legislation, and is important only as advice of great weight voluntarily tendered to the Executive regarding the manner in which he shall exercise his constitutional functions.... The resolution will be without effect and will leave unaltered the attitude of this Government toward the two contending parties in Cuba."

A few days later, Cleveland reportedly told a Congressional delegation that if the Congress declared war on Spain he would refuse to mobilize the Army. In view of Cleveland's intransigent attitude, Congress took no action on the resolution recognizing Cuba's independence.

After McKinley's inauguration, relations with Spain steadily worsened in spite of a series of diplomatic concessions by that country. Following the sinking of the *Maine* in the harbor of Havana in February 1898, it became clear that nothing short of war would satisfy Congressional belligerence. On April 11, McKinley submitted a message to Congress proposing forcible intervention in Cuba. Although Spain had already capitulated to American demands for Cuban autonomy, a resolution declaring that the people of the island "are and of right ought to be free and independent," and authorizing the President to employ the land and naval forces of the United States to expel Spain from Cuba, was adopted in the Senate by a vote of 42 to 35 and in the House, 310 to 6, on April 25. McKinley immediately ordered a blockade of Havana, and the war had begun.

The brevity of the war, the ease with which victory was won and the relatively popular nature of the conflict, both among Members of Congress and among the public, worked to insure a satisfied and wholly cooperative attitude by Congress toward the Executive Branch of the Government. However, opposition to the acquisition of the Philippines led to a month's debate on the treaty of peace, which was consented to April 6, 1899, by the Senate, 57-27, with only one vote to spare.

Congress and World War I

Following the outbreak of war in Europe in August 1914, President Wilson urged upon the people a policy of neutrality. Commencement of German submarine warfare in February 1915, and the sinking of the Lusitania the following May 7 with the loss of 124 American lives, fanned public debate over the twin issues of neutrality and belligerency. Later in 1915 Wilson swung toward limited preparedness—not far enough to satisfy Secretary of War Lindley M. Garrison, yet too far for Secretary of State William Jennings Bryan, both of whom resigned. Wilson's re-election in 1916 was due at least in part to his having kept the country out of war, but the situation changed early in 1917. Two days after Germany resumed unrestricted submarine warfare on Feb. 1, the United States broke off diplomatic relations. Publication of the intercepted Zimmermann telegram, offering pledges of German alliance with Mexico in return for slices of U.S. territory after a German victory, followed on March 1.

While pressure mounted in Congress to require a national referendum before a declaration of war, Wilson ordered the arming of American merchant ships. On April 2, addressing a joint session of Congress, he asked for a declaration of war. In subsequent debate, Sen. Robert M. LaFollette (R Wis.) said that until the President and his supporters were willing to submit the question to the people, "it illy becomes us to offer as an excuse for our entry into the war the unsupported claim that this war was forced upon the German people by their government 'without their previous knowledge or approval.'" Despite such objections, on April 6 the House by a 373-50 vote and the Senate by an 82-6 vote adopted a resolution providing "that the state of war between the United States and the Imperial German Government which has been thrust upon the United States is hereby formally declared."

Extensive Use of Presidential Powers

Woodrow Wilson had no need during World War I to resort to actions beyond the law, but he amassed greater powers than those employed by any previous war President. Many of the extraordinary powers exercised by President Wilson came by delegation from Congress. However, he drew also upon his constitutional powers to implement plans for which Congress denied or delayed legislative authorization.

A week after war was declared, the President used his authority as Commander-in-Chief to create by executive order the Committee on Public Information, under whose direction a system of voluntary news censorship was established and various government publicity services were organized. On April 28, 1917, again acting as Commander-in-Chief, he imposed stringent cable censorship, which was later extended to other forms of communication with foreign countries under authority of the Trading With the Enemy Act of Oct. 6, 1917.

Wilson appointed Herbert Hoover as Food Administrator on May 19, 1917. Then, on June 12, two months before passage of the Food and Fuel Control Act of Aug. 10, 1917, the President gave Hoover "full authority to undertake any steps necessary" for the conservation of food resources. The functions of the War Industries Board, created originally by the Council of National Defense, were expanded and vested almost exclusively in its chairman, Bernard M. Baruch, by a letter of the President to Baruch on March 4, 1918. By an executive order of May 28, 1918, Wilson formally established the War Industries Board "as a separate administrative agency to act for me and under my direction." Although created without statutory authority, the board was able to exert wide

Lincoln's Improvised War Powers

In the early days of the Civil War, Lincoln used not only the war powers at his disposal but also some of the powers reserved to Congress. Without Congressional authorization, he issued a proclamation, May 3, 1861, increasing the size of the Regular Army and the Navy and calling for 80,000 volunteers. Moreover, he ordered 19 vessels added to the Navy and directed the Secretary of the Treasury to advance $2 million to unauthorized persons to cover military and naval requisitions. When Congress convened July 4, 1861, the President declared that some of his emergency measures, "whether strictly legal or not, were ventured upon under what appeared to be a popular demand and a public necessity, trusting then, as now, Congress would readily ratify them."

Congress validated Lincoln's actions by adopting a resolution Aug. 6, 1861, providing that "All the acts, proclamations, and orders of the President respecting the Army and Navy of the United States, and calling out or relating to the militia or volunteers...are hereby approved and in all respects made valid...as if they had been issued and done under the previous express authority and direction of the Congress of the United States."

The Supreme Court, in a group of rulings involving the *Prize Cases* (67 U.S. 635, 1863), gave its blessing to another of Lincoln's improvised war powers. Early in the war, the President had proclaimed a blockade of Confederate ports to prevent the South from selling cotton to England and importing supplies. Vessels attempting to run the blockade were seized and condemned as "prizes"—that is, they were confiscated for having defied the President's order. The owners sued for redress on the ground that no war had ever been declared between North and South.

The Court observed that declarations of war were almost unknown in rebellions and insurrections. The President, charged with seeing that the laws be faithfully executed and armed with the powers of Commander-in-Chief, was entitled to treat the rebellious states as belligerents, to attack them, and to blockade them. The Court said:

"By the Constitution, Congress alone had the power to declare a national or foreign war....(The President) has no power to initiate or declare a war either against a foreign nation or a domestic state....If a war be made by invasion of a foreign nation, the President is not only authorized but is bound to accept the challenge without any legislative act. And whether the hostile party be a foreign invader or states organized in rebellion, it is none the less a war although the declaration be 'unilateral.'"

On the other hand, the Court took a dim view of Lincoln's order authorizing various military commanders to suspend the writ of habeas corpus. Chief Justice Roger Brooke Taney, sitting as a Federal circuit judge at Baltimore in 1861, ordered John Merryman released from military detention to stand trial in civil court. If the President had the power to suspend habeas corpus, Taney argued, "the people of the United States are no longer living under a government of laws, but every citizen holds life, liberty and property at the will and pleasure of the army officer in whose military district he may happen to be found." The Supreme Court supported Taney in *Ex parte Milligan,* a case decided in 1866 (71 U.S. 22). It ruled that civilians might be tried by military tribunal only where civil courts could not function because of invasion or disorder.

---

control over industry; behind its "requests" stood the President's power to commandeer factories or withhold fuel and transportation priorities.

The sweeping control of the economy acquired by Wilson during the war constituted, in the opinion of Rexford G. Tugwell, "the most fantastic expansion of the Executive known to American experience." The numerous powers conferred upon the President by Congress included power:

To take over and operate enemy vessels for use in war.

To regulate and prohibit exports.

To take over and operate the railroads.

To regulate priorities in transportation.

To regulate by a licensing system the importation, manufacture, storage, mining or distribution of any necessaries.

To requisition foods, fuels, and other supplies necessary for any public use connected with national defense.

To fix a reasonable guaranteed price for wheat based upon a statutory minimum.

To fix the price of coal and regulate the method of its production, sale, shipment, distribution and storage.

To prohibit or license transactions in the United States by foreign insurance companies.

Congress was willing to delegate the foregoing powers to the President because it recognized that modern warfare required singleness of direction, unity of command,

and coordination of vital resources. After the war ended, new Republican majorities in Congress reasserted the prerogatives of the Legislative Branch. Feelings on Capitol Hill were ruffled by Wilson's failure to include Senators in the American delegation to the Paris Peace Conference. The Senate twice refused, in 1919 and again in 1920, to consent to ratification of the Treaty of Versailles. *(For details, see Treaty Power above.)*

Roosevelt and World War II

The prevailing mood of isolationism in Congress and the country during the later 1930s sharply limited President Roosevelt's freedom of action in foreign affairs. This mood found expression in such laws as the Neutrality Acts of 1935 and 1937, which prohibited shipments of arms, ammunition or implements of war to belligerent nations. A resolution introduced by Rep. Louis L. Ludlow (D Ind.) in 1935 and again in 1937 would have restricted the war powers of Congress as well as of the President. The resolution proposed a constitutional amendment to require submission of a declaration of war to a popular referendum. Although the Ludlow resolution was pried from committee by a discharge petition, Dec. 14, 1937, a motion to bring it to the House floor for a vote failed to carry.

Following Roosevelt's proclamation of a limited national emergency on Sept. 8, 1939, a week after the outbreak of war in Europe, the United States began to drift from neutrality to engagement. At a special session, Sept.

Declarations of War in 1941

Following are the texts of the war resolutions adopted by Congress against Japan, Germany and Italy in World War II.

Japan

Whereas the Imperial Government of Japan has committed unprovoked acts of war against the Government and the people of the United States of America: Therefore be it

Resolved, etc., That the state of war between the United States and the Imperial Government of Japan which has thus been thrust upon the United States is hereby formally declared; and the President is hereby authorized and directed to employ the entire naval and military forces of the United States and the resources of the Government to carry on war against the Imperial Government of Japan; and, to bring the conflict to a successful termination, all of the resources of the country are hereby pledged by the Congress of the United States.

Germany

Whereas the Government of Germany has formally declared war against the Government and the people of the United States of America: Therefore be it

Resolved, etc., That the state of war between the United States and the Government of Germany, which has thus been thrust upon the United States, is hereby formally declared; and the President is hereby authorized and directed to employ the entire naval and military forces of the United States and the resources of the Government to carry on war against the Government of Germany; and, to bring the conflict to a successful termination, all of the resources of the country are hereby pledged by the Congress of the United States.

Italy

Whereas the Government of Italy has formally declared war against the Government and the people of the United States of America: Therefore be it

Resolved, etc., That the state of war between the United States and the Government of Italy which has thus been thrust upon the United States is hereby formally declared; and the President is hereby authorized and directed to employ the entire naval and military forces of the United States and the resources of the Government to carry on war against the Government of Italy; and, to bring the conflict to a successful termination, all of the resources of the country are hereby pledged by the Congress of the United States.

21-Nov. 3, 1939, Congress revised the Neutrality Act to repeal the arms embargo and allow sale of munitions to belligerents on a cash-and-carry basis. An act of June 15, 1940, authorized military assistance to any Latin American republic that requested it. Almost three months later, on Sept. 3, 1940, the President announced that the United States had entered into an agreement under which Great Britain would receive 50 "over-age" (but reconditioned and recommissioned) destroyers in return for the right to lease certain sites for U.S. naval and air bases on British territory in the western Atlantic. The Attorney General defended the constitutionality of the transaction on the ground that the President's power as Commander-in-Chief enabled him to "dispose" the armed forces of the United States.

Roosevelt cited the same power in 1941 as his authority for ordering American troops to Greenland and Iceland; Congress was not consulted on either occasion. In a special message to Congress, July 7, 1941, the President asserted that the occupation of Iceland by Germany would constitute a serious threat against Greenland and North America, against North Atlantic shipping and against the steady flow of munitions to Britain. While the establishment of bases in Greenland and Iceland was not an act of war, it reflected this nation's hostility toward Germany, which declared war on the United States four days after Japan's attack on Pearl Harbor on Dec. 7, 1941.

Existence of a state of war with Japan was formally declared by Congress on Dec. 8. Existence of a state of war with Germany and Italy was declared on Dec. 11. The resolution declaring war against Japan (S J Res 116) was adopted by the Senate 82 to 0 and by the House 388 to 1. The one negative vote was cast by Jeannette Rankin (R Mont.), who had given a similar vote on the declaration of war against Germany in 1917.

The war declaration against Germany (S J Res 119) was adopted by the Senate 88 to 0 and by the House 393 to 0; the declaration against Italy (S J Res 120) by the Senate 90 to 0 and by the House 399 to 0. Miss Rankin voted "present" on these declarations.

Entry of this country into World War II was accompanied by concentration of virtually all war power in the President's hands. Under his power as Commander-in-Chief and using powers delegated by Congress, Roosevelt created many new emergency agencies and made them responsible to him rather than to existing departments or independent regulatory agencies. By V-J Day, no fewer than 29 war agencies were grouped under the Office for Emergency Management, which had been created by an administrative order of May 25, 1940.

Commitment to Undeclared War in Korea

The war in Korea began with a massive attack on South Korea by North Koreans on June 25 (Korean time), 1950, and continued for three years at a cost of more than 150,000 U.S. casualties. Late on June 26 (U.S. time) President Truman ordered American air and sea forces in the Far East to aid South Korea, a day before the UN Security Council called on UN members for help in repelling the attack. The President on June 30 ordered ground troops into Korea and sent the 7th Fleet to act as a buffer between China and Formosa.

Truman never asked Congress for a declaration of war in Korea, and he waited until Dec. 16, 1950—six months after the outbreak of hostilities—to proclaim the existence of a national emergency. In defense of this course, it was argued that the Russians or Chinese or both had violated post-World War II agreements on Korea, and that emergency powers authorized during World War II could still be applied.

Congress did not mount a serious challenge to Truman's war powers until 1951. At issue then was the President's authority to dispatch troops to Korea and to Western Europe. Sen. Robert A. Taft (R Ohio) opened a three-month-long "great debate" on Jan. 5, 1951, by asserting that Truman had "no authority whatever to commit American troops to Korea without consulting Congress and without Congressional approval." Moreover, Taft said, the President had "no power to agree to send American troops to fight in Europe in a war between the members of the Atlantic Pact and Soviet Russia."

The debate revolved principally around the troops-to-Europe issue. It came to an end on April 4, when the Senate adopted two resolutions approving the dispatch of four divisions to Europe. One of the resolutions stated that it was the sense of the Senate that "no ground troops in addition to such four divisions should be sent to Western Europe...without further Congressional approval."

President Truman hailed the action as a "clear endorsement" of his troop plans, saying "there has never been any real question" about the United States doing its part in the defense of Europe. But he ignored the Senate's claim to a voice in future troop commitments; neither resolution had the force of law.

In essence, the "great debate" had confirmed both the President's power to commit U.S. forces without prior Congressional approval and the decision to defend Western Europe on the ground.

Policy Resolutions as War Authority

Despite the "great debate's" confirmation of Presidential war power, Presidents since Truman in most cases have sought approval from Congress—from the House of Representatives as well as the Senate—when ordering U.S. forces into action. Reliance on such approval in the form of a joint resolution has provoked some Congressional criticism. It has been contended that the resolutions in effect have acted as blank checks to support Presidential war-making. Additional criticism was voiced in Congress when Under Secretary of State Nicholas deB. Katzenbach asserted in 1967 that the Tonkin Gulf Resolution of 1964 was "the functional equivalent" of a declaration of war. Katzenbach made the assertion in testimony before the Senate Foreign Relations Committee during a study of U.S. commitments to foreign powers.

President Eisenhower asked Congress Jan. 24, 1955, for advance approval of the use of American armed force in the event of a Communist attack on Formosa or the nearby Pescadores Islands. However, Eisenhower sent troops to Lebanon in July 1958 strictly on his own authority. In a special message to Congress July 15, he said this action was taken to protect American lives and "to assist the Government of Lebanon in the preservation of Lebanon's territorial integrity and independence, which have been deemed vital to U.S. national interests and world peace."

President Kennedy, responding to Soviet threats to Allied rights in West Berlin, asked Congress on July 26, 1961, for authority to call up Ready Reservists and to extend the enlistments of men already on active duty. Such authority was granted in a joint resolution signed by the President Aug. 1. In September 1962, after learning that Russia was shipping missiles to Cuba, President Kennedy again asked for Congressional authority to call up reservists. Congress granted the request and in October went further by adopting a resolution authorizing the President to take whatever steps were necessary to oppose the deployment of Soviet missiles in Cuba and to defend Latin America against Cuban aggression or subversion. President Kennedy in May 1961 had sent 100 specially trained jungle fighters to South Vietnam in an "advisory" capacity.

President Johnson dispatched additional U.S. troops to South Vietnam in 1964. Following reported attacks on U.S. destroyers in the Gulf of Tonkin, the President ordered a retaliatory air strike and then asked Congress for a resolution of support. Congress promptly adopted the Tonkin Gulf resolution.

In April 1965, President Johnson ordered U.S. troops to the Dominican Republic following the outbreak of political disturbances in Santo Domingo. The Administration later suggested that the danger of a Communist takeover in that country justified the increasingly large involvement of U.S. troops. Mr. Johnson, again without Congressional approval, sent transport aircraft to the Congo in 1964 and 1967. In November 1964, U.S. planes were used to land Belgian paratroopers at Stanleyville to rescue white hostages.

President Nixon ordered U.S. troops into Cambodia in the spring of 1970 to "clean out" border sanctuaries used by North Vietnamese forces at war in South Vietnam. Announced in an April 30 television address to the nation, without prior Congressional approval or consultation, the President's move provoked a volatile reaction in Congress and across the nation.

Commitment to Defend Formosa

On Jan. 18, 1955, Communist forces seized the offshore island of Ichiang, 210 miles north of Formosa, and seemed prepared to invade the nearby Tachen islands. The situation led President Eisenhower to ask Congress, in a special message Jan. 24, for explicit authority to use American armed forces to protect Formosa, the Pescadores Islands and "related positions and territories." It was essential to U.S. security that Formosa "should remain in friendly hands," the President asserted. While "authority for some of the actions which might be required" was clearly his as Commander-in-Chief, he said, Congress should "make clear the unified and serious intentions" of the nation "to fight if necessary." Enactment of the proposed resolution, he added, would "clarify present policy" and help prevent the Communists from "misjudging our firm purpose and national unity."

What neither the President nor Secretary of State Dulles attempted to clarify was their intent regarding Quemoy, Matsu and the other offshore islands. The President said that "we must be alert to any concentration or employment of Chinese Communist forces obviously undertaken to facilitate attack upon Formosa, and be prepared to take appropriate military action." This implied that the President might commit American forces to repel an invasion of Quemoy—the message, essentially, that the Administration wished to give Peking. To a number of Democrats, however, the offshore islands—unlike Formosa—clearly belonged to mainland China, and the question of their disposition, they believed, was beyond the scope of legitimate U.S. security interests. They feared that the Nationalists, in their efforts to regain the mainland, would use this "fatal ambiguity" over the offshore islands to maneuver the United States into a war with Communist China.

But Democratic leaders in Congress hastened to comply with the President's request despite some misgivings. H J Res 159, authorizing him to "employ the armed forces of the United States as he deems necessary" in the defense of Formosa, was reported by the House Foreign

Affairs Committee the same day, unanimously and without amendment. The House adopted it Jan. 25, 410-3, after hearing Speaker Rayburn say that the resolution added nothing to the constitutional powers of the President and should not be taken as a precedent.

On Jan. 26 the Senate Foreign Relations and Armed Services Committees, sitting jointly, voted 27-2 to report the resolution, after rejecting amendments to limit the President's authority. In floor debate Jan. 26-28, Senators Morse (D Ore.) and Flanders (R Vt.) warned of a "preventive war," while Senators Kefauver (D Tenn.), Humphrey (D Minn.) and Lehman (D N.Y.) attacked the resolution's ambiguity regarding the offshore islands. But the Senate, by lopsided margins, rejected three restrictive amendments: by Langer (R N.D.), to prohibit intervention in defense of any island within 12 miles of the Chinese mainland, 3-83; by Kefauver, to substitute language emphasizing UN responsibility for Formosa, 11-75; and by Lehman, to limit the President's authority to Formosa and the Pescadores, 13-74. The Senate then passed H J Res 159, Jan. 28, 85-3. Voting "nay" were Morse, Langer, and Lehman. Sen. Duff (R Pa.) expressed a widely held view in saying that the resolution was "clearly based upon a calculated risk that Russia is unwilling at this time to undertake an all-out war, and since Red China's action is predicated upon Russia's approval or veto, that consequently Red China is not ready at this time for all-out war."

Eisenhower Doctrine in Middle East

At the end of 1956, Secretary of State Dulles was convinced that the Suez crisis had left a dangerous power vacuum in the Middle East into which the Soviets would move unless deterred by the United States. As author of the 1955 Formosa Resolution, Dulles believed that a similar expression of Congressional support for Presidential discretion was needed to convince the Soviets of U.S. determination to block any advance into the Middle East. On Jan. 5, 1957, the President appeared before a joint session of Congress to urge support for a declaration promptly dubbed the Eisenhower Doctrine. Its essence was put as follows:

"In the situation now existing, the greatest risk, as is often the case, is that ambitious despots may miscalculate. If power-hungry Communists should either falsely or correctly estimate that the Middle East is inadequately defended, they might be tempted to use open measures of armed attack. If so, that would start a chain of circumstances which would almost surely involve the United States in military action. I am convinced that the best insurance against this dangerous contingency is to make clear now our readiness to cooperate fully and freely with our friends of the Middle East in ways consonant with the purposes and principles of the United Nations."

To accomplish this, Mr. Eisenhower asked that he be authorized to extend economic aid to nations in the area "dedicated to the maintenance of national independence," to give military aid to nations requesting it and "employ the armed forces of the United States as he deems necessary" to protect the area against "overt armed aggression from any nation controlled by international Communism," and to spend for these purposes $200 million in previously appropriated funds. He announced that he was sending former Chairman James P. Richards (D S.C.) of the House Foreign Affairs Commit-

tee (who had just retired) to the Middle East to "explain the cooperation we are prepared to give."

The Eisenhower Doctrine was greeted with little enthusiasm by Republicans and with some asperity by Democrats. Adlai Stevenson and other Democrats decried the President's request for a "blank check" and complained that it skirted the basic issues of Arab-Israeli hostility and control over the Suez Canal. Former Secretary of State Dean Acheson called the Eisenhower Doctrine "vague, inadequate and not very useful." It was "not a statement of policy," he said, "but an invitation to devise one."

In hearings before the House Foreign Affairs Committee and the combined Senate Foreign Relations and Armed Services Committees during January, Secretary Dulles defended the Administration's draft resolution and urged quick action. Unless the United States moved promptly, he said, "it is our definite belief that this area is very likely to be lost." He defined the Middle East as the area between Libya and Pakistan, Turkey and the Sudan. To the complaints of Senate Majority Leader Lyndon B. Johnson (D Texas) and others that his case rested on generalities with little specific information, Dulles replied: "If we have to pinpoint everything we propose to do, this program will not serve its purpose. If Congress is not willing to trust the President to the extent he asks, we can't win this battle."

Faced with this argument, most Members were unwilling to withhold a vote of confidence. The House Committee on Jan. 25 reported the requested bill with minor amendments limiting to $30 million the amount of economic aid to one country, specifying the right of Congress to terminate the program, and asking the President to work through the UN "to the greatest extent practicable." Fearing more substantive amendments from the floor, the Committee insisted on a closed rule which the House adopted June 30 over strong protests from both sides of the aisle, 262-146 (D 118-95; R 144-51). Then, bearing out the comment of Rep. James Roosevelt (D Calif.) that rarely had there been a bill "which has so few friends that will get so many votes," the House passed H J Res 117, 355-61 (D 188-35; R 167-26).

The Senate's skepticism about Administration policy was indicated when the Foreign Relations and Armed Services Committees voted 30-0, four days later, for a complete review of U.S. policy in the Middle East since 1946. But on Feb. 14 the Committees reported the Administration resolution, amended to state that the United States was prepared to use its armed forces "if the President determines the necessity thereof," and to require 15 days' notice to Congress of intent to use any of the funds authorized for economic aid.

The Senate debated the measure sporadically for 12 days, rejecting a number of amendments but adding an amendment by Mansfield (D Mont.) directing the President to support the UN Emergency Force in maintaining the Suez truce. On March 5 the Senate adopted the amended version of H J Res 117, 72-19 (D 30-16; R 42-3). Action was completed when the House on March 7 agreed to the Senate's amendments, 350-60.

Resolution on Berlin

Unlike other postwar resolutions authorizing the President's use of armed forces to defend certain nations or geographical areas, the Berlin Resolution of 1962 (H Con Res 570) originated in Congress instead of the Administration. Also, unlike the others, it merely expressed the

Commitments Under Congressional Resolutions

Congress has adopted five resolutions since 1945 authorizing the President's use of armed forces to defend certain geographical areas. Following are key passages from four of the resolutions and the complete text of the Tonkin Gulf resolution:

Formosa Straits Resolution

Resolved by the Senate and the House of Representatives of the United States of America in Congress assembled, That the President of the United States be and he hereby is authorized to employ the Armed Forces of the United States as he deems necessary for the specific purpose of securing and protecting Formosa and the Pescadores against armed attack, this authority to include the securing and protection of such related positions and territories of that area now in friendly hands and the taking of such other measures as he judges to be required or appropriate in assuring the defense of Formosa and the Pescadores....

Eisenhower Middle East Doctrine

The President is authorized to undertake, in the general area of the Middle East, military assistance programs with any nation or group of nations of that area desiring assistance. Furthermore, the United States regards as vital to the national interest and world peace the preservation of the independence and integrity of the nations of the Middle East. To this end, if the President determines the necessity thereof, the United States is prepared to use armed forces to assist any such nation or group of such nations requesting assistance against armed aggression from any country controlled by international communism: *Provided,* That such employment shall be consonant with the treaty obligations of the United States and with the Constitution of the United States.

Cuban Resolution

Resolved... That the United States is determined—

(a) to prevent by whatever means may be necessary, including the use of arms, the Marxist-Leninist regime in Cuba from extending, by force or the threat of force, its aggressive or subversive activities to any part of this hemisphere;

(b) to prevent in Cuba the creation or use of an externally supported military capability endangering the security of the United States; and

(c) to work with the Organization of American States and with freedom-loving Cubans to support the aspirations of the Cuban people for self-determination.

Berlin Resolution

Resolved... That it is the sense of the Congress:

(a) that the continued exercise of United States, British, and French rights in Berlin constitutes a fundamental political and moral determination;

(b) that the United States would regard as intolerable any violation by the Soviet Union directly or through others of those rights in Berlin, including the right of ingress and egress;

(c) that the United States is determined to prevent by whatever means may be necessary, including the use of arms, any violation of those rights by the Soviet Union directly or through others, and to fulfill our commitment to the people of Berlin with respect to their resolve for freedom.

Tonkin Gulf Resolution

Whereas naval units of the Communist regime in Vietnam, in violation of the principles of the Charter of the United Nations and of international law, have deliberately and repeatedly attacked United States naval vessels lawfully present in international waters, and have thereby created a serious threat to international peace;

Whereas these attacks are part of a deliberate and systematic campaign of aggression that the Communist regime in North Vietnam has been waging against its neighbors and the nations joined with them in the collective defense of their freedom;

Whereas the United States is assisting the peoples of Southeast Asia to protect their freedom and has no territorial, military or political ambitions in that area, but desires only that these peoples should be left in peace to work out their own destinies in their own way: Now, therefore, be it

Resolved by the Senate and House of Representatives of the United States of America in Congress assembled, That the Congress approves and supports the determination of the President, as Commander-in-Chief, to take all necessary measures to repel any armed attack against the forces of the United States and to prevent further aggression.

SEC. 2. The United States regards as vital to its national interest and to world peace the maintenance of international peace and security in Southeast Asia. Consonant with the Constitution of the United States and the Charter of the United Nations and in accordance with its obligations under the Southeast Asia Collective Defense Treaty, the United States is, therefore, prepared, as the President determines, to take all necessary steps, including the use of armed force, to assist any member or protocol state of the Southeast Asia Collective Defense Treaty requesting assistance in defense of its freedom.

SEC. 3. This resolution shall expire when the President shall determine that the peace and security of the area is reasonably assured by international conditions created by action of the United Nations or otherwise, except that it may be terminated earlier by concurrent resolution of the Congress.

sense of the Congress, lacking the force of law. The resolution was an outgrowth of the 1961 Berlin crisis, which followed erection of the Berlin Wall and led President Kennedy to call up reservists.

H Con Res 570 expressed the sense of Congress that the United States was determined to prevent by whatever means might be necessary, including the use of arms, any Soviet violation of Allied rights in Berlin, "including those of ingress and egress." It affirmed the continued right of the United States to remain in Berlin, pursuant to agreements on four-power rights entered into at the end of World War II. The resolution said it was the purpose of the United States to encourage and support the unification of a democratic Germany.

Congressional objection to the resolution came chiefly from Republicans, who criticized it for failing to mention the Berlin Wall and for not delineating Allied rights in Berlin.

The resolution was adopted Oct. 5 by a 312-0 roll-call vote of the House. During House debate Clement J. Zablocki (D Wis.), sponsor of the resolution, said the Executive Branch had stood up firmly to the Soviet Union on Berlin, and "the only voice that has not been officially heard on this issue is the voice of the U.S. Congress." He said the resolution was designed to let the Soviet Union "know that our nation stands united behind the Administration's firm policy on Berlin."

The Senate Foreign Relations Committee reported an almost identical resolution, but the Senate substituted the House resolution and adopted it by voice vote on Oct. 10.

Definition of Policy on Cuba, 1962

Fidel Castro's open avowal of his attachment to Communism, late in 1961, set the stage for a meeting of the Organization of American States Jan. 31, 1962, at which resolutions were adopted expelling Cuba from the OAS and the Inter-American Defense Board, suspending all arms trade with Cuba, and pledging cooperation in countering Communist subversion in the hemisphere. But the U.S.-led effort to isolate Cuba was paralleled by an increasing flow of Soviet-bloc military as well as economic aid to Castro, and by midsummer political pressure was mounting in Washington for a blockade, an invasion or some other form of direct action against Cuba.

At issue were the kinds and quantities of Soviet military deliveries. Sen. Kenneth B. Keating (R N.Y.) and other Republicans, citing Cuban refugee sources, asserted the presence of Soviet missiles and troops. President Kennedy acknowledged, Sept. 4, that missiles had been delivered, but he said they were short-range weapons of a defensive character. On Sept. 13, the President declared that Soviet arms shipments to Castro "do not constitute a serious threat to any other part of this hemisphere" and that "unilateral military intervention on the part of the United States cannot currently be either required or justified." But he added that "if at any time the Communist buildup in Cuba were to endanger or interfere with our security in any way...or if Cuba should ever attempt to export its aggressive purposes by force or the threat of force against any nation in this hemisphere or become an offensive military base of significant capacity for the Soviet Union, then this country will do whatever must be done to protect its own security and that of its allies."

With a mid-term election approaching, the Administration's wait-and-see attitude became a campaign issue.

On Sept. 7 Minority Leaders Sen. Everett McKinley Dirksen (R Ill.) and Rep. Charles A. Halleck (R Ind.) proposed authorizing the President to use the armed forces to "meet the Cuban problem." Mr. Kennedy swiftly asked for more general authority—similar to that granted after the 1961 Berlin crisis—to call up reservists during the Congressional recess to deal with challenges "in any part of the free world," and the request was quickly granted. But other moves were afoot to commit the United States to some specific course of action against Cuba, and to head off such moves the Administration endorsed a joint resolution modeled on the President's Sept. 13 statement.

As reported Sept. 19, S J Res 230 declared U.S. determination to prevent—with arms if necessary—the Marxist-Leninist regime in Cuba from extending its subversive activities to any part of the hemisphere or the creation in Cuba of an externally supported military capability endangering U.S. security. The Senate adopted the resolution next day, 86-1, with Sen. Winston L. Prouty (R Vt.) opposed on the ground that it was not strong enough. House Republicans voiced the same complaint and moved to insert a provision urging the President to "implement and enforce the Monroe Doctrine"—a euphemism meaning that the Soviet presence in Cuba was already such as to justify direct action. But the motion was rejected on a party-line vote of 140-251 (D 3-238; R 137-13), and the House adopted S J Res 230 on Sept. 26 without change, 384-7, with Republicans voicing all the "nays."

Tonkin Gulf Resolution

Following reported torpedo attacks by North Vietnam PT boats on American destroyers patrolling the Gulf of Tonkin on Aug. 2 and Aug. 4, 1964, President Johnson ordered a retaliatory air strike on their bases that destroyed or damaged 25 boats. On Aug. 5 the President asked Congress to adopt a resolution to "give convincing evidence to the aggressive Communist nations, and to the world as a whole, that our policy in Southeast Asia will be carried forward, and that the peace and security of the area will be preserved."

On Aug. 7, both chambers adopted the resolution (H J Res 1145) by overwhelming majorities—414 to 0 in the House and 88 to 2 in the Senate. The resolution (Joint Resolution To Promote the Maintenance of International Peace and Security in Southeast Asia) recorded Congressional support and approval of the "determination of the President...to take all necessary measures to repel any armed attack against the forces of the United States and to prevent further aggression." The resolution went on to say: "Consonant with the Constitution and the Charter of the United Nations and in accordance with its obligations under the Southeast Asia Collective Defense Treaty, the United States is, therefore, prepared, as the President determines, to take all necessary steps, including the use of armed force, to assist any member or protocol state of... (SEATO) requesting assistance in defense of its freedom."

The meaning of the Tonkin Gulf resolution became a source of intense debate as the Vietnam war grew in scope and as Members of Congress who had supported the resolution became increasingly disillusioned with the progress of the war. Many argued that the resolution did not commit the United States to massive participation in the war. Sen. John C. Stennis (D Miss.) rejected Secretary of State Rusk's defense of the resolution in 1966 as a grant of authority for U.S. action in the war. During hearings before the Preparedness Investigating Subcommittee,

Commager on the War Power

In March 1971, historian Henry Steele Commager testified before the Senate Foreign Relations Committee in support of proposals to limit the war-making powers of the President. Excerpts from his testimony follow:

Great questions of constitutional law are great not because they are complicated legal or technical questions, but because they embody issues of high policy, of public good, of morality. We must consider the problem of the Presidential authority to make war not merely in the light of constitutional precedents but in the light of wisdom and justice....

Let us then turn from the legal and constitutional considerations to more persuasive considerations—considerations, perhaps, of historical experience, of experience not as precedents but as—in the famous words of Lord Bolingbroke—"philosophy teaching by examples."

In 1967, Under Secretary Nicholas Katzenbach assured this Committee that "history has surely vindicated the wisdom of the flexibility of the conduct of our foreign affairs." Two years later the distinguished Senator from Wyoming (Gale W. McGee) stated, in his minority report on S 85 (S Res 85, the "national commitments" resolution adopted by the Senate in 1969), that "the decision-making process may be reduced by events to a single day, or even hours. On more than one occasion the time allotted by crisis incidents to those who must make the decisions has been less than the time it would take to assemble a quorum of the Congress."

We must face squarely the issues raised by Mr. Katzenbach and Sen. McGee: that, after all, history has vindicated the use of the Presidential powers in the realm of war making and that time has been and is of the essence. Has history in fact vindicated the use of armed forces by Presidents? Have Presidents been well advised—again in the light of history—to bypass Congress in using American armed forces overseas? Would consultation with the Congress, would even second thoughts, have made a difference detrimental to national, or world, interests?

I shall not rehearse for you the long list of episodes here but comment on them in passing. Was it really of vital importance that Gen. Jackson pursue the Seminoles and hang Arbuthnot and Ambrister?

Would the fate of Texas have been different had Polk consulted the Congress before launching a war: had he done so he might have escaped the name which has clung to him through history—"Polk the Mendacious." Was it really essential to bombard Greytown in 1854—would we do that now? Grant himself learned what a mistake it was to send troops to the Dominican Republic, for a Senate, perhaps more strong-minded than some later Senates, refused to back him up or allow him to go through with his plans for annexation. Was McKinley wise to commit 5,000 troops to the invasion of China in 1900 and would we do this today in a comparable situation? Our commitment to the provisions of the constitution of the Organization of American States is perhaps sufficient commentary on the wisdom of our many military interventions in the Caribbean, and President Wilson's resort to the ABC Conference—which rescued us from an ugly situation in Mexico—sufficient commentary on the wisdom of the Pershing expedition into Mexico. Once again we may ask, would we do this now? The hapless Abrams was sentenced to jail for distributing leaflets criticizing the Archangel and Siberian Expeditions: at the time he had only the consolation of being the occasion for one of the greatest of all Justice Holmes' opinions. If he were living now, he might have the dubious consolation of knowing that almost everyone agrees with his argument: certainly we have paid a high price in the long-range enmity of the Soviet for that particular folly. Clearly a strong case can be made out for FDR's destroyer-bases exchange and for extending protection to Greenland and Iceland, but is it conceivable that the Congress would have denied him the right to carry through these programs?

If we turn to the many examples of Presidential war making in the past 20 years we are, I submit, impressed by the fact that in almost every instance the Congress was actually in session and available for consultation: thus the Korean intervention, the landing of troops in Lebanon, the Bay of Pigs, the occupation of the Dominican Republic by President Johnson and the successive series of forays into Vietnam, Cambodia and Laos.

I have, to be sure, omitted consideration of Lincoln's use of the Executive power to meet the crisis of secession. Whether Lincoln was wise not to call the Congress into session for four months is still debated: perhaps it can be said that the use of Executive authority to put down a domestic insurrection rests on somewhat stronger constitutional arguments than those used to justify the use of force against China in 1900 or Vietnam in 1964.

There is one further observation that is relevant and may be instructive. Almost every instance of the use of Presidential force in the past has been against small, backward and distraught peoples: the situation today. Call the roll of the victims of Presidential application of force in the past: Spanish Florida, Honduras, Santo Domingo, Nicaragua, Panama, Haiti, Guatemala, a China torn by civil war, a Mexico distraught by civil war, a Russia and a Vietnam riven by war. It is a sobering fact that Presidents do not thus rush in with the weapons of war to bring Britain, France, Italy, Russia or Japan to heel. ...Does it really comport with the honor and dignity of a great nation to indulge its Chief Executive in one standard of conduct for the strong and another for the weak?

I confess that I do not think this record justifies Mr. Katzenbach's rosy view of the use of Presidential authority in this arena of foreign affairs, nor do I find a single instance that bears out Sen. McGee's assertion that "on more than one occasion the time allotted by crisis...has been less than the time it would take to assemble a quorum of the Congress."

Stennis declared: "...you stand on mighty thin ice if you rely on the Tonkin Gulf resolution as a constitutional basis for this war."

Disagreement over the meaning of the resolution surfaced again in 1967 during hearings on U.S. commitments before the Senate Foreign Relations Committee. Under Secretary of State Nicholas deB. Katzenbach described the resolution as the "functional equivalent" of a declaration of war. "What could a declaration of war have done that would have given the President more authority and a clearer voice of the Congress than that did?" Katzenbach asked rhetorically. Katzenbach also maintained that in "limited wars," such as Vietnam, a declaration of war was "inappropriate."

Sen. Albert Gore (D Tenn.) rejected Katzenbach's view. "I did not vote for the resolution with any understanding that it was tantamount to a declaration of war," he said. Sen. Charles H. Percy (R Ill.) and Bourke B. Hickenlooper (R Iowa) expressed doubt that the resolution would have been adopted if it had been known that it would lead to large-scale U.S. military action.

In the Foreign Relations Committee's 1969 report accompanying the National Commitments Resolution, Chairman J. W. Fulbright (D Ark.) said that "in adopting the (Tonkin Gulf) resolution Congress was closer to believing that it was helping to prevent a large-scale war by taking a firm stand than that it was laying down the legal basis for the conduct of such a war." Taking issue with Katzenbach's description of the resolution as a "functional equivalent" of a declaration of war, Fulbright concluded: "The burden of the Under Secretary's remarks seems to have been first, that the Gulf of Tonkin resolution was not a declaration of war but its 'functional equivalent,' and, second, that declarations of war are inappropriate when the nation's purposes are 'limited' and in any case are 'outmoded in the international arena.' The Committee has difficulty reconciling these various observations with each other, much less divining their basis in the Constitution....It is obvious that the question of authority to commit the United States to war is in need of clarification."

In the summer of 1970 the Senate twice voted to repeal the Gulf of Tonkin resolution—on June 24 by attaching a repeal amendment, by a roll-call vote of 81-10, to the so-called Military Sales bill (HR 15628), and a second time on July 10, by adopting a separate repealer, in the form of a Senate concurrent resolution (S Con Res 64), by a roll-call vote of 57-5. Congress on Jan. 2, 1971, cleared HR 15628, with the repeal provision intact, thus enacting it into law. S Con Res 64 never was reported from the House Foreign Affairs Committee.

Authorizations and Appropriations

Development of massive foreign-aid spending—starting with World War II lend-lease—gave Congress a power in foreign affairs not anticipated by the framers of the Constitution.

In almost every instance, the proposals for aid to other countries required consent of Congress to the expenditures. As a result, the House of Representatives, for the first time in its history, shared equal responsibility with the Senate in a fundamental, continuing effort to chart the course of the country's international relations.

Foreign aid—comprised essentially of economic and military assistance programs—became a basic tenet of American policy. For the most part, Congress endorsed the aid proposals advanced by successive postwar Administrations. Much of the continuing Congressional support for foreign aid was ascribed to the authority exercised by the President as Chief Executive, party leader and pre-eminent spokesman on foreign policy.

Congress considered foreign aid in two steps, first by authorizing the appropriation of funds and then by making the actual appropriations. Each step required a separate bill, subject to the normal legislative process of hearings by House and Senate committees, passage by both chambers and reconciliation of any differences between the House and Senate versions. Traditionally, Congress reduced Administration requests by authorizing smaller amounts of money than had been sought by the President and subsequently by appropriating less than both chambers had authorized.

In addition to the basic foreign-aid program, the United States developed a variety of multilateral and specialized programs with significant influence in foreign

---

Cooper-Church Amendment

Following is the final text of the 1970 Cooper-Church Amendment, a precedent-setting attempt by the Senate to use authorizations and appropriations to influence U.S. foreign affairs:

"In concert with the declared objectives of the President of the United States to avoid the involvement of the United States in Cambodia after July 1, 1970, and to expedite the withdrawal of American forces from Cambodia, it is hereby provided that unless specifically authorized by law hereafter enacted, no funds authorized or appropriated pursuant to this act or any other law may be expended after July 1, 1970, for the purpose of—

"(1) retaining United States forces in Cambodia;

"(2) paying the compensation or allowances of, or otherwise supporting, directly or indirectly, any United States personnel in Cambodia who furnish military instruction to Cambodian forces or engage in any combat activity in support of Cambodian forces;

"(3) entering into or carrying out any contract or agreement to provide military instruction in Cambodia or to provide persons to engage in any combat activity in support of Cambodian forces; or

"(4) conducting any combat activity in the air above Cambodia in direct support of Cambodian forces.

"Nothing contained in this section shall be deemed to impugn the constitutional power of the President as Commander-in-Chief, including the exercise of that constitutional power which may be necessary to protect the lives of U.S. armed forces wherever deployed.

"Nothing contained in this section shall be deemed to impugn the constitutional powers of the Congress including the power to declare war and to make rules for the government and regulation of the armed forces of the United States."

affairs. Many of these programs also required specific and recurring authorizations and appropriations. In any one year, for example, Congress might consider funds for the Alliance for Progress, the Peace Corps, the Asian Development Bank, the Inter-American Development Bank or the International Development Association.

Congressional control over funds to provide the salaries and equipment for American military personnel stationed in foreign countries offered still another opportunity to exert power over U.S. international relations. Despite the undisputed existence of such power, it rarely has been used and never has been successfully exercised once the troops overseas have been committed to battle.

A precedent-setting attempt to put the power to use was made in 1970. On June 30 the Senate, by a 58-37 vote, adopted an amendment to the pending Military Sales bill (HR 15628) aimed to shut off the employment of American forces in Cambodia. Sponsored by Senators Frank Church (D Idaho) and John Sherman Cooper (R Ky.), the amendment would have forbidden Government expenditures after July 1, 1970, to support U.S. combat operations in Cambodia or furnish military instruction to Cambodian forces. Conferees dropped the amendment from HR 15628, but the amendment in slightly different form was enacted as part of a supplemental foreign aid authorization bill (HR 19911). Its practical effect was limited, since the ground troops ordered into Cambodia by President Nixon on April 20 were withdrawn by July 1.

Bibliography

Books

Butler, Charles H., *The Treaty Making Power of the United States.* Banks Law Publishing Co., 1902.

Carroll, Holbert N., *The House of Representatives and Foreign Affairs.* Little, Brown & Co., 1966.

Cheever, Daniel S. and Haviland, H. Field Jr., *American Foreign Policy and the Separation of Powers.* Harvard University Press, 1952.

Crandall, Samuel B., *Treaties, Their Making and Enforcement.* Columbia University Press, 1904.

Dahl, Robert A., *Congress and Foreign Policy.* Harcourt, Brace & Co., 1950.

Dangerfield, Royden J., *In Defense of the Senate.* University of Oklahoma Press, 1933.

Dennison, Eleanor E., *The Senate Foreign Relations Committee.* Stanford University Press, 1942.

Farnsworth, David N., *The Senate Committee on Foreign Relations.* University of Illinois Press, 1961.

Fleming, Denna F., *The Treaty Veto of the American Senate.* G. P. Putnam's Sons, 1930.

Hamilton, Alexander; Jay, John; and Madison, James, *The Federalist.* Modern Library Edition, Random House.

Harden, Ralston, *The Senate and Treaties 1789-1817.* Macmillan Co., 1920.

Haynes, George H., *The Senate of the United States.* Houghton, Mifflin Co., 1938.

Robinson, James A., *Congress and Foreign Policy Making.* Dorsey Press, 1962.

Westphal, C. F., *The House Committee on Foreign Affairs.* Columbia University Press, 1942.

Articles

Berry, John M., "Foreign Policy Making and the Congress," *Editorial Research Reports,* April 19, 1967, p. 281-300.

Brewer, F. M., "Advice and Consent of the Senate," *Editorial Research Reports,* June 1, 1943, p. 341-356; "The Treaty Power," *Editorial Research Reports,* Jan. 18, 1943, p. 37-54.

"Congress and Foreign Relations," *Annals of the American Academy of Political and Social Science,* September 1953.

"Congress, the President and the Power to Commit Forces to Combat," *Harvard Law Review,* June 1968.

Humphrey, Hubert H., "The Senate in Foreign Policy," *Foreign Affairs,* July 1959.

Lee, Kendrick, "Congress and the Conduct of War," *Editorial Research Reports,* Aug. 24, 1942, p. 125-140.

Patch, Buel W., "American Policy on the League of Nations and the World Court," *Editorial Research Reports,* Jan. 2, 1935, p. 1-24; "The Power to Declare War," *Editorial Research Reports,* Jan. 6, 1938, p. 1-18; "Treaties and Domestic Law," *Editorial Research Reports,* March 28, 1952, p. 239-256.

Putney, Bryant, "Participation by Congress in Control of Foreign Policy," *Editorial Research Reports,* Nov. 9, 1939, p. 337-355.

Worsnop, Richard L., "War Powers of the President," *Editorial Research Reports,* March 14, 1966, p. 181-200.

Government Publications

Background Information on the Committee on Foreign Relations. Government Printing Office, 1968.

Small, Norman J., editor, *Constitution of the United States of America, Analysis and Interpretation.* Government Printing Office, 1964.

Senate Confirmation of Nominations

LEGISLATIVE participation in the appointment process, an American contribution to governmental practice, has reached a magnitude undreamed of by the framers of the Constitution. In 1969, President Nixon's first year in office, the Senate gave its advice and consent to 72,635 Presidential nominations. This staggering figure reflects the growth of the Federal Government in modern times; in the entire 71st Congress (1929-31) only 16,905 nominations were confirmed.

Obviously, the Senate could not give detailed consideration to upwards of 70,000 nominations, and indeed it did not. In most cases Senate action was only a formality, since nearly 95 percent of these nominations involved routine confirmation of appointments and promotions of military officers, and most of the others were nominations of postmasters and officers in various specialized services. But there remained several hundred nominations to major Federal posts which were subjected to varying degrees of individual scrutiny by the Senate. They included nominations to Cabinet and sub-Cabinet positions, independent boards and agencies, major diplomatic and military posts and the Federal judiciary.

One nomination was rejected. That was President Nixon's nomination of Clement F. Haynsworth Jr. of South Carolina to be an Associate Justice of the Supreme Court. In the debate over the Haynsworth nomination, the Senate considered once more—as it had done so many times in almost two centuries—its proper role in the appointment process.

Controversy Over Senate Role. That role has been a subject of controversy from the very start. The constitutional language governing appointments, itself a compromise between proponents of executive and of legislative supremacy, is full of ambiguities, and relations between the Senate and the President have never been comfortable in this area. History is studded with disputes over nominations, and through these controversies some patterns have emerged.

Although the Haynsworth nomination was the first Supreme Court nomination to meet outright rejection since 1930, the action had sound precedent. The Senate may not be able to dictate Supreme Court appointments, as it does the appointments to some lower Federal courts, but historically it has not been afraid to reject them. Roughly one out of five nominations to the Supreme Court has failed to win Senate confirmation. Although political considerations frequently have played a role in Senate rejection of a Court nominee, in recent years the candidate's economic views and social philosophy have been increasingly subject to scrutiny.

The Constitutional Mandate

"The President...shall nominate, and by and with the Advice and Consent of the Senate, shall appoint Ambassadors, other public Ministers and Consuls, Judges of the supreme Court, and all other Officers of the United States, whose Appointments are not herein otherwise provided for, and which shall be established by Law; but the Congress may by Law vest the Appointment of such inferior Officers, as they think proper, in the President alone, in the Courts of Law, or in the Heads of Departments.

"The President shall have Power to fill up all Vacancies that may happen during the Recess of the Senate, by granting Commissions which shall expire at the End of their next Session." *(Constitution of the United States, Article II, Section 2)*

Cabinet Nominations. By contrast, Cabinet nominations usually are confirmed with little difficulty, on the theory that the President should have great leeway in selecting the members of his official "family." Since 1789, only eight men nominated to the Cabinet have been rejected by the Senate.

Nominations to sub-Cabinet positions, which have multiplied phenomenally in the 20th century, are treated much like Cabinet nominations, although the President is expected to consult in advance with key Members of Congress on appointments in which they have a particular interest, and sub-Cabinet posts frequently are used to reward various party factions. Since 1933 few such nominations have been withdrawn and none rejected.

Appointments to independent boards and commissions offer a somewhat different situation. Usually created by act of Congress and not subordinate to any executive department, they frequently are viewed as an arm of Congress rather than the Executive, and Members of Congress expect to play a greater role in the selection process. Typically, the act of Congress creating an independent agency may require a bipartisan membership or impose geographical or other limitations on the President's selection power. Contests with the Senate over these nominations have been frequent, although few nominees actually have been rejected. Independent agencies with single administrators have fewer problems—these nominations tend to be treated more like Cabinet nominations.

Diplomatic and Other Nominations. Major diplomatic nominations usually encounter little difficulty.

Boxscore of Nominations, 1929-71

	Received	Confirmed	Withdrawn	Rejected	Unconfirmed
71st (1929-31)	17,508	16,905	68	5	530
72nd (1931-33)	12,716	10,909	19	1	1,787
73rd (1933-34)	9,094	9,027	17	3	47
74th (1935-36)	22,487	22,286	51	15	135
75th (1937-38)	15,330	15,193	20	27	90
76th (1939-40)	29,072	28,939	16	21	96
77th (1941-42)	24,344	24,137	33	5	169
78th (1943-44)	21,775	21,371	31	6	367
79th (1945-46)	37,022	36,550	17	3	452
80th (1947-48)	66,641	54,796	153	0	11,692
81st (1949-50)	87,266	86,562	45	6	653
82nd (1951-52)	46,920	46,504	45	2	369
83rd (1953-54)	69,458	68,563	43	0	852
84th (1955-56)	84,173	82,694	38	3	1,438
85th (1957-58)	104,193	103,311	54	0	828
86th (1959-60)	91,476	89,900	30	1	1,545
87th (1961-62)	102,849	100,741	1,279	0	829
88th (1963-64)	122,190	120,201	36	0	1,953
89th (1965-66)	123,019	120,865	173	0	1,981
90th (1967-68)	120,231	118,231	34	0	1,966
91st (1969-71)	134,464	133,797	487	2	178

SOURCES: Floyd M. Riddick, *The United States Congress: Organization and Procedure.* National Capitol Publishers, 1949; and Congressional Record.

Although in the early days of the Republic the Senate attempted to exercise extensive authority over diplomatic appointments, in modern practice the President has been allowed wide discretion in his selection of ambassadors and other persons to assist him in the conduct of foreign relations.

Appointments to lower Federal courts are another matter. By 1840 it had become customary for district court judges to be selected by the Senators from the state in which the district was located, provided the Senators were of the same party as the President. If they were not, the President was expected to consult with state party leaders before making a selection. Senatorial dictation of judicial appointments was reinforced by the institution of Senatorial courtesy; under this unwritten custom, the Senate generally will refuse to confirm a nomination to an office situated within a particular state if the Senators of the President's party from that state oppose it. The President maintains wider discretion in making appointments to circuit court judgeships, since these districts embrace several states, and to other specialized courts such as the tax and customs courts.

Appointees in one other broad group historically were selected by the Legislative Branch. Postmasters of the first, second and third classes constituted the largest group of civilian employees appointed with Senate confirmation. Although it was the Senate that gave its advice and consent, custom decreed that Members of the House—if they were of the same party as the President—make the actual selection of appointees in their districts. This relic of Congressional patronage, which had survived many previous attacks, was finally left by the wayside when President Nixon in 1969 moved to put into effect a thoroughgoing program of postal reform.

U.S. attorneys and marshals continue as patronage appointments. Although appointed, with Senate confirmation, for four-year terms, they actually serve only at the pleasure of the President.

The development of modern attitudes toward the appointment process is traced below, and a historical analysis of the related power of removing Federal officials follows. An explanation of current procedures for handling nominations concludes the subchapter.

History of Appointments

"The President...shall nominate, and by and with the Advice and Consent of the Senate, shall appoint...."

The constitutional language governing the appointment power, hammered out in the final weeks of the Federal Convention of 1787, represented a compromise between those delegates who favored vesting in the Senate sole authority for appointing principal officers of the Government and those who held that the President alone should control appointments as a purely executive function.

As finally adopted, the Constitution required Senate confirmation of principal officers of the Government—"Ambassadors, other public Ministers and Consuls, Judges of the supreme Court" were mentioned specifically—but provided that Congress could "by Law vest the Appointment of such inferior Officers, as they think proper, in the President alone, in the Courts of Law, or in the Heads of Departments."

Approval of the compromise language did not, however, settle the controversy over the Senate's role in the appointment process. What did "the advice and consent of the Senate" entail?

To Hamilton, writing in *The Federalist* (No. 66), the Senate's function did not appear significant: "It will be the office of the President to *nominate*, and with the advice and consent of the Senate to *appoint*. There will, of course, be no exertion of *choice* on the part of the Senate. They may defeat one choice of the Executive and oblige him to make another; but they cannot themselves *choose*—they can only ratify or reject the choice of the President."

John Adams saw it differently. "Faction and distraction," he wrote, "are the sure and certain consequences of giving to the Senate a vote on the distribution of offices." Looking ahead to the emergence of political parties, Adams foresaw the rise of the spoils system and the use of the appointive power as a Senatorial patronage tool.

President Washington regarded the appointment power as "the most irksome part of the executive trust," but his exercise of that power was widely acclaimed and the Senate withheld its consent only five times during his Administration.

Precedents Established by Washington

Methods of handling Presidential nominations had to be established early in the new government. Washington established the precedent of submitting nominations to the Senate in writing, and the Senate after debate on the propriety of the secret ballot determined to take viva voce votes on nominations. The President rejected suggestions that he be present during Senate consideration of appointments: "It could be no pleasing thing, I conceive, for the President, on the one hand to be present and hear the propriety of his nominations questioned; nor for the Senate on the other hand to be under the smallest restraint from his presence from the fullest and freest inquiry into the Character of the Person nominated."

Uncertainty over the extent of the Senate's powers with respect to appointments surfaced early in the Administration. Could the Senate only give its consent to the person named, or could it also rule on the necessity for the post and the grade of the appointee? Washington's nominations of ministers to Paris, London and The Hague in December 1791 were blocked for weeks by Senate debate on a resolution opposing the appointment of "ministers Plenipotentiary to reside permanently at foreign courts." Washington's nominations finally were approved, by narrow votes, on the ground of special need for representation at the three capitals.

Washington maintained high standards for selection of appointees, and although he consulted widely both with Members of Congress and others, he rebuffed all attempts at encroachment on his prerogatives. Thus he refused to appoint Aaron Burr as Minister to France in 1794, despite the recommendation of a caucus of Republican Senators and Representatives, because he questioned Burr's integrity.

Washington was not always successful in resisting Senatorial pressure. Early in the First Congress, the Senate rejected his nomination of Benjamin Fishbourn to the post of naval officer (a customs official handling manifests, clearances, etc.) of the Port of Savannah as a courtesy to the two Georgia Senators, who had a candidate of their own. Washington yielded; he nominated the Senators' choice, and Senatorial courtesy was born.

The practice of inquiring into the political views of a Presidential nominee also had its beginning in the Washington Administration. John Rutledge of South Carolina, nominated in 1795 to succeed John Jay as Chief Justice of the United States, was rejected by the Senate on a 10-14 vote, primarily because of his opposition to the Jay Treaty with Great Britain. Rutledge, one of the original six Supreme Court Justices (1789-91), was already serving as Chief Justice on a recess appointment.

Injection of Politics

John Adams, that vigorous critic of the appointment provisions of the Constitution, found nothing in his experience as President to make him change his views. The Federalist Senate cleared his appointments with Federalist leader Alexander Hamilton (then a private citizen), and Adams later complained that he "soon found that if I had not the previous consent of the heads of departments, and the approbation of Mr. Hamilton, I ran the utmost risk of a dead negative in the Senate."

During Adams' tenure, appointments became increasingly subject to political considerations. The practice of consulting, and bowing to the wishes of, state delegations in Congress upon appointments in their states also grew.

Jefferson had far less trouble with appointments than his predecessor. He was the acknowledged leader of his party, and for most of his term that party was in control of Congress. Perhaps his most embarrassing failure was the unanimous rejection of his final nomination, that of William Short as minister to Russia. However, the opposition apparently was directed more against the establishment of the mission than against Short himself.

Unlike Jefferson, Madison soon found that he had to submit to Senate dictation in the matter of appointments. Thus a small clique of Senators was able to force the appointment of Robert Smith as Secretary of State, although Madison had wanted to give the post to his Secretary of the Treasury, Albert Gallatin.

Gallatin's subsequent appointment as envoy to negotiate a peace treaty with Great Britain also met with difficulty in the Senate. Gallatin was already in Europe when the Senate adopted a resolution declaring that the duties of envoy and Secretary of the Treasury were "incompatible." Subsequently, Gallatin resigned his Treasury post and was confirmed as envoy.

This nomination led to a controversy over the propriety of consultation between the President and a Senate committee on pending nominations. Although previous Presidents had so consulted with committees appointed by the party caucus or by the Senate itself, Madison decided to put an end to the practice. In a message to the Senate, he insisted that if the Senate wanted information on nominations, the correct procedure was to confer with appropriate department heads, not the President. "The appointment of a committee of the Senate to confer immediately with the Executive himself," he said, "appears to lose sight of the coordinate relation between the Executive and the Senate, which the Constitution has established, and which ought therefore to be maintained." In spite of this message, the President received a special committee appointed by the Senate to confer with him about the Gallatin nomination, but he refused to discuss the nomination with them. *(Continued on p. 232)*

Supreme Court...

Name	State	Date of Birth	Nomi-nated by	To Replace	Date of Ap-pointment	Date Confirmed	Other Action	Date Resigned	Date of Death	Years of Service
John Jay*	N.Y.	12/12/1745	Washington		9/24/1789	9/26/1789		6/29/1795	5/17/1829	6
John Rutledge	S.C.	1739	Washington		9/24/1789	9/26/1789		3/5/1791	7/23/1800	1
William Cushing	Mass.	3/1/1732	Washington		9/24/1789	9/26/1789			9/13/1810	21
Robert H. Harrison	Md.	1745	Washington		9/24/1789	9/26/1789	Jan. 1790(D)		4/20/1790	
James Wilson	Pa.	9/14/1742	Washington		9/24/1789	9/26/1789			8/28/1798	9
John Blair	Va.	1732	Washington		9/24/1789	9/26/1789		1/27/1796	8/31/1800	6
James Iredell	N.C.	10/5/1751	Washington	Harrison	2/9/1790	2/10/1790			10/2/1799	9
Thomas Johnson	Md.	11/4/1732	Washington	Rutledge	11/1/1791	11/7/1791		3/4/1793	10/25/1819	1
William Paterson	N.J.	12/24/1745	Washington	Johnson	2/27/1793		2/28/1793(W)**			
William Paterson			Washington	Johnson	3/4/1793	3/4/1793			9/9/1806	13
John Rutledge*			Washington	Jay	7/1/1795		12/15/1795(R)			
William Cushing*			Washington	Jay	1/26/1796	1/27/1796	2/2/1796(D)			
Samuel Chase	Md.	4/17/1741	Washington	Blair	1/26/1796	1/27/1796			6/19/1811	15
Oliver Ellsworth*	Conn.	4/29/1745	Washington	Jay	3/3/1796	3/4/1796		9/30/1800	11/26/1807	4
Bushrod Washington	Va.	6/5/1762	Adams	Wilson	12/19/1798	12/20/1798			11/26/1829	31
Alfred Moore	N.C.	5/21/1755	Adams	Iredell	12/6/1799	12/10/1799		March, 1804	10/15/1810	4
John Jay*			Adams	Ellsworth	12/18/1800	12/19/1800	1/2/1801(D)			
John Marshall*	Va.	9/24/1755	Adams	Ellsworth	1/20/1801	1/27/1801			7/6/1835	34
William Johnson	S.C.	12/27/1771	Jefferson	Moore	3/22/1804	3/24/1804			8/11/1834	30
Henry B. Livingston	N.Y.	11/26/1757	Jefferson	Paterson	12/13/1806	12/17/1806			3/18/1823	16
Thomas Todd	Ky.	1/23/1765	Jefferson	New Seat	2/28/1807	3/3/1807			2/7/1826	19
Levi Lincoln	Mass.	5/15/1749	Madison	Cushing	1/2/1811	1/3/1811	1/20/1811(D)		4/14/1820	
Alexander Wolcott	Conn.	9/15/1758	Madison	Cushing	2/4/1811		2/13/1811(R)		6/26/1828	
John Quincy Adams	Mass.	7/11/1767	Madison	Cushing	2/21/1811	2/22/1811	April, 1811(D)		2/23/1848	
Joseph Story	Mass.	9/18/1779	Madison	Cushing	11/15/1811	11/18/1811			9/10/1845	33
Gabriel Duval	Md.	12/6/1752	Madison	Chase	11/15/1811	11/18/1811		Jan., 1835	3/6/1844	23
Smith Thompson	N.Y.	1/17/1768	Monroe	Livingston	12/8/1823	12/19/1823			12/18/1843	20
Robert Trimble	Ky.	1777	J. Q. Adams	Todd	4/11/1826	5/9/1826			8/25/1828	2
John J. Crittenden	Ky.	9/10/1787	J. Q. Adams	Trimble	12/17/1828		2/12/1829(P)		7/26/1863	
John McLean	Ohio	3/11/1785	Jackson	Trimble	3/6/1829	3/7/1829			4/4/1861	32
Henry Baldwin	Pa.	1/14/1780	Jackson	Washington	1/4/1830	1/6/1830			4/21/1844	14
James M. Wayne	Ga.	1790	Jackson	Johnson	1/7/1835	1/9/1835			7/5/1867	32
Roger B. Taney	Md.	3/17/1777	Jackson	Duval	1/15/1835		3/3/1835(P)			
Roger B. Taney*			Jackson	Marshall	12/28/1835	3/15/1836			10/12/1864	28
Philip P. Barbour	Va.	5/25/1783	Jackson	Duval	12/28/1835	3/15/1836			2/24/1841	5
William Smith	Ala.	1762	Jackson	New Seat	3/3/1837	3/8/1837	March, 1837(D)		6/10/1840	
John Catron	Tenn.	1786	Jackson	New Seat	3/3/1837	3/8/1837			5/30/1865	28
John McKinley	Ala.	5/1/1780	Van Buren	New Seat	9/18/1837	9/25/1837			7/19/1852	15
Peter V. Daniel	Va.	4/24/1784	Van Buren	Barbour	2/26/1841	3/2/1841			6/30/1860	19
John C. Spencer	N.Y.	1/8/1788	Tyler	Thompson	1/9/1844		1/31/1844(R)		5/18/1855	
Reuben H. Walworth	N.Y.	10/26/1788	Tyler	Thompson	3/13/1844		6/17/1844(W)		11/27/1867	
Edward King	Pa.	1/31/1794	Tyler	Baldwin	6/5/1844		6/15/1844(P)			
Edward King			Tyler	Baldwin	12/4/1844		2/7/1845(W)		5/8/1873	
Samuel Nelson	N.Y.	11/10/1792	Tyler	Thompson	2/4/1845	2/14/1845		11/28/1872	12/13/1873	27
John M. Read	Pa.	2/21/1797	Tyler	Baldwin	2/7/1845	No action			11/29/1874	
George W. Woodward	Pa.	3/26/1809	Polk	Baldwin	12/23/1845		1/22/1846(R)		5/10/1875	
Levi Woodbury	N.H.	12/22/1789	Polk	Story	12/23/1845	1/3/1846			9/4/1851	5
Robert C. Grier	Pa.	3/5/1794	Polk	Baldwin	8/3/1846	8/4/1846		1/31/1870	9/26/1870	23
Benjamin R. Curtis	Mass.	11/4/1809	Fillmore	Woodbury	12/11/1851	12/29/1851		9/30/1857	9/15/1874	5
Edward A. Bradford	La.	9/27/1813	Fillmore	McKinley	8/16/1852	No action				
George E. Badger	N.C.	4/13/1795	Fillmore	McKinley	1/10/1853		2/11/1853(P)		5/11/1866	
William C. Micou	La.	1806	Fillmore	McKinley	2/24/1853	No action				
John A. Campbell	Ala.	6/24/1811	Pierce	McKinley	3/21/1853	3/25/1853	April, 1861		3/13/1889	8
Nathan Clifford	Maine	8/18/1803	Buchanan	Curtis	12/9/1857	1/12/1858			7/25/1881	23
Jeremiah S. Black	Pa.	1/10/1810	Buchanan	Daniel	2/5/1861		2/21/1861(R)		8/19/1883	
Noah H. Swayne	Ohio	12/7/1804	Lincoln	McLean	1/21/1862	1/24/1862		1/24/1881	6/8/1884	19
Samuel F. Miller	Iowa	4/5/1816	Lincoln	Daniel	7/16/1862	7/16/1862			10/13/1890	28
David Davis	Ill.	3/9/1815	Lincoln	Campbell	12/1/1862	12/8/1862		3/7/1877	6/26/1886	14
Stephen J. Field	Calif.	11/4/1816	Lincoln	New Seat	3/6/1863	3/10/1863		12/1/1897	4/9/1899	34
Salmon P. Chase*	Ohio	1/13/1808	Lincoln	Taney	12/6/1864	12/6/1864			5/7/1873	8
Henry Stanbery	Ohio	2/20/1803	Johnson	Catron	4/16/1866	No action			6/26/1881	
Ebenezer R. Hoar	Mass.	2/21/1816	Grant	New Seat	12/15/1869		2/3/1870(R)		1/31/1895	
Edwin M. Stanton	Pa.	12/19/1814	Grant	Grier	12/20/1869	12/20/1869			12/24/1869	
William Strong	Pa.	3/6/1808	Grant	Grier	2/7/1870	2/18/1870		12/14/1880	8/19/1895	10
Joseph P. Bradley	N.J.	3/14/1813	Grant	New Seat	2/7/1870	3/21/1870			1/22/1892	21
Ward Hunt	N.Y.	6/14/1810	Grant	Nelson	12/3/1872	12/11/1872		1/7/1882	3/24/1886	9
George H. Williams*	Ore.	3/23/1823	Grant	Chase	12/1/1873		1/8/1874(W)		4/4/1910	
Caleb Cushing*	Mass.	1/17/1800	Grant	Chase	1/9/1874		1/13/1874(W)		1/2/1879	

*Chief Justice　　**Withdrawn for technical reasons　　†Motion to invoke cloture rejected　　D - Declined　　W - Withdrawn　　R - Rejected　　P - Postponed

...Appointments, 1789-1970

Name	State	Date of Birth	Nomi-nated by	To Replace	Date of Ap-pointment	Date Confirmed	Other Action	Date Resigned	Date of Death	Years of Service
Morrison R. Waite*	Ohio	11/29/1816	Grant	Chase	1/19/1874	1/21/1874			3/23/1888	14
John M. Harlan	Ky.	6/1/1833	Hayes	Davis	10/17/1877	11/29/1877			10/14/1911	34
William B. Woods	Ga.	8/3/1824	Hayes	Strong	12/15/1880	12/21/1880			5/14/1887	6
Stanley Matthews	Ohio	7/21/1824	Hayes	Swayne	1/26/1881	No action				
Stanley Matthews			Garfield	Swayne	3/14/1881	5/12/1881			3/22/1889	7
Horace Gray	Mass.	3/24/1828	Arthur	Clifford	12/19/1881	12/20/1881		7/9/1902	9/15/1902	20
Roscoe Conkling	N.Y.	10/30/1829	Arthur	Hunt	2/24/1882	3/2/1882	March, 1882(D)		4/18/1888	
Samuel Blatchford	N.Y.	3/9/1820	Arthur	Hunt	3/13/1882	3/27/1882			7/7/1893	11
Lucius Q. C. Lamar	Miss.	9/17/1825	Cleveland	Woods	12/6/1887	1/16/1888			1/23/1893	5
Melville W. Fuller*	Ill.	2/11/1833	Cleveland	Waite	4/30/1888	7/20/1888			7/4/1910	22
David J. Brewer	Kan.	1/20/1837	Harrison	Matthews	12/4/1889	12/18/1889			3/28/1910	20
Henry B. Brown	Mich.	3/21/1836	Harrison	Miller	12/23/1890	12/29/1890		5/28/1906	9/4/1913	15
George Shiras, Jr.	Pa.	1/26/1832	Harrison	Bradley	7/19/1892	7/26/1892		2/23/1903	8/21/1924	10
Howell E. Jackson	Tenn.	4/8/1832	Harrison	Lamar	2/2/1893	2/18/1893			8/8/1895	2
William B. Hornblower	N.Y.	5/13/1851	Cleveland	Blatchford	9/19/1893		1/15/1894(R)		6/16/1914	
Wheeler H. Peckham	N.Y.	1/1/1833	Cleveland	Blatchford	1/22/1894		2/16/1894(R)		9/27/1905	
Edward D. White	La.	11/3/1845	Cleveland	Blatchford	2/19/1894	2/19/1894				17
Rufus W. Peckham	N.Y.	11/8/1838	Cleveland	Jackson	12/3/1895	12/9/1895			10/24/1909	13
Joseph McKenna	Calif.	8/10/1843	McKinley	Field	12/16/1897	1/21/1898		1/5/1925	11/21/1926	26
Oliver W. Holmes	Mass.	3/8/1841	Roosevelt	Gray	12/2/1902	12/4/1902		1/12/1932	3/6/1935	29
William R. Day	Ohio	4/17/1849	Roosevelt	Shiras	2/19/1903	2/23/1903		11/13/1922	7/9/1923	19
William H. Moody	Mass.	12/23/1853	Roosevelt	Brown	12/3/1906	12/12/1906		11/20/1910	7/2/1917	3
Horace H. Lurton	Tenn.	2/26/1844	Taft	Peckham	12/13/1909	12/20/1909			7/12/1914	4
Edward D. White*			Taft	Fuller	12/12/1910	12/12/1910			5/19/1921	10
Charles E. Hughes	N.Y.	4/11/1862	Taft	Brewer	4/25/1910	5/2/1910		6/10/1916		6
Willis Van Devanter	Wyo.	4/17/1859	Taft	Moody	12/12/1910	12/15/1910		6/2/1937	2/8/1951	26
Joseph R. Lamar	Ga.	10/14/1857	Taft	White	12/12/1910	12/15/1910			1/2/1916	5
Mahlon Pitney	N.J.	2/5/1858	Taft	Harlan	2/19/1912	3/13/1912		12/31/1922	12/9/1924	10
James C. McReynolds	Tenn.	2/3/1862	Wilson	Lurton	8/19/1914	8/29/1914		1/31/1941	8/24/1946	26
Louis D. Brandeis	Mass.	11/13/1856	Wilson	Lamar	1/28/1916	6/1/1916		2/13/1939	10/5/1941	22
John H. Clarke	Ohio	9/18/1857	Wilson	Hughes	7/14/1916	7/24/1916		9/18/1922	3/22/1945	6
William H. Taft*	Conn.	9/15/1857	Harding	White	6/30/1921	6/30/1921		2/3/1930	3/8/1930	8
George Sutherland	Utah	3/25/1862	Harding	Clarke	9/5/1922	9/5/1922		1/17/1938	7/18/1942	15
Pierce Butler	Minn.	3/17/1866	Harding	Day	11/23/1922	12/21/1922			11/16/1939	17
Edward T. Sanford	Tenn.	7/23/1865	Harding	Pitney	1/24/1923	1/29/1923			3/8/1930	7
Harlan F. Stone	N.Y.	10/11/1872	Coolidge	McKenna	1/5/1925	2/5/1925				16
Charles E. Hughes*			Hoover	Taft	2/3/1930	2/13/1930		7/1/1941	8/27/1948	11
John J. Parker	N.C.	11/20/1885	Hoover	Sanford	3/21/1930		5/7/1930(R)		3/17/1958	
Owen J. Roberts	Pa.	5/2/1875	Hoover	Sanford	5/9/1930	5/20/1930		7/31/1945	5/19/1955	15
Benjamin N. Cardozo	N.Y.	5/24/1870	Hoover	Holmes	2/15/1932	2/24/1932			7/9/1938	6
Hugo L. Black	Ala.	2/27/1886	Roosevelt	Van Devanter	8/12/1937	8/17/1937				
Stanley F. Reed	Ky.	12/31/1884	Roosevelt	Sutherland	1/15/1938	1/25/1938		2/25/1957		19
Felix Frankfurter	Mass.	11/15/1882	Roosevelt	Cardozo	1/5/1939	1/17/1939		8/28/1962	2/22/1965	23
William O. Douglas	Conn.	10/16/1898	Roosevelt	Brandeis	3/20/1939	4/4/1939				
Frank Murphy	Mich.	4/13/1890	Roosevelt	Butler	1/4/1940	1/15/1940			7/19/1949	9
Harlan F. Stone*			Roosevelt	Hughes	6/12/1941	6/27/1941			4/22/1946	5
James F. Byrnes	S.C.	5/2/1879	Roosevelt	Stone	6/12/1941	6/12/1941		10/3/1942		1
Robert H. Jackson	N.Y.	2/13/1892	Roosevelt	McReynolds	6/12/1941	7/7/1941			10/9/1954	13
Wiley B. Rutledge	Iowa	7/20/1894	Roosevelt	Byrnes	1/11/1943	2/8/1943			9/10/1949	6
Harold H. Burton	Ohio	6/22/1888	Truman	Roberts	9/19/1945	9/19/1945		10/13/1958	10/28/1964	13
Fred M. Vinson*	Ky.	1/22/1890	Truman	Stone	6/6/1946	6/20/1946			9/8/1953	7
Tom C. Clark	Texas	9/23/1899	Truman	Murphy	8/2/1949	8/19/1949		6/12/1967		18
Sherman Minton	Ind.	10/20/1890	Truman	Rutledge	9/15/1949	10/4/1949		10/15/1956	4/9/1965	7
Earl Warren*	Calif.	3/19/1891	Eisenhower	Vinson	9/30/1953	3/1/1954		6/23/1969		15
John M. Harlan	N.Y.	5/20/1899	Eisenhower	Jackson	1/10/1955	3/16/1955				
William J. Brennan Jr.	N.J.	4/25/1906	Eisenhower	Minton	10/16/1956	3/19/1957				
Charles E. Whittaker	Mo.	2/22/1901	Eisenhower	Reed	3/2/1957	3/19/1957		4/1/1962		5
Potter Stewart	Ohio	1/23/1915	Eisenhower	Burton	1/17/1959	5/5/1959				
Byron R. White	Colo.	6/8/1917	Kennedy	Whittaker	4/3/1962	4/11/1962				
Arthur J. Goldberg	Ill.	8/8/1908	Kennedy	Frankfurter	8/31/1962	9/25/1962		7/25/1965		3
Abe Fortas	Tenn.	6/19/1910	Johnson	Goldberg	7/28/1965	8/11/1965		5/14/1969		4
Thurgood Marshall	N.Y.	6/2/1908	Johnson	Clark	6/13/1967	8/30/1967				
Abe Fortas*			Johnson	Warren	6/26/1968		10/4/1968 (W)†			
Homer Thornberry	Texas	1/9/1909	Johnson	Fortas	6/26/1968		No action			
Warren E. Burger	Minn.	9/17/1907	Nixon	Warren	5/21/1969	6/9/1969				
Clement Haynsworth Jr.	S.C.	10/30/1912	Nixon	Fortas	8/18/1969		11/21/1969(R)			
G. Harrold Carswell	Fla.	12/22/1919	Nixon	Fortas	1/19/1970		4/8/1970(R)			
Harry A. Blackmun	Minn.	11/12/1908	Nixon	Fortas	4/14/1970	5/12/1970				

*Chief Justice   ** Withdrawn for technical reasons.   † Motion to invoke cloture rejected.   D - Declined   W - Withdrawn   R - Rejected   P - Postponed*

Madison in 1811 suffered the second outright rejection of a Supreme Court nomination. Alexander Wolcott was opposed by the Federalists because as collector of customs in Connecticut he had vigorously enforced the unpopular embargo acts passed prior to the War of 1812. He was rejected, 9-24, following charges by the press that he lacked the requisite legal qualifications for service on the Court.

Growth of Spoils System

The Administrations of Monroe and John Quincy Adams were marked by the growth of the spoils system, as Members of the Senate increasingly insisted on control of Federal appointments in their states.

The Four Years Law, enacted in 1820, greatly increased the number of appointments available. This law provided fixed four-year terms for many Federal officers who previously had served at the pleasure of the President. Although its ostensible purpose was to ensure the accountability of appointees, its value as a patronage tool soon became clear. Commented Adams: "The Senate was conciliated by the permanent increase of their power, which was the principal ultimate effect of the Act, and every Senator was flattered by the power conferred upon himself of multiplying chances to provide for his friends and dependents...."

Both Monroe and Adams resisted pressure to use the Four Years Law as a means of introducing rotation in office; they followed the policy of renominating officers upon expiration of their terms, unless they had been guilty of misconduct. Upon taking office as President in 1825, Adams resubmitted all of Monroe's nominations on which the Senate had failed to act; by contrast, Jackson withdrew all of Adams' nominations.

One of Adams' Supreme Court nominations was blocked by the Senate. The name of John J. Crittenden, a Kentucky Whig, had been sent up shortly before Adams' Administration ended in 1829. Jacksonians, who wished to allow the newly elected Democratic President to make the appointment, blocked Senate action on confirmation of Crittenden by a vote of 23-17. Andrew Jackson later filled the seat with a man of his choice.

Jackson, to whom rotation in office was "a leading principle," made full use of the Four Years Act to find places for his supporters. Although he was in constant conflict with the Senate over appointments, such was his popularity in the country that relatively few were rejected.

One of the most significant of the rejections was the appointment of Martin Van Buren as minister to England. Van Buren in 1831 resigned his post as Secretary of State in a Cabinet reorganization, and President Jackson then gave him a recess appointment to the Court of St. James's. He was already in London when the Senate met in December. Clay, Webster and Calhoun, all aspirants for the Presidency who looked on Van Buren as a likely opponent, led the opposition to his appointment. When the nomination came to a vote in January 1832, a tie was contrived so that Vice President Calhoun could vote against Van Buren. Although his opponents thought a Senate rejection would end Van Buren's political career, he returned home a martyr and was soon elected Vice President of the United States.

The Senate twice rejected Jackson's renomination of four incumbent directors of the Bank of the United States.

Senate opposition stemmed from reports critical of the bank that had been submitted to the President by the directors. Efforts to recommit the nominations having failed, the Senate rejected them, 20-24. Jackson thereupon renominated the same persons, and they again were rejected.

The Bank of the United States figured also in rejection of the nomination of Roger B. Taney as Secretary of the Treasury in 1834. Taney was rejected on an 18-28 vote after having served for nine months under a recess appointment. Opposition rested on his withdrawal of Federal funds from the bank, an action which he had recommended as Attorney General and which he had been appointed Secretary of the Treasury to carry out. This was the first outright Senate rejection of a Cabinet appointee in U.S. history, although Madison had been prevented from appointing Gallatin as Secretary of State in 1809 because he feared Gallatin would be rejected.

Early in 1835 Jackson nominated Taney to the Supreme Court. The Senate did not take up that nomination until the closing day of its session, when it voted, 24-21, for an indefinite postponement. Undaunted, the President in December 1835 named Taney to the Chief Justiceship made vacant by the death of Marshall. Notwithstanding charges that the selection was an insult to the Senate, because it had twice rejected the nominee, Taney's appointment was confirmed by a vote of 29-15.

Patronage at a Peak

The 40-year period from 1837 to 1877 marked the high point of Senate efforts to control appointments. During this period, the spoils system reached its peak and all Presidents were subject to intense pressure for patronage appointments. Senatorial courtesy —the practice of permitting Senators of the President's party to control appointments to Federal offices within their states—was firmly entrenched.

President Tyler, a dissident Democrat who had accepted the Whig nomination for Vice President in 1840 and then repudiated the Whigs upon succeeding William Henry Harrison as President, was peculiarly unfortunate in his relations with the Senate. Since he was without a following in either party, both Whigs and Democrats were anxious to embarrass him, and many of his nominees—including four to the Cabinet and four to the Supreme Court—were rejected. In 1843, his nomination of Caleb Cushing as Secretary of the Treasury was rejected three times in one day! Tyler's first Supreme Court rejection came in 1844, when the Senate turned down John C. Spencer, 21-26. Two subsequent Court nominations, of Reuben H. Walworth and Edward King, were postponed and later withdrawn. On a final effort to fill the two Court vacancies, Tyler won approval of one nominee, Samuel Nelson, but the Senate adjourned without acting on the second nominee, John Meredith Read.

Nine months after succeeding Tyler in 1845, President Polk offered the still vacant Supreme Court seat to his Secretary of State, James Buchanan. Buchanan declined, and Polk then named to the Court an obscure but able Pennsylvania judge, George W. Woodward. Polk interpreted the Senate's rejection of the nomination by a vote of 20-29 as an attempt to weaken his Administration.

In the tension-filled decade of the 1850s, President Fillmore was unable to persuade the Senate to approve his southern nominees to the Court. In 1852, the Senate refused to act upon the nomination of Edward A. Bradford of Louisiana. In 1853, Democratic opposition brought postponement, by a 26-25 vote, of action on the nomination of Sen. George E. Badger of North Carolina. Also in 1853, the Democratic Senate failed to act on the Whig President's nomination of William C. Micou of Louisiana.

Weakened by resignations of Senators from seceding states, the Senate in 1861, by a 25-26 vote, rejected President Buchanan's nomination of Jeremiah S. Black of Pennsylvania to the Supreme Court. Black, former Attorney General and Secretary of State, was opposed by Republicans who wished the newly elected President Lincoln to fill the Court seat with his nominee.

Lincoln, a shrewd politician, made masterful use of the appointment power to hold the divided factions of his party together and to advance his legislative goals. Early in his Administration he devoted much of his time to patronage. Most officers subject to Presidential appointment had been removed following the 1860 election, and Lincoln tried to distribute these offices equitably among his various supporters. Only for major posts was a high standard of qualification deemed essential.

Andrew Johnson's bitter struggle with the Senate over appointments, a byproduct of the fight over Reconstruction policy, led to curbs on the President's removal powers in the Tenure of Office Act of 1867 and to Johnson's impeachment trial. *(See Power of Removal.)*

Senate hostility to Johnson blocked the elevation in 1866 of Attorney General Henry Stanbery of Ohio to the Supreme Court. The Senate never acted directly on the nomination but instead passed a bill to reduce the size of the Court from 10 to 8 Justices. The purpose of the bill was to kill the Stanbery nomination by abolishing the seat to which he was named. Stanbery resigned as Attorney General in 1868 to serve as Johnson's chief counsel during the impeachment proceedings. When Johnson subsequently renominated him to the post of Attorney General, the Senate refused, 11-29, to confirm the appointment.

Pressure for Civil Service Reform

Senatorial ascendancy over the President in the matter of appointments and the excesses of the spoils system led, under Grant, to public pressure for civil service reform. In response to this pressure, Congress in 1871 enacted a civil service law but failed to appropriate funds to implement it.

Three of Grant's appointments to the Supreme Court failed to win Senate approval. The first was his Attorney General, Ebenezer Rockwood Hoar, who had earned the enmity of the Senate by refusing to bow to political pressure in the filling of new judgeships created under an 1869 law. Following Hoar's rejection, 24-33, Sen. Simon Cameron of Pennsylvania exclaimed: "What could you expect for a man who has snubbed 70 Senators!" In 1874, Grant was forced to withdraw two successive nominations to the Chief Justiceship, Attorney General George H. Williams and former Attorney General Caleb Cushing. Cushing had been rejected also for the post of Secretary of the Treasury in the Tyler Administration.

The accession to the Presidency of Rutherford B. Hayes in 1877 marked the beginning of Presidential efforts to curb Senatorial control over nominations. Hayes' selection of his own Cabinet members without consulting Sen-

Courtesy of the Senate

Under the unwritten custom of Senatorial courtesy, the Senate generally will refuse to confirm a nomination to an office situated within a particular state unless the nominee has been approved by the Senators of the President's party from that state. The rule is not ordinarily applied to nominations to national office.

A Senator typically invokes the rule of courtesy by stating that the nominee is "personally obnoxious" to him; this may mean that the Senator and the nominee are personal or political foes, or simply that the Senator has another candidate for the post. In effect, the custom permits the Senators of the party in office to control selection of local Federal officials—district court judges, U.S. attorneys, marshals and the like. (By custom, postmasters have been selected by Members of the House.) In states where neither Senator belongs to the President's party, the President has greater freedom of choice, although state party leaders usually make recommendations to him.

The custom of Senatorial courtesy had its beginnings in the Washington Administration, but it did not become firmly established until many years later. Under early practice, the objecting Senator had only to voice the customary formula, but since 1930 he has been expected to explain the reasons for his opposition to the nominee.

The Senate does not invariably sustain appeals to the rule of courtesy. It depends on whether the objecting Senator is in good standing with his colleagues, the nature of his objection and whether the nomination is to a local or national office.

A specialized form of Senatorial courtesy decrees that the nomination of a Senator or former Senator will be confirmed at once, without even being referred to committee. This tradition is not always honored, however. The Supreme Court nominations of Sen. Hugo M. Black in 1937 and of former Sen. Sherman Minton in 1949 were both referred to committee.

ate leaders was viewed as presumptuous by them, and they countered with unprecedented delay in acting upon nominations. However, when public opinion came to the aid of the President, the nominations were rushed to confirmation.

Unable to obtain from Congress the civil service reform legislation he recommended, Hayes nevertheless attempted throughout his one term of office to curb patronage abuses.

The Senate did not consider Hayes' nomination of former Republican Sen. Stanley Matthews of Ohio to the Supreme Court in 1881. There was some feeling that Hayes was rewarding Matthews for his support in the Hayes-Tilden contest in 1876 and for his service as counsel before the commission which dealt with disputed returns from that election. Garfield later resubmitted Matthews' name and he was confirmed by a one-vote margin.

A protracted conflict over the corruption-ridden New York customhouse led to a showdown between Hayes and Sen. Roscoe Conkling of New York over the right of Senators to control nominations. When two Conkling proteges

Senate Rejections of Cabinet Nominations

Nominee	Position	President	Date	Vote
Roger B. Taney	Secretary of Treasury	Jackson	6/23/1834	18-28
Caleb Cushing	Secretary of Treasury	Tyler	3/3/1843	19-27
Caleb Cushing	Secretary of Treasury	Tyler	3/3/1843	10-27
Caleb Cushing	Secretary of Treasury	Tyler	3/3/1843	2-29
David Henshaw	Secretary of Navy	Tyler	1/15/1844	6-34
James M. Porter	Secretary of War	Tyler	1/30/1844	3-38
James S. Green	Secretary of Treasury	Tyler	6/15/1844	Not recorded
Henry Stanbery	Attorney General	Johnson	6/2/1868	11-29
Charles B. Warren	Attorney General	Coolidge	3/10/1925	39-41
Charles B. Warren	Attorney General	Coolidge	3/16/1925	39-46
Lewis L. Strauss	Secretary of Commerce	Eisenhower	6/19/1959	46-49

SOURCE: George H. Haynes, *The Senate of the United States.* Russell & Russell, 1960, 2 v.

—Chester A. Arthur, the customs collector, and Alonzo B. Cornell, the naval officer of the customhouse—refused to comply with a Presidential order prohibiting Federal employees from actively engaging in partisan politics, Hayes asked for their resignations. When they refused to resign, he nominated two other persons to replace them. Conkling appealed to Senatorial courtesy, and the President's nominees were rejected, 25-31. After Congress adjourned, Hayes suspended Arthur and Cornell and made two more appointments to the posts. Despite Conkling's opposition, the Senate in the following session confirmed the President's choices by wide margins.

Conkling was the loser in another showdown, in 1881, with Hayes' successor, James A. Garfield. Garfield's nomination of one of his own supporters, Judge W. H. Robertson, as collector of the New York port infuriated the Senator, who wanted to maintain control of all New York patronage. Conkling invoked the rule of courtesy in his effort to block Robertson's confirmation, and the Republican caucus supported him. However, the Democrats would not agree to vote against the nominee, and Conkling feared a rebuff on the floor. Asserting that they had been "humiliated," he and his New York colleague, Sen. Thomas C. Platt, then took the extraordinary step of resigning from the Senate as a "rebuke" to the President for his presumption in making his own appointment. They expected to be re-elected by the state legislature as a vindication of their position, but they were disappointed. Conkling's political career was at an end, but Platt later returned to the Senate and to leadership of the Republican party in New York.

Meanwhile, the heyday of the spoils system was drawing to a close. Previous efforts at meaningful civil service reform had ended in failure, but public revulsion over Garfield's assassination by a disappointed office-seeker in 1881 provided new impetus for reform. With the rather surprising endorsement of President Chester A. Arthur, a civil service system was established by the Pendleton Act of 1883.

Resistance to Patronage Demands

A test of the President's right to suspend Federal officers, which occurred during Cleveland's first term, was followed by repeal of the Tenure of Office Acts. *(See Power of Removal.)* Few Cleveland nominations were

rejected thereafter. However, in his second term, two conservative appointees to the Supreme Court were rejected upon appeal to the rule of courtesy by Sen. David B. Hill of New York. William B. Hornblower and Wheeler H. Peckham, respected New York attorneys but of a political faction opposed to Hill, lost out by votes of 24-30 and 32-41, respectively. Cleveland then nominated Sen. Edward Douglas White of Louisiana, who was confirmed immediately—an example of the courtesy traditionally accorded by the Senate to one of its own Members.

Theodore Roosevelt, like McKinley before him, tried to avoid patronage fights with Congress. However, Roosevelt, an advocate of civil service reform, insisted on qualification standards for Federal office. Members of Congress, he said, "may ordinarily name the man, but I shall name the standard and the men have got to come up to it." His care in the matter of judicial appointments twice led him to refuse to nominate candidates recommended by Sen. Platt of New York. On one of these occasions he wrote to Platt, "It is, I trust, needless to say that I fully appreciate the right and duty of the Senate to reject or to confirm any appointment according to what its Members conscientiously deem their duty to be; just as it is my business to make an appointment which I conscientiously think is a good one."

President Taft recommended a massive extension of the civil service, to include postmasters and other field officers then subject to Senate confirmation, but Congress did not enact the necessary legislation.

Woodrow Wilson accepted William G. McAdoo's suggestion that he let his department heads handle distribution of patronage, a chore that traditionally had been undertaken by the President himself. Wilson generally tried to get along with the Senate and on occasion yielded to it in the interests of party harmony, but he suffered several notable rejections in contests over local offices.

Noteworthy Nomination Contests

The two most significant nomination contests during Wilson's Administration resulted in the Senate's rejection of the appointment of George Rublee to the Federal Trade Commission and its confirmation of the nomination of Louis D. Brandeis as an Associate Justice of the Supreme Court.

Rublee was rejected in 1916, following a two-year fight led by Sen. Jacob H. Gallinger of New Hampshire, who opposed the nomination on the ground that it was "personally obnoxious" to him. Sen. Robert M. LaFollette of Wisconsin deplored Gallinger's use of the "personally obnoxious" formula against a national appointment; it was the first such application of the rule, he said, since he had been in the Senate. Meanwhile, Rublee actually served on the FTC for a year and a half on a recess appointment.

The confirmation of Brandeis, also in 1916, ended one of the most dramatic appointment contests in the nation's history. The opposition to Brandeis, led by New England business groups that considered him a radical and a crusader because of his unpaid public activities, charged that he was untrustworthy and guilty of unethical conduct. After four months of unusual open hearings by a Senate Judiciary subcommittee—hearings which were twice reopened—and with adjournment of Congress and the national political convention fast approaching, the full Committee still had not acted on the nomination. Finally, after personal appeals by Brandeis and the President to doubtful members, the Committee cleared the nomination by a 10-8 party-line vote. When the Senate voted June 1, Brandeis was confirmed, 47-22, and again the vote followed party lines.

Early in the Harding Administration, the White House announced that Republican Senators would select nominees for local offices and that the President "will hold Republican Senators to account for appointments made by him on their recommendations." Should the appointees prove unworthy or incompetent, he said, the Senators would bear "the responsibility for whatever trouble arises through this means."

Perhaps unfortunately, few of Harding's nominees were rejected. Three of his Cabinet members later became involved in scandals, and his Veterans Administrator was convicted of fraud.

Although Coolidge had few contests with the Senate over appointments, he became the first President since 1868 to have a Cabinet nominee rejected. Coolidge in 1925 nominated Charles Beecher Warren, a prominent Michigan attorney, to be his Attorney General. Little opposition was expected. However, when the nomination reached the Senate floor, where it was considered in unusual open session (until 1929, most nominations were considered in closed session), opponents attacked Warren for association with the "Sugar Trust." Such a man, they said, could not be relied upon to enforce the antitrust laws.

The first vote on Warren was a 40-40 tie, and Vice President Dawes—napping at his hotel—was not present to cast the deciding vote. While efforts were being made to get Dawes to the floor, a Republican Senator changed his vote so that he could offer a motion to reconsider the nomination. This motion was tabled, 41-39, and Warren was rejected. A furious Coolidge promptly renominated Warren, who was again defeated, 39-46. A contributing factor to the second defeat was the President's announcement as debate was in progress that if Warren was not confirmed, he would be given a recess appointment. Warren declined that honor.

President Hoover took a firm line on patronage abuses and refused to nominate candidates simply because they were recommended by party organizations. Hoover also instituted the practice, not followed by his successors, of making public the endorsers of judicial nominees.

Hoover met one notable nomination defeat. The rejection of Judge John J. Parker's nomination to the Supreme Court in 1930 was the first such rejection in 36 years. The Parker case marked the third effort in five years by Senate liberals to block appointments to the Court of persons they thought to be conservative. They had failed to block confirmation of Harlan Fiske Stone in 1925 and of Charles Evans Hughes as Chief Justice earlier in 1930. But, with the aid of a campaign mounted by organized labor and the National Association for the Advancement of Colored People, they were able to defeat Parker, 39-41.

Controversial Roosevelt Appointments

Franklin D. Roosevelt had few problems with appointments in his first years in office, but following the defeat of his Court-packing plan and his unsuccessful effort to purge Democratic opponents in the 1938 primaries, difficulties increased.

The only major appointment controversy of his first term involved Rexford G. Tugwell, a member of the President's "brain trust" who was nominated in 1934 to the newly created post of Under Secretary of Agriculture. Despite opposition based on his liberal philosophy, Tugwell was confirmed, 53-24. In Roosevelt's second term, many more appointees came under attack because of their allegedly radical views. Perhaps the most notable of the second-term contests involved Harry Hopkins, who won confirmation as Secretary of Commerce in 1939 only after a fight in which politics in the Works Progress Administration was the central issue. Hopkins was confirmed, 58-27, but a number of Democrats abstained.

Roosevelt's efforts to cut off patronage of Democratic Senators who opposed his program had mixed success. He succeeded in disciplining Senators Huey P. Long of Louisiana and Rush D. Holt of West Virginia but failed with Senators Harry F. Byrd and Carter Glass of Virginia, Pat McCarran of Nevada and W. Lee O'Daniel of Texas—all of whom successfully invoked Senatorial courtesy to defeat nominations they had not approved.

Of Roosevelt's eight nominees to the Supreme Court, only one—Hugo L. Black—faced serious opposition. Roosevelt appointed Black, a Senator from Alabama who had vigorously supported New Deal programs, in 1937 following the defeat of his Court-packing plan. Although it was traditional for the Senate to confirm one of its own Members immediately without reference to committee, the Black nomination was sent to the Judiciary Committee—the first such action in 50 years. The nomination was cleared by the Committee, 13-4, and the Senate, 66-15, after a debate punctuated by charges that Black had been a member of the Ku Klux Klan and had received Klan support in his 1926 election campaign. Black's confirmation did not end this controversy, and he finally made a public statement that he had once been a member of the Klan but had resigned and severed all ties with the organization.

Partisanship declined during World War II, and the President in the interests of national unity tried to avoid controversial nominations. Most of the emergency agencies were created by executive order, and their heads did not require Senate confirmation.

However, controversy erupted anew in 1945 with the appointment of Henry A. Wallace as Secretary of Commerce to succeed Jesse Jones. Wallace had been dumped from the Democratic ticket in 1944 because of conservative opposition to his "radical" economic views, but he had participated vigorously in the fall campaign and was expected to be rewarded with a Cabinet post. On Inauguration Day 1945, Roosevelt wrote to Jones asking him to step aside for Wallace. "Henry Wallace deserves almost any service which he believes he can satisfactorily perform," the letter said.

Wallace's chief reason for wanting the Commerce post was that it would give him control of the vast lending powers of the Reconstruction Finance Corporation. However, before acting on the Wallace nomination, Congress passed legislation to remove the RFC from the Commerce Department and give it independent status. Jones, testifying on the bill, said the RFC should not be directed by a man who was "willing to jeopardize the country's future with untried ideas and idealistic schemes." Wallace, replying to charges that he was not qualified to supervise the RFC, said: "...it is not a question of my lack of experience. Rather, it is a case of not liking the experience I have."

Following enactment of the RFC removal bill, the Senate on March 1 confirmed Wallace as Secretary of Commerce by a 56-32 vote. Ten Republicans joined 45 Democrats and 1 independent in voting for confirmation; 5 Democrats and 27 Republicans opposed.

Three weeks later the Senate rejected another Roosevelt appointee charged with radical views. Aubrey W. Williams, nominated to be Rural Electrification Administrator, had a background as social worker, administrator of the National Youth Administration and organization director of the National Farmers' Union. Opposition was based on his liberal racial views and on charges that he was an atheist and a Communist sympathizer. Nineteen Democrats joined 33 Republicans to defeat Williams, 36-52.

Truman's Battles With the Senate

President Truman engaged in a number of noteworthy contests with the Senate over appointments. Early in his administration he was widely criticized for appointing "cronies" to important offices. The 1946 appointments of George E. Allen to the RFC and James K. Vardaman to the Federal Reserve Board were subject to this charge, as was the 1949 appointment of Monrad C. Wallgren to the Federal Trade Commission. All three men were confirmed.

In 1946, Truman was forced, after a two-month fight, to withdraw the nomination of Edwin W. Pauley to be Under Secretary of the Navy. Pauley was a California oil man and former treasurer of the Democratic National Committee. In hearings before the Senate Naval Affairs Committee, the opposition, led by Sen. Charles W. Tobey of New Hampshire, presented witnesses who accused Pauley of having used political influence to protect his oil interests. Secretary of the Interior Harold L. Ickes said Pauley had told him, during the 1944 Presidential campaign, that $300,000 in campaign contributions from California oil men could be raised if the Government would drop its suit to establish Federal title to the tidewater oil lands. When Truman said at a press conference that Ickes might be mistaken, Ickes resigned his post, accusing the President of wanting him to commit perjury for the sake of

the Democratic party. Pauley denied categorically all the charges made against him and then requested the President to withdraw his nomination. The Committee was reported to be divided 10-8 against him.

After the 1946 mid-term election, in which the Republicans won control of Congress, Truman tried to avoid controversy by nominating men who would be acceptable to the Senate. The Republican 80th Congress did not actually reject any of Truman's nominees, although 153 names were withdrawn. However, in 1948 the Senate took no action on 11,122 nominations—apparently in the expectation that a Republican President would be able to fill the vacancies with Republican nominees in 1949.

The two most explosive contests that did occur in the 80th Congress concerned nominees who had been named before the 1946 election, David E. Lilienthal and Gordon R. Clapp. In the autumn of 1946, Truman gave Lilienthal, chairman of the Tennessee Valley Authority, a recess appointment to the chairmanship of the newly created Atomic Energy Commission. He appointed Clapp, who had served under Lilienthal, to replace him as TVA chairman.

The opposition to both nominations was led by Sen. Kenneth McKellar of Tennessee, who for years had been engaged in a patronage dispute with the TVA management. During the mid-1940s, McKellar had made several unsuccessful efforts to require Senate confirmation of all TVA employees earning $4,500 a year or more, and he resented TVA's insistence on a merit employment policy. Further, he had locked horns with TVA in 1941 over the location of a dam to be constructed in his state. Although he was not a member of the committees that considered the two nominations, McKellar conducted lengthy interrogations of witnesses and accused both Lilienthal and Clapp of having Communist sympathies. When the nominations finally reached the floor in April 1947, Lilienthal was confirmed, 50-31, and Clapp, 36-31. During the debate on Clapp, McKellar complained that the President had appointed him "without saying beans to me" and declared that he was "hurt beyond expression" that his colleagues should vote for nominees he opposed.

In 1949, President Truman met two outright defeats at the hands of the Senate. Leland Olds, nominated to a third term as member of the Federal Power Commission, was rejected, 15-53, in the face of opposition by oil and natural gas interests. Opponents, led by Sen. Lyndon B. Johnson of Texas, cited articles Olds had written in the 1920s for the labor press as evidence of Communist leanings. As a member of the FPC, Olds had played a key role in the development of Federal regulation of the natural gas industry.

The other 1949 rejection was that of Carl A. Ilgenfritz, who refused to take the chairmanship of the Munitions Board (salary: $14,000) unless he could retain his $70,000 annual salary as a steel executive. The Senate rejected him, 28-40.

Senatorial courtesy played a role in several Truman defeats at the hands of the Senate. In 1950 the Senate rejected, 14-59, the nomination of Martin A. Hutchinson as a member of the Federal Trade Commission. Hutchinson, a foe of Virginia's Byrd machine, was opposed by Senators Byrd and A. Willis Robertson of that state. In 1951 Sen. Paul H. Douglas of Illinois successfully appealed to the courtesy of the Senate to defeat two of President Truman's choices for Federal district judgeships in Illinois.

Douglas said the President should have nominated two candidates recommended by the Senator.

One of the plums of Congressional patronage came to an end in 1952. President Truman proposed, and Congress accepted, a reorganization plan putting all Internal Revenue Bureau jobs except that of Commissioner under civil service. The action followed 1951 Congressional hearings on scandals in the Bureau. The Senate, however, defeated other reorganization plans to put postmasters, customs officials and U.S. marshals under civil service.

Eisenhower and Kennedy Appointments

At the outset of his administration in 1953, President Eisenhower was criticized by conservative Republicans who felt that his Cabinet selections failed to give appropriate recognition to the Taft wing of the party. The President also gave his department and agency heads free rein to select their own subordinates, but when Republican leaders in the Senate complained that their suggestions were being ignored and that even the customary clearances were not being obtained, the Senators were invited to take their recommendations directly to the department heads. Subsequently, more appointments went to Taftites.

Several of Eisenhower's early nominations were opposed on conflict-of-interest grounds. The most celebrated of these cases was the nomination of Charles E. Wilson as Secretary of Defense. Wilson, former president of General Motors, was required to divest himself of all GM stock before the Senate Armed Services Committee consented to recommend his confirmation. Wilson had not planned to give up his stock. Similar issues arose with the nominations of Harold E. Talbott as Secretary of the Air Force and Robert T. Stevens as Secretary of the Army. From this time on, the Senate showed a continuing preoccupation with conflict-of-interest issues in the consideration of Presidential nominations.

One of Eisenhower's subsequent Cabinet nominations was defeated in the Senate in 1959—the first such rejection since 1925. Lewis L. Strauss already was serving under a recess appointment when, after months of hearings, the Senate rejected his nomination as Secretary of Commerce by a 46-49 vote. Opponents accused Strauss of lack of integrity and criticized his "conservative" approach to government. Specific issues raised against him included his role in the Dixon-Yates power contract, viewed by public power advocates as an attempt to undermine the Tennessee Valley Authority; his actions in the J. Robert Oppenheimer security case; and his alleged withholding of information, while chairman of the Atomic Energy Commission, from Congress and the public.

Of President Eisenhower's five appointees to the Supreme Court, three took their seats on the Court under recess appointments before they had been confirmed by the Senate. Chief Justice Earl Warren was unanimously confirmed in 1954 after publication of a 10-point summary of "charges" against him, including allegations that he was at one time connected with a liquor lobbyist and that he lacked judicial experience. William J. Brennan Jr. was confirmed by voice vote in 1957 after Sen. Joseph R. McCarthy protested that Brennan had compared Congressional investigations of Communism to "Salem witch hunts." Potter Stewart was confirmed in 1959, on a 70-17 vote; all opponents were southern Democrats, who criti-

Judgeships as Patronage

The prestige of a Federal judgeship is high, and appointment to the judiciary is considered by most attorneys and politicians to be the apex of a legal and public career.

Federal judgeships are lifetime appointments and pay $42,500 in the circuit court and $40,000 in the district court annually. There is no mandatory retirement age, but judges may retire at full salary at age 65 after 15 years or at 70 after 10 years on the bench.

The following list gives the number of confirmed Federal circuit and district court judges appointed by President Nixon during his first two years in office and by his five immediate predecessors.

	Democrats	Republicans
Roosevelt	188	6
Truman	116	9
Eisenhower	9	165
Kennedy	111†	11
Johnson	159	9
Nixon (1969-70)	3	86*

†*One New York Liberal also was appointed.*
**One judge was appointed from the New Progressive Party of Puerto Rico.*

cized Stewart's concurrence in the Supreme Court's 1954 school desegregation decision.

In 1960, the Senate adopted, 48-37, a Democratic resolution expressing the sense of the Senate that the President should not make recess appointments to the Supreme Court, except to prevent or end a breakdown in the administration of the Court's business; and that a recess appointee should not take his seat on the Court until the Senate had "advised and consented" to the nomination. Proponents claimed it was difficult to investigate the qualifications of a person already sitting on the Court; opponents charged that the Democrats hoped for a victory in the 1960 Presidential election and feared that a vacancy might occur on the Court before January, enabling the Republican President to give a recess appointment to a Republican.

Efforts of the Democratic-controlled Congress to keep judicial appointments out of the hands of the Republican President also led to a four-year delay in enacting legislation to create an unprecedented number of new circuit and district court judgeships. Proposed by Eisenhower in 1957, the bill did not become law until after President Kennedy took office in 1961. The 73 judgeships created by this law, plus 42 judgeship vacancies created by death or resignation, gave Kennedy in his first year in office the largest number of judicial appointments ever available to a President in a single year.

Kennedy participated far more actively than Eisenhower had done in the selection of appointees. Although recruitment of candidates for Federal office was carried out by a well publicized "talent hunt," some care was taken to clear appointments with appropriate Members of Congress.

None of Kennedy's nominations was rejected by the Senate, and few were contested. His two nominees to the

Supreme Court—Byron R. White and Arthur J. Goldberg in 1962—were confirmed without difficulty.

Racial issues figured in several confirmation contests. Despite southern opposition, Robert C. Weaver was confirmed in 1961 by voice vote as Administrator of the Housing and Home Finance Agency. Weaver, a Negro, had been national chairman of the National Association for the Advancement of Colored People. Similarly, Spottswood W. Robinson III, Negro dean of the Howard University Law School, was confirmed as a member of the Civil Rights Commission. But Kennedy's nomination of Thurgood Marshall, Negro civil rights lawyer, to the Second Circuit Court of Appeals was held up by the Senate Judiciary Committee for a year. Marshall was confirmed in 1962, 54-16, with all the dissenting votes cast by southern Democrats.

Fight Over Fortas

Lyndon B. Johnson, with one dramatic exception, had very little trouble with the Senate over nominations. His Cabinet appointees were confirmed without difficulty, and his first two Supreme Court appointments encountered only routine opposition.

The nomination of Abe Fortas to be an Associate Justice was confirmed by voice vote in 1965, although three Republicans raised objections on the floor that he had "put the United States last" in reportedly asking Washington newspaper editors to delay release of a story that Presidential aide Walter W. Jenkins had been arrested on a morals charge shortly before the 1964 Presidential election.

In 1967, President Johnson nominated Thurgood Marshall, then Solicitor General, to be the first Negro Associate Justice of the Supreme Court. Despite criticism from some Senators of Marshall's "activist" views on the role of the judiciary, his nomination was confirmed, 69-11. Ten southern Democrats and one northern Democrat voted "nay."

However, in 1968 Johnson was unsuccessful in his effort to elevate Fortas to the Chief Justiceship in place of Chief Justice Earl Warren, who sought to retire. The Fortas nomination finally was withdrawn in the face of a Senate filibuster, and Warren agreed to remain on the Court through the 1968-69 term—thus assuring that his successor would be appointed by the incoming President. Johnson's nomination of Judge Homer Thornberry of the Fifth Circuit Court of Appeals to replace Fortas as Associate Justice was not acted on, since there was no vacancy for Thornberry to fill.

The fight against Fortas was led by Sen. Robert P. Griffin of Michigan. He charged that the appointment was based on "cronyism" and that Warren had timed his retirement to assure appointment of his successor by a Democratic President. The "lame duck" charge gave way to more serious questions of propriety in the course of hearings held by the Judiciary Committee between July 11 and Sept. 16. One was the question of Fortas' continued involvement in White House affairs after he went on the Court in 1965, an involvement that Fortas admitted but played down in his testimony before the Committee. Toward the end of the hearings, it was disclosed that Fortas had received a fee of $15,000 for conducting a nine-week law seminar at American University in the summer of 1968. The money for the fee and other seminar expenses

had come from five former business associates, one of whom had a son who was involved in a Federal criminal case. During the hearings, as in the subsequent floor debate, attacks were made on the Court in general and on Fortas in particular for decisions on criminal procedural law and obscenity.

By an 11-6 vote, Sept. 17, 1968, the Judiciary Committee ordered the Fortas nomination reported to the Senate with the recommendation that it be confirmed. The majority, made up of eight Democrats and three Republicans, described Fortas as "extraordinarily well qualified for the post" of Chief Justice. His acceptance of a fee for teaching at American University and his participation in White House discussions, the report said, were within his rights and in line with what other Justices had done over the years. Three dissenting Democrats contended that Fortas had shown poor judgment in advising the President on legislative matters and in accepting the $15,000 teaching fee, and that the positions he had taken in Court decisions on crime, obscenity and other matters had been too liberal. One of the three dissenting Republicans (Strom Thurmond of North Carolina) submitted individual views in which he criticized Fortas' positions in decisions on criminal procedure, pornography, Federal-state relations and subversive activities.

In the floor debate, which began Sept. 25, Sen. Griffin pressed the attack relentlessly, and as his following grew, the chances of confirmation became more remote. They virtually vanished Sept. 27 when Minority Leader Everett McKinley Dirksen reversed his position and announced that he was officially "neutral." Majority Leader Mike Mansfield moved to end what was plainly a filibuster by reading to the Senate, Sept. 29, a cloture motion signed by 26 Senators. The motion was rejected Oct. 1 by a roll-call vote of 45-43, which was 14 votes short of the 59 needed for cloture. The next day Fortas requested the President to withdraw his name. Terming the action of the Senate "tragic," Johnson consented. Renewed controversy over Fortas' extra-judicial activities led to his resignation from the Court in 1969. He was the first Justice in history to step down under threat of impeachment.

A further diminution of Senatorial patronage occurred during the Johnson Administration, when Congress acceded to a Presidential reorganization plan placing the Customs Bureau on a career, civil service basis. Previously, appointments of customs collectors and other officers had been made by the President, generally on Senators' recommendations. President Johnson submitted the reorganization plan in 1965, and it was allowed to go into effect. A Senate resolution disapproving the plan was rejected, 17-64.

Nixon's Court Appointments

Early in his first year in office, President Nixon cut off another source of Congressional patronage. He said he was ending the patronage system of appointing postmasters and rural letter carriers, and that henceforth high scores on competitive examinations would be the sole criterion for filling the posts.

The system of choosing postmasters from among the three highest scorers on competitive examinations already was in effect. However, under past practice, the preferred candidate of a Member of Congress or party official was allowed to repeat the test until he gained a place among

Senate Rejections of Supreme Court Nominations

Nominee	Year Nominated	Nominated By	Action
William Paterson [1]	1793	Washington	Withdrawn (for technical reasons)
John Rutledge [2]	1795	Washington	Rejected
Alcxander Wolcott	1811	Madison	Rejected
John J. Crittenden	1828	J. Q. Adams	Postponed, 1829
Roger B. Taney [1]	1835	Jackson	Postponed
John C. Spencer	1844	Tyler	Rejected
Reuben H. Walworth	1844	Tyler	Withdrawn
Edward King	1844	Tyler	Postponed
Edward King [3]	1844	Tyler	Withdrawn, 1845
John M. Read	1845	Tyler	No action
George W. Woodward	1845	Polk	Rejected, 1846
Edward A. Bradford	1852	Fillmore	No action
George E. Badger	1853	Fillmore	Postponed
William C. Micou	1853	Fillmore	No action
Jeremiah S. Black	1861	Buchanan	Rejected
Henry Stanbery	1866	Johnson	No action
Ebenezer R. Hoar	1869	Grant	Rejected, 1870
George H. Williams [2]	1873	Grant	Withdrawn, 1874
Caleb Cushing [2]	1874	Grant	Withdrawn
Stanley Matthews [1]	1881	Hayes	No action
William B. Hornblower	1893	Cleveland	Rejected, 1894
Wheeler H. Peckham	1894	Cleveland	Rejected
John J. Parker	1930	Hoover	Rejected
Abe Fortas [4]	1968	L. B. Johnson	Withdrawn (after motion to invoke cloture was rejected)
Homer Thornberry	1968	L. B. Johnson	No action
Clement F. Haynsworth Jr.	1969	Nixon	Rejected
G. Harrold Carswell	1970	Nixon	Rejected

[1] *Reappointed and confirmed. Taney was confirmed as Chief Justice.*
[2] *Nominated for Chief Justice.*
[3] *Second appointment.*
[4] *Associate Justice nominated for Chief Justice.*

the top three. Under the new system, the test would be given only once, and the Postmaster General would select from among the three leading scorers. Members of Congress would still be consulted, but their recommendations would not necessarily be followed.

Nixon also sought Congressional approval of legislation to end Presidential appointment and Senatorial confirmation of first, second and third-class postmasters. The Senate passed the bill in 1969, but the House did not act. This goal was achieved in the Postal Reorganization Act of 1970, which eliminated all political influence in the selection of postal employees, including postmasters.

President Nixon's early appointments to major policy posts were confirmed with little difficulty, although Interior Secretary Walter J. Hickel's confirmation was delayed briefly in the face of opposition from conservation groups and Deputy Defense Secretary David Packard's confirmation raised conflict-of-interest questions.

Appointments that were never made also generated controversy. Dr. John H. Knowles was slated to get the job of Assistant Secretary of Health, Education and Welfare for health and scientific affairs, but the proposed nomination was blocked after opposition was voiced by Senate Minority Leader Dirksen and the American Medical Association. Franklin Long reportedly was rejected for appointment to head the National Science Foundation because of his opposition to the ABM nuclear defense system.

These controversies paled by comparison with the struggles that arose over President Nixon's efforts to fill one of two vacancies on the Supreme Court. His first Court nomination, that of Warren E. Burger to replace retiring Chief Justice Warren, was quickly confirmed by a 74-3 vote of the Senate. Burger, a judge of the District of Columbia Circuit Court of Appeals, was little known outside of legal circles at the time of his nomination, but he appeared to meet Nixon's standard of judicial conservatism.

It was with his next Court nomination that Nixon ran into a constitutional confrontation with the Senate. In May 1959, Associate Justice Fortas resigned under fire for accepting an outside fee from the family foundation of a convicted stock manipulator. To fill the vacancy thus created, Nixon in August nominated Clement F. Haynsworth Jr. of South Carolina, chief judge of the Fourth Circuit Court of Appeals.

Haynsworth was opposed by labor and civil rights leaders, the same combination that had defeated the Parker nomination in 1930, but as in the Fortas case the debate centered on judicial ethics. Foes of the nomination, led by Democratic Sen. Birch Bayh of Indiana, repeatedly said they did not question Haynsworth's honesty or integrity. But they did question his sensitivity to the appearance of ethical impropriety and his judgment regarding participation in cases in which his financial interests could be said to be involved, if only indirectly.

During committee hearings in September, Haynsworth, his financial affairs and his judicial record were scrutinized more thoroughly and extensively than those of any other Court nominee before him. The Judiciary Committee approved the nomination, Oct. 9, by a 10-7 vote. The 10-man majority asserted that Haynsworth was "extraordinarily well qualified" for the Court post and that the objections raised to his nomination were without substance.

Notwithstanding growing opposition, the President remained steadfast in his refusal to withdraw the nomination. Political pressure to influence the final vote was exerted by both sides. After a week's debate, the Senate on Nov. 21 rejected the Haynsworth nomination by a 45-55 roll-call vote. Republican defections played a decisive role in the outcome. Seventeen Republicans, including the three top GOP leaders in the Senate, joined 38 Democrats in voting against confirmation. Twenty-six Republicans and 19 Democrats—16 of them from the South—voted for it.

Early in 1970, President Nixon tried once more to fill the Supreme Court vacancy. This time he nominated another southerner, G. Harrold Carswell of Florida, a judge of the Fifth Circuit Court of Appeals. Few Senators wanted a repetition of the Haynsworth fight, and opposition to Carswell developed slowly. However, when it came to light that Carswell in a 1948 campaign speech had pledged himself to the principle of white supremacy, resistance to the nomination began to build. Carswell repudiated the views he had expressed more than 20 years earlier, but further charges of a continuing racist attitude were raised against him. Other critics, including many within his own profession, contended that Carswell was a man of mediocre abilities who lacked the judicial competence requisite for service on the High Court.

Carswell won the Judiciary Committee's approval, Feb. 16, 1970, by a vote of 13-4. But when the nomination moved to the Senate floor in March, opponents succeeded in delaying the final vote until after the Easter recess. When the Senate returned to consideration of the nomination at the beginning of April, the opposing sides remained closely matched and the outcome was in doubt.

In this atmosphere, Nixon wrote a letter to a pro-Carswell Republican Senator declaring that rejection of the nomination would impair his constitutional responsibility and the constitutional relationship of the President to Congress.

"What is centrally at issue in this nomination," he said, "is the constitutional responsibility of the President to appoint members of the Court—and whether this responsibility can be frustrated by those who wish to substitute their own philosophy or their own subjective judgment for that of the one person entrusted by the Constitution with the power of appointment. The question arises whether I, as President of the United States, shall be accorded the same right of choice in naming Supreme Court Justices which has been freely accorded to my predecessors of both parties."

Nixon said he respected the right of any Senator to differ with his selection. However, he continued: "The fact remains, under the Constitution, it is the duty of the President to appoint and of the Senate to advise and consent. But if the Senate attempts to substitute its judgment as to who should be appointed, the traditional

constitutional balance is in jeopardy and the duty of the President under the Constitution impaired."

By agreement, the first Senate vote on Carswell came April 6, on a motion to recommit the nomination to the Judiciary Committee. Opponents had hoped originally to defeat the appointment indirectly by burying the matter in committee, but the recommittal effort became instead a diversionary tactic, a preliminary skirmish that was won by the Administration. The recommittal move was rejected, 44-52.

After two days of intensive lobbying, the final vote on Carswell was taken April 8, and the nomination was rejected 45-51. Thirteen Republicans joined 38 Democrats, five of them from the South, in opposition. Not since 1894 had a President suffered similar consecutive rejections of two nominees to a Supreme Court seat.

Nixon responded to the Senate's action with an angry statement that he had "reluctantly" decided that the Senate "as presently constituted" would not confirm a judicial conservative from the South. Thus, he said, he would go elsewhere for his next nominee.

Less than a week later, on April 14, the President nominated Harry A. Blackmun of Minnesota, a judge of the Eighth Circuit Court of Appeals, to fill the Supreme Court vacancy. Blackmun had a reputation as a moderate and scholarly judge, and both liberals and conservatives praised the President's selection. The Senate Judiciary Committee unanimously reported the nomination May 9, and the Senate confirmed it May 12 by a 94-0 vote.

Power of Removal

Controversy over the role of the Senate in the removal of public officers began in the early days of the Republic and continued intermittently into the 20th century.

The Constitution contained no language governing removals except for the impeachment provisions of Article II, Section 4. Hamilton, writing in *The Federalist* (No. 77), contended that the consent of the Senate "would be necessary to displace as well as to appoint," but this view was soon challenged and rejected by Congress.

Debate over the power of removal began in the First Congress, during consideration of a bill to establish the Department of Foreign Affairs. Two principal theories were advanced. One group insisted that since the Constitution gave the Senate a share in the appointment power, the Senate must also give its advice and consent to removals. The other group, led by Madison, maintained that the power of removal was an executive function, necessarily implied in the power to nominate, and that Senate participation would violate the principle of separation of powers.

Madison's view prevailed in the House, which passed the bill by a 29-22 vote after striking out language specifically vesting removal power in the President and substituting a provision that deliberately implied recognition of the President's exclusive power of removal under the Constitution.

After a lengthy and spirited debate in closed session, the Senate narrowly acceded to the House interpretation. A motion to strike out the House language recognizing the President's sole power of removal was rejected on a tie vote, with Vice President Adams—voting for the first time—recorded in opposition. The fact that the Senate agreed to limit its own powers was widely attributed to Senatorial respect for President Washington.

Early Presidents exercised great restraint in use of the removal power, even after the enactment in 1820 of the Four Years Law. This law, ostensibly designed to ensure accountability of Federal officers, established a fixed four-year term for district attorneys, customs collectors and many other officers who previously had served at the pleasure of the President.

Presidents Monroe and John Quincy Adams followed a policy of renominating all such persons when their terms expired unless they had been guilty of misconduct. However, Senatorial pressure for patronage was on the rise, and Adams' self-restraint was met by Senate demands for a broader role in appointments and removals.

Jackson's Clashes With Senate

Andrew Jackson's sweeping and partisan use of the removal power soon brought renewed Senate demands for an increased share in the patronage pie. Controversy over the issue led to a series of Senate resolutions requesting the President to inform the Senate of his reasons for removing various officials. Jackson complied with several of these requests, but by 1835 he had had enough. A Senate resolution, adopted by a 23-22 vote, requesting information on the "charges, if any," against the recently removed Surveyor General of South Tennessee brought the following response:

"It is now, however, my solemn conviction that I ought no longer, from any motive, nor in any degree, to yield to these unconstitutional demands. Their continued repetition imposes on me, as the representative and trustee of the American people, the painful but imperious duty of resisting to the utmost any further encroachment on the rights of the Executive.... The President in cases of this nature possesses the exclusive power of removal from office; and under the sanctions of his official oath, and of his liability to impeachment, he is bound to exercise it whenever the public welfare shall require. On no principle known to our institutions can he be required to account for the manner in which he discharges this portion of his public duties, save only in the mode and under the forms prescribed by the Constitution."

Meanwhile, the Senate had appointed a committee "to inquire into the extent of Executive patronage; the circumstances which contributed to its increase of late; the expediency and practicability of reducing the same, and the means of such reduction." The committee reported a bill to repeal the first two sections of the Four Years Law and to require the President to submit to the Senate the reasons for each removal. John Quincy Adams called this an effort "to cut down the executive power of the President and to grasp it for the Senate." Supported by Calhoun, Webster and Clay, the measure won Senate approval, 31-16, but was never taken up in the House. Webster and Clay disputed the interpretation of the removal power established by the First Congress. Attributing that interpretation largely to Congressional confidence in President Washington, Clay said it had not been reconsidered only because prior to Jackson's administration it had not been abused.

Presidential Opposition to Tenure Acts

The next great clash between Senate and President over the removal power occurred in the administration of Andrew Johnson. Among its consequences were the Tenure of Office Act of 1867 and Johnson's impeachment trial.

The conflict grew out of Johnson's fight with the radical Republican leaders of Congress over Reconstruction policy and his use of the removal power to make places for his own followers.

As passed by the Senate, the Tenure of Office bill enabled civil officers, excluding members of the Cabinet, appointed by and with the advice and consent of the Senate, to remain in office until their successors were appointed by the President and confirmed by the Senate. It permitted the President to suspend an officer during a recess of the Senate and appoint a temporary successor but provided that the suspended officer should resume his post if the Senate failed to approve the suspension. The Senate rejected an amendment to delete the clause excluding Cabinet members, as well as one to require Senate confirmation of the appointment of all officers with salaries exceeding $1,000. However, the House deleted the exclusion for Cabinet members, and in conference it was agreed that Cabinet members should hold office for the term of the President who appointed them and for one month thereafter, subject to removal by and with the advice and consent of the Senate.

President Johnson vetoed the bill on the ground that it would unconstitutionally restrict the President's power of removal, but Congress enacted the measure over the veto—by a 35-11 vote in the Senate and a 133-37 vote in the House.

Johnson promptly put the Tenure of Office Act to the test. First, he suspended Secretary of War Stanton, but the Senate refused to concur in the suspension. Johnson then attempted to dismiss Stanton and make another appointment to the post. The House immediately initiated impeachment proceedings, the principal charge being that Johnson had violated the new law by dismissing Stanton. On this charge, the Senate failed to convict by only one vote; 7 Republicans and 12 Democrats voted for acquittal, while 35 Republicans voted for conviction. A two-thirds majority was required to convict.

Early in Grant's administration in 1869, Congress amended the Tenure of Office Act by repealing its provisions regulating suspensions. The new law provided that the President might suspend officers "in his discretion"—without, as before, reporting to the Senate the reasons for his action—but required prompt nomination of successors. A further dispute between President Cleveland and the Republican-controlled Senate finally led to repeal of what was left of the Tenure of Office Act of 1867 and of the amended 1869 version.

While Congress was in recess in the summer of 1885, Cleveland suspended 643 officers subject to Senatorial confirmation. When Congress reconvened, he submitted to the Senate the names of their replacements to whom he had given recess appointments. The committees handling these nominations then called upon the executive departments for information concerning the reasons for the suspensions, information which the departments refused to give. Action on the nominations was stalled by the dispute.

The climax to the controversy came over the nomination of a U.S. attorney in Alabama. The Justice Department refused demands by the Senate Judiciary Committee for information concerning the reasons for removal of his predecessor. The Senate responded with a resolution, adopted on a party-line vote, censuring the Attorney General for his refusal to transmit the desired papers. A second resolution, adopted by a one-vote margin, said it was "the duty of the Senate to refuse its advice and consent to proposed removals of officers" in cases where information requested by the Senate was withheld.

The Senate debated the resolutions heatedly over a two-week period. While they were pending, Cleveland sent a special message to the Senate reasserting the President's authority:

"The requests and demands which by the score have for nearly three months been presented to the different Departments of the Government, whatever their form, have but one complexion. They assume the right of the Senate to sit in judgment upon the exercise of my exclusive function, for which I am solely responsible to the people from whom I have so lately received the sacred trust of office....

"The pledges I have made were made to the people, and to them I am responsible. I am not responsible to the Senate, and I am unwilling to submit my actions and official conduct to them for judgment...."

Public opinion responded to the President's message, and the nomination logjam was broken. The following year Sen. E. R. Hoar (R Mass.) introduced legislation to repeal the Tenure of Office Acts, and the bill was speedily enacted into law.

Wilson and Coolidge on Removals

Another big controversy over the removal power occurred in 1920, when President Wilson vetoed the forerunner of the Budget and Accounting Act of 1921. That measure, as transmitted to Wilson, provided that the Comptroller General and Assistant Comptroller General were to be appointed by the President subject to Senate confirmation, but were to be subject to removal by "concurrent resolution of Congress." A concurrent resolution does not require the President's approval; thus the President would have had no control over the removal of these officers. Wilson's veto message was emphatic:

"I am convinced that the Congress is without constitutional power to limit the appointing power and its incident power of removal derived from the Constitution."

The following year, the Budget and Accounting Act of 1921 became law with the signature of President Harding. The final legislation, however, differed from the 1920 version in providing for removal of the Comptroller General and Assistant Comptroller General by joint resolution, which requires the signature of the President, or passage over his veto, to go into effect.

Senate pressure for a role in removals does not always take the form of resistance to removals desired by the President. The Senate also has attempted to force removals, although without notable success. President Lincoln was able to head off efforts by a caucus of Republican Senators to force the resignation of Secretary of State Seward in 1862. More recently, in 1924, the Senate adopted a resolution "that it is the sense of the United States Senate that the President of the United States immediately request the resignation of Edwin Denby as Secretary of the Navy." Denby had been implicated in the

naval oil lease scandals, and Senate Democrats hoped to press similar resolutions against other members of President Coolidge's Cabinet. The Denby resolution was adopted on a 47-34 roll call and a copy was sent to the President. Coolidge promptly issued a statement:

"No official recognition can be given to the passage of the Senate resolution relative to their opinion concerning members of the Cabinet or other officers under executive control....

"...The dismissal of an officer of the Government, such as is involved in this case, other than by impeachment, is exclusively an Executive function."

A few days later Denby resigned.

Another Senate removal effort, with a different twist, involved appointees to the newly created Federal Power Commission during the 71st Congress. Dissatisfied with the actions of FPC members it had confirmed shortly before the Christmas recess, the Senate in January 1931 tried to recall the nominations for reconsideration. President Hoover refused, saying:

"I am advised that these appointments were constitutionally made, with the consent of the Senate, formally communicated to me, and that the return of the documents by me and reconsideration by the Senate would be ineffective to disturb the appointees in their offices."

Court Decisions on Power of Removal

The courts upheld the President. After nearly 140 years of controversy over the President's power of removal, the Supreme Court had finally met the issue head on in 1926. In the words of Chief Justice Taft, the Court had "studiously avoided deciding the issue until it was presented in such a way that it could not be avoided."

The case involved a postmaster who had been removed from office by President Wilson in 1920, without consultation with the Senate, although the 1876 law under which the man had been appointed stipulated: "Postmasters of the first, second and third classes shall be appointed and may be removed by the President, by and with the advice and consent of the Senate, and shall hold their offices for four years, unless sooner removed or suspended according to law."

In a 6-3 decision, the Court upheld the President's unrestricted power of removal as inherent in the executive power invested in him by the Constitution. The Court concluded: "It therefore follows that the Tenure of Office Act of 1867, in so far as it attempted to prevent the President from removing executive officers who had been appointed by him by and with the consent of the Senate was invalid, and that subsequent legislation of the same effect was equally so.... The provision of the law of 1876, by which the unrestricted power of removal of first-class postmasters is denied to the President, is in violation of the Constitution and invalid." *(Myers v. U.S.,* 1926)

In a unanimous 1935 decision, the Court modified this position. The 1935 case involved a Federal Trade Commissioner whom President Roosevelt had tried to remove because "I do not feel that your mind and my mind go along together on either the policies or the administration" of the FTC. The Court held that the FTC was "an administrative body created by Congress to carry into effect legislative policies" and thus could not "in any proper sense be characterized as an arm or an eye of the Executive." It continued:

"Whether the power of the President to remove an officer shall prevail over the authority of Congress to condition the power by fixing a definite term and precluding a removal except for cause will depend upon the character of the office; the Myers decision, affirming the power of the President alone to make the removal, is confined to purely executive officers, and as to officers of the kind here under consideration, we hold that no removal can be made during the prescribed term for which the officer is appointed, except for one or more of the causes named in the applicable‾ statute." (*Humphrey's Executor (Rathbun) v. U.S.*, 1935)

Nomination Procedures

It has been customary since the time of Washington for the President to submit nominations to the Senate in written form. By exception, Harding in 1921 proceeded directly from the inaugural ceremonies to the Senate chamber to present his Cabinet nominations in person.

Before submitting a nomination the President normally consults with key Members of Congress, political organizations and special interest groups in an effort to obtain informal clearance for his candidate. Because the President usually wants to avoid a confirmation fight, serious opposition at this stage may lead him to choose another person for the post.

In recent years the Federal Bureau of Investigation has conducted investigations of potential candidates, and there have been frequent controversies between the President and the Senate over access to FBI reports. Potential Supreme Court nominees have been evaluated by the American Bar Association's standing committee on the Federal judiciary. President Nixon abandoned this procedure in 1969 but decided to return to it in 1970, after the Haynsworth and Carswell defeats.

Committee Hearings

Since 1868, most nominations have been referred to committee. The committee, or a subcommittee, may hold hearings at which the nominee and others may testify. Most such hearings are purely routine, although some turn into grueling inquisitions. Nominees have been known to ask the President to withdraw their names rather than face such an ordeal.

Until 30 years or so ago, it was unusual for Supreme Court nominees to be invited to appear before the Judiciary Committee. Felix Frankfurter, who received such an invitation in 1939, noted that on only one previous occasion had a Supreme Court nominee testified before the Committee. Frankfurter originally declined the Committee's invitation but later appeared at the Committee's request. Ten years later the Committee by a 5-4 vote invited Court nominee Sherman Minton to appear before it, but when Minton questioned the propriety of such an appearance, the Committee reversed itself and reported the nomination favorably to the Senate. These precedents notwithstanding, in recent years Supreme Court nominees have been expected to testify at hearings on their nominations. Justice Abe Fortas in 1968 became the first nominee for Chief Justice ever to appear before the Committee and the first sitting Justice, except for recess appointees, ever to do so.

When hearings on a nomination have been completed, the subcommittee votes, usually in executive session, and sends the nomination to the full committee. The committee may report the nomination favorably, unfavorably or without recommendation, or it may simply take no action at all. Nominations that fail to gain approval usually meet defeat at this stage.

Floor Action

Nominations that reach the floor are called up on the executive calendar, frequently en bloc, and usually are approved without objection. The question takes the following form: "Will the Senate advise and consent to this nomination?" Controversial nominations may be debated at length, but few nominations are brought to the floor unless sufficient votes for confirmation can be mustered.

Since 1929, Senate rules (Rule 38) have provided that nominations shall be considered in open session unless the Senate, in closed session and by majority vote, decides to consider a particular nomination in closed session. In such a case any Senator is permitted to make public his own vote.

Prior to 1929, the customary practice was to consider nominations in closed executive session, and the votes taken were not supposed to be made public.

Nominations may not be put to a vote on the day they are received or on the day they are reported from committee, except by unanimous consent. They may be approved, rejected or returned to committee.

All nominations still pending at the end of the session in which they are made die with that session. If the Senate recesses or adjourns for more than 30 days, all pending nominations must be returned to the President; they cannot be considered again unless he resubmits them.

When a nomination has been confirmed or rejected, a motion to reconsider may be made on the day the vote is taken or on either of the next two days of actual executive session.

Recess Appointments

Recess appointments present special problems. The Constitution provides that "the President shall have Power to fill up all Vacancies that may happen during the Recess of the Senate, by granting Commissions which shall expire at the End of their next Session."

The ambiguities of this section have produced repeated controversies between the President and the Senate. Chief point at issue is the constitutional meaning of the word "happen." If it means "happen to occur," then the President can only fill offices that become vacant after the Senate adjourns. If it means "happen to exist," he can fill any vacancy, whatever the cause.

President Washington, taking a strict view of his powers, sought specific Senate authorization to make recess appointments of military officers created by a bill enacted near the end of a session. Madison opted for a broad construction. His recess appointment of envoys to negotiate a peace treaty with Great Britain brought outcries from the Senate that a recess appointment could not be made to an office never before filled. However, resolutions protesting Madison's action never came to a vote, and the appointments ultimately were confirmed.

Although the recess appointment debate continued for years, it gradually became accepted that the President could make recess appointments to fill any vacancies, no matter how they arose. However, Federal law prohibits payment of salary to any person appointed during a recess of the Senate to fill an existing vacancy, if the vacancy existed while the Senate was in session, until the appointee has been confirmed by the Senate. This prohibition does not apply if the vacancy occurred during the last 30 days of the session, or if the Senate failed to act on a nomination submitted to it before adjournment.

Bibliography

Congressional Quarterly, *Congress and the Nation* Vols. I and II, and annual CQ *Almanacs.*

Hamilton, Alexander, *The Federalist*, Nos. 76 and 77.

Harris, Joseph P., *The Advice and Consent of the Senate.* Greenwood Press, 1968.

Harris, Richard, *Decision.* E.P. Dutton & Co., 1971.

Haynes, George H., *The Senate of the United States.* Houghton Mifflin, 1938, and Russell & Russell, 1960.

Mann, Dean E., *The Assistant Secretaries.* Brookings Institution, 1965.

Riddick, Floyd M., *The United States Congress: Organization and Procedure.* National Capitol Publishers, 1949.

Rogers, Lindsay, *The American Senate.* Alfred A. Knopf, 1926.

Warren, Charles, *The Supreme Court in United States History.* Little, Brown and Co., 1935.

Congressional Investigations

THE FIRST Congressional investigation, a House inquiry into an Army disaster in Indian territory, was conducted in 1792. The hearings staked out a major new area of activity which was to become one of the most controversial and highly publicized powers of Congress.

Since 1792, investigating committees of the House and the Senate have left an erratic trail, marked by some of the brightest and darkest moments in Congressional annals. Investigations have led Congress into repeated confrontations with the Executive and Judicial Branches over the constitutional separation of powers. They have elevated comparatively minor political figures to Presidential status, broken the careers of important public men and captured the attention of millions of newspaper readers and, in later years, radio listeners and television viewers. (See box on personalities and investigations.)

Based on the constitutional assignment of "all legislative powers" to Congress, investigations have served as the eyes and ears of the two chambers. Investigations have gathered information on the need for possible future legislation, tested the effectiveness of past legislative action, inquired into the qualifications and performance of Members and laid the groundwork for impeachment proceedings. The Congressional power of investigation has long been regarded as one of the essential functions of the national Legislature. The practices of some committees, however, have led critics to brand investigations as political vehicles for personal publicity and as an extravagant waste of time and money, producing few, if any, useful legislative results.

Woodrow Wilson, writing on Congressional government as a Johns Hopkins University graduate student in 1884, asserted that "The informing function of Congress should be preferred even to its legislative function." Sen. Gerald P. Nye (R N.D.), chairman of the controversial Senate Special Committee Investigating the Munitions Industry (Nye Committee), told a radio audience in 1938 that "Honest investigations, prosecuted by legislators determined to reach and develop the facts, and by legislators who in their work can and will abandon partisanship, are of greatest value to the Government and its people." And President Truman, who achieved national fame as chairman of the World War II Senate Special Committee to Investigate the National Defense Program (Truman Committee), said in the Senate in 1944: "In my opinion, the power of investigation is one of the most important powers of Congress. The manner in which that power is exercised will largely determine the position and prestige of the Congress in the future."

No period of American history has been without investigations. Only the Spanish-American War in 1898,

of all U.S. military engagements, escaped Congressional scrutiny. President McKinley forestalled legislative inquiry into that conflict by appointing the Dodge Commission.

Many early investigations involved traditional legislative privileges, such as charges against a Senator or Representative or trials of Members accused of libels, assaults or bribery attempts. Until toward the end of the 19th century, however, most of the investigations concerned the civil and military activities of the Executive Branch. For example, the Post Office Department was the target of probes in 1820 and 1822, the Bank of the United States in 1832 and 1834, the Smithsonian Institution in 1855, and the General Land Office in 1897.

By 1880 a new field for Congressional investigation was emerging—economic and social problems across the nation. There were studies of Negro migration from South to North (1880), strikebreaking by the railroads (1892) and the concentration of wealth in the "money trust" (1912-13).

Government operations and social conditions served as the principal subjects of Congressional investigation until the period between World Wars I and II, when the threat of subversion from foreign ideologies led to inquiries of a different sort. Investigations of social conditions and Government operations continued but for a time lost much of their former glamor. Meanwhile, probes into possible subversion expanded rapidly, developing new and harsh methods of inquiry. Hearings involved broad-scale intrusions into the thoughts, actions and associations of all manner of persons and institutions, and raised searching legal and moral questions about the power and procedures of Congressional inquiry. (See box on Investigations of Un-Americanism.)

The expanded use of investigations made Congress' investigating power itself a major political issue. To some, the threat to national security posed by Communist subversion was so great as to justify exceptional procedures. To others, the threat to individual liberties from the behavior and authority of some committees appeared a more real danger than that of Communism. The conflict over the powers of the committees and the

Reference

See Appendix table of contents (first thumb tab) for excerpt from Hiss-Chambers testimony in 1948 investigation and texts of two Supreme Court opinions on investigative powers of Congress.

245

Personalities and Investigations

Several leading figures in Congressional investigations were projected into positions of great influence. Sen. Gerald P. Nye (R N.D.) was considered a possible Republican Presidential or Vice Presidential nominee in 1936, after heading the Senate Special Committee Investigating the Munitions Industry. President Truman achieved national prominence as chairman of the World War II Senate Special Committee to Investigate the National Defense Program.

President Nixon first won recognition through his activities on the House Un-American Activities Committee, particularly in its investigation of Alger Hiss. *(See Appendix for partial text of testimony at Hiss-Chambers hearings.)* Sen. Estes Kefauver (D Tenn.) became a leading Presidential contender after the widely viewed televised hearings of his Senate Special Committee to Investigate Organized Crime in Interstate Commerce. In 1956, Kefauver was the Democratic nominee for Vice President. Sen. Robert F. Kennedy (D N.Y.) first achieved a measure of popular recognition while chief counsel of the Senate Select Committee on Improper Activities in the Labor or Management Field.

None of these, however, derived as much authority from Congressional investigations as Sen. Joseph R. McCarthy (R Wis.), whose power was felt—and feared—in Congress, in two Administrations, in the State Department, in the Armed Forces, in universities, and in many other public and private institutions throughout the country.

Not only the investigators achieved fame from committee hearings. Leaders in every segment of the community, from the academic world to the underworld, were thrust into the national spotlight. Though public attention was focused on such varied figures as Gen. Douglas A. MacArthur, teamster boss James R. Hoffa, or ex-Communist Whittaker Chambers, the investigations also paved the way for important legislation, much of which will remain on the statute books when personalities are gone and forgotten.

rights of witnesses continued, with shifting results and varying intensity, throughout the pre-World War II and the postwar period. It was waged in Congress, in the courts, in the Executive Branch, in the councils of both parties, and in public debates and election campaigns.

Power of Congress to Investigate

Congress received its power to investigate along with the legislative functions assigned to it by the Constitution. The investigative power of a legislative body had been established as early as the 16th century by the British House of Commons. The Commons first used its investigative power in determining its membership. It then made increasing use of investigations to assist it in performing its lawmaking functions and in overseeing officials responsible for executing laws and spending the funds made available by Parliament. Investigating committees of the House of Commons had authority to summon witnesses and to examine documents, and the Commons could support its committees by punishing un-

cooperative witnesses for contempt. American colonial legislatures, the Continental Congress and state legislatures relied on these Parliamentary precedents in carrying out their own investigations. Thus the power to investigate, to compel the attendance of witnesses and to demand the production of documents was regarded by most Members of the first Congresses as an intrinsic part of the power to legislate.

Uncertainty arose, despite the precedents, because of the Constitutional assignment to Congress of "all legislative powers herein granted." Strict constructionists asserted that limitation of the authority of Congress to specifically granted powers restricted investigations to clearly defined judicial functions, such as election disputes, impeachment proceedings or cases involving Congressional privileges. Broad constructionists argued that the precedents supported an inherent investigative power in the legislative function. The broad constructionists prevailed, and won approval of the Army investigation in 1792. That first investigation served as a precedent for others. Since then, no serious challenge of the basic authority of Congress to investigate has ever been mounted. However, specific investigations have been challenged, with mixed results; opposition has arisen mainly in the case of investigations that have pried into private affairs, infringed on personal liberties or conflicted with Executive Branch prerogatives.

Power to Punish for Contempt

Like the investigative power which it reinforced, the Congressional power to punish for contempt was based on Parliamentary precedents dating from Elizabethan times. No express power to punish for contempt, except in the case of a Member, was granted Congress in the Constitution. But Congress assumed that it had inherent power to send persons in contempt to jail without a court order, because it regarded such power as necessary for its own protection and for the integrity of its proceedings.

The first use of the Congressional power to punish for contempt was on Dec. 28, 1795, when Robert Randall was summoned to the bar of the House on a charge of having tried to bribe a Member. Following debate, the House on Jan. 4, 1796, voted 78-17 to jail Randall for a week. Both chambers drew on precedents established in the Randall case to punish other non-Members for contemptuous acts. The first committee witness cited for contempt was Nathaniel Rounsavell, editor of the Alexandria, Va., *Herald*, who refused in 1812 to answer questions before a House committee investigating a breach in the security of a secret House session. After a day's confinement in the custody of the House Sergeant at Arms, Rounsavell apologized for his behavior and was discharged.

The Senate first voted a contempt of Congress citation on March 20, 1800, when William Duane was ordered arrested for libeling a Member. On May 14, the Senate by a 13-4 vote sentenced him to 30 days in jail and ordered him to pay costs. The first Senate committee witness to be cited was Thaddeus Hyatt, who had refused a summons by a committee investigating John Brown's raid on Harper's Ferry in 1859. The Senate March 12, 1860, by a 44-10 vote ordered Hyatt jailed. He was released June 15. *(Continued on p. 248)*

Investigations of Un-Americanism

Perhaps the most significant expansion of the investigative function of Congress was the study of subversive movements and other activities alleged to be detrimental to the interests of the United States. Instead of pursuing traditional lines of Congressional inquiry—operations of the Government and national social and economic problems—the probers into subversion or possible subversion regarded the thoughts, actions and associations of all manner of persons and institutions as fit subjects for Congressional inspection.

Early History. The first Congressional investigation of un-American activities was authorized Sept. 19, 1918, two months prior to the armistice in World War I. It was instituted as the result of a statement on the activities of German brewing interests early in September 1918 by A. Mitchell Palmer, then Custodian of Alien Property and later Attorney General. Facts would soon be disclosed, Palmer had said, which would "conclusively show that 12 or 15 German brewers…,in association with the United Brewers Association," secretly furnished the money to purchase a large newspaper in order to fight prohibition. Palmer said the "organized liquor traffic of the country is a vicious interest because it has been unpatriotic, because it has been pro-German, because it has fostered organizations intended to keep young Germans from becoming real American citizens." The investigation, conducted by the Senate Judiciary Committee, was expanded in 1919 to cover "any efforts being made to propagate in this country the principles of any party exercising… authority in Russia…and…to incite the overthrow of the Government of this country or all governments by force or by the destruction of life or property, or the general cessation of industry."

The House on May 12, 1930, set up a Special Committee to Investigate Communist Activities in the United States—the Fish Committee, so-called after its chairman, Rep. Hamilton Fish Jr. (R N.Y.). On March 20, 1934, the House created a Special Committee on Un-American Activities, under Chairman John W. McCormack (D Mass.). On May 26, 1938, three years after the McCormack Committee submitted its report, which covered Nazi as well as Communist activities in the United States, the House set up another Special Committee on Un-American Activities, under Chairman Martin Dies (D Texas).

The controversial path of the Dies Committee, predecessor of the present House Internal Security Committee, began in August 1938 with testimony from John P. Frey, president of the Metal Trades Department of the American Federation of Labor, that the Congress of Industrial Organizations and many of its affiliates were Communist-dominated, and that many CIO leaders were Communists. In October, the Committee heard a string of witnesses testify on the wide extent of Communist influence in California maritime unions and among auto union members who had staged sit-down strikes in Detroit in 1937. An allegation that Michigan Gov. Frank Murphy (D) was receiving strong Communist support in his bid for re-election was followed by his defeat in November 1938.

Witnesses before the Dies Committee accused hundreds of persons of being supporters of Communist activities, but only a few of those named were permitted to testify in rebuttal. The Committee agreed on Aug. 16, 1939, to permit hearings by subcommittees, and Dies on Oct. 2 held in Chicago his first closed hearing as a one-man subcommittee. The next day he told newsmen he had the names of 2,000 of the 4,700 Communists in the Chicago area. This was the beginning of one-man domination of the Committee by Dies. It ushered in his practice of sitting in secret as a subcommittee of one and thereafter issuing highly colored statements. Sensational treatment of these charges by the press was a portent of postwar trends.

Postwar Developments. The Dies Committee was reconstituted in succeeding Congresses until 1945. At the beginning of the 79th Congress, Jan. 3, 1945, Rep. John E. Rankin (D Miss.) offered an amendment to the House rules to make the Dies Committee a standing committee and to rename it the House Committee on Un-American Activities. Opponents of the Committee, caught unprepared by this strategy, failed to muster their forces, and the Rankin proposal carried, 208-186.

Throughout its career, the Committee has been noted chiefly for its wide-ranging investigative activities, directed primarily against Communist activities and influence. The Committee's actions elicited sharp criticism from some Members of Congress, the courts and various liberal groups. Much of the criticism stemmed from charges that the Committee violated the civil liberties of witnesses with inquiries into their political beliefs and associations, and that it resorted to exposure for the sake of exposure.

The Committee's investigation in 1948 of State Department official Alger Hiss and his subsequent conviction for perjury established internal Communism as a leading political issue, and the Committee as a major political force. The Internal Security Subcommittee of the Senate Judiciary Committee, set up in 1951, also regularly conducted probes of Communist activities. Many state legislatures emulated Congress by undertaking investigations of subversion within their respective domains. The most famous investigations of Communism were conducted by Sen. Joseph R. McCarthy (R Wis.) as chairman (1953-54) of the Permanent Investigations Subcommittee of the Senate Government Operations Committee. His behavior in this role intensified concern over the use by Congress of its investigating powers and led in 1954 to his censure by the Senate. After McCarthy's censure, investigations of Communism attracted less public attention. Investigations of un-American activities continued, however, turning to such subjects as the Ku Klux Klan, black militancy and student activists.

On Feb. 18, 1969, the House by a 306-80 roll-call vote adopted a resolution to rename the Un-American Activities Committee the Internal Security Committee and to revise its mandate. Sponsored by Committee Chairman Richard H. Ichord (D Mo.), the resolution in essence changed the emphasis of the Committee from "un-American" activities to "Communist" activities.

Constitutionality of the Power. In 1821 *(Anderson v. Dunn)*, the Supreme Court upheld the constitutionality of summary use of the contempt power by Congress. The Court declared that the power to punish contempts was assumed to be inherent in each chamber, for, without it, Congress would be "exposed to every indignity and interruption that rudeness, caprice, or even conspiracy may mediate against it." The power was limited, however, by the Court "to the least possible power adequate to the end proposed," and imprisonment could not extend beyond the adjournment of Congress.

The case grew out of an attempt by John Anderson to bribe a House Member to help push a land claim through Congress. Anderson was given a summary trial at the bar of the House, at the end of which the Speaker reprimanded Anderson and then freed him. After his release, Anderson brought charges against Sergeant at Arms Thomas Dunn for assault and battery and for false arrest. A lower court ruled against Anderson, and he appealed. The Supreme Court likewise ruled against Anderson, but most of its decision was devoted to upholding the constitutionality of the summary contempt power of Congress. *(See Appendix for text of Court opinion.)*

Passage of Criminal Statute. Considering the limitation of imprisonment only to the end of a legislative session inadequate, Congress in 1857 passed a law, still in effect in amended form (2 USC 192), making it a criminal offense to refuse information demanded by either chamber. Even after passage of the 1857 law, Congress preferred to punish persons in contempt itself, reasoning that a few days of confinement might induce a witness to cooperate, while turning him over to a court would put him out of reach of the inquiring committee. Later, however, as the press of legislative business mounted and as court review of summary Congressional punishment became more frequent, Congress increasingly relied on criminal prosecution for contempt under the 1857 law. Since 1945, all contempt citations have been prosecuted under the criminal statute.

The Congressional power of investigation was further strengthened in 1862 by an amendment to the 1857 law providing that no witness could refuse to testify or to produce documents on the ground that doing so would "tend to disgrace him or otherwise render him infamous."

Use of Contempt Power. Between 1789 and 1969, Congress voted 380 contempt citations in cases where a witness refused to appear before a committee, refused to answer questions before a committee, or refused to produce documents for a committee. (An additional 14 citations were voted in cases involving the privileges of Congress.) Of the 380 cases, 283 have occurred since 1945, primarily as the result of activities by the House Un-American Activities Committee.

Use of the contempt power in Congressional cases has fallen into two general classes: (1) those involving positive acts, such as bribery or libel, which directly or indirectly obstruct the Legislature in carrying out its functions, and (2) those involving refusal to perform acts which the Legislature claims authority to compel, such as testifying or producing documents. Few cases of the first type have occurred in recent years, and the courts have had little opportunity to define positive acts of contempt. The second type, while giving rise to much more extensive judicial interpretation, continues to raise many legal questions because of its greater complexity.

Resorting to the inherent power of Congress to punish for contempt, a committee may introduce a resolution directing the presiding officer of the chamber to issue a warrant for arrest of the witness in contempt by the chamber's Sergeant at Arms. The witness is brought before the bar of the House, or Senate, and questioned. Subsequently, the full chamber may adopt a resolution ordering the confinement of the witness or his discharge, or the witness simply may be reprimanded by the chamber's presiding officer.

When a committee in either chamber wishes to institute criminal proceedings against a contumacious witness, it introduces a resolution in the parent body citing him for contempt. Only simple majority vote is necessary for approval; there seldom is opposition to such a resolution. The matter is then referred to a U.S. attorney for presentation to a grand jury.

Investigative Practices and Procedures

From the beginning, Congress has delegated its power to investigate to committees. Prior to passage of the Legislative Reorganization Act of 1946 (PL 79-601), the majority of investigations were carried out by special or select committees, with subpoena power, established solely to conduct the inquiry. When the investigation was concluded, the committee went out of existence and with it died its power of subpoena. The first attempt to extend subpoena power to a standing committee—the House Committee on Manufactures, for an 1828 tariff investigation—was strongly opposed but was approved Dec. 31, 1827, by a 102-88 vote. Opponents said the proposal was unheard of, since subpoena power previously had been used only by committees acting as judicial bodies.

At first, House committees dominated Congressional investigations. The House, for example, conducted 27 of the 30 inquiries between 1789 and 1814. But as time passed, the Senate pulled in front of the House, conducting about 40 of the 60 investigations between 1900 and 1925. (The Senate first granted subpoena power to a special investigating committee during an 1818 study of the Seminole war.) In the meantime, as the number of standing committees increased in both chambers, it became common practice for them to conduct investigations on their own initiative, without a special authorizing resolution, although specific House or Senate approval was still required to compel testimony and to provide funds. Of the 146 investigations between 1929 and 1938, 89 were made by standing committees and 57 by select committees.

Great Growth of Investigations

The spectacular growth of the Executive Branch during the New Deal and World War II years led to a proliferation of Congressional investigating committees as Congress struggled to fulfill its traditional function of overseeing the administration of laws and the spending of appropriations. By 1945, the House had a total of 111 committees and the Senate, a total of 75; between 1945 and passage of the Reorganization Act in 1946, at least 50 investigations had been voted.

Subpoena Powers in Senate. The 1946 Act attempted to restore the balance by strengthening the Congressional investigative procedures and expanding committee staffs. The Act cut the number of standing committees from 48 to 19 in the House and from 33 to 15 in the Senate. It authorized standing committees of both chambers to "exercise continuous watchfulness of the execution by the administrative agencies concerned of any laws, the subject matter of which is within the jurisdiction" of the respective committees. Further, the Act extended permanent subpoena power to all standing committees of the Senate and authorized $10,000 in investigating funds for each committee during each Congress. The Act also authorized professional staff members for all standing committees.

Subpoena Powers in House. General subpoena power for House committees was blocked by the leadership of Speaker Sam Rayburn (D Texas) and Minority Leader Joseph W. Martin (R Mass.), who feared that such power would make the committees uncontrollable and lead to sensational inquiries motivated by political ambitions. The sole exception was the Un-American Activities Committee, which was authorized to issue subpoenas. Subsequently, general subpoena power was granted to the House Committee on Expenditures in the Executive Departments (Government Operations) in 1947 and to the House Appropriations Committee in 1953. When the Un-American Activities Committee was renamed the House Committee on Internal Security, on Feb. 18, 1969, the new Committee also was given subpoena power. As a result of Rayburn's and Martin's opposition to general subpoena power for House committees, the panels had to seek specific House approval for authority to compel testimony and documents. In practice, the House routinely authorizes broad committee investigatory power and use of the subpoena at the beginning of each Congress.

Cost of Investigations. The combined effect of the Legislative Reorganization Act and Executive Branch expansion was an explosion of investigative activity in the postwar years. Compared to approximately 500 investigations in the century and one-half from 1789 to 1938, the 90th Congress (1967-68) alone authorized 496 investigations. The cost of investigations paralleled the rising number of inquiries. From 1910 to 1919 the Senate spent approximately $330,000 on investigative activities, compared to $2.9 million in the two years 1951 and 1952. In the two years of the 90th Congress the Senate and House together spent $21,994,843 on investigations. The number and cost of the studies rapidly outdistanced the $10,000 per committee authorized in the 1946 Act, and the committees in most cases were again required to seek special funds for investigative activities.

Although Congress continued to establish special investigating committees in postwar years, major investigations were carried on by a handful of standing committees or their subcommittees: the House and Senate Committees on Government Operations, the Internal Security Subcommittee of the Senate Judiciary Committee, the Senate Government Operations Permanent Investigations Subcommittee and the House Internal Security Committee.

Procedural Stages

In essence, Congressional investigations undergo three stages of development: authorization, staff preparation and public hearings.

Authorization. Almost limitless reasons can lead a Senator or Representative to propose an investigation. He may seek to gather facts on widely known public occurrences such as an airline disaster or a missile explosion; he may attempt to confirm reports of improper conduct in the Government, labor unions or private business; or he may pursue a personal interest such as Government silver policy or fees charged ranchers for grazing cattle on Federal range land.

Whatever the reason, the authority and scope of the inquiry are incorporated in a simple resolution for introduction in the House or Senate. Once introduced, the resolution is referred to a committee. In the Senate, resolutions for investigations are considered by the Rules and Administration Committee and by the standing legislative committee having jurisdiction of the subject to be studied. House resolutions are considered by the Rules Committee and by the House Administration Committee. After being reported by the Committees, the resolutions are voted on by the full chamber. Joint House-Senate investigating committees are authorized by a concurrent resolution adopted by both chambers.

Many resolutions to authorize investigations, like bills and resolutions on other matters, are never acted upon by a committee and accordingly die. But if a resolution authorizing an investigation is approved by a committee and adopted on the floor, an investigation almost always follows. One exception occurred in 1933 when an authorized investigation of the Reconstruction Finance Corporation by the Senate Banking and Currency Committee failed to materialize; the Committee reported later that it had had no specific inquiry in mind and had asked for the investigatory power only as a precautionary step.

It has long been a matter of courtesy in both House and Senate that the sponsor of the resolution for an investigation shall preside over the inquiry. When the study is to be made by a standing committee, a subcommittee generally is appointed by the chairman of the full committee, with the sponsor of the resolution being named subcommittee chairman. When a select committee is authorized, the members are chosen by consultation between the Vice President, or the Speaker, and the Majority and Minority Leaders.

Committee Staff. Early Congressional investigations, lacking a committee staff, were undertaken on an informal basis. The investigating committee frequently knew little about the subject under study and simply struck out blindly, asking questions and considering evidence, hoping that something might be found that would be useful to the investigation.

Committee staffs first came into use by investigating committees in the late 1800s and early 1900s. By the 1920s and 1930s the practice of relying on staff members to gather and prepare pertinent information was firmly established. Trained investigators, poring over files and records before the start of public hearings, generally have accumulated most of the information produced by investigations. Occasionally an investigating committee has been authorized access to income tax returns, customarily by Executive Order.

The Nye Committee's staff investigating the munitions industry in the 1930s consisted of three lawyers, two accountants, a specialist in international law, a financial writer, two free-lance newspapermen, and five persons who were doing or had done graduate work in the social sciences. On the staff of the Truman Committee during World War II were a chief counsel, an associate counsel, an assistant counsel, a chief investigator, 12-18 investigators, a committee clerk, an editor and clerical personnel. In 1969, the staff of the Senate Government Operations Permanent Investigations Subcommittee included a general counsel, chief counsel for the majority and for the minority, five assistant counsels, 11 investigators, a staff editor, a chief clerk and nine assistant clerks.

Until the Legislative Reorganization Act of 1946 authorized professional committee staffs, investigating committees frequently borrowed personnel from the administrative agencies. Persons on relief were lent to some investigating committees during the depression. Trained investigators from Government agencies still are used by many committees. For the 12 months ended June 1969, the General Accounting Office reported assigning 65 professional staff members to 12 Congressional committees or subcommittees. For the six months ended December 1968, the House Appropriations Committee reported assistance from 24 FBI investigators, two investigators from the Agriculture Department and one each from the Air Force, Civil Service Commission, Federal Highway Administration, General Services Administration, National Aeronautics and Space Administration, Small Business Administration and the Veterans Administration.

The activities of an investigating committee's staff in a major inquiry are suggested by the scope of the committee's work. The Truman Committee, active from 1941 to 1948, issued 51 reports totaling 1,946 pages and held 432 public hearings at which 1,798 witnesses appeared, filling 27,568 pages of testimony. In addition, the transcript of about 300 private sessions held by the Committee covered 25,000 pages. From 1957 to 1959, the Senate Select Committee on Improper Activities in the Labor or Management Field heard 1,726 witnesses (343 of whom took the 5th Amendment), whose testimony filled 46,150 pages. Staff members traveled nearly 2.5 million miles, forwarded 128,204 documents to the Committee (not counting photostats), conducted 253 active investigations, served more than 8,000 subpoenas in staff investigations and filed more than 19,000 investigative field reports. At its peak, in 1958, the staff numbered 104.

Hearings. Public hearings have been the most visible and controversial element of investigations, but as a rule they have brought forth little material not already uncovered or suggested by staff work. Hearings have helped to act as a check on staff investigators by giving the investigated person a chance to present his case. Procedures have varied from committee to committee, but a witness usually has been allowed to present a prepared statement and to be accompanied by and to consult with a lawyer. Questioning of witnesses has been conducted by members of the committee, frequently the chairman, and by the committee's staff. In some instances, galley proofs of the testimony have been sent to the witness for corrections; this was the practice of the Truman Committee.

Public hearings have provided a method of presenting facts dramatically to the public and a means of influencing public opinion. Public opinion, in turn, has been affected by methods used in the conduct of hearings, particularly when the procedures appeared to infringe on the rights of witnesses.

Rights of Witnesses. Not until the late 1930s did the rights of a witness in a Congressional investigation—and the threat of their infringement—become a serious issue. The potential conflict between the right of Congress to seek information and the right of a witness to protect his privacy always was present; but early legislative investigations were conducted in a comparatively low-key atmosphere, free from the instant mass publicity of television. Witnesses often were allowed to call their own witnesses and to cross-examine hostile witnesses.

The advent in the 1930s of the inquisitorial Congressional panel, typified by the House Special Committee to Investigate Un-American Activities (Dies Committee) aroused new concern. The low-key atmosphere had vanished, replaced by relentless probing questions before massed newsmen and newsreel cameras. Complaints mounted that the procedures of Congressional investigators were exceeding their powers and violating the rights of witnesses.

In fact, as witnesses—and the courts—discovered, investigating committees had virtually free reign to determine their procedures. Challenges of the legality of committee procedures raised sensitive questions. They loomed as a potentially divisive force between two coequal branches of the Government, the Legislative and the Judicial, and the court studiously sought to avoid the issue. They attempted to rule on narrow points of law rather than on the central point, which was the power of a committee to set its own procedures.

The result of the courts' evasiveness was that a witness in essence was at the mercy of the investigating committee, protected only by the general constitutional limitations on Congressional authority and by the Bill of Rights. A 1954 study of Congressional investigative power by the Legislative Reference Service of the Library of Congress concluded: "There are few safeguards for the protection of a witness before a Congressional committee.... In committee, his treatment usually depends upon the skill and attitude of the chairman and the members." That conclusion was foreshadowed clearly by a 1948 comment by House Un-American Activities Committee Chairman J. Parnell Thomas (R N.J.): "The rights you have are the rights given you by this Committee. We will determine what rights you have and what rights you have not got before the committee."

During the postwar era, the rights of witnesses before Congressional investigating committees became a bitter issue. The growing number and broadened scope of investigations, and the increasing use of committee hearings for the purpose of edifying the public rather than informing the Legislature, led to pressure for more precise definitions of committee powers. The advent of television coverage of hearings, first used spectacularly during House Un-American Activities Committee investigations of Communism in 1948, exposed witnesses to vast publicity. The publicity, jeopardizing the privacy of witnesses, their reputations and often their careers, provoked demands for safeguards for those testifying.

In search of protection, witnesses turned repeatedly to the Constitution. Despite the constitutional assignment of only specified powers to Congress, the courts repeatedly had shown reluctance to limit Congressional investigating power. The new search for safeguards led to tests of the effectiveness of the Bill of Rights in protecting the rights of witnesses.

Most frequently cited were the First, Fourth and Fifth Amendments. Efforts by witnesses to invoke the First Amendment in refusing to provide committees with information, on the ground that Congress had no right to probe their private convictions or their political views or propaganda activities, had mixed results. The Fourth Amendment guarantee against unreasonable search and seizure likewise offered irregular protection. The arbitrary power of committees to demand the production of documents was the most used—and disputed—authority throughout the history of Congressional investigations.

Once the courts upheld the right of Congressional committee witnesses to invoke the Fifth Amendment's protection against self-incrimination, use of the Amendment to avoid answering questions became highly controversial. The Fifth Amendment generally stood up as a defense against prosecution for contempt of Congress. However, witnesses could not invoke the privilege partially, answering as to incriminating facts and then refusing further explanation. For this reason, some witnesses repeatedly pleaded the Fifth Amendment in refusing to answer apparently innocuous questions.

Because of the uncertainty and delay in attempting to establish constitutional safeguards for witnesses, pressures mounted both in and out of Congress for reform of committee procedures to protect the rights of witnesses and to give greater assurance that the purposes for which the investigations were instituted would, in fact, be accomplished.

Rules Reforms. Proposals for "fair play" rules for investigations reached flood proportions in the 83rd Congress, when numerous codes of committee procedure were considered. Both the House Rules Committee and the Senate Rules and Administration Committee in 1954 held hearings on a variety of resolutions sponsored by Members of both parties.

House. The House March 23, 1955, adopted by voice vote a resolution (H Res 151) amending House Rules to establish a minimum standard of conduct for House committees. The resolution:

● Required a quorum of no fewer than two members when committees take testimony and receive evidence.

● Allowed witnesses at investigations to be accompanied by counsel.

● Required a committee, if it found that evidence "may tend to defame, degrade, or incriminate any person," to receive the evidence in secret session and to allow the person injured to appear as a witness and to request subpoenas of other witnesses.

● Required committee consent for release of evidence taken in secret session.

The rights of witnesses were also affected by a ruling by House Speaker Sam Rayburn (D Texas), Feb. 25, 1952, that House Rules gave no authority for television, radio or newsreel coverage of hearings or for tape recording of their proceedings. Subsequent resolutions to authorize broadcasting and televising of hearings before House committees received no action.

Senate. The Senate prescribed no "fair play" code for its committees. However, the Senate Republican Policy Committee on March 10, 1954, offered as "suggestions" a set of rules for investigations and sent the proposals to all Senate committee chairmen. The Republican

Use of Fifth Amendment

The right of a witness before a Congressional committee to claim the Fifth Amendment's privilege against self-incrimination never was challenged in the courts until it became widely used during the postwar hearings into Communist subversion.

Once, in 1879, the lawyer for a witness (George E. Seward, consul general in China) summoned to testify at an investigation of the State Department by the House Committee on Expenditures in the State Department claimed protection under the Fifth Amendment clause that "No person...shall be compelled in any criminal case to be a witness against himself...." The Committee's reaction was mixed, but a majority argued that the privilege was not applicable because a Congressional hearing was not a "criminal case." On House approval of a resolution sponsored by the Committee minority, the matter was referred to the House Judiciary Committee, which is authorized to consider important questions of law relating to subjects within the jurisdiction of other committees. After study, the Judiciary Committee reported (H Rept 45-141) that a committee witness was entitled to claim the privilege, and the House approved the Committee's report.

Thereafter, if a witness claimed the privilege and refused to answer a question, the inquiring committee did not press the issue. It shifted its inquiries to another subject. However, few committee witnesses sought to claim the privilege.

A change of tactics took place in the spring of 1950. When the House Un-American Activities Committee held hearings in Hawaii in mid-April, 39 witnesses refused to reply to questions about their membership in the Communist party, and similar queries, on the ground that their replies might tend to incriminate them. They were cited by the House for contempt of Congress, and the case (*United States v. Yukio Abe*) was heard by a Federal judge in Honolulu. In January 1951, a month after the Supreme Court had ruled unanimously in *Blau v. United States* that admission of Communist activity might be incriminating, the Honolulu judge freed all 39 of the witnesses. *Yukio Abe* was the first reported judicial case in which the claim of privilege against self-incrimination was allowed in a Congressional inquiry.

The ruling in *Yukio Abe* was never challenged. Subsequent cases of contempt citations against witnesses who claimed the privilege involved narrower legal issues.

The Supreme Court did not consider any contempt of Congress cases in which a witness had pleaded the Fifth Amendment until 1955. In its decisions then, in *Quinn v. United States; Emspak v. United States;* and *Bart v. United States*, the Court laid down general guidelines for use of the privilege. No special combination of words or ritualistic formula was required of a witness wishing to claim the privilege, the Court said. "Any language" could be used that the committee may "reasonably be expected to understand as an attempt to claim" the Amendment's protection.

proposals would have allowed counsel for witnesses, prohibited release of executive testimony except by majority vote, and strengthened the control of investigations by the majority of the committee.

The Rules Subcommittee of the Senate Rules and Administration Committee on Jan. 6, 1955, issued a unanimous report recommending 12 rules to protect witnesses and to ensure greater majority control of investigations. Among the recommendations were those to:

• Allow a person who felt his reputation had been damaged by other testimony to testify in his own behalf or file a sworn statement.

• Ban public release of testimony given in closed session, except by authorization of the committee.

• Advise each witness, in advance, of the subject of the investigation.

• Allow witnesses to request that television and other cameras and lights not be directed at him during his testimony, and have committee members present at the time to rule on the request.

The report said "elaborate procedural devices" would be unnecessary if there were "courtesy and understanding on the part of committee members and staff," and ineffective if those qualities were lacking. The Subcommittee reported, "What might have been classified decades ago as private opinion of no concern to Congress, takes on a different connotation in the light of world events whose impact Congress may not disregard."

The Senate left investigative procedures to the discretion of individual committees, whose practices varied considerably. The Permanent Investigations Subcommittee of the Senate Government Operations Committee, after Sen. John L. McClellan (D Ark.) replaced McCarthy as chairman, Jan. 18, 1955, adopted rules requiring the presence of two Committee members when testimony was being taken, permitted anyone who was the subject of an investigation to submit questions in writing for cross-examination of other witnesses, and allowed any person adversely affected by testimony to request an appearance or file a statement.

Not only do rules vary from one committee to another in the Senate and, except for the minimum code, in the House, but the strictness with which committees adhere to their own rules is not uniform.

Immunity Statute. Congress in 1954 enacted a bill (S 16—PL 83-600) permitting either chamber of Congress by majority vote, or a Congressional committee by two-thirds vote, to grant immunity to witnesses in national security investigations, provided an order was first obtained from a U.S. district court judge and also provided the Attorney General was notified in advance and given an opportunity to offer objections. The bill also permitted the U.S. district courts to grant immunity to witnesses before the court or grand juries. The bill was aimed at witnesses invoking the Fifth Amendment privilege against self-incrimination. Immunity would have the effect of compelling them to testify or go to jail.

Investigations and the Courts

During the greater part of the 19th century, Congressional investigations were not subjected to judicial review. The Supreme Court ruling in the 1821 case of *Anderson v. Dunn*, that the action of the House must be "presumed" to be in accordance with law, warded off

legal challenges to the power of Congress to punish for contempt.

This precedent was set aside in 1880 by the Court's decision in the important case of *Kilbourn v. Thompson*, which established the principle of judicial review of the investigative activities of Congress. Other cases were to follow. Emerging from the series of judicial decisions since *Kilbourn* was a broad outline of Congressional investigative power:

• The power to conduct investigations and to compel the attendance of witnesses and the production of evidence, under the threat of citation for contempt of Congress, was accepted as a necessary corollary of the power to legislate.

• The investigative power was to be connected with a legislative power authorized by the Constitution, and before a committee could compel a witness to testify, he was to be made aware of the connection between the questions and the legislative purpose.

• Investigations were subject in varying degrees to constitutional protection of individual rights and the Constitution's division of powers among three separate and equal branches of Government.

• The courts had authority to review investigative activities, although committees were allowed to determine their procedures virtually without restraint.

Kilbourn v. Thompson. The *Kilbourn* case originated with the refusal of a witness, Hallet Kilbourn, to produce papers demanded by the House Select Committee on the Real Estate Pool and Jay Cooke Indebtedness, which was investigating the failure of the banking firm of Jay Cooke. Kilbourn, manager of the real estate pool, said he would not acknowledge "the naked, arbitrary power of the House to investigate private business in which nobody but me and my customers have concern." The House ordered that he be jailed for contempt. Released on a writ of habeas corpus, Kilbourn sued the Speaker, members of the investigating committee and Sergeant at Arms John G. Thompson for false arrest. The Supreme Court heard the case and sustained Kilbourn's claim. In its decision, the Court held that the houses of Congress did not have a general power to punish for contempt. A reluctant committee witness could be punished for contempt, the Court ruled, only if the inquiry for which the witness had been called was within the "legitimate cognizance" of Congress.

The *Kilbourn* decision appeared to restrict the Congressional power to investigate to "legitimate" inquiries, without specifying what they were. In deciding the case, the Court declared that investigations of the private affairs of a citizen were not legitimate, but that those made in connection with some specifically granted constitutional power, such a impeachment or the election and qualification of Members, were proper. Later Court decisions have largely removed the limitations imposed in *Kilbourn*; its value has stemmed from the principle of judicial review of Congressional contempt action, which it established.

In Re Chapman. Seventeen years after *Kilbourn*, in 1897, the Supreme Court held *(In Re Chapman)* that investigations were "legitimate" inquiries when they involved the conduct of Members of Congress. This unanimously upheld the constitutionality of the 1857 contempt of Congress statue. Elverton R. Chapman was a New York stockbroker who had refused to answer an investigating committee's questions about Senators' trading in sugar stocks during action on a sugar tariff measure.

McGrain v. Daugherty. In 1927, the Court issued a landmark decision (*McGrain v. Daugherty*) that swept away nearly all the restrictions on the investigating power of Congress left over from the *Kilbourn* decision. The effect of *McGrain v. Daugherty* was to uphold the power of Congress to conduct legislative and oversight investigations. These two types of investigations, together with Membership inquiries, have comprised the vast majority of Congressional investigations since 1789. Thus, in a broad sense, *McGrain v. Daugherty* firmly established the existence of the Congressional power to investigate. *(See Appendix for text of the Court's decision.)*

The *Daugherty* decision grew out of a refusal by Mally S. Daugherty, brother of Attorney General Harry M. Daugherty (1921-24), to testify before a Senate committee investigating the Justice Department. The Senate issued a warrant ordering Deputy Sergeant at Arms John J. McGrain to arrest Mally Daugherty, who had challenged the Senate's power to compel him to testify. The Supreme Court sustained the Senate action.

The Court held that the Senate or the House had power to compel private persons to appear before committees and to answer pertinent questions in aid of the legislative function. "The power of inquiry—with process to enforce it—is an essential and appropriate auxiliary to the legislative function," the Court said. It continued: "A legislative body cannot legislate wisely or effectively in the absence of information respecting the condition which the legislation is intended to affect or change, and where the legislative body does not itself possess the requisite information...recourse must be had to others who possess it. Experience has taught that mere requests for information are often unavailing, and also that information which is volunteered is not always accurate or complete, so some means of compulsion is necessary to obtain what is needed."

The Court indicated further that it would presume a legislative purpose lay behind the authorization of a Congressional investigation, whether indeed that was the purpose of the inquiry or not. "The only legitimate object the Senate could have in ordering the investigation was to aid in legislating; and we think the subject matter was such that the presumption should be indulged that this was the real object," the Court said. "An express avowal of the object would have been better; but in view of the particular subject matter was not indispensable," the Court added.

To this sweeping approval of Congressional investigations, the Court appended two reservations. It cautioned, first, that "Neither house is invested with general power to inquire into private affairs and compel disclosures" and second, that "A witness may rightfully refuse to answer where the bounds of inquiry are exceeded or the questions are not pertinent to the matter under scrutiny."

Sinclair v. United States. In 1929 (*Sinclair v. United States*) the Supeme Court held that a witness who refused to answer questions asked by a Congressional committee could be punished if he were mistaken as to the law on which he based his refusal. The fact that a witness acted in good faith on the advice of counsel was no defense, the Court held. This precedent made any challenge of committee powers a risky proposition, with the possibility of

a jail sentence for any witness seeking to test his rights in court.

The case grew out of an investigation of the Teapot Dome scandals. The Interior Department had leased public lands, containing oil, to the Mammoth Oil Co., the president and sole stockholder of which was Harry F. Sinclair. Sinclair, citing legal arguments, had refused to answer questions of a Senate investigating committee.

Jurney v. MacCracken. In 1935, the Court ruled (*Jurney v. MacCracken*) that an investigating committee had authority to punish for contempt a witness who destroyed papers after the service of a subpoena for them. Several letters had been removed from the office of William P. MacCracken, a Washington lawyer, during a Senate committee investigation of airmail contracts.

Subversive Cases. The wartime and postwar quest to uncover subversion in the United States produced a new style of investigation. The overriding purpose of the antisubversion hearings was exposure. For, as argued by Rep. Martin Dies (D Texas), chairman of the House Special Committee to Investigate Un-American Activities, "I am not in a position to say whether we can legislate effectively in reference to this matter, but I do know that exposure in a democracy of subversive activities is the most effective weapon that we have in our possession."

Committee witnesses balked at the new investigative tactics, and the number of contempt of Congress citations grew, leading to new court tests. To meet the new legal issues raised by the antisubversive inquiries, the courts handed down a number of decisions further defining the rights of witnesses and the powers of investigating committees. Nearly all of the cases originated in hearings by the House Un-American Activities Committee, successor to the Dies Committee.

The Supreme Court ruled (*Blau v. United States,* 1950) that admission of Communist activity might be incriminating, and a lower Federal court ruled (*United States v. Yukio Abe,* 1951), in an unchallenged decision, that committee witnesses had a right to claim the Fifth Amendment's protection against self-incrimination. In another 1951 case (*Rogers v. United States*), the Supreme Court ruled that a witness could not invoke the privilege after once having answered about materially incriminating facts.

In the late 1950s, the Court handed down a pair of decisions which attempted to establish limits to the "exposure power" of a committee. The Court declared in a 1957 case (*Watkins v. United States*) that "there is no Congressional power to expose for the sake of exposure." Conceding that the public was entitled to be informed of the workings of the Government, the Court said: "That cannot be inflated into a general power to expose where the predominant result can only be an invasion of the private rights of individuals." The ruling was praised by many as an important restriction on the procedures of committees investigating subversion.

Yet two years later, in 1959 (*Barenblatt v. United States*), the Court backed away from the Watkins declaration. A challenged Un-American Activities Committee hearing was not unlawful on the ground that its purpose was "exposure," the Court said in the 1959 case. "So long as Congress acts in pursuance of its constitutional power, the Judiciary lacks authority to intervene on the basis of the motives which spurred the exercise of that power," the Court said. In addition, the Court made clear that it would broadly interpret the power of Congress.

Investigations and the Executive Branch

Investigations have often led Congress into conflict with the Executive Branch. The most frequent cause of contention has been refusal by the President to comply with Congressional demands for information.

Though Congress has frequently disputed the Executive privilege to withhold information, the issue has never been tested in the courts. Some have asserted that Executive departments, having been established by Congress and maintained by its appropriations, are the creatures of the Legislature and cannot deny it information regarding their activities. Congress may seek to back up its demands by arousing public support for disclosure, especially if there is any suspicion that an Administration is seeking to protect its political reputation by hiding mistakes or malfeasance. However, the long list of precedents in which Presidents have successfully defied Congressional demands for information, and Congress's reluctance to settle the issue by legislation forcing it into the courts, support claims that the constitutional separation of powers permits the President, at his discretion, to withhold information sought by Congress.

A variety of reasons has been used to justify denying information to Congress. Perhaps the most common has been the need for secrecy in military and diplomatic activities. Presidents have also sought to avoid unwarranted exposure of individuals to unfavorable publicity, especially when documents or files requested contain incomplete, distorted, inaccurate, misleading or unsubstantiated information. The need for confidential exchange of ideas between members of an Administration has been cited as justifying refusal to provide records or describe conversations in the Executive Branch. Fears that disclosures would interfere with criminal or security investigations sometimes have prompted administrative secrecy. Critics of an Administration have frequently charged that its real motive for refusing to divulge information was to escape criticism or scandal.

Presidents who refused demands from investigating committees were Jefferson, Monroe, Jackson, Tyler, Polk, Fillmore, Lincoln, Grant, Hayes, Cleveland, Theodore Roosevelt, Coolidge, Hoover, Franklin D. Roosevelt, Truman, Eisenhower and Kennedy. In some cases the committee has accepted the President's refusal without comment. Other times, the refusal has led to a full-scale constitutional confrontation. A series of selected cases follows.

Early Refusals to Give Information

Washington. The precedent of Executive privilege was first established in 1792 when a select House committee, conducting the first Congressional inquiry, investigated an Indian victory over Maj. Gen. Arthur St. Clair and his men in the Northwest Territory. The committee wrote to War Secretary Henry Knox and asked him to turn over all the documents relating to the St. Clair expedition. Knox asked President Washington for advice; the President raised the subject at a Cabinet meeting. The Cabinet agreed that the House could conduct such an investigation and could call for such papers. It decided, according to the report of Thomas Jefferson, "that the Executive ought to communicate such papers as the public good would permit, and ought to refuse those, the

disclosure of which would endanger the public." As it developed, none of the St. Clair papers were regarded as confidential, and the President on April 4 directed Secretary Knox to make the papers available to the committee.

(Four years later, in 1796, Washington claimed Executive privilege when he refused a House request for correspondence relating to the intensely controversial Jay's Treaty with Great Britain. The House was debating a bill to implement portions of the treaty; the bill eventually was passed.)

Jackson. A House committee appointed "to examine into the conditions of the Executive departments" adopted on Jan. 23, 1837, a series of resolutions that directed President Jackson and members of his Cabinet to furnish lists of Federal appointments made without the concurrence of the Senate, along with information as to the salaries of the appointees and as to whether they were being paid without having taken office. Jackson, backed by a large majority in the House, categorically refused, in what was to become one of the most successful efforts of a President to resist Congressional investigators.

"According to the established rules of law," Jackson replied on Jan. 27, "you request myself and the heads of departments to become our own accusers, and to furnish the evidence to convict ourselves." The President continued: "The heads of departments may answer such a request as they please, provided they do not withdraw their own time and that of the officers under their direction from the public business....For myself, I shall repel all such attempts as an invasion of the principles of justice, as well as of the Constitution; and I shall esteem it my sacred duty to the people of the United States to resist them as I would the establishment of a Spanish inquisition."

After three months of fruitless questioning of some Cabinet officers and others, the committee concluded that it had overstepped its authority in submitting a blanket request for documents, and dropped the inquiry. The Jackson majority on the committee explained that it had gone along with the requests of Chairman Henry A. Wise (D Va.) to avoid charges of protecting the Administration. In a report on March 3, 1837, the committee said: "The condition of the various Executive departments is prosperous, and...they have been conducted with ability and industry."

Tyler. The House on May 18, 1842, adopted a resolution requesting War Secretary J. C. Spencer to make available to the Indian Affairs Committee reports on the Cherokee Indians and alleged frauds committed against them. After consulting with President Tyler, Spencer on June 3 refused, asserting that negotiations to settle claims with the Indians still were in progress. The Committee persisted in its request, and on Aug. 13 the House by an 83-60 vote adopted a Committee resolution requesting the information from Tyler. Tyler took no action on the request. On Dec. 30, the House adopted another resolution asking when the President was going to act.

Tyler replied, Jan. 31, 1843, that the claims negotiations had been concluded in the meantime, and information dealing with the alleged frauds would be submitted. However, the President withheld portions of the reports containing personal comments about Indian negotiators and about recommendations for future action. In doing so, the President argued that the House could not demand information, even if relevant to a House debate, if the information would interfere with the discretion of the Executive Branch. "It cannot be that the only test is whether the information relates to a legitimate subject of deliberation," Tyler said. Also to be considered, he added, were the protection of confidential sources of Government officials and the protection of officials from malicious publicity. The President's message was referred to the Indian Affairs Committee, which submitted a report, Feb. 25, criticizing the President's position but recommending no action.

Cleveland's Brush With the Senate

President Cleveland in 1885 was the first Democrat in the White House since Buchanan in 1861. Democrats also controlled the House, but Republicans had a majority in the Senate. As the new President began replacing holdover Republican officeholders with Democrats, the Senate committees to which the nominations were referred repeatedly requested the information that had led to removal of the Republican incumbents. The standard Department reply was that at the direction of the President it refused, on the ground that the public interest would not be served or that the removal had been a purely executive action.

Some 650 Republican officeholders were replaced. Finally, on Dec. 26, 1885, the Senate Judiciary Committee asked Attorney General A.H. Garland for information on the dismissal of George N. Durskin, U.S. district attorney for the southern district of Alabama. There being no response from Garland, the Senate on Jan. 26, 1886, adopted a Committee resolution directing the Attorney General to furnish the papers. In his reply, Feb. 1, Garland said the President had directed him to report that "the public interest would not be promoted by compliance with the resolution." The Senate responded, Feb. 18, by adopting a resolution refusing to concur in the removal of officeholders when the documents on which the removal was based were withheld.

In a message to the Senate, March 1, Cleveland disclaimed any intent to withhold official papers and asserted that the letters and reports leading to the dismissals were inherently private and confidential. He continued: "I do not suppose that the public offices of the United States are regulated or controlled in their relations to either house of Congress by the fact that they were created by laws enacted by" Congress. Cleveland's argument raised the recurring question of whether Government departments are creatures of the Executive Branch, because they carry out executive functions, or creatures of the Legislative Branch, because they are established and financed through Congressional action. From March 9 to 26 the Senate debated the issue. It concluded by adopting a resolution citing the Attorney General for being "in violation of his official duty and subversive of the fundamental principles of the Government...." President Cleveland stood his ground, however, and the Senate ultimately confirmed his nominee to replace Durskin, John D. Burnett.

Continued Insistence on Executive Privilege

Hoover. During Senate consideration of the London Naval Treaty of 1930, the Foreign Relations Committee asked for the papers relating to the London Conference at which the treaty had been negotiated. Secretary of State Henry L. Stimson submitted some of the papers but withheld others, explaining June 6, 1930, that he had been "directed by the President to say" that their production "would not in his opinion be compatible with the public interest." The Committee adopted a resolution, June 12, asserting that the documents were "relevant and pertinent when the Senate is considering a treaty for the purpose of ratification." On July 10, the Senate, supporting the Committee, adopted by a 53-4 vote a resolution requesting the President to submit the material, "if not incompatible with the public interest." Pleading the next day that the papers were confidential, Hoover again declined to produce them. The Senate on July 21 consented to ratification of the treaty, with "the distinct and explicit understanding" that it contained no secret agreements.

Truman. President Truman in 1948 became involved in a head-on clash between the Executive Branch and an investigating committee of Congress. On March 1 the House Un-American Activities Special Subcommittee on National Security issued a report that called Dr. Edward U. Condon, director of the Bureau of Standards, "one of the weakest links in our national security." The Subcommittee promptly subpoenaed Commerce Department records of loyalty investigations of Condon, but Secretary of Commerce W. Averell Harriman refused to release them on the ground that their publication would be "prejudicial to the public interest."

President Truman took a direct hand in the controversy on March 13 when he issued a directive barring disclosure of any loyalty files to Congress. The President said: "Any subpoena or demand or request for information, reports or files of the nature described, received from sources other than those persons in the Executive Branch ...who are entitled thereto by reason of their special duties, shall be respectfully declined on the basis of this directive, and the subpoena or demand or other request shall be referred to the Office of the President for such response as the President may determine to be in the public interest in the particular case. There shall be no relaxation of this directive except with my express authority."

On April 22 the House by a 302-29 vote adopted a resolution (H Res 522) demanding that Secretary Harriman surrender an FBI report on Condon. The disputed documents were transferred to the White House, and the President refused to release them—despite Condon's request that they be made public. The House on May 12 passed by a 219-152 vote a bill (H J Res 342) "directing all executive departments and agencies of the Federal Government to make available to any and all standing, special or select committees of the House of Representatives and the Senate, information which may be deemed necessary to enable them to properly perform the duties delegated to them by Congress." Refusal to comply was to be considered a misdemeanor, punishable by a fine of up to $1,000 or imprisonment for up to one year, or both. In the Senate, the bill was referred to the Committee on Expenditures in the Executive Departments (Government Operations), where it died upon expiration of the 80th Congress.

Eisenhower. During the Army-McCarthy hearings before the Senate Government Operations Permanent Investigations Subcommittee, President Eisenhower on May 17, 1954, forbade testimony about a Jan. 12 meeting between Attorney General Herbert Brownell Jr. and Army Counsel John Adams. Developments in the aggressively anti-Communist hearings being conducted by Subcommittee Chairman Joseph R. McCarthy (R Wis.) had been discussed at the meeting. In a letter to Defense Secretary Charles E. Wilson imposing the ban on testimony about the meeting, Eisenhower stressed the importance of candid, private communication within the Executive Branch and the "proper separation of power between the Executive and Legislative Branches." When Adams cited the President's order in refusing to answer a question on May 24, McCarthy accused him of using "a type of Fifth Amendment privilege."

McCarthy said three days later that he wanted all Federal workers to know "that I feel it's their duty to give us any information which they have about graft, corruption, Communists, treason, and that there is no loyalty to a superior officer which can tower above and beyond their loyalty to their country." The Senator promised to shield the identity of informants. The Democrats on the Subcommittee protested McCarthy's call for informers, and Brownell on May 28, with the President's approval, issued a statement: "The Executive Branch...has the sole and fundamental responsibility under the Constitution for the enforcement of our laws and Presidential orders.... That responsibility cannot be usurped by an individual who may seek to set himself above the laws of our land or to override orders of the President of the United States to Federal employees of the Executive Branch."

Politics of Investigations

President Truman was a Democrat and the House was controlled by Republicans during the 1948 fight over the loyalty file of Dr. Edward U. Condon, director of the Bureau of Standards. Similar conflicting political forces, at countless other times, have had a profound impact on Congressional investigations. By their very nature, investigating committees have become focal points of partisan political strife.

As an illustration, the three most intensive periods of Congressional investigative activities—the last years of the Grant Administration and the periods immediately following World Wars I and II—coincided with shifts of Congressional majorities that transferred power to a party long in the minority. Grant, a Republican, was President from 1869 to 1877; and when the Democrats in the 1874 election recaptured control of the House for the first time since 1859, the number of investigations soared. In the 1918 election, Republicans gained control of the House and set off on a series of studies of World War I mobilization under President Wilson, a Democrat. In similar fashion, World War II mobilization, and reported infiltration of the Government by Communists during the administrations of Democratic Presidents Roosevelt and Truman, were studied closely by committees of the Republican 80th Congress, elected in 1946.

Maneuvering for Committee Control

A subtler, and potentially far more important form of investigation politics, has taken place in the maneuvering for control of a particular inquiry. The conduct of investigations has depended greatly on the attitude of the investigating committees and of their chairmen. Thus Radical Republicans, gaining control of the joint committee investigating the conduct of the Civil War, used the committee as a platform from which to criticize the moderate policies of President Lincoln and to force more vigorous prosecution of the war.

A similar example, with quite different results, occurred after World War II. The release by President Truman on Aug. 29, 1945, of Army and Navy reports on the Pearl Harbor disaster, brought numerous Republican demands for a Congressional investigation. Through quick maneuvering, the Democrats initiated action. Taking advantage of his right to be recognized first, Senate Majority Leader Alben W. Barkley (D Ky.) obtained unanimous consent, Aug. 29, for consideration of a concurrent resolution to appoint a joint House-Senate committee which, with the Democrats in control of Congress, would have a Democratic majority. The resolution was adopted by both chambers without opposition, though House Republicans made an effort, defeated on a partyline vote, to gain equal membership on the committee. Barkley was named chairman, and the committee conducted hearings. The committee's final report, filed July 20, 1946, absolved President Roosevelt of blame for the Pearl Harbor disaster but held Adm. Harold B. Stark, Chief of Naval Operations, and Maj. Gen. Walter C. Short, Army commander in Hawaii, primarily responsible. A Republican minority report laid the primary blame on Roosevelt, suggesting what might have been the majority view if Republicans had been in command of the inquiry.

When controversy over the Vietnam war was building in Congress during the late 1960s, war-related investigations by the Senate Foreign Relations Committee were critical of the Vietnam policies of the Administration, while House or Senate Armed Services Committee inquiries supported the policies or urged stronger war efforts. The positions of the committees reflected the opposing interests of their chairmen. Sen. J.W. Fulbright (D Ark.) of the Foreign Relations panel opposed the war. Sen. John Stennis (D Miss.) and Rep. L. Mendel Rivers (D S.C.) of the Armed Services groups favored strong military action.

Resort to Select Committees

Occasionally, a proposed investigation has overlapped the jurisdictions of different committees. When, in addition, the committees have held conflicting views on the subject, the impending impasse has been resolved by formation of a select committee, whose members have been drawn from the opposed standing committees. In 1957, for example, both the Labor and Public Welfare Committee and the Government Operations Permanent Investigations Subcommittee of the Senate claimed jurisdiction to investigate labor racketeering and management malpractices uncovered during a Permanent Investigations Subcommittee study of Defense Department procurement. The issue was resolved by the creation of a Select Committee on Improper Activities in the Labor or Management Field. Four members from each party and from each of the two committees were named to the newly formed group.

A decade later, in 1968, a similar dispute over investigation of reports of hunger and malnutrition in the United States involved the Agriculture and Forestry

Committee and the Labor and Public Welfare Committee of the Senate. Government food assistance programs were operated by the Agriculture Department but benefited welfare recipients. Once again, the dispute was resolved by creating a select committee, the Select Committee on Nutrition and Human Needs, comprised of members of both committees plus other Senators not on either panel.

Major Investigations

Following are summaries of selected major Congressional investigations conducted since 1789.

St. Clair Inquiry

The House approved the first Congressional investigation in American history when it adopted on March 27, 1792, by a 44-10 vote, a resolution authorizing a select committee to investigate an Indian victory the previous year over troops commanded by Maj. Gen. Arthur St. Clair. The action came after the House, also on March 27, had rejected, 21-35, a resolution calling upon President Washington to carry out the investigation.

Setting precedents along the way, the Committee, headed by Chairman Thomas Fitzsimmons (Fed Pa.), asked for and received War Department papers on the expedition that had sent St. Clair and about 1,500 soldiers on a road- and fort-building trip through the Northwest Territory. An Indian attack had killed about 600 men and wounded some 300. Witnesses called by the Committee included St. Clair, Secretary of War Henry Knox and Secretary of the Treasury Alexander Hamilton.

The report of the Committee, filed May 8, 1792, completely absolved St. Clair, a former president of the Continental Congress. Blame for the disaster was placed on the War Department, particularly the quartermaster and supply contractors, who were accused of mismanagement, neglect and delay in supplying necessary equipment, clothing and munitions. The House took no action on the report, and Federalists prevented its publication because of its reflections on Knox and Hamilton. Early in 1818, Congress approved a $60 monthly pension for the elderly and by then impoverished St. Clair, who died a few months later. Nearly 40 years later, in 1857, Congress appropriated a substantial sum to be paid to his heirs.

Civil War Study

The Joint Committee on the Conduct of the (Civil) War compiled what was widely considered, at least until the McCarthy era of the 1950s, the worst record of any Congressional investigating unit. It was a political vehicle for Radical Republicans opposed to President Lincoln, and its far-ranging inquiries were used for intensely partisan purposes.

The Senate on Dec. 9, 1861, by a 33-3 vote, and the House on Dec. 10 by a voice vote authorized appointment of the joint Committee simply "to inquire into the conduct of the present war." It was the first time a joint House-Senate panel had been created to conduct a Congressional inquiry. The Committee was set up in the aftermath of the Union defeats at Bull Run in July and Balls Bluff in October. At first, it was thought the panel would investigate those defeats, but the Radical majority

on the Committee, with the leading Senate Radical, Benjamin F. Wade (R Ohio), as chairman, had more ambitious ideas.

In hearings that began Dec. 24, 1861, and continued until early 1865, the Committee examined past and future battle plans, disloyal employees, Navy installations, naval engagements, war supplies and war contracts. It filed its final report May 22, 1865.

In a sense, the Committee took over partial control of Union operations. It harassed conservative and Democratic generals, particularly Gen. George B. McClellan. Typically, when investigating a general, the Committee first would interrogate his subordinate officers, searching for adverse information, With such information in hand, the Committee would summon the general for interrogation, frequently without informing him of the accusations against him or the disclosures made by his subordinates. The Committee's next step would be a meeting with President Lincoln at which the general's resignation or reassignment would be demanded.

Committee sessions were supposed to be closed to the press, but information often would be made public if it suited the purpose of the Radicals. As a result, Confederate Gen. Robert E. Lee was moved to observe that the Committee was worth about two divisions of Confederate troops.

Crédit Mobilier

Two House committees and one in the Senate investigated charges that arose during the 1872 Presidential campaign of wholesale corruption in connection with construction by the Crédit Mobilier of America of the last 667 miles of the Union Pacific Railroad, which had been completed three years earlier. The inquiries disclosed perhaps the most serious legislative scandal in the country's history.

The charges first appeared when the New York *Sun* of Sept. 4, 1872, reported that Rep. Oakes Ames (R Mass.), a principal stockholder in both the Union Pacific and the Crédit Mobilier construction company, had used Crédit Mobilier stock to bribe Vice President Schuyler Colfax, Sen. Henry Wilson (R Mass.), Speaker James G. Blaine (R Maine), Sen. James W. Patterson (R N.H.), Rep. James Brooks (D N.Y.) and Rep. James A. Garfield (R Ohio). The reported bribes represented an attempt to head off a Congressional investigation of railroad transportation rates.

Blaine proposed the first House inquiry, and the House on Dec. 2, 1872, appointed a select committee headed by Rep. Luke P. Poland (R Vt.) "to investigate and ascertain whether any member of this House was bribed by Oakes Ames, or any other person or corporation, in any manner touching his legislative duty." A month later, Jan. 6, 1873, the House appointed another select committee, headed by Rep. Jeremiah M. Wilson (R Ind.), to investigate the financial arrangement between the Union Pacific and the Crédit Mobilier.

As the House investigations proceeded simultaneously, the Poland Committee discovered evidence implicating members of the Senate, and the information was forwarded to the Senate. The result was that the Senate on Feb. 4, 1873, established a select committee of its own to look into the alleged bribery. The committee was headed by Sen. Lot M. Morrill (R Maine).

The Poland Committee's report filed Feb. 18, 1873, cleared Blaine but recommended that both Ames and Brooks be expelled from the House. The Committee said Ames had been "guilty of selling to Members of Congress shares of stock in the Crédit Mobilier of America, for prices much below the true value of such stock, with intent thereby to influence the votes and decisions of such Members in matters to be brought before Congress for action." Brooks, according to the Committee, had purchased stock in his son-in-law's name that was intended for Brooks' own benefit. The House ultimately censured the two Representatives but did not expel them.

In a March 3, 1873, report, the Wilson Committee said the Crédit Mobilier had been making exorbitant profits, and that some persons connected with it were holding bonds illegally. In addition, the Committee recommended that court action be undertaken to eliminate the financial irregularities.

The Senate's Committee reported March 1, 1873, that Sen. Patterson had bought Crédit Mobilier stock from Ames at below-market prices. The Committee recommended Patterson's expulsion, but his term was to expire March 3, and he retired without Senate action to expel him.

Colfax, whose relation to the matter was not satisfactorily explained, had had a falling out with the regular Republicans before the scandal broke and was not renominated in June 1872 for a second term on the Grant ticket. Henry Wilson, who replaced Colfax as Vice President, and Garfield, elected President in 1880, never were able to explain away their connection with the affair.

Study of the Money Trust

The House on Feb. 24, 1912, authorized its Banking and Currency Committee to investigate the concentration of money and credit in the nation. Conducted at a time when the national interest already was turned to such industrial concentrations as the sugar trust, the meat trust and the steel trust, the new inquiry soon became known as the money trust investigation.

Conducted by a Banking and Currency subcommittee, headed by Committee Chairman Arsène P. Pujo (D La.), the inquiry brought to light previously unknown interlocking directorates among two sets of New York banks, controlled by Morgan and Rockefeller interests, and 112 of the country's largest corporations in the fields of banking, public utilities, transportation, insurance, manufacturing and trading.

Witnesses called by Committee Counsel Samuel Untermyer, the real director and principal actor in the hearings, included such financial giants as J.P. Morgan Sr., George F. Baker of the First National Bank of New York, James Stillman of the National City Bank of New York, Jacob H. Schiff of Kuhn, Loeb & Co., and James J. Hill, the railroad magnate. The range of activities investigated by the subcommittee turned the hearings into the most ambitious and far-flung inquiry to date.

The subcommittee filed its report Feb. 28, 1913, summarizing its findings and calling for corrective legislation. Within two years, Congress, prodded by President Wilson, enacted the Federal Reserve Act of 1913, the Clayton Antitrust Act of 1914 and the Federal Trade Commission Act of 1914. Each of these major measures was based on information developed during the investigation.

Teapot Dome

President Harding was inaugurated in 1921 and suspicions of wrongdoing grew and flourished in the first year of his Administration. Oil figured importantly in many rumors. Congress in 1920 had enacted the General Leasing Act, which authorized the Secretary of the Navy under certain conditions to lease naval oil reserves on public lands to private oil operators, and oil interests had been influential at the 1920 Republican Convention. Harding on May 31, 1921, signed an Executive Order transferring jurisdiction over the naval oil reserves to the Interior Department. Early in 1922, Interior leased the Elk Hills reserve in California to Edward L. Doheny of the Pan-American Petroleum and Transport Co. and the Teapot Dome reserve in Wyoming to Harry F. Sinclair's Mammoth Oil Co.

Pressure mounted for a Congressional investigation of the transactions. Tight Republican control blocked action in the House. But Senate Democrats and insurgent Republicans succeeded on April 29, 1922, in pushing through a resolution that authorized the Senate Committee on Public Lands and Surveys (renamed in 1948 the Interior and Insular Affairs Committee) "to investigate this entire subject of leases upon naval oil reserves..." The Committee was headed by a series of Republican chairmen, but a Democrat on the panel, Thomas J. Walsh (Mont.), took charge of the inquiry. All during the remainder of 1922 and into the fall of 1923, Walsh studied the lease arrangements and gathered information. When the hearings opened on Oct. 25, 1923, they concentrated at first on the legality and expediency of the two leases. Then Walsh began probing the sudden wealth of Secretary of the Interior Albert B. Fall. In a sensational national scandal, rivaling the Crédit Mobilier, it was developed that Fall had accepted bribes from Doheny and Sinclair. Doheny had given Fall at least $100,000, and Sinclair had given the Interior Secretary at least $300,000. Both Fall and Navy Secretary Edwin Denby resigned. Fall was later convicted of accepting a bribe in connection with the Elk Hills lease and was sentenced to prison and fined $100,000.

By the time the Committee filed its report, June 6, 1924, Congress already had adopted a joint resolution declaring the leases contrary to the public interest and ordering the President to initiate court action to cancel them. The courts subsequently did cancel the leases and declared invalid Harding's Executive Order transferring jurisdiction over the naval oil reserves from the Navy to the Interior Department.

Acting on information developed in the Teapot Dome inquiry, the Senate on March 4, 1924, created a Select Committee to Investigate the Justice Department. The Committee was headed by Sen. Smith W. Brookhart (R Iowa). Attorney General Harry M. Daugherty's failure to prosecute Fall, Sinclair, Doheny and others led President Coolidge on March 28, 1924, to demand Daugherty's resignation.

Pecora Stock Exchange Probe

The Senate Banking and Currency Committee from 1932 to 1934 conducted an important investigation of the stock exchange and Wall Street financial manipulations, reminiscent of the Pujo hearings 20 years earlier.

Authorized March 4, 1932, while Sen. Peter Norbeck (R S.D.) was chairman of the Committee, the hearings concentrated initially on stock exchanges practices. The 1929 stock market collapse had plunged the nation into a severe depression and a Congressional examination of exchange operations became a political necessity. The hearings began rather inconspicuously, and some observers expected them to become a "whitewash."

Then in January 1933, the Committee hired Ferdinand Pecora as chief counsel. As the country's banking system headed for collapse, the Committee broadened its investigation to include a study of the financial dealings of New York's major banking houses. When the Democrats took over control of the Senate, Sen. Duncan U. Fletcher (D Fla.) became chairman of the Committee.

Chief Counsel Pecora demanded careful research and thorough investigation by the Committee staff. Pecora, in turn, relied on evidence gathered by the staff as he conducted the interrogation of Committee witnesses. Committee members normally listened in silence, asking few questions of their own. Pecora came to dominate the hearings, far overshadowing Fletcher, to the extent that the inquiry was to become known as the Pecora investigation.

As the 1933 hearings progressed under Pecora, they produced spectacular accounts of dubious financial actions. The salary of Charles E. Mitchell, president of the National City Bank of New York, had doubled from $100,000 to $200,000 as the breadlines of the unemployed had lengthened. Albert H. Wiggin, president of the Chase National Bank of New York, had sold short the stock of his own bank. J.P. Morgan Jr. had paid no income tax for several years because his losses offset his gains. Other witnesses recounted the operation of security flotation syndicates and stock market pools. It developed that friends of Morgan, including Cabinet officers, former President Coolidge and top Republican and Democratic party officials, had been profitably let in on the inside of some security flotations.

Practices disclosed in the hearings paved the way for such major Roosevelt Administration measures as the Banking Acts of 1933 and 1935, the Securities Act of 1933 and the Securities Exchange Act of 1934.

By the time the Committee filed its final report, June 16, 1934, the investigation had compiled an unmatchable record for sustained, sensational publicity, for economically significant disclosures and for important resulting regulatory legislation.

Nye Munitions Inquiry

Riding a wave of public sentiment for a Congressional investigation of the munitions industry, the Senate on April 12, 1934, established the Senate Special Committee Investigating the Munitions Industry. The public was firmly convinced before the Committee began hearings that the country's munitions makers were merchants of death, and the Committee accepted the public's verdict and set out to find the proof.

The chief sponsor of the panel had been Sen. Gerald P. Nye (R N.D.). Despite solid Democratic control of the Senate, and a Democratic majority on the Committee, Nye was picked as chairman. A Progressive Republican, he had been appointed to the Senate in 1925. He had earned a measure of public prominence as chairman of

a special Senate campaign expenditures committee to scrutinize spending in the 1930 election contests. The munitions inquiry made Nye a national figure, a leader of the movement to curb the arms traffic and the nation's most eloquent isolationist.

The Nye Committee, as it soon was called, opened hearings on Sept. 4, 1934. The Committee investigated the munitions industry, the shipbuilding industry, and business profits during World War I. Witnesses included leading businessmen, financiers and their associates. Committee investigators gathered documents from Government and diplomatic files and from private corporations. Worldwide attention, carefully cultivated by Nye, focused on the Committee's efforts to prove that arms makers were merchants of death, linked together in a global ring, opposed to disarmament, promoting armed conflicts and reaping enormous profits along the way. The evidence, however, was thin and failed to support general conclusions. Instead of concentrating on a single allegation at a time, the Committee examined separately company after company, thus diffusing its energy. The hearings continued until mid-1935 and were resumed briefly in early 1936.

Controversy was inevitably stirred up by the investigation. Committee disclosures of bribery and arms deals brought sharp responses in Latin America and Great Britain, where the incidents had occurred, and created trouble for the State Department. Some of the disclosures embarrassed President Roosevelt. The Committee was criticized for using as staff aides workers on relief in New York.

In the meantime, public sentiment had shifted from control of the munitions industry to support of U.S. neutrality. The result was that the Senate in 1936 refused to provide the Committee with any more funds than were needed to conclude its activities. In its final report, filed April 20, 1936, the Committee criticized American loans to belligerents during World War I. It recommended a definition of armed merchantmen, a ceiling on wartime exports to belligerents, and restrictions on loans to belligerents. The Committee agreed on the need of strictly controlling the munitions industry but divided on the methods by which control could best be exercised.

World War II Truman Committee

The World War II Senate Special Committee to Investigate the National Defense Program came to be widely regarded as the most effective investigating group in the history of Congress. Created March 1, 1941, nine months before the Japanese attack on Pearl Harbor plunged the United States into the war, the Committee sought to uncover and to halt wasteful practices in war preparations. Its studies were broadened to cover the entire war mobilization effort, once the country entered the conflict.

Closely identified with its first chairman, Sen. Harry S. Truman (D Mo.), the Committee had the broadest possible investigating authority. The Truman Committee was "to make a full and complete study and investigation of the operation of the program for the procurement and construction of supplies, materials, vessels, plants, camps and other articles and facilities in connection with the national defense." The group was comprised largely of freshmen Senators, able to devote much of their time to inquiries.

Confusion in the construction program for training camps, and concentration of war contracts in a few areas of the country and among a few businesses, had led Truman to propose the investigating committee. But the Committee's first hearings, which began April 15, 1941, were devoted to a general investigation of the status of the national defense program. Later studies explored camp construction and other problems of war mobilization; shortages of critical war materials, such as aluminum, rubber, petroleum products, housing and steel; the quality of materials supplied under defense contracts and the distribution of the contracts; and war frauds among contractors, lobbyists and Government officials.

Aware of the excesses of the Civil War investigating committee, Truman scrupulously avoided any attempt to judge military policy or operations. Hearings of the Truman Committee were conducted in a restrained, thoughtful manner, after careful and thorough preparation. Frequently, private meetings or correspondence with contractors or Federal officials led to corrective action, and no public hearings were held. Occasionally, a previously disregarded request of the Committee suddenly would be complied with, once a hearing was scheduled.

The Committee worked closely with Executive Branch departments and agencies. Special liaison officers were assigned to it in the War Department, the Navy Department, the War Production Board, the Maritime Commission and the War Shipping Administration. Reports of Committee findings and recommendations were supported unanimously by Committee members, and most recommendations were put into effect before the findings were published. The record of unanimity on reports was not broken until 1947.

The Truman Committee was not the only Congressional group studying national mobilization, but it was the only one to make a systematic effort to survey the entire war program on a continuing basis. Succeeding Congresses continued the Committee throughout the war and into the early postwar years. Its final report was submitted April 28, 1948.

Truman resigned as chairman Aug. 3, 1944, after receiving the Democratic Vice Presidential nomination. The war was nearing an end when he left the Committee, and its studies turned more and more to problems of reconverting from war to peace. Truman was succeeded as chairman by James M. Mead (D N.Y.) on Aug. 11, 1944, and Mead, in turn, was succeeded on Oct. 1, 1946, by Harley M. Kilgore (D W.Va.). Owen Brewster (R Maine) became Committee chairman on Jan. 6, 1947, when the Republican-controlled 80th Congress took over control on Capitol Hill.

Kefauver Crime Hearings

In 1950 and 1951, the Senate Special Committee to Investigate Organized Crime in Interstate Commerce held hearings around the country, many of which were televised. The TV broadcasts created wide interest and were estimated to have been viewed by 20 million persons.

The Special Committee, approved by the Senate on May 3, 1950, represented a compromise. It grew out of a jurisdictional dispute between the Judiciary Committee and the Interstate and Foreign Commerce Committee over which group should conduct an investigation of

organized crime. Sen. Estes Kefauver (D Tenn.), who first proposed the investigation and supported the Judiciary Committee's jurisdictional claim, was made chairman. Hearings began May 26.

The Committee questioned governors, mayors, sheriffs, and policemen and turned the spotlight on gangsters, gamblers, racketeers and narcotics peddlers. The hearings were full of names of prominent alleged racketeers, including reputed heirs of the Chicago Capone gang and leaders of the Mafia. Many of the alleged criminals proved difficult to locate. Hearings were followed by scores of citations for contempt of Congress and many local indictments for criminal activities.

Kefauver continued as chairman until May 1, 1951, when Sen. Herbert R. O'Conor (D Md.) took the reins. The investigation had been scheduled to end Feb. 28, 1951, but the Committee's life was extended to Aug. 31. The group's records and recommendations then were turned over to the Interstate and Foreign Commerce Committee for further action. The latter Committee decided not to conduct a further crime probe, but various local investigations continued where the Kefauver Committee had left off.

Use of Television. One of the highlights of the hearings was the appearance before the Committee of Frank Costello, reputed underworld king. He refused to have his face televised, so TV audiences viewed only his hands. Many other witnesses likewise complained about testifying before television cameras. Some who refused were cited for contempt, in order to get a court ruling on the use of television and radio by committees. The U.S. District Court for the District of Columbia ruled on Oct. 6, 1952, that two of the contemptuous witnesses, Morris Kleinman and Louis Rothkopf, were "justified" in refusing to testify while television and newsreel cameras were in operation. They were freed of the contempt of Congress charges.

Reports. In a series of reports issued in 1951, the Committee said crime syndicates were operating with the connivance and protection of law enforcement officials, and that the two major syndicates were centered in Chicago and New York. "Shocking" corruption existed, according to one report, "at all levels of government." The Committee recommended creation of a privately financed National Crime Coordinating Committee, a thorough overhauling of state and local laws, a stronger attack on narcotics traffic, legalization of wiretapping, and the adoption by Congress of a code or procedure for the broadcasting or televising of committee hearings.

McCarthy's Investigations

Under the chairmanship of Sen. Joseph R. McCarthy (R Wis.), the Permanent Investigations Subcommittee of the Senate Government Operations Committee conducted a series of wide-ranging and controversial hearings in 1953 and 1954. The hearings were the highwater mark of the McCarthy era and bore the unmistakable scars of the Senator's abrasive and aggressive character. The Subcommittee's activities varied from hearings on Korean War atrocities to investigation of a deal with Greek shipowners, but the State Department and the armed services were the prime targets of the probes. The Subcommittee also investigated the Government Printing Office, Communist infiltration of the United Nations, and the transfer to Russians of occupation currency plates. In 1954, the Subcommittee in an unprecedented move in effect undertook an investigation of itself.

McCarthy tangled with the press, Harvard University and other Senators. The three Democratic members of the Subcommittee—Sens. Henry M. Jackson (Wash.), John L. McClellan (Ark.) and Stuart Symington (Mo.)—resigned July 10, 1953, in protest against the chairman's handling of the group's hired personnel. But after McCarthy on Jan. 25, 1954, announced certain changes in Subcommittee procedure, the three Democrats resumed their places on the panel.

Advent of McCarthy Era. Long before the stormy McCarthy hearings got under way, the Senator himself had become a controversial public figure. The period that was later dubbed the McCarthy era—one of the most controversial periods in American history—began in 1950. On Feb. 9 of that year, McCarthy delivered a speech before the Ohio County Women's Republican Club in Wheeling, W.Va. According to the Wheeling *News Register* and the Wheeling *Intelligencer,* the Senator said at one point: "While I cannot take the time to name all the men in the State Department who have been named as members of the Communist Party and members of a spy ring, I have here in my hand a list of 205 that were known to the Secretary of State as being members of the Communist party and who, nevertheless, are still working and shaping policy in the State Department." The number varied in later versions of the speech, and the text that was read into the *Congressional Record* omitted the paragraph referring to the list of 205 Communists.

A special subcommittee of the Senate Foreign Relations Committee was set up under the chairmanship of Millard E. Tydings (D Md.) to investigate McCarthy's charges. The subcommittee, in one of the most bitterly controversial investigations in the history of Congress, held 31 days of hearings between March 8 and June 28, 1950. During the course of the hearings McCarthy charged 10 individuals by name with varying degrees of Communist activity. One of the persons named was Prof. Owen J. Lattimore of Johns Hopkins University, who in the summer of 1950 published a book, "Ordeal by Slander," defending his record against McCarthy's accusations of disloyalty.

The investigation was a major issue in the 1950 elections. Charges of "softness" toward communism were widely credited with the defeat of Tydings in the Maryland Senatorial contest. On Aug. 6, 1951, after a Senate Rules and Administration Committee report had criticized McCarthy's part in the Maryland election, Sen. William Benton (D Conn.) demanded his expulsion from the Senate. McCarthy on April 10, 1952, demanded an investigation of Benton. The result was a simultaneous investigation of both men by the Privileges and Elections Subcommittee of the Senate Rules and Administration Committee.

The Subcommittee's report on Jan. 2, 1953, asserted that McCarthy had "deliberately set out to thwart" the investigation. Although it did not accuse him of any specific wrongdoing, the report raised a series of questions such as whether McCarthy had diverted to his "personal advantage" funds collected to fight communism. Benton was criticized for accepting a campaign contribution from a former director of the Reconstruction Finance Corporation. By the time the Subcommittee reported, Benton had

been defeated in the 1952 Connecticut Senatorial election; his defeat was widely attributed to his feud with McCarthy.

The 1952 elections gave Republicans a majority in both chambers of the 83rd Congress. Accordingly, at the start of its First Session in January 1953, McCarthy, who had been ranking Republican on the Senate Government Operations Committee, became its chairman and chairman of the Permanent Investigations Subcommittee.

1953 Activities. The Subcommittee on Jan. 25, 1954, filed its annual report summarizing its activities in 1953. The report listed "various actions taken as a result" of its investigations, including: the saving of $18 million through exposure of inefficiency in the International Information Administration and its Voice of America programs; removal of a number of "Fifth Amendment Communists" from Federal jobs and defense plants; removal of incompetent and undesirable persons from Federal employment; and indictment of several witnesses. The report was not signed by the three Democratic members of the Subcommittee who had resigned in July.

Army-McCarthy Dispute. During most of the first half of 1954, McCarthy was involved in controversy with high officials of the Army and, by extension, with the Eisenhower Administration itself. The Permanent Investigations Subcommittee continued its investigation of the armed services, begun in 1953, and the investigation led to a series of charges and countercharges by the Army and McCarthy. At issue was the question of whether or not McCarthy and his staff had used improper means to secure preferential treatment for a former Subcommittee consultant, Private G. David Schine. Also involved was a charge that the Army had tried to pressure McCarthy into calling off his investigation of alleged Communists in the Army.

The Army on April 14, 1954, filed a formal "bill of particulars" detailing charges against McCarthy, Subcommittee chief counsel Roy M. Cohn and Subcommittee staff director Francis P. Carr. The Subcommittee reciprocated April 20 by filing charges against Army Secretary Robert T. Stevens, Army Counsel John G. Adams and Assistant Defense Secretary H. Struve Hensel. To investigate the charges, the Subcommittee held hearings, with Sen. Karl E. Mundt (R S.D.) as acting chairman. McCarthy resigned temporarily from Subcommittee membership. The Subcommittee in effect began an investigation of its own activities.

The 35 days of hearings from April 22 to June 17 attracted, during 187 hours of television coverage, audiences as large as 20 million persons at a time. In addition to the principals charged in the case and the Subcommittee members, the drama featured, as the main interrogators, special Army Counsel Joseph N. Welch and special Subcommittee Counsel Ray H. Jenkins. Several Army officers testified. In its Aug. 31 report, the Subcommittee's Republican majority concluded that the charge of "improper influence" by McCarthy on behalf of Schine "was not established," but that Cohn had been "unduly aggressive and persistent" on Schine's behalf. The Republicans said also that Stevens and Adams had tried "to terminate or influence" investigations of the Army. The Democratic minority asserted that McCarthy had "fully acquiesced in and condoned" the "improper actions" of Cohn, who in turn had "misused and abused the powers of his office and brought disrepute to the Committee." The minority report said also that Stevens "merits severe criticism" for "an inexcusable indecisiveness and lack of sound administrative judgment."

Censure of McCarthy. On June 11, 1954, while the Army-McCarthy hearings were in progress, Sen. Ralph E. Flanders (R Vt.) initiated what was to develop into a six-month controversy over what official attitude the Senate should adopt toward certain of McCarthy's actions. Flanders introduced a resolution to remove McCarthy from the chairmanship of the Government Operations Committee and any of its subcommittees, and to prohibit him from reassuming such posts unless he answered questions raised in 1952 by the Privileges and Elections Subcommittee of the Senate Rules and Administration Committee. After Senate Majority Leader William F. Knowland (R Calif.) had voiced opposition, Flanders on July 30 introduced a substitute resolution, charging McCarthy with "personal contempt" of the Senate. The Flanders and other resolutions were referred to a Select Committee to Study Censure Charges. Following hearings from Aug. 31 to Sept. 13, the Committee on Sept. 27 unanimously recommended adoption of a resolution censuring McCarthy for his attitude toward the Privileges and Elections Subcommittee's Benton-McCarthy investigation in 1952 and toward Army Brig. Gen. Ralph W. Zwicker. At a Permanent Investigations Subcommittee hearing in 1954, McCarthy had told Zwicker that he was "not fit to wear that uniform" and implied that Zwicker did not have "the brains of a five-year-old."

The Senate on Dec. 2, 1954, adopted the resolution censuring McCarthy by a vote of 67 to 22. The resolution condemned McCarthy's abuse of the Privileges and Elections Subcommittee in 1952 and several of his statements about the Select Censure Committee and the special post-election Senate session that had been called to consider the Committee's recommendations. Condemnation of McCarthy's comments on the censure move itself had been substituted, during preliminary action on the final resolution, for condemnation of McCarthy's abuse of Zwicker.

McCarthy lost his committee and subcommittee chairmanships when control of Congress passed to the Democrats in January 1955. His activities no longer attracted any considerable attention in the press, the Senate or elsewhere. He died of a liver ailment on May 2, 1957.

TFX Plane Contract

The Permanent Investigations Subcommittee of the Senate Government Operations Committee in 1963 launched a major investigation of the Defense Department's November 1962 award of a multibillion-dollar TFX fighter plane contract to the General Dynamics Corp., which was in competition with the Boeing Co. The controversial decision by Pentagon civilian officials to award the contract to General Dynamics was made despite the almost unanimous endorsement of the Boeing bid by military technical advisers.

At stake was an aircraft program for which production orders were estimated eventually to total more than $6.5 billion and involve 20,000 jobs and 1,700 planes—the largest tactical airplane contract since World War II. The initial $28-million contract, for which Boeing and General Dynamics were bidding, involved 22 developmental planes for testing, to be delivered within two and one-half years.

Subcommittee hearings were initiated in response to allegations that the contract might have been awarded as a result of political or regional pressure—possibly in conflict with national security and economy interests. General Dynamics planned to build the aircraft at its Convair plant in Fort Worth, Texas, and at the Grumman Aircraft Engineering Corp. plant in Bethpage, Long Island, N.Y. Boeing, whose headquarters is in Seattle, Wash., planned to build the aircraft at its Wichita, Kan., plant.

Sen. Jackson (D Wash.), a member of the Subcommittee, proposed that it look into the circumstances of the award, and Chairman McClellan (D Ark.) decided on a full-scale investigation.

During the long investigation suggestions of political pressure were made concerning Jackson, Rep. K. William Stinson (R Wash.) of Seattle, Rep. Jim Wright (D Texas) of Fort Worth, the Kansas Congressional delegation and then-Vice President Lyndon B. Johnson, among others.

Hearings began Feb. 26, were suspended Nov. 20 and, contrary to expectations, did not resume in 1964. Meanwhile, General Dynamics proceeded with its development of the TFX under a Dec. 21, 1962, "letter contract." Such a contract was common Defense Department procedure for permitting the contractor to get work under way, leaving the details of the more complex, formal contract to be settled later.

Unforeseen obstacles hindered development of the aircraft. Development of the Navy version (F-111B) lagged far behind schedule, and the Defense Department on April 18, 1968, canceled the Navy program. Although the Air Force officially expressed satisfaction with its version of the plane (F-111A), loss of three of the first six F-111As sent to Vietnam in 1968 cast serious doubt on the future of the Air Force's F-111 program. President Nixon in 1969 canceled the Air Force's strategic bomber version of the plane (FB-111).

Bibliography

Books

Barth, Alan, *Government by Investigation.* Viking Press, 1955.

Beck, Carl, *Contempt of Congress.* Hauser Press, 1959.

Chambers, Whittaker, *Witness.* Random House, 1952.

Dimock, Marshall E., *Congressional Investigating Committees.* Johns Hopkins Press, 1929.

Eberling, Ernest J., *Congressional Investigations.* Columbia University Press, 1928.

Galloway, George B., *History of the House of Representatives.* Thomas Y. Crowell Co., 1969.

Goldfarb, Ronald L., *The Contempt Power.* Columbia University Press, 1963.

Harris, Joseph P., *Congressional Control of Administration.* Doubleday & Co., 1964.

McGeary, M. Nelson, *The Development of Congressional Investigative Power.* Octagon Books, Inc., 1966.

Riddle, Donald H., *The Truman Committee.* Rutgers University Press, 1964.

Rovere, Richard H., *Senator Joe McCarthy.* World Publishing Co., 1968.

Taylor, Telford, *Grand Inquest.* Simon & Schuster, Inc., 1955.

Wiltz, John E., *In Search of Peace.* Louisiana State University Press, 1963.

Wilson, Woodrow, *Congressional Government.* World Publishing Co., 1967 edition.

Articles

"Congressional Investigations," *University of Chicago Law Review,* Vol. 18, No. 3, 1951.

Government Publications

Library of Congress, Legislative Reference Service, *Congressional Power of Investigation.* Government Printing Office, 1954.

Power Of Impeachment

IMPEACHMENT is perhaps the most awesome though the least used power of Congress. In essence, it is a political action, couched in legal terminology, directed against a ranking official of the Federal Government. The House of Representatives is the prosecutor. The Senate chamber is the courtroom; and the Senate is the judge and jury. The final penalty is removal from office and disqualification from further office. There is no appeal.

Impeachment proceedings have been initiated in the House some 50 times since 1789, but only 12 cases have reached the Senate. Of these 12, two were dismissed for lack of jurisdiction, six resulted in acquittal and four ended in conviction. All of the convictions involved Federal judges: John Pickering of the district court for New Hampshire, in 1804; West H. Humphreys of the eastern, middle and western districts of Tennessee, in 1862; Robert W. Archbald of the Commerce Court, in 1913; and Halsted L. Ritter of the southern district of Florida, in 1936.

Two of the impeachments traditionally have stood out from all the rest. They involved Justice Samuel Chase of the Supreme Court in 1805 and President Andrew Johnson in 1868, the two most powerful and important Federal officials ever subjected to the process. Both were impeached by the House—Chase for partisan conduct on the bench; Johnson for violating the Tenure of Office Act—and both were acquitted by the Senate after sensational trials. Behind both impeachments lay intensely partisan politics. Chase, a Federalist, was a victim of attacks on the Supreme Court by Jeffersonian Democrats, who had planned to impeach Chief Justice John Marshall if Chase was convicted. President Johnson was a victim of Radical Republicans opposed to his reconstruction policies after the Civil War.

Purpose of Impeachment Process

Based on specific constitutional authority, the impeachment process was designed "as a method of national inquest into the conduct of public men," according to Alexander Hamilton in Federalist No. 65. The Constitution declares that impeachment proceedings may be brought against "the President, Vice President and all civil officers of the United States," without explaining who is, or is not, a "civil officer." In practice, however, the overwhelming majority of impeachment proceedings have been directed against Federal judges, who hold lifetime appointments "during good behavior," and cannot be removed by any other method. Nine of the 12 impeachment cases that have reached the Senate have involved Federal judges. Federal judges have figured in 33 of the approximately fifty impeachment cases that have failed to reach the Senate.

Others whose impeachment has been sought include Cabinet members, diplomats, customs collectors, a Senator and a U.S. district attorney. These officials are subject to removal by dismissal or expulsion as well as by impeachment, and it seldom has been necessary to resort to full-scale impeachment proceedings to bring about their removal. Proceedings against the only Senator to be impeached, William Blount of Tennessee, were dismissed in 1799 after Blount had been expelled from the Senate in 1797. War Secretary William W. Belknap, the only Cabinet member to be tried by the Senate, was acquitted in 1876 largely because Senators questioned their authority to try Belknap, who had resigned as Secretary several months before the trial.

The House Judiciary Committee twice has ruled that certain Federal officials were not subject to impeachment. In 1833, the Committee determined that a territorial judge was not a civil officer within the meaning of the Constitution because he held office for only four years and could be removed at any time by the President. In 1926, the Committee said that a Commissioner of the District of Columbia was immune from impeachment because he was an officer of the District and not a civil officer of the United States.

Debate in Constitutional Convention

The origin of the Congressional impeachment process dates from 14th century England. Under the parliamentary system, an impeachment (indictment) was preferred by the House of Commons and decided by the House of Lords. In America, colonial governments and early state constitutions followed the British pattern of trial before the upper legislative body on charges brought by the lower house.

Despite these precedents, a major controversy arose over the impeachment process in the Constitutional Convention. The issue was whether the Senate should try impeachments. Opposing that role for the Senate, Madison and Pinckney asserted that it would make the President too dependent on the Legislative Branch. Suggested alternative trial bodies included the "national judiciary," the Supreme Court or the assembled chief justices of

---

Reference

See Appendix table of contents (first thumb tab) for text of the Articles of Impeachment against President Andrew Johnson.

The Constitution on Impeachment

Following are provisions of the Constitution that deal with the Congressional power of impeachment:

• The House of Representatives...shall have the sole power of impeachment. (Article I, section 2.)

• The Senate shall have the sole power to try all impeachments. When sitting for that purpose, they shall be on oath or affirmation. When the President of the United States is tried, the Chief Justice shall preside. And no person shall be convicted without the concurrence of two-thirds of the Members present. Judgment in cases of impeachment shall not extend further than to removal from office, and disqualification to hold and enjoy any office of honor, trust or profit under the United States; but the party convicted shall, nevertheless, be liable and subject to indictment, trial, judgment and punishment, according to law. (Article I, section 3.)

• The President...shall have power to grant reprieves and pardons for offenses against the United States, except in cases of impeachment. (Article II, section 2.)

• The President, Vice President and all civil officers of the United States shall be removed from office on impeachment for, and conviction of, treason, bribery or other high crimes and misdemeanors. (Article II, section 4.)

• The trial of all crimes, except in cases of impeachment, shall be by jury....(Article III, section 2.)

state supreme courts. It was argued, however, that such bodies would be too small and perhaps even susceptible to corruption. In the end, the Senate was agreed to. Hamilton (a Senate opponent during the Convention) asked later in the Federalist: "Where else than in the Senate could have been found a tribunal sufficiently dignified, or sufficiently independent?"

A lesser issue was the definition of impeachable crimes. In the original proposals, the President was to be removed on impeachment and conviction "for mal or corrupt conduct," or for "malpractice or neglect of duty." Later, the wording was changed to "treason, bribery or corruption," and then to "treason and bribery" alone. Contending that "treason and bribery" were too narrow, George Mason proposed adding "mal-administration," but switched to "other high crimes and misdemeanors against the state" when Madison said that "mal-administration" was too broad. A final revision made impeachable crimes "treason, bribery or other high crimes and misdemeanors."

The provisions of the Constitution on impeachment were scattered through the first three articles. To the House was given the "sole power of impeachment." The Senate was given "the sole power to try all impeachments." Impeachments could be brought against "the President, Vice President, and all civil officers of the United States" for "treason, bribery or other high crimes or misdemeanors." Conviction meant "removal from office and disqualification to hold" further public office. *(See box.)*

The first attempt to use the impeachment power was made in 1796. A petition from residents of the Northwest Territory, submitted to the House on April 25, accused Judge George Turner of the territorial supreme court of arbitrary conduct. The petition was referred briefly to a special House committee and then was referred to Atty. Gen. Charles Lee. Impeachment proceedings were dropped after Lee said, May 9, that the territorial government would prosecute Turner in the territorial courts.

Procedures in Impeachment Cases

The first impeachment proceedings, against Turner, failed to provide precedents for later impeachments. In fact, the process has been used so infrequently and under such widely varying circumstances that no uniform practice has emerged.

At various times impeachment proceedings have been initiated by the introduction of a resolution by a Member, by a letter or message from the President, by a grand jury action forwarded to the House from a territorial legislature, by a memorial setting forth charges, by a resolution authorizing a general investigation, or by a resolution reported by the House Judiciary Committee. The five cases to reach the Senate since 1900 were based on Judiciary Committee resolutions.

After submission of the charges, a Committee investigation has been undertaken. If the charges have been supported by the investigation, the Committee has reported an impeachment resolution, which in four of the five post-1900 cases has included articles of impeachment. The impeachment resolution has been subject to adoption by majority vote. In earlier cases, the impeachment articles were drafted by a select committee named by the House Speaker or by simple resolution. Like the impeachment resolution, the articles too have been subject to adoption by majority vote.

The next step, after the House has adopted an impeachment resolution and articles of impeachment, has been selection of House managers to direct the proceedings in the Senate. House managers have been chosen by a resolution fixing the number of managers and authorizing the Speaker to appoint them, by a resolution fixing the number and making the appointments, and by ballot, with a majority vote for each candidate. Once selected, the House managers have appeared at the bar of the Senate to inform the upper house of the impending impeachment trial and to present the articles of impeachment. The Senate, in turn, has informed the House when it is ready to proceed.

The full House may attend the trial, but the House managers have been its representatives at the proceedings. Following Senate rules adopted March 2, 1868, the trial has been conducted in a fashion similar to a court trial for a criminal offense. Both sides may present witnesses and evidence, and the defendant has been allowed counsel and the right of cross-examination. If the President is on trial, the Constitution requires the Chief Justice of the Supreme Court to preside. The Constitution is silent on a presiding officer for lesser defendants, but Senate practice has been for the Vice President or the President pro tempore to preside. Procedural questions during trial have been decided by majority vote, but conviction has required, according to the Constitution, approval of two-thirds of the Senators present. A separate vote on each article is required by Senate rules, and a two-thirds vote on a single article is sufficient for conviction. Removal upon conviction is required by the Constitution, although the Senate at times has voted removal after conviction. Disqualification is not mandatory; only two of the four convictions have been accompanied by disqualification, which has been subject to a majority vote.

Controversial Questions

Three major issues have dominated the history of the impeachment power: the definition of impeachable offenses, possible Senatorial conflicts of interest and alternative removal methods for Federal judges.

Impeachable Offenses. "Treason" and "bribery," as constitutionally designated impeachable crimes, have raised little debate, for treason is defined elsewhere in the Constitution and bribery is a well-defined act. "High crimes and misdemeanors," however, have been anything that the prosecution has wanted to make them. An endless debate has surrounded the phrase, pitting broad constructionists, who have viewed impeachment as a political weapon, against narrow constructionists, who have regarded impeachment as being limited to offenses indictable at common law.

The constitutional debates seemed to indicate that impeachment was to be regarded as a political weapon. Narrow constructionists quickly won a major victory, though, when Chase was acquitted, using as a defense the argument that he had committed no indictable offense. The narrow constructionists continued to prevail when President Johnson also was acquitted on a similar defense. His lawyers argued that conviction could result only from commission of high criminal offenses against the United States.

The only two convictions to date in the 20th century suggest that the broad constructionists still have powerful arguments. The 20th century convictions removed Robert W. Archbald, associate judge of the U.S. Commerce Court, in 1913, and Halsted L. Ritter, U.S. judge for the southern district of Florida, in 1936. Archbald was convicted of soliciting for himself and for friends valuable favors from railroad companies, some of which were litigants in his court. It was conceded, however, that he had committed no indictable offense. Ritter was convicted for conduct in a receivership case which raised serious doubts about his integrity.

Ritter's was the last impeachment to reach the Senate. But the debate over impeachable offenses is certain to be revived in future Senate cases.

Conflicts of Interest. An equally controversial issue, particularly in earlier impeachment trials, concerned the partisan political interests of Senators, which raised serious doubt about their impartiality as jurors.

President Johnson's potential successor, for example, was the president pro tempore of the Senate, since there was a vacancy in the Vice Presidency. Sen. Benjamin F. Wade (R Ohio), president pro tempore, took part in the trial and voted—for conviction. On the other hand, Andrew Johnson's son-in-law, Sen. David T. Patterson (D Tenn.), also took part in the trial and voted—for acquittal.

In the Johnson trial and in others, Senators have been outspoken critics or supporters of the defendant, yet have participated in the trial and have voted on the articles. Some Senators who had held seats in the House when the articles of impeachment first came up, and had voted on them there, have failed to disqualify themselves during the trial. On occasion, intense outside lobbying for, and against, the defendant has been aimed at Senators. Senators have testified as witnesses at some trials and then voted on the articles.

Senators may request to be excused from the trial, and in recent cases Senators have disqualified themselves when possible conflicts of interest arose.

Removal of Judges. Two forces have combined in the continuing search for an alternative method of removal for Federal judges. One force has been led by Members of Congress anxious to free the Senate, faced by an enormous legislative workload, from the time-consuming process of sitting as a court of impeachment. The other force has been led by Members anxious to restrict judicial power by providing a simpler and swifter means of removal than the cumbersome and unwieldy impeachment process.

The search to date has been unsuccessful. Efforts to revise and accelerate the impeachment process have failed. So, too, have attempts to amend the Constitution to limit the tenure of Federal judges to a definite term of years. A more recent approach has been to seek legislation providing for a judicial trial and judgment of removal for Federal judges violating "good-behavior" standards. The House passed such a bill on Oct. 22, 1941, by a 124-122 vote, but it died in the Senate.

A 1947 report by the Legislative Reference Service of the Library of Congress concluded:

"1. There is no power in the Executive or Legislative Branches of the Government to remove or limit the tenure of Supreme Court justices, or, indeed, any judges of constitutional courts, except as Congress is expressly authorized to act by impeachment for lack of good behavior....

"2. Means of removal other than impeachment and limitations on tenure could be provided for by constitutional amendment. Among such methods of removal could be that of legislative address.

"3. Congress perhaps can constitutionally provide for judicial removal of Federal judges for lack of good behavior....While the good behavior tenure clause never has been construed by the Supreme Court, it has been contended that the clause must be read with a view to changing needs, and that Congress, therefore, might define the term so as to allow judicial removal for any form of conduct or neglect which according to modern notions tends to corruption or inefficiency."

Attempted Impeachments

Many proposed impeachments have failed to come to a vote in the House because the defendant died or because he resigned or received another appointment, removing him from the disputed office. Among the unsuccessful impeachment attempts have been moves against two Presidents, a Vice President, two Cabinet officers, and a Supreme Court justice.

The House on Jan. 10, 1843, rejected by an 84-127 vote a resolution by Rep. John M. Botts (Henry Clay Whig Va.) to investigate the possibility of initiating impeachment proceedings against President Tyler. Tyler had become a political outcast, ostracized by both Democrats and Whigs, but impeachment apparently was too strong a measure to take against him.

A move developed in 1873 to impeach Vice President Schuyler Colfax because of his involvement in the Credit Mobilier scandal. The matter was dropped when the Judiciary Committee recommended against impeachment on the ground that Colfax had purchased

Senate Rules of Procedure and Practice...

Following are the major provisions of rules used by the Senate during impeachment trials. With the exception of Rule XI, which was adopted May 28, 1935, the rules have remained unchanged since their adoption March 2, 1868, for the trial of President Johnson.

I. Whensoever the Senate shall receive notice from the House of Representatives that managers are appointed on their part to conduct an impeachment against any person and are directed to carry articles of impeachment to the Senate, the Secretary of the Senate shall immediately inform the House of Representatives that the Senate is ready to receive the managers for the purpose of exhibiting such articles of impeachment, agreeably to such notice.

II. When the managers of an impeachment shall be introduced at the bar of the Senate and shall signify that they are ready to exhibit articles of impeachment against any person, the Presiding Officer of the Senate shall direct the Sergeant at Arms to make proclamation...after which the articles shall be exhibited, and then the Presiding Officer of the Senate shall inform the managers that the Senate will take proper order on the subject of the impeachment, of which due notice shall be given to the House of Representatives.

III. Upon such articles being presented to the Senate, the Senate shall, at 1 o'clock afternoon of the day (Sunday excepted) following such presentation, or sooner if ordered by the Senate, proceed to the consideration of such articles and shall continue in session from day to day (Sundays excepted) after the trial shall commence (unless otherwise ordered by the Senate) until final judgment shall be rendered, and so much longer as may, in its judgment, be needful. Before proceeding to the consideration of the articles of impeachment, the Presiding Officer shall administer the oath hereinafter provided to the members of the Senate then present and to the other members of the Senate as they shall appear, whose duty it shall be to take the same.

IV. When the President of the United States or the Vice President of the United States, upon whom the powers and duties of the office of President shall have devolved, shall be impeached, the Chief Justice of the Supreme Court of the United States shall preside; and in a case requiring the said Chief Justice to preside notice shall be given to him by the Presiding Officer of the Senate of the time and place fixed for the consideration of the articles of impeachment, as aforesaid, with a request to attend; and the said Chief Justice shall preside over the Senate during the consideration of said articles and upon the trial of the person impeached therein.

V. The Presiding Officer shall have power to make and issue, by himself or by the Secretary of the Senate, all orders, mandates, writs, and precepts authorized by these rules or by the Senate, and to make and enforce such other regulations and orders in the premises as the Senate may authorize or provide.

VI. The Senate shall have power to compel the attendance of witnesses, to enforce obedience to its orders, mandates, writs, precepts, and judgments, to preserve order, and to punish in a summary way contempts of, and disobedience to, its authority, orders, mandates, writs, precepts, or judgments, and to make all lawful orders, rules, and regulations which it may deem essential or conducive to the ends of justice. And the Sergeant at Arms, under the direction of the Senate, may employ such aid and assistance as may be necessary to enforce, execute and carry into effect the lawful orders, mandates, writs, and precepts of the Senate.

VII. The Presiding Officer of the Senate shall direct all necessary preparations in the Senate Chamber, and the Presiding Officer on the trial shall direct all the forms of proceedings while the Senate is sitting for the purpose of trying an impeachment, and all forms during the trial not otherwise specially provided for. And the Presiding Officer on the trial may rule all questions of evidence and incidental questions, which ruling shall stand as the judgment of the Senate, unless some member of the Senate shall ask that a formal vote be taken thereon, in which case it shall be submitted to the Senate for decision; or he may at his option, in the first instance, submit any such question to a vote of the members of the Senate. Upon all such questions the vote shall be without a division, unless the yeas and nays be demanded by one-fifth of the members present, when the same shall be taken.

VIII. Upon the presentation of articles of impeachment and the organization of the Senate as herein before provided, a writ of summons shall issue to the accused, reciting said articles, and notifying him to appear before the Senate upon a day and at a place to be fixed by the Senate and named in such writ, and file his answer to said articles of impeachment, and to stand to and abide the orders and judgments of the Senate thereon; which writ shall be served by such officer or person as shall be named in the precept thereof, such number of days prior to the day fixed for such appearance as shall be named in such precept, either by the delivery of an attested copy thereof to the person accused, or if that can not conveniently be done, by leaving such copy at the last known place of abode of such person, or at his usual place of business in some conspicuous place therein; or if such service shall be, in the judgment of the Senate, impracticable, notice to the accused to appear shall be given in such other manner, by publication or otherwise, as shall be deemed just; and if the writ aforesaid shall fail of service in the manner aforesaid, the proceedings shall not thereby abate, but further service may be made in such manner as the Senate shall direct. If the accused, after service, shall fail to appear, either in person or by attorney, on the day so fixed therefor as aforesaid, or, appearing, shall fail to file his answer to such articles of impeachment, the trial shall proceed, nevertheless, as upon a plea of not guilty. If a plea of guilty shall be entered, judgment may be entered thereon without further proceedings.

IX. At 12:30 o'clock afternoon of the day appointed for the return of the summons against the person impeached, the legislative and executive business of the Senate shall be suspended, and the Secretary of the Senate shall administer an oath to the returning officer.... Which oath shall be entered at large on the records.

X. The person impeached shall then be called to appear and answer the articles of impeachment against him. If he appear, or any

---

his Credit Mobilier stock before becoming Vice President.

A similar move to impeach Attorney General Harry M. Daugherty in 1922 on account of his action, or lack of action, in the Teapot Dome affair was dropped in 1923 when a Congressional investigation of the scandal got under way. As the Teapot Dome investigation and a separate Justice Department study progressed, Daugherty was forced by President Coolidge to tender his resignation, March 28, 1924.

A running fight between Rep. Wright Patman (D Texas) and Secretary of the Treasury Andrew W. Mellon over Federal economic policy in the depression came to a head in 1932. Patman on Jan. 6 demanded Mellon's impeachment on the ground of conflicting financial interests. To put an end to that move, President Hoover on Feb. 5 nominated Mellon to be ambassador to Great Britain and the Senate confirmed the nomination the same day. Mellon resigned his Treasury post a week later to take on his new duties.

Two depression-era attempts by Rep. Louis T. McFadden (R Pa.) to impeach President Hoover on general charges of usurping legislative powers and violating constitutional and statutory law were rejected by the House. The first attempt was tabled Dec. 13, 1932, by a 361-8 vote; the second attempt was tabled Jan. 17, 1933, by a 344-11 vote.

Associate Justice William O. Douglas of the Supreme Court has been subjected to repeated impeachment attempts. The day after Douglas granted a stay of execution to Soviet spies Julius and Ethel Rosenberg on June 16, 1953, Rep. W. M. Wheeler (D Ga.) introduced a resolution to impeach the justice. The resolution was unanimously tabled by the Judiciary Committee on July

...When Sitting for Impeachment Trials

person for him, the appearance shall be recorded, stating particularly if by himself, or by agent or attorney, naming the person appearing and the capacity in which he appears. If he do not appear, either personally or by agent or attorney, the same shall be recorded.

XI. That in the trial of any impeachment the Presiding Officer of the Senate, upon the order of the Senate, shall appoint a committee of twelve Senators to receive evidence and take testimony at such times and places as the committee may determine, and for such purpose the committee so appointed and the chairman thereof, to be elected by the committee, shall (unless otherwise ordered by the Senate) exercise all the powers and functions conferred upon the Senate and the Presiding Officer of the Senate, respectively, under the rules of procedure and practice in the Senate when sitting on impeachment trials.

Unless otherwise ordered by the Senate, the rules of procedure and practice in the Senate when sitting on impeachment trials shall govern the procedure and practice of the committee so appointed. The committee so appointed shall report to the Senate in writing a certified copy of the transcript of the proceedings and testimony had and given before such committee, and such report shall be received by the Senate and the evidence so received and the testimony so taken shall be considered to all intents and purposes, subject to the right of the Senate to determine competency, relevancy, and materiality, as having been received and taken before the Senate, but nothing herein shall prevent the Senate from sending for any witness and hearing his testimony in open Senate, or by order of the Senate having the entire trial in open Senate.

XII. At 12:30 o'clock afternoon of the day appointed for the trial of an impeachment, the legislative and executive business of the Senate shall be suspended, and the Secretary shall give notice to the House of Representatives that the Senate is ready to proceed upon the impeachment of——, in the Senate Chamber, which chamber is prepared with accommodations for the reception of the House of Representatives.

XIII. The hour of the day at which the Senate shall sit upon the trial of an impeachment shall be (unless otherwise ordered) 12 o'clock m.; and when the hour for such thing shall arrive, the Presiding Officer of the Senate shall so announce; and thereupon the Presiding Officer upon such trial shall cause proclamation to be made, and the business of the trial shall proceed. The adjournment of the Senate sitting in said trial shall not operate as an adjournment of the Senate; but on such adjournment the Senate shall resume the consideration of its legislative and executive business.

XIV. The Secretary of the Senate shall record the proceedings in cases of impeachment as in the case of legislative proceedings, and the same shall be reported in the same manner as the legislative proceedings of the Senate.

XV. Counsel for the parties shall be admitted to appear and be heard upon an impeachment.

XVI. All motions made by the parties or their counsel shall be addressed to the Presiding Officer, and if he, or any Senator, shall re-quire it, they shall be committed to writing, and read at the Secretary's table.

XVII. Witnesses shall be examined by one person on behalf of the party producing them, and then cross-examined by one person on the other side.

XVIII. If a Senator is called as a witness, he shall be sworn, and give his testimony standing in his place.

XIX. If a Senator wishes a question to be put to a witness, or to offer a motion or order (except a motion to adjourn), it shall be reduced to writing, and put by the Presiding Officer.

XX. At all times while the Senate is sitting upon the trial of an impeachment the doors of the Senate shall be kept open, unless the Senate shall direct the doors to be closed while deliberating upon its decisions.

XXI. All preliminary or interlocutory questions, and all motions, shall be argued for not exceeding one hour on each side, unless the Senate shall, by order, extend the time.

XXII. The case, on each side, shall be opened by one person. The final argument on the merits may be made by two persons on each side (unless otherwise ordered by the Senate upon application for that purpose), and the argument shall be opened and closed on the part of the House of Representatives.

XXIII. On the final question whether the impeachment is sustained, the yeas and nays shall be taken on each article of impeachment separately; and if the impeachment shall not, upon any of the articles presented, be sustained by the votes of two-thirds of the members present, a judgment of acquittal shall be entered; but if the person accused in such articles of impeachment shall be convicted upon any of said articles by the votes of two-thirds of the members present, the Senate shall proceed to pronounce judgment, and a certified copy of such judgment shall be deposited in the office of the Secretary of State.

XXIV. All the orders and decisions shall be made and had by yeas and nays, which shall be entered on the record, and without debate, subject, however, to the operation of Rule VII, except when the doors shall be closed for deliberation, and in that case no member shall speak more than once on one question, and for not more than ten minutes on an interlocutory question, and for not more than fifteen minutes on the final question, unless by consent of the Senate, to be had without debate; but a motion to adjourn may be decided without the yeas and nays, unless they be demanded by one-fifth of the members present. The fifteen minutes herein allowed shall be for the whole deliberation on the final question, and not on the final question on each article of impeachment.

XXV. Witnesses shall be sworn....Which oath shall be administered by the Secretary, or any other duly authorized person.

All process shall be served by the Sergeant at Arms of the Senate, unless otherwise ordered by the court.

XXVI. If the Senate shall at any time fail to sit for the consideration of articles of impeachment on the day or hour fixed therefor, the Senate may, by an order to be adopted without debate, fix a day and hour for resuming such consideration.

7, after a one-day hearing at which Wheeler had been the sole witness. In 1970, two resolutions for Douglas's impeachment were introduced in the midst of a bitter conflict between President Nixon and the Senate over Senate rejection of two Supreme Court nominations. One impeachment resolution was introduced April 15 by Rep. Andrew Jacobs Jr. (D Ind.); the other on the same day by a large bipartisan group of sponsors. Among the charges cited were possible financial conflicts similar to those that had led to Senate rejection of the Nixon nominees for the Court. A special House Judiciary Subcommittee on Dec. 3 voted 3-1 that no grounds existed for impeachment.

Impeachment Trials

Sen. William Blount. On July 3, 1797, President John Adams sent to the House and Senate a letter from Sen. William Blount (Tenn.) to James Carey, a U.S. interpreter to the Cherokee Nation of Indians. The letter told of Blount's plans to launch an attack by Indians and frontiersmen, aided by a British fleet, against Louisiana and Spanish Florida to achieve their transfer to British control. Adams' action initiated the first proceedings to result in impeachment by the House and consideration by the Senate.

In the Senate, Blount's letter was referred to a select committee, which recommended his expulsion for "a high misdemeanor, entirely inconsistent with his public trust and duty as a Senator." The Senate expelled Blount on July 8 by a 25-1 vote.

In the House, meanwhile, a special committee had recommended that Blount be impeached. The House on July 7 adopted a committee resolution impeaching Blount, and on the same day it appointed a committee to prepare articles of impeachment. On Jan. 29, 1798, the House adopted five articles accusing Blount of attempting to influence the Indians for the benefit of the British.

Senate proceedings did not begin until Dec. 17, 1798. Blount challenged the proceedings, contending that they violated his right to a trial by jury, that he was not a civil officer within the meaning of the Constitution, that he was not charged with a crime committed while a civil officer, and that courts of common law were competent to try him on the charges. On Jan. 11, 1799, the Senate by a 14-11 vote dismissed the charges for lack of jurisdiction. Citing the Senate vote, Vice President Thomas Jefferson ruled Jan. 14, that the Senate was without jurisdiction in the case, thus ending the proceedings.

Judge John Pickering. In a partisan move to oust a Federalist judge, President Jefferson on Feb. 4, 1803, sent a complaint to the House citing John Pickering, U.S. judge for the district of New Hampshire. The complaint was referred to a special committee, and on March 2 the House adopted a committee resolution impeaching the judge. A committee was appointed Oct. 20 to prepare articles of impeachment, and the House on Dec. 30 by voice vote agreed to four articles charging Pickering with irregular judicial procedures, loose morals and drunkenness. At the time of the trial by the Senate, the judge, born about 1738, was known to be insane. He did not attend the trial, which began March 8, 1804, and ended March 12, with votes of 19-7 for conviction on each of the four articles. The Senate then voted, 20-6, to remove Pickering from office, but it declined to consider disqualifying him from further office.

Justice Samuel Chase. In an equally partisan attack on another Federalist judge, the House on Jan. 7, 1804, by an 81-40 vote adopted a resolution by John Randolph (States Rights Democrat Va.) for an investigation of Samuel Chase, associate justice of the Supreme Court, and of Richard Peters, a U.S. district court judge in Pennsylvania. Ostensibly, the investigation was to study their conduct during a recent treason trial. The House dropped further action against Peters by voice vote on March 12. On the same day, by a 73-32 vote, it adopted a committee resolution to impeach Chase. A committee was appointed to draw up articles, and the House in a series of votes on Dec. 4, 1804, agreed to the articles, charging Chase with harsh and partisan conduct on the bench and with unfairness to litigants.

The trial began Feb. 9, 1805. House managers directing proceedings in the Senate included, in addition to Randolph, Caesar A. Rodney (D Del.), Joseph H. Nicholson (D Md.), Peter Early (Ga.), John Boyle (D Ky.), George W. Campbell (D Tenn.), and Christopher Clark (Jeffersonian Democrat Va.). Chase appeared in person. In addition, he was represented by four lawyers, Robert G. Harper, Luther Martin, Philip B. Key and Joseph Hopkinson. The Senate voting on March 1 failed to produce the two-thirds majority required for conviction on any of the eight articles of impeachment; "not guilty" votes outnumbered the "guilty" votes on five of the articles.

Judge James H. Peck. On Dec. 8, 1826, a memorial from a Missouri man was presented to the House and referred to the Judiciary Committee citing James H. Peck, a U.S. judge for the district of Missouri. The memorial lay dormant until Jan. 7, 1830, when the House adopted a resolution authorizing an investigation of Peck's conduct. On April 24, the House by a 123-49 vote adopted a committee resolution impeaching Peck, and later the same day it appointed a committee to prepare articles of impeachment. A single article was adopted May 1 by voice vote, charging Peck with setting an unreasonable and oppressive penalty for contempt of court. The trial stretched from Dec. 20, 1830, to Jan. 31, 1831, when 21 Senators voted for conviction and 22 for acquittal.

Judge West H. Humphreys. During the Civil War, West H. Humphreys, a U.S. judge for the east, middle and west districts of Tennessee, accepted an appointment as a Confederate judge, without resigning from his Union judicial assignment. Aware of the situation, the House on Jan. 8, 1862, by voice vote adopted a resolution by Horace Maynard (American Tenn.) to authorize a Judiciary Committee investigation of Humphreys. On May 6 the House, also by voice vote, adopted a committee resolution impeaching Humphreys. Articles of impeachment, drafted by a committee appointed May 14, were adopted by voice vote on May 19. The articles charged Humphreys with advocating secession and accepting office as a Confederate judge. In a one-day trial on June 26, the Senate convicted Humphreys on all except one charge, removed him from office by a 38-0 vote and disqualified him from further office on a 36-0 vote.

Johnson's Impeachment and Trial

First Attempt—Radical Republicans in Congress and President Andrew Johnson carried on a running battle over postwar policy toward the Confederate states. Johnson favored a lenient attitude; the Radicals favored repressive tactics. Finally on Jan. 7, 1867, two Radicals, Reps. James M. Ashley (R Ohio) and Benjamin F. Loan (Radical Mo.) introduced a pair of resolutions calling for Judiciary Committee investigations and impeachment of the President. The Committee gathered a mass of general testimony highly critical of Johnson and recommended impeachment. However, the House by a 57-108 vote Dec. 7, rejected a Committee resolution impeaching the President. The resolution was defeated primarily because no specific crime was alleged to have been committed.

Second Attempt—Radical opposition to Johnson continued to run high, and on Jan. 22, 1868, the House by a 99-31 vote adopted a resolution by Rufus P. Spalding (R Ohio) authorizing the Committee on Reconstruction to "inquire what combinations have been made or attempted to be made to obstruct the due execution of the laws...." To help the Committee, the House on Feb. 10 referred to it the impeachment evidence gathered in 1867. Then on Feb. 21, 1868, Johnson formally dismissed Secretary of War Edwin M. Stanton, a leading Radical sympathizer. The dismissal violated the Tenure of Office Act of March 2, 1867, which required Senate concurrence in the removal, as well as the appointment, of certain officers, and which made violation of the Act a "high misdemeanor."

The day after Johnson moved against Stanton, the Committee on Reconstruction recommended impeachment of the President. And on Feb. 24 the House by a

128-47 vote adopted a Committee resolution impeaching Johnson, and by a 124-42 vote appointed a committee to draw up articles of impeachment. In a series of votes March 2 and 3, the House adopted the articles, charging the President with violation of the Tenure of Office Act and with attacking Congress in a series of political speeches. *(See Appendix for complete text of the articles.)*

The impeachment trial opened March 30, 1868. The managers for the House were John A. Bingham (R Ohio), George S. Boutwell (R Mass.), James F. Wilson (R Iowa), Benjamin F. Butler (R Mass.), Thomas Williams (R Pa.), John A. Logan (R Ill.) and Thaddeus Stevens (R Pa.). The President did not appear at the trial. He was represented by a team of lawyers headed by Henry Stanbery, who had resigned as Attorney General to lead the defense. Associated with Stanbery were Benjamin R. Curtis, Jeremiah S. Black, William M. Evarts, Thomas A. R. Nelson and William S. Groesbeck.

After weeks of argument and testimony, the Senate on May 16 took a test vote on Article XI, a general, catch-all charge, thought by the House managers most likely to produce a vote for conviction. The drama of the vote has become legendary. With 36 "guiltys" needed for conviction, the final count was guilty, 35, not guilty, 19. Stunned by the setback, Senate opponents of the President postponed further voting until May 26. Votes were taken then on Article II and Article III. By identical 35-19 votes Johnson was acquitted also on these articles. To head off further defeats for Johnson opponents, Sen. George H. Williams (Union Republican Ore.) moved to adjourn *sine die,* and the motion was adopted 34-16, abruptly ending the trial.

Other Impeachments and Trials

War Secretary William W. Belknap. Faced with widespread corruption and incompetence among high officers of the Grant Administration, the House on Jan. 14, 1876, adopted by voice vote a resolution authorizing various committees to conduct general investigations of Government departments. On March 2 the House by voice vote adopted a resolution from the Committee on Expenditures in the War Department impeaching Secretary of War William W. Belknap. Only hours earlier, Belknap had resigned, and President Grant had accepted the resignation. Despite Belknap's resignation, work by the Judiciary Committee on articles of impeachment was continued, and the House agreed to the articles on April 3. They charged Belknap with graft in connection with the appointment and retention of an Indian post trader at Fort Sill in Oklahoma.

As pre-trial maneuvering proceeded, the Senate on May 29 declared by a vote of 37-29 that it had jurisdiction over Belknap regardless of his resignation. The trial, which ran from July 6 to Aug. 1, 1876, ended in acquittal. The majority of "guilty" votes on each article (35, 36 or 37 as against a constant 25 "not guilty" votes) fell short of the two-thirds necessary for conviction. A number of Senators, explaining their positions, said they had voted against conviction on the ground that the Senate lacked jurisdiction.

Judge Charles Swayne. Rep. William B. Lamar (D Fla.) on Dec. 10, 1903, introduced a resolution, adopted by voice vote, for a Judiciary Committee investigation of Charles Swayne, U.S. judge for the northern

Johnson Impeachment Votes

The Senate voted on only three of the 11 articles of impeachment against President Andrew Johnson. The President was acquitted on each article by identical votes of 35-19, with 36 "guiltys" necessary for conviction. The roll call on the three votes follows:

Guilty: Anthony (R R.I.), Cameron (R Pa.), Cattel (R N.J.), Chandler (R Mich.), Cole (R Calif.), Conkling (Union Republican N.Y.), Conness (Union Republican Calif.), Corbett (Union Republican Ore.), Cragin (American N.H.), Drake (R Mo.), Edmunds (R Vt.), Ferry (R Conn.), Frelinghuysen (R N.J.), Harlan (R Iowa), Howard (R Mich.), Howe (Union Republican Wis.), Morgan (Union Republican N.Y.), Morrill (R Maine), Morrill (Union Republican Vt.), Morton (Union Republican Ind.), Nye (R Nev.), Patterson (R N.H.), Pomeroy (R Kan.), Ramsey (R Minn.), Sherman (R Ohio), Sprague (R R.I.), Stewart (R Nev.), Sumner (R Mass.), Thayer (R Neb.), Tipton (R Neb.), Wade (R Ohio), Willey (R W. Va.), Williams (Union Republican Ore.), Wilson (R Mass.), Yates (Union Republican Ill.).

Not guilty: Bayard (D Del.), Buckalew (D Pa.), Davis (D Ky.), Dixon (R Conn.), Doolittle (R Wis.), Fessenden (R Maine), Fowler (Union Republican Tenn), Grimes (R Iowa), Henderson (D Mo.), Hendricks (D Ind.), Johnson (D Md.), McCreery (D Ky.), Norton (Union Conservative Minn.), Patterson (D Tenn.), Ross (R Kan.), Saulsbury (D Del.), Trumbull (R Ill.), Van Winkle (Unionist W. Va.), Vickers (D Md.).

district of Florida. Months later, the Committee recommended impeachment, and the House on Dec. 13, 1904, adopted by voice vote a Committee resolution impeaching Swayne and authorized a special committee to prepare articles of impeachment. The articles were adopted in a series of votes on Jan. 18, 1905. They charged Swayne with living outside of his district, improperly fining a lawyer for contempt, and using a private railroad car in the hands of a receiver appointed by the judge. Opening arguments in the trial began Feb. 10. The trial ended Feb. 27, when the Senate voted acquittal on all articles; none was given even a simple majority for conviction.

Judge Robert W. Archbald. On May 4, 1912, the House adopted a Judiciary Committee resolution authorizing an investigation of Robert W. Archbald, associate judge of the U.S. Commerce Court. A Committee resolution impeaching Archbald and setting forth articles of impeachment was adopted by the House July 11 by a 223-1 vote. The judge was charged with using improper influence and accepting favors from litigants. The trial, which began Dec. 3, ended Jan. 13, 1913, with Archbald convicted on five of the 13 articles. The Senate on the same day removed him from office by voice vote and, by a 39-35 vote, disqualified him from further office.

Judge George W. English. A resolution asking for an investigation of George W. English, U.S. judge for the eastern district of Illinois, was introduced Jan.

13, 1925, by Rep. Harry B. Hawes (D Mo.). The House on April 1, 1926, adopted by a 306-62 vote a Judiciary Committee resolution to impeach English. The resolution also set forth the articles of impeachment, charging English with partiality, tyranny and oppression. The trial was set to begin Nov. 10, but on Nov. 4 English resigned. Instead of proceeding with the trial, as was done after Belknap's resignation, the Senate on Dec. 13 by a 70-9 vote dismissed the charges at the request of the House managers.

Judge Harold Louderback. A resolution by Rep. Fiorello H. LaGuardia (Republican Progressive N.Y.) for an investigation of Harold Louderback, U.S. judge for the northern district of California, was adopted by a voice vote of the House on June 9, 1932. The Judiciary Committee's study produced mixed results. The majority recommended censuring, but not impeaching Louderback. However, the House on Feb. 24, 1933, by a 183-142 vote adopted a minority resolution by LaGuardia impeaching the judge and specifying the articles. They accused Louderback of favoritism and conspiracy in the appointment of bankruptcy receivers. A trial that lasted from May 15 to May 24 ended in acquittal. The "not guilty" votes outnumbered the "guilty" votes on all except one of the five articles.

Judge Halsted L. Ritter. Rep. J. Mark Wilcox (D Fla.) on May 29, 1933, introduced a resolution for an investigation of Halsted L. Ritter, U.S. judge for the southern district of Florida. The resolution was adopted by a voice vote on June 1. A long delay followed. Then on March 2, 1936, the House by a 181-146 vote adopted a Judiciary Committee impeachment resolution. The articles of impeachment, contained in the resolution,

charged Ritter with a variety of judicial improprieties. The trial lasted from April 6 to April 17. Although there were more "guilty" than "not guilty" votes on all except one of the first six articles, the majorities fell short of the two-thirds required for conviction. However, on the seventh article, with 56 votes necessary for conviction, the vote was 56 guilty and 28 not guilty. Thus, Ritter was convicted. He was ordered removed from office, without a vote. An order to disqualify him from further office was defeated, 0-76.

Bibliography

Books

Dewitt, David M., *Impeachment and Trial of Andrew Johnson.* Russell & Russell, 1967.

Haynes, George H., *The Senate of the United States.* Houghton Mifflin, 1938.

Riddick, Floyd M., *The United States Congress: Organization and Procedure.* National Capitol Publishers Inc., 1949.

Simpson, Alexander Jr., *A Treatise of Federal Impeachments,* 1916.

Government Publications

Cannon, Clarence, *Cannon's Precedents of the House of Representatives.* Government Printing Office, 1935.

Hinds, Asher C., *Hinds' Precedents of the House of Representatives.* Government Printing Office, 1907.

Senate Judiciary Committee, 80th Congress, First Session, *Removal Power of Congress With Respect to the Supreme Court.* Committee Print, 1947.

Power to Regulate Commerce

"The Congress shall have Power...To regulate Commerce with foreign Nations, and among the several States, and with the Indian Tribes." (Article I, Section 8, Clause 3)

WITH this simple grant of authority the Constitution attempted to remedy one of the basic weaknesses of the Federal Government under the Articles of Confederation. The lack of a national power over commerce had been in large part responsible for the drafting of a new Constitution, and the need for such a power was so generally recognized that the provision occasioned comparatively little discussion in the Constitutional Convention.

The constitutional formula is a broad and general one: the positive grant of power to Congress is not coupled with a statement of the powers, if any, reserved to the states, and no definition of terms is offered. Four express limitations on the commerce power are contained in Article I, Section 9, but only one—forbidding Congress to lay a tax or duty on articles exported from any state—has had much practical significance. Thus the extent of Federal power over commerce has been established largely by experience and judicial determination.

The basic Supreme Court decision involving the scope of the commerce clause was *Gibbons v. Ogden* in 1824. In a landmark opinion, Chief Justice John Marshall opted for a broad construction of the term "commerce" and emphatically asserted the supremacy of the Federal power over it. But he rejected the argument—advanced by Daniel Webster, counsel for Gibbons—that the Congressional power over commerce was "complete and entire," holding instead that "the completely internal commerce of a State...may be considered as reserved for the State itself." From this acceptance of a divided authority over commerce has stemmed the concept of interstate as opposed to intrastate commerce, with movement across state lines as the basic test of the distinction.

Although Congress exercised its authority over foreign commerce from its earliest days, for nearly a century it failed to exploit its powers over commerce among the states. Thus most early Supreme Court decisions in the field dealt with state regulations that were challenged as infringements on the constitutional powers of Congress. The limits of state regulatory authority are still a problem for the courts today.

With enactment of the Interstate Commerce Act in 1887, Congress moved decisively into the domestic regulatory field, and in the 20th century the scope of the commerce clause has expanded steadily. For years the Supreme Court held to the view that manufacturing and production were not a part of commerce and that the commerce power extended only to activities that affected commerce directly. Eventually, however, the Court came round to the view that the commerce power embraced activities that had an "effect upon commerce," however indirectly. Application of this doctrine led to a substantial expansion of Congressional authority, and in 1946 the Court concluded that "the Federal commerce power is as broad as the economic needs of the nation."

Early History of Commerce Clause

The necessity for national control over interstate and foreign commerce was the immediate occasion for the calling of the Constitutional Convention in 1787. "Most of our political evils," Madison had written to Jefferson the previous year, "may be traced to our commercial ones." Under the Articles of Confederation, adopted during the Revolutionary War, Congress had power to regulate trade only with the Indians, the control of interstate and foreign commerce having been left to the states. This defect in the Articles was universally recognized. Even those who, like Samuel Adams and Patrick Henry, feared that a Federal Government would be tyrannical, favored more comprehensive regulation of commerce by Congress.

The conditions under which commerce was carried on became increasingly chaotic after the Revolutionary War. Each state attempted to build up its own prosperity at the expense of its neighbors. Justice William Johnson, in a concurring opinion in *Gibbons v. Ogden*, thus described the situation that had developed:

"For a century the states had submitted, with murmurs, to the commercial restrictions imposed by the parent state; and now, finding themselves in the unlimited possession of those powers over their own commerce, which they had so long been deprived of and so earnestly coveted, that selfish principle which, well controlled, is so salutary, and which, unrestricted, is so unjust and tyrannical, guided by inexperience and jealousy, began to show itself in iniquitous laws and impolitic measures, from which grew up a conflict of commercial regulations, destructive to the harmony of the states, and fatal to their commercial interests abroad."

State legislatures imposed tariffs upon goods coming in from other states as well as from foreign countries. Thus, New York levied duties on firewood from Connecticut and cabbages from New Jersey. "The commerce which Massachusetts found it to her interest to encourage," says J. B. McMaster, "Virginia found it to hers to restrict. New York would not protect the trade in indigo

273

and pitch. South Carolina cared nothing for the success of the fur interests."

Seaport states financed their governments through imposts on European goods passing through their harbors but destined for consumption in neighboring states. Madison described the plight of those states not having seaports: "New Jersey placed between Philadelphia and New York was likened to a cask tapped at both ends; and North Carolina, between Virginia and South Carolina, to a patient bleeding at both arms."

Different currencies in each of the 13 states likewise hampered commercial intercourse. And if a merchant were able to carry on an interstate business in spite of tariff and currency difficulties, he often had trouble in collecting his bills. Local courts and juries were less zealous in protecting the rights of distant creditors than those of their neighbors and friends.

The chaotic condition of interstate trade prompted the General Assembly of Virginia, in 1786, to adopt a resolution proposing a joint meeting of commissioners appointed by each of the states "to take into consideration the trade of the United States; to examine the relative situations and trade of the said states; (and) to consider how far a uniform system in their commercial regulations may be necessary to their common interest and their permanent harmony." The action of the Virginia Assembly led to a meeting at Annapolis later in the year of commissioners from five states: Delaware, New Jersey, New York, Pennsylvania and Virginia.

The members of the Annapolis convention, however, "did not conceive it advisable to proceed on the business of their mission, under the circumstance of so partial and defective a representation." They recommended a general meeting of all the states at Philadelphia in 1787 "for the same, and such other purposes, as the situation may be found to require." It was the judgment of the convention that "the power of regulating trade is of such comprehensive extent and will enter so far into the general system of the Federal Government, that to give it efficacy and to obviate questions and doubts concerning its precise nature and limits, may require a correspondent adjustment of other parts of the Federal system."

Adoption of the Commerce Clause

The desirability of uniform regulation of interstate and foreign commerce was so generally recognized that the proposal to give Congress blanket authority in this field occasioned comparatively little discussion at the Philadelphia Convention. Some controversy did arise over an attempt by the South to limit the power of a Congressional majority in regulating commerce. The southern states feared that the North might seek to dominate their commerce. Charles Pinckney of South Carolina proposed, therefore, that "all laws regulating commerce shall require the assent of two-thirds of the Members present in each house," but this proposal was defeated by a vote of seven states to four, Maryland, Virginia, North Carolina and Georgia voting in the affirmative.

"Had Pinckney's proposal been adopted," says Charles Warren, "the course of American history would have been vitally changed. Enactment of protective tariffs might have been practically impossible. The whole political relations between the South and North growing

out of commercial legislation would have been changed. The Nullification movement in the 1830s, which arose out of opposition to a northern tariff, might not have occurred."

In return for the South's acceptance of the unlimited power of the majority in regulation of commerce, the northern states agreed to a ban on export taxes and to a provision that importation of slaves would not be prohibited before the year 1808. This was one of the important compromises reached at Philadelphia.

Many persons consider it remarkable that so important a part of the Constitution as the commerce clause should be so briefly expressed and should leave so much to future determination. "At the time, at least," Warren remarks, "there seems to have been no doubt as to its meaning. The violent differences of opinion which arose during the first half of the 19th century as to what the term 'commerce' included, and as to whether the power to 'regulate' was exclusive in Congress or exercisable by the states until Congress should act, were apparently not in the least foreseen by the members of the Convention." It is generally agreed that nothing more was immediately intended than that Congress should be empowered to prevent commercial wars among the states. Yet it is not to be doubted that the framers were aware of the scope of the power granted to Congress. Monroe pointed out that the commerce clause involved "a radical change in the whole system of our government."

Other Federal Powers Over Commerce

In addition to general regulatory power over interstate commerce, the Convention reposed in the Federal Government the admiralty jurisdiction and the powers to coin money, establish uniform laws of bankruptcy, establish post offices and post roads, regulate weights and measures and grant patents and copyrights. That the taxing power was recognized as an instrument of commercial regulation is indicated by the clause of the Constitution which forbids the Federal Government to give preference to the ports of one state over those of another "by any regulation of commerce or revenue." The importance of these Federal powers was enhanced by provisions expressly forbidding the states to coin money, enact laws impairing the obligation of contracts, lay duties of tonnage or tax exports or imports.

Other specific grants of commercial power were discussed in the Convention. Benjamin Franklin proposed that Congress be given power "to provide for cutting canals," and James Wilson expressed the belief that such power was necessary in order to prevent a single state from obstructing the general welfare. But Franklin's motion was lost because of the sentiment of the Convention that the expense thereby incurred would be a general burden, while the benefit would be local. It was proposed also to give Congress power to grant charters of incorporation in cases where the public good might require them, and where the authority of a single state might be incompetent; to regulate stages on the post roads; to establish institutions for the promotion of agriculture, commerce, trade and manufactures; to make internal improvements, and to charter a national bank. All motions to make these grants in express terms were lost.

Supreme Court Interpretation

The first case involving the scope of the commerce power to reach the Supreme Court was *Gibbons v. Ogden* in 1824. In this case, a New York law granting an exclusive privilege of navigation by steamboat on all waters within the state was held void as repugnant to the commerce clause, so far as the law prohibited vessels licensed by the United States from navigating the same waters. The Court's decision, written by Chief Justice John Marshall, assumed great importance both because of the broad construction of the term "commerce" and because of the Court's emphatic assertion of the supremacy of the Federal power in this field.

"The subject to be regulated is commerce," Marshall said. "To ascertain the extent of the power, it becomes necessary to settle the meaning of the word.

"The counsel for the appellee would limit it to traffic, to buying and selling, or the interchange of commodities, and do not admit that it comprehends navigation. This would restrict a general term, applicable to many objects, to one of its significations. Commerce, undoubtedly, is traffic, but it is something more—it is intercourse. It describes the commercial intercourse between nations, and parts of nations, in all its branches.... All America understands...the word 'commerce' to comprehend navigation...."

The Federal power over commerce, Marshall said, comprehended navigation within the limits of every state, so far as navigation might be in any manner connected with foreign nations, or among the states, and therefore it passed beyond the jurisdiction of New York and included the public waters of the state which were connected with such foreign or interstate commerce.

"The subject to which the power is next applied," Marshall continued, "is to commerce 'among the several states.' The word 'among' means intermingled with.... Commerce among the states cannot stop at the external boundary lines of each state, but may be introduced into the interior. It is not intended to say that these words comprehend that commerce which is completely internal, which is carried on between man and man in a state, or between different parts of the same state, and which does not extend to or affect other states. Such a power would be inconvenient and is certainly unnecessary. Comprehensive as the word 'among' is, it may very properly be restricted to that commerce which concerns more states than one.... The completely internal commerce of a state, then, may be considered as reserved for the state itself."

With regard to the supremacy of the Federal power, the Chief Justice said: "This power, like all others vested in Congress, is complete in itself, may be exercised to its utmost extent and acknowledges no limitations other than are prescribed in the Constitution.... If, as has always been understood, the sovereignty of Congress, though limited to specified objects, is plenary as to those objects, the power over commerce with foreign nations and among the several states is vested in Congress as absolutely as it would be in a single government, having in its constitution the same restrictions on the exercise of the power as are found in the Constitution of the United States."

Justice Johnson's concurring opinion expressed similar conclusions in even more vigorous language. Emphasizing the fact that the necessity for regulation of commerce had been the moving purpose behind the Constitution, Johnson asserted that the power of Congress in this matter "must be exclusive; it can reside but in one potentate; and hence, the grant of this power carries with it the whole subject, leaving nothing for the states to act upon."

With rare foresight, Johnson continued: "Commerce, in its simplest signification, means an exchange of goods; but in the advancement of society, labor, transportation, intelligence, care, and various mediums of exchange, become commodities, and enter into commerce; the subject, the vehicle, the agent, and their various operations, become the objects of commercial regulation. Shipbuilding, the carrying trade, and propagation of seamen, are such vital agents of commercial prosperity, that the nation which could not legislate over these subjects, would not possess power to regulate commerce. That such was the understanding of the framers of the Constitution, is conspicuous from provisions contained in that instrument."

Reactions to Court's Opinion

It is significant that the decision in *Gibbons v. Ogden* was immensely popular. "At the time of its delivery," according to Albert J. Beveridge, "nobody complained of Marshall's opinion except the agents of the steamboat monopoly, the theorists of localism and the slave autocracy. All these influences beheld, in Marshall's statesmanship, their inevitable extinction." Jefferson was "horrified." In 1825, at the age of 82, he wrote that he viewed "with the deepest affliction, the rapid strides with which the Federal branch of our government is advancing towards the usurpation of all the rights reserved to the states.

"Take together the decision of the Federal court, the doctrines of the President, and the misconstructions of the Constitutional Compact acted on by the Legislature of the Federal branch, and it is too evident that the three ruling branches of that department are in combination to strip their colleagues, the state authorities, of the powers reserved by them, and to exercise themselves all functions, foreign and domestic. Under the power to regulate commerce, they assume indefinitely that also over agriculture and manufactures, and call it regulation to take the earnings of one of these branches of industry...and put them in the pocket of the other."

Regulation of Interstate Commerce

In its first century, Congress made little use of its power to regulate interstate commerce. Before the Civil War, it did so in only two classes of subjects—construction of interstate bridges and extension of the admiralty jurisdiction. But with the passage of the Interstate Commerce Act of 1887, Congress moved decisively into the field of domestic regulation.

Both before and after the Civil War, the states attempted in various ways to curb increasing abuses by the railroads. These efforts were generally ineffective. Then, in 1886, the Supreme Court ruled (*Wabash, St. Louis & Pacific Ry. Co. v. Illinois*) that any enterprise engaged in interstate commerce could not be regulated by the states through which it passed. Such regulation, the Court held, was barred by the commerce clause of the Constitution.

Federal Regulatory Agencies: Arms of Congress...

Since the establishment of the Interstate Commerce Commission in 1887, Federal regulatory agencies have come to play a major role in the American economy.

Although the *United States Government Organization Manual* lists almost 50 independent Federal agencies, many of which perform regulatory functions, discussion of Federal regulation usuaully centers on activities of the so-called "Big Seven": in addition to the ICC, these are the Federal Trade Commission, organized in 1915; the Federal Power Commission, established in 1920; and four agencies established during the Administration of President Franklin D. Roosevelt—the Federal Communications Commission (1934), the Securities and Exchange Commission (1934), the National Labor Relations Board (1935) and the Civil Aeronautics Board (1938).

Members of all seven agencies are appointed by the President for fixed terms. Membership ranges from 5 to 11, and no political party may have more than a one-member majority on any of the Big Seven.

The agencies derive their powers from acts of Congress that delegate to them certain regulatory functions that have become too complex for Congress to handle by means of ordinary legislation. Thus they are sometimes described as "arms" of Congress. They also have quasi-judicial functions. When the Civil Aeronautics Board promulgates a rule asserting its primary jurisdiction over airspace for both civil and military purposes, it is exercising its quasi-legislative (or rule-making) power. When it decides which of several commercial airlines shall be awarded a specific airline route, it is exercising quasi-judicial (or adjudicatory) power. Similarly, the FCC is making rules when it sets up criteria for evaluating competing claims for a television license, adjudicating when it awards a license.

"Big Seven" Powers

The powers and influence of the Big Seven regulatory agencies, reaching into virtually every corner of the American economy, give some indication of the scope of the Federal commerce power. The principal functions of these agencies are as follows:

Interstate Commerce Commission. Jurisdiction covers railroads and related carriers, common and contract motor carriers, certain domestic water carriers, pipelines and freight forwarders. ICC fixes rates; sets standards for reasonable service; issues permits or certificates required to engage in interstate transportation; controls consolidations and mergers of carriers, issuance of securities and the accounting systems and records kept by carriers; regulates safety devices and standards.

Federal Trade Commission. FTC may act to prevent practices leading to monopoly or restraint of trade, such as unfair methods of competition (e.g.,

false and misleading advertising), stock acquisitions of competing enterprises and price discrimination. It has power also to investigate and to issue cease-and-desist orders, and it shares anti-monopoly responsibility with the Justice Department.

Federal Power Commission. FPC grants licenses to private power projects on navigable waters subject to Federal jurisdiction; fixes rates on interstate sale of electric energy; prescribes uniform accounting methods; and regulates (1) mergers and security issues of electric utilities, (2) most Federal power projects and (3) interstate sales of natural gas.

Federal Communications Commission. FCC regulates telephone and telegraph common carriers, including their interstate rates; allocates radio frequencies; licenses radio and television stations; licenses radio operators; monitors broadcasts; administers international communications treaties.

Securities and Exchange Commission. SEC regulates security issues; supervises the stock exchanges; regulates holding companies and investment companies—all for the purpose of protecting the investing public.

National Labor Relations Board. NLRB adjudicates charges of unfair labor practices on the part of employers or unions; enforces requirements for collective bargaining; supervises election of bargaining representatives; decides jurisdictional disputes.

Civil Aeronautics Board. CAB licenses domestic air carriers; issues permits to foreign air carriers landing in the United States; fixes passenger, freight and mail rates; controls mergers, pooling and other arrangements between carriers.

Delegation of Power

All of the commissions exercise, to greater or lesser degree, some executive, legislative and judicial power. By the same token, control over the commissions is shared by the President, Congress and the courts, in a system of checks and balances. The President's power to control the regulatory agencies rests largely in his appointive power, while that of Congress rests in its responsibility for appropriations. The courts may review commission orders.

Members of the Legislative Branch nevertheless have insisted periodically that the power of Congress has been delegated, not abdicated, and that in the last analysis the commissions are "creatures of Congress." The classic view of the commissions held by Federal legislators was expressed in 1931 by the late Speaker of the House, Sam Rayburn (D Texas):

"Far from undermining the constitutional authority of Congress, delegation of authority to administrative agencies is one of the surest safeguards to effective legislative action. It is a procedure which conserves the vital power of Congress for vital matters.... (A commission) does not perform any act that Congress has not the authority to perform itself.... Congress...delegated

...Or Headless Fourth Branch of Government?

responsibility to a commission of...trained experts to work out the details for them."

This view has not gone unchallenged. C. Herman Pritchett, a member of the Hoover Commission, wrote in the *American Political Science Review* in October 1949 that "The spurious nature of this 'arm of Congress' claim has long been evident." Pritchett added: "The fact is that Congress has not a single control over any of the regulatory commissions that it does not possess over executive agencies generally.... (The Hoover Commission) wanted to have non-political regulation and at the same time provide for Presidential control."

It has been asserted that every President of the United States from Woodrow Wilson on has tried in one way or another to influence commission activity and has succeeded in doing so. For example, "President Hoover made public statements indicating how he thought the Interstate Commerce Commission ought to exercise certain of its powers, and the commission somewhat reluctantly yielded," wrote Robert E. Cushman. President Roosevelt obtained the resignation of Hoover's chairman of the Federal Power Commission and added two appointees of his own. Four days after his inauguration, President Nixon recalled from the Civil Aeronautics Board "for further review and decision" the awards of new Pacific routes which President Johnson had made to five airlines on Dec. 18, 1968. (Although CAB makes final decisions in domestic route cases, the President has statutory authority to approve or reject CAB recommendations on foreign routes.)

Reorganization Proposals

Regulatory commissions have found it difficult to please simultaneously the Executive Branch, the Legislative Branch and the regulated industry. Commission actions often are criticized as restrictive or permissive, and commission procedures frequently are attacked.

Numerous plans for improving the performance of Federal regulatory agencies have been put forward since World War II, yet few have been adopted. Most reform proposals have foundered because of opposition in Congress. The Legislative Branch tends to be suspicious of any reorganization that might weaken its influence on regulatory agencies. Moreover, the regulated industries evidently prefer a sometimes uncomfortable status quo to a new regulatory environment that might be less to their liking.

The most ambitious attempt to reshape the regulatory agencies took place shortly after John F. Kennedy became President in 1961. Kennedy had asked James M. Landis, a former chairman of the Securities and Exchange Commission, to study the agencies and submit proposals for improving them. Landis' report, which noted the familiar problems of delay, ethical conduct and quality of personnel, made 16 broad recommendations. Among other things, he called for:

● Extensive reorganization of most of the agencies.

● Establishment of special offices in the White House to develop national transportation policy, telecommunications policy and energy resources policy.

● Establishment by Executive order of a Federal employee code of ethics and limitation of off-the-record presentation in regulatory agency cases.

● Creation of a special Office for the Oversight of Regulatory Agencies.

In a special message to Congress on regulatory agencies, April 13, 1961, Kennedy proposed to give agency chairmen "broad managerial powers" to correct the existing, diffused authority of the commissions; provide that all agency chairmen serve in that capacity at the President's pleasure; and authorize delegation of a large proportion of agency responsibilities to inter-agency boards and hearing examiners to eliminate needless work on "unimportant details" at the top level. Congress responded by reviving the Reorganization Act of 1949, which had expired two years earlier, so that the President could submit reorganization plans for the agencies.

Seven such plans were submitted, all of which had the basic aim of speeding up and streamlining agency procedures. The first four plans—those for SEC, FCC, CAB and FTC—contained three basically identical steps. They authorized the agency to delegate some of its functions to certain employees; they empowered the chairman to assign the delegated functions; and they made review of certain lower-level decisions discretionary.

The plan for the National Labor Relations Board was the same as the first four but omitted the chairman's power of assignment; the plan for the Federal Home Loan Bank Board only restored some hiring and firing powers formerly held by the chairman; and in the seventh plan, the Federal Maritime Board was abolished and its functions assigned to other agencies.

Jealous as ever of its authority over the agencies, Congress charged that the Administration planned to create a White House "czar" and establish a "direct chain of political command" over the regulatory agencies. When the smoke of battle cleared, the final score stood: three plans killed, with one replaced by a more limited version; four plans approved. Congress vetoed the reorganization plans for FCC, SEC and NLRB. It upheld those for CAB, FTC, FMB and HLBB.

A scaled-down reorganization bill for FCC allowed the commission to delegate minor functions to employees, but it did not provide the authority requested by the Administration to enable the chairman to make specific work assignments to employees and commissioners. The bill also expedited action by putting oral arguments on exceptions to agency decisions on a discretionary instead of required basis and by giving the commission authority to either accept or deny appeals for over-all review without giving a reason.

The scope of the decision not only nullified state regulation of railroads but also precluded state action in such fields as the curbing of monopolies.

Interstate Commerce Act.

Inability of the states to regulate the railroads led directly to the passage in 1887 of the Interstate Commerce Act, which established the Interstate Commerce Commission. In 1894, the Supreme Court upheld the Act as a necessary and proper means of enforcing Congressional authority. The ICC has served as the prototype for the other great regulatory commissions created by Congress. *(See box.)*

At first the ICC was unable to provide effective regulation because it lacked final legislative and adjudicative power, but subsequent laws strengthened the Commission's authority. In time its jurisdiction was broadened to include all interstate commerce carried on by railroads, trucking companies, bus lines, freight forwarders, water carriers, oil pipelines, transportation brokers and express agencies.

Antitrust Legislation.

In 1890, Congress moved into Federal regulation of commercial enterprise with enactment of the Sherman Antitrust Act, "to protect commerce against unlawful restraints and monopolies." The Act imposed a general prohibition upon "every contract, combination in the form of trust or otherwise, or conspiracy in restraint of trade or commerce." Federal regulation of commerce was further strengthened in 1914 by passage of the Clayton Act and the Federal Trade Commission Act.

Police Power.

Congress entered still another field of regulation in 1895 when it enacted a law prohibiting transportation of lottery tickets in interstate commerce. The Supreme Court upheld this law in 1903 *(Champion v. Ames)* with a decision that, in the words of Charles Warren, "disclosed the existence of a hitherto unsuspected field of national power." Warren said: "The practical result of the case was the creation of a Federal police power—the right to regulate the manner of production, manufacture, sale and transportation of articles and the transportation of persons, through the medium of legislation professing to regulate commerce between the states. Congress took very swift advantage of the new field thus opened to it."

Between 1903 and 1917, Congress enacted laws prohibiting the interstate transportation of explosives, diseased livestock, insect pests, falsely stamped gold and silver articles, narcotics, prostitutes and adulterated or misbranded foods and drugs. Interstate transportation of stolen automobiles was made unlawful in 1925, under the Dyer Act, and the so-called "Lindbergh law" of 1932 made interstate transportation of abducted persons a Federal offense.

The 1910 Mann Act, forbidding the transportation of women in interstate commerce for the purpose of prostitution and debauchery, was upheld by the Supreme Court in 1913. The Court held "that Congress has power over transportation 'among the several States'; that the power is complete in itself, and that Congress, as an incident to it, may adopt not only means necessary but convenient to its exercise, and the means may have the quality of police regulations."

Child Labor Decision.

The same technique of closing the channels of interstate commerce was employed by Congress in enacting the Federal Child Labor Act of 1916. This time, however, the Supreme Court ruled that Congress had exceeded its powers. The 1916 Act prohibited the shipment in interstate commerce of the products of factories, mines or quarries employing children below specified ages. In a historic 5-4 decision in *Hammer v. Dagenhart*, the Court ruled in 1918 that Congress had the power "to control the means by which commerce is carried on," but not the power "to forbid commerce from moving."

Speaking for the majority, Justice William R. Day said: "The thing intended to be accomplished by this statute is the denial of the facilities of interstate commerce to those manufacturers in the states who employ children within the prohibited ages. The Act in its effect does not regulate transportation among the states, but aims to standardize the ages at which children may be employed in mining and manufacturing within the states. The goods shipped are of themselves harmless.... Over interstate transportation, or its incidents, the regulatory power of Congress is ample, but the production of articles, intended for interstate commerce, is a matter of local regulation."

In a classic dissent, Justice Holmes challenged the majority view. Congress clearly had the express power under the commerce clause, he said, to forbid the transportation of goods in interstate commerce. Therefore, if the law was to be declared unconstitutional, it would have to be because of its indirect effects on the states. "But if an Act is within the powers specifically conferred upon Congress, it seems to me that it is not made any less constitutional because of the indirect effects that it may have, however obvious it may be that it will have those effects, and that we are not at liberty upon such grounds to hold it void."

The Court overruled the Hammer decision in 1941 as "a departure from the principles which have prevailed in the interpretation of the commerce clause both before and since" the 1918 decision.

Expansion of Power in 20th Century

Since 1900, Congress has expanded its regulatory authority over commerce into almost every area of the commercial and industrial life of the nation. For the most part, the Supreme Court has gone along with this expansion and even, on occasion, hinted at broader Federal powers than Congress itself claimed.

Many of the great New Deal economic recovery programs were launched under the commerce clause. Until 1937, the Supreme Court tended to view the authorizing laws as unconstitutional, either because the programs were considered to range beyond the bounds of the commerce power or because they were thought to involve too broad a delegation of Congressional authority. Resentment caused by these decisions led to President Roosevelt's plan to enlarge the Court and made the Court a center of controversy.

Two months after the President sent his Court-packing plan to Congress, the Court altered its stance. In a 5-4 decision in 1937, it upheld the constitutionality of the National Labor Relations (Wagner) Act of 1935 and at the same time clarified the scope of the commerce power. The 1935 Act had established the National Labor Relations Board and given it authority to forbid any person from engaging in any unfair labor practice "affecting commerce." The case involved charges of unfair labor practices in one of the Pennsylvania plants of the Jones & Laughlin Corporation, a major steel producer with operations in several states.

Speaking for the Court, Chief Justice Hughes said: "Although activities may be intrastate in character when separately considered, if they have·such a close and substantial relation to interstate commerce that their control is essential or appropriate to protect that commerce from burdens and obstructions, Congress cannot be denied the power to exercise that control.... When industries organize themselves on a national scale, making their relation to interstate commerce the dominant factor in their activities, how can it be maintained that their industrial relations constitute a forbidden field into which Congress may not enter when it is necessary to protect interstate commerce from the paralyzing consequences of industrial war?" (*National Labor Relations Board v. Jones & Laughlin Corp.*)

In a 1941 decision upholding the Fair Labor Standards (Wages and Hours) Act of 1938, the Court reversed its earlier decision in the *Hammer* case. The 1938 Act banned the shipment in interstate commerce of goods produced in violation of the wage-and-hour standards set by the legislation, which included restrictions on child labor. The law was applicable to employees "engaged in commerce or in the production of goods for commerce." Justice Harlan F. Stone, delivering the opinion of the Court, said: "The power of Congress under the commerce clause is plenary to exclude any article from interstate commerce subject only to the specific prohibitions of the Constitution." *(U.S. v. Darby)*

In other decisions the Court upheld application of the commerce clause to such matters as agricultural marketing controls, regulation of the insurance industry and control over navigable waters (including irrigation and flood control) and the hydroelectric power derived from them. In a decision in 1946 upholding the "death sentence" provision of the Public Utility Holding Company Act, the Court concluded: "The Federal commerce power is as broad as the economic needs of the nation."

More recently, the scope of the commerce clause has been enlarged to include civil rights. In the Civil Rights Act of 1964, Congress found sanction in the commerce clause and the "equal protection" clause of the 14th Amendment for a ban on racial discrimination in most public accommodations, such as hotels, motels, restaurants and places of amusement. In two test cases in 1964, the Supreme Court unanimously upheld the law under the commerce power alone.

In 1968, Congress used the commerce clause as the basis for legislation making it a Federal crime to travel in interstate commerce or use the facilities of interstate commerce to incite or participate in a riot. The measure, prompted by rioting in Negro ghettos, was later used to prosecute some of the participants in demonstrations against the Vietnam war.

Regulation of Foreign Commerce

The power to regulate commerce with foreign nations extends to all transportation or communication that crosses the national boundaries. It is inextricably tied to the powers over foreign relations and fiscal affairs. The commerce power may be used to promote, inhibit or simply make rules for trade with other nations. It may be implemented by treaty or international agreement, as well as by Acts of Congress. Such is the breadth of this power that only a suggestion of it can be offered here. *(See Chapter III, Fiscal Powers and Power in Foreign Affairs.)*

Promotion of Trade. Encouragement of foreign trade may take the form of opening up new markets for American goods in other countries or of securing favorable conditions for American traders abroad. The earliest actions in this field were efforts to replace markets lost when the nation won its independence from England. Modern laws have ranged from antitrust exemptions for exporters to use of tariff reductions to stimulate trade.

Efforts to encourage American shipping have ranged from preferential duties for goods imported in American ships (first enacted in 1789) to Federal subsidies for the construction and operation of merchant ships, designed to equalize competition with foreign shipping (since 1936).

Trade Restrictions. The authority to limit or even prohibit foreign trade rests with Congress, although the Legislative Branch frequently delegates this power to the President or executive agencies.

Tariffs. Historically, the predominant mechanism to restrict foreign trade has been the protective tariff. The first major business of the House of Representatives in 1789 was to devise a tariff schedule; unlike many later tariff laws, this one had as its chief object the raising of revenue to finance the new Government. But Congress was not four days old when a Philadelphia Representative offered an amendment proposing additional duties on manufactured articles "to encourage the productions of our country and to protect our infant manufactures." Congress continued to legislate tariffs until 1930, and the pleas of special interests were frequently reflected in the tariff schedules.

The system also had other pitfalls. Members of Congress could hardly hope to master the intricacies of complicated tariff schedules, and tariffs embodied in statutes could not readily be adapted to changing conditions. A measure of flexibility was introduced in 1922, when the Fordney-McCumber Tariff Act gave the President authority to adjust tariff rates on the basis of recommendations by the U.S. Tariff Commission, which previously had had only investigative authority.

Reciprocal Trade Agreements Act. Finally, in 1934, the Roosevelt Administration—hoping to assist economic recovery at home by expanding American exports—proposed that Congress delegate some of its constitutional power to the President by authorizing him to negotiate trade agreements with other nations. The Administration asked authority to cut tariffs by as much as 50 percent in return for equivalent concessions from other nations. Prodded and persuaded by Secretary of State Cordell Hull, the Democratic-controlled 73rd

Congress—over the nearly unanimous opposition of Republicans—made this grant of authority in the Trade Agreements Act of 1934. Thereafter, no serious effort was made to restore Congressional tariff-making in place of the method of Presidential negotiation of bilateral and, after World War II, multilateral trade agreements.

Non-tariff Barriers. Non-tariff barriers to the free flow of trade range from import quotas to embargoes. Although export taxes are forbidden under the Constitution, Congress can control export trade through licensing or other means. Thus it may bar shipment of strategic materials to hostile countries or restrict exports that would deplete essential domestic supplies. Congress has curbed imports that would interfere with domestic regulatory programs (such as agricultural commodities under production-control and price-support programs). It has also enacted "Anti-Dumping," "Buy American" and "Ship American" legislation.

The ultimate restraint on foreign commerce is the embargo, which suspends commerce completely with all or with specified countries. The United States has used the embargo on a number of occasions, beginning in 1794. Trade with mainland China was completely embargoed after that country entered the Korean War. Exports of strategic goods to other Communist countries have long been subject to embargoes of varying severity.

Other Trade Laws. Laws relating to navigation and ship inspection go back to the First Congress. Since 1798, Congress has assumed responsibility for the health care of American merchant seamen; in the La Follette Seamen's Act of 1915, it undertook to safeguard their rights on shipboard as well. Congress also imposes safety regulations on ships using American ports and requires ship owners to prove financial responsibility as a means of protecting passengers from losses.

Bibliography

Books

Bernstein, M. H., *Regulating Business by Independent Commission.* Princeton University Press, 1955.

Beveridge, Albert J., *The Life of John Marshall.* Houghton Mifflin Company, 1919, 4 vols.

Corwin, Edward S., *The Commerce Power versus States Rights.* Princeton University Press, 1936.

Crosskey, William W., *Politics and the Constitution in the History of the United States.* University of Chicago Press, 1953.

Cushman, Robert E., *The Independent Regulatory Commissions.* Oxford University Press, 1941.

Frankfurter, Felix, *The Commerce Clause under Marshall, Taney and Waite.* University of North Carolina Press, 1937.

Haines, Charles Grove, and Foster H. Sherwood, *The Role of the Supreme Court in American Government and Politics, 1835-1864.* University of California Press, 1957.

Hamilton, Walton H., and Douglas Adair, *The Power to Govern: The Constitution—Then and Now.* W. W. Norton & Co., Inc., 1937.

Kallenbach, Joseph E., *Federal Cooperation with the States under the Commerce Clause.* University of Michigan Press, 1942.

Kelly, Alfred H., and Winfred A. Harbison, *The American Constitution: Its Origins and Development.* W. W. Norton & Co., Inc., 1963 (third edition).

Pritchett, C. Herman, *The American Constitution.* McGraw-Hill Book Co., 1968 (second edition).

——, *The Roosevelt Court: A Study in Judicial Politics and Values, 1937-1947.* Macmillan Company, 1948.

Warren, Charles, *The Making of the Constitution.* Little, Brown and Co., 1928.

——, *The Supreme Court in United States History.* Little, Brown and Co., 1926 (revised edition), 2 vols.

Articles

Putney, Bryant, "Federal Powers Under the Commerce Clause," *Editorial Research Reports,* Oct. 4, 1935, p. 289-304.

Worsnop, Richard L., "Federal Regulatory Agencies: Fourth Branch of Government," *Editorial Research Reports,* Feb. 5, 1969, p. 83-102.

The Amending Power

IT WAS THE DIFFICULTY of adapting the Articles of Confederation to changing conditions—a process which required unanimous approval of amendments by the states, as well as the consent of the Continental Congress —which led to the framing of the Constitution. In drafting the amending provision, the delegates to the Philadelphia Convention ot 1787 had little to serve as a guide. Six of the thirteen early state constitutions had been drawn up as "perpetual charters" and made no provision for amendment. In only three states were the legislatures empowered to propose changes. In four, the amending power was vested solely in popular conventions.

The unwritten British Constitution, by contrast, could be effectively amended by act of Parliament. Although the fundamentals of British government were understood as constitutional, and functioned in practice to contain and guide the operation of governing institutions, there was neither a document to define nor an agency to declare what was "unconstitutional." Whatever was enacted in Parliament was the supreme law of the land.

For a variety of reasons the Founding Fathers were unwilling to rely on so flexible a base for their new nation. The 13 independent states could not be expected to resign a part of their newly won sovereignty without a clear, written understanding of what kind of Union they were joining. Furthermore, they would need substantial guarantees that the new national Government would not unilaterally alter the terms of the agreement, in particular by reducing the sovereignty retained by the states. The reliance on separation of powers, and on checks and balances, for protection against arbitrary government required that the arrangement not be subject to easy alteration, lest the separation and the balance be destroyed. Experience with arbitrary acts of Parliament convinced the former colonists that certain rights must be declared inviolable by any agency of government, and must be controlled by a law which no one of those agencies could itself change.

These and other reasons prompted the Constitutional Convention to write a document that was expected to endure as the fundamental law of the land. And yet those assembled in Philadelphia realized that they could not foresee all the future needs of the new nation, nor regard their labors as perfect. They devised, therefore, a Constitution which would be easier to amend than the Articles of Confederation, but more difficult to revise than the British Constitution. They built into the amendment process the principle of checks and balances basic to the Constitution itself, and they reserved to the states the ultimate power to alter the agreement into which they had originally entered.

The Constitutional Convention

The plan for a national government presented by Edmund Randolph of Virginia on May 29, 1787, the fourth day of the Convention, set forth that "provision ought to be made for the amendment of the Articles of Union whensoever it shall seem necessary" and that "the assent of the National Legislature ought not to be required thereto." A plan proposed by Charles Pinckney of South Carolina on the same day provided that amendments "to invest future additional Powers in the United States" should be proposed by conventions and ratified by an unspecified percentage of the state legislatures.

When Randolph's proposal was brought forward in the Convention on June 5, Pinckney expressed doubt as to its "propriety or necessity," while Elbridge Gerry of Massachusetts favored it. "The novelty and difficulty of the experiment requires periodical revision," Gerry said. "The prospect of such a revision would also give intermediate stability to the Government." George Mason of Virginia supported the Randolph proposal, holding that:

"The plan now to be formed will certainly be defective, as the Confederation has been found, on trial, to be. Amendments, therefore, will be necessary and it will be better to provide for them in an easy, regular and constitutional way, than to trust to chance and violence. It would be improper to require the consent of the National Legislature, because they may abuse their power and refuse their consent on that very account."

On June 20, Mason said that "the Convention, though comprising so many distinguished characters, could not be expected to make a faultless government," and that he would prefer "trusting to posterity the amendment of its defects, rather than to push the experiment too far." The Convention agreed, on July 23, that "provisions ought to be made for future amendments... whensoever it shall seem necessary" and referred the matter to the Committee of Detail. In its report of Aug. 6, the committee recommended the provision that: "On the application of the legislatures of two-thirds of the states in the Union, for an amendment of this Constitution, the Legislature of the United States shall call a convention for that purpose." This recommendation was adopted by the Convention on Aug. 30, in spite of the contention of Gouverneur Morris of Pennsylvania that "the Legislature should be left at liberty to call a convention, whenever they please."

Reconsideration of the amendment provision was voted by the Convention on Sept. 10, on the motion of Gerry, who objected to it on the ground that, since the

Constitution was to be paramount to the state constitutions, "two-thirds of the states can bind the Union to innovations that may subvert the state constitutions altogether." Alexander Hamilton of New York likewise favored reconsideration, although he "did not object to the consequence stated by Mr. Gerry."

"There was no greater evil in subjecting the people of the United States to the major voice than the people of a particular state (Hamilton said). It had been wished by many and was much to have been desired that an easier mode for introducing amendments had been provided by the Articles of Confederation. It was equally desirable now that an easy mode should be established for supplying defects which will probably appear in the new system. The mode proposed was not adequate. The state legislatures will not apply for alterations but with a view to increase their own powers. The national Legislature will be most sensible to the necessity of amendments, and ought also to be empowered, whenever two-thirds of each branch should concur, to call a convention." This was one of the few suggestions made by Hamilton which found a place in the finished Constitution.

Roger Sherman of Connecticut moved to add to the provision the following clause: "or the Legislature may propose amendments to the several states for their approbation, but no amendments shall be binding until consented to by the several states." James Wilson of Pennsylvania moved to reduce the requirement of unanimous consent of the states to a two-thirds majority. Six states—Connecticut, Georgia, Massachusetts, New Jersey, North Carolina and South Carolina—voted against this motion and five states—Delaware, Maryland, New Hampshire, Pennsylvania and Virginia—in favor of it, but a later motion by Wilson to permit three-fourths of the states to make an amendment effective was adopted without dissent.

Madison then proposed a substitute for the entire article, and this was adopted with only one state dissenting. Madison's plan provided that amendments should be proposed by Congress whenever two-thirds of both houses considered it necessary or when two-thirds of the state legislatures made application, such amendments to be valid when ratified by three-fourths of the state legislatures or three-fourths of the state conventions, as Congress might designate.

When this provision was reported by the Committee on Style, Sept. 15, Morris and Gerry objected that both methods of amendment depended upon Congress. They urged a provision requiring Congress, when requested by two-thirds of the states, to call a convention to propose amendments. This provision was accepted without dissent.

John Rutledge of South Carolina protested that "he could never agree to give a power by which the articles relating to slaves might be altered by the states not interested in that property and prejudiced against it." The Convention consequently agreed to a provision prohibiting amendment before 1808 of the clauses concerned with slavery (the counting of slaves as three-fifths of the population for assessment of direct taxes and authorization of the slave trade). At the last minute, Sherman voiced the fear that "three-fourths of the states might be brought to do things fatal to particular states, as abolishing them altogether or depriving them of their equality in the Senate." He sought another proviso prohibiting any amend-

ment by which any state would "be affected in its internal policy, or deprived of its equal suffrage in the Senate." Madison warned against adding special provisos restricting the amending power, lest every state insist on protecting its boundaries or exports. However, "the circulating murmurs of the small states" prompted Gouverneur Morris to propose protecting equal representation in the Senate from amendment, a proviso adopted unanimously. These were the only two limitations on the substance of amendments which could be adopted. As finally agreed upon, Article V of the Constitution provided that:

"The Congress, whenever two-thirds of both Houses shall deem it necessary, shall propose Amendments to this Constitution, or, on the Application of the Legislatures of two-thirds of the several States, shall call a Convention for proposing Amendments, which, in either Case, shall be valid to all Intents and Purposes, as Part of this Constitution, when ratified by the Legislatures of three-fourths of the several States, or by Conventions in three-fourths thereof, as the one or the other Mode of Ratification may be proposed by the Congress; Provided that no Amendment which may be made prior to the Year One thousand eight hundred and eight shall in any Manner affect the first and fourth Clauses in the Ninth Section of the first Article; and that no State, without its Consent, shall be deprived of its equal Suffrage in the Senate."

Thus, the Constitution allows either Congress or the state legislatures to initiate the amending process, either Congress or a general convention to propose amendments, and either state legislatures or state conventions to ratify amendments. Congress determines which method of ratification will be employed, and what form a general convention would take if required by the state legislatures.

Ratification

Omission of a bill of rights constituted the principal source of dissatisfaction with the new Constitution in the state ratifying conventions held in 1788. The demand for amendments to establish these rights, and to effect various other changes in the Constitution, made the provisions of Article V an issue in the struggle for ratification. In the Virginia convention, Patrick Henry and George Mason raised vehement objections to the amending process prescribed in Article V.

"When I come to contemplate this part (Henry said), I suppose that I am mad or that my countrymen are so. The way to amendment is, in my conception, shut.... Two-thirds of Congress or of the state legislatures are necessary even to propose amendments. If one-third of these be unworthy men, they may prevent the application for amendments; but what is destructive and mischievous is that three-fourths of the state legislatures, or of the state conventions, must concur in the amendments when proposed.... A bare majority in four small states may hinder the adoption of amendments.... Is this an easy mode of securing the public liberty? It is, sir, a most fearful situation, when the most contemptible minority could prevent the alteration of the most oppressive government, for it may in many respects prove to be such."

Washington admitted that there were defects in the Constitution, but observed that "As a Constitutional door is opened for future amendments and alterations, I think it would be wise in the people to accept what is offered to them...." Jefferson, at first hostile, came to support the Constitution, "contented to travel on towards perfection, step by step."

The Federalist expressed the view that: "The mode (of amendment) preferred by the convention seems to be stamped with every mark of propriety. It guards equally against that extreme facility, which would render the Constitution too mutable; and that extreme difficulty which might perpetuate its discovered faults. It moreover equally enables the general and the state governments to originate the amendment of errors, as they may be pointed out by the experience on one side or the other."

Change Without Amendment

Since the Constitution was drafted, the United States has been transformed beyond recognition. And yet this document remains the fundamental law of the land. The amending process has contributed to the remarkable durability of the Constitution.

But basic changes in the nature of the Constitution are by no means limited to those achieved through the amendment process. Each branch of the national Government has contributed to transformation of the arrangement created at the Constitutional Convention. Following are a few highlights of the alteration of the Constitution outside the formal amendment process.

Interpretation by Supreme Court

The interpretation of the Constitution by the Supreme Court has been a major source of change. The principal of judicial review of legislation established the High Court as the authoritative interpreter of the Constitution.

Chief Justice Marshall, in *Marbury v. Madison* (1803), first asserted the Supreme Court's power to declare acts of Congress unconstitutional. In an *obiter dictum*, Marshall said: "The powers of the Legislature are defined and limited; and that those limits may not be mistaken, or forgotten, the Constitution is written. To what purpose are powers limited, and to what purpose is that limitation committed to writing, if these limits may at any time be passed by those intended to be restrained?"

"It is a proposition too plain to be contested," the Chief Justice continued, "that the Constitution controls any legislative act repugnant to it, or that the Legislature may alter the Constitution by an ordinary act. Between these alternatives there is no middle ground. The Constitution is either a superior paramount law, unchangeable by ordinary means, or it is on a level with ordinary legislative acts, and, like other acts, is alterable when the Legislature shall please to alter it.... If an act of the Legislature, repugnant to the Constitution, is void, does it, notwithstanding its invalidity, bind the courts, and oblige them to give it effect? ...It is emphatically the province and duty of the judicial department to say what the law is.... So if a law be in opposition to the Constitution; if both the law and the Constitution apply to a particular case, so that the Court must either decide that case conformably to the law, disregarding the Constitution; or conformably to the Constitution, disregarding the law; the Court must determine which of these conflicting rules governs the case. This is of the very essence of judicial duty."

Although Marshall's assertion of the Court's power angered Jefferson and the Republicans, Charles Warren pointed out in his *The Making of the Constitution*, that during the first century of the existence of the Supreme Court, the principal controversy was "over the Court's decisions restricting the limits of state authority and not over those restricting the limits of Congressional power." The Court was attacked, not because it invalidated acts of Congress, but because it refused to do so. The Anti-Federalists and early Republicans criticized the Court because it failed to declare the Sedition law, the Bank of the United States charter, and the Judiciary Act unconstitutional. The Democrats later assailed the Court for enunciating doctrines which would sustain the constitutionality of an internal improvement bill, a voluntary bankruptcy bill, a protective tariff bill, and similar measures to which they objected. The Federalists attacked the Court for not invalidating the Embargo Act, while the later Republicans criticized it for sustaining the Fugitive Slave law.

Strict Constructionist Views

The interpretative power of the Supreme Court has found some of its broadest scope in the application of the 14th Amendment *(see below)*. In providing that no state should deprive any person of life, liberty or property without due process of law, the amendment left the meaning of "due process" up to the courts. The interpretations have profoundly affected many aspects of American government.

At first, the Supreme Court showed reluctance to use the clause in reviewing state legislation, disappointing those who had hoped to see the 14th Amendment shift power from the states to the Federal Government. But later, when the states began enacting social legislation in the wake of industrialization, the Court invoked "due process" to overturn these laws. The result not only affected the balance between state and Federal governments; it also enshrined in the Constitution the principles of laissez-faire economics. Legislation seeking to regulate rates, prices, minimum wages, maximum hours and other terms of employment was treated as interference with natural rights of liberty and property. Such control over state regulatory power was not abandoned until the decade of the 1930s.

Federal legislation challenging the principles of laissez-faire was enacted during the Great Depression of the 1930s. In overturning these laws, the Supreme Court ruled that they exceeded the powers delegated to Congress by the Constitution.

In declaring unconstitutional the National Recovery Act (*Schechter Poultry Corp. v. United States*, 1935), the Railroad Retirement Act (*Railroad Retirement Board v. Alton R.R. Co.*, 1935), the Agricultural Adjustment Act (*United States v. Butler*, 1936) and other New Deal legislation, the Supreme Court held that the laws exceeded the constitutional power conferred on Congress by the commerce or the general welfare clauses and invaded areas of legislation reserved exclusively to the states by the 10th Amendment.

In the *Railroad Retirement* case, the majority said: "...a pension plan thus imposed is in no proper sense a regulation of the activity of interstate transportation. It is an attempt for social ends to impose by sheer fiat noncontractual incidents upon the relation of employer and employee, not as a rule or regulation of commerce and transportation between the states, but as a means of assuring a particular class of employees against old-age dependency."

Of the Agricultural Adjustment Act, the Court held: "The Act invades the reserved rights of the states. It is a statutory plan to regulate and control agricultural production, a matter beyond the powers delegated to the Federal Government."

Changes in Court's Views Since 1937

In a series of decisions which followed President Roosevelt's proposals to reform the Supreme Court by adding new judges, New Deal legislation similar to that rejected was found to be constitutional.

In upholding the National Labor Relations Act of 1935 (*National Labor Relations Board v. Jones & Laughlin Steel Corp.*, 1937), the Court said: "The Congressional authority to protect interstate commerce from burdens and obstructions is not limited to transactions which can be deemed to be an essential part of a 'flow' of interstate or foreign commerce.... Although activities may be intrastate in character when separately considered, if they have such a close and substantial relation to interstate commerce that their control is essential or appropriate to protect that commerce from burdens and obstructions, Congress cannot be denied the power to exercise that control."

While the NLRA case and other decisions extended the scope of Federal powers conferred by the commerce clause, in *Helvering v. Davis* (1937) the Court for the first time recognized Congress' power to provide for the general welfare by legislation which did not exercise one of the other enumerated constitutional powers of the Federal Government. The majority held that the old-age benefits provisions of the Social Security Act of 1935 were not an invasion of state powers but a furtherance of the general welfare because, among other reasons, "The problem is plainly national in area and dimensions. Moreover, laws of the separate states cannot deal with it effectively." In determining the boundaries of Federal powers conferred by the general welfare clause, the majority said, "The discretion, however, is not confined to the courts. The discretion belongs to Congress, unless the choice is clearly wrong, a display of arbitrary power, not an exercise of judgment.... Nor is the concept of the general welfare static. Needs that were narrow or parochial a century ago may be interwoven in our day with the well-being of the nation. What is critical or urgent changes with the times."

So fundamental were these decisions for Federal-state relations that in 1956 the Commission on Intergovernmental Relations said: "Under judicial doctrine since 1937 the Supreme Court has largely removed itself as a practical factor in determining the economic policies of the states and the nation." The commission further noted: "...under present judicial interpretations of the Constitution, especially of the spending power and the commerce clause, the boundaries of possible national action are more and more subject to determination by legislative action. In brief, the policymaking authorities of the national Government are for most purposes the arbiters of the Federal system."

A minority on the commission regretted the Supreme Court decisions upholding New Deal legislation on the ground that they upset the division of national and state powers outlined in the 10th Amendment. Former Governor Val Peterson (R Neb. 1947-53), in a statement in which seven other members of the commission joined, said: "The effect of these decisions (*Helvering v. Davis* and others) has been to create a situation under which the Congress may by the expenditure of money enter virtually any sphere of government. There exists little restraint on Congress other than that which it determines to exercise over itself. These decisions have fundamentally altered the balance of power designed by the architects of the Constitution."

Congress, meanwhile, had made full use of the powers ruled available under the commerce and spending clauses, expanding legislation into the realms of health, education, labor, social welfare, agriculture, consumer protection, urban development, environmental protection and other fields undreamt of by the Founding Fathers. Perhaps the most radical innovations under the interstate commerce clause were the prohibitions in the Civil Rights Act of 1964 against racial discrimination in public accommodations and employment.

Application of 14th Amendment

In the years following World War II, the Supreme Court generally left Congress free to determine the boundaries of Federal economic and social powers, and it increasingly restricted state action in the area of civil and political rights. Relying largely on the 14th Amendment's ban against state denial of "equal protection of the laws," the Court attacked state policies of racial segregation and legislative malapportionment with sweeping changes in constitutional doctrine. Under the Amendment's due process clause, the Court also applied many of the Bill of Rights guarantees of civil liberties to state action.

Undoubtedly the most controversial of the Supreme Court's postwar decisions was its 9-0 ruling (*Brown v. Board of Education of Topeka, Kansas*, 1954) that racial segregation in public schools constituted denial of equal protection of the laws. Later, refusing to review lower court opinions, the Supreme Court gave effect to decisions prohibiting segregation in other public facilities. In other decisions, segregation in interstate transportation was prohibited under the commerce clause and the Interstate Commerce Act.

Between 1962 and 1964 the Supreme Court in a series of decisions (*Baker v. Carr*, 1962; *Gray v. Sanders*, 1963; *Reynolds v. Sims* and related cases, 1964) held that unequal apportionment for state legislatures violated the equal protection clause of the 14th Amendment. The effect of these decisions, especially in view of the extent of malapportionment in most states, promised to alter profoundly the character and policies of the state legislatures. In a similar ruling (*Wesberry v. Sanders*, 1964) the Court required that U.S. House of Representatives' districts have approximately equal population, but in this case it did not invoke the 14th Amendment.

The apportionment rulings were criticized as usurpation by Federal authority of states' rights. In a vehement dissent from the 1964 state legislative apportionment decisions, Justice John Marshall Harlan said: "...the aftermath of these cases, however desirable it may be thought in itself, will have been achieved at the cost of a radical alteration in the relationship between the states and the Federal Government, more particularly the Federal judiciary. Only one who has an overbearing impatience with the Federal system and its political processes will believe that cost was not too high or was inevitable."

The Supreme Court in the postwar years continued a trend of interpreting the due process clause of the 14th Amendment to extend to the states the guarantees of civil liberties contained in the first eight amendments to the Constitution. Reversing earlier doctrine, the Court in 1925 (*Gitlow v. New York*) had initiated a series of decisions whose effect was to hold immune from state invasion the First Amendment's freedoms of speech, press, religion, assembly, association and petition for redress of grievances. Decisions culminating in *Mapp v. Ohio* (1961) prohibited admission in state courts of evidence obtained in violation of the Fourth Amendment. The Eighth Amendment's prohibition of cruel and unusual punishment (*Robinson v. California*, 1962), the Sixth Amendment's provision of counsel in criminal cases (*Gideon v. Wainwright*, 1963) and the Fifth Amendment's protection against compulsory self-incrimination (*Malloy v. Hogan*, 1964) were similarly held applicable to state action, though a blanket application of the Bill of Rights to the states was not undertaken by the Court.

President's Powers in Emergencies

In response to the emergencies of the two World Wars and the continuing emergency of the cold war, many changes were made in the fundamentals of American government. Two realms in particular experienced profound change—the power of the President and the civil liberties of private citizens.

The Constitution itself had given extensive authority to Congress to provide for national defense, but great potential powers for dealing with international crises remained with the President in his responsibility for the conduct of foreign affairs and in his role as Commander-in-Chief of the armed forces. Alexis de Tocqueville, in his *Democracy in America* (1835), had noted:

"It is chiefly in its foreign relations that the Executive power of a nation finds occasion to exert its skill and its strength. If the existence of the Union were perpetually threatened, if its chief interests were in daily connection with those of other powerful nations the Executive Government would assume an increased importance in proportion to the measures expected of it and to those which it would execute. The President of the United States, it is true, is the Commander-in-Chief of the army, but the army is composed of only six thousand men; he commands the fleet, but the fleet reckons but few sail; he conducts the foreign relations of the Union, but the United States is a nation without neighbors. Separated from the rest of the world by the ocean, and too weak as yet to aim at the dominion of the seas, it has no enemies, and its interests rarely come into contact with those of any other nation of the globe. This proves that the practical operation of the Government must not be judged by the theory of its Constitution. The President of the United States possesses almost royal prerogatives, which he has no opportunity of exercising; and the privileges which he can at present use are very circumscribed. The laws allow him to be strong, but circumstances keep him weak."

In the early days of the Civil War, President Lincoln used not only the war powers at his disposal, but also some of the powers reserved to Congress. He expanded the armed forces without authorization, but when Congress convened it validated his acts. The Supreme Court, however, took a dim view of Lincoln's order authorizing various military commanders to suspend the writ of habeas corpus. The Court ruled (*Ex Parte Milligan*, 1866) that civilians might be tried by military tribunals only where civil courts could not function because of invasion or disorder.

In the First World War, President Wilson acquired sweeping control of the economy in what Rexford G. Tugwell called "the most fantastic expansion of the Executive known to American experience." The numerous powers conferred upon the President included power:

- To take over and operate enemy vessels for use in the war.
- To regulate and prohibit exports.
- To take over and operate the railroads.
- To regulate priorities in transportation.
- To regulate by a licensing system the importation, manufacture, storage, mining or distribution of any necessaries.
- To requisition foods, fuels, and other supplies necessary for any public use connected with national defense.
- To fix a reasonable guaranteed price for wheat based upon a statutory minimum.
- To fix the price of coal and regulate the method of its production, sale, shipment, distribution and storage.
- To prohibit or license transactions in the United States by foreign insurance companies.

Using his authority as Commander-in-Chief, Wilson had also created by Executive Order the Committee on Public Information, under whose direction a system of voluntary news censorship was established and various Government publicity services were organized.

Entry of this country into World War II was accompanied by concentration of virtually all war power in the President's hands. The experience of total war brought many of the instruments of totalitarianism to the United States for the duration of hostilities. The Government assumed the most extraordinary powers over every aspect of its citizens' lives, through rationing, price and wage controls, censorship, propaganda, resource allocation, and even (for U.S. citizens of Japanese ancestry) concentration camps. None of these had been envisioned by the makers of the Constitution.

When war was followed by "cold war," freedoms guaranteed by the First Amendment were jeopardized by fears of Communist subversion. These freedoms had been limited in earlier emergencies, as by the Alien and Sedition Acts of 1798, by such Civil War actions as suspension of habeas corpus, and by the Espionage Act of 1917. The first peacetime sedition statute since 1798 was the Smith Act of 1940, which made it a crime to advocate violent overthrow of the Government. This law figured prominently in postwar anti-Communist activities, and Congress enacted further legislation impinging on the First Amendment, notably the Internal Security Act of 1950 and the Communist Control Act of 1954. Meanwhile, the thoughts, actions, and associations of all manner of persons and institutions came to be regarded as proper subjects of Congressional investigation.

In balancing the rights of individual witnesses summoned before Congressional committees against the Congressional need for information, the Supreme Court considered (*Barenblatt v. U.S.*, 1959) "world affairs which have determined the whole course of our national policy since the close of World War II, and...the vast burdens which these conditions have entailed for the entire nation." Admitting that the First Amendment "in some circumstances protects an individual from being compelled to disclose his associational relationships," the Court found that the circumstances of the period limited that protection. This limitation of the First Amendment was, according to the Court's majority opinion, ultimately based on "the right of self-preservation, 'the ultimate value of any society.' "

The termination of America's isolation from international danger transformed the elemental conditions under which the institutions of this country had been formed. As a consequence, revision of the Constitution outside the formal amendment process was likely to be grounded upon continuation of the question of "self-preservation." Emergency actions enhancing the powers of the President and restricting the freedoms of individuals stood a chance of becoming permanent elements of the unwritten constitution as emergency conditions became permanent.

Use of Amending Process

While profound changes in the foundations of American Government have been wrought by Congress, the Judiciary and the Executive, formal amendments also have contributed to the process of constitutional transformation. Indeed, some of the amendments, such as the 11th and the 16th, reversed judicial interpretations of the Constitution.

A number of the 25 amendments made only technical adjustments in the mechanisms of government. For example, the 12th Amendment provided for separate balloting for President and Vice President in the electoral college, and the 20th Amendment revised the dates for the beginning of Presidential terms and the convening of Congress. Other amendments advanced the course of democracy by extending the vote to Negroes (15th) and women (19th) and by providing for the direct election of Senators (17th). The economy was profoundly affected by the income tax amendment (16th) and social mores by the Prohibition amendment (18th, repealed by the 21st). The relationship between the national and state governments was altered by the 14th Amendment, the most fundamental formal revision of the Constitution; its consequences are still unfolding in Supreme Court decisions based on the amendment.

The constitutional amendments have come in clusters. The first ten, the Bill of Rights, were practically a part of the original Constitution. Two amendments designed to correct the functioning of the Constitution were soon precipitated by a Supreme Court decision and by a crisis arising from a flaw in the procedure for electing the President and Vice President.

The Civil War prompted the 13th, 14th and 15th Amendments. Apart from those three, which grew out of the nation's gravest crisis, more than a century elapsed between constitutional amendments. From 1913 to 1920,

largely as the culmination of the Progressive movement, four amendments of fundamental importance were ratified—giving the United States the income tax, direct election of Senators, Prohibition, and woman suffrage.

The next two amendments, rescinding Prohibition and altering the dates for the beginning of a new Congress and of the Presidential term, went into effect in 1933. There have been four amendments since the Second World War, none of them profoundly revising the system of government.

Leadership of Congress

Although the Constitutional Convention envisioned a substantial role for the states in the amendment process, Congress has dominated the rewriting of the Constitution. Not once have the states been successful in calling for a convention to propose an amendment, as they are authorized to do by petitions to Congress from two-thirds of the legislatures. The states, while approving 25 amendments proposed by Congress, have failed to ratify only five.

Undoubtedly, the need to obtain the approval of as many as three-fourths of the states has served as a brake on Congressional inclinations to alter the Constitution. On at least one occasion, the prospect that the states might take the initiative drove Congress to act. The 17th Amendment, providing for direct election of Senators, was continually blocked in the Senate until the state legislatures were on the verge of requiring a convention. Even in this case, however, Congress had for years provided the principal public arena for debate of the issue.

Congress has the power to determine by which of the two procedures the states shall ratify a proposed amendment. In every case except one, approval by the state legislatures has been prescribed. Only for the 21st Amendment, the repeal of Prohibition, did Congress call for ratification by state conventions. The provision for ratification by conventions in that instance was primarily the result of three factors: (1) a desire for speedy ratification; (2) the contention of advocates of repeal that the state legislatures ratifying the 18th Amendment had yielded to the pressure tactics of Prohibition forces, had over-represented rural areas favoring Prohibition and had not represented the views of the majority of the people; and (3) the desire to remove permanently from the political arena a question which had divided states, regions and political parties. Submitted to the states in February 1933, the 21st Amendment was ratified by conventions in 36 of the then total of 48 states by December of the same year.

Undecided Questions

Constitutional authorities disagreed on whether Congress or the state legislatures should determine the procedures for ratification by state conventions. Bills were introduced in Congress to spell out procedures, but none of them passed. The state legislatures were divided on this question. At least 21 of them provided by statute that state officials were to follow the procedures specified in a Federal law if Congress should enact one. Sixteen legislatures, assuming that the procedural question was within their jurisdiction, passed laws applicable not merely to the convention summoned for the 21st Amendment, but for all future conventions called to ratify amendments to the U.S. Constitution. One state, New Mexico, claimed exclusive authority on the matter and directed its officials to resist any attempt at Congressional encroachment on that authority.

Even if two-thirds of the states petitioned Congress to summon a national convention to propose constitutional amendments, Congress would retain considerable power and discretion. Because there is no precedent for such a convention, the burden of setting precedents would rest largely with Congress. The Supreme Court has never had occasion to rule on questions involved in such an event and it might refuse to do so. In *Coleman v. Miller* (1939) the Court dismissed an appeal from the Kansas Legislature's ratification of the proposed Child Labor Amendment. The decision was not clear because four opinions were written, no one of which commanded the support of more than four Justices. However, four of the Justices concurred in saying that questions involving the amending process should be left to Congress because the process was " 'political' in its entirety, from submission until an amendment becomes part of the Constitution, and is not subject to judicial guidance, control or interference at any point."

A number of fundamental issues would have to be resolved should two-thirds of the states petition Congress for a convention. In deciding those questions, Congress might determine the outcome of the convention as well as set precedents for future conventions.

The 25 Amendments

The Bill of Rights. Important guarantees of civil liberties were written into the main body of the Constitution. Ex post facto laws and bills of attainder were forbidden, as was suspension of the writ of habeas corpus. A religious test as a qualification for office was prohibited and trial by jury for criminal offenses was guaranteed. Little was said at the Constitutional Convention in favor of a bill of rights. Most delegates were satisfied that the fundamental liberties they cherished would be safe because the Federal Government was limited to powers explicitly granted in the Constitution and thus was denied any authority that could be used against citizens' rights.

But during the campaign for ratification it became clear that many were not content to leave basic rights protected only by inference. The colonists had long claimed the rights guaranteed Englishmen by precedents going back as far as *Magna Carta* (1215), and civil liberties had been included in colonial charters. Since Independence, six states had adopted bills of rights and others had incorporated similar guarantees into their state constitutions. When Massachusetts ratified the new Constitution of the United States, its convention recommended that it be amended to protect basic rights. The Virginia ratifying convention chose a committee to report on amendments for submission in the First Congress. New York attached a bill of rights to its ratification. There was no doubt that action must be taken at once to gain support for the Constitution by adding explicit guarantees of fundamental liberties.

Madison yielded in his view that the grant of only specified powers to the Federal Government was sufficient protection of civil liberties. He proposed amend-

Amendments That Failed

By Jan. 3, 1969, a total of 6,940 proposed amendments to the Constitution had been introduced in Congress. Many of them, of course, were identical or similar proposals; some were introduced repeatedly in successive Congresses. Almost one-third of all the amendments offered since 1789 were introduced in the past 10 years.

Congress has submitted only 30 amendments to the states for ratification; only five were not ratified. Two of the latter were proposed in September 1789, along with the Bill of Rights. The first, which concerned the apportionment of Representatives, was ratified by 10 states—one less than the required number. The second, which provided that no law varying the compensation of Members of Congress should be operative until after the next national election, was ratified by six states and rejected by five, with three states taking no action.

In 1810, an amendment providing for revocation of the citizenship of any American accepting a gift or title of nobility from any foreign power, without the consent of Congress, was submitted to the states for ratification. The amendment was ratified by 12 states and by the senate of the South Carolina Legislature; had it been approved by that Legislature's lower house, it would have become a part of the Constitution. The impression prevailed for nearly a generation that the amendment had been adopted.

A proposed amendment to prohibit interference by Congress with the institution of slavery in the states, offered in 1861 as a last effort to ward off the impending conflict between North and South, was ratified by the legislatures of only two states—Ohio and Maryland. A convention called in Illinois in 1862 to revise the state constitution also ratified the amendment, but since Congress had designated state legislatures as the ratifying bodies, this ratification was manifestly invalid.

The only recent amendment proposed by Congress but not ratified by the states was the Child Labor Amendment. It would have empowered Congress to "limit, regulate, and prohibit the labor of persons under 18 years of age." The amendment sought to reverse rulings by the Supreme Court (*Hammer v. Dagenhart*, 1919; *Bailey v. Drexel Furniture Co.*, 1922) which had struck down child labor laws enacted by Congress.

Submitted to the states June 4, 1924, the amendment had been ratified by 28 of the 48 states by 1938. In that year Congress again enacted a child labor law utilizing its constitutional power to regulate interstate commerce. This time the Supreme Court upheld the law, specifically reversing its 1919 decision. Since then, there have been no further ratifications of the proposed amendment.

ments to be fitted into the Constitution at appropriate points within the document. But the House of Representatives, after a committee had considered and revised Madison's proposals, decided to append the amendments as a supplement to the Constitution. Twelve amendments

33 States Call for Constitutional Convention...

The Constitution's provision for amendment by a convention requested by two-thirds of the states has never been successfully invoked. A movement in behalf of a constitutional amendment that would limit the maximum rate of Federal income, death and gift taxes to 25 percent was actively promoted among state legislatures before and after World War II. More than a score of state legislatures petitioned Congress to call a convention to propose such an amendment to the states for ratification, but a number of the states subsequently rescinded the resolutions and the movement died out.

Petitions to Congress for a convention to propose an amendment in a different field had been made, by 1969, by 33 state legislatures, only one short of the required number. The proposed amendment—to authorize states to apportion one house of a bicameral legislature on a basis of geography or political subdivisions, as well as population—had been prompted by Supreme Court decisions applying the one-man, one-vote rule to state legislatures. Such an amendment had failed to muster in Congress the two-thirds majorities needed for submission of an amendment to the states for ratification. A number of complications made it uncertain whether the alternative route to amendment, by convention, would be adopted even if one more state legislature raised the number seeking a convention to the necessary two-thirds of the total.

Background

A revolution in the apportionment of state legislatures was precipitated by the Supreme Court when it held in *Baker v. Carr* (1962) that the judiciary could entertain suits challenging malapportionment. The decision overturned a line of legal precedent holding that the makeup of state legislatures was not a justiciable matter, but was political in nature, and that citizens had no standing to sue to effect a change.

In subsequent decisions, the Court elaborated on *Baker* and in *Reynolds v. Sims* (1964) applied its "one-man, one-vote" dictum, holding that both houses of a state legislature must be apportioned on a basis of substantial equality of population. That decision struck not only at malapportioned state legislatures, but also

at those apportioned—sometimes by terms of the state constitution—on the basis of one state senator for each city, town or county, for example.

A substantial element in Congress opposed the Court's interpretation of the Constitution. In 1964 the House passed a bill (HR 11926) by a 218-175 roll-call vote which denied Federal courts jurisdiction over state reapportionment. The bill was sponsored by Rep. William M. Tuck (D Va.). In the Senate, Everett McKinley Dirksen (R Ill.) led an unsuccessful move to attach to the foreign aid bill a rider requiring courts to delay reapportionment orders until Congress submitted a proposed constitutional amendment on apportionment.

Sen. Dirksen tried again in 1965. He brought to the floor a minor bill (S J Res 66) which designated the dates for "National American Legion Baseball Week" and then succeeded in substituting for it his proposed constitutional amendment (S J Res 2). The Senate Aug. 4, 1965, by a 57-39 roll-call vote, defeated the substitute. Dirksen had won a majority but lacked by seven votes the two-thirds needed to propose a constitutional amendment.

On Aug. 11, 1965, the Illinois Senator introduced S J Res 103, which required an apportionment of state legislatures in the year following each national census. States with bicameral legislatures would have to apportion one house on the basis of population but could apportion the other house on the basis of "population, geography, and political subdivisions." A key phrase added from *Reynolds v. Sims* said that such apportionment must be "in order to insure effective representation in the state's legislature of the various groups and interests making up the electorate," a phrase Dirksen hoped would mollify opponents who feared racial discrimination in reapportionment schemes.

States having unicameral legislatures (Nebraska currently was the only such state) could apportion their legislatures on the basis of population "with such weight given to" the nonpopulation factors as would insure similar "effective representation."

Finally, S J Res 103 would have required that any such new reapportionment plan be approved at a statewide referendum and that the legislature proposing the reapportionment scheme have at least one house already apportioned on the basis of population. If pro-

were finally approved by Congress and submitted to the states. The first two, which dealt with apportionment of Representatives and compensation of Members of Congress, were not ratified. The others became the first 10 amendments to the Constitution when Virginia, the eleventh state to ratify, approved them on Dec. 15, 1791.

The Supreme Court in 1833 ruled (*Barron v. Baltimore*) that the Bill of Rights was not applicable to the states. However, the 14th Amendment's due process clause was later held to prohibit the states from denying at least some of the freedoms protected by the Bill of Rights (*see below*).

The First Amendment's guarantee of freedoms of religion, speech, press and assembly has proved the

cornerstone of a free society and government. It has also been a source of great controversies. Recently the Supreme Court has outraged segments of American opinion by interpreting the First Amendment to prohibit prayers in public schools and to permit the publication of literature and the showing of films widely viewed as obscene.

Even more controversial have been decisions prompted by efforts to suppress Communism. Justice Holmes in 1919 (*Schenck v. United States*) had first formulated the doctrine that freedom of speech could not be abridged except when "the words are used in such circumstances and are of such a nature as to create a clear and present danger that they will bring about the substantive evils

...To Revise One-Man, One-Vote Ruling

posed by a unicameral legislature, the reapportionment scheme would have required prior court approval. At each submission to the electorate, the proposed scheme would have to be accompanied by an alternative scheme based upon substantial equality of population. The requirement that legislatures ratifying the proposed constitutional amendment have one house already apportioned on the basis of population was another Dirksen concession to critics of his proposal.

State Actions

Despairing of Congressional initiatives, supporters of the Dirksen proposal placed their hopes on constitutional amendment via a convention summoned by Congress upon petition by two-thirds of the states.

In December 1964, the General Assembly of the Council of State Governments published a guide for petitions to Congress by state legislatures. The guide suggested requesting Congress to call a convention on apportionment and permitting one house of a state legislature to be based on factors other than population. This proposed form for a petition was used by state legislatures beginning with the 89th Congress in 1965.

By the end of the 89th Congress in 1966, 28 states had petitioned Congress for a convention. During the 90th Congress (1967-68), four more states joined the list, bringing the total to 32. Iowa, the 33rd, was the only one to do so during the 91st Congress.

Two of the 33 resolutions now before Congress date from the spring of 1963. Washington State adopted its resolution March 30, 1963. Wyoming's resolution was adopted March 25, 1963. The Constitution puts no limit on how long resolutions may remain active. But both of these resolutions would become void if Congress passed S 623, a bill introduced by Sen. Sam J. Ervin Jr. (D N.C.).

Ervin's bill would establish rules governing the call and operation of a constitutional convention. If Congress passed the bill, it would assume jurisdiction in an area where it had never ventured before. The Ervin proposal was approved by the Senate Subcommittee on Separation of Powers June 12, 1969, and awaited action by the Senate Judiciary Committee. As amended,

it would limit to seven years the life of state resolutions requesting a convention.

Legal Challenges. In addition to the time limitation, the legitimacy of the state resolutions might also be challenged on the ground that the legislatures which passed them were malapportioned. Only 5 of the 33 state petitions have emerged from legislatures that meet court definitions of proper apportionment. These are from Colorado, Illinois, Indiana, North Dakota and Iowa.

Other potential legal entanglements are to be found in the wording of the resolutions and in several rescinding resolutions. The Washington and Wyoming resolutions of 1963, for example, are worded differently from the subsequent state petitions. They call for complete removal of Federal court jurisdiction from the apportionment area. In a Congressional showdown, Senate and House liberals might object to the different wording of the two petitions.

Rescinding Actions. Since the original passage of convention resolutions, several state legislative bodies have had second thoughts. Rescinding resolutions have been adopted in one house of each of six legislatures: in Maryland, 1967 and 1969; Texas, North Carolina and Illinois, 1969; Kansas, 1968; and Washington, 1967.

The arrival in Congress of a 34th resolution would not necessarily be decisive. Congressional opponents of a constitutional convention would probably try to delay or kill a convention call. Opponents probably would challenge the validity of state resolutions adopted by malapportioned legislatures, the legality of resolutions from states in which one house of the legislature had approved rescission, and the variables in resolution wordings. And numerous questions would be raised about the manner in which Congress would actually call and conduct a constitutional convention.

Meanwhile, the Supreme Court's order has already had a profound impact on the legislatures. By the end of the decade, every state had reapportioned at least one house, and in most cases both houses. The issue promised to provoke intensified controversy when the 1970 Census figures became available for use in further reapportionment according to the Court's one-man, one-vote rule.

that Congress has a right to prevent." This "clear and present danger" doctrine was modified when the Court in 1951 (*Dennis v. United States*) upheld the Smith Act of 1940, which made it a crime to advocate violent overthrow of the Government. The Court then ruled that freedom of speech must at times give way to other social values, with the courts determining in each case "whether the gravity of the 'evil,' discounted by its improbability, justifies such invasion of free speech as is necessary to avoid the danger." The Court has also ruled against witnesses who have cited the First Amendment in refusing to testify before Congressional investigating committees, balancing their rights to freedom of speech and association against the need of Congress for information. How-

ever, the Fifth Amendment's protection against compulsory self-incrimination has consistently been upheld as constitutional justification for refusing to answer questions in Congressional investigations.

The complex history of judicial interpretations of the first 10 amendments gives an incomplete picture of the role the Bill of Rights has played in the character and development of the United States. It embodies freedoms won through generations of struggle in England and America, and it remains a rallying cry for protecting and extending those freedoms. The Bill of Rights has, in the words of Milton R. Konvitz, "helped mold the American nation as well as its political institutions." He observed: "It has interacted with the people and its governments

Uncertainties About a Convention

Because Congress never has been required, by petitions from two-thirds of the state legislatures, to call a convention "for proposing amendments" to the Constitution, a number of important questions on the procedures to be followed in that event have not been answered:

• What constitutes a valid call of two-thirds of the legislatures? Must their resolutions to Congress be identical in all details or simply relate to one general subject?

• In what time span must the required two-thirds of the states submit their resolutions? The Constitution is silent on this point. In resolutions submitting proposed amendments to the states Congress in recent years has stipulated a seven-year maximum period for ratification. A bill introduced by Sen. Sam J. Ervin Jr. (D N.C.) would apply a seven-year limit to the validity of petitions for a convention.

• Can a state rescind a previous call for a convention? The Constitution says nothing about the legality of a rescinding action. But in 1868, when New Jersey and Ohio attempted to withdraw their ratifications of the 14th Amendment, Congress refused to accept the withdrawals.

• If the required two-thirds of the legislatures issue a convention call, is Congress obligated to call the convention? By the letter of the Constitution, it would appear to have no choice. But Congress might find pretexts for invalidating individual state petitions, and the Supreme Court might consider Congress the final judge of those petitions (see *Coleman v. Miller*, 1939).

• How would Congress act to call a convention? If there were no dispute, the Judiciary Committees of the two houses probably would report appropriate resolutions which the two houses would approve. But what would happen if one of the committees refused to report such a resolution? The resolution might be considered a privileged proposition which could either be referred to committee or considered directly without committee action or recommendation. But what if opponents of the resolution in the Senate blocked action with a filibuster?

• How should a Congressional resolution calling a convention be worded? Should it—or could it—limit the convention to proposing an amendment on the subject named in the petitions from the states? Could it narrowly define that subject? The performance of state constitutional conventions raises serious doubts that a national convention to amend the Constitution could be bound in advance. Moreover, the convention that wrote the U.S. Constitution ignored its original mandate merely to amend the Articles of Confederation. But if amendments were submitted on subjects not specified in the summoning of a convention, they might be subjected to political attack on the ground that the convention had not been authorized, or its members elected, to act in other areas. Many Members of Congress are known to be concerned by the kind of amendments that a "runaway convention" might submit.

• What would be the apportionment of a constitutional convention? The Constitution is also silent on this point. The Constitutional Convention of 1787 had different numbers of delegates from different states but accorded only one vote to each state. Congress presumably could require that a new constitutional convention be apportioned on the same basis as the existing U.S. House, or the House and Senate combined.

• How would delegates be chosen? That question could be left to the discretion of the state legislatures, or Congress might attempt to lay down ground rules requiring the election either by Congressional districts or by statewide balloting, or by a combination of the two.

---

in an amazingly organic way, so that it has become inextricably intertwined with the American character and with the ideals of an open, free, pluralistic society. Other nations, all over the world, have copied its form and words, but have not always succeeded in giving it meaning in the lives, thoughts, and aspirations of their peoples. But even the enemies of freedom pay homage to the virtues of the Bill of Rights by copying its guarantees, even if only as 'parchment barriers,' as Madison would say, against the exercise of power."

Early Amendments After Bill of Rights

11th Amendment. The principle that a sovereign state could not be sued by a private individual, except with its consent, was complicated by the establishment of a Federal union. While state governments might refuse suits in their own courts, the Constitution did not indicate whether or not they could similarly refuse to be sued in a Federal court. Article III of the Constitution gave jurisdiction to Federal courts in cases "between a state and citizens of another state." Although no one doubted that a state could bring a suit against an individual, Article III had not been interpreted in state ratifying conventions as permitting an individual to sue a state without its consent. But the Supreme Court in 1793 (*Chisholm v. Georgia*) upheld the suit of executors of a British creditor against the State of Georgia, which refused to participate in the case.

The ruling gave rise to vigorous agitation on the part of those who opposed a strong Federal Government. The Massachusetts Legislature declared that the power exercised by the Supreme Court was "dangerous to the peace, safety, and independence of the several states and repugnant to the first principles of a Federal Government." The Georgia house of representatives passed a bill providing that any official who attempted to enforce the Court's decision should be declared guilty of a felony and be hanged, without benefit of clergy. Congress immediately proposed an amendment providing that the power of the Federal Judiciary "shall not be construed to extend" to private suits against states. Ratification was completed in February 1795.

12th Amendment. The Constitution provided that Presidential electors chosen in each state were to cast two votes, with no distinction between the votes for President and Vice President. The candidate receiving the highest number of votes, provided they constituted a majority, would be named President. In the absence of a majority, the House of Representatives would choose among the five candidates with the highest number of electoral votes. After selection of the President, the candidate with the next highest number of electoral votes would, in any case, be named Vice President.

The Constitutional Convention had not anticipated the development of political parties, whose candidates for the electoral college would be pledged to register the party choice for President. In 1800 the Republican party won a clear majority, with 73 electors as against 65 Federalist electors. But a deadlock resulted because all the Republicans cast one vote for Jefferson, and one vote for Aaron Burr. They had intended that Jefferson would be President and Burr Vice President, but there was no way of distinguishing the votes cast. Because no candidate had a majority, the election was thrown into the House of Representatives. There many of the Federalists voted for Burr and a deadlock persisted until the 36th ballot. *(See Power to Elect the President, Chapter III.)*

A proposed amendment, providing for separate votes by the electors for President and Vice President, was rejected by the Senate in 1802 after having received the necessary two-thirds majority in the House. In 1803, however, the proposed amendment was approved by both houses, and ratification was completed the following year in time for the election of 1804. Once this adjustment in electoral machinery was made, the two-party system kept election of the President out of the House of Representatives in every election except that of 1824.

One consequence of the change in the manner of choosing the Vice President was to reduce the prestige of that office. When filled by the man with next to the strongest support for the Presidency, the post of Vice President might serve as a platform for national leadership. After the election of 1796, Jefferson, the head of the opposition Republicans, held the office under President Adams, a Federalist. Since ratification of the 12th Amendment, the Vice Presidency has been a singularly powerless position. Statesmen of Presidential caliber often decline to run for the office, while political leaders may seek to get rid of an embarrassing party figure by placing him in the obscurity of the Vice Presidency, as in the case of Theodore Roosevelt.

Post-Civil War Amendments

13th Amendment. Anxious to preserve the Union, most northerners were not demanding abolition of slavery when the South seceded. As the Civil War progressed, however, abolition increasingly became part of the program of the Federal Government. President Lincoln and many Members of Congress at first favored proposals to compensate slave owners for their property loss. In 1862 Congress provided for release of slaves in the District of Columbia, and owners loyal to the Government received up to $300 for each slave freed. Later in the same year, the President recommended a constitutional amendment to authorize Federal aid to states that abolished slavery and provided for compensation to owners.

On Jan. 1, 1863, Lincoln issued his Emancipation Proclamation, which stated that "all persons held as slaves within any state or designated part of a state, the people whereof shall be in rebellion against the United States, shall be then, thenceforward, and forever free...." The proclamation was issued without authorization by Congress, and it had no constitutional basis other than the war powers of the President. Although the legality of the action has been much disputed, subsequent constitutional sanction was provided by the 13th Amendment. The resolution proposing this amendment, which was to abolish slavery throughout the United States, was approved by the Senate on April 8, 1864, but it failed to receive the requisite two-thirds vote in the House. The proposed amendment was an issue in the 1864 election. A Republican victory led in January 1865 to House approval by a vote of 119 to 56; a switch of only three votes would have prevented approval. Ratification was completed in December of the same year.

14th Amendment. "Black codes" adopted by southern state legislatures at the end of the war to limit the civil rights of freed slaves were among the factors leading Congress to propose the 14th Amendment. It was feared that Negro rights established by the 13th Amendment would prove hollow unless further action were taken. The Freedmen's Bureau Act and the Civil Rights Act of 1866 sought to protect basic rights, and the latter attempted to void by legislation the famous Dred Scott decision of 1857 by which the Supreme Court had denied that a free Negro, let alone a slave, could be considered a citizen of the United States. Although the Civil Rights Act was passed by two-thirds votes in both houses to override President Johnson's veto, its constitutionality remained in doubt. The 14th Amendment was intended, among other things, to give the Act constitutional support and accord permanence to the basic rights the Act was intended to guarantee.

The third and fourth sections of the Amendment were of only temporary significance. They prohibited anyone from holding state or Federal office (unless authorized by Congress) who had participated in rebellion after taking an oath to support the U.S. Constitution, and denied the responsibility of Federal or state governments for debts incurred in aid of rebellion. The second section of the Amendment in effect eliminated the clause of Article I, Section 2, of the Constitution, which directed that three-fourths of the slave population of a state was to be counted in apportioning the House of Representatives. This provision had been rendered obsolete by the 13th Amendment, but the 14th did not stop at basing apportionment on total population (exclusive of Indians not taxed). It further provided that if any state abridged the right of its citizens to vote for Federal or state offices, the number of its Representatives in the House should be decreased in proportion to the number of adult male citizens denied the vote. Thaddeus Stevens, leader of the Radicals in the House of Representatives, expected this provision to be the most effective instrument for securing Negro rights, but its inadequacy in guaranteeing the right to vote led later to the 15th Amendment.

The first section of the 14th Amendment declared that all persons born or naturalized in the United States (except those, such as diplomats, not subject to U.S. jurisdiction) were citizens of the United States and of the state in which they resided, thereby nullifying the Dred Scott decision. More importantly, it forbade states to deprive any person of life, liberty or property without due process of law, or to deny anyone equal protection of the laws.

The due process and equal protection clauses, both open to wide differences of interpretation, have served as the basis of controversial shifts in the foundations of American government. The Supreme Court at first frustrated the hopes of those backers of the 14th Amendment who expected to see the Federal Government assume large responsibilities for civil rights. Next, the Court employed the due process clause to frustrate state interference with the principles of laissez faire economics, an approach not abandoned until the New Deal era. Gradually, freedoms guaranteed by the Bill of Rights were extended, by invoking the due process clause, to cover actions by state governments. After the Second World War, the Supreme Court ruled that the equal protection clause prohibited racial segregation in schools, and Congress enacted civil rights legislation sanctioned in part by this section of the 14th Amendment.

The 14th Amendment was submitted to the states in June 1866. Ratification was refused by nine of the former Confederate states until after Congress had enacted a law making such ratification a condition of their restoration to the Union. In announcing adoption of the 14th Amendment in July 1868, Secretary of State Seward declared it had been ratified by the legislatures of 23 states and "by newly constituted and newly established bodies avowing themselves to be and acting as the legislatures" of six southern states.

15th Amendment. When it became apparent that the 14th Amendment's threat of reduced representation in the House had failed to prompt southern states to extend the franchise to Negroes, Congress proposed a more direct approach. The 15th Amendment, submitted to the states in February 1869, prohibited denial of the right to vote on the basis of race, color, or previous condition of servitude. Ratification was completed in February 1870.

Congress in the same year passed an "Enforcement Act" designed to make the Amendment effective. This statute sought to prevent the use of technicalities of registration and voting procedures to confuse and intimidate Negro voters. Heavy penalties were prescribed for state officials convicted of violating the Act. Interference with voting rights by bribery or by threats of violence or economic discrimination was outlawed. Enforcement was to be in Federal courts, and the President was authorized to use military force as necessary to support the judicial process. The Supreme Court in 1876 (*United States v. Reese*) held portions of this Act unconstitutional and in so doing limited the effectiveness of the 15th Amendment. The authority of Congress to enact "appropriate legislation" to enforce the Amendment was construed as limited to legislation to combat outright discrimination on the basis of race; the authority, it was ruled, did not extend to the whole field of obstructions of the right to vote. Nearly a century passed before Congress, in the sweeping Voting Rights Act of 1965, made available effective means for Federal enforcement of the 15th Amendment's attempt to bar racial discrimination in connection with the right to vote.

Income Tax and Election of Senators

16th Amendment. Although the Federal Government had levied an income tax during the Civil War, a similar tax imposed in 1894 was held unconstitutional by the Supreme Court in 1895 (*Pollock v. Farmers' Loan and Trust Co.*). Failure of Congress to submit a remedial amendment during subsequent years was due in part to a belief that such an amendment was unnecessary and that it would be possible to draft an income tax law that would be held constitutional.

Pressure to impose another income tax grew, but President Taft and others opposed action without an authorizing amendment. They feared that to enact a statute similar to one previously declared unconstitutional, in the expectation that the Supreme Court would reverse its earlier decision, would undermine confidence in the Constitution and would subject the Court to the pressures of a public campaign. The amendment to empower Congress to levy taxes on incomes "from whatever source derived" was approved by both houses in 1909, but ratification was not completed until early in 1913. At a special session that year, Congress enacted a graduated personal income tax and converted into a direct income tax a levy on corporation income imposed since 1909 in the guise of an excise tax. *(See Fiscal Powers, Chapter III.)*

17th Amendment. The 17th Amendment is of particular interest because it clearly was forced on Congress, or rather on the Senate, by popular pressure. The Constitution provided for the election of Senators by the state legislatures. But the 17th Amendment, ratified in 1913, changed the Constitution to provide for direct election of Senators. The change was a part of the Progressive Era's movement toward more democratic control of government. Being less immediately dependent on popular sentiment than the House, the Senate did not seek to reform itself. Only persistent pressure from the public, expressed through the House of Representatives, the state governments, pressure groups, petitions, referenda and other means, convinced the Senate that it must participate in its own reform.

In the first 80 years of Congress, only nine resolutions proposing a constitutional amendment for direct election of Senators were introduced in Congress. In the 1870s and 1880s the number increased, and by 1912 a total of not less than 287 such joint resolutions had been introduced. Not until 1892 was a resolution reported favorably from committee in the House. In the next decade such a resolution was carried five times in the House with only a handful in opposition.

Petitions from farmers' associations and other organizations, particularly in the West, and party platforms in state elections pressed the issue until the national parties took it up. Direct election of Senators was a plank in the Populist program at every election, beginning in 1892, and in the Democratic platform in each Presidential election year from 1900 to 1912. Starting in California and Iowa in 1894, state legislatures addressed Congress in favor of a direct election amendment, until by 1905 the legislatures in 31 of the 45 states had taken this step, many of them repeatedly. In 1900, when the House voted 240-15 in favor of submitting such an amendment to the states, it was supported by a majority of the Representatives from every state except Maine and Connecticut. Still the Senate would not act.

The spread of direct primaries in the 1890s led in many states to expressions of a popular choice for Senator on the primary ballot. One-party legislatures in the

South generally ratified the popular choice, though the primary was less effective in putting over the popular choice in other states. Oregon in 1901 adopted a plan under which voters could express their preferences for Senator, though their expression of a preference carried no binding legal force. When the Oregon Legislature nevertheless ignored the popular preference in its next election of a Senator, voters used their new powers of initiative and referendum to approve a new law. Henceforth candidates for the legislature could indicate on the ballot whether or not they would vote for the Senate candidate with the highest popular vote total. This "Oregon system" proved effective and was adopted in other states in modified forms. By December 1910 it was estimated that 14 of the 30 Senators about to be named by state legislatures had already been designated by popular vote.

In 1901 some of the legislatures, no longer content to request Congress to submit a constitutional amendment to the states, began calling for a convention to amend the Constitution. Some Senators, though they opposed a popular election, feared that such a convention, like the original Constitutional Convention, might exceed its original mandate; they preferred to submit to the states a specific amendment for direct election of Senators. A resolution was finally brought to the Senate floor in 1911, but it failed, 54-33, to gain the two-thirds support required. In a special session later that year, the House passed, 296-16, a different version of the resolution. The Senate this time approved its original resolution, 64-24. A deadlock was broken at the next session when the House on May 13, 1912, concurred in the Senate version. By May 1913, three-fourths of the states had ratified the 17th Amendment.

Prohibition and Woman Suffrage

18th Amendment. Prohibition and woman suffrage amendments were first proposed in the platform of the Prohibition party in 1872. Favorable Senate action on the Prohibition Amendment was taken in the special session called in 1917 to declare war on Germany; House approval of the joint resolution followed in December 1917. The vigorous campaign carried on by the Anti-Saloon League had already resulted in the enactment of Prohibition laws in more than half of the states. The war gave impetus to the movement by identifying the attack on alcoholic beverages with patriotism. The effectiveness of the armed forces and the defense industries, it was argued, would be impaired by drunkenness, and the production of alcoholic drinks would divert resources from the war effort. Under war powers granted in the Constitution, Congress enacted legislation to restrict production of liquor and its sale to members of the armed forces.

While the 18th Amendment was before the states, the Wartime Prohibition Act, approved 10 days after the Armistice was signed, prohibited sale of distilled spirits, wine, or beer in the United States from June 30, 1919, until the end of the war. The 18th Amendment was ratified in January 1919, only 13 months after its approval by Congress. Power to enforce the Amendment's prohibition of the manufacture, sale or transportation of intoxicating liquors was granted concurrently to Congress and the states, a provision which hindered enforcement by dividing responsibility. The Volstead Act, which Congress passed on Oct. 28, 1919, over President Wilson's veto, was aimed not only to enforce the Amendment but also to strengthen the Wartime Prohibition Act (which continued in effect because the country was still technically at war) until the Amendment went into force Jan. 16, 1920, one year after its ratification.

Before Prohibition was abandoned in 1933, it profoundly affected the mores of the American people in ways not anticipated by its advocates. Widespread violation of the Amendment and the Volstead Act seriously undermined respect for the law and buttressed the foundations of organized crime.

19th Amendment. Because the Constitution left qualifications for voting in Federal elections to determination by the states, early attempts to authorize woman suffrage focused on the state legislatures. At the time the 14th and 15th Amendments were considered, efforts were made to have their guarantees of voting rights for Negroes extended to women as well. These efforts having proved unsuccessful, a resolution proposing an additional amendment granting the vote to women was introduced in the Senate in 1878. The resolution was reintroduced regularly thereafter until it was finally adopted more than 40 years later.

Meanwhile, some of the states went ahead and gave the vote to women within their jurisdiction. Wyoming, which became a state in 1890, had started blazing the trail toward woman suffrage when it accorded women the right to vote for territorial officials in 1869. By 1914, equal suffrage had been granted in 11 states; New York, considered a center of opposition, joined the procession in 1917.

World War I added impetus to the suffrage movement because it was viewed as a crusade for democracy. President Wilson, who had previously favored attainment of woman suffrage by state action, explained his conversion to the amendment route in terms of the war. The House adopted the resolution proposing the woman suffrage amendment in 1918 by a vote of 274-136, a bare two-thirds majority. Wilson, in a surprise visit to the Senate on Sept. 30, urged adoption of the resolution as "vitally essential to the successful prosecution of the great war of humanity in which we are engaged." The next day, however, the Senate failed, in a 62-34 vote, to supply the necessary margin.

When the Republicans won the November election, Wilson pleaded for approval by the lame-duck Democratic Congress, but a Senate vote of 55-29 in February 1919 again fell short of the required two-thirds majority. But at a special session of the new Congress the proposed amendment was approved within three weeks. Submitted to the states in June 1919, it was ratified in August 1920. A related amendment, to guarantee equal rights to women, has been proposed in every Congress since 1923 *(see box on next page).*

Lame-Duck Amendment

20th Amendment. Like the 12th Amendment, the 20th Amendment effected a mechanical change in the Constitution. It abolished "lame-duck" sessions of Congress and advanced the date of the inauguration of the President from March 4 to Jan. 20. Under the terms of the Amendment, Congress was to convene annually at noon on Jan. 3 unless it "shall by law appoint a different day."

Equal Rights for Women

A perennial proposal for a constitutional amendment to guarantee women equal rights suddenly found its chances momentarily brightened in 1970. A resolution proposing such an amendment had been introduced in every Congress since 1923. In 1950 and 1953, the Senate had approved the proposed amendment. The House, however, had taken no action. The amendment was strenuously opposed by House Judiciary Committee Chairman Emanuel Celler (D N.Y.), who has headed the Committee (except during a Republican majority, 1953-54) since 1949.

On Aug. 10, 1970, the House by a 333-22 roll-call vote agreed to a motion to discharge the Judiciary Committee from further responsibility for the proposal. The resolution proposing the amendment (H J Res 243) was then adopted by the overwhelming vote of 352-15. The Senate took up the proposal in October, following hearings, but revisions on the floor were unacceptable to women's rights organizations and no further action was taken in the 91st Congress.

The proposed amendment would specify that "Equality of rights under the law shall not be denied or abridged by the United States or any state on account of sex. Congress and the several states shall have power, within their respective jurisdictions, to enforce this article by appropriate legislation."

The resolution's sponsor, Rep. Martha W. Griffiths (D Mich.), contended that women were discriminated against by laws covering employment, divorce and alimony, property rights, pensions and inheritances, and by some criminal laws, among other things. Celler called the measure "a blunderbuss amendment" which would do away with necessary protective legislation for women.

Numerous state laws would face court review if the amendment became part of the Constitution. Laws prohibiting women from certain dangerous or strenuous labor might be overturned. Women as well as men might be ordered to provide alimony or child support in divorce cases, and men might challenge the granting of custody of small children to their mothers. The amendment would probably make women subject for the first time to military conscription, though not necessarily for combat assignments.

Prior to this change, the Constitution provided that the terms of Representatives and outgoing Senators were not to end until March 4, four months after the election of a new Congress. While the terms of Members of the new Congress began on March 4, the first regular session did not commence until the first Monday of the following December, 13 months after the election.

Although the President often called Congress into special session in the interim, the long wait between the election and the first regular session of a new Congress, and the potential inequity inherent in actions of a lame-duck Congress at the "short session" (December-March), had drawn criticism for at least a century. Finally, in 1922, a resolution proposing an amendment to correct the situation was taken up on the floor of the Senate.

The proposed amendment was approved by the Senate no less than six times between 1923 and 1932, when the House at last took favorable action.

The reform was so popular that the 20th Amendment was ratified by Virginia on March 4, 1932, the day after it was submitted to the states. Ratification was completed in January 1933. (For the amendment's clauses on procedures to be followed in the event of certain contingencies, such as the death of the President-elect, see p. 321.)

Repeal of Prohibition

21st Amendment. Between 1921 and 1933 more than 130 amendments were proposed in Congress to repeal or modify the 18th Amendment. Prohibition had become so discredited by 1932 that the platforms of both parties favored constitutional revision. The Democrats proposed repeal of the 18th Amendment; the Republicans favored retaining some authority for the Federal Government to control liquor traffic and to protect those states that chose to continue Prohibition.

The landslide victory at the polls of Franklin D. Roosevelt, who unequivocally supported repeal, probably contributed to the decision of the lame-duck Congress at the session convened in December 1932. A joint resolution proposing an amendment to repeal the 18th Amendment was submitted to the states in February 1933 and, following ratification by the necessary 36 states, went into effect on Dec. 5 of the same year.

The 21st was the only Amendment to be ratified by state conventions rather than by the legislatures. Because delegates to these conventions were clearly identified as favoring or opposing repeal of Prohibition, they did not meet to deliberate the issues but simply to execute the will of the voters. The elections to the conventions thus amounted to a national referendum on Prohibition. The result justified the expectations of those who had proposed ratification by conventions; they sought to remove the issue from partisan politics and from organized pressures on rural-dominated legislatures, and to achieve speedy action. (For discussion of this ratification procedure, see above.)

Presidential Tenure and D.C. Vote

22nd Amendment. The first Republican Congress after President Roosevelt's election to four terms quickly approved and sent to the states a proposed amendment to limit Presidential tenure to two terms. The amendment provided that no one might be elected President more than twice; and no one who had served as President for more than two years of a term for which someone else had been elected President was to be elected more than once. The President serving when the amendment was proposed (Truman) was exempted from its provisions, and no one serving on the effective date of ratification was to be prevented from completing his term.

During House floor debate, Republicans insisted that the proposal had nothing to do with politics. The purpose, they said, was merely to incorporate in the Constitution the two-term tradition set by George Washington and maintained until 1940, when Roosevelt was elected to a third term. They urged limitation of tenure as a means of warding off any tendency toward dictatorship.

Democrats contended that the resolution would impose "a limitation upon the people," who had a right to make their own choice of President. Rep. John W. McCormack (D Mass.) declared that Washington, Jefferson and Theodore Roosevelt had stated that an emergency—such as that in 1940 and 1944—might make it advisable for a person to accept more than two terms as President.

The 22nd Amendment, submitted to the states March 24, 1947, was not ratified by the required three-fourths of the state legislatures until Feb. 27, 1951, nearly four years after its submission by Congress. In 1959 a Senate subcommittee approved a proposal to repeal the Amendment, but no further action was taken. At that time, former President Truman said he "never thought well" of the 22nd Amendment. President Eisenhower initially called it "unwise," but he later opposed repeal efforts, saying Congress should "see how it works" for a few years.

23rd Amendment. The 23rd Amendment, giving the citizens of the District of Columbia the right to vote in Presidential elections, was cleared by Congress June 16, 1960. The last time that residents of the District had voted for President was in 1800. The D.C. suffrage amendment, as originally introduced, would have allowed residents of Washington to vote for President and Vice President by giving them three representatives in the electoral college, and also would have given the District a nonvoting delegate in the House of Representatives. In order to ensure House approval and to expedite ratification of the amendment, however, Congress agreed to drop the latter provision, limiting the amendment to national suffrage.

As approved by Congress, the proposed amendment authorized the District of Columbia to appoint a number of electors for President and Vice President equal to the number of Senators and Representatives to which the District would have been entitled if it had been a state (in effect, three electors). It also authorized Congress to prescribe the qualifications of the District's electors and voters. The proposed amendment was submitted to the states June 21, 1960. Ratification was completed 282 days later, on March 29, 1961. No other amendment except the 12th in 1804, which modified the procedure for electing the President and Vice President, had been ratified so quickly.

Most of the opposition to the D.C. suffrage amendment came from the South and was apparently motivated by the race issue. (The District's population was more than 50 percent Negro.) Not a single state of the Deep South was among the ratifying states. Some Republican state legislatures were also reportedly apprehensive about the amendment because they feared the District would automatically vote Democratic. District Republican leaders sought to allay these fears, however, and it was a GOP-controlled legislature (Kansas) which gave the amendment its needed 38th ratification.

In 1961, Congress implemented the 23rd Amendment by enacting legislation spelling out the regulations under which District residents might participate in Presidential elections. Principal discussion on the bill centered on voting age and residence requirements. President Kennedy on May 16 submitted draft legislation which provided both for a 90-day residence requirement and an 18-year-old minimum voting age in the District, but the bill, as enacted, established a one-year residence requirement and a minimum voting age of 21.

Time Taken to Ratify Amendments

The time elapsing between the submission by Congress of a constitutional amendment and its ratification by the requisite number of states has averaged about one and one-half years. The first 10 amendments were proposed and ratified as a group, the process taking two years, two months, and 20 days. The longest time of all—three years, 11 months, and three days—was needed to complete ratification of the 22nd Amendment. In contrast, the 12th Amendment went through in seven months and 16 days, and seven other amendments were ratified in less than one year. The detailed record follows:

Amendment	Proposed	Ratified	Years	Months	Days
1-10 (Bill of Rights)	Sept. 25, 1789	Dec. 15, 1791	2	2	20
11 (Suits Against States)	Mar. 4, 1794	Feb. 7, 1795		11	3
12 (Presidential Electors)	Dec. 9, 1803	July 27, 1804		7	16
13 (Abolition of Slavery)	Jan. 31, 1865	Dec. 9, 1865		10	9
14 (Civil Rights; Due Process)	June 13, 1866	July 9, 1868	2		26
15 (Negro Suffrage)	Feb. 26, 1869	Feb. 17, 1870		11	22
16 (Income Tax)	July 12, 1909	Feb. 3, 1913	3	6	23
17 (Direct Election of Senators)	May 15, 1912	May 9, 1913		11	25
18 (Prohibition)	Dec. 3, 1917	Jan. 17, 1919	1	1	14
19 (Woman Suffrage)	June 5, 1919	Aug. 24, 1920	1	2	19
20 ("Lame-Duck")	Mar. 3, 1932	Jan. 24, 1933		10	21
21 (Prohibition Repeal)	Feb. 20, 1933	Dec. 5, 1933		9	15
22 (Presidential Tenure)	Mar. 24, 1947	Feb. 27, 1951	3	11	3
23 (D.C. Vote)	June 21, 1960	Mar. 29, 1961		9	8
24 (Poll Tax)	Aug. 27, 1962	Jan. 23, 1964	1	4	27
25 (Presidential Disability)	July 6, 1965	Feb. 10, 1967	1	7	3

Poll Taxes and Presidential Disability

24th Amendment. Poll taxes were introduced in some states during the early days of the Republic as a substitute for property qualifications for voting. The intent of the early levies was to enlarge the electorate. These taxes had been eliminated in most states before the Civil War, but between 1889 and 1908 poll taxes were instituted in 11 Southern states. Though ostensibly adopted to "cleanse" elections of mass abuse, the taxes were approved in the South as a means of keeping Negroes and poor whites from the polls. By 1953, however, only five Southern states still required payment of a poll tax as a prerequisite for voting.

Bills to ban such poll taxes by statute, rather than by constitutional amendment, were approved five times between 1942 and 1949 by the House, but died each time in the Senate, with filibusters in 1942, 1944 and 1946. Beginning in 1949, Sen. Holland (D Fla.) introduced a proposed anti-poll tax amendment in every Congress, but it was never reported by the Senate Judiciary Committee. Those who preferred action by legislation feared that reliance on amendment of the Constitution to effect the desired reform would set a precedent that would make other civil rights measures more difficult to enact.

On the theory that poll taxes were not specifically designed to keep Negroes from voting, Holland and most of his supporters argued that there was no language in the Constitution that barred a poll tax and therefore it had to be achieved by the amendment process. To do otherwise, they said, would open the states' control over election machinery to attack by Federal legislation. (Language in Article I, Section 2, and in the 17th Amendment to the Constitution set the "qualifications" for voters in Federal elections as those "requisite" for the electors of the most numerous branch of the state legislature.)

Offered by Holland as a substitute for a minor measure in 1962, the joint resolution proposing the poll tax amendment was approved by the Senate in a 77-16 roll call. The House adopted the resolution, 295-86, on Aug. 27, 1962, and ratification was completed Jan. 23, 1964. The Amendment outlawed payment of "any poll tax or other tax" as a voter qualification only in Federal elections. A move to extend the ban to state and local elections through the Voting Rights Act of 1965 was not successful, but the final compromise version of the Act contained a finding that poll taxes in certain states denied or abridged the right to vote. The Act directed the Attorney General to challenge those taxes in the courts "forthwith." The Supreme Court in 1966 (*Harper v. Virginia State Board of Elections* and *Butts v. Harrison*, decided as one case) struck down Virginia's poll-tax requirement for state elections as a violation of the equal protection clause of the 14th Amendment.

25th Amendment. Congressional consideration of the question of Presidential disability was prompted by President Eisenhower's heart attack in 1955. But ambiguity in the language of the disability clause, Article II, Section I, Clause 6 of the Constitution, had provoked occasional debate ever since the Constitutional Convention of 1787. It had never been agreed how far the term "disability" extended or who was to be the judge of it.

Clause 6 provided that Congress should decide who was to succeed to the Presidency in the event that both the President and the Vice President died, resigned, or became disabled. Congress enacted succession laws three times, but the procedures to follow in the event of Presidential incapacity had not been laid down by statute. Two Presidents had become seriously disabled in office—President Garfield, who lived for 11 weeks after he was shot in 1881, and President Wilson, who suffered a severe stroke in 1919. In each case the Vice President did not assume any duties of the Presidency for fear he would appear to be usurping the powers of that office. After President Eisenhower's series of illnesses in 1955, 1956 and 1957, the President and Vice President Nixon entered into an agreement for an orderly, temporary transfer of power should the President again become incapacitated. Nixon would have become Acting President after "such consultation as it seems to him appropriate under the circumstances." Presidents Kennedy and Johnson made the same agreements with their respective successors, but the legality of these informal arrangements was questioned by some.

The joint resolution proposing the 25th Amendment was introduced in January 1965 and approved by Congress, with scarcely any opposition, six months later. Ratification was completed Feb. 10, 1967. The Amendment provided that the Vice President should become Acting President under either one of two circumstances. If the President informed Congress that he was unable to perform his duties, the Vice President would become Acting President until the President could resume his responsibilities.

If the Vice President and a majority of the Cabinet, or other body designated by Congress, found the President to be incapacitated, the Vice President would become Acting President until the President informed Congress that his disability had ended. Congress was given 21 days to resolve any dispute over the President's disability.

Whenever a vacancy occurred in the office of Vice President, either by death, succession to the Presidency or resignation, the President was to nominate a Vice President to be confirmed by a majority vote of both houses of Congress.

Bibliography

Books

Boorstin, Daniel J., *An American Primer*. University of Chicago Press, 1966.

Burns, James MacGregor, and Peltason, Jack Walter, *Government by the People*. Prentice Hall, 1963 (5th edit.).

Congress and the Nation, 1945-1964 (Vol. I). Congressional Quarterly, 1965.

Congress and the Nation, 1965-1968 (Vol. II). Congressional Quarterly, 1969.

Haynes, George H., *The Senate of the United States*. Houghton Mifflin Co., 1938.

Pritchett, C. Herman, *The American Constitution*. McGraw-Hill, 1968 (2nd edit.).

Warren, Charles, *The Making of the Constitution*. Little, Brown and Co., 1928.

Articles

Forbush, Emory, "The Poll Tax," *Editorial Research Reports*, July 3, 1941, p. 1-18.

Patch, Buel W., "Tax and Debt Limitation," *Editorial Research Reports*, Feb. 13, 1952, p. 121-140.

Putney, Bryant, "Revision of the Constitution," *Editorial Research Reports*, April 21, 1937, p. 285-303.

Government Publications

Ames, Herman V., *The Proposed Amendments to the Constitution of the United States During the First Century of Its History*. House Document 353, pt. 2, 54th Congress (1896).

Library of Congress, Legislative Reference Service, *The Constitution of the United States: Analysis and Interpretation*. Senate Document 39, 88th Congress, 1st Session (1964).

Musmanno, Michael A., *Proposed Amendments to the Constitution of the United States, 1889-1928*. House Document 551, 70th Congress, 2nd Session (1929).

Senate Library, *Proposed Amendments to the Constitution of the United States, 1926-1963*. Senate Document 163, 87th Congress, 2nd Session (1963).

Senate Library, *Proposed Amendments to the Constitution of the United States of America, 1963-1969*. Senate Document 91-38, 91st Congress, 1st Session (1969).

Seating and Disciplining of Members

IN LAYING DOWN the authority of Congress to seat, unseat and punish its Members, the Constitutional Convention of 1787 drew inspiration from its favorite concept, that of checks and balances. The Constitution, while empowering Congress to pass judgment on the qualifications of Members, put bounds on that power by listing certain mandatory qualifications. In carrying out the concept of a balance of power among the branches of the Federal Government, the Judicial Branch has been called on at various times to interpret the authority of Congress under the constitutional clauses on membership qualifications and on punishment of Members' misconduct.

The power of Congress to determine whether a Member-elect fulfills the requirements for service as a national legislator has come into conflict, over the years, with the right of voters in each state to decide who shall represent them. When Congress has ruled on disputed elections, the uncertain citizenship of a Member-elect, or other questions of competence, Senators or Representatives from all over the country have decided whether a state may or may not be represented in Washington by a person certified by the state as the choice of its electorate.

Although Congress has acted often to determine the winner in contested elections, it has rejected the clear choice of the voters, for lack of the requisite qualifications, in fewer than 20 cases since 1789. Congress has shown like restraint in exercise of its constitutional right to punish or expel Members for disorderly or improper conduct. Seven Senators and 18 Representatives have been formally censured by their colleagues for misconduct. Expulsions have numbered 15 in the Senate and three in the House.

Constitutional Provisions

The authority of Congress to judge the qualifications of Members and to punish those who behave improperly rests on two clauses in Article I of the Constitution. The first is Clause 1 of Article I, Section 5, which reads: "Each house shall be the judge of the elections, returns and qualifications of its own Members." This clause would appear to give each house carte blanche in the validation of elections and the seating of Members-elect. However, the election of Members of Congress is regulated elsewhere in Article I and in the 17th Amendment. In addition, the Constitution specifically lists the qualifications required for membership in Congress.

The second clause on seating, unseating, and punishment of Members is Clause 2 of Article I, Section 5, reading: "Each House may determine the rules of its proceedings, punish its Members for disorderly behavior and, with the concurrence of two-thirds, expel a Member." The original draft of this clause did not include the words "with the concurrence of two-thirds." When the clause was considered in the Constitutional Convention, Aug. 10, 1787, James Madison of Virginia said that the right of expulsion was "too important to be exercised by a bare majority of a quorum, and in emergencies might be dangerously abused." He therefore proposed requiring a two-thirds vote for expulsion.

Gouverneur Morris, of Pennsylvania, opposed Madison's proposal. He said: "This power may be safely trusted to a majority. To require more may produce abuses on the side of the minority. A few men from fractious motives may keep in a Member who ought to be expelled." But Edmund Randolph and George Mason of Virginia and Daniel Carroll of Maryland spoke in support of Madison's proposal, and it was adopted by a vote of 10 states in favor, one (Pennsylvania) divided, and none opposed.

Judicial Interpretations

Litigation on the seating and disciplining of Members of Congress reached the Supreme Court in the latter part of the 19th century in suits pivoting mainly on legalistic

---

Constitutional Qualifications for Membership in Congress

- A Senator must be at least 30 years old and have been a citizen of the United States not less than nine years (Article I, Section 3, Clause 3).
- A Representative must be at least 25 years old and have been a citizen not less than seven years (Article I, Section 2, Clause 2).
- Every Member of Congress must be, when elected, an inhabitant of the state that he is to represent (Article I, Section 2, Clause 2, and Section 3, Clause 3).
- No one may be a Member of Congress who holds any other "office under the United States" (Article I, Section 6, Clause 2).
- No person may be a Senator or a Representative who, having previously taken an oath as a Member of Congress to support the Constitution, has engaged in rebellion against the United States or given aid or comfort to its enemies, unless Congress has removed such disability by a two-thirds vote of both houses (14th Amendment, Clause 3).

questions such as the power of Congress to subpoena witnesses when considering the qualifications of Members. These suits afforded the Court an opportunity to indicate bases upon which to judge the qualifications of Members and to suggest the scope of punishment that may be imposed on Members. In cases argued during the present century, the Court has ruled more directly on the nature of the power of Congress to exclude Members-elect and to punish or expel sitting Members.

Application of the constitutional clause on judgment of the qualifications of Members-elect has raised more questions of interpretation than has use of the authority to punish Members. Perhaps the most serious of the issues involved in these cases has been whether exclusion of a Member-elect deprives a state unwarrantedly, even for a short time, of its constitutionally guaranteed representation in Congress. The Court ruled on this question in a case based on the contested election to the Senate in 1926 of William S. Vare of Pennsylvania. It said that exclusion in such a case did not violate a state's rights. But the right of a state to send to Congress anyone it chooses, if he has the constitutionally listed qualifications and is legally elected, was upheld by the Court in a recent case in which it reversed the exclusion of Adam Clayton Powell Jr. of New York from the House of Representatives.

Right to Imprison a Member. The Supreme Court, in its 1880-81 term, handed down a decision which did not involve the seat or good standing of a Member of either house of Congress but which specified a form of punishment which the House of Representatives might impose on a member guilty of misconduct. The case stemmed from an order by the House, March 14, 1876, for the arrest and detention of Hallett Kilbourn, a business broker in the District of Columbia, who had refused to produce papers needed in a House investigation of the bankruptcy of Jay Cooke and Co. Kilbourn brought suit, contending that punishment of an individual in his situation was not included in the powers allotted to Congress by the Constitution.

The year in which the House ordered Kilbourn's arrest was notable for financial scandals allegedly involving House Members. Although the bankruptcy of the Cooke firm raised questions about the conduct of officers in an Executive department rather than Members of Congress, charges which arose in 1876 over trading in Union Pacific Railroad bonds and maneuverings of the Credit Mobilier affected several House Members, including Speaker James G. Blaine (R Maine). The Kilbourn case therefore proceeded in an atmosphere of suspicion about the financial dealings of House Members.

Justice Samuel F. Miller delivered the opinion of the Supreme Court in *Kilbourn v. Thompson (Sergeant-at-Arms)*. The Court denied the right of the House of Representatives to imprison Kilbourn: "No person can be punished for contumacy as a witness before either House, unless his testimony is required in a matter into which that House has jurisdiction to inquire" (103 U.S. 190). The House resolution authorizing the investigation of the Jay Cooke bankruptcy, the Court said, "was in excess of the power conferred on that body by the Constitution." In denying the right of the House to imprison Kilbourn, the Court referred to the power of Congress to judge the qualifications of Members. Speaking in the context of calls for punishment of Members accused of unethical

financial involvement in the businesses under investigation, it said:

- "The Constitution expressly empowers each House to punish its own Members for disorderly behavior. We see no reason to doubt that this punishment may in a proper case be imprisonment."

- "Each House is by the Constitution made the judge of the election and qualifications of its Members. In deciding on these it has an undoubted right to examine witnesses and inspect papers, subject to the usual rights of witnesses in such cases; and it may be that a witness would be subject to like punishment at the hands of the body engaged in trying a contested election, for refusing to testify, that he would if the case were pending before a court of judicature."

Right to Compel Testimony. In Kilbourn's case, the Supreme Court said that each house of Congress had the right to examine witnesses, and punish them for refusal to answer, when the election and qualifications of Members were at issue. Nevertheless, that right was questioned in a subsequent case which centered on legislation enacted prior to the Kilbourn case. An Act of Jan. 24, 1857, as amended Jan. 24, 1862, required witnesses to answer summonses, and respond to questions, on "any matter under inquiry before either House or any committee of either House of Congress." Interpretation of the words "any matter" as used in this Act came into play in an investigation of stock deals of Senators.

Elverton R. Chapman, a New York stockbroker, was indicted, Oct. 1, 1894, for violating the 1857 and 1862 statutes by refusing to answer questions about the accounts of Senators. Chapman's lawyers contended that the statutes were unconstitutional and that the Senate had no right to demand answers to questions about these accounts. The case reached the Supreme Court on appeal. Chief Justice Melville W. Fuller on April 19, 1897, delivered the opinion of the Court, which upheld the constitutionality of the laws in question so long as reasonable limits were placed on the meaning of the words "any matter." On the right of the Senate to pursue the particular inquiry, the Court said:

"Nor will it do to hold that the Senate had no jurisdiction to pursue the particular inquiry because the preamble and resolutions did not specify that the proceedings were taken for the purpose of censure or expulsion, if certain facts were disclosed by the investigation. The matter was within the range of the constitutional powers of the Senate. The resolutions adequately indicated that the transactions referred to were deemed by the Senate reprehensible and deserving of condemnation and punishment. The right to expel extends to all cases where the offense is such as in the judgment of the Senate is inconsistent with the trust and duty of a Member" *(In re Chapman*, 166 U.S. 669-670).

Question of Automatic Expulsion. The reference to expulsion in the Court's opinion of 1897 was supplemented in an opinion handed down in 1906 interpreting an Act of Congress approved June 11, 1864. The Act provided that any Senator or Representative found guilty of illegally receiving compensation for services rendered in connection with a claim, contract, or other proceeding before a Government agency "shall...be rendered forever thereafter incapable of holding any office...under the Government of the United States." Sen. Joseph R. Burton (R Kan.) had been convicted on a charge of illegally receiving such compensation, and the question of his right to retain his seat in the Senate consequently arose. Burton's lawyers contended that the Act of 1864 violated the constitutional right of the Senate to decide on expulsion of its Members.

Justice John M. Harlan, delivering the Court's opinion on May 21, 1906, said: "The final judgment of conviction did not operate, *ipso facto*, to vacate the seat of the convicted Senator nor compel the Senate to expel him or to regard him as expelled by force alone of the judgment" (*Burton v. United States*, 202 U.S. 369). On the following day, the Senate asked its Committee on Privileges and Elections to report what options remained and what further action, if any, should be taken in relation to Burton's seat. Burton resigned on June 4, 1906, before the Committee had prepared a report.

Newberry and Vare Cases

Exclusion for Misconduct in Primary Election. Misconduct, not by sitting Members of Congress, but by a Member-elect was the problem in the next major case requiring the Supreme Court to rule on the power of Congress to judge its Members' qualifications. This case grew out of the Federal Corrupt Practices Act of June 25, 1910, as amended Aug. 19, 1911. The two laws limited the amount of money that a candidate for Congress could spend on his campaign.

Truman H. Newberry and 16 others were found guilty of conspiring to violate the corrupt practices legislation in the Democratic Senatorial primary election of Aug. 27, 1918, in Michigan. Newberry's opponent in the primary was Henry Ford. The conviction was appealed up to the Supreme Court. Here, the issue was whether Congress, despite its lack of express authority to regulate primary elections, might exercise some control over them through its right to pass judgment on its Members' qualifications.

In *Newberry v. United States* (256 U.S. 258), the Court took a restrictive view of the constitutional grant to Congress of power to judge the qualifications of Members. It decided, May 2, 1921, that Congress did not have power to control in any way a state's party primaries or conventions for designating candidates for the Senate or the House. A concurring opinion by Justice Mahlon Pitney, in which Justices Louis D. Brandeis and John H. Clarke joined, went beyond the inapplicability of the Corrupt Practices Act to primaries. On the right of Congress to exclude Newberry, Pitney said: "I am unable to see how, in right reason, it can be held that one of the houses of Congress, on the just exercise of its power, may exclude an elected Member for securing by bribery his nomination at the primary, if the regulation by law of his conduct at the primary is beyond the constitutional power of Congress itself."

The concurring opinion made these additional points: (1) "The power of each house, even if it might rightfully be applied to exclude a Member in the case suggested,... can impose no penal consequences upon the offender"; that is, Newberry and his associates could not be punished by the courts for violating, in a primary election, standards set up by Congress for Congressional elections. (2) The right of either house to exclude a Member-elect "is exerted at the will of but a single house, not by Congress as a law-making body"; in other words, either house, in judging the qualifications of its Members, is

not authorized to set up standards having the effect of legislation.

Twenty years after the Newberry decision, the Supreme Court reversed itself on the right of Congress to legislate on primary elections. Justice Harlan F. Stone on May 26, 1941, delivered the opinion of the Court in *United States v. Classic*. He said that the power to regulate national elections, assigned by the Constitution to Congress, "includes the authority to regulate primary elections when, as in this case, they are a step in the exercise by the people of their choice of representatives in Congress" (313 U.S. 317).

Right to Subpoena Ballot Boxes. Investigatorial powers inherent in the right of each house of Congress to judge the qualifications of its Members, although passed on by the Supreme Court in the Kilbourn and Chapman cases, came up again as an unsettled question following the Senatorial election of Nov. 2, 1926, in Pennsylvania. William S. Vare, Republican, was declared the winner of the election over William B. Wilson, Democrat. But in view of reports of corruption in the election, the Senate established a committee consisting of James A. Reed (D Mo.) and others to investigate the Pennsylvania election campaign. Reed and his committee filed a suit aimed to compel local officials to produce ballot boxes for inspection. The ballot boxes were produced, but the question of the committee's right to sue remained open.

The question reached the Supreme Court in *Reed et al. v. County Commissioners of Delaware County, Pa.* Lawyers for the committee contended that its right to sue was derived from "powers of inquiry auxiliary to the power to judge the elections, returns, and qualifications of the Members of the Senate, or auxiliary to the power to legislate for the regulation of the times and manner of holding Senatorial elections." The Court's opinion, delivered May 28, 1928, by Justice Pierce Butler, reaffirmed the right of each house of Congress to "secure information upon which to decide concerning elections" but ruled that the wording of the resolution setting up the Reed committee did not give it the right to sue. The Senate on Dec. 6, 1929, denied Vare his seat *(see below)*.

Denial of State Representation

Not until 1929 was the Supreme Court required to rule on the question whether a house of Congress, in excluding a Member-elect, deprives a state, though only temporarily, of its right to representation. Presented for decision was a case involving that question in only a secondary way, but the Court took the occasion to state its view on the question. The case arose because Thomas W. Cunningham, member of a William S. Vare-for-Senator organization, refused to answer a Senate committee's questions on the organization's funds. On March 22, 1928, the Senate adopted a resolution ordering Cunningham to be taken into custody. He petitioned for a writ of habeas corpus, contending that the Senate had exceeded its powers.

The case was appealed to the Supreme Court as *Barry, Sergeant-at-Arms of the United States Senate, et al. v. United States ex rel. Cunningham.* In an opinion delivered by Justice George Sutherland on May 27, 1929, the Court pointed out that the Senate's authority "to secure information upon which to decide concerning

elect William S. Vare for lack of a qualification, integrity, not listed in the Constitution. Agreeing essentially with Root, Wickersham wrote: "The vote of a Senator elections," as established in earlier cases, "necessarily involves the ascertainment of facts, the attendance of witnesses, the examination of such witnesses." And it concluded that "the inquiry in which the Senate was engaged, and in respect of which it required the arrest and production of Cunningham, was within its constitutional authority."

The Court referred to the contention that the power which the Constitution conferred on the Senate was the power of judging the elections, returns, and qualifications of its Members and that, the Senate having refused to seat Vare, he was not a Member. "When a candidate is elected to either house, he of course is elected a Member of the body; and when that body determines, upon presentation of his credentials, without first giving him his seat, that the election is void, there would seem to be no real substance in the claim that the election of a 'Member' has not been adjudged. To hold otherwise would be to interpret the word 'Member' with a strictness in no way required by the obvious purpose of the constitutional provisions,...which, so far as the present case is concerned, was to vest the Senate with the authority to exclude persons asserting membership, who either had not been elected or, what amounts to the same thing, had been elected by resort to fraud, bribery, corruption, or other sinister methods having the effect of vitiating the election."

The Supreme Court's decision on this case dealt with two additional questions: (1) whether Congress, in judging election contests, was violating the principle of separation of powers by acting as if it were part of the Judicial Branch of the Government, and (2) whether exclusion or expulsion of a Member of Congress unwarrantedly deprived a state temporarily of its constitutionally guaranteed representation in the national Legislature. On the first question, the Court said that the Constitution, by authorizing Congress to be the judge of its Members' qualifications, conferred on each house "certain powers which are not legislative but judicial in character," including the power "to render a judgment which is beyond the authority of any other tribunal to review."

Taking up the second question, the Court made a pronouncement on the most important issue presented in the case, although the issue was not central to the situation affecting Cunningham: "Nor is there merit in the suggestion that the effect of the refusal of the Senate to seat Vare pending investigation was to deprive the state of its equal representation in the Senate. The equal representation clause is found in Article V, which authorizes and regulates amendments to the Constitution, 'provided, ...that no state, without its consent, shall be deprived of its equal suffrage in the Senate.' This constitutes a limitation upon the power of amendment and has nothing to do with a situation such as the one here presented. The temporary deprivation of equal representation which results from the refusal of the Senate to seat a Member pending inquiry as to his election or qualifications is the necessary consequence of the exercise of a constitutional power, and no more deprives the state of its 'equal suffrage' in the constitutional sense than would a vote of the Senate vacating the seat of a sitting Member or a vote of expulsion" (279 U.S. 615).

The Supreme Court in 1969, while pointing to the right of either house to expel a member for any kind of misconduct, limited the grounds on which a Member-elect might be excluded to those specifically listed in the Constitution. Adam Clayton Powell Jr. (D N.Y.), whose exclusion gave rise to the case, was elected to the House of Representatives in 1944 and every two years thereafter. When the 90th Congress in 1967 denied Powell the seat to which he had been re-elected in 1966, on the ground that he had misappropriated public funds, Powell and 13 voters in his district brought suit against the officers of the House.

The American Civil Liberties Union, submitting a brief as amicus curiae (friend of the court), argued that the House should have confined its inquiry to Powell's constitutional qualifications of age, citizenship, and residence, and that any inquiry into his conduct should have been attended by the rights of due process, including cross-examination. A Federal district judge dismissed the case, but Powell's lawyers filed an appeal. The Circuit Court of Appeals on Feb. 28, 1968, affirmed the lower court's decision. Powell and his fellow plaintiffs then appealed the case to the Supreme Court, which agreed to review it.

The case was entered on the docket as *Adam Clayton Powell Jr. et al., Petitioners, v. John W. McCormack et al.* While the case was pending, the 91st Congress seated Powell, who had been re-elected again in 1968, but the Court felt that the issues that had been raised in the suit, including Powell's claim for back pay, required settlement. Chief Justice Earl Warren on June 16, 1969, delivered the opinion of the Court, in which the following were the main points:

• The Court rejected Speaker McCormack's claim of immunity, which he had based on the constitutional guarantee to Members of both houses against being held to account for what they said in Congress.

• "In judging the qualifications of its Members Congress is limited to the standing qualifications prescribed in the Constitution. Respondents (McCormack et al.) concede that Powell met these.... Therefore, we hold that, since Adam Clayton Powell Jr. was duly elected...and was not ineligible to serve under any provision of the Constitution, the House was without power to exclude him from its membership." (395 U.S. 550)

A claim for back pay was remanded to the U.S. Court for the District of Columbia for further proceedings but was dismissed by Judge George L. Hart Jr., May 14, 1971, when Powell failed to press the matter.

Seating of Members-Elect

The Constitution provides in Article VI that Senators and Representatives "shall be bound by oath or affirmation, to support this Constitution." Congress in implementing that provision, has enacted laws, adopted rules, and made ad hoc decisions. These determinations not only prescribed the form of the oath and procedures for administering it, but also settled such questions as whether a Member whose right to his seat is disputed should take the oath before the dispute is settled or only after it has been settled in his favor. The ad hoc decisions have gone sometimes one way and sometimes another.

The oath of office of members of Congress was worded as follows by an Act of June 1, 1789: "I, A B, do solemnly swear (or affirm) that I will support the Constitution of the United States." In the light of Civil War experience, this language was expanded by an Act of July 11, 1868, to read: "I, A B, do solemnly swear (or affirm) that I will support and defend the Constitution of the United States against all enemies, foreign and domestic; that I will bear true faith and allegiance to the same; that I take this obligation freely, without any mental reservation or purpose of evasion; and that I will well and faithfully discharge the duties of the office on which I am about to enter. So help me God."

Before the first meeting of each Congress, the Secretary of the Senate and the Clerk of the next preceding House of Representatives compile lists of Members-elect on the basis of certifications signed by the state governors and secretaries of state. At the first meeting of each house in the new Congress, the presiding officer administers the oath orally in the form of a question beginning "Do you solemnly swear (or affirm)...?" and the answer by each new Member is "I do." The new Member later receives two printed copies of the oath for signature and retains one copy. New Members chosen by the states between regular elections are similarly sworn in when they take their seats.

The number of new Members who are sworn in together has varied. In the Senate, the oath was administered in some Congresses to groups of four and in later Congresses to all new Members at once; since 1927, the oath again has been administered to groups of four. In the House, the oath was administered for many years by state delegations; since 1929, to all new Members at once.

Challenge Procedure. The right of a Member-elect to take the oath of office and be seated as a Member may be challenged by an already seated Member of Congress or by a private individual or group. A Member-elect whose title to his seat is questioned presents himself in the usual way for the purpose of taking an oath. The presiding officer then, either on his own authority or, more often, on the basis of a motion duly made and carried, may ask the individual to stand aside while the oath is administered to other Members-elect. Sometimes, instead, a Member-elect is permitted to take the oath of office without prejudice, and a resolution calling for investigation of his right to the seat is introduced later.

If a Member-elect has stood aside while others were sworn in, he nevertheless may be accorded the privilege of the floor. The House in particular has accorded to election contestants the privilege of speaking in behalf of their right to be seated. House Rule 33, which lists those who may be "admitted to the Hall of the House," includes "contestants in election cases during the pendency of their cases in the House." The Senate rule on admission to the floor does not include those involved in election contests.

The question whether a claimant to a seat in Congress is entitled to it is usually referred to a committee. Sometimes, a select committee is established for this purpose; at other times, the question is referred to the Senate or House Committee on Administration or another standing committee. Often, the committee assigned such a question conducts hearings. The committee, in reporting its findings, usually presents a draft resolution incorporating its recommendations.

Controversies Over Qualifications

Whether Congress, or either house of Congress, had power to set up qualifications for membership beyond those listed by the Constitution, or power to overlook the lack of one of the constitutional requirements, was a question answered sometimes in the affirmative and sometimes in the negative. Until the Supreme Court gave a negative answer in the Powell case, Congress had acted from time to time as if it was entitled to add qualifications as well as to wink at failure to fulfill a stated qualification.

Alexander Hamilton initiated discussion of the question. In No. 60 of the *Federalist Papers*, he wrote: "The qualifications of the persons who may...be chosen are defined and fixed in the Constitution, and are unalterable by the Legislature." However, later authorities, including a committee of the House of Representatives appointed in 1900 to consider the seating of a Mormon, contended that the Constitutional Convention intended to empower Congress to add to the listed qualifications. Their argument ran as follows:

• The wording of the qualification clauses in preliminary drafts was affirmative, reading, for example, "Every Member of the House of Representatives shall be of the age of 25 years at least."

• On July 26, 1787, James Wilson of Pennsylvania opposed that wording on the ground that "A partial enumeration...(of grounds on which a Member-elect may be challenged) will disable the Legislature from disqualifying odious and dangerous characters."

• The committee on style changed to the supposedly more flexible negative phrasing, so that, for example, the provision on age for a member of the House reads: "No Person shall be a Representative who shall not have attained to the age of twenty-five years."

• The change to the negative, in the opinion of the House committee and others, meant that the constitutional listing was not intended to prevent the addition by Congress of other qualifications. If the Convention had wanted its list of qualifications to be exclusive, the committee said, it would have worded the qualifications clauses affirmatively and categorically, thus: "Every person who has attained...(a certain age, years of citizenship, and so forth) shall be eligible for a seat in the House of Representatives." A minority of the members of the 1900 committee disagreed with this conclusion.

The same question as applying to Senators was widely discussed over an extended period. Sen. Elihu Root (R N.Y.), referring to a contested election in 1911, said: "There exists no power in any Government short of an amendment to the Constitution of the United States to limit or control the evidence we shall receive or the grounds upon which we shall act in judging the qualification and election of members. The sole limit is imposed by our own sense of what is just and right and for the public weal."

In 1927, Price Wickersham, a Kansas City legal scholar, studied the right of the Senate to exclude Senator-

affects every State of the Union. His vote may mean peace or war for the Union. Should not the Union have the right to protect itself against corruption in one of its parts?" However, Sen. Robert A. Taft (R Ohio) asserted in 1946 that the membership qualifications which the two houses may judge are limited to those enumerated in the Constitution.

Congress faced a dilemma on this matter. If it adhered rigidly to the constitutional list of requirements, it would be obligated to seat individuals regarded as obnoxious. If it excluded such individuals, it would be open to the charge of exceeding its powers. Congress grasped the second horn of the dilemma. The issue came to a head at the start of the Civil War.

The two houses added a qualification for membership by enacting a law on the subject in 1862. The Act approved July 2 of that year, known as the "Ironclad Oath Law" or the "Test Oath Law," required Members of the House and Senate to swear, before taking the oath of office, that they had never voluntarily borne arms against the United States or aided, recognized, or supported a jurisdiction hostile to the United States. This law remained in effect until the Fourteenth Amendment was ratified in 1868. Westel W. Willoughby wrote in *The Constitutional Law of the United States* that during the period in which this act was in force, "Congress imposed, in effect, a disqualification for membership in either of its houses which was not imposed by the Constitution."

At the same time, Willoughby pointed out: "Though neither house may formally impose qualifications additional to those mentioned in the Constitution, or waive those that are mentioned, they may, in practice, do either of these things. That is to say, in case these constitutional provisions are disregarded or added to by either of the houses of Congress, there is no judicial means of overruling their action." The Supreme Court found otherwise in the Powell case.

Cases Occurring in the Senate

Three Senators-elect have been denied seats for lack of the requisite qualifications:

(1) Albert Gallatin, born in Geneva, became a citizen of the United States in 1785. When elected to the Senate by the Pennsylvania Legislature in 1793, he had not been a citizen nine years as required by the Constitution. He contended, however, that every man who had taken part in the Revolution was a citizen according to the law of reason and nature. The Senate on Feb. 28, 1794, adopted the following resolution by a vote of 14 yeas to 12 nays: "Resolved, That the election of Albert Gallatin to be a Senator of the United States was void, he not having been a citizen of the United States the term of years required as a qualification to be a Senator of the United States."

(2) James Shields, a native of Ireland, was elected a Senator from Illinois in 1848. When he appeared, March 5, 1849, to take his seat, at a special session of the Senate, the question of whether he had been a citizen the required number of years was raised. Although Shields was seated on March 6, the Senate on March 15 adopted a resolution declaring his election void on the ground of insufficient years of citizenship. Shields then was elected to fill the vacancy thus created and was allowed to serve from Oct. 27, 1849.

(3) Phillip F. Thomas of Maryland had given $100 to his son when the son entered the military service of the Confederacy. When Thomas was elected a U.S. Senator by the Maryland Legislature in 1866, the question of admitting him elicited from Sen. Charles Sumner (R Mass.) the comment that "The 'open sesame' of this chamber must be something more than the oath of a suspected applicant." The Senate voted 27 to 20 to exclude Thomas.

Exclusion proceedings based on the age qualification for Senators were avoided, in two cases, by different means. When Henry Clay (Ind. Ky.) arrived in Washington to take his seat as a Senator, he lacked five months of the required 30 years. The Senate tacitly ignored this fact, and he was sworn in, Nov. 19, 1806. Rush D. Holt (D W.Va.) also had not reached the age of 30 when the time came for him to enter the Senate in 1935. He delayed the presentation of his credentials until his 30th birthday and was then admitted. The Senate later rejected, 62-17, a proposal to declare Holt's election invalid on the ground of age.

Several cases in which exclusion proceedings were begun and failed are noteworthy. John M. Niles, elected to the Senate by the Connecticut Legislature in 1842, was unable to take his seat, owing to severe illness, when the 28th Congress first convened in December 1843. Because Niles showed signs of mental strain when he first appeared with his credentials in April 1844, the Senate appointed a committee to consider his case. After interviewing him, it reported: "The committee are satisfied that Mr. Niles is at this time laboring under mental and physical debility, but is not of unsound mind in the technical sense of that phrase; the faculties of his mind are subject to the control of his will; and there is no sufficient reason why he be not qualified and permitted to take his seat as a member of the Senate." The Senate on May 16, 1844, accepted the committee's conclusion, and Niles took his seat.

Hiram R. Revels (R Miss.), a former slave, was elected to the Senate in 1870. He was challenged on the ground that he had not become a citizen until 1868, when the Fourteenth Amendment was ratified. The Senate ruled that the Amendment made Revels retroactively a citizen, and the oath was administered to him.

On Feb. 23, 1903, Reed Smoot (R Utah) presented his credentials as a Senator-elect. A group of Utah citizens opposed his seating on the ground that as a Mormon he favored polygamy and opposed the separation of church and state. The Senate administered the oath to Smoot on a tentative basis on March 4, 1903. The Senator's eligibility was then studied by the Committee on Privileges and Elections, which on June 11, 1906, reported a resolution which would have declared Smoot not entitled to his seat. Sen. Philander C. Knox (R Pa.) contended, Feb. 14, 1907, that Smoot's case involved expulsion rather than exclusion and therefore required a two-thirds vote: "There is no question as to Sen. Smoot's possessing the qualifications prescribed by the Constitution, and therefore we cannot deprive him of his seat by a majority vote."

Knox's proposed amendment to the Committee's resolution was agreed to as a first step. The amendment consisted of the words "two-thirds of the Senators present concurring," inserted before the words "That Reed Smoot is not entitled to a seat as a Senator of the United States

Senate Cases Involving Qualifications for Membership

Congress	Session	Year	Member-elect	Party	State	Grounds	Disposition
3d	1st	1793	Albert Gallatin	D	Pa.	Citizenship	*Excluded*
11th	1st	1809	Stanley Griswold	D	Ohio	Residence	Admitted
28th	1st	1844	John M. Niles	D	Conn.	Sanity	Admitted
31st	Special Senate	1849	James Shields	D	Ill.	Citizenship	*Excluded*
37th	2d	1861	Benjamin Stark	D	Ore.	Loyalty	Admitted
40th	1st	1867	Phillip F. Thomas	D	Md.	Loyalty	*Excluded*
41st	2d	1870	Hiram R. Revels	R	Miss.	Citizenship	Admitted
41st	2d	1870	Adelbert Ames	R	Miss.	Residence	Admitted
59th	2d	1907	Reed Smoot	R	Utah	Mormonism	Admitted*
69th	2d	1926	Arthur R. Gould	R	Maine	Character	Admitted
74th	1st	1935	Rush D. Holt	D	W.Va.	Age	Admitted
75th	1st	1937	George L. Berry	D	Tenn.	Character	Admitted
77th	2d	1942	William Langer	R	N.D.	Character	Admitted*
80th	1st	1947	Theodore G. Bilbo	D	Miss.	Character	Died before Senate acted

* The Senate decided that a two-thirds majority, as in expulsion cases, would be required for exclusion. The resolution proposing exclusion did not receive a two-thirds majority.

from the State of Utah." A second amendment, substituting the words "Resolved, That Reed Smoot, a Senator from Utah, be expelled from the Senate of the United States," failed, receiving 27 yeas and 43 nays. Then the exclusion resolution, with Knox's amendment, also failed, receiving 28 yeas and 42 nays.

When Arthur R. Gould (R Maine) was elected to the Senate in 1926, various colleagues made an issue of the fact that some 14 years earlier he had been accused of involvement in bribery. Vice President Charles G. Dawes ruled out of order a resolution which would have prevented Gould from being sworn in. Gould later voted for a resolution, which was adopted, directing the Committee on Privileges and Elections to look into his case. In the Committee's hearings on the matter, Gould contended that the attempt to deny him his seat contravened the right of Maine's citizens to send to Washington a Senator of their choice. The Committee on March 4, 1927, reported that Gould's alleged part in the bribery case had not been proved. He was later reimbursed by the Senate for the expenses he had incurred in defending himself before the Committee.

In 1941, the right of William Langer (R N.D.) to a seat in the Senate was challenged. Opponents cited alleged misconduct on Langer's part during his service as Governor of North Dakota and in other posts in that state's government. When an investigating committee recommended that Langer be excluded, the Senate added a two-thirds requirement, as it had done in the case of Reed Smoot, and then on March 27, 1942, voted down the proposed resolution.

The most recent exclusion case involving a Senator-elect arose in January 1947, when Theodore G. Bilbo (D Miss.) presented himself for swearing in. Bilbo had been accused of fraud, violence in preventing Negroes from voting, and other offenses. He was asked to stand aside when other Senators-elect took the oath. In August 1947, before the question of his right to his seat had been settled, Bilbo died.

Cases Occurring in the House

Ten Congressmen-elect have been excluded from the House of Representatives on the ground that they were not qualified to serve. John Bailey of Massachusetts was the first to be excluded. He was challenged on the ground that he was not a resident of the district that he purported to represent. The House, by a resolution of March 18, 1824, declared that Bailey was not entitled to his seat. He returned home, was elected to fill the vacancy created by his exclusion, and was seated Dec. 13, 1824.

In 1867, southern states elected to Congress four citizens whom the House found to be tainted with acts of disloyalty during the Civil War. They were John Y. Brown and John D. Young of Kentucky; W. D. Simpson of South Carolina; and John A. Whimpy of Georgia. The Kentuckians were Democrats; the two others, independents. All four were excluded.

South Carolina had another Representative-elect excluded three years later. Benjamin F. Whittemore, a Republican, was censured by the House in 1870 for selling appointments to the U.S. Military Academy and resigned on Feb. 24 of that year. When Whittemore was re-elected to the same Congress, Rep. John A. Logan (D Ill.) discussed his case on the House floor: "It is said that the constituency has the right to elect such member as they deem proper. I say no. We cannot say that he shall be of a certain politics, or of a certain religion, or anything of that kind; but, Sir, we have the right to say that he shall not be a man of infamous character." The House on June 21, 1870, excluded Whittemore by a vote of 130 to 76.

The House based two exclusions on polygamy. George Q. Cannon was elected in 1872 as a Delegate from Utah Territory. In the first and second sessions of the 43rd Congress, the question of his eligibility was raised and was settled in his favor. However, when Cannon presented

House Cases Involving Qualifications for Membership

Congress	Session	Year	Member-elect	Party	State	Grounds	Disposition
1st	1st	1789	William L. Smith	Fed	S.C.	Citizenship	Admitted
10th	1st	1807	Philip B. Key	Fed	Md.	Residence	Admitted
18th	1st	1823	Gabriel Richard	Ind	Mich. Terr.	Citizenship	Admitted
18th	1st	1823	John Bailey	Ind	Mass.	Residence	*Excluded*
18th	1st	1823	John Forsyth	D	Ga.	Residence	Admitted
27th	1st	1841	David Levy	R	Fla. Terr.	Citizenship	Admitted
40th	1st	1867	William H. Hooper	D	Utah Terr.	Mormonism	Admitted
40th	1st	1867	Lawrence S. Trimble	D	Ky.	Loyalty	Admitted
40th	1st	1867	John Y. Brown	D	Ky.	Loyalty	*Excluded*
40th	1st	1867	John D. Young	D	Ky.	Loyalty	*Excluded*
40th	1st	1867	Roderick R. Butler	R	Tenn.	Loyalty	Admitted
40th	1st	1867	John A. Whimpy	Ind	Ga.	Loyalty	*Excluded*
40th	1st	1867	W. D. Simpson	Ind	S.C.	Loyalty	*Excluded*
41st	1st	1869	John M. Rice	D	Ky.	Loyalty	Admitted
41st	2d	1870	Lewis McKenzie	Unionist	Va.	Loyalty	Admitted
41st	2d	1870	George W. Booker	Conservative	Va.	Loyalty	Admitted
41st	2d	1870	Benjamin F. Whittemore	R	S.C.	Malfeasance	*Excluded*
41st	2d	1870	John C. Conner	D	Texas	Misconduct	Admitted
43rd	1st	1873	George Q. Cannon	R	Utah Terr.	Mormonism	Admitted
43rd	2d	1874	George Q. Cannon	R	Utah Terr.	Polygamy	Admitted
47th	1st	1881	John S. Barbour	D	Va.	Residence	Admitted
47th	1st	1882	George Q. Cannon	R	Utah Terr.	Polygamy	*Seat vacated
50th	1st	1887	James B. White	R	Ind.	Citizenship	Admitted
56th	1st	1899	Robert W. Wilcox	Ind	Hawaii Terr.	Bigamy, treason	Admitted
56th	1st	1900	Brigham H. Roberts	D	Utah	Polygamy	*Excluded*
59th	1st	1905	Anthony Michalek	R	Ill.	Citizenship	Admitted
66th	1st	1919	Victor L. Berger	Socialist	Wis.	Sedition	*Excluded*
66th	2d	1920	Victor L. Berger	Socialist	Wis.	Sedition	*Excluded*
70th	1st	1927	James M. Beck	R	Pa.	Residence	Admitted
71st	1st	1929	Ruth B. Owen	D	Fla.	Citizenship	Admitted
90th	1st	1967	Adam C. Powell Jr.	D	N.Y.	Misconduct	*Excluded*

* Discussions of polygamy and an election contest led to a declaration that the seat was vacant.

himself in 1882 as a Delegate-elect, his election was contested. The House, taking account both of Cannon's practice of polygamy and of doubts about the validity of his election, declared the seat vacant, in effect excluding Cannon.

In 1900, Members of the House questioned the right of Brigham H. Roberts, elected as a Representative from Utah, to take his seat. Roberts had been found guilty some years earlier of violating an 1882 law which prohibited polygamy. This was the case, mentioned earlier, in which an investigating committee argued that the Founding Fathers had not foreclosed the right of Congress to establish qualifications for membership other than those mentioned in the Constitution. The House refused to seat Roberts. There were 268 votes for exclusion, 50 against.

In the 20th century, only Victor L. Berger, Wisconsin Socialist, and Adam Clayton Powell Jr. (D N.Y.) have been excluded from the House. Berger had been convicted in 1919 of violating the Espionage Act of June 15, 1917, by publishing anti-war statements. While an appeal was pending, he was elected to the 66th Congress. By resolution of the House, Nov. 10, 1919, Berger was

declared "not entitled to take the oath of office as a Representative." He was re-elected during the same Congress and excluded again on Jan. 10, 1920. But after the Supreme Court had reversed Berger's conviction, he was elected to the House three times more, in 1922, 1924 and 1926, and was seated without question.

Cases in which House proceedings on exclusion ended in admission of the Representative-elect evoked various memorable exchanges on the floor. An example is the case of John C. Conner (D Texas), who was accused of having whipped Negro soldiers under his command in 1868 and of having boasted in 1869 that he would escape conviction by a military court by bribing witnesses. Rep. James A. Garfield (R Ohio), speaking in the House on March 31, 1870, raised a constitutional question on this case: "Allow me to ask...if anything in the Constitution of the United States...forbids that a 'moral monster' shall be elected to Congress?" Rep. Ebon C. Ingersoll (R Ill.) replied: "I believe the people may elect a moral monster to Congress if they see fit, but I believe that Congress has a right to exclude that moral monster from a seat if they see fit." A resolution allowing Conner to take his seat was adopted the same day.

Case of Adam Clayton Powell Jr.

One of the stormiest episodes of modern Congressional history was the precedent-shattering case of Rep. Adam Clayton Powell Jr. In 1937, Powell succeeded his father as pastor of the Abyssinian Baptist Church in Harlem, one of the largest congregations in the country. The new pastor was elected to the 79th Congress in 1944 with the nomination of both the Democratic and Republican parties. He took his seat with the Democrats, was re-elected regularly by large majorities, served as chairman of the House Committee on Education and Labor from 1961 to 1967, and was considered by many observers the most powerful Negro in the United States. Throughout his legislative career, he retained his pastorate.

Court Suits Against Powell. On the eve of Powell's 1952 re-election bid, he was informed by the Internal Revenue Service that he had underestimated his 1945 income tax by $2,749. A federal grand jury indicted him in 1958 on a charge of tax evasion. In the ensuing trial, held in 1960, the jury was unable to reach a verdict. The case was dismissed the following year, but the I.R.S. continued to dun Powell. In 1966, he paid $27,833.17 in back taxes and penalties.

The Harlem Representative became involved in civil litigation after he had said, in a television interview in 1960, that Mrs. Esther James, a widow in his district, was a "bag woman," or graft collector, for New York City policemen. Mrs. James sued Powell for libel. He was ordered by the court to pay her an amount set originally at $211,739 and reduced, on appeal, to $46,500. That sum plus court costs was paid in 1965-67, in part by Powell directly and in part by a record company from royalties on Powell's record "Keep the Faith, Baby."

A second civil case against Powell was instituted by Mrs. James in 1964 on the basis of an allegation that the Representative had fraudulently transferred property to avoid paying the original libel judgment. In this case, a jury awarded Mrs. James $350,000. That amount was reduced later to $155,785, including $100,000 in punitive damages. The New York Court of Appeals in 1967 eliminated the punitive damages. Powell, after further delays, ultimately paid the remainder. Meanwhile, he had been held in contempt of court on four occasions. To avoid arrest, he found it necessary, while Congress was not in session, to stay out of New York State on all days except Sundays.

Committee Revolt. Powell, as chairman of the Education and Labor Committee, was responsible for shepherding President Johnson's anti-poverty program through the House. After the Committee had reported the bill authorizing the program, Powell delayed bringing it up for floor debate. He favored the program, but by long absences and for personal reasons he put off action. The Committee on Sept. 22, 1966, by a vote of 27 to 1, stripped Powell of his basic powers as chairman by adopting new rules, one of which provided that if the chairman failed to bring a bill to the floor, one of the six subcommittee chairmen could do so. The Committee revolt was initiated by Powell's fellow Democrats.

The House Democratic caucus on Jan. 9, 1967, removed Powell from the chairmanship of the Committee on Education and Labor for the duration of the 90th Congress. This was the first time since 1925 that a committee chairman had been deposed in either house of Congress.

Powell, who attended the caucus, called the action "a lynching, northern style." A few days earlier, the House as a whole had set in motion an action against him which raised the constitutional issue of his qualifications for membership.

Exclusion Proceedings. In the 1950s and the early 1960s, Powell repeatedly went on costly pleasure trips at Government expense. In addition, he incurred criticism for taking a staff member, Corinne A. Huff, on many trips to Bimini Island in the Bahamas. Out of Government funds, he paid his wife $20,578 a year as a clerk while she lived in Puerto Rico. The Special Contracts Subcommittee of the House Committee on Administration on Jan. 3, 1967, recommended that Mrs. Powell be dropped from the payroll, as was done soon thereafter.

The House on Jan. 10, 1967, had before it two resolutions on Powell's right to be seated. A resolution submitted by Rep. Morris K. Udall (D Ariz.) proposed that Powell be seated, pending the result of a 60-day investigation of his conduct by a seven-member select committee. Udall had argued the preceding day that the problem had already been solved by Powell's removal from his committee chairmanship, since his malfeasance was based on misuse of the chairmanship. The House rejected the Udall resolution by a vote of 305 to 126.

Following that vote, the House on the same day adopted a resolution on Powell offered by Minority Leader Gerald R. Ford (R Mich.), which denied Powell his seat pending an investigation by a select committee. On Ford's resolution, there were 363 yeas, 65 nays. The yea votes came from Democrats and Republicans; all of the nay votes were cast by Democrats, including two from the South.

House Judiciary Committee Chairman Emanuel Celler (D N.Y.) was chairman of the select committee appointed to investigate Powell's qualifications for his seat. The Committee conducted hearings beginning Feb. 8, 1967. Its report, submitted Feb. 23, included a recommendation, unprecedented in Congressional history, that Powell be fined. The Committee proposed that he be sworn in; that his seniority be based on the date of his swearing in; that he be censured for "gross misconduct" through misuse of funds of the Committee on Education and Labor, refusal to pay the libel judgment against him, and noncooperation with House investigating committees; and that he be fined $40,000, to be paid to the Clerk of the House in the form of a monthly deduction of $1,000 from Powell's salary, in order to "offset any civil liability of Mr. Powell to the United States."

The House on March 1, 1967, rejected the Committee's proposals and adopted instead a resolution excluding Powell from the 90th Congress—the first exclusion since Victor L. Berger was barred in 1919 and 1920. On the select Committee's proposals, the vote was 202 in favor, 222 against; on the exclusion resolution, 307 in favor, 116 against. Following the vote, Powell spoke to a crowd on the Capitol steps. Recalling the slogan "No taxation without representation," he urged his constituents not to pay any federal, state, or city taxes until his district was again represented in Congress.

As in his ouster from his committee chairmanship, Powell ascribed his downfall to racism. That racial feeling played a part in the vote to exclude Powell seems probable. Rep. Celler said on television and on the House floor that he saw "an element of racism in the vote." Arlen J.

Large, a Washington correspondent, wrote in the *Wall Street Journal*, March 22, 1967: "Disclaimers of race as a factor in Mr. Powell's exclusion don't jibe with the nearly solid anti-Powell votes of southern Congressmen, reflecting the bitterly worded letters from white voters back home."

New York State conducted a special election in Powell's Harlem district to choose a replacement for him in the House. Powell entered his name as a candidate, but he was unable to return to New York City to campaign without being arrested for contempt. However, he was re-elected with 86 per cent of the votes cast. Pending the outcome of his lawsuit against the exclusion, he did not apply to the House to be seated but remained at his vacation retreat on Bimini Island.

Powell Seated. Rep.-elect Powell returned to his district on April 5, 1968. He was arrested, and then released on the theory that the litigation in which he was involved was under appeal. In the general election of 1968, he again became a candidate for a seat in Congress and once more was victorious at the polls. The 91st Congress on Jan. 3, 1969, ended his two-year exile. Powell was sworn in and seated but subjected to loss of seniority and fined $25,000. In the voting on the resolution imposing these penalties, there were 254 yeas, 158 nays.

Contested Elections

Decentralization of control over elections in the United States may have strengthened participatory democracy, but it has led frequently to controversy over election results. Losing candidates and their supporters believe in many cases that more voters were on their side than the official count showed. Floyd M. Riddick wrote in *The United States Congress; Organization and Procedure*: "Seldom if ever has a Congress organized without some losing candidate for a seat in either the Senate or House contesting the right of the Member-elect to be Senator or Representative, as the case might be, as a result of the election in which the losing candidate participated."

To avert partisanship in settling election disputes involving Members of the House, an Act of 1798 established procedures to be followed in handling contested cases; by its own terms the Act expired in 1804. A law approved Feb. 19, 1851, renewed the effort to give the proceedings in contested elections of House members a judicial rather than partisan character, and amendments in 1873 and 1875 improved the procedure for taking testimony in such cases. But despite these efforts, fidelity to party determined the outcome in a large majority of the cases.

The Federal Contested Election Act of Dec. 5, 1969, superseded the earlier legislation. The new law, like those of 1798 and 1851, prescribed procedures for instituting a challenge and presenting testimony, but it did not establish criteria to govern decisions. It was more restrictive than the old laws in providng that only candidates listed on the ballot, or bona fide write-in candidates, might contest election results. Previously, anyone having an interest in a Congressional election could initiate proceedings by filing a petition.

Senators were chosen by state legislatures until the adoption of the Seventeenth Amendment to the Constitution in 1913 (*see The Amending Power, Chapter III*).

Before then, contested Senatorial elections often involved accusations of corruption in the legislatures. Neither before nor after 1913 did Congress enact any law on contested Senate elections comparable to the legislation on contested elections in the House.

Since 1789, the two houses of Congress have ruled on almost 700 election contests, averaging between seven and eight in each Congress. The Senate cases made up about one-fourth of the total, the House cases about three-fourths. Different scholars have come up with different totals of election contests, owing to lack of agreement on what constitutes a contest. George B. Galloway of the Legislative Reference Service stated in 1953 that there had been 136 election contests in the Senate from 1789 to 1952. John T. Dempsey counted only 125 in the Senate from 1789 to 1955. It appears that Galloway included, and Dempsey excluded, contested appointments made by state governors to fill seats vacated by death or otherwise.

Senate Cases

An illustrative 19th century case was that of Henry A. Du Pont (R Del.), who was excluded from the Senate because he had not been duly elected by the Delaware Legislature. Delaware law stated that 15 votes would be sufficient to elect a U.S. Senator if the Legislature consisted of 29 members; 16 votes, if it consisted of 30 members. Du Pont, in an election held in 1895, received 15 votes, but there was a question whether the Legislature consisted of 29 or 30 members. Du Pont admitted that 30 votes had been cast, but he contended that one of the votes had been cast by a person who had no right to participate, because he had succeeded to the governorship through the death of the incumbent. The Senate on May 15, 1895, decided, by a vote of 31 to 30, "That Henry A. Du Pont is not entitled to a seat in the Senate from the State of Delaware."

The more important 20th century cases have included those of Lorimer and Vare. William Lorimer (R Ill.) was elected a Senator by the Illinois Legislature and took his seat in the Senate on June 18, 1909. In May 1910, he requested that the Committee on Privileges and Elections examine allegations made in the press that bribery and corruption had entered into his election. Following an investigation conducted during the 61st Congress (1909-11), the Senate on March 1, 1911, rejected a proposed resolution declaring that Lorimer had not been "duly and legally elected." The vote was 40 for adoption of the resolution, 46 against.

Reopening of the case in the next Congress led to reversal of the earlier decision. A specially appointed committee took further testimony and submitted majority and minority reports. The majority favored dismissing the charges. The minority proposed adoption of the following resolution: "Resolved, That corrupt methods and practices were employed in the election of William Lorimer to the Senate of the United States from the State of Illinois, and that his election was therefore invalid." On June 13, 1912, the Senate adopted the resolution by a vote of 55 to 28.

Corruption was also the crux of the case of William S. Vare. During the primaries in Pennsylvania in 1926, newspapers charged that persons favoring Vare as the Republican nominee for the post of U.S. Senator were engaging in corrupt practices. Vare won the primary contest and the November election. The Senate meanwhile, on May 19, 1926, had appointed a committee to investigate Pennsylvania's senatorial primaries and the fall election. Following the election, Vare's Democratic rival, ex-Secretary of Labor William B. Wilson, charged that Vare had won through corruption. When Congress met, Vare was asked to stand aside while other Senators-elect were sworn in.

Proceedings in Vare's case dragged on for two years, during which time Vare became seriously ill. The Senate received a series of reports on the case, including the report of a special committee, Feb. 22, 1929, asserting that Vare, owing to his excessive use of money to get nominated and elected, was not entitled to a seat in the Senate. Not until December 1929 did the Senate take final action on the matter. On Dec. 5, the Senate Committee on Privileges and Elections reported that Vare had received a plurality of the legal votes cast in the election. But the Senate on the following day voted 58-22 to deny Vare a seat. At the same time, it concluded by a vote of 66 to 15 that Wilson had not been elected.

House Cases

George F. Hoar (R Mass.), who served in both houses, wrote in his *Autobiography of Seventy Years* in 1903: "Whenever there is a plausible reason for making a contest, the dominant party in the House almost always awards the seat to the man of its own side." Thomas B. Reed (R Me.) went farther than Hoar's "almost always." In an article on contested elections published in the *North American Review* in 1890, while he was Speaker of the House, Reed wrote: "Probably there is not an instance on record where the minority was increased by the decision of contested cases." While preparing to write a history of the House of Representatives, De Alva Alexander found, in 1906, that up to that time only three persons not of the dominant party had obtained seats in that chamber through the settlement of some hundreds of election contests.

William F. Willoughby asserted in *Principles of Legislative Organization and Administration* in 1934 that "The whole history of the handling of election contests by the House has constituted one of the major scandals of our political system." Willoughby noted that after enactment of the 1851 law on procedures for adjudicating elections, "for many years the House made little or no pretense of settling election contests on any basis of equity, political considerations in practically all cases determining the decision reached." In 1955, John T. Dempsey, a doctoral candidate at the University of Michigan, made a case-by-case examination of 546 contested election cases in the House. He found that only on 47 occasions, less than 10 per cent of the total, did the controlling party award a contested seat to a member of the minority party.

Perhaps the most dramatic election dispute which the House has settled in recent years was that of the Mississippi Five in 1965. The Governor of Mississippi certified the election to the House in 1964 of four Democrats and one Republican. The Democrats were Thomas G. Abernethy, William M. Colmer, Jamie L. Whitten, and John B. Williams; the Republican was Prentiss Walker. Their right to be seated in the House was contested by a biracial group called the Mississippi Freedom Democratic

---

House Action on Election Contests

In only four Congresses, the 6th (1799-1801), 20th (1827-29), 83rd (1953-54), and 88th (1963-64), has the House of Representatives had no election contests to settle. At the other extreme, the House in the 54th Congress (1895-97) settled 38 such contests.

Where state authorities have declared an individual to be the Representative-elect and a loser contests the validity of the election, the House almost always seats the officially certified Representative-elect. George B. Galloway of the Legislative Reference Service in the Library of Congress counted 126 election contests in the House between 1908 and 1951 and found that the contestant had been seated in only 13 cases; in two, the House found the election void and the seat vacant. Since the mid-1930s, all contests against the declared winner have been unsuccessful.

Party, formed originally to challenge the seating of all-white delegates from the state to the 1964 Democratic National Convention. This group, when unsuccessful in getting its candidates on the 1964 Congressional election ballot, conducted a rump election in which Mrs. Annie Devine, Mrs. Virginia Gray, and Mrs. Fannie L. Hamer were the winners.

The three women, when they sought entrance to the House floor, were barred. However, Speaker John W. McCormack (D Mass.) asked the regular Mississippi Congressmen-elect to stand aside while the other members of the House were sworn in. Rep. William F. Ryan (D N.Y.) was the sponsor of the challenge. He contended that the regular Congressional election in Mississippi was invalid because Negroes had been systematically prevented from voting. A resolution to seat the regular Mississippi delegation was adopted on Jan. 4, 1965, by a voice vote.

During discussion of the resolution, a motion was made to end debate and put the resolution to a vote. In a roll-call vote on this motion, opponents of the resolution voted in the negative. They mustered 149 negative votes, but the motion was carried by 276 affirmative votes. Ryan declared that the number of negative votes on the motion represented a "historic achievement." Five Republican members of the House later issued a statement contending that the Democratic leadership had "effectively condoned the disenfranchisement of more than 400,000 American citizens in Mississippi and missed an opportunity to rectify the wrong." They were John V. Lindsay and Ogden R. Reid (both N.Y.), Silvio O. Conte and F. Bradford Morse (both Mass.), and Charles McC. Mathias (Md.).

The M.F.D.P. on May 16, 1965, filed a brief and petition, with 600 depositions, citing officially inspired harassment of black voters in Mississippi and the admission by state officials of participation in prevention of Negro voting. The House Committee on Administration on Sept. 15 reported, by a vote of 15 to 9, a proposed resolution rejecting the petition, partly because the contestants had not availed themselves of the proper legal steps and because alleged voting discrimination had been made moot by the Voting Rights Act of 1965. The resolution, as presented, dismissed the petition and declared that the Mississippi Congressmen were "entitled to their seats."

Democratic and Republican leaders proposed omitting the latter clause. An amendment to that effect was adopted by voice vote, and the resolution dismissing the petition was approved, Sept. 17, by a vote of 228 to 143.

Censure

For offenses of sufficient gravity, each house of Congress punishes its Members by censure or expulsion. Censure has the advantage that it does not deprive constituents of the services of their elected Senators or Representatives. Grounds for censure usually consist of a Member's actions during his service in Congress. Both houses have distrusted their power to punish a Member for offenses committed prior to his election or for offenses committed during a previous Congress.

For minor transgressions of the rules, the presiding officer of either house may call a Member to order, without a formal move to censure the Member. For example, on Jan. 14, 1955, Sen. Russell B. Long (D La.), while presiding over the Senate, called Sen. Joseph R. McCarthy (R Wis.) to order when McCarthy questioned the motives of some Senators who had voted with him for a resolution continuing an investigation of Communists in Government. Long said: "The statement of the junior Senator from Wisconsin was that other Senators were insincere. In making that statement, the Senator from Wisconsin spoke contrary to the rules of the Senate....He must take his seat." Later on the same day, Long again called McCarthy to order.

In the entire history of Congress, the Senate has censured seven of its Members, the House 18. In the Senate, censure proceedings are carried out with a degree of moderation. The alleged offender, for example, is granted the privilege of speaking in his own behalf. The House often has denied that privilege to a Representative accused of wrongdoing. In most cases in the House, a censured Member is treated like a felon; the Speaker calls him to the bar and makes a solemn pronouncement of censure. The Blanton case is illustrative. Speaker Frederick H. Gillett (R Mass.) on Oct. 27, 1921, directed the Sergeant-at-Arms to bring to the bar of the House Rep. Thomas L. Blanton (D Texas). When the Sergeant-at-Arms had done so, the Speaker made the following statement:

"Mr. Blanton, by a unanimous vote of the House— yeas, 293; nays, none—I have been directed to censure you because, when you had been allowed the courtesy of the House to print a speech which you did not deliver, you inserted in it foul and obscene matter, which you knew you could not have spoken on the floor; and that disgusting matter, which could not have been circulated through the mails in any other publication without violating the law, was transmitted as part of the proceedings of this House to thousands of homes and libraries throughout the country, to be read by men and women, and worst of all by children, whose prurient curiosity it would excite and corrupt. In accordance with the instructions of the House and as its representative, I pronounce upon you its censure."

Censure by the Senate

Timothy Pickering (Fed Mass.) was the first Member to be censured by the Senate. In December 1810, he had

read aloud in the chamber secret documents relating to the 1803 convention with France for the cession of Louisiana. The Senate on Jan. 2, 1811, adopted the following resolution of censure: "Resolved, That Timothy Pickering, a Senator from the State of Massachusetts, having,... whilst the Senate was in session with open doors, read from his place certain documents confidentially communicated by the President of the United States to the Senate, the injunction of secrecy not having been removed, has, in so doing, committed a violation of the rules of this body." Twenty Senators voted for the resolution; seven, against it.

Benjamin Tappan (D Ohio) was similarly censured on May 10, 1844, when the Senate adopted a two-part resolution concerning his release to the press of confidential material relating to a treaty for the annexation of Texas. The resolution read: (1) "Resolved, That Benjamin Tappan, a Senator from the State of Ohio, in furnishing for publication in a newspaper documents directed by an order of the Senate to be printed in confidence for its use, has been guilty of a flagrant violation of the rules of the Senate in disregard of its authority." (2) "Resolved, That in consideration of the acknowledgment and apology tendered by the said Benjamin Tappan for his said offense, no further censure be inflicted on him." The votes on the two parts of the resolution were 35 to 7 and 39 to 3.

Threatened violence was involved in the next censure case in the Senate. On the Senate floor, April 7, 1850, Thomas H. Benton (D Mo.) made menacing gestures and advanced toward Henry S. Foote (Unionist Miss.) while Foote was making a speech. Foote drew a pistol from

Censure Proceedings in the Senate

Congress	Session	Year	Member	Party	State	Grounds	Disposition
11th	3d	1811	Timothy Pickering	Fed.	Mass.	Breach of confidence	*Censured*
28th	1st	1844	Benjamin Tappan	D	Ohio	Breach of confidence	*Censured*
31st	1st	1850	Thomas H. Benton	D	Mo.	Disorderly conduct	Not censured
31st	1st	1850	Henry S. Foote	Unionist	Miss.	Disorderly conduct	Not censured
57th	1st	1902	John L. McLaurin	D	S.C.	Assault	*Censured*
57th	1st	1902	Benjamin R. Tillman	D	S.C.	Assault	*Censured*
71st	1st	1929	Hiram Bingham	R	Conn.	Bringing Senate into disrepute	*Censured*
83rd	2d	1954	Joseph R. McCarthy	R	Wis.	Obstruction of legislative process, insult to Senators, etc.	*Censured*
90th	1st	1967	Thomas J. Dodd	D	Conn.	Financial misconduct	*Censured*

his pocket and cocked it. Before any damage was done, other Senators intervened and restored order. A committee appointed to consider the incident said in its report, July 30, that what the two men had done was deplorable. The committee recommended that Foote be censured, but the Senate took no action. This was the only Senate case in which an investigating committee's recommendation of censure was not adopted.

More than half a century later, on Washington's Birthday in 1902, while the Senate was debating Philippine affairs, Sen. John L. McLaurin (D S.C.) called a statement by Sen. Benjamin R. Tillman (D S.C.) "a willful, malicious and deliberate lie." Tillman advanced toward McLaurin, and they engaged in a brief fistfight. After they had been separated, the Senate by a vote of 61 to 0 declared them to be "in contempt of the Senate" and by a voice vote referred the matter to the Committee on Privileges and Elections for a report on any further action that should be taken.

The Committee on Feb. 27 reported a resolution declaring it to be the judgment of the Senate that the two men, "for disorderly behavior and flagrant violation of the rules of the Senate..., deserve the censure of the Senate, and they are hereby so censured, for their breach of the privileges and dignity of this body." The resolution provided that after its adoption the previous declaration that the two men were in contempt of the Senate "shall be no longer in force and effect." The Senate adopted the resolution by a vote of 54 to 12, with 22 Senators (including the two participants in the affray) not voting.

The remaining Senate censure cases involved Hiram Bingham, Joseph R. McCarthy and Thomas J. Dodd. McCarthy's and Dodd's cases are discussed below. The case of Sen. Hiram Bingham (R Conn.) occurred in 1929 when he placed on the Senate payroll, as a member of his staff, Charles L. Eyanson, a secretary to the president of the Connecticut Manufacturers' Association, to assist him in dealing with tariff questions.

Sen. George W. Norris (R Neb.) introduced a resolution declaring that Bingham's action "is contrary to good morals and Senatorial ethics and tends to bring the Senate into dishonor and disrepute, and such action is hereby condemned." During consideration of the resolution on Nov. 4, 1929, it was agreed that the words "while he placed on the Senate payroll, as a member of

not the result of corrupt motives on the part of the Senator from Connecticut" should be inserted before the words "is contrary to." The resolution as so amended was adopted by a vote of 54 to 22, with 18 Senators (including Bingham) not voting.

Censure by the House

The House in 1789 adopted a rule which, as amended in 1822 and 1880, is still in effect (Rule 14, Section 4). It reads: "If any Member, in speaking or otherwise, transgress the rules of the House, the Speaker shall, or any Member may, call him to order; ...and if the case require it, he shall be liable to censure or such punishment as the House may deem proper." The censure clause of this rule has been invoked 30 times, and censure has been voted 18 times, two-thirds of them in the 1860s and 1870s. Grounds for censure have included assault on a fellow member of the House, insult to the Speaker, treasonable utterance, corruption, and other offenses. Only once in the 20th century has a Representative been censured— Thomas L. Blanton (D Texas) in 1921 for abuse of the leave to print *(see above)*.

The first censure motion in the House was introduced following a physical attack in January 1798 by Rep. Matthew Lyon (Anti-Fed Vt.) on Rep. Roger Griswold (Fed Conn.), who had taunted Lyon on his allegedly poor military record. The censure motion failed. In the following month, Lyon and Griswold engaged in an affray with tongs and cane. Both fracases occurred on the House floor. Following the second incident, a motion was introduced to censure both Members. The motion failed.

The first formal censure by the House was imposed in 1832 on William Stanbery (D Ohio) for saying, in objection to a ruling by the chair, "The eyes of the Speaker are too frequently turned from the chair you occupy toward the White House." There were 93 votes for censuring Stanbery; 44 were opposed. Censure for unacceptable language or offensive publication was imposed in seven other cases. For example, Rep. John W. Hunter (Ind. N.Y.) was censured on Jan. 26, 1867, for saying, about a statement made by a colleague, "So far as I am concerned, it is a base lie." The vote on censure was 77 to 23. One year later, on Jan. 15, 1868, the House by a vote of 114 to 39

Censure Proceedings in the House

Congress	Session	Year	Member	Party	State	Grounds	Disposition
5th	2d	1798	Matthew Lyon	Anti-Fed.	Vt.	Assault on Representative	Not censured
5th	2d	1798	Roger Griswold	Fed.	Conn.	Assault on Representative	Not censured
22nd	1st	1832	William Stanberry	D	Ohio	Insult to Speaker	*Censured*
24th	1st	1836	Sherrod Williams	Whig	Ky.	Insult to Speaker	Not censured
25th	2d	1838	Henry A. Wise	Tyler Dem.	Va.	Service as second in duel	Not censured
25th	3d	1839	Alexander Duncan	Whig	Ohio	Offensive publication	Not censured
27th	2d	1842	John Q. Adams	Whig	Mass.	Treasonable petition	Not censured
27th	2d	1842	Joshua R. Giddings	Whig	Ohio	Offensive paper	*Censured*
34th	2d	1856	Henry A. Edmundson	D	Va.	Complicity in assault	Not censured
34th	2d	1856	Laurence M. Keitt	D	S.C.	on Senator	*Censured*
35th	1st	1858	Orsamus B. Matteson	Whig	N.Y.	Corruption	*Censured*
36th	1st	1860	George S. Houston	D	Ala.	Insult to Representative	Not censured
38th	1st	1864	Alexander Long	D	Ohio	Treasonable utterance	*Censured*
38th	1st	1864	Benjamin G. Harris	D	Md.	Treasonable utterance	*Censured*
39th	1st	1866	John W. Chanler	D	N.Y.	Insult to House	*Censured*
39th	1st	1866	Lovell H. Rousseau	R	Ky.	Assault on Representative	*Censured*
40th	1st	1867	John W. Hunter	Ind.	N.Y.	Insult to Representative	*Censured*
40th	2d	1868	Fernando Wood	D	N.Y.	Offensive utterance	*Censured*
41st	2d	1870	Benjamin F. Whittemore	R	S.C.	Corruption	*Censured*
41st	2d	1870	Roderick R. Butler	R	Tenn.	Corruption	*Censured*
41st	2d	1870	John T. Deweese	D	N.C.	Corruption	*Censured*
42nd	3d	1873	Oakes Ames	R	Mass.	Corruption	*Censured*
42nd	3d	1873	James Brooks	D	N.Y.	Corruption	*Censured*
43rd	2d	1875	John Y. Brown	D	Ky.	Insult to Representative	*Censured*
44th	1st	1876	James G. Blaine	R	Maine	Corruption	Not censured
47th	1st	1882	William D. Kelley	R	Pa.	Offensive utterance	Not censured
47th	1st	1882	John D. White	R	Ky.	Offensive utterance	Not censured
51st	1st	1890	William D. Bynum	D	Ind.	Offensive utterance	*Censured*
63rd	2d	1914	James T. McDermott	D	Ill.	Corruption	Not censured
67th	1st	1921	Thomas L. Blanton	D	Texas	Abuse of leave to print	*Censured*

censured Rep. Fernando Wood (D N.Y.) for describing a bill on the government of the southern states as "a monstrosity, a measure the most infamous of the many infamous acts of this infamous Congress."

In 1842, censure was considered and rejected in the case of one of the most distinguished Representatives in American history, John Quincy Adams, a former President of the United States. Adams had presented to the House, for 46 of his constituents, a petition asking Congress to dissolve the Union and allow the states to go their separate ways. A resolution proposing to censure him for this act was worded so strongly that Adams asserted his right, under the Sixth Amendment to the Constitution, to a trial by jury. He succeeded in putting his opponents on the defensive, and the resolution was not put to a vote.

Rep. Lovell H. Rousseau (R Ky.) during the evening of June 14, 1866, assaulted Rep. Josiah B. Grinnell (R Iowa) with a cane in the portico on the East Front of the Capitol. On the House floor, earlier in the month, Grinnell had imputed cowardice to Rousseau. A committee appointed to report on the case recommended that Rousseau be expelled. That recommendation was rejected, but the House voted on July 17, 1866, that he "be summoned to the bar of this House, and be there publicly reprimanded by the Speaker for his violation of its rights and privi-

leges." The order was carried out July 21, despite Rousseau's announcement that he had sent his resignation to the Governor of Kentucky.

Corruption was the basis for censure or proposed censure in a number of cases. The House on Feb. 27, 1873, by a vote of 182 to 36, censured Reps. Oakes Ames (R Mass.) and James Brooks (D N.Y.) for their part in a financial scandal involving Credit Mobilier stock given to Members of Congress. Three years later, Speaker James G. Blaine (R Maine) was accused of involvement in that scandal as well as of receiving excessive payments from the Union Pacific Railroad Co. for bonds sold to the company. Two months before the convention at which Blaine hoped to be chosen the Republican candidate for President, he spoke in the House on the charges against him. By selective reading of a series of allegedly incriminating letters, Blaine managed to confuse the evidence sufficiently to rout the proponents of censure.

The McCarthy Case

The sixth member of the Senate to be censured was Joseph R. McCarthy (R Wis.). Proceedings on this case began in the 82nd Congress (1951-52) and were concluded in the 83rd (1953-54). Sen. William Benton (D Conn.) in August 1951 offered a resolution calling on the Com-

Assault on Charles Sumner, 1856

Sen. Charles Sumner (R Mass.), in a speech on the Senate floor, May 20, 1856, denounced in scathing language supporters of the Kansas-Nebraska Act of 1854, which repealed the Missouri Compromise of 1820 and permitted the two new territories to decide whether slavery would be allowed there. Two days later, while Sumner was seated at his desk on the Senate floor after the day's session had ended, he heard his name called. Looking up, he saw a tall stranger, who berated him for his speech and then struck him on the head repeatedly with a heavy walking stick, which was broken by the blows. Sumner fell bleeding and unconscious to the floor. He was absent from the Senate, because of the injuries suffered in the assault, for three and one-half years, until Dec. 5, 1859.

The attacker was Rep. Preston S. Brooks (State Rights Dem. S.C.), nephew of one of those whom Sumner had excoriated—Sen. A. P. Butler (State Rights Dem. S.C.). Expulsion proceedings against Brooks failed, on a strictly party vote. He resigned his House seat, July 15, 1856, but was elected to fill the vacancy caused by his resignation.

Rep. Laurence M. Keitt (D S.C.) was censured by the House on July 15, 1856, for having known of Brooks' intention to assault Sumner, for having taken no action to discourage or prevent the assault, and for having been "present on one or more occasions to witness the same." Keitt resigned, July 16, 1856, and was elected to fill the vacancy caused by his resignation. A resolution similar to the one censuring Keitt but directed against Rep. Henry A. Edmundson (D Va.) had failed of adoption, July 15, 1856.

mittee on Rules and Administration to investigate, among other things, McCarthy's participation in the defamation of Sen. Millard E. Tydings (D Md.) during the Maryland Senatorial campaign, in order to determine whether expulsion proceedings should be instituted against McCarthy. On April 10, 1952, McCarthy submitted a resolution calling for investigation by the same Committee of Benton's activities as Assistant Secretary of State, campaign contributions Benton had received, and other matters. Both proposals were referred to the Rules Committee's Privileges and Elections Subcommittee which, after conducting an investigation, submitted an inconclusive report on Jan. 2, 1953.

In the spring of 1954, the Senate Permanent Investigations Subcommittee conducted hearings on mutual accusations of misconduct by McCarthy and Army officials. *(See Congressional Investigations, Chapter III.)* During the hearings, McCarthy told Army Brig. Gen. Ralph W. Zwicker that he was "not fit to wear that uniform" and implied that Zwicker did not have "the brains of a five-year-old." In June, Sens. Ralph E. Flanders (R Vt.) and Herbert H. Lehman (D N.Y.) introduced resolutions to strip McCarthy of his chairmanship of the Senate Permanent Investigations Subcommittee. Both resolutions were referred to the Rules Committee.

The two resolutions became moot when 73-year-old Flanders on July 30 introduced a resolution censuring McCarthy for refusal to testify before a Rules subcommittee in the 1952 Benton-McCarthy exchange of accusations, refusal to repudiate the "frivolous and irresponsible" conduct of Investigations Subcommittee Counsel Roy M. Cohn and consultant G. David Schine on their 1953 subversion-seeking trip to Europe, and "habitual contempt for people." The Senate on Aug. 2 adopted, by a vote of 75 to 12, a proposal to refer Flanders' censure resolution to a select committee. Three days later, Vice President Richard M. Nixon appointed the select committee.

The Select Committee to Study Censure Charges held hearings from Aug. 31 to Sept. 13, 1954. McCarthy, in defending himself before the Committee, contended that the Senate cannot punish a member for what he did in a previous Congress. The Committee rejected that contention and on Sept. 27 submitted a 40,000-word report which included a unanimous recommendation that the Senate adopt a resolution censuring McCarthy. After a recess during the Congressional election campaign, the Senate reconvened Nov. 8 to consider the censure proposal. Proceedings in the next few weeks led to modifications of that proposal and substitution of the word "condemned" for "censured."

The Senate adopted the resolution of condemnation on Dec. 2 by a vote of 67 to 22. Republicans split evenly, 22 favoring and 22 opposing the resolution. All 44 Democrats, together with Sen. Wayne Morse (Ind Ore.), voted for the resolution. McCarthy, when asked whether he believed he had been censured, replied, "It wasn't exactly a vote of confidence." In January 1955, when control of Congress passed to the Democrats, McCarthy lost his committee and subcommittee chairmanships. His activities thereafter attracted less public attention, and he died of a liver ailment May 2, 1957.

The Dodd Case

House Speaker Sam Rayburn (D Texas, 1913-61) often said that the ethics of a Member of Congress should be judged not by his peers but by the voters at re-election time. By the mid-1960s, it had become clear that neither Congress nor the public felt this was enough. In 1964, the Senate was jolted by adverse publicity over charges that Robert G. (Bobby) Baker had used his office as secretary to the Senate majority to promote his business interests. To allay public misgivings, the Senate on July 24 of that year established a Select Committee on Standards and Conduct with responsibility for investigating "allegations of improper conduct" by Senators and Senate employees. In September, however, the Senate assigned jurisdiction over the Baker case to the Rules Committee.

The new Select Committee's first inquiry, instituted in 1966, concerned the Dodd case. On Jan. 24, 1966, and later dates, columnists Drew Pearson and Jack Anderson accused Sen. Thomas J. Dodd (D Conn.) of having (1) used for personal expenses funds contributed to him to help meet the costs of his campaign for re-election in 1964, (2) double-billed the Government for travel expenses, and (3) improperly exchanged favors with Julius Klein, a public relations representative of West German interests. On the last charge, the columnists said that Dodd had gone to Germany for the purpose of interceding with Chancellor Konrad Adenauer on behalf of Klein's accounts, although the trip was supposedly made on Senate business.

Committee Investigation. Dodd on Feb. 23, 1966, requested the Select Committee on Standards and Conduct to investigate his relationship with Klein. The Committee conducted hearings on all three of the Pearson-Anderson charges in June-July 1966 and March 1967. Dodd testified in his own defense.

• On the first charge, Dodd said that the donors of campaign funds had understood the money would be used as he saw fit: "My conscience is clear. I do not believe that anybody can look me in the eye and say I did wrong."

• The second charge, he said, stemmed from "sloppy bookkeeping" by Michael V. O'Hare, who had been an employee of Dodd. O'Hare and other former Dodd employees reportedly had taken documents from Dodd's files and made copies of them available to the Committee. In the course of the hearings, Dodd called O'Hare a liar.

• On charge No. 3, Dodd denied that he had been a mere errand boy for Klein on the trip to Europe.

The Committee on April 27, 1967, submitted its report on the Dodd case. It recommended that Dodd be censured for spending for personal purposes about $116,000 of $450,000 contributed for his re-election campaign, although he and his supporters had said that the money was needed for campaign purposes. The next day, Majority Whip Russell B. Long (D La.) said that the Committee's recommendation could be considered as "making a scapegoat of one man for a practice which may be altogether too prevalent." Censure was also recommended by the Committee on the second (double-billing) charge, but on the third charge the Committee said that while Dodd's relations with Klein were indiscreet, there was not sufficient evidence of wrongdoing to warrant disciplinary action.

Dodd, in a television address on May 15, 1967, said that Pearson, Anderson, and other newsmen had been "after my scalp for many years because of my position on Communism and Communist aggression." The next day William F. Buckley Jr., editor of the conservative *National Review*, and others formed an Ad Hoc National Committee for Justice for Dodd. Majority Whip Long told a newsman, "If we censure Dodd, he will be the second anti-Communist in memory to get that treatment—he and Joe McCarthy."

Censure Voted. In the Senate on June 14, Dodd said: "Does any one of you know that I have ever lied to you? That I have ever cheated?...Get up! If I lied,...if I cheated you,...get up and say so." Sen. James B. Pearson (R Kan.), a member of the Committee which had proposed censuring Dodd, arose and cited the instances of double-billing as cases in which Dodd had cheated.

Voting on the Committee's recommendations, June 23, 1967, the Senate censured Dodd on the first charge, by a vote of 92 to 5, but refused by a vote of 45 yeas to 51 nays to censure him on the second charge. The resolution as adopted recorded the judgment of the Senate that Dodd, "for having engaged in a course of conduct...from 1961 to 1965 of exercising the influence and favor of his office as a United States Senator...to obtain, and use for his personal benefit, funds from the public through political testimonials and a political campaign, deserves the censure of the Senate; and he is so censured for his conduct, which is contrary to accepted morals, derogates from the public trust expected of a Senator, and tends to bring the Senate into dishonor and disrepute." The preponderance of affirmative votes was the largest in the history of censure proceedings in the Senate.

Expulsion

Fifteen Senators have been expelled, one in 1797 and 14 during the Civil War. Expulsion proceedings in the Senate have been instituted 12 times since the Civil War, always without success. In the House, only three Members have been expelled, all of them in 1861. Of the five expulsion cases in the House since the Civil War, all were changed to censure cases, and the accused members were censured. Conspiracy against a foreign country (the 1797 case in the Senate) and support of a rebellion (the Civil War cases of 14 Senators and three Representatives) have been the only grounds on which a Senator or Representative has been expelled. In a few cases, a Senator or Representative escaped expulsion by resigning.

Grounds for Expulsion

In the successful expulsion cases, the grounds were conspiracy or disloyalty. The unsuccessful cases were concerned with the killing of a Representative in a duel, the assaulting of a Senator or a Representative, treasonable or offensive utterances, sedition, corruption and Mormonism. The most important question raised about the validity of grounds for expulsion has been whether a Member of either house may be expelled for offenses committed prior to his election.

John Quincy Adams, while serving in the Senate, submitted a committee report which affirmed the right of the Senate to expel a Member for pre-election conduct that came to light after he had taken his seat. The case was that of John Smith (D Ohio), who allegedly had been connected with Aaron Burr's conspiracy to separate several of the western states from the Union. Adams' committee, in its report of Dec. 31, 1807, said: "When a man whom his fellow citizens have honored with their confidence on the pledge of a spotless reputation has degraded himself by the commission of infamous crimes, which become suddenly and unexpectedly revealed to the world, defective, indeed, would be that institution which should be impotent to discard from its bosom the contagion of such a member."

The expulsion case against Smith was lost by a single vote on April 9, 1808, when 19 yeas, not enough to make up the required two-thirds, were cast for expulsion, against 10 nays. Later Congresses which debated proposals to unseat Members repeatedly took up the question whether acts committed prior to the Member's election furnished legitimate grounds for expulsion. Although no Senator or Representative has ever been expelled for such acts, the question remained alive, surfacing in the 1920s, when cases involving election corruption were under discussion. At that time, Rep. James M. Beck (R Pa.) wrote in a book titled *The Vanishing Rights of the States*:

"It is...clear that the act which would justify (a Senator's) expulsion must have taken place since his election. What he did prior to his election and qualification has been passed upon by the people of his state. In a political sense it is *res adjudicata*. A candidate for the Senate might have been guilty of embezzlement before his election, but the right of the people of that state to send an embezzler to the Senate if it sees fit is clear."

Incompatible Office. The Constitution, in Article I, Section 6, provides: "...no Person holding any Office under the United States, shall be a Member of either House during his continuance in office." When a Senator or Representative has accepted appointment to another "office under the United States," he has jeopardized but not always lost his privilege of remaining in Congress, depending on the type of office he accepted and the attitude of the house in which he was serving. If he lost his

post in Congress by accepting another office, he is not considered to have been expelled; his seat is treated as having been vacated.

The first of two significant cases in which this provision resulted in a sitting Member's loss of his seat was that of Rep. John P. Van Ness (D N.Y.), who in the recess between the first and second sessions of the Seventh Congress was appointed a major in the District of Columbia militia. When the question of the compatibility of holding both that office and a seat in Congress was brought up, Van Ness argued that the pertinent provision of the Constitution was intended to apply only to civil offices, and he pointed out that his militia post carried no pay. On Jan. 11, 1803, however, the House, by a vote of 88 to 0, adopted the following resolution: "Resolved, That John P. Van Ness, one of the Members of this House, having accepted and exercised the office of major of militia, under the authority of the United States, within the Territory of Columbia, has thereby forfeited his right to a seat as a Member of this House."

The second case was that of Rep. Samuel Hammond (Ind. Ga.), who in October 1804 accepted an Army commission as colonel commandant for the District of Louisiana. On Feb. 2, 1805, the House adopted the following resolution: (1) "Resolved, unanimously, That Samuel Hammond, a Member of this House from Georgia, having accepted an Executive appointment, has vacated his seat in this House." (2) "Resolved, That a copy of the foregoing resolution be sent to the Governor of Georgia by the Speaker of this House."

In a similar situation which arose in 1846, the sitting Representative involved, Edward D. Baker (Whig Ill.), resigned before the House had received a report on the matter from the Committee on Elections. Although the case was moot, the Committee felt impelled to raise a hypothetical question. In its report of Feb. 21, 1847, the Committee asked: "Now, suppose that every Member of Congress were a colonel in the Army...and the President, who is by the Constitution the Commander in Chief of that Army, should come into the Halls of Congress and order each individual Member to retire immediately...to his post in the Army, what would become of Congress?"

War Service of Members. Cases arising in the Civil War and subsequent wars in which Members of Congress served in the armed forces generally did not result in vacating of their seats. In the war with Spain, a House committee appointed to investigate the question reported on Feb. 21, 1899: "It cannot be contended that every position held by a Member of Congress is an office within the meaning of the Constitution, even though the term office may usually be applied to many of these positions." The Committee cited as an example the position of official escort representative at the funeral of a public figure. To come under the constitutional prohibition, the Committee said, a position "must not be merely transient, occasional, or incidental."

The Committee recommended adoption of a resolution declaring vacant the seats of four Representatives who had accepted commissions in the Army to serve in the war with Spain. "No mere patriotic sentiment," it said, "should be permitted to override the plain language of the fundamental written law." On March 2, 1899, the House, by a vote of 77 yeas and 163 nays, declined to consider the proposed resolution.

Cases of Expulsion in the Senate

Congress	Session	Year	Member	Party	State	Grounds	Disposition
5th	2d	1797	William Blount	Ind.	Tenn.	Anti-Spanish conspiracy	*Expelled*
10th	1st	1808	John Smith	D	Ohio	Disloyalty	Not expelled
35th	1st	1858	Henry M. Rice	D	Minn.	Corruption	Not expelled
37th	1st	1861	James M. Mason	D	Va.	Support of rebellion	*Expelled*
37th	1st	1861	Robert M. Hunter	D	Va.	Support of rebellion	*Expelled*
37th	1st	1861	Thomas L. Clingman	D	N.C.	Support of rebellion	*Expelled*
37th	1st	1861	Thomas Bragg	D	N.C.	Support of rebellion	*Expelled*
37th	1st	1861	James Chestnut Jr.	State Rights	S.C.	Support of rebellion	*Expelled*
37th	1st	1861	Alfred O. P. Nicholson	D	Tenn.	Support of rebellion	*Expelled*
37th	1st	1861	William K. Sebastian	D	Ark.	Support of rebellion	*Expelled*
37th	1st	1861	Charles B. Mitchel	D	Ark.	Support of rebellion	*Expelled*
37th	1st	1861	John Hemphill	State Rights Dem.	Texas	Support of rebellion	*Expelled*
37th	1st	1861	Louis T. Wigfall	D	Texas	Support of rebellion	Not expelled
37th	1st	1861	Louis T. Wigfall	D	Texas	Support of rebellion	*Expelled*
37th	1st	1861	John C. Breckinridge	D	Ky.	Support of rebellion	*Expelled*
37th	1st	1861	Lazarus W. Powell	D	Ky.	Support of rebellion	Not expelled
37th	2d	1862	Trusten Polk	D	Mo.	Support of rebellion	*Expelled*
37th	2d	1862	Jesse D. Bright	D	Ind.	Support of rebellion	*Expelled*
37th	2d	1862	Waldo P. Johnson	D	Mo.	Support of rebellion	*Expelled*
37th	2d	1862	James F. Simmons	Whig	R.I.	Corruption	Not expelled
42nd	3d	1873	James W. Patterson	R	N.H.	Corruption	Not expelled
53rd	1st	1893	William N. Roach	D	N.D.	Embezzlement	Not expelled
58th	3d	1905	John H. Mitchell	R	Ore.	Corrupation	Not expelled
59th	2d	1907	Reed Smoot	R	Utah	Mormonism	Not expelled
65th	3d	1919	Robert M. La Follette	R	Wis.	Disloyalty	Not expelled
73rd	2d	1934	John H. Overton	D	La.	Corruption	Not expelled
73rd	2d	1934	Huey P. Long	D	La.	Corruption	Not expelled
77th	2d	1942	William Langer	R	N.D.	Corruption	Not expelled

Members of both houses have been appointed to serve as commissioners to negotiate peace, as arbitration commissioners, as members of the World War Debt Commission which functioned in the 1920s, as members of "blue ribbon" boards of inquiry, and so forth, without losing their seats in Congress. The House in 1919 authorized payment to Members who had been absent on military service of "all arrears of salary and clerk allowance" minus their "compensation for service in the Army." Judge Gerhard A. Gesell of the U.S. District Court for the District of Columbia ruled April 2, 1971, that the 117 Members who held commissions in military reserve units were violating the incompatible-office clause of the Constitution. The decision was to be appealed.

Civil War Cases

After the Senate's expulsion of William Blount (Ind Tenn.) in 1797 for conspiracy to incite members of two Indian tribes to attack Spanish Florida and Louisiana *(see Power of Impeachment, Chapter III)*, the only successful expulsion cases were those resulting from the Civil War. On Jan. 21, 1861, Jefferson Davis (D Miss.), like a number of other southern Senators before and after that date, announced his support of secession and withdrew from the Senate. Ten days after Lincoln's inauguration, the Senate adopted a resolution ordering that inasmuch as the seats of these southerners had "become vacant,...the Secretary be directed to omit their names respectively from the roll." Although the southerners had left voluntarily, they had not formally resigned. Hence the Senate's action bore some resemblance to expulsion.

Senate Expulsions. On a single day, July 11, 1861, the Senate actually expelled 10 Members, two each from Arkansas, North Carolina, Texas, and Virginia, and one each from South Carolina and Tennessee, for failure to appear in their seats and for participation in secession. The vote was 32 in favor of expulsion, 10 against. Sen. John C. Breckinridge (D Ky.), who had been Vice President of the United States from 1857 to 1861, was expelled Dec. 4, 1861, by the following resolution: "Whereas John C. Breckinridge, a member of this body from the State of Kentucky, has joined the enemies of his country, and is now in arms against the Government he had sworn to support: Therefore, Resolved, That said John C. Breckinridge, the traitor, be, and he hereby is, expelled from the Senate." On this resolution, the vote was 37 to 0.

The Senate in 1862 expelled two Senators from Missouri, Trusten Polk and Waldo P. Johnson, and one from Indiana, Jesse D. Bright, all Democrats. Debate on the case of Bright focused on determination whether, by giving an arms salesman a letter of introduction to Jefferson Davis, Confederate President, Bright had committed treason. During the debate, the question was raised whether the Senate had a right to make a judicial determination of this kind. Sen. Andrew Johnson (D Tenn.) on Jan. 31, 1862, said that that question was irrelevant: "Mr. President, I hold that under the Constitution of the United States we clearly have the power to expel a Member...without assuming the character of a judicial body.... We have the power and the right to expel any Member from the Senate whenever we deem that the public interests are unsafe in his hands, and that he is unfit to be a Member of the body."

Of the 10 expulsions voted by the Senate on July 11, 1861, one was later annulled. In 1877, the Committee on Privileges and Elections reviewed the expulsion of Sen. William K. Sebastian (D Ark.), decided that the Senate had a right to reverse its earlier action, and recommended such reversal. The Senate on March 3, 1877, adopted the Committee's recommendation, which was based on its finding that the charges made against Sebastian in 1861 were "matters of inference and suspicion, wholly unfounded in fact (except as to absence, which was unavoidable and not an expulsory offense)." Sebastian had died in May 1865, but his children were paid the full amount of his Senate salary from 1861 to the date of his death.

House Expulsions. On July 13, 1861, the House expelled a Member-elect, John B. Clark (D Mo.), who had not yet taken the oath. After a brief debate on Clark's entrance into the Confederate forces, and without referring the case to a committee, the House adopted the following expulsion order by slightly more than a two-thirds vote, 94 to 45: "Resolved, That John B. Clark has forfeited all right to sit as a Representative in the Thirty-seventh Congress, and is hereby expelled and declared to be no longer a Member of this House."

In December of the same year, the House adopted by two-thirds votes the only other expulsions in its history, affecting John W. Reid (D Mo.) and Henry C. Burnett (D Ky.). The first resolution, adopted Dec. 2, read: "Resolved, That John W. Reid, a Member of the House of Representatives from the Fifth District of the State of Missouri, having taken up arms against the Government of the United States, is hereby expelled from the House, and the Speaker of the House is required to notify the Governor of the State of Missouri of this fact." The second, adopted Dec. 3, read:

"Whereas Henry C. Burnett, a Member of this House from the State of Kentucky, is in open rebellion against the Government of the United States; therefore

"Resolved, That said Burnett be, and he is hereby, expelled from this House, and that the Governor of the State of Kentucky be notified of his expulsion.

"Resolved, That the Sergeant at Arms of this House be directed not to pay the said Burnett his salary accrued since the close of the extra session of this Congress."

More Recent Expulsion Efforts

Sen. Robert M. La Follette (R Wis.) made a speech at St. Paul, Minn., Sept. 20, 1917, decrying American

---

Censure for Dueling Withheld

The killing of one Representative by another in a duel in 1838 went uncensured by the House. Rep. Jonathan Cilley (Jackson Dem. Maine) had made statements on the floor reflecting on the character of James W. Webb, prominent editor of a New York City newspaper which was a Whig organ. When Webb sent Cilley a note by the hand of Rep. William J. Graves (Whig Ky.), demanding an explanation of the statements, Cilley refused to receive the note. Further correspondence led to a challenge by Graves and agreement by Cilley to a duel with rifles.

The duel took place on Feb. 24, 1838, on the Marlboro Pike in Maryland, close to the District of Columbia. Graves and Cilley each fired twice, with no result. In the third volley, Cilley was shot fatally in the abdomen. Four days later, the House appointed a committee to investigate the affair. A majority of the committee recommended on April 21 that Graves be expelled from the House and that the seconds in the duel, Rep. Henry A. Wise (Tyler D Va.) and George W. Jones (a member of the Tennessee House of Representatives who served in the national House of Representatives, 1843-59), be censured. One of the minority group on the committee, Rep. Franklin H. Elmore (State Rights Dem S.C.), observed that dueling by Members had been frequent and generally had gone unnoticed by the House. A motion to lay the committee's report on the table and to print the testimony carried on May 10, and an attempt on July 4 to take up the report was unsuccessful. Graves was not expelled and Wise was not censured.

---

participation in the war in Europe. On the basis of that speech, Minnesota's Public Safety Commission petitioned the Senate to expel La Follette for sedition. The petition was referred to the Committee on Privileges and Elections, which held hearings during a 14-month period. On Dec. 2, 1918, three weeks after the World War I armistice, the Committee recommended that the Public Safety Commission's petition be dismissed. The Senate on Jan. 16, 1919, adopted the recommendation by a vote of 50 to 21.

In 1932-34, the two Senators from Louisiana, Huey P. Long and John H. Overton, both Democrats, were accused of fraud and corruption in connection with their nomination and election. Resolutions of expulsion were introduced, and the Committee on Privileges and Elections conducted an investigation. Eventually it asked to be discharged from further consideration of the two cases. The Senate complied with this request on June 16, 1934, in effect burying the expulsion resolutions.

Charges of corruption against Sen.-elect William Langer (R N.D.) led to an effort to prevent his serving in the Senate. The effort took the form in part of a proposal to exclude Langer and in part of a proposal to expel him after he had taken the oath. On March 27, 1942, the Senate first rejected the following resolution submitted by the Committee on Elections: "Resolved, That the case of William Langer does not fall within the constitutional provisions for expulsion by a two-thirds vote." On that proposal, there were 37 yeas and 45 nays. Then the Sen-

Cases of Expulsion in the House

Congress	Session	Year	Member	Party	State	Grounds	Disposition
5th	2d	1798	Matthew Lyonn	Anti-Fed	Vt.	Assault on Representative	Not expelled
5th	2d	1798	Roger Griswold	Fed.	Conn.	Assault on Representative	Not expelled
5th	3d	1799	Matthew Lyon	Anti-Fed	Vt.	Sedition	Not expelled
25th	2d	1838	William J. Graves	Whig	Ky.	Killing of Representative in duel	Not expelled
34th	1st	1856	Preston S. Brooks	State Rights Dem.	S.C.	Assault on Senator	Not expelled
34th	3d	1857	Orsamus B. Matteson	Whig	N.Y.	Corruption	Not expelled
34th	3d	1857	William A. Gilbert		N.Y.	Corruption	Not expelled
34th	3d	1857	William V. Welch		Conn.	Corruption	Not expelled
34th	3d	1857	Francis S. Edwards		N.Y.	Corruption	Not expelled
35th	1st	1858	Orsamus B. Matteson	Whig	N.Y.	Corruption	*Not expelled
37th	1st	1861	John B. Clark	D	Mo.	Support of rebellion	*Expelled*
37th	1st	1861	Henry C. Burnett	D	Ky.	Support of rebellion	*Expelled*
37th	1st	1861	John W. Reid	D	Mo.	Support of rebellion	*Expelled*
38th	1st	1864	Alexander Long	D	Ohio	Treasonable utterance	*Not expelled
38th	1st	1864	Benjamin G. Harris	D	Md.	Treasonable utterance	*Not expelled
39th	1st	1866	Lovell H. Rousseau	R	Ky.	Assault on Representative	*Not expelled
41st	2d	1870	Benjamin F. Whittemore	R	S.C.	Corruption	*Not expelled
41st	2d	1870	Roderick R. Butler	R	Tenn.	Corruption	*Not expelled
43rd	2d	1875	John Y. Brown	D	Ky.	Insult to Representative	*Not expelled
67th	1st	1921	Thomas L. Blanton	D	Texas	Abuse of leave to print	*Not expelled

* Censured after expulsion move failed or was withdrawn.

ate rejected the following resolution, also submitted by the Committee: "Resolved, That William Langer is not entitled to be a Senator of the United States from the State of North Dakota." The vote in this case was 30 in favor and 52 opposed.

Questions in Doubt

In its opinion in the Adam Clayton Powell Jr. case in 1969, the Supreme Court said that·Congress may not add to the qualifications for membership that are set forth in the Constitution. It made no reference in that opinion to previous cases in which one of the houses of Congress had excluded a Member-elect for reasons not listed in the Constitution. Nor did it explicitly deny the right of Congress to require a loyalty oath, as Congress had done from 1862 to 1882.

Some years before the Powell case came up, John T. Dempsey, a political scientist at the University of Michigan, wrote: "There is substantial reason to believe that both houses of Congress would refuse at the present time to admit a declared Communist to a seat, should one be elected. Whether this would be good or bad is not too important. The significant fact is that the power to require Members of the Legislature to fulfill a loyalty qualification could be perverted in such a way as to demand political or social orthodoxy as a qualification for membership in Congress. This would be dangerous."

An unsigned note in the January 1968 *Harvard Law Review* highlighted another aspect of Congressional judgment of Members' qualifications which, although the Powell case touched on it, remains in doubt: "Inherent in this nation's fundamental commitment to a democratic and representative system of government is the right of the electors in each district to choose the individuals who are to represent them in the Congress. Obviously, the effectiveness of this right of choice...is undermined by the decision of a house to exclude an elected candidate."

The author of the unsigned note criticized the clause in the Constitution which regulates judgment of the qualifications of Members of Congress. Taking note of abuses in past decisions on the admission of Members-elect, he wrote: "Since the process of deciding whether a Member is fit to be a Congressman is almost inevitably infected with strong political and partisan feelings, the requirement of a majority vote is an inadequate safeguard against ill-considered or improperly motivated decisions."

Of the various powers of Congress on the seating and disciplining of Members, the one in which partisanship has been most blatant is the power to settle election contests. This is due primarily, according to Dempsey, to "the failure of the Constitution to provide definite standards to guide its exercise." Dempsey listed a number of ways in which Congress might promote objectivity in this area, including relegation to the courts of fact-finding in disputed election cases; equal representation of the major parties on committees which investigate election contests; and establishment of criteria by which to judge the validity of elections.

A move to refuse admission to a Member-elect accused of misconduct has sometimes merged with proposals to censure or expel him. The views of scholars on censure and expulsion of Members of Congress span a broad range. Belittling the exercise of this power, Daniel M. Berman concluded in 1964 that "The power of each house to punish its Members has all but atrophied through disuse." Dempsey struck a somewhat different note: "The power to discipline Members usually has been exercised in a cautious manner.... No instance has been found in which a Member of either house was censured or expelled solely, or even primarily, because of partisan motives. This is a good record."

Bibliography

Books

Beck, James M., *The Vanishing Rights of the States.* George H. Doran Co., 1926.

Berman, Daniel M., *In Congress Assembled; the Legislative Process in the National Government.* Macmillan, 1964.

Galloway, George B., *The Legislative Process in Congress.* Crowell, 1953.

Getz, Robert S., *Congressional Ethics; The Conflict of Interest Issue.* Van Nostrand, 1966. Chap. VI, "Congress and Internal Discipline."

Hoar, George F., *Autobiography of Seventy Years.* Scribner's, 1903, 2 vols.

Remick, Henry C., *The Powers of Congress in Respect to Membership and Elections.* Privately printed, 1929. 2 vols.

Riddick, Floyd M., *The United States Congress; Organization and Procedure.* National Capitol Publishers (Manassas, Va.), 1949.

Weeks, Kent M., *Adam Clayton Powell and the Supreme Court.* University Press of Cambridge, Mass., 1971.

Willoughby, Westel W., *The Constitutional Law of the United States.* 2nd edition. Baker, Voorhis, 1929, 3 vols.

Willoughby, William F., *Principles of Legislative Organization and Administration.* Brookings Institution, 1934.

Wilson, H. Hubert, *Congress; Corruption and Compromise.* Rinehart, 1951.

Articles

"The Power of a House of Congress to Judge the Qualifications of Its Members," *Harvard Law Review,* January 1968, p. 673-684.

Wheildon, L. B., "Challenged Elections to the Senate," *Editorial Research Reports,* Nov. 20, 1946, p. 799-817.

Dissertation

Dempsey, John T., *Control by Congress Over the Seating and Disciplining of Members.* Ph.D. dissertation, University of Michigan, 1956. (Microfilm copy in Library of Congress.)

Government Publications

Hays, Frank E., *Senate Election Cases, 1913-1940.* Government Printing Office, 1940 (Sen. Doc. 147, 76th Congress, 3d Sess.).

Hinds, Asher C., and Clarence Cannon, *Hinds (and Cannon's) Precedents of the House of Representatives of the United States.* Government Printing Office, 1935-41. 11 vols.

Hupman, Richard D., *Senate Election, Expulsion and Censure Cases from 1789 to 1960.* Government Printing Office, 1962 (Sen. Doc. 71, 87th Cong., 2nd Sess.).

Moores, Merrill, *Digest of Contested Election Cases in the House of Representatives, 1901-17.* Government Printing Office, 1917 (House Doc. 2052, 64th Cong., 2d Sess.).

Rowell, Chester H., *A Historical and Legal Digest of All the Contested Election Cases in the House of Representatives from the First to the Fifty-sixth Congress, 1789-1901.* Government Printing Office, 1901 (House Doc. 510, 56th Cong., 2d Sess.).

U.S. Senate, *Compilation of Senate Election Cases from 1789 to 1913.* Government Printing Office, 1913 (Sen. Doc. 1036, 62d Cong., 3d Sess.).

Watkins, Charles L., and Floyd M. Riddick, *Senate Procedure; Precedents and Practices.* Government Printing Office, 1964.

Wickersham, Price. *The Right of the Senate to Determine the Qualifications of Its Members.* Government Printing Office, 1927 (Sen. Doc. 4, 70th Cong., 1st Sess.).

Power to Elect the President

CONGRESS under the Constitution has two key responsibilities relating to the election of the President and Vice President of the United States. First, it is directed to receive and in joint session count the electoral votes certified by the states. Second, if no candidate has a majority of the electoral vote, the House of Representatives must elect the President and the Senate the Vice President.

Although many of the framers of the Constitution apparently thought that most elections would be decided by Congress, the House actually has chosen a President only twice, in 1801 and 1825. But in the course of the nation's history a number of campaigns have been deliberately designed to throw elections into the House, where each state has one vote and a majority of states is needed to elect; apprehension over such an outcome has nurtured electoral reform efforts over the years.

In modern times the formal counting of electoral votes has been largely a ceremonial function, but the Congressional role can be decisive when votes are contested. The preeminent example is the Hayes-Tilden contest of 1876, when Congressional decisions on disputed electoral votes from four states gave the election to Hayes despite the fact that Tilden had a majority of the popular vote.

From the very beginning, the constitutional provisions governing the selection of the President have had few defenders, and many efforts at electoral-college reform have been undertaken. Although prospects for reform seemed favorable following the close 1968 Presidential election, the 91st Congress failed to take final action on a proposed constitutional amendment that would have provided for direct popular election of the President and eliminated the existing provision for contingent election by the House. The plan was endorsed by President Nixon and approved by the House in 1969 but was laid aside by the Senate, Oct. 5, 1970, following two unsuccessful attempts to end a filibuster by southern and small-state Senators who feared that adoption of the amendment would diminish the influence of the less populous states in Presidential elections.

In addition to its role in electing the President, Congress bears responsibility in the related areas of Presidential succession and disability. The 20th Amendment empowers Congress to decide what to do if the President-elect and the Vice President-elect both fail to qualify by the date prescribed for commencement of their terms; it also gives Congress authority to settle problems arising from the death of candidates in cases where the election devolves upon Congress. Under the 25th Amendment, Congress has ultimate responsibility for resolving disputes over Presidential disability. It also must confirm Presidential nominations to fill a vacancy in the Vice Presidency.

Constitutional Background

The method of selecting a President was the subject of long debate at the Constitutional Convention of 1787. Several plans were proposed and rejected before a compromise solution, which was modified only slightly in future years, was adopted (Article II, Section I, Clause 2).

Facing the Convention when it convened May 25 was the question of whether the Chief Executive should be chosen by direct popular election, by the Congress, by state legislatures or by intermediate electors. Direct election was opposed because it was generally felt that the people lacked sufficient knowledge of the character and qualifications of possible candidates to make an intelligent choice. Many delegates also feared that the people of the various states would be unlikely to agree on a single person, usually casting their votes for favorite-son candidates well-known to them. Southerners opposed direct election for the additional reason that suffrage was more widespread in the North than in the South, where Negro slaves did not vote.

The possibility of giving Congress the power to pick the President also received consideration. However, this plan also was rejected, largely because of fear that it would jeopardize the principle of Executive independence. Similarly, a plan favored by many delegates, to let state legislatures choose the President, was turned down because it was feared that the President might feel so indebted to the states as to allow them to encroach on Federal authority.

Unable to agree on a plan, the Convention on Aug. 31 appointed a "Committee of Eleven" to propose a solution to the problem. The Committee on Sept. 4 suggested a compromise under which each state would appoint Presidential electors, equal to the total number of its Representatives and Senators. The electors, chosen in a manner set forth by each state legislature, would meet in their own states and each cast votes for two persons. The votes would be counted in Congress, with the candidate receiving a majority elected President, and the second highest candidate becoming Vice President.

This plan constituted a great concession to the less populous states, since they were assured two extra votes (corresponding to their Senators) regardless of how small their populations might be. The plan also left important powers with the states by giving complete discretion to state legislatures to determine the method of choosing electors.

Only one provision of the Committee's plan aroused serious opposition—that giving the Senate the right to decide elections in which no candidate received a majority of electoral votes. Some delegates feared that the Senate, which already had been given treaty ratification powers and the responsibility to "advise and consent" to all important Executive appointments, might become too powerful. Therefore, a counterproposal was made, and accepted, to let the House decide in instances when the electors failed to give a majority of their votes to a single candidate. The interests of the small states were preserved by giving each delegation only one vote in the House on roll calls to elect a President.

The system adopted by the Constitutional Convention was a compromise born out of problems involved in diverse state voting requirements, the slavery problem, big- versus small-state rivalries and the complexities of the balance of power among different branches of the Government. It also was apparently as close to a direct popular election as the men who wrote the Constitution thought possible and appropriate at the time. Some scholars have suggested that the electoral college, as it came to be called, was a "jerry-rigged improvisation" which really left it to future generations to work out the best form of Presidential election.

Only once since ratification of the Constitution has an amendment been adopted which substantially altered the method of electing the President. In the 1800 Presidential election, the Republican (anti-Federalist) electors inadvertently caused a tie in the electoral college by casting equal numbers of votes for Thomas Jefferson, whom they wished to be elected President, and Aaron Burr, whom they wished to elect Vice President. The election was thrown into the House of Representatives and 36 ballots were required before Jefferson was finally elected President. The 12th Amendment, ratified in 1804, sought to prevent a recurrence of this incident by providing that the electors should vote separately for President and Vice President. *(For text of Amendment, see box.)*

Other changes in the system evolved over the years. The authors of the Constitution, for example, had intended that each state should choose its most distinguished citizens as electors and that they would deliberate and vote as individuals in electing the President. But, as strong political parties began to appear, the electors came to be chosen merely as representatives of the parties; and after 1800 independent voting by electors almost disappeared. From 1820 through 1968, only a handful of electoral votes were cast contrary to "instructions." The only such postwar instances occurred in 1948, when Preston Parks, a Truman elector in Tennessee, voted for Gov. Strom Thurmond (D S.C.); in 1956, when W. F. Turner, a Stevenson elector in Alabama, voted for a local circuit judge, Walter E. Jones; in 1960, when Henry D. Irwin, a Nixon elector in Oklahoma, voted for Sen. Harry F. Byrd (D Va.); and in 1968, when Dr. Lloyd W. Bailey, a Nixon elector in North Carolina, voted for George C. Wallace.

The original system underwent further change as democratic sentiment mounted early in the 19th century, bringing with it the demand that electors should be chosen by direct popular vote of the people, instead of by the state legislatures. By 1804, the majority of state legislatures had adopted popular-vote provisions.

Initially, most "popular-election" states provided that electors should be chosen from districts similar to Congressional districts, with the electoral votes of a state split if the various districts differed in their political sentiment. This "district plan" of choosing electors was supported by the leading statesmen of both parties, including Jefferson, Alexander Hamilton, James Madison, John Quincy Adams, Andrew Jackson, Martin Van Buren and Daniel Webster.

The district plan, however, tended to dilute the power of political bosses and dominant majorities in state legislatures, who found themselves unable to "deliver" their states for one candidate or another. These groups brought pressure for a change and the unit rule system evolved, under which all of a state's electoral votes went to the party which won a plurality of popular votes statewide.

When some states began to adopt the unit vote, the others soon followed suit. Jefferson explained in 1800: "All agree that an election by districts would be the test, if it could be general; but while 10 states choose, either by their legislatures (or by unit-rule popular vote), it is folly and worse for the other six not to follow." A Senate committee report in 1826 said: "When the large states consolidate their votes to overwhelm the small ones, those, in their turn, must concentrate their own strength to resist them. A few states may persevere, for some time, in what they believe to be the fairest system, but when they see the unity of action which others derive from the (unit rule), they cannot resist the temptation of following the same plan."

By 1804, seven of the 10 "popular-election" states cast their electoral votes under the unit rule; by 1824, 13 out of 18. By 1836, the district plan had vanished from the scene. However, no mention of unit-rule voting was ever written into the Constitution, and the state legislatures retained the power to specify any method of choosing Presidential electors and to determine how their votes would be divided. In 1969, Maine adopted a district system for use in the 1972 Presidential election.

Election by Congress

The election of 1800 was the first in which the contingent election procedures of the Constitution were put to the test and the President was elected by the House of Representatives.

The Federalists, a declining but still potent political force, nominated John Adams for a second term and chose Charles Cotesworth Pinckney as his running mate. A Republican Congressional caucus chose Vice President Thomas Jefferson for President and Aaron Burr, who had been instrumental in winning the New York Legislature for the Republicans earlier in 1800, for Vice President.

The bitterly fought campaign was marked by efforts in several states to change for partisan advantage the methods of selecting electors. In New York, where electors previously had been chosen by the legislature, Hamilton proposed that Governor Jay call the lame-duck Federalist legislature into special session to adopt a proposal for popular election of electors under a district system, thus denying the incoming Republicans an opportunity to appoint electors. Jay declined, and in the end the new Republican legislature cast all 12 New York electoral votes for Jefferson and Burr.

The Federalists were more successful in Pennsylvania, another critical state. The state senate, where holdover members maintained Federalist control, refused to

Constitutional Provisions on Selection of President

The following constitutional provisions govern the manner of the selection of the President:

Article II, Section 1, Clause 2: Each state shall appoint, in such a manner as the legislature thereof may direct, a number of electors, equal to the whole number of Senators and Representatives to which the state may be entitled in the Congress; but no Senator or Representative, or person holding an office of trust or profit under the United States, shall be appointed an elector.

Amendment 12 (enacted in 1804, superseding Article II, Sec. 1, Clause 3): The electors shall meet in their respective states, and vote by ballot for President and Vice President, one of whom, at least, shall not be an inhabitant of the same state with themselves; they shall name in their ballots the person voted for as President, and in distinct ballots the person voted for as Vice President, and they shall make distinct lists of all persons voted for as President, and of all persons voted for as Vice President, and of the number of votes for each, which lists they shall sign and certify, and transmit sealed to the seat of the Government of the United States, directed to the President of the Senate;—The President of the Senate shall, in the presence of the Senate and House of Representatives, open all the certificates and the votes shall be counted;—The person having the greatest number of votes for President, shall be the President, if such number be a majority of the whole number of electors appointed; and if no person have such majority, then from the persons having the highest numbers not exceeding three on the list of those voted for as President, the House of Representatives shall choose immediately, by ballot, the President. But in choosing the President, the votes shall be taken by states, the representation from each state having one vote; a quorum for this purpose shall consist of a member or members from two-thirds of the states, and a majority of all the states shall be necessary to a choice. And if the House of Representatives shall not choose a President whenever the right of choice shall devolve upon them, before the fourth day of March* next following, then the Vice President shall act as President, as in

* *Changed to Jan. 20 by the 20th Amendment, ratified in 1933.*

the case of the death or other constitutional disability of the President. The person having the greatest number of votes as Vice President, shall be the Vice President, if such number be a majority of the whole number of Electors appointed, and if no person have a majority, then from the two highest numbers on the list, the Senate shall choose the Vice President; a quorum for the purpose shall consist of two-thirds of the whole number of Senators, and a majority of the whole number shall be necessary to a choice. But no person constitutionally ineligible to the office of President shall be eligible to that of Vice President of the United States.

Article II, Section I, Clause 4: The Congress may determine the time of choosing of the electors, and the day on which they shall give their votes, and the day shall be the same throughout the United States.

Amendment 20, Section 3. If, at the time fixed for the beginning of the term of the President, the President-elect shall have died, the Vice President-elect shall become President. If a President shall not have been chosen before the time fixed for the beginning of his term, or if the President-elect shall have failed to qualify, then the Vice President-elect shall act as President until a President shall have qualified; and the Congress may by law provide for the case wherein neither a President-elect nor a Vice President-elect shall have qualified, declaring who shall then act as President, or the manner in which one who is to act shall be selected, and such person shall act accordingly until a President or Vice President shall have qualified.

Amendment 20, Section 4. The Congress may by law provide for the case of the death of any of the persons from whom the House of Representatives may choose a President whenever the right of choice shall have devolved upon them, and for the case of the death of any of the persons from whom the Senate may choose a Vice President whenever the right of choice shall have devolved upon them.

Statutory provisions implementing the constitutional provisions for election of a President are included in the United States Code, Title 3, Chapter 1—Presidential Elections and Vacancies.

---

renew legislation providing for selection of electors by statewide popular vote. The Republican house of representatives was forced to accept a compromise that gave the Federalists seven electors and the Republicans eight.

Jefferson-Burr Deadlock

The electors met in each state on Dec. 4, and the results gradually became known throughout the country: Jefferson and Burr, 73 electoral votes each; Adams, 65; Pinckney, 64; John Jay, 1. The Federalists had lost, but because the Republicans had neglected to withhold one electoral vote from Burr, their Presidential and Vice Presidential candidates were tied and the election was thrown into the House.

The lame-duck Congress, with a strong Federalist majority, would still be in office for the electoral count, and the possibilities for intrigue were only too apparent. After toying with and rejecting a proposal to block any election until March 4 when Adams' term expired, the Federalists decided to throw their support to Burr and thus elect a cynical and pliant politician over a man they considered a "dangerous radical." Alexander Hamilton opposed this move: "I trust the Federalists will not finally be so mad as to vote for Burr," he wrote. "I speak with intimate and accurate knowledge of his character. His

elevation can only promote the purposes of the desperate and the profligate. If there be a man in the world I ought to hate, it is Jefferson. With Burr I have always been personally well. But the public good must be paramount to every private consideration."

On Feb. 11, 1801, Congress met in joint session— with Jefferson in the chair—to count the electoral vote. This ritual ended, the House retired to its own chamber to elect a President. When the House met, it became apparent that the advice of Hamilton had been rejected. A majority of Federalists in the House insisted on backing Burr over Jefferson, the man they despised more. Indeed, if Burr had given clear assurances he would run the country as a Federalist, he might well have been elected. But Burr was unwilling to make those assurances; and, as one chronicler put it, "no one knows whether it was honor or a wretched indecision which gagged Burr's lips."

In all, there were 106 Members of the House at the time, consisting of 58 Federalists and 48 Republicans. If the ballots had been cast per capita, Burr would have been elected, but the Constitution provided that each state should cast a single vote and that a majority of states was necessary for election.

On the first ballot, Jefferson received the votes of eight states, one short of a majority of the 16 states then in the Union. Six states backed Burr, while the Representatives of Vermont and of Maryland were equally divided, so they lost their votes. By midnight of the first day of voting, 19 ballots had been taken and the deadlock remained.

In all, 36 ballots were taken before the House came to a decision on Feb. 17. Predictably, there were men who sought to exploit the situation for personal gain. Jefferson wrote on Feb. 15: "Many attempts have been made to obtain terms and promises from me. I have declared to them unequivocally that I would not receive the Government on capitulation; that I would not go in with my hands tied."

The impasse was finally broken when Vermont and Maryland switched to support of Jefferson. Delaware and South Carolina also withdrew their support from Burr by casting blank ballots. The final vote: 10 states for Jefferson, 4 (all New England) for Burr. Thus Jefferson became President, and Burr, under the Constitution as it then stood, automatically became Vice President.

Bayard of Delaware, who had played a key role in breaking the deadlock, wrote to Hamilton: "The means existed of electing Burr, but this required his cooperation. By deceiving one man (a great blockhead) and tempting two (not incorruptible), he might have secured a majority of the states. He will never have another chance of being President of the United States; and the little use he has made of the one which has occurred gives me but an humble opinion of the talents of an unprincipled man."

The Jefferson-Burr contest clearly illustrated the dangers of the double-balloting system established by the original Constitution, and pressure began to build for an amendment requiring separate votes for President and Vice President. Congress approved the 12th Amendment in December 1803, and the states—acting with unexpected speed—ratified it in time for the 1804 election.

Election of J. Q. Adams by House

The only other time a President was elected by the House of Representatives was in 1825. There were many contenders for the Presidency in the 1824 election, but four predominated: John Quincy Adams, Henry Clay, William H. Crawford and Andrew Jackson. Crawford, Secretary of the Treasury under Monroe, was the early front-runner, but his candidacy faltered after he suffered a paralytic stroke in 1823.

When the electoral votes were counted, Jackson had 99, Adams 84, Crawford 41 and Clay 37. With 18 of the 24 states choosing their electors by popular vote, Jackson also led in the popular voting, although the significance of the popular vote was open to challenge. Under the 12th Amendment, the names of the three top contenders—Jackson, Adams and the ailing Crawford—were placed before the House. Clay's support was vital to either of the two front-runners.

From the start, Clay apparently intended to support Adams as the lesser of two evils. But before the House voted, a great scandal erupted. A Philadelphia newspaper printed an anonymous letter alleging that Clay had agreed to support Adams in return for being made Secretary of State. The letter alleged also that Clay would have been willing to make the same deal with Jackson. Clay immediately denied the charge and pronounced the writer of the letter "a base and infamous character, a dastard and a liar." But Jackson believed the charges and found his

suspicions vindicated when Adams, after the election, did appoint Clay as Secretary of State. "Was there ever witnessed such a bare-faced corruption in any country before?" Jackson wrote to a friend.

When the House met to vote, Adams was supported by the six New England states and New York and, in large part through Clay's backing, by Maryland, Ohio, Kentucky, Illinois, Missouri and Louisiana. Thus a majority of 13 delegations voted for him—the bare minimum he needed for election, since there were 24 states in the Union at the time. The election was accomplished on the first ballot, but Adams took office under a cloud from which his Administration never recovered.

Jackson's successful 1828 campaign made much of his contention that the House of Representatives had thwarted the will of the people by denying him the Presidency in 1825 even though he had been the leader in popular and electoral votes.

On only one occasion has the Senate chosen the Vice President. That was in 1837, when Van Buren was elected President with 170 of the 294 electoral votes while his Vice Presidential running mate, Richard M. Johnson, received only 147 electoral votes—one less than a majority. This discrepancy occurred because Van Buren electors from Virginia boycotted Johnson, reportedly in protest against his social behavior. The Senate elected Johnson, 33-16, over Francis Granger of New York, the runner-up in the electoral vote for Vice President.

Threat of Election by House

Although only two Presidential elections actually have been decided by the House, a number of others—including those of 1836, 1856, 1860, 1892, 1948, 1960 and 1968—could have been thrown into the House by only a small shift in the popular vote.

The threat of House election was most clearly evident in 1968, when George C. Wallace of Alabama ran as a third-party candidate. For the record, Wallace frequently asserted that he could win an outright majority in the electoral college by the addition of key midwestern and mountain states to his hoped-for base in the Deep South and border states. In reality, the Wallace campaign had a narrower goal: to win the balance of power in electoral college voting, thus depriving either major party of the clear electoral majority required for election. Wallace made it clear that he would then expect one of the major party candidates to make concessions in return for enough votes from Wallace electors to win the election. Wallace indicated that he expected the election to be settled in the electoral college and not in the House of Representatives. At the end of the campaign it was disclosed that Wallace had obtained written affidavits from all of his electors in which they promised to vote for Wallace "or whomsoever he may direct" in the electoral college.

In response to the Wallace challenge, both major party candidates, Republican Richard M. Nixon and Democrat Hubert H. Humphrey, maintained that they would refuse to bargain with Wallace for his electoral vote. Nixon asserted that the House, if the decision rested there, should elect the popular-vote winner. Humphrey said the Representatives should select "the President they believe would be best for the country." Bipartisan efforts to obtain advance agreements from House candidates to vote for the national popular-vote winner if the election should go to the House ended in failure. Neither Nixon nor Humphrey replied to suggestions that they pledge before the election to swing enough electoral votes to the popular-vote winner to assure his election without help from Wallace.

In the end, Wallace received only 13.5 percent of the popular vote and 46 electoral votes (including the vote of one Republican defector), all from southern states. He failed to win the balance of power in the electoral college which he had hoped to use to wring policy concessions from one of the major party candidates. If Wallace had won a few border states, or if a few thousand more Democratic votes had been cast in northern states barely carried by Nixon, thus reducing Nixon's electoral vote below 270, Wallace would have been in a position to bargain off his electoral votes or to throw the election into the House for final settlement.

The near-success of the Wallace strategy provided dramatic impetus for electoral reform efforts in the 91st Congress. *(See below.)*

Counting the Electoral Vote

The Constitution provides that "The President of the Senate shall, in the presence of the Senate and House of Representatives, open all the certificates, and the votes shall then be counted." It offers no guidance on handling disputed ballots.

Before counting the electoral votes in 1865, Congress adopted the 22nd Joint Rule, which provided that no electoral votes objected to in joint session could be counted except by concurrent votes of both the Senate and House. The rule was pushed by Congressional Republicans to ensure rejection of the electoral votes from the newly reconstructed states of Louisiana and Tennessee. Under this rule Congress in 1873 also threw out the electoral votes of Louisiana and Arkansas and three from Georgia.

However, the rule lapsed at the beginning of 1876 when the Senate refused to readopt it because the House was in Democratic control. Thus, following the 1876 election, when it became apparent that for the first time the outcome of an election would be determined by decisions on disputed electoral votes, Congress had no rules to guide it.

Hayes-Tilden Contest

The 1876 campaign pitted Republican Rutherford B. Hayes against Democrat Samuel J. Tilden. Early election night returns indicated that Tilden had been elected. He had won normally Republican Indiana, New York, Connecticut and New Jersey; those states plus his expected southern support would give him the election. However, by the following morning it became apparent that if the Republicans could hold South Carolina, Florida and Louisiana, Hayes would be elected with 185 electoral votes to 184 for Tilden. But if a single elector in any of these states voted for Tilden, he would throw the election to the Democrats. Tilden led in the popular-vote count by more than a quarter of a million votes.

The situation was much the same in each of the three contested states. Historian Eugene H. Rosebloom described it as follows: "The Republicans controlled the state governments and the election machinery, had relied upon the Negro masses for votes, and had practiced frauds as in the past. The Democrats used threats, intimidation, and even violence when necessary, to keep Negroes from the polls; and where they were in a position to do so they resorted to fraud also. The firm determination of the whites to overthrow carpetbag rule contributed to make a full and fair vote impossible; carpetbag hold on the state governments made a fair count impossible. Radical reconstruction was reaping its final harvest."

Both parties pursued the votes of the three states with a fine disregard for propriety or legality, and in the end double sets of elector returns were sent to Congress from all three. Oregon also sent two sets of returns. Although Hayes carried that state, the Democratic Governor discovered that one of the Hayes electors was a postmaster and therefore ineligible to be an elector under the Constitution, so he certified the election of the top-polling Democratic elector. However, the Republican electors met, received the resignation of their ineligible colleague, then reappointed him to the vacancy since he had in the meantime resigned his postmastership.

Had the 22nd Joint Rule remained in effect, the Democratic House of Representatives could have ensured Tilden's election by objecting to any of Hayes' disputed votes. But, since the rule had lapsed, Congress had to find some new method of resolving electoral disputes. A joint committee was created to work out a plan, and the resulting Electoral Commission Law was approved by large majorities and signed into law Jan. 29, 1877—only two days before the date scheduled for counting the electoral votes.

The law, which applied only to the 1876 electoral vote count, established a 15-member Electoral Commission which was to have final authority over disputed electoral votes, unless both houses of Congress agreed to overrule it. The Commission was to consist of five Sena-

House Rules for Election of President

The following rules, reprinted from Hinds' Precedents of the House of Representatives, *were adopted by the House in 1825 for use in deciding the Presidential election of 1824. They would provide a precedent for any future House election of a President, although the House could change them at will.*

1. In the event of its appearing, on opening all the certificates, and counting the votes given by the electors of the several States for President, that no person has a majority of the votes of the whole number of electors appointed, the same shall be entered on the Journals of this House.

2. The roll of the House shall then be called by States; and, on its appearing that a Member or Members from two-thirds of the States are present, the House shall immediately proceed, by ballot, to choose a President from the persons having the highest numbers, not exceeding three, on the list of those voted for as President; and, in case neither of those persons shall receive the votes of a majority of all the States on the first ballot, the House shall continue to ballot for a President, without interruption by other business, until a President be chosen.

3. The doors of the Hall shall be closed during the balloting, except against the Members of the Senate, stenographers, and the officers of the House.

4. From the commencement of the balloting until an election is made no proposition to adjourn shall be received, unless on the motion of one State, seconded by another State, and the question shall be decided by States. The same rule shall be observed in regard to any motion to change the usual hour for the meeting of the House.

5. In balloting the following mode shall be observed, to wit:

The Representatives of each State shall be arranged and seated together, beginning with the seats at the right hand of the Speaker's chair, with the Members from the State of Maine; thence, proceeding with the Members from the States, in the order the States are usually named for receiving petitions,* around the Hall of the House, until all are seated.

A ballot box shall be provided for each State.

The Representatives of each State shall, in the first instance, ballot among themselves, in order to ascertain the vote of their State; and they may, if necessary, appoint tellers of their ballots.

After the vote of each State is ascertained, duplicates thereof shall be made out; and in case any one of the persons from whom the choice is to be made shall receive a majority of the votes given, on any one balloting by the Representatives of a State, the name of that person shall be written on each of the duplicates; and in case the votes so given shall be divided so that neither of said persons shall have a majority of the whole number of votes given by such State, on any one balloting, then the word "divided" shall be written on each duplicate.

After the delegation from each State shall have ascertained the vote of their State, the Clerk shall name the States in the order they are usually named for receiving petitions; and as the name of each is called the Sergeant-at-Arms shall present to the delegation of each two ballot boxes, in each of which shall be deposited, by some Representative of the State, one of the duplicates made as aforesaid of the vote of said State, in the presence and subject to the examination of all the Members from said State then present; and where there is more than one Representative from a State, the duplicates shall not both be deposited by the same person.

When the votes of the States are thus all taken in, the Sergeant-at-Arms shall carry one of said ballot boxes to one table and the other to a separate and distinct table.

One person from each State represented in the balloting shall be appointed by the Representative to tell off said ballots; but, in case the Representatives fail to appoint a teller, the Speaker shall appoint.

The said tellers shall divide themselves into two sets, as nearly equal in number as can be, and one of the said sets of tellers shall proceed to count the votes in one of said boxes, and the other set the votes in the other box.

When the votes are counted by the different sets of tellers, the result shall be reported to the House; and if the reports agree, the same shall be accepted as the true votes of the States; but if the reports disagree, the States shall proceed, in the same manner as before, to a new ballot.

6. All questions arising after the balloting commences, requiring the decision of the House, which shall be decided by the House, voting per capita, to be incidental to the power of choosing a President, shall be decided by States without debate; and in case of an equal division of the votes of States, the question shall be lost.

7. When either of the persons from whom the choice is to be made shall have received a majority of all the States, the Speaker shall declare the same, and that that person is elected President of the United States.

8. The result shall be immediately communicated to the Senate by message, and a committee of three persons shall be appointed to inform the President of the United States and the President-elect of said election.

On February 9, 1825, the election of John Quincy Adams took place in accordance with these rules.

* Petitions are no longer introduced in this way. This old order of calling the States began with Maine and proceeded through the original 13 States and then through the remaining States in the order of their admission.

tors, five Representatives and five Supreme Court Justices. Each chamber was to select its own members of the commission, with the understanding that the majority party would have three members and the minority two.

Four Justices, two from each party, were named in the bill, and these four were to select the fifth. It was expected that they would pick Justice David Davis, who was considered a political independent, but he was disqualified when the Illinois legislature named him to a seat in the Senate. Justice Joseph P. Bradley, a Republican, then was named to the 15th seat on the commission. The Democrats supported his selection, because they considered him the most independent of the remaining Justices, all of whom were Republicans. However, he was to vote with the Republicans on every dispute and thus assure the victory of Hayes.

The electoral vote count began in Congress Feb. 1, and the proceedings continued until March 2. States were called in alphabetical order, and as each disputed state was reached, objections were raised to both the Hayes and Tilden electors. The question was then referred to the Electoral Commission, which in every case voted 8-7 for Hayes. In each case, the Democratic House rejected the Commission's decision, but the Republican Senate upheld it, so the decision stood.

As the count went on, Democrats in the House threatened to launch a filibuster to block resumption of joint sessions so that the count could not be completed before Inauguration Day. The threat was never carried out, because of an agreement reached between the Hayes forces and southern conservatives. The southerners agreed to let the electoral count continue without obstruction. In return Hayes agreed that, as President, he would withdraw Federal troops from the South, end Reconstruction and make other concessions. The southerners, for their part, pledged to respect Negro rights, a pledge they proved unable to carry out.

Thus, at 4 a.m., March 2, 1877, the president of the Senate was able to announce that Hayes had been elected President with 185 electoral votes, as against 184 for Tilden. Later that day Hayes arrived in Washington. The following evening he took the oath of office privately at the White House because March 4 fell on a Sunday. His formal inauguration followed on Monday. The country acquiesced. Thus ended a crisis that easily could have resulted in civil war.

Not until 1887 did Congress enact permanent legislation on the handling of disputed electoral votes. The Electoral Count Act of that year gave each state final authority in determining the legality of its choice of electors and required a concurrent majority of both the Senate and House to reject any electoral votes. It also established procedures for counting electoral votes in Congress.

Application of 1887 Law in 1969

The procedures relating to disputed electoral votes were utilized for the first time following the election of 1968. When Congress met in joint session Jan. 6, 1969, to count the electoral votes, Sen. Edmund S. Muskie (D Maine) and Rep. James G. O'Hara (D Mich.), joined by six other Senators and 37 other Representatives, filed a written objection to the vote cast by a North Carolina elector, Dr. Lloyd W. Bailey of Rocky Mount, who had been elected as a Republican but chose to vote for Wallace and LeMay instead of Nixon and Agnew.

Acting under the 1887 law, Muskie and O'Hara objected to Bailey's vote on the grounds that it was "not properly given" because a plurality of the popular votes in North Carolina were cast for Nixon-Agnew, and the state's voters had chosen electors to vote for Nixon and Agnew only. Muskie and O'Hara asked that Bailey's vote not be counted at all by Congress.

The 1887 statute, currently incorporated in the U.S. Code, Title 3, Section 15, stipulated that "no electoral vote or votes from any state which shall have been regularly given by electors whose appointment has been lawfully certified,...but from which but one return has been received shall be rejected, but the two Houses concurrently may reject the vote or votes when they agree that such vote or votes have not been so certified." The statute did not define the term "regularly given," though at the time of its adoption chief concern centered on problems of dual sets of electoral vote returns from a state, votes cast on an improper day or votes disputed because of uncertainty about whether a state lawfully was in the Union on the day that the electoral vote was cast.

The 1887 statute provided that if written objection to any state's vote was received from at least one Member of both the Senate and House, the two legislative bodies were to retire immediately to separate sessions, debate for two hours with a five-minute limitation on speeches, and that each chamber was to decide the issue by vote before resuming the joint session. The statute made clear that both the Senate and House had to reject a challenged electoral vote (or votes) for such action to prevail. *(For text of law see box.)*

At the Jan. 6 joint session, convened at 1 p.m. in the House Chamber with Senate President Pro Tempore Richard B. Russell (D Ga.) presiding, the counting of the electoral vote proceeded smoothly through the alphabetical order of states until the North Carolina result was announced, at which time O'Hara rose to announce filing of the complaint. The two houses then proceeded to separate sessions, at the end of which the Senate, by 33-58 roll-call vote, and the House, by a 170-228 roll-call vote, refused to sustain the challenge to Bailey's vote. The two houses then reassembled in joint session at which the results of the separate deliberations were announced and the count of the electoral vote by state proceeded without event. At the conclusion, Russell announced the vote and declared Nixon and Agnew elected.

Although Congress did not sustain the challenge to Bailey's vote, the case of the "faithless" elector led to increased pressure for electoral reform. It was the fourth such maverick vote since World War II. *(See Constitutional Background, above.)*

Electoral Reform Proposals

Since Jan. 6, 1797, when Rep. William L. Smith (S.C.) introduced in Congress the first proposed constitutional amendment for reform of the electoral college system, hardly a session of Congress has passed without the introduction of one or more resolutions of this nature. But only one—the 12th Amendment, ratified in 1804—ever has been approved.

In recent years, public interest in a change in the electoral college system was spurred by the close 1960 and 1968 elections, by a series of Supreme Court rulings relating to apportionment and districting and by introduction of unpledged elector systems in the southern states.

Early in 1969, President Nixon asked Congress to take prompt action on electoral college reform. He said he would support any plan that would eliminate individual electors and distribute among the Presidential candidates the electoral vote of every state and the Dis-

Counting Electoral Votes in Congress
(3 USC 15)

Congress shall be in session on the sixth day of January succeeding every meeting of the electors. The Senate and House of Representatives shall meet in the Hall of the House of Representatives at the hour of 1 o'clock in the afternoon on that day, and the President of the Senate shall be their presiding officer. Two tellers shall be previously appointed on the part of the Senate and two on the part of the House of Representatives, to whom shall be handed, as they are opened by the President of the Senate, all the certificates and papers purporting to be certificates of the electoral votes, which certificates and papers shall be opened, presented, and acted upon in the alphabetical order of the States, beginning with the letter A; and said tellers, having then read the same in the presence and hearing of the two Houses, shall make a list of the votes as they shall appear from the said certificates; and the votes having been ascertained and counted according to the rules in this subchapter provided, the result of the same shall be delivered to the President of the Senate, who shall thereupon announce the state of the vote, which announcement shall be deemed a sufficient declaration of the persons, if any, elected President and Vice President of the United States, and, together with a list of the votes, be entered on the Journals of the two Houses. Upon such reading of any such certificate or paper, the President of the Senate shall call for objections, if any. Every objection shall be made in writing, and shall state clearly and concisely, and without argument, the ground thereof, and shall be signed by at least one Senator and one Member of the House of Representatives before the same shall be received. When all objections so made to any vote or paper from a State shall have been received and read, the Senate shall thereupon withdraw, and such objections shall be submitted to the Senate for its decision; and the Speaker of the House of Representatives shall, in like manner, submit such objections to the House of Representatives for its decision; and no electoral vote or votes from any State which shall have been regularly given by electors whose appointment has been lawfully certified to according to section 6* of this title from which but one return has been received shall be rejected, but the two Houses concurrently may reject the vote or votes when they agree that such vote

or votes have not been so regularly given by electors whose appointment has been so certified. If more than one return or paper purporting to be a return from a State shall have been received by the President of the Senate, those votes, and those only, shall be counted which shall have been regularly given by the electors who are shown by the determination mentioned in section 5† of this title to have been appointed, if the determination in said section provided for shall have been made, or by such successors or substitutes, in case of a vacancy in the board of electors so ascertained, as have been appointed to fill such vacancy in the mode provided by the laws of the State; but in case there shall arise the question which of two or more of such State authorities determining what electors have been appointed, as mentioned in section 5 of this title, is the lawful tribunal of such State, the votes regularly given of those electors, and those only, of such State shall be counted whose title as electors the two Houses, acting separately, shall concurrently decide is supported by the decision of such State so authorized by its law; and in such case of more than one return or paper purporting to be a return from a State, if there shall have been no such determination of the question in the State aforesaid, then those votes, and those only, shall be counted which the two Houses shall concurrently decide were cast by lawful electors appointed in accordance with the laws of the State, unless the two Houses, acting separately, shall concurrently decide such votes not to be the lawful votes of the legally appointed electors of such State. But if the two Houses shall disagree in respect of the counting of such votes, then, and in that case, the votes of the electors whose appointment shall have been certified by the executive of the State, under the seal thereof, shall be counted. When the two Houses have voted, they shall immediately again meet, and the presiding officer shall then announce the decision of the questions submitted. No votes or papers from any other State shall be acted upon until the objections previously made to the votes or papers from any State shall have been finally disposed of.

† Section 5 provides that if state law specifies a method for resolving disputes concerning the vote for Presidential electors, Congress must respect any determination so made by a state.

* Section 6 provides for certification of votes by electors by state Governors.

trict of Columbia in a manner more closely approximating the popular vote.

Later that year the House approved, 338-70, a resolution proposing a constitutional amendment to eliminate the electoral college and to provide instead for direct popular election of the President and Vice President. The measure set a minimum of 40 percent of the popular vote as sufficient for election and provided for a runoff election between the two top candidates for the Presidency if no candidate received 40 percent of the vote. Under this plan the House of Representatives could no longer be called upon to select a President. The pro-

posed amendment also authorized Congress to provide a method of filling vacancies caused by the death, resignation or inability of Presidential nominees before the election and a method of filling post-election vacancies caused by the death of the President-elect or Vice President-elect.

Blocking of Proposed Amendment

President Nixon, who previously had favored a proportional plan of allocating each state's electoral votes, endorsed the House resolution and urged the Senate to adopt it. To become effective, the proposed amendment had to be approved by a two-thirds majority in both the

Senate and House and be ratified by the legislatures of three-fourths of the states.

When the proposal reached the Senate floor in September 1970, small-state and southern Senators succeeded in blocking final action on it. The resolution was laid aside Oct. 5, following two unsuccessful efforts to cut off debate by invoking cloture.

Presidential Disability

A decade of Congressional concern over the question of Presidential disability was eased in 1967 by ratification of the 25th Amendment to the Constitution. The Amendment for the first time provided for continuity in carrying out the functions of the Presidency in the event of Presidential disability and for filling a vacancy in the Vice Presidency.

Congressional consideration of the problem of Presidential disability had been prompted by President Eisenhower's heart attack in 1955. The ambiguity of the language of the disability clause (Article II, Section 1, Clause 5) of the Constitution had provoked occasional debate ever since the Constitutional Convention of 1787. But it had never been decided how far the term "disability" extended or who would be the judge of it.

Clause 5 provided that Congress should decide who was to succeed to the Presidency in the event that both the President and the Vice President died, resigned or became disabled. Congress enacted succession laws three times. By the Act of March 1, 1792, it provided for succession (after the Vice President) of the President pro tempore of the Senate, then of the House Speaker; if those offices were vacant, states were to send electors to choose a new President.

That law stood until passage of the Presidential Succession Act of Jan. 19, 1886, which changed the line of succession to run from the Vice President to the Secretary of State, Secretary of the Treasury and so on through the Cabinet in order of rank. Sixty-one years later, the Act of July 18, 1947 (still in force), placed the Speaker of the House and the President pro tempore of the Senate ahead of Cabinet officers in succession after the Vice President.

Prior to ratification of the 25th Amendment in 1967, no procedures had been laid down to govern situations arising in the event of Presidential incapacity or of a vacancy in the office of Vice President. Two Presidents had sustained serious disabilities—President Garfield, who was shot in 1881 and was confined to his bed until he died two and one-half months later, and President Wilson, who suffered a stroke in 1919. In each case the Vice President did not assume any duties of the Presidency for fear he would appear to be usurping the powers of that office. As for a Vice Presidential vacancy, the United States has been without a Vice President 16 times, for a total of 37 years, after the elected Vice President succeeded to the Presidency, died, or, on one occasion, resigned. (John C. Calhoun resigned as Vice President Dec. 28, 1832, to become a U.S. Senator.)

Ratification of the 25th Amendment established procedures that clarified these areas of uncertainty in the Constitution. (For text, see box.) The Amendment provided that the Vice President should become Acting President under either one of two circumstances. If the President informed Congress that he was unable to

---

Text of 25th Amendment

Section 1. In case of the removal of the President from office or his death or resignation, the Vice President shall become President.

Sec. 2. Whenever there is a vacancy in the office of the Vice President, the President shall nominate a Vice President who shall take office upon confirmation by a majority vote of both houses of Congress.

Sec. 3. Whenever the President transmits to the President pro tempore of the Senate and the Speaker of the House of Representatives his written declaration that he is unable to discharge the powers and duties of his office, and until he transmits to them a written declaration to the contrary, such powers and duties shall be discharged by the Vice President as Acting President.

Sec. 4. Whenever the Vice President and a majority of either the principal officers of the Executive departments or of such other body as Congress may by law provide, transmit to the President pro tempore of the Senate and the Speaker of the House of Representatives their written declaration that the President is unable to discharge the powers and duties of his office, the Vice President shall immediately assume the powers and duties of the office as Acting President.

Thereafter, when the President transmits to the President pro tempore of the Senate and the Speaker of the House of Representatives his written declaration that no inability exists, he shall resume the powers and duties of his office unless the Vice President and a majority of either the principal officers of the Executive departments or of such other body as Congress may by law provide, transmit within four days to the President pro tempore of the Senate and the Speaker of the House of Representatives their written declaration that the President is unable to discharge the powers and duties of his office. Thereupon Congress shall decide the issue, assembling within forty-eight hours for that purpose if not in session. If the Congress, within twenty-one days after receipt of the latter written declaration, or, if Congress is not in session, within twenty-one days after Congress is required to assemble, determines by two-thirds vote of both houses that the President is unable to discharge the powers and duties of his office, the Vice President shall continue to discharge the same as Acting President; otherwise, the President shall resume the powers and duties of his office.

---

perform his duties, the Vice President would become Acting President until the President could resume his responsibilities.

If the Vice President and a majority of the Cabinet, or other body designated by Congress, found the President to be incapacitated, the Vice President would become Acting President until the President informed Congress that his disability had ended. Congress was given 21 days to resolve any dispute over the President's disability; a two-thirds vote of both chambers was required to overrule the President's declaration that he was no longer incapacitated.

Whenever a vacancy occurred in the office of Vice President, either by death, succession to the Presidency or resignation, the President was to nominate a Vice President and the nomination was to be confirmed by a majority vote of both houses of Congress.

The proposed 25th Amendment was approved by the Senate and House in 1965. It took effect Feb. 10, 1967, following ratification by 38 states.

Bibliography

Books

Congressional Quarterly, *Congress and the Nation*, Vols. I and II, and CQ *Almanacs.*

McMaster, John Bach, *A History of the People of the United States from the Revolution to the Civil War,* 8 vols. Appleton, 1893-1924.

Peirce, Neal R., *The People's President.* Simon & Schuster, 1968.

Rosebloom, Eugene H., *A History of Presidential Elections.* Macmillan, 1959.

Stanwood, Edward, *A History of the Presidency from 1788 to 1897.* Houghton Mifflin, 1898.

Government Publications

Hinds, Asher C., *Hinds' Precedents of the House of Representatives*, Vol. III. Government Printing Office, 1907.

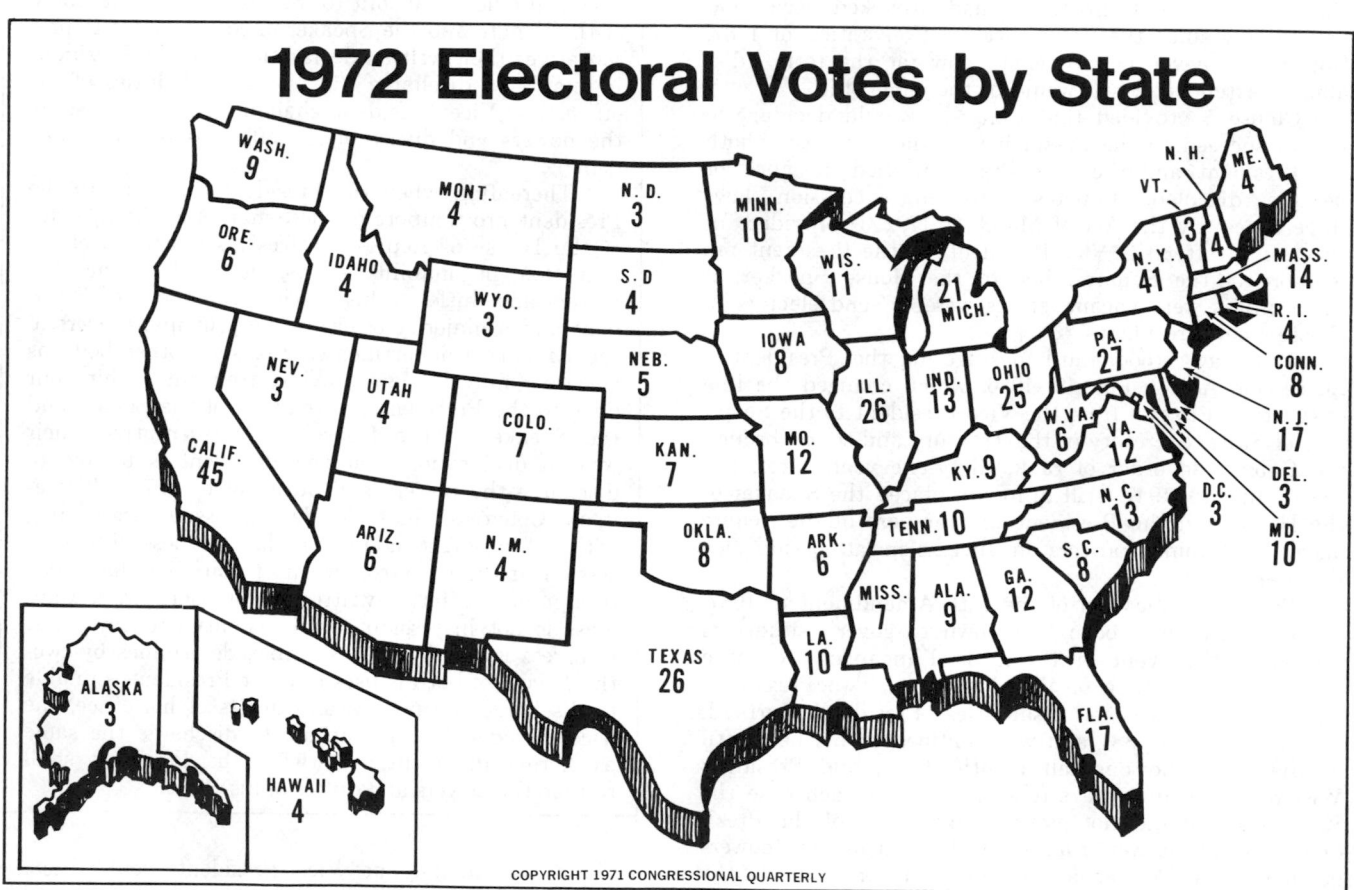

1972 Electoral Votes by State

COPYRIGHT 1971 CONGRESSIONAL QUARTERLY

The Function of Private Bills

HUMAN LAWMAKERS cannot foresee all the border-line cases which a law that they enact will include or exclude contrary to their intention. For this reason, legislative bodies—in ancient Rome, in England, in the United States, and elsewhere—developed the practice of exempting specific individuals, groups, or localities from the application of a law that was not intended to apply to them. A law granting exemption or relief in this way, in the interests of equity, is designated in modern terminology a private law to distinguish it from a law applicable generally, which is called a public law.

Large Number of Private Bills

A significant proportion of the laws enacted by Congress consists of private laws. The ratio of private laws to public laws reached an all-time peak of almost 8 to 1 in the 59th Congress (December 1905-March 1907), which enacted 6,249 private laws as against 775 public laws. The total number of private laws enacted since 1789 constitutes between one-third and one-half of all laws enacted in the same period (see box). The ratio dropped from 54.9 per cent in the 79th Congress (1945-46) to 33.5 per cent in the 80th Congress (1947-48) after the Legislative Reorganization Act of Aug. 2, 1946, banned the introduction of various categories of private bills.

Congress has taken steps, over the years, to avoid excessive allocation of the time of Members and committees to the consideration of bills which directly affect only one person or a small number of persons. These steps have included, in the first place, a series of public laws delegating to Executive agencies the authority to act on cases previously handled by Congress. In the second place, Congress has set up streamlined procedures for investigating the merits of cases which still can be settled only by means of private legislation.

Opportunities for Abuse

The practice of dealing with grievances through enactment of private laws is subject to abuse. Lobbyists able to get private bills introduced reportedly received from $500 to $2,500 a case, during the period 1967-69, in some hundreds of cases of Chinese seamen from Hong Kong and Taiwan. The seamen were ineligible for permanent residence in the United States but sought to remain after overstaying shore leave in New York. Many of them had taken jobs in Chinese restaurants or elsewhere. The lobbyists arranged for introduction of bills designating the individual seamen as exceptions to the immigration laws, on the basis of compassion.

Fewer than 25 private bills had been introduced on behalf of Chinese seamen in the 89th Congress (1965-66). More stringent enforcement of the law by the Immigration and Naturalization Service in 1967, and appeals by the seamen through lawyers and lobbyists led to the introduction of 702 such bills in the 90th Congress (1967-68) and the First Session of the 91st Congress (1969). Sen. Gaylord Nelson (D Wis.) introduced more than 100 bills of this kind; Senators Daniel B. Brewster (D Md.), Daniel K. Inouye (D Hawaii), and Harrison A. Williams Jr. (D N.J.), about 75 each; Senators Lee Metcalf (D Mont.) and Frank E. Moss (D Utah), about 35 each; Senators George McGovern (D S.D.) and Joseph M. Montoya (D N.M.), about 25 each; and a few dozen other Senators, smaller numbers.

Senators rather than Representatives were asked to introduce the bills because the House Judiciary Committee, to which they would have been referred if introduced in the House, followed an unusually strict procedure on bills aimed to save individuals from deportation. Rule 6 of the House Judiciary Subcommittee on Immigration and Nationality (see Appendix) provides that the Subcommittee shall not take preliminary action—which results in a stay of deportation— on bills for the relief of "deserting seamen" unless in a particular case the sponsor of the bill "has secured and filed with the Subcommittee full and complete documentary evidence in support of his request to waive this rule."

The Senate on Sept. 29, 1969, discussed pending private bills for the relief of Chinese seamen. It was brought out, during the debate, that administrative assistants of some Senators had taken the bills to the Secretary of the Senate without the required signature of the Senator, and that the Secretary of the Senate, as a courtesy, had accepted the bills and recorded them as regularly introduced. Sen. Nelson told a newsman that 98 bills for the relief of Chinese seamen had been introduced in his name without his knowledge. Sen. Montoya, on learning at about the same time that his administrative assistant had introduced bills of this kind for him without his knowledge, withdrew four of them which seemed to him particularly questionable.

Sen. Inouye was quoted by the *Washington Daily News,* Sept. 25, 1969, as having said, "I have subsequently received (campaign) contributions from some of these

---

Reference

See Appendix table of contents (first thumb tab) for texts of House Judiciary Committee Rules of Procedure on private bills.

Number of Private and Public Laws

Congress	Private Laws	Public Laws	Total	Ratio of Private to Total (%)
1st 1789-91	10	106	116	8.6
20th 1827-29	101	134	235	43.0
40th 1867-69	415	380	790	52.5
59th 1905-07	6,249	775	7,024	89.0
60th 1907-09	235	411	646	36.4
80th 1947-48	457	906	1,363	33.5
87th 1961-62	684	885	1,569	43.6
88th 1963-64	360	666	1,026	35.1
89th 1965-66	473	810	1,283	36.9
90th 1967-68	362	640	1,002	36.1
91st 1969-71	246	695	941	26.1

SOURCE: *Statutes at Large.*

people." He had told a newsman, regarding the seamen involved, that "My action...(was) limited to ensuring their 'day in court' before appropriate committees of Congress." Staff employees of Senators Birch Bayh (D Ind.) and Charles E. Goodell (R N.Y.) told reporters that they had received and rejected offers of campaign contributions for the Senators from promoters of these bills.

Most active of the lobbyists in the 1967-69 cases of Chinese seamen were Charles A. Murray, son of the late Sen. James E. Murray (D Mont., 1934-61), and Benton Stong, former aide to Sen. McGovern. Murray placed private bills covering more than 200 of the seamen, through Sen. Nelson and others, and received fees totaling in excess of $50,000. He told reporters that estimates that he had earned $250,000 from this source were exaggerated.

Public and Private Bills

Whether a bill applying to a number of individuals or to a moderate-sized locality should be designated a public bill or a private bill, is sometimes hard to decide. The Roman Senate used *ad hoc* criteria rather than agreed definitions to distinguish between ordinary laws, which now would be called public laws, and *constitutionis privilegia*, that is, privileges accorded to specified individuals, under traditional principles of equity, by instruments corresponding to what now are called private laws. In England, for a period following the Norman conquest, the distinction was based on the method by which the legislation was initiated. Laws resulting from the government's initiative and bearing the formula *Le roi le veult* (it is the king's wish) were considered public laws, while those sought by petitioners and carrying the formula *Soit fait comme il est désiré* (let what was requested be granted) were counted as private laws.

Difficulties in Classification

The two houses of the U.S. Congress during the 19th century developed other criteria for differentiating between public and private bills. The identifying characteristics of the two categories of legislation were sorted out more fully by the House of Representatives, in its Rules of Procedure and by on-the-spot rulings of the Speaker, than by the Senate.

Asher C. Hinds, in his *Precedents of the House of Representatives* (1907), quoted the following description of private bills from the House Manual in use at that time: "It has been the practice in Parliament, and also in Congress, to consider as private such (bills) as are 'for the interest of individuals, public companies or corporations, a parish, city, or county, or other locality.' " The language quoted in the Manual, beginning with the words "for the interest of individuals," was adapted from the definition of a private bill given in early editions of Sir Thomas E. May's *A Treatise Upon the Law, Privileges, Proceedings and Usage of Parliament* (1844 and later).

Hinds cited as illustrative of the distinction between public and private a number of bills or kinds of bills which the House had decided from time to time were instances of one or the other category *(see box)*. The decision of the House in these cases normally was made by the Speaker's ruling, but in some cases it was made by the House itself in upholding or reversing the Speaker's ruling. The instances, however, do not conform wholly to the definition which Hinds quoted from the House Manual.

From the examples cited by Hinds, it might be surmised that the classification of these bills was based on the implicit idea that if a bill was important by comparison with many others, it should be counted as public; otherwise, as private. Such a hypothesis finds support in various House decisions on the classification of borderline cases. The House, according to Hinds, designated as public "a bill for the benefit of individuals, but which includes also provisions of general legislation," where the relative importance of the bill consisted in its inclusion of an element of general, or public, legislation; and a bill containing among provisions for the relief of private persons one regarded as important in that it settled a claim made by a sovereign power.

Similarly, the House classed as private "a bill authorizing one tribe of Indians to sue another in the Court of Claims," which presumably was considered unimportant because of the attitude of condescension toward Indians; and "an 'omnibus claim bill,' containing provisions for the payment of many different claimants,...each claimant being specified by name," where a mere compilation of unimportant claims amounted to an unimportant totality.

Types of Public and Private Bills, 1907

Public	Private
Granting pensions to soldiers' widows as a class.	Granting a pension to a particular soldier's widow.
Authorizing payment of money to states or territories.	Authorizing payment of money to counties or cities.
Transferring ownership of public lands to railroads.	Authorizing extension of a particular railroad into the District of Columbia.
Incorporating particular companies which, although operating mainly in the District of Columbia, were authorized to have agencies outside D.C.	Incorporating particular companies whose operations were confined to the District of Columbia.

Source: Asher C. Hinds, *Precedents of the House of Representatives* (1935 reprint), Vol. 4, pp. 247-249.

Hinds noted that, in the classification of bills as public or private, some varieties of bills previously had been counted in one category but were classed in the other category at the time of his writing. For example, bills granting American registration to foreign-built vessels, labeled public in earlier periods, had come to be classed as private, while bills incorporating companies, authorizing construction of bridges, or allowing rights of way through Indian reservations had often been classed as private but were "now generally treated as public."

Hinds gave up completely in the effort to provide a rationale for the classification assigned to two kinds of bills, those authorizing construction of bridges and those "granting the right of way through Indian, military, or other reservations." He wrote that these two categories of bills "partake of both a public and a private character, and it is perhaps an open question whether they should be placed on the Public or the Private Calendar." He also resignedly reported, with reference to a bill to pension a battalion of soldiers, that "it has been held to be private, although the point was much disputed."

In an attempt to summarize the precedents, Hinds proposed the following definition: "A private bill is a bill for the relief of one or several specified persons, corporations, institutions, etc., and is distinguished from a public bill, which relates to public matters and deals with individuals only by classes." However, he quoted the following admonition from the House Manual: "The line of distinction between public and private bills is so difficult to be defined in many cases that it must rest on the opinion of the Speaker and the details of the bill."

Statutory Definition and Court Decisions

The only Federal statutory definition of private laws appears in an Act of Jan. 12, 1895, as amended Jan. 20, 1905. The 1895 Act stated: "The term private bill shall be construed to mean all bills for the relief of private parties, bills granting pensions, and bills removing political disabilities." This definition was embedded in a provision establishing the number of copies of bills of various kinds to be printed and the distribution of those copies in the Senate and the House. In the 1905 Act, which likewise concerned the printing and distribution of bills in Congress, the definition was changed to read: "The term 'private bill' shall be construed to mean all bills for the relief of private parties, bills granting pensions, bills removing political disabilities, and bills for the survey of rivers and habors."

The addition of bills for the survey of rivers and harbors to the category of private bills remained important for only a few years. An Act of March 4, 1913, authorized the Secretary of War to conduct surveys of rivers and harbors at his discretion and to report to Congress periodically on the need for river and harbor improvement work. By this authorization, Congress ended the necessity of introducing private bills for the survey of particular rivers and harbors. Nevertheless, when the compilers of the U.S. Code of Laws codified legislation on Public Printing and Documents, they included the language on the survey of rivers and harbors from the 1905 Act, presumably on the theory that the 1913 law had not expressly repealed that language. The wording of the statutory definition of a private law in the latest edition of the U.S. Code (1964 edition, Title 44, Sec. 189) is identical with the wording in the 1905 Act.

By contrast with statutory determinations, judicial rulings on the distinction between public and private laws have been handed down in the United States in relation not to Federal laws but to state laws. Many state constitutions forbid or restrict the enactment of private legislation. A footnote to the opinion of the U.S. Supreme Court in a case decided March 11, 1940, states: "There are restrictions against the enactment of special legislation in the constitutions of all the states except Connecticut, Massachusetts, New Hampshire and Vermont" (309 U.S. 370). The question whether these restrictions were applicable to particular laws enacted by state legislatures has been raised from time to time in litigation which posed, as the basic issue, whether the laws were public or private.

At least one of these cases reached the U.S. Supreme Court. What the Court had to say in that case, in setting the boundaries between public and private state legislation, may have some bearing on the distinction between public and private Federal legislation.

The case, *Unity v. Burrage* (103 U.S. 447), concerned an Illinois law which authorized a referendum in Unity Township, Ill., on a bond issue to aid railroads operating in the township. Supporters of the bond issue argued that the enabling law, which legalized bond referendums in townships served by the railroads, was public, in applying to all the people in every township affected, and was therefore not forbidden by Article 3 of the state constitution, which prohibited enactment by the General Assembly of any "private or local law." Opponents contended that the law was private, in applying only to certain townships, and therefore in conflict with the state constitution.

The U.S. Supreme Court upheld the law in 1880. The Court stated: "In this country, the disposition has been on the whole to enlarge the limits of this class of public acts (incorporating counties, regulating railroad operations, etc.), and to bring within it all enactments...which in any way affect the community at large."

Senate Rulings

The U.S. Senate, in a series of rulings by the presiding officer, touched the fringes of the question of what distinguishes a public from a private bill. The question as it arose in the Senate concerned the definition not of a private bill as such but of a private-claim amendment to a general appropriation bill. Such an amendment, however, possesses all the features of a private bill with the exception that it is part of a public bill and not a separate piece of legislation.

Senate Rule XVI reads: "No amendment, the object of which is to provide for a private claim, shall be received to any general appropriation bill, unless it be to carry out the provision of an existing law or a treaty stipulation, which shall be cited on the face of the amendment." The earliest case requiring an interpretation of that rule concerned a claim put forward by an attorney for an Indian tribe. The attorney sought payment out of Indian funds, not out of the Federal treasury, for legal services rendered.

On March 23, 1904, during debate on an Indian affairs appropriation bill, Sen. William P. Frye (R Maine), President pro tempore of the Senate, ruled that an amendment providing for payment of the attorney's claim was not a private-claim amendment and therefore was in order. He said that to be barred under Rule XVI a claim must be one which "would take money from the United

---

Publication of Private Laws

In the eight-volume compilation of the *Statutes at Large* covering the first 28 Congresses (1789-1845), Vol. 6 contains the private laws enacted by those Congresses.

In the volumes of the *Statutes at Large* covering the 29th-74th Congresses (1845-1936), there is a separately numbered volume for each Congress, but a volume in this series may consist physically of more than one book. For example, Vol. 49, covering the 74th Congress (1935-36), contains in Part 1 the public laws of that Congress and in Part 2 the private laws along with concurrent resolutions and other papers. Even when the private laws appeared in the same book with the public laws, the private laws were grouped separately.

For many years until 1936, the Federal Government published not only a volume of the *Statutes at Large* for each Congress, but also a paper-bound edition of the laws of each session of Congress, known as the Session Laws. When the Session Laws were published in two parts, the private laws appeared in Part 2.

Since 1937, a volume of the *Statutes at Large* has been published for each session of Congress rather than each Congress. In this series, as previously, the private laws are printed in a separate part if their inclusion in the same book with public laws would make the book unwieldy; and when they are printed in the same book, they are grouped separately.

Each public or private law is published as a separate sheet or pamphlet, depending on its length, as soon as it is enacted. These publications are known as slip laws. They are listed in the *Monthly Catalog, United States Government Publications,* issued by the Superintendent of Documents, Government Printing Office. Private slip laws may be obtained, so long as the supply lasts, from the Document Room of the Senate or the Document Room of the House of Representatives.

States Treasury." A similar ruling was made on Feb. 25, 1913.

A proposed amendment to a deficiency appropriation bill for 1935 raised a comparable question. On July 24, 1935, when the bill was under consideration, Sen. William G. McAdoo (D Calif.) offered an amendment which provided for payment of almost $6.5 million to the State of California for expenditures made in aiding the United States during the Civil War. The question arose whether the amendment concerned a private claim of the kind banned by Rule XVI. Sen. McAdoo observed that "On two occasions it (the Senate) held that this type of claims of states for reimbursement for expenditures during the Civil War were private claims, and on two other occasions it ruled by a majority vote that they were public claims." He contended that they were public claims, and Sen. Key Pittman (D Nev.), President pro tempore, ruled in his favor. This ruling, taken with those of 1904 and 1913, amounted to a liberal interpretation of Rule XVI in that it kept to a narrow span the category of private claims banned by the rule.

Classification for Official Publication

Determination of whether a law is public or private is required in connection with publication of the laws. From the beginning of the nation's history, private laws have been published separately from public laws *(see box)*. Since, however, the engrossed copy of a law, as signed by the President or passed over his veto, does not carry an indication of whether it is public or private, the publishers of the laws must make the determination in each case.

Laurence F. Schmeckebier, while writing the first edition of his book *Government Publications and Their Use* (1936), asked the Department of State, which then was responsible for publishing the *Statutes at Large,* what criteria it used in separating laws into public and private. The Department, in its reply, began by explaining not the criteria but the procedure used in making the determination:

"There are, strictly speaking, no rules which determine automatically the division of laws into public or private acts;...(the principal criterion is) the intent of Congress when the act was passed. The determination of the intent of Congress has come heretofore entirely within the discretion of the Editor of Laws of the Department and is based upon the debate of the legislation as it appears in the *Congressional Record;* the nature of the legislation; its effect and scope; whether it is mandatory of legislation which has been classified previously; and upon personal opinion. In addition, an effort is made to follow precedent in order that certain classes of legislation will appear consistently in the proper part of the *Statutes at Large.*" The Department continued with an effort to specify the attributes which tend to justify classifying a law as public and those which tend to justify classifying one as private:

"Legislation classed generally as public may be listed as that in which the interest of the Government is paramount, particular (sic), or outweighs the other considerations of the act; that in which by the nature and scope of the act, the interest of the public as a whole is affected. Legislation classed generally as private may be stated to include that which is passed for the particular benefit of an individual or group of individuals, in the enactment of which the Government or public has no direct or immediate interest. In borderline cases, the general practice is to classify the law as public."

The responsibility for publishing the *Statutes at Large* was transferred from the Department of State to the National Archives in 1950. Schmeckebier or his collaborator Roy B. Eastin checked with the National Archives in preparing the 1961 edition of the book on Government publications. On the basis of information received from the National Archives, the new edition stated that the procedure followed in classifying laws as public or private was still as described in the two quoted paragraphs, except that the clause referring to the Editor of Laws of the Department was omitted in the 1961 edition.

Unofficial Definitions of Private Bills

Location of the borderline between public and private laws has exercised the ingenuity of numbers of writers on the legislative process. Samuel P. Orth published an article in the *Atlantic Monthly,* January 1906, entitled "Special Legislation." Although the article was concerned more directly with private laws passed by state legislatures than with private acts of Congress, the distinction which Orth made between public and private laws illuminates the classification of Federal as well as state legislation. He wrote:

"A 'public law' is a measure that affects the welfare of the state as a unit; a 'private law' is one that provides an exception to the public rule; the one is an answer to a public need and the other an answer to a private prayer. When it acts upon a public bill, a legislature legislates; when it acts upon a private bill, it adjudicates. It passes from the function of a lawmaker to that of a judge. It is transformed from a tribunal of the people into a justice shop for the seeker after special privilege."

Rep. Robert Luce (R Mass.) was a voluminous writer on the legislative process. In the October 1932 issue of the *American Political Science Review,* he confessed that he despaired of locating with any degree of definiteness "the somewhat arbitrary, finical, and uncertain line drawn between private and public law." Two years later, William F. Willoughby noted in a Brookings Institution study entitled *Principles of Legislative Organization and Administration* that "The determination of what bills shall be deemed to be private bills has always given rise to some difficulties."

Alfred Steinberg said in the August 1951 issue of *Nation's Business* that Congress in passing private bills "sits as a court of last resort for some poor fellow who has a gripe against the Government but doesn't have a legal right to take his claim to a regular court." An analyst writing in Congressional Quarterly's *Weekly Report,* July 3, 1959, described a private bill as one which "seeks relief for an individual who has exhausted his administrative and judicial remedies." This formulation brings out what is probably the essence of private legislation, the fact that it is necessitated by the inadequacy of previous laws or rulings.

Categories of Private Bills

From time to time, various kinds of cases which Congress had previously handled through enactment of private laws have been made ineligible for such treatment. Cases

---

Subjects of Private Bills, 80th Congress (1947-48)

	Introduced	Enacted
Claims	1,346	272
Immigration	833	120
Land	239	38
Military	70	4
Pensions	16	0
Other	28	23
Total	2,532	457

SOURCE: George B. Galloway, "Reform of Private Bill Procedure," *Congressional Record,* Vol. 95 (1949), Appendix, p. A2902.

---

in those areas are now handled by one or another agency in the Executive Branch or by the courts, thereby, reducing the volume of minor bills before Congress. However, each of the main categories of private bills remaining within the purview of Congress is extensive.

Of the kinds of private Congressional legislation which remain alive, two are paramount: claims cases and immigration cases. Bills for the relief of individuals in those two fields have been introduced in large numbers in every session of Congress for many years. Examples of other types of private bills now occur infrequently. Twenty or more years ago, private bills dealing with matters other than claims or immigration were more fully represented *(see box).*

PRIVATE CLAIMS CASES

The Constitution provides in Article I, Section 8, Clause 1, that "The Congress shall have Power...to pay the Debts...of the United States." This provision has been construed broadly to include not only legal but also moral obligations. The Supreme Court stated in 1895 with reference to the cited clause: "The term 'debts' includes those debts or claims which rest upon a merely equitable or honorary obligation, and which would not be recoverable in a court of law if existing against an individual. The nation, broadly speaking, owes a 'debt' to an individual when his claim grows out of general principles of right and justice" (163 U.S. 440).

Interpretation of the term "Debts...of the United States" came up more recently in litigation over the authority of the Court of Claims with respect to private claims against the Government. The litigation concerned the power of Congress to authorize adjudication by the Court of Claims of cases which, at an earlier time, were generally disposed of by private legislation.

The relevant law, enacted March 3, 1911 (U.S. Code, 1964 edition, Title 28, Sec. 2509), provided that when Congress refers a claim to the Court of Claims, the court shall prepare a report to Congress on the facts of the case and "shall also report conclusions sufficient to inform Congress whether the demand is a legal or equitable claim or a gratuity, and the amount, if any, legally or equitably due from the United States to the claimant." In the case of *Burkhardt v. United States* in 1949, the Court of Claims

---

Subjects of Private Bills in the House, 1961-69

(Introduced in House or passed by Senate and referred to House)

Congress	Claims	Immigration and Naturalization	Patents
87th 1961-62	849	3,020	9
88th 1963-64	723	3,003	3
89th 1965-66	847	4,481	2
90th 1967-68	779	4,481	2
*91st 1969-70	529	4,616	0

First Session (1969) only.

SOURCE: House Judiciary Committee, *Legislative Calendars and History of Legislation* (various issues).

---

renewed and extended the Supreme Court's ruling of 1895 by deciding that "The term 'equitable claim' as used in 28 U.S.C., Sec. 2509, is not used in a strict technical sense meaning a claim involving consideration of principles of right and justice as administered by courts of equity, but the broader moral sense based upon general equitable considerations."

The Court of Claims stated further on Jan. 20, 1960, in *B Amusement Co. et al. v. United States,* that the sense of equity intended in the Act of 1911 was a sense "of broad moral responsibility; what the Government ought to do as a matter of good conscience." Marion T. Bennett, chief commissioner of the Court of Claims, wrote in the *U.S. Air Force JAG Law Review* in 1967 that Congress has the constitutional power to pay private claims of equity in a broad sense. He observed: "In this context, equity appears to be ethical rather than jural and not grounded in any sanction of positive law."

French Spoliation Claims

Even when a claim is well grounded, Congress may reject it because of the passage of time or for other reasons. American citizens and companies, for example, have unsuccessfully sought passage of private bills to pay their claims in the French spoliation cases. These cases arose mainly from the fact that the United States remained neutral in the wars between France and Great Britain in the late 18th and early 19th centuries. When American goods were shipped commercially to Great Britain during those wars, the French Navy in many cases seized both the goods and the vessels in which the goods were carried. By treaties of Sept. 30, 1800, and July 4, 1831, the United States Government released the French government from responsibility for paying for the goods or vessels, in exchange for certain intergovernmental payments and concessions on other matters.

Congress in 1885, after many appeals from heirs of the owners of the goods and vessels, authorized the Court of Claims to consider the spoliation claims. Estimates of the total damages incurred by American merchants and shipping companies ranged from $20 million to $40 million. The Court of Claims, from 1886 to 1916, made awards aggregating a little over $7 million. Congress, in 1891, 1899, 1902 and 1905, appropriated sums totaling approximately $3.9 million for payment of the awards. Claims amounting to more than $3 million, although approved by the Court of Claims, remained unpaid. After 1905, Congress was reluctant to pay the remaining sums to heirs so many generations removed from the events that had given rise to the claims.

The Senate Committee on Claims held a hearing, May 8, 1940, on a bill for payment of outstanding French spoliation claims. Sen. David I. Walsh (D Mass.), in supporting the bill, quoted George F. Hoar (R Mass.), who had served in the Senate from 1877 to 1904: "Justice lives more than one generation in this world. Honor is permanent—the public faith of the Government is permanent and if there is anything to which justice, honor, and the public faith is pledged, it is the French spoliation claims." Following Walsh's remarks, Joseph P. Tumulty, who had been President Wilson's secretary, quoted Secretary of State Thomas Jefferson's pledge of Aug. 31, 1793, to traders and shipping companies: "I have it in charge from the President to assure the merchants of the United States concerned in foreign commerce or navigation that

due attention will be paid to any injuries they may suffer on the high seas or in foreign countries contrary to the law of nations."

The bill under consideration in 1940 failed to pass, despite the historical arguments mustered by its advocates. Bills on the spoliation claims continued to be introduced until 1956, without success.

Special Problems, 1890s and After

Private bills for the payment of claims included, toward the end of the 19th century, many cases having dubious foundations. Thomas B. Reed (R Maine), who was Speaker of the House in 1889-91 and 1895-99, showed relentless opposition to most private-claims bills from the time he first came to Congress in 1877. A bill to pay the College of William and Mary for property destroyed by northern forces in the Civil War was under discussion in the House on April 12, 1878. Reed, referring to the eloquence of proponents of the bill, said: "You may bring together Bunker Hill and Yorktown, Massachusetts and Virginia, and tie them together with all the flowers of rhetoric that ever bloomed since the Garden of Eden, but you cannot change the plain, historic fact that no nation on earth ever was so imbecile and idiotic as to establish a principle (reimbursing those who have engaged in hostilities against the Government, for damage done by the Government in resisting them) that would more nearly bankrupt its treasury after victory than after defeat."

Reed continued to oppose private-claims bills after he became Speaker. He was able, by exploiting the House rules, to prevent the calling-up of many of these bills. Sen. Hoar railed against Reed in the April 1897 issue of the *Forum:*

"You go to Mr. Speaker Reed and tell him you are poor, that you have an honest claim against the United States; that it has taken your entire property without compensation; that your claim has been found to be due by the Government's own court, appointed for that very purpose; that it has passed the Senate unanimously ten times; that ten committees of the House have reported in its favor....He will answer you, that he has no doubt all you say is true; but that there are thronging at the gate millions of unjust, corrupt, or extravagant demands against the Treasury, which the House is eager to pass if it can get at them; and that he does not open the door to one honest claimant because, if he should, a hundred dishonest ones would pass in."

Reed eventually took a somewhat more moderate position. The number of private laws enacted actually rose while he was Speaker during the last half-decade of the century, increasing from 514 in the 54th Congress (1895-97) to 885 in the 55th Congress (1897-99). A still further rise, to 1,499, occurred in the 56th Congress (1899-1901). Reed had resigned from his House seat in September 1899.

Two private-claims bills in the 60th Congress (1907-09) attracted wide attention. One was a House bill "To reimburse the estate of General George Washington for certain lands of his in the state of Ohio, lost by conflicting grants made under the authority of the United States." The claim in this case arose from the fact that, through oversight on the part of public land officials, various individuals were permitted to settle on and obtain title to a 3,000-acre tract of which Washington was clearly the owner. When Washington was notified a year before he died that his title to the land might be in danger, he made inquiries and was officially assured that his title would prevail. Nevertheless, those who had located on his land were given rights there and exercised them.

Collateral descendants of Washington, residing in Virginia, other southern states and California, arranged for introduction of the House bill (and a similar bill in the Senate) on the ground that Washington's estate had been deprived of the tract by negligence on the part of public land officers. Col. Robert E. Lee Jr. of Lexington, Va., son of the Confederate general, was administrator of the estate. The House Committee on Claims, of which Charles A. Lindbergh (R Minn.), father of the aviator, was a member, held a hearing on the bill, Jan. 14, 1909. Washington's heirs would have received $305,000 under the bill. However, the committee did not report the bill, and it never reached the floor of either house.

The other famous private-claim bill of the 60th Congress provided for payment of $250,000 to Her Majesty Liliuokalani, former Queen of the Hawaiian Islands. The claim was based on the fact that John L. Stevens, American minister at Honolulu, had collaborated with the American-born revolutionaries who overthrew the Queen in January 1893. Stevens, without authorization from Washington, offered the revolutionaries the support of the American cruiser *Boston,* then in Honolulu harbor. Marines were landed, marched to the palace grounds, and prevented the Queen's forces from resisting the rebels.

Secretary of State Walter Q. Gresham on Oct. 18, 1893, recommended to President Cleveland the restoration of the legitimate government in Honolulu. Cleveland, in his annual message to Congress on Dec. 4, 1893, summarized the report of his special representative to Hawaii, James H. Blount, "showing beyond all question that the constitutional government of Hawaii had been subverted with the active aid of our representative to that government and through the intimidation caused by the presence of an armed naval force of the United States, which was landed for that purpose at the instance of our minister." Cleveland took steps to promote the restoration of the Queen's government, but the steps were unavailing.

The Legislature of the Territory of Hawaii on Feb. 23 and 25, 1907, nine years after the annexation of Hawaii to the United States, adopted a concurrent resolution supporting action in Congress which would result in "the payment to Queen Liliuokalani of an ample sum in settlement of all existing claims on her behalf." The bill for the relief of the Queen died in the Committee on Claims.

Current Categories of Private-Claims Bills

Bills introduced in Congress in recent years for payment of private claims against the Government are of three kinds.

Refund Cases. One kind aims to wipe out the obligation of individuals to refund to the Government payments made to them through error. Typically, in these cases, the money was received in good faith and repayment would cause hardship. The category consists, in large part, of cases in which work was done for the Government in the mistaken belief that it had been authorized.

Also included in the refund category are bills to forgive obligations resulting from the fact that an individual was hired as a Government employee, or given a Government contract, when he was receiving a Government pension or was not a citizen. Although the individual and the responsible Government office both acted in good faith, the wages or other payments made were illegal and therefore subject to refund. Still another example consists of cases in which a Government employee was mistakenly given a promotion, in innocent contravention of the rules.

According to a note in the June 1966 *Harvard Law Review,* a total of one million overpayments in military cases alone, involving $100 million, came to light between 1957 and 1961. The refund obligations in all these military cases were rescinded by private laws, even though no substantial hardship would have been involved in paying back the money.

Waiver Cases. Some private-claims bills provide for waiver of the statute of limitations on the Government's obligation to make a payment to an individual, company, or organization. This kind of bill is considered particularly in order when the claimant, to his own detriment, relied on advice to the effect that the statute of limitations was inapplicable.

Tort Claims. The remaining category of private-claims bills concerns tort claims not covered by the Federal Tort Claims Act of Aug. 2, 1946 (U.S. Code, 1964 edition, Title 28, Chap. 171). That Act, while laying down procedures for the settlement of certain tort claims against the Government, exempted from its provisions claims arising from activities of the Tennessee Valley Authority, the Panama Canal Co., and certain Federal banks; combat activities in time of war; fiscal operations of the U.S. Treasury or regulation of the monetary system; "assault, battery, false imprisonment, false arrest, malicious prosecution, abuse of process, libel, slander, misrepresentation, deceit, or interference with contract rights;" events in a foreign country; establishment of a quarantine by the United States; detention of goods by a customs officer; loss of mail; and certain other situations.

These tort claims, exempted from the Act of 1946 and therefore still eligible for relief by private legislation, may have their origin in injuries caused by Government agents (as in a collision with a Government truck) but not covered by compensation provisions of any applicable laws, or in situations where money was honestly promised by a Government agent but never paid.

Private-claims bills passed by Congress normally are more generous than awards made by courts in comparable cases. However, Alfred Steinberg, writing in *Nation's Business,* August 1951, reported an exception: "Back in 1945, an Army plane crashed into the Empire State Building and killed a man working on the 79th floor. His widow petitioned Congress for a private bill and was in line for a $10,000 award. In the midst of these proceedings, Congress passed the Federal Tort Claims Act, permitting her to transfer her case to Federal court. She did and won an award of $47,000."

The number of private-claims bills introduced in the past two decades has averaged about 2,000 in each Congress. Many such bills in the past prohibited transfer of any part of the settlement amount to an attorney or agent for services rendered in connection with the claim. In recent years, private-claims bills generally have limited the amount that may be transferred to an attorney or agent to 10 percent of the settlement amount.

Private Immigration and Naturalization Bills, 1957-68

Congress	Bills Introduced	Laws Enacted
85th 1957-58	4,364	927
86th 1959-60	3,069	488
87th 1961-62	3,592	544
88th 1963-64	3,647	196
89th 1965-66	5,285	279
90th 1967-68	7,293	218

SOURCE: U.S. Immigration and Naturalization Service, *Annual Report, 1968*, p. 126.

IMMIGRATION AND NATURALIZATION BILLS

Private laws for the relief of aliens are necessitated by the fact that public laws on admission of aliens to the United States, their residence in the United States, and change of nationality do not cover all hardship cases. Some private laws in this area permit aliens residing abroad to come to the United States although technically they are not eligible. Others permit aliens residing in the United State to remain in the country although technically they are not eligible. Still others permit aliens to become citizens although technically they are not eligible.

The number of private bills on immigration and naturalization rose significantly after enactment of strict provisions on both subjects in the Immigration and Nationality Act of June 27, 1952. Such bills, totaling on the average a few hundred in each Congress in the 1940s, reached a crest in the 83rd Congress (1953-54) of 4,797, of which 755 were enacted. The number introduced remained at a comparable level for several years and then increased to 5,285 in the 89th Congress (1965-66) and to 7,293 in the 90th Congress (1967-68).

Private Immigration Bills

Federal statutes on immigration exclude from admission to the United States for permanent residence individuals who have not received a visa in accordance with the statutory provisions on preference in allocation of visas. The laws also exclude individuals having specified mental, physical, or moral defects. They provide for deportation or other penalties if an individual succeeds in entering the United States in violation of these bans. The immigration laws, although providing for exceptions in stated hardship situations, are otherwise stringent and are stringently enforced. In accordance with the clear intent of Congress, the Department of Justice exercises sparingly its authority to grant exceptions.

On the other had, Members of Congress, when faced with hardship cases, have little hesitation in introducing bills aimed at relaxing application of the law in those cases. A foreigner who wishes to move to the United States but is excluded under the moral-defects provision may have close relatives in the country who can effectively explain to a Representative or Senator that the moral defect does not go beyond an offense committed when the applicant was immature. An American couple desiring to

bring in and adopt a Korean or Vietnamese child may be technically ineligible to do so. Often however, a Member of Congress will be glad to seek passage of a bill authorizing an exception in their favor.

Many private immigration bills provide for exceptions in the case of a single individual; some affect more than one person. In 1949, the Immigration and Naturalization Service in the Department of Justice analyzed, from this standpoint, more than 3,500 private immigration bills introduced in the preceding 10 years. The analysis showed that the bills applied to an average of 1.6 persons.

Following enactment of the Immigration and Nationality Act of 1952, requests for relief from immigration restrictions increased markedly. During the fiscal year ended June 30, 1953, the number of private immigration bills introduced was 48 percent greater than in the preceding fiscal year, but, because of restrictive attitudes in Congress, the number of such bills passed declined by 53 percent. Nevertheless, in the fiscal year ended June 30, 1954, almost 43 percent of all private laws enacted had to do with immigration.

President Eisenhower on Jan. 31, 1957, asked Congress to broaden the authority of the Attorney General to exempt deserving individuals from provisions of the immigration laws. He said:

"The large and ever-increasing mass of immigration bills for the relief of aliens continues to place an unnecessary burden upon the Congress and the President. Private immigration laws in recent years have accounted for more than one-third of all enactments, both public and private. Like every other enactment, each case must be separately examined and studied as to its merits by the Congress and the President. The problem presented is usually a determination whether hardships and other factors in the particular case justify an exception from the ordinary provisions of the immigration laws. These determinations could be effected without resort to legislation if the necessary administrative authority is provided."

The President proposed transferring authority from Congress to the Attorney General to grant relief to three classes of persons not likely to become public charges or to be undesirable citizens: "I recommend that the Attorney General be granted authority, subject to such safeguards

Persons Affected by Private Immigration Bills, 1939-49

Congress	No. of Bills Introduced	No. of Persons Affected	Average Number of Persons Per Bill
76th 1939-40	627	892	1.4
77th 1941-42	394	1,031	2.6
78th 1943-44	163	253	1.6
79th 1945-46	423	515	1.2
80th 1947-48	1,157	1,457	1.3
*81st 1949-50	888	1,786	2.0
Total	3,652	5,934	1.6

*To May 3, 1949.

SOURCE: Senate Report No. 1515, 81st Congress, 2nd Session (1950), p. 908-913.

Purpose of Private Immigration and Naturalization Bills in 90th Congress (1967-68)

	Number of Persons Covered by Bills			
	Introduced	**Enacted**	**Rejected**	**Not Acted On**
Permit entry for permanent residence of persons ineligible because of:				
Unavailability of quota	262	52	44	166
Mental or physical defect	20	0	6	14
Criminal or subversive activities	5	1	1	3
Illiteracy	23	2	5	16
Other reasons	38	0	7	31
Grant permanent residence status to aliens deportable for:				
Illegal entry, visa fraud, or violation of nonimmigrant status	7,891	12	1,108	6,771
Mental or physical defect	27	0	10	17
Criminal or subversive activities	105	4	22	79
Immoral activities	4	0	0	4
Other reasons	249	0	2	247
Confer citizenship benefits by:				
Waiver of naturalization requirements	568	150	63	355
Restoration of U.S. citizenship	23	1	14	8
Posthumous bestowal of citizenship	3	3	0	0
Other actions	3	0	0	3

SOURCE: U.S. Immigration and Naturalization Service, *Annual Report, 1968*, p. 127.

as Congress may prescribe, to grant relief from exclusion and expulsion to aliens having close relatives in this country, to veterans, and to functionaries of religious organizations. Generally these are the classes of cases which have been favorably regarded by Congress because of the hardship involved."

Congress adopted amendments to the immigration laws granting additional authority to the Attorney General, but the classes of persons whom the Attorney General was empowered to exempt differed from those recommended by the President. The Act of Sept. 11, 1957, authorized admission, without regard to quotas, of a few categories of relatives previously not eligible for nonquota visas, such as stepchildren. It authorized the Attorney General to let down the bars also for a few additional groups, such as aliens who, though legally admitted, had failed to fulfill the requirements for permanent residence.

Further amendments of this kind were adopted in 1958. The Act of Aug. 8, 1958, authorized the Attorney General to legalize the stay in the United States of persons who had entered the country improperly before June 28, 1940, had resided in the United States continuously since such entry, and were "of good moral character." The Act of Aug. 21, 1958, added to the groups whose status the Attorney General could regularize aliens admitted as non-immigrants who could have been admitted as immigrants.

Private Bills to Avert Deportation

An immigrant who has entered the country illegally and wishes to avoid deportation or other penalties may appeal to a Representative's or Senator's humanitarian feelings and hope for introduction and enactment of a private bill according him status as a legal immigrant. He may plead that he is needed as a breadwinner by members of his family, already legal residents of the United States. There may be medical reasons why he needs to stay in the country. The illegal immigrant may be a widow or widower of an American citizen. Or there may be danger of political persecution in the event of deportation to the country of origin. About 80 percent of all private bills on immigration or naturalization involve threatened deportation.

If an alien is about to be deported, and a private bill is introduced in Congress to allow him to stay in the country, the Immigration and Naturalization Service is placed in a quandary. If it deports the individual and Congress later exempts him, the service will have prevented the Congressional action from achieving its purpose; but if the service refrains from deporting the individual, it may be showing more leniency than Congress itself will show in the ultimate decision on the bill.

In an effort to resolve this dilemma, the Immigration and Naturalization Service reached agreements with the

House and Senate Committees on the Judiciary in 1947-48. The agreement of Feb. 27, 1947, with the House Committee, according to a summary of it published in 1950 by the Senate Judiciary Committee, provided "that deportation proceedings not be stayed upon the introduction of a private bill in the House of Representatives unless the House Committee on the Judiciary addresses some formal communication to the service to stay proceedings." The agreement about a year later with the Senate Committee provided, according to the same summary, "that deportation be stayed in the case of any alien concerning whom a private immigration bill is pending in the Senate on which bill no unfavorable action has been taken by the Senate Committee on the Judiciary by the end of the current session of Congress."

Attorney General James P. McGranery, in a letter of Aug. 21, 1952, to Rep. Francis E. Walter (D Pa.), chairman of the Judiciary Subcommittee on Immigration and Nationality, defined the position of the Department of Justice on this matter as follows: "In the past this Department has generally withheld the deportation of those aliens in whose behalf private bills were pending, when such postponement has been requested by the Senate and House Judiciary Committees. Such deferments represent an administrative courtesy which the Attorney General is glad to extend to Congress. As you know, however, the law reposes in this office the duty to deport aliens who are illegally in the United States, and this Department must reserve the right to determine whether a stay of deportation in any individual case is consistent, in its judgment, with good administration and with the welfare and safety of the United States, a policy with which I am sure that you are in full accord. Such determination, however, will be made only after consultation with the interested committees of the Congress."

Some years later, Charles Gordon and Harry N. Rosenfield, Washington lawyers, wrote in their *Immigration Law and Procedure* (revised edition, 1966-67): "The introduction of a private relief bill does not in itself block deportation. But in many cases it will induce the administrative authorities to stay their hands until Congress can act." The staff of the House Committee on the Judiciary informed *Congressional Quarterly* in 1970 that the substance of the agreements of 1947-48 was reaffirmed in 1969 in an exchange of letters between Rep. Emanuel Celler (D N.Y.), chairman of the Committee, and Raymond F. Farrell, Commissioner of Immigration and Naturalization.

Court Cases on Deportation. Two court cases have involved the question of whether the alien has a legal right to a stay of deportation on the basis of the introduction of a private bill for his relief. Attorneys for the aliens argued that a departure from the general practice of granting a stay would be arbitrary. The first case was that of Ellen Knauff, a German who arrived in New York in 1948 and claimed admission under the War Brides Act of Dec. 28, 1945. When the Attorney General decided to exclude Mrs. Knauff and deport her on the basis of confidential adverse information, Sen. William Langer (R N. Dak.) on Feb. 2, 1950, and Rep. Walter on March 8, 1950, introduced private bills to cancel the deportation proceedings. Rep. Walter's bill passed the House, with amendments, on May 2.

Mrs. Knauff's attorneys sought a stay of deportation while the bills were pending. The Department of Justice declined to hold up deportation for this reason, whereupon the attorneys filed suit. The U.S. Court of Appeals, Second Circuit, on March 28, 1950, decided in Mrs. Knauff's favor. Judge Learned Hand, in a concurring opinion, said:

"The case come to us on a record which...compels us to assume that the Attorney General has hitherto in all cases postponed deportation while a bill to admit the alien has been pending in Congress. This practice may never in fact have covered the case of an alien whose presence the Attorney General has found to be prejudicial to the interests of the United States; and it can be argued that we should not assume that it has gone so far. However, since it is alleged to have been a general practice, we should accept the allegation as it reads, unless the return (reply of the Attorney General) denies that it has ever covered cases like the relator's. The absence of any such denial and of any excuse seems to me to present an unrelieved instance of administrative caprice, which we may not ignore."

The Supreme Court on March 5, 1951, declined to review the decision of the Court of Appeals. Some weeks later, the Department of Justice revived the deportation order, on grounds it considered valid, and was about to put Mrs. Knauff on a plane when on May 17 Supreme Court Justice Robert H. Jackson granted a stay. Rep. Franklin D. Roosevelt Jr. (D N.Y.) told the House the next day that "The latest act in this scandalous situation was played yesterday when the Department of Justice, with unseemly haste, tried to rush Mrs. Knauff out of the country before her legal remedies had been exhausted." The Board of Immigration Appeals later recommended that Mrs. Knauff be allowed to reside in the United States, and Attorney General J. Howard McGrath on Nov. 2, 1951, approved the recommendation.

The second court case involving the right to a stay of deportation while a private bill was pending concerned Mr. and Mrs. Konstantinos Roumeliotis, Greek visitors who had overstayed their visas and were about to be deported. On Feb. 6, 1962, Sen. Everett M. Dirksen (R Ill.) introduced a private bill on their behalf, but the Department of Justice indicated that it nevertheless would go ahead with the deportation. The would-be immigrants' lawyers filed suit. In the course of the proceedings in the U.S. Court of Appeals, Seventh Circuit, the Department of Justice declared: "It is not the policy of the Immigration and Naturalization Service to stay deportation because of the mere filing of a private bill, but rather, the policy of the Immigration and Naturalization Service is to stay deportation only when the Committee on the Judiciary requests a report from the service."

The court, in denying a stay of deportation, noted that the Senate Judiciary Committee had decided on March 7, 1962, not to take action on the bill for the relief of Mr. and Mrs. Roumeliotis, on the ground that, in the words of the Committee's record of the decision, "Similar bills HR 1342 and HR 1343 (for the relief of Mr. and Mrs. Roumeliotis, respectively) were acted on adversely by the House Judiciary Committee on July 25, 1961." Review was denied by the Supreme Court on Dec. 3, 1962.

Mafia Cases. Considerable public attention was focused, from about 1948 to the mid-1950s, on the deportation of individuals considered to be members of the Mafia. Charles (Lucky) Luciano was perhaps the most prominent gangster deported in the period. For some members or supposed members of the Mafia who were facing deportation, private relief bills were introduced in Congress.

Rep. Michael J. Kirwan (D Ohio) on April 20, 1948, introduced a bill directing the Attorney General to cancel deportation proceedings against Francesca Cammarata. The bill failed to pass, but in the next Congress, on March 29, 1949, Kirwan introduced a similar bill. When queried about hostile comments on these bills, July 11, 1950, the Representative replied: "When relatives come to you and plead for you to stop the deportation of a man, you just can't take to word of a police chief (as to the man's criminality)." On Jan. 12, 1954, Kirwan responded to renewed criticism of his 1948 and 1949 actions in the Cammarata case by stating that his purpose had been "to further justice, not to obstruct it." This failed to satisfy Sen. John J. Williams (R Del.), who said in the Senate the following day that Kirwan's activity on behalf of Cammarata was "a disgusting example of gangster coddling."

At least one bill in this general category became a law. Sen. Herbert H. Lehman (D N.Y.) introduced a private bill in 1954 to cancel deportation proceedings against Martin A. Madden, brother of a notorious gangster of the Prohibition era. Lehman told a newspaper reporter, April 20, 1954, that as far as he knew, the beneficiary of the bill had committed no significant crime since serving time for burglary some 35 years earlier. The proposed deportation of Madden, the Senator said, "highlights the injustice of our immigration laws." The Immigration and Naturalization Service contended that Madden had violated a provision of the immigration law in 1953 by claiming American citizenship when he returned from a weekend trip to Cuba. Sen. Lehman reintroduced his private bill in 1955. It passed both houses, and President Eisenhower signed it on August 12, 1955.

Another bill of this sort almost became law. Introduced by Sen. Langer, the bill would have directed the Attorney General to discontinue deportation proceedings against George Pantelas. The bill passed both houses, but President Eisenhower on Aug. 26, 1954, notified the Secretary of the Senate that he had pocket-vetoed it. In his veto memorandum, the President recited the facts of the case and stated his conclusion: "While I am in sympathy with the evident purpose of this legislation to provide support for the family of the alien, the record of bad conduct presented in this case convinces me that the granting of the relief proposed would not be in the best interests of the United States. Accordingly, I am withholding my approval from this bill."

Scripps-Howard newspapers in 1955 carried a number of news stories and editorials on "pressure" exerted by Congressmen on behalf of deportable Mafia members. An editorial of Feb. 8, 1955, read in part:

"Pressure of this sort whether successful or not is a smelly business. It always is possible, of course, that an innocent alien will find himself about to be deported. But there is a last resort of a special act of Congress, few members of which would turn down a deserving case. It is the abuse of that privilege—outright protection of guilty men by Congressmen themselves—that led to current efforts by Rep. Francis E. Walter (D Pa.) to block the so-called "stinker bills." Through some of these bills undesirable aliens have been permitted to remain in the country for years after being ordered deported, even though the bills themselves were never passed by Con-

gress. The 15 bills killed Monday (Feb. 7, 1955)...indicate that we are getting somewhere in the matter. And about time!"

Criticism of such bills continued in 1956. Rep. Walter on March 31, 1956, accused Rep. William H. Ayres (R Ohio) of trying by private immigration bills to block the deportation of alien New York criminals and of a "notorious white slaver from Cleveland."

Private bills introduced on behalf of individuals connected or supposedly connected with the Mafia fell off after a flurry of cases in the early 1950s. The total number of exemptions from deportation was small in comparison with the number of successful deportation efforts. Sen. Dirksen said in a speech at Springfield, Ill., Aug. 18, 1955, that under the Republican Administration 4,000 alien criminals had been deported.

Nationality Cases

Senators and Representatives from time to time introduce private bills in behalf of persons who wish to gain or retain status as American citizens notwithstanding provisions of law which normally would prevent them from doing so. To receive citizenship without waiting the required length of time would enable an alien, in some cases, to work at a job for which only citizens are eligible. If candidates for the job are scarce, and the alien is well qualified, a private bill for relief of the alien may gain quick approval. In other cases, a person who is already an American citizen may be in danger of losing that status. For example, a naturalized American citizen who is a servant of an American ambassador, and therefore resides abroad for extended periods, may be unable to fulfill requirements of the law relating to residence in the United States by naturalized citizens. Congress is likely to view with favor a private bill in such a case.

On grounds of compassion or sentiment, the 90th Congress during its Second Session (1968) enacted seven private laws bestowing American citizenship on individuals who had not strictly fulfilled the residence or physical-presence requirements of the naturalization laws, but who nevertheless were deemed worthy of the privileges of citizenship. Three of these laws conferred citizenship posthumously on men who had joined the U.S. Army in 1965 or 1966 and died while on active duty in Vietnam in 1967: John R. Aneli, native of Italy; John P. Collopy, native of Ireland; and Ivan C. King, native of Germany.

PRIVATE BILLS IN OTHER AREAS

Matters other than claims, immigration, and naturalization call from time to time for private legislation. For one thing, the Constitution provides in Article I, Section 9, Clause 8, that "no Person holding any Office of Profit or Trust under...(the United States), shall, without the Consent of Congress, accept of any present, Emolument, Office, or Title, of any kind whatever, from any King, Prince, or foreign State." Congress grants consent in such cases by private laws.

Gifts and decorations presented to civilian or military employees of the Government are retained by the Department of State until Congress authorizes the individuals concerned to accept them. Originally, the Department of State proposed private laws in these cases while the recipients were still in Government employment, and Congress included in its approval a provision forbidding those awarded foreign decorations to wear them in public.

A private law of Jan. 31, 1881, authorized, with this restriction, a Navy lieutenant to accept the Cross of the Legion of Honor from the French government, in appreciation of services rendered at the 1878 Exposition at Paris; another Navy lieutenant, a pair of vases and a lacquered box from the Japanese government in acknowledgment of his services in rescuing four Japanese seamen; the Superintendent of the Census, a Swedish decoration; and others.

Under current practice, the Department of State retains the decorations and gifts until the recipients have retired from Government employment. A private law of Aug. 27, 1958, authorized certain "named retired personnel of the Government of the United States...to accept and wear such decorations, orders, medals, emblems, presents, and other things as have been tendered...by the foreign government or foreign governments immediately following their names." The list included 114 retired civilian employees and 415 retired members of the armed forces.

Among the individuals named in the 1958 law, and the donor governments, were Col. Harry S Truman (whose date of retirement was given as Jan. 31, 1953), Liberia; Sen. Edwin C. Johnson (D Colo., retired Jan. 2, 1955), Italy; Rep. Ralph O. Brewster (R Maine, retired Dec. 31, 1952), Philippines; Rep. James P. Richards (D S.C., retired Jan. 2, 1957), Greece and Spain; Ambassador to the United Nations Warren R. Austin (retired Jan. 22, 1953), Cuba and the Dominican Republic; Ambassador Joseph C. Grew (retired Oct. 1, 1945), Belgium, Finland, and Peru; and Gen. Mark W. Clark (retired Oct. 31, 1953), Japan.

An additional category of private legislation has developed because Congress, in a number of cases, wanted to reward an inventor or other benefactor. For example, Private Law 86-10, approved May 13, 1959, authorized the payment of $15,000 to Mrs. Paul M. Tedder of Gainesville, Fla., in recognition of the fact that her husband, a research engineer, had, in the words of the law, "conceived many ideas and inventions...which have resulted in savings to the United States of many millions of dollars and for which he received no compensation other than his salary from the University of Florida."

Miscellaneous Private Laws, 1968

Private Law No.	Approved	Subject
90-208	April 11	Authorizing Secretary of the Interior to exchange certain Federal lands for lands owned by Robert S. Latham, Albany, Ore.
90-214	April 29	Exempting from taxation certain property of a religious foundation in District of Columbia.
90-215	May 4	Authorizing documentation of a vessel owned by resident of Port Clyde, Maine, for coastal transportation and fishing despite lack of full compliance with merchant marine laws.
90-264	June 27	Authorizing Secretary of Agriculture to grant easement over certain forest lands in Missouri to specified railroad company.
90-278	July 1	Authorizing Post Office Department to rectify annual leave account of a postal employee for the period 1945-48.

Procedures in Enactment of Private Laws

Alfred Steinberg wrote in *Nation's Business* some years ago that it took nine months to get the average private bill through the process of enactment. The general course of a private bill, from introduction to Presidential approval, is much the same as that of a public bill. But there are some important differences, and they begin to appear at the very outset.

Introduction of Private Bills

A private bill generally is initiated at the instance of the individual, company, group or locality that stands to benefit from its enactment. By contrast, public laws usually originate in the Executive Branch of the Government or in Congress itself. The intended beneficiary of a private bill may get in touch with his Representative or one of his Senators directly, presenting the facts and considerations which he believes will justify introduction of the bill, or he may use the services of a lawyer, lobbyist or other intermediary. Two scholars who studies a series of private bills introduced in the Senate reported that many individuals hesitated to approach a Senator on a matter of this kind. Stephen K. Bailey and Howard D. Samuel wrote in their book *Congress at Work:* "Most applicants looked for influence (influential friends) in the belief that the introduction of a private bill was a weighty affair in which the Senator would only involve himself under pressure. Their belief was mistaken. The Senator regarded the introduction of private immigration bill as a favor easily dispensed."

The same is true in the House of Representatives. Steinberg found that "Most Congressmen feel obliged to introduce any private bill a constituent may petition him for." Daniel M. Berman observed likewise, in his book *In Congress Assembled,* that "Far from considering this burden an onerous chore, most of them relish it as still another golden chance to earn the gratitude of their constituents."

American practice differs from the British at this stage of the process. An American seeking legislative relief approaches a particular Senator or Representative, whereas Parliament has a Private Bill Office to which anyone may direct a request for relief without going to a particular Member of Parliament. The House of Commons on May 26, 1685, adopted a rule, still operative almost 300 years later, which provided "That for the future no private bill be brought into this House, but upon a Petition first presented, truly stating the case, at the peril of the Parties prosecuting the same: and that such Petition shall be signed by the Parties, who are suitors for the Bill." Parliament established the Private Bill Office in 1810 to study these petitions.

Requests of Congress for legislative relief may come from two sources other than the interested party or a Senator or Representative acting in his behalf. By an Act of April 10, 1928 (U.S. Code, 1964 edition, Title 31, Sec. 236), the Comptroller General of the United States was authorized to direct the attention of Congress to cases in which, through error or otherwise, citizens, business concerns, or institutions merited relief not authorized by existing law. Such relief was granted, for example by Private Law 87-39, signed by President Kennedy on June 16, 1961, which authorized the Comptroller General to pay two construction companies for work they had done in 1959 at the American National Exhibition in Moscow.

Congress by various acts has authorized the Attorney General to suspend the deportation of certain classes of deportable aliens and to report to Congress on each case in which he has exercised this authority (U.S. Code, 1964 edition, Title 8, Sec. 1254). Congress may then confirm or end the suspension by measures which are not private laws in the full sense, since they do not require approval by the President, but which are comparable in many respects to private laws. In some cases, either chamber may end the suspension and order the alien deported by adopting a resolution to that effect; if neither House nor Senate does so in a specified period, the deportation proceedings are canceled. In other cases, affirmative approval by Congress is required: both houses must adopt a concurrent resolution confirming the suspension; if they do not do so "prior to the close of the session of Congress next following the session at which...(the) case is reported," the Attorney General is required to deport the alien.

The Department of State, as noted, initiates private bills authorizing retired personnel of the government to accept gifts or decorations from foreign governments. This source of private bills, unlike the two just mentioned, is based on tradition and the general statutory duties of the Department rather than on specific legislation.

A Senator or Representative sponsoring a private bill may have it drafted in his own office or in the office of the Legislative Counsel of the House or Senate as the case may be. If the bill concerns a claim and is to be introduced in the House, assistance is sometimes provided by the staff of the Claims Subcommittee of the House Committee on the Judiciary. The title of the bill often includes the words "for the relief of" and the name of the intended beneficiary.

In the Senate, the rule on introduction of private bills reads as follows (Rule VII, Paragraph 2):

"Senators having petitions, memorials, pension bills, or bills for the payment of private claims to present after the morning hour may deliver them to the Secretary of the Senate, indorsing upon them their names and the reference or disposition to be made of them, and said petitions, memorials, and bills shall, with the approval of the Presiding Officer, be entered on the Journal with the names of the Senators presenting them as having been read twice and referred to the appropriate committees."

In the House, where the majority of private bills originate, the introduction of such a bill is governed by Rule XXII, Section 1, which reads: "Members having petitions or memorials or bills of a private nature to present may deliver them to the Clerk, indorsing their names and the reference or disposition to be made thereof; and said petitions and memorials and bills of a private nature, except such as, in the judgment of the Speaker, are of an obscure or insulting character, shall be entered on the Journal, with the names of the Members presenting them, and the Clerk shall furnish a transcript of such entry to the official reporters of debates for publication in the Record."

Committee Investigations and Reports

Virtually all private bills introduced in the Senate are referred to the Senate Committee on the Judiciary, and private bills introduced in the House are almost always referred to the House Committee on the Judiciary.

The reason in the latter case is that the Legislative Reorganization Act of Aug. 2, 1946, assigned to the House Judiciary Committee the jurisdiction of three former committees which had been responsible for the major topics of private legislation—the Committees on Claims (established 1794), Patents (established 1837), and Immigration and Naturalization (established 1893). The 1946 Act also assigned similar responsibilities to the Senate Judiciary Committee.

One of the few private bills referred to another committee since the Legislative Reorganization Act went into effect was HR 7161, 91st Congress, 1st Session (1969), which was referred to the House Committee on Agriculture. The bill would direct the Secretary of Agriculture to convey title to four tracts of public land in Arizona to certain persons. The land was deeded to the government in 1905 in exchange for other land, but title to the substitute land was subsequently clouded by land legislation which did not take this situation into account. The Committee on Agriculture reported the bill in December 1969, but it was not brought up for floor action.

A private bill usually receives more detailed study in the Judiciary Committee of the chamber in which it originates than in the Judiciary Committee of the other house. This is not to say that the Senate Committee always agrees with a favorable report of the House Committee, or vice versa, but if one of the Committees holds a hearing on a private bill, the other as a rule does not repeat that process if and when the bill comes before it for consideration.

Immigration and Naturalization Cases

Many more private bills on immigration and naturalization originate in the House than in the Senate. The chairman of the House Judiciary Committee refers all bills of this kind to the standing Subcommittee on Immigration and Nationality (Subcommittee No. 1). Under the rules of the Subcommittee (*see Appendix*), no action is taken on a private bill until its sponsor submits a written request. The Subcommittee also holds without action any bills whose passage would be contrary to precedent or to the known attitudes of Congress. The Senate Judiciary Committee conforms in general with the practices of the House Committee in regard to private immigration and naturalization bills.

On April 20, 1950, the Senate Judiciary Committee issued a study of almost 1,000 pages on the immigration and naturalization system. The study described the procedures followed before the Senate or House Judiciary Committee or Subcommittee takes action on a private bill relating to immigration or naturalization:

"When a private bill is introduced, a report is requested from the Immigration and Naturalization Service, which refers the case to the field office in the district in which the alien and his witnesses are located. The field office is required to give top priority to requests for investigations of private bills. Every case is also cleared through the records of the Federal Bureau of Investigation before a report is made to the Congressional committee. The FBI check is made against the existing records, and the security phase of the report is supplemented by further investigation by the Immigration and Naturalization Service. The beneficiary of the bill is questioned in complete detail and persons who appear to have knowledge of the individual are likewise questioned...."

"The Congressional committee also requests reports from the State Department and from the sponsor of each bill. The information requested from the sponsor of each bill concerning a person for whom relief is intended includes: The circumstances surrounding the entry of the person into the United States; his present activities, how the person is presently earning a living or whether dependent on some other person for support; whether or not he is engaged in any activities, political or otherwise, injurious to the American public interest; and whether or not he has been convicted of an offense under any Federal or State law, and if so, what offense."

The report of the Immigration and Naturalization Service usually is received within three weeks of the request. In former years, the report contained a summary of the facts and a recommendation. The recommendation, in almost all cases, was negative. Now, the Immigration and Naturalization Service supplies only a summary of the facts. If the House Immigration and Nationality Subcommittee receives a large number of reports on private immigration and naturalization bills in a short period, they are parceled out among the members of the Subcommittee for study.

The House Subcommittee meets on Thursdays, at which time it takes up private immigration and naturalization bills on which reports have been received and studied. Present, in addition to members of the Subcommittee and its staff, are representatives of the Departments of State and Justice, who often appear in the role of prosecutors, and, in the case of each person seeking relief, his Congressional sponsor and sometimes his attorney. The Subcommittee hears arguments on both sides, but the proceedings are of a nonadversary nature, without formal cross-examination, motions, or other technical courtroom procedures. After the hearing, the Subcommittee goes into executive session and decides what action to take on the bills before it. Recommendations are made accordingly to the full Judiciary Committee as its next weekly meeting.

The House Judiciary Committee, meeting on Tuesdays, generally concurs in the recommendations of the Subcommittee. If the recommendation is favorable, and the Committee agrees, the bill is reported to the House of Representatives and put on the Private Calendar. In the case of a bill introduced originally in the Senate, the procedure is similar. A bill approved by the Senate Judiciary Subcommittee on Immigration and Naturalization and by the full Senate Judiciary Committee goes on the Judiciary Committee Calendar.

Claims Cases. Rule XXI, Clause 3, of the House of Representatives provides: "No bill for the payment or adjudication of any private claim against the Government shall be referred, except by unanimous consent, to any other than the following committees, namely: To the Committee on Foreign Affairs or to the Committee on the Judiciary." This rule is based on the assignment of functions to committees set out in the Legislative Reorganization Act of 1946. The Committee on Foreign Affairs would consider an equity claim of a foreign government or an international organization against the United States. Such claims now are almost nonexistent. Virtually all private claims bills are referred, in the House, to the Committee on the Judiciary.

The chairman of the House Judiciary Committee refers private claims bills to the standing Subcommittee on Claims (Subcommittee No. 2). As in immigration and naturalization cases, the Subcommittee takes no action on a private bill until the sponsor of the bill requests action and, in any case, takes no action if the claim is contrary to the Subcommittee's rules (see Appendix), important precedents, or known attitudes of Congress. On receipt of a request from the sponsor, if there is no obstacle to proceeding, the Subcommittee asks the department or agency of the Federal Government most closely concerned with the claim, or the Comptroller General, for a report on the matter. The report usually is transmitted to the Subcommittee within 90 days. Walter Gellhorn and Louis Lauer, New York lawyers, commended the objectivity of these reports in a *Columbia Law Review* article: "The expectation of full disclosure of evidence, even when adverse to the Government, is well grounded. Our examination of numerous case files convinces us that the agencies do typically attempt to report objectively all the material known to them and to appraise the equities disinterestedly."

The House Subcommittee on Claims meets on Wednesdays, a quorum consisting of five of its nine members. If the report from the interested department or agency (or the Comptroller General) is favorable, the Subcommittee generally approves the bill and sends it to the full Judiciary Committee. If the report is unfavorable, the Subcommittee is likely to hold a hearing on the bill, or may refer it to a single member of the Subcommittee for further study and recommendation. If a hearing is held, the sponsoring Representative, the claimant, and in some cases the claimant's attorney may testify in behalf of the bill. The Subcommittee at this point either reports its conclusions to the full Judiciary Committee or asks the Court of Claims for a study and report on its findings. Eventually, if the Subcommittee favors the bill, it so informs the Judiciary Committee.

At the weekly meeting of the full Judiciary Committee, the chairman of Subcommittee No. 2 presents a synopsis of each case. The Committee generally confirms the recommendations of the Subcommittee, reporting to the House the bills that the Committee recommends for passage. Each bill thus recommended goes on the Private Calendar.

In the Senate, the procedure is similar, except that the Senate Committee on the Judiciary does not have a standing subcommittee on claims. Instead, the chairman of the Committee assigns bills to individual Committee members. A private claims bill approved by the Senate Judiciary Committee goes on the Judiciary Committee Calendar.

Both Judiciary Committees publish reports on private claims bills which they recommend for passage. The Senate Judiciary Committee, in addition, prepares a report on each private claim bill that it deems undeserving of passage. The latter reports are not published, but they may be examined in the Committee's offices.

Floor Consideration; Objector System

House Rule XXIV, Clause 6, provides for calling up private bills as follows:

"On the first Tuesday of each month after disposal of such business on the Speaker's table as requires reference only, the Speaker shall direct the Clerk to call the bills and resolutions on the Private Calendar. Should objection be made by two or more Members to the consideration of any bill or resolution so called, it shall be recommitted to the committee which reported the bill

Chronology of House Decisions on Taking Up Private Bills

1810, Jan. 26. The House adopted a rule reading: "That Friday, in each week, be set apart for the consideration of reports and bills originating from petitions."

1826, Jan. 26. The rule was modified to read: "That Friday and Saturday, in every week, be set apart for the consideration of private bills and private business, in preference to any other, unless otherwise determined by a majority of the House."

1826, Feb. 9. The Speaker decided that the rule did not prevent private bills from being considered on other days.

1828, Apr. 26. The House adopted a rule requiring a two-thirds vote for a change of the order of business as established by the rules. This rule was applied consistently—with one exception noted below—to proposals to dispense with consideration of private bills on Friday or Saturday.

1833, Jan. 18. Speaker Andrew Stevenson (D Va.) ruled that a majority vote was sufficient for a decision to dispense with consideration of private bills on Friday or Saturday.

1874, May 8. The House decided to set aside only Friday, and not Saturday too, for consideration of private bills.

1890, Feb. 14. By this time, Speaker Stevenson's ruling that a majority vote was sufficient to dispense with consideration of private bills on the day or days designated had been accepted. In a revision of the rules adopted on this date, Friday was set aside for private business "unless otherwise determined by the House."

1932, April 23. The House substituted Saturday for Friday as the day for consideration of private bills; eliminated preference for certain classes of private bills in certain weeks (except that the last Saturday of each month was set aside for consideration of private bills previously deferred because of objections); limited debate on each private bill; and decided to take up private bills in their numerical order instead of by committee.

1935, March 27. The House set aside the first and third Tuesdays of each month for consideration of private bills.

or resolution, and no reservation or objection shall be entertained by the Speaker. Such bills and resolutions, if considered, shall be considered in the House as in the Committee of the Whole. No other business shall be in order on this day unless the House, by two-thirds vote on motion to dispense therewith, shall otherwise determine. On such motion debate shall be limited to five minutes for and five minutes against such motion."

Clause 6 provides also that the third Tuesday of each month shall be set aside for consideration of private bills, except that on the third Tuesday (1) the Speaker may (not "shall") direct the Clerk to call the bills and resolutions on the Private Calendar and (2) preference is to be given to "omnibus bills containing bills or resolutions which have previously been objected to on a call of the Private Calendar" *(see box on omnibus private bills).*

When private bills are being considered, whether on the first or third Tuesday, the House sits in Committee of the Whole. The main advantage of this is that only 100 Representatives are required to be present in the Committee of the Whole to constitute a quorum, as distinguished from the ordinary requirement of a majority. In the Committee of the Whole, moreover, no roll-call votes are taken and debate on amendments is limited to five minutes.

When the House has gone into Committee of the Whole, the Speaker asks the Clerk to call the first bill on the Private Calendar. The Clerk reads the title of the bill and then, if there is no objection, he proceeds to the bill. If no amendments are offered, and there is no opposition, the normal procedure is followed, which appears in the *Congressional Record* as follows: "The bill was ordered to be engrossed and read a third time, was read a third time, and passed, and a motion to reconsider was laid on the table."

The sufficiency of two days a month for floor consideration of private bills in the House was questioned by Rep. Fiorello H. La Guardia (Prog N.Y.). He told the House Committee on Rules, Jan. 16, 1932: "I think it would be

a good thing to provide for the consideration of the Private Calendar every week and make it mandatory, so that if the afternoon is devoted to other legislation, a night session would automatically follow, solely for the purpose of consideration of the bills." La Guardia suggested also that "all bills objected to...go on a separate calendar and that calendar be taken up every third Saturday or Friday, whichever day you adopt, limiting the debate to 10 minutes on each side." This procedure was not adopted.

Senate procedures for the calling up of private bills are not so detailed as those of the House of Representatives. The Senate Calendar of Business consists of bills reported by committees. Private bills reported by the Judiciary Committee and placed on the Calendar of Business are taken up in the order in which they are listed in the Calendar, when calendar business is taken up. Calendar business is taken up on any day, after the conclusion of the Morning Hour.

Official Objectors. A memorandum by the Legislative Reference Service of the Library of Congress printed in the *Congressional Record* on Feb. 19, 1957, explained as follows the so-called objector system employed during consideration of private bills in the House:

"Seldom are more than 50 Members present at a time during the consideration of private bills....But the political parties...see to it that some check is placed on the number and nature of private bills to be enacted. If no check existed, many billions of dollars would be drawn from the Treasury to pay off alleged claims. To prevent this, each party has three or more 'official objectors'. The majority floor leader designates three to five official objectors; the minority leader to check the majority party does likewise. In each case these objectors are charged by the leaders of their party with respect to what they should oppose and what they should approve....Those men stay on the floor constantly while the Private Calendar is under consideration."

Omnibus Private Bills

A private bill passed over by the House of Representatives because an official objector or anyone else has expressed opposition to it is reconsidered by the House Committee on the Judiciary. The committee, if it still favors the bill, may include the bill's provisions in a conglomerate piece of legislation called an omnibus bill. House Rule XXIV, Clause 6, governs, among other things, the consideration of omnibus bills. In its present form, adopted May 27, 1935, the clause reads, in part:

"On the third Tuesday of each month after the disposal of such business on the Speaker's table as requires reference only, the Speaker may direct the Clerk to call the bills and resolutions on the Private Calendar, preference to be given to omnibus bills containing bills or resolutions which have previously been objected to on a call of the Private Calendar....

"Omnibus bills shall be read for amendment by paragraph, and no amendment shall be in order except to strike out or to reduce amounts of money stated or to provide limitations. Any item or matter stricken from such an omnibus bill shall not thereafter during the same session of Congress be included in any omnibus bill.

"Upon passage of any such omnibus bill, said bill shall be resolved into the several bills and resolutions of which it is composed, and such original bills and resolutions, with any amendments adopted by the House, shall be engrossed, where necessary, and proceedings thereon had as if said bills and resolutions had been passed in the House severally.

Senate procedure is similar in respect to revival of deferred bills in omnibus bills and floor consideration of omnibus bills. In either house, one objection to a particular bill within an omnibus bill is enough to strike that particular bill.

Rulings on May 7, 1935, and March 17, 1936, were aimed at expediting consideration of omnibus bills. On the former date, John J. O'Connor (D N.Y.) was Speaker pro tempore during the consideration of an omnibus bill. While that bill was being considered, he declined to recognize Representatives requesting unanimous consent to address the House. On the latter date, Speaker James F. Byrnes (D S.C.) ruled that when an omnibus bill was before the House, a motion to strike out the last word was not in order, and a request for extension of time under the five-minute rule laid down in another part of Clause 6 would not be entertained.

The duty of the House objectors is to screen private bills reported by the Judiciary Committee, before the bills are called up on the Calendar. If one of them objects during floor consideration, the bill is passed over for later consideration. If two or more object, the bill is recommitted. Often, this kills the bill.

The objectors do not meet as a group, except on procedural matters. To give themselves time to do the screening, they have obtained agreement in recent years that a bill must be on the Private Calendar for seven days before it can be brought to the floor. The objectors seldom base their decisions on partisan considerations. However, they are not without their prejudices. On Feb. 9, 1934, Marion A. Zioncheck (D Wash.), who was an objector, prevented consideration of a bill for the relief of a bonding company because he did not like bonding companies. Minority Leader Bertrand H. Snell (R N.Y.) then said that he would object to every private bill that came up that day; and he did.

The system by which one Representative or a few Representatives may obstruct passage of a private bill has been criticized and praised. Rep. Abraham W. Lafferty (Prog R Ore.) said in the House on Feb. 14, 1913: "These claims, nearly every one, represent bread and butter in the mouth of some individual, and you place rancor in the heart of every citizen of this country who comes here with a just claim and has it considered by the Committee on Claims, has its merits thoroughly gone over, has it favorably reported and presented to this House, and it is then shut off from any consideration...by an objection of a single capricious individual. That is not the way to make patriotic citizens. That is not the way to do business." The House on April 23, 1932, decided that three objections rather than one would be needed to defer consideration of a private bill. The number of objections required for deferral was changed to two on March 27, 1935.

Rep. Robert Luce (R Mass.), in his book *Legislative Problems,* offered light praise and strong criticism of the objector system. The objectors, he wrote, "deserve praise for their willingness to perform an unpleasant, disagreeable public duty." But, Luce added:

"The objector, with no information at hand other than what appears in the committee report accompanying the bill or on the face of the bill itself, undertakes to say that hard-working, conscientious committees, helped by clerks usually of long experience with the questions involved, have reached wrong conclusions. He may be biased by extraneous considerations—prejudiced, perhaps unwittingly, against the man who introduced the bill or the class (such, for example, as public service corporations) to which the claimant belongs. He may have set up shibboleths that would not be accepted by the great majority of the members if they had a chance."

Luce had written earlier, in the *American Political Science Review,* that an objector "tends to become captious—the danger of all critics....Objectors on the floor have not had the benefit of committee hearings and deliberations....Naturally, the objectors sympathize with each other, and if one objects, two others are likely to back him up for the sake of the morale of the group."

In the Senate, the function which the House assigns to official objectors is carried out by the Democratic and Republican Policy Committees. They screen private bills reported by the Committee on the Judiciary, to ensure that objection will be voiced against bills that conflict with policy objectives.

Referral to Court of Claims. Congress by an act of Feb. 24, 1855, set up the Court of Claims of the United States to consider a narrow range of legal claims against the Government. The court was given the power, if it approved a claim, to have a bill on the subject introduced in Congress. The Bowman Act of March 3, 1883, authorized referral of a claim in the other direction, from Congress to the court. It provided that either house of Congress, or any committee of either house, might refer a claim involving determination of facts to the Court of Claims for investigation.

Referral of additional categories of cases to the court was authorized by the Tucker Act of March 3, 1887. The additional categories included claims "legal or equitable, or for a grant, gift, or bounty to any person." The Tucker Act empowered the court to render judgment in certain cases, Congress reserving the power to appropriate funds for carrying out the judgments. The cases to be so decided were those involving claims based on the Constitution or any law of Congress, except for pensions; a regulation of an executive department; a contract with the Government; or non-tort injury by an agent of the Government.

Senate Rule XV, Paragraph 2, provides: "Whenever a private bill is under consideration, it shall be in order to move, as a substitute for it, a resolution of the Senate referring the case to the Court of Claims, under the provisions of the act approved March 3, 1883." The House, while it does not have a corresponding rule, was authorized by the same law to make such a referral. The latest re-enactment of this authority appears in the Act of Oct. 15, 1966, which provides: "Any bill, except a bill for a pension, may be referred by either House of Congress to the chief commissioner of the Court of Claims for a report."

As stated by Supreme Court Justice Tom Clark, in a concurring opinion on June 25, 1962, "Congress still makes legislative references to the court (Court of Claims), averaging some 10 a year." The court's Chief Commissioner, Marion T. Bennett, said in 1967 that since the end of World War II the court had handled over 100 Congressional reference cases.

Private Amendment to Public Bill. The question of whether it would be in order to amend a general appropriation bill by attaching to it a provision for payment of a particular private claim has arisen in the Senate on a number of occasions. Sen. George F. Edmunds (R Vt.), President pro tempore, decided on May 13, 1884, that an amendment of this kind was subject to a point of order unless it served "to carry out the provisions of an existing law or a treaty stipulation, which shall be cited on the face of the amendment" (quoted from a Senate rule then in effect). This decision was confirmed in 1885, 1925, and 1933, and was included, as still in force, in the officially published 1964 digest of Senate procedure compiled by Charles L. Watkins and Floyd M. Riddick.

On July 2, 1884, less than two months after Edmunds' ruling, an exception was allowed. The Treasury Department, administering a law which entitled various Government employees to extra compensation, had ruled that the law was inapplicable to a particular group, but the Supreme Court decided later that that group was covered by the law. An amendment to a general appropriation bill, authorizing payment to these employees, was ruled in order.

Presidential Approval or Veto

The first private bill vetoed by a President was a bill to incorporate the Protestant Episcopal Church in Alexandria, Va. President Madison's veto of the bill on Feb. 21, 1811, was his first veto of any bill and the third veto in U.S. history. When Madison returned the bill to the House of Representatives, discussion arose as to whether the Constitution required immediate consideration of the returned bill. It was agreed that the bill should

be passed over to the next day. Actually, the bill was taken up two days later, and the veto was sustained.

The question whether a vetoed private bill must be reconsidered immediately under the Constitution arose in another form almost a half-century later. President Buchanan on April 17, 1860, vetoed a bill for the relief of individuals who claimed payment for services rendered in transporting mail. The House, on receiving the veto message, considered referring it to a committee. This proposal was rejected, but no further action on the message was taken until June 7, 1860, when the veto was sustained.

In recent years, a message vetoing a private bill has regularly been referred to the Judiciary Committee of the house receiving the message. Prof. Clarence A. Berdahl wrote, in the *Political Science Quarterly,* December 1937: "Such reference to committee has meant, and has pretty clearly been intended to mean, not merely postponement of consideration but indefinite postponement and final burial. In other words, committee reference in the case of private bill vetoes has been a way of sustaining the veto without the constitutional formality of a roll-call vote." The presiding officer, realizing that referral to a committee is an evasion of the requirement that the vetoed bill be put before the House for reconsideration, has felt, in Berdahl's words, "only an occasional constitutional scruple."

Rule 15 of the House Subcommittee on Claims (*see Appendix*) provides that the Subcommittee will not reconsider a vetoed bill unless there has been a material change in the facts, or unless the Administration withdraws its objection in writing. But this rule may be waived by a two-thirds majority of the Subcommittee.

President Cleveland directly vetoed 301, and pocket-vetoed 181, private bills. Richard M. Boeckel, in a report on "The Veto Power of the President" published in 1932 by Editorial Research Reports, explained the situation:

"Under the Arrears of Pensions Act (1879) it had become profitable for veterans to search for excuses that would put them on the pension lists. They could now receive not only current pensions, as allowed by law, but back pensions from the time of discharge. In many cases these arrears ran into thousands of dollars, and a swarm of attorneys prospered aiding veterans in obtaining pensions on dubious evidence. Congress was willing, with large surpluses accumulating in the Treasury, to pass in the form of private bills many claims that could not be granted through the ordinary channels of the Pension Bureau. Such bills descended upon Cleveland in hundreds and he vetoed them right and left."

Since the time of President Franklin D. Roosevelt, every private bill passed by both Houses has been sent by the White House to the Bureau of the Budget for review prior to action by the President. The fact that an executive department or agency has previously submitted an unfavorable recommendation to Congress on a private bill does not mean that the President will veto the bill. However, a private bill veto in 1954 was clearly founded on an unchanged adverse reaction to a bill in the agency concerned—in this case, the Army. President Eisenhower on June 14, 1954, vetoed a bill for the relief of a woman whose soldier son had committed suicide at a military post while he was under detention for drunkenness. The veto message included the following unqualified generalization: "It is unwise to adjudicate individual cases by private legislation."

Private Bills Vetoed

(through 91st Congress)

President	Formally Vetoed	Vetoes Overridden	Pocket-vetoed
Madison	2	0	0
Van Buren	0	0	1
Buchanan	2	0	0
Lincoln	0	0	1
Johnson, Andrew	0	0	2
Grant	29	3	37
Hayes	1	0	0
Arthur	1	0	8
Cleveland	271	1	82
Harrison, Benjamin	5	0	23
Cleveland	30	2	99
McKinley	4	0	32
Roosevelt, Theodore	27	0	31
Taft	10	0	7
Wilson	7	0	2
Harding	3	0	0
Coolidge	3	0	17
Hoover	4	0	6
Roosevelt, Franklin D.	317	0	180
Truman	137	1	38
Eisenhower	43	0	64
Kennedy	8	0	4
Johnson, Lyndon B.	12	0	4
Nixon, Richard M.	0	0	2
	916	7	640

SOURCES: (1) Clarence A. Berdahl, "The President's Veto of Private Bills," *Political Science Quarterly,* December 1937, p. 508; (2) U.S. Senate Library, *Presidential Vetoes (1969).* (3) Congressional Quarterly staff.

NOTE: For many years, bills were not formally designated public or private until they were enacted and published. Hence the classification of vetoed bills as public or private depends in many cases on interpretation of the criteria generally used for that purpose.

President Eisenhower could hardly have meant that dictum to be taken literally. He himself had approved scores of other private claim bills. Walter Gellhorn and Louis Lauer commented in the *Columbia Law Journal,* January 1955:

"Obviously, despite the quoted language, the President did not veto the legislative proposal before him because of a general feeling that individual cases should not be adjudicated by private legislation....A more likely explanation is that the President thought Congress had unduly extended the scope of Congressional review of final administrative action by substituting its independent judgment for that of the agency."

Of private bills referred by Congress to the Court of Claims for examination, reported favorably by the court, and then passed by Congress, only one has been vetoed. The case arose when Federal officials who had filed a tax lien against a hotel refused to let the tenants pay their rent but failed to collect the rent themselves. The principal stockholder in the corporation that owned the hotel was a horse-race bookmaker. President Kennedy on Oct. 18, 1962, vetoed a bill for the relief of the corporation. He noted in his veto message that the primary beneficiary would be the bookmaker whose fraudulent evasion of taxes had caused the case. Congress later passed the bill again. It was vetoed this time by President Johnson on Aug. 11, 1964; and that ended the efforts of the hotel owners to obtain compensation.

Prof. Berdahl found that the proportion of bills enacted over the President's veto, up to 1937, was only about 1 percent in the case of private bills as against 16 percent in the case of public bills. Berdahl gave two reasons for Congressional acceptance of vetoes of private bills:

"In the first place,...private bills, by their very nature, are the active concern of only a small number, and commonly of only the introducer in each case. Hence, although passed in large numbers, and generally by unanimous consent, this means in most cases that the bills are passed in default of serious opposition rather than because of enthusiastic affirmative support, and probably also as a 'courtesy' to one another or even as the result of 'trading.' ...Secondly, the petty character of private bill legislation has brought an increasing feeling that it is a serious waste of the time of Congress to examine the details of these bills, and this in turn has induced members...to accept the President's judgment."

Berdahl asserted that for Congress to defer to the President's judgment on matters of detail "would seem... to be the most sensible procedure, although, in respect to the veto, there is grave doubt whether it is strictly in accord with the letter and intent of the Constitution."

Only once since the Cleveland administration has Congress overridden a Presidential veto of a private bill. A Tennessee tobacco factory was destroyed by fire in 1945. Internal revenue stamps worth more than $8,000, for which the factory owners had paid the Government in full, reportedly went up in flames. Congress early in 1949 passed a private bill to reimburse the factory owners for the value of the stamps, but President Truman on April 21, 1949, vetoed the bill because evidence was lacking that the stamps had been destroyed. The veto was overridden by the House on May 18 (318 yeas, 49 nays) and by the Senate on Sept. 15 (45 yeas, 6 nays).

Two-thirds of all vetoed bills since 1789 have been private bills. In recent years, a considerable proportion of the private bills vetoed would have waived the statute of limitations, particularly in tax cases. Another sizable category of vetoed private bills has consisted of bills to reverse unfavorable judicial decisions. Presidents generally have felt, in these cases, that the individuals already had had their day in court.

Efforts to Cut Number of Private Laws

In the sultry summer of 1571, the House of Lords faced up to the need to cut down the amount of time the Peers were devoting to private bills pouring in from the House of Commons. According to the Journal of the House of Commons, a committee appointed to confer with the Lords "brought report that, as the season waxed very hot and dangerous for sickness, so the Lords desired that this House would spend the time in proceeding with necessary bills for the commonwealth, and lay aside all private bills in the meantime." The House of Commons acceded to this plea.

The burden of private bills in the U.S. Congress came under attack a few decades after the adoption of the Constitution, but not because of the weather. Justice Joseph

Story, in his *Commentaries on the Constitution,* noted in 1833 that Congress was needlessly dealing with numerous small private claims. He blamed Congress "for not having provided (as it is clearly within their constitutional authority to do) an adequate remedy for all private grievances of this sort in the courts of the United States." Congress responded at a leisurely pace.

The leisurely pace included enactment in 1896 of a public law which eliminated the need for Congress to pass a private bill to authorize every donation of an obsolete Civil War cannon to a town, civic association, or other group. The law, approved May 22, 1896, provided "That the Secretary of War and the Secretary of the Navy are each hereby authorized, in their discretion, to loan or give to soldiers' monument associations, posts of the Grand Army of the Republic, and municipal corporations, condemned ordnance, guns, and cannon balls which may not be needed in the service of either of said Departments." More comprehensive public laws to make unnecessary the passage of private laws followed over an extended period in the field of private claims.

Public Laws for Settling Private Claims

By an act of Feb. 24, 1855, as noted, Congress established the Court of Claims and gave it authority to investigate contractual and other legal claims against the Government and report on them to Congress. An opinion by Supreme Court Justice John M. Harlan, handed down June 25, 1962 (370 U.S. 553), provided a brief history lesson: "The Court of Claims was created...primarily to relieve the pressure on Congress caused by the volume of private bills....By the end of 1861, however, it was apparent that the limited powers conferred on the court were insufficient to relieve Congress from the laborious necessity of examining the merits of private bills."

President Lincoln, in his first annual message to Congress, Dec. 3, 1861, requested that the Court of Claims be given authority to make final decisions:

"It is as much the duty of Government to render prompt justice against itself in favor of its citizens as it is to administer the same between private individuals. The investigation and adjudication of claims in their nature belong to the Judicial department. Besides, it is apparent that the attention of Congress will be more than usually engaged for some time to come with great national questions. It was intended by the organization of the Court of Claims mainly to remove this branch of business from the halls of Congress; but while the court has proved to be an effective and valuable means of investigation, it in great degree fails to effect the object of its creation for want of power to make its judgments final. Fully aware of the delicacy, not to say danger, of the subject, I commend to your careful consideration whether this power of making judgments final may not properly be given to the court, reserving the right of appeal on questions of law to the Supreme Court, with such other provisions as experience may have shown to be necessary." Congress, as has been pointed out, expanded the powers of the Court of Claims by the Bowman Act of 1883 and the Tucker Act of 1887, but not to the extent recommended by Lincoln.

A complication affecting referral of cases to the Court of Claims arose in the 1960s. The situation was summarized in a report submitted to the Senate by the Judiciary Committee on Sept. 22, 1966:

"In 1962,...in the case of *Glidden Co. v. Zdanok,* 370 U.S. 530, the Supreme Court held that the Court of Claims was a court of the United States within the meaning of Article III of the Constitution. It is well settled that an Article III court may only decide cases and controversies, and may not render merely advisory opinions that other branches of the Government are free to disregard. Since the *Glidden* decision, the Court of Claims has regretfully declined to accept any further Congressional reference cases."

The impasse was resolved by the Act of Oct. 15, 1966, which authorized trial commissioners of the Court of Claims, rather than the court as such, to consider and report on Congressional reference cases.

Over the years, Congress has authorized executive departments and agencies in general, or particular departments and agencies, to settle small claims such as previously had required the introduction of private bills. Types of claims thus sloughed off by Congress were supplementary to those that the Court of Claims had been empowered to consider. Sections of the U.S. Code embodying public laws of the kind referred to are cited under the heading "Claims" in the index to the Code. Claims that may be settled under this authority are limited to specified amounts, the maximum being $1 million in the case of claims to be settled by the Secretary of Defense for damage caused by vessels of the U.S. Navy.

Changes Under Legislative Reorganization Act

Congressional committees considering legislative reforms in 1946 found it possible to eliminate three categories of private bills: those to settle certain tort claims, those to authorize construction of bridges, and those to correct military records. The Legislative Reorganization Act of Aug. 2, 1946, prescribed other means of handling such matters.

Tort Claims. The act of 1946 provided, in Title IV, Sec. 403, for settlement by executive departments and agencies of "any claim against the United States for money only...on account of damage to or loss of property or on account of personal injury or death, where the total amount of the claim does not exceed $1,000, caused by the negligent or wrongful act or omission of any employee of the Government, while acting within the scope of his office or employment." Similar claims exceeding $1,000 were authorized to be settled in U.S. district courts. Title IV was called the Federal Tort Claims Act. Twenty years later, by an act of July 18, 1966, Congress eliminated the $1,000 maximum on tort claims to be settled by departments and agencies but added the provision "That any award, compromise, or settlement in excess of $25,000 shall be effected only with the prior written approval of the Attorney General or his designee."

Bridges and Military Records. Title V of the act of 1946 was called the General Bridge Act. In Sec. 502, it provided: "The consent of Congress is hereby granted for the construction, maintenance, and operation of bridges and approaches thereto over the navigable waters of the United States, in accordance with the provisions of this title." Among the provisions specified were approval by the Chief of Engineers and the Secretary of War (now the Secretary of the Army) of the location of such bridges and the plans for them, limitation of privately owned toll bridges, and special requirements for bridges connecting American with foreign territory.

The Act provided in Title II, Sec. 207: "The Secretary of War, the Secretary of the Navy, and the Secretary of the Treasury with respect to the Coast Guard, respectively, under procedures set up by them, and acting through boards of civilian officers or employees of their respective departments, are authorized to correct any military or naval record where in their judgment such action is necessary to correct an error or to remove an injustice."

Prohibition of Private Bills. In Title I, Sec. 131, the Legislative Reorganization Act banned not only private bills which, under the authority granted in the Act's other titles, were no longer necessary, but also private pension bills:

"No private bill or resolution (including so-called omnibus claims or pension bills), and no amendment to any bill authorizing or directing (1) the payment of money for property damages, for personal injuries or death for which suit may be instituted under the Federal Tort Claims Act, or for a pension (other than to carry out a provision of law or treaty stipulation); (2) the construction of a bridge across a navigable stream; or (3) the correction of a military or naval record, shall be received or considered in either the Senate or the House of Representatives."

This provision was made a part of the standing rules of the House of Representatives Jan. 3, 1953, as Rule XXII, Clause 2. As a result of the ban, the number of private bills introduced in Congress decreased from 3,772 in the 79th Congress (1945-46) to 2,532 in the 80th Congress (1947-48). The ratio of private bills to the total number of bills introduced fell off from 32 percent to 21 percent. Rep. Carl Vinson (D Ga.) told the House of Representatives July 2, 1951, that Sec. 207 of the Legislative Reorganization Act had relieved Congress since 1946 of consideration of about 15,000 private bills for the correction of military and naval records by delegating the task of correcting such records to boards in the Department of Defense.

During the First Session of the 84th Congress (1955), Congress overrode one of its own previous strictures on private bills. The Act of 1946 provided that no private bill for the correction of a military or naval record shall be received or considered by Congress. Nevertheless, HR 6232, a bill to correct the military record of Stephen S. Ogletree, was not only received and considered but also passed by both houses. President Eisenhower pocket-vetoed the bill and recorded his disapproval in a memorandum of Aug. 12, 1955. His memorandum cited, among other things, the Congressional ban against such bills.

Criticism and Defense of Private Laws

The idea that public legislative bodies should concern themselves with bills to benefit private individuals has stirred criticism from an early period. And suspicion of favoritism has entered into consideration of the practice. The Roman writer Tacitus, in the section of his *Annals* covering the first half of the first century B.C., wrote: "And now laws were made not for the public only, but for particular men; and it was in the most corrupt period of the commonwealth that the greatest proliferation of laws occurred."

Constitutional Questions

Lawmakers in the United States sometimes have viewed their consideration of private bills as based on the right of individuals, under the First Amendment to the Constitution, to petition Congress for redress of grievances. "But the right to petition," according to an unsigned note in the June 1966 *Harvard Law Review,* "cannot confer upon Congress the power to enact bills dealing with any subject regarding which they are petitioned; otherwise, passage of any bill, no matter how local the subject matter or how far beyond stated constitutional limitations on Congress, might be justified by a mere petition." The note added: "Enactment of private bills no doubt makes meaningful the right to petition, but the constitutional basis for passing such bills must be found elsewhere."

Relevant provisions elsewhere in the Constitution include Article I, Section 8, Clause 1, which authorizes Congress to pay the nation's debts; Article I, Section 8, Clause 4, which authorizes Congress "To establish an uniform Rule of Naturalization, and uniform Laws on the subject of Bankruptcies throughout the United States"; and Article I, Section 9, Clause 8, which requires the consent of Congress for acceptance of a gift or title from a foreign state by a Government employee. As regards the word "uniform" in the clause on naturalization, the note in the *Harvard Law Review* commented, "While there is a constitutional requirement that such laws be 'uniform,' this appears to mean uniform among the states, not among the applicants."

Among the serious constitutional questions which have been raised about private laws, three have been paramount: equal protection, separation of powers, and the ban on bills of attainder.

Equal Protection. In the words of the *Harvard Law Review* note, "unanswered problems related to the notion of 'equal protection' are raised when an individual denied a bill is in all relevant respects in the same position as one for whom a bill has been passed." The Supreme Court ruled on this question in the case of *Paramino Lumber Co. v. Marshall,* which concerned the constitutionality of a private law of April 10, 1936, for the relief of a claimant under the Longshoremen's and Harbor Workers' Compensation Act of March 4, 1927. The private law allowed reconsideration, to raise the award, of an order for compensation under the 1927 Act, despite the statute of limitations and the fact that compensation would be paid by a private party.

Justice Stanley Reed on March 11, 1940, delivered the opinion of the Court (309 U.S. 379) upholding the law: "It is urged by appellant...that the equal protection clause of the Fourteenth Amendment should be read into the due process clause of the Fifth Amendment. If so read, it is argued, this private act violates the rule of equal protection. This conclusion, however, we find untenable. Private acts, as such, are not forbidden by the Constitution."

The decision rested at least in part on refusal to read an equal protection requirement into the due process clause. This refusal was reversed by the Court in its opinion of May 17, 1954, in *Bolling v. Sharpe,* which struck down racial segregation in the public schools of the District of Columbia. Chief Justice Earl Warren delivered the opinion (347 U.S. 499):

"The Fifth Amendment, which is applicable in the District of Columbia, does not contain an equal protection clause as does the Fourteenth Amendment which applies only to states. But the concepts of equal protection and due process, both stemming from our American ideal of fairness, are not mutually exclusive. The 'equal protection of the laws' is a more explicit safeguard of prohibited unfairness than 'due process of law,' and, therefore, we do not imply that the two are always interchangeable phrases. But, as this Court has recognized, discrimination may be so unjustifiable as to be violative of due process.''

On the basis of the 1954 case, the author of the *Harvard Law Review* note wrote that if Congress now were to pass a law abrogating the statute of limitations in relations between private parties, as it did in the Paramino Lumber Co. case, ''it probably would be unconstitutional as a denial of equal protection.''

Private legislation involves another type of equal protection besides the one mentioned. As noted, the question arose in 1950 whether the mere introduction of a private bill to cancel deportation proceedings entitled the beneficiary to a stay of deportation in every case on the equal-protection ground that a stay is granted in most cases. The Second Circuit Court of Appeals in that case ruled in favor of a stay for the beneficiary of the bill because the Department of Justice had not provided special reasons for not granting it in that case.

Separation of Powers. The courts have had to decide whether Congress, in functioning as a court of equity when it deliberates on private bills, is violating the separation of powers by intruding into the judicial function which the Constitution assigns to another branch of the Government. The Supreme Court in 1940 took up this question in *Paramino Lumber Co. v. Marshall.* The appellant in that case contended, with reference to the private law of April 10, 1936, mentioned above: ''The Act is an attempted usurpation by Congress of judicial functions. It is judicial in nature and authorizes a readjudication between individuals of private property rights arising out of past transactions. Legislative grant of a new trial, rehearing or further determination in a cause which has proceeded to final adjudication under existing statutes is an attempted exercise of judicial power....Congress possesses no judicial power.''

The Court's opinion, after rejecting the equal-protection argument, added (309 U.S. 381): ''Nor can we say that this legislation is an excursion of the Congress into the judicial function.'' The reason given by the Court was that in this case the private law affected an administrative order rather than a judicial decision.

Bills of Attainder. A private bill which benefits one individual to the possible detriment of another can plausibly be held to be a bill of attainder and, as such, barred by Article I, Section 9, Clause 3, of the Constitution. In former years especially, many U.S. private laws concerned not only claims against the Government but also relations between private persons. (In England, at one time, a divorce could be obtained only by a private act of Parliament.) The question whether a private bill could successfully be attacked as a bill of attainder has not as such arisen in the courts, but a Supreme Court decision of June 7, 1965, came close to this subject-matter area.

In the context of the cited clause of the Constitution, the author of the *Harvard Law Review* note discussed the constitutionality of private laws which abrogate the statute of limitations in claims cases arising between individuals. He wrote that in the light of recent decisions, especially the 1965 case of *United States v.*

Brown, such a law, if passed now, ''might be taken by the courts to be a bill of attainder against the individual suffering detriment under it.'' The Supreme Court's opinion in *United States v. Brown* declared that the Labor-Management Reporting and Disclosure Act of Sept. 14, 1959, which barred Communists from all except custodial tasks as employees of labor unions, ''plainly constitutes a bill of attainder'' (381 U.S. 449).

Views of Statesmen and Scholars

Intermittently for more than a century, various officeholders, political scientists, and pundits have scrutinized the practice of enacting private legislation. Many of them have disapproved of the practice because it takes up valuable time and is subject to abuse; in some cases, they have suggested ways of either minimizing the need for it or abolishing it. Defenders of the institution of private laws generally have emphasized its potential for good in cases in which rigid application of the laws on the statute books would result in miscarriage of justice.

Ex-Presidents. John Quincy Adams noted in his diary on Feb. 23, 1832, that during the meeting of the House of Representatives on that date two hours had been devoted to debating whether the House should consider private bills on Saturdays alone instead of on Fridays and Saturdays. He then commented: ''There ought to be no private business before Congress....It is judicial business, and legislative assemblies ought to have nothing to do with it. One-half of the time of Congress is consumed by it, and there is no common rule of justice for any two of the cases decided. A deliberative assembly is the worst of all tribunals for the administration of justice.''

A half-century later, Grover Cleveland, in the interval between his two terms as President (1885-89 and 1893-97), took a position on private bills which resembled that of Adams. In a speech of June 27, 1891, to the Commercial Club of Providence, R.I., Cleveland said: ''The people have a right to claim from their representatives their best care and attention to the great subjects of legislation in which the entire country is interested. This is denied them if their representatives take their seats burdened with private bills, in which their immediate neighbors exclusively are interested, and which they feel they must be diligent in advancing, if they would secure their continuance in public life. They are thus led by the exigencies of the situation as they view it, not only to the support of private bills of questionable propriety, but to a neglect of a study and understanding of the important questions involved in general legislation.''

Cleveland charged in the same speech that some sponsors of private bills were guilty of raiding the Treasury to promote their re-election: ''The importance of a successful championship of these private bills, measured by a standard which ought not for a moment to be recognized, seems so vital to those having them in charge that they are easily led to barter their votes for measures as bad as theirs or worse, in order to secure the support of similarly situated colleagues. Thus is inaugurated a system called log-rolling, which comes frightfully near actual legislative corruption; and thus the people at large lose not only the attention to their affairs which is due them, but are often no better than robbed of the money in the public Treasury.''

Members of Congress. Senators and Representatives, unlike former Presidents, have taken opposite positions on the propriety of private legislation. The position of Rep. William M. Springer (D Ill.) on this issue was uncompromisingly negative. Nine times in the period 1876-90, Springer introduced a resolution proposing an amendment to the Constitution that would have effectually prohibited the passage of special legislation. The proposed amendment would have forbidden the enactment by Congress of laws granting to an individual a pension, land, prize money, or relief from an obligation; granting to a corporation an exclusive privilege, subsidy, immunity, or franchise; or paying a claim against the United States except on the judgment of a court or commission. Springer's perennial resolution never mustered a majority in either house.

Rep. Robert Luce (R Mass.), in a 1932 article entitled "Petty Business in Congress," inveighed in particular against the Congressional practice of considering private claims. He wrote: "It is hard to see how any reasonable man with any sense of proportion can find ground for insisting that Congress continue to burden itself with little claims. To do so is penny wise and pound foolish." Luce's suggestion was that the right of decision on private claims be given to Executive agencies and law courts, subject to disapproval by Congress.

Not until 1946 did Congress react seriously to proposals such as Springer's and Luce's. In that year, the Joint Committee on the Organization of Congress, of which Sen. Robert M. La Follette Jr. (Prog Wis.) was chairman and Rep. A. S. Mike Monroney (D Okla.) was vice chairman, agreed with Springer and Luce in principle. The Committee stated, in its report of March 4, 1946: "Congress is poorly equipped to serve as a judicial tribunal for the settlement of private claims against the Government of the United States. This method of handling individual claims does not work well either for the Government or for the individual claimant, while the cost of legislating the settlement in many cases far exceeds the total amounts involved."

The Legislative Reorganization Bill which resulted from the Committee's deliberations was reported shortly thereafter to both houses. As noted earlier, the bill contained provisions for dealing with various categories of private matters administratively and judicially and forbade the introduction of private bills on those matters. After receiving the approval of both houses, the bill was signed by President Truman Aug. 2, 1946.

Rep. Emanuel Celler (D N.Y.) is one of the few who have spoken out in favor of private laws. He defended them in principle at a hearing on the organization and operation of Congress, conducted by the Senate Committee on Government Operations (then called the Committee on Expenditures in the Government Departments), June 13, 1951: "It is...(the) equity factor that will suffer through administrative handling. An administrative body is necessarily hemmed in by the rules and regulations and is equipped to handle the regular rather than the exceptional case. An administrative body will generally err on the side of caution since the use of discretion may be subject to criticism. Thus, the very essence of equity may be lost." Celler's suggestion was that Congress establish a joint standing committee on private legislation, thus making it unnecessary for committees of both houses to go over the same ground.

Fifteen years later, the Senate Committee on the Judiciary also strongly endorsed the principle of private legislation. A report submitted by that Committee on Sept. 22, 1966, stated: "The contention that general legislation is preferable and should be sufficient to cover all cases attributes to the Legislative Branch a degree of omniscience and prescience that this Committee is unwilling to claim for itself. It is impossible, particularly in legislation regulating the relationship between the Government and private parties, to take account of all eventualities."

A pertinent distinction between the impulse of conscience in a Government official and the impulse of conscience in a private individual was brought out by the Committee: "It should also be remembered that in the special area with which private relief legislation deals, factors that in other areas ameliorate the possible harsh effects of general laws may not exist. Government officials are understandably unwilling to spend the taxpayer's money in situations in which they are not clearly authorized by statute to do so, whereas in a comparable situation a private party might well decide that, although under the law his obligation is not clear, he will pay another person what he feels that equity and fair play dictate he pay." The report concluded: "For all these reasons, the Committee is of the opinion that private relief legislation is both useful and necessary."

Congressional Staff Experts. One of the best-known legislative technicians of recent years, George B. Galloway, investigated the problems involved in private legislation. Galloway was a staff member of the Legislative Reference Service, Library of Congress. In his memorandum of May 2, 1949, on reform of private bill procedure, he recommended a reduction in the volume of private legislation. He said: "The duty of Congress is to legislate, not to discharge judicial functions as well. Questions of general policy or expediency are not involved in private-bill legislation. Members are elected to Congress to attend to great questions concerning the nation and the world, to supervise the administration, and to take part in making public laws, but not to spend their time on petty business."

Galloway outlined the advantages and disadvantages of referring additional private cases to non-Congressional agencies. He distinguished between referral to courts or court-like tribunals, which he favored, and referral to Executive or administrative agencies, which he opposed. Of delegation to courts or tribunals, he wrote: "It would ensure uniformity of treatment in private matters and save Congressional time and money." As an argument against delegation to administrative agencies, he noted that "The administrative authority may be at one and the same time a fact-finding, a prosecuting, and an adjudicating authority, and a party in the case."

As a matter of improved housekeeping, Galloway urged the establishment of a standing joint committee of Congress to consider private bills, with a joint staff to aid it. "While this change would not reduce the private work load on Congress," he said, "it would make for simplicity, rapidity, and economy in its disposition by avoiding such duplication as now exists in the consideration of small bills by both houses. There are now 28 stages in the enactment of a law. Joint action would eliminate a dozen of these expensive and time-consuming steps." Neither house took up the recommendation for a joint standing committee. Rep. Celler, as noted, made the same proposal two years later, but it was not adopted.

Ernest S. Griffith, director of the Legislative Reference Service from 1940 to 1958, later offered a mixed evaluation of Congressional intervention by private laws to effect flexible application of existing laws. In the 1961 edition of his book *Congress: Its Contemporary Role,* he wrote: "For the most part, such intervention is based on humane considerations; in some instances it reflects the economic interests of...(the Member's) constituent or his district; in still other instances, campaign contributions or a legal retainer to a Member's firm may have been not without their influence. In any event the practice of private bills is vigorously and widely defended in Congress itself, and in its end results bears a curious resemblance to the effect on specific administrative decisions which British members of Parliament produce through the instrumentality of the question hour."

Scholars and Publicists. Polemicists, academicians, and a research-minded chief commissioner of the Court of Claims have been just as divided on the issue of private laws as Presidents, legislators, and legislative technicians. An editorial writer for the *New Republic* indignantly commented, in the issue of Jan. 6, 1917, that fully 91 percent of the bills introduced in Congress in December 1916 were private bills: "There were three times as many bills authorizing the Secretary of War to donate to the city of————a condemned bronze cannon and complete set of cannon balls, as there were bills touching on the whole question of social integration. There was...a bill to improve a highway near an Asylum for Insane Indians, but none to improve the rules of Congress. This 91 percent of bills was not only local and political, but not even legislative. The awarding of pensions, the erection of public buildings, the settlement of claims, and the correction of military records are administrative functions and not matters for lawmaking."

The writer made two specific suggestions to rectify the imbalance in the attention which Congress devoted to public and private matters: "If the Court of Claims and the Pension Department are incompetent organs, then it is the business of Congress to reconstruct them....As for public buildings and other local improvements, the sooner they are placed in the hands of an administrative commission the sooner Congress will cease to be an assembly of community attorneys."

Stephen R. Bailey and Howard D. Samuel, political scientists, have asserted that limited use of the device of private bills is necessary, but that indiscriminate use is dangerous. They wrote in *Congress at Work:* "If Congress never softened rigid patterns of administrative action, Government might become insensitive to the worthy exception; but if Congress softens too often, administrative efficiency and fairness are destroyed, and the dangerous word becomes spread abroad that the way to happiness is through political pull. This attitude can demoralize a nation theoretically based upon 'Equal Justice under Law.' "

An unsigned note in the June 1966 *Harvard Law Review* listed a number of criticisms of private laws: (1) "There are no means of ensuring regularity of decision —an important component of the equity that Congress purports to dispense." (2) The reasons for approval or rejection of a private bill are not always made clear. "The lack of clear reports gives an impression of obscurity or even secrecy that can serve only to raise doubts about the system's fairness and freedom from political favoritism, while shielding the system from the benefits of scholarly critique." (3) Congress does not have time to give adequate consideration to each private bill. These objections seem to imply that the practice of passing private bills should be reformed, not abolished.

Marion T. Bennett, chief commissioner of the Court of Claims, defended private laws in 1967 on the grounds of equity, as Rep. Celler had done 16 years earlier. Bennett wrote in the *U.S. Air Force JAG Law Review:* "There will always be the unusual and closely contested claims, those suggesting need for an equitable exception to the general law, and claims which an agency is simply not authorized to adjust or will not for policy reasons. It is in this area that the sovereign has reserved its right to exercise its conscience with measures for special relief. The touchstone for such relief is that of moral or honorable treatment in the broadest sense of equity, such as was exercised by the ancient chancellors in equity centuries ago."

In agreement with Bennett's prediction that there will always be cases requiring private legislation, Arlen J. Large wrote in the *Wall Street Journal,* April 14, 1967: "People can run afoul of the Government in the most unpredictable ways, so it's unlikely that single-shot bills to bail them out will ever be entirely abandoned."

Bibliography

Books

Bailey, Stephen K. and Samuel, Howard D., *Congress at Work.* Holt, 1952.

Berman, Daniel M., *In Congress Assembled.* Macmillan, 1964.

Clifford, Frederick, *A History of Private Bill Legislation.* Frank Cass and Co. (London), 1968. 2 vols. (Reprint of 1885 edition.)

Gordon, Charles and Rosenfield, Harry N., *Immigration Law and Procedure.* Banks, 1966 (revised edition).

Griffith, Ernest S., *Congress: Its Contemporary Role.* New York University Press, 1961 edition.

Luce, Robert, *Legislative Problems.* Houghton Mifflin, 1935.

May, Sir Thomas E., *A Treatise Upon the Law, Privileges, Proceedings and Usage of Parliament.* Butterworth and Co. (London), 17th edition, 1964. Book III, "Private Business."

Schmeckebier, Laurence F. and Eastin, Roy B., *Government Publications and Their Use.* Brookings Institution, 1936 (revised edition, 1969).

Story, Joseph, *Commentaries on the Constitution of the United States.* Da Capo Press, 1969 edition. 3 vols.

Williams, Orlo C., *The Historical Development of Private Bill Procedures and Standing Orders in the House of Commons.* H. M. Stationery Office (London), 1948-49. 2 vols.

Willoughby, William F., *Principles of Legislative Organization and Administration.* Brookings Institution, 1934.

Articles

Berdahl, Clarence A., "The President's Veto of Private Bills," *Political Science Quarterly,* December 1937, p. 505-531.

Boeckel, Richard M., "The Veto Power of the President," *Editorial Research Reports,* Dec. 16, 1932, p. 405-423.

Galloway, George B., "Reform of Private Bill Procedure" (memorandum, May 2, 1949); *Congressional Record,* Vol. 95 (81st Congress, 1st Session, 1949), Appendix, p. A 2901-A 2904.

Gellhorn, Walter and Lauer, Louis, "Congressional Settlement of Tort Claims Against the United States," *Columbia Law Review,* January 1955, p. 1-36.

Large, Arlen J., "Drama in the Capitol: Private Bills Assist Lovers and a Cowman." *Wall Street Journal,* April 14, 1967, p. 1, 14.

Luce, Robert, "Petty Business in Congress," *American Political Science Review,* October 1932, p. 815-827.

Orth, Samuel P., "Special Legislation," *Atlantic Monthly,* January 1906, p. 69-76.

"Private Bills and the Immigration Law," *Harvard Law Review,* April 1956, p. 1083-1096.

"Private Bills in Congress," *Harvard Law Review,* June 1966; p. 1684-1706.

Steinberg, Alfred, "When to Use Your Right of Petition," *Nation's Business,* August 1951, p. 56-59.

Government Publications

Bennett, Marion T., *Private Claims Acts and Congressional References.* Government Printing Office, 1968. (Printed for House Judiciary Committee; reprint from *U.S. Air Force JAG Law Review,* November-December 1967.)

Hinds, Asher C., *Hinds' Precedents of the House of Representatives.* Government Printing Office, 1907.

U.S. Congress, Senate. *List of Private Claims Brought Before the Senate of the United States from the Commencement of the Fourteenth to the Close of the Forty-sixth Congress.* Government Printing Office, 1881. 2 vols.

U.S. Congress, Senate. *List of Private Claims Brought Before the Senate of the United States from the Commencement of the Forty-seventh to the Close of the Fifty-first Congress.* Government Printing Office, 1895. 3 vols.

U.S. Congress, Senate, Committee on Claims. *Alphabetical List of Private Claims Which Were Brought Before the Senate of the United States...from December 4, 1899, to March 4, 1903.* Government Printing Office, 1903.

U.S. Congress, Senate, Committee on Claims. *Alphabetical List of Private Claims Which Were Brought Before the Senate of the United States...from November 9, 1903, to March 4, 1905.* Government Printing Office, 1905.

Control of the Seat of Government

THE FOUNDING FATHERS included among the powers of Congress the exclusive right to legislate for the nation's capital. That provision was a source of controversy from the beginning. There was disagreement over whether it meant that Congress should exercise direct control over municipal affairs at the seat of Government, or whether it left leeway for handling of purely local affairs by a locally elected governing body. Limited self-government was granted to the District of Columbia almost as soon as the Government moved from Philadelphia to Washington, and it endured for nearly 70 years. Then, after a brief experiment with a territorial form of government, Congress took back into its own hands virtually all governing authority. There it has rested for almost a century.

At the Constitutional Convention in Philadelphia, James Madison of Virginia, in association with Charles Pinckney of South Carolina, proposed on Aug. 18, 1787, that the "general legislature" under the new Government should exercise legislative authority "at the seat of the General Government, and over a district around the same,...the Consent of the Legislature of the State or States comprising the same, being first obtained." The convention accepted that proposal on Sept. 5. In the Constitution as approved by the Convention on Sept. 17, 1787, Article I, Section 8, Clause 17 provided that the Congress should have power: "To exercise exclusive Legislation in all Cases whatsoever, over such District (not exceeding ten Miles square) as may, by Cession of particular States, and the Acceptance of Congress, become the Seat of Government of the United States." The same clause explicitly granted Congress "like Authority" over places purchased within the new district for the erection of public buildings, dockyards, etc.

During the debate in the Virginia state convention on ratification of the Constitution, June 14, 1788, Patrick Henry referred to the words "in all Cases whatsoever" and asked, "Is there any act, however atrocious, which they cannot do by virtue of this clause?...Is it consistent with any principle of prudence or good government to grant unlimited, unbounded authority?" Madison replied, "Were it possible to delineate on paper all those particular cases and circumstances in which legislation by the general legislature would be necessary,...no gentleman would object to it. But this is not within the limits of human capacity." The Virginia convention, not satisfied with Madison's reply, proposed a constitutional amendment to restrict the power of Congress over "the Federal town and its adjacent district" to "such regulations as respect the police and good government thereof." The other states ignored this proposal.

Madison on a D.C. Legislature

In the *The Federalist* papers, which Madison, Alexander Hamilton, and John Jay published in 1787-88 to promote ratification of the Constitution, Madison wrote (No. 43): "The extent of this Federal district is sufficiently circumscribed to satisfy every jealousy of an opposite nature. And as it is to be appropriated to this use with the consent of the State ceding it;...as the inhabitants will find sufficient inducements of interest to become willing parties to the cession; as they will have had their voice in the election of the government which is to exercise authority over them; as a municipal legislature for local purposes, derived from their own suffrages, will of course be allowed them;...every imaginable objection seems to be obviated."

Madison's reference to a muncipal legislature derived from local suffrage has often been cited by proponents of self-government for the District of Columbia. But in the absence of a constitutional guarantee of such suffrage, the legal situation has stood as Constance McLaughlin Green described it in *Washington, Capital City, 1879-1950*: "All power in Uncle Sam's company town rested ultimately in the company directorate—Congress." The only way for District of Columbia residents to win self-government is to get the company directorate to delegate its authority to them.

D.C. Representation in Congress

The Founding Fathers branded taxation without representation as tyranny. Yet residents of the nation's capital, though taxed by Congress, have no voting representation in Congress. Proponents of a voice in government for the people of the District of Columbia cite Madison's words "as they will have had their voice in the election of the government which is to exercise authority over them." But opponents interpret those words as referring only to residents of the area at the time of its cession to the Federal Government. Historians have concluded from the debates in the Constitutional Convention and from other evidence that one reason why the Convention did not give residents of the seat of Government a voice in Congress was a feeling on the part of the delegates that the capital's representatives would be in position to wrest unwarranted concessions from other Members of Congress.

Nonvoting Delegate in House

Congress has power to authorize the people of areas under American jurisdiction which are not states to elect nonvoting Members of the House of Representatives. It has accorded this degree of representation to territories before they became states, to the Commonwealth of the Philippines before it was given its independence, to Puerto Rico since 1902, and to the District of Columbia on two occasions—in 1871 and in 1970.

The Act of Congress approved Feb. 21, 1871, which established a territorial form of government for the national capital, gave local residents the right to elect a nonvoting delegate to the House of Representatives, who was to serve as a member of the Committee on the District of Columbia. Norton P. Chipman, a brigadier general in the Union Army who had settled in Washington after the Civil War, was elected to the post on the Republican ticket on April 21, 1871, and re-elected on Oct. 14, 1873. The Act of June 20, 1874, which replaced the territorial government of the District of Columbia by a commission form of government included a clause stating that repeal of the earlier legislation "shall not affect the term of office of the present Delegate in Congress." Chipman served as a delegate from the convening of the first regular session of the 42nd Congress on Dec. 4, 1871, to final adjournment of the 43rd Congress on March 4, 1875.

Bills providing for re-establishment of nonvoting representation for the District of Columbia were introduced repeatedly after the demise of the territorial government in 1874, but they made little progress until the 1950s. The Senate passed such bills in 1951, 1953, 1955, 1958 and 1959. Each time, however, the bill was killed in the House Committee on the District of Columbia.

In 1960, House supporters of a bill on the question gained 204 of the 219 signatures needed on a petition to take the bill from the District Committee's hands and bring it to the floor for a vote. Their near-success was hailed as a moral victory, but it led to no legislation. When the Senate passed a similar bill in 1965, the House passed, instead, a bill to set up a complex procedure for determining by referendum whether the people of the District really wanted the suffrage and, if so, what kind of suffrage they wanted. Differences between the two bills were not reconciled.

President Nixon on April 28, 1969, proposed that Congress submit to the states a constitutional amendment to give the District voting representation in Congress. He said: "Until such an amendment is approved by Congress and ratified by the states, I recommend that Congress enact legislation to provide for a nonvoting House delegate for the District." The Senate on Oct. 1, 1969, passed a bill providing for a nonvoting D.C. delegate in the House of Representatives and another bill providing for a "little Hoover Commission" study of the organization of Washington's government.

The House on Aug. 10, 1970, also passed two bills on the District of Columbia government, but they differed from those passed by the Senate in 1969. The House District Committee, irked by frequent Senate passage of bills providing for nonvoting representation in the House, had reported a bill (HR 8002) authorizing nonvoting representation in both the Senate and the House. The House passed that bill and then passed another (HR 18725) providing for a nonvoting District of Columbia representative in the House as well as a "little Hoover Commission" study of the D.C. government.

Three days later, the Senate District Committee reported HR 18725, since it corresponded in substance to the two D.C. bills passed by the Senate in 1969. Floor action

on the bill was held up initially at the request of Sen. Edward M. Kennedy (D Mass.), who explained on Aug. 14 that he was "concerned that the immediate passage of this measure may seriously prejudice the very real prospect we now have in this Congress of achieving the vastly more important goal of full voting representation." Kennedy wanted Senate action on the House bill deferred until after the Senate had acted on a proposed constitutional amendment to provide for voting representation of the District of Columbia in Congress. But on Sept. 9, 1970, he agreed not to hold up voting on HR 18725 any longer. The delay of almost a month, he said, had succeeded in highlighting his contention that "the nonvoting delegate is important, but only as an interim measure." The Senate passed the bill the same day, and President Nixon signed it on Sept. 22.

Moves for Voting Representation

Article I of the Constitution provides that the House of Representatives shall be composed of "Members chosen...by the People of the several States" and that the Senate shall be composed of "two Senators from each State." Supreme Court decisions handed down beginning in 1805 made it clear that the District of Columbia, for constitutional purposes, was not a state and that a constitutional amendment would be required to authorize voting representation of the District in Congress. Arthur Capper (R Kan.), who served in the Senate from 1919 to 1948, was prominent among those who over the years introduced resolutions proposing a constitutional amendment of this kind. In 1960, the Senate adopted such a resolution, but it was not acted on by the House. In 1967, hearings on similar resolutions were held in both houses, but no resolution was reported out of committee.

President Nixon, in his message to Congress on April 28, 1969, said: "It should offend the democratic senses of this nation that the 850,000 citizens of its capital, comprising a population larger than 11 of its states, have no voice in Congress. I urge that Congress approve, and the states ratify, an amendment to the Constitution granting to the District at least one Representative in the House of Representatives, and such additional Representatives in the House as the Congress shall approve, and to provide for the possibility of two Senators." The Senate Judiciary Subcommittee on Constitutional Amendments held hearings in 1970 on resolutions proposing an amendment to the Constitution of the kind suggested, but decided on July 28 to take no action.

Sen. Kennedy said he would move to attach one of the D.C. voting representation resolutions as a rider to some other measure. The measure which he chose initially as a vehicle for this purpose was the resolution proposing a constitutional amendment for direct election of the President and Vice President. The House had adopted that resolution Sept. 18, 1969, and it was debated in the Senate in September 1970. When it became apparent that it would not be adopted there, Kennedy said he might try to attach a D.C. voting representation amendment to the resolution proposing a constitutional amendment on equal rights for women. But the latter resolution was set aside by the crowded lame-duck session of Congress following the November midterm elections.

Creation of District of Columbia

Before there was a District of Columbia, and before the Constitution was adopted, the seat of Government of

Seats of Government

Prior to the selection of Washington, D.C., as the permanent seat of the Federal Government, Congress met in eight cities in four states. Following are the seats of Government under the Continental Congress, the Articles of Confederation and the Constitution:

Continental Congress

Philadelphia	Sept. 5, 1774-Dec. 12, 1776
Baltimore	Dec. 20, 1776-Feb. 27, 1777
Philadelphia	March 4, 1777-Sept. 18, 1777
Lancaster, Pa.	Sept. 27, 1777
York, Pa.	Sept. 30, 1777-June 27, 1778
Philadelphia	July 2, 1778-March 1, 1781

Articles of Confederation

Philadelphia	March 2, 1781-June 21, 1783
Princeton	June 30, 1783-Nov. 4, 1783
Annapolis	Nov. 26, 1783-June 3, 1784
Trenton	Nov. 1, 1784-Dec. 24, 1784
New York	Jan. 11, 1785-March 4, 1789

Constitution

New York	March 4, 1789-Aug. 12, 1790
Philadelphia	Dec. 6, 1790-May 14, 1800
Washington, D.C.	Nov. 17, 1800-

the United States was located wherever the Continental Congress met. There were eight such places: Philadelphia, Lancaster, and York in Pennsylvania; Trenton and Princeton in New Jersey; New York City; and Baltimore and Annapolis in Maryland. The Continental Congress made a number of abortive attempts to agree on a permanent site for the capital, including a decision on Oct. 7, 1783, to establish a Federal town on the Delaware River and a decision 10 days later to set aside Georgetown, on the Potomac River, as a second Federal town.

Decision on the Site

In the light of the constitutional provision on the seat of Government, the general assemblies of Maryland and Virginia on Dec. 23, 1788, and Dec. 3, 1789, adopted resolutions offering up to 10 miles square of any portion of their respective states for use in laying out the Federal city. But opposition to a site in the Maryland-Virginia area developed in the New England and Middle Atlantic states, where a more northerly site was preferred.

On Sept. 22, 1789, the House passed a bill naming a site on the Susquehanna River as the permanent capital and New York as the temporary capital. The Senate on Sept. 24 amended the bill to make Germantown, Pa., the permanent location and Philadelphia the temporary site. The conflicting bills were lost in the rush as the First Session of the First Congress headed for adjournment on Sept. 29. In the ensuing months, southern advocates of a site on the Potomac River rallied their forces.

Meanwhile, another North-South dispute was brewing, and it provided an ingredient for compromise on location of the seat of Government. Northerners favored assumption by the Federal Government of debts which the states had incurred as a result of their participation in the Revolutionary War. These debts in the late 1780s were largely in the form of bonds which northern financiers had bought up at low prices. Since Virginia had already paid its debts of this kind, many Virginians, along with other southerners, objected to assumption of the state debts by the national Government. But in mid-May 1790, Secretary of State Thomas Jefferson, Secretary of the Treasury Alexander Hamilton (who favored the "assumption" proposal), and two Members of Congress from Virginia met around Jefferson's supper table in New York and agreed that, in return for Hamilton's aligning of northern support for a southern capital, the Virginians would vote for assumption.

Jefferson's southern sympathies induced feelings of guilt about his part in this compromise. On Sept. 9, 1792, while vacationing at Monticello, he wrote to President Washington: "The first and only instance of variance from the former part of my resolution (not to meddle in legislative matters), I was duped into by the Secretary of the Treasury, and made a tool for forwarding his schemes, not then sufficiently understood by me; and of all the errors of my political life, this has occasioned me the deepest regret." However, the deal had already gone into effect; an Act of Congress of July 16, 1790, provided that the seat of Government should be located in Philadelphia from 1790 to 1800 and thereafter in "a district...on the river Potomac"; and by an Act of Aug. 4, 1790, the Federal Government had assumed the states' Revolutionary War debts.

Definition of the Boundaries

The Act of July 16, 1790, accepting the offers of land from Maryland and Virginia for a Federal district, bounded it as follows: "...a district of territory, not exceeding ten miles square, to be located as hereafter directed on the river Potomac, at some place between the mouths of the Eastern Branch and Connogocheague." A distance of some 70 miles, as the crow flies, separated the mouth of the Eastern Branch, which is now called the Anacostia River, and the mouth of what is now called Conococheague Creek, a stream that empties into the upper Potomac near Williamsport, Md. Three commissioners, appointed by President Washington and serving under his direction, were to "survey and by proper metes and bounds define and limit a district of territory, under the limitations above mentioned."

The exact boundaries preferred by Washington and the commissioners did not accord with the specifications. The 1790 law required that the district be located wholly to the west of the mouth of Maryland's Eastern Branch. But the area selected lay in part to the east of that stream and extended south along the Potomac to a point opposite Alexandria, Virginia. The area included the latter settlement and a slice of Virginia stretching northward from Alexandria along the west side of the Potomac to a point opposite Georgetown, a settlement that was also included in the district.

By an Act of March 3, 1791, Congress obligingly redefined the area to accord with the preferences of the President and the commissioners. Washington on March 30, 1791, issued a proclamation specifying the boundaries of the Federal district. The boundaries formed a square, 10 miles on each side, comprising the portion on the Maryland side of the Potomac which is the present District of Columbia and a portion on the Virginia side that completed the square.

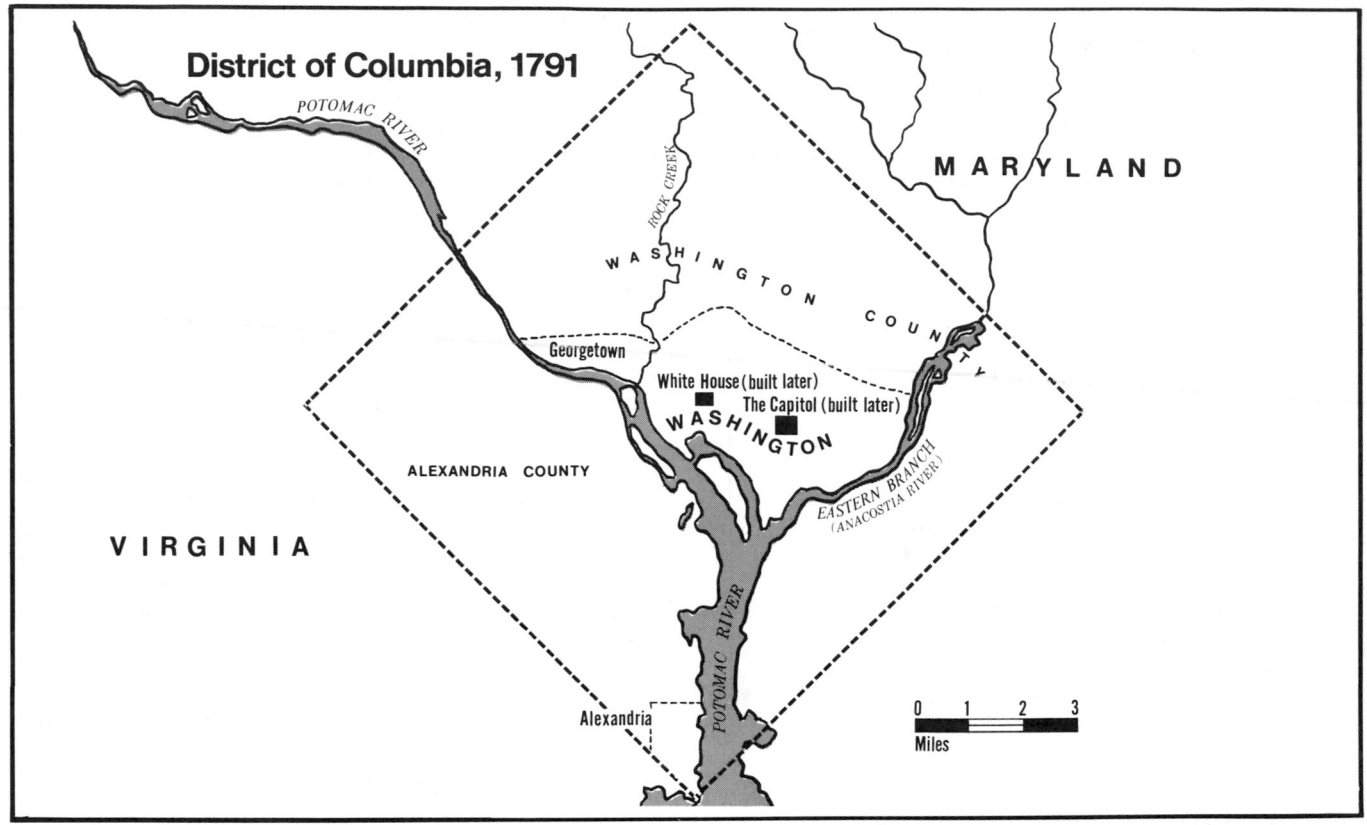

Deal With The Landowners

It was understood by all parties that what Maryland and Virginia were ceding was governmental jurisdiction only. Ownership of land and buildings in the ceded area was to remain in the hands of deedholders. For example, the Virginia law of Dec. 3, 1789, stated: "Nothing herein contained shall be construed to vest in the United States any right of property in the soil, or to affect the rights of individuals therein, otherwise than the same shall or may be transferred by such individuals to the United States."

The Act of Congress of July 16, 1790, provided that the commissioners who were to choose the site of the Federal capital "shall have power to purchase or accept such quantity of land on the eastern side of the said (Potomac) river, within the said district, as the President shall deem proper for the use of the United States." Land for governmental purposes in the new district was actually acquired through an arrangement which Washington, Jefferson and Madison negotiated with landowners in the general area before the decision on an exact site had been made. Washington himself conducted the principal talks with the landowners in a Georgetown tavern in the early part of 1791. On March 30 of that year, he obtained the owners' agreement to a plan under which they might expect to profit handsomely by ceding their land even though the Government would not be required to levy taxes to pay for it. The plan provided:

1. Each landowner would cede one-half of his land to the Federal Government.

2. The Government would keep that portion of the ceded land needed for public buildings, streets and parks, and would sell the remainder.

3. The landowners who had ceded one-half of their holdings would benefit in two ways: First, they would receive $66.67 an acre from the Government for those portions of the ceded land which the Government decided to keep for public buildings, streets and parks; secondly, the value of the one-half of their holdings which they did not sell to the Government was expected to rise because of its proximity to the seat of Government.

4. The Government would benefit in that the money needed to pay for the acreage selected for buildings, streets and parks would have entered its coffers through the sale to private persons of those portions of the ceded land which it did not need. The Treasury stood to benefit also from contributions of $120,000 and $72,000 pledged by Virginia and Maryland, respectively, toward construction of public buildings in the new capital.

Trouble With L'Enfant

President Washington in March 1791 appointed Pierre Charles L'Enfant to prepare a plan of the new capital city and to participate in execution of the plan. Washington regularly called the place "the Federal city." The commissioners whom he had appointed to oversee development of the city called it, in a letter of Sept. 9, 1791, to Major L'Enfant, "the city of Washington" and named the whole district "the Territory of Columbia." Congress formally named the city and the district almost by indirection. An Act of Congress approved May 6, 1796, was entitled "An Act Authorizing a Loan for the City of Washington, in the District of Columbia, and for other purposes therein mentioned." The text of the Act merely referred to "the said city" and did not mention either the city or the district by name.

L'Enfant's design for the capital city, completed in 1791, was greatly admired as combining features of the arrangement of avenues at Versailles with innovations to meet the special needs of an American capital city. However, in moving to carry out the plan, L'Enfant displayed an overbearing temperament. He repeatedly defied the authority of the commissioners and of the President himself. At one point, without waiting for approval, he had a large private dwelling, still under construction, torn down because it would block a proposed street. And he insisted on proceeding with development of the new city at a pace which would have forced the Government into borrowing on a scale it was not prepared to undertake. On Feb. 27, 1792, President Washington asked for his resignation. (See Appendix for text of L'Enfant plan.)

After 1800, L'Enfant haunted the halls of Congress, seeking compensation for his plan for the Federal city. He claimed $95,500, but a public law of March 27, 1804, and a private act of May 1, 1810, authorized payments totaling less than $3,000. The bulk of that amount was paid, under a court order, to one of L'Enfant's creditors. L'Enfant died in poverty. His plan was revived in 1901 and used as a basis for further development of the capital city.

Government's Move to Washington

The Act of July 16, 1790, which established a Federal district on the Potomac, stipulated that during the 10 years in which the seat of Government would be at Philadelphia a three-man commission should "provide suitable buildings for the accommodation of Congress, and of the President, and for the public offices of the Government of the United States" in the district and place laid out on the Potomac, and that on the first Monday in December 1800 "the seat of the Government of the United States shall, by virtue of this act, be transferred to the district and place aforesaid."

Early in 1800 it became clear that the buildings erected in Washington for the Government would be ready long before December. Accordingly Congress, by an Act of April 24, 1800, provided: "That the President of the United States shall be, and hereby is authorized and empowered, to direct the various offices belonging to the several executive departments of the United States, to be removed to the city of Washington, at any time that he shall judge proper, after the adjournment of the present session of Congress, and before the time heretofore appointed by law for such removal."

The First Session of the Sixth Congress adjourned on May 14, 1800. Later that month, sloops carrying Government records from Philadelphia sailed up the Potomac to the new city. President John Adams supervised the opening of Government offices in June, and Abigail Adams, according to contemporary records, hung her washing in the East Room of the unfinished White House. Pursuant to an Act of May 13, 1800, the Second Session of the Sixth Congress, the first session of Congress to be held in Washington, convened Nov. 17.

Congress was not in session during the summer of 1814, when British troops invaded Washington and burned the Capitol and other buildings. A special session of Congress convened on Sept. 19 of that year. On Sept. 26, 1814, Rep. Jonathan Fisk (D N.Y.) offered a resolution proposing a committee to study moving the seat of Government to "a place of greater security and less inconvenience." The resolution was adopted after a short debate, 72-51.

The committee report, submitted by Fisk on Oct. 3, said that it was "inexpedient to remove the seat of Government at this time from the city of Washington." However, Fisk proposed an amendment to substitute the word "expedient" for "inexpedient," and the amendment carried, 69-68, with Speaker Langdon Cheves (D S.C.) casting the tie-breaking vote in favor of moving the Government. House debate on the report continued until Oct. 6 when by a 72-71 vote it adopted the amended report and appointed a committee to prepare a bill for transferring the Government. The committee bill, brought in Oct. 13, provided for moving the Government to another location during the war with Britain.

No alternate sites were mentioned in the bill, but among the possible choices were Philadelphia, New York and Lancaster, Pa. It was widely assumed that such a temporary removal would develop into a permanent absence, and residents of the District of Columbia urged defeat of the measure. Finally on Oct. 15 the debate ended. The House defeated the bill on a 74-83 vote.

Thereafter, continuation of the seat of Government in Washington was not seriously questioned, except that after the national territory had been extended to the Pacific, a feeble voice was occasionally heard in favor of a more centrally located capital.

Return of Alexandria to Virginia

Congress, by an Act of Feb. 21, 1801, created two counties in the District of Columbia: Washington County on the Maryland side of the Potomac and Alexandria County on the Virginia side. Although the general provisions of the Act, especially those concerning courts of law, were set forth for both counties, the two already incorporated communities of the new District—Georgetown and Alexandria—were exempted from the operation of most of these provisions.

In 1840, toward the end of Martin Van Buren's Presidency, Washington in particular and the District of Columbia in general became a battleground between Washington's mayor, William W. Seaton (Whig), and the Democrats, who were dominant in Congress. Because Seaton had been elected under a system which limited the franchise to property holders, the Democrats in Congress initiated a move to extend the franchise in the District of Columbia to all male adults. In addition, Congress virtually legislated D.C. banks out of existence by forbidding them, in an Act of June 3, 1840, to receive deposits, issue checks, or make loans. Renewal of the banks' charters was not effected until Aug. 25, 1841, after the Whigs had gained a majority in Congress.

When the banks of the District were deprived of their privileges, the City of Georgetown and the rural parts of Washington County, as well as the County of Alexandria, sought retrocession to Maryland and Virginia, respectively. The Maryland Legislature was not willing to assume the financial burden of reintegrating Georgetown and the nearby countryside into the state. But much later, on Feb. 3, 1846, the Virginia Legislature indicated its willingness to take back all of Alexandria County.

By an Act of July 9, 1846, Congress agreed to retrocede to Virginia the portion of the District of Columbia which lay in that state, if and when the residents of the County of Alexandria registered their approval. After a referendum resulted in a vote of 763 for retrocession and 222 against, President James K. Polk on Sept. 7, 1846,

Number of Negroes Elected to D.C. Council, 1868-71

	14-man Board of Aldermen	21-man Common Council
1868-69.	1	1
1869-70.	1	7
1870-71.	1	6

SOURCE: W.B. Bryan, *A History of the National Capital*, Vol. II (1916), pp. 559-560.

proclaimed Alexandria County retroceded to Virginia. Since then, the District of Columbia has consisted of about 70 square miles on the Maryland side of the Potomac.

Consolidation of District of Columbia

The three political entities remaining in the District of Columbia after the retrocession of the Virginia section were the City of Washington, the County of Washington, and the City of Georgetown. The first step toward erasing the inner boundaries of the District was taken in 1861, when Congress, by an act approved Aug. 6, established the Metropolitan Police District of the District of Columbia, which included in its jurisdiction the entire 70 square miles. The Act assigned responsibility for law enforcement throughout the District to a board consisting of five commissioners appointed by the President, "three...from the City of Washington, one from Georgetown and one from the County of Washington at large," plus "the mayors of the cities of Washington and Georgetown, ex officio."

The Act of Feb. 21, 1871, establishing a territorial government for the District of Columbia, stated "That all that part of the territory of the United States included within the limits of the District of Columbia be, and the same is hereby, created into a government by the name of the District of Columbia, by which name it is hereby constituted a body corporate for municipal purposes." A later section of the Act repealed the charters of the cities of Washington and Georgetown, with the proviso that "all laws and ordinances of said cities,...not inconsistent with this Act, shall remain in full force until modified or repealed by Congress or the legislative assembly of the said District."

The Act also stated that "That portion of said District included within the present limits of the City of Washington shall continue to be known as the City of Washington; and that portion of said District included within the limits of the City of Georgetown shall continue to be known as the City of Georgetown." The Act further recognized the geographic components of the District by providing that two of the 11 members of the D.C. legislative assembly "shall be residents of the City of Georgetown, and two residents of the County outside of the Cities of Washington and Georgetown."

The City of Washington and the District of Columbia were finally made coterminous by an Act of Feb. 11, 1895. It provided that "from and after the passage of this Act, all that part of the District of Columbia embraced within the bounds and now constituting the City of Georgetown... shall no longer be known by the name and title in law of the City of Georgetown, but the same shall be known as

and shall constitute a part of the City of Washington, the Federal Capital." Taking a backward glance, the legislators provided "That nothing in this Act shall operate to affect or repeal existing law making Georgetown a port of entry, except as to its name."

Changes in Form of D.C. Government

The Act of Feb. 21, 1801, relating to the government of the District of Columbia provided that the laws of Maryland and Virginia should continue to apply respectively in the portions of the District taken from those states. This situation continued in Alexandria city and county until the retrocession of 1846, and in Georgetown and Washington city and county until 1871. Georgetown, which had been governed before 1801 by a popularly elected council and board of aldermen under an appointed mayor, continued to be so governed thereafter; no change was made until 1830, when Congress authorized Georgetown's citizens to elect their mayor. Washington County, formerly governed by a so-called levy court whose members were appointed by the Governor of Maryland, was governed after February 1801 by a levy court whose members were appointed by the President of the United States.

Mayor-Council Government, 1802-71

An act of Congress approved May 3, 1802, set up a government for the City of Washington consisting of a mayor appointed by the President and a 12-member, two-chamber Council elected by the people. Two changes were made in the early years of the century in the direction of fuller self-government. First, an act of May 4, 1812, authorized the popularly elected Council to elect the mayor. Then, by an act of May 15, 1820, Congress authorized the city's residents themselves to elect the mayor.

Slavery was abolished in the District of Columbia on April 16, 1862. By 1866, about 30,000 ex-slaves had made their way to the District, where they constituted less than one-fourth of the population. In 1867, three years before ratification of the Fifteenth Amendment to the Constitution (which prohibited voting discrimination on the basis of race), Congress conferred the franchise "without any distinction on account of color or race" on male citizens over 21 years of age who had resided in the District of Columbia for one year. President Andrew Johnson vetoed the franchise bill, but his veto was overridden by the Senate Jan. 7, 1867, and by the House the next day. Many whites refrained from voting in the election of members of the D.C. Council later that year, and those whites who went to the polls were divided politically. Negroes voted solidly for the Republican ticket, and Republicans—all white—were put in control of both chambers of the Council.

Territorial Government, 1871-74

Early in the 1870s, Alexander Shepherd, a Washington native who had risen from the job of plumber's helper to be the city's leading entrepreneur, suggested a modified territorial form of government for the District of Columbia. Acting on this suggestion, Congress enacted a law, Feb. 21, 1871, providing for a governor appointed by the President; an elected nonvoting delegate in the House of Representatives; a territorial assembly consisting of an 11-member council appointed by the President and a 22-member house of delegates elected by the people; and a five-member board of public works appointed by the President.

These provisions resembled those employed for the government of territories. However, the term "territorial government" was not used formally with reference to the District of Columbia. The reason was that Congress, in establishing the new government, relied on the authority contained in Article I, Section 8, Clause 17 of the Constitution, which accords to Congress legislative authority over the seat of government, rather than on Article 4, Section 3, which refers to the government of territories.

Shepherd was made executive officer of the District of Columbia's board of public works. Under his direction, the city was modernized. Water mains and sewers were laid, streets paved, and parks developed. However, the bill for this work totaled some $20 million, nearly three times the estimate. Shepherd may have been extravagant, but he apparently sought no personal profit. According to *The Nation*, June 25, 1874, he "had never been known to cheat or steal"; but the same could not be said of Shepherd's associates. Martha Derthick wrote in *City Politics in Washington, D.C.*, a study published in 1962, that Shepherd made the city bankrupt but he also made it habitable.

The situation was aggravated in September 1873 when President Ulysses S. Grant named Shepherd to the post of Governor of the District of Columbia. Aggrieved taxpayers presented a memorial to Congress which led to the appointment in February 1874 of a joint Congressional committee to investigate District affairs. The Committee, headed by Sen. William B. Allison (R Iowa), asserted in its report in June 1874 that the existing government of the District of Columbia, ridden by graft and financial mismanagement, was a failure.

The Committee recommended that, for a temporary period, the governorship be replaced by an appointed three-member commission; that the assembly, the board of public works, and the post of D.C. delegate in the House of Representatives be abolished; and that Congress perform legislative functions for the District. Thus, representative government in the District would be brought to an end, but supposedly only for the time being. The investigating committee recommended that Congress appoint a new committee to propose a permanent form of government for the District.

Commission Government, 1874-1967

By an act of Congress approved June 20, 1874, the investigating committee's basic recommendations were put into effect. A furor over the naming of one of the three new commissioners followed. Wilhelmus B. Bryan wrote in his two-volume *History of the National Capital:* "With that sturdy virtue of fidelity to friends that was the admiration of men, even when they did not approve the results, President Grant nominated Shepherd, who was promptly and decisively rejected." The vote in the Senate, June 23, 1874, was 6 in favor of confirmation and 32 opposed. A substitute nominee, William Dennison, one-time Governor of Ohio, was approved. Shepherd, his fortune gone and his name besmirched, moved with his family to Mexico in 1876.

The joint Congressional Committee appointed to propose a permanent government for the District of Columbia recommended in 1875 that the commission form of government be continued, but with provision for popular election of three of the eight members of the school board. Action on this proposal in the next three years was prevented by disagreement over the franchise for District residents. Those favoring the franchise were embarrassed by pilfering of government property by popularly elected Negro members of the D.C. house of delegates when it went out of existence in 1874.

The commission form of government, without any voting rights for District residents, was made permanent from July 1, 1878, by an Act of June 11 of that year, which came to be known as the Organic Act of the District of Columbia. Basic to the decision to prolong the commission form of government were two factors: (1) the desire of the business community to assure the District of a sound financial future and (2) hostility to Negro suffrage. The second factor was of importance not so much among Members of Congress as among white residents of the District, many of whom preferred to do without the franchise rather than share it with the Negro residents.

The new law provided that of the three commissioners two "shall have been actual residents of the District of Columbia for three years next before their appointment"; the third commissioner was to be an officer of the U.S. Army's Corps of Engineers above the rank of captain. The Act specified that "one of said three commissioners shall be chosen president of the Board of Commissioners at their first meeting, and annually and whenever a vacancy shall occur, thereafter."

Congress kept tight control over the manner in which Washington developed. In the late 1890s, construction of a 14-story apartment hotel nine blocks north of the White House (the Cairo, still standing in 1970), caused dismay in Congress, whose Members wanted no private buildings in the capital to overshadow Government structures. An Act of March 1, 1899, limited new residential buildings to five stories or 60 feet in height; buildings of any kind on a residential street to 90 feet; and buildings on a business street to 130 feet. Church spires could go higher with the approval of the District Commissioners. As a rule of thumb, no buildings taller than 12 or 13 stories were allowed. The height limitations on residential buildings were subsequently modified, but the over-all top limit of 130 feet was never relaxed.

Commissioner-Council Government Since 1967

The commission form of government prevailed in the District of Columbia for more than 90 years. In the latter part of that period, sentiment in favor of self-government for the national capital gathered substantial support. Although such sentiment reached a high point in the 1960s, moves in Congress to grant home rule to the District were obstructed, mainly by the House District Committee. Accordingly, strategists turned their attention to other ways of effecting changes in the District's government.

President Lyndon B. Johnson's advisers on District affairs persuaded the Chief Executive to utilize for this purpose his power to submit to Congress government reorganization plans, which would go into effect unless disapproved by either house within 60 days (plus an additional number of days if either house was temporarily in recess). On June 1, 1967, Mr. Johnson sent to Congress a plan to replace the three-member D.C. Board of Commissioners with a single commissioner and an assistant commissioner, appointed by the President, and a nine-member council, also to be appointed by the President, which would have the ordinance-making powers formerly exercised by the Board of Commissioners. The President's appointees would be confirmed by the Senate. The new Commissioner would have the right to veto the Council's actions, but the Council would be empowered to override his veto by a three-fourths vote.

The plan was referred to the Senate and House Committees on Government Operations, but the House District Committee was not inactive. Rep. Thomas G. Abernethy (D Miss.), chairman of the Committee's Subcommittee No. 1, held hearings on the D.C. government between June 27 and Aug. 2, 1967. The full District Committee on Aug. 7 reported to the House a substitute proposal which would continue the three-member Board of Commissioners with a number of changes in the D.C. government structure, including establishment of a department of management and a provision for popular election of the school board. The Committee's report, to which eight of the Committee's 25 members took exception, asserted that the President's plan was "deficient in the major areas wherein administrative difficulty and disagreements lie" and that experience with the three-member Board of Commissioners for 90 years "bears no color of obsolescence."

The House of Representatives on Aug. 9, 1967, nevertheless rejected a resolution to disapprove the plan. The vote was 160 in favor of disapproval and 244 opposed. In the Senate, no disapproval resolution was introduced. The plan went into effect on Aug. 11. President Johnson nominated Walter E. Washington, a Negro, as Commissioner, and included five Negroes among his nine appointees to the Council. At that time, about 65 percent of Washington's inhabitants were black. The Senate confirmed all of the President's nominees. Mr. Johnson soon started calling the new D.C. Commissioner by the title of "Mayor," and the press and others adopted this practice.

Power of Congress Over D.C. Affairs

Since 1874, every significant bill in Congress dealing with District of Columbia affairs has had to run the gauntlet of four committees: the Senate and House Committees on the District of Columbia and the Senate and House Committees on Appropriations. Opposition by a majority in any one of these Committees has been enough to bury a bill. Action has been blocked by disagreement between two of the Committees in the same house or between the District (or Appropriations) Committee of one house and the corresponding Committee of the other house. In the Senate, since 1947, three members of the Committee on the District of Columbia have served ex officio on the Committee on Appropriations when the latter Committee has been considering the annual appropriations for the District. Congressional committees in addition to those on Appropriations and the District of Columbia have jurisdiction over special aspects of D.C. affairs. Among them are the Committees on Government Operations, the Judiciary, Labor, and the Post Office and Civil Service.

Committees on District of Columbia

Matters considered by members of the Senate and House Committees on the District of Columbia have ranged in importance from whether slavery should be abolished in the District to fixing the local license fee for dog tags. Martha Derthick wrote in *City Politics in Washington, D.C.,* "The District Committees routinely receive many requests from District residents or other persons seeking local favors and jobs. Influential persons get parking tickets fixed through the Committees," and ambitious municipal employees, "especially policemen, maintain close relations with Members of Congress." Under a tacit arrangement, "The District police are said to overlook their (Members') parking offenses, and Congressmen are said to take a generous view of police appeals for personnel benefits."

Daniel M. Berman, a professor of government at American University, wrote in his book *In Congress Assembled* (1964): "...there are certain committees on which practically no one wants to serve, notably those that deal with the District of Columbia....The only Congressmen who generally want to serve on...(these committees) are those from nearby Maryland districts, and southern Democrats (whose motive is to block 'home rule' for the residents of the District, a majority of whom are Negroes)."

The District Committees of the two houses often are reproved for taking what their critics regard as a relaxed view of the District's pressing needs. Sen. James B. Allen (D Ala.) on Aug. 17, 1970, defended the Committees during a debate on the proposal to allow the District a nonvoting delegate in the House of Representatives. He said: "We have a very able Senate Committee on the District of Columbia and a very able House Committee on the District of Columbia.... The District is well represented through the District of Columbia Committees in the two bodies."

Senate Committee. An explanatory pamphlet issued by the Senate District Committee in 1969 stated: "In the conduct of its legislative responsibilities over the affairs of the Nation's Capital, the Senate Committee on the District of Columbia in some respects is not unlike a state legislature and city council combined, by virtue of the great variety of problems and proposals that come before it." Martha Derthick noted: "The Senate District Committee is more liberal than its House counterpart. It has repeatedly favored home rule and is more lenient in authorizing taxation and expenditures for the District."

The Senate Committee has established four subcommittees, dealing respectively with matters relating to business and commerce; fiscal affairs; the judiciary; and public health, education, welfare and safety. The Subcommittees consider legislative proposals on these matters in the District of Columbia and submit recommendations to the full Committee.

House Committee. The House D.C. Committee, established Jan. 27, 1808, is the second oldest of the standing committees of the House, next in seniority to the Committee on Interstate and Foreign Commerce, which was established in 1795. That southerners are not only willing but eager to serve on the House D.C. Committee was indicated by Martha Derthick, who wrote in 1962: "The role that veteran southerners play there satisfies the interests of their constituents as few other committee assignments could."

The D.C. Committee has five regular subcommittees, with duties assigned by the Committee chairman, and occasionally it has set up special investigating subcommittees. William L. Morrow wrote in *Congressional Committees* (1969) that the chairman of the House

---

Jurisdiction of D.C. Committees

Sections 102 and 121 of the Legislative Reorganization Act of Aug. 2, 1946, still in force, set forth the jurisdiction of the Senate and House Committees on the District of Columbia, respectively, in identical language, as follows:

"1. All measures relating to municipal affairs of the District of Columbia in general, other than appropriations therefor, including—

"2. Public health and safety, sanitation, and quarantine regulations.

"3. Regulation of sale of intoxicating liquors.

"4. Adulteration of food and drugs.

"5. Taxes and tax sales.

"6. Insurance, executors, administrators, wills, and divorce.

"7. Municipal and juvenile courts.

"8. Incorporation and organization of societies.

"9. Municipal code and amendments to the criminal and corporation laws."

Committee on the District of Columbia was among those who "avoid the problem of entrenched subcommittee power by resorting to the practice of numbering subcommittees without assigning them any specific jurisdiction." *(For changes instituted in 1971, see p. 154-155.)*

Advocates of self-government for the District of Columbia often have felt that their proposals received short shrift from the House District Committee. Martha Derthick wrote: "In the eyes of its many local critics, the Committee plays an obstructionist role in District government, willfully and maliciously frustrating the best interests of the District. It has consistently blocked home rule....In general it acts...to limit the benefits that Negroes derive from government. It is conservative also on issues that have no overt racial implications. It is consistently reluctant to authorize new taxes or expenditures."

Rep. John L. McMillan (D S.C.), chairman of the House District Committee, in August 1970 defended the Committee's and his own policies. Reporting to the House with some hesitation a bill allowing the District to elect a nonvoting delegate to the House of Representatives, McMillan said: "Your chairman, having resided in the nation's capital community during the past 40 years, is of the opinion that he is as well informed on the conditions in the District of Columbia as any man that could be elected to a position as delegate to the House from the District of Columbia."

Committees on Appropriations

The budget of the District of Columbia government goes through the same steps as the budgets of departments of the Federal Government. Units of the District government prepare estimates of receipts and proposed expenditures and submit them to the D.C. Office of Budget and Program Analysis. That office compiles the estimates and submits them to the mayor and the deputy mayor. The latter officials make changes they deem necessary and pass the budget along to the Council, which in turn may make changes. The mayor has au-

thority to overrule the Council's recommendations before transmitting the D.C. budget to the Federal Office of Management and Budget.

Federal officials review and revise the District estimates, usually paring them on the expenditure side, before incorporating the District budget in the President's over-all Budget, which he sends to Congress in January of each year. Later, the D.C. Subcommittees of the House and Senate Appropriations Committees conduct hearings and report, through the full Committees, a D.C. appropriations bill which often is amended after floor discussion in House and Senate.

Members of the Appropriations Subcommittees, as well as of the District Committees, have expressed concern about rising costs for welfare, community development, and recreation in the District and have limited the appropriations for such purposes to amounts which have often been criticized as far from adequate. Stewart Alsop, in a book on Washington entitled *The Center* (1968), wrote: "There are times when the southern Congressmen who control Washington's purse strings seem actually to want bad trouble."

Defending the record of Congress on D.C. appropriations, the House District Committee, in a pamphlet entitled *Legislation Pertaining to the District of Columbia; Summary Report,* said in 1968: "As a result of...appropriations by the Congress, the District for some years has ranked at or near the top of 17 U.S. cities of comparable size (500,000 to 1,000,000 in population) in general expenditures, as well as in expenditures in major categories affecting public welfare, as for police, fire protection, health and hospitals, public welfare, and public education."

The House Appropriations Committee has wielded its power over District affairs not only by controlling appropriations but also by imposing various requirements on the D.C. government. For example, Rep. William H. Natcher (D Ky.), chairman of the Committee's Subcommittee on D.C. Appropriations, had long urged the construction of four highway projects, including an additional bridge across the Potomac, which had been included in the District segment of the Interstate highway system. The District government and local citizen groups opposed the projects on the ground that they would serve

---

Work of House District Committee, 90th Congress (1968-69)

Bills referred to the Committee	339
Originating in the House	306
Passed by Senate and referred to House	33
Bills on which hearings were held	161
Days consumed by hearings	79
Printed pages of hearings	3,975
Bills reported by the Committee	76
Passed by the House	70
Passed also by Senate and signed by the President	47

SOURCE: House D.C. Committee, *Legislation Pertaining to the District of Columbia; Summary Report* (1968), p. 4.

District of Columbia Appropriations

(Financed mostly by D.C. revenues)

Fiscal Year	Millions of Dollars
1960	199.8
1961	223.1
1962	233.6
1963	255.4
1964	265.1
1965	298.1
1966	326.0
1967	368.5
1968	457.4
1969	527.3
1970	592.4

SOURCE: House Appropriations Committee, Report on D.C. Appropriations Bill for Fiscal Year 1971 (House Report No. 1135, 91st Congress, 2d Session, June 1, 1970), p. 5.

the convenience of suburban motorists at the expense of inner city residents. Natcher managed to get inserted in the Federal Aid Highway Act of 1968 a mandate for an immediate start on the D.C. projects, and he vowed to hold back funds for a projected D.C. rapid transit system until the highway and bridge projects had progressed, as he said, "beyond recall."

Carrol W. Cagle, press secretary for Rep. Allard K. Lowenstein (D N.Y.), referred to Natcher as "the capital's invisible despot." Cagle wrote in *The Nation,* Sept. 29, 1969: "He (Natcher) holds enormous control over the 2-million-population metropolitan area of Washington, D.C. ...His actions during the Byzantine freeway-subway controversy illustrate full well that Washington's nominal officials...are powerless if their wishes conflict with one of the Congressional dukedoms."

Federal Payment to the District. Congress for many years has made an annual contribution to the District of Columbia from the Federal treasury. The amount of the contribution is recommended by the Appropriations Committees in association with the Committees on the District of Columbia. The rationale for the contribution includes several factors. In the first place, the Federal Government owns 43.2 per cent of the land area of the District of Columbia as well as many Government buildings and pays no real estate taxes on its holdings. In addition, the seat of government attracts other tax-exempt property owners, such as foreign embassies and the headquarters of patriotic organizations. Further, values of taxable real property are kept down by the Congressional ban on skyscrapers.

The amount of the Federal contribution to the District was set initially, by an act of June 11, 1878, at one-half of the expenses of the D.C. government. The proportion was cut to 40 per cent by an act of June 5, 1920. Four years later, Congress abandoned a fixed percentage and started appropriating a specific amount each year *(see box).* President Johnson on Feb. 2, 1965,

proposed a permanent annual Federal appropriation for the District of Columbia equal to the real estate, personal property, and business income taxes which the Federal Government would pay if it were a taxable entity. The Senate on July 22 and the House on Sept. 29, 1965, passed home rule bills which included provisions along this line, but the differences between the bills were not reconciled and consequently they fell by the wayside.

A different tack was taken by President Nixon. In a message to Congress on reorganization of the District of Columbia, April 28, 1969, he included a proposal "that the Congress authorize a Federal payment formula, fixing the Federal contribution at 30 per cent of local tax and other general fund revenues." Before acting on that proposal, Congress passed, and the President on Oct. 31, 1969, signed a bill authorizing an increase in the annual Federal payment to the District from $90 million to $105 million. Then, in the summer of 1970, the Appropriations and D.C. Committees of the Senate approved the President's proposal to set the contribution at 30 per cent of local revenues, and the Senate on Aug. 13 passed a bill to that effect and sent it to the House, where it died.

Other Committees

Plans which the President submits to Congress for reorganization of the D.C. government are referred to the Senate and House Committees on Government Operations. The plan of 1967 which proposed replacing the commission form of government with a commissioner-council government was so referred. Indeed, President Johnson's strategy in proposing to institute a new form of government for the District of Columbia by means of a reorganization plan was aimed at bypassing the House Committee on the District of Columbia, which strongly supported the existing arrangement. However, a few weeks before submitting the reorganization plan to Congress, Mr. Johnson invited the members of the Senate and House District Committees to the White House to discuss the plan.

Annual Federal Payment to D.C.

Fiscal Year	Authorized (millions of dollars)	Actual (millions of dollars)	Percent of D.C. Government's Ordinary Income*
1960	32	25	12.5
1961	32	25	11.2
1962	32	30	12.8
1963	32	30	11.8
1964	50	37.5	14.2
1965	50	37.5	12.6
1966	50	44.3	13.6
1967	60	58	15.7
1968	70	70	15.3
1969	90	89.4	17.0
1970	105	104.2	17.6
1971	126	108.9	-

The major portion of the D.C. government's ordinary income is derived from local taxes.

SOURCES: House D.C. Committee, *Legislation Pertaining to the District of Columbia; Summary Report* (1968), pp. 36-37; and House Appropriations Committee, Report on D.C. Appropriations Bill for Fiscal Year 1971 (June 1, 1970, p. 5.

The House Committee on Government Operations referred the 1967 plan to its Subcommittee on Executive and Legislative Reorganization, which held hearings on the plan in June. On Aug. 1, the Subcommittee recommended that the plan be allowed to take effect. The full Government Operations Committee voted 26 to 4, Aug. 3, to report to the House a disapproval resolution with the recommendation that the resolution be rejected. Heavy support of the plan by Republican members of the Committee (11 for rejection of the disapproval resolution and 2 in favor of it) surprised and pleased the plan's supporters. The House on Aug. 9 accepted the Committee's recommendation; and the Senate took no action to prevent the plan from going into effect.

Prominent among other Congressional committees which consider D.C. affairs are the Senate and House Committees on the Judiciary. To them are referred proposed constitutional amendments, such as amendments that would expand the franchise for District residents, and bills affecting crime control in the District. A stringent D.C. Anticrime Act, approved July 29, 1970, was passed over the strong opposition of a southern conservative member of the Senate Judiciary Committee, Sam J. Ervin (D N.C.), who threw a curve to strict law-and-order advocates by calling the bill's provisions on preventive detention and "no-knock" searches "unconstitutional, unfair, unjust, and unworkable."

Self-Government for the District

Residents of the national capital area which Maryland and Virginia ceded to the Federal Government voted in 1800, in both national and local elections. Thereafter, they continued to vote in local elections until 1874. In national politics, they were deprived not only of an elected representative in Congress (except for a few years in the early 1870s), but also of participation in the nomination and election of the President and Vice President of the United States. Exclusion of D.C. residents from Presidential politics continued for more than a century and a half.

After World War II, leaders of both major political parties sent up trial balloons on the possibility of permitting residents of the District of Columbia to participate in the quadrennial showpiece of American democracy, the choice of President and Vice President. The reaction was predominantly favorable. Congress took the first step toward implementing the proposal in 1954 and 1955.

Participation in National Politics

The Senate on July 10, 1954, and the House of Representatives on Aug. 9 of that year, passed a bill authorizing residents of the District to elect committeemen to represent them in the councils of the national political parties and delegates to the national nominating conventions. The then President, Dwight D. Eisenhower, vetoed the bill, Aug. 20, because it included a provision to which he was strongly opposed. The provision would have allowed employees of the Federal Government in the District of Columbia to engage in partisan political activities, contrary to the Hatch Act of 1939.

In 1955, both houses of Congress passed a sanitized version of the bill, excluding the provision to which exception had been taken. President Eisenhower signed the bill Aug. 12, 1955. Under its provisions, the District of Columbia for the first time since 1874 set up and operated official election machinery. The act authorized the election by qualified voters in the District of Columbia of members and alternate members of the national committees of the political parties; delegates and alternates to the national nominating conventions; and "such members and officials of local committees of political parties as may be designated by the duly authorized local committees of such parties for election at large in the District of Columbia."

Right to Vote for President

The Constitution provides, in Article II, Section 1, for election of the President and Vice President of the United States by electors chosen in each state. To enable the residents of the District of Columbia to participate in choosing the electors, an amendment to the Constitution was required. A resolution proposing such an amendment was first introduced in Congress in 1890. In the next 70 years, more than 65 amendments on the subject were proposed. They failed to elicit substantial support until after the admission of Alaska and Hawaii to the Union in 1959.

The Senate on Feb. 2, 1960, adopted a resolution proposing to the states an amendment to the Constitution which would grant to the District of Columbia the right to participate in the election of President and Vice President and, in addition, the right to elect a nonvoting delegate in the House of Representatives. In the House, the resolution, amended by removal of any reference to a delegate in Congress, was adopted on June 14. Two days later, the Senate accepted the House change, and the proposal was submitted to the states on June 21. Under the proposed amendment, D.C. voters would elect "a number of electors of President and Vice President equal to the whole number of Senators and Representatives in Congress to which the District would be entitled if it were a State, but in no event more than the least populous State."

Opposition developed on two fronts. Only Tennessee among the southern and border states, where legislatures were disinclined to enfranchise Washington's Negro majority, ratified the amendment; Arkansas went on record against it, the only state in the nation to do so; and others took no action. Opposition in traditionally Republican states reflected fear that the District would regularly vote for Democratic nominees. Success of efforts by D.C. Republican leaders to allay this fear was indicated by the fact that it was a G.O.P.-controlled legislature, that of Kansas, which on March 29, 1961, gave the needed 38th ratification of the amendment. Ratification was completed in 281 days, a shorter period than that required in the case of any other amendment except the 12th, which modified the voting procedures for election of the President and Vice President. *(See Chapter III, Subchapter 6.)*

Congress implemented the new amendment by an act of Oct. 4, 1961. President John F. Kennedy had proposed a 90-day residence requirement and 18 years as the minimum age for D.C. voters. But Sen. Russell B. Long (D La.) fought vigorously for a 21-year minimum, and the act as passed conformed to his position and also established a one-year residence requirement. District of Columbia voters gave their three electoral votes in 1964 to Lyndon B. Johnson and in 1968 to Hubert H. Humphrey.

Election of Board of Education

District residents, having exercised their right to vote in Presidential elections, received a second concession in 1968. Congress, responding to continued pressures for more self-government for the District, and taking account of controversies over Washington's educational programs, authorized direct election of an 11-member D.C. Board of Education. Previously, under an act of June 20, 1906, the board had been chosen by the judges of the U.S. District Court for the District of Columbia. The new law, signed April 22, 1968, provided that eight of the members of the board should be elected from wards and three at large; that the first election should be held on Nov. 5, 1968, and later elections in November of odd-numbered years; and that the members should serve in staggered terms of four years' duration.

In the election of Nov. 5, 1968, a total of 54 candidates competed for the eight ward seats, and nine for the three at-large seats. Run-off elections were necessitated by the fact that none of the ward candidates obtained a majority, and that only one of the at-large candidates obtained the required one-sixth of all at-large votes cast. Julius W. Hobson, who gained an at-large seat on Nov. 5, was a militant black. In the run-off elections on Nov. 26, only about 20 per cent of the eligible voters went to the polls, compared with 75 per cent in the Nov. 5 balloting. Three members of the elected board had served on the previous board, appointed by Federal judges.

Question of Home Rule

Of American cities with a Negro majority, Washington is the largest. The proportion of Negroes in Washington's population was around 25 per cent in Jefferson's time. A substantial influx of Negroes during and after the Civil War lifted the proportion to about 33 per cent by 1879. Nearly a century later, in 1970, it stood at about 66 percent. And in the city's public schools, the proportion of black pupils had risen by 1970 to around 95 percent.

Negroes were granted the suffrage in the District of Columbia in 1867. In the 1868 elections, they helped to replace a conservative Democratic mayor of Washington with a Republican, Sayles J. Bowen. For almost a century, the issue of restoring home rule in the District of Columbia has involved the implicit question, For what kind of candidates will Washington's Negro citizens cast their votes?

Proposals for Restoration of Home Rule. Washingtonians were deprived in 1874 of the right to vote for local officials. Proposals for restoration of that right made no legislative headway and had little impact politically until the 1940s. Evidence of a turnaround in public sentiment on the issue then became apparent. Beginning with Harry S Truman, every President has recommended home rule for the District of Columbia. The Democratic Party platform has favored it since 1940; the Republican Party platform, since 1948.

A bill to grant self-government to the District of Columbia reached the floor of the House of Representatives in 1948 but was killed there by the delaying tactics of southern Members. Between 1949 and 1959 the Senate passed five successive bills providing for home rule, but southerners who dominated the House Committee on the District of Columbia succeeded in burying each one in turn. John L. McMillan (D S.C.), an opponent of home

rule, became chairman of the Committee in 1946 and has served in that capacity since then except in the 80th and 83rd Congresses (1947-49 and 1953-55), when the Republicans were in the majority.

In 1960, supporters of home rule tried to get the necessary 219 names on a petition to force a home rule bill out of the House District Committee. They got 204 signatures. From 1961 to 1964, Senators made no serious attempt to pass such a bill. But public opinion polls in that period showed Americans in favor of self-government for the District of Columbia by 6 to 1. On July 22, 1965, the Senate passed a home rule bill, and on Sept. 3 a discharge petition in the House gained the required number of signatures. The House D.C. Committee reported a bill which differed from the Senate's, and it was passed on Sept. 29, 1965. But the House D.C. Committee effectively killed it by voting, May 11, 1966, not to send the bill to conference for reconciliation of the Senate and House measures.

Congress was occupied in 1967 with President Johnson's reorganization plan for the D.C. government, and in 1968 with the legislation for election of the D.C. Board of Education. Action on home rule remained in abeyance. President Nixon revived the hopes of home rule advocates the following year. In his message to Congress on District affairs, April 28, 1969, he urged enactment of home rule legislation, saying: "At issue is whether the city will be enabled to take hold of its future: whether its institutions will be reformed so that its government can truly represent its citizens and act upon their needs." The President proposed creation of a commission to prepare plans for "meaningful self-government" for the capital city. The Senate on Oct. 1, 1969, passed a bill creating a commission of the kind suggested, but the House took no action.

Arguments of Home Rule Advocates. Sen. Charles E. Goodell (R N.Y.) of the Senate's D.C. Committee presented a statement on behalf of self-government for the District at a Committee hearing on the subject on April 30, 1969. Goodell summarized as follows the chief arguments mustered by home rule advocates:

1. "This nation was founded on the premise that governments derive their powers from the consent of the governed; but the citizens of the District of Columbia have no say in choosing District government officials."

2. "...in Washington democracy is weakest where it should be a great example to the country and the world."

3. "The pressing needs of this city cannot be adequately met by a Congress whose proper concern should be national in scope." Advocates of home rule often formulate this argument differently by saying that officials elected by D.C. residents and politically answerable to them would be more responsive to the city's needs than are Members of Congress dependent for re-election on a constituency not concerned with those needs.

4. "...the local citizens of the District of Columbia are capable of dealing with the issues that confront them. They are eager to accept these responsibilities."

Other proponents of D.C. home rule have cited precedents in support of the constitutionality of home rule. The chief precedent is the Supreme Court's decision of June 8, 1953, in *District of Columbia v. John R. Thompson Co.* (346 U.S. 100), which sustained the validity of anti-segregation ordinances adopted by the District's territorial assembly in 1872-73. The Court's opinion, delivered by Justice William O. Douglas, said: "It would seem then that... there is no constitutional barrier to the delegation by Congress to the District of Columbia of full legislative power, subject of course to constitutional limitations to which all lawmaking is subservient and subject also to the power of Congress at any time to revise, alter or revoke the authority granted."

Arguments Against Home Rule. Jack McGann, a legislative aide of the Liberty Lobby, presented counter-arguments at the 1969 hearing at which Sen. Goodell testified. McGann's arguments may be summarized as follows:

1. Home rule would violate the constitutional provision setting aside the seat of government as a non-partisan oasis.

2. "A grant of 'home rule' to the District, putting the police under the control of an elected city government, dominated by men whose primary motivation seems to be hatred of all police authority, would make a bad crime problem absolutely intolerable."

3. Residents of the District of Columbia have not yet shown the responsibility that is necessary for mature self-government. "The D.C. Elected Board of Education Act of 1968 gave D.C. residents the right to vote for an elected school board....In the first election held under this act, voters of the nation's capital elected Julius Hobson to their school board, with a higher vote than that won by any other candidate....Mr. Hobson has boasted that he is a 'Marxist-Socialist,' meaning a Communist. He has declared that the American free enterprise system 'must be overthrown by force and violence.' "

Additional arguments advanced by opponents of home rule include the following: Home rule led to bankruptcy in the 1870s; Congress would contribute less money for District needs if it did not control D.C. affairs; an elected D.C. government might subordinate the interests of the Federal Government to the desires of local citizens; and home rule probably would end the enviable record that Washington has had of clean municipal government.

Stewart Alsop suggested in *The Center* that home rule opponents were motivated primarily by fear. "What the fearful whites fear more than riots or crime is a take-over of the city administration by Black Power extremists who would make life miserable, economically and in other ways, for the city's white minority."

Bibliography

Books

Alsop, Stewart, *The Center; People and Power in Political Washington.* Harper and Row, 1968.

Bryan, Wilhelmus B., *A History of the National Capital.* Macmillan, 1914-16. 2 vols.

Derthick, Martha, *City Politics in Washington, D.C.* Harvard University Press, 1962. (Prepared for Joint Center for Urban Studies, Massachusetts Institute of Technology and Harvard University.)

Green, Constance McLaughlin, *Washington, Capital City, 1879-1950.* Princeton University Press, 1963.

——, *Washington, Village and Capital, 1800-1878.* Princeton University Press, 1962.

Hendrix, Marcia A., *The Residence Question; The Genesis of Our National Capital.* Coral Gables (Fla.), 1968.

Morrow, William L., *Congressional Committees.* Scribner, 1969.

Schmeckebier, Laurence F., *The District of Columbia; Its Government and Administration.* Johns Hopkins Press, 1928.

Government Publications

Caemmerer, Hans P., *Washington, The National Capital.* Government Printing Office, 1932.

District of Columbia, *District of Columbia Code, Annotated.* Government Printing Office, 1967. 3 vols., with supplements.

Padover, Saul K. (ed.), *Thomas Jefferson and the National Capital, Containing Notes and Correspondence Exchanged Between Jefferson, Washington, L'Enfant... and Others, 1783-1818.* Government Printing Office, 1946.

U.S. House of Representatives, Committee on Government Operations, Subcommittee on Executive and Legislative Reorganization, *Reorganization Plan No. 3 of 1967: Government of the District of Columbia; Hearings...Ninetieth Congress, First Session.* Government Printing Office, 1967.

——, Committee on the District of Columbia, *District of Columbia Reorganization.* House Report No. 540, 90th Congress, 1st Session, August 7, 1967. Government Printing Office, 1967.

——, ——, *Home Rule; Hearings Before Subcommittee No. 5, Eighty-ninth Congress, First Session.* Government Printing Office, 1965.

——, ——, *Legislation Relating to the District of Columbia; Summary Report of the Committee on the District of Columbia, House of Representatives.* Government Printing Office, 1964--. Issued in 1964, 1965, 1966, and 1968.

——, ——, Subcommittee No. 1, *D.C. Reorganization Proposals; Hearings, Ninetieth Congress, First Session.* Government Printing Office, 1967.

U.S. Senate, Committee on Government Operations, *Reorganization Plan No. 3 of 1967, District of Columbia Government; Hearings, Ninetieth Congress, First Session, July 25, 26, and 27, 1967.* Government Printing Office, 1967.

Chapter 4—Housing and Support of Congress

The Capitol and Office Buildings

TO SOME PERSONS, the United States Capitol is the magnificent symbol of a proud nation. It is the seat of government for a great, throbbing, vital country. Spanning in its own history all but a few years of the nation's history, the Capitol, according to this view, has witnessed nearly 200 years of greatness and tragedy. It has seen the United States grow from a string of 13 colonies clinging precariously to the Atlantic seaboard into a continent-sized nation whose influence circles the globe.

To other persons, the Capitol, while heroically scaled, is in essence a functional, public building. It is a meeting place and a forum for national politicians, where legislation can be proposed, debated, altered and enacted or rejected. Designed by men for use by other men, it has been built, remodeled, burned, rebuilt, expanded and expanded again. It has changed, according to this view, as the nation has changed; and it will continue to change, because time forever exacts new demands.

Varied Nature of the Capitol

The fact is that the Capitol is both symbol and building. The profile of the Capitol dome is as typically American as the Eiffel Tower is typically French, or the pyramids are typically Egyptian. Yet in the rotunda under the dome, a President has been shot at; and one floor below the rotunda stands a souvenir concession. Elsewhere in the building, the House, Senate, Library of Congress and Supreme Court have played a form of musical chairs, shifting from room to room in a continuing search for adequate quarters.

Designed originally to be a home for the Senate and the House of Representatives, the Capitol has been pressed into service by others almost from the start. The Library of Congress did not leave until 1897, the Supreme Court until 1935. Presidential inaugurations take place on the East Portico. Presidential funerals have been held in the Rotunda. A vast collection of art, some of it priceless and some of it worthless, crowds the floors, walls, ceilings, corridors and rooms of the Capitol.

Home of House and Senate

As the home of the House and the Senate, the Capitol has been the place where Congress works. It is within the Capitol that Congress has developed and exercised its powers, and enjoyed its perquisites. From the Capitol, Members of succeeding Congresses have gone forth to meet the electorate, some returning to pursue careers of fame and power, others vanishing anonymously into the countryside. On the Capitol have focused all the varied pressures that Americans have devised to apply to Congress.

Controversy has dogged the Capitol from its beginning. Designers failed to produce acceptable plans. Builders quarreled with architects. And in the end, Members of Congress grumbled about the results. More recently, plans to extend the East and West Fronts have aroused strong protests from opponents.

Speaking broadly, the Capitol has undergone four major periods of construction. The first period, which included the original design work and early construction, stretched from 1792 to around 1811. The second period, from 1815 to 1829, involved repair of damage caused by the British in 1814 and completion of the originally planned building, which had been halted by the War of 1812. The third period, covering from 1851 to 1892, included erection of the present wings used by the House and Senate, and landscaping of the grounds. The fourth period, not yet concluded, began in 1949 with extensive repairs to the roofs of the House and Senate wings. Extension of the East Front was completed in 1962. Proposals to extend or to restore the West Front still are under debate.

Early Construction, 1792-1811

Congress had met in makeshift quarters in New York City and Philadelphia. The Act of July 16, 1790, which shifted the seat of Government to the Potomac, made it clear that a new city would have to be laid out, sites selected for the Government buildings, and the buildings themselves designed and erected. *(See box on New York, Philadelphia Capitols.)*

Selection of Capitol Site

The task of selecting a site for the Capitol (referred to at first as the Congress Hall, or Congress House) fell to Pierre Charles L'Enfant, who had been appointed by President Washington in March 1791 to prepare a plan of the new city. *(For background on designation of Washington, D.C., as the capital, see Seat of Government, Chapter III.)*

Reference

See Appendix table of contents (first thumb tab) for Rules for Regulation of the Senate Wing of the U.S. Capitol.

Washington had instructed L'Enfant to locate the city on the Maryland side of the Potomac. L'Enfant made several tours of the area, studied maps of major European cities and developed his plan. In a letter to Washington on June 22, 1791, he outlined a plan for the city which called for a rectangular grid of streets that would be intersected by broad avenues radiating from the "principal places." The Capitol would be one of the "principal places," and L'Enfant recommended putting it "on the west end of Jenkins Heights, which stand as a pedestal waiting for a monument...."

The President accepted L'Enfant's recommendations and on Dec. 13, 1791, forwarded them to Congress for its information. Although L'Enfant was dismissed in February 1792, his plans were used in preparing maps of the city. His recommendation of a site for the Capitol was retained on the maps and appeared as Reservation 2. *(For text of L'Enfant's proposal, see Appendix.)*

The original Capitol grounds were a part of Cerne Abbey Manor, owned by Daniel Carroll of Duddington. Earlier, the area had been occupied by a subtribe of the Algonquin Indians, known as the Powhatans, whose council house had been located at the foot of the hill.

Design Competition

The three commissioners, whom Washington had appointed to oversee development of the city and the public buildings, originally had expected L'Enfant to provide designs for the public buildings as well as for the city. But by early 1792, it had become clear that the commissioners could not rely on L'Enfant for the building designs, and they decided to conduct a public design competition.

On March 8, 1792, Washington wrote to one of the commissioners, Dr. David Stuart of Fairfax Court House, Va.: "A chaste plan sufficiently capacious and convenient for a period not *too* remote, but one to which we may reasonably look forward, would meet my idea in the Capitol." Throughout the month of March the commissioners advertised for designs. They set July 15, 1792, as a deadline for the competition and offered a prize of $500 and a city lot for the winning design.

The specifications laid down by the commissioners called for a brick building to include a conference room and a room for the Representatives, each capable of accommodating 300 persons; a room for the Senate, containing 1,200 square feet; 12 rooms of 600 square feet each for committees and clerks' offices; and appropriate lobbies and anterooms. "It will be a recommendation of any plan," the commissioners added, "if the central part of it may be detached and erected for the present with the appearance of a complete whole, and be capable of admitting the additional parts in future, if they shall be wanted."

Proposed Plans. The results of the competition were disappointing. Some 14 to 16 plans were received, according to different sources. Among them were plans from at least 14 individuals: Stephen Hallet, Judge George Turner, Samuel Blodget, Lamphiere, S.M. McIntire, Jacob Small, James Diamond, Charles Winter Smith, Andrew Mayo, Philip Hart, Abram Farris, Colin Williamson, Carstairs and Hasborough.

There were few trained architects in the United States at the time. Some of the designs pictured oddly proportioned structures or proposed impossible details. A design by James Diamond, for example, included a monstrously oversized weathercock atop the building.

From among the designs that had been received, the commissioners favored Hallet's. Washington favored Turner's. And Blodget's also attracted attention. Each of the three men was asked to revise his drawings and to submit them again. This second competition was not entirely successful either, but the commissioners agreed to ask Hallet to prepare more detailed plans, incorporating some suggested alterations.

Accepted Design. In the meantime, Dr. William Thornton, a Philadelphia physician, had written the commissioners in October 1792 from the island of Tortola, West Indies, asking whether he could submit a design even though the July 15 deadline had passed. The commissioners on Dec. 4, 1792, told Thornton to go ahead. They suggested that he send his proposal directly to Jefferson for study by Washington. Hallet's revisions were to be ready for the President in January 1793.

Washington studied both plans. Commenting on them in a Jan. 31, 1793, letter to the commissioners, the President said that while Hallet's plans "undoubtedly have a great deal of merit," he favored Thornton's. "The grandeur, simplicity and beauty of the exterior; the propriety with which the apartments are distributed, and the economy in the whole mass of the structure will I doubt not give it a preference in your eyes, as it has done in mine...," Washington wrote.

The commissioners agreed with Washington. On April 5, 1793, they wrote Thornton that "the President has given formal approbation of your plans."

Thornton's design, apparently influenced by a glimpse of one of Hallet's plans after Thornton had returned to Philadelphia, called for a stately, three-story building, surmounted by a low dome. For the design, Thornton received the $500 award and lot 15 in square 634.

Thornton's design was merely an elevation sketch. The commissioners hired Hallet, who was a professional French architect, to prepare working drawings. A clash was inevitable. As modifications of Thornton's design (some of them required for structural and practical reasons) crept into Hallet's working drawings, Thornton raised a series of noisy objections. To settle the dispute, Washington called a meeting of Thornton, Hallet, James Hoban (winner of the design competition for the White House), and two builders. The group agreed, as noted in a July 25, 1793, letter from Washington to the commissioners, "that the foundations would be begun upon the plan exhibited by Mr. Hallet," while "preserving the original plan of Dr. Thornton."

Building of the Capitol

The Capitol was laid out on a north-south axis, so that descriptions mention north and south wings (ends) and east and west fronts (sides).

The first cornerstone was laid Sept. 18, 1793, by George Washington amid colorful Masonic rites. Although contemporary accounts put the cornerstone at the southeast corner of the north wing, it was not found during the 1958-62 extension of the East Front.

Hallet was placed in charge of the construction, under the supervision of Hoban. As work progressed, Hallet persisted in altering the agreed-upon design without approval either of the President or of the commissioners. Hallet was tolerated for a year but finally was discharged on Nov. 15, 1794. Two months earlier, on Sept. 12, 1794, Washington had named Thornton to a vacancy on the three-man board of commissioners, putting Thornton for the first time in a place of direct authority over the construction. Congress abolished the board of commissioners in 1802, when its responsibilities for Government buildings were taken over by a superintendent of public buildings.

Nearly a year passed before a successor to Hallet was appointed. In the interval, Hoban superintended construction of both the White House and the Capitol. Then on Oct. 15, 1795, the commissioners appointed as the new construction superintendent George Hadfield, a prize-winning student at the Royal Academy in London. At first, Hadfield quarreled with the commissioners over following the agreed plans, but the quarreling ended abruptly when the commissioners indicated they would instantly accept Hadfield's threatened resignation.

Despite the controversies, work progressed. The work force was composed in large part of Negro slaves hired out by their masters in the District of Columbia and nearby Maryland and Virginia, as was then a common custom. By March 1796, the foundations had been laid, and the north wing was rising above the ground. The roof of the north wing had been boarded, shingled and painted by the fall of 1798. When Con-

gress arrived from Philadelphia in the autumn of 1800, the walls of the south wing had risen a few feet above ground.

The first public function held at the Capitol was a reception given by the citizens of Washington for President Adams on June 5, 1800.

Arrival of Congress

The Act of July 16, 1790, designating a Potomac site as the permanent seat of Government, had set the first Monday in December 1800 as the deadline for moving to the new capital. When it became clear that the Government buildings would be ready before December, Congress by an Act of April 24, 1800, authorized the President to make an earlier transfer of the seat of Government. And by an Act of May 13, 1800, Congress fixed Nov. 17, 1800, as the date of its own Washington opening.

However, Congress was late for its debut. The House could not assemble a quorum until Nov. 18; the Senate

---

Washington's Tomb

In the Capitol basement, two stories below the Rotunda, is an area that was intended to serve as a tomb for George and Martha Washington.

Within a few days after Washington's death on Dec. 14, 1799, Congress adopted a joint resolution providing that the first President was to be honored by placing his body in this special tomb, even though that section of the Capitol had not yet been constructed. Meanwhile, Washington was buried at Mount Vernon in accordance with the terms of his will. But in a letter of Dec. 31, 1799, Martha Washington gave permission to have his body moved to the Capitol.

Interior construction of the Rotunda was completed by 1824, but nearly five years more were needed to finish the whole of the central section. A circular opening was left in the center of the Rotunda floor. The opening was to permit visitors to look down upon a statue of Washington which was to have been placed in the Crypt on the first floor. The tomb itself was to be directly below the statue.

In 1828, the opening in the Rotunda floor was closed, because dampness from the lower floors was damaging the Trumbull paintings already hanging in the Rotunda. In 1830, a House committee recommended that both Washington and his wife be re-interred in the tomb.

As the 1832 centennial of Washington's birth approached, Congress asked John A. Washington, grandnephew of President Washington, and George Washington Parke Custis, Mrs. Washington's grandson, for permission to move the bodies of Washington and his wife to the Capitol. Custis agreed, but John Washington refused. The bodies have remained at Mount Vernon.

The area for the tomb is used at present to store the Lincoln catafalque.

until Nov. 21. On Nov. 22, the Senators and Representatives attending the second session of the Sixth Congress filled the Senate chamber to hear President Adams deliver his annual message.

The citizens of Washington had planned a parade and a formal reception for Congress on the 22nd, but the plans fizzled. Some sources have laid the blame on a dispute over selection of a master of ceremonies, others on a surprise three-inch snowfall. Perhaps both are partly correct. In any event, the Washington welcome for Congress consisted of "a congratulatory letter from sundry inhabitants of the District of Columbia" and a newly written, and long since forgotten, song.

Both the House and the Senate were quartered in the north wing, because it was the only part of the Capitol that had been completed. The wing was three stories high and was faced with sandstone on three sides. President Washington had decided to use sandstone, which was quarried in Virginia, for economy reasons. The fourth (south) side, to be connected later to the center section and south wing, was enclosed temporarily with brick.

Inside the north wing, both the House and Senate chambers were two stories high. The House chamber was on the west side of the second floor. The Senate chamber was on the east side of the first floor, a floor below the space it later was to occupy and still later to turn over to the Supreme Court. On the walls of the Senate chamber hung portraits of Louis XVI and Marie Antoinette, the first art in the Capitol. The portraits had been presented by the King to the Continental Congress in 1784. Both portraits are thought to have been burned by the British in 1814.

Bursting out of its admittedly temporary quarters in the north wing, the House ordered construction of other temporary quarters on the foundations of its own south wing. The result was a one-story, elliptical brick building. Because of its shape and the stifling summer temperatures inside, the structure quickly was dubbed "the oven." The House met in "the oven" from the

beginning of the Seventh Congress on Dec. 7, 1801, until the end of the first session of the Eighth Congress on March 27, 1804, when it returned to its old chamber in the north wing so that construction could continue on the south wing. It met in the old chamber from Nov. 5, 1804, to March 3, 1807.

Continuation of Work Under Latrobe

In the meantime, Jefferson had become President. On March 6, 1803, he appointed Benjamin H. Latrobe, an English architect, as Surveyor of Public Buildings and placed him in charge of finishing the Capitol.

After demolition of "the oven," work was resumed on the south wing. The completed north wing determined the exterior design of the south wing, and the completed foundations of the south wing set the form of the interior. But like Hallet and Hadfield before him, Latrobe, as a professional architect, found flaws in Thornton's design. Thornton answered on Jan. 1, 1805, with an open letter to Members of the House. The bitter pamphlet war that ensued rocked Congress and threatened further construction appropriations. Jefferson supported Latrobe, while cautioning him to "deviate as little as possible from the plan approved by General Washington." Latrobe survived the pamphlet war and remained in charge of the work.

The roof of the south wing was completed during the winter of 1806-07, and by March 1807 construction of the wing was virtually completed. The House moved from the north wing into what was considered its permanent home (later Statuary Hall) for the opening of the 10th Congress on Oct. 26, 1807. Problems arose almost at once. Latrobe had succeeded in changing Thornton's design for an elliptical House chamber into two semicircles joined by parallel lines, and the acoustics were horrible. Hanging curtains between the stone columns helped somewhat, but faulty acoustics plagued the House throughout its tenure of the south wing.

Upon completion of the south wing, Latrobe turned to repairing some of the mediocre construction in the north wing. He replaced with stone some of the wood, plaster and brick interiors. He raised the floor of the two-story Senate chamber, dividing the area into two one-story chambers. As part of the remodeling, he designed in 1809 cornstalk (or corncob) columns and capitals for the vestibule outside the first floor chamber.

During the remodeling, following adjournment of the first session of the 10th Congress on April 25, 1808, the Senate moved into a first floor room on the west side of the north wing. The Supreme Court moved into the old House chamber on the west side of the second floor, sharing the space with the Library of Congress. The Court had moved to Washington for the opening of its February 1801 term and had been sitting in a small room adjoining the south side of the Senate chamber. After the Court adjourned in 1809, the Senate moved upstairs to share the old House quarters with the Library.

By the winter of 1809-10, new quarters were ready for both the Senate and the Court. On Jan. 1, 1810, the Senate moved into its remodeled chamber (later the Supreme Court chamber) on the second floor of the east side. And the Court opened its 1810 term in the first floor chamber (later the Court's law library) beneath the Senate.

Fires, Explosions in Capitol

Aug. 24, 1814. A detachment of British troops led by Maj. Gen. Robert Ross and Rear Adm. Sir George Cockburn set fire to the Capitol, heavily damaging the interior.

Dec. 24, 1851. An accidental fire burned the West Front quarters of the Library of Congress, destroying 35,000 of the Library's 55,000 books.

Nov. 6, 1898. A gas explosion and fire heavily damaged the Supreme Court chamber, the room formerly used by the Senate.

July 2, 1915. The Senate reception room was damaged by the explosion of a homemade bomb, placed there by Erich Muenter (first identified as Frank Holt), a former instructor of German at Harvard who was upset by private sales of American munitions to the Allies in World War I.

Mar. 1, 1971. A bomb explosion at 1:32 a.m. caused substantial damage in a small area on the ground floor of the Senate wing. (See 2-page box at end of chapter.)

Threat of an approaching war with Britain then began to cut into construction appropriations for the Capitol. Work slowed to a halt. The two sections, the north wing and the south wing, stood alone, separated by the unfinished center section. In 1811, before work was completely suspended, a temporary wooden covered walk was built to connect the two wings.

Cost. Estimates of the cost of erecting the two wings are at best tentative. Part of the cost was defrayed by the original contributions of $72,000 from Maryland and $120,000 from Virginia for construction of public buildings at Washington. The first Congressional appropriation for the Capitol, in 1803, provided $50,000, although Congress had appropriated $9,000 in 1800 for furnishings. After studying Treasury records, Glenn Brown, author of a two-volume history of the Capitol published in 1900, put the cost of the north and south wings at $788,077.98.

Reconstruction, 1815-1829

Capitol Burned. Most of the fighting during the War of 1812 took place far from Washington. But in response to American raids into Canada and in hopes of demoralizing the Government, Vice Adm. Sir Alexander Cochrane authorized a series of Atlantic seaboard operations. Carrying out one of those operations, a British force under the command of Maj. Gen. Robert Ross and Rear Adm. Sir George Cockburn moved up the Patuxent River in Maryland in August 1814. The troops were put ashore at Benedict, Md., and marched overland through Upper Marlboro and Bladensburg toward Washington. American troops offered ineffective resistance.

The capital city was nearly deserted. Many residents had fled before the approaching troops. Most Members of Congress, after a routine adjournment April 18, had long since left for their homes.

The British entered Washington around dusk on Aug. 24, 1814. That night a detachment of troops headed by Ross and Cockburn set the Capitol afire. The building was burned, according to tradition, after Cockburn had mounted the Speaker's chair in the House chamber and asked, "Shall this harbor of Yankee democracy be burned?" The soldiers shouted "Aye," tradition adds. Leaving the Capitol in flames, the troops moved through

---

Morse's Telegraph

After Congress had appropriated $30,000 in 1843 for an experimental telegraph line from Washington to Baltimore, Samuel F. B. Morse used the old (first floor) Supreme Court chamber for a test of his invention.

On May 24, 1844, Annie Ellsworth handed Morse a line from the Bible (Numbers 23:23), "What hath God wrought!" Morse tapped out the message to his partner, Alfred Vail, in Baltimore. Vail returned the message correctly, to confirm the transmission, and a short conversation ensued over the wire. Among witnesses to the test were Henry Clay and Dolley Madison.

Inaugural Sites

The inauguration of President Andrew Jackson in 1829 on the newly finished East Portico of the Capitol set a tradition that has been followed by nearly all Presidents since then. Following is a list of other inaugural sites:

Federal Hall, Wall Street, New York.
    1789—George Washington
Congress Hall, Sixth and Chestnut Streets, Philadelphia.
    1793—George Washington
    1797—John Adams
Senate Chamber, Washington, D.C.
    1801—Thomas Jefferson
    1805—Thomas Jefferson
    1909—William Howard Taft
House of Representatives, Washington, D.C.
    1809—James Madison
    1813—James Madison
    1821—James Monroe
    1825—John Quincy Adams
    1833—Andrew Jackson
Brick Capitol, First and A Streets N.E., Washington, D.C.
    1817—James Monroe
South Portico, White House, Washington, D.C.
    1945—Franklin Delano Roosevelt

---

the city and burned the White House and the Treasury building. Later on the night of Aug. 24-25, a violent rainstorm drowned the flames, preventing complete destruction of the buildings. The British again roamed through the city on the 25th. Before withdrawing that night, they also burned buildings used by the State and War Departments and a Government arsenal.

As the President and other government officials returned to Washington, the slow work of reconstruction began.

Task of Rebuilding

On Aug. 8, 1814, President Madison had called a special session of Congress for Sept. 19. The Capitol had been damaged too heavily to meet there, and on Sept. 17 the President announced that Congress would convene in Blodget's Hotel, which had been taken over previously by the Post Office and the Patent Office. The huge structure, on E Street between 7th and 8th Streets, Northwest, was the only Government building not burned by the British.

The special session in Blodget's lasted from Sept. 19, 1814, to March 3, 1815. On Oct. 15, shortly after the session opened, the House by a 74-83 vote defeated a bill to transfer the seat of Government elsewhere. An Act of Feb. 15, 1815, authorized the President to accept a $500,000 loan from Washington banks to pay for rebuilding the Capitol. And on March 14, Latrobe was recalled to oversee the work. According to his reports, damage to the north wing was more extensive than that to the south wing. The wooden covered walk between them had been completely destroyed.

The Capitol Art Collection

Although the Capitol was designed to provide working quarters for Congress, it has acquired a vast collection of works of art and other objects. Some of the art is excellent, some is not. Since 1872, the Joint Committee on the Library has had supervision of all works of art in the Capitol.

The collection, comprised of 744 pieces as of June 1964, includes portraits, paintings, busts, statues, relief portraits, sculptured reliefs, frescoes, murals, lunettes, stained glass windows, plaques and mantles. Also in the Capitol are prized objects like the floors of Minton tile, the Senate desk of Daniel Webster, and the couch on which John Quincy Adams died.

The earliest works of art were portraits of Marie Antoinette and Louis XVI by Madam Vigee Le Brun. Hung in the old Senate chamber, they are thought to have been destroyed by the British in 1814. An early statue, Liberty and the Eagle by Giuseppe Franzoni, is known to have been destroyed in the 1814 fire.

Statuary Hall. When the House moved into new quarters in 1857, its old chamber was left unused. In 1864, Congress designated it a National Statuary Hall. The legislation invited "all the states to provide and furnish statues, in marble or bronze, not exceeding two in number for each state, of deceased persons who have been citizens thereof and illustrious for their historic renown or distinguished civil or military service, such as each state may deem to be worthy of this national commemoration...."

Rhode Island in 1870 supplied the first statue, a marble sculpture of Revolutionary hero Nathanael Greene. Other statues followed. By 1933, the combined weight threatened to collapse the floor, and Congress limited Statuary Hall to a single statue per state, authorizing the placement of other statues throughout the Capitol.

Works by Brumidi. Perhaps no other artist had as great an impact on the Capitol as Constantino Brumidi, an Italian hired in the 1850s to decorate the interior. His works appear in both the House and Senate wings and in the Rotunda.

Brumidi's first work in the Capitol, executed in 1855-56, was the decoration of a House committee room (H-144), used formerly by the Agriculture Committee and now by the Appropriations Committee. The artist worked in fresco, applying paint to the surface of the plaster in its initial wet state. His murals in this room, "Calling of Cincinnatus from the Plow," and "Calling of Putnam from the Plow to the Revolution," were the first frescoes in the Capitol. There were to be many more, and Brumidi was to execute most of them.

In the Rotunda, a Brumidi fresco, "The Apotheosis of George Washington," decorates the canopy of the dome. The sketches were begun in 1863; the actual fresco was started in 1865 and completed in 1866.

The frieze encircling the Rotunda, commenced by Brumidi in 1877, illustrates historical events in American history. Brumidi continued to work on the frieze until his death in 1880. Filippo Costaggini,

Brumidi's assistant, continued the work from 1880 to 1888, executing designs which Brumidi had prepared to circle the frieze. Either because of poor judgment or by his own planning, a 30-foot gap remained undecorated. In 1950, a Congressional resolution provided for completion of the frieze, and Allyn Cox, a New York artist skilled in fresco painting, was commissioned to paint the remaining panels. He finished in 1953. Events depicted in the frieze range from the landing of Columbus in 1492 to the birth of aviation in the United States in 1903.

Bronze Doors. Four cast bronze doors were executed for the major entrances to the Capitol, but only three of the four doors have been installed.

The best known door, sometimes called the Rogers Door or Columbus Door, is located at the eastern entrance to the Rotunda. Designed and modeled by Randolph Rogers in 1858, the door is decorated with scenes that depict events in the life of Christopher Columbus. In November 1863, the door was installed between the old House chamber and the new south wing, but it was moved to the East Portico entrance in 1871.

The bronze doors at the entrance of the east porticoes of the House and Senate wings were designed in 1855-57 by Thomas Crawford. The panels of each door depict great events in American history. The Senate door was installed late in 1868 and the House door in 1905.

The fourth door, designed and modeled by Louis Amateis of Washington, D.C., in 1904, was intended for the western entrance of the Capitol. As enabling legislation for improvements of the West Front had not been enacted, the door could not be installed. It was displayed temporarily at the Corcoran Gallery of Art. Since 1914, the door has been on loan to the Smithsonian Institution. Panels in the door depict allegorical representations, and statuettes and medallions depict famous men.

Other Objects. Two of the most unusual objects in the Capitol art collection are the Centennial Safe and the memorial to the pioneers of woman suffrage.

The Centennial Safe, kept in a storage room off the northeast quadrant of the Crypt, was a gift to the Government by Mrs. A.M. Deihm of New York, publisher of the weekly paper, *Our Second Century.* The safe was displayed at the 1876 Centennial Exposition in Philadelphia and later moved to Statuary Hall. It was closed and locked with a key on Feb. 22, 1879, to be opened on the occasion of the Bicentennial in 1976. However, the key, entrusted to the Smithsonian Institution, is said to have disappeared. The safe is believed to contain photographs of distinguished men, autographs, a silver inkstand and other items.

The suffragist memorial, located in the Crypt, was presented in 1921. Executed by Adelaide Johnson, the monument consists of busts of Elizabeth Cady Stanton, Susan B. Anthony and Lucretia Mott. Because the busts appear to be emerging from a 7-to-8-ton block of Carrara marble, the memorial has acquired the nickname of "Ladies in a Bathtub."

In repairing the interiors, Latrobe again redesigned the House chamber, making it semicircular but failing to improve its acoustics. He designed the tobacco capitals used in the lobby of the small rotunda on the second floor, north of the main rotunda. He designed the wing west of the rotunda and the East Portico and steps. Latrobe's designs changed the main entrance from the west, where Thornton had planned it, to the east.

Resignation of Latrobe. Work on the reconstruction was well under way when Latrobe became entangled in a dispute with Samuel Lane, who had been named in 1816 to the newly created post of Commissioner of Public Buildings and Grounds. Latrobe resigned Nov. 20, 1817.

Meanwhile, Congress had moved from Blodget's Hotel into new quarters. A group of private citizens, mainly principal Washington landowners, had raised $25,000 to build a temporary "Capitol" at 1st Street and Maryland Avenue, Northeast. The cornerstone was laid July 4, 1815, and both the House and the Senate met in the new building at the opening of the 14th Congress on Dec. 4, 1815. Known as the "Brick Capitol," the three-story brick building was rented to Congress for $1,650 per year. The Senate chamber was on the ground floor, the House met on the floor above. (The building later was used as a rooming house, a military prison during the Civil War, and finally as headquarters of the National Woman's Party until set aside as a part of the site of the present Supreme Court building.)

Appointment of Bulfinch. To succeed Latrobe, President Monroe on Jan. 8, 1818, appointed Charles Bulfinch of Boston, the first American-born architect to hold the post.

Bulfinch completed the reconstruction of the north and south wings, enabling Congress to resume meeting in the Capitol at the beginning of the 16th Congress on Dec. 6, 1819. The Supreme Court had returned for the February 1819 term.

The principal contribution of Bulfinch was supervision of work on the center section. The cornerstone for this section was laid Aug. 24, 1818. At first, Bulfinch planned to abandon the idea of an open rotunda and dome and to substitute a grand staircase and salon. He was persuaded to retain the original plans by John Trumbull, the artist, who was working at the time on four paintings to commemorate important events of the American Revolution. Congress had authorized the President to commission the paintings in 1817. As an artist, Trumbull was convinced that the paintings could best be displayed in a large, open rotunda, lighted from a high dome.

Bulfinch also modified Latrobe's plan for the West Front. By October 1824 work on the center section was far enough along for the rotunda to be used for a public reception for Lafayette. Also in 1824, Trumbull's completed paintings were hung in the rotunda. They portray the signing of the Declaration of Independence on July 4, 1776; the surrender of General Burgoyne at Saratoga on Oct. 17, 1777; the surrender of Lord Cornwallis at Yorktown on Oct. 19, 1781; and Washington surrendering his commission at Annapolis on Dec. 23, 1783.

The original dome, made of wood sheathed in copper, was completed in 1827. The pediment over the

---

Final Tributes in Rotunda

There is no law, written rule or regulation governing the question of whose body may lie in state in the Rotunda. Use of the Rotunda is controlled generally by concurrent resolution of the House and the Senate, although it has been used without Congressional action during recesses or between sessions of Congress.

Since Lincoln's time, the simple bier of cloth-covered boards constructed for his coffin has been used for all those whose bodies have lain in state in the Rotunda. The bier was used also for services in the Senate chamber for Chief Justice Salmon P. Chase in 1873 and for services in the House chamber for Rep. Samuel Hooper (R Mass.) in 1875.

Following is a list of persons who have been honored in the Rotunda and the dates on which their bodies lay in state:

Henry Clay	June 30, 1852
Abraham Lincoln	April 19-21, 1865
Thaddeus Stevens	Aug. 13-14, 1868
Charles Sumner	March 13, 1874
Henry Wilson	Nov. 25-26, 1875
James A. Garfield	Sept. 21-23, 1881
John A. Logan	Dec. 30-31, 1886
William McKinley Jr.	Sept. 17, 1901
Pierre Charles L'Enfant (reinterment)	April 28, 1909
Adm. George Dewey	Jan. 20, 1917
Unknown Soldier of World War I	Nov. 9-11, 1921
Warren G. Harding	Aug. 8, 1923
William Howard Taft	March 11, 1930
Gen. John J. Pershing	July 18-19, 1948
Robert A. Taft	Aug. 2-3, 1953
Unknown Soldiers of World War II and Korea[1]	May 28-30, 1958
John F. Kennedy	Nov. 24-25, 1963
Gen. Douglas MacArthur	April 8-9, 1964
Herbert C. Hoover	Oct. 23-25, 1964
Dwight D. Eisenhower	March 30-31, 1969
Everett McKinley Dirksen	Sept. 9-10, 1969

1. *A duplicate catafalque was constructed, and each coffin rested for a time on the historic Lincoln catafalque.*

East Portico (Genius of America), by Luigi Persico, was completed in 1828. Essentially, initial construction of the Capitol was complete.

Cost. Treasury records indicate that the cost of repairing the damage wrought by the British was $687,126. Erection of the center section cost $957,647.36.

Expansion, 1851-1892

Neither the House chamber nor the Senate chamber proved to be very comfortable. In addition to the acoustical problems in the House, both chambers were difficult to heat adequately in winter and were difficult to ventilate.

As the mid-point of the 19th century approached, a new problem arose. The two chambers were becoming overcrowded by additional Members representing newly admitted states. It was clear that the Capitol would have to be expanded.

Search for Designs. In response to a Congressional request in 1843, the War Department prepared plans for an addition to the south wing to provide an enlarged chamber for the House. No further action was taken, however.

In May 1850, another set of requested drawings was rejected. The new drawings had been prepared by Robert Mills, architect of public buildings, at the request of the Senate Public Buildings Committee. Mills had proposed adding two wings and enlarging the dome. (Mills is more widely known as the architect of the Washington Monument, the Treasury and the Patent Building.)

Then in September 1850 a Congressional resolution for a design competition under the supervision of the House and Senate Committees on Public Buildings was adopted. Plans were to be submitted by Dec. 1, 1850, and the winning design would receive a $500 award. As advertised in newspapers, "...these plans and estimates shall provide for the extension of the Capitol, either by additional wings, to be placed on the north and south of the present building, or by the erection of a separate and distinct building" to the east of the existing Capitol.

A variety of plans was submitted. Some merely extended the old building further to the north and the south. Others proposed adding wings to the east and the west. At least one plan called for a duplicate building to the east. Four of the plans were selected, and Mills was asked to prepare a composite, incorporating certain features of each.

Appointment of Walter. In the meantime, a modified Senate amendment had been added to a routine appropriations bill authorizing President Fillmore to select a suitable plan and to appoint an architect. The appropriations measure, approved Sept. 30, 1850, also provided an initial $100,000 for the expansion.

On June 10, 1851, Fillmore approved the general outline of a plan submitted by Thomas U. Walter, a Philadelphia architect who had designed Girard College (considered to be the highwater mark of the Greek Revival style in America). Walter was sworn in as Architect on June 11. His accepted design provided for the erection at either end of the old building of the two wings which have been used for the House and Senate ever since they were built. The House is in the south wing, the Senate in the north.

Building of House and Senate Wings

The cornerstone for the extension was laid by President Fillmore on July 4, 1851, in the northeast corner of the House wing. The ceremonies included an oration by Daniel Webster. Work began immediately, but it was halted almost as soon as it began. Congress blocked further appropriations in the winter of 1851, when a controversy arose over charges of fraud and poor construction. The charges apparently were initiated by unsuccessful contractors and by the Commissioner of Public Buildings and Grounds. President Fillmore had

made the Interior Department responsible for the extensions, leaving the commissioner in charge only of the old, central section. Investigating committees found the charges groundless, and appropriations were resumed in April 1852.

After renewed Congressional sniping at Walter in 1853, President Pierce on March 23 transferred responsibility for the construction from the Interior Department to the War Department. War Secretary Jefferson Davis named Capt. M.C. Meigs of the Corps of Engineers to superintend the construction, and Meigs began a review of Walter's plans.

Meigs' review left Walter's basic design intact, but altered the location of the Senate and House chambers in their respective wings. Walter had put the Senate chamber on the east side of the north wing and arranged it so that the Senators would sit facing east. The House, in the Walter plan, was to be on the east side of the south wing, arranged so that the Representatives would face south. At Meigs' suggestion, Walter redesigned the location of the chambers to place them in the center of their respective wings, with the Senate facing north and the House facing south.

By the fall of 1854, the walls of the House and Senate wings were up to the ceiling level, but the chambers were not covered over until 1856. The present House chamber was occupied Dec. 16, 1857. As had been the case in the past, Members were provided with individual desks and chairs. The desks were replaced by semi-circular benches in 1859, but the benches were removed and the desks reinstalled in 1860. Not until 1913 were the desks replaced by semi-circular rows of seats, similar to the arrangement that exists at present.

Adequate acoustics had remained a problem for the House even when it moved into its new chamber in 1857. Finally, in 1939 a system of microphones and loudspeakers was installed. After years of obstinate opposition, the Senate also had a public address sytem installed in its chamber in 1970.

A delay in receiving certain ironwork held up completion of the north wing in the 1850s, so that the Senate was unable to meet in its chamber until Jan. 4, 1859. The Senate's old desks were moved to the new chamber; new desks were added from time to time as the number of Senators increased.

Marble used in constructing the extensions was quarried in Massachusetts and Maryland.

Replacement of Bulfinch Dome

Although the original plans for extending the Capitol had made no provision for replacing the Bulfinch dome, it soon became apparent that the greatly enlarged building dwarfed the old dome. By an Act of April 4, 1855, Congress authorized replacement of the old dome, and Walter drew up plans.

Work on the dome began in 1856 and continued into the Civil War. President Lincoln insisted that work on the Capitol continue during the war as a symbol of the permanency of the Union.

On Dec. 2, 1863, the last section of the Statue of Freedom atop the dome was bolted into place, crowning the Capitol. Originally designed by sculptor Thomas Crawford as "Armed Liberty," wearing a soft cap of freed Roman slaves, it was modified at the request

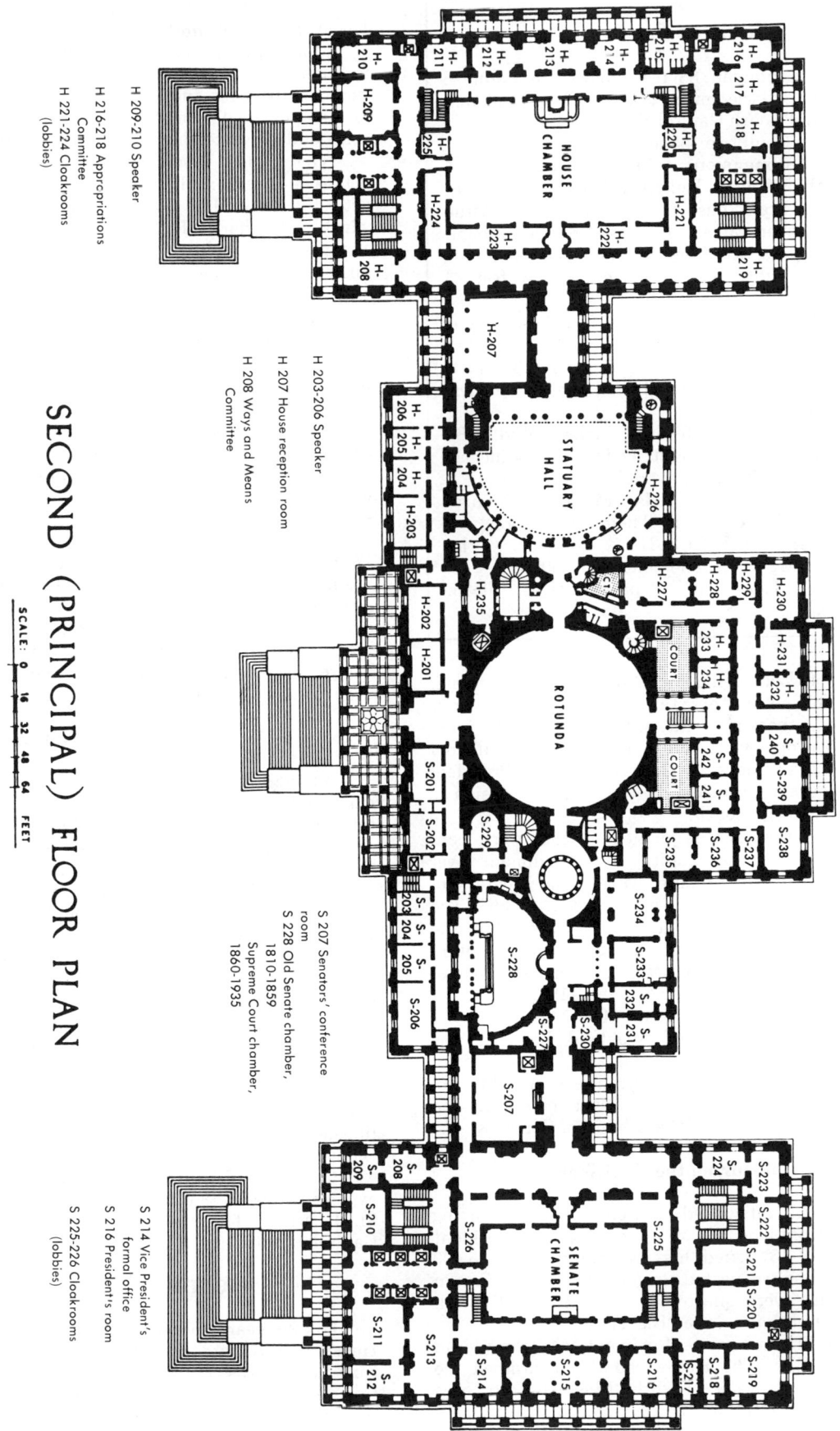

SECOND (PRINCIPAL) FLOOR PLAN

SCALE: 0　16　32　48　64　FEET

H 209-210 Speaker
H 216-218 Appropriations
　Committee
H 221-224 Cloakrooms
　(lobbies)

H 203-206 Speaker
H 207 House reception room
H 208 Ways and Means
　Committee

S 207 Senators' conference
　room
S 228 Old Senate chamber,
　1810-1859
　Supreme Court chamber,
　1860-1935

S 214 Vice President's
　formal office
S 216 President's room
S 225-226 Cloakrooms
　(lobbies)

Capitol Facts

Site. On a plateau 88 feet above the Potomac River. Located at the intersection of The Mall and North, East and South Capitol Streets.

Grounds. Comprise 155 acres.

Over-all dimensions. Length 751 feet, 4 inches. Width 350 feet. Height 287 feet, 5½ inches from the East Front base to the top of the Statue of Freedom. Covers about 4 acres. Provides around 16½ acres of floor space. Contains some 540 rooms.

Rotunda. Width 96 feet. Height 180 feet, 3 inches.

Dome. Width at base 135 feet, 5 inches. Weight 8,909,200 pounds. Made of iron.

Hall of Representatives. Length 139 feet. Width 92 feet. Greatest height 42 feet, 6 inches. Total seating capacity 448.

Senate. Length 113 feet, 3 inches. Width 80 feet, 3 inches. Greatest height 42 feet, 5 3/4 inches.

Statue of Freedom. Height 19 feet, 6 inches. Weight 14,985 pounds. Made of bronze, with iron pedestal. Modeled by Thomas Crawford.

Telephone. 202-224-3121. Connects the Capitol and all Members' and committee offices.

Zip Code. House of Representatives 20515. Senate 20510.

---

of Secretary of War Jefferson Davis. Officially, Davis ordered the change in the statue, in a Jan. 15, 1856, letter to Meigs, because "its history renders it inappropriate to a people who were born free and would not be enslaved." Tradition says that Davis, later President of the Confederacy, considered the original design a threat to slavery in the South.

After installation of the dome's statue, work continued elsewhere on the Capitol. The pediment over the east portico of the Senate wing (The Progress of Civilization), also by Crawford, was erected in 1863. The east portico was finished in the fall of 1864, but the north and west porticoes of the Senate wing were not completed until several years later. The porticoes of the House wing were completed by 1867, but the pediment over the east portico (The Apotheosis of Democracy), designed by Paul Wayland Bartlett, was not unveiled until Aug. 2, 1916.

Thomas Walter resigned as Architect on May 26, 1865, as the result of a conflict over enlarging the quarters, in the West Front, of the Library of Congress.

Capitol During the Civil War

Congress had adjourned March 3, 1861, leaving the Capitol vacant, nearly six weeks before President Lincoln on April 15 issued his proclamation for 75,000 volunteers. As the requested troops began arriving in Washington, they were quartered in the empty Capitol. The troops referred to it as the "Big Tent."

The Sixth Massachusetts Regiment was camped in the Senate chamber. The House chamber contained the Seventh New York. The Eighth Massachusetts was quartered in the Rotunda. In all, some 14 units were bivouacked in the Capitol at one time or another. *(See box on Troops in Capitol.)*

Mock sessions of Congress were a favorite pastime. Basement vaults were turned into storehouses for firewood, flour, beef and pork. Heating furnaces were used for cooking food. Committee rooms were lined with firebrick and converted into giant bread ovens.

The Capitol itself had become a heavily guarded defensive position. It was one of three centers (along with the City Hall hill and the White House) around which Col. Charles P. Stone of the District of Columbia Volunteers had planned his defense of Washington. The doors and windows were blocked with boards, stones and casks of cement. Heavy planking protected paintings and statues. Heavy iron plates, delivered for work on the dome, were erected as breastworks on the porticoes. (Fifty armed men had been hidden beneath the platform erected for Lincoln's inauguration on the East Portico.)

Lincoln's April 15 proclamation for troops also had called a special session of Congress for July 4. As the date for the special session approached, the troops were cleared out, and the Capitol was given a thorough scouring.

In 1862, after the adjournment of Congress on July 17, the Capitol again was temporarily requisitioned, as a hospital for the wounded from the Second Bull Run and Antietam. Hundreds of cots were set up in the corridors, the Rotunda and the House and Senate chambers. The patients were transferred to other hospitals before the return of Congress on Dec. 1, and the Capitol once again was cleaned and refurbished.

Landscaping of Capitol Grounds

As major work on the Capitol expansion drew to a close in the late 1860s, the task of landscaping the Capitol grounds remained. The most prominent landscape architect of the time was Frederick Law Olmsted, the designer of New York's Central Park. By an Act of June 23, 1874, Olmsted was commissioned to landscape the grounds of the Capitol. The results of his work still surround the building.

Initial work on the grounds was carried out from 1875 to 1881. In 1881, additional funds were sought for the grand marble stairway and terraces on the west side of the Capitol, also designed by Olmsted. Congress approved the request, and work began in 1883. Space beneath the terraces was designed for use as committee rooms. Because the landscaping was virtually completed, Olmsted resigned in 1885, and the final work, finished in 1892, was supervised by Architect of the Capitol Edward Clark.

Cost. According to Treasury records, the Capitol expansion cost $8,075,299.04 for the new wings and $1,047,291.89 for the new dome. Landscaping the Capitol grounds cost $3,626,579.83.

Recent Alterations

For 90 years following the initial occupancy of the House and Senate chambers, little important architectural work was done on the Capitol. Then in 1940, Congress authorized remodeling of the chambers and replacement of the old cast iron and glass ceilings with

Violence in the Capitol

From time to time, particularly during the 19th century, violence flared in the Capitol. Strong personal feelings have led to brawls among Members in both chambers. In 1835, Vice President Martin Van Buren adopted the habit of wearing a brace of pistols while presiding over the Senate. The House became known as the "Bear Garden" because of its quarrels. One picture in the files of the Library of Congress shows a wild melee on the House floor during an angry debate in 1858 on the Kansas statehood bill.

Following is a selected list of major incidents:

Attempted Assassination. On Jan. 30, 1835, an assailant later identified as Richard Lawrence fired two pistols at President Jackson as the President stood in the Rotunda. Jackson had come to the Capitol to attend funeral services in the House chamber for Rep. Warren R. Davis (State Rights Democrat S.C.). Both pistols misfired. Lawrence, who was captured immediately, was found to be insane.

Foote-Benton Quarrel. On April 17, 1850, during the controversy surrounding the Compromise of 1850, Sen. Henry S. Foote (Unionist Miss.), a supporter of the Compromise, drew a pistol on Sen. Thomas Hart Benton (D Mo.), an opponent of the Compromise. The incident occurred when Benton rushed threateningly toward Foote after Foote had directed bitter personal abuse at Benton. Other Senators intervened before Foote could fire.

Brooks-Sumner Caning. On May 22, 1856, Rep. Preston Brooks (State Rights Democrat S.C.) used a heavy cane in an attack on Sen. Charles Sumner (R Mass.) in the Senate chamber. The attack came during discussion of the Kansas-Nebraska bill. It followed a May 20 speech in which Sumner had personally denounced Brooks' uncle, Sen. A. P. Butler (State Rights Democrat S.C.). Sumner was beaten unconscious and was not able to resume his Senate duties for more than three years.

Shooting of Taulbee. On Feb. 28, 1890, Charles E. Kincaid, a correspondent for the Louisville *Times,* shot former Rep. William P. Taulbee (D Ky.) on the stairs leading from the eastern corridor of the House to the basement. The shooting apparently stemmed from *Times* stories of a scandal involving Taulbee. Taulbee died of the wounds on March 11, 1890. Kincaid was found innocent after a trial.

House Gunman. On Dec. 13, 1932, a young department store clerk from Allentown, Pa., entered the House gallery, pulled a loaded revolver and began waving it wildly, demanding time to address the House. As bedlam broke loose on the House floor, Rep. Melvin J. Maas (R Minn.) approached the gunman, named Marlin R.M. Kemmerer, and talked him into dropping the gun. Police arrested the gunman without a shot being fired.

Bricker Shooting. On July 12, 1947, Sen. John W. Bricker (R Ohio) was shot at twice as he entered the Senate subway. Both shots missed. The gunman was William L. Kaiser, a former Capitol policeman, who had lost money when an Ohio building and loan firm was liquidated 15 years earlier.

Puerto Rican Shooting. Extreme nationalistic sentiment over Puerto Rico erupted in the House March 1, 1954, when five Representatives were shot on the chamber floor. Their assailants, three pistol-wielding Puerto Ricans of the Nationalist party, fired about 30 shots from a visitors' gallery into a crowd of around 200 Representatives. Wounded were Reps. Alvin M. Bentley (R Mich.), Ben F. Jensen (R Iowa), Clifford Davis (D Tenn.), George H. Fallon (D Md.) and Kenneth A. Roberts (D Ala.). The three assailants, and a fourth member of the group taken later, received prison sentences.

---

new ceilings of stainless steel and plaster. The roofs of the old north and south wings, over Statuary Hall and the old Senate, had been reconstructed and fireproofed in 1902.

Remodeling. In 1940, temporary supports were installed under the old, weakened ceilings of the House and the Senate. Further work was delayed by World War II. The remodeling itself, under appropriations totaling $5,102,000, took place from July 1949 to January 1951.

During the renovation program, the Senate and House vacated their chambers on three occasions to allow the work to progress. The Senate held its sessions in the old Senate chamber, or Supreme Court room. The House met in the caucus room of the Longworth House Office Building.

When the temporary ceiling supports were being installed, the two bodies met in their substitute quarters from Nov. 22, 1940, to Jan. 3, 1941. When the first stage of construction work was being performed, the two bodies met away from their chambers from July 1, 1949, to Jan. 3, 1950. When construction on the final stage was under way, the Senate met in its old chamber from Aug. 11, 1950, to Jan. 3, 1951, and the House met in the Longworth Building from Sept. 1, 1950, to Jan. 1, 1951.

Extension of East Front

The most controversial recent alteration to the Capitol was the 1958-62 extension of the East Front. Although such an extension had been proposed before, and had been discussed for years, its authorization by Congress in 1956 led to a heated dispute.

When Architect Thomas Walter designed the new wings for the House and Senate and the new dome, he had suggested extending the east central section of the Capitol to make it symmetrical with the west central section and avoid any appearance of inadequate support for the new and larger dome. The plan never was executed.

In 1903, the House passed a bill for extension of the East Front, but the bill died in the Senate. Congress in 1904 established a joint commission to study the question. The commission asked the firm of Carrere and Hastings, designers of the original Senate and House office buildings, to prepare plans for a proposed eastern extension. The architects submitted two alternative proposals. One, labeled scheme A, provided for an extension of 12 feet, 10 inches. The other, called scheme B, provided for a 32½-foot extension. Once again, no further action was taken.

In 1935 and in 1937, the Senate passed bills providing for an extension. Both measures died in the House.

Finally in 1955, in the fiscal 1956 Legislative Appropriations Act, Congress authorized the extension of the East Front and provided an initial appropriation of $5 million. The extension was to follow the Carrere and Hastings proposal for a 32½-foot extension (scheme B). The work was to be directed by a Commission for Extension of the United States Capitol, comprised of the President of the Senate, the Speaker of the House, the minority leader of each chamber and the Architect of the Capitol.

Despite the later turmoil, there was little discussion about the project at first. Contributing to its acceptance were the deteriorating condition of the sandstone facing and the need of Congress for additional space. House Speaker Sam Rayburn (D Texas) was one of the strongest advocates of extension.

As public awareness of the impending project grew, however, strong opposition developed among architectural and historical groups. Opponents of the extension said the East Front should be repaired and preserved as it was. They forced a one-day hearing before the Senate Public Works Subcommittee on Public Buildings and Grounds. The hearing was held on Feb. 17, 1958. On Feb. 21, the commission ordered the project to go ahead.

Work began in 1958. On July 4, 1959, President Eisenhower laid the cornerstone. Under the approved plans, a new East Front in marble was constructed 32½ feet east of the old front. The east walls of the connections between the central section of the Capitol and the Senate and House wings also were extended to the east and reproduced in marble. The old sandstone walls were retained as a part of the interior wall construction. The work was completed in 1962, although it was far enough along for President Kennedy's inauguration on the East Front steps in 1961.

The extension added 100,000 gross square feet of space, making room for 54 offices, eight rooms for House and Senate documents, an additional dining room each for the House and Senate, and a private corridor between the House and Senate wings. The total cost, including the extension and some additional repairs and construction, came to $24 million.

Controversy Over West Front

Although the authority of the fiscal 1956 Legislative Appropriations Act was used initially for extension of the East Front, the language was broad enough to cover an extension of the West Front as well.

As work on the East Front drew to a close in 1962, the Commission for Extension of the U.S. Capitol turned its attention to the West Front. The West Front also was faced with sandstone and was deteriorating.

In 1964, Congress appropriated $125,000 for engineering studies of the West Front, and the commission hired a Brookline, Mass., engineering concern, Thompson and Lichtner Co. Inc., to make the studies. They were completed and submitted to the commission early in 1965. The firm recommended "an extended building... as the least hazardous and as causing the least interference with the occupancy of the present structure." Restoration of the existing West Front was specifically not recommended. After a public hearing on the studies on June 24, 1965, the commission agreed to ask Congress for money for preliminary plans, cost estimates and a model. Congress appropriated $300,000 for the project in October.

In a surprise announcement on June 17, 1966, the commission approved a $34-million plan to extend the West Front and add 4.5 acres of new space, including two auditoriums, two cafeterias, four dining rooms, 115 offices and a tourist center. The center section of the Capitol was to be extended westward 44 feet, the two original wings 88 feet, and the corridors connecting the House and Senate wings 56 feet.

A storm of Congressional protest erupted when details of the proposed extension were made public. The objections were based on economic, historical and architectural grounds. Strenuous opposition developed in the Senate where 30 Members, led by A.S. Mike Monroney (D Okla.) and William Proxmire (D Wis.), sponsored bills to block the project. A small but vocal House protest was organized by Samuel S. Stratton (D N.Y.).

Capitol Architect J. George Stewart was criticized almost daily in both House and Senate.

Stewart never made good his announced intention to seek the $34 million in 1966, apparently because of the clearly hostile reception the extension proposal had met. But the debate continued in 1967.

Opposing the extension and favoring in its place a restoration of the west wall, the American Institute of Architects (AIA) said in a special April 1967 report: "The West Front of the Capitol can be restored and its structural weaknesses corrected." While restoration would be costly and "would entail some inconvenience," the AIA said, it was "unlikely that the cost of the restoration would approach the total cost of extension." The AIA, stressing the historical importance of the existing West Front, also called for a "permanent policy prohibiting any further major alteration to the Capitol."

Stratton contended that Stewart had consciously allowed the West Front to deteriorate as part of a campaign to drum up support for its extension. Stewart blamed Congress for failing to provide sufficient maintenance funds. Stratton also said more study should be given to alternatives before proceeding with the extension.

Arguing for the extension project, Speaker McCormack said on June 1, 1967: "It will improve the esthetic quality of the west side, while at the same time preserving its essential characteristics." Furthermore, it would provide critically needed new office space. On the other hand, the Speaker contended, restoration could cost anywhere from $10 million to $50 million and would require that the entire west central section of the Capitol be vacated for 5 to 10 years.

Discussing the AIA-backed restoration plan, Stewart's office told the House Legislative Branch Appropriations Subcommittee in early 1967: "What a shame it would be to butcher this old building in the manner they propose. Their program, if it can be called that,...is an open invitation to endless expense,...continued admittedly poor structural conditions,...a scabby appearance...and stifling any further space growth for Congressional operations in the Capitol."

Debate over the West Front extension marked time in 1968. In 1969, Congress appropriated an additional $2,275,000 for extension of the Capitol but earmarked $250,000 of the total for an independent study on restoring the West Front.

Despite the provision for a restoration study, additional language in the appropriations bill (the fiscal 1970 Legislative Appropriations) made it clear that advocates of expansion still held the upper hand. The bill authorized the commission to proceed with extension of the West Front unless the restoration study met five conditions. Among the conditions was one that limited the cost of restoration to $15 million. Even if all the conditions were met, the commission was left free to make its own choice between restoration and extension.

The restoration study, carried out by the New York architectural firm of Praeger, Kavanagh & Waterbury and made public Jan. 6, 1971, concluded that the west walls of the Capitol could be repaired without impairing their "inherent beauty" at a cost of less than $15 million. The study asserted that the Capitol "survives in relatively good condition, attesting to the excellence of its builders and to the concern of those responsible

Architect of the Capitol

The Architect of the Capitol, who is not required to be a professional architect, has been responsible for the care and maintenance of the building since 1876, when Congress transferred to the Architect the functions previously performed by the Commissioner of Public Buildings and Grounds. The post of Architect is filled by a Presidential appointee.

The Architect is charged with the structural and mechanical care of the following buildings: the Capitol itself and its grounds, the office buildings of the House and the Senate, the Capitol Power Plant, the Senate Garage, the Robert A. Taft Memorial, the buildings and grounds of the Library of Congress, and the building and grounds of the Supreme Court.

The Architect also is charged with the operation of the U.S. Botanic Garden, the House restaurants and the Senate restaurants. He serves as a member of the Capitol Police Board, the Commission for the Extension of the U.S. Capitol, the District Zoning Commission, the President's Commission on Pennsylvania Avenue, and as coordinator of civilian defense for Capitol Hill. In addition, the Architect is charged with acquisition of real property and with the planning and construction of buildings and other improvements committed to his care by Congress.

In connection with the office buildings of the Senate, the Architect is subject in matters of policy to the Senate Rules and Administration Committee. He is subject to the House Building Commission in connection with the Capitol Power Plant and the office buildings of the House. In connection with the Senate Garage, he is subject to the rules and regulations of the Senate Rules and Administration Committee. He is subject to the direction of the Joint Library Committee in connection with the Botanic Garden.

Following is a list of men who have served as Architect of the Capitol, though under other titles prior to 1876:

1793-1794 William Thornton and Stephen Hallet
1794-1795 James Hoban
1795-1798 George Hadfield
1803-1811 and 1815-1817 Benjamin H. Latrobe
1818-1829 Charles Bulfinch
1850-1851 Robert Mills
1851-1865 Thomas U. Walter
1865-1902 Edward Clark
1902-1923 Elliott Woods
1923-1954 David Lynn
1954-1970 J. George Stewart
1971-   George M. White

for maintaining this, the national monument to our republic."

House and Senate Office Buildings

Erection of separate office buildings for Senators and Representatives is a relatively recent occurrence in the history of Congress. The first Congressional office building, for Members of the House, was not ready for use until 1908.

Traditionally, a Member's office consisted of his desk in the House or Senate chamber, or his rented room in a Washington boarding house. His files were carried in his head or the pockets of his jacket. The Capitol was the neatly self-contained home of the Legislative Branch.

The record of change from the traditional situation to the contemporary housing of Congress is in microcosm the broad history of Congress itself.

For years after the organization of the Legislative Branch under the Constitution, serving as a Member of Congress was at most a part-time occupation. Sessions were short. Standing committees were few. And Washington was both inaccessible and inhospitable, protecting Members from visits by constituents.

At the Capitol, if a Member was not actually on the floor, he had virtually no sanctuary, except his boarding house. The lobbies just off the chambers provided some

---

Botanic Garden

Members of Congress may decorate their offices with potted plants and cut flowers from the greenhouses of the U.S. Botanic Garden, located southwest of the Capitol on Maryland Avenue between First and Second Streets, Southwest.

The Garden was founded in 1820 under the auspices of the Columbia Institute for the Promotion of Arts and Sciences. It was operated under the direction of the institute until 1837, when that organization became inactive and the Garden was abandoned.

In 1842, the Government was confronted with the problem of housing the botanical collections brought to Washington from the South Seas by the U.S. Exploring Expedition of 1838-42, under the leadership of Capt. Charles Wilkes. When the expedition returned, the collections were placed temporarily in the Patent Office. Later, a greenhouse was constructed behind the Patent Office Building. The Joint Committee on the Library named the Commissioner of Patents to oversee the collections.

In 1850, the Botanic Garden was moved to the west end of the Capitol grounds, and it was relocated at its present site in 1933. The Joint Committee supervises the Garden through the Capitol Architect, who has been serving as acting director of the Botanic Garden since 1934.

The purpose of the Botanic Garden is to collect, cultivate and grow various plants for public display and for study by students, scientists and garden clubs. The entire collection includes more than 10,000 species and varieties. In the collection are palms, cycads, ferns, cacti, orchids and other tropical and subtropical plants, many of which are rare species.

---

relaxation. But the lobbies were open to the public, and favor-seekers took advantage of the chance to buttonhole legislators; hence the term "lobbying."

Growth of Pressure for Office Space

The first pressure for additional office space came from the Congressional committees. The groups quickly overflowed the rooms allocated to them in the unfinished Capitol. At times, several Senate committees would meet in separate areas of the Senate chamber. Finally, a temporary building for committee rooms was erected on the Capitol grounds, while the central section of the Capitol was under construction. Additional committee space was provided by the expansion of the Capitol in the 1850s and by the later construction of the West Terrace.

The proliferation of committees devoured new space almost as fast as it was provided. Not all of the proliferation, however, was dictated by the press of legislative business. A committee office in the Capitol frequently doubled as a personal office for the committee chairman. The committee clerks doubled as a personal staff. While widely acknowledged, this dual role of committees was occasionally criticized. In 1884, for example, Sen. George G. Vest (D Mo.) complained on the Senate floor: "...There are six of the standing committees of the Senate that have never had a bill, or a resolution or a particle of business before them within the memory of a living man that I know of. They are all sinecure committees. They were created simply to give secretaries to Members of the Senate and a committee room."

Criticized or not, the committees and their perquisites proved attractive. As a result, some committees survived long after their business was completed. The Senate Committee on Revolutionary (War) Claims, for example, still existed in 1921.

As the committees outgrew the space provided even in the expanded Capitol, additional space was rented in nearby Capitol Hill buildings. By 1891, the Maltby Building, for instance, at B Street and New Jersey Avenue, Northwest, had become known as the Senate Annex. It had been converted into some 81 offices.

By the end of the 19th century, the Congress had grown too large for the Capitol, and the use of converted Capitol Hill buildings was judged inconvenient, if not hazardous, because of the danger of fire. Before the Senate left the Maltby Building, it had been condemned as unsafe. An increased membership of the Senate and House produced a demand for additional rooms to accommodate Members. The House authorized its first office building in 1903, the Senate in 1904.

Construction of Office Buildings

Once the first buildings set the precedent, pressure for additional buildings was impossible to resist. The pressure rose as the staffs of Members increased, and as committees (and their expanded staffs) moved out of the Capitol and into the office buildings. The House currently has three office buildings; the Senate has two, and is planning to enlarge one of them. Assignment of space in the buildings is based on seniority.

For years, the House buildings were unnamed, known prosaically as the House Office Building, or, when a second one was built, as the Old House Office Building and the New House Office Building. When a third House building was under construction in 1962, the House decided to name all three. It named each building for the House Speaker in office during a major part of the construction. Thus the Old House Office Building was named for Joseph G. Cannon; the New House Office Building for Nicholas Longworth; and the third building for Sam Rayburn.

The buildings on the Senate side have not been named. They are called simply the Old and New Senate Office Buildings. However, proposals to name them are offered periodically.

Most committees of Congress now have space in one of the office buildings, although a handful of House and joint House-Senate panels have retained rooms in the Capitol. A vast array of miscellaneous groups also have been alloted space in the office buildings. They range from the Democratic Study Group, a loose alliance of liberal House Members, to a branch office of the U.S. Employment Service.

In the meantime, senior Members anxious to escape visiting constituents and lobbyists in the office buildings have been assigned unmarked hideaways in the Capitol. The development of these Capitol offices has brought the housing of Congress nearly full circle, reverting to a past era that preceded construction of the first office building.

The Different Buildings

Cannon House Office Building. Congress authorized construction of the first House offices, later called the Cannon Building, in 1903. Designed by Carrere and Hastings, who later designed the Old Senate Office Building, the building was completed and occupied on Jan. 10, 1908. President Theodore Roosevelt had participated in cornerstone ceremonies on April 14, 1906.

As designed, the office building was large enough for the existing House membership. But Congress in 1911 authorized an increase in the size of the House to 435 Members, and an additional story was erected on the building in 1913-14. The total cost of the building, including site, furnishings, equipment and a subway connecting with the Capitol, was $4,860,155.

As a part of the later Rayburn House Office Building project, the Cannon Building was remodeled in the 1960s under a $5.2-million appropriation.

Old Senate Office Building. In 1904, Congress authorized construction of the Old Senate Office Building. Plans for the Cannon Building were adapted for the Senate building, with the exception that one side of the structure (fronting on First Street, Northeast) was temporarily omitted. The cornerstone was laid July 31, 1906, and the building was occupied March 5, 1909. The First Street side was added in 1931-33. The cost of the completed building was $8,390,892.

Longworth House Office Building. Construction of the Longworth House Office Building was authorized in 1929. The cornerstone was laid June 24, 1932, and the building was completed and ready for occupancy on April 20, 1933. The cost of the building was $7,805,705.

New Senate Office Building. Congress authorized construction of the New Senate Office Building in 1948, but the Korean War delayed groundbreaking ceremonies

<table>
<tr><td>

Senate and House Subways

The office buildings of the Senate and House are linked to the Capitol by underground tunnels. Subway cars have shuttled through the tunnel between the Capitol and the Old Senate Office Building since 1909. The only subway cars on the House side operate between the Capitol and the Rayburn Building. The tunnel between the Capitol and the Cannon and Longworth Buildings is restricted to pedestrian traffic.

Two Studebaker-made, battery-operated electric vehicles with solid rubber tires, each carrying eight passengers, supplied the first subway to and from the Old Senate Office Building. After a few years, faster service was provided by two monorail cars, which drew their power from overhead wires and operated on opposite sides of the tunnel. Two redesigned monorail cars, produced at the Washington Navy Yard and put into service in 1920, remained in use until 1961. At that time, a new Senate subway system, constructed as a part of the New Senate Office Building project, went into full operation.

The new system, connecting both Senate office buildings and the Capitol, consists of four 18-passenger cars and four two-rail tracks. Two cars shuttle between the Capitol and the Old Senate Office Building and two between the Capitol and the New Senate Office Building.

</td></tr>
</table>

to Jan. 26, 1955. The cornerstone was laid July 13, 1956. The building was accepted for occupancy on Oct. 15, 1958. Work on the building was carried out under an authorization of $24,196,000.

Site for Extension—As presently constructed, the New Senate Office Building fills one-half of a Capitol Hill block bounded by First, Second and C Streets and Constitution Avenue, Northeast. Congress in 1969 appropriated $1.25 million to purchase the other half of the block with the exception of the land occupied by the historic 1799 Belmont House, headquarters of the National Woman's Party, at Second Street and Constitution Avenue. The additional land was to be used eventually for more Senate offices.

Rayburn House Office Building

The Rayburn Building was conceived in controversy and completed in conflict. Its legislative history began in 1955 when the New Senate Office Building was under construction, and Speaker Sam Rayburn reminded the House of its own space needs.

At Rayburn's personal request, $25,000 for a study of the need for a third House office structure was inserted in a supplemental appropriations bill in committee. When the bill reached the House floor, March 18, 1955, Rayburn left the chair and moved to strike the $25,000 item from the bill. In its place he offered an amendment authorizing the House Office Building Commission to spend $2 million and "such additional sums as may be necessary" for acquisition of a site and immediate construction of an additional House office building.

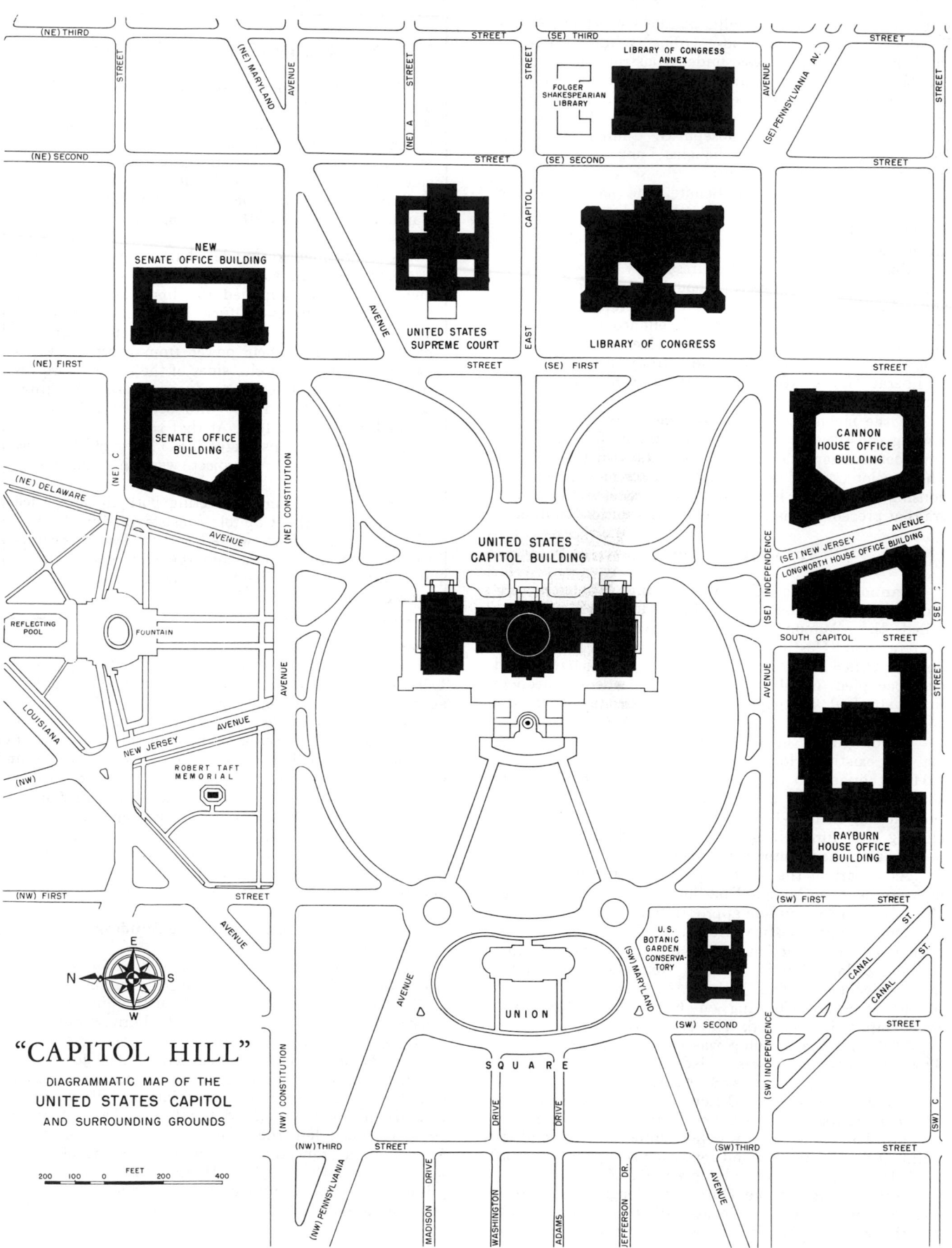

"CAPITOL HILL"

DIAGRAMMATIC MAP OF THE
UNITED STATES CAPITOL
AND SURROUNDING GROUNDS

Group Responsible for Recent Capitol Hill Architecture

The recent history of construction on Capitol Hill revealed that a small number of architects was regularly involved in all major projects.

After the appointment in 1954 of former Rep. J. George Stewart (R Del. 1935-37) as Architect of the Capitol, more than $250 million was spent or authorized for Capitol Hill construction.

Under Stewart, who was not an architect but had experience as a landscape contractor, the East Front of the Capitol was extended, the Rayburn House Office Building was built, remodeling projects were undertaken, parking garages were built and plans were approved for the extension of the Capitol's West Front and for a third Library of Congress building. Without exception, the names of a tiny and sometimes rotating constellation of architects were attached to all these projects. This prompted charges that an architectural monopoly held sway on Capitol Hill.

House Speaker Sam Rayburn, chairman of the three-man House Office Building Commission, started the ball rolling in 1955 when the Philadelphia firm of Harbeson, Hough, Livingston and Larson was chosen to design what was to become the Rayburn Building. Architect John Harbeson was a friend of Stewart.

A little later, three other firms—Roscoe Dewitt and Fred L. Hardison of Dallas, well known to Rayburn; Alfred Easton Poor and Albert Homer Swanke of New York City; and Jesse M. Shelton and Alan G. Stanford of Atlanta, well known to the late Rep. Carl Vinson (D Ga. 1914-65), a member of Rayburn's commission—were brought in to work on related remodeling projects in the future. Dewitt and Hardison got the Cannon House Office Building remodeling job, Poor and Swanke the Longworth House Office Building project, and Shelton and Stanford the garage construction under and behind the Rayburn Building as well as the House-Capitol subway.

Meanwhile, also in 1955, a five-member Commission on the Extension of the U.S. Capitol, composed of the Speaker, the Vice President, the Minority Leaders in both House and Senate and the Capitol Architect, was created to consider expanding the Capitol.

Because no remodeling work had been authorized yet on either the Cannon or Longworth buildings, Stewart hired Dewitt and Hardison, Poor and Swanke and Shelton and Stanford—who joined forces as Dewitt, Poor and Shelton—to draw up plans for extending the Capitol.

For the Capitol job, an advisory panel was established consisting of Harbeson (whose firm would design the Rayburn Building and earlier did the Folger Library) and Henry R. Shepley of Boston and Arthur Brown Jr. of San Francisco, both now dead.

In 1957 Dewitt, Poor and Shelton, who were also to do the design work for remodeling the old Senate and Supreme Court chambers, presented the Capitol Extension Commission plans for extending both the East and West Fronts. After bitter controversy, most of which developed in the Senate, Rayburn in 1958 pushed through the East Front project, which was completed in 1962 at a total cost of $24 million.

Subsequently, Dewitt, Poor and Shelton were picked to design the $75-million James Madison Memorial Library, authorized in 1965. Stewart cited "the highly satisfactory" East Front project as the basis for the selection.

In 1966, the Capitol Extension Commission, then headed by Speaker John W. McCormack (D Mass.), in a surprise move approved a plan for extending the West Front at a cost of $34 million. Again the architects were Dewitt, Poor and Shelton, who contended, with the support of the commission, that they were hired in 1956 for all work (present and future) that might be done on the Capitol.

Clarence Cannon (D Mo.), chairman of the Appropriations Committee, promptly accepted the amendment "in view of the emergency involved and the urgent need of the facility for which the appropriation is proposed."

Under House rules, appropriation bills are supposed to be limited to providing money for projects authorized by previous legislation. No new building had been authorized by Congress. Rep. Clare E. Hoffman (R Mich.) tried to make a point of order that Rayburn's amendment was legislation in an appropriation bill, a point which, if accepted, would have automatically killed the amendment. But Rep. Clark Thompson (D Texas), a trusted lieutenant to whom Rayburn had yielded the chair, ruled that Hoffman had been too late in making the point of order. When Hoffman protested that he had spoken even before the clerk finished reading the amendment, Thompson declared: "That was not the proper time."

During the brief debate that followed, Hoffman received support only from Rep. H. R. Gross (R Iowa). Gross questioned the emergency that compelled construction of a new building, and expressed fears about the eventual cost. Rayburn replied that the matter would be handled by the three-member House Office Building Commission. Rayburn, then age 73, was chairman of this group, and the other members were Rep. Carl Vinson (D Ga.), 72, and Rep. James C. Auchincloss (R N.J.), 70. "I do not think this commission is going to run wild on anything," Rayburn assured the House. His amendment was accepted by voice vote.

While the Act fixed no total cost, the three commission members were given authority to set the limit. The House itself still controlled the appropriations, and it could have stopped the project, especially during the early years, simply by cutting off the funds. Funds were appropriated on 11 occasions from 1955 to 1964. Only in 1957, after $14.9 million had been obligated for the acquisition of land and preliminary work, was the project challenged on the House floor. Rep. Gross objected to a $7.5 million appropriation to carry on the work for the next fiscal year, but his motion to recommit the bill was rejected on a roll-call vote, 206 to 176.

Construction. The company chosen to design the building was the Philadelphia architectural firm of Harbeson, Hough, Livingston & Larson. Architect John Harbeson was a friend of Capitol Architect J. George Stewart. He was a friend also of fellow Philadelphian Matthew H. McCloskey, treasurer and chief fund raiser for the Democratic party. *(See box on Group Responsible for Recent Capitol Hill Architecture.)*

McCloskey's construction firm, McCloskey & Co., was the Rayburn Building's principal contractor, by virtue of submitting the low bid of $6.66 million for excavation and construction of the foundation. Subsequently, the firm also won the contract for construction of the building's superstructure, with a low bid of $50.8 million. Stewart's office supervised all construction work.

The House Office Building Commission, headed by Rayburn until his death in November, 1961, played an active role in design of the building. Writing in Fortune Magazine (March 1965), Harold B. Meyers declared that, "From the start the architects had limited scope for exercising discretion in the design." The building not only had to be large, to provide the desired space, and low, to properly frame the Capitol, but it also had to be built of marble and granite in a classical style.

"Every decision of any moment—including the controversial layout of the suites and such accouterments as the commodious safe in each one—had to be referred to the strongminded, busy members of the commission, with Stewart as intermediary," according to Meyers. Ceiling height, for example, reportedly was set at 13 feet 9 inches after Vinson climbed upon a chair in his high-ceilinged Cannon Building office, pointed at a ventilation grille in the wall, and declared, "I want the ceilings *that* high." Between the time that specifications for the superstructure were drawn and bids were submitted, at least seven time- and money-consuming modifications were made in the plans.

Costs. Confusion over actual costs of the Rayburn Building was compounded not only by design changes and by faulty estimates (as late as 1958 Stewart was still talking about the building as costing $64 million) but by the fact that other remodeling work on Capitol Hill was going on at the same time. According to information provided by the Capitol Architect's office, final cost of the Rayburn Building was $87.4 million, including land acquisition and furnishings. *(See box on Rayburn Building Cost.)*

Various efforts have been made to compare costs of the Rayburn Building with other large office buildings around the nation. Two reporters for the Chicago Daily News, James McCartney and Charles Nicodemus, stated in a series for that newspaper in 1964 that the huge Merchandise Mart in Chicago, completed in 1931, would cost about as much as the Rayburn Building at today's prices. "But the Merchandise Mart has 3,300,000 square feet of rental office space—compared to the Rayburn Building's 935,000 square feet of usable space," they wrote. "The Merchandise Mart houses 25,000 workers, compared to the Rayburn Building's 2,800."

The reporters also sought to compare the Rayburn Building with the 102-story Empire State Building in New York, then the world's tallest building. "By a formula accepted as valid by the builders of the Rayburn Building, the Empire State Building would cost about $84.2 million to build today. The building itself

---

Rayburn Building Cost

Controversy surrounded many aspects of the Rayburn House Office Building. One controversial aspect was its cost. The following figures are a cost breakdown of the Rayburn Building and associated items, as computed in 1967 by the office of the Capitol Architect.

Acquisition of site: Acquisition of land, including appraisals, title search, clearing of site, and protection of property	$ 2,500,000
Preparation of site:	
Rebuilding Tiber Creek sewer	1,392,805
Soils engineering	11,876
Changes in water and sewer lines, streets, and curbings	263,335
Test borings	19,449
Total	1,687,465
Construction and equipment of building:	
Superstructure and equipment	55,111,265
Furnishing and erection of structural steel	7,208,651
Excavation, excavation bracing, foundation piles, and pile caps	8,830,004
Total	71,149,920
Related items:	
Completion of undeveloped areas in the building, as such areas are assigned by the House Office Building Commision	427,915
Occupancy changes	146,899
Landscaping	188,685
Materials tests (by Bureau of Standards and District of Columbia government)	120,221
Street lighting and traffic signals	23,018
Television antenna system for building	14,710
Electrical birdproofing	5,700
Inspection of stone offsite	94,604
Sculptured Rayburn plaque, main entrance	35,000
Paper baling equipment	23,534
Providing sinks for Members' suites	36,318
Miscellaneous	105,073
Total	1,221,677
Architectural and engineering services:	
Architectural and engineering fees (5 ½ percent of cost of work for which services are performed)	4,000,000
Furniture and furnishings	3,299,891
Administration and other costs: Administration, supervision, inspection on site, drawings, blueprints, travel, advertising, stenographic reporting services for contract appeals board, and other miscellaneous costs	3,500,000
Total estimated final cost of Rayburn Building as now occupied, and associated items listed above	$87,358,953

---

cost $24.7 million when completed in 1931. The Empire State Building houses more than 20,000 workers and has 2,158,000 square feet of rentable space—more than twice the usable space in the Rayburn Building." (The complete series of articles was reprinted in the *Congressional Record* of Jan. 28, 1965, p. 1408-1414.)

Rayburn Building Profile. The Rayburn Building is 720 feet long by 450 feet wide (about two square blocks in size) and has 50 acres of floor space under its roof. (One critic has quipped that it could be defended only militarily.) It is served by 25 passenger elevators and 23 escalators. Primary accommodations provided include 169 three-room suites for Members of the House of Representatives (39 percent of the House membership) and nine hearing rooms for standing committees of Congress. Eight of these hearing rooms are two stories high and typically are about 56 feet long and 46 feet wide. Only 130 chairs are provided in each hearing room for the public, an economy dictated by the large rostrum which seats 41 Members and a large "well" where space is provided for witnesses, press and staff members. Committee rooms are provided with adjoining anterooms and staff offices. Underground garage space was built for 1,600 automobiles and takes up 42 percent of the building's gross floor space. Health facilities include a 20-by-60 foot swimming pool, a gymnasium and slumber rooms.

A typical Representative's suite is about 54 feet long and 32 feet wide. It consists of three rooms, one for the Member of Congress, one for his head assistant, and the third for general office work. There is a large reception area.

Critics have noted that only 15 percent of gross floor space in the Rayburn Building actually is used for Congressmen's offices—the original reason for putting up the building. In a detailed reply to such charges, the Capitol Architect's Office used its method of showing space utilization. If the square footage used for the garage floors, plus space taken up with automatic ramps, was subtracted from the gross square footage in the building, a total of 1,189,200 square feet remained. This total was to be used as follows: Congressional offices and files, 34 percent; committee staff rooms, full committee hearing rooms, subcommittee hearing rooms, 13 percent; cafeteria, first aid, health facilities, library, pressroom, television room, public telephone rooms, telegraph rooms, recording studio, mailroom, liaison offices, 9 percent; stairs, escalators, elevators, entrance lobbies, halls, corridors, 21 percent; mechanical and electrical rooms, janitorial and maintenance space, 18 percent; undeveloped office or committee space, 5 percent.

Architectural Criticism. Aside from its cost, most of the criticism leveled at the Rayburn Building was on grounds of style. The building was called "Edifice Rex," "King Hottentot's Temple," and, in tribute to the time taken for its construction, "the ten-year pyramid." Its style, technically "simplified classic," was derided as "Mussolini Modern" and "Texas Penitentiary." Its endless corridors were likened to a rerun of the movie "Last Year at Marienbad." Some specific comments:

Ada Louise Huxtable, in *The New York Times*, March 30, 1965—"Architecturally, the Rayburn Building is a national disaster. Its defects range from profligate mishandling of 50 acres of space to elephantine esthetic banality at record costs.... It is quite possible that this is the worst building for the most money in the history of the construction art. It stuns by sheer mass and boring bulk.

"Stylistically, it is the apotheosis of humdrum. It is hard to label the building, but it might be called Corrupt Classic. Its empty aridity and degraded classical details are vulgarization without drama, and to be both dull and vulgar may be an achievement of sorts....

"The Rayburn Building is the third solid gold turkey in a row to come out of the office of the Architect of the Capitol, J. George Stewart, who is not even an architect, but who picks them for Congress.... He is also responsi-

ble for the ill-advised remodeling of the Capitol's East Front and the construction of the new Senate Office Building. There are no controls or reviews for Mr. Stewart's work, and none for the House committee that authorized the Rayburn Building's construction and appropriations, generally behind closed doors."

Statement by the office of the Architect of the Capitol (published in full in the *Congressional Record* of March 11, 1965, p. 467)—"Esthetics are often matters of opinion. What one person thinks is beautiful, another finds repulsive, and both could be sincere. In architecture, some prefer the classic treatment which has stood the test of time. Presidents Washington and Jefferson did, and our Capital City is the more beautiful today because of their early leadership in this respect. We are not opposed to so-called modern architecture, but the House Office Building Commission wisely determined that it had no place adjoining the U.S. Capitol."

Paul Manship, a New York City sculptor, in a letter to the Architect of the Capitol—"May I say how much I enjoyed the architecture of the building, which impressed me by its beautifully proportioned simplicity. It is modern in its adaptation of grand traditional forms and style. The fenestration, the great entrances with majestic columns and lofty ceilings and their impressive harmony to the whole; just but reticent detailing ornament enhances the architecture. The materials, marble and granite, are beautiful and fitting to this building in the great stately tradition, designed to harmonize with the noble National Capitol which it adjoins and complements."

Columnist Art Buchwald, April 5, 1965—"You can't build a $125-million office building without making a few mistakes, and if there was any hint that the building was really a waste of taxpayers' money, Congressmen would certainly investigate it. Wouldn't they?"

James McCartney and Charles Nicodemus, in the *Chicago Daily News*—"No discussion of the building's opulence would be complete without further mention of the swimming pool. It was supposedly added as an afterthought, but it looks right at home. Finding it in the bowels of the building is like finding a speakeasy in the 1920s....The pool's most curious feature is its ceiling. It's so low that if a diving board is installed—even at floor level—any Congressman taking even the slightest bounce would doubtless crack his cranium on the plaster above. Yet the pool has a deep end—10 feet in depth—which, if not constructed expressly for diving, would scarcely seem to have any utility except for imperiling Congressmen who haven't learned how to keep their heads above water."

Rep. Tom Steed (D Okla.) on the floor of the House, March 11, 1965: "The Rayburn Building is a big building. It is a costly building. It is designed to stand with time—and no one need apologize if it has grandeur and majesty—that is what it ought to have....It is regrettable that many writers have resorted to so many extravagant misstatements and sometimes deliberate inferences which tend to only downgrade the institution of Congress in the eyes of the people."

Harold B. Meyers, in the March 1965 *Fortune* magazine—"What is most outrageous about the Rayburn Building is not its appearance (which is actually well suited to its location); not its cost (which can be defended); nor the fact that Matthew McCloskey, who came into

Text of Baltimore Federal Court Summary

Following is the text of the summary of a Federal grand jury presentment made public June 22, 1970, by Chief Judge Roszel Thomsen of U.S. District Court in Baltimore. The grand jury had been investigating charges of corruption in connection with a Federal Government construction contract.

The proposed indictment charges Victor Frenkil and Baltimore Contractors Inc., the only defendants named therein, with conspiring with Bernard Shepard, a vice president of Baltimore Contractors Inc., and "other persons to the Grand Jury known and unknown," to defraud the United States of its right to have the disinterested services of its officials and employees unimpaired by the exertion of improper pressure and influence.

It is charged that the conspiracy included:

• Seeking to convince the Architect of the Capitol and his officials and employees that, by virtue of Victor Frenkil's allegedly close relationship, association and friendship with high government officials, including Members of both Houses of Congress, he had the ability to affect, either adversely or favorably the employment of officials and employees of the Architect of the Capitol;

• Seeking to obtain the assistance of Members of both houses of Congress, concerning matters of Baltimore Contractors Inc., pending before and to be submitted to the Architect of the Capitol in connection with the Underground Garage Construction Project, and causing them to intercede with the Architect of the Capitol at various times on behalf of defendants with respect to the aforesaid matters;

• Promising employment benefits and advances to various officials in the office of the Architect of the Capitol in return for action favorable to defendants on matters then pending before and to be submitted

to the Architect of the Capitol in connection with the Underground Garage Construction Project; and

• Threatening, directly and indirectly, various officials and employees of the Architect of the Capitol with the loss of their jobs for failing or refusing to act in favor of Baltimore Contractors Inc., on matters then pending before and to be submitted to the Architect of the Capitol in connection with the Underground Garage Construction Project.

It is alleged that it was a further part of said conspiracy that the defendants would offer money to Senator Russell B. Long of Louisiana and another as an inducement for them to bring the prestige, weight and influence of their respective offices to bear upon officials and employees of the Architect of the Capitol so as to further and promote the interests of the defendants in their dealings with the Architect of the Capitol.

It is alleged that it was a further part of said conspiracy that the defendants in an effort to gain the goodwill of Congressman Hale Boggs of Louisiana, and in the hope and expectation that Congressman Boggs would bring the prestige, weight and influence of his office to bear upon the Architect of the Capitol and employees of the Architect of the Capitol, with respect to the matters of Baltimore Contractors Inc., then pending before and to be submitted to the Architect of the Capitol in connection with the Underground Garage Construction Project, would and did cause the Maryland residence of Congressman Boggs, at 5315 Bradley Blvd., Bethesda, Md., to be remodeled at a price to Congressman Boggs substantially below cost.

The indictment lists numerous acts, not in themselves criminal, alleged to have been done in furtherance of the conspiracy. The Grand Jury does not charge that any improper payment was made to any public official.

---

such sharp view in the Bobby Baker investigation, held the major construction contracts (his company won them through competitive bidding). The worst thing about the Rayburn Building is the very thing it symbolizes best: the power system that created it.... The Rayburn House Office Building is in every way a fitting monument to Congressional power and a great Speaker's genius for using it."

Continuing Controversy. Controversy continued to plague the Rayburn project, even after completion of the building itself. A number of claims for associated projects were submitted by contractors. Among the claims were ones totaling more than $5 million from Baltimore Contractors Inc., builder of underground parking garages behind the Rayburn Building. Some of its claims were settled. The rest were challenged and subjected to legal actions.

A summary of a Federal grand jury's investigation of attempts to influence Members of Congress and Congressional employees in connection with settlement of these claims was made public June 22, 1970, by Chief Judge Roszel C. Thomsen of the Federal District Court in Baltimore (*see box above*).

The grand jury and two successive U.S. attorneys recommended the case be prosecuted, but Attorney General John N. Mitchell, citing lack of evidence, refused to authorize signature of the formal indictments.

The judge's summary said the proposed indictment charged Victor H. Frenkil and his firm, Baltimore Contractors Inc., with conspiring with "other persons" to defraud the Government.

The judge said the grand jury report recommended only that Frenkil and his firm be indicted. Bernard Shepard, a vice president of the company, was named as a co-conspirator with Frenkil but was not recommended for indictment.

Frenkil, 61, a prominent Maryland Democrat, was alleged by the grand jury to have conspired to offer money to Sen. Russell B. Long (D La.) as an inducement to help get approval for the claim. The judge's summary also said Frenkil's firm remodeled at a cut-rate price the Bethesda, Md., house of Rep. Hale Boggs (D La.), the House Majority Whip and later Majority Leader. The report said Frenkil also promised employment advances to Capitol employees concerned with the claim in return for favorable action and threatened them with the loss of their jobs if the claim was disapproved.

The judge said he was releasing the summary of the jury report because it concerned public officials, even though formal charges could not be brought. The summary said the jury did not charge any improper payment was made to any public official. On June 23, the judge ordered expunged from court records the grand jury's full report and said the case would not be prosecuted.

Long declined to comment on the matter. He was quoted in *The Washington Post* in 1969 as saying he had asked his administrative assistant, Robert Hunter, to look into the claim because it was "meritorious" and because he had been asked to do so by former Sen. Daniel B. Brewster (D Md.). Boggs issued a statement acknowledging Frenkil's firm performed the remodeling work in 1966, two years before the garage claim, but said he was not aware if it was done below cost. He denied he sought to exert influence on the contractor's claims.

The New York Times on June 21, 1970, and other publications later, reported that the grand jury's secret report stated Long and Brewster were offered bribes of up to $125,000 each, but there was no evidence either accepted the offers. *The Times* also said Reps. Samuel N. Friedel and Clarence Long, both Democrats from Maryland, had urged speedy action on the company's claim. The Representatives told reporters their only involvement in the case was in attempting to hasten the decision on the claim. News reports said House Speaker John W. McCormack (D Mass.) and his long-time friend, Nathan Voloshen, were also named in the grand jury's secret report.

Despite the alleged pressure, the staff of the Capitol Architect recommended the claim be rejected. The Architect, the late J. George Stewart, rejected it. Stewart's successor as Architect of the Capitol, George M. White, rejected in April 1971 renewed Frenkil claims amounting to $3.8 million. The Architect's office said on May 28 that Baltimore Contractors had appealed White's decision to the Contract Appeals Board of the House Office Building Commission.

The grand jury originally (May 28, 1970) returned a sealed document on the case. At that time, the panel said Mitchell personally was blocking it from returning indictments. Chief Judge Thomsen rejected a grand jury request that it be allowed to return an indictment without Justice Department approval. U.S. Attorney George Beall of Baltimore and his predecessor, Stephen H. Sachs, who originated the investigation, had recommended that the case be prosecuted.

Capitol as Target for Protests and Demonstrations

There have been innumerable demonstrations in Washington, D.C., to protest unemployment, poverty and war. Various public buildings have been selected as objectives in different demonstrations, and the Capitol has been a frequent target.

Responsibility for the Capitol is widely shared— among the Capitol Police, the House, the Senate, the Architect of the Capitol and others. Regulations affecting the Capitol are found in statutory law, in official rules of the House and Senate and in precedents established by long-standing practice. *(For text of regulations for Senate wing of the Capitol, see Appendix.)*

Among the major demonstrations in Washington have been those of Coxey's Army in 1894, the Bonus Expeditionary Force in 1932, the 1963 Civil Rights March, the 1968 Poor People's Campaign and numerous anti-Vietnam war protests.

Coxey's Army and the Bonus Marchers

Coxey's Army, which marched on Washington in 1894, was a product of severe unemployment following the economic depression of 1893. An army of the unemployed was organized by Jacob S. Coxey to pressure Congress into authorizing a $500-million highway improvement program and interest-free loans to state and local governments to finance public improvements. Coxey's Army set out from Massillon, Ohio, and similar groups were soon organized in many parts of the West. The total number of men involved has been estimated at 6,000 to 11,000.

Only about 500 men reached Washington. The District of Columbia police department was greatly enlarged for their arrival and Government buildings were heavily guarded. When Coxey and his men arrived May 1 and started to march into the Capitol grounds, the police assaulted the men with clubs. Coxey and two other leaders reached the Senate steps but were arrested and subsequently convicted of trampling the shrubbery and unlawfully displaying banners.

Coxey's Army established camps at various places in and around Washington. The men subsisted on donated food and by begging. By mid-July they had been abandoned by most of their leaders. The demonstration ended when the Virginia militia drove the men out of a large encampment on the Virginia side of the Potomac and burned down their camp. The District of Columbia Government then offered to provide transportation to the West, which most accepted.

The Bonus Expeditionary Force which marched on Washington in 1932 was much larger than Coxey's Army. An estimated 15,000 men participated.

The Bonus marchers, like Coxey's Army, were the product of widespread unemployment. The specific purpose of the Bonus Expeditionary Force was to pressure Congress into providing for immediate payment to World War I veterans of the 1945 matured value of so-called adjusted service certificates (comparable to 20-year endowment insurance policies) that had been issued to the veterans in 1925 to compensate them for the low level of service pay during the war. Late in 1931, Rep. Wright Patman (D Texas) had introduced a bill for immediate payment.

The Bonus marchers, led by Walter W. Waters, started arriving in Washington at the end of May 1932, three weeks after Patman's bill had been reported out unfavorably by the Ways and Means Committee. The Government halted its building program along Pennsylvania Ave. in order to provide shelter in a number of partially razed buildings. The main camp of the Bonus marchers was on the Anacostia Flats and consisted of tents and shacks. Food, clothing and other supplies were donated by private individuals and charities. *(Continued on p. 392)*

1971 Capitol Bombing Causes Extensive Damage;

Early in 1971, the Capitol suffered extensive damage when a powerful bomb exploded in the original part of the building for which George Washington laid the cornerstone in 1793. Damage was estimated at $200,000, but there were no injuries.

Site of the explosion was an unmarked rest room on the ground floor of the Senate wing. The blast demolished the rest room and caused extensive damage to six other rooms, including the Senate barbershop, a hearing room of the Senate Appropriations Committee and hideaway offices used by several Senators.

Telephone Warning

The explosion occurred at 1:32 a.m. on March 1—33 minutes after a telephone caller warned the Capitol switchboard: "This building will blow up in 30 minutes. You will get many calls like this, but this one is real. Evacuate the building. This is in protest against the Nixon involvement in Laos."

Immediately after the warning call, a search of the Capitol building was conducted by the 15 members of the Capitol police force then on duty. Their search took them to the general area of the rest room, but they did not check the room itself, they said, because it had been inspected only a few minutes before the call was received.

Subsequently, an army munitions expert told a Senate subcommittee "it is our belief" that the explosive had been concealed behind a false wall in the rest room. He speculated that the blast could have been caused by 15 to 20 pounds of dynamite connected to a "delayed timing device" and smuggled into the Capitol "in an ordinary briefcase." It was noted that the building had been open to tourists until 4:30 p.m. on the day preceding the bombing, a Sunday, and that while entrances to the Capitol were routinely guarded, no check of visitors or inspection of parcels was customary.

Responsibility for Explosion

Responsibility for the blast was promptly claimed by a group calling itself the Weather Underground. In identical letters to the *New York Times* and the Associated Press, the group wrote: "We have attacked the Capitol because it is, along with the White House and the Pentagon, the worldwide symbol of the Government which is now attacking Indochina."

Some Government officials, however, expressed doubt that the bombing was the result of a conspiracy. Attorney General John Mitchell said March 2 that the evidence pointed to "less than a conspiracy." "Every time we have one of these occurrences there are such communications," he said, "but it doesn't mean they were actually involved." The Federal Bureau of Investigation (FBI), which was investigating the explosion, had no comment.

Meanwhile, FBI questioning of Capitol employees prompted speculation that the bombing might have been the work of a Congressional employee. Although access to the Capitol was free, the rest room where the bomb was placed was not only unmarked but opened off a small corridor not used by the general public. Even the janitor who cleaned the room reportedly did not know that the enclosure where the bomb was thought to have been hidden had a top that could be lifted off.

A week after the explosion, Senate leaders announced that an anonymous donor had offered a $100,000 reward for information leading to the arrest and conviction of the bomber.

The first publicized move in the investigation of the bombing occurred April 27 when Government agents took Leslie Bacon, 19, into custody as a material witness with a personal knowledge of the bombing. The FBI said Miss Bacon was also suspected of participation in the bombing.

Miss Bacon, whose home was in Atherton, Calif., was arrested in Washington, D.C., where she was working on plans for an antiwar protest. She was charged with no crime but was held under $100,000 bond as a witness for a grand jury in Seattle, Wash., which was investigating the bombing.

A letter signed "Weather Underground," made public May 3, said Miss Bacon was "completely innocent of any involvement in the bombing of the U.S. Capitol." The letter, addressed to Miss Bacon's mother, said: "We know this for a fact, because as the FBI and Justice Department well know, our organization did the bombing."

Reactions to Incident

President Nixon and Congressional leaders viewed the bombing as a symbolic attack on the Government itself and agreed on the importance of keeping the Capitol open to the public. The President said that "necessary protective action" should be taken but that "the important thing is that these great buildings not be closed to the public." Senate Majority Leader Mansfield (D Mont.) called the incident "outrageous and sacrilegious." Senate Minority Leader Hugh Scott (R Pa.) said it was a political act of terrorism by groups "who believe that if they cannot persuade by reason or by logic, perhaps they can terrify the American people." Sen. George McGovern (D S.D.) attributed the bombing to "our Vietnam madness."

Tighter Security Proposed

In the wake of the bombing, there was widespread agreement on the need for additional security measures on Capitol Hill. The Capitol was briefly closed to visitors on the morning following the bombing but was reopened at midday. Thereafter Capitol police were instructed to check all briefcases and large packages brought into the Capitol itself and the Senate and House office buildings by employees as well as tourists. The bombing site remained closed pending repairs.

Incident Linked to Antiwar Protests

On March 2, the Senate Public Works Subcommittee on Public Buildings and Grounds held a hearing on the bombing incident at which Senate Sergeant at Arms Robert G. Dunphy and Capitol Police Chief James M. Powell testified on the difficulties of protecting the Capitol. Powell said "200 to 300 bomb threats" had been received at the Capitol in the past few years, and "each call is treated as a real threat." However, said Dunphy, "Remember, we have six large buildings. The Capitol is like a Swiss cheese with all its tunnels and crannies and catacombs. We also have 150 acres of ground. When we say we conduct a search, we do the best we can."

Dunphy said that during the tourist season as many as 25,000 visitors pass through the Rotunda daily and that thorough inspection of all visitors would be extremely difficult. Powell recommended that certain out-of-the-way sections of the Capitol be closed to the public in the interest of security. He also suggested curtailment of patronage appointments to the Capitol police force. Patronage appointees constituted about 25 percent of the authorized force of 622 officers, he said.

The bombing prompted a number of calls by Members of Congress for installation of closed-circuit television systems and electronic devices to detect bombs or dangerous weapons. Dunphy said, however, that the Capitol Police Board had investigated such systems and had not found any that would be satisfactory.

Meanwhile, the incident was expected to give impetus to the work of a special commission directed to plan and oversee the modernization of the House galleries, including the enclosure of the galleries with soundproof glass. The project was authorized under the Legislative Reorganization Act of 1970, but at the time of the bombing commission members had not been named by House Speaker Carl Albert (D Okla.). Although noise reduction was the stated purpose of the enclosure, 1970 House debate on the proposal made it clear that at least some Representatives—recalling the March 1, 1954, shooting of five Members by Puerto Rican nationalists—had security in mind as well.

Extent of Damage

During its March 2 hearings, the Senate Subcommittee also heard testimony on the extent of the bomb damage from George M. White, newly appointed Architect of the Capitol. White said there was apparently no structural damage to the building and that the West Front had "not been damaged in any way," although it was only about 40 feet from the site of the explosion. White's predecessor, J. George Stewart, had contended that the West Front was so structurally weak as to be endangered by vibrations from aircraft flying overhead and had promoted a $34-million project to extend the West Front and add 4.5 acres of new space to the Capitol.

An earlier report by the Architect's Office said, "The damage consists primarily of cracked and otherwise damaged walls, blown-out doors and windows, destruction of trim, paneled jambs, weakened and damaged masonry floor, arch construction and damage to chandeliers." The report said that "Some of the weakened arch construction undoubtedly will require shoring."

Antiwar Protests

The Capitol bombing occurred at a time when antiwar groups were mounting a new series of demonstrations against U.S. involvement in Southeast Asia. Although Washington had been the scene of numerous antiwar protests for several years, prior to 1971 most of the major protests had not focused on the Capitol itself.

The 1971 round of demonstrations began April 18-23 when about 2,300 Vietnam veterans came to Washington to participate in what they called Dewey Canyon III—"a military incursion into the country of Congress." Led by the Vietnam Veterans Against the War, the former soldiers camped on the Mall a quarter of a mile from the Capitol, marched to Arlington Cemetery to pay their respects to war dead, conducted guerrilla theater and a mock search and destroy mission on the steps of the Old Senate Office Building, threw away military medals and ribbons at the foot of the bronze statue of Chief Justice John Marshall on the west side of the Capitol and attempted to visit every Member of Congress.

On April 24, a rally sponsored by the National Peace Action Coalition drew an estimated 175,000 persons to the steps leading to the Capitol's West Front, for what was believed to have been the largest demonstration ever held there. Although the event was peaceful, strict security was maintained at House and Senate office buildings, and the Capitol itself was protected by a barricade.

The April 24 demonstration was followed by 10 days of escalating protests that began April 26 with lobbying of Congress and disruption in the Senate galleries and Congressional office buildings. In the days that followed, the protesters—who called themselves the Mayday Tribe—attempted work stoppages at the Departments of Justice and Health, Education and Welfare, the Internal Revenue Service and Selective Service headquarters. On May 3, the protesters made an unsuccessful attempt to halt morning rush-hour traffic into Washington. They were met by 5,100 Washington policemen, backed by 10,000 Federal troops; the result was an unprecedented mass arrest of approximately 7,000 persons. The following day 2,700 demonstrators were arrested. The protest ended May 5 with the arrest of about 1,200 demonstrators on the steps of the Capitol's East Front.

The House passed the bonus bill June 15 by a 211-176 roll-call vote, but it was rejected by the Senate June 17 on an 18-62 roll-call vote. A contemporary journalist described the Senate action as a "rebuke to what some Senators regarded as practically physical intimidation by the bonus marchers."

The Bonus marchers remained in Washington hoping to pressure the Senate into reversing its vote. Congress adjourned on July 16 without reconsidering the bonus bill, but it authorized $100,000 in loans to veterans to enable them to return home. However, an estimated 11,000 people were still in camps a week after Congress had adjourned.

The Bonus Expeditionary Force was finally dispersed by Federal troops on July 28. Troops were called to quell a riot which broke out when the police tried to evict marchers who were camping out in Federally owned buildings. The Federal troops were led by the Army Chief of Staff, Gen. Douglas MacArthur. Maj. Dwight D. Eisenhower commanded a tank detachment. The marchers were driven towards Anacostia and their encampment was burned that night. The following day President Hoover said of the marchers, "Government cannot be coerced by mob rule."

Civil Rights March, 1963

A disciplined but spontaneously enthusiastic crowd estimated at over 200,000, mostly Negroes but including a number of whites, marched slowly from the Washington Monument on Aug. 28, 1963, toward their symbolic destination, the Lincoln Memorial. The "March on Washington for Jobs and Freedom," was the largest public demonstration ever held in the nation's capital.

The march represented the efforts of 10 national organizations, including labor and religious groups, which joined their forces for the first time in the one-day civil rights demonstration.

The sponsoring groups were: American Jewish Congress, Congress of Racial Equality (CORE), AFL-CIO Industrial Union Department, National Association for the Advancement of Colored People, National Conference of Catholics for Interracial Justice, National Council of Churches of Christ in America, Southern Christian Leadership Conference, Student Nonviolent Coordinating Committee ("Snick"), National Urban League and Negro American Labor Council. A. Philip Randolph of the Negro American Labor Council was the chief promoter and director of the march; he was assisted by deputy director Bayard Rustin.

To maintain order, there was a heavy guard, and most Washingtonians stayed at home. However, fears of trouble never materialized as the march took on a dignified, good-natured air and a threatened white counter-demonstration fizzled.

Demonstrators began to gather early in the morning in the vicinity of the Washington Monument. The leaders held prearranged meetings with Congressional leaders of both parties.

As the march started, the civil rights leaders joined hands and marched to the Lincoln Memorial, preceded and followed by thousands carrying placards, singing and chanting.

The 10 announced goals of the march were:

• Comprehensive and effective civil rights legisla-

tion from the present Congress—without compromise or filibuster—to guarantee all Americans access to all public accommodations; decent housing; adequate and integrated education and the right to vote.

• Withholding of Federal funds from all programs in which discrimination exists.

• Desegregation of all school districts in 1963.

• Enforcement of the 14th Amendment—reducing Congressional representation of states where citizens are disfranchised.

• A new Executive Order banning discrimination in all housing supported by Federal funds.

• Authority for the Attorney General to institute injunctive suits when any constitutional right is violated.

• A massive Federal program to train and place all unemployed workers—Negro and white—in meaningful and dignified jobs at decent wages.

• A national minimum wage act that will give all Americans a decent standard of living. (Government surveys show that anything less than $2 an hour will not meet that goal.)

• A broadened minimum wage law to include all areas of employment still excluded.

• A Federal Fair Employment Practices Act barring discrimination by Federal, state, and municipal governments, and by employers, contractors, employment agencies, and trade unions.

Poor People's Campaign, 1968

Poor people from all over the country converged on Washington in May 1968 in a massive lobbying effort aimed at getting the Federal Government to adopt a far-reaching and costly set of housing, employment, food distribution and welfare programs.

Participants in the "Poor People's Campaign" constructed "Resurrection City," a plywood and canvas shantytown campsite on the Mall near the Lincoln Memorial, which eventually housed more than 3,000 people. The campaign was capped by a huge but orderly "Solidarity Day" rally June 19 at the Lincoln Memorial and Washington Monument which drew an estimated 50,000 demonstrators.

The Poor People's Campaign was conceived by the late Rev. Dr. Martin Luther King Jr., the head of the Southern Christian Leadership Conference (SCLC). King was engaged in organizing the campaign at the time he was assassinated April 4 in Memphis, Tenn. His death forced a postponement of the start of the campaign, which had initially been scheduled to begin in Washington on April 22, the day Congress was to return from its Easter recess.

Led by King's successor as president of the SCLC, the Rev. Ralph David Abernathy, a longtime King lieutenant, 100 leaders of the nation's black, white, Indian and Mexican-American poor arrived in Washington on April 29 to present their demands to the Administration and to Congress.

The legislative demands of the Poor People's Campaign were submitted to key Members of Congress and Cabinet members over the period April 29-May 2. Specific demands were presented to each Cabinet official visited, including the Secretaries of Agriculture, Health,

Education and Welfare, Housing and Urban Development, Interior, Labor, the Secretary of State, the Attorney General and the Director of the Office of Economic Opportunity.

Although new programs were sought in some areas, the principal requests were for more spending on existing programs and for a greater emphasis on meeting the needs of the poor within existing programs. Common to the "must-list" sent to each Department head was a demand that the poor be included in the planning and administration of Federal programs.

The Washington, D.C., headquarters of the Poor People's Campaign was closed July 19. Of all the arrests made during the demonstration, 261 took place on the Capitol grounds to which Abernathy led a band of marchers on June 24 in the hope that he would "be granted the opportunity of speaking to the Congress from its floor...on this hunger question."

Anti-Demonstration Laws. Congress had enacted a bill in 1967 to strengthen laws governing conduct within the Capitol and on the Capitol grounds. The President signed the measure on the eve of a major peace march on Washington.

The bill was designed to supplement and to clarify existing laws, some of which dated from 1892. Clarification had been urged in two 1967 opinions of the U.S. Court of Appeals.

The Court of Appeals had reversed the convictions of two demonstrators at the Capitol who had been sentenced under the general disorderly conduct statute applicable to the District of Columbia. The court had said *(Feeley v. District of Columbia)* that the "defendants could not be required to select from the maze of small statutes here potentially applicable the course probably to be chosen by the prosecutor." The "maze" consisted of:

A 1946 statute which prohibited demonstrations, loud or abusive language and the discharge of firearms on the Capitol grounds but specifically excluded the Capitol buildings from coverage of its provisions.

An 1892 statute covering disorderly conduct in public buildings belonging to the United States, including the Capitol.

A general disorderly conduct statute applicable to the District of Columbia.

Each of the statutes carried different penalties.

Incidents involving demonstrators at the Capitol in 1967 had included forceful entry into the House gallery by supporters of a rat extermination bill, dropping of antiwar leaflets onto the Senate floor from the gallery, and a demonstration by welfare recipients at a committee hearing.

As signed into law, the 1967 bill (PL 90-108):

Made it a felony, subject to a $5,000 fine and/or five years' imprisonment, for unauthorized persons to:

Carry or discharge firearms and other dangerous devices on the Capitol grounds or buildings. (The House report (H Rept 745) made it clear that Members keeping guns for display, protection or sporting use would be exempted under regulations to be drawn up by the Capitol Police Board.)

Knowingly, with force and violence, enter or remain upon the floor of either house of Congress.

Made it a misdemeanor, subject to a $500 fine and/or six months' imprisonment, for unauthorized persons willfully and knowingly to:

Enter or remain on the floor of either house or the cloakrooms, lobbies, or other private rooms, or in the gallery of either house in violation of the rules.

Enter or remain in any room in the Capitol buildings with intent to disrupt the orderly conduct of official business.

Utter loud or abusive language or engage in disorderly conduct on the grounds or in the buildings with intent to disrupt official business.

Obstruct passages or engage in acts of violence in the buildings or grounds or to picket or demonstrate within the Capitol buildings. (A 1946 provision which prohibited standing or moving in processions on the Capitol grounds or displaying the banners of any party, organization or movement except on authorized occasions of "national interest" was left unchanged.)

Precautionary Move in House. In 1970, recurring incidents of violence finally persuaded the House of Representatives to consider breaking with tradition. The Legislative Reorganization Act of 1970 authorized a five-man Special Commission on Modernization of House Gallery Facilities to study enclosing the galleries in glass. The open galleries always have been viewed as symbolic of a democratic society.

Bibliography

Books

Aikman, Lonnelle, *We, the People.* U.S. Capitol Historical Society in cooperation with the National Geographic Society, 1969.

Bryan, Wilhelmus B., *A History of the National Capital.* Macmillan Co., 1914.

Frary, I. T., *They Built the Capitol.* Garrett and Massie, 1940.

Green, Constance McLaughlin, *Washington, Village and Capital, 1800-1878.* Princeton University Press, 1962.

Hazelton, George C. Jr., *The National Capitol.* J.F. Taylor and Co., 1914.

Leech, Margaret, *Reveille in Washington.* Grosset and Dunlap, 1941.

Records of the Columbia Historical Society.

Government Publications

Brown, Glenn, *History of the United States Capitol.* Government Printing Office, 1900.

The Capitol. Government Printing Office, 1970.

Compilation of Works of Art and Other Objects in the U.S. Capitol. Government Printing Office, 1965.

Documentary History of the Construction and Development of the U.S. Capitol Building and Grounds. Government Printing Office, 1904.

The Library Of Congress And The Congressional Research Service

INFORMATION is indispensable to a legislator. Although it cannot take the place of intelligence, judgment or concern, information is essential as a guide to the practical solution of problems of public policy. And it is valuable only if it is accurate. Charles A. Goodrum, an officer of the Library of Congress, wrote in the *Library Journal* in 1965: "Diogenes in his best days never sought truth so vigorously as our legislators."

Senators and Representatives rely on a variety of sources for the information they seek. They read, listen to visitors, fly to problem areas for direct observation, and conduct hearings. They also use the facilities of one of the world's great repositories of information, their own treasury of recorded knowledge, the Library of Congress. Of the two functions of the Library of Congress—to assist Congress and to serve as a national library—the first is probably less well known, but it has a more immediate impact on public affairs. In a radio broadcast on July 21, 1945, Luther H. Evans, then the Librarian of Congress, described the Library's work in assisting Congress as "the inspiring labor of holding a light for the guidance of the nation's leaders."

Service to Congress

No Senator or Representative can keep in his own head or his own office all of the information he requires when making decisions on agricultural policy, consumer needs, the balance of international payments, intercity transportation, labor conditions, missile systems, and an almost endless series of additional subjects. He must turn to published sources for facts, and interpretations of facts, that will help him to make wise judgments. In his choice of published sources, he must go beyond the special pleadings of people with axes to grind. The Library of Congress stands ready to furnish him with unbiased data.

The Library, on request, supplies Members of the two houses and Congressional committees with published material relevant to problems that concern them, finds the answers to specific questions, makes up reading lists, compiles and analyzes pertinent literature, and distills the pros and cons of policy issues. In many cases, it makes available the services of an expert from its staff, who confers with a Senator or Representative or advises him in his conduct of a hearing. It sometimes will write a speech for a Member, but it does its best to remain nonpartisan in politics and impartial on public questions.

The Joint Congressional Committee on the Library has the responsibility of overseeing the Library's services to Congress. The Committee traces its origin to the Act of April 24, 1800, which provided for the purchase of books for the use of Congress at the new seat of Government on the Potomac River, "pursuant to such directions as shall be given...by a joint committee of both houses of Congress to be appointed for that purpose." The Committee consists of five Senators and five Representatives. When a Senator is chairman, a Representative is vice chairman, and vice versa. The Committee oversees every administrative unit of the Library but pays special attention to the Congressional Research Service (formerly the Legislative Reference Service), which has Congress as its sole client.

Service As A National Library

Luther Evans cited statistics in his 1945 broadcast which were soon outdated, but he made a point which is still valid. Referring to the Library's second function, he said: "The Library of Congress is the national library of the United States. This is so in the sense that the Library's work touches the life of every American citizen whether he is aware of it or not. He may never have sat in one of its 20 reading rooms to read one of its six million books, or studied American history in its 10 million manuscripts, or pored over its million and a half maps,...but through the legislation which is enacted by Congress, through the infinite variety of ways in which his life is affected by multitudinous Government agencies, through the research carried on by universities, industrial organizations, and private scholars, he cannot escape its effects."

Conflict of Functions

Sometimes, the Library of Congress is tugged in two directions by its twin functions—to serve as a national library and to serve Congress. On a day in 1949, the following dialogue reportedly took place in the Library's Main Reading Room:

Irate reader. "I've been asking for that book for six weeks now, and they keep telling me, 'It's in use—it's in use.' Wha'dya mean it's in use?"

Joseph Rubin, reference librarian. "It's being used by a Member of Congress."

Irate reader. "A Congressman! Why is a Congressman using it? I thought Congress had its own library!"

Rubin. "You may believe it. They do. And you're in it."

—*Library Journal*, Feb. 1, 1965, p. 572.

Whether the Library of Congress is the greatest library on earth is a matter of opinion. In the number of its holdings, it is probably preeminent, but the ways of measuring quantity in this field are not yet standardized, especially as to manuscript, music, and other nonbook possessions. In measuring greatness, it also is hard to compare objectively the Library's extensive collection of George Washington manuscripts with, say, the British Museum's two signed copies of the Magna Carta. Nevertheless, James Truslow Adams, in his book *The Epic of America,* felt warranted in calling the Library of Congress "a symbol of what democracy can accomplish,...a perfect working-out, in a concrete example, of the American dream."

Origin and Development of the Library

Late in 1784, when the Continental Congress was preparing to move from Trenton to New York City, the New York Society offered to make its library of about 5,000 books available to the legislators. Congress began using the library in January 1785. The First Congress under the Constitution, which convened in New York in 1789, also used the society's library until the seat of the Federal Government was moved to Philadelphia in 1790. From 1790 to 1800, Congress had access to the collection of the Library Company of Philadelphia, the oldest library in America, established in 1731 and superintended for a time by Benjamin Franklin. It had about 7,700 volumes in the 1790s.

The Act of April 24, 1800, on the transfer of Government offices to Washington appropriated $5,000 for purchasing "such books as may be necessary for the use of Congress" and "fitting up a suitable apartment for containing them." About 740 books were bought with these funds and placed in a room in the unfinished Capitol under the supervision of the Secretary of the Senate and the Clerk of the House. Supervision of the library by a single person was intended by an Act of Jan. 26, 1802, which authorized the President of the United States to appoint a Librarian of Congress. But President Thomas Jefferson thought the post was not a full-time job and appointed John Beckley, Clerk of the House, to serve also as Librarian of Congress. Beckley did so until his death in April 1807.

Replacement of Books Burned by British

In November 1807, Jefferson appointed Patrick Magruder to succeed Beckley both as Clerk of the House and as Librarian. Members of Congress were critical of Magruder in 1814 for what they deemed his lack of diligence in removing only a part, not all, of the library when British troops entered Washington. The invaders burned most of the books remaining in the Capitol on Aug. 24, 1814. A newspaper published in Nottingham, England, not long afterward condemned the burning as "an act without example in modern wars." Magruder, insisting that he had done all that was reasonably within his power, resigned as Clerk of the House and automatically gave up his position as Librarian of Congress.

During the fall and winter of 1814-15, while Congress was meeting temporarily in Blodget's Hotel about a mile west of the damaged Capitol, Jefferson, then residing at Monticello, offered to sell his 6,500-volume library

to the Government to make up the loss sustained by Congress in the book-burning. Anti-Jeffersonian Members of Congress opposed the proposition on the ground that Jefferson's library included books by Voltaire and other unorthodox thinkers. But both houses passed a bill appropriating $23,950 to make the purchase. President James Madison signed the bill on Jan. 30, 1815, and Jefferson's books were transported to Washington by horse cart.

First Full-Time Librarian of Congress

The acquisition of Jefferson's library, according to Lucy Salamanca's *Fortress of Freedom; The Story of the Library of Congress,* "proved to be the life-stream that restored energy and enterprise to the expiring... Library of Congress." Whereas the Library's previous collection of books had been narrowly utilitarian, Jefferson's library took all knowledge for its province. Recognizing the new importance in store for the Library, President Madison on Jan. 21, 1815, had appointed the first full-time Librarian of Congress. The man whom he chose, George Watterston, was a lawyer, novelist, playwright and newspaper editor. Watterston, through his wit and zeal, made the Library of Congress the cultural center of life in Washington. In December 1818, the Library was moved from Blodget's Hotel to the Capitol, where it remained, though moved from time to time within the building, until 1897.

Meehan's 32 Years As Librarian

President Andrew Jackson's wholesale displacement of non-Democrats holding Federal jobs reached Watterston, a Whig, less than three months after Inauguration Day. On May 28, 1829, the President dismissed Watterston and appointed as his successor John S. Meehan, publisher of a Washington newspaper, the *United States Telegraph,* which had supported Jackson in the election campaign. Meehan became the first of three Librarians of Congress to stay in the post for more than three decades. He survived changes in the Administration over a period of 32 years.

During Meehan's incumbency, the Library's collection of books in the field of law was notably expanded. A count in 1832 showed that the Library then owned 2,011 law books, of which 639 had been bought from Jefferson. Members of the two houses felt the need for a still larger law library. An Act of July 14, 1832, "to increase and improve the law department of the Library of Congress," provided for the establishment of a separate branch of the Library for law books, with a separate location in the Capitol. The Act appropriated a lump sum of $5,000, and authorized subsequent annual appropriations of $1,000 for five years, for the purchase of additional books in the field of law, in accordance with recommendations to be made by the Chief Justice. After the expiration of the five-year expansion program, money for law books was included in the regular appropriations for the Library of Congress.

Prior to 1846, copyright applicants were required by law to deposit copies of their publications with the Secretary of State and the clerk of the nearest U.S. district court. By an Act of Aug. 10, 1846, Congress provided that one copy of every copyrighted work should be sent to the

Library of Congress. This law, however, contained no teeth and was largely ignored by publishers. It was repealed by an Act of Feb. 5, 1859, which transferred jurisdiction over copyrights from the Department of State to the Department of the Interior. Disappointment in the Library of Congress over the failure of the Act of 1846 to increase its collections significantly had been compounded by a fire on Dec. 24, 1851, which destroyed 35,000 of the Library's 55,000 books.

President Abraham Lincoln, apparently suspecting that Meehan was a southern sympathizer, removed him from office on May 24, 1861, and appointed in his place John G. Stephenson, a legislative aide to Sen. Henry S. Lane (R Ind.). But Stephenson left the work of the Library to his assistants and entered the Union forces, receiving a citation for bravery in the Gettysburg campaign of 1863. He resigned in December 1864 to engage in private business. The meager reputation of the Library in that period is indicated by the fact that an article on American libraries published in *Harper's Monthly* in 1864 made no mention of the Library of Congress.

Term of A. R. Spofford As Librarian

Lincoln in January 1865 appointed as the new Librarian of Congress Ainsworth R. Spofford, a bookseller, publisher, editor, and writer who had served as Assistant Librarian under Stephenson. Congress soon passed a copyright law, the Act of March 3, 1865, which was strong enough in its deposit requirements to result in the building up, in the Library, of a comprehensive collection representative of every trend in American literature and every facet of American thought. By an Act of July 8, 1870, the Government's copyright work

was transferred from the Department of the Interior to the Library of Congress, where it has remained.

Under Spofford's direction, the Library of Congress made a number of sizable additions to its holdings, including the transfer of a large collection of materials from the Smithsonian Institution in 1866-67 and the purchase in 1867 for $100,000 of the Peter Force collection of early American newspapers and other Americana. The Library acquired important publications of foreign governments under a system for the international exchange of official documents authorized by a joint resolution of Congress approved March 2, 1867. The number of books and pamphlets which the Library owned grew from about 100,000 when Spofford took charge to more than one million in 1897. David C. Mearns, Assistant Librarian for the American Collections in the 1960s, referred to Spofford as "the Grand Acquisitor."

When Spofford had completed 33 years as Librarian, in 1897, advancing age led him to resign. President William McKinley on July 1, 1897, appointed John R. Young as Librarian, and Spofford became Young's assistant. Young had been a foreign correspondent in Europe for the *New York Herald* and had served as Minister to China from 1882 to 1885. He supervised the transfer of the Library from the Capitol to its own building during the period from August to November 1897. Young achieved distinction as the first Librarian of Congress to hire women as librarians. He died on Jan. 17, 1899, after only one and one-half years in office.

Herbert Putnam's Long Tenure at Library

After Young's death, McKinley offered the post of Librarian of Congress to Herbert Putnam, 38-year-old member of the Putnam publishing family, lawyer, and librarian of the Boston Public Library. Putnam declined the offer initially but then reconsidered and was appointed on March 13, 1899. He wrote a year later: "The Library of Congress is not now, as a collection, an organic collection, even for the most particular service that it has to render; it is not yet classified, nor equipped with the mechanism necessary to its effective use; the present organization is but partial, and the resources have yet to be provided not merely for the proper development of the collection, but for the work of bringing the existing material into condition for effective service."

Putnam during his long service as Librarian was responsible for innovations, improvements, and enlargements in every area of the Library's work. He organized the Aeronautics, Music, and Orientalia Divisions, as well as other units. On the basis of a special appropriation, he established the Legislative Reference Service (now the Congressional Research Service).

He arranged for "chairs" and consultantships in the Library for specialists in political science, military history, Roman law, poetry, the fine arts, and other fields. He instituted the administration by the Library of funds donated by individuals for expansion of the Library's services.

Noteworthy among the special materials acquired during Putnam's service as Librarian were the G. V. Yudin library of 80,000 books on Russia and Siberia, a Japanese library of 45,000 volumes, the J. B. Thacher collection of 840 European incunabula (books printed before 1500), the library of Harry Houdini on magic and

---

Library Trust Fund Board

An Act of March 3, 1925, created the Library of Congress Trust Fund Board and authorized it to receive and administer gifts and bequests to the Library, apart from money donated or bequeathed for immediate disbursement. The board consists of the Secretary of the Treasury (chairman), the chairman of the Joint Committee on the Library, the Librarian of Congress (secretary), and two persons appointed by the President for terms of five years each. The board may invest its assets in stocks or bonds and may lend money to the U.S. Government and collect interest. Gifts to the Library of Congress, and earnings of the Trust Fund Board, are tax-exempt.

Assets of trust funds administered by the board in 1970 included (1) more than $5 million on loan to the U.S. Treasury at interest and (2) entitlement to one-half of the income of investments valued at $1.2 million. The largest gifts administered by the board up to now have been those received from Mrs. Gertrude Clarke Whittall, amounting to almost $2.5 million, for maintenance of Stradivari instruments donated by Mrs. Whittall, presentation of programs in which those instruments are used, and presentation of poetry and literary programs.

occultism, and one of three extant perfect copies of the Gutenberg Bible. Putnam initiated or supervised projects for the sale of printed catalog cards to other libraries, photocopying of European manuscripts pertaining to American history, distribution of Braille books to the blind, and interlibrary loans of books. Another innovation was the National Union Catalog of books owned by large American libraries, which helps a researcher to locate a book he needs but cannot find in the city where he lives. The Library received, during Putnam's stewardship, a gift of almost $100,000 from Mrs. Elizabeth Sprague Coolidge of Boston which made possible the construction in the Library of· an auditorium for chamber music performances and other uses.

Changes at Library in Past 30 Years

In 1938, when Putnam reached the age of 77, Congress passed an Act, signed June 20, which provided "That upon separation from service, by resignation or otherwise,...Herbert Putnam, the present Librarian of Congress, who has served in that office for 39 years, shall become Librarian Emeritus." Putnam had written to President Franklin D. Roosevelt, June 15, of his satisfaction that the choice of his successor "rests with a President who can fully appreciate the requirements of the position under the recent evolution of the institution." He rounded out 40 years of service in April 1939.

The Regime of the Poet. Roosevelt on May 3, 1939, wrote to his friend and mentor, Supreme Court Justice Felix Frankfurter: "I have had a bad time picking a Librarian to succeed Putnam. What would you think of Archie MacLeish? He is not a professional librarian nor is he a special student of incunabula or ancient manuscripts. Nevertheless, he has lots of qualifications that said specialists have not." Frankfurter favored the choice of MacLeish. His reply of May 11 said in part: "The librarians that have left the most enduring marks have not been technical librarians....What is wanted in the directing head of a great library is imaginative energy and vision. He should be a man who knows books, loves books, and makes books."

The announcement of MacLeish's nomination, June 7, 1939, set off a torrent of opposition. David C. Mearns, Chief of the Manuscript Division, wrote of the affair in the May 1965 issue of the *Atlantic:* "The professional library associations, with degrees of intensity varying from petulance to passion, protested with prideful, proprietary indignation. He was not even a recognized amateur; he had no standing in the guild; whatever his gifts for other callings might be, he was starkly disqualified for a position to which only their own anointed might aspire." The governing body of the American Library Association asked on June 13, 1939, that the Senate reject MacLeish's nomination on the ground that he "could not qualify for the librarianship of any college or public library in America which attempts to maintain professional standards."

The Senate rejected the A.L.A.'s advice and confirmed MacLeish on June 29 by a vote of 64 to 8. MacLeish took office early in October 1939, and Putnam became Librarian Emeritus. The period in the administration of the Library of Congress which followed was called by historian Paul Angle the regime of the poet. Mearns wrote, some 26 years later, "Happily, they (the professionals) were soon conciliated...and when they found their voice again they found that it was his." The Librarian told an audience at the Carnegie Institute in Pittsburgh, two weeks after taking office, that his reason for accepting the Librarianship was his desire to fight with intellectual weapons the growing threat of fascism.

MacLeish set out to strengthen the Library of Congress in three directions. (1) He associated some of the best minds with the Library and with the government by appointing, for example, Allen Tate to the Library's chair of poetry, Thomas Mann as consultant on German literature, and Saint-John Perse as consultant on French poetry. His leadership in these and related measures gave him in some respects the status of a minister of culture. (2) He was active personally, and used the Library as a springboard, in the war for the minds of men that was a part of the World War; concurrently with his librarianship, he served as head of the Office of Facts and Figures and as Assistant Director of War Information. Immediately after the war, when he was Assistant Secretary of State, MacLeish headed the American delegation to the conference which drew up the plans for the U.N. Educational, Scientific and Cultural Organization.

(3) He strengthened the Library's internal organization. Shortly before resigning in 1944 to become Assistant Secretary of State, he wrote in his Annual Report: "To succeed Mr. Putnam was a good deal like inheriting an enormous house...from a wise, well-loved, strong-minded, charming and particular uncle who knew where everything was and how everything worked and what everyone could do but had left no indications in his will." Though best known as a poet, MacLeish was an able administrator. He brought order into the fiscal, personnel and management aspects of the Library's operations. A staff member wrote of MacLeish's service as Librarian, "The brush of the comet gave a new dimension to the Library."

Recent Library Helmsmen. MacLeish's successor as Librarian of Congress was Luther H. Evans, whose career had included service as a teacher of political science at Stanford, Princeton, New York University and Dartmouth; head of the Library's Legislative Reference Service; and Chief Assistant Librarian. President Harry S Truman nominated Evans for the top Library job June 18, 1945, and he was confirmed without opposition June 30. The choice of Evans was applauded by the world of scholarship as well as by the library profession. He had served as Acting Librarian during long periods when MacLeish was otherwise occupied.

Evans presided over the opening to the public at midnight July 26, 1947, of the collection of papers of Abraham Lincoln which had been deposited in the Library in 1919 by Robert Todd Lincoln, the President's son. The opening date, as stipulated by Robert Lincoln, was exactly 21 years after his own death. Evans also saw to the transfer from the main building of the Library of Congress to the National Archives, in 1952, of two documents—the signed originals of the Declaration of Independence and the Constitution of the United States—which had been brought to the Library in 1921 from the Department of State. Although he would have preferred to keep the two documents in the Library, the Joint Committee on the Library decided otherwise.

Evans represented the United States at the founding conference of UNESCO in November 1945 and at general conferences of the organization from 1947 to 1952. At the general conference of 1953 UNESCO selected him as its director general, and he resigned as Librarian of Congress on July 5 of that year. Verner W. Clapp, Chief Assistant Librarian, served as Acting Librarian from then until Sept. 1, 1954, when President Eisenhower's nominee for the post, L. Quincy Mumford, took office.

Mumford had been director of the Cleveland Public Library. The President nominated him as Librarian of Congress April 22, 1954, and the Senate confirmed the nomination on July 29. Mumford was the first graduate of a professional library school to serve as Librarian of Congress. In the course of his service in the post, he has appointed outspoken nonconformists as consultants to the Library. These appointments have served to balance an episode which occurred a little more than a year after he became Librarian. During that episode, Mumford found himself in the middle of a battle between political liberals and those, like Sen. Joseph R. McCarthy (R Wis.), with a propensity to brand liberals as unpatriotic.

The Library invited Dr. Albert Sprague Coolidge, son of one of the Library's principal benefactors, Mrs. Elizabeth Sprague Coolidge, to serve on the advisory committee of the Coolidge Foundation, which played a part in administering the Coolidge gifts to the Library. But when Coolidge's association with ultra-liberal causes came to public attention and aroused criticism, the invitation was withdrawn. The weekly Library of Congress Information Bulletin explained on Feb. 6, 1956: "The Librarian felt that Dr. Coolidge's past associations and activities, entirely aside from the 'loyalty' or 'security' issue, would impair that objectivity in the fulfillment of his duties that one has a right to expect of a public employee, even in an advisory capacity on cultural matters."

Former Librarian MacLeish, in an address at Carleton College in Northfield, Minn., on Sept. 22, 1956, commented acidly on the Library's statement of the preceding February. MacLeish said, "What is clearly implied was that a man is not suitable for work in a library who has taken sides on public issues." But taking sides on issues of freedom to read and freedom to speak one's mind, MacLeish said, was exactly what a librarian should do. "No librarian," he said, "who believes in the freedom guaranteed by the Constitution, and who detests authoritarianism, can avoid taking positions on controversial issues."

Mumford has guided the entrance of the Library of Congress into the age of automation. The Library's program in this field began in 1963 with basic work looking toward mechanical preparation of bibliographies. Later, what is called the Card Automated Reproduction and Distribution System was installed. It is based on a network of electronic hookups dubbed MARC because of its concept of Machine-Readable Cataloging. The format of MARC was worked out in prolonged consultations between the Library of Congress and the American Library Association. Other activities which the Library began to automate during the Mumford regime include identification, storage, and retrieval of single-sheet maps; compilation and publication by the Congressional Research Service of the *Digest of Public General Bills and Resolutions;* and data maintenance and reporting of the Reference Department's National Referral Center for Science and Technology.

The Library in Operation

William A. Slade, a bibliographer in the Library of Congress during the 1920s, described the Library, in a sonnet called *The National Library,* as a place "Where words that glowed of old glow yet again/Gleaming across the bournes of race and clime/Instant to serve the present world of men/Voicing in timeless speech the things of time." The Library aims "to serve the present world of men" by acquiring, organizing, and dispensing physical embodiments of human thought. These embodiments are not confined to the written word. They include many other devices for recording and communicating ideas.

Scope of The Library's Holdings

The Library of Congress possesses about 60 million items, consisting of 30 million manuscript pieces, 15 million books and pamphlets, three million maps, three million volumes and pieces of music, three million photographic items (negatives, prints, slides), three million miscellaneous items, two million "talking books" for the blind (phonograph recordings of read-aloud books), and one million books in raised characters for the blind. The Library has the world's largest collection of published aeronautical literature and the most extensive collection of incunabula in the United States. Of books in foreign languages, its Russian collection is the largest outside the Soviet Union and its Chinese and Japanese collections are the largest outside the Orient.

The manuscript collection includes the papers of most of the Presidents from George Washington through Calvin Coolidge. In the graphic arts, two of the Library's most valued possessions are the Joseph Pennell Collection of Whistleriana and an almost complete set of the Civil War pictures taken by Mathew Brady. The Archive

---

Types of Library of Congress Holdings

Books in the ordinary sense

Books and magazines in raised characters for the blind

Books and magazines recorded for the blind ("talking books")

Drawings, etchings, and other graphic representations and designs

Incunabula

Manuscripts in codex form, scrolls, sheets, and notebooks

Maps

Microfilms and microfiches (films on cards)

Motion pictures, silent and sound

Music in written and printed notations

Music on phonograph records

Music on tapes

Newspapers, loose and in bound volumes

Pamphlets

Photographic negatives, prints, and slides

Posters

Processed materials (material, usually typewritten, reproduced by nearprint processes)

Speeches, recitations, and dramatic performances on film, on phonograph records and on tape

of Recorded Poetry and Literature aims to include recorded readings by every significant living English-speaking poet. In many cases, the Library itself commissions and records the readings. It acquires books from some countries by "open" orders with publishers and book dealers for every important book published.

Administrative Organization

At the top of the pyramid in the Library's work structure is the Office of the Librarian, consisting of the Librarian, the Deputy Librarian, and the Assistant Librarian. Publicity about the library is the responsibility of three specialists attached to the Librarian's Office: the Information, Publications, and Exhibits Officers. Six departments do the major work of the Library, three having primarily reference duties and three primarily technical and housekeeping duties. Supplementing the six departments are a corps of consultants and the Library of Congress Trust Fund Board.

Reference Units. The units of the Library responsible for reference work are the Reference Department, the Congressional Research Service, and the Law Library. In the Reference Department, three divisions are devoted to geographic areas: the Hispanic Foundation, the Slavic and Central European Division, and the Orientalia Division. Two divisions deal with books as such: the Stack and Reader Division and the Rare Book Division. (The Music Division houses both books and nonbook material.) Four others specialize in nonbook material: the Manuscript, Geography and Map, Prints and Photographs, and Serial Divisions. The remaining divisions of the Reference Department deal with general reference and bibliography, federal research, reference work on science and technology, library service for the blind and the physically handicapped, and loans.

The structure of the second reference department, the Congressional Research Service, is described later in this chapter. The third reference component, the Law Library, was created in 1832. Its divisions specialize in five areas of the world: the United States and Great Britain, Europe, the Near East and Africa, the Far East, and Latin America. The bread and butter of their work consists of constitutions, statutes, decrees, and regulations; court cases; and treaties.

Technical and Housekeeping Units. The Library's technical work of facilitating the use of books is centered in the Processing Department. That department contains 17 divisions, or units comparable to divisions. First steps in this work are the selection, ordering, and exchange of books and the receipt of gifts. Subsequent steps include the classification of books by subjects, description of them for the catalog, and the production and sale of catalog cards.

In the Administrative Department, second of the Library's units devoted mainly to technical and housekeeping work, assistant directors are in charge, respectively, of management services for the entire Library, personnel of the Library, and the preservation of Library materials. The unit engaged in preservation tries to cope with "brittle books" (those printed on paper produced since the 1850s, which disintegrates after about 30 years). Some brittle books are microfilmed, while others are salvaged by pasting thin protective sheets over damaged pages. A survey made in 1970 indicated that about 25 per cent of the Library's brittle books were unavailable elsewhere in the United States and were in urgent need of preservation.

The Copyright Office, like the Processing Department, is engaged in technical work. Its implementation of the copyright laws and treaties of the United States is done, under the Register of Copyrights, in the Examining, Cataloging, Reference, and Service Divisions. U.S. copyright law is based on Acts of March 4, 1909, and July 30, 1947, but technological changes in communication have multiplied the difficulty of interpreting those statutes. Planning for thorough revision of U.S. copyright laws was begun in the late 1950s and continued throughout the 1960s but was stalled by differences over the use of copyright material by cable television.

Consultants and Trust Fund Board. In addition to the three reference and three administrative or technical departments are the Library's consultants, including a full-time Consultant in Poetry in English and part-time honorary consultants on 14 subjects. The consultants assist in the systematic development of the collections, furnish expert advice in specialized fields of knowledge, and serve as liaison between the Library and persons conducting intensive research. Consultants in recent years have included Saul Bellow, Ralph Ellison, Charles A. Lindbergh, Stephen Spender, and John Steinbeck. In addition, the Librarian relies on the Library of Congress Trust Fund Board for the administration of endowment funds established for the Library.

Buildings of Library of Congress

The Library of Congress was housed in the Capitol during most of the 19th century. William W. Bishop, librarian of the University of Michigan, writing of the expansion of the Library under Librarian A. R. Spofford in the three decades following the Civil War, remarked: "Dr. Spofford waxed old, and the Frankenstein he had created overwhelmed the Capitol." Congress, by an Act of April 15, 1886, authorized the construction of a separate building for the Library of Congress. In 1888, Gen. Thomas L. Casey, Chief of Engineers of the U.S. Army, was appointed to supervise the construction.

The new edifice, now the Library's main building, was completed in 1897 at a cost of $7 million. The Library's old quarters in the Capitol were closed in July 1897, and the new building was opened on Nov. 1 of that year. During the intervening period, one million books and pamphlets were moved. A test of the time required to locate material in the new building and deliver it by underground belts to the Capitol was conducted Oct. 27. One of the requests, for the issue of the London *Times* containing an account of the Battle of Waterloo, brought the volume of the *Times* for 1815 to the Capitol 12 minutes after receipt of the request.

The Library of Congress building is in the ornate style of the Italian Renaissance, more richly decorated inside than out, with stair, wall, and floor marbles from Tennessee, Siena (Italy), and Algeria. The Main Reading Room is viewed by thousands of tourists annually from the visitors' gallery. In addition to the attendants' counter in the center, the circular room contains about 250 well-lighted individual desk places for readers, the card catalog (which overflows into an adjoining corridor and

Organization of The Library of Congress

(Units arranged alphabetically)

OFFICE OF THE LIBRARIAN

Librarian of Congress
Deputy Librarian of Congress
Assistant Librarian of Congress

American Revolution Bicentennial Office
Chief Internal Auditor
Exhibits Office
Federal Library Committee
General Counsel

ADMINISTRATIVE DEPARTMENT

Office of the Director
  Coordinator of Building Planning
  Information Systems Office
  Photoduplication Service
Assistant Director for Management Services
  Buildings Management Office
  Central Services Division
  Financial Management Office
Assistant Director for Personnel
  Employee Relations Office
  Personnel Operations Office
  Personnel Security Office
  Placement Office
  Position Classification Office
  Training Office
Assistant Director for Preservation
  Binding Office
  Collections Maintenance Office
  Preservation Microfilming Office
  Preservation Research and Testing Office
  Restoration Office

CONGRESSIONAL RESEARCH SERVICE

Office of the Director
  American Law Division
  Congressional Reference Division
  Economics Division
  Education and Public Welfare Division
  Environmental Policy Division
  Foreign Affairs Division
  Government and General Research Division
  Library Services Division
  Science Policy Research Division
  Senior Specialists Division

COPYRIGHT OFFICE

Office of the Register
  Cataloging Division
  Examining Division
  Reference Division
  Service Division

LAW LIBRARY

Office of the Law Librarian
  American-British Law Division

Information Office
Office of the Permanent Committee
  for the Oliver Wendell Holmes
  Devise
Publications Office

European Law Division
Far Eastern Law Division
Hispanic Law Division
Near Eastern and African Law Division

PROCESSING DEPARTMENT

Office of the Director
  MARC Development Office
  National Union Catalog Publication Project
  Technical Processes Research Office
Office of the Assistant Director for Acquisitions and
  Overseas Operations
  Exchange and Gift Division
  Order Division
  Overseas Operations Division
  Selection Office
Office of the Assistant Director for Cataloging
  Decimal Classification Division
  Descriptive Cataloging Division
  MARC Editorial Office
  Office of Cataloging Instruction
  Shared Cataloging Division
  Subject Cataloging Division
Office of the Assistant Director for Processing Services
  Card Division
  Catalog Management Division
  Catalog Publication Division
  Serial Record Division

REFERENCE DEPARTMENT

Office of the Director
  Division for the Blind and Physically Handicapped
  Federal Research Division
  General Reference and Bibliography Division
  Geography and Map Division
  Hispanic Foundation
  Loan Division
  Manuscript Division
  Music Division
  Orientalia Division
  Prints and Photographs Division
  Rare Book Division
  Science and Technology Division
    National Referral Center for Science and Technology
  Serial Division
  Slavic and Central European Division
  Stack and Reader Division

Symbolism in Main Reading Room

The Main Reading Room is circular. Its circumference is divided into eight sections by massive marble pillars. Located behind the pillars, and constituting the boundaries of the room, are alcoves and two balconies containing reference books; above them is a visitors' gallery surmounted by semicircular arches with semicircular stained-glass windows. Separating the arches is one series of statues and within the arches is another. The statues separating the arches represent religion, commerce, history, art, philosophy, poetry, law, and science. Above each is a motto in gold leaf. For example, above the statue of religion are the words "What doth the Lord require of thee, but to do justly, and to love mercy, and to walk humbly with God?"

Within each arch are two bronze portrait statues representing the same eight fields: for religion, Moses and St. Paul; commerce, Columbus and Robert Fulton; history, Herodotus and Gibbon; art, Michelangelo and Beethoven; philosophy, Plato and Bacon; poetry, Homer and Shakespeare; law, Solon and James Kent (American judge and legal scholar); science, Newton and Joseph Henry (American physicist).

Above the arches is a dome of several sections. The lowest section contains 320 blue squares bordered in gold and ivory and containing gold rosettes. Above the squares is a painted collar-like area symbolizing the evolution of civilization, with winged figures corresponding to the following countries (or periods) and contributions to civilization:

Egypt, written records	Italy, fine arts
Judea, religion	Germany, art of printing
Greece, philosophy	Spain, discovery
Rome, administration	England, literature
Islam, physics	France, emancipation
Middle Ages, modern languages	America, science

At the top of the dome, above the collar, is a painting on a blue field of a female figure representing human understanding.

a room beyond), and eight alcoves rising in three tiers which house some 25,000 reference books for handy use by readers. A clock over the entrance is decorated with sculptured figures representing Father Time and the seasons.

The Main Reading Room was closed for the first time for an extended period beginning May 4, 1964, for installation of a new heating system, air-conditioning, and new lighting; improvement of the book-carrying machinery; and other renovation work. During the time when the Main Reading Room was closed, readers were directed to the Thomas Jefferson Reading Room in the annex. The renovated Reading Room in the main building was reopened on Aug. 16, 1965. The Librarian said in his Annual Report for the fiscal year 1966 that temporary offices had been installed "with the greatest regret and only out of sheer necessity, in the mezzanine of the Great Hall of the Main Building for the use of the Legislative Reference Service."

Annexes. The main building, after about three decades of use, was filling its available space faster than had been anticipated. Congress accordingly, by an Act of June 13, 1930, authorized construction of an annex adjacent to the main building. The annex building of gleaming white marble, five stories high with three additional stories below ground and a tunnel to the main building, was completed April 5, 1939, at a cost of $9 million. The main building and the annex, occupying 13 acres of land, contain 36 acres of floor space and 325 miles of book shelves.

About two and one-half decades after the annex was opened, the need for additional space again became evident. An Act of Oct. 19, 1965, authorized the expenditure of $75 million for a building which would serve the double purpose of providing a second annex to the Library of Congress and memorializing President Madison. The James Madison Memorial Building was to consist of six stories above ground and three below, with a tunnel to the main building.

Plans for the Madison Building were to be drawn up, according to the law, "after consultation with the American Institute of Architects." J. George Stewart, Architect of the Capitol (who died in office May 24, 1970), reportedly selected architects to do the work and then consulted the AIA. Hunter Lewis reported in a magazine article in February 1967 that spokesmen for the AIA "predict that one more 'Rayburn Building' is about to rise on the Hill."

Congress put off appropriating the money needed to erect the Madison Building, largely because of the tightness of the budget. At a hearing before the House Subcommittee on Public Buildings and Grounds, Oct. 29, 1969, Rep. Kenneth J. Gray (D Ill.), the Subcommittee chairman, reported that architects had made a new estimate of $90 million as the cost of the building. Librarian Mumford said at the hearing, "We are bursting at the seams in both of these buildings." An Act of March 16, 1970, increased the authorized expenditure to $90 million and thereby released $2.8 million for final plans which had been appropriated for fiscal 1970 on condition that the authorized total was increased. Money was appropriated in fiscal 1971 for excavation and other preliminary construction work.

Meanwhile, some units of the Library had had to find new quarters. The Copyright Office moved to Arlington, Va.; the Geography and Map Division, to Alexandria, Va.; and the Division for the Blind and the Physically Handicapped, to Northwest Washington. Altogether, including the branch of the Law Library in the Capitol, the Library of Congress in 1970 was operating in 15 locations.

Library's Nationwide Services

The White House, Executive Departments, and other Government agencies in Washington have their own libraries. Some of these collections are comprehensive, such as those of the Library of the Department of Agriculture and the National Library of Medicine, but many are narrowly limited in scope. All parts of the Executive Branch depend on the Library of Congress for published information not available in their own buildings. The Library regards the Executive Branch as, next to Congress, its primary client for quick provision of information and for loans of books needed for official business.

Services to Other Libraries. Libraries throughout the United States look to the Library of Congress for many kinds of services, of which five are perhaps the most important: (1) Cataloging of new books and sale of catalog cards; (2) maintenance of the National Union Catalog, which shows the holdings of almost 700 large libraries in the United States; (3) conducting research in library technology; (4) administering a worldwide cooperative acquisitions program; and (5) lending books. In marketing the first of these services, the Library's Card Division sells not only individual cards in the millions annually, but also, as a part of library automation, magnetic tapes, each containing about 1,000 catalog entries in a form which can be fed by a purchaser into a computer for printouts. More than 60 libraries are subscribers for these tapes.

The National Union Catalog, containing about 16 million cards, is being printed in bound volumes by a private firm for sale to libraries that can afford to buy them. The portion of the catalog representing pre-1956 imprints will appear in about 600 volumes, of which about 100 had appeared by the end of 1970. The portion covering the period from 1952 to the present has been published, or is being published, in several partly overlapping series, as follows:

Period	No. of volumes
1952-55	30
1953-57	28
1958-62	54
1963-67	72
1968	12

For 1969 and 1970, the Library has published monthly paperbound volumes, with quarterly cumulations. Supplementing the union catalog of books is a monthly Library of Congress periodical, *New Serial Titles*, which is the only approach to completeness in identifying new periodicals. *New Serial Titles* includes

Sales of Library Catalog Cards
(millions)

Fiscal year	Cards sold	Gross revenue	Net revenue
1960	32.06	$1.84	$1.82
1961	35.68	2.04	2.01
1962	42.39	2.15	2.13
1963	46.02	2.46	2.42
1964	52.51	3.12	3.08
1965	61.49	3.70	3.65
1966	63.21	4.01	3.94
1967	74.50	4.93	4.85
1968	78.77	5.17	5.09
1969	63.40	4.17	4.10
1970	64.55	4.73	4.61

SOURCES: Annual Report of the Librarian of Congress, 1969, p. 111, and Card Division records.

the titles of newly established periodicals and other serials, changes in titles, changes in frequency of issue, and titles of periodicals and serials which have been discontinued; it also shows the major libraries that receive the new periodicals.

In the fiscal year ended June 30, 1969, the Library of Congress loaned more than 250,000 books and other items, of which 48 percent went to other libraries—34 percent to Government libraries in the Washington area, and 14 percent to libraries outside the Washington area. The rest were borrowed by Members of Congress (35 percent) and other authorized borrowers (17 percent). The Librarian, in his Annual Report for the fiscal year 1968, wrote: "As a commentary on changing technologies, it is interesting to note that, while loans of serials decreased 14 percent, loans of microfilms increased 20 percent."

Services to the Public. The Main Reading Room in the main Library of Congress building, the Thomas Jefferson Reading Room in the annex, and more than 20 rooms for use of specialized materials, such as music, maps, and current periodicals, are open to the public. Books requested by readers are delivered to them in the reading rooms, and readers may use the reference books available on the open shelves, without filling in a request slip. Reference librarians are on duty to assist readers.

High school students are not encouraged to use the Library of Congress collections. They are required to present a letter from a school official for admission to the reading rooms. Many elementary and secondary school students from all over the country visit the Library building each year, especially in the spring. Visitors may view the exhibits in the halls of the Library and observe the Main Reading Room from a gallery. Guides conduct 45-minute tours without charge at hourly intervals.

The Library regularly presents, in the Elizabeth Sprague Coolidge Auditorium, concerts, readings, and dramatic performances open to the public. The admission charge for some of these performances is 25 cents. In April 1970, the Library sponsored an International Poetry Festival to which it invited poets, critics, and scholars from France, the Soviet Union, and Yugoslavia in Europe; Israel, Pakistan, and Japan in the Middle and Far East; and Ecuador and Chile in Latin America. The Budapest String Quartet, now disbanded, often played at the Library. The Juilliard String Quartet and the New York Pro Musica are among other well-known musical groups that have performed at the Library.

A service to the public which differs in kind from furnishing books and presenting performances is the registration of copyrights. The Copyright Office, with more than 300 employees, records ownership of literary and other intellectual property in order to secure to the owners any financial fruits which may be derived therefrom. Except for cases involving special problems, the office in the fiscal year ended June 30, 1970, mailed a certificate of copyright registration within three weeks of receipt of the application. Fees and other receipts of the Copyright Office in the fiscal year 1970 totaled $2,049,308.99. This was the second time in the history of the office that receipts had reached the two-million-dollar mark.

Copyright Registrations

1870	5,600	1930	172,792
1880	20,686	1940	176,997
1890	42,794	1950	210,564
1900	94,798	1960	243,926
1910	109,074	1970	316,466
1920	126,562		

Note: 1870-90, calendar year; 1900 and later, fiscal year.

SOURCES: Annual Report of the Librarian of Congress, 1969, p. 96, and Copyright Office records.

Still another form of service which the Library renders is the preparation and issuance of publications, based mainly on the Library's collections. These publications, numbering in the hundreds, span a broad spectrum of subjects. Illustrative of the variety are the 1332-page compilation entitled *American and English Genealogies in the Library of Congress*, published in 1919; the 40-page pamphlet *Long Remembered; Facsimiles of the Five Versions of the Gettysburg Address in the Handwriting of Abraham Lincoln*, published in 1963; and the 349-page *Antarctic Bibliography*, published in 1970. The series entitled *Library of Congress Catalog—Books; Subjects* is published quarterly in paperbound form and cumulated annually; the 1968 set runs to six volumes. Important acquisitions and holdings are discussed in the *Quarterly Journal of the Library of Congress*.

Congressional Research Service

The Legislative Reorganization Act of Oct. 26, 1970, changed the name of the 56-year-old Legislative Reference Service and expanded its responsibilities. The basic function of the service remained as Charles A. Goodrum, Coordinator of Research in the LRS, had described it in the *Library Journal* of Feb. 1, 1965: to provide staff experts who will "act as knowledge brokers to the Members and committees." To serve as honest brokers, the Congressional Research Service's professionals aim to maintain a high degree of objectivity. Goodrum, observing that written material and the spoken word supporting particular solutions of problems pour into the offices of Senators and Representatives, commented: "The Congressman doesn't need more advice. He needs someone who is detached, who has no axe to grind."

One of the difficulties which the CRS encounters in its effort to be objective arises from the fact that the Executive Branch, which generally takes a definite stand on questions of policy, is a prime source of the information that has to be used in gauging the wisdom of those policies. The CRS, in a 1970 pamphlet on its work, noted that inasmuch as "an increasing amount of legislation is generated by the Executive Branch," which is "a thousand times larger than the Legislative," Congress "must struggle constantly to retain some degree of parity in the information sources and technical competence on which its judgments will be based." In that struggle, Congress relies not so much on the number of specialists in its employ as on "the quality of the expertise which it builds into its Congressional office and committee staffs, and into its Legislative Reference (Congressional Research) Service."

The pamphlet added: "The Service does not and should not recommend courses of action. It endeavors to identify such choices, and to the best of its ability attempts to state the apparent strengths and weaknesses of the alternatives—but it must be the legislator who makes the decision." Moreover, the CRS is not an investigative agency. Since it has no powers of subpoena, it limits its sources of information to what is already in the public domain. Within these boundaries, it seeks to provide a sound informational foundation for Congressional decision-making.

Founding and Expansion of the Service

An Act of June 30, 1906, appropriated funds to enable the Library of Congress to prepare law indexes, digests, and compilations for the use of Congress during the fiscal year 1907. Similar appropriations were made for the fiscal years 1908, 1909, and 1910. Hearings were held in 1912-13 on a bill to establish a permanent reference service for analyzing proposed legislation. Sen. Robert M. La Follette (R Wis.), who introduced the bill in the Senate, worked hard for its adoption. Woodrow Wilson, then Governor of New Jersey, wrote in 1912 to Rep. John M. Nelson (R Wis.), who had introduced a similar measure in the House, "It seems to me highly important that a legislative reference department should be established in the Congressional Library." Congress did not pass the La Follette-Nelson bill, but subsequent appropriation bills accomplished its purpose.

An amendment to the Legislative appropriation bill for the fiscal year 1915, adopted during the Senate discussion of the bill and concurred in by the House, provided as follows: "Legislative reference. To enable the Librarian of Congress to employ competent persons to prepare such indexes, digests, and compilations of law as may be required for Congress and other official use pursuant to the Act approved June thirtieth, nineteen hundred and six, $25,000." The bill was signed July 16, 1914, and the Librarian of Congress shortly thereafter established the Legislative Reference Service by administrative order.

The corresponding legislation for the fiscal year 1916, signed March 4, 1915, used the following language adapted from Sen. La Follette's bill: "To enable the Librarian of Congress to employ competent persons to gather, classify, and make available, in translations, indexes, digests, compilations, and bulletins, and otherwise, data for or bearing upon legislation, and to render such data serviceable to Congress and committees and Members thereof." That language, with little change, was repeated annually in the appropriation acts until 1946.

Meanwhile, Congress had given the Legislative Reference Service two specific jobs, of which one was discontinued, and the other has remained on the agenda. Beginning in 1926, the LRS—at the request of Congress—compiled and published a biennial index of state legislation. The last of 12 volumes in the series covered laws enacted in 1947-48. Beginning in 1935, Congress directed LRS to prepare and publish a digest of public bills introduced in Congress. The Legislative Reorganization Act of August 2, 1946, made this task a regular part of the LRS program.

Sec. 203 of the 1946 Act provided as follows: "It shall be the duty of the Legislative Reference Service—

(1) upon request, to advise and assist any committee of either House or any joint committee in the analysis, appraisal, and evaluation of legislative proposals pending before it, or of recommendations submitted to Congress, by the President or any Executive agency, and otherwise to assist in furnishing a basis for the proper determination of measures before the committee;

(2) upon request, or upon its own initiative in anticipation of requests, to gather, classify, analyze, and make available, in translations, indexes, digests, compilations and bulletins, and otherwise, data for or bearing upon legislation, and to render such data serviceable to Congress, and committees and Members thereof, without partisan bias in selection or presentation.

(3) to prepare summaries and digests of public hearings before committees of the Congress, and of bills and resolutions of a public general nature introduced in either House."

The Legislative Reorganization Act of 1970, as noted, transformed LRS into the Congressional Research Service. It assigned to CRS the additional duties of evaluating legislative proposals for committees so as to help them determine the advisability of the proposals, evaluating alternatives, estimating the probable results of the proposals and alternatives, and, at the beginning of each Congress, identifying policy areas which the committees "might profitably analyze in depth." The director of the Congressional Research Service was authorized to prepare the budget for the Service independently, for inclusion in the Library of Congress budget. The 1970 Act directed the Librarian of Congress to accord to CRS "complete research independence and the maximum practicable administrative independence" consistent with the objectives of CRS as a part of the Library.

Kinds of Service Performed by CRS

The 1970 pamphlet which describes CRS says: "An inquiry...may be as simple as the question of the population of California, or as complex as a study of the possible ways to provide care to the aged. The one required a few seconds by one researcher, the other occupied three analysts for a period of six months." However, simplicity or complexity is not the only factor determining how much staff time should be spent on an inquiry and what form the response should take. Other factors are the importance of the need for the information (whether it is wanted, for example, for direct use by a Senator or Representative in considering legislation or for use in answering a schoolboy constituent's letter) and the likelihood that the same question will come up repeatedly.

For factual one-time questions received by telephone, which can be answered while the questioner waits, the CRS has a "hot line" in its Congressional Reference Division. Such questions often are of the who, what, when, or how much variety. The division handled more than 117,000 inquiries in the fiscal year ended June 30, 1970. About 50 percent of the inquiries were answered on the day they were received, and 40 percent more were answered the following day. A rough classification of all requests showed that around 65 percent were routine reference questions, including about 15 percent asked on behalf of constituents.

If an inquiry requires the preparation of a written narrative, projection of statistics, analysis of pros and cons of an issue, evaluation of a Federal program, or subject-oriented research, it is sent to a CRS research division specializing in the subject. Many of the resulting reports are reproduced for use in answering similar inquiries. Some are published as committee prints. At any one time, more than 1,000 such reports are in stock. Each month, CRS sends every Senator and Representative a list of major CRS studies newly available.

CRS issues three documents on a regular basis besides its monthly list of available reports. (1) The weekly *Legislative Status Report* traces 250 to 300 of the most active pieces of legislation. It shows the stage that each important bill has reached, committee actions, amendments under consideration, and, on appropriations, the amounts requested by the President, recommended by Congressional committees, and appropriated. (2) The biweekly *Digest of Public General Bills and Resolutions* contains an abstract of each important bill or resolution introduced in Congress, the name of the sponsor and the status of the proposal. (3) Approximately every 10 years, CRS publishes a new edition of *The Constitution of the United States of America; Analysis and Interpretation—Annotations of Cases Decided by the Supreme Court.*

Variety of CRS Topics and Specialists

The Library of Congress in many of its units employs librarians who know economics, librarians who know political science, librarians who know literature, and so forth. The Legislative Reference Service, now the CRS, by contrast always has hired economists, ecologists, and political scientists as such, without insisting on prior training in librarianship. Its staff consists of about 200 research specialists, assisted by 100 clerical and administrative employees.

The Congressional Reference Division, as noted, is engaged mainly in answering simple inquiries of a

---

CRS Specialists

The Legislative Reorganization Act of Oct. 26, 1970, listed the fields in which the Congressional Research Service is authorized to employ specialists and senior specialists, as follows:

Agriculture	Money and banking
American government and public administration	National defense
American public law	Price economics
Conservation	Science
Engineering and public works	Social welfare
Housing	Taxation and fiscal policy
Industrial organization and corporation finance	Technology
International affairs	Transportation and communications
International trade and economic geography	Urban affairs
Labor and employment	Veterans' affairs
Mineral economics	"Such other broad fields as the Director may consider appropriate"

factual nature. At the other end of the gamut is the work of the Senior Specialists Division. Members of that division are nationally recognized experts in their fields. Most have had extensive experience in government, on the campus or in business, and have made substantial contributions to knowledge. They prepare high-level, comprehensive analyses and evaluations. Their salaries are in the supergrade category of the civil service.

The other CRS divisions overlap, in part, as concerns the topics on which the senior specialists concentrate. Among the newer divisions are the Science Policy Research Division, established in 1964, and the Environmental Policy Division, established in 1969. Other units devoted to topical fields of knowledge are the American Law, Economics, Education and Public Welfare, Foreign Affairs, and Government and General Research Divisions. The Library Services Division maintains a massive filing system in which all past research done in CRS is arranged by subject. The division also clips nine daily newspapers, 350 magazines, government documents and lobbyists' pamphlets. This material, used by the subject divisions of CRS, is arranged under 2,200 subjects, chronologically within each subject; more than 140,000 clippings and other items are filed each year.

Strengths and Shortcomings

Congress often, but not always, has been generous in its appropriations for the Library of Congress. Librarian Luther H. Evans, in his Annual Report for 1951, discussed the effects of reductions ordered that fiscal year in the Library's budget. He said: "Service to the general public was curtailed. The number of hours the reading rooms are kept open for full service has been reduced 18 percent, and only an abridged service is given during evening hours. In fact the Library is now open for full service fewer hours a week than has been the case since 1900." Fuller service was later restored, but some specialized reading rooms still are open fewer hours a week than before the budget cut of the early 1950s.

The Library aims to deliver books to a reader's desk within 20 minutes, but staff shortages sometimes result in a wait of an hour or more. Stack personnel and delivery attendants reportedly make more mistakes than seem reasonable, but readers waiting for books are notoriously impatient. Two Washington newspapers ascribed a part of the problem to overcrowding. An article in the *Washington Star,* Feb. 2, 1969, said: "To the roar of traffic along Independence Ave., S.E., ...a new sound has been added—the ghostly groan of a 70-year-old building suffering from indigestion." Under the heading "U.S. Library Fights the Battle of the Bulge," the *Washington Post,* Nov. 16, 1969, ventured the opinion that the Library was "facing its roughest time since the British reduced its collection of books to ashes."

Good news for the Library came when Congress, by an Act of March 16, 1970, authorized the expenditure of $90 million for the James Madison Memorial Building as a second annex to the Library, released funds previously appropriated for final plans and drawings for the new building, and appropriated $15.6 million for excavation, purchase of stone and similar construction work. Hope for improvement based on erection of another annex does not satisfy those who want better service now. But many users of the Library have found

that the unexcelled comprehensiveness of its collections and the devotion and expertise of many of its staff members counterbalance the annoyance caused by delays and mistakes.

The Library of Congress in general and what then was called the Legislative Reference Service in particular were publicly criticized and defended by Senators and Representatives on a number of occasions in the 1960s. Rep. John Brademas (D Ind.) testified on the subject June 3, 1965, before the Joint Committee on the Organization of Congress. He said: "If I were going to want a first-class paper prepared for a highly intelligent and literate audience on an important public policy problem, the Library of Congress would be the last place in the United States I would go, because I have tried them out and, with rare exceptions, the product has been second-rate....I am appalled by the abysmal quality of productions of the Legislative Reference Service."

Sen. A. S. Mike Monroney (D Okla.), co-chairman of the Joint Committee on the Organization of Congress, commented adversely on LRS three times in the course of the Committee's 1965 hearings. On the first occasion, May 20, he said: "I have asked for a serious study time and time again over the years,...and I get pedestrian types of mimeograph junk that I wouldn't send out to an uninformed constituent." On June 3 he added: "I have never had a paper from them that I would even insert in the *Congressional Record* without putting some of my staff to getting more basic things; and some of it is just absolutely juvenile." On the third occasion, June 9, he said: "I could give the request to my office boy and have him write up a better report than I sometimes get from the Legislative Reference Service."

Congressional users of LRS (CRS) other than Sen. Monroney and Rep. Brademas have been pleased with the service they received. Rep. Thomas B. Curtis (R Mo.) told the Joint Committee June 3, 1965: "From my own experience, I must say in behalf of the Legislative Reference Service, it has been the other way around. We use them in the Joint Economic Committee on a number of projects, and the caliber is topnotch." Rep. Thomas P. O'Neill Jr. (D Mass.) said in the House of Representatives Sept. 1, 1966: "One of the most valuable services at the disposal of Senators and Congressmen is provided by the Legislative Reference Service of the Library of Congress."

In the *Library Journal* of June 15, 1970, Sen. Alan Cranston (D Calif.) argued for expansion of LRS. Noting "the disparity between the small number of experts available to Congress and the immense staffs of Executive departments such as the Department of Defense," Cranston contended that "the greatest potential for closing the expertise gap is the LRS." He recommended use of temporary consultants, use of temporary employees on subjects of temporary interest, increased staff for technological assessment, freeing of more experts for exhaustive research and expanded use of computers. But John Lear, science editor of the *Saturday Review,* wrote in that magazine's issue of April 25, 1970: "My own guess is that LRS cannot take on much more responsibility until Mumford demonstrates to Congress his urgent need for new and comfortable working quarters to replace offices that are jammed into passageways, corridors, and space intended for public display of Library of Congress treasures. With troops of schoolchildren clattering noisily about in the course of holiday tours, the wonder to me is that LRS gets any serious work done."

CRS tried in its 1970 pamphlet to pinpoint the reason why some of the unit's products are not as thorough or as penetrating as those who request them would like: "In the case of the more serious research studies, there is rarely enough time or staff to provide the quality of answer the staff is capable of doing. The demands made on the Service rise every year at a far greater rate than it is possible to provide researchers to cope with them. In the 22 years between 1947 and 1969, the annual receipt of inquiries has risen 514 percent, while the staff has increased only 134 percent."

The Library of Congress is quantitatively superlative in so many ways that occasional failings in the quality of its service to Congress and the public are conspicuous against that background. Increased appropriations for personnel and facilities would enable the Library to improve its service, but whether the level of improvement would be commensurate with the cost, and how to compare the need for improvement with other calls on Federal funds, are questions on which Senators and Representatives must exercise their best judgment.

Bibliography

Books

Adams, James Truslow, *The Epic of America.* Atlantic Monthly Press, 1931.

Angle, Paul M., *The Library of Congress; An Account, Historical and Descriptive.* Kingsport Press, 1958.

Bishop, W. W. and Keogh, Andrew (eds.), *Essays Offered to Herbert Putnam by His Colleagues and Friends on His Thirtieth Anniversary as Librarian of Congress, 5 April 1929.* Yale University Press, 1919.

MacCloskey, Monro, *Our National Attic: The Library of Congress, the Smithsonian Institution, the National Archives.* Richard Rosen Press, 1968.

Salamanca, Lucy, *Fortress of Freedom; The Story of the Library of Congress.* Lippincott, 1942.

Articles

Lewis, Hunter, "Capitol Hill Ugliness Club," *The Atlantic,* February 1967.

Thirteen articles on the Library of Congress in issues of the *Library Journal,* 1965.

Government Publications

Goodrum, Charles A., *The Legislative Reference Service of the United States Congress.* Library of Congress, April 1, 1970.

Johnston, William D., *History of the Library of Congress; Volume I, 1800-1864.* Government Printing Office, 1904. (No more published.)

Mearns, David C., *The Story Up to Now; The Library of Congress, 1800-1946.* Library of Congress, 1947.

U.S. Congress, Joint Committee on the Organization of Congress, *Organization of Congress; Hearings... Eighty-ninth Congress, First Session, Pursuant to S. Con. Res. 2.* Government Printing Office, 1965-66. 16 parts.

U.S. Library of Congress, *Annual Report of the Librarian of Congress.* Government Printing Office, 1866—.

Pay and Perquisites of Members

FOR YEARS, Congress and its Members have been favorite targets of national humor. The origins of this humorous image are obscure but, fair or not, it has persisted. Perhaps the best illustration of the technique comes in Mark Twain's classic commentary: "Suppose you were an idiot. And suppose you were a Member of Congress. But I repeat myself."

While the evidence is uncertain, suspicion has it that not all of the humor is lost on the Members. Rep. Jim Wright (D Texas) in his book *You and Your Congressman* quoted another Member as saying: "I came here to make laws, and what do I do? I send baby books to young mothers, listen to every maladjusted kid who wants out of the service, write sweet replies to pompous idiots who think a public servant is a public footstool, and give tours of the Capitol to visitors who are just as worn out as I am."

In any event, it is clear that among the more dubious perquisites of serving as a Member is the potential for tickling the nation's funny bone. Other perquisites abound. Some are important; others are merely convenient. But they all are designed to ease the burden of what can be a grinding, tedious and frustrating job.

Former Rep. Burr P. Harrison (D Va.) talked about some of the burdens in a 1962 newspaper interview: "The various activities of Congress are in progress at the same time, like a three-ring circus. If one duty is to be done properly, it is likely another must be content with a lick and a promise. Committees sit as the floor debate proceeds and constituents wait in the office. A Member busy in committee will be summoned by the bells to vote on the floor on a measure as to the merits of which he knows little, if anything, and as to the controversial aspects of which he has heard no debate. A Member occupied on the floor or in his office will hurry to committee to propound a series of questions to a witness on points which the witness has discussed fully prior to his arrival.... In general, no one knows this week what Congress is going to do next week.... (This) is an intolerably vexatious, inefficient management of the time of its Members."

A Member's Jobs

The major functions of a Member of Congress are legislative and representational. Some observers also add a third: they believe that a Member should "educate" the public on the major national problems and issues.

While the legislative duties of Members are their most prominent ones, Members are not solely lawmakers. Not only is it their function to act as the representatives of their constituents in the national Government; it is unlikely that they will be re-elected if they neglect to do so. Since most Members consider their own re-election as paramount, scrupulous attention usually is paid to constituent mail and the problems it brings. "You would be surprised at some of the requests we get," the staff manager for one Democratic Senator said. Some Senators and Representatives even make such public relations gestures as congratulating newlyweds, parents of newborn babies and recipients of major scholarship awards.

A widespread complaint is that much of this "case work," as it is known, is trivial, but few Members feel that they can afford to ignore constituents, even non-voting ones who write for help with school assignments. As a result, most of the staff and office facilities of Members are given over to processing mail and running errands for the constituents. Some Congressional staffs pass along constituent requests for information to the Congressional Research Service of the Library of Congress, which consequently has less time to spend on its primary duties. The Member himself at times feels compelled to answer certain letters, introduce and follow private bills, talk to visitors, and even lead high school classes on tours of the Capitol.

Occasionally, a maverick Member will shatter the traditional image of the infinitely patient and courteous public servant. It happens rarely, but when it does occur, the event makes news headlines. Such a maverick was Sen. Stephen M. Young (D Ohio). A liberal, Young was subjected to frequent attacks from conservatives. His acid-tongued replies were widely publicized. When one constituent wrote that Young was an anti-anti-Communist and a worthless showoff, the Senator wrote back to the man that some imposter had written a crackpot letter using his name. "Possibly," Young wrote, "you will wish to see that adequate measures are taken to protect your good name. If some jerk gets away with this one time, he might write even a sillier letter and sign your name." Another Young reply began, "Dear Sir: You are a liar."

The chances of getting a personal reply to a letter depend partly on the size of the state in which the writer lives. A Wyoming resident may receive a personal answer. A New Yorker is more likely to draw a standardized response drafted by a junior staff member, signed by a machine, and only scanned by the Member.

In recent years, a number of machines have been adapted to speed replies to letters. Among them are the Robotype machine and the Autopen. These machines can insert a signature and a heading on form letters while making it appear to the constituent that he has received an individual letter with a personal signature.

The Robotype machine looks like a typewriter. It is capable of reproducing identical copies of form letters without the standardized look of a mimeographed letter. Once it is set up to reproduce the body of a letter, a secretary types only the individual heading for each letter. The Autopen is a console machine with a large wheel. On the wheel is placed a metal plate with an impression of the Member's signature. As the prepared letters revolve around the wheel, the metal plate stamps an imprint of the signature in the proper place on the paper.

Together, these machines make it possible for a Congressional staff to answer letters after scanning them for a few seconds to see what they are about.

A Member's Workload

During the course of hearings held by the Senate Government Operations Committee in 1951 on the organization and operation of Congress, Sen. A. S. Mike Monroney (D Okla.), one of the authors of the 1946 Legislative Reorganization Act, said that "nonlegislative activities" consumed "about 80 percent of the Member's workday." Sen. Hubert H. Humphrey (D Minn.) has said that "many Members of the Senate and the House spend up to 90 percent of their time (and the time of their staffs) answering mail, meeting with constituents and handling individual constituent complaints or requests."

These activities necessarily reduce the resources which Members can bring to bear on legislation. Yet the technical complexities of legislation increase constantly as the code of laws, the economy and the Federal Government grow larger and science, commerce, defense and foreign policy become increasingly interconnected. The problem is perhaps more acute in the Senate than the House, because Senators serve on two and sometimes three major committees, while most Representatives are limited to one major committee.

Caught by the conflicting demands of constituents and legislative duties, few Members have time to perform the "educational" function except sporadically. The constant pressure of elections, however, forces many Members to inform their constituents of their positions on national issues through newsletters, press releases and speeches. This activity, and efforts to promote a particular bill or approach to a national or local problem, of course add that much more to the individual's workload.

The average active Member of Congress—allowing for considerable variation from one office to another—frequently puts in a 10- to 12-hour day at the office and in the Capitol before going home to dinner and two or three hours of reading related to his work. During a typical day he would probably spend time talking to lobbyists and to visiting constituents, possibly show a high school class around the Capitol, read and answer some of the large amount of daily mail, telephone his district or state, answer questions from newsmen, discuss legislation and politics with other Members, attend party or regional meetings, possibly work on a speech or a newsletter to his constituents, read the *Congressional Record,* newspapers, magazines and committee hearings or reports. In addition, he would attend committee meetings in the morning and sometimes the afternoon, attend floor sessions to speak and listen to debate, vote, and wait to vote. He would also spend time overseeing the work of his office staff. If he is the chairman of an active committee or subcommittee, or occupies a leadership post (for example, as a member of the Whip organization), he

Washington's Party Circuit

Official entertaining is widespread in Washington. For the unwary Member of Congress, what began as mere social courtesy can balloon out of control and become a social nightmare. One of the more candid descriptions of Washington's social life—as seen from Capitol Hill—was offered in a 1963 newsletter to constituents by Sen. Stephen M. Young (D Ohio):

People inquire what about social life in Washinton. "Terrific" would be the answer, were a Senator to attend all functions to which he is invited. Frankly, unless a Senator throws in the sponge and accepts only one-fourth of the invitations, he will be out socially five or six evenings weekly. This would be a hardship in many respects. For example, inability to see "Gunsmoke," "Wells Fargo," "The Dakotas," "Wagon Train," to say nothing of wasting time needed to study pending legislation, read committee reports, etc. More than one hundred nations have embassies in Washington. Each holds two large receptions a year plus dinners and cocktail parties to which most Senators are invited. Then there are 17 State dinners. Among other dinners, make a mental note that there are 262 national associations such as the American Legion, American Farm Bureau Federation, American Trucking Associations Inc., Veterans of Foreign Wars, American Medical Association, National Association of Home Builders, U.S. Chamber of Commerce and National Association of Manufacturers. These are registered pressure groups, so-called. They filed reports admitting expenditures in excess of $5,000,000 during 1962. Many of these national associations usually invite all Members of the Congress to at least one dinner a year. In addition, various state associations and citizens' organizations give dinners, cocktail parties, and receptions. They wine and dine Congressmen who attend and individual members and speakers may discuss legislative proposals they are promoting. At least 40 Senators give dinners or luncheons for their colleagues and usually Senators give dinners for their own State Congressional delegations or a Representative throws an affair to which he invites the Senators from his state. In addition, a comparatively new horror has been devised—that is breakfasts to which Senators are invited. The time stated is generally 8:30 a.m. The place, usually a downtown hotel, more than a mile distant from the Capitol. If a Senator attends, he is fortunate to leave by 10 o'clock. Furthermore, quite frequently groups from the Senator's own state visiting in Washington desire him to lunch or dine with them. These are invitations a Senator appreciates receiving and likes to accept; and in turn, a Senator does not keep his own pocketbook padlocked. He "wines and dines" constituents and "throws parties" to repay obligations, and also because this is an American custom we like. Regarding "pressure groups" and various professional and business associations, many Congressmen say "too busy" and are happy to pay for their own meals, and eat at home a couple evenings a week.

would have additional time-consuming duties and additional staff aides. *(See box on Washington's Party Circuit.)*

A Member's Perquisites

Aside from his Congressional salary, a Member's single greatest perquisite is his personal staff. Staff aides multiply the Member's arms, legs, eyes and ears, providing his best hope of meeting the demands on his time. Properly used, a personal staff can function as the Member's strongest ally. Misused, a personal staff becomes little more than a reservoir of wasted talents. And abused, a personal staff can turn traitor; for like the gentleman and his valet, no Member is a hero to his staff.

Among the other formal, statutory perquisites are the franking privilege, immunity from certain legal actions, and allowances for official travel, telephoning, office expenses and office equipment.

In addition, there is a vast, ill-defined collection of informal perquisites based on the deference customarily shown a VIP. Such deference appears typically in delaying the departure of a plane to accommodate the tardy arrival of a Member of Congress.

Are Congressional perquisites abused? Objectively, it is difficult to tell. Probably the best answer is that Members abuse their privileges about as much as such privileges would be abused by the public in general. Large-scale abuses, while rare, are uncovered periodically, touching off widely publicized scandals. The most popular abuse, judging from its recurring appearance, is the employment of a Member's relatives as personal aides.

Pay of Members of Congress

In Article I, Section 6, the Constitution provides that "The Senators and Representatives shall receive a compensation for their services, to be ascertained by law, and paid out of the Treasury of the United States."

The constitutional language settled one sensitive contemporary issue—whether a Member's salary should be drawn from state or national funds—but it left settlement of a far more delicate question up to Congress itself —deciding what the salary should be. The inevitable result was development of the salary issue into a political hot potato.

In attempts to minimize the political impact of periodic salary increases, Congress fell into the practice of wrapping up a pay increase for itself in a general pay increase for other Federal workers, including at times the Judiciary and the President. On a few occasions, even that tactic failed to blunt critical reaction on the part of the public.

Public reaction against Congressional pay increases was strong at times, leading to wholesale election defeats for Members who approved increases that their constituents considered unwarranted. Two controversial salary increases were repealed by succeeding Congresses. Frequently, a few Members would refuse higher pay and return the amount of the increase to the Treasury or donate it to a public charity.

Despite all the turmoil, Congressional pay has risen steadily over the years. From $6 a day in 1789, it has climbed to $42,500 a year at present. Although the salary of Members has remained unchanged for long periods of time, only during the Great Depression of the 1930s was

Retirement Benefits

Congress included in the Legislative Reorganization Act of 1946 a provision, recommended by the Joint Committee on the Organization of Congress, initiating a retirement system for Senators and Representatives. The Act brought Members of Congress under the Civil Service Retirement Act, permitting them, at their option, to contribute 6 percent of their salaries to a retirement fund. (The contribution rose to 7½ percent in 1956.) Retirement annuities were to be calculated at 2½ percent of average salary multiplied by years of service but could not exceed three-fourths of a Member's final Congressional salary. A Member became eligible for benefits upon retirement from Congress if he was at least 62 years old and had served a minimum of six years (except in cases of disability).

In 1954, Congress liberalized the pension law and also adjusted retirement benefits for legislative employees. The basic rate of contribution remained 6 percent of salary, but the bill included the Congressional expense allowance in the salary computation. It also provided for reduced retirement benefits at age 60 and made other minor changes in the program. Further changes were enacted in 1960, although the basic rate of contribution and the basic retirement benefits were left unchanged.

In 1969, Congress again liberalized the pension law for both Members and legislative employees. Retirement benefits were increased by specifying that the annuity computation formula would use an employee's average annual earnings during the highest consecutive three-year period, rather than during a five-year period, as had been required. The method of computing annuities for Congressional employees was liberalized by eliminating a 15-year limitation on number of years of service for which the annuity would be computed at 2½ percent of average pay. Other benefit changes also were made. In addition, the contribution of Members of Congress was increased from 7½ percent to 8 percent, and the contribution of Congressional employees from 6½ percent to 7½ percent, beginning in January 1970.

it ever reduced. And since 1946, Members have been eligible to participate in a retirement system. *(See box on Retirement Benefits.)*

Early Pay Legislation

During the Constitutional Convention, a principal question surrounding compensation for Members of Congress was the source of the funds. Members of the Confederation Congress had been paid by the states; those of the British Parliament were not paid at all. It was felt, however, that Members of Congress should be paid, and paid by the national Government.

Another question raised at the Convention was whether Senators and Representatives should receive equal pay. Charles Pinckney of South Carolina twice moved "that no salary should be allowed" members of the Senate. "As this branch was meant to represent the

Docking of Pay

It is often suggested that the way to curb absenteeism in Congress is to dock a Member's pay for each day he fails to appear on the floor. The Constitution makes no provision for this, saying only that "each House shall be the judge of the elections, returns and qualifications of its own Members, and a majority of each shall constitute a quorum to do business; but a smaller number may adjourn from day to day, and may be authorized to compel the attendance of absent Members, in such manner, and under such penalties as each House may provide." (Article 1, sec. 5)

The first session of the First Congress in 1789 provided for an automatic docking of pay. Salaries were $6 a day for each day of attendance.

The only existing law concerning docking of pay was enacted in 1856. It provided that "The Secretary of the Senate and the Sergeant at Arms of the House, respectively, shall deduct from the monthly payments of each Member or delegate the amount of his salary for each day that he has been absent from the Senate or House,...unless such member or delegate assigns as the reason for such absence the sickness of himself or of some member of his family."

Since then a few rare attempts to compel attendance have cited this law. During the 53rd Congress (1894), after a ruling by the chairman of the Committee of the Whole that the 1856 law was still in force, portions of House Members' salaries were withheld.

The 1894 incident was recalled in 1914 when the House adopted a resolution revoking all leaves of absence granted to Members and directing the Sergeant at Arms to deduct Members' pay for each day they were absent. In debate, Speaker Champ Clark (D Mo.) recalled that "in the summer of 1894, this statute was enforced, and I paid $28 and some cents myself to go down to Virginia to make two speeches, but my recollection about it is that the Sergeant at Arms had some kind of a document down there that you had to sign, and you certified how many days you had been absent. If you did not make the certification, you would have been here every day. Speaker (Thomas B.) Reed (R Maine) sneered at the statute as a 'police court regulation.' Nevertheless it had the effect of keeping a quorum here." Rep. Sereno E. Payne (R N.Y.) added, "My recollection about the enforcement of that statute is that...most of (the Members) certified that they were present during the whole time,...and that nobody suffered after the first month...."

The 1914 resolution, however, was apparently enforced more stringently. Less than two months after it was adopted, Rep. Ben Johnson (D Ky.) stated on the House floor that although he had been present on the floor for the past month, the Sergeant at Arms had withheld his salary because he "declined to certify to his attendance upon the sessions of the House as required."

No docking of pay of absentees has taken place in recent years. The House Parliamentarian's office says there is no way of knowing when a Member is away.

wealth of the country," Pinckney asserted, "it ought to be composed of persons of wealth; and if no allowance was to be made, the wealthy alone would undertake the service." Pinckney's motion was seconded by Benjamin Franklin but was twice rejected, six states to five.

Per Diem Compensation. One of the first—and most controversial—measures enacted by the new Congress in 1789 was a bill fixing the compensation of Members. As originally considered by the House, both Representatives and Senators were to be paid $6 a day. The proposal for equal pay reopened the debate over whether Senators, by reason of greater responsibilities and presumably higher qualifications, should receive a pay differential. At the heart of the debate was an amendment by Rep. Theodore Sedgwick (Federalist Mass.) to lower House pay to $5 per day, thus creating a $1-per-day differential in favor of the Senate. The amendment was defeated by a voice vote. On Aug. 10, 1789, the House by a 30-16 roll call passed a bill providing for payment of $6 a day to Members of both chambers.

In the Senate, the bill was amended to provide that Senators be paid at the $6 rate until March 4, 1795, when their pay would be increased to $8 and the pay of Representatives would remain at $6. The amended bill passed the Senate on Aug. 28, 1789.

Following a House-Senate conference, the House on Sept. 11, by a 29-25 roll call, voted to fix the pay of Senators at $7 a day after March 4, 1795, and by a 28-26 roll call set March 4, 1796, as the expiration date of the legislation. The Senate agreed to the House amendments on Sept. 12, and the bill was signed into law on Sept. 22, 1789, seven days before the end of the first session of Congress.

As enacted, the measure provided also for a travel allowance for Senators and Representatives of $6 per 20 miles, a $6-per-day differential for the House Speaker (making his pay $12 a day), and compensation for a number of lesser House and Senate officials.

When a new pay law was enacted in 1796, only a glancing reference was made to a differential for the Senate. Both the House and the Senate passed a bill equalizing the pay at $6 a day.

Short-Lived Salary Law. In 1816, Congress voted itself a pay increase and a shift from per diem compensation to an annual salary. The Act of March 19, 1816, raised Congressional pay to $1,500 a year and made the raise retroactive to Dec. 4, 1815, when the first session of the 14th Congress convened. The pay raise had passed both houses easily, but it was roundly condemned by the people. A number of Members who had voted for the bill were defeated in the 1816 elections; nine Members resigned over the issue. One of the election victims was Rep. Daniel Webster. He was defeated and was not elected to Congress again until 1822.

Return to Per Diem. The short session of the 14th Congress in 1817 repealed the $1,500 salary act, effective with the end of the Congress on March 3, 1817. An Act of Jan. 22, 1818, restored per diem compensation and set the rate at $8, retroactive to March 3, 1817.

Members' Salaries from 1850s to 1930s

Almost four decades later, a successful conversion to annual Congressional salaries was finally achieved. An Act of Aug. 16, 1856, replaced the $8-per-day rate by a

$3,000 annual salary, retroactive to the start of the 34th Congress on Dec. 3, 1855. Another retroactive pay increase —to $5,000—was approved July 28, 1866, effective Dec. 4, 1865, when the 39th Congress had convened for its first session.

"Salary Grab." In the closing days of the 42nd Congress in 1873, still another retroactive pay raise was enacted, increasing the salary to $7,500. The higher salary was made retroactive to the beginning of the 42nd Congress, in effect providing for Members a $5,000 windfall ($2,500 per year for the two preceding years). Despite precedents for making the increase retroactive, the size of the increase and the windfall effect boomeranged. Congressional critics, already primed by the Credit Mobilier scandal, attacked the pay increase as a "salary grab" and a "back-pay steal." Some Members returned their back pay to the Treasury; others donated it to colleges or charities.

When the 43rd Congress opened in December 1873, scores of bills were introduced to repeal the increase. By an Act of Jan. 20, 1874, Congressional pay reverted to the previous $5,000, and it stayed at that level until a $7,500 salary was at length sanctioned by an Act of Feb. 26, 1907. A raise to $10,000 was provided by an Act of March 4, 1925.

Government austerity was the byword as the Great Depression of the 1930s deepened. Salaries of Federal employees were reduced, and Members of Congress likewise had to take a pay cut. The Economy Act of June 30, 1932, provided for a 10-percent cutback in Members' salaries, dropping them from $10,000 to $9,000. The cutback was increased to 15 percent, meaning a further drop to $8,500, by the Economy Act of March 20, 1933. Gradually the cutbacks were rescinded, and by the end of 1935, Congressional salaries had been restored to the $10,000 level.

Postwar Salaries and Expense Allowances

Congress included in the Legislative Reorganization Act of 1946 a provision increasing Congressional salaries from $10,000 to $12,500 and retaining an existing $2,500 non-taxable expense allowance for all Members. The increases took effect at the beginning of the 80th Congress in 1947. The Joint Committee on the Organization of Congress had recommended a $15,000 annual salary and elimination of the expense allowance, but the bill was amended in the House, and the House provision was retained in the final version of the measure. The Act also provided $20,000 salaries for the Vice President and Speaker of the House.

Provision for the $2,500 expense allowance had been made in 1945. The House Appropriations Committee included in the Legislative Branch appropriation bill for fiscal 1946 an appropriation to cover a $2,500 annual expense allowance for Representatives. Although the bill did not so stipulate, the Committee said the allowance probably would be tax-exempt. When the bill reached the House floor opponents called the allowance an opening wedge for inflation and a pay increase by subterfuge. The key vote came on a resolution to waive all points of order against the bill. (Adoption of this resolution would prevent elimination of the expense allowance section on the ground that it was legislation in an appropriation bill.)

The resolution was adopted, 229-124, so the expense allowance remained in the bill. Other efforts to eliminate or change the proposal failed, and the bill passed by voice vote May 10.

The Senate Appropriations Committee reported the bill with a $2,500 expense allowance for Senators as well. The Committee amendment was defeated on the floor, 9-43, and two compromise amendments also failed. An amendment to strike out the House expense allowance was narrowly defeated, 22-28. The Senate thus passed the bill with the allowance for Representatives, but not for Senators.

The question came up again during Senate consideration of the First Deficiency appropriation bill for fiscal 1946. The Senate Appropriations Committee offered an amendment to extend the expense allowance to Senators, but the Senate rejected the plan, 24-47. Senators finally received the $2,500 expense allowance in 1946, in the fiscal 1947 Legislative Branch Appropriation Act.

In the Revenue Act of 1951, Congress eliminated the tax-free provision on Congressional expense allowances, effective Jan. 3, 1953. Also made subject to taxation were the expense allowances of the President, Vice President and Speaker of the House. The provision was offered as a Senate amendment by Sen. John J. Williams (R Del.) and agreed to on a 77-11 roll call.

Congress in 1953 created a Commission on Judicial and Congressional Salaries to study the salary question and report to Congress by Jan. 15, 1954. As passed by the Senate, the bill would have empowered the Commission to raise salaries. However, the measure was amended in the House to require Congressional approval for any pay increase. The Commission's report recommended a $10,000 salary boost, but Congress took no action.

In 1955, Congress enacted legislation raising Congressional and judicial salaries. The bill increased the salary for Members of Congress to $22,500 (from $12,500 plus a $2,500 expense allowance). It also provided $35,000 for the Speaker and Vice President (up from $30,000), and retained the existing $10,000 taxable expense allowance in both cases. The increases became effective March 1, 1955.

The chief difference between the House and Senate bills was the $2,500 Congressional expense allowance, which the House would have retained. Both the Senate version and the final version deleted this item. The House passed the bill Feb. 16, 283-118, and the Senate passed it Feb. 23, 62-24. The Senate rejected the first conference report Feb. 25, because it contained a compromise expense allowance provision. After that had been deleted, the second conference report was approved by the Senate Feb. 28 and by the House March 1.

Congress again raised its own salaries, and those of other federal personnel, in 1964. Congressmen's salaries were raised by $7,500, to $30,000. Salaries of the Speaker of the House and the Vice President were raised to $43,000. The bill was enacted after the House had first killed another bill raising Congressional salaries by $10,000. The first bill was rejected by the House March 12 on a 184-222 roll-call vote. Election-year worries were believed important in the defeat of the first bill. The second measure was strongly backed by President Johnson and voted upon after most of the 1964 primary elections had been held. It was passed by the House June 11 on a 243-157 roll call and by the Senate July 2 on a 58-21 roll call.

Special Salary Commission

In 1967, Congress modified a bill increasing postal rates and the salaries of Federal employees by adding an amendment creating a nine-member commission to review the salaries of judges, Members of Congress and top officers of the Executive Branch every four years and recommend changes it felt desirable. The amendment originated in the House, was rejected by the Senate, and then reinstated in conference. President Johnson had requested a special joint salary commission, representing all three branches, to examine all Federal pay systems and report to the President and Congress within two years.

The Congressionally established commission was to include three members appointed by the President, two by the President of the Senate, two by the Speaker of the House, and two by the Chief Justice of the United States. Beginning in fiscal 1969, the commission was to submit its recommendations to the President, who was to recommend in his Budget the exact rates of pay "he deems advisable" for Federal executives, judges and Members of Congress. His recommendations could be either higher or lower than those of the commission, or he could propose that salaries not be altered. The recommendations would take effect within 30 days unless Congress either disapproved all or part of them or enacted a separate pay bill. Thus creation of the commission was an attempt to relieve Members of Congress of the politically uncomfortable task of raising their own salaries.

President Johnson announced appointment of the Commission on Executive, Legislative and Judicial Salaries on June 3, 1968. Named to head the Commission was Frederick R. Kappel, former chairman of the American Telephone & Telegraph Co. The commission, reporting in December 1968, recommended salary levels of $50,000 for Members of Congress, $67,500 for the Chief Justice, $65,000 for Associate Justices, $60,000 for Cabinet members, and a scale of $50,000 to $40,000 for Level II-V in the Executive Branch. With the exception of Cabinet members, all salary recommendations were scaled down by Mr. Johnson in his Budget request. The Congressional salary level was reduced to $42,500.

The new salary scales became effective March 1, 1969. Although numerous bills were introduced in 1969 to rescind the Congressional pay increase and to abolish the salary commission, none was enacted.

Personal Staffs of Members

For a century after the organization of Congress, no provision was made in either chamber for personal staff assistance for a Member, unless he was chairman of a committee.

The Senate was first to provide for staff aides. In 1885, a Senator was authorized to employ a clerk when Congress was in session. The rate was set at $6 per day. In 1893, the House first authorized a clerk for its Members and provided $100 monthly for the clerk's salary.

Over the years, the number of aides and the size of their salaries periodically increased. At present, each Senator receives annually from $295,938 to $477,978 for staff aides, depending on the size of his state. He may hire as many aides as he wants within the allotted funds.

A Representative currently receives a flat $141,492 for up to 15 aides, or, if his constituents exceed 500,000, $148,896 for 16 aides.

Problem of Nepotism

Nepotism has been a recurring issue in Congressional annals. Some Members have used their staff allowances to pay relatives and in effect supplement the Member's personal salary.

On May 20, 1932, the House adopted a resolution by Rep. Lindsay C. Warren (D N.C.) which provided that: "The Clerk of the House of Representatives is hereby authorized and directed to keep open for public inspection the payroll records of the disbursing officer of the House." The resolution was adopted without debate. Few Members on the floor understood its import. On the next day, however, stories based upon examinations of the disbursing officer's records were published in all newspapers. They disclosed that 97 Members of the House devoted their clerk-hire allowance, in whole or in part, to payment of persons having the same names as their own. Presumably these persons were relatives. The names were published, and "nepotism in Congress" became a subject of wide public discussion.

Senate payroll information was not opened for public inspection until 1959. On June 26, 1959, the Senate by voice vote adopted a resolution requiring the Secretary of the Senate to make public the name, title, salary and employer of all Senate employees. The resolution was the outgrowth of critical newspaper stories on the withholding of payroll information, coupled with disclosures of Congressional nepotism.

Touching off the new round of disclosures was a Jan. 5, 1959, news story by Scripps-Howard staff writer Vance Trimble, containing a lengthy list of relatives he said were employed by Members in their offices in 1958. Trimble had obtained the names by checking out similar names on available House-Senate records. He filed a court suit to gain access to Senate payroll records.

Adding fuel to the controversy was a Feb. 18, 1959, newspaper report that freshman Rep. Steven V. Carter (D Iowa) had put his 19-year-old son, Steven A. Carter, on his office payroll at a salary of $11,873 a year. Carter at first defended his action, saying his son, a part-time law student, "is the most valuable one in my office." On Feb. 24 Carter disclosed he had been under treatment for cancer and said he needed his son's help in the office while he was hospitalized. He said, Feb. 25, that his own condition had improved enough for him to return to the office and that his son's salary would be cut in half. (Rep. Carter died of cancer Nov. 4.)

The Carter case was followed by several other disclosures. On Feb. 23 the Associated Press published a list of 65 Representatives who had persons with "the same or similar family name" on their January payrolls.

Three Representatives—Clarence J. Brown (R Ohio), Frank E. Smith (D Miss.) and H. Allen Smith (R Calif.)—included on the original AP list of Feb. 25 denied that their payroll namesakes were in any way related to them.

Also on Feb. 25, Richard Martin, son of Sen. Thomas E. Martin (R Iowa), disclosed that he had been on his father's payroll from 1955 to 1958 while he was studying law in Washington. Young Martin said he worked in his father's office "almost every day." The Senator and his son refused to disclose his salary.

Nepotism also was a problem for controversial Rep. Adam Clayton Powell (D N.Y.). From the time of their marriage in December 1960 Powell employed his Puerto Rican wife—Yvette Marjorie Flores—as a paid member of his own Congressional office staff. Mrs. Powell remained in Puerto Rico after the birth of a son in 1962, but she continued to draw a $20,578 annual salary as a clerk whose job was to answer mail to Spanish-speaking constituents. The House in 1964 adopted a resolution aimed specifically at that situation; it forbade Members from hiring employees who did not work either in the Member's home district or in Washington, D.C. That provision was readopted as a part of the Legislative Branch appropriation in 1965. Mrs. Powell, however, remained in Puerto Rico.

In 1967, Congress included in the postal rate-federal pay increase bill a provision to curb nepotism in Federal employment. The provision prohibited public officials, including Members of Congress, from appointing or influencing the appointment of relatives in the agency in which the official served. The ban covered all officials, including the President, but did not cover relatives already employed. And it did not prevent an official in one agency or chamber of Congress from seeking to obtain employment for a relative in another agency or chamber.

Special Allowances

The travel allowance provided in the Act of Sept. 22, 1789, fixing the compensation of Members of Congress was the first of what has become a handful of special allowances that Members have created for themselves through the years. Senators and Representatives still receive a travel allowance. Other special allowances cover office expenses, stationery, postage and telephone and telegraph service.

The various allowances have been a persistent source of trouble for Members. The stationery and other allowances are susceptible to abuse. At the same time, some Members find that the amounts provided by the allowances fail to keep up with rising costs. One answer to the money problem has been for Members to apply campaign contributions to certain incidental expenses.

Senate debate on a code of conduct in 1968 illustrated some of the problems associated with the special allowances. Sen. Clifford P. Case (R N.J.) advocated a ban on the use of political contributions for office expenses. He said that a rule proposed by the Senate Select Committee on Standards and Conduct would give "official sanction" to the practice and would postpone action by the Senate Rules and Administration Committee to increase office allowances. The Committee's recommendations, he added, "not only provide no guide but open the door wider to political pressures."

Sen. John Stennis (D Miss.) agreed that the Rules and Administration Committee ought to review Senate office allowances. He said, however, that "it would be unreasonable and wrong to cut a Senator off and prohibit him from using funds that come into his hands in good faith to be spent in connection with his office." The receipt of such funds, he pointed out, would have to be disclosed.

Aids to Campaigning

In addition to the traditional advantage stemming from the inherent news-making power of a Member of Congress, an incumbent Member enjoys a number of other campaigning advantages over his non-incumbent opponent.

Some of the additional advantages are tied directly to his Congressional perquisites. For example, a Member's staff and his allowances for travel, stationery, postage, office equipment, and telephone and telegraph service may all contribute—at public expense—to his campaign activities. (Members chronically complain of the inadequacy of these allowances.)

One of the greatest advantages—and perhaps a decisive one as electronic campaigning grows in importance—is the availability of radio and television recording facilities. The House Recording Studio, located in the Rayburn House Office Building, and the Senate Recording Studio, located in a former subway tunnel between the Capitol and the Old Senate Office Building, are available to all Members.

In theory the recording studios are designed to help Members communicate with their constituents. Tapes recorded at the studios can be mailed to local stations for use in regular news or public affairs programing. In fact, much of the work performed at the studios is frankly campaign material.

Studio productions are subsidized with public funds. Tapes and films are produced at cost, and the film or tape is available at Congressional stationery rooms.

Howard W. Cannon (D Nev.), however, referred to the proposed ban as "a rich man's amendment," for he pointed out that wealthy Senators could afford to pay for office expenses not covered by official allowances. The amendment was adopted by a 41-40 roll-call vote.

The Case ban was softened the next day when the Senate, by a 43-28 roll-call vote, adopted a second amendment permitting the use of contributions to pay certain politically related office costs. Offered by Jacob K. Javits (R N.Y.) and Ralph W. Yarborough (D Texas), the amendment permitted Senators to use contributions to pay for travel to and from their states, for printing speeches and newsletters to constituents, for radio and television time, telephone, stationery and other expenses over their allowances, and for subscribing to home-state newspapers.

Travel and Office Allowances

The travel allowance of 1789—$6 for each 20 miles—has been altered to reflect the increasing mobility of a nation spanned by air routes as well as by highways. Although the 20-cents-per-mile allowance for an annual round trip to Congress has remained unchanged since 1866, additional funds have been authorized for periodic trips by the Member and his staff.

A Senator at present is authorized 12 round trips a year. His staff is allowed eight round trips a year, or

10 round trips if the Senator represents a state with a population of 10 million or more.

A Representative is allowed one round trip for each month that Congress is in session. If a Representative's district allows him to commute to Congress, he can elect to receive a flat $750 travel allowance. A Representative's staff is allowed two round trips a year.

Office Expenses. In addition to space in one of the Capitol Hill office buildings, each Senator receives certain basic office equipment allocated in accordance with the population of his state and with other conditions set by the Senate Rules and Administration Committee.

Each Senator also is authorized space for two home-state offices. If space is not available in Federal buildings, rental of up to $2,400 per year is allowed for space in private buildings. Expenses at the home-state offices are reimbursed at a rate of $400 quarterly.

A Representative is allowed $2,500 for equipment to furnish his Capitol Hill Office if he represents no more than 500,000 persons, and up to $3,000 if his district is larger. One free electric typewriter is authorized for each Representative.

For his district offices, each Representative has an expense allowance of $300 quarterly. Two district offices are allowed, with $2,400 available for rental of private space if space in a Federal building is unavailable.

One classic example of abuse of the allowance for office expenses came to light in 1959. A Scripps-Howard dispatch on March 4, 1959, disclosed that Rep. Randall S. Harmon (D Ind.) was collecting $100 a month for use of the front porch of his home in Indiana as a district office. The incident was widely publicized and led to further news stories on the use that Members make of their back-home offices. Randall was defeated in the 1960 elections.

Telephone Calls, Postage, Stationery

The Senate Rules and Administration Committee fixes telephone and telegraph allowances for Members of the upper chamber. Each Senator may make 3,000 long-distance calls a year, totaling not more than 15,000 minutes. A Senator from a state of more than 10 million persons is allowed an additional 1,500 calls a year (not more than 7,500 minutes). In addition, a Senator is given a flat $2,200 a year for calls that exceed the per-call allowance. The Senate telegraph allowance includes a $2,000 base amount, plus sums based on state population and Western Union rates from Washington, D.C. Individual allowances in 1970 ranged from $6,000 to $20,000.

The House Administration Committee regulates telephone and telegraph allowances for Representatives. A Representative is assigned 140,000 "units" for long-distance calls, telegrams and cables during each Congress. One minute of a long-distance call is counted as four units. One word of a telegram, cablegram or radiogram is considered a single unit. In a night letter, one word is counted as one-half of a unit. Since 1967, each Representative has been allowed up to $300 quarterly for calls made outside of Washington, D.C.

Beyond these basic telephone and telegraph allowances, many Members have access either to a nationwide, leased-line Federal Telecommunications System (FTS) or to wide-area telephone service (WATS) provided by telephone companies.

Postage Allowance. In addition to the authorized use of the Congressional frank, a Senator is allowed $1,056 and a Representative is allowed $700 a year for airmail and special delivery stamps. Franking covers regular surface mail only.

Stationery Allowance. Regulations permitting Members to withdraw for personal use the funds allowed them for stationery supplies have made the stationery allowance a target of frequent criticism. In extreme cases, Members who have not drawn the stationery allowance for a period of years have directed that the accumulated amount be paid to their estates after they die.

In 1968, Congress included in the fiscal 1969 Legislative appropriations bill a provision limiting the use of Senate stationery funds. The provision, offered on the Senate floor by John J. Williams (R Del.) and accepted by voice vote, required that stationery allowances of Senators be used only for stationery and that any unused funds be returned to the Treasury rather than turned over to individual Senators for their personal use. Williams had offered similar amendments in the past, but they had applied to both chambers and had been rejected in conference.

At present the Senate stationery allowance is $3,600 a year; the House allowance is $3,000. Funds in the House stationery allowance still may be withdrawn for personal use and may be accumulated from year to year.

Franking Privileges

In 1970, Members of Congress, officials of the Senate and House and the Vice President mailed more than 190 million letters and packages under their signatures without being charged postage. The cost to the taxpayer was $11,224,000.

The practice is called "franking" and is defined in the Senate Manual as "the autographic or facsimile signature of persons authorized...to transmit matter through the mail without prepayment of postage." Originally, franking was allowed on mail received, as well as that sent, by Members.

The use of franking privileges by Members has been authorized by law ever since the inception of the Postal Service. One of the first acts of Congress under the Constitution was to continue mailing privileges accorded Members of the Continental Congress. The franking privilege was suspended in 1873 but restored after a few months.

Rules. Title 39 of the U.S. Code, which contains the rules of the franking privilege, limits it to correspondence "in which the Member deals with the addressee as a citizen of the United States or constituent." Members of Congress are not authorized to use the frank for letters in which they are acting as a personal friend, a candidate or a member of a political party.

The Post Office Department keeps records of all franked mail as it passes through the Post Office in Washington. Each year, the Post Office Department sends Congress a bill for the cost of the mail that is sent by its Members. The Post Office computes the bill by weighing a random sample of the sacks of franked mail delivered to it from Congress every day.

Use of the Franking Privilege

Persons authorized to use the frank	Matter that may be franked	Marking required	Period during which the frank may be used
Vice President of the United States, Members of Congress, Resident Commissioners, Secretary of the Senate, Sergeant at Arms of the Senate, and Clerk of the House.	Public documents printed by order of Congress.	The words "Public Document—Free" and the signature and title, either written or printed facsimile, of the person entitled to frank it, must appear on the address side.	Until the 30th day of June following expiration of their respective terms of office.
Members of Congress and Resident Commissioners.	*Congressional Record* or any part of it, or speeches or reports contained in it.	The words, *Congressional Record* or Part of *Congressional Record* —Free" and the signature and title, either written or printed facsimile, of the person entitled to frank it, must appear on the address side.	During term of office only.
Members of Congress.	Seeds and agricultural reports from the Department of Agriculture.	The signature and title, either written or printed facsimile, of the person entitled to frank it, must appear on the address side.	Until the 30th day of June following expiration of their terms of office.
Vice President of the United States, Members and Members-elect of Congress, Resident Commissioners, the Secretary of the Senate, and the Sergeant at Arms of the Senate.	Official correspondence not exceeding 4 ounces in weight. Official correspondence when addressed to a Government official by title may exceed 4 ounces in weight, but must not exceed 4 pounds.		Until the 30th day of June following expiration of their respective terms of office. When the position of Secretary of the Senate or Sergeant at Arms of the Senate is vacant, privilege may be exercised in officer's name by authorized persons.
Vice President-elect.	All mail, including airmail, sent by him in connection with preparation for the assumption of official duties as Vice President.	The signature and title, either written or printed facsimile, of the Vice President-elect must appear on the address side. Matter intended for air service must be marked with the words "Air Mail" on the address side.	Until assumption of duties as the Vice President.
Former Vice President.	All mail, including airmail, sent by him in connection with winding up the affairs of his office.	The signature and title, either written or printed facsimile, of the former Vice President must appear on the address side. Matter intended for air service must be marked with the words "Air Mail" on the address side.	Until 6 months from the date of expiration of his term of office.

The Post Office has never inspected franked mail to determine whether any Members of Congress are abusing the privilege and sending personal or political correspondence postage-free. Until 1968, however, the Post Office issued rulings on specific abuses of the privilege if private citizens made official complaints. In cases where the Post Office ruled that a Member was abusing the privilege, it sent him a bill asking him to pay the postage for the improperly franked letters.

"Many Members paid their bills," said Harvey Hannah, deputy general counsel to the Postmaster General. "There were cases where we collected over $5,000. But we couldn't force them to pay. We had no teeth in the rulings. It wasn't fair for some to pay and others not to."

Junk Mail Controversy

Special uses of the frank occasionally lead to controversy. In 1960, House-Senate conferees on the Treasury-Post Office Department appropriation bill for fiscal 1961 wrangled for more than a month over a House provision, eliminated by a Williams (R Del.) amendment on the Senate floor, that would have permitted delivery of mail in urban areas under the Congressional frank addressed to "Occupant" if the Post Office Department extended the privilege accordingly. Since 1924 the Postmaster General, exercising his discretionary power, had permitted delivery of such mail to rural areas, but not to urban areas. Twice he had extended the privilege to urban areas also, then rescinded it. Proponents of the provision said the privilege would not be a change in law but only an "indication" to the Postmaster General of Congressional sentiment. Opponents held that the Congressional franking privilege already was abused and that the provision would place the Postmaster General in an impossible situation. The House finally yielded to the Senate and the provision was eliminated.

The issue of franked mail addressed to "Occupant" or "Boxholder" was raised again, in connection with the first fiscal 1962 supplemental appropriation. The House had included in the bill, and the Senate Appropriations Committee had deleted, a provision requiring the Post Office to handle such mail for both rural and non-rural areas. House conferees insisted on restoring the provision, which was reported from conference in disagreement. When the conference report came to the floor in the closing hours of the 1961 session, the House quickly adopted this and other disputed provisions and then adjourned for the year. The Senate had no alternative but to agree to the disputed provisions or let the bill die. After protestations, it did agree. The 1961 rider was permanent legislation.

In 1962, the dispute over the franking privilege was resumed during consideration of the Legislative appropriation bill for fiscal 1963. The Senate insisted on curbing delivery of franked mail addressed only to "Occupant," the House on retaining it. Ultimately the Senate won out: the final version of the measure stated that no funds in the bill could be used to deliver franked Congressional mail addressed only to "Occupant" to either rural or non-rural areas. This provision ruled out, for fiscal 1963, not only the expansion of the franking privilege included in the 1961 House rider but also the delivery of franked mail addressed only to "Occupant" in rural areas.

The junk mail controversy was resumed in 1963. In passing its Legislative appropriations bill, the House did not include any language on franking, which meant that the permanent 1961 provision allowing delivery of House and Senate franked "occupant" mail to both rural and urban areas would be in effect. The Senate, however, added a provision forbidding Members of the House or Senate from sending franked mail only to "Occupant." Chairman Tom Steed (D Okla.) of the House Appropriations Legislative Subcommittee refused to send the bill to conference unless the House view on franking privileges for House Members was certain to prevail. Steed charged the Senate with meddling in House affairs and implied he would reveal information on alleged Senatorial misbehavior. After numerous charges and countercharges and Senate rejection of the initial conference report because it yielded to the House position on franking, a compromise franking provision was finally adopted, applying to fiscal 1964. It forbade Senators to send any franked mail in fiscal 1964 addressed only to "Occupant," but permitted House Members to do so, with the limitation that such mail could be sent only to persons within the Representative's own Congressional district. There was no action on "Occupant"-addressed mail in 1964, which left standing the 1961 provision, as modified in 1963.

Restrictions on Franking Privilege

In 1966, the Post Office charged that Sen. Robert Griffin (R Mich.) was using the frank to mail campaign literature to his constituents under the pretext that it was part of a regular newsletter. The Post Office sent Griffin a bill for $25,000, but it had no way of enforcing its collection and the bill was never paid. Griffin said the controversial mailing included material from the *Congressional Record* and therefore constituted "official business." Section 4163, Title 39 of the United States Code authorizes Members of Congress to use the frank to mail any newsletter that is a verbatim reprint of an item that has appeared in the *Record*, even though its content would not otherwise be regarded as official business.

On Dec. 27, 1968, Timothy May, general counsel to Postmaster General Marvin Watson, reversed the franking position of the Post Office Department and ruled that the Department no longer would attempt to collect from individual Members who had allegedly abused the privilege. "Congress never intended that the Post Office should be a collection agency regulating the Congress," May said. "The use of the franking privilege for correspondence on official business is a matter strictly between the Member of Congress and his conscience. Congress... as individuals or as a body must undertake responsibility for determining the use of the Congressional franking privilege."

David A. Nelson, who succeeded May as general counsel to Postmaster General Winton M. Blount, said he agreed with May's policy. Nelson said the Post Office Department would continue to provide advisory opinions on correct use of the frank but would not resume its role as a collection agency.

No person allowed franking privileges may lend his frank to any committee, organization or person (Senate and House committees not included). The fine for lending one's frank to someone else or violating any of the other rules regarding the privilege may be as high as $300.

Travel Abroad—Junketing

Special allowances are available to Members of Congress traveling abroad on Government business. As defined by William L. Safire's *The New Language of Politics,* "An overseas tour by a Congressman or candidate is described by him as a *fact-finding trip,* and as a *junket* by his opponents, who usually add 'at the taxpayer's expense.'"

A Congressional Quarterly survey released July 10, 1970, showed that at least 209 Members of Congress had taken 296 trips abroad during 1969 at a reported cost of $591,550.

In both 1968 and 1969, slightly more than 52 percent of the Members made at least one trip abroad, at either Government or private expense. At least 431 trips were reported in 1968; in 1969 there were at least 449. In 1968, 87 percent of the 431 trips were made at Government expense; of the 449 trips reported in 1969, 66 percent were financed by the Government.

Members generally undertake foreign travel on Congressional (usually committee) business or by Executive request or appointment. Members traveling abroad on committee business or as delegates to meetings of certain parliamentary groups are required by law to make public annually the Government funds used. No public reports are required on other foreign trips.

Defense and Criticism of Members' Trips

As long as Members of Congress have been taking trips abroad at Government expense, there have been arguments between those who say that such travel is valuable and those who say it is a waste of time and money.

Defenders of foreign travel point out that it enables Members to develop insight and to gain first-hand information needed for intelligent legislating and appropriating of funds. They say that such trips help Members to overcome prejudice and provincialism and to spread goodwill, as well as giving them the chance to center their attention on foreign affairs and U.S. programs abroad.

Those who oppose overseas travel argue that trips at Government expense are mainly a waste of the taxpayer's money. They say that visiting Members expect to spend only a minimal amount of time on official business abroad, that they make unreasonable demands on U.S. personnel in the countries they visit, and that they sometimes damage American prestige through tactlessness or give foreign officials the impression that their comments reflect Administration policy.

Efforts to Control Travel Costs

Critics also assert that the true cost of travel can be easily obscured, since expenses are not completely itemized or audited. Sometimes no cost of transportation is reported when flights are furnished by the State Department or the Department of Defense. Commercial airline fares and some other expenses are not always listed if they are defrayed out of Senate and House expense allowances.

Occasionally, prodded by adverse publicity about junketing abuses, Congress moves to enact restrictions. In 1961, a bill raising ship construction subsidies (HR 10644—PL 86-607) included a provision that prohibited shipping companies from giving free or reduced-rate transportation to any Government official or employee, or to members of their families, unless the Government contracted for their transportation. A similar prohibition covering travel on railroads and airlines had been law for some time. The anti-junketing provision was proposed by Sen. John J. Williams (R Del.) and its adoption marked a victory in a campaign Williams had waged since 1954. In 1958 the Senate had agreed to the ban as a rider on a superliner construction bill, but the House rejected it in conference. A similar fate met his proposal in 1959 when it was added to a bill involving Great Lakes passenger vessels. In May 1960 Williams succeeded in adding the anti-junket amendment to a Commerce Department appropriations bill, but it too was dropped in conference. In June, however, a series of magazine articles on Congressional junketing gave considerable impetus to Williams' campaign. The Senate on June 7 adopted his amendment to HR 10644 by an 88-0 vote. House conferees accepted it reluctantly to "protect passage" of the rest of the bill.

Also in 1961, Congress used the Legislative appropriation bill (HR 12232—PL 86-628) as the vehicle for achieving more stringent regulations governing the accounting of Government funds used for domestic and foreign travel by Members of Congress and committee staff members. The Senate on June 20 adopted, 56-23, an amendment requiring Congressional committees to file annual public reports listing both dollar and foreign currency funds spent by individual Congressmen and committee staff members for overseas travel. The House not only accepted the Senate amendment but also added provisions of its own restricting the domestic travel of Members at Government expense. Although the drive for tighter regulations governing the accounting of travel funds was spearheaded by Sen. Williams, long a proponent of stricter accounting procedures, copyrighted articles in Knight newspapers and *Life* magazine played a large part in the Members' eventual decision to accept the reforms.

Sources of Travel Funds

The information regarding expenses contained in the record is usually the minimum required by law. It tells where a Member went, how long he stayed and how much he collected in Government per diem payments. The listings rarely tell why lawmakers went outside the United States. And they do not list all of the sources of money available to Members of Congress when they leave the country on official business.

Some of the funds and facilities used for activities abroad by Members include:

Appropriated Funds. Money is appropriated by Congress to pay the expenses, travel included, of its committees for routine and special investigations. Some committees also have confidential funds, which chairmen may spend without giving taxpayers a specific accounting.

Counterpart Funds. Members traveling abroad are allowed to use American-owned counterpart funds (foreign currencies held by American embassies and credited to the United States in return for aid, and which may be used in the country of origin). This surplus foreign currency generally is disbursed on a $50 per diem basis by embassies. In many "non-surplus" countries, such as France, Germany, Japan and Vietnam, the U.S. Government purchases currency commercially for the use of Members of Congress.

Representational Funds. American embassies and consulates abroad are allocated sums for official entertaining. Some of these funds are used for hospitality purposes in the case of visiting Members of Congress.

Agency Funds. Many Members of Congress travel as guests of Government agencies, which have money appropriated for trips to their overseas posts. The Departments of State and Defense are the agencies most called upon to arrange travel for lawmakers.

Military Transportation. Members often travel without charge on ships of the Military Sea Transportation Service and planes of the Military Airlift Command (formerly MATS).

Areas Visited by Members of Congress

Most of the traveling Members in 1969 visited more than one country while abroad. Geographical areas visited on both Government and non-Government trips are shown below:

Area	Senate	House	Total
Western Europe (including Turkey)	45	130	175
Far East*	21	69	90
Vietnam	5	19	24
Central, South America	15	30	45
Middle East	6	15	21
Australia, New Zealand	0	7	7
Caribbean, Bermuda	10	12	22
Africa	2	9	11
Russia, Eastern Europe	18	15	33
Antarctica	0	7	7
Canada	12	18	30

All trips to Vietnam are included in the Far East category.

Congressional Immunity

The provision of the Constitution that authorized Congressional salaries also established significant special immunities for Members of Congress. "They shall in all cases, except treason, felony and breach of the peace," declares Article I, Section 6, Clause 1, "be privileged from arrest during their attendance at the session of their respective houses, and in going to and returning from the same; and for any speech or debate in either house, they shall not be questioned in any other place." *(See box for Jefferson's comments on Congressional immunity.)*

Court decisions and changing legal practices have rendered the privilege-from-arrest clause virtually obsolete. It has been held to apply only to arrests in civil suits, which were still common in the United States at the time the Constitution was adopted. It has been held inapplicable to service of process in both civil or criminal cases and to arrest in any criminal case. The phrase "treason, felony and breach of the peace" has been broadly interpreted to withdraw all criminal offenses from the operation of the privilege.

The constitutional immunity from prosecution for libel and slander also has been broadly interpreted. As a result of court decisions, the protection of this clause has not been limited only to words spoken in debate; it has been made applicable also to written reports, to pro-

posed resolutions and to all things generally done in Congress by Members in relation to Congressional business.

Court Decisions on Immunity

The practical impact of Congressional immunity is suggested by a selection of examples.

Adam Clayton Powell. In 1958, Rep. Adam Clayton Powell (D N.Y.) was indicted on three counts of tax evasion by a Federal grand jury. In 1960, two counts were dismissed and the trial on the remaining count ended in a hung jury. The Federal Government continued efforts to obtain back taxes from Powell. On June 8, 1966, Powell's attorney announced that Powell had paid $27,833.17 in back taxes and penalties and the Government had withdrawn fraud charges against him. Extensive publicity was given to two suits accusing Powell of libel and to his maneuvers to avoid paying a libel judgment. The suits were brought by Mrs. Esther James, a Harlem widow, whom Powell—in a March 6, 1960, television interview —described as a "bag woman," or graft collector, for New York City police. Mrs. James pursued Powell relentlessly through the courts in an effort to collect the judgment. By the end of 1966, Powell had been held in contempt of court on four separate occasions—three times for civil contempt and once for criminal contempt.

United States v. Johnson. The Supreme Court on Feb. 24, 1966, by a 7-0 vote, held that in prosecuting a former Member of Congress, the Executive Branch may not constitutionally inquire into his motives for making a speech on the floor of Congress, even though the speech was made in consequence of a bribe and was part of an unlawful conspiracy.

The holding in *U.S. v. Johnson* left Members of Congress immune from prosecution for their words and legislative deeds on the floor of Congress, with one exception reserved by the Court—prosecution under a "narrowly drawn" law enacted by Congress itself "to regulate the conduct of its Members."

The *Johnson* case arose out of the conviction of former Rep. Thomas F. Johnson (D Md. 1959-63) on June 13, 1963, by a Federal jury in Baltimore. The Government charged that Johnson, former Rep. Frank W. Boykin (D Ala. 1935-63) and two officers of a Maryland savings and loan company then under indictment, J. Kenneth Edlin and William L. Robinson, entered into a conspiracy whereby Johnson and Boykin would approach the Justice Department to urge a "review" of the indictment and Johnson would make a speech on the floor of the House defending savings and loan institutions. Johnson made the speech June 30, 1960, and it was reprinted by the indicted company and distributed to the public. Johnson and Boykin allegedly received money in the form of "campaign contributions," Johnson's share being more than $20,000.

Johnson was convicted on seven counts of violating the federal conflict-of-interest law (18 U.S.C. 281) and on one count of conspiring to defraud the United States (18 U.S.C. 371); the others were convicted of the same charges. President Johnson on Dec. 17, 1965, granted Boykin a full pardon.

The 4th Circuit Court of Appeals on Sept. 16, 1964, set aside Johnson's conspiracy conviction on the ground that it was unconstitutional under provisions of Article

Jefferson on Immunity

One of the most interesting concise discussions of Congressional immunity is contained in Jefferson's Manual, a compilation of legislative rules and precedents prepared by Thomas Jefferson when he was Vice President. An excerpt from Jefferson's discussion follows:

The privileges of members of Parliament, from small and obscure beginnings, have been advancing for centuries with a firm and never-yielding pace. Claims seem to have been brought forward from time to time, and repeated, till some example of their admission enabled them to build law on that example. We can only, therefore, state the points of progression at which they now are. It is now acknowledged: 1. That they are at all times exempted from question elsewhere, for anything said in their own House; that during the time of privilege. 2. Neither a member himself, his wife, nor his servants *(familiares sui),* for any matter of their own, may be arrested on mesne process in any civil suit. 3. Nor be detained under execution, though levied before time of privilege. 4. Nor impleaded, cited, or subpoenaed in any court. 5. Nor summoned as a witness or juror. 6. Nor may their lands or goods be distrained. 7. Nor their persons assaulted or characters traduced. And the period of time covered by privilege, before and after the session, with the practice of short prorogations under the connivance of the Crown, amounts in fact to a perpetual protection against the course of justice....That these privileges must be continually progressive seems to result from their rejecting all definition of them, the doctrine being that "their dignity and independence are preserved by keeping their privileges indefinite; and that 'the maxims upon which they proceed, together with the method of proceeding, rest entirely in their own breast, and are not defined and ascertained by any particular stated laws.' "

It was probably from this view of the encroaching character of privilege that the framers of our Constitution, in their care to provide that the laws shall bind equally on all, and especially that those who make them shall not exempt themselves from their operation, have only privileged Senators and Representatives themselves from the single act of arrest in all cases except treason, felony, and breach of the peace, during their attendance at the session of their respective Houses, and in going to and returning from the same, and from being questioned in any other place for any speech or debate in either House. Under the general authority to make all laws necessary and proper for carrying into execution the power given them, they may provide by law the details which may be necessary for giving full effect to the enjoyment of this privilege. No such law being as yet made, it seems to stand at present on the following ground: 1. The act of arrest is void *ab initio.* 2. The member arrested may be discharged on motion, or by habeas corpus, under the Federal or State authority, as the case may be; or by a writ of privilege out of the chancery in those States which have adopted that part of the laws of England. 3. The arrest, being unlawful, is a trespass for which the officer and others concerned are liable to action or indictment in the ordinary courts of justice, as in other cases of unauthorized arrest. 4. The court before which the process is returnable is bound to act as in other cases of unauthorized proceeding, and liable, also, as in other similar cases, to have their proceedings stayed or corrected by the superior courts.

The time necessary for going to and returning from Congress not being defined, it will, of course, be judged of in every particular case by those who will have to decide the case. While privilege was understood in England to extend, as it does here, only to exemption from arrest, *eundo, morando, et redeundo,* the House of Commons themselves decided that "a convenient time was to be understood." Nor is the law so strict in point of time as to require the party to set out immediately on his return, but allows him time to settle his private affairs, and to prepare for his journey; and does not even scan his road very nicely, nor forfeit his protection for a little deviation from that which is most direct; some necessity perhaps constraining him to it.

This privilege from arrest, privileges, of course, against all process the disobedience to which is punishable by an attachment of the person, as a *subpoena ad respondendum,* or *testificandum,* or a summons on a jury; and with reason, because a member has superior duties to perform in another place. When a Representative is withdrawn from his seat by summons, the...people whom he represents lose their voice in debate and vote, as they do on his voluntary absence; when a Senator is withdrawn by summons, his State loses half its voice in debate and vote, as it does on his voluntary absence. The enormous disparity of evil admits of no comparison....

I, Section 6. The court ordered a new trial on the other counts on the ground that evidence taken about Johnson's speech on the conspiracy count "infected" the entire case.

The Supreme Court affirmed the lower court's ruling, thus foreclosing further prosecution on the conspiracy count but permitting retrial on the other counts.

Johnson on Jan. 26, 1968, was convicted for the second time on the conflict-of-interest charges by the U.S. District Court in Baltimore, Md. He was sentenced to six months in prison.

Dombrowski v. Eastland. On May 15, 1967, the Supreme Court held a Senator, but not a subcommittee chief counsel, to be immune from civil suit for certain actions. The vote was 8-0, Justice Black not participating. The case involved James A. Dombrowski, executive director of the Southern Conference Education Fund Inc. (SCEF), a civil rights organization operating in Louisiana and elsewhere in the South. In October 1963, police officers, supervised by the staff director of the State Un-American Activities Committee in Louisiana, raided the SCEF offices at gunpoint, ransacked the homes and offices of the group's officers and seized a truckload of files and other materials. Dombrowski and others were arrested and charged with violation of the state subversive activities law. A state judge quashed those indictments as based on evidence illegally obtained, and the Supreme Court, in *Dombrowski v. Pfister* (1965), found sections of the state law invalid and prohibited further prosecution of the SCEF officers. In the meantime, however, the Senate Judiciary Internal Security Subcommittee had subpoenaed the illegally seized records. Sen. James O. Eastland (D Miss.) was chairman of both the full Committee and of the Subcommittee, and J. G. Sourwine was chief counsel to the Subcommittee. Dombrowski sued both men for damages, on the ground that they had entered into a conspiracy with Louisiana officials to seize records by unlawful means in violation of the Fourth Amendment prohibition against illegal search and seizure. A district court in the District of Columbia dismissed the suit on the ground that both Eastland and Sourwine had immunity from suit, and the Circuit Court of Appeals for the District of Columbia upheld the dismissal.

In a *per curiam* (unsigned) opinion, the Supreme Court upheld the Circuit Court as to Eastland but reversed it as to Sourwine. The case was remanded to the district court for further proceedings as to Sourwine.

The Supreme Court said that the doctrine of legislative immunity protected Eastland not only from the consequences of the results of litigation but also from the burden of defending himself. The doctrine applied, the Court said, as long as the Senator or Representative was engaged "in the sphere of legitimate legislative activity,' " quoting its own language in *Tenney v. Brandhove* (1951).

The doctrine of legislative immunity also applies to officials and employees acting on behalf of the legislature, the Court said, but in a less absolute way. Dombrowski had raised substantial questions about Sourwine's involvement in the entire matter, the Court said, and was entitled to go to trial. Dombrowski had alleged that Sourwine actively collaborated with Louisiana officials in setting up the raids. The Court expressed no view on the legal consequences of such collaboration, if there was any, but said the factual dispute as to Sourwine's involvement should be settled at trial first.

Congressional Record

After each daily session of Congress, the Government Printing Office (GPO) publishes the *Congressional Record*—the official report of Congressional proceedings. About 49,000 copies of the *Record*, averaging more than 200 pages a copy, are printed and delivered the following morning.

The *Record* is produced in less than 13 hours and involves the efforts of about 2,500 of the GPO's 8,125 employees. In fiscal 1970, it represented an expenditure of $5,360,000, or 2.3 percent of the gross expenditures of the GPO's massive operation.

The proceedings of Congress were not printed systematically before 1865, when the *Congressional Globe*

—the forerunner of the *Congressional Record*—took on a form and style that later became standard for the *Record.*

According to a 1959 Legislative Reference Service research paper on the *Congressional Record,* "Before 1825, debates in the House of Representatives were not reported except in a haphazard way in some of the better newspapers." The Senate debates, the report said, seldom were reported at all.

Not until 1855 were reporters of Congressional proceedings and debates paid at public expense, and only in 1863 were annual appropriations established in both houses of Congress to cover reporting proceedings.

When the Government contract for publication of the *Congressional Globe* expired in 1873, Congress passed an appropriations act which provided that with the 43rd Congress (March 4, 1873) the *Congressional Record* would be produced by the GPO. *(For forerunners of the* Congressional Record, *see box.)*

Proceedings in both the Senate and the House are taken down by separate staffs of reporters, eight in the Senate and seven in the House. The shorthand notes of the debates are read later into a Dictaphone and typed by a transcriber. The typed copy is then proofread by the reporters, given an appropriate heading and sent to the Members for their own editing and correction.

Reporting in the House is done on a half-hour schedule, requiring that each reporter spend five minutes of each half hour on the floor and the remaining time dictating, transcribing and correcting his notes. The Senate operates under the same procedures, but on an hourly basis. Each Senate reporter spends 10 minutes of each hour on the floor.

Corrected transcripts of debates must be returned to the GPO by 9 p.m. the same day if they are to be included in the following day's *Record.*

Prior Publications

1789-1790—*The Congressional Register.* An early attempt to publish a record of Congressional debates. Taken down in shorthand by Thomas Lloyd of New York. Four volumes.

1790-1825—Debate in House reported in haphazard way by some of better newspapers. Senate debates scarcely reported at all.

1834—Publication of first volume of *Annals of Congress.* Produced by Gales and Seaton. Brought together material from newspapers, magazines and other sources on Congressional proceedings from 1st through 12th Congresses (March 3, 1789, to May 27, 1824.) Forty-two volumes.

1824-1837—*Register of Debate.* Produced by Gales and Seaton; directly reported Congressional proceedings.

1833-1873—*The Congressional Globe.* Published by Blair and Rives; F. and J. Rives; F. and J. Rives and George A. Bailey. Covered 23rd through 42nd Congresses (Dec. 2, 1833, to March 3, 1873). Forty-six volumes.

1873 to Present—*Congressional Record.* Produced by the Government Printing Office. March 4, 1873, to present.

Contents of the *Record*

The *Congressional Record* chronologically reports daily what is said on the floor of both houses of Congress. Biweekly and hard-bound versions also are produced to provide a corrected and permanent record. The proceedings of the House and Senate alternately appear first in each daily printing of the *Record* when schedules permit.

The *Record* contains four separate sections:

- Proceedings of the House.
- Proceedings of the Senate.
- Extensions of Remarks.
- Daily Digest—a summary of the proceedings in both houses, including a calendar of committee meetings for the following day.

At the beginning of each month a resume of Congressional activity is printed in the *Record,* providing statistical data for the preceding month on the following:

- Days Congress was in session.
- Number of pages of proceedings printed in the *Record.*
- Number of pages for extensions of remarks.
- Bills enacted into law.
- Measures reported by committees.
- Reports, quorum calls, votes and bills vetoed by the President.

The summary also provides information on the status of Executive nominations.

Proceedings. Although the *Record* purports to print an exact account of the proceedings on the floor of both chambers, Members of the Senate and the House edit and revise their remarks before they are published.

A Member of Congress may request "unanimous consent to extend my remarks at this point in the *Record*" at any time he is able to gain recognition on the floor. When the request is granted, a Member may include a statement, newspaper article or speech, and it will appear in the body of the *Record* just as if it had been actually spoken on the floor during debate.

Extensions of Remarks. Following the record of floor debate in the two houses is a section for Senators and Representatives to extend their remarks—to add to the *Record* materials not actually presented on the floor. Senators may add extraneous material—such as speeches given outside Congress, selected editorials, magazine articles or letters—to the body of the *Record.* Representatives must place such material in the Extensions of Remarks section.

Daily Digest. The Legislative Reorganization Act of 1946 directed the Joint Committee on Printing, which controls the publication of the *Congressional Record,* to incorporate into the *Record* a list of Congressional committee meetings and hearings, their places and subject matter. This section of the *Record,* titled the Daily Digest, summarizes the following material:

- Highlights of the day's Congressional activities.
- Senate action.
- Senate committee meetings.
- House action.
- House committee meetings.
- Joint committee meetings.
- Time and date of next Senate and House meetings.

The Daily Digest lists also the committee meetings scheduled the day the *Record* is distributed.

Friday issues of the *Record* contain a section outlining the Congressional program for the coming week, including schedules of major floor action and of House and Senate committee meetings.

Index. Published about twice a month, the index is the key to using the *Congressional Record.* It is a guide to the contents and a means of tracing floor action on legislation.

The index consists of two parts: an index to the proceedings, which includes material both in the body and in the Extensions of Remarks section, and an index to the history of bills and resolutions.

Corrections and Additions

Remarks made in heated debates may be judged offensive and edited out of the *Record* by a reporter or the Member who made them. Grammar is often improved and the transcripts are often polished.

In the 1950s, Members of Congress frequently inserted into the transcripts of their own remarks such words as "laughter" and "applause." Such additions have become infrequent. If they appear, the reporter has included them.

On Jan. 8, 1930, one Member of Congress referred to the *Congressional Record* as a "catch-all, ...a burying ground for editorials, articles, speeches and addresses from all parts of the country relating to every conceivable subject...."

Such additions in the body or the Extensions section cost money. According to a staff member of the Joint Committee on Printing, one of the longest *Record* insertions by a Member of the House was made by Rep. Royal C. Johnson (R S.D. 1915-33), who inserted 504 pages of names of World War I slackers. No figures on the cost of this extension are available.

In 1935, a Senate speech opposing the National Recovery Administration by Sen. Huey Long (D La. 1931-35) took up 85 pages of the *Record* and cost $4,493. One of the longest insertions was made by Sen. Robert M. LaFollette (R Wis. 1885-91, 1905-25), who on May 5, 1914, inserted a 365-page speech on railroad rates. The cost of printing this extension, according to figures supplied by the Joint Committee on Printing, was $13,760.85.

Attempts to limit what can be added to the *Record* have not been very successful. New York City Mayor John V. Lindsay, then a Member of the House, in 1962 introduced a bill to require that two type faces be used in printing the *Record*—one for the actual debates and the other for all materials subsequently added to the *Record.* The bill was never reported by a committee.

Costs and Production Schedule

Costs. On June 12, 1970, the subscription price of the *Record* was raised for the first time in 87 years. Since 1883, the *Record* had cost $1.50 a month by mail. The new price is $3.75 per month. Price increases meant nothing to 90 percent of the *Record's* 49,000 subscribers, because they get their copies free.

Schedule. The texts of the Senate and House floor debates, matter for the Extensions and Daily Digest sections are assembled by the GPO each night before printing. The size of the *Record* never can be accurately determined beforehand, since it depends on the length of

Per-Page Cost Of Record

(Per Fiscal Year)
1963-1972

1963	$104.19
1964	96.05
1965	108.50
1966	104.00
1967	110.00
1968	113.00
1969	116.00
1970	119.00
1971	(est.) 128.00
1972	(est.) 140.00

floor proceedings. The only known fact is that the *Record* must be printed and delivered by 8 a.m., regardless of its size or how late Congress remained in session.

GPO officials say that to their knowledge the *Record* never has missed its morning delivery deadline.

Production begins at 6:30 p.m., when "preparers" check incoming copy, note sections to be printed in specific type sizes and ascertain that the material to be printed is in proper sequential order. The copy is set by nearly 400 composing and casting machines, proofed, corrected and readied for sterotyping by 2 a.m. The double-deck, 64-page rotary magazine presses that print the *Record* are supposed to be in operation by 2:15 a.m., running at 18,000 impressions an hour. These presses print 49,000 copies of the *Record* each day, using 36 rolls of paper weighing nearly 21.5 tons.

Approximately 35,000 copies are ready for delivery each morning to Congressional offices: 100 are hand-delivered to the homes of Members requesting such service in the Washington area; 227 are delivered to area libraries, offices and universities; 6,000 to 7,000 are mailed to individual subscribers; and 5,837 go to Federal agencies.

Each Senator is allotted 100 copies of the daily *Record* to distribute free to his personnel and/or constituents; each Representative is allotted 71 copies. In addition to the daily *Record,* each Member receives one subscription to what is called the "Greenbound Record," which is a semi-monthly bound compilation of the dailies. The permanent bound volume of the *Record,* printed on book paper, is published some months after a session ends. Each Member is allotted one complete set.

Legislative Budget

The Legislative Branch, like any Government department or agency, operates on a budget, and the expenditures proposed in the budget have to be authorized and appropriated by Congress. However, there are some distinctive differences.

The Legislative Branch appropriations bill is prepared by Congress and is not subject to revision by the Office of Management and Budget, formerly the Bureau of the Budget. Nor is there a central point at which the legislative budget is screened on Capitol Hill. The Clerk of the House and the Secretary of the Senate are responsible for preparing appropriations requests for offices within their respective jurisdictions. In practice, they do little more than pass along requests submitted to them by others.

Legislative budget requests are reviewed by the Legislative Appropriations Subcommittee of each house. Routine spending is rarely challenged, although large-scale projects—such as extension of the East Front of the Capitol or construction of a new office building—usually undergo close scrutiny. In practice, the power of the Appropriations Committees to control the legislative budget is limited, since the spending has been authorized previously by Congress as a whole. In addition, large portions of the budget are relatively uncontrollable; Legislative Branch salaries, for example, are fixed by law.

A second barrier to tighter budget control in the Legislative Branch is the traditional rule of comity, by which each chamber is considered sovereign over its own affairs. Only rarely will one chamber interfere with a spending proposal for the other chamber. A recent case in which the rule of comity was broken occurred in 1968 when the House rejected a Senate-passed bill authorizing acquisition of land for future expansion of the New Senate Office Building.

The accompanying table shows funds appropriated for the Legislative Branch over a period of 21 years. The appropriations provide funds not only for Congress itself but also for the major Congressional supporting agencies, such as the Library of Congress, the General Accounting Office and others. These are the agencies most commonly funded in the Legislative Branch Appropriations Acts. Figures in the table represent regular appropriations only; sums provided in supplemental appropriations have not been included.

Government Printing Office

The Government Printing Office was established by Congress in 1861 to print for "the Senate and House of Representatives, the executive and judicial departments, and the Court of Claims." Buildings, equipment and machinery were acquired from Cornelius Wendell, a private printer, for $135,000. The original plant stood on the site now occupied by the newest of the GPO's buildings. It was staffed by a work force of 350. At present, the GPO employs 8,000 persons and has an annual payroll of nearly $70 million.

By its own reckoning, the GPO is now one of the largest and best-equipped complete printing plants in the world.

Not only does the Government Printing Office manufacture and buy printing; it also runs a sizable distribution and sales operation. The Public Documents Division, established in 1895 as an organic part of the GPO, performs this function. In 1969, the Public Documents Division distributed nearly 250 million copies of its publications and sold 71 million documents to the public. A Government bookstore and six branch bookstores—three of which are located outside the Washington metropolitan area, in Chicago, Kansas City and San Francisco—ran up sales of more than $1.3 million.

Legislative Branch Appropriations, Fiscal 1951-1971

Fiscal Year	Senate	House of Representatives	Joint Items	Architect of The Capitol	Botanic Garden	Library of Congress	Government Printing Office	General Accounting Office[1]	Total
1951[2]	$12,259,136	$21,574,735	$ 288,715	$ 8,180,400	$196,500	$ 8,590,925	$18,199,800	($34,439,500)	$ 69,290,211
1952	12,395,605	22,822,109	291,265	7,501,868	199,500	8,695,160	21,900,000	(31,494,000)	73,805,507
1953	13,406,396	24,066,513	326,560	7,598,175	218,500	9,440,987	21,817,120	(32,060,000)	76,874,251
1954	14,491,768	24,989,110	345,910	6,600,750	221,000	9,459,293	13,900,000	(31,981,000)	70,007,831
1955	14,665,223	27,424,770	1,542,225	6,115,800	223,100	9,399,636	11,325,000	(31,981,000)	70,695,754
1956	16,315,720	31,123,305	2,542,120	21,163,890	246,000	9,767,937	11,650,000	(31,981,000)	92,808,972
1957	21,226,615	35,499,240	2,598,395	34,998,200	253,600	10,637,608	12,190,400	(34,000,000)	117,404,058
1958	22,271,890	37,827,705	2,638,065	17,009,000	275,500	11,647,500	13,175,000	(36,050,000)	104,844,660
1959	23,473,180	39,337,765	2,468,936	30,638,225	972,500	12,411,591	13,995,190	(37,000,000)	123,297,387
1960	26,406,345	42,398,065	2,929,430	27,412,900	327,500	14,302,790	15,020,350	(41,800,000)	128,797,380
1961	26,643,940	42,492,485	3,508,785	25,493,700	352,300	15,230,000	15,749,200	(41,150,000)	129,470,410
1962	28,421,840	47,856,835	4,090,090	19,256,600	489,000	17,193,700	18,124,000	(43,000,000)	135,432,065
1963	29,601,160	48,150,725	4,255,355	18,252,500	452,000	19,431,930	26,333,600	(43,900,000)	146,477,270
1964	30,675,350	50,131,550	6,271,369	33,279,500	454,500	20,488,800	26,992,000	(45,700,000)	168,293,069
1965	31,397,625	53,777,945	6,319,415	22,010,800	500,000	23,333,100[3]	26,062,000	46,900,000	210,300,885
1966	36,379,790	66,414,730	8,856,977	25,640,100	467,000	25,905,700	26,329,000	46,900,000	189,993,297
1967	39,655,180	77,676,145	9,716,988	14,281,000	504,600	29,974,100	42,655,900	48,500,000	214,463,913
1968	44,125,205	80,368,670	11,311,660	15,308,600	584,500	37,141,400	34,059,000	52,800,000	275,699,035
1969	47,082,247	85,039,420	12,711,299	15,614,700	565,000	40,638,000	39,000,000	57,500,000	298,678,396[4]
1970	54,837,660	104,813,635	13,233,322	24,036,100	599,800	43,856,300	39,950,000	63,000,000	344,733,817[4]
1971	60,929,464	110,526,455	14,558,775	36,568,126	672,800	50,396,600	65,382,000	74,020,000	413,104,220[4]

1 Until fiscal 1968, the General Accounting Office was not regularly funded in the Legislative Branch Appropriations Act. GAO figures in parentheses are for years when appropriations were provided in other bills.

2 Fiscal 1951 appropriations were combined in a single omnibus bill called the General Appropriations Act.

3 Includes $149,000 as a supplemental appropriation for fiscal 1964.

4 Beginning in fiscal 1969, the total includes funds (not included in individual categories for Senate, House, etc.) appropriated to liquidate contract authority. Contract authority allows agencies to enter into contracts ahead of appropriations, but requires appropriations in following years to pay off (liquidate) the contracts. Appropriations to liquidate contract authority were as follows: Fiscal 1969, $527,000; fiscal 1970, $407,000; fiscal 1971, $50,000.

Outside Earnings of Senators

Six Democratic Senators regarded as contenders for the presidential nomination received more than $141,000 for speeches and articles in 1970. Reports filed with the Secretary of the Senate showed Sen. Birch Bayh (Ind.) leading the way with $44,331—more than his Senate salary of $42,500. Sen. Edmund S. Muskie (Maine), considered the current frontrunner for the nomination, earned $40,865. Sen. George McGovern (S.D.) listed honoraria of $24,035.

Next in order of receipts were Senators Harold E. Hughes (Iowa), $20,579; Henry M. Jackson (Wash.), $10,928; and Hubert H. Humphrey (Minn.), $1,000. Sen. Edward M. Kennedy (Mass.), who has said he will not be a candidate for the presidency in 1972, reported a total of $2,200 from speeches and articles in 1970. Sen. Mark O. Hatfield (R Ore.) declared honoraria of $41,956—more than any other Republican and second only to Bayh in total receipts. Muskie reported honoraria of $80,183 for 1969, nearly double his figure for 1970. McGovern earned $63,501 the previous year, nearly three times his 1970 figure. But Bayh increased his total from $38,800 in 1969 to $44,331 in 1970.

Seventy-one Senators and two defeated Senators reported a total of $642,315 from speeches and writing during 1970. This was $1,653 more than the total for 1969, the first full year disclosures of honoraria of $300 or more were required from Senators. Twenty-eight Senators reported no honoraria. One Senator, David H. Gambrell (D Ga.), was appointed to succeed the late Sen. Richard B. Russell (D Ga.) on Feb. 2, 1971, and was not required to file a report.

Speeches to Dairy Groups

The largest single payment for a speech in 1970 went to Hughes who got $5,000 from the Trust for Agricultural Political Education, a dairy industry committee. Dairy groups, organizing a coordinated political offensive for the first time in 1970, paid out $20,500 in speaking fees to eight Senators.

In addition to the $5,000 fee to Hughes, the dairy groups paid Muskie $3,000 and Sens. Thomas F. Eagleton (D Mo.) and Adlai E. Stevenson III (D Ill.) $2,500 for one speech each. Sen. Robert Dole (R Kan.) got $2,500 for two speeches.

Fees From Banking and Other Groups

Banking and financial groups paid out $21,550 to ten Senators—all but four of them members of the Banking, Housing and Urban Affairs Committee. Sen. John Sparkman (D Ala.), chairman of the Committee, received $6,250 for six speeches. He also earned another $3,150 for appearances before housing and building trade associations. The bankers also paid speaking fees to Senate Majority Leader Mike Mansfield (D Mont.) and Minority Leader Hugh Scott (R Pa.).

Labor unions spent $16,450 to have Senators speak before their clubs and political action committees. Sen. Harrison A. Williams Jr. (D N.J.), chairman of the Committee on Labor and Public Welfare, received a total of $3,500 to speak before five labor groups. Other special interests providing large sums as honoraria in 1970 were the housing and building industries, $11,000 to 13 Senators, and medical and pharmaceutical groups, $14,479 to 17 Senators.

Uses of Fee Proceeds

The money brought in from the speeches of Senators is used in a variety of ways. Six Senators indicated on their reports how they used honoraria funds. Senators Herman E. Talmadge (D Ga.), Thomas F. Eagleton (D Mo.) and Strom Thurmond (R S.C.) stated that funds went to help defray office and travel expenses. Sen. Henry M. Jackson (D Wash.) reported $5,400 went to high school scholarship or memorial funds. Sen. Robert C. Byrd (D W.Va.) said his single honorarium was placed in a scholarship fund. Sen. Gaylord Nelson (D Wis.) noted that $7,850 of his honoraria was contributed to Environmental Teach-In Inc., and another $2,700 went to the Wisconsin Nature Conservancy.

Bibliography

Books

Safire, William L., *The New Language of Politics.* Random House, 1968.

Tacheron, Donald G., and Udall, Rep. Morris K., *The Job of the Congressman.* Bobbs-Merrill, 1966.

Wright, Rep. Jim, *You and Your Congressman.* Coward-McCann, 1965.

Article

Boeckel, Richard M., "Wages and Hours of Members of Congress." *Editorial Research Reports*, Oct. 13, 1937, pp. 297-320.

Political Patronage in House and Senate

"O, how wretched is that poor man that hangs on princes' favours," observed Cardinal Wolsey in Shakespeare's Henry VIII.

Members of Congress once pulled the political strings on thousands of Federal jobs. On Capitol Hill and back home, a powerful Member could place scores of his cronies in such jobs as local postmaster, health inspector, tax collector, welfare commissioner and even custodian of public morals. The Congressional patronage empire thus provided Members of Congress with a healthy payoff list for political supporters.

Today on Capitol Hill, the only jobs remaining under patronage are those that generally require no special skills or technical knowledge. Elevator operators, doorkeepers, mail carriers and clerks comprise the bulk of the posts still available to patronage dispensers. As defined by William Safire's *The New Language of Politics,* political patronage means "governmental appointments made so as to increase political strength." All in all, a Member finds the patronage jobs now at his disposal of little help in strengthening his political position or rewarding his campaign supporters.

Andrew Jackson was the first President to give open support to political patronage. In 1829 he said: "The duties of all public offices are, or at least admit of being made, so plain and simple that men of intelligence may readily qualify themselves for their performance; and I cannot but believe that more is lost by the long continuance of men in office than is generally to be gained by experience."

When President Jackson spoke out in favor of patronage, the number of public jobs requiring technical skills was not large. The few misfits who slipped in through patronage appointments seemed to do little damage to the general efficiency of the Government.

But the business of Government grew more complex as it expanded, and the inadequacies of the patronage system became glaringly apparent. The Pendleton Civil Service Act of 1883 made the first assault on the patronage system. Thereafter, successive statutes and executive orders virtually removed patronage rights on the state level from Members of Congress. Ninety-five percent of the persons now employed by Federal agencies are hired under the merit system or Civil Service. *(See box on Civil Service History.)*

Members of Congress do have a voice in Presidential appointments when the President is a member of their party. The Nixon Administration filled about 6,500 jobs when it took office in 1969, and many of the appointments were made after consultation with Members. Jobs filled by the Administration included Cabinet and subcabinet positions, White House staff posts and jobs in Federal regulatory agencies, as well as some lesser positions exempt from Civil Service.

But Congressional influence in these appointments is limited by the discretion of the President. Many of the appointments require Senate confirmation, but none requires prior consultation. A Member's role in White House patronage affairs generally depends on his personal relationship with the President.

Civil Service History

American political patronage reached its peak in the post-Civil War era, when Senators spent much of their time keeping track of patronage in their states and were allowed to dictate major appointments.

In 1881, for example, both of New York's Senators resigned after President James A. Garfield refused to nominate their choice for the lucrative position of Collector of the Port of New York.

Both Senators expected the New York Legislature to express its support by re-electing them. But before the Legislature could meet, Garfield was assassinated by a disappointed patronage seeker.

Public revulsion over the assassination and the excesses of patronage led two years later to passage of the Pendleton Act, the first major attempt at civil service reform in America.

The Pendleton Act set up a three-man bipartisan board, the Civil Service Commission, and empowered it to certify applicants for Federal employment after competitive examinations.

The original Act covered only about 10 percent of Federal employees, but its key provision gave the President power to expand the civil service classifications by Executive order. A series of such orders and additional legislation in the following years removed from politics nearly all nonpolicy-level jobs in the Government.

Following Garfield's assassination, Civil Service received unexpected support from the new President, Chester Alan Arthur.

In 1884, the Pendleton Act produced one more disappointed office seeker—its sponsor, Sen. George H. Pendleton (D Ohio). Pendleton was defeated for re-election by Henry Payne, an outspoken advocate of the patronage system.

Patronage Machinery

There are approximately 1,100 acknowledged patronage jobs on Capitol Hill itself. The 435 Representatives and 100 Senators are responsible for filling these posts. Patronage privileges are meted out to Members of Congress under a puzzling combination of written rules and contradictory traditions. The exceptions to the written procedures are so numerous and diverse that they have all but usurped the rules.

House. Of the two chambers of Congress, the House has the more clearly defined methods for distributing patronage jobs among its Members. The three-man Patronage Committee of the majority party is ostensibly in control of all patronage jobs on the House side.

The Committee assigns a small quota of the jobs to the minority party at the beginning of each session. These are jobs like those of clerk or page in the minority cloakroom. The remaining patronage jobs are divided among the state delegations, and the senior majority member of each delegation is responsible for distributing them among the other Representatives from his state.

The Patronage Committee was first established by a caucus of Democratic Representatives in 1911. Rep. John C. Floyd (D Ark.) informed the House on May 9, 1911, of the methods by which his party would provide for the "equitable" distribution of Capitol patronage. Three members of the Ways and Means Committee would be chosen by the party caucus "to have charge of the proper distribution of all the appointive places in the House organization...except cloakroom men and such other places as are by law or resolution to be filled by the minority." Committee chairmen were excluded from the general distribution of patronage because they already had the power to make appointments to committee staff positions.

When the Republicans won a majority in the House in 1918, they followed the Democrats' example by setting up their own Patronage Committee. In a letter dated March 19, 1918, the temporary chairman of the Republican Committee on Committees announced that his party's Steering Committee would distribute general patronage through state delegations in proportion to the size of the delegation. Again, committee chairmen were excluded because of their other appointive powers.

Current Practice. In outlining the machinery for handling patronage assignments, the parties did not mention how the Speaker of the House might use his influence in the distribution of patronage. They failed also to say how behind-the-scenes bargaining for a crucial vote might involve paying off a reluctant Member with a patronage job or two. Maneuvering of this kind is part of the system of exceptions by which patronage is distributed.

Patronage distribution in the House has become highly informal according to Rep. B.F. Sisk (D Calif.), who was a member of the Patronage Committee in 1970. Sisk told Congressional Quarterly that the Committee has no list of patronage jobs on Capitol Hill and does not know how many exist at any one time. For Members who are not committee chairmen, seniority is a leading factor in obtaining patronage jobs. But this is not a formal rule, Sisk said, and no seniority quota exists. State delegations are still assigned quotas, however, and some of them have worked out their own systems of distribution. Majority members of the New York delegation, for example, pool their patronage jobs in order to obtain what they feel is an equitable distribution.

A veteran House Democrat who has taken a special interest in patronage observed that Members have little knowledge of how the patronage system operates. He agreed with Sisk's contention that the Patronage Committee makes no policy decisions, and he said he believed that many jobs are actually awarded through the Speaker and his office. He said Members rarely discuss patronage among themselves.

"It's sort of a boodle operation," he remarked. "You grab what you can get and you hold on." He said the grabbing is frequently done through the Speaker or other members of the leadership. "When I came here, Rayburn was Speaker. I guess I looked promising, so he gave me an elevator operator—and I have it to this day."

The same Member also controls two patronage jobs on the Capitol police force, one of which he said he obtained through "shakedown tactics." He demanded the

extra jobs in exchange for his vote to expand the force several years ago.

Senate. There is no elaborate committee machinery for distributing patronage jobs among Senators. The Majority Leader is in charge of the process. The minority party is granted about 20 percent of the patronage posts in the minority cloakroom and a like proportion of such jobs as pages and telephone operators for the minority side of the Senate. The other jobs are distributed by seniority and as the Majority Leader may choose.

What Are Patronage Jobs?

Many of the patronage jobs on Capitol Hill are filled by college students needing financial assistance. They work a shift as an elevator operator or chamber doorman and then go to classes. The turnover rate is high, but in most cases it does not greatly affect the efficiency of the operation. *(For an exception, see Capitol Police below.)*

House. The Office of the Doorkeeper controls the largest number of patronage jobs in the House. All except four of the Doorkeeper's 331 employees are hired under patronage, including five officers of the newspaper press gallery, 30 gallery doormen, 13 floor doormen, 50 House pages, 33 custodians, 14 barbers and 122 employees in the "folding room." The folding room, officially called the Publications Distribution Service, is responsible for distributing newsletters, speeches and other material for House Members.

Salaries of the Doorkeeper's 327 patronage employees range from $3,852 for a barbership attendant in the Longworth House Office Building to $21,268 for the superintendent of the House Document Room.

The Office of the Sergeant at Arms of the House employs 370 persons, about 140 of whom are hired under patronage. Members of the Capitol police force account for 131 of the patronage jobs. Several secretaries and clerks in the office of the Sergeant at Arms also are under patronage. The Clerk of the House employs 267 persons, but fewer than 30 are patronage employees.

The House post office has 87 employees, all hired on a patronage basis. Other patronage jobs in the House, less clearly defined, include several in the offices of the Majority and Minority Leaders, the Parliamentarian, the Minority Sergeant at Arms, and the Whips of both political parties.

Senate. The largest number of patronage jobs in the Senate is controlled by the Sergeant at Arms. Of his 750 employees, about 280 are patronage appointees. Included on the patronage rolls of his office are 117 Capitol policemen, 65 employees of the Senate post office, 30 Senate pages, 14 officers of the Senate press galleries, plus several clerks and secretaries assigned to the office of the Sergeant at Arms.

Salaries for these patronage jobs range from $6,800 for a warehouse worker to $20,656 for the Superintendent of the press gallery. The Sergeant at Arms of the Senate is paid $36,000 a year.

The Secretary of the Senate, who is an administrative official, has about 24 patronage employees and a total payroll of 136. And there is a scattering of patronage jobs in the offices of the Majority and Minority secretaries, the Majority and Minority leaders, and the party Whips.

Architect's Office. Of the 2,026 persons working for the Architect of the Capitol, 146 are patronage employees. The latter are all elevator operators in the Capitol and in the Senate and House office buildings. Slightly more than half of the 146 are assigned to the House. Most of them are college students.

On the Periphery of Patronage

Although patronage employment is generally restricted to non-skilled jobs, there is a group of Capitol Hill officials (technically not of patronage status) whose jobs depend on the influence of sponsors or the swing of party control. The House Doorkeeper, the House and Senate Sergeants at Arms, the Secretary of the Senate and the Clerk of the House work for all Members of their respective houses, but are elected by the Members by strict party-line votes.

Party leadership generally plays an important part in the election of these non-patronage officials. For example, the present Secretary of the Senate and the Majority Secretary both are former employees of the Majority Leader. The Clerk of the House is former Rep. W. Pat Jennings (D Va. 1955-67).

The office of the Secretary for the Majority in the Senate received considerable attention in 1963 when it was charged that the incumbent, Robert G. (Bobby) Baker, had used his position to solicit illegal campaign contributions in 1960. Baker resigned under fire in October 1963, and a Senate committee reported in 1965 that he had committed "gross improprieties" but was not guilty of any criminal act in connection with campaign contributions.

In 1967, Baker was convicted by a District of Columbia jury on seven counts of tax evasion, theft and conspiracy to defraud the Government. Baker had been named Majority Secretary in 1955, when Lyndon B. Johnson (D Texas) became Senate Majority Leader.

House Doorkeeper. The Doorkeeper of the House, William M. (Fishbait) Miller, was elected to the post after the Democrats regained control of Congress in the 1948 election. The Mississippian has held the job ever since, except in the two years of the Republican-controlled 83rd Congress (1953-54). The Doorkeeper's salary is now $40,000.

Postmasters. The postmasters of the Senate and House are elected by the Members of each chamber. Senate Postmaster David Longinotti, also a Mississippian, was sponsored by Sen. John Stennis (D Miss.). Although Longinotti was elected to his post, he acknowledges the importance of the Senator's sponsorship. A picture of Stennis hangs on the wall over his desk. "I always feel he is looking over my shoulder," Longinotti once said. His background is in politics, not postal service. Before becoming Senate postmaster, he was administrative assistant to the Joint Committee on Internal Revenue Taxation.

House Printer. An example of the influence of House leaders in patronage appointments was given in 1969 when the job of chief printer became vacant following the death of Truman Ward, who had held the post for 48 years. The print shop had developed into a profitable operation, printing speeches, newsletters and other material needed by House Members. The chief printer receives a salary of more than $10,000 and is allowed to keep all the profits he can make.

Print shop employees and many Members believed the job would go to shop foreman Robert Cutter, a veteran printer who had served as Ward's assistant since 1954 and directed the operation during Ward's illness. But the selection was up to House Majority Leader (now Speaker) Carl Albert (D Okla.), and Albert bypassed Cutter in favor of David R. Ramage, a resident of Wewoka, Okla., in Albert's home district. Ramage was not a professional printer but a loyal Democrat who had served 15 years as a clerk in the House stationery room.

Committee and Personal Staffs

Committees. The selection of committee staffs is supposedly based on a candidate's administrative credentials and his expertise on the subject matter covered by the committee. To a degree this is the case, but an overwhelming preponderance of committee staff jobs are filled by appointees of the majority party. The Senate Appropriations Committee, for example, employs 19 majority and four minority staff personnel, exclusive of stenographers and other clerks in routine jobs. The House Foreign Affairs Committee has two designated minority staff members out of a total of 20.

A Republican task force seeking more minority staff positions estimated in 1966 that 90 percent of all House committee staff personnel were employees of the majority party.

Personal Staffs. The personal staff of a Senator or Representative naturally includes some persons chosen in part for partisan reasons. A Member is hardly likely to appoint a supporter of the opposition party to his staff. House Members are allowed to hire up to 15 staff assistants for their personal offices, with a maximum staff salary of $29,000. The 15th staff member was added in 1971. The few House Members who represent more than 500,000 persons may hire 16 staffers.

Senators are allowed to hire as many staff assistants as they wish but must work within an annual budget of $295,938 if the state population is less than three million and up to $477,978 if the state population is more than 17 million. The maximum salary for a Senate aide is $35,178, and no Senator may employ more than one assistant at that salary.

Debate Over Patronage System

The use of patronage to fill positions requiring special skills or knowledge has been on the decline since 1883, when the Pendleton Civil Service Act removed 10 percent of Federal employees from the system of partisan appointments. Since that time the inequities, inefficiencies and justifications of patronage employment have been debated almost annually in Congress. The Congressional patronage empire has so dwindled that some senior Members count themselves fortunate if they can appoint a Capitol policeman, a few elevator operators and a mailman in the Senate or House post office.

Opposition. The leading spokesman for patronage reform in the House has been Rep. Joel T. Broyhill (R Va.), whose suburban Washington district contains thousands of persons employed in civil service jobs. Broyhill may be besieged by more office-seekers than any other Member of Congress, because so many of his constituents live within easy access of the Capitol.

But in addition to the inconvenience of having his office used as an employment agency, Broyhill considers the patronage system unfair to those who hold patronage jobs. He calls the patronage system "cruel, costly and ugly" and points out that all 31 of the patronage employees he sponsored in 1954 were dismissed the next year when control of the House passed from the Republicans to the Democrats.

Broyhill has advocated a modified merit system for Capitol Hill employees, under which a committee would evaluate and endorse candidates for jobs without regard to political sponsorship. He opposes a full civil service system, because he believes Congress should retain ultimate control over its employees.

Justification. Defenders of patronage argue that most of the jobs remaining under the system require no special ability or training. A merit system for elevator operators or doorkeepers is unnecessary, they say, because one person can handle such jobs as well as the next. Backers of patronage also dispute Broyhill's concern over family hardships inflicted by summary dismissal of employees after a turnabout at the polls.

Few patronage employees, they point out, are young men with families. Most are students in need of money to help them through college, or older people wanting

to supplement retirement income. Salaries for the patronage jobs rarely exceed $6,500, so few can afford to raise families on them.

Supporters of patronage say the turnover in these jobs is high—that most of the employees tend to leave within a short time regardless of what happens to their party at the polls. Few employees have lifetime career plans disrupted by electoral changes, they contend, and the few exceptions are often able to hold their jobs by taking one of the posts allotted to their party after it becomes the minority.

In addition, the relatively precarious nature of patronage jobs is obvious to applicants. Doorkeepers and mailmen know they are likely to lose their jobs if their party loses control of Congress. And the period between an election and the opening of Congress is said to give them plenty of time to find new employment before their replacements take over.

A better objection to patronage may be that it disregards not only merit but also financial need. Critics point out that many Members of Congress fill patronage slots with the children of influential people from their districts. Some do seek out and sponsor disadvantaged scholarship students in the District of Columbia, but there seems to be little evidence that this is a widespread practice.

Capitol's Restaurant Facilities

Perquisites of Members of Congress include extensive dining facilities. Representatives have the use of a coffee shop, two cafeterias, three carry-outs, a private dining room, and a restaurant for Members and their guests. And the Speaker has his own dining room. Senators have two cafeterias, a carry-out service, and two dining rooms, one in the Capitol and one in the New Senate Office Building.

The House restaurant operation had a deficit of between $300,000 and $400,000 in the fiscal year 1971. The financial status of the Senate restaurants was not made public. Rep. Wayne L. Hays (D Ohio) promised to get the service on the House side operating efficiently or, if that proved impossible, to recommend that it be "turned over to some outside company." Hays is chairman of the House Administration Committee, which was given overall responsibility in March 1971 for the House restaurants in the Capitol and the cafeterias and carry-outs in the House office buildings.

Testimony made public May 28, 1971, showed that Hays had told a House Appropriations Subcommittee of

some of the problems involved in supervising the restaurants—one of them being that it has 435 "managers." Hays said: "Many Members store frozen foods in the frozen food storage area, which is already inadequate for the restaurants.... I can issue an order to stop that, but I know it is going to bring down some flak." Among other problems cited were "too many chiefs and not enough Indians," no adequate inventory, "a lot of theft going on," and the personal observation of Hays that "not all the people work." Hays also criticized the auditing of restaurant accounts. Several members of the restaurant staff have been fired since Hays became involved with the restaurant operation.

The Representative testified that he had stopped the food service for evening receptions in Members' offices or committee rooms and was working on the problem of unpaid bills of Members. A Hays order requires bills to be sent at the end of every month. If the bill is not paid within 30 days, "then that Member does not get any more credit." Hays said: "I'm sure that I will get some gripes about it, but that's the way it's going to be."

Security on Capitol Hill

The U.S. Capitol Police is the private security force of Congress. The members of the force are responsible for security inside the Capitol, in the Senate and House office buildings, and on the grounds surrounding the Capitol, the office buildings, the Supreme Court, the Library of Congress, and the Botanic Garden (located near the southwest corner of the Capitol grounds). Because the members of this force are stationed at one of the most popular tourist attractions in the United States, they must be to some extent tour guides and public relations men as well as policemen.

Thirty-nine percent of the men in the spring of 1971 got their jobs as patronage appointees. The others were hired for their professional qualifications. Most of the 248 authorized patronage appointees were college students who rely on their earnings to help finance their education. The rate of turnover is high among these appointees, and their qualifications as policemen have been questioned.

Development of Police Force

From 1800 (when Congress first met in Washington) to 1857, watchmen were hired to guard the inside of the Capitol, and patrol of the Capitol grounds was left to the District of Columbia police. Congress appropriated $200 on March 3, 1857, to pay the watchmen, and for the first time these security men were referred to as the Capitol Police. Five years later, annual appropriations for the Capitol Police totaled $10,225. By 1876, a 31-man force had been organized with one captain, three lieutenants, 22 privates and six watchmen at a cost of $33,700 a year. Salaries ranged from $900 for watchmen to $1,600 for the captain.

The responsibility of selecting men for the force was split evenly between the Sergeants at Arms of the Senate and House. Actually, all the two Sergeants at Arms did was to accept appointments made by Members of Congress. As outlined in an Act of April 29, 1876: "An appointment as a member of the Capitol Police is held subject to the will of the appointing power, which may remove at its pleasure, and both the appointment and the removal may be made informally."

Uniforms. By 1902, the Capitol Police were required to buy uniforms tailored to the specifications of the two Sergeants at Arms. Each man had to pay for his own uniform. A $20 allowance was made for a pistol and gun belt. Although Congress required members of the force to buy a standard uniform, there was no regulation about wearing it. To correct that situation, Congress passed a law two years later (March 18, 1904) stating: "The officers, privates and watchmen of the Capitol shall, when on duty, wear the regulation uniform."

Aid of Metropolitan Police. The District of Columbia Metropolitan Police Department was initially responsible for patrolling the grounds of nearly all Government buildings in Washington. But, as the Federal departments multiplied and expanded, separate security divisions for such areas as the White House, the State Department and the Capitol were organized.

The Capitol Police still rely on the Metropolitan Police for assistance in emergencies and for personnel. Ten of the 59 officers on the Capitol Police force (including the Chief) are technically employed by the Metropolitan Police, although they are permanently assigned to the Hill as working members of the Capitol Police. From 13 (when Congress is out of session) to 49 members of the District of Columbia Police force supplement the Capitol Police. This professional assistance in 1970 cost $900,000—the sum paid to the Metropolitan Police Department.

Capitol Police and Patronage

Until 1967 all members of the Capitol Police were patronage appointees (except for the special officers on loan from the Metropolitan Police). Their continued service as policemen depended on remaining in the good graces of their sponsors and on the sponsor's tenure in office. When a senior Member of Congress lost his seat, his patronage appointees generally left the Capitol with him.

When rising crime pushed the District of Columbia up among the 10 metropolitan centers with the highest crime rates, Members of Congress began speaking out about their patronage-based Capitol Police force and its effectiveness. During Senate Appropriations hearings in 1966, Sen. A. S. Mike Monroney (D Okla.), a member of the Committee, said: "We ought to put real policemen up here instead of boys who are office boys today and policemen tomorrow. I think it is disgraceful that we give these boys absolutely no training, yet expect them to be policemen and to cope with crime situations far beyond their capability. Actually, they're not policemen at all. They are wearing uniforms, maybe they might even be able to direct a little bit of traffic, but I would hate to see this become a patronage-ridden operation where we get nothing but students who will be sitting around studying their lessons instead of doing their police work."

Sen. Monroney continued: "It is the system I am complaining about. Here we have the mightiest capital in the world with the poorest security anywhere. It is a very uneven type of policing, and certainly there's no esprit de corps, such as you find in even the poorest capitals of the world...."

In 1966 the Capitol Police had about 250 men. Although some of them were able to hold their jobs after they lost sponsorship, the annual turnover rate was 82 percent among the privates. The effectiveness of the training program for new men was limited because of the high turnover rate. A college student who was appointed was often put on the beat with an unloaded gun until he could be enrolled in the FBI training school. (Not until 1968 did the Capitol Police have facilities for its own training school.)

Growth of Professionalism Since 1967

The first break with the patronage recruitment tradition came in 1967. The House needed more policemen to handle security for the Rayburn Building, which had opened two years before. Instead of expanding the force through patronage appointments, the House adopted a resolution adding 78 men to the force "without regard to political affiliation and solely on the basis of fitness to perform the duties...."

Since 1967, the Capitol Police Force has more than doubled. The number of patronage appointees has remained unchanged since 1966—177 in the Senate, 131 in the House—but the number of professionals has swelled—150 in the Senate, 223 in the House by 1971.

Misleading Figures. Although 39 percent (248) of the men on the force were still technically patronage appointees, the figure was actually closer to 31 percent. Capitol Police Chief James M. Powell has explained that some of his men came onto the force as Congressional appointees and decided to make police work their career. As their sponsors left Congress over the years, Chief Powell would request that the Patronage Committee allow the men to remain rather than give other Members of Congress the right to appoint replacements.

Since 1967 the Patronage Committees of both chambers have cooperated with the Chief's requests. As a result, some 55 men who initially were patronage appointees have become permanent, professional members of the force. Congress has yet to reduce the authorized number of patronage appointments, but, in fact, the number is dropping.

More Professionals. In 1969, before professional policemen outnumbered the patronage appointees, Chief Powell testified before the Senate Appropriations Committee: "I came up here to do the job and I have said I would not try to interfere with the patronage system. Frankly, the job would be very difficult to do if we did not have these professional men, and I think the time has come that I must be practical about it. The percentage of students is higher than is compatible with maintaining appropriate security."

By 1970, the professional men constituted 59 percent of the force. Again Chief Powell testified before the Senate Appropriations Committee: "I don't think we could operate if we had 100 percent students. It is not that the students are not qualified—usually they are very nice young men and they do a satisfactory job within limits. The problem arises when suddenly, due to no fault of theirs or mine, we are faced with a serious emergency and everybody has to work nights and days, or we cancel days off, and if that happens to be a time when they have examinations, it of course causes hardship on them."

Will the Capitol Police be removed from the patronage system altogether? "By necessity, yes," says Chief Powell. "As the demands for better security increase, the patronage system of appointing men will become incompatible with fulfilling the demands."

Why Patronage Persists. Appointment of a young man to the Capitol Police force may involve reading hundreds of letters from youths seeking financial help. Members of Congress often regard the task of appointing someone to the force as more of a burden than a privilege. Selecting an appointee takes time and the returns for a Member rarely amounts to more than an individual "thank you."

Some Members of Congress nevertheless think the few patronage appointments still available should be retained. For example, Sen. James B. Pearson (R Kan.) a member of the Senate Appropriations Committee, told Chief Powell in 1970: "We have young fellows who come in and join your force and go to school and so forth. This is a patronage assignment here. I had one...and I gave it to a young man who wants to go to school, who doesn't have the money to go. Usually they come in for a year or so and then pass out." "I have mixed emotions about this patronage thing. I have been able to get some awfully fine young men and help them get an education at the law schools and at the graduate schools. I save that job for just that purpose. If they don't make good grades, they don't get the job, or we take it away."

Control of Capitol Police

The first Senate and House offices created to maintain order and security in the chambers were those of the Sergeants at Arms. As the duties of the Sergeant at Arms of the Senate and the Sergeant at Arms of the House were expanded to include more than enforcing good behavior among Members and keeping undesirables from interrupting sessions, the security end of the job was entrusted to others.

The Capitol Police are under the direction and control of the two Sergeants at Arms. The force is technically divided into two parts—one for the House (354 men), one for the Senate (267 men). When one side of Congress needs additional security forces, men are added to the appropriate part of the force.

The Sergeant at Arms in each chamber reviews all recommendations for promotion. When their staffs were smaller, the Sergeants at Arms personally handled promotions. The Act of April 29, 1876, stated: "The Captain and lieutenants shall be selected jointly by the Sergeant at Arms of the Senate and the Sergeant at Arms of the House..." Today the Chief is responsible for recommending promotions, which are then reviewed by the Sergeants at Arms. The Capitol Police are on the payroll of the Sergeant at Arms, in each chamber.

Police Board. The Sergeants at Arms and the Architect of the Capitol are the three members of the Capitol Police Board. The board has a general supervisory function. It reviews recommendations for suspension of an officer, considers requests for more men, and submits reports to Congressional committees.

The Architect of the Capitol is generally responsible for maintenance of the Capitol and the surrounding grounds and buildings. Since Capitol Police duties include protection of the "Capitol grounds and terraces from use as playgrounds..." and protection of the buildings from defacement or destruction, the Architect sits on the Board to make sure that the interests of his office are respected by the Capitol Police.

The Capitol Police Board and the Sergeants at Arms have considerable influence. "I would not fail to carry out any of their orders or to respond immediately to suggestions," says Chief Powell. "As a matter of practice, however, they respect my background in police work and leave the technical handling of police matters to me. Running the force is pretty much my responsibility, but it's one they could take away at any time."

Final authority over the Capitol Police rests, of course, with Congress, but its direct control over individual Capitol policemen is decreasing as the number of patronage appointments declines. Congress is increasingly shifting its responsibility for overseeing the force to the Police Board and the Sergeants at Arms.

The Force Today

At the beginning of 1971, the Capitol Police had an authorized strength of 621 and an actual force of about 595 men. In addition, the force included from 13 to 49 Metropolitan policemen assigned to duty on the Hill. Salaries and expenses for the entire operation (including the $900,000 paid for Metropolitan Police aid) amounted to nearly $6.7 million in 1970. Compensation of members of the force ranged from starting pay of $8,122 a year for privates to $18,567 a year for one of the captains. Chief Powell was paid approximately $22,-000. Plans for a substantial expansion of the force were set in motion after the March 1 bomb explosion in the Capitol *(see p. 390)*.

The philosophy of adequate security has changed at the Capitol. As explained by Chief Powell: "Most people used to respect the law and all the police had to deal with were those few persons who deviated. Now for us to provide adequate security at the Capitol, our men have to be visible everywhere. If people see a policeman, they usually won't try anything."

Requirements and Selection. Both patronage appointees and candidates for professional positions on the force must meet certain physical standards. A man must be at least 5 feet, 7 inches tall; be between the ages of 22 and 50; and be in generally good health. He must also be a high school graduate. If a man meets those requirements and can find a Member of Congress who has patronage rights for a slot on the force, then he would have a chance of getting the job.

Professional standards are somewhat more demanding. A man must have at least one year of police experience, and he is required to write a 500-word essay on why he wants to join the force. His background is thoroughly checked and former employers are contacted as references. If a candidate runs into no trouble up to this point, his employment is at the discretion of the Chief, providing he has approval from one of the Sergeants at Arms. No civil service test is required.

Training. Both patronage appointees and professional members of the force receive the same training during their first six months with the Capitol Police. During the first week, a recruit goes to indoctrination school where he learns the fundamentals of police work and is taught how to use firearms. For the next month the rookie is teamed with a veteran on the force, and together they pull regular duty.

Equipment of Police Force

The Capitol Police have come a long way since the days when a watchman swung a lantern, dressed as he pleased, and carried a gun the Government had bought for him for $20. By 1970 the force had five patrol cars, 12 motor scooters, a 30-passenger bus and seven canine teams (trained police dogs). And each man had been issued $514.83 worth of paraphernalia when he joined the department.

For the working wardrobe, from the head down, a Capitol policeman is issued one cap, one cap cover, two neckties, one scarf, two blouses, six long-sleeved shirts, 12 short-sleeved shirts, one long overcoat, one short overcoat, one raincoat, one visibility jacket (in phosphorescent orange), one pair of visibility gloves, one black belt, two pairs of winter trousers and two pairs of summer trousers. The supplemental equipment includes a gun belt, ammunition, revolver, blackjack, baton, badge, callbox key, flashlight, lock for his locker, manual, whistle and handcuffs. When a man leaves the force, he must return all the equipment.

The Government pays for cleaning of the working wardrobe. Dry cleaning and laundry cost the Capitol Police $27,800 in 1970. General expenses, including the cleaning of uniforms, upkeep on cars, purchase of new equipment, etc., amounted to $134,000 in 1970.

After 30 days, the recruit is given a two-week course in more sophisticated police methods and other basics.

After these two courses, the professionals and patronage policemen are separated. At six months, all professionals and only those patronage men who plan to stay longer than a year are enrolled in "Rookie School." A complete course in law enforcement is offered as well as such related areas as fire control, first aid and crowd control. All the courses of instruction are given at the Capitol Police Training School in the basement of the Rayburn House Office Building. The facilities include two classrooms and a seven-lane firing range. Courses are taught by men already on the force, FBI instructors and firemen.

By early 1971, in addition to the regular training, about 250 men had been instructed in riot control. The Senate appropriated $8,000 for riot control equipment in 1969.

Pages: A Changing Tradition

Serving the needs of the 535 Members of Congress and the nine Justices of the Supreme Court is a force of young patronage appointees called "pages." They range in age from 14 to 18 years and come to the Hill by appointment from a Member of Congress or the Supreme Court Marshal. Starting with the 92nd Congress, 50 pages serve the House of Representatives, 30 the Senate. Four pages serve the Supreme Court.

Five days a week a page reports to the third floor of the Library of Congress, where he goes to school. Classes of the 9th, 10th, 11th and 12th grades begin at 6:30 a.m. and the school day is over by 10 a.m. Then it's off to the Capitol or the Supreme Court. Until early evening a page may answer phones, run errands, deliver messages or distribute information. If there is still unexpended energy by the end of the day, a page can practice with the Capitol Page School varsity basketball team, work for the school newspaper or yearbook, debate school issues in Student Council or simply catch up on the homework from his four courses.

Although the demands on a youngster's time are uncommonly strict, hundreds of boys vie for these select patronage positions each year. The opportunity to observe the highest legislative and judicial bodies in the land is unsurpassed and the pay is good. In 1970, base pay for a Senate page was $6,960 a year; for a House page, $6,383. A Supreme Court page earns $6,548, but one-half of his salary is withheld in a trust fund. The pay is so good, in fact, that a New Jersey school teacher wrote a letter to the *New York Times* (April 23, 1965) pointing out that a 14-year-old page with an eighth grade education was making more money than a teacher with a bachelor's degree.

History of the Pages

Working as a page has not always been so lucrative, and the side benefit of going to school while toiling on the Hill is a relatively new development in the 144-year history of this patronage job. Congress has always used messengers, but the earliest record of boys filling these positions was in 1827. Three youngsters were then employed as "runners" in the House of Representatives, serving as errand boys for the 227 House Members and four delegates.

Runners. Many of the boys who served as runners were orphans or children of poor families. Their plight came to the attention of a Senator or Representative and the boys were given a job running errands. There was apparently no law authorizing the use of young boys for these patronage jobs, yet hundreds have been appointed over the years as a matter of practice. Members often paid the boys a bonus if they performed their duties well, but this practice was discontinued in 1843 after a special review of financial allocations in the House.

The first Senate "runner" was a nine-year-old boy named Grafton Hanson. He was appointed under the august sponsorship of Senators Daniel Webster and Henry Clay. Hanson served his sponsors for 10 years and later became Postmaster of the Senate.

The actual name, "pages," appeared first in the *Congressional Globe,* predecessor of the *Congressional Record,* of the 26th Congress, 1839-41. At about that time, a page was paid $1.50 a day and his activities were restricted to the immediate vicinity of the Capitol.

Riding and Telegraph Pages. Older persons were hired as "riding pages" to carry messages by horseback around Washington and as "telegraph pages" to deliver telegrams that came in through the Capitol telegraph office. There are still riding pages, but they have switched from horses to cars. In addition to the regular Congressional pages, there are also special telephone pages whose only responsibility is answering the phones.

Dress Code. A code of dress was established for pages during the era when knickers were in vogue for young boys. The Supreme Court was the last body to revise its standards. Until 1963 the Court pages would report for duty in knickers, long black stockings and double-breasted jackets. Now all pages wear dark blue suits, four-in-hand black ties, black shoes, black socks and long-sleeved white shirts. Long hair is a ground for dismissal. There is no record, however, of a boy losing his job because of long hair.

House Pages

A page for the House of Representatives works from the office of the Doorkeeper. Each morning after school, the boy reports to either the Democratic or the Republican cloakroom where he begins his daily chores. The actual assignment of tasks is the responsibility of the Chief Pages, who are usually long-time patronage employees reporting directly to the Doorkeeper. One Chief Page serves each party in the House.

A page with less than a year's experience is generally assigned to the floor of the House chamber. Before a session begins, he distributes pertinent documents to each House seat in preparation for the day's business. When the session is called to order, the boy retires to a bench in the rear of the Chamber where he waits for a Representative's call. A button next to a Member's seat triggers a light on a board in the rear of the Chamber when a page is wanted. A page who has served more than a year may be assigned to answer phones in one of the cloakrooms, to work in the Document Room or to run errands from the Doorkeeper's office.

During a normal day, a page who is assigned to the House floor has time to listen to much of the debate while waiting to run errands. March 1, 1954, however, was not a normal day. A woman and three men, members of the militant Nationalist Party of Puerto Rico, rose from their seats in the House visitors' gallery, pulled pistols from their coat pockets and fired 30 shots at the Representatives on the floor. Five Members were hospitalized with bullet wounds. No pages were injured, though one boy said a bullet lodged in the wall just inches from his head. The pages were kept busy ministering to the wounded and helping to carry stretchers.

Selection. As is the case with other patronage appointments in the House, a special three-man committee of the majority party is responsible for rationing page appointments. The Patronage Committee informs a Member, who is usually high on the seniority list, that he is eligible to appoint a page for the coming session. If the Member has a candidate, the appointment is his.

Requirements. Pages for the House must be no more than 16 to 17 years old when they begin serving, and no page turning 18 during a session may serve beyond the end of that session. Since 1970 the minimum appointment period has been two months and, because of the age restrictions, no boy can serve much longer than two years. The length of a page's appointment also depends on his sponsor's tenure in office. If the sponsor loses an election, the page goes out of office with him. House pages must maintain a grade average of C while attending the Capitol Page School, but dismissal for poor academic work is at the discretion of the boy's sponsor and his parents.

Senate Pages

The 26 pages of the Senate are under the direction of the Sergeant at Arms. He assigns pages to the majority and minority cloakrooms and to the Senate floor, where the boys are under the direction of the secretaries of each party. Pages assigned to the Senate floor sit on the rostrum at the front of the Chamber and are called to run errands by the snapping of a Senator's fingers. The duties of the Senate page are virtually the same as those of his counterpart in the House—messages are carried, documents gathered and distributed, telephones answered, etc.

Selection. Senate pages are appointed by high-seniority Members of each party. The distribution of appointments is generally controlled by the Majority Leader. During the 1970 session, a Senate official said that the then 26 Senate pages were appointed by fewer than 20 Senators. Sixteen pages were sponsored by Democrats and ten by Republicans.

Requirements. Before a boy may assume his duties as a Senate page, he must be at least 14 years old and not more than 17. If he turns 18 during a session, he may hold the job only until the session adjourns. He must maintain "adequate" grades at the Capitol Page School. (The interpretation of "adequate" is left up to the boy's sponsor and parents.) The appointee must be willing to serve for at least two months.

Supreme Court Pages

The four pages working in the Supreme Court report each morning to the office of the Marshal of the Court, where they sign in and collect assignments. Before the Court is called to order, the pages place pertinent documents for the day's cases before each Justice's chair. While Court is in session, the pages sit on benches behind the nine Justices and wait to run errands.

Selection. The Marshal reviews all letters of application for the position of Supreme Court page. He then decides on the best-qualified applicants and submits his recommendation to the Chief Justice for approval.

Requirements. Pages appointed by the Court often hold their jobs for four years (from age 14 until they are 18). To qualify for the post, a boy must live in the Washington, D.C., area and be able to commute to work. He must also do "honor roll" work at the Capitol Page School (at least a B average).

Until late in 1950, the Court had a height requirement for its pages. A boy who grew to be taller than 5 feet, 4 inches—the height of the backs of the Justices' chairs—was dismissed. The Justices felt it improper for a page to tower over their heads while they were seated in judgment in the highest Court of the land. But height restrictions have been relaxed. A visitor to the Court today can plainly observe the pages moving around behind the bench and a six-footer is not an uncommon sight.

Capitol Page School

Not until the Legislative Reorganization Act of 1946 became law were pages provided with any kind of uniform schooling. They had to rely on private tutors if they wanted to continue their education while working on the Hill. After Congress established the Capitol Page School, three years passed before semi-permanent quarters were acquired. From 1946 to 1949, pages were bused to the YMCA for classes. In 1949 space was cleared on the third floor of the Library of Congress, classrooms were set up, and the school was officially opened.

The school now has six teachers, a principal who doubles as a counselor, an administrative assistant (secretary) and a part-time basketball coach. According to the principal, costs per student are $1,616 a year or a total of $113,120 annually. When Congress decided to establish a special school for pages, it allocated extra funds to the District of Columbia public school system for administration of the page school's academic program.

The curriculum of the school differs somewhat from that of public schools. The students attend four (or five) 45-minute classes every day with a 30-minute break in the middle of the schedule for a hot breakfast. Because of the time limits, there is no art, music or physical education. Chemistry also is excluded from the curriculum because the Library of Congress forbids laboratory courses that might constitute a hazard to the books and archives on the floors below.

Courses at the Capitol Page School are geared toward college preparation. Ninety-eight percent of the students go on to college, and some even return as Members of Congress. Rep. John D. Dingell Jr. (D Mich. 1955-) and Rep. David H. Pryor (D Ark., 1966-), who were Members of the 92nd Congress, were both pages. Former Rep. Jed Johnson Jr. (D Okla., 1965-67) and former Rep. Compton I. White Jr. (D Idaho, 1963-67) also had been pages.

Questioning of System. Long debate over how the pages are appointed, who supervises them once they arrive in Washington, and the expense of running a special school finally brought action late in 1970. The Legislative Reorganization Act of 1970 instructed the Architect of the Capitol to find land and draw plans for a combination dormitory and school for the pages near the Capitol.

Sen. Olin D. Johnston (D S.C., 1945-65) had introduced a bill with almost identical provisions on Feb. 8, 1955. Sen. Johnston tried again in 1957 and was followed by Rep. William C. Broomfield (R Mich.) in 1960 and Sen. Ralph W. Yarborough (D Texas) in 1963. The Senate Committee on Public Works issued a staff report Nov. 8, 1963, that included blueprints for a dormitory, estimates of costs and suggestions for maintenance of the facility. Still no action was taken.

1964 Hearings. A day of hearings by the Select House Committee on the Welfare and Education of Congressional Pages on Dec. 17, 1964, brought to light many of the questions that had been stalling action for years. One of the broadest questions under debate concerned the possibility of drastically altering the existing page system. Opponents of the school-dormitory asserted that a more economical system could be found. They favored raising the age limit of pages, thus allowing only high school graduates to take the jobs. The expense of running the Capitol Page School would thus be eliminated, and the worry over proper supervision of minors would no longer be a problem.

Those favoring the traditional page system feared that college-age students would not be as eager to do the often menial tasks required of a page. "I am just wondering whether college students are going to react to the snapping of a finger in the Senate?" asked Henry L. DeKeyser, who was principal of the Capitol Page School until 1968.

The most frequently articulated concern expressed by Members of Congress during the years of debate over the dormitory-school concerned the existing lack of supervision of pages during off-duty hours. No single person was responsible for the boys. In school, teachers were in charge. While on the job, the Chief Pages watched over them. Once they left the Capitol, however, the pages were on their own. The Doorkeeper of the House, William "Fishbait" Miller, testified that when pages get off work "they are more or less under the supervision of the Member who brings them here and/or their parents if they live in Washington, or the landlady with whom they stay...We have no way of knowing what they do from the time they leave until the time they come to school." Thirty to 40 percent of the pages usually live at home and commute to work and school.

Part of a report submitted by the Evaluation Committee of the Middle States Association of Colleges and Secondary Schools after a tour of the page school was read into the record of the 1964 hearing. The report said: "It seems inconceivable to the members of this committee...that a 14- or 15-year-old boy should be turned loose in a large metropolis to find his own room, make his own arrangements for eating well balanced and nourishing meals, engage in healthy and moral activities and watch over his own physical and moral well-being."

The John W. McCormack Residential Page School, authorized by the 1970 Act, will be both a home and a school for the pages, and it will have many advantages over the present system. Educationally, the school is expected to offer broader courses that may be taken for extra credit during the evening. Chemistry can be added to the curriculum. The gymnasium included in the new facility will give pages a chance to exercise and it will be easier for the basketball team to practice. (It now borrows another school's gym.)

Having pages all live in one place will cut hours of commuting time from their already crowded schedules. It will give them a sense of community and a central location from which to operate. Most important, some Members of Congress feel, will be improved supervision

for the pages during their off-duty hours. One person, a resident counselor who will live in the building with the boys, will be able to help pages with problems and make sure that all the boys are observing the codes of conduct set for them by Congress.

A code of conduct adopted by the House in 1968 includes study hours on weekday evenings, a 10:30 p.m. bedtime five days a week, room checks for cleanliness, and prohibitions against gambling, drinking and fighting. Pages are also supposed to write or phone their parents once a week. The rules are understandably difficult to enforce when the pages are scattered in private homes and boarding houses in the Capitol Hill area and when no one person is responsible for enforcing them.

The Reorganization Act of 1970 has taken the first step to improve the conditions under which the pages have been living and going to school. No date has been set for the completion of the McCormack Page School, but the major barrier has been overcome—legislative opposition.

Patronage and Discrimination

Finding suitable living accommodations for pages is only one of the debatable questions that have long surrounded this patronage job. By allowing Members of Congress full discretion in selecting pages under the patronage system, the most qualified youngsters have not always been appointed. Outright discrimination has been charged in two particular cases.

Minority Group Pages. Rep. Broomfield felt that the patronage system encouraged racially discriminatory practices. Testifying in 1964 before the Select House Committee on the Welfare and Education of Congressional Pages, he said: "In the history of our country I do not know of one Negro page employed in the House or Senate."

At that time, the only Negro page had been appointed by the Supreme Court. By 1967, however, the House and Senate both had Negroes working as pages. Sen. Jacob K. Javits (R N.Y.) appointed the first black page in 1965.

During 1970, another cry of discrimination was raised. Members of Congress were charged with "sexist" tendencies (discrimination against women). Again it was Javits who broke with a long-standing tradition in December 1970 by selecting a 16-year-old girl from Schenectady, N.Y., to serve as a page. Senators Charles H. Percy (R Ill.) and Fred R. Harris (D Okla.) followed Javits' example and immediately selected girls for page jobs. But selecting a girl for the job proved to be a long step from actually getting the young ladies into the exclusively male ranks of the working pages.

The Senate Rules Committee first considered the question of allowing girls to serve as pages in December 1970. The Committee deliberated on the question intermittently for five months. On May 6, 1971, it finally voted in favor of allowing young women to serve as pages, but only with the understanding that the sponsors had to assume responsibility for the girls' safety while they traveled to and from the Capitol. Pages sometimes work until late evening when the Senate meets in extended session. The Senate approved the Committee's resolution May 13.

Summer Congressional Interns

During the summer of 1970, more than 1,250 college students came to Washington to work in the office of a Senator or Representative. The students generally held down clerical jobs and participated in weekly intern programs addressed by Members of Congress, non-Government newsmakers and newsmen. Topics of the speakers ranged from Vietnam to Congressional reorganization. About 100 students coupled their internship with independent research projects for which they received college credit.

Although students have been working summers in Members' offices for years, the summer intern program did not gain official recognition until 1965. Under PL 89-545 (H Res 416—July 16, 1965), each House Member was authorized to draw $750 from the House contingency fund to employ a student for a 10-week period, or two students for five-week periods. At the same time, the weekly intern-speaker sessions were organized. The Senate still does not provide additional funds for summer interns, but many Senators hire students anyway, paying expenses from clerical allocations.

Controversy Over Interns' Vietnam Protest

During the summer of 1967, various events revolving around intern protests about the war in Vietnam nearly caused abolition of the summer program. A group of interns drafted a letter to President Johnson saying they "could no longer condone this war through silence" and urging the President to make a "new effort to achieve peace."

Rep. Robert H. Michel (R Ill.), who had heard about the letter, told the House on July 20, 1967: "There is at this moment a group of inconspicuous interns organizing a group known as 'The Congressional Interns for Peace.' Their express purpose is to formulate opposition to the Vietnam war." Michel added: "There are about 20 ringleaders of this movement," and they are

using "the prestige of our offices...to foster a given point of view."

The *New York Times* reported, July 30, that a pro-war faction of the interns also had been organized and had sent a letter to the President, signed by 150 interns, voicing support of the war effort.

During the turmoil over drafting of pro-war and anti-war letters to the President, one intern allegedly used his sponsor's name without permission to obtain a conference room for one of the protesting factions. The intern's action, his later dismissal and the annoyance of many Congressmen over the conduct of their youthful charges went largely unreported in the mass media.

The summer intern controversy was discussed for the most part behind closed doors and off the record. However, House Appropriations Committee Chairman George H. Mahon (D Texas) said in the House, Dec. 12, 1967, that "in an effort to reduce expenditures in the Legislative Branch we struck out funds available for the Congressional student intern program." Two days later, Rep. Phillip Burton (D Calif.) told the House: "I doubt that there are many Members in this House who really believe that economy was the motive for killing the summer intern program. Rather, the action smacks of retaliation—an attempt to chastise because a number of interns last summer dared to voice opposition to the war in Vietnam."

The $750 allowance for hiring of a summer intern by a House Member was initially suspended only for the summer of 1968, but it was not until August 1970 that the House Appropriations Committee agreed to restore funds for the program. Despite suspension of the special allowance, college students had continued to work in the offices of many Representatives during the summer. The number of House interns dropped from 630 in 1967 to 275 in 1968, but by 1970 more than 600 students were at work on the House side. Interns were paid from regular clerical allowances, as in the Senate.

Appointments to Service Academies

One remnant of the patronage system has not only survived over the years but has continued to expand. Congressional appointees to the three major service academies account for nearly 75 percent of their enrollment.

Until 1902, the privilege of appointing candidates for admission to the service academies was enjoyed only by Members of the House of Representatives, the idea being to apportion academy enrollment on a national population basis. Each Congressional district was to supply one appointee every four years, thus giving each class maximum geographic variance and allowing equal numbers of appointments from equally populated areas.

By 1970 Senators and Representatives alike were privileged to have as many as five appointees enrolled in each academy at one time. This added up to 8,025 appointments in an available enrollment total of about 13,000.

In appointing young men for cadetships at the academies—U.S. Military Academy, West Point, N.Y.; U.S. Naval Academy, Annapolis, Md.; and U.S. Air Force Academy, Colorado Springs, Colo.—Members of Congress have wide leeway in making their choices. Most Senators and many Representatives do not personally handle the screening of candidates. The job of selecting nominees usually falls to an administrative assistant in the Senator's state office or the Representative's home district.

Selection Methods. It was in 1964 that Congress set the quota of five cadet appointees in each academy at any one time. Either of two methods of selecting appointees may be used, the choice being left to the Member.

• The general listing method allows for only minimal Congressional influence in the selection. A list of as many as 10 candidates is submitted to each of the respective academies. Scholastic and physical tests are given the candidates and the one making the best combined performance wins the appointment.

The principal-alternate method allows the Member far greater discretion over the appointment. Again, a list of as many as 10 candidates is submitted to the academy, but each candidate is ranked in order of the Member's preference. If the first-preference candidate meets the academic and physical entrance requirements, he wins the appointment regardless of how well the other candidates perform. If the first-preference candidate does not fulfill the entrance requirements, then the first-alternate is considered and so on down the list until a qualified candidate is found.

The principal-alternate method may be used by a Member when he feels that a particular young man has outstanding potentialities in some area that is not weighted heavily in the entrance requirements, such as creative talents or outstanding athletic ability. Of course, the method can be used also to ensure the appointment of a Member's son or grandson, if he is qualified, or the son of a political friend, etc.

Requirements. Before a candidate can be considered for appointment, he must submit to scholastic, physical and medical testing. No candidate may be older than 21. He must be of "good moral character" and must never have been married. The candidate must also be a United States citizen unless he is entering one of the academies on a special program. If a person already in the service wishes to attend one of the academies, he may take a competitive examination that is given annually. If he scores well, he will get an appointment.

Other Academies. A Member of Congress may also nominate as many as 10 persons for appointment to the Merchant Marine Academy, New London, Conn. The candidates must take a nationally competitive examination to win an appointment. No nominee on any Member's list is guaranteed appointment. The highest scoring candidates, regardless of who nominated them, are appointed to the freshman class.

No Congressional appointments are made to the Coast Guard Academy. Any interested party must simply contact the Academy and take the national examinations. Highest scoring candidates win the appointments.

Evolution of Appointment System

West Point. The system of Congressional appointments to the three major service academies had an obscure beginning in 1802 when Congress established what is today the U.S. Military Academy at West Point, N.Y. Congress envisioned the academy as an institution that would serve a dual purpose—teach cadets to be both officers and engineers.

Out of the initial class of 10, three had come from civilian backgrounds, the others from the Army. The three civilians were recommended by Representatives and appointed by the Secretary of War. The course of study was unstructured, lasting for as long as a cadet cared to stay. Discipline was virtually nonexistent; compensation consisted of $16 a month and two daily rations.

Congress took an active interest in the Academy when the United States declared war in 1812. Bold plans were drafted that year to create a standing Army of 145,000 men. But Congress had ignored requests from West Point for additional funds, and by 1812 the Academy had graduated only 71 cadets.

After 1812 enrollment was expanded to 250, and Congressmen were told they should appoint only men between the ages of 14 and 20 who had excelled in their preparatory schooling. Officials in Washington, however, had no intention of limiting appointments to these specifications. Thus the Academy had cadets ranging in age from 12 to 25. A Pennsylvania boy who had only one arm was appointed, and a married cadet kept his wife in a boarding house just outside the post and visited her every night.

As the prestige of West Point grew, increasing numbers of young men vied for appointments. By 1820 the President made all appointments to the Academy with recommendations from Congressmen and the Secretary of War. As the Secretary of War explained in 1822, consideration for appointment was based on a boy's poverty and the service his family had rendered the nation.

In 1828 Secretary of War James Barbour said that "in making selections, I have received and treated with great respect, the recommendations of the Members of Congress." Barbour said it was his custom to appoint one cadet from each Congressional district. Congress recognized a chance to increase patronage privileges and changed Barbour's custom into law the same year.

Naval Academy. In 1839 after years of demanding an academy to match the Army's facility at West Point, the Navy started an eight-month school in Philadelphia. Under pressure from the Secretary of the Navy, Congress in 1845 established a permanent facility at an old Army post called Fort Severn in Annapolis, Md. Money was appropriated the following year and a formalized curriculum was drafted. For the next seven years, all cadets at Annapolis were selected by the Secretary of the Navy from the ranks of enlisted men. Not until 1852 did Congress include the Naval Academy in the patronage appointment system. Every member of the House was allowed one appointed cadet in each academy at one time.

In 1862, after the Naval Academy had been moved temporarily to Newport, R.I., when Annapolis was threatened by the Confederacy, a Representative's quota was raised to two appointments to both the Military and Naval Academies. After the Civil War, however, quotas were again cut to one per Congressman.

World War I. The demand for qualified officers in both the Navy and Army continued to grow during the years preceding World War I. In 1900 Congressmen were given two appointive positions and for the first time, Senators and territorial delegates also were granted appointment privileges—a quota of two per Member at each academy. Quotas were increased to three in 1917 and to five, two years later. By 1919 the enrollment at the two academies was being filled also by appointments from the District of Columbia (5), from the ranks of enlisted men (100) and by Presidential selections (25).

World War II. After the First World War, appointments were cut back to three per Member (1923) and the other appointive categories also were reduced. By 1928, however, Congressional quotas were again hiked to four. Presidential appointments were increased to 40 and for the first time (officially), the Vice President was given two places to fill.

During the 1930s, the number of Congressional appointments to the military academies rose and fell in proportion to the size of military appropriations bills, but after the United States became involved in World War II, appointments were raised to five per Member. After the war, the number was again cut to four.

Air Force Academy. When the Air Force Academy was established in 1954, it received a period of grace from the traditional patronage appointment system. During the Academy's first four years in Colorado Springs, candidates were selected for appointment under a strict geographic quota system. Each state was allotted a percentage of appointments in proportion to its population. Members of Congress were to draw up lists of aspiring candidates who were then tested on a statewide basis. The most highly qualified candidates from each state were admitted. By 1958, however, the Air Force Academy was using an appointment system similar to those in use at West Point and Annapolis except that

Distribution of Appointments

The following table gives a breakdown of appointments to one of the three academies during a four-year period. Each institution has slightly different appointment figures for the small-number allotments, but the table is a representative breakdown of the enrollments at all three of the academies.

Noncompetitive:	No. of cadet appointments at one time
Senators	500
Representatives	2,175
Vice President	5
Sons of deceased veterans	40
District of Columbia	5
Guam, Samoa, Virgin Islands	1
Puerto Rico	6
Canal Zone	1
Total:	2,733
Competitive:	
President: sons of regulars	300
Secretary of Army, Navy, Air Force:	
Enlisted regulars	340
Enlisted reserves	340
Honor military schools	80
Congressional: qualified alternates	600
President: Medal of Honor sons	unlimited
Total:	1,660
Specific Foreign Students:	
Philippine Islands	4
American Republics	20
Total:	24
Total basic enrollment of one academy:	4,417

more of the air cadets were Congressional appointees (85 percent).

Changes in 1964

Congress passed a bill in 1964 providing for a virtual doubling of the enrollment at West Point and the Air Force Academy by 1971 (Annapolis already had a substantially larger enrollment than the other two schools). The bill called for an eventual increase of the maximum capacity of each of the two academies from 2,529 cadets to 4,417. To provide for the increase, Members of Congress were again given a five-cadet quota. Another section of the bill provided for appointment of the best qualified 150 of the "alternates" who failed of appointment under the principal-alternate system.

The most recent attempt to remove academy appointments from the patronage system was made in 1969 by Sen. Thomas J. Dodd (D Conn.). When he introduced his bill, Dodd said: "We can no longer afford the luxury of the risk inherent in a procedure where others than the best qualified may be appointed to our service academies. I believe that maintaining the obsolete system of Congressional nominations and appointments to the service academies is totally unjustifiable. It undermines efficiency. It promotes inequity. It defies logic." The Dodd bill provided that any person desiring an appointment would be allowed to take a national examination, but that only the most highly qualified from the entire field would be appointed. Congressional recommendations would no longer be necessary. The bill died in the Senate Armed Services Committee.

Bibliography

Books

Ambrose, Stephen, *Duty, Honor, Country: A History of West Point.* Johns Hopkins Press, 1966.

Beise, J. Arthur, *The Brass Factories.* Public Affairs Press, 1969.

MacCloskey, Monro, *How to Qualify for the Service Academies.* Richards Rosen Press, Inc., 1964.

Government Publications

U.S. Naval Academy, *Naval Academy Register,* 1850-1930.

U.S. Senate Armed Services Committee, *Report Relating to the Nomination and Selection of Candidates for Appointment to the Military, Naval and Air Force Academies,* Feb. 6, 1964.

The General Accounting Office

THE GENERAL Accounting Office (GAO) is an arm of the Legislative Branch that was created to oversee the expenditures of the Executive Branch. Since it was established in 1921, the duties of the GAO have been expanded from routine audits of the accounts of Executive Branch departments to probing analyses of program management and planning, and often to controversial investigations of how Government agencies are spending the taxpayers' money.

The GAO has been called the watchdog of Congress by those who support its actions and the "one-eyed watchdog" by critics who feel it is too responsive to political pressures. The agency has increasingly found itself in the center of controversy between Congress and the Executive Branch. GAO investigative audits have triggered hundreds of well-publicized news stories about everything from multimillion-dollar cost overruns for weapons systems to a $40,000 office remodeling job ordered by former Secretary of the Interior Walter J. Hickel (1969-1970).

Current Activities of GAO

When Congress needs information about a program that will require additional funds, the GAO is contacted to conduct an investigation. When the Appropriations Committees of the Senate and House are working on the annual appropriations bills, GAO staff members act as consultants. The audits and management-analysis reports done by GAO may be used as reference material. If an area of Government activity is of particular interest to a committee or Member, the GAO may be asked to make a special investigation.

During fiscal 1970, at the request of Congress, the GAO sent investigating teams to Vietnam to conduct studies on refugee-camp management by the United States and the South Vietnamese, on the performance of U.S. construction contractors, and on black-market pilfering of American goods from military warehouses. Because of the tremendous expenditures involved in Defense Department programs, the GAO has attempted annually to increase its specific program audits in that field.

Nearly one-half of GAO staff time is devoted to matters relating to Defense. In a controversial GAO report entitled "Acquisition of Major Weapon Systems," released March 18, 1971, the watchdog agency found cost increases of $33.4 billion for 61 weapon systems surveyed. A second report called "Defense Industry Profit Study," released the same day, was harshly criticized by Sen. William Proxmire (D Wis.), who accused the GAO of "softening" its conclusions.

In addition to the routine auditing of all major department budgets, GAO conducted reviews in 1970 of Medicare and Medicaid programs, various community development projects, programs concerning all levels of education, foreign assistance programs, the U.S. balance-of-payments position, and Government shipping, freight and passenger programs. The GAO issued a critical blast at the letting of contracts for water-pollution abatement facilities, accusing the Government of taking a "shotgun" approach lacking in foresight. In other GAO reports, loopholes in military contracting were discussed with emphasis on such projects as the F-111 aircraft, which was originally expected to cost $3 million per plane and was still being tested when the price had reached $13 million per plane.

Organization. During fiscal 1969, the GAO had 68 professional staff members permanently assigned to aid Congressional committees. One-half of that number served with the Senate Committee on Government Operations and its Permanent Subcommittee on Investigations. Of GAO's 4,632 staff members, 1,767 are assigned to the field operations division and work from GAO branch offices in 17 American cities and four foreign cities. The next largest division, with 774 persons, deals with transportation. The bulk of its work concerns routine checks and audits relating to the billions of dollars expended by the Government each year for commercial transportation.

Although GAO has only 322 staff members permanently assigned to the Department of Defense, nearly one-half of the working time of the entire GAO staff of 4,632 persons is spent in defense-related work. According to GAO statistics, 1,100 man-years of staff time were devoted to the Defense Department in 1970 and 1,265 man-years to all other Federal departments and agencies combined.

Work Volume. During fiscal 1969, GAO devoted 2,515 man-years to auditing and investigating Government agencies and projects. During those working hours the agency:

• Conducted more than 2,000 audits and reviews of selected Federal activities and programs in the United States and 45 foreign countries.

• Issued 1,023 reports, including 381 reports to Congress, Congressional committees or individual Members, and 642 reports to Executive Branch officials.

• Audited more than 9.5 million freight shipments and passenger movements for which the Government paid out more than $2.5 billion.

• Collected more than $14 million in transportation overpayments and settled for $16.3 million ($2.5 million less than claimed) almost 14,000 claims from public carriers.

- Disposed of more than 18,690 general claims against the Government for amounts totaling $70.1 million and adjusted and settled an additional 9,750 claims by individuals.
- Handed down approximately 4,900 decisions on legal matters and testified before Congressional committees on 24 occasions.

Background

The authority and influence now enjoyed by the General Accounting Office have been gradually attained through effective response to the needs of Congress. The Bureau of the Budget (known as the Office of Management and Budget since July 1, 1970) and the General Accounting Office both date back to the Budget and Accounting Act of 1921. The Budget Bureau, an arm of the Executive Branch, was given the responsibility of planning how and where Federal funds should be spent. It was the function of GAO, as an agency of the Legislative Branch, to provide Congress with an independent review of Executive expenditures.

The Budget and Accounting Act transferred to GAO the powers formerly vested in the Comptroller of the Treasury and six Treasury auditors. The general audit function, the settlement of claims and the power to review methods of disbursing funds, which were shifted by the 1921 Act from the Executive to the Legislative Branch, gave Congress new means to guard against lax or improper spending of Government funds.

The Comptroller General was empowered to investigage "all matters relating to the receipt, disbursement and application of public funds...making recommendations looking to greater economy or efficiency in public expenditures." "All claims and demands" for and against the Government also were to be settled and adjusted by GAO. As routine procedure, the GAO was required to review the adequacy of the accounting systems employed in all departments.

Early Development of GAO

Although the GAO was established primarily to audit the books of Government agencies, some Members of Congress pointed out during House debate on the bill in 1921 that the agency would have other important functions. Rep. Robert Luce (R Mass.), a sponsor of the Budget and Accounting Act, emphasized that one of the purposes was "to make sure that the Comptroller General shall concern himself not simply with taking in and paying money from an accountant's point of view, but that he shall also concern himself with the questions as to whether it is economically and efficiently applied."

Another supporter of the bill, James W. Good (R Iowa), said: "The Comptroller General should be more than a bookkeeper or accountant.... He should be a real critic and at all times should come to Congress, no matter what the political complexion of Congress or the Executive might be, and point out inefficiency if he found that money was being misapplied. He would bring such facts to the notice of the committees having jurisdiction on appropriations."

What the Budget and Accounting Act of 1921 purported to do was to give the House and Senate a tool by which each chamber could better control the spending of Federal funds once they had been appropriated. With the GAO working as an independent auditing agency responsible to Congress, the audit became an instrument for preventing waste and extravagance as well as fraud.

Despite expression of high hopes by many Members, the value of GAO's work was limited in the early years. Auditing was restricted almost entirely to Washington. Departments and agencies sent the original copies of their financial documents to GAO, and checking was carried out by a centralized desk audit. Major emphasis was placed on detecting illegal expenditures and errors in arithmetic. Only limited numbers of audits in the field were made before World War II.

Congress was generally enthusiastic about the work that GAO did accomplish, but Members made few requests for investigations. When requests were made, the GAO at times tended to be overzealous. (Critics of the agency still maintain that it spends too much time and money on investigating projects that have relatively small budgets while virtually ignoring huge expenditures in more "politically sensitive" areas.) During an investigation of the Tennessee Valley Authority in 1939, TVA Comptroller E.L. Kohler was highly critical of GAO. He told the House-Senate investigating committee:

"It has long been recognized that the Comptroller General regards himself not as an accountant but as a glorified watchdog, and that he has surrounded himself with a narrow-visioned legal staff that recognizes no superior except a decision of the Suprme Court directly in point. In my opinion, he has more than once been sadly out of line with the spirit of the Budget and Accounting Act of 1921....

"A review of his report (1934) and frequent contact this year with the (GAO) field staff, convinced me quickly and decisively that the field staff had made no real audit originally and had made none since; the staff has consisted of persons styled as 'investigators' who have had little accounting training or experience; and the 1934 report was in no sense an audit report, but rather a disorderly miscellany of fact and fancy that could succeed only in misleading the reader, regardless of his skill in auditing, accounting or sleuthing."

Grants of Additional Authority

During the middle and late 1940s, the GAO staff swelled to almost 15,000 persons. Wartime expenditures created masses of vouchers and routine claims that needed to be processed by the GAO. A need arose also for clarification of GAO authority. Disagreement between the General Accounting Office and such Government corporations as the TVA were in part responsible for the passage of the Government Corporation Control Act of 1945. Its primary purpose was to bring Government corporations under the effective control of Congress, thus plugging another loophole in Congressional supervision of Government spending.

Provisions of the Government Corporation Control Act required the GAO to conduct its audits at the location of a Government corporation's place of business. The extent of the audit was left to the discretion of the Comptroller General, who in 1957-61, for example, ordered a complete study of TVA's methods, procedures, programs and management approaches as well as a straight audit. (A Government corporation is funded by Government money but is managed as if it were a private enterprise. President Franklin D. Roosevelt described it as "a corporation clothed with the power of Government, but possessed of the flexibility and initiative of a private enterprise.")

Legislative Reorganization Act of 1946. In 1946 the GAO was accorded new powers intended to facilitate its efforts to bring about greater Government efficiency. Recognizing the financial expertise of GAO, Congress in the Legislative Reorganization Act of 1946, gave the GAO the authority to "make an expenditure analysis of each agency in the Executive Branch of the Government (including corporations), which, in the opinion of the Comptroller General, will enable Congress to determine where public funds have been economically and efficiently administered."

Anti-Kickback Act. Another major piece of legislation in 1946 was the Anti-Kickback Act (later amended by Public Law 86-695, approved Sept. 2, 1960). The Act empowered GAO to "inspect the plants and to audit the books and records of any prime contractor or subcontractor engaged in the performance of a negotiated contract with the Government."

When the General Services Administration was established in 1949 to manage the Government's property holdings, the duties of the GAO were again expanded. The agency was empowered to "audit all types of property accounts," which "as far as practicable shall be conducted at the places where the property or records of the Executive agencies are kept and shall include, but not necessarily be limited to, an evaluation of the effectiveness of internal controls and audits."

Accounting and Auditing Act. A major piece of legislation concerning GAO was the Accounting and Auditing Act of 1950. The Act clarified in specific terms the existing audit authority of GAO. Where the 1921 Act had been vague, the 1950 measure fully outlined the authority granted to, and the restrictions placed on, the agency.

By 1950, GAO was legally in a position to develop its "comprehensive" audit approach. This meant that it could go beyond questions of the legality and propriety of expenditures into other aspects of management. It could reach into nearly every phase of Government spending with an eye to efficiency.

Cost-Benefit Studies. The Legislative Reorganization Act of 1970 expanded GAO authority by specifically empowering the Comptroller General to make cost-benefit studies of Government programs and activities, upon his own initiative or at the request of either chamber or any committee of Congress. The Act also directed the Comptroller General to assist committees in conducting cost-benefit studies themselves and in analyzing any such studies furnished by a Federal agency. In addition, the Comptroller General was directed to cooperate with the Secretary of the Treasury and the Director of the Office of Management and Budget in developing a standardized information and data-processing system for budgetary and fiscal data.

Comptroller General. To isolate the General Accounting Office from political influences, the Budget and Accounting Act of 1921 provided that the Comptroller

---

Comptrollers General

The top positions in the General Accounting Office—Comptroller General and Assistant Comptroller General—are filled by appointment of the President in each case with the advice and consent of the Senate. The appointment is limited to a single term of 15 years. Only one Comptroller General (John R. McCarl) and one Assistant Comptroller General (Frank H. Weitzel) have served the full 15-year term.

Comptrollers General of the United States

John R. McCarl	July 1, 1921—June 30, 1936
Fred H. Brown	April 11, 1939—June 19, 1940
Lindsay C. Warren	Nov. 1, 1940—April 30, 1954
Joseph V. Campbell	Dec. 14, 1954—July 31, 1965
Elmer B. Staats	March 8, 1966—

Assistant Comptrollers General of the United States

Lurtin R. Ginn	July 1, 1921—Nov. 11, 1930
Richard N. Elliott	March 9, 1931—April 30, 1943
Frank L. Yates	May 1, 1943—June 29, 1953
Frank H. Weitzel	Oct. 12, 1953—Jan. 17, 1969*
Robert F. Keller	Sept. 25, 1969—

*Weitzel served as Acting Comptroller General in the period between the resignation of Campbell and the appointment of Staats—time not counted as a part of his 15-year term as Assistant Comptroller General.

General and the Assistant Comptroller General would be appointed for 15-year terms but could serve no more than one term. The appointments would be made by the President, subject to Senate confirmation, and the appointees could be removed from office only by joint resolution of Congress for a specified cause or through impeachment proceedings. Elmer B. Staats was appointed Comptroller general in 1966 by President Johnson, and his term will expire in 1981.

Staats' predecessor, Joseph Campbell, served as Comptroller General for 10 years and then retired for reasons of health. During Campbell's tenure, he sought to upgrade the GAO corps of professionals. He hired only persons with accounting degrees or certificates. The practice thus established still prevails. As of June 30, 1970, the GAO had 2,906 professional employees and of that number 2,372 were accountants.

Other Legislation. A bill was reported to the Senate on Oct. 2, 1970, by the Government Operations Committee that would have changed the name of the General Accounting Office to the Office of the Comptroller General. Other features of the bill would have granted the Comptroller General subpoena power over the records of contractors and subcontractors under negotiated contracts; required the Comptroller General to provide analyses of pending bills at the request of individual Senators or Representatives; authorized additional staff; and required Executive agencies to make available the information needed for GAO analyses. The bill was passed by a voice vote in the Senate Oct. 9, 1970, but it died in the House Government Operations Committee. An identical bill was introduced by Sen. Abraham Ribicoff (D Conn.) in the 92nd Congress.

Philadelphia Plan

Comptroller General Elmer B. Staats used the power of his office in 1960 to challenge the Department of Labor, the Department of Justice and the President. The challenge involved a plan, first agreed to in Philadelphia, under which contractors on Federally assisted construction projects were pledged to make every effort to hire a certain quota of minority-group workers.

The Philadelphia Plan was announced by the Labor Department in June 1969 and went into effect in September. Before the effective date, Comptroller General Staats ruled that the plan, though aimed to promote employment of Negroes, would constitute discrimination in violation of the Civil Rights Act of 1964. Accordingly, Staats said he would sign pay releases to the contractors whether or not they met Labor Department hiring goals. Attorney General John N. Mitchell, on the other hand, denied that the Philadelphia Plan violated the law.

A controversy erupted on the floor of the Senate in December 1969 after the Appropriations Committee had added to a fiscal 1970 supplemental appropriations bill an amendment forbidding use of any Federal funds through contracts or agreements which the Comptroller General "holds to be in contravention of any Federal statute." The Senate nevertheless accepted the amendment, whose effect would have been to nullify the Philadelphia Plan and give the Comptroller General unprecedented power to interpret the law.

After the President threatened to veto the bill, the House refused to accept the Senate amendment. The Senate later agreed to the deletion and the Philadelphia Plan continued in effect despite the objections of the Comptroller General.

By March 1971, the Labor Department's Office of Federal Contract Compliance in Philadelphia had reported more than 50 instances in which building contractors were found in violation of the Plan. The first cutoff of funds for a contractor not complying with the regulations was announced March 27, 1971.

Main Functions of GAO

The General Accounting Office has five broad areas of responsibility—to independently initiate audits and reviews of agencies and programs, to establish accounting standards, provide legal opinions, settle claims for and against the Government and make studies at the request of Congress. The GAO's staff strength for 1971 was estimated to reach 4,800; about 3,000 members of the staff were classified as professionals (accountants, lawyers and specialists in engineering, systems analysis, industrial management, etc.).

Audit and Review

The basic function of the GAO is to audit agency and program spending and to review management ef-

fectiveness. The Budget and Accounting Act of 1921 stated that "the independent audit will...serve to inform Congress at all times as to the actual conditions surrounding the expenditure of public funds in every department of the Government."

The GAO's audit approach is to review the organization, management and controls of each agency system: identify weaknesses; report on conditions found; and recommend improvements. Accordingly, the Comptroller General orders selective reviews of management activities, financial transactions and accounts of 12 Executive departments, about 60 independent agencies and commissions and selected special programs. An example was a report issued Nov. 19, 1970, on the large-scale production of certain weapons systems before the systems had been completely developed. The GAO found that some of the weapons systems did not meet specifications and had been delivered at costs far above original estimates. One of the five systems studied, a classified weapon referred to as Sensor A, had been mass-produced before testing was completed. Changes ordered as a result of subsequent tests on the mass-produced weapon caused a three-year delay in delivery and added costs for refitting that more than doubled the estimated expenditures for the system. The GAO advised that all testing should be completed before the military allowed any of its weapons to be put into production.

Although the auditing and review functions of the GAO are expected to aid the respective departments, Congress also is indirectly benefited by every agency and project audit conducted. The findings of an audit may help Congress in exercising legislative oversight when considering requests by the Executive Branch. The audits may also provide Congressional committees with information necessary to back up requests for further investigations of spending and management. At the same time, it has been asserted that Congress does not use the potentially valuable reports effectively.

The Comptroller General often bases his choice of a selective audit on the interest of Congress in the subject or on whether consideration of proposed legislation will be aided by having authoritative information at the disposal of Members.

The authority to audit and review extends to most Federal activities. However, there are forbidden areas. GAO described them in detail in a 36-page book issued in 1966. The agency has no authority to make analytical audits or reviews in six general areas—the Federal Reserve System, the Office of the Comptroller of the Currency, the operation of the Exchange Stabilization Fund in the Treasury Department, the Federal Land Bank System, Presidential expenditures and most intelligence activities (FBI, CIA and military intelligence). A particular area in which GAO activity is limited comprises Federal grants-in-aid to states for such projects as highway construction. Unless a special clause is included in the appropriations bill, GAO has no authority to audit the handling of Federal funds of this type by the states.

When making an audit, the GAO has the right to demand access to any documents, books, papers or records of any department or office not listed in the book of restrictions. It has the same authority when auditing the accounts of private concerns that have been awarded negotiated contracts of $100,000 or more. Although the

Comptroller General has authority to demand these things, he does not have power to serve a subpoena to obtain records. Subpoenas must be obtained from the Justice Department or the courts. As noted, a bill before Congress in 1970 would have given the Comptroller General the power to subpoena records, but the measure died in the House Government Operations Committee. An identical bill was introduced in the 92nd Congress.

The Federal Government is the largest single user of commercial transportation, paying from $2 billion to $3 billion annually to commercial carriers. Agencies are required to pay transportation bills on presentation, before audit by the GAO. Disbursing officers are relieved of liability for overpayments resulting from improper rates or classifications. Therefore, the GAO is solely responsible for determining the propriety of rates and classifications on which bills and claims for freight and passenger service are based.

Accounting Standards and Claims

The General Accounting Office not only conducts audits but also establishes accounting standards and management guidelines for all Government departments and programs. GAO prescribes the standards, helps the Executive agencies to develop efficient accounting systems and approves the systems when they are deemed adequate.

One criticism of this phase of the GAO's work is that there are no allowances for follow-up. The GAO can make all the recommendations it cares to, but it cannot require them to be put into effect. Once the GAO studies an agency or program and recommends changes, it can do no more. If Congress does not press for the suggested changes, the agency in question can go right on with inefficient management and improper accounting methods which may result in great expense to the taxpayer.

Legal Opinions. The 106 lawyers working for GAO submitted 4,900 legal advisory opinions during fiscal 1970. The bulk of legal work involves interpretations of the law as respects the extent of departmental or agency authority in the expenditure of public funds. Before undertaking new programs or executing contracts, department heads and disbursing officers may request advice from the GAO's legal staff.

Settlement of Claims. As stated in the statutes (31 U.S. Code 71), "All claims and demands whatever by the Government or against it...shall be settled and adjusted in the General Accounting Office." The initial responsibility for collection of debts owed the Government rests with the individual agency involved, but claims involving doubtful legal questions or claims that the agency has been unable to collect are referred to GAO.

Investigation and Analysis

One of the ways in which GAO gives Congress direct assistance is by making special investigative reports either at the request of Congress as a whole or at the request of committees or individual Members. Since 1950, the number of reports issued by special request of Congress has nearly doubled. About 70 professional GAO staff members are permanently assigned to various committees, but they are by no means the only GAO

GAO Savings

Comptroller General Elmer B. Staats told the Senate Legislative Appropriations Subcommittee in 1970 that the GAO estimated it would save the Government $187.6 million in fiscal 1970 by rooting out discrepancies in Government spending and by recommending more economical methods of managing an agency or program. The savings directly attributed by the GAO to its efforts amounted to less than one percent of the Federal budget.

---

staffers who work on the Congressional requests. A report issued Oct. 7, 1970, for example, concerned a specific job training program for the disadvantaged in Los Angeles. The GAO found gross management in the $8.9 million project which was sponsored by the Department of Labor. The report stated that the Department had agreed to pay certain contractors an average of $3,051 for each of a stated number of workers to be trained and hired under the program, but if the stated number was not recruited, the contractor had to refund only $2,500 for each worker not actually taken on. Theoretically, the report pointed out, a company receiving $1 million could buy land, construct a plant, not hire a single disadvantaged employee, and come away with a profit of about $162,500 and an interest-free loan of about $800,000. The report also mentioned that the $8.9 million program had yielded only 526 jobs by the time eight of the 10 contracts had expired.

The GAO increasingly has taken on the job of analyzing legislative proposals under consideration by committees of Congress. GAO staff members provide assistance in drafting bills, give technical advice and provide information based on ongoing work or previous GAO studies. According to Comptroller General Staats, about 20 percent of GAO's work is devoted to direct aid to Congress. In addition to responding to specific Congressional requests, more than half of the GAO studies are conducted in anticipation of Congressional requests.

Criticism of GAO

An analytical study of the GAO itself, conducted in 1970 by the Citizens Advocate Center, a public-interest law firm based in Washington, D.C., concluded that Staats' estimate of 20 percent was too low when the element of GAO anticipation of Congressional requests was considered. The study, "The General Accounting Office: One-Eyed Watchdog?" written by Eliot Stanley, raised two basic questions regarding GAO's increasing emphasis on service as an information agency for Congress on popular issues. Does the priority given to Congressional requests have the effect of diminishing GAO's ability to initiate and plan independent systematic audits and reviews of Federal programs? Does a close interdependence between GAO and Congress mean that GAO must be responsive to the political power structure of Congress? The study indicated that both questions might have to be answered in the affirmative. By anticipating Congressional demands, the study said, the GAO was relinquishing its responsibility for planning independent audits of programs that might hold little interest for

Congress but that were nonetheless recipients of large amounts of Federal money.

Some critics of GAO feel that Congress is to blame for the agency's weak points. They say that GAO is only as strong as the Congress it serves. In some cases GAO has been unable to do complete audits on certain projects because of bureaucratic power plays between branches of the Government and, critics add, because the Comptroller General does not want to offend Members of Congress who control or at least influence appropriations necessary to expand the agency.

During the last six months of 1970, for example, the GAO attempted to audit and review one of the Pentagon's weapons programs—Lockheed Aircraft Corporation's C-5A cargo plane. The Joint Economic Committee had requested a review of Lockheed's financial outlook because the company was requesting an additional $558 million to finish the project. The Committee wanted to know if Lockheed was in danger of going bankrupt even if that sum was paid to the company. Both Lockheed and the Department of Defense at first refused to give the GAO any information. But after receiving a series of letters defining the agency's statutory rights, the Pentagon made a minor concession. The GAO was given permission to look at a Defense Department cash-flow analysis of Lockheed, but the auditors were not allowed to remove the books from the Pentagon, to copy down any figures or to tell anyone what the figures were they had audited. All the Defense Department would allow the auditors to do was to make a judgment on the solvency of Lockheed.

Pentagon officials said the prohibitions were necessary because of the "sensitivity" of the disputed program—the political sensitivity, not that of defense. Neither GAO nor the Joint Economic Committee could enforce GAO's statutory authority to fully audit the defense contractor's cash-flow statement. Neither the Committee nor the GAO had the authority to subpoena Lockheed's books which were in the hands of the Pentagon. The watchdog of Congress was immobilized in the Lockheed dispute because the company insisted that the Government had no right to scrutinize its commercial programs (and, therefore, no broad-based analysis of the company's stability could be conducted).

The GAO has had less difficulty exercising its statutory authority on domestic programs concerning departments other than Defense. It has a record of relentless probing into matters such as job training, education, pollution and numerous others. Critics call many of the unfavorable GAO analyses of domestic programs unfair. They say the agency gets good publicity uncovering minor corruption in the management of comparatively small projects, while making only cursory attempts to root out discrepancies in defense programs.

Bibliography

Brown, Richard, *The GAO; Untapped Source of Congressional Power.* University of Tennessee Press, 1970.

Staats, Elmer B., "The GAO's Long-Range Plans for Military Audits," *The Armed Forces Comptroller,* April 1967, p. 2.

Annual Report of the Comptroller General—1970. Government Printing Office, 1970.

Chapter 5—Congress and the Electorate

Who Elects Congress

FEW GOVERNMENTAL institutions have changed so markedly over the years as has the makeup of the nation's electorate. From the early days of the Republic, when the voting privilege was limited to the upper economic classes, one voting barrier after another has fallen in the face of pressures for wider suffrage. First nonproperty-holding males, then women and the Negro successfully pushed for the franchise. By 1971, almost every restriction on voting had been removed and virtually the entire adult population had won the right to vote.

Actions to expand the electorate have taken place at both the state and Federal levels. (Voting qualifications have varied widely in the states because of a provision of the Federal Constitution (Article I, Section 2) permitting the states to set their own voting standards.) Early in the nation's history, the states dropped their property qualifications for voting but some retained literacy tests as late as 1970.

Constitutional Amendments on Voting

On the Federal level, the Constitution has been amended four times to circumvent state qualifications denying the franchise to certain categories of persons. The 14th Amendment, ratified in 1868, directed Congress to reduce the number of Representatives from any state that disfranchised any adult male citizen for any reason other than commission of a crime, but no such reduction was ever made. The 15th Amendment in 1870 prohibited denial of the right to vote "on account of race, color or previous condition of servitude," while the 19th Amendment in 1920 prohibited denial of that right "on account of sex." Finally, in 1964, the 24th Amendment outlawed denial of the right to vote in any Federal election "by reason of failure to pay any poll tax or other tax."

Congress in the 1950s and 1960s enacted a series of statutes to enforce the 15th Amendment's guaranty against racial discrimination in voting. A law passed in 1970 nullified state residence requirements of longer than 30 days for voting in Presidential elections, suspended literacy tests for a five-year period and lowered the minimum voting age from 21 years (the level in most states) to 18 years. A Supreme Court ruling upheld the voting-age change with respect to Federal elections but invalidated it with respect to state and local elections. In the same decision (*Oregon v. Mitchell*, Dec. 21, 1970) the Court upheld the provision on residence requirements and sustained the suspension of literacy tests with respect to both state and local elections.

The right to vote in Presidential elections was extended to citizens of the District of Columbia by the 23rd Amendment, ratified in 1961. District residents had been disfranchised for national elections except for a brief period in the 1870s, when they elected a nonvoting delegate to the House of Representatives. In 1970, Congress took another step toward full suffrage for District residents by again authorizing the election of a nonvoting delegate to the House, beginning in 1971.

Increases in Persons Voting

Statistics show that each major liberalization of election laws has resulted in a sharp increase in the number of persons voting. From 1824 to 1856, a period in which states gradually relaxed their property and taxpaying qualifications for voting, voter participation in Presidential elections increased from 3.8 percent to 17 percent of the population. From 1912, when women intensified their campaign for the ballot, until 1920, when the Constitution was amended to prohibit voter discrimination against women, participation increased from 15.8 to 25.1 percent. Largely because of growing political awareness by women and passage of new civil rights laws enfranchising Negroes, participation increased to 38.1 percent of the population by 1960 but fell off slightly thereafter. Total voter turnout rose from 356,000 in 1824 to 73,212,000 in 1968.

But despite a steady increase in the numbers of persons voting, voter turnout has actually decreased in terms of percentages of *eligible voters* voting. For the purpose of voting studies, eligible voters normally are defined as all adult civilians of voting age (whether registered or not) except persons housed in penal and other institutions. From 1856 until the turn of the century, the participation rate fell from 83.5 to 73.5 percent. It fell again to 49.1 percent in 1924 before rising gradually, with some fits and starts, to over 64 percent in 1960 and then slumping in 1964 and 1968. Political scientists have attributed the percentage decline in this category of participation to long periods of political stability, the predictable outcome of many races, the lack of appeal of some candidates, and the fact that many eligible voters do not bother to register to vote.

Differences in Voter Participation

Recent U.S. Government studies have shown a marked differential in participation among various classes of voters. In general, the studies found higher participation rates among men, whites, persons 45 to 54 years of age, non-southerners, persons with higher family incomes, and persons in white-collar occupations. Private

Popular Vote in Presidential Elections

Year	Population	Vote for President	% of Population
	(000 omitted)		
1824	9,386	356	3.8
1828	10,228	1,155	11.3
1832	11,733	1,218	10.4
1836	12,936	1,498	11.6
1840	14,633	2,411	16.5
1844	17,082	2,699	15.8
1848	18,202	2,872	15.8
1852	21,707	3,144	14.5
1856	24,258	4,054	16.7
1860	27,559	4,680	17.0
1864	34,863	4,019	*
1868	38,213	5,716	**
1872	41,972	6,466	15.4
1876	46,107	8,431	18.3
1880	50,262	9,219	18.3
1884	55,379	10,050	19.0
1888	60,496	11,392	18.8
1892	65,666	12,150	18.5
1896	70,885	13,813	19.5
1900	76,094	13,965	18.4
1904	82,165	13,524	16.5
1908	88,709	14,887	16.8
1912	95,331	15,031	15.8
1916	101,996	18,529	18.2
1920	106,466	26,705	25.1
1924	114,113	29,022	25.4
1928	120,501	36,879	30.6
1932	124,840	39,814	31.9
1936	128,053	45,648	35.6
1940	131,970	49,901	37.8
1944	138,083	47,974	34.7
1948	146,631	48,794	33.3
1952	157,022	61,552	39.2
1956	168,221	62,026	36.9
1960	180,684	68,838	38.1
1964	192,120	70,644	36.8
1968	201,152	73,211	36.4

* *Population figure for 1864, but not the voting total, includes the Confederate states.*

** *No popular vote was counted for four former Confederate states in 1868.*

SOURCES: U.S. Bureau of the Census; Richard M. Scammon, ed., *America Votes*, Vols. 1-8, Governmental Affairs Institute (1956-70).

studies have shown repeatedly that higher turnout rates generally favor Democrats while lower ones favor Republicans.

As the voting population has grown, political parties have become increasingly important in the electoral process. As the power of the individual's vote became more and more diluted, voters found parties a convenient mechanism for defining political issues and mobilizing the strength to push a particular policy through to enactment and execution. After the rise and fall of numerous different political parties during the first half of the 19th century, most voting strength became and remained polarized in two major parties—the Republican and the Democratic.

What follows is a history of voting qualifications in the United States, together with details of actions by the state and federal governments to expand suffrage. The role of political parties in the process is examined, and details of Government studies on comparative voter participation levels among various identifiable groups are provided.

Expansion of the Electorate

Background. During the first few decades after establishment of the new national government, all 13 of the original states limited the franchise to property holders and taxpayers. Seven of the states required ownership of land (normally a "freehold" or life estate as opposed to a leased estate) as a qualification for voting, while the other six permitted persons to substitute either evidence of ownership of certain amounts of personal property or payment of taxes as a prerequisite to exercise of the franchise. James Madison expressed the prevailing view on the part of the Founding Fathers with respect to this matter in a statement before the Constitutional Convention:

"The freeholders of the country would be the safest depository of republican liberty. In future times a great majority of the people will not only be without land, but any other sort of property. These will either combine under the influence of their common situation; in which case, the rights of property and the public liberty will not be secure in their hands, or, which is more probable, they will become tools of opulence and ambition, in which case there will be equal danger on another side."

The framers of the Constitution were apparently content to have the states limit the right to vote to adult males who had a real stake in good government; this meant, in most cases, persons on the upper economic levels. Not wishing to discriminate against any particular type of property owner (uniform Federal voting standards inevitably would have conflicted with some of the state standards), the convention adopted without dissent the recommendation of its Committee of Detail providing that qualifications for the electors of the House of Representatives "shall be the same...as those of the electors in the several states, of the most numerous branch of their own legislatures."

Under this provision fewer than one-half of the adult white men in the United States were eligible to vote at the outset in Federal elections. Because no state made women eligible (although none was forbidden to do so), only one white adult in four qualified to go to the polls. Slaves, both Negro and Indian, were ineligible, and they comprised almost one-fifth of the American population as enumerated in the census of 1790. Also ineligible were white indentured servants, whose status was little better than that of slaves.

Actually, these early state practices represented a liberalization of restrictions on voting that had prevailed at one time in the colonial period. Roman Catholics had been disfranchised in almost every colony, Jews in most colonies, Quakers and Baptists in some. In Rhode Island, Jews remained legally ineligible to vote until 1842.

Removal of Property Qualifications

For upwards of half a century before the Civil War there was a steady broadening of the electorate. The new western settlements supplied a sharp and continuing stimulus to the principle of universal manhood suffrage, and Jacksonian democracy encouraged its acceptance. Gradually, the seven states making property ownership a condition for voting substituted a taxpaying requirement: Delaware in 1792; Maryland in 1810; Connecticut in 1818; Massachusetts in 1821; New York in 1821; Rhode Island in 1842, and Virginia in 1850. By the mid-19th century, most states had removed even the taxpaying qualifications although some jurisdictions persisted in this practice into the 20th century.

The Negro Vote

In no period of American history have Negroes been totally excluded from the polls. At the time of the Constitutional Convention free Negroes had the right of suffrage in all the original states except Georgia, South Carolina and Virginia. Their right to vote stemmed from the fact that the first Negroes in America had been regarded not as slaves but as indentured servants who could expect freedom after a term of years. By 1800, however, the greater part of the Negro people was held in slavery and, as the institution of slavery for life was more firmly established, disfranchisement of the Negro became widespread. At the time of the outbreak of the Civil War Negroes were disfranchised, solely on the basis of their race, in all except six of the 33 states.

President Lincoln's Emancipation Proclamation of 1863 was the prelude to enfranchisement of former Negro slaves after the Civil War. Lincoln himself preferred to move cautiously in expanding the Negro electorate, however, so as to ease the impact of change on the southern states. In 1864, he wrote a letter for the private consideration of the interim Governor of Louisiana in which he broached the matter of allowing some Negroes to vote, especially the "very intelligent" and those who had fought on the Union side. Lincoln was not disposed to force the southern states to accept all Negroes as qualified voters.

Black Voting in South After Civil War

Soon after Lincoln's assassination, several southern states enacted so-called "Black Codes" barring the newly liberated slaves from voting or holding office. Radical Republicans in Congress responded by passing the Reconstruction Act of 1867, which established provisional military governments in the southern states. Return of control to state officials was made dependent upon ratification of the 14th Amendment, the second section of which provided for reduction of the representation in Congress of any state denying the franchise to any male citizen over 21 years of age in the proportion which the number of the disfranchised bore to the whole adult male population of the state.

The Reconstruction Act conditioned readmission to the Union on extension of the franchise to all adult males "of whatever race, color or previous condition." On Feb. 26, 1869, Congress submitted to the states the 15th Amendment, the first section of which provided: "The right of citizens of the United States to vote shall not be denied or abridged by the United States or by any state on account of race, color or previous condition of servitude." Ratification was completed in less than one year.

The Radical Republican majority in Congress feared that unless the Negro was allowed to vote, Democrats and ex-rebels would quickly regain control of the national government. In the Presidential election of 1868, in fact, Gen. Ulysses S. Grant defeated his Democratic opponent, Horatio Seymour, by a margin of only 306,000 votes, with the new Negro vote probably deciding the election in favor of Grant.

The newly enfranchised Negroes obtained many important posts in the governments formed under the Reconstruction Act of 1867. Louisiana, Mississippi and South Carolina had Negro lieutenant governors. Between 1869 and 1901, 22 Negroes were sent to Congress from southern states. Hiram R. Revels and Blanche Kelso Bruce represented Mississippi in the Senate. Bruce served a full six-year term (1875-1881) and was a presiding officer of the Republican National Convention of 1880.

During the decade of the '70s there was mounting opposition in the South to the participation of former slaves in the electorate. Gunnar Myrdal noted in his landmark study of the Negro in America, *An American Dilemma*, that: "The Fourteenth and Fifteenth Amendments were...looked upon as the supreme foolishness of the North and, worse still, as an expression of ill-will of the Yankees toward the defeated South. The Negro franchise became the symbol of the humiliation of the South."

Loss of Vote After Reconstruction

Congress passed various enforcement acts to protect Negro rights in the South, but the North clearly was growing weary of the crusade for betterment of the condition of Negroes. When the last Federal troops were withdrawn in April 1877, the remaining Radical Reconstruction governments in the South quickly disintegrated. Some Negroes continued to vote but by 1900, according to historian Paul Lewinson in his book *Race, Class and Party*, "all factions united in a white man's party once more, to put the Negro finally beyond the pale of political activity."

Post-War Disfranchisement. Withdrawal of Federal troops from the South in 1877 foreshadowed the end of Negro political power. For about a decade thereafter, the Negro retained his voting rights and was an important source of support for the Populist movement. But tolerance of Negro political activity began to recede after 1883, when the Supreme Court invalidated the Civil Rights Act of 1875.

Mississippi led the way in proscribing Negro political activity. A new state constitution drawn up in 1890 required prospective voters to pay a poll tax of $2 and to demonstrate their ability to read any section of the state constitution or to interpret it when read to them. In Mississippi and the other southern states which adopted voter literacy tests, care was taken not to disfranchise illiterate whites. Five states exempted white voters from literacy and some other requirements by "grandfather clauses"—regulations allowing prospective voters, if not otherwise qualified, to register if they were descended from persons who had voted, or served in the state's military forces, before 1867. Other provisions allowed illiterates to register if they owned a certain amount of property or could show themselves to be of good moral character.

Perhaps the most effective weapon for disfranchising southern Negroes was the "white primary" in which Negroes were excluded from participation in affairs of the Democratic party. Southerners defended the white primary on the ground that the Democratic party was a private organization and hence not subject to the limitations of the 14th and 15th Amendments. Because victory in a southern Democratic primary was for many years tantamount to election, the small numbers of registered Negroes were as effectively stripped of political rights as the vast unregistered majority.

Voter Intimidation. Legal devices to curtail Negro political activity were buttressed by physical and economic intimidation. Gunnar Myrdal, writing of conditions in the South in the early 1940s, noted that "Physical coercion is not so often practiced against the Negro, but the mere fact that it can be used with impunity and that it is devastating in its consequences creates a psychic coercion that exists nearly everywhere in the South."

"A Negro can seldom claim the protection of the police and the courts if a white man knocks him down, or if a mob burns his house or inflicts bodily injury on him or on members of his family. If he defends himself against a minor violence, he may expect a major violence. If he once 'gets in wrong' he may expect the loss of his job or other economic injury, and constant insult or loss of whatever legal rights he may have had. In such circumstances it is no wonder that the great majority of Negroes in the South make no attempt to vote and—if they make attempts which are rebuffed—seldom demand their full rights under the Federal Constitution."

Negroes who summoned up the courage to try to register encountered various forms of delay and harassment. The scornful question "What do you want here, nigger?" often sufficed to send a Negro away from the registration office. If the Negro applicant persisted, the registrar was likely to ignore him, tell him that there were no more registration forms, or direct him to another place of registration which, if it existed, was usually closed. Southern registrars also displayed a tendency to lose registration forms filled out by Negroes. By 1900, the Negro vote in the South had virtually disappeared. In Louisiana, for example, the number of Negro voters fell from 130,334 in 1896 to 5,320 in 1900. Negro voter participation in that state declined even further in subsequent years; between 1900 and 1945, the number of Negroes registered never exceeded 1 per cent of the number potentially qualified to vote.

Supreme Court Decisions. After years of litigation, two of the devices used to curtail Negro voting were struck down by the U.S. Supreme Court in the first half of the 20th century. The "grandfather clause," exempting prospective voters from literacy and certain other qualifications if they or their ancestors had been eligible to vote before Reconstruction, was declared unconstitutional in 1915 *(Guinn v. United States)*. The all-white primary was finally outlawed in 1944 *(Smith v. Allwright)*. The Supreme Court refused, in the white primary case, to accept the contention that a political party was the counterpart of a private club with the right to restrict its membership as it chose and to limit voting for candidates, as for club officers, to members only. In ruling that primaries were essential parts of the electoral process, the Court voided the device that had been the most widely used to keep Negroes from gaining effective political influence. The Supreme Court in 1966 outlawed the poll tax as a condition for voting in state and local elections *(Harper v. Virginia State Board of Education)*. (The 24th Amendment, ratified in 1964, had banned payment of poll taxes for participation in Federal elections.) Justice William O. Douglas wrote the majority opinion in *Harper*, declaring that "Voter qualifications have no relation to wealth nor to paying or not paying this or any other tax. Wealth, like race, creed or color, is not germane to one's ability to participate intelligently in the electoral process."

Civil Rights Legislation

Despite the Supreme Court decisions, actual or threatened intimidation, coupled with discriminatory application of literacy tests, kept Negro political activity at a minimum. It was not until Congress and the White House intervened in behalf of the Negro in the 1950s and 1960s that the tide began to turn.

Acts of 1957, 1960, 1964. The Civil Rights Act of 1957 added to the meager legal weapons previously possessed by the Attorney General the authority to institute civil actions to enjoin any public official or private person from interfering with a citizen's right to vote in any election—Federal, state or local. Other provisions of the statute gave the Federal district courts jurisdiction over such cases; authorized contempt proceedings whenever court orders were disobeyed; provided for appointment of an additional Assistant Attorney General, thus raising the status of the Civil Rights Section of the Justice Department to that of a full division.

The 1957 Act, however, failed to take account of the ingenuity of southern registrars in sidestepping or ignoring the law. Accordingly, the Civil Rights Act of 1960 made states themselves liable to suits for enforcement of voting rights in cases where registrars had resigned and no successors had been appointed. Registration and voting records were declared public records, and it was required that they be preserved for 22 months after any general or special election. Such records thus became available to the U.S. Attorney General prior to institution of any legal proceedings. Instead of providing for appointment of Federal registrars, as the U.S. Civil Rights Commission had recommended, the 1960 Act set up complicated machinery by which Federal voting "referees" might be appointed in cases where state registrars were found to have disqualified applicants on discriminatory grounds.

Title I of the Civil Rights Act of 1964 further strengthened the 1957 statute by prohibiting unequal application of voter registration requirements. Moreover, it enjoined registrars from rejecting registration forms on account of immaterial errors or omissions and required that all literacy tests be administered in writing. Most important of all, the 1964 Act made a sixth-grade education (if in English) a presumption of literacy.

Voting Rights Act of 1965. But the most sweeping piece of Federal voting legislation in a century was yet to come. On March 17, 1965, 10 days after Negro demonstrators were attacked by Alabama law enforcement officers at Selma, President Lyndon B. Johnson sent to Congress a bill aimed at eliminating the remaining obstacles to Negro voting in the South. The Voting Rights Act of 1965 suspended all literacy tests and similar devices in states where less than 50 percent of the population of voting age had been registered or had voted in the 1964 Presidential election. The Act provided also for appointment of Federal examiners with authority to register voters in areas covered by the legislation. The bill's formula applied to all of Alabama, Alaska, Georgia, Louisiana, Mississippi, South Carolina and Virginia, 40 counties in North Carolina and one county in Arizona.

Rise in Negro Registration and Voting

Passage of the Voting Rights Act heralded a significant increase in the numbers of Negroes registered, voting and running for office in the southern states. According to records of the U.S. Civil Rights Commission, Federal examiners had been assigned to 58 countries in southern states through Dec. 31, 1967, and had listed as eligible to vote 158,094 persons, including 150,767 non-whites and 7,327 whites. In addition, officials of the Department of Justice estimated that as of May 3, 1967, an additional 416,000 Negro citizens had been registered by local voting registrars since passage of the Act. In a 1968 report entitled "Political Participation," the Civil Rights Commission noted that Negro registration had climbed to more than 50 percent of the voting-age population in every southern state. (Before the Act, Negro registration had exceeded 50 percent only in Florida, Tennessee and Texas.) The report cited Negro registration gains in the southern states as follows: Mississippi, from 6.7 percent to 59.8 percent of voting-age population; Alabama, from 19.3 to 51.6; Georgia, from 27.4 to 52.6; Louisiana, from 31.6 to 58.9; and South Carolina, from 37.3 to 51.2.

A 1966 report by the Voter Education Project of the Southern Regional Council, a private research group in Atlanta, found that the substantial rise in Negro registration had been coupled with a significant increase in the number of Negroes actually voting. The report estimated that in Arkansas, 80,000 to 90,000 of a total of between 115,000 and 120,000 Negroes registered voted in the November 1966 general election; in South Carolina, 100,000 of 191,000, and in Georgia, 150,000 of 300,000. In Alabama, the Negro turnout for the May 3, 1966, primary was estimated at 74 percent of the total Negro electorate of just under 250,000 (the turnout fell to less than 50 percent in the general election, however, when two segregationists were the principal candidates). In Louisiana, where there were no major statewide contests, a sampling of several Negro precincts indicated turnouts of 50 to 60 percent of those registered.

Poll Taxes and Voting

Payment of poll taxes as a requirement for voting in the United States appeared in two different eras. The levies were introduced in some states during the early days of the Republic as a substitute for property qualifications for voting. The intent of the early levies was to enlarge the electorate. These taxes were gradually eliminated, and by the time of the Civil War, few states still imposed them.

During the second era of the poll tax, which began in the early 1890s, the levy, though imposed in some other states, was used in the South as one of a number of devices to restrict suffrage. Poll taxes tied to the right to vote were adopted in 11 southern states—Florida (1889), Mississippi and Tennessee (1890), Arkansas (1892), South Carolina (1895), Louisiana (1898), North Carolina (1900), Alabama (1901), Virginia and Texas (1902) and Georgia (1908).

The ostensible purpose of the levies was to "cleanse" elections of mass abuse, but the records of constitutional conventions held in five southern states during the period contained statements praising the poll tax as a measure to bar the Negro as well as the poor white from the franchise. Many historians have asserted that the main intent of these measures was to limit the popular base of the agrarian revolution inspired by the Populist party.

State Action to Eliminate Tax

In the years following the Populist era, seven southern states dropped their poll taxes voluntarily. North Carolina, which repealed its tax with the granting of woman suffrage in 1920, was the first. Other states repealing the tax, all during periods of keen interest in political races, were: Louisiana (1934), Florida (1937), Georgia (1945), South Carolina (1951), Tennessee (1953) and Arkansas (1964). In each of the first six states to drop the tax, voter participation increased sharply in the election following repeal, decreased in subsequent elections, and then rose again. In a widely respected 1958 study, *The Poll Tax in the South*, Frederic D. Ogden of the University of Alabama political science faculty estimated that 5 percent of the initial increase in each state could be attributed to repeal of the poll tax.

Constitutional amendments to repeal poll taxes were rejected by Virginia voters in 1949 and Texas voters in both 1949 and 1963. Alabama voters in 1953 amended the state constitution to restrict collection of accumulated unpaid back poll taxes from a maximum of 24 years with a maximum payment of $36 to two years with a ceiling of $3. In May 1965, the Alabama senate voted overwhelmingly to approve a state constitutional amendment repealing the tax; action on a similar amendment in the Alabama house was deferred. The Texas Legislature in May 1965 approved a referendum on the tax for the following year's election. In the meantime, Federal courts outlawed the tax as a voting qualification in a series of legal rulings.

Supreme Court Ban on Poll Tax

On March 24, 1966, the U.S. Supreme Court by a 6-3 vote held that the $1.50 poll tax imposed by Virginia on citizens desiring to vote in state and local elections violated the Equal Protection clause of the Constitution. (The 14th Amendment stated: "...nor shall any State... deny to any person within its jurisdiction the equal protection of the laws.") The Court's decision in *Harper v. Virginia State Board of Elections* and *Butts v. Harrison*, decided as one case, struck down Virginia's poll tax and by extension that of Mississippi. Vermont, by legislation enacted on Feb. 23, 1966, eliminated its poll tax, while three-judge Federal district courts declared unconstitutional the poll taxes in Texas (*U.S. v. Texas*, Feb. 9, 1966) and in Alabama (*U.S. v. Alabama*, March 3, 1966). The rulings completed a series of Federal actions to eliminate the payment of a poll tax as a prerequisite for voting. The 24th Amendment, approved by Congress in 1962 and ratified by the states in 1964, had banned the tax only in Federal elections.

For more than two decades, there had been controversy in Congress over the proper approach to banning the poll tax. Some opponents of the levy favored an outright ban by Congressional statute while others favored court action. The issue came to a head in 1965 when the Senate narrowly rejected (45-49 roll-call vote) an amendment to the Voting Rights Act which would have imposed a flat ban on the tax in all elections. Instead, Congress approved a provision declaring that payment of the poll tax abridged the right to vote and directing the U.S. Attorney General to institute "forthwith" court suits challenging the validity of the tax. The successful cases in Alabama and Texas were filed under that authority. The Virginia case was filed by a private citizen, Mrs. Annie E. Harper.

Woman Suffrage

The drive for woman suffrage, which began in the late 1830s, was closely related in the beginning to the movement for abolition of slavery. Women, because of their extensive legal disadvantages under the common law, often compared their lot to that of slaves and thus directed the bulk of their political activity against proposals for extension of slavery. Women were disfranchised at every level of government. Only in New Jersey did they have a theoretical right to vote, but the right had been included inadvertently in the state constitutions of 1776 and 1797. The state legislature repealed the provision at the outset of the 19th century when some women actually attempted to vote.

Gradual Gains for Woman Suffrage

Early victories for the woman suffrage movement came mostly in connection with school elections. Kentucky in 1838 gave the vote to widows and unmarried women with property subject to taxation for school purposes. Kansas in 1861 gave women the vote on all school questions, and Michigan, Utah, Minnesota, Colorado, New Hampshire and Massachusetts followed by 1880.

Wyoming (then a territory) extended full suffrage to women in 1869 (a right retained when Wyoming became a state in 1890). Three other western states extended the franchise to women before the turn of the century— Colorado in 1893, and Utah and Idaho in 1896. After 1896, advocates of suffrage for women encountered stronger opposition, and it was not until the height of the Progressive movement in 1910 that other states, mostly in the West, gave women full voting rights. Equal suffrage was granted by Washington in 1910, California in 1911, Arizona, Kansas and Oregon in 1912, and Montana and Nevada in 1914. New York followed suit in 1917. After considerable controversy, the matter finally was settled on a national basis by the 19th Amendment, ratified in 1920, which prohibited states from denying the right to vote on account of sex.

Grounds for Opposition

Opposition to female suffrage came on grounds that women were the "weaker sex," that their temperament was unsuited to make the kinds of decisions necessary in casting a ballot, and that their suffrage might alter the relationship between the sexes. A statement by Sen. Joseph E. Brown (D Ga.) in 1884 was typical of these arguments. According to Brown, "The Creator intended that the sphere of the males and females of our race should be different." Man, he argued, was "qualified for the discharge of those duties that require strength and ability to combat with the sterner realities and difficulties of life." The management of government, he contended, was "a laborious task, for which the male sex is infinitely better qualified than the female sex." "On the other hand," Brown continued, "the Creator has assigned to woman very laborious duties, by no means less important than those imposed upon the male sex, though entirely different in their character. In the family she is a queen. She alone is fitted for the discharge of the sacred trust of wife and the endearing relation of mother." How could the wife, he asked, with all "the heavy duties of citizen, politician and officeholder resting upon her shoulders... attend to the more sacred, delicate, refining trust...for which she is peculiarly fitted by nature? Who is to care for and train the children while she is absent in the discharge of these masculine duties?"

Early Tactics of the Suffragists

Direct-action tactics were first applied by suffragists shortly after the Civil War, when Susan B. Anthony urged women to go to the polls and claim the right to vote under terms of the newly adopted 14th Amendment. In the national elections of 1872, Miss Anthony voted in her home city of Rochester, N.Y., and was tried and convicted of the crime of "voting without having a lawful right to vote." For almost a quarter of a century, Miss Anthony and her followers pressed Congress for a constitutional amendment granting woman suffrage. On Jan. 25, 1887, almost 12 years after the suffragists had formally proposed such an amendment to Congress, it finally came up for consideration in the Senate but was rejected by a 16-34 roll-call vote. The suffrage forces then focused the bulk of their effort on the states, where they enjoyed considerable success in the West but little or none in other parts of the country.

Fight for Constitutional Amendment

About the time of the outbreak of World War I in Europe, the advocates of militant tactics, commonly called suffragettes rather than suffragists, took the lead in the national campaign. In the Congressional elections of 1914, in the nine (later in the year, 11) states permitting women to vote, they set out to defeat all Democratic candidates on the ground that the Democrats, as the majority party, were responsible for the failure of Congress to submit to the states a constitutional amendment granting woman suffrage. Suffrage advocates opposed all Democratic candidates regardless of their stand on the suffrage question. In the election, only 20 of the 43 Democratic candidates in the suffrage states were elected. According to Doris Stevens, in her book *Jailed for Freedom*, "It was generally conceded that we had contributed to those defeats." The outcome of the election failed, however, to move President Wilson, who preferred state rather than Federal action on woman suffrage.

Mr. Wilson's opposition to a constitutional amendment prompted a series of stormy demonstrations by the suffragettes around the White House and other sites in Washington after the United States had entered the war. The demonstrators insisted that it was unconscionable for this country to be denying its own female citizens a right to participate in government at the same time it was fighting a war on the premise of "making the world safe for democracy." At the direction of the Administration, thousands of the women demonstrators were arrested and brought to trial. Some were beaten by hostile crowds—often made up of soldiers and sailors who viewed the demonstrations as unpatriotic. At their trials, many of the women stood mute or made speeches advocating suffrage and attacking President Wilson for his refusal to endorse the constitutional amendment. Sentencing of the women to jail caused a severe housing problem for District of Columbia penal authorities and created considerable public sympathy for the suffragettes. Public support for their position was heightened by claims by the prisoners that they had been treated inhumanely and had been subjected to insanitary conditions in prison. To protest such conditions, many of the prisoners went on a hunger strike and the authorities resorted to forced feeding—an action which gave rise to even greater public furor.

On Jan. 9, 1918, President Wilson finally came out for the proposed suffrage amendment. The House of Representatives approved it the next day by a 274-136 roll-call vote, one vote more than the necessary two-thirds majority, but that majority was not attained when the Senate voted in October 1918 or on a second try in February 1919. However, when the new Congress (elected in November 1918) met for the first time (in special session) on May 19, 1919, it took little more than two weeks to gain the required majorities in both House (304-89 on May 21) and Senate (56-25 on June 3). Ratification was completed on Aug. 24, 1920, in time for women to vote in the Presidential election in November. The new 19th Amendment provided simply that "the right of citizens of the United States to vote shall not be denied or abridged by the United States or by any state on account of sex."

Voting in District of Columbia

The right of residents of the District of Columbia to vote in Federal elections was withdrawn in December 1800—shortly after the removal of Congress from Philadelphia to Washington—when the Supreme Court ruled that the constitutional provision granting Congress exclusive jurisdiction over "such district...as may...become the seat of the Government of the United States" had taken effect.

Except for a brief period in the 1870s, when the District of Columbia had a territorial form of government and its citizens elected a nonvoting delegate to Congress,

Suffragettes' 1914 Platform

Following is the program of the Congressional Union for Woman Suffrage (later the American Women's Party)— the leading militant suffrage group—adopted prior to the 1914 Congressional election, in which the suffragettes were instrumental in defeating 23 of 43 Democratic candidates in states where women were permitted to vote:

The dominant party (at that time the Democratic party) is responsible for all action and therefore for action on suffrage.

This party's action had been hostile to this measure.

The dominant party in the approaching election must be convinced, and through it all other parties, that opposition to suffrage is inexpedient.

All parties will be convinced when they see that their opposition costs them votes.

Our fight is a political one.

We must appeal for support to the constituency which is most friendly to suffrage, that constituency being the voting women.

An attempt must be made, no matter how small, to organize the women's vote.

An appeal must be made to the women voters in the nine suffrage states (11 later in 1914) to withhold their support from the Democrats nationally, until the national Democratic party ceases to block the suffrage amendment.

This is non-partisanship in the highest degree, as it calls upon women to forego previous allegiance to a party. If they are Democrats in this instance, they must vote against their party. If the Republican party were in power and pursued a similar course, we would work against that party.

The party which sees votes falling away will change its attitude.

After we have once affected by this means the outcome of a national election, even though slightly, every party will hesitate to trifle with our measure any longer.

All candidates from suffrage states are professing suffragists, and therefore we have nothing to lose by defeating a member of the dominant party in those states. Another suffragist will take his place.

Men will object to being opposed because of their party responsibility in spite of their friendliness individually to suffrage. But women certainly have a right to further through the ballot their wishes on the suffrage question, as well as on other questions like currency, tariff and what not.

This can only be done by considering the party record, for as the individual record and individual pledges go, all candidates are practically equal.

We, as a disfranchised class, consider our right to vote preeminently over any other issue in any party's program.

Political leaders will resent our injecting our issue into their campaign, but the rank and file will be won when they see the loyalty of women to women.

This policy will be called militant and in a sense it is, being strong, positive and energetic.

If it is militant to appeal to women to use their vote to bring suffrage to this country, then it is militant to appeal to men or women to use their vote to any good end.

To the question of 'How will we profit if another party comes in?' our answer will be that adequate political chastisement of one party for its bad suffrage record through a demonstration of power by women voters affecting the result of the national election, will make it easier to get action from any party in power.

they took no part in any Federal election until 1964, after the 23rd Amendment had authorized District voters to participate in Presidential elections. For almost a century, the District itself has been governed in effect by the District Committees of Congress, with day-to-day administration carried out by commissioners and, since 1967, a city council appointed by the President.

Background. The Constitution does not mention Congressional representation in connection with the seat of the Federal Government. Article I, Section 2 reads: "The House of Representatives shall be composed of Members chosen every second year by the people of the several states." Article I, Section 3, reads: "The Senate of the United States shall be composed of two Senators from each state...."

Because the Constitution mentions only Representatives and Senators from the "states," a constitutional amendment would be required to provide full representation for the District of Columbia in Congress. Nonvoting delegates from territories have sat in the House; thus only regular legislation was required to give the District a nonvoting delegate. The Constitution granted Congress the power to exercise "exclusive legislation" over the District. This power, however, can be delegated to local governments by legislation.

The 10-mile-square site for the District of Columbia was chosen by President Washington. It consisted of land ceded by Maryland and Virginia on both banks of the Potomac River. The City of Washington, a much smaller area than the original District, was chartered in 1802. The charter provided for a council of two chambers elected by the people and for a mayor, who was first appointed by the President, later elected by the council, and, after 1820, elected by popular vote. Other cities of the District, Alexandria and Georgetown, also had local self-government.

Conflicts on racial and other issues between District residents and Congress erupted well before the Civil War. In 1846, both Georgetown and Alexandria, unable to obtain money from Congress for improvements, sought retrocession to their respective states, Maryland and Virginia. The Maryland Legislature was unwilling, but Congress, the Commonwealth of Virginia and the citizens of Alexandria agreed that the portion of the District across the Potomac should be returned to Virginia. The District was left with its present area, some 69.2 square miles on the Maryland side of the river. *(See Control of the Seat of Government, Chapter III.)*

Washington was early a center for freed slaves, and, with the grant of universal suffrage in 1867, the Radical Republicans took control of the city. The strain on the city of the Civil War and postwar years led Congress in 1871 to establish a territorial form of government over the entire District.

The new administration included an elected nonvoting delegate to the House of Representatives—Norton P. Chipman, a Republican—as well as an appointed governor, a territorial assembly, with one elected and one appointed chamber and a new board of public works. Gross financial mismanagement by Alexander Shepherd, board member and later the District governor, in his effort to modernize the District, led Congress to place the District under a three-member, appointed board of commis-

sioners in 1874. Chipman's term expired in 1875, and at that point the office of nonvoting delegate was terminated.

23rd Amendment. In 1960, the Senate adopted a resolution to amend the Constitution to allow District residents the right to vote in Presidential and Vice Presidential elections and to elect a delegate to the House of Representatives. Under this proposal, separate legislation would have determined whether or not the District delegate would have a vote. The House approved only the provision for participation in Presidential elections, and the amendment in that form was ratified by the requisite number of states early in 1961.

In 1964, District residents finally were allowed to vote for President and Vice President, for the first time since 1800. The city's three electoral votes went to Lyndon B. Johnson; in 1968, they were cast for Hubert H. Humphrey.

Since 1967, when President Johnson put through a reorganization plan, the local government has been comprised of a commissioner and a nine-member city council. Both the commissioner (generally called the mayor) and council members are nominated by the President and confirmed by the Senate, and both have only limited powers. In 1968, Congress cleared legislation providing for the city's first elected school board.

Nonvoting Delegate. In 1970, Congress enacted legislation enabling the District to elect is first Representative to the House in nearly a century. The bill (PL 91-405), signed into law Sept. 22, 1970, authorized the District, beginning in 1971, to elect a delegate who would have all the privileges of other House Members except that of voting. It was widely expected that the new District delegate would become a full-time lobbyist for a constitutional amendment to give the city voting representatives in both chambers of Congress.

Changes in Voter Qualifications

Special qualifications for voting that have been dropped or modified over the years have included voter literacy, the minimum age for voting, and the period of residence required in a state to qualify as a voter. A single Federal act—a 1970 measure extending and broadening the Voting Rights Act of 1965—made substantial changes in all these requirements. Most of the changes were upheld by the Supreme Court in its decision in the case of *Oregon v. Mitchell* on Dec. 21, 1970.

Suspension of Literacy Tests

Although Negroes and recent immigrants have been the main target of voter literacy tests, such tests have been used also to limit the electorate to persons thought to possess the qualities necessary for responsible citizenship. At one time or another, 21 states have imposed literacy requirements as a condition for voting. The first to do so were Connecticut and Massachusetts (in 1855 and 1857, respectively), which imposed the tests in order to disqualify a flood of European immigrants. Primarily as a means of limiting the Negro electorate, eight southern states imposed the test between 1890 and 1910: Mississippi (1890), South Carolina (1895), Louisiana (1898), North Carolina (1900), Alabama (1901), Virginia (1902), Georgia (1908) and Oklahoma (1910). Other states adopting literacy requirements have been Wyoming (1889), Maine (1892), California (1894), Washington (1896), Delaware (1897), New Hampshire (1902), Arizona (1912), New York (1921), Oregon (1924), Alaska (1959) and Hawaii (1959).

Requirements under the tests have varied widely from state to state. Nineteen of the states applying the tests have required the ability to read and 14 of the states the ability to write. Of the 19 states that imposed reading tests, all except four (New York, Washington, Alaska and Hawaii) required reading of some legal document or passage from the state or Federal constitution. Four states expressly required reading with understanding— New York, Washington, Louisiana and Alabama.

As applied in the southern states, the tests, together with other voting requirements, virtually disfranchised Negroes. Outside the South, the New York test was by far the most stringent although there were seldom any complaints that it was applied in a discriminatory way. In the first six years of its application, 14.9 percent of those who took the New York test failed. Of 472,126 examined over that period, the failures numbered 54,824 —many of them non-English-speaking immigrants in New York City.

Despite pressures by civil libertarians, Congress declined for years to take action to void literacy requirements. Federal action modifying the application of the tests, it was feared, would interfere with the states' constitutional rights to impose their own voting requirements. In the 1950s and 1960s, however, reports of extreme examples of voter discrimination in the South prompted Congress to enact remedial legislation. Basing their actions on authority of the 14th and 15th Amendments, which guarantee due process of law and prohibit voter discrimination on the basis of race, creed or color, Congress passed three civil rights acts dealing in part with voter discrimination (1957, 1960 and 1964). In 1965 it passed a sweeping Voting Rights Act which suspended literacy tests in seven southern states and in a part of another state. *(See section on Negro vote, above.)* Finally, in 1970, the new voting Act suspended all literacy tests, whether discriminatory or not, for a five-year period (through Aug. 6, 1975). The Supreme Court in *Oregon v. Mitchell* upheld the constitutionality of that provision. Suspension of the tests was expected to extend the franchise to about two million previously disfranchised persons in 12 states where the tests still applied—Alaska, Arizona, California, Connecticut, Delaware, Maine, Massachusetts, New Hampshire, New York, North Carolina (only with respect to counties not covered under provisions of the 1965 Voting Rights Act), Washington and Wyoming.

Lowering of Voting Age

In the years before World War II, no state allowed persons to vote before the age of 21. In 1943, during World War II, Georgia lowered the voting age to 18 after suffrage advocates had attracted considerable public support with the slogan, "Fight at 18, vote at 18." In 1946, South Carolina Democrats authorized 18-year-olds

to vote in party primaries, but later they withdrew that privilege. In 1955, Kentucky voters amended the state constitution to permit 18-year-olds to vote. The new states of Alaska and Hawaii, upon entering the union in 1959, adopted minimum voting ages of 19 and 20 years, respectively.

In 1954, President Eisenhower proposed a constitutional amendment granting 18-year-olds the right to vote, but the proposal was rejected by the Senate. Eventually, in 1970, Congress in the Voting Rights Act of 1970 lowered the voting age to 18 for all Federal, state and local elections, effective Jan. 1, 1971. The provision was sustained by the Supreme Court with regard to Federal elections but ruled unconstitutional with regard to state and local elections. The lower voting age for national elections was expected to give about 11 million additional persons the right to vote.

Residence Requirements

At one time or another, every state has imposed a minimum period of residence in the state (and some of them a shorter period of residence is a county or voting district) as a qualification for voting. The rationale for this practice has been that individuals cannot vote intelligently, at least on state and local affairs, until they have lived in an area for a given period of time. In some southern states, unusually long periods of residence were required on the theory that they would help disqualify Negroes.

Most of the states have required one year's residence for voting, but five (Alabama, Louisiana, Mississippi, Rhode Island and South Carolina) have required two years at one time or another. In 1970, 33 states imposed residence requirements of one year, 15 required six months, and two (New York and Pennsylvania) three months.

As a condition for voting in 1970, every state except New Hampshire required residents to have lived in the same county and/or voting district, as well as the state, for a stipulated period of time. The most stringent of these requirements were in Maryland and Texas, where voters had to have resided one year in the state, six months in the county and six months in the voting district. At one time Alabama required two years in the state, one year in the county and three months in the voting district. V. O. Key Jr. estimated in the 1964 edition of his book *Politics, Parties and Pressure Groups* that residence requirements disfranchised as much as 5 percent of the potential electorate.

The Federal voting-rights legislation of 1970 provided that any person could vote in a Presidential election in the place where he had lived for at least 30 days immediately prior to the election. This provision of the law, upheld by the Supreme Court, was expected to extend the franchise to about five million people who might otherwise be disqualified from voting in the 1972 Presidential election.

The changes made by the Voting Rights Act of 1970 had the practical effect of extending the right to vote to almost every citizen of voting age in the country. In general, the only remaining restrictions prevented voting by the insane, convicted felons and otherwise eligible voters unable to meet the remaining residence requirements.

Political Parties and the Electorate

Throughout the nation's history, political parties have played a dominant part in organizing the electorate and thus in shaping the character of the Government. From the outset of the Republic, citizens turned to political parties to define issues, to support or oppose candidates on the basis of those issues, and then to carry out the agreed-upon policies when the party was in power. As one student of government, Prof. E. E. Schattschneider, described the process in his book *Party Government*, "People submit to this assumption of power because they cannot help themselves. The immobility and inertia of large masses are to politics what the law of gravity is to physics. This characteristic compels people to submit to a greater channelization of the expression of their will, and is due to numbers, not to want of intelligence. An electorate of six million Aristotles would be equally restricted. In other words, parties take from the people powers that are merely theoretical. Nature, having first made numbers what they are, limits the effective power of the people, and the parties merely take advantage of the fact.... As interlocutors of the people, the parties frame the question and elicit the answers.... The greater the numbers involved in the scheme, the more necessary become the organization and management of politics by the parties."

Ironically, the Constitution did not provide either authority for or prohibitions against political parties. Historians writing on the subject have pointed out that most of the Founding Fathers had only a dim understanding of the function of political parties and thus were ambivalent on the issue when they laid down the framework of the new Government. In one sense, the delegates to the Constitutional Convention and their successors in Congress ensured a role for parties in the Government when they gave protection to civil rights and the right to organize. But on the other hand, they set up safeguards against excesses of party activity by providing an elaborate governmental system of checks and balances. The prevailing attitude of the Convention on this matter was summed up by James Madison, who wrote in *The Federalist* (No. 10) that the "great object" of the new government was "to preserve the public good and private rights against the action of such a faction (party) and at the same time to preserve the spirit and form of popular government."

Emergence of Parties

The first two great American political parties, the Federalists and the Democratic-Republicans, developed as a result of public sentiment for and against adoption of the Constitution. The Federalist party—a loose association of merchants, shippers, financiers and other business interests—favored the strong central government provided by the Constitution, while the Republicans (at first called Anti-Federalists) were intent upon preservation of state sovereignty. Underlying the controversy was the desire of the interests represented by the Federalists to create a Government with power to guarantee the value of the currency (and thus protect the position of creditors) and the desire of the agrarians and frontiersmen who made up the Anti-Federalist party to maintain easy credit conditions and the power of state legislatures to fend off encroachments by a remote Federal Government.

During the first 12 years of the Republic, Federalists dominated the Government. Largely due to the efforts of President Washington's dynamic Secretary of the Treasury, Alexander Hamilton, Congress enacted a body of landmark fiscal legislation, including provisions for full funding of the national debt, Federal assumption of the war debts of the states, a mild protective tariff, and formation of a Bank of the United States to hold and dispense Federal monies.

These measures drew stiff opposition from the Anti-Federalists, whose ranks grew steadily as the electorate expanded. Despite the growing strength of the opposing party, the Federalists (many of whom openly preferred the European type of monarchy) refused to broaden their power base and thus remained beholden to the leading economic interests of the day. Federalist power continued to slip and by the early 1800s the Anti-Federalists, now called Republicans, had assumed power.

From 1801 until 1829, Republicans held the White House and dominated Congress. Under the leadership of President Jefferson, they promptly reduced the Federal budget, leaving a revenue surplus of $7 million a year to pay off the national debt. Political prisoners sentenced under the Alien and Sedition Acts were pardoned. A whiskey excise tax unpopular with frontiersmen was repealed. Although his party had long opposed the concept of a strong central government, Jefferson stretched his constitutional powers to the limit in approving the Louisiana Purchase and an embargo against trade with the British, who were molesting American shipping on the high seas.

Despite these measures, Jefferson took no action to disturb private capital and actually sought to extend his power base to include former Federalists. In his first inaugural address, in 1801, Jefferson surprised Federalists and Republicans alike by declaring "We are all Republicans, we are all Federalists," pledging the "honest payment of our debts and the sacred preservation of the public faith," and praising commerce as the "handmaid" of agriculture. Although the Federalists continued to put up candidates until 1816, they were never again a serious threat to the Republicans. As Charles A. Beard noted in *The American Party Battle*, active Federalists, deprived of a party of their own, "went into the Republican organization and did what they could to bend it in their direction, while the intransigents of the old generation often sulked in their tents, lamenting the evil days upon which they had fallen."

Unlike the Federalist party, which was never more than a loose alliance of particular interests, the Jeffersonians achieved a high degree of organization. The Federalists, in fact, never considered themselves a political party but rather a gentlemanly coalition of interests representing respectable society. What party management there was, they kept clandestine.

Groundwork for the Republican organization was laid as early as 1792, when Jefferson and Madison traveled to New York state and struck a political alliance between the Virginia planters and New York's professional politicians. By the early 1800s, the party was so tightly unified that Jefferson was able to dominate its Congressional wing through use of the binding legislative caucus. After the election of 1816, the Republican gains were so substantial that even the semblance of a two-party system disappeared. From 1801 to 1825, Republicans held majorities in both houses of Congress.

Split in Democratic-Republican Party

Controversy within the Republican party developed in the second decade of the new century when Henry Clay proposed his famous "American System," a program of extensive internal improvements and a planned economy based on the protective tariff. Clay's plan was never put into effect in toto, but when John Quincy Adams, the former Federalist turned Republican, became President in 1825, he incorporated many of its features, in particular a higher protective tariff, in his legislative program.

The American System infuriated agrarian interests, who blamed Clay and the ruling classes for a severe economic depression that hit the nation in the 1820s. The growing schism in the party became complete in 1828, when Andrew Jackson, who had lost out to Adams when the election of 1824 was thrown into the House of Representatives, won the Presidency as the champion of the rural and urban masses. Clay and his followers adopted the party designation of "National Republicans," while the Jacksonians soon took the name of "Democrats."

The Jacksonian power base consisted of small grain farmers in the South and West, cotton planters of the lesser plantations in the South, southern tobacco growers, almost the entire voting population of the Piedmont region and anti-aristocratic urban voters in the Northeast. "Equal rights for all, special privileges for none" became the slogan of the party. As political scientist Wilfred E. Binkley described the movement in *American Political Parties—Their Natural History*, "The whoop and hurrah of the movement afforded a wholesome psychological release of the accumulated resentments of western small farmers and eastern urban underlings. Everywhere, the less prosperous had been wont to attribute their ill fortune to the ruling oligarchy that had run the Government in its own interest. For this ailment of the body politic the common man had a sovereign remedy, and he now purposed to administer the medicine to the patient in person."

Jackson endeared himself to his constituency by vetoing a bill rechartering the Bank of the United States, vetoing a measure providing for a public highway in Clay's home state of Kentucky, holding the line on tariffs, removing Indians from lands claimed by cotton planters in the South, and opening up new lands in the West for settlement. As Binkley put it, these measures stirred "the common man everywhere—with a new sense of membership in the body politic such as not even Thomas Jefferson had succeeded in doing."

Rise and Decline of the Whigs

Jackson's program evoked strong opposition from the National Republicans—a coalition of eastern manufacturers, large southern plantation owners and westerners who sought greater outlays for internal improvements than the Democrats were willing to provide. The National Republican platform of 1831 declared in favor of "an adequate protection to American industry," "a uniform system of internal improvements sustained and supported by the general Government," the "preservation of the authority and jurisdiction" of the Supreme Court, and the maintenance of the Senate as "preeminently a con-

---

'Minority' Presidents

Under the electoral college system, 15 Presidents have been elected, either by the electoral college itself or by the House of Representatives, who did not receive a majority of the popular votes cast in the election. Three of them—John Quincy Adams, Rutherford B. Hayes and Benjamin Harrison—actually trailed their opponents in the popular vote.

The following table shows the percentage of the popular vote received by candidates in the 15 elections in which a "minority" President was elected:

Year	Elected		Opponents	
1824	Adams 30.54	Jackson 43.13	Clay 13.24	Crawford 13.09
1844	Polk 49.56	Clay 48.13	Birney 2.30	
1848	Taylor 47.35	Cass 42.52	Van Buren 10.13	
1856	Buchanan 45.63	Fremont 33.27	Fillmore 21.08	Smith .01
1860	Lincoln 39.79	Douglas 29.40	Breckinridge 18.20	Bell 12.60
1876	Hayes 48.04	Tilden 50.99	Cooper .97	
1880	Garfield 48.32	Hancock 48.21	Weaver 3.35	Others .12
1884	Cleveland 48.53	Blaine 48.24	Butler 1.74	St. John 1.49
1888	Harrison 47.86	Cleveland 48.66	Fisk 2.19	Streeter 1.29
1892	Cleveland 46.04	Harrison 43.01	Weaver 8.53	Others 2.42
1912	Wilson 41.85	T. Roosevelt 27.42	Taft 23.15	Others 7.58
1916	Wilson 49.26	Hughes 46.12	Benson 3.16	Others 1.46
1948	Truman 49.51	Dewey 45.13	Thurmond 2.40	Wallace 2.38
1960*	Kennedy 49.71	Nixon 49.55	Unpledged .92	Others .27
1968	Nixon 43.42	Humphrey 42.72	Wallace 13.53	Others .33

1960 percentages total more than 100 because of double-counted Alabama votes (both under Kennedy and Unpledged columns).

SOURCES: Library of Congress, Historical Statistics of the U.S. and Congressional Quarterly records.

---

servative branch of the Federal Government." By 1834, the party had become a collecting point for all the elements in the country who were disenchanted with the "mob rule" of the Jacksonians. In that year the National Republicans changed their name to "Whigs"—an English political term signifying antagonism to excessive use of executive prerogative. The party remained in existence until 1856 and won two Presidential elections, in 1840 and 1848, when it ran two popular military figures, William Henry Harrison and Zachary Taylor.

The decline of the Whig party began in 1852, when its overwhelming defeat in that year's Presidential election led to the loss of many party members to the American ("Know-Nothing") party—a party based primarily on opposition to continued immigration of foreigners. Many disenchanted Whigs blamed the party's 1852 defeat on the growing vote of the foreign-born. According to Binkley, the deaths of Whig leaders Henry Clay and Daniel Webster at that time "deprived the Whigs of national leadership when it was most needed and the membership of the disintegrating party went over to the Know-Nothings *en masse*, in many communities both in the North and in the South."

New Republican Party

The next great party schism was precipitated by the issue of extending slavery to the western territories. In 1854, slaveholding interests managed to bring about repeal of the Missouri Compromise of 1820, under which Missouri had been admitted to the Union as a slave state and slavery had been prohibited in all other territories included in the Louisiana Purchase and lying north of the parallel forming the southern boundary of Missouri. The repealer was included in the Kansas-Nebraska Act, a measure providing for formation of territorial governments in Kansas and Nebraska, which lay north of the Missouri Compromise line, and allowing the new territories to decide the slavery question for themselves and subsequently to enter the Union as free or slave states.

Intense northern opposition to the Kansas-Nebraska Act led to the formation of a new political party opposed to the extension of slavery. Four months before passage of the Act, a group of Whigs, Democrats and members of the "Free Soil" factions of both parties met at Ripon, Wis., and resolved, if the Kansas-Nebraska bill became law, "to throw old party organization to the winds and organize a new party on the sole basis of the non-extension of slavery." The new party, which proclaimed itself the logical successor to the Jeffersonian Republicans, adopted the name "Republican" and held its first national convention in Philadelphia in 1856. The party nominated John Charles Fremont on a platform that declared it to be the duty of Congress to outlaw the extension of slavery. Fremont did not win the election, but the party grew substantially over the next four years.

Republicans broadened their constituency by promising a homestead law for the territories and a protective tariff in addition to the party's main objective of blocking the extension of slavery. These programs attracted numerous small farmers from the Democratic party as well as a number of businessmen from the Whig party. After 1856, the Whig party became defunct; party members opposed to slavery became Republicans and the slaveholders became Democrats. In 1860, the Republicans won the Presidential election when Democrats split into two factions—one favoring popular referendums to decide the slavery question in the new states and the other asserting that Congress had no power to prohibit the extension of slavery.

During the Civil War and the Reconstruction period, Republicans (called the National Union party during and just after the war) moved increasingly toward the old Federalist policy of championing the nation's business interests. Tariffs were raised to the highest level in the nation's history. The Republican Congress abolished the depreciated currency created by state banks during the war by taxing it out of existence. In sponsoring the Homestead Act of 1862, authorizing grants of 160 acres of Federally owned land to settlers homesteading the western territories, Republicans endeared themselves to thousands of small farmers. They also pleased railroad promoters and manufacturers by making Government aid available for development of a transcontinental railroad. Except following Democratic victories in the Presidential elections of 1884 and 1892 (by Cleveland) and 1912 and 1916 (by Wilson), Republicans occupied the White House until 1933 and, during much of that period, controlled Congress. *(For political party affiliations in Congress and the Presidency, 1789-1971, see Chapter I, p. 68-69.)*

Party Ups and Downs Since 1930

The great economic depression that followed the stock-market crash of 1929 inevitably brought about a sharp reversal of political fortunes. Democrats gained control of the House of Representatives in the mid-term elections of 1930, and Franklin D. Roosevelt won a sweeping victory in the Presidential election two years later. Roosevelt, whose coalition included the Solid South, small farmers and businessmen, minority groups and intellectuals all over the country, was re-elected in 1936 and went on to break all precedents by winning election for not only a third but also a fourth term.

During the first two terms, prior to the start of World War II, the New Deal Democrats pushed through the most sweeping body of social legislation ever enacted by Congress. It included the Social Security program, tighter regulation of banks, control of securities markets through the Securities and Exchange Commission, regulation of public utility holding companies, aid to farmers through various new Federal agencies, aid to home purchasers and many other measures. President Truman sought after the war to expand on Roosevelt's domestic programs but was largely stymied by hostile Congresses and the Korean War.

A turn by the electorate toward conservatism, coupled with the overwhelming popularity of Gen. Dwight D. Eisenhower, the Republican Presidential candidate in 1952 and 1956, resulted in Republican control of the White House during most of the 1950s. Recurrent economic recessions under Eisenhower and rising concern over the problems of minority groups, helped the old Roosevelt coalition to produce victories for the Democrats in the Presidential elections of 1960 and 1964. The Democratic landslide of 1964 brought a large influx of Democrats to Congress, and the result was a flood of domestic social legislation surpassed only by that of the New Deal. This new tide of social reform was disrupted, however, by the financial demands of the war in Vietnam and its growing unpopularity among the American people.

Dissatisfaction with the Government's war policy on the part of some Democrats and hostility toward the Administration's domestic program on the part of conservative southerners split the Democrats badly in 1968 and led to a Republican takeover of the White House though not of the Congress. The Republican President, Richard M. Nixon, sought to achieve a new party alignment by courting the once solid Democratic South with an essentially conservative domestic program. This policy had mixed results in the 1970 mid-term elections, when Republicans held their own in Congress, though still a minority, but suffered a net loss of 11 state governorships. Democrats have retained control of both the House and the Senate in every Congress since 1933 with the exception of the 80th in 1947-48 and the 83rd in 1953-54.

Nomination of Party Candidates

In pre-Jacksonian times, the legislative caucus was the primary means of nominating party candidates for both state and national offices. From 1800 to 1828, Congressional Republicans even used the caucus to select the party's nominee for the Presidency. In 1824, Jackson's followers, realizing their candidate had no chance of winning the endorsement of the party caucus, set out to discredit "King Caucus" and substitute party conventions as a more democratic means of nomination. By 1832, they had largely succeeded. National conventions were called for the purpose of selecting Presidential candidates, and most states also had shifted to conventions for nominating candidates for state races.

As V. O. Key Jr. put it in *Politics, Parties and Pressure Groups*: "The destruction of the caucus represented more than a mere change in the method of nomination. Its replacement by the convention was regarded as the removal from power of self-appointed oligarchies that had usurped the right to nominate. The new system, the convention, gave, or so it was supposed, the mass of party members an opportunity to participate in nominations. These events occurred as the domestic winds blew in from the growing West, as the suffrage was being broadened, and as the last vestiges of the early aristocratic leadership were disappearing. Sharp alterations in the distribution of power were taking place, and they were paralleled by the shifts in methods of nomination."

From Conventions to Primaries

In the early 1900s, pressures emanated from the Progressive Movement to abolish the convention and replace it with an even more democratic selection process —the direct primary. Proponents of the primary contended that powerful organizations had seized control of the nominating conventions and had frequently ignored the preferences of the party rank and file. Under leadership of Robert M. La Follette, a leading Progressive, Wisconsin in 1903 enacted the first mandatory primary law. In 1907, six other states (Iowa, Nebraska, Missouri, North Dakota, South Dakota and Washington) followed suit. By 1917, the direct primary had been adopted for most nominations in almost every state. Use of the convention persisted only for the selection of Presidential candidates and candidates for a few state offices, and for Republican party nominations in the Democratic South.

Use of the direct primary considerably broadened the range of positions that a given political party might take. V. O. Key Jr. noted: "Rival factions and leaders now could fight out their differences in a campaign directed to the electorate—or a substantial segment of it —rather than be bound by the decisions of an assembly of delegates. Aspirants for nomination could likewise appeal directly to voters—or to those who voted in the primary rather than be limited largely to the cultivation of the professionals who controlled the convention and constituted the operating core of the party. By the same token, new elements of power were introduced into the nominating process. Prominent among them were newspaper publishers and others in control of channels to reach the public."

Primaries have been particularly important in districts (many of them in the South) in which one party is dominant and victory in that party's primary is usually tantamount to election. The U.S. Supreme Court recognized the importance of the party primary when it observed in its opinion in *U.S. v. Classic* (1941) that the primary in many areas determined the choice of the person elected and thus was an integral part of the electoral process. A 1970 study by Congressional Quarterly found that 255 of the 435 House seats (58.6 percent) and 56 of the 100 Senate seats had been controlled by the same party in every general election since 1954. In the 13 southern states, 73.1 percent of all House districts and 20 of 26 Senate seats had remained under one party's control. Outside the South, 53.2 percent of all House seats and 36 of 74 Senate seats had not switched parties since 1954. Turnovers had been most frequent in the West, where 60.9 percent of all House seats had shifted parties at least once.

Political scientists are divided over their assessment of the role of the one-party district. Some see this phenomenon as a stumbling block to orderly change while others view it as a desirable element of stability. Political scientists holding the latter view contend that unless each party dominates a number of Congressional districts, one party might drive the other virtually out of power in the event of a landslide in the elections.

Voter Participation

A precise breakdown to show which identifiable groups of voters (Negroes, women, etc.) have higher turnout rates than others has never been possible. It would require the preparation of an elaborate questionnaire, to be passed out to every eligible voter, asking whether or not he participated in the election under study. In three recent years (1964, 1966 and 1968), however, the Bureau of the Census attempted to determine the relative turnout of various classes of voters on the basis of a random sample of the American electorate.

The studies found that the percentage rates of voting participation were higher for men than for women, for persons 45 to 54 years of age than for those younger or older, for whites than for Negroes, and for northerners and westerners than for southerners. Voter participation rose, moreover, with the extent of education and with the size of family incomes. The Bureau's 1964 and 1966 surveys used random samples of 35,000 households; the 1968 survey increased the number of households to 50,000. All three surveys covered households in all 50 states and the District of Columbia.

Percentages of Voters in Various Groups

Male-Female. The Bureau found that in the 1968 election, 69.8 percent of eligible males voted, against 66 percent of eligible females. Both figures were down from the 1964 levels of 71.9 percent for males and 67 percent for females but were up considerably from the levels of 58.1 percent and 53 percent, respectively, in the 1966 mid-term election. Turnout rates are always higher in Presidential election years.

Age. The 1968 survey showed that persons 45 to 54 years of age had a higher voting rate than those in any other age group, with participation far lower for voters under 35 years of age and for those 75 or older. Rates were as follows: 21 to 24 years, 51.1 percent; 25 to 34, 62.5 percent; 35 to 44, 70.8 percent; 45 to 54, 75.1 percent; 55 to 64, 74.7 percent; 65 to 74, 71.5 percent; and 75 and older, 56.3 percent.

Race. A participation rate in 1968 of 69.1 percent was found for eligible white voters and a rate of 57.6 percent for eligible Negroes. White males participated at a rate of 71.2 percent, Negro males at a rate of 58.2 percent. The rate for white women was 67.2 percent, for Negro women, 57.1 percent.

Regional Turnout. Voting rates in 1968 were considerably higher (71 percent) for the North and West than they were for the South (60.1 percent). In the South, however, Negro voter participation was up markedly from its 1964 level (from 44 percent to 51.6 percent). The Census Bureau's 1968 report attributed the latter trend to "both the effects of Congressional legislation to protect civil and voting rights and increased party competition."

Urban-Rural. Voting rates in 1968 were roughly equal among metropolitan (68 percent) and non-metropolitan voters (67.3 percent). These rates marked a moderate shift from 1964, when the metropolitan turnout rate was 70.8 percent and the non-metropolitan rate 66.5 percent.

Educational Levels. The 1968 figures showed a substantial differential in voter participation on the basis of educational levels. Turnout for college graduates came to 83.1 percent, as compared to 72.5 percent for high school graduates, 52.4 percent for persons with only five to seven years of schooling, and 38.4 percent for persons with none to four years.

Occupational Groups. The 1968 survey showed a considerable differential also in voter participation among occupational groups, with white collar workers participating at a higher rate than other groups. Rates were as follows: white collar, 79.8 percent; manual workers, 62.3 percent; service workers, 62.7 percent; and farm workers, 69.9 percent. The only dramatic change from the 1964 figures was for service workers, who had participated that year at a 72.8 percent rate, more than 10 percentage points higher than the 1968 turnout.

Income Levels. Similar differentials were noted in 1968 on the basis of income levels. Eligible voters whose families had incomes of $15,000 and above turned out at a rate of 84.1 percent, while those whose family income was less than $3,000 participated at a rate of 53.5 percent. The figures were little different than those for the high and low income categories in 1964—family income of $10,000 or more (84.8 percent) and less than $2,000 (49.6 percent).

Conclusion. Although the Census Bureau's studies did not measure participation on the basis of political party affiliation, political scientists long have theorized that low turnout rates favor Republicans while higher rates favor Democrats. In general, the categories of persons with the lowest voting rates (Negroes, blue-collar workers, low-income persons, etc.) have been identified mainly as Democrats while those with higher turnout ratios have been predominantly Republican.

Numerous private studies have shown a higher preference for Democratic candidates among eligible voters who failed to participate in elections. Two of the best-known surveys of this type were a *Fortune* magazine poll in 1940 and a 1952 poll by the Survey Research Center of the University of Michigan. The *Fortune* survey found that persons who did not expect to vote in 1940 preferred President Roosevelt, the incumbent Democrat, by a four-to-one margin over Willkie, the Republican challenger. The Michigan survey found in 1952 that 54 percent of nonvoters in its national sample favored the Democratic candidate, Stevenson, who won only 44.5 percent of the actual vote.

Bibliography

Books

Beard, Charles A., *The American Party Battle*. Macmillan Co., 1928.

Binkley, Wilfred E., *American Political Parties: Their Natural History* (4th ed.). Alfred A. Knopf, Inc., 1962.

Bone, Hugh A., *American Politics and the Party System*. McGraw-Hill, 1955.

----, and Ranney, Austin, *Politics and Voters*. McGraw-Hill, 1963.

Key, V. O. Jr., *Politics, Parties and Pressure Groups* (5th ed.). Thomas Y. Crowell Co., 1964.

----, *The Responsible Electorate*. Belknap Press, 1966.

----, *Southern Politics*, Alfred A. Knopf, Inc., 1950.

Lane, Robert E., *Political Life*. Free Press of Glencoe, Inc., 1959.

Lewinson, Paul, *Race, Class and Party*. Oxford University Press, 1932.

McGovney, Dudley O., *The American Suffrage Medley*. University of Chicago Press, 1949.

Myrdal, Gunnar, *An American Dilemma*. Harper and Row, 1944.

Ogden, Frederic D., *The Poll Tax in the South*. University of Alabama Press, 1958.

Scammon, Richard M. ed., *America Votes* (Vols. 1-8). Governmental Affairs Institute, 1956-70.

Schattschneider, E. E., *Party Government*. Holt, Rinehart and Winston, Inc., 1942.

Stevens, Doris, *Jailed for Freedom*. Boni and Liveright, 1920.

Periodicals

Dickinson, William B. Jr., "Negro Voting," *Editorial Research Reports*, 1964 Vol. II, p. 741-760.

McIntyre, William R., "Right to Vote," *Editorial Research Reports*, 1958 Vol. I, p. 201-219.

Worsnop, Richard L., "Changing Southern Politics," *Editorial Research Reports*, 1966 Vol. I, p. 41-59.

——, "Protection of Voting Rights," *Editorial Research Reports*, 1962 Vol. I, p. 277-295.

Government Publications

U.S. Bureau of the Census, *Current Population Reports*, "Voter Participation in the National Election: November 1964," Oct. 25, 1965.

——, *Current Population Reports*, "Voting and Registration in the Election of November 1966," Aug. 8, 1968.

——, *Current Population Reports*, "Voting and Registration in the Election of November 1968," Dec. 2, 1969.

——, *Historical Statistics of the United States; Continuation to 1962 and Revisions.* 1965.

U.S. Commission on Civil Rights, *Political Participation*, 1968.

Who Gets Elected

IT HAS OFTEN been said that if a Member of Congress closed his eyes and touched the first colleague who walked past him on the House or Senate floor, that Member would be a male in his fifties, Protestant, Caucasian, a veteran of the armed services and law school graduate.

Statistics of recent Congresses bear out this supposition: about 97 to 98 percent of the membership of both houses is male, with average ages fluctuating between 52 and 53 years. Around 75 percent of the Members are Protestants, while about 70 percent are veterans and 60 percent have legal training. As a rule, about 97 percent of the Members are Caucasian; in 1971, for example, there were only 13 Negroes in the 92nd Congress and only four Members of Asian extraction.

Apart from these predominant characteristics, chances are good that a new Senator served earlier in the House, but almost none that a new House Member has served in the Senate. Only two former Presidents have served in Congress after their terms in the White House—John Quincy Adams (Whig Mass.), who was a Representative for 17 years in the 1830s and 1840s, and Andrew Johnson (R Tenn.), who held a seat in the Senate for five months prior to his death in 1875.

Although the legal profession has long been dominant in the occupational background of Members, most other major vocations, including banking, business, journalism, farming and education, also have been well represented. The leading occupational groups that have been under-represented are the clergy and workingmen. No workingman has been elected to Congress in recent years, although some former Members had been manual laborers before taking up the pursuits they followed when elected to Congress.

Only a handful of Protestant ministers have served in Congress, and no Catholic priest had been a full-fledged Member until Rep. Robert F. Drinan (D Mass.), a Jesuit, took his House seat in 1971. (Father Gabriel Richard was the nonvoting delegate of the Territory of Michigan from 1821 to 1823.) There was only one Protestant clergyman in the 92nd Congress—Rep. John H. Buchanan Jr. (R Ala.), a Baptist minister.

The public has tended to be critical of the qualifications of House Members while expressing a much higher regard for those of Senators. An early but still well-known criticism of the House was uttered in 1831, when Alexis de Tocqueville, the French aristocrat and scholar, observed the House in session. In his book, *Democracy in America*, Tocqueville wrote that he was "struck with the vulgar demeanor of that great assembly. The eye frequently does not discover a man of celebrity between its walls. Its members are almost all obscure individuals, whose

names present no associations to the mind; they are mostly village lawyers, men in trade, or even persons belonging to the lower classes of society...."

Tocqueville's views of the House were seconded by a contemporary American, the backwoodsman Davy Crockett, who served three terms as a Representative from Tennessee in the 1820s and 1830s. "We generally lounge or squabble the greater part of the session," Crockett wrote, "and crowd into a few days of the last term three or four times the business done during as many preceding months. You may therefore guess at the deliberations of Congress, when you can't hear, for the soul of you, what's going on, nor no one knows what it is, but three or four, and when it's no use to try to know." In his graduate thesis, *Congressional Government*, Woodrow Wilson found the House in 1885 "a disintegrate mass of jarring elements." Some more recent observers have defended the qualifications of the House membership as a whole, contending that the contrary over-all view has resulted from the rhetoric of a few flamboyant and eccentric Members and the occasional disclosure of questionable conduct by a committee chairman or other influential Member.

With few exceptions, the Senate has fared far better in the public eye than has the House. In his book *Democracy in America*, Tocqueville observed that "The Senate is composed of eloquent advocates, distinguished generals, wise magistrates, and statesmen of note, whose language would at all times do honor to the most remarkable parliamentary debates of Europe." Although there have been cases of misconduct involving Senators, they have been fewer than those involving Representatives. Another factor that has tended to give the Senate greater esteem is its more orderly conduct of business—probably a result of the fact that it is much smaller than the House. *(For the representation of political parties in Senate and House since 1789, see Chapter I, p. 68-69.)*

Characteristics of Members

Age. The average age of Members of Congress went up substantially between the Civil War period and the 1950s, but it remained fairly constant from then to the 1970s. In the 41st Congress (1869-71), the average age of Members was 44.6 years; by the 85th Congress (1957-58), the average had increased by more than nine years, to 53.8. Over the next 13 years, the average fluctuated slightly, and at the outset of the 92nd Congress in 1971 it stood at 52.7 years. Average age for Senators in the 92nd was 56.4 years, that of Representatives, 51.9 years.

Ages of individual Senators in the 92nd ranged from 36 to 80, those of House Members from 30 to 82. The

Members Who Became President

Richard M. Nixon's election to the Presidency in 1968 brought to 22 the number of Presidents who had previous service in the Senate or the House, or both. Of the 22, 6 had served in the House only, 6 in the Senate only, and 10 in both houses. Following is a list of the 22 Presidents, together with the chamber or chambers in which they served. Three other Presidents—George Washington, John Adams and Thomas Jefferson—had served in the Continental Congress, as had two of those listed, James Madison and James Monroe.

House Only	Senate Only
James Madison	James Monroe
James K. Polk	John Quincy Adams
Millard Fillmore	Martin Van Buren
Abraham Lincoln	Benjamin Harrison
Rutherford B. Hayes	Warren G. Harding
William McKinley	Harry S Truman

Both Houses

Andrew Jackson	Andrew Johnson
William Henry Harrison	James A. Garfield
John Tyler	John F. Kennedy
Franklin Pierce	Lyndon B. Johnson
James Buchanan	Richard M. Nixon

youngest Senator was John V. Tunney (D Calif.), while the oldest was Allen J. Ellender (D La.). The youngest Representative was Dawson Mathis (D Ga.), the oldest, Emanuel Celler (D N.Y.).

Proponents of Congressional reform have often contended that the average age level of both Senators and Representatives means that persons under 40 are vastly under-represented while those over 40 are greatly over-represented. In the 79th Congress (1945-46), for example, the average Member of the House was 52, while the average age of eligible voters was only 41. This trend continued to the outset of the 92nd Congress, when the average House Member was 51.9 years old and the average voting-age citizen was a little over 45. Some critics assert that this age differential tends to make Congress more conservative than the country as a whole.

Occupations and Religion

From the early days of the Republic, the legal profession has been the dominant occupational background of Members of Congress—a development that has given that profession substantial over-representation. From a level of 37 percent of the House Members in the First Congress, the proportion of Members with a legal background rose to 70 percent in 1840, then declined slightly in subsequent years and remained at a level of 55 and 60 percent from 1950 to 1971. In the 92nd Congress, 301 of the 535 Members (56 percent) listed law as their primary occupational background.

Other professions that have been prominently represented in recent years have been business and banking, agriculture, journalism and teaching. In 1957, 157 Mem-

bers gave business or banking as their occupation, 68 listed agriculture, 63 teaching, and 40 journalism. By 1971, the number of former businessmen and bankers in Congress had increased to 172 and that of teachers to 72. The ranks of former journalists and farmers had declined to 37 and 49, respectively.

Critics of the structure of Congress frequently contend that the predominance of lawyers and businessmen is another factor, like age, tending to give Congress a conservative tinge. In *American Democracy in Theory and Practice,* Prof. Robert K. Carr points out: "Almost no factory worker or member of the laboring class is ever elected to Congress, although a small number of Congressmen usually claim to hold, or once to have held, union cards. Since a lawyer's business is, after all, with the law and government, it is not strange that so many lawyers should go into politics or ultimately become Congressmen. However, the lawyer's approach to making law is...more often than not, a conservative one because of the strong influence of precedent and tradition in the practice of law...." Carr's book and similar studies have noted that law schools place little emphasis on social and economic approaches to modern-day problems and that most practicing lawyers are closely associated with business interests.

Veterans. Another dominant characteristic of the membership of Congress is former service in the armed forces. In 1971, there were 389 veterans in the House and Senate—more than 70 percent of the combined membership. The high percentage of veterans has prompted critics of alleged waste in military spending to suggest that loyalty of Members to the military has been instrumental

Religious Affiliations in 92nd Congress

	House			Senate			Congress
Religion	D	R	Tot.	D	R	Tot.	Total
Apostolic Christian	0	1	1	0	0	0	1
Baptist	32	10	42	5	3	8	50
Central Schwenkfelder	0	0	0	0	1	1	1
Christian and Missionary Alliance	0	1	1	0	0	0	1
Christian Churches and Churches of Christ	13	5	18	2	0	2	20
Christian Science	1	3	4	0	1	1	5
Eastern Orthodox	5	0	5	0	0	0	5
Episcopal	27	22	49	4	13	17	66
Evangelical Covenant	0	1	1	0	0	0	1
Evangelical Free	0	2	2	0	0	0	2
Jewish	10	2	12	1	1	2	14
Latter-Day Saints	3	3	6	2	2	4	10
Lutheran	2	9	11	3	0	3	14
Methodist	33	32	65	13	7	20	85
Presbyterian	26	41	67	10	6	16	83
Roman Catholic	77	24	101	9	3	12	113
Seventh Day Adventist	0	1	1	0	0	0	1
Society of Friends	0	4	4	0	0	0	4
Unitarian-Universalist	3	0	3	3	2	5	8
United Brethren	1	0	1	0	0	0	1
United Church of Christ and Congregationalist	6	13	19	2	5	7	26
Unspecified Protestant	12	5	17	1	1	12	19
None	3	1	4	0	0	0	4
Total	**254**	**180**	**434***	**55**	**45**	**100**	**534***

One House seat vacant at time of survey.

Women in Congress

At the beginning of the 92nd Congress in 1971, 78 women had held seats in Congress—68 in the House only, 9 in the Senate only, and one—Margaret Chase Smith (R Maine)—in both chambers. Following is a list of the 78 women Members.

Senate

Mrs. Hazel Abel (R Neb. 1954-55)
Mrs. Eva Bowring (R Neb. 1954)
Mrs. Vera Bushfield (R S.D. 1948-49)
Mrs. Hattie W. Caraway (D Ark. 1931-45)
Mrs. Rebecca L. Felton (Independent Democrat Ga. 1922)*
Mrs. Dixie Bibb Graves (D Ala. 1937-38)
Mrs. Rose McConnell Long (D La. 1936-37)
Mrs. Maurine B. Neuberger (D Ore. 1960-67)
Gladys Pyle (R S.D. 1938-39)†
Mrs. Margaret Chase Smith (1949—)

House

Mrs. Bella S. Abzug (D N.Y. 1971—)
Mrs. Howard H. Baker (R Tenn. 1964-65)
Mrs. Iris Blitch (D Ga. 1955-63)
Mrs. Veronica Boland (D Pa. 1942-43)
Mrs. Frances P. Bolton (R Ohio 1940-69)
Mrs. Reva Beck Bosone (D Utah 1949-53)
Mrs. Vera Buchanan (D Pa. 1951-55)
Mrs. Katharine Edgar Byron (D Md. 1941-43)
Mrs. Shirley Chisholm (D N.Y. 1969—)
Mrs. Marguerite Stitt Church (R Ill. 1951-63)
Mrs. Marian Williams Clarke (R N.Y. 1934-35)
Mrs. Emily Taft Douglas (D Ill. 1945-47)
Mrs. Helen Gahagan Douglas (D Calif. 1945-51)
Mrs. Florence P. Dwyer (R N.J. 1957—)
Mrs. Willa B. Eslick (D Tenn. 1932-33)
Mrs. Mary Elizabeth Farrington (R Hawaii 1954-57)
Mrs. Willa E. Fulmer (D S.C. 1944-45)
Mrs. Bessie Hawley Gasque (D S.C. 1938-39)†
Mrs. Florence R. Gibbs (D Ga. 1940-41)
Mrs. Kathryn O. Granahan (D Pa. 1956-63)
Mrs. Ella T. Grasso (D Conn. 1971—)
Mrs. Edith Green (D Ore. 1955—)
Mrs. Isabella Greenway (D Ariz. 1934-37)
Mrs. Martha Griffiths (D Mich. 1955—)
Mrs. Julia Butler Hansen (D Wash. 1960—)
Mrs. Cecil M. Harden (R Ind. 1949-59)

Mrs. Margaret M. Heckler (R Mass. 1967—)
Mrs. Louise Day Hicks (D Mass. 1971—)
Mrs. Nan Wood Honeyman (D Ore. 1937-39)
Mrs. Winnifred Sprague Mason Huck (R Ill. 1922-23)
Mrs. Virginia Ellis Jenckes (D Ind. 1933-39)
Mrs. Florence P. Kahn (R Calif. 1925-37)
Mrs. Elizabeth Kee (D W. Va. 1951-65)
Mrs. Edna F. Kelly (D N.Y. 1949-69)
Mrs. Coya Knutson (D Minn. 1955-59)
Mrs. Katherine Langley (R Ky. 1927-31)
Mrs. Clare Boothe Luce (R Conn. 1943-47)
Mrs. Georgia L. Lusk (D N.M. 1947-49)
Mrs. Ruth Hanna McCormick (R Ill. 1929-31)
Mrs. Clara G. McMillan (D S.C. 1940-41)
Mrs. Helen Douglas Mankin (D Ga. 1946-47)
Mrs. Catherine May (R Wash. 1959-71)
Mrs. Patsy T. Mink (D Hawaii 1965—)
Mrs. Mae Ella Nolan (R Calif. 1923-25)
Mrs. Catherine D. Norrell (D Ark. 1961-63)
Mrs. Mary T. Norton (D N.J. 1925-51)
Mrs. Caroline O'Day (D N.Y. 1935-43)
Mrs. Pearl P. Oldfield (D Ark. 1929-31)
Mrs. Ruth Bryan Owen (D Fla. 1929-33)
Mrs. Gracie Pfost (D Idaho 1953-63)
Eliza Jane Pratt (D N.C. 1946-47)
Mrs. Ruth Baker Pratt (R N.Y. 1929-33)
Jeannette Rankin (R Mont. 1917-19, 1941-43)
Mrs. Louise G. Reece (R Tenn. 1961-63)
Mrs. Charlotte T. Reid (R Ill. 1963—)
Mrs. Corrine Boyd Riley (D S.C. 1962-63)
Alice M. Robertson (R Okla. 1921-23)
Mrs. Edith Nourse Rogers (R Mass. 1925-60)
Mrs. Katherine St. George (R N.Y. 1947-65)
Mrs. Edna Simpson (R Ill. 1959-61)
Mrs. Margaret Chase Smith (R Maine 1940-49)
Winifred C. Stanley (R N.Y. 1943-45)
Mrs. Leonor K. Sullivan (D Mo. 1953—)
Jessie Sumner (R Ill. 1939-47)
Ruth Thompson (R Mich. 1951-57)
Mrs. Jessica McC. Weis (R N.Y. 1959-63)
Mrs. Effiegene Wingo (D Ark. 1930-33)
Mrs. Chase Going Woodhouse (D Conn. 1945-47, 1949-51)

*Mrs. Felton was sworn in Nov. 21, 1922, to fill the vacancy created by the death of Thomas E. Watson (D 1921-22); the next day she gave up her seat to Walter F. George (D 1922-57), the elected candidate for the vacancy.
†Never sworn in because Congress was not in session between election and expiration of term.

in the readiness of Congress to fund weapon systems that the critics consider unnecessary.

Religion. Among religious groups, Protestants have comprised about three-fourths of the membership of both houses in recent years, although Roman Catholic Members have become more numerous than Members belonging to any single Protestant denomination. In the 92nd Congress, there were 113 Catholics—the largest number of Catholics ever to serve in Congress at one time. Catholics had taken the lead from Methodists in 1965 and retained it through 1971.

In the 92nd Congress, Methodists were the second leading denomination with 85 Members. Next were Presbyterians with 83, Episcopalians with 66 and Baptists with 50. There were 14 Jews in the 92nd, a relatively large decrease from 19 at the outset of the 91st Congress two years before.

Women Members

Starting with the first woman Member of Congress, Rep. Jeannette Rankin (R Mont.) in 1916, 69 women had been elected to the House and 10 had been elected or appointed to the Senate through 1971. Only one—Mar-

---

Record of Congressional Service

As of 1971, the record for the longest service in Congress—56 years—was held by Carl Hayden (D Ariz.), who retired from the Senate in 1968 at the age of 91. Hayden gave up his job as a county sheriff to become Arizona's first Representative in 1912. He was sworn in Feb. 19, 1912, five days after Arizona became a state, and served in the House for 15 years. In 1927, he moved to the Senate where he served seven six-year terms. When Hayden retired, he was President pro tempore of the Senate and chairman of the Senate Appropriations Committee.

---

garet Chase Smith (R Maine)—had served in both chambers. In the 92nd Congress there were 12 women in the House and one—Mrs. Smith—in the Senate. This was the largest female contingent in Congress since 1964, when there also were 13.

Of the 78 women who have served in Congress, all but seven have been married (or were widows) at the time of their service. Thirty-three have had husbands who served before them; of these, 31 (4 Senators and 27 House Members) were appointed or elected to fill the unexpired terms of their late husbands. One woman Representative, Emily Taft Douglas (D Ill. 1945-47), preceded her husband, Sen. Paul H. Douglas (D Ill. 1949-67), in Congress. Rep. Charlotte T. Reid (R Ill.) succeeded her husband as the Republican nominee for the House in 1962 when he died between the primary and general elections.

Following the election of Miss Rankin in 1916, the number of women in Congress increased only slightly until 1928, when nine women were elected to the House of the 71st Congress. Membership of women reached a peak in the 87th Congress (1961-62), when there were 17 in the House and two in the Senate. The total fell to 13 in the 88th Congress and had not exceeded that level when the 92nd Congress convened in 1971.

The first woman named to the Senate served there only one day. On Oct. 2, 1922, Mrs. Rebecca L. Felton (Independent Democrat Ga.) was appointed to fill the vacancy created by the death of Sen. Thomas E. Watson (D Ga.); Mrs. Felton was not sworn in until Nov. 21, however, and on the next day she turned the seat over to Walter F. George (D), who had been elected to fill the vacancy. In 1931, Mrs. Hattie W. Caraway (D Ark.) became the second woman Member in the Senate's history when she was named to fill the vacancy created by the death of her husband, Thaddeus H. Caraway (D). In 1932 and 1938, Mrs. Caraway was elected to full six-year terms. Through the election of 1970, only two other woman Senators—Mrs. Maurine B. Neuberger (D Ore. 1960-67) and Mrs. Smith (1949—)had been elected to full Senate terms. No more than two women had ever served in the Senate at any one time.

Although many women elected to Congress on the basis of "widow's mandate" have served only the remainder of the husband's term, some women have gone on to achieve a political reputation of their own. Both Sen. Smith and Rep. Frances P. Bolton (R Ohio 1940-69), who hold the records for the longest service by women in their respective chambers, were elected to the House in 1940 to fill the unexpired terms of their late husbands. Mrs. Smith served in the House until 1948, when she won the first of four terms in the Senate. Mrs. Bolton served in the House until she was defeated in 1968 when redistricting led to a contest with another incumbent, Charles A. Vanik (D).

By the late 1960s, the tradition of "widow's mandate" had apparently declined. Of the 13 women in the 92nd Congress, only Mrs. Smith, Mrs. Reid and Rep. Leonor K. Sullivan (D Mo.), had entered politics as surrogates for their late husbands.

Negro Members

When the 92nd Congress got under way, a total of 39 Negroes had served in Congress—36 in the House and three in the Senate. Of the total, 22 had served during the period of Reconstruction. Thirteen were elected to the 92nd—12 in the House and one in the Senate.

The number of Negroes in Congress had increased gradually since 1928, when Rep. Oscar DePriest (R Ill.) became the first member of his race elected to either house in the 20th century. In the 91st Congress there were 10 Negroes—nine in the House and one in the Senate. The total of 13 for the 92nd was the largest number of Negroes to have served in Congress at one time in the nation's history. Negroes elected to Congress for the first time in 1970 were Ronald V. Dellums (D Calif.), Ralph H. Metcalfe (D Ill.), George W. Collins (D Ill.), Parren J. Mitchell (D Md.) and Charles B. Rangel (D N.Y.). Dellums, Collins and Mitchell had white predecessors.

The first Negro ever elected to Congress was John W. Menard (R La.), who won election in 1868 to an unexpired term in the 40th Congress. Menard's election was disputed, however, and the House denied him his seat. Thus the distinction of being the first Negro actually to serve in Congress went to Hiram Revels (R Miss.), who served in the Senate from Feb. 23, 1870, to March 3, 1871. The first Negro to serve in the House was Joseph H. Rainey (R S.C.), who served from 1870 to 1879.

In 1874, a second Negro, Blanche K. Bruce (R Miss.) was elected to the Senate; Bruce was the first member of his race to serve a full term in the Senate and the last elected to that chamber until Edward W. Brooke (R Mass.) won a six-year term in 1966. The last Negro elected to Congress in the 19th century was George Henry White (R N.C.), who won election in 1896 and 1898, but did not seek renomination in 1900. No other Negro was elected to either chamber until DePriest's successful campaign for a House seat in 1928.

In 1968, Rep. Shirley Chisholm (D N.Y.) became the first Negro woman to be elected to Congress. Earlier in that decade, two other Negroes first elected to the House in the 1940s—Reps. William L. Dawson (D Ill.) and Adam C. Powell (D N.Y.)—had achieved enough seniority to be named chairmen of two important House committees. Dawson served as chairman of the House Government Operations Committee from 1949 until his death in 1970; Powell was chairman of the Education and Labor Committee from 1961 until the House stripped him of the post in 1967 because of alleged misuse of Committee funds. *(See Seating and Disciplining of Members, Chapter III.)*

Decline in Membership Turnover

After experiencing high turnover rates in the 19th and early 20th centuries, the membership of both the House and the Senate has become more stable from one Congress to another. At the outset of the 92nd Congress, only 67 Members of the two houses combined were beginning their first terms, while 61 had served 20 or more years and 13 had served 30 or more years. These records of longevity contrasted sharply with those of a century earlier. In 1869, for example, only 98 of 243 House Members had served in previous Congresses.

Throughout the 19th century, turnover in the House was greater than in the Senate, primarily because of the exigencies of campaign travel every two years and the tendency of state legislatures to continue re-electing the same men to the Senate. For several years after direct election of Senators was instituted by the 17th Amendment in 1913, Senate turnover increased, particularly in the larger states.

Attesting to the difficulty of achieving a long career in the House, DeAlva S. Alexander, a former House Member, noted in 1916 that each new House election rang "the curfew of one-fourth of its Members." He added: "Thus the House, like the heathen goddess, devours its own children. But the rapidity with which the process goes on is a bit startling. Of the 391 members who appeared in March 1911, at the first session of the 62nd Congress, only four belonged to the House in 1891. This represents the havoc usually made every 20 years by death, defeat and other circumstances."

Political scientists have attributed the declining turnover rate in Congress to the increased exposure of incumbents on television and through other media, the spread of one-party states and districts, the rise of big-city political machines, and the tendency of the electorate to favor "experience" over youth in tackling complex national problems. Many students of government expect more incumbents to be defeated in the next few years, however, as a result of legislation enacted in 1970 extending the right to vote to all 18-year-olds. (The Supreme Court in *Oregon v. Mitchell* on Dec. 21, 1970, restricted application of the Act to Federal elections. A proposed constitutional amendment, now awaiting ratification, will lower the voting age to 18 in state and local elections.)

Shifts Between Chambers

From the early days of Congress, there has been shifting of membership from one chamber to another—particularly from the House to the Senate. From 1789 to 1971, a total of 507 former House Members had served in the Senate, while 57 former Senators had become Members of the House. In explaining their decision to move from House to Senate, former Representatives have cited the Senate's greater prestige, its longer term, and their increased effectiveness as legislators in a body of only 100 Members as against one of 435. In recent years, few former Senators have become House Members; those who did have usually done so after having been defeated for re-election to the Senate.

Shifting of Members from one chamber to the other began in the 1790s, when 19 former Representatives became Senators, and three former Senators moved to the House. The number of House Members who became

Negroes in Congress

Upon the convening of the 92nd Congress in 1971, the number of Negroes to have served in Congress reached 39—36 in the House and 3 in the Senate. Of the total, 20 were elected during the Reconstruction period; none was elected after 1898 until 1928. One other was elected during the Reconstruction but was not permitted to take his seat.

Following is a list of the Negroes elected to Congress, together with the years in which they served:

House

John W. Menard (R La.)	(Elected in 1868 but not seated)
Joseph H. Rainey (R S.C.)	1870-79
Jefferson F. Long (R Ga.)	1870-71
Robert B. Elliott (R S.C.)	1871-74
Robert C. DeLarge (R S.C.)	1871-73
Benjamin S. Turner (R Ala.)	1871-73
Josiah T. Walls (R Fla.)	1871-76
Richard H. Cain (R S.C.)	1873-74; 1877-78
John R. Lynch (R Miss.)	1873-77
James T. Rapier (R Ala.)	1873-75
Alonzo J. Ransier (R S.C.)	1873-75
Jeremiah Haralson (R Ala.)	1875-77
John A. Hyman (R N.C.)	1875-77
Charles E. Nash (R La.)	1875-77
Robert Smalls (R S.C.)	1975-79; 1883-87
James E. O'Hara (R N.C.)	1883-87
Henry P. Cheatham (R N.C.)	1889-93
John M. Langston (R Va.)	1890-91
Thomas E. Miller (R S.C.)	1890-91
George W. Murray (R S.C.)	1893-97
George H. White (R S.C.)	1897-1901
Oscar DePriest (R Ill.)	1929-35
Arthur W. Mitchell (D Ill.)	1935-42
William L. Dawson (D Ill.)	1943-70
Adam C. Powell Jr. (D N.Y.)	1945-66; 1969-70
Charles C. Diggs Jr. (D Mich.)	1955 --
Robert N.C. Nix (D Pa.)	1958 --
Augustus F. Hawkins (D Calif.)	1963 --
John Conyers Jr. (D Mich.)	1965 --
Louis Stokes (D Ohio)	1969 --
William Clay D Mo.)	1969 --
Shirley Chisholm (D N.Y.)	1969 --
George W. Collins (D Ill.)	1971 --
Ronald V. Dellums (D Calif.)	1971 --
Ralph H. Metcalfe (D Ill.)	1971 --
Parren J. Mitchell (D Md.)	1971 --
Charles B. Rangel (D N.Y.)	1971 --

Senate

Hiram R. Revels (R Miss.)	1870-71
Blanche K. Bruce (R Miss.)	1875-81
Edward W. Brooke (R Mass.)	1967 --

Senators increased over the next several decades, reaching 55 in the years from 1800 to 1820 and 39 in the 1840s alone. The trend continued through the 1950s and 1960s, when 58 former House Members assumed Senate seats.

By contrast, the greatest number of former Senators to become House Members in any one decade was nine in the years between 1810 and 1820. From 1900 through 1970, only 11 former Senators became Members of the House. The only former Senator in the House at the convening of the 92nd Congress was Rep. Claude Pepper (D Fla.), who had served continuously as a Representative since 1963. Pepper had been a Senator from 1936 through 1951.

Perhaps the most notable shift from the Senate to the House was that of Henry Clay (Democratic Republican Ky.), who gave up his Senate seat in 1811 to assume a House seat. In his first term in the House, Clay was elected Speaker—an office he used successfully to push the country into the War of 1812. After five terms in the House, he returned to the Senate in 1823. Another prominent House Member who had once been a Senator was John Quincy Adams (Whig Mass.), who also was one of only two former Presidents to serve in Congress after his term in the White House. Adams, who was known as "Old Man Eloquent," was one of the most influential members of the Whig opposition in the House to President Jackson in the 1830s. Referring to his election to the House, Adams said, "My election as President of the United States was not half so gratifying to my inmost soul."

Bibliography

Books

Alexander, DeAlva Stanwood, *History and Procedure of the House of Representatives.* Houghton Mifflin Co., 1916.

Carr, Robert K. et. al., *American Democracy in Theory and Practice,* 3rd ed. Rinehart and Co., 1959.

Crockett, David, *Davy Crockett's Own Story as Written by Himself.* Citadel Press, 1955.

Galloway, George B., *Congress at the Crossroads.* Thomas Y. Crowell Co., 1946.

——, *History of the House of Representatives,* Thomas Y. Crowell Co., 1961.·

——, *The Legislative Process in Congress.* Thomas Y. Crowell Co., 1955.

Haynes, George H., *The Senate of the United States,* 2 vols. Houghton Mifflin Co., 1938.

MacNeil, Neil, *Forge of Democracy.* David McKay Co., 1963.

Rothman, David J., *Politics and Power: The United States Senate, 1869-1901.* Harvard University Press, 1966.

Tocqueville, Alexis de, *Democracy in America,* 2 vols. Alfred A. Knopf, Inc., 1945.

White, William S., *Citadel: The Story of the U.S. Senate.* Harper and Bros., 1956.

——, *Home Place: The Story of the U.S. House of Representatives.* Houghton Mifflin Co., 1965.

Wilson, Woodrow, *Congressional Government.* Houghton Mifflin Co., 1885.

Government Publications

Tansill, William R., "Members of Congress Who Have Served in Both Houses," Library of Congress, Legislative Reference Service, 1965.

Van Helden, Morrigene, "Women in the Congress of the United States," Library of Congress, Legislative Reference Service, 1968.

Campaign Financing

THE COST OF RUNNING for the office of Senator or Representative has climbed to such dizzy heights in recent years that the task of bringing it down to something approaching a reasonable level—and keeping it there—has come to seem almost beyond the bounds of legislative ingenuity. Many observers consider regulation of election campaign financing the most important unsolved problem of democracy. John McLaughlin, writing in the Catholic weekly *America* of May 2, 1970, described political campaign spending as "a national disgrace," and Russell D. Hemenway, director of the National Committee for an Effective Congress, told a House subcommittee a month later that "the enormous cost an effective campaign entails is no less than a national scandal."

Issues Raised by Big Expenditures

Americans are concerned over the orgy of political spending mainly because it strikes at the heart of the general assumption that every able and honest citizen of a democracy should have a chance to seek public office whether he is rich, poor or somewhere in between. It follows that an aspirant for public service should not be required to obligate himself, during a campaign, to contributors who will expect him to vote for or against specified measures if he is elected.

There is, however, no simple way to control campaign financing. Regulations to cope effectively with the problem of runaway costs must meet several requirements. The regulations must:

• Be enforceable; that is, they must not have the effect of unreasonably restricting use of the means of publicity necessary for a meaningful election contest. (If the rules are unrealistic, they will encourage evasion.)

• Have as equal an effect as possible on the candidates who are already in office and well known and the candidates not previously in the public eye.

• Be tightly drafted, to guard against loopholes.

• Avoid serious curtailment of freedom of expression.

The problem of regulating campaign costs without violating freedoms guaranteed by the Constitution was spotlighted in 1957 when the Supreme Court, by a majority of five to three, declined to pass on the constitutionality of a prohibition on labor union contributions to political parties and candidates. The Court reinstated an indictment of the United Auto Workers for financing political broadcasts out of its general funds, saying that such action came under the terms of the prohibition. When the case was tried later in district court,

the UAW maintained that the broadcasts had been of an educational nature and the jury did not convict.

Chief Justice Earl Warren and Justices Hugo L. Black and William O. Douglas, in their dissenting Supreme Court opinion, had described prohibition of labor union contributions to election campaigns as equivalent to "burning down the house to roast the pig." They said the majority's ruling "abolishes First Amendment rights on a wholesale basis."

Great Rise of Campaign Costs

The high cost of campaigning was not always a problem in America. In 1846, Abraham Lincoln's friends gave him $200 to help him run for Congress. Since his total campaign costs amounted to 75 cents, spent on a barrel of cider for some farm hands, he returned the remaining $199.25 to the donors. The authenticity of this parable, which was first published in *The Century Magazine,* February 1887, has been questioned by Lincoln scholars. Its point, however, is consistent with Lincoln's political philosophy.

After Lincoln's day, in any case, the price of running for office rose unmanageably. "Robber-baron" capitalists vied for supremacy in financing the campaigns of rival candidates by offering them access to ample "slush funds." Electoral reform legislation enacted during the administrations of Presidents Theodore Roosevelt and Calvin Coolidge failed to stem the rising tide of campaign costs. Will Rogers remarked in his syndicated column of June 28, 1931: "Politics has got so expensive that it takes a lot of money to even get beat with."

Dwight D. Eisenhower, who had been insulated from partisan politics before running for President, expressed his shock at "the outrageous costs of getting elected to public office." He wrote in the *Reader's Digest,* January 1968: "It is generally believed that $100,000 or more is spent every two years to elect a Representative to Congress from a populous and competitive district. The price tag for a seat in the U.S. Senate today averages around $200,000, and in the larger states often runs to a million dollars or more."

Reference

See Appendix table of contents (first thumb tab) for texts of Federal laws on campaign contributions and campaign expenditures.

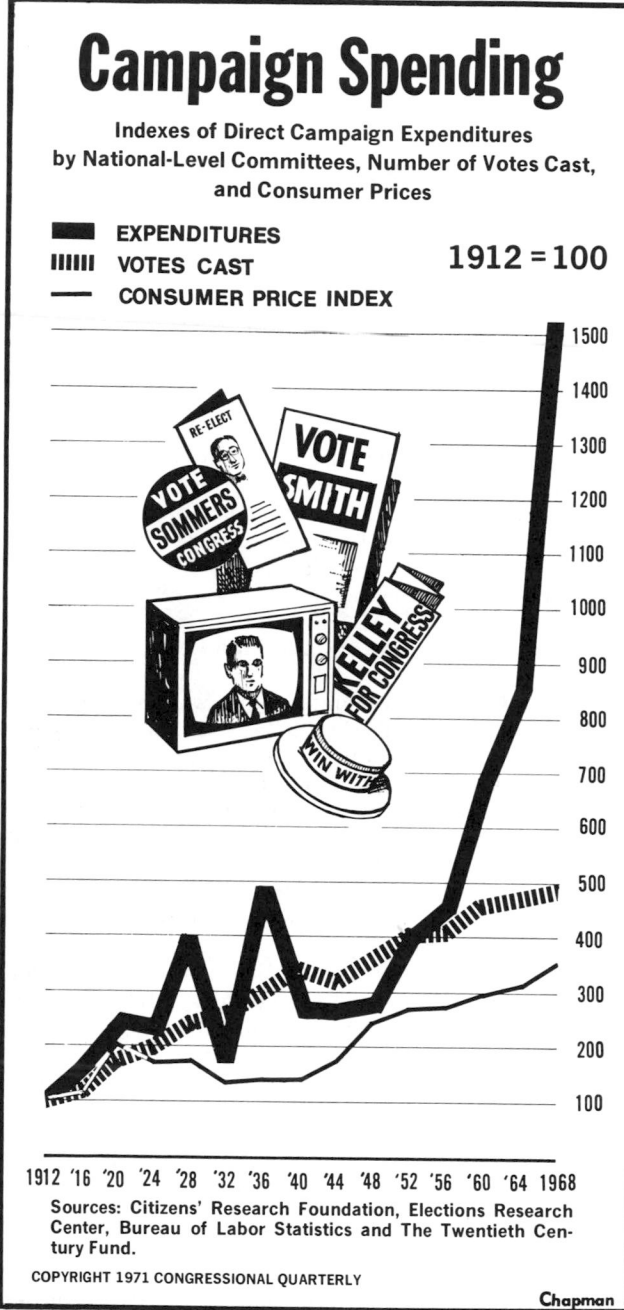

Campaign Spending

Indexes of Direct Campaign Expenditures
by National-Level Committees, Number of Votes Cast,
and Consumer Prices

■ EXPENDITURES
‖‖‖‖ VOTES CAST   **1912 = 100**
— CONSUMER PRICE INDEX

1500
1400
1300
1200
1100
1000
900
800
700
600
500
400
300
200
100

1912 '16 '20 '24 '28 '32 '36 '40 '44 '48 '52 '56 '60 '64 1968

Sources: Citizens' Research Foundation, Elections Research Center, Bureau of Labor Statistics and The Twentieth Century Fund.

COPYRIGHT 1971 CONGRESSIONAL QUARTERLY

Chapman

Unreliability of Reports. Determination of the exact amounts spent in election campaigns is virtually impossible. Legal requirements for reporting campaign receipts and expenditures are riddled with loopholes, which candidates and their supporting committees zealously utilize. The amounts officially reported are only the visible tip of an iceberg extending far below the surface.

In 1962, candidates in Congressional races reported expenditures of $18,404,115, but Congressional Quarterly estimated actual expenditures at almost $100 million. A task force of the Twentieth Century Fund estimated in 1970 that candidates in the 1968 Congressional races spent $50 million and reported only $8,482,857. Candidates for Senator from Pennsylvania in 1968 reported total expenditures of $6,236; their actual expenditures were reported in the *New York Times* for March 17, 1970, to be about $1 million.

Defense of High Expenditures

A well-known writer on the subject of campaign finances believes that today's seemingly astronomical figures are not out of line with the expansion of the American economy as a whole. Alexander Heard said in 1960 in his book *The Costs of Democracy:* "The real costs of political campaigning have *not* soared steadily upward. Despite recent spurts caused by the use of television in some types of elections, the long-run dollar increase appears no greater than rises in the price level and the national income."

Heard asserted that the slice of the national income that goes for political expenses is commensurate with the importance of this activity: "Nothing about the national income nor the scope of expenditures for public and private activities in the United States suggests automatically that Americans pay more for choosing their elective officials than is reasonable. More may be spent in specific instances than required by specific standards of necessity, but the over-all financial burden is light compared with the nation's resources that are deployed for other ends."

David Adamany, a Wesleyan University dean, has supported Heard's view that campaign spending is not excessive. Writing in the April 1970 *National Civic Review,* Adamany referred to a finding by the Citizens' Research Foundation (Princeton, N.J.) that all expenditures in 1968 for Presidential, Congressional, and other U.S. election campaigns, amounting to $300 million, came to an average of $4.10 for each vote cast. He commented: "The sum of $4.10 is not a large burden for each voter in a democratic political system which requires vigorous adversary competition between parties and candidates." The rise in spending per vote between 1952 and 1968, Adamany said, was only 5 percent a year.

Threat To Democratic Ideals

Whether or not the curve of mounting campaign expenditures accords with national economic growth, the influence of large sums of money on the fate of politicians is apt to raise the specter of democracy perverted and stir suspicions of corruption. Elihu Root told the New York State Constitutional Convention in 1894 that campaign contributions of big business were

Available data on Congressional campaign expenditures suggest that Eisenhower's estimates, although approximately accurate for the early and middle 1960s, were greatly exceeded in the latter part of the decade. In 1964, winner Robert F. Kennedy (D) and loser Kenneth B. Keating (R) each spent more than $1 million in the Senatorial campaign in New York State. Kennedy commented, "The mounting cost of elections is rapidly becoming intolerable for a democratic society." In 1966, the unsuccessful campaign of Pierre Salinger (D) for election to the Senate from California cost $1.6 million. The cost of the 1970 Senatorial elections spurted to an aggregate of $5 million for the major candidates in each of three states—California, New York and Texas.

"a constantly growing evil which has done more to shake the confidence of the plain people of small means in our political institutions than any other practice which has ever obtained since the foundation of our Government." Twelve years later, Samuel Gompers, president of the American Federation of Labor, testified before the House Committee on Elections: "It is doubtful to my mind if the contributions and expenditures of vast sums of money in the nominations and elections for our public offices can continue to increase without endangering the endurance of our Republic in its purity and in its essence."

Large contributions and expenditures in election campaigns, however necessary, pose a double-barreled threat to democracy. First, the need to raise a large amount of money to run for office jeopardizes the egalitarian ideal that public service should be open to persons of modest as well as large means. Second, it suggests that elected officials are obligated to dispense favors to interest groups that were campaign contributors. The late Sen. Robert F. Kennedy (D N.Y.) referred to the unseemly alternative of avoiding one of these threats only by succumbing to the other. "We are in danger of creating a situation in which our candidates must be chosen only from among the rich...or those willing to be beholden to others."

A survey made in 1968 showed that one of every five U.S. Senators was a millionaire. Sen. Daniel K. Inouye (D Hawaii), chairman of the Democratic Senatorial Campaign Committee, said in 1969: "I am afraid that realities and practicalities of the election process have, to some extent, developed a new aristocracy of wealth and power." Sen. Edward M. Kennedy (D Mass.) observed in the same year that without restrictions on television spending by candidates "Survival is not of the fittest, but of the wealthiest." In a similar vein, Rep. James C. Wright Jr. (D Texas) wrote in *Harper's Magazine,* April 1967: "It is now, in fact, nearly impossible in most states for men of modest means to seek high elective office—unless they are willing wards of the wealthy."

The Senate Committee on Finance, reporting Nov. 1, 1967, on a bill for Federal sharing of the campaign costs of candidates for Federal offices, said: "Rising campaign costs...are making careers in public life more difficult for any but the rich and the near-rich who can attract the large amounts needed to pay for a successful political campaign." President Lyndon B. Johnson, in a message to Congress on May 26, 1966, said: "For decades we have tolerated the growth of seeds of cynicism from the underbrush surrounding our present methods of financing political campaigns....We have done nothing to insure that able men of modest means can undertake elective office unencumbered by the debts of loyalty to wealthy supporters."

The spiraling costs of getting elected, and the need of candidates to accept contributions from persons interested in the passage or defeat of particular legislative proposals, together strike at the heart of the idea that a legislator should be free to vote according to his conscience. Sen. William E. Borah (R Idaho) said in 1924, "So long as political parties seeking power or control of government accept vast contributions from those who are interested in matters of legislation or administration, you will have sinister and corrupt and controlled government." Sen. Russell B. Long (D La.) in August 1966 told the Senate Committee on Finance that "The

Impact of Campaign Contributions

Many legislators, writers, and civic groups have deplored the erosion of political integrity likely to result from large campaign contributions. Among the more pungent statements on this subject are the following:

"Individuals and organizations providing substantial gifts at critical moments can threaten to place a candidate in moral hock."—President's Commission on Campaign Costs (1962).

"A candidate should not be dependent on shaking down some contractor or gambler or the Mafia or whatever."—Arthur M. Schlesinger Jr., at a 1968 conference in New York City sponsored by the Center for the Study of Democratic Institutions.

"The accelerating cost of campaigning is the single most important factor in corrupting and degrading our politicians."—James M. Perry, political columnist, in *The National Observer,* April 13, 1970.

Acceptance of funds from "labor organizations or other private interests...means that a candidate is placed in the position of being in the pocket of such contributors, or assumed to be by the contributor and by the public."—Sen. John Sherman Cooper (R Ky.), Senate speech, Nov. 23, 1970.

distinction between a campaign contribution and a bribe is almost a hair's line difference."

Sen. Richard L. Neuberger (D Ore., 1955-60) also felt that campaign contributions belonged in the same category as bribes. In his book *Adventures in Politics* (1954), he wrote, with reference to himself and his wife: "If Maureen or I ever would take $100 in cash behind the locked door of a hotel room to cast our vote for or against a specific legislative bill, we would be guilty of receiving a bribe. If apprehended, we would go to jail in disgrace—as we should. But if, at the next election, we accepted not $100 in cash but $1,000 in a check from the same donor, it is all perfectly legal, providing the check is made out to the Neuberger-for-election committee."

In 1956, Congress passed a bill relieving natural gas producers of Federal price regulation. Sen. Francis H. Case (R S.D.) told his colleagues that he had rejected a $2,500 campaign contribution offered him by a lawyer from another state who had made inquiries about his attitude on the bill. President Eisenhower approved the principle embodied in the measure, but he vetoed it because he thought the "highly questionable activities" of the natural gas lobbyists were "so arrogant...as to risk creating doubt among the American people concerning the integrity of governmental processes."

Effects of Using Image-Makers

Some observers have deplored the entry of professional image-makers into the field of political campaigning. Rep. Wright remarked in his 1967 article in *Harper's,* for example, that "In the arena where Lincoln and Douglas once debated great issues, advertising agencies last year hawked candidates like soap flakes."

Reasons for Higher Campaign Costs

Bills for campaigning for public office were higher than ever in the late 1960s and early 1970s chiefly because of the following developments:

• Enlargement of the electorate (the number of persons to be reached in campaigning) by the coming to voting age of the postwar bumper baby crop and by expansion of opportunities for voting by blacks.

• Revitalization of the Republican Party in the South, making it necessary for southern Republicans—and Democrats—to campaign more vigorously.

• Decline in straight-ticket voting; that is, the rise of independent voting, which resulted largely from virtual disappearance of old-style party machines in the precincts. Split-ticket voting requires each candidate for each office to intensify his efforts to get elected.

• Growing use of radio and television to reach prospective voters.

• Increase in numbers of young volunteer workers, whose services, though nominally free, are costly to administer, involving maintenance of headquarters, transportation of canvassers, arrangement of "socials" to sustain enthusiasm, and other expense items.

• Use of computers to categorize voters for specialized appeals.

• Growing reliance on costly public opinion surveys geared to campaigners' needs.

• Use of other new and costly campaign techniques, including "packaged" campaigns managed by political consultants.

• Inflation.

SOURCE: Adapted from David Adamany, "Money for Politics," *National Civic Review*, April 1970, p. 192-193.

The quality of political broadcasts came up at a conference in October 1965 in Washington sponsored by the nongovernmental Fair Campaign Practices Committee. Stimson Bullitt, president of the King Broadcasting Co., suggested that heavy reliance on television by candidates for public office meant "a narrowing of the dialogue, a stagnation of public ideas and a concentration on the proven, the widely popular and the previously successful." Five years later, on Sept. 23, 1970, Sen. John O. Pastore (D R.I.) said: "The idea of the magic of television and radio and newspapers and all the other paraphernalia that money can buy in an election, I am afraid, is going to destroy the very roots of the democratic process."

Advantages of Incumbents

From 1954 to 1968, incumbents in the House—perhaps because they had learned from experience how to cope with the high cost of campaigning—won 92 percent of the primary and general elections in which they sought to be returned to Washington; incumbent Senators in the same period won 85 percent of the primary and general elections in which they ran for reelection.

The Twentieth Century Fund's Task Force on Financing Congressional Campaigns found in 1970 that the high cost of campaigning was an effective deterrent to new entrants in politics: "Many Congressional elections are over before they begin because challengers simply cannot raise the resources they need to overcome the advantages of the incumbents." The task force went on to explain: "Incumbency in Congress gives a person access to campaign resources that make his reelection highly probable....Additionally, he has the perquisites of office—especially his staff, his offices, his almost unlimited free postage—to help his reelection campaign."

Lawsuit on Campaign Controls

Evasion of legal restrictions on campaign financing was the focus of an action taken in 1971 by Common Cause, a lobbying group headed by John W. Gardner, former Secretary of Health, Education and Welfare. Gardner wrote in the *New York Times* of Nov. 23, 1970, on the high cost of political campaigning: "It means final disintegration of the American folk belief that any poor boy can run for office. In most areas today a more correct statement would be that anyone can run for office provided he is wealthy or willing to put himself under obligation to sources of wealth. Could there be a more complete denial of what America stands for?"

Common Cause on Jan. 11, 1971, filed in the U.S. District Court for the District of Columbia a class-action complaint, alleging noncompliance with Federal laws on campaign contributions and spending, with harmful results to members of Common Cause and others, and requesting "declaratory and injunctive relief." Common Cause contended that the Democratic and Republican National Committees and the Conservative Party of New York State, the principal organizations backing winners in the 1970 Congressional elections, had violated, or connived at violation of, the following prohibitions set forth in Federal statutes:

• No campaign contributions of more than $5,000 by an individual to a candidate for Federal office or to a political committee other than a state or local committee.

• No campaign expenditures totaling more than $3 million by a political committee operating in two or more states and supporting candidates for the Presidency or seats in the Senate or the House.

Gardner said at a news conference when the complaint was filed: "The political parties through their national committees have consistently violated and threaten continued violation of the Federal election laws by...subterfuge." Referring to the establishment of a series of committees as a means of evading the law, Gardner added: "The donors are often told that contributions by the same person at the rate of $5,000 each to two or more of the dummy committees are legal. We do not believe that they are."

"The time has come," he said, "to end the dissembling and the flimflam.... We must improve these laws. But we must also seek to enforce compliance with the laws we already have."

Spending in 1970 Campaign

The perils resulting from gigantic campaign costs were exemplified in acute form in the 1970 midterm Congressional election. It was thought that the economic recession that year might hold down political contributions and reduce campaign budgets. However, Edward P. Morgan wrote in his syndicated newspaper column just after the election that the campaign was "the most expensive off-year election campaign in American history." Estimates of total expenditures ran from $100 million to $150 million.

Those staggering amounts were far from fully reflected in the spending reports filed by candidates and their committees with the Secretary of the Senate and the Clerk of the House. Bernard D. Nossiter of the *Washington Post* surmised that officially reported receipts and expenditures in 1970 constituted only 15 to 25 percent of actual campaign contributions and costs. As had happened in the past, some of the biggest-spending candidates officially reported no expenditures at all; that is, none with which they were personally acquainted.

In two states, rival candidates for the Senate agreed to set voluntary limits on their campaign spending. Sen. Philip A. Hart (D Mich.) and his challenger, Mrs. Lenore Romney (R), announced that each would spend on broadcast advertising no more than 7 cents per Michigan vote in the preceding national election and on all campaign advertising, including the broadcasts, no more than $170,755. The two Ohio candidates, Rep. Robert Taft Jr. (R) and Howard M. Metzenbaum (D), agreed to limit their spending on broadcast time to $262,018 apiece. Taft had spent around $200,000 and Metzenbaum about $500,000 to win nomination in the primaries.

Financial Gap Between Parties

The Republican National Committee started the 1970 campaign with a surplus of $1.5 million, and the Democrats with a deficit of $9.3 million. The two committees planned to spend, directly or through other political committees, the following sums for the campaign: Republicans, $6 million; Democrats, $1.6 million. There were similar disparities in the spending plans of the Republican and Democratic campaign committees of the Senate and the House.

The contrast between the campaign chests of the two major parties was not new. Alexander Heard pointed out in 1960 that the Democrats, traditionally behind the eight ball in dollar resources, tried to make a virtue of

Finances of Principal Campaign Committees

(As officially reported Nov. 30, 1970, and aggregated by categories)

Category	Number of Committees	Receipts	Expenditures
Republican	11	$10,644,337	$10,869,307
Democratic	14	3,577,001	3,690,753
Labor	17	3,269,444	3,530,740
Business and professional	5	1,133,297	1,522,450
Conservative	5	1,088,092	1,073,019
Liberal	3	859,069	866,160
Peace	11	564,524	522,224
Agricultural	4	547,103	479,183
Conservation	1	69,775	67,971

SOURCE: Citizens' Research Foundation (Princeton, N.J.).

their necessity: "Democrats," he said, "have seldom lost an opportunity to try to convert their financial disadvantage into a propaganda advantage by emphasizing (and usually exaggerating) the disparity of funds between the two parties."

Among the reasons for Republican opulence in 1970 were the presence of a Republican in the White House; the backing of the business community; and a well-managed, computerized campaign for a flood of small contributions. It is also possible that President Nixon's Vietnam policy enlisted the support of the "silent majority."

Financing of Primaries

Spending in the 1970 primaries by wealthy candidates ranged from $1 to $11 for each vote received. The Senatorial primary campaign of Rep. Richard L. Ottinger (D N.Y.) afforded an example of the effectiveness of heavy spending in lifting a candidate out of obscurity. Ottinger was a member of the family that amassed a fortune from development of plywood. Critics said he built a Senatorial nomination out of plywood.

Ottinger could not make political capital out of campaign issues. On most questions of policy, including the war in Vietnam, the Middle East, civil rights, and the need to prime the pump in the domestic economy, he agreed with his three opponents, all liberals like himself—former Kennedy aide Theodore C. Sorensen, former New York City Councilman Paul O'Dwyer and Rep. Richard D. McCarthy. Another strategy was necessary.

When the campaign began, almost two-thirds of the voters in New York State did not know who Ottinger was. Under the guidance of a media consultant, the managers of Ottinger's campaign spent $1.8 million, including $1 million for production and airing of a flood of televised advertisements projecting him as a man of experience. The expenditure total filed for Ottinger with New York State authorities was six times as great as the combined expenditures reported for Sorensen ($103,000), O'Dwyer ($103,000) and McCarthy ($30,000).

Expenditures of Party Committees, 1970

	Republican	Democratic
National Committee	2,980,308	$1,617,593
Senate Campaign Committee	928,843	568,067
House Campaign Committee	2,444,807	360,471
Other nationwide committees	4,515,339	1,144,622
Total	$10,869,297	$3,690,753

Senate Candidates Reporting No Receipts or Expenditures in 1970 Campaigns

(On basis that they were not personally informed of sums received or spent)

Winning Candidates	State	Party
Lloyd M. Bentsen Jr.	Texas	D
Sen. Vance Hartke	Ind.	D
Sen. Edward M. Kennedy	Mass.	D
Rep. John V. Tunney	Calif.	D
Losing Candidates		
Rep. George Bush	Texas	R
Howard M. Metzenbaum	Ohio	D
Rep. Richard L. Ottinger	N.Y.	D
Rep. Richard L. Roudebush	Ind.	R

SOURCE: Files of the Secretary of the Senate.

After Ottinger had won the Democratic primary, and before he lost in the November election, McCarthy said: "What it boils down to is this: Can you buy a seat in the U.S. Senate?"

The Democratic Senatorial primary in Ohio was another example of a blitz of costly television spots catapulting an unknown figure into millions of living rooms. The primary pitted parking-lot magnate Howard M. Metzenbaum against astronaut John H. Glenn Jr. A poll taken in November 1969 showed that 95 percent of Ohioans knew Glenn, while only 10 percent knew Metzenbaum. The television campaign waged by Metzenbaum cost more than $500,000, and he was victorious in the primary but not in the November election.

In Texas, the candidate who was less well known but spent more was victorious in both the Democratic primary and the election. Sen. Ralph W. Yarborough, who reported spending $275,096, was defeated in the primary by an insurance executive, Lloyd M. Bentsen Jr., whose campaign cost about $800,000. Bentsen won in the November election against Rep. George Bush (R).

Businessmen as Major Contributors

An article in the *Washington Post,* Dec. 6, 1970, pointed out that "Businessmen's contributions of $5,000 and more seemed to fall like confetti into the coffers of Lloyd M. Bentsen Jr. (Democrat), a Houston banking, insurance and mutual funds multimillionaire..., and Republican Rep. George Bush, a Houston oil millionaire who lost to Bentsen in the Nov. 3 general election." Oilmen accounted for 46 percent of individual contributions of $5,000 or more, and bankers, mutual fund managers, and others in the financial world for an additional 19 percent, in the campaigns of various Texas candidates in 1970. The list of those surveyed included several who ran for the governorship, five candidates for the U.S. Senate, and one candidate for the U.S. House of Representatives.

Six candidates in the 1970 Congressional primaries in North Carolina, Pennsylvania and Texas received money from an organized group of businessmen, the Business-Industry Political Action Committee, set up in 1963 by the National Association of Manufacturers. When all six candidates were victorious, the committee's June 1970 newsletter crowed: "BIPAC Bats 1,000 Pct." Edward I. Maher, editor of the newsletter, said his organization avoided direct lobbying. "If you get the right group down there, you don't have to lobby."

BIPAC reported at the end of 1970 that it had received $302,554 during the year. Its expenditures, totaling $539,157, went mostly for donations to the campaigns of Republicans and of southern and conservative Democrats. Among the directors of BIPAC were Robert B. Anderson, Secretary of the Treasury in President Eisenhower's second term; Arthur H. Motley, president of Parade Publications; and H. C. Lumb, vice president of the Republic Steel Corporation.

The Chamber of Commerce of the United States published in 1968 a booklet for the guidance of businessmen wanting to swell the campaign funds of selected candidates for public office without violating the legal ban on political contributions by corporations, a ban in effect since 1907. The booklet said, among other things, that a political action committee set up by a corporation or a trade association should be located elsewhere than in the corporation's or trade association's offices. Brushing aside this advice, the General Foods Corp. provided space in its main office at 250 North St. in White Plains, N.Y., for a political action group, the North Street Good Government Group, made up of the corporation's executives. The group contributed funds in 1970 to three key members of the House Committee on Agriculture. Similarly, the Lone Star Cement Corp.'s headquarters in Greenwich, Conn., were the headquarters also of the Lone Star Executive Voluntary Political Fund, which gave financial help in 1970 to members of the Senate and House Committees on Public Works.

Bankers as Contributors

Another group of capitalists, the Bankers' Political Action Committee, undertook to raise more than $200,000 for Congressional, gubernatorial and other 1970 elections. "The candidates who will receive help from BankPAC," according to the *American Banker,* Oct. 22, 1970, "will be selected candidates of the House Banking and Currency, Ways and Means and Rules Committees and the Senate Banking and Currency and Finance Committees." BankPAC's report of Oct. 29 to the Clerk of the House said the committee had disbursed $55,000 to incumbents of both parties seeking re-election, including 21 members of the House Banking and Currency Committee.

Rep. Wright Patman (D Texas), chairman of the Banking and Currency Committee, received no contribution from BankPAC. For many years, he had been a leading critic of the country's major banks. On Oct. 29, Patman asked the Department of Justice to investigate bankers' campaign contributions. Referring to the Federal Corrupt Practices Act of 1925, which incorporated a 1907 provision prohibiting gifts by national banks to political campaigns, he said that BankPAC and similar

Spending in 1970 Primary Campaigns of Selected Wealthy Candidates

Candidate	State	Party	Office Sought	Votes Received	Estimated Expenses	Cost Per Vote	Outcome of Primary
James H. Scheuer	N.Y.	D	Rep.	11,733	$ 130,000	$11.07	*Won*
Richard L. Ottinger	N.Y.	D	Sen.	370,273	1,800,000	4.86	*Won*
Norton Simon	Calif.	R	Sen.	670,106	1,900,000	2.83	Lost
Howard M. Metzenbaum	Ohio	D	Sen.	430,469	812,900	1.89	*Won*
Lloyd M. Bentsen Jr.	Texas	D	Sen.	814,316	800,000	0.98	*Won*

groups had been "set up in a manner designed to skirt the edges of this statute."

News stories published on the Sunday before the election said that BankPAC had made contributions to the campaigns of various House Members running for re-election. Two of the candidates who were defeated, William O. Cowger (R Ky.) and Chester Mize (R Kan.), said the stories had alienated voters. One who survived, Lawrence G. Williams (R Pa.), said he had never asked for, never received, and would have "rejected as unwanted" the $1,500 contribution to him which BankPAC had listed in its reports. The committee reported, Jan. 1, 1971, that $33,500 in contributions had been returned by the recipients.

BankPAC allegedly delayed disbursal of $46,050 until just before the election, so that the contributions making up that sum would not become publicly known until after the election. These contributions were made Oct. 30, the day after the last pre-election report was required. The $46,050 was contributed to nine members of the House Rules Committee (six Democrats, three Republicans), eight members of the House Committee on Ways and Means (five Democrats, three Republicans), the Senate and House Minority Leaders, and others. BankPAC's report of Jan. 1, 1971, brought the Oct. 30 contributions to light.

Receipts of BankPAC in 1970 totaled $205,428; expenditures, $101,100. The committee's largest contributions, $5,000 each, went to two Senators, Harry F. Byrd (I Va.), a member of the Finance Committee, and Harrison A. Williams Jr. (D N.J.), a member of the Banking and Currency Committee. Byrd ran and won as an Independent. Williams was re-elected. BankPAC's box score in the elections was perfect in the Senate, where it supported five winners (three Democrats and two Republicans), and almost perfect in the House, where 19 of the 21 candidates it supported (11 Democrats, 10 Republicans) were victorious.

The House Special Committee to Investigate Campaign Expenditures, headed by Rep. Thomas P. O'Neill Jr. (D Mass.), looked into BankPAC's activities in the 1970 election, especially its contributions sent to candidates who might not have wanted them and could have been harmed by them. The Committee's report of Jan. 11, 1971, referred to "the explosive situation" created by "the naive belief" of BankPAC that all of its donations would be accepted. The report recommended that the 92d Congress (1971-72) consider legislation to deal with possibly unwanted contributions.

Brokers as Contributors

The Securities Industry Campaign Committee, a group similar to BankPAC, conducted financial appeals in the Wall Street community and received contributions from 13 or more stock brokerage firms. At least eight of the firms were recorded as supplying $5,000 or more each. On Nov. 1, the committee reported having raised $62,-000 up to that date. Candidates who received donations of $1,000 or more from the committee included James F. Buckley (Cons N.Y.), elected to the Senate, and two Republican Senate hopefuls who were defeated—Reps. George Bush (Texas) and William C. Cramer (Fla.).

Groups concerned with clean elections raised questions as to the legality of brokerage firms' participation in financing of the 1970 campaign, in view of the fact that Federal law prohibited political contributions by corporations. The Department of Justice said that most of the contributions were legal because the firms were organized as partnerships, not corporations. Dean Witter and Co., one of the firms which made a $5,000 contribution, was a corporation and therefore could not claim innocence on that score. However, a spokesman for Dean Witter said that its contribution had been made from a special partnership bank account kept separate from corporation funds.

Fund-Raising by Ex-White House Aide

Jack A. Gleason, a member of the staff of White House political adviser Harry Dent, conducted a quiet fund-raising operation during the fall months of 1970 on behalf of selected G.O.P. candidates. The candidates he helped apparently were those whose success in the election President Nixon felt was necessary for enactment of the Republican legislative program. Gleason, originally a professional fund-raiser, had assisted Maurice H. Stans when Stans was financial chairman of Nixon's 1968 Presidential campaign. Before or during the 1970 operation, Gleason was removed from the White House payroll.

Headquarters of the Gleason operation was a basement office in an old Washington house about a mile from the White House. From that office, Gleason solicited contributions and distributed funds on a hush-hush basis. His activity came to light when reporters noted his name in campaign financial reports filed by Republican Senatorial candidates J. Glenn Beall Jr. (Md.), who won an upset victory, and William C. Cramer (Fla.), who was

Ambassadors' Contributions to Republican Candidates for Senate, 1970

Ambassador	Accredited to	Recipient	State	Amount
Annenberg, Walter H.	Great Britain	J. Glenn Beall Jr.	Md.	$2,500
Annenberg, Walter H.	Great Britain	George Murphy	Calif.	2,500
Davis, Shelby C.	Switzerland	J. Glenn Beall Jr.	Md.	2,500
Davis Shelby C.	Switzerland	George Bush	Texas	2,500
Davis, Shelby C.	Switzerland	Robert Taft Jr.	Ohio	2,500
Franzheim, Kenneth II	New Zealand	J. Glenn Beall Jr.	Md.	2,500
Franzheim, Kenneth II	New Zealand	William C. Cramer	Fla.	2,500
Franzheim, Kenneth II	New Zealand	Robert Taft Jr.	Ohio	2,500
Gould, Kingdon Jr.	Luxembourg	J. Glenn Beall Jr.	Md.	1,500
Humes, John P.	Austria	J. Glenn Beall Jr.	Md.	2,500
Middendorf, J. Wm. II	Netherlands	J. Glenn Beall Jr.	Md.	1,000
Middendorf, J. Wm. II	Netherlands	George Bush	Texas	500
Moore, John D. J.	Ireland	J. Glenn Beall Jr.	Md.	2,500

defeated. The reports showed donations from contributors whose address was given as "Care of Jack A. Gleason, 1310 19th St., N.W., Washington, D.C."

The Associated Press reported, Dec. 26, that Gleason had refused to discuss his operation with newsmen. He shouted at one of them, according to the wire service: "Get out! You have 55 seconds to leave, or I'll call the cops!" The White House, when queried about Gleason's activities, said only that he was no longer on its payroll.

The mystery was compounded when Rep. Thomas S. Kleppe, losing G.O.P. Senatorial candidate in North Dakota, was quoted as saying of Gleason: "He was part of our working with the White House. I knew he was working on fund-raising." Kleppe had given up his House seat to run against the incumbent Democrat, Quentin N. Burdick. Reportedly, Gleason asked Kleppe's campaign treasurer for the names of committees to which money could be sent for Kleppe's use. Money thereafter flowed from Gleason to about a dozen committees with names such as Friends of Tom Kleppe.

Another recipient of largesse via Gleason was Rep. Richard L. Roudebush, candidate for the Senate from Indiana. Roudebush received $114,000 in contributions channeled through Gleason. The checks were made out to 40 pro-Roudebush committees. Roudebush's bid to unseat Democratic incumbent Vance Hartke was a cliff-hanger, the outcome of which was not known until days after the election. Hartke won.

Seven ambassadors appointed by President Nixon piped at least a part of their 1970 donations to the Republican cause through Gleason. More than half of their reported $28,000 in contributions coordinated by Gleason went to Maryland Senatorial candidate Beall *(see box).*

Activities of Various Special Groups

Offsetting the mainly pro-Republican business and financial committees in 1970 were numbers of mainly pro-Democratic liberal groups, peace groups and others. Biggest spender of these was the National Committee for an Effective Congress, founded in 1947. In 1970, it spent $830,000, helping to elect 35 House winners, including 16 challengers of incumbents. Largest of the peace groups was the Universities National Anti-War Fund, which collected $214,903 and spent $193,199. Of the 45 candidates backed by the fund, 19 were elected.

In House races in which incumbents were running for re-election, non-incumbents ousted them in only 3 percent of the contests. But 35 percent of the non-incumbents supported by the Universities National Anti-War Fund were victorious (eight victories in 23 races). The Fund, created shortly after the start on April 30, 1970, of U.S. military operations in Cambodia, had coordinators on more than 500 campuses. In all, the Fund supported 15 Democratic candidates for the Senate, of whom seven won, and 30 candidates for the House (26 Democrats, three Republicans, and one Liberal), of whom 12 were elected.

A total of 11 new peace groups collected $564,524 and spent $522,224 on behalf of dovish candidates for Congress. Of the five Senate candidates receiving the largest peace group contributions, all lost; of the five House candidates receiving the largest contributions from these groups, two—Parren J. Mitchell (D Md.) and James Abourezk (D S.D.)—were elected. The Peace Commencement Fund, which had former Attorney General Ramsey Clark and the Rev. William Sloane Coffin on its advisory board, collected $75,133 and spent $74,904. A part of the contributions came from graduating students who, instead of wearing caps and gowns, sent the amount of the rental fee to the Fund.

Labor groups, operating under loopholes in the Federal election laws, spent substantial sums in the 1970 campaign. As of Oct. 29, the AFL-CIO's Committee on Political Education had contributed $988,587, virtually all of it to the campaign funds of liberal Democrats. The Seafarers' International Union, which was under indictment for irregularities in 1968 campaign financing, reported expenditures of $399,341; the United Steelworkers' International Fund, $298,800; one group of the International Association of Machinists, $291,371; another Machinists group, $276,049.

Balancing the labor groups' contributions to liberal candidates were contributions to conservatives by national groups with fewer but more affluent members. Among these was the American Medical Political Action Committee, which had loose ties with the American Medical Association. AMPAC reported income in 1970 totaling $447,309 and expenditures of $666,005. As recipients of its campaign contributions, AMPAC listed only its state affiliates, without showing to what candidates the affiliates donated the funds received from AMPAC.

Filing of Financial Reports

Pre-Election Reports. Candidates and campaign committees are required under the law to file financial reports not later than 10 days before the election and not later than 30 days after the election. A large proportion of the 987 candidates who were running for seats in the House in 1970 failed to file reports by the pre-election deadline, Oct. 24. Among the delinquents were two incumbents who won re-election to the House, Reps. Harold D. Donohue (D Mass.) and Hastings Keith (R Mass.). New Representatives-elect who were delinquent included Bella Abzug (D N.Y.), Herman Badillo (D N.Y.), Charles J. Carney (D Ohio), Louise Day Hicks (D Mass.) and K. Gunn McKay (D Utah).

The relative numbers of candidates who failed to meet the Oct. 24 deadline were especially high in New Jersey and New York. In New Jersey, unsuccessful candidates for the Senate and the House who were delinquent included more than half of those who ran. In New York, 13 of 36 candidates for the House did not file reports by Oct. 24. The proportion of those in other states who did not meet the Oct. 24 deadline was lower but substantial. In Indiana, four of 10 candidates for the House were delinquent; in Michigan, four of 19.

One case of delinquency was intended as a protest against loopholes in the reporting requirements. Dennis J. Morrisseau, candidate of the left-wing Liberal Union Party for Vermont's sole seat in the House of Representatives, wrote to W. Pat Jennings, Clerk of the House, that he would not file the report required by the Federal Corrupt Practices Act. He declined, he said, to fulfill the "empty procedure" set forth in the law, but he added: "I have obeyed the substance of the law in every respect." Morrisseau sent a copy of his letter to Attorney General John N. Mitchell. No steps were taken to prosecute Morrisseau, who was defeated in the election.

A possibly delinquent political committee was the right-wing American Security Council, which reportedly spent $150,000 in 1970 to oppose the election bids of liberal candidates, including Senators Charles E. Goodell (R N.Y.) and Joseph D. Tydings (D Md.), who were defeated, and William Proxmire (D Wis.) and Philip A. Hart (D Mich.), who were re-elected. The Federal Corrupt Practices Act requires financial reports from organizations which accept contributions or make expenditures for the purpose of influencing the outcome of elections. However, John M. Fisher, former F.B.I. agent who is president of the American Security Council, said in October that his organization was engaged in "educational activity" and therefore was not required to file reports under the Act.

Post-Election Reports. Post-election reports were due by December 3, 1970. As of Dec. 9, the Clerk of the House had not received such reports from two winning candidates and 150 defeated candidates. The delinquent winners were Reps. Chet Holifield (D Calif.) and Ray J. Madden (D Ind.), both 28-year Members of the House. In the 35 Senate races, the only winner who was late in filing a report with the Secretary of the Senate was James L. Buckley (Con N.Y.). A considerable number of losing Senatorial candidates also filed late.

The Federal Corrupt Practices Act sets a maximum penalty of one year in prison, a fine of $1,000, or both, for violators. There never have been any convictions in Federal courts for failure to file a campaign financial report. On Jan. 11, 1971, the House Special Committee to Investigate Campaign Expenditures recommended to House Clerk W. Pat Jennings that he transmit to the Attorney General "the names of all those candidates who have failed to file pre-election and post-election statements as of this date." The recommendation did not apply to any re-elected or newly elected Members, since all of them by then had filed reports, although some were late.

Jennings complied with the Committee's recommendation. The Department of Justice, however, decided in February 1971 not to institute any prosecutions on the basis of his list. The reason given was that a Justice Department warning of the risk of prosecution in the event of delinquency had been directed to political committees, whereas the Jennings list was a list of candidates.

Where the Money Comes From

A staff writer for *Business Week* remarked in the issue of Oct. 10, 1970, that "Money is only one ingredient in a candidate's campaign kit, but it is far ahead of whatever is second." In addition to being the pivotal factor in a candidate's kit, money is also chronologically the No. One problem. Before other questions about a campaign can be taken up, someone must know the answer to the question "Where will the cash come from?"

Contributors to Political Campaigns

Alexander Heard wrote in 1960: "Contrary to frequent assertion, American campaign monies are *not* supplied solely by a handful of fat cats. Many millions of people now give to politics. Even those who give several hundred dollars each number in the tens of thousands." However, of adults interviewed at various times in the 1950s and 1960s by the University of Michigan Survey Research Center, only 4 to 12 percent said they had contributed funds to a candidate or a political party. Sen. Joseph D. Tydings (D Md.), defeated for re-election in 1970, once estimated that 90 percent of campaign funds were donated by 1 percent of the population. Because "most mass fund appeals are essentially failures," as David Adamany has pointed out, political managers rely primarily on large gifts from relatively few contributors."

Many individual donors associated with big business, especially with corporations that sell goods or services to the Federal Government, preferred in 1968 to make

Top 10 Political Contributors in 1968

Contributor	Background	Amounts given to Republicans	Democrats
W. Clement Stone	Chicago insurance multimillionaire	$148,916*	
Jack J. Dreyfus Jr.	Former board chairman of investment fund	76,000	$ 63,000
Max M. Fisher	Detroit oil executive and industrialist	105,000	
Rella Factor	Wife of John (Jake the Barber) Factor, who served six years in jail for mail fraud.		100,000
Henry Salvatore	Los Angeles oil executive	95,000	
Margery F. Russell	Daughter of Oregon department store magnate	**	
Mary Lasker	Widow of advertising executive Albert D. Lasker		69,400
J. Howard Pew	Board chairman of Sun Oil Co.	63,834	
Elmer H. Bobst	Executive of Warner-Lambert Pharmaceuticals	63,000	
Richard K. Mellon	Pittsburgh banker	62,000	

*Stone told reporters in January 1971 that he had also given more than $500,000 earmarked for the Nixon-Agnew campaign and that his political contributions to Nixon supporters in 1970 totaled almost $1 million.

**Contributions of $94,613 were made to promote the campaign of ultraconservative Walter S. Blake for election as Oregon's superintendent of schools. Blake was defeated.

SOURCES: Herbert E. Alexander and Caroline D. Jones (eds.), *Political Contributors of $500 or More in 1968*

(Citizens' Research Foundation, 1971).

their campaign contributions to Republicans. A Citizens' Research Foundation study of contributions that year by executives of 49 large companies in the defense, space, and nuclear industries showed that they favored Republicans over Democrats by almost six to one. Eleven officers and directors of Litton Industries gave $151,000 to the Republicans and nothing to the Democrats, according to the study.

Contributions to political campaigns by big business or big labor tend to arouse criticism in many quarters. Jeremiah D. Lambert observed in the December 1965 *New York University Law Review* that "Americans, although extolling wide popular participation in politics, distrust organized and effective political action." The Federal legislation prohibiting direct contributions by corporations, national banks and labor unions is often considered primarily an effort to prevent corruption. But Heard has suggested that "The attempts to regulate the role of corporations and labor organizations in politics come largely from their antagonists."

It is not always clear whether the pertinent laws prohibit or allow various forms of corporation or labor assistance in campaign financing. Leland Hazard, professor of industrial administration and law at the Carnegie Institute of Technology, gave examples, in an article in the February 1960 *Atlantic Monthly:*

"Suppose that a corporation or a union takes a full-page advertisement in a newspaper to state its views on inflation. Such an expenditure is lawful. Congress could not legislate to the contrary because the First Amendment guarantees free speech. But suppose that the corporation or union should want to run the same advertisement and add, 'Congressman X by his record has well exemplified these views, and we hope that he will be re-elected.' The law forbids such an expenditure. The Supreme Court has not yet said whether this restriction also denies free speech."

Corporations and Campaigns

The Tillman Act of Jan. 26, 1907, laid a ban on corporation gifts of money to candidates for Federal elective offices or to committees supporting the candidates. The ban was incorporated in the Federal Corrupt Practices Act of Feb. 28, 1925, which broadened the prohibition to cover contributions of "anything of value." Former President Eisenhower pointed out in the *Reader's Digest,* January 1968, that corporations nevertheless "apply a variety of subterfuges: they lend office equipment and the services of their public relations experts and lawyers; they make it easy, through bonuses and expense accounts, for executives to contribute substantial sums; and they buy advertising space at ridiculously high rates in political pamphlets and program brochures."

Some corporations, prior to 1966, not only placed advertisements in political publications but also deducted the cost of the advertisements as business expenses in their income-tax returns. They paid as much as $15,000 a page for such advertisements. Congress cut the ground out from under this practice by providing in an Act of March 15, 1966, that "No deduction...shall be allowed for any amount paid or incurred for...advertising in a convention program of a political party, or in any other publication if any part of the proceeds of such publication directly or indirectly inures (or is intended to inure) to or for the use of a political party or a political candidate."

Business lobby groups, in addition to businesses themselves, have been a source of campaign funds. The

American Trucking Association in 1966-68 reportedly gave at least $25,000 in campaign contributions to key members of Congressional committees concerned with a bill that the association favored. The bill would have allowed bigger and heavier trucks to operate on the nation's Interstate Highway System. After passing the Senate, the bill foundered in the House because of adverse publicity.

Prosecution of Corporations. In the 62 years following enactment of the 1907 law on campaign financing, the Department of Justice prosecuted only three business concerns for violation of the ban on political gifts by corporations. Then, in the period from May 1969 to January 1970, the Department pressed charges against 14 companies, mostly in California, for violations of the Federal Corrupt Practices Act allegedly committed during the 1968 campaign. The National Brewing Co. of Baltimore and six California companies pleaded guilty and were fined. Others pleaded "no contest" and were fined. One pleaded not guilty and was acquitted. American President Lines and Pacific Far East Lines, both of San Francisco, were fined $50,000 each; other corporations involved were fined smaller amounts. Newsmen made repeated but unsuccessful efforts to learn the names of the candidates, including incumbent members of Congress, who had received the illegal contributions.

Indirect Contributions. To get around the prohibition on political contributions by corporations, the National Association of Manufacturers in 1963 founded the Business-Industry Political Action Committee on the model of the AFL-CIO's Committee on Political Education. BIPAC solicited contributions from individuals in the business world and spent $203,283 in 1964, $294,000 in 1966, $478,675 in 1968, and $498,904 in 1970 in support of business-oriented candidates for Congress. Almost 95 percent of the candidates that BIPAC supported in 1968 were Republicans:

	Republicans	Democrats
Winners		
Senate	12	0
House	70	8
Losers		
Senate	8	0
House	47	1
Totals	137	9

Bad Political Debts. Questions have been raised in recent years as to the legality of a long-standing corporation practice which is tantamount to contributing funds to a candidate or a political committee. The practice involves post-election settlement, by a corporation, of campaign debts, especially those incurred by the loser, at less than 100 cents on the dollar. "Winners pay their debts; losers negotiate theirs," according to an election adage. Hotel bills, debts to airlines for candidates' and newsmen's fares, car rental fees, and telephone bills sometimes are paid off by a loser at 25 to 50 cents on the dollar.

In January 1969, Herbert E. Alexander, director of the Citizens' Research Foundation, commented: "When bills are settled, the corporation is in effect making a form of indirect contribution to the campaign." Others have noted that the Internal Revenue Code prohibits tax deductions for bad debts owed by a political party or a political campaign committee. However, David Ginsberg, former legal counsel of the Democratic National Committee, was quoted in March 1970 to the effect that a corporation could probably win a court test, on a deduction of this kind, by showing that the loss "was incurred in the normal course of business."

Labor and Campaign Contributions

The War Labor Disputes Act of June 25, 1943 (Smith-Connally Act), put labor unions on a par with corporations as to political contributions. One section of the act applied to unions, for the duration of the war, the prohibition enacted in 1907 against campaign contributions by corporations. The Labor-Management Relations (Taft-Hartley) Act of June 23, 1947, made the ban permanent.

Taft-Hartley proscribed all contributions and expenditures by labor unions for candidates for public office, whether the money came from dues or from voluntary donations by members. However, during consideration of the bill in the Senate, Taft said, June 5, 1947: "The prohibition is against labor unions using their members' dues for political purposes." The courts, heeding that statement, have sanctioned political expenditures by unions if the funds are contributed voluntarily by members.

Supreme Court Decisions. Interpretation of the ban on union campaign expenditures came to the fore when the *CIO News,* a weekly publication of the Congress of Industrial Organizations, in its issue of July 14, 1947, urged members to vote for a particular candidate for Congress in a special election. Federal authorities obtained an indictment of the C.I.O. on a charge that it had violated the Taft-Hartley ban. The U.S. District Court for the District of Columbia dismissed the case on the ground that the ban was incompatible with the First Amendment to the Constitution.

When the case, *United States v. C.I.O.,* was appealed, the Supreme Court took into account on the one hand a statement by Senator Taft, during debate on the bill, that endorsement of a candidate in a union publication, "if it were supported by...union dues,...would be a violation of the law" and, on the other hand, the fact that the *CIO News* was circulated primarily among members of the union.

Justice Stanley F. Reed, delivering the five-to-four opinion of the Court on June 21, 1948, stressed the point that the periodical had no general public circulation. The Court said: "If...(the law) were construed to prohibit the publication, by corporations and unions in the regular course of conducting their affairs, of periodicals advising their members, stockholders, or customers of danger or advantage to their interests from the adoption of measures, or the election to office of men espousing such measures, the gravest doubt would arise in our minds as to its constitutionality" (335 U.S. 106).

Taft-Hartley again required interpretation in connection with the 1954 Congressional elections. During the campaign, the United Automobile Workers sponsored and paid for television broadcasts in Detroit which urged the election of named candidates for the Senate and the House. The main issue raised here was whether the broadcasts were intentionally aimed at the public in general or could be taken as an effective way to reach the union's members. However, the union lawyers also raised the question whether the Act invaded constitutional rights of expression.

Both questions were prominent during the argument of the case, *United States v. U.A.W.*, when it reached the Supreme Court on appeal. The Court's majority, six members, refused to rule on the constitutional issue; but three dissenters—Chief Justice Earl Warren and Justices Hugo L. Black and William O. Douglas—asserted that the law was unconstitutional "as construed and applied" in the U.A.W. case. Justice Felix Frankfurter, delivering the majority opinion, March 11, 1957, said that if the government could prove to the satisfaction of a jury, that a union had spent members' dues, or a corporation had spent stockholders' funds, to influence votes of the general public, violation of the law would have occurred, and the constitutional issue would have to be decided (352 U.S. 567). The case was remanded to the U.S. District Court for the Eastern District of Michigan, where a jury found the union not guilty.

Other Cases. Two methods of easing the impact of Taft-Hartley on labor unions were upheld by the courts in 1960-61. George P. Macdonald described the first method in the April 1969 issue of *Prospectus; A Journal of Law Reform:* "A union member simply signs a card designating part of his dues as voluntarily given.... Since that portion of the dues is then construed as a voluntary contribution, it may be directly contributed to Federal candidates." The U.S. District Court for the Eastern District of Missouri ruled in 1960 that this device did not constitute a violation of the Taft-Hartley Act.

"The authorization card plan works well," Macdonald explained, "because regardless of whether the union member authorizes such use of his dues, that portion of his dues will not be refunded to him. Accordingly, he will see little value in refusing such authorization and thereby possibly incurring the displeasure of his union superiors or peers."

In the second case, a union with several locals held a plebiscite among its members on whether to use union dues to finance partisan political activities. A majority voted in the affirmative, and the union executives considered the vote as transforming the money involved into "voluntary funds." The presiding judge of the U.S. District Court for the District of Alaska said in a decision in 1961 on the legality of this maneuver: "Each union decided by a vote of its membership...first, whether they would contribute and second, how much. Surely, that is voluntary; and that, I think, is the crux of the situation here."

Three officials of the Plumbers and Pipefitters Union, Local 562, St. Louis, were indicted May 9, 1968, on charges of conspiring to make political contributions in the 1964 and 1966 elections in violation of the Taft-Hartley ban. The three were found guilty Sept. 27, 1968, and fined $1,000 each and sentenced to one year in jail. In a similar case, the Seafarers International Union and eight of its officials and employees were indicted in New York City, June 30, 1970. Allegedly illegal contributions of $40,000 to Republican and Democratic campaign committees were cited in the indictment as part of a conspiracy involving campaign donations of $750,000 over a period of years. The contributions were funneled through

the Seafarers Political Activity Donation Committee which, the indictment said, existed only on paper.

COPE's Role in Election Financing

When the A.F.L. and the C.I.O. merged in December 1955, the Committee on Political Education was formed as an amalgamation of the A.F.L.'s Labor League for Political Education and the C.I.O.'s Political Action Committee. COPE's funds, coming directly from the treasuries of the A.F.L.-C.I.O. and its affiliated unions, are used for such nonpartisan activities as voter registration drives, publication of candidates' voting records, and exhibits on campaign issues. Funds made available to COPE through voluntary gifts of union members are spent, legally, to support particular candidates. However, even COPE's political education activities often designedly help one candidate more than his rival or rivals, as in get-out-the-vote drives in districts where pro-labor voters predominate.

COPE in 1964 said that of the candidates it had supported in 1960, 57 percent had been elected; in 1962, 60 percent; and in 1964, 68 percent. In 1966, COPE and other labor groups reportedly contributed more than $1 million to candidates for the Senate and the House, with a high percentage of success. An article in the *American Legion Magazine,* August 1966, estimated that well over 90 per cent of labor union election spending had been aimed to benefit Democratic candidates.

Alexander Heard suggested in 1960 that "Much of the concern over organized labor in politics stems from its novelty." He pointed out: "Business interests long dominated the politics of the nation—which is not to say the intent or the results were either bad or good—and more recently a new type of organized interest has entered the arena....It is more realistic to view the debate over labor's political finances as a struggle for the control of government than as a legal or moral issue."

Fund-Raising Methods

The principal methods by which campaign committees raise funds are indicated by Republican National Committee estimates of its anticipated receipts in 1970 from various sources and activities:

Direct mail appeal to small contributors	$3,200,000
Appeals in newsletters of Republican Congressional Campaign Committees and other special mail appeals	2,600,000
Memberships in Republican Victory Associates ($500 or more) and in RN Associates ($1,000 or more)	2,000,000
March 1970 dinner ($1,000 a plate)	2,000,000
Private luncheons sponsored by Republican Boosters	1,300,000
National Committee's fee (10 percent) for local fund-raising appearances by Vice President Agnew and other Cabinet officers	350,000

Fund-Raising Dinners. A fund-raising dinner is now the most effective tool for extracting a hefty check from a well-to-do voter. Where formerly a prospective donor was invited to a dinner and there subjected to give-'em-hell partisan appeals for a contribution or pledge, his gift now is assured in advance by the sale of expensive tickets of admission. President Eisenhower on Jan. 20, 1956, spoke by closed-circuit TV to 53 banquets held simultaneously in 37 states. Ticket sales netted between $4 million and $5 million for the Republican party.

In the 1960s, techniques for holding political dinners were developed further. President Kennedy's Inaugural Eve Gala in Washington, D.C., grossed $1,250,000. Events which Kennedy attended between his inauguration on Jan. 20, 1961, and the final dinner in Houston the night before his assassination on Nov. 22, 1963, raised more than $10 million for the Democratic party. In the administrations of Presidents Kennedy and Lyndon B. Johnson, those who paid $1,000 a plate at major political dinners were known as members of the President's Club.

In 1965, the Republican Senatorial Campaign Committee drew 800 guests at a $500-a-plate dinner honoring Sen. Everett M. Dirksen (R Ill.), Minority Leader. Net proceeds amounted to $380,000, enough to cover the committee's operations for a year. Rep. Charles E. Bennett (D Fla.) on Dec. 1, 1970, told the House Committee on Standards of Official Conduct: "The cost of political filet mignon has jumped from a $100-a-plate donation only five years ago to currently $1,000 for Republicans and $500 for Democrats."

Campaign committees peddle tickets costing from $25 up for other politically oriented meals—breakfast, brunch and lunch. In addition, there are teas, cocktail parties, bean feeds, and snack parties. Favorite invitees are Washington lobbyists and representatives of trade associations, as well as friendly corporation executives and labor union officials. One Washington-based lobbyist reported more than 200 requests for political contributions in the first nine months of 1970.

Other Fund Raising. Democrats in 1965 published a program booklet called *Toward an Age of Greatness.* Large corporations bought advertising space in the booklet at rates approaching those charged by nationally circulated magazines. Democratic coffers were increased by $600,000.

Republicans met to consider strategy in the face of this innovation. Walter Pincus discussed their dilemma in the April 1966 *Atlantic Monthly:* "The choice between attacking the ethics of the 1965 Democratic book...and producing one of their own was decided on the ground that the money was more useful than making an issue of the book." An Act of Congress approved March 15, 1966, put an end to this practice by making outlays for such advertisements nondeductible in calculating taxable income.

In seeking campaign contributions from individuals, political committees often resort to the psychologically effective device of seeing to it that prospective donors are solicited by persons whom they will want to please. A prospective donor's best customer, for example, may be sent to ask him for a contribution. The desire of the donor to stand well with the solicitor may transcend, as a motive for giving, any tangible favors hoped for from the victory of a political candidate or his party.

Appointment of millionaire members of the party to office has long been another standard technique for inducing political contributions. Cabinet posts and other high offices in the Executive Branch, as well as membership on blue-ribbon commissions, are sometimes awarded in recognition of contributions already made or to encourage future contributions. Jerry Landauer observed in the *Wall Street Journal* of Oct. 30, 1970:

"Mr. Nixon is using another traditional fund-raising device far more effectively than either President Johnson or Kennedy: Appointing big donors to prestigious posts....All told, according to available records, 14 Nixon ambassadorial appointees and their wives contributed at least $300,000 to the G.O.P. in 1968. Early this year, within weeks after taking up his new post in Vienna, Ambassador John P. Humes, formerly a New York attorney, sent home a $3,000 check for this fall's G.O.P. Congressional campaign. More recently, he followed up with $3,000 more."

What the Money Goes For

There are major differences between what campaign money went for in former times and what it goes for now. Bruce L. Felknor wrote in his book *Dirty Politics* in 1966: "Budgets that must include the costs of television time and charter planes are 'regulated' by laws conceived for an era of handbills, coal-burner railroad trips, and two-cent stamps." The video tube and travel also were singled out by the Senate Committee on Finance in its report of Nov. 1, 1967, on S 4890, a bill to authorize Federal subsidization of election campaigns: "Rising campaign costs have been brought about largely by increased use of expensive television time and jet air travel."

Soaring TV Expenditures

John F. Kennedy, in the Nov. 14, 1959, issue of *TV Guide,* discussed the dollar-gobbling use of television in politics: "If all candidates and parties are to have equal access to this essential and decisive campaign medium, without becoming deeply obligated to big financial contributors from the world of business, labor or other major lobbies, then the time has come when a solution must be found for this problem of TV costs." More than a decade later, the country had not yet agreed on a solution. The problem was exacerbated in the 1960s.

The number of spot TV commercials purchased by candidates at all levels rose between the midterm elections of 1962 and 1966 from 94,009 to 154,398. In a 1968 poll by Roper Research Associates, 65 percent of those interviewed said that television was the major source of their information about candidates. Stephen Smith, brother-in-law and top campaign adviser of the late Sen. Robert F. Kennedy, said in August 1968: "More and more, the picture tube is where the ball game is won or lost." This medium ate up more than half of the campaign budgets of 73 percent of the Senators who ran for re-election in 1968.

The quality of the product purchased with money set aside for TV has ranged from the highly imaginative and artistic to the inane and barbarous. Among the better spots in 1970 were those produced for unsuccessful Ohio Senatorial candidate Howard M. Metzenbaum (D) by Charles Guggenheim, Washington filmmaker who had won two Academy Awards and dozens of other prizes. At the other end of the spectrum, some producers showed little regard for standards of taste, credibility or honesty.

Edwin P. Morgan wrote in his syndicated newspaper column, Nov. 7, 1970, that "Distorted saturation spots...

came over the air like a blizzard in the 1970 campaign." Morgan added: "Some reform-minded citizens advocate a total ban on political advertising from the air on the ground that it is a special kind of 'pollution' which wealthy candidates and/or wealthy contributors can use to distort the issues and project false images which a less affluent opposition has little or no chance to answer."

Political Consultants' Fees

Other aspects of a candidate's campaign, as well as TV, require special expertise. Professional campaign management has become one of the most expensive elements in American politics, and questions have been raised as to the effectiveness of political consultant firms. Since only one candidate wins, all the others can conclude that they have sent their consultation money down the drain.

The fees charged in 1970 by political consultant firms were high by any standards. Prominent consultants commanded $500 a day for their full-time personal services. One firm of 12 persons charged $80,000 for planning an average campaign for election to the House of Representatives.

The San Francisco public relations firm of Whitaker and Baker pioneered in political consulting. In 1936, the firm began to accept political accounts. What came to be called Madison Avenue techniques were increasingly applied to politics. During the postwar years, the rising demand of politicians for packaged professional campaign services fostered a large increase in the supply of consultant firms. Several score of them advised candidates in the 1970 campaigns for Federal and state offices.

For a large enough fee, professional experts in this field will manage every step in a campaign from the candidate's announcement of availability to the post-election victory party. They will conduct opinion polls to determine what issues most concern the voters and even what kind of clothes it would be advantageous for the candidate to wear. They will accept responsibility for fund-raising, recruitment of volunteers, research, computerization of voting and demographic patterns of the electorate, preparation of brochures and documentaries, speechwriting, advertising, holding of rallies, trips through neighborhoods, and every other activity needed for an effective campaign.

Other Campaign Services

As long as the campaign continues, dollars flow from campaign headquarters not only for broadcasts and professional expertise, but also for a myriad of campaign services of other kinds. Some expenditures are made directly for equipment, supplies and services. Others take the form of contributions by a national committee to a local committee, or vice versa, to help the recipient committee pay its bills. Some costs are peculiar to the process of running for office; others, such as the Social Security tax on payrolls, are common to any business enterprise.

Rep. Charles E. Bennett (D Fla.) on Dec. 1, 1970, compared the relative importance of diverse campaign techniques and services of the past and the present. He told the House Committee on Standards of Official Conduct (sometimes called the Ethics Committee) that the impact of television had made newspaper advertis-

ing as inconsequential as the old-fashioned clambake or fish fry. He said he bought newspaper advertising only "so they won't get mad at me."

Campaign expenses do not end the night before the election. At campaign headquarters, costs continue throughout election day for rent, utilities and salaries of some campaign employees. There will be expenses also for transporting voters to the polls if not enough persons volunteer for such duty. And poll-watchers may have to be paid.

Poll-watching in some areas is serious business. Elsewhere, the duty is nominal. Richard Boeckel's 1926 study of excessive campaign expenditures quoted the following remarks by Charles C. McGovern, a Pittsburgh politician, on the selection of poll-watchers: "Families with the largest numbers of voters in an election district are given preference....In many instances, they never appear near the polls but accept the certificate and later, after the election, have it cashed. That is pure purchase...of the vote."

Cost vs. Benefits of Campaign Spending

Election day in 1970 brought bad news to some of the campaign's biggest spenders, including Democrats Metzenbaum and Ottinger and Republicans Bush, Cramer, Kleppe and Murphy. Many observers wondered whether elaborate campaigns were worth the cost, when those who spent the most had no assurance of success. Alexander Heard had asserted in 1960 that "The old notion that the side with more money will for that reason win, or will usually do so, is *not* correct." Sen. John O. Pastore (D R.I.) said in 1970 that voters probably wondered why a candidate for the Senate was willing to spend millions of dollars—sometimes unsuccessfully—for a job that paid only $42,500 a year.

Douglas L. Bailey, founder of a Washington advertising agency, attempted in a Sunday newspaper article, Nov. 29, 1970, to sort out what the image-makers can and cannot do in an election campaign. "It simply is not possible," he said, "through television advertising... to sell a dunce as a genius, a clown as a sophisticate or a crook as a man of integrity. A talented TV producer... can accentuate the positive, but he cannot eliminate the negative."

Bailey listed a number of benefits of television campaigning that may tend to justify its high cost. He said that widespread use of this technique (1) is producing an electorate "better informed on public issues" and "more self-confident in judging men and issues"; (2) "has taken a massive amount of political power away from the political bosses and given it to the people" by its tendency to break down "the traditional party loyalties which have so long dominated America's politics"; and (3) "may permit bold leadership." As undesirable consequences, he cited television's tendency "to increase the value of some characteristics which are irrelevant to governing, such as good looks and showmanship," to "give more power to the 'image-makers' than they would otherwise have," and to produce "a fickle electorate, a process which undermines political stability."

Despite the sometimes disappointing results, big campaign spenders can point to a better-than-random correlation between financial outlay and victory. A study made in 1968 showed that in eight of 10 cases the man who

State Regulation of Campaign Financing

State	Coverage Office U.S. Sen.	U.S. Rep.	Election Pri-mary	Gen-eral	Expenditures limited By can-didates	For can-didates	Reports required Receipts By can-didates	By com-mittees	Expenditures By can-didates	By com-mittees
Ala.	x	x	x	x	x		x		x	
Alaska										
Ariz.	x	x	x		x		x	x	x	x
Ark.	x	x	x	x					x	
Calif.	x	x	x	x			x	x	x	x
Colo.	x	x	x	x			x	x	x	x
Conn.	x	x	x	x			x	x	x	x
Del.										
Fla.	x	x	x	x			x	x	x	x
Ga.										
Hawaii	x	x	x	x			x		x	x
Idaho	x	x	x		x				x	
Ill.										
Ind.	x	x	x	x	x	x	x	x	x	x
Iowa	x	x	x	x	x		x	x	x	x
Kan.					x		x	x	x	x
Ky.	x	x	x	x			x	x	x	x
La.										
Maine										
Md.	x	x	x	x	x	x	x	x	x	x
Mass.	x	x	x	x	x		x	x	x	x
Mich.	x	x	x	x	x	x	x	x	x	x
Minn.	x	x	x	x	x		x	x	x	x
Miss.	x	x	x		x	x	x		x	
Mo.	x	x	x	x	x				x	x
Mont.	x	x	x	x	x			x	x	x
Neb.	x	x	x	x					x	x
Nev.										
N.H.	x	x	x	x	x	x	x	x	x	x
N.J.	x	x	x	x	x		x	x	x	x
N.M.	x	x	x	x					x	x
N.Y.	x	x	x	x	x	x	x	x	x	x
N.C.	x	x	x	x				x	x	x
N.D.	x	x	x	x	x	x				
Ohio		x	x	x	x		x	x	x	x
Okla.	x	x	x	x		x	x	x	x	x
Ore.	x	x	x	x	x		x	x	x	x
Pa.										
R.I.										
S.C.	x	x	x	x					x	
S.D.	x	x	x	x	x	x	x	x	x	x
Tenn.	x	x	x	x					x	x
Texas	x	x	x	x		x	x		x	
Utah	x	x	x	x			x	x	x	x
Vt.	x	x	x		x	x			x	
Va.	x	x	x	x	x				x	
Wash.	x	x	x				x		x	
W.Va.	x	x	x	x	x	x	x	x	x	x
Wis.	x	x	x	x	x		x	x	x	x
Wyo.	x	x	x	x	x	x	x	x	x	x
Total	39	40	40	35	25	13	31	29	40	31

SOURCE: Adapted from *Book of the States, 1970-71*, p. 44-47.

spent the most was the winner. Some students of the subject analyze the situation as follows:

• The majority of voters have made up their minds, by the start of the campaign, as to the candidate they will vote for. Unswayed by bids for their favor during the campaign, they will vote for their pre-chosen candidate.

• Voters who are undecided when the campaign begins often hold the balance of power.

• The candidate with the most money cannot be sure of winning to his side enough of the undecided voters to give him victory, but the candidate with less money may be unable to present his case adequately to the crucial group of undecided voters.

Attempts to Regulate Spending

Legislation on campaign spending in the United States has had three aims: (1) to limit and regulate donations made to candidates and their campaign committees; (2) to limit and regulate disbursements made by candidates and their committees, and (3) to inform voters of the amounts and sources of the donations and the amounts, purposes and payees of the disbursements. Disclosure, it was felt, would reveal which candidates, if any, were unduly indebted to interest groups, in time to forewarn the voters.

The first provision of Federal law on campaign financing was incorporated in an Act of March 2, 1867, making naval appropriations for the fiscal year 1868. The final section of the Act read: "And be it further enacted, That no officer or employee of the Government shall require or request any workingman in any navy yard to contribute or pay any money for political purposes, nor shall any workingman be removed or discharged for political opinion; and any officer or employee of the Government who shall offend against the provisions of this section shall be dismissed the service of the United States."

Reports circulated in the following year that at least 75 percent of the money raised by the Republican Congressional Committee came from Federal officeholders. Continuing agitation on this and other aspects of the spoils system in Federal employment led to adoption of the Civil Service Reform Act of Jan. 16, 1883, which authorized establishment of Civil Service rules. One of the rules stated "That no person in the public service is for that reason under any obligation to contribute to any political fund...and that he will not be removed or otherwise prejudiced for refusing to do so." The law made it a crime for any Federal employee to solicit campaign funds from another Federal employee. This law is still on the books (U.S. Code, 1964 Edition, Title 18, Section 602).

State Laws on Campaign Financing

New York State in 1883 enacted a law prohibiting solicitation of campaign contributions from state employees and in 1890 required candidates to file sworn financial statements. California in 1893 limited the total amount of money that could be spent on behalf of a candidate and established a list of legitimate campaign expenses. By 1905, some type of regulation of campaign finances was in effect in 14 states. However, Justice

Felix Frankfurter, delivering the opinion of the Supreme Court, March 11, 1957, in *United States v. U.A.W.* (352 U.S. 571), said: "These state publicity laws either became dead letters or were found to be futile."

Florida in 1951 adopted a law on campaign financing which often is cited as a model. It requires each candidate to appoint a campaign treasurer and to designate a single bank as the campaign depository. Contributions to the campaign must be deposited within 24 hours of receipt, with deposit slips showing the names and addresses of donors and the amounts contributed by each. Candidates are required to publish periodic reports of campaign expenditures during the campaign, every week in the case of candidates for the U.S. Senate and the governorship and every month in the case of candidates for all other offices.

By 1971, eight states regulated campaign financing by imposing limits on spending by candidates and political committees and by requiring candidates and committees to report receipts and expenditures. Twelve states made some, but not all, of the foregoing requirements. Twenty-one other states had less comprehensive regulations. Nine states—Alaska, Delaware, Georgia, Illinois, Louisiana, Maine, Nevada, Pennsylvania, Rhode Island—had no regulations. Prosecutions for violation of state laws on campaign financing have been rare.

Federal Corrupt Practices Laws

Muckrakers in the early part of the 20th century highlighted the influence on Government exerted by big business through unrestrained spending on behalf of favored candidates for public office. President Theodore Roosevelt proposed a drastic remedy. In his annual message of Dec. 5, 1905, on the state of the Union, he told Congress: "All contributions by corporations to any political committee or for any political purpose should be forbidden by law." In his State of the Union message of Dec. 3, 1906, he listed as the first item of Congressional business the passage of a law prohibiting political contributions by corporations.

In response to the President's urging, Congress by the Act of Jan. 26, 1907 (Tillman Act), made it unlawful for a corporation or a national bank to make "a money contribution in connection with any election" of candidates for Federal office. Further regulation of campaign financing was provided by an Act of June 25, 1910. The new law required every political committee "which shall in two or more States influence the result or attempt to influence the result of an election at which Representatives in Congress are to be elected" to file with the Clerk of the House of Representatives, within 30 days after the election, the name and address of each contributor of $100 or more, the name and address of each recipient of $10 or more from the committee, and the total amounts that the committee received and disbursed. Individuals who engaged in similar activities outside the framework of committees were also required to submit such reports.

An act of Aug. 19, 1911, extended the filing requirements to committees influencing Senatorial elections and to require filing of financial reports by candidates for the office of either Senator or Representative. In addition, it required statements to be filed both before and after an election. The most important innovation of the

1911 act was the limitation of the amount that a candidate might spend toward his nomination and election: a candidate for the Senate, no more than $10,000 or, if less, the maximum amount permitted in his state; for the House, no more than $5,000 or, if less, the maximum amount permitted in his state.

The basic Federal Corrupt Practices Act now in effect, the Act of Feb. 28, 1925, limited its restrictions to campaigns for election, in view of the unsettled state at that time of the question whether Congress had power to regulate primary elections. Higher maximum amounts that could legally be spent on campaigns for election to Congress resulted from the 1925 Act. Unless a state law prescribed a smaller amount, the Act set the limit of campaign expenditures at (1) $10,000 for a would-be Senator and $2,500 for a would-be member of the House; or (2) an amount equal to three cents for each vote cast in the last preceding election for the office sought, but not more than $25,000 for the Senate and $5,000 for the House.

The 1925 Act incorporated the existing prohibition of campaign contributions by corporations or national banks, the ban on solicitation of political contributions from Federal employees by candidates or other Federal employees and the requirement that reports be filed on campaign finances. It prohibited giving or offering money to anyone in exchange for his vote. In amending the provisions of the Act of 1907 on contributions, the new law substituted for the word "money" the expression "a gift, subscription, loan, advance, or deposit of money, or anything of value."

The Senate in 1927 barred Senator-elect William S. Vare (R Pa.) from taking his seat after reports indicated that his campaign had cost $785,000. In the same year, the Senate refused to seat Senator-elect Frank L. Smith (R Ill.). More than 80 percent of Smith's campaign fund had come from three men who had a direct interest in a decision of the Illinois Commerce Commission, of which Smith continued to be a member throughout the campaign. One of the three donors was Samuel Insull, owner of a controlling interest in a network of utility companies.

In 1934, a case reached the Supreme Court which required the Court to rule on, among other things, the constitutionality of the requirement in the 1925 Act that lists and amounts of campaign contributions and expenditures be filed publicly. The case, *Burroughs and Cannon v. United States,* involved primarily the applicability of the Act to the election of Presidential electors. Justice George Sutherland on Jan. 8, 1934, delivered the opinion of the Court. Applicability of the Act to Presidential campaigns was upheld. The decision included the following statement on disclosure: "Congress reached the conclusion that public disclosure of political contributions, together with the names of contributors and other details, would tend to prevent the corrupt use of money to affect elections. The verity of this conclusion reasonably cannot be denied" (290 U.S. 548).

Clean Politics and Later Acts

The act of Aug. 2, 1939 (Hatch Act, also called the Clean Politics Act), affected campaign financing in only a secondary way. It barred collection of political contributions from persons receiving relief funds provided by the Federal Government. But an amendment to the Hatch Act, approved July 19, 1940, made three significant additions to legislation on campaign financing. It forbade individuals or business concerns doing work for the Federal Government under contract to contribute to any political committee or candidate. It asserted the right of Congress to regulate primary elections for the nomination of candidates for Federal offices and made it unlawful for anyone to contribute more than $5,000 "during any calendar year, or in connection with any campaign for nomination or election, to or on behalf of any candidate for an elective Federal office." However, the Act specifically exempted from this limitation "contributions made to or by a state or local committee." The 1940 amendment also placed a ceiling of $3 million in a calendar year on expenditures by a political committee operating in two or more states. Wartime legislation in 1943 temporarily, and the Taft-Hartley Act of 1947 permanently, as noted, forbade labor unions to contribute to political campaigns.

Proponents of governmental subsidization of election campaigns appeared to have won a major victory in 1966. An act approved Nov. 13 of that year authorized any individual paying Federal income tax to direct that $1 of the tax due in any year be paid into a Presidential Election Campaign Fund. The fund, to be set up in the U.S. Treasury, was to disburse its receipts, on a proportional basis, among political parties whose Presidential candidates had received 5 million or more votes in the preceding Presidential election.

However, an act of June 13 of the following year provided that "Funds which become available under the Presidential Election Campaign Fund Act of 1966 shall be appropriated and disbursed only after the adoption by law of guidelines governing their distribution." As Congress never adopted any guidelines, the 1966 act became a dead letter.

Financing of Primary Campaigns. Application of Federal laws on campaign financing to primary elections has made a complete circuit on the wheel of judicial and legislative fortune. The act of 1911 limiting campaign expenditures in Congressional elections covered primaries as well as general elections. However, the Supreme Court in the Newberry case of 1921 (256 U.S. 232) struck down the application of the law to primaries, on the ground that the power the Constitution gave Congress to regulate the "manner of holding election" did not extend to party primaries and conventions. The Federal Corrupt Practices Act of 1925 exempted primaries from its operation.

The Hatch Act amendments of 1940, as noted, made primaries again subject to Federal restrictions on campaign contributions despite the Newberry decision. This new legislation was upheld in 1941, when the Supreme Court handed down its decision in *United States v. Classic et al.* (313 U.S. 299), which reversed the Newberry decision. The *Classic* decision was confirmed by the Supreme Court in 1944 in *Smith v. Allwright* (321 U.S. 649). When the Taft-Hartley Act was adopted in 1947, its prohibition of political contributions by corporations, national banks and labor organizations was phrased so as to cover primaries as well as general elections.

Enforcement Efforts

In the six decades from 1907 to 1968, the Tillman Act and later legislation on campaign financing was rarely enforced. Alexander Heard wrote in 1960 that the prohibition in the Federal Corrupt Practices Act of direct purchases of goods or advertising for the benefit of a candidate was "manifestly violated right and left"; that the prohibition of campaign contributions by Federal contractors "goes ignored"; and that the prohibition of loans to candidates by banks was "disregarded." Then, in the closing years of the 1960s, Washington's attitude toward enforcement of the Federal Corrupt Practices Act seemed to change. The Nixon Administration successfully pressed charges in 1969 against corporations (mostly in California) that had contributed campaign money in 1968. *(See Corporations and Campaigns above)*

Another form of violation, failure to report or false reporting under the Corrupt Practices Act, was ignored until 1968, despite the fact that newsmen repeatedly uncovered instances of failure to file reports or the filing of incomplete reports. Attorney General Herbert Brownell in 1954 stated as the position of the Department of Justice that the initiative in such cases rested with the Secretary of the Senate and the Clerk of the House.

Public interest in this form of violation grew during the 1960s. When 54 House candidates in the 1962 election failed to file financial reports, Congressional Quarterly asked the Department of Justice whether it would prosecute the delinquents. The Department on Nov. 19, 1963, replied that its policy remained as before—"not to institute investigations into possible violations in the absence of a request from the Clerk of the House of Representatives or the Secretary of the Senate."

Secretaries of the Senate and Clerks of the House for many years winked at violations of the legal requirement that candidates and supporting committees periodically file with them detailed statements of contributions received and disbursements made. Suddenly, the situation changed. W. Pat Jennings, a former Member of the House of Representatives (D Va., 1955-66), was elected Clerk of the House in 1967. In 1968, he broke precedent by sending to the Department of Justice a list of 21 fund-raising committees (20 Republican, one Democratic) with a notation that their treasurers had not complied with "the time requirement as set forth in the Federal Corrupt Practices Act."

The Department of Justice, however, declined to press charges against the committees. In explanation, it said the violators had not been adequately warned of possible prosecution.

Jennings continued his one-man crusade in 1969. In January of that year, he sent to the Justice Department a list of 107 candidates in the 1968 Congressional elections who had failed to file the required financial reports or had missed the post-election deadline of Dec. 5, 1968, for filing final reports. The names of the 107 delinquents were not released, and the Department of Justice did not institute proceedings against them. Reportedly, no incumbents were among the 107 candidates involved.

Assistant Attorney General Will Wilson, in a letter of May 1970 to Members of Congress who had inquired, said that fair play required the Department of Justice to notify candidates and committees in advance of the possibility of prosecution. This requirement was soon fulfilled. A Department of Justice spokesman on July 16, 1970, said the Criminal Division considered that by then those involved had been sufficiently warned of the possibility of prosecution. He indicated that the Department of Justice was ready to undertake prosecutions, provided that in the Department's judgment its own investigations of certified violations warranted court action. However, nothing happened.

Jennings sent a list of delinquents to the Attorney General early in 1971. In mid-February, a Justice Department spokesman first said, "We don't know what we're going to do" about these cases and later added that no prosecutions were contemplated since the 1970 warning had applied to "campaign committees, not candidates," whereas Jennings' list was a list of candidates.

Loopholes in the Legislation

It became common knowledge long ago that the limitations seemingly imposed by campaign financing legislation do not limit, that the prohibitions do not prohibit and that the restrictions do not restrict. Louise Overacker wrote in 1946: "The Hatch Act limitations were included in an act which purported to 'Prohibit Pernicious Political Practices.' One might...parody it to read: 'An Act to *Promote* Pernicious Political Activities.' It defeats its own purpose by encouraging decentralization, evasion and concealment."

Cyrus Eaton appeared before the Senate Subcommittee on Privileges and Elections on March 6, 1952, to explain his gift of $30,000 to an Ohio political committee through intermediaries. Eaton offered no apology for using this loophole in the legal limits on campaign donations by individuals. He said: "It is a long-established custom in Ohio to do it that way."

Rep. James C. Wright Jr. (D Texas), testifying July 21, 1966, before the Subcommittee on Elections of the House Administration Committee, said that legislation on campaign financing was "intentionally evaded by almost every candidate." He added: "I dare say there is not a Member of Congress, myself included, who has not knowingly evaded its purpose in one way or another." If Congress did not act to strengthen the legislation, he said, it would "confirm the shadowy suspicion held by many that Congress is content with the gaping loopholes which make a mockery of our ancient and inadequate campaign spending laws."

An anonymous note in the April 1967 *University of Pennsylvania Law Review* described the "regulation of political finance today" as "more loophole than legislation." This description was echoed in a message which President Johnson sent to Congress May 25, 1967, proposing election reforms. The message said of the Federal Corrupt Practices Act and the Hatch Act: "Inadequate in their scope when enacted, they are now obsolete. More loophole than law, they invite evasion and circumvention."

The citizens' lobby Common Cause, as noted, took legal action on Jan. 11, 1971, to plug loopholes in the Corrupt Practices Act by filing suit in the U.S. District Court for the District of Columbia against the Democratic and Republican National Committees and the Conservative Party of New York State, which had successfully supported candidates for Federal offices in the

November 1970 elections. The suit asked the court to declare illegal, and order a stop to, the giving of large sums by an individual in the names of his wife and children and the setting up of more than one political committee for a single candidate.

Loopholes Available to Donors

The Federal Corrupt Practices Act requires the treasurer of a political committee active in two or more states to report at specified times the name and address of every donor of $100 or more to a campaign. To evade such recording, a donor can give less than $100 to each of numerous committees supporting the candidate of his choice. A Senate subcommittee in 1956 checked the contributions of sums between $50 and $99.99 to one committee. It found that, of 97 contributions in that range, 88 were over $99, including 57 that were exactly $99.99.

Members of the same family can legally contribute up to $5,000 each. A wealthy donor wanting to give more than $5,000 to a candidate or a political committee can privately subsidize gifts by his relatives. Each such subsidized gift can amount to $5,000. In this way, the donor can arrange for his brothers, sisters, uncles, aunts, wife and children to present $5,000 gifts to the favored candidate or committee.

Corporations can skirt the prohibition of contributions to a political campaign by giving bonuses or salary increases to executives in the expectation that the executives as individuals will make corresponding political contributions of the kind the corporation favors. A *Business Week* staffer wrote in the magazine's issue of Nov. 8, 1969: "This kind of sub rosa violation...is almost impossible to prove." In addition, corporations can lend billboards, office furniture, equipment, mailing lists and airplanes to candidates or political committees. If a loan of this kind is deemed a violation of the letter of the law, the corporation can rent these items to a candidate or committee, instead of lending them, and then write off the rental fee as uncollectible.

Labor unions can contribute to a candidate or political committee funds collected from members apart from dues. They can use such funds also for nonpartisan registration and voting drives even if the drives are confined to precincts loaded with voters who favor pro-union candidates. They can emphasize the pro-union or anti-union views of candidates in publications impartially presenting voting records and published statements of candidates. And by nuances, they can introduce a partisan tinge into informational radio and television broadcasts during a campaign.

Loopholes Available to Candidates

Federal or state limitations on the amount of money a candidate may knowingly receive or spend are easily evaded. Former President Eisenhower, in his 1968 *Reader's Digest* article, wrote: "Another gaping loophole in the 1925 law results from the phrase referring to the candidates' 'knowledge or consent.' A Congressional candidate simply makes sure that he 'knows nothing' about the activities created by his backers. One committee, for example, may pay for the use of 100 billboards, but the candidate—and this must be quite a feat—never 'sees' them as he campaigns through his district."

The loophole opened by the law's phrase "knowledge or consent" (U.S. Code, 1964 Edition, Title 2, Section 246; see Appendix) enables numerous candidates to report that they received and spent not one cent on their campaigns. In 1964, four Senators reported that their campaign books showed zero receipts and zero expenditures. They were Vance Hartke (D Ind.), Roman L. Hruska (R Neb.), Edmund S. Muskie (D Maine) and John C. Stennis (D Miss.).

Four years later, when Sen. George McGovern (D S.D.) reported no receipts or expenditures, his executive assistant, George V. Cunningham, said: "We are very careful to make sure that Sen. McGovern never sees the campaign receipts." Two new Senators elected in 1968—William B. Saxbe (R Ohio) and Richard S. Schweiker (R Pa.)—reported general-election expenditures of $769,614 and $664,614, respectively, to their state authorities but expenditures of only $20,962 and $5,736, respectively, to the Secretary of the Senate.

The credibility gap fostered by the "knowledge or consent" loophole is further widened by the fact that the Federal Corrupt Practices Act applies only to political committees operating in two or more states. If a committee operates in one state only and is not a subdivision of a national committee, the law does not apply. If a committee operates in the District of Columbia only, receiving funds there and mailing checks to candidates in a single state, the law does not cover it. Rep. Thomas P. O'Neill Jr. (D Mass.), chairman of the House Special Committee to Investigate Campaign Expenditures, used a District of Columbia committee as the recipient of contributions for his 1970 campaign. The Commonwealth of Massachusetts requires that committees operating there disclose the names of contributors.

Limits on the expenditures that a political committee may make are evaded by establishing more than one committee and apportioning receipts and expenditures among them so that no one committee exceeds the limit. Since the law limits annual spending by a political committee to $3 million, the major parties form committees under various names, each of which is free to spend up to $3 million.

Loopholes in State Laws. A law on campaign finances adopted in Massachusetts in 1962 was hailed as uncommonly tough. It limited the number of committees supporting a candidate to three. The law also required that each committee have a bank account, that the bank report money deposited in the account or paid out from it, and that names and addresses of donors of more than $25, and the addresses of persons whose bills were paid, be made public. Despite the supposed stringency of the law, when Edward M. Kennedy in 1964 reported expenditures of $100,292.45 for his successful bid for the Democratic nomination for the U.S. Senate, newspapers estimated that his staff, billboard, television and other expenses amounted to 10 times that sum.

Some state laws exempt from the ceilings and reporting requirements money spent directly on publicity, such as the costs of television and radio spots, advertisements in newspapers and handbills and booklets. Exemptions apply in other states to renting of halls for meetings, hiring of publicity agents and conveyance of voters to and from the polls. Some states require reports from candidates but not committees, or reports on receipts but not expenditures. Places where reports are to be filed, such as the headquarters of the candidate's party, or the place "where the candidate resides," often constitute obstruction rather than promotion of disclosure.

Rulings on Equal Broadcast Time

Regulation of campaign expenditures entails, among other things, decisions on who may compete for purchase of television time and under what conditions such competition may occur. The basic legislation on the subject, Section 315 (a) of the Communications Act of 1934, apparently raised more questions than it answered. Section 315 (a) provided: "If any licensee shall permit any person who is a legally qualified candidate for any public office to use a broadcasting station, he shall afford equal opportunities to all other such candidates for that office in the use of such broadcasting station."

In 1959, Lar Daly, write-in candidate for Mayor of Chicago, made a demand on Chicago television stations which, if complied with, would have provided him with exposure on the tube without any expenditure on his part. He said that under the Act of 1934 he was entitled to receive as much time on Chicago news broadcasts as was given to Democratic and Republican candidates. He based his demand on a 20-second news shot of Mayor Richard J. Daley, Democratic candidate for re-election, greeting a foreign dignitary, and a one-minute news report on Daley's opening of the March of Dimes campaign. On Feb. 19, 1959, the Federal Communications Commission, in a surprise decision, ruled by a vote of four to three that Daly's demand was justified.

The Commission's application of the equal-time provision to news broadcasts aroused a wave of protests. President Eisenhower on March 19, 1959, called the ruling "ridiculous." Congress, by an act of Sept. 14, 1959, nullified the Commission's ruling. The act inserted, at the end of Section 315 (a), the words: "Appearance by a legally qualified candidate on any (1) bona fide newscast, (2) bona fide news interview, (3) bona fide news documentary (if the appearance of the candidate is incidental to the presentation of the subject or subjects covered by the news documentary), or (4) on-the-spot coverage of bona fide news events (including but not limited to political conventions and activities incidental thereto), shall not be deemed to be use of a broadcasting station within the meaning of this subsection."

Equal-Time Provision in the 1960s. The equal-time provision of the Act of 1934 was suspended in part by an act of Aug. 24, 1960, to make possible a series of television debates between the 1960 Presidential candidates of the two major parties, John F. Kennedy (D) and Richard M. Nixon (R). Congress also considered but did not enact a proposal to suspend Section 315 (a) for the period of the 1962 Congressional campaign. The President's Commission on Campaign Costs recommended in 1962 that Congress allow broadcasters to provide equal time to Presidential and Congressional candidates of the major parties without obligating themselves to provide comparable time to candidates of minor parties. Congress took no definitive action on the recommendation.

During the Senate hearings on the Commission's recommendations, LeRoy Collins, president of the National Association of Broadcasters, said that the equal-opportunities provision had failed "because it assumes that all candidates are bona fide contenders for public office and because it assumes further that a mathematical formula can be substituted for journalistic judgment." But Lawrence Speiser, Washington director of the American Civil Liberties Union, asserted that permanent suspension of the equal-time clause would give the two major parties "a perpetual monopoly" over television.

The Senate and the House in 1964 passed different bills to make possible a television debate between the two major Presidential contenders of that year, President Johnson and Sen. Barry Goldwater (R Ariz.). Although a conference committee reconciled the two bills, the measure was allowed to die, because President Johnson was not inclined to appear with Senator Goldwater on a basis which implied equality of status for the incumbent and the challenger. Similarly, in 1968 there was no television debate between Presidential candidates Richard M. Nixon and Hubert H. Humphrey, partly because the Nixon camp had unpleasant memories of the Kennedy-Nixon television debates of 1960.

The Fair Campaign Practices Committee sponsored a conference in Washington, Oct. 13-14, 1965, on politics and television. A principal conference topic was the complaint of broadcast stations that if they gave free broadcasting time to candidates of major parties, they would be swamped with demands from minor parties for equal amounts of time for their candidates. Hyman H. Goldin, staff member of the Carnegie Commission on Educational Television, disputed that prediction, pointing out that (1) in 20 of the 34 states with Senatorial elections in 1964 there were no minor-party candidates, and (2) the proportion of TV stations that reported campaign-period sustaining time—time for which a station receives no fee—was the same, 29 percent, in the 14 states with minor-party candidates and in the 20 states without them.

Campaigns and First Amendment

Restrictions imposed on campaign financing, if too severe, may trespass on the constitutional rights of individuals. Labor union attorneys in 1956 cited the First Amendment and other provisions of the Constitution in their brief submitted to the Supreme Court in *United States v. U.A.W.* The Department of Justice charged that the U.A.W. had violated the ban on union contributions to election campaigns, as set forth in the U.S. Code, Title 18, Section 610. The alleged violation consisted of an indication, in the union's publicity media, of its preference for a particular election outcome. The union's brief said, "If such an expenditure is prohibited by 18 U.S.C. 610, the statute violates the provisions of the Constitution of the United States in that the statute:

(i) abridges freedom of speech and of the press and the right peaceably to assembly and to petition;

(ii) abridges the right to choose Senators and Representatives granted by Article I, Section 2, and the Seventeenth Amendment;

Proposals to Reform Campaign Financing, 1951-69

Date	Source	Proposal	Outcome
1951, Jan. 3	House Special Committee to Investigate Campaign Expenditures	Raise limits on campaign expenditures; include primaries in the regulations; prohibit committees from receiving and spending funds without the candidate's authorization.	No floor action
1953, Jan. 24	Senate Rules Subcommittee on Elections	Raise limits on campaign expenditures.	S 2081 introduced; no floor action
1955, June 22	Senate Rules and Administration Committee	Raise limits on campaign expenditures and require all committees (not only those active in two or more states) to report.	No floor action
1956, April 7	Senate Select Committee	Consider requiring (1) each candidate to designate a single fiscal agent, who would report fully on campaign financing, and (2) each contributor of more than $5,000 to file a detailed accounting.	No floor action
1957, Aug. 2	Senate Rules and Administration Committee	Raise limits on campaign expenditures.	No floor action
1960, Jan. 25	Senate	Raise limits on campaign expenditures (S 2436 passed Senate).	No House action
1961, April 12	Five Senators	Provide up to one-half of a candidate's broadcasting expenses from Government funds (S 1555, introduced by Sen. Maurine B. Neuberger, D Ore., and four cosponsors).	No floor action
1961, Sept. 15	Senate	Raise limits on campaign expenditures (S 2426 passed Senate).	No House action
1962, April 18	President's Commission on Campaign Costs	Eliminate limits on campaign contributions and expenditures; give income tax credit for small political contributions; establish agency to enforce regulations.	No floor action
1963, April 30	President Kennedy	Give income tax credit for small political contributions.	No floor action
1964, Jan. 28	Senate Finance Committee	Give income tax credit for small political contributions.	Dropped in conference committee considering tax bill approved Feb. 26, 1964.
1965, Oct. 12	Sen. John J. Williams (R Del.)	Prohibit tax deductions for advertisements in political publications.	Included as amendment to excise-tax bill approved March 15, 1966.
1966, Jan. 12	President Johnson	Give income tax credit for small political contributions; raise limits on campaign expenditures; apply regulations to state and local committees; attach severe penalties to violations of disclosure requirements.	Senate Rules Committee reported weaker bill, and House Administration Committee reported stronger bill; no floor action in either case.
1967, June 28	Reps. Robert T. Ashmore (D S.C.) and Charles E. Goodell (R N.Y.)	Apply regulations to primaries and state committees and eliminate restrictions on campaign expenditures.	Reported by subcommittee; stalled in Administration Committee.
1967, Sept. 12	Senate	Apply regulations to primaries and intrastate committees and eliminate restrictions on campaign expenditures (S 1880 passed Senate).	No House action
1967, Nov. 1	Senate Finance Committee	Add to a routine House-passed bill, HR 4890, a rider which would permit income tax credits for campaign contributions and provide Federal subsidies for Presidential and Senatorial campaigns.	No floor action
1969, Jan. 17	Outgoing Attorney General Ramsey Clark	Apply reporting requirements to state committees; limit contributions; eliminate limits on campaign expenditures; require fuller reporting; establish bipartisan enforcement agency.	No floor action

SOURCE: *Congress and the Nation, Vol. II, 1965-1968* (publication of Congressional Quarterly), pp. 443-446, and the *Congressional Record*.

(iii) creates an arbitrary and unlawful classification and discriminates against labor organizations in violation of the Fifth Amendment, and

(iv) is vague and indefinite and fails to provide a reasonably ascertainable standard of guilt in violation of the Fifth and Sixth Amendments" (352 U.S. 589-590).

The Supreme Court on March 11, 1957, remanded the case to a lower court for further finding of facts. But Justice William O. Douglas delivered a dissenting opinion, in which Chief Justice Earl Warren and Justice Hugo L. Black joined. The dissenting opinion said: "Until today, political speech has never been considered a crime....It is startling to learn that a union spokesman or the spokesman for a corporate interest has fewer constitutional rights when he talks to the public than when he talks to members of his group....The First Amendment... protects the impassioned plea of the orator as much as the quiet publication of the tabulations of the statistician or economist."

Three years later, Alexander Heard cited some of the fallout effects of another restriction on campaign financing—the requirement that political contributions be made public: "Many individuals fear reprisals if their political preferences become known....Many contributors protest that to give publicly precludes their having normal business relationships with government and normal personal relations with politicians."

Heard presented the viewpoint of the opposing sides. On the one hand, he said: "Donors with...special stakes in politics realize that if their gifts become known, they, and the recipients, would be harpooned." On the other hand: "Those who advocate full disclosure argue that any gift unable to stand the light of day should not be made. Or, at least, persons making it should pay the penalty of public reaction."

Other Problems. Tight restrictions on campaign financing may interfere with not only the enjoyment of individual rights but also the fulfillment of the democratic process itself. Heard said that the democratic process may properly require more spending than the 1925 law allows: "That legal ceilings on campaign expenditures proved ineffective cannot be attributed simply to the machinations of perverse and ingenious men. Politicans spend money because each, in the situation he finds himself in, cannot avoid it.... Money at work in politics is not, per se, deplorable. It may simply reflect a citizen's political goals and his preferences among candidates, which are, after all, legitimate end products of a democratically organized politics and society."

An anonymous writer in the *University of Pennsylvania Law Review,* April 1967, expressed the view that unduly tight restrictions are unenforceable: "The nature of democracy, with its emphasis on convincing the individual voter, necessarily generates pressures to reach the maximum number of voters with one's message. Any legislation that impedes or attempts to limit this drive will be unenforceable."

David Adamany wrote in the *National Civic Review,* April 1970, that efforts to limit expenditures in election campaigns are of little help in avoiding one of the paramount obstacles to democracy in elections, "the inequality in the resources of parties and candidates." Radical changes in price levels since flat limits on campaign spending were written into law alone have tended to make those limits unrealistic.

Proposals for a Better System

Government officials, political scientists and others have made hundreds of proposals aimed to plug loopholes in campaign legislation, curtail inflation of campaign costs and reduce the jeopardy to democratic ideals arising from the financial demands of campaigning. Some of the recommendations have been introduced as bills in Congress, but resulting legislation has been scanty.

The reform bills which made most headway were of a negative character. Herbert E. Alexander pointed out in *Regulation of Political Finance* (1966) that "In electoral reform, concern with uses of money in politics most often led to legislation designed to deal with unsatisfactory conditions and unsavory practices by prohibition and restriction, rather than by helping candidates and parties to meet their financial needs."

Proposals of Practicing Politicians

Proposals of politicians on campaign financing have run the gamut from complete elimination of top limits on spending to drastic lowering of the limits. Federal financing of all or a part of each candidate's campaign activities, promotion of campaign contributions by tax incentives and fuller disclosure are additional proposals that elected officials and other politicians have supported.

Ideas of Four Presidents. Theodore Roosevelt, John F. Kennedy and Lyndon B. Johnson while they were in office, and Dwight D. Eisenhower after he had left the White House, urged specific reforms in the methods of financing election campaigns. Roosevelt favored, and Eisenhower opposed, provision of campaign funds from the public treasury. Eisenhower and Kennedy urged adoption of tax incentives to encourage wider campaign giving. Johnson proposed that new legislation should limit only donations made to candidates, not expenditures made by candidates.

Theodore Roosevelt. In his annual message to Congress on the state of the Union, Dec. 3, 1907, Roosevelt said: "There is a very radical measure which would, I believe, work a substantial improvement in our system of conducing a campaign, although I am well aware that it will take some time for people so to familiarize themselves with such a proposal as to be willing to consider its adoption. The need for collecting large campaign funds would vanish if Congress provided an appropriation for the proper and legitimate expenses of each of the great national parties....Then the stipulation should be made that no party receiving campaign funds from the Treasury should accept more than a fixed amount from any individual subscriber or donor; and the necessary publicity for receipts and expenditures could without difficulty be provided."

John F. Kennedy. Writing on May 29, 1962, to the President of the Senate and the Speaker of the House transmitting bills to carry out recommendations of the President's Commission on Campaign Costs, Kennedy said: "Although the Commission devoted its attention to the problems of campaign costs for Presidential and Vice Presidential candidates,...the Congress may...wish to consider the applicability of any of the recommended practices to campaigns other than Presidential or Vice Presidential." The Commission recommended that tax incentives be enacted to encourage campaign contributions; that limits on campaign receipts and expenditures be eliminated, and that reporting requirements be strengthened. Kennedy repeated his recommendation on April 20, 1963.

Lyndon B. Johnson. In his State of the Union address to Congress, Jan. 12, 1966, Johnson called for revisions in "present unrealistic restrictions" on campaign contributions. He favored "bringing local and state committees under the Federal Corrupt Practices Act." He also expressed the view that Congress should "attach strong teeth and severe penalties to requirements for full disclosure of contributions."

In the following year, President Johnson sent to Congress, May 5, a message proposing a series of election reforms. His first proposal concerned contributions to candidates: "I recommend that a $5,000 limit be placed on the total amount that could come from any individual, his wife or minor children, to the campaign of any candidate."

On expenditures, Johnson favored elimination of a stipulated maximum. He said: "Legal ceilings on expenditures were enacted many years ago, when the potential of radio in a campaign was virtually unknown, and when television did not exist. They are totally unrealistic and inadequate. They have led to endless proliferation of political committees. I therefore recommend a repeal of the present arbitrary limits on the total expenditures of candidates for Federal office." To "insure full disclosure," he recommended that "Every candidate..and every committee, state, interstate and national, that supports a candidate for Federal office be required to report on every contribution, loan and expense item over $100; (and that) primaries and convention nomination contests be brought within the disclosure laws."

Dwight D. Eisenhower. Former President Eisenhower made three basic proposals in 1968:

(1) Authorization of a deduction from taxable income of campaign contributions up to $100 for each taxpayer, "just as he now deducts charitable, religious and educational contributions."

(2) Limitation of campaign contributions to 1 percent of the donor's adjusted net income, so that "a man who pays tax on an income of $10,000 could give up to $100 a year, the $50,000 man could contribute $500, and so on. Gifts in this range would hardly create difficult obligations for officeseekers. And every such gift would be recorded, by law, on the donor's income-tax return."

(3) Provision of free broadcasting time to candidates. "The air waves belong to the people and are only licensed to the stations; it would not be unreasonable to insist that in return the networks contribute...a reasonable amount of free prime time to candidates for important offices during major campaigns."

Eisenhower voiced dislike of President Theodore Roosevelt's proposal for Government financing of campaigns: "This plan applies compulsion to political giving, which surely is *not* the American way. Our political parties are voluntary organizations of the people, not institutions of government....(A citizen's right to give to the party of his choice) is a right that must not be denied him. And it is also his right *not* to participate in politics if that is his wish."

Ideas of Senators. Members of the Senate on a number of occasions revived Theodore Roosevelt's idea of a campaign subsidy. Early in the 1950s, television was coming into widespread use in election campaigns, and the high cost of broadcasting began to pinch. Sen. William Benton (D Conn.) was among the first to make the suggestion that the Federal Government should pay the costs of providing free radio and television time to candidates in national elections.

Sen. Richard L. Neuberger (D Ore.) on Feb. 20, 1956, introduced a bill authorizing payments from the Federal Treasury to the national committee of each major party. Cosponsors of the bill were Paul H. Douglas (D Ill.), Hubert H. Humphrey (D Minn.), William Langer (R N.D.), Mike Mansfield (D Mont.), Wayne L. Morse (R Ore.), James E. Murray (D Mont.) and John Sparkman (D Ala.)

The Senate Committee on Finance in June 1967 conducted hearings on proposals for financing political campaigns. Chairman Russell B. Long (D La.) advocated a plan under which each Senatorial candidate of a major party would receive from the Federal Treasury an amount equal to the sum of the following: (1) 50 cents multiplied by the number of votes cast in the previous Senatorial election up to 200,000; (2) 35 cents multiplied by the number of votes between 200,000 and 400,000; and (3) 20 cents multiplied by the number of votes over 400,000. Candidates of a minor party, under the Long plan, would receive an amount determined in similar fashion except that the number of cents to be multiplied in each case would be larger than those for candidates of the major parties, but the number of votes included in the multiplication would be only the number of votes received by the party, not the total number of votes cast, in the previous Senatorial election.

Sen. Robert F. Kennedy (D N.Y.), testifying before the Committee, compared the merits of two proposals for campaign financing: (1) Federal subsidization of campaign expenses and (2) a tax credit for campaign contributions. "Tax incentives," he said, "have a number of advantages. They permit aid to candidates and committees at all levels—local, state and Federal. They permit each citizen to determine who will receive his contribution. They can encourage contributions to candidates in primary elections as well as general elections....And they allow for the esprit which comes from getting people out to raise money in small amounts from a large segment of the population."

Kennedy cited as "the most serious objection to direct subsidies" their "potential for centralization of political power." A subsidy fund allocated to a national committee could enable the committee "to enforce party discipline and party ideology by advancing particular local candidates and starving others," and thus "to build a party to the liking of the national committee." Moreover, he said, if a subsidy were accompanied by a ban on private contributions, freedom of expression would be impaired.

Other Suggestions. William Gibbs McAdoo, Secretary of the Treasury in President Wilson's Cabinet (1913-18), a contender for the Democratic nomination for the Presidency (1920 and 1924), and a Senator from California (1933-38), defended in 1920 President Theodore Roosevelt's idea of a Government subsidy for election campaigns. But he added a stiff condition: "The expenses of the national elections should be paid for out of the U.S. Treasury, and it should be made a crime for a man to contribute a dollar to influence an election."

Reps. Abner J. Mikva (D Ill.) and Lawrence J. Hogan (R Md.) were among those who testified in 1970 before the House Committee on Standards of Official Conduct (Ethics Committee). Mikva proposed eliminating unenforceable limits on expenditures: "There can be no more compelling first step in the field of campaign financing than to remove those provisions from the statutes which make every Congressional campaign a living lie." Hogan said: "If every voter would contribute one dollar to the candidate of his or her choice, the campaigns would be adequately financed and the elected Representative would feel no debt of gratitude to special interest groups."

Lawrence F. O'Brien, chairman of the Democratic National Committee, said in a statement on Jan. 11, 1971, that clean campaign financing required Government payment of the costs of candidacy. He proposed that national elections "be Federally financed through a checkoff system for taxpayers to designate whether they are willing for $1 of their income tax to go into a Federal campaign financing pool."

Proposals of Civic Groups and Others

The National Committee for an Effective Congress, a nonpartisan group founded in 1947, repeatedly advocated reforms in campaign spending. It presented the following suggestions to the Senate Committee on Finance, June 6, 1967, when the Committee was considering campaign financing proposals:

- Encourage individual contributions by an income-tax credit.
- Make the credit applicable to contributions to bipartisan and nonpartisan as well as partisan organizations.
- Strengthen pre-election reporting requirements.
- Provide a reduced postage rate "to enable every Congressional candidate to reach every potential voter in his district by mail at least one time before election day."
- Require broadcasters to provide time to candidates free or at reduced rates.

In the following year, the Committee for Economic Development, consisting of 200 business executives and educators, directed its Research and Policy Committee to study campaign financing. On Dec. 30, 1968, the Research and Policy Committee issued a 73-page report, *Financing a Better Election System*. The report's chief recommendations were as follows:

- The Government should pay for informational campaign documents prepared by candidates, allocating an equal aggregate amount of space to each candidate.
- To enable candidates to collect adequate funds for other campaign costs, the Government should provide tax incentives for campaign giving, such as a 50-percent tax credit for gifts up to $50.

- Ceilings on campaign contributions and expenditures should be removed.
- The Government should close the loopholes in requirements for disclosure of campaign contributions and expenditures.

Proposals of Twentieth Century Fund. The Twentieth Century Fund, a New York-based foundation, in 1969 issued a report on campaign costs in general and followed it up the next year with a report specifically addressed to the problem of costs incurred in electing Members of Congress.

The Fund's Task Force on Financing Congressional Campaigns consisted of Herbert E. Alexander, director, Citizens' Research Foundation; two former Members of the House of Representatives, Thomas B. Curtis (R Mo., 1951-68) and Neil Stabler (D Mich., 1963-64); and executives or staff members of the Standard Oil Co. (Ind.), the AFL-CIO Committee for Political Education, the United Negro College Fund and the Charles Edison Youth Fund. The task force issued its final report, *Electing Congress; The Financial Dilemma*, on June 8, 1970. Two months earlier, it had made public 16 recommendations:

"1. Establish a Federal Election Commission; require every political organization or committee that spends money for influencing any Federal election to register with the commission; require every organization that spends $1,000 or more a year to file with the commission quarterly reports and two special reports in the closing days of the campaign; open the commission's records to public examination; impose severe penalties to deter filing of inaccurate, incomplete or late reports.

"2. Authorize the commission to investigate charges of illegal campaign activities and to report violations of campaign ethics.

"3. Eliminate all limits on spending for Congressional election campaigns.

"4. Eliminate all limits on the size of individual political contributions, but require individuals who contribute more than $5,000 a year to candidates for Federal office to file detailed reports on their donations.

"5. Enforce existing prohibitions against corporate, labor union and Government contractor contributions to Federal campaigns. When any such group is prosecuted for a violation of the law, make public the names of the candidates who benefited from the contributions.

"6. Require every candidate for Federal office to designate one official campaign committee. Require that committee to file all income and spending reports for the entire campaign.

"7. Allow an income tax credit up to $25 ($50 on a joint return) for 50 percent of contributions to political committees.

"8. Finance, out of the Federal Treasury, registration of every eligible voter in every state.

"9. Provide free postage for mailing voters' information material prepared by each state.

"10. Authorize national political committees to use the lowest postal rate available to charitable organizations.

"11. Prevent Members of Congress from using their staffs, offices, communication facilities and franking privileges to plan and conduct re-election campaigns.

"12. Provide free postage to every legally qualified candidate for the Senate or the House in a general election for one mail delivery to every voter in the candidate's district (candidates for the House) or state (candidates for the Senate).

"13. Require every commercial broadcaster to bill legally qualified candidates for the Senate and the House, for campaign broadcasts, at no more than 50 percent of the broadcaster's lowest charge for any commercial advertising. Authorize the broadcaster to deduct the dollar value of the discount from his taxable income.

"14. Encourage maximum use of cable television for campaigns in geographically limited constituencies.

"15. Establish a select committee of Congress to recommend legislation for improvements in Congressional campaign finance practices.

"16. Establish an investigating subcommittee to operate throughout the 1970 Congressional election campaigns."

Campaign Subsidy Plan. David Adamany, a Wesleyan University dean, and Washington author and political activist Philip M. Stern were among those who in 1970 urged a Federal subsidy for election campaigns. Adamany called a Federal subsidy "the most promising approach to the problem of political finance." He pointed to apparently good results of subsidies in Oregon, where the state publishes a nonpartisan voter pamphlet; Wisconsin, which gives candidates free television and radio time on the state's educational network; and Puerto Rico, which subsidizes the operations of political parties.

Stern proposed that the Federal Government finance campaigns for Federal offices by payments made directly to vendors of goods and services used by campaigners. The payments would be made from Treasury drawing accounts established for candidates. Each candidate for the Senate or the House would receive drawing accounts equal to 50 cents per vote cast in the average of the previous two elections for the office. Under this system, each New York Senatorial candidate would get about $3.5 million, and an Idaho Senatorial candidate would get $140,000, in drawing accounts.

Action in Congress, 1969-70

Perennial discussions about reforming campaign financing seemed to be coming to a head in the closing years of the 1960s. Both sessions of the 91st Congress (1969-70) showed signs of readiness to take action. However, only one bill (S 3637), which concerned allocation of broadcasting time, was passed by both houses and it was vetoed.

S 2876, 91st Congress, was a bill to provide television time at reduced rates to candidates for the Senate and the House. The bill would have allowed candidates to purchase a limited amount of spot advertising time at 30 percent of commercial rates, and a limited amount of program time at 20 percent of commercial rates. Philip A. Hart (D Mich.) and James B. Pearson (R Kan.) introduced the bill, with 34 additional sponsors. A similar bill, having 34 sponsors, was introduced in the House. The Senate Commerce Subcommittee on Communications in October 1969 conducted hearings on S 2876 but submitted no report to the full committee. There were no hearings on the corresponding bill in the House.

On July 15, 1970, the Senate Committee on Rules and Administration reported the Election Reform Bill of 1970 (S 734), which would allow a tax credit for political contributions, repeal the $3 million limit on spending by a political committee and require the Secretary of the Senate and the Clerk of the House to publicize reports filed by candidates and political committees. No further action was taken.

Rep. John B. Anderson (R Ill.), chairman of the House Republican Conference, made known his views on campaign financing in public statements and in testimony before the House Committee on Standards of Official Conduct. Some of his proposals were aimed at remedying defects which led President Nixon to veto, as noted below, the 1970 bill on campaign television broadcasts. Anderson favored the following measures:

• Limit spending on television on the basis of the number of votes in previous elections, allowing three cents per vote in the primaries and one cent per vote in the general elections.

• Limit total spending, for television and other campaign purposes, to 10 cents, 20 cents and 30 cents per vote, respectively, for Presidential, Senatorial and House elections. (President Nixon criticized the absence of such an over-all limit in the bill he vetoed.)

• Provide Government financing for a fixed number of live television appearances of candidates during prime time.

• Provide Government financing for two mailings during the general election campaign for candidates of the major parties, with lesser benefits going to candidates of minor parties and to all candidates in the primaries. (President Nixon criticized the vetoed bill's discrimination against challengers of incumbents.)

• Grant a 50-percent income tax credit for political contributions up to $50 a year.

• Tighten requirements for reporting of campaign receipts and expenditures.

• Establish an independent agency to monitor campaigns and enforce the legislation.

Ethics Committee Study

The House on July 8, 1970, approved, by a vote of 383-0, a resolution directing its Committee on Standards of Official Conduct (also known as the Ethics Committee) to investigate lobbying and campaign expenditures and to recommend new legislation on those subjects. A number of House Members made specific suggestions in their testimony before the Committee in December 1970. Other Members made public their support of certain reforms. But no legislation resulted.

House Clerk W. Pat Jennings, a former six-term Congressman (D Va.), made the following proposals in his testimony before the Committee: Apply existing laws to primaries and to political committees operating in a single state; allow a candidate for a House seat to spend up to $100,000 on advertising in any or all media; and permit donors of campaign funds to take a tax credit of up to $5 or deduct up to $25 from taxable income. On reporting of campaign finances, Jennings proposed elimination of the loophole which enables a candidate to avoid reporting transactions made without his "knowledge or consent." He would require candidates to list the addresses of donors and recipients of campaign funds.

The Ethics Committee submitted a preliminary report to the House at the end of December 1970. While expressing support for a measure that would establish "equitable and enforceable" ceilings on campaign expenditures, the Committee was unable to recommend "just how such a measure might be devised." It said also that free mailing of limited amounts of campaign literature "merits consideration and examination." Reporting requirements, the Committee stated, should be amended to require listing of all campaign contributions and expenditures without exception.

Bill to Limit Broadcast Spending

The one campaign-financing bill passed by Senate and House in 1970 was limited to political broadcasts. President Nixon vetoed the bill, largely on the ground that it was not more comprehensive. More than half of the Senators voted to override the veto, but their votes were short of the required two-thirds majority.

Passage of the Bill. S 3637 would have limited spending on political broadcasts by candidates for election to the two houses of Congress, the Presidency and the governorship of a state. The limits for Senate and House candidates in the primaries would have been $10,000 or three and one-half cents per vote cast in the previous general election, whichever was greater, and, in the general election, $20,000 or seven cents per vote cast in the previous general election, whichever was greater. The bill also would have made possible television debates between the major parties' candidates for President by repealing the equal-time requirements of the Communications Act of 1934.

The Senate passed S 3637 on Apr. 14, 1970, by a vote of 58-27. The House on Aug. 11 passed the bill with amendments which, among other things, applied the bill's restrictions to primary as well as general elections. Conferees accepted the House version after changing the effective date of the measure from Jan. 1, 1971, to 30 days after enactment. Neither House nor Senate Republican conferees signed the conference report. The House adopted the report, by a vote of 247-112, on Sept. 16. By this time, it was too late for the measure's restrictions to be applied in the 1970 campaign. Final Congressional action came when the Senate on Sept. 23 adopted the conference report by a vote of 60-19.

Unexpected Veto. President Nixon vetoed S 3637 on Oct. 12, 1970, the last day on which he could sign or veto the bill. If he had kept it longer, it would have become law without his signature. Since the President had not made known his opposition, Members of both houses were under the impression that he would sign the bill.

S 3637, the President said in his veto message, represented "a good aim gone amiss." He called it a measure which "plugs only one hole in a sieve," and said he was vetoing it because it:

• "Discriminates against the broadcast media" by imposing spending limits on only one means of communication and leaving unrestricted campaign advertising in print media.

• "Might tend to increase rather than decrease the total amount that candidates spend in their campaigns."

Wealthy candidates "would simply shift their advertising out of radio and television into other media."

• "Unfairly endangers freedom of discussion." By restricting the amount of time a candidate could obtain on television and radio, it "would severely limit the ability of many candidates to get their message to the greatest number of the electorate."

• "Gives an unfair advantage to the famous" over "the worthy but little-known" and to "the incumbent officeholder over the office-seeker." The bill would prevent challengers, who often are less well known than incumbents, from overcoming this handicap by extra television exposure.

Veto Sustained. On Nov. 20, before the Senate voted again on the vetoed bill, the President wrote to Senate Minority Leader Hugh Scott (R Pa.) endorsing Scott's announced plan to propose a comprehensive election reform bill early in 1971. The President's letter said: "Reform is needed in this area, but this issue need not and should not be dealt with in a hurried and contentious fight over a veto. There will be no major elections between now and the time that Congress can consider this legislation in the next session."

The Senate on Nov. 23 sustained the President's veto by a four-vote margin. The vote was 58 for overriding (62 needed) and 34 against. Failure of the Senate to override made a House vote unnecessary.

Action in Congress, 1971

The need for new legislation on campaign financing was acknowledged on all sides when the 92nd Congress convened in 1971. Russell Hemenway, director of the National Committee for an Effective Congress, expressed a widely accepted view when he told the Senate Commerce Subcommittee on Communications: "If money is the propellant of politics, then uncontrolled money has become its chief pollutant." Campaign-financing reforms along several lines were proposed early in the new Congress. A major bill was introduced in the Senate and another in the House:

• S 956, sponsored by Senate Minority Leader Hugh Scott (R Pa.) and cosponsored by Sen. Charles McC. Mathias Jr. (R Md.), would require fuller reporting of campaign contributions and expenditures, provide incentives for small contributors, and repeal for Presidential elections the equal-time provision of the Communications Act of 1934.

• HR 5087, introduced by House Republican Conference Chairman John Anderson (Ill.), Rep. Morris K. Udall (D Ariz.) and a bipartisan group of 63 other Members, would limit total spending not only for broadcasts (as in the vetoed 1970 bill) but also for print media, billboards, telephones and postage. This bill was revised as HR 5098, introduced by Anderson, Udall and Robert T. Stafford (R Vt.).

During discussion of these proposals, two Democratic hopefuls with an eye on the 1972 Presidential election, presented their ideas on campaign reforms. Sen. George McGovern (D S.D.), an announced candidate for the Democratic nomination for President, urged that the Federal Government subsidize both Presidential and Congressional campaigns. Sen. Edmund S. Muskie, considered the front-runner to oppose President Nixon in the 1972 election, favored limitation of spending in all Federal elections, so that no candidate "can buy his way into office."

Then came a historic turnabout on the part of the Administration. Eugene S. Cowan, one of President Nixon's special assistants, visited Rep. Anderson in mid-March and asked him to scrap his own bill, which would limit total campaign expenditures, and support Scott's bill, which would not impose any ceiling on expenditures. However, President Nixon, in a television interview March 22, reversed his course on a spending ceiling. For the first time since his inauguration as President, he endorsed total limitations on campaign expenditures. He added that such limitations should not give an advantage to incumbents over challengers.

In support of the new White House position, Deputy Attorney General Richard G. Kleindienst on March 31 testified before the Senate Commerce Subcommittee on Communications. He said the Department of Justice favored "workable and realistic ceilings" on campaign spending for all media messages, with the candidate free to allocate his budget among the various broadcast and nonbroadcast media within an over-all figure; a tax credit for campaign contributions; repeal of the equal-time provision for Congressional as well as Presidential election campaigns; fuller disclosure of receipts and expenditures, and no limit on the size of individual campaign contributions.

Meanwhile Sen. Scott, apparently alerted to the Administration turnabout, drafted a new bill, reportedly just before the President's surprise announcement, and made it public about April 1. The new bill incorporated spending limits based on a criterion which had been proposed by other Senators—for broadcast spending, seven cents per vote cast in the previous election for the same office; for other media spending, 10 cents per vote cast. Russell Hemenway, suspecting a trap, wondered whether the Administration would "publicly support reform while seeking behind the scenes to render any prospective legislation either toothless or so riddled with controversial provisions as to defy Congressional passage."

Late in the spring of 1971, one bill each in the Senate and the House commanded primary attention. Both bills contained provisions aimed to close loopholes in previous legislation, but their major provisions concerned limits on campaign spending. The bills were:

• The Senate Commerce Committee's revision, reported on May 6, of S 382, which had been introduced in January by Majority Leader Mike Mansfield (D Mont.). The revision established separate but identical upper limits on expenditures for (a) radio and television broadcasts and (b) newspaper, magazine and billboard advertising. It set no limit on other expenditures. The spending limit for each of the two categories, applicable in both the primaries and the general election, was an amount equal to five cents multiplied by the population of voting age in the candidate's constituency (the nation at large, the state and the Congressional district for Presidential, Senatorial and House election campaigns, respectively), but not less than $30,000. Census Bureau estimates would be used in calculating the limits.

• HR 8284, introduced May 11 by Wayne L. Hays (D Ohio), chairman of the Committee on House Ad-

ministration, and Watkins M. Abbitt (D Va.), chairman of the Subcommittee on Elections. This bill, considerably more restrictive than the Senate bill, would limit campaign spending of all kinds by Presidential and Senatorial candidates to a sum equal to six cents multiplied by the population of voting age (in the nation or the state) and a flat $30,000 in each House race. For Presidential candidates, this limit would apply to expenditures in primaries and at the national convention, and the same limit would apply in the general election. For candidates for Senate and House, the limit would apply to primaries and primary runoffs, and the same limit would apply to the general election.

Prospects for New Controls

The Federal Corrupt Practices Act of 1925 seemed ripe in 1971 for a major overhaul. A Gallup poll taken a few years earlier had reported that 73 percent of the public favored additional controls on campaign spending so as to make it easier for the less affluent to run for office. However, it was not at all certain that comprehensive changes actually were in the offing.

Herbert E. Alexander and Harold B. Meyers had cautioned in a *Fortune* article in 1965: "Unfortunately, officeholders—i.e., successful politicians—often seem to resist proposals for making the laws more rational. Having struggled with the existing financial mysteries and emerged victorious, they have little interest in smoothing the way for an opponent who might thereby be helped to turn them out of office."

Even if new legislation were enacted, its effectiveness could not be assured. As Heard wrote: "King Canute could not stay the tides with a royal decree, nor have Americans reduced the financial needs of campaigns by passing laws."

Abraham Lincoln wrote in a letter of March 10, 1860, to Mark W. Delahay: "I say in the main the use of money is wrong; but for certain objects in a political contest, the use of some is both right and indispensable." The questions in this area facing Congress and the American people in the 1970s are:

• For what political objects is the use of money "both right and indispensable"?

• How great is the "some" that is both right and indispensable?

• How should that "some" be made available to candidates?

• What machinery is needed for effective control of campaign receipts and expenditures?

Bibliography

Books and Pamphlets

Alexander, Herbert E., *Money, Politics and Public Reporting.* Citizens' Research Foundation (Princeton, N.J.), 1960.

——,*Regulation of Political Finance.* Published jointly by the Institute of Governmental Studies (University of California, Berkeley) and the Citizens' Research Foundation, 1966.

——(ed.), *Studies in Money in Politics.* Citizens' Research Foundation, 1965-1970. 2 vols.

——and Caroline D. Jones (eds.), *CRF Listing of Contributions of National-Level Political Committees to*

Incumbents and Candidates for Public Offices, 1968 (and) *1969.* Citizens' Research Foundation, 1971. 2 vols.

——and——(eds.), *CRF Listing of Political Contributors of $500 or More in 1968* (and) *1969.* Citizens' Research Foundation, 1971. 2 vols.

Boyd, James, *Above the Law.* New American Library, 1968.

Committee for Economic Development, Research and Policy Committee, *Financing a Better Election System.* Committee for Economic Development, 1968.

Felknor, Bruce L., *Dirty Politics.* Norton, 1966.

Heard, Alexander, *The Costs of Democracy.* University of North Carolina Press, 1960.

Neuberger, Richard L., *Adventures in Politics; We Go to the Legislature.* Oxford University Press, 1954.

Shannon, Jasper B., *Money and Politics.* Random House, 1959.

Stinnett, Ronald F., *Democrats, Dinners, & Dollars.* With an introduction by Hubert H. Humphrey. Iowa State University Press, 1967.

Twentieth Century Fund, Commission on Campaign Costs in the Electronic Era, *Voters' Time; Report.* Twentieth Century Fund, 1969.

——,Task Force on Financing Congressional Campaigns, *Electing Congress; The Financial Dilemma; Report* (and) *Background Paper* by David L. Rosenbloom. Twentieth Century Fund, 1970.

Webster, George D., *Business and Professional Political Action Committees.* Association Department, Chamber of Commerce of the United States, 1968.

Articles

Alexander, Herbert E., and Harold B. Meyers, "A Financial Landslide for the G.O.P.," *Fortune,* March 1970, p. 104-105, 186-189.

——and——, "The Switch in Campaign Giving," *Fortune,* November 1965, p. 170-172, 211-216.

——and others, "The High Costs of TV Campaigns," *Television Quarterly,* Winter 1966, p. 47-65.

Boeckel, Richard, "Excessive Expenditures in Election Campaigns," *Editorial Research Reports,* Aug. 17, 1926, p. 635-658.

"Campaign Spending in the 1968 Elections," *Congressional Quarterly Weekly Report,* Dec. 5, 1969, Part One, p. 2433-2461.

Cerf, Bennett, "The Cerfboard," *This Week,* Oct. 25, 1953, p. 4.

Eisenhower, Dwight D., "The Ticklish Problem of Political Fund-Raising—and Spending," *Reader's Digest,* January 1968, p. 64-69.

Gardner, John W., "To Control Campaign Costs," *The New York Times,* Nov. 23, 1970, p. 37.

Hazard, Leland, "It Takes Money to Get Elected; Should Corporations and Unions Contribute?" *Atlantic Monthly,* February 1960, p. 92-96.

Heard, Alexander, "Political Financing," *International Encyclopedia of the Social Sciences* (Macmillan, 1968, 17 vols.), Vol. 12, p. 235-244.

Kennedy, Sen. John F., "A Force That Has Changed the Political Scene," *TV Guide,* Nov. 14, 1959, p. 5-7.

Lambert, Jeremiah D., "Corporate Political Spending and Campaign Finance," *New York University Law Review,* December 1965, p. 1033-1078.

Lobel, Martin, "Federal Control of Campaign Contributions," *Minnesota Law Review,* 1966-67, p. 1-62.

"Loophole Legislation—State Campaign Finance Laws," *University of Pennsylvania Law Review,* April 1967, p. 983-1006.

Macdonald, George P., "Union Political Involvement and Reform of Campaign Financing Regulation," *Prospectus; A Journal of Law Reform,* April 1969, p. 347-370.

Nicolay, John G., and John Hay, "Abraham Lincoln: A History," *The Century Magazine,* February 1887, p. 515-543.

Peirce, Neal, "The High Cost of High Office," *American Legion Magazine,* August 1966, p. 10-13, 48-50.

Perry, James M., "The National Scandal of Campaign Spending," *The National Observer,* April 13, 1970, p. 12.

Pincus, Walter, "The Fight Over Money," *Atlantic Monthly,* April 1966, p. 71-75.

Rauh, Joseph L. Jr., "Legality of Union Political Expenditures," *Southern California Law Review,* Winter 1961, p. 152-164.

Wright, Rep. James C. Jr., "Clean Money for Congress," *Harper's Magazine,* April 1967, p. 98-106.

Government Publications

U.S. House of Representatives, Committee on House Administration, Subcommittee on Elections, *Election Reform Act of 1966; Hearings...on H.R. 15317 and Related Bills.* Government Printing Office, 1966.

——,Committee on Standards of Official Conduct, *Report...Under the Authority of H. Res. 1031.* Government Printing Office, 1970. (House Report 1803, 91st Congress, 2nd Session.) Deals with lobbying and with campaign funds.

——, ——, *Campaign Finances; Hearings...on H. Res. 1031, Regulation of Lobbying and Management of Campaign Money.* Government Printing Office, 1971.

——,Special Committee to Investigate Campaign Expenditures, *Report.* Government Printing Office, 1964-1971. (Report for 1964, House Report 1946, 88th Congress, 2nd Session; for 1966, House Report 2348, 89th Congress, 2nd Session; for 1968, House Report 2, 91st Congress, 1st Session; for 1970, issued as Committee Print, 92nd Congress, 1st Session.)

U.S. Senate, Committee on Rules and Administration, *Proposed Amendments to and Improvements in the Federal Election Laws; Hearings Before the Subcommittee on Privileges and Elections.* Government Printing Office, 1961. 3 parts.

——, ——, Subcommittee on Privileges and Elections, *1956 Presidential and Senatorial Campaign Contributions and Practices; Hearings.* Government Printing Office, 1956.

——,Committee on Finance, *Political Campaign Financing Proposals; Hearings...on Various Proposals for Financing Political Campaigns.* Government Printing Office, 1967.

——, ——, *Honest Elections Act of 1967...Report.* Government Printing Office, 1967. (Senate Report 714, 90th Congress, 1st Session.)

U.S. President's Commission on Campaign Costs, *Financing Presidential Campaigns; Report.* Government Printing Office, 1962.

Reapportionment and Redistricting

WHEN the 55 delegates to the Constitutional Convention emerged from their remarkable nation-creating endeavor in September 1787, their work was seen to contain many unique features. Among them was a national legislative body (the House of Representatives) whose membership was to be elected by the people and apportioned on the basis of population. But, as with almost everything in the Constitution, only a few basic rules and regulations were laid down. How to interpret and implement the instructions contained in the document was left to the future. Practical reactions to concrete problems would shape the institutions and create the customs by which the new nation would develop and prosper.

Within this framework, many questions soon arose concerning the lower house of Congress. How large was it to be? What mathematical formula was to be used in calculating the distribution of seats to the various states? Were the Representatives to be elected at large or by districts? If by districts, what standards should be used in fixing their boundaries? The Congress and the courts have been wrestling with these questions for almost 200 years.

Nor were such problems considered to be minor or routine. George Washington's only speech at the Constitutional Convention concerned the question of the ratio of population per Representative in the House. Moreover, his first veto as President—and therefore the first Presidential veto in American history—was of the Reapportionment Bill of 1792. Other such prominent figures in American history as Alexander Hamilton, Thomas Jefferson and Daniel Webster played leading roles in reapportionment and redistricting debates.

Until the mid-twentieth century, such questions generally remained in the hands of the legislators. But with growing concentration of the population in urban areas, variations in population between Congressional districts became more pronounced—and more noticeable. Moves in Congress to redress the grievance of heavily populated but under-represented areas proved unsuccessful. So intent were rural legislators on preventing power from slipping out of their hands that they managed to block reapportionment of the House following the Census of 1920. That census showed urban residents in the majority for the first time in American history.

Before long, the focus shifted to the Supreme Court, where litigants tried to get the Court to order the states to revise Congressional district boundaries in line with population shifts. After initial failure, a breakthrough occurred in 1964 in the case of *Wesberry v. Sanders*. The Court declared that the Constitution required that "as nearly as practicable, one man's vote in a Congressional election is to be worth as much as another's."

Background and Early History

Modern legislative bodies are descended from the councils of feudal lords and gentry which meieval kings summoned for the purpose of raising revenues and armies. These councils did not represent a king's subjects in any modern sense; they represented certain groups of subjects, such as the nobility, the clergy, the landed gentry and town merchants. Thus representation was by interest groups and had no relation to equal representation for equal numbers of people. In England, the king's council became Parliament, with the higher nobility and clergy making up the House of Lords and representatives of the gentry and merchants making up the House of Commons.

Beginning as little more than administrative and advisory arms of the throne, royal councils in time developed into lawmaking bodies and acquired powers which eventually eclipsed those of the monarchs they served. The power struggle in England was climaxed during the Cromwellian period when the Crown gave way, temporarily, to the Commonwealth. By 1800, Parliament was clearly the superior branch of Government.

During the 18th and early 19th centuries, as the power of Parliament grew, Englishmen became increasingly concerned about the "representativeness" of their system of apportionment. Newly developing industrial cities had no more representation in the House of Commons than small, almost deserted country towns. Small constituencies were bought and sold. Men from these empty "rotten boroughs" were often sent to Parliament representing a single "patron" landowner or clique of wealthy men. It was not until the Reform Act of 1832 that Parliament curbed such excesses and turned toward a representative system based on population.

The growth of the powers of Parliament as well as the development of Englishmen's ideas of representation during the 17th and 18th centuries had a profound effect on the colonists in America. Representative assemblies were unifying forces behind the breakaway of the colonies from England and the establishment of the newly independent country.

Colonists in America, generally modeling their legislatures after England's, used both population and land units as bases for apportionment. Patterns of early representation varied. "Nowhere did representation bear any uniform relation to the number of electors. Here and there the factor of size had been crudely recognized," Robert Luce pointed out in his book *Legislative Principles*.

In the New England states, the town was usually the basis for representation. In the Middle Atlantic states, the county was frequently used. Some southern states used the county with extra representation for specified cities. In many areas, towns and counties were fairly equal in population. Thus territorial representation afforded roughly equal representation for equal numbers of people. Delaware's three counties, for example, were of almost equal population and had the same representation in the state legislature. But in Virginia the disparity was enormous (from 951 people in one county to 22,015 in another), and Thomas Jefferson criticized the state's constitution on the ground that "among those who share the representation, the shares are unequal."

The Continental Congress, with representation from every colony, proclaimed in the Declaration of Independence in 1776 that Governments derive "their just powers from the consent of the governed" and that "the right of representation in the legislature" is an "inestimable right" of the people. The Constitutional Convention of 1787 included representatives from all the states. However, in neither of these bodies were the state delegations or voting powers proportional to population.

Intentions of Founding Fathers

Andrew Hacker, in his book *Congressional Districting,* said that to ascertain what the framers of the Constitution had in mind when they drew up the section concerning the House of Representatives, it was necessary to study closely (1) the Constitution itself, (2) the recorded discussions and debates at the Constitutional Convention, *(3) The Federalist Papers* (essays written by Alexander Hamilton, John Jay and James Madison in defense of the Constitution) and (4) the deliberations of the state ratifying conventions.

Provisions of Constitution. The Constitution states only that each state is to be allotted a certain number of representatives. It does not state specifically that Congressional districts must be equal or nearly equal in population. Nor does it even require specifically that a state create districts at all. However, it seems clear that the first clause of Article I, Section 2, providing that House Members should be chosen "by the people of the several states," indicated that the House of Representatives, in contrast to the Senate, was to represent people rather than states. "It follows," Hacker believed, "that if the states are to have equal representation in the upper chamber, then individuals are to be equally represented in the lower body."

The third clause of Article I, Section 2, provided that Congressional apportionment among the states must be according to population. But, Hacker argued, "there is little point in giving the states Congressmen 'according to their respective numbers' if the states do not redistribute the members of their delegations on the same principle. For Representatives are not the property of the states, as are the Senators, but rather belong to the people who happen to reside within the boundaries of those states. Thus, each citizen has a claim to be regarded as a political unit equal in value to his neighbors." In this and similar ways, Constitutional scholars have argued the case for single-member Congressional districts deduced from the wording of the Constitution itself.

Constitutional Convention. As for the debates in the Constitutional Convention, the issue of unequal representation arose only once. The occasion was Madi-

son's defense of Article I, Section 4, of the proposed Constitution giving Congress the power to override state regulations on "the times...and manner" of holding elections for United States Senators and Representatives. Madison's argument related to the fact that many state legislatures of the time were badly malapportioned: "The inequality of the representation in the legislatures of particular states would produce a like inequality in their representation in the national legislature, as it was presumable that the counties having the power in the former case would secure it to themselves in the latter."

The implication was twofold: that states would create Congressional districts and that unequal districting was bad and should be prevented.

Provisions of the Constitution on Apportionment and Districting

Article I, Section 2: The House of Representatives shall be composed of Members chosen every second Year by the People of the several States, and the Electors in each State shall have the Qualifications requisite for Electors of the most numerous Branch of the State Legislature....

Representatives and direct Taxes shall be apportioned among the several States which may be included within this Union, according to their respective Numbers, which shall be determined by adding to the whole Number of free Persons, including those bound to Service for a Term of Years, and excluding Indians not taxed, three fifths of all other Persons. The actual Enumeration shall be made within three Years after the first Meeting of the Congress of the United States, and within every subsequent Term of ten Years, in such Manner as they shall by Law direct. The Number of Representatives shall not exceed one for every thirty thousand, but each State shall have at least one Representative....

Article I, Section 4: The Times, Places and Manner of holding Elections for Senators and Representatives, shall be prescribed in each State by the Legislature thereof; but the Congress may at any time by Law make or alter such Regulations, except as to the Place of Chusing Senators....

Article (Amendment) XIV, Section 2: Representatives shall be apportioned among the several States according to their respective numbers, counting the whole number of persons in each State, excluding Indians not taxed. But when the right to vote at any election for the choice of electors for President and Vice President of the United States, Representatives in Congress, the Executive and Judicial officers of a State, or the members of the Legislature thereof, is denied to any of the male inhabitants of such State, being twenty-one years of age, and citizens of the United States, or in any way abridged, except for participation in rebellion, or other crime, the basis of representation therein shall be reduced in the proportion which the number of such male citizens shall bear to the whole number of male citizens twenty-one years of age in such State.

Federalist Papers. Madison made this interpretation even more clear in his contributions to the Federalist Papers. Arguing in favor of the relatively small size of the projected House of Representatives, he wrote in Paper No. 56: "Divide the largest state into ten or twelve districts and it will be found that there will be no peculiar local interests in either which will not be within the knowledge of the Representative of the district."

In the same paper, Madison said: "The Representatives of each State will not only bring with them a considerable knowledge of its laws, and a local knowledge of their respective districts, but will probably in all cases have been members, and may even at the very time be members, of the state legislature, where all the local information and interests of the state are assembled, and from whence they may easily be conveyed by a very few hands into the legislature of the United States." And finally, in the next Federalist Paper (No. 57), Madison made the statement that "...each Representative of the United States will be elected by five or six thousand citizens." In making these arguments, Madison seems to have assumed that all or most Representatives would be elected by districts rather than at large.

State Conventions. In the state ratifying conventions, the grant to Congress by Article I, Section 4, of ultimate jurisdiction over the "times, places and manner of holding elections" (except the places of choosing Senators) held the attention of many delegates. There were differences over the merits of this section, but no justification of unequal districts was prominently used to attack the grant of power. Further evidence that individual districts were the intention of the Founding Fathers was given in the New York ratifying convention, when Alexander Hamilton said: "The natural and proper mode of holding elections will be to divide the state into districts in proportion to the number to be elected. This state will consequently be divided at first into six."

From his study of the sources relating to the question of Congressional districting, Hacker concluded: "There is, then, a good deal of evidence that those who framed and ratified the Constitution intended that the House of Representatives have as its constituency a public in which the votes of all citizens were of equal weight. In the final analysis, the aristocratic pronouncements of Hamilton, Gerry and Morris cannot be regarded as having been written into the document's provisions dealing with the lower chamber of the national legislature. The House of Representatives was designed to be a popular chamber, giving the same electoral power to all who had the vote. And the concern of Madison, King and Pinckney that districts be equal in size was an institutional step in the direction of securing this democratic principle."

The Early Years: 1789-1842

Article I, Section 2, Clause 3, of the Constitution laid down the basic rules for apportionment and reapportionment of seats in the House of Representatives: "Representatives...shall be apportioned among the several states which may be included within this Union, according to their respective numbers, which shall be determined by adding to the whole number of free persons, including those bound to service for a term of years, and excluding

Indians not taxed, three-fifths of all other persons. The actual enumeration shall be made within three years after the first meeting of the Congress of the United States, and within every subsequent term of ten years, in such manner as they shall by law direct. The number of Representatives shall not exceed one for every thirty thousand, but each state shall have at least one Representative...."

Until the first census had been taken, the 13 states were to have the following numbers of Representatives: New Hampshire, three; Massachusetts, eight; Rhode Island and Providence Plantations, one; Connecticut, five; New York, six; New Jersey, four; Pennsylvania, eight; Delaware, one; Maryland, six; Virginia, ten; North Carolina, five; South Carolina, five; and Georgia, three. The apportionment of seats—65 in all—thus mandated by the Constitution remained in effect during the First and Second Congresses (1789-93).

Apparently realizing that apportionment of the House of Representatives was likely to become a major bone of contention, the First Congress submitted to the states a proposed constitutional amendment containing a formula to be used in future reapportionments. The amendment, which was not ratified, provided that following the taking of a decennial census there would be one Representative for every 30,000 persons until the House membership reached 100, "after which the proportion shall be so regulated by Congress that there shall be not less than 100 Representatives, nor less than one Representative for every 40,000 persons, until the number of Representatives shall amount to 200, after which the proportion shall be so regulated by Congress, that there shall not be less than 200 Representatives, nor more than one Representative for every 50,000 persons."

First Apportionment by Congress

The failure to ratify this amendment made it necessary for Congress to enact apportionment legislation after the first census had been taken in 1790. The first apportionment bill was sent to the President on March 23, 1792. Washington, at the urging of Secretary of State Thomas Jefferson, sent the bill back to Congress without his signature—the first Presidential veto.

The bill had incorporated the constitutional minimum of 30,000 as the size of each district. But the population of each state was not a simple multiple of 30,000. Significant fractions were left over when the number of people in each state was divided by 30,000. Thus, for example, Vermont was found to be entitled to 2.851 Representatives, New Jersey to 5.98 and Virginia to 21.018. Therefore, a formula had to be found that would deal in the fairest possible manner with unavoidable variations from exact equality.

Accordingly, Congress proposed in the first apportionment bill to distribute the Members on a fixed ratio of one Representative per 30,000 inhabitants, and give an additional Member to each state with a fraction exceeding one-half. Washington's veto was based on the belief that eight states would receive more than one Representative per 30,000 people under this formula.

A motion to override the veto was unsuccessful. A new bill meeting the President's objections was introduced April 9, 1792, and approved April 14. The Act provided for a ratio of one Member for every 33,000 inhabitants and fixed the exact number of Representatives to which each state was entitled. The total membership of the House was to be 105. In dividing the population of the various states by 33,000, all remainders were to be disregarded. This was known as the Method of Rejected Fractions; it was devised by Thomas Jefferson.

Reapportionment by Jefferson's Method

Jefferson's method of reapportionment resulted in great inequalities between states. A Vermont district would contain 42,766 inhabitants, a New Jersey district 35,911 and a Virginia district only 33,187. Emphasis was placed on what was considered the ideal size of a Congressional district rather than on what the size of the House ought to be. This method was in use until 1840.

The reapportionment act based on the Census of 1800 continued the ratio of 33,000, which provided a House of 141 Members. Debate on the third apportionment bill began in the House on Nov. 22, 1811, and the bill was sent to the President on December 21. The ratio was fixed at 35,000, yielding a House of 181 Members. Following the Census of 1820, Congress approved an apportionment bill providing a ratio of 40,000 inhabitants per district. The sum of the quotas for the various states produced a House of 213 Members.

The Act of May 22, 1832, fixed the ratio at 47,700, resulting in a House of 240 Members. Dissatisfaction with the method in use continued, and Daniel Webster launched a vigorous attack against it. He urged adoption of a method that would assign an additional Representative to each state with a large fraction. His philosophical approach to the reapportionment process was made in a report he submitted to Congress in 1832: "The Constitution, therefore, must be understood not as enjoining an absolute relative equality—because that would be demanding an impossibility—but as requiring of Congress to make the apportionment of Representatives among the several states according to their respective numbers, *as near as may be.* That which cannot be done perfectly must be done in a manner as near perfection as can be... In such a case approximation becomes a rule."

Following the Census of 1840, Congress adopted a reapportionment method similar to that advocated by Webster. The method fixed a ratio of one Representative for every 70,680 persons. This figure was reached by deciding on a fixed size of the House in advance (223), dividing that figure into the total national "Representative population" and using the result (70,680) as the fixed ratio. The population of each state was then divided by this ratio to find the number of its Representatives and assigned an additional Representative for each fraction over one-half.

Redistricting Problems

Another new feature of the legislation following the Census of 1840 was a redistricting provision that became law on June 25, 1842. Under that provision, Representatives were to be "elected by districts composed of contiguous territory equal in number to the Representatives to which said state may be entitled, no one district electing more than one Representative." This provision climaxed a 50-year struggle to enact some sort of districting legislation. Despite substantial evidence of the intent of Congress, many states had not divided themselves into Congressional districts.

In the first few elections to the House, New Hampshire, Pennsylvania, New Jersey and Georgia elected their Representatives at large, as did Rhode Island and Delaware—the two states with only a single Representative. Districts were used in Massachusetts, New York, Maryland, Virginia and South Carolina. In Connecticut, a preliminary election was held to nominate three times as many persons as the number of Representatives to be chosen at large in the subsequent election. In 1840, 22 of the 31 states elected their Representatives by districts. New Hampshire, New Jersey, Georgia, Alabama, Mississippi and Missouri, with a combined representation of 33 out of a total of 232, elected their Representatives at large; three states, Arkansas, Delaware and Florida, had only one Representative each.

Constant efforts had been made during the early 1800s to lay down national rules, by means of a constitutional amendment, for Congressional districting. The first resolution proposing a mandatory division of each state into districts was introduced in Congress in 1800. In 1802 the Legislatures of Vermont and North Carolina adopted resolutions in support of such action. From 1816 to 1826, 22 state resolutions were adopted proposing the election of Representatives by districts.

In Congress, Sen. Mahlon Dickerson (D N.J.) proposed an amendment regularly almost every year from 1817 to 1826. The resolution embodying the Dickerson amendment was adopted by the Senate three times, in 1819, 1820 and 1822, but each time it failed to reach a vote in the House.

Acceptance by most states of the principle of local representation put an end to Congressional efforts in behalf of a constitutional amendment and led to the enactment of the 1842 law requiring contiguous single-member Congressional districts.

When President Tyler signed the bill, he appended to it a memorandum voicing doubt as to the constitutionality of the districting provisions. The memorandum precipitated a minor constitutional crisis. The House, urged on by Rep. John Quincy Adams (Whig Mass.), appointed a select committee to consider the action of the President. Chaired by the aging ex-President, the committee drew up a resolution protesting the President's action as "unwarranted by the Constitution and laws of the United States, injurious to the public interest, and of evil example for the future; and this House do hereby solemnly protest against the said act of the President and against its ever being repeated or adduced as a precedent hereafter." The House took no action on the resolution; several attempts to call it up under suspension of the rules failed to receive the necessary two-thirds vote.

The action of the Congress in enacting districting legislation along with apportionment legislation did stand as a precedent, however. For the next 80 years, some sort of districting requirements were included in successive reapportionment laws.

Another phenomenon encountered—or perhaps only named—in this era, was the gerrymander. Gerrymandering was the practice of drawing district lines so as to maximize the advantage of a political party or interest group. The name originated from a salamander-shaped Congressional district created by the Massachusetts Legislature in 1812 when Elbridge Gerry was Governor.

The Gerrymander

The practice of "gerrymandering"—the excessive manipulation of the shape of a legislative district to benefit a certain incumbent or party—is probably as old as the Republic, but the name originated in 1812.

In that year, the Massachusetts Legislature carved out of Essex County a district which historian John Fiske said had a "dragonlike contour." When the painter Gilbert Stuart saw the misshapen district, he pencilled in a head, wings and claws and exclaimed: "That will do for a salamander!"—to which editor Benjamin Russell replied: "Better say a Gerrymander"—after Elbridge Gerry, then Governor of Massachusetts.

The Middle Years, 1850-1920

The modified reapportionment formula adopted by Congress in 1842 was found more satisfactory than the previous method, but another change was made following the Census of 1850. The new system was proposed by Rep. Samuel F. Vinton (Whig Ohio) and became known as the Vinton method.

Vinton Apportionment Formula

Under this formula, Congress first fixed the size of the House and then distributed the seats. The new method of distribution involved the same procedure as the 1842 system. The total Representative population of the country was divided by the desired number of Representatives and the resulting number became the ratio of population to each Representative. The population of each state was divided by this ratio and each state received the number of Representatives equal to the whole number in the quotient for that state. Then, to reach the required size

of the House, additional Representatives were assigned based on the remaining fractions, beginning with the state having the largest fraction. This procedure differed from the 1842 method only in the last step, which assigned one Representative to every state having a fraction larger than ½. The Vinton method was used from 1850 through 1900.

Advantages and Difficulties

Proponents of the Vinton method pointed out that it had the distinct advantage of making it possible to fix the size of the House in advance and to take into account at least the largest fractions. The concern of the House, grown in size from 65 in 1789 to 240 in 1833, turned from the ideal size of a Congressional district to the ideal size of the House itself. The 1842 legislation resulted in an actual reduction in the size of the House, to 233 Members.

Under the 1842 reapportionment formula, the exact size of the House could not be fixed in advance. If every state with a fraction over ½ were given an additional Representative, the House might wind up with a few more or a few less than the desired number. However, under the Vinton method, only states with the largest fractions were given additional House Members and only up to the desired total size of the House.

Despite the apparent advantages of the Vinton method, certain difficulties began to reveal themselves as the formula was applied. Zechariah Chafee Jr. of the Harvard Law School summarized these difficulties in an article in the *Harvard Law Review* in 1929. The method, he pointed out, suffered from a fatal defect called the "Alabama paradox". Under the paradox, an increase in the total size of the House might be accompanied by an actual loss of a seat by some state, even though there had been no corresponding change in population. This phenomenon first appeared in tables prepared for Congress in 1881, which gave Alabama eight Members in a House of 299 but only seven Members in a House of 300. It could even happen that the state which lost a seat was the one state which had expanded in population, while all the others had fewer people.

Chafee concluded from his study of the Vinton method: "Thus, it is unsatisfactory to fix the ratio of population per Representative before seats are distributed. Either the size of the House comes out haphazard, or, if this be determined in advance the absurdities of the 'Alabama paradox' vitiate the apportionment. Under present conditions, it is essential to determine the size of the House in advance; the problem thereafter is to distribute the required number of seats among the several states as nearly as possible in proportion to their respective populations so that no state is treated unfairly in comparison with any other state."

Reapportionments by Vinton Method

Six reapportionments were carried out under the Vinton method. The 1850 Census Act contained three provisions not included in any previous law. First, it provided not only for reapportionment after the Census of 1850 but also for reapportionment after all subsequent censuses; secondly, it purported to fix the size of the House permanently at 233 Members; and thirdly, it provided in advance for an automatic apportionment by the Secretary of the Interior under the method prescribed in the Act.

Following the Census of 1860, according to the provisions of the Act passed a decade before, an automatic reapportionment was to be carried out by the Interior Department. However, because the size of the House was to remain at the 1850 level, some states faced loss of representation and others would gain less than they expected. To avert these eventualities, an Act was approved March 4, 1862, increasing the size of the House to 241 and giving an extra Representative to eight states—Illinois, Iowa, Kentucky, Minnesota, Ohio, Pennsylvania, Rhode Island and Vermont.

Apportionment legislation following the Census of 1870 contained several new provisions. The Act of Feb. 2, 1872, fixed the size of the House at 283, with the proviso that the number should be increased if new states were admitted. A supplemental Act of May 30, 1872, assigned one additional Representative each to Alabama, Florida, Indiana, Louisiana, New Hampshire, New York, Pennsylvania, Tennessee and Vermont.

Another section of the 1872 Act provided that no state should thereafter be admitted "without having the necessary population to entitle it to at least one Representative fixed by this bill." That provision was found to be unenforceable because no Congress can bind a succeeding Congress.

The Reconstruction era being at its height in the South, the reapportionment legislation of 1872 reflected the desire of Congress to enforce Section 2 of the new 14th Amendment. That section attempted to protect the right of Negroes to vote by providing for reduction of the House representation of a state which interfered with exercise of that right. The number of Representatives of such a state was to be reduced in proportion to the number of inhabitants of voting age whose right to go to the polls was denied or abridged. The reapportionment bill repeated the language of the section, but it was never put into effect because of the difficulty of determining the exact number of persons whose right to vote was being abridged.

The reapportionment Act of Feb. 25, 1882, provided for a House of 325 Members, with additional Members for any new states admitted to the Union. No new apportionment provisions were added. The acts of Feb. 7, 1891, and Jan. 16, 1901, were routine pieces of legislation as far as apportionment was concerned. The 1891 measure provided for a House of 356 Members and the 1901 statute increased the number to 386.

Maximum Membership of House

On Aug. 8, 1911, the membership of the House was fixed at 433. Provision was made in the reapportionment Act of that date for the addition of one Representative each from Arizona and New Mexico, which were expected to become states in the near future. Thus, the size of the House reached 435, where it has remained up to the present with the exception of the brief period 1959-63 when the admission of Alaska and Hawaii raised the total temporarily to 437.

Limiting the size of the House amounted to recognition that the body would soon expand to unmanageable proportions if the practice of adding new seats every 10 years, to match population gains without depriving any

state of its existing representation, were continued. The limitation to a fixed number made the task of reapportionment all the more difficult when the population not only increased but became much more mobile. Population shifts brought Congress up hard against the politically painful necessity of taking seats away from slow-growing states to give the fast-growing adequate representation.

A new mathematical calculation was adopted for the reapportionment following the Census of 1910. Devised by Prof. W. F. Willcox of Cornell University, the new system established a priority list which assigned seats progressively beginning with the first seat above the constitutional minimum of at least one seat per state. When there were 48 states, this method was used to assign the 49th Member, the 50th Member, and so on, until the desired size of the House was reached. The method was called Major Fractions and was used after the Censuses of 1910, 1930 and 1940 *(There was no reapportionment in 1920. See below).*

Districting Legislation, 1850-1910

The districting provisions of the 1842 Act were not repeated in the legislation that followed the Census of 1850. But in 1862 an Act separate from the reapportionment Act revived the provisions of the Act of 1842 requiring districts to be composed of contiguous territory.

The 1872 reapportionment Act again repeated the districting provisions and went even further by adding that districts should contain "as nearly as practicable an equal number of inhabitants." Similar provisions were included in the Acts of 1881 and 1891. In the Act of Jan. 16, 1901, the words "compact territory" were added and the clause then read "contiguous and compact territory and containing as nearly as practicable an equal number of inhabitants." This requirement appeared also in the legislation of Aug. 8, 1911.

Attempts to Enforce Redistricting. Several attempts, none of them successful, were made to enforce redistricting provisions. Despite the districting requirements of the Act of June 25, 1842, New Hampshire, Georgia, Mississippi and Missouri elected their Representatives at large that autumn. When the House elected at that time convened for its first session on Dec. 4, 1843, objection was made to seating the Representatives of the four states. The matter was referred to the Committee on Elections. The majority report of the Committee, made by its chairman, Rep. Stephen A. Douglas (D Ill.), asserted that the Act of 1842 was not binding upon the states and that the Representatives in question were entitled to their seats. A minority report by Rep. Garrett Davis (Whig Ky.) contended that the Members had not been elected according to the Constitution and the laws and were not entitled to their seats.

The matter was debated in the House from Feb. 6 to 14, 1844. With the Democratic party holding a majority of more than 60, and with 18 of the 21 challenged Members being Democrats, the House decided to seat the Members. An amendment to the majority report in the form of a substitute deleted all reference to the apportionment law. However, by 1848, all four states had come around to electing their Representatives by districts.

Methods of Apportioning House Seats

Fixed Ratio With Rejected Fractions, 1790-1830

The Method of Fixed Ratio With Rejected Fractions was devised by Thomas Jefferson at the time of the first reapportionment following the Census of 1790. Under this method, a predetermined ratio of inhibitants per Representative (say 33,000) was divided into the population of each state. The result was the quota for the state. A Representative was assigned for every whole number in the quota and the fractions were disregarded. Thus a state with a quota of 3.9 got three Representatives.

This method was subject to the population paradox. With a fixed ratio of representation, an increase in the total population might result in a decrease in the size of the House. An example was constructed by Edward V. Huntington in *Methods of Apportionment in Congress:* A fixed ratio of 250,000 persons per district would result in a House of 435 members if the population totaled 102,750,113 but in a House of only 391 members if the population rose to 102,958,798.

Fixed Ratio With Major Fractions, 1840

The Method of Fixed Ratio With Major Fractions was used only once—after the Census of 1840. It was based on an idea formulated by Daniel Webster. As under the Method of Fixed Ratio With Rejected Fractions, a predetermined ratio of persons per district was selected and divided into the population of each state. But in this case, the fractions were not discarded.

For every fraction over one half, an additional Representative was assigned. Thus, a state with a quota of 3.51 got four Representatives but a state with a quota of 3.49 got only three. This method also was subject to the population paradox.

Vinton Method, 1850-1900

The Vinton method was based on a fixed ratio and a fixed size of the House. The total population of the country was divided by the number of House members to determine the ratio, or number of persons per district. This ratio was then divided into the population of each state, resulting in the quota for each state. Each state received a Representative for each whole number in its quota (with every state getting at least one Representative, fulfilling the Constitutional requirement). The remaining Representatives were then assigned in order to the states having the highest fractions, until the predetermined size of the House was reached.

The Vinton method was subject to the Alabama paradox, in which a state might lose a Representative even though the size of the House was increased.

Major Fractions, 1910-1940

The Method of Major Fractions, in use after the Censuses of 1910, 1930 and 1940, was based on the same principles as the previous method but some new, complex mathematical formulas were added to make the distribution fairer. Furthermore, a priority list system of ranking states' claims to Representatives was introduced *(See Method of Equal Proportions for explanation of the priority list system).*

SOURCES: Laurence F. Schmeckebier, *Congressional Apportionment;* Edward V. Huntington, *Methods of Apportionment in Congress.*

The next challenge to a Member of the House based on Federal districting laws occurred in 1901. It was charged that the Kentucky redistricting law then in force was contrary to the redistricting provisions of the Federal reapportionment law of Jan. 16, 1901. The specific challenge was to Rep. George G. Gilbert (D) of the eighth Kentucky district. The committee assigned to investigate the matter turned aside the challenge, asserting that the Federal act was not binding on the states. The reasons given were practical and political:

"Your committee are therefore of opinion that a proper construction of the Constitution does not warrant the conclusion that by that instrument Congress is clothed with power to determine the boundaries of Congressional districts, or to revise the acts of a State Legislature in fixing such boundaries; and your committee is further of opinion that even if such power is to be implied from the language of the Constitution, it would be in the last degree unwise and intolerable that it should exercise it. To do so would be to put into the hands of Congress the ability to disfranchise, in effect, a large

body of the electors. It would give Congress the power to apply to all the States, in favor of one party, a general system of gerrymandering. It is true that the same method is to a large degree resorted to by the several states, but the division of political power is so general and diverse that notwithstanding the inherent vice of the system of gerrymandering, some kind of equality of distribution results."

In 1908, the Virginia Legislature transferred Floyd County from the fifth to the sixth Congressional district. As a result, the population of the fifth district was reduced from 175,579 to 160,191 and that of the sixth district was increased from 181,571 to 196,959. The average for the state was 185,418.

When the newly elected Representative from the fifth district, Rep. Edward W. Saunders (D), was challenged by his opponent in the 1908 elections, the majority of the investigating committee upheld the challenge. They concluded that the Virginia law of 1908 was null and void as it did not conform with the Federal law of Jan. 16, 1901, or with the constitution of Virginia, and that the

Malapportionment and Gerrymandering

The prevalence of malapportionment and "gerrymandering" in the creation of U.S. Congressional districts was, to many observers, one of the chief evils in the American system prior to reforms brought about by a Feb. 17, 1964, U.S. Supreme Court decision declaring that "as nearly as is practicable, one man's vote in a Congressional election is to be worth as much as another's."

Malapportionment. Malapportionment involved creating districts of grossly unequal populations—either through actions of state legislatures in establishing new districts or, as was the more frequent practice, simply by failing to redistrict despite major population movements that result in population inequalities. At the time of the 1964 Supreme Court decision, for instance, Louisiana had not redistricted since 1912, nor had Colorado or Georgia since 1931, or South Carolina since 1932.

Examples of great disparity in Congressional district sizes in modern U.S. history: New York (1930) 776,425 in largest district and 90,671 in smallest district; Ohio (1946) 698,650 and 163,561; Illinois (1946) 914,053 and 112,116; Arkansas (1946) 423,152 and 177,476; Texas (1962) 951,527 and 216,371; Michigan (1962) 802,994 and 177,431; Maryland (1962) 711,045 and 243,570; South Dakota (1962) 497,669 and 182,845.

The decennial census and ensuing reapportionment of House seats eventually forced reapportionment in most states, although some resorted to the expedient of electing Members at large (like Texas, Hawaii, Ohio, Michigan and Maryland in 1962) rather than face the process of redrawing district lines.

Gerrymandering. Gerrymandering was the name given to excessive manipulation of the shape of legislative districts. The gerrymander was named after Elbridge Gerry, Governor of Massachusetts in 1812 when the Legislature created a peculiar salamander-shaped district to benefit the Democratic party to which Gerry belonged.

Like malapportionment, gerrymandering was practiced by both political parties. In 1961, for example, Republican redistricters in New York created one gerrymander-like creature stretching across the greater part of upstate New York, his head hanging over Albany in the east and his tail reaching for Rochester in the west. Such salamander, tadpole and fishlike creatures sprang to life on the maps of New York City's boroughs. In California, Democrats in control of the Legislature connected two pockets of strong Republican strength in Los Angeles by a thin strip of land to form an unwieldly district running for miles along the coastline. In North Carolina, Democratic redistricters formed an almost perfect gerrymander shape to throw the state's sole Republican Representative in with a strong Democratic opponent.

The basic intent of practically every gerrymander was political—to create a maximum number of districts which would elect the party candidates or types of candidates favored by the controlling group in the state legislature that did the redistricting. The effect was almost always to increase the political power of the already politically dominant group. Up to the 1950s, this was said to be the Republicans in the North and the Democrats in the South. Growing Democratic strength in many northern states tended to cancel out the Republican advantage in that part of the country, however, and signs of the reverse happening in the South could be detected in the 1950s.

---

district should be regarded as including the counties which were a part of it before enactment of the 1908 state legislation. In that case the contestant would have had a majority of the votes, so the committee recommended that he be seated. Thus, for the first time, it looked as though the districting legislation would be enforced, but the House did not take action on the committee's report and the contestant was not seated.

Reapportionment Struggle of 1920s

Conflict Over Urban Growth. The results of the 14th decennial census were announced Dec. 17, 1920, just after the short session of the 66th Congress convened. The Census of 1920 showed that, for the first time in history, a majority of Americans were urban residents. Disclosure of this fact came as a profound shock to the many persons who were used to emphasizing the nation's rural traditions and the virtues of life on farms and in small towns. Rural legislators immediately mounted an attack on the census results which postponed reapportionment legislation for almost a decade.

Thomas Jefferson once wrote: "Those who labor in the earth are the chosen people of God, if ever He had a chosen people, whose breasts He had made His peculiar deposit for substantial and genuine virtue....The mobs of great cities add just as much to the support of pure government as sores do to the strength of the human body....I think our governments will remain virtuous for many centuries as long as they are chiefly agricultural; and this shall be as long as there shall be vacant lands in any part of America. When they get piled up upon one another in large cities as in Europe, they will become corrupt as in Europe."

As their power waned throughout the latter part of the 19th century and the early part of the 20th, farmers and their spokesmen clung to the Jeffersonian belief that they were somehow more pure and virtuous than the growing number of urban residents. When finally faced with the fact that they were in the minority, they put up a strong rearguard action to prevent the inevitable shift of Congressional districts to the cities.

In the first place, rural Representatives insisted that, since the census was taken as of Jan. 1, the farm population had been undercounted. Supporting this contention, they argued that many farm laborers were seasonally employed in the cities at that time of year. Furthermore, mid-winter road conditions probably had prevented enumerators from visiting many farms; and other farmers were said to have been counted incorrectly because they were absent on winter vacation trips. The change of the census date to Jan. 1 in 1920 had been made to conform

CONGRESSIONAL APPORTIONMENT 1789-1970

	Constitution† (1789)	YEAR OF CENSUS[x]																	
		1790	1800	1810	1820	1830	1840	1850	1860	1870	1880	1890	1900	1910	1930#	1940	1950	1960	1970
Ala.				1*	3	5	7	7	6	8	8	9	9	10	9	9	9	8	7
Alaska																	1*	1	1
Ariz.														1*	1	2	2	3	4
Ark.						1*	1	2	3	4	5	6	7	7	7	7	6	4	4
Calif.							2*	2	3	4	6	7	8	11	20	23	30	38	43
Colo.										1*	1	2	3	4	4	4	4	4	5
Conn.	5	7	7	7	6	6	4	4	4	4	4	4	5	5	6	6	6	6	6
Del.	1	1	1	2	1	1	1	1	1	1	1	1	1	1	1	1	1	1	1
Fla.							1*	1	1	2	2	2	3	4	5	6	8	12	15
Ga.	3	2	4	6	7	9	8	8	7	9	10	11	11	12	10	10	10	10	10
Hawaii																	1*	2	2
Idaho											1*	1	1	2	2	2	2	2	2
Ill.				1*	1	3	7	9	14	19	20	22	25	27	27	26	25	24	24
Ind.				1*	3	7	10	11	11	13	13	13	13	13	12	11	11	11	11
Iowa							2*	2	6	9	11	11	11	11	9	8	8	7	6
Kan.									1	3	7	8	8	8	7	6	6	5	5
Ky.		2	6	10	12	13	10	10	9	10	11	11	11	11	9	9	8	7	7
La.				1*	3	3	4	4	5	6	6	6	7	8	8	8	8	8	8
Maine				7*	7	8	7	6	5	5	4	4	4	4	3	3	3	2	2
Md.	6	8	9	9	9	8	6	6	5	6	6	6	6	6	6	6	7	8	8
Mass.	8	14	17	13‡	13	12	11	11	10	11	12	13	14	16	15	14	14	12	12
Mich.						1*	3	4	6	9	11	12	12	13	17	17	18	19	19
Minn.								2*	2	3	5	7	9	10	9	9	9	8	8
Miss.				1*	1	2	4	5	5	6	7	7	8	8	7	7	6	5	5
Mo.					1	2	5	7	9	13	14	15	16	16	13	13	11	10	10
Mont.											1*	1	1	2	2	2	2	2	2
Neb.									1*	1	3	6	6	6	5	4	4	3	3
Nev.									1*	1	1	1	1	1	1	1	1	1	1
N.H.	3	4	5	6	6	5	4	3	3	3	2	2	2	2	2	2	2	2	2
N.J.	4	5	6	6	6	6	5	5	5	7	7	8	10	12	14	14	14	15	15
N.M.														1*	1	2	2	2	2
N.Y.	6	10	17	27	34	40	34	33	31	33	34	34	37	43	45	45	43	41	39
N.C.	5	10	12	13	13	13	9	8	7	8	9	9	10	10	11	12	12	11	11
N.D.											1*	1	2	3	2	2	2	2	1
Ohio			1*	6	14	19	21	21	19	20	21	21	21	22	24	23	23	24	23
Okla.													5*	8	9	8	6	6	6
Ore.							1*	1	1	1	2	2	3	3	4	4	4	4	4
Pa.	8	13	18	23	26	28	24	25	24	27	28	30	32	36	34	33	30	27	25
R.I.	1	2	2	2	2	2	2	2	2	2	2	2	2	3	2	2	2	2	2
S.C.	5	6	8	9	9	9	7	6	4	5	7	7	7	7	6	6	6	6	6
S.D.											2*	2	2	3	2	2	2	2	2
Tenn.		1	3	6	9	13	11	10	8	10	10	10	10	10	9	10	9	9	8
Texas							2*	2	4	6	11	13	16	18	21	21	22	23	24
Utah												1*	1	2	2	2	2	2	2
Vt.		2	4	6	5	5	4	3	3	3	2	2	2	2	1	1	1	1	1
Va.	10	19	22	23	22	21	15	13	11	9	10	10	10	10	9	9	10	10	10
Wash.											1*	2	3	5	6	6	7	7	7
W.Va.									3	4	4	5	6	6	6	6	5	4	
Wis.							2*	3	6	8	9	10	11	11	10	10	10	10	9
Wyo.											1*	1	1	1	1	1	1	1	1
Total	65	106	142	186	213	242	232	237	243	293	332	357	391	435	435	435	437**	435	435

x *Apportionment effective with Congressional election two years after census.*
† *Original apportionment made in Constitution pending first census.*
# *No apportionment was made in 1920.*
* *These figures are not based on any census, but indicate the provisional representation accorded newly admitted states by the Congress, pending the following census.*

‡ *Twenty Members were assigned to Massachusetts, but seven of these were credited to Maine when that area became a state.*
**Normally 435 but temporarily increased two seats by Congress when Alaska and Hawaii became states.*

SOURCE: Biographical Directory of the American Congress and Bureau of the Census

with recommendations of the Agriculture Department, which had asserted that the census should be taken early in the year if an accurate statistical picture of farming conditions was desired.

Another point raised by rural legislators was that large numbers of unnaturalized aliens were congregated in northern cities, with the result that these cities gained at the expense of constituencies made up mostly of citizens of the United States. Rep. Homer Hoch (R Kan.) submitted a table showing that, in a House of 435 Representatives, exclusion from the census count of persons not naturalized would have altered the allocation of seats to 16 states. Southern and western farming states would have retained the number of seats allocated to them in 1911 or would have gained, while northern industrial states and California would have lost or at least would have gained fewer seats.

A constitutional amendment to exclude all aliens from the enumeration for purposes of reapportionment was proposed during the 70th Congress by Rep. Hoch, Sen. Arthur Capper (R Kan.) and others. During the Senate Commerce Committee's hearings on reapportionment, Sen. Frederic M. Sackett (R Ky.) and Sen. Lawrence D. Tyson (D Tenn.) said they too intended to propose amendments to the same effect. But nothing further came of the proposals.

Lack of Progress on Bills

The first bill to reapportion the House according to the Census of 1920 was drafted by the House Census Committee early in 1921. Proceeding on the theory that no state should have its representation reduced, the Committee proposed to increase the total number of Representatives from 435 to 483. But the House voted 267 to 76 to keep its membership at 435 and passed the bill so amended on Jan. 19, 1921. Under this bill, 11 states would have lost seats and eight would have gained. The Senate sent the bill to a committee where it died when the 66th Congress expired March 4, 1921.

Early in the 67th Congress, the House Census Committee again reported a bill, this time fixing the total membership at 460, an increase of 25. Two states—Maine and Massachusetts—would have lost one Representative each and 16 states would have gained. On the floor of the House an attempt to fix the number at the existing 435 failed, and the House voted to send the bill back to committee, where it remained until that Congress came to an end on March 4, 1923.

During the 68th Congress (1923-25), the House Census Committee failed to report any reapportionment bill, and midway of the 69th Congress (1925-27) it again looked as if no reapportionment measure would come out of the Committee. Accordingly, on April 8, 1926, Rep. Henry E. Barbour (R Calif.) moved that the Committee be discharged from further consideration of a bill identical with that passed by the House in 1921 continuing membership at 435.

Chairman Bertrand H. Snell (R N.Y.) of the House Rules Committee, representing the Republican leadership of the House, raised a point of order against Barbour's motion. The Speaker of the House, Nicholas Longworth (R Ohio), pointed out that decisions of earlier Speakers tended to indicate that reapportionment had been considered a matter of "constitutional privilege,"

and that Rep. Barbour's motion must be held in order if these precedents were followed. But the Speaker said he doubted whether the precedents had been interpreted correctly. He therefore submitted to the House the question of whether the pending motion should be considered privileged. The House sustained the Rules Committee by a vote of 87 to 265.

Intervention by President Coolidge

President Coolidge, who previously had made no reference to reapportionment in his communications to Congress, announced in January 1927 that he favored passage of a new apportionment bill during the short session of the 69th Congress, which would end in less than two months. The House Census Committee refused to act. Its chairman, Rep. E. Hart Fenn (R Conn.) therefore moved in the House on March 2, 1927, to suspend the rules and pass a bill he had introduced authorizing the Secretary of Commerce to reapportion the House immediately after the 1930 census. The motion was voted down 183 to 197.

The Fenn bill was rewritten early in the 70th Congress (1927-29) to give Congress itself a chance to act before the proposed reapportionment by the Secretary of Commerce should go into effect. The bill was submitted to the House, which on May 18, 1928, voted 186 to 165 to recommit it to the Census Committee. After minor changes, the Fenn bill was again reported to the House and was passed on Jan. 11, 1929. No record vote was taken on passage of the bill, but a motion to return it to the Committee was rejected 134-227.

Four days later, the reapportionment bill was reported out of the Senate Committee on Commerce. Repeated efforts to bring it up for floor action ahead of other bills were made in vain. Its supporters gave up the fight on Feb. 27, 1929—five days before the end of the session, when it became evident that Senators from states which would lose representation were ready to carry on a filibuster that would have blocked not only reapportionment but all other measures then awaiting final passage.

Intervention by President Hoover

With the time for the next census rapidly approaching, President Hoover listed provision for the 1930 census and reapportionment as "matters of emergency legislation" that should be acted upon in the special session of the 71st Congress that was convened on April 15, 1929. In response to this urgent request, the Senate June 13 passed, 48 to 37, a combined census-reapportionment bill which had been approved by voice vote of the House two days earlier.

The 1929 law established a permanent system of reapportioning the 435 House seats following each census. It provided that immediately after the convening of the 71st Congress for its short session in December 1930, the President should transmit to Congress a statement showing the apportionment population of each state together with an apportionment of Representatives to each state based on the existing size of the House. Failing enactment of new apportionment legislation, that apportionment would go into effect without further action and would remain in effect for ensuing elections to the House of Repre-

Method of Equal Proportions

The basic problem in reapportionment is to determine the most equitable distribution of the 435 House seats among the states. There is no way of assigning a fractional Representative to a state or of giving a Representative a fractional vote. Nor is there any way by which two states could share the same Representative. To surmount such difficulties and achieve the fairest possible distribution of seats, Congress in 1941 adopted the Method of Equal Proportions. By this method, the proportional differences in the number of persons per Representative for any pair of states are reduced to a minimum.

Under the Constitution, each state is entitled to at least one seat in the House of Representatives. Thus, the first 50 seats are fixed. The question then becomes how to divide the remaining 385—which states are entitled to a second, third, fourth, etc. seat? To make the computation according to the Method of Equal Proportions, the apportionment population of each state is multiplied by the decimal of the fraction $\frac{1}{n(n-1)}$ where "n" is the number of seats for the state. The result of this multiplication is a number called a priority value.

For example, for 1970 the priority value for a second seat for California was determined by multiplying the apportionment population (residents plus residents overseas) of the state for that year, 20,098,863, by $\frac{1}{2(2-1)}$ (or 0.707 10678). The result of this multiplication was 14,212,042. The same computation was then made for New York, which involved multiplying New York's apportionment population, 18,287,529, by the same factor, 0.707 10678. The result was 12,931,236. This operation was repeated for every state. The result for the least populous state, Alaska, was 215,008.

To determine the priority value for each state's claim to a third seat, the population of the state is multiplied by $\frac{1}{3(3-1)}$, or 0.408 24829. The result for California was a priority value of 8,205,326. This process is repeated for every state for any desired number of seats. Thus, to determine the strength of California's claim to a 40th seat, the multiplier was $\frac{1}{40(40-1)}$ or 0.025 31848. The resulting priority value for the state in 1970 was 508,873.

When the necessary priority values for all the states have been computed, they are arranged in order, largest first. California, with the largest priority value for a second seat in 1970, received that seat, which was number 51 for the entire House. New York came next in line for a second seat, which was number 52.

The first 10 and bottom 10 priority values and the states involved, calculated by the Census Bureau on the basis of the 1970 census, were as follows:

Size of House	State	Size of State Delegation	Priority Value
51	California	2	14,212,042
52	New York	2	12,931,236
53	Pennsylvania	2	8,403,479
54	California	3	8,205,326
55	Texas	2	7,989,449
56	Illinois	2	7,908,509
57	Ohio	2	7,587,397
58	New York	3	7,465,852
59	Michigan	2	6,319,552
60	California	4	5,802,042
426	Michigan	19	483,268
427	Texas	24	480,908
428	South Carolina	6	477,855
429	Ohio	23	477,016
430	South Dakota	2	476,058
431	Illinois	24	476,036
432	New York	39	475,041
433	Florida	15	473,088
434	California	43	472,947
435	Oklahoma	6	472,043

The test of fairness of the Method of Equal Proportions is whether the percentage difference in population per Representative is the smallest possible for any pair of states. Again using the Census Bureau calculations for 1970, states can be compared with each other to test the method.

With six seats for Oklahoma, the average number of persons per Representative was 430,914. The state of Connecticut also was allocated six seats. The average number of persons per seat in Connecticut was 508,449, 17.99 percent more than the average for Oklahoma. But if a seat were taken from Oklahoma and given to Connecticut, the difference in the number of persons per Representative would have been 18.65 percent.

South Dakota received two seats, North Dakota only one. The difference was 85.2 percent in population of Congressional districts. However, if the situation had been reversed, North Dakota receiving two and South Dakota one seat, the difference would have been 115.72 percent. In each of these comparisons, the test is met: the proportional difference between the numbers per Representative is smaller for the apportionment as computed than would be the case with alternative methods. A similar comparison could be carried out in relation to the number of Representatives per million of the population, and the results would be the same.

SOURCE: Conrad Taeuber (Associate Director, Bureau of the Census), "Reapportionment," *U.S. Department of Commerce News*, Dec. 7, 1970, p. 1-6.

sentatives until another census had been taken and another reapportionment made.

Because two whole decades had passed between reapportionments, a greater shift than usual took place following the Census of 1930. California's House delegation was almost doubled, rising from 11 to 20. Michigan gained four seats, Texas three, and New Jersey, New York and Ohio two each. Twenty-one states lost a total of 27 seats: Missouri alone lost three and Georgia, Iowa, Kentucky and Pennsylvania each lost two.

The 1929 Act required the President to report the distribution of seats by two methods, major fractions and equal proportions. This was in the nature of a test to see which method yielded the fairest result. However, pending legislation to the contrary, the method of major fractions was to be used.

The two methods gave an identical distribution of seats based on 1930 census figures. However, in 1940 the two methods gave different results: under major fractions, Michigan would have gained a seat lost by Arkansas; under equal proportions, there would have been no change in either state. The automatic reapportionment provisions of the 1929 Act went into effect in January 1941. But the House Census Committee moved to reverse the result, favoring the certain Democratic seat in Arkansas over a possible Republican gain if the seat were shifted to Michigan. Congress went along, adopting Equal Proportions as the method to be used in reapportionment calculations after the 1950 and subsequent censuses, and making this action retroactive to January 1941 in order to save Arkansas its seat.

While politics doubtless played a part in timing of the action taken in 1941, the Method of Equal Proportions had come to be accepted as the best available. It had been worked out by Prof. Edward V. Huntington of Harvard in 1921. At the request of the Speaker of the House, all known methods of apportionment were considered in 1929 by the National Academy of Sciences Committee on Apportionment. The Committee expressed its preference for Equal Proportions.

This method involves complicated mathematical calculations. In brief, each of the states (now 50) is initially assigned the one seat to which every state is entitled by the Constitution. The population of each state then is multiplied by a series of multipliers. There are 59 of these multipliers, each one decreasing in size. The products of all the multiplications are arranged in order of size, beginning with the largest, to form what is known as the priority list. Seats numbered 51 through 435 are then distributed according to that list. *(For full explanation, see box.)*

Court Action on Apportionment

After the long and desultory battle over reapportionment in the 1920s, those who were unhappy over the inaction of Congress or the state legislatures began taking their cases to court. At first, they had no luck. But as the disparity in both Federal and state legislative districts grew, and the Supreme Court began to show a tendency to intervene, plaintiffs were more successful. Finally, in a series of decisions beginning with *Baker v. Carr* in 1962, the Court intervened massively in the redistricting process, ordering that Congressional districts as well as state and local legislative districts be drawn so that their populations would be as nearly equal as possible.

Supreme Court's 1932 Decisions

In 1932 the Supreme Court handed down several important decisions on Congressional redistricting. In each case, petitioners asserted that state legislatures had not complied with the 1911 Act's requirement that districts be separate, compact, contiguous and equally populated. The question was whether that requirement, neither specifically repealed nor reaffirmed in the 1929 Act, was still in effect.

In *Smiley v. Holm* the petitioner also attacked a Minnesota redistricting statute which the Legislature had not repassed over the Governor's veto because it contended that districting legislation was not subject to veto. The Supreme Court, ignoring the question of compliance with the 1911 Act and ruling solely on the issue of the gubernatorial veto, declared that the U.S. Constitution did not exempt districting statutes from a Governor's veto. Two other 1932 Congressional districting cases—*Koenig v. Flynn*, from the New York Court of Appeals, and *Carroll v. Becker*, from the Missouri Supreme Court, were decided by the Supreme Court on similar questions regarding gubernatorial vetoes.

The question of the 1911 Act's applicability was reached in *Wood v. Broom*, a 1932 case challenging the constitutionality of a new Mississippi redistricting law. Speaking for the Court, Chief Justice Charles Evans Hughes ruled that the 1911 Act had, in effect, expired with the approval of the 1929 apportionment Act and that the standards of the 1911 Act were therefore no longer applicable. The Court reversed the decision of a lower Federal court which had permanently enjoined elections under the new Mississippi redistricting act because it violated the standards of the 1911 Act. Later the same year the Court made a similar ruling in *Mahan v. Hume*, a Kentucky Congressional districting case.

Four Members of the Supreme Court—Justices Louis D. Brandeis, Harlan F. Stone, Owen J. Roberts and Benjamin N. Cardozo—while concurring in the majority opinion, said they would have dismissed the Wood suit for "want of equity." The "want-of-equity" phrase in this context suggested a policy of judicial self-limitation with respect to the entire question of judicial involvement in essentially "political" questions.

Court's Decision in 1946 Case

Not until 1946, in *Colegrove v. Green*, did the Court again rule in a significant case dealing with Congressional redistricting. The case was brought by Kenneth Colegrove, a political science professor at Northwestern University, who alleged that Illinois' Congressional districts—varying between 112,116 and 914,053 in population—were so unequal that they violated the 14th Amendment's guarantee of equal protection of the laws. A seven-man Supreme Court divided 4-3 in dismissing the suit.

Justice Felix Frankfurter gave the plurality opinion of the Court, speaking for himself and Justices Stanley F. Reed and Harold H. Burton. Frankfurter's opinion cited *Wood v. Broom* to indicate that Congress had deliberately removed the standard set by the 1911 Act. "We also agree," he said, "with the four Justices (Brandeis, Stone, Roberts and Cardozo) who were of the opinion that the bill in *Wood v. Broom* should be 'dismissed for want of equity.' " The issue, Frankfurter said, was "of a peculiarly political nature and therefore not meet for judicial interpretation....The short of it is that the Constitution has conferred upon Congress exclusive authority to secure fair representation by the states in the popular House and has left to that House determination whether states have fulfilled their responsibility. If Congress failed in exercising its powers, whereby standards of fairness are offended, the remedy lies ultimately with the people...To sustain this action would cut very deep into the very being of Congress. Courts ought not to enter this political thicket. The remedy for unfairness in districting is to secure state legislatures that will apportion properly, or to invoke the ample powers of Congress." Frankfurter said, in addition, that the Court could not affirmatively remap Congressional districts and that elections at large would be politically undesirable.

Justice Hugo L. Black, joined in a dissenting opinion by Justices William O. Douglas and Frank Murphy, expressed the belief that the District Court had jursidiction under a section of the U.S. Code giving district courts the right to redress deprivations of constitutional rights occurring through action of the states. Black's opinion also rested on a previous case in which the Court had indicated that Federal constitutional questions, unless "frivolous," fall under the jursidiction of the Federal courts. Black asserted that the appellants had standing to sue, that the population disparities did violate the equal protection clause of the 14th Amendment, and that relief should be granted. Black specifically rejected the view that *Smiley v. Holm* had set a precedent of non-justiciability. *Smiley v. Holm,* he said, merely decided that the 1911 Act was no longer applicable. Only a minority of the Court, he pointed out, had thought the case should be dismissed for "want of equity."

With the Court split 3-3 on whether the Judiciary had or should exercise jurisdiction, the deciding opinion in *Colegrove v. Green* was that of Justice Wiley B. Rutledge. On the question of justiciability, Rutledge agreed with Black, Douglas and Murphy that the issue could be considered by the Federal courts. "But for the ruling in *Smiley v. Holm,*" Rutledge said, he would have thought that the Constitution specifically reserved the regulation of Congressional elections to the states and Congress. Rutledge believed, however, that Smiley "rules squarely to the contrary." Thus a majority of the Court participating in the Colegrove case felt that Congressional redistricting cases were justiciable.

On the other hand, on the question of granting relief in this specific instance, Rutledge agreed with Frankfurter, Reed and Burton that the case should be dismissed. He pointed out that four of the nine justices in *Wood v. Broom* had felt that dismissal should be for want of equity. Rutledge saw a "want-of-equity" situation in *Colegrove v. Green* as well. "I think the gravity of the constitutional questions raised so great, together with the possibility of collision (with the political departments of the Government), that the admonition (against avoidable constitutional decision) is appropriate to be followed here," Rutledge said. Jurisdiction, he thought, should be exercised "only in the most compelling circumstances." He thought that "the shortness of time remaining (before the forthcoming election) makes it doubtful whether action could or would be taken in time to secure for petitioners the effective relief they seek." Rutledge warned that Congressional elections at large would deprive citizens of representation by districts, "which the prevailing policy of Congress demands." In the case of at-large elections, he warned, "the cure sought may be worse than the disease." For all these reasons he concluded that the case was "one in which the Court may properly, and should, decline to exercise its jurisdiction."

Factors Leading to New Court Position

In the ensuing years, law professors, political scientists and other commentators expressed growing dislike for the Colegrove doctrine and growing impatience with the Supreme Court's position. Yet the membership of the Court was changing, and the new members were more inclined toward judicial action on redistricting. By 1962, only three members of the Colegrove Court remained: Justices Black and Douglas, dissenters in that case, and Justice Frankfurter, aging spokesman for restraint in the exercise of judicial power.

Already in the 1950s, the Court had decided two cases which laid some groundwork for its subsequent reapportionment decisions. The first was *Brown v. Board of Education* (1954), the historic school desegregation case, in which the Court decided that an individual citizen could assert a right to equal protection of the laws under the 14th Amendment, contrary to the "separate but equal" doctrine of public facilities for white and Negro citizens. Six years later, in *Gomillion v. Lightfoot* (1960), the Court held that the Alabama Legislature could not draw the city limits of Tuskegee so as to exclude the Negro community. Justice Frankfurter based his opinion on the 15th Amendment, but Justice Charles E. Whittaker said that the equal protection clause was the proper constitutional basis for the decision. One commentator later remarked that *Gomillion* amounted to a "dragon" in the "political thicket" of *Colegrove*.

With this groundwork already laid, during the years 1962-64 the Supreme Court rendered a series of four landmark decisions in the politically sensitive area of Congressional and state legislative apportionment and districting. The precedent-breaking decisions all had a common theme—that "as nearly as practicable, one man's vote... is to be worth as much as another's." By entering the "political thicket" of apportionment and redistricting, the Court extended its authority far beyond its previous scope and seemed certain to cause a revolution in the complexion of state government and the bases of Congressional power.

A major element causing the reversal of the Court's previous decision on reapportionment and redistricting was the population migration from country to city, which had been under way ever since the turn of the century. By 1960, there was not a single legislative body in a single state in which there was not at least a 2-1 population disparity between the most and the least heavily populated districts. For example, the disparity was 242 to 1 in the Connecticut House, 223 to 1 in the Nevada Senate, 141 to 1 in the Rhode Island Senate and 9 to 1 in the Georgia Senate. Studies of the effective vote of large and small counties in state legislatures between 1910 and 1960 showed that the effective vote of the large counties had slipped while their percentage of the national population had more than doubled. The most lightly populated counties, on the other hand, advanced from a position of slight over-representation to one of extreme over-representation, holding almost twice as many seats as they would be entitled to by population alone. Predictably, the rural-dominated state legislatures resisted every move toward reapportioning districts to reflect new population patterns.

By no means as gross but still substantial was population imbalance among Congressional districts. In Texas, the Census of 1960 showed the most heavily populated district had four times as many inhabitants as the most lightly populated. Arizona, Maryland and Ohio each had at least one district with three times as many inhabitants as the most lightly populated. In a majority of cases, it was rural areas which benefited from Congressional malapportionment. As a result of the postwar population movement out of central cities to the surrounding areas, the suburbs were the most under-represented.

Historic 1962 Decision

It was against this background that a group of Tennessee city dwellers successfully broke the long-standing precedent against Federal court involvement in legislative apportionment problems. For more than half a century, since 1901, the Tennessee Legislature had refused to reapportion itself, even though a decennial reapportionment based on population was specifically required by the state's constitution. In the meantime, Tennessee's population had grown and shifted dramatically to urban areas. By 1960, the House legislative districts ranged from 3,454 to 36,031 in population, while the Senate districts ranged from 39,727 to 108,094. Appeals by urban residents to the rural-controlled Tennesee Legislatures proved fruitless. A suit brought in the state courts to force reapportionment was rejected on the ground that the courts should stay out of legislative matters.

The urban interests then appealed to the Federal courts, stating that they had no redress: the Legislature had refused to act for more than half a century; the state courts had refused to intervene; Tennessee had no referendum or initiative laws. The city dwellers charged that there was "a debasement of their votes by virtue of the incorrect, obsolete and unconstitutional apportionment" to such an extent that they were being deprived of their right to "equal protection of the laws" under the 14th Amendment. (The 14th Amendment reads, in part: "No state shall...deny to any person within its jurisdiction the equal protection of the laws.")

The Supreme Court on March 26, 1962, handed down its historic decision in *Baker v. Carr,* ruling in favor of the Tennessee city dwellers by a 6-2 margin. In the majority opinion, Justice William J. Brennan Jr. emphasized that the Federal judiciary had the power to review the apportionment of state legislatures under the 14th Amendment's equal protection clause. "The mere fact that a suit seeks protection as a political right," Brennan wrote, "does not mean that it presents a political question" which the courts should avoid.

In a vigorous dissent, Justice Frankfurter said the majority decision constituted "a massive repudiation of the experience of our whole past" and was an assertion of "destructively novel judicial power." He contended that the lack of any clear basis for relief "catapults

the lower courts" into a "mathematical quagmire." Frankfurter insisted that "there is not under our Constitution a judicial remedy for every political mischief." Appeal for relief, he maintained, should not be made in the courts, but rather "to an informed civically militant electorate."

One Man, One Vote for Congressmen

Shortly after the Baker decision was handed down, James P. Wesberry Jr., an Atlanta resident and a member of the Georgia Senate, filed suit in a Federal court in Atlanta claiming that gross disparity in the population of Georgia's Congressional districts violated 14th Amendment rights of equal protection of the laws. At the time, Georgia districts ranged in population from 272,154 in the rural 9th district in the northeastern part of the state to 823,860 in the 5th district in Atlanta and its suburbs. District lines had not been changed since 1931. The state's number of House seats remained the same in the interim, but Atlanta's district population—already high in 1931 compared with the others—had more than doubled in 30 years, making a 5th District vote worth about one-third that of a vote in the 9th.

On June 20, 1962, the three-judge Federal court divided 2-1 in dismissing Wesberry's suit. The majority reasoned that the precedent of *Colegrove* still controlled in Congressional district cases. The judges cautioned against Federal judicial interference with Congress and against "depriving others of the right to vote" it the suit should result in at-large elections. They suggested that the Georgia Legislature (under court order to reapportion itself) or the U.S. Congress might better provide relief. Wesberry then appealed to the Supreme Court, which heard arguments on the case in November 1963.

On Feb. 17, 1964, the Supreme Court ruled in the case of *Wesberry v. Sanders* that Congressional districts must be substantially equal in population. The Court, which upheld Wesberry's challenge by a 6-3 decision, based its ruling on the history and wording of Article I, Section 2, of the Constitution providing that Representatives shall be apportioned among the states according to their respective numbers and be chosen by the people of the several states. This language, the Court stated, meant that "as nearly as is practicable, one man's vote in a Congressional election is to be worth as much as another's."

The majority opinion, written by Justice Black and supported by Chief Justice Earl Warren and Justices Brennan, Douglas, Arthur J. Goldberg and Byron R. White, said that "While it may not be possible to draw Congressional districts with mathematical precision, that is no excuse for ignoring our Constitution's plain objective of making equal representation for equal numbers of people the fundamental goal for the House of Representatives."

Predictably, the decision referred to the findings of the Baker case to show that districting questions were justiciable and to the *Gray v. Sanders* case to establish the principle of "one man, one vote." (*Gray v. Sanders,* 1963, overturned Georgia's county unit system of voting in statewide and Congressional primary elections.) Unlike those two decisions, however, the Wesberry decision did not attempt to use the 14th Amendment as its justification.

Conflicting Arguments in Wesberry v. Sanders

Wesberry v. Sanders, the Supreme Court's landmark decision on Congressional redistricting, was handed down Feb. 17, 1964. Justice Hugo L. Black, arguing for the majority, based his reasoning on Article I, Section 2, of the Constitution. Justice John M. Harlan, dissenting, argued that the Supreme Court should not intrude itself into what he saw as primarily a political question.

Justice Black, for the majority: "We agree with the District Court that the 1931 Georgia apportionment grossly discriminates against voters in the Fifth Congressional District. A single Congressman represents from two to three times as many Fifth District voters as are represented by each of the Congressmen from the other Georgia Congressional districts. The apportionment statute thus contracts the value of some votes and expands that of others. If the Federal Constitution intends that when qualified voters elect Members of Congress each vote be given as much weight as any other vote, then this statute cannot stand.

"We hold that, construed in its historical context, the command of Article I, Section 2, that Representatives be chosen 'by the People of the several States' means that as nearly as is practicable one man's vote in a Congressional election is to be worth as much as another's. This rule is followed automatically, of course, when Representatives are chosen as a group on a statewide basis, as was a widespread practice in the first 50 years of our nation's history. It would be extraordinary to suggest that in such statewide elections the votes of inhabitants of some parts of a State, for example, Georgia's thinly populated Ninth District, could be weighed at two or three times the value of the votes of people living in more populous parts of the State, for example, the Fifth District around Atlanta.... We do not believe that the Framers of the Constitution intended to permit the same vote-diluting discrimination to be accomplished through the device of districts containing widely varied numbers of inhabitants. To say that a vote is worth more in one district than in another would not only run counter to our fundamental ideas of democratic government, it would cast aside the principle of a House of Representatives elected 'by the People,' a principle tenaciously fought for and established at the Constitutional Convention. The history of the Constitution, particularly that part of it relating to the adoption of Article I, Section 2, reveals that those who framed the Constitution meant that, no matter what the mechanics of an election, whether statewide or by districts, it was population which was to be the basis of the House of Representatives....

"It would defeat the principle solemnly embodied in the Great Compromise—equal representation in the House of equal numbers of people—for us to hold that, within the states, legislatures may draw the lines of Congressional districts in such a way as to give some voters a greater voice in choosing a Congress-man than others. The House of Representatives, the Convention agreed, was to represent the people as individuals, and on a basis of complete equality for each voter. The delegates were quite aware of what Madison called the 'vicious representation' in Great Britain whereby 'rotten boroughs' with few inhabitants were represented in Parliament on or almost on a par with cities of greater population. Wilson urged that people must be represented as individuals, so that America would escape the evils of the English system under which one man could send two members to Parliament to represent the borough of Old Sarum while London's million people sent but four. The delegates referred to rotten borough apportionments in some of the state legislatures as the kind of objectionable governmental action that the Constitution should not tolerate in the election of Congressional representatives."

Justice John M. Harlan, dissenting: "...the language of Article I Sections 2 and 4, the surrounding text, and the relevant history are all in strong and consistent direct contradiction of the Court's holding. The constitutional scheme vests in the States plenary power to regulate the conduct of elections for Representatives, and, in order to protect the Federal Government, provides for Congressional supervision of the States' exercise of their power. Within this scheme, the appellants do not have the right which they assert, in the absence of provision for equal districts by the Georgia Legislature or the Congress. The constitutional right which the Court creates is manufactured out of whole cloth....

"The claim for judicial relief in this case strikes at one of the fundamental doctrines of our system of government, the separation of powers. In upholding that claim, the Court attempts to effect reforms in a field which the Constitution, as plainly as can be, has committed exclusively to the political process.

"This Court, no less than all other branches of the Government, is bound by the Constitution. The Constitution does not confer on the Court blanket authority to step into every situation where the political branch may be thought to have fallen short. The stability of this institution ultimately depends not only upon its being alert to keep the other branches of government within constitutional bounds but equally upon recognition of the limitations on the Court's own functions in the constitutional system.

"What is done today saps the political process. The promise of judicial intervention in matters of this sort cannot but encourage popular inertia in efforts for political reform through the political process, with the inevitable result that the process is itself weakened. By yielding to the demand for a judicial remedy in this instance, the Court in my view does a disservice both to itself and to the broader values of our system of government."

In a strongly worded dissent, Justice John M. Harlan asserted that the Constitution did not establish population as the only criterion of Congressional districting and that the subject was left in the Constitution to the discretion of the states, subject only to the supervisory power of Congress.

Justice Potter Stewart said he found that the Constitution gave "no mandate to this Court or to any court to ordain that Congressional districts within each state must be equal in population," but he disagreed with Harlan in that he thought the matter was justiciable.

Justice Tom C. Clark also found the matter justiciable but rejected the idea that Article I, Section 2, required a "one man, one vote" standard in Congressional elections. Clark said the case should be returned to the lower court for a hearing on the merits based on the 14th Amendment's equal protection requirements set down in the Baker case.

The Wesberry opinion established no precise standards for districting beyond declaring that districts must be as nearly equal in population "as is practicable." In his dissent, Harlan suggested that a disparity of more than 100,000 between a state's largest and smallest districts would "presumably" violate the equality standard enunciated by the majority. On that basis, Harlan estimated, the districts of 37 states with 398 Representatives would be unconstitutional, "leaving a constitutional House of 37 Members now sitting."

Neither did the Court's decision make any reference to gerrymandering, since it discussed only the population, not the shape of districts. In a separate districting opinion handed down the same day as *Wesberry,* the Court dismissed a challenge to Congressional districts in New York City, which had been brought by voters who charged that Manhattan's 17th "silk-stocking" district had been gerrymandered to exclude Negroes and Puerto Rican citizens.

Decision on Variance in Size of Districts

The next step in the Court's districting rulings came on April 7, 1969. On that date, the Court in a 6-3 decision tightened the "one man, one vote" principle by declaring Missouri's redistricting statute unconstitutional. *(Kirkpatrick v. Preisler).* Justice Brennan, speaking for the Court, said that states must strive to create Congressional districts of precisely equal population. Any variance in population, "no matter how small," must be justified by the state or shown to result in spite of a "good-faith effort."

In *Wesberry v. Sanders,* Brennan pointed out, the Court had held that the Constitution required "as nearly as is practicable one man's vote in a Congressional election...be worth as much as another's." Defining the phrase "as nearly as is practicable," Brennan said there was no fixed population variance small enough to be considered negligible. The Wesberry standard directed states to create districts absolutely equal in population. In the Court's words: "Equal representation for equal numbers of people is a principle designed to prevent debasement of voting power and diminution of access to elected Representatives. Toleration of even small deviations detracts from these purposes."

Maximum Population Variations From State Averages

(At time of Wesberry v. Sanders, *February 1964)*

State*	Maximum Variation	Total Districts
Alabama	+ 21.4%	8
Arizona	− 54.3	3
Arkansas	+ 28.8	4
California	+ 42.4	38
Colorado	− 55.4	4
Connecticut	− 37.1	6
Florida	+ 60.3	12
Georgia	+ 108.9	10
Idaho	22.9 #	2
Illinois	− 33.6	24
Indiana	+ 64.6	11
Iowa	+ 12.3	7
Kansas	+ 23.9	5
Kentucky	+ 40.8	7
Louisiana	− 35.2	8
Maine	4.3 #	2
Maryland	+ 83.5	8
Massachusetts	− 12.3	12
Michigan	+ 84.8	19
Minnesota	− 13.2	8
Mississippi	+ 39.7	5
Missouri	+ 17.3	10
Montana	18.7 #	2
Nebraska	− 14.0	3
New Hampshire	9.3 #	2
New Jersey	+ 44.8	15
New York	+ 15.1	41
North Carolina	− 32.9	11
North Dakota	5.4 #	2
Ohio	+ 72.1	24
Oklahoma	+ 42.5	6
Oregon	− 40.0	4
Pennsylvania	+ 31.9	27
Rhode Island	7.0 #	2
South Carolina	+ 33.9	6
South Dakota	46.3 #	2
Tennessee	+ 58.2	9
Texas	+ 118.5	23
Utah	28.6 #	2
Virginia	+ 36.0	10
Washington	+ 25.2	7
West Virginia	− 18.6	5
Wisconsin	+ 3.4	10

Alaska, Delaware, Hawaii, Nevada, New Mexico, Vermont and Wyoming seats were filled at large and therefore are not listed.

#State has only two districts: thus one district is the stated percentage above the average and the other district is the stated percentage below the average.

The only permissible variances in population, the Court ruled, were those unavoidable despite the effort to achieve absolute equality or those which could be legally justified. The variances in Missouri, which amounted to 3.1 percent between Congressional districts on a statewide basis, could have been avoided, the Court said.

None of Missouri's arguments for the plan qualified as "legally acceptable" justifications. The Court rejected the argument that population variance was necessary to allow representation of distinct interest groups. It held acceptance of such variances in order to produce districts with specific interests as "antithetical" to the basic purpose of equal representation.

The Court also rejected the argument that political reality—legislative compromise or the integrity of existing political boundaries—justified population variance. It dismissed arguments that nonvoting military personnel and students inflated census figures for certain districts, that post-1960 population trends were reflected in the new districts, and that geographical compactness dictated the new boundaries and some population inequality.

Dissenting Opinions. Justice White dissented from the Court's opinion, which he characterized as "an unduly rigid and unwarranted application of the Equal Protection Clause which will unnecessarily involve the courts in the abrasive task of drawing district lines." The Justice added that some "acceptably small" population variance could be established. He indicated that considerations of existing political boundaries and geographical compactness could justify to him some variation from "absolute equality" of population.

Justice Harlan, joined by Justice Stewart, objected that "whatever room remained under this Court's prior decisions for the free play of the political process in matters of reapportionment is now all but eliminated by today's Draconian judgments."

As a result of the Court decisions of the 1960s, nearly every state was forced to redraw its Congressional district lines—sometimes more than once. By the end of the decade, 39 of the 45 states with more than one Representative had made the necessary adjustments.

Congress and Redistricting

Several attempts were made during the period of court action to enact new legislation on redistricting. Only one of the efforts was successful—the passage of a measure to rule out at-large elections in states with more than one Representative.

On Jan. 9, 1951, President Truman, upon presentation of the official state population figures of the Census of 1950, asked for changes in the existing law which would tighten Federal control of state redistricting. Specifically, he asked for a ban on gerrymandering, an end to "at-large" seats in states having more than one Representative, and a sharp reduction in the huge differences in size between Congressional districts in each state.

On behalf of the Administration, Chairman Emanuel Celler (D N.Y.) of the House Judiciary Committee introduced a bill to require compact and contiguous Congressional districts which would not vary by more than 15 per cent between districts within a state. The bill also would have eliminated at-large seats and made redis-

tricting mandatory every 10 years in accordance with population changes. But the House Judiciary Committee took no action on the proposals.

Rep. Celler regularly introduced his bill throughout the 1950s and early 1960s, but it made no headway until the Supreme Court handed down the Wesberry decision in 1964. On June 24 of that year a Celler bill finally was approved by a House Judiciary Subcommittee. But the full Committee did not act on the bill before adjournment.

On March 16, 1965, the House passed a new Celler bill. It established 15 percent as the maximum percentage by which a Congressional district's population might deviate from the average size of the state's districts; prohibited at-large elections for any state with more than one House seat; required that districts be composed of "contiguous territory in as compact form as practicable"; and forbade more than one redistricting of a state between decennial censuses. A major reason for House approval of Celler's bill appeared to be a desire to gain protection from Court imposition of even more rigid criteria. "We're saying to the courts that we're setting guidelines which we expect them to follow," Rep. James C. Corman (D Calif.) said. But the measure encountered difficulties in the Senate Judiciary Committee. After considerable wrangling over its provisions, the Committee voted to report the bill without precise agreement on its wording. No actual report was ever filed by the Senate Judiciary Committee.

In 1967, a redistricting bill was passed by both the Senate and the House but not in the same form. And the bill had a different purpose from that of previous bills dealing with the subject. Instead of trying to establish standards of fairness in drawing district lines, the chief purpose in 1967 was to prevent the courts, until after the House had been reapportioned on the basis of the Census of 1970, from ordering redistricting of House seats or from ordering any state to hold elections at large—a procedure that many incumbent Representatives feared.

A combination of liberal Democrats and Republicans in the Senate managed to defeat the conference report Nov. 8, 1967, by a vote of 22-55. Liberals favored court action which they believed would eliminate many conservative rural districts, while Republicans felt that redistricted areas, especially in the growing suburbs, would elect more Republicans than Democrats.

To avoid at-large elections, the Senate added a rider to a House-passed private bill. Under the rider, at-large elections of U.S. Representatives were banned in all states entitled to more than one Representative, with the exceptions of New Mexico and Hawaii. Those states had a tradition of electing their two Representatives at large. Both of them, however, soon passed districting laws—New Mexico for the 1968 elections and Hawaii for 1970.

Following the Census of 1960, an attempt had been made to increase the size of the House to avoid some of the losses of seats that would otherwise be suffered by several states. By a vote of 12-14 the House Judiciary Committee on Sept. 9, 1961, rejected a motion to recommend enlarging the House to 453 seats. And by a vote of 14-15, the same Committee rejected a bill reported by a subcommittee which would have increased the permanent size of the House to 438. In Committee voting, a majority of Democrats favored the House-increase bills while Republicans were almost unanimous in opposition. Republican National Chairman William E. Miller and other Republican leaders reportedly reached the conclusion that any increase in the size of the House was more likely to benefit Democrats than Republicans.

Bibliography

Books

Congressional Quarterly, *Representation and Apportionment,* 1966.

De Grazia, Alfred, *Essay on Apportionment and Representative Government.* American Enterprise Institute, 1963.

Dixon, Robert J., *Democratic Representation: Reapportionment in Law and Politics.* Oxford University Press, 1968.

Farrand, Max, *Records of the Federal Convention of 1787.* Yale University Press, 1937.

Hacker, Andrew, *Congressional Districting.* Brookings Institution, Revised Edition, 1964.

Hanson, Royce, *The Political Thicket: Reapportionment and Constitutional Democracy.* Prentice-Hall, 1966.

Jewell, Malcolm (ed.), *The Politics of Reapportionment.* Atherton Press, 1962.

Keefe, William J. and Ogul, Morris S., *The American Legislative Process: Congress and the States.* Prentice-Hall, 1964.

Luce, Robert, *Legislative Principles.* Houghton Mifflin, 1930.

McKay, Robert B., *Reapportionment: The Law and Politics of Equal Representation.* Twentieth Century Fund, 1965.

Rossiter, Clinton (ed.), *The Federalist Papers.* The New American Library, 1961.

Schmeckebier, Laurence F., *Congressional Apportionment.* Brookings Institution, 1941.

Schubert, Glendon (ed.), *Reapportionment.* Charles Scribner's Sons, 1965.

Articles

Celler, Emanuel, "Congressional Apportionment—Past, Present, and Future," *Law and Contemporary Problems,* Vol. 17, 1952.

Chafee, Zechariah, "Congressional Reapportionment," *Harvard Law Review,* Vol. 42, 1929.

Farrelly, David, and Ivan Hinderaker, "Congressional Reapportionment and National Political Power," *Law and Contemporary Problems,* Vol. 17, 1952.

Tabor, Neil, "The Gerrymandering of State and Federal Legislative Districts," *Maryland Law Review,* Vol. 16, 1956.

Government Publications

Huntington, Edward V., *Methods of Apportionment in Congress.* Government Printing Office, 1940.

Taeuber, Conrad, "Reapportionment," *U.S. Department of Commerce News,* Dec. 7, 1970.

Chapter 6—Pressures on Congress

Constituency Pressures

T HE RELATIONSHIP between a Member of Congress and his constituents is the crux of self-government in the United States. The vitality of that relationship alone assures that government by laws enacted in Congress is also government by the people. How can the people be said to govern themselves unless they are effectively *represented* in their legislature?

The survival today—in a continental empire embracing 200 million people—of representative institutions created nearly 200 years ago by 13 small colonies is an extraordinary historical phenomenon. But can 200 million people really be said to govern themselves? No one pretends that Senators and Representatives carry out the instructions of the residents of their states or districts. Nor does anyone believe that they completely ignore the will of the voters who choose them. What, then, is the relationship between the lawmaker and the citizen?

The 1960s witnessed a growing sense that government is slipping from the hands of the governed, a sense quite pronounced among a younger generation which demands more "participatory democracy." As this generation inherits the American democracy, the connections between citizen and legislator assume crucial importance. Is the ideal of representative government fading before a new reality?

Representative Government

In a pure, or direct, democracy, there are no constituents; each citizen represents himself. Execution of the laws may be delegated, but the full body of citizens makes the laws. The Athenian city-state and the New England town meeting are the best-known examples approximating this ideal.

The adoption of direct democracy by states with larger populations and extensive territory is a practical impossibility. But where the ideal of popular self-government is cherished, even vast populations can participate in lawmaking by choosing delegates to speak and vote for them. In theory, representative government may be substituted for direct democracy solely as a matter of convenience. Representative government will approach democratic government in direct proportion to the degree of agreement between the representative's acts and his constituents' wishes.

Representative institutions are not necessarily derived from democratic theory. In fact, the English Parliament, from which the United States Congress can trace descent, originated in medieval practice under which the king summoned feudal lords and representa-

tives of towns and counties to provide him with revenues. The lords acted on their own behalf; the Commons consisted of men chosen by a limited franchise and originally viewed as attorneys empowered to execute certain transactions on behalf of their electors. The assembling of peers and commoners was based as much on the ruler's incapacity to raise money through means of his own as it was on theories granting the estates of the realm any share in decision-making. The bureaucratic weakness of the monarchy placed the estates in a position to exact concessions in exchange for revenues. The evolution of the principle of "grievance before supply" into the doctrine of "no taxation without representation" need not be traced here. It is enough to note the development of the representative principle as a check on a government which was still expected to lead, not to follow, its people.

Prior to the American Revolution the colonists were English subjects represented, in theory, in the English Parliament. It was precisely the fictitious character of this representation against which the colonists rebelled. Having experienced government by their own elected representatives in the colonial legislatures, their patience with remote rulers was limited. The frustrations imposed by a government in which they did not participate impressed upon Americans the importance of exercising continuous control over the government. They expected lawmakers to be dominated by their constituents because they were rebelling against a regime too independent of its subjects.

The colonists could derive representative government from the social-contract theories of Englishmen like John Locke, which based legitimate authority on the consent of the governed. Not only consent, but active participation in government could be demanded on the basis of the colonists' experience of creating their own social order out of a state of nature. The absence of hereditary privileges and the prevalence of equal opportunities in a new land encouraged the conviction that representative government should be based on a broad, popular electorate. Thus the experience of the frontier, like the experience of rebellion against unrepresentative government, pushed the Americans toward the view that constituents should control their legislators.

Belief in a right of constituents to instruct their representatives was widespread late in the 18th century. Efforts to instruct Members of Congress and state legislators were not uncommon, and several state constitutions explicitly recognized this right. Members of the Congress of the Confederation considered binding the instructions of their state legislatures.

Instruction of Representatives

In the First Session of the First Congress, an amendment to the Bill of Rights was proposed which would have constitutionally guaranteed the right of the people "to instruct their Representatives." Arguing for the amendment, Rep. Elbridge Gerry of Massachusetts observed: "The friends and patrons of this Constitution have always declared that the sovereignty resides in the people, and that they do not part with it on any occasion. To say the sovereignty vests in the people, and that they have not a right to instruct and control their Representatives, is absurd to the last degree."

Opponents in the House of Representatives argued that variety of instructions could prevent agreement, and that momentary popular sentiment might commit the legislature to action which its deliberation would reveal as shortsighted. Rep. James Madison of Virginia noted that guarantees of speech, press, assembly and petition protected the right to instruct Representatives, but he opposed *binding* a legislator to support specific measures because "from circumstances known to him but not to his constituents he (may be) convinced that they will endanger the public good." Rep. Thomas Hartley of Pennsylvania argued:

"It appears to my mind that the principle of representation is distinct from any agency which may require written instructions. The great end of meeting is to consult for the common good; but can the common good be discerned without the object is reflected and shown in every light? A local or partial view does not necessarily enable any man to comprehend it clearly; this can only result from an inspection into the aggregate. Instructions viewed in this light will be found to embarrass the best and wisest men."

Although the Constitution was not amended to empower constituents to instruct Members of Congress, the character of the Representative's obligations to those he represented remained a live issue. In 1816 a bill providing salaries (in lieu of per diem payments) to Members provoked a storm of criticism and led to the defeat of many of them. Returning after the election in a final session, these Members debated whether the popular response obligated them to repeal the salary bill. Rep. John C. Calhoun (S.C.) scoffed at the idea of "implied instructions," noting that the people had not assembled and deliberated to produce authenticated written instructions. "The Constitution," he said, "is my letter of instruction. Written by the hand of the people, stamped with their authority, it admits of no doubt as to its obligation."

Rep. Lewis Williams (N.C.) agreed with Calhoun that the Representative should not "surrender his judgment in obedience to mere passion or caprice." "But," he insisted, "if the Representative has no rational doubt that the people, in all their integrity of heart and with all the means of judgment before them, would decidedly object to a measure or firmly wish its adoption, then I hold that their will should be obligatory upon him."

Burke on Representation

When Edmund Burke was elected to the British Parliament to represent the city of Bristol, he made a speech to the electors which has since been regarded as the classic statement of the view that a representative should not be bound by instructions from those who choose him. The following is an excerpt from that speech, given Nov. 3, 1774:

"...Certainly, gentlemen, it ought to be the happiness and glory of a representative to live in the strictest union, the closest correspondence, and the most unreserved communication with his constituents. Their wishes ought to have great weight with him; their opinion, high respect; their business, unremitted attention. It is his duty to sacrifice his repose, his pleasures, his satisfactions, to theirs; and above all, ever, and in all cases, to prefer their interest to his own. But his unbiased opinion, his mature judgment, his enlightened conscience, he ought not to sacrifice to you, to any man, or to any set of men living. These he does not derive from your pleasure; no, nor from the law and the constitution. They are a trust from Providence, for the abuse of which he is deeply answerable. Your representative owes you not his industry only, but his judgment; and he betrays, instead of serving you, if he sacrifices it to your opinion.

"My worthy colleague says, his will ought to be subservient to yours. If that be all, the thing is innocent. If government were a matter of will upon any side, yours, without question, ought to be superior. But government and legislation are matters of reason and judgment, and not of inclination; and what sort of reason is that, in which the determination precedes the discussion; in which one set of men deliberate, and another decide; and where those who from the conclusion are perhaps three hundred miles distant from those who hear the arguments?

"To deliver an opinion, is the right of all men; that of constituents is a weighty and respectable opinion, which a representative ought always to rejoice to hear; and which he ought always most seriously to consider. But authoritative instructions; mandates issued, which the member is bound blindly and implicitly to obey, to vote and to argue for, though contrary to the clearest conviction of his judgment and conscience—these are things utterly unknown to the laws of this land, and which arise from a fundamental mistake of the whole order and tenor of our constitution.

"Parliament is not a *congress* of ambassadors from different and hostile interests; which interests each must maintain, as an agent and advocate, against other agents and advocates; but parliament is a *deliberative* assembly of *one* nation, with *one* interest, that of the whole; where, not local purposes, not local prejudices, ought to guide, but the general good, resulting from the general reason of the whole. You choose a member indeed; but when you have chosen him, he is not a member of Bristol, but he is a member of *Parliament....*"

Rep. Thomas P. Grosvenor (N.Y.) asserted that the right of instruction is not necessary to make the people masters over their Representatives because the latter every two years are "stripped of all power and wholly dependent on their will for continued official existence.... Responsibility for conduct, not control over it, while in office, is the real secret of our safety." In fact, Grosvenor saw in the Constitution an obligation *not* to be bound strictly by constituents. He said:

"When a member enters this Hall, he becomes a Representative of the people of this Republic—he becomes a legislator for the whole American community. What are his duties? Do they constitute him merely the guardian of his district? Are they confined to the little corners of townships and counties? No; they embrace the rights, the interests, and happiness of a great Republic. They 'insure domestic tranquility, provide for the common defense, promote the general welfare, and secure the blessings of liberty to ourselves and our posterity'; these are the sublime and comprehensive terms in which the people have taught to all their Representatives the great duties of their stations."

Thus in its earliest years Congress itself took up and debated most of the limitations that might legitimately be placed on control of Representatives by constituents even though the people were recognized as sovereign. The dangers of momentary popular passion or caprice; the priority of considered popular judgment expressed in the Constitution; the practical difficulties of establishing authentic constituent instructions, and of reconciling conflicting ones; the information often available to the Representatives but not to constituents; the need to deliberate, and to combine different viewpoints; the sufficiency of the ballot for controlling legislators; and the priority of the national interest over local interests—all these arguments have been used down to the present to justify independence from constituency pressures.

Senators and State Legislatures

The Senate was deliberately separated from the voters. Its constituents were not the people, but the state governments whose legislators chose them. They came to the seat of Government somewhat in the guise of ambassadors of semi-sovereign states. Their august name suggested the patrician traditions of the Roman Senate, and the analogous upper chamber in Great Britain, the House of Lords, was not elected at all. The functions of Senators included those of an executive council—advice and consent in international affairs and approval of Presidential appointments. At first, their debates were held in closed session, for they were not responsible to the general electorate.

Senators were ultimately dependent on the voters who elected the state legislators. But the legislators inevitably enjoyed great freedom in naming U.S. Senators. The voters had scant means to express their preferences, and even if a legislator cast his vote for an unpopular Senate candidate, it would be but one act among many determining his own popularity in state elections. Senators were further removed from popular control by their six-year terms, and the election of only one-third of the body at a time was designed to make it less dependent on the momentary will of the electorate.

Selection by state legislatures seemed a perfectly normal procedure at the time of the Constitutional Convention. It was the legislatures which had elected the governors and most of the civil and military officials during the revolution. The legislatures had elected members of the Continental Congress, delegates to the Congress of the Confederation, and delegates to the Constitutional Convention itself. In many states they also elected governors and judges. The procedure in the case of U.S. Senators was adopted not merely to separate the Senators from direct influence by the people, but also to recognize the constituent rights of the states agreeing to the Union.

In making Senators less dependent on the general public, the Constitution made them more dependent on their constituents—that is, the legislatures. Instruction of Senators by state legislatures was much more common than attempts to instruct Representatives. Insofar as the Senator was considered an ambassador of his state, the practice of giving instructions seemed perfectly normal. The size and operation of the legislatures made the practice of instruction a simple matter. To strengthen the state's control over its Senators, some urged that legislatures be empowered to recall them. Legislatures had enjoyed such power under the Articles of Confederation, and constitutional amendments to provide such recall were frequently introduced in the early years of the Republic.

Opposition to the view that the Senator was a state, rather than a Federal, official was emphatically expressed by Alexander Hamilton during debates on the Constitution: "That a man should have the power in private life of recalling his agent is proper, because in the business in which he is engaged he has no other object but to gain the approbation of his principal. Is this the case with the Senator? Is he simply the agent of the State: No. He is an agent for the Union, and he is bound to perform services necessary to the good of the whole, though his State should condemn them."

The philosophy behind instruction and recall was expressed in the First Congress by Sen. William Mcclay (Pa.): "Were we chosen with dictatorial powers, or were we sent as servants of the public, to do their business? The latter, clearly, in my opinion. The first question, then, which presented itself was, were my constituents here, what would they do? The answer, if known, was the rule of the Representative."

State legislatures, not surprisingly, were more inclined than the Senators themselves to consider their wishes binding on their Senators' actions. From the First Congress, some of them sent instructions to the men they had chosen for the Senate, a practice which reached a peak in the second quarter of the 19th century. Southern states in particular adopted the practice in the pre-Civil War decades. The distinction between responsibility of Senators and Representatives to legislatures was evident in the formula commonly used, of which one adopted by the Tennessee General Assembly in 1840 serves as an example: "That our Senators to Congress be *instructed* and our Representatives *requested* to vote against the chartering by Congress of a National Bank." (Italics added.)

The force of these instructions was illustrated in 1835 when many states directed their Senators to vote for or against a motion to expunge an 1834 Senate Resolution declaring that President Jackson had "assumed upon himself authority and power not conferred by the Constitution." Virginia instructed its Senators to vote for the expunging resolution, adding: "It is the duty of the representative to obey the instructions of his constituents or resign the trust with which they have clothed him." The previous year the Virginia Legislature, by majorities of more than two to one in each house, had instructed its Senators to vote *for* the resolution they now insisted be expunged. Sen. W. C. Rives had resigned in 1834 rather than obey the instructions; the Senator who replaced him resigned (alleging ill health) after receiving the opposite instructions in 1835. His Virginia colleague, Sen. John Tyler, who had voted for the original resolution, resigned rather than reverse his stand. He was replaced by Rives.

Senators' Position After Civil War

According to George H. Haynes in *The Senate of the United States,* more Senators probably received instructions from their legislatures in the impeachment trial of President Andrew Johnson than have been instructed upon any other matter in American history. But the triumph of the Union in the Civil War vitiated the force attached to legislative instructions in the heyday of the states' rights doctrine. Increasingly, Senators felt as free as Representatives to disregard them. An illustration of the change in attitude was provided by Sen. Lucius Q. C. Lamar (D Miss.), the first of the Confederate generals to gain prominence in Congress. On three major issues Lamar defied the Mississippi Legislature's instructions: to oppose the retirement of Gen. Grant with pay; to oppose the seating of Sen. Frank B. Kellogg of Louisiana; and to support the Bland Silver Bill.

The resentment in Mississippi was so strong that everyone agreed Lamar had committed political suicide. But after he toured the state explaining his actions, the Legislature re-elected him by an overwhelming majority. His first speech after his return to Mississippi typified his rationale for disobeying instructions. He recounted how, when he had been on a ship preparing to run the Union blockade of Savannah Harbor, prominent Confederate officers on board concluded that they could safely proceed. But the captain of the ship sent a sailor to the topmast where, with his telescope, he counted 10 Yankee gunboats in the harbor. The officers conferred and concluded that the sailor must be mistaken because they knew where the Yankee fleet was then located. The captain nevertheless refused to proceed. Although he recognized that the officers knew more of naval affairs than an ordinary seaman, he realized that the topmast provided a much better view of the real situation. By the same token, Lamar said, he made no claim to be wiser than the Mississippi Legislature, but he believed that as a Member of the U.S. Senate he was in a better position to judge what was in the interest of his constituents.

In 1913 the 17th Amendment, requiring direct election of Senators, entirely freed Members of the upper house from the constraints of legislative instructions. They were thenceforth representatives of a different constituency—the people of their states. Indeed, in many states they could have claimed to represent the will of the people more effectively than legislatures elected from malapportioned districts. The shift to direct election did not imply, however, that the popular electorate would instruct Senators as legislatures had done. In-

deed, the foremost leader in the struggle for direct election, Sen. William E. Borah (R Idaho), protested when Sen. David A. Reed (R Pa.) announced some years later his intention of asking his state legislature to conduct a popular referendum on repeal of prohibition. "The fundamental principle upon which this Government was originated," Borah said, "was that of representative government, not referendum or a pure democracy, but that the people select a representative, and that that representative is to represent their views if they are in harmony with his. If he has convictions against them, their remedy is to retire him...."

Decline of Localism

The central issue of representation—whether and to what extent a Member of Congress is bound to follow the wishes of his constituents—has exercised American politicans and theorists from the days of the Founding Fathers to the present. Long-range trends have tended, however, to increase the independence of Members. The growth in population of House districts, and even more the shift of Senate elections from legislatures to the populations of whole states, has made it every more difficult to ascertain what constituents want. The increased volume of legislation in the 20th century reduces opportunities to gauge constituent opinion on each issue.

The variety of issues decided between elections makes Senators and Representatives less dependent on public support on any particular one of them, unless it is judged of overriding importance by the voters. And the growing complexity of legislation widens the gap in information and expertise between the Member and most of his constituents. But, on questions of first importance, Members are subjected to greater pressures than ever by reason of the increased power of the President and the existence of highly organized national lobbies. Both the White House and the lobbies may try to influence them directly and, indirectly, through their constituents.

The relationship between a Senator or Representative and his community has been transformed by the slow growth of a national community. In an age of mass production, nationwide television and jet travel, it is difficult to imagine an earlier American society in which local and state loyalties were more real than the sense of national identity. Heightened awareness of foreign problems, coming particularly from the experience of two World Wars and the Cold War, has deepened the American sense of belonging to one distinct nation. The urgent demands of foreign policy and national defense inevitably shifted the attention of Members of Congress from local toward national and international concerns.

Because foreign and defense issues are the least familiar to constituents, their prominence has compelled Congress to exercise more independence of local opinion. Indeed, the complexity of these issues has tended to make Members dependent to a considerable extent on specialists in the Executive Branch. From representatives making decisions on behalf of their constituents, they have become, rather, mediators between those constituents and the decision-makers. They have the dual responsibility of trying to make the State and Defense Departments understand the mood of the citizens, and the citizens understand the problems faced by those departments. The same mediating role assumes importance also in domestic affairs, as technology and urbanization render the Government increasingly remote and incomprehensible to the common man.

The contrast with the period before the Civil War is striking. Then the fate of the nation rested not on reconciling a national bureaucracy and ordinary citizens, but on reconciling divergent local and regional pressures. Members of Congress were not expected to mediate between those conflicting interests so much as to represent one side or another. Ideological issues of national significance gave way to a bargaining process in which the tie between the Member and his constituents tended to be concrete and specific.

The Washington environment, which now competes with constituent pressures, then tended to reinforce them. At the end of a long, difficult journey, Senators and Representatives arrived from the South, New England and the West to find in Washington colleagues whose differences were much more striking than their similarities. The cultural differences between the regions made it natural for the newcomers in a strange city to seek out their own kind. Frequently they traveled in groups to Washington. While their families remained at home, Representatives and Senators lived in boarding houses with others from the same region. As James Sterling Young has shown in *The Washington Community, 1800-1828,* these boarding house groups not only were the basis of a Member's social life; they also were key voting blocs on legislation.

The close ties among Members from the same region kept their attention focused on the people back home and weakened any impulse to represent national interests. These ties also inhibited development of truly national parties, while the high rate of turnover in Congress inhibited the development there of strong leadership or an *esprit* which could exert pressures counter to those of the constituencies.

Conflicting Pressures

Gradually the development of national party organization and spirit, and the establishment of internal loyalties and leadership in House and Senate, introduced pressures competitive with those of constituents. And other pressures developed that were not entirely separate from the constituency. Lobbies were long viewed as cabals aimed at thwarting the electorate, but in recent years they frequently have exerted their influence not by opposing, but by mobilizing, constituents. Pressure from an increasingly powerful Executive may compete with responsiveness to constituent opinion, but that pressure in part derives from the power of the President to sway constituent opinion through the media and through the granting or withholding of favors for a Member's district.

The relative decline of local pressures in the face of national institutions like political parties, the Presidency, and Congressional leadership reflects the blurring of local and regional differences through mass communication and transportation. It reflects also the growth of problems clearly national in character. When Americans were creating a constitution or waging a civil war, ideological issues and national institutions naturally tended to supplant local interests as the focus of politics. But the primacy of local interests tended to reassert itself in the long lulls between national crises. In the 20th century, national crises have followed one another in a quick succession—World War I, the Great Depression, World War II, the Cold War, Korea, Vietnam, race relations and the upheaval in cities and on campuses. As a consequence a Member of Congress is forced to consider many matters in addition to the immediate concerns of those who send him to Congress.

But it is still the constituents, and not the President, or the party, or the Congressional leadership, who grant and can take away the Member's job. A Senator or Representative popular with his constituency can defy all three in a way unthinkable in a country like England, where the leadership of the legislature, the executive and the party are one and the same. The use of direct primaries in the present century, like the shift from statewide at-large elections to single-member House districts in the first half of the 19th century, have tended to increase the local Congressman's ability to resist nonconstituent pressures.

Looking after his district, however, may make the Congressman dependent on the President and Congressional leaders, who have power to influence the location of Federal projects. In return for their channeling of Federal funds into the district, the Member may be expected to support their positions on national issues. The bargaining, which is often implicit rather than spoken, works both ways. The party leadership is anxious to win friends for key roll calls, and to help its supporter gain re-election, through distribution of Federal projects.

The leadership conserves support thus won by keeping demands to the minimum. When it has more votes than needed on a roll call, Congressmen whose support might alienate their constituents are usually freed to "vote the constituency." One result of this practice is to reduce the statistical evidence of party unity and increase the appearance of effective constituent pressure against the party's influence on its Congressmen.

Decisions affecting constituents have increasingly been transferred to executive agencies. Thus in some programs, guidelines written into legislation leave an element of discretion which can be used to favor selected Congressional districts or states with Federal funds. A classic example of the transfer of bread-and-butter decisions from the Legislative to the Executive Branch is the Trade Agreements Act of 1934. In the setting of tariffs Congress had long responded to special interests and local pressures. By granting President Roosevelt power to negotiate reciprocal tariff agreements with foreign countries, and extending that authority to his successors, the direct tie between legislators and constituents was weakened. Congress continued to place limits on tariff agreements, and when an industry felt injured by foreign competition, the threat of Congressional action was likely to influence policy decisions. But the effect of this and other legislation transferring decisions to administrative agencies was to prompt Members of Congress to function as lobbyists for their constituents before the Executive Branch.

Senators and Representatives have always pressured the Executive on behalf of constituents, but current Congressional patronage is only a feeble vestige of the spoils system of the 19th century. Then, local Federal appointments to inferior posts were considered at the disposal of Representatives, and Senatorial power over nominations to higher positions was exploited for local advantage. Compliance with the patronage system was the price Presidents were expected to pay for support of their programs. With the passage of the Civil Service Act of 1883 and subsequent reforms, this means of serving constituents was gradually restricted. Powerful Members of Congress may still influence a President of their own party in the choice of an ambassador or a top-level official in the Executive Branch. But as a means of rewarding supporters in a Member's constituency, patronage has dwindled to an almost insignificant factor. *(See Chapter IV, Subchapter 2.)*

The 'Pork Barrel'

The process of obtaining jobs for constituents now depends much more on bringing Federal projects into the district. The great expansion of legislation in other realms has reduced the *relative* attention paid to projects for specific Congressional districts and states, but the sums involved has grown beyond the dreams of Members of Congress in the last century. Injection of Federal funds into the local economy often has more effect on a Member's chances for re-election than his votes on controversial issues.

The Member with a reputation for "bringing home the bacon" is very hard to beat. By securing the construction of a dam or preventing the closing of a military base in his constituency, a Representative or Senator contributes directly to the livelihood of both business and labor. The benefits to the voters are tangible and unambiguous in a way that most campaign issues are not. Those who gain from Federal projects attributable to their Congressman or one of their Senators may feel that contributions of effort and funds to his re-election are merely practical investments in their own well-being.

Defense installations and contracts provide the largest share of Federal expenditures. Rivers and harbors bills which periodically authorize Army Corps of Engineers water projects, and programs included in the annual omnibus public works appropriations bills, are most often cited as "pork barrel" legislation. But the types of Federal largesse are unlimited, ranging from a peanut research laboratory to designation of the United States bicentennial city. Members of Congress are not averse to claiming credit for allocation of projects whose location was in fact decided within an executive department, and it was common practice for announcements of new projects to be made by the Member representing the constituency. However, the fiscal 1971 defense procurement bill abolished that custom because it was felt that the practice prompted suspicion of improper Congressional influence in the awarding of contracts.

The publicity gained by project announcements can be considerable. Sen. Joseph S. Clark (D Pa.) observed: "I have made long speeches in the Senate on disarmament, civil rights and the manpower revolution which inspired either a few paragraphs from the wire services or nothing at all in many a paper with less than 25,000 circulation in Pennsylvania. But when I have forwarded the announcement of a new post office or a million-dollar contract award, I have been blessed with streamer headlines, even pictures, and once a special box on the front page of the Pottstown *Mercury* headed, 'Thank You, Senator.' And, usually, I had little if anything to do with the award."

Getting Federal economic aid for one's constituents is not, of course, limited to individual projects or instal-

lations. Much legislation of a general character has a heavy impact only in particular states and districts. Shipbuilding subsidies, oil depletion allowances, or import controls on textiles, for example, would be as important in some districts as construction of a nuclear accelerator or the award of a model cities grant in other constituencies.

Pressuring of the Executive. Members of Congress, of course, have direct control over the location only of projects specified in legislation. The Defense Department is supposed to distribute its installations as national security requires, and other departments are required to award grants impartially according to criteria written into the authorizing legislation. But the opportunities for Congressional pressure are considerable, and the President himself may intercede to help a Senator or Representative from his own party.

Candidates from the President's party sometimes imply that constituents have more to gain by electing them than members of the party that is not in the White House. Thus Sen. Edward M. Kennedy (D Mass.), brother of the President, campaigned in 1962 as "the nan that can do more for Massachusetts." Some Republicans the next year voiced the suspicion that the location of a $50-million electronics research center in Boston was a favor from President Kennedy, and they sought unsuccessfully to block its construction. But the leading Republican Representative from Massachusetts, former Speaker Joseph W. Martin Jr., called allegations of favoritism "a red herring...to defeat the New England proposal."

The stakes can be unusually high in the award of defense contracts. One of the largest contracts, for the F-111 (TFX) tactical aircraft, provoked a storm of Congressional controversy. When the contract was awarded, production orders were estimated to be worth eventually more than $6.5 billion and to involve 20,000 jobs and 1,700 planes. In 1963 the Permanent Investigations Subcommittee of the Senate Government Operations Committee conducted a long and argumentative probe of the decision to give the contract to General Dynamics for construction at Fort Worth, Texas, instead of to the Boeing Co., with headquarters in Seattle, Wash., and construction planned for its Wichita, Kan., plant. During the investigation, suggestions of political pressure were made concerning Sen. Henry M. Jackson (D Wash.), Rep. K. William Stinson (R Wash.) of Seattle, Rep. James C. Wright (D Texas) of Forth Worth, the Kansas Congressional delegation, and then-Vice President Lyndon B. Johnson of Texas, among others.

Powerful figures on the Armed Services and Appropriations Committees may obtain for their states and districts an impressive array of military installations. The late House Armed Services Chairman L. Mendel Rivers (D S.C.), for example, had in his district the big Charleston shipyard, a naval weapons station, a Polaris submarine base, an Air Force base, the Parris Island Marine Corps recruit depot, a Marine Corps air base, an Army supply station and two naval hospitals. The Charleston Chamber of Commerce estimated in 1969 that the military installations alone accounted for more than $317 million in payrolls, and that 55 percent of the area's payrolls came from defense industries attracted to the area.

Rank-and-file Members may find, on the other hand, that there is little they can do to attract, or even keep, defense spending in their constituencies. When Defense Secretary Robert S. McNamara announced in 1964 plans to close 95 military installations in the United States and abroad, eliminating 63,401 military and civilian jobs at estimated annual savings of $477 million, many Members were apprehensive about the economic consequences in their districts. They put through a bill requiring Congressional review of base closings, but it was vetoed by President Johnson as a "fundamental encroachment" on powers of the Executive Branch. A watered-down version was then passed and signed into law.

Public Works. Although Congressional control of the purse strings does not usually extend to precise geographic distribution of Federal funds, rivers and harbors authorizations and some public works bills explicitly designate the location of projects. While these projects constitute only a small portion of the total Federal Budget, their usefulness as aids to re-election makes them important counters in the internal politics of Capitol Hill. Chairmen of committees and subcommittees controlling authorizations and appropriations for such projects are in a position to exert pressure on colleagues eager to obtain similar favors for their own constituents. Votes on questions that have no intrinsic connection with public works may thus be determined by pork-barrel considerations.

Some recent legislation, like the Public Works and Economic Development Act of 1965 and its predecessor, the 1961 Area Redevelopment Act, authorized administrative allocation of funds for depressed areas. But Congress remains jealous of its control over the distribution of public works. When President Kennedy in 1962 pressed for standby Presidential authority to undertake public works when the economy required priming, Congress killed the proposal. Critics insisted that such bypassing of the appropriations process would give the President a political slush fund with which he could reward his friends and buy votes, and that it would utterly remove Congressional control over spending of the money. Some defenders of the President's proposal countered with the charge that Members wanted to keep control of the funds only for logrolling purposes, to distribute projects among constituencies according to political rather than economic criteria.

Constituency Influence

The extent to which a Member of Congress seeks to follow the wishes of his constituents is determined to a considerable extent by the issue at stake. Probably no Member would actively oppose construction in his district of a dam or post office wanted by his constituents. Few, if any, would follow locally popular policies which they were convinced would seriously endanger the nation. Between these extremes lies a full spectrum of different blends of pressure from constituents and from conscience. It is in this grey area that Members must make most of their decisions.

Frequently, of course, a Senator or Representative experiences no conflict between his own views and what he believes are the views of most of his constituents. In Roger H. Davidson's study, *The Role of the Congressman*, 59 percent of the 87 Representatives surveyed in the 80th Congress agreed with the statement: "I seldom have to sound out my constituents because I think so much like them that I know how to react to almost any proposal." Members would be less than human if they did not sometimes rationalize their convictions to fit the demands of voters, or filter their perception of voter demands to fit their convictions. But agreement between the Member and his constituents is more normal than disagreement, especially in homogeneous districts and states, because of the shared experiences of living, working, and usually growing up, in the same environment. Moreover, a Member may readily "vote his constituency" against his own convictions if he knows that he could not change the final result by voting his convictions.

Constituent opinion may set clear limits beyond which the Representative or Senator cannot trespass. Unless he was planning to retire, a southern Senator could not become an ardent advocate of civil rights, nor could a Representative from a farm district push policies designed to lower the price of foods grown by those who elect him. But on most questions the Member has great leeway. The character of his constituency may have more effect on the kinds of questions he gives priority to than on how he votes on them. Thus a Representative from a district with a large ethnic minority might become a champion of immigration reform, and a Senator from a western state might concentrate his efforts on natural resources policies. The committees on which the Senator or Representative seeks membership also are often determined by the type of constituency he serves.

The Representative Role

Electoral Vulnerability. The extent to which a legislator feels obliged to follow the opinion of his constituents depends in part on his own electoral vulnerability. In his House survey, Davidson divided the 87 respondents into three types according to their "style" of representation: "Trustees," who see themselves as following their own knowledge or conscience; "Delegates," who view themselves as following "instructions" (either actual or implied) from their constituents; and "Politicos," who combine the two other viewpoints. Interviews showed 28 percent trustees, 23 percent delegates, 46 percent politicos, and 3 percent undetermined. In safe districts the percentage of trustees rose to 35, while that of delegates fell to 11. Only 19 percent of Representatives holding marginal seats were in the trustee category, compared to 44 percent classified as delegates.

The tendency to emphasize local rather than national concerns increased with the competitiveness of the district. Only 19 percent of Representatives in the marginal group were predominantly concerned with national affairs, while 53 percent focused on local matters. Among those with safe seats, 34 percent emphasized national and 38 percent local considerations. (The remainder in each classification were equally divided on national and local interests, or their interests were primarily nongeographic.)

Davidson found that the relationship between safety of the seat and the ease of assuming trustee and national roles produced the following distinctions among categories of Members: "Trustee and National roles are more common among Democrats, leaders, southerners, and high-seniority members. Delegate and Local roles are more typical of Republicans, nonleaders, nonsoutherners, and freshmen." Other factors appeared to exercise independent influence, but were less clearly identifiable.

To illustrate the limitation of a competitive constituency on a Congressman's independence, Davidson recounted the lament of a California liberal Democrat who was disappointed by the state legislature's failure to redraw his district to enhance his electoral chances. "I would have been a statesman if they had cut off a few of those conservatives. Now I'll have to continue going this way, that way, back and forth. I'm a cracker-ass Congressman—and I could have been a statesman!" Davidson concluded that the combination of safe and marginal districts, however it affects the individual Congressman, produces institutional advantages:

"On the one hand, our political framework requires that legislators, or at least a good portion of them, possess the kind of enforced sensitivity to public attitudes that electoral competition produces. On the other hand, the House is a large and complex institution, requiring the labors of Members whose electoral good fortune allows them to tend to its business. The committee leaders, policy experts, and political entrepreneurs of the House are unquestionably aided, and their time budgets made more manageable, by the fact that many of them have only minimal pressures from the folks back home. In fact, the complicated division of labor that has evolved in the House would most likely be impossible if all the districts were poised at the electoral tipping-point."

Length of Incumbency. Figures comparable to Davidson's are not available for earlier periods. However, the association of safe seats with trustee attitudes and national focus suggests that such attitudes have probably increased as a consequence of a lengthening of the tenure of Representatives. For a variety of reasons the advantages of incumbency have increased *(see Chapter V)*, with the result that the average period the Representative spends in the House has grown longer. In the first 40 years of the Republic, an average of more than 40 percent of House Members were replaced every two years. In the mid-20th century, 15 to 20 percent turnover was typical. The consequent reduction in the proportion of freshman Congressmen, who are the ones most likely to emphasize district and delegate roles, could be expected to increase independence of constituent pressures in the House as a whole.

The average Representative in the 19th century spent two or two and one-half terms in the House. In the 90th Congress, the average period of House service was 5.5 terms, about 11 years. With longer terms and longer sessions, service in the House has taken on most of the characteristics of a career. The professionalism of the Congressman, and the specialized division of labor within the House, has in all probability reduced the Representative's reliance on "instruction" from his constituents. He may feel bound by their basic philosophy, but for guidance amidst the increasing complexity and variety of legislation he is more likely to turn to his own professional experience, the specialized judgment of trusted colleagues or Congressional staff, or expert testimony from the Executive Branch, lobbies, or universities.

The original purpose of two-year terms—to make one branch of the legislature highly responsive to popular opinion—may be somewhat vitiated by the increased security of incumbents. Rep. Herman P. Eberharter (D Pa.) told Lewis Dexter: "You know I am sure you will find out a Congressman can do pretty much what he decides to do and he doesn't have to bother too much about criticism. I've seen plenty of cases since I've been up here where a guy will hold one economic or political position and get along all right; and then he'll die or resign and a guy comes in who holds quite a different economic or political position and he gets along all right, too. That's the fact of the matter."

Dexter's interviews with Congressmen on tariff issues showed them less dependent on constituency pressures than had generally been assumed. The average number of incumbents defeated in an election year during the 1960s was only 32, a figure that gives some statistical support to this view. Davidson found that 42 percent of those he interviewed agreed with the Eberharter statement, but a majority believed he had overstated the freedom of the Congressman to ignore constituent opinion.

Senators and Constituents. The attitudes of Senators toward their constituents have not been scientifically surveyed. A number of factors would be expected to make Senators less concerned than Representatives about constituent opinion. The six-year term, as was originally intended, reduces the Senator's dependence on popularity. He can take stands he expects to be forgotten or forgiven before he seeks re-election. He does not have to spend as much time as a Representative campaigning to persuade constituents to vote for him rather than for another candidate. He imbibes the more relaxed atmosphere of a body two-thirds of whose Members will not face the electorate (or retirement) for at least two years. Many of the traditions and folkways of the Senate originated during the first two-thirds of its history, when it was not elected by the people. The Senate's special concern with foreign relations also encourages its Members to adopt the mantle of the "statesman," pursuing national rather than parochial interests.

The larger constituencies to which most Senators must appeal may give them more choice than Representatives in deciding to which groups in the electorate they will direct their appeal. But party competition in the largest states has made them less secure constituencies than the more homogeneous small states. The average length of service in the Senate in the 90th Congress was 12.6 years, but the average for Senators from the seven largest states combined was 9.2 years. The greater exposure of Senators to publicity may make them more vulnerable than Representatives to public opinion.

A Senator's vulnerability appears to change with length of service. Donald Matthews found that 55 of the 180 Senators in office during the postwar decade served for one full term or less. Seven of the 55 died in office, but the others were defeated or chose to retire, often in anticipation of defeat. Eighty percent of the Senators seeking re-election in the postwar decade were successful in their first bids. The figure rose to 84 percent at the end of their second term and to 88 percent at the end of the third. But only 57 percent of the 15 Senators seeking re-election after four terms were successful. Age, and a new generation of voters, make it more difficult for a Senator to hold on after his fourth term. But so does his growing distance from his constituency. As the Senator gains in seniority and influence, Matthews observes, "his reference groups" change, he becomes more concerned with Senate, national and international problems, and devotes less time and attention to the folks back home." At the height of his power in the Senate, he may be struck down by a challenger stirring up the grass roots.

Power of Constituents

Uninformed Voters. The length of careers in Senate and House and the statistical evidence of the chances of re-election make Congressional awe of constituent power seem somewhat unrealistic. The voters' lack of information about their Senators and Representatives makes some wonder how they can exercise any influence on those who represent them. The Gallup Poll found in 1966 that only 46 percent of American adults could name their Representative. The Survey Research Center of the University of Michigan, immediately following the 1958 Congressional elections, interviewed a sample of constituents in 116 House districts. Where there were contests between a Republican and a Democrat, less than one-fifth of the district's residents said they had read or heard something about both candidates, while well over half admitted they had heard nothing about either. Even among those who indicated that they had voted (slightly over one-half of the sample), 46 percent had heard nothing about either candidate. Describing the survey's results, Warren E. Miller and Donald E. Stokes noted that a respondent classed as having read or heard about a candidate usually only "knew" that "he's a good man," or "he understands the problems." They added: "Of detailed information about policy stands not more than a chemical trace was found."

Among their sample of Representatives opposed for re-election in 1958, Miller and Stokes found that more than four-fifths said the outcome in their districts had been strongly influenced by the voters' response to the records and personal standing of the candidates. The contrast was clear: "Congressmen feel that their individual legislative actions may have considerable impact on the electorate, yet some simple facts about the Representative's salience to his constituents imply that this could hardly be true."

Representatives may overestimate their visibility to the electorate because the part of it with which they deal directly is the most informed sector. More important, those who are informed can have considerable impact on the mass of uninformed voters. As leaders of local party organizations, civic groups, labor unions, business associations, news media, ethnic groups, citizens' lobbies or other groups, they may disseminate their impressions of the Member without necessarily producing a well-informed constituency. As Miller and Stokes explain, a part of the electorate "may get simple positive or negative cues about the Congressman which were provoked by his legislative actions but which no longer have a recognizable issue content."

Potential Opposition. The local leaders are likely to include some who would like to see the Representative replaced. Whether it's a candidate who wants to fill the seat himself, leaders of the opposition party, an opposing faction within his own party, a hostile newspaper publisher, or a powerful interest group which he has antagonized, they will be monitoring his past and current performance in Washington. Any move he makes that might be unpopular in his district or state is likely to be seized upon by his opponents and publicized as widely as possible. The fact that a Congressman is little known may testify to the fact that his record in Congress had given opponents little opportunity to point with alarm at his defiance of his constituents.

In safer constituencies, the advantages enjoyed by an incumbent may discourage potential opponents from trying to unseat him. But even a "safe" Congressman may provoke a challenge if his actions convince local leaders that they should, and can, persuade voters they have been forgotten or betrayed. In most election years, Representatives see a few of their colleagues unpleasantly surprised at the polls, a harsh reminder of the precariousness of their occupation.

Election Margin. Unless a Congressman's behavior outrages opinion at home, his opponents have an uphill struggle to arouse opposition to him. An ill-informed electorate is not exactly tinder waiting for a spark. But a swing of only a small percentage of the voters may spell the difference between a new term and retirement from Congress. Thus the Congressman's concern with constituent response to his actions is not rendered entirely unrealistic by the fact that most constituents are unaware of those actions. The minority which is informed is the minority which is more volatile, and its members may provide the losing margin.

A comfortable margin might encourage indifference to constituent opinion were it not for occasional reversals of normal political trends. A crisis or a combination of events may produce a sharp national swing in voter sentiment and a higher rate of mortality among incumbents of one of the parties. Thus many Democrats accustomed to easy re-election went down in 1946, and well-established Republicans were unseated in the Democratic sweep of 1958. Regional or state conditions may also prompt departures from familiar voter habits. Thus GOP perennials were hurt in 1958 by the extra effort of organized labor in states where "right-to-work" laws were on the ballots. To build up the kind of margin which will enable him to survive such unforeseen hostile trends, the Congressman may be more cautious about alienating voters than his usual election margin would seem to require.

It is not surprising that a Representative sometimes exaggerates his dependence on constituent opinion. Democratic traditions which established, sustain and justify his office insist that constituents ought to exercise control over him. Moreover, his career, prestige, way of life, and opportunity to serve his convictions may be jeopardized by underestimating the power of constituents. Thus both his ideals and his interest may well combine to convince the Congressman that he must be responsive to constituent pressures.

Opportunities For Leadership

In a study of *American Business and Public Policy*, Raymond A. Bauer, Ithiel de Sola Pool, and Lewis Anthony Dexter were impressed by the amount of freedom that Members of Congress have to choose their own activities and policies. Far from belittling the pressures which they (and the political scientists who study them) consider so overwhelming, the authors concluded that the volume of pressures actually functioned to free the Member. "Paradoxical as it may seem, their 'freedom' comes from the excessive demands made on them. The complexity of their environment which seems to rob them of initiative thrusts initiative back on them, for, when the demands on a man's resources clearly exceed his capacity to respond, he *must* select the problems and pressures to which to respond."

Because constituencies contain diverse groups, the Senator or Representative can choose which one he will rely upon for more than passive support, for funds, volunteers, influence, dissemination of news. He may shift his appeal from one group to another, but such shifts are rendered difficult by the initial choice of supporters. They are the ones who communicate most with the Member, and the ones to whom he feels committed. If he thinks he cannot oppose their wishes, he is only responding to pressure which he chose in the first place from several alternatives. A Member may, however, seek to build a base of support in a different interest group in order to give himself more flexibility. A midwestern Congressman said of his district: "It is a good district because, if the farmers are mad at you, the cities won't be; and, if the cities are, the farmers won't be; so you can be free."

On local bread-and-butter issues, interest groups are usually satisified with evidence that the Representative or Senator is attentive to their problems. Indeed, the majority of constituents are less likely to tell him, than to ask him, what is the best solution. Once elected, the Member of Congress is, after all, a prominent figure in his community, and he is looked to for leadership. Moreover, many interest groups have multiple objectives. They do not expect their Representative or Senator to agree to all of them. He can take his pick, and if the group is satisfied with his over-all performance, it is unlikely to withdraw support because of particular disagreements. It may fear losing his support as much, or more, than he fears losing the support of the group.

The Member's local supporters may even revise their priorities in response to his initiative. As Bauer, Pool and Dexter point out: "He is freed from a slavish dependence on the elements in his coalition, not only because he can change it, but, even more, because once he has built a coalition, he tends to lead it. His closest supporters, who may originally have rallied around him because they wanted him to take certain stands, come to be his men. Within very broad limits, when he shifts, they shift. They gain prestige by being close to a Congressman, and they fear to break a relationship which may someday be useful for important purposes. Once the leader has committed himself, his supporters are inclined to go along."

A Member of Congress who attempted only to follow his constituents probably would not remain long in office. Only by anticipating their demands can he establish a record on issues which will appeal to voters when those issues become paramount. The Member must be alert to the earliest portents of change in economic, social and political conditions, and in the mood of his constituents. If he fails to stake out a position before the pressure mounts, his response to a popular movement is likely to be interpreted as insincere expediency. An opponent committed in advance to the popular position will have captured the high ground from which to wage an election campaign.

Indeed, the opponent may himself have stimulated the movement among the voters on an issue whose appeal had only been potential. Challengers are not the only ones to create issues. Like businesses that stimulate demand for new products, Members of Congress often develop a legislative proposal for which they see a potential "market," and then try to drum up interest in it. "They generate the public concerns which come back as pressures on them."

Opportunities for Evasion

Even in the case of those few, but important, questions on which the constituency has definite views to urge on a Member of Congress his opportunities for evasion are considerable. The more complex the proposed legislation, the easier it is for a Representative or Senator to justify either a yea or nay vote in terms that will appeal to his constituents. He or his colleagues may so amend the bill that the original issue is lost to sight.

A controversial proposal sometimes is rendered so innocuous that it carries by huge majorities while at other times, provisions designed to carry out the original intent are so altered that the bill's sponsors are glad to see it recommitted. Special considerations can be raised to excuse an unpopular roll-call vote, as when inflation is said to demand postponing a costly social program, or an international crisis is alleged to necessitate Government intervention in labor-management relations. A Member opposed to a bill desired by his constituents may cast a yea vote only when he is certain the measure will be defeated, or a nay vote on a bill his constituents oppose only when he knows enough votes are available to pass the bill.

Horse-Trading for Constituents

In voting contrary to the apparent wishes of those he represents, a Member of Congress may actually be working in their interest. This is true not only because he sometimes has a clearer perspective on national issues, but also because each vote is but a single act in the complex transactions of Government. Thus, for example, a Representative who offends constituent opinion to support his party's leadership or a powerful committee chairman may later be rewarded for such support with a new post office or dam for his district. Some of his constituents are likely to remember what is built in their community after everyone has forgotten an earlier unpopular vote.

Voters may confront a similar kind of choice. A new candidate may offer more appealing stands on current issues than the man who has represented them for many years in Washington. But their Senator's or Representative's seniority and accumulated influence enable him to serve his state's or district's needs more effectively than any freshman. Particularly in the South constituents have consciously recognized the advantages of re-electing incumbents.

The power of committee chairmen complicates the choice of voters in another way. Because the party winning a majority in each house determines the chairmanship of every committee, a vote for a sympathetic Representative or Senator may also be a vote for a hostile chairman. The victory of a Democratic Senator favoring civil rights legislation might preserve his party's majority, which makes Sen. James O. Eastland of Mississippi chairman of the Judiciary Committee; the victory of a Republican "dove" favoring withdrawal from Vietnam might remove Sen. J. W. Fulbright (D Ark.), a leading dove, from the chairmanship of the Foreign Relations Committee.

Statistical Studies

So many complications intervene between the constituent and Congress that the voters' control of their Government may seem no more than a myth. The view that Congress does, or even could, follow specific instructions of voters is naive. But to assume that Congress is not responsive to fundamental attitudes of the American public would be equally naive. The real question is the degree to which the actions of Congress correspond to the beliefs of the people it represents. It is extremely difficult to measure that correspondence, but recently political scientists have begun to make the effort.

House of Representatives

MacRae. One way to examine constituency impact on Congressional behavior is to correlate characteristics of the constituents—wealth, occupations, ethnic background, population density, etc.—with roll-call votes. Duncan MacRae's *Dimensions of Congressional Voting* (1958) compared House roll-call vote patterns in the 81st Congress with the percentage of district population engaged in farming and in professional or managerial occupations. MacRae concluded, among other things, that Members' votes correpond most closely to interest groups in their constituencies on agricultural matters, in which party, regional and ideological influences have less impact than in the case of other issues. He found that association between interest groups and Congressional voting was less clear-cut on questions related to President Truman's "Fair Deal" and the "Welfare State," and he attributed that fact to the cultivation by the two parties, especially in the urban North, of organized segments of communities rather than the district population as a whole. Among the voting patterns examined, MacRae found that foreign-aid roll calls showed the least relationship to identified constituency characteristics.

Froman. Lewis A. Froman Jr., in his *Congressmen and Their Constituencies* (1963), correlated the voting of nonsouthern Representatives in 1961 with socio-economic status (percentage of owner-occupied dwelling units), race (percentage of nonwhite population), population density (average population per square mile), and place of residence (percentage urban). As expected, he found that northern Democrats tended to represent districts with a smaller percentage of owner-occupied dwellings, higher percentages of nonwhite population and urban residents, and a higher average population density than Republicans. In this way, constituency characteristics tended to reinforce patterns in roll-call voting that followed party lines. Using Congressional Quarterly scores for roll-call support of President Kennedy on domestic issues, Froman found that that support tended to be higher in both parties in districts with greater population density, higher percentages of nonwhites and urban residents, and lower percentages of owner-occupied dwellings.

Froman also examined roll calls on reciprocal trade between 1948 and 1958 to determine whether the character of the particular incumbent influenced voting patterns regardless of constituency and party pressures. He found that in districts represented during that period by more than one Congressman from the same party there was less consistency in voting on reciprocal trade than in districts represented throughout the period by the same Congressman. Republicans from the same district were more likely to vote the same way than were Democrats representing the same district. Individual variation among northern Democrats was greater in the more competitive districts; southern Democrats were more likely to differ with their predecessors' voting in the less competitive districts. Froman concluded also that among northern Democratic Representatives individual views were a more influential factor in districts with more owner-occupied dwelling units; southerners showed greater individual variation when representing districts with smaller nonwhite population. Whether these generalizations hold for other issues than reciprocal trade was not considered.

Shannon. In his study of *Party, Constituency and Congressional Voting* (1968), W. Wayne Shannon likewise found constituency differences reinforcing party differences. He sought to explain deviations from party positions on roll calls by examining characteristics of the constituencies of the Members. For the 86th and 87th Congresses, scores on voting scales for a variety of issues were compared with selected constituency factors—urban population, percentage of blue-collar labor, and median income for the northern Republicans and Democrats, and median income and percentage nonwhite population for southern Democrats.

Shannon found that urban-rural constituency differences did not account for intraparty voting differences. Detailed analysis of socio-economic differences also produced no clear relationship to dissent from party positions. Shannon found evidence casting doubt on an earlier study by Samuel P. Huntingdon which had indicated that Representatives from more competitive districts took more extreme policy positions (Democrats more liberal and Republicans more conservative). In the 86th and 87th Congresses the reverse seemed true—party differences were greatest in the case of Representatives from safe constituencies.

Shannon concluded on a note of dissatisfaction with the results of the statistical analyses published on Congressionl voting: "The several studies that have sought to illuminate factors influencing Congressional voting behavior, while they have clarified some questions, have left many others in doubt....It now seems all too clear, for example, that a major portion of the intraparty variance in voting behavior is left unexplained by the manipulation of aggregate constituency characteristics. Although the easy availability of roll-call and aggregate Congressional district data will continue to recommend their use in the kinds of studies examined here, there would seem to be little doubt today that some of the most important questions dealing with the Congressman, his party, and his constituency can only be settled by others modes of inquiry."

Shannon traces the limitations of the statistical analyses to three major difficulties: the inadequacy of aggregate census data in conveying the opinions, contacts, communications, group activities, etc., which constitute the "real-world" constituency of the Representative; the oversimplified models of the representative process, particularly their failure to consider the Congressman's subjective perception of his constituency; and the neglect of such variables as logrolling and other bargaining behavior, the influence of colleagues, and the actions of formal party leaders and the Executive.

Miller and Stokes. In an article on "Constituency Influence in Congress," *(American Political Science Review,* March 1963), Warren E. Miller and Donald E. Stokes sought to correlate Congressional actions and attitudes with constituent opinion expressed in interviews. Immediately after the 1958 elections the University of Michigan's Survey Research Center studied 116 House districts chosen as a representative sample of the total 435. The incumbent Congressman, his opponent (if any), and a sample of constituents were interviewed to determine their basic attitudes on Federal Government action in three areas: social welfare, U.S. involvement in foreign affairs, and civil rights for Negroes. Miller and Stokes ranked district opinion and the Representative's roll-call votes on these issues and found considerable agreement on social welfare, a high level of agreement on civil rights, and no significant relationship on foreign policy. When attitudes of the constituency majority, rather than the median of the district as a whole, were considered, the majority's agreement with the incumbent it re-elected appeared greater. The disagreement of this majority with the opposing candidate increased its relative agreement with the incumbent.

Miller and Stokes sought to identify the paths through which constituency opinion influenced Congressional voting. The voters' lack of knowledge of their Congressman's actions seriously handicapped the exercise of any control over those actions. However, the importance of small increments of votes in elections, the role of informed local leaders in influencing other voters, and the threat that an opponent will publicize unpopular actions, all tend to bring the Representative's roll-call votes into harmony with the basic attitudes of his constituents. It was found that the agreement was achieved by a combination of two processes: voters tend to select a man whose own attitudes are already similar to theirs; and Representatives are guided by their perceptions of constituent opinion. The perception of constituent views was more influential than the Representatives' own attitude in determining the high correlation between roll-call votes and district opinion on civil rights issues. On social welfare issues, however, the constituency's influence was exercised more through the attitudes of the man it elected than through his estimate of its opinion. On foreign policy Congressmen also tended to vote according to a combination of their own attitudes and their perception of constituent opinion, but the connection of both factors with actual constituent opinion was almost negligible.

Miller and Stokes concluded that on civil rights legislation, representation was secured primarily through the "instructed-delegate" type of connection between voter and Congressman. On social welfare issues, repre-

sentation tended to be secured through the medium of the national parties, whose labels were the principal means voters used to identify the candidate whose attitudes on social questions were closest to their own.

The lack of correlation between constituent opinion and roll-call voting on foreign policy suggested the possibility that on such issues Members are inclined to adopt Edmund Burke's view that the legislator should exercise his own informed judgment rather than carry out instructions from his electorate. Miller and Stokes noted, however, that Congressmen today often look to the Executive for calculation of the public interest for the same reason that Burke urged his constituents to look to Parliament—because the Executive now has much greater resources than Congress for gathering and evaluating information on foreign affairs.

Senate

Matthews. The Senate has attracted much less attention from political scientists than the House. Among other reasons, the extreme variation in the size of Senate constituencies does not lend itself to statistical generalizations about representation. Donald Matthews has attempted to indicate constituency influence in the Senate by comparing the voting records of Senators from the same state. Since they share a single constituency, if the Senators from one state tend to vote together more often than Senators from other states, the tendency can be attributed to the influence of the constituency. Analyzing a Congressional Quarterly study of same-state Senators in 1951, Matthews found that eight of 47 pairs agreed on more than 90 percent of roll calls, 17 pairs agreed on 80-89 percent, and nine agreed on 70-79 percent of the votes. Party affiliation was the principal factor differentiating Senators from the same state who frequently disagreed. All seven pairs which voted in disagreement more than half the time were composed of Senators from different parties; all 25 pairs which agreed more than 80 percent of the time belonged to the same party.

Matthews did not attribute conflicting votes among same-state Senators of different parties simply to the primacy of party pressure over constituent influence. He saw party affiliation rather as influencing which groups in the constituency the Senator would choose to "represent." He also attributed differences among same-state Senators partly to the different years in which they obtained their original "mandate," noting that early commitments tend to be perpetuated in a Senator's later voting patterns. Matthews observed that Senators of the same party were more likely to disagree in one-party states than in two-party states. In the former, conflicting constituent pressures find expression within different factions of the same party, whose label then is a poor indicator of agreement.

Constituent Communications

Whatever the Senator's or Representative's concept of his role, he needs information on the views of his constituents. He also seeks to keep them informed on national issues and his own activities in Congress. A variety of channels of communication between the Member and his constituents are available.

Elections

Election returns are perhaps the most impressive indicators of constituent opinion. A Member of Congress is highly conscious of the margins by which he and his predecessors have been elected. Because so many factors affect voting patterns—candidate personality, party affiliation, specific issues, etc.—the bare figures give only crude hints of local sentiment. Breakdown of these figures by neighborhood may indicate which interest groups supported or opposed a Member, and inferences can be drawn to explain the causes of that support or opposition. Shifts in population and voter registration within a district may indicate shifts in the strength of opinion on some issues.

Ward-by-ward, precinct-by-precinct analysis of voting statistics assumes major significance when state legislatures redistrict House seats. A Representative whose constituency is significantly altered through redistricting may assess the views of his new constituents through consideration of their past voting records as well as their ethnic, occupational, and other characteristics.

Elections for other offices, when held between Congressional races, also serve as indicators of trends within the constituency. Senators, with six-year terms, are in the best position to observe trends in intervening elections.

The fact that the constituents select the Representative functions as an indirect kind of communication—it increases the chances that the Member will know how his constituents feel about an issue because it increases the chances that he agrees with them, that he is their kind of man. The shared experience of the milieu of the district makes it likely that the Congressman and his constituents share the same outlook on public issues. Empathy is not, however, a particularly reliable source of information on constituent sentiment. The Congressman who relies on his subjective sense of what the home-folks are thinking is apt to think that his personal opinions are shared by those who in fact disagree. Senators, whose statewide constituencies usually are less homogeneous than House districts, have less reason to believe that their personal views are a good indicator of the views of their constituents.

Mail

Of all the sources of information about his constituents, their letters to him consume the largest share of the time of the Congressman and his staff. In a survey of the House in 1965, John S. Saloma found an average weekly mail count of 521 pieces, distributed as follows:

a. 64 (12.3%) letters involving casework (constituent problems).

b. 154 (29.6%) pressures or opinion letters (views pro and con issues, legislation).

c. 51 (9.8%) opinion ballots (preprinted by an organization).

d. 44 (8.4%) requests for information (such as Government bulletins, etc.).

e. 77 (14.8%) miscellaneous letters from constituents.

f. 120 (23.0%) letters received from outside the district.

g. 11 (2.1%) letters referred by other Members of Congress.

Answering the mail consumed an average of seven hours a week, or nearly 12 percent of the Representative's time, according to estimates given in the survey.

Volume of Mail

Precise figures on the volume of constituent mail to Members of Congress are not available. However, during hearings on the fiscal 1970 legislative appropriations, the total volume of mail received at the House post office during the 13-month period from March 1968 to April 1969 was estimated at 21,891,000 items (not including 6.8 million papers and flats and 116,000 parcels). A post office official said the Senate received about 9.5 million letters during calendar 1968. The increase over earlier periods is immense, but no figures are available for exact comparison. Figures for franked mail dispatched by Members go back to 1938. An average of 25 million pieces sent per year during the first four postwar years (Fiscal 1946-49) has increased nearly eightfold to an annual average of 190 million in the four years 1966-69.

Franked Mail Sent By Members of Congress

Fiscal Year	Pieces (millions)	Fiscal Year	Pieces (millions)
1938	24	1954	44
1939	36	1955	46
1940	45	1956	58
1941	31	1957	60
1942	24	1958	65
1943	—	1959	85
1944	24	1960	108
1945	24	1961	83
1946	28	1962	110
1947	25	1963	93
1948	29	1964	119
1949	19	1965	121
1950	31	1966	197
1951	35	1967	193
1952	35	1968	178
1953	46	1969	190

His staff spent an average of 88.6 hours a week, which amounted to 40.8 percent of their total working time, handling correspondence. (See box on following page.) A Senator's mail may range from a few hundred to 10,000 or more communications per week.

The volume of correspondence rises and falls with public interest in legislative issues, and it can be suddenly expanded by a pressure group campaign. Mail dealing with the problems of individual constituents tends to remain rather constant. Variation in the volume of mail from one office to another will depend on both the characteristics of the state or district and the policies of the Members. Senators from more populous states naturally get more mail.

Southern Senators and Representatives have usually received less mail in proportion to the number of constituents, perhaps because of their greater political security, the region's large Negro minority, and other factors. However, industrialization, voter registration drives and the growth of two-party politics are increasing

Workload of Representatives and Their Staffs

The following breakdown of the average workweek of Representatives and their offices is drawn from a study by John S. Saloma III, published in his *Congress and the New Politics* in 1969. The study was based on a survey he made in 1965 of 160 Representatives and the members of their staffs.

Average Workweek for a Congressman

Activity	Hours per Week (average)	Percentage of Workweek
On the floor	15.3	26.0%
In committee	7.7	13.1
Answering mail	7.0	11.9
On legislative research and reading	6.9	11.7
Handling constituent problems	5.1	8.6
Visiting with constituents in Washington	4.2	7.1
On committee work outside of committee	3.4	5.8
On writing speeches, articles	2.6	4.4
On leadership or party functions	2.4	4.1
Meeting with lobbyists and lobby groups	2.3	3.9
On press work, radio and television	2.0	3.4
Total	58.9	100.0

Average Workweek Summarized by Function

Function	Hours per Week (average)	Percentage
Legislative	38.0	64.6%
Committee work	(11.1)	(18.9)
General	(26.9)	(45.7)
Constituency service	16.3	27.6
Education / Publicity	4.6	7.8

Average Staff Workweek for a Congressional Office

Activity	Hours per Week (average)	Percentage
With the Member in committee	1.1	0.5%
Handling constituent problems (casework)	40.6	18.7
Visiting with constituents in Washington	12.9	6.0
With lobbyists and special interest groups	4.9	2.3
On press work, radio, and television	13.9	6.4
Writing speech drafts, floor remarks	11.2	5.2
On legislative research, bill drafting	13.6	6.3
On pressure and opinion mail	34.2	15.8
On opinion ballots (preprinted by organizations)	4.4	2.0
On requests for information	14.6	6.7
On letters of congratulation, condolence	9.2	4.2
On correspondence other than described	26.2	12.1
Mailing Government publications	8.5	3.9
Other	21.4	9.0
Total	216.7	100.0%

Average Staff Workweek Summarized by Function

Function	Hours per Week (average)	Percentage
Legislative support	30.8	14.3%
Constituency service	53.5	24.7
Correspondence (mixed constituency service, education)	88.6	40.8
Education and Publicity	22.4	10.3
Other	21.4	9.9

the participation of southerners in politics, including participation through correspondence with Members of Congress.

Generally, a responsiveness to letters tends to generate more correspondence. Although complaints about the volume of mail are commonplace, many Members of Congress actively stimulate correspondence by such devices as mass mailings, soliciting opinions. Those who write are usually put on mailing lists for newsletters, polls, and other literature. One Representative observed: "I wonder how many Congressmen invite (unnecessary) mail by returning to their districts and going to each courthouse or prominent place and saying, 'Now, please bring your problems to me.' Hasn't that become quite a campaign gimmick?"

Personal requests usually involve "casework" with agencies of the Federal Government. But they also cover a wide variety of other services. Requests for theater tickets and hotel or plane reservations are not uncommon, but the Congressman may be asked to perform almost any service—to purchase an outsize pair of overalls or to match a constituent's pair of draperies. Donald R. Matthews observed, in his study of the Senate, that Senators receive pleas from "mental cases, unwed mothers, sufferers from venereal diseases—all kinds of lost and bewildered people who do not know where else to turn." He reports a letter that began, "Dear Senator, I am complaining about my feet that are flat and badly callused and stay like they are on ice all the time."

A Representative who felt that a request to replace broken china was "a little outside the realm of a legislator's responsibility" added: "I don't mean to make fun of these people. I think it is very nice that they turn to us for assistance when they have a problem and feel that we represent them in so many ways. Naturally one must recognize it is their votes which help to return Members of Congress, but even apart from that I think it is wonderful they expect us to help."

Means of Supplying Information

Requests for information are numerous. A telephone call from the Congressman's office to an appropriate executive agency or Congressional committee may quickly supply the desired facts. Some departments make quotas of popular Government publications available to Members for mailing to constituents. The Department of Agriculture annually allots 400 of its yearbooks to each Representative and Senator. Each Member is entitled also to a total of 100,000 farmers' bulletins from more than 400 titles covering subjects of interest to urban as well as rural districts. A wide variety of other Agriculture Department publications are available as a part of this quota, including a special packet of 10 publications designed especially for brides. The Department of Health, Education and Welfare makes available up to 500 copies per month of an infant care publication for new parents. Often a member of the Member's staff clips wedding and birth notices from local papers so that such publications may be sent to the constituent.

The Congressional Research Service of the Library of Congress deals with many requests for specific information. In 1965 the service handled 113,628 inquiries, more than half of which were reference requests from constituents. Students preparing term papers or debates have swollen the demand for information. The service prepares special reports or packets of material for Congressional distribution on subjects of recurrent inquiry, such as the annual national debate topic.

Much legislative mail is "inspired" by pressure groups. Sometimes it takes the form of printed or mimeographed postcards. Identical letters reveal that the writers have been supplied with the message and have given it little consideration. Other letters generated by pressure groups are usually easy to recognize by the recurrence of phrases and arguments, the timing, or even the stationery. Such mail is given less weight than spontaneous communications which reflect individual thought. However, inspired mail may contain an implied threat: If an organization can prompt people to write, it may be able to deliver their votes, though the possibility is usually considered slight. Letters from personal or political friends have the greatest impact.

As an indicator of constituent opinion on business before Congress, the mail has grave limitations. Few Americans ever write their Congressmen. The highly educated, prosperous, and politically active are over-represented. Constituents are more inclined to write to Congressmen with whom they agree than to those with whom they take issue.

In their study of pressures affecting tariff legislation, Bauer, Pool and Dexter found that persons most likely to write were "those who saw the act of writing as part of a recognized professional role, likely to contribute to specific and short-run objectives and contributing effectively to the special interest for which the writer spoke." Neither moral conviction, nor a sense of the question's importance, nor a desire for self-expression differentiated those who wrote to Congressmen from those who did not. "A man was more likely to write on a trivial point if it were part of his job and a practical thing to do than if he were burning with deep conviction about the nation's future welfare." What is true about mail on tariff legislation, however, does not always apply to other matters. An event like the 1970 invasion of Cambodia is apt to produce a tidal wave of mail "burning with deep conviction."

Extreme distortion of constituent opinion may be produced by the mail. President Roosevelt's proposal in 1939 to repeal a provision of the existing Neutrality Act requiring imposition of an embargo on arms shipments to nations at war provoked an unprecedented flood of mail (reaching 487,000 items in a single day). Robert A. Dahl's *Congress and Foreign Policy* noted that the ratio of opposition to repeal ran about five to one in mail sent to the House; the ratio in Senate mail was even higher. Yet a public opinion poll at the time indicated that the public supported repeal by 56 to 44 percent. In this case Congress disregarded the mail, repealing the embargo by majorities of 68 percent in the Senate and 59 percent in the House. A year later, when a large sample of Senate mail showed 90 percent opposition to Selective Service, a public opinion poll indicated 70 percent support for the same measure. It passed the Senate with a 68 percent majority.

And yet Members of Congress normally treat the mail with great respect. That attitude reflects in part the inadequacies of other sources of information. But the mail's distortion of constituent opinion often is an advantage to the Senator or Representative. The views which are over-represented are likely to be those held by the more active, informed, influential and organized voters. They are also the constituents whose votes, and perhaps campaign funds or efforts, may depend on the Member's stand on the question at issue. Many Members periodically tabulate the opinions expressed in the mail on key issues, though "inspired" mail may be discounted or tabulated separately.

No Senator or Representative has time to read all his mail. Usually only complex matters and letters from friends or politically potent individuals are referred to him. Some Members ask to see all significant case mail or all mail concerning legislation. However, when replies drafted by the staff are given to the Member for his signature, often with the previous correspondence attached, he exercises control of his mail. Routine requests may be handled by a staff member authorized to use the Member's signature.

When considerable mail on the same question arrives, a standard reply may be drafted setting forth the Member's position. Special typewriters can produce identical copies of the text that look like individual letters; the clerk himself types the name, address and salutation, then switches to automatic typing for the body of the reply.

Thoughtful, concerned letters from constituents are likely to prompt careful replies. If the issue is complex, additional materials may be enclosed—a speech or article, a committee report, or a bulletin from an executive agency. Some Members of Congress prepare "issue packets" on controversial subjects. One seasoned Congressman suggested to his freshman colleagues that when a particular group wants detailed information or is applying heavy pressure, they send transcripts of committee hearings, which may run to four volumes. The constituents can be told: "Please read this and then if you have any further questions I will be glad to answer them."

Many House and Senate offices keep a record of all correspondents, with the subjects of their letters noted. Such a file may provide addresses for special mailings and serve other purposes. A Representative described how he used it during visits to his district: "As we are driving along touring our district, my wife goes through the card file for the next town. She reads off the names and identifies the kind of correspondence we have had with the various individuals. When we get there, the names of those people are familiar and you can say, 'Oh, yes, you wrote me about public power,' or 'you wrote me about a farm bill,' or something like that. We have a duplicate file. My Washington office files alphabetically and the field office by area."

A special file is often reserved for "crackpots." Most Members of Congress ignore chronic writers of crank mail on whom replies would be wasted. Occasionally a Senator or Representative may respond sharply to abusive mail. "Dear Friend," one replied to a constituent, "I want to call attention to the fact that some crackpot in your city is writing me and signing your name." But some Members of Congress go out of their way to court sharp critics with extra attention, hoping perhaps that the antagonist's surprise will prompt him to report the unexpected courtesy to his acquaintances.

Members often avoid committing themselves precisely in their letters. Support pledged to a bill may prove embarrassing when amendments are added that make it wise to vote against it. A Member may regret taking a stand on a controversial question that will alienate some

voters only to find that he never has to vote on it because a committee kills the bill. Complexities in proposed legislation and the context in which it is considered may be more than the Member can explain to the constituent who asks for a yea or nay vote. One Representative telephoned a random selection of his correspondents to test their knowledge of labor legislation they had written about. He found they had written because they had been told to or because they had gotten excited; they did not know the issues, could not specify what they disliked in the committee bill, and could not compare the competing bills.

Each Senator and Representative is granted allowances for stationery, stamps, and telephone and telegraph messages. All Members of Congress enjoy franking privileges under which all surface mail related to official business is carried free of postage. "Official business" is defined broadly to include all matters related to a Member's work in Congress. However, if personal comments or political appeals are included in the official correspondence, postage must be paid. Public documents printed by order of Congress, such as bills or committee hearings and report, can be mailed under franking privilege. Copies of speeches or of articles reprinted in the *Congressional Record* can be mailed at no charge regardless of the subject. It is not uncommon for Members to have politically useful material inserted in the *Record* so that it can be reproduced and posted under frank.

Office Visitors

Constituents may come to Washington to contact their Representatives or Senators about legislation or to seek their assistance on individual matters. They may request help on business with a Government agency, job hunting, a term paper, introductions to officials, or other matters. But the largest number of visitors from the home state or district are tourists who stop by the Member's office. They may take advantage of the opportunity to make known their views or needs, but they are more likely to seek information and aid as tourists in the nation's capital. Often the visitors appear in groups—high school classes, delegates to conventions held in Washington, tours organized by district organizations, etc.

The staff welcomes constituents, knowing the importance of the direct impression they will take back to the district or state. Information about Washington tourist attractions and the Federal Government are provided in a variety of booklets and brochures; the office staff may prepare calendars of events as well. Passes to House and Senate visitors' galleries are handed out, and special tours of the White House and some executive agencies may be arranged.

Though the staff can usually handle the needs of visitors, some are anxious to see the Congressman himself. He may be reluctant to interrupt his other work, yet even more reluctant to turn down such a request. Unless he is hard-pressed for time, he is likely to speak with the caller or callers. He may arrange to be photographed with a group of constituents, providing them with copies to take home. Some legislators will even conduct groups on a tour of the Capitol or sponsor luncheons with them. Others attempt to keep time spent with visitors to a minimum.

Representatives surveyed by Saloma in 1965 estimated their time spent with visiting constituents at an average of 4.2 hours per week, or 7.1 percent of their workload. Staff time with constituents was estimated at 12.9 hours per week, or 6.0 percent of total staff workload. During the 88th Congress, 89 Representatives received an average of 1,511 visitors, of whom they personally saw an average of 52 percent. Comparable figures are not available for Senators, although the larger number of their constituents reduces the chances that visitors will be able to contact the Senator personally.

The Congressman may actively pursue the role of Washington host, sponsoring an annual busload of schoolchildren or making arrangements for packages tours bringing constituents from home. Some have initiated student intern programs providing, often with wages to cover living costs, opportunities for practical experience in Congressional work. Most intern programs, however, are sponsored by colleges.

Delegates who come from the district or state to lobby for legislation, or to deal with a problem before an administrative agency, usually receive careful attention from Members of Congress. They may represent a municipality or a section of industry, labor or agriculture that considers a pending decision in Congress or the Executive Branch vital to its future. The impression that members of such a delegation take home with them can be quite important.

The visiting constituents may seek commitments that the Representative or Senator is not prepared to give. They usually do not press their cases too hard, though the Member is probably alert to their views. "We go out to lunch," a Congressman observed, "But they don't necessarily talk about anything. (We) just know a good guy may be going out of business because he doesn't get more trade or so. It's the spirit that influences." Such indirection saves a Congressman from the unpleasant business of rejecting requests, and most of them are skilled at avoiding confrontation. "The typical business visitor to a Congressional office," Bauer, Pool and Dexter note, "comes with not one problem, but several, and in general Congressmen are much more experienced and expert at diverting visitors than visitors are in forcing Congressmen on a point."

Visits To The Constituency

Earlier in the century, when sessions of Congress did not take up most of the year, hectic fence-mending trips to the home state or district were not urgent. Today, with Members buried in work in Washington, these trips are much more difficult and much more necessary. The constituents have less opportunity to get acquainted with their Senators or Representatives at a time when, with the growth of legislation affecting their daily lives, they have greater need to know them. The Members, meanwhile, have more voters to woo but less time to devote to that task.

Politicians know that the most effective electioneering is done between campaigns. The officeholder has no opponent at such times, and he carries the aura of his office more than the stigma of a "politician." The Member of Congress who neglects to spend time in his constituency, despite—or indeed because of—his achievements as a legislator, is liable to find himself out of a job.

Tuesday to Thursday

Members of Congress living within easy weekend travel distance of Washington, D.C., form the bulk of the so-called "Tuesday-to-Thursday" group. Often criticized for absence from legislative business, they may feel they have no choice. A Representative from an urban district less than 250 miles from Washington explained:

"Casework takes a lot of time. When you are home, you cannot even go to church in safety. Every time I go, there are 30 to 40 people hiding behind automobiles just waiting to bump into me, always quite by accident. Each thinks his individual problem is the most important in the world. Problems of world peace and international tension pale into insignificance beside some personal problem of many constituents. People knock the Tuesday-to-Thursday group. I agree that it is a problem. I would be very happy if I didn't live so close to Washington. As it is, there is a 100-percent demand on my time. I go to my district on weekends and I hold office hours every Friday evening, beginning at eight o'clock and usually continuing until midnight. This life is no picnic no matter what some people think."— Quoted in Charles L. Clapp, *The Congressman: His Work as He Sees It* (1963), p. 68-69.

Most Members make short home visits during the legislative session, and longer ones during the adjournment of Congress. In 1965, the average Representative spent about six days in his district while the House was in session. The amount of time spent cultivating the grass roots will vary with the constituency's distance from Washington, the proximity of the next election, the precariousness of the seat, the Member's own predilections, and Washington's demands on his time.

In 1970 each Representative was entitled to one paid round trip to his constituency for each month Congress was in session; in addition, a total of two trips a year was available for use by members of his staff. In December 1969, a Senator's annual travel allowance was increased from 6 to 12 trips. Eight trips a year were available for distribution among his staff; 10 trips were allowed for the staffs of Senators from states of more than 10 million population. Representatives, but not Senators, were entitled to use a flat allowance of $750 a year in lieu of the trip quota—an alternative attractive to Representatives from districts near Washington. Members of Congress frequently exceed their travel allowances, paying the added expense out of their own pockets.

Donald R. Matthews observes that "Fence-mending trips help in regaining perspective. 'Ninety-five percent of what happens on Capitol Hill doesn't create a ripple back home,' and all Senators desperately need, from time to time, to relearn this lesson." But Matthews adds: "Without the most stubborn and conscientious efforts, a Senator is almost certain to see and talk mostly with friends and supporters on such a trip. Since both categories are likely to be in general agreement with him, the image of constituency opinion he brings back to

Mobile District Office

Rep. G. Elliott Hagan (D Ga.), when first campaigning for a House seat, found that the "one big complaint" in his district was that the incumbent Congressman "comes home and he sees Bill Smith and John Jones and then drives on out of town." Hagan had made a point of asking voters when they had seen their Congressman. To avoid incurring the same complaint after he gained office, Hagan hit upon the unique idea of a mobile office. Preceded by advance publicity, he managed during a short autumn adjournment in 1962 to visit all 18 counties in his district, answering questions, passing out information, and meeting with high school government classes. He later told a seminar of freshman Representatives that he got his picture, in front of his mobile office, on the front pages of Georgia's major newspapers and also found television stations "happy to carry it."

"I couldn't have bought the publicity. The four sides of this mobile office are white with red, big boxcar letters, with dignity, of course, but with some blue also. Regardless of the direction from which they are traveling into the main part of each of 18 counties in my district, the county seat, they know that Elliott Hagan is in town because the name is there. They can't miss it. I have had as high as 200 people in one day to sit across my office desk asking me questions and, of course, I have a little adjoining office and two or three helpers there. We get the information, and we are still working on it from last fall....I talked to any constituent who wanted to see me, and that is the beautiful part about it. How can anybody in my district say, 'Well, you can't see the Congressman. He never comes around.' " —*Transscript of Seminars for New Members of the 88th Congress, Jan. 14-23, 1963.*

Washington is usually distorted in favor of his own views. This is, no doubt a gratifying consequence of such visits. But the spurious support they provide to the Senator's own patterns of thought can be dangerous."

The majority of Senators and Representatives have offices in their districts. The division of work between the district and Washington offices varies widely. Some Members have a staffer handle substantial amounts of casework in the district, especially if regional offices of Federal agencies are located there. Others prefer to deal with all casework in Washington and use the district office primarily for public relations work or keeping track of events in the district. Former Rep. George W. Grider (D Tenn.) set up "Dial-a-Congressman" hours on Monday afternoons when constituents could visit his Memphis office to place a free telephone call to him in Washington. He observed that "The constituents, when they talk with me personally, know that through me they have a voice in what happens." Some Members have no district office at all, while those within a striking distance of Washington may appear for regular weekend office hours.

According to listings in the 1965 Congressional Directory, 301 Representatives maintained year-round offices with one or more full-time staff members in their constituencies. Of these, 36 Representatives had more than one office. Offices open only when the Congressman returns home, or listing no staff or schedule, accounted for 102 Representatives. Only 32 Representatives had no district offices listed.

One or two district offices may be maintained in Federal Government facilities or, if these are not available and suitable, the Member of Congress is entitled to an allowance of $2,400 per year to rent other space. Senators are allowed an additional $400 per quarter, and Representatives $300 per month, for district office expenses.

Grass Roots Lobbying

Whether contact with a Member of Congress is made through the mail, by telephone or telegraph, through visits to Washington, or during the Member's visits to his state or district, lobbies often seek to influence him through his own constituents. In fact, the trend in lobbying has been to emphasize grassroots efforts rather than Washington contacts by professionals. Often the Washington office of national lobbies functions primarily to feed, stimulate and coordinate pressures by constituents on Senators and Representatives. *(See following subchapter on Lobbies.)*

A Democratic Representative has stressed the significance of the withdrawal of lobbying from Capitol Hill to the constituencies, using the private utility lobby to illustrate his point: "About ten years ago they were here in force with a big office and were working like mad. Soon they realized that the way to get to the Congressman was back home with the voters. Today their real effort is made at the grassroots. And they can control more votes among individual Congressmen than any other special interest lobby."

Stimulating mail is one way national lobbies can activate constituents. Thus four large corporations were credited by Bauer, Pool and Dexter with inspiring 40 percent of the heavy mail on extension of the Reciprocal Trade Agreements Act in 1954, and most of the remainder was attributed to other business interests seeking tariff protection. Three-fourths of the antiprotectionist mail (which was outnumbered about 10 to 1) was attributed directly or indirectly to the League of Women Voters.

Knowing that inspired mail is recognized and largely discounted by Members of Congress, effective national lobbies give more attention to working through the structure of influence in the states and districts. An organization like the American Medical Association, whose members tend to be articulate and influential in their communities, concentrates on alerting doctors on legislative action that may affect them. The American Cotton Manufacturers Institute was highly successful in 1955 in shifting southern Congressmen toward tariff protection by plugging its effort into the local power structures. Acccording to Bauer, Pool and Dexter: "Many of the southern (textile) mills are not southern at all, but parts of northern combines. Yet their local managers, often the old owners, are still part of that relatively small, tightly knit, small-town elite with face-to-face relationships of which the Congressman is a part. Thus, the ACMI's real effectiveness arose not so much from its own testifying, lobbying, or organizing as from the fact that it stimulated action by members who had the ear of their Congressman to a far greater degree than do members of most trade associations. They were geographically localized and politically influential."

The local elite was mobilized by regional meetings in which industry members were warned by the ACMI of the threat of textile imports to their business. The lobby also stimulated a massive letter-writing campaign from workers in the factories. Such mobilization of constituents, standard operating procedures in other regions, was particularly successful in their campaign because southern Congressmen were not familiar with it and were sensitive to local changes being wrought by industrialization.

National offices can be useful to constituents in advising them on the most effective approach to their Congressmen—when the constituent is visiting Washington or the Representative is visiting his district. They can inform constituents about the issues, the effect of legislation on them, the voting record of the Congressman, who are his friends and aides, the etiquette of pressure, and arguments likely to be persuasive. The lobby has to anticipate legislative action in order to alert constituents in time for them to make their weight felt in Washington. A Representative has described how a national lobby activitates its members at the district level: "They are very good at sitting in offices here and figuring out ways to get their people back home scared. I got back to the district, and my wife told me that in five minutes the association against raising the minimum wage would be there. About 15 of them arrived. One fellow served as spokesman and said, "Now, Bob, you tell the Congressman what this minimum wage would do to you." They went around the room, and it took an hour for them to finish. I told them that there was not going to be any minimum wage legislation this year and there was no need to commit ourselves completely now. They said they knew better, that their organization had informed them it was imminent—the corner druggist, the retail stores, etc., would all be covered by the minimum wage."

The Washington lobbyist can also provide the Congressman with information about his constituents. Postal employee and railway labor organizations, for example, produce materials indicating their numerical strength in individual districts.

In a reversal of the stereotype of lobby pressure, a Member of Congress is likely to turn to the lobbies for help in pursuing a legislative campaign on which he is bent. Whether responding to the wants of his own constituents, or inspiring a demand by them that he can meet, or pursuing his own convictions, the Member may prompt a lobby agreeing with him to mobilize action by constituents in the districts and states of other legislators. The lobby has resources for grassroots work which are not available to a Senator or Representative, especially when it comes to such work outside his own constituency.

Newsletters, Special Mailings

The flow of information from a Senator or Representative to his constituents is as important as that in the reverse direction. It is vital not only to the Member's re-election but also to public understanding of the issues and processes of Government. Some of the Con-

---

How Much Candor?

Most legislators doubt the wisdom of consistently loading newsletters with detailed information or exposing one's stand on every issue. There is no unanimity, however. Charles L. Clapp, in The Congressman, His Work as He Sees It *(pp. 91-92), records the following dialogue between two Representatives from the same state (and suggests that the Congressman who produces the detailed newsletter exaggerates its effectiveness):*

A. There are two schools of thought as to whether it is a good idea to let your constituents know your attitude on all subjects and on all votes. Someone has said that every time you vote you are voting against the interests of some group, and your opponent is smart if he brings out your complete voting record because many groups will be antagonized by specific votes. Getting to——'s newsletter, it is a good one, and I read it every week. He, probably more than anyone else in Congress, lets his constituency know how he votes on every single bill that comes up. I don't do that. I don't think constituents are interested. I advised him to stop doing it but he continues. Certainly the fact that he has been re-elected in the toughest district in our large state is to his credit. Perhaps his newsletter is one reason for his success.

B. I would rather let them know where I stand than have any opponent informing them a week before the election.

A. You get into a problem when you are specific. You are voluntarily subjecting yourself to criticism as to why you acted in that way. So unless people raise an issue with you, you don't want to go over every one exhaustively in an effort to educate people as to your views. It may irritate.

B. I am not so sure about that. My newsletters are distributed all over the district. My opponents often have many house meetings and at practically every one of them there is at least one person who has received my report. If my opponent starts taking off on me, somebody is in the room to fight my battle for me.

---

gressional dissemination of information takes one of the forms of communication already discussed—individual responses to mail and direct contacts in Washington or at home. Members also employ instruments of mass communication.

Newsletters. Newsletters have gained great favor in the past two decades. Some Members have come to regard them as their most effective single activity among constituents. In 1965, 122 out of 152 offices of Representatives responding to a survey indicated that they sent newsletters to constituents on a regular basis. An average of 5.7 hours of effort by the Representative and 28.5 staff-hours were invested in preparation and mailing of each newsletter. *(See box for circulation figures.)* Newsletters were published weekly, fortnightly or monthly. Twelve of the offices mailed their newsletters to all postal patrons in the district, and 98 used special mailing lists.

Circulation of Mailings

(152 Representatives Surveyed in 1965)

Circulation	Number of Members *(Newsletters)*	Number of Members *(Questionnaires)*
Less than 5,000	11	1
6,000-15,000	25	3
16,000-30,000	21	3
31,000-60,000	17	11
61,000-90,000	11	14
91,000-120,000	16	19
121,000-150,000	13	19
Over 150,000	4	7

Source: John S. Saloma III, *Congress and the New Politics* (1969).

The format of the newsletter varies from mimeographed sheets stapled together to polished photo offset productions embellished with a picture of the Congressman, and one of the Capitol and a map of the district. The content ranges from resumes of various legislative activities to analysis of a single issue. The Congressman's own activities are usually highlighted. Items of special interest to the district are most likely to be included, and some newsletters list visitors from the district to the Washington office. Some newsletters adopt a chatty tone; others are more formal.

Special Mailings. A mass mailing that does not take the form of a newsletter is often used to publicize a special issue or event. Such mailings may be specially prepared for the occasion or may consist of reproductions of a Government report, a magazine article, or a speech from the *Congressional Record.* The material may be accompanied by a covering news release.

Mailing Lists. Mailing lists for newsletters and special mailings are built from a wide variety of sources. If the target is a particular town or county, the telephone directory may suffice. Cities usually have directories organized by address, permitting ward and precinct lists and concentration on specific ethnic or class neighborhoods. Voter registration lists, tax rolls, specialized directories, and membership lists of clubs, labor unions and voluntary associations can all be used to compile lists. Constituents who write to Congressmen are usually added to mailing lists. People identified as opinion molders—school principals, clergy, newsmen, presidents of local organizations, local officials, etc.—are particularly sought, and the local press is culled for names of newsmakers to be added to the lists. Some Congressmen list doctors' offices, beauty parlors, and barber shops.

Questionnaires and Polls. Increasingly Congressmen mail questionnaires to their constituents. Of 152 Representatives surveyed in 1965, 91 reported using them. They and their staffs said they spent an average of about 20 hours preparing each questionnaire, and 118 hours for processing. Circulation varied, with distribution of most questionnaires ranging between 30,000 and 150,-000. The average constituent response was 16.7 per-

cent. Most Members reported the results to their constituents through their newsletters or press releases.

Questionnaires are distributed by a variety of methods. They may be incorporated in a newsletter, published in newspapers, mailed separately to any of a wide variety of mailing lists, or even handed out at meetings. As a means of determining constituent opinion, Congressional polls have been criticized by social scientists. Unsophisticated sampling methods with consequent distortion of findings have been found to characterize most polls. *(See box.)* Members of Congress are seldom surprised by the results, but their frequent distribution to the press and insertion in the *Congressional Record* may create false impressions.

Use of professional polling organizations by individual Congressmen is rare, largely because of the expense. The national surveys of organizations like the Gallup Poll do not help Members of Congress much, because they are not broken down by state and district. Senators are less likely than Representatives to distribute questionnaires because of their larger constituencies.

The unscientific character of the sampling does not interfere with the Congressman's principal purpose in distributing questionnaires. He considers the device especially useful for establishing a sense of connection between himself and his constituents. Some respondents take pains to elaborate on their answers, and it is not uncommon for them to note that "this is the first time anyone ever asked me for my views." Some make known their doubts that the Member will ever pay any attention to their answers, and most never bother to reply at all, but Congressmen believe questionnaires win friends in their districts.

Constituents have been known to return the blank questionnaire to the Congressman, asking him to fill it out and mail it back. "I got one like that recently," an experienced Member admitted, "and I guess I'm stupid. I don't known how to answer my own questionnaire. I mean you can't answer yes or no."

The Press

Members of Congress have to rely heavily on the press to inform their constituents, but they are not generally satisfied with the performance of the press in this regard. An individual Representative's activities are largely lost in the flood of news competing for space in newspapers and on television. Senators, however, have less difficulty than Representatives in attracting the attention of newspapers and networks.

Members and reporters often differ in their views of what is newsworthy. Members are apt to think that reporters neglect the substance of news in their eagerness for an "angle" that will attract attention. The complexities of public questions and of the legislative process sometimes appear to Members to get less coverage than stories that tend to denigrate the public image of a Senator or Representative. "Much of the press," the late Rep. Clem Miller (D Calif. 1959-62) said in a newsletter to his constituents, "seems to regard its Washington role as it does police reporting. The broader sweep of the meaningful 'why' and the 'wherefore' of government is lost in the welter of what is on the police captain's blotter."

The extent to which Members depend on the press may prompt some of their dissatisfaction with it. At the same time, their dependence makes them normally cordial to reporters, including those they dislike and fear. Reporters are well aware of the politician's quest for publicity, and understandably skeptical of the importance he attaches to keeping constituents aware of what he is doing. In an article on "Government by Publicity" (*The Reporter*, March 19, 1959), Douglass Cater noted that the politician had "always been something of a dramatist in search of an audience." Cater suggested that a new type of Member was emerging who neglects the painstaking work of legislation in favor of "the subtleties of appealing beyond Congress directly to the mass audience." According to this description: "He knows the formula of the news release, the timing, the spoon-feeding necessities of the publicity campaign. He assesses with canny shrewdness the areas of enterprise that will best lend themselves to a sustained publicity buildup. He is a master at shadow play, creating the illusion of magnificent drama from a reality that may be quite mundane."

Some Members of Congress have former newsmen on their staffs to handle press relations. News releases are frequently dispatched to state and district media, often accompanied by the full text of a speech. Telephone calls may be made to direct the attention of the press to the Member's activities. Releases are distributed to the House and Senate press galleries. Weekly newspapers in the constituencies, which have small staffs and tend to welcome stories connecting the community with a larger world, may print the releases verbatim. In the 1965 House survey, 51 Representatives said their newsletters were reprinted in district papers, while 65 indicated that theirs were not. Forty-eight reported that they prepared a separate column for newspapers.

Members rely on the local press as a source, as well as a distributor, of information. The 1965 survey found the average Congressman reading five daily newspapers, eight weekly newspapers, and five or six periodicals. Congressional staff members regularly scan local papers for figures of local prominence to be added to mailing lists, and for weddings, births, honors, elections and other events deserving congratulatory letters.

TV and Radio. Some Members make weekly, biweekly, or monthly reports to their constituents on local TV and radio stations. Typically these reports consume from three to five minutes. Because licensed stations are required to devote a portion of their time to public service broadcasts, they are relatively receptive to such programs. A one-minute commentary on a major news event or item of particular local interest may also be supplied by the Member to fit into newscasts. Interviews, typically lasting 5 to 15 minutes and often including a Federal executive, provide a popular format for current issues of concern to constituents.

Once a Senator or Representative is officially a candidate for re-election, he can no longer obtain free radio or television time. The high cost of TV then reduces most of his broadcasting to spot announcements at peak listening hours. Reports and interviews or panel shows tend during the campaign to give way to documentaries on the candidate's life and achievements. The House and Senate have studios where films and transcripts can be produced at cost to be dispatched to networks and stations.

Polling Samples

An article by Leonard A. Marascuilo and Harriet Amster, "Survey of 1961-62 Congressional Polls" (*Public Opinion Quarterly*, Fall 1964, pp. 497-506), was critical of the sampling techniques of Congressmen. The article included a tabulation of types of populations sampled. The following figures reflect the sampling practices of 39 Representatives who supplied sufficient information in response to the survey (some Representatives used more than one of the population types):

Types of Populations Sampled	Frequency
1. Households in district	6
2. Households of registered voters	4
3. Personal mailing list or newsletter recipients	11
4. Club members and attendants at meetings	2
5. Personal contacts by Congressman or others	5
6. Civic and business leaders	3
7. Specific occupational group (poll workers, druggists, etc.)	2
8. Names in telephone book	4
9. Newspaper advertisement	4
10. Individuals who requested questionnaires	1
11. Residents or constituents of district.	6
12. Registered voters	8

Representatives surveyed in 1965 reported an average of four television and eight radio appearances a month while Congress was in session. Of the 152 participating in the survey, 85 (56 percent) gave regular radio or TV reports to constituents. The weekly five-minute radio report, made by 36 Representatives, was the most popular form of presentation.

Filtered Communication

What goes out of the office of a Member of Congress has a major influence on what comes into it. The role that the Member emphasizes for himself—legislator, caseworker, educator—and the way in which he plays it helps to determine which constituents communicate with him and on what subjects. Thus the Member who assists in immigration cases, or accepts speaking invitations from high schools, or sponsors legislation for senior citizens, or gives speeches on foreign affairs, will be asked to do more of the same.

The Representative, and even more the Senator, cannot appeal to every interest group in his constituency. The groups whose support he most cultivates will provide most of the messages he receives. They will tend to reinforce the views which prompted him to choose these supporters in the first place.

The Member's own views will in any case filter communication from his constituents, helping him to decide what, in the flood of messages, is significant and what he can or should disregard. The greater the diversity of pressures on him, the more freedom the Member has to decide which are really compelling. Observing that experienced Members and their staffs are "quite tough-minded and skilled at assessing their mail," Bauer, Pool and Dexter add: "They are unlikely to feel pressure from the mere existence of numerous demands on them. That being the case, the demands that seem compelling to Congressmen are apt to be those which fit their own psychic needs and their images of the world. Things interior to the Congressman's mind largely determine what events he will perceive as external pressure on him. He unconsciously chooses which pressures to recognize."

Because a Member's predispositions affect his perception of communications from constituents, trends in these communications are more likely to influence the relative importance he assigns an issue than his stand on that issue. "Messages serve more as triggers than as persuaders."

Belief that a Member's mind is already made up, or that other concerns consume all his time, may reduce communication with him on a particular subject. Sen. Joseph R. McCarthy (R Wis.) twice obtained a quota on imported furs, but after he took up the investigation of Communism, it was observed: "None of the Wisconsin dairy or fur people would go to see Joe. He's too busy and out of that world. They'd go see (Senators) Wiley or Thye or Humphrey's assistant, but not Joe—he doesn't follow that sort of thing any more." Noting this tendency, Bauer, Pool and Dexter concluded: "Thus, an anticipatory feedback discourages messages that may not be favorably received from even getting sent. A Congressman very largely gets back what he puts out. In his limited time, he associates more with some kinds of people than with others, listens to some kinds of messages more than others, and as a result hears from some kinds of people more than from others. He controls what he hears both by his attention and by his attitudes. He makes the world to which he thinks he is responding. Congressmen, indeed, do respond to pressures, but they generate the pressures they feel."

But they also respond to pressures which are quite real even though barely visible. A Member of Congress must anticipate what matters might become major grievances with constituents if he were to neglect them. A few voices may influence a Member if he reads them —or misreads them—as the visible tip of an iceberg.

Failure in communication is often caused by false inference, usually based on inadequate information. Constituents, lobbyists and even other Members of Congress not infrequently assume they know a Representative's or Senator's stand on an issue because they know his party affiliation, his region, and perhaps his past views on other questions. A Member may similarly take for granted the viewpoint on specific issues of groups within his own constituency. When either the Member or the constituents are not, in fact, committed to the position attributed to them, opportunities for influential communications are lost. Pressure groups generally pleased with a Member's record may be particularly cautious not to antagonize him by prodding for a particular measure they expect him to oppose. The Member may show similar caution about raising subjects he believes would offend groups that support his stand on most issues.

Members As Educators

"The informing function of Congress," Woodrow Wilson said, "should be preferred even to its legislative function." Unless Congress scrutinized the Government and sifted its acts "by every means of discussion," he wrote, "the country must remain in embarrassing, crippling ignorance of the very affairs which it is most important that it should understand and direct." Since Wilson expressed this view in his Ph.D dissertation in 1884, the Federal Government has grown in size, and its actions in complexity, beyond anything he could then have imagined. With this growth, the difficulty of the informing function has expanded enormously; so has the need.

Constituents today are directly affected by innumerable Federal laws. It is unrealistic to expect most of them to understand the intricacies of each piece of legislation. But unless the broad principles at stake can be identified for them, they can no longer participate in self-government. In making clear to voters the essentials of complicated issues, the Member of Congress performs a function for which he is uniquely suited. He is both a participant in government as lawmaker, and an observer of government in his oversight of the Executive. He has more expert knowledge of national affairs than the ordinary citizen, and more varied concerns than the ordinary expert. He is closer to the grassroots than the bureaucrat, and closer to the problems of governing than the constituent. As a mediator between effective government and democratic government, he is essential to their coexistence.

It is a well-established principle that a Member of Congress must represent his community in the decisions of the Federal Government. But with the growing complexity of the Government, it becomes increasingly urgent that he represent the Government's point of view to his constituents. Men of experience and intelligence and education are gathered in Washington, grappling with problems that most voters never face directly. If voters are not to abdicate, or to sabotage, self-government, then the insight, information and perspective of Washington must be a resource to them.

The fact that Senators and Representatives are specially qualified to explain Government to voters does not necessarily mean that they do so. In fact, the most painful truths are often precisely the ones most necessary to convey to the electorate. Few men seeking re-election relish the role of messenger of unpleasant tidings. It is much easier to gain re-election by conscientiously responding to mail, handling casework, attracting attention, and avoiding controversy.

The high cost of candor may, however, be largely myth. Observing that only 15 incumbent Congressmen had been defeated in the previous general election, journalist David Broder told a seminar of freshmen Congressmen in 1963 that the security of their jobs enabled them to be substantially freer agents than they might suppose under "the prevailing myth that your main problem is getting yourself re-elected." Broder went on to say:

"I think you should be as frank in defining for your constituents the problems and the prospects of the nation, both at home and abroad, as you are in telling the bureaucrats downtown the facts of life about the

Vandenberg's Re-education

Profound changes in America's role in world politics—the realm least familiar to the ordinary voter—have especially challenged the capacity of Members of Congress to re-educate themselves and their constituents. Earl Mazo described for the 1963 freshman House seminar a particularly dramatic case of such re-education, the switch of Sen. Arthur H. Vandenberg (R Mich.) from "a symbol of isolation in the Senate of the United States for over a generation" to a leader of internationalism.

"...when the Germans put up the first V-1 automatic bomber, manless bomber, manless missile, into the community of London, he (Vandenberg) after long conversations with Foster Dulles began to think about this, and to think about the influence of science upon his basic theory. He came to the conclusion that if the Germans could create a small bomb with wings on it and put a certain amount of gas into it that would run out when it got over in London and then came down, it was only a matter of time when they could do the same across the Atlantic. And he changed his views under scientific and political education, went back to his constituency and told them so, and spent the last, I would say, eight years of his life in a totally different position—not as a representative of the State of Michigan alone—but as one of the great figures in the Western world."

problems and wishes of your constituents in matters in which they are concerned. I think you have to take the serious responsibility of telling your people as honestly and as frankly and as fully as you can, what kind of shape we are in as a nation and what kind of world we are living in....And if there were one wish which I could express to you it would be that, as you enjoy the security that your membership in this distinguished body has given you, you will recall your obligation to be a teacher to your people."

Although the Member of Congress gains in Washington new perspectives on issues, he may be reluctant to alter views to which he committed himself when asking constituents to vote for him. Yet new information and changing conditions are precisely what require him to represent Washington to his constituents. Even if he feels obliged to cast a vote according to campaign pledges, he has an obligation to inform those who elected him what he has learned that forces him to revise his views.

The various means by which the individual Congressman can communicate with his own constituents have been described. Congress also communicates as an institution with its national constituency. The House and Senate, by their debate, legislation and resolutions, inform the nation, with the press serving as the principal messenger. One of the most effective educational devices at the disposal of Congress, especially since the Second World War, has been the committee investigation. The use of investigations has helped Congress to

compete with the vastly expanded publicity powers of the Presidency. It has also strengthened the ability of Congress to obtain information it needs to carry on its increasingly complicated tasks, including the task of informing the public.

Investigations have sometimes had great impact in alerting, alarming and educating, or sometimes only misleading or entertaining, the public. Some of the more sensational probes have altered the viewpoints of wide audiences, while less publicized inquiries have affected the key groups most directly involved in the questions investigated, with lobbies often serving as the medium by which the committee's activities are communicated to constituencies which are defined by their special interests.

Perhaps the greatest limitation on the educational performance of the Member of Congress lies in his audience. Through a wide variety of means, Members make an enormous amount of valuable information and ideas easily available to anyone who is interested. Their real problem as educators is not how to disseminate knowledge of the Government, but how to stimulate interest in such knowledge. If many scarcely try, it is at least in part because the response so often proves discouraging.

Services for Constituents

The volume of services which Members of Congress perform for their constituents has grown enormously in recent years. Before 1900, when Senators and Representatives did not have offices of their own, Congress was not in session half of the time, and the population of constituencies was much smaller, requests for help on particular problems demanded little time or effort. With population growth, easier communication, and the spread of education, the volume of private requests expanded. But it is the expansion of the Federal Government into many areas directly affecting the private lives of individuals which has produced a revolution in the volume of services Members perform for their constituents.

Variety of Casework

A Member's dealings with administrative agencies of the Federal Government on behalf of his constituents is usually called "casework." The variety of casework is almost unlimited. Typical requests concern military service, Social Security benefits, veterans' affairs, immigration, passports, unemployment claims, and problems arising from Federal aid programs such as housing. The character of requests also varies widely among constituencies. Thus agricultural districts generate casework related to acreage quotas and delayed crop subsidy checks. But even districts that are much alike sometimes show substantial variation in the type of problems brought to their Representatives.

While some casework involves complaints, a good deal has to do with requests for assistance in approaching Federal agencies. Government contracts, loans, grants, jobs and patents are among the benefits sought by constituents. They may ask only for referral to an appropriate agency, or, at the opposite extreme, they may ask their Congressman to appear before an agency to argue the merits of a specific claim. Some requests are for introductions to Federal officials, ranging from

Types of Communicators

A study of material circulated by Senators and Representatives in the first six months of the 89th Congress sought to determine whether or not Members provided constituents with reasonably objective information on topics of current concern. The study scored written communications to divide Members into five basic types: 1) the promoter (of himself); 2) the persuader; 3) the combined promoter-persuader; 4) the reticent; and 5) the educator. Based on a content analysis of 1,500 separate printed communications to constituents from 149 Representatives and 32 Senators, the study allocated the Members as follows:

House of Representatives Sample

Category	Number	Percent of Total
Promoter	56	38%
Persuader	33	22
Promoter-Persuader	25	17
Reticent	22	15
Educator	13	9
	149	

Senate Sample

Category	Number	Percent of Total
Promoter	14	44%
Persuader	9	28
Promoter-Persuader	6	19
Reticent	2	6
Educator	1	3
	32	

Source: William C. Love Jr., "The Congressman as Educator: A Study in Legislator-Constituent Relationships," M.S.Thesis, M.I.T., 1966. Data used in John S. Saloma III, *Congress and the New Politics* (1969), pp. 175-177.

The data indicated that roles tended to shift with seniority from a promoter orientation for freshman Representatives through a persuader orientation to reticence among Members from safe House districts. Although the impartial educator constituted a small percentage in both houses, the persuader and promoter-persuader also were engaged in education, albeit of a more or less partisan nature. Through their other activities, especially in committee work, many Members participate in educational efforts whatever posture they adopt in direct communications with their constituents.

livered to the Congressman with a letter from the Clerk's office certifying that it has been flown as requested by the specified individual or group.

Some requests are highly unusual. Most Members can recall a number of bizarre cases. Transportation to Antarctica and a gold brick from the vaults of Fort Knox are among those reported. One Congressman went to great lengths to get doors for toilets installed in a Post Office men's room in Milwaukee. Another received the following letter:

"Dear Congressman:

Some ninny working for the government has informed me that under the law, oats are not a feed grain. Would you please explain that to my mule. I sure can't."

Volume of Requests

Statistical data accurately describing the volume and character of casework are, according to a review of the literature on the subject, "virtually nonexistent." Walter Kravitz of the Legislative Reference Service of the Library of Congress, after citing varied and often conflicting descriptions of casework, summarized the confusion as follows: "To sum up, our knowledge about the dimensions of casework amounts to this: Total mail in a Senate office may run from a few hundred to 10,000 or more communications per week, of which case mail may constitute 7.8, 25, 33½, 53, or 65 percent. The weekly mail count for a Representative may be anywhere from a few hundred to 1,000, with cases comprising 7.5, 10, 15, 40, 50, or 56 percent. A busy Senate office may receive 15,000 or more cases per year. In a Representative's office the figures may be 1, 11, 12, 15, 18, or 20 per day, or 7, 51, 66, or 300 per week, or 'thousands' a year. A Representative's staff may spend 100 percent of its time on casework, or 'most' of its time, or 75, 50, over 30, 18.7, or less percent. Representatives devote more time to cases than Senators, and freshman Representatives are apt to spend more time on cases than others. Some Representatives give 90 percent of their working hours to cases, others 66-2/3 per-

Definition of a Congressman

"A Congressman has become an expanded messenger boy, an employment agency, getter-out of the Navy, Army, and Marines, a ward heeler, a wound healer, trouble shooter, law explainer, bill finder, issue translator, resolution interpreter, controversy-oil-pourer, glad-hand extender, business promoter, veterans affairs adjuster, ex-serviceman's champion, watchdog for the underdog, sympathizer for the upperdog, kisser of babies, recoverer of lost baggage, soberer of delegates, adjuster for traffic violations and voters straying into the toils of the law, binder-up of broken hearts, financial wet nurse, a good samaritan, contributor to good causes, cornerstone layer, public building and bridge dedicator and ship christener."—Rep. Luther Patrick (D Ala. 1937-43; 1945-47), reprinted in *Congressional Record*, May 13, 1963, p. A 2978.

the Secretary of the Treasury to "the right man" in the Pentagon about the purchase of surplus goods.

A routine procedure has been worked out for one popular request. Schools and other organizations often ask for an American flag that has flown over the Capitol building. The Congressman may purchase a flag from the House Stationery Room. The page service then has it hoisted to the top of the Capitol, after which it is decent, others 27.6 percent, and still others only 10 percent. The workload of most committee staffs is about 10 to 15 percent casework, but watchdog committee staffs do little else."

One of the broadest surveys, in 1965, asked 160 Representatives and each member of their staffs how their time was distributed during a "typical workweek." Constituency service, broadly defined to include answering mail and visiting with constituents in Washington as well as handling constituent problems, accounted for an average of 27.6 percent (16.3 hours) of the Representatives' workload according to their own estimates. Among those Congressmen who devoted significantly more time to constituent service, its average share of the workweek was 42.7 percent. Congressional staffs devoted 24.7 percent of their time to constituent service, plus 40.8 percent handling correspondence, in which services were mixed with educational and other functions. That portion of services described as "handling constituent problems" comprised 8.6 percent of the average Representative's time, and 18.7 percent of his staff's workweek.

Comparable figures are not available for Senators. Except in the smallest states, they have more constituents, but they also have larger staffs than Representatives to handle casework. The larger constituency of the Senator tends to reduce the relative importance of casework as a means of seeking re-election.

The distribution of types of casework varies considerably from one Member to another, but some notion of its variety can be gained from the following breakdown of case mail received by former Sen. Paul H. Douglas (D Ill.) during a more or less typical week in 1958:

Number and Types of Letters Received in One Week in a U.S. Senator's Office

	From Constituents	From Agencies
Illinois projects (public works, urban renewal)	29	6
Federal welfare programs	20	8
Veterans programs	17	6
Civil Service claims & problems	9	10
Post Office personnel & operations	7	4
Military—personnel	28	17
Military—non-personnel	3	5
Immigration	20	14
Miscellaneous agency problems	24	23
Federal employment	6	4
Complaints about Federal agencies	9	1
Complaints about non-governmental groups	10	1
Totals	182	99

Source: Kenneth G. Olson, "The Service Function of the United States Congress" in *Congress: The First Branch of Government* (American Enterprise Institute for Public Policy Research), p. 352.

Another rough indication of the character of casework is available in a similar breakdown of the entire year's caseload of a fourth-term midwestern Representative.

Casework Sample

Rep. James C. Wright Jr. (D Texas) gave some of the flavor of casework with the following sampling of requests drawn from a week's mail:

"A serviceman, stationed in Greenland, has learned that his father has dropped dead and that his mother is on the verge of nervous collapse. He needs help in getting compassionate leave.

"A small industrial firm wants to offer its products to the Federal Government, but doesn't know which agency to deal with or the proper form in which to prepare its bids.

"A man has suffered a severe heart attack. His wife is somewhere in Europe, but nobody knows exactly where. The Congressman is asked to get word to her so she can fly back to the bedside.

"A disabled veteran needs hospitalization in a hurry. The nearest Veterans Administration hospital is overcrowded and cannot possibly admit him. Arrangements must be made to get him into another.

"An inventor is certain that he has come up with something which will transform the whole technological future of the world. Unfortunately, he can't get anyone to listen to him.

"A homeowner with a Federal Housing Authority loan has made payments regularly for eight years. However, because of illness, he has missed the last two payments and the mortgage company has issued instructions for foreclosure. The Congressman will try to get the FHA to intercede.

"A student preparing a thesis needs some information from the Library of Congress.

"A local manufacturer is in trouble with the Federal Trade Commission because of an advertisement. He feels he is being discriminated against and that the FTC is treating him more harshly than it is treating his competition. He wants a top-level interview with officials.

"The Government has lapsed a veteran's G.I. life insurance policy because he failed to execute and return a certain form. The veteran says he never received the form and he wants his policy reinstated.

"A family is coming to Washington for a visit. Where should they stay, and what should they see?"—Congressman Jim Wright, *You and Your Congressman* (1965), pp. 34-35.

Volume and Character of One Representative's Casework During the Year 1957

	No.	%
Individual cases		
Personnel matters (civilian)	62	16.1
Personnel matters (military)	63	16.3
Veterans' benefits	98	25.4
Social Security, Old Age and Survivors Insurance, and Unemployment Compensation	49	12.7
Immigration	15	3.9
Federal agency programs	58	15.0
Special service requests	41	10.6
Total	386	100.0

Casework (cont.)

Group cases	No.	%
Requests for general information	6	9.8
Requests for specific information	10	16.4
Complaints	12	19.7
Requests to expedite or promote	33	54.1
Total	61	100.0

Source: Same as preceding table, p. 353.

Casework Procedures

Most casework is handled by the staff. A telephone call to the appropriate agency is often sufficient, especially when the request is only for information. More complex matters, or those requiring a record of the transaction, are usually sent to the agency in writing. The constituent's letter, or a restatement of it by the Senator or Representative, may be used. A reply signed by the head of the agency is expected, and the Member often forwards copies of it to the constituent.

To cope with the volume of constituents' problems, 31 Federal agencies and the three military services have liaison offices to assist Members of Congress. The armed services, the Civil Service Commission and the Veterans Administration maintain offices in the House Office Buildings; other agencies send liaison personnel periodically to visit Congressional offices. "We normally try to deal with the liaison officer," Rep. Gerald R. Ford (R Mich.) told a 1963 seminar of freshmen Representatives, "and then if we are unsuccessful and it is a meritorious matter, we then proceed higher up. On the other hand, where an emergency is in question then, on occasion, you will go directly to the top man in the Department." When cases involve agencies which have regional offices—Internal Revenue, Civil Service and the Veterans Administration, for example—Members may urge their constituents to pursue the matter first at that level.

"Service" and "watchdog" committees, like the House and Senate Select Committees on Small Business or the Joint Committee on Defense Production, encourage Members to channel constituents' affairs through

---

Half a Century Ago

"My father served in Congress from 1909 to 1919 from the state of Texas. During his last term I was one of his clerks. Congress sat for six months the first session and three months the second session. A Representative got about 15 letters a week. Only at rare intervals would a constituent come to see him. He had no pressure groups to contend with. Because Congress enacted only a few bills each session, legislation got the deliberative attention it deserved. Every Member had plenty of time to study bills in committee before they came on the floor. Debate was important in the consideration of every bill. A Member did not take the floor until he had carefully got together as many facts as were available. When he spoke, he knew his subject. A good debater had no trouble getting a large audience in the chamber. Most of a Member's time was spent on legislation. There was little else for him to do."—Rep. Martin Dies (D Texas, 1931-45; 1953-59), quoted by Congressman Jim Wright, *You and Your Congressman* (1965).

---

them. Staffs of legislative committees also handle some matters having to do with constituents.

Often one or more members of a Senator's or Representative's staff specialize in casework; and an assistant skilled in handling constituents' affairs with Federal agencies is valued highly. Legal education or experience in the Executive Branch are particularly helpful. In some offices, staff members specialize in problems relating to specific Federal agencies; in others, all persons handle all types of requests, thus avoiding difficulties that would occur should a specialist be absent. Staff members have little opportunity to develop expertise in the wide variety of problems that prompt requests from constituents.

Most Members of Congress deal personally with difficult cases, or those involving personal friends, important supporters, influential figures in the district, or large numbers of constituents. When the Member does intervene personally, he increases the chances of a prompt and favorable response. While some Members will pursue cases to the point of appearing as counsel for constituents, many are reluctant to spend the time or exert the influence required to press individual matters that far. One Congressman explained why he never consented to requests to appear at hearings before the Veterans Appeals Board:

"In the first place, the types that come up on appeals are difficult cases. They have been rejected time and time again, so you might as well recognize the fact that four out of five of them are going to be turned down. Therefore, if you are the one that represents them, you are going to be accused of having it turned down if you go there personally. Secondly, you won't be able to brief yourself adequately.

"Once you accept one of them, then you haven't any means of drawing a line as to others that you can accept, and the only way to handle those properly is just to say that you are here elected by your constituents to serve as a legislative representative. This is not within the province of the duties of a legislative representative; that your assignment that you have been given by your constituents is full-time, and you therefore recommend that they take other steps to see that their case is properly handled." (Quoted by Donald G. Tacheron and Rep. Morris K. Udall, *The Job of the Congressman.*)

Another Congressman observed that when he served as "an unpaid lawyer" for constituents, "Uniformly I have been mildly successful and uniformly my man has been an ingrate at the results, whereas in other kinds of activities for constituents you may make one quick phone call and have a pathetically grateful family and bonded debtor forever." However, even routine matters are apt to rebound against the helpful Congressman. A Representative who expedited passport proceedings for a constituent said: "Next thing I learned he was one of 13 men who had gone to Moscow with one of the 'Peace Forever' groups. I had more letters demanding to know why I helped a Communist get over to Moscow—the incident occurred during the Korean War, and it was terrible." (Quoted by Charles L. Clapp in *The Congressman, His Work as He Sees It.*)

Effectiveness of Members' Efforts

A study by Walter Gellhorn in 1965 found unanimity among Congressional staff members and administrators that "a Congressional referral assures exceptionally quick attention and a courteous response." Most authorities agree also that the chances of favorable action for the constituent improve with the expression of interest by a Senator or Representative. The Committee on Congress of the American Political Science Association observed in 1945 that "these agencies depend on the favor of Congress and are too prone to try to curry favor with the individual Members." Gellhorn's survey, on the other hand, discovered few who believed that administrative decisions were easily or frequently revised at the behest of a Member of Congress. One Representative told Gellhorn: "At least some agencies are becoming pretty sophisticated. They seem to realize that usually all I need or want is a demonstration that I have done everything possible on my constituent's behalf....Some of the other agencies, though, seem to be dazzled by the fact that my office is involved, and then they get distracted from the real merit of the matter." Frequently, however, the official gets no clear indication of the extent of a Congressman's interest in a case. Because matters before Federal agencies often entail an element of discretion, the benefit of the doubt is likely to go to the Congressman's client.

A Member's influence is enhanced if he is on the Appropriations Committee or the legislative committee responsible for the department involved in the case. In his study of the Senate, Donald R. Matthews observed that "A department's special friends and leading enemies in the Senate receive a little more than the usual treatment. ('You can be sure that the State Department used to think twice before turning down a request from Senator (Joseph R.) McCarthy')." But Matthews noted also that day-to-day intervention by Capitol Hill reinforced the "institutionalized suspicion" between administrators and legislators. Bureaucrats view Senators and their staffs as "special pleaders for the narrow interests of their constituents," and in turn are seen as "arbitrary, patronizing, and compulsively attached to formal rules and procedures even to the detriment of 'justice.'"

No precise measure of the effectiveness of Congressional intervention in the Federal bureaucracy is available. Gellhorn accepted a 10-percent success ratio "not because any objective evidence supports it, but because every person who was interviewed asserted it to be accurate. It may be folklore instead of fact; in any event, it seems to be accepted as true."

Political Importance

The value of casework for re-election is a commonplace on Capitol Hill; many consider it more important in garnering votes than the stand the Member takes on legislative matters. As long as he does not outrage the people of his district or state by consistently or blatantly ignoring their opinions on controversial issues, the Representative or Senator who carefully tends to constituents' requests is considered very hard to beat. The cultivation of election support based on services rendered tends to increase the independence of the Member on legislative matters, and may even be justified on those grounds.

Freshman Representatives, in particular, are solemnly warned by experienced hands to devote their energies to responding to constituents. As they discover how little impact they have on legislation in their first

---

The Senator and the Bureaucrat

The following exchange between former Sen. Paul H. Douglas (D Ill.) and an Assistant Secretary of Agriculture was quoted by Donald R. Matthews in U.S. Senators and Their World:

Mr. Appleby. I think perhaps the principal source of troubles with Members of Congress is that they do not recognize how powerful they are.

Sen. Douglas. They feel very impotent and very helpless indeed with the civil service.

Mr. Appleby. So do the bureaucrats with Members of Congress.

Sen. Douglas. We are completely ineffective.

Mr. Appleby. Representations from Members of Congress weigh very much more than Members of Congress know, and that is the reason why I think they sometimes go overboard. They are trying to be effective and they speak with more force than is necessary for them in their position.

Sen. Douglas. I am struck with this air of excessive purity with which people in Washington who are not exposed to the rigors of winning elections put on about politicians....It always reminds me of the superior feeling that staff officers around headquarters had for the foot soldiers out in the field who are dying.

---

term, they may be only too glad to tackle casework, in which they can obtain tangible results for their efforts.

Why is the handling of problems of individual constituents considered to have such valuable political payoff? As already noted, cases may add up to several thousand a year, and over the years a Representative or Senator may build up a substantial personal following, the kind of following which has little incentive to abandon an incumbent for a challenger. In closely contested constituencies, such a following can itself make the difference between victory or defeat, especially because it cuts across party lines. In more homogeneous districts, where rival candidates are likely to agree on basic legislative matters, the Member's effectiveness in serving the interests of constituents may be the principal election issue.

The support gained is not limited to the individuals served. Their families and friends are likely to hear how helpful the Representative or Senator was. Of course, not everyone who has been helped votes for the candidate seeking re-election. But at least he has made himself known directly to individuals through matters of real concern to them. Anyone seeking to replace the incumbent has no such means of making individual voters notice him.

Even small favors are likely to be remembered, as remarks of a Representative quoted by Clapp suggest: "I get my biggest assist from people I have been able to help on *little* things. I was born and reared on a farm where our mail box was a half-mile from home, and because it seemed like every time it rained Dad sent me for the mail as a youngster, I have a feeling about people who have to go far to their mailboxes. I was helpful in getting inserted in Post Office

(Continued on p. 548)

Suggestions on How to Write a Letter . . . .

Citizens with complaints, suggestions and comments on how the Government is being run can voice their views directly to the Executive Branch and to Congress by letters and telegrams.

Both branches of Government are geared to handle and to reply to letters and telegrams, which have been increasing in number in recent years.

Members of Congress also reported receiving a record volume of mail in 1969. The Senate received about 9.5 million letters. This is equal to an average of 260 letters per Senator per day. The House total was 18.7 million, an average of 118 letters per Member per day.

Handling Procedures

The chances of getting a personal reply to a legislative letter depend partly on what state it comes from. Sen. Gale W. McGee (D Wyo.) tries to answer as many of his 30 daily letters as he can. He scrawls personal comments across the margins of some of the rest.

In populous states, where volume of mail in Senate offices is about 1,000 letters a week, constituents are much more likely to receive a standardized reply drafted by a junior staff member, signed by a machine and scanned by the Senator.

In the office of Sen. Harrison A. Williams Jr. (D N.J.), the work is compartmentalized. Legislative letters are answered mostly by a group of research assistants, each familiar with a specific area of legislation. The research assistants are armed with copies of statements the Senator has already made on the issue.

"About 80 percent of the letters are easy to answer and go out right away," said a Williams aide. "If it's an issue he hasn't taken a position on, or hasn't made up his mind on, we'll consult with him before we do anything."

Automated Answers. Among electronic devices introduced in recent years to speed letter response are the Robotype machine and the Autopen.

The Robotype machine looks like a typewriter. It is capable of reproducing identical copies of form letters without the standardized look of a mimeographed letter. Once it is set up to reproduce the body of a letter, a secretary types only the individual heading for each letter.

The Autopen is a console machine with a large wheel. On the wheel is placed a metal plate with an impression of the Member's signature. As the prepared letters revolve around the wheel, the metal plate stamps an imprint of the signature in the proper place on the paper.

Together, these machines make it possible for a Congressional staff to answer letters after scanning them for a few seconds to see what they are about.

Writing Tips

The following hints on how to write a Member of Congress were suggested by Congressional sources and the League of Women Voters.

- Write to your own Senators or Representative. Letters sent to other Members will end up on the desk of Members from your state.
- Write at the proper time, when a bill is being discussed in committee or on the floor.
- Use your own words and your own stationery. Avoid signing and sending a form or mimeographed letter.
- Don't be a pen pal. Don't try to instruct the Representative or Senator on every issue that comes up.
- Don't demand a commitment before all the facts are in. Bills rarely become law in the same form as introduced.
- Whenever possible, identify all bills by their number.
- If possible, include pertinent editorials from local papers.
- Be constructive. If a bill deals with a problem you admit exists but you believe the bill is the wrong approach, tell what you think the right approach is.
- If you have expert knowledge or wide experience in particular areas, share it with the Member. But don't pretend to wield vast political influence.
- Write to the Member when he does something you approve of. A note of appreciation will make him remember you more favorably the next time.
- Feel free to write when you have a question or problem dealing with procedures of Government departments.
- Be brief, write legibly and be sure to use the proper form of address.

A 15-word telegram called a Public Opinion Message (P.O.M.) can be sent to the President, Vice President or a Member of Congress from anywhere in the United States for $1. Name and address are not counted as part of the message unless there are additional signers.

Subject Matter

House staff members have noted an increase in casework mail—constituents' requests for help with a multitude of bureaucratic problems. For example, constituents complain about Selective Service procedures, seek adjustments in Social Security or veterans' benefits and ask for help in obtaining or increasing business loans or in solving immigration difficulties.

In the House, casework mail has been running heavier than mail on legislative issues. Most House and Senate offices employ caseworkers who do nothing but deal with this kind of mail. On smaller House staffs, the ombudsman-like job is often divided among all employees.

Answering casework mail often entails explaining the constituent's problem to the appropriate Executive Branch agency.

On the Senate side, more than half the mail in 1969 was about legislative issues. Staff members said it

. . . . to Your Congressman or Your Senator

fluctuated most of the year, reaching a midsummer peak during the antiballistic missile (ABM) debate. But underlying the swings in volume was a steadily rising tide of mail about economic problems—tax reforms, inflation and the cost of living.

In almost every one of the offices sampled, mail about taxes and inflation exceeded that on any other issue in 1969.

Influx of Mail

Most Senate and House staff members interviewed were unable to recall an instance in which constituent mail had changed a Senator's or Representative's vote on any issue. Among the most unimpressed mail readers was a House administrative assistant who pointed to the pile of tax-reform letters on his desk and said, "Most of them don't even know the House has passed tax reform. Frankly, we don't have the most intelligent district in the country."

Aides to Sen. Jack Miller (R Iowa), however, remembered a 1962 letter that persuaded the Senator to introduce an amendment lifting restrictions on defense-contract bidding for small businesses. The aides said that Small Business Administration officials later called the constituent-proposed amendment "one of the most useful changes we've ever had."

Rep. Morris K. Udall (D Ariz.) told his constituents in a newsletter: "On several occasions I can testify that a single thoughtful, factually persuasive letter did change my mind or cause me to initiate a review of a previous judgment."

Answering Techniques. Most Members of Congress keep in fairly close touch with legislative mail in order to determine the mood of their constituents. Miller reads through a day's worth of mail once every 10 days. Rep. John Brademas (D Ind.) tries to write personal answers to letters that are highly critical of his voting record.

Aides to Sen. James O. Eastland (D Miss.) said the Senator makes personal replies to about 10 percent of the legislative letters he receives.

Perhaps the Senator best known for his blunt replies was Stephen M. Young (D Ohio). Young was known to respond with, "Dear Sir: You are a liar." But with an Ohio constituency of nearly 10 million, Young used prepared letters and signature machines to deal with correspondence on most legislative issues.

Constituents who wrote Young on a controversial issue received one of two prepared replies. Most supporters of the Senator's position got a brief, machine-signed letter thanking them and noting that the Senator agreed. Most opponents received a polite but strongly worded letter, signed on the same machine, explaining that the Senator did not see it that way. Each of these responses was a copy of an initial letter carefully written by the Senator himself. Young retired at the close of the 91st Congress when 81 years old.

Even a smaller office such as McGee's is less likely to respond thoughtfully to a letter if it appears to be part of an organized campaign. "If they take the time to write an individual letter, they'll get an individual letter back," said a McGee aide. "If it's a form letter, the response is usually a form letter."

Correct Form For Writing Government Officials

President

> The President
> The White House
> Washington, D.C. 20500

> Dear Mr. President:

> Very respectfully yours,

Vice President

> The Vice President
> The White House
> Washington, D.C. 20500

> Dear Mr. Vice President:

> Sincerely yours,

Senator

> The Honorable Philip A. Hart
> United States Senate
> Washington, D.C. 20510

> Dear Senator Hart:

> Sincerely yours,

Representative

> The Honorable Silvio O. Conte
> House of Representatives
> Washington, D.C. 20515

> Dear Mr. Conte:

> Sincerely yours,

Member of the Cabinet

> The Honorable William P. Rogers
> The Secretary of State
> Washington, D.C. 20520

> Dear Mr. Secretary:

> Sincerely yours,

regulations a provision that there be extensions (of routes) granted for farmers in certain instances. A survey indicated that I had 3,000 farmers in my district who had to go over half a mile for mail, so I started a campaign. By the last election I had gotten 1,300 extensions. They think of me every time they go to get that mail."

The story may provide an additional clue to the political potency of casework. If well handled, it gives the constituent a feeling that somewhere in the vast impersonal Federal Government a powerful figure takes a personal interest in him. Whether that interest is attributed to the empathy of the legislator or the power of the voter, it is reassuring to the constituent. And such reassurance may win more kind remembrance on election day than specific roll-call votes.

But the same Representative who got closer mailboxes for the farmers reported also that his assistance with certain Small Business Administration appointments got him into "terrible trouble." Inevitably, a few constituents are likely to be alienated by a Congressman's inability to solve their problems or satisfy their demands. Indeed, every patronage job proverbially creates "one ingrate and 20 enemies." But in casework, Members usually are dealing not with activists competing for scarce political plums, but with individuals trying to cope with a personal problem in a political world unfamiliar to them. Their gratitude can pay real dividends. The administrative assistant to one southern Senator recounted: "When we get a positive action of some significance in our casework, we add the man's name and address plus a report on what we have done for him to our card file of friends. The last time ...ran for re-election, we sent this file down to his campaign manager. His manager then wrote a personal letter to every person on that list, informing him that ...was facing opposition in the primary and would he help out. The response was amazing—75-80 percent must have volunteered to help."

Controversy Over Casework

Congressional handling of casework has prompted serious criticism, which can be divided into two basic types. On the one hand, the volume of requests from constituents is said to interfere with the Member's legislative responsibilities. On the other hand, Congressional efforts to meet those requests are said to constitute an inefficient, or positively harmful, means of reviewing administrative decisions and procedures.

Whether or not the portion of a Member's time spent on casework is excessive, it is time taken away from complex and important legislative work. Often valuable time devoted to casework is spent on trivia, though the staff is more likely than the Member to handle the trivial cases. Moreover, what seems trivial to political scientists may be crucial to the individual, or family, or business involved. Whatever the importance of Congressional care for individual cases, their volume is growing. There is no natural upper limit to the demands constituents can make on their Representatives or Senators in Washington. The growth of casework, combined with the growth of legislative responsibilities, will intensify pressures for reforms that would lighten the casework burden on Congress.

The emphasis freshman Members feel obliged to devote to service to constituents may have a formative effect on their concept of their roles. Through the process of active, daily involvement in the problems of individuals, they may be conditioned to view Congressional responsibilities in terms of particular, rather than general, needs. Whether this tendency is the saving grace of the U.S. Congress, or its abiding vice, is a question on which there is no agreement.

On the other hand, building a base of political support on service to constituents may actually free the senior legislator to take national, rather than provincial, stands on legislation. The more certain he is of a personal following, the more safely he can adopt positions dictated by his conscience or his knowledge even though they conflict with opinion back home. At the same time, local support based on service to constituents makes the legislator more independent of the Executive, and of his own political party. And such independence may reduce his concern for national, as opposed to provincial, needs. Among Senators and Representatives who have achieved "safe" seats, one is apt to find men at both extremes—statesmen and ideological spokesmen of national prominence, and parochial figures closely identified with those who send them to Washington.

Casework affects legislation in another way. Defects in existing laws and procedures often come to light through the inconveniences and injustices of which constituents complain. Members of Congress may follow up their casework with legislation to correct these defects. Gellhorn tells how individual complaints in one year stimulated a particularly conscientious Congressional office to undertake the amendment of a tariff law and a successful campaign for enlarged Federal support for education of exceptional children. The same office promoted a statutory redefinition of eligibility requirements in low-cost, Federally aided housing, after investigating a widow's complaint that she had been evicted when her husband died. Gellhorn, however, sees such follow-ups from the particular case to the general problem as the exception rather than the rule, and he explains why:

"Since triumph is the usual goal, casework tends to go no further than the case at hand, leaving untouched the problems that generated it. Ordinarily, investigation is superficial. Implications, if not altogether unperceived, are in any event likely to be ignored. So long as the present case has an appropriately happy outcome, tomorrow's case is left to its own devices; anyway, it may involve some other Congressman's constituent. Always pressed for time and almost always untrained generalists in a world of trained specialists, Congressmen pass on to other things—and so do administrators. Unless the Congressman is pertinaciously reform-minded, casework comes and goes without greatly improving the conduct of public affairs."

Although individual cases may not prompt general reforms, their cumulative effect undoubtedly contributes to the Member's education. Because he is daily forced to consider what laws mean to individuals, he may be more inclined by habit to incorporate in the laws which he makes procedural safeguards for personal rights and needs. Although the causal connection between specific cases and specific laws may be the exception, casework as a part of the Member's way of life may help to explain why, in Gellhorn's own words, "In general, American administrative adjudication and rulemaking are attended by the world's most fully elaborated procedural protections against ill-informed exercises of official judgment."

But the casework of a Senator or Representative may interfere with the safeguards incorporated in the laws. He may disrupt orderly review of administrative decisions by an agency's established procedures. He may accelerate consideration of one case, but in so doing consume agency time that might have been spent on a larger number of cases with prior claims to consideration. He may gain a favor for a client, but at the expense of equal application of the law to all claimants. Recurrent intervention in bureaucratic procedures, especially if it is publicized, may erode the commitment of bureaucrats and citizens alike to impartial service.

Interlocking Interests in Casework

Administrators may show favoritism in response to the clients of a Member of Congress because the Member has political clout unavailable to most citizens with whom the agency deals. "Even a routine expression of interest may prejudice a case." But it is precisely because he combines service to constituents with legislative and budgetary power over executive departments that the Member's constituents have confidence in his capacity to correct abuses. And it is precisely because the constituents have power to work for the Member's re-election or removal, that they have confidence in his willingness to intervene on their behalf.

The agency's vested interest in Congressional favor, and the Senator's or Representative's vested interest in the constituent's favor, may be the most convincing guarantee that the bureaucracy will be attentive to individual citizens. But those very self-interests which guarantee its effectiveness also generate inequalities. Not all Members and not all constituents are feared equally. A senior member of the Senate Appropriations Committee and a freshman Representative are liable to get different levels of attention in matters requiring special bureaucratic effort. A president of a local chamber of commerce may elicit more Congressional interest in his case than a migrant farm laborer.

While the care with which cases are handled is not uncommonly influenced by the position of the supplicant, deliberate weighting of casework decisions to favor the powerful is exceptional. Many Members take special pride in instances where they have been able to help the otherwise helpless. Moreover, the great mass of casework is too routine to warrant application of special pressure for favors. But the connection of casework with re-election unquestionably distorts its achievements as a review procedure for administrative actions. For example, a southern Congressman might hesitate to pursue a Negro constituent's request in a matter related to civil rights, especially if he thought it might attract publicity; other Members might shy away from civil liberties claims of Communists, homosexuals, or members of other highly unpopular minorities.

Of course, appeals to Congress are only one of the recourses available to citizens; review procedures are also available through administrative agencies and the courts. Both the advantages and the disadvantages of the Congressional review of individual cases stem from the fact that the Member of Congress, unlike the bureaucrat or the judge, depends on the petitioner for his job.

Preventive Function

The effectiveness of casework cannot be measured solely in terms of revised decisions. Congressional attention to particular cases serves a preventive as well as a curative function. As former Sen. Joseph S. Clark (D Pa.) observed: "The very knowledge by executive officials that some Congressman is sure to look into a matter affecting his constituents acts as a healthy check against bureaucratic indifference or arrogance." Even when the official does not himself have potential Congressional intervention in the back of his mind, he operates within an institutional framework of procedures, habits, leadership, and standards that have been conditioned by the normality of intervention by elected officials. The result may not be a bureaucracy beloved by the citizens, but the tyrannical officialdom that many nations take for granted has been avoided.

While civil servants are reminded by casework that they are servants, and not masters, of the constituent of a Member of Congress, the constituent is reassured that the bureaucracy is not an uncontrollable giant indifferent to his fate. No doubt the course of American history would not be deflected by neglect of a case here and there. But the accumulation of grievances that would arise in the absence of Congressional casework could produce substantial alienation of the population from the state. The alienation would not be limited to those with grievances of their own, but would spread to all who witnessed the futility of appeals against bureaucracy.

The danger of such a divorce between Government and governed increases as the Government grows in size and as its involvement in the lives of ordinary citizens deepens. The very forces which increase the volume and complexity of casework, then, also increase its urgency. As a generation of Americans matures that is particularly suspicious of impersonal bureaucracy and particularly anxious for individual consideration, Congressional service of constituents may play a crucial role in preserving a direct, convincing, human link between the individual and the state.

Reaction against the impersonality of big government may, however, increase demands for personal favoritism. By catering to private interests at the expense of bureaucratic procedures, Congressional casework could prompt a different kind of alienation. Cynical belief that only those who have powerful connections can protect their rights and pursue their interests with the Government is commonplace in much of the world, and not unknown in the United States. As Government services and controls expand, it will become increasingly difficult for Congressional casework to steer between the opposite evils of impersonal and personal bureaucracy.

Bibliography

Books

Bauer, Raymond A.; Pool, Ithiel de Sola; and Dexter, Lewis Anthony, *American Business and Public Policy: The Politics of Foreign Trade.* Atherton Press, 1963.

Clapp, Charles L., *The Congressman, His Work as He Sees It.* Brookings Institution, 1963.

Dahl, Robert, *Congress and Foreign Policy.* Harcourt Brace and Co., 1950.

Davidson, Roger H., *The Role of the Congressman.* Pegasus, 1969.

DeGrazia, Alfred, *Public and Republic: Political Representation in America.* Alfred A. Knopf, 1951.

Froman, Lewis A. Jr., *Congressmen and their Constituencies.* Rand McNally and Co., 1963.

Gellhorn, Walter, *When Americans Complain: Governmental Grievance Procedures.* Harvard University Press, 1966.

Haynes, George H., *The Senate of the United States: Its History and Practice.* Houghton Mifflin Co., 1938.

Hyneman, Charles S., and Carey, George W. (Eds.), *A Second Federalist.* Appleton-Century-Crofts, 1967.

Key, V.O. Jr., *Public Opinion and American Democracy.* Alfred A. Knopf, 1961.

MacRae, Duncan, Jr., *Dimensions of Congressional Voting: A Statistical Study of the House of Representatives in the Eighty-First Congress.* University of California Press, 1958.

Matthews, Donald R., *U.S. Senators and Their World.* University of North Carolina Press, 1960.

Pennock, J. Roland, and Chapman, John W., *Representation.* Atherton Press, 1968.

Saloma, John S. III, *Congress and the New Politics.* Little, Brown and Co., 1969.

Shannon, W. Wayne, *Party, Constituency, and Congressional Voting.* Louisiana State University Press, 1968.

Tacheron, Donald G., and Udall, Morris K., *The Job of the Congressman: An Introduction to Service in the House of Representatives.* Bobbs-Merrill, 1966.

Truman, David B. (Ed.), *Congress and America's Future.* Prentice-Hall, 1965.

Truman, David B., *The Governmental Process.* Alfred A. Knopf, 1964.

Turner, Julius, *Party and Constituency: Pressures on Congress.* Johns Hopkins Press, 1951.

Wright, James, *You and Your Congressman.* Coward McCann, 1965.

Young, James Sterling, *The Washington Community, 1800-1828.* Columbia University, 1966.

Articles

Cnudde, Charles F., and McCrone, Donald J., "The Linkage Between Constituency Attitudes and Congressional Voting Behavior: A Causal Model," *American Political Science Review,* March 1966.

Dexter, Anthony Lewis, "The Representative and His District," in Robert L. Peabody and Nelson W. Polsby, *New Perspectives on the House of Representatives.* Rand McNally, 1963.

Froman, Lewis A., Jr., "Inter-Party Constituency Differences and Congressional Voting Behavior," *American Political Science Review,* March 1963.

Kravitz, Walter, "Casework by Members of Congress: A Survey of the Literature," The Library of Congress, Legislative Reference Service, May 4, 1965, revised and expanded Jan. 22, 1968.

Huntington, Samuel P., "A Revised Theory of American Party Politics," *American Political Science Review,* September 1950.

Marascuilo, Leonard A. and Amster, Harriet, "Survey of 1961-62 Congressional Polls," *Public Opinion Quarterly,* Fall, 1964.

Miller, Warren E., and Stokes, Donald E., "Constituency Influence in Congress," *American Political Science Review,* Vol. 57 (1963), pp. 45-56.

Olson, Kenneth G., "The Service Function of the United States Congress," in Alfred de Grazia, *Congress: the First Branch,* American Enterprise Institute for Public Policy Research, 1966.

Government Publications

U.S. Congress, Joint Committee on the Organization of Congress, *Hearings,* 1945.

U.S. Congress, Joint Committee on the Organization of Congress, *Hearings,* 1965.

The Lobbies

OF ALL THE PRESSURES on Congress, none has received such widespread publicity and yet is so dimly understood as the role of Washington-based lobbyists and the groups they represent. The popular image of a rotund agent for special interests buying up Members' votes is a vast oversimplification. The role of today's lobbyist is far more subtle, his techniques more refined.

Lobbyists and lobby groups have played an increasingly active part in the modern legislative process. The corps of Washington lobbyists has grown markedly since the 1930s, in line with the expansion of Federal authority into new areas and with the huge increase in Federal spending. Over the last four decades the Federal Government has become a tremendous force in the entire economic life of the nation, and the number of fields in which changes in Federal policy may spell success or failure for special interest groups has been greatly enlarged. Thus commercial and industrial interests, labor unions, ethnic and racial groups, professional organizations, citizen groups and representatives of foreign interests—all from time to time and some continuously—have sought by one method or another to exert pressure on Congress to attain their legislative goals.

The pressure usually has selfish aims—to assert rights or win some special privilege or financial benefit for the group exerting it. But in other cases the objective may be disinterested—to achieve an ideological goal or to further a group's particular conception of the national interest.

Lobbying: Pros and Cons. It is widely recognized that pressure groups, whether operating through general propaganda campaigns designed to sway public opinion or through direct contacts with Members of Congress, perform some important and indispensable functions. Such functions include helping to inform both Congress and the public about problems and issues, stimulating public debate, opening a path to Congress for the wronged and needy, and making known to Congress the practical aspects of proposed legislation—whom it would help, whom it would hurt, who is for it and who against it. The spin-off from this process is considerable technical information produced by research on legislative proposals.

Against benefits to the public that result from pressure activities, critics point to certain serious liabilities. The most important is that in singlemindedly pursuing their own often selfish objectives, the pressure groups are apt to lead Congress into decisions which benefit the pressure group but which do not necessarily serve the public interest. A group's power to influence legislation often is based less on the validity of its arguments than on the size of its membership, the amount of financial and manpower resources it can commit to a legislative pressure campaign, the astuteness of its representatives and the lengths to which it is willing to go in use of trickery, threats, or dishonest methods like mistatements of fact or concealment of information.

Origins of Lobbying. Representatives of special interests haunted the environs of the First Continental Congress, but the word "lobby" was not recorded until 1808 when it appeared in the annals of the 10th Congress. By 1829, the term "lobby-agents" was applied to favor-seekers at the state capitol in Albany, N.Y. By 1832, it had been shortened to "lobbyist" and was in wide use at the U.S. Capitol. Karl Shriftgiesser, an authority on lobbying, has observed that "from the beginning, it was a term of reproach, and throughout the 19th century, it was always so used." Other terms applied by critics included "five-percenters," "fixers," "boodlers" and, collectively, "the third house of Congress" or "the fourth branch of Government."

Although the term had not yet been coined, the right to "lobby" was made implicit by the First Amendment to the Constitution, which provided that "Congress shall make no law...abridging the freedom of speech or of the press; or the right of the people peaceably to assemble and to petition the Government for redress of grievances." Among the Founding Fathers, only James Madison expressed concern over the dangers posed by pressure groups. In his *Federalist* (No. 10), Madison warned against the self-serving activities of "factions." "Among the numerous advantages promised by a well-constructed union," he wrote, "none deserves to be more accurately developed than its tendency to break and control the violence of faction.... By a faction, I understand a number of citizens, whether amounting to a majority or minority of the whole, who are united and actuated by some common impulse of passion, or of interest, adverse to the rights of other citizens, or to the permanent and aggregate interests of the community." A strong Federal Government, Madison concluded, was the only effective counterbalance to the influence of such "factions."

Regulation of Lobbying. In the 19th and early 20th centuries, abundant evidence accumulated that venal, selfish or misguided pressure groups could often succeed in pressing Congress into enacting legislation designed to

---

Reference

See Appendix table of contents (first thumb tab) for additional material on lobbies—a case study, texts, etc.

enrich the pressure group at the expense of the public or to impose the group's own standards on the nation.

Following a series of Congressional investigations, which began in 1913 with a probe of lobbying activities by the National Association of Manufacturers, proposals were repeatedly made for some kind of Congressional regulation of pressure groups and lobbyists in the nation's capital. Bills requiring lobbyists to register and report on their activities were passed by one chamber or the other on several occasions, including 1928, 1935 and 1936, but were not enacted into law.

Laws were passed in 1935 and 1936 which required registration of utilities and shipping representatives who appeared before committees of Congress or specified Federal agencies; and in 1938, Congress enacted the Foreign Agents Registration Act, requiring persons in the United States acting for foreign governments or principals in any capacity to register with the Justice Department. But it was not until 1946 that a general lobbyist registration law was put on the statute books. The measure was full of loopholes, and it was further emasculated by a narrow Supreme Court interpretation.

The problem in gaining the approval of Congress and the courts for Federal legislation regulating lobbying was how to curb dishonest pressure activities without interfering with constitutional rights of free speech and petition. Equally significant was Congressional reluctance to delve into activity that might result in dirtying Congress' own linen. Karl Shriftgiesser observed: "Any investigation of lobbying is, in many respects, an investigation of Congress itself. For Congress is, after all, the party of the second part."

Evolution of Lobby Techniques

Bribery of Members of Congress was a well-documented occurrence in the 19th and early 20th centuries.

When Congress in the 1830s became embroiled in President Andrew Jackson's battle with the Bank of the United States, it was disclosed that Daniel Webster, then a Senator from Massachusetts, enjoyed a retainer from the Bank. On Dec. 21, 1833, Webster complained to Bank President Nicholas Biddle: "My retainer has not been renewed or refreshed as usual. If it is wished that my relation to the Bank should be continued, it may be well to send me the usual retainers." Historian Arthur M. Schlesinger Jr. observed in *The Age of Jackson* that Henry Clay supported the Bank "because it fitted in with his superb vision of America, but Webster was fighting for it in great part because it was a dependable source of private income."

In the biggest scandal of the Grant Administration, it was rumored that 12 Members of Congress had received stock in the Crédit Mobilier, a joint stock company, in return for large Congressional grants for construction of the transcontinental Union Pacific Railroad, which controlled the Crédit Mobilier. Following an investigation, two of the alleged participants were censured by the House.

Col. Martin M. Mulhall, a lobbyist for the National Association of Manufacturers, stated publicly in 1913 that he had bribed Members of Congress for legislative favors, had paid the chief House page $50 a month for inside information from the cloakrooms, and had influenced House leaders to place Members friendly to the NAM on House committees and subcommittees. In a subsequent Congressional probe, six Members were exonerated but one was censured and resigned.

After World War II, direct vote-buying by lobbyists was supplemented by sophisticated techniques. Indirect, grass-roots pressures and promises of political support became the predominant methods. As for direct pressures, political backing was the accepted currency of the time. Usually, the most valuable thing one could offer a Member was re-election.

Who Is A Lobbyist?

In common use, the term "lobbyist" has at least three different meanings.

(1) In its broadest use, the term "lobbyist" is often used interchangeably with the term "pressure group" to mean any organization or person that carries on activities which have as their ultimate aim to influence the decisions of Congress, of the state and local legislatures or of government administrative agencies.

(2) In a somewhat narrower sense, "lobbyist" means any person who, on behalf of some other person or group and usually for pay, attempts to influence legislation through direct contact with legislators. Such a person may meet with the legislators in their home districts or at any other place, but he is most frequently found in the nation's capital while Congress is in session or in the state capitals while the state legislatures are in session. Used in this narrower sense, the term "lobbyist" had its first recorded appearance in 1829, according to H. L. Mencken as reported in Karl Shriftgiesser's book, *The Lobbyists* (Atlantic-Little Brown, 1951). The term first appeared as "lobby-agent" (meaning someone who frequented the lobbies of government buildings in order to speak to officials or legislators)

and was applied to those seeking special privileges from the New York state government in Albany. Shortened to "lobbyist" by journalists, the expression was in frequent use in the nation's capital in Washington by the early 1830s.

The practice of lobbying Congress in this manner was so widespread by the middle of the 19th century that, according to *The Lobbyists*, James Buchanan wrote as follows to Franklin Pierce in 1852:

"The host of contractors, speculators, stock-jobbers and lobby members which haunt the halls of Congress, all desirous...on any and every pretext to get their arms into the public treasury, are sufficient to alarm every friend of his country. Their progress must be arrested."

(3) In a third and still narrower meaning, "lobbyist" denotes anyone who is required to register or report on his spending under the terms of the Federal Regulation of Lobbying Act of 1946. The purpose of the 1946 act was to force anyone who received pay for pressuring Members of Congress on legislation to reveal that fact by registering with the Secretary of the Senate and the Clerk of the House and to reveal on whose behalf he was acting and how much he was receiving and spending in carrying out his pressure activities.

Members' Views on Lobbying

What do Members of Congress think of the activities of lobbyists belonging to what often is termed the "third house of Congress?"

A 1957 Congressional Quarterly poll of Senators and Representatives revealed that Congress found lobbyists helpful to the legislative process. The 122 Members of Congress answering the poll generally agreed they:

• Received enough information to identify lobbyists who pressured them.

• Felt little unreasonable pressure from the lobby corps.

• Received valuable information on complicated issues from the lobbyists.

Questionnaire

A total of 122, or 23 percent, of the 528 Members polled returned their questionnaires with these results (figures will not total since many Members checked more than one item):

• 84, or 69 percent: "I am receiving enough information to enable me to identify lobbyists who contact me."

• 15, or 12 percent: "I am not receiving enough information about lobbyists and therefore favor provisions in the pending bill (S 2191) to direct the General Accounting Office to collect and distribute such information."

• 76, or 62 percent: "Most lobbyists are helpful to me because they supply detailed facts on complicated legislative questions." (Nine other Members, or seven percent, checked the question after amending it to read "some" lobbyists instead of "most" lobbyists.)

• 4, or 3 percent: "Most lobbyists confuse the issue because they distort the facts."

• 50, or 41 percent: "Lobbyists help Congress to legislate with maximum intelligence."

• 6, or 5 percent: "Congress would be better off without lobbyists."

• 21, or 17 percent: "Lobbyists neither help nor hinder me in my work."

• 13, or 11 percent: "I often have felt unreasonable pressure from lobbyists."

• 25, or 21 percent: "I sometimes have felt unreasonable pressure from lobbyists."

• 40, or 33 percent: "I have never felt unreasonable pressure from lobbyists."

Campaign Support

While corporations have been barred since 1907, and labor unions since 1943, from making contributions to campaigns for Federal office, it is widely acknowledged that contributors have found numerous ways to get around the restrictions. Although unions are prohibited from using dues money to assist political candidates in Federal elections, it is legal for them to set up separate political arms, like the AFL-CIO's Committee on Political Education (COPE), which collect voluntary contributions from union members and use the funds for political expenditures calculated to benefit Members friendly to labor. It is also legal for unions to endorse political candidates.

Similarly, while corporations are prohibited from making direct campaign contributions, corporation executives urge subordinate managers to make personal contributions to particular candidates, to spread the word that election of a particular person would be bad for business, or to act through voluntary or political groups to which they belong to help or hurt a Member of Congress.

The same general resources for political support and opposition are available to members of citizens' groups and, indeed, to a wide range of organizations seeking to exert political pressure on Members of Congress.

In approaching the typical Member, a pressure group has no need to tell him outright that its future political support or opposition and perhaps its future political expenditures, and the voluntary campaign efforts of its members, depend on how he votes on a particular bill or whether, over a long period, he acts favorably toward the group. The Member understands this without being told. He understands that, in the nature of the political process, the positions he takes on legislation help to determine which groups will support him and which will not. He understands that when the vital interests of some group are at stake in legislation, his vote for it would normally win him the group's friendship and future support and his vote against it would mean the group's enmity and future opposition.

James Deakin pointed out in *The Lobbyists* that when lobbyists themselves are asked to assess the main value of campaign contributions, "they frequently reply with one word: access." The campaign donation helps them to gain access to the legislator to present their case. "The reasoning is that the other fellow is contributing to the campaign of Congressman Doe and therefore is likely to get a cordial reception when he visits Doe's office, so we had better do the same. This, according to many lobbyists, is all that is gained from a campaign donation—a chance to present facts, figures and arguments to the lawmaker in the privacy of his office."

In the years since World War II, there have been only three known instances of attempted bribery of Members of Congress.

In 1956, it was charged that lobbyists had offered Sen. Francis Case (R S.D.) a $2,500 campaign contribution (which he rejected) to influence his vote on a natural gas bill. Bribery charges against the two lawyers involved in the case were dismissed when they and the Superior Oil Co., their principal, pleaded guilty to the lesser charge of violating the 1946 Federal Regulation of Lobbying Act by failing to register as lobbyists. There was no suggestion that Case had either sought or accepted the contribution or had acted improperly in any way.

In 1963, former Rep. Thomas F. Johnson (D Md.) was accused of receiving money to make a speech on the House floor in 1960 favorable to the persons paying him

Lobbying Act Federal Court Cases Since 1946

The Justice Department in mid-1970 told Congressional Quarterly it knew of only five Federal court cases involving the Federal Regulation of Lobbying Act of 1946. Only four of the cases were prosecuted. Following are summaries of the cases:

NAM Test Suit. The National Association of Manufacturers on Jan. 28, 1948, brought a test suit challenging the validity of the lobbying law. On March 17, 1952, a Federal court in Washington, D.C., ruled that the law was unconstitutional. It held that definitions in the law were too "indefinite and vague to constitute an ascertainable standard of guilt." Eight months later, on Oct. 13, 1952, the U.S. Supreme Court on a technicality reversed the lower court, leaving the 1946 law in full force but open to further challenge.

Harriss Case. The Government on June 16, 1948, obtained indictments of several individuals and an organization for alleged violations of the registration or reporting sections of the 1946 lobbying law. It was charged that, without registering or reporting, New York cotton broker Robert M. Harriss had made payments to Ralph W. Moore, a Washington commodity trader and secretary of the National Farm Committee, for the purpose of pressuring Congress on legislation, and that Moore had made similar payments to James E. McDonald, the agricultural commissioner of Texas, and Tom Linder, the agricultural commissioner of Georgia. A lower court ruling, Jan. 30, 1953, by Judge Alexander Holtzoff held the lobbying law unconstitutional on grounds that it was too vague and indefinite to meet the requirements of due process, that the registration and reporting requirements violated the First Amendment (freedom of speech, assembly, etc.) and that certain of the penalty provisions violated the constitutional right to petition Congress. Holtzoff's ruling was appealed by the Government to the Supreme Court. On June 7, 1954, in a 5-3 decision, the Supreme Court reversed Holtzoff and upheld the constitutionality of the 1946 lobbying law, though construing it narrowly.

In upholding the validity of the lobbying law, the Supreme Court sent the cases of the individual defendants back to the lower court to decide whether the individuals involved were guilty. None of the defendants was found guilty. The case against Harriss was dismissed on the ground that the lobbying law, as construed by the Supreme Court, applied only to those who solicited or received money for the purpose of lobbying, whereas Harriss was charged merely with paying money to Moore. The case against Linder was dismissed because he was exempt from the lobbying law under a specific provision exempting public officials. The charges against McDonald were dropped because of his death earlier in the case. The lower court dismissed the charges against Moore and acquitted the National Farm Committee, Nov. 2, 1955.

The importance of the *Harriss* case lay not in the decisions on the individual defendants but in the Supreme Court's ruling that the 1946 lobbying law was constitutional.

Savings & Loan League. A Federal grand jury in Washington, D.C., March 30, 1948, indicted the U.S. Savings and Loan League for failure to comply with the 1946 lobbying law. The case was dismissed April 19, 1949, by a Federal district court.

Slaughter Case. On Nov. 23, 1948, ex-Rep. Roger C. Slaughter (D Mo. 1943-47), a bitter political foe of then-President Truman, was indicted on charges he had lobbied for the North American Grain Association without registering under the lobbying act. Slaughter's defense was that he had merely acted as an attorney and had helped prepare testimony for witnesses. On April 17, 1950, Slaughter was acquitted, with the judge holding that the specific provision of the lobbying act which exempted persons who merely testified before a Congressional committee applied, also, to those who helped such persons prepare testimony.

Natural Gas Case. On Feb. 3, 1956, Sen. Francis Case (R S.D.) announced on the floor of the Senate that he would vote against the natural gas bill because an out-of-state lawyer who was interested in passage of the bill, and who had learned that Case was favorably inclined to the measure, had left a $2,500 campaign contribution for the Senator. (Case had refused the contribution.) As a result of this incident, President Eisenhower on Feb. 17 vetoed the natural gas bill on the ground that agents of a natural gas producer had made an "arrogant" effort to influence legislation with a campaign contribution. John M. Neff of Lexington, Neb., the man who had offered the contribution to Sen. Case, was indicted, July 24, on charges of violating the Federal Regulation of Lobbying Act. Also indicted were Elmer Patman of Austin, Texas, and the Superior Oil Co. of California. Both Neff and Patman were attorneys for Superior Oil. In a Senate investigation and at court proceedings, Neff and Patman said the $2,500 offered to Case came from the personal funds of Superior Oil President Howard B. Keck. The money was given by Keck to Patman, who in turn gave it to Neff. Neff then offered it to Case. The accused denied any attempt at bribery and said the purpose of the offer was to aid Senators they believed to be of the economic school of thought that would favor the natural gas bill, which would exempt producers from certain Federal regulation.

On Dec. 14, 1956, both Neff and Patman pleaded guilty of violating the lobbying act by failing to register although engaged in lobbying the natural gas bill. They were fined $2,500 each and given one-year suspended sentences by Federal District Judge Joseph C. McGarraghy in Washington, D.C. Superior Oil was fined $5,000 on each of two counts of aiding and abetting Neff and Patman to violate the lobbying law. Bribery charges arising from the case were dropped. The convictions of Neff, Patman and Superior Oil were the first (and through 1970 only) convictions ever obtained under the 1946 lobbying law. There was never any suggestion that Senator Case had sought the campaign contribution or had accepted it or had in any way acted improperly.

the bribe. He was convicted in January 1968 on conflict-of-interest charges and sentenced to jail. The conviction was later upheld on appeal.

In 1969, former Sen. Daniel B. Brewster (D Md.) was indicted by a Federal grand jury on charges of having taken a bribe in return for his support of postage rate legislation favorable to a mail-order house. The charges were dismissed by a U.S. district court judge on Oct. 9, 1970.

Grass-Roots Pressures

Except on obscure or highly specialized legislation, most lobby campaigns now are accompanied by massive propaganda or "educational" drives in which pressure groups seek to mobilize public opinion to support their aims. In most cases, citizens are urged to respond by contacting Members of Congress in support of or opposition to a particular bill.

One of the most notable successes for this technique came in 1962, when the U.S. Savings and Loan League sought to defeat President Kennedy's proposal for withholding the taxes due on interest earned on savings deposits. Because the speedup in collections would have cut back the funds on deposit at the savings and loan institutions, it would have reduced the amount of S & L money available for housing loans.

After the plan had been approved by the House, the League launched a massive effort to generate pressures that would kill the proposal in the Senate. Some of the League's advertisements depicted the plan as a new tax on savings, not a mere speedup in the collection of existing levies on interest from the savings. "The result," James Deakin has said, "was an avalanche, a flood, a torrent of letters to Members of the Senate. So many stacks of letters piled up that Senate staffs had to drop everything else to cope with the deluge. The Senate post office said there had been nothing to compare with it since Truman fired General MacArthur, or possibly the Army-McCarthy hearings." The plan was summarily dropped by the Senate Finance Committee.

Another recent grass-roots effort acknowledged as highly successful came in the mid-1960s, when the National Rifle Association instigated an outpouring of mail against Administration proposals for tighter gun controls. Even after the assassinations of President Kennedy, the Rev. Martin Luther King Jr. and Sen. Robert F. Kennedy (D N.Y. 1965-68), the gun lobby was able to bottle up proposals for tough controls, and all that was passed was watered-down legislation not vigorously opposed by the NRA.

Anti-Saloon League Drive. Sometimes lobbying efforts originate at the grass roots and then attract national attention. The best-known and most successful of these campaigns was the drive by the Anti-Saloon League and associated organizations to bar the sale of alcoholic beverages. After 15 years devoted to building up local support, particularly among Protestant denominations, the League met in Washington in 1911 to map strategy for its assault on Congress. A leading strategist of the League told members what was necessary to win: Lobbying of legislatures and the Congress was important, he said, but "back of all such endeavor there must be a nationwide movement of public opinion, voicing itself in such a way that (it) will be heard by every Congressman." To sway public opinion, the League launched an advertis-

ing campaign that blamed all the evils of society on the saloon.

Although the League's initial effort was not immediately productive, Congress deferred to this increasingly powerful lobby two years later by passing the Webb-Kenyon Act, which outlawed transportation of alcoholic beverages into states where their sale was illegal. Spurred by that victory, the League went on to push through nationwide prohibition. As one of its leaders, Bishop James Cannon Jr., expressed it, "The walls of Jericho were falling down before the armies of the Lord."

Following substantial gains by "dry" candidates in the Congressional election of 1916, Congress the next year submitted the Eighteenth Amendment, prohibiting the sale or consumption of alcoholic beverages, to the states for ratification. Ratification was completed early in 1919, and the amendment went into effect in January 1920 (it was repealed in 1933).

Karl Shriftgiesser has observed that the imposition of prohibition was "almost entirely" the work of the Anti-Saloon League. "Unscrupulous and determined," he said, "willing to use any and every known method of propaganda and lobbying, a minority pressure group had managed to capture the Government. For many years to come few Members of Congress could get elected without submitting to the demands of this lobby. In the end, after years of bloody strife and lawlessness such as the wildest frontier days had not seen, the same methods that the prohibitionists had used were turned against them and the Eighteenth Amendment was repealed."

Disadvantages of Grass-Roots Approach. Despite the frequent success of grass-roots lobbying, such an approach has several inherent limitations which make its use questionable unless it is carefully and cleverly managed. If a Member's mail on an issue appears artificially generated, the Member may feel that the response is not representative of his constituency. Such pressure mail is easily recognized because the letters all arrive at about the same time, are mimeographed or printed, or are identically or similarly worded. Political scientist David B. Truman has observed that "Filling up the legislator's mailbag is essentially a crude device, a shotgun technique which may only wound where a rifle would kill." While Truman concedes that there may be times when a Member will add up the pros and cons and vote with the majority, he cautions that "one fact is clear" in such instances: "The usual channels of access to him are empty or silent."

House Judiciary Committee Chairman Emanuel Celler (D N.Y.) remarked a dozen years ago that grass-roots lobbying is the most annoying of all for the Members of Congress. "Legislators cannot afford to give this kind of message much weight. Nor can they afford to ignore it entirely. The result is a great waste of time counting the individual letters on each side of the question and in perfunctory attempts to reply."

Occasionally, this method may boomerang and leave the lobbyist worse off than when he started. A noteworthy example was the utility fight of 1935, when lobbyists for private utilities sought unsuccessfully to defeat President Roosevelt's proposed curbs on utility holding companies. A Congressional investigation brought out the fact that thousands of phony telegrams to Congress had been financed by utility interests. A resulting wave of adverse publicity helped assure passage of Roosevelt's proposals.

Direct Lobbying

Much lobbying still is conducted on a face-to-face basis. In a study of pressures on the Senate, Donald R. Matthews, a political scientist, observed that the vast majority of such lobbying was directed at Members "who are already convinced." He added: "The services a lobby can provide a friendly Senator are substantial. Few Senators could survive without them. First, they can perform much of the research and speech-writing chores of the Senator's office. This service is especially attractive to the more publicity-oriented Senators. Members of the party that does not control the White House also find this service especially valuable, since they cannot draw upon the research services of the Departments as much as can the other Members. But most Senators find this service at first a convenience and soon a necessity."

Once established, Matthews has said, "Senator-lobbyist friendships also tend to reinforce the Senator's commitment to a particular group and line of policy." "Relatively few Senators are actually changed by lobbyists from a hostile or neutral position to a friendly one. Perhaps a few on every major issue are converted and this handful of votes may carry the day. But quantitatively, the conversion effect is relatively small."

Ensuring continued access to Members of Congress requires considerable tact on the part of the lobbyist. Lobbyists must be particularly wary of overstaying their welcome and appearing overly aggressive. Rep. Celler has written: "The man who keeps his appointment, presents his problem or proposal and lets the Congressman get on with his other work comes to be liked and respected. His message has an excellent chance of being effective. The man who feels that it somehow adds to his usefulness and prestige to be seen constantly in the company of one legislator or another, or who seeks to ingratiate himself with Congressional staffs, gets under foot and becomes a nuisance. He does his principal and cause no good."

Above all, the lobbyist must be certain that the information he gives the Member is accurate and complete. Former White House aide Douglass Cater has said: "The smart lobbyist...knows he can be most effective by being helpful, by being timely, and, not least, by being accurate. According to the testimony of lobbyists themselves, the cardinal sin is to supply faulty information which puts a trusting policy-maker in an exposed position."

Most contemporary lobbyists carefully avoid approaches that the Member may interpret as threatening or as constituting excessive pressure. An adverse reaction by a Member may lead to unfavorable publicity or even a damaging Congressional investigation. Matthews has described the lobbyist as a "sitting duck—their public reputation is so low that public attack is bound to be damaging." "To invite public attack, or even worse a Congressional investigation, is, from the lobbyist's point of view, clearly undesirable. Matthews adds: "(It is the) threat of and use of these countermeasures which help explain why so little lobbying is aimed at conversion. A lobbyist minimizes the risk of his job, the cause which he serves, and his ego by staying away from those Senators clearly against him and his program. For, of all types of lobbying, attempts at conversion are most likely to boomerang."

Information-Gathering Function. Some lobbyists may be of more use to their employers as a conduit of information than as a source of direct pressure on Congress. The late Merriman Smith, longtime White House correspondent for United Press International, wrote a few years ago: "(The typical lobbyist) arises when he feels like it, usually midmorning, in a spacious, comfortable, but definitely unflashy home in the Northwest residential section of town. Over breakfast, he reads four or five major morning newspapers. If interested, he skims through the *Congressional Record* for the day before.... These are the golden hours of his day. He may earn his keep more from intelligent reading than from any other single activity. Years of experience have taught him to read between the lines and to search for indicative but seemingly small details....

"Once 'read' for the day, he may make it to town for luncheon with one or two key men in Government at the Carlton or the Mayflower. Mostly, they talk about golf or fishing. Possibly in parting, he may ask casually, 'You fellows heard anything new on depreciation allowances?'... This man is more effective for his employer than a dozen more energetic fellows patrolling the halls of the Senate and House office buildings.... By being highly selective in his friendships, he manages to keep in touch with virtually any Government move that might help or hinder his company.... Our man's effectiveness would be destroyed if he had to play the lobbyist's conventional role in attempting to push or halt specific bills before Congress."

Strategic Contacts. In fights over a specific bill, most direct approaches by lobbyists are likely to center on a few strategic Members instead of a large part of the membership of the House or Senate. In most lobby battles, approval of a measure by a Congressional committee is tantamount to final passage. Except on highly controversial issues, committee decisions are almost always upheld by the full chamber. Lobby pressures may focus not only on key members of a committee but also on the committee's professional staff. Particularly on legislation involving highly technical matters, such staffs are extremely influential. Lester W. Milbrath has noted that "failure to locate such key persons (Members and staff) may result in the sending of many superfluous messages, and if the key persons cannot be persuaded, there is a high likelihood that the decision will go adversely." Any inroads the lobbyist may have made outside the circle of strategic Members are likely to be negated if these key Members start pushing the other way.

Testimony at Hearings

Another useful technique for lobbyists is testimony at Congressional hearings. The hearing provides the lobbyist with a propaganda forum that has few parallels in Washington. It also provides access to key Members whom the lobbyist may not have been able to contact in any other way. On important legislation, lobbyists normally rehearse their statements before the hearing, seek to ensure a large turnout from their constituency on the hearing day, and may even hand friendly committee members leading questions for the group's witness to answer.

The degree of propaganda success for the hearing, however, is likely to depend on how well the Committee's controlling factions are disposed to the group's position. In his book, *House Out of Order*, Rep. Richard Bolling

(D Mo.) says that within Congressional committees "proponents and opponents of legislation jockey for position—each complementing the activities of their alter egos in lobbies outside." He points out: "Adverse witnesses can be kept to a minimum, for example, or they can be sandwiched among friendly witnesses in scheduled appearances so that their testimony does not receive as much attention from the press as it deserves. Scant attention will be given, for example, to a knowledgeable opponent of the Federal fallout shelter program if he is scheduled to testify on such legislation on the same day as are Dr. Edward Teller, an Assistant Secretary of Defense, and a three-star general. The opponent is neatly boxed in."

Lobby Coalitions

Most major legislation is backed by alliances of interest groups on one side and opposed by alliances on the other. Such lobby coalitions, while having the advantage of bigger memberships and more financial resources for lobbying, are difficult to control because of the differences of viewpoint that are likely within the coalition. Despite these inner tensions, however, lobby coalitions have been instrumental in obtaining the passage of much major legislation in recent years, including Medicare (see Appendix for case study), civil rights bills, and housing legislation. Notable coalition efforts that failed have been a 1967 push for import restrictions, which ran into trouble when too many industries sought protective quotas, and a 1970 drive for cuts in military spending, which lost impact when liberal and conservative critics of Pentagon spending levels fell to quarreling over use of the prospective savings. Liberals sought to earmark the cuts for domestic programs, while the conservatives favored tax reductions.

In a broad sense, lobby coalitions have broken down into liberal and conservative camps, the former usually led by the labor unions and civil rights groups and the latter by business associations such as the Chamber of Commerce of the United States and the National Association of Manufacturers. Disparities within these groups usually lead to shifting of alliances among individual organizations as issues change and to formation of ad hoc coalitions to exert pressure on a particular issue.

Although there is considerable log-rolling, with organizations getting assistance on one issue by promising future support on another, the activity of many groups is limited mainly to matters of immediate concern to them. Thus, the American Medical Association, one of the most powerful pressure groups in the capital, is extremely active on questions of medical practice and health but normally shows little interest in questions like agricultural policy, foreign trade, or economic policy in general.

Defensive Lobby Alignments. While massive promotional campaigns by lobbyists have attracted wide public attention, a large share of lobby activity is defensive or preventive. Lewis Dexter has observed that this is only natural because "it is much easier to get successful people—the kind who finance and initiate most lobbies—excited about having a favorable situation disturbed than to stir them up—at least in American society—about a contingent benefit."

The bicameral structure of the Legislative Branch and the Constitutional separation of powers also gives a considerable natural advantage to defensive lobbying efforts. David B. Truman has written that these structures "operate, as they were designed, to delay or obstruct action rather than to facilitate it." He adds: "Requirement of extensive majorities for particular kinds of measures and the absence of limits on the duration of debate have a like effect as do numerous technical details of the parliamentary rules. Finally, the diffuseness of leadership, and the power and independence of committees and their chairmen, not only provide a multiplicity of points of access...but also furnish abundant activities for obstruction and delay, opportunities that buttress the position of defensive groups."

Famous Lobbyists

Most colorful of all the early Washington lobbyists was Samuel Ward, brother of Julia Ward Howe, author of "The Battle Hymn of the Republic." Ward, known widely as "King of the Lobby," reigned in Washington for 15 years in the period following the Civil War. His clients included the railroads and other financial interests concerned with Federal legislation.

In his study of the House of Representatives, journalist Neil MacNeil described Ward as "a short, stout man with the imperial white beard of a French count...a man of refined education, who sported diamond studs in his shirts and never appeared without a rose in his coat lapel." "He entertained nightly the political leaders of Washington at a table groaning with choice viands and fine wines. Himself a wit and gentleman of culture, Ward lavished on his guests a plentiful bounty with never so much as an indelicate suggestion of his ulterior motives; he never asked a man for a favor at his table. That came later." Ward is reported to have bragged repeatedly that "The way to a man's 'Aye' is through his stomach."

The size of Ward's fees was not a matter of record. On one occasion, however, he wrote his friend Henry Wadsworth Longfellow: "When I see you again, I will tell you how a client, eager to prevent the arrival at a committee of a certain member before it should adjourn, offered me $5,000 to accomplish his purpose, which I did by having his (the Congressman's) boots mislaid while I smoked a cigar and condoled with him until they would be found at 11:45. I had the satisfaction of a good laugh, a good fee in my pocket, and of having prevented a conspiracy." By "conspiracy," Ward is reported to have meant legislation in which he saw no merit.

On other occasions, Ward reportedly received $50,000 for influencing tariff legislation and $1 million for his work on a mail subsidy case. When a Congressional committee asked him what he had done to earn his fee in the mail case, Ward denied that he had bribed anyone to influence the legislation. He supposed he had been retained, he said, because "I am called King of the Lobby, but I am not Treasurer of the Lobby, that is certain."

Edward Pendleton. A lobbyist of the immediate pre-Civil War era who achieved a reputation almost equal to Ward's was Edward Pendleton, who operated a popular gambling house on Pennsylvania Avenue. Pendleton's establishment, known as the "Palace of Fortune" and "Hall of the Bleeding Heart," was elaborately furnished and equipped with a wine cellar in which Pendleton was said to have invested $10,000. Perley Poore, a contemporary of Pendleton's, wrote: "The people who nightly assembled to see and to take part in the entertainments of the house consisted of candidates for the Presidency,

Senators and Representatives, members of the Cabinet, editors and journalists and the master workmen of the third house, the lobby. Pendleton's in its palmiest days might have been called the vestibule of the lobby."

It was reported that the transfer of bribes to Members of Congress in the form of winnings at cards was another of the methods followed at Pendleton's. But lending money to Members who went broke at his tables was Pendleton's main stock in trade. Neil MacNeil has observed that "This was the source of his power as a lobbyist, and he proved successful many times in having bills passed for his clients." Perley Poore said of Pendleton that "A broker in parliamentary notes is an inevitable retainer of broker votes."

Thomas G. Corcoran. Among contemporary lobbyists, one of the best-known and most influential has been Thomas G. Corcoran, a powerful White House adviser in New Deal days who later became a highly paid lobbyist for Washington business interests.

During five years in the White House, Corcoran (dubbed "Tommy the Cork" by President Roosevelt) assisted in writing much of the major New Deal legislation, including the Securities and Exchange Act, the Public Utility Holding Company Act and the Fair Labor Standards Act. Corcoran also helped on Roosevelt's abortive plan to "pack" the Supreme Court with additional justices. He thus became one of the most controversial of the White House staff members, and when he sought the post of Solicitor General in 1940, President Roosevelt declined to nominate him for fear the Senate would deny confirmation. Corcoran resigned his White House job and, almost overnight, reappeared as representative of the same business interests he had opposed as a New Deal crusader. Within a few months, he testified before a Congressional committee that he had received $100,000 in legal fees and was turning away clients "by the hundreds."

Louis W. Koenig has described Corcoran as "an adventurer who...sought to introduce banana-growing on the island fortress of Taiwan and to establish across the length and breadth of Brazil a chain of restaurants under the auspices of the Union News Company." He added: "In reality, he belongs not to the twentieth century, but to another age. He is a medieval character who operated in the era of the New Deal with the fervor, bravado and finesse of a top-notch grand duke of an Italian principality.... 'The way to get ahead,' he would say, 'is to fish in troubled waters.' "

James Deakin has observed that when a 1960 House subcommittee investigating lobbyist contacts with members of the Federal Power Commission began probing the alleged activities of Corcoran, the panel "got out of its league." Deakin went on to say: "This was no plodding political hack caught cozying up to the industry, but a wily old pro who had forgotten more about the regulatory agencies and regulatory law than the Subcommittee members ever knew....Corcoran ran rings around the Subcommittee in some of the stormiest and funniest hearings ever held on Capitol Hill." Following is a partial transcript:

Rep. Derounian: "Just answer the question, Mr. Corcoran. I don't want you to be a long-playing record, because you have been doing that for two days now. Your contacts with Members of the Senate has (sic) gotten you into their habit of filibuster and we have to get through with this hearing."

Corcoran: "Thank you, Mr. Derounian, if you think I am that long-winded that I have talked for two days. I have only been here for a half session."

Derounian: "Yesterday, you talked all morning and you didn't answer one of the eight questions that I was concerned with. I think I am justified in that comment...."

Corcoran: "May I finish, Mr. Derounian. I know I am not like your friend Tom Dewey, I don't come down here in the same kind of a case as your friend Tom Dewey came down, who is also a friend of mine, with a long, long time-sheet justification as to how he charged more than I did in the case. No, I didn't do that."

Derounian: "First of all, Tom Dewey is not my friend. He couldn't care less about what happens to me, and I couldn't care less about what happens to him. He can take care of himself as, apparently, you proved you can."

Corcoran: "I know what you want me to do."

Derounian: "Let's get the record straight about my friendship."

Corcoran: "All right."

Derounian: "And stop winking at the chairman (Rep. Oren Harris, D Ark.) with your left eye. Maybe he is your friend too. That is all right but let's keep this thing strictly business."

Corcoran: "All right, Mr. Derounian."

The Chairman: "The committee will be in order."

Derounian: "I have noticed here, Mr. Corcoran—"

Corcoran: "I am not going to use any right eye on you, it is just that I have been having a little trouble."

Derounian: "It is all right, use your other eye. I will look you straight back. We are trying to get to the facts here, let's not have a filibuster."

Corcoran: "Have I, I assume I have answered the question."

Corcoran later admitted to the panel that he had held off-the-record talks with several members of the FPC while his client's case was pending—a proposal by the Midwestern Gas Transmission Co. to build a $50-million pipeline for four Middle Western states. Corcoran contended, however, that the talks had been "in conformity" with FPC regulations and did not influence the Commission's decision, which favored Midwestern Gas. The Democratic majority on the panel absolved Corcoran of any impropriety, but the Republican minority termed that finding "perhaps the most shocking political whitewash to come out of a Congressional committee in many years." The subcommittee majority and its staff, the minority said, have "sought to exonerate one of Washington's best-known influence peddlers."

Corcoran maintained his relationship with Midwestern, and, according to reports filed with FPC, received a fee of $31,875 from Midwestern two years later and $70,283 from its parent firm, Tennessee Gas Transmission Co. Over the years Corcoran's Washington law firm, Corcoran, Foley, Youngman and Rowe, has registered as lobbyist for such diverse interests as individual gas companies, the Gas Marketers Association, Committee for Broadening Commercial Bank Participation in Public Financing, Committee on Metropolitan Washington Banking, Lilly Endowment Inc., and the Association of Stock Exchange Firms.

Clark M. Clifford. Another highly paid representative for powerful business interests has been Clark M. Clifford, prominent Washington attorney and a former White House aide in the Truman Administration, adviser to

Presidents Kennedy and Johnson, and Secretary of Defense (1968-69) for the last 11 months of the Johnson Administration. Clifford has long been a senior partner in the Washington law firm of Clifford, Warnke, Glass, McIlwain and Finney (formerly Clifford and Miller), which has held retainers from some of the nation's largest corporations. Among them are DuPont, General Electric, Standard Oil of California, Phillips Petroleum Co., Hughes Tool Co., and a number of mutual funds.

Clifford's firm declined for many years to register as a lobby group, contending that it did no actual lobbying. (Finally, in 1969, it did register for Hughes Tool, the Avco Corp. and several smaller clients.) Soon after setting up the firm, Clifford told reporters: "I have not and will not register as a lobbyist, for that is not the kind of work we do. We run a law office here, with a background of experience in the general practice of law, topped off by an intimate knowledge of how the Government operates." Associates of Clifford's firm often said their role in the legislative process was to advise clients on positions to take on legislation and to suggest the tactics that they use in lobbying campaigns. The firm followed the legislation closely for the client, but if the situation called for active lobbying, it recommended someone else for that job.

It was widely rumored that Clifford's firm received a fee of $1 million from the DuPont Co. for its assistance in a stock divestiture case. The firm claimed that the size of the fee was exaggerated and said it had received only its regular retainer as DuPont's Washington counsel. The bulk of the fee, it said, went to the Washington law firm of Cleary, Gottlieb and Steen, which Clifford's firm recommended for the lobbying job.

Andrew J. Biemiller. The most prominent labor lobbyist in Washington has been Andrew J. Biemiller, a former U.S. Representative from Wisconsin (D 1945-47; 1949-51), who registered as a lobbyist for the AFL in 1953, became chief lobbyist for the AFL-CIO when the organizations merged in 1955, and was still in that position in 1970. James Deakin has called Biemiller "one of the best-known men on Capitol Hill" and points out that he has "one of the toughest jobs in Washington (because) he is caught in the occasional crossfire between the AFL and CIO and beset by the prickly personalities of some of labor's top brass." Deakin quotes Biemiller as saying: "The only labor lobbyists over which I have control are those directly employed by the AFL-CIO. There are some 95 other labor lobbyists in Washington. With these, all I can use is suasion."

Despite Biemiller's widely acclaimed skills in mobilizing a united labor front, Congress during his tenure as labor's top lobbyist has passed relatively few of the major bills of direct interest to labor—right-to-work repeal, liberalized rules for picketing, and others. However, Biemiller's over-all effectiveness is not questioned. Many of the flood of labor-supported civil rights and welfare bills that have won approval during that period were at the top of the AFL-CIO's priorities list, right after the bills of exclusive interest to labor.

Ex-Members of Congress as Lobbyists

Among the most influential and active lobbyists in Washington have been former Members of Congress, who,

after leaving office, have been hired as lobbyists for private organizations.

In some cases, former Members become permanently associated with a single organization whose views they share. Thus, Rep. Clyde T. Ellis (D Ark. 1939-43), after leaving Congress, registered Dec. 6, 1946, under the Federal Regulation of Lobbying Act as a lobbyist for the National Rural Electric Cooperative Association, whose representative he remained throughout the following two decades. Similarly, ex-Rep. Andrew J. Biemiller has served as labor's top lobbyist.

On the other hand, some former Members work for many different organizations as lobbyists, frequently changing or adding employers from year to year. Thus, ex-Sen. Scott W. Lucas (D Ill. House 1935-39; Senate 1939-51) registered as a lobbyist for more than 25 different organizations between 1951 and the time of his death in early 1968. *(See Appendix for names of ex-Members who registered as lobbyists from 1946-70 under the Federal Regulation of Lobbying Act.)*

Because of their service in Congress, former Members of the House or Senate enjoy several advantages in lobbying activities. They have an excellent knowledge of the legislative process and frequently a good "feel" for the operations of the House or Senate which tell them precisely when and what kind of pressure to exert on behalf of their clients. They often enjoy easy access to Congressional staff members and Members who are friends and former colleagues. This enables them to see and speak with key legislative personnel, perhaps the chairman of a committee or subcommittee, at the proper time. The ordinary lobbyist might spend weeks trying to obtain an appointment. Former Members also frequently have an expert knowledge of the subject matter of legislation through having dealt with it while in Congress.

The privilege of being admitted to the floor and private lobbies of the House and Senate, which is granted in each chamber to former Members of that chamber, is used relatively little by former Members directly for lobbying purposes, although it is useful for maintaining contacts and old acquaintances. In the House, use of the floor by former Members for lobbying purposes has been circumscribed by House Rule 32 and a chair ruling in 1945 by then-Speaker Sam Rayburn (D Texas). Under the "Rayburn rule," a former Member is forbidden the privilege of the floor at any time the House is debating or voting on legislation in which he is interested, either personally or as an employee of some other person or group.

In the Senate, no similar formal rule exists. But as a matter of custom, it is considered improper for a former Senator, or any other non-Member granted the privilege of the floor, to use the privilege to lobby for legislation in which he is interested either personally or as a representative or lobbyist for another person or organization.

Sources of Lobby Pressure

As noted, the expansion of Federal activity and the increase in Federal spending have resulted in a marked increase in lobby activity. In view of these Government trends, many interests which seldom bothered to exert pressure on Congress found it necessary or advantageous to do so.

The expansion of single-interest groups into multiple-interest groups can be illustrated by the case of a hypothetical manufacturer who, until the 1930s, took interest in Federal legislation only when it concerned tariffs. In the postwar era, he found himself directly affected not only by tariff legislation but also by Federal corporation taxes, minimum wage legislation, Social Security, unemployment insurance tax and benefit levels, the possibility of getting a Government contract, restrictions on the countries from which he might import materials, and other questions.

Changing Patterns

Perhaps the two most important changes in pressure group activities have been the emergence of labor organizations as important pressure groups and the decline in the influence of farm organizations.

Rise of Labor Unions. Before World War II, labor union lobbying was a relatively negligible force in the nation's capital. But there was a remarkable growth in union membership from 1935 to 1945. At the same time, many labor union officials "learned the ropes" in Washington when they came to the capital during the Second World War to serve on the War Labor Board's tripartite dispute settlement sections. These developments set the stage for the emergence of labor unions as the most important pressure group in the nation's capital working for liberal legislation. The unions carried on both grass roots pressure campaigns designed to influence public opinion and active lobbying of Congress (and frequently of the President and other Executive Branch leaders). Their large membership, strength in urban centers, comparatively substantial financial resources, organizational know-how and, in many cases, the liberally oriented idealism of most of their spokesmen made them a formidable force in legislative pressure activities. An important aspect of their influence was that many unions, and notably the two federations (AFL and CIO, which merged into the AFL-CIO in 1955), maintained research and publications staffs which contributed importantly to the development and popularization of many new policy proposals in the welfare and labor fields.

Also important, probably even more than research and propaganda activities, was the willingness of the unions to use political means to achieve their ends. Both the AFL and the CIO maintained political action arms (the AFL Labor's League for Political Education and the CIO Political Action Committee) which, when the two federations merged in 1955, were united to form the AFL-CIO Committee on Political Education (COPE).

Although the 1943 Smith-Connally Act barred political contributions from dues money by unions in connection with Federal elections, the law did not prevent unions from setting up political action arms financed by voluntary political contributions from union members. COPE and its predecessors operated in this fashion, as did a number of other political action groups maintained by unions.

All these factors made labor unions, particularly the two great federations, AFL and CIO, but also large individual unions like the Teamsters, United Mine Workers, United Automobile Workers and International Ladies' Garment Workers' Union, extremely influential with many Members of Congress, particularly liberals and, most notably, northern urban Democrats. The unions' strength was greatest on certain "bread and butter" legislation which directly affected union members—labor-manage-ment relations, wage and hour legislation, Social Security—and was also substantial, though not as great, on non-"bread and butter" issues like foreign aid and Federal aid to education.

The strength of the unions, though very great, should not be exaggerated. Acting alone, the unions were seldom if ever able to get any important legislation enacted. They needed the cooperation of other liberal groups and other economic-interest groups. On the two major labor-management bills of the postwar era—the 1947 Taft-Hartley Act and the 1959 Landrum-Griffin Bill, both of which unions opposed as restricting their rights in collective bargaining—the unions were beaten, in part because there was a powerful coalition of business groups arrayed against them that was stronger than the unions.

For many legislators, fear of union retaliation when the legislator did not vote as the unions wished was lessened by the recognition that union leaders, on many non-"bread and butter" issues, tended to be far more liberal than their members and that union leaders did not always control the votes of members on election day. Moreover, there was a general feeling that the strength of labor unions as a pressure group was greatest in the 1940s and early 1950s and had begun to decline in the later 1950s and 1960s—in part because unions were no longer expanding their membership very rapidly, in part because the experience of the preceding 15-20 years demonstrated that unions alone simply were not strong enough to dominate Congressional elections in a way which once was feared. On some legislative issues, the unions frequently disagreed among themselves.

Decline of Farm Bloc. The declining influence of farm organizations was the product largely of the decline in the farm population. As time went on, fewer and fewer Members of Congress represented true farm districts and the strength of agricultural pressure groups declined accordingly. Another factor in the decline of the farm bloc, however, was increasing disagreement among farm groups on policies. Whereas in the farm crisis of the 1930s most farm organizations supported certain of President Roosevelt's policies to aid the farmer, a sharp split emerged in fights over World War II price controls and the 1949 Brannan Plan.

The American Farm Bureau Federation, the nation's largest farm organization, was one of the major pressure groups behind the Roosevelt Administration's Agricultural Adjustment Act of 1938. But in the postwar era, it opposed the Truman Administration's Brannan Plan and subsequently also opposed most proposals by Presidents Kennedy and Johnson for production controls and high price supports. The National Farmers Union, on the other hand, backed the Brannan Plan and Mr. Kennedy's production-control and price-support proposals. The position of the National Grange varied.

Professional, Urban, State Groups. The postwar expansion of the Federal Government into many new fields of action gave rise to pressure activities by groups whose interest had previously been trifling or nonexistent. This development was particularly noticeable in the fields of scientific research, health, education and medicine, where the Federal Government was becoming heavily engaged in both personnel and financing. Professional organizations of scientists and doctors accordingly developed keen interest in the determination of Federal policy.

For example, an informal ad hoc group of nuclear scientists, alarmed at possible misuse of atomic energy, was widely credited with convincing Congress in the summer of 1946 to set up a Federal civilian authority (the Atomic Energy Commission) to control the development of nuclear energy, rather than putting atomic energy under military control, as some proposed.

Similarly, though less spectacularly, numerous organizations of physicians and research scientists were extremely influential in helping shape legislation in the burgeoning fields of public health, medical research and hospital construction. Federal participation in these activities was negligible before World War II, but the Federal Government in fiscal 1971 was expected to spend about $14.9 million in these fields, including Medicare and Medicaid.

A similar development was evident with regard to municipal, state and regional problems. It became commonplace for city, county or state officials or associations to make regular representations to Congress asking Federal help with different problems. Housing, roads, slum clearance, urban redevelopment, area transportation systems, water pollution, sewage plants—all these became the subject of pressure activites by community and state officials and leaders. Before the 1930s, the Federal Government had not involved itself in most of these problems, and it was not until the postwar era that the heaviest pressure activity got under way. Pressure activities on housing and urban problems not only involved public officials from the localities but also commercial builders, real estate interests, transportation companies (e.g., railroads, buses and trucks), citizen groups, banking groups and unions—anybody who stood to gain or lose from the legislation under consideration.

Military-Industrial Complex

Another important pressure factor in the postwar era was the immense increase, as compared with the prewar period before 1940, in the size of the military establishment and in Federal spending for military and space development, hardware, and supporting goods and services. So great was the level of defense spending that whole companies, whole industries and even whole Congressional districts came to depend on Federal contracts for their economic survival or prosperity. The welfare of millions of workers was involved. Large numbers of armed forces procurement officers also were involved.

From this situation there arose a natural alliance between corporations seeking to maintain or enlarge their Federal contracts and officers whose prestige and possible advancement within the military depended on a continued high level of Government spending for the armed services. Labor unions in defense industries and Representatives and Senators representing areas benefiting from Federal spending for military procurement and construction were similarly interested. It was to the mutual advantage of all these participants to keep Government military spending at a high level in their own fields of interest. The alliance of all these groups, sometimes quite conscious and at other times not planned but simply felt as the sum of individual actions and endeavors, produced great pressure on Congress for continuation of high military spending.

In his Jan. 17, 1961, farewell speech, President Eisenhower warned the nation that the power and influence of

---

Eisenhower's Warning

In his final address to the nation as President, Jan. 17, 1961, Dwight D. Eisenhower noted that the United States had been compelled to "create a permanent armaments industry of vast proportions" and to maintain a defense establishment employing 3.5 million persons and spending huge sums. He continued as follows:

"This conjunction of an immense military establishment and a large arms industry is new in American experience. The total influence—economic, political, even spiritual—is felt in every city, every State House, every office of the Federal Government. We recognize the imperative need for this development. Yet we must not fail to comprehend its grave implications. Our toil, resources and livelihood are all involved; so is the very structure of our society.

"In the councils of government, we must guard against the acquisition of unwarranted influence, whether sought or unsought, by the military-industrial complex. The potential for the disastrous rise of misplaced power exists and will persist. We must never let the weight of this combination endanger our liberties or democratic processes. We should take nothing for granted. Only an alert and knowledgeable citizenry can compel the proper meshing of the huge industrial and military machinery of defense with our peaceful methods and goals, so that security and liberty may prosper together."

---

the "military-industrial complex," as he put it, was "felt in every city, every State House, every office of the Federal Government" and posed serious dangers for democratic government. There was little doubt that this meshing, this alliance of military and industrial interests deeply influenced Congressional policies in the postwar era in a variety of ways—not only through direct pressure on many occasions for continuing military spending on one project or another but also by influencing public opinion, Congress and the White House on strategic and related matters.

Veterans

In the period from World War I to World War II, the veterans' bloc, led by the American Legion, the Disabled American Veterans and the Veterans of Foreign Wars, exercised tremendous influence over legislation within its purview. In legislation enacted in 1930, veterans' groups won extension of World War I veterans' disability compensation to veterans who had become disabled since the war, whether or not the disability was service-connected. In 1924, pressure from veterans' groups pushed Congress into overriding President Coolidge's veto of a bill calling for eventual payment of a World War I veterans' bonus. Similar pressure in 1934 caused Congress to override President Roosevelt's veto of a bill restoring certain veterans' benefits which had been curtailed for economy reasons a year earlier. And in 1936, veterans' groups again got Congress to override Mr. Roosevelt and pass a bill requiring immediate payment of the World War I bonus.

After World War II, veterans' groups (still dominated by the American Legion, Disabled American Veterans and

Veterans of Foreign Wars) did not exhibit the same legislative potency. One reason was that they did not have to. An extremely generous program of veterans' benefits enacted by Congress for World War II and Korean War veterans undermined present and future claims that veterans had been mistreated or forgotten, which had been a major argument after earlier wars. Another reason was that in the context of the increasingly complex over-all national problems, veterans' problems seemed less pressing to Congress and the nation than they had been before World War II.

Protectionist Bloc

The high point of high-tariff sentiment in the United States was reached when the 1930 Smoot-Hawley Act imposed the highest tariff barriers in history. It was not long, however, before the Roosevelt Administration began a move away from protectionism with passage of the Trade Agreements Act of 1934. Successive liberalizations of the Trade Agreements Act followed. It became clear in the post-1945 period that protectionist forces, led by the American Tariff League (renamed Trade Relations Council in 1958), though still powerful were not able to regain the strength and influence they had held before 1934. Despite the efforts of this group and some others, the nation never went back to a position of rigorous protectionism and it maintained, on the whole, a favorable attitude toward the lowering of trade barriers.

The reasons for this development were partly ideological, partly practical. The cold war and the national interest in the development of a Western alliance and Western community of nations led to internationalist attitudes and the need for closer ties with Western Europe and other non-Communist areas—ends which would be served, many believed, by a low-tariff policy. At the same time there was a development within the United States of economic interests which would benefit by liberal trade policies—corporations with large investments and subsidiaries overseas which sought access to the American market, and agricultural interests fearing exclusion from overseas markets if the United States pursued a protectionist policy. The upshot was that the business community in the postwar era was far less united than it had been on many occasions in the past in favor of protectionism. This development was illustrated by the appearance in the postwar era of the business-sponsored Committee for Economic Development, which espoused a liberal trade policy, and the formation in 1953 of the business-sponsored, antiprotectionist Committee for a National Trade Policy.

Civil Rights Groups

Another important development in the postwar era was the growth of a strong civil rights bloc. The bloc was concerned mainly with legislation to foster Negro and minority group rights. No similar bloc had existed before World War II, when civil rights was not the great national issue it later became and when pressure on Congress for civil rights legislation was largely nonexistent. The civil rights organizations worked both through grass-roots techniques, designed to influence public opinion throughout the nation, and through direct pressure activities in the nation's capital.

In Washington pressure activities, the leading group was the National Association for the Advancement of Colored People (NAACP), whose Washington operation was headed by Clarence Mitchell. Also active in the capital was Americans for Democratic Action (ADA), founded in 1947 as a citizens' action group by a number of leading liberals. (The ADA was the sparkplug of many important liberal pressure campaigns, not only those involving civil rights.) Other groups active in Washington in favor of civil rights were some of the trade unions, such as the United Automobile Workers and International Union of Electrical, Radio and Machine Workers, and religious groups such as the American Jewish Congress, American Jewish Committee, Anti-Defamation League, National Council of Catholic Men, various Catholic interracial organizations, and, in the later postwar period, the Protestant National Council of Churches.

In 1949, the leading civil rights organizations formed a loose ad hoc grouping called the Leadership Conference on Civil Rights, with about 30 organizations associated. By 1971, the number of associates had risen to more than 125 organizations. The Leadership Conference was not a membership organization with any strict lines of discipline or formal mechanisms for concerted action but simply, as the name implied, a continuing conference where civil rights groups could meet and coordinate activities as the need arose.

The civil rights organizations, as might be expected, had their greatest strength in northern urban areas where there was a heavy proportion of minority groups, and they exerted increasingly heavy pressure for civil rights legislation on Members of Congress from those areas.

In the 1960s, civil rights groups turned to the tactic of mass petition and produced two of the biggest lobby demonstrations ever assembled in the nation's capital— a 1963 "March on Washington for Jobs and Freedom" and a 1968 "Poor People's Campaign." The 1963 demonstration, participated in by more than 200,000 persons, most of them black, gave support to demands for stronger civil rights laws and tougher enforcement of existing laws. It was considered one of the major factors responsible for passage of a strong civil rights bill in 1964. The Poor People's Campaign, during which an estimated 3,000 persons camped near the Lincoln Memorial for 56 days, was less demonstrably effective. The campaign had three major legislative priorities—repeal of welfare restrictions to the 1967 Social Security Act, passage of an emergency employment bill and passage of an Administration housing bill. Only the latter was enacted, and funds for it were reduced.

Toward the end of the decade, the civil rights movement experienced severe fragmentation, with some elements eschewing peaceful petition and turning to violent demonstrations. Partly in response to such "hardline" pressures, traditional civil rights leaders began seeking measures to increase black economic power instead of merely to assure legal rights. A public backlash to the outbursts of violence, however, jeopardized the outlook in Congress for programs of that kind.

Strength of Business Groups

Business groups, taken in the aggregate, probably have been the single most powerful pressure force seeking to influence Congress in recent years. The business

Mass Pressure Demonstrations in Washington

Over the years, some pressure groups that lacked large financial resources have sought to make their pressure felt by staging demonstrations in the nation's capital. This method was particularly popular among civil rights and anti-war groups in the 1960s and early 70s.

The first of these large demonstrations came in 1894, when an army of the unemployed was organized by Jacob S. Coxey to pressure Congress into authorizing a $500,000,000 highway improvement program and interest-free loans to state and local governments to finance public improvements. Coxey's Army set out from Massillon, Ohio; others were soon organized in many parts of the West. The total number of men involved has been estimated at 6,000 to 11,000.

Only about 500 men reached Washington. The District of Columbia police department was greatly enlarged for their arrival and Government buildings were heavily guarded. When Coxey and his men arrived May 1 and started to march into the Capitol grounds the police assaulted the men with clubs. Coxey and two other leaders reached the Senate steps but were arrested and subsequently convicted of trampling the shrubbery and unlawfully displaying banners.

Coxey's Army established camps at various places in and around Washington. They subsisted on donated food and by begging. By mid-July they had been abandoned by most of their leaders. The demonstration ended when the Virginia militia drove the men out of a large encampment on the Virginia side of the Potomac and burned down their camp. The District of Columbia Government then offered to provide transportation to the West, which most accepted.

The Bonus Expeditionary Force. The Bonus Expeditionary Force which marched on Washington in 1932 was much larger than Coxey's Army. An estimated 15,000 men participated.

The Bonus marchers, like Coxey's Army, were the product of a depression era. The specific purpose of the Bonus Expeditionary Force was to pressure Congress into providing immediate payment to World War I veterans of bonus certificates that were scheduled to mature in 1945. Late in 1931 Rep. Wright Patman (D Texas) had introduced a bill to that end.

The Bonus marchers, led by Walter W. Waters, started arriving in Washington at the end of May 1932, three weeks after Patman's bill had been reported out unfavorably by the Ways and Means Committee. Some of the men found shelter in partly razed buildings along Pennsylvania Ave. The main camp of the Bonus marchers was on the Anacostia Flats and consisted of tents and shacks. Food, clothing and other supplies were donated by private individuals and charities.

The House passed the bonus bill June 15 by a 211-176 roll-call vote but it was rejected by the Senate June 17 on an 18-62 roll-call vote. A contemporary journalist described the Senate action as a "rebuke to what some Senators regarded as practically physical intimidation by the bonus marchers."

The Bonus marchers remained in Washington hoping to pressure the Senate into reversing its vote. Congress adjourned on July 16 without reconsidering the bonus bill, but it authorized $100,000 in loans to veterans to enable them to return home. However, an estimated 11,000 people were still in camps a week after Congress had adjourned.

The Bonus Expeditionary Force was finally dispersed by Federal troops on July 28. Troops were called to quell a riot which broke out when the police tried to evict marchers who were camping out in Federally owned buildings. The Federal troops were led by the Army Chief of Staff, General Douglas MacArthur. Major Dwight D. Eisenhower commanded a tank detachment. The marchers were driven towards Anacostia and the encampment there was burned that night. The following day President Hoover said of the marchers, "Government cannot be coerced by mob rule."

1963 March on Washington. On Aug. 28, 1963, about 200,000 persons descended on the capital for a "March on Washington for Jobs and Freedom." Goals of the massive demonstration included stronger civil rights laws and tougher enforcement of existing laws. A massive Federal training program for the unemployed and a broadened minimum wage law also were demanded.

Lafayette Park Camp-in. A group of about 90 unemployed Mississippi Negroes organized a camp-in in Lafayette Park, across from the White House, in April 1966. The campers were protesting delays in processing their application for poverty funds. Four tents were set up in Lafayette Park April 4-7. The demonstrators took turns living in them. They were given a permit by the Department of the Interior.

Poor People's Campaign. Some 3,000 persons, most of them black, camped near the Lincoln Memorial from April 29 through June 23, 1968, in a demonstration for jobs and welfare legislation. Termed the "Poor People's Campaign," the demonstration was dispersed when Federal officials refused to renew the demonstrators' camping permit.

Anti-War Demonstrations. Crowds estimated in the tens of thousands turned out on numerous occasions from 1966 into 1971 to demonstrate for American withdrawal from the war in Vietnam. Pro-war groups also demonstrated, but turnouts were much smaller.

groups tend to take a conservative position on most legislation.

The two leading business organizations—the Chamber of Commerce of the United States and the National Association of Manufacturers—both have been extremely influential and carried on a high level of legislative pressure activities, though both groups contend they are not lobbying organizations subject to the 1946 lobbying law. Numerous other business groups, representing small businessmen, the retail trades, the building trades, banking and transportation interests, have exerted continual or intermittent pressure on Congress. According to Congressional Quarterly's computations of lobby spending reports filed with the Clerk of the House, business organizations as a group have usually spent more on lobbying than labor organizations, citizens' organizations, farm organizations or any other interest grouping.

Investigations of Lobbying

Alleged wrongdoing or excessive influence on the part of pressure groups has led to a number of Congressional investigations of lobbying over the years. Following are the highlights of lobby probes in the modern era:

House and Senate Probes in 1913

The first Congressional probe of lobbying in the present century took place in 1913, after Col. Martin M. Mulhall, lobbyist for the National Association of Manufacturers, had published a sensational account of his activities in a front-page article in the *New York World*. Among other disclosures, Mulhall said he had paid "between $1,500 and $2,000" to Rep. James T. McDermott (D Ill.) for legislative favors.

A four-month inquiry by a select House panel chaired by Majority Leader Finis J. Garrett (D Tenn.) found that many of Mulhall's allegations were exaggerated. The panel definitely established, however, that Mulhall had set up his own office in the Capitol, had paid the chief House page $50 a month for inside information, had received advance information on pending legislation from McDermott and House Republican leader John Dwight, and had influenced the appointment of members to House committees and subcommittees. Six of seven House Members implicated by Mulhall were exonerated, but the panel recommended that McDermott be "strongly censured." The House adopted the panel's recommendations. Although McDermott was not expelled from the House, he resigned the following year.

The Senate also probed lobbying in 1913, at the request of President Woodrow Wilson, who was enraged over alleged lobbying activity by the NAM and other protectionist groups on the Underwood tariff bill. On May 26, 1913, Wilson denounced the presence of an "insidious lobby" which sought to bring on a new tide of protectionism. "I think the public ought to know," he said, "that extraordinary exertions are being made by the lobby in Washington to gain recognition for certain alterations in the tariff bill.... Washington has seldom seen so numerous, so industrious, or so insidious a lobby.... There is every evidence that money without limit is being spent to sustain this lobby.... The Government ought to be relieved from this intolerable burden and the constant interruption to the calm progress of debate."

In the Senate hearings that followed, testimony disclosed that large amounts had been spent for entertainment and for other lobbying purposes both by the interests seeking high tariff duties and by those interested in low duties, such as the sugar refiners. Following the hearings, a bill for registration of lobbyists was introduced, but farm, labor and other special interests succeeded in warding off a vote on it.

Senate Inquiries in 1920s

Interest in lobbying activities was rekindled in the mid-1920s, after the American Legion and other veterans'

groups had succeeded in obtaining passage of a bonus bill over the veto of President Coolidge. In 1927, an investigating committee under Sen. Thaddeus H. Caraway (D Ark.) conducted extensive public hearings and recommended a sweeping registration bill. The bill defined lobbying as "...any effort in influencing Congress upon any matter coming before it, whether it be by distributing literature, appearing before committees of Congress, or seeking to interview members of either the House or Senate." A lobbyist was defined as "...one who shall engage, for pay, to attempt to influence legislation, or to prevent legislation by the national Congress." The bill passed the Senate by a unanimous vote but was pigeonholed by a House Committee.

Despite failure of the Caraway bill, the Senate Judiciary Committee's report on the measure contributed greatly to the public's knowledge of lobbying. The panel asserted that about 90 percent of the 300 to 400 lobbying associations listed in the Washington telephone directory were "fakes" whose aim was to bilk unwary clients. These organizations, according to the Committee report, included groups that purported to represent scientific, agricultural, religious, temperance, and anti-prohibition interests. "In fact," the panel said, "every activity of the human mind has been capitalized by some grafter." The Committee estimated that $99 of every $100 paid to these groups "go into the pockets of the promoters." Caraway himself disclosed that one of the lobbyists had collected $60,000 in one year from business interests by simply writing them every time a bill favorable to business was passed and claiming sole credit for its passage.

The next Congressional probe of lobbying came in 1929, when a Senate Naval Affairs Subcommittee looked into the activities of William B. Shearer, who represented shipping, electrical, metals, machinery and similar concerns interested in blocking limitation of naval armaments and in obtaining larger appropriations for Navy ships. The path to Shearer's exposure had been paved when he filed a suit in the New York courts to recover $257,655, which he said was owed to him by the New York Shipbuilding Co. Shearer claimed the money was due for lobbying services he had performed in Washington and at the Geneva naval limitation conference of 1927.

Testimony before the Subcommittee showed that Shearer had been sent to Geneva by shipbuilding interests and had done everything he could to torpedo an agreement. Following the conference, at which no agreement was reached, Shearer had led industry lobbying efforts for bigger naval appropriations and for subsidies for the merchant marine. His other activities included preparing pro-Navy articles for the Hearst newspaper chain, writing articles for the 1928 Republican Presidential campaign, in which he characterized peace advocates as traitors, and writing speeches for the American Legion and like-minded lobby groups.

Utility and Munitions Lobbies, 1935

A decade of Congressional concern over the influence exerted by private utilities led to a stormy probe of that industry's lobbying activities in 1935. Although Congress nine years earlier had instructed the Federal Trade Commission to investigate utility lobbying, a two-year probe by the FTC had been largely inconclusive.

After intensive lobbying by the utilities had threatened to emasculate an Administration bill to regulate utility holding companies, President Roosevelt in a special message to Congress described the holding companies as "private empires within the nation" and denounced their lobbying techniques. Congressional supporters of the measure demanded an investigation to bring out the lengths to which the power interests' lobbying had gone.

A special investigative panel was set up in the Senate under the chairmanship of Sen. Hugo L. Black (D Ala.), an Administration stalwart who later was to become an Associate Justice of the Supreme Court. Following a sometimes raucous hearing, Black concluded that the utilities had spent about $4 million to defeat the utility bill and had engaged in massive propagandizing to convince the public that the bill was an iniquitous invasion of private rights and a sharp turn toward socialism. Among other findings, Black's panel stated that the utilities had financed thousands of phony telegrams to Congress, in which the names of the senders had been picked at random from telephone books.

Amid a furor over the telegrams, Congress passed the holding company bill, which carried provisions requiring reports to Federal agencies on utility lobbying activities. The Senate also passed a lobbyist-registration bill sponsored by Black; the measure was passed by the House the next year, but it never emerged from conference.

Also in 1935, the Senate again turned its attention to the "munitions lobby," which had been part of the focus of the 1928 Shearer investigation. Sen. Gerald P. Nye (R S.D.), who had led the demand for such a probe, was named chairman of a special seven-member investigating committee. In its report the Committee asserted that the big three naval powers (United States, Great Britain and Japan) had been in collusion on shipbuilding bids, so that there was no real competition either for naval shipbuilding or merchant marine contracts. The Committee majority called for nationalization of defense industries; its recommendations were ignored by the full Senate.

President Roosevelt's continuing concern over concentration of economic power led to another lobby investigation in 1938. The Temporary National Economic Committee, a Congressional panel under the chairmanship of Sen. Joseph C. O'Mahoney (D Wyo.), studied the question but no legislation resulted. Mr. Roosevelt again called for lobby curbs in 1944, denouncing "the pests who swarm through the lobbies of Congress, and the cocktail bars of Washington, representing special groups as opposed to the basic interests of the nation as a whole." Preoccupied with the war, Congress failed to act on the President's proposals.

After the war, however, the Joint Committee on the Organization of Congress recommended passage of a law requiring lobbyists to register with Congress and to report certain financial information. The recommendation was accepted by both houses with only minor modifications. The Federal Regulation of Lobbying Act (Title III of the Legislative Reorganization Act of 1946) became law on Aug. 2, 1946 *(see below)*.

Postwar Lobbying Probes

A House Select Committee on Lobbying Activities headed by Rep. Frank M. Buchanan (D Pa.) investigated the lobbying and related activities of a wide range of organizations in 1950. The Committee's probe had been prompted largely by the assertion of President Truman that the 80th Congress was "the most thoroughly surrounded...with lobbies in the whole history of this great country of ours." Truman said: "There were more lobbyists in Washington, there was more money spent by lobbyists in Washington, than ever before in the history of the United States. It's disgraceful...." Most of the publicity centered on the efforts of the Committee for Constitutional Government to distribute low-cost or free "right-wing" books and pamphlets designed to influence the public. The House Committee made recommendations for strengthening the 1946 Lobbying Act, but there was no action.

Two separate investigations were initiated in 1956 after Sen. Francis Case (R S.D.) disclosed that a lawyer interested in passage of a natural gas bill had offered him a $2,500 campaign contribution in connection with his vote for the bill.

One of the inquiries, conducted by a Select Committee headed by Sen. Walter F. George (D Ga.), was limited to the offer to Case. The month-long probe ended with a report asserting that the contribution did not constitute a direct attempt to bribe the Senator. (Case had rejected the contribution, and there was no suggestion of any wrongdoing on his part.) The report recommended thorough study of the 1946 law, which the Committee called "too vague." The two lawyers involved in the offer to Case, plus their client, the Superior Oil Co., were eventually absolved of bribery charges but pleaded guilty in Federal court to the lesser charge of violating the 1946 Act.

The second inquiry undertaken in 1956 was conducted by a Senate Special Committee charged with probing corrupt practices involving campaign contributions, lobbying and other influences on Congress. The panel was appointed by Vice President Nixon (R) and was chaired by Sen. John L. McClellan (D Ark.).

Following a long investigation, McClellan on May 31, 1957, introduced a new lobbying registration bill designed to replace the 1946 Act. The bill proposed to tighten the existing law by making the Comptroller General responsible for enforcing it (there was no administrator under the 1946 Act); by eliminating a loophole that required registration of only those lobbyists whose "principal purpose" was lobbying; by extending the coverage to anyone who spent $50,000 or more a year on grass-roots lobbying; and by eliminating an exemption which made the law inapplicable to persons who merely testified on proposed legislation.

The bill was vigorously opposed by the Chamber of Commerce of the United States and was criticized on certain points by the National Association of Manufacturers, the Association of American Railroads and the American Medical Association, although the latter endorsed the measure as a whole. The bill did not reach the floor and died with the close of the 85th Congress.

Retired Military Officers and Foreign Agents

Lobbying next attracted Congressional attention in 1959, when the Special Investigations Subcommittee of the House Armed Services Committee held three months of hearings on the employment of former Army, Navy and Air Force officers by defense contractors, and the influence of the retired officers in obtaining government contracts for their new employers. The Subcommittee found that more than 1,400 retired officers with the rank of major or higher—including 261 of general or flag rank—were employed by the top 100 defense contractors.

In its report in 1960, the Subcommittee said that "The coincidence of contracts and personal contacts with firms represented by retired officers and retired civilian officials sometimes raises serious doubts as to the objectivity of these [contract] decisions." Congress largely accepted Subcommittee recommendations for tighter restrictions on "sales" to the Government by former retired personnel.

Lobbying in connection with the Sugar Act of 1962 led the Senate Foreign Relations Committee to vote, July 6, 1962, to launch an investigation of "foreign lobbies" and "the extent to which they attempt to influence United States policies." At the request of Foreign Relations Committee Chairman J. W. Fulbright (D Ark.) and Sen. Paul H. Douglas (D Ill.), the Senate Finance Committee, which had jurisdiction over the sugar bill, had queried sugar lobbyists on their arrangements with their employers, mostly foreign countries. A compendium of the answers, made public June 26, 1962, showed that some payments to the sugar lobbyists were made on the basis of the size of the sugar quotas granted by Congress.

Such contingent fees were denounced by President Kennedy at a July 5 news conference. "I think it is an unfortunate situation," the President said, "when men are paid large fees by foreign governments to secure quotas, and where, in some cases, there are contingency fees. For every ton of sugar they get allocated to their country, they secure a payment of so much. Well now, that is not satisfactory."

Hearings conducted some months later by the Foreign Relations Committee produced evidence that some lobbyists also lobbied their own clients. Fulbright disclosed, for example, that Michael B. Deane, a Washington public relations man who had been hired by the Dominican Sugar Commission to lobby for its interests before Congress, had "apparently filed exaggerated and sometimes inaccurate reports" to the Commission regarding his effectiveness. Deane admitted that he had falsely reported to Commission officials that he had been "invited by the President" to a White House luncheon and had "talked with" the Secretary of Agriculture. Deane said he occasionally gave himself "too much credit," but "one tends to do that a little bit when they have a client who is outside of Washington." Similar testimony was elicited from other sugar lobbyists.

The Fulbright probe continued well into 1963, and at its conclusion, Fulbright introduced a bill to tighten registration requirements under the Foreign Agents Registration Act of 1938 for persons in the United States representing foreign interests. The bill passed the Senate in 1964 but died in the House. It was revived in the 89th Congress and enacted in 1966.

Failure of New Lobby Bill

The Joint Committee on the Organization of Congress reported a strengthened general lobbying bill in 1966 as part of a proposed new Legislative Reorganization Act. The bill, intact with its lobbying provisions, passed the Senate in 1967 but was pigeonholed in the House. No other attempts to revise lobby statutes were

made up to the end of 1970. *(See Appendix for story on 1967 bill.)*

Attack on Farm Bureau

The functions and activities of the American Farm Bureau Federation (AFBF) in 1967 were the subject of a one-man investigation by Rep. Joseph Y. Resnick (D N.Y.), chairman of the House Agriculture Committee's Rural Development Subcommittee. Other members of the Subcommittee disassociated themselves from the investigation, as did the full Committee.

Resnick, a liberal, was attacking the country's largest and most conservative general farm organization. Of 296 organizations which filed lobby spending reports for 1966, the Farm Bureau ranked fifth in the amount of money spent, with $133,944. Resnick charged on the House floor, June 27 and 28, that the Farm Bureau had "not been representing the American farmer" but had "been using him to build one of the largest insurance and financial empires in the United States, an empire...bringing great profit to a select handful of men."

The House Agriculture Committee, by a 27-1 vote on July 12, rebuked Resnick by disassociating itself from the charges he had made against the AFBF. The action by the full Committee stemmed from a resolution offered by the other five Subcommittee members, stating that the Committee "does in no manner endorse, condone or support the personal attack launched" by Resnick against the Farm Bureau.

In a speech on the House floor, James G. O'Hara (D Mich.) described the Committee's action as "unprecedented" and said it set "a dangerous precedent when a subcommittee chairman cannot question the activities of one of the largest lobbies that operates in Congress."

Regulation of Lobbying

Over the years, a patchwork of Federal statutes has set forth the "rules of the game" for Washington lobbyists and pressure groups. These statutes, most of which resulted from the investigations previously discussed, established guidelines indicating which types of pressure activities were permissible and which were not. In some cases, they also required paid lobbyists or parties interested in proposed legislation to register with the Secretary of the Senate, the Clerk of the House, the Securities and Exchange Commission or some other Federal agency before undertaking pressure activities. The statutes are described below. Citations are to the 1964 edition of the U.S. Code.

Antibribery Statute

Attempting to influence a Member of Congress by offering him a bribe has long been a Federal crime. Similarly, it has long been a crime for the Member to accept a bribe. The version of the law in effect as the postwar era opened was first enacted March 4, 1909. This statute was recodified June 25, 1948, in the general law (HR 3190—PL 80-772) recodifying criminal sections of the U.S. Code. In a bill signed Oct. 23, 1962 (HR 8140—PL 87-849), the antibribery statute was revised and somewhat strengthened, as also were some of the conflict-of-interest laws affecting Congressional Members.

Under the 1962 version, any person who offered a Member a bribe in order to influence his actions and any Member who agreed to accept such a bribe could be fined up to $20,000, imprisoned for up to 15 years and disqualified from "holding any office of honor, trust, or profit under the United States."

The language of the statute (18 USC 201) referred to the corrupt offer or acceptance of "anything of value." It was therefore sufficiently broad to cover bribes in whatever form they were offered, not just outright cash payments. Thus, for an individual to offer or a Member to accept a campaign contribution, a future job for himself or a friend or relative, an inside tip on the commodity market or a fee for a speech to an organization—all of which might be perfectly legal where no corrupt intent was involved—would be punishable as bribery if it could be proved that the offer was really a direct attempt to buy the legislator's vote or otherwise influence his official actions. Such proof, however, was extremely difficult to come by.

Pressure Group Spending

A group's effectiveness in pressuring Congress is intimately linked to the financial resources it can commit to a legislative campaign. Important also is the amount it can spend to elect or defeat Congressional candidates favorable to its cause.

In general, there were no Federal laws in the postwar period to restrict spending by individuals, businesses, unions or organizations on pressure activities. However, there were Federal limitations on contributions to political candidates. Details are given below.

Spending for Pressure Activities

Individuals, corporations, unions and others were free to spend their money to maintain paid lobbyists in the national and state capitals. They could make contributions to trade organizations representing their viewpoint. They could finance and distribute circulars, brochures, pamphlets and newspapers designed to influence their own members, stockholders, Members of Congress, state legislators or the public for or against any legislation or bill. They could do the same through radio and television advertisements. They could advertise and publish their general views as well as their views on legislation.

Although pressure spending by private individuals or groups was not restricted by Federal law, there did exist a Federal statute, first passed in 1919, which attempted to restrict pressure on Congress by the Federal Executive Branch. This statute (18 USC 1913) forbade Federal employees and officials from using appropriated funds to lobby Congress on legislation. This provision was not designed to prevent normal Federal employee communications and contacts with Congress in connection with legislative requests by Executive Branch agencies. Rather, it was designed to prevent flagrant spending to manipulate public opinion or to bombard Members of Congress with letters and telegrams from the Executive Branch. In practice the law did not block high officials from publicly advocating legislation and pressuring Congress.

As stated above, there were no Federal laws in effect after World War II which directly restricted private individuals, unions and corporations from spending money to influence public opinion, to lobby legislatures or to carry on other pressure activities. But a Supreme Court decision in 1961 somewhat limited the financial resources upon which railway labor unions could draw for their lobbying and similar activities.

The decision was handed down by a five-member majority in a Railway Labor Act case *(International Assn. of Machinists v. Street)*. The case involved several employees of the Southern Railway System. They contended their rights were being interfered with because, under a union shop contract sanctioned by a 1951 amendment to the Railway Labor Act, they were required to join a union and pay dues, part of which were used to promote legislation and public policies which they opposed.

The Court majority held that the employees had a valid grievance. The Court held that under the 1951 Railway Labor Act provision, the union could not use an employee's dues to support legislation and general public policies to which he objected. As a remedy, it suggested to the lower Federal courts that they order the return to the complaining employees of that portion of their dues which had been used, not for collective bargaining activities, but for legislative and lobbying activities to which the employees objected.

The decision in the *Street* case had certain broad implications regarding the future use of union dues for support of legislative and public opinion activities carried on by unions. However, these implications should not be exaggerated. The following facts should be kept in mind:

1. The 1961 decision applied only to railroad unions and other unions subject to the Railway Labor Act—a relatively small group. The much larger group of unions subject to the Taft-Hartley Act (National Labor Relations Act, as amended) was not affected.

2. The 1961 decision applied only where a union shop contract was in effect under the Railway Labor Act.

3. The decision applied only with regard to that portion of an individual's dues not used for collective bargaining but for legislative and lobbying purposes or similar purposes.

4. The union was barred from spending an individual's dues on legislative and lobbying activities only when the individual objected. In the absence of a specific objection, the union was free to use portions of dues money for lobbying, legislative activities and, where otherwise legal, for political contributions.

Political Spending Restrictions

The promise of electoral support or opposition has been probably the most effective device available to pressure groups in their attempts to influence Congress on legislation. Precisely for this reason, Congress attempted on several occasions to limit campaign contributions made by corporations, organizations and individuals in connection with Federal elections. The limitations were intended to prevent those with great financial resources from using them to dominate the selection of Members of Congress and thereby the legislative decisions of Congress.

Two major sets of Federal laws have long restricted campaign spending and contributions by pressure groups. The first, the Federal Corrupt Practices Act of 1925, strengthened a 1907 ban on campaign contributions by corporations in connection with Federal elections. This prohibition was extended to labor unions temporarily by the 1943 wartime Smith-Connally (War Labor Disputes) Act and permanently by the 1947 Taft-Hartley Act. The Taft-Hartley Act also broadened the prohibition on both corporations and unions.

The second and probably less important set of restrictions was contained in the second Hatch Act, passed in 1940, which (among other things) limited to $5,000 the amount an individual or group could contribute to any one candidate in a single calendar year in connection with any Federal election campaign.

Had either of these restrictions been truly effective, they might well have sealed off unions, businesses and other pressure groups from any major influence over Federal elections and thus undermined their major weapon in Congressional pressure activities. But loopholes in these laws, coupled with lack of clarity about the applicability and constitutionality of the ban on contributions by unions and corporations, left labor, business and other pressure groups numerous ways to continue effective political activity in Federal elections.

Congress, reacting to criticism of $15,000-a-page advertisements in Democratic party political brochures, in 1966 added an amendment to a tax bill prohibiting all tax deductions for the cost of ads in political journals or programs.

Union, Corporation Spending Ban

Under the Taft-Hartley Act, unions and corporations were forbidden to make contributions to or expenditures on behalf of candidates for Federal elective offices. The ban applied not only in connection with Federal elections but also in connection with primaries, conventions and nominating caucuses held to choose candidates for Federal office. However, the prohibition applied only in connection with Federal elective offices and did not apply to state and local elections or primaries, except for one small category of business—namely, national banks and other corporations organized under the authority of Federal laws. This small group was forbidden to contribute or spend in any election, primary, convention or caucus, regardless of whether it was for state, local or Federal office.

At first glance the Taft-Hartley Act appeared to institute a rather full prohibition against union and corporate participation in Federal elections, primaries, caucuses and conventions. But it soon became clear that both unions and business groups had ways of continuing their political activities without violating the law.

The Taft-Hartley Act prohibition actually consisted of two parts: the ban on campaign contributions and the ban on direct expenditures. With regard to the prohibition on campaign contributions, there was no question that such contributions were barred in connection with Federal elections and primaries if proposed to be made from corporate funds or from general union revenues derived from member dues. The ban applied whether the contribution was made directly to a candidate or to some group which used it on his behalf. But there was nothing in the law which stated that business executives or union members were barred from making voluntary contributions from their own personal funds to candidates for Federal office.

Consequently, business leaders used informal techniques to organize voluntary, personal political giving by businessmen. In some cases, they organized noncorporate associations to solicit businessmen for personal contributions to candidates for Federal office. In others, business executives made the rounds of their co-executives and associates to ask them for personal contributions on behalf of a particular candidate.

In some cases, reportedly, businesses adopted the practice of giving selected employees bonuses, ostensibly for good work, but actually with the tacit understanding that all or part of the bonus would be used to make a "personal" contribution to a particular candidate for Federal office. This bonus practice was illegal, since it was a device to channel corporate funds into Federal political campaigns, but it was extremely difficult to discover and prosecute.

Labor unions developed techniques of their own. The unions set up separate political arms which were technically not labor unions and which received funds not from dues money but from voluntary contributions made by union members. These groups, the best known of which was the AFL-CIO's Committee on Political Education (COPE), were, in effect, simply voluntary political organizations and were not subject to the Taft-Hartley Act prohibition against political contributions by unions in Federal elections. COPE and similar groups were free to make campaign contributions in connection with Federal elections, primaries, conventions and caucuses.

With regard to the second part of the Taft-Hartley prohibition, which barred direct expenditures by corporations and unions in connection with Federal elections, "leakages" developed there too. The reason was, in part, that the ban on direct expenditures had to be construed narrowly lest it run afoul of the guarantees of freedom of speech contained in the First Amendment to the U. S. Constitution. In the years following the Taft-Hartley Act, a long list of expenditures in Federal elections came to be accepted as permissible for corporations and unions.

To begin with, voluntary organizations of businessmen or union members, like COPE, which were not technically corporations nor unions and which were financed by voluntary, personal contributions rather than by corporate funds or union dues money, were not subject to the Taft-Hartley ban on direct expenditures—just as they were not subject to the ban on campaign contributions. Such voluntary organizations were free to purchase advertisements backing a particular candidate in a Federal campaign, to spend money for rallies and to hire political organizers.

In addition, certain expenditures were permitted for corporations and unions even if made directly with corporate funds or union dues money. Following were some of the major types of direct spending and their apparent legal status as of 1970:

General Propaganda. The Taft-Hartley Act prohibition applied only in connection with attempts to aid candidates or parties in Federal elections and primaries. It therefore did not prevent unions and corporations from using dues money and corporate funds to propagandize the public or their own members or stockholders on issues or in favor of legislation. There were, in fact, no Federal laws in operation which restricted this kind of spending.

Nonpartisan Activities. Spending of union dues and corporate funds for nonpartisan activities in connection with Federal elections was permitted. Thus, spending for voter registration drives and get-out-the-vote drives was permitted, provided the drives did not deliberately concentrate on lists of potential voters provided by one party. A union, for example, was free to carry out a get-out-the-vote drive in a neighborhood which it guessed would produce a heavy vote in favor of the Congressional candidate the union favored; but it was not free to send canvassers out to visit only registered Democrats in order to make sure they went to the polls.

Partisan Activities. Even certain types of partisan political activities in Federal elections were permitted to be financed by union dues and corporate funds. In the leading and, in fact, only major Supreme Court decision on this issue, *U.S. v. CIO* (1948), the Supreme Court ruled unanimously that a union could use its union newspaper to endorse a candidate for Congress without violating the Taft-Hartley Act ban on union expenditures in connection with Federal elections. The key factor in the decision was the Court's holding that the union had the right to advise its own members on the merits or failings of candidates for Federal elective offices. The Court indicated that if the Taft-Hartley Act ban should purport to block a union from advising its members on a candidate's merits, then the "gravest doubt would arise in our minds as to its constitutionality."

As a result of this decision, the rule appeared to be established that both corporations and unions were free to use their own funds for circulars, letters and union newspapers which urged their stockholders or members to support or vote for this or that candidate in a Federal election, primary, convention or nominating caucus. The Taft-Hartley Act ban, in effect, was construed as being inapplicable to this type of activity.

However, two other types of direct political activities by unions and corporations using their own funds were generally considered to be forbidden by the Taft-Hartley Act ban, although these two types of activities have not been ruled on by the Supreme Court.

The two forbidden activites:

(A) Using union dues or corporate funds to buy advertisements or broadcast time or to send out letters or circulars designed to persuade the general public to support a specific party or candidate for Federal elective office.

(B) Using union dues or corporate funds to pay a union or corporate employee (or anyone else) for time spent or expenses incurred while working for a candidate or party in a Federal election, primary, caucus or convention. A union or corporate employee was free to work on his own time for a candidate in a Federal election, but not during time for which he was being paid by the union or corporation.

Hatch Act Limitation

The second Hatch Act, passed in 1940, limited to $5,000 per calendar year the aggregate of contributions that any one individual or group could make to any one candidate in a Federal election or nomination campaign. However, it did not apply to labor unions and corporations as such, since these groups were subject to the far more drastic controls in the Federal Corrupt Practices Act, as amended by the Smith-Connally and Taft-Hartley Acts, which barred unions and corporations from making any campaign contributions directly from union dues or corporate funds in connection with Federal elections.

The $5,000 Hatch Act limitation applied to giving by individuals, political groups and other organized groups. It applied to the special political groups (like COPE), set up by labor organizations and financed with voluntary contributions from labor union members, which were not subject to the Taft-Hartley Act ban on direct campaign contributions by unions in Federal elections.

The $5,000 limitation did help to prevent massive spending in small areas by political and pressure organizations. But it was vitiated by several glaring loopholes. The $5,000 limitation did not prevent an individual, his wife, his children and other relatives from giving $5,000 each to the same candidate. Nor did it prevent a single wealthy individual from making contributions of $5,000 each to as many different candidates and political committees as he wished.

On Feb. 3, 1957, the Senate Rules and Administration Privileges and Elections Subcommittee issued a report on its investigation of campaign contributions and spending in the 1956 Federal elections. The Subcommittee, often called the Gore Committee after Chairman Albert Gore (D Tenn.), analyzed written reports on campaign contributions which certain individuals and groups were required to file with the Clerk of the House and Secretary of the Senate under the Federal Corrupt Practices Act.

The Subcommittee found that among persons contributing $500 or more were members of 12 selected families who had contributed over $1 million to Republicans and $107,000 to Democrats; the DuPont, Pew, Rockefeller, Whitney and Mellon families were the leaders. Officials of the largest 25 corporations had contributed $1.8 million to Republicans and $103,000 to Democrats. Labor groups (of the COPE type) had contributed over $1 million to Democrats, only $3,925 to Republicans.

This spending enabled business and labor groups to maintain the threat of political retaliation to backstop their efforts to win from Congress legislation they favored. Moreover, there appeared to be grounds for believing that, in addition to the lawful devices used by business and labor to continue making campaign contributions and expenditures in Federal elections, many illegal but hard-to-stop devices also were used: Campaign activities were carried out by corporation employees and union officials during their regular work time, while they were being paid by the corporation or union. Personal expenses like travel costs, meals, hotel bills in connection with such activities were paid by the union or corporation. The bonus method of channeling corporate funds into campaign contributions was used. Individuals who wished to contribute more than $5,000 to a single Federal candidate gave the additional amounts to friends who then contributed it in their own names. Covert and unrecorded payments were made which were not in accord with the law.

Tax Deductions for Lobbying

Under a 1919 regulation by the Internal Revenue Service interpreting Federal tax laws, money spent by businesses or individuals for lobbying purposes was not deductible from taxable income. The application of the regulation led to protests by businesses and several attempts to upset the regulation. Finally, in the omnibus tax bill of 1962 (HR 10650—PL 87-834), Congress authorized Federal income tax deductions for sums of money spent for lobbying purposes. The authorization permitted a business to deduct the cost of lobbying for legislation—whether Federal, state or local legislatures were involved—if the legislation was of direct interest to the taxpayer concerned. The company's interest had to be truly direct (e.g., tax or labor legislation affecting it) and not remote and speculative. Lobbying for a Presidential disability amendment, for example, was considered remote and therefore not deductible. Deductions were made permissible for any otherwise legal type of direct contact with a legislative body designed to influence the public. Under the legislation, a business could also deduct any portion of the dues it paid to a trade organization or chamber of commerce allocable to lobbying, and an individual union member could deduct union dues allocable to lobbying purposes.

Lobby Spending Reports

Under terms of the 1946 Federal Regulation of Lobbying Act, persons employed for the "principal purpose" of lobbying Congress were required to file financial reports with the Clerk of the House and the Secretary of the Senate. Because of loopholes in the Act, however, the reports filed were scarcely an indication of the amounts spent on lobbying. The largest annual total ever reported for lobby spending was $10,319,671 in 1950. A House investigating committee reported that year that "the business of influencing legislation is a billion-dollar industry."

One of the loopholes in the lobby law results from its vague language on who is to file, what information is to be included and who is to ensure enforcement. Some organizations, after filing reports for the first few years after 1946, stopped reporting on the ground that lobbying was not their "principal purpose." Others, such as the Chamber of Commerce of the United States and the National Association of Manufacturers, filed reports but did so under protest, contending that they were not covered under their interpretations of the Act. Many groups engaged primarily in grass-roots lobbying filed for a time but stopped after the Supreme Court ruled in the *Harriss* decision in 1954 that grass-roots activities were not covered unless the organization, in effect, urged the public to contact Congress on legislation. Some groups that filed began subtracting the amounts they spent on their grass-roots work. For example, the Chamber of Commerce of the United States reportedly spends, but does not report, about $3 million a year on grass-roots lobbying activities.

Loopholes in the filing and recording procedures have come to light over the years. Congressional Quarterly learned in 1967 that spending not reported exactly according to prescribed rules is left out when spending reports are printed in the *Congressional Record*, the source used by CQ in compiling spending reports. Thus, if a lobby group staples an accounting of its receipts and expenditures to the lobby reporting form instead of entering the figures in the appropriate places on the form, the stapled material is omitted from the *Record's* compilation.

The House Clerk does nothing to the forms except to acknowledge their receipt, place them in order and send them on to the Joint Congressional Committee on Printing. The Committee uses only the figures appearing on the official form in preparing the material sent to the Government Printing Office for printing. Attachments are removed. If a lobbyist fills in amounts for various categories of lobby spending (public relations, office overhead, etc.) but fails to add these up and fill in the space where the total belongs, the Joint Committee disregards these figures.

In the years since 1950, the amounts reported for lobby spending have declined sharply. The total dropped from the 1950 level of over $10 million to $4.8 million by 1952, and remained between $4 million and $4.5 million in most of the succeeding years. After the reported spending fell below $5 million in 1952, the only year in which it rose above that amount was 1965, when heavy outlays by the American Medical Association ($1.1 million) for lobbying against the Medicare bill pushed the total to $5.5 million.

The only Congressional study of lobby spending since passage of the 1946 Act came in 1950. In May of that year, the House Select Committee on Lobbying Activities, chaired by Rep. Frank M. Buchanan (D Pa.), sent questionnaires to 173 large corporations, requesting information on their lobby spending. The spending reports on file with Congress showed that only 38 of these corporations had reported lobby spending since passage of the Act and that the total amount they reported in the period from Jan. 1, 1947, to June 30, 1950, was only $776,446. After the returns came in from all except 22 of the 178 corporations, the Committee majority found that a total of $32,124,835 had been spent for activities which it considered lobbying under its interpretation of the Act. On the basis of these figures, the panel made the projection that lobbying was a "billion-dollar business."

Antitrust Action Against Lobbying

An attempt to use the Federal antitrust laws to restrain lobbying activities failed in 1961 when the U.S. Supreme Court held the antitrust laws inapplicable to campaigns for or against legislation. In the case of *Noerr v. Eastern Railroad Presidents' Conference*, the Supreme Court held unanimously, Feb. 21, 1961, that attempts by any group to obtain legislation harmful to a competitor could not be considered a conspiracy in restraint of trade or any other violation of the Federal antitrust laws. The Court, speaking through Justice Hugo L. Black, said that because of the importance of the right to petition in the U.S. constitutional system, the Federal antitrust laws could not be construed as outlawing action that was genuinely aimed at securing legislation—even if the legislation would injure a competitor and reduce competition, even if the legislative campaign had the effect of injuring the competitor's reputation and business or even if the publicity used in the legislative campaign was not wholly ethical.

The *Noerr* case decision appeared to seal off permanently any possibility of using the Federal antitrust laws to restrain lobbying campaigns for or against legislation, whether conducted at the Federal, state or local level and whether conducted through direct contacts with legislators or by grass-roots methods.

The *Noerr* case arose in 1953 when 41 Pennsylvania truck operators and the Pennsylvania Motor Truck Association brought suit against 24 railroads associated in the Eastern Railroad Presidents' Conference. The truckers alleged that the railroads had engaged the Carl Byoir public relations firm to conduct a publicity campaign against truckers designed to foster adoption and retention of laws and law enforcement policies destructive of the trucking industry. The real motive, it was alleged, was to destroy the trucking industry as a competitor of the railroads in the long-haul freight business. It was alleged that the Byoir agency had, among other things, "planted" antitrucker editorials and articles in newspapers and magazines, helped to create supposedly spontaneous grass-roots citizens' organizations, which called for antitrucker legislation, conducted public opinion polls with questions loaded against the trucking industry and publicized the results as if they were unbiased findings. These tactics, it was asserted, resulted in a number of state actions injurious to the trucking industry, including Pennsylvania Gov. John S. Fine's (R) 1951 veto of a state "fair-truck" bill which would have permitted heavier loads on Pennsylvania highways. The truckers contended that this campaign, which, it came out in the original trial, cost the railroads over $350,000, violated the Federal antitrust laws.

A lower court decision on Oct. 10, 1957, by Federal Judge Thomas J. Clary upheld the truckers' position. Judge Clary conceded that legitimate lobbying activities and efforts to influence public opinion were not actionable under the antitrust laws, but he held that in this case the antitrust laws did apply because the objective of the railroad campaign was to destroy competition in the long-haul freight industry, the methods used to secure legislation were deceitful and the result had been to destroy the trucking industry's good will with the public. When the case reached the Supreme Court in 1961, however, it reversed the lower court, holding that the antitrust laws could not be construed as intended to permit injunctions or damage suits in a campaign involving a genuine attempt to obtain legislation, even where the campaign and the legislation sought would be injurious to a particular group.

Lobbyist Registration Laws

As previously indicated, Congress has always been reluctant to curb legislative pressure activities by individuals, groups or paid lobbyists, in large measure because it feared restrictions would interfere with constitutionally guaranteed rights of free speech and petition. The preservation of such rights has always been considered far more important than doing away with lobbying abuses.

In order to block lobbying abuses without imposing direct restrictions on activities permitted to lobbyists and pressure groups, Congress has resorted to laws requiring registration and/or financial reporting by lobbyists operating on the national scene. Attempts to enact such laws were made on several occasions early in the 20th century, but it was not until 1935-36 that the first lobbyist registration laws were passed; and they were only of limited application (utilities and maritime fields only). In the same years, 1935-36, both the House and Senate passed general lobbyist registration laws, but there was no final action. In 1946, Congress finally passed a general lobbyist registration and reporting statute. All the lobbyist registration laws had the objective of forcing individuals seeking to influence legislation (or administrative

Annual Registration, Spending Totals

The total number of persons registering as lobbyists and the total of all reported spending by organizations under the 1946 Federal Regulation of Lobbying Act are shown below. Registration figures, prior to 1964, are computed on a calendar year basis. Since 1964, the adjournment of Congress has marked the end of each year's total. Spending figures computed by the Buchanan Committee, which investigated lobbying in 1950 and which had access to certain spending reports (those filed late or not published in the *Congressional Record*) not available to Congressional Quarterly, are shown in the middle column. The Buchanan group calculations were published in the Committee's final report Jan. 1, 1951 (H Rept 3239, 81st Congress, 2nd Session).

| | | Spending Reported for Year | |
Covered	Registra-tions	Buchanan Calculations	Congressional Quarterly Calculations
1946*	222	$ 2,297,281	
1947	731	$ 6,969,897	$ 5,191,856
1948	447	$ 7,844,669	$ 6,763,480
1949	599	$10,319,671	$ 7,969,710
1950	430		$10,303,204
1951	342		$ 8,771,097
1952	204		$ 4,823,981
1953	296		$ 4,445,841
1954	413		$ 4,286,158
1955	383		$ 4,365,843
1956	347		$ 3,957,120
1957	392		$ 3,818,177
1958	337		$ 4,132,719
1959	393		$ 4,281,468
1960	236		$ 3,854,374
1961	365		$ 3,986,095
1962	375		$ 4,211,304
1963	384		$ 4,223,605
1964	255		$ 4,223,277
1965	450		$ 5,484,413
1966	332		$ 4,656,872
1967	449		$ 4,751,145
1968	266		$ 4,298,387
1969	647		$ 5,114,709

Law effective Aug. 2, 1946, and registrations and reports cover period from then to end of year only.

actions) to disclose whom they represented and what their real interests were.

A brief description of the various lobbyist registration laws follows. Citations are to the 1964 edition of the U.S. Code.

Utilities Holding Company Act

Section 12(i) of the Public Utilities Holding Company Act of 1935 required anyone employed or retained by a registered holding company or a subsidiary to file certain information with the Securities and Exchange Commission before attempting to influence Congress, the Federal Power Commission or the Securities and Exchange Commission on any legislative or administrative matter affect-

---

Registration, Reporting Requirements

The 1946 Federal Regulation of Lobbying Act made a distinction between paid lobbyists (usually individuals or public relations or law firms) and organizations which carried on lobbying.

Any person (or group) that met the general coverage tests of the 1946 law as set forth in Section 307 and who hired himself out for pay as a lobbyist for someone else was required (1) to register as a lobbyist with the House Clerk and Senate Secretary, and (2) to file quarterly reports with the House Clerk and Senate Secretary on his receipts and expenditures for lobbying. Paid lobbyists of this type were covered by Section 308 of the 1946 law.

On the other hand, organizations that met the general coverage tests in Section 307 but which did not hire themselves out as lobbyists for someone else were not required to register as organizations (although some chose to do so). But they were required to file quarterly reports with the House Clerk on their receipts and expenditures for lobbying. They were governed by Section 305.

---

ing any registered companies. Information required to be filed included a statement of the subject matter in which the individual was interested, the nature of his employment, and the nature of his compensation.

This provision of the 1935 Act, 15 USC 79 1(i), remained in effect from 1935 on.

Merchant Marine Act

Section 807 of the Merchant Marine Act of 1936 required any persons employed by or representing firms affected by various Federal shipping laws to file certain information with the Secretary of Commerce before attempting to influence Congress, the Commerce Department and certain Federal shipping agencies on shipping legislation or administrative decisions. The information included a statement of the subject matter in which the person was interested, the nature of his employment and the amount of his compensation.

Foreign Agents Registration Act

The Foreign Agents Registration Act of 1938, as amended, required registration with the Justice Department of anyone in the United States representing a foreign government or principal. Exceptions from the registration requirement were allowed for purely commercial groups and certain other categories. The Act brought to public view many groups, individuals and associations that, while not necessarily engaged in lobbying Congress directly, carried on propaganda activities which might ultimately affect Congressional legislation and national policy. The Foreign Agents Registration Act was amended frequently following its passage in 1938—for example, in 1939, 1942, 1946, 1950, 1956, 1961 and 1966—without changing its broad purposes. From 1950 on, the Justice Department followed the practice of reporting annually to Congress, in the form of a booklet listing registrants under the Act and their receipts and the names of the foreign principals of registrants.

Federal Regulation of Lobbying Act

In 1946, Congress passed the first and only general lobbyist registration law. The measure, called the Federal Regulation of Lobbying Act, was actually passed as part of the Legislative Reorganization Act of 1946 (S 2177—PL 79-601). The lobbying provisions prompted little debate at the time. The Federal Regulation of Lobbying Act was never subsequently amended and only four sets of prosecutions had been brought for violations through 1970.

The 1946 Act did not in any way directly restrict the activities of lobbyists. It simply required any person who was hired by someone else for the principal purpose of lobbying Congress to register with the Secretary of the Senate and Clerk of the House and file certain quarterly financial reports so that his activities would be known to Congress and the public. Organizations which solicited or received money for the principal purpose of lobbying Congress did not necessarily have to register, but they did have to file quarterly spending reports with the Clerk detailing how much they spent to influence legislation. In 1954, in the *Harriss* case, the Supreme Court, 5-3, upheld the constitutionality of the 1946 lobbyist law. *(See Appendix for text of Court opinion and dissenting views.)*

The Court said that the law applied only to groups and individuals which collected or received money for the principal purpose of influencing legislation through direct contacts with Members of Congress. This interpretation, based upon the Court's reading of the legislative history, contained several major loopholes or vague areas permitting various organizations and individuals to avoid registering and/or reporting on spending under the 1946 law.

The first loophole involved collection or receipt of money. Under the language of the law as interpreted by the Court, groups or individuals that merely spent money out of their own funds to finance activities designed to influence legislation apparently were not covered by the law unless they also solicited, collected or received money for that purpose.

The second involved the term "principal purpose." A number of organizations argued that since influencing Congress was not the principal purpose for which they collected or received money, they were not covered by the law regardless of what kind of activities they carried on. This argument was used by both the National Association of Manufacturers and the Chamber of Commerce of the United States as a basis for refusal to report any spending as an organization under the lobbyist law. The lobbyists for these groups personally reported their spending, but they did so under protest.

Still a third loophole, if in this case it might be called one, was the Court's holding that an organization or individual was not covered unless the method used to influence Congress contemplated some direct contact with Members. The significance of this interpretation was that individuals or groups whose activities were confined to influencing the public on legislation or issues (so-called "grass-roots" lobbying) were not subject to the 1946 law.

A fourth weakness in the law was that it left vague precisely what kind of contacts with Congress constituted lobbying subject to the law's reporting and registration requirements. The language of the law itself specifically exempted testimony before a Congressional committee, and in 1950, in the Slaughter case, a lower Federal court held that this exemption applied also to those helping to prepare the testimony. Other direct contacts presumably were covered, but a whole gray area soon emerged, with some groups contending that their contacts with Members of Congress were informational and could not be considered lobbying subject to the law.

Still a fifth weakness was that the law left it up to each group or lobbyist to determine, more or less for himself, what portion of his total expenditures need be reported as spending for lobbying. As a result, some organizations whose budgets for their Washington, D.C., operation ran into the hundreds of thousands of dollars reported only very small amounts for spending on lobbying activities, contending that the remainder of their spending was for general public information purposes, research and other matters. Other organizations, interpreting the law quite differently, reported a much larger percentage of their total budgets as being for lobbying. The result was that some groups which year after year reported a large portion of their budgets gained reputations as "big lobby spenders" when, in fact, they simply were reporting more honestly and fully, at least under a different view of the law, in comparison with other groups spending just as much.

Another weakness in the lobbying law was that it applied only to attempts to influence Congress, not administrative agencies or the Executive Branch where a considerable amount of legislation was generated which was later enacted by Congress, and where many decisions and regulations similar to legislation were put into effect under administrative rule-making and quasi-judicial powers.

Finally, reinforcing all the other weaknesses was the fact that the 1946 law did not designate anyone to investigate the truthfulness of lobbying registrations and reports and to seek enforcement. The Clerk of the House and Secretary of the Senate were to receive registrations and reports but were not directed or empowered to investigate reports or to compel anyone to register. Since violation of the law was made a crime, the Justice Department had power to prosecute violators, but no mandate was given it to investigate reports. In fact, the Justice Department eventually adopted a policy of investigating only when it received complaints and brought only four prosecutions (some involving several individuals) from 1946-70.

Despite the many loopholes and despite the absence of any active enforcement agent, many groups and individuals which might have contested or evaded their obligation to register or report as lobbyists voluntarily did so.

Nevertheless, the inadequacies and vagueness of the law reduced its effectiveness in presenting to Congress and the nation a true picture of what lobbyists and pressure groups were doing and spending in the nation's capital. The registrations and quarterly spending reports gave an incomplete and in some cases quite distorted picture.

These problems led to many proposals, from time to time, both to close the loopholes in the existing law and possibly to impose some direct curbs on the types of lobbying activities that were permissible. But no amendments to the 1946 lobbying law were enacted through 1970.

Bibliography

Books

Bolling, Richard, *House Out of Order*. E. P. Dutton Co., 1965.

Cater, Douglass, *Power in Washington*. Random House, 1964.

Chase, Stuart, *Democracy Under Pressure*. Greenwood Press, 1945.

Crawford, Kenneth G., *The Pressure Boys*. Julian Messner Inc., 1939.

Deakin, James, *The Lobbyists*. Public Affairs Press, 1966.

Dexter, Lewis Anthony, *How Organizations Are Represented in Washington*. Bobbs-Merrill, 1969.

Harriss, Joseph P., *Congress and the Legislative Process*. McGraw Hill, 1963.

Key, V. O., *Politics, Parties and Pressure Groups*, 5th ed. Thomas Y. Crowell Co., 1964.

Koenig, Louis W., *The Invisible Presidency*. Rinehart and Co., Inc., 1960.

MacNeil, Neil, *Forge of Democracy*. David McKay Co., 1963.

Milbrath, Lester W., *The Washington Lobbyists*. Rand McNally Co., 1963.

Poore, Ben Perley, *Perley's Reminiscences of Sixty Years in the National Metropolis*, Vol. II. W. A. Houghton, 1886.

Schlesinger, Arthur M. Jr., *The Age of Jackson*. Little, Brown and Co., 1945.

Shriftgiesser, Karl, *The Lobbyists*. Little, Brown and Co., 1951.

Smith, Merriman, *The Good New Days*. Bobbs-Merrill, 1962.

Truman, David B., *The Governmental Process*, 10th ed. Alfred A. Knopf, 1964.

Articles

Boeckel, Richard, "Regulation of Congressional Lobbies," *Editorial Research Reports*, March 7, 1928, pp. 207-234.

Brewer, F. M., "Congressional Lobbying," *Editorial Research Reports*, May 8, 1946, pp. 314-333.

Celler, Emanuel, "Pressure Groups in Congress," *Annals of the American Academy of Political and Social Science*, September 1958.

Matthews, Donald R., "Senators and Lobbyists," *Congressional Reform*, Joseph Clark ed. Thomas Y. Crowell Co., 1965.

Government Publications

General Interim Report, Select Committee on Lobbying Activities, U.S. House of Representatives, 81st Congress, 2nd session, 1950.

"Lobbying, Direct and Indirect," Hearings, Part 6, Select Committee on Lobbying Activities, U.S. House of Representatives, 81st Congress, 2nd session, 1950.

"The Role of Lobbying in Representative Self-Government," Hearings, Part 1, Select Committee on Lobbying Activities, U.S. House of Representatives, 81st Congress, 2nd session, 1950.

The Executive Branch

THE INFLUENCE of the Washington lobbies on legislation pales beside that of the Executive Branch, particularly the Presidency. Because of the vast powers and prestige of his office, the President has an array of methods at his disposal for securing his legislative aims. He may use his easy access to the news media to mobilize public opinion behind important Administration bills. He may sway some Members' votes by an appeal to party loyalty, or in the case of foreign policy or national security matters, by an appeal to bipartisanship. Other Members may be influenced by hints of Federal jobs and contracts for their constituents or by plain indications that such favors will be withheld if they fail to go along. In the event that Congress pushes a measure the President opposes, he may be able to bottle it up by threatening a veto. Modern Presidents have tended to engage in pressure activities to such an extent that few major bills now emerge from Congress without some degree of Presidential support or at least Presidential acquiescence.

President As Legislative Leader

Although the President's legislative role has always been important, the growing complexity of running the Government has put him at the center of the legislative process. Political scientist Lawrence H. Chamberlain has observed that "When so much of the life of the individual is influenced by Federal legislation, the attitude of the President toward this legislation and his skill in gaining legislative approval of his proposals are matters of practical interest to millions of people...." Former Congressional staff aide Bertram M. Gross has asserted that the President now has become "the most important single legislative leader in the Government." Except in wartime, he believes, "Presidents are judged more by the quality of legislation they propose or succeed in getting enacted than by their record as Executive."

The President's role as legislative leader derives, at least in part, from the Constitution. While the Constitution vests "all legislative powers" in Congress, it also directs the President to "give to the Congress information of the state of the union and recommend to their consideration such measures as he shall judge necessary and expedient." Congress has broadened this function to direct the President to present to Congress each year, in addition to his State of the Union Message, two other general statements of Presidential aims—an Economic Report including proposals directed to the maintenance of maximum employment, and a Budget Message outlining appropriations proposals. During a typical session, the President transmits to Congress scores of other legislative proposals, some on his own initiative and others in conformity with various statutes.

Presidents in recent years have sought to strengthen their legislative activities by establishing "legislative liaison" offices in the various Federal agencies and by designating White House officials as full-time lobbyists to coordinate the Administration's pressure efforts. These officials help the President put heat on Congress and inform him of any obstacles that lie in the path of important Administration bills. Pointing to the emphasis that Presidents now place on direction of this far-flung lobbying apparatus, journalist Neil MacNeil observed in 1963 that the President had become "the chief advocate, the chief lobbyist and the chief legislator of the United States."

Evolution of Presidential Pressures

The hope of strict constructionists that the Executive Branch would remain aloof from Congress was dashed almost at the beginning of the American Republic. Although President Washington carefully avoided pressuring Congress, his chief assistants, Secretary of the Treasury Alexander Hamilton and Secretary of State Thomas Jefferson, had no such scruples. In the House, where the great debates of the day were conducted, Hamilton became so influential on fiscal matters that the chamber established its Ways and Means Committee as a buffer against his pressures. As President, Jefferson held effective control over Congress through influence over his (Democratic Republican) party's Congressional leadership apparatus. Among the landmark events of his term was ratification of the treaty for the Louisiana Purchase—the most significant territorial expansion in American history.

Other early Presidents varied considerably in their approach to the Legislative Branch. The years between Jefferson and Andrew Jackson were not marked by notable instances of executive attempts to pressure Congress. But Jackson, elected in 1828, clashed with Congress repeatedly when he sought to enlarge executive power and make the Presidency responsive to the masses. He vetoed

---

Reference

See Appendix table of contents (first thumb tab) for comments on Executive lobbying by Lawrence F. O'Brien, chairman of the Democratic National Committee.

numerous bills pushed through by special interests and appealed successfully to the public to ensure that the vetoes were sustained. Another forceful President, Abraham Lincoln, found himself on the defensive with Congress, mostly over his conduct of the Civil War. But because of his effective manipulation of public opinion, Lincoln was able for the most part to maintain the upper hand.

For several decades after Lincoln, Congress dominated the Government. As late as 1893, one Washington correspondent, Theron Crawford, wrote: "No one has apparently less influence on Congressional legislation than the President of the United States. His message is treated always as a perfunctory document and while it is regularly and respectfully referred to the proper committees for consideration, it is very rare that any suggestion made by the Executive has any practical result."

Leadership of T. Roosevelt and Wilson

The pendulum swung back toward the Executive at the outset of the 20th century, when President Theodore Roosevelt asked Congress to approve a far-reaching legislative program. This reform package, which Roosevelt called the "Square Deal," was the first formalized Presidential program ever submitted to Congress. (In the past, such programs normally had been submitted by the Speaker of the House, as in the case of Henry Clay's American Plan, a broad program of internal improvements and tariff protection.) Major bills passed at Roosevelt's request included some of the nation's basic conservation and railroad legislation.

The next President to seek a broad legislative program was Woodrow Wilson, who was attracted by the British parliamentary system and thought the country needed a leader like the British Prime Minister, who would be responsible for the enactment of his party's legislative program. Outlining this philosophy, Wilson said in a speech in 1913: "(The President) is expected by the nation to be the leader of his party as well as the chief executive officer of the Government, and the country will take no excuses from him. He must play the part and play it successfully, or lose the country's confidence. He must be Prime Minister, as much concerned with the guidance of legislation as with the just and orderly execution...."

Wilson won passage of broad tariff reforms, legislation reforming the nation's banking system through creation of the Federal Reserve System, a series of statutes strengthening the Sherman Antitrust Act, and a number of other important measures. His record was shattered only by the advent of World War I and the postwar refusal of a hostile Republican Senate to ratify the Treaty of Versailles, which embodied his cherished League of Nations proposal.

Franklin Roosevelt's One Hundred Days

A President even more adept than Wilson at pushing his program through Congress was Franklin D. Roosevelt, whose first 100 days in the White House have no counterpart in U.S. history. Like Wilson, Roosevelt considered the Presidency a sort of Prime Ministership. "The Presidency is not merely an administrative office," he observed during the 1932 campaign. "That is the least of it.... It is preeminently a place of moral leadership...."

Roosevelt scored his first major legislative victory within days after taking office, when he appeared before Congress to ask special powers to ward off the threat of a nationwide banking panic. "In the event that the Congress shall fail to take these courses," he said, "and in the event the national emergency is still critical, I shall not evade the clear course of duty that will then confront me. I shall ask Congress for the one remaining instrument to meet the crisis—broad executive power to wage a war against the emergency as great as the power that would be given me if we were in fact invaded by a foreign foe." The requested powers were granted that day; they were even supported by the Republican Minority Leader, who declared that "The house is burning down, and the President of the United States says this is the way to put out the fire."

Congress went on, in the spring of 1933, to approve a flood of Administration proposals, scarcely pausing to change as much as a comma. At the time, the President's program became known as the "Roosevelt Revolution," but the President said he preferred the term "New Deal." In the first 100 days alone, Congress approved the bank reorganization bill, authority to cut Government operating expenses by 25 percent, a farm relief bill, a massive public works program, relief grants to the states, establishment of a Civilian Conservation Corps, and other important measures. Although the going got much tougher in subsequent sessions of Congress, Roosevelt still won enactment of such landmark measures as the Trade Agreements Act, the Social Security Act, the Public Utilities Holding Company Act and other important legislation.

Postwar Presidents and Congress

The next three Presidents, Harry S. Truman, Dwight D. Eisenhower and John F. Kennedy, all maintained the Executive's initiative in proposing legislation, but none scored the legislative record of a Wilson or a Franklin Roosevelt. Truman dropped legislative proposals on Congress in batches, such as his "21 Points" of 1946, but most of his proposals were emasculated by hostile Congresses. That was particularly true of the Republican-dominated 80th Congress, which carved out its own legislative program over frequent Presidential vetoes.

Eisenhower presented only a modest legislative program but even so was thwarted by three Democratic Congresses. The hallmark of his Administration was use of the veto and the veto threat to stymie the program of the Congressional Democrats. Kennedy recommended enactment of the most vigorous legislative program since the New Deal, and he made unprecedented use of legislative liaison experts to help put on the pressure. However, Republicans and Southern Democrats closed ranks against him, and a trade expansion bill was the only major legislative enactment of his brief Administration. It was left up to Lyndon B. Johnson to push through the Kennedy program.

Johnson's Handling of Congress

No President ever came to office more schooled in the ways of Congress than did Lyndon Johnson. He had worked at the Capitol for 32 years, first as a Congressional secretary, then as a House Member, Senator, Senate

Majority Leader and Vice President. With Johnson applying the pressure, Congress in a single year, 1965, put on the books the broadest domestic legislative program since Roosevelt's first 100 days. Among its landmark enactments were Federal aid to elementary and secondary education, a voting rights act, a comprehensive Federal health care program for the aged, rent supplements for needy families and a major liberalization of the immigration laws.

An important aspect of Johnson's legislative strategy was explained at a meeting of Administration legislative liaison officers in January 1965. "I have watched the Congress from either the inside or the outside, man and boy, for more than 40 years," he said, "and I've never seen a Congress that didn't eventually take the measure of the President it was dealing with." Johnson therefore urged quick enactment of his entire "Great Society" program against the day when relations with Congress should turn sour.

For the most part, the immense Democratic majorities that Johnson swept into office in the 1964 election were eager to do the President's bidding. He was always ready to put on the pressure, however, if a Member stepped out of line. As journalist Jack Bell has written: "Lawmakers were individually needled, cajoled, persuaded, threatened or intimidated...into doing Johnson's bidding. The rewards for going along were as substantial as the punishment for deviation was severe. Always, however, the President tried first to apply his Biblical slogan of 'Come let us reason together.'"

Whatever the pressure method he employed, Johnson was amazingly successful. According to a Congressional Quarterly study, Congress in 1965 approved 68.9 percent of the President's requests, the highest score since CQ began its tabulations in 1953. The figure was in marked contrast to President Kennedy's low of 27.2 percent, recorded only two years earlier.

But just as other strong Presidents had experienced, Congress eventually rebelled at the pressure treatment, and after 1966, the pace of legislation slowed. Divided over the President's Vietnam war policy and the inflation it had wrought on the economy, the nation elected 47 more Republicans to the House in 1966. The next Congress used the better part of two sessions to enact major tax legislation and approved few other important Administration bills.

Johnson's successor, Republican Richard M. Nixon, sought a low profile and did not recommend a broad legislative program in either of his first two years in office.

Presidential Use of Direct Pressure

Probably the most effective method of Presidential pressure on Congress is the direct meeting between the President and Members of Congress, particularly the leaders. As political scientist Nelson W. Polsby has put it: "Only the crustiest and most independent Congressmen and Senators fail to warm to considerate personal treatment by a President of the United States. A private breakfast, a walk in the rose garden, an intimate conference, all duly and widely reported in the press, give a man a sense of importance which may not only flatter his ego but also may remind him of his responsibilities as a national legislator, as a trustee of the common weal. He may then moderate his opposition, or stiffen his resolve to support the President."

The first and one of the most effective practitioners of the direct-pressure method was Thomas Jefferson, who as President participated openly in the selection of the House Speaker and of committee chairmen and instituted the party caucus. Edward S. Corwin and Louis W. Koenig have described Jefferson's tactics as "usually direct, sometimes even furtive." They added: "He induced former colleagues to run for Congress in order to have a corps of sponsors for his measures. Legislative committees were constituted strictly in accordance with his wishes. Messages prepared in Cabinet were forwarded to the committees of Congress by his Secretary of the Treasury, Albert Gallatin, the Administration's watchdog in legislative matters. Jefferson supervised the progress of his measures in Congress at all stages until their enactment. Caucuses were held at his direction, sometimes under his chairmanship.... Floor leaders, an invention of his Administration, cooperated at every turn."

Theodore Roosevelt's Methods

It was not until the early 20th century and the Administration of Theodore Roosevelt that another President used direct pressures on Congress effectively to win enactment of a major legislative program. Roosevelt chose to center his pressures on the House Speaker, Joseph G. Cannon (R Ill.), whom he considered the duly authorized agent of his party's Congressional majority. As Cannon has described their dealings: "The chairmen of committees conferred with the Speaker as to legislation before their committees, and the Speaker's room became a clearing house where the views of the majority were freely discussed, and the Speaker could intelligently present the majority opinion to the President.... I think Mr. Roosevelt talked over with me virtually every serious recommendation to Congress before he made it and requested me to sound out the leaders in the House, for he did not want to recommend legislation simply to write messages. He wanted results and he wanted to secure results with the least friction."

A practical man, Roosevelt was willing to make sacrifices to achieve his legislative goals. To obtain legislation to strengthen regulation of the railroads, for example, he found it necessary to drop an intended move for tariff reform that was strongly opposed by Cannon. Wilfred E. Binkley noted that "On one occasion, a message to Congress containing a recommendation for tariff revision had already been written, printed and even circulated when the President consented to withdraw the recommendation and thereby won Speaker Cannon's backing on the Hepburn Railroad Rate bill, which then passed the House with only seven dissenting votes."

Roosevelt supplemented his pressure on Speaker Cannon with voluminous messages to Congress on a variety of matters. Some of his messages ran to as many as 40,000 words and proposed legislation in almost every area of human activity. As political scientist Lawrence H. Chamberlain put it: "He struck out in all directions, and his enthusiasm was infectious. Through a skillful utilization of the press he was able to monopolize public attention whenever he spoke and this was often...."

Wilson's Direct Pressure Tactics

Woodrow Wilson, the next strong activist to enter the White House used the Presidential message with unprecedented effect in seeking legislation from Congress.

Several weeks after taking office, Wilson summoned Congress in special session, and on April 8, 1913, he addressed a joint session of the two houses to urge action on tariff reform. His appearance before Congress was the first by a President since John Adams, for Wilson's predecessors had adhered to the precedent established by Jefferson of sending Presidential messages to Congress to be read by a clerk. (Washington as well as John Adams had appeared in person on Capitol Hill.) "I am very glad indeed," Wilson said, "to have this opportunity to address the two houses directly and to verify for myself the impression that the President of the United States is a person, not a mere department of the Government hailing Congress from some isolated island of jealous power, sending messages and not speaking naturally and with his own voice—that he is a human being trying to cooperate with other human beings in a common service." The President's address evoked some Congressional concern over "separation of powers;" one Senator spoke of it derisively as "the speech from the throne." Wilson continued the practice, however, personally delivering 24 more messages during his two terms in office.

Wilson took extraordinary steps to persuade Congress to carry out his program, a series of reform proposals which he called the "New Freedom." In the midst of Senate debate on tariff reform, he appeared in the President's Room just off the chamber and conferred with Senate leaders—something that had not been done since the Civil War. In the tariff fight, Rep. Oscar W. Underwood (D Ala.), then House Democratic leader and chairman of the Ways and Means Committee, organized a party caucus where House Democrats were bound by a two-thirds rule and went to the floor primed for united action. The first caucus of Democratic Senators in decades was held on June 20, 1913. At another meeting on July 7, the Senate caucus declared the tariff a party measure and made it the duty of all Senate Democrats to support it. Several weeks later, the bill was enacted into law—the first time since the Polk Administration that the tariff had been revised under a Democratic President.

Unlike Theodore Roosevelt, Wilson preferred to deal with Congressional committee chairmen instead of the party leadership. To assist him with rank-and-file Members, Wilson relied on an unofficial lobby called the "Common Council Club," a group of about 30 officials of sub-Cabinet rank. Among the participants was future President Franklin D. Roosevelt, then Assistant Secretary of the Navy. The group, which met almost every Wednesday from 1913 until the outbreak of World War I, focused on key Administration measures and sent delegations to Capitol Hill to help the President break up legislative logjams.

Direct Pressure by Later Presidents

Franklin Roosevelt, like his cousin Theodore, worked through top party leaders to push through his legislative program. In turn, House leaders strengthened their control by appointing regional whips for each of 15 geographical districts. As Wilfred Binkley has noted, control in the House was so tight in the first 100 days that the chamber spent an average of only 3½ hours of debate on 11 of the President's most important measures.

Undoubtedly, the nation's economic panic was the single most important factor in accounting for Roosevelt's early success. But his reasoned approach to Congress was equally important. "For a hundred days," wrote Bernard Fay, "he kept Congress at work. And for a hundred days, he collaborated with Congress. During these hundred days he avoided all conflicts and all quarrels with both houses. He had innumerable conferences with Congressional leaders and, far from ever adopting a contemptuous attitude toward Congress, he always treated it with the utmost courtesy."

Presidents Kennedy and Johnson also were skilled operators in the use of the direct-pressure tactic. After a walk in the White House rose garden in 1962, Kennedy persuaded House Armed Services Committee Chairman Carl Vinson (D Ga.) to avoid a Constitutional clash by dropping language from a military procurement bill directing the President to spend funds on the purchase of a new Air Force bomber, the B-70, which was opposed by the Administration. Johnson's attention to Senate Minority Leader Everett McKinley Dirksen (R Ill.) was almost legendary. On several occasions when key Administration bills appeared lost, Johnson's intervention with the Minority Leader led to a timely bail-out maneuver.

Case of Direct Pressure Failure

One of the most notable failures of the direct-pressure technique occurred in 1957, when President Eisenhower's foreign aid bill was headed for serious trouble in the House Appropriations Committee. In an attempt to break the logjam, the President sent for Rep. Otto Passman (D La.), chairman of the Foreign Operations Appropriations Subcommittee and the chief House opponent of foreign aid. Columnist Rowland Evans Jr. reported several years later that Passman had told him his White House visit was "...kind of embarrassing." He said: "I refer to it as the Passman trial. They sent for me in a long black Cadillac, I guess the first time I had ever been in one. I felt real important, which is not my usual way of feeling. When I got to the President's study at the White House, all the big shots were there. Admiral Radford and Secretary Dulles and the leaders of Congress. We had tea and little cakes, and they sat me right across from the President. They went around the room, asking for comments, one minute each. When they got to me, I said I would need more than one minute, maybe six or seven minutes to tell what was wrong with their program." According to Evans, "Passman's lecture was complete with footnotes and fine print, figures down to the last thin dime, unobligated balances in the various foreign aid accounts, carryover funds, re-obligated de-obligated obligations, supplies in the pipeline, uncommitted balances, and so on—in that mysterious verbal shorthand that only a man who lives and breathes foreign aid could comprehend.... After everyone left, the President turned to his staff and said, 'Remind me never to invite that fellow down here again.' "

Executive Liaison With Congress

To bolster their direct-pressure efforts, recent Presidents have appointed full-time legislative liaison forces, centered both at the departmental level and on the White House staff. The practice began in 1945, when the

(Continued on p. 580)

Presidential Appearances Before Congress

With the exception of Woodrow Wilson, Franklin D. Roosevelt and Harry S Truman, few Presidents have relied on direct appearances before Congress as a means of promoting their legislative programs. Although Washington and John Adams appeared before Congress to deliver their Annual Messages, the practice was dropped by their successors and was not revived until Wilson addressed a joint session of the House and Senate on April 8, 1913, to urge support of his tariff reform program. In all, Wilson addressed Congress on 25 occasions, Roosevelt on 16 and Truman on 17.

Beginning with Truman in 1947, it became customary for the President to deliver his annual State of the Union Message (formerly called the Annual Message) in person, and all did so each year with the exception of President Eisenhower in 1955 and 1956. Since Truman went to Capitol Hill in 1952 to ask Congress for authority to seize the strike-bound steel industry, Presidents have appeared before Congress only twice to ask support for specific policies—Johnson in 1965 for his voting rights bill and Nixon in 1969 for his Vietnam policy.

Following is a list of the direct appearances by Presidents before Congress through May 1971 (appearances are before joint sessions unless otherwise indicated):

President	Number of Appearances	Occasions
George Washington	10	8 Annual Messages (1789-1796); 2 Inaugural Addresses (1789, 1793—second Inaugural before Senate only).
John Adams	6	4 Annual Messages (1797-1800); Inaugural Address (1797); Relations With France Message (1797).
Woodrow Wilson	25	6 Annual Messages (1913-1918). Also *1913:* Tariff Reform (Apr. 8); Bank Reform (June 23); Relations with Mexico (Aug. 27). *1914:* Antitrust Laws (Jan. 20); Panama Canal Tolls (Mar. 5); New Tax Revenue (Sept. 4). *1916:* Impending Rail Strike (Aug. 29). *1917:* "Peace Without Victory" (Jan. 22, Senate only); Breaking Relations with Germany (Feb. 3); Arming of Merchant Ships (Feb. 26); Request for War Declaration Against Germany (Apr. 2). *1918:* Federal Takeover of Railroads (Jan. 4); "14 Points" for Peace (Jan. 8); Peace Outlook (Feb. 11); Need for New Revenue (May 27); Request for Ratification of Woman Suffrage Amendment (Sept. 30, Senate only); Announcing Armistice (Nov. 11). *1919:* Request for Ratification of Versailles Treaty (July 10, Senate only); High Cost of Living (Aug. 8).
Warren G. Harding	7	2 Annual Messages (1921-22); Federal Problems Message (1921); 2 Merchant Marine Messages (1922); Coal and Railroad Message (1922); Debt Message (1923).
Calvin Coolidge	2	Annual Message (1923); George Washington's Birthday Message (1927).
Franklin D. Roosevelt	16	10 Annual Messages (1934-43); 100th Anniversary of Lafayette's Death (1934); 150th Anniversary of First Congress (1939); Neutrality Address (1939); National Defense Message (1940); Declaration of War (1941); Yalta Conference Report (1945).
Harry S Truman	17	6 State of the Union Messages (1947-52); Prosecution of the War Message (1945); Submission of UN Charter (Senate only, 1945); Congressional Medal of Honor Ceremony (1945); Universal Military Training Message (1945); Railroad Strike Message (1946); Greek-Turkish Aid Policy (1947); Aid to Europe Message (1947); National Security and Conditions in Europe Message (1948); 50th Anniversary of the Liberation of Cuba (1948); Inflation, Housing and Civil Rights Message (1948); Steel Industry Dispute (1952).
Dwight D. Eisenhower	7	6 State of the Union Messages (1953-54; 1957-60); Message on Middle East (1957).
John F. Kennedy	3	State of the Union Messages (1961-63).
Lyndon B. Johnson	8	6 State of the Union Messages (1964-69); Assumption of Office (1963); Voting Rights (1965).
Richard M. Nixon	3	Vietnam Policy (1969—separate addresses before House and Senate); State of the Union Message (1970 and 1971).

White House Legislative Liaison Men

Only five Presidential staff assistants have held the position of top White House liaison man with Congress since President Eisenhower gave the post official status in 1953. Prior to that time, White House officials had met with Congressmen on legislation but on a highly informal basis. No official had ever been specifically designated to handle White House lobbying activities.

First of the White House lobbyists was Bryce N. Harlow, who served in that position throughout the Eisenhower Administration. Harlow, a former staff assistant on the House Armed Services Committee, was given the title "Deputy Assistant to the President for Congressional Affairs," a position that placed him in the second echelon of the White House staff's hierarchy.

Chief White House lobbyist in the Kennedy and a part of the Johnson Administration was Lawrence F. O'Brien, a longtime Kennedy confidant and campaign assistant. O'Brien was designated "Special Assistant for Congressional Affairs," a position coequal with several other top staff posts. Unlike Harlow, O'Brien was given full-time assistants for both the House and the Senate—Mike N. Manatos, former assistant to four Democratic Senators from Wyoming, for the Senate, and Henry Hall Wilson Jr., attorney and former Democratic National Committee member, for the House. O'Brien remained on the job until 1965, when he became Postmaster General. Wilson left in 1967 and Manatos in 1968.

Succeeding O'Brien as chief White House lobbyist (although O'Brien as Postmaster General still retained over-all direction of the Administration's lobbying program) was E. Jake Jacobsen, who was given the title, "Legislative Counsel," a top-ranking White House job. Jacobsen retained the position until early 1967, when he was succeeded by Harold Barefoot Sanders. Sanders held the post during the remainder of President Johnson's term.

In the Nixon Administration, the top lobbying job went first to Bryce Harlow, who returned to the White House after eight years as a lobbyist for the Procter and Gamble Co. Harlow was given the title "Special Assistant for Congressional Relations," a job that carried top-level rank. He was assigned two full-time deputy assistants—Kenneth E. Belieu and Franklyn C. Nofziger.

In a major White House staff reshuffle on Nov. 4, 1969, Harlow was elevated to "Counselor to the President," a new position that carried Cabinet rank. Although Harlow retained over-all direction of the White House lobbying effort, responsibility for day-to-day conduct of Congressional liaison went to William Timmons, who assumed Harlow's old position as Special Assistant for Congressional Relations.

State Department established the Office of Assistant Secretary for Congressional Relations, and by 1955, Congressional liaison offices were operating also in the Post Office and in the Departments of Commerce and of Health, Education and Welfare. By 1963, all Federal departments had such offices, and Congressional liaison directly involved the services of 500 Government employees at a cost that year of $5,432,938.

Eisenhower's Liaison Operation

A big step toward coordinating the liaison function was taken in the early days of the Eisenhower Administration, when the President named one of his special assistants, Bryce N. Harlow, as a full-time White House lobbyist. Harlow, long an employee of the House Armed Services Committee, retained the White House post throughout the Eisenhower Administration.

According to Neil MacNeil, Harlow "normally operated from his White House office, answering and making telephone calls, perhaps as many as 125 a day." MacNeil's account of Harlow's liaison methods continued: "Only rarely did he slip up to the House of Representatives and usually then only to have a private lunch with Charles Halleck of Indiana, one of the Republican leaders.... Harlow kept the Republican party's Congressional leaders informed of forthcoming Eisenhower legislative proposals and kept in touch with the Democratic leaders. Frequently he escorted Speaker Sam Rayburn and Senate Majority Leader Lyndon Johnson into the White House late in the day for a highball and chat with the President.... Harlow tried to satisfy the requests of Members and tried to persuade them to support the President's program. 'In this game,' he said, 'it's what you've done lately that counts.' "

Kennedy-O'Brien Liaison Team

President Kennedy sought to beef up the liaison function, appointing his long-time associate Lawrence F. O'Brien as chief lobbyist and giving O'Brien full authority to speak for him on legislative matters. O'Brien, who was designated "Special Assistant for Congressional Affairs," was given coequal rank with other top White House aides and was assigned assistants for both House and Senate. Neil MacNeil has reported that "to even the most influential Senators who telephoned Kennedy in the first weeks of his Presidency, the President had a stock reply: 'Have you discussed this with Larry O'Brien?' "

At the outset of the Kennedy Administration, O'Brien organized a series of cocktail parties, all held in House committee rooms, in which he sought to meet House Members on a purely social basis. Later, O'Brien invited House Members in groups of 50 for coffee at the the White House. For committee chairmen, he set up private discussions with the President. At a dinner with the Democratic Study Group, a bloc of about 100 House liberals, O'Brien promised that the President would support them for re-election if they backed his legislative program. "The White House certainly remembers who its friends are," he said, "and can be counted on to apply significant assistance in the campaign."

Clearing their activities with O'Brien, Cabinet officials sought to cultivate key Congressional leaders.

Department of Defense created the office of Assistant Secretary for Congressional Liaison, thus centralizing Congressional relations which had been handled separately by the respective military services. In 1949, the

Defense Secretary Robert S. McNamara courted House Armed Services Committee Chairman Carl Vinson (D Ga.), Vinson's Senate counterpart Richard B. Russell (also a Georgia Democrat) and other key members of the House and Senate military committees. Treasury Secretary Douglas Dillon kept in close touch with House Ways and Means Committee Chairman Wilbur D. Mills (D Ark.). Agriculture Secretary Orville L. Freeman consulted frequently with Congressional leaders on the President's farm program. Other Cabinet officers and their liaison staffs made similar contacts.

The Kennedy tactics were often successful in removing major legislative obstacles, but the obstacles appeared so frequently that the President's program foundered in Congress. Some Members, primarily the older, more conservative ones, resented the pressure treatment. As Meg Greenfield reported: "The most widely shared and loudly voiced grievance that Congress has against Administration practices concerns the unremitting attention it receives from those it describes simply and without affection as the 'young men.' They badger, to hear the Members tell it. They hector. They even chase.... Legislators who still cherish the notion that they themselves will decide how to vote appear to have been at various times amused, confused and infuriated by the discombobulation of incoming messages.... 'Why are you calling me, son?' an august legislator asked an all but anonymous Administration phoner not long ago.... To the White House counterclaim that pushing and prodding sometimes helps and never hurts, one Congressman replies by citing the case of a young liaison man, the very sight of whom at the cloakroom door, he claims, is enough to cost the Administration 25 votes. Under questioning, he lowered the figure to three, but this time he seemed serious."

Liaison Under Johnson

The liaison system Kennedy nurtured paid dividends during the Johnson Administration. Loyal Democrats had picked up a working margin of seats in the 1964 election, and with O'Brien still supervising the liaison job, almost all of the old Kennedy measures sailed through Congress. Although President Nixon sought to slow down the furious pace of legislation that had marked the Johnson years, he still relied on a large liaison staff to push key Administration bills. As chief lobbyist, he named Bryce Harlow, who came back to the White House after eight years of lobbying for the Procter and Gamble Co. In Nixon's first two years, his lobby force lost critical battles over two Supreme Court nominations and over restrictions on the Administration's Southeast Asia policy but won a notable victory on funds for deployment of a controversial antiballistic missile system.

Appeals to Public Opinion

Other effective pressure methods available to the President include the manipulation of public opinion through television, radio and the press. Since the early days of the Republic, Presidents have gone over the head of Congress, often successfully, to work up support for their legislative programs.

The most effective practitioner of public relations among the early Presidents was Andrew Jackson, who used the partisan press to considerable advantage in his frequent battles with Congress. Jackson arranged Government printing orders to sustain his favorite publications, a practice that his successors continued until Lincoln's time. James E. Pollard has written: "(Jackson) knew what he wanted, he meant to have his way, and he was fortunate in finding journalists devoted to him and capable of carrying out his desires. The result was the most effective employment of the press for partisan purposes in the long history of the Presidency."

Lincoln, highly sensitive to public opinion, vastly broadened the Presidency's channels for mobilizing grass-roots support. With little regard for partisanship, Lincoln passed out stories to correspondents and editors and wrote numerous letters outlining his views, which eventually found their way into print. His many eloquent addresses received widespread publicity and also helped to galvanize public support for his policies. George Fort Milton has asserted that no President ever surpassed and few equaled Lincoln as "chief of public opinion." He always tried to inform the people of the controlling reasons for his policies and acts. "While he paid some heed to the sanctity of military secrets, he declined to worship at that shrine. He knew that the people had ears, whether the walls had them or not, and took advantage of every appropriate occasion to tell them his innermost thoughts."

Presidents and the Press

Andrew Johnson was the first President to grant a formal interview to the press. Between October 1865 and May 1868, Johnson gave 12 exclusive interviews, most of them dealing with his troubles with Congress. The interviews were ineffective, however, in evoking support for his position.

Presidential relations with the press took a major step forward in Theodore Roosevelt's Administration. The President made himself readily available to newsmen and instituted the practice of systematic White House issuance of news releases.

Roosevelt visualized the Presidency as a "bully pulpit" and used his flair for showmanship to mobilize popular support. When in December 1907 he dispatched the whole U.S. battleship fleet on a 14-month cruise around the world, the Navy lacked funds to pay the costs of such a long voyage. But the public was so impressed by this display of American naval power that Congress lost no time in approving the necessary appropriations.

Roosevelt is credited with having developed the "background" news conference, often called the "trial balloon," a technique later Presidents used extensively for testing public opinion prior to announcing a course of action. According to Jack Bell: "Roosevelt called favorite reporters together, told them of actions he intended to take, and then admonished them not to attribute to him their reports on what the President planned to do.... If the reaction was bad, he himself reacted by denouncing the reporters as liars and consigning them to his 'Ananias (Liars) Club.'"

Presidential newsmaking techniques also advanced under Woodrow Wilson, who instituted the regular and formal White House press conference and increased the frequency of Presidential statements to the public. Until the war in Europe absorbed virtually all of his time and attention, Wilson held press conferences on the average of twice a week.

Of all his opinion-molding techniques, Wilson was most effective with the direct appeal to the public. Several weeks after his inauguration, he issued a statement attacking the "extraordinary exertions" being made by private lobby groups to alter his tariff legislation. "The newspapers are being filled with paid advertisements," he said, "calculated to mislead the judgment of public men, not only, but also the public opinion of the country itself." It was unfair, he added, that "the people at large should have no lobby and be voiceless in these matters, while great bodies of astute men seek to create an artificial public opinion and to overcome the interests of the public for their profit." While usually successful, this technique failed Wilson in 1919. His whistle-stop tour of the country in September, undertaken to generate popular support for the League of Nations, did not arouse enough public backing to force Senate ratification of the Treaty of Versailles, which contained the Covenant of the League.

Fireside Chats

Probably no President in history has used the news media to such advantage as did Franklin D. Roosevelt, particularly in the period of legislative fervor that was his first 100 days. Roosevelt showered attention on White House correspondents, holding 998 news conferences during his 147 months in office. As a result, Pollard has written: "He was on an unprecedented footing with the working press. He knew its ways, he understood many of its problems and he more than held his own in his twice-weekly parry and thrust with the correspondents. In time, of course, some of the glamor wore off and occasionally he was quite out of patience. But on the whole, he made the relationship such an integral part of his working program that any comparison with any previous Administration is futile."

In the nationwide radio hookup, Roosevelt found a powerful new opinion-making tool. At the conclusion of his first week in office, he allayed widespread apprehension with a radio message urging confidence in his banking reforms. Similar messages followed, and they became known as "fireside chats." As Arthur Schlesinger Jr. has put it, these discussions were effective because they "conveyed Roosevelt's conception of himself as a man at ease in his own house talking frankly and intimately to neighbors as they sat in their living rooms." Wilfred Binkley observed: "(Roosevelt) had only to glance toward a microphone or suggest that he might go on the air again and a whole Congressional delegation would surrender. They had no relish for the flood of mail and telegrams they knew would swamp them after another fireside chat to the nation."

Presidential Use of Television

The next innovation in White House public relations techniques occurred in the Eisenhower Administration, when the President permitted increased use of the direct quotation and opened his news conferences to television filming, subject to White House editing. President Kennedy broke new ground by permitting live televising of his news conferences, and Presidents

Johnson and Nixon continued the practice. The live conferences gave them the opportunity to get their views across by "planting" questions with favored newsmen.

All four of these recent Presidents enjoyed almost instant access to television and radio and used those media extensively to communicate their views to the public. *New York Times* columnist James Reston noted in a 1966 book that the energies devoted by the President and top Cabinet officials to public relations functions were almost beyond calculation. "When they are being criticized, they seem all the more eager to argue their case in public. The President not only makes periodic addresses over the television networks, but usually makes himself available every day to repeat some statement for the national newscasters. Not satisfied with the pressures generated in Washington, he calls in the Governors, the mayors, the businessmen and the press in an effort to get their support or at least their understanding."

The Veto and Threat of Veto

From a purely defensive standpoint, the most powerful weapon in the President's arsenal is his authority to veto bills. Under terms of the Constitution, Congress must submit to the President every bill or joint resolution, which he must then approve or else send back to Congress. In the event he disapproves, Congress can override the veto only by a 2/3 vote of both houses. (Under a Supreme Court decision, a quorum must be present for the override to be effective.)

Because a President usually finds it relatively easy to marshal the support of at least one-third plus one Member of the House or the Senate, the veto has been used with deadly effect. Through 1970, 1,310 bills or joint resolutions had been vetoed and returned to Congress with a veto message, but only 77, or 5.9 per cent, of those vetoes had been overridden. In addition, 967 bills had been pocket-vetoed, i.e., allowed to die within a specified period on the eve of or after the adjournment of Congress. *(See box.)*

The concept of *veto* (I forbid) originated in the Roman Empire as a means of protecting the plebeians from injustice at the hands of the patricians. Roman tribunes, representing the masses, were authorized to veto acts of the Senate, dominated by the patricians. English rulers were given absolute veto power, and in 1597, Queen Elizabeth I rejected more parliamentary bills than she accepted. The English veto, which is absolute and cannot be overriden, is still nominally in effect but has not been used since 1707.

Early American Presidents conceived of the veto as a device to be used rarely and then only against legislative encroachment on the prerogatives of another branch of Government. Washington vetoed only two bills; Adams and Jefferson, none. Although Madison and Monroe vetoed seven bills between them, they cited Constitutional grounds for doing so in all except one case. John Quincy Adams, like his father John Adams, did not veto a bill.

Jackson's New View of Veto

The concept of the veto underwent a marked change under Andrew Jackson, who vetoed 12 bills, mostly because he took issue with their content or purpose. His

Vetoes and Vetoes Overridden

Through the first 28 months of the Nixon Administration, Presidents had vetoed a grand total of 2,277 bills, with all except 58 of the vetoes occurring in the years since the Civil War. Of the vetoed bills, only 77, or 3 percent, became law through action by Congress overriding the President's veto. The Presidents who vetoed the most bills were Franklin D. Roosevelt (631 during his 12 years in the White House) and Grover Cleveland (584 during an eight-year period). The President who had the most vetoes overridden was Andrew Johnson (15 of the 28 bills vetoed).

Of the 2,277 bills disapproved, 967 were pocket-vetoed—a procedure under which the President, presented with a bill 10 days or less (Sundays excepted) prior to the adjournment of Congress can merely ignore or "pocket" it, preventing it from becoming law without going through the formality of returning it to Congress with a veto message. The pocket veto, specifically authorized under Article I, Section 7 of the Constitution, deprives Congress of an opportunity to override.

The following list shows the number of bills vetoed by each President, the type of veto used, and the number of vetoes overriden:

President	Bills Vetoed	Direct Veto	Pocket Veto	Vetoes Overriden
Washington	2	2	0	0
J. Adams	0	0	0	0
Jefferson	0	0	0	0
Madison	7	5	2	0
Monroe	2	1	1	1
J.Q. Adams	0	0	0	0
Jackson	12	5	7	0
Van Buren	0	0	0	0
W.H. Harrison	0	0	0	0
Tyler	10	6	4	1
Polk	3	2	1	0
Taylor	0	0	0	0
Fillmore	0	0	0	0
Pierce	9	9	0	5
Buchanan	7	4	3	0
Lincoln	6	2	4	0
A. Johnson	28	21	7	15
Grant	92	44	48	4
Hayes	13	12	1	1
Garfield	0	0	0	0
Arthur	12	4	8	1
Cleveland (1st term)	414	304	110	2
B. Harrison	44	19	25	1
Cleveland (2nd term)	170	42	128	5
McKinley	42	6	36	0
T. Roosevelt	82	42	40	1
Taft	39	30	9	1
Wilson	44	33	11	6
Harding	6	5	1	0
Coolidge	50	20	30	4
Hoover	37	21	16	3
F.D. Roosevelt	631	371	260	9
Truman	250	180	70	12
Eisenhower	201	83	118	3
Kennedy	25	14	11	0
L.B. Johnson	30	16	14	0
Nixon (through May 1971)	9	7	2	2
Total	**2,277**	**1,310**	**967**	**77**

Source: Library of Congress, Congressional Research Service

most noteworthy veto was that of a bill to recharter the Bank of the United States, which Jackson considered a creature of special interests. Binkley has described Jackson's message vetoing that bill "a landmark in the evolution of the Presidency." Binkley said: "For the first time in American history, a veto message was used as an instrument of party warfare. Through it, the Democratic Party, as the Jacksonians were now denominated, dealt a telling blow to their opponents, the National Republicans. Though addressed to Congress, the veto message was an appeal to the nation. Not a single opportunity to discredit the old ruling class was missed."

President John Tyler's veto of a tariff bill in 1843 brought on the first attempt by Congress to impeach a President. An impeachment resolution, introduced in the House by Whig Members, charged the President "with the high crime and misdemeanor of withholding his assent to laws indispensable to the just operation of the government." When the impeachment move failed, Henry Clay proposed a Constitutional amendment to enable Congress to override the President's veto by a simple majority instead of the required two-thirds vote.

Noting that the President's right of veto gave him power equal to that of almost two-thirds of Congress, Clay declared that such power would ultimately make the President "ruler of the nation."

Use of Veto Since Civil War

After the Civil War, the determination of Radical Republican Congresses to write their own reconstruction policy in defiance of the Executive represented a new landmark in Legislative-Executive relations. When President Andrew Johnson vetoed a bill to protect the rights of free slaves, Congress passed the measure over his head —the first time in the nation's history that Congress had overridden the President's veto on a major issue. The civil rights bill was only the first of a number of measures to be passed over Johnson's veto. Among others was the Tenure of Office Act, which led indirectly to Johnson's impeachment. When Johnson refused to abide by the provisions of the Act, which prohibited the President from removing appointed officials from office until their successors had been confirmed, the House initiated impeachment proceedings. Although Johnson was impeached, he escaped conviction by a single vote when tried by the Senate.

During the remainder of the 19th century, the veto was used mainly to prevent corruption through the passage of private bills. Unlike the situation in the case of major legislation, it was difficult for supporters of a private bill to get enough support, even through logrolling, to override a veto. Of President Grant's 44 direct vetoes, 29 were of private bills. President Cleveland vetoed more bills and resolutions than all the Presidents together before him. Most of his 584 vetoes were of private pension bills.

Threatened use of the veto became a powerful tool in the hands of Wilson and Franklin Roosevelt. Wilson told Congress specifically what he wanted in legislation, pointing out what provisions must be included to win his approval of a bill. Roosevelt used the threat of veto not only to exert his influence in Congress but also to remind maverick bureaucrats of his executive control. In 1944, Roosevelt became the first President to veto a tax bill, declaring that the Revenue Act of 1944 would provide tax relief "not for the needy but for the greedy."

President Truman vetoed numerous bills passed by the Republican-dominated 80th Congress, but his vetoes were overridden on several major bills, including the Taft-Hartley Act and a bill reducing individual income taxes. President Eisenhower used the veto and the veto threat to defeat or restrict social programs favored by Democratic Congresses. In the 1959 session alone, he vetoed two major housing measures, a rural electrification bill and two versions of a civil functions appropriations bill; the Democrats were able to override only the second, watered-down version of the civil functions bill. The constant threat of a veto also prompted Democratic frugality in provisions of other measures.

The veto was seldom used or threatened by Presidents Kennedy or Johnson, two Democratic activists whose main concern was getting their own programs through Congress. The principal exception was Johnson's veto in 1965 of a bill requiring advance Congressional review of Presidential decisions to close military bases. President Nixon, confronted in his first two years with a Democratic Congress, used the veto and veto threat much as Eisenhower did, to temper Democratic social programs.

Impounding of Funds by President

An action tantamount to the veto is the President's refusal to spend unwanted appropriations. This method of exerting pressure on Congress, never legally challenged, has been used frequently. In 1949, when Congress approved a 58-group Air Force rather than the 48-group force President Truman sought, the President refused to spend the extra money. Two years later, he ignored a rider to the Omnibus Appropriations Act providing for a loan to Spain. During the Kennedy and Johnson years, Congress provided funds for exotic new weapons systems opposed by Defense Secretary Robert S. McNamara, but in most cases the Administration simply refused to deploy the systems. *(See Fiscal Powers, p. 191.)*

Students of government have expressed doubt that this tactic can be used in connection with any legislation other than appropriations bills. As Bertram M.

Gross has pointed out: "If President Truman had expressed the same disregard for any provision of the Taft-Hartley Act as he expressed toward the Spanish loan provision, ...the result would have been a public uproar of incalculable proportions."

Pressures Through Party and Patronage

Another pressure tool open to the President is the appeal for party support. But only four Presidents—Jefferson, Wilson, Franklin Roosevelt and Lyndon Johnson—have mobilized party pressures to carve out broad legislative programs.

The biggest drawback in the party loyalty appeal is the diverse makeup of American political parties. Because they represent varied shades of political opinion, American parties are not highly disciplined, and the measure of support they give the President's program depends largely on his popularity and persuasive appeal. As Lawrence Chamberlain has put it: "Each Congressman is elected by his particular constituency to work for a program. He may be a member of the President's party but elected on a program quite different from that of his party chieftain.... Just as the President accepts responsibility to his constituency, so does the individual Congressman. There is nothing in our Constitution or in our political and governmental traditions to suggest that the individual Congressman's obligation to the President's program is paramount to his obligation to his own constituency."

In the years since World War II, Democratic Presidents have had more difficulty than Republicans in keeping their party united in Congress. Southern Democrats from conservative constituencies found it expedient to maintain an alliance with Republicans to vote down liberal programs proposed by Democratic Presidents. Until Democratic loyalists won wide margins in the 1964 election, this coalition ruled Congress.

Most Presidents understand the Member's problem with his constituents and are wary of pushing party loyalty too far. Lawrence F. O'Brien, Congressional liaison chief for Presidents Kennedy and Johnson, said that no one on his staff would ever suggest to a Member of Congress that he commit political hara-kari. "That is not the realistic approach to this problem, and as long as we don't reach that point where we feel a Member just must darn well be with us or all bets are off, then, I think we have good mutual understanding and rapport."

Two Presidents who defied this concept and asked Members to vote against constituency interests were notably unsuccessful in their efforts. When some prominent Democrats obstructed Roosevelt's plan for packing the Supreme Court, he campaigned against two of the offending Senators (George of Georgia and Tydings of Maryland) in the 1938 primaries, but both were returned to office by wide margins; the President did succeed in bringing about the defeat of one House Member, Rep. John J. O'Connor of New York, chairman of the Rules Committee. President Johnson lost much of his huge House majority in 1966 after he persuaded Democratic loyalists to vote for an unpopular 1965 bill that would have annulled the authority of states to enact "right-to-work" laws. The bill was filibustered to death in the Senate.

Douglass Cater, a White House aide under President Johnson, has observed that even the President, "while paying lip service to his party...finds himself obliged to bypass it." Cater gave some of the reasons: "With the help of modern communications, he has more direct means of contact with his public than the party's many-layered relay system. On the compelling issues of foreign affairs and defense, he inevitably seeks to clothe his policies in the respectable robes of bipartisanship. Toward such matters as fiscal and monetary policy and even civil rights legislation, he makes constant efforts to maintain an unpartisan position. His appointments to high office often bear little relation to the party which elected him."

Patronage. Dispensation of Federal patronage is one of the President's most powerful means of exerting political pressure. The genesis of this practice appears to go back to the time when Treasury Secretary Alexander Hamilton urged the Chief Executive to use "the loaves and fishes" as an element of executive control. In his 351 civil appointments, Washington made fitness for office the main criterion, but some of his appointments were clearly political. Among them were appointments aimed to build up support for the Federal Government in states that had been lukewarm to federalism, particularly North Carolina.

Andrew Jackson is widely regarded as the founder of the "spoils system." "To the victors belong the spoils," Jackson declared when he took office in 1829 and fired 252 Federal employees, replacing them with the party faithful. However, historians have found that Jefferson, also a strong party leader, dismissed about the same proportion of officeholders.

Despite his reputation for devotion to straight-laced government, President Lincoln once resorted to the spoils system when he needed votes for a key bill. According to D.S. Alexander, Lincoln turned to patronage in 1864 to promote adoption of a Constitutional amendment abolishing slavery. Not sure that enough states would vote to ratify the amendment, Lincoln sought to hasten the admission of a new state, Nevada. With the bill for that purpose bogged down in the House, the President learned that the votes of three Representatives might be up for bargaining. When Assistant Secretary of War Charles A. Dana, whom the President authorized to negotiate with the legislators, asked Lincoln what they expected for their votes, he replied: "I don't know. It makes no difference. We must carry this vote.... Whatever promises you make, I will perform." Dana made a deal with the three Representatives, and Nevada was brought into the Union on Oct. 31, 1864. As Lincoln expected, it ratified the 13th Amendment, which was submitted to the states Feb. 1, 1865, and was proclaimed in effect Dec. 18, 1865.

Perhaps the most successful dispenser of patronage ever to hold the Presidency was Woodrow Wilson, who made patronage an important instrument of his party leadership. Although patronage jobs had been cut back severely under President Cleveland, as part of his civil service reform, Wilson used what patronage was left him with maximum effect. As his patronage chief (and Postmaster General), he installed Albert Burleson, a former Texas Congressman who, as George Fort Milton said, "proved a past master at the combination of entreaty, cajolery and command required by the task." Milton

added that "Some of the White House entourage did not like his (Burleson's) insistence on 'taking care of the boys in the trenches,' but he got enough jobs, campaign contributions and other favors to keep them in the fight."

The next Democrat in the White House, Franklin Roosevelt, also made effective use of his patronage power. His patronage chief, Postmaster General James A. Farley, asked Congressional patronage seekers such questions as "What was your pre-convention position on the Roosevelt candidacy?" and "How did you vote on the economy bill?" As Wilfred Binkley reported, if a Congressman was asked to vote for a Presidential measure against local pressures, the matter was put "on the frank basis of quid pro quo."

The Eisenhower Administration used patronage more as a stick than a carrot. The President's patronage dispenser, Postmaster General Arthur Summerfield, frequently set up shop in the office of House Minority Leader Charles A. Halleck (R Ind.) and berated Republican representatives who broke party ranks. Insurgents were warned that key jobs such as postmasterships might be cut back unless they got behind the President's program. The President himself sought to broaden the spoils, however, by removing some 134,000 classified jobs from the civil service.

Under the Kennedy and Johnson Administrations, patronage was assigned to John Bailey, chairman of the Democratic National Committee. Although clever use of patronage swayed votes on several key bills, Kennedy was not overly enamored of the tactic and preferred the direct pressure technique. But patronage "does give us some influence," he once said.

In recent years, many legislators and government officials have concluded that patronage is overrated as a Presidential pressure tool. Former White House aide Douglass Cater has written that patronage can be "a clumsy instrument" and that "for the senior Member in Congress, it provokes more hostility when withheld than gratitude when bestowed." Rep. Paul J. Kilday (D Texas), said in 1961 that a Representative normally had as many as 100 applicants for every patronage job. "You make 99 fellows mad at you and get one ingrate."

Preferment. A weapon that is usually more effective than patronage is preferment, the selective use of the President's powers to assign Federal contract awards and to choose the location of Government installations. Political scientist Nelson W. Polsby has observed that use of this authority as a pressure tool makes it possible "to reward and punish Congressional friends and foes quite vigorously." Going into particulars, he said: "Small Business Administration and Area Redevelopment Administration loans to certain areas may get more and more difficult to obtain, as applications fail to 'qualify.' Pilot programs and demonstration projects may be funneled here rather than there. Defense contracts and public works may be accelerated in some areas, retarded in others.... These administrative decisions have great potential impact because they affect the prosperity of areas where they are put into effect and they are often of acute concern to local political leaders. And so they can become weapons in the hands of a politically astute President."

Distribution of Federal contracts became increasingly important in the postwar years as Federal budgets grew phenomenally. The greatest beneficiaries were Members of the powerful House and Senate Armed Services Committees and Defense Appropriations Subcommittees, who received defense plants and installations in their districts in return for their support of military requests. Even highly placed members of the opposition party may occasionally win a plum. Former House Minority Leader Joseph W. Martin Jr. (R Mass.) wrote in his memoirs that he told President Roosevelt one day that he needed a new road for the southern part of his district. As Martin recounted the meeting, Roosevelt summoned his aide Louis McHenry Howe. " 'Louis,' he said, 'call McDonald.'— Thomas H. McDonald, head of the Bureau of Public Roads—'and tell him I am sending down a black Republican, and I want him to give him a road.' And I got it...."

Few Presidents have been as skillful in distributing Federal contracts as was Lyndon Johnson, who used preferment to great effect in pushing his Great Society program. When a crucial Administration plan for "model city" grants for urban rehabilitation appeared mired in both houses, Johnson used the bait of program grants for key Members' districts to get the program moving. Several months after passage of the measure, these Members got their grants. Johnson also was reported to have promised a space program installation for one Senator's crucial vote on a civil rights bill, and a special native housing program for an Alaska Senator's vote on funding the Administration's controversial rent supplements program.

Coordination of Administration Pressures

With expansion of the Federal bureaucracy, a President's coordination of his legislative program has become an increasingly complex job. A Congressional act and several administrative reorganizations, however, have helped him to tighten control.

With passage of the Budget and Accounting Act of 1921, Congress ended the right of Federal agencies to decide for themselves what appropriation levels to ask of Congress. The Act set up the Bureau of the Budget which was to serve under the President's direction as a central clearinghouse for Administration budget requests. Another important part of the budget reform was a change of House rules in 1920 that reduced from eight to one the number of committees authorized to act on appropriations; the Senate followed suit in 1922.

Budget Circular 49, approved by President Harding on Dec. 19, 1921, required that all agency proposals for appropriations be submitted to the President prior to presentation to Congress. Agency proposals were to be studied for their relationship to "the President's financial program" and were to be sent on to Capitol Hill only if approved by the President. In 1935, President Roosevelt broadened the clearance function to include other legislation as well as appropriation requests. As his rationale for that action, Roosevelt told the National Emergency Council that he had been "quite horrified— not once but half a dozen times—by reading in the paper that some department or agency was after this, that or the other without my knowledge." The new function, vested at first in the secretariat of the National Emergency Council, was transferred to the Budget Bureau on Dec. 21, 1935.

According to political scientist Richard E. Neustadt, Roosevelt's new clearance system was not a mere extension of the budget process. "On the contrary...this was Roosevelt's creation, intended to protect not just his budget, but his prerogatives, his freedom of action, and his choice of policies in an era of fast-growing Government and of determined Presidential leadership." Neustadt reported that in 1939 the Budget Bureau processed agency reports on 2,448 bills, as compared with only 300 such measures in 1935. It also handled 438 drafts of proposed legislation as compared to only 170 four years earlier.

Roosevelt in 1939 broadened the Bureau's clearance function by making it responsible for coordination of department views on all measures sent to the White House for the President's signature or veto. That responsibility had been limited previously to views on appropriations measures. Any recommendation that the President withhold his approval of a bill was required to be accompanied by a draft veto message or, in the case of a pocket veto, a memorandum of disapproval. These procedures were retained and further strengthened by later Presidents. In addition, Presidents sought to extend their control through centralization of agency legislative liaison forces under top White House officials.

Still, the special interests of separate bureaucracies make effective control extremely difficult. As Douglass Cater explained: "Fierce rivalries for funds and functions go on ceaselessly among the departments and between the agencies. A cunning bureau chief learns to negotiate alliances on Capitol Hill that bypass the central authority of the White House. The senior civil servant senses a power in his tenure able to withstand transient whims." Presidential lobbyist Lawrence O'Brien once commented that "some of these bureaucrats are absolutely frank about it. They tell us 'We're going to be running things in Washington after you're gone.' "

Although Federal departments are required to support the President's Budget, there is nothing to prevent their telling Congressional committees covertly that they disagree with the budgeted levels. The departments employing this technique most effectively are the military services; they are apt to be in close rapport with the Armed Services and Appropriations Committees. The services often use committee hearings as a propaganda forum to tell the public that they disagree with the President's views. Clever, often prearranged dialogues between witnesses and Members of Congress give military officers a chance to admit under questioning that they disagree with the Administration.

Some Federal bureaus are so well-entrenched that they openly defy Presidential control. Among the most powerful of these agencies are the U.S. Forest Service and the Army Corps of Engineers. For years, the Forest Service, supported by mining and lumber interests, was successful in lobbying to prevent Administration-proposed expansion of Federal park and recreation lands. The Army Engineers are in an even stronger position, since the Corps' civil functions—river and harbor development work—are of intense interest to local constituencies and thus to Members of Congress. Consequently, the Corps has been able on occasion to wage a successful struggle against Administration reclamation policy. One of its most notable victories came in a 1944 battle with President Roosevelt, who ordered that the new Kings River reclamation project in California "be built by the Bureau of Reclamation (of the Interior Department) and not by the Army Engineers."

Congress appropriated money for the project but made its use contingent on construction by the Army Engineers.

Regulation of Administration Lobbying

Over the years, Congress has sought to restrict activities of Federal agencies designed to influence legislative action or public opinion. The two major statutes governing these activities were enacted as far back as the Wilson Administration, but they have not been vigorously enforced.

The chief measure restricting agency public relations activities was passed in 1913, following a groundswell of Congressional criticism of Administration plans to hire a "publicity expert" for the Office of Public Roads. The resulting legislation (5 U.S.C. 54) stipulated that "No money appropriated by this or any other act shall be used for the compensation of any publicity expert unless specifically appropriated for that purpose." Although Congress has made no subsequent provision for hiring such officials, Federal agencies have countered by designating public relations officers as "Information Specialist," "Special Assistants," or "Public Affairs Officers." V.O. Key, a political scientist, observed that "The principal effect of the legislation of 1913 has been to outlaw the title, 'publicity expert.' "

Congress in 1919 enacted a law (18 U.S.C. 1913) prohibiting use of public funds "to pay for any personal service, advertisement, telegram, telephone, letter, printed or written matter, or other device, intended or designed to influence in any manner a Member of Congress, to favor or oppose, by vote or otherwise, any legislation or appropriation by Congress." This law has been circumvented by broad interpretation of a clause permitting executive contacts concerning legislation when made through "the proper official channels" at a Member's request. Numerous other laws have sought to block executive agencies from engaging in publicity or propaganda campaigns.

Executive lobbying came under Congressional scrutiny in 1950 in a probe by the House Select Committee on Lobbying Activities. The Committee's ranking minority member, Rep. Charles A. Halleck (R Ind.), proposed that the Federal Regulation of Lobbying Act, requiring lobbyists to register, be extended to officials of the Executive Branch. The proposal was resisted by Committee Democrats, who defended Truman Administration lobbying procedures.

At the 1950 hearings, a high General Accounting Office official testified on the difficulty of enforcing the 1919 law. Frank H. Weitzel, assistant to the Comptroller General, told the panel: "In many cases it is obviously hard, if not impossible, to recognize the unlawful use of Federal funds for lobbying activities from documents submitted with the accounts to the General Accounting Office, except possibly from the context of telegrams included therein. For example, a trip of a Government official to Washington might in fact have been intended and directed because of the official's capacity to enlist the aid of a certain Member or Members of Congress in legislation of interest to the department. The vouchers for the reimbursement of travel expenses covering such a trip will very seldom reveal the true purpose of the trip, which is usually described as being 'for official business.' Concrete evidence of irregular methods on the part of Federal personnel involving either direct or indirect attempts to influence Congressional action, is quite elusive. When personnel of the departments testify before Congressional committees, the General Accounting Office is hardly in a position to say they are lobbying, when in fact their testimony may have been requested, as is usually the case. Also, much necessary liaison work goes on perfectly legitimately between Congressional committees and executive agencies. Any Member of Congress has a perfect right to request an official of the Executive department to come up and advise him, or inform him, or discuss with him the effect of legislation that he may propose to introduce."

Notwithstanding continuing complaints by Members of Congress about Administration "arm-twisting," no laws have been enacted to place new curbs on such activities. Nor has there been a serious court test of the 1913 and 1919 statutes. Consequently, these laws have fallen into disuse, and the bounds of Administration lobbying activities appear to be limited only by the extent to which an Administration thinks Congress will let it go.

Bibliography

Books

Acheson, Dean, *Present at the Creation.* W. W. Norton & Co., Inc., 1969.

Alexander, DeAlva Stanwood, *History and Procedure of the House of Representatives.* Houghton Mifflin Co., 1916.

Bailey, Stephen Kemp, *Congress Makes A Law.* Columbia University Press, 1950.

Bell, Jack, *The Presidency: Office of Power.* Allyn and Bacon Inc., 1967.

Binkley, Wilfred E., *Powers of the President.* Doubleday and Co., 1937.

Binkley, Wilfred E., *President and Congress.* Alfred A. Knopf, 1947.

Cater, Douglass, *Power in Washington.* Random House, 1964.

Chamberlain, Lawrence H., *President, Congress and Legislation.* Columbia University Press, 1946.

Corwin, Edward S., *The President: Office and Powers.* New York University Press, 1948.

Corwin, Edward S., and Koenig, Louis W., *The Presidency Today.* New York University Press, 1956.

Evans, Rowland, Jr., and Novak, Robert, *Lyndon B. Johnson: The Exercise of Power.* The New American Library, 1966.

Gross, Bertram M., *The Legislative Struggle.* McGraw Hill Co., 1953.

Key, V.O., *Politics, Parties and Pressure Groups,* 5th ed. Thomas Y. Crowell Co., 1964.

MacLean, Joan Coyne, ed., *President and Congress: The Conflict of Powers.* H.W. Wilson Co., 1955.

MacNeil, Neil, *Forge of Democracy.* David McKay Co., 1963.

Milton, George Fort, *The Use of Presidential Power.* Little, Brown and Co., 1944.

Neustadt, Richard E., *Presidential Power.* John Wiley and Sons Inc., 1960.

Pollard, James E., *The Presidents and the Press.* The Macmillan Co., 1947.

Pollard, James E., *The Presidents and the Press: Truman to Johnson.* Public Affairs Press, 1964.

Polsby, Nelson W., *Congress and the Presidency.* Prentice Hall Inc., 1964.

Reston, James, *The Artillery of the Press.* Harper and Row, 1966.

Schlesinger, Arthur M. Jr., *The Coming of the New Deal.* Houghton Mifflin Co., 1959.

Truman, David B., *The Governmental Process,* 10th ed. Alfred A. Knopf, 1964.

Articles

Cornwell, Elmer E., Jr., "Wilson, Creel and the Presidency," *Public Opinion Quarterly,* Summer 1959, p. 189-202.

Duscha, Julius, "The Undercover Fight Over the Wilderness," *Harper's,* April 1962, p. 55-59.

Evans, Rowland Jr., "Louisiana's Passman: The Scourge of Foreign Aid," *Harper's,* January 1962, p. 78-83.

Greenfield, Meg, "Why Are You Calling Me, Son?", *The Reporter,* Aug. 16, 1962, p. 29-31.

Miller, Nathan, "The Making of a Majority: The Senate and the ABM," *Washington Monthly,* October 1969, p. 60-72.

Neustadt, Richard E., "President and Legislation: The Growth of Central Clearance," *American Political Science Review,* September 1954, p. 641-671.

Neustadt, Richard E., "President and Legislation: Planning the President's Program," *American Political Science Review,* December 1955, p. 980-1021.

Packman, Martin, "Government Jobs," *Editorial Research Reports,* May 18, 1955, p. 357-375.

Patch, Buel W., "Political Reform and Federal Patronage," *Editorial Research Reports,* July 2, 1934, p. 1-20.

Pipe, G. Russell, "Congressional Liaison; The Executive Branch Consolidates Its Relations With Congress," *Public Administration Review,* March 1966, p. 14-24.

Editorial, "The Spoils System in Congress," *America,* Sept. 11, 1965, p. 252-253.

Government Publications

General Interim Report, Select Committee on Lobbying Activities, U.S. House of Representatives, 81st Congress, 2nd Session, 1950.

"Lobbying, Direct and Indirect," Hearings, Part 6, Select Committee on Lobbying Activities, U.S. House of Representatives, 81st Congress, 2nd Session, 1950.

"The Role of Lobbying in Representative Self-Government," Hearings, Part 1, Select Committee on Lobbying Activities, U.S. House of Representatives, 81st Congress, 2nd Session, 1950.

The Supreme Court

THE SUPREME COURT, great interpreter of the law and guardian of the people against unconstitutional legislative or executive action, exerts a strong restraining influence upon Congress. Although the Constitution did not expressly authorize the Court to strike down acts it deemed unconstitutional, the Court assumed that important authority through its own broad interpretation of its vested powers. Without the process known as judicial review, there would be no assurance (not even the President's veto) against domination of the entire Government by runaway Congressional majorities.

Surprisingly, the incidence of Court rulings overturning acts of Congress is not high; only 85 acts or parts of acts have been declared unconstitutional in the 182 years of the Republic. Among the measures invalidated, many were unimportant and others, such as the measures prohibiting the spread of slavery and those carrying out parts of Franklin D. Roosevelt's New Deal program, were replaced by legislation so revised as to pass muster with the Supreme Court. Most constitutional scholars agree that the significance of judicial review is not in the number or even in the types of statutes the Court has struck down, but in the deterrent effect on Congress of a possible Supreme Court veto.

With few exceptions, the Court has interpreted the right of Congress to enact specific legislation as broadly as it has its own authority to sit in review of the statutes. The Court's approach to its duties was defined in 1827, when Justice Bushrod Washington observed that "it is but a decent respect due to the wisdom, the integrity and the patriotism of the legislative body by which any law is passed to presume in favor of its validity until its violation of the Constitution is proved beyond all reasonable doubt." Justices on almost every Court since Justice Washington's day have reaffirmed that attitude.

Changes in Court's Philosophy

Because Supreme Court Justices are appointed for life terms, the Court's philosophy is much slower to change than is that of the other two branches of the Federal Government. For a century and a half, the Court served primarily as a bulwark against encroachment on property rights, much to the chagrin of Populist-oriented Congresses. This concept was maintained even in the 1930s, when the need was evident for precedent-shattering legislation to grapple with the country's economic crisis. In 1935 and 1936, the Court struck down 11 New Deal statutes—the heart of the recovery program. But after President Roosevelt's overwhelming victory in the 1936 election and his threat to "pack" the Court with additional justices who presumably would favor his program, the Court relented and the remainder of the New Deal legislation was upheld. From that point on, the Court's philosophy leaned more toward a flexible reading of the Constitution to permit achievement of national social goals than it did toward the traditional practice of giving priority to protection of property. This shift of doctrine was completed during the term of Chief Justice Earl Warren (1954-1969), when the Court promulgated a series of sweeping decisions in support of individual rights and human welfare.

Whatever the Court's philosophy, it has always had its share of Congressional critics quick to accuse it of usurping undue powers. The early Anti-Federalists (later known as Democratic Republicans and finally as Democrats) thought the Court nullified the Constitution by a series of rulings strengthening Federal power at the expense of individuals and the states. New Deal Democrats thought the Court was attempting to seize the pre-eminent role in Government by voiding much of their legislative program. And in recent years, Republicans and southern Democrats were driven virtually to despair by the Court's decisions on school desegregation, civil rights, criminal law, internal security and voter representation.

Such criticism of the Court has led to a number of proposals to curb the tribunal's powers. Among the proposals have been a requirement of more than a majority vote to render a statute unconstitutional, removal of justices upon concurrence of the President and both houses of Congress, and restriction of the Court's appellate jurisdiction to exclude certain types of cases in which the Court has made decisions not to the liking of some Members of Congress. Although certain of these proposals have attracted wide support, none has ever been enacted into law. The only effective sanction available to Congress has been the Senate's refusal to confirm Court nominees. The Court's critics have been moderately successful in use of that sanction, blocking 27 of 136 Court nominations submitted by successive Presidents. Eleven of the 27 nominations were rejected outright, and the others were withdrawn or allowed to lapse in the face of Senate opposition. (See p. 230.)

Reference

See Appendix table of contents (first thumb tab) for list of Acts of Congress declared unconstitutional by the Supreme Court and for excerpts from Chief Justice John Marshall's opinion in *Marbury v. Madison*.

Sources of Supreme Court's Power

Unlike the rebels who framed the Declaration of Independence, the men who met at Philadelphia in 1787 to shape the U.S. Constitution represented conservative financial interests. These interests had suffered heavily during the period of national confederation following the Revolution, when state legislatures, controlled mostly by agrarian interests, made repeated assaults on vested rights.

While the framers of the Constitution deprecated the excesses of the legislatures, they held a high respect for the courts, which gave judgments in favor of creditors and sent delinquent debtors to jail. As political scientist Charles A. Beard, a leading constitutional scholar, once put it, "The conservative interests, made desperate by the imbecilities of the Confederation and harried by the state legislatures, roused themselves from their lethargy, drew together in a mighty effort to establish a government that would be strong enough to pay the national debt, regulate interstate and foreign commerce, provide for national defense, prevent fluctuations in the currency created by paper emissions, and control the propensities of legislative majorities to attack private rights."

At the time the Framers met, judicial review had not yet been instituted in any country in the world. And despite considerable discussion of some means to check the excesses of Congress, the matter of a judicial veto never came up for a direct vote. The closest the Convention got to considering such a scheme was when it rejected the Virginia Plan of government. That plan contained a section establishing a Council of Revision, consisting of Supreme Court justices and the President, to consider the constitutionality of proposed acts prior to final Congressional passage. As submitted to the state conventions for ratification, the Constitution was not clear on the final arbiter of constitutional disputes. Wilfred E. Binkley and Malcolm C. Moos have pointed out that there were matters the delegates "dared not baldly assert in the Constitution without imperiling its ratification, but they doubtless hoped that implications would eventually be interpreted to supply the thing desired." Judicial review appeared to be one of those things. Most other constitutional scholars have supported this view.

In *The Federalist*, a series of essays written to promote adoption of the Constitution, Alexander Hamilton made clear that the Framers expected the Judiciary to rule on constitutional issues. In Number 78 of *The Federalist*, Hamilton wrote: "The complete independence of the courts of justice is peculiarly essential in a limited constitution. By a limited constitution, I understand one which contains certain specified exceptions to the legislative authority, such for instance, as that it shall pass no bills of attainder, no ex-post facto laws, and the like. Limitations of this kind can be preserved in practice no other way than through the courts of justice, whose duty it must be to declare all acts contrary to the manifest tenor of the Constitution void. Without this, all the reservations of particular rights or privileges would amount to nothing."

In a 1912 study of the history of judicial review, Beard found that of the 25 members of the Convention who appeared to be most influential in shaping the Constitution, 17 (including Hamilton) were on record as favoring "the proposition that the Judiciary would, in the

normal course of things, pass upon the constitutionality of acts of Congress." Of the less prominent members, Beard said, eight went on record as understanding and approving the doctrine. Opponents of the concept have placed five members of the Convention against judicial review, but only one of these, Pierce Butler of South Carolina, was in the influential group. Beard observed that "The accepted canons of historical criticism warrant the assumption that, when a legal proposition is before a lawmaking body (the Constitutional Convention) and a considerable number of the supporters of that proposition definitely assert that it involves certain important and fundamental implications, and it is nevertheless approved by that body without any protests worthy of mention, these implications must be deemed part of that legal proposition when it becomes law...." Binkley and Moos asserted: "Whether or not the Supreme Court 'usurped' the practice of judicial review is now purely an academic question. So completely has the practice been woven into the warp and woof of our constitutional fabric that the garment could now scarcely endure its elimination."

Acts Declared Unconstitutional

No major constitutional clashes occurred during the Republic's first decade. Congress and the Executive Branch were firmly in the hands of the Federalist party, which was united in its determination to stifle the political opposition—the states'-rights-minded Anti-Federalists. When Congress passed the far-reaching Sedition Act of 1798, which led to the imprisonment of several Anti-Federalist editors for criticizing the Government, the Court refused to strike down the Act despite Anti-Federalist assertions of its probable unconstitutionality.

Only once in that decade did the courts question an act of Congress, and that was on a minor matter. In the *Hayburn Case* of 1792, two Supreme Court Justices sitting on a circuit court (as they then had to do in addition to performing their Supreme Court duties) declined to implement an act requiring the circuit courts to pass upon certain claims of invalid pensioners, subject to later revision by the Secretary of War and Congress. The Justices ruled the act unconstitutional because Congress was not empowered by the Constitution to add to the original jurisdiction of the Court. Article III of the Constitution gave the Supreme Court original jurisdiction over "cases affecting ambassadors, other public ministers and consuls, and those in which a state shall be party." In other cases the Supreme Court was given appellate jurisdiction "both as to law and fact, with such exceptions and under such regulations as the Congress shall make."

Case of Marbury v. Madison

The doctrine of judicial review was first enunciated by the Supreme Court in the famous case of *Marbury v. Madison* (1 Cranch 137) in 1803.

After Republican Presidential candidate Thomas Jefferson had defeated Federalist John Adams in the latter's bid for re-election in 1800—but before the Republicans took office—Adams nominated a number of Federalists to judicial posts created by court-reform legislation passed by the lame-duck Federalist Congress. The nominations of 16 judges and some other officials were confirmed by the Senate and the commissions signed by Adams in the waning days and hours of his Administration. When Adams' term expired at midnight on March 3, 1801, several of the commissions had not been delivered. Jefferson, who entered office at the stroke of midnight, ordered that these commissions be withheld.

One of the appointees whose commission had not been delivered was William Marbury, who had been named to the post of justice of the peace for the District of Columbia. Marbury sought to test Jefferson's executive power by filing suit in the Supreme Court requiring Jefferson's Secretary of State, James Madison, to deliver the commission. Marbury filed the suit under terms of the Judiciary Act of 1789, which empowered the Court to issue writs of mandamus compelling Federal officials to perform their duties.

The Chief Justice at the time of the case was John Marshall, a staunch Federalist who had been Secretary of State in the Adams Administration and had been responsible in that capacity for delivering the commissions to Marbury and the other appointees. Notwithstanding his personal interest, Marshall refused to disqualify himself from participation in the Court's action in the case. On the contrary, he delivered the opinion of the Court.

Marshall first held that Marbury was entitled to his commission and that he should be granted the writ of mandamus if the Court had proper jurisdiction. Although the Judiciary Act of 1789 purported to grant the Supreme Court the jurisdiction necessary in this case, Marshall asserted that that part of the Act was unconstitutional because Congress had no power to enlarge the Court's original jurisdiction.

Under the guise of handing his Jeffersonian foes a political victory, Marshall had laid the cornerstone of Federal judicial power. Charles Warren, a leading constitutional authority, has commented: "Marshall naturally felt that in view of the recent attacks on judicial power, it was important to have the great principle firmly established, and undoubtedly he welcomed the opportunity of fixing the precedent in a case in which his action would necessitate a decision in favor of his political opponents.... In comprehensive and forceful terms, which for over 100 years have never been successfully controverted, he proceeded to lay down the great principles of the supremacy of the Constitution over statute law, and of the duty and power of the Judiciary to act as the arbiter in case of any conflict between the two."

Ironically, the doctrine of Supreme Court authority to strike down unconstitutional legislation, which Marshall established in the Marbury case, attracted little comment at the time. Republicans were critical instead of Marshall's comment that the mandamus should have been granted if the Court held proper jurisdiction. According to Charles Warren, Jefferson felt that Marshall and the other Federalists on the Court had "intentionally gone out of their way to rule on points unnecessary for the decision, and he regarded it as a deliberate assumption of a right to interfere with his executive functions." Jefferson remained indignant about that aspect of the decision until his death in 1826. As late as 1823, he wrote that "the practice of Judge Marshall in travelling out of his case to prescribe what the law would be in a moot case not before the Court" was "very irregular and very censurable" and amounted to an unwarranted lecture to the President from a political opponent on the bench.

Dred Scott Decision

It was not until the eve of the Civil War that the Supreme Court again held an act of Congress unconstitutional. It did so in the case of *Scott v. Sanford* (60 U.S. 393) in 1857, probably the Court's most controversial decision of all time and the one most criticized by students of the Constitution.

Dred Scott, a slave, had been taken by his former master from the slave state of Missouri into territory made free by the act of Congress known as the Missouri Compromise. After returning to Missouri, Scott sued to establish his freedom on the ground that his sojourn in free territory had made him a free man. The Missouri Supreme Court held that he had indeed gained his freedom through being on free soil, but that he had lost it when he returned to the slave state of Missouri.

Since Scott's present master (Sanford) was a citizen of New York, the case could now be considered by a Federal court as a controversy between citizens of different states, provided that Scott was a citizen of Missouri. When the case reached the U.S. Supreme Court, a majority of the Justices decided initially that the case should have been dismissed in lower Federal court for lack of jurisdiction, because no Negro could be a citizen under terms of the Constitution. But the Court did not stop there despite the finding of no jurisdiction. Chief Justice Roger Brooke Taney, who wrote what is considered the majority decision in the case (although nine separate opinions were filed by the Justices), asserted that Scott was a slave because the Missouri Compromise—which had been repealed three years earlier by the Kansas-Nebraska Act—was unconstitutional. Congress, Taney declared, had no authority to limit the extension of slavery. (The decision was voided by the 13th Amendment outlawing slavery.)

The Dred Scott decision aroused tremendous resentment in the North, especially among members of the newly organized Republican party whose cardinal tenet was that Congress should abolish slavery in all of the territories. The *New York Tribune* asserted that the decision was entitled to "just so much moral weight as would be the judgment of a majority of those congregated in any Washington barroom.... Until that remote period when different judges sitting in this same court shall reverse this wicked and false judgment, the Constitution of the United States is nothing better than the bulwark of inhumanity and repression."

Greenback and Tax Cases

Greenback Cases. The Dred Scott decision was a prime example of what a later Supreme Court Chief Justice, Charles Evans Hughes, called the Court's "self-inflicted wounds." As he noted, "It was many years before the Court, even under new judges, was able to retrieve its reputation." Before it had been able to do so, another decision on a constitutional issue brought the Court into further disrepute. In the case of *Hepburn v. Griswold* (8 Wallace 603), the Court by a 4-3 decision in 1870 ruled unconstitutional the provision of a Civil War statute making United States notes, popularly known as "greenbacks," legal tender in payment of debts contracted before passage of the Act.

On the day the opinion was rendered, President Grant, a proponent of the greenback clause, nominated

The Federal Judicial System....

Under the United States system of checks and balances, the Supreme Court stands at the pinnacle of the Federal judicial structure as the final reviewing authority of Congressional legislation and executive action. However, as is implicit in a check and balance system of government, the High Court, and also the lower Federal judiciary, does not function with complete independence. On the one hand, the Judicial Branch is beholden to the Legislative Branch for its size, pay and, most importantly, for its scope of jurisdiction. On the other hand, the Judicial Branch is beholden to the Executive Branch for its membership.

Federal and State Courts. Two types of judicial systems, state and Federal, have provided forums for the resolution of litigated disputes. The state judicial systems are comprised of the state supreme court, or state court of appeals, and a group of lower courts, such as municipal, police and justice-of-the-peace courts. The Federal system forms a tri-level pyramid, comprised of district courts at the bottom, circuit courts of appeals in the middle, and the Supreme Court at the top.

Provision for a Federal judiciary was made by Article III, Section 1, of the Constitution, which stated: "The judicial power of the United States shall be vested in one supreme court, and in such inferior courts as the Congress may from time to time ordain and establish." Thus, aside from the required "supreme court," the structure of the lower Federal judicial system was left entirely to the discretion of Congress.

Congress and Federal Courts

The Judiciary Act of 1789 established the Supreme Court, 13 district courts, each with a single judge, and, above the district courts, three circuit courts, each presided over by one district and two Supreme Court judges. Thereafter, as the nation grew and the Federal judiciary's workload increased, Congress established additional circuit and district courts. There are now 11 circuit courts of appeals, 88 district courts, and four territorial courts (Canal Zone, Guam, Puerto Rico and Virgin Islands).

The influence of Congress over the Federal judiciary went beyond the creation of courts. Although the power to appoint Federal judges resided with the President, by and with the Senate's advice and consent, the power to create judgeships to which appointments could be made resided with Congress. It was in this area that politics historically played its most important role. For example, in 1801, the Federalist Congress created additional circuit court judgeships to be filled by a Federalist President. However, in 1802, when the Jefferson Republicans came into power, the new posts were abolished.

As Federal judges were appointed to serve during good behavior, the power of Congress to abolish judge-ships was limited to providing in the creation of a judgeship that, when it became vacant, it could not be filled. The history of the Supreme Court's size provides the best illustration of the earlier habit of creating and abolishing judgeships. Originally, the Supreme Court was comprised of six justices. Subsequently, however, its membership varied: five justices, 1801-07; seven justices, 1807-37; nine justices, 1837-63; 10 justices, 1863-66; seven justices, 1866-69; and nine justices since 1869.

Jurisdiction of Federal Courts. Article III, Section 2, of the Constitution vested in the Supreme Court original jurisdiction over only a few kinds of cases. The most important of these were suits between two states, which might concern such issues as water rights, offshore lands, etc. Article III, Section 2, also extended to the Court "judicial power" over all cases arising under the Constitution, Federal laws and treaties. This jurisdiction, however, was appellate (i.e., limited to review of decisions from lower courts) and was subject to "such exceptions and...regulations as Congress shall make." Most of the High Court's present jurisdiction is defined by the Judiciary Act of 1925, largely drafted by the Court itself under Chief Justice Taft.

At that time, the Court was falling far behind in its docket—by as much as two years. It was felt that obligatory appellate jurisdiction was bringing before the Court far too many cases of relatively minor significance. In the Judiciary Act of 1925, the exercise of the Court's appellate jurisdiction was made largely discretionary.

Except for certain limited types of cases in which the Court was still "obligated" to take appeals, the Court was allowed to decide whether the decisions from the inferior tribunals presented questions or conflicts important enough or of such a constitutional nature as to warrant the Court's consideration on review.

In the relationship between Federal and state judicial systems, Federal courts had jurisdiction—usually where $10,000 or more was involved—over cases relating to Federal rights or actions in which the parties were citizens of different states. The state courts, on the other hand, were concerned with cases generally involving citizens of the specific states and their own state laws.

There was some overlap of jurisdiction. The state courts were empowered to hear litigation concerning some Federal rights, and Federal constitutional rights often formed the basis of decision in state court cases.

In the Federal courts, where jurisdiction is based on a "diversity of citizenship" (i.e., the litigants are from different states), the court is obliged to find and apply the pertinent law of the state in which the court is sitting. In state court cases, similarly, in those few instances where a "Federal question" might be resolved, the court is obliged to disregard its own precedents and apply appropriate Federal law.

....in the United States

Judicial Appointments

The power to name members of the Federal judiciary is perhaps the strongest and most controversial patronage lever possessed by an incumbent President. As a result, Federal judgeships, which are filled by the President with Senate confirmation, traditionally go to those having the same political affiliation as the President. Throughout the nation's history, however, Presidents generally have indicated their intention to make judicial appointments nonpartisan. Nevertheless, since a judge is appointed for life at a substantial salary, making the position a plum, appointees to the Federal bench, with few exceptions, have been of the same political party as the President appointing them.

Stages of Appointment Process. Two sections of the Constitution govern judicial appointments. Article II, Section 2, Clause 2, provided: The President "...shall nominate, and by and with the advice and consent of the Senate, shall appoint...judges of the Supreme Court, and all other officers of the United States...." Article II, Section 3, provided: The President "...shall commission all officers of the United States...."

From these two sections evolved three stages in the appointment process: (1) the nomination, (2) the appointment, and (3) the commission. The "nomination" was the independent act of the President, and was completely voluntary. In the selection, or nomination, of a prospective district or circuit court judge, however, the President usually took into consideration a number of things—for example, political views and party affiliation, the opinions of Congressional advisers who aided the President on other partisan matters, the recommendations of national, state and local political organizations and the qualification ratings given prospective nominees by national, state and local bar associations. In the selection of Supreme Court nominees, on the other hand, the President usually acted with more independence and gave more weight to political philosophy.

The "appointment" was also the sole act of the President, and was also a voluntary act, but could be performed only with the advice and consent of the Senate. In effect, the appointment was made automatically upon Senate confirmation, unless the President, for some previously unforeseen reason, decided to retract the nomination. Confirmation followed Senate Judiciary Committee approval and an affirmative floor vote in the Senate. Prior to confirmation, a Senator could object to a nominee for patronage or other reasons—for example, when a nomination to a district or circuit judgeship was made without consulting the Senators of the district or circuit concerned. Then a Senator could use the stock, but rare, objection that the nominee was "personally obnoxious" to him. In this case, other Senators usually —but not always—joined in blocking confirmation out of courtesy to their colleague.

The "commission" was also the sole act of the President, although merely a technicality provided for by the Constitution. It simply meant that the appointee was given by the President the authority to carry out the duties of his office.

Under the original agreement between the American Bar Association and the Senate, the ABA worked exclusively with the Senate Judiciary Committee, submitting its evaluation of the prospective nominee when informed by the Committee that hearings were going to be held. In 1952, the Justice Department as well asked for the ABA's evaluation of the candidate. In 1953, at the request of the Justice Department, the ABA stopped submitting the names of lawyers it considered qualified whenever a Federal judicial vacancy occurred. Thereafter it confined its reports to persons under active consideration by the Department.

Types of Appointments. There are two types of judicial appointments, including the regular appointment route outlined above. The other is the "recess" appointment prescribed by the Constitution's Article II, Section 2, Clause 3, which stated: "The President shall have power to fill up all vacancies that may happen during the recess of the Senate, by granting commissions which shall expire at the end of their (the Congress') next session."

The recess appointment is a frequently used and often criticized means of making appointments by temporarily bypassing Senate confirmation. Under this procedure, the President, when a judgeship becomes vacant and when Congress is not in session, can extend a "commission" for a judgeship, and the new judge can then take office without Senate confirmation. However, when Congress reconvenes, the President has to submit the name of his recess nominee for confirmation within 40 days. If he does not do so, the judge's pay is terminated. On the other hand, if the name is submitted in the required time and Congress fails to confirm or reject the nomination during the session, the appointment is good until Congress adjourns. When this happens, the President customarily gives the incumbent judge another recess appointment.

To prevent a President from leaving a vacancy which occurred in mid-session unfilled until Congress adjourns, so that he can make a recess appointment, law requires that the President nominate a person to fill a vacancy within 30 days. If the President fails to do this, he can still wait until Congress adjourns and then make the recess appointment, but the appointee would not be eligible to draw a salary.

William Strong and Joseph P. Bradley to fill two vacant seats on the Court. Soon after their confirmation, the Court ordered reargument of the case and reversed itself. In a 5-4 decision, with Bradley and Strong voting with the majority, the greenback statute was held constitutional. Even Chief Justice Salmon P. Chase joined critics in contending that the President had packed the court in order to win the reversal. The decision worked to the advantage of the railroads, whose long-term bonds were becoming due. The notes could now be paid in depreciated currency instead of gold, as would have been required under the first greenback decision.

In the opinion of Justice Hughes, "The reopening of the case was a serious mistake and the overruling in such a short time, and by one vote, of the previous decision, shook popular confidence in the Court." Hughes concluded: "The argument for reopening was strongly presented in view of the great importance of the question but the effect of such a sudden reversal of judgment might easily have been foreseen. Stability in judicial opinions is of no little importance in maintaining respect for the Court's work."

Income Tax Case. The next controversial overturning of a Congressional statute came in the income tax case of 1895, *Pollock v. Farmer's Loan and Trust Co.* (157 U.S. 429, 158 U.S. 601). Under assault in the case were the income tax provisions of the Tariff Act of 1894, which imposed a tax of 2 percent on incomes of more than $4,000. The Court at first held the statute constitutional by a 4-4 vote but later ruled it void by a vote of 5-4. The Court's reasoning was that the levy was a "direct tax," and the Constitution required that direct taxes be apportioned among the states according to population. The decision was widely interpreted as a predisposition by the Court to the doctrines of rugged individualism and Social Darwinism (survival of the fittest). This theme seemed to run through the concurring opinion of Justice Stephen J. Field, who said: "If the provisions of the Constitution can be set aside by an act of Congress, where is the course of usurpation to end? The present assault upon capital is but the beginning. It will be but the stepping stone to others, larger and more sweeping, till our political contests will become a war of the poor against the rich; a war constantly growing in intensity and bitterness." The decision was bitterly assailed by Democrats in Congress who contended that such protection of wealth was unconscionable in view of the severe depression then afflicting the country. The decision was nullified by the ratification in 1913 of the 16th Amendment empowering Congress to levy taxes on income without apportionment among the states. *(See p. 292.)*

Wave of Invalidations in Taft Court

Solicitude for property rights reached its high-water mark on the Supreme Court during the Chief Justiceship of William Howard Taft, who served from 1921 to 1930. "In the last analysis," the former President once commented, "personal liberty includes the right of property, as it includes the right of contract and the right of labor. Our primary conception of a free man is one who can enjoy what he earns, who can spend it for his comfort or pleasure if he would.... This is the right of property.... Personal liberty and the right of property are indispensable to any possible useful progress to society."

To ward off what it regarded as unwarranted governmental intrusion on property rights, the Taft Court struck down an unusually large number of state and Federal statutes. While the Court had invalidated only two acts of Congress in the period from 1789 to 1865 (in the Marbury and Dred Scott cases), it struck down 22 in the period from 1920 to 1932. Among the Congressional statutes invalidated were curbs on the use of child labor (*Bailey v. Drexel Furniture Co.*, 259 U.S. 20) and a minimum wage for women and children in the District of Columbia *(Adkins v. Children's Hospital,* 261 U.S. 525). In the D.C. minimum wage case, decided in 1923, Justice George Sutherland wrote that the freedom of an individual to make his own labor arrangements was "the general rule and restraint the exception." Taft himself voted with the minority, but he wrote in dissent that "It is a disputable question in the field of political economy how far a statutory requirement of maximum hours or minimum wages may be a useful remedy" for the sweatshop system.

Fate of New Deal Legislation

The appointment in 1930 of Charles Evans Hughes to succeed Taft as Chief Justice seemed at the time to herald a new, less conservative era on the Supreme Court. In his six years on the Court as an Associate Justice (1910-1916), Hughes had become known for his liberal attitude in the field of civil liberties. As it developed, however, the Hughes Court became involved in an unprecedented clash with the Legislative and Executive Branches over the New Deal's intrusion on property rights.

One after another, the depression-born statutes passed by Congress at President Roosevelt's urging were struck down by the Hughes Court. During the 1935 and 1936 terms, laws invalidated by the Court included such key New Deal measures as the Railroad Retirement Act, the National Industrial Recovery Act (NIRA), the Agricultural Adjustment Act (AAA), the Bituminous Coal Conservation (Guffey) Act, a part of the Home Owners' Loan Act, an act providing for readjustment of municipal indebtedness, and the Frazier-Lemke Act designed to delay foreclosures of farm mortgages.

The only major New Deal statute to survive Supreme Court scrutiny (the important Reciprocal Trade Agreements Act did not come up for judicial review) was the Tennessee Valley Authority Act, which created a public regional development authority. In the NIRA and certain other cases, the Court ruled that Congress had made unconstitutional delegations of legislative power to the Executive Branch—unconstitutional because they set no standards to be followed in carrying out the acts or prescribed no findings of fact to be made before invoking the delegated powers. In most of the other cases, the Court narrowly interpreted the authority of Congress to regulate commerce or ruled that Congress was encroaching upon powers reserved to the states. Fear rose that the Court might strike down two 1935 New Deal enactments, the National Labor Relations (Wagner) Act and the Social Security Act, if given the opportunity.

President Roosevelt, stung by the Supreme Court's piecemeal destruction of his legislative program, resolved after the 1936 elections to do something about it. In a surprise message to Congress, Feb. 5, 1937, he asked for legislation that would authorize the President, when any Federal judge who had been in service for 10 years did not retire within six months after becoming 70 years old, to appoint an additional judge to the court in question.

Such a law would have made it possible for the President to add six Justices to the Supreme Court and thus presumably ensure a majority sympathetic to the New Deal. Speaking to the country on radio a month later, Roosevelt declared that he wanted "a Supreme Court that will enforce the Constitution as written—that will refuse to amend the Constitution by the arbitrary exercise of judicial power—amendment by judicial say-so."

Although the Court had come under heavy fire for its anti-New Deal decisions, the Court-packing plan ran into strong opposition within and outside of Congress. Hughes presented an able defense of the Court before the Senate Judiciary Committee, which, on June 14, 1937, submitted an adverse report on the Administration bill. A measure finally approved in August provided only for procedural reforms in the lower courts.

Nonetheless, the President's campaign succeeded in bringing about a change of heart on the part of the Supreme Court. In *West Coast Hotel v. Parrish* (300 U.S. 379), decided soon after the court-packing plan was submitted to Congress, a minimum wage law, similar to one ruled unconstitutional a year before, was held to be valid. Revised versions of several of the other acts struck down by the Hughes Court were passed by Congress and sustained by the Court. On April 12, 1937, the Court in *NLRB v. Jones and Laughlin Steel Corp.* (301 U.S. 1) upheld the constitutionality of the Wagner Act. In that decision, Chief Justice Hughes put forward a broad and encompassing definition of interstate commerce, contending that Congress had power to protect the lifelines of the national economy from private industrial warfare. Arguments that had proved effective in the NIRA and coal cases were unavailing. "These cases," Hughes asserted, "are not controlling here." Of the Court's change of direction, it was said that "A switch in time saved nine."

Civil Rights Cases in Warren Court

The Supreme Court under Chief Justice Earl Warren (1954-1969) clashed repeatedly with Congress over a series of Court rulings protecting individual rights. Although most of the controversy had to do with alleged Court usurpation of states' rights, several of the Court's decisions, including three important ones in the field of internal security, involved reversal of acts of Congress.

The first of the controversial rulings in the security field came in 1956, when the Court curbed dismissal of Government employees who were considered security risks. By a 6-3 decision in *Cole v. Young*, the Court ruled that the term "national security" in PL 81-733, the statute establishing the Government's industrial security program, was not used "in an all-inclusive sense, but was intended to refer only to the protection of 'sensitive' activities. It followed that an employee could be dismissed 'in the interests of the national security' under the Act only if he occupied a 'sensitive' position."

Another controversial decision was handed down the following year in the case of *Yates v. United States*. In that case the Warren Court ruled that the Smith Act of 1940 did not outlaw advocacy of forcible overthrow of the Government as an abstract doctrine but only as an incitement to action. The Court ruled also that the term "organize," as used in the Smith Act's prohibition against organizing a group advocating forcible overthrow, re-ferred only to the initial act of bringing the group into being and not to continued organizing activities such as the recruitment of members. For the American Communist Party, the Court held, the act of organization had taken place in 1945, when the Communist Political Association was dissolved and the party brought into being. In 1962, Congress finally succeeded in enacting legislation to broaden the term "organize" to include continuing organizational activities.

A third major internal security case in which the Warren Court struck down Federal legislation was the 1964 case of *Aptheker v. Secretary of State*, in which the Court held unconstitutional a section of the Subversive Activities Control Act of 1950 depriving all U.S. Communist Party members of passport privileges. The Court, in a 6-3 decision, ruled that the clause was in violation of the due process clause of the Fifth Amendment. Other acts or parts of acts of Congress overturned by the Warren Court included provisions of the Uniform Code of Military Justice; a law depriving of citizenship (1) citizens leaving the country or remaining abroad during wartime in order to escape military service, (2) citizens voting in foreign elections, and (3) naturalized citizens having extended residence in the country of their birth or prior citizenship; a law prohibiting Communists from serving as officers or employees of labor unions; a provision for compulsory registration of Communist Party members; and several other minor statutes.

Congressional Investigations

Alleged abuse of Congressional investigatory powers has produced a number of Supreme Court decisions through the years. After some inconclusive disputes over the power of Congress to penalize contempt, the Supreme Court in 1821 (*Anderson v. Dunn*) upheld the authority of a house of Congress to punish "contempts committed against themselves." The power was limited to "the least possible power adequate to the end proposed," and imprisonment could not extend beyond the adjournment of Congress. Considering the limitation of imprisonment to the legislative session inadequate, Congress in 1857 enacted a law making it a criminal offense to refuse information demanded by either house. This statute is the original version of the law generally used by Congress today to enforce observance of its investigative authority.

In 1881 (*Kilbourn v. Thompson*), the Supreme Court asserted the right of the courts to review the investigative activities of Congress. The decision was an extension of the principle of judicial review established by Chief Justice Marshall in the 1803 Marbury decision. The 1881 decision concerned a House investigation of a private real estate pool, with one of whose bankrupt members the Federal Government had deposited funds. The Court held that "the investigation which the Committee was directed to make was judicial...and could only be properly and successfully made by a court of justice." The House, it said, was pursuing "a fruitless investigation into the personal affairs of individuals," which "could result in no valid legislation on the subject" of the inquiry.

Congress delegated its investigative powers to the Interstate Commerce Commission, established in 1887, and subsequently to other regulatory agencies. The Supreme Court in 1894 (*Interstate Commerce Commission v. Brimson*) sustained the ICC's investigative authority, but in 1906 *(Harriman v. Interstate Commerce Commission)* held that the power was limited to obtaining information connected with possible violations of law.

A series of Supreme Court decisions evolved a balance between the powers of investigating committees and the rights of witnesses. The most important of these decisions was made in 1927 *(McGrain v. Daugherty)*, when the Court ruled that the Senate could require information from Mally S. Daugherty, brother of former Attorney General Harry M. Daugherty. Justice Willis Van Devanter, speaking for the Court, stated that "the only legitimate object the Senate could have in ordering the investigation was to aid it in legislating; and we think the subject matter was such that the presumption should be indulged that this was the real object." Van Devanter sought to balance two general principles which he summarized as follows:

"One, that the two houses of Congress...possess not only such powers as are expressly granted to them by the Constitution, but such auxiliary powers as are necessary and appropriate to make the express powers effective; and the other, that neither house is invested with 'general' power to inquire into private affairs and compel disclosures, but only with such limited power of inquiry as is shown to exist when the rule...just stated is rightly applied."

In 1929 *(Sinclair v. United States)* the Supreme Court held that a witness who refused to answer questions asked by a Congressional committee could be punished if he were mistaken as to the ground on which he based his refusal, even if he acted in good faith on the advice of counsel. This precedent made any challenge of committee powers risky; a jail sentence might be in store for a witness seeking to test his rights in court. *(See p. 252-253.)*

Following World War II, the Supreme Court was far more protective of the rights of witnesses than of the rights of Congressional committees. In the 1953 case of *United States v. Rumely*, the Supreme Court upheld a Court of Appeals decision reversing the conviction for contempt of Congress of Edward A. Rumely. Rumely had refused to tell the House Select Committee on Lobbying Activities the names of individuals making bulk purchases of books distributed by the Committee for Constitutional Government, an arch-conservative organization. He had asserted to the Committee that "under the Bill of Rights, that is beyond the power of your Committee to investigate."

A majority of the Court avoided the constitutional questions by narrowly construing the authority granted by the resolution establishing the Committee. It held that the mandate to investigate "lobbying activities" was limited to "representations made directly to the Congress, its Members, or its committees," and excluded attempts to influence Congress indirectly through public dissemination of literature. Otherwise, the Court said, it would be confronted by "grave constitutional questions." Interpreting the authorizing resolution to include attempts to influence Congress indirectly, Justices William O. Douglas and Hugo L. Black contended that the requirement that a publisher disclose the identity of purchasers would violate the First Amendment guarantees of freedom of speech and the press.

The Court again placed strictures on the investigative powers of Congress in 1957, when it ruled in *Watkins v. United States* that John T. Watkins was not guilty of contempt of Congress for refusing to answer certain questions before the House Un-American Activities Committee. The Court based its decision on a finding that the Committee's legislative mandate was "loosely worded" and "excessively broad" and that the Committee had failed to show that its questions were pertinent to the subject of the inquiry.

The Court backtracked somewhat from this position in its decision in a 1959 case, *Barenblatt v. United States*. By a 5-4 vote, it ruled that First Amendment rights may be limited where the public interest outweighs the private interest. While the Court in that case criticized the "vagueness" of that section of House Rule XI defining the powers and duties of the Un-American Activities Committee (in the language of the resolution establishing the Committee), it concluded that "we may not read it in isolation from its long history in the House." *(See box.)* Shifting gears again, the Court in 1963, by another 5-4 decision, reversed the conviction of Edward Yellin for contempt of Congress on the ground that the Un-American Activities Committee violated its own rules by failing to consider his request for an executive session before he was questioned.

Court-Curbing Proposals

Intermittently throughout American history, Congressional critics of judicial power have sought to impose restrictions on the Supreme Court. The methods have ranged from proposed curbs on the Court's authority to the Senate's rejection of Court nominees.

Early Proposals. The first move against the Court was made in 1802, when the newly elected Congress dominated by Jeffersonian Republicans abolished additional Federal circuit courts set up the year before by the old Congress and staffed with 16 Federalist judges (the "midnight judges") appointed by President Adams on the eve of his departure from office. To delay a decision in the Marbury and controversial cases, Congress also enacted legislation postponing the Supreme Court's term for 14 months, until February 1803. In 1805, Rep. John Randolph, a Virginia Republican, proposed a constitutional amendment providing for removal of Supreme Court Justices by the President upon the approval of both houses of Congress. However, Randolph's proposal attracted little support and was dropped.

Alarmed by a series of Supreme Court decisions strengthening Federal power at the expense of the states, states' rights advocates in Congress introduced a variety of other Court-curbing proposals over the next several decades. In 1807, Republicans proposed a constitutional amendment providing for a limited tenure of office for Federal judges and for their removal by the President upon a two-thirds vote of each house. In 1831, Congressional Democrats (the old Jeffersonian Republican party) launched a determined effort to repeal Section 25 of the Judiciary Act of 1789, which authorized writs of error to the Supreme Court on state court judgments. (A writ of error is a process under which an appellate court may bring up a case from a lower court to examine the trial record as to questions of law but not of fact.) On Jan. 29, 1831, the House rejected this proposal by a 51-158 roll-call vote, with all but six of the minority votes coming from southern and western states. Later that year, Democrats introduced another proposal directing the House Judiciary Committee to study the feasibility of amending the Constitution to limit the tenure of Federal judges. That proposal was rejected by a 61-115 roll-call vote.

Another series of attacks on the Court was launched in the early 1900s by critics of the Court's decisions protecting property rights. In 1923, Sen. William E. Borah (R Idaho) introduced a bill to require concurrence by seven of the nine justices to invalidate an act of Congress. The following year Sen. Robert M. LaFollette (Prog Wis.) proposed a constitutional amendment providing that a statute once struck down by the Supreme Court could be declared constitutional and immune from further Court consideration by a two-thirds majority of both houses of Congress. Neither the Borah nor the LaFollette proposal received serious consideration.

After Congress rejected the Roosevelt court-packing plan in 1937, the Supreme Court experienced a period of relatively placid relations with Congress until the Warren Court launched on its course of judicial activism in the mid-1950s. The only proposed curb on the Court that attracted much support from the mid-1930s to the early 1950s was a 1953 proposal to amend the Constitution to make retirement mandatory for all Federal judges at age 75. The resolution proposing the amendment, suggested by the American Bar Association, was adopted by the Senate in 1954 but was shelved by the House.

Attacks on the Warren Court

Congressional attacks on the Warren Court began in 1954, the year of the Court's famous school desegregation decision. On May 17, 1954, the Court had declared in the case of *Brown v. Board of Education of Topeka, Kansas* that racial segregation in public schools was inherently discriminatory and therefore in contravention of the equal protection clause of the 14th Amendment. The period of the next four years was a time of unusual anti-Court activity in Congress, spurred at first by southern Members. Some 19 Senators and 74 Representatives from the South signed a "Declaration of Constitutional Principles"—the so-called Southern Manifesto—on March 12, 1956, protesting the "decision of the Supreme Court in the school cases as a clear abuse of judicial power." The southerners were joined in time by colleagues from other sections who were dismayed by the Court's decisions in such matters as Federal-state relations, Communist activities, and contempt of Congress.

From 1955 through 1962, Congress considered legislation to curb the Supreme Court's power to strike down state laws under the doctrine of Federal legislative preemption. Under Article VI, Section 2, of the Constitution, making Federal law the "supreme law of the land," the courts had invalidated state laws in cases where: (1) Congress had stated an intention to take over ("preempt") a given field of legislation; (2) there was a direct conflict between a Federal law and a state law; or (3) Congressional intention to preempt a field of legislation could be inferred, even though it had not been specified by Congress (the doctrine of "preemption by implication"). In 1958, a broad anti-preemption bill was passed overwhelmingly by the House and was defeated in the Senate by only one vote.

Jenner-Butler Bill. Still to come in 1958 was another major court-curbing bill. The measure, known as the Jenner-Butler bill (for Republican Senators William E. Jenner of Indiana and John Marshall Butler of Maryland), would have deprived the Supreme Court of authority to review several types of cases, including those concerning contempt of Congress, the Federal loyalty-security program, state anti-subversive statutes, and admission to the practice of law in any state. After lengthy committee hearings and bitter floor debate, the Senate tabled the bill by a vote of 49 to 41 on Aug. 20, 1958.

Attacks on the Supreme Court came not only from Congress but also from the Judiciary itself. Three days after the Jenner-Butler bill was shelved by the Senate, the Conference of State Chief Justices approved a statement asserting that the Court "too often has tended to adopt the rule of policy-maker without proper judicial restraint." The statement added: "We are not alone in our view that the Court, in many cases...has assumed what seem to us primarily legislative powers."

Dirksen Amendments. Congressional attacks on the Court intensified in the early 1960s. The Court in 1962 ruled unconstitutional the use of a 22-word prayer in New York State public schools. Justice Black, speaking for the Court in the case of *Engel v. Vitale* (370 U.S. 421), said the prayer requirement violated the First Amendment's clause forbidding laws "respecting the establishment of religion." Soon afterward, Senate Republican Leader Everett McKinley Dirksen (Ill.) championed a proposed constitutional amendment to legalize voluntary student participation in prayers in public schools. Four years later, the proposal came to a vote in the Senate and fell nine votes short of receiving the necessary two-thirds majority.

Dirksen was also leader of Congressional efforts to modify the Supreme Court's "one man, one vote" doctrine on legislative apportionment. The House passed a bill to deny Federal courts jurisdiction over apportionment of state legislatures, but it was blocked in the Senate. At this juncture, Court foes proposed a constitutional amendment to permit states to apportion one house of their legislatures on some basis other than population. The proposal came to a vote in the Senate in 1965 and again in 1966—each time failing by seven votes to achieve a two-thirds majority. *(See p. 288-289.)*

Court Pay Raises. Anti-Court sentiment triumphed in Congress in 1964 when pay raises of $7,500 were voted for Federal judges—except Supreme Court Justices, whose salaries were raised by only $4,500. The following year, an attempt to restore the pay differential was beaten down. For the next five years, the salary of the Chief Justice remained at $40,000 and that of Associate Justices at $39,500. In 1969, the Chief Justice's salary was raised to $62,500 and the salaries of Associate Justices to $60,000.

Supreme Court and 1968 Crime Act

A recent instance of anti-Court sentiment found expression in the Omnibus Crime and Safe Streets Act of 1968. Much of the publicity that attended final passage of the Act centered on three decisions of the Supreme Court—*Miranda, Mallory* and *Wade.* In *Mallory v.*

Supreme Court 'Balances' Rights of Witnesses...

The leading Supreme Court decisions regarding the question of the First Amendment rights of witnesses and the investigating powers of Congress were Watkins v. United States (1957) *and* Barenblatt v. United States (1959). *A central issue in both cases was that section of House Rule XI defining the powers and duties of the House Un-American Activities Committee. Following are excerpts from Supreme Court opinions in these two cases:*

Watkins Case

(Majority opinion by Chief Justice Earl Warren)

"The controversy thus rests upon fundamental principles of the power of the Congress and the limitations upon that power. We approach the questions presented with conscious awareness of the far-reaching ramifications that can follow from a decision of this nature....

"We start with several basic premises on which there is general agreement. The power of the Congress to conduct investigations is inherent in the legislative process. That power is broad. It encompasses inquiries concerning the administration of existing laws as well as proposed or possibly needed statutes. It includes surveys of defects in our social, economic or political system for the purpose of enabling the Congress to remedy them. It comprehends probes into departments of the Federal Government to expose corruption, inefficiency or waste. But, broad as is this power of inquiry, it is not unlimited. There is no general authority to expose the private affairs of individuals without justification in terms of the functions of the Congress. This was freely conceded by the Solicitor General in his argument of this case. Nor is the Congress a law enforcement or trial agency. These are functions of the Executive and Judicial departments of government. No inquiry is an end in itself; it must be related to, and in furtherance of, a legitimate task of the Congress. Investigations conducted solely for the personal aggrandizement of the investigators or to punish those investigated are indefensible....

"Clearly, an investigation is subject to the command that the Congress shall make no law abridging freedom of speech or press or assembly. While it is true that there is no statute to be reviewed, and that an investigation is not a law, nevertheless an investigation is part of law-making. It is justified solely as an adjunct to the legislative process. The First Amendment may be invoked against infringement of the protected freedoms by law or by law-making.

"Abuses of the investigative process may imperceptibly lead to abridgment of protected freedoms. The mere summoning of a witness and compelling him to testify, against his will, about his beliefs, expressions or associations is a measure of governmental interference. And when those forced revelations concern matters that are unorthodox, unpopular, or even hateful to the general public, the reaction in the life of the witness may be disastrous. This effect is even more harsh when it is past beliefs, expressions or associations that are disclosed and judged by current standards rather than those contemporary with the matters exposed. Nor does the witness alone suffer the consequences. Those who are identified by witnesses and thereby placed in the same glare of publicity are equally subject to public stigma, scorn and obloquy. Beyond that, there is the more subtle and immeasurable effect upon those who tend to adhere to the most orthodox and uncontroversial views and associations in order to avoid a similar fate at some future time. That this impact is partly the result of nongovernmental activity by private persons cannot relieve the investigators of their responsibility for initiating the reaction....

"Accommodation of the Congressional need for particular information with the individual and personal interest in privacy is an arduous and delicate task for any court.... The critical element is the existence of, and the weight to be ascribed to, the interest of the Congress in demanding disclosures from an unwilling witness. We cannot simply assume, however, that every Congressional investigation is justified by a public need that overbalances any private rights to be affected. To do so would be to abdicate the responsibility placed by the Constitution upon the Judiciary to insure that the Congress does not unjustifiably encroach upon an individual's right to privacy nor abridge his liberty of speech, press, religion, or assembly....

"We have no doubt that there is no Congressional power to expose for the sake of exposure. The public is, of course, entitled to be informed concerning the workings of its government. That cannot be inflated into a general power to expose where the predominant result can only be an invasion of the private rights of individuals. But a solution to our problem is not to be found in testing the motives of committee members for this purpose. Such is not our function. Their motives alone would not vitiate an investigation which had been instituted by a house of Congress if that assembly's legislative purpose is being served....

(The Court took note of House Rule XI, which incorporated the resolution establishing the Un-American Activities Committee and authorizing it to investigate: "(1) the extent, character, and objects of un-American propaganda activities in the United States, (2) the diffusion within the United States of subversive and un-American propaganda that is insti-

...and Congressional Investigating Power

gated from foreign countries or of a domestic origin and attacks the principle of the form of government as guaranteed by our Constitution, and (3) all other questions in relation thereto that would aid Congress in any necessary remedial legislation.")

"It would be difficult to imagine a less explicit authorizing resolution. Who can define the meaning of 'un-American?' What is that single, solitary 'principle of the form of government as guaranteed by our Constitution?'....

"An excessively broad charter, like that of the House Un-American Activities Committee, places the courts in an untenable position if they are to strike a balance between the public need for a particular interrogation and the right of citizens to carry on their affairs free from unnecessary governmental interference. It is impossible in such a situation to ascertain whether any legislative purpose justifies the disclosure sought and, if so, the importance of that information to the Congress in furtherance of its legislative function. The reason no court can make this critical judgment is that the House of Representatives itself has never made it."

Barenblatt Case

(Majority opinion by Justice John Marshall Harlan)

"...Granting the vagueness of the Rule (House Rule XI), we may not read it in isolation from its long history in the House of Representatives. Just as legislation is often given meaning by the gloss of legislative reports, administrative interpretation, and long usage, so the proper meaning of an authorization to a Congressional committee is not to be derived alone from its abstract terms unrelated to the definite content furnished them by the course of Congressional actions. The rule comes to us with a 'persuasive gloss of legislative history,'...which shows beyond doubt that in pursuance of its legislative concerns in the domain of 'national security' the House has clothed the Un-American Activities Committee with pervasive authority to investigate Communist activities in this country....

"The precise constitutional issue confronting us is whether the Subcommittee's inquiry into petitioner's past or present membership in the Communist Party transgressed the provisions of the First Amendment, which of course reach and limit congressional investigations.

"The Court's past cases establish sure guides to decision. Undeniably, the First Amendment in some circumstances protects an individual from being compelled to disclose his associational relationships. However, the protections of the First Amendment, unlike a

proper claim of the privilege against self-incrimination under the Fifth Amendment, do not afford a witness the right to resist inquiry in all circumstances. Where First Amendment rights are asserted to bar governmental interrogation, resolution of the issue always involves a balancing by the courts of the competing private and public interests at stake in the particular circumstances shown. These principles were recognized in the Watkins case, where, in speaking of the First Amendment in relation to Congressional inquiries, we said: 'It is manifest that despite the adverse effects which follow upon compelled disclosure of private matters, not all such inquiries are barred.... The critical element is the existence of, and the weight to be ascribed to, the interest of the Congress in demanding disclosures from an unwilling witness....'

"That Congress has wide power to legislate in the field of Communist activity in this country, and to conduct appropriate investigations in aid thereof, is hardly debatable. The existence of such power has never been questioned by this Court, and it is sufficient to say, without particularization, that Congress has enacted or considered in this field a wide range of legislative measures, not a few of which have stemmed from recommendations of the very Committee whose actions have been drawn in question here. In the last analysis this power rests on the right of self-preservation, 'the ultimate value of any society.' Justification for its exercise in turn rests on the long and widely accepted view that the tenets of the Communist party include the ultimate overthrow of the Government of the United States by force and violence, a view which has been given formal expression by the Congress. On these premises, this Court in its constitutional adjudications has consistently refused to view the Communist party as an ordinary political party, and has upheld Federal legislation aimed at the Communist problem which in a different context would certainly have raised constitutional issues of the gravest character....

"To suggest that because the Communist party may also sponsor peaceable political reforms the constitutional issues before us should now be judged as if that party were just an ordinary political party from the standpoint of national security, is to ask this Court to blind itself to world affairs which have determined the whole course of our national policy since the close of World War II, and to the vast burdens which these conditions have entailed for the entire Nation....

"We conclude that the balance between the individual and governmental interests here at stake must be struck in favor of the latter, and that therefore the provisions of the First Amendment have not been offended."

United States (354 U.S. 449), the Court in 1957 ruled that if there was unnecessary delay in bringing a suspect before a judge for arraignment, any confession he made during that period could not be admitted in court as evidence against him. Although the Mallory decision affected only Federal police practices, it worried both Federal and state law enforcement officers. They said it would hamper police investigations. Sen. Strom Thurmond (R S.C.), a leading critic of the Court, denounced the Mallory decision when it was handed down and again, more than a decade later, during hearings before the Senate Judiciary Committee on the nomination of Associate Justice Abe Fortas to be Chief Justice of the Supreme Court.

"Mallory! Mallory! I want those words to ring in your ears," Thurmond told Fortas on July 18, 1968. "He raped a woman and confessed it in court and the Supreme Court turned him loose on a technicality." The Court had held that District of Columbia police violated Rule 5(a) of the Federal Rules of Criminal Procedure—that an arrested person should be arraigned "without unnecessary delay"—when they arrested Andrew Mallory, a 19-year-old Negro, and questioned him seven and one-half hours prior to arraignment. During that time, Mallory submitted to a lie detector test, made a confession and repeated it.

In *Miranda v. Arizona* (384 U.S. 436), the Court in 1966 set rules for stationhouse questioning of suspects. Before the police could conduct an interrogation or obtain a confession, the Court ruled, they must advise the suspect that anything he says may become evidence against him; that he has a right to remain silent, and that he is entitled to have a lawyer present during questioning. The following year, in the case of *United States v. Wade* (354 U.S. 449), the Court held that a pre-trial lineup in which a defendant is exhibited to identifying witnesses constitutes a critical step in a criminal prosecution and that the defendant is entitled to assistance of counsel at the lineup.

Title II of the 1968 Act contains language governing admissibility of evidence and eyewitness testimony which the magazine *Judicature* considered inconsistent with the three Court decisions. "These Supreme Court decisions are based on constitutional principles," the magazine commented in its June-July 1968 issue. "If the law enforcement practices to which *Miranda, Mallory* and *Wade* objected were unconstitutional, it is hard to see how an act of Congress alone can make them constitutional."

Rejection of Court Nominees

Congress exerts influence over the Judiciary in another major way—through the Senate's prerogative to "advise and consent" in the President's selection of candidates for judicial offices, including not only Supreme Court justices but also other Federal court judges. *(See p. 230.)* Starting with George Washington, 15 Presidents have seen 27 of their nominees for the Supreme Court fail to win Senate confirmation—among a total of 136 appointments. In contrast, only eight Cabinet nominees have been rejected by the Senate. The last time a Cabinet nomination was rejected was in 1959, when Senate Democrats refused to approve President Eisenhower's selection of Lewis B. Strauss as Secretary of Commerce.

Although Congress also has authority to remove Federal judges by impeachment, this has been attempted with respect to a Supreme Court justice only once and that attempt failed. In 1804, the House impeached Justice Samuel Chase, a staunch Federalist who had rankled Republicans with his partisan political statements and his vigorous prosecution of the Sedition Act (which had finally been repealed in 1802). But Chase was not convicted by the Senate even though his opponents obtained a majority on three of the eight articles of impeachment. (A total of 23 Senators—two-thirds of the Senate—was necessary for conviction. The greatest number of votes for conviction on any of the articles was 19.) After the trial, President Jefferson, a strong foe of the Federalist-dominated Court, criticized impeachment as "a bungling way of removing judges" and "a farce which will not be tried again." *(See p. 270.)*

Senate rejection of Court nominations was common in the 19th century, when political ideology often colored the confirmation process. But from 1900 to 1968, the Senate refused a seat on the Supreme Court to only one man, John J. Parker in 1930. Then, in a 19-month period from late 1968 to early 1970, the Senate rejected four Supreme Court nominees—Abe Fortas and Homer Thornberry, nominated by President Johnson, and Clement F. Haynsworth Jr. and G. Harrold Carswell, nominated by President Nixon. (Fortas, already an Associate Justice, had been nominated for Chief Justice. Thornberry was to take his place as an Associate Justice. Both nominations were withdrawn when Senate supporters of the nominees were unable to break a Republican-southern Democratic filibuster on the Fortas nomination.)

Despite the low incidence of rejection for most of the 20th century, at least four other Court nominations faced stiff opposition—those of Louis D. Brandeis in 1916, Harlan F. Stone in 1925, Charles Evans Hughes in 1930, and Hugo L. Black in 1937. To this list might be added Thurgood Marshall, the only Negro ever named to the Court. The Senate Judiciary Committee, under the chairmanship of Sen. James O. Eastland (D Miss.), was able to induce President Johnson to hold back his intended nomination of Marshall for a year. When the nomination did come, in 1965, Marshall was confirmed, 54 to 16.

Action on the Brandeis nomination a half-century earlier was delayed for months by the same committee while it pondered the nominee's "radical views." When the nomination of Hughes as Chief Justice was made in 1930, the country was entering the Great Depression and the nominee's views were attacked as too conservative.

Despite the opposition to Hughes, voiced before his confirmation on Feb. 13, 1930, President Hoover thought Parker would be a non-controversial nominee. He was a Federal judge and a Republican from North Carolina. Hoover later wrote in his memoirs that "No member of the Court at that time was from the southern states, and the regional distribution of justices had always been regarded as of some importance." But Hoover misjudged the temper of the times. Social and economic issues were more important than was geography. A bipartisan group in Congress charged that Parker had made anti-Negro statements as a political candidate and an anti-Negro ruling from the bench. His nomination was rejected, 39 to 41, on May 7, 1930.

Hugo L. Black encountered difficulty getting confirmed because he had once been a member of the Ku

Supreme Court Nominations Not Confirmed by the Senate

From 1789 through 1970, 27 Supreme Court nominations have failed to receive Senate confirmation. Of these, 11 have been rejected outright and the remainder withdrawn or allowed to lapse when Senate rejection appeared imminent. Following is the complete list of nominees failing to receive confirmation:

Nominee	President	Date of Nomination	Senate Action	Date of Senate Action
William Paterson	Washington	Feb. 27, 1793	Withdrawn	(Later renominated and confirmed)
John Rutledge (for Chief Justice)	Washington	July 1, 1795	Rejected (10-14)	Dec. 15, 1795
Alexander Wolcott	Madison	Feb. 4, 1811	Rejected (9-24)	Feb. 13, 1811
John J. Crittenden	John Quincy Adams	Dec. 17, 1828	Postponed	Feb. 12, 1829
Roger Brooke Taney	Jackson	Jan. 15, 1835	Postponed	March 3, 1825 (Later nominated for Chief Justice and confirmed)
John C. Spencer	Tyler	Jan. 9, 1844	Rejected (21-26)	Jan. 31, 1844
Reuben H. Walworth	Tyler	March 13, 1844	Withdrawn	
Edward King	Tyler	June 5, 1844	Postponed	June 15, 1844
Edward King	Tyler	Dec. 4, 1844	Withdrawn	
John M. Read	Tyler	Feb. 7, 1845	Not Acted Upon	
George W. Woodward	Polk	Dec. 23, 1845	Rejected (20-29)	Jan. 22, 1846
Edward A. Bradford	Fillmore	Aug. 16, 1852	Not Acted Upon	
George E. Badger	Fillmore	Jan. 10, 1853	Postponed	Feb. 11, 1853
William C. Micou	Fillmore	Feb. 24, 1853	Not Acted Upon	
Jeremiah S. Black	Buchanan	Feb. 5, 1861	Rejected (25-26)	Feb. 21, 1861
Henry Stanbery	Andrew Johnson	April 16, 1866	Not Acted Upon	
Ebenezer R. Hoar	Grant	Dec. 15, 1869	Rejected (24-33)	Feb. 3, 1870
George H. Williams (for Chief Justice)	Grant	Dec. 1, 1873	Withdrawn	
Caleb Cushing (for Chief Justice)	Grant	Jan. 9, 1874	Withdrawn	
Stanley Matthews	Hayes	Jan. 26, 1881	Not Acted Upon	(Later renominated and confirmed)
William B. Hornblower	Cleveland	Sept. 19, 1893	Rejected (24-30)	Jan. 15, 1894
Wheeler H. Peckham	Cleveland	Jan. 22, 1894	Rejected (32-41)	Feb. 16, 1894
John J. Parker	Hoover	March 21, 1930	Rejected (39-41)	May 7, 1930
Abe Fortas (for Chief Justice)	Lyndon Johnson	June 26, 1968	Withdrawn	
Homer Thornberry	Lyndon Johnson	June 26, 1968	Not Acted Upon	
Clement F. Haynsworth Jr.	Nixon	Aug. 18, 1969	Rejected (45-55)	Nov. 21, 1969
G. Harrold Carswell	Nixon	Jan. 19, 1970	Rejected (45-51)	April 8, 1970

SOURCE: Library of Congress, Congressional Research Service.

Klux Klan in his native Alabama. Stone, at the time of his nomination, was U.S. Attorney General and was in the midst of prosecuting Burton K. Wheeler, a recently elected Democratic Senator from Montana. Wheeler was accused, but later acquitted, of charges of participating in an oil-land fraud. Wheeler's home state Democratic colleague, Sen. Thomas J. Walsh, used the committee hearings on Stone's nomination to criticize the Justice Department's handling of the Wheeler case.

The Senate's refusal to take up the Fortas and Thornberry nominations resulted largely from Fortas' affirmative votes in some of the most controversial decisions of the Warren Court and from the desire of Senate Republicans to have a Republican President name the new Chief Justice. The GOP strategy paid off when Republican Presidential candidate Richard M. Nixon won the 1968 election. But after Nixon's nominee for Chief Justice, Warren E. Burger, had been confirmed, Senate Democrats retaliated for the Fortas affair by successfully opposing confirmation of the President's next two Court nominees—Haynsworth and Carswell. *(See p. 239-240.)* Critics of the nominations based their opposition primarily on allegations that both nominees had failed to observe high standards of professional ethics while serving on lower Federal courts. Republicans contended, however, that the avowedly conservative views of both men were responsible for their rejection.

Bibliography

Books

Beard, Charles A., *The Supreme Court and the Constitution*. Macmillan, 1912.

Berger, Raoul, *Congress v. The Supreme Court*. Harvard University Press, 1969.

Berle, Adolf A., *The Three Faces of Power*. Harcourt, Brace and World, 1967.

Bickel, Alexander M., *The Least Dangerous Branch*. Bobbs-Merrill, 1962.

——, *Politics and the Warren Court*. Harper and Row, 1965 ed.

Binkley, Wilfred E. and Malcolm C. Moos, *A Grammar of American Politics*. Alfred A. Knopf, 1958 ed.

Corwin, Edward S., *Court Over Constitution*. Princeton University Press, 1938.

——, *Doctrine of Judicial Review*. Princeton University Press, 1914.

——, *The Twilight of the Supreme Court*. Yale University Press, 1934.

Cushman, Robert Eugene, *Leading Constitutional Decisions*. Appleton-Century-Crofts, 1955.

Harris, Richard, *Decision*. E. P. Dutton & Co., Inc., 1971.

Hughes, Charles Evans, *The Supreme Court of the United States*. Columbia University Press, 1928.

Morgan, Donald G., *Congress and the Constitution*. Belknap Press, 1966.

Schlesinger, Arthur M. Jr., *The Politics of Upheaval*. Houghton Mifflin Co., 1960.

Warren, Charles, *Congress, The Constitution and the Supreme Court*. Little, Brown, 1925.

——, *The Supreme Court in United States History*. Little, Brown, 1922, 1926. Vols. 1 and 2.

Articles

Gimlin, Hoyt, "Challenging of Supreme Court," *Editorial Research Reports*, Oct. 9, 1968, p. 741-760.

Hankin, C. A., "The Supreme Court and the New Deal," *Editorial Research Reports*, June 4, 1935, p. 413-428.

Hankin, Gregory, "The New Deal in the Courts," *Editorial Research Reports*, May 25, 1934, p. 347-362.

Putney, Bryant, "The President, the Constitution and the Supreme Court," *Editorial Research Reports*, June 19, 1935, p. 449-470.

Worsnop, Richard L., "Supreme Court: Legal Storm Center," *Editorial Research Reports*, Sept. 28, 1966, p. 701-720.

Internal Pressures

THE IMPACT of pressures from within Congress often equals or exceeds that of outside pressures on today's legislative process. The Congressional leadership of a Member's political party, his committee chairman, members of his state's delegation and other members of the rank and file all vie with or supplement outside pressures in the contest for the Member's vote.

The significance of internal pressures was summed up succinctly years ago by a powerful House leader, Speaker Sam Rayburn (D Texas), who advised Members that "if you want to get along, go along." Rules and customs of both houses of Congress have placed powerful weapons in the hands of the power structure to help it work its will. Members who cooperate may be rewarded with a choice committee assignment or a coveted public works project, or by a display of personal approval from the leadership—an act that enhances the Member's prestige among his colleagues and his effectiveness as a legislator.

By the same token, Members who refuse to go along on important votes may be relegated to the most insignificant of committees, ignored when the spoils are passed out in "pork barrel" appropriation bills and shunned by the leadership and their fellow Members. The upshot of their refusal to play along may be that they become so ineffective in protecting their constituents' interest that their chances of re-election are endangered. As one House Member put it in a round table discussion conducted by the Brookings Institution, "If you are going to be independent around here, you are going to pay a steep price for it."

Sources of Internal Pressures

Speaker. The main source of pressure in the House is the Speaker, a decidedly partisan official who is nominated by his party's caucus or conference and elected by the whole House, usually on a party-line vote. The Speaker's duties, which spring from the Constitution and from rules and traditions of the House, include presiding over House sessions, recognizing Members to address the House, deciding points of order, referring bills and reports to the appropriate committees and House calendars, appointing the House conferees for House-Senate conferences on legislation, and appointing members of select committees. By virtue of the prestige of his position, the Speaker normally wields considerable influence with his party's committee on committees, which assigns party members to standing committee posts. Although the Constitution does not stipulate that the Speaker must be a Member of the House, no non-Member has ever been

elected to the post. The Speaker, like any other Member, may vote and may lead debate on the floor. *(For detailed description of the Speakership and other leadership posts, see p. 129-148.)*

Over the years, some Speakers have been dominated by committee chairmen or other powerful House Members, while others have run the chamber with their own iron will. According to Hubert Bruce Fuller's study of the Speakership, *The Speakers of the House,* Henry Clay as Speaker in 1811 "so framed his committees as to force an English war." Speaker Thomas B. Reed (R Maine), who served in the 1890s, was so dictatorial in his methods that he became known as "Czar" Reed. Reed stacked his committees with Members sympathetic to his views (at that time the Speaker had authority to appoint committees himself) and made far-reaching parliamentary rulings which broke the power of the minority to filibuster and ensured the right of the majority to transact business in the House.

Champ Clark (D Mo.), Reed's House contemporary who himself became Speaker in 1910, recalled in his memoirs that "no company of soldiers in the regular army was ever more thoroughly drilled" than were the Republicans under Reed. "Time and again I have seen Mr. Reed bring every Republican up standing by waving his hands upward; and just as often, when they had risen inadvertently, I have seen him make them take their seats by waving his hands downwards."

Reed's strong-armed policies were continued in the early 1900s by Speaker Joseph G. Cannon (R Ill.), whose methods came to be known disparagingly as "Cannonism." In *A Grammar of American Politics,* Wilfred E. Binkley and Malcolm C. Moos wrote that Cannon achieved a "dictatorship" in the House "through the Speaker's power of recognition and even more his power to appoint committees whereby he could make or break Members virtually at will." In addition, "As chairman of the Committee on Rules, which he appointed and dominated, the Speaker could determine what measures the House would consider."

Cannon's dictatorial methods and his sponsorship of conservative legislation despite a rising tide of progressive sentiment in the country led to his downfall in 1910 and 1911. First, a combination of Democrats and progressive Republicans succeeded in 1910 in barring the Speaker permanently from a seat on the Rules Committee—one of the major sources of Cannon's power. Then, a year later, Cannon was defeated for the Speakership and the office of the Speaker was permanently deprived of the power to appoint standing committees; that power was given to the full House (in effect, the committees on committees of the two parties). Although these specific powers were never restored to the Speaker, resourceful incumbents of that office in later years were able to restore much of the post's earlier influence through their own personal prestige as head of their party's House majority apparatus.

Floor Leaders. Both the majority and minority parties of the House and Senate appoint officials to shape and direct party strategy on the floor. These officials, known as the Majority and Minority Leaders, devote their efforts to tying together the loose alliances which compose their parties in hopes of shaping them into voting majorities to pass or defeat bills. Majority floor leaders have considerable influence over the scheduling of debate and the selection of Members to speak on bills. The Majority Floor Leader in the House ranks just below the Speaker in importance. In the Senate, the Majority Leader is the most powerful officer, because neither the Vice President nor the President pro tempore hold substantive powers over the chamber's proceedings. In both houses, the floor leaders are in position to wield considerable pressure on Members through their influence over the party apparatus.

Whips. Each party appoints a Whip and a number of Assistant Whips to assist the Floor Leader in execution of the party's legislative program. The main job of the Whip is to canvass party members on a pending issue and give the Floor Leader an accurate picture of the support or opposition he may expect for the measure. Whips also are responsible for making sure that party members are on hand to vote. At the direction of the Floor Leader, the Whips also may apply pressure to ensure that party members follow the leadership line.

Party Caucus. Both major parties over the years have relied periodically on caucuses of party members (called "conferences" by Republicans and recently by Senate Democrats) to adopt party positions on legislation and, in the case of Democrats, to bind party members to support those positions. The concept of the caucus began in the Jefferson Administration, continued under the Speakership of Henry Clay, and was used sporadically in both chambers throughout the 19th century.

Between 1903 and 1916, the caucus or conference type of party government was revived and was used extensively by Democrats in both the House and the Senate. Senate Democrats in 1903 adopted a rule binding Members to follow party positions. House Democrats adopted a similar rule in 1909 and used it frequently until the end of the first Wilson Administration. A rule binding party members to support a Presidentially proposed measure on a majority vote in caucus was adopted at the outset of the New Deal era by Democrats in both chambers. Republicans in the 1940s and 1950s frequently used nonbinding conferences, but never adopted a binding caucus rule. In recent years, caucuses have been used infrequently by Democrats in both chambers except to nominate party officers. Republicans have used the conference more frequently.

Leadership Committees. Both parties maintain extra-legal party committees in each chamber to assist the party leadership and to enable more party members to participate in the leadership process. Steering committees recommend the order in which measures should be taken up and help with floor tactics, while policy committees research proposed legislation and recommend

party positions. By far the most active of these committees in recent years was the House Republican Policy Committee, which from 1959 to 1965 frequently took positions on legislative business and thus became an important instrument of party leadership. The full Republican conference began taking positions in 1965; its influence is generally believed to have exceeded that of the Policy Committee since that year.

Techniques of Applying Pressure

Most Congressional leaders in recent years have preferred to use tact and persuasion rather than overt pressure to win support for party measures. Speaker Sam Rayburn once said: "My experience with the Speakership has been that you can't lead people by driving them. Persuasion and reason are the only ways to lead them. In that way, the Speaker has influence and power in the House." On another occasion, Rayburn said that the Speaker must "feel" his way in the House, "receptive to...rolling waves of sentiment" among House Members. "And if a man can't see and hear and feel, why then, of course, he's lost."

Distribution of Favors

After the revolt of 1910, the House leaders turned to the tactic of passing around enough favors to Members to have a significant number of IOUs to call on in the event of a close vote on an important bill. The master of this tactic was Speaker Rayburn, who had carefully cultivated his personal popularity with other Members during his 25 terms in the House. In his book, *House Out of Order*, Rep. Richard Bolling (D Mo.), a Rayburn protege, wrote: "There was hardly a Member, however strong a political opponent, for whom (Rayburn) had not done a favor—securing a more desirable committee assignment, obtaining a Federal project to help in a difficult re-election campaign, an appointment to a board or commission for prestige purposes, or the assignment of extra space. Rayburn knew that the Speakership had been shorn of much of its substantive power. Therefore, he built up, in place of it, a vast backlog of political IOUs with a compound interest."

Some Congressional leaders have enhanced their influence with rank-and-file Members by withholding pressure in cases where the Member's vote would be against his constituents' interests. Joseph W. Martin Jr. (R Mass.), a contemporary of Rayburn's who served two terms as Speaker and eight more as House Minority Leader, wrote in his memoirs: "Unless it was absolutely necessary, I never asked a man to side with me if his vote would hurt him in his district. Whenever I could spare a man this kind of embarrassment, I did so and saved him for another time when I might need him more urgently. In fact, I often counseled Members against taking positions on legislation that could cost them the next election." John McCormack (D Mass.), Rayburn's successor as Speaker of the House, had much the same philosophy. "I have never asked a man to vote against his conscience," McCormack once said. "If he mentions his conscience— that's all. I don't press him any further."

Expressions of personal friendship toward fellow Members also help Congressional leaders stack up IOUs. One of the most obvious of these tactics is for the House

Speaker to call a young Member to the rostrum to preside over the House in the late afternoon hours while the Members make speeches. If the Speaker permits a Member to preside over the Committee of the Whole House while the House is actively debating major legislation, the Member is likely to be even more appreciative. Another reward is the Speaker's selection of Members to read the House the traditional messages such as Washington's Farewell Address on Washington's Birthday. In his study of the House, *Forge of Democracy,* journalist Neil MacNeil wrote: "Such assignments, denoting the Speaker's approval of a Member, have always been carefully watched by Members of the House. The men receiving them have acquired immediately, in the inner life of the House, recogniton by their fellows as friends of the Speaker with the added influence and prestige that such friendship has always meant. These assignments have denoted that the men receiving them have become members, if only minor members at times, of the Speaker's trusted inner circle. Men frequently called to the chair by the Speaker have even acquired the reputation of being likely successors to the Speaker."

Committee Assignments

When a Congressional leader resorts to overt pressure tactics, one of the most effective methods is the "carrot-and-stick" approach of promising prestigious committee assignments for Members who cooperate and undesirable ones for those who don't.

One of the first and most severe applications of this tactic came in 1858, when Sen. Stephen A. Douglas (D Ill.) was removed from the chairmanship of the Committee on Territories for failure to follow the Democratic stand on the expansion of slavery. Speaker Cannon removed 14 insurgent Republicans from choice committee assignments in 1909, and Speaker Nicholas Longworth (R Ohio) punished 13 Progressive Republicans in the same way in 1925. In 1965, the House Democratic caucus stripped two Democrats—John Bell Williams (Miss.) and Albert W. Watson (S.C.)—of their seniority for supporting the Republican Presidential candidate in the 1964 election. Both retained their committee assignments. The loss of seniority, however, cost Williams the chairmanship of the House Interstate and Foreign Commerce Committee, which he would have been in line to receive in 1966 upon the retirement of Chairman Oren Harris (D Ark.).

No other leader in the history of Congress was more proficient at this tactic than was Lyndon B. Johnson (D Texas), when he served as Senate Democratic floor leader from 1953 through 1960 (Minority Leader 1953-54, Majority Leader 1955-1960).

When Sen. John Stennis (D Miss.) supported Johnson's effort to censure Sen. Joseph R. McCarthy (R Wis.) for misconduct in his stormy probe of suspected Communists in government, Stennis was quickly rewarded with a seat on the prestigious Appropriations Committee. Sen. J. Allen Frear Jr. (D Del.), a conservative who voted a moderate position at Johnson's behest on a number of important bills, was rapidly placed on the Finance Committee, while Sen. Paul H. Douglas (D Ill.), a strong liberal and Johnson foe, waited for nine years to be named to that panel. Freshman Senators who voted with Johnson

in his successful effort in 1959 to resist liberalization of Senate Rule XXII, governing application of cloture on filibusters, were rewarded with choice committee assignments, while those voting for liberalization were given unattractive ones. For example, Sen. Thomas J. Dodd (D Conn.), who voted to uphold Rule XXII, was rewarded with membership on the Appropriations, Judiciary and Aeronautics and Space Sciences Committees—three of the most prestigious in the Senate. And Sen. Vance Hartke (D Ind.), who supported Johnson on Rule XXII, was named to the powerful Finance and Commerce Committees. But Edmund S. Muskie (D Maine), who opposed Johnson on the vote, was relegated to two of the least desirable committees—Government Operations and Public Works.

For years, Johnson and Rayburn teamed up to protect Texas oil interests through careful assignment of Members to the tax-writing Senate Finance and House Ways and Means Committees. Drew Pearson and Jack Anderson asserted in *The Case Against Congress* that no one was admitted to the Ways and Means Committee who couldn't give Rayburn the answer he wanted to one question: "Do you favor the oil depletion allowance?" When a Democratic vacancy occurred on the Finance Committee in 1955, Johnson assumed it himself rather than turn it over to Paul Douglas, a strong foe of percentage depletion. Although Douglas was elected to the Senate in 1948, it was not until 1957 that he finally won a seat on the Finance Committee.

Isolation of Rebels

The threat of unpopularity among their peers stands as a constant deterrent to Members inclined to engage in unpopular activities. As political scientist Randall B. Ripley described it in *Party Leaders of the House of Representatives:* "For most members of the House, the life of an habitual maverick would be intolerable. Acting against the party involves a substantial amount of personal discomfort, which can even be expressed physically. The only Republican to vote against his party's recommittal motion on a major Administration bill in 1963 answered the roll call while crouching behind the rail on the Democratic side of the House chamber. He explained, 'It's 190 degrees over there (pointing to the Republican side).' Another Republican, after voting with the Democrats on the Area Redevelopment Act amendments in 1963, said that he simply refused to go into the Republican cloakroom any more. He indicated that he could no longer talk to his party colleagues: 'Those old men don't ever want to do anything.' "

Another House Member, a Democrat, told Ripley: "When you vote against the leadership it gets sticky over there in the chamber. As a personal matter, you hate teller votes more than roll calls. The pressure on teller votes is meaner: the Speaker, Majority Leader and Whip stand in the aisle where you have to walk by them. That's mean. There's lots of pressure from that stare. And diminished numbers on divisions and teller votes make each vote more important. This is the psychology of the group. You don't really get chewed out. They are polite to me. When the Speaker or Carl Albert (then House Majority Leader) say 'Can't you help us out?' this is worse than if they were nasty. It is tough to refuse."

Distribution of Public Works

Another effective pressure method is the selective distribution of public works projects to Members' states or districts. This can be a powerful lever in the hands of a Congressional leader or committee chairman, because the political success or failure of Members is based at least partly on how much "boodle" the Member can win for his district.

During his eight-year term as Senate Democratic leader, Lyndon B. Johnson frequently employed this tactic in order to win key votes on important Senate bills. As Majority Leader in 1956, Johnson won the crucial vote of conservative Sen. George W. Malone (R Nev.) for a controversial Social Security bill by ramming through legislation providing Government subsidies for tungsten production—a measure vitally important to Malone's state. In effect, Malone's was the swing vote for the Social Security bill. It passed by the narrow margin of 47-45 over the opposition of the Eisenhower Administration and the American Medical Association. A year later, when Johnson needed northern votes on a compromise version of the 1957 civil rights bill, he won IOUs from Senators Margaret Chase Smith (R Maine) and Frank Church (D Idaho) by securing appropriations for important reclamation projects in their states. Later in the year when the civil rights bill came up, both Senators voted with Johnson.

Another expert at the use of the pork-barrel tactic has been Rep. Michael J. Kirwan (D Ohio), the longtime chairman of the House Appropriations Subcommittee on Public Works. When Kirwan experienced opposition in his House district for the first time in more than 20 years, a number of influential House Members who had important public works projects pending for their districts took to the House floor to praise Kirwan for his work in the House.

On an earlier occasion, Kirwan made a public show of his power after his committee's $10-million appropriation for an aquarium for Washington, D.C.—a pet project of Kirwan's—ran into unexpected difficulty in the Senate. Sen. Wayne Morse (D Ore.) attacked the aquarium project—which came to be known as Kirwan's "fish hotel" —as a "luxury the capital cannot afford while there is an acute shortage of classrooms here." Kirwan, then chairman of the Appropriations Subcommittee for the Interior Department, denounced Morse and dropped most Oregon projects from the Interior appropriations bill. "Morse was the cause of it," Kirwan said. "I'll hold up all of Oregon's water projects until Morse learns something about fish." It took President Kennedy's personal intervention to get the Oregon projects restored.

Rivaling Kirwan's expertise as a distributor of public works projects was Sen. Robert S. Kerr (D Okla.), one of the most powerful Members of the Senate from the late 1950s until his death in 1963. According to an account in *Newsweek* by Kenneth G. Crawford, "The base of Kerr's power was never his major committees. Rather, it was his chairmanship of the Rivers and Harbors Subcommittee of the Public Works Committee, an obscure post that makes few national headlines, but much political hay. Kerr not only used it to consolidate his position in Oklahoma by festooning the state with public works but placed practically all Senators under obligation to him by promoting their pet home projects. He never hesitated to collect on these obligations later, when the votes were needed."

Distribution of Campaign Funds

Congressional leaders may also exert pressure on Members through promises of financial aid in the Member's re-election campaign. Both the Democratic and Republican parties have Senate and House Campaign Committees which parcel out funds to party members for help in their campaigns. The committees date from 1866 when Democratic Members of both houses, who were opposing the attempt by Radical Republicans to impeach President Andrew Johnson, appointed their own committees to run the mid-term campaign that year.

The committees do not participate in party primaries but only in the general elections. Their effectiveness as a pressure tool is limited, because party leaders will rarely threaten to cut off funds to a recalcitrant Member if it might mean the election of a candidate of the opposition party. Thus while party leaders can offer the "carrot" of additional campaign money as an inducement to follow the party line, they can scarcely afford to employ the "stick" of cutting off funds altogether.

Careful decisions over how the money is allotted, however, may work to the party leaders' benefit. Just as Lyndon Johnson mastered the other facets of party leadership, he was able also to mold the Senate Campaign Committee into an effective pressure instrument. In their book *Lyndon B. Johnson: The Exercise of Power*, Rowland Evans and Robert Novak wrote:

"De facto control of the Campaign Committee's funds was one of Johnson's least obvious but most effective tools in building his network (of supporters). He controlled the distribution of Committee funds through both its chairmen—first Earle Clements (D Ky.) and later George A. Smathers (D Fla.)—and through its secretary, Bobby Baker. More often than not, the requests for campaign funds were routinely made to Baker, and the money was physically distributed by him. Johnson further tightened his control when Clements was named the Committee's executive director after his Senate defeat in 1956. Johnson got the most out of the Committee's limited funds—at that time a mere four hundred thousand dollars—by shrewdly distributing them where they would do the most work. In the small mountain states like Idaho, a ten-thousand contribution could change the course of an election. But in New York or Pennsylvania, ten thousand dollars was the merest drop in the bucket. Johnson and Baker tried to reduce contributions to Democrats in the industrial northeast to the minimum. Since Senators seldom bite the hand that feeds them, these Westerners were naturally drawn into the Johnson network, while the Eastern liberals tended to remain outside."

Meetings of State Delegations

State party delegations in the House are an effective forum for party pressures. Most state delegations hold informal meetings which are observed closely and sometimes attended by the party leadership. Votes may be swayed at these meetings, and at the very least, the party's whip organization will have a means of gauging the delegation's sentiment on pending issues.

In large delegations whose members have similar constituencies, Members with individual expertise in a given field often are able to sway part, if not all, of the state group. In a study of state delegations, Alan Fiellin found that "A division of labor, corresponding to the committee structure of the House, develops in some groups and provides benefits for the individual." He added: "By virtue of his informal ties, the New York Democrat, for example, has ready access to committees of which he is not a member. Individual Members may, and do, use group connections to check on the status and prospects of legislation in committees other than their own. In the absence of personal ties with members of most House committees, the task of quickly getting trustworthy information on the work of many committees would be most difficult. The New York Democrat may save many hours of legwork, reading and anxious deliberation by holding a brief conversation with a like-minded colleague who knows the material and has previously sifted through it."

Power of Committee Chairmen

Strong pressures come from Congressional committee chairmen, both on committee members and on the full chamber once the committee has acted. A special panel of the American Political Science Association reported in 1945 on the vast powers of the committees. The chairmen, it said, "arrange the schedules of work and the agenda of committee meetings....They parcel out the personnel of subcommittees and determine the scope of their work. They or their subordinate chairmen of the subcommittees report to Congress on decisions for legislation and manage the floor debates in defense of such decisions. In these debates, the committee chairman's word carries great weight because the subject is his peculiar province. In effect, the committee chairmen are able in large measure to dictate what proposals for legislation may be considered by Congress. The ordinary Member proposes, but the chairman disposes."

Neil MacNeil has observed: "The greatest power of a committee chairman in the House has been his ability to impede or hasten any given bill to House passage. The chairman largely has controlled the timing of legislation to be taken up for consideration—and timing alone can determine a bill's fate....This power...has given them the means to intimidate ordinary Members of the House and even to force the Speaker himself to cater to their whims or idiosyncracies. The chairmen have been able to help or hurt the individual Representative's chances of re-election by endorsing or repudiating specific bills. They have been able also, more importantly, to influence and even determine the nature of American law; for they have held the decisive role in the vast screening process through which all legislation has had to pass in the House."

Sometimes a philosophy or tradition springs up around a particular committee which serves as a type of psychological pressure on committee members. In a study of the House Appropriations Committee, Richard F. Fenno Jr. found a consensus among committee members that "all of their House-prescribed tasks can be fulfilled by superimposing upon them one single paramount task—to guard the Federal Treasury." Committee members "state their goals in the essentially negative terms of guardianship—screening requests for money, checking against ill-advised expenditures, and protecting the taxpayer's dollar."

The Committee's official history states that the job of each member is "constantly and courageously to protect the Federal Treasury against thousands of appeals and imperative demands for unnecessary, unwise and excessive expenditures." Fenno found that procedures of the Committee were so rigid that it was frowned upon if a member offered an amendment in the full Committee unless he was a member of the pertinent subcommittee, and that it was frowned on even more if a Committee member failed to support the Committee bill on the House floor. One subcommittee chairman told Fenno: "I tell them (the full Committee) we should have a united front. If there are any objections or changes, we ought to hear it now and not wash our dirty linen out on the floor. If we don't have a bill that we can all agree on and support, we ought not to report it out. To do that is like throwing a piece of meat to a bunch of hungry animals."

Another unwritten policy of the House Appropriations Committee which exerts pressure on Committee members is the tradition against minority reports, both in subcommittee and full committee. Fenno noted that over the period from 1947 to 1957, only nine minority reports had been filed out of a possible 141. Because of the immense prestige of the Appropriations Committee in the House, its unanimous reports serve as a powerful lever on the full House to adopt Committee recommendations.

Logrolling as a Pressure Tool

Because of the diversity of interests in both House and Senate, Members must often trade their votes to get their pet bills enacted. Such maneuvering, which is known as "logrolling," has been practiced in Congress since the early days of the Republic and in state legislatures before that. Two examples of the practice:

• In 1868, former Rep. Ransom Gillet (D N.Y. 1833-37) recalled that the way to enact a tariff bill was to provide protection for the local interests of enough Representatives to ensure the bill's passage. "Interest and not principle," he said, "determines what shall be done. If votes from Louisiana and Texas are needed, sugar will come in for favor. If support is needed from Illinois, Wisconsin, Minnesota and Michigan, lead, copper and pine lumber are provided for. If the votes of Pennsylvania are wanted, coal and iron receive full attention....The principle of protection under a tariff never expands beyond the objects necessary to carry a bill."

• In 1964, liberal Democrats in the House voted for wheat and cotton subsidies in return for the support of rural conservatives for a new food stamp program. Both bills were passed April 8, the food stamp measure by a 229-189 roll-call vote and the wheat-cotton bill by a roll call of 211-203. The Johnson Administration had arranged the trade after both bills appeared to be foundering in the House.

In his book on the House leadership, Randall B. Ripley testified to the success of the trade: "Twelve Democrats," Ripley noted, "were absent for all three votes. Six more were absent for one or more of the three roll calls (two of them on the food stamp bill) but supported the Administration when they voted. One hundred eighty Democrats supported the Administration on all three roll calls and might best be labeled as 'reliable traders.' Twenty-six Members were 'hard-line liberals,' voting with the Administration twice on the food stamp bill and against the wheat-cotton bill. Twelve Members were 'hard-line conservatives,' voting against the food stamp bill twice and for the wheat-cotton bill. Eight Members were 'half-hearted traders,' voting with the Administration on one food stamp roll call and against it on the other and for the wheat-cotton bill. Eight Democrats were against both programs on all three roll calls. The trade was 82 percent successful in that only the hard-line liberals, hard-line conservatives and half-hearted traders explicitly violated the terms of the bargain. Even if only the reliable traders are counted, the trade was 71 percent successful."

Most students of government defend logrolling as a legitimate means of enabling the legislator to protect his constituency's interests. As Neil MacNeil put it, "In the inside struggle to set the House's stance on a question of public policy, rarely has the decision involved for the individual Representative a moral choice between right and wrong....Normally on legislation, there has always been an area of possible compromise, legitimate compromise, and this possibility has caused the bargaining implicit in the formulation of almost all legislation. The adoption of even an amendment of seemingly little or no consequence sometimes has provided the votes needed to pass an entire bill." Political scientists Nelson W. Polsby, another defender of logrolling, notes that cooperative effort of this sort in Congress "dilutes the power of the most entrenched, and enhances tremendously the powers of all Senators, however low on the totem pole."

Power of Voting Coalitions

In addition to logrolling, which entails a Member's voting for proposals which may have little or no relation to his own interests in order to obtain support for his own objections, coalitions of disparate groups of voters often spring up in Congress to work for measures which may accrue to their common interest. The most important of these voting alliances has been the "conservative coalition" of Republicans and southern Democrats—a powerful influence in both the House and the Senate since 1937.

Disillusioned with liberal economic policies, southern Democrats banded together with Republicans to defeat some Roosevelt Administration bills or at least to water them down. Then, under the direction of Rep. Howard W. Smith (D Va.), and House Minority Leader Charles A. Halleck (R Ind.), the coalition dominated the House in the early 1960s, defeating almost every important bill submitted by the Kennedy Administration. It was somewhat less powerful in the Senate, but still had an important impact on the shape of legislation. The coalition lost considerable House strength in the 1964 election, when liberal Democrats won a landslide victory—a factor which largely accounted for the success of President Johnson's "Great Society" program of domestic social legislation. After recouping some of its losses in 1966 and 1968, the coalition again was able to stymie liberal proposals.

The coalition did not function on every House and Senate roll-call vote but only on the major economic or social issues. Neil MacNeil has explained how the coalition took shape before a major vote in the House: "The Republican strategists conferred with the southern Democratic tacticians, and together they agreed on a joint plan of action. The secret of success was for (Joseph

W.) Martin (Halleck's predecessor as Minority Leader) to permit the southern Democrats to carry the fight on the House floor. They would make the main speeches, they would make the motions, they would offer the substitutes and the amendments. The design was to encourage Democrats to join the opposition....The technique once learned proved a major weapon in the conservative coalition's arsenal. Martin used it against Roosevelt measures and Truman measures and Charles Halleck used it against Kennedy bills. It was no accident that Phillip Landrum of Georgia, a conservative Democrat, offered the Eisenhower labor bill in 1959 or that James C. Davis of Georgia, even more conservative than Landrum, offered the Eisenhower airport-construction bill. Both had been chosen by Halleck and Smith as the southerners most likely to encourage other Democrats to join the conservative cause."

Pressure by Informal Groups

Among the more inscrutable elements of internal pressure on Congress are the numerous informal groupings of Senators and Representatives. By definition, the groups operate outside the regular procedures of Congress, and their impact on regular Congressional procedures is frequently hard to discern.

The groups almost defy attempts at generalization. They tend to be short-lived insurgent coalitions. But some, such as the Democratic Study Group in the House, have survived for years; and one of the better known groups, called the Board of Education, served as a strategy council for legislative leaders in the House. The Board of Education was popular with Speakers from Nicolas Longworth to Sam Rayburn.

Many of the groups go unrecorded, organizing temporarily because of a shared interest in a certain bill or amendment, and disbanding once the bill or amendment has been adopted or defeated. Some of the groups consist of little more than a circle of lunch-table companions. Other groups have scores of members, regular assessments for dues, assigned space in a Congressional office building, and paid staff aides.

Underlying all of the groups is the bond of personal friendship that plays such a large part in the functioning of Congress, and a shared desire to short-circuit the more cumbersome regular procedures of House and Senate. In sum, the groups are as powerful, or as harmless, as their members want them to be.

Informal groupings thrive in both chambers, and among staff aides as well as among Members. Two of the better known staff groups are the Bull Elephants, for Republicans, and the Burro Club, for Democrats. When Lyndon Johnson served in 1932-35 as secretary to Rep. Richard M. Kleberg (D Texas), Johnson was elected Speaker of the "Little Congress," a predecessor of the Burro Club.

One of the best known of the many luncheon groups is the Wednesday Club, a loosely knit collection of liberal Republican Senators. House Republicans also have a Wednesday Club. It is similar to the Democratic Study Group in that it researches issues for its members and has a staff, but it lacks the DSG's whip system for notifying members of votes.

Other groups include the Republicans' SOS (Save Our Souls), A-Corns and Marching and Chowder Society;

the Monday Morning Meeting, for staff aides of liberal Democratic Senators; the Sundowners, for older Members; and the Southern Caucus, for southerners and other conservatives in the House.

The Democratic Study Group has developed into the biggest, best organized and potentially most powerful of the informal groupings. Another group, called Members of Congress for Peace through Law, while smaller and less tightly organized than the DSG, has attracted considerable publicity in recent years.

Democratic Study Group

An organization of liberal Democrats in the House of Representatives, the Democratic Study Group was founded in 1959 to counter the roadblocks to liberal legislation erected by the conservative coalition of Republicans and southern Democrats. The DSG played a supporting role for the New Frontier and Great Society legislation of Democratic Administrations from 1961 to 1969. DSG members supplied crucial votes for passage of major education, civil rights and other social welfare legislation. Under the Republican Administration of President Nixon, the group has been trying to carve out a new role.

History. During the Eisenhower years (1953-61), Republicans and southern Democrats frustrated attempts of moderate and liberal Democrats to pass legislation. In the 85th Congress (1957-58), liberals tried to combat the conservative coalition in the House. Based on the 1956 party platform, a legislative program was drafted by Democratic Representatives Eugene J. McCarthy of Minnesota, Lee Metcalf of Montana and Frank Thompson Jr. of New Jersey. The program, presented in 1957 with the support of 80 House Democrats, became known as the "Liberal Manifesto."

During the next two years, efforts to push the program were crippled by lack of organization, by lack of staff and by legislative machinery inadequate to sustain a coordinated operation, according to DSG literature.

In the 1958 Congressional elections, Democrats gained 15 seats in the Senate and 48 in the House, giving them a 2-to-1 majority in both chambers. Many of the newcomers belonged to the liberal wing of the party. With the gains, the liberals' hopes rose. But an unsuccessful attempt in 1959 to liberalize the House Rules Committee—controlled by Republicans and southern Democrats—tightened the conservative alliance. The session produced little action on measures advocated by the progressive Democrats—housing, civil rights, higher minimum wages, aid to education, medical care for the aged.

Because McCarthy drafted much of the "Liberal Manifesto," and because many meetings of those supporting it were held in his office, he was recognized as the leader of the movement. The group described itself as "an informal bloc of 80 liberal Democratic members of the House." Among its nicknames were "McCarthy's Mavericks," "McCarthy's Marauders" and "McCarthy's Mustangs."

The core of that group, according to DSG records, included McCarthy, Metcalf, Thompson and Democratic Representatives Chet Holifield (Calif.), John A. Blatnik (Minn.), Henry S. Reuss (Wis.), James Roosevelt (Calif.), Stewart L. Udall (Ariz.), George M. Rhodes (Pa.), Sidney R. Yates (Ill.), Ray J. Madden (Ind.), John E. Moss (Calif.) and Melvin Price (Ill.).

The group tried to coordinate efforts by using its own informal whip system to alert liberals to key House votes. The bloc operated independently of the House leadership. In the spring of 1959, the group began to call itself the "Congressional Study Group" at Holifield's insistence because of press references to "insurgents" and "young Turks."

Because of the lack of legislative accomplishments, the group decided to put its operations on a more formal basis. A series of meetings was held in September 1959 to discuss the defeat of progressive legislation. Some 70 House Democrats attended the meetings. Metcalf, chairman of the first meeting on Sept. 5, appointed a committee headed by Rep. B. F. Sisk (Calif.) to draw up the group's organizational structure. On Sept. 9, Metcalf was elected chairman of the group, and Thompson was named secretary. Regional vice chairmen were Roosevelt, Blatnik, Yates, Abraham J. Multer (N.Y.), Frank M. Coffin (Maine) and William J. Green (Pa.).

The members named the organization the Democratic Study Group. They stressed the need to avoid words such as "liberal" or "action" because they feared the connotations the press might give these words. On Sept. 12, 1959, Metcalf sent a letter to northern, midwestern and western Democrats who were not members of the DSG, explaining: "Democrats in this Congress are being criticized, unfairly at times, for failure to carry out to a greater extent the legislative program spelled out in the Democratic platform. One reason for lack of success in some of our efforts has been a breakdown of communication among Members who favor such a program. To remedy this lack of communication, and thus to achieve a better record next year than this, a number of us felt that we should have an organization before which we could discuss legislation, both as introduced and as reported, and be able to present the problems of our districts, states and regions to others."

By January 1960, about 120 members from 34 states had been recruited into the DSG. In May 1960, the DSG hired a full-time staff member whose salary and expenses were paid by contributions from several Members' clerk-hire allowance.

The DSG claimed in the months that followed that it had reversed the trend of defeat on legislative issues. The group took credit for beating the conservative coalition in 1960 on 12 of 19 key roll-call votes. According to the DSG, its first major victory came in March 1960, when opposition by its members delayed and finally killed a Treasury-backed bill raising long-term interest rates on Treasury bonds. The bill had been reported by the House Ways and Means Committee.

During the Kennedy and Johnson Administrations, DSG activities included research and voting support for landmark civil rights, education, Medicare and other social welfare legislation, most of which passed the House by narrow margins. On Jan. 31, 1961, House liberals managed to penetrate one of the conservative coalition's bastions—the Rules Committee—and win a majority by enlarging its membership from 12 to 15, paving the way for House consideration of major Democratic programs. The victory gave the liberal Democrats control of the Committee for the first time in 25 years.

In 1965, DSG members persuaded House Speaker McCormack to support stripping of committee seniority from two Democratic supporters of Republican Presidential candidate Barry Goldwater—Representatives Albert W. Watson (S.C.) and John Bell Williams (Miss.). The DSG also succeeded in getting the House leadership to increase the ratio of the Democratic seats on most committees, to revive the 21-day rule for rescuing legislation blocked in the Rules Committee and to institute a new rule permitting a majority to send bills to conference. The 21-day rule made it possible for a committee chairman, with the consent of the Speaker, to call a bill to the House floor if the Rules Committee did not clear it for floor action within 21 days.

Activities of the Study Group

Much of the DSG's mission is to provide information to members on key liberal issues. The group's main function is to help pass liberal legislation by alerting its members to important votes through a whip system. The DSG's importance lies mainly in its research activities and in giving its members an opportunity, through the exchange of information, to find a middle ground on which many of them can agree on certain issues.

In 1969, the DSG published a 67-page fact book on the fiscal 1970 defense budget, including pros and cons of each weapons system; a 50-page booklet on the ABM (antiballistic missile), including arguments for and against; an 81-page analysis of the tax-reform proposals; and a primer for Members of Congress on where to look, whom to talk to and what questions to ask about defense programs.

Publications in 1968 included a book on crime to counter Republican campaign criticism of rising crime rates in years when the Democrats were in power. Other DSG research memoranda included lists of contacts for agency expenditures in Congressional districts, comments on the shortcomings of the welfare system, negative income tax and job-guarantee proposals, and fact sheets on the cigarette advertising issue, surtax extension, education bills, increasing the public debt and revamping the House Un-American Activities Committee (renamed Internal Security Committee in 1969).

The DSG issues a weekly supplement to the House Democratic leadership's "whip notice" listing the weekly House schedule. The supplement points out measures of interest to liberals and summarizes the issues.

The DSG has task forces of members who produce reports and recommendations for legislation. It also operates a "round robin" telephone whip system, through which certain members call certain others to notify them of votes on major issues.

The DSG raises campaign funds for members whose districts are marginal and for liberal Democratic candidates who are running against marginal Republican incumbents. It raised $250,000 in 1968 through direct mail solicitations, group contributions and fund-raising events.

DSG activities are financed by members' dues and donations, contributions from private citizens and an annual fund-raising banquet. Several members contribute part of their office salary allowance to pay DSG staffers. The size of the staff fluctuates. In October 1969 there were eight employees, three of them professionals working on legislative matters.

Chairmen of the DSG have been Metcalf (1959-60), Holifield (1960-62), Blatnik (1962-64), Thompson (1965-66), James G. O'Hara, of Michigan (1967-68), Donald M. Fraser of Minnesota (1969-70) and Phillip Burton of California (1971-).

Membership. The number of DSG members rose from about 80 in 1959 to a high of 180 during the 89th Congress (1965-66). But in the 1966 elections the Democrats suffered a net loss of 47 seats in the House, and in the 1968 election a net loss of 5 seats. As a result, DSG membership dropped sharply and by 1969 stood at only around 120. However, the upturn of Democratic fortunes in 1970 gave the party a net gain of 9 House seats, and DSG membership moved up to an estimated 140 in 1971.

In addition to its 120 dues-paying members in 1969, the DSG contacted about 20 other moderate and liberal House Democrats through its whip system. And 160 House Members were on its mailing list to receive research materials.

There is an agreement among DSG members and supporters not to divulge the names on the lists, except those of the group's officers. The reason, according to Staff Director Richard Conlon, is that publicizing the names might alienate a minority of the members, a few of whom are southerners who might be embarrassed in their conservative districts. For much the same reason—fear of alienating a small number of members on certain issues—the DSG does not officially issue public stands on specific bills. Conlon said the theory is that 90 percent of the time, 90 percent of the group can be counted on to support liberal measures anyway. In a 1963 letter to House Members, Blatnik as DSG chairman pointed out: "No attempt is ever made to bind any Member to any group action pertaining to his responsibilities. No 'membership' lists are kept and no press releases are issued in the name of the DSG endorsing specific legislation or publicizing any position."

DSG leaders frequently have trouble obtaining a group consensus. For example, on the ABM issue there were three factions in the DSG. A majority of the members opposed ABM authorization. A group led by Holifield of California was in favor of ABM. Another group led by Thomas S. Foley (Wash.) was for a limited system. Therefore, about 80 liberals worked as an *ad hoc* group opposing ABM.

Another division occurred in 1968 on the gun-control issue. From one-fourth to one-third of the DSG members opposed strict regulation, and the others supported it. The DSG distributed materials that pointed to a need for gun-control laws but did not take an official stand.

Peace Through Law Group

Members of Congress for Peace through Law may have escaped wide public attention, but to its enthusiastic members it constitutes a valuable addition to the formal structure of Congress.

In the view of one of its more active members, Rep. Morris K. Udall (D Ariz.), "MCPL fills a need that was there, a niche not filled by the existing committee structure. It's someplace you can go with an idea without worrying about whether you're a Republican or Democrat."

"The beauty of MCPL, the great function it performs, is that it gives us a source of knowledge and an opportunity for self-information outside the formal committee work," said Rep. Paul N. McCloskey Jr. (R Calif.), another regular participant. "Essentially, it's a rebel organization. We're rebelling against the close tie between the Administration and committee chairmen who have a monopoly on information."

"MCPL provides an unprecedented forum on foreign policy within Congress," said the organization's former chairman, Rep. F. Bradford Morse (R Mass.). "Through this informal and voluntary effort, Senators and Congressmen can share their views and gain support for joint action. We have already made an impact and the potential is enormous."

In the five years of its formal existence, MCPL has grown from a small luncheon group to a well-established permanent organization of 116 Members of Congress, aided by a staff of four persons full-time. It is unique among the numerous Congressional groupings in that it is both bipartisan and bicameral (there are 29 Senate and 87 House members).

Participants generally feel that the bipartisan-bicameral nature of MCPL is one of its strongest assets. The organization offers "a place where Members of Congress don't feel they'll be chopped up by partisanship" in speaking out on issues, explained Udall.

The diffuseness of the membership has, however, created its own difficulties. MCPL has resolved one of its physical problems—finding a location for its meetings—by frequently holding conferences in Room EF-100 of the Capitol, half-way between the House and Senate sides, with quorum bells ringing for both.

The less tangible problem—that of achieving sufficient coordination to have an impact on Congressional activities —is more difficult to resolve. On the one hand, MCPL's inclusive quality has enhanced its ability to fulfill its primary purpose—"to coordinate Congressional concern for world peace into specific action"—by involving a substantial number of legislators in foreign policy discussions. But because MCPL is far from monolithic, it is difficult to translate such discussion into specific action.

Liberal Slant of Members. Generally, MCPL members comprise the more liberal segments of both houses; they are drawn to join it through a common interest in foreign policy issues. Many—particularly those in the House—are younger Members of Congress who are dissatisfied with the formal committee structure and party leadership. Although there is a broad consensus of views among the membership on issues such as the need for disarmament, closer scrutiny of military spending, strengthening the United Nations and reappraising U.S. Vietnam policy, MCPL has remained a heterogeneous and fluid grouping.

Thus, unlike the 120-member Democratic Study Group in the House (many DSG members also belong to MCPL), MCPL has rarely performed a whip function.

The organization's substantive work is carried on by four standing and several special committees whose members study a wide range of issues, according to their own interests. These committees schedule conferences and luncheon meetings with outside experts and Administration officials to which the entire membership is usually invited. On occasion, the committees may plan to issue a formal report with recommendations; but more often, they have no such objective. Frequently, an individual member or smaller group may use the committee structure as a means to circulate a letter or statement among the membership. Members are free to be as active as they wish; about one-third are regular MCPL participants.

Members' Assessment. "The committee structure of MCPL permits members to work on issues regardless of seniority," said Rep. Abner J. Mikva (D Ill.).

"A Congressman has precious little time to zero in and question policies of the Federal Government which he feels are wrong but doesn't have sufficient specialized knowledge to question," commented McCloskey. "MCPL provides us with a source of information which is essential if we are to have an impact on legislation."

Of particular value to some members is the supportive role given their own efforts by an organization of like-minded (or, at least, receptive) colleagues. "No one of us, alone, could have taken on the problem of waste in military spending," said Sen. Mark O. Hatfield (R Ore.), formerly chairman of MCPL's Military Spending Committee and currently the chairman of MCPL. "By working together, we have found an effective way to carry out our responsibility to the American taxpayer." In Udall's view, this supportive role has been especially useful in debating an issue like Vietnam in the House. "In the Senate, you have a substantial number who are antiwar, particularly in the Foreign Relations Committee," he said. "You aren't bucking the system as much. But (formal) committees are no help in the House, and it's necessary to have an outside organization."

Other MCPL members, however, feel that the organization's principal value and purpose lie in its function as a forum for discussion among members and outside experts. They view it primarily as a source of information rather than as an action-oriented group.

The variety of views among its members is reflected by the range of activities carried on under the umbrella of the organization. During the week of July 9-14, 1970, for example, Members of Congress for Peace through Law:

• Cosponsored an all-day conference on a "Feasible Timetable for Peace" in Indochina, attended by 15 Representatives and 10 Senators (not all were MCPL members). Outside speakers included W. Averell Harriman, former U.S. chief negotiator in Paris, and Townsend Hoopes, former Under Secretary of the Air Force.

• Held a luncheon honoring UN Secretary General U Thant, to which all Members of Congress and—for the first time in MCPL history—members of the press were invited.

• Arranged a press conference at which the second annual MCPL report on military spending was released.

History of MCPL

The precursor of MCPL was an informal lunch group formed in 1959 by Sen. Joseph S. Clark (D Pa., 1957-69), Sen. Jacob K. Javits (R N.Y.), Rep. Robert W. Kastenmeier (D Wis.) and Rep. James G. Fulton (R Pa.). Until it was disbanded in 1963, the group met periodically to discuss foreign policy issues of mutual interest.

In the summer of 1966, Joan McKinney, who became MCPL's executive director, came to Washington to discuss the World Federalist movement with Clark. During their conversation, the idea of forming a joint action group in Congress to coordinate interest in world peace and law was suggested. On Aug. 30, Clark had lunch with Javits, Rep. Donald M. Fraser (D Minn.), Fulton, Sen. George McGovern (D S.D.) and Miss McKinney, and they agreed to start up a formal organization. One month later, MCPL opened an office and began recruiting a staff.

In January 1967, MCPL held its first steering committee meeting, attended by the five original members and Senators John Sherman Cooper (R Ky.), Robert F. Kennedy (D N.Y., 1965-68) and Eugene J. McCarthy (D Minn.) as well as Representatives Richard S. Schweiker (R Pa., 1961-69; Senate 1969-   ), Morse, Jonathan B. Bingham (D N.Y.), Benjamin S. Rosenthal (D N.Y.) and Patsy T. Mink (D Hawaii). They agreed that the organization should serve as an information clearinghouse to keep members abreast of legislation, undertake and promote research through contact with outside experts, arrange formal discussion meetings and provide a liaison with citizens' groups.

The 12 original steering committee participants were asked to contact their Congressional colleagues to find out whether they might be interested in joining. By the end of the year, MCPL had a membership roster of 46 Senators and Representatives. Recruitment still is carried on largely by word of mouth, although an annual letter is sent to all Members of Congress telling them of MCPL's existence.

The formal organization was launched with $10,000 provided by two contributors. The budget for 1967 was $25,000; by 1970, it had increased four-fold, and the funds sought for 1971 were on the same order of magnitude.

Operating expenses are met through membership dues ($10 annually), with the bulk of MCPL revenue coming from individual private contributors. (The steering committee has ruled out contributions from organizations as possibly compromising MCPL independence.) The group has had several fund-raising dinners. Because one of MCPL's objectives is to influence legislation (directly or indirectly), contributions are not tax-deductible.

MCPL has published a list of its officers and steering committee in a small brochure, but has not made public a formal membership list. Some participants—particularly those representing more conservative constituencies—have been reluctant to make public their affiliation. According to one member, "it might involve too much time explaining that MCPL is not some kind of radical or slightly questionable peace group."

In fact, the majority of letters, reports and petitions originating in MCPL committees are not identified as MCPL work as such but simply bear the names of Members of Congress who subscribe to the statement. This allows legislators who do not belong to MCPL but who support a particular activity to sign a statement initiated through MCPL. The relative anonymity may also be helpful in recruiting new participants, since Members of Congress may join without subscribing to a stated set of positions or implicitly pledging to sponsor all MCPL-initiated work.

Organization and Activities

MCPL policymaking is carried on by its steering committee, officers and executive director, who meet approximately once a month. Morse, who became chairman in 1969, succeeded Clark who lost his Senate seat in the 1968 elections. Hatfield succeeded Morse in 1971. Officers

and steering committee members are elected by the entire membership every two years—coinciding with the change in Congress—from a slate presented by a nominating committee. The MCPL professional staff is housed in two rooms of an office-apartment building two blocks from the Capitol. The major function of the staff consultants is to orchestrate the work done by individual Congressional offices. "We want to encourage members to undertake their own research and become actively involved," said Miss McKinney. "We don't want to become another organization which simply provides research services."

In November 1969, the staff began compiling four-page newsletters to the membership; they are printed whenever there is news—on the average of once a month.

An advisory board of five outside experts was formed in November 1969; the organization planned to attract more such experts who, it was hoped, would actively assist in advising the committees.

Committees. The formal MCPL committee structure was initiated by Morse in 1969. As revised in 1971, it consisted of four standing committees and two special committees. The standing committees: (1) Military Spending, Arms Control and Disarmament, headed by Sen. William Proxmire (D Wis.); (2) World Environmental Problems and International Cooperation, with Rep. Gilbert Gude (R Md.) as chairman; (3) United Nations and International Law and Organizations, chaired by Sen. Charles McC. Mathias Jr. (R Md.); and (4) World Trade and Economic Assistance, headed by Sen. Walter F. Mondale (D Minn.). The special committees dealt with Vietnam and United States-China Relations under the chairmanship, respectively, of Rep. Paul N. McCloskey Jr. (R Calif.) and Rep. Patsy T. Mink (D Hawaii).

Conferences. In addition to discussion and study within committees, the organization has arranged several larger conferences. A three-day meeting, held in October 1969 at Airlie House in Warrenton, Va., was attended by about a dozen outside experts (including those who agreed to serve on the MCPL advisory board) and about the same number of members. The conference was entirely off the record and ranged over a wide spectrum of foreign policy issues.

The liberal foreign policy orientation of MCPL made it a rather natural meeting ground for Congressional critics of U.S. policy in Southeast Asia. MCPL did not produce an independent study or report on Vietnam policy but confined its role to sponsoring discussions and conferences, providing background support and coordination for individual members' initiatives and serving as an information clearinghouse for Members of Congress and citizens' groups working to end U.S. military involvement in Southeast Asia.

Bibliography

Books

Anderson, Jack and Drew Pearson. *The Case Against Congress.* Simon & Schuster, 1968.

Binkley, Wilfred E. and Malcolm C. Moos, *A Grammar of American Politics,* 3rd ed. Alfred A. Knopf, 1958.

Bolling, Richard, *House Out of Order.* E. P. Dutton & Co., 1965.

Bone, Hugh A., *American Politics and the Party System,* 3rd ed. McGraw-Hill, 1965.

— —, *Party Committees and National Politics.* University of Washington Press, 1958.

Burns, James MacGregor, *Congress on Trial.* Gordian Press, Inc., 1966.

Clapp, Charles L., *The Congressman: His Work As He Sees It.* Brookings Institution, 1963.

Clark, Champ, *My Quarter Century in American Politics,* Vols. 1 and 2. Harper & Bros., 1920.

Clark, Joseph S., *Congress: The Sapless Branch.* Harper & Row, 1964.

Evans, Rowland and Robert Novak, *Lyndon B. Johnson: The Exercise of Power.* The New American Library, 1966.

Fuller, Hubert Bruce, *The Speakers of the House.* Little, Brown & Co., 1909.

Galloway, George B., *History of the House of Representatives.* Thomas Y. Crowell Co., 1961.

Gross, Bertrand M., *The Legislative Struggle.* McGraw-Hill, 1953.

Harbrouck, Paul DeWitt, *Party Government in the House of Representatives.* Macmillan, 1927.

Haynes, George H., *The Senate of the United States.* Houghton Mifflin, 1938.

MacNeil, Neil, *Forge of Democracy.* David McKay Co., 1963.

Martin, Joe, *My First Fifty Years in Politics.* McGraw-Hill, 1960.

Polsby, Nelson W., *Congress and Presidency.* Prentice-Hall, Inc., 1964.

Riddick, Floyd M., *The United States Congress: Organization and Procedure.* National Capitol Publishers, Inc., 1949.

Ripley, Randall B., *Party Leaders in the House of Representatives.* Brookings Institution, 1967.

Rothman, David J., *Politics and Power: The United States Senate, 1869-1901.* Harvard University Press, 1966.

Truman, David B., *The Governmental Process.* Alfred A. Knopf, 1964.

White, William S., *Citadel.* Harper & Bros., 1955.

Articles

Clark, Kenneth, "The Senate's Ways," *Newsweek,* Jan. 14, 1963, p. 27.

Fenno, Richard F. Jr., "The House of Representatives as a Political System: The Problem of Integration," *American Political Science Review,* June 1962, p. 310-324.

Fiellin, Alan, "The Functions of Informal Groups in Legislative Institutions," *Journal of Politics,* February 1962, p. 72-91.

"The Reorganization of Congress," Report of the Committee on Congress of the American Political Science Association. Public Affairs Press, 1945.

The Press

OF ALL THE PRESSURES on Congress, none is such a two-way proposition as the relationship between Congress and the press. While Members must contend with editorial pressures and constant press scrutiny of their actions, they also must rely on news media coverage to inform the public of their legislative accomplishments. Still another dimension of this relationship is the reliance of the news media on "inside" information from Members and the reluctance of newsmen to displease inside sources lest the pipeline of information be shut off.

In terms of manpower assigned to the "beat," Congress is covered more thoroughly by far than is any other branch of the Federal Government. In 1970, the House and Senate press galleries had a membership of 2,411 accredited reporters (including newspaper, periodical, radio and television reporters and photographers)—several times the size of the White House Correspondents Association. Reporters normally cover every floor session of both chambers and every committee proceeding of any importance except those closed to the public. Reporters usually outnumber the Members on hand for a committee hearing and sometimes even outnumber the legislators present on the House or Senate floor. As the late Rep. Clement W. Miller (D Calif. 1959-62) put it in his book *Member of the House*: "If the press did not report Congress, Congress could hardly function. If the sound of Congressional voices carried no farther than the bare walls of the chambers, Congress could disband."

Most Members of the House and Senate are skilled in public relations and realize that almost every Capitol Hill reporter must file one or more stories each day. That the legislators seek to benefit by this situation is indicated by the stacks of press releases and background statements that almost always inundate both the House and Senate press galleries. Rep. Richard Bolling (D Mo.) said in *House Out of Order*: "...almost any mimeographed statement placed in the gallery is seized upon for news copy. City-reared Members, whose only view of a cow has been on a can of condensed milk, can get their names quoted in the press as experts in agriculture. A House Member whose travels consist of a triangular course between West Witdrip, Washington, and the Army-Navy game in Philadelphia can make the news with outrageous remarks about our foreign aid program simply by getting a press handout to the gallery early in the morning. A Member who can't keep his family accounts in balance can be quoted on the President's economic message to the Congress provided he looks at an advance copy and sends a statement to the gallery first thing in the morning...."

Impact of Press on Government

In exercising their discretion about which news developments to report and how much emphasis to give them, reporters and editors exercise considerable impact on the governmental process. James Reston, a vice president and columnist of the *New York Times*, observed in his book *The Artillery of the Press* that, through the news tickers on Capitol Hill and outside the President's office, "the reporters at the White House are constantly conveying the views of the President to the members of the Federal legislature, and the reporters in the House and Senate press galleries are similarly serving as a link between what is happening on Capitol Hill and the President and his Cabinet members, who also have news tickers in their offices." Reston added: "The politicians at both ends of Pennsylvania Avenue are particularly sensitive to what the reporters select, what is going out on the air and into the headlines, for this often produces strong reactions among the voters outside Washington. In the battle for the appropriation of money, for example, the dramatic news of military requirements tends to get a larger play than the less spectacular news about foreign aid, and this news emphasis on the military undoubtedly helps assure more votes for the armed services than for the foreign aid program."

Some students of government fear that the constant headline-grabbing by legislators creates an imbalance in Washington news coverage at the expense of the other branches of government. Journalist Douglass Cater observed in *The Fourth Branch of Government*: "Collectively, reinforced by the publicity-making mechanisms of the Congressional committees, it (the headline-grabbing) gives a Congressional bias to the news which creates certain advantages for the Legislative Branch of government in its continuing power struggle with the Executive. It contributes at times to a constitutional imbalance that seems to be a recurrent disorder in American government.... When Congress is in session, Capitol Hill becomes a Mecca for large numbers of the press. The syndicated columnist and the reporter for the provincial paper hurry along the long corridors to the committee sessions or crowd into the congested press conferences called by the legislative potentates. Day after day the bulk of the news that flows out of Washington is Congressional-oriented."

Early Fight for Press Freedom

As first conceived, the American form of government provided no legal protection for a press bent on perusing the activities of Government officials. The Constitution, as originally framed, omitted any guaranty of freedom of speech or of the press. This omission came under intense attack by Thomas Jefferson, who did not attend the Constitutional Convention. In early 1787, Jefferson had written from Paris: "The people are the only censors of their governors; and even their errors will tend to keep these to the true principles of their institution. To punish these errors too severely would be to suppress the only safeguard of the public liberty. The way to prevent these irregular interpositions of the people is to give them full information of their affairs through the channel of the public papers, and to contrive that those papers should penetrate the whole mass of the people. The basis of our government being the opinion of the people, the very first object should be to keep that right; and were it left to me to decide whether we should have a government without newspapers or newspapers without a government, I should not hesitate for a moment to prefer the latter...."

The main opposition to a guaranty of press freedom came from Alexander Hamilton, who wrote in *The Federalist* (No. 84): "What signifies a declaration 'that the liberty of the press shall be inviolably preserved'? What is the liberty of the press? Who can give it any definition which would not leave the utmost latitude for evasion? I hold it to be impracticable; and from this, I infer, that its security, whatever fine declarations may be inserted in any Constitution respecting it, must altogether depend on public opinion, and on the general spirit of the people and of the Government." At the Constitutional Convention, Hamilton had been able to repel attempts by James Madison and George Mason to add to the Constitution a Bill of Rights including a guaranty of freedom of the press.

Advocates of constitutional protection of freedom of the press finally won the struggle in 1791, when Virginia became the necessary tenth state to ratify a new Bill of Rights consisting of 10 constitutional amendments. The first of the amendments provided that "Congress shall make no law respecting an establishment of religion, or prohibiting the free exercise thereof; or abridging the freedom of speech, or of the press; or the right of the people peaceably to assemble, and to petition the Government for a redress of grievances."

The rivalry that had developed between Hamilton and Jefferson and their opposing concepts of government grew more intense during the first decade of the Republic. Both Hamilton, the leader of the Federalist party, and Jefferson, who headed the Anti-Federalists or Republicans (later Democrats), relied heavily on the press to advance their own views of government. The result was an era of bitter partisan journalism in which both sides used party organs to keep up a brutal assault on each other. This vigorous press battle, fought mainly by the Federalist *Gazette of the United States* and the Republican *National Gazette* and later the *Aurora*, culminated in the several Alien and Sedition Acts of 1798. One of the main purposes of the Acts passed by the Federalist Congress was to curb the Republican press and to deport some Republican journalists born abroad and not yet naturalized.

The Alien Act, which was never actually enforced and which expired by limitation in 1800, authorized the President to deport all such aliens "as he shall judge dangerous to the peace and safety of the United States,

or shall have reasonable grounds to suspect are concerned in any treasonable or secret machinations against the government." The Alien Enemies Act, aimed at the French, did not go into force because current naval hostilities with France did not lead to a declaration of war. The Sedition Act, among other things, made it a crime, punishable by up to two years' imprisonment and $2,000 in fines, to speak, write or publish any "false, scandalous and malicious" writing against the Government or its high officials with "intent to defame them." Several newspapermen were fined under the Act and a few were sent to prison. All were pardoned, however, when Jefferson became President on March 4, 1801, the day after the Act expired by limitation. Congress eventually reimbursed the journalists for the fines they had paid.

First Press Coverage of Congress

Like the concept of freedom of the press, newspaper coverage of Congress was not envisioned by the Founders of the Republic. Following the example of the British Parliament, which had never admitted reporters to its proceedings (and continued to exclude them until 1834), the U.S. House and Senate both adopted rules in 1789 excluding reporters from their sessions. The rules were short-lived, however, as the House opened its proceedings to press coverage in 1790 and the Senate did the same in 1792. In 1841, the Senate excluded reporters of local Washington newspapers in order to benefit the national party organs then prevalent in the capital. Since that time, neither chamber has sought to exclude correspondents except from executive sessions. However, some individual reporters have been excluded for misconduct or other violation of the standing rules of the press galleries.

The next major step in the evolution of press coverage of Congress was taken in 1802, when Samuel Harrison Smith, editor of a Republican paper, the *National Intelligencer*, obtained permission from the House Speaker to make and publish stenographic reports of House debates. Such permission had been denied Smith the year before when the House was evenly divided between Federalists and Republicans. For years, the reports in the *Intelligencer* were the only printed records of Congressional proceedings. The *Intelligencer* became the official organ of the Republican Administration and remained so until the outset of the John Quincy Adams Administration in 1825, when the *National Journal* became the official organ.

Under the Jackson Administration, *The Globe* was the Administration organ, and it remained so through the Van Buren Administration. While all three of these papers were Administration organs, they received lucrative Government printing contracts. For a time, the owners of the *Intelligencer* did a thriving business in reporting the debates and proceedings of Congress in book form under the name of *Register of Debates*. In 1832, the *Globe* entered this field with a similar publication called the *Congressional Globe*. In 1838, the *Register of Debates* ceased publication, leaving the field to the *Congressional Globe*.

Checks on Votes of Members

In modern times, the *Congressional Record*, a non-partisan publication of Congress, has provided a check for the press and public on the breakdown of roll-call votes. The *Record* has been unreliable, however, as a reference on Congressional debates, because Members are permitted to edit their remarks before the *Record* goes to the printer. In addition, the *Record* did not record the breakdown of teller and standing votes, under which most business is conducted in the House. However, the Legislative Reorganization Act of 1970 required that a breakdown of teller votes be recorded upon request of one-fifth of a House quorum. Previously, the only check on Members who might vote against the interests of their districts on a non-record vote was provided by teams of reporters who watched the vote and published the breakdown.

In the years since World War II, a further check on Members has been made by Congressional Quarterly, which publishes breakdowns of every roll-call vote taken in the House and Senate and provides an annual analysis of each Member's voting record from the standpoint of party support and other considerations. In addition, CQ prints the highlights of Congressional debates, detailed provisions of bills, analyses of legislative strategy and lobbying campaigns, reports on Members' financial interests, reports on the number of committee proceedings held in closed session, and various other analyses of Congressional activities.

Growth of Press Corps at Capitol

Over the years, the number of correspondents covering Congress has increased markedly. In 1813-14, there were only four Congressional correspondents, and in 1823 only 12. By 1868 the number had risen to 58; by 1900 to 171; and by 1930 to 251. By 1960 the size of the Congressional press corps had jumped to 1,326 and by 1970 to 2,411.

Facilities for accommodating the correspondents have been expanded accordingly. Galleries above the House and Senate chambers provide ample room for viewing Congressional debates. A battery of typewriters, telephones and teletype machines makes possible the quick filing of stories. Huge leather couches, coffee and candy machines cater to the relaxation of correspondents when the news is slow. The House gallery has five and the Senate gallery six employees (all paid by Congress), who hand out committee reports and provide other assistance to reporters.

Studios just off the House and Senate floors provide facilities for television and radio broadcasts and interviews. (TV and radio coverage of floor sessions is not allowed in either house; however, exceptions are made in the case of such major events as the President's State of the Union Message and other Presidential appearances.) The Senate long has consented to live television and radio coverage of committee proceedings, but the House banned such coverage from 1952 until late 1970, when the Legislative Reorganization Act carried a provision authorizing it at the discretion of a majority of each House committee.

Congress has made ample provisions to help Members get their message through to the vast press apparatus on Capitol Hill. Virtually every Member has a full-time press specialist, usually an experienced journalist, who is paid out of the Member's staff allowance. These specialists crank out reams of press releases, directed at both the national and the local press.

An equally important public relations tool is provided by the House and Senate recording studios, which enable Members to make low-cost TV and radio reports to their constituents. In these studios, located in the basement of the Capitol, Members can make a five-minute color film for only $35, as compared with $600 to $1,000 for a comparable tape made in a commercial studio. The tapes are sent to television and radio stations in the Member's district or state, which are usually glad to put them on the air. The station not only gets free Washington coverage but applies the air time for the tapes against its obligation to devote a share of its programing to public service broadcasts.

Congressional Use of the Press

The mere size of the Capitol Hill press corps puts such a premium on "exclusive" information that most reporters find themselves pressured to court news sources more assiduously than might be necessary on other beats. As Douglass Cater observed, "A great amount of news is dispensed to...(the reporter) as a favor and must be regarded as such." Reporters who ruffle the feathers of too many Congressional sources are likely to find themselves consistently "beaten" on stories by competing media.

Pressures to conform are a particularly serious problem for the small Washington bureau, which usually centers its coverage on a handful of Congressional offices and relies on legislators to keep it informed of Executive or regulatory agency action concerning its city or state. Pat Munroe, a veteran Washington newsman, observed in a 1966 study, *The Press in Washington*: "To cover Washington effectively for a paper interested in the local angle... (the reporter) is almost compelled to keep the lines to the Congressional office open and friendly. If they are not, he can be effectively frozen out of major news stories, since the Hill is the nerve center for all the Washington news concerning his state. He runs this risk if he writes stories that are critical of the Senator or Congressman from his state. Yet there are always occasions when a good reporter feels compelled to write a story that reveals the legislator as something less than the great white knight. The reporter in this case must have the complete support of his editor. If the editor is not willing to risk getting scooped by the competition at some time in the future because the Congressional source decides to retaliate, the reporter's hands are tied...."

Senator Johnson and the Press

Leaders of both houses of Congress work especially hard to ensure that their own and their party's actions get favorable publicity. For instance, Sen. Lyndon B. Johnson (D Texas) benefited enormously in the mid-1950s from his close relationship with William S. White, a Texan who was covering the Senate for the *New York Times*. James Reston has noted that after White's resignation Johnson became disturbed when Reston, then the *Times* Washington bureau chief, assigned first one reporter and then another to the job. "At this point," Reston said, "Mr. Johnson took me aside and asked what was going on. He had to know who was covering him, he said. He couldn't have one fellow one day and another

Press Galleries

SENATE PRESS GALLERY

Superintendent—Joseph E. Wills
Assistant Superintendents: Don C. Womack, Paul H. Anderson
Wilbur G. De Perini, Herbert L. Hall
Secretary—Sandra H. Hays

HOUSE PRESS GALLERY

Superintendent—Benjamin C. West
Assistant Superintendents: Thayer V. Illsley, Charles F. Marston
James N. Talbert, Jerry L. Gallegos

Standing Committee of Correspondents

Frank Hewlett, Chairman
Richard H. Stewart, Secretary
Steven V. Gerstel
Marjorie Hunter
Dan K. Thomasson

Rules Governing Press Galleries

1. Administration of the press galleries shall be vested in a Standing Committee of Correspondents elected by accredited members of the galleries. The Committee shall consist of five persons elected to serve for terms of 2 years. Provided, however, that at the election in January 1951, the three candidates receiving the highest number of votes shall serve for 2 years and the remaining two for 1 year. Thereafter, three members shall be elected in odd-numbered years and two in even-numbered years. Elections shall be held in January. The Committee shall elect its own chairman and secretary. Vacancies on the Committee shall be filled by special election to be called by the Standing Committee.

2. Persons desiring admission to the press galleries of Congress shall make application in accordance with Rule 34 of the House of Representatives, subject to the direction and control of the Speaker and Rule 34 of the Senate, which rules shall be interpreted and administered by the Standing Committee of Correspondents, subject to the review and approval by the Senate Committee on Rules and Administration.

3. The Standing Committee of Correspondents shall limit membership in the press galleries to bona fide correspondents of repute in their profession, under such rules as the Standing Committee of Correspondents shall prescribe.

4. Provided, however, that the Standing Committee of Correspondents shall admit to the galleries no person who does not establish to the satisfaction of the Standing Committee all of the following:

(a) That his or her principal income is obtained from news correspondence intended for publication in newspapers entitled to second-class mailing privileges.

(b) That he or she is not engaged in paid publicity or promotion work or in prosecuting any claim before Congress or before any department of the Government, and will not become so engaged while a member of the galleries.

(c) That he or she is not engaged in any lobbying activity and will not become so engaged while a member of the galleries.

5. Members of the families of correspondents are not entitled to the privileges of the galleries.

Press Galleries of the....

6. The Standing Committee of Correspondents shall propose no change or changes in these rules except upon petition in writing signed by not less than 100 accredited members of the galleries.

House and Senate Rules No. 34

House

Rule XXXIV
OFFICIAL AND OTHER REPORTERS

1. The appointment and removal, for cause, of the official reporters of the House, including stenographers of committees, and the manner of the execution of their duties shall be vested in the Speaker.

2. Such portion of the gallery over the Speaker's chair as may be necessary to accommodate representatives of the press wishing to report debates and proceedings shall be set aside for their use, and reputable reporters and correspondents shall be admitted thereto under such regulations as the Speaker may from time to time prescribe; and the supervision of such gallery, including the designation of its employees, shall be vested in the standing committee of correspondents, subject to the direction and control of the Speaker; and the Speaker may assign one seat on the floor to Associated Press reporters and one to United Press International, and regulate the occupation of the same. And the Speaker may admit to the floor, under such regulations as he may prescribe, one additional representative of each press association.

3. Such portion of the gallery of the House of Representatives as may be necessary to accommodate reporters of news to be disseminated by radio, television, and similar means of transmission, wishing to report debates and proceedings, shall be set aside for their use, and reputable reporters thus engaged shall be admitted thereto under such regulations as the Speaker may from time to time prescribe; and the supervision of such gallery, including the designation of its employees, shall be vested in the Executive Committee of the Radio and Television Correspondents' Galleries, subject to the direction and control of the Speaker; and the Speaker may admit to the floor, under such regulations as he may prescribe, one representative of the National Broadcasting Company, one of the Columbia Broadcasting System, one of the Mutual Broadcasting System, and one of the American Broadcasting Company.

Senate

Rule XXXIV
REGULATION OF THE SENATE WING OF THE CAPITOL

1. The Senate Chamber shall not be granted for any other purpose than for the use of the Senate; no smoking shall be permitted at any time on the floor of the Senate, or lighted cigars be brought into the Chamber.

2. It shall be the duty of the Committee on Rules and Administration to make all rules and regulations respecting such parts of the Capitol, its passages and galleries, including the restaurant and the Senate Office Building, as are or may be set apart for the use of the Senate and its officers, to be enforced under the direction of the Presiding Officer. They shall make such regulations respecting the reporters' galleries of the Senate, together with the adjoining rooms and facilities, as will confine their occupancy and use to bona fide reporters for

....Senate and the House, 1971....

daily newspapers and periodicals, to bona fide reporters of news or press associations requiring telegraph service to their membership, and to bona fide reporters for daily news dissemination through radio, wire, wireless, and similar media of transmission. These regulations shall so provide for the use of such space and facilities as fairly to distribute their use to all such media of news dissemination.

Press Photographers' Gallery

Superintendent—Maurice J. Johnson
Assistant Superintendent—Joseph M. Darling

Standing Committee of Press Photographers

Henry Burroughs, Chairman
Frank E. Cancellare, Secretary-Treasurer
Walter E. Bennett
Robert Burchette
Henry Griffin
Wallace W. McNamee

Rules Governing Press Photographers' Gallery

1. (a) Administration of the Press Photographers' Gallery is vested in a Standing Committee of Press Photographers consisting of six persons elected by accredited members of the gallery. The Committee shall be composed of one member each from Associated Press Photos, United Press International Newspictures, magazine media, and local newspapers and two "at large" members. At large members may be, but need not be, selected from a media otherwise represented on the Committee.

(b) The term of office of a member of the Committee elected as the Associated Press Photos member, the local newspapers member, or one of the "at large" members shall expire on the day of the election held in the first odd-numbered year following the year in which he was elected, and the term of office of a member of the Committee elected as the United Press International Newspictures member, the magazine media member, or the remaining "at large" member shall expire on the day of the election held in the first even-numbered year following the year in which he was elected, except that a member elected to fill a vacancy occurring prior to the expiration of a term shall serve only for the unexpired portion of such term.

(c) Elections shall be held as early as practicable in each year, and in no case later than March 31. A vacancy in the membership of the Committee occurring prior to the expiration of a term shall be filled by special election called for that purpose by the Committee.

(d) The Standing Committee of the Press Photographers' Gallery shall propose no change or changes in these rules except upon petition in writing signed by not less than 25 accredited members of the gallery.

(e) Notwithstanding the provisions of subsection (b)—

(A) the term of office of the local newspapers member elected in the election held in 1968 shall expire in 1969.

(B) the term of office of the United Press International Newspictures member holding office on January 1, 1968, shall expire in 1969, and

(C) the term of office of the United Press International Newspictures member elected in 1969 shall expire in 1970.

2. Persons desiring admission to the Press Photographers' Gallery of the Senate shall make application in accordance with Rule 34 of the Senate, which rule shall be interpreted and administered by the Standing Committee of Press Photographers subject to the review and approval of the Senate Committee on Rules and Administration.

3. The Standing Committee of Press Photographers shall limit membership in the photographers' gallery to bona fide news photographers of repute in their profession and to Heads of Photographic Bureaus under such rules as the Standing Committee of Press Photographers shall prescribe.

4. Provided, however, that the Standing Committee of Press Photographers shall admit to the gallery no person who does not establish to the satisfaction of the Committee all of the following:

(a) That any member is not engaged in paid publicity or promotion work or in prosecuting any claim before Congress or before any department of the Government, and will not become so engaged while a member of the gallery.

(b) That he or she is not engaged in any lobbying activity and will not become so engaged while a member of the gallery.

The above rules have been approved by the Committee on Rules and Administration.

Radio and Television Correspondents' Galleries

SENATE RADIO AND TELEVISION GALLERY

Superintendent—Robert C. Hough
Assistant Superintendents:
Philip A. Regan, Jane Ruyle, Lawrence J. Janezich

HOUSE RADIO AND TELEVISION GALLERY

Superintendent—Robert M. Menaugh
Assistant Superintendents:
Mike Michaelson, Max M. Barber, C. Larry May

Executive Committee of the Radio and Television Correspondents' Galleries

Joseph F. McCaffrey, Chairman
Robert E. Clark, Vice Chairman
Frank J. Jordan, Secretary
Marya McLaughlin, Treasurer
William Greenwood, Member at Large
Wes Vernon, Member at Large
David Wiegman, Member at Large
Charles Warren, Member Ex Officio

Rules Governing Radio and Television Correspondents' Galleries

1. Persons desiring admission to the Radio and Television Galleries of Congress shall make application to the Speaker, as required by rule XXXIV of the House of Representatives, as amended, and to the Committee on Rules and Administration of the Senate, as required by rule XXXIV, as amended, for the regulation of Senate wing of the Capitol. Applicants shall state in writing the names of all radio stations, television stations, systems, or news-gathering organizations by which they are employed and what other occupation or employment they may have, if any. Applicants shall further declare that they are not engaged in the prosecution of claims or the promotion of legislation pending before Congress, the Departments, or the independent agencies, and that they will not become so employed without resigning from the galleries. They shall further declare that they are not employed in any legislative

....Press Galleries (continued)

or executive department or independent agency of the Government, or by any foreign government or representative thereof; that they are not engaged in any lobbying activities; that they do not and will not, directly or indirectly, furnish special information to any organization, individual, or group of individuals for the influencing of prices on any commodity or stock exchange; that they will not do so during the time they retain membership in the galleries. Holders of visitors cards who may be allowed temporary admission to the galleries must conform to all the restrictions of this paragraph.

2. It shall be prerequisite to membership that the radio station, television station, system, or news-gathering agency which the applicant represents shall certify in writing to the Radio and Television Correspondents' Galleries that the applicant conforms to the foregoing regulations.

3. The applications required by the above rule shall be authenticated in a manner that shall be satisfactory to the Executive Committee of the Radio and Television Correspondents' Galleries who shall see that the occupation of the galleries is confined to bona fide news gatherers and/or reporters of reputable standing in their business who represent radio stations, television stations, systems, or news-gathering agencies engaged primarily in serving radio stations, television stations, or systems. It shall be the duty of the Executive Committee of the Radio and Television Correspondents' Galleries to report, at its discretion, violation of the privileges of the galleries to the Speaker or to the Senate Committee on Rules and Administration, and, pending action thereon, the offending individual may be suspended.

4. Persons engaged in other occupations, whose chief attention is not given to or more than one-half of their earned income is derived from the gathering or reporting of news for radio stations, television stations, systems, or news-gathering agencies primarily serving radio stations or systems, shall not be entitled to admission to the Radio and Television Galleries. The Radio and Television Correspondents' List in the *Congressional Directory* shall be a list only of persons whose chief attention is given to or more than one-half of their earned income is derived from the gathering and reporting of news for radio stations, television stations, and systems engaged in the daily dissemination of news, and of representatives of news-gathering agencies engaged in the daily service of news to such radio stations, television stations, or systems.

5. Members of the families of correspondents are not entitled to the privileges of the galleries.

6. The Radio and Television Galleries shall be under the control of the Executive Committee of the Radio and Television Correspondents' Galleries, subject to the approval and supervision of the Speaker of the House of Representatives and the Senate Committee on Rules and Administration.

Periodical Press Galleries

SENATE PERIODICAL PRESS GALLERY

Superintendent—William M. Perry
Assistant Superintendent—L. Curran Crow

HOUSE PERIODICAL PRESS GALLERY

Superintendent—Clarence T. Day
Assistant Superintendent—Jeanne C. Hundley

Executive Committee

David Secrest, Chairman
Samuel Shaffer, Vice Chairman

Robert Horowitz, Secretary-Treasurer
Earl B. Abrams
George Cullen
Neil MacNeil
Donald Smith

Rules Governing Periodical Press Galleries

1. Persons desiring admission to the Periodical Press Galleries of Congress shall make application to the Speaker, as required by rule XXXIV of the House of Representatives, and to the Committee on Rules and Administration of the Senate, as required by rule VI for the regulation of the Senate wing of the Capitol; and shall state in writing the names of all newspapers or publications or news associations by which they are employed, and what other occupation or employment they may have, if any; and they shall further declare that they are not engaged in the prosecution of claims pending before Congress or the departments, and will not become so engaged while allowed admission to the galleries; that they are not employed in any legislative or executive department of the Government, or by any foreign government or any representative thereof; and that they are not employed, directly or indirectly, by any stock exchange, board of trade, or other organization, or member thereof, or brokerage house or broker, engaged in the buying and selling of any security or commodity, or by any person or corporation having legislation before Congress, and will not become so engaged while retaining membership in the galleries. Holders of visitor's cards who may be allowed temporary admission to the galleries must conform to the restrictions of this rule.

2. The applications required by rule 1 shall be authenticated in a manner that shall be satisfactory to the Executive Committee of the Periodical Correspondents' Gallery who shall see that the occupation of the galleries is confined to bona fide and accredited resident correspondents, newsgatherers, or reporters of reputable standing who represent one or more periodicals which regularly publish a substantial volume of news material of either general or of an economic, industrial, technical or trade character, published for profit and supported chiefly by advertising, and owned and operated independently of any industry, business, association, or institution; and it shall be the duty of the Executive Committee at their discretion to report violation of the privileges of the galleries to the Speaker, or to the Senate Committee on Rules and Administration, and pending action thereon the offending correspondent may be suspended.

3. Persons engaged in other occupations whose chief attention is not given to the gathering or reporting of news for periodicals requiring such continuous service shall not be entitled to admission to the Periodical Press Galleries. The Periodical Correspondents' list in the *Congressional Directory* shall be a list only of persons whose chief attention is given to such service for news periodicals, as described in rule 2, except that admission shall not be denied if his other work is such as to make him eligible to the Press Galleries or Radio Correspondents' Galleries.

4. Members of the families of correspondents are not entitled to the privileges of the galleries.

5. The Periodical Press Galleries shall be under the control of an executive committee elected by members of the Periodical Correspondents' Association, subject to the approval and supervision of the Speaker of the House of Representatives and the Senate Committee on Rules and Administration.

the next. I tried to explain, but it was no use. He simply thought of the job in personal terms...."

Not all Members seek the favor of the press as vigorously as some do. A few Members actually shun publicity because of fears of being misquoted or of having their views oversimplified or taken out of context. Among the Members who have expressed such misgivings was the late Rep. Clement W. Miller, who complained in *Member of the House* that the press expected Members to talk in clichés in order to simplify their reporting job and help them to meet deadlines. "We have become a nation of headline readers," Miller said. "It is not at all surprising that the working press has come to require the same of politicians in its day-to-day reporting. The result is distortion, the inevitable distortion that comes from oversimplification and compression....What all this means in terms of Congress is that the Congressman who tailors his speech and remarks to the strictures of modern reporting is going to get in the news; and he who doesn't is going to have difficult sledding. It means that many capable legislators operate fairly silently, while others who might be of inferior competence are heard from quite frequently."

Publicity Through Investigations

By far the Member's most effective method of achieving publicity is through Congressional investigations, particularly investigations that lend themselves to sensational headlines. As Douglass Cater observed, the investigation "is geared to the production of headlines on a daily and even twice daily basis. It is able to create the news story which lingers week after week on the front pages to form an indelible impression on the public mind. No institution of the Executive Branch is capable of such sustained and well-manipulated publicity."

In the early 1950s, television hearings of (1) the Senate Special Committee to Investigate Organized Crime in Interstate Commerce and (2) the probe by the Permanent Investigations Subcommittee of the Senate Government Operations Committee into alleged Communist infiltration of the Government made national celebrities out of the committee chairmen, Senators Estes Kefauver (D Tenn.) and Joseph R. McCarthy (R Wis.), respectively. *(See p. 260.)* Kefauver was transformed almost instantly from a little-known Senator to a leading competitor for his party's Presidential nomination. McCarthy dominated the headlines for months and became one of the most powerful and most feared Members of the Senate until the public tired of his attacks on Government officials and his colleagues censured him for misconduct.

According to Cater, "the most notable committee investigations are seldom in point of fact 'investigations.' " He said: "They are planned deliberately to move from a preconceived idea to a predetermined conclusion. The skill and resourcefulness of the chairman and a sizable staff are pitted against any effort to alter its destined course. Whatever investigating is done takes place well in advance of the public hearing. The hearing is the final act of the drama. Its intent, by the staging of an arresting spectacle, is to attract public attention, to alarm or to allay, to enlighten, or, yes, sometimes to obscure."

That Members consciously plan such spectacles was documented by a committee memorandum which fell into the hands of the press. This memo, written in 1943 by the counsel of a House committee investigating the Federal Communications Commission, advised committee members as follows:

"(1) Decide what you want the newspapers to hit hardest and then shape each hearing so that the main point becomes the vortex of the testimony. Once that vortex is reached, *adjourn.*

"(2) In handling press releases, first put a release date on them, reading something like this: 'For release at 10 a.m. EST July 6,' etc. If you do this, you can give releases out as much as 24 hours in advance, thus enabling reporters to study them and write better stories.

"(3) Limit the number of people authorized to speak for the committee, to give out press releases or to provide the press with information *to the fewest number possible.* It plugs leaks and helps preserve the concentration of purpose.

"(4) Do not permit distractions to occur, such as extraneous fusses with would-be witnesses, which might provide news that would bury the testimony which you want featured.

"(5) Do not space hearings more than 24 or 48 hours apart when on a controversial subject. This gives the opposition too much opportunity to make all kind of counter-charges and replies by issuing statements to the newspapers.

"(6) Don't ever be afraid to recess a hearing even for five minutes, so that you keep the proceedings completely in control so far as creating news is concerned.

"(7) *And this is most important:* don't let the hearings or the evidence ever descend to the plane of a personal fight between the committee chairman and the head of the agency being investigated. The high plane of a duly authorized committee of the House of Representatives *examining* the operations of an agency of the Executive Branch for constructive purposes should be maintained at all costs."

Impact of Press on Congress

When the press chooses to exert its influence on Congress, the impact is often enormous. Throughout the nation's history, press coverage has mobilized public opinion behind positions—both constructive and otherwise—that have influenced Congressional action. Among the most clear-cut examples:

War With Spain. Newspaper reports by the so-called "yellow press" in New York in the late 1890s created a climate of hostility toward Spain that helped to precipitate the Spanish-American war. For months, the *New York World,* owned by Joseph Pulitzer, and the *New York Journal,* owned by William Randolph Hearst, sought to outdo each other with stories on Spanish atrocities in Cuba, then a possession of Spain. Hearst's *Journal* was generally the more aggressive of the two papers in sensationalizing the Cuban incidents, and Hearst candidly admitted that war would be good for his paper's circulation.

President William McKinley sought to keep the nation out of the war, but the wave of hysteria whipped up by the *World* and the *Journal* eventually proved too much for both Congress and McKinley. The final blow came on Feb. 15, 1898, when the U.S. battleship *Maine* was blown up in Havana harbor. The *Journal's* banner

---

An Exchange of Telegrams

William Randolph Hearst's attitude toward prospects of war with Spain over Cuba was illuminated in 1897 by the following telegraphic exchange between the publisher of the *New York Journal* and Frederic Remington, his special correspondent in Havana:

HEARST, JOURNAL, NY:
     EVERYTHING IS QUIET. THERE IS NO TROUBLE HERE. THERE WILL BE NO WAR. WISH TO RETURN. REMINGTON.

REMINGTON, HAVANA:
     PLEASE REMAIN. YOU FURNISH THE PICTURES AND I'LL FURNISH THE WAR. W. R. HEARST.

---

headline the next day read "Destruction of the Warship Maine Was the Work of an Enemy." Even before a naval court of inquiry could investigate the incident, the Hearst press was contending that the Spanish were responsible. (As it developed, the court of inquiry was unable to fix the blame.) On April 25, 1898, Congress declared war on Spain.

'Muckrakers.' In the early 1900s, a number of investigative articles by magazine reporters, who became known collectively as the "muckrakers," resulted in a large body of reform legislation, including the 17th Amendment (providing for direct election of Senators), the Pure Food and Drug Act and other measures.

Among the most notable of the muckraking reports was a series of articles by David Graham Phillips, appearing in *Cosmopolitan* magazine in 1906, entitled "The Treason of the Senate." In his first article, Phillips charged: "The treason of the Senate! Treason is a strong word, but not too strong, rather too weak, to characterize the situation in which the Senate is eager, resourceful, indefatigable agent of interests as hostile to the American people as any invading Army could be, and vastly more dangerous: interests that manipulate the prosperity produced by all, so that it heaps up riches for the few, interests whose growth and power can only mean the degradation of the people, of the educated into sycophants, of the masses toward serfdom.... The Senators are not elected by the people; they are elected by the 'interests.' " Phillips proceeded to link many of the leading Members of the Senate to large corporations and political machines.

Louis Filler concluded in a book entitled *Crusaders for American Liberalism* that the impact of Phillips' articles had "broken down those adamant walls of the Senate." He then pointed out: "Freer discussion of Senatorial personages and powers followed. A number of Senators were unseated in the next election, and others were dropped from the rolls in succeeding years until, by 1912, the composition of the chamber had changed completely.... An amendment to the Constitution was drafted and triumphantly adopted, and the power of direct election of Senators was at last given to the people."

Muckraking reports by Mark Sullivan in *Collier's* magazine had a similar effect on reform in the House.

Throughout 1909 and 1910, Sullivan, in his weekly column, "Comment About Congress," campaigned for the defeat of Rep. Joseph G. Cannon (R Ill.) in his bid for re-election as Speaker in the 1911 session of Congress. Sullivan's columns showed systematically how Cannon had carried out the will of special interests and had thwarted democratic rule in the House through his exploitation of the House rules and domination of the Rules Committee. This situation, as Sullivan described it, pressured House Members "to act on bills the way Cannon wished them acted upon, to report out for action those that Cannon wanted out, to keep in committee those that Cannon wanted suppressed." With public opinion running strongly against Cannon, Republican "insurgents" banded together with Democrats early in the 1910 session to strip Cannon of much of his power. Cannon was deposed as Speaker after Democrats won control of the House in the next session of Congress. *(See p. 42-43.)*

League of Nations. Press coverage of President Wilson's drive for Senate ratification of the Treaty of Versailles, containing the Covenant of the League of Nations, was believed to have helped tip the scales against ratification in 1919. As journalist Ray Tucker described it in a magazine article in 1933, a small group of correspondents "conspired hourly with the 'irreconcilables,'... tipped off most of the Congressmen to Wilsonian statements and maneuvers, and started Senatorial counterattacks before the war President could unlimber his orators." Tucker continued: "They wrote philippics for the Borahs, Johnsons and Reeds, cooked up interviews,... carried on independent research into the League's implications, dug up secret material. Their dispatches bristled with personal hostility to the League, and the carbon copies which they distributed to pro-Wilson writers affected even the latter's supposedly favorable articles. The Covenant was defeated by the Senate press gallery long before it was finally rejected by the Senate."

Teapot Dome. Investigative reports by the press in 1922 prompted Congressional action that led to full exposure of the Teapot Dome oil scandal and prosecution of the Government officials involved. Reporters from the *Denver Post* and *Albuquerque Morning Journal* traced receipts for racehorses and cattle received by Interior Secretary Albert B. Fall and found that they had been sent by oilman Harry F. Sinclair, whom Fall had permitted, without competitive bidding, to lease the Teapot Dome oil field in east central Wyoming, a reserve long set aside for the Navy. A subsequent investigation by Paul Y. Anderson of the *St. Louis Post-Dispatch* gave Senate investigators the information they needed to fully document the scandal. The Senate investigation led to criminal convictions of Fall and several other prominent officials of the Harding Administration. *(See p. 258.)*

Dodd, Powell Incidents. In the late 1960s, press reports of alleged improprieties by Rep. Adam C. Powell (D N.Y.) and Sen. Thomas J. Dodd (D Conn.) led to Powell's exclusion from the House and Dodd's censure by the Senate. *(See p. 305 and 311.)* In the aftermath of the two incidents, the House and Senate both adopted tougher codes of ethics regarding the conduct of their Members.

Renegotiation Board. In 1968, a single newsman was widely credited with providing the impetus that steered a major bill through Congress. Over a period of several months, Sanford Watzman, Washington correspondent of the *Cleveland Plain Dealer*, filed a series of stories revealing pressures by powerful business interests against renewing the life of the Renegotiation Board, the agency that handles recapture of excessive profits realized by private companies on contracts with Government agencies. The *Plain Dealer* articles spurred four Members of the Ohio delegation—Reps. Jackson E. Betts (R), Michael A. Feighan (D), William E. Minshall (R) and Charles A. Vanik (D) into supporting continuation of the Board.

Two of the Ohio Representatives—Betts and Vanik—were members of the House Ways and Means Committee, which had jurisdiction over the bill. In the Committee, the Ohioans were joined in support of the measure by Reps. Martha W. Griffiths (D Mich.), a former Government procurement officer, and James A. Burke (D Mass.), who also was under pressure from his hometown newspaper, *The Boston Globe*. Together, these four Members pushed the bill through to enactment. Committee sources told Congressional Quarterly that the bill probably would have died in committee without the *Plain Dealer* articles.

Members' Attacks on Newsmen

Despite the constitutional guaranty of freedom of the press, Congress sometimes has attempted to intimidate reporters and editors and to discredit their papers' editorial policies.

One of the most noteworthy of these cases occurred in 1915, when a Senate committee chaired by Sen. Thomas J. Walsh (D Mont.) probed the motives of the *New York Times* in publishing editorials opposing an Administration bill to authorize purchase of foreign ships interned in American harbors at the start of World War I. Charles Ransom Miller, editor-in-chief of the *Times*, and Carr V. Van Anda, managing editor, were brought before the Committee and queried on the *Times'* financial backing and its news and editorial policies. Both editors answered the Committee's questions, but at the close of the hearing Miller said: "I can see no ethical, moral or legal right that you have to put many of the questions you put to me today. Inquisitorial proceedings of this kind would have a very marked tendency, if continued and adopted as a policy, to reduce the press of the United States to the level of the press in some of the Central European empires, the press that has been known as the reptile press, that crawls on its belly every day to the foreign office or to the government officials and ministers to know what it may say or shall say—to receive its orders."

The next major confrontation between a Congressional committee and the press was in 1936. The House Committee on Military Affairs subpoenaed a *Washington Herald* reporter who had linked Rep. John J. McSwain (D S.C.), a member of the Committee, to a group of war-surplus speculators. The reporter, Frank C. Waldrop, declined to answer the Committee's questions on the ground that the panel was proceeding improperly "pursuant to a threat of its chairman and without legislative purpose." J. R. Wiggins, then managing editor of the

Washington Post, gave this account of the proceedings years later in an article in *Nieman Reports*:

"The Committee, particularly its chairman, became enraged at this challenge. The chairman ordered the reporter to take the stand, administered the oath, and then asked, 'Your name is Frank C. Waldrop, is it not?'

"With a smile, the witness replied, 'Upon the advice of counsel, I decline to answer.'

"Then followed one of the most disgraceful exhibitions in the history of Congressional inquisitions...; finally he (Waldrop) was told to stand down, but to hold himself subject to recall.

"The Committee proceeded for several days with its inquiry. As witness after witness gave more and more damaging testimony, its chairman became more and more embarrassed.

"On April 15, a halt was called. At an executive session the Committee voted unanimously to end its inquiry, not to print the record of its proceedings, and to make no report to the House.

"The following day Mr. Waldrop's counsel demanded and obtained a cancellation of his subpoena. Thus did a courageous reporter, in the face of threats, innuendo, and malicious insult, uphold the traditions of American journalism."

An even more stormy episode occurred in 1953, when the McCarthy subcommittee questioned James A. Wechsler, editor of the *New York Post*, on his paper's editorial policy. According to an account by journalist Alan Barth in his book *Government by Investigation*, "Wechsler was led by the subcommittee counsel, Roy Cohn, to acknowledge what was already well known and what he had never attempted to conceal—that he had joined the Young Communist League when he was 18 years old, in his junior year at Columbia University; he managed to say also, what was equally well known, that he had left the Young Communist League and the whole of the Communist movement by the end of 1937, when he was 22, and had been militantly and articulately anti-Communist ever since."

Following this discussion, McCarthy launched a lengthy attack on Wechsler's editorial page, which the Senator contended "always leads the vanguard, with the *Daily Worker*, follows the same line, against anyone who is willing to expose Communists in government." At the close of the hearing, Wechsler retorted: "I regard this proceeding as the first in a long line of attempts to intimidate editors who do not equate McCarthyism with patriotism." The Wechsler incident produced a wave of public animosity toward McCarthy and the committee. Thereafter, Congressional committees were more wary about subpoenaing reporters.

Bibliography

Books

Barth, Alan, *Government by Investigation*. Viking Press, 1955.

Bleyer, Willard Grosvenor, *Main Currents in the History of American Journalism*. Houghton Mifflin Co., 1927.

Bolling, Richard, *House Out of Order*. E. P. Dutton & Co., 1965.

Cater, Douglass, *The Fourth Branch of Government*. Houghton Mifflin Co., 1959.

Clark, Joseph S., *Congress: The Sapless Branch*. Harper & Row, 1964.

Cohen, Bernard C., *The Press and Foreign Policy*. Princeton University Press, 1963.

Daniels, Jonathan, *They Will Be Heard*. McGraw-Hill, 1965.

Edwards, Verne E., Jr., *Journalism in a Free Society*. William C. Brown Co., 1970.

Filler, Louis, *Crusaders for American Liberalism*. Harcourt Brace & Co., 1939.

Hiebert, Ray Eldon, ed., *The Press in Washington*. Dodd Mead & Co., 1966.

Key, V. O., Jr., *Public Opinion and American Democracy*. Alfred A. Knopf, 1961.

Krock, Arthur, *Memoirs: Sixty Years on the Firing Line*. Funk & Wagnalls, 1968.

Miller, Clem, *Member of the House; Letters of a Congressman*. Scribner's, 1962.

Mott, Frank Luther, *American Journalism: A History 1690-1960*. Macmillan Co., 1962.

Phillips, Cabell, ed., *Dateline: Washington*. Doubleday & Co., 1949.

Reston, James, *The Artillery of the Press*. Harper & Row, 1966.

Ross, Ishbel, *Ladies of the Press*. Harper & Bros., 1936.

Rosten, Leo C., *The Washington Correspondents*. Harcourt, Brace & Co., 1937.

Rubin, Bernard, *Political Television*. Wadsworth Publishing Co., Inc., 1967.

Siebert, Fredrick Seaton, *The Rights and Privileges of the Press*. D. Appleton Century Co., 1934.

Sullivan, Mark, *The Education of an American*. Doubleday & Co., 1938.

Swanberg, W. A., *Citizen Hearst*. Scribner's, 1961.

Weinberg, Arthur and Lila, *The Muckrakers*. Simon & Schuster, 1961.

Whale, John, *The Half-Shut Eye; Television and Politics in Britain and America*. Macmillan & Co., Ltd. (London), 1969.

Articles

Gimlin, Hoyt, "First Amendment and Mass Media," *Editorial Research Reports*, 1970 Vol. I, p. 41-60.

Kraft, Joseph, "Politics of the Washington Press Corps," *Harper's*, June 1965, p. 100-105.

Patch, Buel W., "Government and the Press," *Editorial Research Reports*, 1953 Vol. I, p. 317-336.

Tucker, Ray, "Part-Time Statesmen," *Collier's*, Oct. 28, 1933, p. 28-36.

Wiggins, J. R., "Background on Investigations of the Press," *Nieman Reports*, October 1953.

GUIDE TO THE U.S. CONGRESS

Chapter 7—Ethics in Congress

Ethics in Congress

UNDER THE CONSTITUTION, each house of Congress is the judge of the elections and qualifications of its own Members and has the power to punish Members for disorderly behavior. With the concurrence of two-thirds of its membership, either house may expel a Member.

These powers are essential to the functioning of Congress as a co-equal part of the Government, free from harassment and domination by the other branches. They are reinforced by the speech-and-debate clause of the Constitution (Article I, Section 6), which gives Members of Congress immunity from prosecution for statements made within the Capitol.

The failure of the courts to sustain recent criminal prosecutions of Members has appeared to place more of a burden on Congress to police the activities of Members. The historical record shows that this is a responsibility Congress is always reluctant to exercise. Indeed, there is some evidence that Congress is willing to act against an errant Member only when he has acted contemptuously toward Congress itself. The actions taken against Sen. Joseph R. McCarthy (R Wis.), Rep. Adam Clayton Powell Jr. (D N.Y.) and Sen. Thomas J. Dodd (D Conn.) all involved arrogance toward the investigating committees and countercharges against other Members, sins that any club is likely to resent.

Expulsion, Exclusion and Censure

The power to expel Members of Congress has not been exercised since the Civil War. In fact, it was used only once before that traumatic period; Sen. William Blount was expelled in 1797 for dickering with British agents. But during the formation of the Confederacy, three Representatives and 14 Senators, including Jefferson Davis, were expelled. *(See Chapter III, Seating and Disciplining of Members.)*

Exclusion requires only a simple majority vote and usually has been linked to election irregularities. It is exercised at the beginning of a new Congress, when Members-elect present their credentials to the House or Senate.

Unlike exclusion, which applies to Members before they take their seats in a new Congress, censure is exercised against Members already sworn in and seated. This was the form of punishment applied to Sens. McCarthy and Dodd in recent years. Before then only five Senators had been censured. The committee that investigated the conduct of Rep. Powell also recommended censure, only to be overturned by the House, which voted for exclusion instead. In the history of the House of Representatives, only 18 Members have been censured. This total may seem small in view of past scandals that severely tarnished the reputation of Congress. The nadir was in the post-Civil War period, especially during the Administration of President Ulysses S. Grant.

The scholars Rogow and Lasswell wrote in their book *Power, Corruption and Rectitude* in 1963:

"In the House of Representatives, especially, corrupt behavior owes a good deal to the failure of both the leadership and membership to enforce rectitude standards. Although the leaders of the Senate and House after the Civil War were not, for the most part, less able or capable than their pre-War predecessors, unlike them they were largely passive in the face of widespread evidence that much legislative business was transacted in a corrupt fashion. Moreover, an indifferent attitude toward corrupt behavior of Members remains characteristic of both houses."

A committee of the New York City bar, in a 1970 report entitled *Congress and the Public Trust*, also noted the historical reluctance of Congress "to police its Members' ethics by formal discipline." It cited a variety of explanations, including institutional loyalty, political partisanship and a belief that the electoral process should be the "exclusive discipline." The committee offered 29 specific recommendations to improve the "ethical practice and appearance" of Congress *(see below)*, but it also observed: "It is the bane of public life that unspectacular but dedicated and meritorious service, which is the standard of service of the overwhelming majority of today's Members of Congress, is too seldom recognized."

Restrictions on Members

Until World War II, to be a Member of Congress was to hold a part-time job. Consequently, certain occupations which demand almost full-time attention—running a business or teaching school, for example—sent few representatives to Congress while others, notably the law, sent many. For years about 60 percent of all Members of Congress have been lawyers, while few have

---

Reference

See Appendix table of contents (first thumb tab) for comparison of provisions of proposed Omnibus Disclosure Act (S 1885) with existing laws and rules and with other proposed legislation.

Congressional Salaries

1791	$6 per diem	1907	$7,500
*1816	$1,500 a year	1925	$10,000
1856	$3,000	1946	$12,500 plus $2,500 tax-free expense allowance
1866	$5,000	1955	$22,500
1873	$7,500	1965	$30,000
1874	$5,000	1969	$42,500

Repealed in 1817 after hostile reaction from voters, including defeat of all Congressmen from three states and a majority of those from three other states. In 1818, Congress returned to per diem compensation at a rate of $8. (For details, see Chapter IV, Pay and Perquisites of Members.)

been active businessmen (though many have been retired businessmen).

Salaries often have not kept up with the financial demands on Members of Congress, particularly those with children to support. *(See table of salaries.)* Most Members must maintain two residences, one in their home state, one in Washington, D.C., and most have large travel expenses to their home states that are not reimbursed by the Government. Members who do not hold safe seats, moreover, have to spend considerable amounts of money if they wish to be re-elected. This fact explains to a large degree why most legislators who continue to practice law are junior Members of Congress from competitive two-party districts. Among notable exceptions to this finding have been the long-time chairman of the House Judiciary Committee, Rep. Emanuel Celler (D N.Y.), and the late Senate Minority Leader, Everett McKinley Dirksen (R Ill.).

Legal Practice and Past Scandals

Lawyers have never been forbidden to practice law while holding Congressional office, but the combination of the two professions has led to numerous scandals—the case of Robert G. (Bobby) Baker being the most recent example.

Sen. Daniel Webster's retainer from the Bank of the United States is familiar to many. What is not so well known is that Webster's professional relationship with the bank was no secret; he represented the bank in 41 cases before the Supreme Court. It was not an unusual arrangement for the time; neither was it universally condoned. John Quincy Adams, for example, as a Member of Congress declined to practice before Federal courts.

It was not until the 1850s that Members were forbidden to represent claimants against the U.S. Government. This restriction grew out of a scandal surrounding Senator, and later Secretary of the Treasury, Thomas Corwin of Ohio. Corwin successfully recovered half a million dollars (an enormous sum for those days) in a mining case; the scandal erupted when it was revealed that both the claimant and his silver mine were frauds.

Legal practice played a supporting role in the great railroad robbery known as the Credit Mobilier scandal of the Grant Administration. In that case, as brought out in a Congressional hearing, promoters of the Union Pacific Railroad used stock in Credit Mobilier, a joint stock company they controlled, to bribe Members of Congress to keep up the Federal subsidies to the railroad.

The bribe-giver was a Member of Congress, Rep. Oakes Ames of Massachusetts, and among those investigated was the Vice President, Schuyler Colfax, and the Speaker of the House, James G. Blaine. In the end, Ames and another Republican, James Brooks of New York, were censured but not expelled by the House, and censure was recommended but not carried out against Sen. James W. Patterson of New Hampshire. No unfavorable evidence was produced against Speaker Blaine, but Vice President Colfax's political career was ruined.

The early 1900s again brought Congressional ethics to a low spot in public opinion. Heavily promoted by publisher William Randolph Hearst, a series of articles by David Graham Phillips on "The Treason of the Senate" alleged corrupt behavior by 21 Senators. The word "muckraking" was applied to the revelations by Theodore Roosevelt. Even more important, the series played a major role in promoting direct election of Senators.

Only one of the 21 Senators replied publicly to Phillips' charges. He was Sen. Joseph W. Bailey of Texas, who had received more than $225,000 in legal fees for several months' services to a Texas oilman. Bailey vehemently defended his practice of law while serving in the Senate: "I despise those public men who think they must remain poor in order to be considered honest. I am not one of them. If my constituents want a man who is willing to go to the poorhouse in his old age in order to stay in the Senate during his middle age, they will have to find another Senator."

The muckrakers were able to show cases where businessmen had bribed state legislatures to elect U.S. Senators beholden to special interests. This provoked Mark Twain to declare, "I think I can and do say with pride that we have legislatures that bring higher prices than anywhere in the world."

Baker, Dodd and Powell Cases

In the 1960s, ethics cases involving Secretary to the Senate Majority Robert G. (Bobby) Baker, Rep. Adam Clayton Powell Jr. (D N.Y.) and Sen. Thomas J. Dodd (D Conn.) led to the forming of House and Senate committees to oversee, very discreetly, the standards of conduct of Members of Congress. Limited requirements for disclosing financial interests were adopted, but very little of the information was to be made public; most of it was to be filed, in sealed envelopes, with the ethics committees.

Both the Baker and the Dodd cases centered on the use of political campaign funds. Powell got into trouble mainly for flouting court orders and for the age-old practice of payroll padding.

Baker Case. Bobby Baker might never have received notoriety had he not been a protege of Lyndon B. Johnson. An impoverished country boy, he rose from Senate page to right-hand man to the Senate Majority Leader, Johnson. When he resigned his post under fire, Baker had a paper worth of $2 million, most of it gained, the subsequent court records showed, from combining law practice with influence peddling.

Baker resigned from his $19,600 Senate job in 1963 after a civil suit was brought against him, charging that he used his influence to obtain contracts for a vending machine concern in which he had a financial interest. Senate investigations conducted over the next two years concluded that Baker had acted with "gross impropriety." The investigating committee recommended that the Senate require full financial disclosures by Senators and top employees of the Senate. In lieu of doing that, the Senate established a Committee on Standards and Conduct. The Committee did nothing until 1966, when Sen. Dodd asked it to look into charges made against him by columnist Drew Pearson.

Baker meanwhile was brought to trial on charges of income tax evasion, theft and conspiracy to defraud the Government. He was found guilty in January 1967; after appeals had been exhausted, he began his prison term four years later. The major charge on which he was found guilty was that he had collected more than $99,-000 from a group of California savings and loan executives, ostensibly as campaign contributions, but that in reality he had kept about $80,000 of the total for himself.

At the trial two of the California executives testified that in 1962 they gave Baker about $66,000 for campaign contributions to seven Senators and one House Member, Ways and Means Committee Chairman Wilbur D. Mills (D Ark.). Mills and one of the Senators, Foreign Relations Committee Chairman J. W. Fulbright (D Ark.), testified that they had received none of the funds. Defense counsel stipulated that none of the other six Senators had received any of the funds. One of the savings and loan executives testified that Baker told him the California savings and loan associations could improve their standing in Congress with a "very impressive" contribution to certain Senators and House Members and could "win friends" in Congress at a time when a bill was pending to increase taxes on the associations.

Baker testified he turned the money over to Sen. Robert S. Kerr (D Okla.), a power on the Senate Finance Committee, for his re-election campaign. Kerr was dead by the time Baker told his story.

Senate Ethics Committee. The Senate Rules and Administration Committee, which conducted the two investigations of Baker, asked the Senate in 1964 to give it jurisdiction to probe infractions of Senate rules. On the floor of the Senate, however, the request was turned down and the Senate voted instead to establish a six-member bipartisan committee to investigate allegations of improper conduct by Senators and Senate employees. One reason for setting up the special committee was to avoid partisan bickering between the minority of Republicans on the Rules and Administration Committee and the Democratic majority. The Republicans had charged the Democrats with "whitewashing" Bobby Baker.

In establishing the Select Committee on Standards and Conduct the Senate authorized it not only to receive complaints of unethical conduct but also to recommend disciplinary action if needed and to draw up a code of ethical conduct.

The six members of the Select Committee were not appointed until one year later, in July 1965, and their first undertaking, the investigation of charges against Sen. Dodd, did not begin until February 1966.

Dodd Case. For the seventh time in its history, the Senate in 1967 censured one of its Members, Sen.

Conflicts of Interest

Beyond the criminal statutes there is a broad range of opinion on what constitutes conflict of interest. At one extreme is a general consensus that use of an official position to promote or carry on private business is a clear conflict of interest. At another extreme there is the contention that any activity that lessens a Member's attention to official duties constitutes a conflict of interest.

The dilemmas are many, and avoidance of all conflict of interest impossible: Members of Congress, for example, have until recently had to vote on increases in their own salaries.

Critics are fond of citing representatives of oil-producing states as prime examples of unethical conduct. The opposite point of view has been expressed by Sen. Russell B. Long (D La.), chairman of the Senate Finance Committee whose jurisdiction includes the celebrated depletion allowance of the oil industry:

"Most of my income is from oil and gas. I don't regard it as any conflict of interest. My state produces more oil and gas per acre than any state in the Union. If I didn't represent the oil and gas industry, I wouldn't represent the state of Louisiana." (Quoted by Erwin Knoll in the *New York Times Magazine,* March 8, 1970).

In contrast, Texas' two Representatives on the tax-writing House Ways and Means Committee in the 91st Congress, Omar Burleson (D) and George Bush (R), reported in their first official financial disclosures in 1969 that they held no oil or gas stocks. Bush, in fact, disposed of large holdings in oil when he became a member of that Committee.

Thomas J. Dodd (D Conn.). Dodd's troubles began in 1966, when columnists Drew Pearson and Jack Anderson charged that he had misused political campaign funds contributed to him and had committed other offenses. Dodd requested the Senate Select Committee on Standards and Conduct to investigate the charges.

The Committee recommended April 27, 1967, that the Senate censure Dodd for misuse of political funds and for double-billing for official and private travel. The Senate censured Dodd on the first charge June 23, 1967, by a 92-5 roll-call vote but refused, by a 51-45 roll-call vote, to censure him on the second charge.

Before the hearings began, Dodd and the Committee agreed to and released a list of stipulations (facts agreed by both parties to be true), which included statements that funds raised at testimonial dinners for Dodd had in some cases been used for personal expenses and that there had been instances of double billing. In testimony before the Committee, Dodd contended that his continuing financial problems were well known to his constituents, and that persons who bought tickets to testimonial affairs did so on the understanding that he would use the money as he saw fit. Dodd disclaimed responsibility for the double billing.

In recommending censure, the Committee concluded that Dodd or his representatives received a total

Regulations Governing Conduct of Members of Congress

Concern for the ethical conduct of Members of Congress is reflected in the Constitution, Federal statutes and Senate and House rules. Key provisions affecting Members' conduct follow:

Constitutional Provisions

"Each House may determine the Rules of its Proceedings, punish its Members for Disorderly Behavior, and, with the Concurrence of two thirds, expel a Member." (Article I, Section 5, Clause 2)

"They shall in all Cases, except Treason, Felony and Breach of the Peace, be privileged from Arrest during their Attendance at the Session of their respective Houses, and in going to and returning from the same; and for any Speech or Debate in either House, they shall not be questioned in any other Place." (Article I, Section 6, Clause 1)

"No Senator or Representative shall, during the Time for which he was elected, be appointed to any civil Office under the Authority of the United States, which shall have been created, or the Emoluments whereof shall have been encreased during such time; and no Person holding any Office under the United States, shall be a Member of either House during his Continuance in Office." (Article I, Section 6, Clause 2)

"No Title of Nobility shall be granted by the United States; And no Person holding any Office of Profit or Trust under them, shall without the Consent of the Congress, accept of any present, Emolument, Office, or Title, of any kind whatever, from any King, Prince, or foreign •State." (Article I, Section 9, Clause 8)

"The Senators and Representatives before mentioned...shall be bound by Oath or Affirmation, to support this Constitution...." (Article VI, Clause 3)

Criminal Statutes

A series of laws in Title 18 of the U.S. Code make it a Federal crime for Members of Congress to engage in certain actions. Prohibited acts, excluding those relating to campaign spending, include:

Soliciting or receiving a bribe for the performance of any official act, for the violation of an official duty or for participating in or permitting any fraud against the United States. The penalty is a $20,000 fine or three times the monetary equivalent of the thing of value, whichever is greater, or imprisonment for not more than 15 years, or both, plus possible disqualification from holding office. (18 USC 201c)

Soliciting or receiving anything of value for himself or because of any official act performed or to be performed by him. The penalty is a $10,000 fine or imprisonment for not more than two years, or both. (18 USC 201g)

Soliciting or receiving any compensation for services in relation to any proceeding, contract, claim, controversy, etc., in which the United States is a party or has a direct and substantial interest, before any department, agency, court martial, officer or civil or military commission. The penalty is a $10,000 fine and imprisonment for not more than two years, or both, plus disqualification from holding office. (18 USC 203a)

Practicing in the Court of Claims. The penalty is a $10,000 fine and imprisonment for not more than two years, or both, plus disqualification from holding office. (18 USC 204)

Receiving, as a political contribution or otherwise, anything of value for promising use of or using influence to obtain for any person an appointive office or place under the United States. The penalty is a $1,000 fine, or imprisonment for not more than one year, or both. (18 USC 211)

Entering into or benefiting from contracts with the United States or any agency thereof. The penalty is a $3,000 fine and voidance of the contract. (18 USC 431) Numerous exemptions are listed in 18 USC 433 and elsewhere.

Chamber Rules

Prior to the adoption of ethics codes in 1968, the chief ethical curbs on Members' activities related to voting.

In 1801, when he was Vice President and presiding over the Senate, Thomas Jefferson wrote in *Jefferson's Manual:*

"Where the private interests of a Member are concerned in a bill or question he is to withdraw. And where such an interest has appeared, his voice has been disallowed....In a case so contrary, not only to the laws of decency, but to the fundamental principle of the social compact, which denies to any man to be a judge in his own cause, it is for the honor of the House that this rule of immemorial observance should be strictly adhered to."

Jefferson's rule gave rise to Rule 8 of the House, which requires each Member present to vote "unless he has a direct personal or pecuniary interest in the event of such question." In most cases this decision has been left to the Member. Under an 1874 ruling, a Representative may vote for his private interests if the measure is not for his exclusive benefit, but for that of a group.

There is no corresponding rule in the Senate, but under Rule 12 Senators may be excused from voting, provided they give their reasons for abstaining, and Senators have been excused in the past because of such a direct interest in the outcome.

of $450,273 from seven testimonial events between 1961 and 1965 and from contributions to the Senator's re-election campaign in 1964. Of the sum, Dodd used "at least" $116,083 for personal expenses. Dodd "exercised the influence and power of his office as a U.S. Senator to directly or indirectly obtain funds from the public through testimonials which were political in character.... Not one solicitation letter, invitation, ticket...or other written communication informed the public that the funds were to be used for personal purposes."

On the double-billing charge, the Committee found that on seven trips between 1961 and 1965 Dodd "requested and accepted reimbursements from both the Senate and private organizations for the same travel."

The Committee referred a number of allegations brought out in the hearings to the Justice Department and the Internal Revenue Service for review. No legal charges against Dodd resulted. Among the items reviewed for possible violations of law were a contribution of $8,000 to Dodd in 1964 by the International Latex Corp. The company was fined $5,000 in 1970 for making illegal campaign contributions. The IRS was asked to consider the taxability of the funds Dodd received at the testimonial events in his honor; no case was brought against him.

Dodd declined to seek the Democratic nomination for Senator from Connecticut in 1970 but ran in the general election as an independent. He placed third, with 24 percent of the votes, while the Democratic nominee lost to the Republican, Lowell P. Weicker Jr., 34 percent to 42 percent. Dodd had served four years in the House and 12 years in the Senate. He died May 24, 1971.

Powell Case. Adam Clayton Powell Jr. was first elected to the House from his Harlem district in 1944 and was regularly re-elected by huge majorities. By 1961, he had risen through the seniority system to become chairman of the House Education and Labor Committee, only the second Negro chairman in Congressional history. Six years later he was stripped of his chairmanship—the first action of that kind in 42 years—and two months later, on March 1, 1967, the House voted to exclude him from the 90th Congress. This vote led to a historic Supreme Court decision on the power of Congress to exclude a duly elected Representative.

Powell's downfall was brought on in part by his flamboyant personality; contriteness and conciliation were not in his temperament and he was well aware of racial bias on the part of some of his colleagues. "There is no one here who does not have a skeleton in his closet," he told the House as it convened in 1967. "I know, and I know them by name."

Since 1958, Powell had been involved in court cases on income-tax evasion and libel. His Government-paid travels in the company of attractive staff assistants were a delight to the sensationalist press. In 1966 his absenteeism and his bottling-up of bills in his committee led his colleagues on the Education and Labor Committee to strip him of most of his powers.

The caucus of all House Democrats removed him as chairman in 1967, and the full House followed up by naming a special committee to investigate his activities. That committee recommended censure of Powell for "gross misconduct," loss of seniority and a fine of $40,-000. The punishment was considered inadequate by the House, which voted to bar him altogether from

Censure Procedures Contrasted

The two censure proposals of 1967—the Senate resolution to censure Thomas J. Dodd (D Conn.) and the plan, rejected by the House in March, to censure Adam C. Powell (D N.Y.)—illustrated the vast differences in the procedures used by the two chambers in punishing Members. The oddity of a censure proceeding in each chamber in the same year highlighted these differences. Before 1967, only six Senators and 18 Representatives had been censured.

The Senate's courtly observance of the accused Members' privileges contrasted sharply with the tradition of the House, where a censured Member is treated like a felon hearing his sentence pronounced by a judge. Even this harshness was not enough for the House when it considered Powell's case; censure was rejected in favor of the stiffer penalty of exclusion.

Senate. By tradition, Senate censure proceedings were carried out with the moderation which earned that body its reputation as a private gentlemen's club. The accused Senator was considered equal in privilege to his colleagues before and after the censure vote. He had the choice of being present or not, and he was always granted the privilege of debate. The only formal announcement of censure came when the tally clerk stated that the censure resolution had been adopted. After the vote was taken, the issue was closed. Though he suffered the condemnation of his colleagues, the censured Senator suffered no further punishment, such as the loss of seniority or committee assignments.

The six men censured by the Senate before 1967, the date of the action and the cause were:

Senator	Date	Cause
Timothy Pickering (Fed. Mass.)	1811	Security breach
Benjamin Tappan (D Ohio)	1844	Security breach
Benjamin R. Tillman (D S.C.)	1902	Assault
John L. McLaurin (D S.C.)	1902	Assault
Hiram Bingham (R Conn.)	1929	Unethical acts
Joseph R. McCarthy (R Wis.)	1954	Abuse of Senators

Only two of the six—Pickering and Tillman—were re-elected following their censure.

House. As in the Senate, most accused House Members had the choice of being present for the debate on the censure resolution or not. In Powell's case, he was allowed to speak in his own defense, but many other Members were denied this privilege. In most instances, if the censure resolution was adopted, the Member was in effect under arrest until the Speaker "pronounced" censure. Almost all the resolutions after 1875 included a dramatic injunction that the Member "be brought to the bar of the House in the custody of the Sergeant-at-Arms and there publicly censured by the Speaker in the name of the House." The Powell censure resolution which the House rejected included this clause as well as a course of action unprecedented in House tradition: a requirement that he pay a $40,000 fine, and a provision stripping him of his 22-year seniority.

The House by 1967 had censured 18 Members. Ten of the 18 were re-elected.

Ban on Nepotism

In a move that surprised most Members of Congress and reporters, the House voted in 1967 to prohibit nepotism by Federal officials, including Senators and Representatives. The proposal was offered by Rep. Neal Smith (D Iowa) as a floor amendment to the postal rate and Federal pay bill of 1967 and was adopted by a 49-33 standing vote. The Senate accepted the Smith proviso, with language extending it to less immediate relatives (sons-in-law, for example), and the ban was written into permanent law.

In explaining his amendment, Smith said it was aimed in particular at postmasters in small post offices who were inclined to hire their wives as post office clerks.

But nepotism by Members of Congress—the hiring of wives, children, brothers and other close relatives for work on a Member's own staff—was a frequent source of critical press comment. Columns by Drew Pearson and Jack Anderson over the years had charged certain Members with padding their official staffs or district offices with relatives who did no work for their Government paycheck.

The nepotism ban prohibited officers or employees of the Federal or District of Columbia Governments from appointing, or recommending for appointment or promotion, a relative to serve in the same agency or department as the official.

Congress. In recommending censure the special committee asserted that Powell had been guilty of "contumacious conduct" toward the New York courts which had found him guilty of libel and contempt of court; that he had misappropriated public funds by keeping his wife on the Committee payroll while she lived in Puerto Rico and by using Committee funds for trips taken by his family and friends; and that he had refused to cooperate with the special committee by failing to answer inquiries.

In his appearances before the committee, Powell responded only to questions relating to the constitutional requirements for House membership—his age, citizenship and inhabitancy. These were the only questions that the House could properly inquire into, Powell and his lawyers claimed. Upon his exclusion by the House, Powell filed suit in the U.S. District Court for the District of Columbia to test his claim.

The central legal issues in the Powell suit were:

• Could the House add to the Constitution's three qualifications for House membership? The three were that the Member be at least 25 years old, have been a U.S. citizen for at least seven years and be, when elected, an inhabitant of the state from which he was elected.

• Could the courts properly examine the actions of the House in such cases, order the House not to add to the Constitution's qualifications, and enforce this order?

U.S. District Judge George L. Hart Jr. ruled April 7, 1967, that he had no jurisdiction in the case and dismissed the suit.

The U.S. Court of Appeals for the District of Columbia on Feb. 28, 1968, affirmed the action of the lower court in dismissing the suit. The Court of Appeals held that the lower court did have jurisdiction over the subject matter but that the case involved a political question, which, if decided, would constitute a violation of the separation of powers and produce an embarrassing confrontation between Congress and the courts.

The Supreme Court by a 7-1 vote on June 16, 1969, reversed the lower courts. Chief Justice Earl Warren, delivering the opinion of the Court, ruled that the House had improperly excluded Powell, a duly elected Representative who met the constitutional requirements of age, residence and citizenship.

The suit had been brought against the Speaker of the House, the Majority and Minority Leaders, the ranking members of the committee that investigated Powell, and three functionaries of the House who had withheld his pay and denied him such perquisites as an office and staff. The Supreme Court held that under the speech-and-debate clause of the Constitution, the five Members of Congress were immune from prosecution but that the three employees were liable for action. The Court ruling was limited to the case at hand. No ruling was made on the power of a house of Congress to exclude or expel a properly elected Member.

While Powell's case was proceeding through the courts, his constituents re-elected him in a special election to fill his own vacant seat in 1967 and to a regular term in 1968. This time the House agreed to seat Powell but levied on him a $25,000 fine for the past misappropriation of funds. Powell rarely appeared in the House during the 91st Congress and in 1970 was defeated in the Democratic primary in his Congressional district.

House Ethics Committee

Largely in reaction to the Powell case, the House in 1966 took its first step toward achieving an enforceable code of ethics. The effort was minimal, for the select committee empowered to draft a code was in existence only two months before that Congress expired. It could only recommend that the next Congress create a permanent committee that would not only draft a code of ethical practices but would also, like the Senate Select Committee, investigate allegations of improper conduct and recommend disciplinary action.

Still moving slowly, the House the next year, early in the 90th Congress, created a 12-member, bipartisan standing Committee on Standards of Official Conduct. The Committee was given no investigative authority. Its sole function was to recommend a code of conduct and the powers it might need to enforce the code.

In 1968, the House and Senate both finally adopted codes of conduct that required Members of Congress to make confidential reports on some of their outside income and financial interests. *(See below.)* At the same time, the authority of the House Standards Committee was increased.

Committee Powers. The Committee on Standards of Official Conduct was given several specific powers, including the following:

• The Committee may consider measures related to the House Code of Official Conduct or financial disclosure requirements which have been referred to it.

• The Committee may recommend to the House such legislative or administrative actions as it deems appropriate for establishing or enforcing standards of conduct.

• It may investigate, subject to limitations, any alleged violation of the code of official conduct or of any law, rule, regulation, or other standard of conduct applicable to Members, officers or employees in the performance of their duties.

• It may report, with the approval of the House, to appropriate Federal or state authorities, any substantial evidence of a violation of any law by a Member, officer or employee of the House applicable to the discharge of his duties and responsibilities.

• It may consider a request of a Member, officer or employee for an advisory opinion respecting the general propriety of any current or proposed conduct by him.

Limits on Authority. Certain limitations were imposed on the Committee by the resolution creating it. These included:

• No resolution, report, recommendation or advisory opinion may be made, and no investigation of conduct undertaken, unless approved by the vote of not less than 7 of the 12 members. (This assures that no action can be taken unless at least one member of the majority or minority is willing to join with those of the opposite political party.)

• Except when the Committee undertakes an investigation on its own initiative, it may act only upon receipt of a complaint, in writing and under oath, made by a Member. If the complaint is submitted by an individual, not a Member of the House, and as many as three Members of the House have refused, in writing, to transmit the complaint, the Committee may act on it.

• No member of the Committee may participate in any Committee proceeding relating to his own official conduct.

Immunity From Prosecution

"Ex-Senator Is Freed of Bribery Charges—Protected by Congressional Immunity," the newspaper headline reads. Two recent court cases have made clear that under present law a Member of Congress cannot be convicted for legislative activities—speeches, votes or committee actions.

This does not mean immunity from any kind of criminal activity, including bribery. Dealings with Executive agencies, for example, may not confer immunity. Nor have the courts yet held that Congress itself may not regulate the conduct of its Members.

Johnson Case. The Supreme Court by a 7-0 vote, Feb. 24, 1966, held that in prosecuting a former Member of Congress, the Executive Branch may not constitutionally inquire into his motives for making a speech on the floor of Congress, even though the speech was made for a bribe and was part of an unlawful conspiracy.

The holding in *U.S. v. Johnson* left Members of Congress immune from prosecution for their words and legislative deeds on the floor of Congress, with one exception reserved by the Court—prosecution under a "narrowly drawn" law enacted by Congress itself "to regulate the conduct of its Members." Members of Congress already were immune from libel suits for speeches made on the floor.

The Johnson case arose out of the conviction of former Rep. Thomas F. Johnson (D Md.) on June 13,

1963, by a Federal jury in Baltimore. The Government charged that Johnson, former Rep. Frank W. Boykin (D Ala.) and two officers of a Maryland savings and loan company then under indictment, J. Kenneth Edlin and William L. Robinson, had entered into a conspiracy whereby Johnson and Boykin would approach the Justice Department to urge a "review" of the indictment and Johnson would make a speech on the floor of the House defending savings and loan institutions. Johnson made the speech June 30, 1960, and it was reprinted by the indicted company and distributed to the public. Johnson and Boykin allegedly received money in the form of "campaign contributions," Johnson's share being more than $20,000.

Johnson was convicted on seven counts of violating the Federal conflict of interest law (18 U.S.C. 281) and on one count of conspiring to defraud the United States (18 U.S.C. 371); the others were convicted of the same charges. President Johnson on Dec. 17, 1965, granted Boykin a full pardon.

The Fourth Circuit Court of Appeals Sept. 16, 1964, set aside Johnson's conspiracy conviction on the ground that it was unconstitutional under provisions of Article I, Section 6: "...for any speech or debate in either House, they (Senators and Representatives) shall not be questioned in any other place." The court ordered a new trial on the other counts on the ground that evidence taken about Johnson's speech on the conspiracy count "infected" the entire case.

The Supreme Court affirmed the lower court's ruling, thus foreclosing further prosecution on the conspiracy count but permitting retrial on the other counts.

Johnson was convicted Jan. 26, 1968, for the second time on the conflict of interest charges by the U.S. District Court in Baltimore, Md. He was sentenced to six months in prison.

Brewster Case. Another Maryland Democrat, ex-Sen. Daniel B. Brewster, was ruled immune from prosecution for bribery in a U.S. District Court decision on Oct. 9, 1970. The Government appealed the case.

Brewster had been indicted for accepting $24,500 from a mail order house, Spiegel Inc., to vote favorably for the concern's interests in the Senate Post Office and Civil Service Committee. Spiegel and its Washington representative were indicted for allegedly making five illegal payments to Brewster, who was defeated for reelection in 1968, before the charges were brought against him.

In dismissing the case against Brewster, Judge George L. Hart Jr. said that without Congressional immunity Members of Congress would be susceptible to pressure from anyone, particularly the Executive Branch, who wanted particular legislative action.

Dowdy Case. One month before the Brewster decision, the Fourth Circuit Court of Appeals ruled against an immunity plea in another bribery case involving a Congressman.

A Federal grand jury in Baltimore on March 31, 1970, indicted Rep. John Dowdy (D Texas) on charges of conspiracy, perjury and the use of interstate facilities to promote bribery. The indictment alleged that Dowdy had accepted a $25,000 bribe on Sept. 22, 1965, to intervene in a Justice Department investigation of Monarch Construction Co. of Silver Spring, Md.

Ethical Dilemma: Where to Draw the Line

It is a difficult task to establish broad standards of ethical conduct for Members of Congress. In this complex field there are few easy answers, and the legislators themselves frequently do not agree on what constitutes acceptable behavior.

The task of establishing ethical guidelines is complicated by a lack of fundamental agreement on the role of the legislator. Is he, for instance, supposed to act always in the national interest, and if so, by whom is the national interest to be defined? Or is he to act in the local interest, as he defines it with the concurrence of his constituents, on the assumption that the national interest is always the prevailing sum of local interests? And when he serves the local interest, is it or is it not acceptable to serve his own interest at the same time? In his role as representative of a state or district, how far should he go in pressing the case of a constituent before a Federal agency, or in seeking to influence the award of a Government contract?

Is the legislator supposed to give up other business in order to devote his full time to Congressional duties? Or should he, as some maintain, consider himself a part-time legislator and lead an active business or professional career? And when matters arise in which he has a direct economic stake, should he refrain from voting, or should he assume that his vote will be balanced by another legislator with an opposing stake in the matter?

Not only does the lack of agreement on the fundamental role of the legislator complicate the problem of ethical behavior in Congress; the questions of conduct themselves are often only questions of degree: where should the line be drawn?

Major Problem Areas

Misuse of Position. This category includes such problems as those created by the Member with large financial interests who is in a position to influence the outcome of legislation affecting those interests; or the Member who uses official stationery or his influence to gain special advantages or privileges for private law clients or friends; or the Member who uses confidential information for other than official purposes; or the Member who seeks through off-the-record communications to influence the outcome of a case pending before a regulatory agency.

Outside Employment. Problems in this area are closely allied to those involving misuse of position. For example, does the Member who practices law on the side gain undue personal advantage from his Congressional position? Is this advantage based on specialized knowledge or on influence and reputation? In either case, should the Member use it? Should a Member associate with a firm that does business with the Federal Government? Does he make it possible for lobbyists to approach him by doing business with his firm? Does his connection with a firm affect his decisions as a Member?

Relations With Lobbyists and Campaign Contributors. It is illegal to conspire to defraud the Government or to accept or offer gifts or campaign contributions in payment for services or votes. It is frequently difficult, however, to prove a direct cause-and-effect relationship between gifts or contributions and some particular service or vote.

Lobbyists and other pressure groups tend to court those Members who are not basically opposed to their aims. On the other hand, it may occasionally happen that a lobbyist, by his gift or campaign contribution to a Member, makes it appear he has influenced the course of legislation in order to satisfy his employer that he is an effective lobbyist. Thus a Member may appear to be implicated in a conspiracy or conflict of interest that actually does not exist.

Nevertheless, because the legislator with modest means is constantly in need of additional income and campaign funds, he may accept contributions and such assistance from lobbies as large speaking fees in spite of the appearances created. Accepting such favors may place him in a difficult position later on. Sen. Paul H. Douglas (D Ill.) wrote in 1952: "The vast majority of the big donors want something in return for their money. Their gifts are in a sense investments. After election, if their candidates are victorious, they will come around to collect. They will want contracts, insurance policies, jobs for friends and relations, loans, subsidies, privileges, legislation, and so on. Woe betide the office-holders and the party which ignore their claims. For if they do, then the next time the money is likely to be shut off...."

Another problem is that there is no uniform, nationwide system for reporting all campaign expenses. Thus, like a legislator's outside business, campaign contributions sometimes provide lobbyists and other favor-seekers with an unrecorded means of creating— or paying off—an obligation. The inadequacies of Federal regulation of lobbying and campaign financing are described elsewhere in this volume. *(See Chapter V, Campaign Financing, and Chapter VI, The Lobbies.)*

Misuse of Funds. This category includes the handling of all of the various funds entrusted to a Member's management, such as office rental, stationery allowances, staff allowances and travel funds, in addition to campaign funds. Current accounting procedures permit many abuses to be hidden from the public; even when abuses are exposed, there is little that can be done except to retire the offender at the polls. Among such abuses are staff misuse and payroll padding; misuse of the franking privilege; padding rental and stationery allowances; and taking useless or unnecessarily expensive trips (junkets) at Federal expense. *(See Chapter IV, Pay and Perquisites of Members.)*

The grand jury that indicted Dowdy said he had picked up a briefcase containing $25,000 in cash at the Atlanta, Ga., airport in 1965. The briefcase allegedly had been left for Dowdy by officials of the Monarch home-improvement company. Earlier in 1970, the two indicted officials of the then defunct concern had pleaded guilty to charges of defrauding customers.

Dowdy, a former district attorney and high-ranking member of the House Judiciary and District of Columbia Committees, denied wrongdoing. A nine-term Member of Congress, he was re-elected in 1970 against only minor write-in opposition.

Dowdy was the first incumbent Member to face criminal charges since 1962, when Reps. Johnson and Boykin were indicted. After several postponements, Dowdy's trial was scheduled to begin May 3, 1971. However, on April 28, 1971, U.S. District Court Judge Roszel C. Thomsen granted a further postponement on the basis of a medical report stating that Dowdy was "neither physically nor mentally capable of standing trial at this time."

Congressional Codes of Conduct

The House Committee on Standards of Official Conduct, chaired by Rep. Melvin Price (D Ill.), and the Senate's Select Committee on Standards and Conduct, chaired by Sen. John C. Stennis (D Miss.), won adoption in 1968 of separate codes of conduct for Members and top employees of the two chambers. Beginning in 1969, Members of Congress and employees were required to file reports—the bulk of them confidential—on financial interests and sources of outside income.

The House required its Members to make more information public than did the Senate, but even the House provisions left many loopholes. The intent of the disclosure requirements, according to the House Committee's report, was "to acquaint the voters with the areas in which it is possible for a conflict of interest to occur." This good intention, however, was just about nullified by the strict rules the Committee subsequently laid down for members of the press or public who wanted to copy information from the non-confidential reports.

Senate Ethics Rules

The Senate in March 1968 adopted four new rules intended to guide the ethical conduct of Members and employees. Only two of the rules apply to Senators.

Outside Employment (Rule 41). Provides that no officer or employee of the Senate may engage in any other paid activity if the outside interest is inconsistent with his Senate duties. Employees must report outside jobs to their supervisors, including Senators, who are to take action necessary to avoid a conflict of interest by the employee.

Contributions (Rule 42). A Senator or declared candidate for the Senate may accept contributions from a fund-raising event only if he gives the event prior approval and receives an accounting of the sources and amounts of each contribution. Official party functions are exempted from these restrictions.

Senators and candidates may accept funds from an individual or organization provided a complete accounting of the sources and amounts is made by the recipient.

The rule also states a Senator or candidate may use these contributions for campaign expenses and for travel, printing, telephone, and other expenses not covered by Senate allowances.

Gifts of $50 or more from a single, nonfamily source must be disclosed under Rule 44. *(See below.)*

Political Fund Raising (Rule 43). Prohibits employees of the Senate from receiving, soliciting or distributing funds in connection with a campaign for the Senate or any Federal office. The rule exempts Senators' assistants who earn more than $10,000 a year and are designated to engage in such activity. The Senator must file the names of such designated aides with the Secretary of the Senate as public information.

Financial Disclosure (Rule 44). Requires each Senator, declared candidate and Senate employee earning more than $15,000 a year to file with the U.S. Comptroller General by May 15 each year a sealed envelope containing detailed financial disclosure.

The sealed envelope contains a copy of the individual's U.S. income tax returns, the amount and source of each fee of $1,000 or more received from a client, plus the following information:

• The name and address of each business or professional enterprise in which he is an officer or employee, and the amount of compensation received.

• The identity of real or personal property he owns worth $10,000 or more.

• The identity of each trust or fiduciary relation in which he holds a beneficial interest worth $10,000 or more and the identity, if known, of any interest the trust holds in real or personal property over $10,000.

• The identity of each liability of $5,000 or more owed by him or by him and his spouse jointly.

• The source and value of all gifts worth $50 or more received from a single source.

The Senate Select Committee on Standards and Conduct may, by a majority vote, examine the contents of a confidential filing and make the information available for a staff investigation. The confidential reports are held by the Comptroller General for seven years unless returned earlier when a Senator dies or retires.

Under Rule 44, each Senator, candidate and employee earning more than $15,000 a year must file with the Secretary of the Senate by May 15 each year, the following information available to the public:

• The accounting required under Rule 42 of all contributions received in the previous year.

• The amount, value and source of any honorarium of $300 or more.

House Ethics Rules

The House in April 1968 adopted a code of ethical conduct and a limited financial disclosure rule.

Code of Offical Conduct (Rule 43). Stipulates that a Member, officer or employee of the House shall:

1. "...Conduct himself at all times in a manner which shall reflect creditably on the House of Representatives."

Government's Code of Ethics

Congress in 1958 approved the following Code of Ethics (H Con Res 175, 85th Congress, 2nd Session) for all Government employees, including Members of Congress:

Any person in Government service should—

1. Put loyalty to the highest moral principles and to country above loyalty to persons, party or Government department.

2. Uphold the Constitution, laws, and legal regulations of the United States and of all governments therein and never be a party to their evasion.

3. Give a full day's labor for a full day's pay, giving to the performance of his duties his earnest effort and best thought.

4. Seek to find and employ more efficient and economical ways of getting tasks accomplished.

5. Never discriminate unfairly by the dispensing of special favors or privileges to anyone, whether for remuneration or not; and never accept, for himself or his family, favors or benefits under circumstances which might be construed by reasonable persons as influencing the performance of his Governmental duties.

7. Make no private promises of any kind binding upon the duties of office, since a Government employee has no private word which can be binding on public duty.

8. Never use any information coming to him confidentially in the performance of Governmental duties as a means for making private profit.

9. Expose corruption wherever discovered.

10. Uphold these principles, ever conscious that public office is a public trust.

---

2. "...Adhere to the spirit and the letter of the Rules of the House and to the rules of duly constituted committees thereof."

3. "...Receive no compensation nor shall he permit any compensation to accrue to his beneficial interest from any source, the receipt of which would occur by virtue of influence improperly exerted from his position in the Congress."

4. "...Accept no gift of substantial value, directly or indirectly, from any person, organization or corporation having a direct interest in legislation before the Congress."

5. "...Accept no honorarium for a speech, writing for publication, or other similar activity, from any person, organization or corporation in excess of the usual and customary value for such services."

6. "...Keep his campaign funds separate from his personal funds. He shall convert no campaign funds to personal use in excess of reimbursement for legitimate and verifiable prior campaign expenditures. He shall expend no funds from his campaign account not attributable to bona fide campaign purposes."

7. "...Treat as campaign contributions all proceeds from testimonial dinners or other fund-raising events if the sponsors of such affairs do not give clear notice in advance to the donors or participants that the proceeds are intended for other purposes."

8. "...Retain no one from his clerk-hire allowance who does not perform duties commensurate with the compensation he receives."

Financial Disclosure (Rule 44). Requires Members and officers of the House, their principal assistants and professional staff members of committees to file with the Committee on Standards by April 30 each year a report naming the sources of certain financial interests—which are to be available to the public—and a sealed report on the amount of income from each source. The sealed report may be opened by the Committee only if it determines that it is essential to an investigation.

The public listing of financial interests is to include:

• The name of any business in which the filer has a financial interest of over $5,000 or from which he derives income of $1,000 or more, but only if it does substantial business with the Federal Government or is under Federal regulation.

• The name and type of practice of any professional organization from which the filer receives income of $1,000 or more, but only if the filer or his spouse is an officer, director, partner or adviser.

• The source of income exceeding $5,000 from a service rendered (except to the Government) or a capital gain (except sale of the filer's home) and of reimbursement for expenditures exceeding $1,000.

These reports are to be available for public inspection under regulations to be set by the Committee, which may require full identification of the person making the examination and the reason for it and is to notify the Member involved.

The confidential reports are to give the fair market value of the business holdings reported and the amount of income from each source reported publicly.

Persons without financial interests that must be reported are required to file statements to this effect.

Halpern Amendment. In 1969 the *Wall Street Journal* ran articles about the heavy indebtedness of Rep. Seymour Halpern (R N.Y.), third-ranking Republican on the House Banking and Currency Committee. The information showed, according to the *Journal*, that: "First National City Bank of New York extended Mr. Halpern a $40,000 unsecured personal loan 'at our best lending rate' when he was already in debt to 13 other banks for more than $75,000; while that loan was outstanding, First National City's lobbyists were pressing Congress to enact a mild version of the bill bringing one-bank holding companies under Federal regulation."

In 1970, the House added a new financial disclosure rule: It called for public reporting of any loan of $10,000 or more outstanding for 90 days or longer without a pledge of specific collateral. The amount of the indebtedness need not be made public, only the source. The House added also a requirement, matching the existing Senate requirement, for the disclosure of the sources of honoraria of $300 or more. Again, only the sources need be made public; the amounts received would be reported in the sealed file.

CQ Study of Reports

Early in 1969, Congressional Quarterly compiled and analyzed the first year's reports filed under the disclosure regulations. Among its findings were the following:

Senate Reports. The Senate directed its Members to make reports, available to the public, on the amount and source of each honorarium of $300 or more received during the preceding year.

Senators were also asked to list the sources, amounts, and disposition of political contributions received by them, as well as the source and amount of any gift in excess of $50 from persons other than relatives.

The Senate reports produced little information, however, other than fees received by Senators for speeches, writing, television appearances or related activities. In some cases even this information was sketchy because Senators merely listed booking agents as the source of large amounts of income. Sixty-one Senators reported receiving honoraria in 1968.

House Reports. The House required a more detailed financial report which was available for public inspection. Under the new House Rule on disclosure, Members were asked to list (by name, not amount) interests worth more than $5,000 in any enterprise doing a substantial amount of business with the Federal Government or subject to Federal regulatory agencies.

House Members were also directed to disclose publicly the source of any income for services (other than Congressional salaries) exceeding $5,000 and any capital gain from a single source exceeding $5,000. They were required to report associations with any professional organization from which an income of $1,000 or more was received.

House Loopholes. Although the House disclosure reports revealed far more information about Members' outside business activities than the Senate reports, there were a number of large loopholes in the House statements. No House Member reported the source of any honorarium; instructions supplied by the House Committee on Standards of Official Conduct required at that time the disclosure of speech or writing fees only if they exceeded $5,000 in each case.

The House did not require Members to list the amount or value of stock held in companies doing business with the Federal Government. Eighty lawyer Members reported an active interest in law practices, but were not directed to list the names of clients.

Despite the large proportion (21.6 percent) of House Members who reported in 1969 an interest in financial institutions, they were not required under the disclosure rule to reveal the amount of stock held in banks, savings and loan associations or bank holding companies.

Corporate Interests

The Congressional Quarterly study of disclosures was analyzed in a 1970 report by the New York City bar's committee on Congressional ethics. Some of its findings follow:

• Transportation—Ownership interests of Members of Congress in air, rail and trucking concerns are "so few that it appears that Members may deliberately avoid such interests." The committee found "no current evidence that Congressional financial interests in transportation are affecting the substance of legislation or agency administration."

• Defense contractors—Most of the reported holdings in defense contractors' stock were in widely diversified companies such as AT&T, General Electric, IBM and

---

Financial Disclosure

Full public disclosure of the financial interests of each elected official is regarded by many observers as the most effective means of ensuring an ethical standard in government. Appointed officials can be discharged by their superiors; the electorate cannot fill the same role unless it has access to financial data.

A Senate subcommittee headed by Sen. Paul H. Douglas (D Ill.) issued a report in 1951 which described disclosure as "like an antibiotic which can deal with ethical sicknesses in the field of public affairs." In its study of ways to reform Congressional ethics, the subcommittee found that full disclosure met with wide approval from those who had testified. "(Disclosure) is hardly a sanction and certainly not a penalty," the report continued. "It would sharpen men's own judgments of right and wrong since they would be less likely to do wrong things if they knew these acts would be challenged." Douglas wrote in his 1952 book, *Ethics in Government*, that "sunlight is a strong disinfectant."

Over the years, a handful of Members of Congress have made public detailed statements of their financial status. A slightly larger group has pressed for a law requiring such information to be made public by all Members.

In 1967, before adoption by the two chambers of their limited rules for disclosure, the Senate voted three times on amendments calling for full public disclosure. On the closest of the three votes, an amendment offered by Sen. Joseph S. Clark (D Pa.) to a pending legislative reorganization bill, public disclosure lost by only four votes, 42-46.

---

others typical of any blue chip portfolio. "Those usually mentioned as Congressional friends of the military-industrial complex are conspicuously absent from those reporting ownership interests in it."

• Broadcasting—According to figures published by *Broadcasting* magazine between 1961 and 1968, Congressional ownership of broadcasting interests declined from 23 Members to 15. This was a lower figure than that reported by Congressional Quarterly, which included holding companies that control stations, such as RCA, in its tabulation.

The lawyers' committee noted that Members of Congress often feel dependent on broadcasters for publicity and free radio and TV time. It cited a report that 60 to 70 percent receive free broadcasting time for their reports to constituents. Without reaching any conclusion on alleged "softness" toward the broadcasting industry, the committee said, "if Congress is overly friendly to the broadcasting industry, it is *not* because of Congressional ownership of broadcasting interests."

• Banking—Among the four business areas studied, it was only in the banking field that the bar's committee found evidence that "Federal policy or administration suffers substantially from Congressional business interests."

Noting that CQ reported that 96 Representatives acknowledged banking ownership interests and 43 of them held either offices or directorships, the report said:

Model Disclosure Rules

Model disclosure rules recommended by the New York City bar's committee on Congressional ethics in 1970 call for Members of Congress and Congressional employees paid more than $18,000 annually to publicly report:

• The identity of each interest in real or personal property having a value of $5,000 or more. Excluded would be bank deposits, insurance policies, household furnishings, personal effects and principal residence. Dollar amounts would be filed under seal to be opened only by an official investigation.

• Each source of any income, including capital gains, totaling $1,000 or more during the preceding calendar year. The exact value would be specified under seal.

• The identity of any creditor to whom debts of $5,000 or more aggregated during a year, except a debt secured by mortgage on principal residence. The amount of the debts would be cited under seal.

• The source and value of all nonfamily gifts in the aggregate amount of $25 or more received from any single source.

• The amount or value and source of each honorarium of $300 or more received during the preceding calendar year.

• Assets of a spouse, minor child, corporations in which reporting persons or his family own 50 percent or more of the outstanding stock; a proportionate share of assets of any partnership; assets of trusts and estates in which there is a vested beneficial interest; income received by a spouse or minor child.

• Legal fees aggregating more than $1,000 received from a single client during a year by a law firm with which the Member or Congressional employee is associated; names of such clients and the identity of any proceedings in which the United States was an interested party.

• Amounts and sources of contributions received, including by political committees, to defray official or semiofficial expenses related to Member's office.

The reports would be filed and available for public inspection with the House or Senate Ethics Committees and with the clerk of the U.S. District Court of the judicial districts in which the Members' and employees' home residences are located. A copy also would be maintained for public inspection in the office of the Member in his state or House district.

"As high as it seems, this figure is actually lower than the true number because some did not report interests in state-chartered institutions." These had been ruled by the House Standards Committee to be outside the reporting requirements.

The report called attention to the fact that 13 of those with bank holdings were on the House Banking and Currency Committee and six were on the Ways and Means Committee, which is concerned with all tax matters.

"Banks have played a role perhaps equal to that of law practices in generating Congressional scandal," the lawyers noted.

New York Bar Association Proposals

The most recent extensive study of Congressional ethics was conducted in 1967-69 by a committee of the Association of the Bar of the City of New York. Financed by a Ford Foundation grant, the special committee on Congressional ethics was chaired by Louis M. Loeb, former president of the association. The executive director was James C. Kirby Jr., dean-elect of the Ohio State University College of Law and former chief counsel to the Senate Judiciary Subcommittee on Constitutional Amendments. The committee's report, entitled *Congress and the Public Trust*, was published in 1970.

These were the major recommendations of the bar association committee:

Conflicts of Interest. Congress should:

• Adopt a rule declaring that Members must not use their power in Congress for personal gain and should avoid situations where they might appear to be doing so.

• Widen the requirements for public disclosure of Members' financial interests. Model Disclosure Rules were spelled out. *(See box.)*

• Require Congressional committees to adopt rules governing the financial interests of committee members in matters within the jurisdiction of their committees.

Members of Congress should:

• Adopt investment policies that minimize the possibility that their official decisions may be influenced by personal economic interests.

• Abstain from serving as officers, directors, trustees or partners in commercial enterprises.

• Avoid all economic interests which may be specially affected by legislation within their committees' jurisdiction. (Illustrations of situations to be avoided included: a broadcaster on the Commerce Committee; an investor in defense industries on the Armed Services Committee; an oil-well investor on the House Ways and Means or Senate Finance Committee; a subsidized farmer on the Agriculture Committee.)

• Voluntarily abstain from voting on matters in which they have personal economic interests, if it is not feasible to eliminate those interests. They need not abstain if they intend to vote against those economic interests.

Law Practice. Congress should:

• Enact legislation on "double door" law partnerships, forbidding the partners of a Member of Congress from practicing before Federal agencies (just as the Member himself is already forbidden by law).

• Amend the statute on law practice by Members of Congress to forbid them from appearing for compensation in the courts. (The last known instance of such practice was Sen. Sam J. Ervin's (D N.C.) appearance in 1964 before the Supreme Court, representing a North Carolina textile firm (Darlington Manufacturing Co.) in a case against the National Labor Relations Board. Ervin's Judiciary subcommittee later held an investigation of the NLRB.)

Members of Congress should:

• Voluntarily refrain from any form of law practice. The committee conceded that in a few cases where a newly elected Member foresaw little prospect of re-election (e.g., when the opposition party had regularly held his seat), he might ethically retain his law practice. This should apply, however, only to Senators elected or appointed to less than a full, six-year term and to Representatives in their first two terms in Congress.

Campaign Financing. Congress should enact legislation:

- Providing Federal subsidies for the minimum expenses of major and minor party candidates in general elections.
- Authorizing postage-free mailing for all qualified candidates in primary and general elections.
- Requiring television stations to grant substantial discounts for air time for candidates.
- Tightening the reporting requirements and limits on individual contributions to campaigns and establishing a Federal Elections Commission to oversee the campaign regulatory law.

Salaries and Allowances. Finding that the last pay increase, to $42,500, was sufficient for Members with small families to live comfortably, the committee recommended only changes in fringe allowances:

- A rise in the cost-of-living tax deduction from $3,000 to $5,500 a year, authorization for the Federal Salaries Commission to act in areas concerning fringe benefits, and reimbursement for one trip to the home state every month for all Members while Congress is in session.
- Increases in the staff allowances for Senators from the largest states.
- Adoption of rules against payroll padding and misuse of staff.

Gifts, Supplemental Funds and Honoraria. Congress should adopt rules:

- Against acceptance of substantial personal gifts and for public disclosure of gifts worth more than $25.
- Prohibiting personal use of funds from testimonial dinners and other fund-raising events. The House should adopt the Senate's rule forbidding unusually large honoraria.
- Requiring full public disclosure of privately financed funds for office expenses, though it was urged that all Members refrain from such practices.

Bill Introduced

A proposed Omnibus Disclosure Act (S 4202), putting into legislative text a large part of the bar committee's recommendations, was introduced Aug. 7, 1970, by Sen. Birch Bayh (D Ind.). No hearings were held on the bill in 1970. Bayh reintroduced the measure in 1971 (S 1885).

A noteworthy feature of S 4202 was that it required all members of the three branches of Government, Executive, Judicial and Legislative, to file the same disclosure report with the U.S. Comptroller General each year. All the information in the disclosure reports was to be made public.

In introducing the bill, Bayh said: "In a time when the integrity of all of our institutions is under attack, we can no longer settle for only self-regulation, nor for the suspicions inherent in private disclosure." The Senator presented in the *Congressional Record* a comparison of the Omnibus Disclosure Act with the existing rules and regulations covering members of the three branches of the Federal Government. *(See Appendix.)*

Bibliography

Books

Allyn, Paul and Joseph Greene, *See How They Run; The Making of a Congressman.* Chilton Co., 1964.

Association of the Bar of the City of New York, Special Committee on Congressional Ethics, *Congress and the Public Trust.* Atheneum, 1970.

Bolling, Richard, *House Out of Order.* Dutton, 1965.

Clapp, Charles L., *The Congressman.* Brookings Institution, 1963.

Clark, Joseph S., *Congress: The Sapless Branch.* Harper & Row, 1964.

Congressional Quarterly Inc., *Almanacs* for 1967, 1968 and 1969.

——, *Congress and the Nation, 1945-64* (Vol. I).

——, *Congress and the Nation, 1965-68* (Vol. II).

Deakin, James, *The Lobbyists.* Public Affairs Press, 1966.

Douglas, Paul H., *Ethics in Government.* Harvard University Press, 1952.

Galloway, George B., *History of the House of Representatives.* Thomas Y. Crowell Co., 1962.

Kefauver, Estes and Jack Levin, *A Twentieth Century Congress.* Duell, Sloan and Pearce, 1947.

MacNeil, Neil, *Forge of Democracy.* David McKay Co., 1963.

Rienow, Robert and Leona Train Rienow, *Of Snuff, Sin and the Senate.* Follett Publishing Co., 1965.

Rogow, Arnold A. and Harold D. Lasswell, *Power, Corruption and Rectitude.* Prentice-Hall, 1963.

Twentieth Century Fund Task Force on Financing Congressional Campaigns, *Electing Congress: The Financial Dilemma.* The Twentieth Century Fund, 1970.

White, William S., *Citadel.* Harper & Brothers, 1957.

Government Publication

Hupman, Richard D., *Senate Election, Expulsion and Censure Cases from 1789 to 1960.* Government Printing Office, 1962 (Sen. Doc. 71, 87th Congress, 2nd session).

The Appendix

(Texts of documents and other material relating to the subject matter of the respective chapters of this book will be found in the following pages, as indicated below:)

BIOGRAPHICAL INDEX

(Dates of service arc inclusive, starting in year of service and ending as service ends. From 1789 to 1933 terms of service were from March 4 to March 3; since 1934, service has been from Jan. 3 to Jan. 3. Exact date is shown (where available) if Member began or ended his service in mid-term.)

The names in this index include, alphabetically, all Senators, Representatives, Resident Commissioners and Territorial Delegates who served in Congress from March 4, 1789, through May 15, 1971—the 1st through 92nd Congresses. The material is organized as follows: Name, Relationship to other Members and Presidents, Party, State (of service), Date of Birth, Date of Death (if applicable), Congressional Service, Service as President, Vice President, Member of the Cabinet or Supreme Court, Governor, Delegate to the Continental Congress, Speaker of the House, President pro tempore of the Senate and Chairman of the Democratic or Republican National Committee. If Member changed parties during his Congressional service, party designation is that which applied at the end of such service and breakdown is included with Congressional Service. Party designation is multiple only if Member was elected by two or more at the same time. Where service dates are left open, Members were still serving in 1971. A list of party and other abbreviations used follows.

Abbreviation	Party	Abbreviation	Party
AAD	Adams Anti Democrat	FSil.	Free Silver
ABD	Anti Broderick Democrat	FSil.R	Free Silver Republican
AD	Anti Democrat	FSW	Free Soil Whig
Ad.D	Adams Democrat	Fus.	Fusionist
AF	Anti Federalist	Fus.D	Fusionist Democrat
AJD	Anti Jackson Democrat		
AL	American Laborite	G	Greenbacker
Alliance D	Alliance Democrat	GD	Greenback Democrat
AM	Anti Monopolist	GLab.Ref.	Greenback Labor Reformer
AMas.	Anti Mason		
AMas.D	Anti Mason Democrat	HCW	Henry Clay Whig
AMD	Anti Monopoly Democrat	HTW	High Tariff Whig
AND	Anti Nebraska Democrat		
AP	American Party	I	Independent
AR	Adams Republican	ID	Independent Democrat
ASW	Anti Slavery Whig	IR	Independent Republican
ATD	Anti Tammany Democrat	IRad.	Independent Radical
AW	American Whig	IRef.	Independent Reformer
		ISil.R	Independent Silver Republican
C	Conservative	IW	Independent Whig
Cal.D	Calhoun Democrat		
Cal.N	Calhoun Nullifier	JD	Jackson Democrat
CassD	Cass Democrat	Jeff.D	Jefferson Democrat
CD	Clay Democrat	JFSt.	Jackson Free Statesman
Clinton D	Clinton Democrat		
Coal.	Coalitionist	KN	Know Nothing
Con.D	Conservative Democrat		
Const. U	Constitutional Unionist	L	Liberal
CR	Conservative Republican	Lab.	Laborite
CU	Conservative Unionist	LD	Liberal Democrat
CW	Clay Whig	L&O	Law & Order
		L&OW	Law & Order Whig
D	Democrat	LR	Liberal Republican
DD	Douglas Democrat	LW	Liberation Whig
DFL	Democrat Farmer Labor		
DR	Democratic Republican	N	Nullifier
		NAD	Native American Democrat
E	Emancipationist	Nat.	Nationalist
		Nat.A	National American
F	Federalist	Nat.G	National Greenbacker
FA	Farmers Alliance	ND	Nullifier Democrat
FL	Farmer Laborite	New Prog.	New Progressive
FS	Free Soiler	Nonpart.R	Nonpartisan Republican
FSD	Free Soil Democrat	NR	National Republican

1a

Abbreviation	Party	Abbreviation	Party
P	Populist	T	Temperance Party
PD	Popular Democrat	TD	Tariff Democrat
PP	People's Party	Tyler D	Tyler Democrat
PR	Progressive Republican		
Pro.	Progressive	U	Unionist
Prohib.	Prohibitionist	UA	Ultra Abolitionist
Protect.	Protectionist	UC	Union Conservative
Protect.TD	Protective Tariff Democrat	UD	Union Democrat
PSD	Popular Sovereignty Democrat	UL	Union Laborite
		UR	Union Republican
R	Republican	UU	Unconditional Unionist
Rad.	Radical	UW	Union Whig
Read.	Readjuster	UWar	Union War Party
RG	Republican Greenbacker		
RR	Radical Republican	VBD	Van Buren Democrat
		W	Whig
Sil.D	Silver Democrat	WD	War Democrat
Sil.R	Silver Republican		

Other Abbreviations

Abbreviation	Party
Soc.	Socialist
SR	State Rights Party	PI	Philippine Islands
SRD	State Rights Democrat	PR	Puerto Rico
SRFT	State Rights Free Trader	Rep.	Representative
SRW	State Rights Whig	Res.Comm.	Resident Commissioner
SRWD	State Rights War Democrat	Terr.Del.	Territorial Delegate

A

AANDAHL, Fred George (R N.D.) April 9, 1897-April 7, 1966; House 1951-53; Gov. 1945-50.

ABBITT, Watkins Moorman (D Va.) May 21, 1908; House Feb. 17, 1948- .

ABBOTT, Amos (W Mass.) Sept. 10, 1786-Nov. 2, 1868; House 1843-49.

ABBOTT, Jo (Joseph) (D Texas) Jan. 15, 1840-Feb. 11, 1908; House 1887-97.

ABBOTT, Joel (D Ga.) March 17, 1776-Nov. 19, 1826; House 1817-25.

ABBOTT, Joseph Carter (R N.C.) July 15, 1825-Oct. 8, 1881; Senate July 14, 1868-71.

ABBOTT, Josiah Gardner (D Mass.) Nov. 1, 1814-June 2, 1891; House July 28, 1876-77.

ABBOTT, Nehemiah (R Maine) March 29, 1804-July 26, 1877; House 1857-59.

ABEL, Hazel Hempell (R Neb.) July 10, 1888-July 30, 1966; Senate Nov. 8, 1954-Dec. 31, 1954.

ABELE, Homer E. (R Ohio) Nov. 21, 1916; House 1963-65.

ABERCROMBIE, James (UW Ala.) 1795-July 2, 1861; House 1851-55.

ABERCROMBIE, John William (D Ala.) May 17, 1866-July 2, 1940; House 1913-17.

ABERNETHY, Charles Laban (D N.C.) March 18, 1872-Feb. 23, 1955; House Nov. 7, 1922-35.

ABERNETHY, Thomas Gerstle (D Miss.) May 16, 1903; House 1943- .

ABOUREZK, James G. (D S.D.) Feb. 24, 1931; House 1971- .

ABZUG, Bella S. (D N.Y.) July 24, 1920; House 1971- .

ACHESON, Ernest Francis (R Pa.) Sept. 19, 1855-May 16, 1917; House 1895-1909.

ACKER, Ephraim Leister (D Pa.) Jan. 11, 1827-May 12, 1903; House 1871-73.

ACKERMAN, Ernest Robinson (R N.J.) June 17, 1863-Oct. 18, 1931; House 1919-Oct. 18, 1931.

ACKLEN, Joseph Hayes (D La.) May 20, 1850-Sept. 28, 1938; House Feb. 20, 1878-81.

ADAIR, Edwin Ross (R Ind.) Dec. 14, 1907; House 1951-71.

ADAIR, Jackson Leroy (D Ill.) Feb. 23, 1887-Jan. 19, 1956; House 1933-37.

ADAIR, John (D Ky.) Jan. 9, 1757-May 19, 1840; Senate Nov. 8, 1805-Nov. 18, 1806; House 1831-33; Gov. 1820-24.

ADAMS, Alva Blanchard (D Colo.) Oct. 29, 1875-Dec. 1, 1941; Senate May 17, 1923-Nov. 30, 1924 and 1933-Dec. 1, 1941.

ADAMS, Benjamin (F Mass.) Dec. 16, 1764-March 28, 1837; House Dec. 2, 1816-21.

ADAMS, Brock (D Wash.) Jan. 13, 1927; House 1965- .

ADAMS, Charles Francis (son of John Quincy Adams and grandson of President John Adams) (R Mass.) Aug. 18, 1807-Nov. 21, 1886; House 1859-May 1, 1861.

ADAMS, Charles Henry (R N.Y.) April 10, 1824-Dec. 15, 1902; House 1875-77.

ADAMS, George Everett (R Ill.) June 18, 1840-Oct. 5, 1917; House 1883-91.

ADAMS, George Madison (nephew of Green Adams) (D Ky.) Dec. 20, 1837-April 6, 1920; House 1867-75.

ADAMS, Green (uncle of George Madison Adams) (AP Ky.) Aug. 20, 1812-Jan. 18, 1884; House 1847-49 (Whig) and 1859-61 (American Party).

ADAMS, Henry Cullen (R Wis.) Nov. 28, 1850-July 9, 1906; House 1903-July 9, 1906.

ADAMS, John (JD N.Y.) Aug. 26, 1778-Sept. 25, 1854; House March 4-Dec. 26, 1815 (Democrat) and 1833-35 (Jackson Democrat).

ADAMS, John Joseph (ID N.Y.) Sept. 16, 1848-Feb. 16, 1919; House 1883-87.

ADAMS, John Quincy (son of President John Adams and father of Charles Francis Adams) (W Mass.) July 11, 1767-Feb. 23, 1848; Senate 1803-June 8, 1808 (Federalist); House 1831-Feb. 23, 1848 (Whig); Secy. of State 1817-25; President 1825-29.

ADAMS, Parmenio (— N.Y.) Sept. 9, 1776-Feb. 19, 1832; House Jan. 7, 1824-27.

ADAMS, Robert, Jr. (R Pa.) Feb. 26, 1849-June 1, 1906; House Dec. 19, 1893-June 1, 1906.

ADAMS, Robert Huntington (JD Miss.) 1792-July 2, 1830; Senate Jan. 6, 1830-July 2, 1830.

ADAMS, Sherman (R N.H.) Jan. 8, 1899; House 1945-47; Governor 1949-53.

ADAMS, Silas (R Ky.) Feb. 9, 1839-May 5, 1896; House 1893-95.

ADAMS, Stephen (UD Miss.) Oct. 17, 1807-May 11, 1857; House 1845-47 (Democrat); Senate March 17, 1852-1857 (Union Democrat).

ADAMS, Wilbur Louis (D Del.) Oct. 23, 1884-Dec. 4, 1937; House 1933-35.

ADAMSON, William Charles (D Ga.) Aug. 13, 1854-Jan. 3, 1929; House 1897-Dec. 18, 1917.

ADDABBO, Joseph P. (D N.Y.) March 17, 1925; House 1961- .

ADDAMS, William (D Pa.) April 11, 1777-May 30, 1858; House 1825-29.

ADDONIZIO, Hugh Joseph (D N.J.) Jan. 31, 1914; House 1949-62.

ADGATE, Asa (D N.Y.) Nov. 17, 1767-Feb. 15, 1832; House June 7, 1815-17.

ADKINS, Charles (R Ill.) Feb. 7, 1863-March 31, 1941; House 1925-33.

ADRAIN, Garnett Bowditch (D N.J.) Dec. 15, 1815-Aug. 17, 1878; House 1857-61.

AHL, John Alexander (D Pa.) Aug. 16, 1813-April 25, 1882; House 1857-59.

AIKEN, David Wyatt (father of Wyatt Aiken and cousin of William Aiken) (D S.C.) March 17, 1828-April 6, 1887; House 1877-87.

AIKEN, George David (R Vt.) Aug. 20, 1892; Senate Jan. 10, 1941- ; Gov. 1937-41.

AIKEN, William (cousin of David Wyatt Aiken) (D S.C.) Aug. 4, 1806-Sept. 7, 1887; House 1851-57; Gov. 1844-46.

AIKEN, Wyatt (son of David Wyatt Aiken) (D S.C.) Dec. 14, 1863-Feb. 6, 1923; House 1903-17.

AINEY, William David Blakeslee (R Pa.) April 8, 1864-Sept. 4, 1932; House Nov. 7, 1911-15.

AINSLIE, George (D Idaho) Oct. 30, 1838-May 19, 1913; House (Terr. Del.) 1879-83.

AINSWORTH, Lucien Lester (A-M Iowa) June 21, 1831-April 19, 1902; House 1875-77.

AITKEN, David Demerest (R Mich.) Sept. 5, 1853-May 26, 1930; House 1893-97.

AKERS, Thomas Peter (AP Mo.) Oct. 4, 1828-April 3, 1877; House Aug. 18, 1856-1857.

AKIN, Theron (PR N.Y.) May 23, 1855-March 26, 1933; House 1911-13.

ALBAUGH, Walter Hugh (R Ohio) Jan. 2, 1890-Jan. 21, 1942; House Nov. 8, 1938-39.

ALBERT, Carl (D Okla.) May 10, 1908; House 1947- ; Speaker 1971- .

ALBERT, William Julian (R Md.) Aug. 4, 1816-March 29, 1879; House 1873-75.

ALBERTSON, Nathaniel (D Ind.) June 10, 1800-Dec. 16, 1863; House 1849-51.

ALBRIGHT, Charles (R Pa.) Dec. 13, 1830-Sept. 28, 1880; House 1873-75.

ALBRIGHT, Charles Jefferson (R Ohio) May 9, 1816-Oct. 21, 1883; House 1855-57.

ALCORN, James Lusk (R Miss.) Nov. 4, 1816-Dec. 19, 1894; Senate Dec. 1, 1871-77; Gov. 1870-71.

ALDERSON, John Duffy (D W.Va.) Nov. 29, 1854-Dec. 5, 1910; House 1889-95.

ALDRICH, Cyrus (R Minn.) June 18, 1808-Oct. 5, 1871; House 1859-63.

ALDRICH, James Franklin (son of William Aldrich) (R Ill.) April 6, 1853-March 8, 1933; House 1893-97.

ALDRICH, Nelson Wilmarth (father of Richard Steere Aldrich and cousin of William Aldrich) (R R.I.) Nov. 6, 1841-April 16, 1915; House 1879-Oct. 4, 1881; Senate Oct. 5, 1881-1911.

ALDRICH, Richard Steere (son of Nelson Wilmarth Aldrich) (R R.I.) Feb. 29, 1884-Dec. 25, 1941; House 1923-33.

ALDRICH, Truman Heminway (brother of William Farrington Aldrich) (R Ala.) Oct. 17, 1848-April 28, 1932; House June 9, 1896-97.

ALDRICH, William (father of James Franklin Aldrich and cousin of Nelson Wilmarth Aldrich) (R Ill.) Jan. 19, 1820-Dec. 3, 1885; House 1877-83.

ALDRICH, William Farrington (brother of Truman Heminway Aldrich) (R Ala.) March 11, 1853-Oct. 30, 1925; House March 13, 1896-97, Feb. 9, 1898-99 and March 8, 1900-01.

ALESHIRE, Arthur William (D Ohio) Feb. 15, 1900-March 11, 1940; House 1937-39.

ALEXANDER, Adam Rankin (F Tenn.) —-—; House 1823-27.

ALEXANDER, Armstead Milton (D Mo.) May 26, 1834-Nov. 7, 1892; House 1883-85.

ALEXANDER, De Alva Stanwood (R N.Y.) July 17, 1846-Jan. 30, 1925; House 1897-1911.

ALEXANDER, Evan Shelby (cousin of Nathaniel Alexander) (— N.C.) about 1767-Oct. 28, 1809; House Feb. 24, 1806-09.

ALEXANDER, Henry Porteous (W N.Y.) Sept. 13, 1801-Feb. 22, 1867; House 1849-51.

ALEXANDER, Hugh Quincy (D N.C.) August 7, 1911; House 1953-63.

ALEXANDER, James, Jr. (D Ohio) Oct. 17, 1789-Sept. 5, 1846; House 1837-39.

ALEXANDER, John (D Ohio) April 16, 1777-June 28, 1848; House 1813-17.

ALEXANDER, John Grant (R Minn.) July 16, 1893; House 1939-41.

ALEXANDER, Joshua Willis (D Mo.) Jan. 22, 1852-Feb. 27, 1936; House 1907-Dec. 15, 1919; Secy. of Commerce 1919-21.

ALEXANDER, Mark (SRD Va.) Feb. 7, 1792-Oct. 7, 1883; House 1819-33.

ALEXANDER, Nathaniel (cousin of Evan Shelby Alexander) (— N.C.) March 5, 1756-March 7, 1808; House 1803-Nov. 1805; Gov. 1805-07.

ALEXANDER, Sydenham Benoni (D N.C.) Dec. 8, 1840-June 14, 1921; House 1891-95.

ALEXANDER, William Vollie, Jr. (D Ark.) Jan. 16, 1934; House 1969- .

ALFORD, Julius Caesar (W Ga.) May 10, 1799-Jan. 1, 1863; House Jan. 2-March 3, 1837 (State Rights Whig) and 1839-Oct. 1, 1841 (Harrison Whig).

ALFORD, Thomas Dale (D Ark.) January 28, 1916; House 1959-63.

ALGER, Bruce Reynolds (R Texas) June 12, 1918; House 1955-65.

ALGER, Russell Alexander (R Mich.) Feb. 27, 1836-Jan. 24, 1907; Senate Sept. 27, 1902-Jan. 24, 1907; Gov. 1884-86; Secy. of War 1897-99.

ALLAN, Chilton (CD Ky.) April 6, 1786-Sept. 3, 1858; House 1831-37.

ALLEE, James Frank (R Del.) Dec. 2, 1857-Oct. 12, 1938; Senate March 3, 1903-07.

ALLEN, Alfred Gaither (D Ohio) July 23, 1867-Dec. 9, 1932; House 1911-17.

ALLEN, Amos Lawrence (R Maine) March 17, 1837-Feb. 20, 1911; House Nov. 6, 1899-Feb. 20, 1911.

ALLEN, Asa Leonard (D La.) Jan. 5, 1891-Jan. 5, 1969; House 1937-53.

ALLEN, Charles (F-SP Mass.) Aug. 9, 1797-Aug. 6, 1869; House 1849-53.

ALLEN, Charles Herbert (R Mass.) April 15, 1848-April 20, 1934; House 1885-89.

ALLEN, Clarence Emir (R Utah) Sept. 8, 1852-July 9, 1932; House Jan. 4, 1896-97.

ALLEN, Edward Payson (R Mich.) Oct. 28, 1839-Nov. 25, 1909; House 1887-91.

ALLEN, Elisha Hunt (son of Samuel Clesson Allen) (W Maine) Jan. 28, 1804-Jan. 1, 1883; House 1841-43.

ALLEN, Heman (W Vt.) June 14, 1777-Dec. 11, 1844; House 1831-39.

ALLEN, Heman (D Vt.) Feb. 23, 1779-April 7, 1852; House 1817-April 20, 1818.

ALLEN, Henry Crosby (R N.J.) May 13, 1872-March 7, 1942; House 1905-07.

ALLEN, Henry Dixon (D Ky.) June 24, 1854-March 9, 1924; House 1899-1903.

ALLEN, Henry Justin (R Kan.) Sept. 11, 1868-Jan. 17, 1950; Senate April 1, 1929-Nov. 30, 1930; Gov. 1919-23.

ALLEN, James Browning (D Ala.) Dec. 28, 1912; Senate 1969- .

ALLEN, James Cameron (D Ill.) Jan. 29, 1822-Jan. 30, 1912; House 1853-July 18, 1856, Nov. 4, 1856-57 and 1863-65.

ALLEN, John (father of John William Allen) (F Conn.) June 12, 1763-July 31, 1812; House 1797-99.

ALLEN, John Beard (R Wash.) May 18, 1845-Jan. 28, 1903; House (Terr. Del.) March 4-Nov. 11, 1889; Senate Nov. 20, 1889-93.

ALLEN, John Clayton (R Ill.) Feb. 14, 1860-Jan. 12, 1939; House 1925-33.

ALLEN, John James (brother of Robert Allen) (W Va.) Sept. 25, 1797-Sept. 18, 1871; House 1833-35.

ALLEN, John Joseph, Jr. (R Calif.) Nov. 27, 1899; House 1947-59.

ALLEN, John Mills (D Miss.) July 8, 1846-Oct. 30, 1917; House 1885-1901.

ALLEN, John William (son of John Allen) Aug. 1802-Oct. 5, 1887; House 1837-41.

ALLEN, Joseph (F Mass.) Sept. 2, 1749-Sept. 2, 1827; House Oct. 8, 1810-11.

ALLEN, Judson (D N.Y.) April 3, 1797-Aug. 6, 1880; House 1839-41.

ALLEN, Leo Elwood (R Ill.) Oct. 5, 1898; House 1933-61.

ALLEN, Nathaniel (father-in-law of Robert Lawson Rose) (— N.Y.) 1780-Dec. 22, 1832; House 1819-21.

ALLEN, Philip (TD R.I.) Sept. 1, 1785-Dec. 16, 1865; Senate July 20, 1853-59; Gov. 1851-53.

ALLEN, Robert (D Tenn.) June 19, 1778-Aug. 19, 1844; House 1819-27.

ALLEN, Robert (brother of John James Allen) (D Va.) July 30, 1794-Dec. 30, 1859; House 1827-33.

ALLEN, Robert Edward Lee (D W.Va.) Nov. 28, 1865-Jan. 28, 1951; House 1923-25.

ALLEN, Robert Gray (D Pa.) Aug. 24, 1902-Aug. 10, 1963; House 1937-41.

ALLEN, Samuel Clesson (father of Elisha Hunt Allen) (— Mass.) Jan. 5, 1772-Feb. 8, 1842; House 1817-29.

ALLEN, Thomas (D Mo.) Aug. 29, 1813-April 8, 1882; House 1881-April 8, 1882.

ALLEN, William (D Ohio) Dec. 27, 1803-July 11, 1879; House 1833-35; Senate 1837-49; Gov. 1874-76.

ALLEN, William (D Ohio) Aug. 13, 1827-July 6, 1881; House 1859-63.

ALLEN, William Franklin (D Del.) Jan. 19, 1883-June 14, 1946; House 1937-39.

ALLEN, William Joshua (son of Willis Allen) (D Ill.) June 9, 1829-Jan. 26, 1901; House June 2, 1862-65.

ALLEN, William Vincent (P Neb.) Jan. 28, 1847-Jan. 12, 1924; Senate 1893-99 and Dec. 13, 1899-March 28, 1901.

ALLEN, Willis (father of William Joshua Allen) (D Ill.) Dec. 15, 1806-April 15, 1859; House 1851-55.

ALLEY, John Bassett (R Mass.) Jan. 7, 1817-Jan. 19, 1896; House 1859-67.

ALLGOOD, Miles Clayton (D Ala.) Feb. 22, 1878; House 1923-35.

ALLISON, James, Jr. (father of John Allison) (W Pa.) Oct. 4, 1772-June 17, 1854; House 1823-25.

ALLISON, John (son of James Allison, Jr.) (W Pa.) Aug. 5, 1812-March 23, 1878; House 1851-53 and 1855-57.

ALLISON, Robert (W Pa.) March 10, 1777-Dec. 2, 1840; House 1831-33.

ALLISON, William Boyd (R Iowa) March 2, 1829-Aug. 4, 1908; House 1863-71; Senate 1873-Aug. 4, 1908.

ALLOTT, Gordon Llewellyn (R Colo.) Jan. 2, 1907; Senate 1955- .

ALMON, Edward Berton (D Ala.) April 18, 1860-June 22, 1933; House 1915-June 22, 1933.

ALMOND, James Lindsay, Jr. (D Va.) June 15, 1898; House Jan. 22, 1946-April 17, 1948; Gov. 1958-62.

ALSTON, Lemuel James (— S.C.) 1760-1836; House 1807-11.

ALSTON, William Jeffreys (W Ala.) Dec. 31, 1800-June 10, 1876; House 1849-51.

ALSTON, Willis (nephew of Nathaniel Macon) (WD N.C.) 1769-April 10, 1837; House 1799-1815 and 1825-31.

ALVORD, James Church (W Mass.) April 14, 1808-Sept. 27, 1839; House 1839-Sept. 27, 1839.

AMBLER, Jacob A. (R Ohio) Feb. 18, 1829-Sept. 22, 1906; House 1869-73.

AMERMAN, Lemuel (D Pa.) Oct. 29, 1846-Oct. 7, 1897; House 1891-93.

AMES, Adelbert (father of Butler Ames) (R Miss.) Oct. 31, 1835-April 12, 1933; Senate Feb. 23, 1870-Jan. 10, 1874; Gov. 1868-69 and 1874-76.

AMES, Butler (son of Adelbert Ames and grandson of Benjamin Franklin Butler) (R Mass.) Aug. 22, 1871-Nov. 6, 1954; House 1903-13.

AMES, Fisher (F Mass.) April 9, 1758-July 4, 1808; House 1789-97.

AMES, Oakes (R Mass.) Jan. 10, 1804-May 8, 1873; House 1863-73.

AMLIE, Thomas Ryum (Pro. Wis.) April 17, 1897; House Oct. 13, 1931-1933 (Republican Progressive) and 1935-39 (Progressive).

ANCONA, Sydenham Elnathan (D Pa.) Nov. 20, 1824-June 20, 1913; House 1861-67.

ANDERSEN, Herman Carl (R Minn.) Jan. 27, 1897; House 1939-63.

ANDERSON, Albert Raney (IR Iowa) Nov. 8, 1837-Nov. 17, 1898; House 1887-89.

ANDERSON, Alexander Outlaw (son of Joseph Anderson) (D Tenn.) Nov. 10, 1794-May 23, 1869; Senate Feb. 26, 1840-41.

ANDERSON, Carl Carey (D Ohio) Dec. 2, 1877-Oct. 1, 1912; House 1909-Oct. 1, 1912.

ANDERSON, Chapman Levy (D Miss.) March 15, 1845-April 27, 1924; House 1887-91.

ANDERSON, Charles Arthur (D Mo.) Sept. 26, 1899; House 1937-41.

ANDERSON, Charles Marley (D Ohio) Jan. 5, 1845-Dec. 28, 1908; House 1885-87.

ANDERSON, Clinton Presba (D N.M.) October 23, 1895; House 1941-June 30, 1945; Senate 1949- ; Secy. of Agriculture 1945-48.

ANDERSON, George Alburtus (D Ill.) March 11, 1853-Jan. 31, 1896; House 1887-89.

ANDERSON, George Washington (RR Mo.) May 22, 1832-Feb. 26, 1902; House 1865-69.

ANDERSON, Glenn M. (D Calif.) Feb. 21, 1913; House 1969- .

ANDERSON, Hugh Johnston (D Maine) May 10, 1801-May 31, 1881; House 1837-41; Gov. 1844-47.

ANDERSON, Isaac (Jeff.D Pa.) Nov. 23, 1760-Oct. 27, 1838; House 1803-07.

ANDERSON, James Patton (D Wash.) Feb. 16, 1822-Sept. 20, 1872; House (Terr. Del.) 1855-57.

ANDERSON, John (Jeff.D Maine) July 30, 1792-Aug. 21, 1853; House 1825-33.

ANDERSON, John Alexander (R Kan.) June 26, 1834-May 18, 1892; House 1879-91, Republican 1879-87 and 1889-91, Independent 1887-89.

ANDERSON, John B. (R Ill.) Feb. 15, 1922; House 1961- .

ANDERSON, John Zuinglius (R Calif.) March 22, 1904; House 1939-53.

ANDERSON, Joseph (father of Alexander Outlaw Anderson) (— Tenn.) Nov. 5, 1757-April 17, 1837; Senate Sept. 26, 1797-1815; Pres. pro tempore 1804-05.

ANDERSON, Joseph Halstead (D N.Y.) Aug. 25, 1800-June 23, 1870; House 1843-47.

ANDERSON, Josiah McNair (W Tenn.) Nov. 29, 1807-Nov. 8, 1861; House 1849-51.

ANDERSON, LeRoy Hagen (D Mont.) Feb. 2, 1906; House 1957-61.

ANDERSON, Lucian (U Ky.) June 23, 1824-Oct. 18, 1898; House 1863-65.

ANDERSON, Richard Clough, Jr. (— Ky.) Aug. 4, 1788-July 24, 1826; House 1817-21.

ANDERSON, Samuel (— Pa.) 1773-Jan. 17, 1850; House 1827-29.

ANDERSON, Simeon H. (father of William Clayton Anderson) (W Ky.) March 2, 1802-Aug. 11, 1840; House 1839-Aug. 11, 1840.

ANDERSON, Sydney (R Minn.) Sept. 18, 1881-Oct. 8, 1948; House 1911-25.

ANDERSON, Thomas Lilbourne (ID Mo.) Dec. 8, 1808-March 6, 1885; House 1857-61, American Party 1857-59, Independent Democrat 1859-61.

ANDERSON, William (Jeff.D Pa.) 1762-Dec. 16, 1829; House 1809-15 and 1817-19.

ANDERSON, William Black (ID Ill.) April 2, 1830-Aug. 28, 1901; House 1875-77.

ANDERSON, William Clayton (son of Simeon H. Anderson and nephew of Albert Gallatin Talbott) (AP Ky.) Dec. 26, 1826-Dec. 23, 1861; House 1859-61.

ANDERSON, William Coleman (R Tenn.) July 10, 1853-Sept. 8, 1902; House 1895-97.

ANDERSON, William Robert (D Tenn.) June 17, 1921; House 1965- .

ANDRESEN, August Herman (R Minn.) Oct. 11, 1890-Jan. 14, 1958; House 1925-33 and 1935-Jan. 14, 1958.

ANDREW, Abram Piatt, Jr. (R Mass.) Feb. 12, 1873-June 3, 1936; House Sept 27, 1921-June 3, 1936.

ANDREW, John Forrester (D Mass.) Nov. 26, 1850-May 30, 1895; House 1889-93.

ANDREWS, Charles (D Maine) Feb. 11, 1814-April 30, 1852; House 1851-April 30, 1852.

ANDREWS, Charles Oscar (D Fla.) March 7, 1877-Sept. 18, 1946; Senate Nov. 4, 1936-Sept. 18, 1946.

ANDREWS, George Rex (W N.Y.) Sept. 21, 1808-Dec. 5, 1873; House 1849-51.

ANDREWS, George William (D Ala.) Dec. 12, 1906; House March 14, 1944- .

ANDREWS, Glenn (R Ala.) Jan. 15, 1909; House 1965-67.

ANDREWS, John Tuttle (D N.Y.) May 29, 1803-June 11, 1894; House 1837-39.

ANDREWS, Landaff Watson (W Ky.) Feb. 12, 1803-Dec. 23, 1887; House 1839-43.

ANDREWS, Mark (R N.D.) May 19, 1926; House Oct. 22, 1963- .

ANDREWS, Samuel George (R N.Y.) Oct. 16, 1796-June 11, 1863; House 1857-59.

ANDREWS, Sherlock James (W Ohio) Nov. 17, 1801-Feb. 11, 1880; House 1841-43.

ANDREWS, Walter Gresham (R N.Y.) July 16, 1889-March 5, 1949; House 1931-49.

ANDREWS, William Ezekiel (R Neb.) Dec. 17, 1854-Jan. 19, 1942; House 1895-97 and 1919-23.

ANDREWS, William Henry (R N.M.) Jan. 14, 1846-Jan. 16, 1919; House (Terr. Del.) 1905-Jan. 7, 1912.

ANDREWS, William Noble (R Md.) Nov. 13, 1876-Dec. 27, 1937; House 1919-21.

ANDRUS, John Emory (R N.Y.) Feb. 16, 1841-Dec. 26, 1934; House 1905-13.

ANFUSO, Victor L'Episcopo (D N.Y.) March 10, 1905-Dec. 28, 1966; House 1951-53 and 1955-63.

ANGEL, William G. (D N.Y.) July 17, 1790—Aug. 13, 1858; House 1825-27 (John Quincy Adams Democrat) and 1829-33 (Jackson Democrat).

ANGELL, Homer Daniel (R Ore.) Jan. 12, 1875-March 31, 1968; House 1939-55.

ANKENY, Levi (R Wash.) Aug. 1, 1844-March 29, 1921; Senate 1903-09.

ANNUNZIO, Frank (D Ill.) Jan. 12, 1915; House 1965- .

ANSBERRY, Timothy Thomas (D Ohio) Dec. 24, 1871-July 5, 1943; House 1907-Jan. 9, 1915.

ANSORGE, Martin Charles (R N.Y.) Jan. 1, 1882-Feb. 4, 1967; House 1921-23.

ANTHONY, Daniel Read, Jr. (R Kan.) Aug. 22, 1870-Aug. 4, 1931; House May 23, 1907-29.

ANTHONY, Henry Bowen (R R.I.) April 1, 1815-Sept. 2, 1884; Senate 1859-Sept. 2, 1884; President pro tempore 1869-73; Gov. 1850-51.

ANTHONY, Joseph Biles (D Pa.) June 19, 1795-Jan. 10, 1851; House 1833-37.

ANTONY, Edwin Le Roy (D Texas) Jan. 5, 1852-Jan. 16, 1913; House June 14, 1892-93.

APLIN, Henry Harrison (R Mich.) April 15, 1841-July 23, 1910; House Oct. 20, 1901-03.

APPLEBY, Stewart Hoffman (son of Theodore Frank Appleby) (R N.J.) May 17, 1890; House Nov. 3, 1925-27.

APPLEBY, Theodore Frank (father of Stewart Hoffman Appleby) (R N.J.) Oct. 10, 1864-Dec. 15, 1924; House 1921-23.

APPLETON, John (D Maine) Feb. 11, 1815-Aug. 22, 1864; House 1851-53.

APPLETON, Nathan (cousin of William Appleton) (H-TW Mass.) Oct. 6, 1779-July 14, 1861; House 1831-33 and June 9-Sept. 28, 1842.

APPLETON, William (cousin of Nathan Appleton) (W Mass.) Nov. 16, 1786-Feb. 15, 1862; House 1851-55 and March 4-Sept. 27, 1861.

APSLEY, Lewis Dewart (R Mass.) Sept. 29, 1852-April 11, 1925; House 1893-97.

ARCHER, John (father of Stevenson Archer) (D Md.) May 5, 1741-Sept. 28, 1810; House 1801-07.

ARCHER, Stevenson (son of Jonn Archer) (D Md.) Oct. 11, 1786-June 26, 1848; House Oct. 26, 1811-17 and 1819-21.

ARCHER, Stevenson (son of Stevenson Archer and grandson of John Archer) (D Md.) Feb. 28, 1827-Aug. 2, 1898; House 1867-75.

ARCHER, William R., Jr. (R Texas) March 22, 1928; House 1971- .

ARCHER, William Segar (nephew of Joseph Eggleston) (W Va.) March 5, 1789-March 28, 1855; House Jan. 3, 1820-35; Senate 1841-47.

ARENDS, Leslie Cornelius (R Ill.) Sept. 27, 1895; House 1935- .

ARENS, Henry (F-L Minn.) Nov. 21, 1873-Oct. 6, 1963; House 1933-35.

ARENTZ, Samuel Shaw (Ulysses) (R Nev.) Jan. 8, 1879-June 17, 1934; House 1921-23 and 1925-33.

ARMFIELD, Robert Franklin (D N.C.) July 9, 1829-Nov. 9, 1898; House 1879-83.

ARMSTRONG, David Hartley (D Mo.) Oct. 21, 1812-March 18, 1893; Senate Sept. 20, 1877-Jan. 26, 1879.

ARMSTRONG, James (brother of John Armstrong) (F Pa.) Aug. 29, 1748-May 6, 1828; House 1793-95.

ARMSTRONG, John (brother of James Armstrong) (— N.Y.) Nov. 25, 1755-April 1, 1843; Senate Nov. 6, 1800-Feb. 5, 1802 and Nov. 10, 1803-June 30, 1804; Secy. of War 1813-14.

ARMSTRONG, Moses Kimball (D Dakota) Sept. 19, 1832-Jan. 11, 1906; House (Terr. Del.) 1871-75.

ARMSTRONG, Orland Kay (R Mo.) Oct. 2, 1893; House 1951-53.

ARMSTRONG, William (D Va.) Dec. 23, 1782-May 10, 1865; House 1825-33.

ARMSTRONG, William Hepburn (R Pa.) Sept. 7, 1824-May 14, 1919; House 1869-71.

ARNELL, Samuel Mayes (R Tenn.) May 3, 1833-July 20, 1903; House July 24, 1866-71.

ARNOLD, Benedict (brother-in-law of Matthias J. Bovee) (— N.Y.) Oct. 5, 1780-March 3, 1849; House 1829-31.

ARNOLD, Isaac Newton (R Ill.) Nov. 30, 1815-April 24, 1884; House 1861-65.

ARNOLD, Laurence Fletcher (D Ill.) June 8, 1891-Dec. 6, 1966; House 1937-43.

ARNOLD, Lemuel Hastings (great-great-uncle of Theodore Francis Green) (LW R.I.) Jan. 29, 1792-June 27, 1852; House 1845-47; Gov. 1831-32.

ARNOLD, Marshall (D Mo.) Oct. 21, 1845-June 12, 1913; House 1891-95.

ARNOLD, Samuel (D Conn.) June 1, 1806-May 5, 1869; House 1857-59.

ARNOLD, Samuel Greene (granduncle of Theodore Francis Green) (R R.I.) April 12, 1821-Feb. 14, 1880; Senate Dec. 1, 1862-63.

ARNOLD, Samuel Washington (R Mo.) Sept. 21, 1879-Dec. 18, 1961; House 1943-49.

ARNOLD, Thomas Dickens (W Tenn.) May 3, 1798-May 26, 1870; House 1831-33 and 1841-43.

ARNOLD, Warren Otis (R R.I.) June 3, 1839-April 1, 1910; House 1887-91 and 1895-97.

ARNOLD, William Carlile (R Pa.) July 15, 1851-March 20, 1906; House 1895-99.

ARNOLD, William Wright (D Ill.) Oct. 14, 1877-Nov. 23, 1957; House 1923-Sept. 16, 1935.

ARNOT, John, Jr. (D N.Y.) March 11, 1831-Nov. 20, 1886; House 1883-Nov. 20, 1886.

ARRINGTON, Archibald Hunter (uncle of Archibald Hunter Arrington Williams) (D N.C.) Nov. 13, 1809-July 20, 1872; House 1841-45.

ARTHUR, William Evans (D Ky.) March 3, 1825-May 18, 1897; House 1871-75.

ASH, Michael Woolston (— Pa.) March 5, 1789-Dec. 14, 1858; House 1835-37.

ASHBROOK, John Milan (son of William Albert Ashbrook) (R Ohio) Sept. 21, 1928; House 1961- .

ASHBROOK, William Albert (father of John Milan Ashbrook) (D Ohio) July 1, 1867-Jan. 1, 1940; House 1907-21 and 1935-Jan. 1, 1940.

ASHE, John Baptista (uncle of John Baptista Ashe of Tennessee, Thomas Samuel Ashe and William Shepperd Ashe) (F N.C.) 1748-Nov. 27, 1802; House 1789-93; Cont. Cong. 1787.

ASHE, John Baptista (brother of William Shepperd Ashe, nephew of John Baptista Ashe of N.C. and cousin of Thomas Samuel Ashe) (W Tenn.) 1810-Dec. 29, 1857; House 1843-45.

ASHE, Thomas Samuel (nephew of John Baptista Ashe of N.C. and cousin of John Baptista Ashe of Tenn. and of William Shepperd Ashe) (D N.C.) July 21, 1812-Feb. 4, 1887; House 1873-77, 1873-75 Conservative, 1875-77 Democrat.

ASHE, William Shepperd (brother of John Baptista Ashe of Tenn. and nephew of John Baptista Ashe of N.C. and cousin of Thomas Samuel Ashe) (D N.C.) Aug. 12, 1813-Sept. 14, 1862; House 1849-55.

ASHLEY, Chester (D Ark.) June 1, 1790-April 29, 1848; Senate Nov. 8, 1844-April 29, 1848.

ASHLEY, Delos Rodeyn (R Nev.) Feb. 19, 1828-July 18, 1873; House 1865-69.

ASHLEY, Henry (— N.Y.) Feb. 19, 1778-Jan. 14, 1829; House 1825-27.

ASHLEY, James Mitchell (great-grandfather of Thomas William Ludlow Ashley) (R Ohio) Nov. 14, 1824-Sept. 16, 1896; House 1859-69; Gov. Terr. of Montana 1869-70.

ASHLEY, Thomas William Ludlow (great-grandson of James Mitchell Ashley) (D Ohio) Jan. 11, 1923; House 1955- .

ASHLEY, William Henry (W Mo.) 1778-March 26, 1838; House Oct. 31, 1831-37.

ASHMORE, John Durant (D S.C.) Aug. 18, 1819-Dec. 5, 1871; House 1859-Dec. 21, 1860.

ASHMORE, Robert Thomas (D S.C.) Feb. 22, 1904; House June 2, 1953-69.

ASHMUN, Eli Porter (father of George Ashmun) (— Mass.) June 24, 1770-May 10, 1819; Senate June 12, 1816-May 10, 1818.

ASHMUN, George (son of Eli Porter Ashmun) (W Mass.) Dec. 25, 1804-July 16, 1870; House 1845-51.

ASHURST, Henry Fountain (D Ariz.) Sept. 13, 1874-May 31, 1962; Senate March 27, 1912-41.

ASPER, Joel Funk (RR Mo.) April 20, 1822-Oct. 1, 1872; House 1869-71.

ASPIN, Les (D Wis.) July 21, 1938; House 1971- .

ASPINALL, Wayne Norviel (D Colo.) April 3, 1896; House 1949- .

ASWELL, James Benjamin (D La.) Dec. 23, 1869-March 16, 1931; House 1913-March 16, 1931.

ATCHISON, David Rice (W Mo.) Aug. 11, 1807-Jan. 26, 1886; Senate Oct. 14, 1843-55; President pro tempore 1846-54.

ATHERTON, Charles Gordon (son of Charles Humphrey Atherton) (D N.H.) July 4, 1804-Nov. 15, 1853; House 1837-43; Senate 1843-49.

ATHERTON, Charles Humphrey (father of Charles Gordon Atherton) (F N.H.) Aug. 14, 1773-Jan. 8, 1853; House 1815-17.

ATHERTON, Gibson (D Ohio) Jan. 19, 1831-Nov. 10, 1887; House 1879-83.

ATKESON, William Oscar (R Mo.) Aug. 24, 1854-Oct. 16, 1931; House 1921-23.

ATKINS, John DeWitt Clinton (D Tenn.) June 4, 1825-June 2, 1908; House 1857-59 and 1873-83.

ATKINSON, Archibald (D Va.) Sept. 15, 1792-Jan. 7, 1872; House 1843-49.

ATKINSON, George Wesley (R W.Va.) June 19, 1845-April 4, 1925; House Feb. 26, 1890-91; Gov. 1897-1901.

ATKINSON, Louis Evans (R Pa.) April 16, 1841-Feb. 5, 1910; House 1883-93.

ATKINSON, Richard Merrill (D Tenn.) Feb. 6, 1894-April 29, 1947; House 1937-39.

ATWATER, John Wilbur (P N.C.) Dec. 27, 1840-July 4, 1910; House 1899-1901.

ATWOOD, David (R Wis.) Dec. 15, 1815-Dec. 11, 1889; House Feb. 23, 1870-71.

ATWOOD, Harrison Henry (R Mass.) Aug. 26, 1863-Oct. 22, 1954; House 1895-97.

AUCHINCLOSS, James Coats (R N.J.) Jan. 19, 1885; House 1943-65.

AUF DER HEIDE, Oscar Louis (D N.J.) Dec. 8, 1874-March 29, 1945; House 1925-35.

AUSTIN, Albert Elmer (stepfather of Clare Boothe Luce) (R Conn.) Nov. 15, 1877-Jan. 26, 1942; House 1939-41.

AUSTIN, Archibald (D Va.) Aug. 11, 1772-Oct. 16, 1837; House 1817-19.

AUSTIN, Richard Wilson (R Tenn.) Aug. 26, 1857-April 20, 1919; House 1909-19.

AUSTIN, Warren Robinson (R Vt.) Nov. 12, 1877-Dec. 25, 1962; Senate April 1, 1931-Aug. 2, 1946.

AVERETT, Thomas Hamlet (D Va.) July 10, 1800-June 30, 1855; House 1849-53.

AVERILL, John Thomas (R Minn.) March 1, 1825-Oct. 3, 1889; House 1871-75.

AVERY, Daniel (D N.Y.) Sept. 18, 1766-Jan. 30, 1842; House 1811-15 and Sept. 30, 1816-17.

AVERY, John (R Mich.) Feb. 29, 1824-Jan. 21, 1914; House 1893-97.

AVERY, William Henry (R Kan.) Aug. 11, 1911; House 1955-65; Gov. 1965-67.

AVERY, William Tecumsah (D Tenn.) Nov. 11, 1819-May 22, 1880; House 1857-61.

AVIS, Samuel Brashear (R W.Va.) Feb. 19, 1872-June 8, 1924; House 1913-15.

AXTELL, Samuel Beach (D Calif.) Oct. 14, 1819-Aug. 6, 1891; House 1867-71; Gov. Utah Territory (Republican) 1874-75; Gov. Territory of N. Mexico (Republican) 1875.

AYCRIGG, John Bancker (W N.J.) July 9, 1798-Nov. 8, 1856; House 1837-39 and 1841-43.

AYER, Richard Small (R Va.) Oct. 9, 1829-Dec. 14, 1896; House Jan. 31, 1870-71.

AYERS, Roy Elmer (D Mont.) Nov. 9, 1882-May 23, 1955; House 1933-37; Gov. 1937-41.

AYRES, Steven Beckwith (ID N.Y.) Oct. 27, 1861-June 1, 1929; House 1911-13.

AYRES, William Augustus (D Kan.) April 19, 1867-Feb. 17, 1952; House 1915-21 and 1923-Aug. 22, 1934.

AYRES, William Hanes (R Ohio) Feb. 5, 1916; House 1951-71.

B

BABBITT, Clinton (D Wis.) Nov. 16, 1831-March 11, 1907; House 1891-93.

BABBITT, Elijah (R Pa.) July 29, 1795-Jan. 9, 1887; House 1859-63, Unionist 1859-61, Republican 1861-63.

BABCOCK, Alfred (W N.Y.) April 15, 1805-May 16, 1871; House 1841-43.

BABCOCK, Joseph Weeks (grandson of Joseph Weeks) (R Wis.) March 6, 1850-April 27, 1909; House 1893-1907.

BABCOCK, Leander (D N.Y.) March 1, 1811-Aug. 18, 1864; House 1851-53.

BABCOCK, William (— N.Y.) 1785-Oct. 20, 1838; House 1831-33.

BABKA, John Joseph (D Ohio) March 16, 1884-March 22, 1937; House 1919-21.

BACHARACH, Isaac (R N.J.) Jan. 5, 1870-Sept. 5, 1956; House 1915-37.

BACHMAN, Nathan Lynn (D Tenn.) Aug. 2, 1878-April 23, 1937; Senate Feb. 28, 1933-April 23, 1937.

BACHMAN, Reuben Knecht (D Pa.) Aug. 6, 1834-Sept. 19, 1911; House 1879-81.

BACHMANN, Carl George (R W.Va.) May 14, 1890; House 1925-33.

BACON, Augustus Octavius (cousin of William S. Howard) (D Ga.) Oct. 20, 1839-Feb. 14, 1914; Senate 1895-Feb. 14, 1914.

BACON, Ezekiel (son of John Bacon and father of William Johnson Bacon) (D Mass.) Sept. 1, 1776-Oct. 18, 1870; House Sept. 16, 1807-13.

BACON, Henry (D N.Y.) March 14, 1846-March 25, 1915; House Dec. 6, 1886-89 and 1891-93.

BACON, John (father of Ezekiel Bacon and grandfather of William Johnson Bacon) (— Mass.) April 5, 1738-Oct. 25, 1820); House 1801-03.

BACON, Mark Reeves (R Mich.) Feb. 29, 1852-Aug. 20, 1941; House March 4-Dec. 13, 1917.

BACON, Robert Low (R N.Y.) July 23, 1884-Sept. 12, 1938; House 1923-Sept. 12, 1938.

BACON, William Johnson (son of Ezekiel Bacon and grandson of John Bacon) (R N.Y.) Feb. 18, 1803-July 3, 1889; House 1877-79.

BADGER, De Witt Clinton (D Ohio) Aug. 7, 1858-May 20, 1926; House 1903-05.

BADGER, George Edmund (W N.C.) April 17, 1795-May 11, 1866; Senate Nov. 25, 1846-55; Secy. of the Navy March 5-Sept. 11, 1841.

BADGER, Luther (— N.Y.) April 10, 1785-1869; House 1825-27.

BADILLO, Herman (D N.Y.) Aug. 21, 1929; House 1971- .

BAER, George, Jr. (F Md.) 1763-April 3, 1834; House 1797-1801 and 1815-17.

BAER, John Miller (R N.D.) March 29, 1886-Feb. 18, 1970; House July 10, 1917-21, Nonpartisan League 1917-19, Republican 1919-21.

BAGBY, Arthur Pendleton (D Ala.) 1794-Sept. 21, 1858; Senate Nov. 24, 1841-June 16, 1848; Gov. 1837-41.

BAGBY, John Courts (D Ill.) Jan. 24, 1819-April 4, 1896; House 1875-77.

BAGLEY, George Augustus (R N.Y.) July 22, 1826-May 12, 1915; House 1875-79.

BAGLEY, John Holroyd, Jr. (D N.Y.) Nov. 26, 1832-Oct. 23, 1902; House 1875-77 and 1883-85.

BAILEY Alexander Hamilton (R N.Y.) Aug. 14, 1817-April 20, 1874; House Nov. 30, 1867-71.

BAILEY, Cleveland Monroe (D W.Va.) July 15, 1886-July 13, 1965; House 1945-47 and 1949-63.

BAILEY, David Jackson (SRD Ga.) March 11, 1812-June 14, 1897; House 1851-55.

BAILEY, Goldsmith Fox (July 17, 1823-May 8, 1862; House 1861-May 8, 1862.

BAILEY, James Edmund (D Tenn.) Aug. 15, 1822-Dec. 29, 1885; Senate Jan. 19, 1877-81.

BAILEY, Jeremiah (W Maine) May 1, 1773-July 6, 1853; House 1835-37.

BAILEY, John (— Mass.) 1786-June 26, 1835; House Dec. 13, 1824-31.

BAILEY, John Mosher (R N.Y.) Aug. 24, 1838-Feb. 21, 1916; House Nov. 5, 1878-81.

BAILEY, Joseph (D Pa.) March 18, 1810-Aug. 26, 1885; House 1861-65.

BAILEY, Joseph Weldon (father of Joseph Weldon Bailey, Jr.) (D Texas) Oct. 6, 1862-April 13, 1929; House 1891-1901; Senate 1901-Jan. 3, 1913.

BAILEY, Joseph Weldon, Jr. (son of Joseph Weldon Bailey) (D Texas) Dec. 15, 1892-July 17, 1943; House 1933-35.

BAILEY, Josiah William (D N.C.) Sept. 14, 1873-Dec. 15, 1946; Senate 1931-Dec. 15, 1946.

BAILEY, Ralph Emerson (R Mo.) July 14, 1878-April 8, 1948; House 1925-27.

BAILEY, Theodorus (D N.Y.) Oct. 12, 1758-Sept. 6, 1828; House 1793-97, 1799-1801 and Oct. 6, 1801-03; Senate 1803-Jan. 16, 1804.

BAILEY, Warren Worth (D Pa.) Jan. 8, 1855-Nov. 9, 1928; House 1913-17.

BAILEY, Willis Joshua (R Kan.) Oct. 12, 1854-May 19, 1932; House 1899-1901; Gov. 1903-05.

BAIRD, David (father of David Baird, Jr.) (R N.J.) April 7, 1839-Feb. 25, 1927; Senate Feb. 23, 1918-19.

BAIRD, David, Jr. (son of David Baird) (R N.J.) Oct. 10, 1881-Feb. 28, 1955; Senate Nov. 30, 1929-Dec. 1, 1930.

BAIRD, Joseph Edward (R Ohio) Nov. 12, 1865-June 14, 1942; House 1929-31.

BAIRD, Samuel Thomas (D La.) May 5, 1861-April 22, 1899; House 1897-April 22, 1899.

BAKER, Caleb (— N.Y.) 1762-June 26, 1849; House 1819-21.

BAKER, Charles Simeon (R N.Y.) Feb. 18, 1839-April 21, 1902; House 1885-91.

BAKER, David Jewett (D Ill.) Sept. 7, 1792-Aug. 6, 1869; Senate Nov. 12-Dec. 11, 1830.

BAKER, Edward Dickinson (R Ill., Ore.) Feb. 24, 1811-Oct. 21, 1861; House 1845-Jan. 15, 1847 (Whig, Ill.), 1849-51 (R Ill.); Senate Oct. 2, 1860-Oct. 21, 1861 (R Ore.).

BAKER, Ezra (— N.J.) —-—; House 1815-17.

BAKER, Henry Moore (R N.H.) Jan. 11, 1841-May 30, 1912; House 1893-97.

BAKER, Howard Henry (husband of Irene B. Baker, father of Howard Henry Baker, Jr.) (R Tenn.) Jan. 12, 1902-Jan. 7, 1964; House 1951-64.

BAKER, Howard Henry, Jr. (son of Howard Henry Baker and Irene B. Baker, son-in-law of Everett McKinley Dirksen) (R Tenn.) Nov. 15, 1925; Senate 1967- .

BAKER, Irene B. (widow of Howard Henry Baker, Jr. and mother of Howard Henry Baker, Jr.) (R Tenn.) Nov. 17, 1901; House March 10, 1964-65.

BAKER, Jacob Thompson (D N.J.) April 13, 1847-Dec. 7, 1919; House 1913-15.

BAKER, Jehu (R Ill.) Nov. 4, 1822-March 1, 1903; House 1865-69 and 1887-89 (Republican), 1897-99 (Fusionist).

BAKER, John (F Va.) —-Aug. 18, 1823; House 1811-13.

BAKER, John Harris (R Ind.) Feb. 28, 1832-Oct. 21, 1915; House 1875-81.

BAKER, LaMar (R Tenn.) Dec. 19, 1915; House 1971- .

BAKER, Lucien (R Kan.) June 8, 1846-June 21, 1907; Senate 1895-1901.

BAKER, Osmyn (W Mass.) May 18, 1800-Feb. 9, 1875; House Jan. 14, 1840-45.

BAKER, Robert (D N.Y.) April, 1862-June 15, 1943; House 1903-05.

BAKER, Stephen (R N.Y.) Aug. 12, 1819-June 9, 1875; House 1861-63.

BAKER, William (PP Kan.) April 19, 1831-Feb. 11, 1910; House 1891-97.

BAKER, William Benjamin (R Md.) July 22, 1840-May 17, 1911; House 1895-1901.

BAKER, William Henry (R N.Y.) Jan 17, 1827-Nov. 25, 1911; House 1875-79.

BAKEWELL, Charles Montague (R Conn.) April 14, 1867-Sept. 19, 1957; House 1933-35.

BAKEWELL, Claude Ignatius (R Mo.) Aug. 9, 1912; House 1947-49 and March 9, 1951-53.

BALDRIGE, Howard Malcolm (R Neb.) June 23, 1894; House 1931-33.

BALDWIN, Abraham (F Ga.) Nov. 2, 1754-March 4, 1807; House 1789-99; Senate 1799-March 4, 1807; President pro tempore 1801-02; Cont. Cong. 1785, 1787-89.

BALDWIN, Augustus Carpenter (UD Mich.) Dec. 24, 1817-Jan. 21, 1903; House 1863-65.

BALDWIN, Harry Streett (D Md.) Aug. 21, 1894-Oct. 19, 1952; House 1943-47.

BALDWIN, Henry (F Pa.) Jan. 14, 1780-April 21, 1844; House 1817-May 8, 1822; Assoc. Justice U.S. Supreme Court Jan. 6, 1830-April 21, 1844.

BALDWIN, Henry Alexander (R Hawaii) Jan. 12, 1871-Oct. 8, 1946; House (Terr. Del.) March 25, 1922-23.

BALDWIN, Henry Porter (R Mich.) Feb. 22, 1814-Dec. 31, 1892; Senate Nov. 17, 1879-81; Gov. 1869-73.

BALDWIN, John (— Conn.) April 5, 1772-March 27, 1850; House 1825-29.

BALDWIN, John Denison (R Mass.) Sept. 28, 1809-July 8, 1883; House 1863-69.

BALDWIN, John Finley, Jr. (R Calif.) June 28, 1915-March 9, 1966; House 1955-March 9, 1966.

BALDWIN, Joseph Clark (R N.Y.) Jan. 11, 1897-Oct. 27, 1957; House March 11, 1941-47.

BALDWIN, Melvin Riley (D Minn.) April 12, 1838-April 15, 1901; House 1893-95.

BALDWIN, Raymond Earl (R Conn.) Aug. 31, 1893; Senate Dec. 27, 1946-Dec. 16, 1949; Gov. 1939-40, 1943-46.

BALDWIN, Roger Sherman (son of Simeon Baldwin) (W Conn.) Jan. 4, 1793-Feb. 19, 1863; Senate Nov. 11, 1847-51; Gov. 1844-46.

BALDWIN, Simeon (father of Roger Sherman Baldwin) (F Conn.) Dec. 14, 1761-May 26, 1851; House 1803-05.

BALL, Edward (W Ohio) Nov. 6, 1811-Nov. 22, 1872; House 1853-57.

BALL, Joseph Hurst (R Minn.) Nov. 3, 1905; Senate Oct. 14, 1940-Nov. 17, 1942, 1943-49.

BALL, Lewis Heisler (R Del.) Sept. 21, 1861-Oct. 18, 1932; House 1901-03; Senate March 3, 1903-05, 1919-25.

BALL, Thomas Henry (D Texas) Jan. 14, 1859-May 7, 1944; House 1897-Nov. 16, 1903.

BALL, Thomas Raymond (R Conn.) Feb. 12, 1896-June 16, 1943; House 1939-41.

BALL, William Lee (D Va.) Jan. 2, 1781-Feb. 28, 1824; House 1817-Feb. 28, 1824.

BALLENTINE, John Goff (D Tenn.) May 20, 1825-Nov. 23, 1915; House 1883-87.

BALLOU, Latimer Whipple (R R.I.) March 1, 1812-May 9, 1900; House 1875-81.

BALTZ, William Nicolas (D Ill.) Feb. 5, 1860-Aug. 22, 1943; House 1913-15.

BANDSTRA, Bert (D Iowa) Jan. 25, 1922; House 1965-67.

BANKHEAD, John Hollis (father of John Hollis Bankhead 2d and William Brockman Bankhead and grandfather of Walter Will Bankhead) (D Ala.) Sept. 13, 1842-March 1, 1920; House 1887-1907; Senate June 18, 1907-March 1, 1920.

BANKHEAD, John Hollis 2d (son of John Hollis Bankhead, brother of William Brockman Bankhead and father of Walter Will Bankhead) (D Ala.) July 8, 1872-June 12, 1946; Senate 1931-June 12, 1946.

BANKHEAD, Walter Will (son of John Hollis Bankhead 2d, grandson of John Hollis Bankhead and nephew of William Brockman Bankhead) (D Ala.) July 21, 1897; House Jan. 3-Feb. 1, 1941.

BANKHEAD, William Brockman (son of John Hollis Bankhead, brother of John Hollis Bankhead 2d and uncle of Walter Will Bankhead) (D Ala.) April 12, 1874-Sept. 15, 1940; House 1917-Sept. 15, 1940; Speaker June 4, 1936-Sept. 15, 1940.

BANKS, John (W Pa.) Oct. 17, 1793-April 3, 1864; House 1831-36.

BANKS, Linn (D Va.) Jan. 23, 1784-Jan. 13, 1842; House April 28, 1838-Dec. 6, 1841.

BANKS, Nathaniel Prentice (R Mass.) Jan. 30, 1816-Sept. 1, 1894; House 1853-Dec. 24, 1857, Dec. 4, 1865-1873, 1875-79 and 1889-91; 1853-55 (Coalition Democrat), 1855-57 (American Party), Jan. 3-Dec. 24, 1857 (Republican), 1865-67 (Union Republican), 1867-73 (Republican), 1875-79 (Liberal Republican), 1889-91 (Republican); Speaker 1855-57; Gov. 1858-61.

BANNING, Henry Blackstone (D Ohio) Nov. 10, 1836-Dec. 10, 1881; House 1873-79.

BANNON, Henry Towne (R Ohio) June 5, 1867-Sept. 6, 1950; House 1905-09.

BANTA, Parke Monroe (R Mo.) Nov. 21, 1891-May 12, 1970; House 1947-49.

BARBER, Hiram, Jr. (R Ill.) March 24, 1835-Aug. 5, 1924; House 1879-81.

BARBER, Isaac Ambrose (R Md.) Jan. 26, 1852-March 1, 1909; House 1897-99.

BARBER, Joel Allen (R Wis.) Jan. 17, 1809-June 17, 1881; House 1871-75.

BARBER, Laird Howard (D Pa.) Oct. 25, 1848-Feb. 16, 1928; House 1899-1901.

BARBER, Levi (— Ohio) Oct. 16, 1777-April 23, 1833; House 1817-19, 1821-23.

BARBER, Noyes (uncle of Edwin Barbour Morgan and Christopher Morgan) (D Conn.) April 28, 1781-Jan. 3, 1841; House 1821-35.

BARBOUR, Henry Ellsworth (R Calif.) March 8, 1877-March 21, 1945; House 1919-33.

BARBOUR, James (brother of Philip Pendleton Barbour and cousin of John Strode Barbour) (A-D/SR Va.) June 10, 1775-June 7, 1842; Senate Jan. 2, 1815-March 7, 1825; President pro tempore 1819; Gov. 1812-14; Secy. of War 1825-28.

BARBOUR, John Strode (father of John Strode Barbour, cousin of James Barbour and Philip Pendleton Barbour) (SRD Va.) Aug. 8, 1790-Jan. 12, 1855; House 1823-33.

BARBOUR, John Strode (son of John Strode Barbour) (D Va.) Dec. 29, 1820-May 14, 1892; House 1881-87; Senate 1889-May 14, 1892.

BARBOUR, Lucien (FS/T/KN Ind.) March 4, 1811-July 19, 1880; House 1855-57.

BARBOUR, Philip Pendleton (brother of James Barbour and cousin of John Strode Barbour) (D Va.) May 15, 1783-Feb. 25, 1841; House Sept. 19, 1814-25, 1827-Oct. 15, 1830; Speaker 1821-23; Assoc. Justice U.S. Supreme Court 1836-41.

BARBOUR, William Warren (R N.J.) July 31, 1888-Nov. 22, 1943; Senate Dec. 1, 1931-37, Nov. 9, 1938-Nov. 22, 1943.

BARCHFELD, Andrew Jackson (R Pa.) May 18, 1863-Jan. 28, 1922; House 1905-17.

BARCLAY, Charles Frederick (R Pa.) May 9, 1844-March 9, 1914; House 1907-11.

BARCLAY, David (D Pa.) 1823-Sept. 10, 1889; House 1855-57.

BARD, David (— Pa.) 1744-March 12, 1815; House 1795-99, 1803-March 12, 1815.

BARD, Thomas Robert (R Calif.) Dec. 8, 1841-March 5, 1915; Senate Feb. 7, 1900-05.

BARDEN, Graham Arthur (D N.C.) Sept. 25, 1896-Jan. 29, 1967; House 1935-61.

BARHAM, John All (R Calif.) July 17, 1843-Jan. 22, 1926; House 1895-1901.

BARING, Walter Stephan (D Nev.) Sept. 9, 1911; House 1949-53, 1957- .

BARKER, Abraham Andrews (UR Pa.) March 30, 1816-March 18, 1898; House 1865-67.

BARKER, David, Jr. (— N.H.) Jan. 8, 1797-April 1, 1834; House 1827-29.

BARKER, Joseph (D Mass.) Oct. 19, 1751-July 5, 1815; House 1805-09.

BARKLEY, Alben William (D Ky.) Nov. 24, 1877-April 30, 1956; House 1913-27; Senate 1927-Jan. 19, 1949, 1955-April 30, 1956; Vice President 1949-53.

BARKSDALE, Ethelbert (brother of William Barksdale) (D Miss.) Jan. 4, 1824-Feb. 17, 1893; House 1883-87.

BARKSDALE, William (brother of Ethelbert Barksdale) (SRD Miss.) Aug. 21, 1821-July 2, 1863; House 1853-Jan. 12, 1861.

BARLOW, Bradley (NR Vt.) May 12, 1814-Nov. 6, 1889; House 1879-81.

BARLOW, Charles Averill (P/D Calif.) March 17, 1858-Oct. 3, 1927; House 1897-99.

BARLOW, Stephen (D Pa.) June 13, 1779-Aug. 24, 1845; House 1827-29.

BARNARD, Daniel Dewey (W N.Y.) July 16, 1797-April 24, 1861; House 1827-29, 1839-45.

BARNARD, Isaac Dutton (F Pa.) July 18, 1791-Feb. 28, 1834; Senate 1827-Dec. 6, 1831.

BARNARD, William Oscar (R Ind.) Oct. 25, 1852-April 8, 1939; House 1909-11.

BARNES, Demas (D N.Y.) April 4, 1827-May 1, 1888; House 1867-69.

BARNES, George Thomas (D Ga.) Aug. 4, 1833-Oct. 24, 1901; House 1885-91.

BARNES, James Martin (D Ill.) Jan. 9, 1899-June 8, 1958; House 1939-43.

BARNES, Lyman Eddy (D Wis.) June 30, 1855-Jan. 16, 1904; House 1893-95.

BARNETT, William (SRD Ga.) March 4, 1761-April 1832; House Oct. 5, 1812-15.

BARNEY, John (F Md.) Jan. 18, 1785-Jan. 26, 1857; House 1825-29.

BARNEY, Samuel Stebbins (R Wis.) Jan. 31, 1846-Dec. 31, 1919; House 1895-1903.

BARNHART, Henry A. (D Ind.) Sept. 11, 1858-March 26, 1934; House Nov. 3, 1908-19.

BARNITZ, Charles Augustus (W Pa.) Sept. 11, 1780-Jan. 8, 1850; House 1833-35.

BARNUM, William Henry (D Conn.) Sept. 17, 1818-April 30, 1889; House 1867-May 18, 1876; Senate May 18, 1876-79; Chrmn. Dem. Nat. Comm. 1876-89.

BARNWELL, Robert (father of Robert Woodward Barnwell) (F S.C.) Dec. 21, 1761-Oct. 24, 1814; House 1791-93; Cont. Cong. 1788-89.

BARNWELL, Robert Woodward (son of Robert Barnwell) (D S.C.) Aug. 10, 1801-Nov. 24, 1882; House 1829-33; Senate June 4-Dec. 8, 1850.

BARR, Joseph Walker (D Ind.) January 17, 1918; House 1959-61; Secy. of the Treasury 1968-69.

BARR, Samuel Fleming (R Pa.) June 15, 1829-May 20, 1919; House 1881-85.

BARR, Thomas Jefferson (D N.Y.) 1812-March 27, 1881; House Jan. 17, 1859-61.

BARRERE, Granville (nephew of Nelson Barrere) (R Ill.) July 11, 1829-Jan. 13, 1889; House 1873-75.

BARRERE, Nelson (uncle of Granville Barrere) (W Ohio) April 1, 1808-Aug. 20, 1883; House 1851-53.

BARRET, John Richard (D Mo.) Aug. 21, 1825-Nov. 2, 1903; House 1859-June 8, 1860, Dec. 3, 1860-61.

BARRETT, Frank A. (R Wyo.) Nov. 10, 1892-May 30, 1962; House 1943-Dec. 31, 1950; Senate 1953-59; Gov. 1951-53.

BARRETT, William A. (D Pa.) Aug. 14, 1896; House 1945-47, 1949- .

BARRETT, William Emerson (R Mass.) Dec. 29, 1858-Feb. 12, 1906; House 1895-99.

BARRINGER, Daniel Laurens (uncle of Daniel Moreau Barringer) (D N.C.) Oct. 1, 1788-Oct. 16, 1852; House Dec. 4, 1826-35.

BARRINGER, Daniel Moreau (nephew of Daniel Laurens Barringer) (W N.C.) July 30, 1806-Sept. 1, 1873; House 1843-49.

BARROW, Alexander (W La.) March 27, 1801-Dec. 19, 1846; Senate 1841-Dec. 19, 1846.

BARROW, Middleton Pope (grandson of Wilson Lumpkin) (D Ga.) Aug. 1, 1839-Dec. 23, 1903; Senate Nov. 15, 1882-83.

BARROW, Washington (W Tenn.) Oct. 5, 1807-Oct. 19, 1866; House 1847-49.

BARROWS, Samuel June (R Mass.) May 26, 1845-April 21, 1909; House 1897-99.

BARRY, Alexander Grant (R Ore.) Aug. 23, 1892-Dec. 28, 1952; Senate Nov. 9, 1938-39.

BARRY, Frederick George (D Miss.) Jan. 12, 1845-May 7, 1909; House 1885-89.

BARRY, Henry W. (R Miss.) April, 1840-June 7, 1875; House Feb. 23, 1870-75.

BARRY, Robert Raymond (R N.Y.) May 15, 1915; House 1959-65.

BARRY, William Bernard (D N.Y.) July 21, 1902-Oct. 20, 1946; House Nov. 5, 1935-Oct. 20, 1946.

BARRY, William Taylor (D Ky.) Feb. 15, 1784-Aug. 30, 1835; House Aug. 8, 1810-11; Senate Dec. 16, 1814-May 1, 1816; Postmaster General 1829-35.

BARRY, William Taylor Sullivan (D Miss.) Dec. 10, 1821-Jan. 19, 1868; House 1853-55.

BARSTOW, Gamaliel Henry (NR N.Y.) July 20, 1784-March 30, 1865; House 1831-33.

BARSTOW, Gideon (D Mass.) Sept. 7, 1783-March 26, 1852; House 1821-23.

BARTHOLDT, Richard (R Mo.) Nov. 2, 1855-March 19, 1932; House 1893-1915.

BARTINE, Horace Franklin (R Nev.) March 21, 1848-Aug. 27, 1918; House 1889-93.

BARTLETT, Bailey (F Mass.) Jan. 29, 1750-Sept. 9, 1830; House Nov. 27, 1797-1801.

BARTLETT, Charles Lafayette (D Ga.) Jan. 31, 1853-April 21, 1938; House 1895-1915.

BARTLETT, Edward Lewis (Bob) (D Alaska) April 20, 1904-Dec. 11, 1968; House (Terr. Del.) 1945-59; Senate 1959-Dec. 11, 1968.

BARTLETT, Franklin (D N.Y.) Sept. 10, 1847-April 23, 1909; House 1893-97.

BARTLETT, George Arthur (D Nev.) Nov. 30, 1869-June 1, 1951; House 1907-11.

BARTLETT, Ichabod (A-D N.H.) July 24, 1786-Oct. 19, 1853; House 1823-29.

BARTLETT, Josiah, Jr. (— N.H.) Aug. 29, 1768-April 16, 1838; House 1811-13.

BARTLETT, Thomas, Jr. (D Vt.) June 18, 1808-Sept. 12, 1876; House 1851-53.

BARTLEY, Mordecai (— Ohio) Dec. 16, 1783-Oct. 10, 1870; House 1823-31; Gov. 1844-46.

BARTON, Bruce (R N.Y.) Aug. 5, 1886-July 5, 1967; House Nov. 2, 1937-41.

BARTON, David (— Mo.) Dec. 14, 1783-Sept. 28, 1837; Senate Aug. 10, 1821-31.

BARTON, Richard Walker (W Va.) 1800-March 15, 1859; House 1841-43.

BARTON, Samuel (JD N.Y.) July 27, 1785-Jan. 19, 1858; House 1835-37.

BARTON, Silas Reynolds (R Neb.) May 21, 1872-Nov. 7, 1916; House 1913-15.

BARTON, William Edward (cousin of Courtney Walker Hamlin) (D Mo.) April 11, 1868-July 29, 1955; House 1931-33.

BARWIG, Charles (D Wis.) March 19, 1837-Feb. 15, 1912; House 1889-95.

BASHFORD, Coles (I Ariz.) Jan. 24, 1816-April 25, 1878; House (Terr. Del.) 1867-69; Gov. of Wisconsin (Republican) 1855-58.

BASS, Lyman Kidder (R N.Y.) Nov. 13, 1836-May 11, 1889; House 1873-77.

BASS, Perkins (R N.H.) Oct. 6, 1912; House 1955-63.

BASS, Ross (D Tenn.) March 17, 1918; House 1955-Nov. 4, 1964; Senate Nov. 4, 1964-67.

BASSETT, Burwell (D Va.) March 18, 1764-Feb. 26, 1841; House 1805-13, 1815-19, 1821-29.

BASSETT, Edward Murray (D N.Y.) Feb. 7, 1863-Oct. 27, 1948; House 1903-05.

BASSETT, Richard (grandfather of Richard Henry Bayard and James Asheton Bayard, Jr.) (— Del.) April 2, 1745-Aug. 15, 1815; Senate 1789-93; Gov. 1799-1801.

BATE, William Brimage (D Tenn.) Oct. 7, 1826-March 9, 1905; Senate 1887-March 9, 1905; Gov. 1883-86.

BATEMAN, Ephraim (D N.J.) July 9, 1780-Jan. 18, 1829; House 1815-23; Senate Nov. 10, 1826-Jan. 12, 1829.

BATES, Arthur Laban (nephew of John Milton Thayer) (R Pa.) June 6, 1859-Aug. 26, 1934; House 1901-13.

BATES, Edward (brother of James Woodson Bates) (A A-D Mo.) Sept. 4, 1793-March 25, 1869; House 1827-29; Atty. Gen. of the U.S. 1861-64.

BATES, George Joseph (father of William Henry Bates) (R Mass.) Feb. 25, 1891-Nov. 1, 1949; House 1937-Nov. 1, 1949.

BATES, Isaac Chapman (W Mass.) Jan. 23, 1779-March 16, 1845; House 1827-35 (Anti-Jackson); Senate Jan. 13, 1841-March 16, 1845 (Whig).

BATES, James (D Maine) Sept. 24, 1789-Feb. 25, 1882; House 1831-33.

BATES, James Woodson (brother of Edward Bates) (— Ark.) Aug. 25, 1788-Dec. 16, 1846; House (Terr. Del.) Dec. 21, 1819-23.

BATES, Joseph Bengal (D Ky.) Oct. 29, 1893-Sept. 10, 1965; House June 4, 1938-53.

BATES, Martin Waltham (D Del.) Feb. 24, 1787-Jan. 1, 1869; Senate Jan. 14, 1857-59.

BATES, William Henry (son of George Joseph Bates) (R Mass.) April 26, 1917-June 22, 1969; House Feb. 14, 1950-June 22, 1969.

BATHRICK, Elsworth Raymond (D Ohio) Jan. 6, 1863-Dec. 23, 1917; House 1911-15, March 4-Dec. 23, 1917.

BATTIN, James F. (R Mont.) Feb. 13, 1925; House 1961-Feb. 27, 1969.

BATTLE, Laurie Calvin (D Ala.) May 10, 1912; House 1947-55.

BAUMHART, Albert David, Jr. (R Ohio) June 15, 1908; House 1941-Sept. 2, 1942, 1955-61.

BAXTER, Portus (R Vt.) December 4, 1806-March 4, 1868; House 1861-67.

BAY, William Van Ness (D Mo.) Nov. 23, 1818-Feb. 10, 1894; House 1849-51.

BAYARD, James Asheton, Sr. (father of Richard Henry Bayard and James Asheton Bayard, Jr., grandfather of Thomas Francis Bayard, Sr., and great-grandfather of Thomas Francis Bayard, Jr.) (F Del.) July 28, 1767-August 6, 1815; House 1797-1803; Senate Nov. 13, 1804-13.

BAYARD, James Asheton, Jr. (son of James Asheton Bayard, Sr., grandson of Richard Bassett, father of Thomas Francis Bayard, Sr. and grandfather of Thomas Francis Bayard, Jr.) (D Del.) Nov. 15, 1799-June 13, 1880; Senate 1851-Jan. 29, 1864, April 5, 1867-69.

BAYARD, Richard Henry (son of James Asheton Bayard, Sr., and grandson of Richard Bassett) (W Del.) Sept. 23, 1796-March 4, 1868; Senate June 17, 1836-Sept. 19, 1839, Jan. 12, 1841-45.

BAYARD, Thomas Francis, Sr. (son of James Asheton Bayard, Jr., and father of Thomas Francis Bayard, Jr.) (D Del.) Oct. 29, 1828-Sept. 28, 1898; Senate 1869-March 6, 1885; President pro tempore 1881; Secretary of State 1885-89.

BAYARD, Thomas Francis, Jr. (son of Thomas Francis Bayard, Sr.) (D Del.) June 4, 1868-July 12, 1942; Senate Nov. 8, 1922-29.

BAYH, Birch E. (D Ind.) Jan. 22, 1928; Senate 1963- .

BAYLIES, Francis (brother of William Baylies) (— Mass.) Oct. 16, 1784-Oct. 28, 1852; House 1821-27.

BAYLIES, William (brother of Francis Baylies) (WD Mass.) Sept. 15, 1776-Sept. 27, 1865; House March 4-June 28, 1809, 1813-17, 1833-35.

BAYLOR, Robert Emmett Bledsoe (nephew of Jesse Bledsoe) (D Ala.) May 10, 1793-Jan. 6, 1874; House 1829-31.

BAYLY, Thomas (D Md.) Sept. 13, 1775-1829; House 1817-23.

BAYLY, Thomas Henry (son of Thomas Monteagle Bayly) (SRD Va.) Dec. 11, 1810-June 23, 1856; House May 6, 1844-June 23, 1856.

BAYLY, Thomas Monteagle (father of Thomas Henry Bayly) (D Va.) March 26, 1775-Jan. 7, 1834; House 1813-15.

BAYNE, Thomas McKee (R Pa.) June 14, 1836-June 16, 1894; House 1877-91.

BEACH, Clifton Bailey (R Ohio) Sept. 16, 1845-Nov. 15, 1902; House 1895-99.

BEACH, Lewis (D N.Y.) March 30, 1835-Aug. 10, 1886; House 1881-Aug. 10, 1886.

BEAKES, Samuel Willard (D Mich.) Jan. 11, 1861-Feb. 9, 1927; House 1913-March 3, 1917, Dec. 13, 1917-19.

BEALE, Charles Lewis (R N.Y.) March 5, 1824-Jan. 29, 1900; House 1859-61.

BEALE, James Madison Hite (D Va.) Feb. 7, 1786-Aug. 2, 1866; House 1833-37, 1849-53.

BEALE, Joseph Grant (R Pa.) March 26, 1839-May 21, 1915; House 1907-09.

BEALE, Richard Lee Turberville (D Va.) May 22, 1819-April 21, 1893; House 1847-49, Jan. 23, 1879-81.

BEALES, Cyrus William (R Pa.) Dec. 16, 1877-Nov. 14, 1927; House 1915-17.

BEALL, James Andrew (Jack) (D Texas) Oct. 25, 1866-Feb. 12, 1929; House 1903-15.

BEALL, James Glenn (father of James Glenn Beall, Jr.) (R Md.) June 5, 1894-Jan. 14, 1971; House 1943-53; Senate 1953-65.

BEALL, James Glenn, Jr. (son of James Glenn Beall) (R Md.) June 19, 1927; House 1969-71; Senate 1971- .

BEALL, Reasin (W Ohio) Dec. 3, 1769-Feb. 20, 1843; House April 20, 1813-June 7, 1814.

BEAM, Harry Peter (D Ill.) Nov. 23, 1892; House 1931-Dec. 6, 1942.

BEAMAN, Fernando Cortez (R Mich.) June 28, 1814-Sept 27, 1882; House 1861-71.

BEAMER, John Valentine (R Ind.) Nov. 17, 1896-Sept. 8, 1964; House 1951-59.

BEAN, Benning Moulton (D N.H.) Jan. 9, 1782-Feb. 6, 1866; House 1833-37.

BEAN, Curtis Coe (R Ariz.) Jan. 4, 1828-Feb. 1, 1904; House (Terr. Del.) 1885-87.

BEARDSLEY, Samuel (D N.Y.) Feb. 6, 1790-May 6, 1860; House 1831-March 29, 1836, 1843-Feb. 29, 1844.

BEATTY, John (— N.J.) Dec. 10, 1749-May 30, 1826; House 1793-95; Cont. Cong. Jan. 13-June 3, 1784, Nov. 11, 1784-Nov. 7, 1785.

BEATTY, John (R Ohio) Dec. 16, 1828-Dec. 21, 1914; House Feb. 5, 1868-73.

BEATTY, William (VBD Pa.) 1787-April 12, 1851; House 1837-41.

BEATY, Martin (W Ky.) —-—; House 1833-35.

BEAUMONT, Andrew (D Pa.) Jan. 24, 1790-Sept. 30, 1853; House 1833-37.

BECK, Erasmus Williams (D Ga.) Oct. 21, 1833-July 22, 1898; House Dec. 2, 1872-73.

BECK, James Burnie (D Ky.) Feb. 13, 1822-May 3, 1890; House 1867-75; Senate 1877-May 3, 1890.

BECK, James Montgomery (R Pa.) July 9, 1861-April 12, 1936; House Nov. 8, 1927-Sept. 30, 1934.

BECK, Joseph David (R Wis.) March 14, 1866-Nov. 8, 1936; House 1921-29.

BECKER, Frank John (R N.Y.) Aug. 27, 1899; House 1953-65.

BECKHAM, John Crepps Wickliffe (grandson of Charles Anderson Wickliffe and cousin of Robert Charles Wickliffe) (D Ky.) Aug. 5, 1869-Jan. 9, 1940; Senate 1915-21; Gov. Feb. 3, 1900-07.

BECKNER, William Morgan (D Ky.) June 19, 1841-March 14, 1910; House Dec. 3, 1894-95.

BECKWITH, Charles Dyer (R N.J.) Oct. 22, 1838-March 27, 1921; House 1889-91.

BECKWORTH, Lindley Gary (D Texas) June 30, 1913; House 1939-53, 1957-67.

BEDE, James Adam (R Minn.) Jan. 13, 1856-April 11, 1942; House 1903-09.

BEDINGER, George Michael (uncle of Henry Bedinger) (— Ky.) Dec. 10, 1756-Dec. 7, 1843; House 1803-07.

BEDINGER, Henry (nephew of George Michael Bedinger) (D Va.) Feb. 3, 1812-Nov. 26, 1858; House 1845-49.

BEE, Carlos (D Texas) July 8, 1867-April 20, 1932; House 1919-21.

BEEBE, George Monroe (D N.Y.) Oct. 28, 1836-March 1, 1927; House 1875-79.

BEECHER, Philemon (F Ohio) 1775-Nov. 30, 1839; House 1817-21, 1823-29.

BEEDY, Carroll Lynwood (R Maine) Aug. 3, 1880-Aug. 30, 1947; House 1921-35.

BEEKMAN, Thomas (— N.Y.) —-—; House 1829-31.

BEEMAN, Joseph Henry (D Miss.) Nov. 17, 1833-July 31, 1909; House 1891-93.

BEERMANN, Ralph F. (R Neb.) Aug. 13, 1912; House 1961-65.

BEERS, Cyrus (D N.Y.) June 21, 1786-June 5, 1850; House Dec. 3, 1838-39.

BEERS, Edward McMath (R Pa.) May 27, 1877-April 21, 1932; House 1923-April 21, 1932.

BEESON, Henry White (D Pa.) Sept. 14, 1791-Oct. 28, 1863; House May 31, 1841-43.

BEGG, James Thomas (R Ohio) Feb. 16, 1877-March 26, 1963; House 1919-29.

BEGICH, Nicholas J. (D Alaska) April 6, 1932; House 1971- .

BEGOLE, Josiah Williams (R Mich.) Jan. 20, 1815-June 5, 1896; House 1873-75; Gov. 1883-85.

BEIDLER, Jacob Atlee (R Ohio) Nov. 2, 1852-Sept. 13, 1912; House 1901-07.

BEIRNE, Andrew (VBD Va.) 1771-March 16, 1845; House 1837-41.

BEITER, Alfred Florian (D N.Y.) July 7, 1893; House 1933-39, 1941-43.

BELCHER, Hiram (W Maine) Feb. 23, 1790-May 6, 1857; House 1847-49.

BELCHER, Nathan (D Conn.) June 23, 1813-June 2, 1891; House 1853-55.

BELCHER, Page Henry (R Okla.) April 21, 1899; House 1951- .

BELDEN, George Ogilvie (D N.Y.) March 28, 1797-Oct. 9, 1833; House 1827-29.

BELDEN, James Jerome (R N.Y.) Sept. 30, 1825-Jan. 1, 1904; House Nov. 8, 1887-95, 1897-99.

BELFORD, James Burns (R Colo.) Sept. 28, 1837-Jan. 10, 1910; House Oct. 3, 1876-Dec. 13, 1877, 1879-85.

BELFORD, Joseph McCrum (R N.Y.) Aug. 5, 1852-May 3, 1917; House 1897-99.

BELKNAP, Charles Eugene (R Mich.) Oct. 17, 1846-Jan. 16, 1929; House 1889-91, Nov. 3, 1891-93.

BELKNAP, Hugh Reid (R Ill.) Sept. 1, 1860-Nov. 12, 1901; House Dec. 27, 1895-99.

BELL, Alphonzo (R Calif.) Sept. 19, 1914; House 1961- .

BELL, Charles Henry (nephew of Samuel Bell and cousin of James Bell) (R N.H.) Nov. 18, 1823-Nov. 11, 1893; Senate March 13-June 18, 1879; Gov. 1881-83.

BELL, Charles Jasper (D Mo.) Jan. 16, 1885; House 1935-49.

BELL, Charles Keith (nephew of Reese Bowen Brabson) (D Texas) April 18, 1853-April 21, 1913; House 1893-97.

BELL, Charles Webster (PR Calif.) June 11, 1857-April 19, 1927; House 1913-15.

BELL, Hiram (W Ohio) April 22, 1808-Dec. 21, 1855; House 1851-53.

BELL, Hiram Parks (D Ga.) Jan. 19, 1827-Aug. 17, 1907; House 1873-75, March 13, 1877-79.

BELL, James (son of Samuel Bell, uncle of Samuel Newell Bell and cousin of Charles Henry Bell) (W N.H.) Nov. 13, 1804-May 26, 1857; Senate July 30, 1855-May 26, 1857.

BELL, James Martin (D Ohio) Oct. 16, 1796-April 4, 1849; House 1833-35.

BELL, John (W Ohio) June 19, 1796-May 4, 1869; House Jan. 7-March 3, 1851.

BELL, John (W Tenn.) Feb. 15, 1797-Sept. 10, 1869; House 1827-41 (Democrat 1827-29, Whig 1829-41); Senate Nov. 22, 1847-59; Speaker 1834; Secretary of War March 5-Sept. 12, 1841.

BELL, John Calhoun (D Colo.) Dec. 11, 1851-Aug. 12, 1933; House 1893-1903.

BELL, John Junior (D Texas) May 15, 1910-Jan. 24, 1963; House 1955-57.

BELL, Joshua Fry (W Ky.) Nov. 26, 1811-Aug. 17, 1870; House 1845-47.

BELL, Peter Hansbrough (D Texas) March 11, 1810-March 8, 1898; House 1853-57; Gov. 1849-53.

BELL, Samuel (father of James Bell, grandfather of Samuel Newell Bell and uncle of Charles Henry Bell) (— N.H.) Feb. 9, 1770-Dec. 23, 1850; Senate 1823-35; Gov. 1819-23.

BELL, Samuel Newell (grandson of Samuel Bell and nephew of James Bell) (D N.H.) March 25, 1829-Feb. 8, 1889; House 1871-73, 1875-77.

BELL, Theodore Arlington (D Calif.) July 25, 1872-Sept. 4, 1922; House 1903-05.

BELL, Thomas Montgomery (D Ga.) March 17, 1861-March 18, 1941; House 1905-31.

BELLAMY, John Dillard (D N.C.) March 24, 1854-Sept. 25, 1942; House 1899-1903.

BELLINGER, Joseph (— S.C.) 1773-Jan. 10, 1830; House 1817-19.

BELLMON, Henry (R Okla.) Sept. 3, 1921; Senate 1969- ; Gov. 1963-67.

BELMONT, Oliver Hazard Perry (brother of Perry Belmont) (D N.Y.) Nov. 12, 1858-June 10, 1908; House 1901-03.

BELMONT, Perry (brother of Oliver Hazard Perry Belmont) (D N.Y.) Dec. 28, 1851-May 25, 1947; House 1881-Dec. 1, 1888.

BELSER, James Edwin (D Ala.) Dec. 22, 1805-Jan. 16, 1859; House 1843-45.

BELTZHOOVER, Frank Eckels (D Pa.) Nov. 6, 1841-June 2, 1923; House 1879-83, 1891-95.

BENDER, George Harrison (R Ohio) Sept. 29, 1896-June 18, 1961; House 1939-49, 1951-Dec. 15, 1954; Senate Dec. 16, 1954-57.

BENEDICT, Charles Brewster (D N.Y.) Feb. 7, 1828-Oct. 3, 1901; House 1877-79.

BENEDICT, Henry Stanley (R Calif.) Feb. 20, 1878-July 10, 1930; House Nov. 7, 1916-17.

BENET, Christie (D S.C.) Dec. 26, 1879-March 30, 1951; Senate July 6-Nov. 5, 1918.

BENHAM, John Samuel (R Ind.) Oct. 24, 1863-Dec. 11, 1935; House 1919-23.

BENJAMIN, John Forbes (RR Mo.) Jan. 23, 1817-March 8, 1877; House 1865-71.

BENJAMIN, Judah Philip (D La.) Aug. 6, 1811-May 8, 1884; Senate 1853-Feb. 4, 1861 (1853-59 Whig; 1859-Feb. 4, 1861 Democrat).

BENNER, George Jacob (D Pa.) April 13, 1859-Dec. 30, 1930; House 1897-99.

BENNET, Augustus Witschief (son of William Stiles Bennet) (R N.Y.) Oct. 7, 1897; House 1945-47.

BENNET, Benjamin (— N.J.) Oct. 31, 1764-Oct. 8, 1840; House 1815-19.

BENNET, Hiram Pitt (CR Colo.) Sept. 2, 1826-Nov. 11, 1914; House (Terr. Del.) Aug. 19, 1861-65.

BENNET, William Stiles (father of Augustus Witschief Bennet) (R N.Y.) Nov. 9, 1870-Dec. 1, 1962; House 1905-11, Nov. 2, 1915-17.

BENNETT, Charles Edward (D Fla.) Dec. 2, 1910; House 1949- .

BENNETT, Charles Goodwin (R N.Y.) Dec. 11, 1863-May 25, 1914; House 1895-99.

BENNETT, David Smith (R N.Y.) May 3, 1811-Nov. 6, 1894; House 1869-71.

BENNETT, Granville Gaylord (R Dakota) Oct. 9, 1833-June 28, 1910; House (Terr. Del.) 1879-81.

BENNETT, Hendley Stone (D Miss.) April 7, 1807-Dec. 15, 1891; House 1855-57.

BENNETT, Henry (R N.Y.) Sept. 29, 1808-May 10, 1868; House 1849-59 (1849-51 Whig; 1851-59 Republican).

BENNETT, John Bonifas (R Mich.) Jan. 10, 1904-Aug. 9, 1964; House 1943-45, 1947-Aug. 10, 1964.

BENNETT, Joseph Bentley (R Ky.) April 21, 1859-Nov. 7, 1923; House 1905-11.

BENNETT, Marion Tinsley (son of Philip A. Bennett) (R Mo.) June 6, 1914; House Jan. 12, 1943-49.

BENNETT, Philip Allen (father of Marion T. Bennett) (R Mo.) March 5, 1881-Dec. 7, 1942; House 1941-Dec. 7, 1942.

BENNETT, Risden Tyler (D N.C.) June 18, 1840-July 21, 1913; House 1883-87.

BENNETT, Thomas Warren (I Idaho) Feb. 16, 1831-Feb. 2, 1893; House (Terr. Del.) 1875-June 23, 1876; Gov. 1871-75.

BENNETT, Wallace Foster (R Utah) Nov. 13, 1898; Senate 1951- .

BENNY, Allan (D N.J.) July 12, 1867-Nov. 6, 1942; House 1903-05.

BENSON, Alfred Washburn (R Kan.) July 15, 1843-Jan. 1, 1916; Senate June 11, 1906-Jan. 23, 1907.

BENSON, Carville Dickinson (D Md.) Aug. 24, 1872-Feb. 8, 1929; House Nov. 5, 1918-21.

BENSON, Egbert (— N.Y.) June 21, 1746-Aug. 24, 1833; House 1789-93, March 4-Aug. 7, 1813; Cont. Cong. 1784-88.

BENSON, Elmer Austin (F-L Minn.) Sept. 22, 1895; Senate Dec. 27, 1935-Nov. 3, 1936; Gov. 1937-39.

BENSON, Samuel Page (R Maine) Nov. 28, 1804-Aug. 12, 1876; House 1853-57 (1853-55 Whig; 1855-57 Republican).

BENTLEY, Alvin Morell (R Mich.) Aug. 30, 1918-April 10, 1969; House 1953-61.

BENTLEY, Henry Wilbur (D N.Y.) Sept. 30, 1838-Jan. 27, 1907; House 1891-93.

BENTON, Charles Swan (D N.Y.) July 12, 1810-May 4, 1882; House 1843-47.

BENTON, Jacob (R N.H.) Aug. 19, 1814-Sept. 29, 1892; House 1867-71.

BENTON, Lemuel (great-grandfather of George William Dargan) (D S.C.) 1754-May 18, 1818; House 1793-99.

BENTON, Maecenas Eason (D Mo.) Jan. 29, 1848-April 27, 1924; House 1897-1905.

BENTON, Thomas Hart (D Mo.) March 14, 1782-April 10, 1858; Senate Aug. 10, 1821-51; House 1853-55 (Missouri Compromise Democrat).

BENTON, William (D Conn.) April 1, 1900; Senate Dec. 17, 1949-53.

BENTSEN, Lloyd Millard, Jr. (D Texas) Feb. 11, 1921; House Dec. 4, 1948-55; Senate 1971- .

BERGEN, Christopher Augustus (R N.J.) Aug. 2, 1841-Feb. 18, 1905; House 1889-93.

BERGEN, John Teunis (second cousin of Teunis Garret Bergen) (D N.Y.) 1786-March 9, 1855; House 1831-33.

BERGEN, Teunis Garret (second cousin of John Teunis Bergen) (D N.Y.) Oct. 6, 1806-April 24, 1881; House 1865-67.

BERGER, Victor Luitpold (Soc. Wis.) Feb. 28, 1860-Aug. 7, 1929; House 1911-13, 1923-29.

BERGLAND, Bob (D Minn.) July 31, 1928; House 1971- .

BERLIN, William Markle (D Pa.) March 29, 1880-Oct. 14, 1962; House 1933-37.

BERNARD, John Toussaint (F-L Minn.) March 6, 1893; House 1937-39.

BERNHISEL, John Milton (W Utah) July 23, 1799-Sept. 28, 1881; House (Terr. Del.) 1851-59, 1861-63.

BERRIEN, John Macpherson (W Ga.) Aug. 23, 1781-Jan. 1, 1856; Senate 1825-March 9, 1829 (Democrat), 1841-May, 1845 and Nov. 14, 1845-47, Nov. 13, 1847-May 28, 1852 (Whig); Attorney General 1829-31.

BERRY, Albert Seaton (D Ky.) May 13, 1836-Jan. 6, 1908; House 1893-1901.

BERRY, Campbell Polson (cousin of James Henderson Berry) (D Calif.) Nov. 7, 1834-Jan. 8, 1901; House 1879-83.

BERRY, Ellis Yarnal (R S.D.) Oct. 6, 1902; House 1951-71.

BERRY, George Leonard (D Tenn.) Sept. 12, 1882-Dec. 4, 1948; Senate May 6, 1937-Nov. 8, 1938.

BERRY, James Henderson (cousin of Campbell Polson Berry) (D Ark.) May 15, 1841-Jan. 30, 1913; Senate March 20, 1885-1907; Gov. 1882-85.

BERRY, John (D Ohio) April 26, 1833-May 18, 1879; House 1873-75.

BESHLIN, Earl Hanley (D/Prohib. Pa.) April 28, 1870; House Nov. 8, 1917-19.

BETHUNE, Lauchlin (JD N.C.) April 15, 1785-Oct. 10, 1874; House 1831-33.

BETHUNE, Marion (R Ga.) April 8, 1816-Feb. 20, 1895; House Dec. 22, 1870-71.

BETTON, Silas (— N.H.) Aug. 26, 1768-Jan. 22, 1822; House 1803-07.

BETTS, Jackson Edward (R Ohio) May 26, 1904; House 1951- .

BETTS, Samuel Rossiter (D N.Y.) June 8, 1787-Nov. 2, 1868; House 1815-17.

BETTS, Thaddeus (W Conn.) Feb. 4, 1789-April 7, 1840; Senate 1839-April 7, 1840.

BEVERIDGE, Albert Jeremiah (R Ind.) Oct. 6, 1862-April 27, 1927; Senate 1899-1911.

BEVERIDGE, John Lourie (R Ill.) July 6, 1824-May 3, 1910; House Nov. 7, 1871-Jan. 4, 1873; Gov. 1873-77.

BEVILL, Tom (D Ala.) March 27, 1921; House 1967- .

BIAGGI, Mario (D N.Y.) Oct. 26, 1917; House 1969- .

BIBB, George Motier (— Ky.) Oct. 30, 1776-April 14, 1859; Senate 1811-Aug. 23, 1814, 1829-35; Secy. of the Treasury 1844-45.

BIBB, William Wyatt (D Ga.) Oct. 1, 1780-July 9, 1820; House Jan. 26, 1807-Nov. 6, 1813; Senate Nov. 6, 1813-Nov. 9, 1816; Gov. of Ala. 1817-20.

BIBIGHAUS, Thomas Marshal (W Pa.) March 17, 1817-June 18, 1853; House 1851-53.

BIBLE, Alan Harvey (D Nev.) Nov. 20, 1909; Senate Dec. 2, 1954- .

BICKNELL, Bennet (D N.Y.) Nov. 14, 1781-Sept. 15, 1841; House 1837-39.

BICKNELL, George Augustus (D Ind.) Feb. 6, 1815-April 11, 1891; House 1877-81.

BIDDLE, Charles John (nephew of Richard Biddle) (D Pa.) April 30, 1819-Sept. 28, 1873; House July 2, 1861-63.

BIDDLE, John (W Mich.) March 2, 1792-Aug. 25, 1859; House (Terr. Del.) 1829-Feb. 21, 1831.

BIDDLE, Joseph Franklin (R Pa.) Sept. 14, 1871-Dec. 3, 1936; House Nov. 8, 1932-33.

BIDDLE, Richard (uncle of Charles John Biddle) (W Pa.) March 25, 1796-July 6, 1847; House 1837-40.

BIDLACK, Benjamin Alden (D Pa.) Sept. 8, 1804-Feb. 6, 1849; House 1841-45.

BIDWELL, Barnabas (— Mass.) Aug. 23, 1763-July 27, 1833; House 1805-July 13, 1807.

BIDWELL, John (U Calif.) Aug. 5, 1819-April 4, 1900; House 1865-67.

BIEMILLER, Andrew John (D Wis.) July 23, 1906; House 1945-47, 1949-51.

BIERMANN, Frederick Elliott (D Iowa) March 20, 1884-July 1, 1968; House 1933-39.

BIERY, James Soloman (R Pa.) March 2, 1839-Dec. 3, 1904; House 1873-75.

BIESTER, Edward G., Jr. (R Pa.) Jan. 5, 1931; House 1967- .

BIGBY, John Summerfield (R Ga.) Feb. 13, 1832-March 28, 1898; House 1871-73.

BIGELOW, Abijah (F Mass.) Dec. 5, 1775-April 5, 1860; House Oct. 8, 1810-March 3, 1815.

BIGELOW, Herbert Seely (D Ohio) Jan. 4, 1870-Nov. 11, 1951; House 1937-39.

BIGELOW, Lewis (— Mass.) Aug. 18, 1785-Oct. 2, 1838; House 1821-23.

BIGGS, Asa (D N.C.) Feb. 4, 1811-March 6, 1878; House 1845-47; Senate 1855-May 5, 1858.

BIGGS, Benjamin Thomas (D Del.) Oct. 1, 1821-Dec. 25, 1893; House 1869-73; Gov. 1887-91.

BIGGS, Marion (D Calif.) May 2, 1823-Aug. 2, 1910; House 1887-91.

BIGLER, William (D Pa.) Jan. 1, 1814-Aug. 9, 1880; Senate Jan. 14, 1856-61; Gov. 1851.

BILBO, Theodore Gilmore (D Miss.) Oct. 13, 1877-Aug. 21, 1947; Senate 1935-Aug. 21, 1947; Gov. 1916-20, 1928-32.

BILLINGHURST, Charles (R Wis.) July 27, 1818-Aug. 18, 1865; House 1855-59.

BILLMEYER, Alexander (D Pa.) Jan. 7, 1841-May 24, 1924; House Nov. 4, 1902-03.

BINDERUP, Charles Gustav (D Neb.) March 5, 1873-Aug. 19, 1950; House 1935-39.

BINES, Thomas (D N.J.) —April 9, 1826; House Nov. 2, 1814-15.

BINGHAM, Henry Harrison (R Pa.) Dec. 4, 1841-March 22, 1912; House 1879-March 22, 1912.

BINGHAM, Hiram (father of Jonathan B. Bingham) (R Conn.) Nov. 19, 1875-June 6, 1956; Senate Dec. 17, 1924-33; Gov. 1924.

BINGHAM, John Armor (R Ohio) Jan. 21, 1815-March 19, 1900; House 1855-63, 1865-73.

BINGHAM, Jonathan B. (son of Hiram Bingham) (D N.Y.) April 24, 1914; House 1965- .

BINGHAM, Kinsley Scott (R Mich.) Dec. 16, 1808-Oct. 5, 1861; House (Dem.) 1847-51; Senate 1859-Oct. 5, 1861; Gov. 1854-58.

BINGHAM, William (— Pa.) March 8, 1752-Feb. 7, 1804; Senate 1795-1801; President pro tempore 1797; Cont. Cong. 1787-88.

BINNEY, Horace (W Pa.) Jan. 4, 1780-Aug. 12, 1875; House 1833-35.

BIRCH, William Fred (R N.J.) Aug. 30, 1870-Jan. 25, 1946; House Nov. 5, 1918-19.

BIRD, John (D N.Y.) Nov. 22, 1768-Feb. 2, 1806; House 1799-July 25, 1801.

BIRD, John Taylor (D N.J.) Aug. 16, 1829-May 6, 1911; House 1869-73.

BIRD, Richard Ely (R Kan.) Nov. 4, 1878-Jan. 10, 1955; House 1921-23.

BIRDSALL, Ausburn (D N.Y.) —July 10, 1903; House 1847-49.

BIRDSALL, Benjamin Pixley (R Iowa) Oct. 26, 1858-May 26, 1917; House 1903-09.

BIRDSALL, James (D N.Y.) 1783-July 20, 1856; House 1815-17.

BIRDSALL, Samuel (D N.Y.) May 14, 1791-Feb. 8, 1872; House 1837-39.

BIRDSEYE, Victory (W N.Y.) Dec. 25, 1782-Sept. 16, 1853; House 1815-17, 1841-43.

BISBEE, Horatio, Jr. (R Fla.) May 1, 1839-March 27, 1916; House 1877-Feb. 20, 1879, Jan. 22-March 3, 1881, June 1, 1882-85.

BISHOP, Cecil William (Runt) (R Ill.) June 29, 1890; House 1941-55.

BISHOP, James (W N.J.) May 11, 1816-May 10, 1895; House 1855-57.

BISHOP, Phanuel (— Mass.) Sept. 3, 1739-Jan. 6, 1812; House 1799-1807.

BISHOP, Roswell Peter (R Mich.) Jan. 6, 1843-March 4, 1920; House 1895-1907.

BISHOP, William Darius (D Conn.) Sept. 14, 1827-Feb. 4, 1904; House 1857-59.

BISHOP, William Harrison (D Ill.) April 25, 1811-March 18, 1860; House 1849-55; Gov. 1857-60.

BIXLER, Harris Jacob (R Pa.) Sept. 16, 1870-March 29, 1941; House 1921-27.

BLACK, Edward Junius (father of George Robison Black) (D Ga.) Oct. 30, 1806-Sept. 1, 1846; House 1839-41 (States Rights Whig), Jan. 3, 1842-45 (Democrat).

BLACK, Eugene (D Texas) July 2, 1879; House 1915-29.

BLACK, Frank Swett (R N.Y.) March 8, 1853-March 22, 1913; House 1895-Jan. 7, 1897; Gov. 1897-99.

BLACK, George Robison (son of Edward Junius Black) (D Ga.) March 24, 1835-Nov. 3, 1886; House 1881-83.

BLACK, Henry (W Pa.) Feb. 25, 1783-Nov. 28, 1841; House June 28-Nov. 28, 1841.

BLACK, Hugo Lafayette (D Ala.) Feb. 27, 1886; Senate 1927-August 19, 1937; Assoc. Justice U.S. Supreme Court 1937- .

BLACK, James (D Pa.) March 6, 1793-June 21, 1872; House Dec. 5, 1836-37, 1843-47.

BLACK, James Augustus (Cal.D S.C.) 1793-April 3, 1848; House 1843-April 3, 1848.

BLACK, James Conquest Cross (D Ga.) May 9, 1842-Oct. 1, 1928; House 1893-March 4, 1895, Oct. 2, 1895-97.

BLACK, John (— Miss.) —-Aug. 29, 1854; Senate Nov. 12, 1832-March 3, 1833, Nov. 22, 1833-Jan. 22, 1838.

BLACK, John Charles (D Ill.) Jan. 27, 1839-Aug. 17, 1915; House 1893-Jan. 12, 1895.

BLACK, Loring Milton, Jr. (D N.Y.) May 17, 1886-May 21, 1956; House 1923-35.

BLACKBURN, Benjamin B. (R Ga.) Feb. 14, 1927; House 1967- .

BLACKBURN, Edmond Spencer (R N.C.) Sept. 22, 1868-March 10, 1912; House 1901-03, 1905-07.

BLACKBURN, Joseph Clay Stiles (D Ky.) Oct. 1, 1838-Sept 12, 1918; House 1875-85; Senate 1885-97, 1901-07.

BLACKBURN, Robert E. Lee (R Ky.) April 9, 1870-Sept. 20, 1935; House 1929-31.

BLACKBURN, William Jasper (R La.) July 24, 1820-Nov. 10, 1899; House July 18, 1868-69.

BLACKLEDGE, William (father of William Salter Blackledge) (D N.C.) —-Oct. 19, 1828; House 1803-09, 1811-13.

BLACKLEDGE, William Salter (son of William Blackledge) (D N.C.) 1793-March 21, 1857; House Feb. 7, 1821-23.

BLACKMAR, Esbon (W N.Y.) June 19, 1805-Nov. 19, 1857; House Dec. 4, 1848-49.

BLACKMON, Fred Leonard (D Ala.) Sept. 15, 1873-Feb. 8, 1921; House 1911-Feb. 8, 1921.

BLACKNEY, William Wallace (R Mich.) Aug. 28, 1876-March 14, 1963; House 1935-37, 1939-53.

BLACKWELL, Julius W. (VBD Tenn.) —-—; House 1839-41, 1843-45.

BLAINE, James Gillespie (R Maine) Jan. 31, 1830-Jan. 27, 1893; House 1863-July 10, 1876; Speaker 1869-75; Senate July 10, 1876-March 5, 1881; Secy. of State March 5-Dec. 12, 1881, March 7, 1889-June 4, 1892.

BLAINE, John James (R Wis.) May 4, 1875-April 18, 1934; Senate 1927-33; Gov. 1921-27.

BLAIR, Austin (R Mich.) Feb. 8, 1818-Aug. 6, 1894; House 1867-73; Gov. 1861-65.

BLAIR, Bernard (W N.Y.) May 24, 1801-May 7, 1880; House 1841-43.

BLAIR, Francis Preston, Jr. (D Mo.) Feb. 19, 1821-July 8, 1875; House 1857-59 (Free-Soiler) June 8-25, 1860, 1861-July 1862, 1863-June 10, 1864; Senate Jan. 20, 1871-73 (Democrat)

BLAIR, Henry William (R N.H.) Dec. 6, 1834-March 14, 1920; House 1875-79; Senate June 20, 1879-March 3, 1885, March 5, 1885-91; House 1893-95.

BLAIR, Jacob Beeson (U Va. and W.Va.) April 11, 1821-Feb. 12, 1901; House Dec. 2, 1861-63 (Va.), Dec. 7, 1863-65 (W.Va.).

BLAIR, James (D S.C.) 1790-April 1, 1834; House 1821-May 8, 1822 (Democrat), 1829-31 (Union Democrat), 1831-April 1, 1834 (Democrat).

BLAIR, James Gorrall (LR Mo.) Jan. 1, 1825-March 1, 1904; House 1871-73.

BLAIR, John (D Tenn.) Sept. 13, 1790-July 9, 1863; House 1823-35.

BLAIR, Samuel Steel (R Pa.) Dec. 5, 1821-Dec. 8, 1890; House 1859-63.

BLAISDELL, Daniel (F N.H.) Jan. 22, 1762-Jan. 10, 1833; House 1809-11.

BLAKE, Harrison Gray Otis (R Ohio) March 17, 1818-April 16, 1876; House Oct. 11, 1859-63.

BLAKE, John, Jr. (— N.Y.) Dec. 5, 1762-Jan. 13, 1826; House 1805-09.

BLAKE, John Lauris (R N.J.) March 25, 1831-Oct. 10, 1899; House 1879-81.

BLAKE, Thomas Holdsworth (AR Ind.) June 14, 1792-Nov. 28, 1849; House 1827-29.

BLAKENEY, Albert Alexander (R Md.) Sept. 28, 1850-Oct. 15, 1924; House 1901-03, 1921-23.

BLAKLEY, William A. (D Texas) Nov. 17, 1898; Senate Jan. 15-April 28, 1957, Jan. 3-June 14, 1961.

BLANCHARD, George Washington (R Wis.) Jan. 26, 1884-Oct. 2, 1964; House 1933-35.

BLANCHARD, John (W Pa.) Sept. 30, 1787-March 9, 1849; House 1845-49.

BLANCHARD, Newton Crain (D La.) Jan. 29, 1849-June 22, 1922; House 1881-March 12, 1894; Senate March 12, 1894-97; Gov. 1904-08.

BLAND, Oscar Edward (R Ind.) Nov. 21, 1877-Aug. 3, 1951; House 1917-23.

BLAND, Richard Parks (D Mo.) Aug. 19, 1835-June 15, 1899; House 1873-95, 1897-June 15, 1899.

BLAND, Schuyler Otis (D Va.) May 4, 1872-Feb. 16, 1950; House July 2, 1918-Feb. 16, 1950.

BLAND, Theodorick (— Va.) March 21, 1742-June 1, 1790; House 1789-June 1, 1790; Cont. Cong. 1780-83.

BLAND, William Thomas (grandson of John George Jackson and cousin of James Monroe Jackson) (D Mo.) Jan. 21, 1861-Jan. 15, 1928; House 1919-21.

BLANTON, Leonard Ray (D Tenn.) April 10, 1930; House 1967- .

BLANTON, Thomas Lindsay (D Texas) Oct. 25, 1872-Aug. 11, 1957; House 1917-29, May 20, 1930-37.

BLATNIK, John Anton (D Minn.) Aug. 17, 1911; House 1947- .

BLEAKLEY, Orrin Dubbs (R Pa.) May 15, 1854-Dec. 3, 1927; House March 4-April 3, 1917.

BLEASE, Coleman Livingston (D S.C.) Oct. 8, 1868-Jan. 19, 1942; Senate 1925-31; Gov. 1911-15.

BLEDSOE, Jesse (uncle of Robert Emmett Bledsoe Baylor) (— Ky.) April 6, 1776-June 25, 1836; Senate 1813-Dec. 24, 1814.

BLEECKER, Harmanus (F N.Y.) Oct. 9, 1779-July 19, 1849; House 1811-13.

BLISS, Aaron Thomas (R Mich.) May 22, 1837-Sept. 16, 1906; House 1889-91; Gov. 1900-04.

BLISS, Archibald Meserole (D N.Y.) Jan. 25, 1838-March 19, 1923; House 1875-83, 1885-89.

BLISS, George (D Ohio) Jan. 1, 1813-Oct. 24, 1868; House 1853-55, 1863-65.

BLISS, Philemon (R Ohio) July 28, 1813-Aug. 25, 1889; House 1855-59.

BLITCH, Iris Faircloth (D Ga.) April 25, 1912; House 1955-63.

BLODGETT, Rufus (D N.J.) Oct. 9, 1834-Oct. 3, 1910; Senate 1887-93.

BLOODWORTH, Timothy (— N.C.) 1736-Aug. 24, 1814; House April 6, 1790-91; Senate 1795-1801; Cont. Cong 1786-Aug. 13, 1787.

BLOOM, Isaac (— N.Y.) 1716-April 26, 1803; House March 4-April 26, 1803.

BLOOM, Sol (D N.Y.) March 9, 1870-March 7, 1949; House 1923-March 7, 1949.

BLOOMFIELD, Joseph (D N.J.) Oct. 5, 1753-Oct. 3, 1823; House 1817-21; Gov. 1801-12.

BLOUNT, James Henderson (D Ga.) Sept. 12, 1837-March 8, 1903; House 1873-93.

BLOUNT, Thomas (brother of William Blount and uncle of William Grainger Blount) (D N.C.) May 10, 1759-Feb. 7, 1812; House 1793-99, 1805-09, 1811-Feb. 7, 1812.

BLOUNT, William (father of William Grainger Blount and brother of Thomas Blount) (— Tenn.) March 26, 1749-March 21, 1800; Senate Aug. 2, 1796-July 8, 1797; Cont. Cong. (Va.) 1782-83, 1786-87.

BLOUNT, William Grainger (son of William Blount and nephew of Thomas Blount) (D Tenn.) 1784-May 21, 1827; House Dec. 8, 1815-19.

BLOW, Henry Taylor (R Mo.) July 15, 1817-Sept. 11, 1875; House 1863-67.

BLUE, Richard Whiting (R Kan.) Sept. 8, 1841-Jan. 28, 1907; House 1895-97.

BOARDMAN, Elijah (father of William Whiting Boardman) (D Conn.) March 7, 1760-Oct. 8, 1823; Senate 1821-Oct. 8, 1823.

BOARDMAN, William Whiting (son of Elijah Boardman) (W Conn.) Oct. 10, 1794-Aug. 27, 1871; House Dec. 7, 1840-43.

BOARMAN, Alexander (Aleck) (L La.) Dec. 10, 1839-Aug. 30, 1916; House Dec. 3, 1872-73.

BOATNER, Charles Jahleal (D La.) Jan. 23, 1849-March 21, 1903; House 1889-95, June 10, 1896-97.

BOCKEE, Abraham (JD N.Y.) Feb. 3, 1784-June 1, 1865; House 1829-31, 1833-37.

BOCOCK, Thomas Stanhope (D Va.) May 18, 1815-Aug. 5, 1891; House 1847-61.

BODEN, Andrew (— Pa.) —Dec. 20, 1835; House 1817-21.

BODINE, Robert Nall (D Mo.) Dec. 17, 1837-March 16, 1914; House 1897-99.

BODLE, Charles (— N.Y.) 1787-Oct. 31, 1835; House 1833-35.

BOEHNE, John William (father of John William Boehne, Jr.) (D Ind.) Oct. 28, 1856-Dec. 27, 1946; House 1909-13.

BOEHNE, John William, Jr. (son of John William Boehne) (D Ind.) March 2, 1895; House 1931-43.

BOEN, Haldor Erickson (PP Minn.) Jan. 2, 1851-July 23, 1912; House 1893-95.

BOGGS, James Caleb (R Del.) May 15, 1909; House 1947-53; Senate 1961- ; Gov. 1953-60.

BOGGS, Thomas Hale (D La.) Feb. 15, 1914; House 1941-43, 1947- .

BOGY, Lewis Vital (D Mo.) April 9, 1813-Sept. 20, 1877; Senate 1873-Sept. 20, 1877.

BOHN, Frank Probasco (R Mich.) July 14, 1866-June 1, 1944; House 1927-33.

BOIES, William Dayton (R Iowa) Jan. 3, 1857-May 31, 1932; House 1919-29.

BOILEAU, Gerald John (Pro. Wis.) Jan. 15, 1900; House 1931-39; 1931-35 (Republican), 1935-39 (Progressive).

BOKEE, David Alexander (W N.Y.) Oct. 6, 1805-March 15, 1860; House 1849-51.

BOLAND, Edward Patrick (D Mass.) Oct. 1, 1911; House 1953- .

BOLAND, Patrick Joseph (husband of Veronica G. Boland) (D Pa.) Jan. 6, 1880-May 18, 1942; House 1931-May 18, 1942.

BOLAND, Veronica Grace (widow of Patrick J. Boland) (D Pa.) March 18, 1899; House Nov. 19, 1942-43.

BOLES, Thomas (R Ark.) July 16, 1837-March 13, 1905; House June 22, 1868-71, Feb. 9, 1872-73.

BOLLES, Stephen (R Wis.) June 25, 1866-July 8, 1941; House 1939-July 8, 1941.

BOLLING, Richard Walker (D Mo.) May 17, 1916; House 1949- .

BOLTON, Chester Castle (husband of Frances P. Bolton and father of Oliver P. Bolton) (R Ohio) Sept. 5, 1882-Oct. 29, 1939; House 1929-37, Jan. 3-Oct. 29, 1939.

BOLTON, Frances Payne (widow of Chester C. Bolton, grand-daughter of Henry B. Payne and mother of Oliver P. Bolton) (R Ohio) March 29, 1885; House 1940-69.

BOLTON, Oliver Payne (son of Chester Castle Bolton and Frances Payne Bolton and great-grandson of Henry B. Payne) (R Ohio) Feb. 22, 1917; House 1953-57, 1963-65.

BOLTON, William P. (D Md.) July 2, 1885-Nov. 22, 1964; House 1949-51.

BOND, Charles Grosvenor (nephew of Charles Henry Grosvenor) (R N.Y.) May 29, 1877; House 1921-23.

BOND, Shadrack (D Ill.) Nov. 24, 1773-April 12, 1832; House (Terr. Del.) Oct. 10, 1812-Oct. 1814; Gov. 1818-22.

BOND, William Key (W Ohio) Oct. 2, 1792-Feb. 17, 1864; House 1835-41.

BONE, Homer Truett (D Wash.) Jan. 25, 1883-March 11, 1970; Senate 1933-Nov. 13, 1944.

BONHAM, Milledge Luke (SRD S.C.) Dec. 25, 1813-Aug. 27, 1890; House 1857-Dec. 21, 1860; Gov. 1862-64.

BONIN, Edward John (R Pa.) Dec. 23, 1904; House 1953-55.

BONNER, Herbert Covington (D N.C.) May 16, 1891-Nov. 7, 1965; House Nov. 5, 1940-Nov. 7, 1965.

BONYNGE, Robert William (R Colo.) Sept. 8, 1863-Sept. 22, 1939; House Feb. 16, 1904-09.

BOODY, Azariah (W N.Y.) April 21, 1815-Nov. 18, 1885; House March 4-October 1853.

BOODY, David Augustus (D N.Y.) Aug. 13, 1837-Jan. 20, 1930; House March 4-Oct. 13, 1891.

BOOHER, Charles Ferris (D Mo.) Jan. 31, 1848-Jan. 21, 1921; House Feb. 19-March 3, 1889, 1907-Jan. 21, 1921.

BOOKER, George William (C Va.) Dec. 5, 1821-June 4, 1883; House Jan. 26, 1870-71.

BOON, Ratliff (JD Ind.) Jan. 18, 1781-Nov. 20, 1844; House 1825-27, 1829-39; Gov. Sept. 12-Dec. 5, 1822.

BOONE, Andrew Richmond (D Ky.) April 4, 1831-Jan. 26, 1886; House 1875-79.

BOOTH, Newton (A-M Calif.) Dec. 25, 1825-July 14, 1892; Senate 1875-81; Gov. 1871-74.

BOOTH, Walter (F-S Conn.) Dec. 5, 1821-June 4, 1883; House 1849-51.

BOOTHMAN, Melvin Morella (R Ohio) Oct. 16, 1846-March 5, 1904; House 1887-91.

BOOZE, William Samuel (R Md.) Jan. 9, 1862-Dec. 6, 1933; House 1897-99.

BORAH, William Edgar (R Idaho) June 29, 1865-Jan. 19, 1940; Senate 1907-Jan. 19, 1940.

BORCHERS, Charles Martin (D Ill.) Nov. 18, 1869-Dec. 2, 1946; House 1913-15.

BORDEN, Nathaniel Briggs (W Mass.) April 15, 1801-April 10, 1865; House 1835-39 (Van Buren Democrat), 1841-43 (Whig).

BOREING, Vincent (R Ky.) Nov. 24, 1839-Sept. 16, 1903; House 1899-Sept. 16, 1903.

BOREMAN, Arthur Inghram (R W.Va.) July 24, 1823-April 19, 1896; Senate 1869-75; Gov. 1863-69.

BOREN, Lyle H. (D Okla.) May 11, 1909; House 1937-47.

BORLAND, Charles, Jr. (— N.Y.) June 29, 1786-Feb. 23, 1852; House Nov. 8, 1821-23.

BORLAND, Solon (D Ark.) Sept. 21, 1808-Jan. 1, 1864; Senate March 30, 1848-April 3, 1853.

BORLAND, William Patterson (D Mo.) Oct. 14, 1867-Feb. 20, 1919; House 1909-Feb. 20, 1919.

BORST, Peter I. (JD N.Y.) April 24, 1797-Nov. 14, 1848; House 1829-31.

BOSCH, Albert Henry (R N.Y.) Oct. 30, 1908; House 1953-Dec. 31, 1960.

BOSONE, Reva Zilpha Beck (D Utah) —-—; House 1949-53.

BOSS, John Linscom, Jr. (— R.I.) Sept. 7, 1780-Aug. 1, 1819; House 1815-19.

BOSSIER, Pierre Evariste John Baptiste (Cal. D La.) March 22, 1797-April 24, 1844; House 1843-April 24, 1844.

BOTELER, Alexander Robinson (AP Va.) May 16, 1815-May 8, 1892; House 1859-61.

BOTKIN, Jeremiah Dunham (Fus. Kan.) April 24, 1849-Dec. 29, 1921; House 1897-99.

BOTTS, John Minor (HCW Va.) Sept. 16, 1802-Jan. 8, 1869; House 1839-43, 1847-49.

BOTTUM, Joe H. (R S.D.) Aug. 7, 1903; Senate July 11, 1962-63.

BOUCK, Gabriel (nephew of Joseph Bouck) (D Wis.) Dec. 16, 1828-Feb. 21, 1904; House 1877-81.

BOUCK, Joseph (uncle of Gabriel Bouck) (D N.Y.) July 22, 1788-March 30, 1858; House 1831-33.

BOUDE, Thomas (F Pa.) May 17, 1752-Oct. 24, 1822; House 1801-03.

BOUDINOT, Elias (— N.J.) May 2, 1740-Oct. 24, 1821; House 1789-95; Cont. Cong. 1777-78, 1781-83.

BOULDIN, James Wood (brother of Thomas Tyler Bouldin) (JD Va.) 1792-March 30, 1854; House March 15, 1834-39.

BOULDIN, Thomas Tyler (brother of James Wood Bouldin) (D Va.) 1781-Feb. 11, 1834; House 1829-33, Aug. 26, 1833-Feb. 11, 1834.

BOULIGNY, Charles Joseph Dominique (uncle of John Edward Bouligny) (— La.) Aug. 22, 1773-March 6, 1833; Senate Nov. 19, 1824-29.

BOULIGNY, John Edward (nephew of Charles Joseph Dominique Bouligny) (AP La.) Feb. 5, 1824-Feb. 20, 1864; House 1859-61.

BOUND, Franklin (R Pa.) April 9, 1829-Aug. 8, 1910; House 1885-89.

BOURN, Benjamin (F R.I.) Sept. 9, 1755-Sept. 17, 1808; House Aug. 31, 1790-96.

BOURNE, Jonathan, Jr. (R Ore.) Feb. 23, 1855-Sept. 1, 1940; Senate 1907-13.

BOURNE, Shearjashub (— Mass.) June 14, 1746-March 11, 1806; House 1791-95.

BOUTELL, Henry Sherman (R Ill.) March 14, 1856-March 11, 1926; House Nov. 23, 1897-1911.

BOUTELLE, Charles Addison (R Maine) Feb. 9, 1839-May 21, 1901; House 1883-1901.

BOUTWELL, George Sewel (R Mass.) Jan. 28, 1818-Feb. 27, 1905; House 1863-March 12, 1869; Senate March 17, 1873-77; Gov. 1851-52; Secy. of the Treasury March 12, 1869-March 17, 1873.

BOVEE, Matthias Jacob (JD N.Y.) July 24, 1793-Sept. 12, 1872; House 1835-37.

BOW, Frank Townsend (R Ohio) Feb. 20, 1901; House 1951- .

BOWDEN, George Edwin (nephew of Lemuel Jackson Bowden) (R Va.) July 6, 1852-Jan. 22, 1908; House 1887-91.

BOWDEN, Lemuel Jackson (uncle of George Edwin Bowden) (R Va.) Jan. 16, 1815-Jan. 2, 1864; Senate 1863-Jan. 2, 1864.

BOWDLE, Stanley Eyre (D Ohio) Sept. 4, 1868-April 6, 1919; House 1913-15.

BOWDON, Franklin Welsh (uncle of Sydney Johnston Bowie) (D Ala.) Feb. 17, 1817-June 8, 1857; House Dec. 7, 1846-51.

BOWEN, Christopher Columbus (R S.C.) Jan. 5, 1832-June 23, 1880; House July 20, 1868-71.

BOWEN, Henry (son of Rees Tate Bowen, nephew of John Warfield Johnston and cousin of William Bowen Campbell) (R Va.) Dec. 26, 1841-April 29, 1915; House 1883-85 (Readjuster), 1887-89 (Republican).

BOWEN, John Henry (D Tenn.) Sept. 1780-Sept. 25, 1822; House 1813-15.

BOWEN, Rees Tate (father of Henry Bowen) (C Va.) Jan. 10, 1809-Aug. 29, 1879; House 1873-75.

BOWEN, Thomas Mead (R Colo.) Oct. 26, 1835-Dec. 30, 1906; Senate 1883-89; Gov. (Idaho Terr.) 1871.

BOWER, Gustavus Miller (D Va.) Dec. 12, 1790-Nov. 17, 1864; House 1843-45.

BOWER, William Horton (D N.C.) June 6, 1850-May 11, 1910; House 1893-95.

BOWERS, Eaton Jackson (D Miss.) June 17, 1865-Oct. 26, 1939; House 1903-11.

BOWERS, George Meade (R W.Va.) Sept. 13, 1863-Dec. 7, 1925; House May 9, 1916-23.

BOWERS, John Myer (— N.Y.) Sept. 25, 1772-Feb. 24, 1846; House May 26-Dec. 20, 1813.

BOWERS, William Wallace (R Calif.) Oct. 20, 1834-May 2, 1917; House 1891-97.

BOWERSOCK, Justin De Witt (R Kan.) Sept. 19, 1842-Oct. 27, 1922; House 1899-1907.

BOWIE, Richard Johns (W Md.) June 23, 1807-March 12, 1888; House 1849-53.

BOWIE, Sydney Johnston (nephew of Franklin Welsh Bowdon) (D Ala.) July 26, 1865-May 7, 1928; House 1901-07.

BOWIE, Thomas Fielder (grandnephew of Walter Bowie and brother-in-law of Reverdy Johnson) (D Md.) April 7, 1808-Oct. 30, 1869; House 1855-59.

BOWIE, Walter (granduncle of Thomas Fielder Bowie) (D Md.) 1748-Nov. 9, 1810; House March 24, 1802-05.

BOWLER, James Bernard (D Ill.) Feb. 5, 1875-July 18, 1957; House July 7, 1953-July 18, 1957.

BOWLES, Chester Bliss (D Conn.) April 5, 1901; House 1959-61; Gov. 1949-51.

BOWLES, Henry Leland (R Mass.) Jan. 6, 1866-May 17, 1932; House Sept. 19, 1925-29.

BOWLIN James Butler (D Mo.) Jan. 16, 1804-July 19, 1874; House 1843-51.

BOWLING, William Bismarck (D Ala.) Sept. 24, 1870-Dec. 27, 1946; House Dec. 14, 1920-Aug. 16, 1928.

BOWMAN, Charles Calvin (R Pa.) Nov. 14, 1852-July 3, 1941; House 1911-Dec. 12, 1912.

BOWMAN, Frank Llewellyn (R W.Va.) Jan. 21, 1879-Sept. 15, 1936; House 1925-33.

BOWMAN, Selwyn Zadock (R Mass.) May 11, 1840-Sept. 30, 1928; House 1879-83.

BOWMAN, Thomas (D Iowa) May 25, 1848-Dec. 1, 1917; House 1891-93.

BOWNE, Obadiah (W N.Y.) May 19, 1822-April 27, 1874; House 1851-53.

BOWNE, Samuel Smith (VBD N.Y.) April 11, 1800-July 9, 1865; House 1841-43.

BOWRING, Eva Kelly (R Neb.) Jan. 9, 1892; Senate April 16-Nov. 7, 1954.

BOX, John Calvin (D Texas) March 28, 1871-May 17, 1941; House 1919-31.

BOYCE, William Henry (D Del.) Nov. 28, 1855-Feb. 6, 1942; House 1923-25.

BOYCE, William Waters (SRD S.C.) Oct. 24, 1818-Feb. 3, 1890; House 1853-Dec. 21, 1860.

BOYD, Adam (D N.J.) March 21, 1746-Aug. 15, 1835; House 1803-05, March 8, 1808-13.

BOYD, Alexander (W N.Y.) Sept. 14, 1764-April 8, 1857; House 1813-15.

BOYD, John Frank (R Neb.) Aug. 8, 1853-May 28, 1945; House 1907-09.

BOYD, John Huggins (W N.Y.) July 31, 1799-July 2, 1868; House 1851-53.

BOYD, Linn (D Ky.) Nov. 22, 1800-Dec. 17, 1859; House 1835-37, 1839-55; Speaker 1851-55.

BOYD, Sempronius Hamilton (R Mo.) May 28, 1828-June 22, 1894; House 1863-65 (Emancipationist), 1869-71 (Republican).

BOYD, Thomas Alexander (R III.) June 25, 1830-May 28, 1897; House 1877-81.

BOYDEN, Nathaniel (R N.C.) Aug. 16, 1796-Nov. 20, 1873; House 1847-49 (Whig), July 13, 1868-69 (Republican).

BOYER, Benjamin Markley (D Pa.) Jan. 22, 1823-Aug. 16, 1887; House 1865-69.

BOYER, Lewis Leonard (D III.) May 19, 1886-March 12, 1944; House 1937-39.

BOYKIN, Frank William (D Ala.) Feb. 21, 1885-March 12, 1969; House July 30, 1935-63.

BOYLAN, John Joseph (D N.Y.) Sept. 20, 1878-Oct. 5, 1938; House March 4, 1923-Oct. 5, 1938.

BOYLE, Charles Augustus (D III.) Aug. 13, 1907-Nov. 4, 1959; House 1955-Nov. 4, 1959.

BOYLE, Charles Edmund (D Pa.) Feb. 4, 1836-Dec. 15, 1888; House 1883-87.

BOYLE, John (D Ky.) Oct. 28, 1774-Feb. 28, 1834; House 1803-09.

BRABSON, Reese Bowen (uncle of Charles Keith Bell) (D Tenn.) Sept. 16, 1817-Aug. 16, 1863; House 1859-61.

BRACE, Jonathan (F Conn.) Nov. 12, 1754-Aug. 26, 1837; House Dec. 3, 1798-1800.

BRACKENRIDGE, Henry Marie (W Pa.) May 11, 1786-Jan. 18, 1871; House Oct. 13, 1840-41.

BRADBURY, George (F Mass.) Oct. 10, 1770-Nov. 7, 1823; House 1813-17.

BRADBURY, James Ware (D Maine) June 10, 1802-Jan. 7, 1901; Senate 1847-53.

BRADBURY, Theophilus (F Mass.) Nov. 13, 1739-Sept. 6, 1803; House 1795-July 24, 1797.

BRADEMAS, John (D Ind.) March 2, 1927; House 1959- .

BRADFORD, Allen Alexander (R Colo.) July 23, 1815-March 12, 1888; House (Terr. Del.) 1865-67, 1869-71.

BRADFORD, Taul (D Ala.) Jan. 20, 1835-Oct. 28, 1883; House 1875-77.

BRADFORD, William (— R.I.) Nov. 4, 1729-July 6, 1808; Senate 1793-Oct. 1797; President pro tempore 1797.

BRADLEY, Edward (D Mich.) April 1808-Aug. 5, 1847; House March 4-Aug. 5, 1847.

BRADLEY, Frederick Van Ness (R Mich.) April 12, 1898-May 24, 1947; House 1939-May 24, 1947.

BRADLEY, Michael Joseph (D Pa.) May 24, 1897; House 1937-47.

BRADLEY, Nathan Ball (R Mich.) May 28, 1831-Nov. 8, 1906; House 1873-77.

BRADLEY, Stephen Row (father of William Czar Bradley) (D Vt.) Feb. 20, 1754-Dec. 9, 1830; Senate Oct. 17, 1791-95, Oct. 15, 1801-13; President pro tempore 1802-03, 1808.

BRADLEY, Thomas Joseph (D N.Y.) Jan. 2, 1870-April 1, 1901; House 1897-1901.

BRADLEY, Thomas Wilson (R N.Y.) April 6, 1844-May 30, 1920; House 1903-13.

BRADLEY, William Czar (son of Stephen Row Bradley) (D Vt.) March 23, 1782-March 3, 1867; House 1813-15 (War Democrat), 1823-27 (Democrat).

BRADLEY, William O'Connell (R Ky.) March 18, 1847-May 23, 1914; Senate 1909-May 23, 1914; Gov. 1895-99.

BRADLEY, Willis Winter (R Calif.) June 28, 1884-Aug. 27, 1954; House 1947-49.

BRADSHAW, Samuel Carey (W Pa.) June 10, 1809-June 9, 1872; House 1855-57.

BRADY, James Dennis (R Va.) April 3, 1843-Nov. 30, 1900; House 1885-87.

BRADY, James Henry (R Idaho) June 12, 1862-Jan. 13, 1918; Senate Feb. 6, 1913-Jan. 13, 1918; Gov. 1909-11.

BRADY, Jasper Ewing (W Pa.) March 4, 1797-Jan. 26, 1871; House 1847-49.

BRAGG, Edward Stuyvesant (D Wis.) Feb. 20, 1827-June 20, 1912; House 1877-83, 1885-87.

BRAGG, John (SRD Ala.) Jan. 14, 1806-Aug. 10, 1878; House 1851-53.

BRAGG, Thomas (D N.C.) Nov. 10, 1810-Jan. 21, 1872; Senate 1859-March 6, 1861; Gov. 1855-59.

BRAINERD, Lawrence (F-S Vt.) March 16, 1794-May 9, 1870; Senate Oct. 14, 1854-55.

BRAINERD, Samuel Myron (R Pa.) Nov. 13, 1842-Nov. 21, 1898; House 1883-85.

BRAMBLETT, Ernest King (R Calif.) April 25, 1901; House 1947-55.

BRANCH, John (uncle of Lawrence O'Bryan Branch) (D N.C.) Nov. 4, 1782-Jan. 3, 1863; Senate 1823-March 9, 1829; House May 12, 1831-33; Gov. (N.C.) 1817-20; Gov. (Fla.) 1844-45; Secy. of the Navy 1829-31.

BRANCH, Lawrence O'Bryan (father of William Augustus Blount Branch and nephew of John Branch) (D N.C.) Nov. 28, 1820-Sept. 17, 1862; House 1855-61.

BRANCH, William Augustus Blount (son of Lawrence O'Bryan Branch) (D N.C.) Feb. 26, 1847-Nov. 18, 1910; House 1891-95.

BRAND, Charles (R Ohio) Nov. 1, 1871-May 23, 1966; House 1923-33.

BRAND, Charles Hillyer (D Ga.) April 20, 1861-May 17, 1933; House 1917-May 17, 1933.

BRANDEGEE, Augustus (father of Frank Bosworth Brandegee) (R Conn.) July 15, 1828-Nov. 10, 1904; House 1863-67.

BRANDEGEE, Frank Bosworth (son of Augustus Brandegee) (R Conn.) July 8, 1864-Oct. 14, 1924; House Nov. 5, 1902-May 10, 1905; Senate May 10, 1905-Oct. 14, 1904.

BRANTLEY, William Gordon (D Ga.) Sept. 18, 1860-Sept. 11, 1934; House 1897-1913.

BRASCO, Frank J. (D N.Y.) Oct. 15, 1932; House 1967- .

BRATTON, John (D S.C.) March 7, 1831-Jan. 12, 1898; House Dec. 8, 1884-85.

BRATTON, Robert Franklin (D Md.) May 13, 1845-May 10, 1894; House 1893-May 10, 1894.

BRATTON, Sam Gilbert (D N.M.) Aug. 19, 1888-Sept. 22, 1963; Senate 1925-June 24, 1933.

BRAWLEY, William Huggins (cousin of John James Hemphill and great-uncle of Robert Witherspoon Hemphill) (D S.C.) May 13, 1841-Nov. 15, 1916; House 1891 Feb. 12, 1894.

BRAXTON, Elliott Muse (D Va.) Oct. 8, 1823-Oct. 2, 1891; House 1871-73.

BRAY, William Gilmer (R Ind.) April 17, 1903; House 1951- .

BRAYTON, William Daniel (R R.I.) Nov. 6, 1815-June 30, 1887; House 1857-61.

BREAZEALE, Phanor (D La.) Dec. 29, 1858-April 29, 1934; House 1899-1905.

BRECK, Daniel (brother of Samuel Breck) (W Ky.) Feb. 12, 1788-Feb. 4, 1871; House 1849-51.

BRECK, Samuel (brother of Daniel Breck) (F Pa.) July 17, 1771-Aug. 31, 1862; House 1823-25.

BRECKINRIDGE, Clifton Rodes (son of John Cabell Breckinridge and great-grandson of John Breckinridge) (D Ark.) Nov. 22, 1846-Dec. 3, 1932; House 1883-Sept. 5, 1890, Nov. 4, 1890-Aug. 14, 1894.

BRECKINRIDGE, James (brother of John Breckinridge) (F Va.) March 7, 1763-May 13, 1833; House 1809-17.

BRECKINRIDGE, James Douglas (— Ky.) —-May 6, 1849; House Nov. 21, 1821-23.

BRECKINRIDGE, John (brother of James Breckinridge, grandfather of John Cabell Breckinridge and William Campbell Preston Breckinridge and great-grandfather of Clifton Rodes Breckinridge) (D Ky.) Dec. 2, 1760-Dec. 14, 1806; Senate 1801-Aug. 7, 1805; Atty. Gen. of the U.S. 1805-06.

BRECKINRIDGE, John Cabell (grandson of John Breckinridge, father of Clifton Rodes Breckinridge and cousin of Henry Donnel Foster) (D Ky.) Jan. 21, 1821-May 17, 1875; House 1851-55; Senate March 4-Dec. 4, 1861; Vice Pres. 1857-61.

BRECKINRIDGE, William Campbell Preston (grandson of John Breckinridge and uncle of Levin Irving Handy) (D Ky.) Aug. 28, 1837-Nov. 18, 1904; House 1885-95.

BREEDING, James Floyd (D Kan.) Sept. 28, 1901; House 1957-63.

BREEN, Edward F. (D Ohio) June 10, 1908; House 1949-Oct. 1, 1951.

BREESE, Sidney (D Ill.) July 15, 1800-June 28, 1878; Senate 1843-49.

BREHM, Walter Ellsworth (R Ohio) May 25, 1892; House 1943-53.

BREITUNG, Edward (R Mich.) Nov. 10, 1831-March 3, 1887; House 1883-85.

BREMNER, Robert Gunn (D N.J.) Dec. 17, 1874-Feb. 5, 1914; House 1913-Feb. 5, 1914.

BRENGLE, Francis (W Md.) Nov. 26, 1807-Dec. 10, 1846; House 1843-45.

BRENNAN, Martin Adlai (D Ill.) Sept. 21, 1879-July 4, 1941; House 1933-37.

BRENNAN, Vincent Morrison (R Mich.) April 22, 1890-Feb. 4, 1959; House 1921-23.

BRENNER, John Lewis (D Ohio) Feb. 2, 1832-Nov. 1, 1906; House 1897-1901.

BRENT, Richard (uncle of William Leigh Brent and nephew of Daniel Carroll) (— Va.) 1757-Dec. 30, 1814; House 1795-99, 1801-03; Senate 1809-Dec. 30, 1814.

BRENT, William Leigh (nephew of Richard Brent) (— La.) Feb. 20, 1784-July 7, 1848; House 1823-29.

BRENTANO, Lorenzo (R Ill.) Nov. 4, 1813-Sept. 18, 1891; House 1877-79.

BRENTON, Samuel (R Ind.) Nov. 22, 1810-March 29, 1857; House 1851-53 (Whig), 1855-March 29, 1857 (Republican).

BRENTS, Thomas Hurley (R Wash.) Dec. 24, 1840-Oct. 23, 1916; House (Terr. Del.) 1879-85.

BRETZ, John Lewis (D Ind.) Sept. 21, 1852-Dec. 25, 1920; House 1891-95.

BREVARD, Joseph (W S.C.) July 19, 1766-Oct. 11, 1821; House 1819-21.

BREWER, Francis Beattie (R N.Y.) Oct. 8, 1820-July 29, 1892; House 1883-85.

BREWER, John Hart (R N.J.) March 29, 1844-Dec. 21, 1900; House 1881-85.

BREWER, Mark Spencer (R Mich.) Oct. 22, 1837-March 18, 1901; House 1877-81; 1887-91.

BREWER, Willis (D Ala.) March 15, 1844-Oct. 30, 1912; House 1897-1901.

BREWSTER, Daniel Baugh (D Md.) Nov. 23, 1923; House 1959-63; Senate 1963-69.

BREWSTER, David P. (D N.Y.) June 15, 1801-Feb. 20, 1876; House 1839-43.

BREWSTER, Henry Colvin (R N.Y.) Sept. 7, 1845-Jan. 29, 1928; House 1895-99.

BREWSTER, Ralph Owen (R Maine) Feb. 22, 1888-Dec. 25, 1961; House 1935-41; Senate 1941-Dec. 31, 1952; Gov. 1925-29.

BRICE, Calvin Stewart (D Ohio) Sept. 17, 1845-Dec. 15, 1898; Senate 1891-97; Chrmn., Dem. Natl. Comm. 1889.

BRICK, Abraham Lincoln (R Ind.) May 27, 1860-April 7, 1908; House 1899-April 7, 1908.

BRICKER, John William (R Ohio) Sept. 6, 1893; Senate 1947-59; Gov. 1939-45.

BRICKNER, George H. (D Wis.) Jan. 21, 1834-Aug. 12, 1904; House 1889-95.

BRIDGES, George Washington (U Tenn.) Oct. 9, 1825-March 16, 1873; House Feb. 25-March 3, 1863.

BRIDGES, Henry Styles (R N.H.) Sept. 9, 1898-Nov. 26, 1961; Senate 1937-Nov. 26, 1961; Gov. 1934-36.

BRIDGES, Samuel Augustus (D Pa.) Jan. 27, 1802-Jan. 14, 1884; House March 6, 1848-49, 1853-55, 1877-79.

BRIGGS, Clay Stone (D Texas) Jan. 8, 1876-April 29, 1933; House 1919-April 29, 1933.

BRIGGS, Frank Obadiah (son of James Frankland Briggs) (R N.J.) Aug. 12, 1851-May 8, 1913; Senate 1907-13.

BRIGGS, Frank Parks (D Mo.) Feb. 25, 1894; Senate Jan. 18, 1945-47.

BRIGGS, George (AP N.Y.) May 6, 1805-June 1, 1869; House 1849-53 (Whig), 1859-61 (American Party).

BRIGGS, George Nixon (W Mass.) April 12, 1796-Sept. 11, 1861; House 1831-43; Gov. 1844-51.

BRIGGS, James Frankland (father of Frank Obadiah Briggs) (R N.H.) Oct. 23, 1827-Jan. 21, 1905; House 1877-83.

BRIGHAM, Elbert Sidney (R Vt.) Oct. 19, 1877-July 5, 1962; House 1925-31.

BRIGHAM, Elijah (F Mass.) July 7, 1751-Feb. 22, 1816; House 1811-Feb. 22, 1816.

BRIGHAM, Lewis Alexander (R N.J.) Jan. 2, 1831-Feb. 19, 1885; House 1879-81.

BRIGHT, Jesse David (D Ind.) Dec. 18, 1812-May 20, 1875; Senate 1845-Feb. 5, 1862; President pro tempore 1854, 1856, 1860.

BRIGHT, John Morgan (D Tenn.) Jan. 20, 1817-Oct. 3, 1911; House 1871-81.

BRINKERHOFF, Henry Roelif (cousin of Jacob Brinkerhoff) (D Ohio) Sept. 23, 1787-April 30, 1844; House 1843-April 30, 1844.

BRINKERHOFF, Jacob (cousin of Henry Roelif Brinkerhoff) (D Ohio) Aug. 31, 1810-July 19, 1880; House 1843-47.

BRINKLEY, Jack Thomas (D Ga.) Dec. 22, 1930; House 1967- .

BRINSON, Samuel Mitchell (D N.C.) March 20, 1870-April 13, 1922; House 1919-April 13, 1922.

BRISBIN, John (W Pa.) July 13, 1818-Feb. 3, 1880; House Jan. 13-March 3, 1851.

BRISTOW, Francis Marion (W Ky.) Aug. 11, 1804-June 10, 1864; House Dec. 4, 1854-55, 1859-61.

BRISTOW, Henry (R N.Y.) June 5, 1840-Oct. 11, 1906; House 1901-03.

BRISTOW, Joseph Little (R Kan.) July 22, 1861-July 14, 1944; Senate 1909-15.

BRITT, James Jefferson (R N.C.) March 4, 1861-Dec. 26, 1939; House 1915-17, March 1-3, 1919.

BRITTEN, Frederick Albert (R Ill.) Nov. 18, 1871-May 4, 1946; House 1913-35.

BROADHEAD, James Overton (D Mo.) May 29, 1819-Aug. 7, 1898; House 1883-85.

BROCK, Lawrence (D Neb.) Aug. 16, 1906-Aug. 28, 1968; House 1959-61.

BROCK, William Emerson (grandfather of William Emerson Brock, III) (D Tenn.) March 14, 1872-Aug. 5, 1950; Senate Sept. 2, 1929-31.

BROCK, William Emerson, III (grandson of William Emerson Brock) (R Tenn.) Nov. 23, 1930; House 1963-71; Senate 1971- .

BROCKENBROUGH, William Henry (D Fla.) Feb. 23, 1812-Jan. 28, 1850; House Jan. 24, 1846-47.

BROCKSON, Franklin (D Del.) Aug. 6, 1865-March 16, 1942; House 1913-15.

BROCKWAY, John Hall (W Conn.) Jan. 31, 1801-July 29, 1870; House 1839-43.

BRODBECK, Andrew R. (D Pa.) April 11, 1860-Feb. 27, 1937; House 1913-15, 1917-19.

BRODERICK, Case (cousin of David Colbreth Broderick and Andrew Kennedy) (R Kan.) Sept. 23, 1839-April 1, 1920; House 1891-99.

BRODERICK, David Colbreth (cousin of Andrew Kennedy and Case Broderick) (D Calif.) Feb. 4, 1820-Sept. 16, 1859; Senate 1857-Sept. 16, 1859.

BRODHEAD, John (D N.H.) Oct. 5, 1770-April 7, 1838; House 1829-33.

BRODHEAD, John Curtis (D N.Y.) Oct. 27, 1780-Jan. 2, 1859; House 1831-33, 1837-39.

BRODHEAD, Joseph Davis (son of Richard Brodhead) (D Pa.) Jan. 12, 1859-April 23, 1920; House 1907-09.

BRODHEAD, Richard (father of Joseph Brodhead) (D Pa.) Jan. 5, 1811-Sept. 16, 1863; House 1843-49; Senate 1851-57.

BROMBERG, Frederick George (LR/D Ala.) June 19, 1837-Sept. 4, 1930; House 1873-75.

BROMWELL, Henry Pelham Holmes (R Ill.) Aug. 26, 1823-Jan. 7, 1903; House 1865-69.

BROMWELL, Jacob Henry (R Ohio) May 11, 1848-June 4, 1924; House Dec. 3, 1894-1903.

BROMWELL, James E. (R Iowa) March 26, 1920; House 1961-65.

BRONSON, David (W Maine) Feb. 8, 1800-Nov. 20, 1863; House May 31, 1841-43.

BRONSON, Isaac Hopkins (D N.Y.) Oct. 16, 1802 Aug. 13, 1855; House 1837-39.

BROOCKS, Moses Lycurgus (D Texas) Nov. 1, 1864-May 27, 1908; House 1905-07.

BROOKE, Edward W. (R Mass.) Oct. 26, 1919; Senate 1967- .

BROOKE, Walker (W Miss.) Dec. 25, 1813-Feb. 18, 1869; Senate Feb. 18, 1852-53.

BROOKHART, Smith Wildman (PR Iowa) Feb. 2, 1869-Nov. 15, 1944; Senate Nov. 7, 1922-April 12, 1926, 1927-33.

BROOKS, Charles Wayland (R Ill.) March 8, 1897-Jan. 14, 1957; Senate Nov. 22, 1940-49.

BROOKS, David (— N.Y.) 1756-Aug. 30, 1838; House 1797-99.

BROOKS, Edward Schroeder (R Pa.) June 14, 1867-July 12, 1957; House 1919-23.

BROOKS, Edwin Bruce (cousin of Edmund Howard Hinshaw) (R Ill.) Sept. 20, 1868-Sept. 18, 1933; House 1919-23.

BROOKS, Franklin Eli (R Colo.) Nov. 19, 1860-Feb. 7, 1916; House 1903-07.

BROOKS, George Merrick (R Mass.) July 26, 1824-Sept. 22, 1893; House Nov. 2, 1869-May 13, 1872.

BROOKS, Jack Bascom (D Texas) Dec. 18, 1922; House 1953- .

BROOKS, James (D N.Y.) Nov. 10, 1810-April 30, 1873; House 1849-53 (Whig), 1863-April 7, 1866, 1867-April 30, 1873 (Democrat).

BROOKS, Joshua Twing (D Pa.) Feb. 27, 1884-Feb. 7, 1956; House 1933-37.

BROOKS, Micah (— N.Y.) May 14, 1775-July 7, 1857; House 1815-17.

BROOKS, Overton (nephew of John Holmes Overton) (D La.) Dec. 21, 1897-Sept. 16, 1961; House 1937-Sept. 16, 1961.

BROOKS, Preston Smith (SRD S.C.) Aug. 5, 1819-Jan. 17, 1857; House 1853-July 15, 1856, Aug. 1, 1856-Jan. 17, 1857.

BROOKSHIRE, Elijah Voorhees (D Ind.) Aug. 15, 1856-April 14, 1936; House 1889-95.

BROOM, Jacob (son of James Madison Broom) (AW Pa.) July 25, 1808-Nov. 28, 1864; House 1855-57.

BROOM, James Madison (father of Jacob Broom) (F Del.) 1776-Jan. 15, 1850; House 1805-07.

BROOMALL, John Martin (R Pa.) Jan. 19, 1816-June 3, 1894; House 1863-69.

BROOMFIELD, William S. (R Mich.) April 28, 1922; House 1957- .

BROPHY, John Charles (R Wis.) Oct. 8, 1901; House 1947-49.

BROSIUS, Marriott (R Pa.) March 7, 1843-March 16, 1901; House 1889-March 16, 1901.

BROTZMAN, Donald G. (R Colo.) June 28, 1922; House 1963-65, 1967- .

BROUGHTON, Joseph Melville (D N.C.) Nov. 17, 1888-March 6, 1949; Senate Dec. 31, 1948-March 6, 1949; Gov. 1941-45.

BROUSSARD, Edwin Sidney (brother of Robert Foligny Broussard (D La.) Dec. 4, 1874-Nov. 19, 1934; Senate 1921-33.

BROUSSARD, Robert Foligny (brother of Edwin Sidney Broussard) (D La.) Aug. 17, 1864-April 12, 1918; House 1897-1915; Senate 1915-April 12, 1918.

BROWER, John Morehead (R N.C.) July 19, 1845-Aug. 5, 1913; House 1887-91.

BROWN, Aaron Venable (D Tenn.) Aug. 15, 1795-March 8, 1859; House 1839-45; Gov. 1845-47; Postmaster General 1857-59.

BROWN, Albert Gallatin (D Miss.) May 31, 1813-June 12, 1880; House 1839-41, 1847-53; Senate Jan. 7, 1854-Jan. 12, 1861; Gov. 1844-48.

BROWN, Anson (W N.Y.) 1800-June 14, 1840; House 1839-June 14, 1840.

BROWN, Arthur (R Utah) March 8, 1843-Dec. 12, 1906; Senate Jan. 22, 1896-97.

BROWN, Bedford (D N.C.) June 6, 1795-Dec. 6, 1870; Senate Dec. 9, 1829-Nov. 16, 1840.

BROWN, Benjamin (nephew of John Brown) (— Mass.) Sept. 23, 1756-Sept. 17, 1831; House 1815-17.

BROWN, Benjamin Gratz (grandson of John Brown of Virginia and Kentucky) (D Mo.) May 28, 1826-Dec. 13, 1885; Senate Nov. 13, 1863-67; Gov. 1871.

BROWN, Charles (D Pa.) Sept. 23, 1797-Sept. 4, 1883; House 1841-43, 1847-49.

BROWN, Charles Elwood (R Ohio) July 4, 1834-May 22, 1904; House 1885-89.

BROWN, Charles Harrison (D Mo.) Oct. 22, 1920; House 1957-61.

BROWN, Clarence J. (father of Clarence J. Brown, Jr.) (R Ohio) July 14, 1893-Aug. 23, 1965; House 1939-Aug. 23, 1965.

BROWN, Clarence J., Jr. (son of Clarence J. Brown) June 18, 1927; House Nov. 2, 1965- .

BROWN, Elias (W Md.) May 9, 1793-July 7, 1857; House 1829-31.

BROWN, Ernest S. (R Nev.) Sept. 25, 1903-July 23, 1965; Senate Oct. 1-Dec. 1, 1954.

BROWN, Ethan Allen (D Ohio) July 4, 1776-Feb. 24, 1852; Senate Jan. 3, 1822-25; Gov. 1818-22.

BROWN, Foster Vincent (father of Joseph Edgar Brown) (R Tenn.) Dec. 24, 1852-March 26, 1937; House 1895-97.

BROWN, Fred Herbert (D N.H.) April 12, 1879-Feb. 3, 1955; Senate 1933-39; Gov. 1923-24.

BROWN, Garry E. (R Mich.) Aug. 12, 1923; House 1967- .

BROWN, George E., Jr. (D Calif.) March 6, 1920; House 1963-71.

BROWN, George Houston (W N.J.) Feb. 12, 1810-Aug. 1, 1865; House 1851-53.

BROWN, James (brother of John Brown of Virginia and Kentucky) (— La.) Sept. 11, 1776-April 7, 1835; Senate Feb. 5, 1813-17, 1819-Dec. 10, 1823.

BROWN, James Sproat (D Wis.) Feb. 1, 1824-April 15, 1878; House 1863-65.

BROWN, James W. (R Pa.) July 14, 1844-Oct. 23, 1909; House 1903-05.

BROWN, Jason Brevoort (D Ind.) Feb. 26, 1839-March 10, 1898; House 1889-95.

BROWN, Jeremiah (W Pa.) April 14, 1785-March 2, 1858; House 1841-45.

BROWN, John (uncle of Benjamin Brown and grandfather of John Brown Francis) (F R.I.) Jan. 27, 1736-Sept. 20, 1803; House 1799-1801.

BROWN, John (D Md.)— - Dec. 13, 1815; House 1809-10

BROWN, John (brother of James Brown and grandfather of Benjamin Gratz Brown) (— Va./Ky.) Sept. 12, 1757-Aug. 29, 1837; House 1789-June 1, 1792 (Ky. district of Va.); Senate June 18, 1792-1805 (Ky.); President pro tempore 1803-04; Cont. Cong. (Ky. district of Va.) 1787-88.

BROWN, John (— Pa.) Aug. 12, 1772 Oct. 12, 1845; House 1821-25.

BROWN, John Brewer (D Md.) May 13, 1836-May 16, 1898; House Nov. 8, 1892-93.

BROWN, John Robert (IR Va.) Jan. 14, 1842-Aug. 4, 1927; House 1887-89.

BROWN, John W. (D N.Y.) Oct. 11, 1796-Sept. 6, 1875; House 1833-37.

BROWN, John Young (nephew of Bryan Rust Young and William Singleton Young) (D Ky.) June 28, 1835-Jan. 11, 1904; House 1859-61, 1873-77; Gov. 1891-95.

BROWN, John Young (D Ky.) Feb. 1, 1900; House 1933-35.

BROWN, Joseph Edgar (son of Foster Vincent Brown) (R Tenn.) Feb. 11, 1880-June 13, 1939; House 1921-23.

BROWN, Joseph Emerson (D Ga.) April 15, 1821-Nov. 30, 1894; Senate May 26, 1880-91; Gov. 1855-65.

BROWN, Lathrop (D N.Y.) Feb. 26, 1883-Nov. 28, 1959; House 1913-15.

BROWN, Milton (W Tenn.) Feb. 28, 1804-May 15, 1883; House 1841-47.

BROWN, Norris (R Neb.) May 2, 1863-Jan. 5, 1960; Senate 1907-13.

BROWN, Paul (D Ga.) March 31, 1880-Sept. 24, 1961; House July 5, 1933-61.

BROWN, Prentiss Marsh (D Mich.) June 18, 1889; House 1933-Nov. 18, 1936; Senate Nov. 19, 1936-43.

BROWN, Robert (D Pa.) Dec. 25, 1744-Feb. 26, 1823; House Dec. 4, 1798-1815.

BROWN, Seth W. (R Ohio) Jan. 4, 1841-Feb. 24, 1923; House 1897-1901.

BROWN, Titus (— N.H.) Feb. 11, 1786-Jan. 29, 1849; House 1825-29.

BROWN, Webster Everett (R Wis.) July 16, 1851-Dec. 14, 1929; House 1901-07.

BROWN, William (— Ky.) April 19, 1779-Oct. 6, 1833; House 1819-21.

BROWN, William Gay (U/W.Va.) Sept. 25, 1800-April 19, 1884; House 1845-49 (Democrat Va.), 1861-63 (U Va.), Dec. 7, 1863-65 (U W.Va.).

BROWN, William Gay, Jr. (son of William Gay Brown) (D W.A.) April 7, 1856-March 9, 1916; House 1911-March 9, 1916.

BROWN, William John (D Ind.) Aug. 15, 1805-March 18, 1857; House 1843-45, 1849-51.

BROWN, William Ripley (R Kan.) July 16, 1840-March 3, 1916; House 1875-77.

BROWN, William Wallace (R Pa.) April 22, 1836-Nov. 1926; House 1883-87.

BROWNE, Charles (D N.J.) Sept. 28, 1875-Aug. 17, 1947; House 1923-25.

BROWNE, Edward Everts (R Wis.) Feb. 16, 1868-Nov. 23, 1945; House 1913-31.

BROWNE, George Huntington (D R.I.) Jan. 6, 1811-Sept. 26, 1885; House 1861-63.

BROWNE, Thomas Henry Bayly (R Va.) Feb. 8, 1844-Aug. 27, 1892; House 1887-91.

BROWNE, Thomas McLelland (R Ind.) April 19, 1829-July 17, 1891; House 1877-91.

BROWNING, Gordon (D Tenn.) Nov. 22, 1889; House 1923-35; Gov. 1937-39, 1949-53.

BROWNING, Orville Hickman (R Ill.) Feb. 10, 1806-Aug. 10, 1881; Senate June 26, 1861-Jan. 12, 1863; Secy. of the Interior 1866-69; Atty. Gen. 1868.

BROWNING, William John (R N.J.) April 11, 1850-March 24, 1920; House Nov. 7, 1911-March 24, 1920.

BROWNLOW, Walter Preston (nephew of William Gannaway Brownlow) (R Tenn.) March 27, 1851-July 8, 1910; House 1897-July 8, 1910.

BROWNLOW, William Gannaway (uncle of Walter Preston Brownlow) (R Tenn.) Aug. 29, 1805-April 29, 1877; Senate 1869-75; Gov. 1865-68.

BROWNSON, Charles Bruce (R Ind.) Feb. 5, 1914; House 1951-59.

BROYHILL, James T. (R N.C.) Aug. 19, 1927; House 1963- .

BROYHILL, Joel Thomas (R Va.) Nov. 4, 1919; House 1953- .

BRUCE, Blanche Kelso (R Miss.) March 1, 1841-March 17, 1898; Senate 1875-81.

BRUCE, Donald C. (R Ind.) April 27, 1921-Aug. 31, 1969; House 1961-65.

BRUCE, Phineas (— Mass.) June 7, 1762-Oct. 4, 1809; House 1803-05.

BRUCE, William Cabell (D Md.) March 12, 1860-May 9, 1946; Senate 1923-29.

BRUCKER, Ferdinand (D Mich.) Jan. 8, 1858-March 3, 1904; House 1897-99.

BRUCKNER, Henry (D N.Y.) June 17, 1871-April 14, 1942; House 1913-Dec. 31, 1917.

BRUMBAUGH, Clement Laird (D Ohio) Feb. 28, 1863-Sept. 28, 1921; House 1913-21.

BRUMBAUGH, David Emmert (R Pa.) Oct. 8, 1894; House Nov. 2, 1943-47.

BRUMM, Charles Napoleon (father of George Franklin Brumm) (RG Pa.) June 9, 1838-Jan. 11, 1917; House 1881-89, 1895-99, Nov. 6, 1906-Jan. 4, 1909.

BRUMM, George Franklin (son of Charles Napoleon Brumm) (R Pa.) Jan. 24, 1880-May 29, 1934; House 1923-27, 1929-May 29, 1934.

BRUNDIDGE, Stephen, Jr. (D Ark.) Jan. 1, 1857-Jan. 14, 1938; House 1897-1909.

BRUNNER, David B. (D Pa.) March 7, 1835-Nov. 29, 1903; House 1889-93.

BRUNNER, William Frank (D N.Y.) Sept. 15, 1887-April 23, 1965; House 1929-Sept. 27, 1935.

BRUNSDALE, Clarence Norman (R N.D.) July 9, 1891; Senate Nov. 19, 1959-Aug. 7, 1960; Gov. 1951-57.

BRUSH, Henry (— Ohio) June, 1778-Jan. 19, 1855; House 1819-21.

BRUYN, Andrew DeWitt (D N.Y.) Nov. 18, 1790-July 27, 1838; House 1837-July 27, 1838.

BRYAN, Guy Morrison (D Texas) Jan. 12, 1821-June 4, 1901; House 1857-59.

BRYAN, Henry H. (— Tenn.) —-May 7, 1835; House 1819-23.

BRYAN, James Wesley (PR Wash.) March 11, 1874-Aug. 26, 1956; House 1913-15.

BRYAN, John Heritage (W N.C.) Nov. 4, 1798-May 19, 1870; House 1825-29.

BRYAN, Joseph (D Ga.) Aug. 18, 1773-Sept. 12, 1812; House 1803-06.

BRYAN, Joseph Hunter (— N.C.) —-—; House 1815-19.

BRYAN, Nathan (— N.C.) 1748-June 4, 1798; House 1795-June 4, 1798.

BRYAN, Nathan Philemon (brother of William James Bryan) (D Fla.) April 23, 1872-Aug. 8, 1935; Senate 1911-17.

BRYAN, William James (brother of Nathan Philemon Bryan) (D Fla.) Oct. 10, 1876-March 22, 1908; Senate Dec. 26, 1907-March 22, 1908.

BRYAN, William Jennings (father of Ruth Bryan Owen) (D Neb.) March 19, 1860-July 26, 1925; House 1891-95; Secy. of State 1913-15.

BRYCE, Lloyd Stephens (D N.Y.) Sept. 20, 1850-April 2, 1917; House 1887-89.

BRYSON, Joseph Raleigh (D S.C.) January 18, 1893-March 10, 1953; House 1939-March 10, 1953.

BUCHANAN, Andrew (D Pa.) April 8, 1780-Dec. 2, 1848; House 1835-39.

BUCHANAN, Frank (D Ill.) June 14, 1862-April 18, 1930; House 1911-17.

BUCHANAN, Frank (husband of Vera Daerr Buchanan) (D Pa.) Dec. 1, 1902-April 27, 1951; House May 21, 1946-April 27, 1951.

BUCHANAN, Hugh (D Ga.) Sept. 15, 1823-June 11, 1890; House 1881-85.

BUCHANAN, James (D Pa.) April 23, 1791-June 1, 1868; House 1821-31; Senate Dec. 6, 1834-March 5, 1845; Secy. of State 1845-49; President 1857-61.

BUCHANAN, James (R N.J.) June 17, 1839-Oct. 30, 1900; House 1885-93.

BUCHANAN, James Paul (cousin of Edward William Pou) (D Texas) April 30, 1867-Feb. 22, 1937; House April 5, 1913-Feb. 22, 1937.

BUCHANAN, John Alexander (D Va.) Oct. 7, 1843-Sept. 2, 1921; House 1889-93.

BUCHANAN, John H. (R Ala.) March 19, 1928; House 1965- .

BUCHANAN, Vera Daerr (wife of Frank Buchanan) (D Pa.) July 20, 1902-Nov. 26, 1955; House July 24, 1951-Nov. 26, 1955.

BUCHER, John Conrad (— Pa.) Dec. 28, 1792-Oct. 15, 1851; House 1831-33.

BUCK, Alfred Eliab (R Ala.) Feb. 7, 1832-Dec. 4, 1902; House 1869-71.

BUCK, Charles Francis (D La.) Nov. 5, 1841-Jan. 19, 1918; House 1895-97.

BUCK, Clayton Douglas (great-grandnephew of John M. Clayton) (R Del.) March 21, 1890-Jan. 28, 1965; Senate 1943-49; Gov. 1929-37.

BUCK, Daniel (father of Daniel Azro Ashley Buck) (F Vt.) Nov. 9, 1753-Aug. 16, 1816; House 1795-97.

BUCK, Daniel Azro Ashley (son of Daniel Buck) (D Vt.) April 19, 1789-Dec. 24, 1841; House 1823-25, 1827-29.

BUCK, Ellsworth Brewer (R N.Y.) July 3, 1892-Aug. 14, 1970; House June 6, 1944-49.

BUCK, Frank Henry (D Calif.) Sept. 23, 1887-Sept. 17, 1942; House 1933-Sept. 17, 1942.

BUCK, John Ransom (R Conn.) Dec. 6, 1835-Feb. 6, 1917; House 1881-83, 1885-87.

BUCKALEW, Charles Rollin (D Pa.) Dec. 28, 1821-May 19, 1899; Senate 1863-69; House 1887-91.

BUCKBEE, John Theodore (R Ill.) Aug. 1, 1871-April 23, 1936; House 1927-April 23, 1936.

BUCKINGHAM, William Alfred (R Conn.) May 28, 1804-Feb. 5, 1875; Senate 1869-Feb. 5, 1875; Gov. 1856-66.

BUCKLAND, Ralph Pomeroy (R Ohio) Jan. 20, 1812-May 27, 1892; House 1865-69.

BUCKLER, Richard Thompson (F-L Minn.) Oct. 27, 1865-Jan. 23, 1950; House 1935-43.

BUCKLEY, Charles Anthony (D N.Y.) June 23, 1890-Jan. 22, 1967; House 1935-65.

BUCKLEY, Charles Waldron (R Ala.) Feb. 18, 1835-Dec. 4, 1906; House July 21, 1868-73.

BUCKLEY, James L. (C N.Y.) March 9, 1923; Senate 1971- .

BUCKLEY, James Richard (D Ill.) Nov. 18, 1870-June 22, 1945; House 1923-25.

BUCKLEY, James Vincent (D Ill.) May 15, 1894-July 30, 1954; House 1949-51.

BUCKMAN, Clarence Bennet (R Minn.) April 1, 1851-March 1, 1917; House 1903-07.

BUCKNER, Alexander (— Mo.) 1785-June 6, 1833; Senate 1831-June 6, 1833.

BUCKNER, Aylett (son of Richard Aylett Buckner) (W Ky.) July 21, 1806-July 3, 1869; House 1847-49.

BUCKNER, Aylett Hawes (nephew of Aylett Hawes and cousin of Richard Hawes and Albert Gallatin Hawes) (D Mo.) Dec. 14, 1816-Feb. 5, 1894; House 1873-85.

BUCKNER, Richard Aylett (father of Aylette Buckner) (A-D Ky.) July 16, 1763-Dec. 8, 1847; House 1823-29.

BUDD, James Herbert (D Calif.) May 18, 1851-July 30, 1908; House 1883-85.

BUDGE, Hamer Harold (R Idaho) Nov. 21, 1910; House 1951-61.

BUEL, Alexander Woodruff (D Mich.) Dec. 13, 1813-April 19, 1868; House 1849-51.

BUELL, Alexander Hamilton (D N.Y.) July 14, 1801-Jan. 29, 1853; House 1851-Jan. 29, 1853.

BUFFETT, Howard Homan (R Neb.) Aug. 13, 1903-April 29, 1964; House 1943-49, 1951-53.

BUFFINGTON, Joseph (W Pa.) Nov. 27, 1803-Feb. 3, 1872; House 1843-47.

BUFFINGTON, James (R Mass.) March 16, 1817-March 7, 1875; House 1855-63, 1869-March 7, 1875.

BUFFUM, Joseph, Jr. (D N.H.) Sept. 23, 1784-Feb. 24, 1874; House 1819-21.

BUGG, Robert Malone (W Tenn.) Jan. 20, 1805-Feb. 18, 1887; House 1853-55.

BULKELEY, Morgan Gardner (cousin of Edwin Dennison Morgan) (R Conn.) Dec. 26, 1837-Nov. 6, 1922; Senate 1905-11; Gov. 1889-93.

BULKLEY, Robert Johns (D Ohio) Oct. 8, 1880-July 21, 1965; House 1911-15; Senate Dec. 1, 1930-39.

BULL, John (W Mo.) 1803-Feb. 1863; House 1833-35.

BULL, Melville (R R.I.) Sept. 19, 1854-July 5, 1909; House 1895-1903.

BULLARD, Henry Adams (W La.) Sept. 9, 1788-April 17, 1851; House 1831-Jan. 4, 1834, Dec. 5, 1850-51.

BULLOCH, William Bellinger (D Ga.) 1777-May 6, 1852; Senate April 8-Nov. 6, 1813.

BULLOCK, Robert (D Fla.) Dec. 8, 1828-July 27, 1905; House 1889-93.

BULLOCK, Stephen (F Mass.) Oct. 10, 1735-Feb. 2, 1816; House 1797-99.

BULLOCK, Wingfield (— Ky.) —-Oct. 13, 1821; House 1821-Oct. 13, 1821.

BULOW, William John (D S.D.) Jan. 13, 1869-Feb. 26, 1960; Senate 1931-43; Gov. 1927-31.

BULWINKLE, Alfred Lee (D N.C.) April 21, 1883-Aug. 31, 1950; House 1921-29, 1931-Aug. 31, 1950.

BUNCH, Samuel (W Tenn.) Dec. 4, 1786-Sept. 5, 1849; House 1833-37.

BUNDY, Hezekiah Sanford (R Ohio) Aug. 15, 1817-Dec. 12, 1895; House 1865-67, 1873-75, Dec. 4, 1893-95.

BUNDY, Solomon (R N.Y.) May 22, 1823-Jan. 13, 1889; House 1877-79.

BUNKER, Berkeley Lloyd (D Nev.) Aug. 12, 1906; Senate Nov. 27, 1940-Dec. 6, 1942; House 1945-47.

BUNN, Benjamin Hickman (D N.C.) Oct. 19, 1844-Aug. 25, 1907; House 1889-95.

BUNNELL, Frank Charles (R Pa.) March 19, 1842-Sept. 11, 1911; House Dec. 24, 1872-73, 1885-89.

BUNNER, Rudolph (AD N.Y.) Aug. 17, 1779-July 16, 1837; House 1827-29.

BUNTING, Thomas Lathrop (D N.Y.) April 24, 1844-Dec. 27, 1898; House 1891-93.

BURCH, John Chilton (D Calif.) Feb. 1, 1826-Aug. 31, 1885; House 1859-61.

BURCH, Thomas Granville (D Va.) July 3, 1869-March 20, 1951; House 1931-May 31, 1946; Senate May 31-Nov. 5, 1946.

BURCHARD, Horatio Chapin (R Ill.) Sept. 22, 1825-May 14, 1908; House Dec. 6, 1869-79.

BURCHARD, Samuel Dickinson (D Wis.) July 17, 1836-Sept. 1, 1901; House 1875-77.

BURCHILL, Thomas Francis (D N.Y.) Aug. 3, 1882-March 28, 1960; House 1943-45.

BURD, George (— Pa.) 1793-Jan. 13, 1844; House 1831-35.

BURDETT, Samuel Swinfin (R Mo.) Feb. 21, 1836-Sept. 24, 1914; House 1869-73.

BURDICK, Clark (R R.I.) Jan. 13, 1868-Aug. 27, 1948; House 1919-33.

BURDICK, Quentin Northrop (son of Usher L. Burdick and brother-in-law of Robert W. Levering) (D N.D.) June 19, 1908; House 1959-Aug. 8, 1960; Senate Aug. 8, 1960- .

BURDICK, Theodore Weld (R Iowa) Oct. 7, 1836-July 16, 1898; House 1877-79.

BURDICK, Usher Lloyd (father of Quentin N. Burdick and father-in-law of Robert W. Levering) (R N.D.) Feb. 21, 1879-Aug. 19, 1960; House 1935-45, 1949-59.

BURGES, Dempsey (— N.C.) 1751-Jan. 13, 1800; House 1795-99.

BURGES, Tristam (great-great-uncle of Theodore Francis Green) (— R.I.) Feb. 26, 1770-Oct. 13, 1853; House 1825-35.

BURGESS, George Farmer (D Texas) Sept. 21, 1861-Dec. 31, 1919; House 1901-17.

BURGIN, William Olin (D N.C.) July 28, 1877-April 11, 1946; House 1939-April 11, 1946.

BURK, Henry (R Pa.) Sept. 26, 1850-Dec. 5, 1903; House 1901-Dec. 5, 1903.

BURKE, Aedanus (— S.C.) June 16, 1743-March 30, 1802; House 1789-91.

BURKE, Charles Henry (R S.D.) April 1, 1861-April 7, 1944; House 1899-1907, 1909-15.

BURKE, Edmund (D N.H.) Jan. 23, 1809-Jan. 25, 1882; House 1839-45.

BURKE, Edward Raymond (D S.D.) Nov. 28, 1880-Nov. 4, 1968; House 1933-35; Senate 1935-41.

BURKE, Frank Welsh (D Ky.) June 1, 1920; House 1959-63.

BURKE, James Anthony (D Mass.) March 30, 1910; House 1959- .

BURKE, James Francis (R Pa.) Oct. 21, 1867-Aug. 8, 1932; House 1905-15.

BURKE, J. Herbert (R Fla.) Jan. 14, 1913; House 1967- .

BURKE, John Harley (D Calif.) June 2, 1894-May 14, 1951; House 1933-35.

BURKE, Michael Edmund (D Wis.) Oct. 15, 1863-Dec. 12, 1918; House 1911-17.

BURKE, Raymond Hugh (R Ohio) Nov. 4, 1881-Aug. 18, 1954; House 1947-49.

BURKE, Robert Emmet (D Texas) Aug. 1, 1847-June 5, 1901; House 1897-June 5, 1901.

BURKE, Thomas A. (D Ohio) Oct. 30, 1898; Senate Nov. 10, 1953-Dec. 2, 1954.

BURKE, Thomas Henry (D Ohio) May 6, 1904-Sept. 12, 1959; House 1949-51.

BURKE, William Joseph (R Pa.) Sept. 25, 1862-Nov. 7, 1925; House 1919-23.

BURKETT, Elmer Jacob (R Neb.) Dec. 1, 1867-May 23, 1935; House 1899-March 4, 1905; Senate 1905-11.

BURKHALTER, Everett G. (D Calif.) Jan. 19, 1897; House 1963-65.

BURLEIGH, Edwin Chick (R Maine) Nov. 27, 1843-June 16, 1916; House June 21, 1897-1911; Senate 1913-June 16, 1916; Gov. 1889-92.

BURLEIGH, Henry Gordon (R N.Y.) June 2, 1832-Aug. 10, 1900; House 1883-87.

BURLEIGH, John Holmes (son of William Burleigh) (R Maine) Oct. 9, 1822-Dec. 5, 1877; House 1873-77.

BURLEIGH, Walter Atwood (R Dakota) Oct. 25, 1820-March 7, 1896; House (Terr.Del.) 1865-69.

BURLEIGH, William (father of John Holmes Burleigh) (AD Maine) Oct. 24, 1785-July 2, 1827; House 1823-July 2, 1827.

BURLESON, Albert Sidney (D Texas) June 7, 1863-Nov. 24, 1937; House 1899-March 6, 1913; Postmaster General 1913-21.

BURLESON, Omar Truman (D Texas) March 19, 1906; House 1947- .

BURLINGAME, Anson (R Mass.) Nov. 14, 1820-Feb. 23, 1870, House 1855-59 (American Party), 1859-61 (R).

BURLISON, Bill D. (D Mo.) March 15, 1931; House 1969- .

BURNELL, Barker (W Mass.) Jan. 30, 1798-June 15, 1843; House 1841-June 15, 1843.

BURNES, Daniel Dee (D Mo.) Jan. 4, 1851-Nov. 2, 1899; House 1893-95.

BURNES, James Nelson (D Mo.) Aug. 22, 1827-Jan. 23, 1889; House 1883-Jan. 23, 1889.

BURNET, Jacob (F N.J.) Feb. 22, 1770-May 10, 1853; Senate Dec. 10, 1828-31,

BURNETT, Edward (D Mass.) March 16, 1849-Nov. 5, 1925; House 1887-89.

BURNETT, Henry Cornelius (D Ky.) Oct. 5, 1825-Oct. 1, 1866; House 1855-Dec. 3, 1861.

BURNETT, John Lawson (D Ala.) Jan. 20, 1854-May 13, 1919; House 1899-May 13, 1919.

BURNEY, William Evans (D Colo.) Sept. 11, 1893; House Nov. 5, 1940-41.

BURNHAM, Alfred Avery (R Conn.) March 8, 1819-April 11, 1879; House 1859-63.

BURNHAM, George (R Calif.) Dec. 28, 1868-June 28, 1939; House 1933-37.

BURNHAM, Henry Eben (R N.H.) Nov. 8, 1844-Feb. 8, 1917; Senate 1901-13.

BURNS, John Anthony (D Hawaii) March 30, 1909; House (Terr. Del.) 1957-Aug. 21, 1959; Gov. 1963- .

BURNS, Joseph (D Ohio) March 11, 1800-May 12, 1875; House 1857-59.

BURNS, Robert (D N.H.) Dec. 12, 1792-June 26, 1866; House 1833-37.

BURNSIDE, Ambrose Everett (R R.I.) May 23, 1824-Sept. 13, 1881; Senate 1875-Sept. 13, 1881; Gov. 1866-68.

BURNSIDE, Maurice Gwinn (D W.Va.) Aug. 23, 1902; House 1949-53, 1955-57.

BURNSIDE, Thomas (— Pa.) July 28, 1782-March 25, 1851; House Oct. 10, 1815-April, 1816.

BURR, Aaron (cousin of Theodore Dwight) (D N.Y.) Feb. 6, 1756-Sept. 14, 1836; Senate 1791-97; Vice President 1801-05.

BURR, Albert George (D Ill.) Nov. 8, 1829-June 10, 1882; House 1867-71.

BURRELL, Orlando (R Ill.) July 26, 1826-June 7, 1922; House 1895-97.

BURRILL, James, Jr. (great-grandfather of Theodore Francis Green) (— R.I.) April 25, 1772-Dec. 25, 1820; Senate 1817-Dec. 25, 1820.

BURROUGHS, Sherman Everett (R N.H.) Feb. 6, 1870-Jan. 27, 1923; House June 7, 1917-Jan. 27, 1923.

BURROUGHS, Silas Mainville (R N.Y.) July 16, 1810-June 3, 1860; House 1857-June 3, 1860.

BURROWS, Daniel (uncle of Lorenzo Burrows) (D Conn.) Oct. 26, 1766-Jan. 23, 1858, House 1821-23,

BURROWS, Joseph Henry (G Mo.) May 15, 1840-April 28, 1914; House 1881-83.

BURROWS, Julius Caesar (R Mich.) Jan. 9, 1837-Nov. 16, 1915; House 1873-75, 1879-83, 1885-Jan. 23, 1895; Senate Jan. 24, 1895-1911.

BURROWS, Lorenzo (nephew of Daniel Burrows) (W N.Y.) March 15, 1805-March 6, 1885; House 1849-53.

BURSUM, Holm Olaf (R N.M.) Feb. 10, 1867-Aug. 7, 1953; Senate March 11, 1921-25.

BURT, Armistead (D S.C.) Nov. 13, 1802-Oct. 30, 1883; House 1843-53.

BURTNESS, Olger Burton (R N.D.) March 14, 1884-Jan. 20, 1960; House 1921-33.

BURTON, Charles Germman (R Mo.) April 4, 1846-Feb. 25, 1926; House 1895-97.

BURTON, Clarence Godber (D Va.) Dec. 14, 1886; House Nov. 2, 1948-53.

BURTON, Harold Hitz (R Ohio) June 22, 1888-Oct. 28, 1964; Senate 1941-Sept. 30, 1945; Assoc. Justice of the Supreme Court 1945-58.

BURTON, Hiram Rodney (R Del.) Nov. 13, 1841-June 17, 1927; House 1905-09.

BURTON, Hutchins Gordon (A-D N.C.) 1782-April 21, 1836; House Dec. 6, 1819-March 23, 1824; Gov. 1824-27.

BURTON, Joseph Ralph (R Kan.) Nov. 16, 1850-Feb. 27, 1923; Senate 1901-June 4, 1906.

BURTON, Laurence J. (R Utah) Oct. 30, 1926; House 1963-71.

BURTON, Phillip (D Calif.) June 1, 1926; House Feb. 18, 1964- .

BURTON, Theodore Elijah (R Ohio) Dec. 20, 1851-Oct. 28, 1929; House 1889-91, 1895-1909; Senate 1909-15; House 1921-Dec. 15, 1928; Senate Dec. 15, 1928-Oct. 28, 1929.

BURWELL, William Armisted (D Va.) March 15, 1780-Feb. 16, 1821; House Dec. 1, 1806-Feb. 16, 1821.

BUSBEY, Fred Ernst (R Ill.) Feb. 8, 1895-Feb. 11, 1966; House 1943-45, 1947-49, 1951-55.

BUSBY, George Henry (D Ohio) June 10, 1794-Aug. 22, 1869; House 1851-53.

BUSBY, Thomas Jefferson (D Miss.) July 26, 1884-Oct. 18, 1964; House 1923-35.

BUSEY, Samuel Thompson (D Ill.) Nov. 16, 1835-Aug. 12, 1909; House 1891-93.

BUSH, Alvin Ray (R Pa.) June 4, 1893-Nov. 5, 1959; House 1951-Nov. 5, 1959.

BUSH, George Herbert Walker (son of Prescott S. Bush) (R Texas) June 12, 1924; House 1967-71.

BUSH, Prescott Sheldon (father of George Herbert Walker Bush) (R Conn.) May 15, 1895; Senate Nov. 4, 1952-63.

BUSHFIELD, Harlan John (husband of Vera C. Bushfield) (R S.D.) Aug. 6, 1882-Sept. 27, 1948; Senate 1943-Sept. 27, 1948; Gov. 1939-42.

BUSHFIELD, Vera Cahalan (widow of Harlan J. Bushfield) (R S.D.) Aug. 9, 1889; Senate Oct. 6-Dec. 26, 1948.

BUSHNELL, Allen Ralph (D Wis.) July 18, 1833-March 29, 1909; House 1891-93.

BUSHONG, Robert Grey (R Pa.) June 10, 1883-April 6, 1951; House 1927-29.

BUTLER, Andrew Pickens (son of William Butler) (SRD S.C.) Nov. 19, 1796-May 25, 1857; Senate Dec. 4, 1846-May 25, 1857.

BUTLER, Benjamin Franklin (grandfather of Butler Ames) (R Mass.) Nov. 5, 1818-Jan. 11, 1893; House 1867-75, 1877-79; Gov. 1882 (Greenback & Democrat).

BUTLER, Chester Pierce (W Pa.) March 21, 1798-Oct. 5, 1850; House 1847-Oct. 5, 1850.

BUTLER, Ezra (D Vt.) Sept. 24, 1763-July 12, 1838; House 1813-15; Gov. 1826-28.

BUTLER, Hugh Alfred (R Neb.) Feb. 28, 1878-July 1, 1954; Senate 1941-July 1, 1954.

BUTLER, James Joseph (D Mo.) Aug. 29, 1862-May 31, 1917; House 1901-June 28, 1902, Nov. 4, 1902-Feb. 26, 1903, 1903-05.

BUTLER, John Cornelius (R N.Y.) July 2, 1887-Aug. 13, 1953; House April 22, 1941-49, 1951-53.

BUTLER, John Marshall (R Md.) July 21, 1897; Senate 1951-63.

BUTLER, Josiah (D N.H.) Dec. 4, 1779-Oct. 27, 1854; House 1817-23.

BUTLER, Marion (P N.C.) May 20, 1863-June 3, 1938; Senate 1895-1901.

BUTLER, Matthew Calbraith (son of William Butler) (D S.C.) March 8, 1836-April 14, 1909; Senate 1877-95.

BUTLER, Mounce Gore (D Tenn.) May 11, 1849-Feb. 13, 1917; House 1905-07.

BUTLER, Pierce (D S.C.) July 11, 1744-Feb. 15, 1822; Senate 1789-Oct. 25, 1796, Nov. 4, 1802-Nov. 21, 1804; Cont. Cong. 1787-88.

BUTLER, Robert Reyburn (grandson of Roderick Randum Butler) (R Ore.) Sept. 24, 1881-Jan. 7, 1933; House Nov. 6, 1928-Jan. 7, 1933.

BUTLER, Roderick Randum (grandfather of Robert Reyburn Butler) (R Tenn.) April 9, 1827-Aug. 18, 1902; House 1867-75, 1887-89.

BUTLER, Sampson Hale (D S.C.) Jan. 3, 1803-March 16, 1848; House 1839-Sept. 27, 1842.

BUTLER, Thomas (— La.) April 14, 1785-Aug. 7, 1847; House Nov. 16, 1818-21.

BUTLER, Thomas Belden (W Conn.) Aug. 22, 1806-June 8, 1873; House 1849-51.

BUTLER, Thomas Stalker (R Pa.) Nov. 4, 1855-May 26, 1928; House 1897-May 26, 1928.

BUTLER, Walter Halben (D Iowa) Feb. 13, 1852-April 24, 1931; House 1891-93.

BUTLER, William (father of Andrew Pickens Butler) (A-F S.C.) Dec. 17, 1759-Sept. 15, 1821; House 1801-13.

BUTLER, William (son of William Butler, brother of Andrew Pickens Butler and father of Matthew Calbraith Butler) (W S.C.) Feb. 1, 1790-Sept. 25, 1850; House 1841-43.

BUTLER, William Morgan (R Mass.) Jan. 29, 1861-March 29, 1937; Senate Nov. 13, 1924-Dec. 6, 1926; Chrmn. Republican Nat. Comm. 1924.

BUTLER, William Orlando (D Ky.) April 19, 1791-Aug. 6, 1880; House 1839-43.

BUTMAN, Samuel (— Maine) 1788-Oct. 9, 1864; House 1827-31.

BUTTERFIELD, Martin (R N.Y.) Dec. 8, 1790-Aug. 6, 1866; House 1859-61.

BUTTERWORTH, Benjamin (R Ohio) Oct. 22, 1837-Jan. 16, 1898; House 1879-83, 1885-91.

BUTTON, Daniel E. (R N.Y.) Nov. 1, 1917; House 1967-71.

BUTTZ, Charles Wilson (R S.C.) Nov. 16, 1837-July 20, 1913; House Nov. 7, 1876-77.

BYNUM, Jesse Atherton (D N.C.) May 23, 1797-Sept. 23, 1868; House 1833-41.

BYNUM, William Dallas (D Ind.) June 26, 1846-Oct. 21, 1927; House 1885-95.

BYRD, Adam Monroe (D Miss.) July 6, 1859-June 21, 1912; House 1903-11.

BYRD, Harry Flood (father of Harry F. Byrd, Jr., nephew of Henry De La Warr Flood and Joel West Flood) (D Va.) June 10, 1887-Oct. 20, 1966; Senate 1933-Nov. 10, 1965; Gov. 1926-30.

BYRD, Harry F., Jr. (son of Harry Flood Byrd) (D Va.) Dec. 20, 1914; Senate Nov. 12, 1965- .

BYRD, Robert Carlyle (D W.Va.) Jan. 15, 1918; House 1953-59; Senate 1959- .

BYRNE, Emmet Francis (R Ill.) Dec. 6, 1896; House 1957-59.

BYRNE, James Aloysius (D Pa.) June 22, 1906; House 1953- .

BYRNE, William Thomas (D N.Y.) March 6, 1876-Jan. 27, 1952; House 1937-Jan. 27, 1952.

BYRNES, James Francis (D S.C.) May 2, 1879; House 1911-25; Senate 1931-July 8, 1941; Assoc. Justice U.S. Supreme Court July 8, 1941-Oct. 3, 1942; Secy. of State 1945-47; Gov. 1951-55.

BYRNES, John William (R Wis.) June 12, 1913; House 1945- .

BYRNS, Joseph Wellington (father of Joseph Wellington Byrns, Jr.) (D Tenn.) July 20, 1869-June 4, 1936; House 1909-June 4, 1936; Speaker 1935-June 4, 1936.

BYRNS, Joseph Wellington, Jr. (son of Joseph Wellington Byrns) (D Tenn.) Aug. 15, 1903; House 1939-51.

BYRNS, Samuel (D Mo.) March 4, 1848-July 9, 1914; House 1891-93.

BYRON, Goodloe E. (son of Katharine E. Byron and William D. Byron and great-grandson of Louis E. McComas) (D Md.) June 22, 1929; House 1971- .

BYRON, Katharine Edgar (widow of William D. Byron, mother of Goodloe E. Byron and granddaughter of Louis E. McComas) (D Md.) Oct. 25, 1903; House May 27, 1941-43.

BYRON, William Devereux (husband of Katharine E. Byron and father of Goodloe E. Byron) (D Md.) May 15, 1895-Feb. 27, 1941; House 1939-Feb. 27, 1941.

C

CABANISS, Thomas Banks (cousin of Thomas Chipman McRae) (D Ga.) Aug. 31, 1835-Aug. 14, 1915; House 1893-95.

CABELL, Earle (D Texas) Oct. 27, 1906; House 1965- .

CABELL, Edward Carrington (W Fla.) Feb. 5, 1816-Feb. 28, 1896; House Oct. 6, 1845-Jan. 24, 1846, 1847-53.

CABELL, George Craighead (D Va.) Jan. 25, 1836-June 23, 1906; House 1875-87.

CABELL, Samuel Jordan (D Va.) Dec. 15, 1756-Aug. 4, 1818; House 1795-1803.

CABLE, Benjamin Taylor (D Ill.) Aug. 11, 1853-Dec. 13, 1923; House 1891-93.

CABLE, John Levi (gread-grandson of Joseph Cable) (R Ohio) April 15, 1884; House 1921-25, 1929-33.

CABLE, Joseph (great-grandfather of John Levi Cable) (D Ohio) April 17, 1801-May 1, 1880; House 1849-53.

CABOT, George (great-grandfather of Henry Cabot Lodge) (F Mass.) Dec. 16, 1751-April 18, 1823; Senate 1791-June 9, 1796.

CADMUS, Cornelius Andrew (D N.J.) Oct. 7, 1844-Jan. 20, 1902; House 1891-95.

CADWALADER, John (D Pa.) April 1, 1805-Jan. 26, 1879; House 1855-57.

CADWALADER, Lambert (— N.J.) 1742-Sept. 13, 1823; House 1789-91, 1793-95; Cont. Cong. 1784-87.

CADY, Claude Ernest (D Mich.) May 28, 1878-Nov. 30, 1953; House 1933-35.

CADY, Daniel (uncle of John Watts Cady) (F N.Y.) April 29, 1773-Oct. 31, 1859; House 1815-17.

CADY, John Watts (nephew of Daniel Cady) (W N.Y.) June 28, 1790-Jan. 5, 1854; House 1823-25.

CAFFERY, Donelson (grandfather of Patrick Thomson Caffery) (D La.) Sept. 10, 1835-Dec. 30, 1906; Senate Dec. 31, 1892-1901.

CAFFERY, Patrick Thomson (grandson of Donelson Caffery) (D La.) July 6, 1932; House 1969- .

CAGE, Harry (— Miss.) —-1859; House 1833-35.

CAHILL, William Thomas (R N.J.) June 25, 1912; House 1959-Jan. 19, 1970; Gov. 1970- .

CAHOON, William (A-Mas. Vt.) Jan. 12, 1774-May 30, 1833; House 1829-33.

CAIN, Harry Pulliam (R Wash.) Jan. 10, 1906; Senate Dec. 26, 1946-53.

CAIN, Richard Harvey (R S.C.) April 12, 1825-Jan. 18, 1887; House 1873-75, 1877-79.

CAINE, John Thomas (D Utah) Jan. 8, 1829-Sept. 20, 1911; House (Terr. Del.) Nov. 7, 1882-89 (D), 1889-93 (PP).

CAKE, Henry Lutz (R Pa.) Oct. 6, 1827-Aug. 26, 1899; House 1867-71.

CALDER. William Musgrave (R N.Y.) March 3, 1869-March 3, 1945; House 1905-15; Senate 1917-23.

CALDERHEAD, William Alexander (R Kan.) Sept. 26, 1844-Dec. 18, 1928; House 1895-97, 1899-1911.

CALDWELL, Alexander (R Kan.) March 1, 1830-May 19, 1917; Senate 1871-March 24, 1873.

CALDWELL, Andrew Jackson (D Tenn.) July 22, 1837-Nov. 22, 1906; House 1883-87.

CALDWELL, Ben Franklin (D Ill.) Aug. 2, 1848-Dec. 29, 1924; House 1899-1905, 1907-09.

CALDWELL, Charles Pope (D N.Y.) June 18, 1875-July 31, 1940; House 1915-21.

CALDWELL. George Alfred (D Kan.) Oct. 18, 1814-Sept. 17, 1866; House 1843-45, 1849-51.

CALDWELL, Greene Washington (D N.C.) April 13, 1806-July 10, 1864; House 1841-43.

CALDWELL, James (D Ohio) Nov. 30, 1770-May 1838; House 1813-17.

CALDWELL, John Alexander (R Ohio) April 21, 1852-May 24, 1927; House 1889-May 4, 1894.

CALDWELL, John Henry (D Ala.) April 4, 1826-Sept. 4, 1902; House 1873-77.

CALDWELL, John William (D Ky.) Jan. 15, 1837-July 4, 1903; House 1877-83.

CALDWELL, Joseph Pearson (W N.C.) March 5, 1808-June 30, 1853; House 1849-53.

CALDWELL, Millard Fillmore (D Fla.) Feb. 6, 1897; House 1933-41; Gov. 1945-49.

CALDWELL, Patrick Calhoun (SRD S.C.) March 10, 1801-Nov. 22, 1855; House 1841-43.

CALDWELL, Robert Porter (D Tenn.) Dec. 16, 1821-March 12, 1885; House 1871-73.

CALDWELL, William Parker (D Tenn.) Nov. 8, 1832-June 7, 1903; House 1875-79.

CALE, Thomas (I Alaska) Sept. 17, 1848-Feb. 3, 1941; House (Terr. Del.) 1907-09.

CALHOON, John (W Ky.) 1797-—; House 1835-39.

CALHOUN, John Caldwell (cousin of John Ewing Calhoun and Joseph Calhoun) (WD S.C.) March 18, 1782-March 31, 1850; House 1811-Nov. 3, 1817; Senate Dec. 29, 1832-March 3, 1843, Nov. 26, 1845-March 31, 1850; Vice President 1825-Dec. 28, 1832; Secy. of War 1817-25; Secy. of State 1844-45.

CALHOUN, Joseph (cousin of John Caldwell Calhoun and John Ewing Calhoun) (D S.C.) Oct. 22, 1750-April 14, 1817; House June 2, 1807-11.

CALHOUN, William Barron (W Mass.) Dec. 29, 1796-Nov. 8, 1865; House 1835-43.

CALKIN, Hervey Chittenden (D N.Y.) March 23, 1828-April 20, 1913; House 1869-71.

CALKINS, William Henry (R Ind.) Feb. 18, 1842-Jan. 29, 1894; House 1877-Oct. 20, 1884.

CALL, Jacob (— Ind.) —-April 20, 1826; House Dec. 23, 1824-25.

CALL, Richard Keith (uncle of Wilkinson Call) (D Fla.) Oct. 24, 1792-Sept. 14, 1862; House (Terr.Del.) 1823-25; Terr.Gov. 1835-40, 1841-44.

CALL, Wilkinson (nephew of Richard Keith Call and cousin of James David Walker) (D Fla.) Jan. 9, 1834-Aug. 24, 1910; Senate 1879-97.

CALLAHAN, James Yancy (FSil. Okla.) Dec. 19, 1852-May 3, 1935; House 1897-99.

CALLAN, Clair Armstrong (D Neb.) March 20, 1920; House 1965-67.

CALLAWAY, Howard H. (Bo) (R Ga.) May 2, 1927; House 1965-67.

CALLAWAY, Oscar (D Texas) Oct. 2, 1872-Jan. 31, 1947; House 1911-17.

CALLIS, John Benton (R Ala.) Jan. 3, 1828-Sept. 24, 1898; House July 21, 1868-69.

CALVERT, Charles Benedict (UW Md.) Aug. 24, 1808-May 12, 1864; House 1861-63.

CALVIN, Samuel (W Pa.) July 30, 1811-March 12, 1890; House 1849-51.

CAMBRELENG, Churchill Caldom (D N.Y.) Oct. 24, 1786-April 30, 1862; House 1821-39.

CAMDEN, Johnson Newlon (D W.Va.) March 6, 1828-April 25, 1908; Senate 1881-87, Jan. 25, 1893-95.

CAMDEN, Johnson Newlon, Jr. (son of Johnson Newlon Camden (D Ky.) Jan. 5, 1865-Aug. 16, 1942; Senate June 16, 1914-15.

CAMERON, Angus (R Wis.) July 4, 1826-March 30, 1897; Senate 1875-81, March 14, 1881-85.

CAMERON, James Donald (son of Simon Cameron) (R Pa.) May 14, 1833-Aug. 30, 1918; Senate March 20, 1877-97; Secy. of War 1876-77; Chrmn. Rep. Nat. Comm. 1880. 1880.

CAMERON, Ralph Henry (R Ariz.) Oct. 21, 1863-Feb. 12, 1953; House (Terr.Del.) 1909-Feb. 18, 1912; Senate 1921-27.

CAMERON, Ronald Brooks (D Calif.) Aug. 16, 1927; House 1963-67.

CAMERON, Simon (father of James Donald Cameron) (R Pa.) March 8, 1799-June 26, 1889; Senate March 13, 1845-49 (D), 1857-March 4, 1861 and 1867-March 12, 1877 (R); Secy. of War 1861-62.

CAMINETTI, Anthony (D Calif.) July 30, 1854-Nov. 17, 1923; House 1891-95.

CAMP, Albert Sidney (D Ga.) July 26, 1892-July 24, 1954; House Aug. 1, 1939-July 24, 1954.

CAMP, John Henry (R N.Y.) April 4, 1840-Oct. 12, 1892; House 1877-83.

CAMP, John N. Happy (R Okla.) May 11, 1908; House 1969- .

CAMPBELL, Albert James (D Mont.) Dec. 12, 1857-Aug. 9, 1907; House 1899-1901.

CAMPBELL, Alexander (— Ohio) 1779-Nov. 5, 1857; Senate Dec. 11, 1809-13.

CAMPBELL, Alexander (I Ill.) Oct. 4, 1814-Aug. 8, 1898; House 1875-77.

CAMPBELL, Brookins (D Tenn.) 1808-Dec. 25, 1853; House March 4-Dec. 25, 1853.

CAMPBELL, Courtney Warren (D Fla.) April 29, 1895; House 1953-55.

CAMPBELL, Ed Hoyt (R Iowa) March 6, 1882-April 26, 1969; House 1929-33.

CAMPBELL, Felix (D N.Y.) Feb. 28, 1829-Nov. 8, 1902; House 1883-91.

CAMPBELL, George Washington (D Tenn.) Feb. 9, 1769-Feb. 17, 1848; House 1803-09; Senate Oct. 8, 1811-Feb. 11, 1814, Oct. 10, 1815-April 20, 1818; Secy. of the Treasury Feb. 9-Oct. 6, 1814.

CAMPBELL, Guy Edgar (R Pa.) Oct. 9, 1871-Feb. 17, 1940; House 1917-23 (D), 1923-33 (R).

CAMPBELL, Howard Edmond (R Pa.) Jan. 4, 1890; House 1945-47.

CAMPBELL, Jacob Miller (R Pa.) Nov. 20, 1821-Sept. 27, 1888; House 1877-79, 1881-87.

CAMPBELL, James Edwin (nephew of Lewis David Campbell) (D Ohio) July 7, 1843-Dec. 18, 1924; House June 20, 1884-89; Gov. 1889.

CAMPBELL, James Hepburn (W Pa.) Feb. 8, 1820-April 12, 1895; House 1855-57, 1859-63.

CAMPBELL, James Romulus (D Ill.) May 4, 1853-Aug. 12, 1924; House 1897-99.

CAMPBELL, John (F Md.) Sept. 11, 1765-June 23, 1828; House 1801-11.

CAMPBELL, John (brother of Robert Blair Campbell) (SRD S.C.) —-May 19, 1845; House 1829-31 (SRW), 1837-45 (SRD).

CAMPBELL, John Goulder (D Ariz.) June 25, 1827-Dec. 22, 1903; House (Terr. Del.) 1879-81.

CAMPBELL, John Hull (W Pa.) Oct. 10, 1800-Jan. 19, 1868; House 1845-47.

CAMPBELL, John Pierce, Jr. (AP Ky.) Dec. 8, 1820-Oct. 29, 1888; House 1855-57.

CAMPBELL, John Wilson (D Ohio) Feb. 23, 1782-Sept. 24, 1833; House 1817-27.

CAMPBELL, Lewis Davis (uncle of James Edwin Campbell) (D Ohio) Aug. 9, 1811-Nov. 26, 1882; House 1849-May 25, 1858 (W), 1871-73 (D).

CAMPBELL, Philip Pitt (R Kan.) April 25, 1862-May 26, 1941; House 1903-23.

CAMPBELL, Robert Blair (brother of John Campbell of South Carolina) (W S.C.) —-July 12, 1862; House 1823-25 (—), Feb. 27, 1834-35 (Nul.), 1835-37 (W).

CAMPBELL, Samuel (— N.Y.) July 11, 1773-June 2, 1853; House 1821-23.

CAMPBELL, Thomas Jefferson (W Tenn.) 1786-April 13, 1850; House 1841-43.

CAMPBELL, Thompson (D Ill.) 1811-Dec. 6, 1868; House 1851-53.

CAMPBELL, Timothy John (D N.Y.) Jan. 8, 1840-April 7, 1904; House Nov. 3, 1885-89, 1891-95.

CAMPBELL, William Bowen (cousin of Henry Bowen) (D Tenn.) Feb. 1, 1807-Aug. 19, 1867; House 1837-43 (W), July 24, 1866-67 (D); Gov. 1851-53.

CAMPBELL, William W. (AP N.Y.) June 10, 1806-Sept. 7, 1881; House 1845-47.

CAMPBELL, William Wildman (R Ohio) April 2, 1853-Aug. 13, 1927; House 1905-07.

CANBY, Richard Sprigg (W Ohio) Sept. 30, 1808-July 27, 1895; House 1847-49.

CANDLER, Allen Daniel (cousin of Ezekiel Samuel Candler, Jr. and Milton Anthony Candler) (D Ga.) Nov. 4, 1834-Oct. 26, 1910; House 1883-91; Gov. 1898-1902.

CANDLER, Ezekiel Samuel, Jr. (nephew of Milton A. Candler and cousin of Allen Daniel Candler) (D Miss.) Jan. 18, 1862-Dec. 18, 1944; House 1901-21.

CANDLER, John Wilson (R Mass.) Feb. 10, 1828-March 16, 1903; House 1881-83, 1889-91.

CANDLER, Milton Anthony (uncle of Ezekiel Samuel Candler, Jr. and cousin of Allen Daniel Candler) (D Ga.) Jan. 11, 1837-Aug. 8, 1909; House 1875-79.

CANFIELD, Gordon (R N.J.) April 15, 1898; House 1941-61.

CANFIELD, Harry Clifford (D Ind.) Nov. 22, 1875-Feb. 9, 1945; House 1923-33.

CANNON, Arthur Patrick (D Fla.) May 22, 1904-Jan. 23, 1966; House 1939-47.

CANNON, Clarence (D Mo.) April 11, 1879-May 12, 1964; House 1923-May 12, 1964.

CANNON, Frank Jenne (son of George Quayle Cannon) (R Utah) Jan. 25, 1859-July 25, 1933; House (Terr. Del.) 1895-Jan. 4, 1896; Senate Jan. 22, 1896-99.

CANNON, George Quayle (father of Frank Jenne Cannon) (R Utah) Jan. 11, 1827-April 12, 1901; House (Terr. Del.) 1873-81.

CANNON, Howard Walter (D Nev.) Jan. 26, 1912; Senate 1959- .

CANNON, Joseph Gurney (R Ill.) May 7, 1836-Nov. 12, 1926; House 1873-91, 1893-1913, 1915-23; Speaker 1903-11.

CANNON, Marion (PP/D Calif.) Oct. 30, 1834-Aug. 27, 1920; House 1893-95.

CANNON, Newton (D Tenn.) May 22, 1781-Sept. 16, 1841; House Sept. 16, 1814-17, 1819-23; Gov. 1835-39.

CANNON, Raymond Joseph (D Wis.) Aug. 26, 1894-Nov. 15, 1951; House 1933-39.

CANTOR, Jacob Aaron (D N.Y.) Dec. 6, 1854-July 2, 1921; House Nov. 4, 1913-15.

CANTRILL, James Campbell (D Ky.) July 9, 1870-Sept. 2, 1923; House 1909-Sept. 2, 1923.

CAPEHART, Homer Earl (R Ind.) June 6, 1897; Senate 1945-63.

CAPEHART, James (D W.Va.) March 7, 1847-April 28, 1921; House 1891-95.

CAPERTON, Allen Taylor (son of Hugh Caperton) (D W.Va.) Nov. 21, 1810-July 26, 1876; Senate 1875-July 26, 1876.

CAPERTON, Hugh (father of Allen Taylor Caperton) (F Va.) April 17, 1781-Feb. 9, 1847; House 1813-15.

CAPOZZOLI, Louis Joseph (D N.Y.) March 6, 1901; House 1941-45.

CAPPER, Arthur (R Kan.) July 14, 1865-Dec. 19, 1951; Senate 1919-49; Gov. 1915-19

CAPRON, Adin Ballou (R R.I.) Jan. 9, 1841-March 17, 1911; House 1897-1911.

CAPSTICK, John Henry (R N.J.) Sept. 2, 1856-March 17, 1918; House 1915-March 17, 1918.

CARAWAY, Hattie Wyatt (wife of Thaddeus Horatius Carraway) (D Ark.) Feb. 1, 1878-Dec. 21, 1950; Senate Nov. 13, 1931-45.

CARAWAY, Thaddeus Horatius (husband of Hattie Wyatt Caraway) (D Ark.) Oct. 17, 1871-Nov. 6, 1931; House 1913-21; Senate 1921-Nov. 6, 1931.

CARDEN, Cap Robert (D Ky.) Dec. 17, 1866-June 13, 1935; House 1931-June 13, 1935.

CAREW, John Francis (nephew of Thomas Francis Magner) (D N.Y.) April 16, 1873-April 10, 1951; House 1913-Dec. 28, 1929.

CAREY, Hugh L. (D N.Y.) April 11, 1919; House 1961- .

CAREY, John (R Ohio) April 5, 1792-March 17, 1875; House 1859-61.

CAREY, Joseph Maull (father of Robert Davis Carey) (R Wyo.) Jan. 19, 1845-Feb. 5, 1924; House (Terr. Del.) 1885-July 10, 1890; Senate Nov. 15, 1890-95; Gov. 1911-15.

CAREY, Robert Davis (son of Joseph Maull Carey) (R Wyo.) Aug. 12, 1878-Jan. 17, 1937; Senate Dec. 1, 1930-37; Gov. 1919-23.

CARLETON, Ezra Child (D Mich.) Sept. 6, 1838-July 24, 1911; House 1883-87.

CARLETON, Peter (D N.H.) Sept. 19, 1755-April 29, 1828; House 1807-09.

CARLEY, Patrick J. (D N.Y.) Feb. 2, 1866-Feb. 25, 1936; House 1927-35.

CARLILE, John Snyder (U Va.) Dec. 16, 1817-Oct. 24, 1878; House 1855-57 and March 4-July 9, 1861 (AP); Senate July 9, 1861-65 (U).

CARLIN, Charles Creighton (D Va.) April 8, 1866-Oct. 14, 1938; House Nov. 5, 1907-19.

CARLISLE, John Griffin (D Ky.) Sept. 5, 1835-July 31, 1910; House 1877-May 26, 1890; Senate May 26, 1890-Feb. 4, 1893; Speaker 1883-89; Secy. of the Treasury 1893-97.

CARLSON, Frank (R Kan.) Jan. 23, 1893; House 1935-47; Senate Nov. 29, 1950-69; Gov. 1947-50.

CARLTON, Henry Hull (D Ga.) May 14, 1835-Oct. 26, 1905; House 1887-91.

CARLYLE, Frank Ertel (D N.C.) April 7, 1897-Oct. 2, 1960; House 1949-57.

CARMACK, Edward Ward (D Tenn.) Nov. 5, 1858-Nov. 9, 1908; House 1897-1901; Senate 1901-07.

CARMICHAEL, Archibald Hill (D Ala.) June 17, 1864-July 15, 1947; House Nov. 14, 1933-37.

CARMICHAEL, Richard Bennett (JD Md.) Dec. 25, 1807-Oct. 21, 1884; House 1833-35.

CARNAHAN, Albert Sidney Johnson (D Mo.) Jan. 9, 1897-March 24, 1968; House 1945-47, 1949-61.

CARNES, Thomas Petters (— Ga.) 1762-May 5, 1822; House 1793-95.

CARNEY, Charles J. (D Ohio) April 17, 1913; House Nov. 3, 1970- .

CARPENTER, Cyrus Clay (R Iowa) Nov. 24, 1829-May 29, 1898; House 1879-83; Gov. 1872-76.

CARPENTER, Davis (W N.Y.) Dec. 25, 1799-Oct. 22, 1878; House Nov. 8, 1853-55.

CARPENTER, Edmund Nelson (R Pa.) June 27, 1865-Nov. 4, 1952; House 1925-27.

CARPENTER, Levi D. (D N.Y.) Aug. 21, 1802-Oct. 27, 1856; House Nov. 5, 1844-45.

CARPENTER, Lewis Cass (R S.C.) Feb. 20, 1836-March 6, 1908; House Nov. 3, 1874-75.

CARPENTER, Matthew Hale (R Wis.) Dec. 22, 1824-Feb. 24, 1881; Senate 1869-75, 1879-Feb. 24, 1881; President pro tempore 1873-75.

CARPENTER, Terry McGovern (D Neb.) March 28, 1900; House 1933-35.

CARPENTER, William Randolph (D Kan.) April 24, 1894-July 26, 1956; House 1933-37.

CARR, Francis (father of James Carr) (D Mass.) Dec. 6, 1751-Oct. 6, 1821; House April 6, 1812-13.

CARR, James (son of Francis Carr) (— Mass.) Sept. 9, 1777-Aug. 24, 1818; House 1815-17.

CARR, John (D Ind.) April 9, 1793-Jan. 20, 1845; House 1831-37, 1839-41.

CARR, Nathan Tracy (D Ind.) Dec. 25, 1833-May 28, 1885; House Dec. 5, 1876-77.

CARR, Wooda Nicholas (D Pa.) Feb. 6, 1871-June 28, 1953; House 1913-15.

CARRIER, Chester Otto (R Ky.) May 5, 1897; House Nov. 30, 1943-45.

CARRIGG, Joseph Leonard (R Pa.) Feb. 23, 1901; House Nov. 6, 1951-59.

CARROLL, Charles (cousin of Daniel Carroll) (F Md.) Sept. 19, 1737-Nov. 14, 1832; Senate 1789-Nov. 30, 1792; Cont. Cong. 1776-78.

CARROLL, Charles Hobart (great-grandson of Daniel Carroll) (CW N.Y.) May 4, 1794-June 8, 1865; House 1843-47.

CARROLL, Daniel (uncle of Richard Brent, cousin of Charles Carroll and great-grandfather of Charles Hobart Carroll) (F Md.) July 22, 1730-May 7, 1796; House 1789-91; Cont. Cong. 1780-84.

CARROLL, James (D Md.) Dec. 2, 1791-Jan. 16, 1873; House 1839-41.

CARROLL, John Albert (D Colo.) July 30, 1901; House 1947-51; Senate 1957-63.

CARROLL, John Michael (D N.Y.) April 27, 1823-May 8, 1901; House 1871-73.

CARSON, Henderson Haverfield (R Ohio) Oct. 25, 1893; House 1943-45, 1947-49.

CARSON, Samuel Price (D N.C.) Jan. 22, 1798-Nov. 2, 1838; House 1825-33.

CARSS, William Leighton (F-L Minn.) Feb. 15, 1865-May 31, 1931; House 1919-21 (I), 1925-29 (F-L).

CARTER, Albert Edward (R Calif.) July 5, 1881-Aug. 7, 1964; House 1925-45.

CARTER, Charles David (D Okla.) Aug. 16, 1868-April 9, 1929; House Nov. 16, 1907-27.

CARTER, John (— S.C.) Sept. 10, 1792-June 20, 1850; House Dec. 11, 1822-29.

CARTER, Luther Cullen (UR N.Y.) Feb. 25, 1805-Jan. 3, 1875; House 1859-61.

CARTER, Steven V. (D Iowa) Oct. 8, 1915-Nov. 4, 1959; House Jan. 3-Nov. 4, 1959.

CARTER, Thomas Henry (R Mont.) Oct. 30, 1854-Sept. 17, 1911; House (Terr. Del.) March 4,-Nov. 7, 1889, (Representative) Nov. 8, 1889-91; Senate 1895-1901, 1905-11; Chrmn. Rep. Nat. Comm. 1892.

CARTER, Tim Lee (R Ky.) Sept. 2, 1910; House 1965- .

CARTER, Timothy Jarvis (D Maine) Aug. 18, 1800-March 14, 1838; House Sept. 4, 1837-March 14, 1838.

CARTER, Vincent Michael (R Wyo.) Nov. 6, 1891; House 1929-35.

CARTER, William Blount (W Tenn.) Oct. 22, 1792-April 17, 1848; House 1835-41.

CARTER, William Henry (R Mass.) June 15, 1864-April 23, 1955; House 1915-19.

CARTTER, David Kellogg (D Ohio) June 22, 1812-April 16, 1887; House 1849-53.

CARTWRIGHT, Wilburn (D Okla.) Jan. 12, 1892; House 1927-43.

CARUTH, Asher Graham (D Ky.) Feb. 7, 1844-Nov. 25, 1907; House 1887-95.

CARUTHERS, Robert Looney (W Tenn.) July 31, 1800-Oct. 2, 1882; House 1841-43.

CARUTHERS, Samuel (D Mo.) Oct. 13, 1820-July 20, 1860; House 1853-57 (W), 1857-59 (D).

CARVILLE, Edward Peter (D Nev.) May 14, 1885-June 27, 1956; Senate July 25, 1945-47; Gov. 1939-45.

CARY, George (— Ga.) Aug. 7, 1789-Sept. 10, 1843; House 1823-27.

CARY, George Booth (D Va.) 1811-March 5, 1850; House 1841-43.

CARY, Glover H. (D Ky.) May 1, 1885-Dec. 5, 1936; House 1931-Dec. 5, 1936.

CARY, Jeremiah Eaton (D N.Y.) April 30, 1803-June, 1888; House 1843-45.

CARY, Samuel Fenton (R Ohio) Feb. 18, 1814-Sept. 29, 1900; House Nov. 21, 1867-69.

CARY, Shepard (D Maine) July 3, 1805-Aug. 9, 1866; House May 10, 1844-45.

CARY, William Joseph (R Wis.) March 22, 1865-Jan. 2, 1934; House 1907-19.

CASE, Charles (D Ind.) Dec. 21, 1817-June 30, 1883; House Dec. 7, 1857-61.

CASE, Clifford Philip (R N.J.) April 16, 1904; House 1945-Aug. 16, 1953; Senate 1955- .

CASE, Francis Higbee (R S.D.) Dec. 9, 1896-June 22, 1962; House 1937-51; Senate 1951-June 22, 1962.

CASE, Walter (— N.Y.) 1776-Oct. 7, 1859; House 1819-21.

CASEY, John Joseph (D Pa.) May 26, 1875-May 5, 1929; House 1913-17, 1919-21, 1923-25, 1927-May 5, 1929.

CASEY, Joseph (W Pa.) Dec. 17, 1814-Feb. 10, 1879; House 1849-51.

CASEY, Joseph Edward (D Mass.) Dec. 27, 1898; House 1935-43.

CASEY, Levi (— S.C.) about 1752-Feb. 3, 1807; House 1803-Feb. 3, 1807.

CASEY, Lyman Rufus (R N.D.) May 6, 1837-Jan. 26, 1914; Senate Nov. 25, 1889-93.

CASEY, Robert Randolph (Bob) (D Texas) July 27, 1915; House 1959- .

CASEY, Samuel Lewis (R Ky.) Feb. 12, 1821-Aug. 25, 1902; House March 10, 1862-63.

CASEY, Zadoc (JD Ill.) March 7, 1796-Sept. 4, 1862; House 1833-43.

CASKIE, John Samuels (D Va.) Nov. 8, 1821-Dec. 16, 1869; House 1851-59.

CASON, Thomas Jefferson (R Ind.) Sept. 13, 1828-July 10, 1901; House 1873-77.

CASS, Lewis (D Mich.) Oct. 9, 1782-June 17, 1866; Senate 1845-May 29, 1848, 1849-57; Gov. (Mich. Terr.) 1813-31; Secy. of War 1831-36; Secy. of State 1857-60.

CASSEDY, George (D N.J.) Sept. 16, 1783-Dec. 31, 1842; House 1821-27.

CASSEL, Henry Burd (R Pa.) Oct. 19, 1855-April 28, 1926; House Nov. 5, 1901-09.

CASSERLY, Eugene (D Calif.) Nov. 13, 1820-June 14, 1883; Senate 1869-Nov. 29, 1873.

CASSIDY, George Williams (D Nev.) April 25, 1836-June 24, 1892; House 1881-85.

CASSIDY, James Henry (R Ohio) Oct. 28, 1869-Aug. 23, 1926; House April 20, 1909-11.

CASSINGHAM, John Wilson (D Ohio) June 22, 1840-March 14, 1930; House 1901-05.

CASTELLOW, Bryant Thomas (D Ga.) July 29, 1876-July 23, 1962; House Nov. 8, 1932-37.

CASTLE, Curtis Harvey (P/D Calif.) Oct. 4, 1848-July 12, 1928; House 1897-99.

CASTLE, James Nathan (D Minn.) May 23, 1836-Jan. 2, 1903; House 1891-93.

CASTOR, George Albert (R Pa.) Aug. 6, 1855-Feb. 19, 1906; House Feb. 16, 1904-Feb. 19, 1906.

CASWELL, Lucien Bonaparte (R Wis.) Nov. 27, 1827-April 26, 1919; House 1875-83, 1885-91.

CATCHINGS, Thomas Clendinen (D Miss.) Jan. 11, 1847-Dec. 24, 1927; House 1885-1901.

CATE, George Washington (IRef. Wis.) Sept. 17, 1825-March 7, 1905; House 1875-77.

CATE, William Henderson (D Ark.) Nov. 11, 1839-Aug. 23, 1899; House 1889-March 5, 1890, 1891-93.

CATHCART, Charles William (D Ind.) July 24, 1809-Aug. 22, 1888; House 1845-49; Senate Dec. 6, 1852-53.

CATLIN, George Smith (D Conn.) Aug. 24, 1808-Dec. 26, 1851; House 1843-45.

CATLIN, Theron Ephron (R Mo.) May 16, 1878-March 19, 1960; House 1911-Aug. 12, 1912.

CATRON, Thomas Benton (R N.M.) Oct. 6, 1840-May 15, 1921; House (Terr. Del.) 1895-97; Senate March 27, 1912-17.

CATTELL, Alexander Gilmore (R N.J.) Feb. 12, 1816-April 8, 1894; Senate Sept. 19, 1866-71.

CAULFIELD, Bernard Gregory (D Ill.) Oct. 18, 1828-Dec. 19, 1887; House Feb. 1, 1875-77.

CAULFIELD, Henry Stewart (R Mo.) Dec. 9, 1873-May 11, 1966; House 1907-09; Gov. 1929-33.

CAUSEY, John Williams (D Del.) Sept. 19, 1841-Oct. 1, 1908; House 1891-95.

CAUSIN, John M. S. (W Md.) 1811-Jan. 30, 1861; House 1843-45.

CAVALCANTE, Anthony (D Pa.) Feb. 6, 1897-Oct. 29, 1966; House 1949-51.

CAVANAUGH, James Michael (D Minn./ Mont.) July 4, 1823-Oct. 30, 1879; House May 11, 1858-59 (Minn.), 1867-71 (Terr. Del.-Mont.).

CAVICCHIA, Peter Angelo (R N.J.) May 22, 1879-Sept. 11, 1967; House 1931-37.

CEDERBERG, Elford Alfred (R Mich.) March 6, 1918; House 1953- .

CELLER, Emanuel (D N.Y.) May 6, 1888; House 1923- .

CESSNA, John (R Pa.) June 29, 1821-Dec. 13, 1893; House 1869-71, 1873-75.

CHACE, Jonathan (R R.I.) July 22, 1829-June 30, 1917; House 1881-Jan. 26, 1885; Senate Jan. 20, 1885-April 9, 1889.

CHADWICK, E. Wallace (R Pa.) Jan. 17, 1884-Aug. 18, 1969; House 1947-49.

CHAFFEE, Calvin Clifford (AP Mass.) Aug. 28, 1811-Aug. 8, 1896; House 1855-59.

CHAFFEE, Jerome Bunty (R Colo.) April 17, 1825-March 9, 1886; House (Terr. Del.) 1871-75; Senate Nov. 15, 1876-79.

CHALMERS, William Wallace (R Ohio) Nov. 1, 1861-Oct. 1, 1944; House 1921-23, 1925-31.

CHALMERS, James Ronald (son of Joseph Williams Chalmers) (I Miss.) Jan. 12, 1831-April 9, 1898; House 1877-April 29, 1882 (D), June 25, 1884-85 (I).

CHALMERS, Joseph Williams (father of James Ronald Chalmers) (D Miss.) Dec. 20, 1806-June 16, 1853; Senate Nov. 3, 1845-47.

CHAMBERLAIN, Charles Ernest (R Mich.) July 22, 1917; House 1957- .

CHAMBERLAIN, Ebenezer Mattoon (D Ind.) Aug. 20, 1805-March 14, 1861; House 1853-55.

CHAMBERLAIN, George Earle (D Ore.) Jan. 1, 1854-July 9, 1928; Senate 1909-21; Gov. 1903-09.

CHAMBERLAIN, Jacob Payson (R N.Y.) Aug. 1, 1802-Oct. 5, 1878; House 1861-63.

CHAMBERLAIN, John Curtis (F N.H.) June 5, 1772-Dec. 8, 1834; House 1809-11.

CHAMBERLAIN, William (F Vt.) April 27, 1755-Sept. 27, 1828; House 1803-05, 1809-11.

CHAMBERS, David (— Ohio) Nov. 25, 1780-Aug. 8, 1864; House Oct. 9, 1821-23.

CHAMBERS, Ezekiel Forman (W Md.) Feb. 28, 1788-Jan. 30, 1867; Senate Jan. 24, 1826-Dec. 20, 1834.

CHAMBERS, George (W Pa.) Feb. 24, 1786-March 25, 1866; House 1833-37.

CHAMBERS, Henry H. (D Ala.) Oct. 1, 1790-Feb. 24, 1826; Senate 1825-Feb. 24, 1826.

CHAMBERS, John (W Ky.) Oct. 6, 1780-Sept. 21, 1852; House Dec. 1, 1828-29, 1835-39; Gov. of Territory of Iowa 1841-45.

CHAMPION, Edwin Van Meter (D Ill.) Sept. 18, 1890; House 1937-39.

CHAMPION, Epaphroditus (F Conn.) April 6, 1756-Dec. 22, 1834; House 1807-17.

CHAMPLIN, Christopher Grant (— R.I.) April 12, 1768-March 18, 1840; House 1797-1801; Senate June 26, 1809-Oct. 2, 1811.

CHANDLER, Albert Benjamin (D Ky.) July 14, 1898; Senate Oct. 10, 1939-Nov. 1, 1945; Gov. 1935-39, 1955-59.

CHANDLER, John (brother of Thomas Chandler and uncle of Zachariah Chandler) (D Mass./Maine) Feb. 1, 1762-Sept. 25, 1841; House (Mass.) 1805-09; Senate (Maine) June 14, 1820-29.

CHANDLER, Joseph Ripley (W Pa.) Aug. 22, 1792-July 10, 1880; House 1849-55.

CHANDLER, Thomas (brother of John Chandler and uncle of Zachariah Chandler) (D N.H.) Aug. 10, 1772-Jan. 28, 1866; House 1829-33.

CHANDLER, Thomas Alberter (R Okla.) July 26, 1871-June 22, 1953; House 1917-19, 1921-23.

CHANDLER, Walter (Clift) (D Tenn.) Oct. 5, 1887-Oct. 1, 1967; House 1935-Jan. 2, 1940.

CHANDLER, Walter Marion (R N.Y.) Dec. 8, 1867-March 16, 1935; House (Pro.) 1913-19, (R) 1921-23.

CHANDLER, William Eaton (R N.H.) Dec. 28, 1835-Nov. 20, 1917; Senate June 14, 1887-March 3, 1889, June 18, 1889-1901; Secy. of the Navy 1882-85.

CHANDLER, Zachariah (nephew of John Chandler and Thomas Chandler and grandfather of Frederick Hale) (R Mich.) Dec. 10, 1813-Nov. 1, 1879; Senate 1857-75, Feb. 22, 1879-Nov. 1, 1879; Secy. of the Interior 1875-77.

CHANEY, John (JD Ohio) Jan. 12, 1790-April 10, 1881; House 1833-39.

CHANEY, John Crawford (R Ind.) Feb. 1, 1853-April 26, 1940; House 1905-09.

CHANLER, John Winthrop (father of William Astor Chanler) (D N.Y.) Sept. 14, 1826-Oct. 19, 1877; House 1863-69.

CHANLER, William Astor (son of John Winthrop Chanler) (D N.Y.) June 11, 1867-March 4, 1934; House 1899-1901.

CHAPIN, Alfred Clark (D N.Y.) March 8, 1848-Oct. 2, 1936; House Nov. 3, 1891-Nov. 16, 1892.

CHAPIN, Chester Williams (D Mass.) Dec. 16, 1798-June 10, 1883; House 1875-77.

CHAPIN, Graham Hurd (D N.Y.) Feb. 10, 1799-Sept. 8, 1843; House 1835-37.

CHAPMAN, Andrew Grant (son of John Grant Chapman) (D Md.) Jan. 17, 1839-Sept. 25, 1892; House 1881-83.

CHAPMAN, Augustus Alexandria (VBD Va.) March 9, 1803-June 7, 1876; House 1843-47.

CHAPMAN, Bird Beers (D Neb.) Aug. 24, 1821-Sept. 21, 1871; House (Terr. Del.) 1855-57.

CHAPMAN, Charles (W Conn.) June 21, 1799-Aug. 7, 1869; House 1851-53.

CHAPMAN, Henry (D Pa.) Feb. 4, 1804-April 11, 1891; House 1857-59.

CHAPMAN, John (F Pa.) Oct. 18, 1740- Jan. 27, 1800; House 1797-99.

CHAPMAN, John Grant (father of Andrew Grant Chapman) (W Md.) July 5, 1798-Dec. 10, 1856; House 1845-49.

CHAPMAN, Pleasant Thomas (R Ill.) Oct. 8, 1854-Jan. 31, 1931; House 1905-11.

CHAPMAN, Reuben (D Ala.) July 15, 1799-May 16, 1882; House 1835-47; Gov. 1847-49.

CHAPMAN, Virgil Munday (D Ky.) March 15, 1895-March 8, 1951; House 1925-29, 1931-49; Senate 1949-March 8, 1951.

CHAPMAN, William Williams (D Iowa) Aug. 11, 1808-Oct. 18, 1892; House (Terr. Del.) Sept. 10, 1838-Oct. 27, 1840.

CHAPPELL, Absalom Harris (cousin of Lucius Quintus Cincinnatus Lamar) (SRW Ga.) Dec. 18, 1801-Dec. 11, 1878; House Oct. 2, 1843-45.

CHAPPELL, John Joel (SRWD S.C.) Jan. 19, 1782-May 23, 1871; House 1813-17.

CHAPPELL, William V., Jr. (D Fla.) Feb. 3, 1922; House 1969- .

CHARLES, William Barclay (R N.Y.) April 3, 1861-Nov. 25, 1950; House 1915-17.

CHARLTON, Robert Milledge (— Ga.) Jan. 19, 1807-Jan. 18, 1854; Senate May 31, 1852-53.

CHASE, Dudley (uncle of Salmon Portland Chase and Dudley Chase Denison) (JD Vt.) Dec. 30, 1771-Feb. 23, 1846; Senate 1813-Nov. 3, 1817, 1825-31.

CHASE, George William (W N.Y.) —-April 17, 1867; House 1853-55.

CHASE, Jackson Burton (R Neb.) Aug. 19, 1890; House 1955-57.

CHASE, James Mitchell (R Pa.) Dec. 19, 1891-Jan. 1, 1945; House 1927-33.

CHASE, Lucien Bonaparte (D Tenn.) Dec. 5, 1817-Dec. 4, 1864; House 1845-49.

CHASE, Ray P. (R Minn.) March 12, 1880-Sept. 18, 1948; House 1933-35.

CHASE, Salmon Portland (nephew of Dudley Chase and cousin of Dudley Chase Denison) (R Ohio) Jan. 13, 1808-May 7, 1873; Senate 1849-55 (F-S/D), March 4-6, 1861 (R); Governor 1856-60; Secy. of the Treasury 1861-64; Chief Justice of the Supreme Court 1864-73.

CHASE, Samuel (Ad.D N.Y.) —-Aug. 3, 1838; House 1827-29.

CHASTAIN, Elijah Webb (UD Ga.) Sept. 25, 1813-April 9, 1874; House 1851-55.

CHATHAM, Richard Thurmond (D N.C.) Aug. 16, 1896-Feb. 5, 1957; House 1949-57.

CHAVES, Jose Francisco (R N.M.) June 27, 1833-Nov. 26, 1904; House (Terr. Del.) 1865-67, Feb. 20, 1869-71.

CHAVEZ, Dennis (D N.M.) April 8, 1888-Nov. 18, 1962; House 1931-35; Senate May 11, 1935-Nov. 18, 1962.

CHEADLE, Joseph Bonaparte (R Ind.) Aug. 14, 1842-May 28, 1904; House 1887-91.

CHEATHAM, Henry Plummer (R N.C.) Dec. 27, 1857-Nov. 29, 1935; House 1889-93.

CHEATHAM, Richard (W Tenn.) Feb. 20, 1799-Sept. 9, 1845; House 1837-39.

CHELF, Frank Leslie (D Ky.) Sept. 22, 1907; House 1945-67.

CHENEY, Person Colby (R N.H.) Feb. 25, 1828-June 19, 1901; Senate Nov. 24, 1886-June 14, 1887; Gov. 1875-77.

CHENOWETH, John Edgar (R Colo.) Aug. 17, 1897; House 1941-49, 1951-65.

CHESNEY, Chester Anton (D Ill.) March 9, 1916; House 1949-51.

CHESTNUT, James, Jr. (SRD S.C.) Jan. 18 1815-Feb. 1, 1885; Senate Dec. 3, 1858-Nov. 10, 1860.

CHETWOOD, William (JD N.J.) June 17, 1771-Dec. 17, 1857; House Dec. 5, 1836-37.

CHEVES, Langdon (D S.C.) Sept. 17, 1776-June 26, 1857; House Dec. 31, 1810-15; Speaker 1814-15.

CHICKERING, Charles Addison (R N.Y.) Nov. 26, 1843-Feb. 13, 1900; House 1893-Feb. 13, 1900.

CHILCOTT, George Miles (R Colo.) Jan. 2, 1828-March 6, 1891; House (Terr. Del.) 1867-69; Senate April 17, 1882-Jan. 27, 1883.

CHILD, Thomas, Jr. (D N.Y.) March 22, 1818-March 9, 1869; House 1855-57.

CHILDS, Robert Andrew (R Ill.) March 22, 1845-Dec. 19, 1915; House 1893-95.

CHILDS, Timothy (W N.Y.) 1785-Nov. 8, 1847; House 1829-31, 1835-39, 1841-43.

CHILES, Lawton (D Fla.) April 3, 1930; Senate 1971- .

CHILTON, Horace (grandson of Thomas Chilton) (D Texas) Dec. 29, 1853-June 12, 1932; Senate June 10, 1891-March 22, 1892, 1895-1901.

CHILTON, Samuel (W Va.) Sept. 7, 1804-Jan. 14, 1867; House 1843-45.

CHILTON, Thomas (grandfather of Horace Chilton) (W Ky.) July 30, 1798-Aug. 15, 1854; House Dec. 22, 1827-31, 1833-35.

CHILTON, William Edwin (D W.Va.) March 17, 1858-Nov. 7, 1939; Senate 1911-17.

CHINDBLOM, Carl Richard (R Ill.) Dec. 21, 1870-Sept. 12, 1956; House 1919-33.

CHINN, Joseph William (D Va.) Nov. 16, 1798-Dec. 5, 1840; House 1831-35.

CHINN, Thomas Withers (cousin of Robert Enoch Withers) (W La.) Nov. 22, 1791-May 22, 1852; House 1839-41.

CHIPERFIELD, Burnett Mitchell (father of Robert Bruce Chiperfield) (R Ill.) June 14, 1870-June 24, 1940; House 1915-17, 1929-33.

CHIPERFIELD, Robert Bruce (son of Burnett Mitchell Chiperfield) (R Ill.) Nov 20, 1899 April 9, 1971; House 1939-63.

CHIPMAN, Daniel (brother of Nathaniel Chipman) (F Vt.) Oct. 22, 1765-April 23, 1850; House 1815-May 5, 1816.

CHIPMAN, John Logan (grandson of Nathaniel Chipman) (D Mich.) June 5, 1830-Aug. 17, 1893; House 1887-Aug. 17, 1893.

CHIPMAN, John Smith (D Mich.) Aug. 10, 1800-July 27, 1869; House 1845-47.

CHIPMAN, Nathaniel (brother of Daniel Chipman and grandfather of John Logan Chipman) (— Vt.) Nov. 15, 1752-Jan. 15, 1843; Senate Oct. 17, 1797-1803.

CHIPMAN, Norton Parker (R D.C.) March 7, 1836-Feb. 1, 1924; House (Delegate) April 21, 1871-75.

CHISHOLM, Shirley (D N.Y.) Nov. 30, 1924; House 1969- .

CHITTENDEN, Martin (— Vt.) March 12, 1763-Sept. 5, 1840; House 1803-13; Gov. 1814-15.

CHITTENDEN, Simeon Baldwin (R N.Y.) March 29, 1814-April 14, 1889; House Nov. 3, 1874-81.

CHITTENDEN, Thomas Cotton (W N.Y.) Aug. 30, 1788-Aug. 22, 1866; House 1839-43.

CHOATE, Rufus (W Mass.) Oct. 1, 1799-July 13, 1859; House 1831-June 30, 1834; Senate Feb. 23, 1841-45.

CHRISMAN, James Stone (D Ky.) Sept. 14, 1818-July 29, 1881; House 1853-55.

CHRISTGAU, Victor (R Minn.) Sept. 20, 1894; House 1929-33.

CHRISTIANCY, Isaac Peckham (R Mich.) March 12, 1812-Sept. 8, 1890; 1875-Feb. 10, 1879.

CHRISTIANSON, Theodore (R Minn.) Sept. 12, 1883-Dec. 9, 1948; House 1933-37.

CHRISTIE, Gabriel (— Md.) 1755-April 1, 1808; House 1793-97, 1799-1801.

CHRISTOPHER, George Henry (D Mo.) Dec. 9, 1888-Jan. 23, 1959; House 1949-51, 1955-Jan. 23, 1959.

CHRISTOPHERSON, Charles Andrew (R S.D.) July 23, 1871-Nov. 2, 1951; House 1919-33.

CHUDOFF, Earl (D Pa.) Nov. 16, 1907; House 1949-Jan. 5, 1958.

CHURCH, Denver Samuel (D Calif.) Dec. 11, 1862-Feb. 21, 1952; House 1913-19, 1933-35.

CHURCH, Frank Forrester (D Idaho) July 25, 1924; Senate 1957- .

CHURCH, Marguerite Stitt (widow of Ralph Edwin Church) (R Ill.) Sept. 13, 1892; House 1951-63.

CHURCH, Ralph Edwin (husband of Marguerite Stitt Church) (R Ill.) May 5, 1883-March 21, 1950; House 1935-41, 1943-March 21, 1950.

CHURCHILL, George Bosworth (R Mass.) Oct. 24, 1866-July 1, 1925; House March 4-July 1, 1925.

CHURCHILL, John Charles (R N.Y.) Jan. 17, 1821-June 4, 1905; House 1867-71.

CHURCHWELL, William Montgomery (D Tenn.) Feb. 20, 1826-Aug. 18, 1862; House 1851-55.

CILLEY, Bradbury (uncle of Jonathan Cilley and Joseph Cilley) (F N.H.) Feb. 1, 1760-Dec. 17, 1831; House 1813-17.

CILLEY, Jonathan (nephew of Bradbury Cilley and brother of Joseph Cilley) (JD Maine) July 2, 1802-Feb. 24, 1838; House 1837-Feb. 24, 1838.

CILLEY, Joseph (nephew of Bradbury Cilley and brother of Jonathan Cilley) (D N.H.) Jan. 4, 1791-Sept. 12, 1887; Senate June 13, 1846-47.

CITRON, William Michael (D Conn.) Aug. 29, 1896; House 1935-39.

CLAFLIN, William (R Mass.) March 6, 1818-Jan. 5, 1905; House 1877-81; Gov. 1869-71.

CLAGETT, Clifton (— N.H.) Dec. 3, 1762-Jan. 25, 1829; House 1803-05, 1817-21.

CLAGETT, William Horace (uncle of Samuel Barrett Pettengill) (R Mont.) Sept. 21, 1838-Aug. 3, 1901; House (Terr. Del.) 1871-73.

CLAGUE, Frank (R Minn.) July 13, 1865-March 25, 1952; House 1921-33.

CLAIBORNE, James Robert (D Mo.) June 22, 1882-Feb. 16, 1944; House 1933-37.

CLAIBORNE, John (son of Thomas Claiborne) (— Va.) 1777-Oct. 9, 1808; House 1805-Oct. 9, 1808.

CLAIBORNE, John Francis Hamtramck (nephew of William Charles Cole Claiborne and Nathaniel Herbert Claiborne and great-grandfather of Herbert Claiborne Pell, Jr.) (JD Miss.) April 24, 1809-May 17, 1884; House 1835-37, July 18, 1837-Feb. 5, 1838.

CLAIBORNE, Nathaniel Herbert (brother of William Charles Cole Claiborne and uncle of John Francis Hamtramck Claiborne) (R Va.) Nov. 14, 1777-Aug. 15, 1859; House 1825-37.

CLAIBORNE, Thomas (father of John Claiborne and Thomas Claiborne) (— Va.) Feb. 1, 1749-1812; House 1793-99, 1801-05.

CLAIBORNE, Thomas (son of Thomas Claiborne) (D Tenn.) May 17, 1780-Jan. 7, 1856; House 1817-19.

CLAIBORNE, William Charles Cole (brother of Nathaniel Herbert Claiborne and uncle of John Francis Hamtramck Claiborne) (Jeff. D Tenn.; D La.) 1775-Nov. 23, 1817; House 1797-1801 (Tenn.); Senate March 4-Nov. 23, 1817 (La.); Gov. of Terr. of Miss. 1801-03; Gov. of Terr. of Orleans 1804-12; Gov. of La. 1812-16.

CLANCY, Donald D. (R Ohio) July 24, 1921; House 1961- .

CLANCY, John Michael (D N.Y.) May 7, 1837-July 25, 1903; House 1889-95.

CLANCY, John Richard (D N.Y.) March 8, 1859-April 21, 1932; House 1913-15.

CLANCY, Robert Henry (R Mich.) March 14, 1882-April 23, 1962; House 1923-25 (D), 1927-33 (R).

CLAPP, Asa William Henry (D Maine) March 6, 1805-March 22, 1891; House 1847-49.

CLAPP, Moses Edwin (R Minn.) May 21, 1851-March 6, 1929; Senate Jan. 23, 1901-1917.

CLARDY, John Daniel (D Ky.) Aug. 30, 1828-Aug. 20, 1918; House 1895-99.

CLARDY, Kit Francis (R Mich.) June 17, 1892-Sept. 5, 1961; House 1953-55.

CLARDY, Martin Linn (D Mo.) April 26, 1844-July 5, 1914; House 1879-89.

CLARK, Abraham (— N.J.) Feb. 15, 1726-Sept. 15, 1794; House 1791-Sept. 15, 1794; Cont. Cong. 1776-78, 1779-83, 1787-89.

CLARK, Alvah Augustus (cousin of James Nelson Pidcock) (D N.J.) Sept. 13, 1840-Dec. 27, 1912; House 1877-81.

CLARK, Ambrose Williams (R N.Y.) Feb. 19, 1810-Oct. 13, 1887; House 1861-65.

CLARK, Amos, Jr. (R N.J.) Nov. 8, 1828-Oct. 31, 1912; House 1873-75.

CLARK, Charles Benjamin (R Wis.) Aug. 24, 1844-Sept. 10, 1891; House 1887-91.

CLARK, Charles Nelson (R Mo.) Aug. 21, 1827-Oct. 4, 1902; House 1895-97.

CLAY, Matthew (D Va.) March 25, 1754-May 27, 1815; House 1797 1813, March 4-May 27, 1815.

CLAY, William (D Mo.) April 30, 1931; House 1969- .

CLAYPOOL, Harold Kile (son of Horatio Clifford Claypool and cousin of John Barney Peterson) (D Ohio) June 2, 1886-Aug. 2, 1958; House 1937-43.

CLAYPOOL, Horatio Clifford (father of Harold Kile Claypool and cousin of John Barney Peterson) (D Ohio) Feb. 9, 1859-Jan. 19, 1921; House 1911-15, 1917-19.

CLAYTON, Augustin Smith (SRD Ga.) Nov. 27, 1783-June 21, 1839; House Jan. 21, 1832-35.

CLAYTON, Bertram Tracy (brother of Henry De Lamar Clayton) (D N.Y.) Oct. 19, 1862-May 30, 1918; House 1899-1901.

CLAYTON, Charles (R Calif.) Oct. 5, 1825-Oct. 4, 1885; House 1873-75.

CLAYTON, Henry De Lamar (brother of Bertram Tracy Clayton) (D Ala.) Feb. 10, 1857-Dec. 21, 1929; House 1897-May 25, 1914.

CLAYTON, John Middleton (nephew of Joshua Clayton, cousin of Thomas Clayton and great-grand-uncle of C. Douglass Buck) (W Del.) July 24, 1796-Nov. 9, 1856; Senate 1829-Dec. 29, 1836 (NR), 1845-Feb. 23, 1849 and 1853-Nov. 9, 1856 (W); Secy. of State March 7, 1849-July 22, 1850.

CLAYTON, Joshua (father of Thomas Clayton and uncle of John Middleton Clayton) (— Del.) July 20, 1744-Aug. 11, 1798; Senate Jan. 19, 1798-Aug. 11, 1798; Gov. 1793-98.

CLAYTON, Powell (R Ark.) Aug. 7, 1833-Aug. 25, 1914; Senate 1871-77; Gov. 1868.

CLAYTON, Thomas (son of Joshua Clayton and cousin of John Middleton Clayton) (W Del.) March 9, 1778-Aug. 21, 1854; House 1815-17 (F); Senate Jan. 8, 1824-27 (F), Jan. 9, 1837-47 (W).

CLEARY, William Edward (D N.Y.) July 20, 1849-Dec. 20, 1932; House March 5, 1918-21, 1923-27.

CLEMENS, Jeremiah (D Ala.) Dec. 28, 1814-May 21, 1865; Senate Nov. 30, 1849-53.

CLEMENS, Sherrard (D Va.) April 28, 1820-June 30, 1881; House Dec. 6, 1852-53, 1857-61.

CLEMENTE, Louis Gary (D N.Y.) June 10, 1908-May 13, 1968; House 1949-53.

CLEMENTS, Andrew Jackson (U Tenn.) Dec. 23, 1832-Nov. 7, 1913; House 1861-63.

CLEMENTS, Earle C. (D Ky.) Oct. 22, 1896; House 1945-Jan. 6, 1948; Senate Nov. 27, 1950-57; Gov. Jan. 1948-Nov., 1950.

CLEMENTS, Isaac (R Ill.) March 31, 1837-May 31, 1909; House 1873-75.

CLEMENTS, Judson Claudius (D Ga.) Feb. 12, 1846-June 18, 1917; House 1881-91.

CLEMENTS, Newton Nash (— Ala.) Dec. 23, 1837-Feb. 20, 1900; House Dec. 8, 1880-81.

CLENDENIN, David (— Ohio) — - —; House Oct. 11, 1814-17.

CLEVELAND, Chauncey Fitch (D Conn.) Feb. 16, 1799-June 6, 1887; House 1849-53; Gov. 1842-43.

CLEVELAND, James C. (R N.H.) June 13, 1920; House 1963- .

CLEVELAND, Jesse Franklin (UD Ga.) Oct. 25, 1804-June 22, 1841; House Oct. 5, 1835-39.

CLEVELAND, Orestes (D N.J.) March 2, 1829-March 30, 1896; House 1869-71.

CLEVENGER, Cliff (R Ohio) Aug. 20, 1885-Dec. 13, 1960; House 1939-59.

CLEVENGER, Raymond F. (D Mich.) June 6, 1926; House 1965-67.

CLEVER, Charles P. (D N.M.) Feb. 23, 1830-July 8, 1874; House (Terr. Del.) Sept. 2, 1867-Feb. 20, 1869.

CLIFFORD, Nathan (D Maine) Aug. 18, 1803-July 25, 1881; House 1839-43; Atty. Gen. of U.S. Oct. 17, 1846-March 17, 1848; Assoc. Justice of Supreme Court Jan. 28, 1858-July 25, 1881.

CLIFT, Joseph Wales (R Ga.) Sept. 30, 1837-May 2, 1908; House July 25, 1868-69.

CLINCH, Duncan Lamont (W Ga.) April 6, 1787-Nov. 27, 1849; House Feb. 15, 1844-45.

CLINE, Cyrus (D Ind.) July 12, 1856-Oct. 5, 1923; House 1909-17.

CLINGMAN, Thomas Lanier (D N.C.) July 27, 1812-Nov. 3, 1897; House 1843-45 (W), 1847-May 7, 1858 (D); Senate May 7, 1858-March 28, 1861.

CLINTON, De Witt (half brother of James Graham Clinton and cousin of George Clinton) (D N.Y.) March 2, 1769-Feb. 11, 1828; Senate Feb. 9, 1802-Nov. 4, 1803; Gov. 1817-21, 1825-28.

CLINTON, George (cousin of De Witt Clinton and James Graham Clinton) (D N.Y.) June 6, 1771-Sept. 16, 1809; House Feb. 14, 1805-09.

CLINTON, James Graham (half brother of De Witt Clinton and cousin of George Clinton) (D N.Y.) Jan. 2, 1804-May 28, 1849; House 1841-45.

CLIPPINGER, Roy (R Ill.) Jan. 13, 1886-Dec. 24, 1962; House Nov. 6, 1945-49.

CLOPTON, David (SRD Ala.) Sept. 29, 1820-Feb. 5, 1892; House 1859-Jan. 21, 1861.

CLOPTON, John (D Va.) Feb. 7, 1756-Sept. 11, 1816; House 1795-99; 1801-Sept. 11, 1816.

CLOUSE, Wynne F. (R Tenn.) Aug. 29, 1883-Feb. 19, 1944; House 1921-23.

CLOVER, Benjamin Hutchinson (FA Kan.) Dec. 22, 1837-Dec. 30, 1899; House 1891-93.

CLOWNEY, William Kennedy (SRD S.C.) March 21, 1797-March 12, 1851; House 1833-35 (N), 1837-39 (SRD).

CLUETT, Ernest Harold (R N.Y.) July 13, 1874-Feb. 4, 1954; House 1937-43.

CLUNIE, Thomas Jefferson (D Calif.) March 25, 1852-June 30, 1903; House 1889-91.

CLYMER, George (F Pa.) March 16, 1739-Jan. 23, 1813; House 1789-91; Cont. Cong. 1776-78 and 1780-83.

CLYMER, Hiester (nephew of William Hiester and cousin of Isaac Ellmaker Hiester) (D Pa.) Nov. 3, 1827-June 12, 1884; House 1873-81.

COAD, Merwin (D Iowa) Sept. 28, 1924; House 1957-63.

COADY, Charles Pearce (D Md.) Feb. 22, 1868-Feb. 16, 1934; House Nov. 4, 1913-21.

COBB, Amasa (R Wis.) Sept. 27, 1823-July 5, 1905; House 1863-71.

COBB, Clinton Levering (R N.C.) Aug. 25, 1842-April 30, 1879; House 1869-75.

COBB, David (F Mass.) Sept. 14, 1748-April 17, 1830; House 1793-95.

COBB, George Thomas (D N.J.) Oct. 13, 1813-Aug. 12, 1870; House 1861-63.

COBB, Howell (nephew of George T. Cobb) (D Ga.) Sept. 7, 1815-Oct. 9, 1868; House 1843-51, 1855-57; Speaker 1849-51; Gov. 1851-53; Secy. of the Treasury March 6, 1857-Dec. 10, 1860.

COBB, Howell (— Ga.) Aug. 3, 1772-May 26, 1818; House 1807-12.

COBB, James Edward (— Ala.) Oct. 5, 1835-June 2, 1903; House 1887-April 21, 1896.

COBB, Seth Wallace (D Mo.) Dec. 5, 1838-May 22, 1909; House 1891-97.

COBB, Stephen Alonzo (R Kan.) June 17, 1833-Aug. 24, 1878; House 1873-75.

COBB, Thomas Reed (D Ind.) July 2, 1828-June 23, 1892; House 1877-87.

COBB, Thomas Willis (— Ga.) 1784-Feb. 1, 1830; House 1817-21, 1823-Dec. 6, 1824; Senate Dec. 6, 1824-28.

COBB, Williamson Robert Winfield (D Ala.) June 8, 1807-Nov. 1, 1864; House 1847-Jan. 30, 1861.

COBURN, Frank Potter (D Wis.) Dec. 6, 1858-Nov. 2, 1932; House 1891-93.

COBURN, John (R Ind.) Oct. 27, 1825-Jan. 28, 1908; House 1867-75.

COBURN, Stephen (R Maine) Nov. 11, 1817-July 4, 1882; House Jan. 2-March 3, 1861.

COCHRAN, Alexander Gilmore (D Pa.) March 20, 1846-May 1, 1928; House 1875-77.

COCHRAN, Charles Fremont (D Mo.) Sept. 27, 1846-Dec. 19, 1906; House 1897-1905.

COCHRAN, James (grandfather of James Cochrane Dobbin) (D N.C.) about 1767-April 7, 1813; House 1809-13.

COCHRAN, James (— N.Y.) Feb. 11, 1769-Nov. 7, 1848; House 1797-99.

COCHRAN, John Joseph (D Mo.) Aug. 11, 1880-March 6, 1947; House Nov. 2, 1926-47.

COCHRAN, Thomas Cunningham (R Pa.) Nov. 30, 1877-Dec. 10, 1957; House 1927-35.

COCHRANE, Aaron Van Schaick (nephew of Isaac Whitbeck Van Schaick) (R N.Y.) March 14, 1858-Sept. 7, 1943; House 1897-1901.

COCHRANE, Clark Betton (R N.Y.) May 31, 1815-March 5, 1867; House 1857-61.

COCHRANE, John (SRD N.Y.) Aug. 27, 1813-Feb. 7, 1898; House 1857-61.

COCKE, John (son of William Cocke and uncle of William Michael Cocke) (— Tenn.) 1772-Feb. 16, 1854; House 1819-27.

COCKE, William (father of John Cocke and grandfather of William Michael Cocke (— Tenn.) 1747-Aug. 22, 1828; Senate Aug. 2, 1796-Mar 3, 1797, April 22-Sept. 26, 1797, 1799-1805.

COCKE, William Michael (grandson of William Cocke and nephew of John Cocke) (D Tenn.) July 16, 1815-Feb. 6, 1896; House 1845-49.

COCKERILL, Joseph Randolph (D Ohio) Jan. 2, 1818-Oct. 23, 1875; House 1857-59.

COCKRAN, William Bourke (D N.Y.) Feb. 28, 1854-March 1, 1923; House 1887-89, Nov. 3, 1891-95, Feb. 23, 1904-09, 1921-March 1, 1923.

COCKRELL, Francis Marion (brother of Jeremiah Vardaman Cockrell) (D Mo.) Oct. 1, 1834-Dec. 13, 1915; Senate 1875-1905.

COCKRELL, Jeremiah Vardaman (brother of Francis Marion Cockrell) (D Texas) May 7, 1832-March 18, 1915; House 1893-97.

COCKS, William Willets (brother of Frederick Cocks Hicks) (R N.Y.) July 24, 1861-May 24, 1932; House 1905-11.

CODD, George Pierre (R Mich.) Dec. 7, 1869-Feb. 16, 1927; House 1921-23.

CODDING, James Hodge (R Pa.) July 8, 1849-Sept. 12, 1919; House Nov. 5, 1895-99.

COFFEE, Harry Buffington (D Neb.) March 16, 1890; House 1935-43.

COFFEE, John (D Ga.) Dec. 3, 1782-Sept. 25, 1836; House 1833-Sept. 25, 1836.

COFFEE, John Main (D Wash.) Jan. 23, 1897; 1937-47.

COFFEEN, Henry Asa (D Wyo.) Feb. 14, 1841-Dec. 9, 1912; House 1893-95.

COFFEY, Robert Lewis, Jr. (D Pa.) Oct. 21, 1918-April 20, 1949; House Jan. 3-April 20, 1949.

COFFIN, Charles Dustin (W Ohio) Sept. 9, 1805-Feb. 28, 1880; House Dec. 20, 1837-39.

COFFIN, Charles Edward (R Md.) July 18, 1841-May 24, 1912; House Nov. 6, 1894-97.

COFFIN, Frank Morey (D Maine) July 11, 1919; House 1957-61.

COFFIN, Howard Aldridge (R Mich.) June 11, 1877-Feb. 28, 1956; House 1947-49.

COFFIN, Peleg, Jr. (— Mass.) Nov. 3, 1756-March 6, 1805; House 1793-95.

COFFIN, Thomas Chalkley (D Idaho) Oct. 25, 1887-June 8, 1934; House 1933-June 8, 1934.

COFFROTH, Alexander Hamilton (D Pa.) May 18, 1828-Sept. 2, 1906; House 1863-65, Feb. 19-July 18, 1866, 1879-81.

COGHLAN, John Maxwell (R Calif.) Dec. 8, 1835-March 26, 1879; House 1871-73.

COGSWELL, William (R Mass.) Aug. 23, 1838-May 22, 1895; House 1887-May 22, 1895.

COHELAN, Jeffery (D Calif.) June 24, 1914; House 1959-71.

COHEN, John Sanford (D Ga.) Feb. 26, 1870-May 13, 1935; Senate April 25, 1932-Jan. 11, 1933.

COHEN, William Wolfe (D N.Y.) Sept. 6, 1874-Oct. 12, 1940; House 1927-29.

COIT, Joshua (F Conn.) Oct. 7, 1758-Sept. 5, 1798; House 1793-Sept. 5, 1798.

COKE, Richard (nephew of Richard Coke, Jr.) (D Texas) March 13, 1829-May 14, 1897; Senate 1877-95; Gov. Dec. 1873-Dec. 1, 1877.

COKE, Richard, Jr. (uncle of Richard Coke) (JD Va.) Nov. 16, 1790-March 31, 1851; House 1829-33.

COLCOCK, William Ferguson (D S.C.) Nov. 5, 1804-June 13, 1889; House 1849-53.

COLDEN, Cadwallader David (D N.Y.) April 4, 1769-Feb. 7, 1834; House Dec. 12, 1821-23.

COLDEN, Charles J. (D Calif.) Aug. 24, 1870-April 15, 1938; House 1933-April 15, 1938.

COLE, Albert McDonald (R Kan.) Oct. 13, 1901; House 1945-53.

COLE, Cornelius (UR Calif.) Sept. 17, 1822-Nov. 3, 1924; House 1863-65; Senate 1867-73.

COLE, Cyrenus (R Iowa) Jan. 13, 1863-Nov. 14, 1939; House July 19, 1921-33.

COLE, George Edward (D Wash.) Dec. 23, 1826-Dec. 3, 1906; House (Terr. Del.) 1863-65; Terr. Gov. Nov. 1866-March 4, 1867.

COLE, Nathan (R Mo.) July 26, 1825-March 4, 1904; House 1877-79.

COLE, Orsamus (W Wis.) Aug. 23, 1819-May 5, 1903; House 1849-51.

COLE, Ralph Dayton (brother of Raymond Clinton Cole) (R Ohio) Nov. 30, 1873-Oct. 15, 1932; House 1905-11.

COLE, Raymond Clinton (brother of Ralph Dayton Cole) (R Ohio) Aug. 21, 1870-Feb. 8, 1957; House 1919-25.

COLE, William Clay (R Mo.) Aug. 29, 1897-Sept. 23, 1965; House 1943-49, 1953-55.

COLE, William Hinson (D Md.) Jan. 11, 1837-July 8, 1886; House 1885-July 8, 1886.

COLE, William Purington, Jr. (D Md.) May 11, 1889-Sept. 22, 1957; House 1927-29, 1931-Oct. 26, 1942.

COLE, William Sterling (R N.Y.) April 18, 1904; House 1935-Dec. 1, 1957.

COLEMAN, Hamilton Dudley (R La.) May 12, 1845-March 16, 1926; House 1889-91.

COLEMAN, Nicholas Daniel (JD Ky.) April 22, 1800-May 11, 1874; House 1829-31.

COLEMAN, William Henry (R Pa.) Dec. 28, 1871-June 3, 1943; House 1915-17.

COLERICK, Walpole Gillespie (D Ind.) Aug. 1, 1845-Jan. 11, 1911; House 1879-83.

COLES, Isaac (father of Walter Coles) (— Va.) March 2, 1747-June 3, 1813; House 1789-91, 1793-97.

COLES, Walter (son of Isaac Coles) (D Va.) Dec. 8, 1790-Nov. 9, 1857; House 1835-45.

COLFAX, Schuyler (R Ind.) March 23, 1823-Jan. 13, 1885; House 1855-69; Speaker 1863-69; Vice Pres. 1869-73.

COLHOUN, John Ewing (cousin of John Caldwell Calhoun and Joseph Calhoun) (D S.C.) 1750-Oct. 26, 1802; Senate 1801-Oct. 26, 1802.

COLLAMER, Jacob (R Vt.) Jan. 8, 1792-Nov. 9, 1865; House 1843-49 (W); Senate 1855-Nov. 9, 1865; Postmaster General March 7, 1849-July 20, 1850.

COLLIER, Harold Reginald (R Ill.) Dec. 12, 1915; House 1957- .

COLLIER, James William (D Miss.) Sept. 28, 1872-Sept. 28, 1933; House 1909-33.

COLLIER, John Allen (CD NY) Nov. 13, 1787-March 24, 1873; House 1831-33.

COLLIN, John Francis (D N.Y.) April 30, 1802-Sept. 16, 1889; House 1845-47.

COLLINS, Ela (father of William Collins) (D N.Y.) Feb. 14, 1786-Nov. 23, 1848; House 1823-25.

COLLINS, Francis Dolan (D Pa.) March 5, 1841-Nov. 21, 1891; House 1875-79.

COLLINS, George W. (D Ill.) March 5, 1925; House Nov. 3, 1970- .

COLLINS, James M. (R Texas) April 29, 1916; House Aug. 24, 1968- .

COLLINS, Patrick Andrew (D Mass.) March 12, 1844-Sept. 13, 1905; House 1883-89.

COLLINS, Ross Alexander (D Miss.) April 25, 1880-July 14, 1968; House 1921-35, 1937-43.

COLLINS, Samuel LaFort (R Calif.) Aug. 6, 1895-June 26, 1965; House 1933-37.

COLLINS, William (son of Ela Collins) (D N.Y.) Feb. 22, 1818-June 18, 1878; House 1847-49.

COLMER, William Meyers (D Miss.) Feb. 11, 1890; House 1933- .

COLQUITT, Alfred Holt (son of Walter Terry Colquitt) (D Ga.) April 20, 1824-March 26, 1894; House 1853-55; Senate 1883 March 26, 1894; Gov. 1876-82.

COLQUITT, Walter Terry (father of Alfred Holt Colquitt (VBD Ga.) Dec. 27, 1799-May 7, 1855; House 1839-July 21, 1840 (SRW); Jan. 3, 1842-43 (VBD); Senate 1843-Feb., 1848.

COLSON, David Grant (R Ky.) April 1, 1861-Sept. 27, 1904; House 1895-99.

COLSTON, Edward (F Va.) Dec. 25, 1786-April 23, 1852; House 1817-19.

COLT, LeBaron Bradford (R R.I.) June 25, 1846-Aug. 18, 1924; Senate 1913-Aug. 18, 1924.

COLTON, Don Byron (R Utah) Sept. 15, 1876-Aug. 1, 1952; House 1921-33.

COMBS, George Hamilton, Jr. (D Mo.) May 2, 1899; House 1927-29.

COMBS, Jesse Martin (D Texas) July 7, 1889-Aug. 21, 1953; House 1945-53.

COMEGYS, Joseph Parsons (W Del.) Dec. 29, 1813-Feb. 1, 1893; Senate Nov. 19, 1856-Jan. 14, 1857.

COMER, Braxton Bragg (D Ala.) Nov. 7, 1848-Aug. 15, 1927; Senate March 5-Nov. 2, 1920; Gov. 1907-11.

COMINGO, Abram (D Mo.) Jan. 9, 1820-Nov. 10, 1889; House 1871-75.

COMINS, Linus Bacon (R Mass.) Nov. 29, 1817-Oct. 14, 1892; House 1855-57 (AP), 1857-59 (R).

COMPTON, Barnes (great-grandson of Philip Key) (D Md.) Nov. 16, 1830-Dec. 4, 1898; House 1885-March 20, 1890, 1891-May 15, 1894.

COMPTON, Ranulf (R Conn.) Sept. 16, 1881; House 1943-45.

COMSTOCK, Charles Carter (Fus. D Mich.) March 5, 1818-Feb. 20, 1900; House 1885-87.

COMSTOCK, Daniel Webster (R Ind.) Dec. 16, 1840-May 19, 1917; House March 4-May 19, 1917.

COMSTOCK, Oliver Cromwell (D N.Y.) March 1, 1780-Jan. 11, 1860; House 1813-19.

COMSTOCK, Solomon Gilman (R Minn.) May 9, 1842-June 3, 1933; House 1889-91.

CONABLE, Barber B., Jr. (R N.Y.) Nov. 2, 1922; House 1965- .

CONARD, John (D Pa.) Nov. 1773-May 9, 1857; House 1813-15.

CONDICT, Lewis (A-F N.J.) March 3, 1722-May 26, 1862; House 1811-17, 1821-33.

CONDIT, John (father of Silas Condit) (D N.J.) July 8, 1755-May 4, 1834; House 1799-1803; Senate Sept. 1, 1803-March 3, 1809, March 21, 1809-17, House March 4-Nov. 4, 1819.

CONDIT, Silas (son of John Condit) (CD N. J.) Aug. 18, 1778-Nov. 29, 1861; House 1831-33.

CONDON, Francis Bernard (D R.I.) Nov. 11, 1891-Nov. 23, 1965; House Nov. 4, 1930-Jan. 10, 1935.

CONDON, Robert Likens (D Calif.) Nov. 10, 1912; House 1953-55.

CONGER, Edwin Hurd (R Iowa) March 7, 1843-May 18, 1907; House 1885-Oct. 3, 1890.

CONGER, Harmon Sweatland (W N.Y.) April 9, 1816-Oct. 22, 1882; House 1847-51.

CONGER, James Lockwood (F-S W Mich.) Feb. 18, 1805-April 10, 1876; House 1851-53.

CONGER, Omar Dwight (R Mich.) April 1, 1818-July 11, 1898; House 1869-81; Senate 1881-87.

CONKLING, Alfred (father of Frederick Augustus Conkling and Roscoe Conkling) (AJD N.Y.) Oct. 12, 1789-Feb. 5, 1874; House 1821-23.

CONKLING, Frederick Augustus (son of Alfred Conkling and brother of Roscoe Conkling) (R N.Y.) Aug. 22, 1816-Sept. 18, 1891; House 1861-63.

CONKLING, Roscoe (son of Alfred Conkling and brother of Frederick Augustus Conkling (UR N.Y.) Oct. 3, 1829-April 18, 1888; House 1859-63, 1865-March 4, 1867 (R); Senate 1867-May 16, 1881 (UR).

CONN, Charles Gerard (D Ind.) Jan. 29, 1844-Jan. 5, 1931; House 1893-95.

CONNALLY, Thomas Terry (Tom) (D Texas) Aug. 19, 1877-Oct. 28, 1963; House 1917-29; Senate 1929-53.

CONNELL, Charles Robert (son of William Connell) (R Pa.) Sept. 22, 1864-Sept. 26, 1922; House 1921-Sept. 26, 1922.

CONNELL, Richard Edward (D N.Y.) Nov. 6, 1857-Oct. 30, 1912; House 1911-Oct. 30, 1912.

CONNELL, William (father of Charles Robert Connell) (R Pa.) Sept. 10, 1827-March 21, 1909; House 1897-1903, Feb. 10, 1904-05.

CONNELL, William James (R Neb.) July 6, 1846-Aug. 16, 1924; House 1889-91.

CONNELLY, John Robert (D Kan.) Feb. 27, 1870-Sept. 9, 1940; House 1913-19.

CONNER, James Perry (R Iowa) Jan. 27, 1851-March 19, 1924; House Dec. 4, 1900-09.

CONNER, John Cogswell (D Texas) Oct. 14, 1842-Dec. 10, 1873; House March 31, 1870-73.

CONNER, Samuel Shepard (— Mass.) about 1783-Dec. 17, 1820; House 1815-17.

CONNERY, Lawrence Joseph (brother of William Patrick Connery, Jr.) (D Mass.) Oct. 17, 1895-Oct. 19, 1941; House Sept. 28, 1937-Oct. 19, 1941.

CONNERY, William Patrick, Jr. (brother of Lawrence Joseph Connery) (D Mass.) Aug. 24, 1888-June 15, 1937; House 1923-June 15, 1937.

CONNESS, John (UR Calif.) Sept. 22, 1821-Jan. 10, 1909; Senate 1863-69. (*elected as a Douglass D)

CONNOLLY, Daniel Ward (D Pa.) April 24, 1847-Dec. 4, 1894; House 1883-85.

CONNOLLY, James Austin (R Ill.) March 8, 1843-Dec. 15, 1914; House 1895-99.

CONNOLLY, James Joseph (R Pa.) Sept. 24, 1881-Dec. 10, 1952; House 1921-35.

CONNOLLY, Maurice (D Iowa) March 13, 1877-May 28, 1921; House 1913-15.

CONNOR, Henry William (D N.C.) Aug. 5, 1793-Jan. 6, 1866; House 1821-41.

CONOVER, Simon Barclay (R Fla.) Sept. 23, 1840-April 19, 1908; Senate 1873-79.

CONRAD, Charles Mynn (W La.) Dec. 24, 1804-Feb. 11, 1878; Senate April 14, 1842-43; House 1849-August 17, 1850; Secy. of War Aug. 15, 1850-March 7, 1853.

CONRAD, Frederick (F Pa.) 1759-Aug. 3, 1827; House 1803-07.

CONRY, Joseph Aloysius (D Mass.) Sept. 12, 1868-June 22, 1943; House 1901-03.

CONRY, Michael Francis (D N.Y.) April 2, 1870-March 2, 1917; House 1909-March 2, 1917.

CONSTABLE, Albert (D Md.) June 3, 1805-Sept. 18, 1855; House 1845-47.

CONTE, Silvio Otto (R Mass.) Nov. 9, 1921; House 1959- .

CONTEE, Benjamin (uncle of Alexander Contee Hanson and granduncle of Thomas Contee Worthington) (— Md.) 1755-Nov. 30, 1815; House 1789-91; Cont. Cong. 1787-88.

CONVERSE, George Leroy (D Ohio) June 4, 1827-March 30, 1897; House 1879-85.

CONWAY, Henry Wharton (cousin of Ambrose Hendley Sevier) (D Ark.) March 18, 1793-Nov. 9, 1827; House (Terr. Del.) 1823-Nov. 9, 1827.

CONWAY, Martin Franklin (R Kan.) Nov. 19, 1827-Feb. 15, 1882; House Jan. 29, 1861-63.

CONYERS, John, Jr. (D Mich.) May 16, 1929; House 1965- .

COOK, Burton Chauncey (R Ill.) May 11, 1819- Aug. 18, 1894; House 1865-Aug. 16, 1871.

COOK, Daniel Pope (— Ill.) 1794-Oct. 16, 1827; House 1819-27.

COOK, George Washington (R Colo.) Nov. 10, 1851-Dec. 18, 1916; House 1907-09.

COOK, Joel (R Pa.) March 20, 1842-Dec. 15, 1910; House Nov. 5, 1907-Dec. 15, 1910.

COOK, John Calhoun (ID Iowa) Dec. 26, 1846-June 7, 1920; House March 3, 1883 and Oct. 9, 1883-85.

COOK, John Parsons (W Iowa) Aug. 31, 1817-April 17, 1872; House 1853-55.

COOK, Marlow W. (R Ky.) July 27, 1926; Senate Dec. 16, 1968- .

COOK, Orchard (- Mass.) March 24, 1763-Aug. 12, 1819; House 1905-11.

COOK, Philip (D Ga.) July 30, 1817-May 24, 1894; House 1873-83.

COOK, Robert Eugene (D Ohio) May 19, 1920; House 1959-63.

COOK, Samuel Andrew (R Wis.) Jan. 28, 1849-April 4, 1918; House 1895-97.

COOK, Samuel Ellis (D Ind.) Sept. 30, 1860-Feb. 22, 1946; House 1923-25.

COOK, Zadock (— Ga.) Feb. 18, 1769-Aug. 3, 1863; House Dec. 2, 1816-19.

COOKE, Bates (A-Mas. N.Y.) Dec. 23, 1787-May 31, 1841; House 1831-33.

COOKE, Edmund Francis (R N.Y.) April 13, 1885; House 1929-33.

COOKE, Edward Dean (R Ill.) Oct. 17, 1849-June 24, 1897; House 1895-June 24, 1897.

COOKE, Eleutheros (NR Ohio) Dec. 25, 1787-Dec. 17, 1864; House 1831-33.

COOKE, Thomas Burrage (D N.Y.) Nov. 21, 1778-Nov. 20, 1853; House 1811-13.

COOLEY, Harold Dunbar (D N.C.) July 26, 1897; House July 7, 1934-66.

COOLIDGE, Frederick Spaulding (father of Marcus Allen Coolidge) (D Mass.) Dec. 7, 1841-June 8, 1906; House 1891-93.

COOLIDGE, Marcus Allen (son of Frederick Spaulding Coolidge) (D Mass.) Oct. 6, 1865-Jan. 23, 1947; Senate 1931-37.

COOMBS, Frank Leslie (R Calif.) Dec. 27, 1853-Oct. 5, 1934; House 1901-03.

COOMBS, William Jerome (D N.Y.) Dec. 24, 1833-Jan. 12, 1922; House 1891-95.

COON, Samuel Harrison (R Ore.) April 15, 1903; House 1953-57.

COONEY, James (D Mo.) July 28, 1848-Nov. 16, 1904; House 1897-1903.

COOPER, Allen Foster (R Pa.) June 16, 1862-April 20, 1917; House 1903-11.

COOPER, Charles Merian (D Fla.) Jan. 16, 1856-Nov. 14, 1923; House 1893-97.

COOPER, Edmund (brother of Henry Cooper) (C Tenn.) Sept. 11, 1821-July 21, 1911; House July 24, 1866-67.

COOPER, Edward (R W. Va.) Feb. 26, 1873-March 1, 1928; House 1915-19.

COOPER, George Byran (D Mich.) June 6, 1808-Aug. 29, 1866; House 1859-May 15, 1860.

COOPER, George William (D Ind.) May 21, 1851-Nov. 27, 1899; House 1889-95.

COOPER, Henry (brother of Edmund Cooper) (D Tenn.) Aug. 22, 1827-Feb. 3, 1884; Senate 1871-77.

COOPER, Henry Allen (R Wis.) Sept. 8, 1850-March 1, 1931; House 1893-1919, 1921-March 1, 1931.

COOPER, James (W Pa.) May 8, 1810-March 28, 1863; House 1839-43; Senate 1849-55.

COOPER, Jere (D Tenn.) July 20, 1893-Dec. 18, 1957; House 1929-Dec. 18, 1957.

COOPER, John Gordon (R Ohio) April 27, 1872-Jan. 7, 1955; House 1915-37.

COOPER, John Sherman (R Ky.) Aug. 23, 1901; Senate Nov. 6, 1946-49, Nov. 5, 1952-55, Nov. 7, 1956- .

COOPER, Mark Anthony (cousin of Eugenius Aristides Nisbet) (D Ga.) April 20, 1800-March 17, 1885; House 1839-41, Jan. 3, 1842-43 (SRW) and March 4-June 26, 1843 (D).

COOPER, Richard Matlack (— N.J.) Feb. 29, 1768-March 10, 1843; House 1829-33.

COOPER, Samuel Bronson (D Texas) May 30, 1850-Aug. 21, 1918; House 1893-1905, 1907-09.

COOPER, Thomas (F Del.) 1764-1829; House 1813-17.

COOPER, Thomas Buchecker (D Pa.) Dec. 29, 1823-April 4, 1862; House 1861-April 4, 1862.

COOPER, William (F N.Y.) Dec. 2, 1754-Dec. 22, 1809; House 1795-97, 1799-1801.

COOPER, William Craig (R Ohio) Dec. 18, 1832-Aug. 29, 1902; House 1885-91.

COOPER, William Raworth (D N.J.) Feb. 20, 1793-Sept. 22, 1856; House 1839-41.

COPELAND, Oren Sturman (R Neb.) March 16, 1887-April 10, 1958; House 1941-43.

COPELAND, Royal Samuel (D N.Y.), Nov. 7, 1868-June 17, 1938; Senate 1923-June 17, 1938.

COPLEY, Ira Clifton (nephew of Richard Henry Whiting) (R Ill.) Oct. 25, 1864-Nov. 1, 1947; House 1911-23.

CORBERT, Henry Winslow (UR Ore.) Feb. 18, 1827-March 31, 1903; Senate 1867-73.

CORBETT, Robert James (R Pa.) Aug. 25, 1905-April 25, 1971; House 1939-41, 1945-April 25, 1971.

CORDON, Guy (R Ore.) April 24, 1890-June 8, 1969; Senate March 4, 1944-55.

CORDOVA, Jorge Luis (New Prog. P.R.) April 20, 1907; House (Res. Comm.) 1969- .

CORKER, Stephen Alfestus (D Ga.) May 7, 1830-Oct. 18, 1879; House Dec. 22, 1870-1871.

CORLETT, William Wellington (R Wyo) April 10, 1842-July 22, 1890; House (Terr. Del.) 1877-79.

CORLEY, Manuel Simeon (R S.C.) Feb. 10, 1823-Nov. 20, 1902; House July 25, 1868-69.

CORLISS, John Blaisdell (R Mich.) June 7, 1851-Dec. 24, 1929; House 1895-1903.

CORMAN, James C. (D Calif.) Oct. 20, 1920; House 1961- .

CORNELL, Thomas (R N.Y.) Jan. 27, 1814-March 30, 1890; House 1867-69, 1881-83.

CORNING, Erastus (grandfather of Parker Corning) (D N.Y.) Jan. 22, 1874-May 24, 1943; House 1923-37.

CORNING, Parker (grandson of Erastus Corning) (D N.Y.) Jan. 22, 1874-May 24, 1943; House 1923-37.

CORNISH, Johnston (D N.J.) June 13, 1858-June 26, 1920; House 1893-95.

CORWIN, Franklin (nephew of Moses Bledso Corwin and Thomas Corwin) (R Ill.) Jan. 12, 1818-June 15, 1879; House 1873-75.

CORWIN, Moses Bledso (brother of Thomas Corwin and uncle of Franklin Corwin) (W Ohio) Jan. 5, 1790-April 7, 1872; House 1849-51, 1853-55.

CORWIN, Thomas (brother of Moses Bledso Corwin and uncle of Franklin Corwin) (R Ohio) July 29, 1794-Dec. 18, 1865; House 1831-May 30, 1840 (W), 1859-March 12, 1861 (R); Senate 1845-July 20, 1850 (W); Gov. 1840-42; Secy. of the Treasury 1850-53.

COSDEN, Jeremiah (— Md.) 1768-Dec. 5, 1824; House 1821-March 19, 1822.

COSGROVE, John (D Mo.) Sept. 12, 1839-Aug. 15, 1925; House 1883-85.

COSTELLO, John Martin (D Calif.) Jan. 15, 1903; House 1935-45.

COSTELLO, Peter Edward (R Pa.) June 27, 1854-Oct. 23, 1935; House 1915-21.

COSTIGAN, Edward Prentiss (D Colo.) July 1, 1874-Jan. 17, 1939; Senate 1931-37.

COTHRAN, James Sproull (D S.C.) Aug. 8, 1830-Dec. 5, 1897; House 1887-91.

COTTER, William R. (D Conn.) July 18, 1926; House 1971- .

COTTMAN, Joseph Stewart (IW Md.) Aug. 16, 1803-Jan. 28, 1863; House 1851-53.

COTTON, Aylett Rains (R Iowa) Nov. 29, 1826-Oct. 30, 1912; House 1871-75.

COTTON, Norris (R N.H.) May 11, 1900; House 1947-Nov. 7, 1954; Senate Nov. 8, 1954- .

COTTRELL, James La Fayette (D Ala.) Aug. 25, 1808-Sept. 7, 1885; House Dec. 7, 1946-47.

COUDERT, Frederick Rene, Jr. (R N.Y.) May 7, 1898; House 1947-59.

COUDREY, Harry Marcy (R Mo.) Feb. 28, 1867-July 5, 1930; House June 23, 1906-11.

COUGHLIN, Clarence Dennis (R Pa.) July 27, 1883-Dec. 15, 1946; House 1921-23.

COUGHLIN, R. Lawrence (R Pa.) April 11, 1929; House 1969- .

COULTER, Richard (D Pa.) March, 1788-April 21, 1852; House 1827-31 (I) and 1831-35 (D).

COURTNEY, William Wirt (D Tenn.) Sept. 7, 1889-April 6, 1961; House May 11, 1939-49.

COUSINS, Robert Gordon (R Iowa) Jan. 31, 1859-June 20, 1933; House 1893-1909.

COUZENS, James (R Mich.) Aug. 26, 1872-Oct. 22, 1936; Senate Nov. 29, 1922-Oct. 22, 1936.

COVERT, James Way (D N.Y.) Sept. 2, 1842-May 16, 1910; House 1877-81, 1889-95.

COVINGTON, George Washington (D Md.) Sept. 12, 1838-April 6, 1911; House 1881-85.

COVINGTON, James Harry (D Md.) May 3, 1870-Feb. 4, 1942; House 1909-Sept. 30, 1914.

COVINGTON, Leonard (D Md.) Oct. 30, 1768-Nov. 14, 1813; House 1805-07.

COVODE, John (R Pa.) March 18, 1808-Jan. 11, 1871; House 1855-57 (A-Mas. W), 1857-63, 1867-69 and Feb. 9, 1870-Jan. 11, 1871 (R).

COWAN, Edgar (R Pa.) Sept. 19, 1815-Aug. 29, 1885; Senate 1861-67.

COWAN, Jacob Pitzer (D Ohio) March 20, 1823-July 9, 1895; House 1875-77.

COWEN, Benjamin Sprague (W Ohio) Sept. 27, 1793-Sept. 27, 1860; House 1841-43.

COWEN, John Kissig (D Md.) Oct. 28, 1844-April 26, 1904; House 1895-97.

COWGER, William O. (R Ky.) Jan. 1, 1922; House 1967-71.

COWGILL, Calvin (R Ind.) Jan. 7, 1819-Feb. 10, 1903; House 1879-81.

COWHERD, William Strother (D Mo.) Sept. 1, 1860-June 20, 1915; House 1897-1905.

COWLES, Charles Holden (nephew of William Henry Harrison Cowles) (R N.C.) July 16, 1875-Oct. 2, 1957; House 1909-11.

COWLES, George Washington (R N.Y.) Dec. 6, 1823-Jan. 20, 1901; House 1869-71.

COWLES, Henry Booth (— N.Y.) March 18, 1798-May 17, 1873; House 1829-31.

COWLES, William Henry Harrison (uncle of Charles Holden Cowles) (D N.C.) April 22, 1840-Dec. 30, 1901; House 1885-93.

COX, Edward Eugene (D Ga.) April 3, 1880-Dec. 24, 1952; House 1925-Dec. 24, 1952.

COX, Issac Newton (D N.Y.) Aug. 1, 1846-Sept. 28, 1916; House 1891-93.

COX, Jacob Dolson (R Ohio) Oct. 27, 1828-Aug. 4, 1900; House 1877-79; Gov. 1866-68; Secy. of the Interior 1869-70.

COX, James (D N.J.) June 14, 1753-Sept. 12, 1810; House 1809-Sept. 12, 1810.

COX, James Middleton (D Ohio) March 31, 1870-July 15, 1957; House 1909-Jan. 12, 1913; Gov. 1913-15, 1917-21.

COX, Leander Martin (AP Ky.) May 7, 1812-March 19, 1865; House 1853-55 (W), 1855-57 (AP).

COX, Nicholas Nichols (D Tenn.) Jan. 6, 1837-May 2, 1912; House 1891-1901.

COX, Samuel Sullivan (D Ohio/N.Y.) Sept. 30, 1824-Sept. 10, 1889; House (Ohio) 1857-65, (N.Y.) 1869-73, Nov. 4, 1873-May 20, 1885, Nov. 2, 1886-Sept. 10, 1889; Speaker pro tempore 1876.

COX, William Elijah (D Ind.) Sept. 6, 1861-March 11, 1942; House 1907-19.

COX, William Ruffin (D N.C.) March 11, 1831-Dec. 26, 1919; House 1881-87.

COXE, William, Jr. (F N.J.) May 3, 1762-Feb. 25, 1831; House 1813-15.

COYLE, William Radford (R Pa.) July 10, 1878; House 1925-27, 1929-33.

CRABB, George Whitfield (W Ala.) Feb. 22, 1804-Aug. 15, 1846; House Sept. 4, 1838-41.

CRABB, Jeremiah (D Md.) 1760-1800; House 1795-96.

CRADDOCK, John Durrett (R Ky.) Oct. 26, 1881-May 20, 1942; House 1929-31.

CRADLEBAUGH, John (— Nev.) Feb. 22, 1819-Feb. 22, 1872; House (Terr. Del.) Dec. 2, 1861-1863.

CRAFTS, Samuel Chandler (— Vt.) Oct. 6, 1768-Nov. 19, 1853; House 1817-25; Senate April 23, 1842-43; Gov. 1828-31.

CRAGIN, Aaron Harrison (AP N.H.) Feb. 3, 1821-May 10, 1898; House 1855-57 (AP), 1857-59 (R); Senate 1865-77 (AP).

CRAGO, Thomas Spencer (R Pa.) Aug. 8, 1866-Sept. 12, 1925; House 1911-13, 1915-21, Sept. 20, 1921-23.

CRAIG, Alexander Kerr (D Pa.) Feb. 21, 1828-July 29, 1892; House Feb. 6, 1892-July 29, 1892.

CRAIG, George Henry (R Ala.) Dec. 25, 1845-Jan. 26, 1923; House Jan. 9-March 3, 1885.

CRAIG, Hector (JD N.Y.) 1775-Jan. 31, 1842; House 1823-25, 1829-July 12, 1830.

CRAIG, James (D Mo.) Feb. 28, 1818-Oct. 22, 1888; House 1857-61.

CRAIG, Robert (D Va.) 1792-Nov. 25, 1852; House 1829-33, 1835-41.

CRAIG, Samuel Alfred (R Pa.) Nov. 19, 1839-March 17, 1920; House 1889-91.

CRAIG, William Benjamin (D Ala.) Nov. 2, 1877-Nov. 27, 1925; House 1907-11.

CRAIGE, Francis Burton (D N.C.) March 13, 1811-Dec. 30, 1875; House 1853-61.

CRAIK, William (— Md.) Oct. 31, 1761 - prior to 1814; House Dec. 5, 1796-1801.

CRAIL, Joe (R Calif.) Dec. 25, 1877-March 2, 1938; House 1927-33.

CRAIN, William Henry (D Texas) Nov. 25, 1848-Feb. 10, 1896; House 1885-Feb. 10, 1896.

CRALEY, Nathaniel Nieman, Jr. (D Pa.) Nov. 17, 1927; House 1965-67.

CRAMER, John (D N.Y.) May 17, 1779-June 1, 1870; House 1833-37.

CRAMER, William Cato (R Fla.) Aug. 4, 1922; House 1955-71.

CRAMTON, Louis Convers (R Mich.) Dec. 2, 1875-June 23, 1966; House 1913-31.

CRANE, Joseph Halsey (W Ohio) Aug. 31, 1782-Nov. 13, 1851; House 1829-37.

CRANE, Philip M. (R Ill.) Nov. 3, 1930; House Nov. 25, 1969- .

CRANE, Winthrop Murray (R Mass.) April 23, 1853-Oct. 2, 1920; Senate Oct. 12, 1904-1913; Gov. 1900-02.

CRANFORD, John Walter (D Texas) 1862-March 3, 1899; House 1897-March 3, 1899.

CRANSTON, Alan (D Calif.) June 19, 1914; Senate 1969- .

CRANSTON, Henry Young (brother of Robert Bennie Cranston) (W R.I.) Oct. 9, 1789-Feb. 12, 1864; House 1843-47.

CRANSTON, Robert Bennie (brother of Henry Young Cranston) (L&OW R.I.) Jan. 14, 1791-Jan. 27, 1873; House 1837-43 (W), 1847-49 (L&OW)

CRAPO, William Wallace (R Mass.) May 16, 1830-Feb. 28, 1926; House Nov. 2, 1875-83.

CRARY, Isaac Edwin (D Mich.) Oct. 2, 1804-May 8, 1854; House Jan. 26, 1837-41.

CRAVENS, James Addison (second cousin of James Harrison Cravens) (D Ind.) Nov. 4, 1818-June 20, 1893; House 1861-65.

CRAVENS, James Harrison (second cousin of James Addison Cravens) (W Ind.) Aug. 2, 1802-Dec. 4, 1876; House 1841-43.

CRAVENS, Jordan Edgar (cousin of William Ben Cravens) (D Ark.) Nov. 7, 1830-April 8, 1914; House 1877-83.

CRAVENS, William Ben (father of William Fadjo Cravens and cousin of Jordan Cravens) (D Ark.) Jan. 17, 1872-Jan. 13, 1939; House 1907-13, 1933-Jan. 13, 1939.

CRAVENS, William Fadjo (son of William Ben Cravens) (D Ark.) Feb. 15, 1889; House Sept. 12, 1939-49.

CRAWFORD, Coe Isaac (R S.D.) Jan. 14, 1858-April 25, 1944; Senate 1909-15; Gov. 1907-08.

CRAWFORD, Fred Lewis (R Mich.) May 5, 1888-April 13, 1957; House 1935-53.

CRAWFORD, George Washington (W Ga.) Dec. 22, 1798-July 22, 1872; House Jan. 7-March 3, 1843; Gov. 1843-47; Secy. of War 1849-50.

CRAWFORD, Joel (D Ga.) June 15, 1783-April 5, 1858; House 1817-21.

CRAWFORD, Martin Jenkins (D Ga.) March 17, 1820-July 23, 1883; House 1855-Jan. 23, 1861.

CRAWFORD, Thomas Hartley (JD Pa.) Nov. 14, 1786-Jan. 27, 1863; House 1829-33.

CRAWFORD, William (D Pa.) 1760-Oct. 23, 1823; House 1809-17.

CRAWFORD, William Harris (— Ga.) Feb. 24, 1772-Sept. 15, 1834; Senate Nov. 7, 1807-March 23, 1813; President pro tempore 1812; Secy. of War 1815-16; Secy. of the Treasury 1816-25.

CRAWFORD, William Thomas (D N.C.) June 1, 1856-Nov. 16, 1913; House 1891-95, 1899-May 10, 1900, 1907-09.

CREAGER, Charles Edward (R Okla.) April 28, 1873-Jan. 11, 1964; House 1909-11.

CREAL, Edward Wester (D Ky.) Nov. 20, 1883-Oct. 13, 1943; House Nov. 5, 1935-Oct. 13, 1943.

CREAMER, Thomas James (D N.Y.) May 26, 1843-Aug. 4, 1914; House 1873-75, 1901-03.

CREBS, John Montgomery (D Ill.) April 9, 1830-June 26, 1890; House 1869-73.

CREELY, John Vaudain (R Pa.) Nov. 14, 1839-Sept. 28, 1900; House 1871-73.

CREIGHTON, William, Jr. (D Ohio) Oct. 29, 1778-Oct. 8, 1851; House May 4, 1813-17, 1827-28, 1829-33.

CRESWELL, John Andrew Jackson (R Md.) Nov. 18, 1828-Dec. 23, 1891; House 1863-65; Senate March 9, 1865-67; Postmaster General 1869-74.

CRETELLA, Albert William (R Conn.) April 22, 1897; House 1953-59.

CRIPPA, Edward David (R Wyo.) April 8, 1899-Oct. 20, 1960; Senate June 24-Nov. 28, 1954.

CRISFIELD, John Woodland (UR Md.) Nov. 8, 1806-Jan. 12, 1897; House 1847-49 (W), 1861-63 (UR).

CRISP, Charles Frederick (father of Charles Robert Crisp) (D Ga.) Jan. 29, 1845-Oct. 23, 1896; House 1883-Oct. 23, 1896; Speaker 1891-95.

CRISP, Charles Robert (son of Charles Frederick Crisp) (D Ga.) Oct. 19, 1870-Feb. 7, 1937; House Dec. 19, 1896-97, 1913-Oct. 7, 1932.

CRIST, Henry (— Ky.) Oct. 20, 1764-Aug. 11, 1844; House 1809-11.

CRITCHER, John (C Va.) March 11, 1820-Sept. 27, 1901; House 1871-73.

CRITTENDEN, John Jordan (uncle of Thomas Theodore Crittenden) (U Ky.) Sept. 10, 1787-July 26, 1863; Senate 1817-19, 1835-41, March 31, 1842-June 12, 1848, 1855-61, House 1861-63; Gov. 1848-50; Attorney General March 5-Sept. 13, 1841 and 1850-53.

CRITTENDEN, Thomas Theodore (nephew of John Jordan Crittenden) (D Mo.) Jan. 1, 1832-May 29, 1909; House 1873-75, 1877-79; Gov. 1881-85.

CROCHERON, Henry (brother of Jacob Crocheron) (D N.Y.) Dec. 26, 1772-Nov. 8, 1819; House 1815-17.

CROCHERON, Jacob (brother of Henry Crocheron) (JD N.Y.) Aug. 23, 1774-Dec. 27, 1849; House 1829-31.

CROCKER, Samuel Leonard (W Mass.) March 31, 1804-Feb. 10, 1883; House 1853-55.

CROCKETT, David (father of John Wesley Crockett) (W Tenn.) Aug. 17, 1786-March 6, 1836; House 1827-31 (D), 1833-35 (W).

CROCKETT, John Wesley (W Tenn.) July 10, 1807-Nov. 24, 1852; House 1837-41.

CROFT, George William (father of Theodore Gaillard Croft) (D S.C.) Dec. 20, 1846-March 10, 1904; House 1903-March 10, 1904.

CROFT, Theodore Gaillard (son of George William Croft) (D S.C.) Nov. 26, 1874-March 23, 1920; House May 17, 1904-05.

CROLL, William Martin (D Pa.) April 9, 1866-Oct. 21, 1929; House 1923-25.

CROMER, George Washington (R Ind.) May 13, 1856-Nov. 8, 1936; House 1899-1907.

CROOK, Thurman Charles (D Ind.) July 18, 1891; House 1949-51.

CROOKE, Philip Schuyler (R N.Y.) March 2, 1810-March 17, 1881; House 1873-75.

CROSBY, Charles Noel (D Pa.) Sept. 29, 1876-Jan. 26, 1951; House 1933-39.

CROSBY, John Crawford (D Mass.) June 15, 1859-Oct. 14, 1943; House 1891-93.

CROSS, Edward (D Ark.) Nov. 11, 1798-April 6, 1887; House 1839-45.

CROSS, Oliver Harian (D Texas) July 13, 1868-April 24, 1960; House 1929-37.

CROSSER, Robert (D Ohio) June 7, 1874-June 3, 1957; House 1913-19, 1923-55.

CROSSLAND, Edward (D Ky.) June 30, 1827-Sept. 11, 1881; House 1871-75.

CROUCH, Edward (D Pa.) Nov. 9, 1764-Feb. 2, 1827; House Oct. 12, 1813-1815.

CROUNSE, Lorenzo (R Neb.) Jan. 27, 1834-May 13, 1909; House 1873-77; Gov. 1892-95.

CROUSE, George Washington (R Ohio) Nov. 23, 1832-Jan. 5, 1912; House 1887-89.

CROW, Charles Augustus (R Mo.) March 31, 1873-March 20, 1938; House 1909-11.

CROW, William Evans (father of William J. Crow) (R Pa.) March 10, 1870-Aug. 2, 1922; Senate Oct. 24, 1921-Aug. 2, 1922.

CROW, William Josiah (son of William Evans Crow) (R Pa.) Jan. 22, 1902; House 1947-49.

CROWE, Eugene Burgess (D Ind.) Jan. 5, 1878-May 12, 1970; House 1931-41.

CROWELL, John (— Ala.) Sept. 18, 1780-June 25, 1846; House (Terr. Del.) Jan. 29, 1818-1819; (Rep.) Dec. 14, 1819-1821.

CROWELL, John (W Ohio) Sept. 15, 1801-March 8, 1883; House 1847-51.

CROWLEY, Joseph Burns (D Ohio) July 19, 1858-June 25, 1931; House 1899-1905.

CROWLEY, Miles (D Texas) Feb. 22, 1859-Sept. 22, 1921; House 1895-97.

CROWLEY, Richard (R N.Y.) Dec. 14, 1836-July 22, 1908; House 1879-83.

CROWNINSHIELD, Benjamin Williams (brother of Jacob Crowinshield) (D Mass.) Dec. 27, 1772-Feb. 3, 1851; House 1823-31; Secy. of the Navy 1814-18.

CROWTHER, Frank (R N.Y.) July 10, 1870-July 20, 1955; House 1919-43.

CROWTHER, George Calhoun (R Mo.) Jan. 26, 1849-March 18, 1914; House 1895-97.

CROXTON, Thomas (D Va.) March 8, 1822-July 3, 1903; House 1885-87.

CROZIER, John Hervey (W Tenn.) Feb. 10, 1812-Oct. 25, 1889; House 1845-49.

CROZIER, Robert (R Kan.) Oct. 13, 1827-Oct. 2, 1895; House Nov. 24, 1873-Feb. 12, 1874.

CRUDUP, Josiah (W N.C.) Jan. 13, 1791-May 20, 1872; House 1821-23.

CRUGER, Daniel (D N.Y.) Dec. 22, 1780-July 12, 1843; House 1817-19.

CRUMP, Edward Hull (D Tenn.) Oct. 2, 1874-Oct. 16, 1954; House 1931-35.

CRUMP, George William (JD Va.) Sept. 26, 1786-Oct. 1, 1848; House Jan. 21, 1826-27.

CRUMP, Rousseau Owen (R Mich.) May 20, 1843-May 1, 1901; House 1895-May 1, 1901.

CRUMPACKER, Edgar Dean (father of Maurice Edgar Crumpacker and cousin of Shepard J. Crumpacker, Jr.) (R Ind.) May 27, 1851-May 19, 1920; House 1897-1913.

CRUMPACKER, Maurice Edgar (son of Edgar Dean Crumpacker and cousin of Shepard J. Crumpacker, Jr.) (R Ore.) Dec. 19, 1886-July 24, 1927; House 1925-July 24, 1927.

CRUMPACKER, Shepard J., Jr. (cousin of Edgar Dean Crumpacker and Maurice Edgar Crumpacker) (R Ind.) Feb. 13, 1917; House 1951-57.

CRUTCHFIELD, William (R Tenn.) Nov. 16, 1824-Jan. 24, 1890; House 1873-75.

CULBERSON, Charles Allen (son of David Browning Culberson) (D Texas) June 10, 1855-March 19, 1925; Senate 1899-1923; Gov. 1894-98.

CULBERSON, David Browning (father of Charles Allen Culberson) (D Texas) Sept. 29, 1830-May 7, 1900; House 1875-97.

CULBERTSON, William Constantine (R Pa.) Nov. 25, 1825-May 24, 1906; House 1889-91.

CULBERTSON, William Wirt (R Ky.) Sept. 22, 1835-Oct. 31, 1911; House 1883-85.

CULBRETH, Thomas (D Md.) April 13, 1786-April 16, 1843; House 1817-21.

CULKIN, Francis Dugan (R N.Y.) Nov. 10, 1874-Aug. 4, 1943; House Nov. 6, 1928-Aug. 4, 1943.

CULLEN, Elisha Dickerson (AP Del.) April 23, 1799-Feb. 8, 1862; House 1855-57.

CULLEN, Thomas Henry (D N.Y.) March 29, 1868-March 1, 1944; House 1919-March 1, 1944.

CULLEN, William (R Ill.) March 4, 1826-Jan. 17, 1914; House 1881-85.

CULLOM, Alvan (brother of William Cullom and uncle of Shelby Moore Cullom) (D Tenn.) Sept. 4, 1797-July 20, 1877; House 1843-47.

CULLOM, Shelby Moore (nephew of Alvan Cullom and William Cullom) (R Ill.) Nov. 22, 1829-Jan. 28, 1914; House 1865-71; Senate 1883-1913; Gov. 1877-83.

CULLOM, William (brother of Alvan Cullom and uncle of Shelby Moore Cullom) (W Tenn.) June 4, 1810-Dec. 6, 1896; House 1851-55.

CULLOP, William Allen (D Ind.) March 28, 1853-Oct. 9, 1927; House 1909-17.

CULPEPPER, John (F N.C.) 1761-Jan., 1841; House 1807-Jan. 2, 1808, Feb. 23, 1808-09, 1813-17, 1819-21, 1823-25, 1827-29.

CULVER, Charles Vernon (R Pa.) Sept. 6, 1830-Jan. 10, 1909; House 1865-67.

CULVER, Erastus Dean (W N.Y.) March 15, 1803-Oct. 13, 1889; House 1845-47.

CULVER, John C. (D Iowa) Aug. 8, 1932; House 1965- .

CUMBACK, William (R Ind.) March 24, 1829-July 31, 1905; House 1855-57.

CUMMING, Thomas William (D N.Y.) 1814 or 1815-Oct. 13, 1855; House 1853-55.

CUMMINGS, Amos Jay (D N.Y.) May 15, 1841-May 2, 1902; House 1887-89, Nov. 5, 1889-Nov. 21, 1894, Nov. 5, 1895-May 2, 1902.

CUMMINGS, Fred Nelson (D Colo.) Sept. 18, 1864-Nov. 10, 1952; House 1933-41.

CUMMINGS, Henry Johnson Brodhead (R Iowa) May 21, 1831-April 16, 1909; House 1877-79.

CUMMINGS, Herbert Wesley (D Pa.) July 13, 1873-March 4, 1956; House 1923-25.

CUMMINS, Albert Baird (R Iowa) Feb. 15, 1850-July 30, 1926; Senate Nov. 24, 1908-July 30, 1926; President pro tempore 1919-25; Gov. 1902-08.

CUMMINS, John D. (D Ohio) 1791-Sept. 11, 1849; House 1845-49.

CUNNINGHAM, Francis Alanson (D Ohio) Nov. 9, 1804-Aug. 16, 1864; House 1845-47.

CUNNINGHAM, Glenn Clarence (R Neb.) Sept. 10, 1912; House 1957-71.

CUNNINGHAM, Paul Harvey (R Iowa) June 15, 1890-July 16, 1961; House 1941-59.

CURLEY, Edward Walter (D N.Y.) May 23, 1873-Jan. 6, 1940; House Nov. 5, 1935-Jan. 6, 1940.

CURLEY, James Michael (D Mass.) Nov. 20, 1874-Nov. 12, 1958; House 1911-Feb. 4, 1914, 1943-47, Gov. 1935-37.

CURRIE, Gilbert Archibald (R Mich.) Sept. 19, 1882-June 5, 1960; House 1917-21.

CURRIER, Frank Dunklee (R N.H.) Oct. 30, 1853-Nov. 25, 1921; House 1901-13.

CURRY, Charles Forrest (father of Charles Forrest Curry, Jr.) (R Calif.) March 14, 1858-Oct. 10, 1930; House 1913-Oct. 10, 1930.

CURRY, Charles Forrest, Jr. (son of Charles Forrest Curry) (R Calif.) Aug. 13, 1893; House 1931-33.

CURRY, George (R N.M.) April 3, 1863-Nov. 27, 1947; House Jan. 8, 1912-1913; Gov. (Terr. of N.M.) 1907-11.

CURRY, Jabez Lamar Monroe (SRD Ala.) June 5, 1825-Feb. 12, 1903; House 1857-Jan. 21, 1861.

CURTIN, Andrew Gregg (D Pa.) April 22, 1817-Oct. 7, 1894; House 1881-87; Gov. 1861-67.

CURTIN, Willard Sevier (R Pa.) Nov. 28, 1905; House 1957-67.

CURTIS, Carl Thomas (R Neb.) March 15, 1905; House 1939-Dec. 31, 1954, Jan. 1, 1955- .

CURTIS, Carlton Brandaga (R Pa). Dec. 17, 1811-March 17, 1883; House 1851-55 (D), 1873-75 (R).

CURTIS, Charles (R Kan.) Jan. 25, 1860-Feb. 8, 1936; House 1893-Jan. 28, 1907; Senate Jan. 29, 1907-13, 1915-29; President pro tempore 1911; Vice President 1929-33.

CURTIS, Edward (W N.Y.) Oct. 25, 1801-Aug. 2, 1856; House 1837-41.

CURTIS, George Martin (R Iowa) April 1, 1844-Feb. 9, 1921; House 1895-99.

CURTIS, Laurence (R Mass.) Sept. 3, 1893- —; House 1953-63.

CURTIS, Newton Martin (R N.Y.) May 21, 1835-Jan. 8, 1910; House Nov. 3, 1891-97.

CURTIS, Samuel Ryan (R Iowa) Feb. 3, 1805-Dec. 25, 1866; House 1857-Aug. 4, 1861.

CURTIS, Thomas Bradford (R Mo.) May 14, 1911; House 1951-69.

CUSACK, Thomas (D Ill.) Oct. 5, 1858-Nov. 19, 1926; House 1899-1901.

CUSHING, Caleb (W Mass.) Jan. 17, 1800-Jan. 2, 1879; House 1835-43; Attorney General 1853-57.

CUSHMAN, Francis Wellington (R Wash.) May 8, 1867-July 6, 1909; House 1899-July 6, 1909.

CUSHMAN, John Paine (— N.Y.) March 8, 1784-Sept. 16, 1848; House 1817-19.

CUSHMAN, Joshua (D Mass./Maine) April 11, 1761-Jan. 27, 1834; House 1819-21 (Mass.), 1821-25 (Maine).

CUSHMAN, Samuel (D N.H.) June 8, 1783-May 20, 1851; House 1835-39.

CUTCHEON, Byron M. (R Mich.) May 11, 1836-April 12, 1908; House 1883-91.

CUTHBERT, Alfred (brother of John Alfred Cuthbert) (D Ga.) Dec. 23, 1785-July 9, 1856; House Dec. 13, 1813-Nov. 9, 1816, 1821-27; Senate Jan. 12, 1835-43.

CUTHBERT, John Alfred (brother of Alfred Cuthbert) (D Ga.) June 3, 1788-Sept. 22, 1881; House 1819-21.

CUTLER, Augustus William (D N.J.) Oct. 22, 1827-Jan. 1, 1897; House 1875-79.

CUTLER, Manasseh (F Mass.) May 13, 1742-July 28, 1823; House 1801-05.

CUTLER, William Parker (R Ohio) July 12, 1812-April 11, 1889; House 1861-63.

CUTTING, Bronson Murray (R N.M.) June 23, 1888-May 6, 1935; Senate Dec. 29, 1927-Dec. 6, 1928, 1929-May 6, 1935.

CUTTING, Francis Brockholst (D N.Y.) Aug. 6, 1804-June 26, 1870; House 1853-55.

CUTTING, John Tyler (R Calif.) Sept. 7, 1844-Nov. 24, 1911; House 1891-93.

CUTTS, Charles (F N.H.) Jan. 31, 1769-Jan. 25, 1846; Senate June 21, 1810-March 3, 1813, April 2-June 10, 1813.

CUTTS, Marsena Edgar (R Iowa) May 22, 1833-Sept. 1, 1883; House 1881-Sept. 1, 1883.

CUTTS, Richard (D Mass.) June 28, 1771-April 7, 1845; House 1801-13.

D

DADDARIO, Emilio Quincy (D Conn.) Sept. 24, 1918; House 1959-71.

DAGGETT, David (F Conn.) Dec. 31, 1764-April 12, 1851; Senate May 13, 1813-19.

DAGGETT, Rollin Mallory (R Nev.) Feb. 22, 1831-Nov. 12, 1901; House 1879-81.

DAGUE, Paul Bartram (R Pa.) May 19, 1898- —; House 1947-67.

DAHLE, Herman Bjorn (R Wis.) March 30, 1855-April 25, 1920; House 1899-1903.

DAILY, Samuel Gordon (R Neb.) 1823-Aug. 15, 1866; House (Terr. Del.) May 18, 1860-65.

DALE, Harry Howard (D N.Y.) Dec. 3, 1868-Nov. 17, 1935; House 1913-Jan. 6, 1919.

DALE, Porter Hinman (R Vt.) March 1, 1867-Oct. 6, 1933; House 1915-Aug. 11, 1923; Senate Nov. 7, 1923-Oct. 6, 1933.

DALE, Thomas Henry (R Pa.) June 12, 1846-Aug. 21, 1912; House 1905-07.

D'ALESANDRO, Thomas, Jr. (D Md.) Aug. 1, 1903; House 1939-May 16, 1947.

DALLAS, George Mifflin (D Pa.) July 10, 1792-Dec. 31, 1864; Senate Dec. 13, 1831-33; Vice President 1845-49.

DALLINGER, Frederick William (R Mass.) Oct. 2, 1871-Sept. 5, 1955; House 1915-25, Nov. 2, 1926-Oct. 1, 1932.

DALTON, Tristram (— Mass.) May 28, 1738-May 30, 1817; Senate 1789-91.

DALY, John Burrwood (D Pa.) Feb. 13, 1872-March 12, 1939; House 1935-March 12, 1939.

DALY, William Davis (D N.J.) June 4, 1851-July 31, 1900; House 1899-July 31, 1900.

DALZELL, John (R Pa.) April 19, 1845-Oct. 2, 1927; House 1887-1913.

DAMRELL, William Shapleigh (R Mass.) Nov. 29, 1809-May 17, 1860; House 1855-57 (AP), 1857-59 (R).

DANA, Amasa (D N.Y.) Oct. 19, 1792-Dec. 24, 1867; House 1839-41, 1843-45.

DANA, Judah (D Maine) April 25, 1772-Dec. 27, 1845; Senate Dec. 7, 1836-37.

DANA, Samuel (D Mass.) June 26, 1767-Nov. 20, 1835; House Sept. 22, 1814-15.

DANA, Samuel Whittlesey (F Conn.) Feb. 13, 1760-July 21, 1830; House Jan. 3, 1797-May 10, 1810; Senate May 10, 1810-21.

DANAHER, John Anthony (R Conn.) Jan. 9, 1899- —; Senate 1939-45.

DANE, Joseph (F Maine) Oct. 25, 1778-May 1, 1858; House Nov. 6, 1820-23.

DANFORD, Lorenzo (R Ohio) Oct. 18, 1829-June 19, 1899; House 1873-79, 1895-June 19, 1899.

DANFORTH, Henry Gold (R N.Y.) June 14, 1854-April 8, 1918; House 1911-17.

DANIEL, Charles Ezra (D S.C.) Nov. 11, 1895-Sept. 13, 1964; Senate Sept. 6-Dec. 23, 1954.

DANIEL, Henry (JD Ky.) March 15, 1786-Oct. 5, 1873; House 1827-33.

DANIEL, John Reeves Jones (D N.C.) Jan. 13, 1802-June 22, 1868; House 1841-53.

DANIEL, John Warwick (D Va.) Sept. 5, 1842-June 29, 1910; House 1885-87; Senate 1887-June 29, 1910.

DANIEL, Price Marion (D Texas) Oct. 10, 1910; Senate 1953-Jan. 14, 1957; Gov. 1957-63.

DANIEL, W. C. (Dan) (D Va.) May 12, 1914; House 1969- .

DANIELL, Warren Fisher (D N.H.) June 26, 1826-July 30, 1913; House 1891-93.

DANIELS, Charles (R N.Y.) March 24, 1825-Dec. 20, 1897; House 1893-97.

DANIELS, Dominick V. (D N.J.) Oct. 18, 1908; House 1959- .

DANIELS, Milton John (R Calif.) April 18, 1838-Dec. 1, 1914; House 1903-05.

DANIELSON, George E. (D Calif.) Feb. 20, 1915; House 1971- .

DANNER, Joel Buchanan (D Pa.) 1804-July 29, 1885; House Dec. 2, 1850-51.

DARBY, Ezra (D N.J.) June 7, 1768-Jan. 27, 1808; House 1805-Jan. 27, 1808.

DARBY, Harry (R Kan.) Jan. 23, 1895- —; Senate Dec. 2, 1949-Nov. 28, 1950.

DARBY, John Fletcher (W Mo.) Dec. 10, 1803-May 11, 1882; House 1851-53.

DARDEN, Colgate Whitehead, Jr. (D Va.) Feb. 11, 1897- —; House 1933-37, 1939-March 1, 1941; Gov. 1942-46.

DARGAN, Edmund Strother (D Ala.) April 15, 1805-Nov. 22, 1879; House 1845-47.

DARGAN, George William (great-grandson of Lemuel Benton) (D S.C.) May 11, 1841-June 29, 1898; House 1883-91.

DARLING, Mason Cook (D Wis.) May 18, 1801-March 12, 1866; House June 9, 1848-49.

DARLING, William Augustus (R N.Y.) Dec. 27, 1817-May 26, 1895; House 1865-67.

DARLINGTON, Edward (cousin of Isaac Darlington and William Darlington) (A-Mas. Pa.) Sept. 17, 1795-Nov. 21, 1884; House 1833-37 (W), 1837-39 (A-Mas.)

DARLINGTON, Isaac (cousin of Edward Darlington and William Darlington) (F Pa.) Dec. 13, 1781-April 27, 1839; House 1817-19.

DARLINGTON, Smedley (second cousin of Edward Darlington, Isaac Darlington and William Darlington) (R Pa.) Dec. 24, 1827-June 24, 1899; House 1887-91.

DARLINGTON, William (cousin of Edward Darlington and Isaac Darlington) (D Pa.) April 28, 1782-April 23, 1863; House 1815-17; 1819-23.

DARRAGH, Archibald Bard (R Mich.) Dec. 23, 1840-Feb. 21, 1927; House 1901-09.

DARRAGH, Cornelius (W Pa.) 1809-Dec. 22, 1854; House March 26, 1844-47.

DARRALL, Chester Bidwell (R La.) June 24, 1842-Jan. 1, 1908; House 1869-Feb. 20, 1878, 1881-83.

DARROW, George Potter (R Pa.) Feb. 4, 1859-June 7, 1943; House 1915-37, 1939-41.

DAUGHERTY, James Alexander (D Mo.) Aug. 30, 1847-Jan. 26, 1920; House 1911-13.

DAUGHTON, Ralph Hunter (D Va.) Sept. 23, 1885-Dec. 22, 1958; House Nov. 7, 1944-47.

DAVEE, Thomas (D Maine) Dec. 9, 1797-Dec. 9, 1841; House 1837-41.

DAVENPORT, Franklin (— N.J.) Sept., 1755-July 27, 1832; Senate Dec. 5, 1798-99; House 1799-1801.

DAVENPORT, Frederick Morgan (R N.Y.) Aug. 27, 1866-Dec. 26, 1956; House 1925-33.

DAVENPORT, Harry James (D Pa.) Aug. 28, 1902; House 1949-51.

DAVENPORT, Ira (R N.Y.) June 28, 1841-Oct. 6, 1904; House 1885-89.

DAVENPORT, James (brother of John Davenport of Connecticut) (— Conn.) Oct. 12, 1758-Aug. 3, 1797; House Dec. 5, 1796-Aug. 3, 1797.

DAVENPORT, James Sanford (D Okla.) Sept. 21, 1864-Jan. 3, 1940; House Nov. 16, 1907-09, 1911-17.

DAVENPORT, John (brother of James Davenport) (F Conn.) Jan. 16, 1752-Nov. 28, 1830; House 1799-1817.

DAVENPORT, John (— Ohio) Jan. 9, 1788-July 18, 1855; House 1827-29.

DAVENPORT, Samuel Arza (R Pa.) Jan. 15, 1834-Aug. 1, 1911; House 1897-1901.

DAVENPORT, Stanley Woodward (D Pa.) July 21, 1861-Sept. 26, 1921; House 1899-1901.

DAVENPORT, Thomas (F Va.) - —; Nov. 18, 1838; House 1825-35.

DAVEY, Martin Luther (D Ohio) July 25, 1884-March 31, 1946; House Nov. 5, 1918-21, 1923-29; Gov. 1935-39.

DAVEY, Robert Charles (D La.) Oct. 22, 1853-Dec. 26, 1908; House 1893-95, 1897-Dec. 26, 1908.

DAVIDSON, Alexander Caldwell (D Ala.) Dec. 26, 1826-Nov. 6, 1897; House 1885-89.

DAVIDSON, Irwin Delmore (D/L N.Y.) Jan. 2, 1906; House 1955-Dec. 31, 1956.

DAVIDSON, James Henry (R Wis.) June 18, 1858-Aug. 6, 1918; House 1897- 1913, 1917-Aug. 6, 1918.

DAVIDSON, Robert Hamilton McWhorta (D Fla.) Sept. 23, 1832-Jan. 18, 1908; House 1877-91.

DAVIDSON, Thomas Green (D La.) Aug. 3, 1805-Sept. 11, 1883; House 1855-61.

DAVIDSON, William (F N.C.) Sept. 12, 1778-Sept. 16, 1857; House Dec. 2, 1818-21.

DAVIES, Edward (W Pa.) Nov., 1779-May 18, 1853; House 1837-41.

DAVIES, John Clay (D N.Y.) May 1, 1920; House 1949-51.

DAVILA, Felix Cordova (U P.R.), Nov. 20, 1878-Dec. 3, 1938; House (Res Comm.) Aug. 7, 1917-April 11, 1932.

DAVIS, Alexander Mathews (- Va.) Jan. 17, 1833-Sept. 25, 1889; House 1873-March 5, 1874.

DAVIS, Amos (brother of Garrett Davis) (W Ky.) Aug. 15, 1794-June 11, 1835; House 1833-35.

DAVIS, Charles Russell (R Minn.) Sept. 17, 1849-July 29, 1930; House 1903-25.

DAVIS, Clifford (D Tenn.) Nov. 18, 1897-June 8, 1970; House Feb. 15, 1940-65.

DAVIS, Cushman Kellogg (R Minn.) June 16, 1838-Nov. 27, 1900; Senate 1887-Nov. 17, 1900; Gov. 1874-75.

DAVIS, David (cousin of Henry Winter Davis) (I/D Ill.) March 9, 1815-June 26, 1886; Senate 1877-83; President pro tempore 1881-83; Asso. Justice of Supreme Court 1862-77.

DAVIS, Ewin Lamar (D Tenn.) Feb. 5, 1876-Oct. 23, 1949; House 1919-33.

DAVIS, Garrett (brother of Amos Davis) (D Ky.) Sept. 10, 1801-Sept. 22, 1872; House 1839-47 (HCW); Senate Dec. 10, 1861-67 (W), 1867-Sept. 22, 1872 (D).

DAVIS, George Royal (R Ill.) Jan. 3, 1840-Nov. 25, 1899; House 1879-85.

DAVIS, George Thomas (W Mass.) Jan. 12, 1810-June 17, 1877; House 1851-53.

DAVIS, Glenn R. (R Wis.) Oct. 28, 1914; House April 22, 1947-57, 1965- .

DAVIS, Henry Gassaway (brother of Thomas Beall Davis and grandfather of Davis Elkins) (D W. Va.) Nov. 16, 1823-March 11, 1916; Senate 1871-83.

DAVIS, Henry Winter (cousin of David Davis) (UU Md.) Aug. 16, 1817-Dec. 30, 1865; House 1855-57 (AP), 1857-61 (R), 1863-65 (UU).

DAVIS, Horace (R Calif.) March 16, 1831-July 12, 1916; House 1877-81.

DAVIS, Jacob Cunningham (D Ill.) Sept. 16, 1820-Dec. 25, 1883; House Nov. 4, 1856-57.

DAVIS, Jacob Erastus (D Ohio) Oct. 31, 1905; House 1941-43.

DAVIS, James Curran (D Ga.) May 17, 1895- —; House 1947-63.

DAVIS, James Harvey (Cyclone) (D Texas) Dec. 24, 1853-Jan. 31, 1940; House 1915-17.

DAVIS, James John (R Pa.) Oct. 27, 1873-Nov. 22, 1947; Senate Dec. 2, 1930-45; Secy of Labor 1921-30.

DAVIS, Jeff (D Ark.) May 6, 1862-Jan. 3, 1913; Senate 1907-Jan. 3, 1913; Gov. 1901-06.

DAVIS, Jefferson (D Miss.) June 3, 1808-Dec. 6, 1889; House 1845-June, 1846; Senate Aug. 10, 1847-Sept. 23, 1851, 1857-Jan. 21, 1861; Secy. of War 1853-57.

DAVIS, John (W Mass.) Jan. 13, 1787-April 19, 1854; House 1825-Jan. 14, 1834 (NR); Senate 1835-Jan. 5, 1841, March 24, 1845-53; Gov. 1834-35, 1841-43.

DAVIS, John (D Pa.) Aug. 7, 1788-April 1, 1878; House 1839-41.

DAVIS, John (PP Kan.) Aug. 9, 1826-Aug. 1, 1901; House 1891-95.

DAVIS, John Givan (D Ind.) Oct. 10, 1810-Jan. 18, 1866; House 1851-55, 1857-61.

DAVIS, John James (father of John William Davis) (D W. Va.) May 5, 1835-March 19, 1916; House 1871-75.

DAVIS, John Wesley (D Ind.) April 16, 1799-Aug. 22, 1859; House 1835-37, 1839-41, 1843-47; Speaker 1845-47; Gov. of Oregon Terr. 1853-54.

DAVIS, John William (son of John James Davis) (D W. Va.) April 13, 1873-March 24, 1955; House 1911-Aug. 29, 1913.

DAVIS, John William (D Ga.) Sept. 12, 1916; House 1961- .

DAVIS, Joseph Jonathan (D N.C.) April 13, 1828-Aug. 7, 1892; House 1875-81.

DAVIS, Lowndes Henry (D Mo.) Dec. 13, 1836-Feb. 4, 1920; House 1879-85.

DAVIS, Mendel J. (D S.C.) Oct. 23, 1942; House 4/27/71- .

DAVIS, Noah (R N.Y.) Sept. 10, 1818-March 20, 1902; House 1869-July 15, 1870.

DAVIS, Reuben (D Miss.) Jan. 18, 1813-Oct. 14, 1890; House 1857-Jan. 12, 1861.

DAVIS, Richard David (D N.Y.) 1799-June 17, 1871; House 1841-45.

DAVIS, Robert Lee (R Pa.) Oct. 29, 1893- —; House Nov. 8, 1932-33.

DAVIS, Robert Thompson (R Mass.) Aug. 28, 1823-Oct. 29, 1906; 1883-89.

DAVIS, Robert Wyche (D Fla.) March 15, 1849-Sept. 15, 1929; House 1897-1905.

DAVIS, Roger (D Pa.) Oct. 2, 1762-Nov. 20, 1815; House 1811-15.

DAVIS, Samuel (F Mass.) 1774-April 20, 1831; House 1813-15.

DAVIS, Thomas (D R.I.) Dec. 18, 1806-July 26, 1895; House 1853-55.

DAVIS, Thomas Beall (brother of Henry Gassaway Davis) (D W. Va.) April 25, 1828-Nov. 26, 1911; House June 6, 1905-07.

DAVIS, Thomas Terry (— Ky.) - —; Nov. 15, 1807; House 1797-1803.

DAVIS, Thomas Treadwell (grandson of Thomas Tredwell) (U N.Y.) Aug. 22, 1810-May 2, 1872; House 1863-67.

DAVIS, Timothy (W Iowa) March 29, 1794-April 27, 1872; House 1857-59.

DAVIS, Timothy (R Mass.) April 12, 1821-Oct. 23, 1888; House 1855-57 (AP), 1857-59 (R).

DAVIS, Warren Ransom (SRD S.C.) May 8, 1793-Jan. 29, 1835; House 1827-Jan. 29, 1835.

DAVIS, William Morris (R Pa.) Aug. 16, 1815-Aug. 5, 1891; House 1861-63.

DAVISON, George Mosby (R Ky.) March 23, 1855-Dec. 18, 1912; House 1897-99.

DAVY, John Madison (R N.Y.) June 29, 1835-April 21, 1909; House 1875-77.

DAWES, Henry Laurens (R Mass.) Oct. 30, 1816-Feb. 5, 1903; House 1857-75; Senate 1875-93

DAWES, Rufus (father of Vice President Charles Gates Dawes and Beman Gates Dawes) (R Ohio) July 4, 1838-Aug. 2, 1899; House 1881-83.

DAWSON, Albert Foster (R Iowa) Jan. 26, 1872-March 9, 1949; House 1905-11.

DAWSON, John (D Va.) 1762-March 31, 1814; House 1797-March 31, 1814; Cont. Cong. 1788-89.

DAWSON, John Bennett (D La.) March 17, 1798-June 26, 1845; House 1841-June 26, 1845.

DAWSON, John Littleton (D Pa.) Feb. 7, 1813-Sept. 18, 1870; House 1851-55, 1863-67.

DAWSON, William (D Mo.) March 17, 1848-Oct. 12, 1949; House 1885-87.

DAWSON, William Adams (R Utah) Nov. 5, 1903; House 1947-49; 1953-59.

DAWSON, William Crosby (SRW Ga.) Jan. 4, 1798-May 6, 1956; House Nov. 7, 1836-Nov. 13, 1841; Senate 1849-55.

DAWSON, William Levi (D Ill.) April 26, 1886-Nov. 9, 1970; House 1943-Nov. 9, 1970.

DAY, Rowland (D N.Y.) March 6, 1779-Dec. 23, 1853; House 1823-25, 1833-35.

DAY, Stephen Albion (R Ill.) July 13, 1882-Jan. 5, 1950; House 1941-45.

DAY, Timothy Crane (R Ohio) Jan. 8, 1819-April 15, 1869; House 1855-57.

DAYAN, Charles (D N.Y.) July 8, 1792-Dec. 25, 1877; House 1831-33.

DAYTON, Alston Gordon (R W. Va.) Oct. 18, 1857-July 30, 1920; House 1895-March 16, 1905.

DAYTON, Jonathan (R N.J.) Oct. 16, 1760-Oct. 9, 1824; House 1791-99; Speaker 1795-99; Senate 1799-1805; Cont. Cong. 1787-89.

DAYTON, William Lewis (W N.J.) Feb. 17, 1807-Dec. 1, 1864; Senate July 2, 1842-1851.

DEAL, Joseph Thomas (D Va.) Nov. 19, 1860-March 7, 1942; House 1921-29.

DEAN, Benjamin (D Mass.) Aug. 14, 1824-April 9, 1897; House March 28, 1878-79.

DEAN, Ezra (D Ohio) April 9, 1795-Jan. 25, 1872; House 1841-45.

DEAN, Gilbert (D N.Y.) Aug. 14, 1819-Oct. 12, 1870; House 1851-July 3, 1854.

DEAN, Josiah (D Mass.) March 6, 1748-Oct. 14, 1818; House 1807-09.

DEAN, Sidney (R Conn.) Nov. 16, 1818-Oct. 29, 1901; House 1855-57 (AP), 1857-59 (R).

DEANE, Charles Bennett (D N.C.) Nov. 1, 1898-Nov. 24, 1969; House 1947-57.

DEAR, Cleveland (D La.) Aug. 22, 1888-Dec. 30, 1950; House 1933-37.

DEARBORN, Henry (father of Henry Alexander Scammell Dearborn) (D Mass.) Feb. 23, 1751-June 6, 1829; House 1793-97; Secy. of War 1801-09.

DEARBORN, Henry Alexander Scammell (son of Henry Dearborn) (— Mass.) March 3, 1783-July 29, 1851; House 1831-33.

DE ARMOND, David Albaugh (D Mo.) March 18, 1844-Nov. 23, 1909; House 1891-Nov. 23, 1909.

DEBERRY, Edmund (W N.C.) Aug. 14, 1787-Dec. 12, 1859; House 1829-31, 1833-45, 1849-51.

DEBOE, William Joseph (R Ky.) June 30, 1849-June 15, 1927; Senate 1897-1903.

DE BOLT, Rezin A. (D Mo.) Jan. 20, 1828-Oct. 30, 1891; House 1875-77.

DECKER, Perl D. (D Mo.) Sept. 10, 1875-Aug. 22, 1934; House 1913-19.

DEEMER, Elias (R Pa.) Jan. 3, 1838-March 29, 1918; House 1901-07.

DEEN, Braswell Drue (D Ga.) June 28, 1893- —; House 1933-39.

DEERING, Nathaniel Cobb (R Iowa) Sept. 2, 1827-Dec. 11, 1887; House 1877-83.

DE FOREST, Henry Schermerhorn (R N.Y.) Feb. 16, 1847-Feb. 13, 1917; House 1911-13.

DE FOREST, Robert Elliott (D Conn.) Feb. 20, 1845-Oct. 1, 1924; House 1891-95.

DEFREES, Joseph Hutton (R Ind.) May 13, 1812-Dec. 21, 1885; House 1865-67.

DEGENER, Edward (R Texas) Oct. 20, 1809-Sept. 11, 1890; House March 31, 1870-71.

DEGETAU, Federico (R P.R.) Dec. 5, 1862-Jan. 20, 1914; House (Res Comm.) 1901-05.

DE GRAFF, John Isaac (D N.Y.) Oct. 2, 1783-July 26, 1848; House 1827-29; 1837-39.

DE GRAFFENREID, Reese Calhoun (D Texas) May 7, 1859-Aug. 29, 1902; House 1897-Aug. 29, 1902.

deGRAFFENRIED, Edward (D Ala.) June 30, 1899- —; House 1949-53.

DE HAVEN, John Jefferson (R Calif.) March 12, 1849-Jan. 26, 1913; House 1889-Oct. 1, 1890.

DEITRICK, Frederick Simpson (D Mass.) April 9, 1875-May 24, 1948; House 1913-15.

DE JARNETTE, Daniel Coleman (D Va.) Oct. 18, 1822-Aug. 20, 1881; House 1859-61.

DE LACY, Emerson Hugh (D Wash.) May 9, 1910; House 1945-47.

de la GARZA, Eligio (D Texas) Sept. 22, 1927; House 1965- .

DE LA MATYR, Gilbert (Nat./D Ind.) July 8, 1825-May 17, 1892; House 1879-81.

DE LA MONTANYA, James (D N.Y.) March 20, 1798-April 29, 1849; House 1839-41.

DELANEY, James Joseph (D N.Y.) March 19, 1901; House 1945-47, 1949- .

DELANEY, John Joseph (D N.Y.) Aug. 21, 1878-Nov. 18, 1948; House March 5, 1918-19, 1931-Nov. 18, 1948.

DELANO, Charles (R Mass.) June 24, 1820-Jan. 23, 1883; House 1859-63.

DELANO, Columbus (R Ohio) June 4, 1809-Oct. 23, 1896; House 1845-47 (W), (R) 1865-67, June 3, 1868-69; Secy. of the Interior 1870-75.

DE LANO, Milton (R N.Y.) Aug. 11, 1844-Jan. 2, 1922; House 1887-91.

DELAPLAINE, Isaac Clason (Fus. N.Y.) Oct. 27, 1817-July 17, 1866; House 1861-63.

DE LARGE, Robert Carlos (R S.C.) March 15, 1842-Feb. 14, 1874; House 1871-Jan. 24, 1873.

DELGADO, Francisco A. (Nat. P.I.) Jan. 25, 1886-House (Res. Comm.) 1935-Feb. 14, 1936.

DELLAY, Vincent John (D N.J.) June 23, 1907; House 1957-59 (1957 (R), 1958 (D)).

DELLENBACK, John R. (R Ore.) Nov. 6, 1918; House 1967- .

DELLET, James (W Ala.) Feb. 18, 1788-Dec. 21, 1848; House 1839-41, 1843-45.

DELLUMS, Ronald V. (D Calif.) Nov. 24, 1935; House 1971- .

DEMING, Benjamin F. (W Vt.) 1790-July 11, 1834; House 1833-July 11, 1834.

DEMING, Henry Champion (R Conn.) May 23, 1815-Oct. 8, 1872; House 1863-67.

DE MOTT, John (D N.Y.) Oct. 7, 1790-July 31, 1870; House 1845-47.

DE MOTTE, Mark Lindsey (R Ind.) Dec. 28, 1832-Sept. 23, 1908; House 1881-83.

DEMPSEY, John Joseph (D N.M.) June 22, 1879-March 11, 1958; House 1935-41, 1951-March 11, 1958; Gov. 1943-47.

DEMPSEY, Stephen Wallace (R N.Y.) May 8, 1862-March 1, 1949; House 1915-31.

DE MUTH, Peter Joseph (D Pa.) Jan. 1, 1892- —; House 1937-39.

DENBY, Edwin (grandson of Graham Newell Fitch) (R Mich.) Feb. 18, 1870-Feb. 8, 1929; House 1905-11; Secy. of the Navy 1921-24.

DENEEN, Charles Samuel (R Ill.) May 4, 1863-Feb. 5, 1940; Senate Feb. 26, 1925-31; Gov. 1905-13.

DENHOLM, Frank E. (D S.C.) Nov. 29, 1923; House 1971- .

DENISON, Charles (nephew of George Denison) (D Pa.) Jan. 23, 1818-June 27, 1867; House 1863-June 27, 1867.

DENISON, Dudley Chase (nephew of Dudley Chase and cousin of Salmon Portland Chase) (R Vt.) Sept. 13, 1819-Feb. 10, 1905; House 1875-79.

DENISON, Edward Everett (R Ill.) Aug. 28, 1873-June 17, 1953; House 1915-31.

DENISON, George (uncle of Charles Denison) (D Pa.) Feb. 22, 1790-Aug. 20, 1831; House 1819-23.

DE NIVERNAIS, Edward James (see: LIVERNASH, Edward James).

DENNEY, Robert V. (R Neb.) April 11, 1916; House 1967-71.

DENNING, William (— N.Y.) April 1740-Oct. 30, 1819; House 1809-10.

DENNIS, David W. (R Ind.) June 7, 1912; House 1969- .

DENNIS, George Robertson (D Md.) April 8, 1822-Aug. 13, 1882; Senate 1873-79.

DENNIS, John (father of John Dennis and uncle of Littleton Purnell Dennis) (F Md.) Dec. 17, 1771-Aug. 17, 1806; House 1797-1805.

DENNIS, John (son of John Dennis) (W Md.) 1807-Nov. 1, 1859; House 1837-41.

DENNIS, Littleton Purnell (nephew of John Dennis) (W Md.) July 21, 1786-April 14, 1834; House 1833-April 14, 1834.

DENNISON, David Short (R Ohio) July 29, 1918; House 1957-59.

DENNY, Arthur Armstrong (R Wash.) June 20, 1822-Jan. 9, 1899; House (Terr. Del.) 1865-67.

DENNY, Harmar (great-grandfather of Harmar Denny Denny, Jr.) (W Pa.) May 13, 1794-Jan. 29, 1852; House Dec. 15, 1829-35 (A-Mas.), 1835-37 (W).

DENNY, Harmar Denny, Jr. (great grandson of Harmar Denny) (R Pa.) July 2, 1886-Jan. 6, 1966; House 1951-53.

DENNY, James William (D Md.) Nov. 20, 1838-April 12, 1923; House 1899-1901, 1903-05.

DENNY, Walter McKennon (D Miss.) Oct. 28, 1853-Nov. 5, 1926; House 1895-97.

DENOYELLES, Peter (— N.Y.) 1766-May 6, 1829; House 1813-15.

DENSON, William Henry (D Ala.) March 4, 1846-Sept. 26, 1906; House 1893-95.

DENT, George (D Md.) 1756-Dec. 2, 1813; House 1793-1801.

DENT, John Herman (D Pa.) March 10, 1908; House Jan. 21, 1958- .

DENT, Stanley Hubert, Jr. (D Ala.) Aug. 16, 1869-Oct. 6, 1938; House 1909-21.

DENT, William Barton Wade (D Ga.) Sept. 8, 1806-Sept. 7, 1855; House 1853-55.

DENTON, George Kirkpatrick (D Ind.) Nov. 17, 1864-Jan. 4, 1926; House 1917-19.

DENTON, Winfield Kirkpatrick (D Ind.) Oct. 28, 1896- —; House 1949-53, 1955-Dec. 30, 1966.

DENVER, James William (father of Matthew Rombach Denver) (A-BD Calif.) Oct. 23, 1817-Aug. 9, 1892; House 1855-57; Gov. of Terr. of Kansas 1857-58.

DENVER, Matthew Rombach (son of James William Denver) (D Ohio) Dec. 21, 1870-May 13, 1954; House 1907-13.

DEPEW, Chauncey Mitchell (R N.Y.) April 23, 1834-April 5, 1928; Senate 1899-1911.

DE PRIEST, Oscar (R Ill.) March 9, 1871-May 12, 1951; House 1929-35.

DE ROUEN, Rene Louis (D La.) Jan. 7, 1874-March 27, 1942; House Aug. 23, 1927-41.

DEROUNIAN, Steven Boghos (R N.Y.) April 6, 1918; House 1953-65.

DERSHEM, Franklin Lewis (D Pa.) March 5, 1865-Feb. 14, 1950; House 1913-15.

DERWINSKI, Edward Joseph (R Ill.) Sept. 15, 1926; House 1959- .

DE SAUSSURE, William Ford (D S.C.) Feb. 22, 1792-March 13, 1870; Senate May 10, 1852-53.

DESHA, Joseph (brother of Robert Desha) (D Ky.) Dec. 9, 1768-Oct. 11, 1842; House 1807-19; Gov. 1824-28.

DESHA, Robert (brother of Joseph Desha) (— Tenn.) Jan. 14, 1791-Feb. 6, 1849; House 1827-31.

DESTREHAN, John Noel (—La.) 1780-1824; Senate Sept. 3-Oct. 1, 1812.

DEUSTER, Peter Victor (D Wis.) Feb. 13, 1831-Dec. 31, 1904; House 1879-85.

DEVEREUX, James Patrick Sinnott (R Md.) Feb. 20, 1903; House 1951-59.

DE VEYRA, Jaime Carlos (Nat. P.I.) Nov. 4, 1873-March 7, 1963; House (Res. Comm.) 1917-23.

DEVINE, Samuel Leeper (R Ohio) Dec. 21, 1915; House 1959- .

DEVITT, Edward James (R Minn.) May 5, 1911; House 1947-49.

DE VRIES, Marion (D Calif.) Aug. 15, 1865-Sept. 11, 1939; House 1897-Aug. 20, 1900.

DEWALT, Arthur Granville (D Pa.) Oct. 11, 1854-Oct. 26, 1931; House 1915-21.

DEWART, Lewis (father of William Lewis Dewart) (JD Pa.) Nov. 14, 1780-April 26, 1852; House 1831-33.

D'EWART, Wesley Abner (R Mont.) Oct. 1, 1889-House June 5, 1945-55.

DEWART, William Lewis (son of Lewis Dewart) (D Pa.) June 21, 1821-April 19, 1888; House 1857-59.

DEWEESE, John Thomas (D N.C.) June 4, 1835-July 4, 1906; House July 6, 1868-Feb. 28, 1870.

DEWEY, Charles Schuveldt (R Ill.) Nov. 10, 1882- —; House 1941-45.

DEWEY, Daniel (W Mass.) Jan 29, 1766-May 26, 1815; House 1813-Feb. 24, 1814.

DE WITT, Alexander (AP Mass.) April 2, 1798-Jan. 13, 1879; House 1853-57.

DE WITT, Charles Gerrit (JD N.Y.) Nov. 7, 1789-April 12, 1839; House 1829-31.

DE WITT, David Miller (D N.Y.) Nov. 25, 1837-June 23, 1912; House 1873-75.

DE WITT, Francis Byron (R Ohio) March 11, 1849-March 21, 1929; House 1895-97.

DE WITT, Jacob Hasbrouck (Clinton D N.Y.) Oct. 2, 1784-Jan. 30, 1867; House 1819-21.

DE WOLF, James (D R.I.) March 18, 1764-Dec. 21, 1837; Senate 1821-Oct. 31, 1825.

DEXTER, Samuel (F Mass.) May 14, 1761-May 3, 1816; House 1793-95; Senate 1799-May 30, 1800; Secy. of War May 13-Dec. 31, 1800; Secy. of the Treasury Jan. 1-May 6, 1801.

DEZENDORF, John Frederick (R Va.) Aug. 10, 1834-June 22, 1894; House 1881-83.

DIAL, Nathaniel Barksdale (D S.C.) April 24, 1862-Dec. 11, 1940; Senate 1919-25.

DIBBLE, Samuel (D S.C.) Sept. 16, 1837-Sept. 16, 1913; House June 9, 1881-May 31, 1882, 1883-91.

DIBRELL, George Gibbs (D Tenn.) April 12, 1822-May 9, 1888; House 1875-85.

DICK, Charles William Frederick (R Ohio) Nov. 3, 1858-March 13, 1945; House Nov. 8, 1898-March 23, 1904; Senate March 23, 1904-11.

DICK, John (father of Samuel Bernard Dick) (R Pa.) June 17, 1794-May 29, 1872; House 1853-55 (W), 1855-59 (R).

DICK, Samuel Bernard (son of John Dick) (R Pa.) Oct. 26, 1836-May 10, 1907; House 1879-81.

DICKENS, Samuel (— N.C.) — -1840; House Dec. 2, 1816-17.

DICKERMAN, Charles Heber (D Pa.) Feb. 3, 1843-Dec. 17, 1915; House 1903-05.

DICKERSON, Mahlon (brother of Philemon Dickerson) (D N.J.) April 17, 1770-Oct. 5, 1853; Senate 1817-33; Gov. 1815-17; Secy. of the Navy 1834-38.

DICKERSON, Philemon (brother of Mahlon Dickerson) (JD N.J.) Jan. 11, 1788-Dec. 10, 1862; House 1833-Nov. 3, 1836 (D), 1839-41 (JD); Gov. 1836-37.

DICKERSON, William Worth (D Ky.) Nov. 29, 1851-Jan. 31, 1923; House June 21, 1890-93.

DICKEY, Henry Luther (D Ohio) Oct. 29, 1832-May 23, 1910; House 1877-81.

DICKEY, Jesse Column (W Pa.) Feb. 27, 1808-Feb. 19, 1890; House 1849-51.

DICKEY, John (father of Oliver James Dickey) (W Pa.) June 23, 1794-March 14, 1853; House 1843-45, 1847-49.

DICKEY, Oliver James (son of John Dickey) (R Pa.) April 6, 1823-April 21, 1876; House Dec. 7, 1868-73.

DICKINSON, Clement Cabell (D Mo.) Dec. 6, 1849-Jan. 14, 1938; House Feb. 1, 1910-21, 1923-29, 1931-35.

DICKINSON, Daniel Stevens (D N.Y.) Sept. 11, 1800-April 12, 1866; Senate Nov. 30, 1844-51.

DICKINSON, David W. (nephew of William Hardy Murfree) (W Tenn.) June 10, 1808-April 27, 1845; House 1833-35 (D), 1843-45 (W).

DICKINSON, Edward (W Mass.) Jan. 1, 1803-June 16, 1874; House 1853-55.

DICKINSON, Edward Fenwick (D Ohio) Jan. 21, 1829-Aug. 25, 1891; House 1869-71.

DICKINSON, John Dean (W N.Y.) June 28, 1767-Jan. 28, 1841; House 1819-23 (F), 1827-31 (W).

DICKINSON, Lester Jesse (cousin of Fred Dickinson Letts) (R Iowa) Oct. 29, 1873-June 4, 1968; House 1919-31; Senate 1931-37.

DICKINSON, Philemon (— N.J.) April 5, 1739-Feb. 4, 1809; Senate Nov. 23, 1790-93; Cont. Cong. (Del.) 1782-83.

DICKINSON, Rodolphus (D Ohio) Dec. 28, 1797-March 20, 1849; House 1847-March 20, 1849.

DICKINSON, William Louis (R Ala.) June 5, 1925; House 1965- .

DICKSON, David (D Miss.) — -July 31, 1836; House 1835-July 31, 1836.

DICKSON, Frank Stoddard (R Ill.) Oct. 6, 1876-Feb. 24, 1953; House 1905-07.

DICKSON, John (W N.Y.) June 1, 1783-Feb. 22, 1852; House 1831-35.

DICKSON, Joseph (F N.C.) April 1745-April 14, 1825; House 1799-1801.

DICKSON, Samuel (W N.Y.) March 29, 1807-May 3, 1858; House 1855-57.

DICKSON, William (— Tenn.) May 5, 1770-Feb. 1816; House 1801-07.

DICKSON, William Alexander (D Miss.) July 20, 1861-Feb. 25, 1940; House 1909-13.

DICKSTEIN, Samuel (D N.Y.) Feb. 5, 1885-April 22, 1954; House 1923-Dec. 30, 1945.

DIEKEMA, Gerrit John (R Mich.) March 27, 1859-Dec. 20, 1930; House March 17, 1908-11.

DIES, Martin, Jr. (son of Martin Dies) (D (D Texas) March 13, 1870-July 13, 1922; House 1909-19.

DIES, Martin, Jr. (son of Martin Dies (D Texas) Nov. 5, 1900; House 1931-45, 1953-59.

DIETERICH, William Henry (D Ill.) March 31, 1876-Oct. 12, 1940; House 1931-33; Senate 1933-39.

DIETRICH, Charles Elmer (D Pa.) July 30, 1889-May 20, 1942; House 1935-37.

DIETRICH, Charles Henry (R Neb.) Nov. 26, 1853-April 10, 1924; Senate March 28, 1901-05; Gov. Jan. 3-May 1, 1901.

DIETZ, William (D N.Y.) June 28, 1778-Aug. 24, 1848; House 1825-27.

DIFFENDERFER, Robert Edward (D Pa.) June 7, 1849-April 27, 1923; House 1911-15.

DIGGS, Charles Coles, Jr. (D Mich.) Dec. 2, 1922; House 1955- .

DILL, Clarence Cleveland (D Wash.) Sept. 21, 1884- —; House 1915-19; Senate 1923-35.

DILLINGHAM, Paul, Jr. (father of William Paul Dillingham) (D Vt.) Aug. 10, 1799-July 26, 1891; House 1843-47; Gov. 1865-66.

DILLINGHAM, William Paul (son of Paul Dillingham, Jr.) (R Vt.) Dec. 12, 1843-July 12, 1923; Senate Oct. 18, 1900-July 12, 1923; Gov. 1888-90.

DILLON, Charles Hall (R S.D.) Dec. 18, 1853-Sept. 15, 1929; House 1913-19.

DILWEG, La Vern Ralph (D Wis.) Nov. 1, 1903-Jan. 2, 1968; House 1943-45.

DIMMICK, Milo Melankthon (brother of William Harrison Dimmick) (D Pa.) Oct. 30, 1811-Nov. 22, 1872; House 1849-53.

DIMMICK, William Harrison (brother of Milo Melankthon Dimmick) (D Pa.) Dec. 20, 1815-Aug. 2, 1861; House 1857-61.

DIMOCK, Davis, Jr. (D Pa.) Sept. 17, 1801-Jan. 13, 1842; House 1841-Jan. 13, 1842.

DIMOND, Anthony Joseph (D Alaska) Nov. 30, 1881-May 28, 1953; House (Terr. Del.) 1933-45.

DINGELL, John David (father of John David Dingell, Jr. (D Mich.) Feb. 2, 1894-Sept. 19, 1955; House 1933-Sept. 19, 1955.

DINGELL, John David, Jr. (son of John Dingell) (D Mich.) July 8, 1926; House Dec. 13, 1955- .

DINGLEY, Nelson, Jr. (R Maine) Feb. 15, 1832-Jan. 13, 1899; House Sept. 12, 1881-Jan. 13, 1899; Gov. 1874.

DINSMOOR, Samuel (WD N.H.) July 1, 1766-March 15, 1835; House 1811-13; Gov. 1831-33.

DINSMORE, High Anderson (D Ark.) Dec. 24, 1850-May 2, 1930; House 1893-1905.

DIRKSEN, Everett McKinley (R Ill.) Jan. 4, 1896-Sept. 7, 1969; House 1933-49; Senate 1951-Sept. 7, 1969.

DISNEY, David Tiernan (D Ohio) Aug. 25, 1803-March 14, 1857; House 1849-55.

DISNEY, Wesley Ernest (D Okla.) Oct. 31, 1883-March 26, 1961; House 1931-45.

DITTER, John William (R Pa.) Sept. 5, 1888-Nov. 21, 1943; House 1933-Nov. 21, 1943.

DIVEN, Alexander Samuel (R N.Y.) Feb. 10, 1809-June 11, 1896; House 1861-63.

DIX, John Adams (son-in-law of John Jordan Morgan) (D N.Y.) July 24, 1798-April 21, 1879; Senate Jan. 27, 1845-49; Secy. of the Treasury Jan. 11-March 3, 1861; Gov. (R) 1873-75.

DIXON, Archibald (W Ky.) April 2, 1802-April 23, 1876; Senate Sept. 1, 1852-55.

DIXON, Henry Aldous (R Utah) June 29, 1890-Jan. 22, 1967; House 1955-61.

DIXON, James (R Conn.) Aug. 5, 1814-March 27, 1873; House 1845-49 (W); Senate 1857-69 (R).

DIXON, Joseph (R N.C.) April 9, 1828-March 3, 1883; House Dec. 5, 1870-71.

DIXON, Joseph Andrew (D Ohio) June 3, 1879-July 4, 1942; House 1937-39.

DIXON, Joseph Moore (R Mont.) July 31, 1867-May 22, 1934; House 1903-07; Senate 1907-13; Gov. 1921-25.

DIXON, Lincoln (D Ind.) Feb. 9, 1860-Sept. 16, 1932; House 1905-19.

DIXON, Nathan Fellows (father of Nathan Fellows Dixon) (W R.I.) Dec. 13, 1774-Jan. 29, 1842; Senate 1839-Jan. 19, 1842.

DIXON, Nathan Fellows (son of Nathan Fellows Dixon) (R R.I.) May 1, 1812-April 11, 1881; House 1849-51 (W), 1863-71 (R).

DIXON, Nathan Fellows (son of the preceding) (R R.I.) Aug. 28, 1847-Nov. 8, 1897; House Feb. 12-March 3, 1885; Senate April 10, 1889-95.

DIXON, William Wirt (D Mont.) June 3, 1838-Nov. 13, 1910; House 1891-93.

DOAN, Robert Eachus (R Ohio) July 23, 1831-Feb. 24, 1919; House 1891-93.

DOAN, William (D Ohio) April 4, 1792-June 22, 1847; House 1839-43.

DOBBIN, James Cochrane (grandson of James Cochran of North Carolina) (D N.C.) Jan. 17, 1814-Aug. 4, 1857; House 1845-47; Secy. of the Navy 1853-57.

DOBBINS, Donald Claude (D Ill.) March 20, 1878-Feb. 14, 1943; House 1933-37.

DOBBINS, Samuel Atkinson (R N.J.) April 14, 1814-May 26, 1886; House 1873-77.

DOCKERY, Alexander Monroe (D Mo.) Feb. 11, 1845-Dec. 26, 1926; House 1883-99; Gov. 1901-05.

DOCKERY, Alfred (father of Oliver Hart Dockery) (W N.C.) Dec. 11, 1797-Dec. 7, 1875; House 1845-47, 1851-53.

DOCKERY, Oliver Hart (son of Alfred Dockery) (R N.C.) Aug. 12, 1830-March 21, 1906; House July 13, 1868-71.

DOCKWEILER, John Francis (D Calif.) Sept. 19, 1895-Jan. 31, 1943; House 1933-39.

DODD, Edward (W N.Y.) Aug. 25, 1805-March 1, 1891; House 1855-59.

DODD, Thomas Joseph (D Conn.) May 15, 1907-May 24, 1971; House 1953-57; Senate 1959-71.

DODDRIDGE, Philip (— Va.) May 17, 1773-Nov. 19, 1832; House 1829-Nov. 19, 1832.

DODDS, Francis Henry (R Mich.) June 9, 1858-Dec. 23, 1940; House 1909-13.

DODDS, Ozro John (D Ohio) March 22, 1840-April 18, 1882; House Oct. 8, 1872-73.

DODGE, Augustus Caesar (son of Henry Dodge) (D Iowa) Jan. 2, 1812-Nov. 20, 1883; House (Terr. Del.) Oct. 28, 1840-Dec. 28, 1846; Senate Dec. 7, 1848-Feb. 22, 1855.

DODGE, Grenville Mellen (R Iowa) April 12, 1831-Jan. 3, 1916; House 1867-69.

DODGE, Henry (father of Augustus Caesar Dodge) (D Wis.) Oct. 12, 1782-June 19, 1867; House (Terr. Del.) 1841-45; Senate June 8, 1848-57; Gov. (Terr.) 1836-41, 1845-48.

DODGE, William Earle (R N.Y.) Sept. 4, 1805-Feb. 9, 1883; House April 7, 1866-67.

DOE, Nicholas Bartlett (W N.Y.) June 16, 1786-Dec. 6, 1856; House Dec. 7, 1840-41.

DOIG, Andrew Wheeler (D N.Y.) July 24, 1799-July 11, 1875; House 1839-43.

DOLE, Robert J. (R Kan.) July 22, 1923; House 1961-69; Senate 1969- .

DOLLINGER, Isidore (D N.Y.) Nov. 13, 1903; House 1949-Dec. 31, 1959.

DOLLIVER, James Isaac (nephew of Jonathan Prentiss Dolliver) (R Iowa) Aug. 31, 1894- —; House 1945-57.

DOLLIVER, Jonathan Prentiss (uncle of James Isaac Dolliver) (R Iowa) Feb. 6, 1858-Oct. 15, 1910; House 1889-Aug. 22, 1900; Senate Aug. 22, 1900-Oct. 15, 1910.

DOLPH, Joseph Norton (uncle of Frederick William Mulkey) (R Ore.) Oct. 19, 1835-March 10, 1897; Senate 1883-95.

DOMENGEAUX, James (D La.) Jan. 6, 1907; House 1941-April 15, 1944; Nov. 7, 1944-49.

DOMINICK, Frederick Haskell (D S.C.) Feb. 20, 1877-March 11, 1960; House 1917-33.

DOMINICK, Peter H. (R Colo.) July 7, 1915; House 1961-63; Senate 1963- .

DONAHEY, Alvin Victor (D Ohio) July 7, 1873-April 8, 1946; Senate 1935-41; Gov. 1923-29.

DONDERO, George Anthony (R Mich.) Dec. 16, 1883-Jan. 29, 1968; House 1933-57.

DONLEY, Joseph Benton (R Pa.) Oct. 10, 1838-Jan. 23, 1917; House 1869-71.

DONNAN, William G. (R Iowa) June 30, 1834-Dec. 4, 1908; House 1871-75.

DONNELL, Forrest C. (R Mo.) Aug. 20, 1884- —; Senate 1945-51; Gov. 1941-45.

DONNELL, Richard Spaight (grandson of Richard Dobbs Spaight) (W N.C.) Sept. 20, 1820-June 3, 1867; House 1847-49.

DONNELLY, Ignatius (R Minn.) Nov. 3, 1831-Jan. 1, 1901; House 1863-69.

DONOHOE, Michael (D Pa.) Feb. 22, 1864-Jan. 17, 1958; House 1911-15.

DONOHUE, Harold Daniel (D Mass.) June 18, 1901; House 1947- .

DONOVAN, Dennis D. (D Ohio) Jan. 31, 1859-April 21, 1941; House 1891-95.

DONOVAN, James George (D/R/L N.Y.) Dec. 15, 1898- —; House 1951-57.

DONOVAN, Jeremiah (D Conn.) Oct. 18, 1857-April 22, 1935; House 1913-15.

DONOVAN, Jerome Francis (D N.Y.) Feb. 1, 1872-Nov. 2, 1949; House March 5, 1918-21.

DOOLEY, Edwin Benedict (R N.Y.) April 13, 1905; House 1957-63.

DOOLING, Peter Joseph (D N.Y.) Feb. 15, 1857-Oct. 18, 1931; House 1913-21.

DOOLITTLE, Dudley (D Kan.) June 21, 1881-Nov. 14, 1957; House 1913-19.

DOOLITTLE, James Rood (R Wis.) Jan. 3, 1815-July 23, 1897; Senate 1857-69.

DOOLITTLE, William Hall (R Wash.) Nov. 6, 1848-Feb. 26, 1914; House 1893-97.

DOREMUS, Frank Ellsworth (D Mich.) Aug. 31, 1865-Sept. 4, 1947; House 1911-21.

DORN, Francis Edwin (R N.Y.) April 18, 1911; House 1953-61.

DORN, William Jennings Bryan (D S.C.) April 14, 1916; House 1947-49; 1951- .

DORR, Charles Philips (R W. Va.) Aug. 12, 1852-Oct. 8, 1914; House 1897-99.

DORSEY, Clement (— Md.) 1778-Aug. 6, 1848; House 1825-31.

DORSEY, Frank Joseph Gerard (D Pa.) April 26, 1891-July 13, 1949; House 1935-39.

DORSEY, George Washington Emery (R Neb.) Jan. 25, 1842-June 12, 1911; House 1885-91.

DORSEY, John Lloyd, Jr. (D Ky.) Aug. 10, 1891-March 22, 1960; House Nov. 4, 1930-31.

DORSEY, Stephen Wallace (R Ark.) Feb. 28, 1842-March 20, 1916; Senate 1873-79.

DORSHEIMER, William (D N.Y.) Feb. 5, 1832-March 26, 1888; House 1883-85.

DOTY, James Duane (cousin of Morgan Lewis Martin) (F-S Wis.) Nov. 5, 1799-June 13, 1865; House (Terr. Del.) Jan. 14, 1839-41) (D), (Rep.) 1849-51 (D), 1851-53 (F-S); Gov. (Terr. of Wis.) 1841-44, (Terr. of Utah) 1863-65.

DOUBLEDAY, Ulysses Freeman (JD N.Y.) Dec. 15, 1792-March 11, 1866; House 1831-33, 1835-37.

DOUGHERTY, Charles (D Fla.) Oct. 15, 1850-Oct. 11, 1915; House 1885-89.

DOUGHERTY, John (D Mo.) Feb. 25, 1857-Aug. 1, 1905; House 1899-1905.

DOUGHTON, Robert Lee (D N.C.) Nov. 7, 1863 Oct. 1, 1954; House 1911-53.

DOUGLAS, Albert (R Ohio) April 25, 1852-March 14, 1935; House 1907-11.

DOUGLAS, Beverly Browne (D Va.) Dec. 21, 1822-Dec. 22, 1878; House 1875-77 (C), 1877-Dec. 22, 1878 (D).

DOUGLAS, Emily Taft (wife of Senator Paul H. Douglas) (D Ill.) April 10, 1899; House 1945-47.

DOUGLAS, Fred James (R N.Y.) Sept. 14, 1869-Jan. 1, 1949; House 1937-45.

DOUGLAS, Helen Gahagan (D Calif.) Nov. 25, 1900; House 1945-51.

DOUGLAS, Lewis Williams (D Ariz.) July 2, 1894- —; House 1927-March 4, 1933.

DOUGLAS, Paul Howard (husband of Emily Taft Douglas) (D Ill.) March 26, 1892- —; Senate 1949-67.

DOUGLAS, Stephen Arnold (PSD Ill.) April 23, 1813-June 3, 1861; House 1843-47 (D); Senate 1847-53 (D), 1853-June 3, 1861 (PSD).

DOUGLAS, William Harris (R N.Y.) Dec. 5, 1853-Jan. 27, 1944; House 1901-05.

DOUGLASS, John Joseph (D Mass.) Feb. 9, 1873-April 5, 1939; House 1925-35.

DOUTRICH, Isaac Hoffer (R Pa.) Dec. 19, 1871-May 28, 1941; House 1927-37.

DOVENER, Blackburn Barrett (R W. Va.) April 20, 1842-May 9, 1914; House 1895-1907.

DOW, John Goodchild (D N.Y.) May 6, 1905; House 1965-69; 1971- .

DOWD, Clement (D N.C.) Aug. 27, 1832-April 15, 1898; House 1881-85.

DOWDELL, James Ferguson (SRD Ala.) Nov. 26, 1818-Sept. 6, 1871; House 1853-59.

DOWDNEY, Abraham (D N.Y.) Oct. 31, 1841-Dec. 10, 1886; House 1885-Dec. 10, 1886.

DOWDY, John Vernard (D Texas) Feb. 11, 1912; House Sept. 23, 1952- .

DOWELL, Cassius Clay (R Iowa) Feb. 29, 1864-Feb. 4, 1940; House 1915-35, 1937-Feb. 4, 1940.

DOWNEY, Sheridan (son of Stephen Wheeler Downey) (D Calif.) March 11, 1884-Oct. 25, 1961; Senate 1939-Nov. 30, 1950.

DOWNEY, Stephen Wheeler (father of Sheridan Downey) (R Wyo.) July 25, 1839-Aug. 3, 1902; House (Terr. Del.) 1879-81.

DOWNING, Charles (— Fla.) — -; 1845; House (Terr. Del.) 1837-41.

DOWNING, Finis Ewing (D Ill.) Aug. 24, 1846-March 8, 1936; House 1895-June 5, 1896.

DOWNING, Thomas Nelms (D Va.) Feb. 1, 1919; House 1959- .

DOWNS, Le Roy Donnelly (D Conn.) April 11, 1900-Jan. 18, 1970; House 1941-43.

DOWNS, Solomon Weathersbee (D La.) 1801-Aug. 14, 1854; Senate 1847-53.

DOWSE, Edward (D Mass.) Oct. 22, 1756-Sept. 3, 1828; House 1819-May 26, 1820.

DOX, Peter Myndert (grandson of John Nicholas) (D Ala.) Sept. 11, 1813-April 2, 1891; House 1869-73.

DOXEY, Charles Taylor (R Ind.) July 13, 1841-April 30, 1898; House Jan. 17-March 3, 1883.

DOXEY, Wall (D Miss.) Aug. 8, 1892- ; House 1929-Sept. 28, 1941; Senate Sept. 29, 1941-43.

DOYLE, Clyde Gilman (D Calif.) July 11, 1887-March 14, 1963; House 1945-47, 1949-March 14, 1963.

DOYLE, Thomas Aloysius (D Ill.) Jan. 9, 1886-Jan. 29, 1935; House Nov. 6, 1923-31.

DRAKE, Charles Daniel (R Mo.) April 11, 1811-April 1, 1892; Senate 1867-Dec. 19, 1870.

DRAKE, John Reuben (— N.Y.) Nov. 28, 1782-March 21, 1857; House 1817-19.

DRANE, Herbert Jackson (D Fla.) June 20, 1863-Aug. 11, 1947; House 1917-33.

DRAPER, Joseph (— Va.) Dec. 25, 1794-June 10, 1834; House Dec. 6, 1830-31, Dec. 6, 1832-33.

DRAPER, William Franklin (R Mass.) April 9, 1842-Jan. 28, 1910; House 1893-97.

DRAPER, William Henry (R N.Y.) June 24, 1841-Dec. 7, 1921; House 1901-13.

DRAYTON, William (UD S.C.) Dec. 30, 1776-May 24, 1846; House May 17, 1825-33.

DRESSER, Solomon Robert (R Pa.) Feb. 1, 1842-Jan. 21, 1911; House 1903-07.

DREW, Ira Walton (D Pa.) Aug. 31, 1878- —; House 1937-39.

DREW, Irving Webster (R N.H.) Jan. 8, 1845-April 10, 1922; Senate Sept. 2-Nov. 5, 1918.

DREWRY, Patrick Henry (D Va.) May 24, 1875-Dec. 21, 1947; House April 27, 1920-Dec. 21, 1947.

DRIGGS, Edmund Hope (D N.Y.) May 2, 1865-Sept. 27, 1946; House Dec. 6, 1897-1901.

DRIGGS, John Fletcher (R Mich.) March 8, 1813-Dec. 17, 1877; House 1863-69.

DRINAN, Robert F. (D Mass.) Nov. 15, 1920; House 1971- .

DRISCOLL, Daniel Angelus (D N.Y.) March 6, 1875-June 5, 1955; House 1909-17.

DRISCOLL, Denis Joseph (D Pa.) March 27, 1871-Jan. 18, 1958; House 1935-37.

DRISCOLL, Michael Edward (R N.Y.) Feb. 9, 1851-Jan. 19, 1929; House 1899-1913.

DRIVER, William Joshua (D Ark.) March 2, 1873-Oct. 1, 1948; House 1921-39.

DROMGOOLE, George Coke (uncle of Alexander Drumgoole Sims) (D Va.) May 15, 1797-April 27, 1847; House 1835-41, 1843-April 27, 1847.

DRUKKER, Dow Henry (R N.J.) Feb. 7, 1872-Jan. 11, 1963. House April 7, 1914-19.

DRUM, Augustus (D Pa.) Nov. 26, 1815-Sept. 15, 1858; House 1853-55.

DRYDEN, John Fairfield (R N.J.) Aug. 7, 1839-Nov. 24, 1911; Senate Jan. 29, 1902-07.

DUBOIS, Fred Thomas (D Idaho) May 29, 1851-Feb. 14, 1930; House (Terr. Del.) 1887-July 3, 1890 (R); Senate 1891-97 (R), 1901-07 (Sil. R 1901, D 1901-07).

DU BOSE, Dudley McIver (D Ga.) Oct. 28, 1834-March 2, 1883; House 1871-73.

DUDLEY, Charles Edward (D N.Y.) May 23, 1780-Jan. 23, 1841; Senate Jan. 15, 1829-33.

DUDLEY, Edward Bishop (NR N.C.) Dec. 15, 1769-Oct. 30, 1855; House Nov. 10, 1829-31; Gov. 1837-41.

DUELL, Rodolphus Holland (R N.Y.) Dec. 20, 1824-Feb. 11, 1891; House 1859-63, 1871-75.

DUER, William (W N.Y.) May 25, 1805-Aug. 25, 1879; House 1847-51.

DUFF, James Henderson (R Pa.) Jan. 21, 1883-Dec. 20, 1969; Senate Jan. 16, 1951-57; Gov. 1947-51.

DUFFEY, Warren Joseph (D Ohio) Jan. 24, 1886-July 7, 1936; House 1933-July 7, 1936.

DUFFY, Francis Ryan (D Wis.) June 23, 1888- —; Senate 1933-39.

DUFFY, James Patrick Bernard (D N.Y.) Nov. 25, 1878-Jan. 8, 1969; House 1935-37.

DUGRO, Philip Henry (D N.Y.) Oct. 3, 1855-March 1, 1920; House 1881-83.

DUKE, Richard Thomas Walker (C Va.) June 6, 1822-July 2, 1898; House Nov. 8, 1870-73.

DULLES, John Foster (R N.Y.) Feb. 25, 1888-May 24, 1959; Senate July 7-Nov. 8, 1949; Secy. of State 1953-59.

DULSKI, Thaddeus J. (D N.Y.) Sept. 27, 1915; House 1959- .

DUMONT, Ebenezer (U Ind.) Nov. 23, 1814-April 16, 1871; House 1863-67.

DUNBAR, James Whitson (R Ind.) Oct. 17, 1860-May 19, 1943; House 1919-23, 1929-31.

DUNBAR, William (D La.) 1805-March 18, 1861; House 1853-55.

DUNCAN, Alexander (W Ohio) 1788-March 23, 1853; House 1837-41, 1843-45.

DUNCAN, Daniel (W Ohio) July 22, 1806-May 18, 1849; House 1847-49.

DUNCAN, James (— Pa.) 1756-June 24, 1844; House 1821.

DUNCAN, James Henry (W Mass.) Dec. 5, 1793-Feb. 8, 1869; House 1849-53.

DUNCAN, John J. (R Tenn.) March 24, 1919; House 1965- .

DUNCAN, Joseph (JD Ill.) Feb. 22, 1794-Jan. 15, 1844; House 1827-Sept. 21, 1834; Gov. 1834-38.

DUNCAN, Richard Meloan (D Mo.) Nov. 10, 1889- —; House 1933-43.

DUNCAN, Robert B. (D Ore.) Dec. 4, 1920; House 1963-67.

DUNCAN, William Addison (D Pa.) Feb. 2, 1836-Nov. 14, 1884; House 1883-Nov. 14, 1884.

DUNCAN, (William) Garnett (W Ky.) March 2, 1800-May 25, 1875; House 1847-49.

DUNGAN, James Irvine (D Ohio) May 29, 1844-Dec. 28, 1931; House 1891-93.

DUNHAM, Cyrus Livingston (D Ind.) Jan. 16, 1817-Nov. 21, 1877; House 1849-55.

DUNHAM, Ransom Williams (R Ill.) March 21, 1838-Aug. 19, 1896; House 1883-89.

DUNLAP, George Washington, (U Ky.) Feb. 22, 1813-June 6, 1880; House 1861-63.

DUNLAP, Robert Pickney (D Maine) Aug. 17, 1794-Oct. 20, 1859; House 1843-47; Gov. 1834-38.

DUNLAP, William Claiborne (D Tenn.) Feb. 25, 1798-Nov. 16, 1872; House 1833-37.

DUNN, Aubert Culberson (D Miss.) Nov. 20, 1896- —; House 1935-37.

DUNN, George Grundy (R Ind.) Dec. 20, 1812-Sept. 4, 1857; House 1847-49 (W), 1855-57 (R).

DUNN, George Hedford (W Ind.) Nov. 15, 1794-Jan. 12, 1854; House 1837-39.

DUNN, John Thomas (D N.J.) June 4, 1838-Feb. 22, 1907; House 1893-95.

DUNN, Matthew Anthony (D Pa.) Aug. 15, 1886-Feb. 13, 1942; House 1933-41.

DUNN, Poindexter (D Ark.) Nov. 3, 1834-Oct. 12, 1914; House 1879-89.

DUNN, Thomas Byrne (R N.Y.) March 16, 1853-July 2, 1924; House 1913-23.

DUNN, William McKee (R Ind.) Dec. 12, 1814-July 24, 1887; House 1859-63.

DUNNELL, Mark Hill (R Minn.) July 2, 1823-Aug. 9, 1904; House 1871-83, 1889-91.

DUNPHY, Edward John (D N.Y.) May 12, 1856-July 29, 1926; House 1889-95.

DUNWELL, Charles Tappan (R N.Y.) Feb. 13, 1852-June 12, 1908; House 1903-June 12, 1908.

DU PONT, Henry Algernon (cousin of Thomas Coleman du Pont) (R Del.) July 30, 1838-Dec. 31, 1926; Senate June 13, 1906-17.

du PONT, Pierre S., IV (R Del.) Jan. 22, 1935; House 1971- .

DU PONT, Thomas Coleman (cousin of Henry Algernon du Pont) (R Del.) Dec. 11, 1863-Nov. 11, 1930; Senate July 7, 1921-Nov. 7, 1922; 1925-Dec. 9, 1928.

DUPRÉ, Henry Garland (D La.) July 28, 1873-Feb. 21, 1924; House Nov. 8, 1910-Feb. 21, 1924.

DURAND, George Harman (D Mich.) Feb. 21, 1838-June 8, 1903; House 1875-77.

DURBOROW, Alan Cathcard, Jr. (D Ill.) Nov. 10, 1857-March 10, 1908; House 1891-95.

DURELL, Daniel Meserve (— N.H.) July 20, 1769-April 29, 1841; House 1807-09.

DUREY, Cyrus (R N.Y.) May 16, 1864-Jan. 4, 1933; House 1907-11.

DURFEE, Job (D R.I.) Sept. 20, 1790-July 26, 1847; House 1821-23 (PP), 1823-25 (D).

DURFEE, Nathaniel Briggs (R R.I.) Sept. 29, 1812-Nov. 9, 1872; House 1855-57 (AP), 1857-59 (R).

DURGAN, George Richard (D Ind.) Jan. 20, 1872-Jan. 13, 1942; House 1933-35.

DURHAM, Carl Thomas (D N.C.) Aug. 28, 1892- —; House 1939-61.

DURHAM, Milton Jameson (D Ky.) May 16, 1824-Feb. 12, 1911; House 1873-79.

DURKEE, Charles (R Wis.) Dec. 10, 1805-Jan. 14, 1870; House 1849-53 (F-S); Senate 1855-61 (R); Gov. of Utah Terr. 1865- —.

DURNO, Edwin R. (R Ore.) Jan. 26, 1899- —; House 1961-63.

DUVAL, Isaac Harding (R W. Va.) Sept. 1, 1824-July 10, 1902; House 1869-71.

DUVAL, William Pope (D Ky.) 1784-March 19, 1854; House 1813-15; Gov. of Terr. of Fla. 1822-34.

DUVALL, Gabriel (D Md.) Dec. 6, 1752-March 6, 1844; House Nov. 11, 1794-March 28, 1796; Asso. Justice, U.S. Supreme Court 1812-35.

DWIGHT, Henry Williams (— Mass.) Feb. 26, 1788-Feb. 21, 1845; House 1821-31.

DWIGHT, Jeremiah Wilbur (father of John Wilbur Dwight) (R N.Y.) April 17, 1819-Nov. 26, 1885; House 1877-83.

DWIGHT, John Wilbur (son of Jeremiah Wilbur Dwight) (R N.Y.) May 24, 1859-Jan. 19, 1928; House Nov. 2, 1902-13.

DWIGHT, Theodore (cousin of Aaron Burr) (F Conn.) Dec. 15, 1764-June 12, 1846; House Dec. 1, 1806-07.

DWIGHT, Thomas (F Mass.) Oct. 29, 1758-Jan. 2, 1819; House 1803-05.

DWINELL, Justin (— N.Y.) Oct. 28, 1785-Sept. 17, 1850; House 1823-25.

DWORSHAK, Henry Clarence (R Idaho) Aug. 29, 1894-July 23, 1962; House 1939-Nov. 5, 1946; Senate Nov. 6, 1946-49, Oct. 14, 1949-July 23, 1962.

DWYER, Florence Price (R N.J.) July 4, 1902; House 1957- .

DYAL, Kenneth Warren (D Calif.) July 9, 1910; House 1965-67.

DYER, David Patterson (uncle of Leonidas Carstarphen Dyer) (R Mo.) Feb. 12, 1838-April 29, 1924; House 1869-71.

DYER, Leonidas Carstarphen (nephew of David Patterson Dyer) (R Mo.) June 11, 1871-Dec. 15, 1957; House 1911-June 19, 1914, 1915-33.

E

EAGAN, John Joseph (D N.J.) Jan. 22, 1872-June 13, 1956; House 1913-21, 1923-25.

EAGER, Samuel Watkins (R N.Y.) April 8, 1789-Dec. 23, 1860; House Nov. 2, 1830-31.

EAGLE, Joe Henry (D Texas) Jan. 23, 1870-Jan. 10, 1963; House 1913-21, 1933-37.

EAGLETON, Thomas F. (D Mo.) Sept. 4, 1929; Senate Dec. 28, 1968- .

EAMES, Benjamin Tucker (R R.I.) June 4, 1818-Oct. 6, 1901; House 1871-79.

EARHART, Daniel Scofield (D Ohio) May 28, 1907; House Nov. 3, 1936-37.

EARLE, Elias (uncle of Samuel Earle and John Baylis Earle and great-grandfather of John Laurens Manning Irby and Joseph Haynsworth Earle) (D S.C.) June 19, 1762-May 19, 1823; House 1805-07, 1811-15, 1817-21.

EARLE, John Baylis (nephew of Elias Earle and cousin of Samuel Earle) (— S.C.) Oct. 23, 1766-Feb. 3, 1863; House 1803-05.

EARLE, Joseph Haynsworth (great-grandson of Elias Earle, cousin of John Laurens Manning Irby and nephew of William Lowndes Yancey) (D S.C.) April 30, 1847-May 20, 1897; Senate March 4-May 20, 1897.

EARLE, Samuel (nephew of Elias Earle and cousin of John Baylis Earle) (— S.C.) Nov. 28, 1760-Nov. 24, 1833; House 1795-97.

EARLL, Jonas, Jr. (cousin of Nehemiah Hezekiah Earll) (D N.Y.) 1786-Oct. 28, 1846; House 1827-31.

EARLL, Nehemiah Hezekiah (cousin of Jonas Earll, Jr.) (D N.Y.) Oct. 5, 1787-Aug. 26, 1872; House 1839-41.

EARLY, Peter (— Ga.) June 20, 1773-Aug. 15, 1817; House Jan. 10, 1803-07; Gov. 1813-15.

EARNSHAW, Manuel (I P.I.) Nov. 19, 1862-Feb. 13, 1936; House (Res. Comm.) 1913-17.

EARTHMAN, Harold Henderson (D Tenn.) April 13, 1900; House 1945-47.

EASTLAND, James Oliver (D Miss.) Nov. 28, 1904; Senate June 30-Sept. 18, 1941, 1943- .

EASTMAN, Ben C. (D Wis.) Oct. 24, 1812-Feb. 2, 1856; House 1851-55.

EASTMAN, Ira Allen (nephew of Nehemiah Eastman) (D N.H.) Jan. 1, 1809-March 21, 1881; House 1839-43.

EASTMAN, Nehemiah (uncle of Ira Allen Eastman) (D N.H.) June 16, 1782-Jan. 11, 1856; House 1825-27.

EASTON, Rufus (D Mo.) May 4, 1774-July 5, 1834; House (Terr. Del.) Sept. 17, 1814-Aug. 5, 1816.

EATON, Charles Aubrey (uncle of William Robb Eaton) (R N.J.) March 29, 1868-Jan. 23, 1953; House 1925-53.

EATON, John Henry (D Tenn.) June 18, 1790-Nov. 17, 1856; Senate Sept. 5, 1818-21, Sept. 27, 1821-March 9, 1829; Secy. of War 1829-31; Gov. of Fla. Terr. 1834-36.

EATON, Lewis (— N.Y.) - — —; House 1823-25.

EATON, Thomas Marion (R Calif.) Aug. 3, 1896-Sept. 16, 1939; House Jan. 3-Sept. 16, 1939.

EATON, William Robb (nephew of Charles Aubrey Eaton) (R Colo.) Dec. 17, 1877-Dec. 16, 1942; House 1929-33.

EATON, William Wallace (D Conn.) Oct. 11, 1816-Sept. 21, 1898; Senate Feb. 5, 1875-1881; House 1883-85.

EBERHARTER, Herman Peter (D Pa.) April 29, 1892-Sept. 9, 1958; House 1937-Sept. 9, 1958.

ECHOLS, Leonard Sidney (R W. Va.) Oct. 30, 1871-May 9, 1946; House 1919-23.

ECKERT, Charles Richard (D Pa.) Jan. 20, 1868-Oct. 26, 1959; House 1935-39.

ECKERT, George Nicholas (W Pa.) July 4, 1802-June 28, 1865; House 1847-49.

ECKHARDT, Bob (D Texas) July 16, 1913; House 1967- .

ECKLEY, Ephraim Ralph (R Ohio) Dec. 9, 1811-March 27, 1908; House 1863-69.

ECTON, Zales Nelson (R Mont.) April 1, 1898-March 3, 1961; Senate 1947-53.

EDDY, Frank Marion (R Minn.) April 1, 1856-Jan. 13, 1929; House 1895-1903.

EDDY, Norman (D Ind.) Dec. 10, 1810-Jan. 28, 1872; House 1853-55.

EDDY, Samuel (D R.I.) March 31, 1769-Feb. 3, 1839; House 1819-25.

EDELSTEIN, Morris Michael (D N.Y.) Feb. 5, 1888-June 4, 1941; House Feb. 6, 1940-June 4, 1941.

EDEN, John Rice (D Ill.) Feb. 1, 1826-June 9, 1909; House 1863-65, 1873-79, 1885-87.

EDGE, Walter Evans (R N.J.) Nov. 20, 1873-Oct. 29, 1956; Senate 1919-Nov. 21, 1929; Gov. 1917-19, 1944-47.

EDGERTON, Alfred Peck (brother of Joseph Ketchum Edgerton (D Ohio) Jan. 11, 1813-May 14, 1897; House 1851-55.

EDGERTON, Alonzo Jay (R Minn.) June 7, 1827-Aug. 9, 1896; Senate March 12-Oct. 30, 1881.

EDGERTON, Joseph Ketchum (brother of Alfred Peck Edgerton) (D Ind.) Feb. 16, 1818-Aug. 25, 1893; House 1963-65.

EDGERTON, Sidney (R Ohio) Aug. 17, 1818-July 19, 1900; House 1859-63; Gov. of Montana Terr. 1865-66.

EDIE, John Rufus (W Pa.) Jan. 14, 1814-Aug. 27, 1888; House 1855-59.

EDMANDS, John Wiley (W Mass.) March 1, 1809-Jan. 31, 1877; House 1853-55.

EDMISTON, Andrew (D W. Va.) Nov. 13, 1892-Aug. 28, 1966; House Nov. 28, 1933-43.

EDMOND, William (F Conn.) Sept. 28, 1755-Aug. 1, 1838; House Nov. 13, 1797-1801.

EDMONDS, George Washington (R Pa.) Feb. 22, 1864-Sept. 28, 1939; House 1913-25, 1933-35.

EDMONDSON, Edmond Augustus (brother of J. Howard Edmondson) (D Okla.) April 7, 1919; House 1953- .

EDMONDSON, J. Howard (brother of Edmond Augustus Edmondson) (D Okla.) Sept. 27, 1925; Senate Jan. 9, 1963-Nov. 3, 1964, Gov. 1959-63.

EDMUNDS, George Franklin (R Vt.) Feb. 1, 1828-Feb. 27, 1919; Senate April 3, 1866-Nov. 1, 1891, President pro tempore 1883-85.

EDMUNDS, Paul Carrington (D Va.) Nov. 1, 1836-March 12, 1899; House 1889-95.

EDMUNDSON, Henry Alonzo (D Va.) June 14, 1814-Dec. 16, 1890; House 1849-61.

EDSALL, Joseph E. (D N.J.) 1789-1865; House 1845-49.

EDWARDS, Benjamin (father of Ninian Edwards) (— Md.) Aug. 12, 1753-Nov. 13, 1829; House Jan. 2-March 3, 1795.

EDWARDS, Caldwell, (D-P Mont.) Jan. 8, 1814-July 23, 1922; House 1901-03.

EDWARDS, Charles Gordon (D Ga.) July 2, 1878-July 13, 1931; House 1907-17, 1925-July 13, 1931.

EDWARDS, Don (D Calif.) Jan. 6, 1915; House 1963- .

EDWARDS, Don Calvin (R Ky.) July 13, 1861-Sept. 19, 1938; House 1905-11.

EDWARDS, Edward Irving (D N.J.) Dec. 1, 1863-Jan. 26, 1931; Senate 1923-29; Gov. 1920-23.

EDWARDS, Edwin W. (D La.) Aug. 7, 1927; House Oct. 2, 1965- .

EDWARDS, Francis Smith (AP N.Y.) May 28, 1817-May 20, 1899; House 1855-Feb. 28, 1857.

EDWARDS, Henry Waggaman (D Conn.) Oct. 1779-July 22, 1847; House 1819-23; Senate Oct. 8, 1823-27; Gov. 1833, 1835-37.

EDWARDS, Jack (R Ala.) Sept. 20, 1928; House 1965- .

EDWARDS, John (— Ky.) 1748-1837; Senate June 18, 1792-95.

EDWARDS, John (D N.Y.) Aug. 6, 1781-Dec. 28, 1850; House 1837-39.

EDWARDS, John (granduncle of John Edwards Leonard) (W Pa.) 1786-June 26, 1843; House 1839-43.

EDWARDS, John (LR Ark.) Oct. 24, 1805-April 8, 1894; House 1871-Feb. 9, 1872.

EDWARDS, John Cummins (D Mo.) June 24, 1804-Oct. 14, 1888; House 1841-43; Gov. 1844-48.

EDWARDS, Ninian (son of Benjamin Edwards) (D Ill.) March 17, 1775-July 20, 1833; Senate Dec. 3, 1818-24; Terr. Gov. 1809-18; Gov. 1826-31.

EDWARDS, Samuel (F Pa.) March 12, 1785-Nov. 21, 1850; House 1819-27.

EDWARDS, Thomas McKey (R N.H.) Dec. 16, 1795-May 1, 1875; House 1859-63.

EDWARDS, Thomas Owen (W Ohio) March 29, 1810-Feb. 5, 1876; House 1847-49.

EDWARDS, Weldon Nathaniel (D N.C.) Jan. 25, 1788-Dec. 18, 1873; House Feb. 7, 1816-27.

EDWARDS, William Posey (R Ga.) Nov. 9, 1835-June 28, 1900; House July 25, 1868-69.

EFNER, Valentine (D N.Y.) May 5, 1776-Nov. 20, 1865; House 1835-37.

EGBERT, Albert Gallatin (D Pa.) April 13, 1828-March 28, 1896; House 1875-77.

EGBERT, Joseph (D N.Y.) April 10, 1807-July 7, 1888; House 1841-43.

EGE, George (— Pa.) March 9, 1748-Dec. 14, 1829; House Dec. 8, 1796-Oct. 1797.

EGGLESTON, Benjamin (R Ohio) Jan. 3, 1816-Feb. 8, 1888; House 1865-69.

EGGLESTON, Joseph (uncle of William Segar Archer) (D Va.) Nov. 24, 1754-Feb. 13, 1811; House Dec. 3, 1798-1801.

EICHER, Edward Clayton (D Iowa) Dec. 16, 1878-Nov. 29, 1944; House 1933-Dec. 2, 1938.

EICKHOFF, Anthony (D N.Y.) Sept. 11, 1827-Nov. 5, 1901; House 1877-79.

EILBERG, Joshua (D Pa.) Feb. 12, 1921; House 1967- .

EINSTEIN, Edwin (R N.Y.) Nov. 18, 1842-Jan. 24, 1905; House 1879-81.

EKWALL, William Alexander (R Ore.) June 14, 1887-Oct. 16, 1956; House 1935-37.

ELA, Jacob Hart (R N.H.) July 18, 1820-Aug. 21, 1884; House 1867-71.

ELAM, Joseph Barton (D La.) June 12, 1821-July 4, 1885; House 1877-81.

ELDER, James Walter (D La.) Oct. 5, 1882-Dec. 16, 1941; House 1913-15.

ELDREDGE, Charles Augustus (D Wis.) Feb. 27, 1820-Oct. 26, 1896; House 1863-75.

ELDREDGE, Nathaniel Buel (D Mich.) March 28, 1813-Nov. 27, 1893; House 1883-87.

ELIOT, Samuel Atkins (great-grandfather of Thomas Hopkinson Eliot) (W Mass.) March 5, 1798-Jan. 29, 1862; House Aug. 22, 1850-51.

ELIOT, Thomas Dawes (R Mass.) March 20, 1808-June 14, 1870; House April 17, 1854-1855 (W), 1859-69 (R).

ELIOT, Thomas Hopkinson (great-grandson of Samuel Atkins Eliot) (D Mass.) June 14, 1907; House 1941-43.

ELIZALDE, Joaquin Miguel (— P.I.) Aug. 2, 1896-Feb. 9, 1965; House (Res. Comm.) Sept. 29, 1938-Aug. 9, 1944.

ELKINS, Davis (son of Stephen Benton Elkins and grandson of Henry Gassaway Davis) (R W. Va.) Jan. 24, 1876-Jan. 5, 1959; Senate Jan. 9-Jan. 31, 1911, 1919-25.

ELKINS, Stephen Benton (father of Davis Elkins) (R N.M./ W. Va.) Sept. 26, 1841-Jan. 4, 1911; House (Terr. Del. N.M.) 1873-77; Senate (W. Va.) 1895-Jan. 4, 1911; Secy. of War 1891-93.

ELLENBOGEN, Henry (D Pa.) April 3, 1900; House 1933-Jan. 3, 1938.

ELLENDER, Allen Joseph (D La.) Sept. 24, 1891; Senate 1937- ; President pro tempore 1971- .

ELLERBE, James Edwin (D S.C.) Jan. 12, 1867-Oct. 24, 1917; House 1905-13.

ELLERY, Christopher (D R.I.) Nov. 1, 1768-Dec. 2, 1840; Senate May 6, 1801-05.

ELLETT, Henry Thomas (D Miss.) March 8, 1812-Oct. 15, 1887; House Jan. 26-March 3, 1847.

ELLETT, Tazewell (D Va.) Jan. 1, 1856-May 19, 1914; House 1895-97.

ELLICOTT, Benjamin (D N.Y.) April 17, 1765-Dec. 10, 1827; House 1817-19.

ELLIOTT, Alfred James (D Calif.) June 1, 1895- —; House May 4, 1937-49.

ELLIOTT, Carl Atwood (D Ala.) Dec. 20, 1913; House 1949-65.

ELLIOTT, Douglas Hemphill (R Pa.) June 3, 1921-June 19, 1960; House April 26-June 19, 1960.

ELLIOTT, James (F Vt.) Aug. 18, 1775-Nov. 10, 1839; House 1803-09.

ELLIOTT, James Thomas (R Ark.) April 22, 1823-July 28, 1875; House Jan. 13-March 3, 1869.

ELLIOTT, John (— Ga.) Oct. 24, 1773-Aug. 9, 1827; Senate 1819-25.

ELLIOTT, John Milton (D Ky.) May 20, 1820-March 26, 1879; House 1853-59.

ELLIOTT, Mortimer Fitzland (D Pa.) Sept. 24, 1839-Aug. 5, 1920; House 1883-85.

ELLIOTT, Richard Nash (R Ind.) April 25, 1873-March 21, 1948; House June 26, 1917-31.

ELLIOTT, Robert Brown (R S.C.) Aug. 11, 1842-Aug. 9, 1884; House 1871-Nov. 1, 1874.

ELLIOTT, William (D S.C.) Sept. 3, 1838-Dec. 7, 1907; House 1887-Sept. 23, 1890, 1891-93, 1895-June 4, 1896, 1897-1903.

ELLIS, Caleb (— N.H.) April 16, 1767-May 6, 1816; House 1805-07.

ELLIS, Chesselden (D N.Y.) 1808-May 10, 1854; House 1843-45.

ELLIS, Clyde Taylor (D Ark.) Dec. 21, 1908; House 1939-43.

ELLIS, Edgar Clarence (R Mo.) Oct. 2, 1854-March 15, 1947; House 1905-09, 1921-23, 1925-27, 1929-31.

ELLIS, Ezekiel John (D La.) Oct. 15, 1840-April 25, 1889; House 1875-85.

ELLIS, Hubert Summers (R W. Va.) July 6, 1887-Dec. 3, 1959; House 1943-49.

ELLIS, Powhatan (D Miss.) Jan. 17, 1790-March 18, 1863; Senate Sept. 28, 1825-Jan. 28, 1826; 1827-July 16, 1832.

ELLIS, William Cox (F Pa.) May 5, 1787-Dec. 13, 1871; House 1821, 1823-25.

ELLIS, William Russell (R Ore.) April 23, 1850-Jan. 18, 1915; House 1893-99, 1907-11.

ELLIS, William Thomas (D Ky.) July 24, 1845-Jan. 8, 1925; House 1889-95.

ELLISON, Andrew (D Ohio) 1812-about 1860; House 1853-55.

ELLISON, Daniel (R Md.) Feb. 14, 1886-Aug. 20, 1960; House 1943-45.

ELLMAKER, Amos (— Pa.) Feb. 2, 1787-Nov. 28, 1851; House March 3-July 3, 1815.

ELLSBERRY, William Wallace (D Ohio) Dec. 18, 1833-Sept. 7, 1894; House 1885-87.

ELLSWORTH, Charles Clinton (R Mich.) Jan. 29, 1824-June 25, 1899; House 1877-79.

ELLSWORTH, Franklin Fowler (R Minn.) July 10, 1879-Dec. 23, 1942; House 1915-21.

ELLSWORTH, Matthew Harris (R Ore.) Sept. 17, 1899- —; House 1943-57.

ELLSWORTH, Oliver (father of William Wolcott Ellsworth) (F Conn.) April 29, 1745-Nov. 26, 1807; Senate 1789-March 8, 1796; Cont. Cong. 1777-84; Chief Justice, U.S. Supreme Court 1796-99.

ELLSWORTH, Robert F. (R Kan.) June 11, 1926; House 1961-67.

ELLSWORTH, Samuel Stewart (D N.Y.) Oct. 13, 1790-June 4, 1863; House 1845-47.

ELLSWORTH, William Wolcott (son of Oliver Ellsworth) (W Conn.) Nov. 10, 1791-Jan. 15, 1868; House 1829-July 8, 1834; Gov. 1838-42.

ELLWOOD, Reuben (R Ill.) Feb. 21, 1821-July 1, 1885; House 1883-July 1, 1885.

ELLZEY, Lawrence Russell (D Miss.) March 20, 1891- —; House March 15, 1932-35.

ELMENDORF, Lucas Conrad (D N.Y.) 1758-Aug. 17, 1843; House 1797-1803.

ELMER, Ebenezer (brother of Jonathan Elmer and father of Lucius Quintius Cincinnatus Elmer) (D N.J.) Aug. 23, 1752-Oct. 18, 1843; House 1801-07.

ELMER, Jonathan (brother of Ebenezer Elmer and uncle of Lucius Quintius Cincinnatus Elmer) (F N.J.) Nov. 29, 1745-Sept. 3, 1817; Senate 1789-91; Cont. Cong. 1776-78, 1781-84, 1787-88.

ELMER, Lucius Quintius Cincinnatus (son of Ebenezer Elmer and nephew of Jonathan Elmer) (D N.J.) Feb. 3, 1793-March 11, 1883; House 1843-45.

ELMER, William Price (R Mo.) March 2, 1871-May 11, 1956; House 1943-45.

ELMORE, Franklin Harper (SRD S.C.) Oct. 15, 1799-May 28, 1850; House Dec. 10, 1836-39; Senate April 11-May 28, 1850.

ELSAESSER, Edward Julius (R N.Y.) March 10, 1904; House 1945-49.

ELSTON, Charles Henry (R Ohio) Aug. 1, 1891- —; House 1939-53.

ELSTON, John Arthur (PR Calif.) Feb. 10, 1874-Dec. 15, 1921; House 1915-Dec. 15, 1921.

ELTSE, Ralph Roscoe (R Calif.) Sept. 13, 1885- —; House 1933-35.

ELVINS, Politte (R Mo.) March 16, 1878-Jan. 14, 1943; House 1909-11.

ELY, Alfred (R N.Y.) Feb. 15, 1815-May 18, 1892; House 1859-63.

ELY, Frederick David (R Mass.) Sept. 24, 1838-Aug. 6, 1921; House 1885-87.

ELY, John (D N.Y.) Oct. 8, 1774-Aug. 20, 1849; House 1839-41.

ELY, Smith, Jr. (D N.Y.) April 17, 1825-July 1, 1911; House 1871-73, 1875-Dec. 11, 1876.

ELY, William (F Mass.) Aug. 14, 1765-Oct. 9, 1817; House 1805-15.

EMBREE, Elisha (W Ind.) Sept. 28, 1801-Feb. 28, 1863; House 1847-49.

EMERICH, Martin (D Ill.) April 27, 1846-Sept. 27, 1922; House 1903-05.

EMERSON, Henry Ivory (R Ohio) March 15, 1871-Oct. 28, 1953; House 1915-21.

EMERSON, Louis Woodard (R N.Y.) July 25, 1857-June 10, 1924; House 1899-1903.

EMOTT, James (F N.Y.) March 9, 1771-April 7, 1850; House 1809-13.

EMRIE, Jonas Reece (R Ohio) April 25, 1812-June 5, 1869; House 1855-57.

ENGEL, Albert Joseph (R Mich.) Jan. 1, 1888-Dec. 2, 1959; House 1935-51.

ENGLAND, Edward Theodore (R W. Va.) Sept. 29, 1869-Sept. 9, 1934; House 1927-29.

ENGLE, Clair (D Calif.) Sept. 21, 1911-July 30, 1964; House Aug. 31, 1943-59; Senate 1959-July 30, 1964.

ENGLEBRIGHT, Harry Lane (son of William F. Englebright) (R Calif.) Jan. 2, 1884-May 13, 1943; House Aug. 31, 1926-May 13, 1943.

ENGLEBRIGHT, William Fellows (father of Harry Lane Englebright) (R Calif.) Nov. 23, 1855-Feb. 10, 1915; House Nov. 6, 1906-11.

ENGLISH, James Edward (D Conn.) March 13, 1812-March 2, 1890; House 1861-65; Senate Nov. 27, 1875-May 17, 1876; Gov. 1867-68, 1870.

ENGLISH, Thomas Dunn (D N.J.) June 29, 1819-April 1, 1902; House 1891-95.

ENGLISH, Warren Barkley (D Calif.) May 1, 1840-Jan. 9, 1913; House April 1894-95.

ENGLISH, William Eastin (son of William Hayden English) (D Ind.) Nov. 3, 1850-April 29, 1926; House May 22, 1884-85.

ENGLISH, William Hayden (father of William Eastin English) (D Ind.) Aug. 27, 1822-Feb. 7, 1896; House 1853-61.

ENLOE, Benjamin Augustine (D Tenn.) Jan. 18, 1848-July 8, 1922; House 1887-95.

ENOCHS, William Henry (R Ohio) March 29, 1842-July 13, 1893; House 1891-July 13, 1893.

EPES, James Fletcher (cousin of Sydney Parham Epes) (D Va.) May 23, 1842-Aug. 24, 1910; House 1891-95.

EPES, Sydney Parham (cousin of James Fletcher Epes) (D Va.) Aug. 20, 1865-March 3, 1900; House 1897-March 23, 1898, 1899-March 3, 1900.

EPPES, John Wayles (D Va.) April 7, 1773-Sept. 13, 1823; House 1803-11, 1813-15; Senate 1817-Dec. 4, 1819.

ERDMAN, Constantine Jacob (grandson of Jacob Erdman) (D Pa.) Sept. 4, 1846-Jan. 15, 1911; House 1893-97.

ERDMAN, Jacob (grandfather of Constantine Jacob Erdman) (D Pa.) Feb. 22, 1801-July 20, 1867; House 1845-47.

ERICKSON, John Edward (D Mont.) March 14, 1863-May 25, 1946; Senate March 13, 1933-Nov. 6, 1934; Gov. 1925-33.

ERK, Edmund Frederick (R Pa.) April 17, 1872-Dec. 14, 1953; House Nov. 4, 1930-33.

ERLENBORN, John N. (R Ill.) Feb. 8, 1927; House 1965- .

ERMENTROUT, Daniel (D Pa.) Jan. 24, 1837-Sept. 17, 1899; House 1881-89, 1897-Sept. 17, 1899.

ERNST, Richard Pretlow (R Ky.) Feb. 28, 1858-April 13, 1934; Senate 1921-27.

ERRETT, Russell (R Pa.) Nov. 10, 1817-April 7, 1891; House 1877-83.

ERVIN, James (Protect. S.C.) Oct. 17, 1778-July 7, 1841; House 1817-21.

ERVIN, Joseph Wilson (brother of Samuel James Ervin, Jr.) (D N.C.) March 3, 1901-Dec. 25, 1945; House Jan. 3-Dec. 25, 1945.

ERVIN, Samuel James, Jr. (brother of Joseph Wilson Ervin (D N.C.) Sept. 27, 1896; House Jan. 22, 1946-47; Senate June 5, 1954- .

ESCH, John Jacob (R Wis.) March 20, 1861-April 27, 1941; House 1899-1921.

ESCH, Marvin L. (R Mich.) Aug. 4, 1927; House 1967- .

ESHLEMAN, Edwin D. (R Pa.) Dec. 4, 1920; House 1967- .

ESLICK, Edward Everett (husband of Willa McCord Eslick) (D Tenn.) April 19, 1872-June 14, 1932; House 1925-June 14, 1932.

ESLICK, Willa McCord Blake (wife of Edward Everett Eslick) (D Tenn.) Sept. 8, 1878-Feb. 18, 1961; House Aug. 4, 1932-33.

ESSEN, Frederick (R Mo.) April 22, 1863-Aug. 18, 1946; House Nov. 5, 1918-19.

ESTABROOK, Experience (— Neb.) April 30, 1813-March 26, 1894; House (Terr. Del.) 1859-May 18, 1860.

ESTEP, Harry Allison (R Pa.) Feb. 1, 1884-Feb. 28, 1968; House 1927-33.

ESTERLY, Charles Joseph (R Pa.) Feb. 8, 1888-Sept. 3, 1940; House 1925-27, 1929-31.

ESTIL, Benjamin (— Va.) March 13, 1780-July 14, 1853; House 1825-27.

ESTOPINAL, Albert (D La.) Jan. 30, 1845-April 28, 1919; House Nov. 3, 1908-April 28, 1919.

ESTY, Constantine Canaris (R Mass.) Dec. 26, 1824-Dec. 27, 1912; House Dec. 2, 1872-73.

ETHERIDGE, Emerson (W Tenn.) Sept. 28, 1819-Oct. 21, 1902; House 1853-57, 1859-61.

EUSTIS, George, Jr. (brother of James Biddle Eustis) (AP La.) Sept. 28, 1828-March 15, 1872; House 1855-59.

EUSTIS, James Biddle (brother of George Eustis, Jr.) (D La.) Aug. 27, 1834-Sept. 9, 1899; Senate Jan. 12, 1876-79, 1885-91.

EUSTIS, William (D Mass.) June 10, 1753-Feb. 6, 1825; House 1801-05, Aug. 21, 1820-23; Secy. of War 1809-13; Gov. 1823-25.

EVANS, Alexander (W Md.) Sept. 13, 1818-Dec. 5, 1888; House 1847-53.

EVANS, Alvin (R Pa.) Oct. 4, 1845-June 19, 1906; House 1901-05.

EVANS, Charles Robley (D Nev.) Aug. 9, 1866-Nov. 30, 1954; House 1919-21.

EVANS, David Ellicott (D N.Y.) March 19, 1788-May 17, 1850; House March 4-May 2, 1827.

EVANS, David Reid (D S.C.) Feb. 20, 1769-March 8, 1843; House 1813-15.

EVANS, Frank Edwards (D Colo.) Sept. 6, 1923; House 1965- .

EVANS, George (W Maine) Jan. 12, 1797-April 6, 1867; House July 20, 1829-41; Senate 1841-47.

EVANS, Henry Clay (R Tenn.) June 18, 1843-Dec. 12, 1921; House 1889-91.

EVANS, Hiram Kinsman (R Iowa) March 17, 1863-July 9, 1941; House June 4, 1923-25.

EVANS, Isaac Newton (R Pa.) July 29, 1827-Dec. 3, 1901; House 1877-79, 1883-87.

EVANS, James La Fayette (R Ind.) March 27, 1825-May 28, 1903; House 1875-79.

EVANS, John Morgan (D Mont.) Jan. 7, 1863-March 12, 1946; House 1913-21, 1923-33.

EVANS, Joshua, Jr. (D Pa.) Jan. 20, 1777-Oct. 2, 1846; House 1829-33.

EVANS, Josiah James (SRD S.C.) Nov. 27, 1786-May 6, 1858; Senate 1853-May 6, 1858.

EVANS, Lemuel Dale (AP Texas) Jan. 8, 1810-July 1, 1877; House 1855-57.

EVANS, Lynden (D Ill.) June 28, 1858-May 6, 1926; House 1911-13.

EVANS, Marcellus Hugh (D N.Y.) Sept. 22, 1884-Nov. 21, 1953; House 1935-41.

EVANS, Nathan (W Ohio) June 24, 1804-Sept. 27, 1879; House 1847-51.

EVANS, Robert Emory (R Neb.) July 15, 1856-July 8, 1925; House 1919-23.

EVANS, Thomas (— Va.) - — —; House 1797-1801.

EVANS, Walter (nephew of Burwell Clark Ritter) (R Ky.) Sept. 18, 1842-Dec. 30, 1923; House 1895-99.

EVANS, William Elmer (R Calif.) Dec. 14, 1877-Nov. 12, 1959; House 1927-35.

EVARTS, William Maxwell (grandson of Roger Sherman) (R N.Y.) Feb. 6, 1818-Feb. 28, 1901; Senate 1885-91; Atty. Gen. 1868-69; Secy. of State 1877-81.

EVERETT, Edward (father of William Everett) (NR Mass.) April 11, 1794-Jan. 15, 1865; House 1825-35; Senate 1853-June 1, 1954; Gov. 1836-40; Secy. of State 1852-53.

EVERETT, Horace (W Vt.) July 17, 1779-Jan. 30, 1851; House 1829-43.

EVERETT, Robert Ashton (D Tenn.) Feb. 24, 1915-Jan. 26, 1969; House Feb. 1, 1958-Jan. 26, 1969.

EVERETT, Robert William (D Ga.) March 3, 1839-Feb. 27, 1915; House 1891-93.

EVERETT, William (son of Edward Everett) (D Mass.) Oct. 10, 1839-Feb. 16, 1910; House April 25, 1893-95.

EVERHART, James Bowen (son of William Everhart) (R Pa.) July 26, 1821-Aug. 23, 1888; House 1883-87.

EVERHART, William (father of James Bowen Everhart) (W Pa.) May 17, 1785-Oct. 30, 1868; House 1853-55.

EVINS, John Hamilton (D S.C.) July 18, 1830-Oct. 20, 1884; House 1877-Oct. 20, 1884.

EVINS, Joseph Landon (Joe) (D Tenn.) Oct. 24, 1910; House 1947- .

EWART, Hamilton Glover (R N.C.) Oct. 23, 1849-April 28, 1918; House 1889-91.

EWING, Andrew (brother of Edwin Hickman Ewing) (D Tenn.) June 17, 1813-June 16, 1864; House 1849-51.

EWING, Edwin Hickman (brother of Andrew Ewing) (W Tenn.) Dec. 2, 1809-April 24, 1902; House 1845-47.

EWING, John (W Ind.) May 19, 1789-April 6, 1858; House 1833-35, 1837-39.

EWING, John Hoge (W Pa.) Oct. 5, 1796-June 9, 1887; House 1845-47.

EWING, Presley Underwood (W Ky.) Sept. 1, 1822-Sept. 27, 1854; House 1851-Sept. 27, 1854.

EWING, Thomas (W Ohio) Dec. 28, 1789-Oct. 26, 1871; Senate 1831-37; July 20, 1850-51; Secy. of the Treasury 1841; Secy. of the Interior 1849-50.

EWING, William Lee Davidson (JD Ill.) Aug. 31, 1795-March 25, 1846; Senate Dec. 30, 1835-37; Gov. Nov. 1834.

F

FADDIS, Charles I. (D Pa.) June 13, 1890-—; House 1933-Dec. 4, 1942.

FAIR, James Graham (D Nev.) Dec. 3, 1831-Dec. 28, 1894; Senate 1881-87.

FAIRBANKS, Charles Warren (R Ind.) May 11, 1852-June 4, 1918; Senate 1897-1905; Vice President 1905-09.

FAIRCHILD, Benjamin Lewis (R N.Y.) Jan. 5, 1863-Oct. 25, 1946; House 1895-97; 1917-19; 1921-23; Nov. 6, 1923-27.

FAIRCHILD, George Winthrop (R N.Y.) May 6, 1854-Dec. 31, 1924; House 1907-19.

FAIRFIELD, John (D Maine) Jan. 30, 1797-Dec. 24, 1847; House 1835-Dec. 24, 1838; Senate 1843-Dec. 24, 1847; Gov. 1839-43.

FAIRFIELD, Louis William (R Ind.) Oct. 15, 1858-Feb. 20, 1930; House 1917-25.

FAISON, John Miller (D N.C.) April 17, 1862-April 21, 1915; House 1911-15.

FALCONER, Jacob Alexander (Pro Wash.) Jan. 26, 1869-July 1, 1928; House 1913-15.

FALL, Albert Bacon (R N.M.) Nov. 26, 1861-Nov. 30, 1944; Senate March 27, 1912-March 4, 1921; Secy. of the Interior 1921-23.

FALLON, George Hyde (D Md.) July 24, 1902; House 1945-71.

FANNIN, Paul Jones (R Ariz.) Jan. 29, 1907; Senate 1965- —; Gov. 1958-64.

FARAN, James John (D Ohio) Dec. 29, 1808-Dec. 12, 1892; House 1945-49.

FARBSTEIN, Leonard (D N.Y.) Oct. 12, 1902; House 1957-71.

FARIS, George Washington (R Ind.) June 9, 1854-April 17, 1914; House 1895-1901.

FARLEE, Isaac Gray (— N.J.) May 18, 1787-Jan. 12, 1855; House 1843-45.

FARLEY, Ephraim Wilder (W Maine) Aug. 29, 1817-April 3, 1880; House 1853-55.

FARLEY, James Indus (D Ind.) Feb. 24, 1871-June 16, 1948; House 1933-39.

FARLEY, James Thompson (D Calif.) Aug. 6, 1829-Jan. 22, 1886; Senate 1879-85.

FARLEY, Michael Francis (D N.Y.) March 1, 1863-Oct. 8, 1921; House 1915-17.

FARLIN, Dudley (D N.Y.) Sept. 2, 1777-Sept. 26, 1837; House 1835-37.

FARNSLEY, Charles Rowland Peaslee (D Ky.) March 28, 1907; House 1965-67.

FARNSWORTH, John Franklin (R Ill.) March 27, 1820-July 14, 1897; House 1857-61, 1863-73.

FARNUM, Billie Sunday (D Mich.) April 11, 1916; House 1965-67.

FARQUHAR, John Hanson (R Ind.) Dec. 20, 1818-Oct. 1, 1873; House 1865-67.

FARQUHAR, John McCreath (R N.Y.) April 17, 1832-April 24, 1918; House 1885-91.

FARR, Evarts Worcester (R N.H.) Oct. 10, 1840-Nov. 30, 1880; House 1879-Nov. 30, 1880.

FARR, John Richard (R Pa.) July 18, 1857-Dec. 11, 1933; House 1911-19, Feb. 25-March 3, 1921.

FARRELLY, John Wilson (son of Patrick Farrelly) (W Pa.) July 7, 1809-Dec. 20, 1860; House 1847-49.

FARRELLY, Patrick (father of John Wilson Farrelly) (D Pa.) 1770-Jan. 12, 1826; House 1821-Jan. 12, 1826.

FARRINGTON, James (D N.H.) Oct. 1, 1791-Oct. 29, 1859; House 1837-39.

FARRINGTON, Joseph Rider (husband of Mary Elizabeth Pruett Farrington) (R Hawaii) Oct. 15, 1897-June 19, 1954; House (Terr. Del.) 1943-June 19, 1954.

FARRINGTON, Mary Elizabeth Pruett (widow of Joseph Rider Farrington) (R Hawaii) May 30, 1898- —; House (Terr. Del.) July 31, 1954-57.

FARROW, Samuel (WD S.C.) 1759-Nov. 18, 1824; House 1813-15.

FARWELL, Charles Benjamin (R Ill.) July 1, 1823-Sept. 23, 1903; House 1871-May 6, 1876, 1881-83; Senate Jan. 19, 1887-91.

FARWELL, Nathan Allen (cousin of Owen Lovejoy) (R Maine) Feb. 24, 1812-Dec. 9, 1893; Senate Oct. 27, 1864-65.

FARWELL, Sewall Spaulding (R Iowa) April 26, 1834-Sept. 21, 1909; House 1881-83.

FASCELL, Dante Bruno (D Fla.) March 9, 1917; House 1955- .

FASSETT, Jacob Sloat (R N.Y.) Nov. 13, 1853-April 21, 1924; House 1905-11.

FAULKNER, Charles James (D Va./ W. Va.) July 6, 1806-Nov. 1, 1884; House 1851-59) (Va.), 1875-77 (W. Va.).

FAULKNER, Charles James (son of the preceding) (D W. Va.) Sept. 21, 1847-Jan. 13, 1929; Senate 1887-99.

FAUST, Charles Lee (R Mo.) April 24, 1879-Dec. 17, 1928; House 1921-Dec. 17, 1928.

FAVROT, George Kent (D La.) Nov. 26, 1868-Dec. 26, 1934; House 1907-09, 1921-25.

FAY, Francis Ball (W Mass.) June 12, 1793-Oct. 6, 1876; House Dec. 13, 1852-53.

FAY, James Herbert (D N.Y.) April 29, 1899-Sept. 10, 1948; House 1939-41, 1943-45.

FAY, John (D N.Y.) Feb. 10, 1773-June 21, 1855; House 1819-21.

FEARING, Paul (F N.W. Terr.) Feb. 28, 1762-Aug. 21, 1822; House (Terr. Del.) 1801-03.

FEATHERSTON, Winfield Scott (D Miss.) Aug. 8, 1820-May 28, 1891; House 1847-51.

FEATHERSTONE, Lewis Porter (UL Ark.) July 28, 1851-March 14, 1922; House March 5, 1890-91.

FEAZEL, William Crosson (D La.) June 10, 1895-March 16, 1965; Senate May 18-Dec. 30, 1948.

FEELY, John Joseph (D Ill.) Aug. 1, 1875-Feb. 15, 1905; House 1901-03.

FEIGHAN, Michael Aloysius (D Ohio) Feb. 16, 1905; House 1943-71.

FELCH, Alpheus (D Mich.) Sept. 28, 1804-June 13, 1896; Senate 1847-53; Gov. 1846-47.

FELDER, John Myers (D S.C.) July 7, 1782-Sept. 1, 1851; House 1831-35.

FELLOWS, Frank (R Maine) Nov. 7, 1889-Aug. 27, 1951; House 1941-Aug. 27, 1951.

FELLOWS, John R. (D N.Y.) July 29, 1832-Dec. 7, 1896; House 1891-Dec. 31, 1893.

FELTON, Charles Norton (R Calif.) Jan. 1, 1828-Sept. 13, 1914; House 1885-89; Senate March 19, 1891-93.

FELTON, Rebecca Latimer (wife of William Harrell Felton) (D Ga.) June 10, 1835-Jan. 24, 1930; Senate Oct. 3-Nov. 22, 1922.

FELTON, William Harrell (husband of Rebecca Latimer Felton) (D Ga.) June 19, 1823-Sept. 24, 1909; House 1875-81.

FENERTY, Clare Gerald (R Pa.) July 25, 1895-July 1, 1952; House 1935-37.

FENN, Edward Hart (R Conn.) Sept. 12, 1856-Feb. 23, 1939; House 1921-31.

FENN, Stephen Southmyd (D Idaho) March 28, 1820-April 13, 1892; House (Terr. Del.) June 23, 1876-79.

FENNER, James (D R.I.) Jan. 22, 1771-April 17, 1846; Senate 1805-Sept. 1807; Gov. 1807-11, 1824-31, 1843-45.

FENTON, Ivor David (R Pa.) Aug. 3, 1889- —; House 1939-63.

FENTON, Lucien Jerome (R Ohio) May 7, 1844-June 28, 1922; House 1895-99.

FENTON, Reuben Eaton (R N.Y.) July 4, 1819-Aug. 25, 1885; House 1853-55, 1857-Dec. 20, 1864; Senate 1869-75; Gov. 1865-68.

FERDON, John William (R N.Y.) Dec. 13, 1826-Aug. 5, 1884; House 1879-81.

FERGUSON, Fenner (D Neb.) April 25, 1814-Oct. 11, 1859; House (Terr. Del.) 1857-59.

FERGUSON, Homer (R Mich.) Feb. 25, 1889- —; Senate 1943-55.

FERGUSON, Phillip Colgan (D Okla.) Aug. 15, 1903; House 1935-41.

FERGUSSON, Harvey Butler (D N.M.) Sept. 9, 1848-June 10, 1915; House (Terr. Del.) 1897-99; (Rep.) Jan. 8, 1912-15.

FERNALD, Bert Manfred (R Maine) April 3, 1858-Aug. 23, 1926; Senate Sept. 12, 1916-Aug. 23, 1926; Gov. 1909-11.

FERNANDEZ, Antonio Manuel (D N.M.) Jan. 17, 1902-Nov. 7, 1956; House 1943-Nov. 7, 1956.

FERNANDEZ, Joachim Octave (D La.) Aug. 14, 1896- —; House 1931-41.

FERNOS-ISERN, Antonio (PD P.R.) May 10, 1895- —; House (Res. Comm.) Sept. 11, 1946-65.

FERRELL, Thomas Merrill (D N.J.) June 20, 1844-Oct. 20, 1916; House 1883-85.

FERRIS, Charles Goadsby (JD N.Y.) about 1796-June 4, 1848; House Dec. 1, 1834-35, 1841-43.

FERRIS, Scott (D Okla.) Nov. 3, 1877-June 8, 1945; House Nov. 16, 1907-21.

FERRIS, Woodbridge Nathan (D Mich.) Jan. 6, 1853-March 23, 1928; Senate 1923-March 23, 1928; Gov. 1913-16.

FERRISS, Orange (R N.Y.) Nov. 26, 1814-April 11, 1894; House 1867-71.

FERRY, Orris Sanford (IR/D Conn.) Aug. 15, 1823-Nov. 21, 1875; House 1859-61 (R); Senate 1867-74 (R), 1874-Nov. 21, 1875 (IR/D).

FERRY, Thomas White (R Mich.) June 10, 1827-Oct. 13, 1896; House 1865-71; Senate 1871-83; President pro tempore 1875-79.

FESS, Simeon Davison (R Ohio) Dec. 11, 1861-Dec. 23, 1936; House 1913-23; Senate 1923-35; Chrmn. Rep. Nat. Comm. 1930-32.

FESSENDEN, Samuel Clement (brother of Thomas Amory Deblois Fessenden and William Pitt Fessenden) (R Maine) March 7, 1815-April 18, 1882; House 1861-63.

FESSENDEN, Thomas Amory Deblois (brother of Samuel Clement Fessenden and William Pitt Fessenden) (R Maine) Jan. 23, 1826-Sept. 28, 1868; House Dec. 1, 1862-63.

FESSENDEN, William Pitt (brother of Samuel Clement Fessenden and Thomas Amory Deblois Fessenden) (W Maine) Oct. 16, 1806-Sept. 9, 1869; House 1841-43; Senate Feb. 10, 1854-July 1, 1864, 1865-Sept. 9, 1869; Secy. of the Treasury 1864-65.

FEW, William (D Ga.) June 8, 1748–July 16, 1828; Senate 1789-93; Cont. Cong. 1780-88.

FICKLIN, Orlando Bell (D Ill.) Dec. 16, 1808-May 5, 1886; House 1843-49, 1851-53.

FIEDLER, William Henry Frederick (D N.J.) Aug. 25, 1847–Jan. 1, 1919; House 1883-85.

FIELD, David Dudley (D N.Y.) Feb. 13, 1805-April 13, 1894; House Jan. 11-March 3, 1877.

FIELD, Moses Whelock (R Mich.) Feb. 10, 1828-March 14, 1889; House 1873-75.

FIELD, Richard Stockton (R N.J.) Dec. 31, 1803-May 25, 1870; Senate Nov. 21, 1862-Jan. 14, 1863.

FIELD, Scott (D Texas) Jan. 26, 1847-Dec. 20, 1931; House 1903-07.

FIELD, Walbridge Abner (R Mass.) April 26, 1833–July 15, 1899; House 1877-March 28, 1878, 1879-81.

FIELDER, George Bragg (D N.J.) July 24, 1842-Aug. 14, 1906; House 1893-95.

FIELDS, William Craig (R N.Y.) Feb. 13, 1804-Oct. 27, 1882; House 1867-69.

FIELDS, William Jason (D Ky.) Dec. 29, 1874-Oct. 21, 1954; House 1911-Dec. 11, 1923; Gov. 1923-27.

FIESINGER, William Louis (D Ohio) Oct. 25, 1877-Sept. 11, 1953; House 1931-37.

FILLMORE, Millard (W N.Y.) Jan. 7, 1800-March 8, 1874; House 1833-35, 1837-43; Vice President 1849–July 9, 1850; President July 9, 1850-53.

FINCH, Isaac (D N.Y.) Oct. 13, 1783–June 23, 1845; House 1829-31.

FINCK, William Edward (D Ohio) Sept. 1, 1822–Jan. 25, 1901; House 1863-67, Dec. 7, 1874-75.

FINDLAY, James (brother of John Findlay and William Findlay) (JD Ohio) Oct. 12, 1770-Dec. 28, 1835; House 1825-33.

FINDLAY, John (brother of James Findlay and William Findlay) (D Pa.) March 31, 1766-Nov. 5, 1838; House Oct. 9, 1821-27.

FINDLAY, John Van Lear (D Md.) Dec. 21, 1839-April 19, 1907; House 1883-87.

FINDLAY, William (brother of James Findlay and John Findlay) (D Pa.) June 20, 1768-Nov. 12, 1846; Senate Dec. 10, 1821-27; Gov. 1817-20.

FINDLEY, Paul (R Ill.) June 23, 1921; House 1961- .

FINDLEY, William (D Pa.) 1741 or 1742 April 4, 1821; House 1791-99, 1803-17.

FINE, John (D N.Y.) Aug. 26, 1794–Jan. 4, 1867; House 1839-41.

FINE, Sidney Asher (D N.Y.) Sept. 14, 1903; House 1951–Jan. 2, 1956.

FINERTY, John Frederick (ID Ill.) Sept. 10, 1846–June 10, 1908; House 1883-85.

FINKELNBURG, Gustavus Adolphus (LR Mo.) April 6, 1837-May 18, 1908; House 1869-71 (R), 1871-73 (LR).

FINLEY, Charles (son of Hugh Franklin Finley) (R Ky.) March 26, 1865-March 18, 1941; House Feb. 15, 1930-33.

FINLEY, David Edward (D S.C.) Feb. 28, 1861–Jan. 26, 1917; House 1899–Jan. 26, 1917.

FINLEY, Ebenezer Byron (nephew of Stephen Ross Harris) (D Ohio) July 31, 1833-Aug. 22, 1916; House 1877-81.

FINLEY, Hugh Franklin (father of Charles Finley) (R Ky.) Jan. 18, 1833-Oct. 16, 1909; House 1887-91.

FINLEY, Jesse Johnson (D Fla.) Nov. 18, 1812-Nov. 6, 1904; House April 19, 1876-77, Feb. 20-March 3, 1879, 1881-June 1, 1882.

FINNEGAN, Edward R. (D Ill.) June 5, 1905-Feb. 2, 1971; House 1961-Dec. 6, 1964.

FINNEY, Darwin Abel (R Pa.) Aug. 11, 1814-Aug. 25, 1868; House 1867-Aug. 25, 1868.

FINO, Paul Albert (R N.Y.) Dec. 15, 1913; House 1953-Dec. 31, 1968.

FISCHER, Israel Frederick (R N.Y.) Aug. 17, 1858-March 16, 1940; House 1895-99.

FISH, Hamilton (great-grandfather of Hamilton Fish, Jr.) (W N.Y.) Aug. 3, 1808-Sept. 7, 1893; House 1843-45; Senate 1851-57; Gov. 1849-50; Secy. of State 1869-77.

FISH, Hamilton (son of the preceding and grandfather of Hamilton Fish, Jr.) (R N.Y.) April 17, 1849-Jan. 15, 1936; House 1909-11.

FISH, Hamilton (son of the preceding, grandson of Hamilton Fish and father of Hamilton Fish, Jr.) (R N.Y.) Dec. 7, 1888- —; House Nov. 2, 1920-45.

FISH, Hamilton, Jr. (son of the preceding) (R N.Y.) June 3, 1926; House 1969- .

FISHBURNE, John Wood (cousin of Fontaine Maury Maverick) (D Va.) March 8, 1868–June 24, 1937; House 1931-33.

FISHER, Charles (D N.C.) Oct. 20, 1789-May 7, 1849; House Feb. 11, 1819-21, 1839-41.

FISHER, David (W Ohio) Dec. 3, 1794-May 7, 1886; House 1847-49.

FISHER, George (— N.Y.) March 17, 1788-March 26, 1861; House 1829-Feb. 5, 1830.

FISHER, George Purnell (UR Del.) Oct. 13, 1817-Feb. 10, 1899; House 1861-63.

FISHER, Horatio Gates (R Pa.) April 21, 1838-May 8, 1890; House 1879-83.

FISHER, Hubert Frederick (D Tenn.) Oct. 6, 1877–June 16, 1941; House 1917-31.

FISHER, John (R N.Y.) March 13, 1806-March 28, 1882; House 1869-71.

FISHER, Ovie Clark (D Texas) Nov. 22, 1903; House 1943- .

FISHER, Spencer Oliver (D Mich.) Feb. 3, 1843–June 1, 1919; House 1885-89.

FISK, James (D Vt.) Oct. 4, 1763-Nov. 17, 1844; House 1805-09, 1811-15; Senate Nov. 4, 1817–Jan. 8, 1818.

FISK, Jonathan (D N.Y.) Sept. 26, 1778-July 13, 1832; House 1809-11, 1813-March 1815.

FITCH, Asa (F N.Y.) Nov. 10, 1765-Aug. 24, 1843; House 1811-13.

FITCH, Ashbel Parmelee (D N.Y.) Oct. 8, 1838-May 4, 1904; House 1887-89 (R), 1889-Dec. 26, 1893 (D).

FITCH, Graham Newell (grandfather of Edwin Denby) (D Ind.) Dec. 5, 1809-Nov. 29, 1892; House 1849-53; Senate Feb. 4, 1857-61.

FITCH, Thomas (R Nev.) Jan. 27, 1838-Nov. 12, 1923; House 1869-71.

FITE, Samuel McClary (D Tenn.) June 12, 1816-Oct. 23, 1875; House March 4-Oct. 23, 1875.

FITHIAN, George Washington (D Ill.) July 4, 1854–Jan. 21, 1921; House 1889-95.

FITZGERALD, Frank Thomas (D N.Y.) May 4, 1857-Nov. 25, 1907; House March 4-Nov. 4, 1889.

FITZGERALD, John Francis (grandfather of John F. Kennedy, Robert F. Kennedy and Edward Kennedy) (D Mass.) Feb. 11, 1863-Oct. 2, 1950; House 1895-1901; March 4-Oct. 23, 1919.

FITZGERALD, John Joseph (D N.Y.) March 10, 1872-May 13, 1952; House 1899-Dec. 31, 1917.

FITZGERALD, Roy Gerald (R Ohio) Aug. 25, 1875-Nov. 16, 1962; House 1921-31.

FITZGERALD, Thomas (D Mich.) April 10, 1796-March 25, 1855; Senate June 8, 1848-49.

FITZGERALD, William (JD Tenn.) Aug. 6, 1799-March 1864; House 1831-33.

FITZGERALD, William Joseph (D Conn.) March 2, 1887-May 6, 1947; House 1937-39, 1941-43.

FITZGERALD, William Thomas (R Ohio) Oct. 13, 1858-Jan. 12, 1939; House 1925-29.

FITZGIBBONS, John (D N.Y.) July 10, 1868-Aug. 4, 1941; House 1933-35.

FITZHENRY, Louis (D Ill.) June 13, 1870-Nov. 18, 1935; House 1913-15.

FITZPATRICK, Benjamin (SRD Ala.) June 30, 1802-Nov. 25, 1869; Senate Nov. 25, 1848-Nov. 30, 1849, Jan. 14, 1853-55, Nov. 26, 1855-Jan. 21, 1861; President pro tempore 1857-61; Gov. 1841-45.

FITZPATRICK, James Martin (D N.Y.) June 27, 1869-April 10, 1949; House 1927-45.

FITZPATRICK, Morgan Cassius (D Tenn.) Oct. 29, 1868-June 25, 1908; House 1903-05.

FITZPATRICK, Thomas Young (D Ky.) Sept. 20, 1850-Jan. 21, 1906; House 1897-1901.

FITZSIMONS, Thomas (F Pa.) 1741-Aug. 26, 1811; House 1789-95; Cont. Cong. 1782-83.

FJARE, Orvin Benonie (R Mont.) April 16, 1918; House 1955-57.

FLACK, William Henry (R N.Y.) March 22, 1861-Feb. 2, 1907; House 1903-Feb. 2, 1907.

FLAGLER, Thomas Thorn (W N.Y.) Oct. 12, 1811-Sept. 6, 1897; House 1853-57.

FLAHERTY, Lawrence James (R Calif.) July 4, 1878-June 13, 1926; House 1925-June 13, 1926.

FLAHERTY, Thomas Aloysius (D Mass.) Dec. 21, 1898-April 28, 1965; House Dec. 14, 1937-43.

FLANAGAN, De Witt Clinton (D N.J.) Dec. 28, 1870-Jan. 15, 1946; House June 18, 1902-03.

FLANAGAN, James Winright (R Texas) Sept. 5, 1805-Sept. 28, 1887; Senate March 30, 1870-75.

FLANDERS, Alvan (R Wash.) Aug. 2, 1825-March 14, 1884; House (Terr. Del.) 1867-69; Gov. of Terr. 1869-70.

FLANDERS, Benjamin Franklin (U La.) Jan. 26, 1816-March 13, 1896; House Dec. 3, 1862-63; Military Gov. 1867-68.

FLANDERS, Ralph Edward (R Vt.) Sept. 28, 1880-Feb. 19, 1970; Senate Nov. 1, 1946-59.

FLANNAGAN, John William, Jr. (D Va.) Feb. 20, 1885-April 27, 1955; House 1931-49.

FLANNERY, John Harold (D Pa.) April 19, 1898-June 3, 1961; House 1937-42.

FLEEGER, George Washington (R Pa.) March 13, 1839-June 25, 1894; House 1885-87.

FLEETWOOD, Frederick Gleed (R Vt.) Sept. 27, 1868-Jan. 28, 1938; House 1923-25.

FLEGER, Anthony Alfred (D Ohio) Oct. 21, 1900-July 16, 1963; House 1937-39.

FLEMING, William Bennett (D Ga.) Oct. 29, 1803-Aug. 19, 1886; House Feb. 10-March 3, 1879.

FLEMING, William Henry (D Ga.) Oct. 18, 1856-June 9, 1944; House 1897-1903.

FLETCHER, Charles Kimball (R Calif.) Dec. 15, 1902; House 1947-49.

FLETCHER, Duncan Upshaw (D Fla.) Jan. 6, 1859-June 17, 1936; Senate 1909-June 17, 1936.

FLETCHER, Isaac (A-Mas. D Vt.) Nov. 22, 1784-Oct. 19, 1842; House 1837-41.

FLETCHER, Loren (R Minn.) April 10, 1833-April 15, 1919; House 1893-1903, 1905-07.

FLETCHER, Richard (W Mass.) Jan. 8, 1788-June 21, 1869; House 1837-39.

FLETCHER, Thomas (— Ky.) Oct. 21, 1779- —; House Dec. 2, 1816-17.

FLETCHER, Thomas Brooks (D Ohio) Oct. 10, 1879-July 1, 1945; House 1925-29, 1933-39.

FLICK, James Patton (R Iowa) Aug. 28, 1845-Feb. 25, 1929; House 1889-93.

FLINT, Frank Putnam (R Calif.) July 15, 1862-Feb. 11, 1929; Senate 1905-11.

FLOOD, Daniel John (D Pa.) Nov. 26, 1903; House 1945-47, 1949-53, 1955- .

FLOOD, Henry De La Warr (brother of Joel West Flood and uncle of Harry Flood Byrd (D Va.) Sept. 2, 1865-Dec. 8, 1921; House 1901-Dec. 8, 1921.

FLOOD, Joel West (brother of Henry De La Warr Flood and uncle of Harry Flood Byrd) (D Va.) Aug. 2, 1894-April 27, 1964; House Nov. 8, 1932-33.

FLOOD, Thomas Schmeck (R N.Y.) April 12, 1844-Oct. 28, 1908; House 1887-91.

FLORENCE, Elias (W Ohio) Feb. 15, 1797-Nov. 21, 1880; House 1843-45.

FLORENCE, Thomas Birch (D Pa.) Jan. 26, 1812-July 3, 1875; House 1851-61.

FLOURNOY, Thomas Stanhope (W Va.) Dec. 15, 1811-March 12, 1883; House 1847-49.

FLOWER, Roswell Pettibone (D N.Y.) Aug. 7, 1835-May 12, 1899; House Nov. 8, 1881-83, 1889-Sept. 16, 1891; Gov. 1891-95.

FLOWERS, Walter (D Ala.) April 12, 1933; House 1969- .

FLOYD, Charles Albert (D N.Y.) 1791-Feb. 20, 1873; House 1841-43.

FLOYD, John (— Ga.) Oct. 3, 1769-June 24, 1839; House 1827-29.

FLOYD, John (D Va.) April 24, 1783-Aug. 17, 1837; House 1817-29; Gov. 1830-34.

FLOYD, John Charles (D Ark.) April 14, 1858-Nov. 4, 1930; House 1905-15.

FLOYD, John Gelston (D N.Y.) Feb. 5, 1806-Oct. 5, 1881; House 1839-43, 1851-53.

FLOYD, William (— N.Y.) Dec. 17, 1734-Aug. 4, 1821; House 1789-91; Cont. Cong. 1774-77, 1778-83.

FLYE, Edwin (R Maine) March 4, 1817-July 12, 1886; Dec. 4, 1876-77.

FLYNN, Dennis Thomas (R Okla.) Feb. 13, 1861-June 19, 1939; House 1893-97, 1899-1903.

FLYNN, Gerald Thomas (D Wis.) Oct. 7, 1910; House 1959-61.

FLYNN, Joseph Vincent (D N.Y.) Sept. 2, 1883-Feb. 6, 1940; House 1915-19.

FLYNT, John James, Jr. (D Ga.) Nov. 8, 1914; House Nov. 2, 1954- .

FOCHT, Benjamin Kurtz (R Pa.) March 12, 1863-March 27, 1937; House 1907-13, 1915-23, 1933-March 27, 1937.

FOELKER, Otto Godfrey (R N.Y.) Dec. 29, 1875-Jan. 18, 1943; House Nov. 3, 1908-11.

FOERDERER, Robert Hermann (R Pa.) May 16, 1860-July 26, 1903; House 1901-July 26, 1903.

FOGARTY, John Edward (D R.I.) March 23, 1913-Jan. 10, 1967; House 1941-Dec. 7, 1944; 1945-Jan. 10, 1967.

FOGG, George Gilman (R N.H.) May 26, 1813-Oct. 5, 1881; Senate Aug. 31, 1866-67.

FOLEY, James Bradford (D Ind.) Oct. 18, 1807-Dec. 5, 1886; House 1857-59.

FOLEY, John Robert (D Md.) Oct. 16, 1917; House 1959-61.

FOLEY, Thomas Stephen (D Wash.) March 6, 1929; House 1965- .

FOLGER, Alonzo Dillard (brother of John Hamlin Folger) (D N.C.) July 9, 1888-April 30, 1941; House 1939-April 30, 1941.

FOLGER, John Hamlin (brother of Alonzo D. Folger) (D N.C.) Dec. 18, 1880-July 19, 1963; House June 14, 1941-49.

FOLGER, Walter, Jr. (D Mass.) June 12, 1765-Sept. 8, 1849; House 1817-21.

FOLLETT, John Fassett (D Ohio) Feb. 18, 1831-April 15, 1902; House 1883-85.

FONG, Hiram Leong (R Hawaii) Oct. 1, 1907; Senate Aug. 21, 1959- .

FOOT, Solomon (R Vt.) Nov. 19, 1802-March 28, 1866; House 1943-47 (W); Senate 1851-57 (W), 1857-March 28, 1866 (R); President pro tempore 1860-64.

FOOTE, Charles Augustus (D N.Y.) April 15, 1785-Aug. 1, 1828; House 1823-25.

FOOTE, Ellsworth Bishop (R Conn.) Jan. 12, 1898; House 1947-49.

FOOTE, Henry Stuart (U Miss.) Feb. 28, 1804-May 19, 1880; Senate 1847-Jan. 8, 1852; Gov. 1852-54.

FOOTE, Samuel Augustus (W Conn.) Nov. 8, 1780-Sept. 15, 1846; House 1819-21, 1823-25, 1833-May 9, 1834; Senate 1827-33; Gov. 1834-35.

FOOTE, Wallace Turner, Jr. (R N.Y.) April 7, 1864-Dec. 17, 1910; House 1895-99.

FORAKER, Joseph Benson (R Ohio) July 5, 1846-May 10, 1917; Senate 1897-1909; Gov. 1885-89.

FORAN, Martin Ambrose (D Ohio) Nov. 11, 1844-June 28, 1921; House 1883-89.

FORAND, Aime Joseph (D R.I.) May 23, 1895; House 1937-39, 1941-61.

FORD, Aaron Lane (D Miss.) Dec. 21, 1903; House 1935-43.

FORD, George (D Ind.) Jan. 11, 1846-Aug. 30, 1917; House 1885-87.

FORD, Gerald R., Jr. (R Mich.) July 14, 1913; House 1949- .

FORD, James (JD Pa.) May 4, 1783-Aug. 18, 1859; House 1829-33.

FORD, Leland Merritt (R Calif.) March 8, 1893-November 27, 1965; House 1939-43.

FORD, Melbourne Haddock (D Mich.) June 30, 1849-April 20, 1891; House 1887-89; March 4-April 20, 1891.

FORD, Nicholas (LR Mo.) June 21, 1833-June 18, 1897; House 1879-83.

FORD, Thomas Francis (D Calif.) Feb. 18, 1873-Dec. 26, 1958; House 1933-45.

FORD, William D. (D N.Y.) 1779-Oct. 1, 1833; House 1819-21.

FORD, William D. (D Mich.) Aug. 6, 1927; House 1965- .

FORDNEY, Joseph Warren (R Mich.) Nov. 5, 1853-Jan. 8, 1932; House 1899-23.

FOREMAN, Ed (R Texas/N.M.) Dec. 22, 1933; House 1963-65 (Texas), 1969-71 (N.M.).

FORESTER, John B. (— Tenn.) — -Aug. 31, 1845; House 1833-37.

FORKER, Samuel Carr (D N.J.) March 16, 1821-Feb. 10, 1900; House 1871-73.

FORMAN, William St. John (D Ill.) Jan. 20, 1847-June 10, 1908; House 1889-95.

FORNANCE, Joseph (D Pa.) Oct. 18, 1804-Nov. 24, 1852; House 1839-43.

FORNES, Charles Vincent (D N.Y.) Jan. 22, 1844-May 22, 1929; House 1907-13.

FORNEY, Daniel Munroe (son of Peter Forney) (— N.C.) May 1784-Oct. 15, 1847; House 1815-18.

FORNEY, Peter (father of Daniel Munroe Forney) (D N.C.) April 21, 1756-Feb. 1, 1834; House 1813-15.

FORNEY, William Henry (grandson of Peter Forney) (D Ala.) Nov. 9, 1823-Jan. 16, 1894; House 1875-93.

FORREST, Thomas (— Pa.) 1747-March 20, 1825; House 1819-21, Oct. 8, 1822-23.

FORREST, Uriah (F Md.) 1756-July 6, 1805; House 1793-Nov. 8, 1794; Cont. Cong. 1786-87.

FORRESTER, Elijah Lewis (D Ga.) Aug. 16, 1896-March 19, 1970; House 1951-65.

FORSYTH, John (D Ga.) Oct. 22, 1780-Oct. 21, 1841; House 1813-Nov. 23, 1818, 1823-Nov. 7, 1827; Senate Nov. 23, 1818-Feb. 17, 1819, Nov. 9, 1829-June 27, 1834; Gov. 1827-29; Secy. of State 1834-41.

FORSYTHE, Edwin B. (R N.J.) Jan. 17, 1916; House Nov. 3, 1970- .

FORSYTHE, Albert Palaska (R Ill.) May 24, 1830-Sept. 2, 1906; House 1879-81.

FORT, Franklin William (R N.J.) March 30, 1880-June 20, 1937; House 1925-31.

FORT, Greenbury Lafayette (R Ill.) Oct. 17, 1825-Jan. 13, 1883; House 1873-81.

FORT, Tomlinson (D Ga.) July 14, 1787-May 11, 1859; House 1827-29.

FORWARD, Chauncey (brother of Walter Forward) (D Pa.) Feb. 4, 1793-Oct. 19, 1839; House Dec. 4, 1826-31.

FORWARD, Walter (brother of Chauncey Forward) (D Pa.) Jan. 24, 1783-Nov. 24, 1852; House Oct. 8, 1822-25; Secy. of the Treasury 1841-43.

FOSDICK, Nicoll (W N.Y.) Nov. 9, 1785-May 7, 1868; House 1825-27.

FOSS, Eugene Noble (brother of George Edmund Foss) (D Mass.) Sept. 14, 1858-Sept. 13, 1939; House March 22, 1910-Jan. 4, 1911; Gov. 1911-13.

FOSS, Frank Herbert (R Mass.) Sept. 20, 1865-Feb. 15, 1947; House 1925-35.

FOSS, George Edmund (brother of Eugene Noble Foss) (R Ill.) July 2, 1863-March 15, 1936; House 1895-1913, 1915-19.

FOSTER, A. Lawrence (W N.Y.) — - —; House 1841-43.

FOSTER, Abiel (— N.H.) Aug. 8, 1735-Feb. 6, 1806; House 1789-91, 1795-1803; Cont. Cong. 1783-85.

FOSTER, Addison Gardner (R Wash.) Jan. 28, 1837-Jan. 16, 1917; Senate 1899-1905.

FOSTER, Charles (R Ohio) April 12, 1828-Jan. 9, 1904; House 1871-79; Gov. 1880-84; Secy. of the Treasury 1891-93.

FOSTER, David Johnson (R Vt.) June 27, 1857-March 21, 1912; House 1901-March 21, 1912.

FOSTER, Dwight (brother of Theodore Foster) (F Mass.) Dec. 7, 1757-April 29, 1823; House 1793-June 6, 1800; Senate June 6, 1800-March 2, 1803.

FOSTER, Ephraim Hubbard (W Tenn.) Sept. 17, 1794-Sept. 14, 1854; Senate Sept. 17, 1838-1839; Oct. 17, 1843-45.

FOSTER, George Peter (D Ill.) April 3, 1858-Nov. 11, 1928; House 1899-1905.

FOSTER, Henry Allen (D N.Y.) May 7, 1800-May 11, 1889; House 1837-39; Senate Nov. 30, 1844 Jan. 27, 1845.

FOSTER, Henry Donnel (cousin of John Cabell Breckinridge) (D Pa.) Dec. 19, 1808-Oct. 16, 1880; House 1843-47, 1871-73.

FOSTER, Israel Moore (R Ohio) Jan. 12, 1873-June 10, 1950; House 1919-25.

FOSTER, John Hopkins (R Ind.) Jan. 31, 1862-Sept. 5, 1917; House May 16, 1905-09.

FOSTER, Lafayette Sabine (R Conn.) Nov. 22, 1806-Sept. 19, 1880; Senate 1855-67; President pro tempore 1865-67.

FOSTER, Martin David (D Ill.) Sept. 3, 1861-Oct. 20, 1919; House 1907-19.

FOSTER, Murphy James (D La.) Jan. 12, 1849-June 12, 1921; Senate 1901-13; Gov. 1892-1900.

FOSTER, Nathaniel Greene (D Ga.) Aug. 25, 1809-Oct. 19, 1869; House 1855-57 (elected as AP candidate).

FOSTER, Stephen Clark (R Maine) Dec. 24, 1799-Oct. 5, 1872; House 1857-61.

FOSTER, Theodore (brother of Dwight Foster) (L&O R.I.) April 29, 1752-Jan. 13, 1828; Senate June 7, 1790-1803.

FOSTER, Thomas Flournoy (D Ga.) Nov. 23, 1790-Sept. 14, 1848; House 1829-35, 1841-43.

FOSTER, Wilder De Ayr (R Mich.) Jan. 8, 1819-Sept. 20, 1873; House Dec. 4, 1871-Sept. 20, 1873.

FOUKE, Philip Bond (D Ill.) Jan. 23, 1818-Oct. 3, 1876; House 1859-63.

FOULKES, George Ernest (D Mich.) Dec. 25, 1878-Dec. 13, 1960; House 1933-35.

FOULKROD, William Walker (R Pa.) Nov. 22, 1846-Nov. 13, 1910; House 1907-Nov. 13, 1910.

FOUNTAIN, Lawrence H. (D NC.) April 23, 1913; House 1953- .

FOWLER, Charles Newell (R N.J.) Nov. 2, 1852-May 27, 1932; House 1895-1911.

FOWLER, Hiram Robert (D Ill.) Feb. 7, 1851-Jan. 5, 1926; House 1911-15.

FOWLER, John (— Ky.) 1755-Aug. 22, 1840; House 1797-1807.

FOWLER, John Edgar (P N.C.) Sept. 8, 1866-July 4, 1930; House 1897-99.

FOWLER, Joseph Smith (UR Tenn.) Aug. 31, 1820-April 1, 1902; Senate July 24, 1866-71.

FOWLER, Orin (F-SW Mass.) July 19, 1791-Sept. 3, 1852; House 1849-Sept. 3, 1852.

FOWLER, Samuel (JD N.J.) Oct. 30, 1779-Feb. 20, 1844; House 1833-37.

FOWLER, Samuel (grandson of the preceding) (D N.J.) March 22, 1851-March 17, 1919; House 1889-93.

FOX, Andrew Fuller (D Miss.) April 26, 1849-Aug. 29, 1926; House 1897-1903.

FOX, John (D N.Y.) June 30, 1835-Jan. 17, 1914; House 1867-71.

FRANCE, Joseph Irvin (R Md.) Oct. 11, 1873-Jan. 26, 1939; Senate 1917-23.

FRANCHOT, Richard (R N.Y.) June 2, 1816-Nov. 23, 1875; House 1861-63.

FRANCIS, George Blinn (R N.Y.) Aug. 12, 1883-May 20, 1967; House 1917-19.

FRANCIS, John Brown (grandson of John Brown of Rhode Island) (L&O R.I.) May 31, 1791-Aug. 9, 1864; Senate Jan. 25, 1844-45; Gov. 1833-38.

FRANCIS, William Bates (D Ohio) Oct. 25, 1860-Dec. 5, 1954; House 1911-15.

FRANK, Augustus (nephew of William Patterson of N.Y.) (R N.Y.) July 17, 1826-April 29, 1895; House 1859-65.

FRANK, Nathan (R/UL Mo.) Feb. 23, 1852-April 5, 1931; House 1889-91.

FRANKHAUSER, William Horace (R. Mich.) March 5, 1863-May 9, 1921; House March 4-May 9, 1921.

FRANKLIN, Benjamin Joseph (D Mo.) March 1839-May 18, 1898; House 1875-79; Gov. of Terr. of Ariz. 1896-97.

FRANKLIN, Jesse (brother of Meshack Franklin) (D N.C.) March 24, 1760-Aug. 31, 1823; House 1795-97; Senate 1799-1805, 1807-13; President pro tempore 1804-05; Gov. 1820-21.

FRANKLIN, John Rankin (W Md.) May 6, 1820-Jan. 11, 1878; House 1853-55.

FRANKLIN, Meshack (brother of Jesse Franklin) (D N.C.) 1772-Dec. 18, 1839; House 1807-15.

FRASER, Donald MacKay (D-F-L Minn.) Feb. 20, 1924; House 1963- .

FRAZIER, James Beriah (D Tenn.) Oct. 18, 1856-March 28, 1937; Senate March 21, 1905-1911; Gov. 1902-05.

FRAZIER, James Beriah, Jr. (son of the preceding) (D Tenn.) June 23, 1890; House 1949-63.

FRAZIER, Lynn Joseph (R N.D.) Dec. 21, 1874-Jan. 11, 1947; Senate 1923-41; Gov. 1917-21.

FREAR, James Archibald (R Wis.) Oct. 24, 1861-May 28, 1939; House 1913-35.

FREAR, Joseph Allen, Jr. (D Del.) March 7, 1903; Senate 1949-61.

FREDERICK, Benjamin Todd (D Iowa) Oct. 5, 1834-Nov. 3, 1903; House March 3, 1885-87.

FREDERICKS, John Donnan (R Calif.) Sept. 10, 1869-Aug. 26, 1945; House May 1, 1923-27.

FREE, Arthur Monroe (R Calif.) Jan. 15, 1879-April 1, 1953; House 1921-33.

FREEDLEY, John (W Pa.) May 22, 1793-Dec. 8, 1851; House 1847-51.

FREEMAN, Chapman (R Pa.) Oct. 8, 1832-March 22, 1904; House 1875-79.

FREEMAN, James Crawford (R Ga.) April 1, 1820-Sept. 3, 1885; House 1873-75.

FREEMAN, John D. (U Miss.) — Jan. 17, 1886; House 1851-53.

FREEMAN, Jonathan (uncle of Nathaniel Freeman, Jr.) (F N.H.) March 21, 1745-Aug. 20, 1808; House 1797-1801.

FREEMAN, Nathaniel, Jr. (nephew of Jonathan Freeman) (— Mass.) May 1, 1766-Aug. 22, 1800; House 1795-99.

FREEMAN, Richard Patrick (R Conn.) April 24, 1869-July 8, 1944; House 1915-33.

FREER, Romeo Hoyt (R W. Va.) Nov. 9, 1846-May 9, 1913; House 1899-1901.

FRELINGHUYSEN, Frederick (father of Theodore Frelinghuysen and great-great-great-grandfather of Peter Hood Ballantine Frelinghuysen, Jr.) (F N.J.) April 13, 1753-April 13, 1804; Senate 1793-Nov. 12, 1796; Cont. Cong. 1778-79, 1782-83.

FRELINGHUYSEN, Frederick Theodore (nephew and adopted son of Theodore Frelinghuysen, uncle of Joseph Sherman Frelinghuysen and great-grandfather of Peter Hood Ballantine Frelinghuysen, Jr.) (R N.J.) Aug. 4, 1817-May 20, 1885; Senate Nov. 12, 1866-69, 1871-77; Secy. of State 1881-85.

FRELINGHUYSEN, Joseph Sherman (nephew of Frederick Theodore Frelinghuysen and cousin of Peter Hood Ballantine Frelinghuysen, Jr.) (R N.J.) March 12, 1869-Feb. 8, 1948; Senate 1917-23.

FRELINGHUYSEN, Peter Hood Ballantine, Jr. (cousin of Joseph Sherman Frelinghuysen, great-grandson of Frederick T. Frelinghuysen, great-great-great-nephew of Theodore Frelinghuysen and great-great-great-grandson of Frederick Frelinghuysen) (R N.J.) Jan. 17, 1916; House 1953- .

FRELINGHUYSEN, Theodore (son of Frederick Frelinghuysen and great-great-great-uncle of Peter Hood Ballantine Frelinghuysen, Jr.) (Ad. D N.J.) March 28, 1787-April 12, 1862; Senate 1829-35.

FREMONT, John Charles (F-SD Calif.) Jan. 21, 1813-July 13, 1890; Senate Sept. 9, 1850-51; Gov. of Ariz. Terr. 1878-81.

FRENCH, Burton Lee (R Idaho) Aug. 1, 1875-Sept. 12, 1954; House 1903-09, 1911-15, 1917-33.

FRENCH, Carlos (D Conn.) Aug. 6, 1835-April 14, 1903; House 1887-89.

FRENCH, Ezra Bartlett (R Maine) Sept. 23, 1810-April 24, 1880; House 1859-61.

FRENCH, John Robert (R N.C.) May 28, 1819-Oct. 2, 1890; House July 6, 1868-69.

FRENCH, Richard (D Ky.) June 20, 1792-May 1, 1854; House 1835-37, 1843-45, 1847-49.

FRENZEL, William E. (R Minn.) July 31, 1928; House 1971- .

FREY, Louis, Jr. (R Fla.) Jan. 11, 1934; House 1969- .

FREY, Oliver Walter (D Pa.) Sept. 7, 1887-Aug. 26, 1939; House Nov. 7, 1933-39.

FRICK, Henry (W Pa.) March 17, 1795-March 1, 1844; House 1843-March 1, 1844.

FRIEDEL, Samuel Nathaniel (D Md.) April 18, 1898; House 1953-71.

FRIES, Frank William (D Ill.) May 1, 1893; House 1937-41.

FRIES, George (D Ohio) 1799-Nov. 13, 1866; House 1845-49.

FROMENTIN, Eligius (— La.) — -Oct. 6, 1822; Senate 1813-19.

FROST, Joel (— N.Y.) — - —; House 1823-25.

FROST, Richard Graham (D Mo.) Dec. 29, 1851-Feb. 1, 1900; House 1879-March 2, 1883.

FROST, Rufus Smith (R Mass.) July 18, 1826-March 6, 1894; House 1875-July 28, 1876.

FROTHINGHAM, Louis Adams (R Mass.) July 13, 1871-Aug. 23, 1928; House 1921-Aug. 23, 1928.

FRY, Jacob, Jr. (D Pa.) June 10, 1802-Nov. 28, 1866; House 1935-39.

FRY, Joseph, Jr. (D Pa.) Aug. 4, 1781-Aug. 15, 1860; House 1827-31.

FRYE, William Pierce (grandfather of Wallace Humphrey White, Jr.) (R Maine) Sept. 2, 1830-Aug. 8, 1911; House 1871-March 17, 1881; Senate March 18, 1881-Aug. 8, 1911, President pro tempore 1896-1911.

FUGATE, Thomas Bacon (D Va.) April 10, 1899; House 1949-53.

FULBRIGHT, James Franklin (D Mo.) Jan. 24, 1877-April 5, 1948; House 1923-25, 1927-29, 1931-33.

FULBRIGHT, James William (D Ark.) April 9, 1905; House 1943-45; Senate 1945- .

FULKERSON, Abram (D Va.) May 13, 1834-Dec. 17, 1902; House 1881-83 (elected as a Readjuster)

FULKERSON, Frank Ballard (R Mo.) March 5, 1866-Aug. 30, 1936; House 1905-07.

FULLER, Alvan Tufts (R Mass.) Feb. 27, 1878-April 30, 1958; House 1917-Jan. 5, 1921; Gov. 1925-29.

FULLER, Benoni Stinson (D Ind.) Nov. 13, 1825-April 14, 1903; House 1875-79.

FULLER, Charles Eugene (R Ill.) March 31, 1849-June 25, 1926; House 1903-13, 1915-June 25, 1926.

FULLER, Claude Albert (D Ark.) Jan. 20, 1876-Jan. 8, 1968; House 1929-39.

FULLER, George (D Pa.) Nov. 7, 1802-Nov. 24, 1888; House Dec. 2, 1844-45.

FULLER, Hadwen Carlton (R N.Y.) Aug. 28, 1895; House Nov. 2, 1943-49.

FULLER, Henry Mills (W Pa.) Jan. 3, 1820-Dec. 26, 1860; House 1851-53, 1855-57.

FULLER, Philo Case (W N.Y.) Aug. 14, 1787-Aug. 16, 1855; House 1833-Sept. 2, 1836.

FULLER, Thomas James Duncan (D Maine) March 17, 1808-Feb. 13, 1876; House 1849-57.

FULLER, Timothy (D Mass.) July 11, 1778-Oct. 1, 1835; House 1817-25.

FULLER, William Elijah (R Iowa) March 30, 1846-April 23, 1918; House 1885-89.

FULLER, William Kendall (D N.Y.) Nov. 24, 1792-Nov. 11, 1883; House 1833-37.

FULLERTON, David (uncle of David Fullerton Robison) (— Pa.) Oct. 4, 1772-Feb. 1, 1843; House 1819-May 15, 1820.

FULMER, Hampton Pitts (husband of Willa L. Fulmer) (D S.C.) June 23, 1875-Oct. 19, 1944; House 1921-Oct. 19, 1944.

FULMER, Willa Lybrand (widow of Hampton P. Fulmer) (D S.C.) Feb. 3, 1884-May 13, 1968; House Nov. 7, 1944-45.

FULTON, Andrew Steele (brother of John H. Fulton) (W Va.) Sept. 29, 1800-Nov. 22, 1884; House 1847-49.

FULTON, Charles William (brother of Elmer Lincoln Fulton) (R Ore.) Aug. 24, 1853-Jan. 27, 1918; Senate 1903-09.

FULTON, Elmer Lincoln (brother of Charles William Fulton) (D Okla.) April 22, 1865-Oct. 4, 1939; House Nov. 16, 1907-09.

FULTON, James Grove (R Pa.) March 1, 1903; House Feb. 2, 1945- .

FULTON, John Hall (brother of Andrew Steele Fulton) (W Va.) — -Jan. 28, 1836; House 1833-35.

FULTON, Richard (D Tenn.) Jan. 27, 1927; House 1963- .

FULTON, William Savin (D Ark.) June 2, 1795-Aug. 15, 1844; Senate Sept. 18, 1836-Aug. 15, 1844; Gov. (Terr.) 1835-36.

FUNK, Benjamin Franklin (father of Frank Hamilton Funk) (R Ill.) Oct. 17, 1838-Feb. 14, 1909; House 1893-95.

FUNK, Frank Hamilton (son of Benjamin Franklin Funk) (R Ill.) April 5, 1869-Nov. 24, 1940; House 1921-27.

FUNSTON, Edward Hogue (R Kan.) Sept. 16, 1836-Sept. 10, 1911; House March 21, 1884-Aug. 2, 1894.

FUQUA, Don (D Fla.) Aug. 20, 1933; House 1963- .

FURCOLO, Foster (D Mass.) July 29, 1911; House 1949-Sept. 30, 1952; Gov. 1957-61.

FURLONG, Robert Grant (D Pa.) Jan. 4, 1886; House 1943-45.

FURLOW, Allen John (R Minn.) Nov. 9, 1890-Jan. 29, 1954; House 1925-29.

FYAN, Robert Washington (D Mo.) March 11, 1835-July 28, 1896; House 1883-85, 1891-95.

G

GABALDON, Isauro (Nat. P.I.) Dec. 8, 1875-Dec. 21, 1942; House (Res. Comm.) 1920-July 16, 1928.

GAGE, Joshau (D Mass.) Aug. 7, 1763-Jan. 24, 1831; House 1817-19.

GAHN, Harry Conrad (R Ohio) April 26, 1880-Nov. 2, 1962; House 1921-23.

GAILLARD, John (uncle of Theodore Gaillard Hunt) (D S.C.) Sept. 5, 1765-Feb. 26, 1826; Senate Dec. 6, 1804-Feb. 26, 1826; President pro tempore 1809-10, 1814-18, 1819-25.

GAINES, John Pollard (W Ky.) Sept. 22, 1795-Dec. 9, 1857; House 1847-49; Gov. of Ore. Terr. 1850-53.

GAINES, John Wesley (D Tenn.) Aug. 24, 1860-July 4, 1926; House 1897-1909.

GAINES, Joseph Holt (R W. Va.) Sept. 3, 1864-April 12, 1951; House 1901-11.

GAINES, William Embre (R Va.) Aug. 30, 1844-May 4, 1912; House 1887-89.

GAITHER, Nathan (D Ky.) Sept. 15, 1788-Aug. 12, 1862; House 1829-33.

GALBRAITH, John (D Pa.) Aug. 2, 1794-June 15, 1860; House 1933-37, 1839-41.

GALE, George (father of Levin Gale) (- Md.) June 3, 1756-Jan. 2, 1815; House 1789-91.

GALE, Levin (son of George Gale) (- Md.) April 24, 1784-Dec. 18, 1834; House 1827-29.

GALE, Richard Pillsbury (R Minn.) Oct. 30, 1900; House 1941-45.

GALIFIANAKIS, Nick (D N.C.) July 22, 1928; House 1967- .

GALLAGHER, Cornelius Edward (D N.J.) March 2, 1921; House 1959- .

GALLAGHER, James A. (R Pa.) Jan. 16, 1869-Dec. 8, 1957; House 1943-45, 1947-49.

GALLAGHER, Thomas (D Ill.) July 6, 1850-Feb. 24, 1930; House 1909-21.

GALLAGHER, William James (D Minn.) May 13, 1875-Aug. 13, 1946; House 1945-Aug. 13, 1946.

GALLATIN, Albert (D Pa.) Jan. 29, 1761-Aug. 12, 1849; Senate Dec. 2, 1793-Feb. 28, 1794; House 1795-1801; Secy. of the Treasury 1802-14.

GALLEGOS, Jose Manuel (D N.M.) Oct. 30, 1815-April 21, 1875; House (Terr. Del.) 1853-July 23, 1856, 1871-73.

GALLINGER, Jacob Harold (R N.H.) March 28, 1837-Aug. 17, 1918; House 1885-89; Senate 1891-Aug. 17, 1918.

GALLIVAN, James Ambrose (D Mass.) Oct. 22, 1866-April 3, 1928; House April 7, 1914-April 3, 1928.

GALLOWAY, Samuel (R Ohio) March 20, 1811-April 5, 1872; House 1855-57.

GALLUP, Albert (D N.Y.) Jan. 30, 1796-Nov. 5, 1851; House 1837-39.

GAMBLE, James (D Pa.) Jan. 28, 1809-Feb. 22, 1883; House 1851-55.

GAMBLE, John Rankin (brother of Robert Jackson Gamble and uncle of Ralph Abernethy Gamble) (R S.D.) Jan. 15, 1848-Aug. 14, 1891; House March 4-Aug. 14, 1891.

GAMBLE, Ralph Abernethy (son of Robert Jackson Gamble and nephew of John Rankin Gamble) (R N.Y.) May 6, 1885-March 4, 1959; House Nov. 2, 1937-57.

GAMBLE, Robert Jackson (brother of John Rankin Gamble and father of Ralph Aberenthy Gamble) (R S.D.) Feb. 7, 1851-Sept. 22, 1924; House 1895-97; 1899-1901; Senate 1901-13.

GAMBLE, Roger Lawson (W Ga.) 1787-Dec. 20, 1847; House 1833-35 (D); 1841-43 (W).

GAMBRELL, David Henry (D Ga.) Dec. 20, 1929; Senate Feb. 2, 1971- .

GAMBRILL, Stephen Warfield (D Md.) Oct. 2, 1873-Dec. 19, 1938; House Nov. 4, 1924-Dec. 19, 1938.

GANDY, Harry Luther (D S.C.) Aug. 13, 1881-Aug. 15, 1957; House 1915-21.

GANLY, James Vincent (D N.Y.) Sept. 13, 1878-Sept. 7, 1923; House 1919-21; March 4-Sept. 7, 1923.

GANNETT, Barzillai (D Mass.) June 17, 1764-1832; House 1809-12.

GANSON, John (D N.Y.) Jan. 1, 1818-Sept. 28, 1874; House 1863-65.

GANTZ, Martin Kissinger (D Ohio) Jan. 28, 1862-Feb. 10, 1916; House 1891-93.

GARBER, Harvey Cable (D Ohio) July 6, 1866-March 23, 1938; House 1903-07.

GARBER, Jacob Aaron (R Va.) Jan. 25, 1879-Dec. 2, 1953; House 1929-31.

GARBER, Milton Cline (R Okla.) Nov. 30, 1867-Sept. 12, 1948; House 1923-33.

GARD, Warren (D Ohio) July 2, 1873-Nov. 1, 1929; House 1913-21.

GARDENIER, Barent (R N.Y.) - —; Jan. 10, 1822; House 1807-11.

GARDNER, Augustus Peabody (R Mass.) Nov. 5, 1865-Jan. 14, 1918; House Nov. 3, 1902-May 15, 1917.

GARDNER, Edward Joseph (D Ohio) Aug. 7, 1898-Dec. 7, 1950; House 1945-47.

GARDNER, Francis (- N.H.) Dec. 27, 1771-June 25, 1835; House 1807-09.

GARDNER, Frank (D Ind.) May 8, 1872-Feb. 1, 1937; House 1923-29.

GARDNER, Gideon (- Mass.) May 30, 1759-March 22, 1832; House 1809-11.

GARDNER, James Carson (R N.C.) April 8, 1933; House 1967-69.

GARDNER, John James (R N.J.) Oct. 17, 1845-Feb. 7, 1921; House 1893-1913.

GARDNER, Mills (R Ohio) Jan. 30, 1830-Feb. 20, 1910; House 1877-79.

GARDNER, Obadiah (D Maine) Sept. 13, 1850-July 24, 1938; Senate Sept. 23, 1911-13.

GARDNER, Washington (R Mich.) Feb. 16, 1845-March 31, 1928; House 1899-1911.

GARFIELD, James Abram (R Ohio) Nov. 19, 1831-Sept. 19, 1881; House 1863-Nov. 8, 1880; President March 4-July 2, 1881.

GARFIELDE, Selucius (R Wash.) Dec. 8, 1822-April 13, 1881; House (Terr. Del.) 1969-73.

GARLAND, Augustus Hill (D Ark.) June 11, 1832-Jan. 26, 1899; Senate 1877-March 6, 1885; Gov. 1874-76; Attorney General 1885-89.

GARLAND, David Shepherd (D Va.) Sept. 27, 1769-Oct. 7, 1841; House Jan. 17, 1810-11.

GARLAND, James (D Va.) June 6, 1761-Aug. 8, 1885; House 1835-41.

GARLAND, Mahlon Morris (R Pa.) May 4, 1856-Nov. 19, 1920; House 1915-Nov. 19, 1920.

GARLAND, Peter Adams (R Maine) June 16, 1923; House 1961-63.

GARLAND, Rice (W La.) about 1795-1861; House April 28, 1834-July 21, 1840.

GARMATZ, Edward Alexander (D Md.) Feb. 7, 1903; House July 15, 1947- .

GARNER, Alfred Buckwalter (R Pa.) March 4, 1873-July 30, 1930; House 1909-11.

GARNER, John Nance (D Texas) Nov. 22, 1868-Nov. 7, 1967; House 1903-33; Speaker 1931-33; Vice President 1933-41.

GARNETT, James Mercer (brother of Robert Selden Garnett and grandfather of Muscoe Russell Hunter Garnett) (D Va.) June 8, 1770-April 23, 1843; House 1805-09.

GARNETT, Muscoe Russell Hunter (grandson of James Mercer Garnett) (D Va.) July 25, 1821-Feb. 14, 1864; House Dec. 1, 1856-61.

GARNETT, Robert Selden (brother of James Mercer Garnett and cousin of Charles Fenton Mercer) (D Va.) April 26, 1789-Aug. 15, 1840; House 1817-27.

GARNSEY, Daniel Greene (JD N.Y.) June 17, 1779-May 11, 1851; House 1825-29.

GARRETT, Abraham Ellison (D Tenn.) March 6, 1830-Feb. 14, 1907; House 1871-73.

GARRETT, Clyde Leonard (D Texas) Dec. 16, 1885-Dec. 18, 1959; House 1937-41.

GARRETT, Daniel Edward (D Texas) April 28, 1869-Dec. 13, 1932; House 1913-15; 1917-19; 1921-Dec. 13, 1932.

GARRETT, Finis James (D Tenn.) Aug. 26, 1875-May 25, 1956; House 1905-29.

GARRISON, Daniel (D N.J.) April 3, 1782-Feb. 13, 1851; House 1823-27.

GARRISON, George Tankard (D Va.) Jan. 14, 1835-Nov. 14, 1889; House 1881-83; March 20, 1884-85.

GARROW, Nathaniel (D N.Y.) April 25, 1780-March 3, 1841; House 1827-29.

GARTH, William Willis (D Ala.) Oct. 28, 1828-Feb. 25, 1912; House 1877-79.

GARTNER, Fred Christian (R Pa.) March 14, 1896- —; House 1939-41.

GARTHRELL, Lucius Jeremiah (uncle of Choice Boswell Randell) (D Ga.) Jan. 7, 1821-April 7, 1891; House 1857-Jan. 23, 1861.

GARVIN, William Swan (D Pa.) July 25, 1806-Feb. 20, 1883; House 1945-47.

GARY, Frank Boyd (D S.C.) March 9, 1860-Dec. 7, 1922; Senate March 6, 1908-09.

GARY, Julian Vaughan (D Va.) Feb. 25, 1892- —; House March 6, 1945-65.

GASQUE, Allard Henry (husband of Elizabeth (Bessie) Hawley Gasque) (D S.C.) March 8, 1873-June 17, 1938; House 1923-June 17, 1938.

GASQUE, Elizabeth Hawley (widow of Allard Henry Gasque—later Mrs. A. J. Van Exem) (D S.C.) - —; House Sept. 13, 1938-39.

GASSAWAY, Percy Lee (D Okla.) Aug. 30, 1885-May 15, 1937; House 1935-37.

GASTON, Athelston (D Pa.) April 24, 1838-Sept. 23, 1907; House 1899-1901.

GASTON, William (F N.C.) Sept. 19, 1778-Jan. 23, 1844; House 1813-17.

GATES, Seth Merrill (A-SW N.Y.) Oct. 10, 1800-Aug. 24, 1877; House 1839-43.

GATHINGS, Ezekiel Candler (D Ark.) Nov. 10, 1903; House 1939-69.

GATLIN, Alfred Moore (- N.C.) April 20, 1790- —; House 1823-25.

GAUSE, Lucien Coatsworth (D Ark.) Dec. 25, 1836-Nov. 5, 1880; House 1875-79.

GAVAGAN, Joseph Andrew (D N.Y.) Aug. 20, 1892-Oct. 18, 1968; House Nov. 5, 1929-Dec. 30, 1943.

GAVIN, Leon Harry (R Pa.) Feb. 25, 1893-Sept. 15, 1963; House 1943-Sept. 15, 1963.

GAY, Edward James (D La.) Feb. 3, 1816-May 30, 1889; House 1885-May 30, 1889.

GAY, Edward James (grandson of the preceding) (D La.) May 5, 1878-Dec. 1, 1952; Senate Nov. 6, 1918-21.

GAYDOS, Joseph M. (D Pa.) July 3, 1926; House Nov. 5, 1968- .

GAYLE, John (W Ala.) Sept. 11, 1792-July 28, 1859; House 1847-49; Gov. 1831-35.

GAYLE, June Ward (D Ky.) Feb. 22, 1865-Aug. 5, 1942; House Jan. 15, 1900-01.

GAYLORD, James Madison (- Ohio) May 29, 1811-June 14, 1874; House 1851-53.

GAZLAY, James William (JF-St. Ohio) July 23, 1784-June 8, 1874; House 1823-25.

GEAR, John Henry (R Iowa) April 7, 1825-July 14, 1900; House 1887-91; 1893-95; Senate 1895-July 14, 1900; Gov. 1878-81.

GEARHART, Bertrand Wesley (R Calif.) May 31, 1890-Oct. 11, 1955; House 1935-49.

GEARIN, John McDermeid (D Ore.) Aug. 15, 1851-Nov. 12, 1930; House Dec. 13, 1905-Jan. 23, 1907.

GEARY, Thomas J. (D/AP Calif.) Jan. 18, 1854-July 6, 1929; House Dec. 9, 1890-95.

GEBHARD, John (— N.Y.) Feb. 22, 1782-Jan. 3, 1854; House 1821-23.

GEDDES, George Washington (D Ohio) July 16, 1824-Nov. 9, 1892; House 1879-87.

GEDDES, James (F N.Y.) July 22, 1763-Aug. 19, 1838; House 1813-15.

GEELAN, James Patrick (D Conn.) Aug. 11, 1901; House 1945-47.

GEHRMANN, Bernard John (Pro. Wis.) Feb. 13, 1880-July 12, 1958; House 1935-43.

GEISSENHAINER, Jacob Augustus (D N.J.) Aug. 28, 1839-July 20, 1917; House 1889-95.

GENSMAN, Lorraine Michael (R Okla.) Aug. 26, 1878-May 27, 1954; House 1921-23.

GENTRY, Brady Preston (D Texas) March 25, 1896-Nov. 9, 1966; House 1953-57.

GENTRY, Meredith Poindexter (W Tenn.) Sept. 15, 1809-Nov. 2, 1866; House 1839-43; 1845-53.

GEORGE, Henry, Jr. (D N.Y.) Nov. 3, 1862-Nov. 14, 1916; House 1911-15.

GEORGE, James Zachariah (D Miss.) Oct. 20, 1826-Aug. 14, 1897; Senate 1881-Aug. 14, 1897.

GEORGE, Melvin Clark (R Ore.) May 13, 1849-Feb. 22, 1933; House 1881-85.

GEORGE, Myron Virgil (R Kan.) Jan. 6, 1900; House Nov. 7, 1950-59.

GEORGE, Newell A. (D Kan.) Sept. 24, 1904; House 1959-61.

GEORGE, Walter Franklin (D Ga.) Jan. 19, 1878-Aug. 4, 1957; Senate Nov. 22, 1922-57.

GERAN, Elmer Hendrickson (D N.J.) Oct. 24, 1875-Jan. 12, 1954; House 1923-25.

GERLACH, Charles Lewis (R Pa.) Sept. 14, 1895-May 5, 1947; House 1939-May 5, 1947.

GERMAN, Obadiah (D N.Y.) April 22, 1766-Sept. 24, 1842; Senate 1809-15.

GERNERD, Fred Benjamin (R Pa.) Nov. 22, 1879-Aug. 7, 1948; House 1921-23.

GERRY, Elbridge (great-grandfather of Peter Goelet Gerry) (A-F Mass.) July 17, 1744-Nov. 23, 1814; House 1789-93; Cont. Cong. 1776-81 and 1782-85; (D) Gov. 1810-11; Vice President 1813-14 (D).

GERRY, Elbridge (grandson of the preceding) (D Maine) Dec. 6, 1813-April 10, 1886; House 1849-51.

GERRY, James (D Pa.) Aug. 14, 1796-July 19, 1873; House 1839-43.

GERRY, Peter Goelet (great-grandson of Elbridge Gerry) (D R.I.) Sept. 18, 1879-Oct. 31, 1957; House 1913-15; Senate 1917-29; 1935-47.

GEST, William Harrison (R Ill.) Jan. 7, 1838-Aug. 9, 1912; House 1887-91.

GETTYS, Thomas Smithwick (D S.C.) June 19, 1912; House Nov. 3, 1964- .

GETZ, James Lawrence (D Pa.) Sept. 14, 1821-Dec. 25, 1891; House 1867-73.

GEYER, Henry Sheffie (D Mo.) Dec. 9, 1790-March 5, 1859; Senate 1851-57.

GEYER, Lee Edward (D Calif.) Sept. 9, 1888-Oct. 11, 1941; 1939-Oct. 11, 1941.

GHOLSON, James Herbert (D Va.) 1798-July 2, 1848; House 1833-35.

GHOLSON, Samuel Jameson (D Miss.) May 19, 1808-Oct. 16, 1883; House Dec. 1, 1836-37; July 18, 1837-Feb. 5, 1838.

GHOLSON, Thomas, Jr. (D Va.) - —; July 4, 1816; House Nov. 7, 1808-July 4, 1816.

GIAIMO, Robert Nicholas (D Conn.) Oct. 15, 1919; House 1959- .

GIBBONS, Sam M. (D Fla.) Jan. 20, 1920; House 1963- .

GIBBS, Florence Reville (widow of Willis Benjamin Gibbs) (D Ga.) April 4, 1890-Aug. 19, 1964; House Oct. 1, 1940-41.

GIBBS, Willis Benjamin (husband of Florence Reville Gibbs) (D Ga.) April 15, 1889-Aug. 7, 1940; House 1939-Aug. 7, 1940.

GIBSON, Charles Hopper (cousin of Henry Richard Gibson) (D Md.) Jan. 19, 1842-March 31, 1900; House 1885-91; Senate Nov. 19, 1891-97.

GIBSON, Ernest Willard (father of Ernest William Gibson) (R Vt.) Dec. 29, 1872-June 20, 1940; House Nov. 6, 1923-Oct. 19, 1933; Senate Nov. 21, 1933-June 20, 1940.

GIBSON, Ernest William (R Vt.) March 6, 1901-Nov. 4, 1969; Senate June 24, 1940-41; Gov. 1947-50.

GIBSON, Eustace (D W. Va.) Oct. 4, 1842-Dec. 10, 1900; House 1883-87.

GIBSON, Henry Richard (cousin of Charles Hopper Gibson) (R Tenn.) Dec. 24, 1837-May 25, 1938; House 1895-1905.

GIBSON, James King (D Va.) Feb. 18, 1812-March 30, 1879; House Jan. 28, 1870-71.

GIBSON, John Strickland (D Ga.) Jan. 3, 1893-Oct. 19, 1960; House 1941-47.

GIBSON, Paris (D Mont.) July 1, 1830-Dec. 16, 1920; Senate March 7, 1901-05.

GIBSON, Randall Lee (D La.) Sept. 10, 1832-Dec. 15, 1892; House 1875-83; Senate 1883-Dec. 15, 1892.

GIDDINGS, De Witt Clinton (D Texas) July 18, 1827-Aug. 19, 1903; House May 13, 1872-75; 1877-79.

GIDDINGS, Joshua Reed (A-SW Ohio) Oct. 6, 1795-May 27, 1864; House Dec. 3, 1838-March 22, 1842; Dec. 5, 1842-59.

GIDDINGS, Napoleon Bonaparte (D Neb.) Jan. 2, 1816-Aug. 3, 1897; House (Terr. Del.) Jan. 5-March 3, 1855.

GIFFORD, Charles Laceille (R Mass.) March 15, 1871-Aug. 23, 1947; House Nov. 7, 1922-Aug. 23, 1947.

GIFFORD, Oscar Sherman (R SD) Oct. 20, 1842-Jan. 16, 1913; House: Terr. Del. for Dakota 1885-89; Rep. Nov. 2, 1889-91.

GILBERT, Abijah (R Fla.) June 18, 1806-Nov. 23, 1881; Senate 1869-75.

GILBERT, Edward (D Calif.) about 1819-Aug. 2, 1852; House Sept. 11, 1850-51.

GILBERT, Ezekiel (— N.Y.) March 25, 1756-July 17, 1841; House 1793-97.

GILBERT, George Gilmore (father of Ralph Waldo Emerson Gilbert) (D Ky.) Dec. 24, 1849-Nov. 9, 1909; House 1899-1907.

GILBERT, Jacob H. (D N.Y.) June 17, 1920; House March 8, 1960- .

GILBERT, Newton Whiting (R Ind.) May 24, 1862-July 5, 1939; House 1905- —; Nov. 6, 1906.

GILBERT, Ralph Waldo Emerson (son of George Gilmore Gilbert) (D Ky.) Jan. 17, 1882-July 30, 1939; House 1921-29; 1931-33.

GILBERT, Sylvester (— Conn.) Oct. 20, 1755-Jan. 2, 1846; House Nov. 16, 1818-19.

GILBERT, William Augustus (W N.Y.) Jan. 25, 1815-May 25, 1875; House 1855-Feb. 27, 1857.

GILCHRIST, Fred Cramer (R Iowa) June 2, 1868-March 10, 1950; House 1931-45.

GILDEA, James Hilary (D Pa.) Oct. 21, 1890- —; House 1935-39.

GILES, William Branch (D Va.) Aug. 12, 1762-Dec. 4, 1830; House Dec. 7, 1790-Oct. 2, 1798 (A-F); 1801-03 (D); Senate Aug. 11, 1804-15; Gov. 1827-30.

GILES, William Fell (D Md.) April 8, 1807-March 1879; House 1845-47.

GILFILLAN, Calvin Willard (R Pa.) Feb. 20, 1832-Dec. 2, 1901; House 1869-71.

GILFILLAN, John Bachop (R Minn.) Feb. 11, 1835-Aug. 19, 1924; House 1885-87.

GILHAMS, Clarence Chauncey (R Ind.) April 11, 1860-June 5, 1912; House Nov. 6, 1906-09.

GILL, John, Jr. (D Md.) June 9, 1850-Jan. 27, 1918; House 1905-11.

GILL, Joseph John (R Ohio) Sept. 21, 1846-May 22, 1920; House Dec. 4, 1899- —; Oct. 31, 1903.

GILL, Michael Joseph (D Mo.) Dec. 5, 1864-Nov. 1, 1918; House June 19, 1914-15.

GILL, Patrick Francis (D Mo.) Aug. 16, 1868-May 21, 1923; House 1909-11; Aug. 12, 1912-13.

GILL, Thomas P. (D Hawaii) April 21, 1922; House 1963-65.

GILLEN, Courtland Craig (D Ind.) July 3, 1880-Sept. 1, 1954; House 1931-33.

GILLESPIE, Dean Milton (R Colo.) May 3, 1884-Feb. 2, 1949; House March 7, 1944-47.

GILLESPIE, Eugene Pierce (D Pa.) Sept. 24, 1852-Dec. 16, 1899; House 1891-93.

GILLESPIE, James (— N.C.) - —; Jan. 11, 1805; House 1793-99; 1803-Jan. 11, 1805.

GILLESPIE, James Frank (D Ill.) April 18, 1869-Nov. 26, 1954; House 1933-35.

GILLESPIE, Oscar William (D Texas) June 20, 1858-Aug. 23, 1927; House 1903-11.

GILLET, Charles William (R N.Y.) Nov. 26, 1840-Dec. 31, 1908; House 1893-1905.

GILLET, Ransom Hooker (D N.Y.) Jan. 27, 1800-Oct. 24, 1876; House 1833-37.

GILLETT, Frederick Huntington (R Mass.) Oct. 16, 1851-July 31, 1935; House 1893-1925; Speaker 1919-25; Senate 1925-31.

GILLETT, James Norris (R Calif.) Sept. 20, 1860-April 20, 1937; House 1903-Nov. 4, 1906; Gov. 1907-11.

GILLETTE, Edward Hooker (son of Francis Gillette) (G Iowa) Oct. 1, 1840-Aug. 14, 1918; House 1879-81.

GILLETTE, Francis (father of Edward Hooker Gillette) (F-SW Conn.) Dec. 14, 1807-Sept. 30, 1879; Senate May 24, 1854-55.

GILLETTE, Guy Mark (D Iowa) Feb. 3, 1879- —; House 1933-Nov. 3, 1936; Senate Nov. 4, 1936-45; 1949-55.

GILLETTE, Wilson Darwin (R Pa.) July 1, 1880-Aug. 7, 1951; House Nov. 4, 1941-Aug. 7, 1951.

GILLIE, George W. (R Ind.) Aug. 15, 1880-July 3, 1963; House 1939-49.

GILLIGAN, John J. (D Ohio) March 22, 1921; House 1965-67; Gov. 1971- .

GILLIS, James Lisle (D Pa.) Oct. 2, 1792-July 8, 1881; House 1857-59.

GILLON, Alexander (— S.C.) 1741-Oct. 6, 1794; House 1793-Oct. 6, 1794.

GILMAN, Charles Jervis (grandnephew of Nicholas Gilman) (R Maine) Feb. 26, 1824-Feb. 5, 1901; House 1857-59.

GILMAN, Nicholas (granduncle of Charles Jervis Gilman) (D N.H.) Aug. 3, 1755-May 2, 1814; House 1789-97 (F); Senate 1805-May 2, 1814 (D); Cont. Cong. 1786-88.

GILMER, George Rockingham (D Ga.) April 11, 1790-Nov. 16, 1859; House 1821-23; Oct. 1, 1827-29; 1833-35; Gov. 1829-31; 1837-39.

GILMER, John Adams (AP N.C.) Nov. 4, 1805-May 14, 1868; House 1857-61.

GILMER, Thomas Walker (D Va.) April 6, 1802-Feb. 28, 1844; House 1841-43 (W); 1843-Feb. 16, 1844 (D); Gov. 1840-41; Secy. of the Navy Feb. 15-Feb. 28, 1844.

GILMER, William Franklin (Dixie) (D Okla.) June 7, 1901-June 9, 1954; House 1949-51.

GILMORE, Alfred (son of John Gilmore (D Pa.) June 9, 1812-June 29, 1890; House 1849-53.

GILMORE, Edward (D Mass.) Jan. 4, 1867-April 10, 1924; House 1913-15.

GILMORE, John (father of Alfred Gilmore) (JD Pa.) Feb. 18, 1780-May 11, 1845; House 1829-33.

GILMORE, Samuel Louis (D La.) July 30, 1859-July 18, 1910; House March 30, 1909-July 18, 1910.

GINGERY, Don (D Pa.) Feb. 19, 1884 - —; House 1935-39.

GIST, Joseph (D S.C.) Jan. 12, 1775-March 8, 1836; House 1821-27.

GITTENS, Robert Henry (D N.Y.) Dec. 14, 1869- —; House 1913-15.

GLASCOCK, John Raglan (D Calif.) Aug. 25, 1845-Nov. 10, 1913; House 1883-85.

GLASCOCK, Thomas (UD Ga.) Oct. 21, 1790-May 19, 1841; House Oct. 5, 1835-39.

GLASGOW, Hugh (— Pa.) Sept. 8, 1769-Jan. 31, 1818; House 1813-17.

GLASS, Carter (D Va.) Jan. 4, 1858-May 28, 1946; House Nov. 4, 1902-Dec. 16, 1918; Senate Feb. 2, 1920-May 28, 1946; Secy. of the Treasury 1918-20.

GLASS, Presley Thornton (D Tenn.) Oct. 18, 1824-Oct. 9, 1902; House 1885-89.

GLATFELTER, Samuel Feiser (D Pa.) April 7, 1858-April 23, 1927; House 1923-25.

GLEN, Henry (— N.Y.) July 13, 1739-Jan. 6, 1814; House 1793-1801.

GLENN, Milton Willits (R N.J.) June 18, 1903-Dec. 14, 1967; House Nov. 5, 1957-65.

GLENN, Otis Ferguson (R Ill.) Aug. 27, 1879-March 11, 1959; Senate Dec. 3, 1928-33.

GLENN, Thomas Louis (P Idaho) Feb. 2, 1847-Nov. 18, 1918; House 1901-03.

GLONINGER, John (D Pa.) Sept. 19, 1758-Jan. 22, 1836; House March 4-Aug. 2, 1813.

GLOSSBRENNER, Adam John (D Pa.) Aug. 31, 1810-March 1, 1889; House 1865-69.

GLOVER, David Delano (D Ark.) Jan. 18, 1868-April 5, 1952; House 1929-35.

GLOVER, John Milton (nephew of John Montgomery Glover) (D Mo.) June 23, 1852-Oct. 20, 1929; House 1885-89.

GLOVER, John Montgomery (uncle of John Milton Glover) (D Mo.) Sept. 4, 1822-Nov. 15, 1891; House 1873-79.

GLYNN, James Peter (R Conn.) Nov. 12, 1867-March 6, 1930; House 1915-23; 1925-March 6, 1930.

GLYNN, Martin Henry (D N.Y.) Sept. 27, 1871-Dec. 14, 1924; House 1899-1901; Gov. 1913-14.

GODDARD, Calvin (F Conn.) July 17, 1768-May 2, 1842; House May 14, 1801-05.

GODSHALK, William (R Pa.) Oct. 25, 1817-Feb. 6, 1891; House 1879-83.

GODWIN, Hannibal Lafayette (D N.C.) Nov. 3, 1873-June 9, 1929; House 1907-21.

GOEBEL, Herman Philip (R Ohio) April 5, 1853-May 4, 1930; House 1903-11.

GOEKE, John Henry (D Ohio) Oct. 28, 1869-March 25, 1930; House 1911-15.

GOFF, Abe McGregor (R Idaho) Dec. 21, 1899- —; House 1947-49.

GOFF, Guy Despard (son of Nathan Goff and father of Mrs. Louise Goff (Reece) (R W. Va.) Sept. 13, 1866-Jan. 7, 1933; Senate 1925-31.

GOFF, Nathan (father of Guy Despard Goff and grandfather of Mrs. Louise Goff Reece) (R W. Va.) Feb. 9, 1843-April 24, 1920; House 1883-89; Senate April 1, 1913-19; Secy. of the Navy Jan. 6-March 5, 1881.

GOGGIN, William Leftwich (W Va.) May 31, 1807-Jan. 3, 1870; House 1839-43; April 25, 1844-45; 1847-49.

GOLD, Thomas Ruggles (F N.Y.) Nov. 4, 1764-Oct. 24, 1827; House 1809-13; 1815-17.

GOLDEN, James Stephen (R Ky.) Sept. 10, 1891- —; House 1949-55.

GOLDER, Benjamin Martin (R Pa.) Dec. 23, 1891-Dec. 30, 1946; House 1925-33.

GOLDFOGLE, Henry Mayer (D N.Y.), May 23, 1956-June 1, 1929; House 1901-15; 1919-21.

GOLDSBOROUGH, Charles (great-grandfather of Thomas Alan Goldsborough and Winder Laird Henry) (F Md.) July 15, 1765-Dec. 13, 1834; House 1805-17; Gov. 1818-19.

GOLDSBOROUGH, Phillips Lee (R Md.) Aug. 6, 1865-Oct. 22, 1946; Senate 1929-35; Gov. 1912-15.

GOLDSBOROUGH, Robert Henry (great-grandfather of Winder Laird Henry) (W Md.) Jan. 4, 1779-Oct. 5, 1836; Senate May 21, 1813-19 (F); Jan. 13, 1835-Oct. 5, 1836 (W).

GOLDSBOROUGH, Thomas Alan (great-grandson of Charles Goldsborough) (D Md.) Sept. 16, 1877-June 16, 1951; House 1921-April 5, 1939.

GOLDTHWAITE, George Thomas (D Ala.) Dec. 10, 1809-March 18, 1879; Senate 1871-77.

GOLDWATER, Barry Morris (R Ariz.) Jan. 1, 1909; Senate 1953-65, 1969- .

GOLDWATER, Barry M., Jr. (son of the preceding) (R Calif.) July 15, 1938; House April 29, 1969- .

GOLDZIER, Julius (D Ill.) Jan. 20, 1854-Jan. 20, 1925; House 1893-95.

GOLLADAY, Edward Isaac (brother of Jacob Shall Golladay) (D Tenn.) Sept. 9, 1830-July 11, 1897; House 1871-73.

GOLLADAY, Jacob Shall (brother of Edward Isaac Golladay) (D Ky.) Jan. 19, 1819-May 20, 1887; House Dec. 5, 1867-Feb. 28, 1870.

GONZALEZ, Henry B. (D Texas) May 3, 1916; House Nov. 4, 1961- .

GOOCH, Daniel Linn (D Ky.) Oct. 28, 1853-April 12, 1913; House 1901-05.

GOOCH, Daniel Wheelwright (R Mass.) Jan. 8, 1820-Nov. 11, 1891; House Jan. 31, 1858-Sept. 1, 1865, 1873-75.

GOOD, James William (R Iowa) Sept. 24, 1866-Nov. 18, 1929; House 1909-June 15, 1921; Secy. of War March 5-Nov. 18, 1929.

GOODALL, Louis Bertrand (R Maine) Sept. 23, 1851-June 26, 1935; House 1917-21.

GOODE, John, Jr. (D Va.) May 27, 1829-July 14, 1909; House 1875-81.

GOODE, Patrick Gaines (W Ohio) May 10, 1798-Oct. 17, 1862; House 1837-43.

GOODE, Samuel (— Va.) March 21, 1756-Nov. 14, 1822; House 1799-1801.

GOODE, William Osborne (D Va.) Sept. 16, 1798-July 3, 1859; House 1841-43, 1853-July 3, 1859.

GOODELL, Charles Ellsworth (R N.Y.) March 16, 1926; House May 26, 1959-Sept. 10, 1968; Senate Sept. 10, 1968-71.

GOODENOW, John Milton (JD Ohio) 1782-July 20, 1838; House 1829-April 9, 1830.

GOODENOW, Robert (brother of Rufus King Goodenow) (W Maine) April 19, 1800-May 15, 1874; House 1851-53.

GOODENOW, Rufus King (brother of Robert Goodnow) (W Maine) April 24, 1790-March 24, 1863; House 1849-51.

GOODHUE, Benjamin (—Mass.) Sept. 20, 1748-July 28, 1814; House 1789-June 1796; Senate June 11, 1796-Nov. 8, 1800.

GOODIN, John Randolph (D Kan.) Dec. 14, 1836-Dec. 18, 1885; House 1875-77.

GOODING, Frank Robert (R Idaho) Sept. 16, 1859-June 24, 1928; Senate Jan. 15, 1921-June 24, 1928; Gov. 1905-09.

GOODLING, George A. (R Pa.) Sept. 26, 1896; House 1961-65, 1967- .

GOODNIGHT, Isaac Herschel (D Ky.) Jan. 31, 1849-July 24, 1901; House 1889-95.

GOODRICH, Chauncey (brother of Elizur Goodrich) (F Conn.) Oct. 20, 1759-Aug. 18, 1815; House 1795-1801; Senate Oct. 25, 1807-May 1813.

GOODRICH, Elizur (brother of Chauncey Goodrich) (F Conn.) March 24, 1761-Nov. 1, 1849; House 1799-1801.

GOODRICH, John Zacheus (W Mass.) Sept. 27, 1804-April 19, 1885; House 1851-55.

GOODRICH, Milo (R N.Y.) Jan. 3, 1814-April 15, 1881; House 1871-73.

GOODWIN, Angier Louis (R Mass.) Jan. 30, 1881- —; House 1943-55.

GOODWIN, Forrest (R Maine) June 14, 1862-May 28, 1913; House March 4-May 28, 1913.

GOODWIN, Godfrey Gummer (R Minn.) Jan. 11, 1873-Feb. 16, 1933; House 1925-Feb. 16, 1933.

GOODWIN, Henry Charles (R N.Y.) June 25, 1824-Nov. 12, 1860; House Nov. 7, 1854-55, 1857-59.

GOODWIN, John Noble (R Maine/Ariz.) Oct. 18, 1824-April 29, 1887; House (Rep. Maine) 1861-63, (Terr. Del. Ariz.) 1865-67; Gov. of Ariz. Terr. 1863-65.

GOODWIN, Philip Arnold (R N.Y.) Jan. 20, 1882-June 6, 1937; House 1933-June 6, 1937.

GOODWIN, Robert Kingman (F Iowa) May 23, 1905; House March 5, 1940-41.

GOODWIN, William Shields (D Ark.) May 2, 1866-Aug. 9, 1937; House 1911-21.

GOODWYN, Albert Taylor (D Ala.) Dec. 17, 1842-July 2, 1931; House April 22, 1896-97.

GOODWYN, Peterson (D Va.) 1745-Feb. 21, 1818; House 1803-Feb. 21, 1818.

GOODYEAR, Charles (D N.Y.) April 26, 1804-April 9, 1876; House 1845-47, 1865-67.

GOODYKOONTZ, Wells (R W. Va.) June 3, 1872-March 2, 1944; House 1919-23.

GORDON, George Washington (D Tenn.) Oct. 5, 1836-Aug. 9, 1911; House 1907-Aug. 9, 1911.

GORDON, James (F N.Y.) Oct. 31, 1739-Jan. 17, 1810; House 1791-95.

GORDON, James (— Miss.) Dec. 6, 1833-Nov. 28, 1912; Senate Dec. 27, 1909-Feb. 22, 1910.

GORDON, John Brown (D Ga.) Feb. 6, 1832-Jan. 9, 1904; Senate 1873-May 26, 1880, 1891-97; Gov. 1886-90.

GORDON, Robert Bryarly (D Ohio) Aug. 6, 1855-Jan. 3, 1923; House 1899-1903.

GORDON, Samuel (D N.Y.) April 28, 1802-Oct. 28, 1873; House 1841-43, 1845-47.

GORDON, Thomas Sylvy (D Ill.) Dec. 17, 1893-Jan. 22, 1959; House 1943-59.

GORDON, William (— N.H.) April 12, 1763-May 8, 1802; House 1797-June 12, 1800.

GORDON, William (D Ohio) Dec. 15, 1862-Jan. 16, 1942; House 1913-19.

GORDON, William Fitzhugh (D Va.) Jan. 13, 1787-Aug. 28, 1858; House Jan. 25, 1830-35.

GORE, Albert Arnold (D Tenn.) Dec. 26, 1907; House 1939-Dec. 4, 1944, 1945-53; Senate 1953-71.

GORE, Christopher (— Mass.) Sept. 21, 1758-March 1, 1827; Senate May 5, 1813-May 30, 1816; Gov. 1809.

GORE, Thomas Pryor (D Okla.) Dec. 10, 1870-March 16, 1949; Senate Dec. 11, 1907-21, 1931-37.

GORHAM, Benjamin (— Mass.) Feb. 13, 1775-Sept. 27, 1855; House Nov. 6, 1820-23, July 23, 1827-31, 1833-35.

GORMAN, Arthur Pue (D Md.) March 11, 1839-June 4, 1906; Senate 1881-99, 1903-June 4, 1906.

GORMAN, George Edmund (D Ill.) April 13, 1873-Jan. 13, 1935; House 1913-15.

GORMAN, James Sedgwick (D Mich.) Dec. 28, 1850-May 27, 1923; House 1891-95.

GORMAN, John Jerome (R Ill.) June 2, 1883-Feb. 24, 1949 - —; House 1921-23, 1925-27.

GORMAN, Willis Arnold (D Ind.) Jan. 12, 1816-May 20, 1876; House 1849-53; Terr. Gov. of Minn. 1853-57.

GORSKI, Chester Charles (D N.Y.) June 22, 1906; House 1949-51.

GORSKI, Martin (D Ill.) Oct. 30, 1886-Dec. 4, 1949; House 1943-Dec. 4, 1949.

GOSS, Edward Wheeler (R Conn.) April 27, 1893 - —; House Nov. 4, 1930-35.

GOSS, James Hamilton (R S.C.) Aug. 9, 1820-Oct. 31, 1886; House July 18, 1868-69.

GOSSETT, Charles Clinton (D Idaho) Sept. 2, 1888- —; Senate Nov. 17, 1945-1947; Gov. Jan.-Nov. 16, 1945.

GOSSETT, Ed Lee (D Texas) Jan. 27, 1902; House 1939-July 31, 1951.

GOTT, Daniel (W N.Y.) July 10, 1794-July 6, 1864; House 1847-51.

GOULD, Arthur Robinson (R Maine) March 16, 1857-July 24, 1946; Senate Nov. 30, 1926-31.

GOULD, Herman Day (W N.Y.) Jan. 16, 1799-Jan. 26, 1852; House 1849-51.

GOULD, Norman Judd (grandson of Norman Buel Judd) (R N.Y.) March 15, 1877-Aug. 20, 1964 - —; House Nov. 2, 1915-23.

GOULD, Samuel Wadsworth (D Maine) Jan. 1, 1852-Dec. 19, 1935; House 1911-13.

GOULDEN, Joseph Aloysius (D N.Y.) Aug. 1, 1844-May 3, 1915; House 1903-11; 1913-May 3, 1915.

GOURDIN, Theodore (D S.C.) March 20, 1764-Jan. 17, 1826; House 1813-15.

GOVAN, Andrew Robison (— S.C.) Jan. 13, 1794-June 27, 1841; House Dec. 4, 1822-27.

GOVE, Samuel Francis (R Ga.) March 9, 1822-Dec. 3, 1900; House June 25, 1868-69.

GRABOWSKI, Bernard F. (D Conn.) June 11, 1923; House 1963-67.

GRADY, Benjamin Franklin (D N.C.) Oct. 10, 1831-March 6, 1914; House 1891-95.

GRAFF, Joseph Verdi (R Ill.) July 1, 1854-Nov. 10, 1921; House 1895-11.

GRAHAM, Frank Porter (D N.C.) Oct. 14, 1886 - —; Senate March 29, 1949-Nov. 26, 1950.

GRAHAM, George Scott (R Pa.) Sept. 13, 1850-July 4, 1931; House 1913-July 4, 1931.

GRAHAM, James (brother of William Alexander Graham) (W N.C.) Jan. 7, 1793-Sept. 25, 1851; House 1833-March 29, 1836; Dec. 5, 1836-1843; 1845-47.

GRAHAM, James Harper (R N.Y.) Sept. 18, 1812-June 23, 1881; House 1859-61.

GRAHAM, James McMahon (D Ill.) April 14, 1852-Oct. 23, 1945; House 1909-15.

GRAHAM, John Hugh (D N.Y.) April 1, 1835-July 11, 1895; House 1893-95.

GRAHAM, Louis Edward (R Pa.) Aug. 4, 1880-Nov. 9, 1965; House 1939-55.

GRAHAM, William (W Ind.) March 16, 1782-Aug. 17, 1858; House 1837-39.

GRAHAM, William Alexander (brother of James Graham) (W N.C.) Sept. 5, 1804-Aug. 11, 1875; Senate Nov. 25, 1840-43; Gov. 1845-49; Secy. of the Navy 1850-52.

GRAHAM, William Harrison (R Pa.) Aug. 3, 1844-March 2, 1923; House Nov. 29, 1898-1903; 1905-11.

GRAHAM, William Johnson (R Ill.) Feb. 7, 1872-Nov. 10, 1937; House 1917-June 7, 1924.

GRAMMER, Elijah Sherman (R Wash.) April 3, 1868-Nov. 19, 1936; Senate Nov. 22, 1932-33.

GRANAHAN, Kathryn Elizabeth (widow of William Thomas Granahan) (D Pa.) Dec. 7, 1906- —; House Nov. 6, 1956-63.

GRANAHAN, William Thomas (husband of Kathryn Elizabeth Granahan) (D Pa.) July 26, 1895-May 25, 1956; House 1945-47; 1949-May 25, 1956.

GRANATA, Peter Charles (R Ill.) Oct. 28, 1898- —; House 1931-April 5, 1932.

GRANFIELD, William Joseph (D Mass.) Dec. 18, 1889-May 28, 1959; House Feb. 11, 1930-37.

GRANGER, Amos Phelps (cousin of Francis Granger) (W N.Y.) June 3, 1789-Aug. 20, 1866; House 1855-59.

GRANGER, Bradley Francis (D Mich.) March 12, 1825-Nov. 4, 1882; House 1861-63.

GRANGER, Daniel Larned Davis (D R.I.) May 30, 1852-Feb. 14, 1909; House 1903-Feb. 14, 1909.

GRANGER, Francis (cousin of Amos Phelps Granger) (W N.Y.) Dec. 1, 1792-Aug. 31, 1868; House 1835-37; 1839-March 5, 1841; Nov. 27, 1841-1843; Postmaster General March 6-Sept. 18, 1841.

GRANGER, Miles Tobey (D Conn.) Aug. 12, 1817-Oct. 21, 1895; House 1887-89.

GRANGER, Walter Kiel (D Utah) Oct. 11, 1888- —; House 1941-53.

GRANT, Abraham Phineas (D N.Y.) April 5, 1804-Dec. 11, 1871; House 1837-39.

GRANT, George McInvale (D Ala.) July 11, 1897- —; House June 14, 1938-65.

GRANT, John Gaston (R N.C.) Jan. 1, 1858-June 21, 1923; House 1909-11.

GRANT, Robert Allen (R Ind.) July 31, 1905; House 1939-49.

GRANTLAND, Seaton (U Ga.) June 8, 1782-Oct. 18, 1864; House 1835-39.

GRASSO, Ella T. (D Conn.) May 10, 1919; House 1971- .

GRAVEL, Mike (D Alaska) May 13, 1930; Senate 1969- .

GRAVELY Joseph Jackson (R Mo.) Sept. 25. 1828-April 28, 1872; House 1867-69.

GRAVES, Alexander (D Mo.) Aug. 25, 1844-Dec. 23, 1916; House 1883-85.

GRAVES, Dixie Bibb (D Ala.) July 26, 1882- —; Senate Aug. 19, 1937-Jan. 10, 1938.

GRAVES, William Jordan (W Ky.) 1805-Sept. 27, 1848; House 1835-41.

GRAY, Edward Winthrop (R N.J.) Aug. 18, 1870-June 10, 1942; House 1915-19.

GRAY, Edwin (— Va.) July 18, 1743- —; House 1799-1813.

GRAY, Finly Hutchinson (D Ind.) July 21, 1863-May 8, 1947; House 1911-17; 1933-39.

GRAY, George (D Del.) May 4, 1840-Aug. 7, 1925; Senate March 18, 1885-99.

GRAY, Hiram (D N.Y.) July 10, 1801-May 6, 1890; House 1837-39.

GRAY, John Cowper (— Va.) 1783-May 18, 1823; House Aug. 28, 1820-21.

GRAY, Joseph Anthony (D Pa.) Feb. 25, 1884-May 8, 1966 - —; House 1935-39.

GRAY, Kenneth James (D Ill.) Nov. 14, 1924; House 1955- .

GRAY, Oscar Lee (D Ala.) July 2, 1865-Jan. 2, 1936; House 1915-19.

GRAYSON, William (father of William John Grayson and uncle of Alexander Dalrymple Orr) (— Va.) 1740-March 12, 1790; Senate 1789-March 12, 1790; Cont. Cong. 1784-87.

GRAYSON, William John (son of William Grayson and cousin of Alexander Dalrymple Orr) (W S.C.) Nov. 2, 1788-Oct. 4, 1863; House 1833-37.

GREELEY, Horace (W N.Y.) Feb. 3, 1811-Nov. 29, 1872; House Dec. 4, 1848-49.

GREEN, Byram (— N.Y.) April 15, 1786-Oct. 18, 1865; House 1843-45.

GREEN, Edith (D Ore.) Jan. 17, 1910; House 1955- .

GREEN, Frederick William (D Ohio) Feb. 18, 1816-June 18, 1879; House 1851-55.

GREEN, Henry Dickinson (D Pa.) May 3, 1857-Dec. 29, 1929; House Nov. 7, 1899-1903.

GREEN, Innis (D Pa.) Feb. 26, 1776-Aug. 4, 1839; House 1827-31.

GREEN, Isaiah Lewis (—Mass.) Dec. 28, 1761-Dec. 5, 1841; House 1805-09; 1811-13.

GREEN, James Stephen (D Mo.) Feb. 28, 1817-Jan. 19, 1870; House 1847-51; Senate Jan. 12, 1857-61.

GREEN, Robert Alexis (D Fla.) Feb. 10, 1892- —; House 1925-Nov. 25, 1944.

GREEN, Robert Stockton (D N.J.) March 25, 1831-May 7, 1895; House 1885-Jan. 17, 1887; Gov. 1887-89.

GREEN, Theodore Francis (grandnephew of Samuel Greene Arnold, great-grand-nephew of Tristam Burges, great-grand-son of James Burrill, Jr., great-great-nephew of Lemuel Hastings Arnold) (D R.I.) Oct. 2, 1867-May 19, 1966; Senate 1937-61; Gov. 1933-36.

GREEN, Wharton Jackson (grandson of Jesse Wharton and cousin of Matt Whitaker Ransom) (D N.C.) Feb. 28, 1831-Aug. 6, 1910; House 1883-87.

GREEN, William Joseph, Jr. (D Pa.) March 5, 1910-Dec. 21, 1963; House 1945-47; 1949-Dec. 21, 1963.

GREEN, William J. III (son of the preceding) (D Pa.) June 24, 1938; House April 28, 1964- .

GREEN, William Raymond (R Iowa) Nov. 7, 1856-June 11, 1947; House June 5, 1911-March 31, 1928.

GREEN, Willis (W Ky.) — - —; House 1839-45.

GREENE, Albert Collins (W R.I.) April 15, 1791-Jan. 8, 1863; Senate 1845-51.

GREENE, Frank Lester (R Vt.) Feb. 10, 1870-Dec. 17, 1930; House July 30, 1912-1923; Senate 1923-Dec. 17, 1930.

GREENE, George Woodward (D N.Y.) July 4, 1831-July 21, 1895; House 1869-Feb. 17, 1870.

GREENE, Ray (— R.I.) Feb. 2, 1765-Jan. 11, 1829; Senate Nov. 13, 1797-1801.

GREENE, Thomas Marston (— Miss.) Feb. 26, 1758-Feb. 7, 1813; House (Terr. Del.) Dec. 6, 1802-03.

GREENE, William Laury (P Neb.) Oct. 3, 1849-March 11, 1899; House 1897-March 11, 1889.

GREENE, William Stedman (R Mass.) April 28, 1841-Sept. 22, 1924; House May 31, 1898-Sept. 22, 1924.

GREENHALGE, Frederic Thomas (R Mass.) July 19, 1842-March 5, 1896; House 1889-91; Gov. 1894-96.

GREENLEAF, Halbert Stevens (D N.Y.) April 12, 1827-Aug. 25, 1906; House 1883-85; 1891-93.

GREENMAN, Edward Whitford (D N.Y.) Jan. 26, 1840-Aug. 3, 1908; House 1887-89.

GREENUP, Christopher (— Ky.) 1750-April 27, 1818; House Nov. 9, 1792-1797; Gov. 1804-08.

GREENWAY, Isabella Selmes (later Mrs. Harry Orland King) (D Ariz.) March 22, 1886-Dec. 18, 1953; House Oct. 3, 1933-37.

GREENWOOD, Alfred Burton (D Ark.) July 11, 1811-Oct. 4, 1889; House 1853-59.

GREENWOOD, Arthur Herbert (D Ind.) Jan. 31, 1880-April 26, 1963; House 1923-39.

GREENWOOD, Ernest (D N.Y.) Nov. 25, 1884-June 15, 1955; House 1951-53.

GREEVER, Paul Ranous (D Wyo.) Sept. 28, 1891-Feb. 16, 1943; House 1935-39.

GREGG, Alexander White (D Texas) Jan. 31, 1855-April 30, 1919; House 1903-19.

GREGG, Andrew (grandfather of James Xavier McLanahan) (— Pa.) June 10, 1755-May 20, 1835; House 1791-1807; Senate 1807-13; President pro tempore 1809.

GREGG, Curtis Hussey (D Pa.) Aug. 9, 1865-Jan. 18, 1933; House 1911-13.

GREGG, James Madison (D Ind.) June 26, 1806-June 16, 1869; House 1857-59.

GREGORY, Dudley Sanford (W N.J.) Feb. 5, 1800-Dec. 8, 1874; House 1847-49.

GREGORY, Noble Jones (brother of William Voris Gregory) (D Ky.) Aug. 30, 1897- —; House 1937-59.

GREGORY, William Voris (brother of Noble Jones Gregory) (D Ky.) Oct. 21, 1877-Oct. 10, 1936; House 1927-Oct. 10, 1936.

GREIG, John (W N.Y.) Aug. 6, 1779-April 9, 1858; House May 21-Sept. 25, 1841.

GREIGG, Stanley Lloyd (D Iowa) May 7, 1931; House 1965-67.

GRENNELL, George, Jr. (— Mass.) Dec. 25, 1786-Nov. 19, 1877; House 1829-39.

GRESHAM, Walter (D Texas) July 22, 1841-Nov. 6, 1920; House 1893-95.

GREY, Benjamin Edwards (grandson of Benjamin Edwards) (W Ky.) — - —; House 1851-55.

GRIDER, George William (D Tenn.) Oct. 1, 1912; House 1965-67.

GRIDER, Henry (W Ky.) July 16, 1796-Sept. 7, 1866; House 1843-47; 1861-Sept. 7, 1866.

GRIEST, William Walton (R Pa.) Sept. 22, 1858-Dec. 5, 1929; House 1909-Dec. 5, 1929.

GRIFFIN, Anthony Jerome (D N.Y.) April 1, 1866-Jan. 13, 1935; House March 5, 1918-Jan. 13, 1935.

GRIFFIN, Charles H. (D Miss.) May 9, 1926; House March 12, 1968- .

GRIFFIN, Daniel Joseph (D N.Y.) March 26, 1880-Dec. 11, 1926; House 1913-Dec. 31, 1917.

GRIFFIN, Isaac (great-grandfather of Eugene McLanahan Wilson) (D Pa.) Feb. 27, 1756-Oct. 12, 1827; House Feb. 16, 1813-17.

GRIFFIN, John King (SRW S.C.) Aug. 13, 1789-Aug. 1, 1841; House 1831-41.

GRIFFIN, Levi Thomas (D Mich.) May 23, 1837-March 17, 1906; House Dec. 4, 1893-95.

GRIFFIN, Michael (R Wis.) Sept. 9, 1842-Dec. 29, 1899; House Nov. 5, 1894-99.

GRIFFIN, Robert Paul (R Mich.) Nov. 6, 1923; House 1957-May 10, 1966; Senate May 11, 1966- .

GRIFFIN, Samuel (— Va.) — -Nov. 3, 1810; House 1789-95.

GRIFFIN, Thomas (— Va.) 1773-Oct. 7, 1837; House 1803-05.

GRIFFITH, Francis Marion (D Ind.) Aug. 21, 1849-Feb. 8, 1927; House Dec. 6, 1897-1905.

GRIFFITH, John Keller (D La.) Oct. 16, 1882-Sept. 25, 1942; House 1937-41.

GRIFFITH, Samuel (D Pa.) Feb. 14, 1816-Oct. 1, 1893; House 1871-73.

GRIFFITHS, Martha Wright (D Mich.) Jan. 29, 1912; House 1955- .

GRIFFITHS, Percy Wilfred (R Ohio) March 30, 1893- —; House 1943-49.

GRIGGS, James Mathews (D Ga.) March 29, 1861-Jan. 5, 1910; House 1897-Jan. 5, 1910.

GRIGSBY, George Barnes (D Alaska) Dec. 2, 1874-May 14, 1962; House (Terr. Del.) June 3, 1920-March 1, 1921.

GRIMES, James Wilson (R Iowa) Oct. 20, 1816-Feb. 7, 1872; Senate 1859-Dec. 6, 1869; Gov. 1854-58.

GRIMES, Thomas Wingfield (D Ga.) Dec. 18, 1844-Oct. 28, 1905; House 1887-91.

GRINNELL, Joseph (brother of Moses Hicks Grinnell) (W Mass.) Nov. 17, 1788-Feb. 7, 1885; House Dec. 7, 1843-51.

GRINNELL, Josiah Bushnell (R Iowa) Dec. 22, 1821-March 31, 1891; House 1863-67.

GRINNELL, Moses Hicks (brother of Joseph Grinnell) (W N.Y.) March 3, 1803-Nov. 24, 1877; House 1839-41.

GRISWOLD, Dwight Palmer (R Neb.) Nov. 27, 1893-April 12, 1954; Senate Nov. 5, 1952-April 12, 1954; Gov. 1941-46.

GRISWOLD, Gaylord (F N.Y.) Dec. 18, 1767-March 1, 1809; House 1803-05.

GRISWOLD, Glenn Hasenfratz (D Ind.) Jan. 20, 1890-Dec. 5, 1940; House 1931-39.

GRISWOLD, Harry Wilbur (R Wis.) May 19, 1886-July 4, 1939; House Jan. 3-July 4, 1939.

GRISWOLD, John Ashley (D N.Y.) Nov. 18, 1822-Feb. 22, 1902; House 1869-71.

GRISWOLD, John Augustus (R N.Y.) Nov. 11, 1822-Oct. 31, 1872; House 1863-65 (D); 1865-69 (R).

GRISWOLD, Matthew (grandson of Roger Griswold) (R Pa.) June 6, 1833-May 19, 1919; House 1891-93; 1895-97.

GRISWOLD, Roger (grandfather of Matthew Griswold) (R Conn.) May 21, 1762-Oct. 25, 1812; House 1795-1805; Gov. 1811-12.

GRISWOLD, Stanley (— Ohio) Nov. 14, 1763-Aug. 21, 1815; Senate May 18-Dec. 11, 1809.

GROESBECK, William Slocum (D Ohio) July 24, 1815-July 7, 1897; House 1857-59.

GRONNA, Asle Jorgenson (R N.D.) Dec. 10, 1858-May 4, 1922; House 1905-Feb. 2, 1911; Senate Feb. 2, 1911-21.

GROOME, James Black (D Md.) April 4, 1838-Oct. 5, 1893; Senate 1879-85; Gov. 1874-76.

GROSS, Chester Heilman (R Pa.) Oct. 13, 1888- —; House 1939-41; 1943-49.

GROSS, Ezra Carter (D N.Y.) July 11, 1787-April 9, 1829; House 1819-21.

GROSS, Harold Royce (R Iowa) June 30, 1899- —; House 1949- .

GROSS, Samuel (D Pa.) 1774-March 19, 1844; House 1819-23.

GROSVENOR, Charles Henry (uncle of Charles Grosvenor Bond) (R Ohio) Sept. 20, 1833-Oct. 30, 1917; House 1885-91; 1893-1907.

GROSVENOR, Thomas Peabody (F N.Y.) Dec. 20, 1778-April 24, 1817; House Jan. 29, 1813-17.

GROUT, Jonathan (D Mass.) July 23, 1737-Sept. 8, 1807; House 1787-91.

GROUT, William Wallace (R Vt.) May 24, 1836-Oct. 7, 1902; House 1881-83; 1885-1901.

GROVE, William Barry (F N.C.) Jan. 15, 1764-March 30, 1818; House 1791-1803.

GROVER, Asa Porter (D Ky.) Feb. 18, 1819-July 20, 1887; House 1867-69.

GROVER, James R. Jr. (R N.Y.) March 5, 1919; House 1963- .

GROVER, La Fayette (D Ore.) Nov. 29, 1823-May 10, 1911; House Feb. 15-March 3, 1859; Senate 1877-83; Gov. 1870-77.

GROVER, Martin (NAD N.Y.) Oct. 20, 1811-Aug. 23, 1875; House 1845-47.

GROW, Galusha Aaron (R Pa.) Aug. 31, 1823-March 31, 1907; House 1851-57 (F-SD); 1857-63 (R); Feb. 26, 1894-1903 (R); Speaker 1861-63.

GRUENING, Ernest (D Alaska) Feb. 6, 1887- —; Senate 1959-69; Gov. (Terr.) 1939-53.

GRUNDY, Felix (WD Tenn.) Sept. 11, 1777-Dec. 19, 1840; House 1811-14; Senate Oct. 19, 1829-July 4, 1838; Nov. 19, 1839-Dec. 19, 1840; Atty. Gen. 1838-39.

GRUNDY, Joseph Ridgway (R Pa.) Jan. 13, 1863-March 3, 1961; Senate Dec. 11, 1929-Dec. 1, 1930.

GUBSER, Charles Samuel (R Calif.) Feb. 1, 1916; House 1953- .

GUDE, Gilbert (R Md.) March 9, 1923; House 1967- .

GUDGER, James Madison, Jr. (father of Katherine Gudger Langley) (D N.C.) Oct. 22, 1855-Feb. 29, 1920; House 1903-07; 1911-15.

GUENTHER, Richard William (R Wis.) Nov. 30, 1845-April 5, 1913; House 1881-89.

GUERNSEY, Frank Edward (R Maine) Oct. 15, 1866-Jan. 1, 1927; House Nov. 3, 1908-17.

GUEVARA, Pedro (Nat. P.I.) Feb. 23, 1879-Jan. 19, 1937; House (Res. Comm.) 1923-Feb. 14, 1936.

GUFFEY, Joseph F. (D Pa.) Dec. 29, 1870-March 6, 1959; Senate 1935-47.

GUGGENHEIM, Simon (R Colo.) Dec. 30, 1867-Nov. 2, 1941; Senate 1907-13.

GUILL, Ben Hugh (R Texas) Sept. 8, 1909; House May 6, 1950-51.

GUION, Walter (D La.) April 3, 1849-Feb. 7, 1927; Senate April 22-Nov. 5, 1918.

GUNCKEL, Lewis B. (R Ohio) Oct. 15, 1826-Oct. 3, 1903; House 1873-75.

GUNN, James (— Ga.) March 13, 1753-July 30, 1801; Senate 1789-1801; Cont. Cong. 1788-89.

GUNN, James (P Idaho) March 6, 1843-Nov. 5, 1911; House 1897-99.

GUNTER, Thomas Montague (D Ark.) Sept. 18, 1826-Jan. 12, 1904; House June 16, 1874-83.

GURLEY, Henry Hosford (W La.) May 20, 1788-March 16, 1833; House 1823-31.

GURLEY, John Addison (R Ohio) Dec. 9, 1813-Aug. 19, 1863; House 1859-63.

GURNEY, Chan (John Chandler) (R S.D.) May 21, 1896- —; Senate 1939-51.

GURNEY, Edward John (R Fla.) Jan. 12, 1914; House 1963-69; Senate 1969- .

GUSTINE, Amos (D Pa.) 1789-March 3, 1844; House May 4, 1841-43.

GUTHRIE, James (D Ky.) Dec. 5, 1792-March 13, 1869; Senate 1865-Feb. 7, 1868; Secy. of the Treasury 1853-57.

GUYER, Ulysses Samuel (R Kan.) Dec. 13, 1868-June 5, 1943; House Nov. 4, 1924-1925; 1927-June 5, 1943.

GUYON, James, Jr. (F N.Y.) Dec. 24, 1778-March 9, 1846; House Jan. 14, 1820-21.

GWIN, William McKendree (D Miss./Calif.) Oct. 9, 1805-Sept. 3, 1885; House 1841-43 (Miss.); Senate Sept. 9, 1850-1855; Jan. 13, 1857-1861 (Calif.).

GWINN, Ralph Waldo (R N.Y.) March 29, 1884; House 1945-59.

GWYNNE, John William (R Ohio) Oct. 20, 1889; House 1935-49.

H

HABERSHAM, Richard Wylly (SRD Ga.) Dec. 1786-Dec. 2, 1842; House 1839-Dec. 2, 1842.

HACKETT, Richard Nathaniel (D N.C.) Dec. 4, 1866-Nov. 22, 1923; House 1907-09.

HACKETT, Thomas C. (D Ga.) — -Oct. 8, 1851; House 1849-51.

HACKLEY, Aaron, Jr. (— N.Y.) May 6, 1783-Dec. 28, 1868; House 1819-21.

HACKNEY, Thomas (D Mo.) Dec. 11, 1861-Dec. 24, 1946; House 1907-09.

HADLEY, Lindley Hoag (R Wash.) June 19, 1861-Nov. 1, 1948; House 1915-33.

HADLEY, William Flavius Lester (R Ill.) June 15, 1847-April 25, 1901; House Dec. 2, 1895-97.

HAGAN, G. Elliott (D Ga.) May 24, 1916; House 1961- .

HAGANS, John Marshall (R W. Va.) Aug. 13, 1838-June 17, 1900; House 1873-75.

HAGEN, Harlan Francis (D Calif.) Oct. 8, 1914; House 1953-67.

HAGEN, Harold Christian (R Minn.) Nov. 10, 1901-March 19, 1957; House 1943-45 (F-L); 1945-55 (R).

HAGER, Alva Lysander (R Iowa) Oct. 29, 1850-Jan. 29, 1923; House 1893-99.

HAGER, John Sharpenstein (A-MD Calif.) March 12, 1818-March 19, 1890; Senate Dec. 23, 1873-75.

HAGGOTT, Warren Armstrong (R Colo.) May 18, 1864-April 29, 1958; House 1907-09.

HAHN, John (D Pa.) Oct. 30, 1776-Feb. 26, 1823; House 1815-17.

HAHN, Michael (R La.) Nov. 24, 1830-March 15, 1886; House Dec. 3, 1862-1863 (U); 1885-March 15, 1886 (R); Gov. 1864-65.

HAIGHT, Charles (D N.J.) Jan. 4, 1838-Aug. 1, 1891; House 1867-71.

HAIGHT, Edward (D N.Y.) March 26, 1817-Sept. 15, 1885; House 1861-63.

HAILE, William (— Miss.) 1797-March 7, 1837; House July 10, 1826-Sept. 12, 1828.

HAILEY, John (D Idaho) Aug. 29, 1835-April 10, 1921; House (Terr. Del.) 1873-75; 1885-87.

HAINER, Eugene Jerome (R Neb.) Aug. 16, 1851-March 17, 1929; House 1893-97.

HAINES, Charles Delemere (D N.Y.) June 9, 1856-April 11, 1929; House 1893-95.

HAINES, Harry Luther (D Pa.) Feb. 1, 1880-March 29, 1947; House 1931-39; 1941-43.

HALDEMAN, Richard Jacobs (D Pa.) May 19, 1831-Oct. 1, 1886; House 1869-73.

HALE, Artemas (W Mass.) Oct. 20, 1783-Aug. 3, 1882; House 1845-49.

HALE, Eugene (father of Frederick Hale) (R Maine) June 9, 1836-Oct. 28, 1918; House 1869-79; Senate 1881-1911.

HALE, Fletcher (R N.H.) Jan. 22, 1883-Oct. 22, 1931; House 1925-Oct. 22, 1931.

HALE, Frederick (son of Eugene Hale, grandson of Zachariah Chandler and cousin of Robert Hale) (R Maine) Oct. 7, 1874-Sept. 28, 1963; Senate 1917-41.

HALE, James Tracy (R Pa.) Oct. 14, 1810-April 6, 1865; House 1859-65.

HALE, John Blackwell (D Mo.) Feb. 27, 1831-Feb. 1, 1905; House 1885-87.

HALE, John Parker (F-S N.H.) March 31, 1806-Nov. 19, 1873; House 1843-45 (D); Senate 1847-53; July 30, 1855-1865 (F-S).

HALE, Nathan Wesley (R Tenn.) Feb. 11, 1860-Sept. 16, 1941; House 1905-09.

HALE, Robert (cousin of Frederick Hale) (R Maine) Nov. 29, 1889- —; House 1943-59.

HALE, Robert Safford (R N.Y.) Sept. 24, 1822-Dec. 14, 1881; House Dec. 3, 1866-1867; 1873-75.

HALE, Salma (D N.H.) March 7, 1787-Nov. 19, 1866; House 1817-19.

HALE, William (F N.H.) Aug. 6, 1765-Nov. 8, 1848; House 1809-11; 1813-17.

HALEY, Elisha (D Conn.) Jan. 21, 1776-Jan. 22, 1860; House 1835-39.

HALEY, James Andrew (D Fla.) Jan. 4, 1899; House 1953- .

HALL, Albert Richardson (R Ind.) Aug. 27, 1884-Nov. 29, 1969; House 1925-31.

HALL, Augustus (D Iowa) April 29, 1814-Feb. 1, 1861; House 1855-57.

HALL, Benton Jay (D Iowa) Jan. 13, 1835-Jan. 5, 1894; House 1885-87.

HALL, Bolling (WD Ga.) Dec. 25, 1767-Feb. 25, 1836; House 1811-17.

HALL, Chapin (R Pa.) July 12, 1816-Sept. 12, 1879; House 1859-61.

HALL, Darwin Scott (R Minn.) Jan. 23, 1844-Feb. 23, 1919; House 1889-91.

HALL, David McKee (D N.C.) May 16, 1819-Jan. 29, 1960; House 1959-Jan. 29, 1960.

HALL, Durward Gorham (R Mo.) Sept. 14, 1910; House 1961- .

HALL, Edwin Arthur (R N.Y.) Feb. 11, 1909; House Nov. 7, 1939-53.

HALL, George (D N.Y.) May 12, 1770-March 20, 1840; House 1819-21.

HALL, Hiland (W Vt.) July 20, 1795-Dec. 18, 1885; House Jan. 1, 1833-1843; Gov. 1858-60.

HALL, Homer William (R Ill.) July 22, 1870-Sept. 22, 1954; House 1927-33.

HALL, James Knox Polk (D Pa.) Sept. 30, 1844-Jan. 5, 1915; House 1899-Nov. 29, 1902.

HALL, Joseph (D Maine) June 26, 1793-Dec. 31, 1859; House 1833-37.

HALL, Joshua Gilman (R N.H.) Nov. 5, 1828-Oct. 31, 1898; House 1879-83.

HALL, Lawrence Washington (D Ohio) 1819-Jan. 18, 1863; House 1857-59.

HALL, Leonard Wood (R N.Y.) Oct. 2, 1900; House 1939-Dec. 31, 1952; Chrmn. Rep. Nat. Comm. 1952-57.

HALL, Nathan Kelsey (W N.Y.) March 28, 1810-March 2, 1874; House 1847-49; Postmaster General 1850-52.

HALL, Norman (D Pa.) Nov. 17, 1829-Sept. 29, 1917; House 1887-89.

HALL, Obed (D N.H.) Dec. 23, 1757-April 1, 1828; House 1811-13.

HALL, Osee Matson (D Minn.) Sept. 10, 1847-Nov. 26, 1914; 1891-95.

HALL, Phila (R S.D.) Dec. 31, 1865-Oct. 7, 1938; House 1907-09.

HALL, Robert Bernard (R Mass.) Jan. 28, 1812-April 15, 1868; House 1855-57 (AP); 1857-59 (R).

HALL, Robert Samuel (D Miss.) March 10, 1879-June 10, 1941; House 1929-33.

HALL, Thomas (R N.D.) June 6, 1869-Dec. 4, 1958; House Nov. 4, 1924-33.

HALL, Thomas H. (D N.C.) June 1773-June 30, 1853; House 1817-25; 1827-35.

HALL, Uriel Sebree (son of William Augustus Hall and nephew of Willard Preble Hall) (D Mo.) April 12, 1852-Dec. 30, 1932; House 1893-97.

HALL, Willard (D Del.) Dec. 24, 1780-May 10, 1875; House 1817-Jan. 22, 1821.

HALL, Willard Preble (brother of William Augustus Hall and uncle of Uriel Sebree Hall) (D Mo.) May 9, 1820-Nov. 2, 1882; House 1847-53; Gov. 1864-65.

HALL, William (D Tenn.) Feb. 11, 1775-Oct. 7, 1856; House 1831-33; Gov. 1829.

HALL, William Augustus (father of Uriel Sebree Hall and brother of Willard Preble Hall) (D Mo.) Oct. 15, 1815-Dec. 15, 1888; House Jan. 20, 1862-65.

HALL, Wilton Earle (D S.C.) March 11, 1901; Senate Nov. 20, 1944-45.

HALLECK, Charles Abraham (R Ind.) Aug. 22, 1900; House Jan. 29, 1935-69.

HALLOCK, John, Jr. (D N.Y.) July 1783-Dec. 6, 1840; House 1825-29.

HALLOWAY, Ransom (W N.Y.) about 1793-April 6, 1851; House 1849-51.

HALLOWELL, Edwin (D Pa.) April 2, 1844-Sept. 13, 1916; House 1891-93.

HALPERN, Seymore (R N.Y.) Nov. 19, 1913; House 1959- .

HALSELL, John Edward (D Ky.) Sept. 11, 1826-Dec. 26, 1899; House 1883-87.

HALSEY, George Armstrong (R N.J.) Dec. 7, 1827-April 1, 1894; House 1867-69; 1871-73.

HALSEY, Jehiel Howell (son of Silas Halsey) (JD N.Y.) Oct. 7, 1788-Dec. 5, 1867; House 1829-31.

HALSEY, Nicoll (son of Silas Halsey (D N.Y.) March 8, 1782-March 3, 1865; House 1833-35.

HALSEY, Silas (father of Jehiel Howell Halsey and Nicoll Halsey) (D N.Y.) Oct. 16, 1743-Nov. 19, 1832; House 1805-07.

HALSEY, Thomas Jefferson (R Mo.) May 4, 1863-March 17, 1951; House 1929-31.

HALSTEAD, William (W N.J.) June 4, 1794-March 4, 1878; House 1837-39; 1841-43.

HALTERMAN, Frederick (R Pa.) Oct. 22, 1831-March 22, 1907; House 1895-97.

HALVORSON, Kittel (FA/Prohib. Minn.) Dec. 15, 1846-July 12, 1936; House 1891-93.

HAMBLETON, Samuel (D Md.) Jan. 8, 1812-Dec. 9, 1886; House 1869-73.

HAMER, Thomas Lyon (uncle of Thomas Ray Hamer) (D Ohio) July 1800-Dec. 2, 1846; House 1833-39.

HAMER, Thomas Ray (nephew of Thomas Lyon Hamer) (R Idaho) May 4, 1864-Dec. 22, 1950; House 1909-11.

HAMILL, James Alphonsus (D N.J.) March 30, 1877-Dec. 15, 1941; House 1907-21.

HAMILL, Patrick (D Md.) April 28, 1817-Jan. 15, 1895; House 1869-71.

HAMILTON, Andrew Holman (D Ind.) June 7, 1834-May 9, 1895; House 1875-79.

HAMILTON, Andrew Jackson (brother of Morgan Calvin Hamilton) (ID Texas) Jan. 28, 1815-April 11, 1875; House 1859-61; Military Gov. 1862-65; Provisional Gov. 1865-66.

HAMILTON, Charles Mann (R N.Y.) Jan. 23, 1874-Jan. 3, 1942; House 1913-19.

HAMILTON, Charles Memorial (R Fla.) Nov. 1, 1840-Oct. 22, 1875; House July 1, 1868-1871.

HAMILTON, Cornelius Springer (R Ohio) Jan. 2, 1821-Dec. 22, 1867; House March 4-Dec. 22, 1867.

HAMILTON, Daniel Webster (D Iowa) Dec. 20, 1861-Aug. 21, 1936; House 1907-09.

HAMILTON, Edward La Rue (R Mich.) Dec. 9, 1857-Nov. 2, 1923; House 1897-1921.

HAMILTON, Finley (D Ky.) June 19, 1886-Jan. 10, 1940; House 1933-35.

HAMILTON, James, Jr. (SRFT S.C.) May 8, 1786-Nov. 15, 1857; House Dec. 13, 1822-29; Gov. 1830-32.

HAMILTON, John (D Pa.) Nov. 25, 1754-Aug. 22, 1837; House 1805-07.

HAMILTON, John M. (D W. Va.) March 16, 1855-Dec. 27, 1916; House 1911-13.

HAMILTON, John Taylor (D Iowa) Oct. 16, 1843-Jan. 25, 1925; House 1891-93.

HAMILTON, Lee Herbert (D Ind.) April 20, 1931; House 1965-

HAMILTON, Morgan Calvin (brother of Andrew Jackson Hamilton) (R Texas) Feb. 25, 1809-Nov. 21, 1893; Senate March 30, 1870-77.

HAMILTON, Norman Rond (D Va.) Nov. 13, 1877-March 26, 1964; House 1937-39.

HAMILTON, Robert (D N.J.) Dec. 9, 1809-March 14, 1878; House 1873-77.

HAMILTON, William Thomas (D Md.) Sept. 8, 1820-Oct. 26, 1888; House 1849-55; Senate 1869-75; Gov. 1879-83.

HAMLIN, Courtney Walker (cousin of William Edward Barton) (D Mo.) Oct. 27, 1858-Feb. 16, 1950; House 1903-05; 1907-19.

HAMLIN, Edward Stowe (W Ohio) July 6, 1808-Nov. 23, 1894; House Oct. 8, 1844-45.

HAMLIN, Hannibal (R Maine) Aug. 27, 1809-July 4, 1891; House 1843-47 (D); Senate June 8, 1848-Jan. 7, 1857 (D); 1857-Jan. 17, 1961 and 1869-81 (R); Gov. Jan. 8-Feb. 20, 1857; Vice President 1861-65.

HAMLIN, Simon Moulton (D Maine) Aug. 10, 1866-July 27, 1939; House 1935-37.

HAMMER, William Cicero (D N.C.) March 24, 1865-Sept. 26, 1930; House 1921-Sept. 26, 1930.

HAMMERSCHMIDT, John Paul (R Ark.) May 4, 1922; House 1967- .

HAMMETT, William H. (D Miss.) — -—; House 1843-45.

HAMMOND, Edward (D Md.) March 17, 1812-Oct. 19, 1882; House 1849-53.

HAMMOND, Jabez Delno (D N.Y.) Aug. 2, 1778-Aug. 18, 1855; House 1815-17.

HAMMOND, James Henry (SRD S.C.) Nov. 15, 1807-Nov. 13, 1964; House 1835-Feb. 26, 1836 (SRFT); Senate Dec. 7, 1857-Nov. 11, 1860 (SRD); Gov. 1842-44.

HAMMOND, John (R N.Y.) Aug. 17, 1827-May 28, 1889; House 1879-83.

HAMMOND, Nathaniel Job (D Ga.) Dec. 26, 1833-April 20, 1899; House 1879-87.

HAMMOND, Peter Francis (D Ohio) June 30, 1887; House Nov. 30, 1936-37.

HAMMOND, Robert Hanna (VBD Pa.) April 28, 1791-June 2, 1847; House 1837-41.

HAMMOND, Samuel (D Ga.) Sept. 21, 1757-Sept. 11, 1842; House 1803-Feb. 2, 1805; Gov. - - —.

HAMMOND, Thomas (D Ind.) Feb. 27, 1843-Sept. 21, 1909; House 1893-95.

HAMMOND, Winfield Scott (D Minn.) Nov. 17, 1863-Dec. 30, 1915; House 1907-Jan. 6, 1915; Gov. Jan. 7, 1914-Dec. 30, 1915.

HAMMONS, David (D Maine) May 12, 1808-Nov. 7, 1888; House 1847-49.

HAMMONS, Joseph (JD N.H.) March 3, 1787-March 29, 1836; House 1829-33

HAMPTON, James Giles (W N.J.) June 13, 1814-Sept. 22, 1861; House 1845-49.

HAMPTON, Moses (W Pa.) Oct. 28, 1803-June 27, 1878; House 1847-51.

HAMPTON, Wade (D S.C.) 1752-Feb. 4, 1835; House 1795-97; 1803-05.

HAMPTON, Wade (D S.C.) (grandson of the preceding) March 28, 1818-April 11, 1902; Senate 1879-91; Gov. 1876-79.

HANBACK, Lewis (R Kan.) March 27, 1839-Sept. 7, 1897; House 1883-87.

HANBURY, Harry Alfred (R N.Y.) Jan. 1, 1863-Aug. 22, 1940; House 1901-03.

HANCHETT, Luther (R Wis.) Oct. 25, 1825-Nov. 24, 1862; House 1861-Nov. 24, 1862.

HANCOCK, Clarence Eugene (R N.Y.) Feb. 13, 1885-Jan. 3, 1948; House Nov. 8, 1927-47.

HANCOCK, Franklin Wills, Jr. (D N.C.) Nov. 1, 1894-Jan. 23, 1969; House Nov. 4, 1930-39.

HANCOCK, George (D Va.) June 13, 1754-July 18, 1820; House 1793-97.

HANCOCK, John (D Texas) Oct. 24, 1824-July 19, 1893; House 1871-77; 1883-85.

HAND, Augustus Cincinnatus (D N.Y.) Sept. 4, 1803-March 8, 1878; House 1839-41.

HAND, Thomas Millet (R N.J.) July 7, 1902-Dec. 26, 1956; House 1945-Dec. 26, 1956.

HANDLEY, William Anderson (D Ala.) Dec. 15, 1834-June 23, 1909; House 1871-73.

HANDY, Levin Irving (nephew of William Campbell Preston Breckinridge) (D Del.) Dec. 24, 1861-Feb. 3, 1922; House 1897-99.

HANKS, James Millander (D Ark.) Feb. 12, 1833-May 24, 1909; House 1871-73.

HANLEY, James M. (D N.Y.) July 19, 1920; House 1965- .

HANLY, James Franklin (R Ind.) April 4, 1863-Aug. 1, 1920; House 1895-97; Gov. 1905-09.

HANNA, John (R Ind.) Sept. 3, 1827-Oct. 24, 1882; House 1877-79.

HANNA, John Andre (grandfather of Archibald McAllister) (A-F Pa.) 1762-July 23, 1805; House 1797-July 23, 1805.

HANNA, Louis Benjamin (R N.D.) Aug. 9, 1861-April 23, 1948; House 1909-Jan. 7, 1913; Gov. 1913-17.

HANNA, Marcus Alonzo (father of Ruth Hanna McCormick) (R Ohio) Sept. 24, 1837-Feb. 15, 1904; Senate March 5, 1897-Feb. 15, 1904.

HANNA, Richard T. (D Calif.) June 9, 1914; House 1963- .

HANNA, Robert (W Ind.) April 6, 1786-Nov. 16, 1858; Senate Aug. 19, 1831-Jan. 3, 1832.

HANNEGAN, Edward Allen (D Ind.) June 25, 1807-Feb. 25, 1859; House 1833-37; Senate 1843-49.

HANSEN, Clifford Peter (R Wyo.) Oct. 16, 1912; Senate 1967- —; Gov. 1963-67.

HANSEN, George Vernon (R Idaho) Sept. 14, 1930; House 1965-69.

HANSEN, John Robert (D Iowa) Aug. 24, 1901; House 1965-67.

HANSEN, Julia Butler (D Wash.) June 14, 1907; House Nov. 8, 1960- .

HANSEN, Orval (R Idaho) Aug. 3, 1926; House 1969- .

HANSON, Alexander Contee (grandnephew of Benjamin Contee) (F Md.) Feb. 27, 1786-April 23, 1819; House 1813-16; Senate Dec. 20, 1816-April 23, 1819.

HARALSON, Hugh Anderson (D Ga.) Nov. 13, 1805-Sept. 25, 1854; House 1843-51.

HARALSON, Jeremiah (R Ala.) April 1, 1846-about 1916; House 1875-77.

HARD, Gideon (W N.Y.) April 29, 1797-April 27, 1885; House 1833-37.

HARDEMAN, Thomas, Jr. (D Ga.) Jan. 12, 1825-March 6, 1891; House 1859-Jan. 23, 1861; 1883-85.

HARDEN, Cecil Murray (R Ind.) Nov. 21, 1894- —; House 1949-59.

HARDENBERGH, Augustus Albert (D N.J.) May 18, 1830-Oct. 5, 1889; House 1875-79; 1881-83.

HARDIN, Benjamin (cousin of Martin Davis Hardin) (W Ky.) Feb. 29, 1784-Sept. 24, 1852; House 1815-17; 1819-23; 1833-37.

HARDIN, John J. (son of Martin Davis Hardin) (W Ill.) Jan. 6, 1810-Feb. 23, 1847; House 1843-45.

HARDIN, Martin Davis (cousin of Benjamin Hardin and father of John J. Hardin) (D Ky.) June 21, 1780-Oct. 8, 1823; Senate Nov. 13, 1816-17.

HARDING, Aaron (UD Ky.) Feb. 20, 1805-Dec. 24, 1875; House 1861-67.

HARDING, Abner Clark (R Ill.) Feb. 10, 1807-July 19, 1874; House 1865-69.

HARDING, Benjamin Franklin (R Ore.) Jan. 4, 1823-June 16, 1899; Senate Sept. 12, 1862-65.

HARDING, John Eugene (R Ohio) June 27, 1877-July 26, 1959; House 1907-09.

HARDING, Warren Gamaliel (R Ohio) Nov. 2, 1865-Aug. 2, 1923; Senate 1915-Jan. 13, 1921; President 1921-Aug. 2, 1923.

HARDING, Ralph R (D Idaho) Sept. 9, 1929; House 1961-65.

HARDWICK, Thomas William (D Ga.) Dec. 9, 1872-Jan. 31, 1944; House 1903-Nov. 2, 1914; Senate Nov. 4, 1914-19; Gov. 1921-23.

HARDY, Alexander Merrill (R Ind.) Dec. 16, 1847-Aug. 31, 1927; House 1895-97.

HARDY, Guy Urban (R Colo.) April 4, 1872-Jan. 26, 1947; House 1919-33.

HARDY, John (D N.Y.) Sept. 19, 1835-Dec. 9, 1913; House Dec. 5, 1881-85.

HARDY, Porter, Jr. (D Va.) June 1, 1903; House 1947-69.

HARDY, Rufus (D Texas) Dec. 16, 1855-March 13, 1943; House 1907-23.

HARE, Butler Black (father of James Butler Hare) (D S.C.) Nov. 25, 1875-Dec. 30, 1967; House 1925-33; 1939-47.

HARE, Darius Dodge (D Ohio) Jan. 9, 1843-Feb. 10, 1897; House 1891-95.

HARE, James Butler (son of Butler Black Hare) (D S.C.) Sept. 4, 1918-July 16, 1966; House 1949-51.

HARE, Silas (D Texas) Nov. 13, 1827-Nov. 26, 1907; House 1887-91.

HARGIS, Denver David (D Kan.) July 22, 1921; House 1959-61.

HARLAN, Aaron (cousin of Andrew Jackson Harlan) (W Ohio) Sept. 8, 1802-Jan. 8, 1868; House 1853-59.

HARLAN, Andrew Jackson (cousin of Aaron Harlan) (D Ind.) March 29, 1815-May 19, 1907; House 1849-51; 1853-55.

HARLAN, Byron Berry (D Ohio) Oct. 22, 1886-Nov. 11, 1949; House 1931-39.

HARLAN, James (W Ky.) June 22, 1800-Feb. 18, 1863; House 1835-39.

HARLAN, James (R Iowa) Aug. 26, 1820-Oct. 5, 1899; Senate Dec. 31, 1855-Jan. 12, 1857 (W); Jan. 29, 1857-May 15, 1865; 1867-73; Secy. of the Interior May 15, 1865-July 27, 1866.

HARLESS, Richard Fielding (D Ariz.) Aug. 6, 1905-Nov. 24, 1970; House 1943-49.

HARMANSON, John Henry (D La.) Jan. 15, 1803-Oct. 24, 1850; House 1845-Oct. 24, 1850.

HARMER, Alfred Crout (R Pa.) Aug. 8, 1825-March 6, 1900; House 1871-75; 1877-March 6, 1900.

HARMON, Randall S. (D Ind.) July 19, 1903; House 1959-61.

HARNESS, Forest Arthur (R Ind.) June 24, 1895- —; House 1939-49.

HARPER, Alexander (W Ohio) Feb. 5, 1786-Dec. 1, 1860; House 1837-39; 1843-47; 1851-53.

HARPER, Francis Jacob (D Pa.) March 5, 1800-March 18, 1837; House March 4-18, 1837.

HARPER, James (W Pa.) March 28, 1780-March 31, 1873; House 1833-35 (CD); 1835-37 (W).

HARPER, James Clarence (C N.C.) Dec. 6, 1819-Jan. 8, 1890; House 1871-73.

HARPER, John Adams (WD N.H.) Nov. 2, 1779-June 18, 1816; House 1811-13.

HARPER, Joseph Morrill (D N.H.) June 21, 1787-Jan. 15, 1865; House 1831-35.

HARPER, Robert Goodloe (F S.C./Md.) Jan. 1765-Jan. 14, 1825; House Feb. 5, 1795-1801 (S.C.); Senate Jan. 29-Dec. 6, 1816 (Md.)

HARPER, William (SRD S.C.) Jan. 17, 1790-Oct. 10, 1847; Senate March 8-Nov. 29, 1826.

HARRELD, John William (R Okla.) Jan. 24, 1872-Dec. 26, 1950; House Nov. 8, 1919-21; Senate 1921-27.

HARRIES, William Henry (D Minn.) Jan. 15, 1843-July 23, 1921; House 1891-93.

HARRINGTON, Henry William (D Ind.) Sept. 12, 1825-March 20, 1882; House 1863-65.

HARRINGTON, Michael J. (D Mass.) Sept. 2, 1936; House Sept. 30, 1969- .

HARRINGTON, Vincent Francis (D Iowa) May 16, 1903-Nov. 29, 1943; House 1937-Sept. 5, 1942.

HARRIS, Benjamin Gwinn (D Md.) Dec. 13, 1805-April 4, 1895; House 1863-67.

HARRIS, Benjamin Winslow (father of Robert Orr Harris) (R Mass.) Nov. 10, 1823-Feb. 7, 1907; House 1873-83.

HARRIS, Charles Murray (D Ill.) April 10, 1821-Sept. 20, 1896; House 1863-65.

HARRIS, Christopher Columbus (D Ala.) Jan. 28, 1842-Dec. 28, 1935; House May 11, 1914-15.

HARRIS, Fred R. (D Okla.) Nov. 13, 1930; Senate Nov. 4, 1964- .

HARRIS, George Emrick (R Miss.) Jan. 6, 1827-March 19, 1911; House Feb. 23, 1870-73.

HARRIS, Henry Richard (D Ga.) Feb. 2, 1828-Oct. 15, 1909; House 1873-79; 1885-87.

HARRIS, Henry Schenck (D N.J.) Dec. 27, 1850-May 2, 1902; House 1881-83.

HARRIS, Ira (grandfather of Henry Riggs Rathbone) (R N.Y.) May 31, 1802-Dec. 2, 1875; Senate 1861-67.

HARRIS, Isham Green (D Tenn.) Feb. 10, 1818-July 8, 1897; House 1849-53; Senate 1877-July 8, 1897; President pro tempore 1893-95; Governor 1858-64.

HARRIS, James Morrison (AP Md.) Nov. 20, 1817-July 16, 1898; House 1855-61.

HARRIS, John (cousin of Robert Harris) (— N.Y.) Sept. 26, 1760-Nov., 1824; House 1807-09.

HARRIS, John Spafford (R La.) Dec. 18, 1825-Jan. 25, 1906; Senate July 9, 1868-71.

HARRIS, John Thomas (cousin of John Hill, of Virginia) (D Va.) May 8, 1823-Oct. 14, 1899; House 1859-61; 1871-81.

HARRIS, Mark (— Maine) Jan. 27, 1779-March 2, 1843; House Dec. 2, 1822-23.

HARRIS, Oren (D Ark.) Dec. 20, 1903; House 1941-Feb. 2, 1966.

HARRIS, Robert (cousin of John Harris) (— Pa.) Sept. 5, 1768-Sept. 3, 1851; House 1823-27.

HARRIS, Robert Orr (son of Benjamin Winslow Harris) (R Mass.) Nov. 8, 1854-June 13, 1926; House 1911-13.

HARRIS, Sampson Willis (D Ala.) Feb. 23, 1809-April 1, 1857; House 1847-57.

HARRIS, Stephen Ross (uncle of Ebenezer Byron Finley) (R Ohio) May 22, 1824-Jan. 15, 1905; House 1895-97.

HARRIS, Thomas K. (D Tenn.) — -March 18, 1816; House 1813-15.

HARRIS, Thomas Langrell (D Ill.) Oct. 29, 1816-Nov. 24, 1858; House 1849-51; 1855-Nov. 24, 1858.

HARRIS, Wiley Pope (D Miss.) Nov. 9, 1818-Dec. 3, 1891; House 1853-55.

HARRIS, William Alexander (D Va.) Aug. 24, 1805-March 28, 1864; House 1841-43.

HARRIS, William Alexander (son of the preceding) (D Kan.) Oct. 29, 1841-Dec. 20, 1909; House 1893-95 (P); Senate 1897-1903 (D).

HARRIS, William Julius (great-grandson of Charles Hooks) (D Ga.) Feb. 3, 1868-April 18, 1932; Senate 1919-April 18, 1932.

HARRIS, Winder Russell (D Va.) Dec. 3, 1888- —; House April 8, 1931-Sept. 15, 1944.

HARRISON, Albert Galliton (VBD Mo.) June 26, 1800-Sept. 7, 1839; House 1835-39.

HARRISON, Benjamin (grandson of President William Henry Harrison; son of John Scott Harrison of Ohio; and grandfather of William Henry Harrison of Wyoming) (R Ind.) Aug. 20, 1833-March 13, 1901; Senate 1881-87; President 1889-93.

HARRISON, Burr Powell (son of Thomas Walter Harrison) (D Va.) July 2, 1904; House Nov. 6, 1946-63.

HARRISON, Byron Patton (Pat) (D Miss.) Aug. 29, 1881-June 22, 1941; House 1911-19; Senate 1919-June 22, 1941; President pro tempore 1941.

HARRISON, Carter Bassett (brother of President William Henry Harrison) (— Va.) — -April 18, 1808; House 1793-99.

HARRISON, Carter Henry (D Ill.) Feb. 15, 1825-Oct. 28, 1893; House 1875-79.

HARRISON, Francis Burton (D N.Y.) Dec. 18, 1873-Nov. 21, 1957; House 1903-05; 1907-Sept. 1, 1913.

HARRISON, George Paul (D Ala.) March 19, 1841-July 17, 1922; House Nov. 6, 1894-97.

HARRISON, Horace Harrison (R Tenn.) Aug. 7, 1829-Dec. 20, 1885; House 1873-75.

HARRISON, John Scott (son of President William Henry Harrison, and father of President Benjamin Harrison) (W Ohio) Oct. 4, 1804-May 25, 1878; House 1853-57.

HARRISON, Richard Almgill (UD Ohio) April 8, 1824-July 30, 1904; House July 4, 1861-63.

HARRISON, Robert Dinsmore (R Neb.) Jan. 26, 1897- —; House Dec. 4, 1951-59.

HARRISON, Samuel Smith (D Pa.) 1780-April, 1853; House 1833-37.

HARRISON, Thomas Walter (father of Burr Powell Harrison) (D Va.) Aug. 5, 1856-May 9, 1935; House Nov. 7, 1916-Dec. 15, 1922; 1923-29.

HARRISON, William Henry (father of John Scott Harrison, brother of Carter Basset Harrison, grandfather of Benjamin Harrison and great-great-grandfather of William Henry Harrison of Wyoming) (W Ohio); Feb. 9, 1773-April 4, 1841; House (Terr. Del.) 1799-May 14, 1800; (Rep.) Oct. 8, 1816-19; Senate 1825-May 20, 1828; President March 4-April 4, 1841; Terr. Gov. of Indiana 1801-13.

HARRISON, William Henry (great-great-grandson of President William Henry Harrison and grandson of President Benjamin Harrison and Alvin Saunders) (R Wyo.) Aug. 10, 1896; House 1951-55, 1961-65, 1967-69.

HARSHA, William H. (R Ohio) Jan. 1, 1921; House 1961- .

HART, Alphonso (R Ohio) July 4, 1830-Dec. 23, 1910; House 1883-85.

HART, Archibald Chapman (D N.J.) Feb. 27, 1873-July 24, 1935; House Nov. 5, 1912-March 3, 1913; July 22, 1913-17.

HART, Edward Joseph (D N.J.) March 25, 1893-April 20, 1961; House 1935-55.

HART, Elizur Kirke (D N.Y.) April 8, 1841-Feb. 18, 1893; House 1877-79.

HART, Emanuel Bernard (D N.Y.) Oct. 27, 1809-Aug. 29, 1897; House 1851-53.

HART, Joseph Johnson (D Pa.) April 18, 1859-July 13, 1926; House 1895-97.

HART, Michael James (D Mich.) July 16, 1877-Feb. 14, 1951; House Nov. 3, 1931-35.

HART, Philip A. (D Mich.) Dec. 10, 1912; Senate 1959- .

HART, Roswell (R N.Y.) Aug. 4, 1824-April 20, 1883; House 1865-67.

HART, Thomas Charles (R Conn.) June 12, 1877- —; Senate Feb. 15, 1945-Nov. 5, 1946.

HARTER, Dow Watters (D Ohio) Jan. 2, 1885- —; House 1933-43.

HARTER, John Francis (R N.Y.) Sept. 1, 1897-Dec. 20, 1947; House 1939-41.

HARTER, Michael Daniel (grandson of Robert Moore) (D Ohio) April 6, 1846-Feb. 22, 1896; House 1891-95.

HARTKE, Rupert Vance (D Ind.) May 31, 1919; Senate 1959- .

HARTLEY, Fred Allan, Jr. (R N.J.) Feb. 22, 1902-May 11, 1969; House 1929-49.

HARTLEY, Thomas (— Pa.) Sept. 7, 1748-Dec. 21, 1800; House 1789-Dec. 21, 1800.

HARTMAN, Charles Sampson (R Mont.) March 1, 1861-Aug. 3, 1929; House 1893-97 (R); 1897-99 (Sil. R).

HARTMAN, Jesse Lee (R Pa.) June 18, 1853-Feb. 17, 1930; House 1911-13.

HARTRIDGE, Julian (D Ga.) Sept. 9, 1829-Jan. 8, 1879; House 1875-Jan. 8, 1879.

HARTZELL, William (D Ill.) Feb. 20, 1837-Aug. 14, 1903; House 1875-79.

HARVEY, David Archibald (R Okla.) March 20, 1845-May 24, 1916; House (Terr. Del.) Nov. 4, 1890-93.

HARVEY, James (R Mich.) July 4, 1922; House 1961- .

HARVEY, James Madison (R Kan.) Sept. 21, 1833-April 15, 1894; Senate Feb. 2, 1874-77; Gov. 1868-72.

HARVEY, Jonathan (brother of Matthew Harvey) (— N.H.) Feb. 25, 1780-Aug. 23, 1859; House 1825-31.

HARVEY, Matthew (brother of Jonathan Harvey) (D N.H.) June 21, 1781-April 7, 1866; House 1821-25; Gov. 1830.

HARVEY, Ralph (R Ind.) Aug. 9, 1901; House Nov. 4, 1947-59; 1961-Dec. 30, 1966.

HASBROUCK, Abraham Bruyn (cousin of Abraham Joseph Hasbrouck) (NR N.Y.) Nov. 29, 1791-Feb. 24, 1879; House 1825-27.

HASBROUCK, Abraham Joseph (cousin of Abraham Bruyn Hasbrouck) (Clinton D N.Y.) Oct. 16, 1773-Jan. 12, 1845; House 1813-15.

HASBROUCK, Josiah (— N.Y.) March 5, 1755-March 19, 1821; House April 28, 1803-05, 1817-19.

HASCALL, Augustus Porter (W N.Y.) June 24, 1800-June 27, 1872; House 1851-53.

HASKELL, Dudley Chase (grandfather of Otis Halbert Holmes) (R Kan.) March 23, 1842-Dec. 16, 1883; House 1877-Dec. 16, 1883.

HASKELL, Harry Garner, Jr. (R Del.) May 27, 1921; House 1957-59.

HASKELL, Reuben Locke (R N.Y.) Oct. 5, 1878- —; House 1915-Dec. 31, 1919.

HASKELL, William T. (nephew of Charles Ready) (W Tenn.) July 21, 1818-March 12, 1859; House 1847-49.

HASKIN, John Bussing (D N.Y.) Aug. 27, 1821-Sept. 18, 1895; House 1857-61.

HASKINS, Kittredge (R Vt.) April 8, 1836-Aug. 7, 1916; House 1901-09.

HASTINGS, Daniel Oren (R Del.) March 5, 1874-May 9, 1966; Senate Dec. 10, 1928-37.

HASTINGS, George (D N.Y.) March 13, 1807-Aug. 29, 1866; House 1853-55.

HASTINGS, James F. (R N.Y.) April 10, 1926; House 1969- .

HASTINGS, John (JD Ohio) 1778-Dec. 8, 1854; House 1839-43.

HASTINGS, Serranus Clinton (D Iowa) Nov. 14, 1813-Feb. 18, 1893; House Dec. 28, 1846-47.

HASTINGS, Seth (father of William Soden Hastings) (F Mass.) April 8, 1762-Nov. 19, 1831; House Aug. 24, 1801-07.

HASTINGS, William Soden (son of Seth Hastings) (D Mass.) June 3, 1798-June 17, 1842; House 1837-June 17, 1842.

HASTINGS, William Wirt (D Okla.) Dec. 31, 1866-April 8, 1938; House 1915-21; 1923-35.

HATCH, Carl Atwood (D N.M) Nov. 27, 1889-Sept. 12, 1963; Senate Oct. 10, 1933-49.

HATCH, Herschel Harrison (R Mich.) Feb. 17, 1837-Nov. 30, 1920; House 1883-85.

HATCH, Israel Thompson (D N.Y.) June 30, 1808-Sept. 24, 1875; House 1857-59.

HATCH, Jethro Ayers (R Ind.) June 18, 1837-Aug. 3, 1912; House 1895-97.

HATCH, William Henry (D Mo.) Sept. 11, 1833-Dec. 23, 1896; House 1879-95.

HATCHER, Robert Anthony (D Mo.) Feb. 24, 1819-Dec. 4, 1886; House 1873-79.

HATFIELD, Henry Drury (R W. Va.) Sept. 15, 1875-Oct. 23, 1962; Senate 1929-35; Gov. 1913-17.

HATFIELD, Mark O. (R Ore.) July 12, 1922; Senate Jan. 10, 1967- ; Gov. 1959-67.

HATHAWAY, Samuel Gilbert (D N.Y.) July 18, 1780-May 2, 1867; House 1833-35.

HATHAWAY, William Dodd (D Maine) Feb. 21, 1924; House 1965- .

HATHORN, Henry Harrison (R N.Y.) Nov. 28, 1813-Feb. 20, 1887; House 1873-77.

HATHORN, John (F N.Y.) Jan. 9, 1749-Feb. 19, 1825; House 1789-91; 1795-97; Cont. Cong. 1788.

HATTON, Robert Hopkins (AP Tenn.) Nov. 2, 1826-May 31, 1862; House 1859-61.

HAUGEN, Gilbert Nelson (R Iowa) April 21, 1859-July 18, 1933; House 1899-1933.

HAUGEN, Nils Pederson (R Wis.) March 9, 1849-April 23, 1931; House 1887-95.

HAUGHEY, Thomas (R Ala.) 1826-Aug. 1869; House July 21, 1868-69.

HAUN, Henry Peter (D Calif.) Jan. 18, 1815-June 6, 1860; Senate Nov. 3, 1859-60.

HAVEN, Nathaniel Appleton (F N.H.) July 19, 1762-March 13, 1831; House 1809-11.

HAVEN, Solomon George (W N.Y.) Nov. 27, 1810-Dec. 24, 1861; House 1851-57.

HAVENNER, Franck Roberts (D Calif.) Sept. 20, 1882-July 24, 1967; House 1937-39 (Pro.); 1939-41 and 1945-53 (D).

HAVENS, Harrison Eugene (R Mo.) Dec. 15, 1837-Aug. 16, 1916; House 1871-75.

HAVENS, James Smith (D N.Y.) May 28, 1859-Feb. 27, 1927; House April 19, 1910-11.

HAVENS, Jonathan Nicoll (D N.Y.) June 18, 1757-Oct. 25, 1799; House 1795-Oct. 25, 1799.

HAWES, Albert Gallatin (brother of Richard Hawes, nephew of Aylett Hawes, grand-uncle of Harry Bartow Hawes, and cousin of Aylett Hawes Buckner) (JD Ky.) April 1, 1804-March 14, 1849; House 1831-37.

HAWES, Aylett (uncle of Richard Hawes, Albert Gallatin Hawes, and Aylett Hawes Buckner) (D Va.) April 21, 1768-Aug. 31, 1833; House 1811-17.

HAWES, Harry Bartow (grandnephew of Albert Gallatin Hawes) (D Mo.) Nov. 15, 1869-July 31, 1937; House 1921-Oct. 15, 1926; Senate Dec. 6, 1926-Feb. 3, 1933.

HAWES, Richard (brother of Albert Gallatin Hawes, nephew of Aylett Hawes and cousin of Aylett Hawes Buckner) (W Ky.) Feb. 6, 1797-May 25, 1877; House 1837-41.

HAWK, Robert Moffett Allison (R Ill.) April 23, 1839-June 29, 1882; House 1879-June 29, 1882.

HAWKES, Albert Wahl (R N.J.) Nov. 20, 1878-May 9, 1971; Senate 1943-49.

HAWKES, James (— N.Y.) Dec. 13, 1776-Oct. 2, 1865; House 1821-23.

HAWKINS, Augustus F. (D Calif.) Aug. 31, 1907; House 1963- .

HAWKINS, Benjamin (uncle of Micajah Thomas Hawkins) (F N.C.) Aug. 15, 1754-June 6, 1816; Senate Nov. 27, 1789-1795; Cont. Cong. 1791-84, 1786-87.

HAWKINS, George Sydney (D Fla.) 1808-March 15, 1878; House 1857-Jan. 21, 1861.

HAWKINS, Isaac Roberts (R Tenn.) May 16, 1818-Aug. 12, 1880; House July 24, 1866-71.

HAWKINS, Joseph (Ad. D N.Y.) Nov. 14, 1781-April 20, 1832; House 1829-31.

HAWKINS, Joseph H. (F Ky.) — -1823; House March 29, 1814-15.

HAWKINS, Micajah Thomas (nephew of Benjamin Hawkins and Nathaniel Macon) (D N.C.) May 20, 1790-Dec. 22, 1858; House Dec. 15, 1831-41.

HAWKS, Charles, Jr. (R Wis.) July 7, 1899-Jan. 6, 1960; House 1939-41.

HAWLEY, John Baldwin (R Ill.) Feb. 9, 1831-May 24, 1895; House 1869-75.

HAWLEY, Joseph Roswell (R Conn.) Oct. 31, 1826-March 17, 1905; House Dec. 2, 1872-75, 1879-81; Senate 1881-1905; Gov. 1866.

HAWLEY, Robert Bradley (R Texas) Oct. 25, 1849-Nov. 28, 1921; House 1897-1901.

HAWLEY, Willis Chatman (R Ore.) May 5, 1864-July 24, 1941; House 1907-33.

HAWS, John Henry Hobart (W N.Y.) 1809-Jan. 27, 1858; House 1851-53.

HAY, Andrew Kessler (W N.J.) Jan. 19, 1809-Feb. 7, 1881; House 1849-51.

HAY, James (D Va.) Jan. 9, 1856-June 12, 1931; House 1897-Oct. 1, 1916.

HAY, John Breese (R Ill.) Jan. 8, 1834-June 16, 1916; House 1869-73.

HAYDEN, Carl (D Ariz.) Oct. 2, 1877; House Feb. 19, 1912-27; Senate 1927-69; President pro tempore 1957-69.

HAYDEN, Edward Daniel (R Mass.) Dec. 27, 1833-Nov. 15, 1908; House 1885-89.

HAYDEN, Moses (— N.Y.) 1786-Feb. 13, 1830; House 1823-27.

HAYES, Everis Anson (R Calif.) March 10, 1855-June 3, 1942; House 1905-19.

HAYES, Cornelius (R Ill.) Feb. 3, 1833-July 13, 1916; House 1877-81.

HAYES, Rutherford Birchard (R Ohio) Oct. 4, 1822-Jan. 17, 1893; House 1865-July 20, 1867; President 1877-81; Gov. 1868-72, 1876-77.

HAYES, Walter Ingalls (D Iowa) Dec. 9, 1841-March 14, 1901; House 1887-95.

HAYMOND, Thomas Sherwood (W Va.) Jan. 15, 1794-April 5, 1869; House Nov. 8, 1849-51.

HAYMOND, William Summerville (D/L Ind.) Feb. 20, 1823-Dec. 24, 1885; House 1875-77.

HAYNE, Arthur Peronneau (brother of Robert Young Hayne) (D S.C.) March 12, 1790-Jan. 7, 1867; Senate May 11-Dec. 2, 1858.

HAYNE, Robert Young (TD S.C.) Nov. 10, 1791-Sept. 24, 1839; Senate 1823-Dec. 13, 1832; Gov. 1832-34.

HAYNES, Charles Eaton (U Ga.) April 15, 1784-Aug. 29, 1841; House 1825-31 (D), 1835-39 (U).

HAYNES, Martin Alonzo (R N.H.) July 30, 1842-Nov. 28, 1919; House 1883-87.

HAYNES, William Elisha (cousin of George William Palmer) (D Ohio) Oct. 19, 1829-Dec. 5, 1914; House 1889-93.

HAYS, Charles (R Ala.) Feb. 2, 1834-June 24, 1879; House 1869-77.

HAYS, Edward Dixon (R Mo.) April 28, 1872-July 25, 1941; House 1919-23.

HAYS, Edward Retilla (R Iowa) May 26, 1847-Feb. 28, 1896; House Nov. 4, 1890-91.

HAYS, Lawrence Brooks (D Ark.) Aug. 9, 1898; House 1943-59.

HAYS, Samuel (D Pa.) Sept. 10, 1783-July 1, 1868; House 1843-45.

HAYS, Samuel Lewis (D Va.) Oct. 20, 1794-March 17, 1871; House 1841-43.

HAYS, Wayne Levere (D Ohio) May 13, 1911; House 1949- .

HAYWARD, Monroe Leland (R Neb.) Dec. 22, 1840-Dec. 5, 1899; Senate March 8-Dec. 5, 1899.

HAYWARD, William, Jr. (D Md.) 1787-Oct. 19, 1836; House 1823-25.

HAYWOOD, William Henry, Jr. (D N.C.) Oct. 23, 1801-Oct. 7, 1852; Senate 1843-July 25, 1846.

HAYWORTH, Donald (D Mich.) Jan. 13, 1898; House 1955-57.

HAZARD, Nathaniel (D R.I.) 1776-Dec. 17, 1820; House 1819-Dec. 17, 1820.

HAZELTINE, Abner (W N.Y.) June 10, 1793-Dec. 20, 1879; House 1833-37.

HAZELTINE, Ira Sherwin (RG Mo.) July 13, 1821-Jan. 13, 1899; House 1881-83.

HAZELTON, George Cochrane (brother of Gerry Whiting Hazelton and nephew of Clark Betton Cochrane) (R Wis.) Jan. 3, 1832-Sept. 4, 1922; House 1877-83.

HAZELTON, Gerry Whiting (brother of George Cochrane Hazelton and nephew of Clark Betton Cochrane) (R Wis.) Feb. 24, 1899-Sept. 19, 1920; House 1871-75.

HAZELTON, John Wright (R N.J.) Dec. 10, 1814-Dec. 20, 1878; House 1871-75.

HAZLETT, James Miller (R Pa.) Oct. 14, 1864-Nov. 8, 1940; House March 4-Oct. 20, 1927.

HEALD, William Henry (R Del.) Aug. 17, 1864-June 3, 1939; House 1909-13.

HEALEY, Arthur Daniel (D Mass.) Dec. 29, 1889-Sept. 16, 1948; House 1933-Aug. 3, 1942.

HEALEY, James Christopher (D N.Y.) Dec. 24, 1909; House Feb. 7, 1956-65.

HEALY, Joseph (D N.H.) Aug. 21, 1776-Oct. 10, 1861; House 1825-29.

HEALY, Ned R. (D Calif.) Aug. 9, 1905; House 1945-47.

HEARD, John Thaddeus (D Mo.) Oct. 29, 1840-Jan. 27, 1927; House 1885-95.

HEARST, George (father of William Randolph Hearst) (D Calif.) Sept. 3, 1820-Feb. 28, 1891; Senate March 23-Aug. 4, 1886, 1887-Feb. 28, 1891.

HEARST, William Randolph (son of George Hearst) (D N.Y.) April 29, 1863-Aug. 14, 1951; House 1903-07.

HEATH, James P. (D Md.) Dec. 21, 1777-June 12, 1854; House 1833-35.

HEATH, John (R Va.) May 8, 1758-Oct. 13, 1810; House 1793-97.

HEATON, David (R N.C.) March 10, 1823-June 25, 1870; House July 15, 1868-June 25, 1870.

HEATON, Robert Douglas (R Pa.) July 1, 1873-June 11, 1933; House 1915-19.

HEATWOLE, Joel Prescott (R Minn.) Aug. 22, 1856-April 4, 1910; House 1895-1903.

HEBARD, William (W Vt.) Nov. 29, 1800-Oct. 20, 1875; House 1849-53.

HEBERT, Felix (R R.I.) Dec. 11, 1874-December 14, 1969; Senate 1929-35.

HEBERT, Felix Edward (D La.) Oct. 12, 1901; House 1941- .

HECHLER, Kenneth (D W. Va.) Sept. 20, 1914; House 1959- .

HECKLER, Margaret M. (R Mass.) June 21, 1931; House 1967- .

HEDGE, Thomas (R Iowa) June 24, 1844-Nov. 28, 1920; 1899-1907.

HEDRICK, Erland Harold (D W. Va.) Aug. 9, 1894-Sept. 20, 1954; House 1945-53.

HEFFERNAN, James Joseph (D N.Y.) Nov. 8, 1888-Jan. 27, 1967; House 1941-53.

HEFLIN, James Thomas (nephew of Robert Stell Heflin) (D Ala.) April 9, 1869-April 22, 1951; House May 10, 1904-Nov. 1, 1920; Senate Nov. 3, 1920-31.

HEFLIN, Robert Stell (uncle of James Thomas Heflin) (R Ala.) April 15, 1815-Jan. 24, 1901; House 1869-71.

HEIDINGER, James Vandaveer (R Ill.) July 17, 1882-March 22, 1945; House 1941-March 22, 1945.

HEILMAN, William (great-grandfather of Charles Marion LaFollette) (R Ind.) Oct. 11, 1824-Sept. 22, 1890; House 1879-83.

HEINER, Daniel Brodhead (R Pa.) Dec. 30, 1854-Feb. 14, 1944; House 1893-97.

HEINKE, George Henry (R Neb.) July 22, 1882-Jan. 2, 1940; House 1939-January 2, 1940.

HEINTZ, Victor (R Ohio) Nov. 20, 1876-Dec. 27, 1968; House 1917-19.

HEISKELL, John Netherland (D Ark.) Nov. 2, 1872; Senate Jan. 6-Jan. 29, 1913.

HEITFELD, Henry (P Idaho) Jan. 12, 1859-Oct. 21, 1938; Senate 1897-1903.

HELGESEN, Henry Thomas (R N.D.) June 26, 1857-April 10, 1917; House 1911-April 10, 1917.

HELLER, Louis Benjamin (D N.Y.) Feb. 10, 1905; House Feb. 15, 1949-July 21, 1954.

HELM, Harvey (D Ky.) Dec. 2, 1865-March 3, 1919; House 1907-March 3, 1919.

HELMICK, William (R Ohio) Sept. 6, 1817-March 31, 1888; House 1859-61.

HELMS, William (D N.J.) — - 1813; House 1801-11.

HELSTOSKI, Henry (D N.J.) March 21, 1925; House 1965- .

HELVERING, Guy Tresillian (D Kan.) Jan. 10, 1878-July 4, 1946; House 1913-19.

HEMENWAY, James Alexander (R Ind.) March 8, 1860-Feb. 10, 1923; House 1895-1905; Senate 1905-09.

HEMPHILL, John (uncle of John James Hemphill and great-great-uncle of Robert Witherspoon Hemphill) (SRD Texas) Dec. 18, 1803-Jan. 7, 1862; Senate 1859-July 11, 1861.

HEMPHILL, John James (cousin of William Huggins Brawley, nephew of John Hemphill and great-uncle of Robert Witherspoon Hemphill) (D S.C.) Aug. 25, 1849-May 11, 1912; House 1883-93.

HEMPHILL, Joseph (JD Pa.) Jan. 7, 1770-May 29, 1842; House 1801-03, 1819-26 (F), 1829-31 (JD).

HEMPHILL, Robert Witherspoon (great-great nephew of John Hemphill, great-nephew of John J. Hemphill and William Huggins Brawley, and great-great-grandson of Robert Witherspoon) (D S.C.) May 10, 1915; House 1957-May 1, 1964.

HEMPSTEAD, Edward (— Mo.) June 3, 1780-Aug. 10, 1817; House (Terr. Del.) Nov. 9, 1812-Sept. 17, 1814.

HENDEE, George Whitman (R Vt.) Nov. 30, 1832-Dec. 6, 1906; House 1873-79.

HENDERSON, Archibald (F N.C.) Aug. 7, 1768-Oct. 21, 1822; House 1799-1803.

HENDERSON, Bennett H. (—Tenn.) Sept. 5, 1784- —; House 1815-17.

HENDERSON, Charles Belknap (D Nev.) June 8, 1873-Nov. 8, 1954; Senate Jan. 12, 1918-21.

HENDERSON, David Bremner (R Iowa) March 14, 1840-Feb. 25, 1906; House 1883-1903; Speaker 1899-1903.

HENDERSON, David Newton (D N.C.) April 16, 1921; House 1961- .

HENDERSON, James Henry Dickey (UR Ore.) July 23, 1810-Dec. 13, 1885; House 1865-67.

HENDERSON, James Pinckney (SRD Texas) March 31, 1808-June 4, 1858; Senate Nov. 9, 1857-June 4, 1858; Gov. 1846.

HENDERSON, John (W Miss.) 1795-Sept. 13, 1866; Senate 1839-45.

HENDERSON, John Brooks (D Mo.) Nov. 16, 1826-April 12, 1913; Senate Jan. 17, 1862-69.

HENDERSON, John Earl (R Ohio) Jan. 4, 1917; House 1955-61.

HENDERSON, John Steele (D N.C.) Jan. 6, 1846-Oct. 9, 1916; House 1885-95.

HENDERSON, Joseph (— Pa.) Aug. 2. 1791-Dec. 25, 1863; House 1833-37.

HENDERSON, Samuel (R Pa.) Nov. 27, 1764-Nov. 17, 1841; House Oct. 11, 1814-15.

HENDERSON, Thomas (— N.J.) Aug. 15, 1743-Dec. 15, 1824; House 1795-97.

HENDERSON, Thomas Jefferson (R Ill.) Nov. 29, 1824-Feb. 6, 1911; House 1875-95.

HENDRICK, John Kerr (D Ky.) Oct. 10, 1849-June 20, 1921; House 1895-97.

HENDRICKS, Joseph Edward (D Fla.) Sept. 24, 1903; House 1937-49.

HENDRICKS, Thomas Andrews (nephew of William Hendricks) (D Ind.) Sept. 7, 1819-Nov. 25, 1885; House 1851-55; Senate 1863-69; Gov. 1872; Vice Pres. March 4-Nov. 25, 1885.

HENDRICKS, William (uncle of Thomas Andrews Hendricks) (D Ind.) Nov. 12, 1782-May 16, 1850; House Dec. 11, 1816-July 25, 1822; Senate 1825-37; Gov. 1822-25.

HENDRICKSON, Robert Clymer (R N.J.) Aug. 12, 1898-Dec. 7, 1964; Senate 1949-55.

HENDRIX, Joseph Clifford (D N.Y.) May 25, 1853-Nov. 9, 1904; House 1893-95.

HENKLE, Eli Jones (D Md.) Nov. 24, 1828-Nov. 1, 1893; House 1875-81.

HENLEY, Barclay (son of Thomas Jefferson Henley) (D Calif.) March 17, 1843-Feb. 15, 1914; House 1883-87.

HENLEY, Thomas Jefferson (father of Barclay Henley) (D Ind.) April 2, 1810-Jan. 2, 1865; House 1843-49.

HENN, Bernhart (D Iowa) 1817-Aug. 30, 1865; House 1851-55.

HENNEY, Charles William Francis (D Wis.) Feb. 2, 1884-Nov. 16, 1969; House 1933-35.

HENNINGS, Thomas Carey, Jr. (D Mo.) June 25, 1903-Sept. 13, 1960; House 1935-Dec. 31, 1940; Senate 1951-Sept. 13, 1960.

HENRY, Charles Lewis (R Ind.) July 1, 1849-May 2, 1927; House 1895-99.

HENRY, Daniel Maynadier (D Md.) Feb. 19, 1823-Aug. 31, 1899; House 1877-81.

HENRY, Edward Stevens (R Conn.) Feb. 10, 1836-Oct. 10, 1921; House 1895-1913.

HENRY, John (D Md.) Nov. 1750-Dec. 16, 1798; Senate 1789-Dec. 10, 1797; Cont. Cong. 1778-81, 1784-87; Gov. 1797-98.

HENRY, John (W Ill.) Nov. 1, 1800-April 28, 1882; House Feb. 5-March 3, 1847.

HENRY, John Flournoy (— Ky.) Jan. 17, 1793-Nov. 12, 1873; House Dec. 11, 1826-27.

HENRY, Lewis (R N.Y.) June 8, 1885-July 23, 1941; House April 11, 1922-23.

HENRY, Patrick (D Miss.) Feb. 12, 1843-May 18, 1930; House 1897-1901.

HENRY, Patrick (nephew of the preceding) (D Miss.) Feb. 15, 1861-Dec. 28, 1933; House 1901-03.

HENRY, Robert Kirkland (R Wis.) Feb. 9, 1890-Nov. 20, 1946; House 1945-Nov. 20, 1946.

HENRY, Robert Lee (D Texas) May 12, 1864-July 9, 1931; House 1897-1917.

HENRY, Robert Pryor (CD Ky.) Nov. 24, 1788-Aug. 25, 1826; House 1823-Aug. 25, 1826.

HENRY, Thomas (W Pa.) 1779-July 20, 1849; House 1837-43.

HENRY, William (W Vt.) March 22, 1788-April 16, 1861; House 1847-51.

HENRY, Winder Laird (great-grandson of Charles Goldsborough and Robert Henry Goldsborough) (D Md.) Dec. 20, 1864-July 5, 1940; House Nov. 6, 1894-95.

HENSLEY, Walter Lewis (D Mo.) Sept. 3, 1871-July 18, 1946; House 1911-19.

HEPBURN, William Peters (great-grandson of Matthew Lyon) (R Iowa) Nov. 4, 1833-Feb. 7, 1916; House 1881-87; 1893-1909.

HERBERT, Hilary Abner (D Ala.) March 12, 1834-March 5, 1919; House 1877-93; Secy. of the Navy 1893-97.

HERBERT, John Carlyle (F Md.) Aug. 16, 1775-Sept. 1, 1846; House 1815-19.

HERBERT, Philemon Thomas (D Calif.) Nov. 1, 1825-July 23, 1864; House 1855-57.

HEREFORD, Frank (D W. Va.) July 4, 1825-Dec. 21, 1891; House 1871-Jan. 31, 1877; Senate Jan. 31, 1877-81.

HERKIMER, John (D N.Y.) 1773-June 8, 1848; House 1817-19, 1823-25.

HERLONG, Albert Sydney, Jr. (D Fla.) Feb. 14, 1909; House 1949-69.

HERMANN, Binger (R Ore.) Feb. 19, 1843-April 15, 1926; House 1885-97, June 1, 1903-07.

HERNANDEZ, Benigno Cardenas (R N.M.) Feb. 13, 1862-Oct. 18, 1954; House 1915-17, 1919-21.

HERNANDEZ, Joseph Marion (— Fla.) Aug. 4, 1793-June 8, 1857; House (Terr. Del.) Sept. 30, 1822-23.

HERNDON, Thomas Hord (D Ala.) July 1, 1828-March 28, 1883; House 1879-March 28, 1883.

HERNDON, William Smith (D Texas) Nov. 27, 1835-Oct. 11, 1903; House 1871-75.

HEROD, William (W Ind.) March 31, 1801-Oct. 20, 1871; House Jan. 25, 1837-39.

HERRICK, Anson (son of Ebenezer Herrick) (D N.Y.) Jan. 21, 1812-Feb. 6, 1868; House 1863-65.

HERRICK, Ebenezer (father of Anson Herrick) (— Maine) Oct. 21, 1785-May 7, 1839; House 1821-27.

HERRICK, Joshua (D Maine) March 18, 1793-Aug. 30, 1874; House 1843-45.

HERRICK, Manuel (R Okla.) Sept. 20, 1876-Feb. 29, 1952; House 1921-23.

HERRICK, Richard Platt (W N.Y.) March 23, 1791-June 20, 1846; House 1845-June 20, 1846.

HERRICK, Samuel (D Ohio) April 14, 1779-June 4, 1852; House 1817-21.

HERRING, Clyde LaVerne (D Iowa) May 3, 1879-Sept. 15, 1945; Senate Jan. 15, 1937-43; Gov. 1933-37.

HERSEY, Ira Greenlief (R Maine) March 31, 1858-May 6, 1943; House 1917-29.

HERSEY, Samuel Freeman (R Maine) April 12, 1812-Feb. 3, 1875; House 1873-Feb. 3, 1875.

HERSMAN, Hugh Steel (D Calif.) July 8, 1872-March 7, 1954; House 1919-21.

HERTER, Christian Archibald (R Mass.) March 28, 1895-Dec. 30, 1966; House 1943-53; Gov. 1953-57; Secy. of State 1959-61.

HESELTON, John Walter (R Mass.) March 17, 1900-Aug. 19, 1962; House 1945-59.

HESS, William Emil (R Ohio) Feb. 13, 1898; House 1929-37, 1939-49, 1951-61.

HEWITT, Abram Stevens (D N.Y.) July 31, 1822-Jan. 18, 1903; House 1875-79, 1881-Dec. 30, 1886.

HEWITT, Goldsmith Whitehouse (D Ala.) Feb. 14, 1834-May 27, 1895; House 1875-79, 1881-85.

HEYBURN, Weldon Brinton (R Idaho) May 23, 1852-Oct. 17, 1912; Senate 1903-Oct. 17, 1912.

HIBBARD, Ellery Albee (cousin of Harry Hibbard) (D N.H.) July 31, 1826-July 24, 1903; House 1871-73.

HIBBARD, Harry (cousin of Ellery Albee Hibbard) (D N.H.) June 1, 1816-July 28, 1872; House 1849-55.

HIBSHMAN, Jacob (R Pa.) Jan. 31, 1772-May 19, 1852; House 1819-21.

HICKENLOOPER, Bourke Blakemore (R Iowa) July 21, 1896; Senate 1945-69; Gov. 1943-44.

HICKEY, Andrew James (R Ind.) Aug. 27, 1872-Aug. 20, 1942; House 1919-31.

HICKEY, John Joseph (D Wyo.) Aug. 22, 1911-Sept. 22, 1970; Senate Jan. 2, 1961-Nov. 7, 1962; Gov. 1959-61.

HICKMAN, John (R Pa.) Sept. 11, 1810-March 23, 1875; House 1855-59 (D), 1859-61 (DD), 1861-63 (R).

HICKS, Floyd V. (D Wash) May 29, 1915; House 1965- .

HICKS, Frederick Cocks (original name, Frederick Hicks Cocks, brother of William Willets Cocks) (R N.Y.) March 6, 1872-Dec. 14, 1925; House 1915-23.

HICKS, Josiah Duane (R Pa.) Aug. 1, 1844-May 9, 1923; House 1893-99.

HICKS, Louise Day (D Mass.) Oct. 16, 1923; House 1971- .

HICKS, Thomas Holliday (R Md.) Sept. 2, 1798-Feb. 14, 1865; Senate Dec. 29, 1862-Feb. 14, 1865; Gov. 1862.

HIESTAND, Edgar Willard (R Calif.) Dec. 3, 1888-Aug. 19, 1970; House 1953-63.

HIESTAND, John Andrew (R Pa.) Oct. 2, 1824-Dec. 13, 1890; House 1885-89.

HIESTER, Daniel (brother of John Hiester, cousin of Joseph Hiester and uncle of William Hiester) (— Pa./Md.) June 25, 1747-March 7, 1804; House 1789-July 1, 1796 (Pa.), 1801-March 7, 1804 (Md.).

HIESTER, Daniel (son of John Hiester and nephew of the preceding) (— Pa.) 1774-March 8, 1834; House 1809-11.

HIESTER, Isaac Ellmaker (son of William Hiester and cousin of Hiester Clymer) (W Pa.) May 29, 1824-Feb. 6, 1871; House 1853-55.

HIESTER, John (brother of Daniel Hiester, cousin of Joseph Hiester, and uncle of William Hiester) (— Pa.) April 9, 1745-Oct. 15, 1821; House 1807-09.

HIESTER, Joseph (cousin of John Hiester and Daniel Hiester and grandfather of Henry Augustus Muhlenberg) (F Pa.) Nov. 18, 1752-June 10, 1832; House Dec. 1, 1797-1805, 1815-Dec. 1820; Gov. 1820-24.

HIESTER, William (father of Isaac Ellmaker Hiester, uncle of Hiester Clymer, and nephew of John Hiester and Daniel Hiester) (W Pa.) Oct. 10, 1790-Oct. 13, 1853; House 1831-37.

HIGBY, William (R Calif.) Aug. 18, 1813-Nov. 27, 1887; House 1863-69.

HIGGINS, Anthony (R Del.) Oct. 1, 1840-June 26, 1912; Senate 1889-95.

HIGGINS, Edwin Werter (R Conn.) July 2, 1874-Sept. 24, 1954; House Oct. 2, 1905-13.

HIGGINS, John Patrick (D Mass.) Feb. 19, 1893-Aug. 2, 1955; House 1935-Sept. 30, 1937.

HIGGINS, William Lincoln (R Conn.) March 8, 1867-Nov. 19, 1951; House 1933-37.

HILBORN, Samuel Greeley (R Calif.) Dec. 9, 1834-April 19, 1899; House Dec. 5, 1892-April 4, 1894, 1895-99.

HILDEBRANDT, Fred Herman (D S.D.) Aug. 2, 1874-Jan. 26, 1956; House 1933-39.

HILDEBRANT, Charles Quinn (R Ohio) Oct. 17, 1864-March 31, 1953; House 1901-05.

HILL, Benjamin Harvey (cousin of Hugh Lawson White Hill) (D Ga.) Sept. 14, 1823-Aug. 16, 1882; House May 5, 1875-77; Senate 1877-Aug. 16, 1882.

HILL, Charles Augustus (R Ill.) Aug. 23, 1833-May 29, 1902; House 1889-91.

HILL, Clement Sidney (ID Ky.) Feb. 13, 1813-Jan. 5, 1892; House 1853-55.

HILL, David Bennett (D N.Y.) Aug. 29, 1843-Oct. 20, 1910; Senate Jan. 7, 1892-97; Gov. 1885-92.

HILL, Ebenezer J. (R Conn.) Aug. 4, 1845-Sept. 27, 1917; House 1895-1913, 1915-Sept. 17, 1917.

HILL, Hugh Lawson White (cousin of Benjamin Harvey Hill) (D Tenn.) March 1, 1810-Jan. 18, 1892; House 1847-49.

HILL, Issac (D N.Y.) April 6, 1788-March 22, 1851; Senate 1831-May 30, 1836; Gov. 1836-39.

HILL, John (D N.C.) April 9, 1797-April 24, 1861: House 1839-41.

HILL, John (cousin of John Thomas Harris) (W Va.) July 18, 1800-April 19, 1880; House 1839-41.

HILL, John (R N.J.) June 10, 1821-July 24, 1884; House 1867-73, 1881-83.

HILL, John Boynton Philip Clayton (R Md.) May 2, 1879-May 23, 1941; House 1921-27.

HILL, Joshua (UR Ga.) Jan. 10, 1812-March 6, 1891; House 1857-Jan. 23, 1861 (AP); Senate July 28, 1868-73 (UR).

HILL, Knute (D Wash.) July 31, 1876-Dec. 3, 1963; House 1933-43.

HILL, Lister (D Ala.) Dec. 29, 1894; House Aug. 14, 1923-Jan. 11, 1938; Senate Jan. 11, 1938-69.

HILL, Mark Langdon (— Mass./Maine) June 30, 1772-Nov. 26, 1842; House 1819-21 (Mass.), 1821-23 (Maine).

HILL, Nathaniel Peter (R Colo.) Feb. 18, 1832-May 22, 1900; Senate 1879-85.

HILL, Ralph (R Ind.) Oct. 12, 1827-Aug. 20, 1899; House 1865-67.

HILL, Robert Potter (D Ill./Okla.) April 18, 1874-Oct. 29, 1937; House 1913-15 (Ill.), Jan. 3-Oct. 29, 1937 (Okla.).

HILL, Samuel Billingsley (D Wash.) April 2, 1875-March 16, 1958; House Sept. 25, 1923-June 25, 1936.

HILL, William David (D Ohio) Oct. 1, 1833-Dec. 26, 1906; House 1879-81, 1833-87.

HILL, William Henry (F N.C.) May 1, 1767-1809; House 1799-1803.

HILL, William Henry (R N.Y.) March 23, 1877; House 1919-21.

HILL, William Luther (D Fla.) Oct. 17, 1873-Jan. 5, 1951; Senate July 1-November 3, 1936.

HILL, William Silas (R Colo.) Jan. 20, 1866; House 1941-59.

HILL, Wilson Shedric (D Miss.) Jan. 19, 1863-Feb. 14, 1921; House 1903-09.

HILLELSON, Jeffrey Paul (R Mo.) March 9, 1919; House 1953-55.

HILLEN, Solomon, Jr. (D Md.) July 10, 1810-June 26, 1873; House 1839-41.

HILLHOUSE, James (F Conn.) Oct. 21, 1754-Dec. 29, 1832; House 1791-96; Senate Dec. 6, 1796-June 10, 1810; President pro tempore 1801.

HILLIARD, Benjamin Clark (D Colo.) Jan. 9, 1868-Aug. 7, 1951; House 1915-19.

HILLIARD, Henry Washington (W Ala.) Aug. 4, 1808-Dec. 17, 1892; House 1845-51.

HILLINGS, Patrick Jerome (R Calif.) Feb. 19, 1923; House 1951-59.

HILLIS, Elwood H. (R Ind.) March 6, 1926; House 1971- .

HILLYER, Junius (D Ga.) April 23, 1807-June 21, 1886; House 1851-55.

HIMES, Joseph Hendrix (R Ohio) Aug. 15, 1885-Sept. 9, 1960; House 1921-23.

HINDMAN, Thomas Carmichael (D Ark.) Jan. 28, 1828-Sept. 27, 1868; House 1859-61.

HINDMAN, William (— Md.) April 1, 1743-Jan. 19, 1822; House Jan. 30, 1793-1799; Senate Dec. 12, 1800-Nov. 19, 1801; Cont. Cong. 1784-88.

HINDS, Asher Crosby (R Maine) Feb. 6, 1863-May 1, 1919; House 1911-17.

HINDS, James (R Ark.) Dec. 5, 1833-Oct. 22, 1868; House June 22-Oct. 22, 1868.

HINDS, Thomas (D Miss.) Jan. 9, 1780-Aug. 23, 1840; House Oct. 21, 1828-31.

HINEBAUGH, William Henry (Pro. Ill.) Dec. 16, 1867-Sept. 22, 1943; House 1913-15.

HINES, Richard (D N.C.) — -; Nov. 20, 1851; House 1825-27.

HINES, William Henry (D Pa.) March 15, 1856-Jan. 17, 1914; House 1893-95.

HINRICHSEN, William Henry (D Ill.) May 27, 1850-Dec. 18, 1907; House 1897-99.

HINSHAW, Edmund Howard (cousin of Edwin Bruce Brooks) (R Neb.) Dec. 8, 1860-June 15, 1932; House 1903-11.

HINSHAW, John Carl Williams (R Calif.) July 28, 1894-Aug. 5, 1956; House 1939-Aug. 5, 1956.

HIRES, George (R N.J.) Jan. 26, 1835-Feb. 16, 1911; House 1885-89.

HISCOCK, Frank (R N.Y.) Sept. 6, 1834-June 18, 1914; House 1877-87; Senate 1887-93.

HISE, Elijah (D Ky.) July 4, 1802-May 8, 1867; House Dec. 3, 1866, May 8, 1867.

HITCHCOCK, Gilbert Monell (son of Phineas Warren Hitchcock) (D Neb.) Sept. 18, 1859-Feb. 3, 1934; House 1903-05, 1907-11; Senate 1911-23.

HITCHCOCK, Herbert Emery (D S.D.) Aug. 22, 1867-Feb. 17, 1958; Senate Dec. 29, 1936-Nov. 8, 1938.

HITCHCOCK, Peter (— Ohio) Oct. 19, 1781-March 4, 1854; House 1817-19.

HITCHCOCK, Phineas Warren (father of Gilbert Monell Hitchcock) (R Neb.) Nov. 30, 1831-July 10, 1881; House (Terr. Del.) 1865-March 1, 1867; Senate 1871-77.

HITT, Robert Roberts (R Ill.) Jan. 16, 1834-Sept. 19, 1906; House Nov. 7, 1882-Sept. 19, 1906.

HOAG, Truman Harrison (D Ohio) April 9, 1816-Feb. 5, 1870; House 1869-Feb. 5, 1870.

HOAGLAND, Moses (D Ohio) June 19, 1812-April 16, 1865; House 1849-51.

HOAR, Ebenezer Rockwood (son of Samuel Hoar, brother of George Frisbie Hoar, and father of Sherman Hoar) (R Mass.) Feb. 21, 1816-Jan. 31, 1895; House 1873-75; Atty. Gen. 1869-70.

HOAR, George Frisbie (son of Samuel Hoar, brother of Ebenezer Rockwood Hoar, and father of Rockwood Hoar) (R Mass.) Aug. 29, 1826-Sept. 30, 1904; House 1869-77; Senate 1877-Sept. 30, 1904.

HOAR, Rockwood (son of George Frisbie Hoar) (R Mass.) Aug. 24, 1855-Nov. 1, 1906; House 1905-Nov. 1, 1906.

HOAR, Samuel (father of Ebenezer Rockwood Hoar and George Frisbie Hoar) (W Mass.) May 18, 1778-Nov. 2, 1856; House 1835-37.

HOAR, Sherman (son of Ebenezer Rockwood Hoar) (D Mass.) July 30, 1860-Oct. 7, 1898; House 1891-93.

HOARD, Charles Brooks (R N.Y.) June 5, 1805-Nov. 20, 1886; House 1857-61.

HOBART, Aaron (D Mass.) June 26, 1787-Sept. 19, 1858; House Nov. 24, 1820-27.

HOBART, John Sloss (— N.Y.) May 6, 1738-Feb. 4, 1805; Senate Jan. 11-April 16, 1798.

HOBBIE, Selah Reeve (JD N.Y.) March 10, 1797-March 23, 1854; House 1827-29.

HOBBS, Samuel Francis (Sam) (D Ala.) Oct. 5, 1887-May 31, 1952; House 1935-51.

HOBLITZELL, Fetter Schrier (D Md.) Oct. 7, 1838-May 2, 1900; House 1881-85.

HOBLITZELL, John Dempsey, Jr. (R W. Va.) Dec. 30, 1912; Senate Jan. 25-Nov. 4, 1958.

HOBSON, Richmond Pearson (D Ala.) Aug. 17, 1870-March 16, 1937; House 1907-15.

HOCH, Daniel Knabb (D Pa.) Jan. 31, 1866-Oct. 11, 1960; House 1943-47.

HOCH, Homer (R Kan.) July 4, 1879-Jan. 30, 1949; House 1919-33.

HODGES, Asa (R Ark.) Jan. 22, 1822-June 6, 1900; House 1873-75.

HODGES, Charles Drury (D Ill.) Feb. 4, 1810-April 1, 1884; House Jan. 4-March 3, 1859.

HODGES, George Tisdale (R Vt.) July 4, 1789-Aug. 9, 1860; House Dec. 1, 1856-57.

HODGES, James Leonard (— Mass.) April 24, 1790-March 8, 1846; House 1827-33.

HOEPPEL, John Henry (D Calif.) Feb. 10, 1881; House 1933-37.

HOEVEN, Charles Bernard (R Iowa) March 30, 1895; House 1943-65.

HOEY, Clyde Roark (D N.C.) Dec. 11, 1877-May 12, 1954; House Dec. 16, 1919-21; Senate 1945-May 12, 1954; Gov. 1937-41.

HOFFECKER, John Henry (father of Walter Oakley Hoffecker) (R Del.) Sept. 12, 1827-June 16, 1900; House 1899-June 16, 1900.

HOFFECKER, Walter Oakley (son of John Henry Hoffecker) (R Del.) Sept. 20, 1854-Jan. 23, 1934; House Nov. 6, 1900-01.

HOFFMAN, Carl Henry (R Pa.) Aug. 12, 1896; House May 21, 1946-47.

HOFFMAN, Clare Eugene (R Mich.) Sept. 10, 1875-Nov. 3, 1967; House 1935-63.

HOFFMAN, Elmer Joseph (R Ill.) July 7, 1899; House 1959-65.

HOFFMAN, Harold Giles (R N.J.) Feb. 7, 1896-June 4, 1954; House 1927-31; Gov. 1935-38.

HOFFMAN, Henry William (AP Md.) Nov. 10, 1825-July 28, 1895; House 1855-57.

HOFFMAN, Josiah Ogden (W N.Y.) May 3, 1793-May 1, 1856; House 1837-41.

HOFFMAN, Michael (D N.Y.) Oct. 11, 1787-Sept. 27, 1848; House 1825-33.

HOFFMAN, Richard William (R Ill.) Dec. 23, 1893; House 1949-57.

HOGAN, Earl Lee (D Ind.) March 13, 1920; House 1959-61.

HOGAN, John (D Mo.) Jan. 2, 1805-Feb. 5, 1892; House 1865-67.

HOGAN, Lawrence J. (R Md.) Sept. 30, 1928; House 1969- .

HOGAN, Michael Joseph (R N.Y.) April 22, 1871-May 7, 1940; House 1921-23.

HOGAN, William (JD N.Y.) July 17, 1792-Nov. 25, 1874; House 1831-33.

HOGE, John (brother of William Hoge) (D Pa.) Sept. 10, 1760-Aug. 4, 1824; House Nov. 2, 1804-05.

HOGE, John Blair (D W. Va.) Feb. 2, 1825-March 1, 1896; House 1881-83.

HOGE, Joseph Pendleton (D Ill.) Dec. 15, 1810-Aug. 14, 1891; House 1843-47.

HOGE, Solomon Lafayette (R S.C.) July 11, 1836-Feb. 23, 1909; House April 8, 1869-71, 1875-77.

HOGE, William (brother of John Hoge) (F Pa.) 1762-Sept. 25, 1814; House 1801-Oct. 15, 1804, 1807-09.

HOGEBOOM, James Lawrence (W N.Y.) Aug. 25, 1766-Dec. 23, 1839; House 1823-25.

HOGG, Charles Edgar (father of Robert Lynn Hogg) (D W. Va.) Dec. 21, 1852-June 14, 1935; House 1887-89.

HOGG, David (R Ind.) Aug. 21, 1886; House 1925-33.

HOGG, Herschel Millard (R Colo.) Nov. 21, 1853-Aug. 27, 1934; House 1903-07.

HOGG, Robert Lynn (son of Charles Edgar Hogg) (R W. Va.) Dec. 30, 1893; House Nov. 4, 1930-33.

HOGG, Samuel (D Tenn.) April 18, 1783-May 28, 1842; House 1817-19.

HOLIDALE, Einar (D Minn.) Aug. 17, 1870-Dec. 5, 1952; House 1933-35.

HOLADAY, William Perry (R Ill.) Dec. 14, 1882-Jan. 29, 1946; House 1923-33.

HOLBROCK, Greg John (D Ohio) June 21, 1906; House 1941-43.

HOLBROOK, Edward Dexter (D Idaho) May 6, 1836-June 18, 1870; House (Terr. Del.) 1865-69.

HOLCOMBE, George (D N.J.) March 1786-Jan. 14, 1828; House 1821-Jan. 14, 1828.

HOLIFIELD, Chet (D Calif.) Dec. 3, 1903; House 1943- .

HOLLADAY, Alexander Richmond (D Va.) Sept. 18, 1811-Jan. 29, 1877; House 1849-53.

HOLLAND, Cornelius (D Maine) July 9, 1783-June 2, 1870; House Dec. 6, 1830-33.

HOLLAND, Edward Everett (D Va.) Feb. 26, 1861-Oct. 23, 1941; House 1911-21.

HOLLAND, Elmer Joseph (D Pa.) Jan. 8, 1894-Aug. 9, 1968; House May 19, 1942-43; Jan. 24, 1956-Aug. 9, 1968.

HOLLAND, James (A-F N.C.) 1754-May 19, 1823; House 1795-97, 1801-11.

HOLLAND, Spessard Lindsey (D Fla.) July 10, 1892; Senate Sept. 25, 1946-71; Gov. 1941-45.

HOLLEMAN, Joel (VBD Va.) Oct. 1, 1799-Aug. 5, 1844; House 1839-40.

HOLLEY, John Milton (W N.Y.) Nov. 10, 1802-March 8, 1848; House 1847-March 8, 1848.

HOLLIDAY, Elias Selah (R Ind.) March 5, 1842-March 13, 1936; House 1901-09.

HOLLINGS, Ernest F. (D S.C.) Jan. 1, 1922; Senate Nov. 9, 1966; Gov. 1959-63.

HOLLINGSWORTH, David Adams (R Ohio) Nov. 21, 1844-Dec. 3, 1929; House 1909-11, 1915-19.

HOLLIS, Henry French (D N.H.) Aug. 30, 1869-July 7, 1949; Senate March 13, 1913-19.

HOLLISTER, John Baker (R Ohio) Nov. 7, 1890; House Nov. 3, 1931-37.

HOLLOWAY, David Pierson (PP Ind.) Dec. 7, 1809-Sept. 9, 1883; House 1855-57.

HOLMAN, Rufus Cecil (R Ore.) Oct. 14, 1877-Nov. 27, 1959; Senate 1939-45.

HOLMAN, William Steele (D Ind.) Sept. 6, 1822-April 22, 1897; House 1859-65, 1867-77, 1881-95, March 4-April 22, 1897.

HOLMES, Adoniram Judson (R Iowa) March 2, 1842-Jan. 21, 1902; House 1883-89.

HOLMES, Charles Horace (R N.Y.) Oct. 24, 1827-Oct. 2, 1874; House Dec. 6, 1870-71.

HOLMES, David (— Va./Miss.) March 10, 1769-Aug. 20, 1832; House 1797-1809 (Va.); Senate Aug. 30, 1820-Sept. 25, 1825 (Miss.); Gov. 1809-17 (Terr. of Miss), 1817-20 (Miss.).

HOLMES, Elias Bellows (W N.Y.) May 22, 1807-July 31, 1866; House 1845-49.

HOLMES, Gabriel (— N.C.) 1769-Sept. 26, 1829; House 1825-Sept. 26, 1829; Gov. 1821-24.

HOLMES, Isaac Edward (D S.C.) April 6, 1796-Feb. 24, 1867; House 1839-51.

HOLMES, John (D Mass./Maine) March 14, 1773-July 7, 1843; House 1817-March 15, 1820 (Mass.); Senate June 13, 1820-27, Jan. 15, 1829-33 (Maine)

HOLMES, Otis Halbert (Hal) (grandson of Dudley Chase Haskell) (R Wash.) Feb. 22, 1902; House 1943-59.

HOLMES, Pehr Gustaf (R Mass.) April 9, 1881-Dec. 19, 1952; House 1931-47.

HOLMES, Sidney Tracy (R N.Y.) Aug. 14, 1815-Jan. 16, 1890; House 1865-67.

HOLMES, Uriel (F Conn.) Aug. 26, 1764-May 18, 1827; House 1817-18.

HOLSEY, Hopkins (UD Ga.) Aug. 25, 1779-March 31, 1859; House Oct. 5, 1835-39.

HOLT, Hines (W Ga.) April 27, 1805-Nov. 4, 1865; House Feb. 1-March 3, 1841.

HOLT, Joseph Franklin, 3d (R Calif.) July 6, 1924; House 1953-61.

HOLT, Orrin (D Conn.) March 13, 1792-June 20, 1855; House Dec. 5, 1836-39.

HOLT, Rush Dew (D W. Va.) June 19, 1905-Feb. 8, 1955; Senate June 21, 1935-41.

HOLTEN, Samuel (— Mass.) June 9, 1738-Jan. 2, 1816; House 1793-95; Cont. Cong. 1778-80, 1782-87.

HOLTON, Hart Benton (R Md.) Oct. 13, 1835-Jan. 4, 1907; House 1883-85.

HOLTZMAN, Lester (D N.Y.) June 1, 1913; House 1953-Dec. 31, 1961.

HONEYMAN, Nan Wood (D Ore.) July 15, 1881-Dec. 10, 1970; House 1937-39.

HOOD, George Ezekial (D N.C.) Jan. 25, 1875-March 8, 1960; House 1915-19.

HOOK, Enos (D Pa.) Dec. 3, 1804-July 15, 1841; House 1839-April 18, 1841.

HOOK, Frank Eugene (D Mich.) May 26, 1893- —; House 1935-43, 1945-47.

HOOKER, Charles Edward (D Miss.) 1825-Jan. 8, 1914; House 1875-83, 1887-95, 1901-03.

HOOKER, James Murray (D Va.) Oct. 29, 1873-Aug. 6, 1940; House Nov. 8, 1921-25.

HOOKER, Warren Brewster (R N.Y.) Nov. 24, 1856-March 5, 1920; House 1891-Nov. 10, 1898.

HOOKS, Charles (great-grandfather of William Julius Harris) (D N.C.) Feb. 20, 1768-Oct. 18, 1843; House Dec. 2, 1816-17, 1819-25.

HOOPER, Benjamin Stephen (Read. Va.) March 6, 1835-Jan. 17, 1898; House 1883-85.

HOOPER, Joseph Lawrence (R Mich.) Dec. 22, 1877-Feb. 22, 1934; House Aug. 18, 1925-Feb. 22, 1934.

HOOPER, Samuel (R Mass.) Feb. 3, 1808-Feb. 14, 1875; House Dec. 2, 1861-Feb. 14, 1875.

HOOPER, William Henry (D Utah) Dec. 25, 1813-Dec. 30, 1882; House (Terr. Del.) 1859-61, 1865-73.

HOPE, Clifford Ragsdale (R Kan.) June 9, 1893-May 16, 1970; House 1927-57.

HOPKINS, Albert Cole (R Pa.) Sept. 15, 1837-June 9, 1911; House 1891-95.

HOPKINS, Albert Jarvis (R Ill.) Aug. 15, 1846-Aug. 23, 1922; House Dec. 7, 1885-1903; Senate 1903-09.

HOPKINS, Benjamin Franklin (R Wis.) April 22, 1829-Jan. 1, 1870; House 1867-Jan. 1, 1870.

HOPKINS, David William (R Mo.) Oct. 31, 1897-Oct. 14, 1968; House Feb. 5, 1929-33.

HOPKINS, Francis Alexander (Frank) (D Ky.) May 27, 1853-June 5, 1918; House 1903-07.

HOPKINS, George Washington (D Va.) Feb. 22, 1804-March 1, 1861; House 1835-47, 1857-59.

HOPKINS, James Herron (D Pa.) Nov. 3, 1832-June 17, 1904; House 1875-77, 1883-85.

HOPKINS, Nathan Thomas (R Ky.) Oct. 27, 1852-Feb. 11, 1927; House Feb. 18- March 3, 1897.

HOPKINS, Samuel (D Ky.) April 9, 1753-Sept. 16, 1819; House 1813-15.

HOPKINS, Samuel Isaac (D Va.) Dec. 12, 1843-Jan. 15, 1914; House 1887-89.

HOPKINS, Samuel Miles (— N.Y.) May 9, 1772-March 9, 1837; House 1813-15.

HOPKINS, Stephen Tyng (R N.Y.) March 25, 1849-March 3, 1892; House 1887-89.

HOPKINSON, Joseph (F Pa.) Nov. 12, 1770-Jan. 15, 1842; House 1815-19.

HOPWOOD, Robert Freeman (R Pa.) July 24, 1856-March 1, 1940; House 1915-17.

HORAN, Walter Franklin (R Wash.) Oct. 15, 1898-Dec. 20, 1966; House 1943-65.

HORN, Henry (JD Pa.) 1786-Jan. 12, 1862; House 1831-33.

HORNBECK, John Westbrook (W Pa.) Jan. 24, 1804-Jan. 16, 1848; House 1847-Jan. 16, 1848.

HORNOR, Lynn Sedwick (D W. Va.) Nov. 3, 1874-Sept. 23, 1933; House 1931-Sept. 23, 1933

HORR, Ralph Ashley (R Wash.) Aug. 12, 1884-Jan. 26, 1960; House 1931-33.

HORR, Roswell Gilbert (R Mich.) Nov. 26, 1830-Dec. 19, 1896; House 1879-85.

HORSEY, Outerbridge (F Del.) March 5, 1777-June 9, 1842; Senate Jan. 12, 1810-21.

HORSFORD, Jerediah (W N.Y.) March 8, 1791-Jan. 14, 1875; House 1851-53.

HORTON, Frank (R N.Y.) Dec. 12, 1919; House 1963- .

HORTON, Frank Ogilvie (R Wyo.) Oct. 18, 1882-Aug. 17, 1948; House 1939-41.

HORTON, Thomas Raymond (R N.Y.) April 1822-July 26, 1894; House 1855-57.

HORTON, Valentine Baxter (W Ohio) Jan. 29, 1802-Jan. 14, 1888; House 1855-59, 1861-63.

HOSKINS, George Gilbert (R N.Y.) Dec. 24, 1824-June 12, 1893; House 1873-77.

HOSMER, Craig (R Calif.) May 6, 1915; House 1953- .

HOSMER, Hezekiah Lord (—N.Y.) June 7, 1765-June 9, 1814; House 1797-99.

HOSTETLER, Abraham Jonathan (D Ind.) Nov. 22, 1818-Nov. 24, 1899; House 1879-81.

HOSTETTER, Jacob (D Pa.) May 9, 1754-June 29, 1831; House Nov. 16, 1818-21.

HOTCHKISS, Giles Waldo (R N.Y.) Oct. 25, 1815-July 5, 1878; House 1863-67, 1869-71.

HOTCHKISS, Julius (R Conn.) July 11, 1810-Dec. 23, 1878; House 1867-69.

HOUCK, Jacob Jr. (D N.Y.) Jan. 14, 1801-Oct. 2, 1857; House 1841-43.

HOUGH, David (—N.H.) March 13, 1753-April 18, 1831; House 1803-07.

HOUGH, William Jervis (D N.Y.) March 20, 1795-Oct. 4, 1869; House 1845-47.

HOUGHTON, Alanson Bigelow (R N.Y.) Oct. 10, 1863-Sept. 15, 1941; House 1919-Feb. 28, 1922.

HOUGHTON, Sherman Otis (R Calif.) April 10, 1828-Aug. 31, 1914; House 1871-75.

HOUK, George Washington (D Ohio) Sept. 25, 1825-Feb. 9, 1894; House 1891-Feb. 9, 1894.

HOUK, John Chiles (son of Leonidas Campbell Houk) (R Tenn.) Feb. 26, 1860-June 3, 1923; House Dec. 7, 1891-95.

HOUK, Leonidas Campbell (father of John Chiles Houk) (R Tenn.) June 8, 1836-May 25, 1891; House 1879-May 25, 1891.

HOUSE, John Ford (D Tenn.) Jan. 9, 1827-June 28, 1904; House 1875-83.

HOUSEMAN, Julius (D Mich.) Dec. 8, 1832-Feb. 8, 1891; House 1883-85.

HOUSTON, Andrew Jackson (son of Samuel Houston) (D Texas) June 21, 1854-June 26, 1941; Senate April 21-June 26, 1941.

HOUSTON, George Smith (D Ala.) Jan. 17, 1808-Dec. 31, 1879; House 1841-49, 1851-Jan. 21, 1861; Senate March 4-Dec. 31, 1879; Gov. 1874-78.

HOUSTON, Henry Aydelotte (D Del.) July 10, 1847-April 5, 1925; House 1903-05.

HOUSTON, John Mills (D Kan.) Sept. 15, 1890; House 1935-43.

HOUSTON, John Wallace (uncle of Robert Griffith Houston) (W Del.) May 4, 1814-April 26, 1896; House 1845-51.

HOUSTON, Robert Griffith (nephew of John Wallace Houston) (R Del.) Oct. 13, 1867-Jan. 29, 1946; House 1925-33.

HOUSTON, Samuel (father of Andrew Jackson Houston and cousin of David Hubbard) (D Tenn./Texas) March 2, 1793-July 26, 1863; House 1823-27 (Tenn.); Senate Feb. 21, 1846-59 (Texas), Gov. 1827-April 16, 1829 (Tenn.); 1859-61 (Texas).

HOUSTON, Victor Stewart Kaleoaloha (R Hawaii) July 22, 1876-July 31, 1959; House (Terr. Del.) 1927-33.

HOUSTON, William Cannon (D Tenn.) March 17, 1852-Aug. 30, 1931; House 1905-19.

HOVEY, Alvin Peterson (R Ind.) Sept. 6, 1821-Nov. 23, 1891; House 1887-Jan. 17, 1889; Gov. 1889-91.

HOWARD, Benjamin (—Ky.) 1760-Sept. 18, 1814; House 1807-April 10, 1810; Gov. Terr. of Louisiana 1810-12.

HOWARD, Benjamin Chew (son of John Eager Howard) (D Md.) Nov. 5, 1791-March 6, 1872; House 1829-33, 1835-39.

HOWARD, Edgar (D Neb.) Sept. 16, 1858-July 19, 1951; House 1923-35.

HOWARD, Everette Burgess (D Okla.) Sept. 19, 1873-April 3, 1950; House 1919-21, 1923-25, 1927-29.

HOWARD, Guy Victor (R Minn.) Nov. 28, 1879-Aug. 20, 1954; Senate Nov. 4, 1936-37.

HOWARD, Jacob Merritt (R Mich.) July 10, 1805-April 2, 1871; House 1841-43 (W); Senate Jan. 17, 1862-71 (R).

HOWARD, James J. (D N.J.) July 24, 1927; House 1965- .

HOWARD, John Eager (father of Benjamin Chew Howard) (F Md.) June 4, 1752-Oct. 12, 1827; Senate Nov. 30, 1796-1803; Cont. Cong. 1784-88; Gov. 1789-91.

HOWARD, Jonas George (D Ind.) May 22, 1825-Oct. 5, 1911; House 1885-89.

HOWARD, Milford Wriarson (P Ala.) Dec. 18, 1862-Dec. 28, 1937; House 1895-99.

HOWARD, Tilghman Ashurst (D Ind.) Nov. 14, 1787-Aug. 16, 1844; House Aug. 5, 1839-July 1, 1840.

HOWARD, Volney Erskine (D Texas) Oct. 22, 1809-May 14, 1889; House 1849-53.

HOWARD, William (D Ohio) Dec. 31, 1817-June 1, 1891; House 1859-61.

HOWARD, William Alanson (R Mich.) April 8, 1813-April 10, 1880; House 1855-59, May 15, 1860-61; Gov. of Dakota Terr. 1878-80.

HOWARD, William Marcellus (D Ga.) Dec. 6, 1857-July 5, 1932; House 1897-1911.

HOWARD, William Schley (cousin of Augustus O. Bacon) (D Ga.) June 29, 1875-Aug. 1, 1953; House 1911-19.

HOWE, Albert Richards (R Miss.) Jan. 1, 1840-June 1, 1884; House 1873-75.

HOWE, James Robinson (R N.Y.) Jan. 27, 1839-Sept. 21, 1914; House 1895-99.

HOWE, John W. (F-SW Pa.) 1801-Dec. 1, 1873; House 1849-53.

HOWE, Thomas Marshall (father-in-law of James W. Brown) (W Pa.) April 20, 1808-July 20, 1877; House 1851-55.

HOWE, Thomas Y., Jr. (D N.Y.) 1801-July 15, 1860; House 1851-53.

HOWE, Timothy Otis (UR Wis.) Feb. 24, 1816-March 25, 1883; Senate 1861-79; Postmaster General 1882-83.

HOWELL, Benjamin Franklin (R N.J.) Jan. 27, 1844-Feb. 1, 1933; House 1895-1911.

HOWELL, Charles Robert (D N.J.) April 23, 1904; House 1949-55.

HOWELL, Edward (D N.Y.) Oct. 16, 1792-Jan. 30, 1871; House 1833-35.

HOWELL, Elias (father of James Bruen Howell) (W Ohio) 1792-May 1844; House 1835-37.

HOWELL, Evan (George) (R Ill.) Sept. 21, 1905; House 1941-Oct. 5, 1947.

HOWELL, George (R Pa.) June 28, 1859-Nov. 19, 1913; House 1903-Feb. 10, 1904.

HOWELL, James Bruen (son of Elias Howell) (R Iowa) July 4, 1816-June 17, 1880; Senate Jan. 18, 1870-71.

HOWELL, Jeremiah Brown (F R.I.) Aug. 28, 1771-Feb. 5, 1822; Senate 1811-17.

HOWELL, Joseph (R Utah) Feb. 17, 1857-July 18, 1918; House 1903-17.

HOWELL, Nathaniel Woodhull (—N.Y.) Jan. 1, 1770-Oct. 15, 1851; House 1813-15.

HOWELL, Robert Beecher (R Neb.) Jan. 21, 1864-March 11, 1933; Senate 1923-March 11, 1933.

HOWEY, Benjamin Franklin (nephew of Charles Creighton Stratton) (R N.J.) March 17, 1828-Feb. 6, 1895; House 1883-85.

HOWLAND, Benjamin (D R.I.) July 27, 1755-May 1, 1821; Senate Oct. 29, 1804-09.

HOWLAND, Leonard Paul (R Ohio) Dec. 5, 1865-Dec. 23, 1942; House 1907-13.

HOXWORTH, Stephen Arnold (D Ill.) May 1, 1860-Jan. 25, 1930; House 1913-15.

HRUSKA, Roman Lee (R Neb.) Aug. 16, 1904; House 1953-Nov. 8, 1954; Senate Nov. 8, 1954- .

HUBARD, Edmund Wilcox (D Va.) Feb. 20, 1806-Dec. 9, 1878; House 1841-47.

HUBBARD, Asahel Wheeler (father of Elbert Hamilton Hubbard) (R Iowa) Jan. 19, 1819-Sept. 22, 1879; House 1863-69.

HUBBARD, Chester Dorman (father of William Pallister Hubbard) (R W. Va.) Nov. 25, 1814-Aug. 23, 1891; House 1865-69.

HUBBARD, David (cousin of Samuel Houston) (SRD Ala.) 1792-Jan. 20, 1874; House 1839-41, 1849-51.

HUBBARD, Demas, Jr. (R N.Y.) Jan. 17, 1806-Sept. 2, 1873; House 1865-67.

HUBBARD, Elbert Hamilton (son of Asahel Wheeler Hubbard) (R Iowa) Aug. 19, 1849-June 4, 1912; House 1905-June 4, 1912.

HUBBARD, Henry (D N.H.) May 3, 1784-June 5, 1857; House 1829-35; Senate 1835-41; Gov. 1841-43.

HUBBARD, Joel Douglas (R Mo.) Nov. 6, 1860-May 26, 1919; House 1895-97.

HUBBARD, John Henry (R Conn.) March 24, 1804-July 30, 1872; House 1863-67.

HUBBARD, Jonathan Hatch (F Vt.) May 7, 1768-Sept. 20, 1849; House 1809-11.

HUBBARD, Levi (D Mass.) Dec. 19, 1762-Feb. 18, 1836; House 1813-15.

HUBBARD, Richard Dudley (D Conn.) Sept. 7, 1818-Feb. 28, 1884; House 1867-69; Gov. 1878-79.

HUBBARD, Samuel Dickinson (W Conn.) Aug. 10, 1799-Oct. 8, 1855; House 1845-49; Postmaster General 1852-53.

HUBBARD, Thomas Hill (D N.Y.) Dec. 5, 1781-May 21, 1857; House 1817-19, 1821-23.

HUBBARD, William Pallister (son of Chester Dorman Hubbard) (R W. Va.) Dec. 24, 1843-Dec. 5, 1921; House 1907-11.

HUBBELL, Edwin Nelson (D N.Y.) Aug. 13, 1815-—; House 1865-67.

HUBBELL, James Randolph (R Ohio) July 13, 1824-Nov. 26, 1890; House 1865-67.

HUBBELL, Jay Abel (R Mich.) Sept. 15, 1829-Oct. 13, 1900; House 1873-83.

HUBBELL, William Spring (D N.Y.) Jan. 17, 1801-Nov. 16, 1873, House 1843-45.

HUBBS, Orlando (R N.C.) Feb. 18, 1840-Dec. 5, 1930; House 1881-83.

HUBER, Walter B. (D Ohio) June 29, 1903; House 1945-51.

HUBLEY, Edward Burd (JD Pa.) 1792-Feb. 23, 1856; House 1835-39.

HUCK, Winnifred Sprague Mason (daughter of William Ernest Mason) (R Ill.) Sept. 14, 1882-Aug. 24, 1936; House Nov. 7, 1922-23.

HUDD, Thomas Richard (D Wis.) Oct. 2, 1835-June 22, 1896; House March 8, 1886-89.

HUDDLESTON, George (D Ala.) Nov. 11, 1869-Feb. 29, 1960; House 1915-37.

HUDDLESTON, George, Jr. (son of the preceding) (D Ala.) March 19, 1920; House 1955-65.

HUDSON, Charles (W Mass.) Nov. 14, 1795-May 4, 1881; House May 3, 1841-49.

HUDSON, Grant Martin (R Mich.) July 23, 1868-Oct. 26, 1955; House 1923-31.

HUDSON, Thomas Jefferson (P Kan.) Oct. 30, 1839-Jan. 4, 1923; House 1893-95.

HUDSPETH, Claude Benton (D Texas) May 12, 1877-March 19, 1941; House 1919-31.

HUFF, George Franklin (R Pa.) July 16, 1842-April 18, 1912; House 1891-93, 1895-97, 1903-11.

HUFFMAN, James Wylie (D Ohio) Sept. 13, 1894; Senate Oct. 8, 1945-Nov. 5, 1946.

HUFTY, Jacob (D N.J.) —-May 20, 1814; House 1808-May 20, 1814.

HUGER, Benjamin (—S.C.) 1768-July 7, 1823; House 1799-1805, 1815-17.

HUGER, Daniel (father of Daniel Elliott Huger) (—S.C.) Feb. 20, 1742-July 6, 1799; House 1789-93; Cont. Cong. 1786-88.

HUGER, Daniel Elliott (son of the preceding) SRD S.C.) June 28, 1779-Aug. 21, 1854; Senate 1843-45.

HUGHES, Charles (D N.Y.) Feb. 27, 1822-Aug. 10, 1887; House 1853-55.

HUGHES, Charles James Jr. (D Colo.) Feb. 16, 1853-Jan. 11, 1911; Senate 1909-Jan. 11, 1911.

HUGHES, Dudley Mays (D Ga.) Oct. 10, 1848-Jan. 20, 1927; House 1909-17.

HUGHES, George Wurtz (D Md.) Sept. 30, 1806-Sept. 3, 1870; House 1859-61.

HUGHES, Harold Everett (D Iowa) Feb. 10, 1922; Senate 1969- ; Gov. 1963-69.

HUGHES, James (D Ind.) Nov. 24, 1823-Oct. 24, 1873; House 1857-59.

HUGHES, James Anthony (R W. Va.) Feb. 27, 1861-March 2, 1930; House 1901-15, 1927-March 2, 1930.

HUGHES, James Frederic (D Wis.) Aug. 7, 1883-Aug. 9, 1940; House 1933-35.

HUGHES, James Hurd (D Del.) Jan. 14, 1867-Aug. 29, 1953; Senate 1937-43.

HUGHES, James Madison (D Mo.) April 7, 1809-Feb. 26, 1861; House 1843-45.

HUGHES, Thomas Hurst (W N.J.) Jan. 10, 1769-Nov. 10, 1839; House 1829-33.

HUGHES, William (D N.J.) April 3, 1872-Jan. 30, 1918; House 1903-05, 1907-Sept. 27, 1912; Senate 1913-Jan. 30, 1918.

HUGHSTON, Jonas Abbott (W N.Y.) 1808-Nov. 10, 1862; House 1855-57.

HUGUNIN, Daniel, Jr. (—N.Y.) Feb. 6, 1790-June 21, 1850; House Dec. 15, 1825-27.

HUKRIEDE, Theodore Waldemar (R Mo.) Nov. 9, 1878-April 14, 1945; House 1921-23.

HULBERT, George Murray (D N.Y.) May 14, 1881-April 26, 1950; House 1915-Jan. 1, 1918.

HULBERT, John Whitefield (F Mass.) June 1, 1770-Oct. 19, 1831; House Sept. 26, 1814-17.

HULBURD, Calvin Tilden (R N.Y.) June 5, 1809-Oct. 25, 1897; House 1863-69.

HULICK, George Washington (R Ohio) June 29, 1833-Aug. 13, 1907; House 1893-97.

HULING, James Hall (R W. Va.) March 24, 1844-April 23, 1918; House 1895-97.

HULINGS, Willis James (R Pa.) July 1, 1850-Aug. 8, 1924; House 1913-15 (Pro.), 1919-21 (R).

HULL, Cordell (D Tenn.) Oct. 2, 1871-July 23, 1955; House 1907-21, 1923-31; Senate 1931-March 3, 1933; Secy. of State 1933-44.

HULL, Harry Edward (R Iowa) March 12, 1864-Jan. 16, 1938; House 1915-25.

HULL, John Albert Tiffin (R Iowa) May 1, 1841-Sept. 26, 1928; House 1891-1911.

HULL, Merlin (R Wis.) Dec. 18, 1870-May 17, 1953; House 1929-31 (R), 1935-47 (Pro), 1947-May 17, 1953 (R).

HULL, Morton Denison (R Ill.) Jan. 13, 1867-Aug. 20, 1937; House April 3, 1923-33.

HULL, Noble Andrew (D Fla.) March 11, 1827-Jan. 28, 1907; House 1879-Jan. 22, 1881.

HULL, William Edgar (R Ill.) Jan. 13, 1866-May 30, 1942; House 1923-33.

HULL, William Raleigh, Jr. (D Mo.) April 17, 1906; House 1955- .

HUMPHREY, Augustin Reed (R Neb.) Feb. 18, 1859-Dec. 10, 1937; House Nov. 7, 1922-23.

HUMPHREY, Charles (D N.Y.) Feb. 14, 1792-April 17, 1850; House 1825-27.

HUMPHREY, Herman Leon (R Wis.) March 14, 1830-June 10, 1902; House 1877-83.

HUMPHREY, Hubert Horatio, Jr. (D Minn.) May 27, 1911; Senate 1949-Dec. 29, 1964, 1971- ; Vice President 1965-69.

HUMPHREY, James (R N.Y.) Oct. 9, 1811-June 16, 1866; House 1859-61, 1865-June 16, 1866.

HUMPHREY, James Morgan (D N.Y.) Sept. 21, 1819-Feb. 9, 1899; House 1865-69.

HUMPHREY, Reuben (—N.Y.) Sept. 2, 1757-Aug. 10, 1832; House 1807-09.

HUMPHREY, William Ewart (R Wash) March 31, 1862-Feb. 14, 1934; House 1903-17.

HUMPHREYS, Andrew (D Ind.) March 30, 1821-June 14, 1904; House Dec. 5, 1876-77.

HUMPHREYS, Benjamin Grubb (father of William Yerger Humphreys) (D Miss.) Aug. 17, 1865-Oct. 16, 1923; House 1903-Oct. 16, 1923.

HUMPHREYS, Parry Wayne (D Tenn.) 1778-Feb. 12, 1839; House 1813-15.

HUMPHREYS, Robert (D Ky.) Aug. 20, 1893; Senate June 21-Nov. 6, 1956.

HUMPHREYS, William Yerger (son of Benjamin Grubb Humphreys) (D Miss.) Sept. 9, 1890-Feb. 26, 1933; House Nov. 27, 1923-25.

HUNGATE, William Leonard (D Mo.) Dec. 14, 1922; House Nov. 3, 1964- .

HUNGERFORD, John Newton (R N.Y.) Dec. 31, 1825-April 2, 1883; House 1877-79.

HUNGERFORD, John Pratt (D Va.) Jan. 2, 1761-Dec. 21, 1833; House March 4-Nov. 29, 1811, 1813-17.

HUNGERFORD, Orville (D N.Y.) Oct. 29, 1790-April 6, 1851; House 1843-47.

HUNT, Carleton (nephew of Theodore Gaillard Hunt) (D La.) Jan. 1, 1836-Aug. 14, 1921; House 1883-85.

HUNT, Hiram Paine (W N.Y.) May 23, 1796-Aug. 14, 1865; House 1835-37, 1839-43.

HUNT, James Bennett (D Mich.) Aug. 13, 1799-Aug. 15, 1857; House 1843-47.

HUNT, John E. (R N.J.) Nov. 25, 1908; House 1967- .

HUNT, John Thomas (D Mo.) Feb. 2, 1860-Nov. 30, 1916; House 1903-07.

HUNT, Jonathan (NR Vt.) Aug. 12, 1787-May 15, 1932; House 1827-May 15, 1832.

HUNT, Lester Callaway (D Wyo.) July 8, 1892-June 19, 1954; Senate 1949-June 19, 1954; Gov. 1943-49.

HUNT, Samuel (—N.H.) July 8, 1765-July 7, 1807; House Dec. 6, 1802-05.

HUNT, Theodore Gaillard (nephew of John Gaillard and uncle of Carleton Hunt) (W La.) Oct. 23, 1805-Nov. 15, 1893; House 1853-55.

HUNT, Washington (W N.Y.) Aug. 5, 1811-Feb. 2, 1867; House 1843-49; Gov. 1850-52.

HUNTER, Allan Oakley (R Calif.) June 15, 1916; House 1951-55.

HUNTER, Andrew Jackson (D Ill.) Dec. 17, 1831-Jan. 12, 1913; House 1893-95, 1897-99.

HUNTER, John (F S.C.) 1732-1802; House 1793-95; Senate Dec. 8, 1796-Nov. 26, 1798.

HUNTER, John Feeney (D Ohio) Oct. 19, 1896-Dec. 19, 1957; House 1937-43.

HUNTER, John Ward (—N.Y.) Oct. 15, 1807-April 16, 1900; House Dec. 4, 1866-67.

HUNTER, Morton Craig (R Ind.) Feb. 5, 1825-Oct. 25, 1896; House 1867-69, 1873-79.

HUNTER, Narsworthy (— Miss.)— -March 11, 1802; House (Terr. Del.) 1801-March 11, 1802.

HUNTER, Richard Charles (D Neb.) Dec. 3, 1884-Jan. 23, 1941; Senate Nov. 7, 1934-35.

HUNTER, Robert Mercer Taliaferro (D Va.) April 21, 1809-July 18, 1887; House 1837-43, 1845-47; Senate 1847-March 28, 1861; Speaker 1839-41.

HUNTER, Whiteside Godfrey (R Ky.) Dec. 25, 1841-Nov. 2, 1917; House 1887-89, 1895-97, Nov. 10, 1903-05.

HUNTER, William (R Vt.) Jan. 3, 1754-Nov. 30, 1827; House 1817-19.

HUNTER, William (F R.I.) Nov. 26, 1774-Dec. 3, 1849; Senate Oct. 28, 1811-21.

HUNTER, William Forrest (W Ohio) Dec. 10, 1808-March 30, 1874; House 1849-53.

HUNTER, William H. (D Ohio) — -1842; House 1837-39.

HUNTINGTON, Abel (D N.Y.) Feb. 21, 1777-May 18, 1858; House 1833-37.

HUNTINGTON, Benjamin (—Conn.) April 19, 1736-Oct. 16, 1800; House 1789-91; Cont. Cong. 1780-84, 1787-88.

HUNTINGTON, Ebenezer (W Conn.) Dec. 26, 1754-June 17, 1834; House Oct. 11, 1810-11, 1817-19.

HUNTINGTON, Jabez Williams (W Conn.) Nov. 8, 1788-Nov. 1, 1847; House 1829-Aug. 16, 1834; Senate May 4, 1840-Nov. 1, 1847.

HUNTON, Eppa (D Va.) Sept. 24, 1822-Oct. 11, 1908; House 1873-81; Senate May 28, 1892-95.

HUNTSMAN, Adam (JD Tenn.)-—; House 1835-37.

HUOT, J. Oliva (D N.H.) Aug. 11, 1917; House 1965-67.

HURD, Frank Hunt (D Ohio) Dec. 25, 1840-July 10, 1896; House 1875-77, 1879-81, 1883-85.

HURLBUT, Stephen Augustus (R Ill.) Nov. 29, 1815-March 27, 1882; House 1873-77.

HURLEY, Denis Michael (R N.Y.) March 14, 1843-Feb. 26, 1899; House 1895-Feb. 26, 1899.

HUSTED, James William (R N.Y.) March 16, 1870-Jan. 2, 1925; House 1915-23.

HUSTING, Paul Oscar (D Wis.) April 25, 1866-Oct. 21, 1917; Senate 1915-Oct. 21, 1917.

HUTCHESON, Joseph Chappell (D Texas) May 18, 1842-May 25, 1924; House 1893-97.

HUTCHINS, John (cousin of Wells Andrews Hutchins) (R Ohio) July 25, 1812-Nov. 20, 1891; House 1859-63.

HUTCHINS, Waldo (D N.Y.) Sept. 30, 1822-Feb. 8, 1891; House Nov. 4, 1879-85.

HUTCHINS, Wells Andrews (cousin of John Hutchins) (D Ohio) Oct. 8, 1818-Jan. 25, 1895; House 1863-65.

HUTCHINSON, Edward (R Mich.) Oct. 13, 1914; House 1963- .

HUTCHINSON, Elijah Cubberley (R N.J.) Aug. 7, 1855-June 25, 1932; House 1915-23.

HUTTON, John Edward (D Mo.) March 28, 1828-Dec. 28, 1893; House 1885-89.

HUYLER, John (D N.J.) April 9, 1808-Jan. 9, 1870; House 1857-59.

HYDE, DeWitt Stephen (R Md.) March 21, 1909; House 1953-59.

HYDE, Ira Barnes (R Mo.) Jan. 18, 1838-Dec. 6, 1926; House 1873-75.

HYDE, Samuel Clarence (R Wash.) April 22, 1842-March 7, 1922; House 1895-97.

HYMAN, John Adams (R N.C.) July 23, 1840-Sept. 14, 1891; House 1875-77.

HYNEMAN, John M. (D Pa.) April 25, 1771-April 16, 1816; House 1811-Aug. 2, 1813.

HYNES, William Joseph (D Ark.) March 31, 1843-April 2, 1915; House 1873-75.

I

ICHORD, Richard H. (D Mo.) June 27, 1926; House 1961- .

IGLESIAS, Santiago (formerly Santiago Iglesias Pantin) (Coal. P.R.) Feb. 22, 1872-Dec. 5, 1939; House (Res. Comm.) 1933-Dec. 5, 1939.

IGOE, James Thomas (D Ill.) Oct. 23, 1883; House 1927-33.

IGOE, Michael Lambert (D Ill.) April 16, 1885-Aug. 21, 1967; House Jan. 3-June 2, 1935.

IGOE, William Leo (D Mo.) Oct. 19, 1879-April 20, 1953; House 1913-21.

IHRIE, Peter, Jr. (JD Pa.) Feb. 3, 1796-March 29, 1871; House Oct. 13, 1829-33.

IKARD, Frank Neville (D Texas) Jan. 30, 1914; House Sept. 8, 1951-Dec. 15, 1961.

IKIRT, George Pierce (D Ohio) Nov. 3, 1852-Feb. 12, 1927; House 1893-95.

ILSLEY, Daniel (D Mass.) May 30, 1740-May 10, 1813; House 1807-09.

IMHOFF, Lawrence E. (D Ohio) Dec. 28, 1895; House 1933-39, 1941-43.

IMLAY, James Henderson (—N.J.) Nov. 26, 1764-March 6, 1823; House 1797-1801.

INGALLS, John James (R Kan.) Dec. 29, 1833-Aug. 16, 1900; Senate 1873-91; President pro tempore 1887-91.

INGE, Samuel Williams (nephew of William Marshall Inge) (D Ala.) Feb. 22, 1817-June 10, 1868; House 1847-51.

INGE, William Marshall (uncle of Samuel Williams Inge) (D Tenn.) 1802-46; House 1833-35.

INGERSOLL, Charles Jared (brother of Joseph Reed Ingersoll) (D Pa.) Oct. 3, 1782-May 14, 1862; House 1813-15, 1841-49.

INGERSOLL, Colin Macrae (son of Ralph Isaacs Ingersoll) (D Conn.) March 11, 1819-Sept. 13, 1903; House 1851-55.

INGERSOLL, Ebon Clark (R Ill.) Dec. 12, 1831-May 31, 1879; House May 20, 1864-71.

INGERSOLL, Joseph Reed (brother of Charles Jared Ingersoll) (W Pa.) June 14, 1786-Feb. 20, 1868; House 1835-37, Oct. 12, 1841-49.

INGERSOLL, Ralph Isaacs (father of Colin Macrae Ingersoll) (D Conn.) Feb. 8, 1789-Aug. 26, 1872; House 1825-33.

INGHAM, Samuel (D Conn.) Sept. 5, 1793-Nov. 10, 1881; House 1835-39.

INGHAM, Samuel Delucenna (Jeff. D Pa.) Sept. 16, 1779-June 5, 1860; House 1813-July 6, 1818, Oct. 8, 1822-29; Secy. of the Treasury 1829-31.

INOUYE, Daniel Ken (D Hawaii) Sept. 7, 1924; House Aug. 21,1959-63; Senate 1963- .

IRBY, John Laurens Manning (great-grandson of Elias Earle) (D S.C.) Sept. 10, 1854-Dec. 9, 1900; Senate 1891-97.

IREDELL, James (D N.C.) Nov. 2, 1788-April 13, 1853; Senate Dec. 15, 1828-31; Gov. 1828.

IRELAND, Clifford Cady (R Ill.) Feb. 14, 1878-May 24, 1930; House 1917-23.

IRION, Alfred Briggs (D La.) Feb. 18, 1833-May 21, 1903; House 1885-87.

IRVIN, Alexander (W Pa.) Jan. 18, 1800-March 20, 1874; House 1847-49.

IRVIN, James (W Pa.) Feb. 18, 1800-Nov. 28, 1862; House 1841-45.

IRVIN, William W. (D Ohio) 1778-March 28, 1842; House 1829-33.

IRVINE, William (— Pa.) Nov. 3, 1741-July 29, 1804; House 1793-95; Cont. Cong. 1786-88.

IRVINE, William (R N.Y.) Feb. 14, 1820-Nov. 12, 1882; House 1859-61.

IRVING, Theodore Leonard (D Mo.) March 24, 1898; House 1949-53.

IRVING, William (D N.Y.) Aug. 15, 1766-Nov. 9, 1821; House Jan. 22, 1814-19.

IRWIN, Donald J. (D Conn.) Sept. 7, 1926; House 1959-61, 1965-69.

IRWIN, Edward Michael (R Ill.) April 14, 1869-Jan. 30, 1933; House 1925-31.

IRWIN, Harvey Samuel (R Ky.) Dec. 10, 1844-Sept. 3, 1916; House 1901-03.

IRWIN, Jared (D Pa.) Jan. 19, 1768-—; House 1813-17.

IRWIN, Thomas (D Pa.) Feb. 22, 1785-May 14, 1870; House 1829-31.

IRWIN, William Wallace (W Pa.) 1803-Sept. 15, 1856; House 1841-43.

ISACKS, Jacob C. (— Tenn.) — - —; House 1823-33.

ISACSON, Leo (AL N.Y.) April 20, 1910; House Feb. 17, 1948-49.

ITTNER, Anthony Friday (R Mo.) Oct. 8, 1837-Feb. 22, 1931; House 1877-79.

IVERSON, Alfred, Sr. (D Ga.) Dec. 3, 1798-March 5, 1873; House 1847-49; Senate 1855-Jan. 28, 1861.

IVES, Irving McNeil (R N.Y.) Jan. 24, 1896-Feb. 24, 1962; Senate 1947-59.

IVES, Willard (D N.Y.) July 7, 1806-April 19, 1896; House 1851-53.

IZAC, Edouard Victor Michel (D Calif.) Dec. 18, 1891; House 1937-47.

IZARD, Ralph (— S.C.) Jan. 23, 1742-May 30, 1804; Senate 1789-95; President pro tempore 1794-95; Cont. Cong. 1782-83.

IZLAR, James Ferdinand (D S.C.) Nov. 25, 1832-May 26, 1912; House April 12, 1894-95.

J

JACK, Summers Melville (R Pa.) July 18, 1852-Sept. 16, 1945; House 1899-1903.

JACK, William (D Pa.) July 19, 1788-Feb. 28, 1852; House 1841-43.

JACKSON, Alfred Metcalf (D Kan.) July 14, 1860-June 11, 1924; House 1901-03.

JACKSON, Amos Henry (R Ohio) May 10, 1846-Aug. 30, 1924; House 1903-05.

JACKSON, Andrew (D Tenn.) March 15, 1767-June 8, 1845; House Dec. 5, 1796-97; Senate Sept. 26, 1797-April 1798, March 4, 1823-Oct. 14, 1825; Gov. of Florida March 10-July 18, 1821; President 1829-37.

JACKSON, David Sherwood (D N.Y.) 1813-Jan. 20, 1872; House 1847-April 19, 1848.

JACKSON, Donald L. (R Calif.) Jan. 23, 1910; House 1947-61.

JACKSON, Ebenezer, Jr. (W Conn.) Jan. 31, 1796-Aug. 17, 1874; House Dec. 1, 1834-35.

JACKSON, Edward Brake (son of George Jackson and brother of John George Jackson) (D Va.) Jan. 25, 1793-Sept. 8, 1826; House Oct. 23, 1820-23.

JACKSON, Fred Schuyler (R Kan.) April 19, 1868-Nov. 21, 1931; House 1911-13.

JACKSON, George (father of John George Jackson and Edward Brake Jackson) (—Va.) Jan. 9, 1757-May 17, 1831; House 1795-97, 1799-1803.

JACKSON, Henry Martin (D Wash.) May 31, 1912; House 1941-53; Senate 1953- ; Chairman, Dem. Nat. Comm. 1960-61.

JACKSON, Howell Edmunds (D Tenn) April 8, 1832-Aug. 8, 1895; Senate 1881-April 14, 1886; Assoc. Justice Supreme Court 1894-95.

JACKSON, Jabez Young (son of Senator James Jackson and uncle of Representative James Jackson) (UD Ga.) July 1790- —; House Oct. 5, 1835-39.

JACKSON, James (father of Jabez Y. Jackson and grandfather of James Jackson) (— Ga.) Sept. 21, 1757-March 19, 1806; House 1789-91; Senate 1793-95, 1801-March 19, 1806; Gov. 1798-1801.

JACKSON, James (grandson of the preceding and nephew of Jabez Y. Jackson) (D Ga.) Oct. 18, 1819-Jan. 13, 1887; House 1857-Jan. 23, 1861.

JACKSON, James Monroe (cousin of William Thomas Bland) (D W.Va.) Dec. 3, 1825-Feb. 14, 1901; House 1889-Feb. 3, 1890.

JACKSON, James Streshly (U Ky.) Sept. 27, 1823-Oct. 8, 1862; House March 4-Dec. 13, 1861.

JACKSON, John George (son of George Jackson, brother of Edward Brake Jackson and grandfather of William Thomas Bland) (D Va.) Sept. 22, 1777-March 28, 1825; House 1803-Sept. 28, 1810, 1813-17.

JACKSON, Joseph Webber (D Ga.) Dec. 6, 1796-Sept. 29, 1854; House March 4, 1850-53.

JACKSON, Oscar Lawrence (R Pa.) Sept. 2, 1840-Feb. 16, 1920; House 1885-89.

JACKSON, Richard, Jr. (F R.I.) July 3, 1764-April 18, 1838; House Nov. 11, 1808-15.

JACKSON, Samuel Dillon (D Ind.) May 28, 1895-March 8, 1951; Senate Jan. 28-Nov. 13, 1944.

JACKSON, Thomas Birdsall (D N.Y.) March 24, 1797-April 23, 1881; House 1837-41.

JACKSON, William (W Mass.) Sept. 2, 1783-Feb. 26, 1855; House 1833-37.

JACKSON, William Humphreys (father of William Purnell Jackson) (R Md.) Oct. 15, 1839-April 3, 1915; House 1901-05, 1907-09.

JACKSON, William Purnell (Son of William Humphreys Jackson) (R Md.) Jan. 11, 1868-March 7, 1939; Senate Nov. 29, 1912-Jan. 28, 1914.

JACKSON, William Terry (W N.Y.) Dec. 29, 1794-Sept. 15, 1882; House 1849-51.

JACOBS, Andrew, Sr. (D Ind.) Feb. 22, 1906; House 1949-51.

JACOBS, Andrew Jr. (D Ind.) Feb. 24, 1932; House 1965- .

JACOBS, Ferris, Jr. (R N.Y.) March 20, 1836-Aug. 30, 1886; House 1881-83.

JACOBS, Israel (— Pa.) June 9, 1726-about Dec. 10, 1796; House 1791-93.

JACOBS, Orange (R Wash.) May 2, 1827-May 21, 1914; House (Terr. Del.) 1875-79.

JACOBSEN, Bernhard Martin (father of William Sebastian Jacobsen) (D Iowa) March 26, 1862-June 30, 1936; House 1931-June 30, 1936.

JACOBSEN, William Sebastian (son of Bernhard Martin Jacobsen) (D Iowa) Jan. 15, 1887-April 10, 1955; House 1937-43.

JACOBSTEIN, Meyer (D N.Y.) Jan. 25, 1880-April 18, 1963; House 1923-29.

JACOWAY, Henderson Madison (D Ark.) Nov. 7, 1870-Aug. 4, 1947; House 1911-23.

JADWIN, Cornelius Comegys (R Pa.) March 27, 1835-Aug. 17, 1913; House 1881-83.

JAMES, Addison Davis (grandfather of John Albert Whitaker) (R Ky.) Feb. 27, 1850-June 10, 1947; House 1907-09.

JAMES, Amaziah Bailey (R N.Y.) July 1, 1812-July 6, 1883; House 1877-81.

JAMES, Benjamin Franklin (R Pa.) Aug. 1, 1885-Jan. 26, 1961; House 1949-59.

JAMES, Charles Tillinghast (Protect. TD) Sept. 15, 1805-Oct. 17, 1862; Senate 1851-57.

JAMES, Darwin Rush (R N.Y.) May 14, 1834-Nov. 19, 1908; House 1883-87.

JAMES, Francis (W Pa.) April 4, 1799-Jan. 4, 1886; House 1839-41.

JAMES, Hinton (D N.C.) April 24, 1884-Nov. 3, 1948; House Nov. 4, 1930-31.

JAMES, Ollie Murray (D Ky.) July 27, 1871-Aug. 28, 1918; House 1903-13; Senate 1913-Aug. 28, 1918.

JAMES, Rorer Abraham (D Va.) March 1, 1859-Aug. 6, 1921; House June 15, 1920-Aug. 6, 1921.

JAMES, William Francis (Frank) (R Mich.) May 23, 1873-Nov. 17, 1945; House 1915-35.

JAMESON, John (D Mo.) March 6, 1802-Jan. 24, 1857; House Dec. 12, 1839-41, 1843-45, 1847-49.

JAMIESON, William Darius (D Iowa) Nov. 9, 1873-Nov. 18, 1949; House 1909-11.

JANES, Henry Fisk (W/A-M Vt.) Oct. 10, 1792-June 6, 1879; House Dec. 2, 1834-37.

JARMAN, John (D Okla.) July 17, 1915; House 1951- .

JARMAN, Pete (D Ala.) Oct. 31, 1892-Feb. 17, 1955; House 1937-49.

JARNAGIN, Spencer (W Tenn.) 1792-June 25, 1853; Senate Oct. 17, 1843-47.

JARRETT, Benjamin (R Pa.) July 1881-July 20, 1944; House 1937-43.

JARRETT, William Paul (D Hawaii) Aug. 22, 1877-Nov. 10, 1929; House (Terr. Del.) 1923-27.

JARVIS, Leonard (D Maine) Oct. 19, 1781-Oct. 18, 1854; House 1829-37.

JARVIS, Thomas Jordan (D N.C.) Jan. 18, 1836-June 17, 1915; Senate April 19, 1894-Jan. 23, 1895; Gov. 1879-85.

JAVITS, Jacob Koppel (R N.Y.) May 18, 1904; House 1947-Dec. 31, 1954; Senate Jan. 9, 1957- .

JAYNE, William (— Dakota) Oct. 8, 1826-March 20, 1916; House (Terr. Del.) 1863-June 17, 1864; Gov. 1861-63.

JEFFERIS, Albert Webb (R Neb.) Dec. 7, 1868-Sept. 14, 1942; House 1919-23.

JEFFERS, Lamar (D Ala.) April 16, 1888; House June 7, 1921-35.

JEFFORDS, Elza (R Miss.) May 23, 1826-March 19, 1885; House 1883-85.

JEFFREY, Harry Palmer (R Ohio) Dec. 26, 1901; House 1943-45.

JEFFRIES, Walter Sooy (R N.J.) Oct. 16, 1893-Oct. 11, 1954; House 1939-41.

JENCKES, Thomas Allen (R R.I.) Nov. 2, 1818-Nov. 4, 1875; House 1863-71.

JENCKES, Virginia Ellis (D Ind.) Nov. 6, 1882; House 1933-39.

JENIFER, Daniel (NR Md.) April 15, 1791-Dec. 18, 1855; House 1831-33, 1835-41.

JENISON, Edward Halsey (R Ill.) July 27, 1907; House 1947-53.

JENKINS, Albert Gallatin (D Va.) Nov. 10, 1830-May 21, 1864; House 1857-61.

JENKINS, John James (R Wis.) Aug. 24, 1843-June 8, 1911; House 1895-1909.

JENKINS, Lemuel (D N.Y.) Oct. 20, 1789-Aug. 18, 1862; House 1823-25.

JENKINS, Mitchell (R Pa.) Jan. 24, 1896; House 1947-49.

JENKINS, Robert (— Pa.) July 10, 1769-April 18, 1848; House 1807-11.

JENKINS, Thomas Albert (R Ohio) Oct. 28, 1880-Dec. 21, 1959; House 1925-59.

JENKINS, Timothy (D N.Y.) Jan. 29, 1799-Dec. 24, 1859; House 1945-49, 1851-53.

JENKS, Arthur Byron (R N.H.) Oct. 15, 1866-Dec. 14, 1947; House 1937-June 9, 1938, 1939-43.

JENKS, George Augustus (D Pa.) March 26, 1836-Feb. 10, 1908; House 1875-77.

JENKS, Michael Hutchinson (W Pa.) May 21, 1795-Oct. 16, 1867; House 1843-45.

JENNER, William Ezra (R Ind.) July 21, 1908; Senate Nov. 14, 1944-45, 1947-59.

JENNESS, Benning Wentworth (D N.H.) July 14, 1806-Nov. 16, 1879; Senate Dec. 1, 1845-June 13, 1846.

JENNINGS, David (— Ohio) 1787-1834; House 1825-May 25, 1826.

JENNINGS, John, Jr. (R Tenn.) June 6, 1880-Feb. 27, 1956; House Dec. 30, 1939-51.

JENNINGS, Jonathan (D Ind.) 1784-July 26, 1834; House (Terr. Del.) Nov. 27, 1809-Dec. 11, 1816, (Rep.) Dec. 2, 1822-31; Gov. 1816-22.

JENNINGS, William Pat (D Va.) Aug. 20, 1919; House 1955-67.

JENSEN, Benton Franklin (Ben) (R Iowa) Dec. 16, 1892-Feb. 5, 1970; House 1939-65.

JETT, Thomas Marion (D Ill.) May 1, 1862-Jan. 10, 1939; House 1897-1903.

JEWETT, Daniel Tarbox (R Mo.) Sept. 14, 1807-Oct. 7, 1906; Senate Dec. 19, 1870-Jan. 20, 1871.

JEWETT, Freeborn Garrettson (JD N.Y.) Aug. 4, 1791-Jan. 27, 1858; House 1831-33.

JEWETT, Hugh Judge (brother of Joshua Husband Jewett) (D Ohio) July 1, 1817-March 6, 1898; House 1873- June 23, 1874.

JEWETT, Joshua Husband (brother of Hugh Judge Jewett) (D Ky.) Sept. 30, 1815-July 14, 1861; House 1855-59.

JEWETT, Luther (F Vt.) Dec. 24, 1772-March 8, 1860; House 1815-17.

JOELSON, Charles S. (D N.J.) Jan. 27, 1916; House 1961-Sept. 4, 1969.

JOHANSEN, August Edgar (R Mich.) July 21, 1905; House 1955-65.

JOHNS, Joshua Leroy (R Wis.) Feb. 27, 1881-March 16, 1947; House 1939-43.

JOHNS, Kensey, Jr. (F Del.) Dec. 10, 1791-March 28, 1857; House Oct. 2, 1827-31.

JOHNSON, Adna Romulus (R Ohio) Dec. 14, 1860-June 11, 1938; House 1909-11.

JOHNSON, Albert (R Wash.) March 5, 1869-Jan. 17, 1957; House 1913-33.

JOHNSON, Albert W. (R Pa.) April 17, 1906; House Nov. 5, 1963- .

JOHNSON, Andrew (R Tenn.) Dec. 29, 1808-July 31, 1875; House 1843-53 (D); Senate Oct. 8, 1857-March 4, 1862 (D), March 4-July 31, 1875 (R); Gov. 1853-57 (D); Vice Pres. March 4-April 15, 1865; Pres. April 15, 1865-69 (R).

JOHNSON, Anton Joseph (R Ill.) Oct. 20, 1878-April 16, 1958; House 1939-49.

JOHNSON, Ben (D Ky.) May 20, 1858-June 4, 1950; House 1907-27.

JOHNSON, Byron Lindberg (D Colo.) Oct. 12, 1917; House 1959-61.

JOHNSON, Calvin Dean (R Ill.) Nov. 22, 1898; House 1943-45.

JOHNSON, Cave (D Tenn.) Jan. 11, 1793-Nov. 23, 1866; House 1829-37, 1839-45; Postmaster Gen. 1845-49.

JOHNSON, Charles (— N.C.) — July 23, 1802; House 1801-July 23, 1802.

JOHNSON, Charles Fletcher (D Maine) Feb. 14, 1859-Feb. 15, 1930; Senate 1911-17.

JOHNSON, Dewey William (F-L Minn.) March 14, 1899-Sept. 18, 1941; House 1937-39.

JOHNSON, Edwin Carl (D Colo.) Jan. 1, 1884-May 30, 1970; Senate 1937-55; Gov. 1933-37, 1955-57.

JOHNSON, Edwin Stockton (D S.D.) Feb. 26, 1857-July 19, 1933; Senate 1915-21.

JOHNSON, Francis (Ad. D Ky.) June 19, 1776-May 16, 1842; House Nov. 13, 1820-27.

JOHNSON, Frederick Avery (— N.Y.) Jan. 2, 1833-July 17, 1893; House 1883-87.

JOHNSON, Fred Gustus (R Neb.) Oct. 16, 1876-April 30, 1951; House 1929-31.

JOHNSON, George William (D W. Va.) Nov. 10, 1869-Feb. 24, 1944; House 1923-25, 1933-43.

JOHNSON, Glen Dale (D Okla.) Sept. 11, 1911; House 1947-49.

JOHNSON, Grove Lawrence (father of Hiram Warren Johnson) (R Calif.) March 27, 1841-Feb. 1, 1926; House 1895-97.

JOHNSON, Harold Terry (D Calif.) Dec. 2, 1907; House 1959- .

JOHNSON, Harvey Hull (D Ohio) Sept. 7, 1808-Feb. 4, 1896; House 1853-55.

JOHNSON, Henry (W La.) Sept. 14, 1783-Sept. 4, 1864; Senate Jan. 12, 1818-May 27, 1824, Feb. 12, 1844-49; House Sept. 25, 1834-39; Gov. 1824-28.

JOHNSON, Henry Underwood (R Ind.) Oct. 28, 1850-June 4, 1939; House 1891-99.

JOHNSON, Herschel Vespasian (D Ga.) Sept. 18, 1812-Aug. 16, 1880; Senate Feb. 4, 1848-49; Gov. 1853-57.

JOHNSON, Hiram Warren (son of Grove Lawrence Johnson) (R Calif.) Sept. 2, 1866-Aug. 6, 1945; Senate March 16, 1917-Aug. 6, 1945; Gov. 1911-17.

JOHNSON, Jacob (R Utah) Nov. 1, 1847-Aug. 15, 1925; House 1913-15.

JOHNSON, James (D Va.)— Dec. 7, 1825; House 1813-Feb. 1, 1820.

JOHNSON, James (brother of Richard Mentor Johnson and John Telemachus Johnson and uncle of Robert Ward Johnson) (D Ky.) Jan. 1, 1774-Aug. 14, 1826; House 1825-Aug. 14, 1826.

JOHNSON, James (U Ga.) Feb. 12, 1811-Nov. 20, 1891; House 1851-53; Provisional Gov. 1865.

JOHNSON, James Augustus (D Calif.) May 16, 1829-May 11, 1896; House 1867-71.

JOHNSON, James Hutchins (— N.H.) June 3, 1802-Sept. 2, 1887; House 1845-49.

JOHNSON, James Leeper (W Ky.) Oct. 30, 1818-Feb. 12, 1877; House 1849-51.

JOHNSON, Jed Joseph (D Okla.) July 31, 1888-May 7, 1963; House 1927-47.

JOHNSON, Jed, Jr. (son of the preceding) (D Okla.) Dec. 17, 1939; House 1965-67.

JOHNSON, Jeromus (D N.Y.) Nov. 2, 1775-Sept. 7, 1846; House 1825-29.

JOHNSON, John (I Ohio) 1805-Feb. 5, 1867; House 1851-53.

JOHNSON, John Telemachus (brother of James Johnson and Richard Mentor Johnson and uncle of Robert Ward Johnson) (JD Ky.) Oct. 5, 1788-Dec. 17, 1856; House 1821-25.

JOHNSON, Joseph (uncle of Waldo Porter Johnson) (D Va.) Dec. 19, 1785-Feb. 17, 1877; House 1823-27, Jan. 21-March 3, 1833, 1835-41, 1845-47; Gov. 1852-56.

JOHNSON, Joseph Travis (D S.C.) Feb. 28, 1858-May 8, 1919; House 1901-April 19, 1915.

JOHNSON, Justin Leroy (R Calif.) April 8, 1888-March 26, 1961; House 1943-57.

JOHNSON, Lester R. (D Wis.) June 16, 1901; House Oct. 13, 1953-65.

JOHNSON, Luther Alexander (D Texas) Oct. 29, 1875-June 6, 1965; House 1923-July 17, 1946.

JOHNSON, Lyndon Baines (D Texas) Aug. 27, 1908; House April 10, 1937-49; Senate 1949-61; Vice Pres. 1961-Nov. 22, 1963; President Nov. 22, 1963-69.

JOHNSON, Magnus (F-L Minn.) Sept. 19, 1871-Sept. 13, 1936; Senate July 16, 1923-25; House 1933-35.

JOHNSON, Martin Nelson (R N.D.) March 3, 1950-Oct. 21, 1909; House 1891-99, March 4-Oct. 21, 1909.

JOHNSON, Noadiah (D N.Y.) 1795-April 4, 1839; House 1833-35.

JOHNSON, Noble Jacob (R Ind.) Aug. 23, 1887-March 17, 1968; House 1925-31, 1939-July 1, 1948.

JOHNSON, Paul Burney (D Miss.) March 23, 1880-Dec. 26, 1943; House 1919-23; Gov. 1939-43.

JOHNSON, Perley Brown (W Ohio) Sept. 8, 1798-Feb. 9, 1870; House 1843-45.

JOHNSON, Philip (R Pa.) Jan. 17, 1818-Jan. 29, 1867; House 1861-Jan. 29, 1867.

JOHNSON, Reverdy (brother-in-law of Thomas Fielder Bowie) (D Md.) May 21, 1796-Feb. 10, 1876; Senate 1845-March 7, 1849 (W), 1863-July 10, 1868 (D); Attorney Gen. 1849-50.

JOHNSON, Richard Mentor (brother of James Johnson and John Telemachus Johnson and uncle of Robert Ward Johnson) (D Ky.) Oct. 17, 1781-Nov. 19, 1850; House 1807-19, 1829-37; Senate Dec. 10, 1819-29 (JD); Vice Pres. 1837-41.

JOHNSON, Robert Davis (D Mo.) Aug. 12, 1883-Oct. 23, 1961; House Sept. 29, 1931-33.

JOHNSON, Robert Ward (nephew of James Johnson, John Telemachus Johnson and Richard Mentor Johnson) (D Ark.) July 22, 1814-July 26, 1879; House 1847-53; Senate July 6, 1853-61.

JOHNSON, Royal Cleaves (R S.D.) Oct. 3, 1882-Aug. 2, 1939; House 1915-33.

JOHNSON, Thomas F. (D Md.) June 26, 1909; House 1959-63.

JOHNSON, Tom Loftin (D Ohio) July 18, 1854-April 10, 1911; House 1891-95.

JOHNSON, Waldo Porter (nephew of Joseph Johnson) (D Mo.) Sept. 16, 1817-Aug. 14, 1885; Senate March 17, 1861- Jan. 10, 1862.

JOHNSON, William Cost (W Md.) Jan. 14, 1806-April 14, 1860; House 1833-35, 1837-43.

JOHNSON, William Richard (R Ill.) May 15, 1875-Jan. 2, 1938; House 1925-33.

JOHNSON, William Samuel (—Conn.) Oct. 7, 1727-Nov. 14, 1819; Senate 1789-March 4, 1791; Cont. Cong. 1784-87.

JOHNSON, William Ward (R Calif.) March 9, 1892-June 10, 1963; House 1941-45.

JOHNSTON, Charles (W N.Y.) Feb. 14, 1793-Sept. 1, 1845; House 1839-41.

JOHNSTON, Charles Clement (brother of Joseph Eggleston Johnston and uncle of John Warfield Johnston) (SRD Va.) April 30, 1795-June 17, 1832; House 1831-June 17, 1832.

JOHNSTON, David Emmons (D W. Va.) April 10, 1845-July 7, 1917; House 1899-1901.

JOHNSTON, James Thomas (R Ind.) Jan. 19, 1839-July 19, 1904; House 1885-89.

JOHNSTON, John Brown (D N.Y.) July 10, 1882-Jan. 11, 1960; House 1919-21.

JOHNSTON, John Warfield (uncle of Henry Bowen and nephew of Charles Clement Johnston and Joseph Eggleston Johnston) (C Va.) Sept. 9, 1818-Feb. 27, 1889; Senate Jan. 26, 1870-March 3, 1871, March 15, 1871-83.

JOHNSTON, Joseph Eggleston (brother of Charles Clement Johnston and uncle of John Warfield Johnston) (D Va.) Feb. 3, 1807-March 21, 1891; House 1879-81.

JOHNSTON, Joseph Forney (D Ala.) March 23, 1843-Aug. 8, 1913; Senate Aug. 6, 1907-Aug. 8, 1913; Gov. 1896-1900.

JOHNSTON, Josiah Stoddard (D La.) Nov. 24, 1784-May 19, 1833; House 1821-23; Senate Jan. 15, 1824-May 19, 1833.

JOHNSTON, Olin DeWitt Talmadge (D S.C.) Nov. 18, 1896-April 18, 1965; Senate 1945-April 18, 1965; Gov. 1935-39; 1943-45.

JOHNSTON, Rienzi Melville (cousin of Benjamin Edward Russell) (D Texas) Sept. 9, 1849-Feb. 28, 1926; Senate Jan. 4-Feb. 2, 1913.

JOHNSTON, Rowland Louis (R Mo.) April 23, 1872-Sept. 22, 1939; House 1929-31.

JOHNSTON, Samuel (F N.C.) Dec. 15, 1733-Aug. 18, 1816; Senate Nov. 27, 1789-93; Cont. Cong. 1780-82.

JOHNSTON, Thomas Dillard (D N.C.) April 1, 1840-June 22, 1902; House 1885-89.

JOHNSTON, William (D Ohio) 1819-May 1, 1866; House 1863-65.

JOHNSTONE, George (D S.C.) April 18, 1846-March 8, 1921; House 1891-93.

JOLLEY, John Lawlor (R S.D.) July 14, 1840-Dec. 14, 1926; House Dec. 7, 1891-93.

JONAS, Benjamin Franklin (D La.) July 19, 1834-Dec. 21, 1911; Senate 1879-85.

JONAS, Charles Andrew (father of Charles Raper Jonas) (R N.C.) Aug. 14, 1876-May 25, 1955; House 1929-31.

JONAS, Charles Raper (son of Charles Andrew Jonas) (R N.C.) Dec. 9, 1904; House 1953- .

JONAS, Edgar Allan (R Ill.) Oct. 14, 1885-Nov. 14, 1965; House 1949-55.

JONES, Alexander Hamilton (R N.C.) July 21, 1822-Jan. 29, 1901; House July 6, 1868-71.

JONES, Andrieus Aristieus (D N.M.) May 16, 1862-Dec. 20, 1927; Senate 1917-Dec. 10, 1927.

JONES, Benjamin (D Ohio) April 13, 1787-April 24, 1861; House 1833-37.

JONES, Burr W. (D Wis.) March 9, 1846-Jan. 7, 1935; House 1883-85.

JONES, Charles William (D Fla.) Dec. 24, 1834-Oct. 11, 1897; Senate 1875-87.

JONES, Daniel Terryll (D N.Y.) Aug. 17, 1800-March 19, 1861; House 1851-55.

JONES, Ed (D Tenn.) April 20, 1912; House March 25, 1969- .

JONES, Evan John (R Pa.) Oct. 23, 1872-Jan. 9, 1952; House 1919-23.

JONES, Francis (— Tenn.) — - —; House 1817-23.

JONES, Frank (D N.H.) Sept. 15, 1832-Oct. 2, 1902; House 1875-79.

JONES, George (—Ga.) Feb. 25, 1766-Nov. 13, 1838; Senate Aug. 27-Nov. 7, 1807.

JONES, George Wallace (—Mich./ Wis./ Iowa) April 12, 1804-July 22, 1896; House (Terr. Del.) 1835-April 1836 (Mich.), April 1836-Jan. 14, 1839 (Wis.); Senate Dec. 7, 1848-59 (Iowa)

JONES, George Washington (D Tenn.) March 15, 1806-Nov. 14, 1884; House 1843-59.

JONES, George Washington (G Texas) Sept. 5, 1828-July 11, 1903; House 1879-83.

JONES, Hamilton Chamberlain (D N.C.) Sept. 26, 1884-Aug. 10, 1957; House 1947-53.

JONES, Homer Raymond (R Wash.) Sept. 3, 1893-Nov. 26, 1970; House 1947-49.

JONES, Isaac Dashiell (W Md.) Nov. 1, 1806-July 5, 1893; House 1841-43.

JONES, James (R Ga.) — -Jan. 11, 1801; House 1799-Jan. 11, 1801.

JONES, James (D Va.) Dec. 11, 1772-April 25, 1848; House 1819-23.

JONES, James Chamberlain (W Tenn.) April 20, 1809-Oct. 29, 1859; Senate 1851-57; Gov. 1841-45.

JONES, James Henry (D Texas) Sept. 13, 1830-March 22, 1904; House 1883-87.

JONES, James Kimbrough (D Ark.) Sept. 29, 1839-June 1, 1908; House 1881-Feb. 19, 1885; Senate March 4, 1885-1903.

JONES, James Taylor (D Ala.) July 20, 1832-Feb. 15, 1895; House 1877-79, Dec. 3, 1883-89.

JONES, Jehu Glancy (D Pa.) Oct. 7, 1811-March 24, 1878; House 1851-53, Feb. 4, 1854-Oct. 30, 1858.

JONES, John James (D Ga.) Nov. 13, 1824-Oct. 19, 1898; House 1859-Jan. 23, 1861.

JONES, John Percival (R Nev.) Jan. 27, 1829-Nov. 27, 1912; Senate 1873-1903.

JONES, John Sills (R Ohio) Feb. 12, 1836-April 11, 1903; House 1877-79.

JONES, John William (W Ga.) April 14, 1806-April 27, 1871; House 1847-49.

JONES, John Winston (D Va.) Nov. 22, 1791-Jan. 29, 1848; House 1835-45; Speaker 1843-45.

JONES, Marvin (D Texas) Feb. 26, 1886; House 1917-Nov. 20, 1940.

JONES, Morgan (D N.Y.) Feb. 26, 1830-July 13, 1894; House 1865-67.

JONES, Nathaniel (D N.Y.) Feb. 17, 1788-July 20, 1866; House 1837-41.

JONES, Owen (D Pa.) Dec. 29, 1819-Dec. 25, 1878; House 1857-59.

JONES, Paul Caruthers (D Mo.) March 12, 1901; House Nov. 2, 1948-69.

JONES, Phineas (R N.J.) April 18, 1819-April 19, 1884; House 1881-83.

JONES, Robert Emmett, Jr. (D Ala.) June 12, 1912; House Jan. 28, 1947- .

JONES, Robert Franklin (R Ohio) June 25, 1907-June 22, 1968; House 1939-Sept. 2, 1947.

JONES, Roland (D La.) Nov. 18, 1813-Feb. 5, 1869; House 1853-55.

JONES, Seaborn (D Ga.) Feb. 1, 1788-March 18, 1864; House 1833-35; 1845-47.

JONES, Thomas Laurens (D Ky.) Jan. 22, 1819-June 20, 1887; House 1867-71, 1875-77.

JONES, Walter (D Va.) Dec. 18, 1745-Dec. 31, 1815; House 1797-99, 1803-11.

JONES, Walter B. (D N.C.) Aug. 19, 1913; House Feb. 5, 1966- .

JONES, Wesley Livcoy (R Wash.) Oct. 9, 1863-Nov. 19, 1932; House 1899-1909; Senate 1909- Nov. 19, 1932.

JONES, William (D Pa.) 1760-Sept. 6, 1831; IIouse 1801-03; Secy. of the Navy 1813-14.

JONES, William Atkinson (D Va.) March 21, 1849-April 17, 1918; House 1891-April 17, 1918.

JONES, William Carey (FSil. R Wash.) April 5, 1855-June 14, 1927; House 1897-99.

JONES, William Theopilus (R Wyo) Feb. 20,1842-Oct. 9, 1882; House (Terr. Del.) 1871-73.

JONES, Woodrow Wilson (D N.C.) Jan. 26, 1914; House Nov. 7, 1950-57.

JONKMAN, Bartel John (R Mich.) April 28, 1884-June 13, 1955; House Feb. 19, 1940-49.

JORDAN, B. Everett (D N.C.) Sept. 8, 1896; Senate April 19, 1958- .

JORDAN, Isaac M. (D Ohio) May 5, 1835-Dec. 3, 1890; House 1883-85.

JORDAN, Len B. (R Idaho) May 15, 1899; Senate Aug. 6, 1962- ; Gov. 1951-55.

JORDEN, Edwin James (R Pa.) Aug. 30, 1863-Sept. 7, 1903; House Feb. 23-March 4, 1895.

JORGENSEN, Joseph (R Va.) Feb. 11, 1844-Jan. 21, 1888; House 1877-83.

JOSEPH, Antonio (D N.M.) Aug. 25, 1846-April 19, 1910; House (Terr. Del.) 1885-95.

JOST, Henry Lee (D Mo.) Dec. 6, 1873-July 13, 1950; House 1923-25.

JOY,Charles Frederick (R Mo.)Dec.11,1849-April 13,1921;House 1893-April 3, 1894, 1895-1903.

JOYCE, Charles Herbert (R Vt.) Jan. 30, 1830-Nov. 22, 1916; House 1875-83.

JOYCE, James (R Ohio) July 2, 1870-March 25, 1931; House 1909-11.

JUDD, Norman Buel (grandfather of Norman Judd Gould) R Ill.) Jan. 10, 1815-Nov. 10, 1878; House 1867-71.

JUDD, Walter Henry (R Minn.) Sept. 25, 1898—House 1943-63.

JUDSON, Andrew Thompson (D Conn.) Nov. 29, 1784-March 17, 1853; House 1835-July 4, 1836.

JULIAN, George Washington (R Ind.) May 5, 1817-July 7, 1899; House 1849-51 (F-S); 1861-71 (R).

JUNKIN, Benjamin Franklin (R Pa.) Nov. 12, 1822-Oct. 9, 1908; House 1859-61.

JUUL, Niels (R Ill.) April 27, 1859-Dec. 4, 1929; House 1917-21.

K

KADING, Charles August (R Wis.) Jan. 14, 1874-June 19, 1956; House 1927-33.

KAHN, Florence Prag (wife of Julius Kahn) (R Calif.) Nov. 9, 1868-Nov. 16, 1948; House 1925-37.

KAHN, Julius (husband of Florence Prag Kahn) (R Calif.) Feb. 28, 1861-Dec. 18, 1924; House 1899-1903, 1905-Dec. 18, 1924.

KALANIANAOLE, Jonah Kuhio (R Hawaii) March 26, 1871-Jan. 7, 1922; House (Terr. Del.) 1903-Jan. 7, 1922.

KALBFLEISCH, Martin (D N.Y.) Feb. 8, 1804-Feb. 12, 1873; House 1863-65.

KANE, Elias Kent (D Ill.) June 7, 1794-Dec. 12, 1835; Senate 1825-Dec. 12, 1835.

KANE, Nicholas Thomas (D N.Y.) Sept.12,1846-Sept.14,1887; House March 4-Sept.14,1887.

KARCH, Charles Adam (D Ill.) March 17, 1875-Nov. 6,1932; House 1931-Nov. 6, 1932.

KARST, Raymond Willard (D Mo.) Dec. 31, 1902; House 1949-51.

KARSTEN, Frank Melvin (D Mo.) Jan. 7, 1913; House 1947-69.

KARTH, Joseph Edward (D Minn.) Aug. 26, 1922; House 1959- .

KASEM, George Albert (D Calif.) April 6, 1919; House 1959-61.

KASSON, John Adam (R Iowa) Jan. 11, 1822-May 19, 1910; House 1863-67, 1873-77, 1881-July 13, 1884.

KASTENMEIER, Robert William (D Wis.) Jan. 24, 1924; House 1959- .

KAUFMAN, David Spangler (D Texas) Dec. 18, 1813-Jan. 31, 1851; House March 30, 1846-Jan. 31, 1851.

KAVANAGH, Edward (D Maine) April 27,1795-Jan. 20, 1844; House 1831-35; Gov. 1843-44.

KAVANAUGH, William Marmaduke (D Ark.) March 3, 1866-Feb. 21, 1915; Senate Jan. 29-March 3, 1913.

KAYNOR, William Kirk (R Mass.) Nov. 29,1884-Dec. 20,1929; House March 4-Dec.20,1929.

KAZEN, Abraham, Jr. (D Texas) Jan. 17, 1919; House 1967- .

KEAN, Hamilton Fish (father of Robert Winthrop Kean, brother of John Kean) (R N.J.) Feb. 27,1862-Dec. 27,1941; Senate 1929-35.

KEAN, John (brother of Hamilton Fish Kean and uncle of Robert Winthrop Kean) (R N.J.) Dec. 4, 1852-Nov. 4, 1914; House 1883-85, 1887-89; Senate 1899-1911.

KEAN, Robert Winthrop (son of Hamilton Fish Kean, nephew of John Kean) (R N.J.) Sept. 28, 1893; House 1939-59

KEARNEY, Bernard William (R N.Y.) May 23, 1889; House 1943-59.

KEARNS, Carroll Dudley (R Pa.) May 7, 1900; House 1947-63.

KEARNS, Charles Cyrus (R Ohio) Feb. 11, 1869-Dec. 17, 1931; House 1915-31.

KEARNS, Thomas (R Utah) April 11, 1862-Oct. 18, 1918; Senate Jan. 23, 1901-05.

KEATING, Edward (D Colo.) July 9, 1875-March 18, 1965; House 1913-19.

KEATING, Kenneth Barnard (R N.Y.) May 18, 1900; House 1947-59; Senate 1959-65.

KEATING, William J. (R Ohio) March 30, 1927; House 1971- .

KEE, James (son of John and Maude Elizabeth Kee) (D W. Va.) April 15, 1917; House 1965- .

KEE, John (husband of Maude Elizabeth Kee and father of James Kee) (D W. Va.) Aug. 22, 1874-May 8, 1951; House 1933-May 8, 1951.

KEE, Maude Elizabeth (widow of John Kee and mother of James Kee) (D W. Va.); House July 17, 1951-65.

KEEFE, Frank Bateman (R Wis.) Sept. 23, 1887-Feb. 5, 1952; House 1939-51.

KEENEY, Russell Watson (R Ill.) Dec. 29, 1897-Jan. 11. 1958; House 1957-Jan. 11, 1958.

KEESE, Richard (D N.Y.) Nov. 23, 1794-Feb. 7, 1883; House 1827-29.

KEFAUVER, Carey Estes (D Tenn.) July 26, 1903-Aug. 10, 1963; House Sept. 13, 1939-49; Senate 1949-Aug. 10, 1963.

KEHOE, James Nicholas (D Ky.) July 15, 1862-June 16, 1945; House 1901-05.

KEHOE, James Walter (D Fla.) April 25, 1870-Aug. 20, 1938; House 1917-19.

KEHR, Edward Charles (D Mo.) Nov. 5, 1837-April 20, 1918; House 1875-77.

KEIFER, Joseph Warren (R Ohio) Jan. 30, 1836-April 22, 1932; House 1877-85, 1905-11; Speaker 1881-83.

KEIGHTLEY, Edwin William (R Mich.) Aug. 7, 1843-May 4, 1926; House 1877-79.

KEIM, George May (uncle of William High Keim) (D Pa.) March 23, 1805-June 10, 1861; House March 17, 1838-43.

KEIM, William High (nephew of George May Keim) (D Pa.) June 13, 1813-May 18, 1862; House Dec. 7, 1858-59.

KEISTER, Abraham Lincoln (R Pa.) Sept. 10, 1852-May 26, 1917; House 1913-17.

KEITH, Hastings (R Mass.) Nov. 22, 1915; House 1959- .

KEITT, Laurence Massillon (D S.C.) Oct. 4, 1824-June 4, 1864; House 1853-July 16, 1856; Aug. 6, 1856-Dec. 1860.

KELIHER, John Austin (D Mass.) Nov. 6, 1866-Sept. 20, 1938; House 1903-11.

KELLER, Kent Ellsworth (D Ill.) June 4, 1867-Sept. 3, 1954; House 1931-41.

KELLER, Oscar Edward (IR Minn.) July 30, 1878-Nov. 21, 1927; House July 1, 1919-27.

KELLEY, Augustine Bernard (D Pa.) July 9, 1883-Nov. 20, 1957; House 1941-Nov. 20, 1957.

KELLEY, Harrison (R Kan.) May 12, 1836-July 24, 1897; House Dec. 2, 1889-91.

KELLEY, John Edward (D/PP S.D.) March 27, 1853-Aug. 5, 1941; House 1897-99.

KELLEY, Patrick Henry (R Mich.) Oct. 7, 1867-Sept. 11, 1925; House 1913-23.

KELLEY, William Darrah (R Pa.) April 12, 1814-Jan. 9, 1890; House 1861-Jan. 9, 1890.

KELLOGG, Charles (—N.Y.) Oct. 3, 1773-May 11, 1842; House 1825-27.

KELLOGG, Francis William (R Mich./Ala.) May 30, 1810-Jan. 13, 1879; House 1859-65 (Mich.); July 22, 1868-69 (Ala.).

KELLOGG, Frank Billings (R Minn.) Dec. 22, 1856-Dec. 21, 1937; Senate 1917-23; Secy. of State 1925-29.

KELLOGG, Orlando (W N.Y.) June 18, 1809-Aug. 24, 1865; House 1847-49; 1863-Aug. 24, 1865.

KELLOGG, Stephen Wright (R Conn.) April 5, 1822-Jan. 27, 1904; House 1869-73.

KELLOGG, William (R Ill.) July 8, 1814-Dec. 20, 1872; House 1857-63.

KELLOGG, William Pitt (R La.) Dec. 8, 1831-Aug. 10, 1918; Senate July 9, 1868-Nov. 1, 1872, 1877-83; House 1883-85; Gov. 1873-77.

KELLY, Edna Flannery (D N.Y.) Aug. 20, 1906; House Nov. 8, 1949-69.

KELLY, Edward Austin (D Ill.) April 3, 1892-Aug. 30, 1969; House 1931-43, 1945-47.

KELLY, George Bradshaw (D N.Y.) Dec. 12, 1900; House 1937-39.

KELLY, James (—Pa.) July 17, 1760-Feb. 4, 1819; House 1805-09.

KELLY, James Kerr (D Ore.) Feb. 16, 1819-Sept. 15, 1903; Senate 1871-77.

KELLY, John (D N.Y.) April 21, 1821-June 1, 1886; House 1855-Dec. 25, 1858.

KELLY, Melville Clyde (R Pa.) Aug. 4, 1883-April 29, 1935; House 1913-15, 1917-35.

KELLY, William (—Ala.) 1770-1832; Senate Dec. 12, 1822-25.

KELSEY, William Henry (R N.Y.) Oct. 2, 1812-April 20, 1879; House 1855-59 (W), 1867-71 (R).

KELSO, John Russell (IRad. Mo.) March 23, 1831-Jan. 26, 1891; House 1865-67.

KEM, James Preston (R Mo.) April 2, 1890-Feb. 24, 1965; Senate 1947-53.

KEM, Omer Madison (P Neb.) Nov. 13, 1855-Feb. 13, 1942; House 1891-97.

KEMBLE, Gouverneur (D N.Y.) Jan. 25, 1786-Sept. 16, 1875; House 1837-41.

KEMP, Bolivar Edwards (D La.) Dec. 28, 1871-June 19, 1933; House 1925-June 19, 1933.

KEMP, Jack F. (R N.Y.) July 13, 1935; House 1971- .

KEMPSHALL, Thomas (W N.Y.) about 1796-Jan. 14, 1865; House 1839-41.

KENAN, Thomas (D N.C.) Feb. 26, 1771-Oct. 22, 1843; House 1805-11.

KENDALL, Charles West (D Nev.) April 22, 1828-June 25, 1914; House 1871-75.

KENDALL, Elva Roscoe (R Ky.) Feb. 14, 1893; House 1929-31.

KENDALL, John Wilkerson (father of Joseph Morgan Kendall) (D Ky.) June 26, 1834-March 7, 1892; House 1891-March 7, 1892.

KENDALL, Jonas (father of Joseph Gowing Kendall) (F Mass.) Oct. 27, 1757-Oct. 22, 1844; House 1819-21.

KENDALL, Joseph Gowing (son of Jonas Kendall) (—Mass.) Oct. 27, 1788-Oct. 2, 1847; House 1829-33.

KENDALL, Joseph Morgan (son of John Wilkerson Kendall) (D Ky.) May 12, 1863-Nov. 5, 1933; House April 21, 1892-93, 1895-Feb. 18, 1897.

KENDALL, Nathan Edward (R Iowa) March 17, 1868-Nov. 5, 1936; House 1909-13; Gov. 1921-25.

KENDALL, Samuel Austin (R Pa.) Nov. 1, 1859-Jan. 8, 1933; House 1919-Jan. 8, 1933.

KENDRICK, John Benjamin (D Wyo.) Sept. 6, 1857-Nov. 3, 1933; Senate 1917-Nov. 3, 1933; Gov. 1915-17.

KENNA, John Edward (D W. Va.) April 10, 1848-Jan. 11, 1893; House 1877-83; Senate 1883-Jan. 11, 1893.

KENNEDY, Ambrose (R R.I.) Dec. 1, 1875-March 11, 1967; House 1913-23.

KENNEDY, Ambrose Jerome (D Md.) Jan. 6, 1893-Aug. 29, 1950; House Nov. 8, 1932-41.

KENNEDY, Andrew (cousin of Case Broderick) (D Ind.) July 24, 1810-Dec. 31, 1847; House 1841-47.

KENNEDY, Anthony (brother of John Pendleton Kennedy) (U Md.) Dec. 21, 1810-July 4, 1892; Senate 1857-63.

KENNEDY, Charles Augustus (R Iowa) March 24, 1869-Jan. 10, 1951; House 1907-21.

KENNEDY, Edward Moore (brother of John Fitzgerald Kennedy and Robert Francis Kennedy and grandson of John Francis Fitzgerald) (D Mass.) Feb. 22, 1932; Senate Nov. 7, 1962- .

KENNEDY, James (R Ohio) Sept. 3, 1853-Nov. 9, 1928; House 1903-11.

KENNEDY, John Fitzgerald (brother of Edward Moore Kennedy and Robert Francis Kennedy and grandson of John Francis Fitzgerald) (D Mass.) May 29, 1917-Nov. 22, 1963; House 1947-53; Senate 1953-Dec. 22, 1960; President 1961-Nov. 22, 1963.

KENNEDY, John Lauderdale (R Neb.) Oct. 27, 1854-Aug. 30, 1946; House 1905-07.

KENNEDY, John Pendleton (brother of Anthony Kennedy) (W Md.) Oct. 25, 1795-Aug. 18, 1870; House April 25, 1838-39, 1841-45; Secy. of the Navy 1852-53.

KENNEDY, Martin John (D N.Y.) Aug. 29, 1892-Oct. 27, 1955; House March 11, 1930- 45.

KENNEDY, Michael Joseph (D N.Y.) Oct. 25, 1897-Nov. 1, 1949; House 1939-43.

KENNEDY, Robert Francis (brother of Edward Moore Kennedy and John Fitzgerald Kennedy and grandson of John Francis Fitzgerald) (D N.Y.) Nov. 20, 1925-June 6, 1968; Senate 1965-June 6, 1968; Atty. Gen. 1961-64.

KENNEDY, Robert Patterson (R Ohio) Jan. 23, 1840-May 6, 1918; House 1887-91.

KENNEDY, William (F N.C.) July 31, 1768-Oct. 11, 1834; House 1803-05, 1809-11, Jan. 30, 1813-15.

KENNEDY, William (D Conn.) Dec. 19, 1854-June 19, 1918; House 1913-14.

KENNETT, Luther Martin (AP Mo.) March 15, 1807-April 12, 1873; House 1855-57.

KENNEY, Edward Aloysius (D N.J.) Aug. 11, 1884-Jan. 27, 1938; House 1933-Jan. 17, 1938.

KENNEY, Richard Rolland (D Del.) Sept. 9, 1856-Aug. 14, 1931; Senate Jan. 19, 1897-1901.

KENNON, William, Sr. (cousin of William Kennon, Jr.) (D Ohio) May 14, 1793-Nov. 2, 1881; House 1829-33, 1835-37.

KENNON, William, Jr. (cousin of William Kennon, Sr.) (D Ohio) June 12, 1802-Oct. 19, 1867; House 1847-49.

KENT, Everett (D Pa.) Nov. 15, 1888-Oct. 13, 1963; House 1923-25, 1927-29.

KENT, Joseph (NR Md.) Jan. 14, 1779-Nov. 24, 1837; House 1811-15 (F); 1819-Jan. 6, 1826 (D); Senate 1833-Nov. 24, 1837 (NR); Gov. 1826-29.

KENT, Moss (F N.Y.) April 3, 1766-May 30, 1838; House 1813-17.

KENT, William (I Calif.) March 29, 1864-March 13, 1928; House 1911-13 (PR), 1913-17 (I).

KENYON, William Scheuneman (R N.Y.) Dec. 13, 1820-Feb. 10, 1896; House 1859-61.

KENYON, William Squire (R Iowa) June 10, 1869-Sept. 9, 1933; Senate April 12, 1911-Feb. 24, 1922.

KEOGH, Eugene James (D N.Y.) Aug. 30, 1907; House 1937-67.

KERN, Frederick John (D Ill.) Sept. 6, 1864-Nov. 9, 1931; House 1901-03.

KERN, John Worth (D Ind.) Dec. 20, 1849-Aug. 17, 1917; Senate 1911-17.

KERNAN, Francis (D N.Y.) Jan. 14, 1816-Sept. 7, 1892; House 1863-65.; Senate 1875-81.

KERR, Daniel (R Iowa) June 18, 1836-Oct. 8, 1916; House 1887-91.

KERR, James (D Pa.) Oct. 2, 1851-Oct. 31, 1908; House 1889-91.

KERR, John (father of John Kerr, Jr., cousin of Bartlett Yancey, and grand-uncle of John Hosea Kerr) (D Va.) Aug. 4, 1782-Sept. 29, 1842; House 1813-15, Oct. 30, 1815-17.

KERR, John, Jr. (son of John Kerr) (W N.C.) Feb. 10, 1811-Sept. 5, 1879; House 1853-55.

KERR, John Bozman (son of John Leeds Kerr) (W Md.) March 5, 1809-Jan. 27, 1878; House 1849-51.

KERR, John Hosea (grandnephew of John Kerr) (D N.C.) Dec. 31, 1873-June 21, 1958; House Nov. 6, 1923-53.

KERR, John Leeds (father of John Bozman Kerr) (W Md.) Jan. 15, 1780-Feb. 21, 1844; House 1825-29, 1831-33; Senate Jan. 5, 1841-43.

KERR, Joseph (D Ohio) 1765-Aug. 22, 1837; Senate Dec. 10, 1814-15.

KERR, Josiah Leeds (R Md.) Jan. 10, 1861-Sept. 27, 1920; House Nov. 6, 1900-01.

KERR, Michael Crawford (D Ind.) March 15, 1827-Aug. 19, 1876; House 1865-73, 1875-Aug. 19, 1876; Speaker 1875-76.

KERR, Robert Samuel (D Okla.) Sept. 11, 1896-Jan. 1, 1963; Senate 1949-Jan. 1, 1963; Gov. 1943-47.

KERR, Winfield Scott (R Ohio) June 23, 1852-Sept. 11, 1917; House 1895-1901.

KERRIGAN, James (D N.Y.) Dec. 25, 1828-Nov. 1, 1899; House 1861-63.

KERSHAW, John (D S.C.) Sept. 12, 1765-Aug. 4, 1829; House 1813-15.

KERSTEN, Charles J. (R Wis.) May 26, 1902; House 1947-49; 1951-55.

KETCHAM, John Clark (R Mich.) Jan. 1, 1873-Dec. 4, 1941; House 1921-33.

KETCHAM, John Henry (R N.Y.) Dec. 21, 1832-Nov. 4, 1906; House 1865-73, 1877-93, 1897-Nov. 4, 1906.

KETCHUM, Winthrop Welles (R Pa.) June 29, 1820-Dec. 6, 1879; House 1875-July 19, 1876.

KETTNER, William (D Calif.) Nov. 20, 1864-Nov. 11, 1930; House 1913-21.

KEY, David McKendree (D Tenn.) Jan. 27, 1824-Feb. 3, 1900; Senate Aug. 18, 1875-Jan. 19, 1877; Postmaster Gen. 1877-80.

KEY, John Alexander (D Ohio) Dec. 30, 1871-March 4, 1954; House 1913-19.

KEY, Philip (cousin of Philip Barton Key and great-grandfather of Barnes Compton) (—Md.) 1750-Jan. 4, 1820; House 1791-93.

KEY, Philip Barton (cousin of Philip Key) (F Md.) April 12, 1757-July 28, 1815; House 1807-13.

KEYES, Elias (R Vt.) April 14, 1758-July 9, 1844; House 1821-23.

KEYES, Henry Wilder (R N.H.) May 23, 1863-June 19, 1938; Senate 1919-37; Gov. 1917-19.

KIDDER, David (W Maine) Dec. 8, 1787-Nov. 1, 1860; House 1823-27.

KIDDER, Jefferson Parish (R Dakota) June 4, 1815-Oct. 2, 1883; House (Terr. Del.) 1875-79.

KIDWELL, Zedekiah (D Va.) Jan. 4, 1814-April 27, 1872; House 1853-57.

KIEFER, Andrew Robert (R Minn.) May 25, 1832-May 1, 1904; House 1893-97.

KIEFNER, Charles Edward (R Mo.) Nov. 25, 1869-Dec. 13, 1942; House 1925-27, 1929-31.

KIESS, Edgar Raymond (R Pa.) Aug. 26, 1875-July 20, 1930; House 1913-July 20, 1930.

KILBOURNE, James (D Ohio) Oct. 19, 1770-April 9, 1850; House 1813-17.

KILBURN, Clarence Evans (R N.Y.) April 13, 1893; House Feb. 13, 1940-65.

KILDAY, Paul Joseph (D Texas) March 29, 1900-Oct. 12, 1968; House 1939-Sept. 24, 1961.

KILGORE, Constantine Buckley (D Texas) Feb. 20, 1835-Sept. 23, 1897; House 1887-95.

KILGORE, Daniel (D Ohio) 1793-Dec. 12, 1851; House Dec. 1, 1834-July 4, 1838.

KILGORE, David (R Ind.) April 3, 1804-Jan. 22, 1879; House 1857-61.

KILGORE, Harley Martin (D W. Va.) Jan. 11, 1893-Feb. 28, 1956; Senate 1941-Feb. 28, 1956.

KILGORE, Joe Madison (D Texas) Dec. 10, 1918; House 1955-65.

KILLE, Joseph (D N.J.) April 12, 1790-March 1, 1865; House 1839-41.

KILLINGER, John Weinland (R Pa.) Sept. 18, 1824-June 30, 1896; House 1859-63, 1871-75, 1877-81.

KIMBALL, Alanson Mellen (R Wis.) March 12, 1827-May 26, 1913; House 1875-77.

KIMBALL, Henry Mahlon (R Mich.) Aug. 27, 1878-Oct. 19, 1935; House Jan. 3-Oct. 19, 1935.

KIMBALL, William Preston (D Ky.) Nov. 4, 1857-Feb. 24, 1926; House 1907-09.

KIMMEL, William (D Md.) Aug. 15, 1812-Dec. 28, 1886; House 1877-81.

KINCAID, John (D Ky.) Feb. 15, 1791-Feb. 7, 1873; House 1829-31.

KINCHELOE, David Hayes (D Ky.) April 9, 1877-April 16, 1950; House 1915-Oct. 5, 1930.

KINDEL, George John (D Colo.) March 2, 1855-Feb. 28, 1930; House 1913-15.

KINDRED, John Joseph (D N.Y.) July 15, 1864-Oct. 23, 1937; House 1911-13, 1921-29.

KING, Adam (D Pa.) 1790-May 6, 1835; House 1827-33.

KING, Andrew (D Mo.) March 20, 1812-Nov. 18, 1895; House 1871-73.

KING, Austin Augustus (UD Mo.) Sept. 21, 1802-April 22, 1870; House 1863-65; Gov. 1848-53.

KING, Carleton James (R N.Y.) June 15, 1904; House 1961- .

KING, Cecil Rhodes (D Calif.) Jan. 13, 1898; House Aug. 25, 1942-69.

KING, Cyrus (half brother of Rufus King) Sept. 6, 1772-April 25, 1817; House 1813-17.

KING, Daniel Putnam (W Mass.) Jan. 8, 1801-July 25, 1850; House 1843-July 25, 1850.

KING, David Sjodahl (son of William H. King) (D Utah) June 20, 1917; House 1959-63, 1965-67.

KING, Edward John (R Ill.) July 1, 1867-Feb. 17, 1929; House 1915-Feb. 17, 1929.

KING, George Gordon (W R.I.) June 9, 1807-July 17, 1870; House 1849-53.

KING, Henry (brother of Thomas Butler King and uncle of John Floyd King) (D Pa.) July 6, 1790-July 13, 1861; House 1831-35.

KING, James Gore (son of Rufus King and brother of John Alsop King) (W N.J.) May 8, 1791-Oct. 3, 1853; House 1849-51.

KING, John (D N.Y.) 1775-Sept. 1, 1836; House 1831-33.

KING, John Alsop (son of Rufus King and brother of James Gore King) (W N.Y.) Jan. 3, 1788-July 7, 1867; House 1849-51.

KING, John Floyd (son of Thomas Butler King and nephew of Henry King) (D La.) April 20, 1842-May 8, 1915; House 1879-87.

KING, John Pendleton (D Ga.) April 3, 1799-March 19, 1888; Senate Nov. 21, 1833-Nov. 1, 1837.

KING, Karl Clarence (R Pa.) Jan. 26, 1897; House Nov. 6, 1951-57.

KING, Perkins (D N.Y.) Jan. 12, 1784-Nov. 29, 1875; House 1829-31.

KING, Preston (R N.Y.) Oct. 14, 1806-Nov. 12, 1865; House 1843-47, 1849-53 (D); Senate 1857-63 (R).

KING, Rufus (half brother of Cyrus King and father of John Alsop King and James Gore King) (F N.Y.) March 24, 1755-April 29, 1827; Senate July 16, 1789-May 23, 1796; 1813-25; Cont. Cong. (Mass.) 1784-87.

KING, Rufus H. (W N.Y.) Jan. 20, 1820-Sept. 13, 1890; House 1855-57.

KING, Samuel Wilder (R Hawaii) Dec. 17, 1886-March 24, 1959; House (Terr. Del.) 1935-43; Gov. 1953-57.

KING, Thomas Butler (brother of Henry King and father of John Floyd King) (W Ga.) Aug. 27, 1800-May 10, 1864; House 1839-43, 1845-50.

KING, William Henry (father of David S. King) (D Utah) June 3, 1863-Nov. 27, 1949; House 1897-99, April 2, 1900-01; Senate 1917-41.

KING, William Rufus deVane (D N.C./Ala.) April 7, 1786-April 18, 1853; House 1811-Nov. 4, 1816 (N.C.); Senate Dec. 14, 1819-April 15, 1844, July 1, 1848-Dec. 20, 1852 (Ala.); President pro tempore 1835-41, 1849-52; Vice President March 4-April 18, 1853.

KING, William Smith (R Minn.) Dec. 16, 1828-Feb. 24, 1900; House 1875-77.

KINGSBURY, William Wallace (D Minn.) June 4, 1828-April 17, 1892; House (Terr. Del.) 1857-May 11, 1858.

KINKAID, Moses Pierce (R Neb.) Jan. 24, 1856-July 6, 1922; House 1903-July 6, 1922.

KINKEAD, Eugene Francis (D N.J.) March 27, 1876-Sept. 6, 1960; House 1909-Feb. 4, 1915.

KINNARD, George L. (D Ind.) 1803-Nov. 26, 1836; House 1833-Nov. 26, 1836.

KINNEY, John Fitch (D Utah) April 2, 1816-Aug. 16, 1902; House (Terr. Del.) 1863-65.

KINSELLA, Thomas (D N.Y.) Dec. 31, 1832-Feb. 11, 1884; House 1871-73.

KINSEY, Charles (—N.J.) 1773-June 25, 1849; House 1817-19, Feb. 2, 1820-21.

KINSEY, William Medcalf (R Mo.) Oct. 28, 1846-June 20, 1931; House 1889-91.

KINSLEY, Martin (—Mass.) June 2, 1754-June 20, 1835; House 1819-21.

KINZER, John Roland (R Pa.) March 28, 1874-July 25, 1955; House Jan. 28, 1930-47.

KIPP, George Washington (D Pa.) March 28, 1847-July 24, 1911; House 1907-09, March 4-July 24, 1911.

KIRBY, William Fosgate (D Ark.) Nov. 16, 1867-July 26, 1934; Senate Nov. 8, 1916-21.

KIRK, Andrew Jackson (R Ky.) March 19, 1866-May 25, 1933; House Feb. 13, 1926-27.

KIRKLAND, Joseph (—N.Y.) Jan. 18, 1770-Jan. 26, 1844; House 1821-23.

KIRKPATRICK, Littleton (D N.J.) Oct. 19, 1797-Aug. 15, 1859; House 1843-45.

KIRKPATRICK, Sanford (D Iowa) Feb. 11, 1842-Feb. 13, 1932; House 1913-15.

KIRKPATRICK, Snyder Solomon (R Kan.) Feb. 21, 1848-April 5, 1909; House 1895-97.

KIRKPATRICK, William (D N.Y.) Nov. 7, 1769-Sept. 2, 1832; House 1807-09.

KIRKPATRICK, William Huntington (son of William Sebring Kirkpatrick) (R Pa.) Oct. 2, 1885-Nov. 28, 1970; House 1921-23.

KIRKPATRICK, William Sebring (father of William Huntington Kirkpatrick) (R Pa.) April 21, 1844-Nov. 3, 1932; House 1897-99.

KIRKWOOD, Samuel Jordan (R Iowa) Dec. 20, 1813-Sept. 1, 1894; Senate Jan. 13, 1866-67, 1877-March 7, 1881; Gov. 1860-64, 1876-77; Secy. of the Interior 1881-82.

KIRTLAND, Dorrance (—N.Y.) July 28, 1770-May 23, 1840; House 1817-19.

KIRWAN, Michael Joseph (D Ohio) Dec. 2, 1886-July 27, 1970; House 1937-July 27, 1970.

KISSEL, John (R N.Y.) July 31, 1864-Oct. 3, 1938; House 1921-23.

KITCHELL, Aaron (D N.J.) July 10, 1744- June 25, 1820; House 1791-93, Jan. 29, 1795-97, 1799-1801; Senate 1805-March 12, 1809.

KITCHEN, Bethuel Middleton (R W. Va.) March 21, 1812-Dec. 15, 1895; House 1867-69.

KITCHENS, Wade Hampton (D Ark.) Dec. 26, 1878-Aug. 22, 1966; House 1937-41.

KITCHIN, Alvin Paul (nephew of Claude Kitchin and William Walton Kitchin and grandson of William Hodges Kitchin) (D N.C.) Sept. 13, 1908; House 1957-63.

KITCHIN, Claude (son of William Hodges Kitchin, brother of William Walton Kitchin and uncle of A. Paul Kitchin) (D N.C.) March 24, 1869-May 31, 1923; House 1901-May 31, 1923.

KITCHIN, William Hodges (father of Claude Kitchin and William Walton Kitchin, and grandfather of A. Paul Kitchin) (D N.C.) Dec. 22, 1837-Feb. 2, 1901; House 1879-81.

KITCHIN, William Walton (son of William Hodges Kitchin, brother of Claude Kitchin, and uncle of A. Paul Kitchin) (D N.C.) Oct. 9, 1866-Nov. 9, 1924; House 1897-Jan. 11, 1909; Gov. 1909-13.

KITTERA, John Wilkes (father of Thomas Kittera) (F Pa.) Nov. 1752–June 6, 1801; House 1791-1801.

KITTERA, Thomas (son of John Wilkes Kittera) (F Pa.) March 21, 1789–June 16, 1839; House Oct. 10, 1826-27.

KITTREDGE, Alfred Beard (R S.D.) March 28,1861-May 4,1911;Senate July 11,1901-09.

KITTREDGE, George Washington (A-ND N.H.) Jan. 31, 1805-March 6, 1881; House 1853-55.

KLEBERG, Richard Mifflin, Sr. (nephew of Rudolph Kleberg) (D Texas) Nov. 18, 1887-May 8, 1955; House Nov. 24, 1931-45.

KLEBERG, Rudolph (uncle of Richard Mifflin Kleberg, Sr.)(D Texas) June 26, 1847-Dec. 28, 1924; House April 7, 1896-1903.

KLECZKA, John Casimir (R Wis.) May 6, 1885-April 21, 1959; House 1919-23.

KLEIN, Arthur George (D N.Y.) Aug. 8, 1904-Feb. 20, 1968; House July 29, 1941-45, Feb. 19, 1946-Dec. 31, 1956.

KLEINER, John Jay (D Ind.) Feb. 8, 1845-April 8, 1911; House 1883-87.

KLEPPE, Thomas S. (R N.D.) July 1, 1919; House 1967-71.

KLEPPER, Frank B. (R Mo.) June 22, 1864-Aug. 4, 1933; House 1905-07.

KLINE, Ardolph Loges (R N.Y.) Feb. 21, 1858-Oct. 13, 1930; House 1921-23.

KLINE, Isaac Clinton (R Pa.) Aug. 18, 1858-Dec. 2, 1947; House 1921-23.

KLINE, Marcus Charles Lawrence (D Pa.) March 26, 1855-March 10, 1911; House 1903-07.

KLINGENSMITH, John, Jr. (D Pa.) 1785-—; House 1835-39.

KLOEB, Frank LeBlond (grandson of Francis C. LeBlond) (D Ohio) June 16, 1890; House 1933-Aug. 19, 1937.

KLOTZ, Robert (D Pa.) Oct. 27, 1819-May 1, 1895; House 1879-83.

KLUCZYNSKI, John Carl (D Ill.) Feb. 15, 1896; House 1951- .

KLUTTZ, Theodore Franklin (D N.C.) Oct. 4, 1848-Nov. 18, 1918; House 1899-1905.

KNAPP, Anthony Lausett (brother of Robert McCarty Knapp) (D Ill.) June 14, 1828-May 24, 1881; House Dec. 12, 1861-65.

KNAPP, Charles (father of Charles Junius Knapp) (R N.Y.) Oct. 8, 1787-May 14, 1880; House 1869-71.

KNAPP, Charles Junius (son of Charles Knapp) (R N.Y.) June 30, 1845–June 1, 1916; House 1889-91.

KNAPP, Charles Luman (R N.Y.) July 4, 1847-Jan. 3, 1929; House Nov. 5, 1901-11.

KNAPP, Chauncey Langdon (R Mass.) Feb. 26, 1809-May 31,1898; House 1855-57 (AP), 1857-59 (R).

KNAPP, Robert McCarty (brother of Anthony Lausett Knapp) (D Ill.) April 21, 1831–June 24, 1889; House 1873-75, 1877-79.

KNICKERBOCKER, Herman (F N.Y.) July 27, 1779–Jan. 30, 1855; House 1809-11.

KNIFFIN, Frank Charles (D Ohio) April 26, 1894-April 30, 1968; House 1931-39.

KNIGHT, Charles Landon (R Ohio) June 18, 1867-Sept. 26, 1933; House 1921-23.

KNIGHT, Jonathan (W Pa.) Nov. 22, 1787-Nov. 22, 1858; House 1855-57.

KNIGHT, Nehemiah (father of Nehemiah Rice Knight) (A-F R.I.) March 23, 1746–June 13, 1808; House 1803–June 13, 1808.

KNIGHT, Nehemiah Rice (son of Nehemiah Knight) (D R.I.) Dec. 31, 1780-April 18, 1854; Senate Jan. 9, 1821-35 (A-F), 1835-41 (D); Gov. 1817-21 (A-F).

KNOPF, Philip (R Ill.) Nov. 18, 1847-Aug. 14, 1920; House 1903-09.

KNOTT, James Proctor (D Ky.) Aug. 29, 1830–June 18, 1911; House 1867-71, 1875-83; Gov. 1883-87.

KNOWLAND, Joseph Russell (father of William Fife Knowland) (R Calif.) Aug. 5, 1873-Feb. 1, 1966; House Nov. 8, 1904-15.

KNOWLAND, William Fife (son of Joseph Russell Knowland) (R Calif.) June 26, 1908; Senate Aug. 26, 1945-59.

KNOWLES, Freeman Tulley (P S.D.) Oct. 10, 1846–June 1, 1910; House 1897-99.

KNOWLTON, Ebenezer (R Maine) Dec. 6, 1815-Sept. 10, 1874; House 1855-57.

KNOX, James (W Ill.) July 4, 1807-Oct. 8, 1876; House 1853-57.

KNOX, Philander Chase (R Pa.) May 6, 1853-Oct. 12, 1921; Senate June 10, 1904-March 4, 1909, 1917-Oct. 12, 1921; Atty. Gen. 1901-04; Secy. of State 1909-13.

KNOX, Samuel (R Mo.) March 21, 1815-March 7, 1905; House June 10, 1864-65.

KNOX, Victor Alfred (R Mich.) Jan. 13, 1899; House 1953-65.

KNOX, William Shadrach (R Mass.) Sept. 10, 1843-Sept. 21, 1914; House 1895-1903.

KNUTSON, Coya Gjesdal (D-FL Minn.) Aug. 22, 1912; House 1955-59.

KNUTSON, Harold (R Minn.) Oct. 20, 1880-Aug. 21, 1953; House 1917-49.

KOCH, Edward I. (D/L N.Y.) Dec. 12, 1924; House 1969- .

KOCIALKOWSKI, Leo Paul (D Ill.) Aug. 16, 1882-Sept. 27, 1958; House 1933-43.

KONIG, George (D Md.) Jan. 26, 1865-May 31, 1913; House 1911-May 31, 1913.

KONOP, Thomas Frank (D Wis.) Aug. 17, 1879-Oct. 17, 1964; House 1911-17.

KOONTZ, William Henry (R Pa.) July 15, 1830–July 4, 1911; House July 18, 1866-69.

KOPP, Arthur William (R Wis.) Feb. 28, 1874–June 2, 1967; House 1909-13.

KOPP, William Frederick (R Iowa) June 20, 1869-Aug. 24, 1938; House 1921-33.

KOPPLEMANN, Herman Paul (D Conn.) May 1, 1880-Aug. 11, 1957; House 1933-39, 1941-43, 1945-47.

KORBLY, Charles Alexander (D Ind.) March 24, 1871–July 26, 1937; House 1909-15.

KORELL, Franklin Frederick (R Ore.) July 23, 1889–June 7, 1965; House Oct. 18, 1927-31.

KORNEGAY, Horace Robinson (D N.C.) March 12, 1924; House 1961-69.

KOWALSKI, Frank (D Conn.) Oct. 18, 1907; House 1959-63.

KRAMER, Charles (D Calif.) April 18, 1879-Jan. 20, 1943; House 1933-43.

KRAUS, Milton (R Ind.) June 26, 1866-Nov. 18, 1942; House 1917-23.

KREBS, Jacob (D Pa.) March 13, 1782-Sept. 26, 1847; House Dec. 4, 1826-March 3, 1827.

KREBS, Paul J. (D N.J.) May 26, 1912; House 1965-67.

KREIDER, Aaron Shenk (R Pa.) June 26, 1863-May 19, 1929; House 1913-23.

KREMER, George (— Pa.) Nov. 21, 1775-Sept. 11, 1854; House 1823-29.

KRIBBS, George Frederic (D Pa.) Nov. 8, 1846-Sept. 8, 1938; House 1891-95.

KRONMILLER, John (R Md.) Dec. 6, 1858-June 19, 1928; House 1909-11.

KRUEGER, Otto (R N.D.) Sept. 7, 1890-June 10, 1963; House 1953-59.

KRUSE, Edward H., Jr. (D Ind.) Oct. 22, 1918; House 1949-51.

KUCHEL, Thomas Henry (R Calif.) Aug. 15, 1910; Senate Jan. 2, 1953-69.

KUHNS, Joseph Henry (W Pa.) Sept. 1800-Nov. 16, 1883; House 1851-53.

KULP, Monroe Henry (R Pa.) Oct. 23, 1858-Oct. 19, 1911; House 1895-99.

KUNKEL, Jacob Michael (D Md.) July 13, 1822-April 7, 1870; House 1857-61.

KUNKEL, John Christian (grandfather of John Crain Kunkel) (W Pa.) Sept. 18, 1816-Oct. 14, 1870; House 1855-59.

KUNKEL, John Crain (grandson of John Christian Kunkel, great-grandson of John Sergeant, and great-great-grandson of Robert Whitehill) (R Pa.) July 21, 1898-July 27, 1970; House 1939-51, May 16, 1961-Dec. 30, 1966.

KUNZ, Stanley Henry (D Ill.) Sept. 26, 1864-April 23, 1946; House 1921-31, April 5, 1932-33.

KUPFERMAN, Theodore R. (R N.Y.) May 12, 1920; House Feb. 8, 1966-69.

KURTZ, Jacob Banks (R Pa.) Oct. 31, 1867-Sept. 18, 1960; House 1923-35.

KURTZ, William Henry (D Pa.) Jan. 31, 1804-June 24, 1868; House 1851-55.

KUSTERMANN, Gustav (R Wis.) May 24, 1850-Dec. 25, 1919; House 1907-11.

KUYKENDALL, Andrew Jackson (R Ill.) March 3, 1815-May 11, 1891; House 1865-67.

KUYKENDALL, Dan H. (R Tenn.) July 9, 1924; House 1967- .

KVALE, Ole Juulson (father of Paul John Kvale) (F-L Minn.) Feb. 6, 1869-Sept. 11, 1929; House 1923-25 (IR), 1925-Sept. 11, 1929 (F-L).

KVALE, Paul John (son of Ole Juulson Kvale) (F-L Minn.) March 27, 1896-June 14, 1960; House Oct. 16, 1929-39.

KYL, John Henry (R Iowa) May 9, 1919; House Dec. 15, 1959-65, 1967- .

KYLE, James Henderson (I S.D.) Feb. 24, 1854-July 1, 1901; Senate 1891-July 1, 1901.

KYLE, John Curtis (D Miss.) July 17, 1851-July 6, 1913; House 1891-97.

KYLE, Thomas Barton (R Ohio) March 10, 1856-Aug. 13, 1915; House 1901-05.

KYROS, Peter N. (D Maine) July 11, 1925; House 1967- .

L

LA BRANCHE, Alcee Louis (D La.) 1806-Aug. 17, 1861; House 1843-45.

LACEY, Edward Samuel (R Mich.) Nov. 26, 1835-Oct. 2, 1916; House 1881-85.

LACEY, John Fletcher (R Iowa) May 30, 1841-Sept. 29, 1913; House 1889-91, 1893-1907.

LACOCK, Abner (D Pa.) July 9, 1770-April 12, 1837; House 1811-13; Senate 1813-19.

LADD, Edwin Freemont (Nonpart. R N.D.) Dec. 13, 1859-June 22, 1925; Senate 1921-June 22, 1925.

LADD, George Washington (D/G Maine) Sept. 28, 1818-Jan. 30, 1892; House 1879-83.

LA DOW, George Augustus (D Ore.) March 18, 1826-May 1, 1875; House March 4-May 1, 1875.

LAFEAN, Daniel Franklin (R Pa.) Feb. 7, 1861-April 18, 1922; House 1903-13, 1915-17.

LAFFERTY, Abraham Walter (PR Ore.) June 10, 1875-Jan. 15, 1964; House 1911-15.

LAFFOON, Polk (D Ky.) Oct. 24, 1844-Oct. 22, 1906; House 1885-89.

LAFLIN, Addison Henry (R N.Y.) Oct. 24, 1823-Sept. 24, 1878; House 1865-71.

LA FOLLETTE, Charles Marion (great-grandson of William Heilman) (R Ind.) Feb. 27, 1898; House 1943-47.

LA FOLLETTE, Robert Marion (R Wis.) June 14, 1855-June 18, 1925; House 1885-91; Senate Jan. 2, 1906-June 18, 1925; Gov. 1901-06.

LA FOLLETTE, Robert Marion, Jr. (son of the preceding) (Prog. Wis.) Feb. 6, 1895-Feb. 24, 1953; Senate Sept. 30, 1925-35 (R/Prog.), 1935-47 (Prog.).

LA FOLLETTE, William Leroy (R Wash.) Nov. 30, 1860-Dec. 20, 1934; House 1911-19.

LAFORE, John Armand, Jr. (R Pa.) May 25, 1905; House Nov. 5, 1957-61.

LAGAN, Matthew Diamond (D La.) June 20, 1829-April 8, 1901; House 1887-89, 1891-93.

LA GUARDIA, Fiorello Henry (R/Prog. N.Y.) Dec. 11, 1882-Sept. 20, 1947; House 1917-Dec. 31, 1919, 1923-25 (R), 1925-27 (Soc.), 1927-33 (R/Prog.).

LAHM, Samuel (D Ohio) April 22, 1812-June 16, 1876; House 1847-49.

LAIDLAW, William Grant (R N.Y.) Jan. 1, 1840-Aug. 19, 1908; House 1887-91.

LAIRD, James (R Neb.) June 20, 1849-Aug. 17, 1889; House 1883-Aug. 17, 1889.

LAIRD, Melvin Robert (R Wis.) Sept. 1, 1922; House 1953-Jan. 21, 1969; Secy. of Defense 1969- .

LAIRD, William Robert, III (D W. Va.) June 2, 1916; Senate March 13-Nov. 6, 1956.

LAKE, William Augustus (W Miss.) Jan. 6, 1808-Oct. 15, 1861; House 1855-57.

LAMAR, Henry Graybill (D Ga.) July 10, 1798-Sept. 10, 1861; House Dec. 7, 1829-33.

LAMAR, James Robert (D Mo.) March 28, 1866-Aug. 11, 1923; House 1903-05; 1907-09.

LAMAR, John Basil (D Ga.) Nov. 5, 1812-Sept. 15, 1862; House March 4-July 29, 1843.

LAMAR, Lucius Quintus Cincinnatus (uncle of William Bailey Lamar and cousin of Absalom Harris Chappell) (D Miss.) Sept. 17, 1825-Jan. 23, 1893; House 1857-December 1860, 1873-77; Senate 1877-March 6, 1885; Secy. of the Int. 1885-88, Assoc. Justice of the Supreme Court 1888-93.

LAMAR, William Bailey (nephew of Lucius Quintus Cincinnatus Lamar) (D Fla.) June 12, 1853-Sept. 26, 1928; House 1903-09.

LAMB, Alfred William (D Mo.) March 18, 1824-April 29, 1888; House 1853-55.

LAMB, John (D Va.) June 12, 1840-Nov. 21, 1924; House 1897-1913.

LAMB, John Edward (D Ind.) Dec. 26, 1852-Aug. 23, 1914; House 1883-85.

LAMBERT, John (D N.J.) Feb. 24, 1746-Feb. 4, 1823; House 1805-09; Senate 1809-15.

LAMBERTSON, William Purnell (R Kan.) March 23, 1880-Oct. 26, 1957; House 1929-45.

LAMBETH, John Walter (D N.C.) Jan. 10, 1896-Jan. 12, 1961; House 1931-39.

LAMISON, Charles Nelson (D Ohio) 1826-April 24, 1896; House 1871-75.

LAMNECK, Arthur Philip (D Ohio) March 12, 1880-April 23, 1944; House 1931-39.

LAMPERT, Florian (R Wis.) July 8, 1863-July 18, 1930; House Nov. 5, 1918-July 18, 1930.

LAMPORT, William Henry (R N.Y.) May 27, 1811-July 21, 1891; House 1871-75.

LANCASTER, Columbia (D Wash.) Aug. 26, 1803-Sept. 15, 1893; House (Terr. Del.) April 12, 1854-55.

LANDERS, Franklin (D Ind.) March 22, 1825-Sept. 10, 1901; House 1875-77.

LANDERS, George Marcellus (D Conn.) Feb. 22, 1813-March 27, 1895; House 1875-79.

LANDES, Silas Zephaniah (D Ill.) May 15, 1842-May 23, 1910; House 1885-89.

LANDGREBE, Earl F. (R Ind.) Jan. 21, 1916; House 1969- .

LANDIS, Charles Beary (brother of Frederick Landis) (R Ind.) July 9, 1858-April 24, 1922; House 1897-1909.

LANDIS, Frederick (brother of Charles Beary Landis) (R Ind.) Aug. 18, 1872-Nov. 15, 1934; House 1903-07.

LANDIS, Gerald Wayne (R Ind.) Feb. 23, 1895; House 1939-49.

LANDRUM, John Morgan (D La.) July 3, 1815-Oct. 18, 1861; House 1859-61.

LANDRUM, Phillip Mitchell (D Ga.) Sept. 10, 1909; House 1953- .

LANDRY, Joseph Aristide (W La.) July 10, 1817-March 9, 1881; House 1851-53.

LANDY, James (D Pa.) Oct. 13, 1813-July 25, 1875; House 1857-59.

LANE, Amos (father of James Henry Lane) (D Ind.) March 1, 1778-Sept. 2, 1849; House 1833-37.

LANE, Edward (D Ill.) March 27, 1842-Oct. 30, 1912; House 1887-95.

LANE, Harry (grandson of Joseph Lane and nephew of LaFayette Lane) (D Ore.) Aug. 28, 1855-May 23, 1917; Senate 1913-May 23, 1917.

LANE, Henry Smith (R Ind.) Feb. 24, 1811-June 18, 1881; House Aug. 3, 1840-43 (W); Senate 1861-67 (R); Gov. Jan. 1861 (R).

LANE, James Henry (son of Amos Lane) (D Ind./R Kan.) June 22, 1814-July 11, 1866; House 1853-55 (D Ind.); Senate April 4, 1861-July 11, 1866 (R Kan.).

LANE, Joseph (father of LaFayette Lane and grandfather of Harry Lane) (D Ore.) Dec. 14, 1801-April 19, 1881; House (Terr. Del.) 1851-Feb. 14, 1859; Senate Feb. 14, 1859-61; Gov. (Terr.) 1849-50, May 16-19, 1853.

LANE, Joseph Reed (R Iowa) May 6, 1858-May 1, 1931; House 1899-1901.

LANE, LaFayette (son of Joseph Lane and uncle of Harry Lane) (D Ore.) Nov. 12, 1842-Nov. 23, 1896; House Oct. 25, 1875-77.

LANE, Thomas Joseph (D Mass.) July 6, 1898; House Dec. 30, 1941-63.

LANGDON, Chauncey (F Vt.) Nov. 8, 1763-July 23, 1830; House 1815-17.

LANGDON, John (D N.H.) June 25, 1741-Sept. 18, 1819; Senate 1789-1801; President pro tempore 1789, 1792-94; Cont. Cong. 1775-76, 1783; Gov. 1788, 1805, 1809-11.

LANGEN, Odin (R Minn.) Jan. 5, 1913; House 1959-71.

LANGER, William (R N.D.) Sept. 30, 1886-Nov. 8, 1959; Senate 1941-Nov. 8, 1959; Gov. 1933-34, 1937-39.

LANGHAM, Jonathan Nicholas (R Pa.) Aug. 4, 1861-May 21, 1945; House 1909-15.

LANGLEY, John Wesley (husband of Katherine Gudger Langley) (R Ky.) Jan. 14, 1868-Jan. 17, 1932; House 1907-Jan. 11, 1926.

LANGLEY, Katherine Gudger (wife of John Wesley Langley and daughter of James Madison Gudger, Jr.) (R Ky.) Feb. 14, 1888-Aug. 15, 1948; House 1927-31.

LANGSTON, John Mercer (R Va.) Dec. 14, 1829-Nov. 15, 1897; House Sept. 23, 1890-91.

LANHAM, Fritz Garland (son of Samuel Willis Tucker Lanham) (D Texas) Jan. 3, 1880-July 31, 1965; House April 19, 1919-47.

LANHAM, Henderson Lovelace (D Ga.) Sept. 14, 1888-Nov. 10, 1957; House 1947-Nov. 10, 1957.

LANHAM, Samuel Willis Tucker (father of Fritz Garland Lanham) (D Texas) July 4, 1846-July 19, 1908; House 1883-93, 1897-Jan. 15, 1903; Gov. 1903-07.

LANING, Jay Ford (R Ohio) May 15, 1853-Sept. 1, 1941; House 1907-09.

LANKFORD, Menalcus (R Va.) March 14, 1833-Dec. 17, 1937; House 1929-33.

LANKFORD, Richard Estep (D Md.) July 22, 1914; House 1955-65.

LANKFORD, William Chester (D Ga.) Dec. 7, 1877-Dec. 10, 1964; House 1919-33.

LANMAN, James (D Conn.) June 14, 1767-Aug. 7, 1841; Senate 1819-25.

LANNING, William Mershon (R N.J.) Jan. 1, 1849-Feb. 16, 1912; House 1903-June 6, 1904.

LANSING, Frederick (R N.Y.) Feb. 16, 1838-Jan. 31, 1894; House 1889-91.

LANSING, Gerrit Yates (JD N.Y.) Aug. 4, 1783-Jan. 3, 1862; House 1831-37.

LANSING, William Esselstyne (R N.Y.) Dec. 29, 1821-July 29, 1883; House 1861-63, 1871-75.

LANTAFF, William Courtland (D Fla.) July 31, 1913-Jan. 29, 1970; House 1951-55.

LANZETTA, James Joseph (D N.Y.) Dec. 21, 1894-Oct. 27, 1956; House 1933-35, 1937-39.

LAPHAM, Elbridge Gerry (R N.Y.) Oct. 18, 1814-Jan. 8, 1890; House 1875-July 29, 1881; Senate Aug. 2, 1881-85.

LAPHAM, Oscar (D R.I.) June 29, 1837-March 29, 1926; House 1891-95.

LAPORTE, John (— Pa.) Nov. 4, 1798-Aug. 22, 1862; House 1833-37.

LARCADE, Henry Dominique, Jr. (D La.) July 12, 1890-March 14, 1966; House 1943-53.

LARNED, Simon (— Mass.) Aug. 3, 1753-Nov. 16, 1817; House Nov. 5, 1804-05.

LARRABEE, Charles Hathaway (D Wis.) Nov. 9, 1820-Jan. 20, 1883; House 1859-61.

LARRABEE, William Henry (D Ind.) Feb. 21, 1870-Nov. 16, 1960; House 1931-43.

LARRAZOLO, Octaviano Ambrosio (R N.M.) Dec. 7, 1859-April 7, 1930; Senate Dec. 7, 1928-29; Gov. 1919-21.

LARRINAGA, Tulio (U P.R.) Jan. 15, 1847-April 28, 1917; House (Res. Comm.) 1905-11.

LARSEN, William Washington (D Ga.) Aug. 12, 1871-Jan. 5, 1938; House 1917-33.

LARSON, Oscar John (R Minn.) May 20, 1871-Aug. 1, 1957; House 1921-25.

LA SERE, Emile (D La.) 1802-Aug. 14, 1882; House Jan. 29, 1846-51.

LASH, Israel George (R N.C.) Aug. 18, 1810-April 1, 1878; House July 20, 1868-71.

LASSITER, Francis Rives (great-nephew of Francis Everod Rives) (D Va.) Feb. 18, 1866-Oct. 31, 1909; House April 19, 1900-03, 1907-Oct. 31, 1909.

LATHAM, George Robert (R W. Va.) March 9, 1832-Dec. 16, 1917; House 1865-67.

LATHAM, Henry Jepson (R N.Y.) Dec. 10, 1908; House 1945-Dec. 31, 1958.

LATHAM, Louis Charles (D N.C.) Sept. 11, 1840-Oct. 16, 1895; House 1881-83, 1887-89.

LATHAM, Milton Slocum (D Calif.) May 23, 1827-March 4, 1882; House 1853-55; Senate March 5, 1860-63; Gov. Jan. 9-Jan. 14, 1860.

LATHROP, Samuel (R Mass.) May 1, 1772-July 11, 1846; House 1819-27.

LATHROP, William (R Ill.) April 17, 1825-Nov. 19, 1907; House 1877-79.

LATIMER, Asbury Churchwell (D S.C.) July 31, 1851-Feb. 20, 1908; House 1893-1903; Senate 1903-Feb. 20, 1908.

LATIMER, Henry (— Del.) April 24, 1752-Dec. 19, 1819; House Feb. 14, 1794-Feb. 7, 1795; Senate Feb. 7, 1795-Feb. 28, 1801.

LATTA, Delbert Leroy (R Ohio) March 5, 1920; House 1959- .

LATTA, James Polk (D Neb.) Oct. 31, 1844-Sept. 11, 1911; House 1909-Sept. 11, 1911.

LATTIMORE, William (— Miss.) Feb. 9, 1774-April 3, 1843; House (Terr. Del.) 1803-07, 1813-17.

LAURANCE, John (— N.Y.) 1750-Nov. 11, 1810; House 1789-93; Senate Nov. 9, 1796-August 1800; President pro tempore 1798-99; Cont. Cong 1785-87.

LAUSCHE, Frank John (D Ohio) Nov. 14, 1895; Senate 1957-69; Gov. 1945-47, 1949-57.

LAW, Charles Blakeslee (R N.Y.) Feb. 5, 1872-Sept. 15, 1929; House 1905-11.

LAW, John (son of Lyman Law and grandson of Amasa Learned) (D Ind.) Oct. 28, 1796-Oct. 7, 1873; House 1861-65.

LAW, Lyman (father of John Law) (F Conn.) Aug. 19, 1770-Feb. 3, 1842; House 1811-17.

LAWLER, Frank (D Ill.) June 25, 1842-Jan. 17, 1896; House 1885-91.

LAWLER, Joab (W Ala.) June 12, 1796-May 8, 1838; House 1835-May 8, 1838.

LAWRENCE, Abbott (W Mass.) Dec. 16, 1792-Aug. 18, 1855; House 1835-37, 1839-Sept. 18, 1840.

LAWRENCE, Cornelius Van Wyck (cousin of Effingham Lawrence) (JD N.Y.) Feb. 28, 1791-Feb. 20, 1861; House 1833-May 14, 1834.

LAWRENCE, Effingham (cousin of Cornelius Van Wyck Lawrence) (D La.) March 2, 1820-Dec. 9, 1878; House March 3, 1875.

LAWRENCE, George Pelton (R Mass.) May 19, 1859-Nov. 21, 1917; House Nov. 2, 1897-1913.

LAWRENCE, George Van Eman (son of Joseph Lawrence) (R Pa.) Nov. 13, 1818-Oct. 2, 1904; House 1865-69 (W), 1883-85 (R).

LAWRENCE, Henry Franklin (R Mo.) Jan. 31, 1868-Jan. 12, 1950; House 1921-23.

LAWRENCE, John Watson (D N.Y.) Aug. 1800-Dec. 20, 1888; House 1845-47.

LAWRENCE, Joseph (father of George Van Eman Lawrence) (W Pa.) 1786-April 17, 1842; House 1825-29, 1841-April 17, 1842.

LAWRENCE, Samuel (brother of William Thomas Lawrence) (— N.Y.) May 23, 1773-Oct. 20, 1837; House 1823-25.

LAWRENCE, Sidney (D N.Y.) Dec. 31, 1801-May 9, 1892; House 1847-49.

LAWRENCE, William (D Ohio) Sept. 2, 1814-Sept. 8, 1895; House 1857-59.

LAWRENCE, William (R Ohio) June 26, 1819-May 8, 1899; House 1865-71, 1873-77.

LAWRENCE, William Thomas (brother of Samuel Lawrence) (— N.Y.) May 7, 1788-Oct. 25, 1859; House 1847-49.

LAWS, Gilbert Lafayette (R Neb.) March 11, 1838-April 25, 1907; House Dec. 2, 1889-91.

LAWSON, John Daniel (R N.Y.) Feb. 18, 1816-Jan. 24, 1896; House 1873-75.

LAWSON, John William (D Va.) Sept. 13, 1837-Feb. 21, 1905; House 1891-93.

LAWSON, Thomas Graves (D Ga.) May 2, 1835-April 16, 1912; House 1891-97.

LAWYER, Thomas (— N.Y.) Oct. 14, 1785-May 21, 1868; House 1817-19.

LAY, Alfred Morrison (D Mo.) May 20, 1836-Dec. 8, 1879; House March 4-Dec. 8, 1879.

LAY, George Washington (W N.Y.) July 26, 1798-Oct. 21, 1860; House 1833-37.

LAYTON, Caleb Rodney (R Del.) Sept. 8, 1851-Nov. 11, 1930; House 1919-23.

LAYTON, Fernando Coello (D Ohio) April 11, 1847-June 22, 1926; House 1891-97.

LAZARO, Ladislas (D La.) June 5, 1872-March 30, 1927; House 1913-March 30, 1927.

LAZEAR, Jesse (D Pa.) Dec. 12, 1804-Sept. 2, 1877; House 1861-65.

LEA, Clarence Frederick (D/R Calif.) July 11, 1874-June 20, 1964; House 1917-19 (D), 1919-49 (D/R).

LEA, Luke (brother of Pryor Lea) (UD Tenn.) Jan. 21, 1783-June 17, 1851; House 1833-37.

LEA, Luke (great-grandson of the preceding) (D Tenn.) April 12, 1879-Nov. 18, 1945; Senate 1911-17.

LEA, Pryor (brother of Luke Lea) (JD Tenn.) Aug. 31, 1794-Sept. 14, 1879; House 1827-31.

LEACH, DeWitt Clinton (R Mich.) Nov. 23, 1822-Dec. 21, 1909; House 1857-61.

LEACH, James Madison (C N.C.) Jan. 17, 1815—June 1, 1891; House 1859-61 (W), 1871-75 (C).

LEACH, Robert Milton (R Mass.) April 2, 1879-Feb. 18, 1952; House Nov. 4, 1924-25.

LEADBETTER, Daniel Parkhurst (JD Ohio) Sept. 10, 1797-Feb. 26, 1870; House 1837-41.

LEAHY, Edward Laurence (D R.I.) Feb. 9, 1886-July 22, 1953; Senate Aug. 24, 1949-Dec. 18, 1950.

LEAKE, Eugene Walter (D N.J.) July 13, 1877-Aug. 23, 1959; House 1907-09.

LEAKE, Shelton Farrar (D Va.) Nov. 30, 1812-March 4, 1884; House 1845-47, 1859-61.

LEAKE, Walter (D Miss.) May 25, 1762-Nov. 17, 1825; Senate Dec. 10, 1817-May 15, 1820; Gov. 1821-25.

LEARNED, Amasa (grandfather of John Law) (— Conn.) Nov. 15, 1750-May 4, 1825; House 1791-95.

LEARY, Cornelius Lawrence Ludlow (U Md.) Oct. 22, 1813-March 21, 1893; House 1861-63.

LEATHERWOOD, Elmer O. (R Utah) Sept. 4, 1872-Dec. 24, 1929; House 1921-Dec. 24, 1929.

LEAVENWORTH, Elias Warner (R N.Y.) Dec. 20, 1803-Nov. 25, 1887; House 1875-77.

LEAVITT, Humphrey Howe (JD Ohio) June 18, 1796-March 15, 1873; House Dec. 6, 1830-July 10, 1834.

LEAVITT, Scott (R Mont.) June 16, 1879-Oct. 19, 1966; House 1923-33.

LEAVY, Charles Henry (D Wash.) Feb. 16, 1884-Sept. 25, 1952; House 1937-Aug. 1, 1942.

LE BLOND, Francis Celeste (grandfather of Frank LeBlond Kloeb) (D Ohio) Feb. 14, 1821-Nov. 9, 1902; House 1863-67.

LECOMPTE, Joseph (D Ky.) Dec. 15, 1797-April 25, 1851; House 1825-33.

LE COMPTE, Karl Miles (R Iowa) May 25, 1887; House 1939-59.

LEE, Blair (D Md.) Aug. 9, 1857-Dec. 25, 1944; Senate Jan. 28, 1914-17.

LEE, Frank Hood (D Mo.) March 29, 1873-Nov. 20, 1952; House 1933-35.

LEE, Gideon (JD N.Y.) April 27, 1778-Aug. 21, 1841; House Nov. 4, 1835-37.

LEE, Gordon (D Ga.) May 29, 1859-Nov. 7, 1927; House 1905-27.

LEE, Henry (brother of Richard Bland Lee and grandfather of William Henry Fitzhugh Lee) (F Va.) Jan. 29, 1756-March 25, 1818; House 1799-1801; Cont. Cong. 1785-88; Gov. 1791-94.

LEE, John (D Md.) Jan. 30, 1788-May 17, 1871; House 1823-25.

LEE, Joshua (D N.Y.) 1783-Dec. 19, 1842; House 1835-37.

LEE, Joshua Bryan (D Okla.) Jan. 23, 1892-Aug. 10, 1967; House 1935-37; Senate 1937-43.

LEE, Moses Lindley (R N.Y.) May 29, 1805-May 19, 1876; House 1859-61.

LEE, Richard Bland (brother of Henry Lee) (— Va.) Jan. 20, 1761-March 12, 1827; House 1789-95.

LEE, Richard Henry (— Va.) Jan. 20, 1732-June 19, 1794; Senate 1789-Oct. 8, 1792; Cont. Cong. 1774-80, 1784-87.

LEE, Robert Emmett (D Pa.) Oct. 12, 1868-Nov. 19, 1916; House 1911-15.

LEE, Robert Quincy (D Texas) Jan. 12, 1869-April 18, 1930; House 1929-April 18, 1930.

LEE, Silas (F Mass.) July 3, 1760-March 1, 1814; House 1799-Aug. 20, 1801.

LEE, Thomas (D N.J.) Nov. 28, 1780-Nov. 2, 1856; House 1833-37.

LEE, Warren Isbell (R N.Y.) Feb. 5, 1876-Dec. 25, 1955; House 1921-23.

LEE, William Henry Fitzhugh (grandson of Henry Lee) (D Va.) May 31, 1837-Oct. 15, 1891; House 1887-Oct. 15, 1891.

LEECH, James Russell (R Pa.) Nov. 19, 1888-Feb. 5, 1952; House 1927-Jan. 19, 1932.

LEEDOM, John Peter (D Ohio) Dec. 20, 1847-March 18, 1895; House 1881-83.

LEET, Isaac (D Pa.) 1801-June 10, 1844; House 1839-41.

LE FEVER, Jacob (father of Frank Jacob LeFevre) (R N.Y.) April 20, 1830-Feb. 4, 1905; House 1893-97.

LE FEVER, Joseph (D Pa.) April 3, 1760-Oct. 17, 1826; House 1811-13.

LE FEVRE, Benjamin (D Ohio) Oct. 8, 1838-March 7, 1922; House 1879-87.

LE FEVRE, Frank Jacob (son of Jacob Le Fever) (R N.Y.) Nov. 30, 1874-April 29, 1941; House 1905-07.

LE FEVRE, Jay (R N.Y.) Sept. 6, 1893-April 26, 1970; House 1943-51.

LEFFERTS, John (D N.Y.) Dec. 17, 1785-Sept. 18, 1829; House 1813-15.

LEFFLER, Isaac (brother of Shepherd Leffler) (— Va.) Nov. 7, 1788-March 8, 1866; House 1827-29.

LEFFLER, Shepherd (brother of Isaac Leffler) (D Iowa) April 24, 1811-Sept. 7, 1879; House Dec. 28, 1846-51.

LEFTWICH, Jabez (— Va.) Sept. 22, 1765-June 22, 1855; House 1821-25.

LEFTWICH, John William (D Tenn.) Sept. 7, 1826-March 6, 1870; House July 24, 1866-67.

LEGARDA Y TUASON, Benito (— P.I.) Sept. 27, 1853-Aug. 27, 1915; House (Res. Comm.) Nov. 22, 1907-13.

LEGARE, George Swinton (D S.C.) Nov. 11, 1869-Jan. 31, 1913; House 1903-Jan. 31, 1913.

LEGARE, Hugh Swinton (UD S.C.) Jan. 2, 1797-June 20, 1843; House 1837-39; Atty. Gen. 1841-43; Secy. of State 1843.

LEGGETT, Robert L. (D Calif.) July 26, 1926; House 1963- .

LEHLBACH, Frederick Reimold (nephew of Herman Lehlbach) (R N.J.) Jan. 31, 1876-Aug. 4, 1937; House 1915-37.

LEHLBACH, Herman (uncle of Frederick Reimold Lehlbach) (R N.J.) July 3, 1845-Jan. 11, 1904; House 1885-91.

LEHMAN, Herbert Henry (D N.Y.) March 28, 1878-Dec. 5, 1963; Senate Nov. 9, 1949-57; Gov. 1933-42.

LEHMAN, William Eckart (D Pa.) Aug. 21, 1821-July 19, 1895; House 1861-63.

LEHR, John Camillus (D Mich.) Nov. 18, 1878-Feb. 17, 1958; House 1933-35.

LEIB, Michael (D Pa.) Jan. 8, 1760-Dec. 22, 1822; House 1799-Feb. 14, 1806; Senate Jan. 9, 1809-Feb. 14, 1814.

LEIB, Owen D. (D Pa.) —June 17, 1848; House 1845-47.

LEIDY, Paul (D Pa.) Nov. 13, 1813-Sept. 11, 1877; House Dec. 7, 1857-59.

LEIGH, Benjamin Watkins (W Va.) June 18, 1781-Feb. 2, 1849; Senate Feb. 26, 1834-July 4, 1836.

LEIGHTY, Jacob D. (R Ind.) Nov. 15, 1839-Oct. 18, 1912; House 1895-97.

LEIPER, George Gray (D Pa.) Feb. 3, 1786-Nov. 18, 1868; House 1829-31.

LEISENRING, John (R Pa.) June 3, 1853-Jan. 19, 1901; House 1895-97.

LEITER, Benjamin Franklin (R Ohio) Oct. 13, 1813-June 17, 1866; House 1855-59.

LEMKE, William (R N.D.) Aug. 13, 1878-May 30, 1950; House 1933-41 (Nonpart. R), 1943-May 30, 1950 (R).

LE MOYNE, John Valcoulon (D Ill.) Nov. 17, 1828-July 27, 1918; House May 6, 1876-77.

LENAHAN, John Thomas (D Pa.) Nov. 15, 1852-April 28, 1920; House 1907-09.

L'ENGLE, Claude (D Fla.) Oct. 19, 1868-Nov. 6, 1919; House 1913-15.

LENNON, Alton Asa (D N.C.) Aug. 17, 1906; Senate July 10, 1953-Nov. 28, 1954; House 1957- .

LENROOT, Irvine Luther (R Wis.) Jan. 31, 1869-Jan. 26, 1949; House 1909-April 17, 1918; Senate April 18, 1918-27.

LENT, James (JD N.Y.) 1782-Feb. 22, 1833; House 1829-Feb. 22, 1833.

LENT, Norman F. (R N.Y.) March 23, 1931; House 1971- .

LENTZ, John Jacob (D Ohio) Jan. 27, 1856-July 27, 1931; House 1897-1901.

LEONARD, Fred Churchill (R Pa.) Feb. 16, 1856-Dec. 5, 1921; House 1895-97.

LEONARD, George (— Mass.) July 4, 1729-July 26, 1819; House 1789-91, 1795-97.

LEONARD, John Edwards (grandnephew of John Edwards of Pa.) (R La.) Sept. 22, 1845-March 15, 1878; House 1877-March 15, 1878.

LEONARD, Moses Gage (D N.Y.) July 10, 1809-March 20, 1899; House 1843-45.

LEONARD, Stephen Banks (D N.Y.) April 15, 1793-May 8, 1876; House 1835-37, 1839-41.

LESHER, John Vandling (D Pa.) July 27, 1866-May 3, 1932; House 1913-21.

LESINSKI, John (D Mich.) Jan. 3, 1885-May 27, 1950; House 1933-May 27, 1950.

LESINSKI, John, Jr. (son of the preceding) (D Mich.) Dec. 28, 1914; House 1951-65.

LESSLER, Montague (R N.Y.) Jan. 1, 1869-Feb. 17, 1938; House Jan. 7, 1902-03.

LESTER, Posey Green (D Va.) March 12, 1850-Feb. 9, 1929; House 1889-93.

LESTER, Rufus Ezekiel (D Ga.) Dec. 12, 1837-June 16, 1906; House 1889-June 16, 1906.

LETCHER, John (D Va.) March 29, 1813-Jan. 26, 1884; House 1851-59; Gov. 1860-64.

LETCHER, Robert Perkins (W Ky.) Feb. 10, 1788-Jan. 24, 1861; House 1823-27 (CD), 1827-33, Aug. 6, 1834-35 (W); Gov. 1840-44.

LETTS, Fred Dickinson (cousin of Lester Jesse Dickinson) (R Iowa) April 26, 1875-Jan. 19, 1965; House 1925-31.

LEVER, Asbury Francis (D S.C.) Jan. 5, 1875-April 28, 1940; House Nov. 5, 1901-Aug. 1, 1919.

LEVERING, Robert Woodrow (son-in-law of Usher L. Burdick and brother-in-law of Quentin N. Burdick) (D Ohio) Oct. 3, 1914; House 1959-61.

LEVIN, Lewis Charles (AP Pa.) Nov. 10, 1808-March 14, 1860; House 1845-51.

LEVY, David (R Fla.) (See YULEE, David Levy.)

LEVY, Jefferson Monroe (D N.Y.) April 16, 1852-March 6, 1924; House 1899-1901, 1911-15.

LEVY, William Mallory (D La.) Oct. 31, 1827-Aug. 14, 1882; House 1875-77.

LEWIS, Abner (W N.Y.)——; House 1845-47.

LEWIS, Barbour (R Tenn.) Jan. 5, 1818-July 15, 1893; House 1873-75.

LEWIS, Burwell Boykin (D Ala.) July 7, 1838-Oct. 11, 1885; House 1875-77, 1879-Oct. 1, 1880.

LEWIS, Charles Swearinger (D Va.) Feb. 26, 1821-Jan. 22, 1878; House Dec. 4, 1854-55.

LEWIS, Clarke (D Miss.) Nov. 8, 1840-March 13, 1896; House 1889-93.

LEWIS, David John (D Md.) May 1, 1869-Aug. 12, 1952; House 1911-17, 1931-39.

LEWIS, Dixon Hall (D Ala.) Aug. 10, 1802-Oct. 25, 1848; House 1829-April 22, 1844 (SRD); Senate April 22, 1844-Oct. 24, 1848 (D).

LEWIS, Earl Ramage (R Ohio) Feb. 22, 1887-Feb. 1, 1956; House 1939-41, 1943-49.

LEWIS, Edward Taylor (D La.) Oct. 26, 1834-April 26, 1927; House 1883-85.

LEWIS, Elijah Banks (D Ga.) March 27, 1854-Dec. 10, 1920; House 1897-1909.

LEWIS, Fred Ewing (R Pa.) Feb. 8, 1865-June 27, 1949; House 1913-15.

LEWIS, James Hamilton (D Wash./Ill.) May 18, 1863-April 9, 1939; House 1897-99 (Wash.); Senate March 26, 1913-19, 1931-April 9, 1939 (Ill.).

LEWIS, John Francis (R Va.) March 1, 1818-Sept. 2, 1895; Senate Jan. 26, 1870-75.

LEWIS, John Henry (R Ill.) July 21, 1830-Jan. 6, 1929; House 1881-83.

LEWIS, John William (R Ky.) Oct. 14, 1841-Dec. 20, 1913; House 1895-97.

LEWIS, Joseph, Jr. (F Va.) 1772-March 30, 1834; House 1803-17.

LEWIS, Joseph Horace (D Ky.) Oct. 29, 1824-July 6, 1904; House May 10, 1870-73.

LEWIS, Lawrence (D Colo.) June 22, 1879-Dec. 9, 1943; House 1933-Dec. 9, 1943.

LEWIS, Robert Jacob (R Pa.) Dec. 30, 1864-July 24, 1933; House 1901-03.

LEWIS, Thomas (— Va.) ——; House 1803-March 5, 1804.

LEWIS, William (R Ky.) Sept. 22, 1868-Aug. 8, 1959; House April 24, 1948-49.

LEWIS, William J. (D Va.) July 4, 1766-Nov. 1, 1828; House 1817-19.

LIBBEY, Harry (R Va.) Nov. 22, 1843-Sept. 30, 1913; House 1883-87.

LIBONATI, Roland Victor (D Ill.) Dec. 29, 1900; House Dec. 31, 1957-65.

LICHTENWALNER, Norton Lewis (D Pa.) June 1, 1889-May 3, 1960; House 1931-33.

LICHTENWALTER, Franklin Herbert (R Pa.) March 28, 1910;House Sept. 9, 1947-51.

LIEB, Charles (D Ind.) May 20, 1852-Sept. 1, 1928; House 1913-17.

LIEBEL, Michael, Jr. (D Pa.) Dec. 12, 1870-Aug. 8, 1927; House 1915-17.

LIGON, Robert Fulwood (D Ala.) Dec. 16, 1823-Oct. 11, 1901; House 1877-79.

LIGON, Thomas Watkins (D Md.) May 10, 1810-Jan. 12, 1881; House 1845-49; Gov. 1854-58.

LILLEY, George Leavens (R Conn.) Aug. 3, 1859-April 21, 1909; House 1903-Jan. 5, 1909; Gov. 1909.

LILLEY, Mial Eben (R Pa.) May 30, 1850-Feb. 28, 1915; House 1905-07.

LILLY, Samuel (D N.J.) Oct. 28, 1815-April 3, 1880; House 1853-55.

LILLY, Thomas Jefferson (D W. Va.) June 3, 1878-April 2, 1956; House 1923-25.

LILLY, William (R Pa.) June 3, 1821-Dec. 1, 1893; House March 4-Dec. 1, 1893.

LINCOLN, Abraham (W Ill.) Feb. 12, 1809-April 14, 1865; House 1847-49 (W); President 1861-April 14, 1865.

LINCOLN, Enoch (son of Levi Lincoln and brother of Levi Lincoln) (— Mass./Maine) Dec. 28, 1788-Oct. 8, 1829; House Nov. 4, 1818-21 (Mass.), 1821-26 (Maine); Gov. of Maine 1827-Oct. 8, 1829.

LINCOLN, Levi (father of Enoch Lincoln and Levi Lincoln) (D Mass.) May 15, 1749-April 14, 1820; House Dec. 15, 1800-March 5, 1801; Atty. Gen. 1801-04; Gov. 1808-09.

LINCOLN, Levi (son of the preceding and brother of Enoch Lincoln) (W Mass.) Oct. 25, 1782-May 29, 1868; House Feb. 17, 1834-March 16, 1841; Gov. 1825-34.

LINCOLN, William Slosson (R N.Y.) Aug. 13, 1813-April 21, 1893; House 1867-69.

LIND, James Francis (D Pa.) Oct. 17, 1900; House 1949-53.

LIND, John (D Minn.) March 25, 1854-Sept. 18, 1930; House 1887-93 (R), 1903-05 (D); Gov. 1898-1900 (D).

LINDBERGH, Charles Augustus (R Minn.) Jan. 20, 1859-May 24, 1924; House 1907-17.

LINDLEY, James Johnson (W Mo.) Jan. 1, 1822-April 18, 1891; House 1853-57.

LINDQUIST, Francis Oscar (R Mich.) Sept. 27, 1869-Sept. 25, 1924; House 1913-15.

LINDSAY, George Henry (father of George Washington Lindsay) (D N.Y.) Jan. 7, 1837-May 25, 1916; House 1901-13.

LINDSAY, George Washington (son of George Henry Lindsay) (D N.Y.) March 28, 1865-March 15, 1938; House 1923-35.

LINDSAY, John Vliet (R N.Y.) Nov. 24, 1921; House 1959-Dec. 31, 1965.

LINDSAY, William (D Ky.) Sept. 4, 1835-Oct. 15, 1909; Senate Feb. 15, 1893-1901.

LINDSEY, Stephen Decatur (R Maine) March 3,1828-April 26,1884; House 1877-83.

LINDSLEY, James Girard (R N.Y.) March 19, 1819-Dec. 4, 1898; House 1885-87.

LINDSLEY, William Dell (D Ohio) Dec. 25, 1812-March 11, 1890; House 1853-55.

LINEBERGER, Walter Franklin (R Calif.) July 20, 1883-Oct. 9, 1943; House 1921-27.

LINEHAN, Neil Joseph (D Ill.) Sept. 23, 1895-Aug. 23, 1967; House 1949-51.

LINK, Arthur A. (D N.D.) May 24, 1914; House 1971- .

LINK, William Walter (D Ill.) Feb. 12, 1884-Sept. 23, 1950; House 1945-47.

LINN, Archibald Ladley (W N.Y.) Oct. 15, 1802-Oct. 10, 1857; House 1841-43.

LINN, James (D N.J.) 1749–Jan. 5, 1821; House 1799-1801.

LINN, John (— N.J.) Dec. 3, 1763–Jan. 5, 1821; House 1817–Jan. 5, 1821.

LINN, Lewis Fields (D Mo.) Nov. 5, 1796-Oct. 3, 1843; Senate Oct. 25, 1833-Oct. 3, 1843.

LINNEY, Romulus Zachariah (R N.C.) Dec. 26, 1841-April 15, 1910; House 1895-1901.

LINTHICUM, John Charles (D Md.) Nov. 26, 1867-Oct. 5, 1932; House 1911-Oct. 5, 1932.

LINTON, William Seelye (R Mich.) Feb. 4, 1856-Nov. 22, 1927; House 1893-97.

LIPPITT, Henry Frederick (R R.I.) Oct. 12, 1856-Dec. 28, 1933; Senate 1911-17.

LIPSCOMB, Glenard Paul (R Calif.) Aug. 19, 1915-Feb. 1, 1970; House Nov. 10, 1953-Feb. 1, 1970.

LISLE, Marcus Claiborne (D Ky.) Sept. 23, 1862-July 7, 1894; House 1893–July 7, 1894.

LITCHFIELD, Elisha (D N.Y.) July 12, 1785-Aug. 4, 1859; House 1821-25.

LITTAUER, Lucius Nathan (R N.Y.) Jan. 20, 1859-March 2, 1944; House 1897-1907.

LITTLE, Chauncey Bundy (D Kan.) Feb. 10, 1877-Sept. 29, 1952; House 1925-27.

LITTLE, Edward Campbell (R Kan.) Dec. 14, 1858-June 27, 1924; House 1917–June 27, 1924.

LITTLE, Edward Preble (D Mass.) Nov. 7, 1791-Feb. 6, 1875; House Dec. 13, 1852-53.

LITTLE, John (R Ohio) April 25, 1837-Oct. 18, 1900; House 1885-87.

LITTLE, John Sebastian (D Ark.) March 15, 1853-Oct. 29, 1916; House Dec. 3, 1894–Jan. 14, 1907; Gov. 1907.

LITTLE, Joseph James (D N.Y.) June 5, 1841-Feb. 11, 1913; House Nov. 3, 1891-93.

LITTLE, Peter (D Md.) Dec. 11, 1775-Feb. 5, 1830; House 1811-13, Sept. 2, 1816-29.

LITTLEFIELD, Charles Edgar (R Maine) June 21, 1851-May 2, 1915; House June 19, 1899-Sept. 30, 1908.

LITTLEFIELD, Nathaniel Swett (D Maine) Sept. 20, 1804-Aug. 15, 1882; House 1841-43 (D), 1849-51 (Cass D).

LITTLEJOHN, DeWitt Clinton (R N.Y.) Feb. 7, 1818-Oct. 27, 1892; House 1863-65.

LITTLEPAGE, Adam Brown (D W. Va.) April 14, 1859–June 29, 1921; House 1911-13, 1915-19.

LITTLETON, Martin Wiley (D N.Y.) Jan. 12, 1872-Dec. 19, 1934; House 1911-13.

LIVELY, Robert Maclin (D Texas) Jan. 6, 1855–Jan. 15, 1929; House July 23, 1910-11.

LIVERMORE, Arthur (son of Samuel Livermore and brother of Edward St. Loe Livermore) (D N.H.) July 29, 1766–July 1, 1853; House 1817-21, 1823-25.

LIVERMORE, Edward St. Loe (son of Samuel Livermore and brother of Arthur Livermore) (F Mass.) April 5, 1762-Sept. 15, 1832; House 1807-11.

LIVERMORE, Samuel (father of Arthur Livermore and Edward St. Loe Livermore) (— N.H.) May 14, 1732-May 18, 1803; House 1789-93; Senate 1793–June 12, 1801; Cont. Cong. 1780-82 and 1785.

LIVERNASH, Edward James (subsequently Edward James de Nivernais) (UL/D Calif.) Feb. 14, 1866–June 1, 1938; House 1903-05.

LIVINGSTON, Edward (D N.Y./La.) May 26, 1764-May 23, 1836; House 1795-1801 (N.Y.), 1823-29 (La.); Senate 1829-May 24, 1831 (La.); Secy. of State 1831-33.

LIVINGSTON, Henry Walter (— N.Y.) 1768-Dec. 22, 1810; House 1803-07.

LIVINGSTON, Leonidas Felix (D Ga.) April 3, 1832-Feb. 11, 1912; House 1891-1911.

LIVINGSTON, Robert LeRoy (F N.Y.) — -—; House 1809-May 6, 1812.

LLOYD, Edward (D Md.) July 22, 1779-June 2, 1834; House Dec. 3, 1806-09; Senate 1819–Jan. 14, 1826; Gov. 1809-11.

LLOYD, James (D Md.) 1745-1820; Senate Dec. 11, 1797-Dec. 1, 1800.

LLOYD, James (F Mass.) Dec. 1769-April 5, 1831; Senate June 9, 1808-May 1, 1813, June 5, 1822-May 23, 1826.

LLOYD, James Tilghman (D Mo.) Aug. 28, 1857-April 3, 1944; House June 1, 1897-1917.

LLOYD, Sherman Parkinson (R Utah) Jan. 11, 1914; House 1963-65, 1967- .

LLOYD, Wesley (D Wash.) July 24, 1883-Jan. 10, 1936; House 1933–Jan. 10, 1936.

LOAN, Benjamin Franklin (Rad. Mo.) Oct. 4, 1819-March 30, 1881; House 1863-67 (E), 1867-69 (Rad.).

LOBECK, Charles Otto (D Neb.) April 6, 1852–Jan. 30, 1920; House 1911-19.

LOCHER, Cyrus (D Ohio) March 8, 1878-Aug. 17, 1929; Senate April 5-Dec. 14, 1928.

LOCKE, Francis (nephew of Matthew Locke) (D N.C.) Oct. 31, 1776–Jan. 8, 1823; Senate 1814-Dec. 5, 1815.

LOCKE, John (— Mass.) Feb. 14, 1764-March 29, 1855; House 1823-29.

LOCKE, Matthew (uncle of Francis Locke and great-great-great-grandfather of Effiegene (Locke) Wingo) (D N.C.) 1730-Sept. 7, 1801; House 1793-99.

LOCKHART, James (D Ind.) Feb. 13, 1806-Sept. 7, 1857; House 1851-53, March 4-Sept. 7, 1857.

LOCKHART, James Alexander (D N.C.) June 2, 1850-Dec. 24, 1905; House 1895-June 5, 1896.

LOCKWOOD, Daniel Newton (D N.Y.) June 1, 1844–June 1, 1906; House 1877-79, 1891-95.

LODGE, Henry Cabot (great-grandson of George Cabot) (R Mass.) May 12, 1850-Nov. 9, 1924; House 1887-93; Senate 1893-Nov. 9, 1924.

LODGE, Henry Cabot, Jr. (grandson of the preceding, brother of John Davis Lodge and nephew of Augustus P. Gardner) (R Mass.) July 5, 1902; Senate 1937-Feb. 3, 1944, 1947-53.

LODGE, John Davis (grandson of Henry Cabot Lodge, brother of Henry Cabot Lodge, Jr., nephew of Augustus P. Gardner) (R Conn.) Oct. 20, 1903; House 1947-51; Gov. 1951-55.

LOFLAND, James Rush (R Del.) Nov. 2, 1823-Feb. 10, 1894; House 1873-75.

LOFT, George William (D N.Y.) Feb. 6, 1865-Nov. 6, 1943; House Nov. 4, 1913-17.

LOFTIN, Scott Marion (D Fla.) Sept. 14, 1878-Sept. 22, 1953; Senate May 26-Nov. 3, 1936.

LOGAN, George (D Pa.) Sept. 9, 1753-April 9, 1821; Senate July 13, 1801-07.

LOGAN, Henry (D Pa.) April 14, 1784-Dec. 26, 1866; House 1835-39.

LOGAN, John Alexander (R Ill.) Feb. 9, 1826-Dec. 26, 1886; House 1859-April 2, 1862 (D), 1867-71 (R); Senate 1871-77, 1879-Dec. 26, 1886 (R).

LOGAN, Marvel Mills (D Ky.) Jan. 7, 1875-Oct. 3, 1939; Senate 1931-Oct. 3, 1939.

LOGAN, William (D Ky.) Dec. 8, 1776-Aug. 8, 1822; Senate 1819-May 28, 1820.

LOGAN, William Turner (D S.C.) June 21, 1874-Sept. 15, 1941; House 1921-25.

LOGUE, James Washington (D Pa.) Feb. 22, 1863-Aug. 27, 1925; House 1913-15.

LONDON, Meyer (Soc. N.Y.) Dec. 29, 1871-June 6, 1926; House 1915-19, 1921-23.

LONERGAN, Augustine (D Conn.) May 20, 1874-Oct. 18, 1947; House 1913-15, 1917-21, 1931-33; Senate 1933-39.

LONG, Alexander (D Ohio) Dec. 24, 1816-Nov. 28, 1886; House 1863-65.

LONG, Chester Isaiah (R Kan.) Oct. 12, 1860-July 1, 1934; House 1895-97, 1899-March 4, 1903; Senate 1903-09.

LONG, Clarence Dickinson (D Md.) Dec. 11, 1908; House 1963- .

LONG, Edward Henry Carroll (W Md.) Sept. 28, 1808-Oct. 16, 1865; House 1845-47.

LONG, Edward Vaughn (D Mo.) July 18, 1908; Senate Sept. 23, 1960-69.

LONG, George Shannon (brother of Huey Pierce Long, brother-in-law of Rose McConnell Long and uncle of Russell Billiu Long) (D La.) Sept. 11, 1883-March 22, 1958; House 1953-March 22, 1958.

LONG, Gillis William (D La.) May 4, 1923; House 1963-65.

LONG, Huey Pierce (husband of Rose McConnell Long, father of Russell B. Long and brother of George S. Long) (D La.) Aug. 30, 1893-Sept. 10, 1935; Senate Jan. 25, 1932-Sept. 10, 1935; Gov. 1928-32.

LONG, Jefferson Franklin (R Ga.) March 3, 1836-Feb. 5, 1900; House Dec. 22, 1870-71.

LONG, John (W N.C.) Feb. 26, 1785-Aug. 11, 1857; House 1821-29.

LONG, John Benjamin (D Texas) Sept. 8, 1843-April 27, 1924; House 1891-93.

LONG, John Davis (R Mass.) Oct. 27, 1838-Aug. 28, 1915; House 1883-89; Gov. 1880-82; Secy. of the Navy 1897-1902.

LONG, Lewis Marshall (D Ill.) June 22, 1883-Sept. 9, 1957; House 1937-39.

LONG, Oren Ethelbirt (D Hawaii) March 4, 1889-May 6, 1965; Senate Aug. 21, 1959-63; Gov. (Terr.) 1951-53.

LONG, Rose McConnell (widow of Huey Pierce Long, mother of Russell B. Long and sister-in-law of George S. Long) (D La.) April 8, 1892-May 27, 1970; Senate Jan. 31, 1936-37.

LONG, Russell Billiu (son of Huey Pierce Long and Rose McConnell Long and nephew of George S. Long) (D La.) Nov. 3, 1918; Senate Dec. 31, 1948- .

LONG, Speedy O. (D La.) June 16, 1928; House 1965- .

LONGFELLOW, Stephen (F Maine) June 23, 1775-Aug. 2, 1849; House 1823-25.

LONGNECKER, Henry Clay (R Pa.) April 17, 1820-Sept. 16, 1871; House 1859-61.

LONGWORTH, Nicholas (nephew of Bellamy Storer) (R Ohio) Nov. 5, 1869-April 9, 1931; House 1903-13, 1915-April 9, 1931; Speaker 1925-31.

LONGYEAR, John Wesley (R Mich.) Oct. 22, 1820-March 11, 1875; House 1863-67.

LOOFBOUROW, Frederick Charles (R Utah) Feb. 8, 1874-July 8, 1949; House Nov. 4, 1930-38.

LOOMIS, Andrew Williams (W Ohio) June 27, 1797-Aug. 24, 1873; House March 4-Oct. 20, 1837.

LOOMIS, Arphaxed (D N.Y.) April 9, 1798-Sept. 15, 1885; House 1837-39.

LOOMIS, Dwight (R Conn.) July 27, 1821-Sept. 17, 1903; House 1859-63.

LORD, Frederick William (W N.Y.) Dec. 11, 1800-May 24, 1860; House 1847-49.

LORD, Henry William (R Mich.) March 8, 1821-Jan. 25, 1891; House 1881-83.

LORD, Scott (D N.Y.) Dec. 11, 1820-Sept. 10, 1885; House 1875-77.

LORE, Charles Brown (D Del.) March 16, 1831-March 6, 1911; House 1883-87.

LORIMER, William (R Ill.) April 27, 1861-Sept. 13, 1934; House 1895-1901, 1903-June 17, 1909; Senate June 18, 1909-July 13, 1912.

LORING, George Bailey (R Mass.) Nov. 8, 1817-Sept. 13, 1891; House 1877-81.

LOSER, Joseph Carlton (D Tenn.) Oct. 1, 1892; House 1957-63.

LOUD, Eugene Francis (R Calif.) March 12, 1847-Dec. 19, 1908; House 1891-1903.

LOUD, George Alvin (R Mich.) June 18, 1852-Nov. 13, 1925; House 1903-13, 1915-17.

LOUDENSLAGER, Henry Clay (R N.J.) May 22, 1852-Aug. 12, 1911; House 1893-Aug. 12, 1911.

LOUGHRIDGE, William (R Iowa) July 11, 1827-Sept. 26, 1889; House 1867-71, 1873-75.

LOUNSBERY, William (D N.Y.) Dec. 25, 1831-Nov. 8, 1905; House 1879-81.

LOUTTIT, James Alexander (R Calif.) Oct. 16, 1848-July 26, 1906; House 1885-87.

LOVE, Francis Johnson (R W. Va.) Jan. 23, 1901; House 1947-49.

LOVE, James (— Ky.) May 12, 1795-June 12, 1874; House 1833-35.

LOVE, John (D Va.) — -Aug. 17, 1822; House 1807-11.

LOVE, Peter Early (D Ga.) July 7, 1818-Nov. 8, 1866; House 1859-Jan. 23, 1861.

LOVE, Rodney Marvin (D Ohio) July 18, 1908; House 1965-67.

LOVE, Thomas Cutting (W N.Y.) Nov. 30, 1789-Sept. 15, 1853; House 1835-37.

LOVE, William Carter (D N.C.) 1784-1835; House 1815-17.

LOVE, William Franklin (D Miss.) March 29, 1850-Oct. 16, 1898; House 1897-Oct. 16, 1898.

LOVEJOY, Owen (cousin of Nathan Allen Farwell) (R Ill.) Jan. 6, 1811-March 25, 1864; House 1857-March 25, 1864.

LOVERING, Henry Bacon (D Mass.) April 8, 1841-April 5, 1911; House 1883-87.

LOVERING, William Croad (R Mass.) Feb. 25, 1835-Feb. 4, 1910; House 1897-Feb. 5, 1910.

LOVETT, John (F N.Y.) Feb. 20, 1761-Aug. 12, 1818; House 1813-17.

LOVETTE, Oscar Byrd (R Tenn.) Dec. 20, 1871-July 6, 1934; House 1931-33.

LOVRE, Harold Orrin (R S.D.) Jan. 30, 1904; House 1949-57.

LOW, Frederick Ferdinand (R Calif.) June 30, 1828-July 21, 1894; House June 3, 1862-63; Gov. 1863-67.

LOW, Philip Burrill (R N.Y.) May 6, 1836-Aug. 23, 1912; House 1895-99.

LOWDEN, Frank Orren (R Ill.) Jan. 26, 1861-March 20, 1943; House Nov. 6, 1906-11; Gov. 1917-21.

LOWE, David Perley (R Kan.) Aug. 22, 1823-April 10, 1882; House 1871-75.

LOWE, William Manning (GD Ala.) June 12, 1842-Oct. 12, 1882; House 1879-81, June 3, 1882-Oct. 12, 1882.

LOWELL, Joshua Adams (D Maine) March 20, 1801-March 13, 1874; House 1839-43.

LOWENSTEIN, Allard K. (D-L N.Y.) Jan. 16, 1929; House 1969-71.

LOWER, Christian (D Pa.) Jan. 7, 1740-Dec. 19, 1806; House 1805-Dec. 19, 1806.

LOWNDES, Lloyd, Jr. (R Md.) Feb. 21, 1845-Jan. 8, 1905; House 1873-75; Gov. 1895-99.

LOWNDES, Thomas (brother of William Lowndes) (F S.C.) Jan. 22, 1766-July 8, 1843; House 1801-05.

LOWNDES, William (brother of Thomas Lowndes) (D S.C.) Feb. 11, 1782-Oct. 27, 1822; House 1811-May 8, 1822.

LOWREY, Bill Green (D Miss.) May 25, 1862-Sept. 2, 1947; House 1921-29.

LOWRIE, Walter (D Pa.) Dec. 10, 1784-Dec. 14, 1868; Senate 1819-25.

LOWRY, Robert (D Ind.) April 2, 1824-Jan. 27, 1904; House 1883-87.

LOYALL, George (D Va.) May 29, 1789-Feb. 24, 1868; House March 9, 1830-31, 1833-37.

LOZIER, Ralph Fulton (D Mo.) Jan. 28, 1866-May 28, 1945; House 1923-35.

LUCAS, Edward (brother of William Lucas) (D Va.) Oct. 20, 1780-March 4, 1858; House 1833-37.

LUCAS, John Baptiste Charles (D Pa.) Aug. 14, 1758-Aug. 17, 1842; House 1803-05.

LUCAS, Scott Wike (D Ill.) Feb. 19, 1892-Feb. 22, 1968; House 1935-39; Senate 1939-51.

LUCAS, William (brother of Edward Lucas) (D Va.) Nov. 30, 1800-Aug. 29, 1877; House 1839-41, 1843-45.

LUCAS, William Vincent (R S.D.) July 3, 1835-Nov. 10, 1921; House 1893-95.

LUCAS, Wingate Hezekiah (D Texas) May 1, 1908; House 1947-55.

LUCE, Clare Boothe (stepdaughter of Albert E. Austin) (R Conn.) April 10, 1903; House 1943-47.

LUCE, Robert (R Mass.) Dec. 2, 1862-April 7, 1946; House 1919-35, 1937-41.

LUCKEY, Henry Carl (D Neb.) Nov. 22, 1868-Dec. 31, 1956; House 1935-39.

LUCKING, Alfred (D Mich.) Dec. 18, 1856-Dec. 1, 1929; House 1903-05.

LUDLOW, Louis Leon (D Ind.) June 24, 1873-Nov. 28, 1950; House 1929-49.

LUECKE, John Frederick (D Mich.) July 4, 1889-March 21, 1952; House 1937-39.

LUFKIN, Willfred Weymouth (R Mass.) March 10, 1879-March 28, 1934; House Nov. 6, 1917-June 30, 1921.

LUHRING, Oscar Raymond (R Ind.) Feb. 11, 1879-Aug. 20, 1944; House 1919-23.

LUJAN, Manuel, Jr. (R N.M.) May 12, 1928; House 1969- .

LUKENS, Donald E. (Buz) (R Ohio) Feb. 11, 1931; House 1967-71.

LUMPKIN, Alva Moore (D S.C.) Nov. 13, 1886-Aug. 1, 1941; Senate July 22-Aug. 1, 1941.

LUMPKIN, John Henry (nephew of Wilson Lumpkin) (D Ga.) June 13, 1812-July 10, 1860; House 1843-49, 1855-57.

LUMPKIN, Wilson (uncle of John Henry Lumpkin and grandfather of Middleton Pope Barrow) (D Ga.) Jan. 14, 1783-Dec. 28, 1870; House 1815-17, 1827-31; Senate Nov. 22, 1837-41; Gov. 1831-35.

LUNA, Tranquillino (R N.M.) Feb. 25, 1849-Nov. 20, 1892; House (Terr. Del.) 1881-March 5, 1884.

LUNDEEN, Ernest (F-L Minn.) Aug. 4, 1878-Aug. 31, 1940; House 1917-19 (R), 1933-37 (F-L); Senate 1937-Aug. 31, 1940 (F-L).

LUNDIN, Frederick (R Ill.) May 18, 1868-Aug. 20, 1947; House 1909-11.

LUNN, George Richard (D N.Y.) June 23, 1873-Nov. 27, 1948; House 1917-19.

LUSK, Georgia L. (D N.M.) May 12, 1893-Jan. 5, 1971; House 1947-49.

LUSK, Hall Stoner (D Ore.) Sept. 21, 1883; Senate March 16-Nov. 8, 1960.

LUTTRELL, John King (D Calif.) June 27, 1831-Oct. 4, 1893; House 1873-79.

LYBRAND, Archibald (R Ohio) May 23, 1840-Feb. 7, 1910; House 1897-1901.

LYLE, Aaron (D Pa.) Nov. 17, 1759-Sept. 24, 1825; House 1809-17.

LYLE, John Emmett, Jr. (D Texas) Sept. 4, 1910; House 1945-55.

LYMAN, Joseph (R Iowa) Sept. 13, 1840-July 9, 1890; House 1885-89.

LYMAN, Joseph Stebbins (— N.Y.) Feb. 14, 1785-March 21, 1821; House 1819-21.

LYMAN, Samuel (— Mass.) Jan. 25, 1749-June 5, 1802; House 1795-Nov. 6, 1800.

LYMAN, Theodore (I Mass.) Aug. 23, 1833-Sept. 9, 1897; House 1883-85.

LYMAN, William (D Mass.) Dec. 7, 1755-Sept. 2, 1811; House 1793-97.

LYNCH, John (R Maine) Feb. 18, 1825-July 21, 1892; House 1865-73.

LYNCH, John (D Pa.) Nov. 1, 1843-Aug. 17, 1910; House 1887-89.

LYNCH, John Roy (R Miss.) Sept. 10, 1847-Nov. 2, 1939; House 1873-77, April 29, 1882-83.

LYNCH, Thomas (D Wis.) Nov. 21, 1844-May 4, 1898; House 1891-95.

LYNCH, Walter Aloysius (D N.Y.) July 7, 1894-Sept. 10, 1957; House Feb. 20, 1940-51.

LYNDE, William Pitt (D Wis.) Dec. 16, 1817-Dec. 18, 1885; House June 5, 1848-49, 1875-79.

LYON, Asa (F Vt.) Dec. 31, 1763-April 4, 1841; House 1815-17.

LYON, Caleb (I N.Y.) Dec. 7, 1822-Sept. 8, 1875; House 1853-55; Gov. of Idaho (Terr.) 1864-66.

LYON, Chittenden (son of Matthew Lyon) (D Ky.) Feb. 22, 1787-Nov. 23, 1842; House 1827-35.

LYON, Francis Strother (W Ala.) Feb. 25, 1800-Dec. 31, 1882; House 1835-39.

LYON, Homer Le Grand (D N.C.) March 1, 1879-May 31, 1956; House 1921-29.

LYON, Lucius (D Mich.) Feb. 26, 1800-Sept. 24, 1851; House (Terr. Del.) 1833-35, (Rep.) 1843-45; Senate Jan. 26, 1837-39.

LYON, Matthew (father of Chittenden Lyon and great grandfather of William Peters Hepburn (— Vt./Ky.) July 14, 1746-Aug. 1, 1822; House 1797-1801 (Vt.), 1803-11 (Ky.).

LYTLE, Robert Todd (nephew of John Rowan) (JD Ohio) May 19, 1804-Dec. 22, 1839; House 1833-March 10, 1934, Dec. 27, 1834-35.

M

MAAS, Melvin Joseph (R Minn.) May 14, 1898-April 14, 1964; House 1927-33, 1935-45.

MacCRATE, John (R N.Y.) March 29, 1885; House 1919-Dec. 30, 1920.

MacDONALD, John Lewis (D Minn.) Feb. 22, 1838-July 13, 1903; House 1887-89.

MACDONALD, Moses (D Maine) April 8, 1815-Oct. 18, 1869; House 1851-55.

MACDONALD, Torbert Hart (D Mass.) June 6, 1917; House 1955- .

MacDONALD, William Josiah (Pro. Mich.) Nov. 17, 1873-March 29, 1946; House Aug. 26, 1913-15.

MacDOUGALL, Clinton Dugald (R N.Y.) June 14, 1839-May 24, 1914; House 1873-77.

MACE, Daniel (R Ind.) Sept. 5, 1811-July 26, 1867; House 1851-55 (D), 1855-57 (R).

MacGREGOR, Clarence (R N.Y.) Sept. 16, 1872-Feb. 18, 1952; House 1919-Dec. 31, 1928.

MacGREGOR, Clark (R Minn.) July 12, 1922; House 1961-71.

MACHEN, Hervey Gilbert (D Md.) Oct. 14, 1916; House 1965-69.

MACHEN, Willis Benson (D Ky.) April 10, 1810-Sept. 29, 1893; Senate Sept. 27, 1872-73.

MACHIR, James (— Va.) —June 25, 1827; House 1797-99.

MACHROWICZ, Thaddeus Michael (D Mich.) Aug. 21, 1899-Feb. 17, 1970; House 1951-Sept. 18, 1961.

MACIEJEWSKI, Anton Frank (D Ill.) Jan. 3, 1893-Sept. 25, 1949; House 1939-Dec. 8, 1942.

MacINTYRE, Archibald Thompson (D Ga.) Oct. 27, 1822-Jan. 1, 1900; House 1871-73.

MACIORA, Lucien John (D Conn.) Aug. 17, 1902; House 1941-43.

MACK, Peter Francis, Jr. (D Ill.) Nov. 1, 1916; House 1949-63.

MACK, Russell Vernon (R Wash.) June 13, 1891-March 28, 1960; House June 7, 1947-March 28, 1960.

MACKAY, James Armstrong (D Ga.) June 25, 1919; House 1965-67.

MACKEY, Edmund William McGregor (R S.C.) March 8, 1846-Jan. 27, 1884; House 1875-July 19, 1876 (IR), May 31, 1882-Jan. 27, 1884 (R).

MACKEY, Levi Augustus (D Pa.) Nov. 25, 1819-Feb. 8, 1889; House 1875-79.

MACKIE, John C. (D Mich.) June 1, 1920; House 1965-67.

MacKINNON, George Edward (R Minn.) April 22, 1906; House 1947-49.

MacLAFFERTY, James Henry (R Calif.) Feb. 27, 1871-June 9, 1937; House Nov. 7, 1922-25.

MACLAY, Samuel (brother of William Maclay and father of William Plunkett Maclay) (— Pa.) June 17, 1741-Oct. 5, 1811; House 1795-97; Senate 1803-Jan. 4, 1809.

MACLAY, William (brother of Samuel Maclay) (D Pa.) July 20, 1737-April 16, 1804; Senate 1789-91.

MACLAY, William (— Pa.) March 22, 1765-Jan. 4, 1825; House 1815-19.

MACLAY, William Brown (D N.Y.) March 20, 1812-Feb. 19, 1882; House 1843-49, 1857-61.

MACLAY, William Plunkett (son of Samuel Maclay) (D Pa.) Aug. 23, 1774-Sept. 2, 1842; House Oct. 8, 1816-21.

MACON, Nathaniel (uncle of Willis Alston and Micajah Thomas Hawkins and great-grandfather of Charles Henry Martin) (D N.C.) Dec. 17, 1757-June 29, 1837; House 1791-Dec. 13, 1815; Senate Dec. 13, 1815-Nov. 14, 1828; Speaker 1801-07; President pro tempore 1825-27.

MACON, Robert Bruce (D Ark.) July 6, 1859-Oct. 9, 1925; House 1903-13.

MACY, John B. (D Wis.) March 25, 1799-Sept. 24, 1856; House 1853-55.

MACY, William Kingsland (R N.Y.) Nov. 21, 1889-July 15, 1961; House 1947-51.

MADDEN, Martin Barnaby (R Ill.) March 20, 1855-April 27, 1928; House 1905-April 27, 1928.

MADDEN, Ray John (D Ind.) Feb. 25, 1892; House 1943- .

MADDOX, John W. (D Ga.) June 3, 1848-Sept. 27, 1922; House 1893-1905.

MADISON, Edmond Haggard (R Kan.) Dec. 18, 1865-Sept. 18, 1911; House 1907-Sept. 18, 1911.

MADISON, James (D Va.) March 16, 1751-June 28, 1836; House 1789-97; Cont. Cong. 1780-83, 1786-88; Secretary of State 1801-09; President 1809-17.

MAFFETT, James Thompson (R Pa.) Feb. 2, 1837-Dec. 19, 1912; House 1887-89.

MAGEE, Clare (D Mo.) March 31, 1899-Aug. 7, 1969; House 1949-53.

MAGEE, James McDevitt (R Pa.) April 5, 1877-April 16, 1949; House 1923-27.

MAGEE, John (D N.Y.) Sept. 3, 1794-April 5, 1868; House 1827-31.

MAGEE, John Alexander (D Pa.) Oct. 14, 1827-Nov. 18, 1903; House 1873-75.

MAGEE, Walter Warren (R N.Y.) May 23, 1861-May 25, 1927; House 1915-May 25, 1927.

MAGINNIS, Martin (D Mont.) Oct. 27, 1841-March 27, 1919; House (Terr.Del.) 1873-85.

MAGNER, Thomas Francis (uncle of John Francis Carew) (D N.Y.) March 8, 1860-Dec. 22, 1945; House 1889-95.

MAGNUSON, Donald Hammer (D Wash.) March 7, 1911; House 1953-63.

MAGNUSON, Warren Grant (D Wash.) April 12, 1905; House 1937-Dec. 13, 1944; Senate Dec. 14, 1944- .

MAGOON, Henry Sterling (R Wis.) Jan. 31, 1832-March 3, 1889; House 1875-77.

MAGRADY, Frederick William (R Pa.) Nov. 24, 1863-Aug. 27, 1954; House 1925-33.

MAGRUDER, Allan Bowie (D La.) 1775-April 16, 1822; Senate Sept. 3, 1812-13.

MAGRUDER, Patrick (— Md.) 1768-Dec. 24, 1819; House 1805-07.

MAGUIRE, James George (D Calif.) Feb. 22, 1853-June 20, 1920; House 1893-99.

MAGUIRE, John Arthur (D Neb.) Nov. 29, 1870-July 1, 1939; House 1909-15.

MAHAN, Bryan Francis (D Conn.) May 1, 1856-Nov. 16, 1923; House 1913-15.

MAHANY, Rowland Blennerhassett (R N.Y.) Sept. 28, 1864-May 2, 1937; House 1895-99.

MAHER, James Paul (D N.Y.) Nov. 3, 1865-July 31, 1946; House 1911-21.

MAHON, Gabriel Heyward, Jr. (D S.C.) Nov. 11, 1889-June 11, 1962; House Nov. 3, 1936-39.

MAHON, George Herman (D Texas) Sept. 22, 1900; House 1935- .

MAHON, Thaddeus Maclay (R Pa.) May 21, 1840-May 31, 1916; House 1893-1907.

MAHONE, William (Read. Va.) Dec. 1, 1826-Oct. 8, 1895; Senate 1881-87.

MAHONEY, Peter Paul (D N.Y.) June 25, 1848-March 27, 1889; House 1885-89.

MAHONEY, William Frank (D Ill.) Feb. 22, 1856-Dec. 27, 1904; House 1901-Dec. 27, 1904.

MAILLIARD, William Somers (R Calif.) June 10, 1917; House 1953- .

MAIN, Verner Wright (R Mich.) Dec. 16, 1885-July 6, 1965; House Dec. 17, 1935-37.

MAISH, Levi (D Pa.) Nov. 22, 1837-Feb. 26, 1899; House 1875-79, 1887-91.

MAJOR, James Earl (D Ill.) Jan. 5, 1887; House 1923-25, 1927-29, 1931-Oct. 6, 1933.

MAJOR, Samuel Collier (D Mo.) July 2, 1869-July 28, 1931; House 1919-21, 1923-29, March 4-July 28, 1931.

MAJORS, Thomas Jefferson (R Neb.) June 25, 1841-July 11, 1932; House Nov. 5, 1878-79.

MALBONE, Francis (F R.I.) March 20, 1759-June 4, 1809; House 1793-97; Senate March 4-June 4, 1809.

MALBY, George Roland (R N.Y.) Sept. 16, 1857-July 5, 1912; House 1907-July 5, 1912.

MALLARY, Rollin Carolas (— Vt.) May 27, 1784-April 16, 1831; House Jan. 13, 1820-April 16, 1831.

MALLORY, Francis (W Va.) Dec. 12, 1807-March 26, 1860; House 1837-39, Dec. 28, 1840-43.

MALLORY, Meredith (D N.Y.) —-—; House 1839-41.

MALLORY, Robert (UD Ky.) Nov. 15, 1815-Aug. 11, 1885; House 1859-65.

MALLORY, Rufus (UR Ore.) Jan. 10, 1831-April 30, 1914; House 1867-69.

MALLORY, Stephen Russell (D Fla.) 1812-Nov. 9, 1873; Senate 1851-Jan. 21, 1861.

MALLORY, Stephen Russell (son of the preceding) (D Fla.) Nov. 2, 1848-Dec. 23, 1907; House 1891-95; Senate May 15, 1897-Dec. 23, 1907.

MALONE, George Wilson (R Nev.) Aug. 7, 1890-May 19, 1961; Senate 1947-59.

MALONEY, Francis Thomas (D Conn.- March 31, 1894-Jan. 16, 1945; House 1933-35; Senate 1935-Jan. 16, 1945.

MALONEY, Franklin John (R Pa.) March 29, 1899-Sept. 15, 1958; House 1947-49.

MALONEY, Paul Herbert (D La.) Feb. 14, 1876-March 26, 1967; House 1931-Dec. 15, 1940, 1943-47.

MALONEY, Robert Sarsfield (R Mass.) Feb. 3, 1881-Nov. 8, 1934; House 1921-23.

MANAHAN, James (R Minn.) March 12, 1866-Jan. 8, 1932; House 1913-15.

MANASCO, Carter (D Ala.) Jan. 3, 1902; House June 24, 1941-49.

MANDERSON, Charles Frederick (R Neb.) Feb. 9, 1837-Sept. 28, 1911; Senate 1883-95; President pro tempore 1891-93.

MANGUM, Willie Person (W N.C.) May 10, 1792-Sept. 7, 1861; House 1823-March 18, 1826; Senate 1831-Nov. 26, 1836, Nov. 25, 1840-53; President pro tempore 1842-45.

MANKIN, Helen Douglas (D Ga.) Sept. 11, 1896-July 25, 1956; House Feb. 12, 1946-47.

MANLOVE, Joe Jonathan (R Mo.) Oct. 1, 1876-Jan. 31, 1956; House 1923-33.

MANN, Abijah, Jr. (D N.Y.) Sept. 24, 1793-Sept. 6, 1868; House 1833-37.

MANN, Edward Coke (D S.C.) Nov. 21, 1880-Nov. 11, 1931; House Oct. 7, 1919-21.

MANN, Horace (F-S Mass.) May 4, 1796-Aug. 2, 1859; House April 3, 1848-51 (W), 1851-53 (F-S).

MANN, James (D La.) June 22, 1822-Aug. 26, 1868; House July 18-Aug. 26, 1868.

MANN, James Robert (R Ill.) Oct. 20, 1856-Nov. 30, 1922; House 1897-Nov. 30, 1922.

MANN, James Robert (D S.C.) April 27, 1920; House 1969- .

MANN, Job (D Pa.) March 31, 1795-Oct. 8, 1873; House 1835-37, 1847-51.

MANN, Joel Keith (D Pa.) Aug. 1, 1780-Aug. 28, 1857; House 1831-35.

MANNING, John, Jr. (D N.C.) July 30, 1830-Feb. 12, 1899; House Dec. 7, 1870-71.

MANNING, Richard Irvine (D S.C.) May 1, 1789-May 1, 1836; House Dec. 8, 1834-May 1, 1836; Gov. 1824-26.

MANNING, Vannoy Hartrog (D Miss.) July 26, 1839-Nov. 3, 1892; House 1877-83.

MANSFIELD, Joseph Jefferson (D Texas) Feb. 9, 1861-July 12, 1947; House 1917-July 12, 1947.

MANSFIELD, Michael Joseph (Mike) (D Mont.) March 16, 1903; House 1943-53; Senate 1953- .

MANSON, Mahlon Dickerson (D Ind.) Feb. 20, 1820-Feb. 4, 1895; House 1871-73.

MANSUR, Charles Harley (D Mo.) March 6, 1835-April 16, 1895; House 1887-93.

MANTLE, Lee (R Mont.) Dec. 13, 1851-Nov. 18, 1934; Senate Jan. 16, 1895-99.

MANZANARES, Francisco Antonio (D N.M.) Jan. 25, 1843-Sept. 17, 1904; House (Terr. Del.) March 5, 1884-85.

MAPES, Carl Edgar (R Mich.) Dec. 26, 1874-Dec. 12, 1939; House 1913-Dec. 12, 1939.

MARABLE, John Hartwell (NR Tenn.) Nov. 18, 1786-April 11, 1844; House 1825-29.

MARCANTONIO, Vito (AL N.Y.) Dec. 10, 1902-Aug. 9, 1954; House 1935-37 (R), 1939-51 (AL).

MARCHAND, Albert Gallatin (son of David Marchand) (D Pa.) Feb. 27, 1811-Feb. 5, 1848; House 1839-43.

MARCHAND, David (father of Albert Gallatin Marchand) (— Pa.) Dec. 10, 1776-March 11, 1832; House 1817-21.

MARCY, Daniel (D N.H.) Nov. 7, 1809-Nov. 3, 1893; House 1863-65.

MARCY, William Learned (JD N.Y.) Dec. 12, 1786-July 4, 1857; Senate 1831-Jan. 1, 1833; Gov. 1833-39; Secy. of War 1845-49; Secy. of State 1853-57.

MARDIS, Samuel Wright (D Ala.) June 12, 1800-Nov. 14, 1836; House 1831-35.

MARION, Robert (— S.C.) —-—; House 1805-Dec. 4, 1810.

MARKELL, Henry (son of Jacob Markell) (D N.Y.) Feb. 7, 1792-Aug. 30, 1831; House 1825-29.

MARKELL, Jacob (father of Henry Markell) (F N.Y.) May 8, 1770-Nov. 26, 1852; House 1813-15.

MARKHAM, Henry Harrison (R Calif.) Nov. 16, 1840-Oct. 9, 1923; House 1885-87; Gov. 1891-95.

MARKLEY, Philip Swenk (D Pa.) July 2, 1789-Sept. 12, 1834; House 1823-27.

MARKS, William (D Pa.) Oct. 13, 1778-April 10, 1858; Senate 1825-31.

MARLAND, Ernest Whitworth (D Okla.) May 8, 1874-Oct. 4, 1941; House 1933-35; Gov. 1935-39.

MARQUETTE, Turner Mastin (R Neb.) July 19, 1831-Dec. 22, 1894; House March 2-3, 1867.

MARR, Alem (D Pa.) June 18, 1787-March 29, 1843; House 1829-31.

MARR, George Washington Lent (— Tenn.) May 25, 1779-Sept. 5, 1856; House 1817-19.

MARSALIS, John Henry (D Colo.) May 9, 1904; House 1949-51.

MARSH, Benjamin Franklin (R Ill.) 1839-June 2, 1905; House 1877-83, 1893-1901, 1903-June 2, 1905.

MARSH, Charles (father of George Perkins Marsh) (F Vt.) July 10, 1765-Jan. 11, 1849; House 1815-17.

MARSH, George Perkins (son of Charles Marsh) (W Vt.) March 15, 1801-July 24, 1882; House 1843-May 1849.

MARSH, John O., Jr. (D Va.) Aug. 7, 1926; House 1963-71.

MARSHALL, Alexander Keith (AP Ky.) Feb. 11, 1808-April 28, 1884; House 1855-57.

MARSHALL, Alfred (D Maine) 1797-Oct. 2, 1868; House 1841-43.

MARSHALL, Edward Chauncey (D Calif.) June 29, 1821-July 9, 1893; House 1851-53.

MARSHALL, Fred (D Minn.) March 13, 1906; House 1949-63.

MARSHALL, George Alexander (D Ohio) Sept. 14, 1851-April 21, 1899; House 1897-99.

MARSHALL, Humphrey (father of Thomas Alexander Marshall and cousin of John Marshall) (F Ky.) 1760-July 1, 1841; Senate 1795-1801.

MARSHALL, Humphrey (grandson of the preceding) (AP Ky.) Jan. 13, 1812-March 28, 1872; House 1849-Aug. 4, 1852 (W), 1855-59 (AP).

MARSHALL, James William (D Va.) March 31, 1844-Nov. 27, 1911; House 1893-95.

MARSHALL, John (uncle of Thomas Francis Marshall and cousin of Humphrey Marshall) (— Va.) Sept. 24, 1755-July 6, 1835; House 1799-June 7, 1800; Secy. of State June 6, 1800-March 4, 1801; Chief Justice of the Supreme Court Feb. 4, 1801-July 6, 1835.

MARSHALL, Leroy Tate (R Ohio) Nov. 8, 1883-Nov. 22, 1950; House 1933-37.

MARSHALL, Lycurgus Luther (R Ohio) July 9, 1888-Jan. 12, 1958; House 1939-41.

MARSHALL, Samuel Scott (D Ill.) March 12, 1821-July 26, 1890; House 1855-59, 1865-75.

MARSHALL, Thomas Alexander (son of Humphrey Marshall) (W Ky.) Jan. 15, 1794-April 17, 1871; House 1831-35.

MARSHALL, Thomas Francis (nephew of John Marshall) (— Ky.) June 7, 1801-Sept. 22, 1864; House 1841-43.

MARSHALL, Thomas Frank (R N.D.) March 7, 1854-Aug. 20, 1921; House 1901-09.

MARSTON, Gilman (R N.H.) Aug. 20, 1811-July 3, 1890; House 1859-63, 1865-67; Senate March 4-June 18, 1889.

MARTIN, Alexander (— N.C.) 1740-Nov. 10, 1807; Senate 1793-99; Gov. 1782-84, 1789-92.

MARTIN, Augustus Newton (D Ind.) March 23, 1847-July 11, 1901; House 1889-95.

MARTIN, Barclay (uncle of Lewis Tillman) (D Tenn.) Dec. 17, 1802-Nov. 8, 1890; 1845-47.

MARTIN, Benjamin Franklin (D W.Va.) Oct. 2, 1828-Jan. 20, 1895; House 1877-81.

MARTIN, Charles (D Ill.) May 20, 1856-Oct. 28, 1917; House March 4-Oct. 28, 1917.

MARTIN, Charles Drake (D Ohio) Aug. 5, 1829-Aug. 27, 1911; House 1859-61.

MARTIN, Charles Henry (great-grandson of Nathaniel Macon) (P N.C.) Aug. 28, 1848-April 19, 1931; House June 5, 1896-99.

MARTIN, Charles Henry (D Ore.) Oct. 1, 1863-Sept. 22, 1946; House 1931-35; Gov. 1935-39.

MARTIN, David Thomas (R Neb.) July 9, 1907; House 1961- .

MARTIN, Eben Wever (R S.D.) April 12, 1855-May 22, 1932; House 1901-07, Nov. 3, 1908-15.

MARTIN, Edward (R Pa.) Sept. 18, 1879-March 19, 1967; Senate 1947-59; Gov. 1943-46.

MARTIN, Edward Livingston (D Del.) March 29, 1837-Jan. 22, 1897; House 1879-83.

MARTIN, Elbert Sevier (brother of John Preston Martin) (AP Va.) about 1829-Sept. 3, 1876; House 1859-61.

MARTIN, Frederick Stanley (W N.Y.) April 25, 1794-June 28, 1865; House 1851-53.

MARTIN, George Brown (grandson of John Preston Martin) (D Ky.) Aug. 18, 1876-Nov. 12, 1945; Senate Sept. 7, 1918-19.

MARTIN, James D. (R Ala.) Sept. 1, 1918; House 1965-67.

MARTIN, James Stewart (R Ill.) Aug. 19, 1826-Nov. 20, 1907; House 1873-75.

MARTIN, John (D Kan.) Nov. 12, 1833-Sept. 3, 1913; Senate 1893-95.

MARTIN, John Andrew (D Colo.) April 10, 1868-Dec. 23, 1939; House 1909-13, 1933-Dec. 23, 1939.

MARTIN, John Cunningham (D Ill.) April 29, 1880-Jan. 27, 1952; House 1939-41.

MARTIN, John Mason (son of Joshua Lanier Martin) (D Ala.) Jan. 20, 1837-June 16, 1898; House 1885-87.

MARTIN, John Preston (brother of Elbert Sevier Martin and grandfather of George Brown Martin) (D Ky.) Oct. 11, 1811-Dec. 23, 1862; House 1845-47.

MARTIN, Joseph John (R N.C.) Nov. 21, 1833-Dec. 18, 1900; House 1879-Jan. 19, 1881.

MARTIN, Joseph William, Jr. (R Mass.) Nov. 3, 1884-March 6, 1968; House 1925-67; Speaker 1947-49, 1953-55; Chrmn. Rep. Nat. Comm. 1940-42.

MARTIN, Joshua Lanier (father of John Mason Martin) (D Ala.) Dec. 5, 1799-Nov. 2, 1856; House 1835-39; Gov. 1845-47.

MARTIN, Lewis J. (D N.J.) Feb. 22, 1844-May 5, 1913; House March 4-May 5, 1913.

MARTIN, Morgan Lewis (cousin of James Duane Doty) (D Wis.) March 31, 1805-Dec. 10, 1887; House (Terr.Del.) 1845-47.

MARTIN, Patrick Minor (R Calif.) Nov. 25, 1924-July 18, 1968; House 1963-65.

MARTIN, Robert Nicols (D Md.) Jan. 14, 1798-July 20, 1870; House 1825-27.

MARTIN, Thomas Ellsworth (R Iowa) Jan. 18, 1893-June 27, 1971; House 1939-55; Senate 1955-61.

MARTIN, Thomas Staples (D Va.) July 29, 1849-Nov. 12, 1919; Senate 1895-Nov. 12, 1919.

MARTIN, Whitmell Pugh (D La.) Aug. 12, 1867-April 6, 1929; House 1915-19 (Pro.), 1919-April 6, 1929 (D).

MARTIN, William Dickinson (D S.C.) Oct. 20, 1789-Nov. 17, 1833; House 1827-31.

MARTIN, William Harrison (D Texas) May 23, 1823-Feb. 3, 1898; House Nov. 4, 1887-91.

MARTINDALE, Henry Clinton (W N.Y.) May 6, 1780-April 22, 1860; House 1823-31, 1833-35.

MARTINE, James Edgar (D N.J.) Aug. 25, 1850-Feb. 26, 1925; Senate 1911-17.

MARVIN, Dudley (Ad.D N.Y.) May 9, 1786-June 25, 1856; House 1823-29, 1847-49.

MARVIN, Francis (R N.Y.) March 8, 1828-Aug. 14, 1905; House 1893-95.

MARVIN, James Madison (U N.Y.) Feb. 27, 1809-April 25, 1901; House 1863-69.

MARVIN, Richard Pratt (W N.Y.) Dec. 23, 1803-Jan. 11, 1892; House 1837-41.

MASON, Armistead Thomson (son of Stevens Thomson Mason) (D Va.) Aug. 4, 1787-Feb. 6, 1819; Senate Jan. 3, 1816-17.

MASON, Harry Howland (D Ill.) Dec. 16, 1873-March 10, 1946; House 1935-37.

MASON, James Brown (F R.I.) January 1775-Aug. 31, 1819; House 1815-19.

MASON, James Murray (JD Va.) Nov. 3, 1798-April 28, 1871; House 1837-39; Senate Jan. 21, 1847-March 28, 1861.

MASON, Jeremiah (F N.H.) April 27, 1768-Oct. 14, 1848; Senate June 10, 1813-June 16, 1817.

MASON, John Calvin (JD Ky.) Aug. 4, 1802-Aug. 1865; House 1849-53, 1857-59.

MASON, John Thomson (D Md.) May 9, 1815-March 28, 1873; House 1841-43.

MASON, John Young (D Va.) April 18, 1799-Oct. 3, 1859; House 1831-Jan. 11, 1837; Secy. of the Navy 1844-45 and 1846-49; Atty. Gen. 1845-46.

MASON, Jonathan (F Mass.) Aug. 30, 1752-Nov. 1, 1831; Senate Nov. 14, 1800-03; House 1817-May 15, 1820.

MASON, Joseph (R N.Y.) March 30, 1828-May 31, 1914; House 1879-83.

MASON, Moses, Jr. (D Maine) June 2, 1789-June 25, 1866; House 1833-37.

MASON, Noah Morgan (R Ill.) July 19, 1882-March 29, 1965; House 1937-63.

MASON, Samson (W Ohio) July 24, 1793-Feb. 1, 1869; House 1835-43.

MASON, Stevens Thomson (father of Armistead Thomson Mason) (D Va.) Dec. 29, 1760-May 10, 1803; Senate Nov. 18, 1794-May 10, 1803.

MASON, William (D N.Y.) Sept. 10, 1786-Jan. 13, 1860; House 1835-37.

MASON, William Ernest (father of Winnifred Sprague Mason Huck) (R Ill.) July 7, 1850-June 16, 1921; House 1887-91, 1917-June 16, 1921; Senate 1897-1903.

MASSEY, William Alexander (R Nev.) Oct. 7, 1856-March 5, 1914; Senate July 1, 1912-Jan. 29, 1913.

MASSEY, Zachary David (R Tenn.) Nov. 14, 1864-July 13, 1923; House Nov. 8, 1910-11.

MASSINGALE, Samuel Chapman (D Okla.) Aug. 2, 1870-Jan. 17, 1941; House 1935-Jan. 17, 1941.

MASTERS, Josiah (D N.Y.) Nov. 22, 1763-June 30, 1822; House 1805-09.

MATHEWS, Frank Asbury, Jr. (R N.J.) Aug. 3, 1890-Feb. 5, 1964; House Nov. 6, 1945-49.

MATHEWS, George (— Ga.) Aug. 30, 1739-Aug. 30, 1812; House 1789-91; Gov. 1787, 1793-96.

MATHEWS, George Arthur (R Dakota) June 4, 1852-April 19, 1941; House March 4-Nov. 2, 1889.

MATHEWS, James (D Ohio) June 4, 1805-March 30, 1887; House 1841-45.

MATHEWS, Vincent (F N.Y.) June 29, 1766-Aug. 23, 1846; House 1809-11.

MATHEWSON, Elisha (D R.I.) April 18, 1767-Oct. 14, 1853; Senate Oct. 26, 1807-11.

MATHIAS, Charles McC., Jr. (R Md.) July 24, 1922; House 1961-69; Senate 1969- .

MATHIAS, Robert B. (R Calif.) Nov. 17, 1930; House 1967- .

MATHIOT, Joshua (W Ohio) April 4, 1800-July 30, 1849; House 1841-43.

MATHIS, Dawson (D Ga.) Nov. 30, 1940; House 1971- .

MATLACK, James (— N.J.) Jan. 11, 1775-Jan. 16, 1840; House 1821-25.

MATSON, Aaron (— N.H.) 1770-July 18, 1855; House 1821-25.

MATSON, Courtland Cushing (D Ind.) April 25, 1841-Sept. 4, 1915; House 1881-89.

MATSUNAGA, Spark Masayuki (D Hawaii) Oct. 8, 1916; House 1963- .

MATTESON, Orsamus Benajah (W N.Y.) Aug. 28, 1805-Dec. 22, 1889; House 1849-51, 1853-Feb. 27, 1857, March 4, 1857-59.

MATTHEWS, Charles (R Pa.) Oct. 15, 1856-Dec. 12, 1932; House 1911-13.

MATTHEWS, Donald Ray (Billy) (D Fla.) Oct. 3, 1907; House 1953-67.

MATTHEWS, Nelson Edwin (R Ohio) April 14, 1852-Oct. 13, 1917; House 1915-17.

MATTHEWS, Stanley (uncle of Henry Watterson) (R Ohio) July 21, 1824-March 22, 1889; Senate March 21, 1877-79; Assoc. Justice of Supreme Court 1881-89.

MATTHEWS, William (— Md.) April 26, 1755-—; House 1797-99.

MATTOCKS, John (W Vt.) March 4, 1777-Aug. 14, 1847; House 1821-23, 1825-27, 1841-43; Gov. 1843-44.

MATTOON, Ebenezer (F Mass.) Aug. 19, 1755-Sept. 11, 1843; House Feb. 2, 1801-03.

MAURICE, James (D N.Y.) Nov. 7, 1814-Aug. 4, 1884; House 1853-55.

MAURY, Abram Poindexter (cousin of Fontaine Maury Maverick) (W Tenn.) Dec. 26, 1801-July 22, 1848; House 1835-39.

MAVERICK, Fontaine Maury (cousin of Abram P. Maury, nephew of James L. Slayden, and cousin of John W. Fishburne) (D Texas) Oct. 23, 1895-June 7, 1954; House 1935-39.

MAXEY, Samuel Bell (D Texas) March 30, 1825-Aug. 16, 1895; Senate 1875-87.

MAXWELL, Augustus Emmett (grandfather of Emmett Wilson) (D Fla.) Sept. 21, 1820-May 5, 1903; House 1853-57.

MAXWELL, George Clifford (father of John Patterson Bryan Maxwell) (— N.J.) May 31, 1771-March 16, 1816; House 1811-13.

MAXWELL, John Patterson Bryan (son of George Clifford Maxwell and uncle of George Maxwell Robeson) (W N.J.) Sept. 3, 1804-Nov. 14, 1845; House 1837-39, 1841-43.

MAXWELL, Lewis (N R Va.) April 17, 1790-Feb. 13, 1862; House 1827-33.

MAXWELL, Samuel (Fus. Neb.) May 20, 1825-Feb. 11, 1901; House 1897-99.

MAXWELL, Thomas (D N.Y.) Feb. 16, 1792-Nov. 4, 1864; House 1829-31.

MAY, Andrew Jackson (D Ky.) June 24, 1875-Sept. 6, 1959; House 1931-47.

MAY, Catherine Dean (Barnes) (R Wash.) May 18, 1914; House 1959-71.

MAY, Edwin Hyland, Jr. (R Conn.) May 28, 1924; House 1957-59.

MAY, Henry (D Md.) Feb. 13, 1816-Sept. 25, 1866; House 1853-55, 1861-63.

MAY, Mitchell (D N.Y.) July 10, 1870-March 24, 1961; House 1899-1901.

MAY, William L. (D Ill.) about 1793-Sept. 29, 1849; House Dec. 1, 1834-39.

MAYALL, Samuel (D Maine) June 21, 1816-Sept. 17, 1892; House 1853-55.

MAYBANK, Burnet Rhett (D S.C.) March 7, 1899-Sept. 1, 1954; Senate Nov. 5, 1941-Sept. 1, 1954; Gov. 1939-41.

MAYBURY, William Cotter (D Mich.) Nov. 20, 1848-May 6, 1909; House 1883-87.

MAYFIELD, Earle Bradford (D Texas) April 12, 1881-June 23, 1964; Senate 1923-29.

MAYHAM, Stephen Lorenzo (D N.Y.) Oct. 8, 1826-March 3, 1908; House 1869-71, 1877-79.

MAYNARD, Harry Lee (D Va.) June 8, 1861-Oct. 23, 1922; House 1901-11.

MAYNARD, Horace (R Tenn.) Aug. 30, 1814-May 3, 1882; House 1857-63 (AP), July 24, 1866-75 (R); Postmaster General 1880-81.

MAYNARD, John (W N.Y.) 1810-March 24, 1850; House 1827-29, 1841-43.

MAYNE, Wiley (R Iowa) Jan. 19, 1917; House 1967- .

MAYO, Robert Murphy (Read. Va.) April 28, 1836-March 29, 1896; House 1883-March 20, 1884.

MAYRANT, William (— S.C.) —-—; House 1815-Oct. 21, 1816.

MAYS, Dannite Hill (D Fla.) April 28, 1852-May 9, 1930; House 1909-13.

MAYS, James Henry (D Utah) June 29, 1868-April 19, 1926; House 1915-21.

MAZZOLI, Romano L. (D Ky.) Nov. 2, 1932; House 1971- .

McADOO, William (D N.J.) Oct. 25, 1853-June 7, 1930; House 1883-91.

McADOO, William Gibbs (D Calif.) Oct. 31, 1863-Feb. 1, 1941; Senate 1933-Nov. 8, 1938; Secy. of the Treasury 1913-18.

McALEER, William (D Pa.) Jan. 6, 1838-April 19, 1912; House 1891-95, 1897-1901.

McALLISTER, Archibald (grandson of John Andre Hanna) (D Pa.) Oct. 12, 1813-July 18, 1883; House 1863-65.

McANDREWS, James (D Ill.) Oct. 22, 1862-Aug. 31, 1942; House 1901-05, 1913-21, 1935-41.

McARDLE, Joseph A. (D Pa.) June 29, 1903-Dec. 27, 1967; House 1939-Jan. 5, 1942.

McARTHUR, Clifton Nesmith (grandson of James Willis Nesmith) (R Ore.) June 10, 1879-Dec. 9, 1923; House 1915-23.

McARTHUR, Duncan (D Ohio) June 14, 1772-April 29, 1839; House March 4-April 5, 1813, 1823-25; Gov. 1830-32.

McBRIDE, George Wycliffe (brother of John Rogers McBride) (R Ore.) March 13, 1854-June 18, 1911; Senate 1895-1901.

McBRIDE, John Rogers (brother of George Wycliffe McBride) (R Ore.) Aug. 22, 1832-July 20, 1904; House 1863-65.

McBRYDE, Archibald (D N.C.) Sept. 28, 1766-Feb. 15, 1816; House 1809-13.

McCALL, John Ethridge (R Tenn.) Aug. 14, 1859-Aug. 8, 1920; House 1895-97.

McCALL, Samuel Walker (R Mass.) Feb. 28, 1851-Nov. 4, 1923; House 1893-1913; Gov. 1916-18.

McCANDLESS, Lincoln Loy (D Hawaii) Sept. 18, 1859-Oct. 5, 1940; House (Terr.Del.) 1933-35.

McCARRAN, Patrick Anthony (Pat) (D Nev.) Aug. 8, 1876-Sept. 28, 1954; Senate 1933-Sept. 28, 1954.

McCARTHY, Dennis (R N.Y.) March 19, 1814-Feb. 14, 1886; House 1867-71.

McCARTHY, Eugene Joseph (D Minn.) March 29, 1916; House 1949-59; Senate 1959-71.

McCARTHY, John Henry (D N.Y.) Nov. 16, 1850-Feb. 5, 1908; House 1889-Jan. 14, 1891.

McCARTHY, John Jay (R Neb.) July 19, 1857-March 30, 1943; House 1903-07.

McCARTHY, Joseph Raymond (R Wis.) Nov. 14, 1908-May 2, 1957; Senate 1947-May 2, 1957.

McCARTHY, Kathryn O'Loughlin (see O'LOUGHLIN, Kathryn Ellen.)

McCARTHY, Richard Dean (D N.Y.) Sept. 24, 1927; House 1965-71.

McCARTY, Andrew Zimmerman (W N.Y.) July 14, 1808-April 23, 1879; House 1855-57.

McCARTY, Johnathan (W Ind.) Aug. 3, 1795-March 30, 1852; House 1831-37.

McCARTY, Richard (D N.Y.) Feb. 19, 1780-May 18, 1844; House 1821-23.

McCARTY, William Mason (W Va.) about 1789-Dec. 20, 1863; House Jan. 25, 1840-41; Terr. Gov. of Fla. 1827.

McCAUSLEN, William Cochran (D Ohio) 1796-March 13, 1863; House 1843-45.

McCLAMMY, Charles Washington (D N.C.) May 29, 1839-Feb. 26, 1896; House 1887-91.

McCLEAN, Moses (D Pa.) June 17, 1804-Sept. 30, 1870; House 1845-47.

McCLEARY, James Thompson (R Minn.) Feb. 5, 1853-Dec. 17, 1924; House 1893-1907.

McCLEERY, James (R La.) Dec. 2, 1837-Nov. 5, 1871; House March 4-Nov. 5, 1871.

McCLELLAN, Abraham (D Tenn.) Oct. 4, 1789-May 3, 1866; House 1837-43.

McCLELLAN, Charles A. O. (D Ind.) May 25, 1835-Jan. 31, 1898; House 1889-93.

McCLELLAN, George (D N.Y.) Oct. 10, 1856-Feb. 20, 1927; House 1913-15.

McCLELLAN, George Brinton (D N.Y.) Nov. 23, 1865-Nov. 30, 1940; House 1895-Dec. 21, 1903.

McCLELLAN, John Little (D Ark.) Feb. 25, 1896; House 1935-39; Senate 1943- .

McCLELLAN, Robert (D N.Y.) Oct. 2, 1806-June 28, 1860; House 1837-39, 1841-43.

McCLELLAND, Robert (D Mich.) Aug. 1, 1807-Aug. 30, 1880; House 1843-49; Gov. 1851-53; Secy. of the Interior 1853-57.

McCLELLAND, William (D Pa.) March 2, 1842-Feb. 7, 1892; House 1871-73.

McCLENACHAN, Blair (— Pa.) —-May 8, 1812; House 1797-99.

McCLERNAND, John Alexander (D Ill.) May 30, 1812-Sept. 20, 1900; House 1843-51, Nov. 8, 1859-Oct. 28, 1861.

McCLINTIC, James Vernon (D Okla.) Sept. 8, 1878-April 22, 1948; House 1915-35.

McCLINTOCK, Charles Blaine (R Ohio) May 25, 1886-Feb. 1, 1965; House 1929-33.

McCLORY, Robert (R Ill.) Jan. 31, 1908; House 1963- .

McCLOSKEY, Augustus (D Texas) Sept. 23, 1878-July 21, 1950; House 1929-Feb. 10, 1930.

McCLOSKEY, Paul N. (Pete), Jr. (R Calif.) Sept. 29, 1927; House Dec. 12, 1967- .

McCLURE, Addison S. (R Ohio) Oct. 10, 1839-April 17, 1903; House 1881-83, 1895-97.

McCLURE, Charles (D Pa.) 1804-Jan. 10, 1846; House 1837-39, Dec. 7, 1840-41.

McCLURE, James A. (R Idaho) Dec. 27, 1924; House 1967- .

McCLURG, Joseph Washington (Rad. Mo.) Feb. 22, 1818-Dec. 2, 1900; House 1863-65 (E), 1865-68 (Rad); Gov. 1869-71 (R).

McCOID, Moses Ayers (R Iowa) Nov. 5, 1840-May 19, 1904; House 1879-85.

McCOLLISTER, John Y. (R Neb.) June 10, 1921; House 1971- .

McCOMAS, Louis Emory (grandfather of Katharine E. Byron and great-grandfather of Goodloe E. Byron) (R Md.) Oct. 28, 1846-Nov. 10, 1907; House 1883-91; Senate 1899-1905.

McCOMAS, William (W Va.) 1795-June 3, 1865; House 1833-37.

McCONNELL, Felix Grundy (D Ala.) April 1, 1809-Sept. 10, 1846; House 1843-Sept. 10, 1846.

McCONNELL, Samuel Kerns, Jr. (R Pa.) April 6, 1901; House Jan. 18, 1944-Sept. 1, 1957.

McCONNELL, William John (R Idaho) Sept. 18, 1839-March 30, 1925; Senate Dec. 18, 1890-91; Gov. 1892-96.

McCOOK, Anson George (R N.Y.) Oct. 10, 1835-Dec. 30, 1917; House 1877-83.

McCORD, Andrew (— N.Y.) about 1754-1808; House 1803-05.

McCORD, James Nance (D Tenn.) March 17, 1879-Sept. 2, 1968; House 1943-45; Gov. 1945-49.

McCORD, Myron Hawley (R Wis.) Nov. 26, 1840-April 27, 1908; House 1889-91; Gov. (Ariz. Terr.) 1897-98.

McCORKLE, Joseph Walker (D Calif.) June 24, 1819-March 18, 1884; House 1851-53.

McCORKLE, Paul Grier (D S.C.) Dec. 19, 1863-June 2, 1934; House Feb. 24-March 3, 1917.

McCORMACK, John William (D Mass.) Dec. 21, 1891; House Nov. 6, 1928-71; Speaker 1962-71.

McCORMACK, Mike (D Wash.) Dec. 14, 1921; House 1971- .

McCORMICK, Henry Clay (R Pa.) June 30, 1844-May 26, 1902; House 1887-91.

McCORMICK, James Robinson (D Mo.) Aug. 1, 1824-May 19, 1897; House Dec. 17, 1867-73.

McCORMICK, John Watts (R Ohio) Dec. 20, 1831-June 25, 1917; House 1883-85.

McCORMICK, (Joseph) Medill (husband of Ruth Hanna McCormick) (R Ill.) May 16, 1877-Feb. 25, 1925; House 1917-19; Senate 1919-Feb. 25, 1925.

McCORMICK, Nelson B. (P Kan.) Nov. 20, 1847-April 10, 1914; House 1897-99.

McCORMICK, Richard Cunningham (U Ariz. & R N.Y.) May 23, 1832-June 2, 1901; House (Terr. Del. Ariz.) 1869-75, (Rep. N.Y.) 1895-97; Gov. (Ariz. Terr.) 1866.

McCORMICK, Ruth Hanna (daughter of Marcus Alonzo Hanna, wife of Joseph Medill McCormick and of Albert Gallatin Simms) (R Ill.) March 27, 1880-Dec. 31, 1944; House 1929-31.

McCORMICK, Washington Jay (R Mont.) Jan. 4, 1884-March 7, 1949; House 1921-23.

McCOWEN, Edward Oscar (R Ohio) June 29, 1877-Nov. 4, 1953; House 1943-49.

McCOY, Robert (— Pa.) —June 7, 1849; House Nov. 22, 1831-33.

McCOY, Walter Irving (D N.J.) Dec. 8, 1859-July 17, 1933; House 1911-Oct. 3, 1914.

McCOY, William (D Va.) —-1864; House 1811-33.

McCRACKEN, Robert McDowell (R Idaho) March 5, 1874-May 16, 1934; House 1915-17.

McCRARY, George Washington (R Iowa) Aug. 29, 1835-June 23, 1890; House 1869-77; Secy. of War 1877-79.

McCRATE, John Dennis (D Maine) Oct. 1, 1802-Sept. 11, 1879; House 1845-47.

McCREARY, George Deardorff (R Pa.) Sept. 28, 1846-July 26, 1915; House 1903-13.

McCREARY, James Bennett (D Ky.) July 8, 1838-Oct. 8, 1913; House 1885-97; Senate 1903-09; Gov. 1875-79, 1912-16.

McCREARY, John (— S.C.) 1761-Nov. 4, 1833; House 1819-21.

McCREDIE, William Wallace (R Wash.) April 27, 1862-May 10, 1935; House Nov. 2, 1909-11.

McCREERY, Thomas Clay (D Ky.) Dec. 12, 1816-July 10, 1890; Senate Feb. 19, 1868-71, 1873-79.

McCREERY, William (— Md.) 1750-March 8, 1814; House 1803-09.

McCREERY, William (D Pa.) May 17, 1786-Sept. 27, 1841; House 1829-31.

McCULLOCH, George (D Pa.) Feb. 22, 1792-April 6, 1861; House Nov. 20, 1839-41.

McCULLOCH, John (W Pa.) Nov. 15, 1806-May 15, 1879; House 1853-55.

McCULLOCH, Philip Doddridge, Jr. (D Ark.) June 23, 1851-Nov. 26, 1928; House 1893-1903.

McCULLOCH, Roscoe Conkling (R Ohio) Nov. 27, 1880-March 17, 1958; House 1915-21; Senate Nov. 5, 1929-Nov. 30, 1930.

McCULLOCH, William Moore (R Ohio) Nov. 24, 1901; House Nov. 4, 1947- .

McCULLOGH, Welty (R Pa.) Oct. 10, 1847-Aug. 31, 1889; House 1887-89.

McCULLOUGH, Hiram (D Md.) Sept. 26, 1813-March 4, 1885; House 1865-69.

McCULLOUGH, Thomas Grubb (— Pa.) April 20, 1785-Sept. 10, 1848; House Oct. 17, 1820-21.

McCUMBER, Porter James (R N.D.) Feb. 3, 1858-May 18, 1933; Senate 1899-1923.

McDADE, Joseph Michael (R Pa.) Sept. 29, 1931; House 1963- .

McDANIEL, William (D Mo.) —-about 1854; House Dec. 7, 1846-47.

McDANNOLD, John James (D Ill.) Aug. 29, 1851-Feb. 3, 1904; House 1893-95.

McDEARMON, James Calvin (D Tenn.) June 13, 1844-July 19, 1902; House 1893-97.

McDERMOTT, Allan Langdon (D N.J.) March 30, 1854-Oct. 26, 1908; House Dec. 3, 1900-07.

McDERMOTT, James Thomas (D Ill.) Feb. 13, 1872-Feb. 7, 1938; House 1907-July 21, 1914, 1915-17.

McDILL, Alexander Stuart (R Wis.) March 18, 1822-Nov. 12, 1875; House 1873-75.

McDILL, James Wilson (R Iowa) March 4, 1834-Feb. 28, 1894; House 1873-77; Senate March 8, 1881-83.

McDONALD, Alexander (R Ark.) April 10, 1832-Dec. 13, 1903; Senate June 22, 1868-71.

McDONALD, Edward Francis (D N.J.) Sept. 21, 1844-Nov. 5, 1892; House 1891-Nov. 5, 1892.

McDONALD, Jack H. (R Mich.) June 28, 1932; House 1967- .

McDONALD, John (R Md.) May 24, 1837-Jan. 30, 1917; House 1897-99.

McDONALD, Joseph Ewing (D Ind.) Aug. 29, 1819-June 21, 1891; House 1849-51; Senate 1875-81.

McDONOUGH, Gordon Leo (R Calif.) Jan. 2, 1895-June 25, 1968; House 1945-63.

McDOUGALL, James Alexander (D Calif.) Nov. 19, 1817-Sept. 3, 1867; House 1853-55; Senate 1861-67.

McDOWELL, Alexander (R Pa.) March 4, 1845-Sept. 30, 1913; House 1893-95.

McDOWELL, Harris Brown, Jr. (D Del.) Feb. 10, 1906; House 1955-57, 1959-67.

McDOWELL, James (D Va.) Oct. 13, 1796-Aug. 24, 1851; House March 6, 1846-51; Gov. 1842-46.

McDOWELL, James Foster (D Ind.) Dec. 3, 1825-April 18, 1887; House 1863-65.

McDOWELL, John Anderson (D Ohio) Sept. 25, 1853-Oct. 2, 1927; House 1897-1901.

McDOWELL, John Ralph (R Pa.) Nov. 6, 1902-Dec. 11, 1957; House 1939-41, 1947-49.

McDOWELL, Joseph (father of Joseph Jefferson McDowell and cousin of Joseph McDowell (P G)) (— N.C.) Feb. 15, 1756-Feb. 5, 1801; House 1797-99.

McDOWELL, Joseph (P G) (cousin of Joseph McDowell) (— N.C.) Feb. 25, 1758-March 7, 1799; House 1793-95.

McDOWELL, Joseph Jefferson (son of Joseph McDowell) (D Ohio) Nov. 13, 1800-Jan. 17, 1877; House 1843-47.

McDUFFIE, George (D S.C.) Aug. 10, 1790-March 11, 1851; House 1821-34; Senate Dec. 23, 1842-Aug. 17, 1846; Gov. 1834-36.

McDUFFIE, John (D Ala.) Sept. 25, 1883-Nov. 1, 1950; House 1919-March 2, 1935.

McDUFFIE, John Van (R Ala.) May 16, 1841-Nov. 18, 1896; House June 4, 1890-91.

McENERY, Samuel Douglas (D La.) May 28, 1837-June 28, 1910; Senate 1897-June 28, 1910; Gov. 1881-88.

McETTRICK, Michael Joseph (D Mass.) June 22, 1848-Dec. 31, 1921; House 1893-95.

McEWAN, Robert Cameron (R N.Y.) Jan. 5, 1920; House 1965- .

McEWAN, Thomas, Jr. (R N.J.) Feb. 26, 1854-Sept. 11, 1926; House 1895-99.

McFADDEN, Louis Thomas (R Pa.) July 25, 1876-Oct. 1, 1936; House 1915-35.

McFADDEN, Obadiah Benton (D Wash.) Nov. 18, 1815-June 25, 1875; House (Terr. Del.) 1873-75.

McFALL, John Joseph (D Calif.) Feb. 20, 1918; House 1957- .

McFARLAN, Duncan (— N.C.) —Sept. 7, 1816; House 1805-07.

McFARLAND, Ernest William (D Ariz.) Oct. 9, 1894; Senate 1941-53; Gov. 1955-59.

McFARLAND, William (D Tenn.) Sept. 15, 1821-April 12, 1900; House 1875-77.

McFARLANE, William Doddridge (D Texas) July 17, 1894; House 1933-39.

McGANN, Lawrence Edward (D Ill.) Feb. 2, 1852-July 22, 1928; House 1891-Dec. 2, 1895.

McGARVEY, Robert Neill (R Pa.) Aug. 14, 1888-June 28, 1952; House 1947-49.

McGAUGHEY, Edward Wilson (W Ind.) Jan. 16, 1817-Aug. 6, 1852; House 1845-47, 1849-51.

McGAVIN, Charles (R Ill.) Jan. 10, 1874-Dec. 17, 1940; House 1905-09.

McGEE, Gale William (D Wyo.) March 17, 1915; Senate 1959- .

McGEHEE, Daniel Rayford (D Miss.) Sept. 10, 1883-Feb. 9, 1962; House 1935-47.

McGILL, George (D Kan.) Feb. 12, 1879-May 14, 1963; Senate Dec. 1, 1930-39.

McGILLICUDDY, Daniel John (D Maine) Aug. 27, 1859-July 30, 1936; House 1911-17.

McGINLEY, Donald Francis (D Neb.) June 30, 1920; House 1959-61.

McGLENNON, Cornelius Augustine (D N.J.) Dec. 10, 1878-June 13, 1931; House 1919-21.

McGLINCHEY, Herbert Joseph (D Pa.) Nov. 7, 1904; House 1945-47.

McGOVERN, George Stanley (D S.D.) July 19, 1922; House 1957-61; Senate 1963- .

McGOWAN, Jonas Hartzell (R Mich.) April 2, 1837-July 5, 1909; House 1877-81.

McGRANERY, James Patrick (D Pa.) July 8, 1895-Dec. 23, 1962; House 1937-Nov. 17, 1943; Atty. Gen. 1952-53.

McGRATH, Christopher Columbus (D N.Y.) May 15, 1902; House 1949-53.

McGRATH, James Howard (D R.I.) Nov. 28, 1903-Sept. 2, 1966; Senate 1947-Aug. 23, 1949; Chrmn. Dem. Nat. Comm. 1947-49; Gov. 1941-45; Atty. Gen. 1949-52.

McGRATH, John Joseph (D Calif.) July 23, 1872-Aug. 25, 1951; House 1933-39.

McGRATH, Thomas C., Jr. (D N.J.) April 22, 1927; House 1965-67.

McGREGOR, J. Harry (R Ohio) Sept. 30, 1896-Oct. 7, 1958; House Feb. 27, 1940-Oct. 7, 1958.

McGREW, James Clark (R W.Va.) Sept. 14, 1813-Sept. 18, 1910; House 1869-73.

McGROARTY, John Steven (D Calif.) Aug. 20, 1862-Aug. 7, 1944; House 1935-39.

McGUGIN, Harold Clement (R Kan.) Nov. 22, 1893-March 7, 1946; House 1931-35.

McGUIRE, Bird Segle (cousin of William Neville) (R Okla.) Oct. 13, 1865-Nov. 9, 1930; House (Terr. Del.) 1903-07, (Rep.) Nov. 16, 1907-15.

McGUIRE, John Andrew (D Conn.) Feb. 28, 1906; House 1949-53.

McHATTON, Robert Lytle (JD Ky.) Nov. 17, 1788-May 20, 1835; House Dec. 7, 1826-29.

McHENRY, Henry Davis (son of John Hardin McHenry) (D Ky.) Feb. 27, 1826-Dec. 17, 1890; House 1871-73.

McHENRY, John Geiser (D Pa.) April 26, 1868-Dec. 27, 1912; House 1907-Dec. 27, 1912.

McHENRY, John Hardin (father of Henry Davis McHenry) (W Ky.) Oct. 13, 1797-Nov. 1, 1871; House 1845-47.

McILVAINE, Abraham Robinson (W Pa.) Aug. 14, 1804-Aug. 22, 1863; House 1843-49.

McILVAINE, Joseph (D N.J.) Oct. 2, 1769-Aug. 19, 1826; Senate Nov. 12, 1823-Aug. 19, 1826.

McINDOE, Walter Duncan (R Wis.) March 30, 1819-Aug. 22, 1872; House Jan. 26, 1863-67.

McINTIRE, Clifford Guy (R Maine) May 4, 1908; House Oct. 22, 1951-65.

McINTIRE, Rufus (JD Maine) Dec. 19, 1784-April 28, 1866; House Sept. 10, 1827-35.

McINTIRE, William Watson (R Md.) June 30, 1850-March 30, 1912; House 1897-99.

McINTOSH, Robert John (R Mich.) Sept. 16, 1922; House 1957-59.

McINTYRE, John Joseph (D Wyo.) Dec. 17, 1904; House 1941-43.

McINTYRE, Thomas James (D N.H.) Feb. 20, 1915; Senate Nov. 7, 1962- .

McJUNKIN, Ebenezer (R Pa.) March 28, 1819-Nov. 10, 1907; House 1871-Jan. 1, 1875.

McKAIG, William McMahon (D Md.) July 29, 1845-June 6, 1907; House 1891-95.

McKAY, James Iver (D N.C.) 1793-Sept. 4, 1853; House 1831-49.

McKAY, K. Gunn (D Utah) Feb. 23, 1925; House 1971- .

McKEAN, James Bedell (nephew of Samuel McKean) (R N.Y.) Aug. 5, 1821-Jan. 5, 1879; House 1859-63.

McKEAN, Samuel (uncle of James Bedell McKean) (D Pa.) April 7, 1787-Dec. 14, 1841; House 1823-29; Senate 1833-39.

McKEE, George Colin (R Miss.) Oct. 2, 1837-Nov. 17, 1890; House 1869-75.

McKEE, John (— Ala.) 1771-Aug. 12, 1832; House 1823-29.

McKEE, Samuel (D Ky.) Oct. 13, 1774-Oct. 16, 1826; House 1809-17.

McKEE, Samuel (R Ky.) Nov. 5, 1833-Dec. 11, 1898; House 1865-67, June 22, 1868-69.

McKEIGHAN, William Arthur (I Neb.) Jan. 19, 1842-Dec. 15, 1895; House 1891-93 (D), 1893-95 (I).

McKELLAR, Kenneth Douglas (D Tenn.) Jan. 29, 1869-Oct. 25, 1957; House Nov. 9, 1911-17; Senate 1917-53; President pro tempore 1945-47, 1949-53.

McKENNA, Joseph (R Calif.) Aug. 10, 1843-Nov. 21, 1926; House 1885-92; Atty. Gen. 1897-98; Assoc. Justice of Supreme Court 1898-1925.

McKENNAN, Thomas McKean Thompson (W Pa.) March 31, 1794-July 9, 1852; House 1831-39, May 30, 1842-43; Secy. of the Interior Aug. 15-Sept. 12, 1850.

McKENNEY, William Robertson (D Va.) Dec. 2, 1851-Jan. 3, 1916; House 1895-May 2, 1896.

McKENTY, Jacob Kerlin (D Pa.) Jan. 19, 1827-Jan. 3, 1866; House Dec. 3, 1860-61.

McKENZIE, Charles Edgar (D La.) Oct. 3, 1896-June 7, 1956; House 1943-47.

McKENZIE, James Andrew (uncle of John McKenzie Moss) (D Ky.) Aug. 1, 1840-June 25, 1904; House 1877-83.

McKENZIE, John Charles (R Ill.) Feb. 18, 1860-Sept. 17, 1941; House 1911-25.

McKENZIE, Lewis (UC Va.) Oct. 7, 1810-June 28, 1895; House Feb. 16-March 3, 1863 (U); Jan. 31, 1870-71 (UC).

McKEON, John (D N.Y.) March 29, 1808-Nov. 22, 1883; House 1835-37, 1841-43.

McKEOUGH, Raymond Stephen (D Ill.) April 29, 1888; House 1935-43.

McKEOWN, Thomas Deitz (D Okla.) June 4, 1878-Oct. 22, 1951; House 1917-21, 1923-35.

McKEVITT, James D. (R Colo.) Oct. 26, 1928; House 1971- .

McKIBBIN, Joseph Chambers (D Calif.) May 14, 1824-July 1, 1896; House 1857-59.

McKIM, Alexander (uncle of Isaac McKim) (D Md.) Jan. 10, 1748-Jan. 18, 1832; House 1809-15.

McKIM, Isaac (nephew of Alexander McKim) (D Md.) July 21, 1775-April 1, 1838; House Jan. 4, 1823-25, 1833-April 1, 1838.

McKINIRY, Richard Francis (D N.Y.) March 23, 1878-May 30, 1950; House 1919-21.

McKINLAY, Duncan E. (R Calif.) Oct. 6, 1862-Dec. 30, 1914; House 1905-11.

McKINLEY, John (JD Ala.) May 1, 1780-July 19, 1852; Senate Nov. 27, 1826-31, March 4-April 22, 1837; House 1833-35; Assoc. Justice of Supreme Court 1837-52.

McKINLEY, William (D Va.) —-—; House Dec. 21, 1810-11.

McKINLEY, William, Jr. (R Ohio) Jan. 29, 1843-Sept. 14, 1901; House 1877-May 27, 1884, 1885-91; Gov. 1892-96; President 1897-1901.

McKINLEY, William Brown (R Ill.) Sept. 5, 1856-Dec. 7, 1926; House 1905-13, 1915-21; Senate 1921-Dec. 7, 1926.

McKINNEY, James (R Ill.) April 14, 1852-Sept. 29, 1934; House Nov. 7, 1905-13.

McKINNEY, John Franklin (D Ohio) April 12, 1827-June 13, 1903; House 1863-65, 1871-73.

McKINNEY, Luther Franklin (D N.H.) April 25, 1841-July 30, 1922; House 1887-89, 1891-93.

McKINNEY, Stewart B. (R Conn.) Jan. 30, 1931; House 1971- .

McKINNON, Clinton Dotson (D Calif.) Feb. 5, 1906; House 1949-53.

McKISSOCK, Thomas (W N.Y.) April 17, 1790-June 26, 1866; House 1849-51.

McKNEALLY, Martin B. (R N.Y.) Dec. 31, 1914; House 1969-71.

McKNIGHT, Robert (R Pa.) Jan. 20, 1820-Oct. 25, 1885; House 1859-63.

McLACHLAN, James (R Calif.) Aug. 1, 1852-Nov. 21, 1940; House 1895-97, 1901-11.

McLAIN, Frank Alexander (D Miss.) Jan. 29, 1852-Oct. 10, 1920; House Dec. 12, 1898-1909.

McLANAHAN, James Xavier (grandson of Andrew Gregg) (D Pa.) 1809-Dec. 16, 1861; House 1849-53.

McLANE, Louis (father of Robert Milligan McLane) (F Del.) May 28, 1786-Oct. 7, 1857; House 1817-27; Senate 1827-April 16, 1829; Secy. of the Treasury 1831-33; Secy. of State 1833-34.

McLANE, Patrick (D Pa.) March 14, 1875-Nov. 13, 1946; House 1919-Feb. 25, 1921.

McLANE, Robert Milligan (son of Louis McLane) (D Md.) June 23, 1815-April 16, 1898; House 1847-51, 1879-93; Gov. 1884-85.

McLAUGHLIN, Charles Francis (D Neb.) June 19, 1887; House 1935-43.

McLAUGHLIN, James Campbell (R Mich.) Jan. 26, 1858-Nov. 29, 1932; House 1907-Nov. 29, 1932.

McLAUGHLIN, Joseph (R Pa.) June 9, 1867-Nov. 21, 1926; House 1917-19, 1921-23.

McLAUGHLIN, Melvin Orlando (R Neb.) Aug. 8, 1876-June 18, 1928; House 1919-27.

McLAURIN, Anselm Joseph (D Miss.) March 26, 1848-Dec. 22, 1909; Senate Feb. 7, 1894-95, 1901-Dec. 22, 1909; Gov. 1895-1900.

McLAURIN, John Lowndes (D S.C.) May 9, 1860-July 29, 1934; House Dec. 5, 1892-May 31, 1897; Senate June 1, 1897-1903.

McLEAN, Alney (— Ky.) June 10, 1779-Dec. 30, 1841; House 1815-17, 1819-21.

McLEAN, Donald Holman (R N.J.) March 18, 1884; House 1933-45.

McLEAN, Finis Ewing (W Ky.) Feb. 19, 1806-April 12, 1881; House 1849-51.

McLEAN, George Payne (R Conn.) Oct. 7, 1857-June 6, 1932; Senate 1911-29; Gov. 1901-02.

McLEAN, James Henry (R Mo.) Aug. 13, 1829-Aug. 12, 1886; House Dec. 15, 1882-83.

McLEAN, John (brother of William McLean) (WD Ohio) March 11, 1785-April 4, 1861; House 1813-16; Postmaster Gen. 1823-29; Assoc. Justice of Supreme Court 1829-61.

McLEAN, John (uncle of James David Walker) (D Ill.) Feb. 4, 1791-Oct. 14, 1830; House Dec. 3, 1818-19; Senate Nov. 23, 1824-25, 1829-Oct. 14, 1830.

McLEAN, Samuel (D Mont.) Aug. 7, 1826-July 16, 1877; House (Terr. Del.) Jan. 6, 1865-67.

McLEAN, William (brother of John McLean) (— Ohio) Aug. 10, 1794-Oct. 12, 1839; House 1823-29.

McLEAN, William Pinkney (D Texas) Aug. 9, 1836-March 13, 1925; House 1873-75.

McLEMORE, Atkins Jefferson (Jeff) (D Texas) March 13, 1857-March 4, 1929; House 1915-19.

McLENE, Jeremiah (D Ohio) 1767-March 19, 1837; House 1833-37.

McLEOD, Clarence John (R Mich.) July 3, 1895-May 15, 1959; House Nov. 2, 1920-21, 1923-37, 1939-41.

McLOSKEY, Robert Thaddeus (R Ill.) June 26, 1907; House 1963-65.

McMAHON, Gregory (R N.Y.) March 19, 1915; House 1947-49.

McMAHON, James O'Brien (Brien) (D Conn.) Oct. 6, 1903-July 28, 1952; Senate 1945-July 28, 1952.

McMAHON, John A. (nephew of Clement Laird Vallandigham) (D Ohio) Feb. 19, 1833-March 8, 1923; House 1875-81.

McMANUS, William (— N.Y.) 1780-Jan. 18, 1835; House 1825-27.

McMASTER, William Henry (R S.D.) May 10, 1877-Sept. 14, 1968; Senate 1925-31; Gov. 1921-24.

McMILLAN, Alexander (— N.C.) —-1817; House 1817.

McMILLAN, Clara Gooding (widow of Thomas S. McMillan) (D S.C.) Aug. 17, 1894-July 31, 1957; House Nov. 7, 1939-41.

McMILLAN, James (R Mich.) May 12, 1838-Aug. 10, 1902; Senate 1889-Aug. 10, 1902.

McMILLAN, John Lanneau (D S.C.) April 22, 1898; House 1939- .

McMILLAN, Samuel (R N.Y.) Aug. 6, 1850-May 6, 1924; House 1907-09.

McMILLAN, Samuel James Renwick (R Mich.) Feb. 22, 1826-Oct. 3, 1897; Senate 1875-87.

McMILLAN, Thomas Sanders (husband of Clara Gooding McMillan) (D S.C.) Nov. 27, 1888-Sept. 29, 1939; House 1925-Sept. 19, 1939.

McMILLAN, William (— N.W. Terr.) March 2, 1764-May 1804; House (Terr. Del.) Nov. 24, 1800-01.

McMILLEN, Rolla Coral (R Ill.) Oct. 5, 1880-May 6, 1961; House June 13, 1944-51.

McMILLIN, Benton (D Tenn.) Sept. 11, 1845-Jan. 8, 1933; House 1879-Jan. 6, 1899; Gov. 1899-1903.

McMORREN, Henry Gordon (R Mich.) June 11, 1844-July 19, 1929; House 1903-13.

McMULLEN, Chester Bartow (D Fla.) Dec. 6, 1902-Nov. 3, 1953; House 1951-53.

McMULLEN, Fayette (D Va.) May 18, 1805-Nov. 8, 1880; House 1849-57; Gov. of Wash. Terr. 1857-61.

McMURRAY, Howard Johnstone (D Wis.) March 3, 1901-Aug. 14, 1961; House 1943-45.

McNAGNY, William Forgy (D Ind.) April 19, 1850-Aug. 24, 1923; House 1893-95.

McNAIR, John (D Pa.) June 8, 1800-Aug. 12, 1861; House 1851-55.

McNAMARA, Patrick Vincent (D Mich.) Oct. 4, 1894-April 30, 1966; Senate 1955-April 30, 1966.

McNARY, Charles Linza (R Ore.) June 12, 1874-Feb. 25, 1944; Senate May 29, 1917-Nov. 5, 1918, Dec. 18, 1918-Feb. 25, 1944.

McNARY, William Sarsfield (D Mass.) March 29, 1863-June 26, 1930; House 1903-07.

McNEELY, Thompson Ware (D Ill.) Oct. 5, 1835-July 23, 1921; House 1869-73.

McNEILL, ARCHIBALD (— N.C.) —-1849; House 1821-23, 1825-27.

McNULTA, John (R Ill.) Nov. 9, 1837-Feb. 22, 1900; House 1873-75.

McNULTY, Frank Joseph (D N.J.) Aug. 10, 1872-May 26, 1926; House 1923-25.

McPHERSON, Edward (R Pa.) July 31, 1830-Dec. 14, 1895; House 1859-63.

McPHERSON, Isaac Vanbert (R Mo.) March 8, 1868-Oct. 31, 1931; House 1919-23.

McPHERSON, John Rhoderic (D N.J.) May 9, 1833-Oct. 8, 1897; Senate 1877-95.

McPHERSON, Smith (R Iowa) Feb. 14, 1848-Jan. 17, 1915; House 1899-June 6, 1900.

McQUEEN, John (D S.C.) Feb. 9, 1804-Aug. 30, 1867; House Feb. 12, 1849-Dec. 21, 1860.

McRAE, John Jones (SRD Miss.) Jan. 10, 1815-May 31, 1868; Senate Dec. 1, 1851-March 17, 1852 (D); House Dec. 7, 1858-Jan. 12, 1861 (SRD); Gov. 1854-58.

McRAE, Thomas Chipman (cousin of Thomas Banks Cabaniss) (D Ark.) Dec. 21, 1851-June 2, 1929; House Dec. 7, 1885-1903; Gov. 1921-25.

McREYNOLDS, Samuel Davis (D Tenn.) April 16, 1872-July 11, 1939; House 1923-July 11, 1939.

McROBERTS, Samuel (D Ill.) April 12, 1799-March 27, 1843; Senate 1841-March 27, 1843.

McRUER, Donald Campbell (R Calif.) March 10, 1826-Jan. 29, 1898; House 1865-67.

McSHANE, John Albert (D Neb.) Aug. 25, 1850-Nov. 10, 1923; House 1887-89.

McSHERRY, James (— Pa.) July 29, 1776-Feb. 3, 1849; House 1821-23.

McSWAIN, John Jackson (D S.C.) May 1, 1875-Aug. 6, 1936; House 1921-Aug. 6, 1936.

McSWEEN, Harold Barnett (D La.) July 19, 1926; House 1959-63.

McSWEENEY, John (D Ohio) Dec. 19, 1890-Dec. 13, 1969; House 1923-29, 1937-39, 1949-51.

McVEAN, Charles (D N.Y.) 1802-Dec. 22, 1848; House 1833-35.

McVEY, Walter Lewis (R Kan.) Feb. 19, 1922; House 1961-63.

McVEY, William Estus (R Ill.) Dec. 13, 1885-Aug. 10, 1958; House 1951-Aug. 10, 1958.

McVICKER, Roy Harrison (D Colo.) Feb. 20, 1924; House 1965-67.

McWILLIAMS, John Dacher (R Conn.) July 23, 1891; House 1943-45.

McWILLIE, William (D Miss.) Nov. 17, 1795-March 3, 1869; House 1849-51; Gov. 1858-60.

MEACHAM, James (W Vt.) Aug. 16, 1810-Aug. 23, 1856; House Dec. 3, 1849-Aug. 23, 1856.

MEAD, Cowles (— Ga.) Oct. 18, 1776-May 17, 1844; House March 4-Dec. 24, 1805.

MEAD, James Michael (D N.Y.) Dec. 27, 1885-March 15, 1964; House 1919-Dec. 2, 1938; Senate Dec. 3, 1938-47.

MEADE, Edwin Ruthven (D N.Y.) July 6, 1836-Nov. 28, 1889; House 1875-77.

MEADE, Hugh Allen (D Md.) April 4, 1907-July 8, 1949; House 1947-49.

MEADE, Richard Kidder (D Va.) July 29, 1803-April 20, 1862; House Aug. 5, 1847-53.

MEADE, Wendell Howes (R Ky.) Jan. 18, 1912; House 1947-49.

MEADER, George (R Mich.) Sept. 13, 1907; House 1951-65.

MEANS, Rice William (R Colo.) Nov. 16, 1877-Jan. 30, 1949; Senate Dec. 1, 1924-27.

MEBANE, Alexander (— N.C.) Nov. 26, 1744-July 5, 1795; House 1793-95.

MECHEM, Edwin Leard (R N.M.) July 2, 1912; Senate Nov. 30, 1962-Nov. 3, 1964; Gov. 1951-54, 1957-58, 1961-62.

MEDILL, William (D Ohio) 1802-Sept. 2, 1865; House 1839-43; Gov. 1853-55.

MEECH, Ezra (D Vt.) July 26, 1773-Sept. 23, 1856; House 1819-21, 1825-27.

MEEDS, Lloyd (D Wash.) Dec. 11, 1927; House 1965- .

MEEKER, Jacob Edwin (R Mo.) Oct. 7, 1878-Oct. 16, 1918; House 1915-Oct. 16, 1918.

MEEKISON, David (D Ohio) Nov. 14, 1849-Feb. 12, 1915; House 1897-1901.

MEEKS, James Andrew (D Ill.) March 7, 1864-Nov. 10, 1946; House 1933-39.

MEIGS, Henry (D N.Y.) Oct. 28, 1782-May 20, 1861; House 1819-21.

MEIGS, Return Jonathan, Jr. (D Ohio) Nov. 16, 1764-March 29, 1825; Senate Dec. 12, 1808-May 1, 1810; Gov. 1810-14; Postmaster Gen. 1814-23.

MEIKLEJOHN, George de Rue (R Neb.) Aug. 26, 1857-April 19, 1929; House 1893-97.

MELCHER, John (D Mont.) Sept. 6, 1924; House June 24, 1969- .

MELLEN, Prentiss (— Mass.) Oct. 11, 1764-Dec. 31, 1840; Senate June 5, 1818-May 15, 1820.

MELLISH, David Batcheller (R N.Y.) Jan. 2, 1831-May 23, 1874; House 1873-May 23, 1874.

MENEFEE, Richard Hickman (W Ky.) Dec. 4, 1809-Feb. 21, 1841; House 1837-39.

MENGES, Franklin (R Pa.) Oct. 26, 1858-May 12, 1956; House 1925-31.

MENZIES, John William (U Ky.) April 12, 1819-Oct. 3, 1897; House 1861-63.

MERCER, Charles Fenton (cousin of Robert Selden Garnett) (D Va.) June 16, 1778-May 4, 1858; House 1817-Dec. 26, 1839.

MERCER, David Henry (R Neb.) July 9, 1857-Jan. 10, 1919; House 1893-1903.

MERCER, John Francis (D Md.) May 17, 1759-Aug. 30, 1821; House Feb. 5, 1792-April 13, 1794; Cont. Cong. (Va.) 1782-85; Gov. of Md. 1801-03.

MERCUR, Ulysses (R Pa.) Aug. 12, 1818-June 6, 1887; House 1865-Dec. 2, 1872.

MEREDITH, Elisha Edward (D Va.) Dec. 26, 1848-July 29, 1900; House Dec. 9, 1891-97.

MERIWETHER, David (father of James Meriwether) (D Ga.) April 10, 1755-Nov. 16, 1822; House Dec. 6, 1802-07.

MERIWETHER, David (D Ky.) Oct. 30, 1800-April 4, 1893; Senate July 6-Aug. 31, 1852; Gov. of N.M. Terr. 1853-55.

MERIWETHER, James (son of David Meriwether and uncle of James A. Meriwether (— Ga.) 1789-1854; House 1825-27.

MERIWETHER, James A. (nephew of James Meriwether) (W Ga.) Sept. 20, 1806-April 18, 1852; House 1841-43.

MERRIAM, Clinton Levi (R N.Y.) March 25, 1824-Feb. 18, 1900; House 1871-75.

MERRICK, William Duhurst (father of William Matthew Merrick) (W Md.) Oct. 25, 1793-Feb. 5, 1857; Senate Jan. 4, 1838-45.

MERRICK, William Matthew (son of William Duhurst Merrick) (D Md.) Sept. 1, 1818-Feb. 4, 1889; House 1871-73.

MERRILL, D. Bailey (R Ind.) Nov. 22, 1912; House 1953-55.

MERRILL, Orsamus Cook (D Vt.) June 18, 1775-April 12, 1865; House 1817-Jan. 12, 1820.

MERRIMAN, Truman Adams (D N.Y.) Sept. 5, 1839-April 16, 1892; House 1885-89.

MERRIMON, Augustus Summerfield (D N.C.) Sept. 15, 1830-Nov. 14, 1892; Senate 1873-79.

MERRITT, Edwin Albert (R N.Y.) July 25, 1860-Dec. 4, 1914; House Nov. 5, 1912-Dec. 4, 1914.

MERRITT, Matthew Joseph (D N.Y.) April 2, 1895-Sept. 29, 1946, House 1935-45.

MERRITT, Samuel Augustus (D Idaho) Aug. 15, 1827-Sept. 8, 1910; House (Terr. Del.) 1871-73.

MERRITT, Schuyler (R Conn.) Dec. 16, 1853-April 1, 1953; House Nov. 6, 1917-31, 1933-37.

MERROW, Chester Earl (R N.H.) Nov. 15, 1906; House 1943-63.

MERWIN, Orange (— Conn.) April 7, 1777-Sept. 4, 1853; House 1825-29.

MESICK, William Smith (R Mich.) Aug. 26, 1856-Dec. 1, 1942; House 1897-1901.

MESKILL, Thomas J. (R Conn.) Jan. 30, 1928; House 1967-71; Gov. 1971- .

METCALF, Arunah (D N.Y.) Aug. 15, 1771-Aug. 15, 1848; House 1811-13.

METCALF, Jesse Houghton (R R.I.) Nov. 16, 1860-Oct. 9, 1942; Senate Nov. 5, 1924-37.

METCALF, Lee (D Mont.) Jan. 28, 1911; House 1953-61; Senate 1961- .

METCALF, Victor Howard (R Calif.) Oct. 10, 1853-Feb. 20, 1936; House 1899-July 1, 1904; Secy. of Commerce & Labor 1904-06; Secy. of the Navy 1906-08.

METCALFE, Henry Bleecker (D N.Y.) Jan. 20, 1805-Feb. 7, 1881; House 1875-77.

METCALFE, Lyne Shackelford (R Mo.) April 22, 1822-Jan. 31, 1906; House 1877-79.

METCALFE, Ralph H. (D Ill.) May 29, 1910; House 1971- .

METCALFE, Thomas (D Ky.) March 20, 1780-Aug. 18, 1855; House 1819-June 1, 1828; Senate June 23, 1848-49; Gov. 1829-33.

METZ, Herman August (D N.Y.) Oct. 19, 1867-May 17, 1934; House 1913-15.

MEYER, Adolph (D La.) Oct. 19, 1842-March 8, 1908; House 1891-March 8, 1908.

MEYER, Herbert Alton (R Kan.) Aug. 30, 1886-Oct. 2, 1950; House 1947-Oct. 2, 1950.

MEYER, John Ambrose (D Md.) May 15, 1899-Oct. 2, 1969; House 1941-43.

MEYER, William Henry (D Vt.) Dec. 29, 1914; House 1959-61.

MEYERS, Benjamin Franklin (D Pa.) July 6, 1833-Aug. 11, 1918; House 1871-73.

MICHAELSON, Magne Alfred (R Ill.) Sept. 7, 1878-Oct. 26, 1949; House 1921-31.

MICHALEK, Anthony (R Ill.) Jan. 16, 1878-Dec. 21, 1916; House 1905-07.

MICHEL, Robert Henry (R Ill.) March 2, 1923; House 1957- .

MICHENER, Earl Cory (R Mich.) Nov. 30, 1876-July 4, 1957; House 1919-33, 1935-51.

MICKEY, J. Ross (D Ill.) Jan. 5, 1856-March 20, 1928; House 1901-03.

MIDDLESWARTH, Ner (W Pa.) Dec. 12, 1783-June 2, 1865; House 1853-55.

MIDDLETON, George (D N.J.) Oct. 14, 1800-Dec. 31, 1888; House 1863-65.

MIDDLETON, Henry (D S.C.) Sept. 28, 1770-June 14, 1846; House 1815-19; Gov. 1811-12.

MIERS, Robert Walter (D Ind.) Jan. 27, 1848-Feb. 20, 1930; House 1897-1905.

MIKVA, Abner J. (D Ill.) Jan. 21, 1926; House 1969- .

MILES, Frederick (R Conn.) Dec. 19, 1815-Nov. 20, 1896; House 1879-83, 1889-91.

MILES, John Esten (D N.M.) July 28, 1884-—; House 1949-51; Gov. 1939-42.

MILES, Joshua Weldon (D Md.) Dec. 9, 1858-March 4, 1929; House 1895-97.

MILES, William Porcher (D S.C.) July 4, 1822-May 11, 1899; House 1857-Dec. 1860.

MILLARD, Charles Dunsmore (R N.Y.) Dec. 1, 1873-Dec. 11, 1944; House 1931-Sept. 29, 1937.

MILLARD, Joseph Hopkins (R Neb.) April 20, 1836-Jan. 13, 1922; Senate 1901-07.

MILLARD, Stephen Columbus (R N.Y.) Jan. 14, 1841-June 21, 1914; House 1883-87.

MILLEDGE, John (— Ga.) 1757-Feb. 9, 1818; House Nov. 22, 1792-93, 1795-99, 1801-May 1802; Senate June 19, 1806-Nov. 14, 1809; President pro tempore 1809; Gov. 1802-06.

MILLEN, John (D Ga.) 1804-Oct. 15, 1843; House March 4-Oct. 15, 1843.

MILLER, Arthur Lewis (R Neb.) May 24, 1892-March 16, 1967; House 1943-59.

MILLER, Bert Henry (D Idaho) Dec. 15, 1879-Oct. 8, 1949; Senate Jan. 3-Oct. 8, 1949.

MILLER, Clarence Benjamin (R Minn.) March 13, 1872-Jan. 10, 1922; House 1909-19.

MILLER, Clarence E. (R Ohio) Nov. 1, 1917; House 1967- .

MILLER, Clement Woodnutt (nephew of Thomas W. Miller) (D Calif.) Oct. 28, 1916-Oct. 7, 1962; House 1959-Oct. 2, 1962.

MILLER, Daniel Fry (W Iowa) Oct. 4, 1814-Dec. 9, 1895; House Dec. 20, 1850-51.

MILLER, Daniel H. (JD Pa.) —-1846; House 1823-31.

MILLER, Edward Edwin (R Ill.) July 22, 1880-Aug. 1, 1946; House 1923-25.

MILLER, Edward Tylor (R Md.) Feb. 1, 1895-Jan. 20, 1968; House 1947-59.

MILLER, George Funston (R Pa.) Sept. 5, 1809-Oct. 21, 1885; House 1865-69.

MILLER, George Paul (D Calif.) Jan. 15, 1891; House 1945- .

MILLER, Homer Virgil Milton (D Ga.) April 29, 1814-May 31, 1896; Senate Feb. 24-March 3, 1871.

MILLER, Howard Shultz (D Kan.- Feb. 27, 1879-Jan. 2, 1970; House 1953-55.

MILLER, Jack Richard (R Iowa) June 6, 1916; Senate 1961- .

MILLER, Jacob Welsh (W N.J.) Aug. 29, 1800-Sept. 30, 1862; Senate 1841-53.

MILLER, James Francis (D Texas) Aug. 1, 1830-July 3, 1902; House 1883-87.

MILLER, James Monroe (R Kan.) May 6, 1852-Jan. 20, 1926; House 1899-1911.

MILLER, Jesse (father of William Henry Miller (D Pa.) 1800-Aug. 20, 1850; House 1833-Oct. 30, 1836.

MILLER, John (— N.Y.) Nov. 10, 1774-March 31, 1862; House 1825-27.

MILLER, John (VBD Mo.) Nov. 25, 1781-March 18, 1846; House 1837-43; Gov. 1825-32.

MILLER, John Elvis (D Ark.) May 15, 1888-—; House 1931-Nov. 14, 1937; Senate Nov. 15, 1937-March 31, 1941.

MILLER, John Franklin (R Calif.) Nov. 21, 1831-March 8, 1886; Senate 1881-March 8, 1886.

MILLER, John Franklin (nephew of the preceding) (R Wash.) June 9, 1862-May 28, 1936; House 1917-31.

MILLER, John Gaines (W Mo.) Nov. 29, 1812-May 11, 1856; House 1851-May 11, 1856.

MILLER, John Krepps (D Ohio) May 25, 1819-Aug. 11, 1863; House 1847-51.

MILLER, Joseph (D Ohio) Sept. 9, 1819-May 27, 1862; House 1857-59.

MILLER, Killian (W N.Y.) July 30, 1785-Jan. 9, 1859; House 1855-57.

MILLER, Louis Ebenezer (R Mo.) April 30, 1899-Nov. 1, 1952; House 1943-45.

MILLER, Lucas Miltiades (D Wis.) Sept. 15, 1824-Dec. 4, 1902; House 1891-93.

MILLER, Morris Smith (father of Rutger Bleecker Miller) (F N.Y.) July 31, 1779-Nov. 16, 1824; House 1813-15.

MILLER, Orrin Larrabee (R Kan.) Jan. 11, 1856-Sept. 11, 1926; House 1895-97.

MILLER, Pleasant Moorman (— Tenn.) —-1849; House 1809-11.

MILLER, Rutger Bleecker (son of Morris Smith Miller) (D N.Y.) July 28, 1805-Nov. 12, 1877; House Nov. 9, 1836-37.

MILLER, Samuel Franklin (R N.Y.) May 27, 1827-March 16, 1892; House 1863-65, 1875-77.

MILLER, Samuel Henry (R Pa.) April 19, 1840-Sept. 4, 1918; House 1881-85, 1915-17.

MILLER, Smith (D Ind.) May 30, 1804-March 21, 1872; House 1853-57.

MILLER, Stephen Decatur (N S.C.) May 8, 1787-March 8, 1838; House Jan. 2, 1817-19 (D); Senate 1831-March 2, 1833 (N); Gov. 1828-30.

MILLER, Thomas Byron (R Pa.) Aug. 11, 1896-—; House May 9, 1942-45.

MILLER, Thomas Ezekiel (R S.C.) June 17, 1849-April 8, 1938; House Sept. 24, 1890-91.

MILLER, Thomas Woodnutt (uncle of Clement W. Miller) (R Del.) June 26, 1886-—; House 1915-17.

MILLER, Ward MacLaughlin (R Ohio) Nov. 29, 1902; House Nov. 8, 1960-61.

MILLER, Warner (R N.Y.) Aug. 12, 1838-March 21, 1918; House 1879-July 26, 1881; Senate July 27-1881-87.

MILLER, Warren (R W.Va.) April 2, 1847-Dec. 29, 1920; House 1895-99.

MILLER, William Edward (R N.Y.) March 22, 1914; House 1951-65; Chrmn. Rep. Nat. Comm. 1961-64.

MILLER, William Henry (son of Jesse Miller) (D Pa.) Feb. 28, 1829-Sept. 12, 1870; House 1863-65.

MILLER, William Jennings (R Conn.) March 12, 1899-Nov. 22, 1950; House 1939-41, 1943-45, 1947-49.

MILLER, William Starr (— N.Y.) Aug. 22, 1793-Nov. 9, 1854; House 1845-47.

MILLIGAN, Jacob Le Roy (D Mo.) March 9, 1889-March 9, 1951; House Feb. 14, 1920-21, 1923-35.

MILLIGAN, John Jones (W Del.) Dec. 10, 1795-April 20, 1875; House 1831-39.

MILLIKEN, Charles William (D Ky.) Aug. 15, 1827-Oct. 16, 1915; House 1873-77.

MILLIKEN, Seth Llewellyn (R Maine) Dec. 12, 1831-April 18, 1897; House 1883-April 18, 1897.

MILLIKEN, William H., Jr. (R Pa.) Oct. 19, 1897-July 4, 1969; House 1959-65.

MILLIKIN, Eugene Donald (R Colo.) Feb. 12, 1891-July 26, 1958; Senate Dec. 20, 1941-57.

MILLINGTON, Charles Stephen (R N.Y.) March 13, 1855-Oct. 25, 1913; House 1909-11.

MILLS, Daniel Webster (R Ill.) Feb. 25, 1838-Dec. 16, 1904; House 1897-99.

MILLS, Elijah Hunt (F Mass.) Dec. 1, 1776-May 5, 1829; House 1815-19; Senate June 12, 1820-27.

MILLS, Newt Virgus (D La.) Sept. 27, 1899-—; House 1937-43.

MILLS, Ogden Livingston (R N.Y.) Aug. 23, 1884-Oct. 11, 1937; House 1921-27; Secy. of the Treasury 1932-33.

MILLS, Roger Quarles (D Texas) March 30, 1832-Sept. 2, 1911; House 1873-March 28, 1892; Senate March 29, 1892-99.

MILLS, Wilbur Daigh (D Ark.) May 24, 1909; House 1939- .

MILLSON, John Singleton (D Va.) Oct. 1, 1808-March 1, 1874; House 1849-61.

MILLSPAUGH, Frank Crenshaw (R Mo.) Jan. 14, 1872-July 8, 1947; House 1921-Dec. 5, 1922.

MILLWARD, William (W Pa.) June 30, 1822-Nov. 28, 1871; House 1855-57, 1859-61.

MILNES, Alfred (R Mich.) May 28, 1844-Jan. 15, 1916; House Dec. 2, 1895-97.

MILNES, William, Jr. (C Va.) Dec. 8, 1827-Aug. 14, 1889; House Jan. 27, 1870-71.

MILNOR, James (F Pa.) June 20, 1773-April 8, 1844; House 1811-13.

MILNOR, William (F Pa.) June 26, 1769-Dec. 13, 1848; House 1807-11, 1815-17, 1821-May 8, 1822.

MILTON, John Gerald (D N.J.) Jan. 21, 1881- —; Senate Jan. 18-Nov. 8, 1938.

MILTON, William Hall (D Fla.) March 2, 1864-Jan. 4, 1942; Senate March 27, 1908-09.

MINAHAN, Daniel Francis (D N.J.) Aug. 8, 1877-April 29, 1947; House 1919-21, 1923-25.

MINER, Ahiman Louis (Whig Vt.) Sept. 23, 1804-July 19, 1886; House 1851-53.

MINER, Charles (F Pa.) Feb. 1, 1780-Oct. 26, 1865; House 1825-29.

MINER, Henry Clay (D N.Y.) March 23, 1842-Feb. 22, 1900; House 1895-97.

MINER, Phineas (W Conn.) Nov. 27, 1777-Sept. 15, 1839; House Dec. 1, 1834-35.

MINISH, Joseph George (D N.J.) Sept. 1, 1916; House 1963- .

MINK, Patsy Takemoto (D Hawaii) Dec. 6, 1927; House 1965- .

MINOR, Edward Sloman (R Wis.) Dec. 13, 1840-July 26, 1924; House 1895-1907.

MINSHALL, William Edwin, Jr. (R Ohio) Oct. 24, 1911; House 1955- .

MINTON, Sherman (D Ind.) Oct. 20, 1890-April 8, 1965; Senate 1935-41; Assoc. Justice of the Supreme Court 1949-56.

MITCHEL, Charles Burton (D Ark.) Sept. 19, 1815-Sept. 20, 1864; Senate March 4-July 11, 1861.

MITCHELL, Alexander (father of John Lendrum Mitchell) (D Wis.) Oct. 18, 1817-April 19, 1887; House 1871-75.

MITCHELL, Alexander Clark (R Kan.) Oct. 11, 1860-July 7, 1911; House March 4-July 7, 1911.

MITCHELL, Anderson (W N.C.) June 13, 1800-Dec. 24, 1876; House April 27, 1842-43.

MITCHELL, Arthur Wergs (D Ill.) Dec. 22, 1883-May 9, 1968; House 1935-43.

MITCHELL, Charles F. (W N.Y.) about 1808- —; House 1837-41.

MITCHELL, Charles Le Moyne (D Conn.) Aug. 6, 1844-March 1, 1890; House 1883-87.

MITCHELL, Edward Archibald (R Ind.) Dec. 2, 1910; House 1947-49.

MITCHELL, George Edward (D Md.) March 3, 1781-June 28, 1832; House 1823-27, Dec. 7, 1829-June 28, 1832.

MITCHELL, Harlan Erwin (D Ga.) Aug. 17, 1924; House Jan. 8, 1958-61.

MITCHELL, Henry (JD N.Y.) 1784-Jan. 12, 1856; House 1833-35.

MITCHELL, Hugh Burnton (D Wash.) March 22, 1907; Senate Jan. 10, 1945-Dec. 25, 1946; House 1949-53.

MITCHELL, James Coffield (— Tenn.) March 1786-Aug. 7, 1843; House 1825-29.

MITCHELL, James S. (D Pa.) 1784-1844; House 1821-27.

MITCHELL, John (D Pa.) March 8, 1781-Aug. 3, 1849; House 1825-29.

MITCHELL, John Hipple (R Ore.) June 22, 1835-Dec. 8, 1905; Senate 1873-79, Nov. 18, 1885-97, 1901-Dec. 8, 1905.

MITCHELL, John Inscho (R Pa.) July 28, 1838-Aug. 20, 1907; House 1877-81; Senate 1881-87.

MITCHELL, John Joseph (D Mass.) May 9, 1873-Sept. 13, 1925; House Nov. 8, 1910-11, April 15, 1913-15.

MITCHELL, John Lendrum (son of Alexander Mitchell) (D Wis.) Oct. 19, 1842-June 29, 1904; House 1891-93; Senate 1893-99.

MITCHELL, John Murray (R N.Y.) March 18, 1858-May 31, 1905; House June 2, 1896-99.

MITCHELL, John Ridley (D Tenn.) Sept. 26, 1877-—; House 1931-39.

MITCHELL, Nahum (F Mass.) Feb. 12, 1769-Aug. 1, 1853; House 1803-05.

MITCHELL, Parren J. (D Md.) April 29, 1922; House 1971- .

MITCHELL, Robert (D Ohio) 1778-Nov. 13, 1848; House 1833-35.

MITCHELL, Stephen Mix (F Conn.) Dec. 9, 1743-Sept. 30, 1835; Senate Dec. 2, 1793-95; Cont. Cong. 1783-88.

MITCHELL, Thomas Rothmaler (— S.C.) May 1783-Nov. 2, 1837; House 1821-23; 1825-29, 1831-33.

MITCHELL, William (R Ind.) Jan. 19, 1807-Sept. 11, 1865; House 1861-63.

MITCHILL, Samuel Latham (D N.Y.) Aug. 20, 1764-Sept. 7, 1831; House 1801-Nov. 22, 1804, Dec. 4, 1810-13; Senate Nov. 23, 1804-09.

MIZE, Chester L. (R Kan.) Dec. 25, 1917; House 1965-71.

MIZELL, Wilmer David (R N.C.) Aug. 13, 1930; House 1969- .

MOBLEY, William Carlton (D Ga.) Dec. 7, 1906, House March 2, 1932-33.

MOELLER, Walter Henry (D Ohio) March 15, 1910; House 1959-63, 1965-67.

MOFFATT, Seth Crittenden (R Mich.) Aug. 10, 1841-Dec. 22, 1887; House 1885-Dec. 22, 1887.

MOFFET, John (D Pa.) April 5, 1831-June 19, 1884; House March 4-April 9, 1869.

MOFFITT, Hosea (F N.Y.) Nov. 17, 1757-Aug. 31, 1825; House 1813-17.

MOFFITT, John Henry (R N.Y.) Jan. 8, 1843-Aug. 14, 1926; House 1887-91.

MOLLOHAN, Robert Homer (D W.Va.) Sept. 18, 1909; House 1953-57, 1969- .

MOLONY, Richard Sheppard (D Ill.) June 28, 1811-Dec. 14, 1891; House 1851-53.

MONAGAN, John Stephen (D Conn.) Dec. 23, 1911; House 1959- .

MONAGHAN, Joseph Patrick (D Mont.) March 26, 1906; House 1933-37.

MONAHAN, James Gideon (R Wis.) Jan. 12, 1855-Dec. 5, 1923; House 1919-21.

MONAST, Louis (R R.I.) July 1, 1863-April 16, 1936; House 1927-29.

MONDALE, Walter F. (D-FL Minn.) Jan. 5, 1928; Senate Dec. 30, 1964- .

MONDELL, Franklin Wheeler (R Wyo.) Nov. 6, 1860-Aug. 6, 1939; House 1895-97, 1899-1923.

MONELL, Robert (— N.Y.) 1786-Nov. 29, 1860; House 1819-21, 1829-Feb. 21, 1831.

MONEY, Hernando De Soto (D Miss.) Aug. 26, 1839-Sept. 18, 1912; House 1875-85, 1893-97; Senate Oct. 8, 1897-1911.

MONKIEWICZ, Boleslaus Joseph (R Conn.) Aug. 8, 1898-—; House 1939-41, 1943-45.

MONROE, James (— Va.) April 28, 1758-July 4, 1831; Senate Nov. 9, 1790-May 27, 1794; Cont. Cong. 1783-86; Gov. 1799-1802, 1811; Secy. of State 1811-17; President 1817-25.

MONROE, James (nephew of the preceding) (W N.Y.) Sept. 10, 1799-Sept. 7, 1870; House 1839-41.

MONROE, James (R Ohio) July 18, 1821-July 6, 1898; House 1871-81.

MONRONEY, Almer Stillwell Mike (D Okla.) March 2, 1902; House 1939-51; Senate 1951-69.

MONTAGUE, Andrew Jackson (D Va.) Oct. 3, 1862-Jan. 24, 1937; House 1913-Jan. 24, 1937; Gov. 1902-06.

MONTET, Numa Francois (D La.) Sept. 17, 1892-—; House Aug. 6, 1929-37.

MONTGOMERY, Alexander Brooks (D Ky.) Dec. 11, 1837-Dec. 27, 1910; House 1887-95.

MONTGOMERY, Daniel, Jr. (D Pa.) Oct. 30, 1765-Dec. 30, 1831; House 1807-09.

MONTGOMERY, Gillespie V. (D Miss.) Aug. 5, 1920; House 1967- .

MONTGOMERY, John (D Md.) 1764-July 17, 1828; House 1807-April 29, 1811.

MONTGOMERY, John Gallagher (D Pa.) June 27, 1805-April 24, 1857; House March 4-April 24, 1857.

MONTGOMERY, Samuel James (R Okla.) Dec. 1, 1896-June 4, 1957; House 1925-27.

MONTGOMERY, Thomas (D Ky.) 1779-April 2, 1828; House 1813-15, Aug. 1, 1820-23.

MONTGOMERY, William (— Pa.) Aug. 3, 1736-May 1, 1816; House 1793-95; Cont. Cong. 1784-85.

MONTGOMERY, William (D N.C.) Dec. 29, 1789-Nov. 27, 1844; House 1835-41.

MONTGOMERY, William (D Pa.) April 11, 1818-April 28, 1870; House 1857-61.

MONTOYA, Joseph Manuel (D N.M.) Sept. 24, 1915; House April 9, 1957-Nov. 3, 1964; Senate Nov. 4, 1964- .

MONTOYA, Nestor (R N.M.) April 14, 1862-Jan. 13, 1923; House 1921-Jan. 13, 1923.

MOODY, Arthur Edson Blair (D Mich.) Feb. 13, 1902-July 20, 1954; Senate April 23, 1951-Nov. 4, 1952.

MOODY, Gideon Curtis (R S.D.) Oct. 16, 1832-March 17, 1904; Senate Nov. 2, 1889-91.

MOODY, James Montraville (R N.C.) Feb. 12, 1858-Feb. 5, 1903; House 1901-Feb. 5, 1903.

MOODY, Malcolm Adelbert (R Ore.) Nov. 30, 1854-March 19, 1925; House 1899-1903.

MOODY, William Henry (R Mass.) Dec. 23, 1853-July 2, 1917; House Nov. 5, 1895-May 1, 1902; Secy. of the Navy 1902-04; Atty. Gen. 1904-06; Assoc. Justice of Supreme Court 1906-10.

MOON, John Austin (D Tenn.) April 22, 1855-June 26, 1921; House 1897-1921.

MOON, John Wesley (R Mich.) Jan. 18, 1836-April 5, 1898; House 1893-95.

MOON, Reuben Osborne (R Pa.) July 22, 1847-Oct. 25, 1919; House Nov. 2, 1903-13.

MOONEY, Charles Anthony (D Ohio) Jan. 5, 1879-May 29, 1931; House 1919-21, 1923-May 29, 1931.

MOONEY, William Crittenden (R Ohio) June 15, 1855-July 24, 1918; House 1915-17.

MOOR, Wyman Bradbury Seavy (D Maine) Nov. 11, 1811-March 10, 1869; Senate Jan. 5-June 7, 1848.

MOORE, Allen Francis (R Ill.) Sept. 30, 1869-Aug. 18, 1945; House 1921-25.

MOORE, Andrew (father of Samuel McDowell Moore) (— Va.) 1752-April 14, 1821; House 1789-97, March 5-Aug. 11, 1804; Senate Aug. 11, 1804-09.

MOORE, Arch Alfred, Jr. (R W.Va.) April 16, 1923; House 1957-69; Gov. 1969- .

MOORE, Arthur Harry (D N.J.) July 3, 1879-Nov. 18, 1952; Senate 1935-Jan. 17, 1938; Gov. 1926-28, 1932-34, 1938-40.

MOORE, Charles Ellis (R Ohio) Jan. 3, 1884-April 2, 1941; House 1919-33.

MOORE, Edward Hall (R Okla.) Nov. 19, 1871-Sept. 2, 1950; Senate 1943-49.

MOORE, Eliakim Hastings (R Okla.) June 19, 1812-April 4, 1900; House 1869-71.

MOORE, Ely (D N.Y.) July 4, 1798-Jan. 27, 1861; House 1835-39.

MOORE, Gabriel (— Ala.) 1785-June 9, 1845; House 1821-29; Senate 1831-37; Gov. 1829-31.

MOORE, Heman Allen (D Ohio) Aug. 27, 1809-April 3, 1844; House 1843-April 3, 1844.

MOORE, Henry Dunning (W Pa.) April 13, 1817-Aug. 11, 1887; House 1849-53.

MOORE, Horace Ladd (D Kan.) Feb. 25, 1837-May 1, 1914; House Aug. 2, 1894-95.

MOORE, Jesse Hale (R Ill.) April 22, 1817-July 11, 1883; House 1869-73.

MOORE, John (W La.) 1788-June 17, 1867; House Dec. 17, 1840-43, 1851-53.

MOORE, John Matthew (D Texas) Nov. 18, 1862-Feb. 3, 1940; House June 6, 1905-13.

MOORE, John William (D Ky.) June 9, 1877-Dec. 11, 1941; House Nov. 3, 1925-29, June 1, 1929-33.

MOORE, Joseph Hampton (R Pa.) March 8, 1864-May 2, 1950; House Nov. 6, 1906-Jan. 4, 1920.

MOORE, Laban Theodore (Nat. A. Ky.) Jan. 13, 1829-Nov. 9, 1892; House 1859-61.

MOORE, Littleton Wilde (D Texas) March 25, 1835-Oct. 29, 1911; House 1887-93.

MOORE, Nicholas Ruxton (D Md.) July 21, 1756-Oct. 7, 1816; House 1803-11, 1813-15.

MOORE, Orren Cheney (R N.H.) Aug. 10, 1839-May 12, 1893; House 1889-91.

MOORE, Oscar Fitzallen (R Ohio) Jan. 27, 1817-June 24, 1885; House 1855-57.

MOORE, Paul John (D N.J.) Aug. 5, 1868-Jan. 10, 1938; House 1927-29.

MOORE, Robert (grandfather of Michael Daniel Harter) (— Pa.) March 30, 1778-Jan. 14, 1831; House 1817-21.

MOORE, Robert Lee (D Ga.) Nov. 27, 1867-Jan. 14, 1940; House 1923-25.

MOORE, Robert Walton (D Va.) Feb. 6, 1859-Feb. 8, 1941; House May 27, 1919-31.

MOORE, Samuel (D Pa.) Feb. 8, 1774-Feb. 18, 1861; House Oct. 13, 1818-May 20, 1822.

MOORE, Samuel McDowell (son of Andrew Moore) (W Va.) Feb. 9, 1796-Sept. 17, 1875; House 1833-35.

MOORE, Sydenham (D Ala.) May 25, 1817-May 31, 1862; House 1857-Jan. 21, 1861.

MOORE, Thomas (— S.C.) 1759-July 11, 1822; House 1801-13, 1815-17.

MOORE, Thomas Love (— Va.) —-1862; House Nov. 13, 1820-23.

MOORE, Thomas Patrick (D Ky.) 1797-July 21, 1853; House 1823-29.

MOORE, William (R N.J.) Dec. 25, 1810-April 26, 1878; House 1867-71.

MOORE, William Robert (R Tenn.) March 28, 1830-June 12, 1909; House 1881-83.

MOORE, William Sutton (R Pa.) Nov. 18, 1822-Dec. 30, 1877; House 1873-75.

MOOREHEAD, Tom Van Horne (R Ohio) April 12, 1898; House 1961-63.

MOORES, Merrill (R Ind.) April 21, 1856-Oct. 21, 1929; House 1915-25.

MOORHEAD, James Kennedy (R Pa.) Sept. 7, 1806-March 6, 1884; House 1859-69.

MOORHEAD, William Singer (D Pa.) April 8, 1923; House 1959- .

MOORMAN, Henry DeHaven (D Ky.) June 9, 1880-Feb. 3, 1939; House 1927-29.

MORAN, Edward Carleton, Jr. (D Maine) Dec. 29, 1894-July 12, 1967; House 1933-37.

MORANO, Albert Paul (R Conn.) Jan. 18, 1908; House 1951-59.

MOREHEAD, Charles Slaughter (W Ky.) July 7, 1802-Dec. 21, 1868; House 1847-51; Gov. (AP) 1855-59.

MOREHEAD, James Turner (W Ky.) May 24, 1797-Dec. 28, 1854; Senate 1841-47; Gov. 1834-36.

MOREHEAD, James Turner (W N.C.) Jan. 11, 1799-May 5, 1875; House 1851-53.

MOREHEAD, John Henry (D Neb.) Dec. 3, 1861-May 31, 1942; House 1923-35; Gov. 1913-17.

MOREHEAD, John Motley (R N.C.) July 20, 1866-Dec. 13, 1923; House 1909-11.

MOREY, Frank (R La.) July 11, 1840-Sept. 22, 1889; House 1869-June 8, 1876.

MOREY, Henry Lee (R Ohio) April 8, 1841-Dec. 29, 1902; House 1881-June 20, 1884, 1889-91.

MORGAN, Charles Henry (R Mo.) July 5, 1842-Jan. 4, 1912; House 1875-79, 1883-85, 1893-95 (D), 1909-11 (R).

MORGAN, Christopher (brother of Edwin Barbour Morgan and nephew of Noyes Barber) (W N.Y.) June 4, 1808-April 3, 1877; House 1839-43.

MORGAN, Daniel (F Va.) 1736-July 6, 1802; House 1797-99.

MORGAN, Dick Thompson (R Okla.) Dec. 6, 1853-July 4, 1920; House 1909-July 4, 1920.

MORGAN, Edwin Barbour (brother of Christopher Morgan and nephew of Noyes Barber) (R N.Y.) May 2, 1806-Oct. 13, 1881; House 1853-59.

MORGAN, Edwin Dennison (cousin of Morgan Gardner Bulkeley) (UR N.Y.) Feb. 8, 1811-Feb. 14, 1883; Senate 1863-69; Chrmn. Rep. Nat. Comm. 1856-64, 1872; Gov. 1859-62.

MORGAN, George Washington (D Ohio) Sept. 20, 1820-July 26, 1893; House 1867-June 3, 1868, 1869-73.

MORGAN, James (F N.J.) Dec. 29, 1756-Nov. 11, 1822; House 1811-13.

MORGAN, James Bright (D Miss.) March 14, 1833-June 18, 1892; House 1885-91.

MORGAN, John Jordan (father-in-law of John Adams Dix) (D N.Y.) 1770-July 29, 1849; House 1821-25, Dec. 1, 1834-35.

MORGAN, John Tyler (D Ala.) June 20, 1824-June 11, 1907; Senate 1877-June 11, 1907.

MORGAN, Lewis Lovering (D La.) March 2, 1876-June 10, 1950; House Nov. 5, 1912-17.

MORGAN, Stephen (R Ohio) Jan. 25, 1854-Feb. 9, 1928; House 1899-1905.

MORGAN, Thomas Ellsworth (D Pa.) Oct. 13, 1906; House 1945- .

MORGAN, William Mitchell (R Ohio) Aug. 1, 1870-Sept. 17, 1935; House 1921-31.

MORGAN, William Stephen (D Va.) Sept. 7, 1801-Sept. 3, 1878; House 1835-39.

MORIN, John Mary (R Pa.) April 18, 1868-March 3, 1942; House 1913-29.

MORITZ, Theodore Leo (D Pa.) Feb. 10, 1892-—; House 1935-37.

MORPHIS, Joseph Lewis (R Miss.) April 17, 1831-July 29, 1913; House Feb. 23, 1870-73.

MORRELL, Daniel Johnson (R Pa.) Aug. 8, 1821-Aug. 20, 1885; House 1867-71.

MORRELL, Edward de Veaux (R Pa.) Aug. 7, 1863-Sept. 1, 1917; House Nov. 6, 1900-07.

MORRIL, David Lawrence (Ad.D N.H.) June 10, 1772-Jan. 28, 1849; Senate 1817-23; Gov. 1824-27.

MORRILL, Anson Peaslee (brother of Lot Myrick Morrill) (R Maine) June 10, 1803-July 4, 1887; House 1861-63; Gov. 1855.

MORRILL, Edmund Needham (R Kan.) Feb. 12, 1834-March 14, 1909; House 1883-91; Gov. 1895-97.

MORRILL, Justin Smith (UR Vt.) April 14, 1810-Dec. 28, 1898; House 1855-67 (W); Senate 1867-Dec. 28, 1898.

MORRILL, Lot Myrick (brother of Anson Peaslee Morrill) (R Maine) May 3, 1813-Jan. 10, 1883; Senate Jan. 17, 1861-69; Oct. 30, 1869-July 7, 1876; Gov. 1858-60; Secy. of the Treasury 1876-77.

MORRILL, Samuel Plummer (R Maine) Feb. 11, 1816-Aug. 4, 1892; House 1869-71.

MORRIS, Calvary (W Ohio) Jan. 15, 1798-Oct. 13, 1871; House 1837-43.

MORRIS, Daniel (R N.Y.) Jan. 4, 1812-April 22, 1889; House 1863-67.

MORRIS, Edward Joy (W Pa.) July 16, 1815-Dec. 31, 1881; House 1843-45; 1857-June 8, 1861.

MORRIS, Gouverneur (uncle of Lewis Robert Morris) (F N.Y.) Jan. 31, 1752-Nov. 6, 1816; Senate April 3, 1800-03; Cont. Cong. 1777-78.

MORRIS, Isaac Newton (son of Thomas Morris and brother of Jonathan David Morris) (D Ill.) Jan. 22, 1812-Oct. 29, 1879; House 1857-61.

MORRIS, James Remley (son of Joseph Morris) (D Ohio) Jan. 10, 1819-Dec. 24, 1899; House 1861-65.

MORRIS, Jonathan David (son of Thomas Morris and brother of Isaac Newton Morris (D Ohio) Oct. 8, 1804-May 16, 1875; House 1847-51.

MORRIS, Joseph (father of James Remley Morris) (D Ohio) Oct. 16, 1795-Oct. 23, 1854; House 1843-47.

MORRIS, Joseph Watkins (D Ky.) Feb. 26, 1879-Dec. 21, 1837; House Nov. 30, 1923-25.

MORRIS, Lewis Robert (nephew of Gouverneur Morris) (F Vt.) Nov. 2, 1760-Dec. 29, 1825; House 1797-1803.

MORRIS, Mathias (W Pa.) Sept. 12, 1787-Nov. 9, 1839; House 1835-39.

MORRIS, Robert (father of Thomas Morris) (— Pa.) Jan. 20, 1734-May 8, 1806; Senate 1789-95; Cont. Cong. 1776-78.

MORRIS, Robert Page Walter (R Minn.) June 30, 1853-Dec. 16, 1924; House 1897-1903.

MORRIS, Samuel Wells (D Pa.) Sept. 1, 1786-May 25, 1847; House 1837-41.

MORRIS, Thomas (son of Robert Morris) (— N.Y.) Feb. 26, 1771-March 12, 1849; House 1801-03.

MORRIS, Thomas (father of Isaac Newton Morris and Jonathan David Morris) (D Ohio) Jan. 3, 1776-Dec. 7, 1844; Senate 1833-39.

MORRIS, Thomas Gayle (D N.M.) Aug. 20, 1919; House 1959-69.

MORRIS, Toby (D Okla.) Feb. 28, 1899-—; House 1947-53, 1957-61.

MORRISON, Cameron A. (D N.C.) Oct. 5, 1869- Aug. 20, 1953; Senate Dec. 13, 1930-Dec. 4, 1932; House 1943-45; Gov. 1921-25.

MORRISON, George Washington (D N.H.) Oct. 16, 1809-Dec. 21, 1888; House Oct. 8, 1850-51, 1853-55.

MORRISON, James Hobson (D La.) Dec. 8, 1908; House 1943-67.

MORRISON, James Lowery Donaldson (D Ill.) April 12, 1816-Aug. 14, 1888; House Nov. 4, 1856-57.

MORRISON, John Alexander (D Pa.) Jan. 31, 1814-July 25, 1904; House 1851-53.

MORRISON, Martin Andrew (D Ind.) April 15, 1862-July 9, 1944; House 1909-17.

MORRISON, William Ralls (D Ill.) Sept. 14, 1825-Sept. 29, 1909; House 1863-65, 1873-87.

MORRISSEY, John (D N.Y.) Feb. 12, 1831-May 1, 1878; House 1867-71.

MORROW, Dwight Whitney (R N.J.) Jan. 11, 1873-Oct. 5, 1931; Senate Dec. 3, 1930-Oct. 5, 1931.

MORROW, Jeremiah (W Ohio) Oct. 6, 1771-March 22, 1852; House Oct. 17, 1803-13 (D) Oct. 13, 1840-43 (W); Senate 1813-19 (D); Gov. 1822-26.

MORROW, John (— Va.) —-—; House 1805-09.

MORROW, John (D N.M.) April 19, 1865-Feb. 25, 1935; House 1923-29.

MORROW, William W. (R Calif.) July 15, 1843-July 24, 1929; House 1885-91.

MORSE, Elijah Adams (R Mass.) May 25, 1841-June 5, 1898; House 1889-97.

MORSE, Elmer Addison (R Wis.) May 11, 1870-Oct. 4, 1945; House 1907-13.

MORSE, F. Bradford (R Mass.) Aug. 7, 1921; House 1961- .

MORSE, Freeman Harlow (R Maine) Feb. 19, 1807-Feb. 5, 1891; House 1843-45 (W), 1857-61 (R).

MORSE, Isaac Edward (D La.) May 22, 1809-Feb. 11, 1866; House Dec. 2, 1844-51.

MORSE, Leopold (D Mass.) Aug. 15, 1831-Dec. 15, 1892; House 1877-85, 1887-89.

MORSE, Oliver Andrew (R N.Y.) March 26, 1815-April 20, 1870; House 1857-59.

MORSE, Wayne Lyman (D Ore.) Oct. 20, 1900; Senate 1945-Oct. 24, 1952 (R), Oct. 24, 1952-Feb. 17, 1955 (I), Feb. 17, 1955-69 (D).

MORTON, Jackson (brother of Jeremiah Morton) (W Fla.) Aug. 10, 1794-Nov. 20, 1874; Senate 1849-55.

MORTON, Jeremiah (brother of Jackson Morton) (W Va.) Sept. 3, 1799-Nov. 28, 1878; House 1849-51.

MORTON, Levi Parsons (R N.Y.) May 16, 1824-May 16, 1920; House 1879-March 21, 1881; Vice President 1889-93; Gov. 1895-97.

MORTON, Marcus (D Mass.) Dec. 19, 1784-Feb. 6, 1864; House 1817-21; Gov. 1840-41, 1843-44.

MORTON, Oliver Hazard Perry Throck (UR Ind.) Aug. 4, 1823-Nov. 1, 1877; Senate 1867-Nov. 1, 1877; Gov. 1861-69.

MORTON, Rogers Clark Ballard (brother of Thruston Ballard Morton) (R Md.) Sept. 19, 1914; House 1963-Jan. 29, 1971; Chrmn. Rep. Nat. Comm. 1969-71; Secy. of Interior 1971- .

MORTON, Thruston Ballard (brother of Rogers Clark Ballard Morton) (R Ky.) Aug. 19, 1907; House 1947-53; Senate 1957-Dec. 16, 1968; Chrmn. Rep. Nat. Comm. 1959-61.

MOSELEY, Jonathan Ogden (R Conn.) April 9, 1762-Sept. 9, 1838; House 1805-21.

MOSELEY, William Abbott (W N.Y.) Oct. 20, 1798-Nov. 19, 1873; House 1843-47.

MOSER, Guy Louis (D Pa.) Jan. 23, 1886-May 9, 1961; House 1937-43.

MOSES, Charles Leavell (D Ga.) May 2, 1856-Oct. 10, 1910; House 1891-97.

MOSES, George Higgins (R N.H.) Feb. 9, 1869-Dec. 20, 1944; Senate Nov. 6, 1918-33; President pro tempore 1925-33.

MOSES, John (D N.D.) June 12, 1885-March 3, 1945; Senate Jan. 3-March 3, 1945; Gov. 1939-45.

MOSGROVE, James (D/G Pa.) June 14, 1821-Nov. 27, 1900; House 1881-83.

MOSHER, Charles Adams (R Ohio) May 7, 1906; House 1961- .

MOSIER, Harold Gerard (D Ohio) July 24, 1889-—; House 1937-39.

MOSS, Frank Edward (D Utah) Sept. 23, 1911; Senate 1959- .

MOSS, Hunter Holmes, Jr. (R W.Va.) May 26, 1874-July 15, 1916; House 1913-July 15, 1916.

MOSS, John Emerson, Jr. (D Calif.) April 13, 1913; House 1953- .

MOSS, John McKenzie (nephew of James Andrew McKenzie) (R Ky.) Jan. 3, 1868-June 11, 1929; House March 25, 1902-03.

MOSS, Ralph Wilbur (D Ind.) April 21, 1862-April 26, 1919; House 1909-17.

MOTT, Gordon Newell (R Nev.) Oct. 21, 1812-April 27, 1887; House (Terr. Del.) 1863-Oct. 31, 1864.

MOTT, James (D N.J.) Jan. 18, 1739-Oct. 18, 1823; House 1801-05.

MOTT, James Wheaton (R Ore.) Nov. 12, 1883-Nov. 12, 1945; House 1933-Nov. 12, 1945.

MOTT, Luther Wright (R N.Y.) Nov. 30, 1874-July 10, 1923; House 1911-July 10, 1923.

MOTT, Richard (R Ohio) July 21, 1804-Jan. 22, 1888; House 1855-59.

MOULDER, Morgan Moore (D Mo.) Aug. 31, 1904; House 1949-63.

MOULTON, Mace (D N.H.) May 2, 1796-May 5, 1867; House 1845-47.

MOULTON, Samuel Wheeler (D Ill.) Jan. 20, 1821-June 3, 1905; House 1865-67, 1881-85.

MOUSER, Grant Earl (R Ohio) Sept. 11, 1868-May 6, 1949; House 1905-09.

MOUSER, Grant Earl, Jr. (son of the preceding) (R Ohio) Feb. 20, 1895-Dec. 21, 1943; House 1929-33.

MOUTON, Alexander (D La.) Nov. 19, 1804-Feb. 12, 1885; Senate Jan. 12, 1837-March 1, 1842; Gov. 1842-46.

MOUTON, Robert Louis (D La.) Oct. 20, 1892-Nov. 26, 1956; House 1937-41.

MOXLEY, William James (R Ill.) May 22, 1851-Aug. 4, 1938; House Nov. 23, 1909-11.

MOYNIHAN, Patrick Henry (R Ill.) Sept. 25, 1869-May 20, 1946; House 1933-35.

MOZLEY, Norman Adolphus (R Mo.) Dec. 11, 1865-May 9, 1922; House 1895-97.

MRUK, Joseph (R N.Y.) Nov. 6, 1903; House 1943-45.

MUDD, Sydney Emanuel (R Md.) Feb. 12, 1858-Oct. 21, 1911; House March 20, 1890-91, 1897-1911.

MUDD, Sydney Emanuel (son of the preceding) (R Md.) June 20, 1885-Oct. 11, 1924; House 1915-Oct. 11, 1924.

MUHLENBERG, Francis Swaine (son of John Peter Gabriel Muhlenberg and nephew of Frederick Augustus Conrad Muhlenberg) (NR Ohio) April 22, 1795-Dec. 17, 1831; House Dec. 19, 1828-29.

MUHLENBERG, Frederick Augustus (great-great-grandson of Frederick Augustus Conrad Muhlenberg, great-great-grand-nephew of John Peter Gabriel Muhlenberg) (R Pa.) Sept. 25, 1887-—; House 1947-49.

MUHLENBERG, Frederick Augustus Conrad (brother of John Peter Gabriel Muhlenberg, uncle of Francis Swaine Muhlenberg and of Henry Augustus Philip Muhlenberg and great-great-grandfather of Frederick Augustus Muhlenberg) (— Pa.) Jan. 1, 1750-June 5, 1801; House 1789-97; Speaker 1789-91, 1793-95; Cont. Cong. 1779-80.

MUHLENBERG, Henry Augustus (son of Henry Augustus Philip Muhlenberg and grandson of Joseph Hiester) (D Pa.) July 21, 1823-Jan. 9, 1854; House 1853-Jan. 9, 1854.

MUHLENBERG, Henry Augustus Philip (father of Henry Augustus Muhlenberg and nephew of John Peter Gabriel Muhlenberg and of Frederick Augustus Conrad Muhlenberg) (JD Pa.) May 13, 1782-Aug. 11, 1844; House 1829-Feb. 9, 1838.

MUHLENBERG, John Peter Gabriel (father of Francis Swaine Muhlenberg, brother of Frederick Augustus Conrad Muhlenberg, and uncle of Henry Augustus Philip Muhlenberg and great-great-granduncle of Frederick Augustus Muhlenberg) (D Pa.) Oct. 1, 1746-Oct. 1, 1807; House 1789-91, 1793-95, 1799-1801; Senate March 4-June 30, 1801.

MULDOWNEY, Michael Joseph (R Pa.) Aug. 10, 1889-March 30, 1947; House 1933-35.

MULDROW, Henry Lowndes (D Miss.) Feb. 8, 1837-March 1, 1905; House 1877-85.

MULKEY, Frederick William (nephew of Joseph Norton Dolph) (R Ore.) Jan. 6, 1874-May 5, 1924; Senate Jan. 23-March 3, 1907, Nov. 6-Dec. 17, 1918.

MULKEY, William Oscar (D Ala.) July 27, 1871-June 30, 1943; House June 29, 1914-15.

MULLER, Nicholas (D N.Y.) Nov. 15, 1836-Dec. 12, 1917; House 1877-81, 1883-87, 1899-Dec. 1, 1902.

MULLIN, Joseph (R N.Y.) Aug. 6, 1811-May 17, 1882; House 1847-49.

MULLINS, James (R Tenn.) Sept. 15, 1807-June 26, 1873; House 1867-69.

MULTER, Abraham Jacob (D N.Y.) Dec. 24, 1900; House Nov. 4, 1947-Dec. 31, 1967.

MUMFORD George (D N.C.) —-Dec. 31, 1818; House 1817-Dec. 31, 1818.

MUMFORD, Gurdon Saltonstall (F N.Y.) Jan. 29, 1764-April 30, 1831; House 1805-11.

MUMMA, Walter Mann (R Pa.) Nov. 20, 1890-Feb. 25, 1961; House 1951-Feb. 25, 1961.

MUNDT, Karl Earl (R S.D.) June 3, 1900; House 1939-Dec. 30, 1948; Senate Dec. 31, 1948- .

MUNGEN, William (D Ohio) May 12, 1821-Sept. 9, 1887; House 1867-71.

MURCH, Thompson Henry (G Lab.Ref. Maine) March 29, 1838-Dec. 15, 1886; House 1879-83.

MURDOCK, John Robert (D Ariz.) April 20, 1885-—; House 1937-53.

MURDOCK, Orrice Abram, Jr. (Abe) (D Utah) July 18, 1893; House 1933-41; Senate 1941-47.

MURDOCK, Victor (R Kan.) March 18, 1871-July 8, 1945; House May 26, 1903-15; Chrmn. Progressive Party Nat. Comm. 1915-16.

MURFREE, William Hardy (uncle of David W. Dickinson) (D N.C.) Oct. 2, 1781-Jan. 19, 1827; House 1813-17.

MURPHEY, Charles (D Ga.) May 9, 1799-Jan. 16, 1861; House 1851-53.

MURPHY, Arthur Phillips (R Mo.) Dec. 10, 1870-Feb. 1, 1914; House 1905-07; 1909-11.

MURPHY, Benjamin Franklin (R Ohio) Dec. 24, 1867-March 6, 1938; House 1919-33.

MURPHY, Edward, Jr. (D N.Y.) Dec. 15, 1836-Aug. 3, 1911; Senate 1893-99.

MURPHY, Everett Jerome (R Ill.) July 24, 1852-April 10, 1922; House 1895-97.

MURPHY, George Lloyd (R Calif.) July 4, 1902; Senate Dec. 31, 1964-Jan. 2, 1971.

MURPHY, Henry Cruse (D N.Y.) July 5, 1810-Dec. 1, 1882; House 1843-45, 1847-49.

MURPHY, James Joseph (D N.Y.) Nov. 3, 1898-Oct. 19, 1962; House 1949-53.

MURPHY, James William (D Wis.) April 17, 1858-July 11, 1927; House 1907-09.

MURPHY, Jeremiah Henry (D Iowa) Feb. 19, 1835-Dec. 11, 1893; House 1883-87.

MURPHY, John (D Ala.) 1786-Sept. 21, 1841; House 1833-35; Gov. 1825-29.

MURPHY, John Michael (D N.Y.) Aug. 3, 1926; House 1963- .

MURPHY, John William (D Pa.) April 26, 1902; House 1943-July 17, 1946.

MURPHY, Maurice J., Jr. (R N.H.) Oct. 3, 1927; Senate Dec. 7, 1961-Nov. 7, 1962.

MURPHY, Morgan F., Jr. (D Ill.) April 16, 1932; House 1971- .

MURPHY, Nathan Oakes (R Ariz.) Oct. 14, 1849-Aug. 22, 1908; House (Terr. Del.) 1895-97; Gov. (Terr.) 1892-94, 1898-1902.

MURPHY, Richard Louis (D Iowa) Nov. 6, 1875-July 16, 1936; Senate 1933-July 16, 1936.

MURPHY, William Thomas (D Ill.) Aug. 7, 1899; House 1959-71.

MURRAY, Ambrose Spencer (brother of William Murray (R N.Y.) Nov. 27, 1807-Nov. 8, 1885; House 1855-59.

MURRAY, George Washington (R S.C.) Sept. 22, 1853-April 21, 1926; House 1893-95, June 4, 1896-97.

MURRAY, James Cunningham (D Ill.) May 16, 1917; House 1955-57.

MURRAY, James Edward (D Mont.) May 3, 1876-March 23, 1961; Senate Nov. 7, 1934-61.

MURRAY, John (cousin of Thomas Murray, Jr.) (— Pa.) 1768-March 7, 1834; House Oct. 14, 1817-21.

MURRAY, John L. (D Ky.) Jan. 25, 1806-Jan. 31, 1842; House 1837-39.

MURRAY, Reid Fred (R Wis.) Oct. 16, 1887-April 29, 1952; House 1939-April 29, 1952.

MURRAY, Robert Maynard (D Ohio) Nov. 28, 1841-Aug. 2, 1913; House 1883-85.

MURRAY, Thomas, Jr. (cousin of John Murray) (D Pa.) 1770-Aug. 26, 1823; House Oct. 9, 1821-23.

MURRAY, Thomas Jefferson (D Tenn.) Aug. 1, 1894; House 1943-Dec. 30, 1966.

MURRAY, William (brother of Ambrose Spencer Murray) (D N.Y.) Oct. 1, 1803-Aug. 25, 1875; House 1851-55.

MURRAY, William Francis (D Mass.) Sept. 7, 1881-Sept. 21, 1918; House 1911-Sept. 28, 1914.

MURRAY, William Henry (D Okla.) Nov. 21, 1869-Oct. 15, 1956; House 1913-17; Gov. 1931-35.

MURRAY, William Vans (F Md.) Feb. 9, 1760-Dec. 11, 1803; House 1791-97.

MUSKIE, Edmund Sixtus (D Maine) March 28, 1914; Senate 1959-—; Gov. 1955-59.

MUSSELWHITE, Harry Webster (D Mich.) May 23, 1868-Dec. 14, 1955; House 1933-35.

MUTCHLER, Howard (son of William Mutchler) (D Pa.) Feb. 12, 1859-Jan. 4, 1916; House Aug. 7, 1893-95, 1901-03.

MUTCHLER, William (father of Howard Mutchler) (D Pa.) Dec. 21, 1831-June 23, 1893; House 1875-77, 1881-85, 1889-June 23, 1893.

MYERS, Amos (R Pa.) April 23, 1824-Oct. 18, 1893; House 1863-65.

MYERS, Francis John (D Pa.) Dec. 18, 1901-July 5, 1956; House 1939-45; Senate 1945-51.

MYERS, Henry Lee (D Mont.) Oct. 9, 1862-Nov. 11, 1943; Senate 1911-23.

MYERS, John Thomas (R Ind.) Feb. 8, 1927; House 1967- .

MYERS, Leonard (R Pa.) Nov. 13, 1827-Feb. 11, 1905; House 1863-69, April 9, 1869-75.

MYERS, William Ralph (D Ind.) June 12, 1836-April 18, 1907; House 1879-81.

N

NABERS, Benjamin Duke (U Miss.) Nov. 7, 1812-Sept. 6, 1878; House 1851-53.

NAPHEN, Henry Francis (D Mass.) Aug. 14, 1852-June 8, 1905; House 1899-1903.

NAREY, Harry Elsworth (R Iowa) May 15, 1885-Aug. 19, 1962; House Nov. 3, 1942-43.

NASH, Charles Edmund (R La.) May 23, 1844-June 2, 1913; House 1875-77.

NATCHER, William Huston (D Ky.) Sept. 11, 1909; House Aug. 1, 1953- .

NAUDAIN, Arnold (— Del.) Jan. 6, 1790-Jan. 4, 1872; Senate Jan. 13, 1830-June 16, 1836.

NAYLOR, Charles (W Pa.) Oct. 6, 1806-Dec. 24, 1872; House June 29, 1837-41.

NEAL, Henry Safford (R Ohio) Aug. 25, 1828-July 13, 1906; House 1877-83.

NEAL, John Randolph (D Tenn.) Nov. 26, 1836-March 26, 1889; House 1885-89.

NEAL, Lawrence Talbot (D Ohio) Sept. 22, 1844-Nov. 2, 1905; House 1873-77.

NEAL, William Elmer (R W.Va.) Oct. 14, 1875-Nov. 12, 1959; House 1953-55, 1957-59.

NEALE, Raphael (— Md.) —-Oct. 19, 1833; House 1819-25.

NEDZI, Lucien Norbert (D Mich.) May 28, 1925; House Nov. 7, 1961- .

NEECE, William Henry (D Ill.) Feb. 26, 1831-Jan. 3, 1909; House 1883-87.

NEEDHAM, James Carson (R Calif.) Sept. 17, 1864-July 11, 1942; House 1899-1913.

NEELEY, George Arthur (D Kan.) Aug. 1, 1879-Jan. 1, 1919; House Nov. 11, 1912-15.

NEELY, Matthew Mansfield (D W.Va.) Nov. 9, 1874-Jan. 18, 1958; House Oct. 14, 1913-21, 1945-47; Senate 1923-29, 1931-Jan. 12, 1941, 1949-Jan. 18, 1958; Gov. 1941-45.

NEGLEY, James Scott (R Pa.) Dec. 22, 1826-Aug. 7, 1901; House 1869-75, 1885-87.

NEILL, Robert (D Ark.) Nov. 12, 1838-Feb. 16, 1907; House 1893-97.

NELSEN, Ancher (R Minn.) Oct. 11, 1904; House 1959- .

NELSON, Adolphus Peter (R Wis.) March 28, 1872-Aug. 21, 1927; House Nov. 5, 1918-23.

NELSON, Arthur Emanuel (R Minn.) May 10, 1892-April 11, 1955; Senate Nov. 18, 1942-43.

NELSON, Charles Pembroke (son of John E. Nelson) (R Maine) July 2, 1907-June 8, 1962; House 1949-57.

NELSON, Gaylord (D Wis.) June 4, 1916; Senate 1963- ; Gov. 1959-63.

NELSON, Homer Augustus (D N.Y.) Aug. 31, 1829-April 25, 1891; House 1863-65.

NELSON, Hugh (D Va.) Sept. 30, 1768-March 18, 1836; House 1811-Jan. 14, 1823.

NELSON, Jeremiah (F Mass.) Sept. 14, 1769-Oct. 2, 1838; House 1805-07, 1815-25, 1831-33.

NELSON, John (son of Roger Nelson) (D Md.) June 1, 1794-Jan. 18, 1860; House 1821-23; Atty. Gen. 1843-45; Secy. of State 1844.

NELSON, John Edward (father of Charles Pembroke Nelson (R Maine) July 12, 1874-April 11, 1955; House March 27, 1922-33.

NELSON, John Mandt (R Wis.) Oct. 10, 1870-Jan. 29, 1955; House Sept. 4, 1906-19, 1921-33.

NELSON, Knute (R Minn.) Feb. 2, 1843-April 28, 1923; House 1883-89; Senate 1895-April 28, 1923; Gov. 1893-95.

NELSON, Roger (father of John Nelson) (D Md.) 1759-June 7, 1815; House Nov. 6, 1804-May 14, 1810.

NELSON, Thomas Amos Rogers (U Tenn.) March 19, 1812-Aug. 24, 1873; House 1859-61.

NELSON, Thomas Maduit (D Va.) Sept. 27, 1782-Nov. 10, 1853; House Dec. 4, 1816-19.

NELSON, William (W N.Y.) June 29, 1784-Oct. 3, 1869; House 1847-51.

NELSON, William Lester (D Mo.) Aug. 4, 1875-Dec. 31, 1946; House 1919-21, 1925-33, 1935-43.

NES, Henry (I Pa.) May 20, 1799-Sept. 10, 1850; House 1843-45, 1847-Sept. 10, 1850.

NESBIT, Walter (D Ill.) May 1, 1878-Dec. 6, 1938; House 1933-35.

NESBITT, Wilson (D S.C.) —-May 13, 1861; House 1817-19.

NESMITH, James Willis (cousin of Joseph Gardner Wilson and grandfather of Clifton Nesmith McArthur) (D Ore.) July 23, 1820-June 17, 1885; Senate 1861-67; House Dec. 1, 1873-75.

NEUBERGER, Maurine Brown (widow of Richard L. Neuberger) (D Ore.) Jan. 9, 1907; Senate Nov. 9, 1960-67.

NEUBERGER, Richard Lewis (husband of Maurine B. Neuberger) (D Ore.) Dec. 26, 1912-March 9, 1960; Senate 1955-March 9, 1960.

NEVILLE, Joseph (— Va.) 1730-March 4, 1819; House 1793-95.

NEVILLE, William (cousin of Bird Segle McGuire) (P Neb.) Dec. 29, 1843-April 5, 1909; House Dec. 4, 1899-1903.

NEVIN, Robert Murphy (R Ohio) May 5, 1850-Dec. 17, 1912; House 1901-07.

NEW, Anthony (D Va./Ky.) 1747-March 2, 1833; House 1793-1805 (Va.), 1811-13, 1817-19 and 1821-23 (Ky.).

NEW, Harry Stewart (R Ind.) Dec. 31, 1858-May 9, 1937; Senate 1917-23; Chrmn. Rep. Nat. Comm. 1907-08; Postmaster Gen. 1923-29.

NEW, Jeptha Dudley (D Ind.) Nov. 28, 1830-July 9, 1892; House 1875-77, 1879-81.

NEWBERRY, John Stoughton (father of Truman Handy Newberry) (R Mich.) Nov. 18, 1826-Jan. 2, 1887; House 1879-81.

NEWBERRY, Truman Handy (son of John Stoughton Newberry) (R Mich.) Nov. 5, 1864-Oct. 3, 1945; Senate 1919-Nov. 18, 1922; Secy. of the Navy 1908-09.

NEWBERRY, Walter Cass (D Ill.) Dec. 23, 1835-July 20, 1912; House 1891-93.

NEWBOLD, Thomas (D N.J.) Aug. 2, 1760-Dec. 18, 1823; House 1807-13.

NEWCOMB, Carman Adam (R Mo.) July 1, 1830-April 6, 1902; House 1867-69.

NEWELL, William Augustus (R N.J.) Sept. 5, 1817-Aug. 8, 1901; House 1847-51 (W), 1865-67 (R); Gov. (N.J.) 1857-60; Terr. Gov. (Wash.) 1880-84.

NEWHALL, Judson Lincoln (R Ky.) March 26, 1870-July 23, 1952; House 1929-31.

NEWHARD, Peter (D Pa.) July 26, 1783-Feb. 19, 1860; House 1839-43.

NEWLANDS, Francis Griffith (D Miss.) Aug. 28, 1848-Dec. 24, 1917; House 1893-1903; Senate 1903-Dec. 24, 1917.

NEWMAN, Alexander (D Va.) Oct. 5, 1804-Sept. 8, 1849; House March 4-Sept. 8, 1849.

NEWNAN, Daniel (SRD Ga.) about 1780-Jan. 16, 1851; House 1831-33.

NEWSHAM, Joseph Parkinson (R La.) May 24, 1837-Oct. 22, 1919; House July 18, 1868-69, May 23, 1870-71.

NEWSOME, John Parks (D Ala.) Feb. 13, 1893-Nov. 10, 1961; House 1943-45.

NEWTON, Cherubusco (D La.) May 15, 1848-May 26, 1910; House 1887-89.

NEWTON, Cleveland Alexander (R Mo.) Sept. 3, 1873-Sept. 17, 1945; House 1919-27.

NEWTON, Eben (W Ohio) Oct. 16, 1795-Nov. 6, 1885; House 1851-53.

NEWTON, Thomas, Jr. (D Va.) Nov. 21, 1768-Aug. 5, 1847; House 1801-29, 1829-March 9, 1830, 1831-33.

NEWTON, Thomas Willoughby (W Ark.) Jan. 18, 1804-Sept. 22, 1853; House Feb. 6-March 3, 1847.

NEWTON, Walter Hughes (R Minn.) Oct. 10, 1880-Aug. 10, 1941; House 1919-June 30, 1929.

NEWTON, Willoughby (W Va.) Dec. 2, 1802-May 23, 1874; House 1843-45.

NIBLACK, Silas Leslie (cousin of William Ellis Niblack) (D Fla.) March 17, 1825-Feb. 13, 1883; House Jan. 19-March 3, 1873.

NIBLACK, William Ellis (cousin of Silas Leslie Niblack) (D Ind.) May 19, 1822-May 7, 1893; House Dec. 7, 1857-61, 1865-75.

NICHOLAS, John (brother of Wilson Cary Nicholas and uncle of Robert Carter Nicholas) (D Va.) about 1757-Dec. 31, 1819; House 1793-1801.

NICHOLAS, Robert Carter (nephew of John Nicholas and Wilson Cary Nicholas) (D La.) 1793-Dec. 24, 1857; Senate Jan. 13, 1836-41.

NICHOLAS, Wilson Cary (brother of John Nicholas and uncle of Robert Carter Nicholas) (D Va.) Jan. 31, 1761-Oct. 10, 1820; Senate Dec. 5, 1799-May 22, 1804; House 1807-Nov. 27, 1809; Gov. 1814-17.

NICHOLLS, John Calhoun (D Ga.) April 25, 1834-Dec. 25, 1893; House 1879-81, 1883-85.

NICHOLLS, Samuel Jones (D S.C.) May 7, 1885-Nov. 23, 1937; House Sept. 14, 1915-21.

NICHOLLS, Thomas David (ID Pa.) Sept. 16, 1870-Jan. 19, 1931; House 1907-11.

NICHOLS, Charles Archibald (R Mich.) Aug. 25, 1876-April 25, 1920; House 1915-April 25, 1920.

NICHOLS, John (I N.C.) Nov. 14, 1834-Sept. 22, 1917; House 1887-89.

NICHOLS, John Conover (Jack) (D Okla.) Aug. 31, 1896-Nov. 7, 1945; House 1935-July 3, 1943.

NICHOLS, Matthias H. (R Ohio) Oct. 3, 1824-Sept. 15, 1862; House 1853-55 (W), 1855-59 (R).

NICHOLS, William (D Ala.) Oct. 16, 1918; House 1967- .

NICHOLSON, Alfred Osborn Pope (D Tenn.) Aug. 31, 1808-March 23, 1876; Senate Dec. 25, 1840-Feb. 7, 1842, 1859-61.

NICHOLSON, Donald William (R Mass.) Aug. 11, 1888-Feb. 16, 1968; House Nov. 18, 1947-59.

NICHOLSON, John (D N.Y.) 1765-Jan. 20, 1820; House 1809-11.

NICHOLSON, John Anthony (D Del.) Nov. 17, 1827-Nov. 4, 1906; House 1865-69.

NICHOLSON, Joseph Hopper (D Md.) May 15, 1770-March 4, 1817; House 1799-March 1, 1806.

NICHOLSON, Samuel Danford (R Colo.) Feb. 22, 1859-March 24, 1923; Senate 1921-March 24, 1923.

NICOLL, Henry (D N.Y.) Oct. 23, 1812-Nov. 28, 1879; House 1847-49.

NIEDRINGHAUS, Frederick Gottlieb (uncle of Henry Frederick Niedringhaus) (R Mo.) Oct. 21, 1837-Nov. 25, 1922; House 1889-91.

NIEDRINGHAUS, Henry Frederick (nephew of Frederick Gottlieb Niedringhaus) (R Mo.) Dec. 15, 1864-Aug. 3, 1941; House 1927-33.

NILES, Jason (R Miss.) Dec. 19, 1814-July 7, 1894; House 1873-75.

NILES, John Milton (D Conn.) Aug. 20, 1787-May 31, 1856; Senate Dec. 21, 1835-39, 1843-49; Postmaster Gen. 1840-41.

NILES, Nathaniel (— Vt.) April 3, 1741-Oct. 31, 1828; House Oct. 17, 1791-95.

NIMTZ, F. Jay (R Ind.) Dec. 1, 1915; House 1957-59.

NISBET, Eugenius Aristides (cousin of Mark Anthony Cooper) (W Ga.) Dec. 7, 1803-March 18, 1871; House 1839-Oct. 12, 1841.

NIVEN, Archibald Campbell (D N.Y.) Dec. 8, 1803-Feb. 21, 1882; House 1845-47.

NIX, Robert Nelson Cornelius, Sr. (D Pa.) Aug. 9, 1905; House May 20, 1958- .

NIXON, George Stuart (R Nev.) April 2, 1860-June 5, 1912; Senate 1905-June 5, 1912.

NIXON, John Thompson (R N.J.) Aug. 31, 1820-sept. 28, 1889; House 1859-63.

NIXON, Richard Milhous (R Calif.) Jan. 9, 1913; House 1947-Nov. 30, 1950; Senate Dec. 1, 1950-Jan. 1, 1953; Vice Pres. 1953-61; Pres. 1969- .

NOBLE, David Addison (D Mich.) Nov. 9, 1802-Oct. 13, 1876; House 1853-55.

NOBLE, James (— Ind.) Dec. 16, 1785-Feb. 26, 1831; Senate Dec. 11, 1816-Feb. 26, 1831.

NOBLE, Warren Perry (D Ohio) June 14, 1820-July 9, 1903; House 1861-65.

NOBLE, William Henry (D N.Y.) Sept. 22, 1788-Feb. 5, 1850; House 1837-39.

NODAR, Robert Joseph, Jr. (R N.Y.) March 23, 1916; House 1947-49.

NOELL, John William (father of Thomas Estes Noell) (D Mo.) Feb. 22, 1816-March 14, 1863; House 1859-March 14, 1863.

NOELL, Thomas Estes (son of John William Noell) (Rad. Mo.) April 3, 1839-Oct. 3, 1867; House 1865-Oct. 3, 1867.

NOLAN, John Ignatius (husband of Mae Ella Nolan) (R Calif.) Jan. 14, 1874-Nov. 18, 1922; House 1913-Nov. 18, 1922.

NOLAN, Mae Ella (widow of John Ignatius Nolan) (R Calif.) Sept. 20, 1886; House Jan. 23, 1923-25.

NOLAN, Michael Nicholas (D N.Y.) May 4, 1833-May 31, 1905; House 1881-83.

NOLAN, William Ignatius (R Minn.) May 14, 1874-Aug. 3, 1943; House June 17, 1929-33.

NOLAND, James E. (D Ind.) April 22, 1920; House 1949-51.

NOONAN, Edward Thomas (D Ill.) Oct. 23, 1861-Dec. 19, 1923; House 1899-1901.

NOONAN, George Henry (R Texas) Aug. 20, 1828-Aug. 17, 1907; House 1895-97.

NORBECK, Peter (R S.D.) Aug. 27, 1870-Dec. 20, 1936; Senate 1921-Dec. 20, 1936; Gov. 1917-21.

NORBLAD, Albin Walter, Jr. (R Ore.) Sept. 12, 1908-Sept. 20, 1964; House Jan. 11, 1946-Sept. 20, 1964.

NORCROSS, Amasa (R Mass.) Jan. 26, 1824-April 2, 1898; House 1877-83.

NORMAN, Fred Barthold (R Wash.) March 21, 1882-April 18, 1947; House 1943-45, Jan. 3-April 18, 1947.

NORRELL, Catherine Dorris (widow of William Frank Norrell) (D Ark.) March 30, 1901; House April 18, 1961-63.

NORRELL, William Frank (husband of Catherine D. Norrell (D Ark.) Aug. 29, 1896-Feb. 15, 1961; House 1939-Feb. 15, 1961.

NORRIS, Benjamin White (R Ala.) Jan. 22, 1819-Jan. 26, 1873; House July 21, 1868-69.

NORRIS, George William (R Neb.) July 11, 1861-Sept. 2, 1944; House 1903-13; Senate 1913-37 (R), 1937-43 (R).

NORRIS, Moses, Jr. (D N.H.) Nov. 8, 1799-Jan. 11, 1855; House 1843-47; Senate 1849-Jan. 11, 1855.

NORTH, Solomon Taylor (R Pa.) May 24, 1853-Oct. 19, 1917; House 1915-17.

NORTH, William (F N.Y.) 1755-Jan. 3, 1836; Senate May 5-Aug. 17, 1798.

NORTHWAY, Stephen Asa (R Ohio) June 19, 1833-Sept. 8, 1898; House 1893-Sept. 8, 1898.

NORTON, Daniel Sheldon (UC Minn.) April 12, 1829-July 13, 1870; Senate 1865-July 13, 1870.

NORTON, Ebenezer Foote (D N.Y.) Nov. 7, 1774-May 11, 1851; House 1829-31.

NORTON, Elijah Hise (D Mo.) Nov. 24, 1821-Aug. 5, 1914; House 1861-63.

NORTON, James (D S.C.) Oct. 8, 1843-Oct. 14, 1920; House Dec. 6, 1897-1901.

NORTON, James Albert (D Ohio) Nov. 11, 1843-July 24, 1912; House 1897-1903.

NORTON, Jesse Olds (R Ill.) Dec. 25, 1812-Aug. 3, 1875; House 1853-57, 1863-65.

NORTON, John Nathaniel (D Neb.) May 12, 1878-Oct. 5, 1960; House 1927-29, 1931-33.

NORTON, Mary Teresa (D N.J.) March 7, 1875-Aug. 2, 1959; House 1925-51.

NORTON, Miner Gibbs (R Ohio) May 11, 1857-Sept. 7, 1926; House 1921-23.

NORTON, Nelson Ira (R N.Y.) March 30, 1820-Oct. 28, 1887; House Dec. 6, 1875-77.

NORTON, Patrick Daniel (R N.D.) May 17, 1876-Oct. 14, 1953; House 1913-19.

NORTON, Richard Henry (D Mo.) Nov. 6, 1849-March 15, 1918; House 1889-93.

NORVELL, John (D Mich.) Dec. 21, 1789-April 24, 1850; Senate Jan. 26, 1837-41.

NORWOOD, Thomas Manson (D Ga.) April 26, 1830-June 19, 1913; Senate Nov. 14, 1871-77; House 1885-89.

NOTT, Abraham (F S.C.) Feb. 5, 1768-June 19, 1830; House 1799-1801.

NOURSE, Amos (— Maine) Dec. 17, 1794-April 7, 1877; Senate Jan. 16-March 3, 1857.

NOYES, John (F Vt.) April 2, 1764-Oct. 26, 1841; House 1815-17.

NOYES, Joseph Cobham (W Maine) Sept. 22, 1798-July 28, 1868; House 1837-39.

NUCKOLLS, Stephen Friel (D Wyo.) Aug. 16, 1825-Feb. 14, 1879; House (Terr. Del.) Dec. 6, 1869-71.

NUCKOLLS, William Thompson (— S.C.) Feb. 23, 1801-Sept. 27, 1855; House 1827-33.

NUGEN, Robert Hunter (D Ohio) July 16, 1809-Feb. 28, 1872; House 1861-63.

NUGENT, John Frost (D Idaho) June 28, 1868-Sept. 18, 1931; Senate Jan. 22, 1918-Jan. 14, 1921.

NUNN, David Alexander (R Tenn.) July 26, 1833-Sept. 11, 1918; House 1867-69, 1873-75.

NUTE, Alonzo (R N.H.) Feb. 12, 1826-Dec. 24, 1892; House 1889-91.

NUTTING, Newton Wright (R N.Y.) Oct. 22, 1840-Oct. 15, 1889; House 1883-85, 1887-Oct. 15, 1889.

NYE, Frank Mellen (R Minn.) March 7, 1852-Nov. 29, 1935; House 1907-13.

NYE, Gerald Prentice (R N.D.) Dec. 19, 1892; Senate Nov. 14, 1925-45.

NYE, James Warren (R Nev.) June 10, 1815-Dec. 25, 1876; Senate Dec. 16, 1864-73; Gov. (Terr.) 1861-64.

NYGAARD, Hjalmar (R N.D.) March 24, 1906-July 18, 1963; House 1961-July 18, 1963.

O

OAKEY, Peter Davis (R Conn.) Feb. 25, 1861-Nov. 18, 1920; House 1915-17.

OAKLEY, Thomas Jackson (Clinton D N.Y.) Nov. 10, 1783-May 11, 1857; House 1813-15 (F), 1827-May 9, 1828 (Clinton D).

OAKMAN, Charles G. (R Mich.) Sept. 4, 1903; House 1953-55.

OATES, William Calvin (D Ala.) Nov. 30, 1835-Sept. 9, 1910; House 1881-Nov. 5, 1894; Gov. 1894-96.

OBEY, David R. (D Wis.) Oct. 3, 1938; House April 1, 1929- .

O'BRIEN, Charles Francis Xavier (D N.J.) March 7, 1879-Nov. 14, 1940; House 1921-25.

O'BRIEN, George Donoghue (D Mich.) Jan. 1, 1900-Oct. 25, 1957; House 1937-39, 1941-47, 1949-55.

O'BRIEN, James (A-TD N.Y.) March 13, 1841-March 5, 1907; House 1879-81.

O'BRIEN, James Henry (D N.Y.) July 15, 1860-Sept. 2, 1924; House 1913-15.

O'BRIEN, Jeremiah (D Maine) Jan. 21, 1778-May 30, 1858; House 1823-29.

O'BRIEN, Joseph John (R N.Y.) Oct. 9, 1897-Jan. 23, 1953; House 1939-45.

O'BRIEN, Leo William (D N.Y.) Sept. 21, 1900; House April 1, 1952-Dec. 30, 1966.

O'BRIEN, Thomas Joseph (D Ill.) April 30, 1878-April 14, 1964; House 1933-39, 1943-April 14, 1964.

O'BRIEN, William James (D Md.) May 28, 1836-Nov. 13, 1905; House 1873-77.

O'BRIEN, William Smith (D W.Va.) Jan. 8, 1862-Aug. 10, 1948; House 1927-29.

OCAMPO, Pablo (— P.I.) Jan. 25, 1853-Feb. 5, 1925; House (Res.Comm.) Nov. 22, 1907-Nov. 22, 1909.

OCHILTREE, Thomas Peck (I Texas) Oct. 26, 1837-Nov. 25, 1902; House 1883-85.

O'CONNELL, David Joseph (D N.Y.) Dec. 25, 1868-Dec. 29, 1930; House 1919-21, 1923-Dec. 29, 1930.

O'CONNELL, Jeremiah Edward (D R.I.) July 8, 1883-Sept. 18, 1964; House 1923-27, 1929-May 9, 1930.

O'CONNELL, Jerry Joseph (D Mont.) June 14, 1909-Jan. 16, 1956; House 1937-39.

O'CONNELL, John Matthew (D R.I.) Aug. 10, 1872-Dec. 6, 1941; House 1933-39.

O'CONNELL, Joseph Francis (D Mass.) Dec. 7, 1872-Dec. 10, 1942; House 1907-11.

O'CONNOR, Charles (R Okla.) Oct. 26, 1878-Nov. 15, 1940; House 1929-31.

O'CONNOR, James (D La.) April 4, 1870-Jan. 7, 1941; House June 5, 1919-31.

O'CONNOR, James Francis (D Mont.) May 7, 1878-Jan. 15, 1945; House 1937-Jan. 15, 1945.

O'CONNOR, John Joseph (D N.Y.) Nov. 23, 1885-Jan. 26, 1960; House Nov. 6, 1923-39.

O'CONNOR, Michael Patrick (D S.C.) Sept. 29, 1831-April 26, 1881; House 1879-April 26, 1881.

O'CONOR, Herbert Romulus (D Md.) Nov. 17, 1896-March 4, 1960; Senate 1947-53; Gov. 1939-46.

O'DANIEL, Wilbert Lee (D Texas) March 11, 1890-May 11, 1969; Senate Aug. 4, 1941-49; Gov. 1939-41.

O'DAY, Caroline Love Goodwin (D N.Y.) June 22, 1875-Jan. 4, 1943; House 1935-43.

ODDIE, Tasker Lowndes (R Nev.) Oct. 24, 1870-Feb. 17, 1950; Senate 1921-33; Gov. 1911-15.

ODELL, Benjamin Baker, Jr. (R N.Y.) Jan. 14, 1854-May 9, 1926; House 1895-99; Gov. 1901-03.

ODELL, Moses Fowler (D N.Y.) Feb. 24, 1818-June 13, 1866; House 1861-65.

ODELL, Nathaniel Holmes (D N.Y.) Oct. 10, 1828-Oct. 30, 1904; House 1875-77.

O'DONNELL, James (R Mich.) March 25, 1840-March 17, 1915; House 1885-93.

O'FERRALL, Charles Triplett (D Va.) Oct. 21, 1840-Sept. 22, 1905; House May 5, 1884-Dec. 28, 1893; Gov. 1894-98.

OGDEN, Aaron (F N.J.) Dec. 3, 1756-April 19, 1838; Senate Feb. 28, 1801-03; Gov. 1812.

OGDEN, Charles Franklin (R Ky.) —-April 10, 1933; House 1919-23.

OGDEN, David A. (F N.Y.) Jan. 10, 1770-June 9, 1829; House 1817-19.

OGDEN, Henry Warren (D La.) Oct. 21, 1842-July 23, 1905; House May 12, 1894-99.

OGLE, Alexander (father of Charles Ogle and grandfather of Andrew Jackson Ogle) (D Pa.) Aug. 10, 1766-Oct. 14, 1832; House 1817-19.

OGLE, Andrew Jackson (grandson of Alexander Ogle) (W Pa.) March 25, 1822-Oct. 14, 1852; House 1849-51.

OGLE, Charles (son of Alexander Ogle) (W Pa.) 1798-May 10, 1841; House 1837-May 10, 1841.

OGLESBY, Richard James (cousin of Woodson Ratcliffe Oglesby) (R Ill.) July 25, 1824-April 24, 1899; Senate 1873-79; Gov. 1865-69; Jan. 13-23, 1873; 1885-89.

OGLESBY, Woodson Ratcliffe (cousin of Richard James Oglesby) (D N.Y.) Feb. 9, 1867-April 30, 1955; House 1913-17.

O'GORMAN, James Aloysius (D N.Y.) May 5, 1860-May 17, 1943; Senate 1911-17.

O'GRADY, James Mary Early (R N.Y.) March 31, 1863-Nov. 3, 1928; House 1899-1901.

O'HAIR, Frank Trimble (D Ill.) March 12, 1870-Aug. 3, 1932; House 1913-15.

O'HARA, Barratt (D Ill.) April 28, 1882-Aug. 11, 1969; House 1949-51; 1953-69.

O'HARA, James Edward (R N.C.) Feb. 26, 1844-Sept. 15, 1905; House 1883-87.

O'HARA, James Grant (D Mich.) Nov. 8, 1925; House 1959- .

O'HARA, Joseph Patrick (R Minn.) Jan. 23, 1895-—; House 1941-59.

OHLIGER, Lewis Phillip (D Ohio) Jan. 3, 1843-Jan. 9, 1923; House Dec. 5, 1892-93.

O'KONSKI, Alvin Edward (R Wis.) May 26, 1904; House 1943- .

OLCOTT, Jacob Van Vechten (R N.Y.) May 17, 1856-June 1, 1940; House 1905-11.

OLCOTT, Simeon (F N.H.) Oct. 1, 1735-Feb. 22, 1815; Senate June 17, 1801-05.

OLDFIELD, Pearl Peden (widow of William Allan Oldfield) (D Ark.) Dec. 2, 1876-April 12, 1962; House Jan. 9, 1929-31.

OLDFIELD, William Allan (husband of Pearl Peden Oldfield) (D Ark.) Feb. 4, 1874-Nov. 19, 1928; House 1909-Nov. 19, 1928.

OLDS, Edson Baldwin (D Ohio) June 3, 1802-Jan. 24, 1869; House 1849-55.

O'LEARY, Denis (D N.Y.) Jan. 22, 1863-Sept. 27, 1943; House 1913-Dec. 31, 1914.

O'LEARY, James Aloysius (D N.Y.) April 23, 1889-March 16, 1944; House 1935-March 16, 1944.

OLIN, Abram Baldwin (son of Gideon Olin) (R N.Y.) Sept. 21, 1808-July 7, 1879; House 1857-63.

OLIN, Gideon (father of Abram Baldwin Olin and uncle of Henry Olin) (D Vt.) Nov. 2, 1743-Jan. 21, 1823; House 1803-07.

OLIN, Henry (nephew of Gideon Olin) (Jeff. D Vt.) May 7, 1768-Aug. 16, 1837; House Dec. 13, 1824-25.

OLIVER, Andrew (D N.Y.) Jan. 16, 1815-March 6, 1889; House 1853-57.

OLIVER, Daniel Charles (D N.Y.) Oct. 6, 1865-March 26, 1924; House 1917-19.

OLIVER, Frank (D N.Y.) Oct. 2, 1883-Jan. 1, 1968; House 1923-June 18, 1934.

OLIVER, George Tener (R Pa.) Jan. 26, 1848-Jan. 22, 1919; Senate March 17, 1909-17.

OLIVER, James Churchill (D Maine) Aug. 6, 1895-—; House 1937-43 (R); 1959-61 (D).

OLIVER, Mordecai (W Mo.) Oct. 22, 1819-April 25, 1898; House 1853-57.

OLIVER Samuel Addison (R Iowa) July 21, 1833-July 7, 1912; House 1875-79.

OLIVER, William Bacon (cousin of Sydney Parham Epes) (D Ala.) May 23, 1867-May 27, 1948; House 1915-37.

OLIVER, William Morrison (D N.Y.) Oct. 15, 1792-July 21, 1863; House 1841-43.

OLMSTED, Marlin Edgar (R Pa.) May 21, 1847-July 19, 1913; House 1897-1913.

OLNEY, Richard (D Mass.) Jan. 5, 1871-Jan. 15, 1939; House 1915-21.

O'LOUGHLIN, Kathryn Ellen (after election was married to Daniel M. McCarthy and thereupon served under the name of Kathryn O'Loughlin McCarthy) (D Kan.) April 24, 1894-Jan. 16, 1952; House 1933-35.

OLPP, Archibald Ernest (R N.J.) May 12, 1882-July 26, 1949; House 1921-23.

OLSEN, Arnold (D Mont.) Dec. 17, 1916; House 1961-71.

OLSON, Alec G. (D Minn.) Sept. 11, 1930; House 1963-67.

O'MAHONEY, Joseph Christopher (D Wyo.) Nov. 5, 1884-Dec. 1, 1962; Senate Jan. 1, 1934-53; Nov. 29, 1954-61.

O'MALLEY, Matthew Vincent (D N.Y.) June 26, 1878-May 26, 1931; House March 4-May 26, 1931.

O'MALLEY, Thomas David Patrick (D Wis.) March 24, 1903; House 1933-39.

O'NEAL, Emmet (D Ky.) April 14, 1887-July 18, 1967; House 1935-47.

O'NEAL, Maston Emmett, Jr. (D Ga.) July 19, 1907; House 1965-71.

O'NEALL, John Henry (D Ind.) Oct. 30, 1838-July 15, 1907; House 1887-91.

O'NEIL, Joseph Henry (D Mass.) March 23, 1853-Feb. 19, 1935; House 1889-95.

O'NEILL, Charles (R Pa.) March 21, 1821-Nov. 25, 1893; House 1863-71; 1873-Nov. 25, 1893.

O'NEILL, Edward Leo (D N.J.) July 10, 1903-Dec. 12, 1948; House 1937-39.

O'NEILL, Harry Patrick (D Pa.) Feb. 10, 1889-June 24, 1953; House 1949-53.

O'NEILL, John (D Ohio) Dec. 17, 1822-May 25, 1905; House 1863-65.

O'NEILL, John Joseph (D Mo.) June 25, 1846-Feb. 19, 1898; House 1883-89; 1891-93; April 3, 1894-95.

O'NEILL, Thomas Phillip, Jr. (D Mass.) Dec. 9, 1912; House 1953- .

O'REILLY, Daniel (ID N.Y.) June 3, 1838-Sept. 23, 1911; House 1879-81.

ORMSBY, Stephen (D Ky.) 1759-1844; House 1811-13; April 20, 1813-17.

ORR, Alexander Dalrymple (nephew of William Grayson and cousin of William John Grayson) (— Ky.) Nov. 6, 1761-June 21, 1835; House Nov. 8, 1792-97.

ORR, Benjamin (F Mass.) Dec. 1, 1772-Sept. 3, 1828; House 1817-19.

ORR, Jackson (R Iowa) Sept. 21, 1832-March 15, 1926; House 1871-75.

ORR, James Lawrence (D S.C.) May 12, 1822-May 5, 1873; House 1849-59; Speaker 1857-59; Gov. 1867 (R).

ORR, Robert, Jr. (D Pa.) March 5, 1786-May 22, 1876; House Oct. 11, 1825-29.

ORTH, Godlove Stein (R Ind.) April 22, 1817-Dec. 16, 1882; House 1863-71, 1873-75; 1879-Dec. 16, 1882.

OSBORN, Thomas Ward (R Fla.) March 9, 1836-Dec. 18, 1898; Senate June 25, 1868-73.

OSBORNE, Edwin Sylvanus (R Pa.) Aug. 7, 1839-Jan. 1, 1900; House 1885-91.

OSBORNE, Henry Zenas (R Calif.) Oct. 4, 1848-Feb. 8, 1923; House 1917-Feb. 8, 1923.

OSBORNE, John Eugene (D Wyo.) June 19, 1858-April 24, 1943; House 1897-99; Gov. 1893-95.

OSBORNE, Thomas Burr (W Conn.) July 8, 1798-Sept. 2, 1869; House 1839-43.

OSGOOD, Gayton Pickman (D Mass.) July 4, 1797-June 26, 1861; House 1833-35.

O'SHAUNESSY, George Francis (D R.I.) May 1, 1868-Nov. 28, 1934; House 1911-19.

OSIAS, Camilo (Nat. P.I.) March 23, 1889-—; House (Res. Comm.) 1929-35.

OSMER, James H. (R Pa.) Jan. 23, 1832-Oct. 3, 1912; House 1879-81.

OSMERS, Frank Charles, Jr. (R N.J.) Dec. 30, 1907; House 1939-43; Nov. 6, 1951-65.

OSTERTAG, Harold Charles (R N.Y.) June 22, 1896-—; House 1951-65.

O'SULLIVAN, Eugene Daniel (D Neb.) May 31, 1883-Feb. 7, 1968; House 1949-51.

O'SULLIVAN, Patrick Brett (D Conn.) Aug. 11, 1887-—; House 1923-25.

OTERO, Mariano Sabino (nephew of Miguel Antonio Otero) (R N.M.) Aug. 29, 1844-Feb. 1, 1904; House (Terr. Del.) 1879-81.

OTERO, Miguel Antonio (uncle of Mariano Sabino Otero) (D N.M.) June 21, 1829-May 30, 1882; House (Terr. Del.) July 23, 1856-61.

OTEY, Peter Johnston (D Va.) Dec.22, 1840-May 4, 1902; House 1895-May 4, 1902.

OTIS, Harrison Gray (F Mass.) Oct. 8, 1765-Oct. 28, 1848; House 1797-1801; Senate 1817-May 30, 1822.

OTIS, John (W Maine) Aug. 3, 1801-Oct. 17, 1856; House 1849-51.

OTIS, John Grant (PP Kan.) Feb. 10, 1838-Feb. 22, 1916; House 1891-93.

OTIS, Norton Prentiss (R N.Y.) March 18, 1840-Feb. 20, 1905; House 1903-Feb. 20, 1905.

OTJEN, Theobald (R Wis.) Oct. 27, 1851-April 11, 1924; House 1895-1907.

O'TOOLE, Donald Lawrence (D N.Y.) Aug. 1, 1902-Sept. 13, 1964; House 1937-53.

OTTINGER, Richard Lawrence (D N.Y.) Jan. 27, 1929; House 1965-71.

OURY, Granville Henderson (D Ariz.) March 12, 1825-Jan. 11, 1891; House (Terr. Del.) 1881-85.

OUTHWAITE, Joseph Hodson (D Ohio) Dec. 5, 1841-Dec. 9, 1907; House 1885-95.

OUTLAND, George Elmer (D Calif.) Oct. 8, 1906; House 1943-47.

OUTLAW, David (cousin of George Outlaw) (W N.C.) Sept. 14, 1806-Oct. 22, 1868; House 1847-53.

OUTLAW, George (cousin of David Outlaw) (JD N.C.) —-Aug. 15, 1825; House Jan. 19-March 3, 1825.

OVERMAN, Lee Slater (D N.C.) Jan. 3, 1854-Dec. 12, 1930; Senate 1903-Dec. 12, 1930.

OVERMYER, Arthur Warren (D Ohio) May 31, 1879-March 8, 1952; House 1915-19.

OVERSTREET, James (— S.C.) Feb. 11, 1773-May 24, 1822; House 1819-May 24, 1822.

OVERSTREET, James Whetstone (D Ga.) Aug. 28, 1866-Dec. 4, 1938; House Oct. 3, 1906-07, 1917-23.

OVERSTREET, Jesse (R Ind.) Dec. 14, 1859-May 27, 1910; House 1895-1909.

OVERTON, Edward, Jr. (R Pa.) Feb. 4, 1836-Sept. 18, 1903; House 1877-81.

OVERTON, John Holmes (uncle of Overton Brooks) (D La.) Sept. 17, 1875-May 14, 1948; House May 12, 1931-33; Senate 1933-May 14, 1948.

OVERTON, Walter Hampden (D La.) 1788-Dec. 24, 1845; House 1829-31.

OWEN, Allen Ferdinand (W Ga.) Oct. 9, 1816-April 7, 1865; House 1849-51.

OWEN, Emmett Marshall (D Ga.) Oct. 19, 1877-June 21, 1939; House 1933-June 21, 1939.

OWEN, George Washington (— Ala.) Oct. 20, 1796-Aug. 18, 1837; House 1823-29.

OWEN, James (D N.C.) Dec. 7, 1784-Sept. 4, 1865; House 1817-19.

OWEN, Robert Dale (D Ind.) Nov. 9, 1800-June 24, 1877; House 1843-47.

OWEN, Robert Latham (D Okla.) Feb. 3, 1856-July 19, 1947; Senate Dec. 11, 1907-25.

OWEN, Ruth Bryan (later Mrs. Borge Rohde; daughter of William Jennings Bryan) (D Fla.) Oct. 2, 1885-July 26, 1954; House 1929-33.

OWEN, William Dale (R Ind.) Sept. 6, 1846-1906; House 1885-91.

OWENS, George Welshman (U Ga.) Aug. 29, 1786-March 2, 1856; House 1835-39.

OWENS, James W. (D Ohio) Oct. 24, 1837-March 30, 1900; House 1889-93.

OWENS, Thomas Leonard (R Ill.) Dec. 21, 1897-June 7, 1948; House 1947-June 7, 1948.

OWENS, William Claiborne (D Ky.) Oct. 17, 1849-Nov. 18, 1925; House 1895-97.

OWSLEY, Bryan Young (W Ky.) Aug. 19, 1798-Oct. 27, 1849; House 1841-43.

P

PACE, Stephen (D Ga.) March 9, 1891-April 5, 1970; House 1937-51.

PACHECO, Romualdo (R Calif.) Oct. 31, 1831-Jan. 23, 1899; House 1877-Feb. 7, 1878; 1879-83; Gov. 1875.

PACKARD, Jasper (R Ind.) Feb. 1, 1832-Dec. 13, 1899; House 1869-75.

PACKER, Asa (D Pa.) Dec. 29, 1805-May 17, 1879; House 1853-57.

PACKER, Horace Billings (R Pa.) Oct. 11, 1851-April 13, 1940; House 1897-1901.

PACKER, John Black (R Pa.) March 21, 1824-July 7, 1891; House 1869-77.

PACKWOOD, Robert William (R Ore.) Sept. 11, 1932; Senate 1969- .

PADDOCK, Algernon Sidney (R Neb.) Nov. 9, 1830-Oct. 17, 1897; Senate 1875-81, 1887-93.

PADDOCK, George Arthur (R Ill.) March 24, 1885-Dec. 29, 1964; House 1941-43.

PADGETT, Lemuel Phillips (D Tenn.) Nov. 28, 1855-Aug. 2, 1922; House 1901-Aug. 2, 1922.

PAGAN, Bolivar (Coal. P.R.) May 16, 1897-Feb. 9, 1961; House (Res. Comm.) Dec. 26, 1939-45.

PAGE, Carroll Smalley (R Vt.) Jan. 10, 1843-Dec. 3, 1925; Senate Oct. 21, 1908-23; Gov. 1890-92.

PAGE, Charles Harrison (D R.I.) July 19, 1843-July 21, 1912; House Feb. 21-March 3, 1887, 1891-93, April 5, 1893-95.

PAGE, Henry (D Md.) June 28, 1841-Jan. 7, 1913; House 1891-Sept. 3, 1892.

PAGE, Horace Francis (R Calif.) Oct. 20, 1833-Aug. 23, 1890; House 1873-83.

PAGE, John (D Va.) April 17, 1744-Oct. 11, 1808; House 1789-97; Gov. 1802-05.

PAGE, John (D N.H.) May 21, 1787-Sept. 8, 1865; Senate June 8, 1836-37; Gov. 1840-42.

PAGE, Robert (F Va.) Feb. 4, 1765-Dec. 8, 1840; House 1799-1801.

PAGE, Robert Newton (D N.C.) Oct. 26, 1859-Oct. 3, 1933; House 1903-17.

PAGE, Sherman (JD N.Y.) May 9, 1779-Sept. 27, 1853; House 1833-37.

PAIGE, Calvin DeWitt (R Mass.) May 20, 1848-April 24, 1930; House Nov. 26, 1913-25.

PAIGE, David Raymond (D Ohio) April 8, 1844-June 30, 1901; House 1883-85.

PAINE, Elijah (F Vt.) Jan. 21, 1757-April 28, 1842; Senate 1795-Sept. 1, 1801.

PAINE, Halbert Eleazer (R Wis.) Feb. 4, 1826-April 14, 1905; House 1865-71.

PAINE, Robert Treat (AP N.C.) Feb. 18, 1812-Feb. 8, 1872; House 1855-57.

PAINE, William Wiseham (D Ga.) Oct. 10, 1817-Aug. 5, 1882; House Dec. 22, 1870-71.

PALEN, Rufus (W N.Y.) Feb. 25, 1807-April 26, 1844; House 1839-41.

PALFREY, John Gorham (W Mass.) May 2, 1796-April 26, 1881; House 1847-49.

PALMER, Alexander Mitchell (D Pa.) May 4, 1872-May 11, 1936; House 1909-15; Atty. Gen. 1919-21.

PALMER, Beriah (— N.Y.) 1740-May 20, 1812; House 1803-05.

PALMER, Cyrus Maffet (R Pa.) Feb. 12, 1887-Aug. 16, 1959; House 1927-29.

PALMER, Francis Wayland (Frank) (R Iowa) Oct. 11, 1827-Dec. 3, 1907; House 1869-73.

PALMER, George William (nephew of John Palmer and cousin of William Elisha Haynes) (R N.Y.) Jan. 13, 1818-March 2, 1916; House 1857-61.

PALMER, Henry Wilber (R Pa.) July 10, 1839-Feb. 15, 1913; House 1901-07, 1909-11.

PALMER, John (uncle of George William Palmer) (D N.Y.) Jan. 29, 1785-Dec. 8, 1840; House 1817-19, 1837-39.

PALMER, John McAuley (D Ill.) Sept. 13, 1817-Sept. 25, 1900; Senate 1891-97; Gov (R) 1869-73.

PALMER, John William (R Mo.) Aug. 20, 1866-Nov. 3, 1958; House 1929-31.

PALMER, Thomas Witherell (R Mich.) Jan. 25, 1830-June 1, 1913; Senate 1883-89.

PALMER, William Adams (D Vt.) Sept. 12, 1781-Dec. 3, 1860; Senate Oct. 20, 1818-25; Gov. 1831-35.

PALMISANO, Vincent Luke (D Md.) Aug. 5, 1882-Jan. 12, 1953; House 1927-39.

PANTIN, Santiago Iglesias (see IGLESIAS, Santiago).

PAREDES, Quintin (Nat. P.I.) Sept. 9, 1884-—; House (Res. Comm.) Feb. 14, 1936-Sept. 29, 1938.

PARK, Frank (D Ga.) March 3, 1864-Nov. 20, 1925; House Nov. 5, 1913-25.

PARKE, Benjamin (D Ind.) Sept. 22, 1777-July 12, 1835; House (Terr. Del.) Dec. 12, 1805-March 1, 1808.

PARKER, Abraham X. (R N.Y.) Nov. 14, 1831-Aug. 9, 1909; House 1881-89.

PARKER, Amasa Junius (D N.Y.) June 2, 1807-May 13, 1890; House 1837-39.

PARKER, Andrew (D Pa.) May 21, 1805-Jan. 15, 1864; House 1851-53.

PARKER, Homer Cling (D Ga.) Sept. 25, 1885-June 22, 1946; House Sept. 10, 1931-35.

PARKER, Hosea Washington (D N.H.) May 30, 1833-Aug. 21, 1922; House 1871-75.

PARKER, Isaac (— Mass.) June 17, 1768-July 26, 1830; House 1797-99.

PARKER, Isaac Charles (R Mo.) Oct. 15, 1838-Nov. 17, 1896; House 1871-75.

PARKER, James (D Mass.) 1768-Nov. 9, 1837; House 1813-15, 1819-21.

PARKER, James (grandfather of Richard Wayne Parker) (D N.J.) March 3, 1776-April 1, 1868; House 1833-37.

PARKER, James Southworth (R N.Y.) June 3, 1867-Dec. 19, 1933; House 1913-Dec. 19, 1933.

PARKER, John Mason (W N.Y.) June 14, 1805-Dec. 16, 1873; House 1855-59.

PARKER, Josiah (— Va.) May 11, 1751-March 18, 1810; House 1789-1801.

PARKER, Nahum (— N.H.) March 4, 1760-Nov. 12, 1839; Senate 1807-June 1, 1810.

PARKER, Richard (D Va.) Dec. 22, 1810-Nov. 10, 1893; House 1849-51.

PARKER, Richard Elliott (D Va.) Dec. 27, 1783-Sept. 6, 1840; Senate Dec. 12, 1836-March 13, 1837.

PARKER, Richard Wayne (grandson of James Parker) (R N.J.) Aug. 6, 1848-Nov. 28, 1923; House 1895-1911, Dec. 1, 1914-19, 1921-23.

PARKER, Samuel Wilson (W Ind.) Sept. 9, 1805-Feb. 1, 1859; House 1851-55.

PARKER, Severn Eyre (— Va.) July 19, 1787-Oct. 21, 1836; House 1819-21.

PARKER, William Henry (— S.D.) May 5, 1847-June 26, 1908; House 1907-June 26, 1908.

PARKS, Gorham (D Maine) May 27, 1794-Nov. 23, 1877; House 1833-37.

PARKS, Tilman Bacon (D Ark.) May 14, 1872-Feb. 12, 1950; House 1921-37.

PARMENTER, William (D Mass.) March 30, 1789-Feb. 25, 1866; House 1837-45.

PARRAN, Thomas (R Md.) Feb. 12, 1860-March 29, 1955; House 1911-13.

PARRETT, William Fletcher (D Ind.) Aug. 10, 1825-June 30, 1895; House 1889-93.

PARRIS, Albion Keith (cousin of Virgil Delphini Parris) (D Mass./Maine) Jan. 19, 1788-Feb. 22, 1857; House (Mass.) 1815-Feb. 3, 1818; Senate (Maine) 1827-Aug. 26, 1828; Gov. (Maine) 1822-27.

PARRIS, Virgil Delphini (cousin of Albion Keith Parris) (SRD Maine) Feb. 18, 1807-June 13, 1874; House May 29, 1838-41.

PARRISH, Isaac (D Ohio) March 1804-Aug. 9, 1860; House 1839-41; 1845-47.

PARRISH, Lucian Walton (D Texas) Jan. 10, 1878-March 27, 1922; House 1919-March 27, 1922.

PARROTT, John Fabyan (D N.H.) Aug. 8, 1767-July 9, 1836; House 1817-19; Senate 1819-25.

PARROTT, Marcus Junius (R Kan.) Oct. 27, 1828-Oct. 4, 1879; House (Terr. Del.) 1857-Jan. 29, 1861.

PARSONS, Glaude VanCleve (D Ill.) Oct. 7, 1895-May 23, 1941; House Nov. 4, 1930-41.

PARSONS, Edward Young (D Ky.) Dec. 12, 1842-July 8, 1876; House 1875-July 8, 1876.

PARSONS, Herbert (R N.Y.) Oct. 28, 1869-Sept. 16, 1925; House 1905-11.

PARSONS, Richard Chappel (R Ohio) Oct. 10, 1826-Jan. 9, 1899; House 1873-75.

PARTRIDGE, Donald Barrows (R Maine) June 7, 1891-June 5, 1946; House 1931-33.

PARTRIDGE, Frank Charles (R Vt.) May 7, 1861-March 2, 1943; Senate Dec. 23, 1930-March 31, 1931.

PARTRIDGE, George (— Mass.) Feb. 8, 1740-July 7, 1828; House 1789-Aug. 14, 1790; Cont. Cong. 1779-82; 1783-85.

PARTRIDGE, Samuel (D N.Y.) Nov. 29, 1790-March 30, 1883; House 1841-43.

PASCHAL, Thomas Moore (D Texas) Dec. 15, 1845-Jan. 28, 1919; House 1893-95.

PASCO, Samuel (D Fla.) June 28, 1834-March 13, 1917; Senate May 19, 1887-April 19, 1899.

PASSMAN, Otto Ernest (D La.) June 27, 1900; House 1947- .

PASTORE, John Orlando (D R.I.) March 17, 1907; Senate Dec. 19, 1950- ; Gov. 1945-50.

PATERSON, John (— N.Y.) 1744-July 19, 1808; House 1803-05.

PATERSON, William (F N.J.) Dec. 24, 1745-Sept. 9, 1806; Senate 1789-Nov. 13, 1790; Cont. Cong. 1780-81; 1787; Gov. 1790-93; Asso. Justice of Supreme Court 1793-1806.

PATMAN, Wright (D Texas) Aug. 6, 1893- ; House 1929- .

PATRICK, Luther (D Ala.) Jan. 23, 1894-May 26, 1957; House 1937-43; 1945-47.

PATTEN, Edward James (D N.J.) Aug. 22, 1905; House 1963- .

PATTEN, Harold Ambrose (D Ariz.) Oct. 6, 1907-Sept. 6, 1969; House 1949-55.

PATTEN, John (— Del.) April 26, 1746-Dec. 26, 1800; House 1793-Feb. 14, 1794; 1795-97; Cont. Cong. 1785-86.

PATTEN, Thomas Gedney (D N.Y.) Sept. 12, 1861-Feb. 23, 1939; House 1911-17.

PATTERSON, David Trotter (D Tenn.) Feb. 28, 1818-Nov. 3, 1891; Senate July 24, 1866-69.

PATTERSON, Edward White (D Kan.) Oct. 4, 1895-March 6, 1940; House 1935-39.

PATTERSON, Ellis Ellwood (D Calif.) Nov. 28, 1897- ; House 1945-47.

PATTERSON, Francis Ford, Jr. (R N.J.) July 30, 1867-Nov. 30, 1935; House Nov. 2, 1920-27.

PATTERSON, George Robert (R Pa.) Nov. 9, 1863-March 21, 1906; House 1901-March 21, 1906.

PATTERSON, George Washington (brother of William Patterson) (R N.Y.) Nov. 11, 1799-Oct. 15, 1879; House 1877-79.

PATTERSON, Gilbert Brown (D N.C.) May 29, 1863-Jan. 26, 1922; House 1903-07.

PATTERSON, James O'Hanlon (D S.C.) June 25, 1857-Oct. 25, 1911; House 1905-11.

PATTERSON, James Thomas (R Conn.) Oct. 20, 1908; House 1947-59.

PATTERSON, James Willis (R N.H.) July 2, 1823-May 4, 1893; House 1863-67; Senate 1867-73.

PATTERSON, John (half brother of Thomas Patterson) (D Ohio) Feb. 10, 1771-Feb. 7, 1848; House 1823-25.

PATTERSON, John James (R S.C.) Aug. 8, 1830-Sept. 28, 1912; Senate 1873-79.

PATTERSON, Josiah (father of Malcolm Rice Patterson) (D Tenn.) April 14, 1837-Feb. 10, 1904; House 1891-97.

PATTERSON, Lafayette Lee (D Ala.) Aug. 23, 1888- ; House Nov. 6, 1828-33.

PATTERSON, Malcolm Rice (son of Josiah Patterson) (D Tenn.) June 7, 1861-March 8, 1935; House 1901-Nov. 5, 1906; Gov. 1906-10.

PATTERSON, Roscoe Conkling (R Mo.) Sept. 15, 1876-Oct. 22, 1954; House 1921-23; Senate 1929-35.

PATTERSON, Thomas (half brother of John Patterson) (D Pa.) Oct. 1, 1764-Nov. 16, 1841; House 1817-25.

PATTERSON, Thomas J. (W N.Y.) about 1808- ; House 1843-45.

PATTERSON, Thomas MacDonald (D Colo.) Nov. 4, 1839-July 23, 1916; House (Terr. Del.) 1875-Aug. 1, 1876; (Rep.) Dec. 13, 1877-79; Senate 1901-07.

PATTERSON, Walter (— N.Y.) —-— ; House 1821-23.

PATTERSON, William (brother of George Washington Patterson and uncle of Augustus Frank) (W N.Y.) June 4, 1789-Aug. 14, 1838; House 1837-Aug. 14, 1838.

PATTERSON, William (D Ohio) 1790-Aug. 17, 1868; House 1833-37.

PATTISON, John M. (D Ohio) June 13, 1847-June 18, 1906; House 1891-93; Gov. 1906.

PATTON, Charles Emory (son of John Patton and brother of John Patton, Jr.) (— Pa.) July 5, 1859-Dec. 15, 1937; House 1911-15.

PATTON, David Henry (D Ind.) Nov. 26, 1837-Jan. 17, 1914; House 1891-93.

PATTON, John (father of Charles Emory Patton and John Patton, Jr. and uncle of William Irvin Swoope) (R Pa.) Jan. 6, 1823-Dec. 23, 1897; House 1861-63; 1887-89.

PATTON, John, Jr. (son of the preceding and brother of Charles Emory Patton) (R Mich.) Oct. 30, 1850-May 24, 1907; Senate May 5, 1894-Jan. 14, 1895.

PATTON, John Denniston (D Pa.) Nov. 28, 1829-Feb. 22, 1904; House 1883-85.

PATTON, John Mercer (D Va.) Aug. 10, 1797-Oct. 29, 1858; House Nov. 25, 1830-April 7, 1838.

PATTON, Nat (D Texas) Feb. 26, 1884-July 27, 1957; House 1935-45.

PAUL, John (Read. Va.) June 30, 1839-Nov. 1, 1901; House 1881-Sept. 5, 1883.

PAUL, John (son of the preceding) (R Va.) Dec. 9, 1883—Feb. 13, 1964; House Dec. 15, 1922-23.

PAULDING, William, Jr. (D N.Y.) March 7, 1770-Feb. 11, 1854; House 1811-13.

PAWLING, Levi (D Pa.) July 25, 1773-Sept. 7, 1845; House 1817-19.

PAYNE, Frederick George (R Maine) July 24, 1900; Senate 1953-59; Gov. 1949-53.

PAYNE, Henry B. (grandfather of Frances P. Bolton) (D Ohio) Nov. 30, 1810-Sept. 9, 1896; House 1875-77; Senate 1885-91.

PAYNE, Sereno Elisha (R N.Y.) June 26, 1843-Dec. 10, 1914; House 1883-87; 1889-Dec. 10, 1914.

PAYNE, William Winter (D Ala.) Jan. 2, 1807-Sept. 2, 1874; House 1841-47.

PAYNTER, Lemuel (D Pa.) 1788-Aug. 1, 1863; House 1837-41.

PAYNTER, Thomas Hanson (D Ky.) Dec. 9, 1851-March 8, 1921; House 1889-Jan. 5, 1895; Senate 1907-13.

PAYSON, Lewis Edwin (R Ill.) Sept. 17, 1840-Oct. 4, 1909; House 1881-91.

PEACE, Roger Craft (D S.C.) May 19, 1899-Aug. 20, 1968; Senate Aug. 5-Nov. 4, 1941.

PEARCE, Charles Edward (R Mo.) May 29, 1842-Jan. 30, 1902; House 1897-1901.

PEARCE, Dutee Jerauld (D R.I.) April 3, 1789-May 9, 1849; House 1825-37.

PEARCE, James Alfred (D Md.) Dec. 8, 1804-Dec. 20, 1862; House 1835-39; 1841-43 (W); Senate 1843-62 (W); March 4-Dec. 20, 1862 (D).

PEARCE, John Jamison (W Pa.) Feb. 28, 1826-May 26, 1912; House 1855-57.

PEARRE, George Alexander (R Md.) July 16, 1860-Sept. 19, 1923; House 1899-1911.

PEARSON, Albert Jackson (D Ohio) May 20, 1846-May 15, 1905; House 1891-95.

PEARSON, Herron Carney (D Tenn.) July 31, 1890-April 24, 1953; House 1935-43.

PEARSON, James Blackwood (R Kan.) May 7, 1920; Senate Jan. 31, 1962- .

PEARSON, John James (W Pa.) Oct. 25, 1800-May 30, 1888; House Dec. 5, 1836-37.

PEARSON, Joseph (F N.C.) 1776-Oct. 27, 1834; House 1809-15.

PEARSON, Richmond (R N.C.) Jan. 26, 1852-Sept. 12, 1923; House 1895-99; May 10, 1900-01.

PEASE, Henry Roberts (R Miss.) Feb. 19, 1835-Jan. 2, 1907; Senate Feb. 3, 1874-75.

PEASLEE, Charles Hazen (D N.H.) Feb. 6, 1804-Sept. 18, 1866; House 1847-53.

PEAVEY, Hubert Haskell (R Wis.) Jan. 12, 1881-Nov. 21, 1937; House 1923-35.

PECK, Erasmus Darwin (R Ohio) Sept. 16, 1808-Dec. 25, 1876; House April 23, 1870-73.

PECK, George Washington (D Mich.) June 4, 1818-June 30, 1905; House 1855-57.

PECK, Jared Valentine (D N.Y.) Sept. 21, 1816-Dec. 25, 1891; House 1853-55.

PECK, Lucius Benedict (D Vt.) Nov. 17, 1802-Dec. 28, 1866; House 1847-51.

PECK, Luther Christopher (W N.Y.) Jan. 1800-Feb. 5, 1876; House 1837-41.

PECKHAM, Rufus Wheeler (D N.Y.) Dec. 20, 1809-Nov. 22, 1873; House 1853-55.

PEDDIE, Thomas Baldwin (R N.J.) Feb. 11, 1808-Feb. 16, 1889; House 1877-79.

PEDEN, Preston Elmer (D Okla.) June 28, 1914; House 1947-49.

PEEK, Harmanus (— N.Y.) June 24, 1782-Sept. 27, 1838; House 1819-21.

PEEL, Samuel West (D Ark.) Sept. 13, 1831-Dec. 18, 1924; House 1883-93.

PEELLE, Stanton Judkins (R Ind.) Feb. 11, 1843-Sept. 4, 1928; House 1881-May 22, 1884.

PEERY, George Campbell (D Va.) Oct. 28, 1873-Oct. 14, 1952; House 1923-29; Gov. 1934-38.

PEFFER, William Alfred (P Kan.) Sept. 10, 1831-Oct. 7, 1912; Senate 1891-97.

PEGRAM, John (— Va.) Nov. 16, 1773-April 8, 1831; House April 21, 1818-19.

PEIRCE, Joseph (— N.H.) June 25, 1748-Sept. 12, 1812; House 1801-02.

PEIRCE, Robert Bruce Fraser (R Ind.) Feb. 17, 1843-Dec. 5, 1898; House 1881-83.

PELHAM, Charles (R Ala.) March 12, 1835-Jan. 18, 1908; House 1873-75.

PELL, Claiborne de Borda (son of Herbert Claiborne Pell, Jr.) (D R.I.) Nov. 22, 1918; Senate 1961- .

PELL, Herbert Claiborne, Jr. (great-grandson of John Francis Hamtramck Claiborne, great-great-grandnephew of William Charles Cole Claiborne and Nathaniel Herbert Claiborne and father of Claiborne de Borda Pell) (D N.Y.) Feb. 16, 1884-July 17, 1961; House 1919-21.

PELLY, Thomas Minor (R Wash.) Aug. 22, 1902; House 1953- .

PELTON, Guy Ray (W N.Y.) Aug. 3, 1824-July 24, 1890; House 1855-57.

PENCE, Lafayette (P/Sil.D Colo.) Dec. 23, 1857-Oct. 22, 1923; House 1893-95.

PENDLETON, Edmund Henry (W N.Y.) 1788-Feb. 25, 1862; House 1831-33.

PENDLETON, George Cassety (D Texas) April 23, 1845-Jan. 19, 1913; House 1893-97.

PENDLETON, George Hunt (son of Nathaniel Greene Pendleton) (D Ohio) July 19, 1825-Nov. 24, 1889; House 1857-65; Senate 1879-85.

PENDLETON, James Monroe (R R.I.) Jan. 10, 1822-Feb. 16, 1889; House 1871-75.

PENDLETON, John Overton (D W.Va.) July 4, 1851-Dec. 24, 1916; House 1889-Feb. 26, 1890; 1891-95.

PENDLETON, John Strother (W Va.) March 1, 1802-Nov. 19, 1868; House 1845-49.

PENDLETON, Nathanael Greene (father of George Hunt Pendleton) (W Ohio) Aug. 25, 1793-June 16, 1861; House 1841-43.

PENINGTON, John Brown (D Del.) Dec. 20, 1825-June 1, 1902; House 1887-91.

PENN, Alexander Gordon (D La.) May 10, 1799-May 7, 1866; House Dec. 30, 1850-53.

PENNIMAN, Ebenezer Jenckes (W/F-S Mich.) Jan. 11, 1804-April 12, 1890; House 1851-53.

PENNINGTON, Alexander Cumming McWhorter (cousin of William Pennington) (W N.J.) July 2, 1810-Jan. 25, 1867; House 1853-57.

PENNINGTON, William (cousin of Alexander Cumming McWhorter Pennington) (W N.J.) May 4, 1796-Feb. 16, 1862; House 1859-61; Speaker 1859-61; Gov. 1837-43.

PENNYBACKER, Isaac Samuels (cousin of Green Berry Samuels) (D Va.) Sept. 3, 1805-Jan. 12, 1847; House 1837-39; Senate Dec. 3, 1845-Jan. 12, 1847.

PENROSE, Boies (R Pa.) Nov. 1, 1860-Dec. 31, 1921; Senate 1897-Dec. 31, 1921.

PEPPER, Claude Denson (D Fla.) Sept. 8, 1900; Senate Nov. 4, 1936-51; House 1963- .

PEPPER, George Wharton (R Pa.) March 16, 1867-May 24, 1961; Senate Jan. 9, 1922-27.

PEPPER, Irvin St. Clair (D Iowa) June 10, 1876-Dec. 22, 1913; House 1911-Dec. 22, 1913.

PERCE, Legrand Winfield (R Miss.) June 19, 1836-March 16, 1911; House Feb. 23, 1870-73.

PERCY, Charles Harting (R Ill.) Sept. 27, 1919; Senate 1967- .

PERCY, Le Roy (D Miss.) Nov. 9, 1860-Dec. 24, 1929; Senate Feb. 23, 1910-13.

PEREA, Francisco (cousin of Pedro Perea) (R N.M.) Jan. 9, 1830-May 21, 1913; House (Terr. Del.) 1863-65.

PEREA, Pedro (cousin of Francisco Perea) (R N.M.) April 22, 1852-Jan. 11, 1906; House (Terr. Del.) 1899-1901.

PERHAM, Sidney (R Maine) March 27, 1819-April 10, 1907; House 1863-69; Gov. 1871-74.

PERKINS, Bishop (D N.Y.) Sept. 5, 1787-Nov. 20, 1866; House 1853-55.

PERKINS, Bishop Walden (R Kan.) Oct. 18, 1841-June 20, 1894; House 1883-91; Senate Jan. 1, 1892-93.

PERKINS, Carl Dewey (D Ky.) Oct. 15, 1912; House 1949- .

PERKINS, Elias (F Conn.) April 5, 1767-Sept. 27, 1845; House 1801-03.

PERKINS, George Clement (R Calif.) Aug. 23, 1839-Feb. 26, 1923; Senate July 26, 1893-1915; Gov. 1879-83.

PERKINS, George Douglas (R Iowa) Feb. 29, 1840-Feb. 3, 1914; House 1891-99.

PERKINS, James Breck (R N.Y.) Nov. 4, 1847-March 11, 1910; House 1901-March 11, 1910.

PERKINS, Jared (W N.H.) Jan. 5, 1793-Oct. 15, 1854; House 1851-53.

PERKINS, John, Jr. (D La.) July 1, 1819-Nov. 28, 1885; House 1853-55.

PERKINS, Randolph (R N.J.) Nov. 30, 1871-May 25, 1936; House 1921-May 25, 1936.

PERKY, Kirtland Irving (D Idaho) Feb. 8, 1867-Jan. 9, 1939; Senate Nov. 18, 1912-Feb. 5, 1913.

PERLMAN, Nathan David (R N.Y.) Aug. 2, 1887-June 29, 1952; House Nov. 2, 1920-27.

PERRILL, Augustus Leonard (D Ohio) Jan. 20, 1807-June 2, 1882; House 1845-47.

PERRY, Aaron Fyfe (R Ohio) Jan. 1, 1815-March 11, 1893; House 1871-72.

PERRY, Eli (D N.Y.) Dec. 25, 1799-May 17, 1881; House 1871-75.

PERRY, John Jasiel (R Maine) Aug. 2, 1811-May 2, 1897; House 1855-57; 1859-61.

PERRY, Nehemiah (Const.U N.J.) March 30, 1816-Nov. 1, 1881; House 1861-65.

PERRY, Thomas Johns (D Md.) Feb. 17, 1807-June 27, 1871; House 1845-47.

PERRY, William Hayne (D S.C.) June 9, 1839-July 7, 1902; House 1885-91.

PERSON, Seymour Howe (R Mich.) Feb. 2, 1879-April 7, 1957; House 1931-33.

PERSONS, Henry (D Ga.) Jan. 30, 1834-June 17, 1910; House 1879-81.

PESQUERA, Jose Lorenzo (Nonpart. P.R.) Aug. 10, 1882-July 25, 1950; House (Res. Comm.) April 15, 1932-33.

PETER, George (D Md.) Sept. 28, 1779-June 22, 1861; House Oct. 7, 1816-19; 1825-27.

PETERS, Andrew James (D Mass.) April 3, 1872-June 26, 1938; House 1907-Aug. 15, 1914.

PETERS, John Andrew (R Maine) Oct. 9, 1822-April 2, 1904; House 1867-73.

PETERS, John Andrew (nephew of the preceding) (R Maine) Aug. 13, 1864-Aug. 22, 1953; House Sept. 8, 1913-Jan. 2, 1922.

PETERS, Mason Summers (D/P Kan.) Sept. 3, 1844-Feb. 14, 1914; House 1897-99.

PETERS, Samuel Ritter (R Kan.) Aug. 16, 1842-April 21, 1910; House 1883-91.

PETERSEN, Andrew Nicholas (R N.Y.) March 10, 1870-Sept. 28, 1952; House 1921-23.

PETERSON, Hugh (D Ga.) Aug. 21, 1898-Oct. 3, 1961; House 1935-47.

PETERSON, James Hardin (D Fla.) Feb. 11, 1894-——; House 1933-51.

PETERSON, John Barney (cousin of Horation Clifford Claypool and Harold Kile Claypool) (D Ind.) July 4, 1850-July 16, 1944; House 1913-15.

PETERSON, Morris Blaine (D Utah) March 26, 1906; House 1961-63.

PETRIE, George (R N.Y.) Sept. 8, 1793-May 8, 1879; House 1847-49.

PETRIKIN, David (D Pa.) Dec. 1, 1788-March 1, 1847; House 1837-41.

PETTENGILL, Samuel Barrett (nephew of William Horace Clagett) (D Ind.) Jan. 19, 1886-——; House 1931-39.

PETTIBONE, Augustus Herman (R Tenn.) Jan. 21, 1835-Nov. 26, 1918; House 1881-87.

PETTIGREW, Ebenezer (W N.C.) March 10, 1783-July 8, 1848; House 1835-37.

PETTIGREW, Richard Franklin (R S.D.) July 23, 1848-Oct. 5, 1926; House (Terr. Del.) 1881-83; Senate Nov. 2, 1889-1901.

PETTIS, Jerry L. (R Calif.) July 18, 1916; House 1967- .

PETTIS, Solomon Newton (R Pa.) Oct. 10, 1827-Sept. 18, 1900; House Dec. 7, 1868-69.

PETTIS, Spencer Darwin (D Mo.) 1802-Aug. 28, 1831; House 1829-Aug. 28, 1831.

PETTIT, John (D Ind.) June 24, 1807-Jan. 17, 1877; House 1843-49; Senate Jan. 11, 1853-55.

PETTIT, John Upfold (R Ind.) Sept. 11, 1820-March 21, 1811; House 1855-61.

PETTUS, Edmund Winston (D Ala.) July 6, 1821-July 27, 1907; Senate 1897-July 27, 1907.

PEYSER, Peter A. (R N.Y.) Sept. 7, 1921; House 1971- .

PEYSER, Theodore Albert (D N.Y.) Feb. 18, 1873-Aug. 8, 1937; House 1933-Aug. 8, 1937.

PEYTON, Balie (brother of Joseph Hopkins Peyton) (W Tenn.) Nov. 26, 1803-Aug. 18, 1878; House 1833-37.

PEYTON, Joseph Hopkins (brother of Balie Peyton) (W Tenn.) May 20, 1808-Nov. 11, 1845; House 1843-Nov. 11, 1845.

PEYTON, Samuel Oldham (D Ky.) Jan. 8, 1804-Jan. 4, 1870; House 1847-49; 1857-61.

PFEIFER, Joseph Lawrence (D N.Y.) Feb. 6, 1892-——; House 1935-51.

PFEIFFER, William Louis (R N.Y.) May 29, 1907; House 1949-51.

PFOST, Gracie Bowers (D Idaho) March 12, 1906-Aug. 11, 1965; House 1953-63.

PHEIFFER, William Townsend (R N.Y.) July 15, 1898-—— House 1941-43.

PHELAN, James (D Tenn.) Dec. 7, 1856-Jan. 30, 1891; House 1887-Jan. 30, 1891.

PHELAN, James Duval (D Calif.) April 20, 1861-——; Senate 1915-21.

PHELAN, Michael Francis (D Mass.) Oct. 22, 1875-Oct. 12, 1941; House 1913-21.

PHELPS, Charles Edward (UC Md.) May 1, 1833-Dec. 27, 1908; House 1865-67 (U War); 1867-69 (UC).

PHELPS, Darwin (R Pa.) April 17, 1807-Dec. 14, 1879; House 1869-71.

PHELPS, Elisha (father of John Smith Phelps) (D Conn.) Nov. 16, 1779-April 6, 1847; House 1819-21; 1825-29.

PHELPS, James (son of Lancelot Phelps) (D Conn.) Jan. 12, 1822-Jan. 15, 1900; House 1875-83.

PHELPS, John Smith (son of Elisha Phelps) (D Mo.) Dec. 22, 1814-Nov. 20, 1886; House 1845-63; Gov. 1877-81.

PHELPS, Lancelot (father of James Phelps) (D Conn.- Nov. 9, 1784-Sept. 1, 1866; House 1835-39.

PHELPS, Oliver (D N.Y.) Oct. 21, 1749-Feb. 21, 1809; House 1803-05.

PHELPS, Samuel Shethar (W Vt.) May 13, 1793-March 25, 1855; Senate 1839-51; Jan. 17, 1853-March 16, 1854.

PHELPS, Timothy Guy (R Calif.) Dec. 20, 1824-June 11, 1899; House 1861-63.

PHELPS, William Wallace (D Minn.) June 1, 1826-Aug. 3, 1873; House May 11, 1858-59.

PHELPS, William Walter (R N.J.) Aug. 24, 1839-June 17, 1894; House 1873-75; 1883-89.

PHILBIN, Philip Joseph (D Mass.) May 29, 1898-—; House 1943-71.

PHILIPS, John Finis (D Mo.) Dec. 31, 1834-March 13, 1919; House 1875-77; Jan. 10, 1880-81.

PHILLIPS, Alfred Noroton (D Conn.) April 23, 1894-Jan. 18, 1970; House 1937-39.

PHILLIPS, Dayton Edward (R Tenn.) March 29, 1910; House 1947-51.

PHILLIPS, Fremont Orestes (R Ohio) March 16, 1856-Feb. 21, 1936; House 1899-1901.

PHILLIPS, Henry Myer (D Pa.) June 30, 1811-Aug. 28, 1884; House 1857-59.

PHILLIPS, John (F Pa.) —-—; House 1821-23.

PHILLIPS, John (R Calif.) Sept. 11, 1887-—; House 1943-57.

PHILLIPS, Philip (D Ala.) Dec. 13, 1807-Jan. 14, 1884; House 1853-55.

PHILLIPS, Stephen Clarendon (W Mass.) Nov. 4, 1801-June 26, 1857; House Dec. 1, 1834-Sept. 28, 1838.

PHILLIPS, Thomas Wharton (father of Thomas Wharton Phillips, Jr.) (R Pa.) Feb. 23, 1835-July 21, 1912; House 1893-97.

PHILLIPS, Thomas Wharton, Jr. (son of the preceding) (R Pa.) Nov. 21, 1874-Jan. 2, 1956; House 1923-27.

PHILLIPS, William Addison (R Kan.) Jan. 14, 1824-Nov. 30, 1893; House 1873-79.

PHILSON, Robert (— Pa.) 1759-July 25, 1831; House 1819-21.

PHIPPS, Lawrence Cowle (R Colo.) Aug. 30, 1862-March 1, 1958; Senate 1919-31.

PHISTER, Elijah Conner (D Ky.) Oct. 8, 1822-May 16, 1887; House 1879-83.

PHOENIX, Jonas Phillips (W N.Y.) Jan. 14, 1788-May 4, 1859; House 1843-45; 1849-51.

PICKENS, Andrew (grandfather of Francis Wilkinson Pickens) (D S.C.) Sept. 13, 1739-Aug. 11, 1817; House 1793-95.

PICKENS, Francis Wilkinson (grandson of Andrew Pickens) (ND S.C.) April 7, 1805-Jan. 25, 1869; House Dec. 8, 1834-43; Gov. 1860-62.

PICKENS, Israel (D N.C./Ala.) Jan. 30, 1780-April 24, 1827; House (N.C.) 1811-17; Senate (Ala.) Feb. 17, 1826-Nov. 27, 1826; Gov. (Ala.) 1821-25.

PICKERING, Timothy (F Mass.) July 17, 1745-Jan. 29, 1829; Senate 1803-11; House 1813-17; Postmaster Gen. 1791-95; Secy. of War 1795-96; Secy. of State 1795-1800.

PICKETT, Charles Edgar (R Iowa) Jan. 14, 1866-July 20, 1930; House 1909-13.

PICKETT, Thomas Augustus (Tom) (D Texas) Aug. 14, 1906; House 1945-June 30, 1952.

PICKLE, J. J. (Jake) (D Texas) Oct. 11, 1913; House Dec. 21, 1963— .

PICKLER, John Alfred (R S.D.) Jan. 24, 1844-June 13, 1910; House Nov. 2, 1889-97.

PICKMAN, Benjamin, Jr. (— Mass.) Sept. 30, 1763-Aug. 16, 1843; House 1809-11.

PIDCOCK, James Nelson (cousin of Alvah Augustus Clark) (D N.J.) Feb. 8, 1836-Dec. 17, 1899; House 1885-89.

PIERCE, Charles Wilson (D Ala.) Oct. 7, 1823-Feb. 18, 1907; House July 21, 1868-69.

PIERCE, Franklin (D N.H.) Nov. 23, 1804-Oct. 8, 1869; House 1833-37; Senate 1837-Feb. 28, 1842; President 1853-57.

PIERCE, Gilbert Ashville (R N.D.) Jan. 11, 1839-Feb. 15, 1901; Senate Nov. 21, 1889-91; Gov. (Terr.) 1884-86.

PIERCE, Henry Lillie (R Mass.) Aug. 23, 1825-Dec. 17, 1896; House Dec. 1, 1873-77.

PIERCE, Ray Vaughn (R N.Y.) Aug. 6, 1840-Feb. 4, 1914; House 1879-Sept. 18, 1880.

PIERCE, Rice Alexander (D Tenn.) July 3, 1848-July 12, 1936; House 1883-85; 1889-93; 1897-1905.

PIERCE, Wallace Edgar (R N.Y.) Dec. 9, 1881-Jan. 3, 1940; House 1939-Jan. 3, 1940.

PIERCE, Walter Marcus (D Ore.) May 30, 1861-March 27, 1954; House 1933-43; Gov. 1923-27.

PIERSON, Isaac (W N.J.) Aug. 15, 1770-Sept. 22, 1833; House 1827-31.

PIERSON, Jeremiah Halsey (F N.Y.) Sept. 13, 1766-Dec. 12, 1855; House 1821-23.

PIERSON, Job (D N.Y.) Sept. 23, 1791-April 9, 1860; House 1831-35.

PIGOTT, James Protus (D Conn.) Sept. 11, 1852-July 1, 1919; House 1893-95.

PIKE, Austin Franklin (R N.H.) Oct. 16, 1819-Oct. 8, 1886; House 1873-75; Senate 1883-Oct. 8, 1886.

PIKE, Frederick Augustus (R Maine) Dec. 9, 1816-Dec. 2, 1886; House 1861-69.

PIKE, James (AP N.H.) Nov. 10, 1818-July 26, 1895; House 1855-59.

PIKE, Otis G. (D N.Y.) Aug. 31, 1921; House 1961- .

PILCHER, John Leonard (D Ga.) Aug. 27, 1898-—; House Feb. 4, 1953-65.

PILE, William Anderson (R Mo.) Feb. 11, 1829-July 7, 1889; House 1867-69; Gov. of New Mexico 1869-70.

PILES, Samuel Henry (R Wash.) Dec. 28, 1858-March 11, 1940; Senate 1905-11.

PILLION, John Raymond (R N.Y.) Aug. 10, 1904; House 1953-65.

PILSBURY, Timothy (Cal.D Texas) April 12, 1789-Nov. 23, 1858; House March 30, 1846-49.

PINCKNEY, Charles (father of Henry Laurens Pinckney) (D S.C.) Oct. 26, 1757-Oct. 29, 1824; Senate Dec. 6, 1798-1801; House 1819-21; Cont. Cong. 1777-78; 1784-87; Gov. 1789-92; 1796-98; 1806-08.

PINCKNEY, Henry Laurens (son of Charles Pinckney) (D S.C.) Sept. 24, 1794-Feb. 3, 1863; House 1833-37.

PINCKNEY, John McPherson (D Texas) May 4, 1845-April 24, 1905; House Nov. 17, 1903-April 24, 1905.

PINCKNEY, Thomas (F S.C.) Oct. 23, 1750-Nov. 2, 1828; House Nov. 23, 1797-1801; Gov. 1787-89.

PINDALL, James (F Va.) about 1783-Nov. 22, 1825; House 1817-July 26, 1820.

PINDAR, John Sigsbee (D N.Y.) Nov. 18, 1835-June 30, 1907; House 1885-87; Nov. 4, 1890-91.

PINE, William Bliss (R Okla.) Dec. 30, 1877-Aug. 25, 1942; Senate 1925-31.

PINERO, Jesus T. (PD P.R.) April 16, 1897-Nov. 19, 1952; House (Res.Comm.) 1945-Sept. 2, 1946; Gov. 1946-48.

PINKNEY, William (— Md.) March 17, 1764-Feb. 25, 1822; House March 4-Nov. 1791; 1815-April 18, 1816; Senate Dec. 21, 1819-Feb. 25, 1822; Atty. Gen. 1811-14.

PIPER, William (— Pa.) Jan. 1, 1774-1852; House 1811-17.

PIPER, William Adam (D Calif.) May 21, 1826-Aug. 5, 1899; House 1875-77.

PIRCE, William Almy (R R.I.) Feb. 29, 1824-March 5, 1891; House 1885-Jan. 25, 1887.

PIRNIE, Alexander (R N.Y.) April 16, 1903; House 1959- .

PITCHER, Nathaniel (D N.Y.) 1777-May 25, 1836; House 1819-23, 1831-33.

PITKIN, Timothy (F Conn.) Jan. 21, 1766-Dec. 18, 1847; House Sept. 16, 1805-19.

PITMAN, Charles Wesley (W Pa.) —June 8, 1871; House 1849-51.

PITNEY, Mahlon (R N.J.) Feb. 5, 1858-Dec. 9, 1924; House 1895-Jan. 10, 1899; Assoc. Justice of Supreme Court 1912-22.

PITTENGER, William Alvin (R Minn.) Dec. 29, 1885-Nov. 26, 1951; House 1929-33, 1935-37, 1939-47.

PITTMAN, Key (D Nev.) Sept. 19, 1872-Nov. 10, 1940; Senate Jan. 29, 1913-Nov. 10, 1940; President pro tempore March 9, 1933-Nov. 10, 1940.

PLAISTED, Harris Merrill (R Maine) Nov. 2, 1828-Jan. 31, 1898; House Sept. 13, 1875-77; Gov. 1881-83.

PLANT, David (NR Conn.) March 29, 1783-Oct. 18, 1851; House 1827-29.

PLANTS, Tobias Avery (R Ohio) March 17, 1811-June 19, 1887; House 1865-69.

PLATER, Thomas (—Md.) May 9, 1769-May 1, 1830; House 1801-05.

PLATT, Edmund (R N.Y.) Feb. 2, 1865-Aug. 7, 1939; House 1913-June 7, 1920.

PLATT, James Henry, Jr. (R Va.) July 13, 1837-Aug. 13, 1894; House Jan. 26, 1870-75.

PLATT, Jonas (F N.Y.) June 30, 1769-Feb. 22, 1834; House 1799-1801.

PLATT, Orville Hitchcock (R Conn.) July 19, 1827-April 21, 1905; Senate 1879-April 21, 1905.

PLATT, Thomas Collier (R N.Y.) July 15, 1833-March 6, 1910; House 1873-77; Senate March 4-May 16, 1881; 1897-1909.

PLAUCHE, Vance (D La.) Aug. 25, 1897-—; House 1941-43.

PLEASANTS, James (D Va.) Oct. 24, 1769-Nov. 9, 1836; House 1811-Dec. 14, 1819; Senate Dec. 14, 1819-Dec. 15, 1822; Gov. 1822-25.

PLOESER, Walter Christian (R Mo.) Jan. 7, 1907; House 1941-49.

PLOWMAN, Thomas Scales (D Ala.) June 8, 1843-July 26, 1919; House 1897-Feb. 9, 1898.

PLUMB, Preston B. (R Kan.) Oct. 12, 1837-Dec. 20, 1891; Senate 1877-Dec. 20, 1891.

PLUMB, Ralph (R Ill.) March 29, 1816-April 8, 1903; House 1885-89.

PLUMER, Arnold (D Pa.) June 6, 1801-April 28, 1869; House 1837-39, 1841-43.

PLUMER, George (D Pa.) Dec. 5, 1762-June 8, 1843; House 1821-27.

PLUMER, William (father of William Plumer, Jr.) (F N.H.) June 25, 1759-Dec. 22, 1850; Senate June 17, 1802-07; Gov. (D) 1812-13, 1816-19.

PLUMER, William, Jr. (son of William Plumer) (D N.H.) Feb. 9, 1789-Sept. 18, 1854; House 1819-25.

PLUMLEY, Charles Albert (son of Frank Plumley) (R Vt.) April 14, 1875-Oct. 31, 1964; House Jan. 16, 1934-51.

PLUMLEY, Frank (father of Charles Albert Plumley) (R Vt.) Dec. 17, 1844-April 30, 1924; House 1909-15.

PLUMMER, Franklin E. (— Miss.) —Sept. 24, 1847; House 1831-35.

POAGE, William Robert (D Texas) Dec. 28, 1899; House 1937- .

PODELL, Bertram L. (D N.Y.) Dec. 27, 1925; House Feb. 28, 1968- .

POEHLER, Henry (D Minn.) Aug. 22, 1833-July 18, 1912; House 1879-81.

POFF, Richard Harding (R Va.) Oct. 19, 1923; House 1953- .

POINDEXTER, George (— Miss.) 1779-Sept. 5, 1855; House (Terr. Del.) 1807-13; (Rep.) Dec. 10, 1817-19; Senate Oct. 15, 1830-35; Gov. 1819-21.

POINDEXTER, Miles (R Wash.) April 22, 1868-Sept. 21, 1946; House 1909-11; Senate 1911-23.

POINSETT, Joel Roberts (D S.C.) March 2, 1779-Dec. 12, 1851; House 1821-March 7, 1825; Secy. of War 1837-41.

POLANCO-ABREU, Santiago (PD P.R.) Oct. 30, 1920; House 1965-69.

POLAND, Luke Potter (R Vt.) Nov. 1, 1815-July 2, 1887; Senate Nov. 21, 1865-67; House 1867-75, 1883-85.

POLK, Albert Fawcett (D Del.) Oct. 11, 1869-Feb. 14, 1955; House 1917-19.

POLK, James Gould (D Ohio) Oct. 6, 1896-April 28, 1959; House 1931-41, 1949-April 28, 1959.

POLK, James Knox (brother of William Hawkins Polk) (D Tenn.) Nov. 2, 1795-June 15, 1849; House 1825-39; Speaker 1835-39; Gov. 1839-41; President 1845-49.

POLK, Rufus King (D Pa.) Aug. 23, 1866-March 5, 1902; House 1899-March 5, 1902.

POLK, Trusten (D Mo.) May 29, 1811-April 16, 1876; Senate 1857-Jan. 10, 1862; Gov. 1857.

POLK, William Hawkins (brother of James Knox Polk) (D Tenn.) May 24, 1815-Dec. 16, 1862; House 1851-53.

POLLARD, Ernest Mark (R Neb.) April 15, 1869-Sept. 24, 1939; House July 18, 1905-09.

POLLARD, Henry Moses (R Mo.) June 14, 1836-Feb. 24, 1904; House 1877-79.

POLLOCK, Howard W. (R Ark.) April 11, 1920; House 1967-61.

POLLOCK, James (W Pa.) Sept. 11, 1810-April 19, 1890; House April 5, 1844-49; Gov. 1855-58.

POLLOCK, William Pegues (D S.C.) Dec. 9, 1870-June 2, 1922; Senate Nov. 6, 1918-19.

POLSLEY, Daniel Haymond (R W.Va.) Nov. 28, 1803-Oct. 14, 1877; House 1867-69.

POMERENE, Atlee (D Ohio) Dec. 6, 1863-Nov. 12, 1937; Senate 1911-23.

POMEROY, Charles (R Iowa) Sept. 3, 1825-Feb. 11, 1891; House 1869-71.

POMEROY, Samuel Clarks (R Kan.) Jan. 3, 1816-Aug. 27, 1891; Senate April 4, 1861-73.

POMEROY, Theodore Medad (R N.Y.) Dec. 31, 1824-March 23, 1905; House 1861-69; Speaker March 3, 1869.

POND, Benjamin (D N.Y.) 1768-Oct. 6, 1814; House 1811-13.

POOL, Joe Richard (D Texas) Feb. 18, 1911-July 14, 1968; House 1963-July 14, 1968.

POOL, John (uncle of Walter Freshwater Pool) (W N.C.) June 16, 1826-Aug. 16, 1884; Senate July 4, 1868-73.

POOL, Walter Freshwater (nephew of John Pool) (R N.C.) Oct. 10, 1850-Aug. 25, 1883; House March 4-Aug. 25, 1883.

POOLE, Theodore Lewis (R N.Y.) April 10, 1840-Dec. 23, 1900; House 1895-97.

POPE, James Pinckney (D Idaho) March 31, 1884-Jan. 23, 1966; Senate 1933-39.

POPE, John (D Ky.) 1770-July 12, 1845; Senate 1807-13; House 1837-43; President pro tempore 1810-11; Terr. Gov. of Ark. 1829-35.

POPE, Nathaniel (— Ill.) Jan. 5, 1784-Jan. 22, 1850; House (Terr. Del.) Sept. 5, 1816-Sept. 5, 1818.

POPE, Patrick Hamilton (D Ky.) March 17, 1806-May 4, 1841; House 1833-35.

POPPLETON, Earley Franklin (D Ohio) Sept. 29, 1834-May 6, 1899; House 1875-77.

PORTER, Albert Gallatin (R Ind.) April 20, 1824-May 3, 1897; House 1859-63; Gov. 1881-85.

PORTER, Alexander (W La.) 1786-Jan. 13, 1844; Senate Dec. 19, 1833-Jan. 5, 1837.

PORTER, Augustus Seymour (nephew of Peter Buell Porter) (W Mich.) Jan. 18, 1798-Sept. 18, 1872; Senate Jan. 20, 1840-45.

PORTER, Charles Howell (R Va.) June 21, 1833-July 9, 1897; House Jan. 26, 1870-73.

PORTER, Charles Orlando (D Ore.) April 4, 1919; House 1957-61.

PORTER, Gilchrist (W Mo.) Nov. 1, 1817-Nov. 1, 1894; House 1851-53; 1855-57.

PORTER, Henry Kirke (— Pa.) Nov. 24, 1840-April 10, 1921; House 1903-05.

PORTER, James (D N.Y.) April 18, 1787-Feb. 7, 1839; House 1817-19.

PORTER, John (— Pa.) —-—; House Dec. 8, 1806-11.

PORTER, Peter Augustus (grandson of Peter Buell Porter) (IR/D Oct. 10, 1853-Dec. 15, 1925; House 1907-09.

PORTER, Peter Buell (grandfather of Peter Augustus Porter and uncle of Augustus Seymour Porter (D N.Y.) Aug. 4, 1773-March 20, 1844; House 1809-13, 1815-Jan. 23, 1816; Secy. of War 1828-29.

PORTER, Stephen Geyer (R Pa.) May 18, 1869-June 27, 1930; House 1911-June 27, 1930.

PORTER, Timothy H. (— N.Y.) —-about 1840; House 1825-27.

POSEY, Francis Blackburn (R Ind.) April 28, 1848-Oct. 31, 1915; House Jan. 29-March 3, 1889.

POSEY, Thomas (— La.) July 9, 1750-March 19, 1818; Senate Oct. 8, 1812-Feb. 4, 1813; Gov. of Ind. Terr. 1813-16.

POST, George Adams (D Pa.) Sept. 1, 1854-Oct. 31, 1925; House 1883-85.

POST, James Douglass (D Ohio) Nov. 25, 1863-April 1, 1921; House 1911-15.

POST, Jotham, Jr. (F N.Y.) April 4, 1771-May 15, 1817; House 1813-15.

POST, Morton Everel (D Wyo.) Dec. 25, 1840-March 19, 1933; House (Terr.Del.) 1881-85.

POST, Philip Sidney (R Ill.) March 19, 1833-Jan. 6, 1895; House 1887-Jan. 6, 1895.

POSTON, Charles Debrille (R Ariz.) April 20, 1825-June 24, 1902; House (Terr.Del.) Dec. 5, 1864-65.

POTTER, Allen (I Mich.) Oct. 2, 1818-May 8, 1885; House 1875-77.

POTTER, Charles Edward (R Mich.) Oct. 30, 1916; House Aug. 26, 1947-Nov. 4, 1952; Senate Nov. 5, 1952-59.

POTTER, Clarkson Nott (D N.Y.) April 25, 1825-Jan. 23, 1882; House 1869-75; 1877-79.

POTTER, Elisha Reynolds (F R.I.) Nov. 5, 1764-Sept. 26, 1835; House Nov. 15, 1796-97; 1809-15.

POTTER, Elisha Reynolds (son of the preceding) (W R.I.) June 20, 1811-April 10, 1882; House 1843-45.

POTTER, Emery Davis (D Ohio) Oct. 7, 1804-Feb. 12, 1896; House 1843-45; 1849-51.

POTTER, John Fox (R Wis.) May 11, 1817-May 18, 1899; House 1857-63.

POTTER, Orlando Brunson (UD N.Y.) March 10, 1823-Jan. 2, 1894; House 1883-85.

POTTER, Robert (JD N.C.) about 1800-March 2, 1841; House 1829-Nov. 1831.

POTTER, Samuel John (— R.I.) June 29, 1753-Oct. 14, 1804; Senate 1803-Oct. 14, 1804.

POTTER, William Wilson (D Pa.) Dec. 18, 1792-Oct. 28, 1839; House 1837-Oct. 28, 1839.

POTTLE, Emory Bemsley (R N.Y.) July 4, 1815-April 18, 1891; House 1857-61.

POTTS, David, Jr. (W Pa.) Nov. 27, 1794-June 1, 1863; House 1831-39.

POTTS, David Matthew (R N.Y.) March 12, 1906; House 1947-49.

POTTS, Richard (F Md.) July 19, 1753-Nov. 26, 1808; Senate Jan. 10, 1793-Oct. 24, 1796; Cont. Cong. 1781-82.

POU, Edward William (cousin of James Paul Buchanan) (D N.C.) Sept. 9, 1863-April 1, 1934; House 1901-April 1, 1934.

POULSON, Norris (R Calif.) July 23, 1895-—; House 1943-45; 1947-June 11, 1953.

POUND, Thaddeus Coleman (R Wis.) Dec. 6, 1833-Nov. 21, 1914; House 1877-83.

POWELL, Adam Clayton, Jr. (D N.Y.) Nov. 29, 1908; House 1945-71.

POWELL, Alfred H. (— Va.) March 6, 1781-1831; House 1825-27.

POWELL, Cuthbert (son of Levin Powell) (W Va.) March 4, 1775-May 8, 1849; House 1841-43.

POWELL, Joseph (D Pa.) June 23, 1828-April 24, 1904; House 1875-77.

POWELL, Lazarus Whitehead (D Ky.) Oct. 6, 1812-July 3, 1867; Senate 1859-65; Gov. 1851-55.

POWELL, Levin (father of Cuthbert Powell) (F Va.) 1737-Aug. 23, 1810; House 1799-1801.

POWELL, Paulus (D Va.) 1809-June 10, 1874; House 1849-59.

POWELL, Samuel (— Tenn.) July 10, 1776-Aug. 2, 1841; House 1815-17.

POWELL, Walter E. (R Ohio) April 25, 1931; House 1971- .

POWER, Thomas Charles (R Mont.) May 22, 1839-Feb. 16, 1923; Senate Jan 2, 1890-95.

POWERS, Caleb (R Ky.) Feb. 1, 1869-July 25, 1932; House 1911-19.

POWERS, David Lane (R N.J.) July 29, 1896-March 28, 1968; House 1933-Aug. 30, 1945.

POWERS, Gershom (JD N.Y.) July 11, 1789-June 25, 1831; House 1829-31.

POWERS, Horace Henry (R Vt.) May 29, 1835-Dec. 8, 1913; House 1891-1901.

POWERS, Llewellyn (R Maine) Oct. 14, 1836-July 28, 1908; House 1877-79; April 8, 1901-July 28, 1908; Gov. 1896-1900.

POWERS, Samuel Leland (R Mass.) Oct. 26, 1848-Nov. 30, 1929; House 1901-05.

POYDRAS, Julien de Lallande (— Orleans) April 3, 1740-June 14, 1824; House (Terr. Del.) 1809-11.

PRACHT, Charles Frederick (R Pa.) Oct. 20, 1880-Dec. 22, 1950; House 1943-45.

PRALL, Anning Smith (D N.Y.) Sept. 17, 1870-July 23, 1937; House Nov. 6, 1923-35.

PRATT, Charles Clarence (R Pa.) April 23, 1854-Jan. 27, 1916; House 1909-11.

PRATT, Daniel Darwin (R Ind.) Oct. 26, 1813-June 17, 1877; Senate 1869-75.

PRATT, Eliza Jane (D N.C.) March 5, 1902; House May 25, 1946-47.

PRATT, Harcourt Joseph (R N.Y.) Oct. 23, 1866-May 21, 1934; House 1925-33.

PRATT, Harry Hayt (R N.Y.) Nov. 11, 1864-Nov. 13, 1932; House 1915-19.

PRATT, Henry Otis (R Iowa) Feb. 11, 1838-May 22, 1931; House 1873-77.

PRATT, James Timothy (D Conn.) Dec. 14, 1802-April 11, 1887; House 1853-55.

PRATT, Joseph Marmaduke (R Pa.) Sept. 4, 1891-July 19, 1946; House Jan. 18, 1944-45.

PRATT, Le Gage (D N.J.) Dec. 14, 1852-March 9, 1911; House 1907-09.

PRATT, Ruth Sears Baker (R N.Y.) Aug. 24, 1877-Aug. 23, 1965; House 1929-33.

PRATT, Thomas George (W Md.) Feb. 18, 1804-Nov. 9, 1869; Senate Jan. 12, 1850-57; Gov. 1845-48.

PRATT, Zadock (D N.Y.) Oct. 30, 1790-April 6, 1871; House 1837-39; 1843-45.

PRAY, Charles Nelson (R Mont.) April 6, 1868-Sept. 12, 1963; House 1907-13.

PRENTISS, John Holmes (brother of Samuel Prentiss) (D N.Y.) April 17, 1784-June 26, 1861; House 1837-41.

PRENTISS, Samuel (brother of John Holmes Prentiss) (W Vt.) March 31, 1782-Jan. 15, 1857; Senate 1831-April 11, 1842.

PRENTISS, Sergeant Smith (— Miss.) Sept. 30, 1808-July 1, 1850; House May 30, 1838-39.

PRESCOTT, Cyrus Dan (R N.Y.) Aug. 15, 1836-Oct. 23, 1902; House 1879-83.

PRESTON, Francis (father of William Campbell Preston and uncle of William Ballard Preston and William Preston) (— Va.) Aug. 2, 1765-May 26, 1836; House 1793-97.

PRESTON, Jacob Alexander (W Md.) March 12, 1796-Aug. 2, 1868; House 1843-45.

PRESTON, Prince Hulon, Jr. (D Ga.) July 5, 1908-Feb. 8, 1961; House 1947-61.

PRESTON, William (nephew of Francis Preston) (W Ky.) Oct. 16, 1816-Sept. 21, 1887; House Dec. 6, 1852-55.

PRESTON, William Ballard (nephew of Francis Preston) (W Va.) Nov. 25, 1805-Nov. 16, 1862; House 1847-49; Secy. of the Navy 1849-50.

PRESTON, William Campbell (son of Francis Preston) (Cal.N S.C.) Dec. 27, 1794-May 22, 1860; House Nov. 26, 1833-Nov. 29, 1842.

PREYER, Lunsford Richardson (D N.C.) Jan 11, 1919; House 1969- .

PRICE, Andrew (D La.) April 2, 1854-Feb. 5, 1909; House Dec. 2, 1889-97.

PRICE, Charles Melvin (D Ill.) Jan. 1, 1905; House 1945- .

PRICE, Emory Hilliard (D Fla.) Dec. 3, 1899- —; House 1943-49.

PRICE, Hiram (R Iowa) Jan. 10, 1814-May 30, 1901; House 1863-69; 1877-81.

PRICE, Hugh Hiram (son of William Thompson Price) (R Wis.) Dec. 2, 1859-Dec. 25, 1904; House Jan. 18-March 3, 1887.

PRICE, Jesse Dashiell (D Md.) Aug. 15, 1863-May 14, 1939; House Nov. 3, 1914-19.

PRICE, Robert Dale (Bob) (R Texas) Sept. 7, 1927; House 1967- .

PRICE, Rodman McCamley (D N.J.) May 5, 1816-June 7, 1894; House 1851-53; Gov. 1854-57.

PRICE, Samuel (— W.Va.) July 28, 1805-Feb. 25, 1884; Senate Aug. 26, 1876-Jan. 26, 1877.

PRICE, Sterling (D Mo.) Sept. 20, 1809-Sept. 29, 1867; House 1845-Aug. 12, 1846; Gov. 1853-57.

PRICE, Thomas Lawson (D Mo.) Jan. 19, 1809-July 15, 1870; House Jan. 21, 1862-63.

PRICE, William Pierce (D Ga.) Jan. 29, 1835-Nov. 4, 1908; House Dec. 22, 1870-73.

PRICE, William Thompson (father of Hugh Hiram Price) (R Wis.) June 17, 1824-Dec. 6, 1886; House 1883-Dec. 6, 1886.

PRIDEMORE, Auburn Lorenzo (D Va.) June 27, 1837-May 17, 1900; House 1877-79.

PRIEST, James Percy (D Tenn.) April 1, 1900-Oct. 12, 1956; House 1941-Oct. 12, 1956.

PRINCE, Charles Henry (R Ga.) May 9, 1837-April 3, 1912; House July 25, 1868-69.

PRINCE, George Washington (R Ill.) March 4, 1854-Sept. 26, 1939; House Dec. 2, 1895-1913.

PRINCE, Oliver Hillhouse (— Ga.) 1787-Oct. 9, 1837; Senate Nov. 7, 1828-29.

PRINCE, William (— Ind.) 1772-Sept. 8, 1824; House 1823-Sept. 8, 1824.

PRINDLE, Elizur H. (R N.Y.) May 6, 1829-Oct. 7, 1890; House 1871-73.

PRINGEY, Joseph Colburn (R Okla.) May 22, 1858-Feb. 11, 1935; House 1921-23.

PRINGLE, Benjamin (W N.Y.) Nov. 9, 1807-June 7, 1887; House 1853-57.

PRITCHARD, George Moore (son of Jeter Connelly Pritchard) (R N.C.) Jan. 4, 1886-April 24, 1955; House 1929-31.

PRITCHARD, Jeter Connelly (father of George Moore Pritchard) (R N.C.) July 12, 1857-April 10, 1921; Senate Jan. 23, 1895-1903.

PROCTOR, Redfield (R Vt.) June 1, 1831-March 4, 1908; Senate Nov. 2, 1891-March 4, 1908; Gov. 1878-80; Secy. of War 1889-91.

PROFFIT, George H. (W Ind.) Sept. 7, 1807-Sept. 7, 1847; House 1839-43.

PROKOP, Stanley A. (D Pa.) —-—; House 1959-61.

PROSSER, William Farrand (R Tenn.) March 16, 1834-Sept. 23, 1911; House 1869-71.

PROUTY, Solomon Francis (R Iowa) Jan. 17, 1854-July 16, 1927; House 1911-15.

PROUTY, Winston Lewis (R Vt.) Sept. 1, 1906; House 1951-59; Senate 1959- .

PROXMIRE, William (D Wis.) Nov. 11, 1915; Senate Aug. 28, 1957- .

PRUYN, John Van Schaick Lansing (D N.Y.) June 22, 1811-Nov. 21, 1877; House Dec. 7, 1863-65; 1867-69.

PRYOR, David (D Ark.) Aug. 29, 1934; House Nov. 8, 1966- .

PRYOR, Luke (D Ala.) July 5, 1820-Aug. 5, 1900; Senate Jan. 7-Nov. 23, 1880; House 1883-85.

PRYOR, Roger Atkinson (D Va.) July 19, 1828-March 14, 1919; House Dec. 7, 1859-61.

PUCINSKI, Roman Conrad (D Ill.) May 13, 1919; House 1959- .

PUGH, George Ellis (D Ohio) Nov. 28, 1822-July 19, 1876; Senate 1855-61.

PUGH, James Lawrence (D Ala.) Dec. 12, 1820-March 9, 1907; House 1859-Jan. 21, 1861; Senate Nov. 24, 1880-97.

PUGH, John (D Pa.) June 2, 1761-July 13, 1842; House 1805-09.

PUGH, John Howard (R N.J.) June 23, 1827-April 30, 1905; House 1877-79.

PUGH, Samuel Johnson (R Ky.) Jan. 28, 1850-April 17, 1922; House 1895-1901.

PUGSLEY, Cornelius Amory (D N.Y.) July 17, 1850-Sept. 10, 1936; House 1901-03.

PUGSLEY, Jacob Joseph (R Ohio) Jan. 25, 1838-Feb. 5, 1920, House 1887-91.

PUJO, Arsene Paulin (D La.) Dec. 16, 1861-Dec. 31, 1939; House 1903-13.

PULITZER, Joseph (D N.Y.) April 10, 1847-Oct. 29, 1911; House 1885-April 10, 1886.

PURCELL, Graham (D Texas) May 5, 1919; House Jan. 27, 1962- .

PURCELL, William Edward (D N.D.) Aug. 3, 1856-Nov. 23, 1928; Senate Feb. 1, 1910-Feb. 1, 1911.

PURDY, Smith Meade (D N.Y.) July 31, 1796-March 30, 1870; House 1843-45.

PURMAN, William James (R Fla.) April 11, 1840-Aug. 14, 1928; House 1873-Jan. 25, 1875, March 4, 1875-77.

PURNELL, Fred Sampson (R Ind.) Oct. 25, 1882-Oct. 21, 1939; House 1917-33.

PURTELL, William Arthur (R Conn.) May 6, 1897-—; Senate Aug. 29-Nov. 4, 1952, 1953-59.

PURVIANCE, Samuel Anderson (W Pa.) Jan. 10, 1809-Feb. 14, 1882; House 1855-59.

PURVIANCE, Samuel Dinsmore (F N.C.) Jan. 7, 1774-about 1806; House 1803-05.

PURYEAR, Richard Clauselle (W N.C.) Feb. 9, 1801-July 30, 1867; House 1853-57.

PUSEY, William Henry Mills (D Iowa) July 29, 1826-Nov. 15, 1900; House 1883-85.

PUTNAM, Harvey (W N.Y.) Jan. 5, 1793-Sept. 20, 1855; House Nov. 7, 1838-39, 1847-51.

PYLE, Gladys (R S.D.) Oct. 4, 1890-—; Senate Nov. 9, 1938-39.

Q

QUACKENBUSH, John Adam (R N.Y.) Oct. 15, 1828-May 11, 1908; House 1889-93.

QUARLES, James Minor (W Tenn.) Feb. 8, 1823-March 3, 1901; House 1859-61.

QUARLES, Joseph Very (R Wis.) Dec. 16, 1843-Oct. 7, 1911; Senate 1899-1905.

QUARLES, Julian Minor (D Va.) Sept. 25, 1848-Nov. 18, 1929; House 1899-1901.

QUARLES, Tunstall (D Ky.) about 1770-Jan. 7, 1855; House 1817-June 15, 1820.

QUAY, Matthew Stanley (R Pa.) Sept. 30, 1833-May 28, 1904; Senate 1887-99, Jan. 16, 1901-May 28, 1904; Chrmn. Rep. Nat. Comm. 1888.

QUAYLE, John Francis (D N.Y.) Dec. 1, 1868-Nov. 27, 1930; House 1923-Nov. 27, 1930.

QUEZON, Manuel Luis (Nat. P.I.) Aug. 19, 1878-Aug. 1, 1944; House (Res. Comm.) Nov. 23, 1909-Oct. 15, 1916; President of P.I. 1935-44.

QUIE, Albert Harold (R Minn.) Sept. 18, 1923; House Feb. 18, 1958- .

QUIGG, Lemuel Ely (R N.Y.) Feb. 12, 1863-July 1, 1919; House Jan. 30, 1894-99.

QUIGLEY, James Michael (D Pa.) March 30, 1918; House 1955-57, 1959-61.

QUILLEN, James H. (Jimmy) (R Tenn.) Jan. 11, 1916; House 1963- .

QUIN, Percy Edwards (D Miss.) Oct. 30, 1872-Feb. 4, 1932; House 1913-Feb. 4, 1932.

QUINCY, Josiah (F Mass.) Feb. 4, 1772-July 1, 1864; House 1805-13.

QUINN, James Leland (D Pa.) Sept. 8, 1875-Nov. 12, 1960; House 1935-39.

QUINN, John (D N.Y.) Aug. 9, 1839-Feb. 23, 1903; House 1889-91.

QUINN, Peter Anthony (D N.Y.) May 10, 1904; House 1945-47.

QUINN, Terence John (D N.Y.) Oct. 16, 1836-June 18, 1878; House 1877-June 18, 1878.

QUINN, Thomas Vincent (D N.Y.) March 16, 1903; House 1949-Dec. 30, 1951.

QUITMAN, John Anthony (D Miss.) Sept. 1, 1799-July 17, 1858; House 1855-July 17, 1858; Gov. 1850-51.

R

RABAUT, Louis Charles (D Mich.) Dec. 5, 1886-Nov. 12, 1961; House 1935-47, 1949-Nov. 12, 1961.

RABIN, Benjamin J. (D N.Y.) June 3, 1896-Feb. 22, 1969; House 1945-Dec. 31, 1947.

RACE, John Abner (D Wis.) May 12, 1914; House 1965-67.

RADCLIFFE, Amos Henry (R N.J.) Jan. 16, 1870-Dec. 29, 1950; House 1919-23.

RADCLIFFE, George L. (D Md.) Aug. 22, 1877-—; Senate 1935-47.

RADFORD, William (D N.Y.) June 24, 1814-Jan. 18, 1870; House 1863-67.

RADWAN, Edmund Patrick (R N.Y.) Sept. 22, 1911-Sept. 7, 1959; House 1951-59.

RAGON, Heartsill (D Ark.) March 20, 1885-Sept. 15, 1940; House 1923-June 16, 1933.

RAGSDALE, James Willard (D S.C.) Dec. 14, 1872-July 23, 1919; House 1913-July 23, 1919.

RAILSBACK, Thomas F. (R Ill.) Jan. 22, 1932; House 1967- .

RAINES, John (R N.Y.) May 6, 1840-Dec. 16, 1909; House 1889-93.

RAINEY, Henry Thomas (D Ill.) Aug. 20, 1860-Aug. 19, 1934; House 1903-21, 1923-Aug. 19, 1934; Speaker 1933-34.

RAINEY, John William (D Ill.) Dec. 21, 1880-May 4, 1923; House April 2, 1918-May 4, 1923.

RAINEY, Joseph Hayne (R S.C.) June 21, 1832-Aug. 2, 1887; House Dec. 12, 1870-79.

RAINEY, Lilius Bratton (D Ala.) July 27, 1876-Sept. 27, 1959; House Sept. 30, 1919-23.

RAINS, Albert M. (D Ala.) March 11, 1902; House 1945-65.

RAKER, John Edward (D Calif.) Feb. 22, 1863-Jan. 22, 1926; House 1911-Jan. 22, 1926.

RALSTON, Samuel Moffett (D Ind.) Dec. 1, 1857-Oct. 14, 1925; Senate 1923-Oct. 14, 1925; Gov. 1913-17.

RAMEY, Frank Marion (R Ill.) Sept. 23, 1881-March 27, 1942; House 1929-31.

RAMEY, Homer Alonzo (R Ohio) March 2, 1891-April 13, 1960; House 1943-49.

RAMSAY, Robert Lincoln (D W.Va.) March 24, 1877-Nov. 14, 1956; House 1933-39, 1941-43, 1949-53.

RAMSEY, Alexander (W Pa./R Minn.) Sept. 8, 1815-April 22, 1903; House (W Pa.) 1843-47; Senate (R Minn.) 1863-75; Gov. (Terr. of Minn.) 1849-53, (State of Minn.) 1860-63; Secy. of War 1879-81.

RAMSEY, John Rathbone (R N.J.) April 25, 1862-April 10, 1933; House 1917-21.

RAMSEY, Robert (W Pa.) Feb. 15, 1780-Dec. 12, 1849; House 1833-35, 1841-43.

RAMSEY, William (D Pa.) Sept. 7, 1779-Sept. 29, 1831; House 1827-Sept. 19, 1831.

RAMSEY, William Sterrett (D Pa.) June 12, 1810-Oct. 17, 1840; House 1839-Oct. 17, 1840.

RAMSEYER, Christian William (R Iowa) March 13, 1875-Nov. 1, 1943; House 1915-33.

RAMSPECK, Robert C. Word (D Ga.) Sept. 5, 1890-—; House Oct. 2, 1929-Dec. 31, 1945.

RANDALL, Alexander (W Md.) Jan. 3, 1803-Nov. 21, 1881; House 1841-43.

RANDALL, Benjamin (W Maine) Nov. 14, 1789-Oct. 11, 1859; House 1839-43.

RANDALL, Charles Hiram (Prohib./D/R/Pro. Calif.) July 23, 1865-Feb. 18, 1951; House 1915-21.

RANDALL, Charles Sturtevant (R Mass.) Feb. 20, 1824-Aug. 17, 1904; House 1889-95.

RANDALL, Clifford Ellsworth (R Wis.) Dec. 25, 1876-Oct. 16, 1934; House 1919-21.

RANDALL, Samuel Jackson (D Pa.) Oct. 10, 1828-April 13, 1890; House 1863-April 13, 1890; Speaker 1876-81.

RANDALL, William Harrison (R Ky.) July 15, 1812-Aug. 1, 1881; House 1863-67.

RANDALL, William Joseph (D Mo.) July 16, 1909; House March 3, 1959- .

RANDELL, Choice Boswell (nephew of Lucius Jeremiah Gartrell) (D Texas) Jan. 1, 1857-Oct. 19, 1945; House 1901-13.

RANDOLPH, James Fitz (father of Theodore Fitz Randolph) (— N.J.) June 26, 1791-Jan. 25, 1872; House Dec. 1, 1827-33.

RANDOLPH, James Henry (R Tenn.) Oct. 18, 1825-Aug. 22, 1900; House 1877-79.

RANDOLPH, Jennings (D W.Va.) March 8, 1902; House 1933-47; Senate Nov. 5, 1958- .

RANDOLPH, John (SRD Va.) June 2, 1773-May 24, 1833; House 1799-1813, 1815-17, 1819-Dec. 26, 1825, 1827-29, March 4-May 24, 1833; Senate Dec. 26, 1825-27.

RANDOLPH, Joseph Fitz (W N.J.) March 14, 1803-March 20, 1873; House 1837-43.

RANDOLPH, Theodore Fitz (son of James Fitz Randolph) (D N.J.) June 24, 1826-Nov. 7, 1883; Senate 1875-81; Gov. 1869-72.

RANDOLPH, Thomas Mann (D Va.) Oct. 1, 1768-June 20, 1828; House 1803-07; Gov. 1819-22.

RANEY, John Henry (R Mo.) Sept. 28, 1849-Jan. 23, 1928; House 1895-97.

RANGEL, Charles B. (D N.Y.) June 11, 1930; House 1971- .

RANKIN, Christopher (D Miss.) 1788-March 14, 1826; House 1819-March 14, 1826.

RANKIN, Jeannette (R Mont.) June 11, 1880-—; House 1917-19, 1941-43.

RANKIN, John Elliott (D Miss.) March 29, 1882-Nov. 26, 1960; House 1921-53.

RANKIN, Joseph (D Wis.) Sept. 25, 1833-Jan. 24, 1886; House 1883-Jan. 24, 1886.

RANNEY, Ambrose Arnold (R Mass.) April 17, 1821-March 5, 1899; House 1881-87.

RANSDELL, Joseph Eugene (D La.) Oct. 7, 1858-July 27, 1954; House Aug. 29, 1899-1913; Senate 1913-31.

RANSIER, Alonzo Jacob (R S.C.) Jan. 3, 1834-Aug. 17, 1882; House 1873-75.

RANSLEY, Harry Clay (R Pa.) Feb. 5, 1863-Nov. 7, 1941; House Nov. 2, 1920-37.

RANSOM, Matt Whitaker (cousin of Wharton Jackson Green) (D N.C.) Oct. 8, 1826-Oct. 8, 1904; Senate Jan. 30, 1872-95.

RANTOUL, Robert, Jr. (D Mass.) Aug. 13, 1805-Aug. 7, 1852; Senate Feb. 1-March 3, 1851; House March 4, 1851-Aug. 7, 1852.

RAPIER, James Thomas (R Ala.) Nov. 13, 1837-May 31, 1883; House 1873-75.

RARICK, John R. (D La.) Jan. 29, 1924; House 1967- .

RARIDEN, James (W Ind.) Feb. 14, 1795-Oct. 20, 1856; House 1837-41.

RATHBONE, Henry Riggs (grandson of Ira Harris) (R Ill.) Feb. 12, 1870-July 15, 1928; House 1923-July 15, 1928.

RATHBUN, George Oscar (D N.Y.) 1803-Jan. 5, 1870; House 1843-47.

RAUCH, George Washington (D Ind.) Feb. 22, 1876-Nov. 4, 1940; House 1907-17.

RAUM, Green Berry (R Ill.) Dec. 3, 1829-Dec. 18, 1909; House 1867-69.

RAWLINS, Joseph Lafayette (D Utah) March 28, 1850-May 24, 1926; House (Terr.Del.) 1893-95; Senate 1897-1903.

RAWLS, Morgan (D Ga.) June 29, 1829-Oct. 18, 1906; House 1873-March 24, 1874.

RAWSON, Charles Augustus (R Iowa) May 29, 1867-Sept. 2, 1936; Senate Feb. 24-Dec. 1, 1922.

RAY, George Washington (R N.Y.) Feb. 3, 1844-Jan. 10, 1925; House 1883-85, 1891-Sept. 11, 1902.

RAY, John Henry (R N.Y.) Sept. 27, 1886-—; House 1953-63.

RAY, Joseph Warren (R Pa.) May 25, 1849-Sept. 15, 1928; House 1889-91.

RAY, Ossian (R N.H.) Dec. 13, 1835-Jan. 28, 1892; House Jan. 8, 1881-85.

RAY, William Henry (R Ill.) Dec. 14, 1812-Jan. 25, 1881; House 1873-75.

RAYBURN, Sam (D Texas) Jan. 6, 1882-Nov. 16, 1961; House 1913-Nov. 16, 1961; Speaker 1940-47, 1949-53, 1955-61.

RAYFIEL, Leo Frederick (D N.Y.) March 22, 1888-—; House 1945-Sept. 13, 1947.

RAYMOND, Henry Jarvis (R N.Y.) Jan. 24, 1820-June 18, 1869; House 1865-67.

RAYMOND, John Baldwin (R Dakota) Dec. 5, 1844-Jan. 3, 1886; House (Terr.Del.) 1883-85.

RAYNER, Isidor (D Md.) April 11, 1850-Nov. 25, 1912; House 1887-89, 1891-95; Senate 1905-Nov. 25, 1912.

RAYNER, Kenneth (W N.C.) June 20, 1808-March 4, 1884; House 1839-45.

REA, David (D Mo.) Jan. 19, 1831-June 13, 1901; House 1875-79.

REA, John (D Pa.) Jan. 27, 1755-Feb. 26, 1829; House 1803-11, May 11, 1813-15.

READ, Almon Heath (D Pa.) June 12, 1790-June 3, 1844; House March 18, 1842-June 3, 1844.

READ, George (— Del.) Sept. 18, 1733-Sept. 21, 1798; Senate 1789-Sept. 18, 1793; Cont. Cong. 1774-77.

READ, Jacob (F S.C.) 1751-July 17, 1816; Senate 1795-1801; Cont. Cong. 1783-85.

READ, Nathan (F Mass.) July 2, 1759-Jan. 20, 1849; House Nov. 25, 1800-03.

READ, William Brown (D Ky.) Dec. 14, 1817-Aug. 5, 1880; House 1871-75.

READE, Edwin Godwin (AP N.C.) Nov. 13, 1812-Oct. 18, 1894; House 1855-57.

READING, John Roberts (D Pa.) Nov. 1, 1826-Feb. 14, 1886; 1869-April 13, 1870.

READY, Charles (uncle of William T. Haskell) (W Tenn.) Dec. 22, 1802-June 4, 1878; House 1853-59.

REAGAN, John Henninger (D Texas) Oct. 8, 1818-March 6, 1905; House 1857-61, 1875-March 4, 1887; Senate March 4, 1887-June 10, 1891.

REAMES, Alfred Evan (D Ore.) Feb. 5, 1870-March 4, 1943; Senate Feb. 1-Nov. 8, 1938.

REAMS, Henry Frazier (I Ohio) Jan. 15, 1897-—; House 1951-55.

REAVIS, Charles Frank (R Neb.) Sept. 5, 1870-May 26, 1932; House 1915-June 3, 1922.

REBER, John (R Pa.) Feb. 1, 1858-Sept. 26, 1931; House 1919-23.

REDDEN, Monroe Minor (D N.C.) Sept. 24, 1901; House 1947-53.

REDFIELD, William Cox (D N.Y.) June 18, 1858-June 13, 1932; House 1911-13; Secy. of Commerce 1913-19.

REDING, John Randall (D N.H.) Oct. 18, 1805-Oct. 8, 1892; House 1841-45.

REDLIN, Rolland (D N.D.) Feb. 29, 1920; House 1965-67.

REECE, Brazilla Carroll (husband of Louise G. Reece) (R Tenn.) Dec. 22, 1889-March 19, 1961; House 1921-31, 1933-47, 1951-March 19, 1961; Chrmn. Rep. Nat. Comm. 1946-48.

REECE, Louise Goff (widow of B. Carroll Reece, daughter of Guy Despard Goff and granddaughter of Nathan Goff) (R Tenn.) Nov. 6, 1898-May 14, 1970; House May 16, 1961-63.

REED, Charles Manning (W Pa.) April 3, 1803-Dec. 16, 1871; House 1843-45.

REED, Chauncey William (R Ill.) June 2, 1890-Feb. 9, 1956; House 1935-Feb. 9, 1956.

REED, Clyde Martin (R Kan.) Oct. 19, 1871-Nov. 8, 1949; Senate 1939-Nov. 8, 1949; Gov. 1929-31.

REED, Daniel Alden (R N.Y.) Sept. 15, 1875-Feb. 19, 1959; House 1919-Feb. 19, 1959.

REED, David Aiken (R Pa.) Dec. 21, 1880-Feb. 10, 1953; Senate Aug. 8, 1922-35.

REED, Edward Cambridge (D N.Y.) March 8, 1793-May 1, 1883; House 1831-33.

REED, Eugene Elliott (D N.H.) April 23, 1866-Dec. 15, 1940; House 1913-15.

REED, Isaac (W Maine) Aug. 22, 1809-Sept. 19, 1887; House June 25, 1852-53.

REED, James Alexander (D Mo.) Nov. 9, 1861-Sept. 8, 1944; Senate 1911-29.

REED, James Byron (D Ark.) Jan. 2, 1881-April 17, 1935; House Oct. 20, 1923-29.

REED, John (F Mass.) Nov. 11, 1751-Feb. 17, 1831; House 1795-1801.

REED, John (son of the preceding) (W Mass.) Sept. 2, 1781-Nov. 25, 1860; House 1813-17 (F), 1821-41 (W).

REED, Joseph Rea (R Iowa) March 12, 1835-April 2, 1925; House 1889-91.

REED, Philip (— Md.) 1760-Nov. 2, 1829; Senate Nov. 25, 1806-13; House 1817-19, March 19, 1822-23.

REED, Robert Rentoul (W Pa.) March 12, 1807-Dec. 14, 1864; House 1849-51.

REED, Stuart Felix (R W.Va.) Jan. 8, 1866-July 4, 1935; House 1917-25.

REED, Thomas Brackett (R Maine) Oct. 18, 1839-Dec. 7, 1902; House 1877-Sept. 4, 1899; Speaker 1889-91, 1895-99.

REED, Thomas Buck (D Miss.) May 7, 1787-Nov. 26, 1829; Senate Jan. 28, 1826-27, March 4-Nov. 26, 1829.

REED, William (F Mass.) June 6, 1776-Feb. 18, 1837; House 1811-15.

REEDER, William Augustus (R Kan.) Aug. 28, 1849-Nov. 7, 1929; House 1899-1911.

REES, Edward Herbert (R Kan.) June 3, 1886-Oct. 25, 1969; House 1937-61.

REES, Rollin Raymond (R Kan.) Jan. 10, 1865-May 30, 1935; House 1911-13.

REES, Thomas M. (D Calif.) March 26, 1925; House Dec. 15, 1965- .

REESE, David Addison (W Ga.) March 3, 1794-Dec. 16, 1871; House 1853-55.

REESE, Seaborn (D Ga.) Nov. 28, 1846-March 1, 1907; House Dec. 4, 1882-87.

REEVES, Albert Lee, Jr. (R Mo.) May 31, 1906; House 1947-49.

REEVES, Henry Augustus (D N.Y.) Dec. 7, 1832-March 4, 1916; House 1869-71.

REEVES, Walter (R Ill.) Sept. 25, 1848-April 9, 1909; House 1895-1903.

REGAN, Kenneth Mills (D Texas) March 6, 1893-Aug. 15, 1959; House Aug. 23, 1947-55.

REID, Charles Chester (D Ark.) June 15, 1868-May 20, 1922; House 1901-11.

REID, Charlotte T. (R Ill.) Sept. 27, 1913; House 1963- .

REID, David Settle (nephew of Thomas Settle) (D N.C.) April 19, 1813-June 19, 1891; House 1843-47; Senate Dec. 6, 1854-59; Gov. 1851-54.

REID, Frank R. (R Ill.) April 18, 1879-Jan. 25, 1945; House 1923-35.

REID, James Wesley (D N.C.) June 11, 1849-Jan. 1, 1902; House Jan. 28, 1885-Dec. 31, 1886.

REID, John William (D Mo.) June 14, 1821-Nov. 22, 1881; House March 4-Aug. 3, 1861.

REID, Robert Raymond (D Ga.) Sept. 8, 1789-July 1, 1841; House Feb. 18, 1819-23; Gov. of Terr. of Fla. 1839-41.

REID, Ogden Rogers (R N.Y.) June 24, 1925; House 1963- .

REIFEL, Benjamin (R S.D.) Sept. 19, 1906; House 1961-71.

REILLY, James Bernard (D Pa.) Aug. 12, 1845-May 14, 1924; House 1875-79, 1889-95.

REILLY, John (D Pa.) Feb. 22, 1836-April 19, 1904; House 1875-77.

REILLY, Michael Kieran (D Wis.) July 15, 1869-Oct. 14, 1944; House 1913-17, Nov. 4, 1930-39.

REILLY, Thomas Lawrence (D Conn.) Sept. 20, 1858-July 6, 1924; House 1911-15.

REILLY, Wilson (D Pa.) Aug. 8, 1811-Aug. 26, 1885; House 1857-59.

REILY, Luther (D Pa.) Oct. 17, 1794-Feb. 20, 1854; House 1837-39.

REINECKE, Ed (R Calif.) Jan. 7, 1924; House 1965-Jan. 21, 1969.

RELFE, James Hugh (D Mo.) Oct. 17, 1791-Sept. 14, 1863; House 1843-47.

REMANN, Frederick (R Ill.) May 10, 1847-July 14, 1895; House March 4-July 14, 1895.

RENCHER, Abraham (D N.C.) Aug. 12, 1798-July 6, 1883; House 1829-39, 1841-43; Gov. of N.M. 1857-61.

RESA, Alexander John (D Ill.) Aug. 4, 1887-July 4, 1964; House 1945-47.

RESNICK, Joseph Y. (D N.Y.) July 13, 1924-Oct. 6, 1969; House 1965-69.

REUSS, Henry Schoellkopf (D Wis.) Feb. 22, 1912; House 1955- .

REVELS, Hiram Rhodes (R Miss.) Sept. 27, 1827-Jan. 16, 1901; Senate Feb. 23, 1870-71.

REVERCOMB, William Chapman (R W.Va.) July 20, 1895- —;Senate 1942-49, Nov. 7, 1956-59.

REYBURN, John Edgar (father of William Stuart Reyburn) (R Pa.) Feb. 7, 1845-Jan. 4, 1914; House Feb. 18, 1890-97, Nov. 6, 1906-March 31, 1907.

REYBURN, William Stuart (son of John Edgar Reyburn) (R Pa.) Dec. 17, 1882-July 25, 1946; House May 23, 1911-13.

REYNOLDS, Edwin Ruthvin (R N.Y.) Feb. 16, 1816-July 4, 1908; House Dec. 5, 1860-61.

REYNOLDS, Gideon (W N.Y.) Aug. 9, 1813-July 13, 1896; House 1847-51.

REYNOLDS, James B. (D Tenn.) 1779-June 10, 1851; House 1815-17, 1823-25.

REYNOLDS, John (D Ill.) Feb. 26, 1789-May 8, 1865; House Dec. 1, 1834-37, 1839-43; Gov. 1830-34.

REYNOLDS, John Hazard (R N.Y.) June 21, 1819-Sept. 24, 1875; House 1859-61.

REYNOLDS, John Merriman (R Pa.) March 5, 1848-Sept. 14, 1933; House 1905-Jan. 17, 1911.

REYNOLDS, Joseph (D N.Y.) Sept. 14, 1785-Sept. 24, 1864; House 1835-37.

REYNOLDS, Robert Rice (D N.C.) June 18, 1884-Feb. 13, 1963; Senate Dec. 5, 1932-45.

REYNOLDS, Samuel Williams (R Neb.) Aug. 11, 1890-—; Senate July 3-Nov. 7, 1954.

RHEA, John (D Tenn.) 1753-May 27, 1832; House 1803-15, 1817-23.

RHEA, John Stockdale (D/P Ky.) March 9, 1855-July 29, 1924; House 1897-March 25, 1902, 1903-05.

RHEA, William Francis (D Va.) April 20, 1858-March 23, 1931; House 1899-1903.

RHETT, Robert Barnwell (formerly Robert Barnwell Smith) (D S.C.) Dec. 24, 1800-Sept. 14, 1876; House 1837-49; Senate Dec. 18, 1850-May 7, 1852.

RHINOCK, Joseph Lafayette (D Ky.) Jan. 4, 1863-Sept. 20, 1926; House 1905-11.

RHODES, George Milton (D Pa.) Feb. 24, 1898-—; House 1949-69.

RHODES, John Jacob (R Ariz.) Sept. 18, 1916; House 1953- .

RHODES, Marion Edwards (R Mo.) Jan. 4, 1868-Dec. 25, 1928; House 1905-07, 1919-23.

RIBICOFF, Abraham A. (D Conn.) April 9, 1910; House 1949-53; Senate 1963- ; Gov. 1955-61; Secy. of H.E.W. 1961-62.

RICAUD, James Barroll (AP Md.) Feb. 11, 1808-Jan. 24, 1866; House 1855-59.

RICE, Alexander Hamilton (R Mass.) Aug. 30, 1818-July 22, 1895; House 1859-67; Gov. 1876-78.

RICE, Americus Vespucius (D Ohio) Nov. 18, 1835-April 4, 1904; House 1875-79.

RICE, Benjamin Franklin (R Ark.) May 26, 1828-Jan. 19, 1905; Senate June 23, 1868-73.

RICE, Edmund (brother of Henry Mower Rice) (D Minn.) Feb. 14, 1819-July 11, 1889; House 1887-89.

RICE, Edward Young (D Ill.) Feb. 8, 1820-April 16, 1883; House 1871-73.

RICE, Henry Mower (brother of Edmund Rice) (D Minn.) Nov. 29, 1817-Jan. 15, 1894; House (Terr. Del.) 1853-57; Senate May 11, 1858-63.

RICE, John Birchard (R Ohio) June 23, 1832-Jan. 14, 1893; House 1881-83.

RICE, John Blake (R Ill.) May 28, 1809-Dec. 17, 1874; House 1873-Dec. 17, 1874.

RICE, John Hovey (R Maine) Feb. 5, 1816-March 14, 1911; House 1861-67.

RICE, John McConnell (D Ky.) Feb. 19, 1831-Sept. 18, 1895; House 1869-73.

RICE, Theron Moses (Natl.G Mo.) Sept. 21, 1829-Nov. 7, 1895; House 1881-83.

RICE, Thomas (— Mass.) March 30, 1768-Aug. 25, 1854; House 1815-19.

RICE, William Whitney (R Mass.) March 7, 1826-March 1, 1896; House 1877-87.

RICH, Carl W. (R Ohio) Sept. 12, 1898-—; House 1963-65.

RICH, John Tyler (R Mich.) April 23, 1841-March 28, 1926; House April 5, 1881-83; Gov. 1892-96.

RICH, Robert Fleming (R Pa.) June 23, 1883-April 28, 1968; House Nov. 4, 1930-43, 1945-51.

RICHARD, Gabriel (— Mich.) Oct. 15, 1767-Sept. 13, 1832; House (Terr.Del.) 1823-25.

RICHARDS, Charles Lenmore (D Nev.) Oct. 3, 1877-Dec. 22, 1953; House 1923-25.

RICHARDS, Jacob (D Pa.) 1773-July 20, 1816; House 1803-09.

RICHARDS, James Alexander Dudley (D Ohio) March 22, 1845-Dec. 4, 1911; House 1893-95.

RICHARDS, James Prioleau (D S.C.) Aug. 31, 1894-—; House 1933-57.

RICHARDS, John (brother of Matthias Richards) (— Pa.) April 18, 1753-Nov. 13, 1822; House 1795-97.

RICHARDS, John (— N.Y.) April 13, 1765-April 18, 1850; House 1823-25.

RICHARDS, Mark (D Vt.) July 15, 1760-Aug. 10, 1844; House 1817-21.

RICHARDS, Matthias (brother of John Richards) (— Pa.) Feb. 26, 1758-Aug. 4, 1830; House 1807-11.

RICHARDSON, David Plunket (R N.Y.) May 28, 1833-June 21, 1904; House 1879-83.

RICHARDSON, George Frederick (D Mich.) July 1, 1850-March 1, 1923; House 1893-95.

RICHARDSON, Harry Alden (R Del.) Jan. 1, 1853-June 16, 1928; Senate 1907-13.

RICHARDSON, James Daniel (D Tenn.) March 10, 1843-July 24, 1914; House 1885-1905.

RICHARDSON, James Montgomery (D Ky.) July 1, 1858-Feb. 9, 1925; House 1905-07.

RICHARDSON, John Peter (SRD S.C.) April 14, 1801-Jan. 24, 1864; House Dec. 19, 1836-39; Gov. 1840-42.

RICHARDSON, John Smythe (D S.C.) Feb. 29, 1828-Feb. 24, 1894; House 1879-83.

RICHARDSON, Joseph (— Mass.) Feb. 1, 1778-Sept. 25, 1871; House 1827-31.

RICHARDSON, William (D Ala.) May 8, 1839-March 31, 1914; House Aug. 6, 1900-March 31, 1914.

RICHARDSON, William Alexander (D Ill.) Jan. 16, 1811-Dec. 27, 1875; House Dec. 6, 1847-Aug. 25, 1856, 1861-Jan. 29, 1863; Senate Jan. 30, 1863-65.

RICHARDSON, William Emanuel (D Pa.) Sept. 3, 1886-Nov. 3, 1948; House 1933-37.

RICHARDSON, William Merchant (F Mass.) Jan. 4, 1774-March 15, 1838; House Nov. 4, 1811-April 18, 1814.

RICHMOND, Hiram Lawton (R Pa.) May 17, 1810-Feb. 19, 1885; House 1873-75.

RICHMOND, James Buchanan (D Va.) Feb. 27, 1842-April 30, 1910; House 1879-81.

RICHMOND, Jonathan (— N.Y.) July 31, 1774-July 28, 1853; House 1819-21.

RICKETTS, Edwin Darlington (R Ohio) Aug. 3, 1867-July 3, 1937; House 1915-17, 1919-23.

RIDDICK, Carl Wood (R Mont.) Feb. 25, 1872-July 9, 1960; House 1919-23.

RIDDLE, Albert Gallatin (R Ohio) May 28, 1816-May 16, 1902; House 1861-63.

RIDDLE, George Read (D Del.) 1817-March 29, 1867; House 1851-55; Senate Feb. 2, 1864-March 29, 1867.

RIDDLE, Haywood Yancey (D Tenn.) June 20, 1834-March 28, 1879; House Dec. 14, 1875-79.

RIDDLEBERGER, Harrison Holt (Read. Va.) Oct. 4, 1844-Jan. 24, 1890; Senate 1883-89.

RIDER, Ira Edgar (D N.Y.) Nov. 17, 1868-May 29, 1906; House 1903-05.

RIDGELY, Edwin Reed (PP/D Kan.) May 9, 1844-April 23, 1927; House 1897-1901.

RIDGELY, Henry Moore (F Del.) Aug. 6, 1779-Aug. 6, 1847; House 1811-15; Senate Jan. 12, 1827-29.

RIDGWAY, Joseph (W Ohio) May 6, 1783 Feb. 1, 1861; House 1837-43.

RIDGWAY, Robert (C Va.) April 21, 1823-Oct. 16, 1870; House Jan. 27-Oct. 16, 1870.

RIEGLE, Donald W., Jr. (R Mich.) Feb. 4, 1938; House 1967- .

RIEHLMAN, Roy Walter (R N.Y.) Aug. 26, 1899; House 1947-65.

RIFE, John Winebrenner (R Pa.) Aug. 14, 1846-April 17, 1908; House 1889-93.

RIGGS, James Milton (D Ill.) April 17, 1839-Nov. 18, 1933; House 1883-87.

RIGGS, Jetur Rose (D N.J.) June 20, 1809-Nov. 5, 1869; House 1859-61.

RIGGS, Lewis (D N.Y.) Jan. 16, 1789-Nov. 6, 1870; House 1841-43.

RIGNEY, Hugh McPheeters (D Ill.) July 31, 1873-Oct. 12, 1950; House 1937-39.

RIKER, Samuel (— N.Y.) April 8, 1743-May 19, 1823; House Nov. 5, 1804-05, 1807-09.

RILEY, Corinne Boyd (widow of John J. Riley) (D S.C.) July 4, 1894; House April 12, 1962-63.

RILEY, John Jacob (husband of Corinne Boyd Riley) (D S.C.) Feb. 1, 1895-Jan. 2, 1962; House 1945-49, 1951-Jan. 2, 1962.

RINAKER, John Irving (R Ill.) Nov. 1, 1830-Jan. 15, 1915; House June 5, 1896-97.

RINGGOLD, Samuel (D Md.) Jan. 15, 1770-Oct. 18, 1829; House Oct. 15, 1810-15, 1817-21.

RIORDAN, Daniel Joseph (D N.Y.) July 7, 1870-April 28, 1923; House 1899-1901, Nov. 6, 1906-April 28, 1923.

RIPLEY, Eleazar Wheelock (brother of James Wheelock Ripley) (D La.) April 15, 1782-March 2, 1839; House 1835-March 2, 1839.

RIPLEY, James Wheelock (brother of Eleazar Wheelock Ripley) (D Maine) March 12, 1786-June 17, 1835; House Sept. 11, 1826-March 12, 1830.

RIPLEY, Thomas C. (— N.Y.) —-—; House Dec. 7, 1846-47.

RISK, Charles Francis (R R.I.) Aug. 19, 1897-Dec. 26, 1943; House Aug. 6, 1935-37, 1939-41.

RISLEY, Elijah (W N.Y.) May 7, 1787-Jan. 9, 1870; House 1849-51.

RITCHEY, Thomas (D Ohio) Jan. 19, 1801-March 9, 1863; House 1847-49, 1853-55.

RITCHIE, Byron Foster (son of James Monroe Ritchie) (D Ohio) Jan. 29, 1853-Aug. 22, 1928; House 1893-95.

RITCHIE, David (R Pa.) Aug. 19, 1812-Jan. 24, 1867; House 1853-59.

RITCHIE, James Monroe (father of Byron Foster Ritchie) (R Ohio) July 28, 1829-Aug. 17, 1918; House 1881-83.

RITCHIE, John (D Md.) Aug. 12, 1831-Oct. 27, 1887; House 1871-73.

RITTER, Burwell Clark (uncle of Walter Evans) (C Ky.) Jan. 6, 1810-Oct. 1, 1880; House 1865-67.

RITTER, John (D Pa.) Feb. 6, 1779-Nov. 24, 1851; House 1843-47.

RIVERA, Luis Munoz (U P.R.) July 17, 1859-Nov. 15, 1916; House (Res. Comm.) 1911-Nov. 15, 1916.

RIVERS, Lucius Mendel (D S.C.) Sept. 28, 1905-Dec. 28, 1970; House 1941-Dec. 28, 1970.

RIVERS, Ralph Julian (D Alaska) May 23, 1903; House 1959-Dec. 30, 1966.

RIVERS, Thomas (AP Tenn.) Sept. 18, 1819-March 18, 1863; House 1855-57.

RIVES, Francis Everod (great uncle of Francis Rives Lassiter) (D Va.) Jan. 14, 1792-Dec. 26, 1861; House 1837-41.

RIVES, William Cabell (W Va.) May 4, 1792-April 25, 1868; House 1823-29 (D); Senate Dec. 10, 1832-Feb. 22, 1834, March 4, 1836-39 (D), 1839-45 (W).

RIVES, Zeno John (R Ill.) Feb. 22, 1874-Sept. 2, 1939; House 1905-07.

RIXEY, John Franklin (D Va.) Aug. 1, 1854-Feb. 8, 1907; House 1897-Feb. 8, 1907.

RIZLEY, Ross (R Okla.) July 5, 1892-March 4, 1969; House 1941-49.

ROACH, Sidney Crain (R Mo.) July 25, 1876-June 29, 1934; House 1921-25.

ROACH, William Nathaniel (D N.D.) Sept. 25, 1840-Sept. 7, 1902; Senate 1893-99.

ROANE, John (father of John Jones Roane) (D Va.) Feb. 9, 1766-Nov. 15, 1838; House 1809-15, 1827-31, 1835-37.

ROANE, John Jones (son of John Roane) (D Va.) Oct. 31, 1794-Dec. 18, 1869; House 1831-33.

ROANE, William Henry (grandson of Patrick Henry) (D Va.) Sept. 17, 1787-May 11, 1845; House 1815-17; Senate March 14, 1837-41.

ROARK, Charles Wickliffe (R Ky.) Jan. 22, 1887-April 5, 1929; House March 4-April 5, 1929.

ROBB, Edward (D Mo.) March 19, 1857-March 13, 1934; House 1897-1905.

ROBBINS, Asher (W R.I.) Oct. 26, 1757-Feb. 25, 1845; Senate Oct. 31, 1825-39.

ROBBINS, Edward Everett (R Pa.) Sept. 27, 1860-Jan. 25, 1919; House 1897-99, 1917-Jan. 25, 1919.

ROBBINS, Gaston Ahi (D Ala.) Sept. 26, 1858-Feb. 22, 1902; House 1893-March 13, 1896, 1899-March 8, 1900.

ROBBINS, George Robbins (W N.J.) Sept. 24, 1808-Feb. 22, 1875; House 1855-59.

ROBBINS, John (D Pa.) 1808-April 27, 1880; House 1849-55, 1875-77.

ROBBINS, William McKendree (D N.C.) Oct. 26, 1828-May 5, 1905; House 1873-79.

ROBERTS, Anthony Ellmaker (grandfather of Robert Grey Bushong) (W Pa.) Oct. 29, 1803-Jan. 25, 1885; House 1855-59.

ROBERTS, Brigham Henry (D Utah) March 13, 1857-Sept. 27, 1933; House 1899-Jan. 25, 1900.

ROBERTS, Charles Boyle (D Md.) April 19, 1842-Sept. 10, 1899; House 1875-79.

ROBERTS, Edwin Ewing (R Nev.) Dec. 12, 1870-Dec. 11, 1933; House 1911-19.

ROBERTS, Ellis Henry (R N.Y.) Sept. 30, 1827-Jan. 8, 1918; House 1871-75.

ROBERTS, Ernest William (R Mass.) Nov. 22, 1858-Feb. 27, 1924; House 1899-1917.

ROBERTS, Jonathan (R Pa.) Aug. 16, 1771-July 24, 1854; House 1811-Feb. 24, 1814; Senate Feb. 24, 1814-21.

ROBERTS, Kenneth Allison (D Ala.) Nov. 1, 1912; House 1951-65.

ROBERTS, Ray (D Texas) March 28, 1913; House Jan. 30, 1962- .

ROBERTS, Robert Whyte (D Miss.) Nov. 28, 1784-Jan. 4, 1865; House 1843-47.

ROBERTS, William Randall (D N.Y.) Feb. 6, 1830-Aug. 9, 1897; House 1871-75.

ROBERTSON, Alice Mary (R Okla.) Jan. 2, 1854-July 1, 1931; House 1921-23.

ROBERTSON, A. Willis (D Va.) May 27, 1887; House 1933-Nov. 5, 1946; Senate Nov. 6, 1946-Dec. 30, 1966.

ROBERTSON, Charles Raymond (R N.D.) Sept. 5, 1889-Feb. 18, 1951; House 1941-43, 1945-49.

ROBERTSON, Edward Vivian (R Wyo.) May 27,1881-April 15,1963; Senate 1943-49.

ROBERTSON, Edward White (father of Samuel Matthews Robertson) (D La.) June 13, 1823-Aug. 2, 1887; House 1877-83, March 4-Aug. 2, 1887.

ROBERTSON, George (—Ky.) Nov. 18, 1790-May 16, 1874; House 1817-21.

ROBERTSON, John (brother of Thomas Bolling Robertson) (W Va.) April 13, 1787-July 5, 1873; House Dec. 8, 1834-39.

ROBERTSON, Samuel Matthews (son of Edward White Robertson) (D La.) Jan. 1, 1852-Dec. 24, 1911; House Dec. 5, 1887-1907.

ROBERTSON, Thomas Austin (D Ky.) Sept. 9, 1848-July 18, 1892; House 1883-87.

ROBERTSON, Thomas Bolling (brother of John Robertson) (D La.) Feb. 27, 1779-Oct. 5, 1828; House April 30, 1812-April 20, 1818; Gov. 1820-22.

ROBERTSON, Thomas James (R S.C.) Aug. 3, 1823-Oct. 13, 1897; Senate July 15, 1868-77.

ROBERTSON, William Henry (R N.Y.) Oct. 10, 1823-Dec. 7, 1898; House 1867-69.

ROBESON, Edward John, Jr. (D Va.) Aug. 9,1890-March 10, 1966; House May 2, 1950-59.

ROBESON, George Maxwell (nephew of George Clifford Maxwell) (R N.J.) March 16, 1829-Sept. 27, 1897; House 1879-83; Secy. of the Navy 1869-77.

ROBIE, Reuben (D N.Y.) July 15, 1799-Jan. 21, 1872; House 1851-53.

ROBINSON, Arthur Raymond (R Ind.) March 12, 1881-March 17, 1961; Senate Oct. 20, 1925-35.

ROBINSON, Christopher (AP R.I.) May 15, 1806-Oct. 3, 1889; House 1859-61.

ROBINSON, Edward (W Maine) Nov. 25, 1796-Feb. 19, 1857; House April 28, 1838-39.

ROBINSON, George Dexter (R Mass.) Jan. 20, 1834-Feb. 22, 1896; House 1877-Jan. 7, 1884; Gov. 1884-87.

ROBINSON, James Carroll (D Ill.) Aug. 19, 1823-Nov. 3, 1886; House 1859-65, 1871-75.

ROBINSON, James McClellan (D Ind.) May 31, 1861-Jan. 16, 1942; House 1897-1905.

ROBINSON, James Sidney (R Ohio) Oct. 14, 1827-Jan. 14, 1892; House 1881-Jan. 12, 1885.

ROBINSON, James Wallace (R Ohio) Nov. 26, 1826-June 28, 1898; House 1873-75.

ROBINSON, James William (D Utah) Jan. 19, 1878-Dec. 2, 1964; House 1933-47.

ROBINSON, J. Kenneth (R Va.) May 14, 1916; House 1971- .

ROBINSON, John Buchanan (R Pa.) May 23, 1846-Jan. 28, 1933; House 1891-97.

ROBINSON, John Larne (D Ind.) May 3, 1813-March 21, 1860; House 1847-53.

ROBINSON, John McCracken (D Ill.) April 10, 1794-April 25, 1843; Senate Dec. 11, 1830-41.

ROBINSON, John Seaton (D Neb.) May 4, 1856-May 25, 1903; House 1899-1903.

ROBINSON, Jonathan (brother of Moses Robinson) (—Vt.) Aug. 11, 1756-Nov. 3, 1819; Senate Oct. 10, 1807-15.

ROBINSON, Joseph Taylor (D Ark.) Aug. 26, 1872-July 14, 1937; House 1903-Jan. 14, 1913; Senate 1913-July 14, 1937; Gov. Jan. 16-March 8, 1913.

ROBINSON, Leonidas Dunlap (D N.C.) April 22, 1867-Nov. 7, 1941; House 1917-21.

ROBINSON, Milton Stapp (R Ind.) April 20, 1832-July 28, 1892; House 1875-79.

ROBINSON, Moses (brother of Jonathan Robinson) (D Vt.) March 20, 1741-May 26, 1813; Senate Oct. 17, 1791-Oct. 15, 1796; Gov. 1789-90.

ROBINSON, Orville (D N.Y.) Oct. 28, 1801-Dec. 1, 1882; House 1843-45.

ROBINSON, Thomas, Jr. (D Del.) 1800-Oct. 28, 1843; House 1839-41.

ROBINSON, Thomas John Bright (R Iowa) Aug. 12, 1868-Jan. 27, 1958; House 1923-33.

ROBINSON, William Erigena (D N.Y.) May 6, 1814-Jan. 23, 1892; House 1867-69, 1881-85.

ROBISON, David Fullerton (nephew of David Fullerton) (W Pa.) May 28, 1816-June 24, 1859; House 1855-57.

ROBISON, Howard Winfield (R N.Y.) Oct. 30, 1915; House Jan. 14, 1958- .

ROBSION, John Marshall (R Ky.) Jan. 2, 1873-Feb. 17, 1948; House 1919-Jan. 10, 1930, 1935-Feb. 17, 1948; Senate Jan. 11-Nov. 30, 1930.

ROBSION, John Marshall, Jr. (son of the preceding) (R Ky.) Aug. 28, 1904; House 1953-59.

ROCHESTER, William Beatty (D N.Y.) Jan. 29, 1789-June 14, 1838; House 1821-April, 1823.

ROCKEFELLER, Lewis Kirby (R N.Y.) Nov. 25, 1875-Sept. 18, 1948; House Nov. 2, 1937-43.

ROCKHILL, William (D Ind.) Feb. 10, 1793-Jan. 15, 1865; House 1847-49.

ROCKWELL, Francis Williams (son of Julius Rockwell) (R Mass.) May 26, 1844-June 26, 1929; House Jan. 17, 1884-91.

ROCKWELL, Hosea Hunt (D N.Y.) May 31, 1840-Dec. 18, 1918; House 1891-93.

ROCKWELL, John Arnold (W Conn.) Aug. 27, 1803-Feb. 10, 1861; House 1845-49.

ROCKWELL, Julius (father of Francis Williams Rockwell) (W Mass.) April 26, 1805-May 19, 1888; House 1843-51; Senate June 3, 1854-Jan. 31, 1855.

ROCKWELL, Robert Fay (R Colo.) Feb. 11, 1886-Sept. 29, 1950; House Dec. 9, 1941-49.

RODDENBERY, Seaborn Anderson (D Ga.) Jan. 12, 1870-Sept. 25, 1913; House Feb. 16, 1910-Sept. 25, 1913.

RODENBERG, William August (R Ill.) Oct. 30, 1865-Sept. 10, 1937; House 1899-1901, 1903-13, 1915-23.

RODEY, Bernard Shandon (R N.M.) March 1, 1856-March 10, 1927; House (Terr. Del.) 1901-05.

RODGERS, Robert Lewis (R Pa.) June 2, 1875-May 9, 1960; House 1939-47.

RODINO, Peter Wallace, Jr. (D N.J.) June 7, 1909; House 1949- .

RODMAN, William (D Pa.) Oct. 7, 1757-July 27, 1824; House 1811-13.

RODNEY, Caesar Augustus (cousin of George Brydges Rodney) (D Del.) Jan. 4, 1772-June 10, 1824; House 1803-05, 1821-Jan. 24, 1822; Senate Jan. 24, 1822-Jan. 29, 1823; Atty. Gen. 1807-11.

RODNEY, Daniel (F Del.) Sept. 10, 1764-Sept. 2, 1846; House Oct. 1, 1822-23; Senate Nov. 8, 1826-Jan. 12, 1827; Gov. 1814-17.

RODNEY, George Brydges (cousin of Caesar Augustus Rodney) (W Del.) April 2, 1803-June 18, 1883; House 1841-45.

ROE, Dudley George (D Md.) March 23, 1881-Jan. 4, 1970; House 1945-47.

ROE, James A. (D N.Y.) July 9, 1896-April 22, 1967; House 1945-47.

ROE, Robert A. (D N.J.) Feb. 28, 1924; House Nov. 4, 1969- .

ROGERS, Andrew Jackson (D N.J.) July 1, 1828-May 22, 1900; House 1863-67.

ROGERS, Anthony Astley Cooper (D Ark.) Feb. 14, 1821-July 27, 1899; House 1869-71.

ROGERS, Byron Giles (D Colo.) Aug. 1, 1900; House 1951-71.

ROGERS, Charles (W N.Y.) April 30, 1800-Jan. 13, 1874; House 1843-45.

ROGERS, Dwight Laing (father of Paul G. Rogers) (D Fla.) Aug. 17, 1886-Dec. 1, 1954; House 1945-Dec. 1, 1954.

ROGERS, Edith Nourse (wife of John Jacob Rogers) (R Mass.) 1881-Sept. 10, 1960; House June 30, 1925-Sept. 10, 1960.

ROGERS, Edward (D N.Y.) May 30, 1787-May 29, 1957; House 1839-41.

ROGERS, George Frederick (D N.Y.) March 19, 1887-Nov. 20, 1948; House 1945-47.

ROGERS, James (D S.C.) Oct. 24, 1795-Dec. 12, 1873; House 1835-37, 1839-43.

ROGERS, John (D N.Y.) May 9, 1813-May 11, 1879; House 1871-73.

ROGERS, John Henry (D Ark.) Oct. 9, 1845-April 16, 1911; House 1883-91.

ROGERS, John Jacob (husband of Edith Nourse Rogers) (R Mass.) Aug. 18, 1881-March 28, 1925; House 1913-March 28, 1925.

ROGERS, Paul Grant (son of Dwight L. Rogers) (D Fla.) June 4, 1921; House Jan. 11, 1955- .

ROGERS, Sion Hart (D N.C.) Sept. 30, 1825-Aug. 14, 1874; House 1853-55 (W), 1871-73 (D).

ROGERS, Thomas Jones (father of William Findlay Rogers) (D Pa.) 1781-Dec. 7, 1832; House March 3, 1818-April 20, 1824.

ROGERS, Walter Edward (D Texas) July 19, 1908; House 1951-67.

ROGERS, Will (D Okla.) Dec. 12, 1898; House 1933-43.

ROGERS, Will, Jr. (D Calif.) Oct. 20, 1911; House 1943-May 23, 1944.

ROGERS, William Findlay (son of Thomas Jones Rogers) (D N.Y.) March 1, 1820-Dec. 16, 1899; House 1883-85.

ROGERS, William Nathaniel (D N.H.) Jan. 10, 1892-Sept. 25, 1945; House 1923-25, Jan. 5, 1932-37.

ROHRBOUGH, Edward Gay (R W.Va.) 1874-Dec. 12, 1956; House 1943-45, 1947-49.

ROLLINS, Edward Henry (R N.H.) Oct. 3, 1824-July 31, 1889; House 1861-67; Senate 1877-83.

ROLLINS, James Sidney (C Mo.) April 19, 1812-Jan. 9, 1888; House 1861-65.

ROLPH, Thomas (R Calif.) Jan. 17, 1885-May 10, 1956; House 1941-45.

ROMAN, James Dixon (W Md.) Aug. 11, 1809-Jan. 19, 1867; House 1847-49.

ROMEIS, Jacob (R Ohio) Dec. 1, 1835-March 8, 1904; House 1885-89.

ROMERO, Trinidad (R N.M.) June 15, 1835-Aug. 28, 1918; House (Terr. Del.) 1877-79.

ROMJUE, Milton Andrew (D Mo.) Dec. 5, 1874-Jan. 23, 1968; House 1917-21, 1923-43.

ROMULO, Carlos Pena (—P.I.) Jan. 14, 1901; House (Res. Comm.) Aug. 10, 1944-July 4, 1946.

RONAN, Daniel J. (D Ill.) July 13, 1914-Aug. 13, 1969; House 1965-Aug. 13, 1969.

RONCALIO, Teno (D Wyo.) March 23, 1916; House 1965-67, 1971- .

ROONEY, Fred B. (D Pa.) Nov. 6, 1925; House July 30, 1963- .

ROONEY, John James (D N.Y.) Nov. 29, 1903; House June 6, 1944- .

ROOSEVELT, Franklin Delano, Jr. (son of President Franklin D. Roosevelt and brother of James Roosevelt) (D N.Y.) Aug. 17, 1914; House May 17, 1949-51 (L/Four Freedoms Party), 1951-55 (D).

ROOSEVELT, James (son of President Franklin D. Roosevelt and brother of Franklin Delano Roosevelt, Jr.) (D Calif.) Dec. 23, 1907; House 1955-Sept. 30, 1965.

ROOSEVELT, James I. (uncle of Robert Barnwell Roosevelt) (D N.Y.) Dec. 14, 1795-April 5, 1875; House 1841-43.

ROOSEVELT, Robert Barnwell (nephew of James I. Roosevelt and uncle of President Theodore Roosevelt) (D N.Y.) Aug. 7, 1829-June 14, 1906; House 1871-73.

ROOT, Elihu (R N.Y.) Feb. 15, 1845-Feb. 7, 1937; Senate 1909-15; Secy. of War 1899-1904; Secy. of State 1905-09.

ROOT, Erastus (D N.Y.) March 16, 1773-Dec. 24, 1846; House 1803-05, 1809-11, Dec. 26, 1815-17, 1831-33.

ROOT, Joseph Mosley (W Ohio) Oct. 7, 1807-April 7, 1879; House 1845-51.

ROOTS, Logan Holt (R Ark.) March 26, 1841-May 30, 1893; House June 22, 1868-71.

ROSE, John Marshall (R Pa.) May 18, 1856-April 22, 1923; House 1917-23.

ROSE, Robert Lawson (son of Robert Seldon Rose and son-in-law of Nathaniel Allen) (W N.Y.) Oct. 12, 1804-March 14, 1877; House 1847-51.

ROSE, Robert Selden (father of Robert Lawson Rose) (—N.Y.) Feb. 24, 1774-Nov. 24, 1835; House 1823-27, 1829-31.

ROSECRANS, William Starke (D Calif.) Sept. 6, 1819-March 11, 1898; House 1881-85.

ROSENBLOOM, Benjamin Louis (R W. Va.) June 3, 1880-March 22, 1965; House 1921-25.

ROSENTHAL, Benjamin S. (D/L N.Y.) June 8, 1923; House Feb. 20, 1962- .

ROSIER, Joseph (D W. Va.) Jan. 24, 1870-Oct. 7, 1951; Senate Jan. 13, 1941-Nov. 17, 1942.

ROSS, Edmund Gibson (R Kan.) Dec. 7, 1826-May 8, 1907; Senate July 19, 1866-71; Gov. of N.M. Terr. (D) 1885-89.

ROSS, Henry Howard (W N.Y.) May 9, 1790-Sept. 14, 1862; House 1825-27.

ROSS, James (F Pa.) July 12, 1762-Nov. 27, 1847; Senate April 24, 1794-1803.

ROSS, John (father of Thomas Ross) (—Pa.) Feb. 24, 1770-Jan. 31, 1834; House 1809-11, 1815-Feb. 24, 1818.

ROSS, Jonathan (R Vt.) April 30, 1826-Feb. 23, 1905; Senate Jan. 11, 1899-Oct. 18, 1900.

ROSS, Lewis Winans (D Ill.) Dec. 8, 1812-Oct. 20, 1895; House 1863-69.

ROSS, Miles (D N.J.) April 30, 1827-Feb. 22, 1903; House 1875-83.

ROSS, Robert Tripp (R N.Y.) June 4, 1903; House 1947-49, Feb. 19, 1952-53.

ROSS, Sobieski (R Pa.) May 16, 1828-Oct. 24, 1877; House 1873-77.

ROSS, Thomas (son of John Ross) (D Pa.) Dec. 1, 1806-July 7, 1865; House 1849-53.

ROSS, Thomas Randolph (D Ohio) Oct. 26, 1788-June 28, 1869; House 1819-25.

ROSSDALE, Albert Berger (R N.Y.) Oct. 23, 1878; House 1921-23.

ROSTENKOWSKI, Daniel David (Dan) (D Ill.) Jan. 2, 1928; House 1959- .

ROTH, William V., Jr. (R Del.) July 22, 1921; House 1967-Dec. 31, 1970; Senate Jan. 1, 1971- .

ROTHERMEL, John Hoover (D Pa.) March 7, 1856-Aug., 1922; House 1907-15.

ROTHWELL, Gideon Frank (D Mo.) April 24, 1836-Jan. 18, 1894; House 1879-81.

ROUDEBUSH, Richard Lowell (R Ind.) Jan. 18, 1918; House 1961-71.

ROUSE, Arthur Blythe (D Ky.) June 20, 1874-Jan. 25, 1956; House 1911-27.

ROUSH, John Edward (D Ind.) Sept. 12, 1920; House 1959-69, 1971- .

ROUSSEAU, Lovell Harrison (R Ky.) Aug. 4, 1818-Jan. 7, 1869; House 1865-July 21, 1866, Dec. 3, 1866-67.

ROUSSELOT, John Harbin (R Calif.) Nov. 1, 1927; House 1961-63, June 30, 1970- .

ROUTZOHN, Harry Nelson (R Ohio) Nov. 4, 1881-April 14, 1953; House 1939-41.

ROWAN, John (uncle of Robert Todd Lytle) (D Ky.) July 12, 1773-July 13, 1843; House 1807-09; Senate 1825-31.

ROWAN, Joseph (D N.Y.) Sept. 8, 1870-Aug. 3, 1930; House 1919-21.

ROWAN, William A. (D Ill.) Nov. 24, 1882-May 31, 1961; House 1943-47.

ROWBOTTOM, Harry Emerson (R Ind.) Nov. 3, 1884-March 22, 1934; House 1925-31.

ROWE, Edmund (Ed) (R Ohio) Dec. 21, 1892; House 1943-45.

ROWE, Frederick William (R N.Y.) March 19, 1863-June 20, 1946; House 1915-21.

ROWE, Peter (D N.Y.) March 10, 1807-April 17, 1876; House 1853-55.

ROWELL, Jonathan Harvey (R Ill.) Feb. 10, 1833-May 15, 1908; House 1883-91.

ROWLAND, Alfred (D N.C.) Feb. 9, 1844-Aug. 2, 1898; House 1887-91.

ROWLAND, Charles Hedding (R Pa.) Dec. 20, 1860-Nov. 24, 1921; House 1915-19.

ROY, Alphonse (D N.H.) Oct. 26, 1897-Oct. 5, 1967; House June 9, 1938-39.

ROY, William R., Sr. (D Kan.) Feb. 23, 1926; House 1971- .

ROYBAL, Edward R. (D Calif.) Feb. 10, 1916; House 1963- .

ROYCE, Homer Elihu (R Vt.) June 14, 1819-April 24, 1891; House 1857-61.

ROYSE, Lemuel Willard (R Ind.) Jan. 19, 1847-Dec. 18, 1946; House 1895-99.

RUBEY, Thomas Lewis (D Mo.) Sept. 27, 1862-Nov. 2, 1928; House 1911-21, 1923-Nov. 2, 1928.

RUCKER, Atterson Walden (D Colo.) April 3, 1847-July 19, 1924; House 1909-13.

RUCKER, Tinsley White (D Ga.) March 24, 1848-Nov. 18, 1926; House Jan. 11-March 3, 1917.

RUCKER, William Waller (D Mo.) Feb. 1, 1855-May 30, 1936; House 1899-1923.

RUDD, Stephen Andrew (D N.Y.) Dec. 11, 1874-March 31, 1936; House 1931-March 31, 1936.

RUFFIN, James Edward (D Mo.) July 24, 1893; House 1933-35.

RUFFIN, Thomas (D N.C.) Sept. 9, 1820-Oct. 13, 1863; House 1853-61.

RUGGLES, Benjamin (D Ohio) Feb. 21, 1783-Sept. 2, 1857; Senate 1815-33.

RUGGLES, Charles Herman (—N.Y.) Feb. 10, 1789-June 16, 1865; House 1821-23.

RUGGLES, John (D Maine) Oct. 8, 1789-June 20, 1874; Senate Jan. 20, 1835-41.

RUGGLES, Nathaniel (F Mass.) Nov. 11, 1761-Dec. 19, 1819; House 1813-19.

RUMPLE, John Nicholas William (R Iowa) March 4, 1841-Jan. 31, 1903; House 1901-Jan. 31, 1903.

RUMSEY, David (W N.Y.) Dec. 25, 1810-March 12, 1883; House 1847-51.

RUMSEY, Edward (W Ky.) Nov. 5, 1796-April 6, 1868; House 1837-39.

RUMSFELD, Donald (R Ill.) July 9, 1932; House 1963-May 25, 1969.

RUNK, John (W N.J.) July 3, 1791-Sept. 22, 1872; House 1845-47.

RUNNELS, Harold L. (D N.M.) March 17, 1924; House 1971- .

RUPLEY, Arthur Ringwalt (PR Pa.) Nov. 13, 1868-Nov. 11, 1920; House 1913-15.

RUPPE, Philip E. (R Mich.) Sept. 29, 1926; House 1967- .

RUPPERT, Jacob, Jr. (D N.Y.) Aug. 5, 1867-Jan. 13, 1939; House 1899-1907.

RUSK, Harry Welles (D Md.) Oct. 17, 1852-Jan. 28, 1926; House Nov. 2, 1886-97.

RUSK, Jeremiah McLain (R Wis.) June 17, 1830-Nov. 21, 1893; House 1871-77; Gov. 1882-89; Secy. of Agric. 1889-93.

RUSK, Thomas Jefferson (D Texas) Dec. 5, 1803-July 29, 1857; Senate Feb. 21, 1846-July 29, 1857; President pro tempore 1857.

RUSS, John (D Conn.) Oct. 29, 1767-June 22, 1833; House 1819-23.

RUSSELL, Benjamin Edward (cousin of Rienzi Melville Johnston) (D Ga.) Oct. 5, 1845-Dec. 4, 1909; House 1893-97.

RUSSELL, Charles Addison (R Conn.) March 2, 1852-Oct. 23, 1902; House 1887-Oct. 23, 1902.

RUSSELL, Charles Hinton (R Nev.) Dec. 27, 1903; House 1947-49; Gov. 1951-59.

RUSSELL, Daniel Lindsay (R N.C.) Aug. 7, 1845-May 14, 1908; House 1879-81; Gov. 1896-1900.

RUSSELL, David Abel (W N.Y.) 1780-Nov. 24, 1861; House 1835-41.

RUSSELL, Donald Stuart (D S.C.) Feb. 22, 1906; Senate April 22, 1965-Nov. 8, 1966; Gov. 1963-65.

RUSSELL, Gordon James (D Texas) Dec. 22, 1859-Sept. 14, 1919; House Nov. 4, 1902-June 14, 1910.

RUSSELL, James McPherson (father of Samuel Lyon Russell) (W Pa.) Nov. 10, 1786-Nov. 14, 1870; House Dec. 21, 1841-43.

RUSSELL, Jeremiah (D N.Y.) Jan. 26, 1786-Sept. 30, 1867; House 1843-45.

RUSSELL, John (— N.Y.) Sept. 7, 1772-Aug. 2, 1842; House 1805-09.

RUSSELL, John Edwards (D Mass.) Jan. 20, 1834-Oct. 28, 1903; House 1887-89.

RUSSELL, Jonathan (D Mass.) Feb. 27, 1771-Feb. 16, 1832; House 1821-23.

RUSSELL, Joseph (D N.Y.)—-—; House 1845-57, 1851-53.

RUSSELL, Joseph James (D Mo.) Aug. 23, 1854-Oct. 22, 1922; House 1907-09, 1911-19.

RUSSELL, Joshua Edward (R Ohio) Aug. 9, 1867-June 21, 1953; House 1915-17.

RUSSELL, Leslie W. (—N.Y.) April 15, 1840-Feb. 3, 1903; House March 4-Sept. 11, 1891.

RUSSELL, Richard Brevard (D Ga.) Nov. 2, 1897-Jan. 21, 1971; Senate Jan. 12, 1933-Jan. 21, 1971; Gov. 1931-33.

RUSSELL, Richard Manning (D Mass.) March 3, 1891; House 1935-37.

RUSSELL, Sam Morris (D Texas) Aug. 9, 1889; House 1941-47.

RUSSELL, Samuel Lyon (son of James McPherson Russell) (W Pa.) July 30, 1816-Sept. 27, 1891; House 1853-55.

RUSSELL, William (W Ohio) 1782-Sept. 28, 1845; House 1827-33 (JD), 1841-43 (W).

RUSSELL, William Augustus (R Mass) April 22, 1831-Jan. 10, 1899; House 1879-85.

RUSSELL, William Fiero (D N.Y.) Jan. 14, 1812-April 29, 1896; House 1857-59.

RUST, Albert (D Ark.)—April 3, 1870; House 1855-57; 1859-61.

RUTH, Earl B. (R N.C.) Feb. 7, 1916; House 1969- .

RUTHERFORD, Albert Greig (R Pa.) Jan. 3, 1879-Aug. 10, 1941; House 1937-Aug. 10, 1941.

RUTHERFORD, J. T. (D Texas) May 30, 1920; House 1955-63.

RUTHERFORD, Robert (—Va.) Oct. 20, 1728-Oct. 1803; House 1793-97.

RUTHERFORD, Samuel (D Ga.) March 15, 1870-Feb. 4, 1932; House 1925-Feb. 4, 1932.

RUTHERFURD, John (F N.J.) Sept. 20, 1760-Feb. 23, 1840; Senate 1791-Dec. 5, 1798.

RUTLEDGE, John, Jr. (F S.C.) 1766-Sept. 1, 1819; House 1797-1803.

RYALL, Daniel Bailey (D N.J.) Jan. 30, 1798-Dec. 17, 1864; House 1839-41.

RYAN, Elmer James (D Minn.) May 26, 1907-Feb. 1, 1958; House 1935-41.

RYAN, Harold M. (D Mich.) Feb. 6, 1911; House Feb. 13, 1962-65.

RYAN, James Wilfrid (D Pa.) Oct. 16, 1858-Feb. 26, 1907; House 1899-1901.

RYAN, Thomas (R Kan.) Nov. 25, 1837-April 5, 1914; House 1877-April 4, 1889.

RYAN, Thomas Jefferson (R N.Y.) June 17, 1890-Nov. 10, 1968; House 1921-23.

RYAN, William (D N.Y.) March 8, 1840-Feb. 18, 1925; House 1893-95.

RYAN, William F. (D/L N.Y.) June 28, 1922; House 1961- .

RYAN, William Henry (D N.Y.) May 10, 1860-Nov. 18, 1939; House 1899-1909.

RYON, John Walker (D Pa.) March 4, 1825-March 12, 1901; House 1879-81.

RYTER, Joseph Francis (D Conn.) Feb. 4, 1914; House 1945-47.

S

SABATH, Adolph Joachim (D Ill.) April 4, 1866-Nov. 6, 1952; House 1907-Nov. 6, 1952.

SABIN, Alvah (W Vt.) Oct. 23, 1793-Jan. 22, 1885; House 1853-57.

SABIN, Dwight May (R Minn.) April 25, 1843-Dec. 22, 1902; Senate 1883-89; Chrmn. Rep. Nat. Comm. 1883-84.

SABINE, Lorenzo (W Mass.) Feb. 28, 1803-April 14, 1877; House Dec. 13, 1852-53.

SACKETT, Frederick Mosley (R Ky.) Dec. 17, 1868-May 18, 1941; Senate 1925-Jan. 9, 1930.

SACKETT, William Augustus (W N.Y.) Nov. 18, 1811-Sept. 6, 1895; House 1849-53.

SACKS, Leon (D Pa.) Oct. 7, 1902; House 1937-43.

SADLAK, Antoni Nicholas (R Conn.) June 13, 1908-Oct. 18, 1969; House 1947-59.

SADLER, Thomas William (D Ala.) April 17, 1831-Oct. 29, 1896; House 1885-87.

SADOWSKI, George Gregory (D Mich.) March 12, 1903-Oct. 9, 1961; House 1933-39, 1939-51.

SAGE, Ebenezer (D N.Y.) Aug. 16, 1755-Jan. 20, 1834; House 1809-15.

SAGE, Russell (W N.Y.) Aug. 4, 1816-July 22, 1906; House 1853-57.

SAILLY, Peter (D N.Y.) April 20, 1754-March 16, 1826; House 1805-07.

ST. GEORGE, Katharine Price Collier (R N.Y.) July 12, 1896-—; House 1947-65.

ST. GERMAIN, Fernand Joseph (D R.I.) Jan. 9, 1928; House 1961- .

ST. JOHN, Charles (R N.Y.) Oct. 8, 1818-July 6, 1891; House 1871-75.

ST. JOHN, Daniel Bennett (W N.Y.) Oct. 8, 1808-Feb. 18, 1890; House 1847-49.

ST. JOHN, Henry (D Ohio) July 16, 1783-May 1869; House 1843-47.

ST. MARTIN, Louis (D La.) May 17, 1820-Feb. 9, 1893; House 1851-53, 1885-57.

ST. ONGE, William Leon (D Conn.) Oct. 9, 1914-May 1, 1970; House 1963-May 1, 1970.

SALINGER, Pierre Emil George (D Calif.) June 14, 1925; Senate Aug. 5-Dec. 31, 1964.

SALMON, Joshua S. (D N.J.) Feb. 2, 1846-May 6, 1902; House 1899-May 6, 1902.

SALMON, William Charles (D Tenn.) April 3, 1868-May 13, 1925; House 1923-25.

SALTONSTALL, Leverett (W Mass.) June 13, 1783-May 8, 1845; House Dec. 5, 1838-43.

SALTONSTALL, Leverett (great-grandson of the preceding) (R Mass.) Sept. 1, 1892-—; Senate Jan. 4, 1945-67; Gov. 1939-44.

SAMFORD, William James (D Ala.) Sept. 16, 1844-June 11, 1901; House 1879-81; Gov. 1900-01.

SAMMONS, Thomas (grandfather of John Henry Starin) (D N.Y.) Oct. 1, 1762-Nov. 20, 1838; House 1803-07, 1809-13.

SAMPLE, Samuel Caldwell (W Ind.) Aug. 15, 1796-Dec. 2, 1855; House 1843-45.

SAMPSON, Ezekiel Silas (R Iowa) Dec. 6, 1831-Oct. 7, 1892; House 1875-79.

SAMPSON, Zabdiel (D Mass.) Aug. 22, 1781-July 19, 1828; House 1817-July 26, 1820.

SAMUEL, Edmund William (R Pa.) Nov. 27, 1857-March 7, 1930; House 1905-07.

SAMUELS, Green Berry (cousin of Isaac Samuels Pennybacker) (D Va.) Feb. 1, 1806-Jan. 5, 1859; House 1839-41.

SANBORN, John Carfield (R Idaho) Sept. 28, 1885-May 16, 1968; House 1947-51.

SANDAGER, Harry (R R.I.) April 12, 1887-Dec. 24, 1955; House 1939-41.

SANDERS, Archie Dovell (R N.Y.) June 17, 1857-July 15, 1941; House 1917-33.

SANDERS, Everett (R Ind.) March 8, 1882-May 12, 1950; House 1917-25; Chrmn. Rep. Nat. Comm. 1932-34.

SANDERS, Jared Young (D La.) Jan. 29, 1869-March 23, 1944; House 1917-21; Gov. 1908-12.

SANDERS, Jared Young, Jr. (son of the preceding) (D La.) April 20, 1892-Nov. 29, 1960; House May 1, 1934-37, 1941-43.

SANDERS, Morgan Gurley (D Texas) July 14, 1878-Jan. 7, 1956; House 1921-39.

SANDERS, Newell (R Tenn.) July 12, 1850-Jan. 26, 1939; Senate April 11, 1912-Jan. 24, 1913.

SANDERS, Wilbur Fiske (R Mont.) May 2, 1834-July 7, 1905; Senate Jan. 1, 1890-93.

SANDFORD, James T. (— Tenn.) —-—; House 1823-25.

SANDFORD, Thomas (D Ky.) 1762-Dec. 10, 1808; House 1803-07.

SANDIDGE, John Milton (D La.) Jan. 7, 1817-March 30, 1890; House 1855-59.

SANDLIN, John Nicholas (D La.) Feb. 24, 1872-Dec. 25, 1957; House 1921-37.

SANDMAN, Charles W., Jr. (R N.J.) Oct. 23, 1921; House 1967- .

SANDS, Joshua (— N.Y.) Oct. 12, 1757-Sept. 13, 1835; House 1803-05, 1825-27.

SANFORD, John (father of Stephen Sanford) (D N.Y.) June 3, 1803-Oct. 4, 1857; House 1841-43.

SANFORD, John (son of Stephen Sanford and grandson of the preceding) (R N.Y.) Jan. 18, 1851-Sept. 26, 1939; House 1889-93.

SANFORD, John W. A. (UD Ga.) Aug. 28, 1798-Sept. 12, 1870; House March 4-July 25, 1835.

SANFORD, Jonah (great-grandfather of Rollin Brewster Sanford) (JD N.Y.) Nov. 30, 1790-Dec. 25, 1867; House Nov. 3, 1830-31.

SANFORD, Nathan (D N.Y.) Nov. 5, 1777-Oct. 17, 1838; Senate 1815-21, Jan. 14, 1826-31.

SANFORD, Rollin Brewster (great-grandson of Jonah Sanford) (R N.Y.) May 18, 1874-May 16, 1957; House 1915-21.

SANFORD, Stephen (son of John Sanford born in 1803 and father of John Sanford born in 1851) (R N.Y.) May 26, 1826-Feb. 13, 1913; House 1869-71.

SANTANGELO, Alfred Edward (D N.Y.) June 4, 1912; House 1957-63.

SAPP, William Fletcher (nephew of William R. Sapp) (R Iowa) Nov. 20, 1824-Nov. 22, 1890; House 1877-81.

SAPP, William Robinson (uncle of William F. Sapp) (W Ohio) March 4, 1804-Jan. 3, 1875; House 1853-57.

SARBACHER, George William Jr. (R Pa.) Sept. 30, 1919; House 1947-49.

SARBANES, Paul S. (D Md.) Feb. 3, 1933; House 1971- .

SARGENT, Aaron Augustus (R Calif.) Sept. 28, 1827-Aug. 14, 1887; House 1861-63, 1869-73; Senate 1873-79.

SASSCER, Lansdale Ghiselin (D Md.) Sept. 30, 1893-Nov. 5, 1964; House Feb. 3, 1939-53.

SATTERFIELD, Dave Edward, Jr. (D Va.) Sept. 11, 1894-Dec. 27, 1946; House Nov. 2, 1937-Feb. 15, 1945.

SATTERFIELD, David Edward, III (son of the preceding) (D Va.) Dec. 2, 1920; House 1965- .

SAUERHERING, Edward (R Wis.) June 24, 1864-March 1, 1924; House 1895-99.

SAULSBURY, Eli (brother of Willard Saulsbury) (D Del.) Dec. 29, 1817-March 22, 1893; Senate 1871-89.

SAULSBURY, Willard (brother of Eli Saulsbury) (D Del.) June 2, 1820-April 6, 1892; Senate 1859-71.

SAULSBURY, Willard (son of the preceding) (D Del.) April 17, 1861-Feb. 20, 1927; Senate 1913-19; President pro tempore 1916-19.

SAUND, Dalip Singh (D Calif.) Sept. 20, 1899-—; House 1957-63.

SAUNDERS, Alvin (grandfather of William Henry Harrison of Wyoming) (R Neb.) July 12, 1817-Nov. 1, 1899; Senate March 5, 1877-83; Gov. (Neb. Terr.) 1861-67.

SAUNDERS, Edward Watts (D Va.) Oct. 20, 1860-Dec. 16, 1921; House Nov. 6, 1906-Feb. 29, 1920.

SAUNDERS, Romulus Mitchell (D N.C.) March 3, 1791-April 21, 1867; House 1821-27, 1841-45.

SAUTHOFF, Harry (Pro. Wis.) June 3, 1879-June 16, 1966; House 1935-39, 1941-45.

SAVAGE, Charles Raymon (D Wash.) April 12, 1906; House 1945-47.

SAVAGE, John (D N.Y.) Feb. 22, 1779-Oct. 19, 1863; House 1815-19.

SAVAGE, John Houston (— Tenn.) Oct. 9, 1815-April 5, 1904; House 1849-53, 1855-59.

SAVAGE, John Simpson (D Ohio) Oct. 30, 1841-Nov. 24, 1884; House 1875-77.

SAWTELLE, Cullen (D Maine) Sept. 25, 1805-Nov. 10, 1887; House 1845-47, 1849-51.

SAWYER, Frederick Adolphus (R S.C.) Dec. 12, 1822-July 31, 1891; Senate July 16, 1868-73.

SAWYER, John Gilbert (R N.Y.) June 5, 1825-Sept. 5, 1898; House 1885-91.

SAWYER, Lemuel (D N.C.) 1777-Jan. 9, 1852; House 1807-13, 1817-23, 1825-29.

SAWYER, Lewis Ernest (D Ark.) June 24, 1867-May 5, 1923; House March 4-May 5, 1923.

SAWYER, Philetus (R Wis.) Sept. 22, 1816-March 29, 1900; House 1865-75; Senate 1881-93.

SAWYER, Samuel Locke (D Mo.) Nov. 27, 1813-March 29, 1890; House 1879-81.

SAWYER, Samuel Tredwell (D N.C.) 1800-Nov. 29, 1865; House 1837-39.

SAWYER, William (D Ohio) Aug. 5, 1803-Sept. 18, 1877; House 1845-49.

SAXBE, William B. (R Ohio) June 24, 1916; Senate 1969- .

SAY, Benjamin (— Pa.) 1756-April 23, 1813; House Nov. 16, 1808-June, 1809.

SAYERS, Joseph Draper (D Texas) Sept. 23, 1841-May 15, 1929; House 1885-Jan. 16, 1899; Gov. 1899-1903.

SAYLER, Henry Benton (cousin of Milton Sayler) (R Ind.) March 31, 1836-June 18, 1900; House 1873-75.

SAYLER, Milton (cousin of Henry Benton Sayler) (D Ohio) Nov. 4, 1831-Nov. 17, 1892; House 1873-79.

SAYLOR, John Phillips (R Pa.) July 23, 1908; House Sept. 13, 1949- .

SCALES, Alfred Moore (D N.C.) Nov. 26, 1827-Feb. 9, 1892; House 1857-59, 1875-Dec. 30, 1884; Gov. 1884-88.

SCAMMAN, John Fairfield (D Maine) Oct. 24, 1786-May 22, 1858; House 1845-47.

SCANLON, Thomas Edward (D Pa.) Sept. 18, 1896-Aug. 9, 1955; House 1941-45.

SCARBOROUGH, Robert Bethea (D S.C.) Oct. 29, 1861-Nov. 23, 1927; House 1901-05.

SCHADEBERG, Henry C. (R Wis.) Oct. 12, 1913; House 1961-65, 1967-71.

SCHAEFER, Edwin Martin (D Ill.) May 14, 1887-Nov. 8, 1950; House 1933-43.

SCHAFER, John Charles (R Wis.) May 7, 1893-June 12, 1962; House 1923-33, 1939-41.

SCHALL, Thomas David (R Minn.) June 4, 1878-Dec. 22, 1935; House 1915-25; Senate 1925-Dec. 22, 1935.

SCHELL, Richard (D N.Y.) May 15, 1810-Nov. 10, 1879; House Dec. 7, 1874-75.

SCHENCK, Abraham Henry (uncle of Isaac Teller) (D N.Y.) Jan. 22, 1775-June 1, 1831; House 1815-17.

SCHENCK, Ferdinand Schureman (JD N.J.) Feb. 11, 1790-May 16, 1860; House 1833-37.

SCHENCK, Paul Fornshell (R Ohio) April 19, 1899-Nov. 30, 1968; House Nov. 6, 1951-65.

SCHENCK, Robert Cumming (R Ohio) Oct. 4, 1809-March 23, 1890; House 1843-51 (W), 1863-Jan. 5, 1871 (R).

SCHERER, Gordon Harry (R Ohio) Dec. 26, 1906; House 1953-63.

SCHERLE, William J. (R Iowa) March 14, 1923; House 1967- .

SCHERMERHORN, Abraham Maus (W N.Y.) Dec. 11, 1791-Aug. 22, 1855; House 1849-53.

SCHERMERHORN, Simon Jacob (D N.Y.) Sept. 25, 1827-July 21, 1901; House 1893-95.

SCHEUER, James H. (D N.Y.) Feb. 6, 1920; House 1965- .

SCHIFFLER, Andrew Charles (R W.Va.) Aug. 10, 1889-March 27, 1970; House 1939-41, 1943-45.

SCHIRM, Charles Reginald (R Md.) Aug. 12, 1864-Nov. 2, 1918; House 1901-03.

SCHISLER, Gale (D Ill.) March 2, 1933; House 1965-67.

SCHLEICHER, Gustave (D Texas) Nov. 19, 1823-Jan. 10, 1879; House 1875-Jan. 10, 1879.

SCHLEY, William (D Ga.) Dec. 15, 1786-Nov. 20, 1858; House 1833-July 1, 1835; Gov. 1835-37.

SCHMIDHAUSER, John Richard (D Iowa) Jan. 3, 1922; House 1965-67.

SCHMITZ, John G. (R Calif.) Aug. 12, 1930; House June 30, 1970- .

SCHNEEBELI, Gustav Adolphus (R Pa.) May 23, 1853-Feb. 6, 1923; House 1905-07.

SCHNEEBELI, Herman T. (R Pa.) July 7, 1907; House April 26, 1960- .

SCHNEIDER, George John (Pro. Wis.) Oct. 30, 1877-March 12, 1939; House 1923-33 (R), 1935-39 (Pro.).

SCHOEPPEL, Andrew Frank (R Kan.) Nov. 23, 1894-Jan. 21, 1962; Senate 1949-Jan. 21, 1962; Gov. 1943-47.

SCHOOLCRAFT, John Lawrence (W N.Y.) 1804-July 7, 1860; House 1849-53.

SCHOONMAKER, Cornelius Corneliusen (grandfather of Marius Schoonmaker) (— N.Y.) June 1745-96; House 1791-93.

SCHOONMAKER, Marius (grandson of Cornelius Corneliusen Schoonmaker) (W N.Y.) April 24, 1811-Jan. 5, 1894; House 1851-53.

SCHUETZ, Leonard William (D Ill.) Nov. 16, 1887-Feb. 13, 1944; House 1931-Feb. 13, 1944.

SCHULTE, William Theodore (D Ind.) Aug. 19, 1890-Dec. 7, 1966; House 1933-43.

SCHUMAKER, John Godfrey (D N.Y.) June 27, 1826-Nov. 23, 1905; House 1869-71, 1873-77.

SCHUNEMAN, Martin Gerretsen (D N.Y.) Feb. 10, 1764-Feb. 21, 1827; House 1805-07.

SCHUREMAN, James (F N.J.) Feb. 12, 1756-Jan. 22, 1824; House 1789-91, 1797-99, 1813-15; Senate 1799-Feb. 16, 1801; Cont. Cong. 1786-87.

SCHURZ, Carl (R Mo.) March 2, 1829-May 14, 1906; Senate 1869-75; Secy. of the Interior 1877-81.

SCHUYLER, Karl Cortlandt (R Colo.) April 3, 1877-July 31, 1933; Senate Dec. 7, 1932-33.

SCHUYLER, Philip Jeremiah (son of Philip John Schuyler) (— N.Y.) Jan. 21, 1768-Feb. 21, 1835; House 1817-19.

SCHUYLER, Philip John (father of Philip Jeremiah Schuyler) (F N.Y.) Nov. 20, 1733-Nov. 18, 1804; Senate 1789-91, 1797-Jan. 3, 1798; Cont. Cong. 1775-81.

SCHWABE, George Blaine (brother of Max Schwabe) (R Okla.) July 26, 1886-April 2, 1952; House 1945-49, 1951-April 2, 1952.

SCHWABE, Max (brother of George Blaine Schwabe) (R Mo.) Dec. 6, 1905; House 1943-49.

SCHWARTZ, Henry Herman (Harry) (D Wyo.) May 18, 1869-April 24, 1955; Senate 1937-43.

SCHWARTZ, John (D Pa.) Oct. 27, 1793-June 20, 1860; House 1859-June 20, 1860.

SCHWEIKER, Richard Schultz (R Pa.) June 1, 1926; House 1961-69; Senate 1969- .

SCHWELLENBACH, Lewis Baxter (D Wash.) Sept. 20, 1894-June 10, 1948; Senate 1935-Dec. 16, 1940; Secy. of Labor 1945-48.

SCHWENGEL, Frederick Delbert (R Iowa) May 28, 1907; House 1955-65, 1967- .

SCHWERT, Pius Louis (D N.Y.) Nov. 22, 1892-March 11, 1941; House 1939-March 11, 1941.

SCOBLICK, James Paul (R Pa.) May 10, 1909; House Nov. 5, 1946-49.

SCOFIELD, Glenni William (R Pa.) March 11, 1817-Aug. 30, 1891; House 1863-75.

SCOTT, Byron Nicholson (D Calif.) March 21, 1903; House 1935-39.

SCOTT, Charles Frederick (R Kan.) Sept. 7, 1860-Sept. 18, 1938; House 1901-11.

SCOTT, Charles Lewis (D Calif.) Jan. 23, 1827-April 30, 1899; House 1857-61.

SCOTT, David (— Pa.) ——-; House 1817.

SCOTT, Frank Douglas (R Mich.) Aug. 25, 1878-Feb. 12, 1951; House 1915-27.

SCOTT, George Cromwell (R Iowa) Aug. 8, 1864-Oct. 6, 1948; House Nov. 5, 1912-15, 1917-19.

SCOTT, Hardie (son of John Roger Kirkpatrick Scott) (R Pa.) June 7, 1907; House 1947-53.

SCOTT, Harvey David (R Ind.) Oct. 18, 1818-July 11, 1891; House 1855-57.

SCOTT, Hugh Doggett, Jr. (R Pa.) Nov. 11, 1900; House 1941-45, 1947-59; Senate 1959- ; Chrmn. Rep. Nat. Comm. 1948-49.

SCOTT, John (— Mo.) May 18, 1785-Oct. 1, 1861; House (Terr. Del.) Aug. 6, 1816-Jan. 13, 1817, Aug. 4, 1817-March 3, 1821, (Rep.) Aug. 10, 1821-27.

SCOTT, John (— Pa.) Dec. 25, 1784-Sept. 22, 1850; House 1829-31.

SCOTT, John (son of the preceding) (R Pa.) July 24, 1824-Nov. 29, 1896; Senate 1869-75.

SCOTT, John Guier (D Mo.) Dec. 26, 1819-May 16, 1892; House Dec. 7, 1863-65.

SCOTT, John Roger Kirkpatrick (father of Hardie Scott) (R Pa.) July 6, 1873-Dec. 9, 1945; House 1915-Jan. 5, 1919.

SCOTT, Lon Allen (R Tenn.) Sept. 25, 1888-Feb. 11, 1931; House 1921-23.

SCOTT, Nathan Bay (R W.Va.) Dec. 18, 1842-Jan. 2, 1924; Senate 1899-1911.

SCOTT, Owen (D Ill.) July 6, 1848-Dec. 21, 1928; House 1891-93.

SCOTT, Ralph James (D N.C.) Oct. 15, 1905; House 1957-67.

SCOTT, Thomas (— Pa.) 1739-March 2, 1796; House 1789-91, 1793-95.

SCOTT, William Kerr (D N.C.) April 17, 1896-April 16, 1958; Senate Nov. 29, 1954-April 16, 1958; Gov. 1949-52.

SCOTT, William Lawrence (D Pa.) July 2, 1828-Sept. 19, 1891; House 1885-89.

SCOTT, William Lloyd (R Va.) July 1, 1915; House 1967- .

SCOVILLE, Jonathan (D N.Y.) July 14, 1830-March 4, 1891; House Nov. 12, 1880-83.

SCRANTON, George Whitfield (second cousin of Joseph Augustine Scranton) (R Pa.) May 11, 1811-March 24, 1861; House 1859-March 24, 1861.

SCRANTON, Joseph Augustine (second cousin of George Whitfield Scranton) (R Pa.) July 26, 1838-Oct. 12, 1908; House 1881-83, 1885-87, 1889-91, 1893-97.

SCRANTON, William Warren (R Pa.) July 19, 1917; House 1961-63; Gov. 1963-67.

SCRIVNER, Errett Power (R Kan.) March 20, 1898-——; House Sept. 14, 1943-59.

SCROGGY, Thomas Edmund (R Ohio) March 18, 1843-March 6, 1915; House 1905-07.

SCRUGHAM, James Graves (D Nev.) Jan. 19, 1880-June 23, 1945; House 1933-Dec. 7, 1942; Senate Dec. 7, 1942-June 23, 1945; Gov. 1923-27.

SCUDDER, Henry Joel (uncle of Townsend Scudder) (R N.Y.) Sept. 18, 1825-Feb. 10, 1886; House 1873-75.

SCUDDER, Hubert Baxter (R Calif.) Nov. 5, 1888-July 4, 1968; House 1949-59.

SCUDDER, Isaac Williamson (R N.J.) 1816-Sept. 10, 1881; House 1873-75.

SCUDDER, John Anderson (D N.J.) March 22, 1759-Nov. 6, 1835; House Oct. 31, 1810-11.

SCUDDER, Townsend (nephew of Henry Joel Scudder) (D N.Y.) July 26, 1865-Feb. 22, 1960; House 1899-1901, 1903-05.

SCUDDER, Tredwell (— N.Y.) Jan. 1, 1778-Oct. 31, 1834; House 1817-19.

SCUDDER, Zeno (W Mass.) Aug. 18, 1807-June 26, 1857; House 1851-March 4, 1854.

SCULL, Edward (R Pa.) Feb. 5, 1818-July 10, 1900; House 1887-93.

SCULLY, Thomas Joseph (D N.J.) Sept. 19, 1868-Dec. 14, 1921; House 1911-21.

SCURRY, Richardson (D Texas) Nov. 11, 1811-April 9, 1862; House 1851-53.

SEAMAN, Henry John (AP N.Y.) April 16, 1805-May 3, 1861; House 1845-47.

SEARING, John Alexander (D N.Y.) May 14, 1805-May 6, 1876; House 1857-59.

SEARS, William Joseph (D Fla.) Dec. 4, 1874-March 30, 1944; House 1915-29, 1933-37.

SEARS, Willis Gratz (R Neb.) Aug. 16, 1860-June 1, 1949; House 1923-31.

SEATON, Frederick Andrew (R Neb.) Dec. 11, 1909; Senate Dec. 10, 1951-Nov. 4, 1952; Secy. of the Interior 1956-61.

SEAVER, Ebenezer (D Mass.) July 5, 1763-March 1, 1844; House 1803-13.

SEBASTIAN, William King (D Ark.) 1812-May 20, 1865; Senate May 12, 1848-July 11, 1861.

SEBELIUS, Keith G. (R Kan.) Sept. 10, 1916; House 1969- .

SECCOMBE, James (R Ohio) Feb. 12, 1893-Aug. 23, 1970; House 1939-41.

SECREST, Robert Thompson (D Ohio) Jan. 22, 1904; House 1933-Aug. 3, 1942, 1949-Sept. 26, 1954, 1963-Dec. 30, 1966.

SEDDON, James Alexander (D Va.) July 13, 1815-Aug. 19, 1880; House 1845-47, 1849-51.

SEDGWICK, Charles Baldwin (R N.Y.) March 15, 1815-Feb. 3, 1883; House 1859-63.

SEDGWICK, Theodore (F Mass.) May 9, 1746-Jan. 24, 1813; House 1789-June 1796, 1799-1801; Senate June 11, 1796-99; Speaker 1799-1801; President pro tempore 1798; Cont. Cong. 1785-88.

SEELEY, John Edward (R N.Y.) Aug. 1, 1810-March 30, 1875; House 1871-73.

SEELY-BROWN, Horace, Jr. (R Conn.) May 12, 1908; House 1947-49, 1951-59, 1961-63.

SEELYE, Julius Hawley (I Mass.) Sept. 14, 1824-May 12, 1895; House 1875-77.

SEERLEY, John Joseph (D Iowa) March 13, 1852-Feb. 23, 1931; House 1891-93.

SEGAR, Joseph Eggleston (U Va.) June 1, 1804-April 30, 1880; House March 15, 1862-63.

SEGER, George Nicholas (R N.J.) Jan. 4, 1866-Aug. 26, 1940; House 1923-Aug. 26, 1940.

SEIBERLING, Francis (R Ohio) Sept. 20, 1870-Feb. 1, 1945; House 1929-33.

SEIBERLING, John F. (D Ohio) Sept. 8, 1918; House 1971- .

SELBY, Thomas Jefferson (D Ill.) Dec. 4, 1840-March 10, 1917; House 1901-03.

SELDEN, Armistead Inge, Jr. (D Ala.) Feb. 20, 1921; House 1953-69.

SELDEN, Dudley (D N.Y.) —-Nov. 7, 1855; House 1833-July 1, 1834.

SELDOMRIDGE, Harry Hunter (D Colo.) Oct. 1, 1864-Nov. 2, 1927; House 1913-15.

SELLS, Sam Riley (R Tenn.) Aug. 2, 1871-Nov. 2, 1935; House 1911-21.

SELVIG, Conrad George (R Minn.) Oct. 11, 1877-Aug. 2, 1953; House 1927-33.

SELYE, Lewis (I N.Y.) July 11, 1803-Jan. 27, 1883; House 1867-69.

SEMMES, Benedict Joseph (D Md.) Nov. 1, 1789-Feb. 10, 1863; House 1829-33.

SEMPLE, James (D Ill.) Jan. 5, 1798-Dec. 20, 1866; Senate Dec. 4, 1843-47.

SENER, James Beverley (R Va.) May 18, 1837-Nov. 18, 1903; House 1873-75.

SENEY, George Ebbert (D Ohio) May 29, 1832-June 11, 1905; House 1883-91.

SENEY, Joshua (— Md.) March 4, 1756-Oct. 20, 1798; House 1789-May 1, 1792; Cont. Cong. 1787-88.

SENNER, George Frederick Jr. (D Ariz.) Nov. 24, 1921; House 1963-67.

SENTER, William Tandy (W Tenn.) May 12, 1801-Aug. 28, 1848; House 1843-45.

SERGEANT, John (grandfather of John Sergeant Wise and Richard Alsop Wise, and great-grandfather of John Crain Kunkel) (F Pa.) Dec. 5, 1779-Nov. 23, 1852; House Oct. 10, 1815-23, 1827-29, 1837-Sept. 15, 1841.

SESSINGHAUS, Gustavus (R Mo.) Nov. 8, 1838-Nov. 16, 1887; House March 2-3, 1883.

SESSIONS, Walter Loomis (R N.Y.) Oct. 4, 1820-May 27, 1896; House 1871-75, 1885-87.

SETTLE, Evan Evans (D Ky.) Dec. 1, 1848-Nov. 16, 1899; House 1897-Nov. 16, 1899.

SETTLE, Thomas (uncle of David Settle Reid) (D N.C.) March 9, 1789-Aug. 5, 1857; House 1817-21.

SETTLE, Thomas (grandson of the preceding) (R N.C.) March 10, 1865-Jan. 20, 1919; House 1893-97.

SEVERANCE, Luther (W Maine) Oct. 26, 1797-Jan. 25, 1855; House 1843-47.

SEVIER, Ambrose Hundley (cousin of Henry Wharton Conway) (D Ark.) Nov. 10, 1801-Dec. 31, 1848; House (Terr. Del.) Feb. 13, 1828-June 15, 1836 (W); Senate Sept. 18, 1836-March 15, 1848 (D).

SEVIER, John (D N.C./Tenn.) Sept. 23, 1745-Sept. 24, 1815; House 1789-91 (N.C.), 1811-Sept. 24, 1815 (Tenn.); Gov. of Tenn. 1796-1801, 1803-09.

SEWALL, Charles S. (— Md.) 1779-Nov. 3, 1848; House Oct. 1, 1832-33, Jan. 2-March 3, 1843.

SEWALL, Samuel (— Mass.) Dec. 11, 1757-June 8, 1814; House Dec. 7, 1796-Jan. 10, 1800.

SEWARD, James Lindsay (D Ga.) Oct. 30, 1813-Nov. 21, 1886; House 1853-59.

SEWARD, William Henry (R N.Y.) May 16, 1801-Oct. 16, 1872; Senate 1849-55 (W), 1855-61 (R); Secy. of State 1861-69.

SEWELL, William Joyce (R N.J.) Dec. 6, 1835-Dec. 27, 1901; Senate 1881-87, 1895-Dec. 27, 1901.

SEXTON, Leonidas (R Ind.) May 19, 1827-July 4, 1880; House 1877-79.

SEYBERT, Adam (D Pa.) May 16, 1773-May 2, 1825; House Oct. 10, 1809-15, 1817-19.

SEYMOUR, David Lowrey (D N.Y.) Dec. 2, 1803-Oct. 11, 1867; House 1843-45, 1851-53.

SEYMOUR, Edward Woodruff (son of Origen Storrs Seymour) (D Conn.) Aug. 30, 1832-Oct. 16, 1892; House 1883-87.

SEYMOUR, Henry William (R Mich.) July 21, 1834-April 7, 1906; House Feb. 14, 1888-89.

SEYMOUR, Horatio (uncle of Origen Storrs Seymour) (CD Vt.) May 31, 1778-Nov. 21, 1857; Senate 1821-33.

SEYMOUR, Origen Storrs (father of Edward Woodruff Seymour and nephew of Horatio Seymour) (D Conn.) Feb. 9, 1804-Aug. 12, 1881; House 1851-55.

SEYMOUR, Thomas Hart (D Conn.) Sept. 29, 1807-Sept. 3, 1868; House 1843-45; Gov. 1850-53.

SEYMOUR, William (D N.Y.) about 1780-Dec. 28, 1848; House 1835-37.

SHACKELFORD, John Williams (D N.C.) Nov. 16, 1844-Jan. 18, 1883; House 1881-Jan. 18, 1883.

SHACKLEFORD, Dorsey William (D Mo.) Aug. 27, 1853-July 15, 1936; House Aug. 29, 1899-1919.

SHAFER, Jacob K. (D Idaho) Dec. 26, 1823-Nov. 22, 1876; House (Terr. Del.) 1869-71.

SHAFER, Paul Werntz (R Mich.) April 27, 1893-Aug. 17, 1954; House 1937-Aug. 17, 1954.

SHAFFER, Joseph Crockett (R Va.) Jan. 19, 1880-Oct. 19, 1958; House 1929-31.

SHAFROTH, John Franklin (D Colo.) June 9, 1854-Feb. 20, 1922; House 1895-97 (R), 1897-1903 (Sil.R/D), 1903-Feb. 15, 1904 (D); Senate 1913-19; Gov. 1908-12.

SHALLENBERGER, Ashton Cokayne (D Neb.) Dec. 23, 1862-Feb. 22, 1938; House 1901-03, 1915-19, 1923-29, 1931-35; Gov. 1908-11.

SHALLENBERGER, William Shadrack (R Pa.) Nov. 24, 1839-April 15, 1914; House 1877-83.

SHANKLIN, George Sea (D Ky.) Dec. 23, 1807-April 1, 1883; House 1865-67.

SHANKS, John Peter Cleaver (R Ind.) June 17, 1826-Jan. 23, 1901; House 1861-63, 1867-75.

SHANLEY, James Andrew (D Conn.) April 1, 1896-April 5, 1965; House 1935-43.

SHANNON, Joseph Bernard (D Mo.) March 17, 1867-March 28, 1943; House 1931-43.

SHANNON, Richard Cutts (R N.Y.) Feb. 12, 1839-Oct. 5, 1920; House 1895-99.

SHANNON, Thomas (brother of Wilson Shannon) (D Ohio) Nov. 15, 1786-March 16, 1843; House Dec. 4, 1826-27.

SHANNON, Thomas Bowles (R Calif.) Sept. 21, 1827-Feb. 21, 1897; House 1863-65.

SHANNON, Wilson (brother of Thomas Shannon) (D Ohio) Feb. 24, 1802-Aug. 31, 1877; House 1853-55; Gov. of Ohio 1838-40, 1842-44; Gov. Kansas Terr. 1855-56.

SHARON, William (R Nev.) Jan. 9, 1821-Nov. 13, 1885; Senate 1875-81.

SHARP, Edgar Allan (R N.Y.) June 3, 1876-Nov. 27, 1948; House 1945-47.

SHARP, Solomon P. (D Ky.) 1780-Nov. 7, 1825; House 1813-17.

SHARP, William Graves (D Ohio) March 14, 1859-Nov. 17, 1922; House 1909-July 23, 1914.

SHARPE, Peter (— N.Y.) —-—; House 1823-25.

SHARTEL, Cassius McLean (R Mo.) April 27, 1860-Sept. 27, 1943; House 1905-07.

SHATTUC, William Bunn (R Ohio) June 11, 1841-July 13, 1911; House 1897-1903.

SHAW, Aaron (D Ill.) Dec. 19, 1811-Jan. 7, 1887; House 1857-59, 1883-85.

SHAW, Albert Duane (R N.Y.) Dec. 21, 1841-Feb. 10, 1901; House Nov. 6, 1900-Feb. 10, 1901.

SHAW, Frank Thomas (D Md.) Oct. 7, 1841-Feb. 24, 1923; House 1885-89.

SHAW, George Bullen (R Wis.) March 12, 1854-Aug. 27, 1894; House 1893-Aug. 27, 1894.

SHAW, Guy Loren (R Ill.) May 16, 1881-May 19, 1950; House 1921-23.

SHAW, Henry (son of Samuel Shaw) (F Mass.) 1788-Oct. 17, 1857; House 1817-21.

SHAW, Henry Marchmore (D N.C.) Nov. 20, 1819-Nov. 1, 1864; House 1853-55, 1857-59.

SHAW, John Gilbert (D N.C.) Jan. 16, 1859-July 21, 1932; House 1895-97.

SHAW, Samuel (father of Henry Shaw) (D Vt.) Dec. 1768-Oct. 23, 1827; House Sept. 6, 1808-13.

SHAW, Tristram (— N.H.) May 23, 1786-March 14, 1843; House 1839-43.

SHEAFE, James (F N.H.) Nov. 16, 1755-Dec. 5, 1829; House 1799-1801; Senate 1801-June 14, 1802.

SHEAKLEY, James (D Pa.) April 24, 1829-Dec. 10, 1917; House 1875-77; Gov. of Alaska 1893-97.

SHEATS, Charles Christopher (R Ala.) April 10, 1839-May 27, 1904; House 1873-75.

SHEEHAN, Timothy Patrick (R Ill.) Feb. 21, 1909; House 1951-59.

SHEFFER, Daniel (D Pa.) May 24, 1783-Feb. 16, 1880; House 1837-39.

SHEFFEY, Daniel (F Va.) 1770-Dec. 3, 1830; House 1809-17.

SHEFFIELD, William Paine (R R.I.) Aug. 30, 1820-June 2, 1907; House 1861-63; Senate Nov. 19, 1884-Jan. 20, 1885.

SHEFFIELD, William Paine (son of the preceding) (R R.I.) June 1, 1857-Oct. 19, 1919; House 1909-11.

SHELDEN, Carlos Douglas (R Mich.) June 10, 1840-June 24, 1904; House 1897-1903.

SHELDON, Lionel Allen (R La.) Aug. 30, 1828-Jan. 17, 1917; House 1869-75; Gov. Terr. of N.M. 1881-85.

SHELDON, Porter (R N.Y.) Sept. 29, 1831-Aug. 15, 1908; House 1869-71.

SHELL, George Washington (D S.C.) Nov. 13, 1831-Dec. 15, 1899; House 1891-95.

SHELLABARGER, Samuel (R Ohio) Dec. 10, 1817-Aug. 7, 1896; House 1861-63, 1865-69, 1871-73.

SHELLEY, Charles Miller (D Ala.) Dec. 28, 1833-Jan. 20, 1907; House 1877-81, Nov. 7, 1882-Jan. 9, 1885.

SHELLEY, John Francis (D Calif.) Sept. 3, 1905; House Nov. 8, 1949-Jan. 7, 1964.

SHELTON, Samuel Azariah (R Mo.) Sept. 3, 1858-Sept. 13, 1948; House 1921-23.

SHEPARD, Charles Biddle (D N.C.) Dec. 5, 1807-Oct. 31, 1843; House 1837-41.

SHEPARD, William (— Mass.) Dec. 1, 1737-Nov. 16, 1817; House 1797-1803.

SHEPARD, William Biddle (NR N.C.) May 14, 1799-June 20, 1852; House 1829-37.

SHEPLER, Matthias (D Ohio) Nov. 11, 1790-April 7, 1863; House 1837-39.

SHEPLEY, Ether (D Maine) Nov. 2, 1789-Jan. 15, 1877; Senate 1833-March 3, 1836.

SHEPPARD, Harry Richard (D Calif.) Jan. 10, 1885-April 28, 1969; House 1937-65.

SHEPPARD, John Levi (father of Morris Sheppard) (D Texas) April 13, 1852-Oct. 11, 1902; House 1899-Oct. 11, 1902.

SHEPPARD, Morris (son of John Levi Sheppard) (D Texas) May 28, 1875-April 9, 1941; House Nov. 15, 1902-Feb. 3, 1913; Senate Feb. 3, 1913-April 9, 1941.

SHEPPERD, Augustine Henry (W N.C.) Feb. 24, 1792-July 11, 1864; House 1827-39, 1841-43, 1847-51.

SHERBURNE, John Samuel (— N.H.) 1757-Aug. 2, 1830; House 1793-97.

SHEREDINE, Upton (D Md.) 1740-Jan. 14, 1800; House 1791-93.

SHERIDAN, George Augustus (L La.) Feb. 22, 1840-Oct. 7, 1896; House 1873-75.

SHERIDAN, John Edward (D Pa.) Sept. 15, 1902; House Nov. 7, 1939-47.

SHERLEY, Joseph Swagar (D Ky.) Nov. 28, 1871-Feb. 13, 1941; House 1903-19.

SHERMAN, James Schoolcraft (R N.Y.) Oct. 24, 1855-Oct. 30, 1912; House 1887-91, 1893-1909; Vice Pres. 1909-Oct. 30, 1912.

SHERMAN, John (R Ohio) May 10, 1823-Oct. 22, 1900; House 1855-March 21, 1861; Senate March 21, 1861-March 8, 1877, 1881-March 4, 1897; Secy. of the Treasury 1877-81; Secy. of State 1897-98.

SHERMAN, Judson W. (R N.Y.) 1808-Nov. 12, 1881; House 1857-59.

SHERMAN, Lawrence Yates (R Ill.) Nov. 8, 1858-Sept. 15, 1939; Senate March 26, 1913-21.

SHERMAN, Roger (— Conn.) April 19, 1721-July 23, 1793; House 1789-91; Senate June 13, 1791-July 23, 1793; Cont. Cong. 1774-81, 1783-84.

SHERMAN, Socrates Norton (R N.Y.) July 22, 1801-Feb. 1, 1873; House 1861-63.

SHERRILL, Eliakim (W N.Y.) Feb. 16, 1813-July 4, 1863; House 1847-49.

SHERROD, William Crawford (D Ala.) Aug. 17, 1835-March 24, 1919; House 1869-71.

SHERWIN, John Crocker (R Ill.) Feb. 8, 1838-Jan. 1, 1904; House 1879-83.

SHERWOOD, Henry (D Pa.) Oct. 9, 1813-Nov. 10, 1896; House 1871-73.

SHERWOOD, Isaac R. (D Ohio) Aug. 13, 1835-Oct. 15, 1925; House 1873-75 (R), 1907-21, 1923-25 (D).

SHERWOOD, Samuel (F N.Y.) April 24, 1779-Oct. 31, 1862; House 1813-15.

SHERWOOD, Samuel Burr (F Conn.) Nov. 26, 1767-April 27, 1833; House 1817-19.

SHIEL, George Knox (D Ore.) 1825-Dec. 12, 1893; House July 30, 1861-63.

SHIELDS, Benjamin Glover (W Ala.) 1808-—; House 1841-43.

SHIELDS, Ebenezer J. (W Tenn.) Dec. 22, 1778-April 21, 1846; House 1835-39.

SHIELDS, James (JD Ohio) April 13, 1762-Aug. 13, 1831; House 1829-31.

SHIELDS, James (nephew of the preceding) (D Ill./Minn./Mo.) May 10, 1810-June 1, 1879; Senate March 6-15, 1849, Oct. 27, 1849-55 (Ill.), May 11, 1858-59 (Minn.), Jan. 27-March 3, 1879 (Mo.).

SHIELDS, John Knight (D Tenn.) Aug. 15, 1858-Sept. 30, 1934; Senate 1913-25.

SHINN, William Norton (JD N.J.) Oct. 24, 1782-Aug. 18, 1871; House 1833-37.

SHIPHERD, Zebulon Rudd (F N.Y.) Nov. 15, 1768-Nov. 1, 1841; House 1813-15.

SHIPLEY, George Edward (D Ill.) April 21, 1927; House 1959- .

SHIPSTEAD, Henrik (R Minn.) Jan. 8, 1881-June 26, 1960; Senate 1923-41 (F-L), 1941-47 (R).

SHIRAS, George, 3d (IR Pa.) Jan. 1, 1859-March 24, 1942; House 1903-05.

SHIVELY, Benjamin Franklin (D Ind.) March 20, 1857-March 14, 1916; House Dec. 1, 1884-85 (Nat. AM), 1887-93 (D); Senate 1909-March 14, 1916 (D).

SHOBER, Francis Edwin (father of Francis Emanuel Shober) (D N.C.) March 12, 1831-May 29, 1896; House 1869-73.

SHOBER, Francis Emanuel (son of Francis Edwin Shober) (D N.Y.) Oct. 24, 1860-Oct. 7, 1919; House 1903-05.

SHOEMAKER, Francis Henry (F-L Minn.) April 25, 1889-July 24, 1958; House 1933-35.

SHOEMAKER, Lazarus Denison (R Pa.) Nov. 5, 1819-Sept. 9, 1893; House 1871-75.

SHONK, George Washington (R Pa.) April 26, 1850-Aug. 14, 1900; House 1891-93.

SHORT, Dewey (R Mo.) April 7, 1898-—; House 1929-31, 1935-57.

SHORT, Don Levingston (R N.D.) June 22, 1903; House 1959-65.

SHORTER, Eli Sims (D Ala.) March 15, 1823-April 29, 1879; House 1855-59.

SHORTRIDGE, Samuel Morgan (R Calif.) Aug. 3, 1861-Jan. 15, 1952; Senate 1921-33.

SHOTT, Hugh Ike (R W.Va.) Sept. 3, 1866-Oct. 12, 1953; House 1929-33; Senate Nov. 18, 1942-43.

SHOUP, George Laird (grandfather of Richard G. Shoup) (R Idaho) June 15, 1836-Dec. 21, 1904; Senate Dec. 18, 1890-1901; Terr. Gov. 1889-90; Gov. Oct. 1-Dec. 1890.

SHOUP, Richard G. (grandson of George Laird Shoup) (R Mont.) Nov. 29, 1923; House 1971- .

SHOUSE, Jouett (D Kan.) Dec. 10, 1879-June 2, 1968; House 1915-19.

SHOWALTER, Joseph Baltzell (R Pa.) Feb. 11, 1851-Dec. 3, 1932; House April 20, 1897-1903.

SHOWER, Jacob (I Md.) Feb. 22, 1803-May 25, 1879; House 1853-55.

SHREVE, Milton William (R Pa.) May 3, 1858-Dec. 23, 1939; House 1913-15, 1919-33.

SHRIVER, Garner E. (R Kan.) July 6, 1912; House 1961- .

SHUFORD, Alonzo Craig (P N.C.) March 1, 1858-Feb. 8, 1933; House 1895-99.

SHUFORD, George Adams (D N.C.) Sept. 5, 1895-Dec. 8, 1962; House 1953-59.

SHULL, Joseph Horace (D Pa.) Aug. 17, 1848-Aug. 9, 1944; House 1903-05.

SHULTZ, Emanuel (R Ohio) July 25, 1819-Nov. 5, 1912; House 1881-83.

SIBAL, Abner Woodruff (R Conn.) April 11, 1921; House 1961-65.

SIBLEY, Henry Hastings (son of Solomon Sibley) (— Wis./Minn.) Feb. 20, 1811-Feb. 18, 1891; House (Terr. Del.) Oct. 30, 1848-49 (Wis.), July 7, 1849-53 (Minn.); Gov. of Minn. 1858-60.

SIBLEY, Jonas (D Mass.) March 7, 1762-Feb. 5, 1834; House 1823-25.

SIBLEY, Joseph Crocker (R Pa.) Feb. 18, 1850-May 19, 1926; House 1893-95 (D/PP/Prohib), 1899-1901 (D), 1901-07 (R).

SIBLEY, Mark Hopkins (W N.Y.) 1796-Sept. 8, 1852; House 1837-39.

SIBLEY, Solomon (father of Henry Hastings Sibley) (— Mich.) Oct. 7, 1769-April 4, 1846; House (Terr. Del.) Nov. 20, 1820-23.

SICKLES, Carlton R. (D Md.) June 15, 1921; House 1963-67.

SICKLES, Daniel Edgar (D N.Y.) Oct. 20, 1825-May 3, 1914; House 1857-61, 1893-95.

SICKLES, Nicholas (D N.Y.) Sept. 11, 1801-May 13, 1845; House 1835-37.

SIEGEL, Isaac (R N.Y.) April 12, 1880-June 29, 1947; House 1915-23.

SIEMINSKI, Alfred Dennis (D N.J.) Aug. 23, 1911; House 1951-59.

SIKES, Robert Louis Fulton (D Fla.) June 3, 1906; House 1941-Oct. 19, 1944, 1945- .

SILER, Eugene (R Ky.) June 26, 1900; House 1955-65.

SILL, Thomas Hale (NR Pa.) Oct. 11, 1783-Feb. 7, 1856; House March 14, 1826-27, 1829-31.

SILSBEE, Nathaniel (D Mass.) Jan. 14, 1773-July 14, 1850; House 1817-21; Senate May 31, 1826-35.

SILVESTER, Peter (grandfather of Peter Henry Silvester) (— N.Y.) 1734-Oct. 15, 1808; House 1789-93.

SILVESTER, Peter Henry (grandson of Peter Silvester) (W N.Y.) Feb. 17, 1807-Nov. 29, 1882; House 1847-51.

SIMKINS, Eldred (D S.C.) Aug. 30, 1779-Nov. 17, 1831; House Jan. 24, 1818-21.

SIMMONS, Furnifold McLendel (D N.C.) Jan. 20, 1854-April 30, 1940; House 1887-89; Senate 1901-31.

SIMMONS, George Abel (W N.Y.) Sept. 8, 1791-Oct. 27, 1857; House 1853-57.

SIMMONS, James Fowler (W R.I.) Sept. 10, 1795-July 10, 1864; Senate 1841-47, 1857-Aug. 15, 1862.

SIMMONS, James Samuel (nephew of Milton George Urner) (R N.Y.) Nov. 25, 1861-Nov. 28, 1935; House 1909-13.

SIMMONS, Robert Glenmore (R Neb.) Dec. 25, 1891-Dec. 27, 1969; House 1923-33.

SIMMS, Albert Gallatin (husband of Ruth Hanna McCormick) (R N.M.) Oct. 8, 1882-Dec. 29, 1964; House 1929-31.

SIMMS, William Emmett (D Ky.) Jan. 2, 1822-June 25, 1898; House 1859-61.

SIMON, Joseph (R Ore.) Feb. 7, 1851-Feb. 14, 1935; Senate Oct. 8, 1898-1903.

SIMONDS, William Edgar (R Conn.) Nov. 24, 1842-March 14, 1903; House 1889-91.

SIMONS, Samuel (D Conn.) 1792-Jan. 13, 1847; House 1843-45.

SIMONTON, Charles Bryson (D Tenn.) Sept. 8, 1838-June 10, 1911; House 1879-83.

SIMONTON, William (W Pa.) Feb. 12, 1788-May 17, 1846; House 1839-43.

SIMPKINS, John (R Mass.) June 27, 1862-March 27, 1898; House 1895-March 27, 1898.

SIMPSON, Edna Oakes (widow of Sidney E. Simpson) (R Ill.) Oct. 28, 1891-—; House 1859-61.

SIMPSON, James, Jr. (R Ill.) Jan. 7, 1905-Feb. 29, 1960; House 1933-35.

SIMPSON, Jeremiah (Jerry) (P Kan.) March 31, 1842-Oct. 23, 1905; House 1891-95, 1897-99.

SIMPSON, Kenneth Farrand (R N.Y.) May 4, 1895-Jan. 25, 1941; House Jan. 3-Jan. 25, 1941.

SIMPSON, Milward Lee (R Wyo.) Nov. 12, 1897-—; Senate Nov. 7, 1962-67; Gov. 1955-59.

SIMPSON, Richard Franklin (D S.C.) March 24, 1798-Oct. 28, 1882; House 1843-49.

SIMPSON, Richard Murray (R Pa.) Aug. 30, 1900-Jan. 7, 1960; House May 11, 1937-Jan. 7, 1960.

SIMPSON, Sidney Elmer (Sid) (husband of Edna Oakes Simpson) (R Ill.) Sept. 20, 1894-Oct. 26, 1958; House 1943-Oct. 26, 1958.

SIMS, Alexander Dromgoole (nephew of George Coke Dromgoole) (D S.C.) June 12, 1803-Nov. 22, 1848; House 1845-Nov. 22, 1848.

SIMS, Hugo Sheridan, Jr. (D S.C.) Oct. 14, 1921; House 1949-51.

SIMS, Leonard Henly (D Mo.) Feb. 6, 1807-Feb. 28, 1886; House 1845-47.

SIMS, Thetus Willrette (D Tenn.) April 25, 1852-Dec. 17, 1939; House 1897-1921.

SINCLAIR, James Herbert (R N.D.) Oct. 9, 1871-Sept. 5, 1943; House 1919-35.

SINGISER, Theodore Frelinghuysen (R Idaho) March 15, 1845-Jan. 23, 1907; House (Terr. Del.) 1883-85.

SINGLETON, James Washington (D Ill.) Nov. 23, 1811-April 4, 1892; House 1879-83.

SINGLETON, Otho Robards (D Miss.) Oct. 14, 1814-Jan. 11, 1889; House 1853-55, 1857-Jan. 12, 1861, 1875-87.

SINGLETON, Thomas Day (N S.C.) —-Nov. 25, 1833; House March 3-Nov. 25, 1833.

SINNICKSON, Clement Hall (grandnephew of Thomas Sinnickson) (R N.J.) Sept. 16, 1834-July 24, 1919; House 1875-79.

SINNICKSON, Thomas (granduncle of Clement Hall Sinnickson) (— N.J.) Dec. 21, 1744-May 15, 1817; House 1789-91, 1797-99.

SINNICKSON, Thomas (nephew of the preceding) (— N.J.) Dec. 13, 1786-Feb. 17, 1873; House Dec. 1, 1828-29.

SINNOTT, Nicholas John (R Ore.) Dec. 6, 1870-July 20, 1929; House 1913-May 31, 1928.

SIPE, William Allen (D Pa.) July 1, 1844-Sept. 10, 1935; House Dec. 5, 1892-95.

SIROVICH, William Irving (D N.Y.) March 18, 1882-Dec. 17, 1939; house 1927-Dec. 17, 1939.

SISK, Bernice Frederic (D Calif.) Dec. 14, 1910; House 1955- .

SISSON, Frederick James (D N.Y.) March 31, 1879-Oct. 20, 1949; House 1933-37.

SISSON, Thomas Upton (D Miss.) Sept. 22, 1869-Sept. 26, 1923; House 1909-23.

SITES, Frank Crawford (D Pa.) Dec. 24, 1864-May 23, 1935; House 1923-25.

SITGREAVES, Charles (D N.J.) April 22, 1803-March 17, 1878; House 1865-69.

SITGREAVES, Samuel (F Pa.) March 16, 1764-April 4, 1827; House 1795-98.

SITTLER, Edward Lewis, Jr. (R Pa.) April 21, 1908; House 1951-53.

SKELTON, Charles (D N.J.) April 19, 1806-May 20, 1879; House 1851-55.

SKILES, William Woodburn (R Ohio) Dec. 11, 1849-Jan. 9, 1904; House 1901-Jan. 9, 1904.

SKINNER, Charles Rufus (R N.Y.) Aug. 4, 1844-June 30, 1928; House Nov. 8, 1881-85.

SKINNER, Harry (brother of Thomas Gregory Skinner) (P N.C.) May 25, 1855-May 19, 1929; House 1895-99.

SKINNER, Richard (D Vt.) May 30, 1778-May 23, 1833; House 1813-15; Gov. 1820-23.

SKINNER, Thomas Gregory (brother of Harry Skinner) (D N.C.) Jan. 22, 1842-Dec. 22, 1907; House Nov. 20, 1883-87, 1889-91.

SKINNER, Thomson Joseph (D Mass.) May 24, 1752-Jan. 20, 1809; House Jan. 27, 1797-99, 1803-Aug. 10, 1804.

SKUBITZ, Joe (R Kan.) May 6, 1906; House 1963- .

SLACK, John Mark, Jr. (D W.Va.) March 18, 1915; House 1959- .

SLADE, Charles (D Ill.) —July 26, 1834; House 1833-July 26, 1834.

SLADE, William (W Vt.) May 9, 1786-Jan. 18, 1859; House Nov. 1, 1831-43; Gov. 1844-46.

SLATER, James Harvey (D Ore.) Dec. 28, 1826-Jan. 28, 1899; House 1871-73; Senate 1879-85.

SLATTERY, James Michael (D Ill.) July 29, 1878-Aug. 28, 1948; Senate April 14, 1939-Nov. 21, 1940.

SLAUGHTER, Roger Caldwell (D Mo.) July 17, 1905; House 1943-47.

SLAYDEN, James (uncle of Maury Maverick) (D Texas) June 1, 1853-Feb. 24, 1924; House 1897-1919.

SLAYMAKER, Amos (— Pa.) March 11, 1755-June 12, 1837; House Oct. 11, 1814-15.

SLEMONS, William Ferguson (D Ark.) March 15, 1830-Dec. 10, 1918; House 1875-81.

SLEMP, Campbell (father of Campbell Bascom Slemp) (R Va.) Dec. 2, 1839-Oct. 13, 1907; House 1903-Oct. 13, 1907.

SLEMP, Campbell Bascom (son of Campbell Slemp) (R Va.) Sept. 4, 1870-Aug. 7, 1943; House Dec. 17, 1907-23.

SLIDELL, John (SRD La.) 1793-July 26, 1871; House 1843-Nov. 10, 1845; Senate Dec. 5, 1853-Feb. 4, 1861.

SLINGERLAND, John I. (R N.Y.) March 1, 1804-Oct. 26, 1861; House 1847-49.

SLOAN, Andrew (R Ga.) June 10, 1845-Sept. 22, 1883; House March 24, 1874-75.

SLOAN, Andrew Scott (brother of Ithamar Conkey Sloan) (R Wis.) June 12, 1820-April 8, 1895; House 1861-63.

SLOAN, Charles Henry (R Neb.) May 2, 1863-June 2, 1946; House 1911-19, 1929-31.

SLOAN, Ithamar Conkey (brother of Andrew Scott Sloan) (R Wis.) May 9, 1822-Dec. 24, 1898; House 1863-67.

SLOAN, James (— N.J.) —-Nov. 1811; House 1803-09.

SLOANE, John (W Ohio) 1779-May 15, 1856; House 1819-29.

SLOANE, Jonathan (W Ohio) Nov. 1785-April 25, 1854; House 1833-37.

SLOCUM, Henry Warner (D N.Y.) Sept. 24, 1827-April 14, 1894; House 1869-73, 1883-85.

SLOCUMB, Jesse (F N.C.) 1780-Dec. 20, 1820; House 1817-Dec. 20, 1820.

SLOSS, Joseph Humphrey (Con.D Ala.) Oct. 12, 1826-Jan. 27, 1911; House 1871-75.

SMALL, Frank, Jr. (R Md.) July 15, 1896-—; House 1953-55.

SMALL, John Humphrey (D N.C.) Aug. 29, 1858-July 13, 1946; House 1899-1921.

SMALL, William Bradbury (R N.H.) May 17, 1817-April 7, 1878; House 1873-75.

SMALLS, Robert (R S.C.) April 5, 1839-Feb. 22, 1915; House 1875-79, July 19, 1882-83, March 18, 1884-87.

SMART, Ephraim Knight (D Maine) Sept. 3, 1813-Sept. 29, 1872; House 1847-49, 1851-53.

SMART, James Stevenson (R N.Y.) June 14, 1842-Sept. 17, 1903; House 1873-75.

SMATHERS, George Armistead (nephew of William H. Smathers) (D Fla.) Nov. 14, 1913; House 1947-51; Senate 1951-69.

SMATHERS, William Howell (uncle of George A. Smathers) (D N.J.) Jan. 7, 1891-Sept. 24, 1955; Senate April 15, 1937-43.

SMELT, Dennis (— Ga.) about 1750-—; House Sept. 1, 1806-11.

SMILIE, John (D Pa.) 1741-Dec. 30, 1812; House 1793-95, 1799-Dec. 30, 1812.

SMITH, Abraham Herr (R Pa.) March 7, 1815-Feb. 16, 1894; House 1873-85.

SMITH, Addison Taylor (R Idaho) Sept. 5, 1862-July 5, 1956; House 1913-33.

SMITH, Albert (D Maine) Jan. 3, 1793-May 29, 1867; House 1839-41.

SMITH, Albert (R N.Y.) June 22, 1805-Aug. 27, 1870; House 1843-47.

SMITH, Arthur (— Va.) Nov. 15, 1785-March 30, 1853; House 1821-25.

SMITH, Ballard (— Va.) —-—; House 1815-21.

SMITH, Benjamin A., II (D Mass.) March 26, 1916; Senate Dec. 27, 1960-Nov. 7, 1962.

SMITH, Bernard (— N.Y.) July 5, 1776-July 16, 1835; House 1819-21.

SMITH, Caleb Blood (W Ind.) April 16, 1808-Jan. 7, 1864; House 1843-49; Secy. of the Interior 1861-63.

SMITH, Charles Bennett (D N.Y.) Sept. 14, 1870-May 21, 1939; House 1911-19.

SMITH, Charles Brooks (R W.Va.) Feb. 24, 1844-Dec. 7, 1899; House Feb. 3, 1890-91.

SMITH, Clyde Harold (husband of Margaret Chase Smith) (R Maine) June 9, 1876-April 8, 1940; House 1937-April 8, 1940.

SMITH, Daniel (— Tenn.) Oct. 28, 1748-June 6, 1818; Senate Oct. 6, 1798-99, 1805-March 31, 1809.

SMITH, David Highbaugh (D Ky.) Dec. 19, 1854-Dec. 17, 1928; House 1897-1907.

SMITH, Delazon (D Ore.) Oct. 5, 1816-Nov. 19, 1860; Senate Feb. 14-March 3, 1859.

SMITH, Dietrich Conrad (R Ill.) April 4, 1840-April 18, 1914; House 1881-83.

SMITH, Edward Henry (D N.Y.) May 5, 1809-Aug. 7, 1885; House 1861-63.

SMITH, Ellison DuRant (D S.C.) Aug. 1, 1866-Nov. 17, 1944; Senate 1909-Nov. 17, 1944.

SMITH, Frances Ormand Jonathan (D Maine) Nov. 23, 1806-Oct. 14, 1876; House 1833-39.

SMITH, Francis Raphael (D Pa.) Sept. 25, 1911; House 1941-43.

SMITH, Frank Ellis (D Miss.) Feb. 21, 1918; House 1951-Nov. 14, 1962.

SMITH, Frank Leslie (R Ill.) Nov. 24, 1867-Aug. 30, 1950; House 1919-21; Senate Dec. 16, 1926-Feb. 9, 1928.

SMITH, Frank Owens (D Md.) Aug. 27, 1859-Jan. 29, 1924; House 1913-15.

SMITH, Frederick Cleveland (R Ohio) July 29, 1884-July 16, 1956; House 1939-51.

SMITH, George (— Pa.) —-—; House 1809-13.

SMITH, George Joseph (R N.Y.) Nov. 7, 1859-Dec. 2, 1913; House 1903-05.

SMITH, George Luke (R La.) Dec. 11, 1837-July 9, 1884; House Nov. 24, 1873-75.

SMITH, George Ross (R Minn.) May 28, 1864-Nov. 7, 1952; House 1913-17.

SMITH, George Washington (R Ill.) Aug. 18, 1846-Nov. 30, 1907; House 1889-Nov. 30, 1907.

SMITH, Gerrit (UA N.Y.) March 6, 1797-Dec. 28, 1874; House 1853-Aug. 7, 1854.

SMITH, Gomer Griffith (D Okla.) July 11, 1896-May 26, 1953; House Dec. 10, 1937-39.

SMITH, Green Clay (son of John Speed Smith) (U Ky.) July 4, 1826-June 29, 1895; House 1863-July 13, 1866; Gov. of Montana Terr. 1866-69.

SMITH, H. Allen (R Calif.) Oct. 8, 1909; House 1957- .

SMITH, Henry (PP Wis.) July 22, 1838-Sept. 16, 1916; House 1887-89.

SMITH, Henry Cassorte (R Mich.) June 2, 1856-Dec. 7, 1911; House 1899-1903.

SMITH, Henry P., III (R N.Y.) Sept. 29, 1911; House 1965- .

SMITH, Hezekiah Bradley (D/G N.J.) July 24, 1816-Nov. 3, 1887; House 1879-81.

SMITH, Hiram Ypsilanti (R Iowa) March 22, 1843-Nov. 4, 1894; House Dec. 2, 1884-85.

SMITH, Hoke (D Ga.) Sept. 2, 1855-Nov. 27, 1931; Senate Nov. 16, 1911-21; Secy. of the Interior 1893-96; Gov. 1907-09, 1911.

SMITH, Horace Boardman (R N.Y.) Aug. 18, 1826-Dec. 26, 1888; House 1871-75.

SMITH, Howard Alexander (R N.J.) Jan. 30, 1880-Oct. 27, 1966; Senate Dec. 7, 1944-59.

SMITH, Howard Worth (D Va.) Feb. 2, 1883- —; House 1931-67.

SMITH, Isaac (F N.J.) 1740-Aug. 29, 1807; House 1795-97.

SMITH, Isaac (D Pa.) Jan. 4, 1761-April 4, 1834; House 1813-15.

SMITH, Israel (D Vt.) April 4, 1759-Dec. 2, 1810; House Oct. 17, 1791-1797, 1801-03; Senate 1803-Oct. 1, 1807; Gov. 1807-08.

SMITH, James, Jr. (D N.J.) June 12, 1851-April 1, 1927; Senate 1893-99.

SMITH, James Strudwick (D N.C.) Oct. 15, 1790-Aug. 1859; House 1817-21.

SMITH, James V. (R Okla.) July 23, 1926; House 1967-69.

SMITH, Jedediah Kilburn (— N.H.) Nov. 7, 1770-Dec. 17, 1828; House 1807-09.

SMITH, Jeremiah (brother of Samuel Smith of N.H. and uncle of Robert Smith) (F N.H.) Nov. 29, 1759-Sept. 21, 1842; House 1791-July 26, 1797; Gov. 1809-10.

SMITH, John (D Ohio) 1735-June 10, 1816; Senate April 1, 1803-April 25, 1808.

SMITH, John (D Va.) May 7, 1750-March 5, 1836; House 1801-15.

SMITH, John (D N.Y.) Feb. 12, 1752-Aug. 12, 1816; House Feb. 6, 1800-Feb. 23, 1804; Senate Feb. 23, 1804-13.

SMITH, John (father of Worthington Curtis Smith) (D Vt.) Aug. 12, 1789-Nov. 26, 1858; House 1839-41.

SMITH, John Ambler (R Va.) Sept. 23, 1847-Jan. 6, 1892; House 1873-75.

SMITH, John Armstrong (R Ohio) Sept. 23, 1814-March 7, 1892; House 1869-73.

SMITH, John Cotton (F Conn.) Feb. 12, 1765-Dec. 7, 1845; House Nov. 17, 1800-Aug. 1806; Gov. 1813-18.

SMITH, John Hyatt (IR/D N.Y.) April 10, 1824-Dec. 7, 1886; House 1881-83.

SMITH, John Joseph (D Conn.) Jan. 25, 1904; House 1935-Nov. 4, 1941.

SMITH, John M. C. (R Mich.) Feb. 6, 1853-March 30, 1923; House 1911-21, June 28, 1921-March 30, 1923.

SMITH, John Quincy (R Ohio) Nov. 5, 1824-Dec. 30, 1901; House 1873-75.

SMITH, John Speed (father of Green Clay Smith) (D Ky.) July 1, 1792-June 6, 1854; House Aug. 6, 1821-23.

SMITH, John T. (D Pa.) —-—; House 1843-45.

SMITH, John Walter (D Md.) Feb. 5, 1845-April 19, 1925; House 1899-Jan. 12, 1900; Senate March 25, 1908-21; Gov. 1900-04.

SMITH, Joseph Luther (D W.Va.) May 22, 1880-Aug. 23, 1962; House 1929-45.

SMITH, Joseph Showalter (D Ore.) June 20, 1824-July 13, 1884; House 1869-71.

SMITH, Josiah (— Mass.) Feb. 26, 1738-April 4, 1803; House 1801-03.

SMITH, Lawrence Henry (R Wis.) Sept. 15, 1892-Jan. 22, 1958; House Aug. 29, 1941-Jan. 22, 1958.

SMITH, Madison Roswell (D Mo.) July 9, 1850-June 18, 1919; House 1907-09.

SMITH, Marcus Aurelius (D Ariz.) Jan. 24, 1851-April 7, 1924; House (Terr. Del.) 1887-95, 1897-99, 1901-03, 1905-09; Senate March 27, 1912-21.

SMITH, Margaret Chase (widow of Clyde Harold Smith) (R Maine) Dec. 14, 1897; House June 3, 1940-49; Senate 1949- .

SMITH, Martin Fernand (D Wash.) May 28, 1891-Oct. 25, 1954; House 1933-43.

SMITH, Nathan (brother of Nathaniel Smith and uncle of Truman Smith) (W Conn.) Jan. 8, 1770-Dec. 6, 1835; Senate 1833-Dec. 6, 1835.

SMITH, Nathaniel (brother of Nathan Smith and uncle of Truman Smith) (F Conn.) Jan. 6, 1762-March 9, 1822; House 1795-99.

SMITH, Neal Edward (D Iowa) March 23, 1920; House 1959- .

SMITH, O'Brien (— S.C.) about 1756-April 27, 1811; House 1805-07.

SMITH, Oliver Hampton (W Ind.) Oct. 23, 1794-March 19, 1859; House 1827-29 (JD), Senate 1837-43 (W).

SMITH, Perry (D Conn.) May 12, 1783-June 8, 1852; Senate 1837-43.

SMITH, Ralph Tyler (R Ill.) Oct. 6, 1915; Senate Sept. 17, 1969-Nov. 16, 1970.

SMITH, Robert (nephew of Jeremiah Smith and Samuel Smith of N.H.) (D Ill.) June 12, 1802-Dec. 21, 1867; House 1843-49, 1857-59.

SMITH, Robert Barnwell (see RHETT, Robert Barnwell).

SMITH, Samuel (D Md.) July 27, 1752-April 22, 1839; House 1793-1803, Jan. 31, 1816-Dec. 17, 1822; Senate 1803-15, Dec. 17, 1822-33; President pro tempore 1805-08.

SMITH, Samuel (— Pa.)— - —; House Nov. 7, 1805-11.

SMITH, Samuel (brother of Jeremiah Smith and uncle of Robert Smith) (F N.H.) Nov. 11, 1765-April 25, 1842; House 1813-15.

SMITH, Samuel A. (ID Pa.) 1795-May 15, 1861; House Oct. 13, 1829-33.

SMITH, Samuel Axley (D Tenn.) June 26, 1822-Nov. 25, 1863; House 1853-59.

SMITH, Samuel William (R Mich.) Aug. 23, 1852-June 19, 1931; House 1897-1915.

SMITH, Sylvester Clark (R Calif.) Aug. 26, 1858-Jan. 26, 1913; House 1905-Jan. 26, 1913.

SMITH, Thomas (F Pa.) — -Jan. 29, 1846; House 1815-17.

SMITH, Thomas (D Ind.) May 1, 1799-April 12, 1876; House 1839-41, 1843-47.

SMITH, Thomas Alexander (D Md.) Sept. 3, 1850-May 1, 1932; House 1905-07.

SMITH, Thomas Francis (D N.Y.) July 24, 1865-April 11, 1923; House April 12, 1917-21.

SMITH, Thomas Vernor (D Ill.) April 26, 1890-May 24, 1964; House 1939-41

SMITH, Truman (nephew of Nathan Smith and Nathaniel Smith) (W Conn.) Nov. 27, 1791-May 3, 1884; House 1839-43, 1845-49; Senate 1849-May 24, 1854.

SMITH, Walter Inglewood (R Iowa) July 10, 1862-Jan. 27, 1922; House Dec. 3, 1900-March 15, 1911.

SMITH, William (F Md.) April 12, 1728-March 27, 1814; House 1789-91; Cont. Cong. 1777-78.

SMITH, William (D S.C.) 1762-June 26, 1840; Senate Dec. 4, 1816-23, Nov. 29, 1826-31.

SMITH, William (— S.C.) Sept. 20, 1751-June 22, 1837; House 1797-99.

SMITH, William (— Va.)—-—; House 1821-27.

SMITH, William (D Va.) Sept. 6, 1797-May 18, 1887; House 1841-43, 1853-61; Gov. 1846-49, 1864.

SMITH, William Alden (R Mich.) May 12, 1859-Oct. 11, 1932; House 1895-Feb. 9, 1907; Senate Feb. 9, 1907-19.

SMITH, William Alexander (R N.C.) Jan. 9, 1828-May 16, 1888; House 1873-75.

SMITH, William Ephraim (D Ga.) March 14, 1829-March 11, 1890; House 1875-81.

SMITH, William Jay (R Tenn.) Sept. 24, 1823-Nov. 29, 1913; House 1869-71.

SMITH, William Loughton (F S.C.) 1758-Dec. 19, 1812; House 1789-July 10, 1797.

SMITH, William Nathan Harrell (D N.C.) Sept. 24, 1812-Nov. 14, 1889; House 1859-61.

SMITH, William Orlando (R Pa.) June 13, 1859-May 12, 1932; House 1903-07.

SMITH, William Robert (D Texas) Aug. 18, 1863-Aug. 16, 1924; House 1903-17.

SMITH, William Russell (AP Ala.) March 27, 1815-Feb. 26, 1896; House 1851-55 (UW), 1855-57 (AP).

SMITH, William Stephens (F N.Y.) Nov. 8, 1755-June 10, 1816; House 1813-15.

SMITH, Willis (D N.C.) Dec. 19, 1887-June 26, 1953; Senate Nov. 27, 1950-June 26, 1953.

SMITH, Wint (R Kan.) Oct. 7, 1893; House 1947-61.

SMITH, Worthington Curtis (son of John Smith of Vt.) (R Vt.) April 23, 1823-Jan. 2, 1894; House 1867-73.

SMITHERS, Nathaniel Barratt (R Del.) Oct. 8, 1818-Jan. 16, 1896; House Dec. 7, 1863-65.

SMITHWICK, John Harris (D Fla.) July 17, 1872-Dec. 2, 1948; House 1919-27.

SMOOT, Reed (R Utah) Jan. 10, 1862-Feb. 9, 1941; Senate 1903-33.

SMYSER, Martin Luther (R Ohio) April 3, 1851-May 6, 1908; House 1889-91, 1905-07.

SMYTH, Alexander (— Va.) 1765-April 17, 1830; House 1817-25, 1827-April 17, 1830.

SMYTH, George Washington (D Texas) May 16, 1803-Feb. 21, 1866; House 1853-55.

SMYTH, William (R Iowa) Jan. 3, 1824-Sept. 30, 1870; House 1869-Sept. 30, 1870.

SNAPP, Henry (father of Howard Malcolm Snapp) (R Ill.) June 30, 1822-Nov. 26, 1895; House Dec. 4, 1871-73.

SNAPP, Howard Malcolm (son of Henry Snapp) (R Ill.) Sept. 27, 1855-Aug. 14, 1938; House 1903-11.

SNEED, William Henry (AP Tenn.) Aug. 27, 1812-Sept. 18, 1869; House 1855-57.

SNELL, Bertrand Hollis (R N.Y.) Dec. 9, 1870-Feb. 2, 1958; House Nov. 2, 1915-39.

SNIDER, Samuel Prather (R Minn.) Oct. 9, 1845-Sept. 24, 1928; House 1889-91.

SNODGRASS, Charles Edward (nephew of Henry Clay Snodgrass) (D Tenn.) Dec. 28, 1866-Aug. 3, 1936; House 1899-1903.

SNODGRASS, Henry Clay (uncle of Charles Edward Snodgrass) (D Tenn.) March 29, 1848-April 22, 1931; House 1891-95.

SNODGRASS, John Fryall (D Va.) March 2, 1804-June 5, 1854; House 1853-June 5, 1854.

SNOOK, John Stout (D Ohio) Dec. 18, 1862-Sept. 19, 1952; House 1901-05, 1917-19.

SNOVER, Horace Greeley (R Mich.) Sept. 21, 1847-July 21, 1924; House 1895-99.

SNOW, Donald Francis (R Maine) Sept. 6, 1877-Feb. 12, 1958; House 1929-33.

SNOW, Herman Wilber (D Ill.) July 3, 1836-Aug. 25, 1914; House 1891-93.

SNOW, William W. (D N.Y.) April 27, 1812-Sept. 3, 1886; House 1851-53.

SNYDER, Adam Wilson (VBD Ill.) Oct. 6, 1799-May 14, 1842; House 1837-39.

SNYDER, Charles Philip (D W. Va.) June 9, 1847-Aug. 21, 1915; House May 15, 1883-89.

SNYDER, Homer Peter (R N.Y.) Dec. 6, 1863-Dec. 30, 1937; House 1915-25.

SNYDER, John (— Pa.) Jan. 29, 1793-Aug. 15, 1850; House 1841-43.

SNYDER, John Buell (D Pa.) July 30, 1877-Feb. 24, 1946; House 1933-Feb. 24, 1946.

SNYDER, Melvin Claude (R W. Va.) Oct. 29, 1898; House 1947-49.

SNYDER, Marion Gene (R Ky.) Jan. 26, 1928; House 1963-65, 1967- .

SNYDER, Oliver P. (R Ark.) Nov. 13, 1833-Nov. 22, 1882; House 1871-75.

SOLLERS, Augustus Rhodes (W Md.) May 1, 1814-Nov. 26, 1862; House 1841-43, 1853- 55.

SOMERS, Andrew Lawrence (D N.Y.) March 21, 1895-April 6, 1949; House 1925-April 6, 1949.

SOMERS, Peter J. (D Wis.) April 12, 1850-Feb. 15, 1924; House Aug. 27, 1893-95.

SOMES, Daniel Eton (R Maine) May 20, 1815-Feb. 13, 1888; House 1859-61.

SORG, Paul John (D Ohio) Sept. 23, 1840-May 28, 1902; House May 21, 1894-97.

SOSNOWSKI, John Bartholomew (R Mich.) Dec. 8, 1883-July 16, 1968; House 1925-27.

SOULE, Nathan (— N.Y.)—-—; House 1831-33.

SOULE, Pierre (SRD La.) Aug. 28, 1801-March 26, 1870; Senate Jan. 21-March 3, 1847, 1849-April 11, 1853.

SOUTH, Charles Lacy (D Texas) July 22, 1892-Dec. 20, 1965; House 1935-43.

SOUTHALL, Robert Goode (D Va.) Dec. 26, 1852-May 25, 1924; House 1903-07.

SOUTHARD, Henry (father of Isaac Southard and Samuel Lewis Southard) (D N.J.) Oct. 7, 1747-May 22, 1842; House 1801-11, 1815-21.

SOUTHARD, Isaac (son of Henry Southard and brother of Samuel Lewis Southard) (CD N.J.) Aug. 30, 1783-Sept. 18, 1850; House 1831-33.

SOUTHARD, James Harding (R Ohio) Jan. 20, 1851-Feb. 20, 1919; House 1895-1907.

SOUTHARD, Milton Isaiah (D Ohio) Oct. 20, 1836-May 4, 1905; House 1873-79.

SOUTHARD, Samuel Lewis (son of Henry Southard and brother of Isaac Southard) (W N.J.) June 9, 1787-June 26, 1842; Senate Jan. 26, 1821-March 3, 1823 (D), 1833-June 26, 1842 (W); President pro tempore 1841-42; Secy. of the Navy 1823-29; Secy. of War 1824; Secy. of the Treasury 1825; Gov. 1832-33.

SOUTHGATE, William Wright (W Ky.) Nov. 27, 1800-Dec. 26, 1849; House 1837-39.

SOUTHWICK, George Newell (R N.Y.) March 7, 1863-Oct. 17, 1912, House 1895-99, 1901-11.

SOWDEN, William Henry (D Pa.) June 6, 1840-March 3, 1907; House 1885-89.

SPAIGHT, Richard Dobbs (grandfather of Richard Spaight Donnell) (D N.C.) March 25, 1758-Sept. 6, 1802; House Dec. 10, 1798-1801; Cont. Cong. 1782-85; Gov. 1792-95.

SPAIGHT, Richard Dobbs, Jr. (son of the preceding) (D N.C.) 1796-May 2, 1850; House 1823-25; Gov. 1835-37.

SPALDING, Burleigh Folsom (R N.D.) Dec. 3, 1853-March 17, 1934; House 1899-1901, 1903-05.

SPALDING, George (R Mich.) Nov. 12, 1836-Sept. 13, 1915; House 1895-99.

SPALDING, Rufus Paine (WD Ohio) May 3, 1798-Aug. 29, 1886; House 1863-69.

SPALDING, Thomas (— Ga.) March 26, 1774-Jan. 5, 1851; House Dec. 24, 1805-06.

SPANGLER, David (W Ohio) Dec. 2, 1796-Oct. 18, 1856; House 1833-37.

SPANGLER, Jacob (F Pa.) Nov. 28, 1767-June 17, 1843; House 1817-April 20, 1818.

SPARKMAN, John Jackson (D Ala.) Dec. 20, 1899; House 1937-Nov. 5, 1946; Senate Nov. 6, 1946- .

SPARKMAN, Stephen Milancthon (D Fla.) July 29, 1849-Sept. 26, 1929; House 1895-1917.

SPARKS, Charles Isaac (R Kan.) Dec. 20, 1872-April 30, 1937; House 1929-33.

SPARKS, William Andrew Jackson (D Ill.) Nov. 19, 1828-May 7, 1904; House 1875-83.

SPAULDING, Elbridge Gerry (U N.Y.) Feb. 24, 1809-May 5, 1897; House 1849-51 (W); 1859-63 (U).

SPAULDING, Oliver Lyman (R Mich.) Aug. 2, 1833-July 30, 1922; House 1881-83.

SPEAKS, John Charles (R Ohio) Feb. 11, 1859-Nov. 6, 1945; House 1921-31.

SPEARING, James Zacharie (D La.) April 23, 1864-Nov. 2, 1942; House April 22, 1924-31.

SPEED, Thomas (— Ky.) Oct. 25, 1768-Feb. 20, 1842; House 1817-19.

SPEER, Emory (I Ga.) Sept. 3, 1848-Dec. 13, 1918; House 1879-81 (D), 1881-83 (I).

SPEER, Peter Moore (R Pa.) Dec. 29, 1862-Aug. 3, 1933; House 1911-13.

SPEER, Robert Milton (D Pa.) Sept. 8, 1838-Jan. 17, 1890; House 1871-75.

SPEER, Thomas Jefferson (R Ga.) Aug. 31, 1837-Aug. 18, 1872; House 1871-Aug. 18, 1872.

SPEIGHT, Jesse (D N.C./Miss.) Sept. 22, 1795-May 1, 1847; House 1829-37 (N.C.); Senate 1845-May 1, 1847 (Miss.).

SPENCE, Brent (D Ky.) Dec. 24, 1874-Sept. 18, 1967; House 1931-63.

SPENCE, Floyd D. (R S.C.) April 9, 1928; House 1971- .

SPENCE, John Selby (uncle of Thomas Ara Spence) (D Md.) Feb. 29, 1788-Oct. 24, 1840; House 1823-25, 1831-33; Senate Dec. 31, 1836-Oct. 24, 1840.

SPENCE, Thomas Ara (nephew of John Selby Spence) (W Md.) Feb. 20, 1810-Nov. 10, 1877; House 1843-45.

SPENCER, Ambrose (father of John Canfield Spencer) (D N.Y.) Dec. 13, 1765-March 13, 1848; House 1829-31.

SPENCER, Elijah (D N.Y.) 1775-Dec. 15, 1852; House 1821-23.

SPENCER, George Eliphaz (R Ala.) Nov. 1, 1836-Feb. 19, 1893; Senate July 13, 1868-79.

SPENCER, George Lloyd (D Ark.) March 27, 1893; Senate April 1, 1941-43.

SPENCER, James Bradley (D N.Y.) April 26, 1781-March 26, 1848; House 1837-39.

SPENCER, James Grafton (D Miss.) Sept. 13, 1844-Feb. 22, 1926; House 1895-97.

SPENCER, John Canfield (son of Ambrose Spencer) (D N.Y.) Jan. 8, 1788-May 18, 1855; House 1817-19; Secy. of War 1841-43; Secy of the Treasury 1843-44.

SPENCER, Richard (D Md.) Oct. 29, 1796-Sept. 3, 1868; House 1829-31.

SPENCER, Selden Palmer (R Mo.) Sept. 16, 1862-May 16, 1925; Senate Nov. 6, 1918-May 16, 1925.

SPENCER, William Brainerd (D La.) Feb. 5, 1835-Feb. 12, 1882; House June 8, 1876-Jan. 8, 1877.

SPERRY, Lewis (D Conn.) Jan. 23, 1848-June 22, 1922; House 1891-95.

SPERRY, Nehemiah Day (R Conn.) July 10, 1827-Nov. 13, 1911; House 1895-1911.

SPIGHT, Thomas (D Miss.) Oct. 25, 1841-Jan. 5, 1924; House July 5, 1898-1911.

SPINK, Cyrus (R Ohio) March 24, 1793-May 31, 1859; House March 4-May 31, 1859.

SPINK, Solomon Lewis (R Dakota) March 20, 1831-Sept. 22, 1881; House (Terr. Del.) 1869-71.

SPINNER, Francis Elias (D N.Y.) Jan. 21, 1802-Dec. 31, 1890; House 1855-61.

SPINOLA, Francis Barretto (D N.Y.) March 19, 1821-April 14, 1891; House 1887-April 14, 1891.

SPONG, William Belser, Jr. (D Va.) Sept. 29, 1920; Senate Dec. 31, 1966- .

SPOONER, Henry Joshua (R R.I.) Aug. 6, 1839-Feb. 9, 1918; House Dec. 5, 1881-91.

SPOONER, John Coit (R Wis.) Jan. 6, 1843-June 11, 1919; Senate 1885-91, 1897-April 30, 1907.

SPRAGUE, Charles Franklin (grandson of Peleg Sprague) (R Mass.) June 10, 1857-Jan. 30, 1902; House 1897-1901.

SPRAGUE, Peleg (— N.H.) Dec. 10, 1756-April 20, 1800; House Dec. 15, 1797-99.

SPRAGUE, Peleg (grandfather of Charles Franklin Sprague) (NR Maine) April 27, 1793-Oct. 13, 1880; House 1825-29; Senate 1829-Jan. 1, 1835.

SPRAGUE, William (W Mich.) Feb. 23, 1809-Sept. 19, 1868; House 1849-51.

SPRAGUE, William (W R.I.) Nov. 3, 1799-Oct. 19, 1856; House 1835-37; Senate Feb. 18, 1842-Jan. 17, 1844; Gov. 1838-39.

SPRAGUE, William (nephew of the preceding) (R R.I.) Sept. 12, 1830-Sept. 11, 1915; Senate 1863-75; Gov. 1860-63 (U).

SPRAGUE, William Peter (R Ohio) May 21, 1827-March 3, 1899; House 1871-75.

SPRIGG, James Cresap (brother of Michael Cresap Sprigg) (— Ky.) 1802-Oct. 3, 1852; House 1841-43.

SPRIGG, Michael Cresap (brother of James Cresap Sprigg) (D Md.) July 1, 1791-Dec. 18, 1845; House 1827-31.

SPRIGG, Richard, Jr. (nephew of Thomas Sprigg) (— Md.)—-—; House May 5, 1796-99, 1801-Feb. 11, 1802.

SPRIGG, Thomas (uncle of Richard Sprigg, Jr.) (— Md.) 1747-Dec. 13, 1809; House 1793-97.

SPRIGGS, John Thomas (D N.Y.) April 5, 1825-Dec. 23, 1888; House 1883-87.

SPRINGER, Raymond Smiley (R Ind.) April 26, 1882-Aug. 28, 1947; House 1939-Aug. 28, 1947.

SPRINGER, William Lee (R Ill.) April 12, 1909; House 1951- .

SPRINGER, William McKendree (D Ill.) May 30, 1836-Dec. 4, 1903; House 1875-95.

SPROUL, Elliott Wilford (R Ill.) Dec. 28, 1856-June 22, 1935; House 1921-31.

SPROUL, William Henry (R Kan.) Oct. 14, 1867-Dec. 27, 1932; House 1923-31.

SPRUANCE, Presley (W Del.) Sept. 11, 1785-Feb. 13, 1863; Senate 1847-53.

SQUIRE, Watson Carvosso (R Wash.) May 18, 1838-June 7, 1926; Senate Nov. 20, 1889-97; Gov. (Terr.) 1884-87.

STACK, Edmund John (D Ill.) Jan. 31, 1874-April 12, 1957; House 1911-13.

STACK, Michael Joseph (D Pa.) Sept. 29, 1888-Dec. 14, 1960; House 1935-39.

STACKHOUSE, Eli Thomas (D S.C.) March 27, 1824-June 14, 1892; House 1891-June 14, 1892.

STAEBLER, Neil (D Mich.) July 11, 1905; House 1963-65.

STAFFORD, Robert Theodore (R Vt.) Aug. 8, 1913; House 1961- ; Gov. 1959-61.

STAFFORD, William Henry (R Wis.) Oct. 12, 1869-April 22, 1957; House 1903-11, 1913-19, 1921-23, 1929-33.

STAGGERS, Harley Orrin (D W. Va.) Aug. 3, 1907; House 1949- .

STAHLE, James Alonzo (R Pa.) Jan. 11, 1829-Dec. 21, 1912; House 1895-97.

STAHLNECKER, William Griggs (D N.Y.) June 20, 1849-March 26, 1902; House 1885-93.

STALBAUM, Lynn Ellsworth (D Wis.) May 15, 1920; House 1965-67.

STALKER, Gale Hamilton (R N.Y.) Nov. 7, 1889; House 1923-35.

STALLINGS, Jesse Francis (D Ala.) April 4, 1856-March 18, 1928; House 1893-1901.

STALLWORTH, James Adams (D Ala.) April 7, 1822-Aug. 31, 1861; House 1857-Jan. 21, 1861.

STANARD, Edwin Obed (R Mo.) Jan. 5, 1832-March 12, 1914; House 1873-75.

STANBERY, William (JD Ohio) Aug. 10, 1788-Jan. 23, 1873; House Oct. 9, 1827-33.

STANDIFER, James (W Tenn.)—-Aug. 20, 1837; House 1823-25, 1829-Aug. 20, 1837.

STANDIFORD, Elisha David (D Ky.) Dec. 28, 1831-July 26, 1887; House 1873-75.

STANFIELD, Robert Nelson (R Ore.) July 9, 1877-April 13, 1945; Senate 1921-27.

STANFIL, William Abner (R Ky.) Jan. 16, 1892; Senate Nov. 19, 1945-Nov. 5, 1946.

STANFORD, Leland (R Calif.) March 9, 1824-June 21, 1893; Senate 1885-June 21, 1893; Gov. 1861-63.

STANFORD, Richard (grandfather of William Robert Webb) (D N.C.) March 2, 1767-April 9, 1816; House 1797-April 9, 1816.

STANLEY, Augustus Owsley (D Ky.) May 21, 1867-Aug. 13, 1958; House 1903-15; Senate May 19, 1919-25; Gov. 1915-19.

STANLEY, Thomas Bahnson (D Va.) July 16, 1890-July 10, 1970; House Nov. 5, 1946-Feb. 3, 1953; Gov. 1954-58.

STANLEY, Winifred Claire (R N.Y.) Aug. 14, 1909; House 1943-45.

STANLY, Edward (son of John Stanly) (W N.C.) July 13, 1810-July 12, 1872; House 1837-43, 1849-53.

STANLY, John (father of Edward Stanly) (— N.C.) April 9, 1774-Aug. 2, 1834; House 1801-03, 1809-11.

STANTON, Benjamin (W Ohio) June 4, 1809-June 2, 1872; House 1851-53, 1855-61.

STANTON, Frederick Perry (D Tenn.) Dec. 22, 1814-June 4, 1894; House 1845-55; Gov. of Kansas Terr. 1858-61.

STANTON, James V. (D Ohio) Feb. 27, 1932; House 1971- .

STANTON, John William (R Ohio) Feb. 20, 1924; House 1965- .

STANTON, Joseph, Jr. (D R.I.) July 19, 1739-1807; Senate June 7, 1790-93; House 1801-07.

STANTON, Richard Henry (D Ky.) Sept. 9, 1812-March 20, 1891; House 1849-55.

STANTON, William Henry (D Pa.) July 28, 1843-March 28, 1900; House Nov. 7, 1876-77.

STARIN, John Henry (grandson of Thomas Sammons) (R N.Y.) Aug. 27, 1825-March 21, 1909; House 1877-81.

STARK, Benjamin (D Ore.) June 26, 1820-Oct. 10, 1898; Senate Oct. 29, 1861-Sept. 12, 1862.

STARK, William Ledyard (D Neb.) July 29, 1853-Nov. 11, 1922; House 1897-1903.

STARKEY, Frank Thomas (D Minn.) Feb. 18, 1892-May 14, 1968; House 1945-47.

STARKWEATHER, David Austin (D Ohio) Jan. 21, 1802-July 12, 1876; House 1839-41, 1845-47.

STARKWEATHER, George Anson (D N.Y.) May 19, 1794-Oct. 15, 1879; House 1847-49.

STARKWEATHER, Henry Howard (R Conn.) April 29, 1826-Jan. 28, 1876; House 1867-Jan. 28, 1876.

STARNES, Joe (D Ala.) March 31, 1895; House 1935-45.

STARR, John Farson (R N.J.) March 25, 1818-Aug. 9, 1904; House 1863-67.

STAUFFER, S. Walter (R Pa.) Aug. 13, 1888; House 1953-55, 1957-59.

STEAGALL, Henry Bascom (D Ala.) May 19, 1873-Nov. 22, 1943; House 1915-Nov. 22, 1943.

STEARNS, Asahel (F Mass.) June 17, 1774-Feb. 5, 1839; House 1815-17.

STEARNS, Foster Waterman (R N.H.) July 29, 1881-June 4, 1956; House 1939-45.

STEARNS, Ozora Pierson (R Minn.) Jan. 15, 1831-June 2, 1896; Senate Jan. 23-March 3, 1871.

STEBBINS, Henry George (WD N.Y.) Sept. 15, 1811-Dec. 9, 1881; House 1863-Oct. 24, 1864.

STECK, Daniel Frederick (D Iowa) Dec. 16, 1881-Dec. 31, 1950; Senate April 12, 1926-31.

STEDMAN, Charles Manly (D N.C.) Jan. 29, 1841-Sept. 23, 1930; House 1911-Sept. 23, 1930.

STEDMAN, William (F Mass.) Jan. 21, 1765-Aug. 31, 1831; House 1803-July 16, 1810.

STEED, Thomas Jefferson (D Okla.) March 2, 1904; House 1949- .

STEELE, George Washington (R Ind.) Dec. 13, 1839-July 12, 1922; House 1881-89, 1895-1903; Gov. Okla. Terr. 1890-91.

STEELE, Henry Joseph (D Pa.) May 10, 1860-March 19, 1933; House 1915-21.

STEELE, John (F N.C.) Nov. 1, 1764-Aug. 14, 1815; House 1789-93.

STEELE, John Benedict (D N.Y.) March 28, 1814-Sept. 24, 1866; House 1861-65.

STEELE, John Nevett (W Md.) Feb. 22, 1796-Aug. 13, 1853; House May 29, 1834-37.

STEELE, Leslie Jasper (D Ga.) Nov. 21, 1868-July 24, 1929; House 1927-July 24, 1929.

STEELE, Robert H. (R Conn.) Nov. 3, 1938; House Nov. 3, 1970- .

STEELE, Thomas Jefferson (D Iowa) March 19, 1853-March 20, 1920; House 1915-17.

STEELE, Walter Leak (D N.C.) April 18, 1823-Oct. 16, 1891; House 1877-81.

STEELE, William Gaston (D N.J.) Dec. 17, 1820-April 22, 1892; House 1861-65.

STEELE, William Randolph (D Wyo.) July 24, 1842-Nov. 30, 1901; House (Terr. Del.) 1873-77.

STEENERSON, Halvor (R Minn.) June 30, 1852-Nov. 22, 1926; House 1903-23.

STEENROD, Lewis (D Va.) May 27, 1810-Oct. 3, 1862; House 1839-45.

STEFAN, Karl (R Neb.) March 1, 1884-Oct, 2, 1951; House 1935-Oct. 2, 1951.

STEIGER, Sam (R Ariz.) March 10, 1929; House 1967- .

STEIGER, William A. (R Wis.) May 15, 1938; House 1967- .

STEIWER, Frederick (R Ore.) Oct. 13, 1883-Feb. 3, 1939; Senate 1927-Jan. 31, 1938.

STENGER, William Shearer (D Pa.) Feb. 13, 1840-March 29, 1918; House 1875-79.

STENGLE, Charles Irwin (D N.Y.) Dec. 5, 1869-Nov. 23, 1953; House 1923-25.

STENNIS, John Cornelius (D Miss.) Aug. 3, 1901; Senate Nov. 5, 1947- .

STEPHENS, Abraham P. (D N.Y.) Feb. 18, 1796-Nov. 25, 1859; House 1851-53.

STEPHENS, Alexander Hamilton (D Ga.) Feb. 11, 1812-March 4, 1883; House Oct. 2, 1843-59, Dec. 1, 1873-Nov. 4, 1882; Gov. 1882-83.

STEPHENS, Ambrose Everett Burnside (R Ohio) June 3, 1862-Feb. 12, 1927; House 1919-Feb. 12, 1927.

STEPHENS, Dan Voorhees (D Neb.) Nov. 4, 1868-Jan. 13, 1939; House Nov. 7, 1911-19.

STEPHENS, Hubert Durrett (D Miss.) July 2, 1875-March 14, 1946; House 1911-21; Senate 1923-35.

STEPHENS, John Hall (D Texas) Nov. 22, 1847-Nov. 18, 1924; House 1897-1917.

STEPHENS, Philander (JD Pa.) 1788-July 8, 1842; House 1829-33.

STEPHENS, Robert Grier, Jr. (D Ga.) Aug. 14, 1913; House 1961- .

STEPHENS, William Dennison (R Calif.) Dec. 26, 1859-April 25, 1944; House 1911-July 22, 1916; Gov. 1917-23.

STEPHENSON, Benjamin (D Ill.)—Oct. 10, 1822; House (Terr. Del.) Sept. 3, 1814-16.

STEPHENSON, Isaac (brother of Samuel Merritt Stephenson) (R Wis.) June 18, 1829-March 15, 1918; House 1883-89; Senate May 17, 1907-15.

STEPHENSON, James (F Va.) March 20, 1764-Aug. 7, 1833; House 1803-05, 1809-11, Oct. 28, 1822-25.

STEPHENSON, Samuel Merritt (brother of Isaac Stephenson) (R Mich.) Dec. 23, 1831-July 31, 1907; House 1889-97.

STERETT, Samuel (A-F Md.) 1758-July 12, 1833; House 1791-93.

STERIGERE, John Benton (D Pa.) July 31, 1793-Oct. 13, 1852; House 1827-31.

STERLING, Ansel (brother of Micah Sterling) (— Conn.) Feb. 3, 1782-Nov. 6, 1853; House 1821-25.

STERLING, Bruce Foster (D Pa.) Sept. 28, 1870-April 26, 1945; House 1917-19.

STERLING, John Allen (brother of Thomas Sterling) (R Ill.) Feb. 1, 1857-Oct. 17, 1918; House 1903-14, 1915-Oct. 17, 1918.

STERLING, Micah (brother of Ansel Sterling) (F N.Y.) Nov. 5, 1784-April 11, 1844; House 1821-23.

STERLING, Thomas (brother of John Allen Sterling) (R S.D.) Feb. 21, 1851-Aug. 26, 1930; Senate 1913-25.

STETSON, Charles (D Maine) Nov. 2, 1801-March 27, 1863; House 1849-51.

STETSON, Lemuel (D N.Y.) March 13, 1804-May 17, 1868; House 1843-45.

STEVENS, Aaron Fletcher (R N.H.) Aug. 9, 1819-May 10, 1887; House 1867-71.

STEVENS, Bradford Newcomb (D Ill.) Jan. 3, 1813-Nov. 10, 1885; House 1871-73.

STEVENS, Charles Abbot (brother of Moses Tyler Stevens and cousin of Isaac Ingalls Stevens) (R Mass.) Aug. 9, 1816-April 7, 1892; House Jan. 27-March 3, 1875.

STEVENS, Frederick Clement (R Minn.) Jan. 1, 1861-July 1, 1923; House 1897-1915.

STEVENS, Hestor Lockhart (D Mich.) Oct. 1, 1803-May 7, 1864; House 1853-55.

STEVENS, Hiram Sanford (D Ariz.) March 20, 1832-March 22, 1893; House (Terr. Del.) 1875-79.

STEVENS, Isaac Ingalls (cousin of Charles Abbot Stevens and cousin of Isaac Ingalls (D Wash.) March 25, 1818-Sept. 1, 1862; House (Terr. Del.) 1857-61; Terr. Gov. 1853-57.

STEVENS, James (D Conn.) July 4, 1768-April 4, 1835; House 1819-21.

STEVENS, Moses Tyler (brother of Charles Abbot Stevens and cousin of Isaac Ingalls Stevens) (D Mass.) Oct. 10, 1825-March 25, 1907; House 1891-95.

STEVENS, Raymond Bartlett (D N.H.) June 18, 1874-May 18, 1942; House 1913-15.

STEVENS, Robert Smith (D N.Y.) March 27, 1824-Feb. 23, 1893; House 1883-85.

STEVENS, Thaddeus (R Pa.) April 4, 1792-Aug. 11, 1868; House 1849-53 (W), 1859-Aug. 11, 1868 (R).

STEVENS, Theodore F. (Ted) (R Alaska) Nov. 18, 1923; Senate Dec. 24, 1968- .

STEVENSON, Adlai Ewing (D Ill.) Oct. 23, 1835-June 14, 1914; House 1875-77, 1879-81; Vice Pres. 1893-97.

STEVENSON, Adlai Ewing, III (grandson of the preceding) (D Ill.) Oct. 10, 1930; Senate Nov. 17, 1970- .

STEVENSON, Andrew (father of John White Stevenson) (D Va.) Jan. 21, 1784-Jan. 25, 1857; House 1821-June 2, 1834; Speaker 1827-34.

STEVENSON, James S. (— Pa.) 1780-Oct. 16, 1831; House 1825-29.

STEVENSON, Job Evans (R Ohio) Feb. 10, 1832-July 24, 1922; House 1869-73.

STEVENSON, John White (son of Andrew Stevenson) (D Ky.) May 4, 1812-Aug. 10, 1886; House 1857-61; Senate 1871-77; Gov. 1867-71.

STEVENSON, William Francis (D S.C.) Nov. 23, 1861-Feb. 12, 1942; House 1917-33.

STEVENSON, William Henry (R Wis.) Sept. 23, 1891; House 1941-49.

STEWARD, Lewis (D Ill.) Nov. 21, 1824-Aug. 27, 1896; House 1891-93.

STEWART, Alexander (R Wis.) Sept. 12, 1829-May 24, 1912; House 1895-1901.

STEWART, Andrew (W Pa.) June 11, 1791-July 16, 1872; House 1821-29, 1831-35 (D), 1843-49 (W).

STEWART, Andrew (son of the preceding) (R Pa.) April 6, 1836-Nov. 9, 1903; House 1891-Feb. 26, 1892.

STEWART, Arthur Thomas (Tom) (D Tenn.) Jan. 11, 1892; Senate Jan. 16, 1939-49.

STEWART, Charles (D Texas) May 30, 1836-Sept. 21, 1895; House 1883-93.

STEWART, David (W Md.) Sept. 13, 1800-Jan. 5, 1858; Senate Dec. 6, 1849-Jan. 12, 1850.

STEWART, David Wallace (R Iowa) Jan. 22, 1887; Senate Aug. 7 1926-27.

STEWART, Jacob Henry (R Minn.) Jan. 15, 1829-Aug. 25, 1884; House 1877-79.

STEWART, James (— N.C.) Nov. 11, 1775-Dec. 29, 1821; House Jan. 5, 1818-19.

STEWART, James Augustus (D Md.) Nov. 24, 1808-April 3, 1879; House 1855-61.

STEWART, James Fleming (R N.J.) June 15, 1851-Jan. 21, 1904; House 1895-1903.

STEWART, John (D Pa.)—-1820; House Jan. 15, 1801-05.

STEWART, John (D Conn.) Feb. 10, 1795-Sept. 16, 1860; House 1843-45.

STEWART, John David (D Ga.) Aug. 2, 1833-Jan. 28, 1894; House 1887-91.

STEWART, John George (R Del.) June 2, 1890-May 24, 1970; House 1935-37.

STEWART, John Knox (R N.Y.) Oct. 20, 1853-June 27, 1919; House 1899-1903.

STEWART, John Wolcott (R Vt.) Nov. 24, 1825-Oct. 29, 1915; House 1883-91; Senate March 24-Oct. 21, 1908; Gov. 1870-72.

STEWART, Paul (D Okla.) Feb. 27, 1892-Nov. 13, 1950; House 1943-47.

STEWART, Percy Hamilton (D N.J.) Jan. 10, 1867-June 30, 1951; House Dec. 1, 1931-33.

STEWART, Thomas Elliott (CR N.Y.) Sept. 22, 1824-Jan. 9, 1904; House 1867-69.

STEWART, William (R Pa.) Sept. 10, 1810-Oct. 17, 1876; House 1857-61.

STEWART, William Morris (R Nev.) Aug. 9, 1827-April 23, 1909; Senate Dec. 15, 1864-75, 1887-1905.

STIGLER, William Grady (D Okla.) July 7, 1891-Aug. 21, 1952; House March 28, 1944-Aug. 21, 1952.

STILES, John Dodson (D Pa.) Jan. 15, 1822-Oct. 29, 1896; House June 3, 1862-65, 1869-71.

STILES, William Henry (D Ga.) Jan. 1, 1808-Dec. 20, 1865; House 1843-45.

STILLWELL, Thomas Neel (R Ind.) Aug. 29, 1830-Jan. 14, 1874; House 1865-67.

STINESS, Walter Russell (R R.I.) March 13, 1854-March 17, 1924; House 1915-23.

STINSON, K. William (Bill) (R Wash.) April 20, 1930; House 1963-65.

STIVERS, Moses Dunning (R N.Y.) Dec. 30, 1828-Feb. 2, 1895; House 1889-91.

STOBBS, George Russell (R Mass.) Feb. 7, 1877-Dec. 23, 1966; House 1925-31.

STOCKBRIDGE, Francis Brown (R Mich.) April 9, 1826-April 30, 1894; Senate 1887-April 30, 1894.

STOCKBRIDGE, Henry, Jr. (R Md.) Sept. 18, 1856-March 22, 1924; House 1889-91.

STOCKDALE, Thomas Ringland (D Miss.) March 28, 1828-Jan. 8, 1899; House 1887-95.

STOCKMAN, Lowell (R Ore.) April 12, 1901-Aug. 10, 1962; House 1943-53.

STOCKSLAGER, Strother Madison (D Ind.) May 7, 1842-June 1, 1930; House 1881-85.

STOCKTON, John Potter (son of Robert Field Stockton) Aug. 2, 1826-Jan. 22, 1900; Senate March 15, 1865-March 27, 1866, 1869-75.

STOCKTON, Richard (father of Robert Field Stockton) (F N.J.) April 17, 1764-March 7, 1828; Senate Nov. 12, 1796-99; House 1813-15.

STOCKTON, Robert Field (son of the preceding and father of John Potter Stockton) (D N.J.) Aug. 20, 1795-Oct. 7, 1866; Senate 1851-Jan. 10, 1853.

STODDARD, Ebenezer (— Conn.) May 6, 1785-Aug. 19, 1847; House 1821-25.

STODDERT, John Truman (JD Md.) Oct. 1, 1790-July 19, 1870; House 1833-35.

STOKELY, Samuel (W Ohio) Jan. 25, 1796-May 23, 1861; House 1841-43.

STOKES, Edward Lowber (R Pa.) Sept. 29, 1880-Nov. 8, 1964; House Nov. 3, 1931-35.

STOKES, James William (D S.C.) Dec. 12, 1853-July 6, 1901; House 1895-June 1, 1896; Nov. 3, 1896-July 6, 1901.

STOKES, Louis (D Ohio) Feb. 23, 1925; House 1969- .

STOKES, Montfort (D N.C.) March 12, 1762-Nov. 4, 1842; Senate Dec. 4, 1816-23; Gov. 1830-32.

STOKES, William Brickly (R Tenn.) Sept. 9, 1814-March 14, 1897; House 1859-61 (W); July 24, 1866-71.

STOLL, Philip Henry (D S.C.) Nov. 5, 1874-Oct. 29, 1958; House Oct. 7, 1919-23.

STONE, Alfred Parish (D Ohio) June 28, 1813-Aug. 2, 1865; House Oct. 8, 1844-45.

STONE, Charles Warren (R Pa.) June 29, 1843-Aug. 15, 1912; House Nov. 4, 1890-99.

STONE, Claudius Ulysses (D Ill.) May 11, 1879-Nov. 13, 1957; House 1911-17.

STONE, David (D N.C.) Feb. 17, 1770-Oct. 7, 1818; House 1799-1801; Senate 1801-Feb. 17, 1807, 1813-Dec. 24, 1814; Gov. 1808-10.

STONE, Eben Francis (R Mass.) Aug. 3, 1822-Jan. 22, 1895; House 1881-87.

STONE, Frederick (grandson of Michael Jenifer Stone) (D Md.) Feb. 7, 1820-Oct. 17, 1899; House 1867-71.

STONE, James W. (D Ky.) 1813-Oct. 13, 1854; House 1843-45, 1851-53.

STONE, John Wesley (R Mich.) July 18, 1838-March 24, 1922; House 1877-81.

STONE, Joseph Champlin (R Iowa) July 30, 1829-Dec. 3, 1902; House 1877-79.

STONE, Michael Jenifer (grandfather of Frederick Stone) (— Md.) 1747-1812; House 1789-91.

STONE, Ulysses Stevens (R Okla.) Dec. 17, 1878-Dec. 8, 1962; House 1929-31.

STONE, William (W Tenn.) Jan. 26, 1791-Feb. 18, 1853; House Sept. 14, 1837-39.

STONE, William Alexis (R Pa.) April 18, 1846-March 1, 1920; House 1891-Nov. 9, 1898; Gov. 1899-1903.

STONE, William Henry (D Mo.) Nov. 7, 1828-July 9, 1901; House 1873-77.

STONE, William Joel (D Mo.) May 7, 1848-April 14, 1918; House 1885-91; Senate 1903-April 14, 1918; Gov. 1893-97.

STONE, William Johnson (D Ky.) June 26, 1841-March 12, 1923; House 1885-95.

STORER, Bellamy (W Ohio) March 26, 1796-June 1, 1875; House 1835-37.

STORER, Bellamy (son of the preceding and uncle of Nicholas Longworth) (R Ohio) Aug. 28, 1847-Nov. 12, 1922; House 1891-95.

STORER, Clement (— N.H.) Sept. 20, 1760-Nov. 21, 1830; House 1807-09; Senate June 27, 1817-19.

STORKE, Thomas More (D Calif.) Nov. 23, 1876; Senate Nov. 9, 1938-39.

STORM, Frederic (R N.Y.) July 2, 1844-June 9, 1935; House 1901-03.

STORM, John Brutzman (D Pa.) Sept. 19, 1838-Aug. 13, 1901; House 1871-75, 1883-87.

STORRS, Henry Randolph (brother of William Lucius Storrs) (F N.Y.) Sept. 3, 1787-July 29, 1837; House 1817-21, 1823-31.

STORRS, William Lucius (brother of Henry Randolph Storrs) (W Conn.) March 25, 1795-June 25, 1861; House 1829-33, 1839-June 1840.

STORY, Joseph (D Mass.) Sept. 18, 1779-Sept. 10, 1845; House May 23, 1808-09; Assoc. Just. of Supreme Court 1811-Sept. 10, 1845.

STOUGHTON, William Lewis (R Mich.) March 20, 1827-June 6, 1888; House 1869-73.

STOUT, Byron Gray (D Mich.) Jan. 12, 1829-June 19, 1896; House 1891-93.

STOUT, Lansing (D Ore.) March 27, 1828-March 4, 1871; House 1859-61.

STOUT, Tom (D Mont.) May 20, 1879-Dec. 26, 1965; House 1913-17.

STOVER, John Hubler (R Mo.) April 24, 1833-Oct. 27, 1889; House Dec. 7, 1868-69.

STOW, Silas (F N.Y.) Dec. 21, 1773-Jan. 19, 1827; House 1811-13.

STOWELL, William Henry Harrison (R Va.) July 26, 1840-April 27, 1922; House 1871-77.

STOWER, John G. (JD N.Y.)——; House 1827-29.

STRADER, Peter Wilson (D Ohio) Nov. 6, 1818-Feb. 25, 1881; House 1869-71.

STRAIT, Horace Burton (R Minn.) Jan. 26, 1835-Feb. 25, 1894; House 1873-79, 1881-87.

STRAIT, Thomas Jefferson (Alliance D S.C.) Dec. 25, 1846-April 18, 1924; House 1893-99.

STRANAHAN, James Samuel Thomas (W N.Y.) April 25, 1808-Sept. 3, 1898; House 1855-57.

STRANGE, Robert (D N.C.) Sept. 20, 1796-Feb. 19, 1854; Senate Dec. 5, 1836-Nov. 16, 1840.

STRATTON, Charles Creighton (uncle of Benjamin Franklin Howey) (W N.J.) March 6, 1796-March 30, 1859; House 1837-39, 1841-43; Gov. 1845-48.

STRATTON, John (— Va.) Aug. 19, 1769-May 10, 1804; House 1801-03.

STRATTON, John Leake Newbold (R N.J.) Nov. 27, 1817-May 17, 1899; House 1859-63,

STRATTON, Nathan Taylor (D N.J.) March 17, 1813-March 9, 1887; House 1851-55.

STRATTON, Samuel Studdiford (D N.Y.) Sept. 27, 1916; House 1959- .

STRATTON, William Grant (R Ill.) Feb. 26, 1914; House 1941-43, 1947-49; Gov. 1953-61.

STRAUB, Christian Markle (D Pa.) 1804-—; House 1853-55.

STRAUS, Isidor (D N.Y.) Feb. 6, 1845-April 15, 1912; House Jan. 30, 1894-95.

STRAWBRIDGE, James Dale (R Pa.) April 7, 1824-July 19, 1890; House 1873-75.

STREET, Randall S. (D N.Y.) 1780-Nov. 21, 1841; House 1819-21.

STRICKLAND, Randolph (R Mich.) Feb. 4, 1823-May 5, 1880; House 1869-71.

STRINGER, Lawrence Beaumont (D Ill.) Feb. 24, 1866-Dec. 5, 1942; House 1913-15.

STRINGFELLOW, Douglas (R Utah) Sept. 24, 1922-Oct. 19, 1966; House 1953-55.

STRODE, Jesse Burr (R Neb.) Feb. 18, 1845-Nov. 10, 1924; House 1895-99.

STROHM, John (W Pa.) Oct. 16, 1793-Sept. 12, 1884; House 1845-49.

STRONG, Caleb (F Mass.) Jan. 9, 1745-Nov. 7, 1819; Senate 1789-June 1, 1796; Gov. 1800-07, 1812-16.

STRONG, James (F N.Y.) 1783-Aug. 8, 1847; House 1819-21, 1823-31.

STRONG, James George (R Kan.) April 23, 1870-Jan. 11, 1938; House 1919-33.

STRONG, Julius Levi (R Conn.) Nov. 8, 1828-Sept. 7, 1872; House 1869-Sept. 7, 1872.

STRONG, Luther Martin (R Ohio) June 23, 1838-April 26, 1903; House 1893-97.

STRONG, Nathan Leroy (R Pa.) Nov. 12, 1859-Dec. 14, 1939; House 1917-35.

STRONG, Selah Brewster (D N.Y.) May 1, 1792-Nov. 29, 1872; House 1843-45.

STRONG, Solomon (F Mass.) March 2, 1780-Sept. 16, 1850; House 1815-19.

STRONG, Stephen (D N.Y.) Oct. 11, 1791-April 15, 1866; House 1845-47.

STRONG, Sterling Price (D Texas) Aug. 17, 1852-March 28, 1936; House 1933-35.

STRONG, Theron Rudd (cousin of William Strong of Pa.) (D N.Y.) Nov. 7, 1802-May 14, 1873; House 1839-41.

STRONG, William (D Vt.) 1763-Jan. 28, 1840; House 1811-15, 1819-21.

STRONG, William (cousin of Theron Rudd Strong) (D Pa.) May 6, 1808-Aug. 19, 1895; House 1847-51; Assoc. Justice of Supreme Crt. 1870-80.

STROTHER, George French (father of James French Strother) (D Va.) 1783-Nov. 28, 1840; House 1817-Feb. 10, 1820.

STROTHER, James French (son of George French Strother) (W Va.) Sept. 4, 1811-Sept. 20, 1860; House 1851-53.

STROTHER, James French (grandson of the preceding) (R W. Va.) June 29, 1868-April 10, 1930; House 1925-29.

STROUSE, Myer (D Pa.) Dec. 16, 1825-Feb. 11, 1878; House 1863-67.

STROWD, William Franklin (P N.C.) Dec. 7, 1832-Dec. 12, 1911; House 1895-99.

STRUBLE, Isaac S. (R Iowa) Nov. 3, 1843-Feb. 17, 1913; House 1883-91.

STRUDWICK, William Francis (F N.C.) —-1812; House Nov. 28, 1796-97.

STUART, Alexander Hugh Holmes (cousin of Archibald Stuart) (W W.Va.) April 2, 1807-Feb. 13, 1891; House 1841-43; Secy. of the Interior 1850-53.

STUART, Andrew (D Ohio) Aug. 3, 1823-April 30, 1872; House 1853-55.

STUART, Archibald (cousin of Alexander Hugh Holmes Stuart) (W W.Va.) Dec. 2, 1795-Sept. 20, 1855; House 1837-39.

STUART, Charles Edward (D Mich.) Nov. 25, 1810-May 19, 1887; House Dec. 6, 1847-49, 1851-53; Senate 1853-59.

STUART, David (D Mich.) March 12, 1816-Sept. 12, 1868; House 1853-55.

STUART, John Todd (D Ill.) Nov. 10, 1807-Nov. 23, 1885; House 1839-43 (W), 1863-65 (D).

STUART, Philip (F Md.) 1760-Aug. 14, 1830; House 1811-19.

STUBBLEFIELD, Frank Albert (D Ky.) April 5, 1907; House 1959- .

STUBBS, Henry Elbert (D Calif.) March 4, 1881-Feb. 28, 1937; House 1933-Feb. 28, 1937.

STUCKEY, Williamson Sylvester, Jr. (D Ga.) May 25, 1935; House 1967- .

STUDLEY, Elmer Ebenezer (R N.Y.) Sept. 24, 1869-Sept. 6, 1942; House 1933-35.

STULL, Howard William (R Pa.) April 11, 1876-April 22, 1949; House April 26, 1932-33.

STUMP, Herman (D Md.) Aug. 8, 1837-Jan. 9, 1917; House 1889-93.

STURGEON, Daniel (D Pa.) Oct. 27, 1789-July 3, 1878; Senate Jan. 14, 1840-51.

STURGES, Jonathan (father of Lewis Burr Sturges) (— Conn.) Aug. 23, 1740-Oct. 4, 1819; House 1789-93; Cont. Cong. 1774-87.

STURGES, Lewis Burr (son of Jonathan Sturges) (F Conn.) March 15, 1763-March 30, 1844; House Sept. 16, 1805-17.

STURGISS, George Cookman (R W. Va.) Aug. 16, 1842-Feb. 26, 1925; House 1907-11.

STURTEVANT, John Cirby (R Pa.) Feb. 20, 1835-Dec. 20, 1912; House 1897-99.

SULLIVAN, Christopher Daniel (D N.Y.) July 14, 1870-Aug. 3, 1942; House 1917-41.

SULLIVAN, George (— N.H.) Aug. 29, 1771-April 14, 1838; House 1811-13.

SULLIVAN, John Andrew (D Mass.) May 10, 1868-May 31, 1927; House 1903-07.

SULLIVAN, John Berchmans (husband of Leonor Kretzer Sullivan) (D Mo.) Oct. 10, 1897-Jan. 29, 1951; House 1941-43, 1945-47, 1949-Jan. 19, 1951.

SULLIVAN, Leonor Kretzer (widow of John Berchmans Sullivan) (D Mo.) Aug. 21, 1903; House 1953- .

SULLIVAN, Maurice Joseph (D Nev.) Dec. 7, 1884-Aug. 9, 1953; House 1943-45.

SULLIVAN, Patrick Joseph (R Wyo.) March 17, 1865-April 8, 1935; Senate Dec. 5, 1929-Nov. 20, 1930.

SULLIVAN, Patrick Joseph (R Pa.) Oct. 12, 1877-Dec. 31, 1946; House 1929-33.

SULLIVAN, Timothy Daniel (D N.Y.) July 23, 1862-Aug. 31, 1913; House 1903-July 27, 1906, March 4-Aug. 31, 1913.

SULLIVAN, William Van Amberg (D Miss.) Dec. 18, 1857-March 21, 1918; House 1897-May 31, 1898; Senate May 31, 1898-1901.

SULLOWAY, Cyrus Adams (R N.H.) June 8, 1839-March 11, 1917; House 1895-1913, 1915-March 11, 1917.

SULZER, Charles August (brother of William Sulzer) (D Alaska) Feb. 24, 1879-April 28, 1919; House (Terr. Del.) 1917-Jan. 7, 1919, March 4-April 28, 1919.

SULZER, William (brother of Charles August Sulzer) (D N.Y.) March 18, 1863-Nov. 6, 1941; House 1895-Dec. 31, 1912; Gov. 1913.

SUMMERS, George William (W Va.) March 4, 1804-Sept. 19, 1868; House 1841-45.

SUMMERS, John William (R Wash.) April 29, 1870-Sept. 25, 1937; House 1919-33.

SUMNER, Charles (R Mass.) Jan. 6, 1811-March 11, 1874; Senate April 24, 1851-57 (D/FS), 1857-March 11, 1874 (R).

SUMNER, Charles Allen (D Calif.) Aug. 2, 1835-Jan. 31, 1903; House 1883-85.

SUMNER, Daniel Hadley (D Wis.) Sept. 15, 1837-May 29, 1903; House 1883-85.

SUMNER, Jessie (R Ill.) July 17, 1898; House 1939-47.

SUMNERS, Hatton William (D Texas) May 30, 1875-April 19, 1962; House 1913-47.

SUMTER, Thomas (grandfather of Thomas De Lage Sumter) (D S.C.) Aug. 14, 1734-June 1, 1832; House 1789-93, 1797-Dec. 15, 1801; Senate Dec. 15, 1801-Dec. 16, 1810.

SUMTER, Thomas De Lage (grandson of Thomas Sumter) (D S.C.) Nov. 14, 1809-July 2, 1874; House 1839-43.

SUNDSTROM, Frank Leander (R N.J.) Jan. 5, 1901; House 1943-49.

SUTHERLAND, Daniel Alexander (R Alaska) April 17, 1869-March 24, 1955; House (Terr. Del.) 1921-31.

SUTHERLAND, George (R Utah) March 25, 1862-July 18, 1942; House 1901-03; Senate 1905-17; Assoc. Justice of Supreme Crt. 1922-38.

SUTHERLAND, Howard (R W. Va.) Sept. 8, 1865-March 12, 1950; House 1913-17; Senate 1917-23.

SUTHERLAND, Jabez Gridley (D Mich.) Oct. 6, 1825-Nov. 20, 1902; House 1871-73.

SUTHERLAND, Joel Barlow (JD Pa.) Feb. 26, 1792-Nov. 15, 1861; House 1827-37.

SUTHERLAND, Josiah (D N.Y.) June 12, 1804-May 25, 1887; House 1851-53.

SUTHERLAND, Roderick Dhu (P Neb.) April 27, 1862-Oct. 18, 1915; House 1897-1901.

SUTPHIN, William Halstead (D N.J.) Aug. 30, 1887; House 1931-43.

SUTTON, James Patrick (Pat) (D Tenn.) Oct. 31, 1915; House 1949-55.

SWAN, Samuel (— N.J.) 1771-Aug. 24, 1844; House 1821-31.

SWANK, Fletcher B. (D Okla.) April 24, 1875-March 16, 1950; House 1921-29, 1931-35.

SWANN, Edward (D N.Y.) March 10, 1862-Sept. 19, 1945; House Nov. 4, 1902-03.

SWANN, Thomas (D Md.) Feb. 3, 1809-July 24, 1883; House 1869-79; Gov. 1865-69 (U).

SWANSON, Charles Edward (R Iowa) Jan. 3, 1879; House 1929-33.

SWANSON, Claude Augustus (D Va.) March 31, 1862-July 7, 1939; House 1893-Jan. 30, 1906; Senate Aug. 1, 1910-33; Gov. 1906-10; Secy. of the Navy 1933-39.

SWANWICK, John (D Pa.) 1740-Aug. 1, 1798; House 1795-Aug. 1, 1798.

SWART, Peter (— N.Y.) July 5, 1752-Nov. 3, 1829; House 1807-09.

SWARTZ, Joshua William (R Pa.) June 9, 1867-May 27, 1959; House 1925-27.

SWASEY, John Philip (R Maine) Sept. 4, 1839-May 27, 1928; House Nov. 3, 1908-11.

SWEARINGEN, Henry (D Ohio) about 1792-—; House Dec. 3, 1838-41.

SWEAT, Lorenzo De Medici (D Maine) May 26, 1818-July 26, 1898; House 1863-65.

SWEENEY, Martin Leonard (father of Robert E. Sweeney) (D Ohio) April 15, 1885-May 1, 1960; House Nov. 3, 1931-43.

SWEENEY, Robert E. (son of Martin L. Sweeney) (D Ohio) Nov. 4, 1924; House 1965-67.

SWEENEY, William Northcut (D Ky.) May 5, 1832-April 21, 1895; House 1869-71.

SWEENY, George (— Ohio) Feb. 22, 1796-Oct. 10, 1877; House 1839-43.

SWEET, Burton Erwin (R Iowa) Dec. 10, 1867-Jan. 3, 1957; House 1915-23.

SWEET, Edwin Forrest (D Mich.) Nov. 21, 1847-April 2, 1935; House 1911-13.

SWEET, John Hyde (R Neb.) Sept. 1, 1880-April 4, 1964; House April 9, 1940-41.

SWEET, Thaddeus C. (R N.Y.) Nov. 16, 1872-May 1, 1928; House Nov. 6, 1923-May 1, 1928.

SWEET, Willis (R Idaho) Jan. 1, 1856-July 9, 1925; House Oct. 1, 1890-95.

SWEETSER, Charles (D Ohio) Jan. 22, 1808-April 14, 1864; House 1849-53.

SWENEY, Joseph Henry (R Iowa) Oct. 2, 1845-Nov. 11, 1918; House 1889-91.

SWICK, Jesse Howard (R Pa.) Aug. 6, 1879-Nov. 17, 1952; House 1927-35.

SWIFT, Benjamin (F Vt.) April 3, 1781-Nov. 11, 1847; House 1827-31; Senate 1833-39.

SWIFT, George Robinson (D Ala.) Dec. 19, 1887; Senate June 15-Nov. 5, 1946.

SWIFT, Oscar William (R N.Y.) April 11, 1869-June 30, 1940; House 1915-19.

SWIFT, Zephaniah (F Conn.) Feb. 27, 1759-Sept. 27, 1823; House 1793-97.

SWINBURNE, John (R N.Y.) May 30, 1820-March 28, 1889; House 1885-87.

SWINDALL, Charles (R Okla.) Feb. 13, 1876-June 19, 1939; House Nov. 2, 1920-21.

SWING, Philip David (R Calif.) Nov. 30, 1884-Aug. 8, 1963; House 1921-33.

SWITZER, Robert Mauck (R Ohio) March 6, 1863-Oct. 28, 1952; House 1911-19.

SWOOPE, Jacob (F Va.)—1832; House 1809-11.

SWOOPE, William Irvin (nephew of John Patton) (R Pa.) Oct. 3, 1862-Oct. 9, 1930; House 1923-27.

SWOPE, Guy Jacob (D Pa.) Dec. 26, 1892-July 25, 1969; House 1937-39; Gov. of Puerto Rico 1941.

SWOPE, John Augustus (D Pa.) Dec. 25, 1827-Dec. 6, 1910; House Dec. 23, 1884-March 3, 1885, Nov. 3, 1885-87.

SWOPE, King (R Ky.) Aug. 10, 1893-April 23, 1961; House Aug. 2, 1919-21.

SWOPE, Samuel Franklin (R Ky.) March 1, 1809-April 19, 1865; House 1855-56 (AP), 1856-57 (R).

SYKES, George (D N.J.) Sept. 20, 1802-Feb. 25, 1880; House 1843-45, Nov. 4, 1845-47.

SYMES, George Gifford (R Colo.) April 28, 1840-Nov. 3, 1893; House 1885-89.

SYMINGTON, James Wadsworth (son of William Stuart Symington) (D Mo.) Sept. 28, 1927; House 1969- .

SYMINGTON, William Stuart (father of James Wadsworth Symington) (D Mo.) June 26, 1901; Senate 1953- ; Secy. of the Air Force 1947-50.

SYPHER, Jacob Hale (R La.) June 22, 1837-May 9, 1905; House July 18, 1868-69, Nov. 7, 1870-75.

TABER, John (R N.Y.) May 5, 1880-Nov. 22, 1965; House 1923-63.

TABER, Stephen (son of Thomas Taber 2d) (D N.Y.) March 7, 1821-April 23, 1886; House 1865-69.

TABER, Thomas 2d (father of Stephen Taber) (D N.Y.) May 19, 1785-March 21, 1862; House Nov. 5, 1828-29.

TABOR, Horace Austin Warner (R Colo.) Nov. 26, 1830-April 10, 1899; Senate Jan. 27-March 3, 1883.

TACKETT, Boyd (D Ark.) May 9, 1911; House 1949-53.

TAFFE, John (R Neb.) Jan. 30, 1827-March 14, 1884; House 1867-73.

TAFT, Charles Phelps (uncle of Robert Alphonso Taft) (R Ohio) Dec. 21, 1843-Dec. 31, 1929; House 1895-97.

TAFT, Kingsley Arter (R Ohio) July 19, 1903-March 28, 1970; Senate Nov. 5, 1946-47.

TAFT, Robert Alphonso (son of President William Howard Taft, father of Robert Taft, Jr., and nephew of Charles Phelps Taft) (R Ohio) Sept. 8, 1889-July 31, 1953; Senate 1939-July 31, 1953.

TAFT, Robert, Jr. (son of the preceding) (R Ohio) Feb. 26, 1917; House 1963-65, 1967-71; Senate 1971- .

TAGGART, Joseph (D Kan.) June 15, 1867-Dec. 3, 1938; House Nov. 7, 1911-17.

TAGGART, Samuel (F Mass.) March 24, 1754-April 25, 1825; House 1803-17.

TAGGART, Thomas (D Ind.) Nov. 17, 1856-March 6, 1929; Senate March 20-Nov. 7, 1916; Chrmn. Dem. Nat. Comm. 1900-08.

TAGUE, Peter Francis (D Mass.) June 4, 1871-Sept. 17, 1941; House 1915-19, Oct. 23, 1919-25.

TAIT, Charles (D Ga.) Feb. 1, 1768-Oct. 7, 1835; Senate Nov. 27, 1809-19.

TALBERT, William Jasper (D S.C.) Oct. 6, 1846-Feb. 5, 1931; House 1893-1903.

TALBOT, Isham (— Ky.) 1773-Sept. 25, 1837; Senate Jan. 3, 1815-19, Oct. 19, 1820-25.

TALBOT, Joseph Edward (R Conn.) March 18, 1901-April 30, 1966; House Jan. 20, 1942-47.

TALBOT, Silas (F N.Y.) Jan. 11, 1751-June 30, 1813; House 1793-95.

TALBOTT, Albert Gallatin (uncle of William Clayton Anderson) (D Ky.) April 4, 1808-Sept. 9, 1887; House 1855-59.

TALBOTT, Joshua Frederick Cockey (D Md.) July 29, 1843-Oct. 5, 1918; House 1879-85, 1893-95, 1903-Oct. 5, 1918.

TALCOTT, Burt L. (R Calif.) Feb. 22, 1920; House 1963- .

TALCOTT, Charles Andrew (D N.Y.) June 10, 1857-Feb. 27, 1920; House 1911-15.

TALIAFERRO, Benjamin (— Ga.) 1750-Sept. 3, 1821; House 1799-1802.

TALIAFERRO, James Piper (D Fla.) Sept. 30, 1847-Oct. 6, 1934; Senate April 20, 1899-1911.

TALIAFERRO, John (W Va.) 1768-Aug. 12, 1852; House 1801-03, Nov. 29, 1811-13, March 24, 1924-31 (D); 1835-43 (W).

TALLE, Henry Oscar (R Iowa) Jan. 12, 1892-March 14, 1969; House 1939-59.

TALLMADGE, Benjamin (father of Frederick Augustus Tallmadge) (F Conn.) Feb. 25, 1754-March 7, 1835; House 1801-17.

TALLMADGE, Frederick Augustus (son of Benjamin Tallmadge) (W N.Y.) Aug. 29, 1792-Sept. 17, 1869; House 1847-49.

TALLMADGE, James, Jr. (D N.Y.) Jan. 20, 1778-Sept. 29, 1853; House June 6, 1817-19.

TALLMADGE, Nathaniel Pitcher (D N.Y.) Feb. 8, 1795-Nov. 2, 1864; Senate 1833-June 17, 1844; Gov. of Wis. Terr. 1844-45.

TALLMAN, Peleg (D Mass.) July 24, 1764-March 12, 1840; House 1811-13.

TALMADGE, Herman Eugene (D Ga.) Aug. 9, 1913; Senate 1957-—; Gov. 1947, 1948-55.

TANNEHILL, Adamson (D Pa.) May 23, 1750-Dec. 23, 1820; House 1813-15.

TANNER, Adolphus Hitchcock (R N.Y.) May 23, 1833-Jan. 14, 1882; House 1869-71.

TAPPAN, Benjamin (D Ohio) May 25, 1773-April 12, 1857; Senate 1839-45.

TAPPAN, Mason Weare (R N.H.) Oct. 20, 1817-Oct. 25, 1886; House 1855-61.

TARBOX, John Kemble (D Mass.) May 6, 1838-May 28, 1887; House 1875-77.

TARR, Christian (— Pa.) May 25, 1765-Feb. 24, 1833; House 1817-21.

TARSNEY, John Charles (D Mo.) Nov. 7, 1845-Sept. 4, 1920; House 1889-Feb. 17, 1896.

TARSNEY, Timothy Edward (D Mich.) Feb. 4, 1849-June 8, 1909; House 1885-89.

TARVER, Malcolm Connor (D Ga.) Sept. 25, 1885-March 5, 1960; House 1927-47.

TATE, Farish Carter (D Ga.) Nov. 20, 1856-Feb. 7, 1922; House 1893-1905.

TATE, Magnus (F Va.) 1760-March 30, 1823; House 1815-17.

TATGENHORST, Charles, Jr. (R Ohio) Aug. 19, 1883-Jan. 13, 1961; House Nov. 8, 1927-29.

TATOM, Absalom (R N.C.) 1742-Dec. 20, 1802; House 1795-June 1, 1796.

TATTNALL, Edward Fenwick (—Ga.) 1788-Nov. 21, 1832; House 1821-27.

TATTNALL, Josiah (— Ga.) 1764-June 6, 1803; Senate Feb. 20, 1796-99; Gov. 1801-02.

TAUL, Micah (grandfather of Taul Bradford) (D Ky.) May 14, 1785-May 27, 1850; House 1815-17.

TAULBEE, William Preston (D Ky.) Oct. 22, 1851-March 11, 1890; House 1885-89.

TAURIELLO, Anthony Francis (D N.Y.) Aug. 14, 1899-—; House 1949-51.

TAVENNER, Clyde Howard (D Ill.) Feb. 4, 1882-Feb. 6, 1942; House 1913-17.

TAWNEY, James Albertus (R Minn.) Jan. 3, 1855-June 12, 1919; House 1893-1911.

TAYLER, Robert Walker (R Ohio) Nov. 26, 1852-Nov. 25, 1910; House 1895-1903.

TAYLOR, Abner (R Ill.) 1829-April 13, 1903; House 1889-93.

TAYLOR, Alexander Wilson (R Pa.) March 22, 1815-May 7, 1893; House 1873-75.

TAYLOR, Alfred Alexander (son of Nathaniel Green Taylor and brother of Robert Love Taylor) (R Tenn.) Aug. 6, 1848-Nov. 25, 1931; House 1889-95; Gov. 1921-23.

TAYLOR, Arthur Herbert (D Ind.) Feb. 29, 1852-Feb. 20, 1922; House 1893-95.

TAYLOR, Benjamin Irving (D N.Y.) Dec. 21, 1877-Sept. 5, 1946; House 1913-15.

TAYLOR, Caleb Newbold (R Pa.) July 27, 1813-Nov. 15, 1887; House 1867-69, April 13, 1870-71.

TAYLOR, Chester William (son of Samuel Mitchell Taylor) (D Ark.) July 16, 1883-July 17, 1931; House Oct. 31, 1921-23.

TAYLOR, Dean Park (R N.Y.) Jan. 1, 1902; House 1943-61.

TAYLOR, Edward Livingston, Jr. (R Ohio) Aug. 10, 1869-March 10, 1938; House 1905-13.

TAYLOR, Edward Thomas (D Colo.) June 19, 1858-Sept. 3, 1941; House 1909-Sept. 3, 1941.

TAYLOR, Ezra Booth (R Ohio) July 9, 1823-Jan. 29, 1912; House Dec. 13, 1880-93.

TAYLOR, George (D N.Y.) Oct. 19, 1820-Jan. 18, 1894; House 1857-59.

TAYLOR, George Washington (D Ala.) Jan. 16, 1849-Dec. 21, 1932; House 1897-1915.

TAYLOR, Glen Hearst (D Idaho) April 12, 1904; Senate 1945-51.

TAYLOR, Herbert Worthington (R N.J.) Feb. 19, 1869-Oct. 15, 1931; House 1921-23, 1925-27.

TAYLOR, Isaac Hamilton (R Ohio) April 18, 1840-Dec. 18, 1936; House 1885-87.

TAYLOR, James Alfred (D W.Va.) Sept. 25, 1878-June 9, 1956; House 1923-27.

TAYLOR, James Willis (R Tenn.) Aug. 28, 1880-Nov. 14, 1939; House 1919-Nov. 14, 1939.

TAYLOR, John (D Va.) May 17, 1754-Aug. 20, 1824; Senate Oct. 18, 1792-May 11, 1794; June 4-Dec. 7, 1803; Dec. 18, 1822-Aug. 20, 1824.

TAYLOR, John (D S.C.) May 4, 1770-April 16, 1832; House 1807-Dec. 30, 1810; Senate Dec. 31, 1810-Nov. 1816; Gov. 1826-28.

TAYLOR, John (— S.C.)—-—; House 1815-17.

TAYLOR, John Clarence (D S.C.) March 2, 1890-—; House 1933-39.

TAYLOR, John James (D N.Y.) April 27, 1808-July 1, 1892; House 1853-55.

TAYLOR, John Lampkin (W Ohio) March 7, 1805-Sept. 6, 1870; House 1847-55.

TAYLOR, John May (D Tenn.) May 18, 1838-Feb. 17, 1911; House 1883-87.

TAYLOR, John W. (D N.Y.) March 26, 1784-Sept. 8, 1854; House 1813-33; Speaker 1820-21, 1825-27.

TAYLOR, Jonathan (D Ohio) 1796-April 1848; House 1839-41.

TAYLOR, Joseph Danner (R Ohio) Nov. 7, 1830-Sept. 19, 1899; House Jan. 2, 1883-85, 1887-93.

TAYLOR, Miles (D La.) July 16, 1805-Sept. 23, 1873; House 1855-Feb. 5, 1861.

TAYLOR, Nathaniel Green (father of Alfred Alexander Taylor and Robert Love Taylor) (W Tenn.) Dec. 29, 1819-April 1, 1887; House March 30, 1854-55, July 24, 1866-67.

TAYLOR, Nelson (D N.Y.) June 8, 1821-Jan. 16, 1894; House 1865-67.

TAYLOR, Robert (— Va.) April 29, 1763-July 3, 1845; House 1825-27.

TAYLOR, Robert Love (D Tenn.) (son of Nathaniel Green Taylor and brother of Alfred Alexander Taylor) (July 31, 1850-March 31, 1912; House 1879-81; Senate 1907-March 31, 1912; Gov. 1887-91, 1897-99.

TAYLOR, Roy Arthur (D N.C.) Jan. 31, 1910; House June 25, 1960- .

TAYLOR, Samuel Mitchell (father of Chester William Taylor) (D Ark.) May 25, 1852-Sept. 13, 1921; House Jan. 15, 1913-Sept. 13, 1921.

TAYLOR, Vincent Albert (R Ohio) Dec. 6, 1845-Dec. 2, 1922; House 1891-93.

TAYLOR, Waller (D Ind.) before 1786-Aug. 26, 1826; Senate Dec. 11, 1816-25.

TAYLOR, William (D N.Y.) Oct. 12, 1791-Sept. 16, 1865; House 1833-39.

TAYLOR, William (D Va.) April 5, 1788-Jan. 17, 1846; House 1843-Jan. 17, 1846.

TAYLOR, William Penn (W Va.)—-—; House 1833-35.

TAYLOR, Zachary (R Tenn.) May 9, 1849-Feb. 19, 1921; House 1885-87.

TAZEWELL, Henry (father of Littleton Waller Tazewell) (—Va.) Nov. 15, 1753-Jan. 24, 1799; Senate Dec. 29, 1794-Jan. 24, 1799; President pro tempore 1794-96.

TAZEWELL, Littleton Waller (son of Henry Tazewell) (D Va.) Dec. 17, 1774-May 6, 1860; House Nov. 26, 1800-01; Senate Dec. 7, 1824-July 16, 1832; President pro tempore 1832; Gov. 1834-36.

TEAGUE, Charles McKevett (R Calif.) Sept. 18, 1909; House 1955- .

TEAGUE, Olin Earl (D Texas) April 6, 1910; House Aug. 24, 1946- .

TEESE, Frederick Halstead (D N.J.) Oct. 21, 1823-Jan. 7, 1894; House 1875-77.

TEIGAN, Henry George (F-L Minn.) Aug. 7, 1881-March 12, 1941; House 1937-39.

TELFAIR, Thomas (D Ga.) March 2, 1780-Feb. 18, 1818; House 1813-17.

TELLER, Henry Moore (D Colo.) May 23, 1830-Feb. 23, 1914; Senate Nov. 15, 1876-April 17, 1882, 1885-97 (R), 1897-1903 (ISil.R), 1903 09 (D); Secy. of the Interior 1882-85.

TELLER, Isaac (nephew of Abraham Henry Schenck) (D N.Y.) Feb. 7, 1799-April 30, 1868; House Nov. 7, 1854-55.

TELLER, Ludwig (D N.Y.) June 22, 1911-Oct. 4, 1965; House 1957-61.

TEMPLE, Henry Wilson (R Pa.) March 31, 1864-Jan. 11, 1955; House 1913-15 (PR), Nov. 2, 1915-33 (R).

TEMPLE, William (D Del.) Feb. 28, 1814-May 28, 1863; House March 4-May 28, 1863.

TEMPLETON, Thomas Weir (R Pa.) Nov. 8, 1867-Sept. 5, 1935; House 1917-19.

TENER, John Kinley (R Pa.) July 25, 1863-May 19, 1946; House 1909-Jan. 16, 1911; Gov. 1911-15.

TENEROWICZ, Rudolph Gabriel (D Mich.) June 14, 1890-Aug. 31, 1963; House 1939-43.

TEN EYCK, Egbert (— N.Y.) April 18, 1779-April 11, 1844; House 1823-Dec. 15, 1825.

TEN EYCK, John Conover (R N.J.) March 12, 1814-Aug. 24, 1879; Senate 1859-65.

TEN EYCK, Peter Gansevoort (D N.Y.) Nov. 7, 1873-Sept. 2, 1944; House 1913-15, 1921-23.

TENNEY, Samuel (— N.H.) Nov. 27, 1748-Feb. 6, 1816; House Dec. 8, 1800-07.

TENZER, Herbert (D N.Y.) Nov. 1, 1905; House 1965-69.

TERRELL, George Butler (D Texas) Dec. 5, 1862-April 18, 1947, House 1933-35.

TERRELL, James C. (UD Ga.) Nov. 7, 1806-Dec. 1, 1835; House March 4-July 8, 1835.

TERRELL, Joseph Meriwether (D Ga.) June 6, 1861-Nov. 17, 1912; Senate Nov. 17, 1910-July 14, 1911; Gov. 1902-07.

TERRELL, William (D Ga.) 1778-July 4, 1855; House 1817-21.

TERRY, David Dickson (son of William Leake Terry) (D Ark.) Jan. 31, 1881-Oct. 7, 1963; House Dec. 19, 1933-43.

TERRY, John H. (R N.Y.) Nov. 14, 1924; House 1971- .

TERRY, Nathaniel (— Conn.) Jan. 30, 1768-June 14, 1844; House 1817-19.

TERRY, William (C Va.) Aug. 14, 1824-Sept. 5, 1888; House 1871-73, 1875-77.

TERRY, William Leake (father of David Dickson Terry) (D Ark.) Sept. 27, 1850-Nov. 4, 1917; House 1891-1901.

TEST, John (W Ind.) Nov. 12, 1771-Oct. 9, 1849; House 1823-27 (CD), 1829-31 (W).

TEWES, Donald Edgar (R Wis.) Aug. 4, 1916; House 1957-59.

THACHER, George (F Mass.) April 12, 1754-April 6, 1824; House 1789-1801; Cont. Cong. 1787.

THACHER, Thomas Chandler (D Mass.) July 20, 1858-April 11, 1945; House 1913-15.

THATCHER, Maurice Hudson (R Ky.) Aug. 15, 1870-—; House 1923-33.

THATCHER, Samuel (D Mass.) July 1, 1776-July 18, 1872; House Dec. 6, 1802-05.

THAYER, Andrew Jackson (D Ore.) Nov. 27, 1818-April 28, 1873; House March 4-July 30, 1861.

THAYER, Eli (father of John Alden Thayer) (R Mass.) June 11, 1819-April 15, 1899; House 1857-61.

THAYER, Harry Irving (R Mass.) Sept. 10, 1869-March 10, 1926; House 1925-March 10, 1926.

THAYER, John Alden (son of Eli Thayer) (D Mass.) Dec. 22, 1857-July 31, 1917; House 1911-13.

THAYER, John Milton (uncle of Arthur Laban Bates) (R Neb.) Jan. 24, 1820-March 19, 1906; Senate March 1, 1867-71; Gov. (Wyo. Terr.) 1875-79, (Neb.) 1887-91.

THAYER, John Randolph (D Mass.) March 9, 1845-Dec. 19, 1916; House 1899-1905.

THAYER, Martin Russell (R Pa.) Jan. 27, 1819-Oct. 14, 1906; House 1863-67.

THEAKER, Thomas Clarke (R Ohio) Feb. 1, 1812-July 16, 1883; House 1859-61.

THIBODEAUX, Bannon Goforth (— La.) Dec. 22, 1812-March 5, 1866; House 1845-49.

THILL, Lewis Dominic (R Wis.) Oct. 18, 1903; House 1939-43.

THISTLEWOOD, Napoleon Bonaparte (R Ill.) March 30, 1837-Sept. 15, 1915; House Feb. 15, 1908-13.

THOM, William Richard (D Ohio) July 7, 1885-Aug. 28, 1960; House 1933-39, 1941-43, 1945-47.

THOMAS, Albert (husband of Lera M. Thomas) (D Texas) April 12, 1898-Feb. 15, 1966; House 1937-Feb. 15, 1966.

THOMAS, Benjamin Franklin (CU Mass.) Feb. 12, 1813-Sept. 27, 1878; House June 11, 1861-63.

THOMAS, Charles Randolph (R N.C.) Feb. 7, 1827-Feb. 18, 1891; House 1871-75.

THOMAS, Charles Randolph (son of the preceding) (D N.C.) Aug. 21, 1861-March 8, 1931; House 1899-1911.

THOMAS, Charles Spalding (D Colo.) Dec. 6, 1849-June 24, 1934; Senate Jan. 15, 1913-21; Gov. 1899-1901.

THOMAS, Christopher Yancy (R Va.) March 24, 1818-Feb. 11, 1879; House March 5, 1874-75.

THOMAS, David (D N.Y.) June 11, 1762-Nov. 11, 1831; House 1801-May 1, 1808.

THOMAS, Elbert Duncan (D Utah) June 17, 1883-Feb. 11, 1953; Senate 1933-51.

THOMAS, Francis (UR Md.) Feb. 3, 1799-Jan. 22, 1876; House 1831-41 (D); 1861-69 (UR); Gov. 1841-44 (D).

THOMAS, George Morgan (R Ky.) Nov. 23, 1828-Jan. 7, 1914; House 1887-89.

THOMAS, Henry Franklin (R Mich.) Dec. 17, 1843-April 16, 1912; House 1893-97.

THOMAS, Isaac (D Tenn.) Nov. 4, 1784-Feb. 2, 1859; House 1815-17.

THOMAS, James Houston (D Tenn.) Sept. 22, 1808-Aug. 4, 1876; House 1847-51, 1859-61.

THOMAS, Jesse Burgess (W Ind./Ill.) 1777-May 4, 1853; House (Terr. Del.) Oct. 22, 1808-09 (Ind.); Senate Dec. 3, 1818-29 (Ill.).

THOMAS, John (R Idaho) Jan. 4, 1874-Nov. 10, 1945; Senate June 30, 1928-33, Jan. 27, 1940-Nov. 10, 1945.

THOMAS, John Chew (F Md.) Oct. 15, 1764-May 10, 1836; House 1799-1801.

THOMAS, John Lewis, Jr. (R Md.) May 20, 1835-Oct. 15, 1893; House Dec. 4, 1865-67.

THOMAS, John Parnell (R N.J.) Jan. 16, 1895-Nov. 19, 1970; House 1937-Jan. 2, 1950.

THOMAS, John Robert (R Ill.) Oct. 11, 1846-Jan. 19, 1914; House 1879-89.

THOMAS, John William Elmer (D Okla.) Sept. 8, 1876-Sept. 19, 1965; House 1923-27; Senate 1927-51.

THOMAS, Lera M. (widow of Albert Thomas) (D Texas) April 4, 1898-—; House March 30, 1966-67.

THOMAS, Lot (R Iowa) Oct. 17, 1843-March 17, 1905; House 1899-1905.

THOMAS, Ormsby Brunson (R Wis.) Aug. 21, 1832-Oct. 24, 1904; House 1885-91.

THOMAS, Philemon (D La.) Feb. 9, 1763-Nov. 18, 1847; House 1831-35.

THOMAS, Phillip Francis (D Md.) Sept. 12, 1810-Oct. 2, 1890; House 1839-41, 1875-77; Gov. 1848-51; Secy. of the Treasury 1860-61.

THOMAS, Richard (F Pa.) Dec. 30, 1744-Jan. 19, 1832; House 1795-1801.

THOMAS, Robert Young, Jr. (D Ky.) July 13, 1855-Sept. 3, 1925; House 1909-Sept. 3, 1925.

THOMAS, William Aubrey (R Ohio) June 7, 1866-Sept. 8, 1951; House Nov. 8, 1904-11.

THOMAS, William David (R N.Y.) March 22, 1880-May 17, 1936; House Jan. 30, 1934-May 17, 1936.

THOMASON, Robert Ewing (D Texas) May 30, 1879-—; House 1931-July 31, 1947.

THOMASSON, William Poindexter (W Ky.) Oct. 8, 1797-Dec. 29, 1882; House 1843-47.

THOMPSON, Albert Clifton (R Ohio) Jan. 23, 1842-Jan. 26, 1910; House 1885-91.

THOMPSON, Benjamin (W Mass.) Aug. 5, 1798-Sept. 24, 1852; House 1845-47, 1851-Sept. 24, 1852.

THOMPSON, Charles James (R Ohio) Jan. 24, 1862-March 27, 1932; House 1919-31.

THOMPSON, Charles Perkins (D Mass.) July 30, 1827-Jan. 19, 1894; House 1875-77.

THOMPSON, Charles Winston (D Ala.) Dec. 30, 1860-March 20, 1904; House 1901-March 20, 1904.

THOMPSON, Chester Charles (D Ill.) Sept. 19, 1893-Jan. 30, 1971; House 1933-39.

THOMPSON, Clark Wallace (D Texas) Aug. 6, 1896-—; House June 24, 1933-35, Aug. 23, 1947-Dec. 30, 1966.

THOMPSON, Fletcher (R Ga.) Feb. 5, 1925; House 1967- .

THOMPSON, Fountain Land (D N.D.) Nov. 18, 1854-Feb. 4, 1942; Senate Nov. 10, 1909-Jan. 31, 1910.

THOMPSON, Frank, Jr. (D N.J.) July 26, 1918; House 1955- .

THOMPSON, George Western (D Va.) May 14, 1806-Feb. 24, 1888; House 1851-July 30, 1852.

THOMPSON, Hedge (— N.J.) Jan. 28, 1780-July 23, 1828; House 1827-July 23, 1828.

THOMPSON, Jacob (D Miss.) May 15, 1810-March 24, 1885; House 1839-51; Secy. of the Interior 1857-61.

THOMPSON, James (D Pa.) Oct. 1, 1806-Jan. 28, 1874; House 1845-51.

THOMPSON, Joel (F N.Y.) Oct. 3, 1760-Feb. 8, 1843; House 1813-15.

THOMPSON, John (D N.Y.) March 20, 1749-1823; House 1799-1801, 1807-11.

THOMPSON, John (R N.Y.) July 4, 1809-June 1, 1890; House 1857-59.

THOMPSON, John Burton (W Ky.) Dec. 14, 1810-Jan. 7, 1874; House Dec. 7, 1840-43, 1847-51; Senate 1853-59.

THOMPSON, John McCandless (brother of William George Thompson) (R Pa.) Jan. 4, 1829-Sept. 3, 1903; House Dec. 22, 1874-75, 1877-79.

THOMPSON, Joseph Bryan (D Okla.) April 29, 1871-Sept. 18, 1919; House 1913-Sept. 18, 1919.

THOMPSON, Philip (— Ky.) Aug. 20, 1789-Nov. 25, 1836; House 1823-25.

THOMPSON, Philip Burton, Jr. (D Ky.) Oct. 15, 1845-Dec. 15, 1909; House 1879-85.

THOMPSON, Philip Rootes (D Va.) March 26, 1766-July 27, 1837; House 1801-07.

THOMPSON, Richard Wigginton (W Ind.) June 9, 1809-Feb. 9, 1900; House 1841-43, 1847-49; Secy. of the Navy 1877-80.

THOMPSON, Robert Augustine (father of Thomas Larkin Thompson) (D Va.) Feb. 14, 1805-Aug. 31, 1876; House 1847-49.

THOMPSON, Ruth (R Mich.) Sept. 15, 1887-April 5, 1970; House 1951-57.

THOMPSON, Theo Ashton (D La.) March 31, 1916-July 1, 1965; House 1953-July 1, 1965.

THOMPSON, Thomas Larkin (son of Robert Augustine Thompson) (D Calif.) May 31, 1838-Feb. 1, 1898; House 1887-89.

THOMPSON, Thomas Weston (— N.H.) March 15, 1766-Oct. 1, 1821; House 1805-07; Senate June 24, 1814-17.

THOMPSON, Waddy, Jr. (W S.C.) Jan. 8, 1798-Nov. 23, 1868; House Sept. 10, 1835-41.

THOMPSON, Wiley (D Ga.) Sept. 23, 1781-Dec. 28, 1835; House 1821-33.

THOMPSON, William (D Iowa) Nov. 10, 1813-Oct. 6, 1897; House 1847-June 29, 1850.

THOMPSON, William George (brother of John McCandless Thompson) (R Iowa) Jan. 17, 1830-April 2, 1911; House Oct. 14, 1879-83.

THOMPSON, William Henry (D Neb.) Dec. 14, 1853-June 6, 1937; Senate May 24, 1933-Nov. 6, 1934.

THOMPSON, William Howard (D Kan.) Oct. 14, 1871-Feb. 9, 1928; Senate 1913-19.

THOMSON, Alexander (— Pa.) Jan. 12, 1788-Aug. 2, 1848; House Dec. 6, 1824-May 1, 1826.

THOMSON, Charles Marsh (PR Ill.) Feb. 13, 1877-Dec. 30, 1943; House 1913-15.

THOMSON, Edwin Keith (R Wyo.) Feb. 8, 1919-Dec. 9, 1960; House 1955-Dec. 9, 1960.

THOMSON, John (D Ohio) Nov. 20, 1780-Dec. 2, 1852; House 1825-27, 1829-37.

THOMSON, John Renshaw (D N.J.) Sept. 25, 1800-Sept. 12, 1862; Senate 1853-Sept. 12, 1862.

THOMSON, Mark (F N.J.) 1739-Dec. 14, 1803; House 1795-99.

THOMSON, Vernon Wallace (R Wis.) Nov. 5, 1905; House 1961- ; Gov. 1957-58.

THONE, Charles (R Neb.) Jan. 4, 1924; House 1971- .

THORINGTON, James (W Iowa) May 7, 1816-June 13, 1887; House 1855-57.

THORKELSON, Jacob (R Mont.) Sept. 24, 1876-Nov. 20, 1945; House 1939-41.

THORNBERRY, William Homer (D Texas) Jan. 9, 1909; House 1949-Dec. 20, 1963.

THORNBURGH, Jacob Montgomery (R Tenn.) July 3, 1837-Sept. 19, 1890; House 1873-79.

THORNTON, Anthony (D Ill.) Nov. 9, 1814-Sept. 10, 1904; House 1865-67.

THORNTON, John Randolph (D La.) Aug. 25, 1846-Dec. 28, 1917; Senate Dec. 7, 1910-15.

THORP, Robert Taylor (R Va.) March 12, 1850-Nov. 26, 1938; House May 2, 1896-97, March 23, 1898-99.

THORPE, Roy Henry (R Neb.) Dec. 13, 1874-Sept. 19, 1951; House Nov. 7, 1922-23.

THROCKMORTON, James Webb (D Texas) Feb. 1, 1825-April 21, 1894; House 1875-79, 1883-87; Gov. 1866-67.

THROOP, Enos Thompson (D N.Y.) Aug. 21, 1784-Nov. 1, 1874; House 1815-June 4, 1816; Gov. 1829-33.

THROPP, Joseph Earlston (R Pa.) Oct. 4, 1847-July 27, 1927; House 1899-1901.

THRUSTON, Buckner (D Ky.) Feb. 9, 1764-Aug. 30, 1845; Senate 1805-Dec. 18, 1809.

THURMAN, Allen Granberry (D Ohio) Nov. 13, 1813-Dec. 12, 1895; House 1845-47; Senate 1869-81.

THURMAN, John Richardson (W N.Y.) Oct. 6, 1814-July 24, 1854; House 1849-51.

THURMOND, James Strom (R S.C.) Dec. 5, 1902; Senate Dec. 24, 1954-April 4, 1956, Nov. 7, 1956-Sept. 16, 1964 (D), Sept. 16, 1964- (R); Gov. 1947-51.

THURSTON, Benjamin Babock (D R.I.) June 29, 1804-May 17, 1886; House 1847-49, 1851-57.

THURSTON, John Mellen (R Neb.) Aug. 21, 1847-Aug. 9, 1916; Senate 1895-1901.

THURSTON, Lloyd (R Iowa) March 27, 1880-May 7, 1970; House 1925-39.

THURSTON, Samuel Royal (D Ore.) April 15, 1816-April 9, 1851; House (Terr. Del.) 1849-51.

THYE, Edward John (R Minn.) April 26, 1896-Aug. 28, 1969; Senate 1947-59; Gov. 1943-47.

TIBBATTS, John Wooleston (D Ky.) June 12, 1802-July 5, 1852; House 1843-47.

TIBBITS, George (F N.Y.) Jan. 14, 1763-July 19, 1849; House 1803-05.

TIBBOTT, Harve (R Pa.) May 27, 1885-Dec. 31, 1969; House 1939-49.

TICHENOR, Isaac (F Vt.) Feb. 8, 1754-Dec. 11, 1838; Senate Oct. 18, 1796-Oct. 17, 1797, 1815-21; Gov. 1797-1806, 1808.

TIERNAN, Robert Owens (D R.I.) Feb. 24, 1929; House March 28, 1967- .

TIERNEY, William Laurence (D Conn.) Aug. 6, 1876-April 13, 1958; House 1931-33.

TIFFIN, Edward (D Ohio) June 19, 1766-Aug. 9, 1829; Senate 1807-09; Gov. 1803-07.

TIFT, Nelson (D Ga.) July 23, 1810-Nov. 21, 1891; House July 25, 1868-69.

TILDEN, Daniel Rose (W Ohio) Nov. 5, 1804-March 4, 1890; House 1843-47.

TILLINGHAST, Joseph Leonard (great-grandson of Thomas Tillinghast) (W R.I.) 1791-Dec. 30, 1844; House 1837-43.

TILLINGHAST, Thomas (great-grandfather of Joseph Leonard Tillinghast) (— R.I.) Aug. 21, 1742-Aug. 26, 1821; House Nov. 13, 1797-99, 1801-03.

TILLMAN, Benjamin Ryan (brother of George Dionysius Tillman) (D S.C.) Aug. 11, 1847-July 3, 1918; Senate 1895-July 3, 1918; Gov. 1890-94.

TILLMAN, George Dionysius (brother of Benjamin Ryan Tillman) (D S.C.) Aug. 21, 1826-Feb. 2, 1902; House 1879-June 19, 1882, 1883-93.

TILLMAN, John Newton (D Ark.) Dec. 13, 1859-March 9, 1929; House 1915-29.

TILLMAN, Lewis (nephew of Barclay Martin) (R Tenn.) Aug. 18, 1816-May 3, 1886; House 1869-71.

TILLOTSON, Thomas (— N.Y.) 1750-May 5, 1832; House March 4-Aug. 10, 1801.

TILSON, John Quillin (R Conn.) April 5, 1866-Aug. 14, 1958; House 1909-13, 1915-Dec. 3, 1932.

TIMBERLAKE, Charles Bateman (R Colo.) Sept. 25, 1854-May 31, 1941; House 1915-33.

TINCHER, Jasper Napoleon (R Kan.) Nov. 2, 1878-Nov. 6, 1951; House 1919-27.

TINKHAM, George Holden (R Mass.) Oct. 29, 1870-Aug. 28, 1956; House 1915-43.

TIPTON, John (D Ind.) Aug. 14, 1786-April 5, 1839; Senate Jan. 3, 1832-39.

TIPTON, Thomas Foster (R Ill.) Aug. 29, 1833-Feb. 7, 1904; House 1877-79.

TIPTON, Thomas Weston (R Neb.) Aug. 5, 1817-Nov. 26, 1899; Senate March 1, 1867-75.

TIRRELL, Charles Quincy (R Mass.) Dec. 10, 1844-July 31, 1910; House 1901-July 31, 1910.

TITUS, Obadiah (D N.Y.) Jan. 20, 1789-Sept. 2, 1854; House 1837-39.

TOBEY, Charles William (R N.H.) July 22, 1880-July 24, 1953; House 1933-39; Senate 1939-July 24, 1953; Gov. 1929-30.

TOD, John (D Pa.) 1779-March 1830; House 1821-24.

TODD, Albert May (Fus. Mich.) June 3, 1850-Oct. 6, 1931; House 1897-99.

TODD, John Blair Smith (D Dakota) April 4, 1814-Jan. 5, 1872; House (Terr. Del.) Dec. 9, 1861-63, June 17, 1864-65.

TODD, Lemuel (R Pa.) July 29, 1817-May 12, 1891; House 1855-57, 1873-75.

TODD, Paul H., Jr. (D Mich.) Sept. 22, 1921; House 1965-67.

TOLAN, John Harvey (D Calif.) Jan. 15, 1877-June 30, 1947; House 1937-47.

TOLAND, George Washington (W Pa.) Feb. 8, 1796-Jan. 30, 1869; House 1837-43.

TOLL, Herman (D Pa.) March 15, 1907-July 26, 1967; House 1959-67.

TOLLEFSON, Thor Carl (R Wash.) May 2, 1901; House 1947-65.

TOLLEY, Harold Sumner (R N.Y.) Jan. 16, 1894-May 20, 1956; House 1925-27.

TOMLINSON, Gideon (D Conn.) Dec. 31, 1780-Oct. 8, 1854; House 1819-27; Senate 1831-37; Gov. 1827-31.

TOMLINSON, Thomas Ash (W N.Y.) March 1802-June 18, 1872; House 1841-43.

TOMPKINS, Arthur Sidney (R N.Y.) Aug. 26, 1865-Jan. 20, 1938; House 1899-1903.

TOMPKINS, Caleb (— N.Y.) Dec. 22, 1759-Jan. 1, 1846; House 1817-21.

TOMPKINS, Christopher (— Ky.) March 24, 1780-Aug. 9, 1858; House 1831-35.

TOMPKINS, Cydnor Bailey (father of Emmett Tompkins) (R Ohio) Nov. 8, 1810-July 23, 1862; House 1857-61.

TOMPKINS, Emmett (son of Cydnor Bailey Tompkins) (R Ohio) Sept. 1, 1853-Dec. 18, 1917; House 1901-03.

TOMPKINS, Patrick Watson (W Miss.) 1804-May 8, 1853; House 1847-49.

TONGUE, Thomas H. (R Ore.) June 23, 1844-Jan. 11, 1903; House 1897-Jan. 11, 1903.

TONRY, Richard Joseph (D N.Y.) Sept. 30, 1893-Jan. 18, 1971; House 1935-37.

TOOLE, Joseph Kemp (D Mont.) May 12, 1851-March 11, 1929; House (Terr. Del.) 1885-89; Gov. 1889-93, 1901-08.

TOOMBS, Robert (SRD Ga.) July 2, 1810-Dec. 15, 1885; House 1845-53; Senate 1853-Feb. 4, 1861.

TORRENS, James H. (D N.Y.) Sept. 12, 1874-April 5, 1952; House Feb. 29, 1944-47.

TOUCEY, Isaac (D Conn.) Nov. 5, 1796-July 30, 1869; House 1835-39; Senate May 12, 1852-57; Gov. 1846-47; Atty. Gen. 1848-49; Secy. of the Navy 1857-61.

TOU VELLE, William Ellsworth (D Ohio) Nov. 23, 1862-Aug. 14, 1951; House 1907-11.

TOWE, Harry Lancaster (R N.J.) Nov. 3, 1898-—; House 1943-Sept. 7, 1951.

TOWER, John Goodwin (R Texas) Sept. 29, 1925; Senate June 15, 1961- .

TOWEY, Frank William, Jr. (D N.J.) Nov. 5, 1895-—; House 1937-39.

TOWNE, Charles Arnette (D Minn./N.Y.) Nov. 21, 1858-Oct. 22, 1928; House 1895-97 (R Minn.), 1905-07 (D N.Y.); Senate Dec. 5, 1900-Jan. 28, 1901 (D Minn.).

TOWNER, Horace Mann (R Iowa) Oct. 23, 1855-Nov. 23, 1937; House 1911-April 1, 1923; Gov. of Puerto Rico 1923-29.

TOWNS, George Washington Bonaparte (D Ga.) May 4, 1801-July 15, 1854; House 1835-Sept. 1, 1836, 1837-39 (UD), Jan. 5, 1846-47 (D); Gov. 1847-51.

TOWNSEND, Amos (R Ohio) 1821-March 17, 1895; House 1877-83.

TOWNSEND, Charles Champlain (R Pa.) Nov. 24, 1841-July 10, 1910; House 1889-91.

TOWNSEND, Charles Elroy (R Mich.) Aug. 15, 1856-Aug. 3, 1924; House 1903-11; Senate 1911-23.

TOWNSEND, Dwight (D N.Y.) Sept. 26, 1826-Oct. 29, 1899; House Dec. 5, 1864-65, 1871-73.

TOWNSEND, Edward Waterman (D N.J.) Feb. 10, 1855-March 15, 1942; House 1911-15.

TOWNSEND, George (D N.Y.) 1769-Aug. 17, 1844; House 1815-19.

TOWNSEND, Hosea (R Colo.) June 16, 1840-March 4, 1909; House 1899-93.

TOWNSEND, John Gillis, Jr. (R Del.) May 31, 1871-April 10, 1964; Senate 1929-41; Gov. 1917-21.

TOWNSEND, Martin Ingham (R N.Y.) Feb. 6, 1810-March 8, 1903; House 1875-79.

TOWNSEND, Washington (R Pa.) Jan. 20, 1813-March 18, 1894; House 1869-77.

TOWNSHEND, Norton Strange (D Ohio) Dec. 25, 1815-July 13, 1895; House 1851-53.

TOWNSHEND, Richard Wellington (D Ill.) April 30, 1840-March 9, 1889; House 1877-March 9, 1889.

TRACEWELL, Robert John (R Ind.) May 7, 1852-July 28, 1922; House 1895-97.

TRACEY, Charles (D N.Y.) May 27, 1847-March 24, 1905; House Nov. 8, 1887-95.

TRACEY, John Plank (R Mo.) Sept. 18, 1836-July 24, 1910; House 1895-97.

TRACY, Albert Haller (brother of Phineas Lyman Tracy) (D N.Y.) June 17, 1793-Sept. 19, 1859; House 1819-25.

TRACY, Andrew (W Vt.) Dec. 15, 1797-Oct. 28, 1868; House 1853-55.

TRACY, Henry Wells (IR Pa.) Sept. 24, 1807-April 11, 1886; House 1863-65.

TRACY, Phineas Lyman (brother of Albert Haller Tracy) (W N.Y.) Dec. 25, 1786-Dec. 22, 1876; House Nov. 5, 1827-33.

TRACY, Uri (D N.Y.) Feb. 8, 1764-July 21, 1838; House 1805-07, 1809-13.

TRACY, Uriah (F Conn.) Feb. 2, 1755-July 19, 1807; House 1793-Oct. 13, 1796; Senate Oct. 13, 1796-July 19, 1807; President pro tempore 1800.

TRAEGER, William Isham (R Calif.) Feb. 26, 1880-Jan. 20, 1935; House 1933-35.

TRAFTON, Mark (AP Mass.) Aug. 1, 1810-March 8, 1901; House 1855-57.

TRAIN, Charles Russell (R Mass.) Oct. 18, 1817-July 28, 1885; House 1859-63.

TRAMMELL, Park (D Fla.) April 9, 1876-May 8, 1936; Senate 1917-May 8, 1936; Gov. 1913-17.

TRANSUE, Andrew Jackson (D Mich.) Jan. 12, 1903; House 1937-39.

TRAYNOR, Philip Andrew (D Del.) May 31, 1874-Dec. 5, 1962; House 1941-43, 1945-47.

TREADWAY, Allen Towner (R Mass.) Sept. 16, 1867-Feb. 16, 1947; House 1913-45.

TREDWAY, William Marshall (D Va.) Aug. 24, 1807-May 1, 1891; House 1845-47.

TREDWELL, Thomas (grandfather of Thomas Treadwell Davis) (— N.Y.) Feb. 6, 1743-Dec. 30, 1831; House May 1791-95.

TRELOAR, William Mitchellson (R Mo.) Sept. 21, 1850-July 3, 1935; House 1895-97.

TREMAIN, Lyman (R N.Y.) June 14, 1819-Nov. 30, 1878; House 1873-75.

TREZVANT, James (—Va.) —Sept. 2, 1841; House 1825-31.

TRIBBLE, Samuel Joelah (D Ga.) Nov. 15, 1869-Dec. 8, 1916; House 1911-Dec. 8, 1916.

TRIGG, Abram (brother of John Johns Trigg) (— Va.) 1750-—; House 1797-1809.

TRIGG, Connally Findlay (D Va.) Sept. 18, 1847-April 23, 1907; House 1885-87.

TRIGG, John Johns (brother of Abram Trigg) (— Va.) 1748-May 17, 1804; House 1797-May 17, 1804.

TRIMBLE, Carey Allen (R Ohio) Sept. 13, 1813-May 4, 1887; House 1859-63.

TRIMBLE, David (D Ky.) June 1782-Oct. 20, 1842; House 1817-27.

TRIMBLE, James William (D Ark.) Feb. 3, 1894-—; House 1945-67.

TRIMBLE, John (R Tenn.) Feb. 7, 1812-Feb. 23, 1884; House 1867-69.

TRIMBLE, Lawrence Strother (D Ky.) Aug. 26, 1825-Aug. 9, 1904; House 1865-71.

TRIMBLE, South (D Ky.) April 13, 1864-Nov. 23, 1946; House 1901-07.

TRIMBLE, William Allen (—Ohio) April 4, 1786-Dec. 13, 1821; Senate 1819-Dec. 13, 1821.

TRIPLETT, Philip (W Ky.) Dec. 24, 1799-March 30, 1852; House 1839-43.

TRIPPE, Robert Pleasant (W Ga.) Dec. 21, 1819-July 22, 1900; House 1855-59.

TROTTER, James Fisher (D Miss.) Nov. 5, 1802-March 9, 1866; Senate Jan. 22-July 10, 1838.

TROTTI, Samuel Wilds (— S.C.) July 18, 1810-June 24, 1856; House Dec. 17, 1842-43.

TROUP, George Michael (SRD Ga.) Sept. 8, 1780-April 26, 1856; House 1807-15 (D); Senate Nov. 13, 1816-Sept. 23, 1818, 1829-Nov. 8, 1833 (SRD); Gov. 1823-27.

TROUT, Michael Carver (D Pa.) Sept. 30, 1810-June 25, 1873; House 1853-55.

TROUTMAN, William Irvin (R Pa.) Jan. 13, 1905; House 1943-Jan. 2, 1945.

TROWBRIDGE, Rowland Ebenezer (R Mich.) June 18, 1821-April 20, 1881; House 1861-63, 1865-69.

TRUAX, Charles Vilas (D Ohio) Feb. 1, 1887-Aug. 9, 1935; House 1933-Aug. 9, 1935.

TRUMAN, Harry S (D Mo.) May 8, 1884-—; Senate 1935-Jan. 17, 1945; Vice Pres. Jan. 20-April 12, 1945; Pres. April 12, 1945-53.

TRUMBO, Andrew (W Ky.) Sept. 15, 1797-Aug. 21, 1871; House 1845-47.

TRUMBULL, Jonathan (F Conn.) March 26, 1740-Aug. 7, 1809; House 1789-95; Senate 1795-June 10, 1796; Speaker 1791-93; Gov. 1797-1809.

TRUMBULL, Joseph (W Conn.) Dec. 7, 1782-Aug. 4, 1861; House Dec. 1, 1834-35, 1839-43; Gov. 1849-50.

TRUMBULL, Lyman (R Ill.) Oct. 12, 1813-June 25, 1896; Senate 1855-73.

TUCK, Amos (I N.H.) Aug. 2, 1810-Dec. 11, 1879; House 1847-53.

TUCK, William Munford (D Va.) Sept. 28, 1896-—; House April 14, 1953-69; Gov. 1946-50.

TUCKER, Ebenezer (— N.J.) Nov. 15, 1758-Sept. 5, 1845; House 1825-29.

TUCKER, George (cousin of Henry St. George Tucker) (D Va.) Aug. 20, 1775-April 10, 1861; House 1819-25.

TUCKER, Henry St. George (father of John Randolph Tucker, cousin of George Tucker and nephew of Thomas Tudor Tucker) (— Va.) Dec. 29, 1780-Aug. 28, 1848; House 1815-19.

TUCKER, Henry St. George (son of John Randolph Tucker and grandson of the preceding) (D Va.) April 5, 1853-July 23, 1932; House 1889-97, March 21, 1922-July 23, 1932.

TUCKER, John Randolph (son of Henry St. George Tucker) (D Va.) Dec. 24, 1823-Feb. 13, 1897; House 1875-87.

TUCKER, Starling (— S.C.) 1770-Jan. 3, 1834; House 1817-31.

TUCKER, Thomas Tudor (uncle of Henry St. George Tucker) (F S.C.) June 25, 1745-May 2, 1828; House 1789-93; Cont. Cong. 1787-88.

TUCKER, Tilghman Mayfield (D Miss.) Feb. 5, 1802-April 3, 1859; House 1843-45; Gov. 1841-43.

TUFTS, John Quincy (R Iowa) July 12, 1840-Aug. 10, 1908; House 1875-77.

TULLY, Pleasant Britton (D Calif.) March 21, 1829-March 24, 1897; House 1883-85.

TUMULTY, Thomas James (D N.J.) March 2, 1913; House 1955-57.

TUNNELL, James Miller (D Del.) Aug. 2, 1879-Nov. 14, 1957; Senate 1941-47.

TUNNEY, John Varick (D Calif.) June 26, 1934; House 1965-Jan. 2, 1971; Senate Jan. 2, 1971- .

TUPPER, Stanley R. (R Maine) Jan. 25, 1921; House 1961-67.

TURLEY, Thomas Battle (D Tenn.) April 5, 1845-July 1, 1910; Senate July 20, 1897-1901.

TURNBULL, Robert (D Va.) Jan. 11, 1850-Jan. 22, 1920; House March 8, 1910-13.

TURNER, Benjamin Sterling (R Ala.) March 17, 1825-March 21, 1894; House 1871-73.

TURNER, Charles, Jr. (WD Mass.) June 20, 1760-May 16, 1839; House June 28, 1809-13.

TURNER, Charles Henry (D N.Y.) May 26, 1861-Aug. 31, 1913; House Dec. 9, 1889-91.

TURNER, Clarence Wyly (D Tenn.) Oct. 22, 1866-March 23, 1939; House Nov. 7, 1922-23, 1933-March 23, 1939.

TURNER, Daniel (son of James Turner) (D N.C.) Sept. 21, 1796-July 21, 1860; House 1827-29.

TURNER, Erastus Johnson (R Kan.) Dec. 26, 1846-Feb. 10, 1933; House 1887-91.

TURNER, George (Fus. Wash.) Feb. 25, 1850-Jan. 26, 1932; Senate 1897-1903.

TURNER, Henry Gray (D Ga.) March 20, 1839-June 9, 1904; House 1881-97.

TURNER, James (father of Daniel Turner) (D N.C.) Dec. 20, 1766-Jan. 15, 1824; Senate 1805-Nov. 21, 1816; Gov. 1802-05.

TURNER, James (D Md.) Nov. 7, 1783-March 28, 1861; House 1833-37.

TURNER, Oscar (ID Ky.) Feb. 3, 1825-Jan. 22, 1896; House 1879-85.

TURNER, Oscar (son of the preceding) (D Ky.) Oct. 19, 1867-July 17, 1902; House 1899-1901.

TURNER, Smith Spangler (D Va.) Nov. 21, 1842-April 8, 1898; House Jan. 30, 1894-97.

TURNER, Thomas (D Ky.) Sept. 10, 1821-Sept. 11, 1900; House 1877-81.

TURNER, Thomas Johnston (D Ill.) April 5, 1815-April 4, 1874; House 1847-49.

TURNEY, Hopkins Lacy (D Tenn.) Oct. 3, 1797-Aug. 1, 1857; House 1837-43; Senate 1845-51.

TURNEY, Jacob (D Pa.) Feb. 18, 1825-Oct. 4, 1891; House 1875-79.

TURPIE, David (D Ind.) July 8, 1828-April 21, 1909; Senate Jan. 14-March 3, 1863, 1887-99.

TURPIN, Charles Murray (R Pa.) March 4, 1878-June 4, 1946; House June 4, 1929-37.

TURPIN, Louis Washington (D Ala.) Feb. 22, 1849-Feb. 3, 1903; House 1889-June 4, 1890, 1891-95.

TURRILL, Joel (JD N.Y.) Feb. 22, 1794-Dec. 28, 1859; House 1833-37.

TUTEN, James Russell (D Ga.) July 23, 1911-Aug. 16, 1968; House 1963-67.

TUTHILL, Joseph Hasbrouck (nephew of Selah Tuthill) (D N.Y.) Feb. 25, 1811-July 27, 1877; House 1871-73.

TUTHILL, Selah (uncle of Joseph Hasbrouck Tuthill) (— N.Y.) Oct. 26, 1771-Sept. 7, 1821; House March 4-Sept. 7, 1821.

TUTTLE, William Edgar, Jr. (D N.J.) Dec. 10, 1870-Feb. 11, 1923; House 1911-15.

TWEED, William Marcy (D N.Y.) April 3, 1823-April 12, 1878; House 1853-55.

TWEEDY, John Hubbard (W Wis.) Nov. 9, 1814-Nov. 12, 1891; House (Terr. Del.) 1847-May 29, 1848.

TWEEDY, Samuel (W Conn.) March 8, 1776-July 1, 1868; House 1833-35.

TWICHELL, Ginery (R Mass.) Aug. 26, 1811-July 23, 1883; House 1867-73.

TWYMAN, Robert Joseph (R Ill.) June 18, 1897-—; House 1947-49.

TYDINGS, Joseph Davies (son of Millard Evelyn Tydings) (D Md.) May 4, 1928; Senate 1965-71.

TYDINGS, Millard Evelyn (father of Joseph Davies Tydings) (D Md.) April 6, 1890-Feb. 9, 1961; House 1923-27; Senate 1927-51.

TYLER, Asher (W N.Y.) May 10, 1798-Aug. 1, 1875; House 1843-45.

TYLER, David Gardiner (son of John Tyler) (D Va.) July 12, 1846-Sept. 5, 1927; House 1893-97.

TYLER, James Manning (R Vt.) April 27, 1835-Oct. 13, 1926; House 1879-83.

TYLER, John (father of David Gardiner Tyler) (D-R Va.) March 29, 1790-Jan. 18, 1862; House Dec. 16, 1817-21; Senate 1827-Feb. 29, 1836; President pro tempore 1834-35; Gov. 1825-27; Vice Pres. March 4-April 4, 1841; President April 6, 1841-45.

TYNDALL, William Thomas (R Mo.) Jan. 16, 1862-Nov. 26, 1928; House 1905-07.

TYNER, James Noble (R Ind.) Jan. 17, 1826-Dec. 5, 1904; House 1869-75; Postmaster General 1876-77.

TYSON, Jacob (— N.Y.) Oct. 8, 1773-July 16, 1848; House 1823-25.

TYSON, Joe Roberts (W Pa.) Feb. 8, 1803-June 27, 1858; House 1855-57.

TYSON, John Russell (D Ala.) Nov. 28, 1856-March 27, 1923; House 1921-March 27, 1923.

TYSON, Lawrence Davis (D Tenn.) July 4, 1861-Aug. 24, 1929; Senate 1925-Aug. 24, 1929.

U

UDALL, Morris K. (brother of Stewart Lee Udall) (D Ariz.) June 15, 1922; House May 2, 1961- .

UDALL, Stewart Lee (brother of Morris K. Udall) (D Ariz.) Jan. 31, 1920; House 1955-Jan. 18, 1961; Secy. of the Interior 1961-69.

UDREE, Daniel (— Pa.) Aug. 5, 1751-July 15, 1828; House Oct. 12, 1813-15, Dec. 26, 1820-21, Dec. 10, 1822-25.

ULLMAN, Albert Conrad (D Ore.) March 9, 1914; House 1957- .

UMSTEAD, William Bradley (D N.C.) May 13, 1895-Nov. 7, 1954; House 1933-39; Senate Dec. 18, 1946-Dec. 30, 1948; Gov. 1953-54.

UNDERHILL, Charles Lee (R Mass.) July 20, 1867-Jan. 28, 1946; House 1921-33.

UNDERHILL, Edwin Stewart (D N.Y.) Oct. 7, 1861-Feb. 7, 1929; House 1911-15.

UNDERHILL, John Quincy (D N.Y.) Feb. 19, 1848-May 21, 1907; House 1899-1901.

UNDERHILL, Walter (W N.Y.) Sept. 12, 1795-Aug. 17, 1866; House 1849-51.

UNDERWOOD, John William Henderson (D Ga.) Nov. 20, 1816-July 18, 1888; House 1859-Jan. 23, 1861.

UNDERWOOD, Joseph Rogers (brother of Warner Lewis Underwood and grandfather of Oscar Wilder Underwood) (W Ky.) Oct. 24, 1791-Aug. 23, 1876; House 1835-43; Senate 1847-53.

UNDERWOOD, Mell Gilbert (D Ohio) Jan. 30, 1892- —; House 1923-April 10, 1936.

UNDERWOOD, Oscar Wilder (grandson of Joseph Rogers Underwood) (D Ala.) May 6, 1862-Jan. 25, 1929; House 1895-June 9, 1896, 1897-1915; Senate 1915-27.

UNDERWOOD, Thomas Rust (D Ky.) March 3, 1898-June 29, 1956; House 1949-March 17, 1951; Senate March 19, 1951-Nov. 4, 1952.

UNDERWOOD, Warner Lewis (brother of Joseph Rogers Underwood) (AP Ky.) Aug. 7, 1808-March 12, 1872; House 1855-59.

UPDEGRAFF, Jonathan Taylor (R Ohio) May 13, 1822-Nov. 30, 1882; House 1879-Nov. 30, 1882.

UPDEGRAFF, Thomas (R Iowa) April 3, 1834-Oct. 4, 1910; House 1879-83, 1893-99.

UPDIKE, Ralph Eugene (R Ind.) May 27, 1894-Sept. 16, 1953; House 1925-29.

UPHAM, Charles Wentworth (cousin of George Baxter Upham and Jabez Upham) (W Mass.) May 4, 1802-June 15, 1875; House 1853-55.

UPHAM, George Baxter (brother of Jabez Upham and cousin of Charles Wentworth Upham) (— N.H.) Dec. 27, 1768-Feb. 10, 1848; House 1801-03.

UPHAM, Jabez (brother of George Baxter Upham and cousin of Charles Wentworth Upham) (— Mass.) Aug. 23, 1764-Nov. 8, 1811; House 1807-10.

UPHAM, Nathaniel (D N.H.) June 9, 1774-July 10, 1829; House 1817-23.

UPHAM, William (W Vt.) Aug. 5, 1792-Jan. 14, 1853; Senate 1843-Jan. 14, 1853.

UPSHAW, William David (D Ga.) Oct. 15, 1866-Nov. 21, 1952; House 1919-27.

UPSON, Charles (R Mich.) March 19, 1821-Sept. 5, 1885; House 1863-69.

UPSON, Christopher Columbus (D Texas) Oct. 17, 1829-Feb. 8, 1902; House April 15, 1879-83.

UPSON, William Hanford (R Ohio) Jan. 11, 1823-April 13, 1910; House 1869-73.

UPTON, Charles Horace (R Va.) Aug. 23, 1812-June 17, 1877; House May 23, 1861-Feb. 27, 1862.

UPTON, Robert William (R N.H.) Feb. 3, 1884- —; Senate Aug. 14, 1953-Nov. 7, 1954.

URNER, Milton George (uncle of James Samuel Simmons) (R Md.) July 29, 1839-Feb. 9, 1926; House 1879-83.

UTT, James Boyd (R Calif.) March 11, 1899-March 1, 1970; House 1953-March 1, 1970.

UTTER, George Herbert (R R.I.) July 24, 1854-Nov. 3, 1912; House 1911-Nov. 3, 1912; Gov. 1905-06.

UTTERBACK, Hubert (cousin of John Gregg Utterback) (D Iowa) June 28, 1880-May 12, 1942; House 1935-37.

UTTERBACK, John Gregg (cousin of Hubert Utterback) (D Maine) July 12, 1872-July 11, 1955; House 1933-35.

V

VAIL, George (D N.J.) July 21, 1809-May 23, 1875; House 1853-57.

VAIL, Henry (D N.Y.) 1782-June 25, 1853; House 1837-39.

VAIL, Richard Bernard (R Ill.) Aug. 31, 1895-July 29, 1955; House 1947-49, 1951-53.

VAILE, William Newell (R Colo.) June 22, 1876-July 2, 1927; House 1919-July 2, 1927.

VALENTINE, Edward Kimble (R Neb.) June 1, 1843-April 11, 1916; House 1879-85.

VALK, William Weightman (AP N.Y.) Oct. 12, 1806-Sept. 20, 1879; House 1855-57.

VALLANDIGHAM, Clement Laird (uncle of John A. McMahon) (D Ohio) July 29, 1820-June 17, 1871; House May 25, 1858-63.

VAN AERNAM, Henry (R N.Y.) March 11, 1819-June 1, 1894; House 1865-69, 1879-83.

VAN ALEN, James Isaac (half brother of Martin Van Buren) (F N.Y.) 1776-Dec. 23, 1870; House 1807-09.

VAN ALEN, John Evert (— N.Y.) 1749-March 1807; House 1793-99.

VAN ALSTYNE, Thomas Jefferson (D N.Y.) July 25, 1827-Oct. 26, 1903; House 1883-85.

VAN AUKEN, Daniel Myers (D Pa.) Jan. 15, 1826-Nov. 7, 1908; House 1867-71.

VAN BUREN, John (D N.Y.) May 13, 1799-Jan. 16, 1855; House 1841-43.

VAN BUREN, Martin (half-brother of James Isaac Van Alen) (D N.Y.) Dec. 5, 1782-July 24, 1862; Senate 1821-Dec. 20, 1828; Gov. 1829; Secy. of State 1829-31; Vice Pres. 1833-37; President 1837-41.

VANCE, John Luther (D Ohio) July 19, 1839-June 10, 1921; House 1875-77.

VANCE, Joseph (W Ohio) March 21, 1786-Aug. 24, 1852; House 1821-35 (D), 1843-47 (W); Gov. 1836-38.

VANCE, Robert Brank (uncle of Zebulon Baird Vance) (D N.C.) 1793-1827; House 1823-25.

VANCE, Robert Brank (nephew of the preceding and brother of Zebulon Baird Vance) (D N.C.) April 24, 1828-Nov. 28, 1899; House 1873-85.

VANCE, Robert Johnstone (D Conn.) March 15, 1854-June 15, 1902; House 1887-89.

VANCE, Zebulon Baird (brother of Robert Brank Vance) (D N.C.) May 13, 1830-April 14, 1894; House Dec. 7, 1858-61; Senate 1879-April 14, 1894; Gov. 1862-66, 1876-78.

VAN CORTLANDT, Philip (brother of Pierre Van Cortlandt, Jr.) (D N.Y.) Aug. 21, 1749-Nov. 1, 1831; House 1793-1809.

VAN CORTLANDT, Pierre, Jr. (brother of Philip Van Cortlandt) (D N.Y.) Aug. 29, 1762-July 13, 1848; House 1811-13.

VAN DEERLIN, Lionel (D Calif.) July 25, 1914; House 1963- .

VANDENBERG, Arthur Hendrick (R Mich.) March 22, 1884-April 18, 1951; Senate March 31, 1928-April 18, 1951; President pro tempore 1947-49.

VANDER JAGT, Guy Adrian (R Mich.) Aug. 26, 1931; House Nov. 8, 1966- .

VANDERPOEL, Aaron (D N.Y.) Feb. 5, 1799-July 18, 1870; House 1833-37, 1839-41.

VANDERVEER, Abraham (D N.Y.) 1781-July 21, 1839; House 1837-39.

VANDEVER, Wiliam (R Iowa/Calif.) March 31, 1817-July 23, 1893; House 1859-Sept. 24, 1861 (Iowa), 1887-91 (Calif.).

VANDIVER, Willard Duncan (D Mo.) March 30, 1854-May 30, 1932; House 1897-1905.

VAN DUZER, Clarence Dunn (D Nev.) May 4, 1866-Sept. 28, 1947; House 1903-07.

VAN DYKE, Carl Chester (D Minn.) Feb. 18, 1881-May 20, 1919; House 1915-May 20, 1919.

VAN DYKE, John (W N.J.) April 3, 1807-Dec. 24, 1878; House 1847-51.

VAN DYKE, Nicholas (F Del.) Dec. 20, 1769-May 21, 1826; House Oct. 6, 1807-11; Senate 1817-May 21, 1826.

VAN EATON, Henry Smith (D Miss.) Sept. 14, 1826-May 30, 1898; House 1883-87.

VAN GAASBECK, Peter (A-F N.Y.) Sept. 27, 1754-1797; House 1793-95.

VAN HORN, Burt (R N.Y.) Oct. 28, 1823-April 1, 1896; House 1861-63, 1865-69.

VAN HORN, George (D N.Y.) Feb. 5, 1850-May 3, 1904; House 1891-93.

VAN HORN, Robert Thompson (R Mo.) May 19, 1824-Jan. 3, 1916; House 1865-71, 1881-83, Feb. 27, 1896-97.

VAN HORNE, Archibald (— Md.) — -1817; House 1807-11.

VAN HORNE, Espy (D Pa.) 1795-Aug. 25, 1829; House 1825-29.

VAN HORNE, Isaac (D Pa.) Jan. 13, 1754-Feb. 2, 1834; House 1801-05.

VAN HOUTEN, Isaac B. (D N.Y.) June 4, 1776-Aug. 16, 1850; House 1833-35.

VANIK, Charles Albert (D Ohio) April 7, 1913; House 1955- .

VANMETER, John Inskeep (W Ohio) Feb. 1798-Aug. 3, 1875; House 1843-45.

VAN NESS, John Peter (D N.Y.) 1770-March 7, 1846; House Oct. 6, 1801-Jan. 17, 1803.

VAN NUYS, Frederick (D Ind.) April 16, 1874-Jan. 25, 1944; Senate 1933-Jan. 25, 1944.

VAN PELT, William K. (R Wis.) March 10, 1905; House 1951-65.

VAN RENSSELAER, Henry Bell (son of Stephen Van Rensselaer) (W N.Y.) May 14, 1810-March 23, 1864; House 1841-43.

VAN RENSSELAER, Jeremiah (father of Solomon Van Vechten Van Rensselaer and cousin of Killian Killian Van Rensselaer) (— N.Y.) Aug. 27, 1738-Feb. 19, 1810; House 1789-91.

VAN RENSSELAER, Killian Killian (cousin of Jeremiah Van Rensselaer and uncle of Solomon Van Vechten Van Rensselaer) (D N.Y.) June 9, 1763-June 18, 1845; House 1801-11.

VAN RENSSELAER, Solomon Van Vechten (son of Jeremiah Van Rensselaer and nephew of Killian Killian Van Rensselaer) (F N.Y.) Aug. 6, 1774-April 23, 1852; House 1819-Jan. 14, 1822.

VAN RENSSELAER, Stephen (father of Henry Bell Van Rensselaer) (— N.Y.) Nov. 1, 1764-Jan. 26, 1839; House Feb. 27, 1822-29.

VAN SANT, Joshua (D Md.) Dec. 31, 1803-April 8, 1884; House 1853-55.

VAN SCHAICK, Isaac Whitbeck (uncle of Aaron Van Schaick Cochrane) (R Wis.) Dec. 7, 1817-Aug. 22, 1901; House 1885-87, 1889-91.

VAN SWEARINGEN, Thomas (— Va.) May 5, 1784-Aug. 19, 1822; House 1819-Aug. 19, 1822.

VAN TRUMP, Philadelph (D Ohio) Nov. 15, 1810-July 31, 1874; House 1867-73.

VAN VALKENBURGH, Robert Bruce (R N.Y.) Sept. 4, 1821-Aug. 1, 1888; House 1861-65.

VAN VOORHIS, Henry Clay (R Ohio) May 11, 1852-Dec. 12, 1927; House 1893-1905.

VAN VOORHIS, John (R N.Y.) Oct. 22, 1826-Oct. 20, 1905; House 1879-83, 1893-95.

VAN VORHES, Nelson Holmes (R Ohio) Jan. 23, 1822-Dec. 4, 1882; House 1875-79.

VAN WINKLE, Marshall (grandnephew of Peter G. Van Winkle) (R N.J.) Sept. 28, 1869-May 10, 1957; House 1905-07.

VAN WINKLE, Peter Godwin (granduncle of Marshall Van Winkle) (U W. Va.) Sept. 7, 1808-April 15, 1872; Senate Aug. 4, 1863-69.

VAN WYCK, Charles Henry (R N.Y./Neb.) May 10, 1824-Oct. 24, 1895; House 1859-63, 1867-69, Feb. 17, 1870-71 (N.Y.); Senate 1881-87 (Neb.).

VAN WYCK, William William (D N.Y.) Aug. 9, 1777-Aug. 27, 1840; House 1821-25.

VAN ZANDT, James Edward (R Pa.) Dec. 18, 1898- —; House 1939-Sept. 24, 1943, 1947-63.

VARDAMAN, James Kimble (D Miss.) July 26, 1861-June 25, 1930; Senate 1913-19; Gov. 1904-08.

VARE, William Scott (R Pa.) Dec. 24, 1867-Aug. 7, 1934; House April 24, 1912-Jan. 2, 1923, March 4, 1923-27; Senate 1927-Dec. 6, 1929.

VARNUM, John (F Mass.) June 25, 1778-July 23, 1836; House 1825-31.

VARNUM, Joseph Bradley (— Mass.) Jan. 29, 1750-Sept. 21, 1821; House 1795-June 29, 1811; Senate June 8, 1811-17; Speaker 1807-11; President pro tempore 1813-14.

VAUGHAN, Horace Worth (D Texas) Dec. 2, 1867-Nov. 10, 1922; House 1913-15.

VAUGHAN, William Wirt (D Tenn.) July 2, 1831-Aug. 19, 1878; House 1871-73.

VAUGHN, Albert Clinton, Sr. (R Pa.) Oct. 9, 1894-Sept. 1, 1951; House Jan. 3-Sept. 1, 1951.

VAUX, Richard (D Pa.) Dec. 19, 1816-March 22, 1895; House May 20, 1890-91.

VEEDER, William Davis (D N.Y.) May 19, 1835-Dec. 2, 1910; House 1877-79.

VEHSLAGE, John Herman George (D N.Y.) Dec. 20, 1842-July 21, 1904; House 1897-99.

VELDE, Harold Himmel (R Ill.) April 1, 1910; House 1949-57.

VENABLE, Abraham Bedford (uncle of Abraham Watkins Venable) (— Va.) Nov. 20, 1758-Dec. 26, 1811; House 1791-99; Senate Dec. 7, 1803-June 7, 1804.

VENABLE, Abraham Watkins (nephew of Abraham Bedford Venable) (D N.C.) Oct. 17, 1799-Feb. 24, 1876; House 1847-53.

VENABLE, Edward Carrington (D Va.) Jan. 31, 1853-Dec. 8, 1908; House 1889-Sept. 23, 1890.

VENABLE, William Webb (D Miss.) Sept. 25, 1880-Aug. 2, 1948; House Jan. 4, 1916-21.

VERPLANCK, Daniel Crommelin (father of Gulian Crommelin Verplanck) (F N.Y.) March 19, 1762-March 29, 1834; House Oct. 17, 1803-09.

VERPLANCK, Gulian Crommelin (son of Daniel Crommelin Verplanck) (D N.Y.) Aug. 6, 1786-March 18, 1870; House 1825-33.

VERREE, John Paul (R Pa.) March 9, 1817-June 27, 1889; House 1859-63.

VEST, George Graham (D Mo.) Dec. 6, 1830-Aug. 9, 1904; Senate 1879-1903.

VESTAL, Albert Henry (R Ind.) Jan. 18, 1875-April 1, 1932; House 1917-April 1, 1932.

VEYSEY, Victor V. (R Calif.) April 14, 1915; House 1971- .

VIBBARD, Chauncey (D N.Y.) Nov. 11, 1811-June 5, 1891; House 1861-63.

VICKERS, George (D Md.) Nov. 19, 1801-Oct. 8, 1879; Senate March 7, 1868-73.

VIDAL, Michel (R La.) Oct. 1, 1824- —; House July 18, 1868-69.

VIELE, Egbert Ludoricus (D N.Y.) June 17, 1825-April 22, 1902; House 1885-87.

VIGORITO, Joseph Phillip (D Pa.) Nov. 10, 1918; House 1965- .

VILAS, William Freeman (D Wis.) July 9, 1840-Aug. 28, 1908; Senate 1891-97; Postmaster General 1885-88; Secy. of the Interior 1888-89.

VINCENT, Beverly Mills (D Ky.) March 28, 1890-—; House 1937-45.

VINCENT, Bird J. (R Mich.) March 6, 1880-July 18, 1931; House 1923-July 18, 1931.

VINCENT, Earl W. (R Iowa) March 27, 1886-May 22, 1953; House June 4, 1928-29.

VINCENT, William Davis (P Kan.) Oct. 11, 1852-Feb. 28, 1922; House 1897-99.

VINING, John (— Del.) Dec. 23, 1758-Feb. 1802; House 1797-93; Senate 1793-Jan. 19, 1798; Cont. Cong. 1784-86.

VINSON, Carl (D Ga.) Nov. 18, 1883- —; House Nov. 3, 1914-65.

VINSON, Frederick Moore (Fred) (D Ky.) Jan. 22, 1890-Sept. 8, 1953; House Jan. 12, 1924-29, 1931-May 12, 1938; Secy. of the Treasury 1945-46; Chief Justice of Supreme Court 1946-53.

VINTON, Samuel Finley (W Ohio) Sept. 25, 1792-May 11, 1862; House 1823-37, 1843-51.

VIVIAN, Weston Edward (D Mich.) Oct. 25, 1924; House 1965-67.

VOIGT, Edward (R Wis.) Dec. 1, 1873-Aug. 26, 1934; House 1917-27.

VOLK, Lester David (R N.Y.) Sept. 17, 1884-April 30, 1962; House Nov. 2, 1920-23.

VOLLMER, Henry (D Iowa) July 28, 1867-Aug. 25, 1930; House Feb. 10, 1914-15.

VOLSTEAD, Andrew John (R Minn.) Oct. 31, 1860-Jan. 20, 1947; House 1903-23.

VOORHEES, Charles Stewart (son of Daniel Wolsey Voorhees) (D Wash.) June 4, 1853-Dec. 26, 1909; House (Terr. Del.) 1885-89.

VOORHEES, Daniel Wolsey (father of Charles Stewart Voorhees) (D Ind.) Sept. 26, 1827-April 9, 1897; House 1861-Feb. 23, 1866, 1867-73; Senate Nov. 6, 1877-97.

VOORHIS, Charles Henry (R N.J.) March 13, 1833-April 15, 1896; House 1879-81.

VOORHIS, Horace Jerry (D Calif.) April 6, 1901; House 1937-47.

VORYS, John Martin (R Ohio) June 16, 1896-Aug. 25, 1968; House 1939-59.

VOSE, Roger (F N.H.) Feb. 24, 1763-Oct. 26, 1841; House 1813-17.

VREELAND, Albert Lincoln (R N.J.) July 2, 1901; House 1939-43.

VREELAND, Edward Butterfield (R N.Y.) Dec. 7, 1856-May 8, 1936; House Nov. 7, 1899-1913.

VROOM, Peter Dumont (D N.J.) Dec. 12, 1791-Nov. 18, 1873; House 1839-41; Gov. 1830-32, 1834-37.

VURSELL, Charles Wesley (R Ill.) Feb. 8, 1881- —; House 1943-59.

W

WACHTER, Frank Charles (R Md.) Sept. 16, 1861-July 1, 1910; House 1899-1907.

WADDELL, Alfred Moore (D N.C.) Sept. 16, 1834-March 17, 1912; House 1871-79.

WADDILL, Edmund, Jr. (R Va.) May 22, 1855-April 9, 1931; House April 12, 1890-91.

WADDILL, James Richard (D Mo.) Nov. 22, 1842-June 14, 1917; House 1879-81.

WADE, Benjamin Franklin (brother of Edward Wade) (R Ohio) Oct. 27, 1800-March 2, 1878; Senate March 15, 1851-57 (W), 1857-69 (R); President pro tempore 1867-69.

WADE, Edward (brother of Benjamin Franklin Wade) (R Ohio) Nov. 22, 1802-Aug. 13, 1866; House 1853-55 (F-S), 1855-61 (R).

WADE, Martin Joseph (D Iowa) Oct. 20, 1861-April 16, 1931; House 1903-05.

WADE, William Henry (R Mo.) Nov. 3, 1835-Jan. 13, 1911; House 1885-91.

WADLEIGH, Bainbridge (R N.H.) Jan. 4, 1831-Jan. 24, 1891; Senate 1873-79.

WADSWORTH, James Wolcott (R N.Y.) Oct. 12, 1846-Dec. 24, 1926; House Nov. 8, 1881-85, 1891-1907.

WADSWORTH, James Wolcott, Jr. (son of the preceding) (R N.Y.) Aug. 12, 1877-June 21, 1952; Senate 1915-27; House 1933-51.

WADSWORTH, Jeremiah (F Conn.) July 12, 1743-April 30, 1804; House 1789-95; Cont. Cong. 1787-88.

WADSWORTH, Peleg (— Mass.) May 6, 1748-Nov. 12, 1829; House 1793-1807.

WADSWORTH, William Henry (R Ky.) July 4, 1821-April 2, 1893; House 1861-65 (U), 1885-87 (R).

WAGENER, David Douglas (D Pa.) Oct. 11, 1792-Oct. 1, 1860; House 1833-41.

WAGGAMAN, George Augustus (NR La.) 1790-March 22, 1843; Senate Nov. 15, 1831-35.

WAGGONNER, Joe D., Jr. (D La.) Sept. 7, 1918; House Dec. 19, 1961- .

WAGNER, Earl Thomas (D Ohio) April 27, 1908; House 1949-51.

WAGNER, Peter Joseph (W N.Y.) Aug. 14, 1795-Sept. 13, 1884; House 1839-41.

WAGNER, Robert Ferdinand (D N.Y.) June 8, 1877-May 4, 1953; Senate 1927-June 28, 1949.

WAGONER, George Chester Robinson (R Mo.) Sept. 3, 1863-April 27, 1946; House Feb. 26-March 3, 1903.

WAINWRIGHT, Jonathan Mayhew (R N.Y.) Dec. 10, 1864-June 3, 1945; House 1923-31.

WAINWRIGHT, Stuyvesant (R N.Y.) March 16, 1921; House 1953-61.

WAIT, John Turner (R Conn.) Aug. 27, 1811-April 21, 1899; House April 12, 1876-87.

WAKEFIELD, James Beach (R Minn.) March 21, 1825-Aug. 25, 1910; House 1883-87.

WAKEMAN, Abram (W N.Y.) May 31, 1824-June 29, 1889; House 1855-57.

WAKEMAN, Seth (R N.Y.) Jan. 15, 1811-Jan. 4, 1880; House 1871-73.

WALBRIDGE, David Safford (R Mich.) July 30, 1802-June 15, 1868; House 1855-59.

WALBRIDGE, Henry Sanford (cousin of Hiram Walbridge) (W N.Y.) April 8, 1801-Jan. 27, 1869; House 1851-53.

WALBRIDGE, Hiram (cousin of Henry Sanford Walbridge) (D N.Y.) Feb. 2, 1821-Dec. 6, 1870; House 1853-55.

WALCOTT, Frederic Collin (R Conn.) Feb. 19, 1869-April 27, 1949; Senate 1929-35.

WALDEN, Hiram (D N.Y.) Aug. 21, 1800-July 21, 1880; House 1849-51.

WALDEN, Madison Miner (R Iowa) Oct. 6, 1836-July 24, 1891; House 1871-73.

WALDIE, Jerome R. (D Calif.) Feb. 15, 1925; House June 7, 1966- .

WALDO, George Ernest (R N.Y.) Jan. 11, 1851-June 16, 1942; House 1905-09.

WALDO, Loren Pinckney (D Conn.) Feb. 2, 1802-Sept. 8, 1881; House 1849-51.

WALDO, William Frederick (R N.Y.) Aug. 26, 1882-April 16, 1930; House 1917-19.

WALDRON, Alfred Marpole (R Pa.) Sept. 21, 1865-June 28, 1952; House 1933-35.

WALDRON, Henry (R Mich.) Oct. 11, 1819-Sept. 13, 1880; House 1855-61, 1871-77.

WALES, George Edward (— Vt.) May 13, 1792-Jan. 8, 1860; House 1825-29.

WALES, John (— Del.) July 31, 1783-Dec. 3, 1863; Senate Feb. 3, 1849-51.

WALKER, Amasa (R Mass.) May 4, 1799-Oct. 29, 1875; House Dec. 1, 1862-63.

WALKER, Benjamin (D N.Y.) 1753-Jan. 13, 1818; House 1801-03.

WALKER, Charles Christopher Brainerd (D N.Y.) June 27, 1824-Jan. 26, 1888; House 1875-77.

WALKER, David (brother of George Walker and grandfather of James David Walker) (— Ky.) — - March 1, 1820; House 1817-March 1, 1820.

WALKER, E. S. Johnny (D N.M.) June 18, 1911; House 1965-69.

WALKER, Felix (D N.C.) July 19, 1753-1828; House 1817-23.

WALKER, Francis (brother of John Walker) (— Va.) June 22, 1764-March 1806; House 1793-95.

WALKER, Freeman (D Ga.) Oct. 25, 1780-Sept. 23, 1827; Senate Nov. 6, 1819-Aug. 6, 1821.

WALKER, George (brother of David Walker) (— Ky.) 1763-1819; Senate Aug. 30-Dec. 16, 1814.

WALKER, Gilbert Carlton (D Va.) Aug. 1, 1883-May 11, 1885; House 1875-77 (C), 1877-79 (D); Gov. 1869-74.

WALKER, Isaac Pigeon (D Wis.) Nov. 2, 1815-March 29, 1872; Senate June 8, 1848-55.

WALKER, James Alexander (R Va.) Aug. 27, 1832-Oct. 21, 1901; House 1895-99.

WALKER, James David (grandson of David Walker, nephew of John McLean of Ill., and cousin of Wilkinson Call) (D Ark.) Dec. 13, 1830-Oct. 17, 1906; Senate 1879-85.

WALKER, James Peter (D Mo.) March 14, 1851-July 19, 1890; House 1887-July 19, 1890.

WALKER, John (brother of Francis Walker) (— Va.) Feb. 13, 1744-Dec. 2, 1809; Senate March 31-Nov. 9, 1790; Cont. Cong. 1780.

WALKER, John Randall (D Ga.) Feb. 23, 1874- —; House 1913-19.

WALKER, John Williams (father of Percy Walker) (D Ala.) Aug. 12, 1783-April 23, 1823; Senate Dec. 14, 1819-Dec. 12, 1822.

WALKER, Joseph Henry (R Mass.) Dec. 21, 1829-April 3, 1907; House 1889-99.

WALKER, Lewis Leavell (R Ky.) Feb. 15, 1873-June 30, 1944; House 1929-31.

WALKER, Percy (son of John Williams Walker) (AP Ala.) Dec. 1812-Dec. 31, 1880; House 1855-57.

WALKER, Prentiss Lafayette (R Miss.) Aug. 23, 1918; House 1965-67.

WALKER, Robert James (D Miss.) July 23, 1801-Nov. 11, 1869; Senate 1835-March 5, 1845; Secy. of the Treasury 1845-49; Gov. of Kan. 1857.

WALKER, Robert Jarvis Cochran (R Pa.) Oct. 20, 1838-Dec. 19, 1903; House 1881-83.

WALKER, Walter (D Colo.) April 3, 1883-Oct. 8, 1956; Senate Sept. 26-Dec. 6, 1932.

WALKER, William Adams (D N.Y.) June 5, 1805-Dec. 18, 1861; House 1853-55.

WALL, Garret Dorset (father of James Walter Wall) (D N.J.) March 10, 1783-Nov. 22, 1850; Senate 1835-41.

WALL, James Walter (son of Garret Dorset Wall) (D N.J.) May 26, 1820-June 9, 1872; Senate Jan. 14-March 3, 1863.

WALL, William (R N.Y.) March 20, 1800-April 20, 1872; House 1861-63.

WALLACE, Alexander Stuart (R S.C.) Dec. 30, 1810-June 27, 1893; House May 27, 1870-77.

WALLACE, Daniel (W S.C.) May 9, 1801-May 13, 1859; House June 12, 1848-53.

WALLACE, David (W Ind.) April 4, 1799-Sept. 4, 1859; House 1841-43; Gov. 1837-40.

WALLACE, James M. (— Pa.) 1750-Dec. 17, 1823; House Oct. 10, 1815-21.

WALLACE, John Winfield (R Pa.) Dec. 20, 1818-June 24, 1889; House 1861-63, 1875-77.

WALLACE, Jonathan Hasson (D Ohio) Oct. 31, 1824-Oct. 28, 1892; House May 27, 1884-85.

WALLACE, Nathaniel Dick (D La.) Oct. 27, 1845-July 16, 1894; House Dec. 9, 1886-87.

WALLACE, Robert Minor (D Ark.) Aug. 6, 1856-Nov. 9, 1942; House 1903-11.

WALLACE, Rodney (R Mass.) Dec. 21, 1823-Feb. 27, 1903; House 1889-91.

WALLACE, William Andrew (D Pa.) Nov. 28, 1827-May 22, 1896; Senate 1875-81.

WALLACE, William Copeland (R N.Y.) May 21, 1856-Sept. 4, 1901; House 1889-91.

WALLACE, William Henson (R Wash./Idaho) July 19, 1811-Feb. 7, 1879; House (Terr. Del.) 1861-63 (Wash.), Feb. 1, 1864-65 (Idaho); Gov. of Idaho Terr. 1863.

WALLEY, Samuel Hurd (W Mass.) Aug. 31, 1805-Aug. 27, 1877; House 1853-55.

WALLGREN, Monrad Charles (D Wash.) April 17, 1891-Sept. 18, 1961; House 1933-Dec. 19, 1940; Senate Dec. 19, 1940-Jan. 9, 1945; Gov. 1945-49.

WALLHAUSER, George Marvin (R N.J.) Feb. 10, 1900; House 1959-65.

WALLIN, Samuel (R N.Y.) July 31, 1856-Dec. 1, 1917; House 1913-15.

WALLING, Ansel Tracy (D Ohio) Jan. 10, 1824-June 22, 1896; House 1875-77.

WALLS, Josiah Thomas (R Fla.) Dec. 30, 1842-May 5, 1905; House 1871-Jan. 29, 1873, March 4, 1873-April 19, 1876.

WALN, Robert (F Pa.) Feb. 22, 1765-Jan. 24, 1836; House Dec. 3, 1798-1801.

WALSH, Allan Bartholomew (D N.J.) Aug. 29, 1874-Aug. 5, 1953; House 1913-15.

WALSH, Arthur (D N.J.) Feb. 26, 1896-Dec. 13, 1947; Senate Nov. 26, 1943-Dec. 7, 1944.

WALSH, David Ignatius (D Mass.) Nov. 11, 1872-June 11, 1947; Senate 1919-25, Dec. 6, 1926-47; Gov. 1914-15.

WALSH, James Joseph (D N.Y.) May 22, 1858-May 8, 1909; House 1895-June 2, 1896.

WALSH, John Richard (D Ind.) May 22, 1913; House 1949-51.

WALSH, Joseph (R Mass.) Dec. 16, 1875-Jan. 13, 1946; House 1915-Aug. 2, 1922.

WALSH, Michael (D N.Y.) March 8, 1810-March 18, 1859; House 1853-55.

WALSH, Patrick (D Ga.) Jan. 1, 1840-March 19, 1899; Senate April 2, 1894-95.

WALSH, Thomas James (D Mont.) June 12, 1859-March 2, 1933; Senate 1913-March 2, 1933.

WALSH, Thomas Yates (W Md.) 1809-Jan. 20, 1865; House 1851-53.

WALSH, William (D Md.) May 11, 1828-May 17, 1892; House 1875-79.

WALTER, Francis Eugene (D Pa.) May 26, 1894-May 31, 1963; House 1933-May 31, 1963.

WALTERS, Anderson Howell (R Pa.) May 18, 1862-Dec. 7, 1927; House 1913-15, 1919-23, 1925-27.

WALTERS, Herbert S. (D Tenn.) Nov. 17, 1891- —; Senate Aug. 27, 1963-Nov. 3, 1964.

WALTHALL, Edward Cary (D Miss.) April 4, 1831-April 21, 1898; Senate March 9, 1885-Jan. 24, 1894; 1895-April 21, 1898.

WALTON, Charles Wesley (R Maine) Dec. 9, 1819-Jan. 24, 1900; House 1861-May 26, 1862.

WALTON, Eliakim Persons (R Vt.) Feb. 17, 1812-Dec. 19, 1890; House 1857-63.

WALTON, George (cousin of Matthew Walton) (— Ga.) 1750-Feb. 2, 1804; Senate Nov. 16, 1795-Feb. 20, 1796; Cont. Cong. 1776-78, 1780-81, 1787-88; Gov. 1779, 1789.

WALTON, Matthew (cousin of George Walton) (D Ky.) — - Jan. 18, 1819; House 1803-07.

WALTON, William Bell (D N.M.) Jan. 23, 1871-April 14, 1939; House 1917-19.

WALWORTH, Reuben Hyde (D N.Y.) Oct. 26, 1788-Nov. 27, 1867; House 1821-23.

WAMPLER, Fred (D Ind.) Oct. 15, 1909; House 1959-61.

WAMPLER, William Creed (R Va.) April 21, 1926; House 1953-55, 1967- .

WANGER, Irving Price (R Pa.) March 5, 1852-Jan. 14, 1940; House 1893-1911.

WARBURTON, Herbert Birchby (R Del.) Sept. 21, 1916; House 1953-55.

WARBURTON, Stanton (R Wash.) April 13, 1865-Dec. 24, 1926; House 1911-13.

WARD, Aaron (uncle of Elijah Ward) (D N.Y.) July 5, 1790-March 2, 1867; House 1825-29, 1831-37, 1841-43.

WARD, Andrew Harrison (D Ky.) Jan. 3, 1815-April 16, 1904; House Dec. 3, 1866-67.

WARD, Artemas (F Mass.) Nov. 26, 1727-Oct. 28, 1800; House 1791-95; Cont. Cong. 1780-82.

WARD, Artemas, Jr. (son of the preceding) (F Mass.) Jan. 9, 1762-Oct. 7, 1847; House 1813-17.

WARD, Charles Bonnell (R N.Y.) April 27, 1879-May 27, 1946; House 1915-25.

WARD, David Jenkins (D Md.) Sept. 17, 1871-Feb. 18, 1961; House June 6, 1939-45.

WARD, Elijah (nephew of Aaron Ward) (D N.Y.) Sept. 16, 1816-Feb. 7, 1882; House 1857-59, 1861-65, 1875-77.

WARD, Hallett Sydney (D N.C.) Aug. 31, 1870-March 31, 1956; House 1921-25.

WARD, Hamilton (R N.Y.) July 3, 1829-Dec. 28, 1898; House 1865-71.

WARD, James Hugh (D Ill.) Nov. 30, 1853-Aug. 15, 1916; House 1885-87.

WARD, Jasper Delos (R Ill.) Feb. 1, 1829-Aug. 6, 1902; House 1873-75.

WARD, Jonathan (D N.Y.) Sept. 21, 1768-Sept. 28, 1842; House 1815-17.

WARD, Marcus Lawrence (R N.J.) Nov. 9, 1812-April 25, 1884; House 1873-75; Gov. 1866-69; Chrmn. Rep. Nat. Comm. 1866.

WARD, Matthias (D Texas) Oct. 13, 1805-Oct. 5, 1861; Senate Sept. 27, 1858-Dec. 5, 1859.

WARD, Thomas (D N.J.) about 1759-March 4, 1842; House 1813-17.

WARD, Thomas Bayless (D Ind.) April 27, 1835-Jan. 1, 1892; House 1883-87.

WARD, William (R Pa.) Jan. 1, 1837-Feb. 27, 1895; House 1877-83.

WARD, William Lukens (R N.Y.) Sept. 2, 1856-July 16, 1933; House 1897-99.

WARD, William Thomas (W Ky.) Aug. 9, 1808-Oct. 12, 1878; House 1851-53.

WARDWELL, Daniel (R N.Y.) May 28, 1791-March 27, 1878; House 1831-37.

WARE, John H. (R Pa.) Aug. 29, 1908; House Nov. 3, 1970- .

WARE, Nicholas (— Ga.) 1767-Sept. 7, 1824; Senate Nov. 10, 1821-Sept. 7, 1824.

WARE, Orie S. (D Ky.) May 11, 1882- —; House 1927-29.

WARFIELD, Henry Ridgely (F Md.) Sept. 14, 1774-March 18, 1839; House 1819-25.

WARNER, Adoniram Judson (D Ohio) Jan. 13, 1834-Aug. 12, 1910; House 1879-81; 1883-87.

WARNER, Hiram (D Ga.) Oct. 29, 1802-June 30, 1881; House 1855-57.

WARNER, John De Witt (D N.Y.) Oct. 30, 1851-May 27, 1925; House 1891-95.

WARNER, Levi (brother of Samuel Larkin Warner) (D Conn.) Oct. 10, 1831-April 12, 1911; House Dec. 4, 1876-79.

WARNER, Richard (D Tenn.) Sept. 19, 1835-March 4, 1915; House 1881-85.

WARNER, Samuel Larkin (brother of Levi Warner) (R Conn.) June 14, 1828-Feb. 6, 1893; House 1865-67.

WARNER, Vespasian (R Ill.) April 23, 1842-March 31, 1925; House 1895-1905.

WARNER, Willard (R Ala.) Sept. 4, 1826-Nov. 23, 1906; Senate July 13, 1868-71.

WARNER, William (R Mo.) June 11, 1840-Oct. 4, 1916; House 1885-89; Senate March 18, 1905-11.

WARNOCK, William Robert (R Ohio) Aug. 29, 1838-July 30, 1918; House 1901-05.

WARREN, Cornelius (W N.Y.) March 15, 1790-July 28, 1849; House 1847-49.

WARREN, Edward Allen (D Ark.) May 2, 1818-July 2, 1875; House 1853-55, 1857-59.

WARREN, Francis Emroy (R Wyo.) June 20, 1844-Nov. 24, 1929; Senate Nov. 18, 1890-1893; 1895-Nov. 24, 1929; Gov. 1885-86, 1889-90 (Terr.); 1890.

WARREN, Joseph Mabbett (D N.Y.) Jan. 28, 1813-Sept. 9, 1896; House 1871-73.

WARREN, Lindsay Carter (D N.C.) Dec. 16, 1889- —; House 1925-Oct. 31, 1940.

WARREN, Lott (W Ga.) Oct. 30, 1797-June 17, 1861; House 1839-43.

WARREN, William Wirt (D Mass.) Feb. 27, 1834-May 2, 1880; House 1875-77.

WARWICK, John George (D Ohio) Dec. 23, 1830-Aug. 14, 1892; House 1891-Aug. 14, 1892.

WASHBURN, Cadwallader Colden (brother of Israel Washburn, Jr., Elihu Benjamin Washburne, and William Drew Washburn) (R Wis.) April 22, 1818-May 15, 1882; House 1855-61, 1867-71; Gov. 1872-74.

WASHBURN, Charles Grenfill (R Mass.) Jan. 28, 1857-May 25, 1928; House Dec. 18, 1906-11.

WASHBURN, Henry Dana (R Ind.) March 28, 1832-Jan. 26, 1871; House Feb. 23, 1866-69.

WASHBURN, Israel, Jr. (brother of Elihu Benjamin Washburne, Cadwallader Colden Washburn and William Drew Washburn) (R Maine) June 6, 1813-May 12, 1883; House 1851-55 (W); 1855-Jan. 1, 1861 (R); Gov. 1861-62.

WASHBURN, William Barrett (R Mass.) Jan. 31, 1820-Oct. 5, 1887; House 1863-Dec. 5, 1871; Senate April 17, 1874-75; Gov. 1872-74.

WASHBURN, William Drew (brother of Israel Washburn, Jr., Elihu Benjamin Washburne and Cadwallader Colden Washburn) (R Minn.) Jan. 14, 1831-July 29, 1912; House 1879-85; Senate 1889-95.

WASHBURNE, Elihu Benjamin (brother of Israel Washburn, Jr., Cadwallader Colden Washburn and William Drew Washburn) (W Ill.) Sept. 23, 1816-Oct. 22, 1887; House 1853-March 6, 1869; Secy. of State 1869.

WASHINGTON, George Corbin (grand-nephew of President George Washington) (— Md.) Aug. 20, 1789-July 17, 1854; House 1827-33, 1835-37.

WASHINGTON, Joseph Edwin (D Tenn.) Nov. 10, 1851-Aug. 28, 1915; House 1887-97.

WASHINGTON, William Henry (W N.C.) Feb. 7, 1813-Aug. 12, 1860; House 1841-43.

WASIELEWSKI, Thaddeus Francis Boleslaw (D Wis.) Dec. 2, 1904; House 1941-47.

WASKEY, Frank Hinman (D Alaska) April 20, 1875-Jan. 25, 1964; House (Terr. Del.) Aug. 14, 1906-07.

WASON, Edward Hills (R N.H.) Sept. 2, 1865-Feb. 6, 1941; House 1915-33.

WATERMAN, Charles Winfield (R Colo.) Nov. 2, 1861-Aug. 27, 1932; Senate 1927-Aug. 27, 1932.

WATERS, Russell Judson (R Calif.) June 6, 1843-Sept. 25, 1911; House 1899-1901.

WATKINS, Albert Galiton (D Tenn.) May 5, 1818-Nov. 9, 1895; House 1849-53 (W), 1855-59 (D).

WATKINS, Arthur Vivian (R Utah) Dec. 18, 1886-—; Senate 1947-59.

WATKINS, Elton (D Ore.) July 6, 1881-June 24, 1956; House 1923-25.

WATKINS, G. Robert (R Pa.) May 21, 1903-Aug. 7, 1970; House 1965-Aug. 7, 1970.

WATKINS, John Thomas (D La.) Jan. 15, 1854-April 25, 1925; House 1905-21.

WATMOUGH, John Goddard (— Pa.) Dec. 6, 1793-Nov. 27, 1861; House 1831-35.

WATRES, Laurence Hawley (R Pa.) July 18, 1882-Feb. 6, 1964; House 1923-31.

WATSON, Albert William (R S.C.) Aug. 30, 1922; House 1963-Feb. 1, 1965 (D), June 15, 1965-1971 (R).

WATSON, Clarence Wayland (D W.Va.) May 8, 1864-May 24, 1940; Senate Feb. 1, 1911-13.

WATSON, Cooper, Kinderdine (F-S Ohio) June 18, 1810-May 20, 1880; House 1855-57.

WATSON, David Kemper (R Ohio) June 18, 1849-Sept. 28, 1918; House 1895-97.

WATSON, Henry Winfield (R Pa.) June 24, 1856-Aug. 27, 1933; House 1915-Aug. 27, 1933.

WATSON, James (D N.Y.) April 6, 1750-May 15, 1806; Senate Aug. 17, 1798-March 19, 1800.

WATSON, James Eli (R Ind.) Nov. 2, 1863-July 29, 1948; House 1895-97, 1899-1909; Senate Nov. 8, 1916-33.

WATSON, Lewis Findlay (R Pa.) April 14, 1819-Aug. 25, 1890; House 1877-79, 1881-83, 1889-Aug. 25, 1890.

WATSON, Thomas Edward (D Ga.) Sept. 5, 1856-Sept. 26, 1922; House 1891-93 (P); Senate 1921-Sept. 26, 1922 (D).

WATSON, Walter Allen (D Va.) Nov. 25, 1867-Dec. 24, 1919; House 1913-Dec. 24, 1919.

WATTERSON, Harvey Magee (father of Henry Watterson) (D Tenn.) Nov. 23, 1811-Oct. 1, 1891; House 1839-43.

WATTERSON, Henry (son of Harvey Magee Watterson and nephew of Stanley Matthews) (D Ky.) Feb. 16, 1840-Dec. 22, 1921; House Aug. 12, 1876-77.

WATTS, John (— N.Y.) Aug. 27, 1749-Sept. 3, 1836; House 1793-95.

WATTS, John Clarence (D Ky.) July 9, 1902; House April 14, 1951- .

WATTS, John Sebrie (R N.M.) Jan. 19, 1816-June 11, 1876; House (Terr. Del.) 1861-63.

WAUGH, Daniel Webster (R Ind.) March 7, 1842-March 14, 1921; House 1891-95.

WAYNE, Anthony (father of Issac Wayne) (— Ga.) Jan. 1, 1745-Dec. 15, 1796; House 1791-March 21, 1792.

WAYNE, Isaac (son of Anthony Wayne) (F Pa.) 1772-Oct. 25, 1852; House 1823-25.

WAYNE, James Moore (JD Ga.) 1790-July 5, 1867; House 1829-Jan. 13, 1835; Assoc. Justice of Supreme Court 1835-67.

WEADOCK, Thomas Addis Emmet (D Mich.) Jan. 1, 1850-Nov. 18, 1938; House 1891-95.

WEAKLEY, Robert (— Tenn.) July 20, 1764-Feb. 4, 1845; House 1809-11.

WEARIN, Otha Donner (D Iowa) Jan. 10, 1903; House 1933-39.

WEATHERFORD, Zadoc Lorenzo (D Ala.) Feb. 4, 1888-—; House Nov. 5, 1940-41.

WEAVER, Archibald Jerard (grandfather of Phillip H. Weaver) (R Neb.) April 15, 1844-April 18, 1887; House 1883-87.

WEAVER, Claude (D Okla.) March 19, 1867-May 19, 1954; House 1913-15.

WEAVER, James Baird (D/G-Lab. Iowa) June 12, 1833-Feb. 6, 1912; House 1879-81; 1885-87 (G), 1887-89 (D/G-Lab).

WEAVER, James Dorman (R Pa.) Sept. 27, 1920; House 1963-65.

WEAVER, Phillip Hart (grandson of Archibald Jerard Weaver) (R Neb.) April 9, 1919; House 1955-63.

WEAVER, Walter Lowrie (R Ohio) April 1, 1851-May 26, 1909; House 1897-1901.

WEAVER, Zebulon (D N.C.) May 12, 1872-Oct. 29, 1948; House 1917-March 1, 1919, March 4, 1919-29; 1931-47.

WEBB, Edwin Yates (D N.C.) May 23, 1872-Feb. 7, 1955; House 1903-Nov. 10, 1919.

WEBB, William Robert (grandson of Richard Slanford) (D Tenn.) Nov. 11, 1842-Dec. 19, 1926; Senate Jan. 24-March 3, 1913.

WEBBER, Amos Richard (R Ohio) Jan. 21, 1852-Feb. 25, 1948; House Nov. 8, 1904-07.

WEBBER, George Washington (R Mich.) Nov. 25, 1825-Jan. 15, 1900; House 1881-83.

WEBER, John Baptiste (R N.Y.) Sept. 21, 1842-Dec. 18, 1926; House 1885-89.

WEBSTER, Daniel (W N.H./Mass.) Jan. 18, 1782-Oct. 24, 1852; House 1813-17 (F N.H.); 1823-May 30, 1827 (F Mass.); Senate May 30, 1827-Feb. 22, 1841 (F Mass.) 1845-July 22, 1850 (W Mass.); Secy. of State 1841-43, 1850-52.

WEBSTER, Edwin Hansom (R Md.) March 31, 1829-April 24, 1893; House 1859-July 1865.

WEBSTER, John Stanley (R Wash.) Feb. 22, 1877-Dec. 24, 1962; House 1919-May 8, 1923.

WEBSTER, Taylor (JD Ohio) Oct. 1, 1800-April 27, 1876; House 1833-39.

WEDEMEYER, William Walter (R Mich.) March 22, 1873-Jan. 2, 1913; House 1911-Jan. 2, 1913.

WEEKS, Edgar (cousin of John Wingate Weeks) (R Mich.) Aug. 3, 1839-Dec. 17, 1904; House 1899-1903.

WEEKS, John Eliakim (R Vt.) June 14, 1853-Sept. 10, 1949; House 1931-33; Gov. 1927-31.

WEEKS, John Wingate (great uncle of John Wingate Weeks) (— N.H.) March 31, 1781-April 3, 1853; House 1829-33.

WEEKS, John Wingate (father of Sinclair Weeks and cousin of Edgar Weeks) (R Mass.) April 11, 1860-July 12, 1926; House 1905-March 4, 1913; Senate March 4, 1913-1919; Secy. of War 1921-25.

WEEKS, Joseph (grandfather of Joseph Weeks Babcock) (D N.H.) Feb. 13, 1773-Aug. 4, 1845; House 1835-39.

WEEKS, Sinclair (son of John Wingate Weeks) (R Mass.) June 15, 1893; Senate Feb. 8-Dec. 19, 1944; Secy. of Commerce 1953-58.

WEEMS, Capell Lane (R Ohio) July 7, 1860-Jan. 5, 1913; House Nov. 3, 1903-09.

WEEMS, John Crompton (D Md.) 1778-Jan. 20, 1862; House Feb. 1, 1826-29.

WEFALD, Knud (F-L Minn.) Nov. 3, 1869-Oct. 25, 1936; House 1923-27.

WEICHEL, Alvin F. (R Ohio) Sept. 11, 1891-Nov. 27, 1956; House 1943-55.

WEICKER, Lowell P., Jr. (R Conn.) May 16, 1931; House 1969-71; Senate 1971- .

WEIDEMAN, Carl May (D Mich.) March 5, 1898-—; House 1933-35.

WEIGHTMAN, Richard Hanson (D N.M.) Dec. 28, 1816-Aug. 10, 1861; House (Terr. Del.) 1851-53.

WEIS, Jessica McCullough (R N.Y.) July 8, 1901-May 1, 1963; House 1959-63.

WEISS, Samuel Arthur (D Pa.) April 15, 1902; House 1941-Jan. 7, 1936.

WEISSE, Charles Herman (D Wis.) Oct. 24, 1866-Oct. 8, 1919; House 1903-11.

WELBORN, John (R Mo.) Nov. 20, 1857-Oct. 27, 1907; House 1905-07.

WELCH, Adonijah Strong (R Fla.) April 12, 1821-March 14, 1889; Senate June 25, 1868-69.

WELCH, Frank (R Neb.) Feb. 10, 1835-Sept. 4, 1878; House 1877-Sept. 4, 1878.

WELCH, John (W Ohio) Oct. 28, 1805-Aug. 5, 1891; House 1851-53.

WELCH, Philip James (D Mo.) April 4, 1895-April 26, 1963; House 1949-53.

WELCH, Richard Joseph (R Calif.) Feb. 13, 1869-Sept. 10, 1949; House Aug. 31, 1926-Sept. 10, 1949.

WELCH, William Wickham (AP Conn.) Dec. 10, 1818-July 30, 1892; House 1855-57.

WELKER, Herman (R Idaho) Dec. 11, 1906-Oct. 30, 1957; Senate 1951-57.

WELKER, Martin (R Ohio) April 25, 1819-March 15, 1902; House 1965-71.

WELLBORN, Marshall Johnson (D Ga.) May 29, 1808-Oct. 16, 1874; House 1849-51.

WELLBORN, Olin (D Texas) June 18, 1843-Dec. 6, 1921; House 1879-87.

WELLER, John B. (UD Ohio/Calif.) Feb. 22, 1812-Aug. 17, 1875; House 1839-45 (D Ohio); Senate Jan. 30, 1852-57 (UD Calif.); Gov. of Calif. 1858-60.

WELLER, Luman Hamlin (Nat. G/D Iowa) Aug. 24, 1833-March 2, 1914; House 1883-85.

WELLER, Ovington Eugene (R Md.) Jan. 23, 1862-Jan. 5, 1947; Senate 1921-27.

WELLER, Royal Hurlburt (D N.Y.) July 2, 1881-March 1, 1929; House 1923-March 1, 1929.

WELLING, Milton Holmes (D Utah) Jan. 25, 1876-May 28, 1947; House 1917-21.

WELLINGTON, George Louise (R Md.) Jan. 28, 1852-March 20, 1927; House 1895-97; Senate 1897-1903.

WELLS, Alfred (R N.Y.) May 27, 1814-July 18, 1867; House 1859-61.

WELLS, Daniel, Jr. (D Wis.) July 16, 1808-March 18, 1902; House 1853-57.

WELLS, Erastus (D Mo.) Dec. 2, 1823-Oct. 2, 1893; House 1869-77; 1879-81.

WELLS, Guilford Wiley (R Miss.) Feb. 14, 1840-March 21, 1909; House 1875-77.

WELLS, John (W N.Y.) July 1, 1817-May 30, 1877; House 1851-53.

WELLS, John Sullivan (— N.H.) Oct. 18, 1803-Aug. 1, 1860; Senate Jan. 16-March 3, 1855.

WELLS, Owen Augustine (D Wis.) Feb. 4, 1844-Jan. 29, 1935; House 1893-95.

WELLS, William Hill (— Del.) Jan. 7, 1769-March 11, 1829; Senate Jan. 17, 1799-Nov. 6, 1804, May 28, 1813-17.

WELSH, George Austin (R Pa.) Aug. 9, 1878-Oct. 22, 1970; House 1923-May 31, 1932.

WELTNER, Charles Longstreet (D Ga.) Dec. 17, 1927; House 1963-67.

WELTY, Benjamin Franklin (D Ohio) Aug. 9, 1870-Oct. 23, 1962; House 1917-21.

WEMPLE, Edward (D N.Y.) Oct. 23, 1843-Dec. 18, 1920; House 1883-85.

WENDOVER, Peter Hercules (D N.Y.) Aug. 1, 1768-Sept. 24, 1834; House 1815-21.

WENE, Elmer H. (D N.J.) May 1, 1892-Jan. 25, 1957; House 1937-39, 1941-45.

WENTWORTH, John (R Ill.) March 5, 1815-Oct. 16, 1888; House 1843-51, 1853-55 (D); 1865-67 (R).

WENTWORTH, Tappan (W Mass.) Feb. 24, 1802-June 12, 1875; House 1853-55.

WERDEL, Thomas Harold (R Calif.) Sept. 13, 1905-Sept. 30, 1966; House 1949-53.

WERNER, Theodore B. (D S.D.) June 2, 1892; House 1933-37.

WERTZ, George M. (R Pa.) July 19, 1856-Nov. 19, 1928; House 1923-25.

WEST, Charles Franklin (D Ohio) Jan. 12, 1895-Dec. 27, 1955; House 1931-35.

WEST, George (R N.Y.) Feb. 17, 1823-Sept. 20, 1901; 1881-83, 1885-89.

WEST, Joseph Rodman (R La.) Sept. 19, 1822-Oct. 31, 1898; Senate 1871-77.

WEST, Milton Horace (D Texas) June 30, 1888-Oct. 28, 1948; House April 22, 1933-Oct. 28, 1948.

WEST, William Stanley (D Ga.) Aug. 23, 1849-Dec. 22, 1914; Senate March 2-Nov. 3, 1914.

WESTBROOK, John (D Pa.) Jan. 9, 1789-Oct. 8, 1852; House 1841-43.

WESTBROOK, Theodoric Romeyn (D N.Y.) Nov. 20, 1821-Oct. 6, 1885; House 1853-55.

WESTCOTT, James Diament, Jr. (D Fla.) May 10, 1802-Jan. 19, 1880; Senate July 1, 1845-49.

WESTERLO, Rensselaer (F N.Y.) April 29, 1776-April 18, 1851; House 1817-19.

WESTLAND, Alfred John (Jack) (R Wash) Dec. 14, 1904; House 1953-65.

WETHERED, John (D Md.) May 8, 1809-Feb. 15, 1888; House 1843-45.

WETMORE, George Peabody (R R.I.) Aug. 2, 1846-Sept. 11, 1921; Senate 1895-1907; Jan. 22, 1908-1913; Gov. 1885-86.

WEVER, John Madison (R N.Y.) Feb. 24, 1847-Sept. 27, 1914; House 1891-95.

WEYMOUTH, George Warren (R Mass.) Aug. 25, 1850-Sept. 7, 1910; House 1897-1901.

WHALEN, Charles W., Jr. (R Ohio) July 31, 1920; House 1967- .

WHALEY, Kellian Van Rensalear (R Va./W.Va.) May 6, 1821-May 20, 1876; House 1861-63 (Va.); Dec. 7, 1863-67 (W.Va.).

WHALEY, Richard Smith (D S.C.) July 15, 1874-Nov. 8, 1951; House April 29, 1913-21.

WHALLEY, John Irving (R Pa.) Sept. 14, 1902; House Nov. 8, 1960- .

WHALLON, Reuben (JD N.Y.) Dec. 7, 1776-April 15, 1843; House 1833-35.

WHARTON, Charles Stuart (R Ill.) April 22, 1875-Sept. 4, 1939; House 1905-07.

WHARTON, James Ernest (R N.Y.) Oct. 4, 1899; House 1951-65.

WHARTON, Jesse (grandfather of Wharton Jackson Green) (— Tenn.) July 29, 1782-July 22, 1833; House 1807-09; Senate March 17, 1814-Oct. 10, 1815.

WHEAT, William Howard (R Ill.) Feb. 19, 1879-Jan. 16, 1944; House 1939-Jan. 16, 1944.

WHEATON, Horace (D N.Y.) Feb. 24, 1803-June 23, 1882; House 1843-47.

WHEATON, Laban (F Mass.) March 13, 1754-March 23, 1846; House 1809-17.

WHEELER, Burton Kendall (D Mont.) Feb. 27, 1882; Senate 1923-47.

WHEELER, Charles Kennedy (D Ky.) April 18, 1863-June 15, 1933; House 1897-1903.

WHEELER, Ezra (D Wis.) Dec. 23, 1820-Sept. 19, 1871; House 1863-65.

WHEELER, Frank Willis (R Mich.) March 2, 1853-Aug. 9, 1921; House 1889-91.

WHEELER, Grattan Henry (— N.Y.) Aug. 25, 1783-March 11, 1852; House 1831-33.

WHEELER, Hamilton Kinkaid (R Ill.) Aug. 5, 1848-July 19, 1918; House 1893-95.

WHEELER, Harrison H. (D Mich.) March 22, 1839-July 28, 1896; House 1891-93.

WHEELER, John (D N.Y.) Feb. 11, 1823-April 1, 1906; House 1853-57.

WHEELER, Joseph (D Ala.) Sept. 10, 1836-Jan. 25, 1906; House 1881-June 3, 1882; Jan. 15-March 3, 1883; 1885-April 20, 1900.

WHEELER, Loren Edgar (R Ill.) Oct. 7, 1862-Jan. 8, 1932; House 1915-23, 1925-27.

WHEELER, Nelson Platt (R Pa.) Nov. 4, 1841-March 3, 1920; House 1907-11.

WHEELER, William Almon (R N.Y.) June 19, 1819-June 4, 1887; House 1861-63, 1869-77; Vice Pres. 1877-81.

WHEELER, William McDonald (D Ga.) July 11, 1915; House 1947-55.

WHELCHEL, Benjamin Frank (D Ga.) Dec. 16, 1895-May 11, 1954; House 1935-45.

WHERRY, Kenneth Spicer (R Neb.) Feb. 28, 1892-Nov. 29, 1951; Senate 1943-Nov. 29, 1951.

WHIPPLE, Thomas, Jr. (— N.H.) 1787-Jan. 23, 1835; House 1821-29.

WHITACRE, John Jefferson (D Ohio) Dec. 28, 1860-Dec. 2, 1938; House 1911-15.

WHITAKER, John Albert (grandson of Addison Davis James) (D Ky.) Oct. 31, 1901-Dec. 15, 1951; House April 17, 1948-Dec. 15, 1951.

WHITCOMB, James (D Ind.) Dec. 1, 1795-Oct. 4, 1852; Senate 1849-Oct. 4, 1852; Gov. 1843-49.

WHITE, Addison (cousin of John White) (W Ky.) May 1, 1824-Feb. 4, 1909; House 1851-53.

WHITE, Albert Smith (R Ind.) Oct. 24, 1803-Sept. 24, 1864; House 1837-39 (W); 1861-63 (R); Senate 1839-45 (W).

WHITE, Alexander (F Va.) 1738-Sept. 19, 1804; House 1789-93.

WHITE, Alexander (R Ala.) Oct. 16, 1816-Dec. 13, 1893; House 1851-53 (UW); 1873-75(R).

WHITE, Alexander Colwell (R Pa.) Dec. 12, 1833-June 11, 1906; House 1885-87.

WHITE, Allison (D Pa.) Dec. 21, 1816-April 5, 1886; House 1857-59.

WHITE, Bartow (— N.Y.) Nov. 7, 1776-Dec. 12, 1862; House 1825-27.

WHITE, Benjamin (D Maine) May 13, 1790-June 7, 1860; House 1860; House 1843-45.

WHITE, Campbell Patrick (JD N.Y.) Nov. 30, 1787-Feb. 12, 1859; House 1829-35.

WHITE, Cecil Fielding (D Calif.) Dec. 12, 1900; House 1949-51.

WHITE, Chilton Allen (D Ohio) Feb. 6, 1826-Dec. 7, 1900; House 1861-65.

WHITE, Compton Ignatius (D Idaho) July 31, 1877-March 31, 1956; House 1933-47, 1949-51.

WHITE, Compton, Ignatius, Jr. (son of the preceding) (D Idaho) Dec. 19, 1920; House 1963-67.

WHITE, David (— Ky.) 1785-Oct. 19, 1834; House 1823-25.

WHITE, Dudley Allen (R Ohio) Jan. 3, 1901-Oct. 14, 1957; House 1937-41.

WHITE, Edward Douglass (son of James White) (W La.) March 1795-April 18, 1847; House 1829-Nov. 15, 1834, 1839-43; Gov. 1834-38.

WHITE, Edward Douglass (son of the preceding) (D La.) Nov. 3, 1845-May 19, 1921; Senate 1891-March 12, 1894; Supreme Court Assoc. Justice 1894-1910; Chief Justice 1910-21.

WHITE, Francis (— Va.) — -Nov. 1826; House 1813-15.

WHITE, Francis Shelley (Frank) (D Ala.) March 13, 1847-Aug. 1, 1922; Senate May 11, 1914-15.

WHITE, Frederick Edward (D Iowa) Jan. 19, 1844-Jan. 14, 1920; House 1891-93.

WHITE, George (D Ohio) Aug. 21, 1872-Dec. 15, 1953; House 1911-15, 1917-19; Chrmn. Dem. Nat. Comm. 1920-21; Gov. 1931-35.

WHITE, George Elon (R Ill.) March 7, 1848-May 17, 1935; House 1895-99.

WHITE, George Henry (R N.C.) Dec. 18, 1852-Dec. 28, 1918; House 1897-1901.

WHITE, Harry (R Pa.) Jan. 12, 1834-June 23, 1920; House 1877-81.

WHITE, Hays Baxter (R Kan.) Sept. 21, 1855-Sept. 29, 1930; House 1919-29.

WHITE, Hugh (R N.Y.) Dec. 25, 1798-Oct. 6, 1870; House 1945-51.

WHITE, Hugh Lawson (— Tenn.) Oct. 30, 1773-April 10, 1840; Senate Oct. 28, 1825-Jan. 13, 1840; President pro tempore 1832-33.

WHITE, James (father of Edward Douglass White) (— Tenn.) June 16, 1749-Oct. 1809; House (Terr. Del.) Sept. 3, 1794-June 1, 1796; Cont. Cong. (N.C.) 1786-88.

WHITE, James Bain (R Ind.) June 26, 1835-Oct. 9, 1897; House 1887-89.

WHITE, James Bamford (D Ky.) June 6, 1842-March 25, 1931; House 1901-03.

WHITE, John (cousin of Addison White and uncle of John Daughterty White) (W Ky.) Feb. 14, 1802-Sept. 22, 1845; House 1835-45; Speaker 1841-43.

WHITE, John Daugherty (nephew of John White) (R Ky.) Jan. 16, 1849-Jan. 5, 1920; House 1875-77, 1881-85.

WHITE, Joseph Livingston (W Ind.)— -Jan. 12, 1861; House 1841-43.

WHITE, Joseph M. (D Fla.) May 10, 1781-Oct. 19, 1839; House (Terr. Del.) 1825-37.

WHITE, Joseph Worthington (D Ohio) Oct. 2, 1822-Aug. 6, 1892; House 1863-65.

WHITE, Leonard (D Mass.) May 3, 1767-Oct. 10, 1849; House 1811-13.

WHITE, Michael Doherty (R Ind.) Sept. 8, 1827-Feb. 6, 1917; House 1877-79.

WHITE, Milo (R Minn.) Aug. 17, 1830-May 18, 1913; House 1883-87.

WHITE, Phineas (D Vt.) Oct. 30, 1770-July 6, 1847; House 1821-23.

WHITE, Richard Crawford (D Texas) April 29, 1923; House 1965- .

WHITE, Samuel (F Del.) 1770-Nov. 4, 1809; Senate Feb. 28, 1801-Nov. 4, 1809.

WHITE, Sebastian Harrison (D Colo.) Dec. 24, 1864-Dec. 21, 1945; House Nov. 15, 1927-29.

WHITE, Stepehn Mallory (D Calif.) Jan. 19, 1853-Feb. 21, 1901; Senate 1893-99.

WHITE, Stephen Van Culen (R N.Y.) Aug. 1, 1831-Jan. 18, 1913; House 1887-89.

WHITE, Wallace Humphrey, Jr. (grandson of William Pierce Frye) (R Maine) Aug. 6, 1877-March 31, 1952; House 1917-31; Senate 1931-49.

WHITE, Wilbur McKee (R Ohio) Feb. 22, 1890-—; House 1931-33.

WHITE, William John (R Ohio) Oct. 7, 1850-Feb. 16, 1923; House 1893-95.

WHITEAKER, John (D Ore.) May 4, 1820-Oct. 2, 1902; House 1879-81; Gov. 1858-62.

WHITEHEAD, Joseph (D Va.) Oct. 31, 1867-July 8, 1938; House 1925-31.

WHITEHEAD, Thomas (C Va.) Dec. 27, 1825-July 1, 1901; House 1873-75.

WHITEHILL, James (son of John Whitehill and nephew of Robert Whitehill) (— Pa.) Jan. 31, 1762-Feb. 26, 1822; House 1813-Sept. 1, 1814.

WHITEHILL, John (father of James Whitehill and brother of Robert Whitehill) (—Pa.) Dec. 11, 1729-Sept. 16, 1815; House 1803-07.

WHITEHILL, Robert (brother of John Whitehill and uncle of James Whitehill) (— Pa.) July 21, 1738-April 8, 1813; House Nov. 7, 1805-April 8, 1813.

WHITEHOUSE, John Osborne (LD N.Y.) July 19, 1817-Aug. 24, 1881; House 1873-77.

WHITEHURST, G. William (R Va.) March 12, 1925; House 1969- .

WHITELAW, Robert Henry (D Mo.) Jan. 30, 1854-July 27, 1937; House Nov. 4, 1890-91.

WHITELEY, Richard Henry (R Ga.) Dec. 22, 1830-Sept. 26, 1890; House Dec. 22, 1870-75.

WHITELEY, William Gustavus (D Del.) Aug. 7, 1819-April 23, 1886; House 1857-61.

WHITENER, Basil Lee (D N.C.) May 14, 1915; House 1957-69.

WHITESIDE, Jenkin (— Tenn.) 1772-Sept. 25, 1822; Senate April 11, 1809-Oct. 8, 1811.

WHITESIDE, John (D Pa.) 1773-July 28, 1830; House 1815-19.

WHITEFIELD, John Wilkins (D Kan.) March 11, 1818-Oct. 27, 1879; House (Terr. Del.) Dec. 20, 1854-Aug. 1, 1856; Dec. 9, 1856-57.

WHITING, Justin Rice (D/G Mich.) Feb. 18, 1847-Jan. 31, 1903; House 1887-95.

WHITING, Richard Henry (uncle of Ira Clifton Copley) (R Ill.) Jan. 17, 1826-May 24, 1888; House 1875-77.

WHITING, William (R Mass.) March 3, 1813-June 29, 1873; House March 4-June 29, 1873.

WHITING, William (R Mass.) May 24, 1841-Jan. 9, 1911; House 1883-89.

WHITLEY, James Lucius (R N.Y.) May 24, 1872-May 17, 1959; House 1929-35.

WHITMAN, Ezekiel (F Mass./Maine) March 9, 1776-Aug. 1, 1866; House 1809-11; 1817-21 (Mass.); 1821-June 1, 1822 (Maine).

WHITMAN, Lemuel (D Conn.) June 8, 1780-Nov. 13, 1841; House 1823-25.

WHITMORE, Elias (D N.Y.) March 2, 1772-Dec. 26, 1853; House 1825-27.

WHITMORE, George Washington (R Texas) Aug. 26, 1824-Oct. 14, 1876; House March 30, 1870-71.

WHITNEY, Thomas Richard (AP N.Y.) May 2, 1807-April 12, 1858; House 1855-57.

WHITTEMORE, Benjamin Franklin (R S.C.) May 18, 1824-Jan. 25, 1894; House July 18, 1868-Feb. 24, 1870.

WHITTEN, Jamie Lloyd (D Miss.) April 18, 1910; House Nov. 4, 1941- .

WHITTHORNE, Washington Curran (D Tenn.) April 19, 1825-Sept. 21, 1891; House 1871-83, 1887-91; Senate April 16, 1886-87.

WHITTINGTON, William Madison (D Miss.) May 4, 1878-Aug. 20, 1962; House 1925-51.

WHITTLESEY, Elisha (uncle of William Augustus Whittlesey and cousin of Frederick Whittlesey and Thomas Tucker Whittlesey) (— Ohio) Oct. 19, 1783-Jan. 7, 1863; House 1823-July 9, 1838.

WHITTLESEY, Frederick (cousin of Elisha Whittlesey and Thomas Tucker Whittlesey) (W N.Y.) June 12, 1799-Sept. 19, 1851; House 1831-35.

WHITTLESEY, Thomas Tucker (VBD Conn.) Dec. 8, 1798-Aug. 20, 1868; House April 29, 1836-39.

WHITTLESEY, William Augustus (nephew of Elisha Whittlesey) (D Ohio) July 14, 1796-Nov. 6, 1866; House 1849-51.

WHYTE, William Pinkney (D Md.) Aug. 9, 1824-March 17, 1908; Senate July 13, 1868-69, 1875-81, June 8, 1906-March 17, 1908; Gov. 1872-74.

WICK, William Watson (D Ind.) Feb. 23, 1796-May 19, 1868; House 1839-41; 1845-49.

WICKERSHAM, James (R Alaska) Aug. 24, 1857-Oct. 24, 1939; House (Terr. Del.) 1909-17, Jan. 7-March 3, 1919, March 1-3, 1921, 1931-33.

WICKERSHAM, Victor Eugene (D Okal.) Feb. 9, 1906; House April 1, 1941-47, 1949-57, 1961-65.

WICKES, Eliphalet (— N.Y.) April 1, 1769-June 7, 1850; House 1805-07.

WICKHAM, Charles Preston (R Ohio) Sept. 15, 1836-March 18, 1925; House 1887-91.

WICKLIFFE, Charles Anderson (grandfather of Robert Charles Wickliffe and John Crepps Wickliffe Beckham) (UW Ky.) June 8, 1788-Oct. 31, 1869; House 1923-33 (D); 1861-63 (UW); Gov. 1839-40; Postmaster Gen. 1841-45.

WICKLIFFE, Robert Charles (grandson of Charles Anderson Wickliffe and cousin of John Crepps Wickliffe Beckham) (D La.) May 1, 1874-June 11, 1912; House 1909-June 11, 1912.

WIDGERY, William (D Mass.) about 1753-July 31, 1822; House 1811-13.

WIDNALL, William Beck (R N.J.) March 17, 1906; House Feb. 6, 1950- .

WIER, Roy William (D Minn.) Feb. 25, 1888-June 27, 1963; House 1949-61.

WIGFALL, Louis Tresvant (D Texas) April 21, 1816-Feb. 18, 1874, Senate Dec. 5, 1859-March 23, 1861.

WIGGINS, Charles E. (R Calif.) Dec. 3, 1927; House 1967- .

WIGGINTON, Peter Dinwiddie (D Calif.) Sept. 6, 1839-July 7, 1890; House 1875-77, Feb. 7, 1878-79.

WIGGLESWORTH, Richard Bowditch (R Mass.) April 25, 1891-Oct. 22, 1960; House Nov. 6, 1928-Nov. 13, 1958.

WIKE, Scott (D Ill.) April 6, 1834-Jan. 15, 1901; House 1875-77, 1889-93.

WILBER, David (father of David Forrest Wilber) (R N.Y.) Oct. 5, 1820-April 1, 1890; House 1873-75; 1879-81; 1887-April 1, 1890.

WILBER, David Forrest (son of David Wilber) (R N.Y.) Dec. 7, 1859-Aug. 14, 1928; House 1895-99.

WILBOUR, Isaac (F R.I.) April 25, 1763-Oct. 4, 1837; House 1807-09.

WILCOX, James Mark (D Fla.) May 21, 1890-Feb. 3, 1956; House 1933-39.

WILCOX, Jeduthun (father of Leonard Wilcox) (F N.H.) Nov. 18, 1768-July 18, 1838; House 1813-17.

WILCOX, John A. (UW Miss.) April 18, 1819-Feb. 7, 1864; House 1851-53.

WILCOX, Leonard (son of Jeduthum Wilcox) (D N.H.) Jan. 29, 1799-June 18, 1850; Senate March 1, 1842-43.

WILCOX, Robert William (— Hawaii) Feb. 15, 1855-Oct. 23, 1903; House (Terr. Del.) Nov. 6, 1900-03.

WILDE, Richard Henry (D Ga.) Sept. 24, 1789-Sept. 10, 1847; House 1815-17; Feb. 7-March 3, 1825; Nov. 17, 1827-35.

WILDER, Abel Carter (R Kan.) March 18, 1828-Dec. 22, 1875; House 1863-65.

WILDER, William Henry (R Mass.) May 14, 1855-Sept. 11, 1913; House 1911-Sept. 11, 1913.

WILDMAN, Zalmon (D Conn.) Feb. 16, 1775-Dec. 10, 1835; House March 4-Dec. 10, 1835.

WILDRICK, Isaac (D N.J.) March 3, 1803-March 22, 1892; House 1849-53.

WILEY, Alexander (R Wis.) May 26, 1884-Oct. 26, 1967; Senate 1939-63.

WILEY, Ariosto Appling (brother of Oliver Cicero Wiley) (D Ala.) Nov. 6, 1848-June 17, 1908; House 1901-June 17, 1908.

WILEY, James Sullivan (D Maine) Jan. 22, 1808-Dec. 21, 1891; House 1847-49.

WILEY, John McClure (D N.Y.) Aug. 11, 1846-Aug. 13, 1912; House 1889-91.

WILEY, Oliver Cicero (brother of Ariosto Appling Wiley) (D Ala.) Jan. 30, 1851-Oct. 18, 1917; House Nov. 3, 1908-09.

WILEY, William Halsted (R N.J.) July 10, 1842-May 2, 1925; House 1903-07, 1909-11.

WILFLEY, Xenophon Pierce (D Mo.) March 18, 1871-May 4, 1931; Senate April 30-Nov. 5, 1918.

WILKIN, James Whitney (father of Samuel Jones Wilkin) (D N.Y.) 1762-Feb. 23, 1845; House June 7, 1815-19.

WILKIN, Samuel Jones (son of James Whitney Wilkin) (D N.Y.) Dec. 17, 1793-March 11, 1866; House 1831-33.

WILKINS, Beriah (D Ohio) July 10, 1846-June 7, 1905; House 1883-89.

WILKINS, William (D Pa.) Dec. 20, 1779-June 23, 1865; Senate 1831-June 30, 1834 (D/A-M); House 1843-Feb. 14, 1844; Secy. of War 1844-45.

WILKINSON, Morton Smith (R Minn.) Jan. 22, 1819-Feb. 4, 1894; Senate 1859-65; House 1869-71.

WILKINSON, Theodore Stark (D La.) Dec. 18, 1847-Feb. 1, 1921; House 1887-91.

WILLARD, Charles Wesley (R Vt.) June 18, 1827-June 8, 1880; House 1869-75.

WILLARD, George (R Mich.) March 20, 1824-March 26, 1901; House 1873-77.

WILLCOX, Washington Frederick (D Conn.) Aug. 22, 1834-March 8, 1909; House 1889-93.

WILLETT, William Forte, Jr. (D N.Y.) Nov. 27, 1869-Feb. 12, 1938; House 1907-11.

WILLEY, Calvin (D Conn.) Sept. 15, 1776-Aug. 23, 1858; Senate May 4, 1825-31.

WILLEY, Earle Dukes (R Del.) July 21, 1889-March 17, 1950; House 1943-45.

WILLEY, Waitman Thomas (— Va./W.Va.) Oct. 18, 1811-May 2, 1900; Senate July 9, 1861-63 (Va.);, Aug. 4, 1863-71 (W.Va.).

WILLFORD, Albert Clinton (D Iowa) Sept. 21, 1877-March 10, 1937; House 1933-35.

WILLIAMS, Abram Pease (R Calif.) Feb. 3, 1832-Oct. 17, 1911; Senate Aug. 4, 1886-87.

WILLIAMS, Alpheus Starkey (D Mich.) Sept. 20, 1810-Dec. 20, 1878; House 1875-Dec. 20, 1878.

WILLIAMS, Andrew (R N.Y.) Aug. 27, 1828-Oct. 6, 1907; House 1875-79.

WILLIAMS, Archibald Hunter Arrington (nephew of Archibald Hunter Arrington) (D N.C.) Oct. 22, 1842-Sept. 5, 1895; House 1891-93.

WILLIAMS, Arthur Bruce (R Mich.) Jan. 27, 1872-May 1, 1925; House June 19, 1923-May 1, 1925.

WILLIAMS, Benjamin (— N.C.) Jan. 1, 1751-July 20, 1814; House 1793-95; Gov. 1799-1802, 1807-08.

WILLIAMS, Charles Grandison (R Wis.) Oct. 18, 1829-March 30, 1892; House 1873-83.

WILLIAMS, Christopher Harris (grandfather of John Sharp Williams) (W Tenn.) Dec. 18, 1798-Nov. 27, 1857; House 1837-43, 1849-53.

WILLIAMS, Clyde (D Mo.) Oct. 13, 1873-Nov. 12, 1954; House 1927-29; 1931-43.

WILLIAMS, David Rogerson (D S.C.) March 8, 1776-Nov. 17, 1830; House 1805-09, 1811-13; Gov. 1814-16.

WILLIAMS, Elihu Stephen (R Ohio) Jan. 24, 1835-Dec. 1, 1903; House 1887-91.

WILLIAMS, George Fred (D Mass.) July 10, 1852-July 11, 1923; House 1891-93.

WILLIAMS, George Henry (UR Ore.) March 23, 1823-April 4, 1910; Senate 1865-71; Atty. Gen. 1872-75.

WILLIAMS, George Howard (R Mo.) Dec. 1, 1871-Nov. 25, 1963; Senate May 25, 1925-Dec. 5, 1926.

WILLIAMS, George Short (R Del.) Oct. 21, 1877-; House 1939-41.

WILLIAMS, Guinn (D Texas) April 22, 1871-Jan. 9, 1948; House May 13, 1922-33.

WILLIAMS, Harrison Arlington, Jr. (D N.J.) Dec. 10, 1919; House Nov. 3, 1953-57; Senate 1959- .

WILLIAMS, Henry (D Mass.) Nov. 30, 1805-May 8, 1887; House 1839-41, 1843-45.

WILLIAMS, Hezekiah (D Maine) July 28, 1798-Oct. 23, 1856; House 1845-49.

WILLIAMS, Isaac, Jr. (D N.Y.) April 5, 1777-Nov. 9, 1860; House Dec. 20, 1813-1815, 1817-19, 1823-25.

WILLIAMS, James (D Del.) Aug. 4, 1825-April 12, 1899; House 1875-79.

WILLIAMS, James Douglas (D Ind.) Jan. 16, 1808-Nov. 20, 1880; House 1875-Dec. 1, 1876; Gov. 1877-1880.

WILLIAMS, James Robert (D Ill.) Dec. 27, 1850-Nov. 8, 1923; House Dec. 2, 1889-95, 1899-1905.

WILLIAMS, James Wray (D Md.) Oct. 8, 1792-Dec. 2, 1842; House 1841-Dec. 2, 1842.

WILLIAMS, Jared (JD Va.) March 4, 1766-Jan. 2, 1831; House 1819-25.

WILLIAMS, Jared Warner (D N.H.) Dec. 22, 1796-Sept. 29, 1864; House 1837-41; Senate Nov. 29, 1853-July 15, 1854; Gov. 1847-49.

WILLIAMS, Jeremiah Norman (D Ala.) May 29, 1829-May 8, 1915; House 1875-70.

WILLIAMS, John (— N.Y.) Sept. 1752-July 22, 1806; House 1795-99.

WILLIAMS, John (brother of Lewis Williams and Robert Williams, father of Joseph Lanier Williams and cousin of Marmaduke Williams) (— Tenn.) Jan. 29, 1778-Aug. 10, 1837; Senate Oct. 10, 1815-23.

WILLIAMS, John (D N.Y.) Jan. 7, 1807-March 26, 1875; House 1855-57.

WILLIAMS, John Bell (D Miss.- Dec. 4, 1918; House 1947-Jan. 16, 1968; Gov. 1968- .

WILLIAMS, John James (R Del.) May 17, 1904; Senate 1947-Dec. 31, 1970.

WILLIAMS, John McKeown Snow (R Mass.) Aug. 13, 1818-March 19, 1886; House 1873-75.

WILLIAMS, John Sharp (grandson of Christopher Harris Williams) (D Miss.) July 30, 1854-Sept. 27, 1932; House 1893-1909; Senate 1911-23.

WILLIAMS, John Stuart (D Ky.) July 10, 1818-July 17, 1898; Senate 1879-85.

WILLIAMS, Jonathan (— Pa.) May 20, 1750-May 16, 1815; House March 4-May 16, 1815.

WILLIAMS, Joseph Lanier (son of John Williams of Tenn.) (W Tenn.) Oct. 23, 1810-Dec. 14, 1865; House 1837-43.

WILLIAMS, Lawrence G. (R Pa.) Sept. 15, 1913; House 1967- .

WILLIAMS, Lemuel (— Mass.) June 18, 1747-Nov. 8, 1828; House 1799-1805.

WILLIAMS, Lewis (brother of John Williams of Tenn. and Robert Williams and cousin of Marmaduke Williams) (— N.C.) Feb. 1, 1782-Feb. 23, 1842; House 1815-Feb. 23, 1842.

WILLIAMS, Marmaduke (cousin of John Williams of Tenn., Lewis Williams and Robert Williams) (D N.C.) April 6, 1774-Oct. 29, 1850; House 1803-09.

WILLIAMS, Morgan B. (R Pa.) Sept. 17, 1831-Oct. 13, 1903; House 1897-99.

WILLIAMS, Nathan (D N.Y.) Dec. 19, 1773-Sept. 25, 1835; House 1805-07.

WILLIAMS, Reuel (D Maine) June 2, 1783-July 25, 1862; Senate 1837-Feb. 15, 1843.

WILLIAMS, Richard (R Ore.) Nov. 15, 1836-June 19, 1914; House 1877-79.

WILLIAMS, Robert (brother of John Williams of Tenn. and Lewis Williams and cousin of Marmaduke Williams) (— N.C.) July 12, 1773-Jan. 25, 1836; House 1797-1803; Gov. of Miss. Terr. 1805-09.

WILLIAMS, Seward Henry (R Ohio) Nov. 7, 1870-Sept. 2, 1922; House 1915- 17.

WILLIAMS, Sherrod (W Ky.) 1804-—; House 1835-41.

WILLIAMS, Thomas (R Pa.) Aug. 28, 1806-June 16, 1872; House 1863-69.

WILLIAMS, Thomas (D Ala.) Aug. 11, 1825-April 13, 1903; House 1879-85.

WILLIAMS, Thomas Hickman (D Miss.) Jan. 20, 1801-May 3, 1851; Senate Nov. 12, 1838-39.

WILLIAMS, Thomas Hill (D Miss.) 1780-1840; Senate Dec. 10, 1817-29.

WILLIAMS, Thomas Scott (— Conn.) June 26, 1777-Dec. 22, 1861; House 1817-19.

WILLIAMS, Thomas Sutler (R Ill.) Feb. 14, 1872-April 5, 1940; House 1915-Nov. 11, 1929.

WILLIAMS, Thomas Wheeler (W Conn.) Sept. 28, 1789-Dec. 31, 1874; House 1939-43.

WILLIAMS, William (D N.Y.) Sept. 6, 1815-Sept. 10, 1876; House 1871-73.

WILLIAMS, William (R Ind.) May 11, 1821-April 22, 1896; House 1867-75.

WILLIAMS, William Brewster (R Mich.) July 28, 1826-March 4, 1905; House Dec. 1, 1873-77.

WILLIAMS, William Elza (D Ill.) May 5, 1857-Sept. 13, 1921; House 1899-1901 1913-17.

WILLIAMS, William Robert (R N.Y.) Aug. 11, 1884-—; House 1951-59.

WILLIAMSON, Ben Mitchell (D Ky.) Oct. 16, 1864-June 23, 1941; Senate Dec. 1, 1930-31.

WILLIAMSON, Hugh (F N.C.) Dec. 5, 1735-May 22, 1819; House 1789-93; Cont. Cong. 1782-85, 1787-88.

WILLIAMSON, John Newton (R Ore.) Nov. 8, 1855-Aug. 29, 1943; House 1903-07.

WILLIAMSON, William (R S.D.) Oct. 7, 1875-—; House 1921-33.

WILLIAMSON, William Durkee (D Maine) July 31, 1779-May 27, 1846; House 1821-23; Gov. 1821.

WILLIE, Asa Hoxie (D Texas) Oct. 11, 1829-March 16, 1899; House 1873-75.

WILLIS, Albert Shelby (D Ky.) Jan. 22, 1843-Jan. 6, 1897; House 1877-87.

WILLIS, Benjamin Albertson (D N.Y.) March 24, 1840-Oct. 14, 1886; House 1875-79.

WILLIS, Edwin Edward (D La.) Oct. 2, 1904; House 1949-69.

WILLIS, Francis (— Ga.) Jan. 5, 1745-Jan. 25, 1829; House 1791-93.

WILLIS, Frank Bartlett (R Ohio) Dec. 28, 1871-March 30, 1928; House 1911-Jan. 9, 1915; Senate Jan. 14, 1921-March 30, 1928; Gov. 1915-17.

WILLIS, Jonathan Spencer (R Del.) April 5, 1830-Nov. 24, 1903; House 1895-97.

WILLIS, Raymond Eugene (R Ind.) Aug. 11, 1875-March 21, 1956; Senate 1941-47.

WILLITS, Edwin (R Mich.) April 24, 1830-Oct. 22, 1896; House 1877-83.

WILLOUGHBY, Westel, Jr. (D N.Y.) Nov. 20, 1769-Oct. 3, 1844; House Dec. 13, 1815-17.

WILMOT, David (R Pa.) Jan. 20, 1814-March 16, 1868; House 1845-51 (D); Senate March 14, 1861-63 (R).

WILSHIRE, William Wallace (C Ark.) Sept. 8, 1830-Aug. 19, 1888; House 1873-June 16, 1874 (R), 1875-77 (C).

WILSON, Alexander (— Va.)———; House Dec. 4, 1804-09.

WILSON, Benjamin (D W.Va.) April 30, 1825-April 26, 1901; House 1875-83.

WILSON, Charles H. (D Calif.) Feb. 15, 1917; House 1963- .

WILSON, Earl (R Ind.) April 18, 1906; House 1941-59; 1961-65.

WILSON, Edgar (Sil. R/D Idaho) Feb. 25, 1861-Jan. 3, 1915; House 1895-97 (R), 1899-1901 (Sil. R/D).

WILSON, Edgar Campbell (son of Thomas Wilson of Va. and father of Eugene McLanahan Wilson) (W Va.) Oct. 18, 1800-April 24, 1860; House 1833-35.

WILSON, Emmett (grandson of Augustus Emmett Maxwell) (D Fla.) Sept. 17, 1882-May 29, 1918; House 1913-17.

WILSON, Ephraim King (D Md.) Sept. 15, 1771-Jan. 2, 1834; House 1827-31.

WILSON, Ephraim King (son of the preceding) (D Md.) Dec. 22, 1821-Feb. 24, 1891; House 1873-75; Senate 1885-Feb. 24, 1891.

WILSON, Eugene McLanahan (son of Edgar Campbell Wilson, grandson of Thomas Wilson of Va. and great-grandson of Isaac Griffin) (D Minn.) Dec. 25, 1833-April 10, 1890; House 1869-71.

WILSON, Francis Henry (R N.Y.) Feb. 11, 1844-Sept. 25, 1910; House 1895-Sept. 30, 1897.

WILSON, Frank Eugene (D N.Y.) Dec. 22, 1857-July 12, 1935; House 1899-1905, 1911-15.

WILSON, George Allison (R Iowa) April 1, 1884-Sept. 8, 1953; Senate Jan. 14, 1943-49; Gov. 1939-43.

WILSON, George Howard (D Okla.) Aug. 21, 1905; House 1949-51.

WILSON, George Washington (R Ohio) Feb. 22, 1840-Nov. 27, 1909; House 1893-97.

WILSON, Henry (D Pa.) 1778-Aug. 14, 1826; House 1823-Aug. 14, 1826.

WILSON, Henry (F-S/AP/D Mass.) Feb. 16, 1812-Nov. 22, 1875; Senate Jan. 31, 1855-73; Vice Pres. (R) 1873-75.

WILSON, Isaac (— N.Y.) June 25, 1780-Oct. 25, 1848; House 1823-Jan. 7, 1824.

WILSON, James (F N.H.) Aug. 16, 1766-Jan. 4, 1839; House 1809-11.

WILSON, James (son of the preceding) (W N.H.) March 18, 1797-May 29, 1881; House 1847-Sept. 9, 1850.

WILSON, James (D Pa.) April 28, 1779-July 19, 1868; House 1823-29.

WILSON, James (father of John Lockwood Wilson) (R Ind.) April 9, 1825-Aug. 8, 1867; House 1857-61.

WILSON, James (R Iowa) Aug. 26, 1835-Aug. 26, 1920; House 1873-77; 1883-85; Secy. of Agriculture 1897-1913.

WILSON, James Clifton (D Texas) June 21, 1874-Aug. 3, 1951; House 1917-19.

WILSON, James Falconer (R Iowa) Oct. 19, 1828-April 22, 1895; House Oct. 8, 1861-69; Senate 1883-95.

WILSON, James Jefferson (D N.J.) 1775-July 28, 1824; Senate 1815-Jan. 8, 1821.

WILSON, Jeremiah Morrow (R Ind.) Nov. 25, 1828-Sept. 24, 1901; House 1871-75.

WILSON, John (— S.C.) Aug. 11, 1773-Aug. 13, 1828; House 1821-27.

WILSON, John (F Mass.) Jan. 10, 1777-Aug. 9, 1848; House 1813-15, 1817-19.

WILSON, John Frank (D Ark.) May 7, 1846-April 7, 1911; House (Terr. Del.) 1899-1901, 1903-05.

WILSON, John Haden (D Pa.) Aug. 20, 1867-Jan. 28, 1946; House 1919-21.

WILSON, John Henry (R Ky.) Jan. 30, 1846-Jan. 14, 1923; House 1889-93.

WILSON, John Lockwood (son of James Wilson of Ind.) (R Wash.) Aug. 7, 1850-Nov. 6, 1912; House Nov. 20, 1889-Feb. 18, 1895; Senate Feb. 19, 1895-99.

WILSON, John Thomas (R Ohio) April 16, 1811-Oct. 6, 1891; House 1867-73.

WILSON, Joseph Franklin (D Texas) March 18, 1901-Oct. 13, 1968; House 1947-55.

WILSON, Joseph Gardner (cousin of James Willis Nesmith) (R Ore.) Dec. 13, 1826-July 2, 1873; House March 4-July 2, 1873.

WILSON, Nathan (D N.Y.) Dec. 23, 1758-July 25, 1834; House June 3, 1808-09.

WILSON, Riley Joseph (D La.) Nov. 12, 1871-Feb. 23, 1946; House 1915-37.

WILSON, Robert (U Mo.) Nov. 1803-May 10, 1870; Senate Jan. 17, 1862-Nov. 13, 1863.

WILSON, Robert Carleton (Bob) (R Calif.) April 5, 1916; House 1953- .

WILSON, Robert Patterson Clark (D Mo.) Aug. 8, 1834-Dec. 21, 1916; House Dec. 2, 1889-93.

WILSON, Stanyarne (D S.C.) Jan. 10, 1860-Feb. 14, 1928; House 1895-1901.

WILSON, Stephen Fowler (R Pa.) Sept. 4, 1821-March 30, 1897; House 1865-69.

WILSON, Thomas (father of Egard Campbell Wilson and grandfather of Eugene McLanahan Wilson) (F Va.) Sept. 11, 1765-Jan. 24, 1826; House 1811-13.

WILSON, Thomas (D Pa.) 1772-Oct. 4, 1824; House May 4, 1813-17.

WILSON, Thomas (D Minn.) May 16, 1827-April 3, 1910; House 1887-89.

WILSON, Thomas Webber (D Miss.) Jan. 24, 1893-Jan. 31, 1948; House 1923-29.

WILSON, William (— Pa.)—-—; House 1815-19.

WILSON, William (— Ohio) March 19, 1773-June 6, 1827; House 1823-June 6, 1827.

WILSON, William Bauchop (D Pa.) April 2, 1862-May 25, 1934; House 1907-13; Secy of Labor 1913-21.

WILSON, William Edward (D Ind.) March 9, 1870-Sept. 29, 1948; House 1923-25.

WILSON, William Henry (R Pa.) Dec. 6, 1877-Aug. 11, 1937; House 1935-37.

WILSON, William Lyne (D W.Va.) May 3, 1843-Oct. 17, 1900; House 1883-95; Postmaster Gen. 1895-97.

WILSON, William Warfield (R Ill.) March 2, 1868-July 22, 1942; House 1903-13, 1915-21.

WINANS, Edwin Baruch (D Mich.) May 16, 1826-July 4, 1894; House 1883-87; Gov. 1891-93.

WINANS, James January (R Ohio) June 7, 1818-April 28, 1879; House 1869-71.

WINANS, John (ID Wis.) Sept. 27, 1831-Jan. 17, 1907; House 1883-85.

WINCHESTER, Boyd (D Ky.) Sept. 23, 1836-May 18, 1923; House 1869-73.

WINDOM, William (R Minn.) May 10, 1827-Jan. 29, 1891; House 1859-69; Senate July 15, 1870-Jan. 22, 1871; March 4, 1871-March 7, 1881; Nov. 15, 1881-83; Secy. of the Treasury 1881, 1889-91.

WINFIELD, Charles Henry (D N.Y.) April 22, 1822-June 10, 1888; House 1863-67.

WING, Austin Eli (W Mich.) Feb. 3, 1792-Aug. 27, 1849; House (Terr. Del.) 1825-29, 1831-33.

WINGATE, Joseph Ferdinand (D Maine) June 29, 1786-—; House 1827-31.

WINGATE, Paine (F N.H.) May 14, 1739-March 7, 1838; Senate 1789-93; House 1793-95; Cont. Cong. 1787-88.

WINGO, Effiegene (Locke) (widow of Otis Theodore Wingo and great-great-great-granddaughter of Matthew Locke) (D Ark.) April 13, 1883-Sept. 19, 1962; House Nov. 4, 1930-33.

WINGO, Otis Theodore (husband of Effiegene Wingo) (D Ark.) June 18, 1877-Oct. 21, 1930; House 1913-Oct. 21, 1930.

WINN, Larry, Jr. (R Kan.) Aug. 22, 1919; House 1967- .

WINN, Richard (D S.C.) 1750-Dec. 19, 1818; House 1793-97, Jan. 24, 1803-13.

WINN, Thomas Elisha (Alliance D Ga.) May 21, 1839-June 5, 1925; House 1891-93.

WINSLOW, Samuel Ellsworth (R Mass.) April 11, 1862-July 11, 1940; House 1913-25.

WINSLOW, Warren (D N.C.) Jan. 1, 1810-Aug. 16, 1862; House 1855-61.

WINSTEAD, William Arthur (D Miss.) Jan. 6, 1904; House 1943-65.

WINSTON, Joseph (D N.C.) June 17, 1746-April 21, 1815; House 1793-95, 1803-07.

WINTER, Charles Edwin (R Wyo.) Sept. 13, 1870-April 22, 1948; House 1923-29.

WINTER, Elisha I. (F N.Y.) July 15, 1781-June 30, 1849; House 1813-15.

WINTER, Thomas Daniel (R Kan.) July 7, 1896-Nov. 7, 1951; House 1939-47.

WINTHROP, Robert Charles (W Mass.) May 12, 1809-Nov. 16, 1894; House Nov. 9, 1840-May 25, 1842, Nov. 29, 1842-July 30, 1850; Senate July 30, 1850-Feb. 1, 1851; Speaker 1847-49.

WISE, George Douglas (cousin of John Sergeant Wise and Richard Alsop Wise and nephew of Henry Alexander Wise) (D Va.) June 4, 1831-Feb. 4, 1898; House 1881-April 10, 1890, 1891-95.

WISE, Henry Alexander (father of John Sergeant Wise and Richard Alsop Wise and uncle of George Douglas Wise) (Tyler D Va.) Dec. 3, 1806-Sept. 12, 1876; House 1833-37 (JD), 1837 (Whig), 1843-Feb. 12, 1844 (Tyler D); Gov. 1856-60.

WISE, James Walter (D Ga.) March 3, 1868-Sept. 8, 1925; House 1915-25.

WISE, John Sergeant (son of Henry Alexander Wise, grandson of John Sergeant, brother of Richard Alsop Wise and cousin of George Douglas Wise) (Read. Va.) Dec. 27, 1846-May 12, 1913; House 1883-85.

WISE, Morgan Ringland (D Pa.) June 7, 1825-April 13, 1903; House 1879-83.

WISE, Richard Alsop (son of Henry Alexander Wise, grandson of John Sergeant, brother of John Sergeant Wise and cousin of George Douglas Wise) (R Va.) Sept. 2, 1843-Dec. 21, 1900; House April 26, 1898-99, March 12-Dec. 21, 1900.

WITCHER, John Seashoal (R W. Va.) July 15, 1839-July 8, 1906; House 1869-71.

WITHERELL, James (D Vt.) June 16, 1759-Jan. 9, 1838; House 1807-May 1, 1808.

WITHERS, Garrett Lee (D Ky.) June 21, 1884-April 30, 1953; Senate Jan. 20, 1949-Nov. 26, 1950; House Aug. 2, 1952-April 30, 1953.

WITHERS, Robert Enoch (cousin of Thomas Withers Chinn) (C Va.) Sept. 18, 1821-Sept. 21, 1907; Senate 1875-81.

WITHERSPOON, Robert (great-great-grandfather of Robert Witherspoon Hemphill) (D S.C.) Jan. 29, 1767-Oct. 11, 1837; House 1809-11.

WITHERSPOON, Samuel Andrew (D Miss.) May 4, 1855-Nov. 24, 1915; House 1911-Nov. 24, 1915.

WITHROW, Gardner Robert (R Wis.) Oct. 5, 1892-Sept. 22, 1964; House 1931-35 (R), 1935-39 (Pro.), 1949-61 (R).

WITTE, William Henry (D Pa.) Oct. 4, 1817-Nov. 24, 1876; House 1853-55.

WOFFORD, Thomas Albert (D S.C.) Sept. 27, 1908; Senate April 5-Nov. 6, 1956.

WOLCOTT, Edward Oliver (R Colo.) March 26, 1848-March 1, 1905; Senate 1889-1901.

WOLCOTT, Jesse Paine (R Mich.) March 3, 1893-Jan. 28, 1969; House 1931-57.

WOLCOTT, Josiah Oliver (D Del.) Oct. 31, 1877-Nov. 11, 1938; Senate 1917-July 2, 1921.

WOLD, John S. (R Wyo.) Aug. 31, 1916; House 1969-71.

WOLF, George (D Pa.) Aug. 12, 1777-March 11, 1840; House Dec. 9, 1824-29; Gov. 1829-35.

WOLF, Harry Benjamin (D Md.) June 16, 1880-Feb. 17, 1944; House 1907-09.

WOLF, Leonard George (D Iowa) Oct. 29, 1925-March 28, 1970; House 1959-61.

WOLF, William Penn (R Iowa) Dec. 1, 1833-Sept. 19, 1896; House Dec. 6, 1870-71.

WOLFE, Simeon Kalfius (D Ind.) Feb. 14, 1824-Nov. 18, 1888; House 1873-75.

WOLFENDEN, James (R Pa.) July 25, 1889-April 8, 1949; House Nov. 6, 1928-47.

WOLFF, Joseph Scott (D Mo.) June 14, 1878-Feb. 27, 1958; House 1923-25.

WOLFF, Lester Lionel (D N.Y.) Jan. 4, 1919; House 1965- .

WOLFORD, Frank Lane (D Ky.) Sept. 2, 1817-Aug. 2, 1895; House 1883-87.

WOLVERTON, Charles Anderson (R N.J.) Oct. 24, 1880-May 16, 1969; House 1927-59.

WOLVERTON, John Marshall (R W.Va.) Jan. 31, 1872-Aug. 19, 1944; House 1925-27, 1929-31.

WOLVERTON, Simon Peter (D Pa.) Jan. 28, 1837-Oct. 25, 1910; House 1891-95.

WOOD, Abiel (F Mass.) July 22, 1772-Oct. 26, 1834; House 1813-15.

WOOD, Alan, Jr. (nephew of John Wood) (R Pa.) July 6, 1834-Oct. 31, 1902; House 1875-77.

WOOD, Amos Eastman (D Ohio) Jan. 2, 1810-Nov. 19, 1850; House Dec. 3, 1849-Nov. 19, 1850.

WOOD, Benjamin (brother of Fernando Wood) (D N.Y.) Oct. 13, 1820-Feb. 21, 1900; House 1861-65; 1881-83.

WOOD, Benson (R Ill.) March 31, 1839-Aug. 27, 1915; House 1895-97.

WOOD, Bradford Ripley (D N.Y.) Sept. 3, 1800-Sept. 26, 1889; House 1845-47.

WOOD, Ernest Edward (D Mo.) Aug. 24, 1875-Jan. 10, 1952; House 1905-June 23, 1906.

WOOD, Fernando (brother of Benjamin Wood) (D N.Y.) June 14, 1812-Feb. 13, 1881; House 1841-43 (Tammany D), 1863-65, 1867-Feb. 13, 1881 (D).

WOOD, Ira Wells (R N.J.) June 19, 1856-Oct. 5, 1931; House Nov. 8, 1904-13.

WOOD, John (uncle of Alan Wood, Jr.) (R Pa.) Sept. 6, 1816-May 28, 1898; House 1859-61.

WOOD, John Jacob (JD N.Y.) Feb. 16, 1784-May 20, 1874; House 1827-29.

WOOD, John M. (R Maine) Nov. 17, 1813-Dec. 24, 1864; House 1855-59.

WOOD, John Stephens (D Ga.) Feb. 8, 1885-Sept. 12, 1968; House 1931-35, 1945-53.

WOOD, John Travers (R Idaho) Nov. 25, 1878-Nov. 2, 1954; House 1951-53.

WOOD, Reuben Terrell (D Mo.) Aug. 7, 1884-July 16, 1955; House 1933-41.

WOOD, Silas (D N.Y.) Sept. 14, 1769-March 2, 1847; House 1819-29.

WOOD, Thomas Jefferson (D Ind.) Sept. 30, 1844-Oct. 13, 1908; House 1883-85.

WOOD, Walter Abbott (R N.Y.) Oct. 23, 1815-Jan. 15, 1892; House 1879-83.

WOOD, William Robert (R Ind.) Jan. 5, 1861-March 7, 1933; House 1915-33.

WOODARD, Frederick Augustus (D N.C.) Feb. 12, 1854-May 8, 1915; House 1893-97.

WOODBRIDGE, Frederick Enoch (R Vt.) Aug. 29, 1818-April 25, 1888; House 1863-69.

WOODBRIDGE, William (W/D Mich.) Aug. 20, 1780-Oct. 20, 1861; House (Terr. Del.) 1819-Aug. 9, 1820; Senate 1841-47; Gov. 1840-41.

WOODBURN, William (R Nev.) April 14, 1838-Jan. 15, 1915; House 1875-77, 1885-89.

WOODBURY, Levi (D N.H.) Dec. 22, 1789-Sept. 4, 1851; Senate March 16, 1825-31, 1841-Nov. 20, 1845; Gov. 1823-24; Secy. of the Navy 1831-34; Secy. of the Treasury 1834-41; Asso. Justice of Supreme Court 1845-51.

WOODCOCK, David (D N.Y.) 1785-Sept. 18, 1835; House 1821-23, 1827-29.

WOODFORD, Stewart Lyndon (R N.Y.) Sept. 3, 1835-Feb. 14, 1913; House 1873-July 1, 1874.

WOODHOUSE, Chase Going (D Conn.) House 1945-47, 1949-51.

WOODMAN, Charles Walhart (R Ill.) March 11, 1844-March 18, 1898; House 1895-97.

WOODRUFF, George Catlin (D Conn.) Dec. 1, 1805-Nov. 21, 1885; House 1861-63.

WOODRUFF, John (AP Conn.) Feb. 12, 1826-May 20, 1868; House 1855-57; 1859-61.

WOODRUFF, Roy Orchard (R Mich.) March 14, 1876-Feb. 12, 1953; House 1913-15 (Pro. R) 1921-53 (R).

WOODRUFF, Thomas M. (D N.Y.) May 3, 1804-March 28, 1855; House 1845-47.

WOODRUM, Clifton Alexander (D Va.) April 27, 1887-Oct. 6, 1950; House 1923-Dec. 31, 1945.

WOODS, Frank Plowman (R Iowa) Dec. 11, 1868-April 25, 1944; House 1909-19.

WOODS, Henry (brother of John Woods) (— Pa.) 1764-1826; House 1799-1803.

WOODS, James Pleasant (D Va.) Feb. 4, 1868-July 7, 1948; House Feb. 25, 1919-23.

WOODS, John (brother of Henry Woods) (F Pa.) 1761-Dec. 16, 1816; House 1815-17.

WOODS, John (W Ohio) Oct. 18, 1794-July 30, 1855; House 1825-29.

WOODS, Samuel Davis (R Calif.) Sept. 19, 1845-Dec. 24, 1915; House Dec. 3, 1900-03.

WOODS, William (D N.Y.) 1790-Aug. 7, 1837; House Nov. 3, 1823-25.

WOODSON, Samuel Hughes (— Ky.) Sept. 15, 1777-July 28, 1827; House 1821-23.

WOODSON, Samuel Hughes (son of the preceding) (AP Mo.) Oct. 24, 1815-June 23, 1881; House 1857-61.

WOODWARD, George Washington (D Pa.) March 26, 1809-May 10, 1875; House Nov. 21, 1867-71.

WOODWARD, Gilbert Motier (D Wis.) Dec. 25, 1835-March 13, 1913; House 1883-85.

WOODWARD, Joseph Addison (D S.C.) April 11, 1806-Aug. 3, 1885; House 1943-53.

WOODWARD, William (— S.C.)—-—; House 1815-17.

WOODWORTH, James Hutchinson (R Ill.) Dec. 4, 1804-March 26, 1869; House 1855-57.

WOODWORTH, Laurin Dewey (R Ohio) Sept. 10, 1837-March 13, 1897; House 1873-77.

WOODWORTH, William W. (D N.Y.) March 16, 1807-Feb. 13, 1873; House 1845-47.

WOODYARD, Harry Chapman (R W. Va.) Nov. 13, 1867-June 21, 1929; House 1903-11, Nov. 7, 1916-23, 1925-27.

WOOMER, Ephraim Milton (R Pa.) Jan. 14, 1844-Nov. 29, 1897; House 1893-97.

WOOTEN, Dudley Goodall (D Texas) June 19, 1860-Feb. 7, 1929; House July 13, 1901-03.

WORCESTER, Samuel Thomas (R Ohio) Aug. 30, 1804-Dec. 6, 1882; House July 4, 1861-63.

WORD, Thomas Jefferson (W Miss.)—-—; House May 30, 1938-39.

WORKS, John Downey (R Calif.) March 29, 1847-June 6, 1928; Senate 1911-17.

WORLEY, Francis Eugene (D Texas) Oct. 10, 1908; House 1941-April 3, 1950.

WORMAN, Ludwig (F Pa.) 1761-Oct. 17, 1822; House 1821-Oct. 17, 1822.

WORTENDYKE, Jacob Reynier (D N.J.) Nov. 27, 1818-Nov. 7, 1868; House 1857-59.

WORTHINGTON, Henry Gaither (R Nev.) Feb. 9, 1828-July 29, 1909; House Oct. 31, 1864-65.

WORTHINGTON, John Tolley Hood (D Md.) Nov. 1, 1788-April 27, 1849; House 1831-33, 1837-41.

WORTHINGTON, Nicholas Ellsworth (D Ill.) March 30, 1836-March 4, 1916; House 1883-87.

WORTHINGTON, Thomas (D Ohio) July 16, 1773-June 20, 1827; Senate April 1, 1803-07, Dec. 15, 1810-Dec. 1, 1814; Gov. 1814-18.

WORTHINGTON, Thomas Contee (nephew of Benjamin Contee) (D Md.) Nov. 25, 1782-April 12, 1847; House 1825-27.

WREN, Thomas (R Nev.) Jan. 2, 1826-Feb. 5, 1904; House 1877-79.

WRIGHT, Ashley Bascom (R Mass.) May 25, 1841-Aug. 14, 1897; House 1893-Aug. 14, 1897.

WRIGHT, Augustus Romaldus (D Ga.) June 16, 1813-March 31, 1891; House 1857-59.

WRIGHT, Charles Frederick (brother of Myron Benjamin Wright) (R Pa.) May 3, 1856-Nov. 10, 1925; House 1899-1905.

WRIGHT, Daniel Boone (D Miss.) Feb. 17, 1812-Dec. 27, 1887; House 1853-57.

WRIGHT, Edwin Ruthvin Vincent (D N.J.) Jan. 2, 1812-Jan. 21, 1871; House 1865-67; Gov. 1869.

WRIGHT, George Grover (brother of Joseph Albert Wright) (R Iowa) March 24, 1820-Jan. 11, 1896; Senate 1871-77.

WRIGHT, George Washington (I Calif.) June 4, 1816-April 7, 1885; House Sept. 11, 1850-51.

WRIGHT, Hendrick Bradley (D Pa.) April 24, 1808-Sept. 2, 1881; House 1853-55; July 4, 1861-63, 1877-81.

WRIGHT, James Assion (D Pa.) Aug. 11, 1902-Nov. 7, 1963; House 1941-45.

WRIGHT, James Claud, Jr. (D Texas) Dec. 22, 1922, House 1955- .

WRIGHT, John Crafts (ad.D Ohio) Aug. 17, 1783-Feb. 13, 1861; House 1823-29.

WRIGHT, John Vines (D Tenn.) June 28, 1828-June 11, 1908; House 1855-61.

WRIGHT, Joseph Albert (brother of George Grover Wright) (D Ind.) April 17, 1810-May 11, 1867; House 1843-45; Senate Feb. 24, 1862-Jan. 14, 1863; Gov. 1849-57.

WRIGHT, Myron Benjamin (brother of Charles Frederick Wright) (R Pa.) June 12, 1847-Nov. 13, 1894; House 1889-Nov. 13, 1894.

WRIGHT, Robert (D Md.) Nov. 20, 1752-Sept. 7, 1826; Senate Nov. 19, 1801-Nov. 12, 1806; House Nov. 29, 1810-17, 1821-23; Gov. 1806-09.

WRIGHT, Samuel Gardiner (W N.J.) Nov. 18, 1781-July 30, 1845; House March 4-July 30, 1845.

WRIGHT, Silas, Jr. (D N.Y.) May 24, 1795-Aug. 27, 1847; House 1827-Feb. 16, 1829; Senate Jan. 4, 1833-Nov. 26, 1844; Gov. 1844-46.

WRIGHT, William (D N.J.) Nov. 13, 1790-Nov. 1, 1866; House 1843-47 (CW); Senate 1853-59, 1863-Nov. 1, 1866 (D).

WRIGHT, William Carter (D Ga.) Jan. 6, 1866-June 11, 1933; House Jan. 24, 1918-33.

WURTS, John (NR Pa.) Aug. 13, 1792-April 23, 1861; House 1825-27.

WURZBACH, Harry McLeary (R Texas) May 19, 1874-Nov. 6, 1931; House 1921-29, Feb. 10, 1930-Nov. 6, 1931.

WYANT, Adam Martin (R Pa.) Sept. 15, 1869-Jan. 5, 1935; House 1921-33.

WYATT, Wendell (R Ore.) June 15, 1917; House Nov. 3, 1964- .

WYDLER, John W. (R N.Y.) June 9, 1924; House 1963- .

WYLIE, Chalmers Pangburn (R Ohio) Nov. 23, 1920; House 1967- .

WYMAN, Louis Crosby (R N.H.) March 16, 1917; House 1963-65, 1967- .

WYNKOOP, Henry (— Pa.) March 2, 1737-March 25, 1816; House 1789-91; Cont. Cong. 1779-83.

WYNN, William Joseph (UL/D Calif.) June 12, 1860-Jan. 4, 1935; House 1903-05.

WYNNS, Thomas (F N.C.) 1764-June 3, 1825; House Dec. 7, 1802-07.

Y

YANCEY, Bartlett (cousin of John Kerr) (— N.C.) Feb. 19, 1785-Aug. 30, 1828; House 1813-17.

YANCEY, Joel (D Ky.) Oct. 21, 1773-April 1838; House 1827-31.

YANCEY, William Lowndes (uncle of Joseph Haynsworth Earle) (D Ala.) Aug. 10, 1814-July 28, 1963; House Dec. 2, 1844-Sept. 1, 1846.

YANGCO, Teodoro Rafael (Nat. P.I.) Nov. 9, 1861-April 20, 1939; House (Res. Comm.) 1917-20.

YAPLE, George Lewis (U Mich.) Feb. 20, 1851-Dec. 16, 1939; House 1883-85.

YARBOROUGH, Ralph Webster (D Texas) June 8, 1903; Senate April 29, 1957-71.

YARDLEY, Robert Morris (R Pa.) Oct. 9, 1850-Dec. 8, 1902; House 1887-91.

YATES, John Barentse (D N.Y.) Feb. 1, 1784-July 10, 1836; House 1815-17.

YATES, Richard (UR Ill.) Jan. 18, 1818-Nov. 27, 1873; House 1851-55 (W); Senate 1865-71 (UR); Gov. 1861-65.

YATES, Richard (son of the preceding) (R Ill.) Dec. 12, 1860-April 11, 1936; House 1919-33; Gov. 1901-04.

YATES, Sidney Richard (D Ill.) Aug. 27, 1909; House 1949-63, 1965- .

YATRON, Gus (D Pa.) Oct. 16, 1927; House 1969- .

YEAMAN, George Helm (U Ky.) Nov. 1, 1829-Feb. 23, 1908; House Dec. 1, 1862-65.

YEATES, Jesse Johnson (D N.C.) May 29, 1829-Sept. 5, 1892; House 1875-79; Jan. 29-March 3, 1881.

YELL, Archibald (VBD Ark.) 1797-Feb. 22, 1847; House Aug. 1, 1836-39; 1845-July 1, 1846; Gov. 1840-44.

YOAKUM, Charles Henderson (D Texas) July 10, 1849-Jan. 1, 1909; House 1895-97.

YOCUM, Seth Hartman (R Pa.) Aug. 2, 1834-April 19, 1895; House 1879-81.

YODER, Samuel S. (D Ohio) Aug. 16, 1841-May 11, 1921; House 1887-91.

YON, Thomas Alva (D Fla.) March 14, 1882-Feb. 16, 1971; House 1927-33.

YORK, Tyre (LD N.C.) May 4, 1836-Jan. 28, 1916; House 1883-85.

YORKE, Thomas Jones (W N.J.) March 25, 1801-April 4, 1882; House 1837-39, 1841-43.

YORTY, Samuel William (D Calif.) Oct. 1, 1909; House 1951-55.

YOST, Jacob (R Va.) April 1, 1853-Jan. 25, 1933; House 1887-89, 1897-99.

YOST, Jacob Senewell (D Pa.) July 29, 1801-March 7, 1872; House 1843-47.

YOUMANS, Henry Melville (D Mich.) May 15, 1832-July 8, 1920; House 1891-93.

YOUNG, Augustus (W Vt.) March 20, 1784-June 17, 1857; House 1841-43.

YOUNG, Bryan Rust (brother of William Singleton Young and uncle of John Young Brown) (D Ky.) Jan. 14, 1800-May 14, 1882; House 1845-47.

YOUNG, Clarence Clifton (R Nev.) Nov. 7, 1922; House 1953-57.

YOUNG, C. W. Bill (R Fla.) Dec. 16, 1930; House 1971- .

YOUNG, Ebenezer (F Conn.) Dec. 25, 1783-Aug. 18, 1851; House 1829-35.

YOUNG, George Morley (R N.D.) Dec. 11, 1870-May 27, 1932; House 1913-Sept. 2, 1924.

YOUNG, Hiram Casey (D Tenn.) Dec. 14, 1828-Aug. 17, 1899; House 1875-81, 1833-85.

YOUNG, Horace Olin (R Mich.) Aug. 4, 1850-Aug. 5, 1917; House 1903-May 16, 1913.

YOUNG, Isaac Daniel (R Kan.) March 29, 1849-Dec. 10, 1927; House 1911-13.

YOUNG, James (D Texas) July 18, 1866-April 29, 1942; House 1911-21.

YOUNG, James Rankin (R Pa.) March 10, 1847-Dec. 18, 1924; House 1897-1903.

YOUNG, John (W N.Y.) June 12, 1802-April 23, 1852; House Nov. 9, 1836-37, 1841-43; Gov. 1847-49.

YOUNG, John Andrew (D Texas) Nov. 10, 1916; House 1957- .

YOUNG, John Duncan (D Ky.) Sept. 22, 1823-Dec. 26, 1910; House 1873-75.

YOUNG, John Smith (D La.) Nov. 4, 1834-Oct. 11, 1916; House Nov. 5, 1878-79.

YOUNG, Lafayette (R Iowa) May 10, 1848-Nov. 15, 1926; Senate Nov. 12, 1910-April 11, 1911.

YOUNG, Milton Ruben (R N.D.) Dec. 6, 1897; Senate March 12, 1945- .

YOUNG, Pierce Manning Butler (D Ga.) Nov. 15, 1836-July 6, 1896; House July 25, 1868-69, Dec. 22, 1870-75.

YOUNG, Richard (R N.Y.) Aug. 6, 1846-June 9, 1935; House 1909-11.

YOUNG, Richard Montgomery (D Ill.) Feb. 20, 1798-Nov. 28, 1861; Senate 1837-43.

YOUNG, Stephen Marvin (D Ohio) May 4, 1889; House 1933-37, 1941-43, 1949-51; Senate 1959-71.

YOUNG, Thomas Lowry (R Ohio) Dec. 14, 1832-July 20, 1888; House 1879-83.

YOUNG, Timothy Roberts (D Ill.) Nov. 19, 1811-May 12, 1898; House 1949-51.

YOUNG, William Albin (D Va.) May 17, 1860-March 12, 1928; House 1897-April 26, 1898, 1899-March 12, 1900.

YOUNG, William Singleton (brother of Bryan Rust Young and uncle of John Young Brown) (D Ky.) April 10, 1790-Sept. 20, 1827; House 1825-Sept. 20, 1827.

YOUNGBLOOD, Harold Francis (R Mich.) Aug. 7, 1907; House 1947-49.

YOUNGDAHL, Oscar Ferdinand (R Minn.) Oct. 13, 1893-Feb. 3, 1946; House 1939-43.

YOUNGER, Jesse Arthur (R Calif.) April 11, 1893-June 20, 1967; House 1953-June 20, 1967.

YULEE, David Levy (formerly David Levy) (R Fla.) June 12, 1810-Oct. 10, 1886; House (Terr. Del.) 1841-45; Senate July 1, 1845-51, 1855-Jan. 21, 1861.

Z

ZABLOCKI, Clement John (D Wis.) Nov. 18, 1912; House 1949- .

ZELENKO, Herbert (D N.Y.) March 16, 1906; House 1955-63.

ZENOR, William Taylor (D Ind.) April 30, 1846-June 2, 1916; House 1897-1907.

ZIEGLER, Edward Danner (D Pa.) March 3, 1844-Dec. 21, 1931; House 1899-1901.

ZIHLMAN, Frederick Nicholas (R Md.) Oct. 2, 1879-April 22, 1935; House 1917-31.

ZIMMERMAN, Orville (D Mo.) Dec. 31, 1880-April 7, 1948; House 1935-April 7, 1948.

ZION, Roger H. (R Ind.) Sept. 17, 1921; House 1967- .

ZIONCHECK, Marion Anthony (D Wash.) Dec. 5, 1901-Aug. 7, 1936; House 1933-Aug. 7, 1936.

ZOLLICOFFER, Felix Kirk (SRW Tenn.) May 19, 1812-Jan. 19, 1862; House 1853-59.

ZWACH, John M. (R Minn.) Feb. 8, 1907; House 1967- .

Appendix—The Constitutional Beginnings

Documents Relating to Chapter 1

Declaration of Independence

When in the Course of human events, it becomes necessary for one people to dissolve the political bands which have connected them with another, and to assume among the powers of the earth, the separate and equal station to which the Laws of Nature and of Nature's God entitle them, a decent respect to the opinions of mankind requires that they should declare the causes which impel them to the separation.

We hold these truths to be self-evident, that all men are created equal, that they are endowed by their Creator with certain unalienable Rights, that among these are Life, Liberty and the pursuit of Happiness. That to secure these rights, Governments are instituted among Men, deriving their just powers from the consent of the governed. That whenever any Form of Government becomes destructive of these ends, it is the Right of the People to alter or to abolish it, and to institute new Government, laying its foundation on such principles and organizing its powers in such form, as to them shall seem most likely to effect their Safety and Happiness. Prudence, indeed, will dictate that Governments long established should not be changed for light and transient causes; and accordingly all experience hath shewn that mankind are more disposed to suffer, while evils are sufferable, than to right themselves by abolishing the forms to which they are accustomed. But when a long train of abuses and usurpations, pursuing invariably the same Object evinces a design to reduce them under absolute Despotism, it is their right, it is their duty, to throw off such Government, and to provide new Guards for their future security. Such has been the patient sufferance of these Colonies; and such is now the necessity which constrains them to alter their former Systems of Government. The history of the present King of Great Britain is a history of repeated injuries and usurpations, all having in direct object the establishment of an absolute Tyranny over these States. To prove this, let Facts be submitted to a candid world.

He has refused his Assent to Laws, the most wholesome and necessary for the public good.

He has forbidden his Governors to pass Laws of immediate and pressing importance, unless suspended in their operation till his Assent should be obtained; and when so suspended he has utterly neglected to attend to them.

He has refused to pass other Laws for the accommodation of large districts of people, unless those people would relinquish the right of Representation in the Legislature, a right inestimable to them and formidable to tyrants only.

He has called together legislative bodies at places unusual, uncomfortable, and distant from the depository of their public Records, for the sole purpose of fatiguing them into compliance with his measures.

He has dissolved Representative Houses repeatedly, for opposing with manly firmness his invasion on the rights of the people.

He has refused for a long time, after such dissolutions, to cause others to be elected; whereby the Legislative powers, incapable of Annihilation, have returned to the People at large for their exercise; the State remaining in the mean time exposed to all the dangers of invasion from without, and convulsions within.

He has endeavoured to prevent the population of these States; for that purpose obstructing the Laws for Naturalization of Foreigners; refusing to pass others to encourage their migrations hither, and raising the conditions of new Appropriations of Lands.

He has obstructed the Administration of Justice, by refusing his Assent to Laws for establishing Judiciary powers.

He has made Judges dependent on his Will alone, for the tenure of their offices, and the amount and payment of their salaries.

He has erected a multitude of New Offices, and sent hither swarms of Officers to harrass our people, and eat out their substance.

He has kept among us, in times of peace, Standing Armies without the Consent of our legislatures.

He has affected to render the Military independent of and superior to the Civil power.

He has combined with others to subject us to a jurisdiction foreign to our constitution, and unacknowledged by our laws; giving his Assent to their Acts of pretended Legislation:

For quartering large bodies of armed troops among us:

For protecting them, by a mock Trial, from punishment for any Murders which they should commit on the Inhabitants of these States:

For cutting off our Trade with all parts of the world:

For imposing Taxes on us without our Consent:

For depriving us in many cases, of the benefits of Trial by Jury:

For transporting us beyond Seas to be tried for pretended offences:

For abolishing the free System of English Laws in a neighbouring Province, establishing therein an Arbitrary government, and enlarging its Boundaries so as to render it at once an example and fit instrument for introducing the same absolute rule into these Colonies:

For taking away our Charters, abolishing our most valuable Laws, and altering fundamentally the Forms of our Governments:

For suspending our own Legislatures, and declaring themselves invested with power to legislate for us in all cases whatsoever.

He has abdicated Government here, by declaring us out of his Protection and waging War against us.

He has plundered our seas, ravaged our Coasts, burnt our towns, and destroyed the lives of our people.

He is at this time transporting large Armies of foreign Mercenaries to compleat the works of death, desolation and tyranny, already begun with circumstances of Cruelty & perfidy scarcely paralleled in the most barbarous ages, and totally unworthy of the Head of a civilized nation.

He has constrained our fellow Citizens taken Captive on the high Seas to bear Arms against their Country, to become the executioners of their friends and Brethren, or to fall themselves by their Hands.

He has excited domestic insurrections amongst us, and has endeavoured to bring on the inhabitants of our frontiers, the merciless Indian Savages, whose known rule of warfare is an undistinguished destruction of all ages, sexes and conditions.

In every stage of these Oppressions We have Petitioned for Redress in the most humble terms: Our repeated Petitions have been answered only by repeated injury. A Prince, whose character is thus marked by every act which may define a Tyrant, is unfit to be the ruler of a free people.

Nor have We been wanting in attentions to our British brethren. We have warned them from time to time of attempts by their legislature to extend an unwarrantable jurisdiction over us. We have reminded them of the circumstances of our emigration and settlement here. We have appealed to their native justice and magnanimity, and we have conjured them by the ties of our common kindred to disavow these usurpations, which would inevitably interrupt our connections and correspondence. They too have been deaf to the voice of justice and of consanguinity. We must, therefore, acquiesce in the necessity, which denounces our Separation, and hold them, as we hold the rest of mankind, Enemies in War, in Peace Friends.

We, therefore, the Representatives of the United States of America, in General Congress, Assembled, appealing to the Supreme Judge of the world for the rectitude of our intentions, do, in the Name, and by authority of the good People of these Colonies, solemnly publish and declare, That these United Colonies are, and of Right ought to be Free and Independent States; that they are Absolved from all Allegiance to the British Crown, and that all political connection between them and the State of Great Britain, is and ought to be totally dissolved; and that as Free and Independent States, they have full Power to levy War, conclude Peace, contract Alliances, establish Commerce, and do all other Acts and Things which Independent States may of right do. And for the support of this Declaration, with a firm reliance on the protection of divine Providence, we mutually pledge to each other our Lives, our Fortunes, and our sacred Honor.

July 4, 1776   John Hancock

New Hampshire: Josiah Bartlett, William Whipple, Matthew Thornton.

Massachusetts Bay: Samuel Adams, John Adams, Robert Treat Paine, Elbridge Gerry.

Rhode Island: Stephen Hopkins, William Ellery.

Connecticut: Roger Sherman, Samuel Huntington, William Williams, Oliver Wolcott.

New York: William Floyd, Philip Livingston, Francis Lewis, Lewis Morris.

New Jersey: Richard Stockton, John Witherspoon, Francis Hopkinson, John Hart, Abraham Clark.

Pennsylvania: Robert Morris, Benjamin Rush, Benjamin Franklin, John Morton, George Clymer, James Smith, George Taylor, James Wilson, George Ross.

Delaware: Caesar Rodney, George Read, Thomas McKean.

Maryland: Samuel Chase, William Paca, Thomas Stone, Charles Carroll of Carrollton.

Virginia: George Wythe, Richard Henry Lee, Thomas Jefferson, Benjamin Harrison, Thomas Nelson Jr., Francis Lightfoot Lee, Carter Braxton.

North Carolina: William Hooper, Joseph Hewes, John Penn.

South Carolina: Edward Rutledge, Thomas Heyward Jr., Thomas Lynch Jr., Arthur Middleton.

Georgia: Button Gwinnett, Lyman Hall, George Walton.

Articles of Confederation

To all to whom these Presents shall come, we the undersigned Delegates of the States affixed to our Names, send greetings. Whereas the Delegates of the United States of America in Congress assembled did on the 15th day of November in the Year of our Lord One Thousand Seven Hundred and Seventy seven, and in the Second Year of the Independence of America agree to certain articles of Confederation and perpetual Union between the states of Newhampshire, Massachusetts-bay, Rhodeisland and Providence Plantations, Connecticut, New York, New Jersey, Pennsylvania, Delaware, Maryland, Virginia, North Carolina, South Carolina and Georgia in the Words following, viz. "Articles of Confederation and perpetual Union between the states of Newhampshire, Massachusetts-bay, Rhodeisland and Providence Plantations, Connecticut, New York, New Jersey, Pennsylvania, Delaware, Maryland, Virginia, North Carolina, South Carolina and Georgia.

Article I. The Stile of the confederacy shall be "The United States of America."

Article II. Each State retains its Sovereignty, freedom and independence, and every Power, Jurisdiction and right, which is not by this confederation expressly delegated to the United States in Congress assembled.

Article III. The said states hereby severally enter into a firm league of friendship with each other, for their common defence, the security of their Liberties, and their mutual and general welfare, binding themselves to assist each other, against all force offered to, or attacks made upon them, or any of them, on account of religion, sovereignty, trade, or any other pretence whatever.

Article IV. The better to secure and perpetuate mutual friendship and intercourse among the people of the different states in this union, the free inhabitants of each of these states, paupers, vagabonds and fugitives from Justice excepted, shall be entitled to all privileges and immunities of free citizens in the several states, and the people of each state shall have free ingress and regress to and from any other state, and shall enjoy therein all the privileges of trade and commerce, subject to the same duties, impositions and restrictions as the inhabitants thereof respectively, provided that such restrictions shall not extend so far as to prevent the removal of property imported into any state, to any other state of which the Owner is an inhabitant, provided also that no imposition, duties or restriction shall be laid by any state, on the property of the united states, or either of them.

If any Person guilty of, or charged with treason, felony or other high misdemeanor in any state, shall flee from Justice, and be found in any of the united states, he shall upon demand of the Governor or executive power, of the state from which he fled, be delivered up and removed to the state having jurisdiction of his offence.

Full faith and credit shall be given in each of these states to the records, acts and judicial proceedings of the courts and magistrates of every other state.

Article V. For the more convenient management of the general interest of the united states, delegates shall be annually appointed in such manner as the legislature of each state shall direct, to meet in Congress on the first Monday in November, in every year, with a power reserved to each state, to recall its delegates, or any of them, at any time within the year, and to send others in their stead, for the remainder of the Year.

No state shall be represented in Congress by less than two, nor by more than seven Members; and no person shall be capable of being a delegate for more than three years in any term of six years; nor shall any person, being a delegate, be capable of holding any office under the united states, for which he, or another for his benefit receives any salary, fees or emolument of any kind.

Each state shall maintain its own delegates in a meeting of the states, and while they act as members of the committee of the states.

In determining questions in the united states, in Congress assembled, each state shall have one vote.

Freedom of speech and debate in Congress shall not be impeached or questioned in any Court, or place out of Congress, and the members of congress shall be protected in their persons from arrests and imprisonments, during the time of their going to and from and attendance on congress, except for treason, felony, or breach of the peace.

Article VI. No state without the Consent of the united states in congress assembled, shall send any embassy to, or receive any embassy from, or enter into any conference, agreement, alliance or treaty with any King, prince or state; nor shall any person holding any office of profit or trust under the united states, or any of them, accept of any present, emolument, office or title of any kind whatever from any king, prince or foreign state; nor shall the united states in congress assembled, or any of them, grant any title of nobility.

No two or more states shall enter into any treaty, confederation or alliance whatever between them, without the consent of the united states in congress assembled, specifying accurately the purposes for which the same is to be entered into, and how long it shall continue.

No state shall lay any imposts of duties, which may interfere with any stipulations in treaties, entered into by the united states in congress assembled with any king, prince or state, in pursuance of any treaties already proposed by congress to the courts of France and Spain.

No vessels of war shall be kept up in time of peace by any state, except such number only, as shall be deemed necessary by the united states in congress assembled, for the defence of such state, or its trade; nor shall any body of forces be kept up by any state, in time of peace, except such number only, as in the judgment of the united states, in congress assembled, shall be deemed requisite to garrison the forts necessary for the defence of such state; but every state shall always keep up a well regulated and disciplined militia, sufficiently armed and accoutred, and shall provide and constantly have ready for use, in public stores, a due number of field-pieces and tents, and a proper quantity of arms, ammunition and camp equipage.

No state shall engage in any war without the consent of the united states in congress assembled, unless such state be actually invaded by enemies, or shall have received certain advice of a resolution being formed by some nation of Indians to invade such state, and the danger is so imminent as not to admit of a delay, till the united states in congress assembled can be consulted: nor shall any state grant commissions to any ships or vessels of war, nor letters of marque or reprisal, except it be after a declaration of war by the united states in Congress assembled, and then only against the kingdom or state and the subjects thereof, against which war has been so declared, and under such regulations as shall be established by the united states in congress assembled, unless such state be infested by pirates, in which case vessels of war may be fitted out for that occasion, and kept so long as the danger shall continue, or until the united states in congress assembled shall determine otherwise.

Article VII. When land-forces are raised by any state for the common defence, all officers of or under the rank of colonel, shall be appointed by the legislature of each state respectively by whom such forces shall be raised, or in such manner as such state shall direct, and all vacancies shall be filled up by the state which first made the appointment.

Article VIII. All charges of war, and all other expences that shall be incurred for the common defence or general welfare, and allowed by the united states in congress assembled, shall be defrayed out of a common treasury, which shall be supplied by the several states, in proportion to the value of all land within each state, granted to or surveyed for any Person, as such land and the buildings and improvements thereon shall be estimated according to such mode as the united states in congress assembled, shall from time to time direct and appoint.

The taxes for paying that proportion shall be laid and levied by the authority and direction of the legislature of the several states within the time agreed upon by the united states in congress assembled.

Article IX. The united states in congress assembled, shall have the sole and exclusive right and power of determining on peace and war, except in the cases mentioned in the sixth article—of sending and receiving embassadors—entering into treaties and alliances, provided that no treaty of commerce shall be made whereby the legislative power of the respective states shall be restrained from imposing such imposts and duties on foreigners, as their own people are subjected to, or from prohibiting the exportation or importation of any species of goods or commodities whatsoever—of establishing rules for deciding in all cases, what captures on land or water shall be legal, and in what manner prizes taken by land or naval forces in the service of the united states shall be divided or appropriated—of granting letters of marque and reprisal in times of peace—appointing courts for the trial of piracies and felonies committed on the high seas and establishing courts for receiving and determining finally appeals in all cases of captures, provided that no member of congress shall be appointed a judge of any of the said courts.

The united states in congress assembled shall also be the last resort on appeal in all disputes and differences now subsisting or that hereafter may arise between two or more states concerning boundary, jurisdiction or any other cause whatever, which authority shall always be exercised in the manner following. Whenever the legislative or executive authority or lawful agent of any state in controversy with another shall present a petition to congress stating the matter in question and praying for a hearing, notice thereof shall be given by order of congress to the legislative or executive authority of the other state in controversy, and a day assigned for the appearance of the parties by their lawful agents, who shall then be directed to appoint by joint consent, commissioners or judges to constitute a court for hearing and determining the matter in question: but if they cannot agree, congress shall name three persons out of each of the united states, and from the list of such persons each party shall alternately strike out one, the petitioners beginning, until the number shall be reduced to thirteen; and from that number not less than seven, nor more than nine names as congress shall direct, shall in the presence of congress be drawn out by lot, and the persons whose names shall be so drawn or any five of them, shall be commissioners or judges, to hear and finally determine the controversy, so always as a major part of the judges who shall hear the cause shall agree in the determination: and if either party shall neglect to attend at the day appointed, without showing reasons, which congress shall judge sufficient, or being present shall refuse to strike, the congress shall proceed to nominate three persons out of each State, and the secretary of congress shall strike in behalf of such party absent or refusing; and the judgment and sentence of the court to be appointed, in the manner before prescribed, shall be final and conclusive; and if any of the parties shall refuse to submit to the authority of such court, or to appear or defend their claim or cause, the court shall nevertheless proceed to pronounce sentence, or judgment, which shall in like manner be final and decisive, the judgment or sentence and other proceedings being in either case transmitted to congress, and lodged among the acts of congress for the security of the parties concerned: provided that every commissioner, before he sits in judgment, shall take an oath to be administered by one of the judges of the supreme or superior court of the state, where the cause shall be tried, "well and truly to hear and determine the matter in question, according to the best of his judgment without favour, affection or hope of reward": provided also that no state shall be deprived of territory for the benefit of the united states.

All controversies concerning the private right of soil claimed under different grants of two or more states, whose jurisdiction as they may respect such lands, and the states which passed such grants are adjusted, the said grants or either of them being at the same time claimed to have originated antecedent to such settlement of jurisdiction, shall on the petition of either party to the congress of the united states, be finally determined as near as may be in the same manner as is before prescribed for deciding disputes respecting territorial jurisdiction between different states.

The united states in congress assembled shall also have the sole and exclusive right and power of regulating the alloy and value of coin struck by their own authority, or by that of the respective states—fixing the standard of weights and measures throughout the united states—regulating the trade and managing all affairs with the Indians, not members of any of the states, provided that the legislative right of any state within its own limits be not infringed or violated—establishing and regulating post-offices from one state to another, throughout all the united states, and exacting such postage on the papers passing thro' the same as may be requisite to defray the expenses of the said office—appointing all officers of the land forces, in the service of the united states, excepting regimental officers—appointing all the officers of the naval forces, and commissioning all officers whatever in the service of the united states—making rules for the government and regulation of the said land and naval forces, and directing their operations.

The united states in congress assembled shall have authority to appoint a committee, to sit in the recess of congress, to be denominated "A Committee of the States," and to consist of one delegate from each state; and to appoint such other committees and civil officers as may be necessary for managing the general affairs of the united states under their direction—to appoint one of their number to preside, provided that no person be allowed to serve in the office of president more than one year in any term of three years; to ascertain the necessary sums of Money to be raised for the service of the united states, and to appropriate and apply the same for defraying the public expences—to borrow money, or emit bills on the credit of the united states, transmitting every half year to the respective states an account of the sums of moneys so borrowed or emitted,—to build and equip a navy—to agree upon the number of land forces, and to make requisitions from each state for its quota, in proportion to the number of white inhabitants in such state; which requisitions shall be binding, and thereupon the legislature of each state shall appoint the regimental officers, raise the men and cloath, arm and equip them in a soldier like manner, at the expence of the united states; and the officers and men so cloathed, armed and equipped shall march to the place appointed, and within the time agreed on by the united states in congress assembled: But if the united states in congress assembled shall, on consideration of circumstances judge proper that any state should not raise men, or should raise a smaller number than its quota, and that any other state should raise a greater number of men than the quota thereof, such extra number shall be raised, officered, cloathed, armed and equipped in the same manner as the quota of such state, unless the legislature of such state shall judge that such extra number cannot be safely spared out of the same, in which case they shall raise, officer, cloath, arm and equip as many of such extra number as they

judge can be safely spared. And the officers and men so cloathed, armed and equipped, shall march to the place appointed, and within the time agreed on by the united states in congress assembled.

The united states in congress assembled shall never engage in a war, nor grant letters of marque and reprisal in time of peace, nor enter into any treaties or alliances, nor coin money, nor regulate the value thereof, nor ascertain the sums and expences necessary for the defence and welfare of the united states, or any of them, nor emit bills, nor borrow money on the credit of the united states, nor appropriate money, nor agree upon the number of vessels of war, to be built or purchased, or the number of land or sea forces to be raised, nor appoint a commander-in-chief of the army or navy, unless nine states assent to the same; nor shall a question on any other point, except for adjourning from day to day be determined, unless by the votes of a majority of the united states in congress assembled.

The Congress of the united states shall have power to adjourn to any time within the year, and to any place within the united states, so that no period of adjournment be for a longer duration than the space of six Months, and shall publish the Journal of their proceedings monthly, except such parts thereof relating to treaties, alliances or military operations as in their judgment require secrecy; and the yeas and nays of the delegates of each state on any question shall be entered on the Journal, when it is desired by any delegate; and the delegates of a state, or any of them, at his or their request shall be furnished with a transcript of the said Journal, except such parts as are above excepted, to lay before the legislatures of the several states.

Article X. The committee of the states, or any nine of them, shall be authorized to execute, in the recess of congress such of the powers of congress as the united states in congress assembled, by the consent of nine states, shall from time to time think expedient to vest them with; provided that no power be delegated to the said committee, for the exercise of which, by the articles of confederation, the voice of nine states in the congress of the united states assembled is requisite.

Article XI. Canada acceding to this confederation, and joining in the measures of the united states, shall be admitted into, and entitled to all the advantages of this union: but no other colony shall be admitted into the same, unless such admission be agreed to by nine states.

Article XII. All bills of credit emitted, monies borrowed and debts contracted by, or under the authority of congress, before the assembling of the united states, in pursuance of the present confederation, shall be deemed and considered as a charge against the united states, for payment and satisfaction whereof the said united states, and the public faith are hereby solemnly pledged.

Article XIII. Every state shall abide by the determinations of the united states in congress assembled, on all questions which by this confederation are submitted to them. And the Articles of this confederation shall be inviolably observed by every state, and the union shall be perpetual; nor shall any alteration at any time hereafter be made in any of them; unless such alteration be agreed to in a congress of the united states, and be afterwards confirmed by the legislatures of every state.

And whereas it has pleased the Great Governor of the World to incline the hearts of the legislatures we respectively represent in congress, to approve of, and to authorize us to ratify the said articles of confederation and perpetual union. Know ye that we the undersigned delegates, by virtue of the power and authority to us given for that purpose, do by these presents, in the name and in behalf of our respective constituents, fully and entirely ratify and confirm each and every of the said articles of confederation and perpetual union, and all and singular the matters and things therein contained: And we do further solemnly plight and engage the faith of our respective constituents, that they shall abide by the determinations of the united states in congress assembled, on all questions, which by the said confederation are submitted to them. And that the articles thereof shall be inviolably observed by the states we respectively represent, and that the union shall be perpetual.

In witness whereof we have hereunto set our hands in Congress. Done at Philadelphia in the state of Pennsylvania the ninth Day of July in the Year of our Lord one Thousand seven Hundred and Seventy-eight, and in the third year of the independence of America.

New Hampshire: Josiah Bartlett, John Wentworth Jr.

Massachusetts Bay: John Hancock, Samuel Adams, Elbridge Gerry, Francis Dana, James Lovell, Samuel Holten.

Rhode Island: William Ellery, Henry Marchant, John Collins.

Connecticut: Roger Sherman, Samuel Huntington, Oliver Wolcott, Titus Hosmer, Andrew Adams.

New York: James Duane, Francis Lewis, William Duer, Gouverneur Morris.

New Jersey: John Witherspoon, Nathaniel Scudder.

Pennsylvania: Robert Morris, Daniel Roberdeau, Jonathan Bayard Smith, William Clingan, Joseph Reed.

Delaware: John Dickinson, Nicholas Van Dyke, Thomas McKean.
Maryland: John Hanson, Daniel Carroll.
Virginia: Richard Henry Lee, John Banister, Thomas Adams, John Harvie, Francis Lightfoot Lee.

North Carolina: John Penn, Cornelius Harnett, John Williams.
South Carolina: Henry Laurens, William Henry Drayton, John Mathews, Richard Hutson, Thomas Heyward Jr.
Georgia: John Walton, Edward Telfair, Edward Langworthy.

Constitution of the United States

We the People of the United States, in Order to form a more perfect Union, establish Justice, insure domestic Tranquility, provide for the common defence, promote the general Welfare, and secure the Blessings of Liberty to ourselves and our Posterity, do ordain and establish this Constitution for the United States of America.

Article I

Section 1. All legislative Powers herein granted shall be vested in a Congress of the United States, which shall consist of a Senate and House of Representatives.

Section 2. The House of Representatives shall be composed of Members chosen every second Year by the People of the several States, and the Electors in each State shall have the Qualifications requisite for Electors of the most numerous Branch of the State Legislature.

No Person shall be a Representative who shall not have attained to the age of twenty five Years, and been seven Years a Citizen of the United States, and who shall not, when elected, be an Inhabitant of that State in which he shall be chosen.

Representatives and direct Taxes shall be apportioned among the several States which may be included within this Union, according to their respective Numbers, which shall be determined by adding to the whole Number of free Persons, including those bound to Service for a Term of Years, and excluding Indians not taxed, three fifths of all other Persons. The actual Enumeration shall be made within three Years after the first Meeting of the Congress of the United States, and within every subsequent Term of ten Years, in such Manner as they shall by Law direct. The Number of Representatives shall not exceed one for every thirty Thousand, but each State shall have at Least one Representative; and until such enumeration shall be made, the State of New Hampshire shall be entitled to chuse three, Massachusetts eight, Rhode-Island and Providence Plantations one, Connecticut five, New-York six, New Jersey four, Pennsylvania eight, Delaware one, Maryland six, Virginia ten, North Carolina five, South Carolina five, and Georgia three.

When vacancies happen in the Representation from any State, the Executive Authority thereof shall issue Writs of Election to fill such Vacancies.

The House of Representatives shall chuse their Speaker and other Officers; and shall have the sole Power of Impeachment.

Section 3. The Senate of the United States shall be composed of two Senators from each State, chosen by the Legislature thereof, for six Years; and each Senator shall have one Vote.

Immediately after they shall be assembled in Consequence of the first Election, they shall be divided as equally as may be into three Classes. The Seats of the Senators of the first Class shall be vacated at the Expiration of the second Year, of the second Class at the Expiration of the fourth Year, and of the third Class at the Expiration of the sixth Year, so that one third may be chosen every second Year, and if Vacancies happen by Resignation, or otherwise, during the Recess of the Legislature of any State, the Executive thereof may make temporary Appointments until the next Meeting of the Legislature, which shall then fill such Vacancies.

No Person shall be a Senator who shall not have attained to the Age of thirty Years, and been nine Years a Citizen of the United States, and who shall not, when elected, be an Inhabitant of that State for which he shall be chosen.

The Vice President of the United States shall be President of the Senate, but shall have no Vote, unless they be equally divided.

The Senate shall chuse their other Officers, and also a President pro tempore, in the Absence of the Vice President, or when he shall exercise the Office of President of the United States.

The Senate shall have the sole Power to try all Impeachments. When sitting for that Purpose, they shall be on Oath or Affirmation. When the President of the United States is tried the Chief Justice shall preside: And no Person shall be convicted without the Concurrence of two thirds of the Members present.

Judgment in Cases of Impeachment shall not extend further than to removal from Office, and disqualification to hold and enjoy any Office of honor, Trust or Profit under the United States: but the Party convicted shall nevertheless be liable and subject to Indictment, Trial, Judgment and Punishment, according to Law.

Section 4. The Times, Places and Manner of holding Elections for Senators and Representatives, shall be prescribed in each State by the Legislature thereof; but the Congress may at any time by Law make or alter such Regulations, except as to the Places of chusing Senators.

The Congress shall assemble at least once in every Year, and such Meeting shall be on the first Monday in December, unless they shall by Law appoint a different Day.

Section 5. Each House shall be the Judge of the Elections, Returns and Qualifications of its own Members, and a Majority of each shall constitute a Quorum to do Business; but a smaller Number may adjourn from day to day, and may be authorized to compel the Attendance of absent Members in such Manner, and under such Penalties as each House may provide.

Each House may determine the Rules of its Proceedings, punish its Members for disorderly Behaviour, and, with the Concurrence of two thirds, expel a Member.

Each House shall keep a Journal of its Proceedings, and from time to time publish the same, excepting such Parts as may in their Judgment require Secrecy; and the Yeas and Nays of the Members of either House on any question shall, at the Desire of one fifth of those Present, be entered on the Journal.

Neither House, during the Session of Congress, shall, without the Consent of the other, adjourn for more than three days, nor to any other Place than that in which the two Houses shall be sitting.

Section 6. The Senators and Representatives shall receive a Compensation for their Services, to be ascertained by Law, and paid out of the Treasury of the United States. They shall in all Cases, except Treason, Felony and Breach of the Peace, be privileged from Arrest during the Attendance at the Session of their respective Houses, and in going to and returning from the same; and for any Speech or Debate in either House, they shall not be questioned in any other Place.

No Senator or Representative shall, during the Time for which he was elected, be appointed to any civil Office under the Authority of the United States, which shall have been created, or the Emoluments whereof shall have been encreased during such time; and no Person holding any Office under the United States, shall be a Member of either House during his Continuance in Office.

Section 7. All Bills for raising Revenue shall originate in the House of Representatives; but the Senate may propose or concur with amendments as on other Bills.

Every Bill which shall have passed the House of Representatives and the Senate, shall, before it become a Law, be presented to the President of the United States; If he approve he shall sign it, but if not he shall return it, with his Objections to that House in which it shall have originated, who shall enter the Ojbections at large on their Journal, and proceed to reconsider it. If after such Reconsideration two thirds of that House shall agree to pass the Bill, it shall be sent, together with the Objections, to the other House, by which it shall likewise be reconsidered, and if approved by two thirds of that House, it shall become a Law. But in all such Cases the Votes of both Houses shall be determined by yeas and Nays, and the Names of the Persons voting for and against the Bill shall be entered on the Journal of each House respectively. If any Bill shall not be returned by the President within ten Days (Sunday excepted) after it shall have been presented to him, the Same shall be a Law, in like Manner as if he had signed it, unless the Congress by their Adjournment prevent its Return, in which Case it shall not be a Law.

Every Order, Resolution, or Vote to which the Concurrence of the Senate and House of Representatives may be necessary (except on a question of Adjournment) shall be presented to the President of the United States; and before the Same shall take Effect, shall be approved by him, or being disapproved by him, shall be repassed by two thirds of the Senate and House of Representatives, according to the Rules and Limitations prescribed in the Case of a Bill.

Section 8. The Congress shall have Power To lay and collect Taxes, Duties, Imposts and Excises, to pay the Debts and provide for the common Defence and general Welfare of the United States; but all Duties, Imposts and Excises shall be uniform throughout the United States;

To borrow Money on the credit of the United States;

To regulate Commerce with foreign Nations, and among the several States, and with the Indian Tribes;

To establish an uniform Rule of Naturalization, and uniform Laws on the subject of Bankruptcies throughout the United States;

To coin Money, regulate the Value thereof, and of foreign Coin, and fix the Standard of Weights and Measures;

To provide for the Punishment of counterfeiting the Securities and current Coin of the United States;

To establish Post Offices and post Roads;

To promote the Progress of Science and useful Arts, by securing for limited Times to Authors and Inventors the exclusive Right to their respective Writings and Discoveries;

To constitute Tribunals inferior to the supreme Court;

To define and punish Piracies and Felonies committed on the high Seas, and Offences against the Law of Nations;

To declare War, grant Letters of Marque and Reprisal, and make Rules concerning Captures on Land and Water;

To raise and support Armies, but no Appropriation of Money to that Use shall be for a longer Term than two Years;

To provide and maintain a Navy;

To make Rules for the Government and Regulation of the land and naval Forces;

To provide for calling forth the Militia to execute the Laws of the Union, suppress Insurrections and repel Invasions;

To provide for organizing, arming, and disciplining, the Militia, and for governing such Part of them as may be employed in the Service of the United States, reserving to the states respectively, the Appointment of the Officers and the Authority of training the Militia according to the discipline prescribed by Congress;

To exercise exclusive Legislation in all Cases whatsoever, over such District (not exceeding ten Miles square) as may, by Cession of Particular States, and the Acceptance of Congress, become the Seat of the Government of the United States, and to exercise like Authority over all Places purchased by the Consent of the Legislature of the State in which the Same shall be, for the Erection of Forts, Magazines, Arsenals, dock-Yards, and other needful Buildings;—And

To make all Laws which shall be necessary and proper for carrying into Execution the foregoing Powers, and all other Powers vested by this Constitution in the Government of the United States, or in any Department or Officer thereof.

Section 9. The Migration or Importation of such Persons as any of the States now existing shall think proper to admit, shall not be prohibited by the Congress prior to the Year one thousand eight hundred and eight, but a Tax or duty may be imposed on such Importation, not exceeding ten dollars for each Person.

The Privilege of the Writ of Habeas Corpus shall not be suspended, unless when in Cases of Rebellion or Invasion the public Safety may require it.

No Bill of Attainder or ex post facto Law shall be passed.

No Capitation, or other direct, Tax shall be laid, unless in Proportion to the Census of Enumeration herein before directed to be taken.

No Tax or Duty shall be laid on Articles exported from any State.

No Preference shall be given by any Regulation of Commerce or Revenue to the Ports of one State over those of another, nor shall Vessels bound to, or from, one State, be obliged to enter, clear or pay Duties in another.

No Money shall be drawn from the Treasury, but in Consequence of Appropriations made by Law; and a regular Statement and Account of the Receipts and Expenditures of all public Money shall be published from time to time.

No Title of Nobility shall be granted by the United States: And no Person holding any Office of Profit or Trust under them, shall, without the Consent of the Congress, accept of any present, Emolument, Office, or Title, of any kind whatever, from any King, Prince or foreign State.

Section 10. No State shall enter into any Treaty, Alliance, or Confederation; grant Letters of Marque and Reprisal; coin Money; emit Bills of Credit; make any Thing but gold and silver Coin a Tender in Payment of Debts; pass any Bill of Attainder, ex post facto Law, or Law impairing the Obligation of Contracts, or grant any Title of Nobility.

No State shall, without the Consent of the Congress, lay any Imposts or Duties on Imports or Exports, except what may be absolutely necessary for executing it's inspection Laws: and the net Produce of all Duties and Imposts, laid by any State on Imports or Exports, shall be for the Use of the Treasury of the United States; and all such Laws shall be subject to the Revision and Controul of the Congress.

No State shall, without the Consent of Congress, lay any Duty of Tonnage, keep Troops, or Ships of War in time of Peace, enter into any Agreement or Compact with another State, or with a foreign Power, or engage in War, unless actually invaded, or in such imminent Danger as will not admit of delay.

Article II

Section 1. The executive Power shall be vested in a President of the United States of America. He shall hold his Office during the Term of four Years, and, together with the Vice President, chosen for the same Term, be elected, as follows

Each State shall appoint, in such Manner as the Legislature thereof may direct, a Number of Electors, equal to the whole Number of Senators and Representatives to which the State may be entitled in the Congress: but no Senator or Representative, or Person holding an Office of Trust or Profit under the United States, shall be appointed an Elector.

The Electors shall meet in their respective States, and vote by Ballot for two Persons, of whom one at least shall not be an Inhabitant of the same State with themselves. And they shall make a List of all the Persons voted for, and of the Number of Votes for each; which List they shall sign and certify, and transmit sealed to the Seat of the Government of the United States, directed to the President of the Senate. The President of the Senate shall, in the Presence of the Senate and House of Representatives, open all the Certificates, and the Votes shall then be counted. The Person having the greatest Number of Votes shall be the President, if such Number be a Majority of the whole Number of Electors appointed; and if there be more than one who have such Majority, and have an equal Number of Votes, then the House of Representatives shall immediately chuse by Ballot one of them for President; and if no Person have a Majority, then from the five highest on the List the said House shall in like Manner chuse the President. But in chusing the President, the Votes shall be taken by States, the Representation from each State having one Vote; a quorum for this Purpose shall consist of a Member or Members from two thirds of the States, and a Majority of all the States shall be necessary to a Choice. In every Case, after the Choice of the President, the Person having the greatest Number of Votes of the Electors shall be the Vice President. But if there should remain two or more who have equal Votes, the Senate shall chuse from them by Ballot the Vice President.

The Congress may determine the Time of chusing the Electors, and the Day on which they shall give their Votes; which Day shall be the same throughout the United States.

No Person except a natural born Citizen, or a Citizen of the United States, at the time of the Adoption of this Constitution, shall be eligible to the Office of President; neither shall any person be eligible to that Office who shall not have attained to the Age of thirty five Years, and been fourteen Years a Resident within the United States.

In Case of the Removal of the President from Office, or of his Death, Resignation, or Inability to discharge the Powers and Duties of the said Office, the Same shall devolve on the Vice President, and the Congress may by Law provide for the Case of Removal, Death, Resignation or Inability, both of the President and Vice President, declaring what Officer shall then act as President, and such Officer shall act accordingly, until the Disability be removed, or a President shall be elected.

The President shall, at stated Times, receive for his Services, a Compensation, which shall neither be encreased nor diminished during the Period for which he shall have been elected, and he shall not receive within that Period any other Emolument from the United States, or any of them.

Before he enter on the Execution of his Office, he shall take the following Oath or Affirmation:—"I do solemnly swear (or affirm) that I will faithfully execute the Office of President of the United States, and will to the best of my Ability, preserve, protect and defend the Constitution of the United States."

Section 2. The President shall be Commander in Chief of the Army and Navy of the United States, and of the Militia of the several States, when called into the actual service of the United States; he may require the Opinion, in writing, of the principal Officer in each of the executive Departments, upon any Subject relating to the Duties of their respective Offices, and he shall have Power to grant Reprieves and Pardons for Offenses against the United States, except in Cases of Impeachment.

He shall have Power, by and with the Advice and Consent of the Senate, to make Treaties, provided two thirds of the Senators present concur; and he shall nominate, and by and with the Advice and Consent of the Senate, shall appoint Ambassadors, other public Ministers and Consuls, Judges of the supreme Court, and all other Officers of the United States, whose Appointments are not herein otherwise, provided for, and which shall be established by Law: but the Congress may by Law vest the Appointment of such inferior Officers, as they think proper, in the President alone, in the Courts of Law, or in the Heads of Departments.

The President shall have Power to fill up all Vacancies that may happen during the Recess of the Senate, by granting Commissions which shall expire at the End of their next Session.

Section 3. He shall from time to time give to the Congress Information of the State of the Union, and recommend to their Consideration such Measures as he shall judge necessary and expedient; he may, on extraordinary Occasions, convene both Houses, or either of them, and in Case of Disagreement between them, with Respect to the Time of Adjournment, he may adjourn them to such Time as he shall think proper; he shall receive Ambassadors and other public Ministers; he shall take Care that the Laws be faithfully executed, and shall Commission all the Officers of the United States.

Section 4. The President, Vice President and all Civil Officers of the United States, shall be removed from Office on Impeachment for, and Conviction of, Treason, Bribery, or other high Crimes and Misdemeanors.

Article III

Section 1. The judicial Power of the United States, shall be vested in one supreme Court, and in such inferior Courts as the Congress may from time to time ordain and establish. The Judges, both of the supreme and inferior Courts, shall hold their Offices during good Behavior, and shall, at stated Times, receive for their Services, a Compensation, which shall not be diminished during their Continuance in Office.

Section 2. The judicial Power shall extend to all Cases, in Law and Equity, arising under this Constitution, the Laws of the United States, and Treaties made, or which shall be made, under their Authority;—to all Cases affecting Ambassadors, other public Ministers and Consuls;—to all Cases of admiralty and maritime Jurisdiction;—to Controversies to which the United States shall be a Party;—to Controversies between two or more States;—between a State and Citizens of another State;—between Citizens of different states;—between Citizens of the same State claiming Lands under Grants of different States, and between a State, or the Citizens thereof, and foreign States, Citizens or Subjects.

In all Cases affecting Ambassadors, other public Ministers and Consuls, and those in which a State shall be Party, the supreme Court shall have original Jurisdiction. In all the other Cases before mentioned, the supreme Court shall have appellate Jurisdiction, both as to Law and Fact, with such Exceptions, and under such Regulations as the Congress shall make.

The Trial of all Crimes, except in cases of Impeachment, shall be by Jury; and such Trial shall be held in the State where the said Crimes shall have been committed; but when not committed within any State, the Trial shall be at such Place or Places as the Congress may by Law have directed.

Section 3. Treason against the United States, shall consist only in levying War against them, or in adhering to their Enemies, giving them Aid and Comfort. No Person shall be convicted of Treason unless on the Testimony of two Witnesses in the same overt Act, or on Confession in open Court.

The Congress shall have Power to declare the Punishment of Treason, but no Attainder of Treason shall work Corruption of Blood, or Forfeiture except during the Life of the Person attainted.

Article IV

Section 1. Full Faith and Credit shall be given in each State to the public Acts, Records, and judicial Proceedings of every other State. And the Congress may by general Laws prescribe the Manner in which such Acts, Records and Proceedings shall be proved, and the Effect thereof.

Section 2. The Citizens of each State shall be entitled to all Privileges and Immunities of Citizens in the several States.

A Person charged in any State with Treason, Felony, or other Crime, who shall flee from Justice, and be found in another State, shall on Demand of the executive Authority of the State from which he fled, be delivered up, to be removed to the State having Jurisdiction of the Crime.

No Person held to Service of Labour in one State, under the Laws thereof, escaping into another, shall, in Consequence of any Law or Regulation therein, be discharged from such Service or Labour, but shall be delivered up on Claim of the Party to whom such Service or Labour may be due.

Section 3. New States may be admitted by the Congress into this Union; but no new State shall be formed or erected within the Jurisdiction of any other State; nor any State be formed by the Junction of two or more States, or Parts of States, without the Consent of the Legislatures of the States concerned as well as of the Congress.

The Congress shall have Power to dispose of and make all needful Rules and Regulations respecting the Territory or other Property belonging to the United States; and nothing in this Constitution shall be so construed as to Prejudice any Claims of the United States, or of any particular State.

Section 4. The United States shall guarantee to every State in this Union a Republican Form of Government, and shall protect each of them against Invasion; and on Application of the Legislature, or of the Executive (when the Legislature cannot be convened) against domestic Violence.

Article V

The Congress, whenever two thirds of both Houses shall deem it necessary, shall propose Amendments to this Constitution, or, on the Application of the Legislatures of two thirds of the several States, shall call a Convention for proposing Amendments, which, in either Case, shall be valid to all Intents and Purposes, as Part of this Constitution, when ratified by the Legislatures of three fourths of the several States, or by Conventions in three fourths thereof, as the one or the other Mode of Ratification may be proposed by the Congress; Provided that no Amendment which may be made prior to the Year One thousand eight hundred and eight shall in any Manner affect the first and fourth Clauses in the Ninth Section of the First Article; and that no State, without its Consent, shall be deprived of its equal Suffrage in the Senate.

Article VI

All Debts contracted and Engagements entered into, before the Adoption of this Constitution, shall be as valid against the United States under this Constitution, as under the Confederation.

This Constitution, and the Laws of the United States which shall be made in Pursuance thereof; and all Treaties made or which shall be made, under the Authority of the United States, shall be the supreme Law of the Land; and the Judges in every State shall be bound thereby, any Thing in the Constitution or Laws of any State to the Contrary notwithstanding.

The Senators and Representatives before mentioned, and the Members of the several State Legislatures, and all executive and judicial Officers, both of the United States and of the several States, shall be bound by Oath or Affirmation, to support this Constitution; but no religious Test shall ever be required as a Qualification to any Office or public Trust under the United States.

Article VII

The Ratification of the Conventions of nine States, shall be sufficient for the Establishment of this Constitution between the States so ratifying the Same. Done in Convention by the Unanimous Consent of the States present the Seventeenth Day of September in the Year of our Lord one thousand seven hundred and Eighty seven and of the Independence of the United States of America the Twelfth In witness whereof We have hereunto subscribed our Names.

George Washington

New Hampshire: John Langdon, Nicholas Gilman.
Massachusetts: Nathaniel Gorham, Rufus King.
Connecticut: William Samuel Johnson, Roger Sherman.
New York: Alexander Hamilton.
New Jersey: William Livingston, David Brearley, William Paterson, Jonathan Dayton.
Pennsylvania: Benjamin Franklin, Thomas Mifflin, Robert Morris, George Clymer, Thomas Fitzsimons, Jared Ingersoll, James Wilson, Gouverneur Morris.
Delaware: George Read, Gunning Bedford Jr., John Dickinson, Richard Bassett, Jacob Broom.
Maryland: James McHenry, Daniel of St. Thomas Jenifer, Daniel Carroll.
Virginia: John Blair, James Madison Jr.
North Carolina: William Blount, Richard Dobbs Spaight, Hugh Williamson.
South Carolina: John Rutledge, Charles Cotesworth Pinckney, Charles Pinckney, Pierce Butler.
Georgia: William Few, Abraham Baldwin.

AMENDMENTS

(Dates given are dates of proclamations declaring the amendments ratified. The proclamation in some cases lagged far behind completion of ratification by the required number of states.)

Amendment I
(First ten amendments ratified Dec. 15, 1791.)

Congress shall make no law respecting an establishment of religion, or prohibiting the free exercise thereof; or abridging the freedom of speech, or of the press; or the right of the people peaceably to assemble, and to petition the Government for a redress of grievances.

Amendment II

A well regulated Militia, being necessary to the security of a free State, the right of the people to keep and bear Arms, shall not be infringed.

Amendment III

No Soldier shall, in time of peace be quartered in any house, without the consent of the Owner, nor in time of war, but in a manner to be prescribed by law.

Amendment IV

The right of the people to be secure in their persons, houses, papers, and effects, against unreasonable searches and seizures, shall not be violated, and no Warrants shall issue, but upon probable cause, supported by Oath or affirmation, and particularly describing the place to be searched, and the persons or things to be seized.

Amendment V

No person shall be held to answer for a capital, or otherwise infamous crime, unless on a presentment or indictment of a Grand Jury, except in cases arising in the land or naval forces, or in the Militia, when in actual service in time of War or public danger; nor shall any person be subject for the same offence to be twice put in jeopardy of life or limb; nor shall be compelled in any criminal case to be a witness against himself, nor be deprived of life, liberty, or property, without due process of law; nor shall private property be taken for public use without just compensation.

Amendment VI

In all criminal prosecutions, the accused shall enjoy the right to a speedy and public trial, by an impartial jury of the State and district wherein the crime shall have been committed, which district shall have been previously ascertained by law, and to be informed of the nature and cause of the accusation; to be confronted with the witnesses against him; to have compulsory process for obtaining witnesses in his favor, and to have the Assistance of Counsel for his defence.

Amendment VII

In suits at common law, where the value in controversy shall exceed twenty dollars, the right of trial by jury shall be preserved, and no fact tried by a jury, shall be otherwise re-examined in any Court of the United States, than according to the rules of the common law.

Amendment VIII

Excessive bail should not be required, nor excessive fines imposed, nor cruel and unusual punishments inflicted.

Amendment IX

The enumeration in the Constitution, of certain rights, shall not be construed to deny or disparage others retained by the people.

Amendment X

The powers not delegated to the United States by the Constitution, nor prohibited by it to the States, are reserved to the States respectively, or to the people.

Amendment XI *(Ratified Jan. 8, 1798)*

The Judicial power of the United States shall not be construed to extend to any suit in law or equity, commenced or prosecuted against one of the United States by Citizens of another State, or by Citizens or Subjects of any Foreign State.

Amendment XII *(Ratified Sept. 25, 1804)*

The Electors shall meet in their respective states and vote by ballot for President and Vice-President, one of whom, at least, shall not be an inhabitant of the same state with themselves; they shall name in their ballots the person voted for as President, and in distinct ballots the person voted for as Vice-President, and they shall make distinct lists of all persons voted for as President, and of all persons voted for as Vice-President, and of the number of votes for each, which lists they shall sign and certify, and transmit sealed to the seat of the government of the United States, directed to the President of the Senate;—The President of the Senate shall, in the presence of the Senate and House of Representatives open all the certificates and the votes shall then be counted; The person having the greatest number of votes for President, shall be the President, if such number be a majority of the whole number of Electors appointed; and if no person have such majority, then from the persons having the highest numbers not exceeding three on the list of those voted for as President, the House of Representatives shall choose immediately, by ballot, the President. But in choosing the President, the votes shall be taken by states, the representation from each state having one vote; a quorum for this purpose shall consist of a member or members from two-thirds of the states, and a majority of all the states shall be necessary to a choice. And if the House of Representatives shall not choose a President whenever the right of choice shall devolve upon them, before the fourth day of March next following, then the Vice-President shall act as President, as in the case of the death or other constitutional disability of the President—The person having the greatest number of votes as Vice-President, shall be the Vice-President, if such number be a majority of the whole number of electors appointed, and if no person have a majority, then from the two highest numbers on the list, the Senate shall choose the Vice-President; a quorum for the purpose shall consist of two-thirds of the whole number of Senators, and a majority of the whole number shall be necessary to a choice. But no person constitutionally ineligible to the office of President shall be eligible to that of Vice-President of the United States.

Amendment XIII *(Ratified Dec. 18, 1865)*

Section 1. Neither slavery nor involuntary servitude, except as a punishment for crime whereof the party shall have been duly convicted, shall exist within the United States, or any place subject to their jurisdiction.

Section 2. Congress shall have power to enforce this article by appropriate legislation.

Amendment XIV *(Ratified July 28, 1868)*

Section 1. All persons born or naturalized in the United States and subject to the jurisdiction thereof, are citizens of the United States and of the States wherein they reside. No State shall make or enforce any law which shall abridge the privileges or immunities of citizens of the United States; or shall any State deprive any person of life, liberty, or property, without due process of law; nor deny to any person within its jurisdiction the equal protection of the laws.

Section 2. Representatives shall be apportioned among the several States according to their respective numbers, counting the whole number of persons in each State, excluding Indians not taxed. But when the right to vote at any election for the choice of electors for President and Vice President of the United States, Representatives in Congress, the Executive and Judicial officers of a State, or the members of the Legislature thereof, is denied to any of the male inhabitants of such State, being twenty-one years of age, and citizens of the United States, or in any way abridged, except for participation in rebellion, or other crime, the basis of representation therein shall be reduced in the proportion which the number of such male citizens shall bear to the whole number of male citizens twenty-one years of age in such State.

Section 3. No person shall be a Senator or Representative in Congress, or elector of President and Vice President, or hold any office, civil or military, under the United States, or under any State, who, having previously taken an oath, as a member of Congress, or as an officer of the United States, or as a member of any State legislature, or as an executive or judicial officer of any State, to support the Constitution of the United States, shall have engaged in insurrection or rebellion against the same, or given aid or comfort to the enemies thereof. But Congress may by a vote of two-thirds of each House, remove such disability.

Section 4. The validity of the public debt of the United States, authorized by law, including debts incurred for payment of pensions and bounties for services in suppressing insurrection or rebellion, shall not be questioned. But neither the United States nor any State shall assume or pay any debt or obligation incurred in aid of insurrection or rebellion against the United States, or any claim for the loss or emancipation of any slave; but all such debts, obligations and claims shall be held illegal and void.

Section 5. The Congress shall have power to enforce, by appropriate legislation, the provisions of this article.

Amendment XV *(Ratified March 30, 1870)*

Section 1. The right of citizens of the United States to vote shall not be denied or abridged by the United States or by any State on account of race, color, or previous condition of servitude.

Section 2. The Congress shall have power to enforce this article by appropriate legislation.

Amendment XVI *(Ratified Feb. 25, 1913)*

The Congress shall have power to lay and collect taxes on incomes, from whatever source derived, without apportionment among the several States, and without regard to any census or enumeration.

Amendment XVII *(Ratified May 31, 1913)*

The Senate of the United States shall be composed of two Senators from each State, elected by the people thereof, for six years; and each Senator shall have one vote. The electors in each State shall have the qualifications requisite for electors of the most numerous branch of the State legislatures.

When vacancies happen in the representation of any State in the Senate, the executive authority of such State shall issue writs of election to fill such vacancies: *Provided*, That the legislature of any State may empower the executive thereof to make temporary appointments until the people fill the vacancies by election as the legislature may direct.

This amendment shall not be so construed as to affect the election or term of any Senator chosen before it becomes valid as part of the Constitution.

Amendment XVIII *(Ratified Jan. 29, 1919)*

Section 1. After one year from the ratification of this article the manufacture, sale, or transportation of intoxicating liquors within, the importation thereof into, or the exportation thereof from the United States and all territory subject to the jurisdiction thereof for beverage purposes is hereby prohibited.

Sec. 2. The Congress and the several States ahall have concurrent power to enforce this article by appropriate legislation.

Sec. 3. This article shall be inoperative unless it shall have been ratified as an amendment to the Constitution by the legislatures of the several States, as provided in the Constitution, within seven years from the date of the submission hereof to the States by the Congress.

Amendment XIX *(Ratified Aug. 26, 1920)*

The right of citizens of the United States to vote shall not be denied or abridged by the United States or by any State on account of sex.

Congress shall have power to enforce this article by appropriate legislation.

Amendment XX *(Ratified Feb. 6, 1933)*

Section 1. The terms of the President and Vice President shall end at noon on the 20th day of January, and the terms of Senators and Representatives at noon on the 3rd day of January, of the years in which such terms would have ended if this article had not been ratified; and the terms of their successors shall then begin.

Sec. 2. The Congress shall assemble at least once in every year, and such meeting shall begin at noon on the 3rd day of January, unless they shall by law appoint a different day.

Sec. 3. If, at the time fixed for the beginning of the term of the President, the President elect shall have died, the Vice President elect shall become President. If a President shall not have been chosen before the time fixed for the beginning of his term, or if the President elect shall have failed to qualify, then the Vice President elect shall act as President until a President shall have qualified; and the Congress may by law provide for the case wherein neither a President elect nor a Vice President elect shall have qualified, declaring who shall then act as President, or the manner in which one who is to act shall be selected, and such person shall act accordingly until a President or Vice President shall have qualified.

Sec. 4. The Congress may by law provide for the case of the death of any of the persons from whom the House of Representatives may choose a President whenever the right of choice shall have devolved upon them, and for the case of the death of any of the persons from whom the Senate may choose a Vice President whenever the right of choice shall have devolved upon them.

Sec. 5. Sections 1 and 2 shall take effect on the 15th day of October following the ratification of this article.

Sec. 6. This article shall be inoperative unless it shall have been ratified as an amendment to the Constitution by the legislatures of three-fourths of the several States within seven years from the date of its submission.

Amendment XXI *(Ratified Dec. 5, 1933)*

Section 1. The eighteenth article of amendment to the Constitution of the United States is hereby repealed.

Sec. 2. The transportation or importation into any State, Territory or possession of the United States for delivery or use therein of intoxicating liquors, in violation of the laws thereof, is hereby prohibited.

Sec. 3. This article shall be inoperative unless it shall have been ratified as an amendment to the Constitution by conventions in the several States, as provided in the Constitution, within seven years from the date of the submission hereof to the States by the Congress.

Amendment XXII *(Ratified March 1, 1951)*

Section 1. No person shall be elected to the office of the President more than twice, and no person who has held the office of President, or acted as President, for more than two years of a term to which some other person was elected President shall be elected to the office of the President more than once. But this Article shall not apply to any person holding the office of President when this Article was proposed by the Congress, and shall not prevent any person who may be holding the office of President, or acting as President, during the term within which this Article becomes operative from holding the office of President or acting as President during the remainder of such term.

Sec. 2. This Article shall be inoperative unless it shall have been ratified as an amendment to the Constitution by the legislatures of three-fourths of the several States within seven years from the date of its submission to the States by the Congress.

Amendment XXIII *(Ratified April 3, 1961)*

Section 1. The District constituting the seat of Government of the United States shall appoint in such manner as the Congress may direct:

A number of electors of President and Vice President equal to the whole number of Senators and Representatives in Congress to which the District would be entitled if it were a State, but in no event more than the least populous State; they shall be in addition to those appointed by the States, but they shall be considered, for the purposes of the election of President and Vice President, to be electors appointed by a State, and they shall meet in the District and perform such duties as provided by the twelfth article of amendment.

Sec. 2. The Congress shall have power to enforce this article by appropriate legislation.

Amendment XXIV *(Ratified Feb. 4, 1964)*

Section 1. The right of citizens of the United States to vote in any primary or other election for President or Vice President, for electors for President or Vice President, or for Senator or Representative in Congress, shall not be denied or abridged by the United States or any State by reason of failure to pay any poll tax or other tax.

Section 2. The Congress shall have power to enforce this article by appropriate legislation.

Amendment XXV *(Ratified Feb. 23, 1967)*

Section 1. In case of the removal of the President from office or of his death or resignation, the Vice President shall become President.

Sec. 2. Whenever there is a vacancy in the office of the Vice President, the President shall nominate a Vice President who shall take office upon confirmation by a majority vote of both Houses of Congress.

Sec. 3 Whenever the President transmits to the President pro tempore of the Senate and the Speaker of the House of Representatives his written declaration that he is unable to discharge the powers and duties of his office, and until he transmits to them a written declaration to the contrary, such powers and duties shall be discharged by the Vice President as Acting President.

Sec. 4. Whenever the Vice President and a majority of either the principal officers of the Executive departments or of such other body as Congress may by law provide transmit to the President pro tempore of the Senate and the Speaker of the House of Representatives their written declaration that the President is unable to discharge the powers and duties of his office, the Vice President shall immediately assume the powers and duties of the office as Acting President.

Thereafter, when the President transmits to the President pro tempore of the Senate and the Speaker of the House of Representatives his written declaration that no inability exists, he shall resume the powers and duties of his office unless the Vice President and a majority of either the principal officers of the executive departments or of such other body as Congress may by law provide transmit within four days to the President pro tempore of the Senate and the Speaker of the House of Repre- sentatives their written declaration that the President is unable to discharge the powers and duties of his office. Thereupon Congress shall decide the issue, assembling within forty-eight hours for that purpose if not in session. If the Congress, within twenty-one days after receipt of the latter written declaration, or, if Congress is not in session, within twenty-one days after Congress is required to assemble, determines by two-thirds vote of both houses that the President is unable to discharge the powers and duties of his office, the Vice President shall continue to discharge the same as Acting President; otherwise, the President shall resume the powers and duties of his office.

Subsidiary Documents of the Pre-Constitutional Period

Source: *Documents of American History*, Henry Steele Commager, ed.

The Albany Plan of Union 1754

It is proposed that humble application be made for an act of Parliament of Great Britain, by virtue of which one general government may be formed in America, including all the said colonies, within and under which government each colony may retain its present constitution, except in the particulars wherein a change may be directed by the said act, as hereafter follows.

1. That the said general government be administered by a President-General, to be appointed and supported by the crown; and a Grand Council, to be chosen by the representatives of the people of the several Colonies met in their respective assemblies.

2. That within — months after the passing such act, the House of Representatives that happen to be sitting within that time, or that shall be especially for that purpose convened, may and shall choose members for the Grand Council, in the following proportion, that is to say,

Massachusetts Bay	7
New Hampshire	2
Connecticut	5
Rhode Island	2
New York	4
New Jersey	3
Pennsylvania	6
Maryland	4
Virginia	7
North Carolina	4
South Carolina	4
	48

3. —who shall meet for the first time at the city of Philadelphia, being called by the President-General as soon as conveniently may be after his appointment.

4. That there shall be a new election of the members of the Grand Council every three years; and, on the death or resignation of any member, his place should be supplied by a new choice at the next sitting of the Assembly of the Colony he represented.

5. That after the first three years, when the proportion of money arising out of each Colony to the general treasury can be known, the number of members to be chosen for each Colony shall, from time to time, in all ensuing elections, be regulated by that proportion, yet so as that the number to be chosen by any one Province be not more than seven, nor less than two.

6. That the Grand Council shall meet once in every year, and oftener if occasion require, at such time and place as they shall adjourn to at the last preceding meeting, or as they shall be called to meet at by the President-General on any emergency; he having first obtained in writing the consent of seven of the members to such call, and sent duly and timely notice to the whole.

7. That the Grand Council have power to choose their speaker; and shall neither be dissolved, prorogued, nor continued sitting longer than six weeks at one time, without their own consent or the special command of the crown.

8. That the members of the Grand Council shall be allowed for their service ten shillings sterling per diem, during their session and journey to and from the place of meeting; twenty miles to be reckoned a day's journey.

9. That the assent of the President-General be requisite to all acts of the Grand Council, and that it be his office and duty to cause them to be carried into execution.

10. That the President-General, with the advice of the Grand Council, hold or direct all Indian treaties, in which the general interest of the Colonies may be concerned; and make peace or declare war with Indian nations.

11. That they make such laws as they judge necessary for regulating all Indian trade.

12. That they make all purchases from Indians, for the crown, of lands not now within the bounds of particular Colonies, or that shall not be within their bounds when some of them are reduced to more convenient dimensions.

13. That they make new settlements on such purchases, by granting lands in the King's name, reserving a quitrent to the crown for the use of the general treasury.

14. That they make laws for regulating and governing such new settlements, till the crown shall think fit to form them into particular governments.

15. That they raise and pay soldiers and build forts for the defence of any of the Colonies, and equip vessels of force to guard the coasts and protect the trade on the ocean, lakes, or great rivers; but they shall not impress men in any Colony, without the consent of the Legislature.

16. That for these purposes they have power to make laws, and lay and levy such general duties, imposts, or taxes, as to them shall appear most equal and just (considering the ability and other circumstances of the inhabitants in the several Colonies), and such as may be collected with the least inconvenience to the people; rather discouraging luxury, than loading industry with unnecessary burdens.

17. That they may appoint a General Treasurer and Particular Treasurer in each government when necessary; and, from time to time, may order the sums in the treasuries of each government into the general treasury; or draw on them for special payments, as they find most convenient.

18. Yet no money to issue but by joint orders of the President-General and Grand Council; except where sums have been appropriated to particular purposes, and the President-General is previously empowered by an act to draw such sums.

19. That the general accounts shall be yearly settled and reported to the several Assemblies.

20. That a quorum of the Grand Council, empowered to act with the President-General, do consist of twenty-five members; among whom there shall be one or more from a majority of the Colonies.

21. That the laws made by them for the purposes aforesaid shall not be repugnant, but, as near as may be, agreeable to the laws of England, and shall be transmitted to the King in Council for approbation, as soon as may be after their passing; and if not disapproved within three years after presentation, to remain in force.

22. That, in case of the death of the President-General, the Speaker of the Grand Council for the time being shall succeed, and be vested with the same powers and authorities, to continue till the King's pleasure be known.

23. That all military commission officers, whether for land or sea service, to act under this general constitution, shall be nominated by the President-General; but the approbation of the Grand Council is to be obtained, before they receive their commissions. And all civil officers are to be nominated by the Grand Council, and to receive the President-General's approbation before they officiate.

24. But, in case of vacancy by death or removal of any officer, civil or military, under this constitution, the Governor of the Province in which such vacancy happens may appoint, till the pleasure of the President-General and Grand Council can be known.

25. That the particular military as well as civil establishments in each Colony remain in their present state, the general constitution notwithstanding; and that on sudden emergencies any Colony may defend it-

self, and lay the accounts of expense thence arising before the President-General and General Council, who may allow and order payment of the same, as far as they judge such accounts just and reasonable.

Resolutions of the Stamp Act Congress October 19, 1765

The members of this Congress, sincerely devoted with the warmest sentiments of affection and duty to His Majesty's person and Government, inviolably attached to the present happy establishment of the Protestant succession, and with minds deeply impressed by a sense of the present and impending misfortunes of the British colonies on this continent; having considered as maturely as time will permit the circumstances of the said colonies, esteem it our indispensable duty to make the following declarations of our humble opinion respecting the most essential rights and liberties of the colonists, and of the grievances under which they labour, by reason of several late Acts of Parliament.

I. That His Majesty's subjects in these colonies owe the same allegiance to the Crown of Great Britain that is owing from his subjects born within the realm, and all due subordination to that august body the Parliament of Great Britain.

II. That His Majesty's liege subjects in these colonies are intitled to all the inherent rights and liberties of his natural born subjects within the kingdom of Great Britain.

III. That it is inseparably essential to the freedom of a people, and the undoubted right of Englishmen, that no taxes be imposed on them but with their own consent, given personally or by their representatives.

IV. That the people of these colonies are not, and from their local circumstances cannot be, represented in the House of Commons in Great Britain.

V. That the only representatives of the people of these colonies are persons chosen therein by themselves, and that no taxes ever have been, or can be constitutionally imposed on them, but by their respective legislatures.

VI. That all supplies to the Crown being free gifts of the people, it is unreasonable and inconsistent with the principles and spirit of the British Constitution, for the people of Great Britain to grant to His Majesty the property of the colonists.

VII. That trial by jury is the inherent and invaluable right of every British subject in these colonies.

VIII. That the late Act of Parliament, entitled *An Act for granting and applying certain stamp duties, and other duties, in the British colonies and plantations in America, etc.*, by imposing taxes on the inhabitants of these colonies; and the said Act, and several other Acts, by extending the jurisdiction of the courts of Admiralty beyond its ancient limits, have a manifest tendency to subvert the rights and liberties of the colonists.

IX. That the duties imposed by several late Acts of Parliament, from the peculiar circumstances of these colonies, will be extremely burthensome and grievous; and from the scarcity of specie, the payment of them absolutely impracticable.

X. That as the profits of the trade of these colonies ultimately center in Great Britain, to pay for the manufactures which they are obliged to take from thence, they eventually contribute very largely to all supplies granted there to the Crown.

XI. That the restrictions imposed by several late Acts of Parliament on the trade of these colonies will render them unable to purchase the manufactures of Great Britain.

XII. That the increase, prosperity, and happiness of these colonies depend on the full and free enjoyments of their rights and liberties, and an intercourse with Great Britain mutually affectionate and advantageous.

XIII. That it is the right of the British subjects in these colonies to petition the King or either House of Parliament.

Lastly, That it is the indispensable duty of these colonies to the best of sovereigns, to the mother country, and to themselves, to endeavor by a loyal and dutiful address to His Majesty, and humble applications to both Houses of Parliament, to procure the repeal of the Act for granting and applying certain stamp duties, of all clauses of any other Acts of Parliament, whereby the jurisdiction of the Admiralty is extended as aforesaid, and of the other late Acts for the restriction of American commerce.

Declaration and Resolves of the First Continental Congress October 14, 1774

Whereas, since the close of the last war, the British parliament, claiming a power of right to bind the people of America by statute in all cases whatsoever, hath, in some acts expressly imposed taxes on them, and in others, under various pretences, but in fact for the purpose of raising a revenue, hath imposed rates and duties payable in these colonies, established a board of commissioners with unconstitutional powers, and extended the jurisdiction of courts of Admiralty not only for collecting the said duties, but for the trial of causes merely arising within the body of a county.

And whereas, in consequence of other statutes, judges who before held only estates at will in their offices, have been made dependent on the Crown alone for their salaries, and standing armies kept in times of peace. And it has lately been resolved in Parliament, that by force of a statute made in the thirty-fifth year of the reign of king Henry the Eighth, colonists may be transported to England, and tried there upon accusations for treasons and misprisions, or concealment of treasons committed in the colonies; and by a late statute, such trials have been directed in cases therein mentioned.

And whereas, in the last session of Parliament, three statutes were made...(the Boston Port Act, the Massachusetts Government Act, the Administration of Justice Act), and another statute was then made (the Quebec Act).... All which statutes are impolitic, unjust, and cruel, as well as unconstitutional, and most dangerous and destructive of American rights.

And whereas, Assemblies have been frequently dissolved, contrary to the rights of the people, when they attempted to deliberate on grievances; and their dutiful, humble, loyal, and reasonable petitions to the crown for redress, have been repeatedly treated with contempt, by His Majesty's ministers of state:

The good people of the several Colonies of New-hampshire, Massachusetts-bay, Rhode-island and Providence plantations, Connecticut, New-York, New-Jersey, Pennsylvania, Newcastle Kent and Sussex on Delaware, Maryland, Virginia, North-Carolina, and South-Carolina, justly alarmed at these arbitrary proceedings of parliament and administration, have severally elected, constituted, and appointed deputies to meet, and sit in general Congress, in the city of Philadelphia, in order to obtain such establishment, as that their religion, laws, and liberties, may not be subverted:

Whereupon the deputies so appointed being now assembled, in a full and free representation of these Colonies, taking into their most serious consideration the best means of attaining the ends aforesaid, do in the first place, as Englishmen their ancestors in like cases have usually done, for asserting and vindicating their rights and liberties, declare,

That the inhabitants of the English Colonies in North America, by the immutable laws of nature, the principles of the English constitution, and the several charters or compacts, have the following Rights:

Resolved, N.C.D.

1. That they are entitled to life, liberty, and property, and they have never ceded to any sovereign power whatever, a right to dispose of either without their consent.

2. That our ancestors, who first settled these colonies, were at the time of their emigration from the mother country, entitled to all the rights, liberties, and immunities of free and natural-born subjects within the realm of England.

3. That by such emigration they by no means forfeited, surrendered, or lost any of those rights, but that they were, and their descendants now are entitled to the exercise and enjoyment of all such of them, as their local and other circumstances enable them to exercise and enjoy.

4. That the foundation of English liberty, and of all free government, is a right in the people to participate in their legislative council; and as the English colonists are not represented, and from their local and other circumstances, cannot properly be represented in the British parliament, they are entitled to a free and exclusive power of legislation in their several provincial legislatures, where their right of representation can alone be preserved, in all cases of taxation and internal polity, subject only to the negative of their sovereign, in such manner as has been heretofore used and accustomed. But, from the necessity of the case, and a regard to the mutual interest of both countries, we cheerfully consent to the operation of such acts of the British parliament, as are bona fide restrained to the regulation of our external commerce, for the purpose of securing the commercial advantages of the whole empire to the mother country, and the commercial benefits of its respective members excluding every idea of taxation, internal or external, for raising a revenue on the subjects in America without their consent.

5. That the respective colonies are entitled to the common law of England, and more especially to the great and inestimable privilege of being tried by their peers of the vicinage, according to the course of that law.

6. That they are entitled to the benefit of such of the English statutes, as existed at the time of their colonization; and which they have, by experience, respectively found to be applicable to their several local and other circumstances.

7. That these, his majesty's colonies, are likewise entitled to all the immunities and privileges granted and confirmed to them by royal charters, or secured by their several codes of provincial laws.

8. That they have a right peaceably to assemble, consider of their grievances, and petition the King; and that all prosecutions, prohibitory proclamations, and commitments for the same, are illegal.

9. That the keeping a Standing army in these colonies, in times of peace, without the consent of the legislature of that colony in which such army is kept, is against law.

10. It is indispensably necessary to good government, and rendered essential by the English constitution, that the constituent branches of the legislature be independent of each other; that, therefore, the exercise of legislative power in several colonies, by a council appointed during pleasure, by the crown, is unconstitutional, dangerous, and destructive to the freedom of American legislation.

All and each of which the aforesaid deputies, in behalf of themselves, and their constituents, do claim, demand, and insist on, as their indubitable rights and liberties; which cannot be legally taken from them, altered or abridged by any power whatever, without their own consent, by their representatives in their several provincial legislatures.

In the course of our inquiry, we find many infringments and violations of the foregoing rights, which, from an ardent desire that harmony and mutual intercourse of affection and interest may be restored, we pass over for the present, and proceed to state such acts and measures as have been adopted since the last war, which demonstrate a system formed to enslave America.

Resolved, That the following acts of Parliament are infringements and violations of the rights of the colonists; and that the repeal of them is essentially necessary, in order to restore harmony between Great Britain and the American colonies,...viz.:

The several Acts of 4 Geo. 3, ch. 15 & ch. 34; 5 Geo. 3, ch. 25; 6 Geo. 3, ch. 52; 7 Geo. 3, ch. 41 & 46; 8 Geo. 3, ch. 22; which impose duties for the purpose of raising a revenue in America, extend the powers of the admiralty courts beyond their ancient limits, deprive the American subject of trial by jury, authorize the judges' certificate to indemnify the prosecutor from damages that he might otherwise be liable to, requiring oppressive security from a claimant of ships and goods seized before he shall be allowed to defend his property; and are subversive of American rights.

Also the 12 Geo. 3, ch. 24, entitled "An act for the better preserving his Majesty's dock-yards, magazines, ships, ammunition, and stores," which declares a new offense in America, and deprives the American subject of a constitutional trial by jury of the vicinage, by authorizing the trial of any person charged with the committing any offense described in the said act, out of the realm, to be indicted and tried for the same in any shire or county within the realm.

Also the three acts passed in the last session of parliament, for stopping the port and blocking up the harbour of Boston, for altering the charter and government of the Massachusetts-bay, and that which is entitled "An Act for the better administration of Justice," &c.

Also the act passed the same session for establishing the Roman Catholick Religion in the province of Quebec, abolishing the equitable system of English laws, and erecting a tyranny there, to the great danger, from so great a dissimilarity of Religion, law, and government, of the neighboring British colonies....

Also the act passed the same session for the better providing suitable quarters for officers and soldiers in his Majesty's service in North America.

Also, that the keeping a standing army in several of these colonies, in time of peace, without the consent of the legislature of that colony in which the army is kept, is against law.

To these grievous acts and measures Americans cannot submit, but in hopes that their fellow subjects in Great-Britain will, on a revision of them, restore us to that state in which both countries found happiness and prosperity, we have for the present only resolved to pursue the following peaceable measures: 1st. To enter into a non-importation, non-consumption, and non-exportation agreement or association. 2. To prepare an address to the people of Great-Britain, and a memorial to the inhabitants of British America, & 3. To prepare a loyal address to his Majesty, agreeable to resolutions already entered into.

The Virginia or Randolph Plan Presented to the Federal Convention May 29, 1787

1. Resolved that the Articles of Confederation ought to be so corrected and enlarged as to accomplish the objects proposed by their institution; namely "common defence, security of liberty and general welfare."

2. Resolved therefore that the rights of suffrage in the National Legislature ought to be proportioned to the Quotas of contribution, or to the number of free inhabitants, as the one or the other rule may seem best in different cases.

3. Resolved that the National Legislature ought to consist of two branches.

4. Resolved that the members of the first branch of the National Legislature ought to be elected by the people of the several States every... for the terms of...; to be of the age of ...years at least; to receive liberal stipends for the devotion of their time to public service, to be ineligible to any office established by a particular State, or under the authority of the United States, except those peculiarly belonging to the functions of the first branch, during the term of service, and for the space of...after its expiration; to be incapable of reelection for the space of...after the expiration of their term of service, and to be subject to recall.

5. Resolved that the members of the second branch of the National Legislature ought to be elected by those of the first, out of a proper number of persons nominated by the individual Legislatures, to be of the age of...years at least; to hold their offices for a term sufficient to ensure their independency; to receive liberal stipends, by which they may be compensated for the devotion of their time to public service; and to be ineligible to any office established by a particular State, or under the authority of the United States, except those peculiarly belonging to the functions of the second branch, during the term of service, and for the space of...after the expiration thereof.

6. Resolved that each branch ought to possess the right of originating Acts; that the National Legislature ought to be impowered to enjoy the Legislative Rights vested in Congress by the Confederation and moreover to legislate in all cases to which the separate States are incompetent, or in which the harmony of the United States may be interrupted by the exercise of individual Legislation; to negative all laws passed by the several States, contravening in the opinion of the National Legislature the articles of Union; and to call forth the force of the Union against any member of the Union failing in its duty under the articles thereof.

7. Resolved that a National Executive be instituted; to be chosen by the National Legislature for the term of...years; to receive punctually, at stated times, a fixed compensation for the services rendered, in which no increase or diminution shall be made so as to affect the Magistracy, existing at the time of the increase or diminution, and to be ineligible a second time; and that besides a general authority to execute the National laws, it ought to enjoy the Executive rights vested in Congress by the Confederation.

8. Resolved that the Executive and a convenient number of the National Judiciary, ought to compose a Council of revision with authority to examine every act of the National Legislature before it shall operate, and every act of a particular Legislature before a Negative thereon shall be final; and that the dissent of the said Council shall amount to a rejection, unless the Act of the National Legislature be passed again, or that of a particular Legislature be again negatived by...of the members of each branch.

9. Resolved that a National Judiciary be established to consist of one or more supreme tribunals, and of inferior tribunals to be chosen by the National Legislature, to hold their offices during good behavior; and to receive punctually at stated times fixed compensation for their services, in which no increase or diminution shall be made so as to affect the persons actually in office at the time of such increase or diminution. That the jurisdiction of the inferior tribunals shall be to hear and determine in the first instance, and of the supreme tribunal to hear and determine in the dernier resort, all piracies and felonies on the high seas, captures from an enemy; cases in which foreigners or citizens of other States applying to such jurisdictions may be interested, or which respect the collection of the National revenue; impeachments of any National officers, and questions which may involve the national peace and harmony.

10. Resolved that provision ought to be made for the admission of States lawfully arising within the limits of the United States, whether from a voluntary junction of Government and Territory or otherwise, with the consent of a number of voices in the National legislature less than the whole.

11. Resolved that a Republican Government and the territory of each State, except in the instance of a voluntary junction of Government and territory, ought to be guaranteed by the United States to each State.

12. Resolved that provision ought to be made for the continuance of Congress and their authorities and privileges, until a given day after the reform of the articles of Union shall be adopted, and for the completion of all their engagements.

13. Resolved that provision ought to be made for the amendment of the Articles of Union whensoever it shall seem necessary, and that the assent of the National Legislature ought not to be required thereto.

14. Resolved that the Legislative, Executive and Judiciary powers within the several States ought to be bound by oath to support the articles of Union.

15. Resolved that the amendments which shall be offered to the Confederation, by the Convention ought at a proper time, or times, after the approbation of Congress to be submitted to an assembly or assemblies of Representatives, recommended by the several Legislatures to be expressly chosen by the people, to consider and decide thereon.

The Paterson or New Jersey Plan Presented to the Federal Convention June 15, 1787

1. Resolved that the Articles of Confederation ought to be so revised, corrected, and enlarged as to render the federal Constitution adequate to the exigencies of Government, and the preservation of the Union.

2. Resolved that in addition to the powers vested in the United States in Congress, by the present existing articles of Confederation, they be authorized to pass acts for raising a revenue, by levying a duty or duties on all goods or merchandizes of foreign growth or manufacture, imported into any part of the United States, by Stamps on paper, vellum or parchment, and by a postage on all letters or packages passing through the general post-office, to be applied to such federal purposes as they shall deem proper and expedient; to make rules and regulations for the collection thereof; and the same from time to time, to alter and amend in such manner as they shall think proper; to pass Acts for the regulation of trade and commerce as well with foreign nations as with each other; provided that all punishments, fines, forfeitures and penalties to be incurred for contravening such acts, rules and regulations shall be adjudged by the Common law Judiciaries of the State in which any offence contrary to the true intent and meaning of such Acts, rules and regulations shall have been committed or perpetrated, with liberty of commencing in the first instance all suits and prosecutions for that purpose, in the superior common law Judiciary in such state, subject nevertheless, for the correction of errors, both in law and fact in rendering Judgement, to an appeal to the Judiciary of the United States.

3. Resolved that whenever requisitions shall be necessary, instead of the rule for making requisitions mentioned in the articles of Confederation, the United States in Congress be authorized to make such requisitions in proportion to the whole number of white and other free citizens and inhabitants of every age, sex and condition including those bound to servitude for a term of years and three fifths of all other persons not comprehended in the foregoing description, except Indians not paying taxes; that if such requisitions be not complied with, in the time specified therein, to direct the collection thereof in the non-complying States and for that purpose to devise and pass acts directing and authorizing the same; provided that none of the powers hereby vested in the United States in Congress shall be exercised without the consent of at least... States and in that proportion if the number of Confederated States should hereafter be increased or diminished.

4. Resolved that the United States in Congress be authorized to elect a federal Executive to consist of...persons, to continue in office for the term of...years, to receive punctually at stated times a fixed compensation for their services, in which no increase or diminution shall be made so as to affect the persons composing the Executive at the time of such increase or diminution, to be paid out of the federal treasury; to be incapable of holding any other office or appointment during their time of service and for...years thereafter; to be ineligible a second time, and removeable by Congress on application by a majority of the Executives of the several States; that the Executives besides their general authority to execute the federal acts ought to appoint all federal officers not otherwise provided for, and to direct all military operations; provided that none of the persons composing the federal Executive shall on any occasion take command of any troops so as personally to conduct any enterprise as General or in other capacity.

5. Resolved that a federal Judiciary be established to consist of a supreme tribunal of Judges of which to be appointed by the Executive, and to hold their offices during good behavior, to receive punctually at stated times a fixed compensation for their services in which no increase or diminution shall be made so as to affect persons actually in office at the time of such increase or diminution; that the Judiciary so established shall have authority to hear and determine in the first instance on all impeachments of federal officers, and by way of appeal in the dernier resort in all cases touching the rights of Ambassadors, in all cases of captures from an enemy, in all cases of piracies and felonies on the high Seas, in all cases in which foreigners may be interested, in the construction of any treaty or treaties, or which may arise on any of the Acts for regulation of trade, or the collection of the federal Revenue: that none of the Judiciary shall during the time they remain in office be capable of receiving or holding any other office or appointment during the time of service, or for thereafter.

6. Resolved that all Acts of the United States in Congress made by virtue and in pursuance of the powers hereby and by the articles of Confederation vested in them, and all Treaties made and ratified under the authority of the United States, shall be the supreme law of the respective States so far forth as those Acts or Treaties shall relate to the said States or their Citizens, and that the Judiciary of the several States shall be bound thereby in their decisions, any thing in the respective laws of the Individual States to the contrary notwithstanding; and that if any State, or any body of men in any State shall oppose or prevent carrying into execution such acts or treaties, the federal Executive shall be authorized to call forth the power of the Confederated States, or so much thereof as may be necessary to enforce and compel an obedience to such Acts or an observance of such Treaties.

7. Resolved that provision be made for the admission of new States into the Union.

8. Resolved the rule for naturalization ought to be the same in every State.

9. Resolved that a Citizen of one State committing an offence in another State of the Union, shall be deemed guilty of the same offence as if it had been committed by a Citizen of the State in which the offence was committed.

Appendix—Congress at Work

Texts and Other Material Relating to Chapter 2

SESSIONS OF CONGRESS

Congress	Session	Date of beginning	Date of adjournment	Length in days	President pro tempore of the Senate *1*	Speaker of the House of Representatives
1st	1	Mar. 4, 1789 *2*	Sept. 29, 1789	210	John Langdon of New Hampshire	Frederick A. C. Muhlenberg of Pennsylvania
	2	Jan. 4, 1790	Aug. 12, 1790	221		
	3	Dec. 6, 1790	Mar. 3, 1791 *3*	88		
2nd	1	Oct. 24, 1791	May 8, 1792	197	Richard Henry Lee of Virginia	Jonathan Trumbull of Connecticut
	2	Nov. 5, 1792	Mar. 2, 1793	119	John Langdon of New Hampshire	
3rd	1	Dec. 2, 1793	June 9, 1794	190	do.	Frederick A. C. Muhlenberg of Pennsylvania
					Ralph Izard of South Carolina	
	2	Nov. 3, 1794	Mar. 3, 1795	121	Henry Tazewell of Virginia	
4th	1	Dec. 7, 1795	June 1, 1796	177	do.	Jonathan Dayton of New Jersey
					Samuel Livermore of New Hampshire	
	2	Dec. 5, 1796	Mar. 3, 1797	89	William Bingham of Pennsylvania	
5th	1	May 15, 1797	July 10, 1797	57	William Bradford of Rhode Island	Do.
	2	Nov. 13, 1797	July 16, 1798	246	Jacob Read of South Carolina	George Dent of Maryland
					Theodore Sedgwick of Massachusetts	
	3	Dec. 3, 1798	Mar. 3, 1799	91	John Laurence of New York	
					James Ross of Pennsylvania	
6th	1	Dec. 2, 1799	May 14, 1800	164	Samuel Livermore of New Hampshire	Theodore Sedgwick of Massachusetts
					Uriah Tracy of Connecticut	
	2	Nov. 17, 1800	Mar. 3, 1801	107	John E. Howard of Maryland	
					James Hillhouse of Connecticut	
7th	1	Dec. 7, 1801	May 3, 1802	148	Abraham Baldwin of Georgia	Nathaniel Macon of North Carolina
	2	Dec. 6, 1802	Mar. 3, 1803	88	Stephen R. Bradley of Vermont	

1 Until within recent years the appointment or election of a President pro tempore was held by the Senate to be for the occasion only, so that more than one appears in several sessions and in others none was chosen. Since March 12, 1890, they have served until "the Senate otherwise ordered."

2 The Constitution (art. I, sec. 4) provided that "The Congress shall assemble at least once in every year***on the first Monday in December, unless they shall by law appoint a different day." Pursuant to a resolution of the Continental Congress, the first session of the First Congress convened March 4, 1789. Up to and including May 20, 1820, 18 Acts were passed providing for the meeting of Congress on other days in the year. After 1820, Congress met regularly on the first Monday in December until 1934, when the 20th Amendment to the Constitution became effective, changing the meeting date to Jan. 3. Until then, brief special sessions of the Senate only were held at the beginning of each Presidential term to confirm Cabinet and other nominations—and occasionally at other times for other purposes. The Senate last met in special session from March 4 to March 6, 1933.

3 Until adoption of the 20th Amendment, the deadline for adjournment of Congress in odd-numbered years was March 3. However, the expiring Congress often extended the "legislative day" of March 3 up to noon of March 4, when the new Congress came officially into being.

The first and second sessions of the First Congress were held in New York City; subsequently, including the first session of the Sixth Congress, Philadelphia was the meeting place; since then, Congress has convened in Washington.

SESSIONS OF CONGRESS

Congress	Session	Date of beginning	Date of adjournment	Length in days	President pro tempore of the Senate *¹*	Speaker of the House of Representatives
8th	1	Oct. 17, 1803	Mar. 27, 1804	163	John Brown of Kentucky	Do.
					Jesse Franklin of North Carolina	
	2	Nov. 5, 1804	Mar. 3, 1805	119	Joseph Anderson of Tennessee	
9th	1	Dec. 2, 1805	Apr. 21, 1806	141	Samuel Smith of Maryland	Do.
	2	Dec. 1, 1806	Mar. 3, 1807	93	do.	
10th	1	Oct. 26, 1807	Apr. 25, 1808	182	Samuel Smith of Maryland	Joseph B. Varnum of Massachusetts
	2	Nov. 7, 1808	Mar. 3, 1809	117	Stephen R. Bradley of Vermont	
					John Milledge of Georgia	
11th	1	May 22, 1809	June 28, 1809	38	Andrew Gregg of Pennsylvania	Do.
	2	Nov. 27, 1809	May 1, 1810	156	John Gaillard of South Carolina	
	3	Dec. 3, 1810	Mar. 3, 1811	91	John Pope of Kentucky	
12th	1	Nov. 4, 1811	July 6, 1812	245	William H. Crawford of Georgia	Henry Clay of Kentucky
	2	Nov. 2, 1812	Mar. 3, 1813	122	do.	
13th	1	May 24, 1813	Aug. 2, 1813	71		Do.
	2	Dec. 6, 1813	Apr. 18, 1814	134	Joseph B. Varnum of Massachusetts	
	3	Sept. 19, 1814	Mar. 3, 1815	166	John Gaillard of South Carolina	Langdon Cheves of South Carolina
14th	1	Dec. 4, 1815	Apr. 30, 1816	148	do.	Henry Clay of Kentucky
	2	Dec. 2, 1816	Mar. 3, 1817	92	do.	
15th	1	Dec. 1, 1817	Apr. 20, 1818	141	do.	Do.
	2	Nov. 16, 1818	Mar. 3, 1819	108	James Barbour of Virginia	
16th	1	Dec. 6, 1819	May 15, 1820	162	John Gaillard of South Carolina	Do.
	2	Nov. 13, 1820	Mar. 3, 1821	111	do.	John W. Taylor of New York
17th	1	Dec. 3, 1821	May 8, 1822	157	do.	Philip P. Barbour of Virginia
	2	Dec. 2, 1822	Mar. 3, 1823	92	do.	
18th	1	Dec. 1, 1823	May 27, 1824	178	do.	Henry Clay of Kentucky
	2	Dec. 6, 1824	Mar. 3, 1825	88	do.	
19th	1	Dec. 5, 1825	May 22, 1826	169	Nathaniel Macon of North Carolina	John W. Taylor of New York
	2	Dec. 4, 1826	Mar. 3, 1827	90	do.	
20th	1	Dec. 3, 1827	May 26, 1828	175	Samuel Smith of Maryland	Andrew Stevenson of Virginia
	2	Dec. 1, 1828	Mar. 3, 1829	93	do.	
21st	1	Dec. 7, 1829	May 31, 1830	176	do.	Do.
	2	Dec. 6, 1830	Mar. 3, 1831	88	Littleton Waller Tazewell of Virginia	
22nd	1	Dec. 5, 1831	July 16, 1832	225	do.	Do.
	2	Dec. 3, 1832	Mar. 2, 1833	91	Hugh Lawson White of Tennessee	
23rd	1	Dec. 2, 1833	June 30, 1834	211	George Poindexter of Mississippi	Do.
	2	Dec. 1, 1834	Mar. 3, 1835	93	John Tyler of Virginia	John Bell of Tennessee

SESSIONS OF CONGRESS

Congress	Session	Date of beginning	Date of adjournment	Length in days	President pro tempore of the Senate [1]	Speaker of the House of Representatives
24th	1	Dec. 7, 1835	July 4, 1836	211	William R. King of Alabama	James K. Polk of Tennessee
	2	Dec. 5, 1836	Mar. 3, 1837	89	do.	
25th	1	Sept. 4, 1837	Oct. 16, 1837	43	do.	Do.
	2	Dec. 4, 1837	July 9, 1838	218	do.	
	3	Dec. 3, 1838	Mar. 3, 1839	91	do.	
26th	1	Dec. 2, 1839	July 13, 1840	233	do.	Robert M. T. Hunter of Virginia
	2	Dec. 7, 1840	Mar. 3, 1841	87		
27th	1	May 31, 1841	Sept. 13, 1841	106	Samuel L. Southard of New Jersey	John White of Kentucky
	2	Dec. 6, 1841	Aug. 31, 1842	269	Willie P. Mangum of North Carolina	
	3	Dec. 5, 1842	Mar. 3, 1843	89	do.	
28th	1	Dec. 4, 1843	June 17, 1844	196	do.	John W. Jones of Virginia
	2	Dec. 2, 1844	Mar. 3, 1845	92	do.	
29th	1	Dec. 1, 1845	Aug. 10, 1846	253	David R. Atchison of Missouri	John W. Davis of Indiana
	2	Dec. 7, 1846	Mar. 3, 1847	87	do.	
30th	1	Dec. 6, 1847	Aug. 14, 1848	254	do.	Robert C. Winthrop of Massachusetts
	2	Dec. 4, 1848	Mar. 3, 1849	90	do.	
31st	1	Dec. 3, 1849	Sept. 30, 1850	302	William R. King of Alabama	Howell Cobb of Georgia
	2	Dec. 2, 1850	Mar. 3, 1851	92	do.	
32nd	1	Dec. 1, 1851	Aug. 31, 1852	275	William R. King of Alabama	Linn Boyd of Kentucky
	2	Dec. 6, 1852	Mar. 3, 1853	88	David R. Atchison of Missouri	
33rd	1	Dec. 5, 1853	Aug. 7, 1854	246	do.	Do.
	2	Dec. 4, 1854	Mar. 3, 1855	90	Jesse D. Bright of Indiana	
34th	1	Dec. 3, 1855	Aug. 18, 1856	260	Lewis Cass of Michigan Jesse D. Bright of Indiana	Nathaniel P. Banks of Massachusetts
	2	Aug. 21, 1856	Aug. 30, 1856	10	do.	
	3	Dec. 1, 1856	Mar. 3, 1857	93	James M. Mason of Virginia Thomas J. Rusk of Texas	
35th	1	Dec. 7, 1857	June 14, 1858	189	Benjamin Fitzpatrick of Alabama	James L. Orr of South Carolina
	2	Dec. 6, 1858	Mar. 3, 1859	88	do.	
36th	1	Dec. 5, 1859	June 25, 1860	202	do.	William Pennington of New Jersey
	2	Dec. 3, 1860	Mar. 3, 1861	93	Jesse D. Bright of Indiana Solomon Foot of Vermont	
37th	1	July 4, 1861	Aug. 6, 1861	34	do.	Galusha A. Grow of Pennsylvania
	2	Dec. 2, 1861	July 17, 1862	228	do.	
	3	Dec. 1, 1862	Mar. 3, 1863	93	do.	
38th	1	Dec. 7, 1863	July 4, 1864	209	do.	Schuyler Colfax of Indiana
	2	Dec. 5, 1864	Mar. 3, 1865	89	Daniel Clark of New Hampshire do.	

SESSIONS OF CONGRESS

Congress	Session	Date of beginning	Date of adjournment	Length in days	President pro tempore of the Senate [1]	Speaker of the House of Representatives
39th	1	Dec. 4, 1865	July 28, 1866	237	Lafayette S. Foster of Connecticut	Do.
	2	Dec. 3, 1866	Mar. 3, 1867	91	Benjamin F. Wade of Ohio	
40th	1	Mar. 4, 1867	Dec. 2, 1867	274	do.	Do.
	2	Dec. 2, 1867	Nov. 10, 1868	345	do.	
	3	Dec. 7, 1868	Mar. 3, 1869	87	do.	Theodore M. Pomeroy of New York
41st	1	Mar. 4, 1869	Apr. 10, 1869	38	Henry B. Anthony of Rhode Island	James G. Blaine of Maine
	2	Dec. 6, 1869	July 15, 1870	222	do.	
	3	Dec. 5, 1870	Mar. 3, 1871	89	do.	
42nd	1	Mar. 4, 1871	Apr. 20, 1871	48	do.	Do.
	2	Dec. 4, 1871	June 10, 1872	190	do.	
	3	Dec. 2, 1872	Mar. 3, 1873	92	do.	
43rd	1	Dec. 1, 1873	June 23, 1874	204	Matthew H. Carpenter of Wisconsin	Do.
	2	Dec. 7, 1874	Mar. 3, 1875	87	do. Henry B. Anthony of Rhode Island	
44th	1	Dec. 6, 1875	Aug. 15, 1876	254	Thomas W. Ferry of Michigan	Michael C. Kerr of Indiana Samuel S. Cox of New York, pro tempore Milton Sayler of Ohio, pro tempore
	2	Dec. 4, 1876	Mar. 3, 1877	90	do.	Samuel J. Randall of Pennsylvania
45th	1	Oct. 15, 1877	Dec. 3, 1877	50	do.	Do.
	2	Dec. 3, 1877	June 20, 1878	200	do.	
	3	Dec. 2, 1878	Mar. 3, 1879	92	do.	
46th	1	Mar. 18, 1879	July 1, 1879	106	Allen G. Thurman of Ohio	Do.
	2	Dec. 1, 1879	June 16, 1880	199	do.	
	3	Dec. 6, 1880	Mar. 3, 1881	88	do.	
47th	1	Dec. 5, 1881	Aug. 8, 1882	247	Thomas F. Bayard of Delaware David Davis of Illinois	J. Warren Keifer of Ohio
	2	Dec. 4, 1882	Mar. 3, 1883	90	George F. Edmunds of Vermont	
48th	1	Dec. 3, 1883	July 7, 1884	218	do.	John G. Carlisle of Kentucky
	2	Dec. 1, 1884	Mar. 3, 1885	93	do.	
49th	1	Dec. 7, 1885	Aug. 5, 1886	242	John Sherman of Ohio	Do.
	2	Dec. 6, 1886	Mar. 3, 1887	88	John J. Ingalls of Kansas	
50th	1	Dec. 5, 1887	Oct. 20, 1888	321	do.	Do.
	2	Dec. 3, 1888	Mar. 3, 1889	91	do.	
51st	1	Dec. 2, 1889	Oct. 1, 1890	304	do.	Thomas B. Reed of Maine
	2	Dec. 1, 1890	Mar. 3, 1891	93	Charles F. Manderson of Nebraska	
52nd	1	Dec. 7, 1891	Aug. 5, 1892	251	do.	Charles F. Crisp of Georgia
	2	Dec. 5, 1892	Mar. 3, 1893	89	Isham G. Harris of Tennessee	

SESSIONS OF CONGRESS

Congress	Session	Date of beginning	Date of adjournment	Length in days	President pro tempore of the Senate [1]	Speaker of the House of Representatives
53rd	1	Aug. 7, 1893	Nov. 3, 1893	89	do.	Do.
	2	Dec. 4, 1893	Aug. 28, 1894	268	do.	
	3	Dec. 3, 1894	Mar. 3, 1895	97	Matt W. Ransom of North Carolina Isham G. Harris of Tennessee	
54th	1	Dec. 2, 1895	June 11, 1896	193	William P. Frye of Maine	Thomas B. Reed of Maine
	2	Dec. 7, 1896	Mar. 3, 1897	87	do.	
55th	1	Mar. 15, 1897	July 24, 1897	131	do.	Do.
	2	Dec. 6, 1897	July 8, 1898	215	do.	
	3	Dec. 5, 1898	Mar. 3, 1899	89	do.	
56th	1	Dec. 4, 1899	June 7, 1900	186	do.	David B. Henderson of Iowa
	2	Dec. 3, 1900	Mar. 3, 1901	91	do.	
57th	1	Dec. 2, 1901	July 1, 1902	212	do.	Do.
	2	Dec. 1, 1902	Mar. 3, 1903	93	do.	
58th	1	Nov. 9, 1903	Dec. 7, 1903	29	do.	Joseph G. Cannon of Illinois
	2	Dec. 7, 1903	Apr. 28, 1904	144	do.	
	3	Dec. 5, 1904	Mar. 3, 1905	89	do.	
59th	1	Dec. 4, 1905	June 30, 1906	209	do.	Do.
	2	Dec. 3, 1906	Mar. 3, 1907	91	do.	
60th	1	Dec. 2, 1907	May 30, 1908	181	do.	Do.
	2	Dec. 7, 1908	Mar. 3, 1909	87	do.	
61st	1	Mar. 15, 1909	Aug. 5, 1909	144	do.	Do.
	2	Dec. 6, 1909	June 25, 1910	202	do.	Do.
	3	Dec. 5, 1910	Mar. 3, 1911	89	do.	
62nd	1	Apr. 4, 1911	Aug. 22, 1911	141	*4*	Champ Clark of Missouri
	2	Dec. 4, 1911	Aug. 26, 1912	267	*4*	
	3	Dec. 2, 1912	Mar. 3, 1913	92	*4*	
63rd	1	Apr. 7, 1913	Dec. 1, 1913	239	James P. Clarke of Arkansas	Do.
	2	Dec. 1, 1913	Oct. 24, 1914	328	do.	
	3	Dec. 7, 1914	Mar. 3, 1915	87	do.	
64th	1	Dec. 6, 1915	Sept. 8, 1916	278	do.	Do.
	2	Dec. 4, 1916	Mar. 3, 1917	90	Willard Saulsbury of Delaware	
65th	1	Apr. 2, 1917	Oct. 6, 1917	188	do.	Do.
	2	Dec. 3, 1917	Nov. 21, 1918	354	do.	
	3	Dec. 2, 1918	Mar. 3, 1919	92	do.	
66th	1	May 19, 1919	Nov. 19, 1919	185	Albert B. Cummins of Iowa	Frederick H. Gillett of Massachusetts
	2	Dec. 1, 1919	June 5, 1920	188	do.	
	3	Dec. 6, 1920	Mar. 3, 1921	88	do.	
67th	1	Apr. 11, 1921	Nov. 23, 1921	227	do.	Do.
	2	Dec. 5, 1921	Sept. 22, 1922	292	do.	
	3	Nov. 20, 1922	Dec. 4, 1922	15	do.	
	4	Dec. 4, 1922	Mar. 3, 1923	90	do.	
68th	1	Dec. 3, 1923	June 7, 1924	188	do.	Do.
	2	Dec. 1, 1924	Mar. 3, 1925	93	do.	

4 After Sen. Frye resigned as President pro tempore on April 27, 1911, the office was held successively, during the remainder of the 62nd Congress, by five Senators—Charles Curtis of Kansas, Augustus O. Bacon of Georgia, Jacob H. Gallinger of New Hampshire, Henry Cabot Lodge of Massachusetts, and Frank B. Brandegee of Connecticut. Curtis, Lodge and Brandegee each served only one brief period. Bacon and Gallinger each held the office a number of different times, and at still other times it was left vacant.

SESSIONS OF CONGRESS

Congress	Session	Date of beginning	Date of adjournment	Length in days	President pro tempore of the Senate [1]	Speaker of the House of Representatives
69th	1	Dec. 7, 1925	July 3, 1926	209	George H. Moses of New Hampshire	Nicholas Longworth of Ohio
	2	Dec. 6, 1926	Mar. 3, 1927	88	do.	
70th	1	Dec. 5, 1927	May 29, 1928	177	do.	Do.
	2	Dec. 3, 1928	Mar. 3, 1929	91	do.	
71st	1	Apr. 15, 1929	Nov. 22, 1929	222	do.	Do.
	2	Dec. 2, 1929	July 3, 1930	214	do.	
	3	Dec. 1, 1930	Mar. 3, 1931	93	do.	
	1	Dec. 7, 1931	July 16, 1932	223	do.	John N. Garner of Texas
	2	Dec. 5, 1932	Mar. 3, 1933	89	do.	
73rd	1	Mar. 9, 1933	June 15, 1933	99	Key Pittman of Nevada	Henry T. Rainey of Illinois
	2	Jan. 3, 1934	June 18, 1934	167	do.	
74th	1	Jan. 3, 1935	Aug. 26, 1935	236	do.	Joseph W. Byrns of Tennessee
	2	Jan. 3, 1936	June 20, 1936	170	do.	William B. Bankhead of Alabama
75th	1	Jan. 5, 1937	Aug. 21, 1937	229	do.	Do.
	2	Nov. 15, 1937	Dec. 21, 1937	37	do.	
	3	Jan. 3, 1938	June 16, 1938	165	do.	
76th	1	Jan. 3, 1939	Aug. 5, 1939	215	do.	Do.
	2	Sept. 21, 1939	Nov. 3, 1939	44	do.	
	3	Jan. 3, 1940	Jan. 3, 1941	366	do.	Sam Rayburn of Texas
					William H. King of Utah	
77th	1	Jan. 3, 1941	Jan. 2, 1942	365	Pat Harrison of Mississippi; Carter Glass of Virginia	Do.
	2	Jan. 5, 1942	Dec. 16, 1942	346	Carter Glass of Virginia	
78th	1	Jan. 6, 1943	Dec. 21, 1943	350	do.	Do.
	2	Jan. 10, 1944	Dec. 19, 1944	345	do.	
79th	1	Jan. 3, 1945	Dec. 21, 1945	353	Kenneth McKellar of Tennessee	Do.
	2	Jan. 14, 1946	Aug. 2, 1946	201	do.	
80th	1	Jan. 3, 1947	Dec. 19, 1947	351	Arthur H. Vandenberg of Michigan	Joseph W. Martin Jr. of Massachusetts
	2	Jan. 6, 1948	Dec. 31, 1948	361	do.	
81st	1	Jan. 3, 1949	Oct. 19, 1949	290	Kenneth McKellar of Tennessee	Sam Rayburn of Texas
	2	Jan. 3, 1950	Jan. 2, 1951	365	do.	
82nd	1	Jan. 3, 1951	Oct. 20, 1951	291	do.	Do.
	2	Jan. 8, 1951	July 7, 1952	182	do.	
83rd	1	Jan. 3, 1953	Aug. 3, 1953	213	Styles Bridges of New Hampshire	Joseph W. Martin Jr. of Massachusetts
	2	Jan. 6, 1954	Dec. 2, 1954	331	do.	
84th	1	Jan. 5, 1955	Aug. 2, 1955	210	Walter F. George of Georgia	Sam Rayburn of Texas
	2	Jan. 3, 1956	July 27, 1956	207	do.	
85th	1	Jan. 3, 1957	Aug. 30, 1957	239	Carl Hayden of Arizona	Do.
	2	Jan. 7, 1958	Aug. 24, 1958	230	do.	
86th	1	Jan. 7, 1959	Sept. 15, 1959	252	do.	Do.
	2	Jan. 6, 1960	Sept. 1, 1960	240	do.	
87th	1	Jan. 3, 1961	Sept. 27, 1961	268	do.	Do.
	2	Jan. 10, 1962	Oct. 13, 1962	277	do.	John W. McCormack of Massachusetts

SESSIONS OF CONGRESS

Congress	Session	Date of beginning	Date of adjournment	Length in days	President pro tempore of the Senate [1]	Speaker of the House of Representatives
88th	1	Jan. 9, 1963	Dec. 30, 1963	356	do.	Do.
	2	Jan. 7, 1964	Oct. 3, 1964	270	do.	
89th	1	Jan. 4, 1965	Oct. 23, 1965	293	do.	Do.
	2	Jan. 10, 1966	Oct. 22, 1966	286	do.	
90th	1	Jan. 10, 1967	Dec. 15, 1967	340	do.	Do.
	2	Jan. 15, 1968	Oct. 14, 1968	274	do.	
91st	1	Jan. 3, 1969	Dec. 23, 1969	355	Richard B. Russell of Georgia	Do.
	2	Jan. 19, 1970	Jan. 2, 1971	349	do.	Do.
92nd	1	Jan. 21, 1971			Allen J. Ellender of Louisiana	Carl Albert of Oklahoma

Rules of the House of Representatives

(Adopted by the 92nd Congress.)

Rule I

Duties of the Speaker

1. The Speaker shall take the chair on every legislative day precisely at the hour to which the House shall have adjourned at the last sitting and immediately call the Members to order. On the appearance of a quorum, the Speaker, having examined the Journal of the proceedings of the last day's sitting and approved the same, shall announce to the House his approval of the Journal; whereupon, unless the Speaker, in his discretion, orders the reading of the Journal, the Journal shall be considered as read. However, it shall then be in order to offer one motion that the Journal be read and such motion is of the highest privilege and shall be determined without debate.

2. He shall preserve order and decorum, and, in case of disturbance or disorderly conduct in the galleries, or in the lobby, may cause the same to be cleared.

3. He shall have general control, except as provided by rule or law, of the Hall of the House, and of the corridors and passages and the disposal of the unappropriated rooms in that part of the Capitol assigned to the use of the House, until further order.

4. He shall sign all acts, addresses, joint resolutions, writs, warrants, and subpenas of, or issued. by order of, the House, and decide all questions of order, subject to an appeal by any Member, on which appeal no Member shall speak more than once, unless by permission of the House.

5. He shall rise to put a question, but may state it sitting; and shall put questions in this form, to wit: "As many as are in favor (as the question may be), say Aye;" and after the affirmative voice is expressed, "As many as are opposed, say No;" if he doubts, or a division is called for, the House shall divide; those in the affirmative of the question shall first rise from their seats, and then those in the negative; if he still doubts, or a count is required by at least one-fifth of a quorum, he shall name one or more from each side of the question to tell the Members in the affirmative and negative; which being reported, he shall rise and state the decision. If before tellers are named any Member requests tellers with clerks and that request is supported by at least one-fifth of a quorum, the names of those voting on each side of the question and the names of those not voting shall be recorded by clerks or by electronic device, and shall be entered in the Journal. Members shall have not less than twelve minutes from the naming of tellers with clerks to be counted.

6. He shall not be required to vote in ordinary legislative proceedings, except where his vote would be decisive, or where the House is engaged in voting by ballot; and in cases of a tie vote the question shall be lost.

7. He shall have the right to name any Member to perform the duties of the Chair, but such substitution shall not extend beyond three legislative days: *Provided, however,* That in case of his illness, he may make such appointment for a period not exceeding ten days, with the approval of the House at the time the same is made; and in his absence and omission to make such appointment, the House shall proceed to elect a Speaker pro tempore to act during his absence.

Rule II

Election of Officers

There shall be elected by a viva voce vote, at the commencement of each Congress, to continue in office until their successors are chosen and qualified, a Clerk, Sergeant at Arms, Doorkeeper, Postmaster, and Chaplain, each of whom shall take an oath to support the Constitution of the United States, and for the true and faithful discharge of the duties of his office to the best of his knowledge and ability, and to keep the secrets of the House; and each shall appoint all of the employees of his department provided for by law.

Rule III

Duties of the Clerk

1. The Clerk shall, at the commencement of the first session of each Congress, call the Members to order, proceed to call the roll of Members by States in alphabetical order, and, pending the election of a Speaker or Speaker pro tempore, preserve order and decorum, and decide all questions of order subject to appeal by any Member.

2. He shall make and cause to be printed and delivered to each Member, or mailed to his address, at the commencement of every regular session of Congress, a list of the reports which it is the duty of any officer or Department to make to Congress, referring to the act or resolution and page of the volume of the laws or Journal in which it may be contained, and placing under the name of each officer the list of reports required of him to be made.

3. He shall note all questions of order, with the decisions thereon, the record of which shall be printed as an appendix to the Journal of each session; and complete, as soon after the close of the session as possible, the printing and distribution to Members, the Delegate from the District of Columbia, and the Resident Commissioner from Puerto Rico of the Journal of the House, together with an accurate and complete index; retain in the library at his office, for the use of the Members, the Delegate from the District of Columbia, the Resident Commissioner from Puerto Rico and officers of the House, and not to be withdrawn therefrom, two copies of all the books and printed documents deposited there; send, at the end of each session, a printed copy of the Journal thereof to the executive and to each branch of the legislature of every State; deliver or mail to any Member, the Delegate from the District of Columbia, or the Resident Commissioner from Puerto Rico an extra copy, in binding of good quality, of each document requested by that Member, the Delegate from the District of Columbia, or the Resident Commissioner which has been printed, by order of either House of the Congress, in any Congress in which he served; attest and affix the seal of the House to all writs, warrants, and subpenas issued by order of the House, certify to the passage of all bills and joint resolutions, make or approve all contracts, bargains, or agreements relative to furnishing any matter or thing, or for the performance of any labor for the House of Representatives, in pursuance of law or order of the House, keep full and accurate accounts of the disbursements out of the contingent fund of the House, keep the stationery account of Members, the Delegate from the District of Columbia, and the Resident Commissioner from Puerto Rico, and pay them as provided by law. He shall pay to the officers and employees of the House of Representatives the amount of their salaries that shall be due them.

4. He shall, in case of temporary absence or disability, designate an official in his office to sign all papers that may require the official signature of the Clerk of the House, and to do all other acts, except such as are provided for by statute, that may be required under the rules and practice of the House to be done by the Clerk. Such official acts, when so done by the designated official, shall be under the name of the Clerk of the House. The said designation shall be in writing, and shall be laid before the House and entered on the Journal.

Rule IV

Duties of the Sergeant at Arms

1. It shall be the duty of the Sergeant at Arms to attend the House during its sittings, to maintain order under the direction of the Speaker or Chairman, and, pending the election of a Speaker or Speaker pro tempore, under the direction of the Clerk, execute the commands of the House, and all processes issued by authority thereof, directed to him by the Speaker; keep the accounts for the pay and mileage of Members, the Delegate from the District of Columbia, and the Resident Commissioner from Puerto Rico, and pay them as provided by law.

2. The symbol of his office shall be the mace, which shall be borne by him while enforcing order on the floor.

Rule V

Duties of the Doorkeeper

1. The Doorkeeper shall enforce strictly the rules relating to the privileges of the Hall and be responsible to the House for the official conduct of his employees.

2. He shall allow no person to enter the room over the Hall of the House during its sittings; and fifteen minutes before the hour of the meeting of the House each day he shall see that the floor is cleared of all persons except those privileged to remain; and kept so until ten minutes after adjournment.

Rule VI

Duties of the Postmaster

The Postmaster shall superintend the post office in the Capitol and in the respective office buildings of the House for the accommodation of Representatives, the Delegate from the District of Columbia, the Resident Commissioner from Puerto Rico, and officers of the House and shall be held responsible for the prompt and safe delivery of their mail.

Rule VII

Duties of the Chaplain

The Chaplain shall attend at the commencement of each day's sitting of the House and open the same with prayer.

Rule VIII

Of the Members

1. Every Member shall be present within the Hall of the House during its sittings, unless excused or necessarily prevented; and shall vote on each question put, unless he has a direct personal or pecuniary interest in the event of such question.
2. Pairs shall be announced by the Clerk, after the completion of the second roll call, from a written list furnished him, and signed by the Member making the statement to the Clerk, which list shall be published in the Record as a part of the proceedings, immediately following the names of those not voting: *Provided,* pairs shall be announced but once during the same legislative day.

Rule IX

Questions of Privilege

Questions of privileges shall be, first, those affecting the rights of the House collectively, its safety, dignity, and the integrity of its proceedings; second, the rights, reputation, and conduct of Members, individually, in their representative capacity only; and shall have precedence of all other questions, except motions to adjourn.

Rule X

Standing Committees

1. There shall be elected by the House, at the commencement of each Congress, the following standing committees:
(a) Committee on Agriculture, to consist of twenty-seven Members.
(b) Committee on Appropriations, to consist of forty-three Members.
(c) Committee on Armed Services, to consist of thirty-three Members.
(d) Committee on Banking and Currency, to consist of twenty-seven Members.
(e) Committee on the District of Columbia, to consist of twenty-five Members.
(f) Committee on Education and Labor, to consist of twenty-five Members.
(g) Committee on Foreign Affairs, to consist of twenty-five Members.
(h) Committee on Government Operations, to consist of twenty-five Members.
(i) Committee on House Administration, to consist of twenty-five Members.
(j) Committee on Interior and Insular Affairs, to consist of twenty-five Members.
(k) Committee on Internal Security, to consist of nine Members.
(l) Committee on Interstate and Foreign Commerce, to consist of twenty-seven Members.
(m) Committee on the Judiciary, to consist of twenty-seven Members.
(n) Committee on Merchant Marine and Fisheries to consist of twenty-five Members.
(o) Committee on Post Office and Civil Service, to consist of twenty-five Members.

(p) Committee on Public Works, to consist of twenty-seven Members.
(q) Committee on Rules, to consist of fifteen Members.
(r) Committee on Science and Astronautics, to consist of twenty-five Members.
(s) Committee on Standards of Official Conduct, to consist of twelve Members as follows: Six Members of the majority party and six Members of the minority party.
(t) Committee on Veterans' Affairs, to consist of twenty-seven Members.
(u) Committee on Ways and Means, to consist of twenty-five Members.
2. The Speaker shall appoint all select and conference committees which shall be ordered by the House from time to time.
3. The Select Committee on Small Business *(shall)* be a permanent select committee of the House without legislative jurisdiction except to make investigations and reports.
4. At the commencement of each Congress, the House shall elect as chairman of each standing committee one of the Members thereof, in the temporary absence of the chairman the Member next in rank in the order named in the election of the committee, and so on, as often as the case shall happen, shall act as chairman; and in case of a permanent vacancy in the chairmanship of any such committee the House shall elect another chairman.
5. All vacancies in standing committees in the House shall be filled by election by the House.

Rule XI

Powers and Duties of Committees

All proposed legislation, messages, petitions, memorials, and other matters relating to the subject listed under the standing committees named below shall be referred to such committees, respectively:
1. **Committee on Agriculture.**
(a) Adulteration of seeds, insect pests, and protection of birds and animals in forest reserves.
(b) Agriculture generally.
(c) Agricultural and industrial chemistry.
(d) Agricultural colleges and experiment stations.
(e) Agricultural economics and research.
(f) Agricultural education extension services.
(g) Agricultural production and marketing and stabilization of prices of agricultural products.
(h) Animal industry and diseases of animals.
(i) Crop insurance and soil conservation.
(j) Dairy industry.
(k) Entomology and plant quarantine.
(l) Extension of farm credit and farm security.
(m) Forestry in general, and forest reserves other than those created from the public domain.
(n) Human nutrition and home economics.
(o) Inspection of livestock and meat products.
(p) Plant industry, soils, and agricultural engineering.
(q) Rural electrification.
2. **Committee on Appropriations.**
(a) Appropriation of the revenue for the support of the Government.
(b) The committee is authorized, acting as a whole or by any subcommittee thereof appointed by the chairman for the purposes hereof and in accordance with procedures authorized by the committee by a majority vote, to conduct studies and examinations of the organization and operation of any executive department or other executive agency (including any agency the majority of the stock of which is owned by the Government of the United States) as it may deem necessary to assist it in the determination of matters within its jurisdiction; and for this purpose the committee or any subcommittee thereof is authorized to sit and act at such times and places within the United States, whether the House is in session, has recessed, or has adjourned, to hold such hearings, to require the attendance of such witnesses, and the production of such books or papers or documents or vouchers by subpena or otherwise, and to take such testimony and records as it deems necessary. Subpenas may be issued over the signature of the chairman of the committee or subcommittee, or by any person designated by him, and shall be served by such person or persons as the chairman of the committee or subcommittee may designate. The chairman of the committee or subcommittee, or any member thereof, may administer oaths to witnesses.
3. **Committee on Armed Services.**
(a) Common defense generally.
(b) The Department of Defense generally, including the Departments of the Army, Navy, and Air Force generally.

(c) Ammunition depots; forts; arsenals; Army, Navy, and Air Force reservations and establishments.

(d) Conservation, development, and use of naval petroleum and oil shale reserves.

(e) Pay, promotion, retirement, and other benefits and privileges of members of the armed forces.

(f) Scientific research and development in support of the armed services.

(g) Selective service.

(h) Size and composition of the Army, Navy, and Air Force.

(i) Soldiers' and sailors' homes.

(j) Strategic and critical materials necessary for the common defense.

4. Committee on Banking and Currency.

(a) Banking and currency generally.

(b) Control of price of commodities, rents, or services.

(c) Deposit insurance.

(d) Federal Reserve System.

(e) Financial aid to commerce and industry, other than matters relating to such aid which are specifically assigned to other committees under this rule.

(f) Gold and silver, including the coinage thereof.

(g) Issuance of notes and redemption thereof.

(h) Public and private housing.

(i) Valuation and revaluation of the dollar.

5. Committee on the District of Columbia.

(a) All measures relating to the municipal affairs of the District of Columbia in general, other than appropriations therefor, including—

(b) Adulteration of foods and drugs.

(c) Incorporation and organization of societes.

(d) Insurance, executors, administrators, wills, and divorce.

(d) Municipal code and amendments to the criminal and corporation laws.

(f) Municipal and juvenile courts.

(g) Public health and safety, sanitation, and quarantine regulations.

(h) Regulation of sale of intoxicating liquors.

(i) Taxes and tax sales.

6. Committee on Education and Labor.

(a) Measures relating to education or labor generally.

(b) Child labor.

(c) Columbia Institution for the Deaf, Dumb, and Blind; (Gallaudet College) Howard University; Freedmen's Hospital; and Saint Elizabeths Hospital.

(d) Convict labor and the entry of goods made by convicts into interstate commerce.

(e) Labor standards.

(f) Labor statistics.

(g) Mediation and arbitration of labor disputes.

(h) Regulation or prevention of importation of foreign laborers under contract.

(i) School-lunch program.

(j) United States Employees' Compensation Commission.

(k) Vocational rehabilitation.

(l) Wages and hours of labor.

(m) Welfare of miners.

7. Committee on Foreign Affairs.

(a) Relations of the United States with foreign nations generally.

(b) Acquisition of land and buildings for embassies and legations in foreign countries.

(c) Establishment of boundary lines between the United States and foreign nations.

(d) Foreign loans.

(e) International conferences and congresses.

(f) Intervention abroad and declarations of war.

(g) Measures relating to the diplomatic service.

(h) Measures to foster commercial intercourse with foreign nations and to safeguard American business interests abroad.

(i) Neutrality.

(j) Protection of American citizens abroad and expatriation.

(k) The American National Red Cross.

(l) United Nations Organization and international financial and monetary organizations.

8. Committee on Government Operations.

(a) Budget and accounting measures, other than appropriations.

(b) Reorganizations in the executive branch of the Government.

(c) Such committee shall have the duty of—

(1) receiving and examining reports of the Comptroller General of the United States and of submitting such recommendations to the House as it deems necessary or desirable in connection with the subject matter of such reports;

(2) studying the operation of Government activities at all levels with a view to determining its economy and efficiency;

(d) evaluating the effects of laws enacted to reorganize the legislative and executive branches of the Government;

(4) studying intergovernmental relationships between the United States and the States and municipalities, and between the United States and international organizations of which the United States is a member.

(d) For the purpose of performing such duties the committee, or any subcommittee thereof when authorized by the committee, is authorized to sit, hold hearings, and act at such times and places within the United States, whether or not the House is in session, is in recess, or has adjourned, to require by subpena or otherwise the attendance of such witnesses and the production of such papers, documents, and books, and to take such testimony as it deems necessary. Subpenas may be issued under the signature of the chairman of the committee or of any subcommittee, or by any member designated by any such chairman, and may be served by any person designated by any such chairman or member.

9. Committee on House Administration.

(a) Appropriations from the contingent fund.

(b) Auditing and settling of all accounts which may be charged to the contingent fund.

(c) Employment of persons by the House, including clerks for Members and committees, and reporters of debates.

(d) Except as provided in clause 16 (d), matters relating to the Library of Congress and the House Library; statuary and pictures; acceptance or purchase of works of art for the Capitol; the Botanic Gardens; management of the Library of Congress; purchase of books and manuscripts; erection of monuments to the memory of individuals.

(e) Except as provided in clause 16 (d), matters relating to the Smithsonian Institution and the incorporation of similar institutions.

(f) Expenditure of contingent fund of the House.

(g) Matters relating to printing and correction of the Congressional Record.

(h) Measures relating to accounts of the House generally.

(i) Measures relating to assignment of office space for Members and committees.

(j) Measures relating to the disposition of useless executive papers.

(k) Measures relating to the election of the President, Vice President, or Members of Congress; corrupt practices; contested elections; credentials and qualifications; and Federal elections generally.

(l) Measures relating to services to the House, including the House Restaurant and administration of the House Office Buildings and of the House wing of the Capitol.

(m) Measures relating to the travel of Members of the House.

(n) Such committee shall also have the duty of—

(1) arranging a suitable program for each day observed by the House of Representatives as a memorial day in memory of Members of the Senate and House of Representatives who have died during the preceding period, and to arrange for the publication of the proceedings thereof;

(2) examining all bills, amendments, and joint resolutions after passage by the House; and in cooperation with the Senate, of examining all bills and joint resolutions which shall have passed both Houses, to see that they are correctly enrolled; and when signed by the Speaker of the House and the President of the Senate, shall forthwith present the same, when they shall have originated in the House, to the President of the United States in person, and report the fact and date of such presentation to the House;

(3) reporting to the Sergeant at Arms of the House the travel of Members of the House.

10. Committee on Interior and Insular Affairs.

(a) Forest reserves and national parks created from the public domain.

(b) Forfeiture of land grants and alien ownership, including alien ownership of mineral lands.

(c) Geological Survey.

(d) Interstate compacts relating to apportionment of waters for irrigation purposes.

(e) Irrigation and reclamation, including water supply for reclamation projects, and easements of public lands for irrigation projects, and acquisition of private lands when necessary to complete irrigation projects.

(f) Measures relating to the care, education, and management of Indians, including the care and allotment of Indian lands and general and special measures relating to claims which are paid out of Indian funds.

(g) Measures relating generally to Hawaii, Alaska, and the insular possessions of the United States, except those affecting the revenue and appropriations.

(h) Military parks and battlefields; national cemeteries administered by the Secretary of the Interior.

(i) Mineral land laws and claims and entries thereunder.

(j) Mineral resources of the public lands.

(k) Mining interests generally.

(l) Mining schools and experimental stations.

(m) Petroleum conservation on the public lands and conservation of the radium supply in the United States.

(n) Preservation of prehistoric ruins and objects of interest on the public domain.

(o) Public lands generally, including entry, easements, and grazing thereon.

(p) Relations of the United States with the Indians and the Indian tribes.

11. Committee on Internal Security.

(a) Communist and other subversive activities affecting the internal security of the United States.

(b) The Committee on Internal Security, acting as a whole or by subcommittee, is authorized to make investigations from time to time in the establishment of, a totalitarian dictatorship within the United States of organizations or groups, whether of foreign or domestic origin, their members, agents, and affiliates, which seek to establish, or assist in the establishment of, a totaliarian dictatorship within the United States, or to overthrow or alter, or assist in the overthrow or alteration of, the form of government of the United States or of any State thereof, by force, violence, treachery, espionage, sabotage, insurrection, or any unlawful means, (2) the extent, character, objectives, and activities within the United States of organizations or groups, their members, agents and affiliates, which incite or employ acts of force, violence, terrorism, or any unlawful means, to obstruct or oppose the lawful authority of the Government of the United States in the execution of any law or policy affecting the internal security of the United States, and (3) all other questions, including the administration and execution of any law of the United States, or any portion of law, relating to the foregoing that would aid the Congress or any committee of the House in any necessary remedial legislation.

The Committee on Internal Security shall report to the House (or to the Clerk of the House if the House is not in session) the results of any such investigation, together with such recommendations as it deems advisable.

For the purpose of any such investigation, the Committee on Internal Security, or any subcommittee thereof, is authorized to sit and act at such times and places within the United States, whether the House is in session, has recessed, or has adjourned, to hold such hearings, and to require, by subpena or otherwise, the attendance and testimony of such witnesses and the production of such books, records, correspondence, memorandums, papers, and documents, as it deems necessary. Subpenas may be issued under the signature of the chairman of the committee or any subcommittee, or by any member designated by any such chairman, and may be served by any person designated by any such chairman or member.

12. Committee on Interstate and Foreign Commerce.

(a) Interstate and foreign commerce generally.

(b) Civil aeronautics.

(c) Inland waterways.

(d) Interstate oil compacts and petroleum and natural gas, except on the public lands.

(e) Public health and quarantine.

(f) Railroad labor and railroad retirement and unemployment, except revenue measures relating thereto.

(g) Regulation of interstate and foreign communications.

(h) Regulation of interstate and foreign transportation, except transportation by water not subject to the jurisdiction of the Interstate Commerce Commission.

(i) Regulation of interstate transmission of power, except the installation of connections between Government water-power projects.

(j) Securities and exchanges.

(k) Weather Bureau.

13. Committee on the Judiciary.

(a) Judicial proceedings, civil and criminal generally.

(b) Apportionment of Representatives.

(c) Bankruptcy, mutiny, espionage, and counterfeiting.

(d) Civil liberties.

(e) Constitutional amendments.

(f) Federal courts and judges.

(g) Holidays and celbrations.

(h) Immigration and naturalization.

(i) Interstate compacts generally.

(j) Local courts in the Territories and possessions.

(k) Measures relating to claims against the United States.

(l) Meetings of Congress, attendance of Members and their acceptance of incompatible offices.

(m) National penitentiaries.

(n) Patent Office.

(o) Patents, copyrights, and trade-marks.

(p) Presidential succession.

(q) Protection of trade and commerce against unlawful restraints and monopolies.

(r) Revision and codification of the Statutes of the United States.

(s) State and Territorial boundary lines.

14. Committee on Merchant Marine and Fisheries.

(a) Merchant marine generally.

(b) Coast and Geodetic Survey.

(c) Coast Guard, including lifesaving service, lighthouses, lightships, and ocean derelicts.

(d) Fisheries and Wildlife, including research, restoration, refuges, and conservation.

(e) Measures relating to the regulation of common carriers by water (except matters subject to the jurisdiction of the Interstate Commerce Commission) and to the inspection of merchant marine vessels, lights and signals, lifesaving equipment, and fire protection on such vessels.

(f) Merchant marine officers and seamen.

(g) Navigation and the laws relating thereto, including pilotage.

(h) Panama Canal and the maintenance and operation of the Panama Canal, including the administration, sanitation, and government of the Canal Zone; and interoceanic canals generally.

(i) Registering and licensing of vessels and small boats.

(j) Rules and international arrangements to prevent collisions at sea.

(k) United States Coast Guard and Merchant Marine Academies.

15. Committee on Post Office and Civil Service.

(a) Census and the collection of statistics generally.

(b) Federal Civil Service generally.

(c) National Archives.

(d) Postal-savings banks.

(e) Postal service generally, including the railway mail service, and measures relating to ocean mail and pneumatic-tube service; but excluding post roads.

(f) Status of officers and employees of the United States, including their compensation, classification, and retirement.

16. Committee on Public Works.

(a) Flood control and improvement of rivers and harbors.

(b) Measures relating to the Capitol Building and the Senate and House Office Buildings.

(c) Measures relating to the construction or maintenance of roads and post roads, other than appropriations therefor; but it shall not be in order for any bill providing general legislation in relation to roads to contain any provision for any specific road, nor for any bill in relation to a specific road to embrace a provision in relation to any other specific road.

(d) Measures relating to the construction or reconstruction, maintenance, and care of the buildings and grounds of the Botanic Gardens, the Library of Congress, and the Smithsonian Institution.

(e) Measures relating to the purchase of sites and construction of post offices, customhouses, Federal courthouses, and Government buildings within the District of Columbia.

(f) Oil and other pollution of navigable waters.

(g) Public buildings and occupied or improved grounds of the United States generally.

(h) Public reservations and parks within the District of Columbia, including Rock Creek Park and the Zoological Park.

(i) Public works for the benefit of navigation, including bridges and dams (other than international bridges and dams).

(j) Water power.

17. Committee on Rules.

(a) The rules, joint rules (other than rules or joint rules relating to the Code of Official Conduct or relating to financial disclosure by a Member, officer, or employee of the House of Representatives), and order of business of the House.

(b) Recesses and final adjournments of Congress.

(c) The Committee on Rules is authorized to sit and act whether or not the House is in session.

18. Committee on Science and Astronautics.

(a) Astronautical research and development, including resources, personnel, equipment, and facilities.

(b) Bureau of Standards, standardization of weights and measures and the metric system.

(c) National Aeronautics and Space Administration.

(d) National Aeronautics and Space Council.

(e) National Science Foundation.

(f) Outer space, including exploration and control thereof.

(g) Science Scholarships.

(h) Scientific research and development.

19. **Committee on Standards of Official Conduct.**

(a) Measures relating to the Code of Official Conduct.

(b) Measures relating to financial disclosure by Members, officers, and employees of the House of Representatives.

(c) Measures relating to activities designed to (1) assist in defeating, passing, or amending any legislation by the House or (2) influence, directly or indirectly, the passage or defeat of any legislation by the House.

(d) Measures relating to the raising, reporting, and use of campaign contributions for candidates for the office of Representative in the House of Representatives and of Resident Commissioner to the United States from Puerto Rico.

(e) The committee is authorized (1) to recommend to the House of Representatives, from time to time, such legislative or administrative actions as the committee may deem appropriate to establish or enforce standards of official conduct for Members, officers, and employees of the House of Representatives; (2) to investigate, subject to paragraph (f) of this clause, any alleged violation, by a Member, officer, or employee of the House of Representatives, of the Code of Official Conduct or of any law, rule, regulation, or other standard of conduct applicable to the conduct of such Member, officer, or employee in the performance of his duties or the discharge of his responsibilities and, after notice and a hearing, shall recommend to the House of Representatives, by resolution or otherwise, such action as the committee may deem appropriate in the circumstances; (3) to report to the appropriate Federal or State authorities, with approval of the House of Representatives, any substantial evidence of a violation, by a Member, officer, or employee of the House of Representatives of any law applicable to the performance of his duties or the discharge of his responsibilities, which may have been disclosed in a committee investigation; and (4) to give consideration to the request of a Member, officer, or employee of the House of Representatives, for an advisory opinion with respect to the general propriety of any current or proposed conduct of such Member, officer, or employee and, with appropriate deletions to assure the privacy of the individual concerned, to publish such opinion for the guidance of other Members, officers, and employees of the House of Representatives.

(f) (1) No resolution, report, recommendation, or advisory opinion relating to the official conduct of a Member, officer, or employee of the House of Representatives shall be undertaken, unless approved by the affirmative vote of not less than seven members of the committee. (2) Except in the case of an investigation undertaken by the committee on its own initiative, the committee may undertake an investigation relating to the official conduct of an individual Member, officer, or employee of the House of Representatives only (A) upon receipt of a complaint, in writing and under oath, made by or submitted to a Member of the House of Representatives and transmitted to the committee by such Member, or (B) upon receipt of a complaint, in writing and under oath, directly from an individual not a Member of the House of Representatives if the committee finds that such complaint has been submitted by such individual to not less than three Members of the House of Representatives who have refused, in writing, to transmit such complaint to the committee. (3) No investigation shall be undertaken of any alleged violation of a law, rule, regulation, or standard of conduct not in effect at the time of the alleged violation. (4) A member of the committee shall be ineligible to participate as a member of the committee, in any committee proceeding relating to his official conduct. In any case in which a member of the committee is ineligible to act as a member of the committee under the preceding sentence, the Speaker of the House of Representatives shall designate a Member of the House of Representatives from the same political party as the ineligible member of the committee to act as a member of the committee in any committee proceeding relating to the official conduct of such ineligible member.

(g) The Committee on Standards of Official Conduct, acting as a whole or by subcommittee, is authorized to conduct investigations and studies, from time to time, of the laws, rules, regulations, procedures, practices, and activities pertaining to (1) lobbying activities as described in subparagraphs (1) and (2) of paragraph (c) of this clause, or (2) the raising, reporting, and use of political campaign contributions as described in paragraph (d) of this clause, or (3) both. Each such investigation and study may include all pertinent matters which would assist the Congress in connection with necessary remedial legislation. The committee may obtain the views of all parties familiar with the subject matter covered by the investigation and study. The committee shall report to the House (or to the Clerk of the House if the House is not in session) the results of each such investigation and study, together with such recommendations as the committee considers advisable.

(h) For the purpose of carrying out the foregoing provisions of this clause, the committtee, or any subcommittee thereof, is authorized to sit and act at such times and places within the United States, whether the House is in session, has recessed, or has adjourned, to hold such hearings,

and to require, by subpena or otherwise, the attendance and testimony of such witnesses and the production of such books, records, correspondence, memorandums, papers, and documents, as it deems necessary. Subpenas may be issued under the signature of the chairman of the committee or any member of the committee designated by him, and may be served by any person designated by such chairman or member.

20. **Committee on Veterans' Affairs.**

(a) Veterans' measures generally.

(b) Cemeteries of the United States in which veterans of any war or conflict are or may be buried, whether in the United States or abroad, except cemeteries administered by the Secretary of the Interior.

(c) Compensation, vocational rehabilitation, and education of veterans.

(d) Life insurance issued by the Government on account of service in the armed forces.

(e) Pensions of all the wars of the United States, general and special.

(f) Readjustment of servicemen to civil life.

(g) Soldiers' and sailor's civil relief.

(h) Veterans' hospitals, medical care, and treatment of veterans.

21. **Committee on Ways and Means.**

(a) Customs, collection districts, and ports of entry and delivery.

(b) National social security.

(c) Reciprocal trade agreements.

(d) Revenue measures generally.

(e) Revenue measures relating to the insular possessions.

(f) The bonded debt of the United States.

(g) The deposit of public moneys.

(h) Transportation of dutiable goods.

22. The following-named committees shall have leave to report at any time on the matters herein stated, namely: the Committee on Appropriations—on the general appropriation bills; the Committee on House Administration—on the right of a Member to his seat, enrolled bills, on all matters referred to it of printing for the use of the House or the two Houses, and on all matters of expenditure of the contingent fund of the House; the Committee on Interior and Insular Affairs—on bills for the forfeiture of land grants to railroad and other corporations, bills preventing speculation in the public lands, bills for the reservation of the public lands for the benefit of actual and bona fide settlers, and bills for the admission of new States; the Committee on Public Works—on bills authorizing the improvement of rivers and harbors; the Committee on Rules—on rules, joint rules, and order of business; the Committee on Standards of Official Conduct—on resolutions recommending action by the House of Representatives with respect to an individual Member, officer, or employee of the House of Representatives as a result of any investigation by the committee relating to the official conduct of such Member, officer, or employee of the House of Representatives; the Committee on Veterans' Affairs—on general pension bills; the Committee on Ways and Means—on bills raising revenue.

23. It shall always be in order to call up for consideration a report from the Committee on Rules (except it shall not be called up for consideration on the same day it is presented to the House, unless so determined by a vote of not less than two-thirds of the Members voting, but this provision shall not apply during the last three days of the session), and, pending the consideration thereof, the Speaker may entertain one motion that the House adjourn; but after the result is announced he shall not entertain any other dilatory motion until the said report shall have been fully disposed of. The Committee on Rules shall not report any rule or order which shall provide that business under clause 7 of the rule XXIV shall be set aside by a vote of less than two-thirds of the Members present; nor shall it report any rule or order which shall operate to prevent the motion to recommit being made as provided in clause 4 of rule XVI.

24. The Committee on Rules shall present to the House reports concerning rules, joint rules and order of business, within three legislative days of the time when ordered reported by the committee. If such rule or order is not considered immediately, it shall be referred to the calendar and, if not called up by the Member making the report within seven legislative days thereafter, any member of the Rules Committee may call it up as a question of privilege and the Speaker shall recognize any member of the Rules Committee seeking recognition for that purpose. If the Committee on Rules shall make an adverse report on any resolution pending before the committee, providing for an order of business for the consideration by the House of any public bill or joint resolution, on days when it shall be in order to call up motions to discharge committees it shall be in order for any Member of the House to call up for consideration by the House any such adverse report, and it shall be in order to move the adoption by the House of said resolution adversely reported notwithstanding the adverse report of the Committee on Rules, and the Speaker shall recognize the Member seeking recognition for that purpose as a question of the highest privilege.

25. The Committee on House Administration shall make final report to the House in each contested-election case at such time as the committee considers practicable in that Congress to which the contestee is elected.

26. (a) Each standing committee of the House shall fix, by written rule adopted by the committee, regular meeting days of the committee, not less frequent than monthly, for the conduct of its business. Each such committee shall meet, for the consideration of any bill or resolution pending before the committee or for the transaction of other committee business, on all regular meeting days fixed by the committee, unless otherwise provided by written rule adopted by the committee.

(b) The chairman of each standing committee may call and convene, as he considers necessary, additional meetings of the committee for the consideration of any bill or resolution pending before the committee or for the conduct of other committee business. The committee shall meet for such purpose pursuant to that call of the chairman.

(c) If at least three members of any standing committee desire that a special meeting of the committee be called by the chairman, those members may file in the offices of the committee their written request to the chairman for that special meeting. Such request shall specify the measure or matter to be considered. Immediately upon the filing of the request, the clerk of the committee shall notify the chairman of the filing of the request. If, within three calendar days after the filing of the request, the chairman does not call the requested special meeting, to be held within seven calendar days after the filing of the request, a majority of the members of the committee may file in the offices of the committee their written notice that a special meeting of the committee will be held, specifying the date and hour of, and the measure or matter to be considered at, that special meeting. The committee shall meet on that date and hour. Immediately upon the filing of the notice, the clerk of the committee shall notify all members of the committee that such special meeting will be held and inform them of its date and hour and the measure or matter to be considered; and only the measure or matter specified in that notice may be considered at that special meeting.

(d) If the chairman of any standing committee is not present at any regular, additional, or special meeting of the committee, the ranking member of the majority party on the committee who is present shall preside at that meeting.

(e) For the purposes of this clause, "chairman" includes a Member acting as chairman under clause 3 (now clause 4) of Rule X.

(f) Meetings for the transaction of business of each standing committee shall be open to the public except when the committee, by majority vote, determines otherwise. This paragraph does not apply to open committee hearings which are provided for by paragraphs (f)(2) and (g)(3) of clause 27 of this Rule.

27. (a) The Rules of the House are the rules of its committees and subcommittees so far as applicable, except that a motion to recess from day to day is a motion of high privilege in committees and subcommittees. Committees shall adopt written rules not inconsistent with the Rules of the House and those rules shall be binding on each subcommittee of that committee. Each subcommittee of a committee is a part of that committee and is subject to the authority and direction of that committee.

(b) Each committee shall keep a complete record of all committee action. Such record shall include a record of the votes on any question on which a record vote is demanded. The result of each rollcall vote in any meeting of any committee shall be made available by that committee for inspection by the public at reasonable times in the offices of that committee. Information so available for public inspection shall include a description of the amendment, motion, order, or other proposition and the name of each Member voting for and each Member voting against such amendment, motion, order, or proposition, and whether by proxy or in person, and the names of those Members present but not voting. With respect to each record vote by any committee on each motion to report any bill or resolution of a public character, the total number of votes cast for, and the total number of votes cast against, the reporting of such bill or resolution shall be included in the committee report.

(c) All committee hearings, records, data, charts, and files shall be kept separate and distinct from the congressional office records of the Member serving as chairman of the committee; and such records shall be the property of the House and all Members of the House shall have access to such records. Each committee is authorized to have printed and bound testimony and other data presented at hearings held by the committee.

(d)(1) It shall be the duty of the chairman of each committee to report or cause to be reported promptly to the House any measure approved by his committee and to take or cause to be taken necessary steps to bring the matter to a vote.

(2) In any event, the report of any committee on a measure which has been approved by the committee shall be filed within seven calendar days (exclusive of days on which the House is not in session) after the day on which there has been filed with the clerk of the committee a written request, signed by a majority of the members of the committee, for the reporting of that measure. Upon the filing of any such request, the clerk of the committee shall transmit immediately to the chairman of the committee notice of the filing of that request. This subparagraph does

not apply to a report of the Committee on Rules with respect to the rules, joint rules, or order of business of the House or to the reporting of a resolution of inquiry addressed to the head of an executive department.

(3) If, at the time of approval of any measure or matter by any committee (except the Committee on Rules) any member of the committee, gives notice of intention to file supplemental, minority, or additional views, that member shall be entitled to not less than three calendar days (excluding Saturdays, Sundays, and legal holidays), in which to file such views, in writing and signed by that member, with the clerk of the committee. All such views so filed by one or more members of the committee shall be included within, and shall be a part of, the report filed by the committee with respect to that measure or matter. The report of the committee upon that measure or matter shall be printed in a single volume which—

(A) shall include all supplemental, minority, or additional views which have been submitted by the time of the filing of the report, and

(B) shall bear upon its cover a recital that supplemental, minority, or additional views are included as part of the report.
This subparagraph does not preclude—

(i) the immediate filing or printing of a committee report unless timely request for the opportunity to file supplemental, minority, or additional views has been made as provided by this subparagraph; or

(ii) the filing by any such committee of any supplemental report upon any measure or matter which may be required for the correction of any technical error in a previous report made by that committee upon that measure or matter.

(4) A measure or matter reported by any committee (except the Committee on Appropriations, the Committee on House Administration, the Committee on Rules, and the Committee on Standards of Official Conduct) shall not be considered in the House unless the report of that committee upon that measure or matter has been available to the Members of the House for at least three calendar days (excluding Saturdays, Sundays, and legal holidays) prior to the consideration of that measure or matter in the House. If hearings have been held on any such measure or matter so reported, the committee reporting the measure or matter shall make every reasonable effort to have such hearings printed and available for distribution to the Members of the House prior to the consideration of such measure or matter in the House. This subparagraph shall not apply to—

(A) any measure for the declaration of war, or the declaration of a national emergency, by the Congress; and

(B) any executive decision, determination, or action which would become, or continue to be, effective unless disapproved or otherwise invalidated by one or both Houses of Congress.

(5) If, within seven calendar days after a measure has, by resolution, been made in order for consideration by the House, no motion has been offered that the House consider that measure, the Speaker may, in his discretion, recognize any member of the committee which reported that measure to offer a motion that the House shall consider that measure, if that committee has duly authorized that member to offer that motion.

(e) No measure or recommendation shall be reported from any committee unless a majority of the committee were actually present. No vote by any member of any committee with respect to any measure or matter may be cast by proxy unless such committee, by written rule adopted by the committee, permits voting by proxy and requires that the proxy authorization shall be in writing, shall designate the person who is to execute the proxy authorization, and shall be limited to a specific measure or matter and any amendments or motions pertaining thereto.

(f)(1) Each committee of the House (except the Committee on Rules) shall make public announcement of the date, place, and subject matter of any hearing to be conducted by the committee on any measure or matter at least one week before the commencement of that hearing, unless the committee determines that there is good cause to begin such hearing at an earlier date. If the committee makes that determination, the committee shall make such public announcement at the earliest possible date. Such public announcement also shall be published in the Daily Digest portion of the Congressional Record as soon as possible after such public announcement is made by the committee.

(2) Each hearing conducted by each committee shall be open to the public except when the committee, by majority vote, determines otherwise.

(3) Each committee shall require, so far as practicable, each witness who is to appear before it to file with the committee, in advance of his appearance, a written statement of his proposed testimony and to limit his oral presentation at his appearance to a brief summary of his argument.

(4) Whenever any hearing is conducted by any committee upon any measure or matter, the minority party members on the committee shall be entitled, upon request to the chairman by a majority of those minority party members before the completion of such hearing, to call witnesses selected by the minority to testify with respect to that measure

or matter during at least one day of hearing thereon. All committees shall provide in their rules of procedure for the application of the five-minute rule in the interrogation of witnesses until such time as each member of the committee who so desires has had an opportunity to question the witness.

(5) No point of order shall lie with respect to any measure reported by any committee on the ground that hearings upon such measure were not conducted in accordance with the provisions of this clause; except that a point of order on that ground may be made by any member of the committee which has reported the measure if, in the committee, such point of order was (A) timely made and (B) improperly overruled or not properly considered.

(6) The preceding provisions of this paragraph do not apply to hearings on the Budget by the Committee on Appropriations under paragraph (g) of this clause.

(g)(1) The Committee on Appropriations shall, within thirty days after the transmittal of the Budget to the Congress each year, hold hearings on the Budget as a whole with particular reference to—

(A) the basic recommendations and budgetary policies of the President in the presentation of the Budget; and

(B) the fiscal, financial, and economic assumptions used as bases in arriving at total estimated expenditures and receipts.

(2) In holding hearings pursuant to subparagraph (1) of this paragraph, the committee shall receive testimony from the Secretary of the Treasury, the Director of the Office of Management and Budget, the Chairman of the Council of Economic Advisers, and such other persons as the committee may desire.

(3) Hearings pursuant to subparagraph (1) of this paragraph shall be held in open session, except when the committee determines that the testimony to be taken at that hearing may relate to a matter of national security. A transcript of all such hearings shall be printed and a copy thereof furnished to each Member and the Resident Commissioner from Puerto Rico.

(4) Hearings pursuant to subparagraph (1) of this paragraph, or any part thereof, may be held before joint meetings of the committee and the Committee on Appropriations of the Senate in accordance with such procedures as the two committees jointly may determine.

(h) Each committee may fix the number of its members to constitute a quorum for taking testimony and receiving evidence, which shall be not less than two.

(i) The chairman at an investigative hearing shall announce in an opening statement the subject of the investigation.

(j) A copy of the committee rules, if any, and this clause of this rule shall be made available to the witness.

(k) Witnesses at investigative hearings may be accompanied by their own counsel for the purpose of advising them concerning their constitutional rights.

(l) The chairman may punish breaches of order and decorum, and of professional ethics on the part of counsel, by censure and exclusion from the hearings; and the committee may cite the offender to the House for contempt.

(m) If the committee determines that evidence or testimony at an investigative hearing may tend to defame, degrade, or incriminate any person, it shall—

(1) receive such evidence or testimony in executive session;

(2) afford such person an opportunity voluntarily to appear as a witness; and

(3) receive and dispose of requests from such person to subpena additional witnesses.

(n) Except as provided in paragraph (m), the chairman shall receive and the committee shall dispose of requests to subpena additional witnesses.

(o) No evidence or testimony taken in executive session may be released or used in public sessions without the consent of the committee.

(p) In the discretion of the committee, witnesses may submit brief and pertinent sworn statements in writing for inclusion in the record. The committee is the sole judge of the pertinency of testimony and evidence adduced at its hearing.

(q) Upon payment of the cost thereof, a witness may obtain a transcript copy of his testimony given at a public session or, if given at an executive session, when authorized by the committee.

28. (a) In order to assist the House in—

(1) its analysis, appraisal, and evaluation of the application, administration, and execution of the laws enacted by the Congress, and

(2) its formulation, consideration, and enactment of such modifications of or changes in those laws, and of such additional legislation, as may be necessary or appropriate,

each standing committee shall review and study, on a continuing basis, the application, administration, and execution of those laws, or parts of laws, the subject matter of which is within the jurisdiction of that committee.

(b) Each standing committee shall submit to the House, not later than January 2 of each odd-numbered year beginning on or after January 1, 1973, a report on the activities of that committee under this clause during the Congress ending at noon on January 3 of such year.

(c) The preceding provisions of this clause do not apply to the Committee on Appropriations, the Committee on House Administration, the Committee on Rules, and the Committee on Standards of Official Conduct.

(d) Each standing committee of the House shall, in its consideration of all bills and joint resolutions of a public character within its jurisdiction, endeavor to insure that—

(1) all continuing programs of the Federal Government, and of the government of the District of Columbia, within the jurisdiction of that committee, are designed; and

(2) all continuing activities of Government agencies, within the jurisdiction of that committee, are carried on;

so that, to the extent consistent with the nature, requirements, and objectives of those programs and activities, appropriations therefor will be made annually. For the purposes of this paragraph, a Government agency includes the organizational units of government listed in paragraph (d) of clause 7 of Rule XIII.

(e) Each standing committee of the House shall review, from time to time, each continuing program within its jurisdiction for which appropriations are not made annually in order to ascertain whether such program could be modified so that appropriations therefor would be made annually.

29. (a)(1) Subject to subparagraph (2) of this paragraph and paragraph (f) of this clause, each standing committee may appoint, by majority vote of the committee, not more than six professional staff members. Each professional staff member appointed under this subparagraph shall be assigned to the chairman and the ranking minority party member of such committee, as the committee considers advisable.

(2) Subject to paragraph (f) of this clause, whenever a majority of the minority party members of a standing committee (except the Committee on Standards of Official Conduct) so request, not more than two persons may be selected, by majority vote of the minority party members, for appointment by the committee as professional staff members from among the number authorized by subparagraph (1) of this paragraph. The committee shall appoint any persons so selected whose character and qualifications are acceptable to a majority of the committee. If the committee determines that the character and qualifications of any person so selected are unacceptable to the committee, a majority of the minority party members may select other persons for appointment by the committee to the professional staff until such appointment is made. Each professional staff member appointed under this subparagraph shall be assigned to such committee business as the minority party members of the committee consider advisable.

(3) The professional staff members of each standing committee—

(A) shall be appointed on a permanent basis, without regard to political affiliation, and solely on the basis of fitness to perform the duties of their respective positions;

(B) shall not engage in any work other than committee business; and

(C) shall not be assigned any duties other than those pertaining to committee business.

(4) Services of the professional staff members of each standing committee may be terminated by majority vote of the committee.

(5) The foregoing provisions of this paragraph do not apply to the Committee on Appropriations.

(b)(1) The clerical staff of each standing committee shall consist of not more than six clerks, to be attached to the office of the chairman, to the ranking minority party member, and to the professional staff, as the committee considers advisable. Subject to subparagraph (2) of this paragraph and paragraph (f) of this clause, the clerical staff shall be appointed by majority vote of the committee. Except as provided by subparagraph (2) of this paragraph, the clerical staff shall handle committee correspondence and stenographic work both for the committee staff and for the chairman and the ranking minority party member on matters related to committee work.

(2) Subject to paragraph (f) of this clause, whenever a majority of the minority party members of a standing committee (except the Committee on Standards of Official Conduct) so request, one person may be selected, by majority vote of the minority party members, for appointment by the committee to a position on the clerical staff from among the number of clerks authorized by subparagraph (1) of this paragraph. The committee shall appoint to that position any person so selected whose character and qualifications are acceptable to a majority of the committee. If the committee determines that the character and qualifications of any person so selected are unacceptable to the committee, a majority of the minority party members may select other persons for appointment by the committee to that position on the clerical staff until such appoint-

ment is made. Each clerk appointed under this subparagraph shall handle committee correspondence and stenographic work for the minority party members of the committee and for any members of the professional staff appointed under subparagraph (2) of paragraph (a) of this clause on matters related to committee work.

(3) Services of the clerical staff members of each standing committee may be terminated by majority vote of the committee.

(4) The foregoing provisions of this paragraph do not apply to the Committee on Appropriations.

(c) Each employee on the professional staff, and each employee on the clerical staff, of each standing committee, is entitled to pay at a single per annum gross rate, to be fixed by the chairman, which does not exceed the highest rate of basic pay, as in effect from time to time, of the General Schedule of section 5332(a) of title 5, United States Code.

(d) Subject to appropriations hereby authorized, the Committee on Appropriations may appoint such staff, in addition to the clerk thereof and assistants for the minority, as it by majority vote determines to be necessary, such personnel, other than minority assistants, to possess such qualifications as the committee may prescribe.

(e) No committee shall appoint to its staff any experts or other personnel detailed or assigned from any department or agency of the Government, except with the written permission of the Committee on House Administration.

(f) If a request for the appointment of a minority professional staff member under paragraph (a), or a minority clerical staff member under paragraph (b), of this clause, is made when no vacancy exists to which that appointment may be made, the committee nevertheless shall appoint, under paragraph (a) or paragraph (b), as applicable, the person selected by the minority and acceptable to the committee. The person so appointed shall serve as an additional member of the professional staff or the clerical staff, as the case may be, of the committee, and shall be paid from the contingent fund, until such time as such a vacancy (other than a vacancy in the position of head of the professional staff, by whatever title designated) occurs, at which time that person shall be deemed to have been appointed to that vacancy. If such vacancy occurs on the professional staff when two persons have been so appointed who are eligible to fill that vacancy, a majority of the minority party members shall designate which of those persons shall fill that vacancy.

(g) Each staff member appointed pursuant to a request by minority party members under paragraph (a) or (b) of this clause, and each staff member appointed to assist minority party members of a committee pursuant to House resolution, shall be accorded equitable treatment with respect to the fixing of his rate of pay, the assignment to him of work facilities, and the accessibility to him of committee records.

(h) Paragraphs (a) and (b) of this clause shall not be construed to authorize the appointment of additional professional or clerical staff members of a committee pursuant to request under either of such paragraphs by the minority party members of that committee if two or more professional staff members or one or more clerical staff members, provided for in paragraph (a)(1) or paragraph (b)(1) of this clause, as the case may be, who are satisfactory to a majority of the minority party members, are otherwise assigned to assist the minority party members.

30. Each committee shall report to the Clerk of the House within fifteen days after December 31 and June 30 of each year the name, profession, and total salary of each person employed by such committee or any subcommittee thereof during the period covered by such report, and shall make an accounting of funds made available to and expended by such committee or subcommittee during such period, and such information when reported shall be published in the Congressional Record.

31. No committee of the House (except the Committee on Appropriations, the Committee on Government Operations, the Committee on Internal Security, the Committee on Rules, and the Committee on Standards of Official Conduct) may sit, without special leave, while the House is reading a measure for amendment under the five-minute rule.

32. (a) Whenever any standing committee (except the Committee on Appropriations) is to be granted authorization for the payment, from the contingent fund of the House, of its expenses in any year, other than those expenses to be paid from appropriations provided by statute, such authorization initially shall be procured by one primary expense resolution for that committee providing funds for the payment of the expenses of the committee for that year from the contingent fund of the House. Any such primary expense resolution reported to the House shall not be considered in the House unless a printed report on that resolution has been available to the Members of the House for at least one calendar day prior to the consideration of that resolution in the House. Such report shall, for the information of the House—

(1) state the total amount of the funds to be provided to the committee under the primary expense resolution for all anticipated activities and programs of the committee; and

(2) to the extent practicable, contain such general statements regarding the estimated foreseeable expenditures for the respective anticipated

activities and programs of the committee as may be appropriate to provide the House with basic estimates with respect to the expenditure generally of the funds to be provided to the committee under the primary expense resolution.

(b) After the date of adoption by the House of any such primary expense resolution for any such standing committee for any year, authorization for the payment from the contingent fund of additional expenses of such committee in that year, other than those expenses to be paid from appropriations provided by statute, may be procured by one or more additional expense resolutions for that committee, as necessary. Any such additional expense resolution reported to the House shall not be considered in the House unless a printed report on that resolution has been available to the Members of the House for at least one calendar day prior to the consideration of that resolution in the House. Such report shall, for the information of the House—

(1) state the total amount of additional funds to be provided to the committee under the additional expense resolution and the purpose or purposes for which those additional funds are to be used by the committee; and

(2) state the reason or reasons for the failure to procure the additional funds for the committee by means of the primary expense resolution.

(c) The minority party on any such standing committee is entitled to and shall receive fair consideration in the appointment of committee staff personnel pursuant to each such primary or additional expense resolution.

(d) The preceding provisions of this clause do not apply to—

(1) any resolution providing for the payment from the contingent fund of the House of sums necessary to pay compensation for staff services performed for, or to pay other expenses of, any standing committee at any time from and after the beginning of any year and before the date of adoption by the House of the primary expense resolution providing funds to pay the expenses of that committee for that year; and

(2) any resolution providing in any Congress, for all of the standing committees of the House, additional office equipment, airmail and special delivery postage stamps, supplies, staff personnel, or any other specific item for the operation of the standing committees, and containing an authorization for the payment from the contingent fund of the House of the expenses of any of the foregoing items provided by that resolution, subject to and until enactment of the provisions of the resolution as permanent law.

33. (a) It is the purpose of this clause to provide a means, in conformity with acceptable standards of dignity, propriety, and decorum, by which committee hearings which are open to the public may be covered, by television broadcast, radio broadcast, and still photography, or by any of such methods of coverage—

(1) for the education, enlightenment, and information of the general public, on the basis of accurate and impartial news coverage, regarding the operations, procedures, and practices of the House as a legislative and representative body and regarding the measures, public issues, and other matters before the House and its committees, the consideration thereof, and the action taken thereon; and

(2) for the development of the perspective and understanding of the general public with respect to the role and function of the House under the Constitution of the United States as an organ of the Federal Government.

(b) In addition, it is the intent of this clause that radio and television tapes and television film of any coverage under this clause shall not be used, or made available for use, as partisan politican campaign material to promote or oppose the candidacy of any person for elective public office.

(c) It is, further, the intent of this clause that the general conduct of each meeting of any hearing or hearings covered, under authority of this clause, by television broadcast, radio broadcast, and still photography, or by any of such methods of coverage, and the personal behavior of the committee members and staff, other Government officials and personnel, witnesses, television, radio, and press media personnel, and the general public at the hearing shall be in strict conformity with and observance of the acceptable standards of dignity, propriety, courtesy, and decorum traditionally observed by the House in its operations and shall not be such as to—

(A) distort the objects and purposes of the hearing or the activities of committee members in connection with that hearing or in connection with the general work of the committee or of the House; or

(B) cast discredit or dishonor on the House, the committee, or any Member or bring the House, the committee, or any Member into disrepute.

(d) The coverage of committee hearings by television broadcast, radio broadcast, or still photography is a privilege made available by the House and shall be permitted and conducted only in strict conformity with the purposes, provisions, and requirements of this clause.

(e) Whenever any hearing conducted by any committee of the House is open to the public, that committee may permit, by majority vote of the committee, that hearing to be covered, in whole or in part, by television broadcast, radio broadcast, and still photography, or by any of such methods of coverage, but only under such written rules as the committee may adopt in accordance with the purposes, provisions, and requirements of this clause.

(f) The written rules which may be adopted by a committee under paragraph (e) of this clause shall contain provision to the following effect:

(1) If the television or radio coverage of the hearing is to be presented to the public as live coverage, that coverage shall be conducted and presented without commercial sponsorship.

(2) No witness served with a subpena by the committee shall be required against his will to be photographed at any hearing or to give evidence or testimony while the broadcasting of that hearing, by radio or television, is being conducted. At the request of any such witness who does not wish to be subjected to radio, television, or still photography coverage, all lenses shall be covered and all microphones used for coverage turned off. This subparagraph is supplementary to paragraph (m) of clause 27 of this rule, relating to the protection of the rights of witnesses.

(3) Not more than four television cameras, operating from fixed positions, shall be permitted in a hearing room. The allocation among the television media of the positions of the number of television cameras permitted in a hearing room shall be in accordance with fair and equitable procedures devised by the Executive Committee of the Radio and Television Coorespondents' Galleries.

(4) Television cameras shall be placed so as not to obstruct in any way the space between any witness giving evidence or testimony and any member of the committee or the visibility of that witness and that member to each other.

(5) Television cameras shall not be placed in positions which obstruct unnecessarily the coverage of the hearing by the other media.

(6) Equipment necessary for coverage by the television and radio media shall not be installed in, or removed from, the hearing room while the committee is in session.

(7) Floodlights, spotlights, strobelights, and flashguns shall not be used in providing any method of coverage of the hearing, except that the television media may install additional lighting in the hearing room, without cost to the Government, in order to raise the ambient lighting level in the hearing room to the lowest level necessary to provide adequate television coverage of the hearing at the then current state of the art of television coverage.

(8) Not more than five press photographers shall be permitted to cover a hearing by still photography. In the selection of these photographers, preference shall be given to photographers from Associated Press Photos and United Press International Newspictures. If request is made by more than five of the media for coverage of the hearing by still photography, that coverage shall be made on the basis of a fair and equitable pool arrangement devised by the Standing Committee of Press Photographers.

(9) Photographers shall not position themselves, at any time during the course of the hearing, between the witness table and the members of the committee.

(10) Photographers shall not place themselves in positions which obstruct unnecessarily the coverage of the hearing by the other media.

(11) Personnel providing coverage by the television and radio media shall be then currently accredited to the Radio and Television Correspondents' Galleries.

(12) Personnel providing coverage by still photography shall be then currently accredited to the Press Photographers' Gallery.

(13) Personnel providing coverage by the television and radio media and by still photography shall conduct themselves and their coverage activities in an orderly and unobtrusive manner.

Rule XII

Resident Commissioner from Puerto Rico and Delegate from the District of Columbia

1. The Resident Commissioner to the United States from Puerto Rico shall be elected to serve on standing committees in the same manner as Members of the House and shall possess in such committees the same powers and privileges as the other Members.

2. The Delegate from the District of Columbia shall be elected to serve as a member of the Committee on the District of Columbia and shall be elected to serve on other standing committees of the House in the same manner as Members of the House and shall possess in all committees on which he serves the same powers and privileges as the other Members.

Rule XIII

Calendars and Reports of Committees

1. There shall be three calendars to which all business reported from committees shall be referred, viz:

First. A Calendar of the Committee of the Whole House on the state of the Union, to which shall be referred bills raising revenue, general appropriation bills, and bills of a public character directly or indirectly appropriating money or property.

Second. A House Calendar, to which shall be referred all bills of a public character not raising revenue nor directly or indirectly appropriating money or property.

Third. A Calendar of the Committee of the Whole House, to which shall be referred all bills of a private character.

2. All reports of committees, except as provided in clause 22 of Rule XI, together with the views of the minority, shall be delivered to the Clerk for printing and reference to the proper calendar under the direction of the Speaker in accordance with the foregoing clause, and the titles or subject therof shall be entered on the Journal and printed in the Record: *Provided,* That bills reported adversely shall be laid on the table, unless the committee reporting a bill, at the time, or any Member within three days thereafter, shall request its reference to the calendar, when it shall be referred, as provided in clause 1 of this rule.

3. Whenever a committee reports a bill or a joint resolution repealing or amending any statute or part thereof it shall include in its report or in an accompanying document—

(1) The text of the statute or part thereof which is proposed to be repealed; and

(2) A comparative print of that part of the bill or joint resolution making the amendment and of the statute or part thereof proposed to be amended, showing by stricken-through type and italics, parallel columns, or other appropriate typographical devices the omissions and insertions proposed to be made: *Provided, however,* That if a committee reports such a bill or joint resolution with amendments or an amendment in the nature of a substitute for the entire bill; such report shall include a comparative print showing any changes in existing law proposed by the amendments or substitute instead of as in the bill as introduced.

4. After a bill has been favorably reported and shall be upon either the House or Union Calendar any Member may file with the Clerk a notice that he desires such bill placed upon a special calendar to be known as the "Consent Calendar." On the first and third Mondays of each month immediately after the reading of the Journal, the Speaker shall direct the Clerk to call the bills in numerical order, which have been for three legislative days upon the "Consent Calendar." Should objection be made to the consideration of any bill so called it shall be carried over on the calendar without prejudice to the next day when the "Consent Calendar" is again called, and if objected to by three or more Members it shall immediately be stricken from the Calendar, and shall not thereafter during the same session of that Congress be placed again thereon: *Provided,* That no bill shall be called twice on the same legislative day.

5. There shall also be a Calendar of Motions to Discharge Committees, as provided in clause 4 of Rule XXVII.

6. Calendars shall be printed daily.

7. (a) The report accompanying each bill or joint resolution of a public character reported by any committee shall contain—

(1) an estimate, made by such committee, of the costs which would be incurred in carrying out such bill or joint resolution in the fiscal year in which it is reported and in each of the five fiscal years following such fiscal year (or for the authorized duration of any program authorized by such bill or joint resolution, if less than five years), except that, in the case of measures affecting the revenues, such reports shall require only an estimate of the gain or loss in revenues for a one-year period; and

(2) a comparison of the estimate of costs described in subparagraph (1) of this paragraph made by such committee with any estimate of such costs made by any Government agency and submitted to such committee.

(b) It shall not be in order to consider any such bill or joint resolution in the House if the report of the committee which reported that bill or joint resolution does not comply with paragraph (a) of this clause.

(c) For the purposes of this clause, the members of the Joint Committee on Atomic Energy who are Members of the House shall be deemed to be a committee of the House.

(d) For the purposes of subparagraph (2) of paragraph (a) of this clause, a Government agency includes any department, agency, establishment, wholly owned Government corporation, or instrumentality of the Federal Government or the government of the District of Columbia.

(e) The preceding provisions of this clause do not apply to the Committee on Appropriations, the Committee on House Administration, the Committee on Rules, and the Committee on Standards of Official Conduct.

Rule XIV

Of Decorum and Debate

1. When any Member desires to speak or deliver any matter to the House, he shall rise and respectfully address himself to "Mr. Speaker," and, on being recognized, may address the House from any place on the floor or from the Clerk's desk, and shall confine himself to the question under debate, avoiding personality.

2. When two or more Members rise at once, the Speaker shall name the Member who is first to speak; and no Member shall occupy more than one hour in debate on any question in the House or in committee, except as further provided in this rule.

3. The Member reporting the measure under consideration from a committee may open and close, where general debate has been had thereon; and if it shall extend beyond one day, he shall be entitled to one hour to close, notwithstanding he may have used an hour in opening.

4. If any Member, in speaking or otherwise, transgress the rules of the House, the Speaker shall, or any Member may, call him to order; in which case he shall immediately sit down, unless permitted, on motion of another Member, to explain, and the House shall, if appealed to, decide on the case without debate; if the decision is in favor of the Member called to order, he shall be at liberty to proceed, but not otherwise; and, if the case require it, he shall be liable to censure or such punishment as the House may deem proper.

5. If a Member is called to order for words spoken in debate, the Member calling him to order shall indicate the words excepted to, and they shall be taken down in writing at the Clerk's desk and read aloud to the House; but he shall not be held to answer, nor be subject to the censure of the House therefor, if further debate or other business has intervened.

6. No Member shall speak more than once to the same question without leave of the House, unless he be the mover, proposer, or introducer of the matter pending, in which case he shall be permitted to speak in reply, but not until every Member choosing to speak shall have spoken.

7. While the Speaker is putting a question or addressing the House no Member shall walk out of or across the hall, nor, when a Member is speaking, pass between him and the Chair; and during the session of the House no Member shall wear his hat, or remain by the Clerk's desk during the call of the roll or the counting of ballots, or smoke upon the floor of the House; and the Sergeant at Arms and Doorkeeper are charged with the strict enforcement of this clause. Neither shall any person be allowed to smoke upon the floor of the House at any time.

8. It shall not be in order for any Member to introduce to or to bring to the attention of the House during its sessions any occupant in the galleries of the House; nor may the Speaker entertain a request for the suspension of this rule by unanimous consent or otherwise.

Rule XV

On Calls of the Roll and House

1. Upon every roll call the names of the Members shall be called alphabetically by surname, except when two or more have the same surname, in which case the name of the State shall be added; and if there be two such Members from the same State, the whole name shall be called, and after the roll has been once called, the Clerk shall call in their alphabetical order the names of those not voting. Members appearing after the second call, but before the result is announced, may vote or announce a pair.

2. (a) In the absence of a quorum, fifteen Members, including the Speaker, if there is one, shall be authorized to compel the attendance of absent Members, and in all calls of the House the doors shall be closed, the names of the Members shall be called by the Clerk, and the absentees noted, but the doors shall not be closed except when so ordered by the Speaker; and those for whom no sufficient excuse is made may, by order of a majority of those present, be sent for an arrested, wherever they may be found, by offficers to be appointed by the Sergeant at Arms for that purpose, and their attendance secured and retained; and the House shall determine upon what condition they shall be discharged. Members who voluntarily appear shall, unless the House otherwise direct, be immediately admitted to the Hall of the House, and they shall report their names to the Clerk to be entered upon the Journal as present.

(b) When a call of the House in the absence of a quorum is ordered, the Speaker of the House or the Chairman of the Committee of the Whole House, as the case may be, in his discretion may order the Clerk of the House to lay out tally sheets on which the presence of the Members shall be recorded by the Clerk or the respective Members. When a quorum has been recorded, which in the Committee of the Whole House shall be one hundred Members, the Clerk shall advise the Speaker or Chairman of this fact, after which it shall be in order to entertain a motion, which is privileged and shall be decided without debate, to dispense with further proceedings under the call, and the business of the House or the Committee of the Whole shall then resume. However, for a period of thirty minutes following the commencement of such quorum call, Members who are present before the expiration of such thirty-minute period may have their presence recorded on such tally sheets. Absent Members shall be recorded in the Journal of the House.

3. On the demand of any Member, or at the suggestion of the Speaker, the names of Members sufficient to make a quorum in the Hall of the House who do not vote shall be noted by the Clerk and recorded in the Journal, and reported to the Speaker with the names of the Members voting, and be counted and announced in determining the presence of a quorum to do business.

4. Whenever a quorum fails to vote on any question, and a quorum is not present and objection is made for that cause, unless the House shall adjourn there shall be a call of the House, and the Sergeant at Arms shall forthwith proceed to bring in absent Members, and the yeas and nays on the pending question shall at the same time be considered as ordered. The Clerk shall call the role, and each Member as he answers to his name may vote on the pending question, and, after the roll call is completed, each Member arrested shall be brought by the Sergeant at Arms before the House, whereupon he shall be noted as present, discharged from arrest, and given an opportunity to vote and his vote shall be recorded. If those voting on the question and those who are present and decline to vote together make a majority of the House, the Speaker shall declare that a quorum is constituted, and the pending question shall be decided as the majority of those voting shall appear. And thereupon further proceedings, under the call shall be considered as dispensed with. At any time after the roll call has been completed, the Speaker may entertain a motion to adjourn, if seconded by a majority of those present, to be ascertained by actual count by the Speaker; and if the House adjourns, all proceedings under this section shall be vacated.

5. In lieu of the calling of the names of Members in the manner provided for under the preceding provisions of this Rule, upon any roll call or quorum call, the names of such Members voting or present may be recorded through the use of appropriate electronic equipment. In any such case, the Clerk shall enter in the Journal and publish in the Congressional Record, in alphabetical order in each category, a list of the names of those Members recorded as voting in the affirmative, of those Members recorded as voting in the negative, and of those Members voting present, as the case may be, as if their names had been called in the manner provided for under such preceding provisions.

Rule XVI

On Motions, Their Precedence

1. Every motion made to the House and entertained by the Speaker shall be reduced to writing on the demand of any Member, and shall be entered on the Journal with the name of the Member making it, unless it is withdrawn the same day.

2. When a motion has been made, the Speaker shall state it or (if it be in writing) cause it to be read aloud by the Clerk before being debated, and it shall then be in possession of the House, but may be withdrawn at any time before a decision or amendment.

3. When any motion or proposition is made, the question, Will the House now consider it? shall not be put unless demanded by a Member.

4. When a question is under debate, no motion shall be received but to adjourn, to lay on the table, for the previous question (which motions shall be decided without debate), to postpone to a day certain, to refer, or to amend, or postpone indefinitely; which several motions shall have precedence in the foregoing order; and no motion to postpone to a day certain, to refer, or to postpone indefinitely, being decided, shall be again allowed on the same day at the same stage of the question. After the previous question shall have been ordered on the passage of a bill or joint resolution one motion to recommit shall be in order, and the Speaker shall give preference in recognition for such purpose to a Member who is opposed to the bill or joint resolution. However, with respect to any motion to recommit with instructions after the previous question shall have been ordered, it always shall be in order to debate such motion for ten minutes before the vote is taken on that motion, one half of such time to be given to debate by the mover of the motion and one half to debate in opposition to the motion.

5. The hour at which the House adjourns shall be entered on the Journal.

6. On the demand of any Member, before the question is put, a question shall be divided if it include propositions so distinct in substance that one being taken away a substantive proposition shall remain: *Provided,* That any motion or resolution to elect the members or any portion of the members of the standing committees of the House and the joint standing committees shall not be divisible nor shall any resolution or order reported by the Committee on Rules, providing a special order of business be divisible.

7. A motion to strike out and insert is indivisible, but a motion to strike out being lost shall neither preclude amendment nor motion to strike out and insert; and no motion or proposition on a subject different from that under consideration shall be admitted under color of amendment.

8. Pending a motion to suspend the rules, the Speaker may entertain one motion that the House adjourn; but after the result thereon is announced he shall not entertain any other motion till the vote is taken on suspension.

9. At any time after the reading of the Journal it shall be in order, by direction of the appropriate committees, to move that the House resolve itself into the Committee of the Whole House on the state of the Union for the purpose of considering bills raising revenue, or general appropriation bills.

10. No dilatory motion shall be entertained by the Speaker.

Rule XVII

Previous Question

1. There shall be a motion for the previous question, which, being ordered by a majority of Members voting, if a quorum be present, shall have the effect to cut off all debate and bring the House to a direct vote upon the immediate question or questions on which it has been asked and ordered. The previous question may be asked and ordered upon a single motion, a series of motions allowable under the rules, or an amendment or amendments, or may be made to embrace all authorized motions or amendments and include the bill to its passage or rejection. It shall be in order, pending the motion for, or after the previous question shall have been ordered on its passage, for the Speaker to entertain and submit a motion to commit, with or without instructions, to a standing or select committee.

2. A call of the House shall not be in order after the previous question is ordered, unless it shall appear upon an actual count by the Speaker that a quorum is not present.

3. All incidental questions of order arising after a motion is made for the previous question, and pending such motion, shall be decided, whether on appeal or otherwise, without debate.

Rule XVIII

Reconsideration

1. When a motion has been made and carried or lost, it shall be in order for any member of the majority, on the same or suceeding day, to move for the reconsideration thereof, and such motion shall take precedence of all other questions except the consideration of a conference report or a motion to adjourn, and shall not be withdrawn after the said succeeding day without the consent of the House, and thereafter any Member may call it up for consideration: *Provided,* That such motion, if made during the last six days of a session, shall be disposed of when made.

2. No bill, petition, memorial, or resolution referred to a committee, or reported therefrom for printing and recommittment, shall be brought back into the House on a motion to reconsider; and all bills, petitions, memorials, or resolutions reported from a committee shall be accompanied by reports in writing, which shall be printed.

Rule XIX

Of Amendments

When a motion or proposition is under consideration a motion to amend and a motion to amend that amendment shall be in order, and it shall also be in order to offer a further amendment by way of substitute, to which one amendment may be offered, but which shall not be voted on until the original matter is perfected, but either may be withdrawn before amendment or decision is had thereon. Amendments to the title of a bill or resolution shall not be in order until after its passage, and shall be decided without debate.

Rule XX

Of Amendments of the Senate

1. Any amendment of the Senate to any House bill shall be subject to the point of order that it shall first be considered in the Committee of the Whole House on the state of the Union, if, originating in the House, it would be subject to that point: *Provided, however,* That a motion to disagree with the amendments of the Senate to a House bill or resolution and request or agree to a conference with the Senate, or a motion to insist on the House amendments to a Senate bill or resolution and request or agree to a conference with the State, shall always be in order if the Speaker, in his discretion, recognizes for that purpose and if the motion is made by direction of the committee having jurisdiction of the subject matter of the bill or resolution. Such a motion, and any motion, rule, or order to dispose of amendments between the two Houses to any House or Senate bill or resolution (other than a motion to request or agree to a conference), shall require for adoption, on demand of any Member, a separate vote on each amendment to be disposed of if, originating in the House, such amendment would be subject to a point of order on a question of germaneness under clause 7 of Rule XVI. Before such separate vote is taken, it shall be in order to debate such amendment for forty minutes, one-half of such time to be given to debate in favor of, and one-half to debate in opposition to, the amendment.

2. No amendment of the Senate to a general appropriation bill which would be in violation of the provisions of clause 2 of Rule XXI, if said amendment had originated in the House, nor any amendment of the Senate providing for an appropriation upon any bill other than a general appropriation bill, shall be agreed to by the managers on the part of the House unless specific authority to agree to such amendment shall be first given by the House by a separate vote on every such amendment.

3. No amendment of the Senate which would be in violation of the provisions of clause 7 of Rule XVI, if such amendment had been offered in the House, shall be agreed to by the managers on the part of the House unless specific authority to agree to such amendment shall be first given by the House by a separate vote on every such amendment.

Rule XXI

On Bills

1. Bills and joint resolutions on their passage shall be read the first time by title and the second time in full, when, if the previous question is ordered, the Speaker shall state the question to be: Shall the bill be engrossed and read a third time? and, if decided in the affirmative, it shall be read the third time by title, and the question shall then be put upon its passage.

2. No appropriation shall be reported in any general appropriation bill, or be in order as an amendment thereto, for any expenditure not previously authorized by law, unless in continuation of appropriations for such public works and objects as are already in progress. Nor shall any provision in any such bill or amendment thereto changing existing law be in order, except such as being germane to the subject matter of the bill shall retrench expenditures by the reduction of the number and salary of the officers of the United States, by the reduction of the compensation of any person paid out of the Treasury of the United States, or by the reduction of amounts of money covered by the bill: *Provided,* That it shall be in order further to amend such bill upon the report of the committee or any joint commission authorized by law or the House Members of any such commission having jurisdiction of the subject matter of such amendment, which amendment being germane to the subject matter of the bill shall retrench expenditures.

3. No bill for the payment or adjudication of any private claim against the Government shall be referred, except by unanimous consent, to any other than the following committees, namely: To the Committee on Foreign Affairs or to the Committee on the Judiciary.

4. No bill or joint resolution carrying appropriations shall be reported by any committee not having jurisdiction to report appropriations, nor shall an amendment proposing an appropriation be in order during the consideration of a bill or joint resolution reported by a committee not having that jurisdiction. A question of order on an appropriation in any such bill, joint resolution, or amendment thereto may be raised at any time.

5. No general appropriation bill or amendment thereto shall be received or considered if it contains a provision reappropriating unexpended balances of appropriations; except that this provision shall not apply to appropriations in continuation of appropriations for public works on which work has commenced.

6. No general appropriation bill shall be considered in the House until printed committee hearings and a committee report thereon have been available for the Members of the House for at least three calendar days (excluding Saturdays, Sundays, and legal holidays).

Rule XXII

Of Petitions, Memorials, Bills, and Resolutions

1. Members having petitions or memorials or bills of a private nature to present may deliver them to the Clerk, indorsing their names and the reference or disposition to be made thereof; and said petitions and memorials and bills of a private nature, except such as, in the judgment of the Speaker, are of an obscene or insulting character, shall be entered on the Journal, with the names of the Members presenting them, and the Clerk shall furnish a transcript of such entry to the official reporters of debates for publication in the Record.

2. No private bill or resolution (including so-called omnibus claims or pension bills), and no amendment to any bill or resolution, authorizing or directing (1) the payment of money for property damages, for personal injuries or death for which suit may be instituted under the Tort Claims Procedure as provided in Title 28, United States Code, or for a pension (other than to carry out a provision of law or treaty stipulation); (2) the construction of a bridge across a navigable stream; or (3) the correction of a military or naval record, shall be received or considered in the House.

3. Any petition or memorial or private bill excluded under this rule shall be returned to the Member from whom it was received; and petitions and private bills which have been inappropriately referred may, by the direction of the committee having possession of the same, be properly referred in the manner originally presented; and an erroneous reference of a petition or private bill under this clause shall not confer jurisdiction upon the committee to consider or report the same.

4. All other bills, memorials, and resolutions may, in like manner, be delivered, indorsed with the names of Members introducing them, to the Speaker, to be by him referred, and the titles and references thereof and of all bills, resolutions, and documents referred under the rules shall be entered on the Journal and printed in the Record of the next day, and correction in case of error of reference may be made by the House, without debate, in accordance with Rule XI, on any day immediately after the reading of the Journal, by unanimous consent, or on motion of a committee claiming jurisdiction, or on the report of the committee to which the bill has been erroneously referred. Two or more but not more than twenty-five Members may introduce jointly any bill, memorial, or resolution to which this paragraph applies.

5. All resolutions of inquiry addressed to the heads of executive departments shall be reported to the House within one week after presentation.

6. When a bill, resolution, or memorial is introduced "by request," these words shall be entered upon the Journal and printed in the Record.

Rule XXIII

Of Committees of the Whole House

1. In all cases, in forming a Committee of the Whole House, the Speaker shall leave his chair after appointing a Chairman to preside, who shall, in case of disturbance or disorderly conduct in the galleries or lobby, have power to cause the same to be cleared.

2. Unless the Chairman invokes the procedure for the call of the roll under paragraph (b) of clause 2 of Rule XV, whenever a Committee of the Whole House or of the Whole House on the state of the Union finds itself without a quorum, which shall consist of one hundred Members, the Chairman shall cause the roll to be called, and thereupon the committee shall rise, and the Chairman shall report the names of the absentees to the House, which shall be entered on the Journal; but if on such call a quorum shall appear, the committee shall thereupon resume its sitting without further order of the House.

3. All motions or propositions involving a tax or charge upon the people, all proceedings touching appropriations of money, or bills making appropriations of money or property, or requiring such appropriation to be made, or authorizing payments out of appropriations already made, or releasing any liability to the United States for money or property, or referring any claim to the Court of Claims, shall be first considered in a Committee of the Whole, and a point of order under this rule shall be good at any time before the consideration of a bill has commenced.

4. In Committees of the Whole House business on their calendars may be taken up in regular order, or in such order as the committee may determine, unless the bill to be considered was determined by the House

at the time of going into committee, but bills for raising revenue, general appropriation bills, and bills for the improvement of rivers and harbors shall have precedence.

5. When general debate is closed by order of the House, any Member shall be allowed five minutes to explain any amendment he may offer, after which the Member who shall first obtain the floor shall be allowed to speak five minutes in opposition to it, and there shall be no further debate thereon, but the same privilege of debate shall be allowed in favor of and against any amendment that may be offered to an amendment; and neither an amendment nor an amendment to an amendment shall be withdrawn by the mover thereof unless by the unanimous consent of the committee. Upon the offering of any amendment by a Member, when the House is meeting in the Committee of the Whole, the Clerk shall promptly transmit to the majority committee table five copies of the amendment and five copies to the minority committee table. Further, the Clerk shall deliver at least one copy of the amendment to the majority cloak room and at least one copy to the minority cloak room.

6. The committee may, by the vote of a majority of the members present, at any time after the five minutes' debate has begun upon proposed amendments to any section or paragraph of a bill, close all debate upon such section or paragraph or, at its election, upon the pending amendments only (which motion shall be decided without debate); but this shall not preclude further amendment, to be decided without debate. However, if debate is closed on any section or paragraph under this clause before there has been debate on any amendment which any Member shall have caused to be printed in the Congressional Record after the reporting of the bill by the committee but at least one day prior to floor consideration of such amendment, the Member who caused such amendment to be printed in the Record shall be given five minutes in which to explain such amendment, after which the first person to obtain the floor shall be given five minutes in opposition to it, and there shall be no further debate thereon; but such time for debate shall not be allowed when the offering of such amendment is dilatory.

7. A motion to strike out the enacting words of a bill shall have precedence of a motion to amend, and, if carried, shall be considered equivalent to its rejection. Whenever a bill is reported from a Committee of the Whole with an adverse recommendation and such recommendation is disagreed to by the House, the bill shall stand recommitted to the said committee without further action by the House, but before the question of concurrence is submitted it is in order to entertain a motion to refer the bill to any committee, with or without instructions, and when the same is again reported to the House it shall be referred to the Committee of the Whole without debate.

8. The rules of proceeding in the House shall be observed in Committees of the Whole House so far as they may be applicable.

Rule XXIV

Order of Business

1. The daily order of business shall be as follows:
First. Prayer by the Chaplain.
Second. Reading and approval of the Journal.
Third. Correction of reference of public bills.
Fourth. Disposal of business on the Speaker's table.
Fifth. Unfinished business.
Sixth. The morning hour for the consideration of bills called up by committees.
Seventh. Motions to go into Committee of the Whole House on the state of the Union.
Eighth. Orders of the day.

2. Business on the Speaker's table shall be disposed of as follows:
Messages from the President shall be referred to the appropriate committees without debate. Reports and communications from heads of departments, and other communications addressed to the House, and bills, resolutions, and messages from the Senate may be referred to the appropriate committees in the same manner and with the same right of correction as public bills presented by Members; but House bills with Senate amendments which do not require consideration in a Committee of the Whole may be at once disposed of as the House may determine, as may also Senate bills substantially the same as House bills already favorably reported by a committee of the House, and not required to be considered in Committee of the Whole, be disposed of in the same manner on motion directed to be made by such committee.

3. The consideration of the unfinished business in which the House may be engaged at an adjournment, except business in the morning hour, shall be resumed as soon as the business on the Speaker's table is finished, and at the same time each day thereafter until disposed of, and

the consideration of all other unfinished business shall be resumed whenever the class of business to which it belongs shall be in order under the rules.

4. After the unfinished business has been disposed of, the Speaker shall call each standing committee in regular order, and then select committees, and each committee when named may call up for consideration any bill reported by it on a previous day and on the House Calendar, and if the Speaker shall not complete the call of the Committees before the House passes to other business, he shall resume the next call where he left off, giving preference to the last bill under consideration: *Provided,* That whenever any committee shall have occupied the morning hour on two days, it shall not be in order to call up any other bill until the other committees have been called in their turn.

5. After one hour shall have been devoted to the consideration of bills called up by committees, it shall be in order, pending consideration or discussion thereof, to entertain a motion to go into Comitee of the Whole House on the state of the Union, or, when authorized by a committee, to go into the Committee of the Whole House on the state of the Union to consider a particular bill, to which motion one amendment only, designating another bill, may be made; and if either motion be determined in the negative, it shall not be in order to make either motion again until the disposal of the matter under consideration or discussion.

6. On the first Tuesday of each month after disposal of such business on the Speaker's table as requires reference only, the Speaker shall direct the Clerk to call the bills and resolutions on the Private Calendar. Should objection be made by two or more Members to the consideration of any bill or resolution so called, it shall be recommitted to the committee which reported the bill or resolution, and no reservation of objection shall be entertained by the Speaker. Such bills and resolutions, if considered, shall be considered in the House as in the Committee of the Whole. No other business shall be in order on this day unless the House, by two-thirds vote on motion to dispense therewith, shall otherwise determine. On such motion debate shall be limited to five minutes for and five minutes against said motion.

On the third Tuesday of each month after the disposal of such business on the Speaker's table as requires reference only, the Speaker may direct the Clerk to call the bills and resolutions on the Private Calendar, preference to be given to omnibus bills containing bills or resolutions which have previously been objected to on a call of the Private Calendar. All bills and resolutions on the Private Calendar so called, if considered, shall be considered in the House as in the Committee of the Whole. Should objection be made by two or more members to the consideration of any bill or resolution other than an omnibus bill, it shall be recommitted to the committee which reported the bill or resolution and no reservation of objection shall be entertained by the Speaker.

Omnibus bills shall be read for amendment by paragraph, and no amendment shall be in order except to strike out or to reduce amounts of money stated or to provide limitations. Any item or matter stricken from an omnibus bill shall not thereafter during the same session of Congress be included in any omnibus bill.

Upon passage of any such omnibus bill, said bill shall be resolved into the several bills and resolutions of which it is composed, and such original bills and resolutions, with any amendments adopted by the House shall be engrossed, where necessary, and proceedings thereon had as if said bills and resolutions had been passed in the House severally.

In the consideration of any omnibus bill the proceedings as set forth above shall have the same force and effect as if each Senate and House bill or resolution therein contained or referred to were considered by the House as a separate and distinct bill or resolution.

7. On Wednesday of each week no business shall be in order except as provided by clause 4 of this rule unless the House by a two-thirds vote on motion to dispense therewith shall otherwise determine. On such a motion there may be debate not to exceed five minutes for and against. On a call of committees under this rule bills may be called up from either the House or the Union Calendar, excepting bills which are privileged under the rules; but bills called up from the Union Calendar shall be considered in Committee of the Whole House on the state of the Union. This rule shall not apply during the last two weeks of the session. It shall not be in order for the Speaker to entertain a motion for a recess on any Wednesday except during the last two weeks of the session: *Provided,* That not more than two hours of general debate shall be permitted on any measure called up on Calendar Wednesday, and all debate must be confined to the subject matter of the bill, the time to be equally divided between those for and against the bill: *Provided further,* That whenever any committee shall have occupied one Wednesday it shall not be in order, unless the House by a two-thirds vote shall otherwise determine, to consider any unfinished business previously called up by such committee, unless the previous question had been ordered thereon, upon any succeeding Wednesday until the other committees have been called in their turn under this rule: *Provided,* That when, during any one session of Congress, all of the committees of the House are not called under the Calendar

Wednesday rule, at the next session of Congress the call shall commence where it left off at the end of the preceding session.

8. The second and fourth Mondays in each month, after the disposition of motions to discharge committees and after the disposal of such business on the Speaker's table as requires reference only, shall, when claimed by the Committee on the District of Columbia, be set apart for the consideration of such business as may be presented by said committee.

Rule XXV

Priority of Business

All questions relating to the priority of business shall be decided by a majority without debate.

Rule XXVI

Unfinished Business of the Session

All business before committees of the House at the end of one session shall be resumed at the commencement of the next session of the same Congress in the same manner as if no adjournment had taken place.

Rule XXVII

Change or Suspension of Rules

1. No rule shall be suspended except by a vote of two-thirds of the Members voting, a quorum being present; nor shall the Speaker entertain a motion to suspend the rules except on the first and third Mondays of each month, preference being given on the first Monday to individuals and on the third Monday to committees, and during the last six days of a session.

2. All motions to suspend the rules shall, before being submitted to the House, be seconded by a majority by tellers, if demanded.

3. When a motion to suspend the rules has been seconded, it shall be in order, before the final vote is taken thereon, to debate the proposition to be voted upon for forty minutes, one-half of such time to be given to debate in favor of, and one-half to debate in opposition to, such proposition; and the same right of debate shall be allowed whenever the previous question has been ordered on any proposition on which there has been no debate.

4. A Member may present to the Clerk a motion in writing to discharge a committee from the consideration of a public bill or resolution which has been referred to it thirty days prior thereto (but only one motion may be presented for each bill or resolution). Under this rule it shall also be in order for a Member to file a motion to discharge the Committee on Rules from further consideration of any resolution providing either a special order of business, or a special rule for the consideration of any public bill or resolution favorably reported by a standing committee, or a special rule for the consideration of a public bill or resolution which has remained in a standing committee thirty or more days without action: *Provided,* That said resolution from which it is moved to discharge the Committee on Rules has been referred to that committee at least seven days prior to the filing of the motion to discharge. The motion shall be placed in the custody of the Clerk, who shall arrange some convenient place for the signature of Members. A signature may be withdrawn by a Member in writing at any time before the motion is entered on the Journal. When a majority of the total membership of the House shall have signed the motion, it shall be entered on the Journal, printed with the signatures thereto in the Congressional Record, and referred to the Calendar of Motions to Discharge Committees.

On the second and fourth Mondays of each month, except during the last six days of any session of Congress, immediately after the approval of the Journal, any Member who has signed a motion to discharge which has been on the calendar at least seven days prior thereto, and seeks recognition, shall be recognized for the purpose of calling up the motion, and the House shall proceed to its consideration in the manner herein provided without intervening motion except one motion to adjourn. Recognition for the motions shall be in the order in which they have been entered on the Journal.

When any motion under this rule shall be called up, the bill or resolution shall be read by title only. After twenty minutes' debate, one-half in favor of the proposition and one-half in opposition thereto, the House shall proceed to vote on the motion to discharge. If the motion prevails to discharge the Committee on Rules from any resolution pending before the committee, the House shall immediately vote on the adoption of said resolution, the Speaker not entertaining any dilatory or other intervening motion except one motion to adjourn, and, if said resolution is adopted, then the House shall immediately proceed to its execution. If the motion prevails to discharge one of the standing committees of the House from any public bill or resolution pending before the committee, it shall then be in order for any Member who signed the motion to move that the House proceed to the immediate consideration of such bill or resolution (such motion not being debatable), and such motion is hereby made of high privilege; and if it shall be decided in the affirmative, the bill shall be immediately considered under the general rules of the House, and if unfinished before adjournment of the day on which it is called up it shall remain the unfinished business until it is fully disposed of. Should the House by vote decide against the immediate consideration of such bill or resolution, it shall be referred to its proper calendar and be entitled to the same rights and privileges that it would have had had the committee to which it was referred duly reported same to the House for its consideration: *Provided,* That when any perfected motion to discharge a committee from the consideration of any public bill or resolution has once been acted upon by the House it shall not be in order to entertain during the same session of Congress any other motion for the discharge from that committee of said measure, or from any other committee of any other bill or resolution substantially the same, relating in substance to or dealing with the same subject matter, or from the Committee on Rules of a resolution providing a special order of business for the consideration of any other such bill or resolution, in order that such action by the House on a motion to discharge shall be res adjudicata for the remainder of that session: *Provided further,* That if before any one motion to discharge a committee has been acted upon by the House there are on the Calendar of Motions to Discharge Committees other motions to discharge committees from the consideration of bills or resolutions substantially the same, relating in substance to or dealing with the same subject matter, after the House shall have acted on one motion to discharge, the remaining said motions shall be stricken from the Calendar of Motions to Discharge Committees and not acted on during the remainder of that session of Congress.

Rule XXVIII

Conference Reports

1 (a) The presentation of reports of committees of conference shall always be in order, except when the Journal is being read, while the roll is being called, or the House is dividing on any proposition.

(b) After House conferees on any bill or resolution in conference between the House and Senate shall have been appointed for twenty calendar days and shall have failed to make a report, it is hereby declared to be a motion of the highest privilege to move to discharge said House conferees and to appoint new conferees, or to instruct said House conferees; and, further, during the last six days of any session of Congress, it shall be a privileged motion to move to discharge, appoint, or instruct, House conferees after House conferees shall have been appointed thirty-six hours without having made a report.

(c) Each report made by a committee of conference to the House shall be printed as a report of the House. As so printed, such report shall be accompanied by an explanatory statement prepared jointly by the conferees on the part of the House and the conferees on the part of the Senate. Such statement shall be sufficiently detailed and explicit to inform the House as to the effect which the amendments or propositions contained in such report will have upon the measure to which those amendments or propositions relate.

2. It shall not be in order to consider the report of a committee of conference unless such report and the accompanying statement shall have been printed in the Record, at least three calendar days (excluding Saturdays, Sundays, and legal holidays) prior to the consideration of such report by the House; but this provision does not apply during the last six days of the session. Nor shall it be in order to consider any conference report unless copies of the report and accompanying statement are then available on the floor. The time allotted for debate in the consideration of any such report shall be equally divided between the majority party and the minority party.

3. Whenever a disagreement to an amendment in the nature of a substitute has been committed to a conference committee it shall be in order for the Managers on the part of the House to propose a substitute which is a germane modification of the matter in disagreement, but the introduction of any language in that substitute presenting a specific additional topic, question, issue, or proposition not committed to the conference committee by either House shall not constitute a germane modification of the matter in disagreement. Moreover, their report shall not include matter not committed to the conference committee by either House, nor shall their report include a modification of any specific topic, question, issue, or proposition committed to the conference committee by either or both Houses if that modification is beyond the scope of that

specific topic, question, issue, or proposition as so committed to the conference committee.

Rule XXIX

Secret Session

Whenever confidential communications are received from the President of the United States, or whenever the Speaker or any Member shall inform the House that he has communications which he believes ought to be kept secret for the present, the House shall be cleared of all persons except the Members and officers thereof, and so continue during the reading of such communications, the debates and proceedings thereon, unless otherwise ordered by the House.

Rule XXX

Reading of Papers

When the reading of a paper other than one upon which the House is called to give a final vote is demanded, and the same is objected to by any Member, it shall be determined without debate by a vote of the House.

Rule XXXI

Hall of the House

The Hall of the House shall be used only for the legislative business of the House and for the caucus meetings of its Members, except upon occasions where the House by resolution agrees to take part in any ceremonies to be observed therein; and the Speaker shall not entertain a motion for the suspension of this rule.

Rule XXXII

Of Admission to the Floor

1. The persons hereinafter named, and none other, shall be admitted to the Hall of the House or rooms leading thereto, viz: The President and Vice President of the United States and their private secretaries, judges of the Supreme Court, Members of Congress and Members-elect, contestants in election cases during the pendency of their cases in the House, the Secretary and Sergeant at Arms of the Senate, heads of departments, foreign ministers, governors of States, the Architect of the Capitol, the Librarian of Congress and his assistant in charge of the Law Library, the Resident Commissioner to the United States from Puerto Rico, the Delegate from the District of Columbia, such persons as have, by name, received the thanks of Congress, ex-Members of the House of Representatives who are not interested in any claim or directly in any bill pending before Congress, and clerks of committees when business from their committee is under consideration; and it shall not be in order for the Speaker to entertain a request for the suspension of this rule or to present from the chair the request of any Member for unanimous consent.

2. There shall be excluded at all times from the Hall of the House of Representatives and the cloakrooms all persons not entitled to the privilege of the floor during the session, except that until fifteen minutes of the hour of the meeting of the House persons employed in its service, accredited members of the press entitled to admission to the press gallery, and other persons on request of Members, by card or in writing, may be admitted.

Rule XXXIII

Of Admission to the Galleries

The Speaker shall set aside a portion of the west gallery for the use of the President of the United States, the members of his Cabinet, justices of the Supreme Court, foreign ministers and suites, and the members of their respective families, and shall also set aside another portion of the same gallery for the accommodation of persons to be admitted on the card of Members. The southerly half of the east gallery shall be assigned exclusively for the use of the families of Members of Congress, in which the Speaker shall control one bench, and on request of a Member the Speaker shall issue a card of admission to his family, which shall include their visitors, and no other person shall be admitted to this section.

Rule XXXIV

Official and Other Reporters

1. The appointment and removal, for cause, of the official reporters of the House, including stenographers of committees, and the manner of the execution of their duties shall be vested in the Speaker.

2. Such portion of the gallery over the Speaker's chair as may be necessary to accommodate representatives of the press wishing to report debates and proceedings shall be set aside for their use, and reputable reporters and correspondents shall be admitted thereto under such regulations as the Speaker may from time to time prescribe; and the supervision of such gallery, including the designation of its employees, shall be vested in the standing committee of correspondents, subject to the direction and control of the Speaker; and the Speaker may assign one seat on the floor to Associated Press reporters and one to United Press International, and regulate the occupation of the same. And the Speaker may admit to the floor, under such regulations as he may prescribe, one additional representative of each press association.

3. Such portion of the gallery of the House of Representatives as may be necessary to accommodate reporters of news to be disseminated by radio, television, and similar means of transmission, wishing to report debates and proceedings, shall be set aside for their use, and reputable reporters thus engaged shall be admitted thereto under such regulations as the Speaker may from time to time prescribe; and the supervision of such gallery, including the designation of its employees, shall be vested in the Executive Committee of the Radio and Television Correspondents' Galleries, subject to the direction and control of the Speaker; and the Speaker may admit to the floor, under such regulations as he may prescribe, one representative of the National Broadcasting Company, one of the Columbia Broadcasting System, one of the Mutual Broadcasting System, and one of the American Broadcasting Company.

Rule XXXV

Pay of Witnesses

The rule for paying witnesses subpenaed to appear before the House or any of its committees shall be as follows: For each day a witness shall attend, the sum of twenty dollars; and actual expenses of travel in coming to or going from the place of examination, not to exceed twelve cents per mile; but nothing shall be paid for travel when the witness has been summoned at the place of examination.

Rule XXXVI

Papers

1. The clerks of the several committees of the House shall, within three days after the final adjournment of a Congress, deliver to the Clerk of the House all bills, joint resolutions, petitions, and other papers referred to the committee, together with all evidence taken by such committee under the order of the House during the said Congress and not reported to the House; and in the event of the failure or neglect of any clerk of a committee to comply with this rule the Clerk of the House shall, within three days thereafter, take into his keeping all such papers and testimony.

2. At the close of each Congress the Clerk of the House shall obtain all noncurrent records of the House and each committee thereof and transfer them to the General Services Administration for preservation subject to the order of the House. In making the transfer, the Clerk may act jointly with the Secretary of the Senate.

Rule XXXVII

Withdrawal of Papers

No memorial or other paper presented to the House shall be withdrawn from its files without its leave, and if withdrawn therefrom certified copies thereof shall be left in the office of the Clerk; but when an act may pass for the settlement of a claim, the Clerk is authorized to transmit to the officer in charge with the settlement thereof the papers on file in his office relating to such claim, or may loan temporarily to an officer or bureau of the executive departments any papers on file in his office relating to any matter pending before such officer or bureau, taking proper receipt therefor.

Rule XXXVIII

Ballot

In all cases of ballot a majority of the votes given shall be necessary to an election, and where there shall not be such a majority on the first ballot the ballots shall be repeated until a majority be obtained; and in all balloting blanks shall be rejected and not taken into the count in enumeration of votes or reported by the tellers.

Rule XXXIX

Messages

Messages received from the Senate and the President of the United States, giving notice of bills passed or approved, shall be entered in the Journal and published in the Record of that day's proceedings.

Rule XL

Executive Communications

Estimates of appropriations and all other communications from the executive departments, intended for the consideration of any committees of the House, shall be addressed to the Speaker, and by him referred as provided by clause 2 of Rule XXIV.

Rule XLI

Qualifications of Officers and Employees

No person shall be an officer of the House, or continue in its employment, who shall be an agent for the prosecution of any claim against the Government, or be interested in such claim otherwise than as an original claimant; and it shall be the duty of the Committee on House Administration to inquire into and report to the House any violation of this rule.

Rule XLII

General Provisions

The rules of parliamentary practice comprised in Jefferson's Manual and the provisions of the Legislative Reorganization Act of 1946, as amended, shall govern the House in all cases to which they are applicable, and in which they are not inconsistent with the standing rules and orders of the House and joint rules of the Senate and House of Representatives.

Rule XLIII

Code of Official Conduct

There is hereby established (4/3/1968) by and for the House of Representatives the following code of conduct, to be known as the "Code of Official Conduct":

1. A Member, officer, or employee of the House of Representatives shall conduct himself at all times in a manner which shall reflect creditably on the House of Representatives.

2. A Member, officer, or employee of the House of Representatives shall adhere to the spirit and the letter of the Rules of the House of Representatives and to the rules of duly constituted committees thereof.

3. A Member, officer, or employee of the House of Representatives shall receive no compensation nor shall he permit any compensation to accrue to his beneficial interest from any source, the receipt of which would occur by virtue of influence improperly exerted from his position in the Congress.

4. A Member, officer, or employee of the House of Representatives shall accept no gift of substantial value, directly or indirectly, from any person, organization, or corporation having a direct interest in legislation before the Congress.

5. A Member, officer, or employee of the House of Representatives shall accept no honorarium for a speech, writing for publication, or other similar activity, from any person, organization, or corporation in excess of the usual and customary value for such services.

6. A Member of the House of Representatives shall keep his campaign funds separate from his personal funds. He shall convert no campaign funds to personal use in excess of reimbursement for legitimate and verifiable prior campaign expenditures. He shall expend no funds from his campaign account not attributable to bona fide campaign purposes.

7. A Member of the House of Representatives shall treat as campaign contributions all proceeds from testimonial dinners or other fund-raising events if the sponsors of such affairs do not give clear notice in advance to the donors or participants that the proceeds are intended for other purposes.

8. A Member of the House of Representatives shall retain no one from his clerk hire allowance who does not perform duties commensurate with the compensation he receives.

As used in this Code of Official Conduct of the House of Representatives—(a) the terms "Member" and "Member of the House of Representatives" include the Resident Commissioner from Puerto Rico and the Delegate from the District of Columbia; and (b) the term "officer or employee of the House of Representatives" means any individual whose compensation is disbursed by the Clerk of the House of Representatives.

Rule XLIV

Financial Disclosure

Members, officers, principal assistants to Members and officers, and professional staff members of committees shall, not later than April 30, 1969, and by April 30 of each year thereafter, file with the Committee on Standards of Official Conduct a report disclosing certain financial interests as provided in this rule. The interest of a spouse or any other party, if constructively controlled by the person reporting, shall be considered to be the same as the interest of the person reporting. The report shall be in two parts as follows:

Part A

1. List the name, instrument of ownership, and any position of management held in any business entity doing a substantial business with the Federal Government or subject to Federal regulatory agencies, in which the ownership is in excess of $5,000 fair market value as of the date of filing or from which income of $1,000 or more was derived during the preceding calendar year. Do not list any time or demand deposit in a financial institution, or any debt instrument having a fixed yield unless it is convertible to an equity instrument.

2. List the name, address, and type of practice of any professional organization in which the person reporting, or his spouse, is an officer, director, or partner, or serves in any advisory capacity, from which income of $1,000 or more was derived during the preceding calendar year.

3. List the source of each of the following items received during the preceding calendar year: (a) Any income for services rendered (other than from the United States Government) exceeding $5,000. (b) Any capital gain from a single source exceeding $5,000, other than from the sale of a residence occupied by the person reporting. (c) Reimbursement for expenditures (other than from the United States Government) exceed-

ing $1,000 in each instance. (d) Honorariums from a single source aggregating $300 or more.

4. List each creditor to whom the person reporting was indebted for a period of ninety consecutive days or more during the preceding calendar year in an aggregate amount in excess of $10,000, excluding any indebtedness specifically secured by the pledge of assets of the person reporting of appropriate value.

Campaign receipts shall not be included in this report.

Information filed under part A shall be maintained by the Committee on Standards of Official Conduct and made available at reasonable hours to responsible public inquiry, subject to such regulations as the committee may prescribe including, but not limited to, regulations requiring identification by name, occupation, address, and telephone number of each person examining information filed under part A, and the reason for each such inquiry.

The committee shall promptly notify each person required to file a report under this rule of each instance of an examination of his report. The committee shall also promptly notify a Member of each examination of the reports filed by his principal assistants and of each examination of the reports of professional staff members of committees who are responsible to such Member.

Part B

1. List the fair market value (as of the date of filing) of each item listed under paragraph 1 of part A and the income derived therefrom during the preceding calendar year.

2. List the amount of income derived from each item listed under paragraphs 2 and 3 of part A, and the amount of indebtedness owed to each creditor listed under paragraph 4 of part A.

The information filed under this part B shall be sealed by the person filing and shall remain sealed unless the Committee on Standards of Official Conduct, pursuant to its investigative authority, determines by a vote of not less than seven members of the committee that the examination of such information is essential in an official investigation by the committee and promptly notifies the Member concerned of any such determination. The committee may, by a vote of not less than seven members of the committee, make public any portion of the information unsealed by the committee under the preceding sentence and which the committee deems to be in the public interest.

Any person required to file a report under this rule who has no interests covered by any of the provisions of this rule shall file a report so stating.

In any case in which a person required to file a sealed report under part B of this rule is no longer required to file such a report, the committee shall return to such person, or his legal representative, all sealed reports filed by such person under part B and remaining in the possession of the committee.

As used in this rule—(1) the term "Members" includes the Resident Commissioner from Puerto Rico and the Delegate from the District of Columbia; and (2) the term "committees" includes any committee or subcommittee of the House of Representatives and any joint committee of Congress, the expenses of which are paid from the contingent fund of the House of Representatives.

Standing Rules of the Senate

(In use by the 92nd Congress.)

Rule I

Appointment of a Senator to the Chair

1. In the absence of the Vice President, the Senate shall choose a President pro tempore. (On March 12, 1890, the Senate agreed to the following: *Resolved,* That it is competent for the Senate to elect a President pro tempore, who shall hold the office during the pleasure of the Senate and until another is elected, and shall execute the duties thereof during all future absences of the Vice President until the Senate otherwise order.)

2. In the absence of the Vice President, and pending the election of a President pro tempore, the Secretary of the Senate, or in his absence the Chief Clerk, shall perform the duties of the Chair.

3. The President pro tempore shall have the right to name in open Senate, or, if absent, in writing, a Senator to perform the duties of the Chair; but such substitution shall not extend beyond an adjournment, except by unanimous consent.

4. In event of a vacancy in the office of the Vice President, or whenever the powers and duties of the President shall devolve on the Vice President, the President pro tempore shall have the right to name, in writing, a Senator to perform the duties of the Chair during his absence; and the Senator so named shall have the right to name in open session, or in writing, if absent, a Senator to perform the duties of the Chair, but such substitution shall not extend beyond adjournment, except by unanimous consent. (On Jan. 4, 1905, the Senate agreed to the following: *Resolved,* That whenever a Senator shall be designated by the President pro tempore to perform the duties of the Chair during his temporary absence he shall be empowered to sign, as acting President pro tempore, the enrolled bills and joint resolutions coming from the House of Representatives for presentation to the President of the United States.)

Rule II

Oaths

The oaths or affirmations required by the Constitution and prescribed by law shall be taken and subscribed by each Senator, in open Senate, before entering upon his duties.

Rule III

Commencement of Daily Sessions

1. The Presiding Officer having taken the chair, and a quorum being present, the Journal of the preceeding day shall be read, and any mistake made in the entries corrected. The reading of the Journal shall not be suspended unless by unanimous consent; and when any motion shall be made to amend or correct the same, it shall be deemed a privileged question, and proceeded with until disposed of.

2. A quorum shall consist of a majority of the Senators duly chosen and sworn. (On Feb. 6, 1939, the Senate agreed to the following: *Resolved,* That the Chaplain shall open each calendar day's session of the Senate with prayer.)

Rule IV

Journal

1. The proceedings of the Senate shall be briefly and accurately stated on the Journal. Messages of the President in full; titles of bills and joint resolutions, and such parts as shall be affected by proposed amendments; every vote, and a brief statement of the contents of each petition, memorial, or paper presented to the Senate, shall be entered.

2. The legislative, the executive, the confidential legislative proceedings, and the proceedings when sitting as a Court of Impeachment, shall each be recorded in a separate book.

Rule V

Quorum—Absent Senators May be Sent For

1. No Senator shall absent himself from the service of the Senate without leave.

2. If, at any time during the daily sessions of the Senate, a question shall be raised by any Senator as to the presence of a quorum, the Presiding Officer shall forthwith direct the Secretary to call the roll and shall announce the result, and these proceedings shall be without debate.

3. Whenever upon such roll call it shall be ascertained that a quorum is not present, a majority of the Senators present may direct the Sergeant at Arms to request, and, when necessary, to compel the attendance of the absent Senators, which order shall be determined without debate; and pending its execution, and until a quorum shall be present, no debate nor motion, except to adjourn, shall be in order.

Rule VI

Presentation of Credentials

1. The presentation of the credentials of Senators elect and other questions of privilege shall always be in order, except during the reading and correction of the Journal, while a question of order or a motion to adjourn is pending, or while the Senate is dividing; and all questions and motions arising or made upon the presentation of such credentials shall be proceeded with until disposed of.

2. The Secretary shall keep a record of the certificates of election of Senators by entering in a well-bound book kept for that purpose the date of the election, the name of the person elected and the vote given at the election, the date of the certificate, the name of the governor and the secretary of state signing and countersigning the same, and the State from which such Senator is elected.

Rule VII

Morning Business

1. After the Journal is read, the Presiding Officer shall lay before the Senate messages from the President, reports and communications from the heads of Departments, and other communications addressed to the Senate, and such bills, joint resolutions, and other messages from the House of Representatives as may remain upon his table from any previous day's session undisposed of. The Presiding Officer shall then call for, in the following order: the presentation of petitions and memorials; reports of standing and select committees; the introduction of bills and joint resolutions; concurrent and other resolutions. All of which shall be received and disposed of in such order, unless unanimous consent shall be otherwise given. (On Jan. 16, 1908, the Senate agreed to the following: *Resolved,* That no communications from heads of departments, commissioners, chiefs of bureaus, or other Executive officers, except when authorized or required by law, or when made in response to a resolution of the Senate, will be received by the Senate unless such communications shall be transmitted to the Senate by the President. On Dec. 17, 1885, the Senate agreed to the following: *Ordered,* That until otherwise ordered, the Chair shall proceed with the call for resolutions to be newly offered before laying before the Senate resolutions which came over from a former day.)

2. Senators having petitions, memorials, pension bills, or bills for the payment of private claims to present after the morning hour may deliver them to the Secretary of the Senate, indorsing upon them their names and the reference or disposition to be made thereof, and said petitions, memorials, and bills shall, with the approval of the Presiding Officer, be entered on the Journal with the names of the Senators presenting them as having been read twice and referred to the appropriate committees, and the Secretary of the Senate shall furnish a transcript of such entries to the official reporter of debates for publication in the Record.

It shall not be in order to interrupt a Senator having the floor for the purpose of introducing any memorial, petition, report of a committee, resolution, or bill. It shall be the duty of the Chair to enforce this rule without any point of order hereunder being made by a Senator.

3. Until the morning business shall have been concluded, and so announced from the Chair, or until the hour of 1 o'clock has arrived, no motion to proceed to the consideration of any bill, resolution, report of a committee, or other subject upon the Calendar shall be entertained by the Presiding Officer, unless by unanimous consent; and if such consent be given, the motion shall not be subject to amendment, and shall be decided

without debate upon the merits of the subject proposed to be taken up: *Provided, however,* That on Mondays the Calendar shall be called under Rule VIII, and during the morning hour no motion shall be entertained to proceed to the consideration of any bill, resolution, report of a committee, or other subject upon the Calendar except the motion to continue the consideration of a bill, resolution, report of a committee, or other subject against objection as provided in Rule VIII.

4. Every petition or memorial shall be referred, without putting the question, unless objection to such reference is made; in which case all motions for the reception or reference of such petition, memorial, or other paper shall be put in the order in which the same shall be made, and shall not be open to amendment, except to add instructions.

5. Every petition or memorial shall be signed by the petitioner or memorialist and have indorsed thereon a brief statement of its contents, and shall be presented and referred without debate. But no petition or memorial or other paper signed by citizens or subjects of a foreign power shall be received, unless the same be transmitted to the Senate by the President.

6. Only a brief statement of the contents, as provided for in Rule VII, paragraph five, of such communications as are presented under the order of business "Presentation of petitions and memorials" shall be printed in the Congressional Record; and no other portion of such communications shall be inserted in the Record unless specifically so ordered by vote of the Senate, as provided for in Rule XXIX, paragraph one; except that communications from the legislatures or conventions, lawfully called, of the respective States, Territories, and insular possessions shall be printed in full in the Record whenever presented, and the original copies of such communications shall be retained in the files of the Secretary of the Senate. (On Feb. 7, 1887, the Senate agreed to the following: *Ordered,* That when petitions and memorials are ordered printed in the Congressional Record the order shall be deemed to apply to the body of the petition only, and the names attached to said petition or memorial shall not be printed unless specially ordered by the Senate.)

7. The Presiding Officer may at any time lay, and it shall be in order at any time for a Senator to move to lay, before the Senate, any bill or other matter sent to the Senate by the President or the House of Representatives, and any question pending at that time shall be suspended for this purpose. Any motion so made shall be determined without debate.

Rule VIII

Order of Business

1. At the conclusion of the morning business for each day, unless upon motion the Senate shall at any time otherwise order, the Senate will proceed to the consideration of the Calendar of Bills and Resolutions, and continue such consideration until 2 o'clock; and bills and resolutions that are not objected to shall be taken up in their order, and each Senator shall be entitled to speak once and for five minutes only upon any question; and the objection may be interposed at any stage of the proceedings, but upon motion the Senate may continue such consideration; and this order shall commence immediately after the call for "concurrent and other resolutions," and shall take precedence of the unfinished business and other special orders. But if the Senate shall proceed with the consideration of any matter notwithstanding an objection, the foregoing provisions touching debate shall not apply.

2. All motions made before 2 o'clock to proceed to the consideration of any matter shall be determined without debate.

3. At the conclusion of the morning hour or after the unfinished business or pending business has first been laid before the Senate on any calendar day, and until after the duration of three hours, except as determined to the contrary by unanimous consent or on motion without debate, all debate shall be germane and confined to the specific question then pending before the Senate. (On August 10, 1888, the Senate agreed to the following: *Resolved,* That after to-day, unless otherwise ordered, the morning hour shall terminate at the expiration of two hours after the meeting of the Senate.)

Rule IX

Order of Business

Immediately after the consideration of cases not objected to upon the Calendar is completed, and not later than 2 o'clock if there shall be no special orders for that time, the Calendar of General Orders shall be taken up and proceeded with in its order, beginning with the first subject on the Calendar next after the last subject disposed of in proceeding with the Calendar; and in such case the following motions shall be in order at any time as privileged motions, save as against a motion to adjourn, or

to proceed to the consideration of executive business, or questions of privilege, to wit:

First. A motion to proceed to the consideration of an appropriation or revenue bill.

Second. A motion to proceed to the consideration of any other bill on the Calendar, which motion shall not be open to amendment.

Third. A motion to pass over the pending subject, which if carried shall have the effect to leave such subject without prejudice in its place on the Calendar.

Fourth. A motion to place such subject at the foot of the Calendar.

Each of the foregoing motions shall be decided without debate and shall have precedence in the order above named, and may be submitted as in the nature and with all the rights of questions of order.

Rule X

Special Orders

1. Any subject may, by a vote of two-thirds of the Senators present, be made a special order; and when the time so fixed for its consideration arrives the Presiding Officer shall lay it before the Senate, unless there be unfinished business of the preceding day, and if it is not finally disposed of on that day it shall take its place on the Calendar of Special Orders in the order of time at which it was made special, unless it shall become by adjournment the unfinished business.

2. When two or more special orders have been made for the same time, they shall have precedence according to the order in which they were severally assigned, and that order shall only be changed by direction of the Senate.

And all motions to change such order, or to proceed to the consideration of other business, shall be decided without debate.

Rule XI

Objection To Reading A Paper

When the reading of a paper is called for, and objected to, it shall be determined by a vote of the Senate, without debate.

Rule XII

Voting

1. When the yeas and nays are ordered, the names of Senators shall be called alphabetically; and each Senator shall, without debate, declare his assent or dissent to the question, unless excused by the Senate; and no Senator shall be permitted to vote after the decision shall have been announced by the Presiding Officer, but may for sufficient reasons, with unanimous consent, change or withdraw his vote. No motion to suspend this rule shall be in order, nor shall the Presiding Officer entertain any request to suspend it by unanimous consent.

2. When a Senator declines to vote on call of his name, he shall be required to assign his reasons therefor, and having assigned them, the Presiding Officer shall submit the question to the Senate: "Shall the Senator, for the reasons assigned by him, be excused from voting?" which shall be decided without debate; and these proceedings shall be had after the roll call and before the result is announced; and any further proceedings in reference thereto shall be after such announcement.

3. No request by a Senator for unanimous consent for the taking of a final vote on a specified date upon the passage of a bill or joint resolution shall be submitted to the Senate for agreement thereto until, upon a roll call ordered for the purpose by the Presiding Officer, it shall be disclosed that a quorum of the Senate is present; and when a unanimous consent is thus given the same shall operate as the order of the Senate, but any unanimous consent may be revoked by another unanimous consent granted in the manner prescribed above upon one day's notice.

Rule XIII

Reconsideration

1. When a question has been decided by the Senate, any Senator voting with the prevailing side or who has not voted may, on the same day or on either of the next two days of actual session thereafter, move a reconsideration; and if the Senate shall refuse to reconsider, or upon reconsideration shall affirm its first decision, no further motion to reconsider shall be in order unless by unanimous consent. Every motion to reconsider shall be decided by a majority vote, and may be laid on the

table without affecting the question in reference to which the same is made, which shall be a final disposition of the motion.

2. When a bill, resolution, report, amendment, order, or message, upon which a vote has been taken, shall have gone out of the possession of the Senate and been communicated to the House of Representatives, the motion to reconsider shall be accompanied by a motion to request the House to return the same; which last motion shall be acted upon immediately, and without debate, and if determined in the negative shall be a final disposition of the motion to reconsider.

Rule XIV

Bills, Joint Resolutions, and Resolutions

1. Whenever a bill or joint resolution shall be offered, its introduction shall, if objected to, be postponed for one day.

2. Every bill and joint resolution shall receive three readings previous to its passage, which readings shall be on three different days, unless the Senate unanimously direct otherwise; and the Presiding Officer shall give notice at each reading whether it be the first, second, or third: *Provided,* That the first or second reading of each bill may be by title only, unless the Senate in any case shall otherwise order.

3. No bill or joint resolution shall be committed or amended until it shall have been twice read, after which it may be referred to a committee; bills and joint resolutions introduced on leave, and bills and joint resolutions from the House of Representatives, shall be read once, and may be read twice, on the same day, if not objected to, for reference, but shall not be considered on that day nor debated, except for reference, unless by unanimous consent.

4. Every bill and joint resolution reported from a committee, not having previously been read, shall be read once, and twice, if not objected to, on the same day, and placed on the Calendar in the order in which the same may be reported; and every bill and joint resolution introduced on leave, and every bill and joint resolution of the House of Representatives which shall have received a first and second reading without being referred to a committee, shall, if objection be made to further proceeding thereon, be placed on the Calendar.

5. The Secretary of the Senate shall examine all bills, amendments, and joint resolutions before they go out of the possession of the Senate, and shall examine all bills and joint resolutions which shall have passed both Houses, to see that the same are correctly enrolled, and, when signed by the Speaker of the House and the President of the Senate, shall forthwith present the same, when they shall have originated in the Senate, to the President of the United States and report the fact and date of such presentation to the Senate.

6. All resolutions shall lie over one day for consideration, unless by unanimous consent the Senate shall otherwise direct.

Rule XV

Bills

1. When a bill or resolution shall have been ordered to be read a third time, it shall not be in order to propose amendments, unless by unanimous consent, but it shall be in order at any time before the passage of any bill or resolution to move its commitment; and when the bill or resolution shall again be reported from the committee it shall be placed on the Calendar.

2. Whenever a private bill is under consideration, it shall be in order to move, as a substitute for it, a resolution of the Senate referring the case to the Court of Claims, under the provisions of the act approved March 3, 1883.

Rule XVI

Amendments to Appropriation Bills

1. All general appropriation bills shall be referred to the Committee on Appropriations, and no amendments shall be received to any general appropriation bill the effect of which will be to increase an appropriation already contained in the bill, or to add a new item of appropriation, unless it be made to carry out the provisions of some existing law, or treaty stipulation, or act, or resolution previously passed by the Senate during that session; or unless the same be moved by direction of a standing or select committee of the Senate, or proposed in pursuance of an estimate submitted in accordance with law.

2. The Committee on Appropriations shall not report an appropriation bill containing amendments proposing new or general legislation or any restriction on the expenditure of the funds appropriated which

proposes a limitation not authorized by law if such restriction is to take effect or cease to be effective upon the happening of a contingency, and if an appropriation bill is reported to the Senate containing amendments proposing new or general legislation or any such restriction, a point of order may be made against the bill, and if the point is sustained, the bill shall be recommitted to the Committee on Appropriations.

3. All amendments to general appropriation bills moved by direction of a standing or select committee of the Senate, proposing to increase an appropriation already contained in the bill, or to add new items of appropriation, shall, at least one day before they are considered, be referred to the Committee on Appropriations, and when actually proposed to the bill no amendment proposing to increase the amount stated in such amendment shall be received; in like manner, amendments proposing new items of appropriation to river and harbor bills, establishing post roads, or proposing new post roads, shall, before being considered, be referred to the Committee on Public Works.

4. No amendment which proposes general legislation shall be received to any general appropriation bill, nor shall any amendment not germane or relevant to the subject matter contained in the bill be received; nor shall any amendment to any item or clause of such bill be received which does not directly relate thereto; nor shall any restriction on the expenditure of the funds appropriated which proposes a limitation not authorized by law be received if such restriction is to take effect or cease to be effective upon the happening of a contingency; and all questions of relevancy of amendments under this rule, when raised, shall be submitted to the Senate and be decided without debate; and any such amendment or restriction to a general appropriation bill may be laid on the table without prejudice to the bill.

5. No amendment, the object of which is to provide for a private claim, shall be received to any general appropriation bill, unless it be to carry out the provisions of an existing law or a treaty stipulation, which shall be cited on the face of the amendment.

6. (a) Three members of the following-named committees, to be selected by their respective committees, shall be ex officio members of the Committee on Appropriations, to serve on said committee when the annual appropriation bill making appropriations for the purposes specified in the following table opposite the name of the committee is being considered by the Committee on Appropriations:

Name of committee	Purpose of appropriation
Committee on Agriculture and Forestry.	For the Department of Agriculture.
Committee on Post Office and Civil Service.	For the Post Office Department.
Committee on Armed Services.	For the Department of War; for the Department of the Navy.
Committee on the District of Columbia.	For the District of Columbia.
Committee on Public Works.	For rivers and harbors.
Committee on Foreign Relations.	For the Diplomatic and Consular Service.
Senate members of the Joint Committee on Atomic Energy (to be selected by said members).	For the development and utilization of atomic energy.
Committee on Aeronautical and Space Sciences.	For aeronautical and space activities and matters relating to the scientific aspects thereof, except those peculiar to or primarily associated with the development of weapons systems or military operations.

(b) At least one member of each committee enumerated in subparagraph (a), to be selected by his or their respective committees, shall be a member of any conference committee appointed to confer with the House upon the annual appropriation bill making appropriations for the purposes specified in the foregoing table opposite the name of his or their respective committee.

7. When a point of order is made against any restriction on the expenditure of funds appropriated in a general appropriation bill on the ground that the restriction violates this rule, the rule shall be construed strictly and, in case of doubt, in favor of the point of order.

8. Every report on general appropriation bills filed by the Committee on Appropriations shall identify with particularity each recommended amendment which proposes an item of appropriation which is not made to carry out the provisions of an existing law, a treaty stipulation, or an act or resolution previously passed by the Senate during the session.

Rule XVII

Amendment May be Laid on the Table without Prejudice to the Bill

When an amendment proposed to any pending measure is laid on the table, it shall not carry with it, or prejudice, such measure.

Rule XVIII

Amendments—Division of a Question

If the question in debate contains several propositions, any Senator may have the same divided, except a motion to strike out and insert, which shall not be divided; but the rejection of a motion to strike out and insert one proposition shall not prevent a motion to strike out and insert a different proposition; nor shall it prevent a motion simply to strike out; nor shall the rejection of a motion to strike out prevent a motion to strike out and insert. But pending a motion to strike out and insert, the part to be stricken out and the part to be inserted shall each be regarded for the purpose of amendment as a question; and motions to amend the part to be stricken out shall have precedence.

Rule XIX

Debate

1. When a Senator desires to speak, he shall rise and address the Presiding Officer, and shall not proceed until he is recognized, and the Presiding Officer shall recognize the Senator who shall first address him. No Senator shall interrupt another Senator in debate without his consent, and to obtain such consent he shall first address the Presiding Officer, and no Senator shall speak more than twice upon any one question in debate on the same day without leave of the Senate, which shall be determined without debate.

2. No Senator in debate shall, directly or indirectly, by any form of words impute to another Senator or to other Senators any conduct or motive unworthy or unbecoming a Senator.

3. No Senator in debate shall refer offensively to any State of the Union.

4. If any Senator, in speaking or otherwise, in the opinion of the Presiding Officer transgress the rules of the Senate the Presiding Officer shall, either on his own motion or at the request of any other Senator, call him to order; and when a Senator shall be called to order he shall take his seat, and may not proceed without leave of the Senate, which, if granted, shall be upon motion that he be allowed to proceed in order, which motion shall be determined without debate. Any Senator directed by the Presiding Officer to take his seat, and any Senator requesting the Presiding Officer to require a Senator to take his seat, may appeal from the ruling of the Chair, which appeal shall be open to debate.

5. If a Senator be called to order for words spoken in debate, upon the demand of the Senator or of any other Senator, the exceptionable words shall be taken down in writing, and read at the table for the information of the Senate.

6. Whenever confusion arises in the Chamber or the galleries, or demonstrations of approval or disapproval are indulged in by the occupants of the galleries, it shall be the duty of the Chair to enforce order on his own initiative and without any point of order being made by a Senator.

7. No Senator shall introduce to or bring to the attention of the Senate during its sessions any occupant in the galleries of the Senate. No motion to suspend this rule shall be in order, nor may the Presiding Officer entertain any request to suspend it by unanimous consent.

8. Former Presidents of the United States shall be entitled to address the Senate upon appropriate notice to the Presiding Officer who shall thereupon make the necessary arrangements.

Rule XX

Questions of Order

1. A question of order may be raised at any stage of the proceedings, except when the Senate is dividing, and, unless submitted to the Senate, shall be decided by the Presiding Officer without debate, subject to an appeal to the Senate. When an appeal is taken any subsequent question of order which may arise before the decision of such appeal shall be decided by the Presiding Officer without debate; and every appeal therefrom shall be decided at once, and without debate; and any appeal may be laid on the table without prejudice to the pending proposition,

and thereupon shall be held as affirming the decision of the Presiding Officer.

2. The Presiding Officer may submit any question of order for the decision of the Senate.

Rule XXI

Motions

1. All motions shall be reduced to writing, if desired by the Presiding Officer or by any Senator, and shall be read before the same shall be debated.

2. Any motion or resolution may be withdrawn or modified by the mover at any time before a decision, amendment, or ordering of the yeas and nays, except a motion to reconsider, which shall not be withdrawn without leave.

Rule XXII

Precedence of Motions

1. When a question is pending, no motion shall be received but to adjourn; to adjourn to a day certain, or that when the Senate adjourn it shall be to a day certain; to take a recess; to proceed to the consideration of executive business; to lay on the table; to postpone indefinitely; to postpone to a day certain; to commit; to amend. Which several motions shall have precedence as they stand arranged; and the motions relating to adjournment, to take a recess, to proceed to the consideration of executive business, to lay on the table, shall be decided without debate.

2. Notwithstanding the provisions of rule III or rule VI or any other rule of the Senate, at any time a motion signed by sixteen Senators, to bring to a close the debate upon any measure, motion, or other matter pending before the Senate, or the unfinished business, is presented to the Senate, the Presiding Officer shall at once state the motion to the Senate, and one hour after the Senate meets on the following calendar day but one, he shall lay the motion before the Senate and direct that the Secretary call the roll, and, upon the ascertainment that a quorum is present, the Presiding Officer shall, without debate, submit to the Senate by a yea-and-nay vote the question:

"Is it the sense of the Senate that the debate shall be brought to a close?"

And if that question shall be decided in the affirmative by two-thirds of the Senators present and voting, then said measure, motion, or other matter pending before the Senate, or the unfinished business, shall be the unfinished business to the exclusion of all other business until disposed of.

Thereafter no Senator shall be entitled to speak in all more than one hour on the measure, motion, or other matter pending before the Senate, or the unfinished business, the amendments thereto, and motions affecting the same, and it shall be the duty of the Presiding Officer to keep the time of each Senator who speaks. Except by unanimous consent, no amendment shall be in order after the vote to bring the debate to a close, unless the same has been presented and read prior to that time. No dilatory motion, or dilatory amendment, or amendment not germane shall be in order. Points of order, including questions of relevancy, and appeals from the decision of the Presiding Officer, shall be decided without debate.

3. The provisions of the last paragraph of rule VIII (prohibiting debate on motions made before 2 o'clock (rule VIII, para. 2)) shall not apply to any motion to proceed to the consideration of any motion, resolution, or proposal to change any of the Standing Rules of the Senate.

Rule XXIII

Preambles

When a bill or resolution is accompanied by a preamble, the question shall first be put on the bill or resolution and then on the preamble, which may be withdrawn by a mover before an amendment of the same, or ordering of the yeas and nays; or it may be laid on the table without prejudice to the bill or resolution, and shall be a final disposition of such preamble.

Rule XXIV

Appointment of Committees

1. In the appointment of the standing committees, the Senate, unless otherwise ordered, shall proceed by ballot to appoint severally the chairman of each committee, and then, by one ballot, the other members

necessary to complete the same. A majority of the whole number of votes given shall be necessary to the choice of a chairman of a standing committee, but a plurality of votes shall elect the other members thereof. All other committees shall be appointed by ballot, unless otherwise ordered, and a plurality of votes shall appoint.

2. When a chairman of a committee shall resign or cease to serve on a committee, and the Presiding Officer be authorized by the Senate to fill the vacancy in such committee, unless specially otherwise ordered, it shall be only to fill up the number of the committee.

Rule XXV

Standing Committees

1. The following standing committees shall be appointed at the commencement of each Congress, with leave to report by bill or otherwise:

(a) (1) **Committee on Aeronautical and Space Sciences**, to which committee shall be referred all proposed legislation, messages, petitions, memorials, and other matters relating primarily to the following subjects:

(A) Aeronautical and space activities, as that term is defined in the National Aeronautics and Space Act of 1958, except those which are peculiar to or primarily associated with the development of weapons systems or military operations.

(B) Matters relating generally to the scientific aspects of such aeronautical and space activities, except those which are peculiar to or primarily associated with the development of weapons systems or military operations.

(C) National Aeronautics and Space Administration.

(2) Such committee also shall have jurisdiction to survey, and review, and to prepare studies and reports upon, aeronautical and space activities of all agencies of the United States, including such activities which are peculiar to or primarily associated with the development of weapons systems or military operations.

(b) **Committee on Agriculture and Forestry**, to which committee shall be referred all proposed legislation, messages, petitions, memorials, and other matters relating to the following subjects:

1. Agriculture generally.
2. Inspection of livestock and meat products.
3. Animal industry and diseases of animals.
4. Adulteration of seeds, insect pests, and protection of birds and animals in forest reserves.
5. Agricultural colleges and experiment stations.
6. Forestry in general, and forest reserves other than those created from the public domain.
7. Agricultural economics and research.
8. Agricultural and industrial chemistry.
9. Dairy industry.
10. Entomology and plant quarantine.
11. Human nutrition and home economics.
12. Plant industry, soils, and agricultural engineering.
13. Agricultural educational extension services.
14. Extension of farm credit and farm security.
15. Rural electrification.
16. Agricultural production and marketing and stabilization of prices of agricultural products.
17. Crop insurance and soil conservation.

(c) **Committee on Appropriations**, to which committee shall be referred all proposed legislation, messages, petitions, memorials, and other matters relating to appropriation of the revenue for the support of the Government.

(d) **Committee on Armed Services**, to which committee shall be referred all proposed legislation, messages, petitions, memorials, and other matters relating to the following subjects:

1. Common defense generally.
2. The Department of Defense, the Department of the Army, the Department of the Navy, and the Department of the Air Force generally.
3. Soldiers' and sailors' homes.
4. Pay, promotion, retirement, and other benefits and privileges of members of the Armed Forces.
5. Selective service.
6. Size and composition of the Army, Navy, and Air Force.
7. Forts, arsenals, military reservations, and navy yards.
8. Ammunition depots.
9. Maintenance and operation of the Panama Canal, including the administration, sanitation, and government of the Canal Zone.
10. Conservation, development, and use of naval petroleum and oil shale reserves.
11. Strategic and critical materials necessary for the common defense.
12. Aeronautical and space activities peculiar to or primarily associated with the development of weapons systems or military operations.

(e) **Committee on Banking, Housing and Urban Affairs**, to which committee shall be referred all proposed legislation, messages, petitions, memorials, and other matters relating to the following subjects:

1. Banking and currency generally.
2. Financial aid to commerce and industry, other than matters relating to such aid which are specifically assigned to other committees under this rule.
3. Deposit insurance.
4. Public and private housing.
5. Federal Reserve System.
6. Gold and silver, including the coinage thereof.
7. Issuance of notes and redemption thereof.
8. Valuation and revaluation of the dollar.
9. Control of prices of commodities, rents, or services.
10. Urban affairs generally.

(f) **Committee on Commerce**, to which committee shall be referred all proposed legislation, messages, petitions, memorials, and other matters relating to the following subjects:

1. Interstate and foreign commerce generally.
2. Regulations of interstate railroads, busses, trucks, and pipe lines.
3. Communication by telephone, telegraph, radio, and television.
4. Civil aeronautics, except aeronautical and space activities of the National Aeronautics and Space Administration.
5. Merchant marine generally.
6. Registering and licensing of vessels and small boats.
7. Navigation and the laws relating thereto, including pilotage.
8. Rules and international arrangements to prevent collisions at sea.
9. Merchant marine officers and seamen.
10. Measures relating to the regulation of common carriers by water and to the inspection of merchant marine vessels, lights and signals, life-saving equipment, and fire protection on such vessels.
11. Coast and Geodetic Survey.
12. The Coast Guard, including lifesaving service, lighthouses, lightships, and ocean derelicts.
13. The United States Coast Guard and Merchant Marine Academies.
14. Weather Bureau.
15. Except as provided in paragraph (d), the Panama Canal and interoceanic canals generally.
16. Inland waterways.
17. Fisheries and wildlife, including research, restoration, refuges, and conservation.
18. Bureau of Standards, including standardization of weights and measures and the metric system.

(g) **Committee on the District of Columbia**, to which committee shall be referred all proposed legislation, messages, petitions, memorials, and other matters relating to the following subjects:

1. All measures relating to the municipal affairs of the District of Columbia in general, other than appropriations therefor, including—
2. Public health and safety, sanitation, and quarantine regulations.
3. Regulation of sale of intoxicating liquors.
4. Adulteration of food and drugs.
5. Taxes and tax sales.
6. Insurance, executors, administrators, wills, and divorce.
7. Municipal and juvenile courts.
8. Incorporation and organization of societies.
9. Municipal code and amendments to the criminal and corporation laws.

(h) **Committee on Finance**, to which committee shall be referred all proposed legislation, messages, petitions, memorials, and other matters relating to the following subjects:

1. Revenue measures generally.
2. The bonded debt of the United States.
3. The deposit of public moneys.
4. Customs, collection districts, and ports of entry and delivery.
5. Reciprocal trade agreements.
6. Transportation of dutiable goods.
7. Revenue measures relating to the insular possessions.
8. Tariffs and import quotas, and matters related thereto.
9. National social security.

(i) **Committee on Foreign Relations**, to which committee shall be referred all proposed legislation, messages, petitions, memorials, and other matters relating to the following subjects:

1. Relations of the United States with foreign nations generally.
2. Treaties.
3. Establishment of boundary lines between the United States and foreign nations.
4. Protection of American citizens abroad and expatriation.
5. Neutrality.
6. International conferences and congresses.
7. The American National Red Cross.
8. Intervention abroad and declarations of war.

9. Measures relating to the diplomatic service.

10. Acquisition of land and buildings for embassies and legations in foreign countries.

11. Measures to foster commercial intercourse with foreign nations and to safeguard American business interests abroad.

12. United Nations Organization and international financial and monetary organizations.

13. Foreign loans.

(j) (1) **Committee on Government Operations**, to which committee shall be referred all proposed legislation, messages, petitions, memorials, and other matters relating to the following subjects:

(A) Budget and accounting measures, other than appropriations.

(B) Reorganizations in the executive branch of the Government.

(2) Such committee shall have the duty of—

(A) receiving and examining reports of the Comptroller General of the United States and of submitting such recommendations to the Senate as it deems necessary or desirable in connection with the subject matter of such reports;

(B) studying the operation of Government activities at all levels with a view to determining its economy and efficiency;

(C) evaluating the effects of laws enacted to reorganize the legislative and executive branches of the Government;

(D) studying the intergovernmental relationships between the United States and the States and municipalities, and between the United States and international organizations of which the United States is a member.

(k) **Committee on Interior and Insular Affairs**, to which committee shall be referred all proposed legislation, messages, petitions, memorials, and other matters relating to the following subjects:

1. Public lands generally, including entry, easements, and grazing thereon.

2. Mineral resources of the public lands.

3. Forfeiture of land grants and alien ownership, including alien ownership of mineral lands.

4. Forest reserves and national parks created from the public domain.

5. Military parks and battlefields.

6. Preservation of prehistoric ruins and objects of interest on the public domain.

7. Measures relating generally to the insular possessions of the United States, except those affecting their revenue and appropriations.

8. Irrigation and reclamation, including water supply for reclamation projects, and easements of public lands for irrigation projects.

9. Interstate compacts relating to apportionment of waters for irrigation purposes.

10. Mining interests generally.

11. Mineral land laws and claims and entries thereunder.

12. Geological survey.

13. Mining schools and experimental stations.

14. Petroleum conservation and conservation of the radium supply in the United States.

15. Relations of the United States with the Indians and the Indian tribes.

16. Measures relating to the care, education, and management of Indians, including the care and allotment of Indian lands and general and special measures relating to claims which are paid out of Indian funds.

(l) **Committee on the Judiciary**, to which committee shall be referred all proposed legislation, messages, petitions, memorials, and other matters relating to the following subjects:

1. Judicial proceedings, civil and criminal, generally.

2. Constitutional amendments.

3. Federal courts and judges.

4. Local courts in the territories and possessions.

5. Revision and codification of the statutes of the United States.

6. National penitentiaries.

7. Protection of trade and commerce against unlawful restraints and monopolies.

8. Holidays and celebrations.

9. Bankruptcy, mutiny, espionage, and counterfeiting.

10. State and territorial boundary lines.

11. Meetings of Congress, attendance of Members, and their acceptance of incompatible offices.

12. Civil liberties.

13. Patents, copyrights, and trademarks.

14. Patent Office.

15. Immigration and naturalization.

16. Apportionment of Representatives.

17. Measures relating to claims against the United States.

18. Interstate compacts generally.

(m) **Committee on Labor and Public Welfare**, to which committee shall be referred all proposed legislation, messages, petitions, memorials, and other matters relating to the following subjects:

1. Measures relating to education, labor, or public welfare generally.

2. Mediation and arbitration of labor disputes.

3. Wages and hours of labor.

4. Convict labor and the entry of goods made by convicts into interstate commerce.

5. Regulation or prevention of importation of foreign laborers under contract.

6. Child labor.

7. Labor statistics.

8. Labor standards.

9. School-lunch program.

10. Vocational rehabilitation.

11. Railroad labor and railroad retirement and unemployment, except revenue measures relating thereto.

12. United States Employees' Compensation Commission.

13. Columbia Institution for the Deaf, Dumb, and Blind (Gallaudet College); Howard University; Freedmen's Hospital; and St. Elizabeths Hospital.

14. Public health and quarantine.

15. Welfare of miners.

(n) **Committee on Post Office and Civil Service**, to which committee shall be referred all proposed legislation, messages, petitions, memorials, and other matters relating to the following subjects:

1. The Federal civil service generally.

2. The status of officers and employees of the United States, including their compensation, classification, and retirement.

3. The postal service generally, including the railway mail service, and measures relating to ocean mail and pneumatic-tube service; but excluding post roads.

4. Postal-savings banks.

5. Census and the collection of statistics generally.

6. The National Archives.

(o) **Committee on Public Works**, to which committee shall be referred all proposed legislation, messages, petitions, memorials, and other matters relating to the following subjects:

1. Flood control and improvement of rivers and harbors.

2. Public works for the benefit of navigation, and bridges and dams (other than international bridges and dams).

3. Water power.

4. Oil and other pollution of navigable waters.

5. Public buildings and occupied or improved grounds of the United States generally.

6. Measures relating to the purchase of sites and construction of post offices, customhouses, Federal courthouses, and Government buildings within the District of Columbia.

7. Measures relating to the Capitol Building and the Senate and House Office Buildings.

8. Measures relating to the construction or reconstruction, maintenance, and care of the buildings and grounds of the Botanic Gardens, the Library of Congress, and the Smithsonian Institution.

9. Public reservations and parks within the District of Columbia, including Rock Creek Park and the Zoological Park.

10. Measures relating to the construction or maintenance of roads and post roads.

(p) (1) **Committee on Rules and Administration**, to which committee shall be referred all proposed legislation, messages, petitions, memorials, and other matters relating to the following subjects:

(A) Matters relating to the payment of money out of the contingent fund of the Senate or creating a charge upon the same; except that any resolution relating to substantive matter within the jurisdiction of any other standing committee of the Senate shall be first referred to such committee.

(B) Except as provided in paragraph (o) 8, matters relating to the Library of Congress and the Senate Library; statuary and pictures; acceptance or purchase of works of art for the Capitol; the Botanic Gardens; management of the Library of Congress; purchase of books and manuscripts; erection of monuments to the memory of individuals.

(C) Except as provided in paragraph (o) 8, matters relating to the Smithsonian Institution and the incorporation of similar institutions.

(D) Matters relating to the election of the President, Vice President, or Members of Congress; corrupt practices; contested elections; credentials and qualifications; Federal elections generally; Presidential succession.

(E) Matters relating to parliamentary rules; floor and gallery rules; Senate Restaurant; administration of the Senate Office Buildings and of the Senate wing of the Capitol; assignment of office space: and services to the Senate.

(F) Matters relating to printing and correction of the Congressional Record.

(2) Such committee shall also have the duty of assigning office space in the Senate wing of the Capitol and in the Senate Office Buildings.

(q) Committee on Veterans' Affairs, to which committee shall be referred all proposed legislation, messages, petitions, memorials, and other matters relating to the following subjects:
1. Veterans' measures generally.
2. Pensions of all wars of the United States, general and special.
3. Life insurance issued by the Government on account of service in the armed forces.
4. Compensation of veterans.
5. Vocational rehabilitation and education of veterans.
6. Veterans' hospitals, medical care and treatment of veterans.
7. Soldiers' and sailors' civil relief.
8. Readjustment of servicemen to civil life.
9. National cemeteries.

2. Except as otherwise provided by paragraph 6 of this rule, each of the following standing committees shall consist of the number of Senators set forth in the following table on the line on which the name of that committee appears:

Committee	Members
Aeronautical and Space Sciences	14
Agriculture and Forestry	13
Appropriations	24
Armed Services	15
Banking, Housing, and Urban Affairs	15
Commerce	17
Finance	15
Foreign Relations	15
Government Operations	14
Interior and Insular Affairs	14
Judiciary	15
Labor and Public Welfare	15
Public Works	14

3. Except as otherwise provided by paragraph 6 of this rule, each of the following standing committees shall consist of the number of Senators set forth in the following table on the line on which the name of that committee appears:

Committee	Members
District of Columbia	7
Post Office and Civil Service	9
Rules and Administration	9
Veterans' Affairs	9

4. The said committees shall continue and have the power to act until their successors are appointed.

5. (a) Except as provided in paragraph (b) of this subsection, each standing committee, and each subcommittee of any such committee, is authorized to fix the number of its members (but not less than one-third of its entire membership) who shall constitute a quorum thereof for the transaction of such business as may be considered by said committee, subject to the provisions of section 133(d) of the Legislative Reorganization Act of 1946.

(b) Each standing committee, and each subcommittee of any such committee, is authorized to fix a lesser number than one-third of its entire membership who shall constitute a quorum thereof for the purpose of taking sworn testimony.

6. (a) Except as otherwise provided by this paragraph, each Senator shall serve on two and no more of the standing committees named in paragraph 2. Except as otherwise provided by this paragraph, no Senator shall serve on more than one committee included within the following classes: standing committees named in paragraph 3; select and special committees of the Senate; and joint committees of the Congress.

(b) Each Senator who on the day preceding the effective date of section 132 of the Legislative Reorganization Act of 1970 was serving as a member of any standing committee shall be entitled to continue to serve on each such committee of which he was a member on that day as long as his service as a member of such committee remains continuous after that day. Each Senator who (1) on that day was serving as a member of the Committee on Aeronautical and Space Sciences or the Committee on Government Operations, (2) on that date was entitled, under the proviso contained in the first sentence of paragraph 4 of this rule as such rule existed on that day, to serve on three committees named in that sentence, and (3) on June 30, 1971, is serving on three such committees, of which at least one is the Committee on Aeronautical and Space Sciences or the Committee on Government Operations, shall be entitled to continue to serve on each of the committees of which he is a member on June 30, 1971, so long as his service as a member of each such committee remains continuous thereafter. Each Senator who, on the day preceding the effective date of section 132 of the Legislative Reorganization Act of 1970, was a member of more than one committee of the

classes described in the second sentence of subparagraph (a) shall be entitled to serve on each such committee of which he was a member on that day as long as his service as a member of that committee remains continuous after that day. Each Senator who on that day was a member of more than one committee of those classes may be assigned during the 92d Congress to other committees included within those classes, except that no Senator may serve on a number of committees of those classes greater than the number of such committees on which he was serving on the day preceding such effective date. Notwithstanding the provisions of paragraphs 2 and 3, each committee of the Senate shall be temporarily increased in membership by such number as may be required to carry into effect the provisions of this subparagraph.

(c) By agreement entered into by the majority leader and the minority leader, the membership of one or more of the standing committees named in paragraph 2 or paragraph 3 of this rule may be increased temporarily from time to time by such number or numbers as may be required to accord to the majority party a majority of the membership of all standing committees. When any such temporary increase is necessary to accord to the majority party a majority of the membership of all standing committees, members of the majority party in such number as may be required for that purpose may serve as members of three standing committees named in paragraph 2. No such temporary increase in the membership of one or more standing committees under this subparagraph or subparagraph (b) shall be continued in effect after the need therefor has ended. No standing committee may be increased in membership under this subparagraph or subparagraph (b) by more than four members in excess of the number prescribed for that committee by paragraph 2 or paragraph 3 of this rule.

(d) Notwithstanding the limitations contained in subparagraph (a), a Senator may serve at any time on one additional committee included within the following classes: a temporary committee of the Senate or a temporary joint committee of the Congress which, by the terms of the measure by which it was established as initially agreed to, will not continue in existence for more than one Congress; or a joint committee of the Congress having jurisdiction with respect to a subject matter which is directly related to the jurisdiction of a committee named in paragraph 3 of which that Senator is a member.

(e) No Senator shall serve at any time on more than one of the following committees: Committee on Appropriations, Committee on Armed Services, Committee on Finance, and Committee on Foreign Relations. Notwithstanding the limitation contained in this subparagraph, a Senator who on the day preceding the effective date of section 132 of the Legislative Reorganization Act of 1970 was a member of more than one such committee may continue to serve as a member of each such committee of which he was a member on that day as long as his service on that committee remains continuous after that day.

(f) No Senator shall serve at any time as chairman of more than one committee included within the following classes: standing, select, and special committees of the Senate; and joint committees of the Congress except that—

(1) A Senator may serve as chairman of a joint committee of the Congress having jurisdiction with respect to a subject matter which is directly related to the jurisdiction of a committee named in paragraph 2 or paragraph 3 of which that Senator is the chairman;

(2) A Senator who on the day preceding the effective date of section 132 of the Legislative Reorganization Act of 1970 was serving as chairman of more than one committee included within the classes described in this subparagraph may continue to serve as chairman of each such committee of which he was chairman on that day as long as his service as chairman of that committee remains continuous after that day; and

(3) A Senator who is serving at any time as chairman of a committee included within the classes described in this subparagraph may at the same time serve also as chairman of one temporary committee of the Senate or temporary joint committee of the Congress which, by the terms of the measure by which it was established as originally agreed to, will not continue in existence for more than one Congress.

(g) No Senator shall serve at any time as chairman of more than one subcommittee of the same committee if that committee is named in paragraph 2. Notwithstanding the limitation contained in this subparagraph, a Senator who on the day preceding the effective date of section 132 of the Legislative Reorganization Act of 1970 was serving as chairman of more than one such subcommittee may continue to serve as chairman of each such subcommittee of which he was chairman on that day as long as his service as chairman of that subcommittee remains continuous after that day.

7. No standing committee shall sit without special leave while the Senate is in session after (1) the conclusion of the morning hour, or (2) the Senate has proceeded to the consideration of unfinished business, pending business, or any other business except private bills and the routine morning business, whichever is earlier. (The Legislative Reorganization Act of 1970 amended section 134(c) of the Legislative Reor-

ganization Act of 1946 to provide: Except as otherwise provided in this subsection, no standing committee of the Senate shall sit, without special leave, while the Senate is in session. The prohibition contained in the preceding sentence shall not apply to the Committee on Appropriations of the Senate. Any other standing committee of the Senate may sit for any purpose while the Senate is in session if consent therefor has been obtained from the majority leader and the minority leader of the Senate. In the event of the absence of either such leaders, the consent of the absent leader may be given by a Senator designated by such leader for that purpose. Notwithstanding the provisions of this subsection, any standing committee of the Senate may sit without special leave for any purpose as authorized by paragraph 7 of rule XXV of the Standing Rules of the Senate.)

Rule XXVI

Reference to Committees; Motions To Discharge, and Reports of Committees To Lie Over

1. When motions are made for reference of a subject to a select committee, or to a standing committee, the question of reference to a standing committee shall be put first; and a motion simply to refer shall not be opened to amendment, except to add instructions.

2. All reports of committees and motions to discharge a committee from the consideration of a subject, and all subjects from which a committee shall be discharged, shall lie over one day for consideration, unless by unanimous consent the Senate shall otherwise direct.

Rule XXVII

Reports of Conference Committees

1. The presentation of reports of committees of conference shall always be in order, except when the Journal is being read or a question of order or a motion to adjourn is pending, or while the Senate is dividing; and when received the question of proceeding to the consideration of the report, if raised, shall be immediately put, and shall be determined without debate.

2. Conferees shall not insert in their report matter not committed to them by either House, nor shall they strike from the bill matter agreed to by both Houses. If new matter is inserted in the report, or if matter which was agreed to by both Houses is stricken from the bill, a point of order may be made against the report, and if the point of order is sustained, the report shall be recommitted to the committee of conference.

3. (a) In any case in which a disagreement to an amendment in the nature of a substitute has been referred to conferees, it shall be in order for the conferees to report a substitute on the same subject matter; but they may not include in the report matter not committed to them by either House. They may, however, include in their report in any such case matter which is a germane modification of subjects in disagreement.

(b) In any case in which the conferees violate subsection (a), the conference report shall be subject to a point of order.

Rule XXVIII

Messages

1. Messages from the President of the United States or from the House of Representatives may be received at any stage of proceedings, except while the Senate is dividing, or while the Journal is being read, or while a question of order or a motion to adjourn is pending.

2. Messages shall be sent to the House of Representatives by the Secretary, who shall previously certify the determination of the Senate upon all bills, joint resolutions, and other resolutions which may be communicated to the House, or in which its concurrence may be requested; and the Secretary shall also certify and deliver to the President of the United States all resolutions and other communications which may be directed to him by the Senate.

Rule XXIX

Printing of Papers

1. Every motion to print documents, reports, and other matter transmitted by either of the executive departments, or to print memorials, petitions, accompanying documents, or any other paper, except bills of the Senate or House of Representatives, resolutions submitted by a Senator, communications from the legislatures or conventions, lawfully called, of the respective States, and motions to print by order of the standing or select committees of the Senate, shall, unless the Senate otherwise order,

be referred to the Committee on Rules and Administration. When a motion is made to commit with instructions, it shall be in order to add thereto a motion to print.

2. Motions to print additional numbers shall also be referred to the Committee on Rules and Administration; and when the committee shall report favorably, the report shall be accompanied by an estimate of the probable cost thereof; and when the cost of printing such additional numbers shall exceed the sum of five hundred dollars, the concurrence of the House of Representatives shall be necessary for an order to print the same. (By Act of Apr. 19, 1949, the limitation on printing extra copies was increased from $500 to $1,200.)

3. Every bill and joint resolution introduced on leave or reported from a committee, and all bills and joint resolutions received from the House of Representatives, and all reports of committees, shall be printed, unless, for the dispatch of the business of the Senate, such printing may be dispensed with.

4. Whenever a committee reports a bill or a joint resolution repealing or amending any statute or part thereof it shall make a report thereon and shall include in such report or in an accompanying document (to be prepared by the staff of such committee) (a) the text of the statute or part thereof which is proposed to be repealed; and (b) a comparative print of that part of the bill or joint resolution making the amendment and of the statute or part thereof proposed to be amended, showing by stricken-through type and italics, parallel columns, or other appropriate typographical devices the omissions and insertions which would be made by the bill or joint resolution if enacted in the form recommended by the committee. This subsection shall not apply to any such report in which it is stated that, in the opinion of the committee, it is necessary to dispense with the requirements of this subsection to expedite the business of the Senate.

Rule XXX

Withdrawal of Papers

1. No memorial or other paper presented to the Senate, except original treaties finally acted upon, shall be withdrawn from its files except by order of the Senate. But when an act may pass for the settlement of any private claim, the Secretary is authorized to transmit to the officer charged with the settlement the papers on file relating to the claim.

2. No memorial or other paper upon which an adverse report has been made shall be withdrawn from the files of the Senate unless copies thereof shall be left in the office of the Secretary.

Rule XXXI

Reference of Claims Adversely Reported

Whenever a committee of the Senate, to whom any claim has been referred, reports adversely, and the report is agreed to, it shall not be in order to move to take the papers from the files for the purpose of referring them at a subsequent session, unless the claimant shall present a petition therefor, stating that new evidence has been discovered since the report, and setting forth the substance of such new evidence. But when there has been no adverse report it shall be the duty of the Secretary to transmit all such papers to the committee in which such claims are pending.

Rule XXXII

Business Continued from Session to Session

1. At the second or any subsequent session of a Congress, the legislative business of the Senate which remained undetermined at the close of the next preceding session of that Congress shall be resumed and proceeded with in the same manner as if no adjournment of the Senate had taken place; and all papers referred to committees and not reported upon at the close of a session of Congress shall be returned to the office of the Secretary of the Senate, and be retained by him until the next succeeding session of that Congress, when they shall be returned to the several committees to which they had previously been referred.

2. The rules of the Senate shall continue from one Congress to the next Congress unless they are changed as provided in these rules.

Rule XXXIII

Privilege of the Floor

No person shall be admitted to the floor of the Senate while in session, except as follows: the President of the United States and his private secretary; the President-elect and Vice President-elect of the United States; ex-Presidents and Vice Presidents of the United States; Judges of the Supreme Court; ex-Senators and Senators-elect; the officers and employees of the Senate in the discharge of their official duties; ex-Secretaries and ex-Sergeants at Arms of the Senate; Members of the House of Representatives and Members-elect; ex-Speakers of the House of Representatives; the Sergeant at Arms of the House and his chief deputy and the Clerk of the House and his deputy; heads of the Executive Departments; Ambassadors and Ministers of the United States; Governors of States and Territories; the General Commanding the Army; the Senior Admiral of the Navy on the active list; members of National Legislatures of foreign countries; judges of the Court of Claims; the Commissioner of the District of Columbia; the Librarian of Congress and the Assistant Librarian in charge of the Law Library; the Architect of the Capitol; the Secretary of the Smithsonian Institution; clerks to Senate committees and clerks to Senators when in the actual discharge of their official duties. Clerks to Senators, to be admitted to the floor, must be regularly appointed and borne upon the rolls of the Secretary of the Senate as such.

Rule XXXIV

Regulation of the Senate Wing of the Capitol

1. The Senate Chamber shall not be granted for any other purpose than for the use of the Senate; no smoking shall be permitted at any time on the floor of the Senate, or lighted cigars be brought into the Chamber.

2. It shall be the duty of the Committee on Rules and Administration to make all rules and regulations respecting such parts of the Capitol, its passages and galleries, including the restaurant and the Senate Office Building, as are or may be set apart for the use of the Senate and its officers, to be enforced under the direction of the Presiding Officer. They shall make such regulations respecting the reporters' galleries of the Senate, together with the adjoining rooms and facilities, as will confine their occupancy and use to bona fide reporters for daily newspapers and periodicals, to bona fide reporters of news or press associations requiring telegraph service to their membership, and to bona fide reporters for daily news dissemination through radio, wire, wireless, and similar media of transmission. These regulations shall so provide for the use of such space and facilities as fairly to distribute their use to all such media of news dissemination.

Rule XXXV

Session with Closed Doors

On a motion made and seconded to close the doors of the Senate, on the discussion of any business which may, in the opinion of a Senator, require secrecy, the Presiding Officer shall direct the galleries to be cleared; and during the discussion of such motion the doors shall remain closed.

Rule XXXVI

Executive Sessions

1. When the President of the United States shall meet the Senate in the Senate Chamber for the consideration of Executive business, he shall have a seat on the right of the Presiding Officer. When the Senate shall be convened by the President of the United States to any other place, the Presiding Officer of the Senate and the Senators shall attend at the place appointed, with the necessary officers of the Senate.

2. When acting upon confidential or Executive business, unless the same shall be considered in open executive session, the Senate Chamber shall be cleared of all persons except the Secretary, the Chief Clerk, the Principal Legislative Clerk, the Executive Clerk, the Minute and Journal Clerk, the Sergeant at Arms, the Assistant Doorkeeper, and such other officers as the Presiding Officer shall think necessary; and all such officers shall be sworn to secrecy. (On May 2, 1892, the Senate agreed to the following: *Resolved,* That until otherwise ordered there shall be admitted to the floor of the Senate during executive sessions such clerks, not exceeding three in number, as may be assigned by the Secretary of the Senate to Executive duties.)

3. All confidential communications made by the President of the United States to the Senate shall be by the Senators and the officers of the Senate kept secret; and all treaties which may be laid before the Senate, and all remarks, votes, and proceedings thereon shall also be kept secret, until the Senate shall, by their resolution, take off the injunction of secrecy, or unless the same shall be considered in open executive session. (On Feb. 8, 1900, the Senate agreed to the following: *Ordered,* Whenever

the injunction of secrecy shall be removed from any part of the proceedings of the Senate in executive session, or secret legislative session, the order of the Senate removing the same shall be entered by the Secretary in the Legislative Journal as well as in the Executive Journal, and shall be published in the Record.)

4. Any Senator or officer of the Senate who shall disclose the secret or confidential business or proceedings of the Senate shall be liable, if a Senator, to suffer expulsion from the body; and if an officer, to dismissal from the service of the Senate, and to punishment for contempt.

5. Whenever, by the request of the Senate or any committee thereof, any documents or papers shall be communicated to the Senate by the President or the head of any department relating to any matter pending in the Senate, the proceedings in regard to which are secret or confidential under the rules, said documents and papers shall be considered as confidential, and shall not be disclosed without leave of the Senate.

Rule XXXVII

Executive Session—Proceedings on Treaties

1. When a treaty shall be laid before the Senate for ratification, it shall be read a first time; and no motion in respect to it shall be in order, except to refer it to a committee, to print it in confidence for the use of the Senate, to remove the injunction of secrecy, or to consider it in open executive session.

When a treaty is reported from a committee with or without amendment, it shall, unless the Senate unanimously otherwise direct, lie one day for consideration; after which it may be read a second time and considered as in Committee of the Whole, when it shall be proceeded with by articles, and the amendments reported by the committee shall be first acted upon, after which other amendments may be proposed; and when through with, the proceedings had as in Committee of the Whole shall be reported to the Senate, when the question shall be, if the treaty be amended, "Will the Senate concur in the amendments made in Committee of the Whole?" And the amendment may be taken separately, or in gross, if no Senator shall object; after which new amendments may be proposed. At any stage of such proceedings the Senate may remove the injunction of secrecy from the treaty, or proceed with its consideration in open executive session.

The decisions thus made shall be reduced to the form of a resolution of ratification, with or without amendments, as the case may be, which shall be proposed on a subsequent day, unless, by unanimous consent, the Senate determine otherwise; at which stage no amendment shall be received unless by unanimous consent.

On the final question to advise and consent to the ratification in the form agreed to, the concurrence of two-thirds of the Senators present shall be necessary to determine it in the affirmative; but all other motions and questions upon a treaty shall be decided by a majority vote, except a motion to postpone indefinitely, which shall be decided by a vote of two-thirds.

2. Treaties transmitted by the President to the Senate for ratification shall be resumed at the second or any subsequent session of the same Congress at the stage in which they were left at the final adjournment of the session at which they were transmitted; but all proceedings on treaties shall terminate with the Congress, and they shall be resumed at the commencement of the next Congress as if no proceedings had previously been had thereon.

3. All treaties concluded with Indian tribes shall be considered and acted upon by the Senate in its open or legislative session, unless the same shall be transmitted by the President to the Senate in confidence, in which case they shall be acted upon with closed doors.

Rule XXXVIII

Executive Session—Proceedings on Nominations

1. When nominations shall be made by the President of the United States to the Senate, they shall, unless otherwise ordered, by referred to appropriate committees; and the final question on every nomination shall be, "Will the Senate advise and consent to this nomination?" which question shall not be put on the same day on which the nomination is received, nor on the day on which it may be reported by a committee, unless by unanimous consent.

2. Hereafter all business in the Senate shall be transacted in open session, unless the Senate in closed session by a majority vote shall determine that a particular nomination, treaty, or other matter shall be considered in closed executive session, in which case all subsequent proceedings with respect to said nomination, treaty, or other matter shall be kept secret: *Provided,* That the injunction of secrecy as to the whole or any part of proceedings in closed executive session may be removed on motion adopted by a majority vote of the Senate in closed executive

session: *Provided further*, That rule XXXV shall apply to open executive session: *And provided further*, That any Senator may make public his vote in closed executive session.

Anything in the rules of the Senate inconsistent with the foregoing is hereby repealed.

3. When a nomination is confirmed or rejected, any Senator voting in the majority may move for a reconsideration on the same day on which the vote was taken, or on either of the next two days of actual executive session of the Senate; but if a notification of the confirmation or rejection of a nomination shall have been sent to the President before the expiration of the time within which a motion to reconsider may be made, the motion to reconsider shall be accompanied by a motion to request the President to return such notification to the Senate. Any motion to reconsider the vote on a nomination may be laid on the table without prejudice to the nomination, and shall be a final disposition of such motion.

4. Nominations confirmed or rejected by the Senate shall not be returned by the Secretary to the President until the expiration of the time limited for making a motion to reconsider the same, or while a motion to reconsider is pending unless otherwise ordered by the Senate.

5. When the Senate shall adjourn or take a recess for more than thirty days, all motions to reconsider a vote upon a nomination which has been confirmed or rejected by the Senate, which shall be pending at the time of taking such adjournment or recess, shall fall; and the Secretary shall return all such nominations to the President as confirmed or rejected by the Senate, as the case may be.

6. Nominations neither confirmed nor rejected during the session at which they are made shall not be acted upon at any succeeding session without being again made to the Senate by the President; and if the Senate shall adjourn or take a recess for more than thirty days, all nominations pending and not finally acted upon at the time of taking such adjournment or recess shall be returned by the Secretary to the President, and shall not again be considered unless they shall again be made to the Senate by the President. (On Dec. 16, 1885, the Senate agreed to the following: *Resolved,* All nominations to office shall be prepared for the printer by the Official Reporter, and printed in the Record, after the proceedings of the day in which they are received, also nominations recalled, and confirmed. On Dec. 17, 1885, the Senate agreed to the following: *Ordered,* The Secretary shall furnish the Official Reporters with a list of nominations to office after the proceedings of the day on which they are received, and a like list of all confirmations and rejections. On May 2, 1894, the Senate agreed to the following: *Resolved,* The Secretary shall furnish to the press, and to the public upon request, the names of nominees confirmed or rejected on the day on which a final vote shall be had, except when otherwise ordered by the Senate.)

Rule XXXIX

The President Furnished with Copies of Records of Executive Sessions

The President of the United States shall, from time to time, be furnished with an authenticated transcript of the executive records of the Senate, but no further extract from the Executive Journal shall be furnished by the Secretary, except by special order of the Senate; and no paper, except original treaties transmitted to the Senate by the President of the United States, and finally acted upon by the Senate, shall be delivered from the office of the Secretary without an order of the Senate for that purpose.

Rule XL

Suspension and Amendment of the Rules

No motion to suspend, modify, or amend any rule, or any part thereof, shall be in order, except on one day's notice in writing, specifying precisely the rule or part proposed to be suspended, modified, or amended, and the purpose thereof. Any rule may be suspended without notice by the unanimous consent of the Senate, except as otherwise provided in clause 1, Rule XII.

Rule XLI

Outside Business or Professional Activity or Employment by Officers or Employees

1. No officer or employee whose salary is paid by the Senate may engage in any business or professional activity or employment for compensation unless—

(a) the activity or employment is not inconsistent nor in conflict with the conscientious performance of his official duties; and

(b) he has reported in writing when this rule takes effect or when his office or employment starts and on the 15th day of May in each year thereafter the nature of any personal service activity or employment to his supervisor. The supervisor shall then, in the discharge of his duties, take such action as he considers necessary for the avoidance of conflict of interest or interference with duties to the Senate.

2. For the purpose of this rule—

(a) a Senator or the Vice President is the supervisor of his administrative, clerical, or other assistants;

(b) a Senator who is the chairman of a committee is the supervisor of the professional, clerical, or other assistants to the committee except that minority staff members shall be under the supervision of the ranking minority Senator on the committee;

(c) a Senator who is a chairman of a subcommittee which has its own staff and financial authorization is the supervisor of the professional, clerical, or other assistants to the subcommittee except that minority staff members shall be under the supervision of the ranking minority Senator on the subcommittee;

(d) the President pro tempore is the supervisor of the Secretary of the Senate, Sergeant at Arms and Doorkeeper, the Chaplain, and the employees of the Office of the Legislative Counsel;

(e) The Secretary of the Senate is the supervisor of the employees of his office;

(f) the Sergeant at Arms and Doorkeeper is the supervisor of the employees of his office;

(g) the Majority and Minority Leaders and the Majority and Minority Whips are the supervisors of the research, clerical, or other assistants assigned to their respective offices;

(h) the Majority Leader is the supervisor of the Secretary for the Majority. The Secretary for the Majority is the supervisor of the employees of his office; and

(i) the Minority Leader is the supervisor of the Secretary for the Minority. The Secretary for the Minority is the supervisor of the employees of his office.

3. This rule shall take effect ninety days after adoption (adopted 3/22/68).

Rule XLII

Contributions

1. A Senator or person who has declared or otherwise made known his intention to seek nomination or election, or who has filed papers or petitions for nomination or election, or on whose behalf a declaration or nominating paper or petition has been made or filed, or who has otherwise, directly or indirectly, manifested his intention to seek nomination or election, pursuant to State law, to the office of United States Senator, may accept a contribution from—

(a) a fund-raising event organized and held primarily in his behalf, provided—

(1) he has expressly given his approval of the fund-raising event to the sponsors before any funds were raised; and

(2) he receives a complete and accurate accounting of the source, amounts, and disposition of the funds raised; or

(b) an individual or an organization, provided the Senator makes a complete and accurate accounting of the source, amount, and disposition of the funds received; or

(c) his political party when such contributions were from a fund-raising event sponsored by his party, without giving his express approval for such fund-raising event when such fund-raising event is for the purpose of providing contributions for candidates of his party and such contributions are reported by the Senator or candidate for Senator as provided in paragraph (b).

2. The Senator may use the contribution only to influence his nomination for election, or his election, and shall not use, directly or indirectly, any part of any contribution for any other purpose, except as otherwise provided herein.

3. Nothing in this rule shall preclude the use of contributions to defray expenses for travel to and from each Senator's home state; for printing and other expenses in connection with the mailing of speeches, newsletters, and reports to a Senator's constituents; for expenses of radio, television, and news media methods of reporting to a Senator's constituents; for telephone, telegraph, postage, and stationery expenses in excess of allowance; and for newspaper subscriptions from his home state.

4. All gifts in the aggregate amount or value of $50 or more received by a Senator from any single source during a year, except a gift from his spouse, child, or parent, and except a contribution under sections 1 and 2, shall be reported under rule XLIV.

5. This rule shall take effect ninety days after adoption (adopted 3/22/68).

Rule XLIII

Political Fund Activity by Officers and Employees

1. No officer or employee whose salary is paid by the Senate may receive, solicit, be the custodian of, or distribute any funds in connection with any campaign for the nomination for election, or the election of any individual to be a Member of the Senate or to any other Federal office. This prohibition does not apply to any assistant to a Senator who has been designated by that Senator to perform any of the functions described in the first sentence of this paragraph and who is compensated at a rate in excess of $10,000 per annum if such designation has been made in writing and filed with the Secretary of the Senate. The Secretary of the Senate shall make the designation available for public inspection.

2. This rule shall take effect sixty days after adoption (adopted 3/22/68).

Rule XLIV

Disclosure of Financial Interests

1. Each Senator or person who has declared or otherwise made known his intention to seek nomination or election, or who has filed papers or petitions for nomination or election, or on whose behalf a declaration or nominating paper or petition has been made or filed, or who has otherwise, directly or indirectly, manifested his intention to seek nomination or election, pursuant to State law, to the office of United States Senator, and each officer or employee of the Senate who is compensated at a rate in excess of $15,000 a year, shall file with the Comptroller General of the United States, in a sealed envelope marked "Confidential Personal Financial Disclosure of _____(Name)_____," before the 15th day of May in each year, the following reports of his personal financial interests:

(a) a copy of the returns of taxes, declarations, statements, or other documents which he, or he and his spouse jointly, made for the preceding year in compliance with the income tax provisions of the Internal Revenue Code;

(b) the amount or value and source of each fee or compensation of $1,000 or more received by him during the preceding year from a client;

(c) the name and address of each business or professional corporation, firm, or enterprise in which he was an officer, director, partner, proprietor, or employee who received compensation during the preceding year and the amount of each compensation;

(d) the identity of each interest in real or personal property having a value of $10,000 or more which he owned at any time during the preceding year;

(e) the identity of each trust or other fiduciary relation in which he held a beneficial interest having a value of $10,000 or more, and the identity if known of each interest of the trust or other fiduciary relation in real or personal property in which the Senator, officer, or employee held a beneficial interest having a value of $10,000 or more, at any time during the preceding year. If he cannot obtain the identity of the fiduciary interests, the Senator, officer, or employee shall request the fiduciary to report that information to the Comptroller General in the same manner that reports are filed under this rule;

(f) the identity of each liability of $5,000 or more owed by him, or by him and his spouse jointly, at any time during the preceding year; and

(g) the source and value of all gifts in the aggregate amount or value of $50 or more from any single source received by him during the preceding year.

2. Except as otherwise provided by this section, all papers filed under section 1 of this rule shall be kept by the Comptroller General for not less than seven years, and while so kept shall remain sealed. Upon receipt of a resolution of the Select Committee on Standards and Conduct, adopted by a recorded majority vote of the full committee, requesting the transmission to the committee of any of the reports filed by any individual under section 1 of this rule, the Comptroller General shall transmit to the committee the envelopes containing such reports. Within a reasonable time after such recorded vote has been taken, the individual concerned shall be informed of the vote to examine and audit, and shall be advised of the nature and scope of such examination. When any sealed envelope containing any such report is received by the committee, such envelope may be opened and the contents thereof may be examined only by members of the committee in executive session. If, upon such examination, the committee determines that further consideration by the committee is warranted and is within the jurisdiction of the committee, it may make the contents of any such envelope available for any use by any member of the committee, or any member of the staff of the committee, which is required for the discharge of his official duties. The committee may receive the papers as evidence, after giving to the individual concerned due notice and opportunity for hearing in a closed session. The Comptroller General shall report to the Select Committee on Standards and Conduct not later than the 1st day of June in each year the names of Senators, officers, and employees who have filed a report. Any paper which has been filed with the Comptroller General for longer than seven years, in accordance with the provisions of this section, shall be returned to the individual concerned or his legal representative. In the event of the death or termination of service of a Member of the Senate, an officer or employee, such papers shall be returned unopened to such individual, or to the surviving spouse or legal representative of such individual within one year of such death or termination of service.

3. Each Senator or person who has declared or otherwise made known his intention to seek nomination or election, or who has filed papers or petitions for nomination or election, or on whose behalf a declaration or nominating paper or petition has been made or filed, or who has otherwise, directly or indirectly, manifested his intention to seek nomination or election, pursuant to State law, to the office of United States Senator, and each officer or employee of the Senate who is compensated at a rate in excess of $15,000 a year, shall file with the Secretary of the Senate, before the 15th day of May in each year, the following reports of his personal financial interests:

(a) the accounting required by rule XLII for all contributions received by him during the preceding year, except that contributions in the aggregate amount or value of less than $50 received from any single source during the reporting period may be totaled without further itemization; and

(b) the amount or value and source of each honorarium of $300 or more received by him during the preceding year.

4. All papers filed under section 3 of this rule shall be kept by the Secretary of the Senate for not less than three years and shall be made available promptly for public inspection and copying.

5. This rule shall take effect on July 1, 1968. No reports shall be filed for any period before office or employment was held with the Senate, or during a period of office or employment with the Senate of less than ninety days in a year; except that the Senator, or officer or employee of the Senate, may file a copy of the return of taxes for the year 1968, or a report of substantially equivalent information for only the effective part of the year 1968.

Standing Orders of the Senate

Committee Personnel and Expenditure Reports

Resolved, That the Senate shall not (1) authorize the payment from the contingent fund of the Senate of the expenses, in excess of $5,000, of any inquiry or investigation hereafter authorized, or (2) increase the amount heretofore authorized to be paid from the contingent fund of the Senate in connection with any inquiry or investigation, unless, prior to adoption of the resolution authorizing such payment or providing for such increase, the committee or subcommittee thereof authorized to conduct such inquiry or investigation shall have submitted to the Committee on Rules and Administration a budget, in such form as the committee may require, setting forth its estimates of expenses proposed to be incurred for personal services, hearings, and travel, and such other information as the committee may require.

Sec. 2. Whenever the head of any department or agency of the Government shall have detailed or assigned personnel of such department or agency to the staff of any Senate committee or subcommittee thereof, the appropriations of such department or agency from which the personnel so assigned or detailed is paid shall be reimbursed from funds available to the committee or subcommittee at the end of each quarterly period in the amount of the salaries of such personnel while on such detail or assignment; and the services of any personnel so detailed or assigned shall not be accepted or utilized unless, at the time of such detail or assignment, funds are available to such committee or subcommittee for the reimbursement of appropriations, as herein provided, for the period of such detail or assignment.

Sec. 3. The foregoing provisions of this resolution shall become effective on April 1, 1946.

Sec. 4. The Committee on Rules and Administration of the Senate is authorized to make such studies as may be necessary to enable it to prescribe uniform requirements as to the form and content of budgets required to be submitted under the first section of this resolution and otherwise to carry out its functions under such section.

(Adopted 6/28/1945.)

Printing in Congressional Record

Resolved, That hereafter no written or printed matter shall be received for printing in the body of the Congressional Record as a part of the remarks of any Senator unless such matter (1) shall have been read orally by such Senator on the floor of the Senate, or (2) shall have been offered and received for printing in such manner as to indicate clearly that the contents thereof were not read orally by such Senator on the floor of the Senate. All such matter shall be printed in the Record in accordance with the rules prescribed by the Joint Committee on Printing. No request shall be entertained by the Presiding Officer to suspend by unanimous consent the requirements of this resolution.

(Adopted 7/23/1947.)

Special Deputies

Resolved, That the Sergeant at Arms of the Senate is authorized and empowered from time to time to appoint such special deputies as he may think necessary to serve process or perform other duties devolved upon the Sergeant at Arms by law or the rules or orders of the Senate, or which may hereafter be devolved upon him, and in such case they shall be officers of the Senate; and any act done or return made by the deputies so appointed shall have like effect and be of the same validity as if performed or made by the Sergeant at Arms in person.

(Adopted 12/17/1889.)

Persons Not Full-time Employees of Senate

Resolved, That hereafter, standing or select committees employing the services of persons who are not full-time employees of the Senate or any committee thereof shall submit monthly reports to the Senate (or to the Secretary during a recess or adjournment) showing (1) the name and address of any such person; (2) the name and address of the department or organization by whom his salary is paid; and (3) the annual rate of compensation in each case.

(Adopted 8/23/1944.)

Flowers in the Senate Chamber

Resolved, That until further orders the Sergeant at Arms is instructed not to permit flowers to be brought into the Senate Chamber.

(Adopted 2/24/1905.)

Length of Service and Age of Senate Pages

Resolved, That it shall be the duty of the Sergeant at Arms to classify the pages of the Senate, so that at the close of the present and each succeeding Congress, one-half the number shall be removed * * *.

(Adopted 7/17/1854.)

Resolved, * * * That in no case shall a page of the Senate be appointed for duty in the Senate Chamber who is younger than fourteen years of age and who has not completed the eighth grade of school, or is seventeen years of age or older, except that those enrolled in the Senate page school who attain age seventeen may serve as pages through the session of the Senate in which the page-school year terminates.

(First adopted 1/13/1949.)

Seal of the Senate

Resolved, That the Secretary shall have the custody of the seal, and shall use the same for the authentication of process transcripts, copies, and certificates whenever directed by the Senate; and may use the same to authenticate copies of such papers and documents in his office as he may lawfully give copies of.

(Adopted 1/20/1886.)

Marble Busts of Vice Presidents

Resolved, That marble busts of those who have been Vice Presidents of the United States shall be placed in the Senate wing of the Capitol from time to time, that the Architect of the Capitol is authorized, subject to the advice and approval of the Senate Committee on Rules and Administration, to carry into execution the object of this resolution, and the

expenses incurred in doing so shall be paid out of the contingent fund of the Senate.

(First adopted 1/6/1898.)

Reading of Washington's Farewell Address

Ordered, That, unless otherwise directed, on the twenty-second day of February in each year, or if that day shall be on Sunday, then on the day following, immediately after the reading of the Journal, Washington's Farewell Address shall be read to the Senate by a Senator to be designated for the purpose by the Presiding Officer; and that thereafter the Senate will proceed with its ordinary business.

(Adopted 1/24/1901.)

Payment of Witnesses

Resolved, That witnesses summoned to appear before the Senate or any of its committees shall be entitled to a witness fee rated at not to exceed $16 for each full day spent in traveling to and from the place of examination and for each full day in attendance. A witness shall also be entitled to reimbursement of the actual and necessary transportation expenses incurred by him in traveling to and from the place of examination, in no case to exceed 12 cents a mile for the distance actually traveled by him for the purpose of appearing as a witness.

(First adopted 5/23/1951.)

Select Committee on Small Business

Resolved, That there is hereby created a select committee to be known as the Committee on Small Business and to consist of seventeen Senators to be appointed in the same manner and at the same time as the chairmen and members of the standing committees of the Senate at the beginning of each Congress.

It shall be the duty of such committee to study and survey by means of research and investigation all problems of American small-business enterprises, and to obtain all facts possible in relation thereto which would not only be of public interest, but which would aid the Congress in enacting remedial legislation, and to report to the Senate from time to time the the results of such studies and surveys. No proposed legislation shall be referred to such committee and such committee shall not have power to report by bill or otherwise have legislative jurisdiction.

(First adopted 2/20/1950.)

Select Committee on Small Business—Additional Powers

Resolved, That the Select Committee on Small Business, created by Senate Resolution 58, agreed to February 20, 1950, or any duly authorized subcommittee thereof, is authorized to sit and act at such places and times during the sessions, recesses, and adjourned periods of the Senate, to require by subpena or otherwise the attendance of such witnesses and the production of such books, papers, and documents, to administer such oaths, to take such testimony, to procure such printing and binding, and to make such expenditures as it deems advisable. The cost of stenographic services to report such hearings shall not be in excess of 25 cents per 100 words.

Sec. 2. A majority of the members of the committee, or any subcommittee thereof, shall constitute a quorum for the transaction of business, except that a lesser number, to be fixed by the committee, shall constitute a quorum for the purpose of taking sworn testimony.

Sec. 3. The committee shall have power to employ and fix the compensation of such officers, experts, and employees as it deems necessary in the performance of its duties, but the compensation so fixed shall not exceed the compensation prescribed under the Classification Act of 1949 for comparable duties. The committee is authorized to utilize the services, information, facilities, and personnel of the various departments and agencies of the Government to the extent that such services, information, facilities, and personnel, in the opinion of the heads of such departments and agencies, can be furnished without undue interference with the performance of the work and duties of such departments and agencies.

Sec. 4. Until an appropriation shall be made for payment of expenses of the committee, such expenses, in an amount not to exceed $10,000 shall be paid from the contingent fund of the Senate upon vouchers approved by the chairman.

(Adopted 5/26/1950.)

Pay of Clerical and Other Assistants as Affected by Resignation of Senator

Resolved, That in the case of the resignation of a Senator during his term of office, his clerical and other assistants on the payroll of the Senate on the date of such resignation shall be continued on such payroll at their respective salaries for a period of not to exceed thirty days, such sums to be paid from the contingent fund of the Senate: *Provided,* That any such assistants continued on the payroll, while so continued, shall perform their duties under the direction of the Secretary of the Senate, and he hereby is authorized and directed to remove from such payroll any such assistants who are not attending to the duties for which their services are continued: *Provided further,* That this shall not operate to continue such assistants on such payroll beyond the expiration of their Senator's term of service.

(Adopted 4/11/1951.)

Pay of Clerical and Other Assistants as Affected by Termination of Service of Appointed Senators

Resolved, That in any case in which (1) a Senator is appointed to fill any portion of an unexpired term, (2) an election is thereafter held to fill the remainder of such unexpired term, and (3) the Senator so appointed is not a candidate or if a candidate is not elected at such election, his clerical and other assistants on the payroll of the Senate on the date of termination of his service shall be continued on such roll at their respective salaries until the expiration of thirty days following such date or until they become otherwise gainfully employed, whichever is earlier, such sums to be paid from the contingent fund of the Senate. A statement in writing by any such employee that he was not gainfully employed during such period or the portion thereof for which payment is claimed shall be accepted as prima facie evidence that he was not so employed. The provisions of this resolution shall not apply to an employee of any such Senator if on or before the date of termination of his service he notifies the Disbursing Office of the Senate in writing that he does not wish the provisions of this resolution to apply to such employee.

(Adopted 6/28/1960.)

Hearings before Senate Members of Joint Committee on Atomic Energy

Resolved, That the Senate members of the Joint Committee on Atomic Energy, appointed by the President of the Senate as provided in Public Law 585, Seventy-ninth Congress, approved August 1, 1946, shall have the same power and authority, in connection with the holding of hearings and the conduct of investigations and reporting to the Senate thereon, with reference to appointments under said Public Law 585 that require the advice and consent of the Senate, as are possessed by the standing committees of the Senate in other matters requiring the advice and consent of the Senate.

(Adopted 1/20/1947.)

Printing of the Executive Journal

Resolved, That, beginning with the first session, Ninetieth Congress, the Secretary of the Senate is authorized to have printed not more than one hundred and fifty copies of the Executive Journal for a session of the Congress.

(Adopted 2/17/1967.)

Loyalty Checks on Senate Employees

Resolved, That hereafter when any person is appointed as an employee of any committee of the Senate, of any Senator, or of any office of the Senate the committee, Senator, or officer having authority to make such appointment shall transmit the name of such person to the Federal Bureau of Investigation, together with a request that such committee, Senator, or officer be informed as to any derogatory and rebutting information in the possession of such agency concerning the loyalty and reliability for security purposes of such person, and in any case in which such derogatory information is revealed such committee, Senator, or officer shall make or cause to be made such further investigation as shall have been considered necessary to determine the loyalty and reliability for security purposes of such person.

Every such committee, Senator, and officer shall promptly transmit to the Federal Bureau of Investigation a list of the names of the incumbent employees of such committee, Senator, or officer together with a request that such committee, Senator, or officer be informed of any derogatory and rebutting information contained in the files of such agency concerning the loyalty and reliability for security purposes of such employee.

(Adopted 3/6/1953.)

Authorizing Suit by Senate Committees

Resolved, That hereafter any committee of the Senate is hereby authorized to bring suit on behalf of and in the name of the United States in any court of competent jurisdiction if the committee is of the opinion that the suit is necessary to the adequate performance of the powers vested in it or the duties imposed upon it by the Constitution, resolution of the Senate, or other law. Such suit may be brought and prosecuted to final determination irrespective of whether or not the Senate is in session at time the suit is brought or thereafter. The committee may be represented in the suit either by such attorneys as it may designate or by such officers of the Department of Justice as the Attorney General may designate upon the request of the committee. No expenditures shall be made in con-

nection with any such suit in excess of the amount of funds available to the said committee. As used in this resolution, the term "committee" means any standing or special committee of the Senate, or any duly authorized subcommittee thereof, or the Senate members of any joint committee.

(Adopted 5/28/1928.)

Senate Youth Program

Resolved, That, until otherwise directed by the Senate, the Senate youth program authorized by S. Res. 324 of the Eighty-seventh Congress, agreed to May 17, 1962, and extended by S. Res. 147, agreed to May 27, 1963, may be continued at the discretion of and under such conditions as may be determined by the Committee on Rules and Administration.

(Adopted 4/16/1964.)

Select Committee on Standards and Conduct

Resolved, That (a) there is hereby established a permanent select committee of the Senate to be known as the Select Committee on Standards and Conduct (referred to hereinafter as the "Select Committee") consisting of six Members of the Senate, of whom three shall be selected from members of the majority party and three shall be selected from members of the minority party. Members thereof shall be appointed by the President of the Senate. The Select Committee shall select a chairman and a vice chairman from among its members.

(b) Vacancies in the membership of the Select Committee shall not affect the authority of the remaining members to execute the functions of the committee, and shall be filled in the same manner as original appointments thereto are made.

(c) A majority of the members of the Select Committee shall constitute a quorum for the transaction of business, except that the Select Committee may fix a lesser number as a quorum for the purpose of taking sworn testimony. The Select Committee shall adopt rules of procedure not inconsistent with the rules of the Senate governing standing committees of the Senate.

Sec. 2. (a) It shall be the duty of the Select Committee to—

(1) receive complaints and investigate allegations of improper conduct which may reflect upon the Senate, violations of law, and violations of rules and regulations of the Senate, relating to the conduct of individuals in the performance of their duties as Members of the Senate, or as officers or employees of the Senate, and to make appropriate findings of fact and conclusions with respect thereto;

(2) recommend to the Senate by report or resolution by a majority vote of the full committee disciplinary action to be taken with respect to such violations which the Select Committee shall determine, after according to the individuals concerned due notice and opportunity for hearing, to have occurred;

(3) recommend to the Senate, by report or resolution, such additional rules or regulations as the Select Committee shall determine to be necessary or desirable to insure proper standards of conduct by Members of the Senate, and by officers or employees of the Senate, in the performance of their duties and the discharge of their responsibilities; and

(4) report violations by a majority vote of the full committee of any law to the proper Federal and State authorities.

(b) The Select Committee from time to time shall transmit to the Senate its recommendation as to any legislative measures which it may consider to be necessary for the effective discharge of its duties.

Sec. 3. (a) The Select Committee is authorized to (1) make such expenditures; (2) hold such hearings; (3) sit and act at such times and places during the sessions, recesses, and adjournment periods of the Senate; (4) require by subpena or otherwise the attendance of such witnesses and the production of such correspondence, books, papers, and documents; (5) administer such oaths; (6) take such testimony orally or by deposition; and (7) employ and fix the compensation of such technical, clerical, and other assistants and consultants as it deems advisable.

(b) Upon request made by the members of the Select Committee selected from the minority party, the committee shall appoint one assistant or consultant designated by such members. No assistant or consultant appointed by the Select Committee may receive compensation at an annual gross rate which exceeds by more than $1,600 the annual gross rate of compensation of any individual so designated by the members of the committee who are members of the minority party.

(c) With the prior consent of the department or agency concerned, the Select Committee may (1) utilize the services, information, and facilities of the General Accounting Office or any department or agency in the executive branch of the Government, and (2) employ on a reimbursable basis or otherwise the services of such personnel of any such department or agency as it deems advisable. With the consent of any other committee of the Senate, or any subcommittee thereof, the Select Committee may utilize the facilities and the services of the staff of such other committee or subcommittee whenever the chairman of the Select Committee determines that such action is necessary and appropriate.

(d) Subpenas may be issued by the Select Committee over the signature of the chairman or any other member designated by him, and may be served by any person designated by such chairman or member. The chairman of the Select Committee or any member thereof may administer oaths to witnesses.

Sec. 4. The expenses of the Select Committee under this resolution shall be paid from the contingent fund of the Senate upon vouchers approved by the chairman of the Select Committee.

Sec. 5. As used in this resolution, the term "officer or employee of the Senate" means—

(1) an elected officer of the Senate who is not a Member of the Senate;

(2) an employee of the Senate, any committee or subcommittee of the Senate, or any Member of the Senate;

(3) the Legislative Counsel of the Senate or any employee of his office;

(4) an Official Reporter of Debates of the Senate and any person employed by the Official Reporters of Debates of the Senate in connection with the performance of their official duties;

(5) a member of the Capitol Police force whose compensation is disbursed by the Secretary of the Senate;

(6) an employee of the Vice President if such employee's compensation is disbursed by the Secretary of the Senate;

(7) an employee of a joint committee of the Congress whose compensation is disbursed by the Secretary of the Senate.

(Adopted 7/24/1964.)

Award of Service Pins or Emblems to Employees in Legislative Branch

Resolved, That the Committee on Rules and Administration is hereby authorized to provide for the awarding of service pins or emblems to Members, officers, and employees of the Senate, and to promulgate regulations governing the awarding of such pins or emblems. Such pins or emblems shall be of a type appropriate to be attached to the lapel of the wearer, shall be of such appropriate material and design, and shall contain such characters, symbols, or other matter, as the committee shall select.

Sec. 2. The Secretary of the Senate, under direction of the committee and in accordance with regulations promulgated by the committee, shall procure such pins or emblems and award them to Members, officers, and employees of the Senate who are entitled thereto.

Sec. 3. The expenses incurred in procuring such pins or emblems shall be paid from the contingent fund of the Senate on vouchers signed by the chairman of the committee.

(Adopted 9/10/1965.)

Acceptance of Decorations Tendered by Foreign Governments

Resolved, That the Committee on Rules and Administration is hereby authorized to grant approval, for the purposes of section 7342 of title 5, United States Code, and regulations prescribed thereunder, of the acceptance, retention, and wearing by a Member, officer, or employee of the Senate of a decoration tendered by a foreign government in recognition of active field service in time of combat operations or awarded for other outstanding or unusually meritorious service.

(Adopted 7/19/1968.)

Commission on Art and Antiquities of the United States Senate

Resolved, That (a) there is hereby established a Commission on Art and Antiquities of the United States Senate (hereinafter referred to as "the Commission") consisting of the President pro tempore of the Senate, the chairman and ranking minority member of the Committee on Rules and Administration of the Senate, and the majority and minority leaders of the Senate.

(b) The Commission shall elect a Chairman and a Vice Chairman at the beginning of each Congress. Three members of the Commission shall constitute a quorum for the transaction of business, except that the Commission may fix a lesser number which shall constitute a quorum for the taking of testimony.

(c) The Commission shall select a Curator of Art and Antiquities of the Senate who shall be appointed by and be an employee of the Secretary of the Senate. The Curator shall serve at the pleasure of the Commission, shall perform such duties as it may prescribe, and shall receive compensation at a gross rate, not to exceed $22,089 per annum to be fixed by the Commission. At the request of the Commission the Secretary of

the Senate shall detail to the Commission such additional professional, clerical, and other assistants as, from time to time, it deems necessary.

(d) The Commission shall be empowered to hold hearings, summon witnesses, administer oaths, employ reporters, request the production of papers and records, take such testimony, and adopt such rules for the conduct of its hearings and meetings, as it deems necessary.

Sec. 2. (a) The Commission is hereby authorized and, directed to supervise, hold, place, and protect all works of art, historical objects, and exhibits within the Senate wing of the Capitol, and in all rooms, spaces, and corridors thereof, which are the property of the United States, and in its judgment to accept any works of art, historical objects, or exhibits which may hereafter be offered, given, or devised to the Senate, its committees, and its officers for placement and exhibition in the Senate wing of the Capitol, the Senate Office Buildings, or in rooms, spaces, or corridors thereof.

(b) The Commission shall prescribe such regulations as it deems necessary for the care, protection, and placement of such works of art, exhibits, and historical objects in the Senate wing of the Capitol and the Senate Office Buildings and for their acceptance on behalf of the Senate, its committees, and officers. Such regulations shall be published in the Congressional Record at such time or times as the Commission may deem necessary for the information of the Members of the Senate and the public.

(c) Regulations authorized by the provisions of section 1820 of the Revised Statutes (40 U.S.C. 193) to be issued by the Sergeant at Arms of the Senate for the protection of the Capitol, and any regulations issued, or activities undertaken, by the Committee on Rules and Administration of the Senate, or the Architect of the Capitol, in carrying out duties relating to the care, preservation, and protection of the Senate wing of the Capitol and the Senate Office Buildings, shall be consistent with such rules and regulations as the Commission may issue pursuant to subsection (b).

(d) The Committee on Rules and Administration of the Senate in consultation with the Architect of the Capitol and consistent with regulations prescribed by the Commission under subsection (b), shall have responsibility for the supervision, protection, and placement of all works of art, historical objects, and exhibits which shall have been accepted on behalf of the Senate by the Commission or acknowledged as United States property by inventory of the Commission, and which may be lodged in the Senate wing of the Capitol or the Senate Office Buildings by the Commission.

Sec. 3. The Commission shall have responsibility for the supervision and maintenance of the Old Senate Chamber on the principal floor of the Senate wing of the Capitol insofar as it is to be preserved as a patriotic shrine in the Capitol for the benefit of the people of the United States.

Sec. 4. The Commission shall, from time to time, but at least once every ten years, publish as a Senate document a list of all works of art, historical objects, and exhibits currently within the Senate wing of the Capitol and the Senate Office Buildings, together with their description, location, and with such notes as may be pertinent to their history.

Sec. 5. There is hereby authorized to be appropriated out of the contingent fund of the Senate for the expenses of the Commission the sum of $15,000 each fiscal year, to be disbursed by the Secretary of the Senate on vouchers signed by the Chairman or Vice Chairman of the Commission: *Provided,* That no payment shall be made from such appropriation as salary.

(Adopted 10/1/1968.)

Response by Senate to Official Invitations from Foreign Governments

Resolved, That the President of the Senate is authorized to appoint as members of official Senate delegations such Members of the Senate as may be necessary to respond to invitations received officially from foreign governments or parliamentary bodies and associations (including the Commonwealth Parliamentary Association) during the Ninetieth Congress, and to designate the chairmen of said delegations.

Sec. 2. (a) The expenses of the delegations, including staff members designated by the chairmen to assist said delegations, shall not exceed $25,000 for each such delegation, and shall be paid from the contingent fund of the Senate upon vouchers approved by the chairmen of said delegations.

(b) The expenses of each delegation shall include such special expenses as the chairman may deem appropriate to carry out this resolution, including reimbursements to agencies for compensation of employees detailed to each delegation, and expenses incurred in connection with providing appropriate hospitality to foreign delegates.

(c) Each member or employee of each delegation shall receive subsistence expenses in an amount not to exceed the maximum per diem rate set forth in section 502(b) of the Mutual Security Act of 1954, as amended by Public Law 88-633, approved October 7, 1964.

(Adopted 5/19/1967.)

Resolved, It is declared to be the policy of the Senate that—

(a) The ideal concept of public office, expressed by the words, "A public office is a public trust," signifies that the officer has been entrusted with public power by the people; that the officer holds this power in trust to be used only for their benefit and never for the benefit of himself or of a few; and that the officer must never conduct his own affairs so as to infringe on the public interest. All official conduct of Members of the Senate should be guided by this paramount concept of public office.

(b) These rules, as the written expression of certain standards of conduct, complement the body of unwritten but generally accepted standards that continue to apply to the Senate. (Adopted 3/22/1968.)

Leaders of the House and Senate

Speakers of the House

Congress	Speaker	Party and State
1st (1789-91)	Frederick A. C. Muhlenberg	Fed. Pa.
2nd (1791-93)	Jonathan Trumbull	Fed. Conn.
3rd (1793-95)	Frederick A. C. Muhlenberg	Fed. Pa.
4th (1795-97)	Jonathan Dayton	Fed. N.J.
5th (1797-99)	Dayton; George Dent	Dem.-Rep. Md.
6th (1799-1801)	Theodore Sedgwick	Fed. Mass.
7th-9th (1801-07)	Nathaniel Macon	D-R N.C.
10th-11th (1807-11)	Joseph B. Varnum	D-R Mass.
12th (1811-13)	Henry Clay	D-R Ky.
13th (1813-15)	Clay; Langdon Cheves	D-R S.C.
14th-15th (1815-19)	Henry Clay	D-R Ky.
16th (1819-21)	Clay; John W. Taylor	D-R N.Y.
17th (1821-23)	Philip P. Barbour	D-R Va.
18th (1823-25)	Henry Clay	D-R Ky.
19th (1825-27)	John W. Taylor	D-R N.Y.
20th-22nd (1827-33)	Andrew Stevenson	D Va.
23rd (1833-35)	Stevenson; John Bell	Whig Tenn.
24th-25th (1835-39)	James K. Polk	D Tenn.
26th (1839-41)	Robert M. T. Hunter	D Va.
27th (1841-43)	John White	Whig Ky.
28th (1843-45)	John W. Jones	D Va.
29th (1845-47)	John W. Davis	D Ind.
30th (1847-49)	Robert C. Winthrop	Whig Mass.
31st (1849-51)	Howell Cobb	D Ga.
32nd-33rd (1851-55)	Linn Boyd	D Ky.
34th (1855-57)	Nathaniel P. Banks	American Mass.
35th (1857-59)	James L. Orr	D S.C.
36th (1859-61)	William Pennington	Whig N.J.
37th (1861-63)	Galusha A. Grow	R Pa.
38th-39th (1863-67)	Schuyler Colfax	R Ind.
40th (1867-69)	Colfax; Theodore M. Pomeroy	R N.Y.
41st-43rd (1869-75)	James G. Blaine	R Maine
44th (1875-77)	Michael C. Kerr	D Ind.
	Samuel S. Cox (pro tempore)	D N.Y.
	Milton Saylor (pro tempore)	D Ohio
	Samuel J. Randall	D Pa.
45th-46th (1877-81)	Randall	
47th (1881-83)	J. Warren Keifer	R Ohio
48th-50th (1883-89)	John G. Carlisle	D Ky.
51st (1889-91)	Thomas B. Reed	R Maine
52nd-53rd (1891-95)	Charles F. Crisp	D Ga.
54th-55th (1895-99)	Thomas B. Reed	R Maine
56th-57th (1899-1903)	David B. Henderson	R Iowa
58th-61st (1903-11)	Joseph G. Cannon	R Ill.
62nd-65th (1911-19)	Champ Clark	D Mo.
66th-68th (1919-25)	Frederick H. Gillett	R Mass.
69th-71st (1925-31)	Nicholas Longworth	R Ohio
72nd (1931-33)	John N. Garner	D Texas
73rd (1933-35)	Henry T. Rainey	D Ill.
74th (1935-37)	Joseph W. Byrns	D Tenn.
	William B. Bankhead	D Ala.
75th (1937-39)	Bankhead	
76th (1939-41)	Bankhead; Sam Rayburn	D Texas
77th-79th (1941-47)	Rayburn	
80th (1947-49)	Joseph W. Martin Jr.	R Mass.
81st-82nd (1949-53)	Sam Rayburn	D Texas
83rd (1953-55)	Joseph W. Martin Jr.	R Mass.
84th-86th (1955-61)	Sam Rayburn	D Texas
87th (1961-63)	Rayburn; John W. McCormack	D Mass.
88th-91st (1963-71)	McCormack	
92nd (1971-　)	Carl Albert	D Okla.

House Floor Leaders

Congress	Majority Leader	Minority Leader
56th-57th (1899-1903)	Sereno E. Payne (R N.Y.)	James D. Richardson (D Tenn.)
58th-60th (1903-09)	Payne	John Sharp Williams (D Miss.)
61st (1909-11)	Payne	Champ Clark (D Mo.)
62nd-63rd (1911-15)	Oscar W. Underwood (D Ala.)	James R. Mann (R Ill.)
64th-65th (1915-19)	Claude Kitchin (D N.C.)	Mann
66th (1919-21)	Franklin W. Mondell (R Wyo.)	Champ Clark (D Mo.)
67th (1921-23)	Mondell	Claude Kitchin (D N.C.)
68th (1923-25)	Nicholas Longworth (R Ohio)	Finis J. Garrett (D Tenn.)
69th-70th 1925-29	John Q. Tilson (R Conn.)	Garrett
71st (1929-31)	Tilson	John N. Garner (D Texas)
72nd (1931-33)	Henry T. Rainey (D Ill.)	Bertrand H. Snell (R N.Y.)
73rd (1933-35)	Joseph W. Byrns (D Tenn.)	Snell
74th (1935-37)	William B. Bankhead (D Ala.)	Snell
75th (1937-39)	Sam Rayburn (D Texas)	Snell
76th (1939-41)	Rayburn; John W. McCormack (D Mass.)	Joseph W. Martin Jr. (R Mass.)
77th-79th (1941-47)	McCormack	Martin
80th (1947-49)	Charles A. Halleck (R Ind.)	Sam Rayburn (D Texas)
81st-82nd (1949-53)	John W. McCormack (D Mass.)	Joseph W. Martin Jr. (R Mass.)
83rd (1953-55)	Charles A. Halleck (R Ind.)	Sam Rayburn (D Texas)
84th-85th (1955-59)	John W. McCormack (D Mass.)	Joseph W. Martin Jr. (R Mass.)
86th (1959-61)	McCormack	Charles A. Halleck (R Ind.)
87th (1961-63)	McCormack; Carl Albert (D Okla.)	Halleck
88th (1963-65)	Albert	Halleck
89th-91st (1965-71)	Albert	Gerald R. Ford (R Mich.)
92nd (1971-　)	Hale Boggs (D La.)	Ford

House Whips

Congress	Majority Whip	Minority Whip
56th (1899-1901)	James A. Tawney (R Minn.)	Oscar W. Underwood (D Ala.)
57th-58th (1901-05)	Tawney	James T. Lloyd (D Mo.)
59th-60th (1905-09)	James E. Watson (R Ind.)	Lloyd
61st (1909-11)	John W. Dwight (R N.Y.)	None
62nd (1911-13)	None	Dwight
63rd (1913-15)	Thomas M. Bell (D Ga.)	Charles H. Burke (R S.D.)
64th-65th (1915-19)	None	Charles M. Hamilton (R N.Y.)
66th (1919-21)	Harold Knutson (R Minn.)	None
67th (1921-23)	Knutson	William A. Oldfield (D Ark.)
68th-69th (1923-27)	Albert H. Vestal (R Ind.)	Oldfield

70th (1927-29)	Vestal	Oldfield; John McDuffie (D Ala.)
71st (1929-31)	Vestal	McDuffie
72nd (1931-33)	McDuffie	Carl G. Bachmann (R W.Va.)
73rd (1933-35)	Arthur H. Greenwood (D Ind.)	Harry L. Englebright (R Calif.)
74th-76th (1935-41)	Patrick J. Boland (D Pa.)	Englebright
77th (1941-43)	Boland; Robert Ramspeck (D Ga.)	Englebright
78th (1943-45)	Ramspeck	Leslie C. Arends (R Ill.)
79th (1945-47)	John J. Sparkman (D Ala.)	Arends
80th (1947-49)	Arends	John W. McCormack (D Mass.)
81st-82nd (1949-53)	J. Percy Priest (D Tenn.)	Arends
83rd (1953-55)	Arends	John W. McCormack (D Mass.)
84th-86th (1955-61)	Carl Albert (D Okla.)	Arends
87th (1961-63)	Albert; Hale Boggs (D La.)	Arends
88th-91st (1963-71)	Boggs	Arends
92nd (1971-)	Thomas P. O'Neill Jr. (D Mass.)	Arends

67th (1921-23)	Lodge	Underwood
68th (1923-25)	Lodge; Charles Curtis (R Kan.)	Joseph T. Robinson (D Ark.)
69th-70th (1925-29)	Curtis	Robinson
71st (1929-31)	Curtis; James E. Watson (R Ind.)	Robinson
72nd (1931-33)	Watson	Robinson
73rd-74th (1933-37)	Robinson	Charles L. McNary (R Ore.)
75th-78th (1937-45)	Alben W. Barkley (D Ky.)	McNary
79th (1945-47)	Barkley	Wallace H. White Jr. (R Maine)
80th (1947-49)	White	Barkley
81st (1949-51)	Scott W. Lucas (D Ill.)	Kenneth S. Wherry (R Neb.)
82nd (1951-53)	Ernest W. McFarland (D Ariz.)	Wherry; Styles Bridges (R N.H.)
83rd (1953-55)	Robert A. Taft (R Ohio); William F. Knowland (R Calif.)	Lyndon B. Johnson (D Texas)
84th-85th (1955-59)	Johnson	Knowland
86th (1959-61)	Johnson	Everett McKinley Dirksen (R Ill.)
87th-90th (1961-69)	Mike Mansfield (D Mont.)	Dirksen
91st (1969-71)	Mansfield	Dirksen; Hugh Scott (R Pa.)
92nd (1971-)	Mansfield	Scott

Senate Presidents Pro Tempore

Congress	President Pro Tem
51st (1889-91)*	Charles F. Manderson (R Neb.)
52nd (1891-93)	Manderson, Isham G. Harris (D Tenn.)
53rd (1893-95)	Harris; Matt W. Ransom (D N.C.); Harris
54th-61st (1895-1911)	William P. Frye (R Maine)
62nd (1911-13)**	Frye; Augustus O. Bacon (D Ga.); Frank B. Brandegee (R Conn.); Charles Curtis (R Kan.); Jacob H. Gallinger (R N.H.); Henry Cabot Lodge (R Mass.)
63rd (1913-15)	James P. Clarke (D Ark.)
64th (1915-17)	Clarke; Willard Saulsbury (D Del.)
65th (1917-19)	Saulsbury
66th-68th (1919-25)	Albert B. Cummins (R Iowa)
69th-72nd (1925-33)	George H. Moses (R N.H.)
73rd-75th (1933-39)	Key Pittman (D Nev.)
76th (1939-41)	Pittman; William H. King (D Utah)
77th (1941-43)	Pat Harrison (D Miss.); Carter Glass (D Va.)
78th (1943-45)	Glass
79th (1945-47)	Kenneth McKellar (D Tenn.)
80th (1947-49)	Arthur H. Vandenberg (R Mich.)
81st-82nd (1949-53)	Kenneth McKellar (D Tenn.)
83rd (1953-55)	Styles Bridges (R N.H.)
84th (1955-57)	Walter F. George (D Ga.)
85th-90th (1957-69)	Carl Hayden (D Ariz.)
91st (1969-71)	Richard B. Russell (D Ga.)
92nd (1971-)	Allen J. Ellender (D La.)

Senate Floor Leaders

Congress	Majority Leader	Minority Leader
62nd (1911-13)	Shelby M. Cullom (R Ill.)	Thomas S. Martin (D Va.)
63rd-64th (1913-17)	John W. Kern (D Ind.)	Jacob H. Gallinger (R N.H.)
65th (1917-19)	Thomas S. Martin (D Va.)	Henry Cabot Lodge (R Mass.)
66th (1919-21)	Lodge	Martin; Oscar W. Underwood (D Ala.)

Senate Whips

Congress	Majority Whip	Minority Whip
63rd (1913-15)	J. Hamilton Lewis (D Ill.)	None
64th (1915-17)	Lewis	James W. Wadsworth Jr. (R N.Y.); Charles Curtis (R Kan.)
65th (1917-19)	Lewis	Curtis
66th-67th (1919-23)	Curtis	Peter G. Gerry (D R.I.)
68th (1923-25)	Curtis; Wesley L. Jones (R Wash.)	Gerry
69th-70th (1925-29)	Jones	Gerry
71st-72nd (1929-33)	Simeon D. Fess (R Ohio)	Morris Sheppard (D Texas)
73rd (1933-35)	J. Hamilton Lewis (D Ill.)	Felix Hebert (R R.I.)
74th-75th (1935-39)	Lewis	None
76th (1939-41)	Sherman Minton (D Ind.)	None
77th (1941-43)	Lister Hill (D Ala.)	None
78th-79th (1943-47)	Hill	Kenneth Wherry (R Neb.)
80th (1947-49)	Wherry	Scott W. Lucas (D Ill.)
81st (1949-51)	Francis J. Myers (D Pa.)	Leverett Saltonstall (R Mass.)
82nd (1951-53)	Lyndon B. Johnson (D Texas)	Saltonstall
83rd (1953-55)	Saltonstall	Earle C. Clements (D Ky.)
84th (1955-57)	Clements	Saltonstall
85th (1957-59)	Mike Mansfield (D Mont.)	Everett McKinley Dirksen (R Ill.)
86th (1959-61)	Mansfield	Thomas H. Kuchel (R Calif.)
87th-88th (1961-65)	Hubert H. Humphrey (D Minn.)	Kuchel
89th-90th (1965-69)	Russell B. Long (D La.)	Kuchel
91st (1969-71)	Edward M. Kennedy (D Mass.)	Hugh Scott (R Pa.); Robert P. Griffin (R Mich.)
92nd (1971-)	Robert C. Byrd (D W.Va.)	Griffin

CONGRESSIONAL COMMITTEES

A list of Congressional committees and subcommittees, their functions and membership appears on the following pages. The membership is complete as of April 25, 1971 (92nd Congress, first session).

- **LISTING**—Democrats are listed on the left, Republicans on the right, in order of their seniority on the committee. In the case of party leadership committees, members are listed alphabetically.

- **KEY**—Full committee names are in boldface type while subcommittee names are in bold capitals. Asterisk (*) following the name of the committee chairman or ranking minority member indicates ex officio member of all subcommittees. Dagger (†) indicates ex officio member from another committee. Double dagger (‡) indicates a member waived seniority to the next in line.

Capitol Telephone
CA 4-3121
DIRECT DIAL: CA 5 PLUS EXTENSION

OFFICERS OF THE SENATE

President . . . . Spiro T. Agnew
President pro tempore . . . . Sen. Allen J. Ellender (D La.)
Secretary . . . . Francis R. Valeo
Chief Clerk . . . . Darrell St. Clair
Sergeant at Arms . . . . Robert G. Dunphy
Secretary for the Majority . . . . J.S. Kimmitt
Secretary for the Minority . . . . J. Mark Trice
Press Gallery Superintendent . . . . Joseph E. Wills
Chaplain . . . . Rev. Edward L. R. Elson, D.D.

Parliamentarian . . . . Floyd M. Riddick

OFFICERS OF THE HOUSE

Speaker . . . . Rep. Carl Albert (D Okla.)
Clerk . . . . W. Pat Jennings
Sergeant at Arms . . . . Zeake W. Johnson Jr.
Doorkeeper . . . . William M. Miller
Postmaster . . . . H.H. Morris
Press Gallery Superintendent . . . . Benjamin C. West
Chaplain . . . . Rev. Edward G. Latch, D.D.

Parliamentarian . . . . Lewis Deschler

JOINT COMMITTEES, 92nd CONGRESS, FIRST SESSION

Following is a list of eight major joint congressional committees and their subcommittees. Joint committees are set up to examine specific questions and are established by public law. Membership is drawn from both chambers and both parties. When a Senator serves as chairman, the vice chairman is usually a Representative, and vice versa. The chairmanship usually rotates from one chamber to the other at the beginning of each Congress.

Atomic Energy

Atomic Energy Commission; development, use and control of atomic energy generally. Reports legislation to House and Senate. *Ext. 6171.*

Sen. John O. Pastore (D R.I.), *Chairman*
Rep. Melvin Price (D Ill.), *Vice Chairman*

Senate Members

Clinton P. Anderson (N.M.)‡	George D. Aiken (Vt.)
Henry M. Jackson (Wash.)	Wallace F. Bennett (Utah)
Stuart Symington (Mo.)	Peter H. Dominick (Colo.)
Alan Bible (Nev.)	Howard H. Baker Jr. (Tenn.)

House Members

Chet Holifield (Calif.)	Craig Hosmer (Calif.)
Wayne N. Aspinall (Colo.)	John B. Anderson (Ill.)
John Young (Texas)	William M. McCulloch (Ohio)
Ed Edmondson (Okla.)	Orval Hansen (Idaho)

AGREEMENTS FOR COOPERATION

Holifield-*Chairman*

Anderson (N.M.)	Bennett
Price	Dominick
	Baker

COMMUNITIES

Young - *Chairman*

Jackson	Aiken
Edmondson	McCulloch
	Baker
	Hansen

LEGISLATION

Price - *Chairman*

Holifield	Hosmer
Aspinall	Anderson (Ill.)
Pastore	Aiken
Jackson	
Bible	

MILITARY APPLICATIONS

Jackson - *Chairman*

Anderson (N.M.)	Hosmer
Pastore	Anderson (Ill.)
Holifield	Baker
Symington	
Bible	

RAW MATERIALS

Aspinall - *Chairman*

Holifield	Bennett
Anderson (N.M.)	McCulloch
Young	Dominick
Edmondson	

RESEARCH, DEVELOPMENT AND RADIATION

Price - *Chairman*

Holifield	Hosmer
Pastore	Aiken
Jackson	Bennett
Bible	Dominick
	Baker
	Hansen

SECURITY

Anderson (N.M.) - *Chairman*

Pastore	McCulloch
Jackson	Hansen
Young	

Congressional Operations

Oversees activities of Congress generally. *Ext. 6564.*

Rep. Jack Brooks (D Texas), *Chairman*
Sen. Lee Metcalf (D Mont.), *Vice Chairman*

Senate Members

Mike Gravel (Alaska)	Clifford P. Case (N.J.)
Lawton Chiles (Fla.)	Richard S. Schweiker (Pa.)

House Members

Robert N. Giaimo (Conn.)	Durward G. Hall (Mo.)
James G. O'Hara (Mich.)	James C. Cleveland (N.H.)

No standing subcommittees.

Defense Production

Studies and investigates programs authorized by the Defense Production Act and reports findings and recommendations to the House and Senate. *Ext. 2337.*

Rep. Wright Patman (D Texas), *Chairman*
Sen. John Sparkman (D Ala.), *Vice Chairman*

Senate Members

William Proxmire (Wis.)	Wallace F. Bennett (Utah)
Harrison A. Williams Jr. (N.J.)	John G. Tower (Texas)

House Members

William A. Barrett (Pa.)	William B. Widnall (N.J.)
Leonor K. Sullivan (Mo.)	Garry Brown (Mich.)

No standing subcommittees.

Economic

Studies and investigates all recommendations included in the President's annual Economic Report to Congress and reports findings and recommendations to the House and Senate. *Ext. 5171.*

Sen. William Proxmire (D Wis.), *Chairman*
Rep. Wright Patman (D Texas), *Vice Chairman*

Senate Members

John Sparkman (Ala.)‡	Jacob K. Javits (N.Y.)
J.W. Fulbright (Ark.)‡	Jack Miller (Iowa)
Abraham Ribicoff (Conn.)	Charles H. Percy (Ill.)
Hubert H. Humphrey (Minn.)	James B. Pearson (Kan.)
Lloyd Bentsen (Texas)	

House Members

Richard Bolling (Mo.)
Hale Boggs (La.)
Henry S. Reuss (Wis.)
Martha W. Griffiths (Mich.)
William S. Moorhead (Pa.)

William B. Widnall (N.J.)
Barber B. Conable Jr. (N.Y.)
Clarence J. Brown (Ohio)
Ben B. Blackburn (Ga.)

ECONOMIC PROGRESS

Patman - *Chairman*

Griffiths
Moorhead
Proxmire
Fulbright
Bentsen

Brown
Blackburn
Pearson
Percy

ECONOMIC STATISTICS

Ribicoff - *Chairman*

Fulbright
Bolling
Griffiths

Miller
Brown
Blackburn

FISCAL POLICY

Griffiths - *Chairman*

Proxmire
Boggs
Moorhead
Bolling
Ribicoff
Humphrey

Javits
Widnall
Miller
Percy
Conable

FOREIGN ECONOMIC POLICY

Boggs - *Chairman*

Reuss
Moorhead
Sparkman
Fulbright
Ribicoff
Humphrey
Bentsen

Javits
Miller
Widnall
Conable
Brown
Percy

INTER-AMERICAN ECONOMIC RELATIONSHIPS

Sparkman - *Chairman*

Boggs
Fulbright
Ribicoff
Griffiths
Bentsen

Javits
Conable
Blackburn
Pearson

INTERNATIONAL EXCHANGE AND PAYMENTS

Reuss - *Chairman*

Boggs
Moorhead
Proxmire
Humphrey
Bentsen

Widnall
Javits
Percy
Conable

PRIORITIES AND ECONOMY IN GOVERNMENT

Proxmire - *Chairman*

Sparkman
Patman
Griffiths
Moorhead
Humphrey

Percy
Conable
Brown
Pearson

URBAN AFFAIRS

Bolling - *Chairman*

Reuss
Griffiths
Moorhead
Ribicoff
Proxmire
Humphrey

Widnall
Javits
Percy
Brown
Blackburn

Internal Revenue Taxation

Studies tax policies and makes recommendations to House Ways and Means and Senate Finance Committees. *Ext. 3621.*

Rep. Wilbur D. Mills (D Ark.), *Chairman*
Sen. Russell B. Long (D La.), *Vice Chairman*

Senate Members

Clinton P. Anderson (N.M.)
Herman E. Talmadge (Ga.)

Wallace F. Bennett (Utah)
Carl T. Curtis (Neb.)

House Members

John C. Watts (Ky.)
Al Ullman (Ore.)

John W. Byrnes (Wis.)
Jackson E. Betts (Ohio)

No standing subcommittees.

Library

Ext. 6352

Rep. Wayne L. Hays (D Ohio), *Chairman*
Sen. B. Everett Jordan (D N.C.), *Vice Chairman*

Senate Members

Claiborne Pell (R.I.)
Howard W. Cannon (Nev.)

John Sherman Cooper (Ky.)
Hugh Scott (Pa.)

House Members

Lucien N. Nedzi (Mich.)
John Brademas(Ind.)

James Harvey (Mich.)
Fred Schwengel (Iowa)

No standing subcommittees.

Printing

Government printing generally, standards of paper, efficiency, distribution, Congressional Directory. *Ext. 5241.*

Sen. B. Everett Jordan (D N.C.), *Chairman*
Rep. Wayne L. Hays (D Ohio), *Vice Chairman*

Senate Members

James B. Allen (Ala.)   Robert P. Griffin (Mich.)

House Members

John Brademas (Ind.)   Samuel L. Devine (Ohio)

No standing subcommittees.

Reduction of Federal Expenditures

Studies and recommends reductions in federal spending. *Ext. 3750.*

Rep. George Mahon (D Texas), *Chairman*

Senate Members

Allen J. Ellender (La.)   Wallace F. Bennett (Utah)
Russell B. Long (La.)   Vacancy
Clinton P. Anderson (N.M.)
John L. McClellan (Ark.)

House Members

Wilbur D. Mills (Ark.)   John W. Byrnes (Wis.)
John C. Watts (Ky.)   Frank T. Bow (Ohio)
Jamie L. Whitten (Miss.)

John B. Connally, *Secretary of the Treasury*
George P. Shultz, *Director, Office of Management and Budget*

SENATE COMMITTEES, 92nd CONGRESS, FIRST SESSION

Aeronautical and Space Sciences

Aeronautical and space activities and matters relating to the scientific aspects of these activities, except those peculiar to or primarily associated with the development of weapons systems or military operations; National Aeronautics and Space Administration. *Ext. 6477.*

D 6 - R 5

Clinton P. Anderson (D N.M.), *Chairman*

Warren G. Magnuson (Wash.)‡	Carl T. Curtis (Neb.)
Stuart Symington (Mo.)	Margaret Chase Smith (Maine)‡
John C. Stennis (Miss.)	Barry Goldwater (Ariz.)
Howard W. Cannon (Nev.)	Lowell P. Weicker Jr. (Conn.)
David H. Gambrell (Ga.)	James L. Buckley (N.Y.)

No standing subcommittees.

Agriculture and Forestry

Agriculture in general, including farm credit and security, crop insurance, soil conservation and rural electrification; forestry in general. *Ext. 2035.*

D 8 - R 6

Herman E. Talmadge (D Ga.), *Chairman**

Allen J. Ellender (La.)‡	Jack Miller (Iowa)*
James O. Eastland (Miss.)‡	George D. Aiken (Vt.)‡
B. Everett Jordan (N.C.)	Milton R. Young (N.D.)‡
George McGovern (S.D.)	Carl T. Curtis (Neb.)
James B. Allen (Ala.)	Robert Dole (Kan.)
Hubert H. Humphrey (Minn.)	Henry Bellmon (Okla.)
Lawton Chiles (Fla.)	

AGRICULTURAL CREDIT AND RURAL ELECTRIFICATION
McGovern - *Chairman*

Allen	Aiken
Ellender	Miller
Humphrey	Dole

AGRICULTURAL EXPORTS
Chiles - *Chairman*

Jordan	Miller
McGovern	Bellmon

AGRICULTURAL PRODUCTION, MARKETING AND STABILIZATION OF PRICES
Jordan - *Chairman*

McGovern	Young
Eastland	Miller
Ellender	Curtis
Humphrey	Bellmon

AGRICULTURAL RESEARCH AND GENERAL LEGISLATION
Allen - *Chairman*

Jordan	Dole
Eastland	Young
Chiles	Curtis

ENVIRONMENT, SOIL CONSERVATION AND FORESTRY
Eastland - *Chairman*

Jordan	Bellmon
Chiles	Aiken

RURAL DEVELOPMENT
Humphrey - *Chairman*

Ellender	Curtis
Eastland	Dole
Allen	Bellmon

Appropriations

Appropriations of government revenues. *Ext. 3471.*

D 13 - R 11

Allen J. Ellender (D La.), *Chairman**

John L. McClellan (Ark.)	Milton R. Young (N.D.)*
Warren G. Magnuson (Wash.)	Karl E. Mundt (S.D.)
John C. Stennis (Miss.)	Margaret Chase Smith (Maine)
John O. Pastore (R.I.)	Roman L. Hruska (Neb.)
Alan Bible (Nev.)	Gordon Allott (Colo.)
Robert C. Byrd (W.Va.)	Norris Cotton (N.H.)
Gale W. McGee (Wyo.)	Clifford P. Case (N.J.)
Mike Mansfield (Mont.)	Hiram L. Fong (Hawaii)
William Proxmire (Wis.)	J. Caleb Boggs (Del.)
Joseph M. Montoya (N.M.)	Charles H. Percy (Ill.)
Daniel K. Inouye (Hawaii)	Edward W. Brooke (Mass.)
Ernest F. Hollings (S.C.)	

AGRICULTURE, ENVIRONMENTAL AND CONSUMER PROTECTION
McGee - *Chairman*

Stennis	Hruska
Proxmire	Young
Byrd	Mundt
Mansfield	Fong
Inouye	Boggs
Talmadge†	Miller†
Eastland†	

DEFENSE
Ellender - *Chairman 1*

McClellan *1*	Young *1*
Stennis *1*	Smith *1*
Pastore	Allott
Magnuson	Hruska
Mansfield	Cotton
Bible	Case
Symington†	Thurmond†
Jackson†	

1 Members of the Defense Subcommittee's subcommittee on Intelligence Operations.

DISTRICT OF COLUMBIA
Inouye - *Chairman*

Montoya	Percy
Hollings	Boggs
Eagleton†	Mathias†
Stevenson†	

FOREIGN OPERATIONS
Proxmire - *Chairman*

McGee	Fong
Ellender	Cotton
McClellan	Brooke

HOUSING AND URBAN DEVELOPMENT, SPACE, SCIENCE
Pastore - *Chairman*

Magnuson	Allott
Ellender	Smith
Stennis	Hruska
Mansfield	Case
McGee	Percy

Also on Aeronautical and Space Activities:

Anderson†	Curtis†
Symington†	

INTERIOR
Bible - *Chairman*

McClellan	Percy
Byrd	Mundt
McGee	Young
Montoya	Boggs
Inouye	Fong

LABOR; HEALTH, EDUCATION AND WELFARE
Magnuson - *Chairman*

Stennis	Cotton
Bible	Case
Byrd	Fong
Proxmire	Boggs
Montoya	Percy
Hollings	Brooke

LEGISLATIVE
Hollings - *Chairman*

Ellender	Cotton
Inouye	Brooke

MILITARY CONSTRUCTION
Mansfield - *Chairman*

Proxmire	Brooke
Montoya	Boggs
Hollings	Percy
Symington†	Tower†
Cannon†	

PUBLIC WORKS
Stennis - *Chairman*

Ellender	Mundt
McClellan	Young
Magnuson	Hruska
Bible	Smith
Byrd	Allott
Pastore	Case
McGee	Cotton

Also on Rivers and Harbors items:

Randolph†	Cooper†
Muskie†	

Also on Atomic Energy items:

Anderson†	Aiken†
Jackson†	

STATE, JUSTICE, COMMERCE, THE JUDICIARY
McClellan - *Chairman*

Ellender	Smith
Pastore	Hruska
Mansfield	Fong
Hollings	Brooke

Also on Diplomatic and Consular items:

Fulbright†	Aiken†
Sparkman†	

TRANSPORTATION
Byrd - *Chairman*

Stennis	Case
Magnuson	Mundt
Pastore	Smith
Bible	Allott
Proxmire	Percy

TREASURY, POST OFFICE, GENERAL GOVERNMENT
Montoya - *Chairman*

Ellender	Boggs
Inouye	Allott

Also on Post Office items:

McGee†	Fong†
Randolph†	

Armed Services

Military affairs, Panama Canal and Canal Zone, conservation of petroleum resources, strategic and critical materials; aeronautical and space activities peculiar to or primarily associated with development of weapons systems or military operations. *Ext. 3871.*

D 9 - R 7

John C. Stennis (D Miss.), *Chairman*

Stuart Symington (Mo.)	Margaret Chase Smith (Maine)
Henry M. Jackson (Wash.)	Strom Thurmond (S.C.)
Sam J. Ervin Jr. (N.C.)	John G. Tower (Texas)
Howard W. Cannon (Nev.)	Peter H. Dominick (Colo.)
Thomas J. McIntyre (N.H.)	Barry Goldwater (Ariz.)
Harry F. Byrd Jr. (Va.)	Richard S. Schweiker (Pa.)
Harold E. Hughes (Iowa)	William B. Saxbe (Ohio)
Lloyd Bentsen (Texas)	

CENTRAL INTELLIGENCE
Stennis - *Chairman*

Symington	Dominick
Jackson	Goldwater

GENERAL LEGISLATION
Byrd - *Chairman*

McIntyre	Saxbe
Hughes	Schweiker
Bentsen	Dominick

MILITARY CONSTRUCTION AUTHORIZATION
Symington - *Chairman*

Jackson	Tower
Ervin	Thurmond
Cannon	Dominick
Byrd	

NATIONAL STOCKPILE AND NAVAL PETROLEUM RESERVES
Cannon - *Chairman*

Symington	Goldwater
Ervin	Thurmond
Bentsen	Saxbe

NUCLEAR TEST BAN TREATY SAFEGUARDS
Jackson - *Chairman*

Symington	Smith

PREPAREDNESS INVESTIGATING
Ext. 2127
Stennis - *Chairman* [1]

Symington	Thurmond [1]
Jackson	Tower
Cannon	Goldwater
McIntyre [1]	Schweiker
Byrd [1]	Dominick [1]

[1] *Members of Preparedness Subcommittee's subcommittee to review bomber defense.*

STATUS OF FORCES
Ervin - *Chairman*

McIntyre	Schweiker
Byrd	Saxbe

STRATEGIC ARMS LIMITATION TALKS
Jackson - *Chairman*

Stennis	Tower
Symington	Schweiker
Byrd	Saxbe
Hughes	

Ad Hoc Subcommittees

RESEARCH AND DEVELOPMENT
McIntyre - *Chairman*

Byrd	Dominick
Bentsen	Goldwater

TACTICAL AIR POWER
Cannon - *Chairman*

Symington	Thurmond
Jackson	Tower
Hughes	Goldwater

Special Subcommittee

CLOSE AIR SUPPORT AIRCRAFT, AX AND CHEYENNE
Cannon - *Chairman*

Symington	Thurmond
McIntyre	Tower
Byrd	Goldwater
Hughes	Dominick

Banking, Housing and Urban Affairs

Banking and currency generally; financial matters other than taxes and appropriations; public and private housing and economic controls; urban affairs. *Ext. 7391.*

D 8 - R 7

John Sparkman (D Ala.), *Chairman*

William Proxmire (Wis.)	John G. Tower (Texas)
Harrison A. Williams Jr. (N.J.)	Wallace F. Bennett (Utah)‡

Thomas J. McIntyre (N.H.)	Edward W. Brooke (Mass.)
Walter F. Mondale (Minn.)	Robert W. Packwood (Ore.)
Alan Cranston (Calif.)	William V. Roth Jr. (Del.)
Adlai E. Stevenson III (Ill.)	Bill Brock (Tenn.)
David H. Gambrell (Ga.)	Robert Taft Jr. (Ohio)

FINANCIAL INSTITUTIONS
Proxmire - *Chairman*

Sparkman	Bennett
Williams	Tower
McIntyre	Brooke
Mondale	Packwood
Cranston	Brock

HOUSING AND URBAN AFFAIRS
Ext. 6348
Sparkman - *Chairman*

Proxmire	Tower
Williams	Bennett
McIntyre	Brooke
Mondale	Packwood
Cranston	Roth
Stevenson	Brock
Gambrell	Taft

INTERNATIONAL FINANCE
Mondale - *Chairman*

Sparkman	Packwood
Williams	Bennett
Cranston	Brooke
Stevenson	Roth
Gambrell	Taft

PRODUCTION AND STABILIZATION
Cranston - *Chairman*

Sparkman	Brock
Proxmire	Tower
McIntyre	Bennett
Stevenson	Packwood
Gambrell	Taft

SECURITIES
Williams - *Chairman*

Proxmire	Brooke
Mondale	Tower
McIntyre	Bennett
Cranston	Packwood
Stevenson	Roth

SMALL BUSINESS
McIntyre - *Chairman*

Sparkman	Roth
Proxmire	Tower
Williams	Brooke
Mondale	Brock
Gambrell	Taft

Commerce

Regulation of interstate transportation, communications, inland waterways, Coast Guard, merchant marine, civil aeronautics except activities of the National Aeronautics and Space Administration; fisheries and wildlife, Weather Bureau, Coast and Geodetic Survey, Bureau of Standards. *Ext. 5115.*

D 10 - R 8

Warren G. Magnuson (D Wash.), *Chairman***

John O. Pastore (R.I.)	Norris Cotton (N.H.)*
Vance Hartke (Ind.)	Winston L. Prouty (Vt.)
Philip A. Hart (Mich.)	James B. Pearson (Kan.)
Howard W. Cannon (Nev.)	Robert P. Griffin (Mich.)
Russell B. Long (La.)	Howard H. Baker Jr. (Tenn.)
Frank E. Moss (Utah)	Marlow W. Cook (Ky.)
Ernest F. Hollings (S.C.)	Mark O. Hatfield (Ore.)
Daniel K. Inouye (Hawaii)	Ted Stevens (Alaska)
William B. Spong Jr. (Va.)	

AVIATION
Cannon - *Chairman*

Magnuson	Pearson
Hart	Cotton
Hartke	Prouty
Hollings	Baker
Inouye	Griffin
Moss	Cook
Spong	Stevens

COMMUNICATIONS
Pastore - *Chairman*

Hartke	Baker
Hart	Griffin
Long	Cook
Moss	Pearson
Cannon	Stevens

CONSUMER
Moss - *Chairman*
Hart - *Vice Chairman*

Pastore	Cook
Hartke	Pearson
Inouye	Hatfield
Spong	Stevens
	Cotton

ENVIRONMENT
Hart - *Chairman*
Moss - *Vice Chairman*

Pastore	Hatfield
Long	Baker
Spong	Cook
	Pearson

FOREIGN COMMERCE AND TOURISM
Inouye - *Chairman*

Hartke	Prouty
Cannon	Griffin
Long	Baker
Moss	Stevens

MERCHANT MARINE
Long - *Chairman*

Pastore	Griffin
Hollings	Prouty
Inouye	Hatfield
Spong	Stevens

OCEANS AND ATMOSPHERE
Hollings - *Chairman*

Pastore	Stevens
Hart	Griffin
Long	Cook
Inouye	Hatfield
Spong	

SURFACE TRANSPORTATION
Hartke - *Chairman*

Cannon	Prouty
Moss	Pearson
Hollings	Baker
Long	Hatfield

Special Subcommittees

FREIGHT CAR SHORTAGE
Hartke - *Chairman*

Cannon	Prouty
Moss	Pearson
Magnuson	Hatfield

TRANSPORTATION ON THE GREAT LAKES-ST. LAWRENCE SEAWAY
Hartke - *Chairman*

Hart	Griffin
Long	Stevens

District of Columbia

All measures relating to municipal affairs of the District of Columbia, except appropriations for its operation. *Ext. 4161.*

D 4 - R 3

Thomas F. Eagleton (D Mo.), *Chairman*

Daniel K. Inouye (Hawaii)	Charles McC. Mathias Jr. (Md.)
Adlai E. Stevenson III (Ill.)	Lowell P. Weicker Jr. (Conn.)
John V. Tunney (Calif.)	James L. Buckley (N.Y.)

BUSINESS, COMMERCE AND THE JUDICIARY
Stevenson - *Chairman*

Tunney	Mathias

FISCAL AFFAIRS
Eagleton - *Chairman*

Inouye	Weicker

PUBLIC HEALTH, EDUCATION, WELFARE AND SAFETY
Tunney - *Chairman*

Stevenson	Buckley

Finance

Taxes, tariffs, import quotas, social security. *Ext. 4515.*

D 9 - R 7

Russell B. Long (D La.), *Chairman*

Clinton P. Anderson (N.M.)	Wallace F. Bennett (Utah)
Herman E. Talmadge (Ga.)	Carl T. Curtis (Neb.)
Vance Hartke (Ind.)	Jack Miller (Iowa)
J. W. Fulbright (Ark.)	Len B. Jordan (Idaho)
Abraham Ribicoff (Conn.)	Paul J. Fannin (Ariz.)
Fred R. Harris (Okla.)	Clifford P. Hansen (Wyo.)
Harry F. Byrd Jr. (Va.)	Robert P. Griffin (Mich.)
Gaylord Nelson (Wis.)	

No standing subcommittees.

Foreign Relations

Relations of United States with foreign nations generally; treaties, Red Cross, diplomatic service, United Nations, foreign loans. *Ext. 4651.*

D 9 - R 7

J. W. Fulbright (D Ark.), *Chairman**

John Sparkman (Ala.)	George D. Aiken (Vt.)
Mike Mansfield (Mont.)	Karl E. Mundt (S.D.)
Frank Church (Idaho)	Clifford P. Case (N.J.)
Stuart Symington (Mo.)	John Sherman Cooper (Ky.)
Claiborne Pell (R.I.)	Jacob K. Javits (N.Y.)
Gale W. McGee (Wyo.)	Hugh Scott (Pa.)
Edmund S. Muskie (Maine)	James B. Pearson (Kan.)
William B. Spong Jr. (Va.)	

AFRICAN AFFAIRS
McGee - *Chairman*

Mundt
Pearson

ARMS CONTROL, INTERNATIONAL LAW AND ORGANIZATION
Muskie - *Chairman*

Church	Case
Pell	Cooper
McGee	Javits
	Pearson

EUROPEAN AFFAIRS
Sparkman - *Chairman*

Symington	Case
Pell	Cooper
Spong	Javits
	Pearson

FAR EASTERN AFFAIRS
Mansfield - *Chairman*

Sparkman	Aiken
McGee	Mundt
Muskie	Cooper
	Scott

GENOCIDE CONVENTION
Church - *Chairman*

Symington	Cooper
Pell	Javits

NEAR EASTERN AND SOUTH ASIAN AFFAIRS
Symington - *Chairman*

Mansfield	Aiken
	Mundt
	Scott
	Pearson

OCEANS AND INTERNATIONAL ENVIRONMENT
Pell - *Chairman*

Church	Case
Spong	Scott

U.S. SECURITY AGREEMENTS AND COMMITMENTS ABROAD
Symington - *Chairman*

Fulbright	Aiken
Sparkman	Case
Mansfield	Cooper
	Javits

WESTERN HEMISPHERE AFFAIRS
Church - *Chairman*

Sparkman	Aiken
Mansfield	Case
Muskie	Javits
Spong	

Government Operations

Budget and accounting measures; reorganization of the Executive Branch; general governmental and administrative problems; intergovernmental relationships between the federal government and the states and municipalities, and between the United States and international organizations of which the United States is a member. *Ext. 4751.*

D 10 - R 8

John L. McClellan (D Ark.), *Chairman*

Henry M. Jackson (Wash.)	Karl E. Mundt (S.D.)
Sam J. Ervin Jr. (N.C.)	Jacob K. Javits (N.Y.)
Edmund S. Muskie (Maine)	Charles H. Percy (Ill.)
Abraham Ribicoff (Conn.)	Edward J. Gurney (Fla.)
Fred R. Harris (Okla.)	Charles McC. Mathias Jr. (Md.)
Lee Metcalf (Mont.)	William B. Saxbe (Ohio)
James B. Allen (Ala.)	William V. Roth Jr. (Del.)
Hubert H. Humphrey (Minn.)	Bill Brock (Tenn.)
Lawton Chiles (Fla.)	

EXECUTIVE REORGANIZATION AND GOVERNMENT RESEARCH
Ext. 2308
Ribicoff - *Chairman*

Harris	Javits
Metcalf	Percy
Allen	Mathias
Humphrey	Saxbe

INTERGOVERNMENTAL RELATIONS
Ext. 4718
Muskie - *Chairman*

Ervin	Gurney
Metcalf	Saxbe
McClellan	Roth
Chiles	Brock

NATIONAL SECURITY AND INTERNATIONAL OPERATIONS
Ext. 3381
Jackson - *Chairman*

Muskie	Mathias
Harris	Mundt
Humphrey	Brock
Chiles	Roth

PERMANENT INVESTIGATIONS
Ext. 3721
McClellan - *Chairman*

Jackson	Mundt
Ervin	Percy
Ribicoff	Javits
Allen	Gurney

Interior and Insular Affairs

Public lands, natural resources, territorial possessions of the United States, Indian affairs. *Ext. 4971.*

D 9 - R 7

Henry M. Jackson (D Wash.), *Chairman*

Clinton P. Anderson (N.M.)‡   Gordon Allott (Colo.)
Alan Bible (Nev.)   Len B. Jordan (Idaho)
Frank Church (Idaho)   Paul J. Fannin (Ariz.)
Frank E. Moss (Utah)   Clifford P. Hansen (Wyo.)
Quentin N. Burdick (N.D.)   Mark O. Hatfield (Ore.)
George McGovern (S.D.)   Ted Stevens (Alaska)
Lee Metcalf (Mont.)   Henry Bellmon (Okla.)
Mike Gravel (Alaska)

INDIAN AFFAIRS
McGovern - Chairman

Jackson	Fannin
Anderson	Hansen
Burdick	Stevens
Metcalf	Bellmon
Gravel	Allott

MINERALS, MATERIALS AND FUELS
Moss - Chairman

Jackson	Jordan
Bible	Bellmon
McGovern	Allott
Gravel	Stevens

PARKS AND RECREATION
Bible - Chairman

Jackson	Hansen
Anderson	Fannin
Church	Hatfield
Moss	Bellmon

PUBLIC LANDS
Church - Chairman

Jackson	Hatfield
Bible	Allott
Metcalf	Fannin
Gravel	Bellmon

TERRITORIES AND INSULAR AFFAIRS
Burdick - Chairman

Jackson	Stevens
McGovern	Jordan
Metcalf	Hansen

WATER AND POWER RESOURCES
Anderson - Chairman

Jackson	Allott
Church	Jordan
Moss	Fannin
Burdick	Hansen
Metcalf	Hatfield

Special Subcommittee

LEGISLATIVE OVERSIGHT
Jackson - Chairman

Anderson	Allott

Judiciary

Federal courts and judges, civil rights, civil liberties, constitutional amendments, interstate compacts, immigration and naturalization, apportionment of Representatives, meetings of Congress and attendance of members, claims against the United States, Patent Office. *Ext. 5225.*

D 9 - R 7

James O. Eastland (D Miss.), *Chairman*

John L. McClellan (Ark.)   Roman L. Hruska (Neb.)
Sam J. Ervin Jr. (N.C.)   Hiram L. Fong (Hawaii)
Philip A. Hart (Mich.)   Hugh Scott (Pa.)
Edward M. Kennedy (Mass.)   Strom Thurmond (S.C.)
Birch Bayh (Ind.)   Marlow W. Cook (Ky.)
Quentin N. Burdick (N.D.)   Charles McC. Mathias Jr. (Md.)
Robert C. Byrd (W.Va.)   Edward J. Gurney (Fla.)
John V. Tunney (Calif.)

ADMINISTRATIVE PRACTICE AND PROCEDURE
Ext. 5617
Kennedy - Chairman

Hart	Thurmond
Bayh	Mathias
Burdick	Gurney
Tunney	

ANTITRUST AND MONOPOLY
Ext. 5573
Hart - Chairman

McClellan	Hruska
Ervin	Fong
Kennedy	Thurmond
Tunney	Gurney

CONSTITUTIONAL AMENDMENTS
Ext. 3018
Bayh - Chairman

Eastland	Fong
Ervin	Hruska
Byrd	Thurmond
Burdick	Cook
Tunney	Gurney

CONSTITUTIONAL RIGHTS
Ext. 8191
Ervin - Chairman

McClellan	Hruska
Kennedy	Fong
Bayh	Thurmond
Byrd	Scott
Tunney	

FEDERAL CHARTERS, HOLIDAYS AND CELEBRATIONS
Ext. 5225
Hruska - Chairman

McClellan

IMMIGRATION AND NATURALIZATION
Ext. 2347
Eastland - Chairman

McClellan	Fong
Ervin	Thurmond
Kennedy	Cook
Hart	

IMPROVEMENTS IN JUDICIAL MACHINERY
Ext. 3618
Burdick - Chairman

McClellan	Hruska
Hart	Scott
Ervin	Gurney
Byrd	

PATENTS, TRADEMARKS AND COPYRIGHTS
Ext. 2268
McClellan - *Chairman*

Hart	Scott
Burdick	Fong

PENITENTIARIES
Ext. 8994
Burdick - *Chairman*

Hart	Cook
Bayh	Mathias

REVISION AND CODIFICATION
Ext. 3318
Ervin - *Chairman*

Hart	Scott

Special Subcommittees

CRIMINAL LAWS AND PROCEDURES
Ext. 3281
McClellan - *Chairman*

Ervin	Hruska
Hart	Scott
Eastland	Thurmond
Kennedy	Cook
Byrd	

INTERNAL SECURITY
Ext. 6241
Eastland - *Chairman*

McClellan	Scott
Ervin	Thurmond
Bayh	Cook
Byrd	Gurney

JUVENILE DELINQUENCY
Ext. 2951
Bayh - *Chairman*

Hart	Cook
Burdick	Hruska
Kennedy	Fong
Byrd	Mathias

REFUGEES AND ESCAPEES
Ext. 4118
Kennedy - *Chairman*

McClellan	Fong
Hart	Mathias

SEPARATION OF POWERS
Ext. 4434
Ervin - *Chairman*

McClellan	Mathias
Burdick	Gurney

Labor and Public Welfare

Education, labor, welfare, medical care. *Ext. 5375.*

D 10 - R 7

Harrison A. Williams Jr. (N.J.), *Chairman*

Jennings Randolph (W.Va.)‡	Jacob K. Javits (N.Y.)
Claiborne Pell (R.I.)	Winston L. Prouty (Vt.)
Edward M. Kennedy (Mass.)	Peter H. Dominick (Colo.)
Gaylord Nelson (Wis.)	Richard S. Schweiker (Pa.)
Walter F. Mondale (Minn.)	Robert W. Packwood (Ore.)
Thomas F. Eagleton (Mo.)	Robert Taft Jr. (Ohio)
Alan Cranston (Calif.)	J. Glenn Beall Jr. (Md.)

Harold E. Hughes (Iowa)
Adlai E. Stevenson III (Ill.)

AGING
Ext. 7653
Eagleton - *Chairman*

Cranston	Beall
Kennedy	Prouty
Randolph	Schweiker
Williams	Taft
Hughes	Packwood
Stevenson	

ALCOHOLISM AND NARCOTICS
Ext. 8386
Hughes - *Chairman*

Randolph	Packwood
Williams	Javits
Kennedy	Dominick
Mondale	Schweiker
Cranston	

CHILDREN AND YOUTH
Ext. 4538
Mondale - *Chairman*

Williams	Taft
Randolph	Schweiker
Kennedy	Packwood
Nelson	Beall
Cranston	Javits
Stevenson	

EDUCATION
Ext. 7666
Pell - *Chairman*

Randolph	Prouty
Williams	Javits
Kennedy	Dominick
Mondale	Schweiker
Eagleton	Beall
Cranston	

EMPLOYMENT, MANPOWER AND POVERTY
Ext. 3968
Nelson - *Chairman*

Kennedy	Schweiker
Mondale	Javits
Cranston	Prouty
Hughes	Dominick
Stevenson	Taft
Randolph	

HANDICAPPED WORKERS
Ext. 7672
Randolph - *Chairman*

Cranston	Prouty
Williams	Packwood

HEALTH
Ext. 7675
Kennedy - *Chairman*

Williams	Dominick
Nelson	Javits
Eagleton	Prouty
Cranston	Schweiker
Hughes	Packwood
Pell	Beall
Mondale	

LABOR
Ext. 3674
Williams - *Chairman*

Randolph	Javits
Pell	Prouty
Nelson	Schweiker
Eagleton	Packwood
Stevenson	Taft
Hughes	

MIGRATORY LABOR
Ext. 4538
Stevenson - *Chairman*

Williams	Taft
Mondale	Beall
Kennedy	Javits
Hughes	

RAILROAD RETIREMENT
Ext. 7651
Cranston - *Chairman*

Pell	Schweiker
Nelson	Taft
Hughes	Beall
Stevenson	

Special Subcommittees

ARTS AND HUMANITIES
Pell - *Chairman*

Nelson	Javits
Eagleton	Packwood

EVALUATION AND PLANNING OF SOCIAL PROGRAMS
Mondale - *Chairman*

Nelson	Javits
Eagleton	Taft
Stevenson	Beall

HUMAN RESOURCES
Cranston - *Chairman*

Randolph	Packwood
Nelson	Schweiker

INTERNATIONAL HEALTH, EDUCATION AND LABOR PROGRAMS
Hughes - *Chairman*

Williams	Dominick
Pell	Prouty

NATIONAL SCIENCE FOUNDATION
Kennedy - *Chairman*

Pell	Prouty
Eagleton	Dominick
Cranston	Packwood

Post Office and Civil Service

Postal and federal civil services; census, National Archives. Ext. 5451.

D 5 - R 4

Gale W. McGee (D Wyo.), *Chairman**

Jennings Randolph (W.Va.)‡	Hiram L. Fong (Hawaii)*
Quentin N. Burdick (N.D.)	J. Caleb Boggs (Del.)
Ernest F. Hollings (S.C.)	Ted Stevens (Alaska)
Frank E. Moss (Utah)	Henry Bellmon (Okla.)

CIVIL SERVICE POLICIES AND PRACTICES
Randolph - *Chairman*

Burdick	Stevens
Moss	Boggs

COMPENSATION AND EMPLOYMENT BENEFITS
Burdick - *Chairman*

Hollings	Boggs
Moss	Stevens

POSTAL OPERATIONS
Hollings - *Chairman*

Moss	Bellmon
Randolph	Boggs

Public Works

Public buildings, roads; flood control, rivers and harbors, stream pollution, water power. Ext. 6176.

D 9 - R 7

Jennings Randolph (D W.Va.), *Chairman*

Edmund S. Muskie (Maine)	John Sherman Cooper (Ky.)
B. Everett Jordan (N.C.)	J. Caleb Boggs (Del.)
Birch Bayh (Ind.)	Howard H. Baker Jr. (Tenn.)
Joseph M. Montoya (N.M.)	Robert Dole (Kan.)
Thomas F. Eagleton (Mo.)	J. Glenn Beall Jr. (Md.)
Mike Gravel (Alaska)	James L. Buckley (N.Y.)
John V. Tunney (Calif.)	Lowell P. Weicker Jr. (Conn.)
Lloyd Bentsen (Texas)	

AIR AND WATER POLLUTION
Muskie - *Chairman*

Randolph	Boggs
Bayh	Cooper
Montoya	Baker[1]
Eagleton[1]	Dole
Tunney[1]	Beall
Bentsen[1]	Buckley[1]

[1]*Members of Air and Water Pollution Subcommittee's Panel on Environmental Science and Technology.*

ECONOMIC DEVELOPMENT
Montoya - *Chairman*

Randolph	Baker
Muskie	Cooper
Eagleton	Dole
Gravel	Beall
Tunney	Buckley
Bentsen	

FLOOD CONTROL—RIVERS AND HARBORS
Jordan - *Chairman*

Bayh	Dole
Eagleton	Cooper
Tunney	Beall
Bentsen	Weicker

PUBLIC BUILDINGS AND GROUNDS
Gravel - *Chairman*

Jordan	Weicker
Tunney	Boggs

ROADS
Bayh - *Chairman*

Randolph	Cooper
Jordan	Boggs
Montoya	Baker
Gravel	Buckley
Muskie	Weicker

Rules and Administration

Senate administration generally; management of the Library of Congress, the Smithsonian Institution, etc. Ext. 6352.

D 5 - R 4

B. Everett Jordan (D N.C.), *Chairman*

Howard W. Cannon (Nev.)	Winston L. Prouty (Vt.)
Claiborne Pell (R.I.)	John Sherman Cooper (Ky.)
Robert C. Byrd (W.Va.)	Hugh Scott (Pa.)
James B. Allen (Ala.)	Robert P. Griffin (Mich.)

COMPUTER SERVICES
Jordan - *Chairman*

Cannon	Prouty

LIBRARY
Jordan - *Chairman*

Pell	Scott

PRINTING
Jordan - *Chairman*

Allen	Griffin

PRIVILEGES AND ELECTIONS
Ext. 5647
Cannon - *Chairman*

Byrd	Prouty

RESTAURANT
Allen - *Chairman*

Byrd	Griffin

SMITHSONIAN INSTITUTION
Pell - *Chairman*

Byrd	Cooper

STANDING RULES OF THE SENATE
Byrd - *Chairman*

Cannon	Cooper

Select Equal Educational Opportunity

Studies and investigates all aspects of school segregation. Ext. 8701.

D 9 - R 6

Walter F. Mondale (D Minn.), *Chairman*

John L. McClellan (Ark.)	Roman L. Hruska (Neb.)
Warren G. Magnuson (Wash.)	Jacob K. Javits (N.Y.)
Jennings Randolph (W.Va.)	Peter H. Dominick (Colo.)
Daniel K. Inouye (Hawaii)	Edward W. Brooke (Mass.)
Birch Bayh (Ind.)	Mark O. Hatfield (Ore.)
William B. Spong Jr. (Va.)	Marlow W. Cook (Ky.)
Sam J. Ervin Jr. (N.C.)	
Adlai E. Stevenson III (Ill.)	

No standing subcommittees.

Select Nutrition and Human Needs

Studies and investigates poverty and hunger in the United States. Ext. 7326.

D 8 - R 6

George McGovern (D S.D.), *Chairman*

Allen J. Ellender (La.)	Charles H. Percy (Ill.)
Herman E. Talmadge (Ga.)	Marlow W. Cook (Ky.)
Philip A. Hart (Mich.)	Robert Dole (Kan.)
Walter F. Mondale (Minn.)	Henry Bellmon (Okla.)
Edward M. Kennedy (Mass.)	Richard S. Schweiker (Pa.)
Gaylord Nelson (Wis.)	Robert Taft Jr. (Ohio)
Alan Cranston (Calif.)	

No standing subcommittees.

Select Small Business

Studies and investigates problems of small business and reports findings and makes recommendations to the Senate, but cannot report legislation. Ext. 5175.

D 9 - R 8

Alan Bible (D Nev.), *Chairman**

John Sparkman (Ala.)‡	Jacob K. Javits (N.Y.)*
Russell B. Long (La.)‡	Peter H. Dominick (Colo.)
Harrison A. Williams, Jr. (N.J.)	Mark O. Hatfield (Ore.)
Gaylord Nelson (Wis.)	Robert Dole (Kan.)
Joseph M. Montoya (N.M.)	Edward J. Gurney (Fla.)
Fred R. Harris (Okla.)	William B. Saxbe (Ohio)
Thomas J. McIntyre (N.H.)	J. Glenn Beall Jr. (Md.)
David H. Gambrell (Ga.)	Robert Taft Jr. (Ohio)

FINANCING AND INVESTMENT
Sparkman - *Chairman*

Long	Saxbe
Williams	Dominick
McIntyre	Beall

GOVERNMENT PROCUREMENT
Montoya - *Chairman*

Long	Gurney
Sparkman	Beall
Gambrell	Dole

GOVERNMENT REGULATION
McIntyre - *Chairman*

Nelson	Dominick
Harris	Gurney
Gambrell	Hatfield

MONOPOLY
Nelson - *Chairman*

Sparkman	Dole
Long	Taft
McIntyre	Gurney

RETAILING, DISTRIBUTION AND MARKETING PRACTICES
Harris - *Chairman*

Williams	Taft
Nelson	Dole
Montoya	Hatfield

SCIENCE AND TECHNOLOGY
Gambrell - *Chairman*

Montoya	Hatfield
Harris	Saxbe
Williams	Dominick

Select Standards and Conduct

Studies and investigates standards and conduct of Senate members and employees and may recommend remedial action. *Ext. 2981.*

D 3 - R 3

John C. Stennis (D Miss.), *Chairman*
Wallace F. Bennett (R Utah), *Vice Chairman*

Herman E. Talmadge (Ga.)	John Sherman Cooper (Ky.)
Vacancy	Len B. Jordan (Idaho)

No standing subcommittees.

Special Committee on Aging

Studies and investigates problems of the aging and reports findings and makes recommendations to the Senate, but cannot report legislation. *Ext. 5364.*

D 11 - R 9

Frank Church (D Idaho), *Chairman**

Harrison A. Williams Jr. (N.J.)‡	Winston L. Prouty (Vt.)
Alan Bible (Nev.)‡	Hiram L. Fong (Hawaii)
Jennings Randolph (W.Va.)	Jack Miller (Iowa)
Edmund S. Muskie (Maine)	Clifford P. Hansen (Wyo.)
Frank E. Moss (Utah)	Paul J. Fannin (Ariz.)
Edward M. Kennedy (Mass.)	Edward J. Gurney (Fla.)
Walter F. Mondale (Minn.)	William B. Saxbe (Ohio)
Vance Hartke (Ind.)	Edward W. Brooke (Mass.)
Claiborne Pell (R.I.)	Charles H. Percy (Ill.)
Thomas F. Eagleton (Mo.)	

CONSUMER INTERESTS OF THE ELDERLY
Church - *Chairman*

Williams	Fong
Muskie	Hansen
Kennedy	Gurney
Mondale	Saxbe
Hartke	Brooke
Eagleton	Percy

EMPLOYMENT AND RETIREMENT INCOMES
Randolph - *Chairman*

Church	Prouty
Bible	Hansen
Moss	Fannin
Mondale	Gurney
Hartke	Percy

FEDERAL, STATE AND COMMUNITY SERVICES
Kennedy - *Chairman*

Bible	Hansen
Hartke	Miller
Pell	Brooke
Eagleton	Percy

HEALTH OF THE ELDERLY
Muskie - *Chairman*

Moss	Saxbe
Williams	Prouty
Kennedy	Fong
Mondale	Hansen
Hartke	Fannin
Pell	Brooke
Eagleton	Percy

HOUSING FOR THE ELDERLY
Williams - *Chairman*

Church	Fannin
Muskie	Prouty
Kennedy	Gurney
Mondale	Saxbe
Pell	Brooke

LONG-TERM CARE
Moss - *Chairman*

Williams	Miller
Church	Fong
Muskie	Hansen
Kennedy	Fannin
Pell	Saxbe
Eagleton	Brooke

RETIREMENT AND THE INDIVIDUAL
Mondale - *Chairman*

Kennedy	Gurney
Bible	Prouty
Hartke	Fong
Pell	Miller
Eagleton	Fannin

Veterans' Affairs

Veterans' measures generally; pensions, armed forces life insurance, rehabilitation, education, medical care and treatment of veterans, veterans' hospitals. *Ext. 9126.*

D 5 - R 4

Vance Hartke (D Ind.), *Chairman**

Herman E. Talmadge (Ga.)	Strom Thurmond (S.C.)*
Jennings Randolph (W.Va.)	Clifford P. Hansen (Wyo.)
Harold E. Hughes (Iowa)	Marlow W. Cook (Ky.)
Alan Cranston (Calif.)	Ted Stevens (Alaska)

COMPENSATION AND PENSIONS
Talmadge - *Chairman*

Randolph	Hansen
Hughes	Thurmond

HEALTH AND HOSPITALS
Cranston - *Chairman*

Randolph	Thurmond
Hughes	Hansen

HOUSING AND INSURANCE
Hughes - *Chairman*

Talmadge	Cook
Cranston	Stevens

READJUSTMENT, EDUCATION AND EMPLOYMENT

Hartke - *Chairman*

Talmadge	Stevens
Cranston	Cook

SENATE DEMOCRATIC LEADERSHIP

Chairman of the Conference—Mike Mansfield (Mont.)
Secretary of the Conference—Frank E. Moss (Utah)
Floor Leader—Mansfield
Whip—Robert C. Byrd (W. Va.)
Assistant Whips—Ernest F. Hollings (S.C.), Harold E. Hughes (Iowa), Daniel K. Inouye (Hawaii), Edmund S. Muskie (Maine).

Policy Committee

Scheduling of legislation. *Ext. 5551.*

Mike Mansfield (Mont.), *Chairman*

Robert C. Byrd (W. Va.)†	Frank E. Moss (Utah)†
Allen J. Ellender (La.)†	John O. Pastore (R.I.)
J.W. Fulbright (Ark.)	Stuart Symington (Mo.)
Philip A. Hart (Mich.)	Herman E. Talmadge (Ga.)
Warren G. Magnuson (Wash.)	

Legislative Review

Ext. 5551

Edmund S. Muskie (Maine), *Chairman*

Daniel K. Inouye (Hawaii)	Harold E. Hughes (Iowa)
Ernest F. Hollings (S.C.)	

Steering Committee

Makes Democratic committee assignments. *Ext. 5556.*

Mike Mansfield (Mont.), *Chairman*

Clinton P. Anderson (N.M.)	Edward M. Kennedy (Mass.)
Alan Bible (Nev.)	John L. McClellan (Ark.)
Quentin N. Burdick (N.D.)	Frank E. Moss (Utah)†
Robert C. Byrd (W.Va.)†	William Proxmire (Wis.)
Lawton Chiles (Fla.)	John Sparkman (Ala.)
Allen J. Ellender (La.)	William B. Spong Jr. (Va.)
Vance Hartke (Ind.)	Stuart Symington (Mo.)
Henry M. Jackson (Wash.)	Harrison A. Williams Jr. (N.J.)

Senatorial Campaign Committee

Ext. 2447

Ernest F. Hollings (S.C.), *Chairman*
Daniel K. Inouye (Hawaii), *Vice Chairman*

Lloyd Bentsen (Texas)	Warren G. Magnuson (Wash.)
Lawton Chiles (Fla.)	Gaylord Nelson (Wis.)
Alan Cranston (Calif.)	John O. Pastore (R.I.)
Thomas F. Eagleton (Mo.)	Abraham Ribicoff (Conn.)
Edward M. Kennedy (Mass.)	John V. Tunney (Calif.)
Russell B. Long (La.)	Harrison A. Williams Jr. (N.J.)

SENATE REPUBLICAN LEADERSHIP

Chairman of the Conference—Margaret Chase Smith (Maine)
Secretary of the Conference—Norris Cotton (N.H.)
Floor Leader—Hugh Scott (Pa.)
Whip—Robert P. Griffin (Mich.)
Regional Whips—Henry Bellmon (Okla.), Edward J. Gurney (Fla.), Charles McC. Mathias Jr. (Md.), Robert W. Packwood (Ore.), William B. Saxbe (Ohio)

Policy Committee

Counterpart of Democratic Policy Committee. *Ext. 2946.*

Gordon Allott (Colo.), *Chairman*

Wallace F. Bennett (Utah)	Robert P. Griffin (Mich.)
J. Caleb Boggs (Del.)	Roman L. Hruska (Neb.)
Clifford P. Case (N.J.)	Karl E. Mundt (S.D.)
John Sherman Cooper (Ky.)	Hugh Scott (Pa.)
Norris Cotton (N.H.)	Margaret Chase Smith (Maine)
Carl T. Curtis (Neb.)	Strom Thurmond (S.C.)
Peter H. Dominick (Colo.)	John G. Tower (Texas)

Committee on Committees

Makes Republican committee assignments. *Ext. 2441.*

Wallace F. Bennett (Utah), *Chairman*

George D. Aiken (Vt.)	Jack Miller (Iowa)
Henry Bellmon (Okla.)	Robert W. Packwood (Ore.)
Edward W. Brooke (Mass.)	James B. Pearson (Kan.)
Marlow W. Cook (Ky.)	Charles H. Percy (Ill.)
Edward J. Gurney (Fla.)	Winston L. Prouty (Vt.)
Clifford P. Hansen (Wyo.)	Richard S. Schweiker (Pa.)
Mark O. Hatfield (Ore.)	Ted Stevens (Alaska)
Jacob K. Javits (N.Y.)	Milton R. Young (N.D.)
Len B. Jordan (Idaho)	

Senatorial Campaign Committee

Ext. 2351

Peter H. Dominick (Colo.), *Chairman*

J. Glenn Beall Jr. (Md.)	Barry Goldwater (Ariz.)
Bill Brock (Tenn.)	Charles McC. Mathias Jr. (Md.)
James L. Buckley (N.Y.)	William V. Roth Jr. (Del.)
Robert Dole (Kan.)	William B. Saxbe (Ohio)
Paul J. Fannin (Ariz.)	Robert Taft Jr. (Ohio)
Hiram L. Fong (Hawaii)	Lowell P. Weicker Jr. (Conn.)

Personnel Committee

Ext. 3324

Roman L. Hruska (Neb.), *Chairman*
Howard H. Baker Jr. (Tenn.)

Calendar Committee

Ext. 4521

Paul J. Fannin (Ariz.), *Chairman*

Howard H. Baker Jr. (Tenn.)	Lowell P. Weicker Jr. (Conn.)

HOUSE COMMITTEES, 92nd CONGRESS, FIRST SESSION

Agriculture

Agriculture and forestry in general; farm credit and security, crop insurance, soil conservation and rural electrification. *Ext. 2171.*

D 22 - R 14

W.R. Poage (D Texas), *Chairman**
John L. McMillan (D S.C.), *Vice Chairman*

Thomas G. Abernethy (Miss.)	Page Belcher (Okla.)*
Watkins M. Abbitt (Va.)	Charles M. Teague (Calif.)
Frank A. Stubblefield (Ky.)	William C. Wampler (Va.)
Graham Purcell (Texas)	George A. Goodling (Pa.)
Thomas S. Foley (Wash.)	Clarence E. Miller (Ohio)
Eligio de la Garza (Texas)	Robert B. (Bob) Mathias (Calif.)
Joseph P. Vigorito (Pa.)	Wiley Mayne (Iowa)
Walter B. Jones (N.C.)	John M. Zwach (Minn.)
B. F. Sisk (Calif.)	Robert Price (Texas)
Bill Alexander (Ark.)	Keith G. Sebelius (Kan.)
Bill D. Burlison (Mo.)	Wilmer Mizell (N.C.)
John R. Rarick (La.)	Paul Findley (Ill.)
Ed Jones (Tenn.)	John Kyl (Iowa)
John Melcher (Mont.)	J. Kenneth Robinson (Va.)
John G. Dow (N.Y.)	Jorge L. Cordova (P.R.) √
Dawson Mathis (Ga.)	
Bob Bergland (Minn.)	√ *Resident Commissioner*
Arthur A. Link (N.D.)	
Frank E. Denholm (S.D.)	
Spark M. Matsunaga (Hawaii)	

CONSERVATION AND CREDIT
Poage - *Chairman*

Stubblefield	Teague
de la Garza	Goodling
Alexander	Mayne
Bergland	

COTTON

Abernethy - *Chairman*

de la Garza	Mathias
Sisk	Price
Burlison	Mizell
Jones (Tenn.)	

DAIRY AND POULTRY

Stubblefield - *Chairman*

Vigorito	Wampler
Jones (Tenn.)	Miller
Dow	Zwach
Abbitt	

DOMESTIC MARKETING AND CONSUMER RELATIONS

Foley - *Chairman*

Sisk	Goodling
Denholm	Zwach
Link	Robinson
Matsunaga	

FAMILY FARMS AND RURAL DEVELOPMENT

Vigorito - *Chairman*

Purcell	Goodling
Melcher	Miller
Mathis	Kyl
Dow	

DEPARTMENT OPERATIONS

de la Garza - *Chairman*

Abernethy	Mathias
Purcell	Sebelius
Jones (Tenn.)	Mayne
Matsunaga	

FORESTS

McMillan - *Chairman*

Foley	Teague
Burlison	Kyl
Vigorito	Robinson
Dow	

LIVESTOCK AND GRAINS

Purcell - *Chairman*

Foley	Mayne
Rarick	Zwach
Abbitt	Price
Jones (N.C.)	Sebelius
Sisk	Findley
Melcher	Kyl
Bergland	
Link	
Denholm	

OILSEEDS AND RICE

Jones (N.C.) - *Chairman*

Rarick	Wampler
Alexander	Mizell
Burlison	Findley
Mathis	

TOBACCO

Abbitt - *Chairman*

McMillan	Wampler
Stubblefield	Miller
Jones (N.C.)	Mizell
Mathis	

Appropriations

Appropriations of government revenues. *Ext. 2771.*

D 33 - R 22

George Mahon (D Texas), *Chairman*

Jamie L. Whitten (Miss.)	Frank T. Bow (Ohio)
George W. Andrews (Ala.)	Charles Raper Jonas (N.C.)

John J. Rooney (N.Y.)
Robert L. F. Sikes (Fla.)
Otto E. Passman (La.)
Joe L. Evins (Tenn.)
Edward P. Boland (Mass.)
William H. Natcher (Ky.)
Daniel J. Flood (Pa.)
Tom Steed (Okla.)
George E. Shipley (Ill.)
John M. Slack (W.Va.)
John J. Flynt Jr. (Ga.)
Neal Smith (Iowa)
Robert N. Giaimo (Conn.)
Julia Butler Hansen (Wash.)
Joseph P. Addabbo (N.Y.)
John J. McFall (Calif.)
W. R. Hull Jr. (Mo.)
Edward J. Patten (N.J.)
Clarence D. Long (Md.)
Sidney R. Yates (Ill.)
Bob Casey (Texas)
David Pryor (Ark.)
Frank E. Evans (Colo.)
David R. Obey (Wis.)
Edward R. Roybal (Calif.)
William D. Hathaway (Maine)
Nick Galifianakis (N.C.)
Louis Stokes (Ohio)
J. Edward Roush (Ind.)
K. Gunn McKay (Utah)

Elford A. Cederberg (Mich.)
John J. Rhodes (Ariz.)
William E. Minshall (Ohio)
Robert H. Michel (Ill.)
Silvio O. Conte (Mass.)
Glenn R. Davis (Wis.)
Howard W. Robison (N.Y.)
Garner E. Shriver (Kan.)
Joseph M. McDade (Pa.)
Mark Andrews (N.D.)
Louis C. Wyman (N.H.)
Burt L. Talcott (Calif.)
Charlotte T. Reid (Ill.)
Donald W. Riegle Jr. (Mich.)
Wendell Wyatt (Ore.)
Jack Edwards (Ala.)
Del Clawson (Calif.)
William J. Scherle (Iowa)
Robert C. McEwen (N.Y.)
John T. Myers (Ind.)

AGRICULTURE-ENVIRONMENTAL AND CONSUMER PROTECTION
Ext. 2638
Whitten - *Chairman*

Natcher	Andrews
Hull	Michel
Shipley	Scherle
Evans	

DEFENSE
Ext. 2847
Mahon - *Chairman*

Sikes	Minshall
Whitten	Rhodes
Andrews	Davis
Flood	Wyman
Addabbo	
McFall	

DISTRICT OF COLUMBIA
Ext. 5338
Natcher - *Chairman*

Giaimo	Davis
Pryor	Scherle
Obey	McEwen
Stokes	Myers
McKay	

FOREIGN OPERATIONS
Ext. 2041
Passman - *Chairman*

Rooney	Shriver
Long	Reid
Roybal	Riegle
Hathaway	McEwen
Galifianakis	

HOUSING AND URBAN DEVELOPMENT
Ext. 3241
Boland - *Chairman*

Evins	Jonas
Shipley	Talcott
Giaimo	McDade
Pryor	Clawson
Roush	

INTERIOR
Ext. 3081
Hansen - *Chairman*

Flynt	McDade
Obey	Wyatt
Yates	Clawson
Galifianakis	

LABOR-HEALTH, EDUCATION AND WELFARE
Ext. 3508
Flood - *Chairman*

Natcher	Michel
Smith	Shriver
Hull	Reid
Casey	Conte
Patten	

LEGISLATIVE
Ext. 5338
Andrews (Ala.) - *Chairman*

Casey	Bow
Evans	Cederberg
Hathaway	Rhodes
Roush	Wyatt

MILITARY CONSTRUCTION
Ext. 3047
Sikes - *Chairman*

Patten	Cederberg
Long	Jonas
Hansen	Talcott
McKay	

PUBLIC WORKS
Ext. 3421
Evins - *Chairman*

Boland	Rhodes
Whitten	Davis
Andrews	Robison
Slack	

STATE, JUSTICE, COMMERCE AND JUDICIARY
Ext. 3421
Rooney - *Chairman*

Sikes	Bow
Slack	Cederberg
Smith	Andrews
Flynt	

TRANSPORTATION
Ext. 2141
McFall - *Chairman*

Boland	Conte
Yates	Minshall
Steed	Edwards

TREASURY-POST OFFICE-GENERAL GOVERNMENT
Ext. 5834
Steed - *Chairman*

Passman	Robison
Addabbo	Edwards
Roybal	Riegle
Stokes	Myers

Armed Services

All matters relating to the national military establishment; conservation of petroleum resources; strategic and critical materials; scientific research and development in support of the armed services. *Ext. 4151.*

D 25 - R 16

F. Edward Hebert (D La.), *Chairman**

Melvin Price (Ill.)	Leslie C. Arends (Ill.)*
O. C. Fisher (Texas)	Alvin E. O'Konski (Wis.)
Charles E. Bennett (Fla.)	William G. Bray (Ind.)
James A. Byrne (Pa.)	Bob Wilson (Calif.)
Samuel S. Stratton (N.Y.)	Charles S. Gubser (Calif.)
Otis G. Pike (N.Y.)	Alexander Pirnie (N.Y.)
Richard H. Ichord (Mo.)	Durward G. Hall (Mo.)
Lucien N. Nedzi (Mich.)	Donald D. Clancy (Ohio)
Alton Lennon (N.C.)	Robert T. Stafford (Vt.)
William J. Randall (Mo.)	Carleton J. King (N.Y.)
G. Elliott Hagan (Ga.)	William L. Dickinson (Ala.)
Charles H. Wilson (Calif.)	Charles W. Whalen Jr. (Ohio)
Robert L. Leggett (Calif.)	John E. Hunt (N.J.)
Floyd V. Hicks (Wash.)	G. William Whitehurst (Va.)
Speedy O. Long (La.)	Floyd Spence (S.C.)
Richard C. White (Texas)	C. W. Bill Young (Fla.)
Bill Nichols (Ala.)	Jorge L. Cordova (P.R.) √
Jack Brinkley (Ga.)	
Robert H. Mollohan (W.Va.)	√ *Resident Commissioner*
W.C. (Dan) Daniel (Va.)	
G.V. (Sonny) Montgomery (Miss.)	
Michael Harrington (Mass.)	
Harold Runnels (N.M.)	
Les Aspin (Wis.)	

SUBCOMMITTEE NO. 1

Price - *Chairman*

Pike	O'Konski
Ichord	Hall
Leggett	Stafford
Hicks	Whalen
Montgomery	

SUBCOMMITTEE NO. 2

Fisher - *Chairman*

Nedzi	Bray
Lennon	Pirnie
Hagan	Clancy
Long	Young
Daniel	
Runnels	

SUBCOMMITTEE NO. 3

Bennett - *Chairman*

Stratton	Wilson
Randall	King
White	Dickinson
Mollohan	Spence
Harrington	

SUBCOMMITTEE NO. 4

Byrne - *Chairman*

Wilson	Gubser
Nichols	Hunt
Brinkley	Whitehurst
Aspin	

Special Subcommittees

ARMED SERVICES INVESTIGATING
Ext. 4221
Hebert - *Chairman*

Stratton	Arends
Pike	Gubser
Lennon	Pirnie
Randall	Hall
Mollohan	Dickinson
Daniel	Hunt

REAL ESTATE

Bennett - *Chairman*

Byrne	Bray
Stratton	King
Daniel	Whitehurst

Banking and Currency

Banking and currency generally; financial matters other than taxes and appropriations; public and private housing. *Ext. 4247.*

D 22 - R 15

Wright Patman (D Texas), *Chairman*

William A. Barrett (Pa.)	William B. Widnall (N.J.)
Leonor K. Sullivan (Mo.)	Florence P. Dwyer (N.J.)
Henry S. Reuss (Wis.)	Albert W. Johnson (Pa.)
Thomas L. Ashley (Ohio)	J. William Stanton (Ohio)
William S. Moorhead (Pa.)	Ben B. Blackburn (Ga.)
Robert G. Stephens Jr. (Ga.)	Garry Brown (Mich.)
Fernand J. St Germain (R.I.)	Lawrence G. Williams (Pa.)
Henry B. Gonzalez (Texas)	Chalmers P. Wylie (Ohio)
Joseph G. Minish (N.J.)	Margaret M. Heckler (Mass.)
Richard T. Hanna (Calif.)	Philip M. Crane (Ill.)
Tom S. Gettys (S.C.)	John H. Rousselot (Calif.)
Frank Annunzio (Ill.)	Stewart B. McKinney (Conn.)
Thomas M. Rees (Calif.)	Norman F. Lent (N.Y.)
Tom Bevill (Ala.)	Bill Archer (Texas)
Charles H. Griffin (Miss.)	Bill Frenzel (Minn.)
James M. Hanley (N.Y.)	
Frank J. Brasco (N.Y.)	
Bill Chappell Jr. (Fla.)	
Edward I. Koch (N.Y.)	
William R. Cotter (Conn.)	
Parren J. Mitchell (Md.)	

BANK SUPERVISION AND INSURANCE

St Germain - *Chairman*

Moorhead	Johnson
Annunzio	Wylie
Bevill	Crane
Griffin	Rousselot
Brasco	Archer
Chappell	Lent
Koch	
Cotter	

CONSUMER AFFAIRS
Ext. 8400

Sullivan - *Chairman*

Stephens	Dwyer
Gonzalez	Wylie
Minish	Williams
Hanna	Heckler
Annunzio	Archer
Hanley	McKinney
Chappell	
Koch	

DOMESTIC FINANCE

Patman - *Chairman*

Minish	Widnall
Hanna	Blackburn
Gettys	Crane
Annunzio	Brown
Rees	Williams
Hanley	Frenzel
Brasco	
Mitchell	

HOUSING
Ext. 7054

Barrett - *Chairman*

Sullivan	Widnall
Ashley	Dwyer
Moorhead	Brown
Stephens	Stanton
St Germain	Blackburn
Gonzalez	Heckler
Reuss	
Minish	

INTERNATIONAL FINANCE
Ext. 4247

Gonzalez - *Chairman*

Reuss	Johnson
Ashley	Stanton
Moorhead	Crane
Hanna	Frenzel
Rees	Lent
Hanley	Archer
Brasco	
Cotter	

INTERNATIONAL TRADE
Ext. 4146

Ashley - *Chairman*

St Germain	Blackburn
Gettys	Brown

Rees	Johnson
Bevill	Rousselot
Griffin	McKinney
Hanna	Lent
Koch	
Mitchell	

SMALL BUSINESS

Stephens - *Chairman*

Barrett	Stanton
Sullivan	Williams
Gettys	Wylie
Bevill	Heckler
Griffin	Rousselot
Cotter	McKinney
Mitchell	

District of Columbia

All measures relating to municipal affairs of the District of Columbia except its appropriations. *Ext. 4457.*

D 15 - R 10

John L. McMillan (D S.C.), *Chairman*

Thomas G. Abernethy (Miss.)	Ancher Nelsen (Minn.)
John Dowdy (Texas)	William L. Springer (Ill.)
Charles C. Diggs Jr. (Mich.)	Alvin E. O'Konski (Wis.)
G. Elliott Hagan (Ga.)	William H. Harsha (Ohio)
Donald M. Fraser (Minn.)	Joel T. Broyhill (Va.)
Andrew Jacobs Jr. (Ind.)	Gilbert Gude (Md.)
William L. Hungate (Mo.)	Vernon W. Thomson (Wis.)
Earle Cabell (Texas)	Henry P. Smith III (N.Y.)
Ray Blanton (Tenn.)	Earl F. Landgrebe (Ind.)
W.S. (Bill) Stuckey (Ga.)	Stewart B. McKinney (Conn.)
Abner J. Mikva (Ill.)	
Arthur A. Link (N.D.)	
Ronald V. Dellums (Calif.)	
Walter E. Fauntroy (D.C.) √	

√ Delegate

BUSINESS, COMMERCE AND FISCAL AFFAIRS

Cabell - *Chairman*

Abernethy	O'Konski
Dowdy	Harsha
Fraser	Broyhill
Blanton	Gude
Mikva	Thomson
Link	

EDUCATION

Dowdy - *Chairman*

Fraser	Springer
Hagan	O'Konski
Jacobs	Gude
Hungate	Smith
Blanton	McKinney

HOUSING AND YOUTH AFFAIRS

The members of this subcommittee had not been named at the time of publication.

JUDICIARY

Hungate - *Chairman*

Abernethy	Harsha
Jacobs	Broyhill
Stuckey	Thomson
Mikva	Smith
Link	Landgrebe

PUBLIC HEALTH AND WELFARE

Hagan - *Chairman*

Cabell	Broyhill
Blanton	Gude
Stuckey	Smith
Dellums	Landgrebe
	McKinney

Education and Labor

Education, labor and welfare matters. *Ext. 4527.*

D 22 - R 16

Carl D. Perkins (D Ky.), *Chairman**

Edith Green (Ore.)	Albert H. Quie (Minn.)*
Frank Thompson Jr. (N.J.)	John M. Ashbrook (Ohio)
John H. Dent (Pa.)	Alphonzo Bell (Calif.)
Roman C. Pucinski (Ill.)	Ogden R. Reid (N.Y.)
Dominick V. Daniels (N.J.)	John N. Erlenborn (Ill.)
John Brademas (Ind.)	John Dellenback (Ore.)
James G. O'Hara (Mich.)	Marvin L. Esch (Mich.)
Augustus F. Hawkins (Calif.)	Edwin D. Eshleman (Pa.)
William D. Ford (Mich.)	William A. Steiger (Wis.)
Patsy T. Mink (Hawaii)	Earl F. Landgrebe (Ind.)
James H. Scheuer (N.Y.)	Orval Hansen (Idaho)
Lloyd Meeds (Wash.)	Earl B. Ruth (N.C.)
Phillip Burton (Calif.)	Edwin B. Forsythe (N.J.)
Joseph M. Gaydos (Pa.)	Victor V. Veysey (Calif.)
William (Bill) Clay (Mo.)	Jack F. Kemp (N.Y.)
Shirley Chisholm (N.Y.)	Peter A. Peyser (N.Y.)
Mario Biaggi (N.Y.)	
Ella T. Grasso (Conn.)	
Louise Day Hicks (Mass.)	
Romano L. Mazzoli (Ky.)	
Herman Badillo (N.Y.)	

GENERAL EDUCATION
Ext. 4368
Pucinski - *Chairman*

Ford	Bell
Meeds	Ashbrook

Hawkins	Ruth
Mink	Forsythe
Chisholm	Veysey
Biaggi	Kemp
Hicks	Peyser
Mazzoli	
Badillo	
Green	

SELECT EDUCATION
Ext. 5954
Brademas - *Chairman*

Mink	Reid
Meeds	Bell
Scheuer	Landgrebe
Gaydos	Hansen
Clay	Eshleman
Chisholm	Kemp
Grasso	Peyser
Mazzoli	
O'Hara	
Dent	

SPECIAL EDUCATION
Ext. 4958
Green - *Chairman*

Burton	Dellenback
Scheuer	Erlenborn
Brademas	Esch
Daniels	Steiger
Pucinski	Ruth
Dent	
Thompson	

AGRICULTURAL LABOR
Ext. 8881
O'Hara - *Chairman*

Chisholm	Eshleman
Grasso	Ashbrook
Badillo	Veysey
Thompson	

GENERAL LABOR
Ext. 5331
Dent - *Chairman*

Hawkins	Erlenborn
Mink	Bell
Burton	Esch
Clay	Landgrebe
Gaydos	Hansen
Ford	Steiger
Biaggi	Kemp
Mazzoli	
Pucinski	
Brademas	

SELECT LABOR
Ext. 6876
Daniels - *Chairman*

Meeds	Esch
Ford	Steiger
Burton	Eshleman

Hawkins
Gaydos
Scheuer
Biaggi
Grasso
Hicks
Green

Ruth
Forsythe
Veysey
Peyser

SPECIAL LABOR
Ext. 5768
Thompson - *Chairman*

Clay
Hicks
Badillo
O'Hara

Ashbrook
Reid
Dellenback

Foreign Affairs

Relations of the United States with other nations and international organizations and movements. *Ext. 5021.*

D 21 - R 17

Thomas E. Morgan (D Pa.), *Chairman**

Clement J. Zablocki (Wis.)
Wayne L. Hays (Ohio)
L. H. Fountain (N.C.)
Dante B. Fascell (Fla.)
Charles C. Diggs Jr. (Mich.)
Cornelius E. Gallagher (N.J.)
Robert N.C. Nix (Pa.)
John S. Monagan (Conn.)
Donald M. Fraser (Minn.)
Benjamin S. Rosenthal (N.Y.)
John C. Culver (Iowa)
Lee H. Hamilton (Ind.)
Abraham Kazen Jr. (Texas)
Lester L. Wolff (N.Y.)
Jonathan B. Bingham (N.Y.)
Gus Yatron (Pa.)
Roy A. Taylor (N.C.)
John W. Davis (Ga.)
Morgan F. Murphy (Ill.)
Ronald V. Dellums (Calif.)

William S. Mailliard (Calif.)*
Peter H.B. Frelinghuysen (N.J.)
William S. Broomfield (Mich.)
J. Irving Whalley (Pa.)
H. R. Gross (Iowa)
Edward J. Derwinski (Ill.)
F. Bradford Morse (Mass.)
Vernon W. Thomson (Wis.)
James G. Fulton (Pa.)
Paul Findley (Ill.)
John Buchanan (Ala.)
Sherman P. Lloyd (Utah)
J. Herbert Burke (Fla.)
Seymour Halpern (N.Y.)
Guy Vander Jagt (Mich.)
Robert H. Steele (Conn.)
Pierre S. (Pete) du Pont (Del.)

AFRICA
Diggs - *Chairman*

Nix
Culver
Yatron
Dellums

Whalley
Broomfield
Derwinski
Vander Jagt

ASIAN AND PACIFIC AFFAIRS
Gallagher - *Chairman*

Hamilton
Diggs
Wolff
Kazen
Davis
Murphy

Broomfield
Whalley
Thomson
Burke
Halpern
du Pont

EUROPE
Rosenthal - *Chairman*

Hays
Gallagher
Monagan
Hamilton
Yatron
Taylor
Murphy

Frelinghuysen
Fulton
Findley
Burke
Buchanan
Lloyd
Vander Jagt

FOREIGN ECONOMIC POLICY
Culver - *Chairman*

Nix
Zablocki
Yatron
Wolff
Fraser
Davis

Derwinski
Burke
Steele
du Pont

INTER-AMERICAN AFFAIRS
Fascell - *Chairman*

Monagan
Kazen
Rosenthal
Culver
Taylor
Dellums

Morse
Whalley
Gross
Frelinghuysen
Steele

INTERNATIONAL ORGANIZATIONS AND MOVEMENTS
Fraser - *Chairman*

Fascell
Gallagher
Fountain
Rosenthal
Kazen
Bingham
Dellums

Gross
Frelinghuysen
Derwinski
Findley
Halpern

NATIONAL SECURITY POLICY AND SCIENTIFIC DEVELOPMENTS
Zablocki - *Chairman*

Hays
Nix
Fountain
Fraser
Bingham
Davis

Findley
Broomfield
Thomson
Fulton
Morse

NEAR EAST
Hamilton - *Chairman*

Fountain
Monagan
Wolff
Bingham
Taylor

Fulton
Gross
Buchanan
Lloyd
Halpern

STATE DEPARTMENT ORGANIZATION AND FOREIGN OPERATIONS

Hays - *Chairman*

Zablocki	Thomson
Fraser	Morse
Fascell	Lloyd
Kazen	Buchanan
Culver	Vander Jagt
Murphy	

Special Subcommittee

REVIEW OF FOREIGN AID PROGRAMS

Morgan - *Chairman*

Zablocki	Mailliard
Hays	Frelinghuysen
Fountain	Broomfield
Fascell	Whalley

Government Operations

Budget and accounting measures; reorganization in the Executive Branch; intergovernmental relationships. *Ext. 5051.*

D 23 - R 16

Chet Holifield (D Calif.), *Chairman**

Jack Brooks (Texas)	Florence P. Dwyer (N.J.)*
L. H. Fountain (N.C.)	Ogden R. Reid (N.Y.)
Robert E. Jones (Ala.)	Frank Horton (N.Y.)
Edward A. Garmatz (Md.)	John N. Erlenborn (Ill.)
John E. Moss (Calif.)	John W. Wydler (N.Y.)
Dante B. Fascell (Fla.)	Clarence J. Brown (Ohio)
Henry S. Reuss (Wis.)	Guy Vander Jagt (Mich.)
John S. Monagan (Conn.)	Gilbert Gude (Md.)
Torbert H. Macdonald (Mass.)	Paul N. McCloskey Jr. (Calif.)
William S. Moorhead (Pa.)	John Buchanan (Ala.)
Cornelius E. Gallagher (N.J.)	Sam Steiger (Ariz.)
William J. Randall (Mo.)	Garry Brown (Mich.)
Benjamin S. Rosenthal (N.Y.)	Barry M. Goldwater Jr. (Calif.)
Jim Wright (Texas)	J. Kenneth Robinson (Va.)
Fernand J. St Germain (R.I.)	Walter E. Powell (Ohio)
John C. Culver (Iowa)	Charles Thone (Neb.)
Floyd V. Hicks (Wash.)	
George W. Collins (Ill.)	
Don Fuqua (Fla.)	
John Conyers Jr. (Mich.)	
Bill Alexander (Ark.)	
Bella S. Abzug (N.Y.)	

CONSERVATION AND NATURAL RESOURCES
Ext. 6427
Reuss - *Chairman*

Moss	Vander Jagt
Fascell	Gude
Hicks	McCloskey
Conyers	Steiger
Abzug	

FOREIGN OPERATIONS AND GOVERNMENT INFORMATION
Ext. 3741
Moorhead - *Chairman*

Moss	Reid
Macdonald	Horton
Wright	Erlenborn
Conyers	McCloskey
Alexander	

GOVERNMENT ACTIVITIES
Ext. 3252
Brooks - *Chairman*

Jones	Reid
Macdonald	Buchanan
Culver	Gude
Hicks	Goldwater
Monagan	

INTERGOVERNMENTAL RELATIONS
Ext. 2548
Fountain - *Chairman*

Jones	Dwyer
Rosenthal	Brown (Ohio)
Culver	Vander Jagt
Fuqua	Buchanan
Alexander	Robinson

LEGAL AND MONETARY AFFAIRS
Ext. 4407
Monagan - *Chairman*

Fascell	Steiger
Gallagher	Brown (Mich.)
St Germain	Powell
Collins	Thone
Randall	

LEGISLATION AND MILITARY OPERATIONS
Ext. 5147
Holifield - *Chairman*

Garmatz	Horton
Rosenthal	Erlenborn
Wright	Wydler
St Germain	Brown (Ohio)
Fuqua	
Moorhead	

SPECIAL STUDIES
Ext. 6751
Randall - *Chairman*

Garmatz	Wydler
Gallagher	Brown (Mich.)
Collins	Goldwater
Abzug	Robinson
Reuss	

House Administration

House administration generally; printing and correction of the *Congressional Record;* federal elections generally, management of the Library of Congress, supervision of the Smithsonian Institution, etc. *Ext. 2061.*

D 15 - R 10

Wayne L. Hays (D Ohio), *Chairman**

Frank Thompson Jr. (N.J.)	Samuel L. Devine (Ohio)*
Watkins M. Abbitt (Va.)	William L. Dickinson (Ala.)
John H. Dent (Pa.)	James C. Cleveland (N.H.)
Lucien N. Nedzi (Mich.)	Fred Schwengel (Iowa)
John Brademas (Ind.)	James Harvey (Mich.)
Kenneth J. Gray (Ill.)	Orval Hansen (Idaho)
Augustus F. Hawkins (Calif.)	Philip M. Crane (Ill.)
Tom S. Gettys (S.C.)	John Ware (Pa.)
Jonathan B. Bingham (N.Y.)	Victor V. Veysey (Calif.)
Bertram L. Podell (N.Y.)	Bill Frenzel (Minn.)
Frank Annunzio (Ill.)	
Joseph M. Gaydos (Pa.)	
Ed Jones (Tenn.)	
Robert H. Mollohan (W.Va.)	

ACCOUNTS

Thompson - *Chairman*

Dent	Dickinson
Hawkins	Cleveland
Gettys	Crane
Podell	
Annunzio	

ELECTIONS

Abbitt - *Chairman*

Gray	Harvey
Dent	Ware
Jones	Frenzel
Mollohan	

LIBRARY AND MEMORIALS

Nedzi - *Chairman*

Gray	Schwengel
Brademas	Harvey
Bingham	Frenzel
Gaydos	
Thompson	

PRINTING
Ext. 2063
Brademas - *Chairman*

Gettys	Cleveland
Bingham	Hansen
Gaydos	Veysey
Jones	

Special Subcommittees

CONTRACTS

Hawkins - *Chairman*

Abbitt	Cleveland

ELECTRICAL AND MECHANICAL OFFICE EQUIPMENT

Dent - *Chairman*

Nedzi	Schwengel
Podell	Harvey
Brademas	Dickinson
Gray	Crane
Gaydos	
Mollohan	

POLICE

Gray - *Chairman*

Hawkins	Dickinson
Gettys	Ware
Annunzio	Veysey
Gaydos	

Interior and Insular Affairs

Public lands, natural resources, territorial possessions of the United States, Indian affairs. *Ext. 2761.*

D 23 - R 15

Wayne N. Aspinall (D Colo.), *Chairman**

James A. Haley (Fla.)	John P. Saylor (Pa.)*
Ed Edmondson (Okla.)	Craig Hosmer (Calif.)
Walter S. Baring (Nev.)	Joe Skubitz (Kan.)
Roy A. Taylor (N.C.)	John Kyl (Iowa)
Harold T. Johnson (Calif.)	Sam Steiger (Ariz.)
Morris K. Udall (Ariz.)	James A. McClure (Idaho)
Phillip Burton (Calif.)	Don H. Clausen (Calif.)
Thomas S. Foley (Wash.)	Philip E. Ruppe (Mich.)
Robert W. Kastenmeier (Wis.)	John N. Happy Camp (Okla.)
James G. O'Hara (Mich.)	Manuel Lujan (N.M.)
William F. Ryan (N.Y.)	Sherman P. Lloyd (Utah)
Patsy T. Mink (Hawaii)	John Dellenback (Ore.)
James Kee (W.Va.)	Keith G. Sebelius (Kan.)
Lloyd Meeds (Wash.)	James D. (Mike) McKevitt (Colo.)
Abraham Kazen Jr. (Texas)	John H. Terry (N.Y.)
Bill D. Burlison (Mo.)	Jorge L. Cordova (P.R.) √
Robert G. Stephens Jr. (Ga.)	√ *Resident Commissioner*
Joseph P. Vigorito (Pa.)	
John Melcher (Mont.)	
Teno Roncalio (Wyo.)	
Nick Begich (Alaska)	
James Abourezk (S.D.)	

ENVIRONMENT

Aspinall - *Chairman*

Haley	Saylor
Edmondson	Hosmer
Baring	Kyl
Taylor	Steiger
Johnson	McClure
Udall	Ruppe
Kastenmeier	Lloyd
O'Hara	Dellenback
Ryan	Sebelius
Kee	Terry
Burlison	
Vigorito	
Roncalio	
Melcher	

INDIAN AFFAIRS

Haley - *Chairman*

Edmondson	Steiger
Taylor	Kyl
Mink	Camp
Meeds	Lujan
Stephens	Sebelius
Melcher	Terry
Begich	
Abourezk	

IRRIGATION AND RECLAMATION

Johnson - *Chairman*

Haley	Hosmer
Edmondson	McClure
Baring	Clausen
Udall	Camp
Foley	Lujan
Meeds	Dellenback
Kazen	McKevitt
Stephens	
Roncalio	
Abourezk	

MINES AND MINING

Edmondson - *Chairman*

Baring	McClure
Burton	Hosmer
Foley	Skubitz
Kastenmeier	Steiger
Kee	Camp
Kazen	McKevitt
Burlison	Cordova
Vigorito	
Melcher	

NATIONAL PARKS AND RECREATION

Taylor - *Chairman*

Johnson	Skubitz
Udall	Kyl
Kastenmeier	McClure
O'Hara	Clausen
Ryan	Ruppe
Mink	Lloyd
Meeds	Sebelius
Kazen	McKevitt
Burlison	Terry
Stephens	Cordova
Melcher	
Roncalio	
Begich	
Abourezk	

PUBLIC LANDS

Baring - *Chairman*

Edmondson	Kyl
Johnson	Steiger
Udall	Clausen
Burton	Ruppe
Kastenmeier	Camp
O'Hara	Lujan
Kee	Lloyd
Melcher	Dellenback
Roncalio	
Begich	
Abourezk	

TERRITORIAL AND INSULAR AFFAIRS

Burton - *Chairman*

Haley	Clausen
Taylor	Hosmer

Foley	Skubitz
Ryan	Ruppe
Mink	Lujan
Meeds	Sebelius
Burlison	McKevitt
Stephens	Cordova
Vigorito	
Roncalio	
Begich	

Internal Security

Investigation of activities to determine if they are subversive. *Ext. 3051.*

D 5 - R 4

Richard H. Ichord (D Mo.), *Chairman*

Claude Pepper (Fla.)	John M. Ashbrook (Ohio)
Edwin W. Edwards (La.)	Roger H. Zion (Ind.)
Richardson Preyer (N.C.)	Fletcher Thompson (Ga.)
Robert F. Drinan (Mass.)	John G. Schmitz (Calif.)

No standing subcommittees.

Interstate and Foreign Commerce

Regulation of interstate and foreign commerce and communications, regulations of interstate transmission of power (except between government projects), inland waterways, railroad labor, civil aeronautics, Weather Bureau, securities and exchanges, interstate oil compacts, natural gas and public health. *Ext. 2927.*

D 25 - R 18

Harley O. Staggers (D W.Va.), *Chairman**

Torbert H. Macdonald (Mass.)	William L. Springer (Ill.)*
John Jarman (Okla.)	Samuel L. Devine (Ohio)
John E. Moss (Calif.)	Ancher Nelsen (Minn.)
John D. Dingell (Mich.)	Hastings Keith (Mass.)
Paul G. Rogers (Fla.)	James T. Broyhill (N.C.)
Lionel Van Deerlin (Calif.)	James Harvey (Mich.)
J. J. Pickle (Texas)	Tim Lee Carter (Ky.)
Fred B. Rooney (Pa.)	Clarence J. Brown (Ohio)
John M. Murphy (N.Y.)	Dan Kuykendall (Tenn.)
David E. Satterfield III (Va.)	Joe Skubitz (Kan.)
Brock Adams (Wash.)	Fletcher Thompson (Ga.)
Ray Blanton (Tenn.)	James F. Hastings (N.Y.)
W. S. (Bill) Stuckey (Ga.)	John G. Schmitz (Calif.)
Peter N. Kyros (Maine)	James M. Collins (Texas)
Bob Eckhardt (Texas)	Louis Frey Jr. (Fla.)
Robert O. Tiernan (R.I.)	John Ware (Pa.)
Richardson Preyer (N.C.)	John Y. McCollister (Neb.)
Bertram L. Podell (N.Y.)	Richard G. Shoup (Mont.)
Henry Helstoski (N.J.)	
James W. Symington (Mo.)	
Charles J. Carney (Ohio)	
Ralph H. Metcalfe (Ill.)	
Goodloe E. Byron (Md.)	
William R. Roy (Kan.)	

COMMERCE AND FINANCE

Moss - *Chairman*

Stuckey	Broyhill
Eckhardt	Ware
Carney	McCollister

COMMUNICATIONS AND POWER

Macdonald - *Chairman*

Van Deerlin	Keith
Rooney	Brown
Tiernan	Collins
Byron	Frey

PUBLIC HEALTH AND ENVIRONMENT

Rogers - *Chairman*

Satterfield	Nelsen
Kyros	Carter
Preyer	Hastings
Symington	Schmitz
Roy	

TRANSPORTATION AND AERONAUTICS

Jarman - *Chairman*

Dingell	Devine
Pickle	Harvey
Murphy	Kuykendall
Adams	Skubitz
Podell	Thompson
Metcalfe	

Special Subcommittee
INVESTIGATIONS
Ext. 4441
Staggers - *Chairman*

Blanton	Springer
Helstoski	Shoup

Judiciary

Judicial proceedings generally, constitutional amendments, civil rights, interstate compacts, immigration and naturalization, apportionment of Representatives, meetings of Congress and attendance of members, Presidential succession. *Ext. 3951.*

D 22 - R 16

Emanuel Celler (D N.Y.), *Chairman*

Peter W. Rodino Jr. (N.J.)	William M. McCulloch (Ohio)
Harold D. Donohue (Mass.)	Richard H. Poff (Va.)
Jack Brooks (Texas)	Edward Hutchinson (Mich.)
John Dowdy (Texas)	Robert McClory (Ill.)
Robert W. Kastenmeier (Wis.)	Henry P. Smith III (N.Y.)
Don Edwards (Calif.)	Charles W. Sandman Jr. (N.J.)
William L. Hungate (Mo.)	Tom Railsback (Ill.)
John Conyers Jr. (Mich.)	Edward G. Biester Jr. (Pa.)
Andrew Jacobs Jr. (Ind.)	Charles E. Wiggins (Calif.)
Joshua Eilberg (Pa.)	David W. Dennis (Ind.)
William F. Ryan (N.Y.)	Hamilton Fish Jr. (N.Y.)
Jerome R. Waldie (Calif.)	R. Lawrence Coughlin (Pa.)
Edwin W. Edwards (La.)	Wiley Mayne (Iowa)
Walter Flowers (Ala.)	Lawrence J. Hogan (Md.)
James R. Mann (S.C.)	William J. Keating (Ohio)

Abner J. Mikva (Ill.)	James D. (Mike) McKevitt (Colo.)
Paul S. Sarbanes (Md.)	
John F. Seiberling Jr. (Ohio)	
James Abourezk (S.D.)	
George E. Danielson (Calif.)	
Robert F. Drinan (Mass.)	

SUBCOMMITTEE NO. 1
Ext. 5727
Rodino - *Chairman*

Dowdy	Dennis
Eilberg	Mayne
Ryan	Hogan
Seiberling	McKevitt

SUBCOMMITTEE NO. 2
Ext. 5741
Donohue - *Chairman*

Waldie	Smith
Flowers	Sandman
Mann	Railsback
Danielson	

SUBCOMMITTEE NO. 3
Ext. 3927
Kastenmeier - *Chairman*

Conyers	Railsback
Ryan	Biester
Mikva	Fish
Drinan	Coughlin

SUBCOMMITTEE NO. 4
Ext. 7709
Edwards (Calif.) - *Chairman*

Conyers	Wiggins
Jacobs	Sandman
Waldie	Keating
Edwards (La.)	McClory
Sarbanes	

SUBCOMMITTEE NO. 5
Ext. 4853
Celler - *Chairman*

Brooks	McCulloch
Hungate	Poff
Jacobs	Hutchinson
Mikva	McClory
Abourezk	

Merchant Marine and Fisheries

Merchant marine generally, Coast Guard, Coast and Geodetic Survey, maintenance and operation of Panama Canal and administration of Canal Zone, fisheries and wildlife. *Ext. 4047.*

D 22 - R 15

Edward A. Garmatz (D Md.), *Chairman**

Leonor K. Sullivan (Mo.)	Thomas M. Pelly (Wash.)*
Frank M. Clark (Pa.)	William S. Mailliard (Calif.)
Thomas L. Ashley (Ohio)	Charles A. Mosher (Ohio)
John D. Dingell (Mich.)	James A. Grover Jr. (N.Y.)
Alton Lennon (N.C.)	Hastings Keith (Mass.)
Thomas N. Downing (Va.)	Philip E. Ruppe (Mich.)
James A. Byrne (Pa.)	George A. Goodling (Pa.)
Paul G. Rogers (Fla.)	William G. Bray (Ind.)

Frank A. Stubblefield (Ky.)
John M. Murphy (N.Y.)
Joseph E. Karth (Minn.)
Walter B. Jones (N.C.)
Robert L. Leggett (Calif.)
Speedy O. Long (La.)
Mario Biaggi (N.Y.)
Charles H. Griffin (Miss.)
Glenn M. Anderson (Calif.)
Eligio de la Garza (Texas)
Peter N. Kyros (Maine)
Robert O. Tiernan (R.I.)
James V. Stanton (Ohio)

Paul N. McCloskey Jr. (Calif.)
Jack H. McDonald (Mich.)
M. G. (Gene) Snyder (Ky.)
Robert H. Steele (Conn.)
Edwin B. Forsythe (N.J.)
Pierre S. (Pete) du Pont (Del.)
Vacancy

COAST GUARD, COAST AND GEODETIC SURVEY, AND NAVIGATION

Clark - *Chairman*

Lennon	Keith
Byrne	Grover
Sullivan	Ruppe
Rogers	McDonald
Jones	Bray
Stubblefield	Snyder
Biaggi	Steele
Griffin	du Pont
de la Garza	
Tiernan	
Stanton	

FISHERIES AND WILDLIFE CONSERVATION

Dingell - *Chairman*

Lennon	Pelly
Downing	Keith
Karth	Goodling
Rogers	McCloskey
Leggett	McDonald
Long	Mailliard
Biaggi	Ruppe
Anderson	Forsythe
de la Garza	
Kyros	
Tiernan	

MERCHANT MARINE

Garmatz - *Chairman*

Ashley	Mailliard
Downing	Mosher
Rogers	Grover
Stubblefield	Ruppe
Murphy	Bray
Dingell	McCloskey
Byrne	Steele
Sullivan	du Pont
Clark	Vacancy
Lennon	
Karth	
Jones	
Leggett	

OCEANOGRAPHY

Lennon - *Chairman*

Rogers	Mosher
Ashley	Keith
Downing	Goodling
Karth	Mailliard
Clark	Steele
Jones	Forsythe
Leggett	du Pont
Griffin	Vacancy
Anderson	Vacancy
Biaggi	
de la Garza	
Tiernan	
Kyros	

PANAMA CANAL

Murphy - *Chairman*

Sullivan	Grover
Clark	Mosher
Byrne	Bray
Stubblefield	Snyder
Jones	McDonald
Karth	Forsythe
Long	
Stanton	

Special Subcommittee

MARITIME EDUCATION AND TRAINING

Long - *Chairman*

Downing	McCloskey
Murphy	Snyder
Anderson	Vacancy
de la Garza	Vacancy
Kyros	
Stanton	

Post Office and Civil Service

Postal and federal civil services, census, National Archives. Ext. 4057.

D 15 - R 11

Thaddeus J. Dulski (D N.Y.), *Chairman**

David N. Henderson (N.C.)	H. R. Gross (Iowa)*
Morris K. Udall (Ariz.)	Edward J. Derwinski (Ill.)
Dominick V. Daniels (N.J.)	Albert W. Johnson (Pa.)
Robert N. C. Nix (Pa.)	William Lloyd Scott (Va.)
James M. Hanley (N.Y.)	James A. McClure (Idaho)
Charles H. Wilson (Calif.)	Lawrence J. Hogan (Md.)
Jerome R. Waldie (Calif.)	John H. Rousselot (Calif.)
Richard C. White (Texas)	Elwood Hillis (Ind.)
William D. Ford (Mich.)	Walter E. Powell (Ohio)
Lee H. Hamilton (Ind.)	C. W. Bill Young (Fla.)
Frank J. Brasco (N.Y.)	Vacancy
Graham Purcell (Texas)	
Tom Bevill (Ala.)	
Bill Chappell Jr. (Fla.)	

CENSUS AND STATISTICS
Ext. 3718
Wilson - *Chairman*

Bevill	Rousselot
Hanley	McClure
Chappell	Young
Udall	

EMPLOYEE BENEFITS
Ext. 6295
Hanley - *Chairman*

Brasco	Hogan
Udall	Hillis
Wilson	Powell
White	

INVESTIGATIONS
Ext. 7620
Dulski - *Chairman*

Daniels	Johnson
Hamilton	Gross
Purcell	Scott
Henderson	

MANPOWER AND CIVIL SERVICE
Ext. 2821
Henderson - *Chairman*

White	Derwinski
Ford	Gross
Bevill	Rousselot
Chappell	

POSTAL FACILITIES AND MAIL
Ext. 6741
Nix - *Chairman*

Purcell	McClure
Henderson	Johnson
Hanley	Young
Bevill	

POSTAL SERVICE
Ext. 7620
Udall - *Chairman*

Ford	Gross
Nix	Derwinski
Waldie	Hillis
Hamilton	

RETIREMENT, INSURANCE AND HEALTH BENEFITS
Ext. 6831
Waldie - *Chairman*

Chappell	Scott
Daniels	Hogan
White	Powell
Brasco	

Public Works

Public buildings and roads, flood control, improvement of rivers and harbors, water power, stream pollution. *Ext. 4472.*

D 23 - R 14

John A. Blatnik (D Minn.), *Chairman**

Robert E. Jones (Ala.)	William H. Harsha (Ohio)*
John C. Kluczynski (Ill.)	James R. Grover Jr. (N.Y.)
Jim Wright (Texas)	James C. Cleveland (N.H.)
Kenneth J. Gray (Ill.)	Don H. Clausen (Calif.)
Frank M. Clark (Pa.)	Fred Schwengel (Iowa)
Ed Edmondson (Okla.)	M. G. (Gene) Snyder (Ky.)
Harold T. Johnson (Calif.)	Roger H. Zion (Ind.)
William Jennings Bryan	Jack H. McDonald (Mich.)
Dorn (S.C.)	John Paul Hammerschmidt (Ark.)

David N. Henderson (N.C.)	Clarence E. Miller (Ohio)
Ray Roberts (Texas)	Wilmer Mizell (N.C.)
James Kee (W. Va.)	John H. Terry (N.Y.)
James J. Howard (N.J.)	Charles Thone (Neb.)
Glenn M. Anderson (Calif.)	LaMar Baker (Tenn.)
Patrick T. Caffery (La.)	
Robert A. Roe (N.J.)	
George W. Collins (Ill.)	
Teno Roncalio (Wyo.)	
Nick Begich (Alaska)	
Mike McCormack (Wash.)	
Charles B. Rangel (N.Y.)	
James V. Stanton (Ohio)	
Bella S. Abzug (N.Y.)	

FLOOD CONTROL AND INTERNAL DEVELOPMENT
Jones - *Chairman*

Wright	Clausen
Gray	Grover
Clark	Schwengel
Johnson	Snyder
Edmondson	Zion
Dorn	McDonald
Henderson	Hammerschmidt
Roberts	Miller
Kee	Mizell
Andeson	Baker
Roe	
Caffery	
Begich	
McCormack	

INVESTIGATIONS AND OVERSIGHT
Ext. 3274
Wright - *Chairman*

Jones	Cleveland
Kluczynski	Harsha
Gray	Grover
Clark	Clausen
Edmondson	Snyder
Johnson	Zion
Dorn	McDonald
Howard	Hammerschmidt
Caffery	Mizell
Roe	Terry
Collins	Thone
McCormack	
Rangel	
Stanton	
Abzug	

PUBLIC BUILDINGS AND GROUNDS
Gray - *Chairman*

Jones	Grover
Kluczynski	Cleveland
Wright	Schwengel
Roberts	Snyder
Kee	McDonald
Johnson	Miller
Howard	Mizell
Anderson	Terry
Caffery	Thone
Roe	Baker
Collins	
Roncalio	
Rangel	
Abzug	

RIVERS AND HARBORS
Roberts - *Chairman*

Johnson	Snyder
Gray	Harsha
Wright	Grover
Henderson	Cleveland
Dorn	Clausen
Howard	Zion
Anderson	McDonald
Caffery	Hammerschmidt
Roe	Terry
Clark	Thone
Roncalio	Baker
Begich	
McCormack	
Stanton	
Abzug	

ROADS
Kluczynski - *Chairman*

Jones	Harsha
Clark	Cleveland
Edmondson	Clausen
Wright	Schwengel
Howard	Zion
Dorn	McDonald
Henderson	Hammerschmidt
Roberts	Mizell
Anderson	Terry
Collins	Thone
Roncalio	
McCormack	
Rangel	
Stanton	

WATERSHED DEVELOPMENT
Kee - *Chairman*

Kluczynski	Schwengel
Edmondson	Grover
Dorn	Snyder
Anderson	Zion
Caffery	Miller
Roncalio	Baker
Begich	
McCormack	

Special Subcommittee

ECONOMIC DEVELOPMENT PROGRAMS
Ext. 6151
Blatnik - *Chairman*

Edmondson	Hammerschmidt
Henderson	Harsha
Roberts	Cleveland
Kee	Clausen
Howard	Schwengel
Roe	Miller
Gray	Mizell
Johnson	Terry
Collins	Thone
Roncalio	Baker
Begich	
Rangel	
Stanton	
Abzug	

Rules

Rules and order of business of the House. *Ext. 4121.*

D 10 - R 5

William M. Colmer (D Miss.), *Chairman*

Ray J. Madden (Ind.)	H. Allen Smith (Calif.)
James J. Delaney (N.Y.)	John B. Anderson (Ill.)
Richard Bolling (Mo.)	Dave Martin (Neb.)
Thomas P. O'Neill Jr. (Mass.)	James H. Quillen (Tenn.)
B. F. Sisk (Calif.)	Delbert L. Latta (Ohio)
John Young (Texas)	
Claude Pepper (Fla.)	
Spark M. Matsunaga (Hawaii)	
William R. Anderson (Tenn.)	
No standing subcommittees.	

Science and Astronautics

Scientific and astronautical research and development generally, National Aeronautics and Space Administration, National Aeronautics and Space Council, National Science Foundation, outer space, science scholarships, Bureau of Standards. *Ext. 6371.*

D 18 - R 12

George P. Miller (D Calif.), *Chairman**

Olin E. Teague (Texas)	James G. Fulton (Pa.)*
Joseph E. Karth (Minn.)	Charles A. Mosher (Ohio)
Ken Hechler (W.Va.)	Alphonzo Bell (Calif.)
John W. Davis (Ga.)	Thomas M. Pelly (Wash.)
Thomas N. Downing (Va.)	John W. Wydler (N.Y.)
Don Fuqua (Fla.)	Larry Winn Jr. (Kan.)
Earle Cabell (Texas)	Robert Price (Texas)
James W. Symington (Mo.)	Louis Frey Jr. (Fla.)
Richard T. Hanna (Calif.)	Barry M. Goldwater Jr. (Calif.)
Walter Flowers (Ala.)	Marvin L. Esch (Mich.)
Robert A. Roe (N.J.)	R. Lawrence Coughlin (Pa.)
John F. Seiberling Jr. (Ohio)	John N. Happy Camp (Okla.)
William R. Cotter (Conn.)	
Charles B. Rangel (N.Y.)	
Morgan F. Murphy (Ill.)	
Mike McCormack (Wash.)	
Vacancy	

ADVANCED RESEARCH AND TECHNOLOGY
Hechler - *Chairman*

Davis	Pelly
Cotter	Wydler
Rangel	Goldwater
McCormack	Esch

INTERNATIONAL COOPERATION IN SCIENCE AND SPACE
Fuqua - *Chairman*

Davis	Fulton [1]
Roe	Mosher [1]
Cotter	Bell
Murphy	Winn

MANNED SPACE FLIGHT
Teague - *Chairman*

Fuqua	Fulton
Cabell	Bell
Hanna	Winn
Flowers	Price
Roe	Frey

NASA OVERSIGHT
Downing - *Chairman*

Teague	Wydler[1]
Karth	Price[1]
Hechler	Goldwater
Flowers	Camp
Rangel	

SCIENCE, RESEARCH AND DEVELOPMENT
Davis - *Chairman*

Cabell	Bell
Symington	Mosher
Hanna	Frey
Seiberling	Esch
McCormack	Coughlin

SPACE SCIENCES AND APPLICATIONS
Karth - *Chairman*

Downing	Mosher
Symington	Winn
Seiberling	Price
Murphy	Goldwater

1 Ranking minority position shared by both members.

Select Crime Investigation

Investigation of all aspects of crime. *Ext. 4504.*

D 6 - R 5

Claude Pepper (D Fla.), *Chairman*

Jerome R. Waldie (Calif.)	Charles E. Wiggins (Calif.)
Frank J. Brasco (N.Y.)	Sam Steiger (Ariz.)
James R. Mann (S.C.)	Larry Winn Jr. (Kan.)
Morgan F. Murphy (Ill.)	Charles W. Sandman Jr. (N.J.)
Charles B. Rangel (N.Y.)	William J. Keating (Ohio)

No standing subcommittees.

Select Small Business

Studies and investigates problems of small business and reports findings and makes recommendations to the House, but cannot report legislation. *Ext. 5821.*

D 12 - R 7

Joe L. Evins (D Tenn.), *Chairman**

Tom Steed (Okla.)	Silvio O. Conte (Mass.)*
John C. Kluczynski (Ill.)	James T. Broyhill (N.C.)
John D. Dingell (Mich.)	Frank J. Horton (N.Y.)
Neal Smith (Iowa)	J. William Stanton (Ohio)
James C. Corman (Calif.)	Joseph M. McDade (Pa.)
Joseph P. Addabbo (N.Y.)	Manuel Lujan Jr. (N.M.)
William L. Hungate (Mo.)	James D. (Mike) McKevitt (Colo.)
Fernand J. St Germain (R.I.)	
Charles J. Carney (Ohio)	
Parren J. Mitchell (Md.)	
Bob Bergland (Minn.)	

ACTIVITIES OF REGULATORY AGENCIES RELATING TO SMALL BUSINESS
Ext. 4351
Dingell - *Chairman*

Hungate	Conte
St Germain	Broyhill

ENVIRONMENTAL PROBLEMS AFFECTING SMALL BUSINESS
Hungate - *Chairman*

Smith	McKevitt
Carney	Horton

FOUNDATIONS: THEIR IMPACT ON SMALL BUSINESS
Ext. 3851
Patman - *Chairman*

St Germain	Stanton
Mitchell	Lujan

GOVERNMENT PROCUREMENT
Ext. 4881
Corman - *Chairman*

Smith	Broyhill
Addabbo	Horton

MINORITY SMALL BUSINESS ENTERPRISE
Addabbo - *Chairman*

Corman	Lujan
Mitchell	Conte

SMALL BUSINESS PROBLEMS IN SMALLER TOWNS AND URBAN AREAS
Ext. 4351
Kluczynski - *Chairman*

Corman	Horton
Carney	Stanton

SPECIAL SMALL BUSINESS PROBLEMS
Smith - *Chairman*

Addabbo	McDade
Hungate	Broyhill

TAXATION, OIL IMPORTS AND MARKETING
Steed - *Chairman*

Kluczynski	Stanton
Dingell	McKevitt

Standards of Official Conduct

Studies and investigates standards of conduct of House members and employees and may recommend remedial action. *Ext. 7103.*

D 6 - R 6

Melvin Price (D Ill.), *Chairman*

Olin E. Teague (Texas)	Jackson E. Betts (Ohio)
Watkins M. Abbitt (Va.)	Robert T. Stafford (Vt.)
Wayne N. Aspinall (Colo.)	James H. (Jimmy) Quillen (Tenn.)
F. Edward Hebert (La.)	Lawrence G. Williams (Pa.)
Chet Holifield (Calif.)	Edward Hutchinson (Mich.)
	Charlotte T. Reid (Ill.)

No standing subcommittees.

Veterans' Affairs

Veterans' measures generally; pensions, armed forces life insurance, rehabilitation, education, medical care and treatment of veterans, veterans' hospitals. *Ext. 3527.*

D 16 - R 10

Olin E. Teague (D Texas), *Chairman**

William Jennings Bryan Dorn (S.C.)	Charles M. Teague (Calif.)*
James A. Haley (Fla.)	John P. Saylor (Pa.)
Walter S. Baring (Nev.)	John Paul Hammerschmidt (Ark.)
Thaddeus J. Dulski (N.Y.)	William Lloyd Scott (Va.)
Ray Roberts (Texas)	Margaret M. Heckler (Mass.)
David E. Satterfield III (Va.)	John M. Zwach (Minn.)
Henry Helstoski (N.J.)	Chalmers P. Wylie (Ohio)
Roman C. Pucinski (Ill.)	Larry Winn Jr. (Kan.)
Don Edwards (Calif.)	Earl B. Ruth (N.C.)
G. V. (Sonny) Montgomery (Miss.)	Elwood Hillis (Ind.)
Charles J. Carney (Ohio)	
Louise Day Hicks (Mass.)	
George E. Danielson (Calif.)	
Ella T. Grasso (Conn.)	
Lester L. Wolff (N.Y.)	

The Committee's subcommittees had not been organized at the time of publication.

Ways and Means

Revenue measures generally, tariffs and reciprocal trade agreements, Social Security. *Ext. 3625.*

D 15 - R 10

Wilbur D. Mills (D Ark.), *Chairman*

John C. Watts (Ky.)	John W. Byrnes (Wis.)
Al Ullman (Ore.)	Jackson E. Betts (Ohio)
James A. Burke (Mass.)	Herman T. Schneebeli (Pa.)
Martha W. Griffiths (Mich.)	Harold R. Collier (Ill.)
Dan Rostenkowski (Ill.)	Joel T. Broyhill (Va.)
Phil M. Landrum (Ga.)	Barber B. Conable Jr. (N.Y.)
Charles A. Vanik (Ohio)	Charles E. Chamberlain (Mich.)
Richard Fulton (Tenn.)	Jerry L. Pettis (Calif.)
Omar Burleson (Texas)	John J. Duncan (Tenn.)
James C. Corman (Calif.)	Donald G. Brotzman (Colo.)
William J. Green (Pa.)	
Sam Gibbons (Fla.)	
Hugh L. Carey (N.Y.)	
Joe D. Waggonner Jr. (La.)	

No standing subcommittees.

HOUSE DEMOCRATIC LEADERSHIP

Chairman of the Caucus - Olin E. Teague (Texas)
Secretary of the Caucus - Leonor K. Sullivan (Mo.)
Floor Leader - Hale Boggs (La.)
Whip - Thomas P. O'Neill Jr. (Mass.)
  Floor Whips - John Brademas (Ind.), John J. McFall (Calif.)
  Assistant Whips, by zone numbers:
  1. Torbert H. Macdonald (Mass.) - Massachusetts, Connecticut, Maine, Rhode Island.
  2. Samuel S. Stratton (N.Y.) - New York State.
     Hugh L. Carey (N.Y.) - New York City.
  3. William S. Moorhead (Pa.) - Pennsylvania.
  4. Peter W. Rodino Jr. (N.J.) - New Jersey, Maryland.
  5. David E. Satterfield III (Va.) - Virginia, North Carolina.

  6. John J. Flynt Jr. (Ga.) - Georgia, South Carolina.
  7. Clement J. Zablocki (Wis.) - Wisconsin, Michigan, Minnesota.
  8. Lee H. Hamilton (Ind.) - Indiana, Alaska.
  9. Harley O. Staggers (W.Va.) - West Virginia, Ohio.
  10. Richard Fulton (Tenn.) - Tennessee, Arkansas, Kentucky.
  11. G. V. (Sonny) Montgomery (Miss.) - Mississippi, Louisiana.
  12. Tom Bevill (Ala.) - Alabama, Florida.
  13. Leonor K. Sullivan (Mo.) - Missouri, Iowa.
  14. Dan Rostenkowski (Ill.) - Illinois.
  15. Jim Wright (Texas) - Texas.
  16. Ed Edmondson (Okla.) - Oklahoma, Hawaii, Kansas, North Dakota, South Dakota.
  17. Edith Green (Ore.) - Oregon, Arizona, Colorado, Montana, Nevada, New Mexico, Utah, Washington, Wyoming.
  18. George E. Danielson (Calif.) - California.

The five states not covered—Delaware, Idaho, Nebraska, New Hampshire and Vermont—have no Democratic Representatives.

Committee on Committees

The Democratic members of the House Ways and Means Committee comprise the Democratic Committee on Committees.

Democratic National Congressional Committee

The Committee had not completed its organization at the time of publication.

Steering Committee

Ext. 7187

Ray J. Madden (Ind.), *Chairman*

Watkins M. Abbitt (Va.)	John S. Monagan (Conn.)
Carl Albert (Okla.)†	Thomas P. O'Neill Jr. (Mass.)†
Bill Alexander (Ark.)	Wright Patman (Texas)
Thomas L. Ashley (Ohio)	Bertram L. Podell (N.Y.)
John Brademas (Ind.)†	Melvin Price (Ill.)
Hale Boggs (La.)†	Peter W. Rodino Jr. (N.J.)
John H. Dent (Pa.)	Paul G. Rogers (Fla.)
William Jennings Bryan Dorn (S.C.)	Teno Roncalio (Wyo.)
Julia Butler Hansen (Wash.)	Neal Smith (Iowa)
Chet Holifield (Calif.)	Leonor K. Sullivan (Mo.)†
Joseph E. Karth (Minn.)	Olin E. Teague (Texas)†
John J. McFall (Calif.)†	Joe D. Waggonner (La.)
Spark M. Matsunaga (Hawaii)	

Patronage Committee

Ext. 4068

Joe L. Evins (Tenn.), *Chairman*

Augustus F. Hawkins (Calif.)	B. F. Sisk (Calif.)
Thomas E. Morgan (Pa.)	James W. Symington (Mo.)

HOUSE REPUBLICAN LEADERSHIP

Chairman of the Conference - John B. Anderson (Ill.)
Secretary of the Conference - Richard H. Poff (Va.)
Floor Leader - Gerald R. Ford (Mich.)
Whip - Leslie C. Arends (Ill.)

The assistant minority whips are divided into three divisions, each with an over-all regional whip and assistant whips in charge of specific states as follow:

Eastern Division—Robert T. Stafford (Vt.)
Silvio O. Conte (Mass.)—Connecticut, Delaware, Massachusetts, New Hampshire, Vermont.
John W. Wydler (N.Y.)—New York.
Albert W. Johnson (Pa.)—New Jersey, Pennsylvania.
James T. Broyhill (N.C.)—Florida, Georgia, Maryland, North Carolina, South Carolina, Virginia.

Midwest Division—Jackson E. Betts (Ohio)
Robert H. Michel (Ill.)—Illinois.
John T. Myers (Ind.)—Indiana.
Elford A. Cederberg (Mich.)—Michigan, Wisconsin.
Samuel L. Devine (Ohio)—Ohio.
John H. Kyl (Iowa)—Iowa, Minnesota, Missouri, Montana, North Dakota.
Joe Skubitz (Kan.)—Kansas, Nebraska, Oklahoma.

Western and Southern Division—Burt L. Talcott (Calif.)
Jack Edwards (Ala.)—Alabama, Arkansas, Kentucky, Tennessee, Texas.
James A. McClure (Idaho)—Arizona, Colorado, Idaho, New Mexico, Oregon, Utah, Washington.
Victor V. Veysey (Calif.)—California.
The ten states not covered—Alaska, Hawaii, Louisiana, Maine, Mississippi, Nevada, Rhode Island, South Dakota, West Virginia and Wyoming—do not have Republican Representatives.

Policy Committee

Advises on party action and policy. *Ext. 6168.*

John J. Rhodes (Ariz.), *Chairman*

John B. Anderson (Ill.)	Delbert L. Latta (Ohio)
Leslie C. Arends (Ill.)	Thomas M. Pelly (Wash.)
Page Belcher (Okla.)	Alexander Pirnie (N.Y.)
James T. Broyhill (N.C.)	Richard H. Poff (Va.)
John W. Byrnes (Wis.)	J. Kenneth Robinson (Va.)
Barber B. Conable Jr. (N.Y.)	H. Allen Smith (Calif.)
Jack Edwards (Ala.)	William L. Springer (Ill.)
Hamilton Fish Jr. (N.Y.)	Robert T. Stafford (Vt.)
Gerald R. Ford (Mich.)	J. William Stanton (Ohio)
Peter H. B. Frelinghuysen (N.J.)	Charles M. Teague (Calif.)
James R. Grover Jr. (N.Y.)	Bob Wilson (Calif.)
James Harvey (Mich.)	Vacancy
John H. Kyl (Iowa)	

Committee on Committees

Makes Republican committee assignments. *Ext. 3831.*

Gerald R. Ford (Mich.), *Chairman*

Mark Andrews (N.D.)	James A. McClure (Idaho)

Leslie C. Arends (Ill.)
Frank T. Bow (Ohio)
William G. Bray (Ill.)
John N. Happy Camp (Okla.)
Tim Lee Carter (Ky.)
Elford A. Cederberg (Mich.)
William L. Dickinson (Ala.)
Pierre S. (Pete) du Pont (Del.)
Peter H. B. Frelinghuysen (N.J.)
Louis Frey Jr. (Fla.)
James G. Fulton (Pa.)
H. R. Gross (Iowa)
Gilbert Gude (Md.)
Durward G. Hall (Mo.)
John Paul Hammerschmidt (Ark.)
Hastings Keith (Mass.)
Sherman P. Lloyd (Utah)
Manuel Lujan Jr. (N.M.)
Dave Martin (Neb.)

James A. McClure (Idaho)
James D. (Mike) McKevitt (Colo.)
Ancher Nelsen (Minn.)
Thomas M. Pelly (Wash.)
Robert D. Price (Texas)
James H. (Jimmy) Quillen (Tenn.)
John J. Rhodes (Ariz.)
Howard W. Robison (N.Y.)
Earl B. Ruth (N.C.)
Garner E. Shriver (Kan.)
H. Allen Smith (Calif.)
Floyd Spence (S.C.)
Robert T. Stafford (Vt.)
Robert H. Steele (Conn.)
Fletcher Thompson (Ga.)
Vernon W. Thomson (Wis.)
William C. Wampler (Va.)
Wendell Wyatt (Ore.)
Louis C. Wyman (N.H.)

National Republican Congressional Committee

LI 4-3010

Bob Wilson (Calif.), *Chairman*

Mark Andrews (N.D.)	Dan Kuykendall (Tenn.)
Page Belcher (Okla.)	Sherman P. Lloyd (Utah)
Ben B. Blackburn (Ga.)	Manuel Lujan Jr. (N.M.)
William S. Broomfield (Mich.)	William M. McCulloch (Ohio)
Donald G. Brotzman (Colo.)	Stewart B. McKinney (Conn.)
Joel T. Broyhill (Va.)	Wilmer Mizell (N.C.)
John Buchanan (Ala.)	Thomas M. Pelly (Wash.)
J. Herbert Burke (Fla.)	Albert H. Quie (Minn.)
Del Clawson (Calif.)	John P. Saylor (Pa.)
James C. Cleveland (N.H.)	Fred Schwengel (Iowa)
James M. Collins (Texas)	Richard G. Shoup (Mont.)
Silvio O. Conte (Mass.)	Joe Skubitz (Kan.)
Glenn R. Davis (Wis.)	Floyd Spence (S.C.)
John R. Dellenback (Ore.)	William L. Springer (Ill.)
Pierre S. (Pete) du Pont (Del.)	M. G. (Gene) Snyder (Ky.)
Durward G. Hall (Mo.)	Robert T. Stafford (Vt.)
John Paul Hammerschmidt (Ark.)	Sam Steiger (Ariz.)
Orval Hansen (Idaho)	Charles Thone (Neb.)
Lawrence J. Hogan (Md.)	William B. Widnall (N.J.)
Carleton J. King (N.Y.)	Roger H. Zion (Ind.)

Research Committee

Ext. 5107

Barber B. Conable Jr. (N.Y.), *Chairman*

John B. Anderson (Ill.)†	F. Bradford Morse (Mass.)
Leslie C. Arends (Ill.)†	Richard H. Poff (Vat.)†
Elford A. Cederberg (Mich.)	John J. Rhodes (Ariz.)†
Samuel L. Devine (Ohio)	H. Allen Smith (Calif.)†
Jack Edwards (Ala.)	Robert T. Stafford (Vt.)†
John N. Erlenborn (Ill.)	William A. Steiger (Wis.)
Gerald R. Ford (Mich.)†	Victor V. Veysey (Calif.)
John H. Kyl (Iowa)	Bob Wilson (Calif.)†

CLOSED AND OPEN COMMITTEE MEETINGS, 1953-1970

Forty-one percent of all congressional committee meetings were held behind closed doors during 1970, an increase of five percentage points over 1969.

This is the third highest incidence of executive (closed) sessions since Congressional Quarterly started keeping records in 1953. The record was 43 percent in 1968.

The 91st Congress passed reform legislation—the first in 24 years—aimed, in part, as opening up its proceedings to public scrutiny. Still, closed meetings rose from 36 percent in 1969 to 41 percent in 1970 in that same 91st Congress.

The committees in the House, as usual, had the highest percentage of secret meetings. Forty-eight percent of all House committee meetings were held in executive session, as compared to 42 percent in 1969.

Senate committees barred the public from 33 percent of their meetings, an increase of five percentage points over the 28 percent recorded in the first session of the 91st Congress.

Joint Congressional committees continued to open most of their meetings to the public. During 1970, only 17 of 102 such meetings were held in executive session.

Statistics on open and closed committee meetings since 1953, when Congressional Quarterly began its annual study, are given below. (*Standards used in compiling the study, box next column.*)

Year	Total Meetings	Number Closed	Percent Closed
1953	2,640	892	35%
1954	3,002	1,243	41
1955	2,940	1,055	36
1956	3,120	1,130	36
1957	2,517	854	34
1958	3,472	1,167	34
1959	3,152	940	30
1960	2,424	840	35
1961	3,159	1,109	35
1962	2,929	991	34
1963	3,868	1,463	38
1964	2,393	763	32
1965	3,903	1,537	39
1966	3,869	1,626	42
1967	4,412	1,716	39
1968	3,080	1,328	43
1969	4,029	1,470	36
1970	4,506	1,865	41
Total*	59,415	21,989	37%

*Meetings of the House Appropriations Committee, all reported closed, were not included in the study until 1965.

House Committees. The House Appropriations Committee remained true to tradition—all of the 379 sessions reported in the *Congressional Record* were closed. (Committee staff members reported one open meeting on the District of Columbia appropriations and eight open meetings on public works. However, since these were reported as closed in the Daily Digest, they were carried as executive sessions in CQ tabulations.)

Among other committees holding more than 100 meetings, high scorers in the secrecy column included Agriculture, which closed 76 percent of its 131 meetings; Ways and Means, 70 percent of 120 meetings; Armed Services, 57 percent of 215 meetings.

Several other committees which met frequently, but in open session, helped the House to achieve its more balanced over-all score of 48 percent. The leader among these was the Committee on Education and Labor which held only 15 of its 220 meetings, or seven percent, in executive session. Both the Foreign Affairs Committee and the Interior and Insular Affairs Committee closed only 24 percent of their meetings; Banking and Currency, 27 percent; Merchant Marine and Fisheries, 34 percent.

Of committees which met fewer than 100 times, those secluding themselves more often than not were the House Administration Committee, Select Committee on Crime and Committee on Standards of Official Conduct.

The Select Committee on Small Business welcomed the public to all of its 26 meetings.

Senate Committees. Of those Senate committees which met more than 100 times in 1970, only two held more than half of their meetings in executive session. The Armed Services Committee held 94 of its 120 meetings, or 78 percent, in executive session. The Foreign Relations Committee closed 65 of its 127 meetings, or 51 percent.

Notable among those Senate committees which met more than 100 times, frequently in open session, was the Appropriations Committee. In sharp contrast to its counterpart in the House, the Senate committee closed only 76 of its 258 meetings, or 29 percent. Other low scorers were the Judiciary Committee which closed only 17 percent of its sessions; Commerce, 20 percent; Labor and Public Welfare, 28 percent; Interior and Insular Affairs, 30 percent; Public Works, 32 percent.

The Committee on Rules and Administration was the leader of Senate committees which met fewer than 100 times and often in closed session. The public was barred from 14 of its 19 meetings. The Post Office and Civil Service Committee closed 15 of its 21 meetings. Agriculture and Forestry held 57 percent of its meetings in executive session.

The Senate Special Committee on Aging opened all of its 16 meetings.

Congressional Reform. Since 1953, 37 percent of Congressional committee meetings have been held in executive session. Over the years several attempts have been made to reduce committee secrecy.

The 1946 Legislative Reorganization Act—the first of its kind in Congressional history—required that all hearings held by standing committees or their subcommittees be open, except sessions for marking up bills or for voting or meetings in which a majority of the committee votes for an executive session.

Proponents of reform began to seek more effective rules regarding committee proceedings in recent years. The Joint Committee on the Organization of Congress was created in 1965. Reporting in July 1966, the Committee made several recommendations to reduce secrecy. In 1967, the Senate passed S 355 which contained provisions similar to the suggestions of the Joint Committee on the Organization of Congress. The bill died the following year in the House Rules Committee.

In the second session of the 91st Congress, the first reform law since 1946 was enacted. The measure (HR 17654, PL 91-510) contained several provisions affecting the conduct of committee meetings. They included:

● Business meetings of Senate standing committees shall be open to the public except for marking up bills or for voting or when the committee, by majority vote, orders an executive session.

● Business meetings of House standing committees shall be open to the public except when the committee, by majority vote, determines otherwise.

● All roll-call votes taken in the meetings of Senate standing committees on any measure or amendment shall be included in the committee report on the measure, unless previously announced.

Ground Rules

Tabulations in CQ's open-closed committee study were derived mainly from information appearing in the Daily Digest section of the *Congressional Record*, the official journal of Congressional proceedings. Section 221 of the Legislative Reorganization Act of 1946 states that the Joint Printing Committee "is authorized and directed to provide for printing in the Daily Record...a list of Congressional committee hearings and meetings, the place of meeting and the subject matter; and to cause a brief resume of Congressional activities for the previous day to be incorporated in the *Record.*"

In practice, however, not all committee meetings were listed in the *Record*. Committees used different criteria as to what constituted a meeting. Some did not report their meetings regularly to the *Record;* some said they reported their meetings but they were not carried in the *Record.*

Open meetings followed by closed meetings are counted twice—once in each category. Joint meetings of separate committees are counted as one meeting for each committee. A meeting of a subcommittee is counted as a meeting of the full committee.

The tabulations exclude meetings when Congress was not in regular session; meetings outside of Washington, D.C.; meetings of conference committees to reconcile conflicting Senate and House versions of bills; informal meetings without official status; and meetings of the House Rules Committee to consider sending legislation to the floor (but Rules Committee meetings for other purposes are included).

Meetings held by the House Appropriations Committee were not reported to the *Record*. The CQ tally for the Appropriations Committee was made from a *Record* list of meetings scheduled. The Senate Select Committee on Standards and Conduct had not reported its meetings, all closed, to the *Record* nor stated the number of times it met.

• Roll-call votes in House committee meetings shall be made available in the offices of that committee and, if pertaining to a particular bill, shall be included in the committee report of that bill.

• House and Senate committees must announce the date, place and subject of hearings at least one week in advance, unless the committee finds good cause for beginning them earlier. This provision does not apply to the Senate Committee on Appropriations or the House Committee on Rules.

• Senate committee hearings shall be open except when the committee determines that testimony may relate to national security, may tend to reflect adversely on the character or reputation of an individual or may divulge matters deemed confidential under other provisions of law or government regulation.

• House hearings shall be open except when the committee, by majority vote, determines otherwise.

• Open committee hearings may be covered by radio and television, under such rules as the committee may adopt. (Radio and television coverage had been permitted in the Senate, but not in the House.)

• Hearings on the Budget as a whole in the House Appropriations Committee shall be in open session except when the Committee determines that the testimony to be taken at that hearing may relate to a matter of national security.

Outlook. Whether the 1970 Reorganization Act will in reality give the public greater access to proceedings remains to be seen.

There are certain provisions which probably will be absorbed into committee practice because they are either unobjectionable or cannot be circumvented. The announcement of committee roll calls is an example. However, others—particularly those dealing with the opening of business meetings and hearings—infringe on both tradition and the authority of chairmen. Their implementation is less certain. Several factors must be considered.

Most of the provisions limiting executive sessions are accompanied by exceptions to the rule. Certain hearings and meetings must necessarily be closed. These would involve confidential material, matters of national security and evidence reflecting on the character of an individual.

Most hearings and meetings can be closed by a majority vote of the committee. It is at this point that the influence of committee chairmen enters. In the past committees have rarely opposed the wishes of their leaders.

There has been only one change among chairmen of committees that met more than 100 times and often in closed session. And the newcomer does not appear to be out of place. F. Edward Hebert (D La.), new chairman of the House Armed Services Committee, told Congressional Quarterly, "I believe in having open hearings as often as we can." He said that the Committee will follow the rules of the House. However, he feels the issue has been exaggerated" by the news media and finds that the "only disadvantage to a closed meeting is lack of understanding on the part of the public."

Open and Closed Congressional Committee Meetings

91st Congress

Senate Committees	1969				1970			
	Open	Closed	Total	Percent Closed	Open	Closed	Total	Percent Closed
Astronautics and Space Science	7	7	14	50%	12	3	15	20%
Agriculture and Forestry	25	10	35	29	20	27	47	57
Appropriations	176	59	235	25	182	76	258	29
Armed Services	30	38	68	56	26	94	120	78
Banking and Currency	86	27	113	24	60	29	89	33
Commerce	91	20	111	18	130	32	162	20
District of Columbia	54	6	60	10	29	6	35	17
Finance	41	28	69	41	50	36	86	42
Foreign Relations	63	63	126	50	62	65	127	51
Government Operations	95	14	109	13	45	12	57	21
Interior and Insular Affairs	60	30	90	33	88	37	125	30
Judiciary	78	14	92	15	138	29	167	17
Labor and Public Welfare	127	48	175	27	129	49	178	28
Post Office and Civil Service	33	12	45	27	6	15	21	71
Public Works	46	31	77	40	91	43	134	32
Rules and Administration	4	15	19	79	5	14	19	74
Select Equal Educational Opportunity		(Not in existence)			45	4	49	8
Select Small Business	34	1	35	3	24	1	25	4
Select Standards and Conduct		(Not available)				(Not available)		
Special Aging	23	3	26	12	16	0	16	0
Special Nutrition and Human Needs	12	1	13	8	18	4	22	18
TOTAL	1,085	427	1,512	28%	1,176	576	1,752	33%
House Committees								
Agriculture	83	45	128	35%	32	99	131	76%
Appropriations	0	330	330	100	0	379	379 [1]	100
Armed Services	59	105	164	64	92	123	215	57
Banking and Currency	70	22	92	24	73	27	100	27
District of Columbia	50	23	73	32	49	35	84	42
Education and Labor	180	20	200	10	205	15	220	7
Foreign Affairs	79	73	152	48	133	43	176	24
Government Operations	90	29	119	24	69	19	88	22
House Administration	5	36	41	88	7	58	65	89
Interior and Insular Affairs	85	25	110	23	111	36	147	24
Internal Security	24	4	28	14	41	8	49	16
Interstate and Foreign Commerce	122	45	167	27	144	113	257	44
Judiciary	94	66	160	41	97	77	174	44
Merchant Marine and Fisheries	86	21	107	20	69	36	105	34
Post Office and Civil Service	90	35	125	28	45	30	75	40
Public Works	52	27	79	34	57	41	98	42
Rules	27	15	42	36	24	6	30	20
Science and Astronautics	64	21	85	25	38	14	52	27
Select Crime [2]	14	5	19	26	4	6	10	60
Select Small Business	31	0	31	0	26	0	26	0
Standards of Official Conduct	0	14	14	100	8	12	20	60
Veterans' Affairs	20	13	33	39	20	11	31	35
Ways and Means	65	50	115	43	36	84	120	70
TOTAL	1,390	1,024	2,414	42%	1,380	1,272	2,652	48%
Joint Committees								
Atomic Energy	28	12	40	30%	21	15	36	42%
Defense Production	0	1	1	100	0	0	0	0
Economic	56	5	61	8	64	0	64	0
Others [3]	0	1	1	100	0	2	2	100
TOTAL	84	19	103	18%	85	17	102	17%
GRAND TOTAL	2,559	1,470	4,029	36%	2,641	1,865	4,506	41%

1 Committee staff members reported one open meeting on the District of Columbia appropriations and eight open meetings on public works. However, since these were reported as closed in the Daily Digest, they were carried as executive sessions in tabulations.

2 Established May, 1969.
3 Includes Joint Committees on Internal Revenue Taxation, Library, Printing, Reduction of Nonessential Federal Expenditures and Disposition of Executive Papers.

Appendix—The Powers of Congress

Texts and Other Materials Relating to Chapter 3

Katzenbach Testimony on U.S. Foreign Commitments

Following is the text of a statement by Under Secretary of State Nicholas deB. Katzenbach before the Senate Foreign Relations Committee on Aug. 17, 1967. The Committee was holding hearings on a resolution to limit the involvement of U.S. troops in hostilities overseas.

Mr. KATZENBACH. Thank you, Mr. Chairman. I am delighted to be here and I am accompanied by Mr. Jared Carter, special assistant to the legal adviser.

Mr. Chairman and members of the committee, despite its brevity, the resolution before this committee grapples simultaneously with two of the most important, most enduring, and most complex issues of state in American history.

One of these issues is the allocation of governmental powers, as shaped by our Constitution and by nearly 200 years of experience.

The second issue is the changing role of this nation in the affairs of a changing world.

It is not possible to comment intelligently on the proposed resolution in only a current context. I would like, therefore, to begin my statement of the Administration's views with a few thoughts on the nature and history of both of these issues.

The Constitution and Constitutional Practice

The framers of the Constitution recognized the impossibility of compressing the idea of the separation of powers into a simple formula. They did not attempt to engrave clear lines of demarcation.

With respect to diplomacy, they recognized the complexity of foreign affairs even in the far calmer climate of our nation's childhood—a time when we took as our watchword Washington's declaration that, "It is our true policy to steer clear of permanent alliances, with any portion of the foreign world."

Hence the Constitution contains relatively few details about how foreign policy decisions shall be made and foreign relations conducted. It recognized that the voice of the United States in foreign affairs was, of necessity, the voice of the President. Consistent with that basic necessity, it also provided for the participation of Congress in a number of ways, direct and indirect.

John Jay observed in The Federalist that the Presidency possesses great inherent strengths in the direction of foreign affairs: The unity of the office, its capacity for secrecy and speed, and its superior sources of information.

But, as Professor Corwin has said:

"Despite all this, actual practice under the Constitution has shown that while the President is usually in a position to propose, the Senate and Congress are often in a technical position at least to dispose. The verdict of history, in short, is that the power to determine the substantive content of American foreign policy is a divided power, with the lion's share falling usually to the President, though by no means always."

The Constitution left to the judgment and wisdom of the Executive and the Congress the task of working out the details of their relationships. Disagreements susceptible of decision by the Supreme Court have been rare. As a result, controversies over the line of demarcation in foreign affairs have been settled, in the end, by the instinct of the nation and its leaders for political responsibility.

This has not been an easy formula to apply, even early in our history. President John Adams' use of troops in the Mediterranean, President Monroe's announcement of his renowned doctrine, President Jefferson's Louisiana Purchase, all were criticized at the time as exceeding the power of the Executive acting without the support of a Congressional vote.

Similarly, Presidents have frequently criticized actions by Congress as invasions of their responsibility for the conduct of our foreign affairs.

But if the constitutional formula of flexibility was not an easy one, it has surely proved to be a practical and useful one. It has always seemed to me that the genius of our Constitution rests on the recognition of its drafters that they could not provide precise resolution for all future problems, foreseen and unforeseen. And I think that the conduct of foreign affairs demonstrates the validity of this approach.

Despite occasional differences and debates, history has surely vindicated the wisdom of this flexibility—of this essentially political approach to the conduct of our foreign affairs.

In the world we now live in, answers have not become easier. And yet the constitutional allocation of powers continues to work well today.

Our Changing Role in a Changing World

Let me turn to the nature of our foreign policy and the role of the United States in the world today—to the commitments of this nation in foreign affairs.

The basic objective of our foreign policy is the security of the United States and the preservation of our freedoms. How this objective is achieved obviously depends upon the kind of world in which we live and the extent to which we can bring American power and influence to bear upon it.

For most of our history, we had only spasmodic foreign business. We lived in relative isolation, content to allow the European powers to maintain the balance of power on which, in fact, our national security depended.

In recent years, there has been a revolutionary change in the political structure of the world—and of the relative importance of foreign affairs to the United States. What has been perceived by all—by Presidents, by the Congress, and by the people—is that our independence and our security can no longer be assured by default. They depend in large measure on our capacity to lead in the achievement of a system of assured world peace. Within the broad horizons of such a framework—and only within such horizons—can American democracy and American society be safe.

This framework, I believe, rests on three propositions. The first is that events elsewhere can have critical effects on this country; hence our security is bound up with that of other countries.

The second is that we must heed more than power politics. For if we are true to our domestic ideals and are concerned for our domestic security, we cannot ignore the conditions in which people around the world must live—conditions which can and do fuel reverberating political explosions.

The third is that we cannot and should not meet these first two needs alone, any more than we could or should seek unilaterally to establish a pax Americana. We must develop international instrumentalities to help provide collective security and to help create social progress and eliminate the flammable conditions of misery that embrace so much of the world's population.

The United States has made serious, substantial, and enduring efforts to act on all three of these propositions. I do not think it is susceptible of proof, but I firmly believe that the crises we have avoided as a result of imaginative military and political action are at least as important as the crises we have survived.

Coordinate Action by Congress and President

The progress in our efforts has been substantial—and it has been the result of a national commitment. And this has been possible in large measure because of two factors.

This commitment has not been one of administration or of party, but of bipartisanship. One of the remarkable aspects of American foreign policy in the past 20 years is that it has become bipartisan. Partisan politics have, in fact, stopped at the water's edge.

The second factor is the consistent, coordinate action of the Executive and Legislative Branches, each in their proper sphere, to propose and dispose, to create and carry out a national commitment.

As America's role in the world has mushroomed, so have the foreign affairs responsibilities of both branches. Nothing could have made this more clear than the Vandenberg resolution of 1948 which established an enduring base for the conduct of our foreign relations.

There is a long series of other examples:

The resolution to support Greece and Turkey was passed by the Congress. Under that resolution, the administration provided military and economic aid, with funds appropriated by the Congress. It also sent military advisers to help the Greek Army become a more effective force and to conduct successful operations against Communist guerrillas. Without this action, the vast investment authorized by the Congress might not have paid off.

The Marshall Plan was the result both of Congressional and Executive action—in specifying self-help conditions, in appointing U.S. missions to advise aid recipients, and in agreeing to European proposals regarding apportionment of our aid.

The NATO treaty was approved by the Senate and within its framework, the Executive Branch has joined other nations in creating an integrated military structure, in contributing to the cost of jointly owned military facilities, and in other actions needed to translate that treaty into effective deterrence.

Important to President Eisenhower's decision to use the U.S. fleet in the Straits of Taiwan and his decision to send Marines to Lebanon in 1958 were Congressional resolutions expressing the security interests of the United States in those areas.

President Kennedy's decision to call up reserve and National Guard units at the time of the Berlin crisis accorded not only with our NATO obligations, but also a series of Congressional actions in support of the security of Western Europe.

Beyond specific instances, the underlying framework concerning collective security in the past 20 years has been a series of treaty obligations and legislative provisions—the United Nations Charter, coupled with treaties with 42 countries. On each of these the President sought and secured the advice and consent of the Senate.

Constitutional Quality of Commitments

Let me emphasize the constitutional quality of these commitments. By their nature, they set only the boundaries within which the United States will act. They cannot and do not spell out the precise actions which the United States would take in a variety of contingencies. That is left for further decision by the President and the Congress.

In short, none of these incur automatic response. But they do make clear our pledge to take actions we regard as appropriate in the light of all the circumstances—our view that we are not indifferent to the actions of others which disturb the peace of the world and threaten the security of the United States.

Congress has been a full partner, as well, in the great national effort to accelerate the pace of economic and social progress elsewhere in the world:

We have participated in global and regional organizations like the various agencies of the United Nations, the World Bank, the International Monetary Fund, the Asian Development Bank, the International Development Association, and others.

We have revised our trade policies and we have supported regional economic planning, common markets, and other forms of development.

We have sent our young people abroad in the Peace Corps, our food abroad under the Public Law 480 program, and our technical, financial, and development assistance abroad in the AID program.

In all of these actions, the various committees of Congress and the Congress as a whole have participated fully in a variety of ways. In each, there has been express approval and authorization for Executive action.

Frequently, in adopting legislation related to the conduct of foreign affairs, the Congress makes findings and declarations of policy, which express its views on broad policy issues and offer guidance to the Executive Branch.

On several occasions the Congress has adopted joint or concurrent resolutions declaring U.S. defense and foreign policy in relation to particular troubled areas of the world.

The Congress also has a key role in international agreements. In the case of treaties, the Senate's advice and consent is required. In the case of legislation to implement treaty commitments, or to authorize subsequent executive agreements, both Houses give approval.

Consultation Between the Two Branches

Finally, there is the central fiscal power. In the exercise of its annual appropriations functions, the Congress reviews and debates the foreign policies of the Administration.

Beyond these formal methods of Congressional participation in foreign policy, there is the process of informal consultation between the Executive and the Congress. There are literally thousands of contacts each year between officers of the Executive Branch and Members of Congress.

Not only do the Secretary and other high officials of the Department of State consult regularly and frequently with Congressional leaders and committees; the President has often conducted such consultations personally and extensively.

Importance of Coordinate Action

As I noted at the outset, the drafters of the Constitution recognized that the voice of the United States in foreign affairs was that of the President. Throughout our history the focus has always been upon the Presi-

dency, and it is difficult to imagine how it could be otherwise. Jefferson put it succinctly: "The transaction of business with foreign nations is Executive altogether."

I think it is fair to say, as virtually every commentator has in fact said throughout our history, that under our constitutional system the source of an effective foreign policy is Presidential power. His is the sole authority to communicate formally with foreign nations; to negotiate treaties; to command the armed forces of the United States. His is a responsibility born of the need for speed and decisiveness in an emergency. His is the responsibility for controlling and directing all the external aspects of the nation's power. To him flow all of the vast intelligence and information connected with national security. The President, of necessity, has a preeminent responsibility in this field.

But to say this is not to denigrate the role of Congress. Whatever the powers of the President to act alone on his own authority—and I doubt that any President has ever acted to the full limits of that authority—there can be no question that he acts most effectively when he acts with the support and authority of the Congress.

And so it is that every President seeks in various ways—formal and informal—the support of Congress for the policies which the United States pursues in its foreign relations.

Powers of President and Congress

In part, the Constitution compels such support. It gives the President the responsibilities for leadership. It also gives the Congress specific powers which can on the one hand frustrate and distort and on the other hand support and implement.

Obviously, then, there are great advantages to the nation in the conduct of its foreign policy when circumstances permit the President and the Congress to act together. The commitments of this nation to the United Nations Charter and to our allies are more than a matter of constitutional process. It is essential that these basic commitments should be clear, both to our friends and to our potential adversaries. Fitfulness of policy and unpredictability of action make for serious international instability, disorder, and danger.

In short, our safety and our success depend in large measure on the confidence of other nations that they can rely on our conduct and our assurances.

It is, therefore, as important that the Congress fill its constitutional role as it is that the President fill his. The Congress is and must be a participant in formulating the broad outlines of our foreign policy, in supporting those fundamental and enduring commitments on which the conduct of day-to-day diplomacy depend.

But to say this is not to say that the Congress can or should seek to substitute itself for the President or even to share in those decisions which are his to make.

As I have said, the Constitution relies not on express delineation to set the powers of the Executive and the Congress in this field, but depends instead on the practical interaction between the two branches. Today, these considerations require that the President fill the preeminent role:

He alone has the support of the administrative machinery required to deal with the sheer volume of our foreign affairs problems.

He alone is the focus of diplomatic communications, intelligence sources and other information that are the tools for the conduct of foreign affairs.

He alone can act, when necessary, with the speed and decisiveness required to protect our national security.

Conclusion

I see no need to revise the experience of our history, or to seek to alter the boundaries of Presidential or Congressional prerogative regarding foreign affairs. The need, as always, is to make the constitutional scheme and the experience of history continue to work.

"For myself," President Johnson has observed, "I believe that this is the way our system was intended to function—not with Presidents and Congresses locked in battle with each other—but locked arm in arm instead, battling for the people that we serve together."

Thank you, Mr. Chairman.

Testimony at 1948 Hiss-Chambers Hearings

Following is an abridged excerpt of testimony before the House Un-American Activities Committee on Aug. 25, 1948. The Committee was then investigating charges by Whittaker Chambers, a former Communist and later (until December 1948) a senior editor of Time *magazine. The charges concerned alleged Communist activites by Alger Hiss, former director of the State Department's Office of Special Political Affairs and, from 1947-1949, president of the Carnegie Endowment for International Peace.*

The subject under discussion was the fate of a car once owned by Hiss. Hiss had testified that he "threw it into" a deal for Chambers' lease of the Hiss residence in Georgetown; Chambers asserted that Hiss gave the car to a member of the Communist party. The disposal of the car proved crucial in the hearings, for it was one of the few questions at issue between Hiss and Chambers that could be settled by documentary evidence rather than being left to mere recollection of past events.

In addition to Hiss and Chambers, other participants in the hearing were Robert Stripling, the Committee's chief investigator; Benjamin Mandel, Committee research director; John F. Davis, Hiss's counsel; and Committee members Richard M. Nixon (R Calif.), Chairman J. Parnell Thomas (R N.J.), Karl E. Mundt (R S.D.) and F. Edward Hebert (D La.).

MR. STRIPLING: ...In the meantime, Mr. Chairman, I should like now to refer to the testimony of Whittaker Chambers, which he gave on August 7th in New York City in the Federal Building.

"MR. NIXON: Did they have a car?—" (referring to Mr. and Mrs. Alger Hiss).

"MR. CHAMBERS: Yes; they did. When I first knew them they had a car. Again I am reasonably sure, I am almost certain it was a Ford, and that it was a roadster. It was black, and it was very dilapidated. There is no question about that. I remember very clearly that it had hand windshield wipers. I remember that because I drove it one rainy day and had to work those windshield wipers by hand.

"MR. NIXON: Do you recall any other car?

"MR. CHAMBERS: It seems to me in 1936 probably he got a new Plymouth.

"MR. NIXON: Do you recall its type?

"MR. CHAMBERS: It was a sedan, a two-seated car.

"MR. MANDEL: What did he do with the old car?

"MR. CHAMBERS: The Communist party had in Washington a service station; that is, the man in charge or owner of this station was a Communist, or it may have been a car lot.

"MR. NIXON: But the owner was a Communist?

"MR. CHAMBERS: The owner was a Communist. I never knew who he was or where he was. It was against all the rules of the underground organization for Hiss to do anything with his old car but trade it in, and I think this investigation has proved how right the Communists are in such matters, but Hiss insisted that he wanted that car turned over to the open party so it could be of use to some poor organizer in the West or somewhere. Much against my better judgment, and much against Peters' better judgment, he finally got us to permit him to do this thing. Peters knew where this lot was, and he either took Hiss there or he gave Hiss the address, and Hiss went there, and to the best of my recollection of his description of that happening, he left the car there and simply went away, and the man in charge of the station took care of the rest of it for him. I should think the records of that transfer would be traceable.

"MR. NIXON: Where was that?

"MR. CHAMBERS: In Washington, D.C., I believe; certainly somewhere in the District."

Now, Mr. Chairman, I have here a certificate of title, a photostatic copy of a certificate of title, District of Columbia, Director of Vehicles and Traffic. It shows that on July 23, 1936, Alger Hiss assigned the title of this car to the Cherner Motor Co., and I now ask that Mr. Hiss step aside, and that Mr. Russell take the stand. (Louis J. Russell was the Committee's assistant chief investigator.)

MR. STRIPLING: Mr. Russell, I hand you a photostatic copy of an assignment of title, as recorded in the District of Columbia, and ask you to give the Committee details of your investigation regarding this sale and assignment of title (handing photostatic copy of document to witness).

MR. RUSSELL: The space on the back of the document called the certificate of title of a motor vehicle, as issed by the Director of Vehicles and Traffic for the District of Columbia, reflects that on July 23, 1936, one Alger Hiss sold to the Cherner Motor Co. of 1781 Florida Avenue, NW, a motor vehicle.

MR. STRIPLING: Mr. Russell, is there any evidence that he sold the motor vehicle, on the face of that?

MR. RUSSELL: On the face, under the section which reads as follows: "The motor vehicle described on the reverse side of this certificate, and the undersigned hereby warrants that the title to the said motor vehicle, and certifies that at the time of delivery the same is subject to the following liens or encumbrances and none other."

Under that, in typewriting, is the word "None." There is no indication as to the amount of money involved in the transaction.

MR. STRIPLING: Now, did you proceed to the Cherner Motor Co. with a subpoena, and examine their records and subpoena all of their sales records for this date?

MR. RUSSELL: I did.

MR. STRIPLING: Do you have those records with you?

MR. RUSSELL: Yes.

MR. STRIPLING: Is there any evidence of a sale on that date from the records that we have obtained?

MR. RUSSELL: In the records which we obtained, which were the only ones available, there is no evidence that a sale or the subsequent sale of a 1929 Ford roadster was made by the Cherner Motor Co. on that date.

MR. STRIPLING: Now, just a moment. Going back to the assignment of title, does the photostatic document reflect that the car was sold or assigned on the same date that Mr. Hiss turned it in to the Cherner Motor Co.?

MR. RUSSELL: Yes; the reassignment of title reflects that on July 23, 1936, which is the same date that the car was turned over to Cherner Motor Co., by Mr. Hiss, that one William Rosen, of 5403 Thirteenth Street, NW, was the purchaser of the same motor vehicle involved for the amount—the amount is not given. However, it states, or there is a statement on this document, that there was a chattel mortgage of $25.

MR. STRIPLING: Did you go to the address listed there, 5405 Thirteenth Street, NW?

MR. RUSSELL: No; but investigators attached to my division did.

MR. STRIPLING: Who were the investigators?

MR. RUSSELL: Mr. William A. Wheeler and Mr. Benjamin Mandel and Mrs. Howard also visited that address.

MR. STRIPLING: Did any person by the name of William Rosen reside at that address during 1936?

MR. RUSSELL: No.

MR. STRIPLING: Was there any record of a William Rosen having resided at that address?

MR. RUSSELL: No.

MR. NIXON: Who was the—who resides at that address at the present time?

MR. RUSSELL: Mrs. Howard would have to mention that. I am not familiar with the persons presently residing there.

MR. NIXON: You do not have the information as to that?

MR. RUSSELL: No; Mrs. Howard has that.

MR. NIXON: But what your record shows, I understand, Mr. Russell, is that this car was transferred by Mr. Hiss on what date?

MR. RUSSELL: July 23, 1936.

MR. NIXON: That is a year after the transfer to Chambers is supposed to have taken place?

MR. RUSSELL: Yes.

MR. NIXON: Is that in the handwriting of Mr. Hiss?

MR. RUSSELL: According to an identification of certain handwriting specimens consisting of the known handwriting of Mr. Hiss on the questioned document which is this assignment of title, the handwriting experts have testified that the signature appearing on the back of this document, called assignment of title, was written by Alger Hiss.

MR. STRIPLING: Here is the report of the handwriting experts at this time.

MR. NIXON: Is it true also that the words "Cherner Motor Co.," had been written in by Mr. Hiss, or are in the same handwriting?

MR. RUSSELL: Whether the handwriting examination shows that, I do not know. I do not believe that it does.

MR. NIXON: Mr. Stripling, you have information on that fact?

MR. STRIPLING: We have not made a determination on that point. I want to ask Mr. Hiss.

MR. NIXON: I see. Do the files of the Committee on Un-American Activities or the files which you have consulted disclose any information concerning the William Rosen who gave this address?

MR. STRIPLING: There are two William Rosens. This committee is now checking. We find no William Rosen who ever resided at that address. There are two Rosens. We are checking one in California and the other in Detroit. We are not prepared at this time to state definitely concerning these two William Rosens.

Could I clear up one point, Mr. Nixon?

MR. NIXON: Yes.

MR. STRIPLING: Now, Mr. Russell, you have the sales slips of the Cherner Motor Co. for the date on which this car was sold to William Rosen.

MR. RUSSELL: I have.

MR. STRIPLING: Do you have the slips for the day before?

MR. RUSSELL: Yes.

MR. STRIPLING: And the following day?

MR. RUSSELL: Yes.

MR. STRIPLING: Would you explain to the committee the numbering system of those sales slips, and tell them whether or not the sales slips, as contained there in the files which were subpoenaed, reflect that this car was sold to William Rosen.

MR. RUSSELL: These sales invoices are numbered in consecutive order. The last sales invoice for the date July 21, 1936, bore the number 7879.

The first sales invoice for the following day, which was the day before the transaction was recorded on the assignment of title, begins with the number 7880, and ends with the number 7897. There were no invoices missing on that day.

On the following day, July 23, 1936, the date of the transaction, the number was 7898. The last invoice on that date was 7908, and on the following day, July 24, 1936, the invoices begin with the number 7909, and end with number 7923.

If you follow the numbers in consecutive order from the last number of July 2 through July 24, 1936, you will find that there are no sales invoices missing, which indicates that no sales invoice for the sale of this automobile to William Rosen was made out by the Cherner Motor Co. on the day before the sale was recorded on the assignment of title, on the day that the sale was recorded, on the assignment of title, nor on the day following the assignment of title, which was July 24, 1936.

MR. STRIPLING: Now, Mr. Chairman, I think this point should be an occasion for Mr. Nixon, who is chairman of a subcommittee, to state clearly for the record the investigation to this point regarding the Cherner Motor Co.

Yesterday Mr. Cherner, who is head of the motor company, was before the committee, as well as the treasurer, and the vice president in charge of used cars, I believe—three officials of the Cherner Motor Co., who were before the committee. There is no evidence at this time that any of these three officials or that the Cherner Motor Co. might have been a party to any such transaction. It is very possible that a person who was with the Cherner Motor Co. at that time is involved. We expect to have something on that later in the day.

MR. NIXON: Mr. Chairman, the subcommittee yesterday heard Mr. Cherner, of the Cherner Motor Co., and Mr. Mensh, who was the sales manager of the Cherner Motor Co., at the time this transaction occurred. Both witnesses testified at length. Their testimony will, of course, be made public, and I want to say for the record that, as far as both of them were concerned, they had no recollection whatever of this particular transaction, and that, as far as the investigation of the subcommittee is concerned, there is no implication at all that they were involved in the transaction from the basis of their testimony. I want that to be made absolutely clear, because the record of their testimony, which will be made public, will bear out what I have just said.

Do I understand, first of all, that you do have the records of the Cherner Motor Co. for the day of that particular transaction?

MR. RUSSELL: Yes, sir.

MR. NIXON: And you find nothing in those records at all bearing on this transaction?

MR. RUSSELL: Yes, sir.

MR. NIXON: You have searched the records carefully to see whether possibly the invoice might have been misplaced?

MR. RUSSELL: Yes, sir. The invoices are numbered in consecutive order; and if you take the day before the transaction occurred, and find that number and trace that through, and the following day, and then take the first invoice for the day after the transaction, you will find that those numbers are in consecutive order, so there could not be a sales invoice for that day missing.

MR. NIXON: I see. And as far as Mr. William Rosen is concerned, the investigations of your staff have shown that the address that he gave was an address which the occupants of the home at that time deny was his at that time?

MR. RUSSELL: Yes, sir; that is true.

MR. NIXON: That is all I have at this time.

MR. STRIPLING: I ask that Mr. Hiss be recalled.

THE CHAIRMAN: Mr. Hebert.

MR. HEBERT: I just want to ask one clarifying question.

In other words, this transfer of title which the Cherner Motor Co. supposedly gave to the man Rosen does not appear officially at all in their files or in their invoices?

MR. RUSSELL: That is right.

MR. STRIPLING: The point we are making is that Mr. Hiss, according to this document, delivered the Ford automobile to the Cherner Motor Co. on July 23, 1936. On that same date the car was sold or transferred to one William Rosen, but there is no evidence in the sales records of this particular transaction.

MR. HEBERT: It was an unusual case.

MR. STRIPLING: I believe that the officials—one of the officials of the Cherner Motor Co.—testified yesterday that it was a very unusual case.

(Alger Hiss was called to the stand.)

MR. STRIPLING: Mr. Hiss, I show you this photostatic copy of assignment of title, title No. 245647, for a Ford used, model A, 1929 roadster, and the numbers are A-21888119-19-33—that was the date on which it was originally registered in the District of Columbia. The tag, I believe, was 245647, in the name of Alger Hiss, 3411 O Street NW, Washington, D.C.

Now, Mr. Hiss, is this your signature which appears on the reverse side of this assignment of title? (showing witness photostatic copy).

MR. HISS: Mr. Stripling, it certainly looks like my signature to me. Do you have the original document?

MR. STRIPLING: No; I do not.

MR. HISS: This is a photostat. I would prefer to have the original. Do you have the original?

MR. STRIPLING: The original document, Mr. Chairman, cannot be removed from the Department of Motor Vehicles. They keep it in their possession.

MR. HISS: They have it in their possession now?

MR. STRIPLING: I assume they do.

MR. DAVIS: Could it be subpoenaed?

MR. STRIPLING: It might be possible to subpoena it here if they bring it up themselves.

THE CHAIRMAN: Well, Mr. Hiss, can't you tell from the photostat what this signature is? Whether it is your signature or not?

MR. HISS: It looks like my signature to me, Mr. Chairman.

THE CHAIRMAN: Well, if that were the original, would it look any more like your signature? (Laughter.) So, it is just reasonable to believe that you can tell from that whether or not it is your signature.

MR. HISS: I think if I saw the original document I would be able to see whether this photostat is an exact reproduction of the original document. I would just rather deal with originals than with copies.

MR. HEBERT: Mr. Stripling, may I interrupt? In other words, in order to give Mr. Hiss every opportunity—if we recall what he did with the photograph, that he did not recognize Mr. Chambers for some time, and he finally recognized him. I suggest that the Committee issue a subpoena duces tecum to the motor-vehicle people and let them come in here with the original, and it will be just a matter of hours, and he will have to admit it is his signature.

MR. HISS: The reason I asked was that we had not been able to get access to the original. I just wondered what had happened to it.

THE CHAIRMAN: We will try, and Mr. Stripling, you try at noontime, if we ever reach noontime.

MR. STRIPLING: I think we can reach it this way. Do you recall ever signing the assignment, Mr. Hiss?

MR. HISS: I do not at the moment recall signing this.

MR. STRIPLING: Is this your handwriting? There is written here, "Cherner Motor Co., 1781 Florida Avenue NW." Did you write that?

MR. HISS: I could not be sure from the outline of the letters in this photostatic copy. That also looks not unlike my own handwriting.

MR. MUNDT: Could you be sure if you saw the original document?

MR. HISS: I could be surer. (Laughter.)

MR. STRIPLING: Now, Mr. Hiss and Mr. Chairman, yesterday the committee subpoenaed before it W. Marvin Smith, who was the notary public who notarized the signature of Mr. Hiss. Mr. Smith is an attorney in the Department of Justice in the Solicitor General's office. He has been employed there for 35 years. He testified that he knew Mr. Hiss; he does not recall notarizing this particular document, but he did testify that this was his signature.

MR. HISS: I know Mr. Marvin Smith.

THE CHAIRMAN: You know who?

MR. HISS: I say I know Mr. Marvin Smith.

MR. STRIPLING: The man who notarized this.

MR. NIXON: Mr. Hiss, you knew Mr. Smith, the notary, who signed this in 1936, did you not?

MR. HISS: I did....

MR. NIXON: On the basis—in other words, you would not want to say now that you question the fact that Mr. Smith might have violated his oath as a notary public in notarizing a forged signature?

MR. HISS: Definitely not.

MR. NIXON: Then, as far as you are concerned, this is your signature?

MR. HISS: As far as I am concerned, with the evidence that has been shown to me, it is.

MR. NIXON: All right; you are willing to testify now then that since Mr. Smith did notarize your signature as of that time, that it is your signature?

MR. HISS: On the basis of the assumptions you state, the answer is "Yes."

MR. HEBERT: Mr. Hiss, now that your memory has been refreshed by the development of the last few minutes, do you recall the transaction whereby you disposed of that Ford that you could not remember this morning?

MR. HISS: No; I have no present recollection of the disposition of the Ford, Mr. Hebert.

MR. HEBERT: In view of the refreshing of your memory that has been presented here this morning?

MR. HISS: In view of that, and in view of all the other developments.

MR. HEBERT: You are a remarkable and agile young man, Mr. Hiss.

Supreme Court Opinion in *Anderson v. Dunn*

Following is the complete text of the Supreme Court opinion in Anderson v. Dunn, *affirming the constitutionality of Congress' summary use of the contempt power. The opinion, handed down March 2, 1821, marked the first time the Court had ruled on the power of Congress to send contemptuous persons to jail without a court order. The case grew out of assault and battery and false arrest charges by John Anderson against House Sergeant at Arms Thomas Dunn, after Dunn had arrested Anderson for contempt of Congress.*

JOHNSON, Justice, delivered the opinion of the Court. Notwithstanding the range which has been taken by the plaintiff's counsel, in the discussion of this cause, the merits of it really lie in a very limited compass. The pleadings have narrowed them down to the simple inquiry, whether the House of Representatives can take cognizance of contempts committed against themselves, under any circumstances? The duress complained of was sustained under a warrant issued to compel the party's appearance, not for the actual infliction of punishment for an offense committed. Yet it cannot be denied that the power to institute a prosecution must be dependent upon the power to punish. If the House of Representatives possessed no authority to punish for contempt, the initiating process issued in the assertion of that authority must have been illegal; there was a want of jurisdiction to justify it.

It is certainly true that there is no power given by the Constitution to either house to punish for contempts, except when committed by their own members. Nor does the judicial or criminal power given to the United States, in any part, expressly extend to the infliction of punishment for contempt of either house, or any one coordinate branch of the government. Shall we, therefore, decide, that no such power exists?

It is true that such a power, if it exists, must be derived from implication, and the genius and spirit of our institutions are hostile to the exercise of implied powers. Had the faculties of man been competent to the framing of a system of government which would have left nothing to implication, it cannot be doubted that the effort would have been made by the framers of the Constitution. But what is the fact? There is not in the whole of that admirable instrument a grant of powers which does not draw after it others, not expressed, but vital to their exercise; not substantive and independent, indeed, but auxiliary and subordinate. The idea is Utopian that government can exist without leaving the exercise of discretion somewhere. Public security against the abuse of such discretion must rest on responsibility, and stated appeals to public approbation. Where all power is derived from the people, and public functionaries, at short intervals, deposit it at the feet of the people, to be resumed again only at their will, individual fears may be alarmed by the monsters of imagination, but individual liberty can be in little danger. No one is so visionary as to dispute the assertion, that the sole end and aim of all our institutions is the safety and happiness of the citizen. But the relation between the action and the end is not always so direct and palpable as to strike the eye of every observer. The science of government is the most abstruse of all sciences; if, indeed, that can be called a science which has but few fixed principles and practically consists in little more than the exercise of a sound discretion, applied to the exigencies of the state as they arise. It is the science of experiment.

But if there is one maxim which necessarily rides over all others, in the practical application of government, it is that the public functionaries must be left at liberty to exercise the powers which the people have intrusted to them. The interests and dignity of those who created them require the exertion of the powers indispensable to the attainment of the ends of their creation. Nor is a casual conflict with the rights of particular individuals any reason to be urged against the exercise of such powers. The wretch beneath the gallows may repine at the fate which awaits him, and yet it is no less certain that the laws under which he suffers were made for his security. The unreasonable murmurs of individuals against the restraints of society have a direct tendency to produce that worst of all despotisms, which makes every individual the tyrant over his neighbor's rights. That "the safety of the people is the supreme law," not only comports with, but is indispensable to, the exercise of those powers in their public functionaries without which that safety cannot be guarded. On this principle it is that courts of justice are universally acknowledged to be vested, by their very creation, with power to impose silence, respect and decorum in their presence, and submission to their lawful mandates, and as a corollary to this proposition, to preserve themselves and their officers from the approach and insults of pollution.

It is true, that the courts of justice of the United States are vested, by express statute provision, with power to fine and imprison for contempts; but it does not follow, from this circumstance, that they would not have exercised that power, without the aid of the statute, or not in cases, if such should occur, to which such statute provision may not extend; on the contrary, it is a legislative assertion of this right, as incidental to a grant of judicial power, and can only be considered, only as an instance of abundant caution, or a legislative declaration, that the power of punishing for contempt shall not extend beyond its known and acknowledged limits of fine and imprisonment.

But it is contended that if this power in the House of Representatives is to be asserted on the plea of necessity, the ground is too broad, and the result too indefinite; that the Executive, and every coordinate, and even subordinate, Branch of the Government may resort to the same justification, and the whole assume to themselves, in the exercise of this power, the most tyranical licentiousness. This is, unquestionably, an evil to be guarded against, and if the doctrine may be pushed to that extent, it must be a bad doctrine, and is justly denounced. But what is the alternative? The argument obviously leads to the total annihilation of the power of the House of Representatives to guard itself from contempts, and leaves it exposed to every indignity and interruption that rudeness, caprice, or even conspiracy may meditate against it. This result is fraught with too much absurdity, not to bring into doubt the soundness of any argument from which it is derived. That a deliberate assembly, clothed with the majesty of the people, and charged with the care of all that is dear to them; composed of the most distinguished citizens, selected and drawn together from every quarter of a great nation; whose deliberations are required, by public opinion, to be conducted under the eye of the public, and whose decisions must be clothed with all that sanctity which unlimited confidence in their wisdom and purity can inspire; that such an assembly should not possess the power to suppress rudeness, or repel insult, is a supposition too wild to be suggested. And accordingly, to avoid the pressure of these considerations, it has been argued, that the right of the respective houses to exclude from their presence, and their absolute control within their own walls, carry with them the right to punish contempts committed in their presence; while the absolute legislative power given to Congress within this District enables them to provide by law against all other insults against which there is any necessity for providing.

It is to be observed that so far as the issue of this cause is implicated, this argument yields all right of the plaintiff in error to a decision in his favor; for, *non constat*, from the pleadings, but that this warrant issued for an offense committed in the immediate presence of the house. Nor is it immaterial to notice what difficulties the negation of this right in the House of Representatives draws after it, when it is considered that the concession of the power, if exercised within their walls, relinquishes the great grounds of the argument, to wit, the want of an express grant, and the unrestricted and undefined nature of the power here set up. For why should the House be at liberty to exercise an ungranted, an unlimited, and undefined power, within their walls, any more than without them? If the analogy with individual right and power be resorted to, it will reach no further than to exclusion; and it requires no exuberance of imagination, to exhibit the ridiculous consequences which might result from such a restriction, imposed upon the conduct of a deliberative assembly.

Nor would their situation be materially relieved, by resorting to their legislative power within the District. That power may, indeed, be applied to many purposes, and was intended by the Constitution to extend to many purposes indispensable to the security and dignity of the general Government; but they are purposes of a more grave and general character than the offences which may be denominated contempts, and which, from their very nature, admit of no precise definition. Judicial gravity will not admit of the illustrations which this remark would admit of. Its correctness is easily tested by pursuing, in imagination, a legislative attempt at defining the cases to which the epithet contempt might be reasonably applied.

But althouth the offences be held undefinable, it is justly contended that the punishment need not be indefinite. Nor is it so. We are not now considering the extent to which the punishing power of Congress, by a legislative act, may be carried. On that subject, the bounds of their power are to be found in the provisions of the Constitution. The present question is, what is the extent of the punishing power which the deliberative assemblies of the Union may assume and exercise on the principle of self-preservation?

Analogy, and the nature of the case, furnish the answer—"the least possible power adequate to the end proposed"; which is the power of imprisonment. It may, at first view, and from the history of the practice of our legislative bodies, be thought to extend to other inflictions. But every other will be found to be mere commutation for confinement; since commitment alone is the alternative where the individual proves contumacious. And even to the duration of imprisonment a period is imposed, by the nature of things, since the existence of the power that imprisons is indispensable to its continuance: and although the legislative power continues perpetual, the legislative body ceases to exist on the moment of its adjournment or periodical dissolution. It follows that imprisonment must terminate with that adjournment.

This view of the subject necessarily sets bounds to the exercise of a caprice which has sometimes disgraced deliberative assemblies, when under the influence of strong passions or wicked leaders, but the instances of which have long since remained on record only as historical facts, not as precedents for imitation. In the present fixed and settled state of English institutions, there is no more danger of their being revived, probably, than in our own. But the American legislative bodies have never possessed, or pretended to, the omnipotence which constitutes the leading feature in the legislative assembly of Great Britain, and which may have led occasionally to the exercise of caprice, under the specious appearance of merited resentment.

If it be inquired what security is there, that with an officer avowing himself devoted to their will, the House of Representatives will confine its punishing power to the limits of imprisonment, and not push it to the infliction of corporal punishment, or even death, and exercise it in cases affecting the liberty of speech and of the press? the reply is to be found in the consideration, that the Constitution was formed in and for an advanced state of society and rests at every point on received opinions and fixed ideas. It is not a new creation, but a combination of existing materials whose properties and attributes were familiarly understood and had been determined by reiterated experiments. It is not, therefore, reasoning upon things as they are, to suppose that any deliberative assembly, constituted under it, would ever assert any other rights and powers than those which had been established by long practice and conceded by public opinion. Melancholy, also, would be that state of distrust which rests not a hope upon a moral influence. The most absolute tyranny could not

subsist where men could not be trusted with power, because they might abuse it, much less a government which has no other basis than the sound morals, moderation, and good sense of those who compose it. Unreasonable jealousies not only blight the pleasures, but dissolve the very texture of society.

But it is argued, that the inference, if any, arising under the Constitution, is against the exercise of the powers here asserted by the House of Representatives; that the express grant of power to punish their members, respectively, and to expel them, by the application of a familiar maxim, raises an implication against the power to punish any other than their own members. This argument proves too much; for its direct application would lead to the annihilation of almost every power of Congress. To enforce its laws upon any subject, without the sanction of punishment, is obviously impossible. Yet there is an express grant of power to punish in one class of cases, and one only, and all the punishing power exercised by Congress, in any cases, except those which relate to piracy and offenses against the laws of nations, is derived from implication. Nor did the idea ever occur to any one that the express grant in one class of cases repelled the assumption of the punishing power in any other. The truth is that the exercise of the powers given over their own members was of such a delicate nature that a constitutional provision became necessary to assert or communicate it. Constituted, as that body is, of the delegates of confederated states, some such provision was necessary to guard against their mutual jealousy, since every proceeding against a Representative would indirectly affect the honor or interests of the state which sent him.

In reply to the suggestion that, on this same foundation of necessity, might be raised a superstructure of implied powers in the Executive, and every other department, and even ministerial officer, of the Government, it would be sufficient to observe that neither analogy nor precedent would support the assertion of such powers in any other than a legislative or judicial body. Even corruption anywhere else would not contaminate the source of political life. In the retirement of the cabinet, it is not expected that the Executive can be approached by indignity or insult; nor can it ever be necessary to the Executive, or any other department, to hold a public deliberative assembly. These are not arguments; they are visions which mar the enjoyment of actual blessings, with the attack or feint of the harpies of imagination.

As to the minor points made in this case, it is only necessary to observe that there is nothing on the face of this record from which it can appear on what evidence this warrant was issued. And we are not to presume that the House of Representatives would have issued it without duly establishing the fact charged on the individual. And as to the distance to which the process might reach, it is very clear that there exists no reason for confining its operation to the limits of the District of Columbia; after passing those limits, we know no bounds that can be prescribed to its range but those of the United States. And why should it be restricted to other boundaries? Such are the limits of the legislating powers of that body; and the inhabitant of Louisiana or Maine may as probably charge them with bribery and corruption, or attempt, by letter, to induce the commission of either, as the inhabitant of any other section of the Union. If the inconvenience be urged, the reply is obvious: there is no difficulty in observing that respectful deportment which will render all apprehensions chimerical.

Judgment affirmed.

Supreme Court Opinion in *McGrain v. Daugherty*

Following is the complete text of the Supreme Court's opinion in McGrain v. Daugherty. *The case grew out of a Senate investigation of the Justice Department in the 1920s. Mally S. Daugherty, brother of Atty. Gen. Harry M. Daugherty, challenged a subpoena served by Deputy Sergeant at Arms John J. McGrain. The decision, handed down Jan. 17, 1927, was a landmark in the development of Congressional investigating power.*

Mr. Justice Van Devanter delivered the opinion of the court.

This is an appeal from the final order in a proceeding in *habeas corpus* discharging a recusant witness held in custody under process of attachment issued from the United States Senate in the course of an investigation which it was making of the administration of the Department of Justice. A full statement of the case is necessary.

The Department of Justice is one of the great executive departments established by congressional enactment and has charge, among other things, of the initiation and prosecution of all suits, civil and criminal, which may be brought in the right and name of the United States to compel obedience or punish disobedience to its laws, to recover property

obtained from it by unlawful or fraudulent means, or to safeguard its rights in other respects; and also of the assertion and protection of its interests when it or its officers are sued by others. The Attorney General is the head of the department, and its functions are all to be exercised under his supervision and direction.

Harry M. Daugherty became the Attorney General March 5, 1921, and held that office until March 28, 1924, when he resigned. Late in that period various charges of misfeasance and nonfeasance in the Department of Justice after he became its supervising head were brought to the attention of the Senate by individual senators and made the basis of an insistent demand that the department be investigated to the end that the practices and deficiencies which, according to the charges, were operating to prevent or impair its right administration might be definitely ascertained and that appropriate and effective measures might be taken to remedy or eliminate the evil. The Senate regarded the charges as grave and requiring legislative attention and action. Accordingly it formulated, passed and invited the House of Representatives to pass (and that body did pass) two measures taking important litigation then in immediate contemplation out of the control of the Department of Justice and placing the same in charge of special counsel to be appointed by the President; and also adopted a resolution authorizing and directing a select committee of five senators—

"to investigate circumstances and facts, and report the same to the Senate, concerning the alleged failure of Harry M. Daugherty, Attorney General of the United States, to prosecute properly violators of the Sherman Anti-trust Act and the Clayton Act against monopolies and unlawful restraint of trade; the alleged neglect and failure of the said Harry M. Daugherty, Attorney General of the United States, to arrest and prosecute Albert B. Fall, Harry F. Sinclair, E. L. Doheny, C. R. Forbes, and their co-conspirators in defrauding the Government, as well as the alleged neglect and failure of the said Attorney General to arrest and prosecute many others for violations of Federal statutes, and his alleged failure to prosecute properly, efficiently, and promptly, and to defend, all manner of civil and criminal actions wherein the Government of the United States is interested as a party plaintiff or defendant. And said committee is further directed to inquire into, investigate and report to the Senate the activities of the said Harry M. Daugherty, Attorney General, and any of his assistants in the Department of Justice which would in any manner tend to impair their efficiency or influence as representatives of the Government of the United States."

The resolution also authorized the committee to send for books and papers, to subpoena witnesses, to administer oaths, and to sit at such times and places as it might deem advisable.

In the course of the investigation the committee issued and caused to be duly served on Mally S. Daugherty—who was a brother of Harry M. Daugherty and president of the Midland National Bank of Washington Court House, Ohio,—a subpoena commanding him to appear before the committee for the purpose of giving testimony bearing on the subject under investigation, and to bring with him the "deposit ledgers of the Midland National Bank since November 1, 1920; also note files and transcript of owners of every safety vault; also records of income drafts; also records of any individual account or accounts showing withdrawals of amounts of $25,000 or over during above period." The witness failed to appear.

A little later in the course of the investigation the committee issued and caused to be duly served on the same witness another subpoena commanding him to appear before it for the purpose of giving testimony relating to the subject under consideration—nothing being said in this subpoena about bringing records, books or papers. The witness again failed to appear; and no excuse was offered by him for either failure.

The committee then made a report to the Senate stating that the subpoenas had been issued, that according to the officer's returns—copies of which accompanied the report—the witness was personally served; and that he had failed and refused to appear. After a reading of the report, the Senate adopted a resolution reciting these facts and proceeding as follows:

"Whereas the appearance and testimony of the said M. S. Daugherty is material and necessary in order that the committee may properly execute the functions imposed upon it and may obtain information necessary as a basis for such legislative and other action as the Senate may deem necessary and proper: Therefore be it

Resolved, That the President of the Senate pro tempore issue his warrant commanding the Sergeant at Arms or his deputy to take into custody the body of the said M. S. Daugherty wherever found, and to bring the said M. S. Daugherty before the bar of the Senate, then and there to answer such questions pertinent to the matter under inquiry as the Senate may order the President of the Senate pro tempore to propound; and to keep the said M. S. Daugherty in custody to await the further order of the Senate."

It will be observed from the terms of the resolution that the warrant was to be issued in furtherance of the effort to obtain the personal testimony of the witness and, like the second subpoena, was not intended to exact from him the production of the various records, books and papers named in the first subpoena.

The warrant was issued agreeably to the resolution and was addressed simply to the Sergeant at Arms. That officer on receiving the warrant endorsed thereon a direction that it be executed by John J. McGrain, already his deputy, and delivered it to him for execution.

The deputy, proceeding under the warrant, took the witness into custody at Cincinnati, Ohio, with the purpose of bringing him before the bar of the Senate as commanded; whereupon the witness petitioned the federal district court in Cincinnati for a writ of *habeas corpus*. The writ was granted and the deputy made due return setting forth the warrant and the cause of the detention. After a hearing the court held the attachment and detention unlawful and discharged the witness, the decision being put on the ground that the Senate in directing the investigation and in ordering the attachment exceeded its powers under the Constitution, 299 Fed. 620. The deputy prayed and was allowed a direct appeal to this Court under Section 238 of the Judicial Code as then existing.

We have given the case earnest and prolonged consideration because the principal questions involved are of unusual importance and delicacy. They are (a) whether the Senate—or the House of Representatives, both being on the same plane in this regard—has power, through its own process, to compel a private individual to appear before it or one of its committees and give testimony needed to enable it efficiently to exercise a legislative function belonging to it under the Constitution, and (b) whether it sufficiently appears that the process was being employed in this instance to obtain testimony for that purpose.

Other questions are presented which in regular course should be taken up first.

The witness challenges the authority of the deputy to execute the warrant on two grounds—that there was no provision of law for a deputy, and that, even if there were such a provision, a deputy could not execute the warrant because it was addressed simply to the Sergeant at Arms. We are of opinion that neither ground is tenable.

The Senate adopted in 1889 and has retained ever since a standing order declaring that the Sergeant at Arms may appoint deputies "to serve process or perform other duties" in his stead, that they shall be "officers of the Senate," and that acts done and returns made by them "shall have like effect and be of the same validity as if performed or made by the Sergeant at Arms in person." In actual practice the Senate has given full effect to the order; and Congress has sanctioned the practice under it by recognizing the deputies—sometimes called assistants—as officers of the Senate, by fixing their compensation and by making appropriations to pay them. Thus there was ample provision of law for a deputy.

The fact that the warrant was addressed simply to the Sergeant at Arms is not of special significance. His authority was not to be tested by the warrant alone. Other criteria were to be considered. The standing order and the resolution under which the warrant was issued plainly contemplated that he was to be free to execute the warrant in person or to direct a deputy to execute it. They expressed the intention of the Senate; and the words of the warrant were to be taken, as they well could be, in a sense which would give effect to that intention. Thus understood, the warrant admissibly could be executed by a deputy if the Sergeant at Arms so directed, which he did.

The case of *Sanborn v. Carleton* 15 Gray 399, on which the witness relies, related to a warrant issued to the Sergeant at Arms in 1860, which he deputed another to execute. At that time there was no standing rule or statute permitting him to act through a deputy; nor was there anything in the resolution under which the warrant was issued indicative of a purpose to permit him to do so. All that was decided was that in the absence of a permissive provision, in the warrant or elsewhere, he could not commit its execution to another. The provision which was absent in that case and deemed essential is present in this.

The witness points to the provision in the Fourth Amendment to the Constitution declaring "no warrants shall issue but upon probable cause supported by oath or affirmation" and contends that the warrant was void because the report of the committee on which it was based was unsworn. We think the contention overlooks the relation of the committee to the Senate and to the matters reported, and puts aside the accepted interpretation of the constitutional provision.

The committee was a part of the Senate, and its members were acting under their oath of office as senators. The matters reported pertained to their proceedings and were within their own knowledge. They had issued the subpoenas, had received and examined the officer's returns thereon (copies of which accompanied the report), and knew the witness had not obeyed either subpoena or offered any excuse for his failure to do so.

The constitutional provision was not intended to establish a new principle but to affirm and preserve a cherished rule of the common law designed to prevent the issue of groundless warrants. In legislative practice committee reports are regarded as made under the sanction of the oath of office of its members; and where the matters reported are within the committee's knowledge and constitute probable cause for an attachment such reports are acted on and given effect without requiring that they be supported by further oath or affirmation. This is not a new practice but one which has come down from an early period. It was well recognized before the constitutional provision was adopted, has been followed ever since, and appears never to have been challenged until now. Thus it amounts to a practical interpretation, long continued, of both the original common law rule and the affirming constitutional provision, and should be given effect accordingly.

The principle underlying the legislative practice has also been recognized and applied in judicial proceedings. This is illustrated by the settled rulings that courts in dealing with contempts committed in their presence may order commitments without other proof than their own knowledge of the occurrence, and that they may issue attachments, based on their own knowledge of the default, where intended witnesses or jurors fail to appear in obedience to process shown by the officer's return to have been duly served. A further illustration is found in the rulings that grand jurors, acting under the sanction of their oaths as such, may find and return indictments based solely on their own knowledge of the particular offenses, and that warrants may be issued on such indictments without further oath or affirmation; and still another is found in the practice which recognizes that where grand jurors, under their oath as such, report to the court that a witness brought before them has refused to testify, the court may act on that report, although otherwise unsworn, and order the witness brought before it by attachment.

We think the legislative practice, fortified as it is by the judicial practice, shows that the report of the committee—which was based on the committee's own knowledge and made under the sanction of the oath of office of its members—was sufficiently supported by oath to satisfy the constitutional requirement.

The witness also points to the provision in the warrant and in the resolution under which it was issued requiring that he be "brought before the bar of the Senate, then and there" to give testimony "pertinent to the subject under inquiry," and contends that an essential prerequisite to such an attachment was wanting, because he neither had been subpoenaed to appear and testify before the Senate nor had refused to do so. The argument in support of the contention proceeds on the assumption that the warrant of attachment "is to be treated precisely the same as if no subpoena had been issued by the committee, and the same as if the witness had not refused to testify before the committee." In our opinion the contention and the assumption are both untenable. The committee was acting for the Senate and under its authorization; and therefore the subpoenas which the committee issued and the witness refused to obey are to be treated as if issued by the Senate. The warrant was issued as an auxiliary process to compel him to give the testimony sought by the subpoenas; and its nature in this respect is not affected by the direction that his testimony be given at the bar of the Senate instead of before the committee. If the Senate deemed it proper, in view of his contumacy, to give that direction it was at liberty to do so.

The witness sets up an interlocutory injunction granted by a state court at Washington Court House, Ohio, in a suit brought by the Midland National Bank against two members of the investigating committee, and contends that the attachment was in violation of that injunction and therefore unlawful. The contention is plainly ill-founded. The injunction was granted the same day the second subpoena was served, but whether earlier or later in the day does not appear. All that the record discloses about the injunction is comprised in the paragraph copied in the margin from the witness's petition for *habeas corpus*. But it is apparent from what is disclosed that the injunction did not purport to place any restraint on the witness, nor to restrain the committee from demanding that he appear and testify personally to what he knew respecting the subject under investigation; and also that what the injunction did purport to restrain has no bearing on the power of the Senate to enforce that demand by attachment.

In approaching the principal questions, which remain to be considered, two observations are in order. One is that we are not now concerned with the direction in the first subpoena that the witness produce various records, books and papers of the Midland National Bank. That direction was not repeated in the second subpoena; and is not sought to be enforced by the attachment. This was recognized by the court below, 299 Fed. 623, and is conceded by counsel for the appellant. The other is that we are not now concerned with the right of the Senate to propound or the duty of the witness to answer specific questions, for as yet no questions have been propounded to him. He is asserting—and is standing on his assertion—that the Senate is without power to interrogate him, even if the questions propounded be pertinent and otherwise legitimate —which for present purposes must be assumed.

The first of the principal questions—the one which the witness particularly presses on our attention—is, as before shown, whether the Senate—or the House of Representatives, both being on the same plane in this regard—has power, through its own process, to compel a private individual to appear before it or one of its committees and give testimony needed to enable it efficiently to exercise a legislative function belonging to it under the Constitution.

The Constitution provides for a Congress consisting of a Senate and House of Representatives and invests it with "all legislative powers" granted to the United States, and with power "to make all laws which shall be necessary and proper" for carrying into execution these powers and "all other powers" vested by the Constitution in the United States or in any department or officer thereof. Art. I, secs. 1, 8. Other provisions show that, while bills can become laws only after being considered and passed by both houses of Congress, each house is to be distinct from the other, to have its own officers and rules, and to exercise its legislative function independently. Art. I, secs. 2, 3, 5, 7. But there is no provision expressly investing either house with power to make investigations and exact testimony to the end that it may exercise its legislative function advisedly and effectively. So the question arises whether this power is so far incidental to the legislative function as to be implied.

In actual legislative practice power to secure needed information by such means has long been treated as an attribute of the power to legislate. It was so regarded in the British Parliament and in the Colonial legislatures before the American Revolution; and a like view has prevailed and been carried into effect in both houses of Congress and in most of the state legislatures.

This power was both asserted and exerted by the House of Representatives in 1792, when it appointed a select committee to inquire into the St. Clair expedition and authorized the committee to send for necessary persons, papers and records. Mr. Madison, who had taken an important part in framing the Constitution only five years before, and four of his associates in that work, were members of the House of Representatives at the time, and all voted for the inquiry. 3 Cong. Ann. 494. Other exertions of the power by the House of Representatives, as also by the Senate, are shown in the citations already made. Among those by the Senate, the inquiry ordered in 1859 respecting the raid by John Brown and his adherents on the armory and arsenal of the United States at Harper's Ferry is of special significance. The resolution directing the inquiry authorized the committee to send for persons and papers, to inquire into the facts pertaining to the raid and the means by which it was organized and supported, and to report what legislation, if any, was necessary to preserve the peace of the country and protect the public property. The resolution was briefly discussed and adopted without opposition. Cong. Globe, 36th Cong., 1st Sess., pp. 141, 152. Later on the committee reported that Thaddeus Hyatt, although subpoenaed to appear as a witness, had refused to do so; whereupon the Senate ordered that he be attached and brought before it to answer for his refusal. When he was brought in he answered by challenging the power of the Senate to direct the inquiry and exact testimony to aid it in exercising its legislative function. The question of power thus presented was thoroughly discussed by several senators—Mr. Sumner of Massachusetts taking the lead in denying the power and Mr. Fessenden of Maine in supporting it. Sectional and party lines were put aside and the question was debated and determined with special regard to principle and precedent. The vote was taken on a resolution pronouncing the witness's answer insufficient and directing that he be committed until he should signify that he was ready and willing to testify. The resolution was adopted—44 senators voting for it and 10 against. Cong. Globe, 36th Cong., 1st Sess., pp. 1100-1109, 3006-3007. The arguments advanced in support of the power are fairly reflected by the following excerpts from the debate:

Mr. Fessenden of Maine. "Where will you stop? Stop, I say, just at that point where we have gone far enough to accomplish the purposes for which we were created; and these purposes are defined in the Constitution. What are they? The great purpose is legislation. There are some other things, but I speak of legislation as the principal purpose. Now, what do we propose to do here? We propose to legislate upon a given state of facts, perhaps, or under a given necessity. Well, sir, proposing to legislate, we want information. We have it not ourselves. It is not to be presumed that we know everything; and if any body does presume it, it is a very great mistake, as we know by experience. We want information on certain subjects. How are we to get it? The Senator says, ask for it. I am ready to ask for it; but suppose the person whom we ask will not give it to us: what then? Have we not power to compel him to come before us? Is this power, which has been exercised by Parliament, and by all legislative bodies down to the present day without dispute—the power to inquire into subjects upon which they are disposed to legislate— lost to us? Are we not in the possession of it? Are we deprived of it simply because we hold our power here under a Constitution which defines what our duties are, and what we are called upon to do?

"Congress have appointed committees after committees, time after time, to make inquiries on subjects of legislation. Had we not power to do it? Nobody questioned our authority to do it. We have given them authority to send for persons and papers during the recess. Nobody questioned our authority. We appoint committees during the session, with power to send for persons and papers. Have we not that authority, if necessary to legislation?

"Sir, with regard to myself, all I have to inquire into is: is this a legitimate and proper object, committed to me under the Constitution; and then, as to the mode of accomplishing it, I am ready to use judiciously, calmly, moderately, all the power which I believe is necessary and inherent in order to do that which I am appointed to do; and, I take it, I violate no rights, either of the people generally or of the individual, by that course."

Mr. Crittenden of Kentucky. "I come now to a question where the cooperation of the two branches is not necessary. There are some things that the Senate may do. How? According to a mode of its own. Are we to ask the other branch of the Legislature to concede by law to us the power of making such an inquiry as we are now making? Has not each branch the right to make what inquiries and investigation it thinks proper to make for its own action? Undoubtedly. You say we must have a law for it. Can we have a law? Is it not, from the very nature of the case, incidental to you as a Senate, if you, as a Senate, have the power of instituting an inquiry and of proceeding with that inquiry? I have endeavored to show that we have that power. We have a right, in consequence of it, a necessary incidental power, to summon witnesses, if witnesses are necessary. Do we require the concurrence of the other House to that? It is a power of our own. If you have a right to do the thing of your own motion, you must have all powers that are necessary to do it.

"The means of carrying into effect by law all the granted powers, is given where legislation is applicable and necessary; but there are subordinate matters, not amounting to laws; there are inquiries of the one House or the other House, which each House has a right to conduct; which each has, from the beginning, exercised the power to conduct; and each has, from the beginning, summoned witnesses. This has been the practice of the Government from the beginning; and if we have a right to summon the witness, all the rest follows as a matter of course."

The deliberate solution of the question on that occasion has been accepted and followed on other occasions by both houses of Congress, and never has been rejected or questioned by either.

The state courts quite generally have held that the power to legislate carries with it by necessary implication ample authority to obtain information needed in the rightful exercise of that power, and to employ compulsory process for the purpose.

In *Burnham v. Morrisey*, 14 Gray 226, 239, the Supreme Judicial Court of Massachusetts, in sustaining an exertion of this power by one branch of the legislature of that Commonwealth, said:

"The house of representatives has many duties to perform, which necessarily require it to receive evidence and examine witnesses.... It has often occasion to acquire certain knowledge of facts, in order to the proper performance of legislative duties. We therefore think it clear that it has the constitutional right to take evidence, to summon witnesses, and to compel them to appear and testify. This power to summon and examine witnesses it may exercise by means of committees."

In *Wilckens v. Willet*, 1 Keyes 521, 525, a case which presented the question whether the House of Representatives of the United States possesses this power, the Court of Appeals of New York said:

"That the power exists there admits of no doubt whatever. It is a necessary incident to the sovereign power of making laws; and its exercise is often indispensable to the great end of enlightened, judicious and wholesome legislation."

In *People v. Keeler*, 99 N.Y. 463, 482, 483, where the validity of a statute of New York recognizing and giving effect to this power was drawn in question, the Court of Appeals approvingly quoted what it had said in *Wilckens v. Willet*, and added:

"It is difficult to conceive any constitutional objection which can be raised to the provision authorizing legislative committees to take testimony and to summon witnesses. In many cases it may be indispensable to intelligent and effectual legislation to ascertain the facts which are claimed to give rise to the necessity for such legislation, and the remedy required, and, irrespective of the question whether in the absence of a statute to that effect either house would have the power to imprison a recusant witness, I cannot yield to the claim that a statute authorizing it to enforce its process in that manner is in excess of the legislative power. To await the slow process of indictment and prosecution for a misdemeanor, might prove quite ineffectual, and necessary legislation might be obstructed, and perhaps defeated, if the legislative body had no other and more summary means of enforcing its right to obtain the required information. That the power may be abused, is no ground for denying its existence. It is a limited power, and should be kept within its proper bounds; and, when these are exceeded, a jurisdictional question is presented which is cognizable in the courts." ..."Throughout this Union the practice of legislative bodies, and in this State, the statutes existing at the time the present Constitution was adopted, and whose validity has never before been questioned by our courts, afford strong arguments in favor of the recognition of the right of either house to compel the attendance of witnesses for legislative purposes, as one which has been generally conceded to be an appropriate adjunct to the power of legislation, and one which, to say the least, the State legislature has constitutional authority to regulate and enforce by statute."

Other decisions by state courts recognizing and sustaining the legislative practice are found in *Falvey v. Massing*, 7 Wis. 630, 635-638; *State v. Frear*, 138 Wis. 173; *Exparte Parker*, 74 S.C. 466, 470; *Sullivan v. Hill*, 73 W.Va. 49, 53; *Lowe v. Summers*, 69 Mo. App. 637, 649-650. An instructive decision on the question is also found in *Exparte Dansereau* (1875), 19 L. C. Jur. 210, where the legislative assembly of the Province of Quebec was held to possess this power as a necessary incident of its power to legislate.

We have referred to the practice of the two houses of Congress; and we now shall notice some significant congressional enactments. May 3, 1798, c. 36, 1 Stat. 554, Congress provided that oaths or affirmations might be administered to witnesses by the President of the Senate, the Speaker of the House of Representatives, the chairman of a committee

of the whole, or the chairman of a select committee, "in any case under their examination." February 8, 1817, c. 10, 3 Stat. 345, it enlarged that provision so as to include the chairman of a standing committee. January 24, 1857, c. 19, 11 Stat. 155, it passed "An Act more effectually to enforce the attendance of witnesses on the summons of either house of Congress, and to compel them to discover testimony." This act provided, first, that any person summoned as a witness to give testimony or produce papers in any matter under inquiry before either house of Congress, or any committee of either house, who should wilfully make default, or, if appearing, should refuse to answer any question pertinent to the inquiry, should, in addition to the pains and penalties then existing, be deemed guilty of a misdemeanor and be subject to indictment and punishment as there prescribed; and secondly, that no person should be excused from giving evidence in such an inquiry on the ground that it might tend to incriminate or disgrace him, nor be held to answer criminally, or be subjected to any penalty or forfeiture, for any fact or act as to which he was required to testify, excepting that he might be subjected to prosecution for perjury committed while so testifying. January 24, 1862, c. 11, 12 Stat. 333, Congress modified the immunity provision in particulars not material here. These enactments are now embodied in Sections 101-104 and 859 of Revised Statutes. They show very plainly that Congress intended thereby (a) to recognize the power of either house to institute inquiries and exact evidence touching subjects within its jurisdiction and on which it was disposed to act; (b) to recognize that such inquiries may be conducted through committees; (c) to subject defaulting and contumacious witnesses to indictment and punishment in the courts, and thereby to enable either house to exert the power of inquiry "more effectually"; and (d) to open the way for obtaining evidence in such an inquiry, which otherwise could not be obtained, by exempting witnesses required to give evidence therein from criminal and penal prosecutions in respect of matters disclosed by their evidence.

Four decisions of this Court are cited and more or less relied on, and we now turn to them.

The first decision was in *Anderson v. Dunn*, 6 Wheat. 204. The question there was whether, under the Constitution, the House of Representatives has power to attach and punish a person other than a member for contempt of its authority—in fact, an attempt to bribe one of its members. The Court regarded the power as essential to the effective exertion of other powers expressly granted, and therefore as implied. The argument advanced to the contrary was that as the Constitution expressly grants to each house power to punish or expel its own members and says nothing about punishing others, the implication or inference, if any, is that power to punish one who is not a member is neither given nor intended. The Court answered this by saying:

(p. 225) "There is not in the whole of that admirable instrument, a grant of powers which does not draw after it others, not expressed, but vital to their exercise; not substantive and independent, indeed, but auxiliary and subordinate."

(p. 233) "This argument proves too much; for its direct application would lead to annihilation of almost every power of Congress. To enforce its laws upon any subject without the sanction of punishment is obviously impossible. Yet there is an express grant of power to punish in one class of cases and one only, and all the punishing power exercised by Congress in any cases, except those which relate to piracy and offenses against the laws of nations, is derived from implication. Nor did the idea ever occur to any one, that the express grant in one class of cases repelled the assumption of the punishing power in any other. The truth is, that the exercise of the powers given over their own members, was of such a delicate nature, that a constitutional provision became necessary to assert or communicate it. Constituted, as that body is, of the delegates of confederated States, some such provision was necessary to guard against their mutual jealousy, since every proceeding against a representative would indirectly affect the honour or interests of the state which sent him."

The next decision was in *Kilbourn v. Thompson*, 103 U.S. 168. The question there was whether the House of Representatives had exceeded its power in directing one of its committees to make a particular investigation. The decision was that it had. The principles announced and applied in the case are—that neither house of Congress possesses a "general power of making inquiry into the private affairs of the citizen"; that the power actually possessed is limited to inquiries relating to matters of which the particular house "has jurisdiction" and in respect of which it rightfully may take other action; that if the inquiry relates to "a matter wherein relief or redress could be had only by a judicial proceeding" it is not within the range of this power, but must be left to the courts, conformably to the constitutional separation of governmental powers; and that for the purpose of determining the essential character of the inquiry recourse may be had to the resolution or order under which it is made. The court examined the resolution which was the basis of the particular inquiry, and ascertained therefrom that the inquiry related to a private real-estate pool or partnership in the District of Columbia. Jay Cooke & Co. had had an interest in the pool, but had become bankrupts, and their estate was in course of administration in a federal bankruptcy court in Pennsylvania. The United States was one of their creditors. The trustee in the bankruptcy proceeding had effected a settlement of the bankrupts' interest in the pool, and of course his action was subject to examination and approval or disapproval by the bankruptcy court. Some of the creditors, including the United States, were dissatisfied with the settlement. In these circumstances, disclosed in the preamble, the resolution directed the committee "to inquire into the matter and history of said real-estate pool and the character of said settlement, with the amount of property involved in which Jay Cooke & Co. were interested, and the amount paid or to be paid in said settlement, with power to send for persons and papers and report to the House." The Court pointed out that the resolution contained no suggestion of contemplated legislation; that the matter was one in respect to which no valid legislation could be had; that the bankrupts' estate and the trustee's settlement were still pending in the bankruptcy court; and that the United States and other creditors were free to press their claims in that proceeding. And on these grounds the Court held that in undertaking the investigation "the House of Representatives not only exceeded the limit of its own authority, but assumed power which could only be properly exercised by another branch of the government, because it was in its nature clearly judicial."

The case has been cited at times, and is cited to us now, as strongly intimating, if not holding, that neither house of Congress has power to make inquiries and exact evidence in aid of contemplated legislation. There are expressions in the opinion which, separately considered, might bear such an interpretation; but that this was not intended is shown by the immediately succeeding statement (p. 189) that "This later proposition is one which we do not propose to decide in the present case because we are able to decide the case without passing upon the existence or non-existence of such a power in aid of the legislative function."

Next in order is *In re Chapman*, 166 U.S. 661. The inquiry there in question was conducted under a resolution of the Senate and related to charges, published in the press, that senators were yielding to corrupt influences in considering a tariff bill then before the Senate and were speculating in stocks the value of which would be affected by pending amendments to the bill. Chapman appeared before the committee in response to a subpoena, but refused to answer questions pertinent to the inquiry, and was indicted and convicted under the act of 1857 for his refusal. The Court sustained the constitutional validity of the act of 1857, and, after referring to the constitutional provision empowering either house to punish its members for disorderly behavior and by a vote of two-thirds to expel a member, held that the inquiry related to the integrity and fidelity of senators in the discharge of their duties, and therefore to a matter "within the range of the constitutional powers of the Senate" and in respect of which it could compel witnesses to appear and testify. In overruling an objection that the inquiry was without any defined or admissible purpose, in that the preamble and resolution made no reference to any contemplated expulsion, censure, or other action by the Senate, the Court held that they adequately disclosed a subject-matter of which the Senate had jurisdiction, that it was not essential that the Senate declare in advance what it meditated doing, and that the assumption could not be indulged that the Senate was making the inquiry without a legitimate object.

The case is relied on here as fully sustaining the power of either house to conduct investigations and exact testimony from witnesses for legislative purposes. In the course of the opinion (p. 671) it is said that disclosures by witnesses may be compelled constitutionally "to enable the respective bodies to discharge their legitimate functions, and that it was to effect this that the act of 1857 was passed"; and also "We grant that Congress could not divest itself, or either of its houses, of the essential and inherent power to punish for contempt, in cases to which the power of either house properly extended; but, because Congress, by the act of 1857, sought to aid each of the houses in the discharge of its constitutional functions, it does not follow that any delegation of the power in each to punish for contempt was involved." The terms "legitimate functions" and "constitutional functions" are broad and might well be regarded as including the legislative function, but as the case in hand did not call for any expression respecting that function, it hardly can be said that these terms were purposely used as including it.

The latest case is *Marshall v. Gordon*, 243 U.S. 521. The question there was whether the House of Representatives exceeded its power in punishing, as for a contempt of its authority, a person—not a member—who had written, published and sent to the chairman of one of its committees an ill-tempered and irritating letter respecting the action and purposes of the committee. Power to make inquiries and obtain evidence by compulsory process was not involved. The Court recognized distinctly that the House of Representatives has implied power to punish a person not a member for contempt, as was ruled in *Anderson v. Dunn, supra*, but held that its action in this instance was without constitutional justification. The decision was put on the ground that the letter, while offensive

and vexatious, was not calculated or likely to affect the House in any of its proceedings or in the exercise of any of its functions—in short, that the act which was punished as a contempt was not of such a character as to bring it within the rule that an express power draws after it others which are necessary and appropriate to give effect to it.

While these cases are not decisive of the question we are considering, they definitely settle two propositions which we recognize as entirely sound and having a bearing on its solution: One, that the two houses of Congress, in their separate relations, possess not only such powers as are expressly granted to them by the Constitution, but such auxiliary powers as are necessary and appropriate to make the express powers effective; and, the other, that neither house is invested with "general" power to inquire into private affairs and compel disclosures, but only with such limited power of inquiry as is shown to exist when the rule of constitutional interpretation just stated is rightly applied. The latter proposition has further support in *Harriman v. Interstate Commerce Commission*, 211 U.S. 407, 417-419, and *Federal Trade Commission v. American Tobacco Company*, 264 U.S. 298, 305-306.

With this review of the legislative practice, congressional enactments and court decisions, we proceed to a statement of our conclusions on the question.

We are of opinion that the power of inquiry—with process to enforce it—is an essential and appropriate auxiliary to the legislative function. It was so regarded and employed in American legislatures before the Constitution was framed and ratified. Both houses of Congress took this view of it early in their history—the House of Representatives with the approving votes of Mr. Madison and other members whose service in the convention which framed the Constitution gives special significance to their action—and both houses have employed the power accordingly up to the present time. The acts of 1798 and 1857, judged by their comprehensive terms, were intended to recognize the existence of this power in both houses and to enable them to employ it "more effectually" than before. So, when their practice in the matter is appraised according to the circumstances in which it was begun and to those in which it has been continued, it falls nothing short of a practical construction, long continued, of the constitutional provisions respecting their powers, and therefore should be taken as fixing the meaning of those provisions, if otherwise doubtful.

We are further of opinion that the provisions are not of doubtful meaning, but, as was held by this Court in the cases we have reviewed, are intended to be effectively exercised, and therefore to carry with them such auxiliary powers as are necessary and appropriate to that end. While the power to exact information in aid of the legislative function was not involved in those cases, the rule of interpretation applied there is applicable here. A legislative body cannot legislate wisely or effectively in the absence of information respecing the conditions which the legislation is intended to affect or change; and where the legislative body does not itself possess the requisite information—which not infrequently is true—recourse must be had to others who do possess it. Experience has taught that mere requests for such information often are unavailing, and also that information which is volunteered is not always accurate or complete; so some means of compulsion are essential to obtain what is needed. All this was true before and when the Constitution was framed and adopted. In that period the power of inquiry—with enforcing process—was regarded and employed as a necessary and appropriate attribute of the power to legislate—indeed, was treated as inhering in it. Thus there is ample warrant for thinking, as we do, that the constitutional provisions which commit the legislative function to the two houses are intended to include this attribute to the end that the function may be effectively exercised.

The contention is earnestly made on behalf of the witness that this power of inquiry, if sustained, may be abusively and oppressively exerted. If this be so, it affords no ground for denying the power. The same contention might be directed against the power to legislate, and of course would be unavailing. We must assume, for present purposes, that neither house will be disposed to exert the power beyond its proper bounds, or without due regard to the rights of witnesses. But if, contrary to this assumption, controlling limitations or restrictions are disregarded, the decisions in *Kilbourn v. Thompson* and *Marshall v. Gordon* point to admissible measures of relief. And it is a necessary deduction from the decisions in *Kilbourn v. Thompson* and *In re Chapman* that a witness rightfully may refuse to answer where the bounds of the power are exceeded or the questions are not pertinent to the matter under inquiry.

We come now to the question whether it sufficiently appears that the purpose for which the witness's testimony was sought was to obtain information in aid of the legislative function. The court below answered the question in the negative and put its decision largely on this ground, as is shown by the following excerpts from its opinion (299 Fed. 638, 639, 640):

"It will be noted that in the second resolution the Senate has expressly avowed that the investigation is in aid of other action than legislation. Its purpose is to 'obtain information necessary as a basis for such legislative and other action as the Senate may deem necessary and proper.' This indicates that the Senate is contemplating the taking of action other than legislative, as the outcome of the investigation, at least the possibility of so doing. The extreme personal cast of the original resolutions; the spirit of hostility towards the then Attorney General which they breathe; that it was not avowed that legislative action was had in view until after the action of the Senate had been challenged; and that the avowal then was coupled with an avowal that other action was had in view—are calculated to create the impression that the idea of legislative action being in contemplation was an afterthought.

"That the Senate has in contemplation the possibility of taking action other than legislation as an outcome of the investigation, as thus expressly avowed, would seem of itself to invalidate the entire proceeding. But, whether so or not, the Senate's action is invalid and absolutely void, in that, in ordering and conducting the investigation, it is exercising the judicial function, and power to exercise that function, in such a case as we have here, has not been conferred upon it expressly or by fair implication. What it is proposing to do is to determine the guilt of the Attorney General of the shortcomings and wrongdoings set forth in the resolutions. It is 'to hear, adjudge, and condemn.' In so doing it is exercising the judicial function.

"What the Senate is engaged in doing is not investigating the Attorney General's office; it is investigating the former Attorney General. What it has done is to put him on trial before it. In so doing it is exercising the judicial function. This it has no power to do."

We are of opinion that the court's ruling on this question was wrong, and that it sufficiently appears, when the proceedings are rightly interpreted, that the object of the investigation and of the effort to secure the witness's testimony was to obtain information for legislative purposes.

It is quite true that the resolution directing the investigation does not in terms avow that it is intended to be in aid of legislation; but it does show that the subject to be investigated was the administration of the Department of Justice—whether its functions were being properly discharged or were being neglected or misdirected and particularly whether the Attorney General and his assistants were performing or neglecting their duties in respect of the institution and prosecution of proceedings to punish crimes and enforce appropriate remedies against the wrongdoers—specific instances of alleged neglect being recited. Plainly the subject was one on which legislation could be had and would be materially aided by the information which the investigation was calculated to elicit. This becomes manifest when it is reflected that the functions of the Department of Justice, the powers and duties of the Attorney General and the duties of his assistants, are all subject to regulation by congressional legislation, and that the department is maintained and its activities are carried on under such appropriations as in the judgment of Congress are needed from year to year.

The only legitimate object the Senate could have in ordering the investigation was to aid it in legislating; and we think the subject-matter was such that the presumption should be indulged that this was the real object. An express avowal of the object would have been better; but in view of the particular subject-matter was not indispensable. In the *Chapman* case, where the resolution contained no avowal, this Court pointed out that it plainly related to a subject-matter of which the Senate had jurisdiction, and said "We cannot assume on this record that the action of the Senate was without a legitimate object;" and also that "it was certainly not necessary that the resolutions should declare in advance what the Senate meditated doing when the investigation was concluded." (166 U.S. 669-670) In *People v. Keeler*, 99 N.Y. 463, where the Court of Appeals of New York sustained an investigation ordered by the Senate of that state where the resolution contained no avowal, but disclosed that it definitely related to the administration of a public office the duties of which were subject to legislative regulation, the court said (pp. 485, 487): "Where public institutions under the control of the State are ordered to be investigated it is generally with the view of some legislative action respecting them, and the same may be said in respect of public officers." And again: "We are bound to presume that the action of the legislative body was with a legitimate object if it is capable of being so construed, and we have no right to assume that the contrary was intended."

While we rest our conclusion respecting the object of the investigation on the grounds just stated, it is well to observe that this view of what was intended is not new, but was shown in the debate on the resolution.

Of course, our concern is with the substance of the resolution and not with any nice questions of propriety respecting its direct reference to the then Attorney General by name. The resolution, like the charges which prompted its adoption, related to the activites of the department while he was its supervising officer; and the reference to him by name served to designate the period to which the investigation was directed.

We think the resolution and proceedings give no warrant for thinking the Senate was attempting or intending to try the Attorney General at its bar or before its committee for any crime or wrongdoing. Nor do we think it a valid objection to the investigation that it might possibly disclose crime or wrongdoing on his part.

The second resolution—the one directing that the witness be attached—declares that his testimony is sought with the purpose of obtaining "information necessary as a basis for such legislative and other action as the Senate may deem necessary and proper." This avowal of contemplated legislation is in accord with what we think is the right interpretation of the earlier resolution directing the investigation. The suggested possibility of "other action" if deemed "necessary or proper" is of course open to criticism in that there is no other action in the matter which would be within the power of the Senate. But we do not assent to the view that this indefinite and untenable suggestion invalidates the entire proceeding. The right view in our opinion is that it takes nothing from the lawful object avowed in the same resolution and rightly inferable from the earlier one. It is not as if an inadmissible or unlawful object were affirmatively and definitely avowed.

We conclude that the investigation was ordered for a legitimate object; that the witness wrongfully refused to appear and testify before the committee and was lawfully attached; that the Senate is entitled to have him give testimony pertinent to the inquiry, either at its bar or before the committee; and that the district court erred in discharging him from custody under the attachment.

Another question has arisen which should be noticed. It is whether the case has become moot. The investigation was ordered and the committee appointed during the Sixty-eighth Congress. That Congress expired March 4, 1925. The resolution ordering the investigation in terms limited the committee's authority to the period of the Sixty-eighth Congress; but this apparently was changed by a later and amendatory resolution authorizing the committee to sit at such times and places as it might deem advisable or necessary. It is said in Jefferson's Manual: "Neither House can continue any portion of itself in any parliamentary function beyond the end of the session without the consent of the other two branches. When done, it is by a bill constituting them commissioners for the particular purpose." But the context shows that the reference is to the two houses of Parliament when adjourned by prorogation or dissolution by the King. The rule may be the same with the House of Representatives whose members are all elected for the period of a single Congress; but it cannot well be the same with the Senate, which is a continuing body whose members are elected for a term of six years and so divided into classes that the seats of one-third only become vacant at the end of each Congress, two-thirds always continuing into the next Congress, save as vacancies may occur through death or resignation.

Mr. Hinds in his collection of precedents says: "The Senate, as a continuing body, may continue its committees through the recess following the expiration of a Congress;" and, after quoting the above statement from Jefferson's Manual, he says: "The Senate, however, being a continuing body, gives authority to its committees during the recess after the expiration of a Congress." So far as we are advised the select committee having this investigation in charge has neither made a final report nor been discharged; nor has it been continued by an affirmative order. Apparently its activities have been suspended pending the decision of this case. But, be this as it may, it is certain that the committee may be continued or revived now by motion to that effect, and, if continued or revived, will have all its original powers. This being so, and the Senate being a continuing body, the case cannot be said to have become moot in the ordinary sense. The situation is measurably like that in *Southern Pacific Terminal Co. v. Interstate Commerce Commission*, 219 U.S. 498, 514-516, where it was held that a suit to enjoin the enforcement of an order of the Interstate Commerce Commission did not become moot through the expiration of the order where it was capable of repetition by the commission and was a matter of public interest. Our judgment may yet be carried into effect and the investigation proceeded with from the point at which it apparently was interrupted by reason of the *habeas corpus* proceedings. In these circumstances we think a judgment should be rendered as was done in the case cited.

What has been said requires that the final order in the district court discharging the witness from custody be reversed.

Final order reversed.

Mr. Justice Stone did not participate in the consideration or decision of the case.

Article of Impeachment Against President Andrew Johnson

Following is the complete text of the articles of impeachment against President Andrew Johnson:

Articles exhibited by the House of Representatives of the United States, in the name of themselves and all the people of the United States, against Andrew Johnson, President of the United States, in maintenance and support of their impeachment against him for high crimes and misdemeanors in office.

Article I

That said Andrew Johnson, President of the United States, on the 21st day of February, in the year of our Lord 1868, at Washington, in the District of Columbia, unmindful of the high duties of his office, of his oath of office, and of the requirement of the Constitution that he should take care that the laws be faithfully executed, did unlawfully, and in violation of the Constitution and laws of the United States, issue an order in writing for the removal of Edwin M. Stanton from the office of Secretary for the Department of War, said Edwin M. Stanton having been theretofore duly appointed and commissioned, by and with the advice and consent of the Senate of the United States, as such Secretary, and said Andrew Johnson, President of the United States, on the 12th day of August, in the year of our Lord 1867, and during the recess of said Senate, having suspended by his order Edwin M. Stanton from said office, and within twenty days after the first day of the next meeting of said Senate—that is to say, on the 12th day of December, in the year last aforesaid—having reported to said Senate such suspension, with the evidence and reasons for his action in the case and the name of the person designated to perform the duties of such office temporarily until the next meeting of the Senate, and said Senate thereafterwards, on the 13th day of January, in the year of our Lord 1868, having duly considered the evidence and reasons reported by said Andrew Johnson for said suspension, and having refused to concur in said suspension, whereby and by force of the provisions of an act entitled "An act regulating the tenure of certain civil offices," passed March 2, 1867, said Edwin M. Stanton did forthwith resume the functions of his office, whereof the said Andrew Johnson had then and there due notice, and said Edwin M. Stanton, by reason of the premises, on said 21st day of February, being lawfully entitled to hold said office of Secretary for the Department of War, which said order for the removal of said Edwin M. Stanton is, in substance, as follows, that is to say:

"Executive Mansion,
"Washington, D.C., February 21, 1868.
"Sir: By virtue of the power and authority vested in me as President by the Constitution and laws of the United States you are hereby removed from office as Secretary for the Department of War, and your functions as such will terminate upon receipt of this communication.
"You will transfer to Brevet Maj. Gen. Lorenzo Thomas, Adjutant-General of the Army, who has this day been authorized and empowered to act as Secretary of War ad interim, all records, books, papers, and other public property now in your custody and charge.
"Respectfully, yours,

ANDREW JOHNSON.
"Hon. Edwin M. Stanton, *Washington, D.C.*"
Which order was unlawfully issued with intent then and there to violate the act entitled "An act regulating the tenure of certain civil offices," passed March 2, 1867; and with the further intent, contrary to the provisions of said act, in violation thereof, and contrary to the provisions of the Constitution of the United States, and without the advice and consent of the Senate of the United States, the said Senate then and there being in session, to remove said Edwin M. Stanton from the office of Secretary for the Department of War, the said Edwin M. Stanton being then and there Secretary of War, and being then and there in the due and lawful execution and discharge of the duties of said office, whereby said Andrew Johnson, President of the United States, did then and there commit, and was guilty of a high misdemeanor in office.

Article II

That on said 21st day of February, in the year of our Lord 1868, at Washington, in the District of Columbia, said Andrew Johnson, President of the United States, unmindful of the high duties of his office, of his oath of office, and in violation of the Constitution of the United States, and contrary to the provisions of an act entitled "An act regulating the tenure of certain civil offices," passed March 2, 1867, without the advice and consent of the Senate of the United States, said Senate then and there being in session, and without authority of law, did, with intent to violate the Constitution of the United States and the act aforesaid, issue and deliver to one Lorenzo Thomas a letter of authority, in substance as follows, that is to say:

"Executive Mansion,
"Washington, D.C., February 21, 1968.
"Sir: Hon. Edwin M. Stanton having been this day removed from office as Secretary for the Department of War, you are hereby authorized and empowered to act as Secretary of War ad interim, and will immediately enter upon the discharge of the duties pertaining to that office.
"Mr. Stanton has been instructed to transfer to you all the records, books, papers, and other public property now in his custody and charge.
"Respectfully, yours,

ANDREW JOHNSON.
"To Brevet Maj. Gen. Lorenzo Thomas,
"Adjutant-General United States Army, Washington, D.C."
Then and there being no vacancy in said office of Secretary for the Department of War, whereby said Andrew Johnson, President of the United States, did then and there commit, and was guilty of a high misdemeanor in office.

Article III

That said Andrew Johnson, President of the United States, on the 21st day of February, in the year of our Lord 1868, at Washington, in the District of Columbia, did commit and was guilty of a high misdemeanor in office in this, that, without authority of law, while the Senate of the United States was then and there in session, he did appoint one Lorenzo Thomas to be Secretary for the Department of War ad interim, without the advice and consent of the Senate and with intent to violate the Constitution of the United States, no vacancy having happened in said office of Secretary for the Department of War during the recess of the Senate, and no vacancy existing in said office at the time, and which said appointment, so made by said Andrew Johnson, of said Lorenzo Thomas, is in substance as follows, that is to say:

"Executive Mansion,
"Washington, D.C., February 21, 1868.
"Sir: Hon. Edwin M. Stanton having been this day removed from office as Secretary for the Department of War, you are hereby authorized and empowered to act as Secretary of War ad interim, and will immediately enter upon the discharge of the duties pertaining to that office.
"Mr. Stanton has been instructed to transfer to you all the records, books, papers, and other public property now in his custody and charge.
"Respectfully, yours,

ANDREW JOHNSON.
"To Brevet Maj. Gen. Lorenzo Thomas,
"Adjutant-General United States Army, Washington, D.C."

Article IV

That said Andrew Johnson, President of the United States, unmindful of the high duties of his office and of his oath of office, in violation of the Constitution and laws of the United States, on the 21st day of February, in the year of our Lord 1868, at Washington, in the District of Columbia, did unlawfully conspire with one Lorenzo Thomas, and with other persons to the House of Representatives unknown, with intent, by intimidation and threats, unlawfully to hinder and prevent Edwin M. Stanton, then and there the Secretary for the Department of War, duly appointed under the laws of the United States, from holding said office of Secretary for the Department of War, contrary to and in violation of the Constitution of the United States and of the provisions of an act entitled "An act to define and punish certain conspiracies," approved July 31, 1861, whereby said Andrew Johnson, President of the United States, did then and there commit, and was guilty of a high crime in office.

Article V

That said Andrew Johnson, President of the United States, unmindful of the high duties of his office and of his oath of office, on the 21st day of February, in the year of our Lord 1868, and on divers other days and times in said year, before the 2d day of March, A.D. 1868, at Washington, in the District of Columbia, did unlawfully conspire with one Lorenzo Thomas, and with other persons to the House of Representatives unknown, to prevent and hinder the execution of an act entitled "An act regulating the tenure of certain civil offices," passed March 2, 1867, and in pursuance of said conspiracy did unlawfully attempt to prevent Edwin M. Stanton, then and there being Secretary for the Department of War, duly appointed and commissioned under the laws of the United States, from holding said office, whereby the said Andrew Johnson, President of the United States, did then and there commit and was guilty of a high misdemeanor in office.

Article VI

That said Andrew Johnson, President of the United States, unmindful of the high duties of his office and of his oath of office, on the 21st day of February, in the year of our Lord 1868, at Washington, in the District of Columbia, did unlawfully conspire with one Lorenzo Thomas, by force to seize, take, and possess the property of the United States in the Department of War, and then and there in the custody and charge of Edwin M. Stanton, Secretary for said Department, contrary to the provisions of an act entitled "An act to define and punish certain conspiracies," approved July 31, 1861, and with intent to violate and disregard an act entitled "An act regulating the tenure of certain civil offices," passed March 2, 1867, whereby said Andrew Johnson, President of the United States, did then and there commit a high crime in office.

Article VII

That said Andrew Johnson, President of the United States, unmindful of the high duties of his office and of his oath of office, on the 21st day of February, in the year of our Lord 1868, at Washington, in the District of Columbia, did unlawfully conspire with one Lorenzo Thomas with intent unlawfully to seize, take, and possess the property of the United States in the Department of War, in the custody and charge of Edwin M. Stanton, Secretary for said Department, with intent to violate and disregard the act entitled "An act regulating the tenure of certain civil offices," passed March 2, 1867, whereby said Andrew Johnson, President of the United States, did then and there commit a high misdemeanor in office.

Article VIII

That said Andrew Johnson, President of the United States, unmindful of the high duties of his office and of his oath of office, with intent unlawfully to control the disbursements of the moneys appropriated for the military service and for the Department of War, on the 21st day of February, in the year of our Lord 1868, at Washington, in the District of Columbia, did unlawfully and contrary to the provisions of an act entitled "An act regulating the tenure of certain civil offices," passed March 2, 1867, and in violation of the Constitution of the United States, and without the advice and consent of the Senate of the United States, and while the Senate was then and there in session, there being no vacancy in the office of Secretary for the Department of War, with intent to violate and disregard the act aforesaid, then and there issue and deliver to one Lorenzo Thomas a letter of authority in writing, in substance as follows, that is to say:

"Executive Mansion,

"Washington, D.C., February 21, 1868.

"Sir: Hon. Edwin M. Stanton having been this day removed from office as Secretary for the Department of War, you are hereby authorized and empowered to act as Secretary of War ad interim, and will immediately enter upon the discharge of the duties pertaining to that office.

"Mr. Stanton has been instructed to transfer to you all the records, books, papers, and other public property now in his custody and charge.

"Respectfully, yours,

ANDREW JOHNSON.

"Brevet Maj. Gen. Lorenzo Thomas,

"Adjutant-General United States Army, Washington, D.C.

whereby said Andrew Johnson, President of the United States, did then and there commit and was guilty of a high misdemeanor in office.

Article IX

That said Andrew Johnson, President of the United States, on the 22d day of February, in the year of our Lord 1868, at Washington, in the District of Columbia, in disregard of the Constitution and the laws of the United States, duly enacted, as Commander in Chief of the Army of the United States, did bring before himself then and there William H. Emory, a major-general by brevet in the Army of the United States, actually in command of the Department of Washington and the military forces thereof, and did then and there, as such Commander in Chief, declare to

and instruct said Emory that part of a law of the United States, passed March 2, 1867, entitled "An act making appropriations for the support of the Army for the year ending June 30, 1868, and for other purposes," especially the second section thereof which provides among other things, that "all orders and instructions relating to military operations issued by the President or Secretary of War shall be issued through the General of the Army, and, in case of his inability, through the next in rank," was unconstitutional and in contravention of the commission of said Emory, and which said provision of law had been theretofore duly and legally promulgated by general order for the government and direction of the Army of the United States, as the said Andrew Johnson then and there well knew, with intent thereby to induce said Emory, in his official capacity as commander of the Department of Washington, to violate the provisions of said act, and to take and receive, act upon, and obey such orders as he, the said Andrew Johnson, might make and give, and which should not be issued through the General of the Army of the United States, according to the provisions of said act, and with the further intent thereby to enable him, the said Andrew Johnson, to prevent the execution of an act entitled "An act regulating the tenure of certain civil offices," passed March 2, 1867, and to unlawfully prevent Edwin M. Stanton, then being Secretary for the Department of War, from holding said office and discharging the duties thereof, whereby said Andrew Johnson, President of the United States, did then and there commit and was guilty of a high misdemeanor in office.

Article X

That said Andrew Johnson, President of the United States, unmindful of the high duties of his office and the dignity and proprieties thereof, and of the harmony and courtesies which ought to exist and be maintained between the executive and legislative branches of the Government of the United States, designing and intending to set aside the rightful authority and powers of Congress, did attempt to bring into disgrace, ridicule, hatred, contempt, and reproach the Congress of the United States and the several branches thereof, to impair and destroy the regard and respect of all the good people of the United States for the Congress and legislative power thereof (which all officers of the Government ought inviolably to preserve and maintain), and to excite the odium and resentment of all the good people of the United States against Congress and the laws by it duly and constitutionally enacted; and in pursuance of his said design and intent, openly and publicly, and before divers assemblages of the citizens of the United States convened in divers parts thereof to meet and receive said Andrew Johnson as the Chief Magistrate of the United States, did, on the 18th day of August, in the year of our Lord 1866, and on divers other days and times, as well before as afterwards, make and deliver with a loud voice certain intemperate, inflammatory, and scandalous harangues, and did therein utter loud threats and bitter menaces as well against Congress as the laws of the United States duly enacted thereby, amid the cries, jeers, and laughter of the multitudes then assembled and within hearing, which are set forth in the several specifications hereinafter written, in substance and effect, that is to say:

Specification first.—In this, that at Washington, in the District of Columbia, in the Executive Mansion, to a committee of citizens who called upon the President of the United States, speaking of and concerning the Congress of the United States, said Andrew Johnson, President of the United States, heretofore, to wit, on the 18th day of August, in the year of our Lord 1866, did, in a loud voice, declare in substance and effect, among other things, that is to say:

"So far as the executive department of the Government is concerned, the effort has been made to restore the Union, to heal the breach, to pour oil into the wounds which were consequent upon the struggle, and (to speak in common phrase) to prepare, as the learned and wise physician would, a plaster healing in character and coextensive with the wound. We thought, and we think, that we had partially succeeded; but as the work progresses, as reconstruction seemed to be taking place and the country was becoming reunited, we found a disturbing and marring element opposing us. In alluding to that element, I shall go no further than your convention and the distinguished gentleman who has delivered to me the report of its proceedings. I shall make no reference to it that I do not believe the time and the occasion justify.

"We have witnessed in one department of the Government every endeavor to prevent the restoration of peace, harmony, and union. We have seen hanging upon the verge of the Government, as it were, a body called, or which assumes to be, the Congress of the United States, while in fact it is a Congress of only a part of the States. We have seen this Congress pretend to be for the Union when its every step and act tended to perpetrate disunion and make a disruption of the States inevitable. *** We have seen Congress gradually encroach step by step upon constitutional rights and violate, day after day and month after month, fundamental principles of the Government. We have seen a Congress that seemed to forget that there was a limit to the sphere and scope of legislation. We have seen a Congress in a minority assume to exercise power which, allowed to be consummated, would result in despotism or monarchy itself."

Specification second.—In this, that at Cleveland, in the State of Ohio, heretofore, to wit, on the 3d day of September, in the year of our Lord 1866, before a public assemblage of citizens and others, said Andrew Johnson, President of the United States, speaking of and concerning the Congress of the United States did, in a loud voice, declare in substance and effect among other things, that is to say:

"I will tell you what I did do. I called upon your Congress that is trying to break up the Government...."

"In conclusion, beside that, Congress had taken much pains to poison their constituents against him. But what had Congress done? Have they done anything to restore the union of these States? No; on the contrary, they had done everything to prevent it; and because he stood now where he did when the rebellion commenced he had been denounced as a traitor. Who had run greater risks or made greater sacrifices than himself? But Congress, factious and domineering, had undertaken to poison the minds of the American people."

Specification third.—In this, that at St. Louis, in the State of Missouri, heretofore, to wit, on the 8th day of September, in the year of our Lord 1866, before a public assemblage of citizens and others, said Andrew Johnson, President of the United States, speaking of and concerning the Congress of the United States, did, in a loud voice, declare, in substance and effect, among other things, that is to say:

"Go on. Perhaps if you had a word or two on the subject of New Orleans you might understand more about it than you do. And if you will go back—if you will go back and ascertain the cause of the riot at New Orleans, perhaps you will not be so promt in calling out 'New Orleans.' If you will take up the riot at New Orleans and trace it back to its source or its immediate cause, you will find out who was responsible for the blood that was shed there. If you will take up the riot at New Orleans and trace it back to the Radical Congress, you will find that the riot at New Orleans was substantially planned. If you will take up the proceedings in their caucuses, you will understand that they there knew that a convention was to be called which was extinct by its power having expired; that it was said that the intention was that a new government was to be organized, and on the organization of that government the intention was to enfranchise one portion of the population, called the colored population, who had just been emancipated, and at the same time disenfranchise white men. When you design to talk about New Orleans you ought to understand what you are talking about. When you read the speeches that were made, and take up the facts on the Friday and Saturday before that convention sat, you will there find that speeches were made incendiary in their character, exciting that portion of the population, the black population, to arm themselves and prepare for the shedding of blood. You will also find that that convention did assemble in violation of law, and the intention of that convention was to supersede the reorganized authorities in the State government of Louisiana, which had been recognized by the Government of the United States; and every man engaged in that rebellion in that convention, with the intention of superseding and upturning the civil government which had been recognized by the Government of the United States, I say that he was a traitor to the Constitution of the United States, and hence you find that another rebellion was commenced having its origin in the Radical Congress....

"So much for the New Orleans riot. And there was the cause and the origin of the blood that was shed; and every drop of blood that was shed is upon their skirts, and they are responsible for it. I could test this thing a little closer, but will not do it here tonight. But when you talk about the causes and consequences that resulted from proceedings of that kind, perhaps as I have been introduced here and you have provoked questions of this kind, though it does not provoke me, I will tell you a few wholesome things that have been done by this Radical Congress in connection with New Orleans and the extension of the elective franchise.

"I know that I have been traduced and abused. I know it has come in advance of me here, as elsewhere, that I have attempted to exercise an arbitrary power in resisting laws that were intended to be forced upon the Government; that I had exercised that power; that I had abandoned the party that elected me, and that I was a traitor because I exercised the veto power in attempting and did arrest for a time a bill that was called a 'Freedman's Bureau' bill; yes, that I was a traitor. And I have been traduced, I have been slandered, I have been maligned, I have been called Judas Iscariot, and all that. Now, my countrymen here tonight, it is very easy to indulge in epithets; it is easy to call a man a Judas and cry out traitor; but when he is called upon to give arguments and facts he is very easy to indulge in epithets; it is easy to call a man a Judas and and he was one of the twelve apostles. Oh yes; the twelve apostles had a Christ. The twelve apostles had a Christ, and he never could have had a Judas unless he had had twelve apostles. If I have played the Judas,

who has been my Christ that I have played the Judas with? Was it Thad. Stevens? Was it Wendell Philips? Was it Charles Sumner? These are the men that stop and compare themselves with the Saviour; and everybody that differs with them in opinion, and to try and stay and arrest the diabolical and nefarious policy, is to be denounced as a Judas....

"Well, let me say to you, if you will stand by me in this action; if you will stand by me in trying to give the people a fair chance, soldiers and citizens, to participate in these offices, God being willing, I will kick them out. I will kick them out just as fast as I can.

"Let me say to you, in concluding, that what I have said I intended to say. I was not provoked into this, and I care not for their menaces, the taunts, and the jeers. I care not for threats. I do not intend to be bullied by my enemies nor overawed by my friends. But, God willing, with your help I will veto their measures whenever any of them come to me."

Which said utterances, declarations, threats, and harangues, highly censurable in any, are peculiarly indecent and unbecoming in the Chief Magistrate of the United States, by means whereof said Andrew Johnson has brought the high office of the President of the United States into contempt, ridicule, and disgrace, to the great scandal of all good citizens, whereby said Andrew Johnson, President of the United States, did commit, and was then and there guilty of, a high misdemeanor in office.

Article XI

That said Andrew Johnson, President of the United States, unmindful of the high duties of his office and of his oath of office, and in disregard of the Constitution and laws of the United States, did heretofore, to wit, on the 18th day of August, 1866, at the city of Washington, and the District of Columbia, by public speech, declare and affirm, in substance, that the Thirty-ninth Congress of the United States was not a Congress of the United States authorized by the Constitution to exercise legislative power under the same; but, on the contrary, was a Congress of only part of the States, thereby denying and intending to deny that the legislation of said Congress was valid or obligatory upon him, the said Andrew Johnson, except in so far as he saw fit to approve the same, and also thereby denying and intending to deny the power of the said Thirty-ninth Congress to propose amendments to the Constitution of the United States; and, in pursuance of said declaration, the said Andrew Johnson, President of the United States, afterwards, to wit, on the 21st day of February, 1868, at the city of Washington, in the District of Columbia, did unlawfully and in disregard of the requirements of the Constitution, that he should take care that the laws be faithfully executed, attempt to prevent the execution of an act entitled "An act regulating the tenure of certain civil offices," passed March 2, 1867, by unlawfully devising and contriving, and attempting to devise and contrive, means by which he should prevent Edwin M. Stanton from forthwith resuming the functions of the office of the office of Secretary for the Department of War, notwithstanding the refusal of the Senate to concur in the suspension theretofore made by said Andrew Johnson, of said Edwin M. Stanton from said office of Secretary for the Department of War, and also by further unlawfully devising and contriving, and attempting to devise and contrive, means then and there to prevent the execution of an act entitled "An act making appropriations for the support of the Army for the fiscal year ending June 30, 1868, and for other purposes," approved March 2, 1867, and also to prevent the execution of an act entitled "An act to provide for the more efficient government of the rebel States," passed March 2, 1867; whereby the said Andrew Johnson, President of the United States, did then, to wit, on the 21st day of February, 1868, at the city of Washington, commit and was guilty of a high misdemeanor in office.

And the House of Representatives, by protestation, saving to themselves the liberty of exhibiting at any time hereafter any further articles or other accusation or impeachment against the said Andrew Johnson, President of the United States, and also of replying to his answers which he shall make unto the articles herein preferred against him, and of offering proof to the same and every part thereof, and to all and every other article, accusation, or impeachment which shall be exhibited by them, as the case shall require, do demand that the said Andrew Johnson may be put to answer the high crimes and misdemeanors in office herein charged against him, and that such proceedings, examinations, trials, and judgments may be thereupon had and given as may be agreeable to law and justice.

SCHUYLER COLFAX,
Speaker of the House of Representatives.

Attest:
Edward McPherson,
Clerk of the House of Representatives.

House Judiciary Committee Rules of Procedure on Private Bills

Subcommittee No. 1
(Immigration and Nationality)

1. The regular meeting day of the Subcommittee will be Thursday or upon the call of the chairman.

2. All meetings of the Subcommittee shall be public except on the order of the chairman or a majority of the members present.

3. A quorum of the Subcommittee shall consist of one member for the purpose of holding hearings on private bills and four members for the purpose of making recommendations to the Committee.

4. Requests for reports on private bills from the Departments shall be made only upon a written request addressed to the chairman of the Subcommittee or the chairman of the Committee on the Judiciary by the author of such bill. That request shall contain the following information which shall be submitted to the Committee in triplicate:

(a) In the case of aliens who are physically in the United States:

The date and place of the alien's entry into the United States; his immigration status at that time (visitor, student, exchange student, seaman, stowaway, illegal border crosser, etc.); his age; place of birth; address in the United States; and the location of the United States Consulate at which he obtained his visa, if any.

(b) In the case of aliens who are residing outside of the United States:

The alien's age; place of birth; address; and the location of the United States Consulate before which his application for a visa is pending; and the address and relationship of the person primarily interested in the alien's admission to the United States.

5. The staff of the Subcommittee shall not receive nor forward to the Subcommittee for action any requests for reports which do not comply fully with the provisions of Rule 4.

6. The Subcommittee shall not address to the Attorney General communications designed to defer deportation of beneficiaries of private bills who have entered the United States as visitors, exchange visitors, students, stowaways, in transit, or deserting seamen, or by surreptitiously entering without inspection through the land or sea borders of the United States.

Exemption from this rule may be granted by the Subcommittee in cases where the bill is designed to prevent extreme hardship. However, no such exemption may be granted unless the author of the bill has secured and filed with the Subcommittee full and complete documentary evidence in support of his request to waive this rule.

7. No private bill shall be considered if an administrative remedy exists, or where court proceedings are pending for the purpose of adjusting or changing the immigration status of the beneficiary.

8. No favorable consideration shall be given to any private bill until the proper Department has had a reasonable time to submit a report.

9. Upon the receipt of reports from the Departments, private bills shall be scheduled for Subcommittee consideration in the chronological order of their introduction, except that priority shall be given to bills introduced earliest in any of the previous Congresses.

10. Consideration of private bills designed to adjust the status of aliens who are in the United States shall not be deferred due to nonappearance at Subcommittee hearings of the author of the bill or persons authorized to represent him.

11. Bills previously tabled shall not be reconsidered unless new evidence is introduced showing a material change of the facts known to the Committee.

Approved by the Committee on the Judiciary March 11, 1969.

SOURCE: U.S. House of Representatives, Committee on the Judiciary, Subcommittee No. 1, *Rules of Procedure (Private Legislation)* (4-page leaflet, 1970).

Subcommittee No. 2 (Claims)

1. The meeting of the Subcommittee shall be held on Wednesday of each week at 10 A.M., unless otherwise ordered by the chairman.

2. All meetings of the Subcommittee shall be executive except on the order of the chairman or a majority of the members present.

3. A quorum of the Subcommittee shall consist of five members.

4. No consideration shall be given to any bill unless request is made by the author or sponsor thereof, who shall file sufficient evidence in its support, and until the report of the Government Department or office has been secured. The clerk will secure said report upon request.

5. Upon completion of the file, the staff shall present the bill to the Subcommittee. The chairman may then refer the bill to a special Subcommittee which may consist of one or more members.

6. Presentation of oral evidence at hearings on private bills shall be limited to 15 minutes for each side. This rule may be modified by order of the chairman in his discretion.

7. The chairman is authorized to report favorably bills favorably reported in a preceding Congress by the Committee and passed by the House, but if it shall appear to the chairman that the bill requires further consideration, rule 5 shall apply.

8. The chairman is authorized to report favorably bills appropriating not more than $500, when such bills are recommended for enactment by the Government Department or office involved.

9. The Subcommittee shall not consider any claim which accrued prior to Jan. 1, 1954, unless the claim was favorably reported during the 90th Congress, but this rule will not bar the consideration of those claims which were finally disposed of after that date by a court or Government agency. This rule may be waived only upon order of two-thirds of the Subcommittee, present and voting. (Note by the Subcommittee staff in the pamphlet containing the rules: "In accordance with established practice, the Subcommittee advanced the date two years from that fixed during the 90th Congress.")

10. The Subcommittee shall not consider any claim adversely reported or rejected by it at a prevsious consideration, except upon presentation of new or additional evidence disclosing a material change in the facts which, in the chairman's opinion, is sufficient to warrant reopening the case.

11. The Subcommittee shall not consider any claim filed with the Bureau of Employees' Compensation, Department of Labor, considered on its merits and disallowed; or any bill awarding or increasing compensation to an employee or his dependents in lieu of that prescribed by Chapter 81, Compensation for Work Injuries, of Title 5, United States Code (formerly the Federal Employees' Compensation Act of Sept. 7, 1916, as amended), or otherwise interfering with the provisions and compensation of that chapter, except bills to waive the limitations of time contained in Sections 8119, 8121 and 8122, of Chapter 81 ot Title 5 (or of Sections 15 to 20, inclusive, of the previous act), and these sections may be waived only upon order of two-thirds of the Subcommittee, present and voting.

12. The Subcommittee shall not consider any claim for retirement benefits, compensation, or gratuity by an employee of the Government, or a member of the Armed Forces or the Reserves, or by his dependents, when the retirement benefits, compensation, pension, or gratuity to which such person claims to be entitled is specifically covered by statutes, which apply in a uniform manner to all similarly situated individuals.

13. The Subcommittee shall not consider any claim for injuries or damage, either to a member or to third persons, resulting from service in or activities by the National Guard maintained within the several States.

14. The Subcommittee shall not consider any claim over which another tribunal, court, or Department has jurisdiction, until all remedies under such jurisdiction are exhausted.

15. The Subcommittee shall not consider any claim approved by the Congress and vetoed by the President, except upon a material change in the facts or written evidence that Administration disapproval has been withdrawn; and this rule may be waived only upon order of two-thirds of the Subcommittee, present and voting.

16. In all bills carrying an appropriation, a provision shall be added limiting any attorney's fees to not more than 10 percent. This limitation shall not apply to claims based upon findings of the Chief Commissioner of the Court of Claims, court decisions, or where extraordinary services have been rendered. In such cases the Committee will determine the amount of fee to be allowed.

17. The Subcommittee shall not consider any claim for retirement benefits, compensation, pension, or gratuity under the Railroad Retirement Act when such claim has been considered on its merits and disallowed, or otherwise conflicts with the provisions and compensation of that Act, except bills to waive the limitation of time. This rule may be waived only upon order of two-thirds of the Subcommittee, present and voting.

18. The Subcommittee shall not consider any claims bill for benefits under the Social Security Act, as amended, when an application for such benefits has been considered on its merits and disallowed or the provisions of the bill otherwise modify or extend the provisions or benefits payable under that Act, but this prohibition shall not apply to bills to waive limitations of time. This rule may be waived only upon order of two-thirds of the Subcommittee, present and voting.

19. The Subcommittee shall not consider a bill which has twice passed the House and been rejected by a Senate Committee, unless and until the bill has first passed the Senate. Such rule shall be waived only upon a vote of two-thirds of the Subcommittee.

Approved by the Committee on the Judiciary March 11, 1969.

SOURCE: U.S. House of Representatives, Committee on the Judiciary, Subcommittee No. 2, *Rules* (46-page pamphlet, 1970).

Text of L'Enfant's Plan of Washington

Following is the text of a proposal by Pierre Charles L'Enfant to George Washington for laying out the national capital. This proposal was one of three submitted by L'Enfant. Washington rejected the two others and submitted this one to Congress on Dec. 13, 1791. It contains L'Enfant's proposal, which later was carried out, to locate the Capitol on Jenkins Hill, which stood "as a pedestal waiting for a monument."

Georgetown, Jun 22—1791

Sir. In framing the plan here anexed, for the intended Federal City I regreted much being indered by the shortness of time from making any particular drawing of the several buildings—squars—and every other improvement which the smallness of the scale of the general map together with the hurry with which I had it drawn could not admit of having so correctly lay down as necessary to give a perfect Idea of the effect of the whole in the execution.

My whole attention was given to the combination of the general distribution of the grand local(e) as to an object of most immediate moment and of importance to this I yielded every other consideration and have in consequence to sollicite again your Indulgence in submitting to you my Ideas in an incomplete drawing only correct as to the situation and distance of objects all of which were determined after a local(e) well ascertained having for more accuracy had several lines run on the ground cleared the wood and afterwards measured with posts fixed all along, to serve me as certain bases from after the which I might arrange the whole with a certainty of making every part fit to the various grounds.

having first determined some principal points to which I wished making the rest subordinate I next made the distribution regular with streets at right angle *north-south* and *east-west* but afterwards I opened others on various directions as avenues to and from every principal places, wishing by this not mearly to contrast with the general regularity nor to afford a greater variety of pleasant seats and prospect as will be obtained from the advantageous ground over the which the avenues are mostly directed but principally to connect each part of the city with more efficacy by, if I may so express, making the real distance less from place to place in menaging on them a reisprocity of sight and making them thus seemingly connected promot a rapide stellement over the whole so that the most remot may become an adition to the principal while without the help of these divurgents communications such settlements if at all attempted would be languid, and lost in the Extant would become detremental to the main establishment.

Several of these avenues were also necessary to effect the junction of of several out road which I concluded essential to bring central to the city in rendering these road shorter as is done with respect to the bladensburg and Eastern branche Road made above a mile shorter besides the advantage of their leading from the direction given immediately on the warfs of georgetown without passing the hilly ground of that place whose agrandissement it will consequently check while it will accelerate those over Wik creek on the city side the which cannot help spreading soon all along of these avenues forming of themselves a variety of pleasant ride and being combined to injure (insure) a rapide Intercourse with all the part of the City to which they will serve as does the main vains in the animal body to diffuse life through smaller vessels in quickening the action motion to the heart.

as to on what point it is most expedient first to begone the main Establishment, I believe the question may be easily reply if not viewing by part embracing under one sight the whole extant from the Eastern branch to Georgetown and from the branch on the Potowmack across toward the mountains. for considering impartially this whole extant and reflecting it is that of the Intended city than only one position will appear capable of promoting the rapid agrandizement and settlement of the whole.

across the tiber of above were the tide water come lay certainly the elligible spot to lay the Foundation of an establishment of the nature of the one in view, not because this point being central is most likely to diffuse an Equallity of advantages trough the whole territory and in turn to devise a benefit proportional to the rise of its value but because the nature of the local(e) is such as will made everything concur to render a settlement there prosperous—there it will benefit of the natural jalousie which most stimulate establishments on each of its opposed limits it will become necessarily the point of reunion of both and soon become populouz. a canal being easy to open from the eastern branch and to be lead across the first settlement and carried toward the mouth of the tiber where it will again give an issue into the Potowmack and at a distance not to far off for to admit the boats from the grand navigation canal from getting in, will undoubtedly facilitate a conveyance most advantageous to trading Interest it will insure the storing of marketts which,

as lay down on the map, being erected all along the canal and over grounds proper to shelter any number of boats will serve of Mart Houses from were when the city is grown to its fullest extent the most distant markets will be supplied at command.

to these advantages of first necessity to consider to determine the seat of a City is added that of the propositions which there offer and the which are the most susceptible of any within the limits of the intended city of leading to those grand improvements of publique magnitude and as may serve as models for all subsequent undertaking and stand to future ages a monument to national genious and munificence.

After much menutial search for an elligible situation, prompted I may say from a fear of being prejudiced in favour of a first opinion I could discover no one so advantageously to greet the congressional building as is that on the west end of Jenkins heights which stand as a pedestal waiting for a monument, and I am confident, were all the wood cleared from the ground no situation could stand in competition with this. some might perhaps require less labour to be rendered agreeable but after all assistance of arts none ever would be made so grand and all other would appear but of secondary nature.

that were I determine the seat of the presidial palace, in its difference of nature may be view of advantageous to the object of ading to the sumptuousness of a palace the convenience of a house and the agreeableness of country seat situated on that ridge which attracted your attention at the first inspection of the ground on the west side of the tiber entrance it will see 10 or 12 miles down the Potowmack front the town and harbor of Alexandria and stand to the view of the whole city and have the most improved part of it made by addition to those grand Improvements for which the ground in the dependely of the palace is to proper.

fixed as expressed on the map the distance from the Congressional House will not be to great as what the activity of business may be no mesage to nor from the president is to be made without a sort of decorum which will doubtless point out the propriety of committee waiting on him in carriage should his palace be even contiguous to Congress.

to mak however the distance less to other officers I placed the three grand Departments of State contigous to the principle Palace and on the way leading to the Congressional House the gardens of the one together with the park and other improvement on the dependency are connected with the publique walk and avenue to the Congress house in a manner as most form a whole as grand as it will be agreeable and convenient to the whole city which form the distribution of the local(e) will have an early access to this place of general resort and all along side of which may be placed play houses, room of assembly, accademies and all such sort of places as may be attractive to the learned and afford diversion to the idle.

I proposed continuing the canal much further up but this being not to be effectual but with the aid of lock, and from a level obtained of the height of the spring of the tiber the greatest facility being to bring those waters over the flat back of Jenkins I gave the more readily a preference to avail of this water to supply that part of the city as it will promot the execution of a plan which I propose in this map, of leting the tiber return in its proper channel by a fall which issuing from under the base of the Congress building may there form a cascade of forty feet heigh or more than one hundred waide which would produce the most happy effect in rolling down to fill up the canall and discharge itself in the Potowmack of which it would then appear as the main spring when seen through that grand and majestic avenue intersecting with the prospect from the palace at a point which being seen from both I have designated as the proper for to erect a grand Equestrian figure.

in the present unimproved state of the local(e) it will appear that the height were is marked that monument does intercept the view of the water from the palace and in fact it is partly the case but it most be observed that having to bound the entrance of the tiber at the breadth of a canal of 200 ft. which is the utmost breadth that can be preserve to avoid its being drained at low water. it will require much ground to be trown in to feel up, and at least as much as will enable to levell that point of heigh ground between the tiber and P Yong House to almost a level with the tide water and of course to procure to the palace and all other houses from that place to congress a prospect of the Potowmack the which will acquire new swithess being laid over the green of a field well level and made brilant by shade of few tree artfully planted

I am with respectfull submission

Your most humble & obedient servant,

P. C. L'ENFANT.

Per

To the President of the United States.

Appendix—Housing and Support of Congress

Material Relating to Chapter 4

Rules for Regulation of Senate Wing of U.S. Capitol

Responsibility for the Capitol is widely shared. One of the groups sharing the responsibility is the Senate Committee on Rules and Administration. Its regulations governing the Senate wing of the Capitol are an example of the control exercised over the building. Following is the text of the regulations adopted by the Committee.

Rule I

Sergeant At Arms

The Sergeant at Arms of the Senate, under the direction of the Presiding Officer, shall be the Executive Officer of the body for the enforcement of all rules made by the Committee on Rules and Administration for the regulation of the Senate wing of the Capitol and the Senate Office Buildings. The Senate floor shall be at all times under his immediate supervision, and he shall see that the various subordinate officers of his department perform the duties to which they are especially assigned.

Rule II

Majority and Minority Secretaries

The secretary for the majority and the secretary for the minority shall be assigned, during the daily sessions of the Senate, to duty upon the Senate floor. They shall see that the messengers assigned to the doors upon the Senate floor are at their posts, and that the floor and cloakrooms are cleared at least five minutes before the opening of daily sessions of all persons not entitled to remain there. In the absence of the Sergeant at Arms the duties of his office, so far as they pertain to the enforcement of rules, shall devolve upon the secretary for the majority and the secretary for the minority in the order of their rank.

Rule III

Use of the Senate Chamber

In order to secure and protect the Senate Chamber and its furniture and furnishings, the language contained in paragraph numbered one of rule XXXIV of the Standing Rules of the Senate, which reads "The Senate Chamber shall not be granted for any other purpose than for the use of the Senate," shall be interpreted to mean that when the Senate is not sitting in session or otherwise using the Chamber for some function of the Senate, no Senator shall seat any person or persons in chairs of Senators other than the chair assigned to him (other persons shall not seat anyone in a chair of a Senator); and lectures, talks, or speeches shall not be given at such times to groups on the floor by Senators or others except for the purpose of explaining the Chamber.

Rule IV

Taking of Pictures Prohibited

The taking of pictures of any kind is prohibited in the Senate Chamber, the Senate Reading Rooms (Marble Room and Lobby), the Senate Cloakrooms, and the Private Dining Room of the Senate.

Rule V

Messengers Acting As Assistant Doorkeepers

The messengers acting as Assistant Doorkeepers shall be assigned to their duties by the Sergeant at Arms.

Rule VI

Galleries

The Sergeant at Arms shall keep the aisles of the galleries clear, and shall not allow admittance into the galleries of more than their seating capacity. He shall not permit any person to enter a gallery with or carrying any package, bundle, suitcase, briefcase, or camera; he shall not permit any person in any gallery to smoke, applaud, or commit any other type of demonstration either by sound or sign; except in the press and correspondents' galleries he shall not permit any person to read (except the Senate seating diagram) or to write or take notes; he shall not permit any person to take any picture or photograph or to sketch or draw; and he shall not permit any person to place any object whatsoever or portion of his person on any railing, or any male to wear a hat.

The galleries of the Senate shall be set apart and occupied as follows:

Press Gallery

The gallery in the rear of the Vice President's chair shall be set apart for reporters of daily newspapers.

The administration of the Press Gallery shall be vested in a Standing Committee of Correspondents elected by accredited members of the gallery. The committee shall consist of five persons elected to serve for terms of two years: *Provided, however,* That at the election in January 1951, the three candidates receiving the highest number of votes shall serve for two years and the remaining two for one year. Thereafter, three members shall be elected in odd-numbered years and two in even-numbered years. Elections shall be held in January. The committee shall elect its own chairman and secretary. Vacancies on the committee shall be filled by special election to be called by the Standing Committee.

Persons desiring admission to the Press Gallery in the Senate wing shall make application in accordance with rule XXXIV, as amended, for the regulation of the Senate wing of the Capitol, which rule shall be interpreted and administered by the Standing Committee of Correspondents, subject to the review and approval by the Senate Committee on Rules and Administration.

The Standing Committee of Correspondents shall limit membership in the Press Gallery to bona fide correspondents of repute in their profession, under such rules as the Standing Committee of Correspondents shall prescribe: *Provided, however,* That the Standing Commiteee of Correspondents shall admit to the Press Gallery no person who does not establish to the satisfaction of the Standing Committee all of the following:

a. That his or her principal income is obtained from news correspondence intended for publication in newspapers entitled to second-class mailing privileges.

b. That he or she is not engaged in paid publicity or promotion work or in prosecuting any claim before Congress or before any department of the Government, and will not become so engaged while a member of the Press Gallery.

c. That he or she is not engaged in any lobbying activity and will not become so engaged while a member of the Press Gallery.

Members of the families of correspondents are not entitled to the privileges of the Press Gallery.

The Standing Committee of Correspondents shall propose no change or changes in these rules except upon petition in writing signed by not less than 100 accredited members of the Press Gallery.

Radio and Television Correspondents' Gallery

The front row in the northeast public gallery shall be set apart for the use of the radio-television correspondents.

Persons desiring admission to the Radio and Television Correspondents' Gallery of the Senate shall make application to the Committee on Rules and Administration of the Senate, as required by rule XXXIV, as amended, for the regulation of the Senate wing of the Capitol; and shall also state, in writing, the names of all radio stations, television stations, systems, or news-gathering organizations by which they are employed; and what other occupation or employment they may have, if any; and shall further declare that they are not engaged in the prosecution of claims or promotion of legislation pending before Congress, the departments, or the independent agencies, and that they will not become so employed without resigning from the gallery. They shall further declare that they are not employed in any legislative or executive department or independent agency of the Government, or by any foreign government or representative thereof; that they are not engaged in any lobbying activities; that they do not and will not, directly or indirectly, furnish special information to any organization, individual, or group of individuals, for the influencing of prices on any commodity or stock exchange; that they will not do so during the time they retain membership in the gallery. Holders of visitors' cards who may be allowed temporary admission to the gallery must conform to all the restrictions of this paragraph.

It shall be prerequisite to membership that the radio station, television station, system, or news-gathering agencies which the applicants represent shall certify, in writing, to the Radio and Television Correspondents' Gallery that the applicants conform to the foregoing regulations.

The applications required by the above rule shall be authenticated in a manner that shall be satisfactory to the Executive Committee of the Radio and Television Correspondents' Gallery, which shall see that the occupation of the gallery is confined to bona fide news gatherers and/or reporters of reputable standing in their business who represent radio stations, television stations, systems, or news-gathering agencies engaged primarily in serving radio stations, television stations, or systems. It shall be the duty of the Executive Committee of the Radio and Television Correspondents' Gallery to report, at its discretion, violation of privileges of the gallery to the Senate Committee on Rules and Administration, and, pending action thereon, the offending individual may be suspended.

Persons engaged in other occupations, whose chief attention is not given to or more than one-half of their earned income is derived from gathering or reporting of news for radio stations, television stations, systems, or news-gathering agencies primarily serving radio stations, television stations, or systems, shall not be entitled to admission to the Radio and Television Correspondents' Gallery. The Radio and Television Correspondents' list in the Congressional Directory shall be a list only of persons whose chief attention is given to the gathering and reporting of news for radio stations, television stations, and systems engaged in the daily dissemination of news, and of representatives of news-gathering agencies engaged in the daily service of news to such radio stations, television stations, or systems.

Members of the families of correspondents are not entitled to the privileges of the gallery.

The Radio and Television Correspondents' Gallery shall be under the control of the Executive Committee of the Radio and Television Correspondents' Gallery, subject to the approval and supervision of the Senate Committee on Rules and Administration.

Periodical Press Gallery

The front row in the northwest public gallery shall be set aside for the use of the periodical press.

Persons desiring admission to the Periodical Press Gallery of the Senate shall make application to the Committee on Rules and Administration of the Senate, as required by rule XXXIV, as amended, for the regulation of the Senate wing of the Capitol; and shall state in writing the names of all newspapers or publications or news associations by which they are employed, and what other occupation or employment they may have, if any; and they shall further declare that they are not engaged in the prosecution of claims pending before Congress or the departments, and will not become so engaged while allowed admission to the galleries; that they are not employed in any legislative or executive department of the Government, or by any foreign government or any representative thereof; and that they are not employed, directly or indirectly, by any stock exchange, board of trade, or other organization, or member thereof, or brokerage house or broker, engaged in the buying and selling of any security or commodity, or by any person or corporation having legislation before Congress, and will not become so engaged while retaining membership in the galleries. Holders of visitors' cards who may be allowed temporary admission to the galleries must conform to the restrictions of this rule.

The applications required by the foregoing paragraph shall be authenticated in a manner that shall be satisfactory to the executive committee of the Periodical Correspondents' Association who shall see that the occupation of the galleries is confined to bona fide and accredited resident correspondents, news gatherers, or reporters of reputable standing who represent one or more periodicals which regularly publish a substantial volume of news material of either general or of an economic, industrial, technical, or trade character, published for profit and supported chiefly by advertising, and owned and operated independently of any industry, business, association, or institution; and it shall be the duty of the executive committee at their discretion to report violation of the privileges of the galleries to the Senate Committee on Rules and Administration, and pending action thereon the offending correspondent may be suspended.

Persons engaged in other occupations whose chief attention is not given to the gathering or reporting of news for periodicals requiring such continuous service shall not be entitled to admission to the Periodical Press Gallery. The Periodical Correspondents' list in the Congressional Directory shall be a list only of persons whose chief attention is given to such service for news periodicals as described in the foregoing paragraph except that admission shall not be denied if his other work is such as to make him eligible to the Press Galleries or Radio and Television Correspondents' Galleries.

Members of the families of correspondents are not entitled to the privileges of the galleries.

The Periodical Press Gallery in the Senate shall be under the control of an executive committee elected by members of the Periodical Correspondents' Gallery, subject to the approval and supervision of the Senate Committee on Rules and Administration.

Press Photographers' Gallery

1. (a) Administration of the Press Photographers' Gallery is vested in a Standing Committee of Press Photographers consisting of six persons elected by accredited members of the gallery. The Committee shall be composed of one member each from Associated Press Photos, United Press International Newspictures, magazine media, and local newspapers and two "at large" members. "At large" members may be, but need not be, selected from a media otherwise represented on the Committee.

(b) The term of office of a member of the Committee elected as the Associated Press Photos member, the local newspapers member, or one of the "at large" members shall expire on the day of the election held in the first odd-numbered year following the year in which he was elected, and the term of office of a member of the Committee elected as the United Press International Newspictures member, the magazine media member, or the remaining "at large" member shall expire on the day of the election held in the first even-numbered year following the year in which he was elected, except that a member elected to fill a vacancy occurring prior to the expiration of a term shall serve only for the unexpired portion of such term.

(c) Elections shall be held as early as practicable in each year, and in no case later than March 31. A vacancy in the membership of the Committee occurring prior to the expiration of a term shall be filled by special election called for that purpose by the Committee.

(d) The Standing Committee of the Press Photographers' Gallery shall propose no change or changes in these rules except upon petition in writing signed by not less than 25 accredited members of the gallery.

(e) Notwithstanding the provisions of subsection (b)—

(A) the term of office of the local newspapers member elected in the election held in 1968 shall expire in 1969,

(B) the term of office of the United Press International Newspictures member holding office on January 1, 1968, shall expire in 1969, and

(C) the term of office of the United Press International Newspictures member elected in 1969 shall expire in 1970.

2. Persons desiring admission to the Press Photographers' Gallery of the Senate shall make application in accordance with Rule 34 of the Senate, which rule shall be interpreted and administered by the Standing Committee of Press Photographers subject to the review and approval of the Senate Committee on Rules and Administration.

3. The Standing Committee of Press Photographers shall limit membership in the photographers' gallery to bona fide news photographers of repute in their profession and to heads of Photographic Bureaus under such rules as the Standing Committee of Press Photographers shall prescribe.

4. *Provided, however,* That the Standing Committee of Press Photographers shall admit to the gallery no person who does not establish to the satisfaction of the Committee all of the following:

(a) That any member is not engaged in paid publicity or promotion work or in prosecuting any claim before Congress or before any department of the Government, and will not become so engaged while a member of the gallery.

(b) That he or she is not engaged in any lobbying activity and will not become so engaged while a member of the gallery.

Presidential and Diplomatic Gallery

The southern gallery over the main entrance to the Senate Chamber, except the first two rows on the eastern side of the aisle, shall be set apart for the use of the Diplomatic Corps, and no person shall be admitted to it excepting the Secretary of State, foreign ministers, their families and suites, and Senators.

The cards of admission to said gallery shall be issued by the Secretary of State, or the chairman of the Committee on Rules and Administration, to such persons as are entitled to its privileges.

The first row on the eastern side of this gallery shall be set apart for the use of the President and the second row on the eastern side of this gallery shall be set apart for the use of the Vice President.

Senate Gallery

The first two rows of the gallery over the east entrance to the Senate shall be set apart for the exclusive use of the wives and other members of the immediate families of Senators.

The remainder of the gallery shall be set apart for the exclusive use of the families of Senators and guests visiting their families who shall be designated by some member of the Senator's family, and for the families of ex-Presidents of the United States, as well as families of incumbent Secretary and Sergeant at Arms of the Senate.

Employees of the Senate, except those on duty at the gallery door, shall be excluded.

Visitors' Galleries

The visitors' galleries shall be governed by the following rule:

The galleries over the western entrance to the Senate Chamber and over the southeastern, northwestern, and northeastern corners of said Chamber shall be set apart for the use of persons holding a card issued by a Senator. The period to which such card of admission shall be limited rests entirely in the discretion of the Senator issuing it, except that such cards shall expire at the end of each session and cards of a different color shall be furnished by the Sergeant at Arms for the following session. The Sergeant at Arms shall in his discretion limit occupancy of the visitors' galleries to such periods as may be required to accommodate with reasonable expediency all card bearers who are seeking admission.

Special Gallery

The gallery adjoining and west of the Diplomatic Gallery shall be reserved for guided tours and other special parties.

Rule VII

Marble Room

The anteroom known as the Marble Room is a part of the floor of the Senate.

Rule VIII

Cloakrooms

No persons shall be admitted to the cloakrooms adjoining the Senate Chamber excepting those entitled to the privileges of the Senate floor under Standing Rule XXXIII.

Rule IX

Heating and Ventilating Department

No person shall be admitted to the heating and ventilating department of the Senate wing of the Capitol, except upon a pass from the Sergeant at Arms, or unless accompanied by an officer of the Senate.

Rule X

Barber Shop and Bathrooms

The barber shop, and bathrooms connected therewith, shall be reserved exclusively for the use of Senators. The bathroom in the heating and ventilating department of the Senate wing shall be for the use of employees of the Senate; and no other persons shall be entitled to its privileges.

Rule XI

Senate Restaurants

The management of the Senate Restaurants and all matters connected therewith are under the jurisdiction, control, and direction of the Committee on Rules and Administration.

NOTE—Pursuant to Public Law 87-82 (75 Stat. 199, July 6, 1961) the management of the Senate Restaurants was transferred to the Architect of the Capitol, subject to approval by the Committee on Rules and Administration as to matters of general policy.

Rule XII

Corridors, Etc.

The corridors and passageways of the Senate wing of the Capitol shall be kept open and free from obstructions and free from any person or persons loitering or loafing in or around such places without any visible or lawful business and not giving a good account of themselves; and no stands, booths, or counters for the exhibition or sale of any article shall be placed therein.

Rule XIII

Peddling, Begging, Etc.

Peddling, begging, and the solicitation of book or other subscriptions are strictly forbidden in the Senate wing of the Capitol, and no portion of said wing shall be occupied by signs or other devices for advertising any article whatsoever excepting timetables in the Post Office and such signs as may be necessary to designate the entrances to the Senate Restaurant.

Rule XIV

Cards and Communications in the Morning Hour

No cards, letters, or other communications, except letters from Senators' families, and official communications, shall be sent to a Senator in the Chamber during the daily sessions of the Senate before 2 o'clock p.m., unless he shall so direct.

Rule XV

Cards and Communications During Executive Sessions

No cards, letters, or other communications shall be sent to Senators in the Chamber when the Senate is in executive session, except cards of

Rule XVI

Sweeping, Cleaning

All sweeping, cleaning, and dusting of the Senate wing of the Capitol shall be done, as far as practicable, immediately after the adjournment of each day's session of the Senate, and must, in any event, be completed before 8 o'clock a.m.

Members of the House of Representatives, calls from the Supreme Court of the United States, letters from Senators' families, official communications and telegrams, unless Senators shall direct the messenger at the main door of the Senate Chamber otherwise.

Rule XVII

Legislative Buzzers and Signal Lights

Effective May 1, 1964, the system of legislative buzzers and signal lights shall be as follows:

Pre-session signals: One long ring at hour of convening.
One red light to remain lighted at all times while Senate is in actual session.

Session signals: One ring—Yeas and nays.
Two rings—Quorum call.
Three rings—Call of absentees.
Four rings—Adjournment or recess.
Six rings—Morning business concluded.

Effective July 13, 1967, the legislative call system shall be used for alerting Members of Congress, Congressional employees, and visitors of enemy attack or other major disaster conditions. There will be two signals:

1. *Attack warning.*—Notification to all occupants that the United States is under attack and that there is real danger of loss of life. This warning would be given by a sequence of two-second sounds of the legislative bells separated by two-second silent intervals. This signal would be repeated for 3 to 5 minutes.

2. *Attention signal.*—Notification of peacetime disasters, such as accidental presence of radioactive materials or severe weather or natural disaster conditions. This signal would be given by a series of 16-second bell sounds separated by 16-second silent intervals, repeated for 3 to 5 minutes.

(Where lights exist they will correspond with rings.)

Rule XVIII

Senate Office Buildings and Other Senate Buildings

All provisions of the foregoing rules so far as practicable are made applicable to the Senate Office Buildings, the buildings used for the storage of Senate documents, and the Senate garage.

# Appendix—Congress and the Electorate

Texts Relating to Chapter 5

Federal Laws Relating to Campaign Financing

1. UNITED STATES CODE (1964 EDITION,) TITLE 2, "THE CONGRESS," CHAPTER 8, "FEDERAL CORRUPT PRACTICES" (EXCERPTS)

Section 241. Definitions.

When used in this chapter and section 602 of Title 18—

(a) The term "election" includes a general or special election, but does not include a primary election or convention of a political party;

(b) The term "candidate" means an individual whose name is presented at an election for election as Senator or Representative in, or Resident Commissioner to, the Congress of the United States, whether or not such individual is elected;

(c) The term "political committee" includes any committee, association, or organization which accepts contributions or makes expenditures for the purposes of influencing or attempting to influence the election of candidates or presidential and vice presidential electors (1) in two or more States, or (2) whether or not in more than one State if such committee, association, or organization (other than a duly organized State or local committee of a political party) is a branch or subsidiary of a national committee, association, or organization;

(d) The term "contribution" includes a gift, subscription, loan, advance, or deposit, of money, or anything of value, and includes a contract, promise or agreement, whether or not legally enforceable to make a contribution;

(e) The term "expenditure" includes a payment, distribution, loan, advance, deposit, or gift, of money or anything of value, and includes a contract, promise, or agreement, whether or not legally enforceable, to make an expenditure;

(f) The term "person" includes an individual, partnership committee, association, corporation, and any other organization or group of persons;

(g) The term "Clerk" means the Clerk of the House of Representatives of the United States;

(h) The term "Secretary" means the Secretary of the Senate of the United States;

(i) The term "State" includes Territory and possession of the United States. (Feb. 28, 1925, ch. 368, title III, S 302, 43 Stat. 1070; Proc. No. 2695, July 4, 1946, II F.R. 7517, 60 Stat. 1352.)

Section 242. Chairman and treasurer of political committee; duties as to contributions; accounts and receipts.

(a) Every political committee shall have a chairman and a treasurer. No contribution shall be accepted, and no expenditure made, by or on behalf of a political committee for the purpose of influencing an election until such chairman and treasurer have been chosen.

(b) It shall be the duty of the treasurer of a political committee to keep a detailed and exact account of—

(1) All contributions made to or for such committee;

(2) The name and address of every person making any such contribution, and the date thereof;

(3) All expenditures made by or on behalf of such committee; and

(4) The name and address of every person to whom any such expenditure is made, and the date thereof.

(c) It shall be the duty of the treasurer to obtain and keep a receipted bill, stating the particulars, for every expenditure by or on behalf of a political committee exceeding $10 in amount. The treasurer shall preserve all receipted bills and accounts required to be kept by this section for a period of at least two years from the date of the filing of the statement containing such items. (Feb. 28, 1925, ch. 368, title III, S 303, 43 Stat. 1071.)

Section 243. Accounts of contributions received.

Every person who receives a contribution for a political committee shall, on demand of the treasurer, and in any event within five days after the receipt of such contribution, render to the treasurer a detailed account thereof, including the name and address of the person making such contribution, and the date on which received. (Feb. 28, 1925, ch. 368, title III, S 304, 43 Stat. 1071.)

Section 244. Statements by treasurer filed with Clerk of House of Representatives.

(a) The treasurer of a political committee shall file with the Clerk between the 1st and 10th days of March, June, and September, in each year, and also between the 10th and 15th days, and on the 5th day, next preceding the date on which a general election is to be held, at which candidates are to be elected in two or more States, and also on the 1st day of January, a statement containing complete as of the day next preceding the date of filing—

(1) The name and address of each person who has made a contribution to or for such committee in one or more items of the aggregate amount or value, within the calendar year, of $100 or more, together with the amount and date of such contribution.

(2) The total sum of the contributions made to or for such committee during the calendar year and not stated under paragraph (1);

(3) The total sum of all contributions made to or for such committee during the calendar year;

(4) The name and address of each person to whom an expenditure in one or more items of the aggregate amount or value, within the calendar year, of $10 or more has been made by or on behalf of such committee, and the amount, date, and purpose of such expenditure;

(5) The total sum of all expenditures made by or on behalf of such committee during the calendar year and not stated under paragraph (4);

(6) The total sum of expenditures made by or on behalf of such committee during the calendar year.

(b) The statements required to be filed by subdivision (a) of this section shall be cumulative during the calendar year to which they relate, but where there has been no change in an item reported in a previous statement only the amount need be carried forward.

(c) The statement filed on the 1st day of January shall cover the preceding calendar year. (Feb. 28, 1925, ch. 368, title III, S 305, 43 Stat. 1071.)

Section 245. Statements by others than political committee filed with Clerk of House of Representatives.

Every person (other than a political committee) who makes an expenditure in one or more items, other than by contribution to a political committee, aggregating $50 or more within a calendar year for the purpose of influencing in two or more States the election of candidates, shall file with the Clerk an itemized detailed statement of such expenditure in the same manner as required of the treasurer of a political committee by section 244 of this title. (Feb. 28, 1925, ch. 368, title III, S 306, 43 Stat. 1072.)

Section 246. Statements by candidates for Senator, Representative, or Resident Commissioner filed with Secretary of Senate and Clerk of House of Representatives.

(a) Every candidate for Senator shall file with the Secretary and every candidate for Representative, or Resident Commissioner shall file with the Clerk not less than ten nor more than fifteen days before, and also within thirty days after the date on which an election is to be held, a statement containing, complete as of the day next preceding the date of filing—

(1) A correct and itemized account of each contribution received by him or by any person for him with his knowledge or consent from any source, in aid or support of his candidacy for election, or for the purpose of influencing the result of the election, together with the name of the person who had made such contribution;

(2) A correct and itemized account of each expenditure made by him or by any person for him with his knowledge or consent, in aid or support of his candidacy for election, or for the purpose of influencing the result of the election, together with the name of the person to whom such expenditure was made; except that only the total sum of expenditures for items specified in subdivision (c) of section 248 of this title need be stated;

(3) A statement of every promise or pledge made by him or by any person for him with his consent, prior to the closing of the polls on the day of the election, relative to the appointment or recommendation for appointment of any person to any public or private position or employment for the purpose of procuring support in his candidacy, and the name, address, and occupation of every person to whom any such promise or pledge has been made, together with the description of any such position. If no such promise or pledge has been made, that fact shall be specifically stated.

(b) The statements required to be filed by subdivision (a) of this section shall be cumulative, but where there has been no change in an item reported in a previous statement only the amount need be carried forward.

(c) Every candidate shall inclose with his first statement a report, based upon the records of the proper State official, stating the total number of votes cast for all candidates for the office which the candidate seeks, at the general election next preceding the election at which he is a candidate. (Feb. 28, 1925, ch. 368, title III, S 307, 43 Stat. 1072.)

Section 247. Statements; verification filing; preservation; inspection.

A statement required by this chapter to be filed by a candidate or treasurer of a political committee or other person with the Clerk or Secretary, as the case may be—

(a) Shall be verified by the oath or affirmation of the person filing such statement, taken before any officer authorized to administer oaths;

(b) Shall be deemed properly filed when deposited in an established post office within the prescribed time, duly stamped, registered, and directed to the Clerk or Secretary at Washington, District of Columbia, but in the event it is not received, a duplicate of such statment shall be promptly filed upon notice by the Clerk or Secretary of its nonreceipt;

(c) Shall be preserved by the Clerk or Secretary for a period of two years from the date of filing, shall constitute a part of the public records of his office, and shall be open to public inspection. (Feb. 28, 1925, ch. 368, title III, S 308, 43 Stat. 1072.)

Section 248. Limitation upon amount of expenditures by candidate.

(a) A candidate, in his campaign for election, shall not make expenditures in excess of the amount which he may lawfully make under the laws of the State in which he is a candidate, nor in excess of the amount which he may lawfully make under the provisions of this chapter and section 602 of Title 18.

(b) Unless the laws of his State prescribe a less amount as the maximum limit of campaign expenditures, a candidate may make expenditures up to—

(1) The sum of $10,000 if a candidate for Senator, or the sum of $2,500 if a candidate for Representative or Resident Commissioner; or

(2) An amount equal to the amount obtained by multiplying three cents by the total number of votes cast at the last general election for all candidates for the office which the candidate seeks, but in no event exceeding $25,000 if a candidate for Senator or $5,000 if a candidate for Representative or Resident Commissioner.

(c) Money expended by a candidate to meet and discharge any assessment, fee, or charge made or levied upon candidates by the laws of the State in which he resides, or expended for his necessary personal, traveling, or subsistence expenses, or for stationery, postage, writing or printing (other than for use on billboards or in newspapers), for distributing letters, circulars, or posters, or for telegraph or telephone service, shall not be included in determining whether his expenditures have exceeded the sum fixed by paragraph (1) or (2) of subdivision (b) of this section as the limit of campaign expenses of a candidate. (Feb. 28, 1925, ch. 368, title III, S 309, 43 Stat. 1073.)

Section 252. General penalties for violations.

(a) Any person who violates any of the foregoing provisions of this chapter, except those for which a specific penalty is imposed by section 602 of Title 18, and section 251 of this title, shall be fined not more than $1,000 or imprisoned not more than one year, or both.

(b) Any person who willfully violates any of the foregoing provisions of this chapter, except those for which a specific penalty is imposed by section 602 of Title 18, and section 251 of this title, shall be fined not more than $10,000 and imprisoned not more than two years. (Feb. 28, 1925, ch. 368, title III, S 314, 43 Stat. 1074).

Section 253. Expenses of election contests.

This chapter and section 602 of Title 18 shall not limit or affect the right of any person to make expenditures for proper legal expenses in contesting the results of an election. (Feb. 28, 1925, ch. 368, title III, S 315, 43 Stat. 1074.)

Section 254. State laws not affected.

This chapter and section 602 of Title 18 shall not be construed to annul the laws of any State relating to the nomination or election of candidates, unless directly inconsistent with the provisions of this chapter and section 602 of Title 18, or to exempt any candidate from complying with such State laws. (Feb. 28, 1925, ch. 368, title III, S 316, 43 Stat. 1074.)

Section 255. Partial invalidity.

If any provision of this chapter and section 602 of Title 18, or the application thereof to any person or circumstance is held invalid, the validity of the remainder of said chapter and section and of the application of such provision to other persons and circumstances shall not be affected thereby. (Feb. 28, 1925, ch. 368, title III, S 317, 43 Stat. 1074.)

Section 256. Citation.

This chapter and section 602 of Title 18 may be cited as the "Federal Corrupt Practices Act." (Feb. 28, 1925, ch. 368, title III, S 301, 43 Stat. 1070.)

2. UNITED STATES CODE (1964 EDITION), TITLE 5, "EXECUTIVE DEPARTMENTS AND GOVERNMENT OFFICERS AND EMPLOYEES," CHAPTER 1,"PROVISIONS APPLICABLE TO DEPARTMENTS AND OFFICERS GENERALLY" (EXCERPTS)

Section 118k. Employees of State or local agencies financed by loans or grants from United States.

(a) Influencing elections....

No officer or employee of any State or local agency whose principal employment is in connection with any activity which is financed in whole or in part by loans or grants made by the United States or by any Federal agency shall...directly or indirectly coerce, attempt to coerce, command, or advise any other such officer or employee to pay, lend, or contribute any part of his salary or compensation or anything else of value to any party, committee, organization, agency, or person for political purposes....(Aug. 2, 1939, ch. 410, S 12, as added July 19, 1940, ch. 640, S4, 54 Stat. 767....)

Section 118o. Removal from office for soliciting or accepting political contributions.

Any executive officer or employee of the United States not appointed by the President, with the advice and consent of the Senate, who shall request, give to, or receive from, any other officer or employee of the Government any money or property or other thing of value for political purposes shall be at once discharged from the service of the United States. (Aug. 15, 1876, ch. 287, S 6, 19 Stat. 169.)

3. UNITED STATES CODE (1964 EDITION), TITLE 18, "CRIMES AND CRIMINAL PROCEDURE," CHAPTER 29, "ELECTIONS AND POLITICAL ACTIVITIES" (EXCERPTS)

Section 591. Definitions.

When used in sections 597, 599, 602, 609 and 610 of this title—

The term "election" includes a general or special election, but does not include a primary election or convention of a political party;

The term "candidate" means an individual whose name is presented for election as Senator or Representative in, or Delegate or Resident Commissioner to, the Congress of the United States, whether or not such individual is elected;

The term "political committee" includes any committee, association, or organization which accepts contributions or makes expenditures for the purpose of influencing or attempting to influence the election of candidates or presidential and vice presidential electors (1) in two or more States, or (2) whether or not in more than one State if such committee, association, or organization (other than a duly organized State or local committee of a political party) is a branch or subsidiary of a national committee, association, or organization;

The term "contribution" includes a gift, subscription, loan, advance, or deposit, of money, or anything of value; and includes a contract, promise, or agreement to make a contribution, whether or not legally enforceable;

The term "expenditure" includes a payment, distribution, loan, advance, deposit, or gift, of money, or anything of value, and includes a contract, promise, or agreement to make an expenditure, whether or not legally enforceable;

The term "person" or the term "whoever" includes an individual, partnership, committee, association, corporation, and any other organization or group of persons;

The term "State" includes Territory and possession of the United States. (June 25, 1948, ch. 645, 62 Stat. 719; May 24, 1949, ch. 139, S 9, 63 Stat. 90.)

Section 597. Expenditures to influence voting.

Whoever makes or offers to make an expenditure to any person, either to vote or withhold his vote, or to vote for or against any candidate; and

Whoever solicits, accepts, or receives any such expenditure in consideration of his vote or the withholding of his vote—

Shall be fined not more than $1,000 or imprisoned not more than one year, or both; and if the violation was willful, shall be fined not more than $10,000 or imprisoned not more than two years, or both. (June 25, 1948, ch. 645, 62 Stat. 721.)

Section 602. Solicitation of political contributions.

Whoever, being a Senator or Representative in, or Delegate or Resident Commissioner to, or a candidate for Congress, or individual elected as, Senator, Representative, Delegate, or Resident Commissioner, or an officer or employee of the United States or any department or agency thereof, or a person receiving any salary or compensation for services from money derived from the Treasury of the United States, directly or indirectly solicits, receives, or is in any manner concerned in soliciting or receiving, any assessment, subscription, or contribution for any political purpose whatever, from any other such officer, employee, or person, shall be fined not more than $5,000 or imprisoned not more than three years or both. (June 25, 1948, ch. 645, 62 Stat. 722.)

Section 603. Place of solicitation.

Whoever, in any room or building occupied in the discharge of official duties by any person mentioned in section 602 of this title, or in any navy yard, fort, or arsenal, solicits or receives any contribution of money or other thing of value for any political purpose, shall be fined not more than $5,000 or imprisoned not more than three years, or both. (June 25, 1948, ch. 645, 62 Stat. 722; Oct. 31, 1951, ch. 655, S 20 (b), 65 Stat. 718.)

Section 604. Solicitation from persons on relief.

Whoever solicits or receives or is in any manner concerned in soliciting or receiving any assessment, subscription, or contribution for any political purpose from any person known by him to be entitled to, or receiving compensation, employment, or other benefit provided for or made possible by any Act of Congress appropriating funds for work relief or relief purposes, shall be fined not more than $1,000 or imprisoned not more than one year, or both. (June 25, 1948, ch. 645, 62 Stat. 722.)

Section 606. Intimidation to secure political contributions.

Whoever, being one of the officers or employees of the United States mentioned in section 602 of this title discharges, or promotes, or degrades, or in any manner changes the official rank or compensation of any other officer or employee, or promises or threatens so to do, for giving or withholding or neglecting to make any contribution of money or other valuable thing for any political purpose, shall be fined not more than $5,000 or imprisoned not more than three years, or both. (June 25, 1948, ch. 645, 62 Stat. 722.)

Section 607. Making political contributions.

Whoever, being an officer, clerk, or other person in the service of the United States or any department or agency thereof, directly or indirectly gives or hands over to any other officer, clerk, or person in the service of the United States, or to any Senator or Member of or Delegate to Congress, or Resident Commissioner, any money or other valuable thing on account of or to be applied to the promotion of any political object, shall be fined not more than $5,000 or imprisoned not more than three years, or both. (June 25, 1948, ch. 645, 62 Stat. 722.)

Section 608. Limitations on political contributions and purchases.

(a) Whoever, directly or indirectly, makes contributions in an aggregate amount in excess of $5,000 during any calendar year, or in connection with any campaign for nomination or election, to or on behalf of any candidate for an elective Federal office, including the offices of President of the United States and Presidential and Vice Presidential electors, or to or on behalf of any committee or other organization engaged in furthering, advancing, or advocating the nomination or election of any candidate for any such office or the success of any national political party, shall be fined not more than $5,000 or imprisoned not more than five years, or both.

This subsection shall not apply to contributions made to or by a State or local committee or other State or local organization or to similar committees or organizations in the District of Columbia or in any Territory or Possession of the United States.

(b) Whoever purchases or buys any goods, commodities, advertising, or articles of any kind or description, the proceeds of which, or any portion thereof, directly or indirectly inures to the benefit of or for any candidate for an elective Federal office including the offices of President of the United States, and Presidential and Vice Presidential electors or any political com-

mittee or other political organization engaged in furthering, advancing, or advocating the nomination or election of any candidate for any such office or the success of any national political party, shall be fined not more than $5,000 or imprisoned not more than five years, or both.

This subsection shall not interfere with the usual and known business, trade, or profession of any candidate.

(c) In all cases of violations of this section by a partnership, committee, association, corporation, or other organization or group of persons, the officers, directors, or managing heads thereof who knowingly and willfully participate in such violation, shall be punished as herein provided.

(d) The term "contribution," as used in this section, shall have the same meaning prescribed by section 591 of this title. (June 25, 1948, ch. 645, 62 Stat. 723.)

Section 609. Maximum contributions and expenditures.

No political committee shall receive contributions aggregating more than $3,000,000, or make expenditures aggregating more than $3,000,000, during any calendar year.

For the purposes of this section, any contributions received and any expenditures made on behalf of any political committee with the knowledge and consent of the chairman or treasurer of such committee shall be deemed to be received or made by such committee.

Any violation of this section by any political committee shall be deemed also to be a violation by the chairman and the treasurer of such committee and by any other person responsible for such violation and shall be punishable by a fine of not more than $1,000 or imprisonment of not more than one year, or both; and, if the violation was willful by a fine of not more than $10,000 or imprisonment of not more than two years, or both. (June 25, 1948, ch. 645, 62 Stat. 723.)

Section 610. Contributions or expenditures by national banks, corporations or labor organizations.

It is unlawful for any national bank, or any corporation organized by authority of any law of Congress, to make a contribution or expenditure in connection with any election to any political office, or in connection with any primary election or political convention or caucus held to select candidates for any political office, or for any corporation whatever, or any labor organization to make a contribution or expenditure in connection with any election at which Presidential and Vice Presidential electors or a Senator or Representative in, or a Delegate or Resident Commissioner to Congress are to be voted for, or in connection with any primary election or political convention or caucus held to select candidates for any of the foregoing offices, or for any candidate, political committee, or other person to accept or receive any contribution prohibited by this section.

Every corporation or labor organization which makes any contribution or expenditure in violation of this section shall be fined not more than $5,000; and every officer or director of any corporation, or officer of any labor organization, who consents to any contribution or expenditure by the corporation or labor organization, as the case may be, and any person who accepts or receives any contribution, in violation of this section, shall be fined not more than $1,000 or imprisoned not more than one year, or both; and if the violation was willful, shall be fined not more than $10,000 or imprisoned not more than two years, or both.

For the purposes of this section "labor organization" means any organization of any kind, or any agency or employee representation committee or plan, in which employees participate and which exist for the purpose, in whole or in part, of dealing with employers concerning grievances, labor disputes, wages, rates of pay, hours of employment, or conditions of work. (June 25, 1943, ch. 645, 62 Stat. 723; May 24, 1949, ch. 139, S 10, 63 Stat. 90; Oct. 31, 1951, ch. 655, S 20 (c), 65 Stat. 718.)

Section 611. Contributions by firms or individuals contracting with the United States.

Whoever, entering into any contract with the United States or any department or agency thereof, either for the rendition of personal services or furnishing any material, supplies, or equipment to the United States or any department or agency thereof, or selling any land or building to the United States or any department or agency thereof, if payment for the performance of such contract or payment for such material, supplies, equipment, land, or building is to be made in whole or in part from funds appropriated by the Congress, during the period of negotiations for, or performance under such contract or furnishing of material, supplies, equipment, land or buildings, directly or indirectly makes any contribution of money or any other thing of value, or promises expressly or impliedly to make any such contribution, to any political party, committee, or candidate for public office or to any person for any political purpose or use; or

Whoever knowingly solicits any such contribution from any such person or firm, for any such purpose during any such period—

Shall be fined not more than $5,000 or imprisoned not more than five years; or both. (June 25, 1948, ch. 645, 62 Stat. 724.)

Appendix—Pressures on Congress

Texts and Other Material Relating to Chapter 6

Case Study on Lobbying: For and Against Medicare

Enactment of the Johnson Administration's Social Security health-care-for-the-aged bill, which was signed into law July 30, 1965 (HR 6675 —PL 89-97), climaxed a bitter, 30-year dispute dating back to 1935 over the proper role of the Federal Government in health care for the general population.

The key issue in the dispute was this: Should the federal role be limited in assisting the indigent, by means of federal grants to the states under the public assistance (welfare) programs? Or should the Federal Government assume a broader responsibility and undertake to pay for the medical and hospital costs of the entire population, or at least specified age groups, without regard to the financial status or ability to pay of the aid recipient?

BACKGROUND OF DISPUTE

Organized labor, many Northern Democratic Members of Congress and liberal organizations, as well as major organizations of the elderly, long favored federal assumption of very broad responsibility. In the 1940s, they backed proposals for a compulsory national health insurance system that was to be financed by a federal payroll tax (like the existing Social Security Old-Age and Survivors Insurance payroll tax) and that was to pay the costs of nearly all health services for most of the population, without regard to age or need of the beneficiary.

Proposals in the 1940s for compulsory national health insurance failed to win enactment, despite the repeated pleas of President Truman (D 1945-53), in part because of sharp opposition from the medical profession.

Consequently, in the 1950s national health insurance proponents shifted their support to a narrower version: a compulsory national health insurance program, to be financed by raising the Social Security payroll tax, that would pay for the health care only of persons 65 or older—the age group with the heaviest doctor bills, nursing bills and hospital costs and the lowest average income.

This proposal was opposed by President Eisenhower and the medical profession, as well as insurance industry spokesmen and other groups. It won the endorsement of Presidents Kennedy and Johnson.

It was defeated on the Senate floor in 1960 and 1962 by a coalition of Republicans and Southern Democrats, passed the Senate in 1964 but failed to win final enactment that year because of House refusal to accept the health care provision. It was finally enacted in 1965.

Major Features of 1965 Act. Two notable features of the 1965 legislation were that the health benefits plan covered all persons 65 or over, not just those eligible for Social Security old-age or survivor benefits as was the case with many of the earlier proposals; and that, in addition to providing a list of basic hospital care and nursing home benefits to which all persons 65 or over were entitled as a matter of right, the legislation provided for a supplementary, voluntary plan, which anyone 65 or over could purchase for $3 a month to cover doctor bills.

LOBBYING ON MEDICAL CARE ISSUE

Over the years, the Social Security health care dispute was one of the most fiercely lobbied issues to come before Congress. The lobbying involved not only attempts to convince and pressure Members of Congress through visits by agents of interested organizations but also attempts to convince the public, one way or the other, by means of radio and television broadcasts, public meetings and rallies, and repeated advertising campaigns in newspapers and magazines.

1949 Campaign. One of the great early public clashes on the issue occurred in 1949-50 after President Truman, in his Jan. 5, 1949, State of the Union Message and his April 22, 1949, health message, repeated earlier requests for compulsory national health insurance for persons of all ages, to be financed by a federal payroll tax.

Mr. Truman's compulsory national health insurance proposals were among the hardest fought of all issues before Congress in 1949 and 1950. In the end, the bloc opposed to the Truman plan won out, and there was no action on his requests in either chamber of Congress. The AMA's campaign against "socialized medicine" was generally credited with being a major factor in the outcome.

The campaign was costly. According to reports filed by the AMA with the Clerk of the House under the 1946 Federal Regulation of Lobbying Act, the AMA spent $1,522,683 in 1949 and $1,326,078 in 1950 for lobbying purposes, the great bulk of it for the campaign against the Truman medical care proposals. These have been the two highest lobby spending reports filed by any organization since lobby spending reports began in 1946.

1957-65 Campaign. Following the defeat of the Truman proposals, the medical care issue faded from public view for a while. However, in a Feb. 26, 1952, speech in New York, Federal Security Administrator Oscar Ewing, head of the agency administering Social Security, proposed that the Social Security old-age and survivors insurance system begin paying for the medical and hospital costs of persons retired on Social Security old-age and survivors pensions.

Although announced in Congress, these proposals at first received relatively little attention. In 1957, however, the AFL-CIO began a strong campaign for a Social Security health care for the aged bill (HR 9467) sponsored by Rep. Aime J. Forand (D R.I.). Most of the same groups which had backed Mr. Truman's broader earlier proposals got behind the Forand bill. The AMA, as in the past, became the chief opponent.

There then began a prolonged campaign on the issue. A new factor came into play when, in 1961, several persons who had led the Senior Citizens for Kennedy political group during the previous year's Presidential campaign set up a National Council of Senior Citizens for Health Care Through Social Security, headed by Forand, who had retired from Congress. The new group sought to bring into play the political voice of the nation's 16 million and more elderly persons (65 or over), and so force through the Forand proposals.

On Aug. 23, 1960, a Social Security health care amendment backed by both members of the Democratic Presidential ticket—Sens. John F. Kennedy (D Mass.) and Lyndon B. Johnson (D Texas)—and opposed by President Eisenhower and GOP Presidential candidate Richard M. Nixon (R) was beaten on the Senate floor, 44-51 (D 43-19; R 1-32).

The AFL-CIO, National Council of Senior Citizens and others kept up their campaign, despite the 1960 defeat. In 1962, a Kennedy Administration measure was offered as a floor amendment and beaten on the Senate floor July 17.

Finally, in 1965, the House April 8, by a 313-115 (D 248-42; R 65-73) vote, passed HR 6675, a comprehensive Social Security bill including the Johnson Administration medical care program. The Senate subsequently passed the bill July 9, 68-21 (D 55-7; R 13-14).

Although the massive Democratic victory in the 1964 Presidential and Congressional elections, coupled with President Johnson's commitment to the Social Security health care bill, made its passage almost a foregone conclusion in the 89th Congress (1965-66), there was heavy lobbying and publicity in late 1964 and 1965.

The groups most actively working for the bill were the AFL-CIO and several independent unions; the National Council of Senior Citizens; the Group Health Assn. of America (spokesman for community group health service plans); the National Farmers Union's Senior Citizens Council; the National Medical Assn. (an organization of 5,000 Negro physicians); the American Nurses' Assn.; the Ad Hoc Physicians' Committee for Health Care for the Aged through Social Security (founded in 1962), headed by Dr. Caldwell Esselstyn and including among its members the famous baby doctor, Benjamin Spock; the Social Welfare Council of the National Council of Churches; the National Conference of Catholic Charities; the National Social Welfare Assembly; the American Public Health Assn.; the American Public Welfare Assn.; the Women's Division of Christian Service of the Methodist Church Board of Missions; the National Council of Jewish Women; the Council of Jewish Federations and Welfare Funds; the Family Service Assn.; the National Assn. of Social Workers, and Americans for Democratic Action.

Leading opponent of the bill was, once again, the American Medical Assn., which lobbied both in the nation's capital and at the grass roots, mounting two major nationwide publicity campaigns in newspapers, radio and television broadcasts. The AMA reported spending $1.2 million in 1965 to oppose the bill, chiefly for broadcasts and advertisements. It was the third highest amount ever recorded for lobby spending, exceeded only by the AMA's spending in 1949-50.

Other major opponents reported as actively working against the bill in 1964-65 were: the Chamber of Commerce of the U.S. and state chambers of commerce and junior chambers; state associations of manufacturers; some drug companies, many of whose salesmen, according to one source, included statements against the bill in speeches made to local trade groups and community organizations; the American Farm Bureau Federation and National Grange; and insurance organizations, particularly the Health Insurance Assn., which was reported as particularly active. Blue Cross in 1964 said it favored having the Government produce funds to enable individuals to purchase Blue Cross coverage instead of the plan in the Social Security medical care bill.

PROFILES OF MAJOR PRESSURE GROUPS

American Medical Assn. By far the most active and vociferous opponent of the Social Security health care proposals over the years was the American Medical Assn., an organization which in June 1965 had as members 202,404 of the nation's 284,271 physicians. Of the 202,404, a total of 159,781 were dues-paying members (dues then were $45 a year). A doctor became a member of the AMA by joining a state or county medical society and paying the $45 annual AMA dues. Dues-paying members receive free numerous journals, such as the *Journal of the AMA*, *Today's Health*, and the *AMA News*.

Throughout the entire major period of dispute over Social Security health care proposals, the AMA opposed the measures as likely to lead to socialized medicine, as unnecessary and as likely to bring about bureaucratic interference with the practice of medicine and reduce the quality of medical care in the nation.

Various sources told CQ that physicians' fears of the legislation stemmed from fears that Government bureaucrats administering the program would begin making medical decisions (what kind of drugs could be used, what kind of treatment the Government would pay for in a given situation, etc.) that would be detrimental to good medical practice; from fears that doctors would be reduced to the status of paid Government functionaries, and thus lose their community prestige, which was very high; from fears that the Government would begin to regulate the physicians' fees and thus reduce their income (which averaged $17,000 a year after taxes and expenses in 1961 for general practitioners, $20,900 for specialists, according to one survey); and from natural conservatism and opposition to "big government" on the part of doctors as a group. Whatever the reason, there was little doubt that the AMA's opposition to the Social Security health care proposals was supported by most doctors, though not all.

On legislative matters, the AMA exerted its pressure largely through activity in the localities (talking up the issue at local medical society meetings, in community groups, etc.). The high prestige of doctors greatly helped the AMA to influence others—including the public. One of the chief functions was to activate the local physician. The AMA maintained a staff of 900 persons, most of them in the Chicago headquarters but 23 in the AMA's Washington office, which had four registered lobbyists working on a regular basis to defeat the Social Security health care proposals. The AMA's 1964 budget was $23 million, of which about 45 percent came from advertising in its publications and 32 percent from membership dues. A large portion of its budget went for publications, many of which were used to attack the Social Security health care bill.

Aside from the direct lobbying carried on by its Washington staff against the bill, the AMA opposed the bill by:

• Urging local physician members to write Members of Congress and to activate other local people to write Members.

• Creating several groups designed to improve health care for the aged with the objective, in part, of making federal legislation unnecessary. In 1959 the AMA, with the American Dental Assn., American Hospital and American Nursing Home Assn., set up a National Joint Council to Improve the Health of the Aged. In 1961, it initiated a Joint Commission for Promotion of Voluntary Non-Profit Prepayment Health Plans (which included also Blue Cross, Blue Shield and the American Hospital Assn.).

• Creating a political arm, the American Medical Political Action Committee (AMPAC), to receive voluntary contributions which were then used to support Congressional candidates favorable to the AMA position on the medical care bill and/or other legislation. AMPAC, which began its first full year of action in 1962, also sponsored educational courses. It received $301,311 in 1964 (only a portion of total resources; state units of AMPAC raised additional funds, the total of which was not available). An AMPAC spokesman said that in several campaigns AMPAC funds were used primarily to support House Ways and Means Committee members who had opposed the Social Security health care bill in the past. (The Committee had jurisdiction over the bill.)

• Conducting national publicity campaigns, in newspapers and over radio and television.

In October 1964, the AMA conducted a press, radio and television campaign against the bill, the cost of which was not reported as lobby spending because the public was not directly urged to communicate with Congress on the issue. The campaign included a series of spot dramatized television announcements over the ABC network intended to reach 142 major population areas. It also included spot broadcasts over radio stations and a series of advertisements in 8,000 daily and weekly newspapers. In one typical advertisement, *Life* magazine (Oct. 16, 1964), the text stated, "The supporters of the proposed medicare tax would have you believe that passage of this controversial bill is urgent...that persons over 65 are deprived of needed medical care because they can't pay for it. Nothing could be further from the truth." The advertisement then went on to discuss existing federal medical programs.

Early in 1965, the AMA conducted another press, radio and television campaign, this one designed to push the AMA's own "eldercare" bill as an alternative to the Johnson Administration proposals and to urge public opposition to the latter.

In describing the 1965 campaign, the Feb. 22 *AMA News* said advertisements already had or would appear in *Reader's Digest*, *TV Guide*, *Time*, *Newsweek*, *U.S. News & World Report*, *Broadcasting*, *Editor and Publisher*, *Life*, *Saturday Evening Post*, *Saturday Review*, *Nation's Agriculture and Southern State Farm Unit*, *Grit*, *Christian Science Monitor*, *Wall Street Journal* and *National Observer*. The *AMA News* said radio and television broadcasts also were planned.

On June 9, 1965, the AMA ran advertisements in about 100 major daily newspapers opposing the Administration Social Security health care bill, and on June 17 it made a nationwide broadcast over ABC television called "Health Care at the Crossroads." The newspaper advertisements said that passage of the Administration bill would mean "lower quality medical care" and urged the public to "let your Senators, your Congressman and the President know your views on this vital issue."

For the first quarter of 1965, the AMA spent $829,484 for the press, radio and television campaign.

AFL-CIO. The major pressure group over the years working for passage of Social Security health care proposals was the AFL-CIO. The AFL-CIO executive council in 1957 formally determined to make passage of the Social Security health-care-for-the-aged bill a major legislative issue, and the labor federation worked ceaselessly from that time on for passage.

To accomplish its goal, the AFL-CIO was able to muster impressive resources. In 1965, it had 129 affiliated national and international unions with a total membership of 13.5 million persons, numerous union newspapers and publications, a large headquarters in Washington with many lobbyists and thousands of paid union officials all over the country.

Major methods of exerting pressure included: publicity in union publications for members to write Congress; encouragement of members to pay personal visits to their Members in Congress or form delegations; visits to city councils and state and county government bodies for the purpose of getting them to adopt resolutions requesting Congressional action on the bill; mass public letter-writing campaigns; the use of union radio shows to publicize the issue; the use of the commercials on AFL-CIO-sponsored news broadcasts, such as the Edward P. Morgan show; direct lobbying in Washington, D.C.; production of pamphlets and other written materials for the general public; and public statements by union leaders, such as AFL-CIO President George Meany, which normally received wide general coverage in the press.

Through the Committee on Political Education (COPE), a political organization supported by volunteer contributions, the AFL-CIO conducted hard campaigns in 1958, 1960 and subsequent years to defeat opponents of the Social Security health care bill, particularly on the House Ways and Means Committee.

In the 1964 primaries and elections for federal offices (Congress, the Presidency), COPE made contributions of about $900,000.

In the last years, the AFL-CIO campaign for the Social Security health care proposal was masterminded by a five-member working committee consisting of Alexander Barkan, director of COPE; ex-Rep. Andrew J. Biemiller (D Wis. 1945-47; 1949-51), the AFL-CIO's director of legislation; Nelson Cruikshank, the AFL-CIO Social Security director; Lane Kirkland, assistant to AFL-CIO President George Meany; and Al Zack, the AFL-CIO publicity director.

Many individual unions also were active in the labor campaign on the issue.

Senior Citizens Council. Another organization which worked actively for passage of the Social Security health care bill was the National Council of Senior Citizens, which in 1965 claimed a membership of 2 million elderly persons in the various local "golden ring" and senior citizens clubs affiliated with it.

The Council was first formed in 1961 by ex-leaders of the Senior Citizens for Kennedy organization that had operated during the 1960 Presidential campaign. At the time of its creation, the Council had the name "National Council of Senior Citizens for Health Care Through Social Security."

Its first head was ex-Rep. Aime J. Forand (D R.I.), long the House sponsor of medical-care-for-the-aged bills. He was succeeded by John W. Edelman.

From the beginning, the Council's chief objective was to win passage of the medical care bill. Over the years, it put out a large number of pamphlets and other written materials explaining and pushing the measure, produced radio and television shows backing the bill and organized public rallies for the bill.

On one notable occasion, May 20, 1962, it helped organize 35 mass rallies for the bill all over the country, topped by president Kennedy's appearance at Madison Square Garden in New York.

It also helped develop petitions and letter-writing campaigns to Members of Congress and set up visits to the nation's capital by delegations of the elderly in favor of the "medicare" bill.

On several occasions, the Council persuaded radio and television stations to give it free time to answer broadcasts against the "medicare" bill made by the American Medical Assn.

During 1963-65, the Council's budget ran about $150,000 to $160,000 annually. About two-thirds of this came from dues and contributions by affiliated organizations. The remainder, a third of the budget or somewhat more, was supplied in some years by donations from the Democratic party and the AFL-CIO—a fact which led Dr. F. J. L. Blasingame of the AMA to charge June 12 that the Council was "nothing more than a lobbying appendage of the Democratic National Committee and the AFL-CIO."

William R. Hutton, deputy director of the Council, said the Council and its employees had never registered as lobbyists under the 1946 federal lobbying law because the Council regarded its function as primarily to conduct educational and informational work among the elderly and general public rather than to lobby Congress directly.

Aside from Hutton, the organization's paid staff in 1965 included one full-time and one part time person working on membership matters, a bookkeeper, an administrative assistant and a half-dozen clerical employees. It had numerous non-paid volunteers.

Ex-Members of Congress as Lobbyists

The following former or present Members of Congress **or their law firms** have registered under the Federal Regulation of Lobbying Act at one time or another since its enactment in 1946.

Former Senators

Joseph H. Ball (R Minn. 1940-49). Registered for the Assn. of American Ship Owners, Sept. 29, 1949.

Ross Bass (D Tenn. House 1955-65; Senate 1964-66). Registered for the Record Industry Assn. of America, March 15, 1967.

Prentiss M. Brown (D Mich. House 1933-36; Senate 1936-43; served as OPA administrator in 1943). Brown's law firm, Brown, Lund & Levin (formerly Brown and Lund) registered for the National Assn. of Electric Companies, May 31, 1949; American and Foreign Power Co., July 10, 1954; the Dow-Chemical-Detroit Edison and Associates Atomic Power Development Project, Aug. 8, 1954; Power Reactor Development Co., June 4, 1956; Montana Power Co., Sept. 17, 1962; Washington Water Power Co., Sept. 17, 1962; Electric Bond and Share Co., June 3, 1963; Cuban Electric Co., Jan. 15, 1966; General Public Utilities Corp., July 3, 1968, March 4, 1969; Montana Power Co., March 12, 1970; Cominco American Inc., March 19, 1970; Pacific Northwestern Power Co., May 27, 1970.

Edward R. Burke (D Neb. House 1933-35; Senate 1935-41). Registered for the Hawaii Statehood Commission, April 22, 1948.

Joseph S. Clark (D Pa. 1957-69). Registered for the United World Federalists, May 14, 1969.

Earle C. Clements (D Ky. House 1945-48; Senate 1950-57). Registered for the American Merchant Marine Institute Inc., April 12, 1961; Superior Oil Co., June 28, 1963; six tobacco companies, Feb. 25, 1964; The Tobacco Institute, April 19, 1966.

John Sherman Cooper (R Ky. Senate 1946-49; Senate 1952-55 and 1956-). Registered for the Lehigh Valley Railroad Co., Aug. 22, 1949; Oceanic Steamship Co., July 17, 1950. Cooper's lobbying activities ceased before he entered the Senate.

John A. Danaher (R Conn. 1939-45). Registered for Revere Copper & Brass Inc., Feb. 4, 1947; Fuller Brush Co., Jan. 26, 1949; B. F. Goodrich Co., April 19, 1949; Firestone Tire & Rubber Co., April 21, 1949. Danaher subsequently was appointed a federal circuit judge and took office Nov. 20, 1953. His lobbying activities had ceased before then.

Sheridan Downey (D Calif. 1939-50). Registered for the Board of Harbor Commissioners of the city of Long Beach, Calif., 1951. Died Oct. 25, 1961.

Sam J. Ervin Jr. (D N.C. House 1946-47; Senate 1954-). Registered for the Southern Railway Co., June 26, 1947. In 1959 Ervin told CQ he received no compensation for his service as lobbyist and only appeared in Washington for one day. He said: "For my 24 hours of lobbying, it took me five years to convince the Justice Department that I was not doing it permanently for a living."

Felix Hebert (R R.I. 1929-35). Registered for the Associated Factory Mutual Fire Insurance Companies, April 14, 1948.

J. J. Hickey (D Wyo. 1961-62). Registered for the Union Pacific Railroad, Aug. 9, 1965.

Edwin C. Johnson (D Colo. 1937-55). Registered for the Committee for Oil Shale Development, May 20, 1957.

Kenneth B. Keating (R N.Y. House 1947-59; Senate 1959-65). Registered for the Population Crisis Committee, Sept. 2, 1965.

James P. Kem (R Mo. 1947-53). Registered for the American Merchant Marine Institute, May 13, 1953; the Texas Gulf Sulphur Co., May 13, 1953; American Metal Co., July 13, 1953; Washington Gas Light Co., 2nd quarter 1953; Estate of Mary Clark deBrabant and Katherine C. Williams, Jan. 13, 1954; T. H. Mastin & Co., Feb. 26, 1954; Field Enterprises, Educational Division, May 20, 1954; Field Foundation, May 20, 1954; Conference for Inland Waterways Dry-Bulk Regulation, May 26, 1954; Johnson, Lemon & Co., July 6, 1954; Tariff Committee

of the Woven Felt Industry, April 28, 1955; National Committee for Insurance Taxation, April 3, 1957. Died Feb. 24, 1965.

Thomas H. Kuchel (R Calif. 1953-69). Kuchel's law firm, Wyman, Bautzer, Finell, Rothman & Kuchel, registered for the Copyright Owners Negotiating Committee and the New York law firm of Paul, Weiss, Goldberg, Rifkind, Wharton & Garrison, Sept. 4, 1969; Unionamerica Inc., and City of Palm Springs, Nov. 17, 1969; Associacion Nacional De Cultivadores De Cana d'Azucar and Association of Motion Picture and Television Producers, March 3, 1970. Kuchel was Senate Minority Whip, 1959-68.

Scott W. Lucas (D Ill. House 1935-39; Senate 1939-51). Registered for the following groups as a partner of Lucas & Thomas:

American Finance Conference, March 22, 1951; Brunswick-Balke-Collender Co., et al., March 22, 1951; Trailer Coach Manufacturers Assn., March 22, 1951; Acacia Mutual Life Insurance Co., May 2, 1951; Radar-Radio Industries of Chicago Inc., July 10, 1951; National Assn. of Retail Druggists, June 13, 1952; Adolph Mon Von Zedlitz (American Finance Conference), April 9, 1953; Revere Copper and Brass Inc., Feb. 5, 1954; Mobile Homes Manufacturers Assn., June 4, 1954; Cook Electric Co., Feb. 2, 1955.

Lucas registered as an individual for the following: E. J. Albrecht Co., Aug. 2, 1955; State Loan & Finance Corp., Feb. 27, 1956; Republic of Panama, April 11, 1956; Bicycle of Manufacturing Assn. of America, April 27, 1956; Roadside Business Assn., Feb. 5, 1957; Emmco Insurance Co., Feb. 28, 1957; Marian Diane Delphine Sachs, and Arthur Sachs, March 15, 1957; Regular Common Carrier Conference of the American Trucking Assns. Inc., May 1, 1957; Western Medical Corp., April 29, 1957; Joseph E. Seagram & Sons Inc., July 5, 1957; World Commerce Corp., Jan. 27, 1958; Outdoor Advertising Assn., March 5, 1959; Western National Life Insurance Co. of Texas, March 5, 1959; St. James Lumber Co., Aug. 7, 1959; Pinewood Acres Inc., Aug. 7, 1959; Gaylord Inc., Aug. 7, 1960; Group Hospitalization Inc., June 17, 1960; National Assn. of Chain Drug Stores, April 28, 1961; Illinois Bell Telephone Co., Jan. 18, 1962; U.S. Sugar Refiners Assn., June 28, 1962; Algonquin Investment Co., Oct. 17, 1963; Texaco Inc., Dec. 11, 1963; U.S. Cane Sugar Refiners Assn., July 21, 1964; District of Columbia Bankers Assn., Jan. 31, 1966; Robert W. Johnson, Jr., Johnson & Johnson, July 11, 1968; Financial General Corp., Oct. 5, 1967. Died Feb. 22, 1968.

Ernest W. McFarland (D Ariz. 1941-53). Registered for the American Cable & Radio Corp., April 22, 1953; RCA Communications Inc., April 22, 1953; Western Union Telegraph Co., April 22, 1953. In 1954 and 1956, McFarland was elected Governor of Arizona. He served as Governor from 1955-59. His lobbying activities had ceased by the time he ran for Governor.

Francis J. Myers (D Pa. House 1939-45; Senate 1945-51). Registered for the National Foundation for Consumer Credit, Inc., May 28, 1951; Transamerica, March 8, 1956. Died July 5, 1956.

Herbert R. O'Conor (D Md. 1947-53). Registered for the American Merchant Marine Institute Inc., Jan. 6, 1954; Worthington Corp., May 7, 1954. Died March 4, 1960.

Joseph C. O'Mahoney (D Wyo. 1934-53; 1954-61). Registered for the Upper Missouri Development Assn., 2nd quarter 1953; North American Airlines, 2nd quarter 1953. Died Dec. 1, 1962.

Charles E. Potter (R Mich. House 1947-52; Senate 1952-59). Registered for the Committee of American Tanker Owners Inc., Jan. 22, 1960.

George A. Smathers (D Fla. House 1947-51; Senate 1951-69). Smathers' law firm, Smathers, Merrigan & O'Keefe, registered for the American Institute of Merchant Shipping, Apr. 29, 1969; American Horse Council, Aug. 12, 1969; Vance Sanders Company Inc., Jan. 20, 1970.

Kingsley A. Taft (R Ohio 1946-47). Taft was a member of the law firm of McKeehan, Merrick, Arter and Stewart which registered for the Holstein-Friesian Assn. of America, June 4, 1947; Lincoln Electric Co., July 2, 1947.

Edward J. Thye (R Minn. 1947-59). Registered for the Spring Air Co., March 3, 1961.

Burton K. Wheeler (D Mont. 1923-47). Registered for the Shore Line Oil Co., and Craw Co., June 2, 1948; Emil Schultz and group of farmers, April 18, 1949; Jacob Neubauer, April 18, 1949.

Former Representatives

Howard M. Baldrige (R Neb. 1931-33). Registered for the U.S. Cane Sugar Refiners Assn., Feb. 8, 1947.

James M. Barnes (D Ill. 1939-43). Registered for the following 18 organizations on March 2, 1949; Advance Aluminum Castings Corp.; American Hosiery Mills; Atlas Raincoat Co. Inc.; The C. & D. Co.; The Charis Corp.; Fairbanks Tailoring Co.; Fashion Frocks Inc.; George Master Garment Corp.; The Hoover Manufacturing and Sales Co.; J. B. Simpson Inc.; J. R. Watkins Co.; Mason Shoe Manufacturing Co.; Morton Manufacturing Co.; Progress Tailoring Co.; Spirella Co. Inc.; Stayform Co.; Wallace Brown Inc.; Zanol Products.

Also registered for the Lehigh Valley R.R. Co., Aug. 22, 1949; Agency for Canadian Car & Foundry Co. Ltd., Aug. 22, 1949; Kingsland Underwriters Group, Aug. 22, 1949; Reciprocal Inter-insurer's Federal Tax Committee, Feb. 18, 1955; National Assn. of Retired Civil Employees, April 5, 1957. Died June 8, 1958.

Laurie C. Battle (D Ala. 1947-55). Registered for the National Assn. of Manufacturers, Jan. 14, 1959.

John V. Beamer (R Ind. 1951-59). Registered for the Fine Hardwoods Assn., Jan. 19, 1960. Died Sept. 8, 1964.

James T. Begg (R Ohio 1919-29). Registered for the National St. Lawrence Project Conference, Feb. 27, 1951. Died March 26, 1963.

Alfred F. Beiter (D N.Y. 1933-39; 1941-43). Registered for the National Customs Service Assn., May 9, 1949.

C. Jasper Bell (D Mo. 1935-49). Registered for the estate of George A. Carden Sr., April 6, 1949; Philippine-American Committee, Feb. 21, 1950; National Institute of Oil Seed Products, Aug. 10, 1951.

John T. Bernard (Farmer-Labor Minn. 1937-39). Registered for the United Electrical, Radio and Machine Workers of America, Dist. Council #11, Sept. 5, 1950; National Committee to Defeat the Mundt Bill, Sept. 5, 1950.

Andrew J. Biemiller (D Wis. 1945-47; 1949-51). Registered for the American Federation of Labor, 1st quarter 1953.

Loring M. Black Jr. (D N.Y. 1923-35). Registered for William Henry Lyster, Feb. 25, 1952. Died May 21, 1956.

John W. Boehne Jr. (D Ind. 1931-43). Registered for the National Assn. of Employees of Collectors of Internal Revenue, Jan. 16, 1947.

Lyle H. Boren (D Okla. 1937-47). Registered for the Assn. of Western Railways, Feb. 7, 1955.

Charles H. Brown (D Mo. 1957-61). Registered for the American Society of Composers, Authors, and Publishers, May 22, 1961; National Education Assn., May 22, 1961; Colonial Sugar Refining Co., May 22, 1961; National Education Assn., May 12, 1969; the Washington, D.C., law firm of Cleary, Gottlieb, Steen & Hamilton, May 13, 1969. On Sept. 23, 1963, Luke C. Quinn Jr. registered for Charles H. Brown Inc., a public relations firm of ex-Rep. Brown.

Donald C. Bruce (R Ind. 1961-65). Registered for the American Conservative Union, April 29, 1965.

Thomas H. Burke (D Ohio 1949-51). Registered for the United Automobile Workers of America, 1st quarter 1953. Died Sept. 12, 1959.

John L. Cable (R Ohio 1921-25; 1929-33). Registered for the Lima City Lines Inc., March 24, 1949.

Henderson H. Carson (R Ohio 1943-45; 1947-49). Registered for the East Ohio Gas Co., Feb. 7, 1950; Con-Gas Service Corp., April 5, 1962.

Albert E. Carter (R Calif. 1925-45). Registered for the Pacific Gas & Electric Co., Jan. 2, 1947. Died Aug. 7, 1964.

Joseph E. Casey (D Mass. 1935-43). Registered for the Committee for Equalization of Tobacco Taxes, April 9, 1948; Radio-Television Manufacturers Assn., Feb. 14, 1950; Radio Manufacturers Assn., 1st quarter 1950; James, Lofland, March 1, 1962; Paramount Airlines, March 20, 1962; Jerry Maiatico, Aug. 6, 1962.

Frank Chelf (D Ky. 1945-67). Registered for the Conwood Corp., Dec. 2, 1969.

Albert M. Cole (R Kan. 1945-52). Registered for the California Savings & Loan League, July 6, 1959.

John M. Costello (D Calif. 1935-45). Registered for the American League for an Undivided Ireland, March 4, 1948.

Fred L. Crawford (R Mich. 1935-53). Registered for the Richardson Vista Corp., 1st quarter 1953; Panoramic View Corp., 1st quarter 1953; Hollywood Vista Apartments, 1st quarter 1953; Legislative Assembly of the Virgin Islands, 2nd quarter 1953. Died April 13, 1957.

Clifford Davis (D Tenn. 1940-65). Registered for the Louisville Gas and Electricity Co., Aug. 20, 1965; Shawnee Coal Co., Aug. 20, 1965.

Steven B. Derounian (R N.Y. 1953-65). Registered for the Amperex Electronic Corp., Oct. 19, 1967; American Courier Corp., Amperex Electronic Corp., and the Town of Hempstead, L.I., N.Y., Feb. 27, 1968.

Wesley A. D'Ewart (R Mont. 1945-55). Registered for the Montana Reclamation Assn., Sept. 7, 1962.

La Vern R. Dilweg (D Wis. 1943-45). Registered for the Philippine Veterans' Mission to the United States of America, June 7, 1948; Brown County Airport Committee, May 28, 1952. Ceased lobbying before being appointed to the Foreign Claims Settlement Commission in 1961.

Wesley E. Disney (D Okla. 1931-45). Registered for the International Talc Co. Inc. and Eastern Magnesium Talc Co., et. al., Feb. 26, 1947; Independent Natural Gas Assn. of America, March 7, 1947; Fluorspar Mining Group, March 7, 1947. Registered for the following six groups on April 6, 1948: American Hotel Assn.; Lowell Liquidation Corp.; Marlboro Cotton Mills Inc.; Penobscot Chemical Fiber Co.; Wilcox Oil Co.; Wurlitzer Co. Also registered for Henry B. Cleerman, May 13, 1948; Western Oil and Gas Assn., April 8, 1949; American Potash & Chemical Corp., Aug. 22, 1949; National Building Granite Quarries Assn., Sept. 23, 1949; Ozark-Mahoning Co., 4th quarter 1950; West End Chemical Co., July 10, 1951; American Zinc Co., July 30, 1953; Thomas J. Green and Edward Simone, Aug. 18, 1953. Died March 26, 1961.

James G. Donovan (D N.Y. 1951-57). Registered for Customs Brokers & Forwarders Assn. of America Inc., Dec. 28, 1959.

Alfred J. Elliott (D Calif. 1937-49). Registered for County of Tulare, Calif., March 27, 1956.

Carl Elliott (D Ala. 1949-65). Elliott's law firm, Elliott and Naftalin, registered for the South Potomac Citizens' Crises Committee, Feb. 18, 1966; Ethyl Corp., April 4, 1966; National Audio-Visual Assn., Sept. 8, 1966; United Business Schools Assn., April 17, 1967; Council of Savings and Loan Stock Cos., May 22, 1967; Scientific Apparatus Makers Assn., July 27, 1967; American Vocational Assn., March 11, 1968; Bell & Howell, May 7, 1968.

Clyde T. Ellis (D Ark. 1939-43). Registered for the National Rural Electric Cooperative Assn., Dec. 6, 1946.

Aaron L. Ford (D Miss. 1935-43). Registered for Nicholas B. Perry, Oct. 4, 1951; Otho F. Hipkins, 2nd quarter 1953; Joseph Abrams, April 10, 1959.

J. Vaughan Gary (D Va. 1945-65). Registered for the U.S. Coast Guard Selected Reserves Association, May 1, 1970.

George M. Grant (D Ala. 1937-65). Registered for the National Forest Products Assn., Oct. 6, 1965; Sept. 1, 1966, Feb. 1, 1967; Ministry of Industry, Thailand Govt., Oct. 6, 1965.

Robert A. Grant (R Ind. 1939-49). Registered for the Ethanol Committee, Aug. 22, 1949; Associated Railways of Indiana, July 30, 1957.

Ben. H. Guill (R Texas 1950-51). Registered for the following five groups on April 13, 1960: American Smelting & Refining Co., American Zinc, Lead & Smelting Co., Athletic Mining & Smelting Co., Matthiessen & Hegeler, and National Zinc Co. Registered for National Automobile Dealers Assn., July 8, 1960.

Robert Hale (R Maine 1943-59). Registered for the American Assn. for the Advancement of Science, July 31, 1959; Wisconsin Avenue Committee on Transportation Problems, June 23, 1960.

Leonard W. Hall (R N.Y. 1939-52). Hall's law firm, Scribner, Hall, Casey, Thornburg and Thompson (formerly Scribner, Hall & Casey), registered for the Connecticut General Life Insurance Co., April 20, 1962; Committee for an Interstate Taxation Act, June 10, 1966; Aerospace Industries Assn. of America Inc., Oct. 5, 1966; Jefferson Standard Life Insurance Co., April 26, 1967; Record Industry Assn. of America, Oct. 14, 1967; New Process Co., June 10, 1968; Provident Life and Accident Insurance Co., Oct. 17, 1969; Realty Committee on Taxation, Oct. 26, 1969; Transamerica Corp., Oct. 29, 1969.

Richard F. Harless (D Ariz. 1943-49). Registered for the Atlantic Union Committee, March 10, 1951.

Winder R. Harris (D Va. 1941-44). Registered for the Shipbuilders' Council of America, Feb. 11, 1947.

Burr P. Harrison (D Va. 1946-63). Registered for 34 cement companies, Jan. 21, 1964; Household Finance Corp., March 17, 1964; Savage Arms and other gunsight firms, July 7, 1965.

Don W. Harter (D Ohio 1933-43). Registered for the B. F. Goodrich Co., Jan. 16, 1947. Harter's law firm, Harter & Calhoun, registered for Avon Products Inc., 3rd quarter, 1951; Beauty Counselors Inc., 3rd quarter, 1951.

Fred A. Hartley Jr. (R N.J. 1929-49). Registered for the Tool Owners Union Inc., March 25, 1949; Western Medical Corp., Sept. 28, 1951.

A. S. Herlong Jr. (D Fla. 1949-69). Registered for the Association of Southeastern Railroads, May 12, 1969.

Patrick J. Hillings (R Calif. 1951-59). Registered for the California-Portland Cement Co., Aug. 21, 1959; Los Angeles City Employees Section of the Calif. Public Employees for Social Security, Sept. 29, 1961.

Robert L. Hogg (R W.Va. 1930-33). Registered for the American Life Convention, March 10, 1949.

John F. Hunter (D Ohio 1937-43). Registered for Ritter & Boesel, Feb. 12, 1949. Died Dec. 19, 1957.

DeWitt S. Hyde (R Md. 1953-59). Registered for the Laundry & Dry Cleaners Assn., Feb. 6, 1959. On Sept. 23, 1959, Hyde became a judge of the District of Columbia Court of General Sessions (Municipal Court). His lobbying activities had ceased before he took office.

Frank Ikard (D Texas 1951-61). Registered for the American Petroleum Institute, April 16, 1962.

Frank M. Karsten (D Mo. 1947-68). Registered for Affiliated Government Organizations, a federation of organizations representing Federal Government employees in the New York City area, Oct. 27, 1969.

Victor A. Knox (R Mich. 1953-65). Registered for the Committee for Automobile Excise Tax Repeal, May 18, 1965; College of American Pathologists, March 1, 1965.

Horace R. Kornegay (D N.C. 1961-69). Registered for the Tobacco Institute Inc., Feb. 5, 1969.

Edward H. Kruse Jr. (D Ind. 1949-51). Registered for the Wayne Pump Co., June 26, 1951.

Gerald W. Landis (R Ind. 1939-49). Registered for William Ingles, Feb. 3, 1949.

Fritz G. Lanham (D Texas 1919-47). Registered for the American Fair Trade Council Inc., Jan. 8, 1947; National Patent Council Inc., Jan. 8, 1947; Trinity Improvement Assn. Inc., Jan. 8, 1947; State Tax Assn., July 14, 1947; American Chamber of Commerce of Mexico, July 15, 1947; Quality Brands Associates of America Inc., Feb. 23, 1960.

William C. Lantaff (D Fla. 1951-55). Registered for the U.S. Cuban Sugar Council, June 9, 1955.

Clarence F. Lea (D Calif. 1917-49). Registered for the Transportation Assn. of America, March 1, 1949. Lea's official biography indicates he discontinued Washington, D.C., activities after 1954. Died June 20, 1964.

Harold O. Lovre (R S.D. 1949-57). Registered for the American Trucking Assns. Inc., April 10, 1957; National Milk Producers Federation, April 11, 1957; Chicago Mercantile Exchange, Jan. 8, 1958; Porter Brothers Corp., June 23, 1958; American Football League, Sept. 14, 1961. Lovre's law firm, Lovre and DeVany, registered for the Fine Hardwoods Assn., Nov. 26, 1963; American Football League, March 3, 1964; Anti-Friction Bearing Manufacturers Assn. Foreign Trade Committee, May 19, 1964; Major Professional Football, July 20, 1967; National Board of Fur Farm Organizations, May 10, 1967.

John E. Lyle Jr. (D Texas 1945-55). Registered for the Shell Oil Co., July 30, 1958.

George E. MacKinnon (R Minn. 1947-49). Registered for the Farmers & Mechanics Savings Bank, May 2, 1951; four mutual funds, Aug. 23, 1967.

Carter Manasco (D Ala. 1941-49). Registered for the National Coal Assn., Feb. 5, 1949; National Business Publications Inc., March 12, 1949; Southern Pine Industry Committee, Jan. 6, 1955.

Frank A. Mathews Jr. (R N.J. 1945-49). Registered for the Delaware River Valley Assn., Aug. 10, 1954. Died Feb. 5, 1964.

Gordon L. McDonough (R Calif. 1945-63). Registered for David S. Moir "and a group of retired U.S. Army officers," Jan. 7, 1966.

Clifford G. McIntire (R Maine 1951-64). Registered for the American Farm Bureau Federation, Feb. 20, 1970.

Albert P. Morano (R Conn. 1951-59). Registered for the GERLI Company—Cheney Division, June 18, 1969.

Harold G. Mosier (D Ohio 1937-39). Registered for the Glenn L. Martin Co., Jan. 3, 1947; Aircraft Industries Assn., Sept. 12, 1952.

Leo O'Brien (D N.Y. 1952-66). Registered for the Virgin Islands Home Rule Committee, July 10, 1967.

John J. O'Connor (D N.Y. 1923-39). Registered for the Society of Marine Inspectors, May 26, 1947; Isbrandtsen Co. Inc., June 9, 1958. Died Jan. 26, 1961.

Donald L. O'Toole (D N.Y. 1937-53). Registered for the U.S. Cuban Sugar Council, March 1, 1955. Died Sept. 3, 1964.

Hugh Peterson (D Ga. 1935-47). Registered for the U.S. Cane Sugar Refiners Assn., 4th quarter 1951. Died Oct. 3, 1961.

J. Hardin Peterson (D Fla. 1933-51). Registered for the Government of Guam, Jan. 9, 1952; Alaska Statehood Committee, Jan. 16, 1952; U.S. Air Lines, March 26, 1952; Fort Lauderdale, Fla., Air Lines, 1st quarter 1952; Florida Citrus Mutual, Dec. 18, 1953; West Coast (Fla.) Inland Navigation District, June 8, 1954; Tomoka Land Co., July 2, 1954; Gene Salentine, Jan. 27, 1955; Howard L. Shannon, July 11, 1955; Peoples Lobby Inc., Jan. 9, 1956; C. C. Woodward, J. W. Keen, Luke & Eleanor Flood, J. Allen Brown, March 6, 1959; Florida Fruit & Vegetables Assn., March 28, 1964.

Tom Pickett (D Texas 1945-52). Registered for the Assn. of American Railroads, May 1, 1961.

Walter C. Ploeser (R Mo. 1941-49). Registered for the Mississippi Valley Assn., Feb. 27, 1950.

Albert Rains (D Ala. 1945-65). Registered for Mayer, Friedlich, Spiess, Tierney, Brown and Platt, July 12, 1965; Simpson, Thatcher and Bartlett, July 12, 1965.

Robert Ramspeck (D Ga. 1929-45). Registered for the Air Transport Assn. of America, Jan. 2, 1947. Not active as a lobbyist in 1951-52, when he was a member of the Civil Service Commission.

Brazilla Carroll Reece (R Tenn. 1921-31; 1933-47; 1951-61). Reece was a member of the National Advisory Council of the China Emergency Committee which registered April 18, 1949. Died March 19, 1961.

Albert L. Reeves Jr. (R Mo. 1947-49). Registered for the estate of George A. Carden Sr., Jan. 14, 1949; Grace Lines Inc., May 24, 1949; American President Lines, Ltd., May 24, 1949; the following four on May 25, 1949: American Export Lines Inc., Farrell Lines Inc., United States Lines Co., and Lykes Bros. Steamship Co. Inc. All were inactive as of Dec. 31, 1949. Registered for the Estate of Anne Peyton, May 25, 1949; Wilcox Electric Co., June 14, 1949; New Process Co., Sept. 30, 1949. Reeves became a member of the partnership of Cummings, Stanley, Truitt & Cross during the 1st quarter of 1950.

Kenneth M. Regan (D Texas 1947-55). Registered for 19 Texas railroads, Jan. 16, 1959. Died Aug. 15, 1959.

James P. Richards (D S.C. 1933-57). Registered for the Tobacco Institute, Feb. 11, 1959.

Kenneth A. Roberts (D Ala. 1951-65). Registered for the U.S. Plywood Corp., May 24, 1965; American Optometric Assn., April 14, 1965; Animal Health Institute, April 29, 1965; Proprietary Association, June 12, 1970.

Walter Rogers (D Texas 1951-66). Registered for 12 natural gas and pipeline companies, April 28, 1967; Independent Natural Gas Assn. of America, Jan. 11, 1969.

Richard M. Russell (D Mass. 1935-37). Registered for the Estate of Charles W. Taintor, July 11, 1947. Inactive as of Dec. 31, 1949.

J. T. Rutherford (D Texas 1955-63). Registered for the American Trucking Assns., Jan. 16, 1963; South Padre Investment Corp., May 13, 1969. His firm, J. T. Rutherford and Associates, registered for the National Creative Arts Committee for Better Copyright Laws, Feb. 4, 1963; American College of Radiology, March 1, 1965; National Grain Producers, Handlers & Processors Assn., April 2, 1965; Central Arizona Project Assn. (including the Hualapai Indians), Aug. 26, 1966; Central Arizona Project Assn., April 8, 1968.

Elmer J. Ryan (D Minn. 1935-41). Registered for 2,500 individual former employees of Northwest Airlines, March 7, 1947; Josten Manufacturing Co., Feb. 27, 1950. Died Feb. 1, 1958.

Gordon H. Scherer (R Ohio 1953-63). Registered for the Research and Public Relations Committee of the National Panhellenic Conference, Jan. 27, 1964.

Byron N. Scott (D Calif. 1935-39). Registered for the Metropolitan Water District of Southern Calif., March 6, 1950. Employed until March 20, 1950.

Jouett Shouse (D Kan. 1915-19). Registered for the Thornhill Broome estate, June 26, 1947. Inactive as of Dec. 31, 1949. Died June 2, 1968.

Abner W. Sibal (R Conn. 1961-65). Sibal's law firm, Gadsby & Hannah, registered for Vance Sanders Company Inc., Jan. 28, 1970; Boston Stock Exchange, April 16, 1970.

Edward L. Sittler Jr. (R Pa. 1951-53). Registered for the Home Rule Headquarters and Home Rule Committee, 1st quarter 1953.

Lynn E. Stalbaum (D Wis. 1965-67). Registered for the National Rural Electric Cooperative Assn., Jan. 18, 1967; Associated Dairymen Inc., July 7, 1969. Stalbaum was a member of the House Agriculture Committee.

Frank L. Sundstrom (R N.J. 1943-49). Registered for Schenley Industries Inc., May 20, 1955; Tobacco Institute Inc., Feb. 6, 1969, Feb. 24, 1969.

Malcolm C. Tarver (D Ga. 1927-47). Registered for the Committee on Taxation of the Barytes Industry of United States, Jan. 30, 1947. Inactive as of Dec. 31, 1949. Died March 5, 1960.

Clark W. Thompson (D Texas 1933-35; 1947-66). Registered for the United States Independent Telephone Assn., April 20, 1967; National Board of Fur Farm Organizations, May 5, 1967; Tenneco Inc., May 7, 1968.

Harry L. Towe (R N.J. 1943-51). Registered for the Associated Railroads of N.J., March 6, 1956.

Ralph E. Updike (R Ind. 1925-29). Registered for the National Customs Service Assn., Dec. 13, 1948. Died Sept. 16, 1953.

Jerry Voorhis (D Calif. 1937-47). Registered for the Cooperative League of the United States of America, June 26, 1947.

Clifton A. Woodrum (D Va. 1923-45). Registered for the American Plant Food Council, 1st quarter 1949. Died Oct. 6, 1950.

Legislative Reorganization Act of 1946

(S 2177—PL 79-601)

Title III—Regulation of Lobbying Act

SHORT TITLE

SEC 301. This title may be cited as the "Federal Regulation of Lobbying Act."

DEFINITIONS

SEC. 302. When used in this title—

(a) The term "contribution" includes a gift, subscription, loan, advance, or deposit of money or anything of value and includes a contract, promise, or agreement, whether or not legally enforceable, to make a contribution.

(b) The term "expenditure" includes a payment, distribution, loan, advance, deposit, or gift of money or anything of value, and includes a contract, promise, or agreement, whether or not legally enforceable, to make an expenditure.

(c) The term "person" includes an individual, partnership, committee, association, corporation, and any other organization or group of persons.

(d) The term "Clerk" means the Clerk of the House of Representatives of the United States.

(e) The term "legislation" means bills, resolutions, amendments, nominations, and other matters pending or proposed in either house of Congress and includes any other matter which may be the subject of action by either house.

DETAILED ACCOUNTS OF CONTRIBUTIONS

SEC. 303 (a) It shall be the duty of every person who shall in any manner solicit or receive a contribution to any organization or fund for the purposes hereinafter designated to keep a detailed and exact account of—

(1) all contributions of any amount or of any value whatsoever;

(2) the name and address of every person making any such contribution of $500 or more and the date thereof;

(3) all expenditures made by or on behalf of such organization or fund; and

(4) the name and address of every person to whom any such expenditure is made and the date thereof.

(b) It shall be the duty of such person to obtain and keep a receipted bill, stating the particulars, for every expenditure of such funds exceeding $10 in amount, and to preserve all receipted bills and accounts required to be kept by this section for a period of at least two years from the date of the filing of the statement containing such items.

RECEIPTS FOR CONTRIBUTIONS

SEC. 304. Every individual who receives a contribution of $500 or more for any of the purposes hereinafter designated shall within five days after receipt thereof render to the person or organization for which such contribution was received a detailed account thereof, including the name and address of the person making such contribution and the date on which received.

STATEMENTS TO BE FILED WITH CLERK OF HOUSE

SEC. 305. (a) Every person receiving any contributions or expending any money for the purposes designated in subparagraph (a) or (b) of section 307 shall file with the Clerk between the first and tenth day of each calendar quarter, a statement containing complete as of the day next preceding the date of filing—

(1) the name and address of each person who has made a contribution of $500 or more not mentioned in the preceding report; except that the first report filed pursuant to this title shall contain the name and address of each person who has made any contribution of $500 or more to such person since the effective date of this title;

(2) the total sum of the contributions made to or for such person during the calendar year and not stated under paragraph (1);

(3) the total sum of all contributions made to or for such person during the calendar year;

(4) the name and address of each person to whom an expenditure in one or more items of the aggregate amount or value, within the calendar year, of $10 or more has been made by or on behalf of such person, and the amount, date, purpose of such expenditure;

(5) the total of all expenditures made by or on behalf of such person during the calendar year and not stated under paragraph (4);

(6) the total sum of expenditures made by or on behalf of such person during the calendar year.

(b) The statements required to be filed by subsection (a) shall be cumulative during the calendar year to which they relate, but where there has been no change in an item reported in a previous statement only the amount need be carried forward.

STATEMENT PRESERVED FOR TWO YEARS

SEC. 306. A statement required by this title to be filed with the Clerk—

(a) shall be deemed properly filed when deposited in an established post office within the prescribed time, duly stamped, registered, and directed to the Clerk of the House of Representatives of the United States, Washington, District of Columbia, but in the event it is not received, a duplicate of such statement shall be promptly filed upon notice by the Clerk of its nonreceipt;

(b) shall be preserved by the Clerk for a period of two years from the date of filing, shall constitute part of the public records of his office, and shall be open to public inspection.

PERSONS TO WHOM APPLICABLE

SEC. 307. The provisions of this title shall apply to any person (except a political committee as defined in the Federal Corrupt Practices Act, and duly organized state or local committees of a political party), who by himself, or through any agent or employee or other persons in any manner whatsoever, directly or indirectly, solicits, collects, or receives money or any other thing of value to be used principally to aid, or the principal purpose of which person is to aid, in the accomplishment of any of the following purposes:

(a) The passage or defeat of any legislation by the Congress of the United States.

(b) To influence, directly or indirectly, the passage or defeat of any legislation by the Congress of the United States.

REGISTRATION WITH SECRETARY OF THE SENATE AND CLERK OF THE HOUSE

SEC. 308. (a) Any person who shall engage himself for pay or for any consideration for the purpose of attempting to influence the passage or defeat of any legislation by the Congress of the United States shall, before doing anything in furtherance of such object, register with the Clerk of the House of Representatives and the Secretary of the Senate and shall give to those officers in writing and under oath, his name and business address, the name and address of the person by whom he is employed, and in whose interest he appears or works, the duration of such employment, how much he is paid and is to receive, by whom he is paid or is to be paid, how much he is to be paid for expenses, and what expenses are to be included. Each such person so registering, shall, between the first and tenth day of each calendar quarter, so long as his activity continues, file with the Clerk and Secretary a detailed report under oath of all money received and expended by him during the preceding calendar quarter in carrying on his work; to whom paid; for what purposes; and the names of any papers, periodicals, magazines, or other publications in which he has caused to be published any articles or editorials; and the proposed legislation he is employed to support or oppose. The provisions of this section shall not apply to any person who merely appears before a committee of the Congress of the United States in support of or opposition to legislation; nor to any public official acting in his official capacity; nor in the case of any newspaper or other regularly published periodical (including any individual who owns, publishes, or is employed by any such newspaper or periodical) which in the ordinary course of business publishes news items, editorials, or other comments, or paid advertisements, which directly or indirectly urge the passage or defeat of legislation, if such newspaper, periodical, or individual, engages in no further or other activities in connection with the passage or defeat of such legislation, other than to appear before a committee of the Congress of the United States in support of or in opposition to such legislation.

(b) All information required to be filed under the provisions of this section with the Clerk of the House shall be compiled by said Clerk and Secretary, acting jointly, as soon as practicable after the close of the calendar quarter with respect to which such information is filed and shall be printed in the Congressional Record.

REPORTS AND STATEMENTS TO BE MADE UNDER OATH

SEC. 309. All reports and statements required under this title shall be made under oath, before an officer authorized by law to administer oaths.

PENALTIES

SEC. 310. (a) Any person who violates any of the provisions of this title, shall, upon conviction, be guilty of a misdemeanor, and shall be punished by a fine of not more than $5,000 or imprisonment for not more than twelve months, or by both such fine and imprisonment.

(b) In addition to the penalties provided for in subsection (a), any person convicted of the misdemeanor specified therein is prohibited, for a period of three years from the date of such conviction, from attempting to influence, directly or indirectly, the passage or defeat of any proposed legislation or from appearing before a committee of the Congress in support of or opposition to proposed legislation; and any person who violates any provision of this subsection shall, upon conviction thereof, be guilty of a felony, and shall be punished by a fine of not more than $10,000, or imprisonment for not more than five years, or by both such fine and imprisonment.

EXEMPTION

SEC. 311. The provisions of this title shall not apply to practices or activities regulated by the Federal Corrupt Practices Act nor be construed as repealing any portion of said Federal Corrupt Practices Act.

Text of Supreme Court Lobby Law Ruling and Dissents

Majority Opinion

Following is the text of the majority opinions of the Supreme Court in the Harriss-Moore-Linder case, United States v. Harriss, handed down by Chief Justice Earl Warren, June 7, 1954:

I.

The constitutional requirement of definiteness is violated by a criminal statute that fails to give a person of ordinary intelligence fair notice that his contemplated conduct is forbidden by the statute. The underlying principle is that no man shall be held criminally responsible for conduct which he could not reasonably understand to be proscribed.

On the other hand, if the general class of offenses to which the statute is directed is plainly within its terms, the statute will be struck down as vague even though marginal cases could be put where doubts might arise. *United States v. Petrillo*, 332 U.S. 1, 7. *Cf Jordan v. DeGeorge*, 341 U.S. 223, 231. And if this general class of offenses can be made constitutionally definite by a reasonable construction of the statute, this Court is under a duty to give the statute that construction. This was the course adopted in *Screws v. United States*, 325 U.S. 91, upholding the definiteness of the Civil Rights Act.

The same course is appropriate here. The key section of the Lobbying Act is Sec. 307, entitled "Persons to Whom Applicable." Section 307 provides:

"The provisions of this title shall apply to any person (except a political committee as defined in the Federal Corrupt Practices Act, and duly organized State or local committees of a political party), who by himself, or through any agent or employee or other persons in any manner whatsoever, directly or indirectly, solicits, collects, or receives money or any other thing of value to be used principally to aid, or the principal purpose of which person is to aid, in the accomplishment of any of the following purposes:

"(a) The passage or defeat of any legislation by the Congress of the United States.

"(b) To influence, directly or indirectly, the passage or defeat of any legislation by the Congress of the United States."

This section modifies the substantive provisions of the Act, including Sec. 305 and Sec. 308. In other words, unless a "person" falls within the category established by Sec. 307, the disclosure requirements of Sec. 305 and Sec. 308 are inapplicable. Thus coverage under the Act is limited to those persons (except for the specified political committees) who solicit, collect, or receive contributions of money or other thing of value, and then only if the principal purpose of either the persons or the contributions is to aid in the accomplishment of the aims set forth in Sec. 307 (a) and (b). In any event, the solicitation, collection, or receipt of money or other thing of value is a prerequisite to coverage under the Act.

The Government urges a much broader construction—namely, that under Sec. 305 a person must report his expenditures to influence legislation even though he does not solicit, collect, or receive contributions as provided in Sec. 307. Such a construction, we believe, would do violence to the title and language of Sec. 307 as well as its legislative history. If the construction urged by the Government is to become law, that is for Congress to accomplish by further legislation.

We now turn to the alleged vagueness of the purposes set forth in Sec. 307 (a) and (b). As in *United States v. Rumely*, 341 U.S. 41, 47, which involved the interpretation of similar language, we believe this language should be construed to refer only to "lobbying in its commonly accepted sense"—to direct communication with members of Congress on pending or proposed federal legislation.

The legislative history of the Act makes clear that, at the very least, Congress sought disclosure of such direct pressures, exerted by the lobbyists themselves or through their hirelings or through an artificially stimulated letter campaign. It is likewise clear that Congress would have intended the Act to operate on this narrower basis, even if a broader application to organizations seeking to propagandize the general public were not permissible.

There remains for our consideration the meaning of "the principal purpose" and "to be used principally to aid." The legislative history of the Act indicates that the term "principal" was adopted merely to exclude from the scope of Sec. 307 those contributions and persons having only an "incidental" purpose of influencing legislation. Conversely, the "principal purpose" requirement does not exclude a contribution which in substantial part is to be used to influence legislation through direct communication with Congress or a person whose activities in substantial part are directed to influencing legislation through direct communication with Congress. If it were otherwise—if an organization, for example, were exempted because lobbying was only one of its main activities—the Act would in large measure be reduced to a mere exhortation against abuse of the legislative process. In construing the Act narrowly to avoid constitutional doubts, we must also avoid a construction that would seriously impair the effectiveness of the Act in coping with the problem it was designed to alleviate.

To summarize, therefore, there are three prerequisites to coverage under Sec. 307: (1) the "person" must have solicited, collected, or received contributions; (2) one of the main purposes of such "person," or one of the main purposes of such contributions, must have been to influence the passage or defeat of legislation by Congress; (3) the intended method of accomplishing this purpose must have been through direct communication with members of Congress. And since Sec. 307 modifies the substantive provisions of the Act, our construction of Sec. 307 will of necessity also narrow the scope of Sec. 305 and Sec. 308 in this case. Thus Sec. 305 is limited to those persons who are covered by Sec. 307; and when so covered, they must report all contributions and expenditures having the purpose of attempting to influence legislation through direct communication with Congress. Similarly, Sec. 308 is limited to those persons (with the stated exceptions) who are covered by Sec. 307 and who, in addition, engage themselves for pay or for any other valuable consideration for the purpose of attempting to influence legislation through direct communication with Congress. Construed in this way, the Lobbying Act meets the constitutional requirement of definiteness.

II.

Thus construed, Secs. 305 and 308 also do not violate the freedoms guaranteed by the First Amendment—freedom to speak, publish, and petition the Government.

Present-day legislative complexities are such that individual members of Congress cannot be expected to explore the myriad pressures to which they are regularly subjected. Yet full realization of the American ideal of government by elected representatives depends to no small extent on their ability to properly evaluate such pressures. Otherwise the voice of the people may all too easily be drowned out by the voice of special interest groups seeking favored treatment while masquerading as proponents of the public weal. This is the evil which the Lobbying Act was designed to help prevent.

Toward that end, Congress has not sought to prohibit these pressures. It has merely provided for a modicum of information from those who for hire attempt to influence legislation or who collect or spend funds for that purpose. It wants only to know who is being hired, who is putting up the money, and how much. It acted in the same spirit and for a similar purpose in passing the Federal Corrupt Practices Act—to maintain the integrity of a basic governmental process. See *Burroughs and Cannon v. United States*, 290 U.S. 534. 545.

Under these circumstances, we believe that Congress at least within the bounds of the Act as we have construed it, is not constitutionally forbidden to require the disclosure of lobbying activities. To do so would be to deny Congress in large measure the power of self-protection. And here Congress has used that power in a manner restricted to its appropriate end. We conclude that Secs. 305 and 308, as applied to persons defined in Sec. 307, do not offend the First Amendment.

It is suggested, however, that the Lobbying Act, with respect to persons other than those defined in Sec. 307, may as a practical matter act as a deterrent to their exercise of First Amendment rights. Hypothetical borderline situations are conjured up in which such persons choose to remain silent because of fear of possible prosecution for failure to comply with the Act. Our narrow construction of the Act, precluding as it does reasonable fears, is calculated to avoid such restraint. But, even assuming some such deterrent effect, the restraint is at most an indirect one resulting from self-censorship, comparable in many ways to the restraint resulting from criminal libel laws. The hazard of such restraint is too remote to require striking down a statute which on its face is otherwise plainly within the area of congressional power and is designed to safeguard a vital national interest.

III.

The appellees further attack the statute on the ground that the penalty provided in Sec. 310 (b) is unconstitutional. That section provides:

"(b) In addition to the penalties provided for in subsection (a), any person convicted of the misdemeanor specified therein is prohibited, for a period of three years from the date of such conviction, from attempting to influence, directly or indirectly, the passage or defeat of any proposed legislation or from appearing before a committee of the Congress in support of or opposition to proposed legislation; and any person who violates any provision of this subsection shall, upon conviction thereof, be guilty of a felony, and shall be punished by a fine of not more than $10,000, or imprisonment for not more than five years, or by both such fine and imprisonment."

This section, the appellees argue, is a patent violation of the First Amendment guarantees of freedom of speech and the right to petition the Government.

We find it unnecessary to pass on this contention. Unlike Secs. 305, 307, and 308 which we have judged on their face, Sec. 310 (b) has not yet been applied to the appellees, and it will never be so applied if the appellees are found innocent of the charges against them. See *United States v. Wurzbach*, 280 U.S. 396, 399; *United States v. Petrillo*, 322 U.S. 1, 9-12.

Moreover, the Act provides for the separability of any provision found invalid. If Sec. 310 (b) should ultimately be declared unconstitutional, its elimination would still leave a statute defining specific duties and providing a specific penalty for violation of any such duty. The prohibition of Sec. 310 (b) is expressly stated to be "In addition to the penalties provided for in subsection (a)..."; subsection (a) makes a violation of Sec. 305 or Sec. 308 a misdemeanor, punishable by fine or imprisonment or both. Consequently there would seem to be no obstacle to giving effect to the separability clause as to Sec. 310 (b), if this should ever prove necessary. Compare *Electric Bond & Share Co. v. Securities & Exchange Commission*, 303 U.S. 419, 433-437.

The judgment below is reversed and the cause is remanded to the District Court for further proceedings not inconsistent with this opinion.

Reversed.

Mr. JUSTICE CLARK took no part in the consideration or decision of this case.

Dissent—Justice Jackson

Here is the dissenting opinion of Justice Robert H. Jackson in the Harriss-Moore-Linder case:

MR. JUSTICE JACKSON, dissenting.

Several reasons lead me to withhold my assent from this decision.

The clearest feature of this case is that it begins with an Act so mischievously vague that the Government charged with its enforcement does not understand it, for some of its important assumptions are rejected by the Court's interpretation. The clearest feature of the Court's decision is that it leaves the country under an Act which is not much like any Act passed by Congress. Of course, when such a question is before us, it is easy to differ as to whether it is more appropriate to strike out or to strike down. But I recall few cases in which the Court has gone so far in rewriting an Act.

The Act passed by Congress would appear to apply to all persons who (1) solicit or receive funds for the purpose of lobbying, (2) receive and expend funds for the purpose of lobbying, or (3) merely expend funds for the purpose of lobbying. The Court at least eliminates this last category from coverage of the Act, though I should suppose that more serious evils affecting the public interest are to be found in the way lobbyists spend their money than in the ways they obtain it. In the present indictments, six counts relate exclusively to failures to report expenditures while only one appears to rest exclusively on failure to report receipts.

Also, Congress enacted a statute to reach the raising and spending of funds for the purpose of influencing congressional action directly or indirectly. The Court entirely deletes "indirectly" and narrows "directly" to mean "direct communication with members of Congress." These two constructions leave the Act touching only a part of the practices Congress deemed sinister.

Finally, as if to compensate for its deletions from the Act, the Court expands the phrase "the principal purpose" so that it now refers to any contribution which "in substantial part" is used to influence legislation.

I agree, of course, that we should make liberal interpretations to save legislative Acts, including penal statutes which punish conduct traditionally recognized as morally "wrong." Whoever kidnaps, steals, kills, or commits similar acts of violence upon another is bound to know that he is inviting retribution by society, and many of the statutes which define these long-established crimes are traditionally and perhaps necessarily vague. But we are dealing with a novel offense that has no established bounds and no such moral basis. The criminality of the conduct dealt with here depends entirely upon a purpose to influence legislation. Though there may be many abuses in pursuit of this purpose, this Act does not deal with corruption. These defendants, for example, are indicted for failing to report their activities in raising and spending money to influence legislation in support of farm prices, with no charge of corruption, bribery, deception, or other improper action. This may be a selfish business and against the best interests of the nation as a whole, but it is in an area where legal penalties should be applied only by formulae as precise and clear as our language will permit.

The First Amendment forbids Congress to abridge the right of the people "to petition the Government for a redress of grievances." If this right is to have an interpretation consistent with that given to other First Amendment rights, it confers a large immunity upon activities of persons, organizations, groups and classes to obtain what they think is due them from government. Of course, their conflicting claims and propaganda are confusing, annoying and at times, no doubt, deceiving and corrupting. But we may not forget that our constitutional system is to allow the greatest freedom of access to Congress, so that the people may press for their selfish interests, with Congress acting as arbiter of their demands and conflicts.

In matters of this nature, it does not seem wise to leave the scope of a criminal Act, close to impinging on the right of petition, dependent upon judicial construction for its limitations. Judicial construction, constitutional or statutory, always is subject to hazards of judicial reconstruction. One may rely on today's narrow interpretation only at his peril, for some later Court may expand the Act to include, in accordance with its terms, what today the Court excludes. This recently happened with the antitrust laws, which the Court cites as being similarly vague. This Court, in a criminal case, sustained an indictment by admittedly changing repeated and long-established constitutional and statutory interpretations. *United States v. South-Eastern Underwriters Assn.*, 322 U.S. 533. The ex post facto provision of our Constitution has not been held to protect the citizen against a retroactive change in decisional law, but it does against such a prejudicial change in legislation. As long as this statute stands on the books, its vagueness will be a contingent threat to activities which the Court today rules out, the contingency being a change of views by the Court as hereafter constituted.

The Court's opinion presupposes, and I do not disagree, that Congress has power to regulate lobbying for hire as a business or profession and to require such agents to disclose their principals, their activities, and their receipts. However, to reach the real evils of lobbying without cutting into the constitutional right of petition is a difficult and delicate task for which the Court's action today gives little guidance. I am in doubt whether the Act as construed does not permit applications which would abridge the right of petition, for which clear, safe and workable channels must be maintained. I think we should point out the defects and limitations which condemn this Act so clearly that the Court cannot sustain it as written, and leave its rewriting to Congress. After all, it is Congress that should know from experience both the good in the right of petition and the evils of professional lobbying.

Dissent—Justices Douglas, Black

The dissenting opinion of Justices William O. Douglas and Hugo L. Black in the Harriss-Moore-Linder case follows:

MR. JUSTICE DOUGLAS, with whom MR. JUSTICE BLACK concurs, dissenting.

I am in sympathy with the effort of the Court to save this statute from the charge that it is so vague and indefinite as to be unconstitutional. My inclinations were that way at the end of the oral argument. But further study changed my mind. I am now convinced that the formula adopted to save this Act is too dangerous for use. It can easily ensnare people who have done no more than exercise their constitutional rights of speech, assembly and press.

We deal here with the validity of a criminal statute. To use the test of *Connally v. General Construction Co.*, 269 U.S. 385, 391, the question is whether this statute "either forbids or requires the doing of an act in terms so vague that men of common intelligence must necessarily guess at its meaning and differ as to its application." If it is so vague, as I think this one is, then it fails to meet the standards required by due process of law. See *United States v. Petrillo*, 332 U.S. 1. In determining that question we consider the statute on its face. As stated in *Lanzetta v. New Jersey*, 306 U.S. 451, 453:

"If on its face the challenged provision is repugnant to the due process clause, specification of details of the offense intended to be charged would not serve to validate it.... It is the statute, not the accusation under it, that prescribes the rule to govern conduct and warns against transgression.... No one may be required at peril of life, liberty or property to speculate as to the meaning of penal statutes. All are entitled to be informed as to what the State commands or forbids."
And see *Winters v. New York*, 333 U.S. 507, 515.

The question therefore is not what the information charges nor what the proof might be. It is whether the statute itself is sufficiently narrow and precise as to give fair warning.

It is contended that the Act plainly applies
—to persons who pay others to present views to Congress either in committee hearings or by letters or other communications to Congress or Congressmen and
—to persons who spend money to induce others to communicate with Congress.
The Court adopts that view, with one minor limitation which the Court places on the Act—that only persons who solicit, collect, or receive money are included.

The difficulty is that the Act has to be rewritten and words actually added and subtracted to produce that result.

Section 307 makes the Act applicable to anyone who "directly or indirectly" solicits, collects, or receives contributions "to be used principally to aid, or the principal purpose of which person is to aid" in either
—the "passage or defeat of any legislation" by Congress, or
—"To influence, directly or indirectly, the passage or defeat of any legislation" by Congress.
We start with an all-inclusive definition of "legislation" contained in Sec. 302 (e). It means "bills, resolutions, amendments, nominations, and other matters pending or proposed in either House of Congress, and includes any other matter which may be the subject of action by either House." What is the scope of "any other matter which may be the subject of action" by Congress? It would seem to include not only pending or proposed legislation but any matter within the legitimate domain of Congress.

What contributions might be used "principally to aid" in influencing "directly or indirectly, the passage or defeat" of any such measure by Congress? When is one retained for the purpose of influencing the "passage or defeat of any legislation"?

(1) One who addresses a trade union for repeal of a labor law certainly hopes to influence legislation.

(2) So does a manufacturers' association which runs ads in newspapers for a sales tax.

(3) So does a farm group which undertakes to raise money for an educational program to be conducted in newspapers, magazines and on radio and television, showing the need for revision of our attitude on world trade.

(4) So does a group of oil companies which puts agents in the Nation's capital to sound the alarm at hostile legislation, to exert influence on Congressmen to defeat it, to work on the Hill for the passage of laws favorable to the oil interests.

(5) So does a business, labor, farm, religious, social, racial, or other group which raises money to contact people with the request that they write their Congressman to get a law repealed or modified, to get a proposed law passed, or themselves to propose a law.

Are all of these activities covered by the Act? If one is included why are not the others? The Court apparently excludes the kind of activities listed in categories (1), (2), and (3) and includes part of the activities in (4) and (5)—those which entail contacts with the Congress.

There is, however, difficulty in that course, a difficulty which seems to me to be insuperable. I find no warrant in the Act for drawing the line, as the Court does, between "direct communication with Congress" and other pressures on Congress. The Act is as much concerned with one, as with the other.

The words "direct communication with Congress" are not in the Act. Congress was concerned with the raising of money to aid in the passage or defeat of legislation, whatever tactics were used. But the Court not only strikes out one whole group of activities—to influence "indirectly—but substitutes a new concept for the remaining group—to influence "directly." To influence "directly" the passage or defeat of legislation includes any number of methods—for example, nationwide radio, television or advertising programs promoting a particular measure, as well as the "button holing" of Congressmen. To include the latter while excluding the former is to rewrite the Act.

This is not the case where one or more distinct types of "lobbying" are specifically proscribed and another and different group defined in such loose, broad terms as to make its definition vague and uncertain. Here, if we give the words of the Act their ordinary meaning, we do not know what the terminal points are. Judging from the words Congress used, one type of activity which I have enumerated is as much proscribed as another.

The importance of the problem is emphasized by reason of the fact that this legislation is in the domain of the First Amendment. That Amendment provides that "Congress shall make no law...abridging the freedom of speech, or of the press; or the right of the people...to petition the Government for a redress of grievances."

Can Congress require one to register before he writes an article, makes a speech, files an advertisement, appears on radio or television, or writes a letter seeking to influence existing, pending, or proposed legislation? That would pose a considerable question under the First Amendment, as *Thomas v. Collins*, 323 U.S. 516, indicates. I do not mean to intimate that Congress is without power to require disclosure of the real principals behind those who come to Congress (or get others to do so) and speak as though they represent the public interest, when in fact they are undisclosed agents of special groups. I mention the First Amendment to emphasize why statutes touching this field should be "narrowly drawn to prevent the supposed evil" (see *Cantwell v. Connecticut*, 310 U.S. 296, 307) and not be cast in such vague and indefinite terms as to cast a cloud on the exercise of constitutional rights. Cf. *Stromberg v. California*, 283 U.S. 359, 369; *Thornhill v. Alabama*, 310 U.S. 88, 97-98; *Winters v. New York*, 333 U.S. 507, 509; *Joseph Burstyn, Inc. v. Wilson*, 343 U.S. 495, 504-505.

If that rule were relaxed, if Congress could impose registration requirements on the exercise of First Amendment rights, saving to the courts the salvage of the good from the bad, and meanwhile causing all who might possibly be covered to act at their peril, the law would in practical effect be a deterrent to the exercise of First Amendment rights. The Court seeks to avoid that consequence by construing the law narrowly as applying only to those who are paid to "button hole" Congressmen or who collect and expend moneys to get others to do so. It may be appropriate in some cases to read a statute with the gloss a court has placed on it in order to save it from the charge of vagueness. See *Fox v. Washington*, 236 U.S. 273, 277. But I do not think that course is appropriate here.

The language of the Act is so broad that one who writes a letter or makes a speech or publishes an article or distributes literature or does many of the other things with which appellees are charged has no fair notice when he is close to the prohibited line. No construction we give it today will make clear retroactively the vague standards that confronted appellees when they did the acts now charged against them as criminal. Cf. *Pierce v. United States*, 314 U.S. 306, 311. Since the Act touches on the exercise of First Amendment rights, and is not narrowly drawn to meet precise evils, its vagueness has some of the evils of a continuous and effective restraint.

Proposal To Revise Lobby Law, 1967

Title V of the Legislative Reorganization Act of 1967 (S 355) constituted the first full-scale Congressional effort to strengthen the 1946 Federal Regulation of Lobbying Act. An effort to strip Title V from the bill was defeated in the Senate March 7, 1967, on a 30-53 roll-call vote. Further opposition developed in the House, and the bill remained stalled in the House Rules Committee for the remainder of the 90th Congress. When Congress enacted the Legislative Reorganization Act of 1970 (PL 91-510), no lobbying provisions were included in the measure.

Proposed Lobby Provisions

Numerous proposals were made from time to time in the 1946-66 period to close the loopholes in the 1946 Lobby Act. In June 1965, the Senate Rules and Administration Committee reported a bill (S 2233—S Rept 419) to tighten up administration of the 1946 Lobbying Act by placing administration in the hands of the Comptroller General of the United States and empowering him to check lobby reports for accuracy and to determine possible violations of the law. The bill was never brought up for Senate debate.

The appointment of a Joint Committee on the Organization of the Congress in 1965—the first since 1946—provided an appropriate forum for the discussion of lobbying reforms. The possibility of tightening the lobby law was first raised in the Joint Committee's hearings by a representative of *Congressional Quarterly* June 23, 1965. In its final report (S Rept 1414), the Joint Committee July 28, 1966, noted that current lobbying "registrations reveal only a small fraction of the money paid and received for lobbying activities" and that the Act "tends to penalize the more conscientious registrant and reward the individual or organization less candid about legislative activities."

Five significant changes were proposed:

1. The provision requiring registration by those who had as "their principal purpose" the influencing of the passage or defeat of legislation should be amended to require registration by those having such activity as a "substantial purpose." The Joint Committee said the new language would significantly widen the area of coverage while continuing to exempt individuals and organizations whose lobbying activities were merely incidental to other functions.

2. Organizations which contended that it was impossible for them to separate expenditures for lobbying purposes should be required to file their total receipts and expenditures under oath and estimate the percentage properly allocable to lobbying activities. The Committee noted that many organizations had claimed they could not separate lobbying expenditures and thus either refused to register or reported their entire budgets without meaningful breakdowns. "In either event," the Committee said, "the public is not informed and the intention of the Act is subverted." Under the proposed new law, organizations would have to make a good faith estimate of the percentage of total receipts and expenditures allocable to lobbying.

3. Lobby registration and spending information should be filed with the General Accounting Office (GAO), rather than with the Clerk of the House and Secretary of the Senate. The GAO was given five specific responsibilities:

(a) Develop and prescribe standard methods and forms for filing of reports. (New provision.)

(b) Make all lobby registration and spending reports available for public inspection for five years. (Current law stipulated two years.)

(c) Provide for enforcement. The specific language of the bill: "Ascertain whether any persons have failed to file reports or statements as required by this title, or have filed incomplete or inaccurate reports or statements under this title and notify such persons that they are obligated to file such reports or statements in compliance with the requirements of this title. Refer to the Justice Department for appropriate action any information coming to his (the Comptroller General's) attention, through complaints or otherwise, of any failure to register, or the filing of any false, improper or incomplete registration and information...." (New provision)

(d) Deliver to the Congress quarterly records of lobby registrations and spending reports for publication in the *Congressional Record*. (Old provision)

(e) Send Congress an annual "full and complete report on the administration" of the law. (New provision)

4. Lobbyists receiving contingent fees for their activities—fees dependent on success or failure in the passage or defeat of legislation—would be required to state the terms of their fees in detail. The Joint Committee said it wanted to emphasize its "opinion that the interests of the

legislative process can be served only by full disclosure of such arrangements to Members of Congress, the press and the public."

5. Extend to television and radio media the specific exemptions previously granted to newspapers and other periodicals which publish news items, editorials or paid advertisements urging the passage or defeat of legislation.

Senate Debate

S 355 was brought up for Senate debate Jan. 25, 1967, but it was not until March 7, the final day of debate in that chamber, that the lobbying provisions were considered. Sen. Roman L. Hruska (R Neb.), joined by Senate Minority Leader Everett McKinley Dirksen (R Ill.), offered a motion to strike Title V from the bill altogether, saying that action on a new lobby registration law should be delayed until the Justice Department completed a study of the subject pursuant to the President's general recommendation, in his State of the Union address, for tightening the laws regulating lobbying. Hruska said he had been informed by Attorney General Ramsey Clark that the Department's proposals would be "wider in scope" than Title V. At the suggestion of Robert P. Griffin (R Mich.), the Hruska amendment was modified to provide that the Senate and House Judiciary Committees study the matter with the view to recommending amendments which would make the 1946 Act "more adequate and effective in its operation."

Hruska argued that Title V was a "patchwork of an Act which has a dismal judicial and enforcement history." He said the title failed to "come to grips with the basic difficulty" of the 1946 Act, the "lack of definition as to what is meant by the language 'to influence directly or indirectly the passage or defeat of any legislation by the Congress of the United States'." Without clear definitions of the intent of Congress, Hruska said, the change from "principal" to "substantial" purpose could only lead to more confusion in administration of the law. Hruska also complained that Title V gave the Comptroller General the power to promulgate regulations which could have the force of criminal statutes "in a field heavily fraught with serious and substantial constitutional implications" and without bringing the GAO under the detailed requirements for regulatory activity spelled out in the Administrative Procedure Act.

Dirksen complained that only one witness—a representative of *Congressional Quarterly*—had appeared before the joint Committee to testify on the lobby law. Title V, Dirksen said, did nothing to perfect the Foreign Agents Registration Act, was silent on "lobbying in the Executive Branch, which dispenses hundreds of billions of dollars," and failed to treat the problem of lobbying by the 24 colleges and institutes that he said "keep a full-time man in Washington to make sure that they get in on the gravy train for grants-in-aid." Nor did the title contain any language that could force compliance with the existing law against lobbying of Congress by Government agents and bureaus, a provision of law Dirksen said he had never seen enforced. Dirksen suggested that a package bill could be devised incorporating all these problems after testimony by the Attorney General and others.

A. S. Mike Monroney (D Okla.), floor manager and co-author of S 355, acknowledged that Title V made no effort to reverse the Supreme Court decision in the *Harriss* case and that only direct lobbying was covered—thus excluding most "grass-roots" campaigns for or against certain bills. But the step-up from "principal" to "substantial" purpose, he said, would widen the threshold of the Act, closing an "escape hatch" by which many multipurpose organizations with major legislative interests had avoided registration. The term "substantial," Monroney said, had long been a criterion in many areas of federal law, including the Internal Revenue Code. It was also a criterion, he said, in determining applicability of such legislation as the Fair Labor Standards Act and the Taft-Hartley Act. The definition was chosen in place of a set formula on dollars spent or a precise percentage of an organization's outlays going for lobby activities so that an intelligent determination could be made on a case-by-case basis.

One of the most important features of Title V, Monroney said, was the transferral of responsibility for receiving reports and reporting violations to the General Accounting Office. Public access to the lobby reports would be much easier, he said, than in the offices of the Secretary of the Senate and Clerk of the House. The failure to establish clear-cut responsibility for administration and enforcement in the 1946 Act, Monroney said, had been "an almost fatal defect." But Monroney saw no need for bringing the GAO under the Administrative Procedure Act. "The Comptroller General," he said, "is only the administrator of the act—not its enforcer." His duties under the new law would be concerned primarily with the mechanics of registration and making reports available for public inspection. Monroney read a letter from Comptroller General Elmer B. Staats stating that his office was "agreeable to taking on the administrative responsibilities" of the Lobbying Act.

"Responsibility for enforcement lies with the Department of Justice," Monroney said. The Comptroller General would be limited to notification of persons who had filed incomplete or inaccurate reports of the flaws in their reports, and referring cases where there appeared to be actual violation of the law to the Justice Department.

The Hruska amendment, with Griffin's modification, was rejected on a 30-53 roll-call vote, with Republicans splitting 22-8 for the amendment and Democrats 8-45 against it. S 355, with Title V retained without change, passed later March 7 by a 75-9 roll-call vote.

Lobbying by the Executive Branch

O'BRIEN TV INTERVIEW

Following is the transcript of a 1965 television interview in which one of President Johnson's key assistants discussed the role of the Administration in initiating and lobbying for legislation in Congress. The interview was with Lawrence F. O'Brien, then special assistant to the President for Congressional affairs; O'Brien served in that post from the beginning of the Kennedy Administration, until late 1965, when he became Postmaster General. The National Educational Television Network produced the show, titled "From the White House to the Hill," as part of its series entitled "The Changing Congress." The complete interview with O'Brien is printed below; not all of the material was used in the television program. Paul Duke conducted the interview.

Function, Scope of Liaison

Q. Larry, how do you see the function and scope of the White House liaison?

A. Well, it's certainly developed into an important element, the operation of the White House, when you think back on the history of Congressional relations, the fact that to some extent it was not only non-existent White House-to-the-Hill in the days of Wilson and through a period following President Wilson we had the situation of no rapport between the two branches of Government. They seemed to be at cross purposes, and in the era of Roosevelt, the first hundred days, of course, a massive legislative program was enacted. The situation at the moment called for it, and following that, however, after the so-called "court-packing" period, there was a slackening off again in this area. I think this went on to a considerable extent until a point in the Eisenhower Administration, where it was, if you will, reformalized and put on a departmental level in the White House.

With us, of course, it was the problem that we were faced with after the 1960 election, while we had secured the White House; nevertheless, we lost 21 seats. Solid, voting Democrats had been defeated in the '60 election, and it was immediately apparent that we were going to have great difficulties. So we had to take a very close look at the type of operation we might put into effect, and what procedures we could follow. We were hard put to it—the realities of the situation were that the New Frontier Program was massive, and we were in a tight bind in the Congress, particularly in the House.

So my view now in the fifth legislative year I've been in the White House is that it has been awfully productive to us. It really made an impact on the program, and I think finally it has been determined that within the constitutional limitations, it is feasible and proper to have a close rapport with the Legislative Branch of Government; that this doesn't in any sense violate the constitutional provisions or the historic concept, if you will, of the relationship of the two branches. It's just the human element is present, as it is in all activities of life, and the closer the relationship, the better the understanding, the greater the possibilities of ultimate enactment of the White House proposals.

After all, we recognize that the President proposes and it is up to the Legislative Branch of the Government to dispose. But certainly there is no known barrier to constantly advocating our program...to the people and to the Congress.

So I would have to say that in retrospect—viewing the situation in January '61 and thinking back today to that period—that obviously there has been real progress. I don't think perhaps there's been a five-year period in our history similar to the five years here in the White House in this Democratic Administration. I think not only in the number of legislative proposals that have been enacted, but when you look at the substance of these proposals, the far-reaching impact of many of the bills that have been enacted during the period—hopefully will be enacted before this session comes to an end—it all points to a permanency, I think, in relationships of this nature. It is a department of the White House, it involves a variety of individual contact with Members of Congress, and I must say it's developed into a two-way street up and down Pennsylvania Avenue. There's not any hesitancy I'm able to observe on the part of the Member of House or Senate to contact the White House

to discuss matters of mutual interest, nor is there any hesitancy on our part to do the same. And as far as I can determine, it's worked out quite well.

Liaison Office Formalized

Q. You mentioned the formalization of the liaison office under President Kennedy. I think it's quite true. How did he come to do this? How did he come to set up a liaison chief with one man delegated for the House and one man delegated for the Senate under you? Were there any recommendations for this...any studies made that this would be a feasible thing to do?

A. There were discussions involving Professor Dick Neustadt and others. I think, however, that the President's judgment to a great extent, as I indicated, was based, if you will, on the political reality of the situation when we moved into this building—that we had a difficult situation ahead of us and just what conceivably could be done about it. And I recall President Kennedy at one time saying to me, "I see a great deal—Members of Congress individually and in groups—we seem to have a great deal of contact with them;" and he said, "I recall my 14 years on the Hill, and I cannot recall during that 14-year period having any direct or meaningful contact with a Member of the White House staff."

Now, when you think about it for a moment, his years on the Hill were split between the House and the Senate—I believe six and eight. And I can see how that would occur, that in that period the concentration contact-wise was pretty much confined to the top leadership, and the average Member, if you will, seniority-wise, probably wasn't exposed to any great extent to this type of contact. And I think it struck President Kennedy that on this end of the Avenue he found that this was a meaningful, daily activity. And when you looked at the statistics of contact and realize the extent of this activity, I imagine he thought back to his years on the Hill and wondered just what took place during those years.

But I think if he had been a committee chairman, or had, say, 14 years plus seniority in one body, perhaps he would have been exposed to the White House contact. But that wasn't the case, at least, as he remembered the years, and it intrigued him. And then furthermore, it was, as we have said, rather informal, and it was not departmentalized and placed on the level operationally that it has been placed over the last five years.

And again I feel that there are pluses and minuses in the views of observers, some political scientists and others in this activity, but we feel the pluses far outweigh the minuses that conceivably could be conjured up. And I therefore think that as the years go on, this type of contact and relationship will continue—perhaps be further refined—but I think it's here to stay now. It represents an historic breakthrough in this relationship.

Use of Agency Personnel

Q. Well, with a limited staff and more than 500 members, how can you keep up with your job?

A. Well, that entered our minds when we started this operation, but of course there are Congressional liaison chiefs in each department and agency of the Government. Our feeling was that we had to unify this activity, we had to centralize it in the sense that it would be a team effort, and we inaugurated a new procedure. And that is that each department and agency would provide to us by Monday noon of each week a written report of the department's activity with the Congress over the prior week and the projection for the current week.

Now, we take those reports and review them on Monday afternoon and present an analysis to the President for his night reading on Monday, along with a suggested agenda for his use, if he so desires, of the leadership meetings that are held on Tuesday mornings.

In addition, we have these Congressional relations people—there are about 40 of them—they're in these key roles in departments and agencies—in periodically to the White House to discuss our mutual legislative problems. And the emphasis constantly is on the President's program, that all elements of this program really in the final analysis are part of a single program, that the downtown in this building...the only man I'm aware of who's been elected to office is the President of the United States. And he has proposed to the people what he conceives his program to be. The people made a determination that he should be their President. Furthermore, you have the Democratic party platform, and it is, as we see it, a mandate for action.

So by establishing this team and working very, very closely with these people in the departments and agencies, it gave us additional manpower, and it insured that our activities would be properly channeled for maximum results, and we would not have cross-wires and individuals going off in separate directions and working with the Congress.

Now, President Johnson has emphasized and re-emphasized this, as you know, and on many occasions at Cabinet meetings he re-states his concern about the progress of his program, the Great Society program: his intention that every member of the Executive Branch be involved, the responsibility of the Cabinet member in this area. He has stated to them on several occasions in my presence that no person in his respective department could ever be any more important than the head of the Congressional relations activity. And he places the responsibility directly on the Cabinet member in that regard.

So there is a total awareness that we've developed over these years that as I said is re-emphasized constantly by President Johnson—awareness that this team effort is a continuing day-in and day-out effort.

For example, we would anticipate that the Secretary of Agriculture would have a great interest in our education program, although it does not come directly under his activities in his department. Nevertheless, he has friends and associates on the Hill, and he would be an advocate of our educational legislation whenever an opportunity presented itself. And likewise across the board the entire program.

And in addition to that, even here on the White House staff, the special assistants to the President who are working in other areas are under Presidential direction always available to us for assistance and support as we move along through the legislative year. Nothing has a greater priority in the President's view than the legislative program, and I think when you look at the program and analyze it, you can understand that, because we are at this moment engaged in most meaningful legislative activity, again in the field of education—with all the progress that we have made, with the great elementary-secondary education bill that was enacted earlier this year. We still have additional proposals in this area. There will always be an unfinished agenda.

We are still working on our "medicare" program, and our voting rights legislation. And we have several meaningful proposals in the field of health and research. And all of this is so important that you have to bring into focus every element of potential that you can possibly bring in to help promote the program.

'Arm-Twisting...Does Not Exist'

Now, they talk about arm-twisting and all that sort of thing. And I read these stories with great interest, because this just does not exist. The fact of the matter is that what we have by way of strength, if we do have anything in promoting the program, is the attitude of the average Member of Congress toward the President. This has applied to President Kennedy, and it applies to President Johnson, that there is a good feeling on the Hill, if you will, toward the President. There is a realization of his massive problems, there is an attitude of general acceptance of his basic proposals in the legislative area, and therefore we find that doors are open to us. The Members are interested in hearing our views, we are equally interested in having their views, and their views are extremely important.

So I think that basically is what you have going for you, to use the vernacular. This suggestion that you trade the bridge for the dam or some project for a vote, and that sort of thing, well, it's just not the case.

I think that we can continue to make progress in this area and our relationships with the Congress if we never lose sight of one important factor (the fellows on the staff here remind themselves constantly of this, and all those in key roles in the Executive Branch remind themselves constantly) that there are on the Hill 535 elected officials. They have been elected by the people; they have been in the ballot box, so to speak, and we must recognize this. All of us are appointed, and in our form of government we must constantly be aware of the role of the elected officeholder, appreciate his problems, understand his responsibilities. And as long as we continue to have that clearly in mind, we're in no position, nor should we be, nor would we want to be, to dictate in any sense—that this is a matter of firm belief in a program that affects all of America—and that belief in this program is shared generally on the Hill. Individual Members have individual views relating to various aspects of the program, but we can work together, and again, we can only propose and advocate. The decision is made on the other end of Pennsylvania Avenue, and we recognize and respect it.

Powers Available; Rules Committee Fight

Q. Well, you certainly have certain powers that you can use to help get your program across. James McGregor Burns once said that a President not only has the right but the duty to use political power in getting his program through, and I recall the instance of 1961 when the Rules Committee fight came along, and the Administration became involved in that. So isn't it true even if there isn't the over-arm-twisting, that every Administration has certain power which it can use? A President can go out and make a speech for a Member of Congress, for example.

A. Yes, of course, I think that what you are really saying, however, is that, is the President a strong advocate? Is he firm in his convictions? Is he, therefore, a man that the elected officeholders on the Hill respect in the sense that he is the nation's leader, elected by all the people of the country? And, if they can be sure that he means it, they can be sure that therefore it's in the national interest, and he can persuade, in that context.

I think in the final analysis, that is what you have going for you, as I suggested, and I think that you could court disaster in a relationship such as this if at any time the average Member of Congress determined that we were trying to move beyond our constitutional situation, that we felt that the Congress should be a "rubber-stamp" Congress, for example (you hear that reference often). This Congress is not a "rubber-stamp" Congress, I can assure you. And anyone that works with the Congress on the subcommittee and committee level, day in and day out, knows that the independent judgments and views of those Members are expressed without reluctance, and oftentimes we are pressed back a few yards in the struggle. But I think basically they have to be convinced, and that they look to the President for leadership, and I think that many times these decisions are made up on the Hill, when they're very close, on the basis of a feeling of loyalty, desire to support their own leaders on the Hill in the House and the Senate, support the President in his proposals. And you mention the Rules fight of 1961. It was our first struggle, and it was a close one. And as a matter of fact, my recollection is that the vote was postponed twice until we felt we had sufficient troops marshaled. It was a real challenge to us; it was a real test. It was, however, sort of a blessing in disguise, because, having been put through that and winning it, I believe by five votes after a great deal of activity on our part and on the part of our leaders on the Hill, it certainly was the evidence that we needed to show what we had suspected was the case. And that is that we were in for a continuing struggle, and all decisions would be made by very, very, very small margins. But also, if we had lost the Rules struggle in '61, obviously the opportunity to have the Kennedy program voted up or down would have disappeared, and you would have seen a Congress spend two legislative years here with no progress.

So a great deal was at stake, and thank goodness we got by that first one, because we wouldn't be able to point with pride, as I think we can legitimately do, to the progress of the last several years, if the first one hadn't been won.

Reaction of Leadership

Q. The Administration was heavily involved in the Rules Committee fight right after it came into power in 1961, and you obviously spent a lot of your time on the House side then. What was the reaction of the leadership toward your lobbying activities.?

A. Well, of course first of all, this activity was all new to me. And we moved cautiously and carefully. We had to explore reaction. And the distinguished Speaker at that time, Speaker Rayburn, was of course a major point of contact. And I can remember in those early days and weeks as I went to the Hill (being somewhat concerned that we would be accepted, that we would have the freedom of movement in contact with the leadership and the Members, that we would not step on someone's toes), and as I recall those early days, it was not unusual to have a considerable wait to see the Speaker. And I think I was always filled with a certain degree of concern, trepidation, if you will—I found as time went on that there was a warm relationship, one of the great periods of my time here has been in the association that I always remember with Speaker Rayburn. But I must say at the outset I don't know how the Speaker felt about us, but I do know that we were very, very careful not to cross that barrier that we felt existed constitutionally. I don't think we ever have crossed it, but we have found you can talk across it, if you will. You can get together quite easily. But the early days—it wasn't that the Speaker made it difficult—I think we were concerned, nervous about the whole thing, and perhaps the Speaker was wondering a little bit about us, because he hadn't had the experience as a leader up there of having that kind of continuing contact from the White House and the President on down. But it worked out awfully well, and during the Rules fight, of course, it put us to the test, because we had to press. We were awfully concerned; so was the Speaker and the other leaders.

But I think that it was one of the, as I see it, one of the break-throughs, and I think the awfully warm relationship between President Kennedy and Speaker Rayburn developed over those years, until the Speaker's death, is the best evidence that I have that it worked out without any serious problems coming about.

Role of Media, Citizen's Groups

But there's another area of contact. We've talked about the departments and agencies, trying to put as vigorous and able a team as you can—numerically strong team into the field from day to day. But of course we have a reliance upon the activities oftentimes of citizens' groups, you might call them. The great trade bill struggle during the course of that period we were aided tremendously by the citizens' group that was established here in Washington and spread throughout the country.

Media is awfully important to us. If the media generally in the country determines to support our position, that of course can be helpful. The trade bill was a good example of the combination of media support, citizen support across the board, which without question made a real impact on that legislation, had a great deal to do with its ultimate passage.

And you have a variety of citizen activity, and many legislative proposals are made by us—bring into action interested groups throughout the country that can be helpful. The business community on the tax cut is another example in that area.

And then we do have a close and continuing relationship with the labor groups here in Washington. They're represented legislatively by former Congressman Biemiller; President Meany of the AFL-CIO maintains a full-time interest in the legislative program. Generally speaking, labor is in support of most every—all elements of our program. We have a lot in common, so oftentimes it's really a joint effort, and we're coming into labor legislation a little later on this session, and in the meantime, labor's working closely with (us) on "medicare" and voting rights, and pretty much the entire program, so that a citizens' group, if you will, representing millions of members throughout the country has a continuing relationship with us. But I think of all of that is important. And we try to cultivate it, we try to cooperate with these groups, because after all, they are grass roots, and their interests at a given moment mean much to us, and by the same token, the President's interest in their specific problem of the moment means a great deal to them. And so it can be mutually cooperative and helpful.

Influence of the President

Q. Why is the Administration's help needed to get most major legislation through these days?

A. Why, I think that over this five years you have to go back again to a strong President who exerts leadership, who was willing to step out and propose, who was willing to put the weight of his office behind the proposals, who was at all times attempting to encourage the average citizen to join with him. All of this places you, I think, in a much stronger position, because with—the President, after all, gets the attention of the people to a far greater extent than any other leader, and they are interested in his views. They will listen to him. He commands massive audiences on television and radio, and public appearances. And I think that it's an important element in legislative success, the success of the program, to have a President not only advocating initially, but constantly reminding, if you will, everyone of the program and its meaning, and giving proof positive that he is not only proposing, but he is vitally concerned personally.

And that transmits to the public, and in turn, from our point of view, is helpful to us on the hill, because we have to anticipate that these Members, as I've said before, elected to office, are going to react to the views of their constituency. And that's in the nature of things the way it should be,

and we can only hope the constituency view transmitted to them by letter and personal contact will be more often than not our view, and therefore becomes everyone's view.

I think the difference between initiating on the Hill and intiating here is obvious, because the initiation by the President makes for greater impact, greater citizen interest, and consequently, I think ultimately, closer attention on the Hill.

Problems of Members

Q. Larry, one final question. You get hundreds of calls coming in here from Members of Congress. Your office is really a kind of reservoir of complaints and problems. What's a typical problem or complaint you have to deal with?

A. Well, oftentimes a Member has a problem that is serious in his view, because it involves constituent interests. This is a rather massive Government, many departments and agencies and subdivisions, and we find at times we can encourage quicker action, an earlier decision, or perhaps we can express the Presidential view directly to his constituents. It would indicate what his close relationship is to the White House. That type of thing is a daily occurrence. The Member of Congress does not contact us and say: "This is important to me; I want it done this way. The contacts we get generally are: Gosh, it's been a long period of time has elapsed. I have a difficult situation, because my constituents can't understand why this decision hasn't been rendered before this. Can you help us move it along to a decision? And also, interestly enough, during the course of an average day you have Members who contact us on matters such as—simple matters such as a White House tour.

As you know, we have tremendous numbers of people going through the White House daily. There are tours in the early morning that are conducted that we try to be helpful to Members of Congress, having their constituents join in these tours. And you can understand, the Congressman on the Hill would have half a dozen important constituents arriving in Washington, and he has difficulty setting a schedule for them so they can view the White House at their leisure—that could be an embarrassment to him.

Those things don't sound awfully important, but I mentioned earlier human relations, the human element, and we are constantly aware of the need and the right of the Congressman to receive reasonable service from the Executive Branch. After all, most of those fellows give us great service, because they support the program, and again—always recognize—recognizing they're elected to office. It provides a variety of opportunities here to be of some meaningful service, but as I say, there's no single element of it that is overridingly important, but the over-all activity day to day in putting the package together over a period of years can only hope the Member up there has the view that the White House is interested in him and his problems. That's really—and therefore when we have our problems—we will get favorable reaction at least from the sense of giving us a hearing, seriously considering our viewpoint, if he fells that we in turn understand his problems.

Well, to sum it up, and I think you can succinctly, why let me just say that no one here in this building will ever suggest to a Member of Congress that he commit political hari kari. That's not the realistic approach to this problem, and as long as we don't reach that point where we feel a Member just must darn well be with us or all bets are off—then, I think that we have good mutual understanding and rapport.

We just have to recognize the problems of the Members of Congress, their constituent, or, if you want to term it that way, political problem. As long as we have a clear understanding of that, and most of us here have been engaged over a long period of time in the political arena, and I think we do have that understanding, and that is the major asset that we have, in my view, in working with them.

Acts of Congress Held Unconstitutional in Whole or in Part by the Supreme Court

1. Act of September 24, 1789 (1 Stat. 81, sec. 13, in part).

Provision that "...(the Supreme Court) shall have power to issue... writs of mandamus, in cases warranted by the principles and usages of law, to any...persons holding office, under authority of the United States" as applied to the issue of mandamus to the Secretary of State requiring him to deliver to plaintiff a commission (duly signed by the President) as justice of the peace in the District of Columbia, *held* an attempt to enlarge the original jurisdiction of the Supreme Court, fixed by Article III, section 2.

Marbury v. Madison, 1 Cr. 137 (February 24, 1803).

2. Act of February 20, 1812 (2 Stat. 677).

Provisions establishing board of revision to annul titles conferred many years previously by governors of the Northwest Territory were *held* violative of the due process clause of the Fifth Amendment.

Reichart v. Felps, 6 Wall. 160 (March 16, 1868).

3. Act of March 6, 1820 (3 Stat. 548, sec. 8, proviso).

The Missouri Compromise, prohibiting slavery within the Louisiana Territory north of 36 30', except Missouri, *held* not warranted as a regulation of Territory belonging to the United States under Article IV, section 3, clause 2 (and *see* Fifth Amendment).

Dred Scott v. Sandford, 10 How. 303 (March 6, 1857).

4. Act of February 25, 1862 (12 Stat. 345, sec. 1); July 11, 1862 (12 Stat. 532, sec. 1); March 3, 1803 (12 Stat. 711, sec. 3), each in part only.

"Legal tender clauses," making noninterest-bearing United States notes legal tender in payment of "all debts, public and private," so far as applied to debts contracted before passage of the act, *held* not within express or implied powers of Congress under Article I, section 8, and inconsistent with Article I, section 10, and Fifth Amendment.

Hepburn v. Griswold, 8 Wall. 603 (February 7, 1870; overruled in *Knox v. Lee* (Legal Tender Cases), 12 Wall. 457 (May 1, 1871).

5. Act of March 3, 1863 (12 Stat. 756, sec. 5).

"So much of the fifth section...as provides for the removal of a judgment in a State court, and in which the cause was tried by a jury to the circuit court of the United States for a retrial on the facts and law, is not in pursuance of the Constitution, and is void" under the Seventh Amendment.

The Justices v. Murray, 9 Wall. 274 (March 14, 1870).

6. Act of March 3, 1963 (12 Stat. 766, sec. 5).

Provision for an appeal from the Court of Claims to the Supreme Court—there being, at the time, a further provision (sec. 14) requiring an estimate by the Secretary of the Treasury before payment of final judgments, *held* to contravene the judicial finality intended by the Constitution, Article III.

Gordon v. United States, 2 Wall. 561 (March 10, 1865). (Case was dismissed without opinion; the grounds upon which this decision was made were stated in a posthumous opinion by Chief Justice Taney printed in the appendix to volume 117 of the U.S. Reports at p. 697.)

7. Act of June 30, 1864 (13 Stat. 311, sec. 13).

Provision that "any prize cause now pending in any circuit court shall, on the application of all parties in interest...be transferred by that court to the Supreme Court...," as applied in a case where no action had been taken in the Circuit Court on the appeal from the district court, *held* to propose an appeal procedure not within Article III, section 2.

The Alicia, 7 Wall. 571 (January 25, 1869).

8. Act of January 24, 1865 (13 Stat. 424).

Requirement of a test oath (disavowing actions in hostility to the United States) before admission to appear as attorney in a federal court by virtue of any previous admission, *held* invalid as applied to an attorney who had been pardoned by the President for all offenses during the Rebellion—as *ex post facto* (Article I, section 9, clause 3) and an interference with the pardoning power (Article II, section 2, clause 1).

Ex parte Garland, 4 Wall. 833 (January 14, 1867).

9. Act of March 2, 1867 (14 Stat. 484, sec. 29).

General prohibition on sale of naphtha, etc., for illuminating purposes, if inflammable at less temperature than 110 F., *held* invalid "except so far as the section named operates within the United States, but without the limits of any State," as being a mere police regulation.

United States v. Dewitt, 9 Wall. 41 (February 21, 1870).

10. Act of May 31, 1870 (16 Stat. 140, secs. 3, 4).

Provisions penalizing (1) refusal of local election officials to permit voting by persons offering to qualify under State laws, applicable to any citizens; and (2) hindering of any person from qualifying or voting, *held* invalid under Fifteenth Amendment.

United States v. Reese et al., 92 U.S. 214 (March 27, 1876).

11. Act of July 12, 1870 (16 Stat. 235).

Provisions making Presidential pardons inadmissible in evidence in Court of Claims, prohibiting their use by that court in deciding claims or appeals, and requiring dismissal of appeals by the Supreme Court in cases where proof of loyalty had been made otherwise than as prescribed by law, *held* an interference with judicial power under Article III, section 1, and with the pardoning power under Article II, section 2, clause 1.

United States v. Klein, 13 Wall. 128 (January 29, 1872).

12. Act of June 22, 1874 (18 Stat. 1878, sec. 4).

Provision authorizing federal courts, in suits for forfeitures under revenue and custom laws, to require production of documents, with allegations expected to be proved therein to be taken as proved on failure to produce such documents, was *held* violative of the search and seizure provision of the Fourth Amendment and the self-incrimination clause of the Fifth Amendment.

Boyd v. United States, 116 U.S. 616 (February 1, 1886).

13. Revised Statutes 1077 (Act of May 31, 1870, 16 Stat. 144).

Provision that "all persons within the jurisdiction of the United States shall have the same right in every State and Territory to make and enforce contracts...as is enjoyed by white citizens...," *held* invalid under the Thirteenth Amendment.

Hodges v. United States, 203 U.S. 1 (May 28, 1906).

14. Revised Statutes 4937-4947 (Act of July 8, 1870, 16 Stat. 210), and Act of August 14, 1876 (19 Stat. 141).

Original trademark law, applying to marks "for exclusive use within the United States," and a penal act designed solely for the protection of rights defined in the earlier measure, *held* not supportable by Article I, section 8, clause 8 (copyright clause), nor Article I, section 8, clause 3, by reason of its application to intrastate as well as interstate commerce.

Trade-Mark Cases, 100 U.S. 82 (November 17, 1879).

15. Revised Statutes 5132, subdivision 9 (Act of March 2, 1867, 14 Stat. 539).

Provision penalizing "any person respecting whom bankruptcy proceedings are commenced...who, within 3 months before the commencement of proceedings in bankruptcy, under the false color and pretense of carrying on business and dealing in the ordinary course of trade, obtains on credit from any person any goods or chattels with intent to defraud...," *held* a police regulation not within the bankruptcy power (Article I, section 4, clause 4).

United States v. Fox, 95 U.S. 670 (January 7, 1878).

16. Revised Statutes 5507 (Act of May 31, 1870, 16 Stat. 141, sec. 4).

Provision penalizing "every person who prevents, hinders, controls, or intimidates another from exercising...the right of suffrage, to whom that right is guaranteed by the Fifteenth Amendment to the Constitution of the United States, by means of bribery...," *held* not authorized by the said Fifteenth Amendment.

James v. Bowman, 190 U.S. 127 (May 4, 1903).

17. Revised Statutes 5519 (Act of April 20, 1871, 17 Stat. 13, sec. 2).

Section providing punishment in case "two or more persons in any State...conspire...for the purpose of depriving...any person...of the equal protection of the laws...or for the purpose of preventing or hindering the constituted authorities of any State...from giving or securing to all persons within each State...the equal protection of the laws...," *held* invalid as not being directed at State action proscribed by the Fourteenth Amendment.

United States v. Harris, 106 U.S. 629 (January 22, 1883).

In *Baldwin v. Franks*, 120 U.S. 678 (March 17, 1887), an attempt was made to distinguish the Harris case and to apply the statute to a conspiracy directed at aliens within a State, but the provision was held not enforceable in such limited manner.

18. Revised Statutes of the District of Columbia, section 1064 (Act of June 17, 1870, 16 Stat. 154, sec. 3).

Provision that "prosecutions in the police court (of the District of Columbia) shall be by information under oath, without indictment by grand jury or trial by petit jury," as applied to punishment for conspiracy, *held* to contravene Article III, section 2, clause 3, requiring jury trial of all crimes.

Callan v. Wilson, 127 U.S. 540 (May 14, 1888).

19. Act of March 1, 1875 (18 Stat. 336, secs. 1,2).

Provision "That all persons within the jurisdiction of the United States shall be entitled to the full and equal enjoyment of the accommodations...of inns, public conveyances on land or water, theaters, and other places of public amusement; subject only to the conditions and limitations established by law, and applicable alike to citizens of every race and color, regardless of any previous condition of servitude"—subject to penalty, *held* not to be supported by the Thirteenth or Fourteenth Amendments.

Civil Rights Cases, 109 U.S. 3 (October 15, 1883), as to operation within States.

20. Act of March 3, 1875 (18 Stat. 479, sec. 2).

Provision that "if the party (i.e., a person stealing property from the United States) has been convicted, then the judgment against him shall be conclusive evidence in the prosecution against (the) receiver that the property of the United States therein described has been embezzled, stolen, or purloined," *held* to contravene the Sixth Amendment.

Kirby v. United States, 174 U.S. 47 (April 11, 1899).

21. Act of July 12, 1876 (10 Stat. 80, sec. 6, in part).

Provision that "postmasters of the first, second, and third classes... may be removed by the President by and with the advice and consent of the Senate," *held* to infringe the executive power under Article II, section 1, clause 1.

Myers v. United States, 272 U.S. 52 (October 25, 1926).

22. Act of August 14, 1876 (19 Stat. 141, trademark act), *see* Revised Statutes 4937, above, No. 14.

23. Act of August 11, 1888 (25 Stat. 411).

Clause, in a provision for the purchase or condemnation of a certain lock and dam in the Monongahela River, that "...in estimating the sum to be paid by the United States, the franchise of said corporation to collect tolls shall not be considered or estimated...," *held* to contravene the Fifth Amendment.

Monongahela Navigation Co. v. United States, 148 U.S. 312 (March 27, 1893).

24. Act of May 5, 1892 (27 Stat. 25, sec. 4).

Provision of a Chinese exclusion act, that Chinese persons "convicted and adjudged to be not lawfully entitled to be or remain in the United States shall be imprisoned at hard labor for a period not exceeding 1 year and thereafter removed from the United States..." (such conviction and judgment being had before a justice, judge, or commissioner upon a summary hearing), *held* to contravene the Fifth and Sixth Amendments.

Wong Wing v. United States, 163 U.S. 228 (May 18, 1896).

25. Joint Resolution of August 4, 1894 (28 Stat. 1018, No. 41).

Provision authorizing the Secretary of the Interior to approve a second lease of certain land by an Indian chief in Minnesota (granted to lessor's ancestor by art. 9 of a treaty with the Chippewa Indians), *held* an interference with judicial interpretation of treaties under Article III, section 2, clause 1 (and repugnant to the Fifth Amendment).

Jones v. Meehan 175 U.S. 1 (October 30, 1899).

26. Act of August 27, 1894 (28 Stat. 553-560, secs. 27-37).

Income tax provisions of the tariff act of 1894. "The tax imposed by sections 27 and 37, inclusive...so far as it falls on the income of real estate and of personal property, being a direct tax within the meaning of the Constitution, and, therefore, unconstitutional and void because not apportioned according to representation (Article I, section 2, clause 3), all those sections, constituting one entire scheme of taxation, are necessarily invalid" (158 U.S. 601, 637).

Pollock v. Farmers' Loan & Trust Co., 157 U.S. 429 (April 8, 1895) and rehearing, 158 U.S. 601 (May 20, 1895).

27. Act of January 30, 1897 (29 Stat. 506).

Prohibition on sale of liquor "...to any Indian to whom allotment of land has been made while the title to the same shall be held in trust by the Government...," *held* a police regulation infringing State powers, and not warranted by the commerce clause, Article I, section 8, clause 3.

Matter of Heff, 197 U.S. 488 (April 10, 1905), *overruled* in United States v. Nice, 241 U.S. 591 (1916).

28. Act of June 1, 1898 (30 Stat. 428).

Section 10, penalizing "any employer subject to the provisions of this act" who should "threaten any employee with loss of employment... because of his membership in...a labor corporation, association or organization" (the act being applicable "to any common carrier...engaged in the transportation of passengers or property...from one State...to another State...," etc.), *held* an infringement of the Fifth Amendment, and not supported by the commerce clause.

Adair v. United States, 208 U.S. 161 (January 27, 1908).

29. Act of June 13, 1898 (30 Stat. 451, 459).

Stamp tax on foreign bills of lading, *held* a tax on exports in violation of Article I, section 9.

Fairbank v. United States, 181 U.S. 283 (April 15, 1901).

30. Same (30 Stat. 451, 460).

Tax on charter parties, as applied to shipments exclusively from ports in United States to foreign ports, *held* a tax on exports in violation of Article I, section 9.

United States v. Hvoslef, 237 U.S. 1 (March 22, 1915).

31. Act of June 6, 1900 (31 Stat. 359, sec. 171).

Section of the Alaska Code providing for a six-person jury in trials for misdemeanors, *held* repugnant to the Sixth Amendment, requiring "jury" trial of crimes.

Rassmussen v. United States, 197 U.S. 516 (April 10, 1905).

32. Act of March 3, 1901 (31 Stat. 1341, sec. 935).

Section of the District of Columbia Code granting the same right of appeal, in criminal cases, to the United States or the District of Columbia as to the defendant, but providing that a verdict was not to be set aside for error found in rulings during trial, *held* an attempt to take an advisory opinion, contrary to Article III, section 2.

United States v. Evans, 213 U.S. 297 (April 19, 1909).

33. Act of June 11, 1906 (34 Stat. 232).

Act providing that "every common carrier engaged in trade or commerce in the District of Columbia...or between the several States...shall be liable to any of its employees...for all damages which may result from the negligence of any of its officers...or by reason of any defect...due to its negligence in its cars, engines...roadbed," etc., *held* not supportable under Article I, section 8, clause 3 because it extended to intrastate as well as interstate commercial activities.

The Employers' Liability Cases, 207 U.S. 463 (January 6, 1908). (The act was upheld as to the District of Columbia in *Hyde v. Southern R. Co.,* 31 App. D.C. 466 (1908); and as to the Territories, in *El Paso & N.E.Ry. v. Gutierrez,* 215 U.S. 87 (1909).

34. Act of June 16, 1906 (34 Stat. 269, sec. 2).

Provision of Oklahoma Enabling Act restricting relocation of the State capital prior to 1913, *held* not supportable by Article IV, section 3, authorizing admission of new States.

Coyle v. Oklahoma, 221 U.S. 559 (May 29, 1911).

35. Act of February 20, 1907 (34 Stat. 889, sec. 3).

Provision in the Immigration Act of 1907 penalizing "whoever...shall keep, maintain, control, support, or harbor in any house or other place, for the purpose of prostitution...any alien woman or girl, within 3 years after she shall have entered the United States," *held* an exercise of police power not within the control of Congress over immigration (whether drawn from the commerce clause or based on inherent sovereignty).

Keller v. United States, 213 U.S. 138 (April 5, 1909).

36. Act of March 1, 1907 (34 Stat. 1028).

Provisions authorizing certain Indians "to institute their suits in the Court of Claims to determine the validity of any acts of Congress passed since...1902, insofar as said acts...attempt to increase or extend the restrictions upon alienation...of allotments of lands of Cherokee citizens...," and giving a right of appeal to the Supreme Court, *held* an attempt to enlarge the judicial power restricted by Article III, section 2, to cases and controversies.

Muskrat v. United States, 219 U.S. 346 (January 23, 1911).

37. Act of May 27, 1908 (35 Stat. 313, sec. 4).

Provision making locally taxable "all land (of Indians of the Five Civilized Tribes) from which restrictions have been or shall be removed," *held* a violation of the Fifth Amendment, in view of the Atoka Agreement, embodied in the Curtis Act of June 28, 1898, providing tax-exemption for allotted lands while title in original allottee, not exceeding 21 years.

Choate v. Trapp, 224 U.S. 665 (May 13, 1912).

38. Act of August 19, 1911 (37 Stat. 28).

A proviso in section 8 of the Federal Corrupt Practices Act fixing a maximum authorized expenditure by a candidate for Senator "in any campaign for his nomination and election," as applied to a primary election, *held* not supported by Article I, section 4, giving Congress power to regulate the manner of holding elections for Senators and Representatives.

Newberry v. United States, 256 U.S. 232 (May 2, 1921).

39. Act of June 18, 1912 (37 Stat. 136, sec. 8).

Part of section 8 giving the Juvenile Court of the District of Columbia (proceeding upon information) concurrent jurisdiction of desertion cases (which were, by law, punishable by fine or imprisonment in the workhouse at hard labor for 1 year), *held* invalid under the Fifth Amendment, which gives right to presentment by a grand jury in case of infamous crimes.

United States v. Moreland, 258 U.S. 433 (April 17, 1922).

40. Act of March 4, 1913 (37 Stat. 988, part of par. 64).

Provision of the District of Columbia Public Utility Commission Act authorizing appeal to the United States Supreme Court from decrees of the District of Columbia Court of Appeals modifying valuation decisions of the Utilities Commission, *held* an attempt to extend the appellate jurisdiction of the Supreme Court to cases not strictly judicial within the meaning of Article III, section 2.

Keller v. Potomac Elec. Co., 261 U.S. 428 (April 9, 1923).

41. Act of September 1, 1916 (39 Stat. 675).

The original Child Labor Law, providing "that no producer...shall ship...in interstate commerce...any article or commodity the product of any mill...in which within 30 days prior to the removal of such product therefrom children under the age of 14 years have been employed or permitted to work more than 8 hours in any day or more than 6 days in any week...," *held* not within the commerce power of Congress.

Hammer v. Dagenhart, 247 U.S. 251 (June 3, 1918).

42. Act of September 8, 1916 (39 Stat. 757, sec. 2(a), in part).

Provision of the income tax law of 1916, that a "stock dividend shall be considered income, to the amount of its cash value," *held* invalid (in spite of the Sixteenth Amendment) as an attempt to tax something not actually income, without regard to apportionment under Article I, section 2, clause 3.

Eisner v. Macomber, 252 U.S. 189 (March 8, 1920).

43. Act of October 6, 1917 (40 Stat. 305).

The amendment of sections 24 and 256 of the Judicial Code (which prescribe the jurisdiction of district courts) "saving...to claimants the rights and remedies under the workmen's compensation law of any State," *held* an attempt to transfer federal legislative power to the States—the Constitution, by Article III, section 2, and Article I, section 8, having adopted rules of general maritime law.

Knickerbocker Ice Co. v. Stewart, 253 K.S. 149 (May 17, 1920).

44. Act of September 19, 1918 (40 Stat. 960).

Specifically, that part of the Minimum Wage Law of the District of Columbia which authorized the Wage Board "to ascertain and declare... (a) Standards of minimum wages for women in any occupation within the District of Columbia, and what wages are inadequate to supply the necessary cost of living to any such women workers to maintain them in good health and to protect their morals...," *held* to interfere with freedom of contract under the Fifth Amendment.

Adkins et al. v. Children's Hospital and Adkins et al. v. Lyons, 261 U.S. 525 (April 9, 1923), *overruled* in West Coast Hotel Co. v. Parrish, 300 U.S. 379 (March 29, 1937).

45. Act of February 24, 1919 (40 Stat. 1065, sec. 213, in part).

That part of section 213 of the Revenue Act of 1918 which provided that "...for the purposes of this title...the term 'gross income'...includes gains, profits, and income derived from salaries, wages, or compensation for personal service (including in the case of...judges of the Supreme and inferior courts of the United States...the compensation received as such)..." as applied to a judge in office when the act was passed, *held* a violation of the guaranty of judges' salaries, in Article III, section 1.

Evans v. Gore, 253 U.S. 245 (June 1, 1920).

Miles v. Graham, 268 U.S. 501 (June 1, 1925), held it invalid as applied to a judge taking office subsequent to the date of the act.

46. Act of February 24, 1919 (40 Stat. 1097, sec. 402(c)).

That part of the estate tax law providing that "gross estate" of a decedent should include value of all property "to the extent of any interest therein of which the decedent has at any time made a transfer or with respect to which he had at any time created a trust, in contemplation of or intended to take effect in possession or enjoyment at or after his death (whether such transfer or trust is made or created before or after the passage of this act), except in case of a *bona fide* sale..." as applied to a transfer of property made prior to the act and intended to take effect "in possession or enjoyment" at death of grantor, but not in fact testamentary or designed to evade taxation, *held* confiscatory, contrary to Fifth Amendment.

Nicholas v. Coolidge, 274 U.S. 531 (May 31, 1927).

47. Act of February 24, 1919, title XII (40 Stat. 1138, entire title).

The Child Labor Tax Act, providing that "every person...operating... any...factory (etc.)...in which children under the age of 14 years have been employed or permitted to work...shall pay...in addition to all other taxes imposed by law, an excise tax equivalent to 10 percent of the entire net profits received...for such year from the sale...of the product of such... factory...," *held* beyond the taxing power under Article I, section 8, clause 1, and an infringement of State authority.

Bailey v. Drexel Furniture Co. (Child Labor Tax Case), 259 U.S. 20 (May 15, 1922).

48. Act of October 22, 1919 (41 Stat. 298, sec. 2), amending Act of August 10, 1917 (40 Stat. 277, sec. 4).

(a) Section 4 of the Lever Act, providing in part "that it is hereby made unlawful for any person willfully...to make any unjust or unreasonable rate or charge in handling or dealing in or with any necessaries..." and fixing a penalty, *held* invalid to support an indictment for charging an unreasonable price on sale—as not setting up an ascertainable standard of guilt within the requirement of the Sixth Amendment.

United States v. Cohen Grocery Co., 255 U.S. 81 (February 28, 1921).

(b) That provision of section 4 making it unlawful "to conspire, combine, agree, or arrange with any other person to...exact excessive prices for any necessaries" and fixing a penalty, *held* invalid to support an indictment, on the reasoning of the Cohen Grocery case.

Weeds, Inc. v. United States, 255 U.S. 109 (February 28, 1921).

49. Act of August 24, 1921 (42 Stat. 187, Future Trading Act).

(a) Section 4 (and interwoven regulations) providing a "tax of 20 cents a bushel on every bushel involved therein, upon each contract of sale of grain for future delivery, except...where such contracts are made by or through a member of a board of trade which has been designated by the Secretary of Agriculture as a 'contract market'...," *held* not within the taxing power under Article I, section 8.

Hill v. Wallace, 259 U.S. 44 (May 15, 1922).

(b) Section 3, providing "That in addition to the taxes now imposed by law there is hereby levied a tax amounting to 20 cents per bushel on each bushel involved therein, whether the actual commodity is intended to be delivered or only nominally referred to, upon each...option for a contract either of purchase or sale of grain...," *held* invalid on the same reasoning.

Trusler v. Crooks, 269 U.S. 475 (January 11, 1926).

50. Act of November 23, 1921 (42 Stat. 261, sec. 245, in part).

Provision of Revenue Act of 1921 abating the deduction (4 percent of mean reserves) allowed from taxable income of life insurance companies in general by the amount of interest on their tax-exempts, and so according no relative advantage to the owners of the tax-exempt securities, *held* to destroy a guaranteed exemption. (*See* Fifth Amendment.)

National Life Ins. v. United States, 277 U.S. 508 (June 4, 1928).

51. Act of June 10, 1922 (42 Stat. 634).

A second attempt to amend sections 24 and 256 of the Judicial Code, relating to jurisdiction of district courts, by saving "to claimants for compensation for injuries to or death of persons other than the master or members of the crew of a vessel, their rights and remedies under the workmen's compensation law of any State...," *held* invalid on authority of Knickerbocker Ice Co. v. Stewart.

Washington v. Dawson & Co., 264 U.S. 219 (February 25, 1924).

52. Act of June 2, 1924 (43 Stat. 313).

The gift tax provisions of the Revenue Act of 1924, applicable to gifts made during the calendar year, were *held* invalid under the Fifth Amendment insofar as they applied to gifts made before passage of the act.

Untermeyer v. Anderson, 276 U.S. 440 (April 9, 1928).

53. Act of February 26, 1926 (44 Stat. 70, sec. 302, in part).

Stipulation creating a conclusive presumption that gifts made within two years prior to the death of the donor were made in contemplation of death of donor and requiring the value thereof to be included in computing the death transfer tax on decedent's estate was *held* to effect an invalid deprivation of property without due process.

Heiner v. Donnan, 285 U.S. 312 (March 21, 1932).

54. Act of February 26, 1926 (44 Stat. 95, sec. 701).

Provision imposing a special excise tax of $1,000 on liquor dealers operating in States where such business is illegal, was *held* a penalty, without constitutional support following repeal of the Eighteenth Amendment.

United States v. Constantine, 296 U.S. 287 (December 9, 1935).

55. Act of March 20, 1933 (48 Stat. 11, sec. 17, in part).

Clause in the Economy Act of 1933 providing "...all laws granting or pertaining to yearly renewable term war risk insurance are hereby repealed," *held* invalid to abrogate an outstanding contract of insurance, which is a vested right protected by the Fifth Amendment.

Lynch v. United States, 292 U.S. 571 (June 4, 1934).

56. Act of May 12, 1933 (48 Stat. 31).

Agricultural Adjustment Act providing for processing taxes on agricultural commodities and benefit payments therefrom to farmers, *held* not within the taxing power under Article I, section 8, clause 1.

United States v. Butler, 207 U.S. 1 (January 6, 1936).

57. Joint Resolution of June 5, 1933 (48 Stat. 113, sec. 1).

Abrogation of gold clause in Government obligations, *held* a repudiation of the pledge implicit in the power to borrow money (Article I, section 8, clause 2), and within the prohibition of the Fourteenth Amendment, against questioning the validity of the public debt. (The majority of the Court, however, held plaintiff not entitled to recover under the circumstances.)

Perry v. U.S., 294 U.S. 830 (February 18, 1935).

58. Act of June 16, 1933 (48 Stat. 195, the National Industrial Recovery Act).

(a) Title I, except section 9.

Provisions relating to codes of fair competition, authorized to be approved by the President in his discretion "to effectuate the policy" of the act, *held* invalid as a delegation of legislative power (Article I, section 1) and not within the commerce power (Article I, section 8, clause 3).

Schechter Corp. v. United States, 295 U.S. 495 (May 27, 1935).

(b) Section 9(c).

Clause of the oil regulation section authorizing the President "to prohibit the transportation in interstate...commerce of petroleum...produced or withdrawn from storage in excess of the amount permitted...by any State law..." and prescribing a penalty for violation of orders issued thereunder, *held* invalid as a delegation of legislative power.

Panama Refining Co. v. Ryan, 293 U.S. 388 (January 7, 1935).

59. Act of June 16, 1933 (48 Stat. 307, sec. 13).

Temporary reduction of 15 percent in retired pay of judges, retired from service but subject to performance of judicial duties under the Act of March 1, 1929 (45 Stat. 1422), was *held* a violation of the guaranty of judges' salaries in Article III, section 1.

Booth v. United States, 291 U.S. 839 (February 5, 1934).

60. Act of April 27, 1934 (48 Stat. 646, sec. 6), amending section 5(i) of Home Owners' Loan Act of 1933.

Provision for conversion of State building and loan associations into federal associations, upon vote of 51 percent of the votes cast at a meeting of stockholders called to consider such action, *held* an encroachment on reserved powers of State (Amendment 10).

Hopkins Savings Assn. v. Cleary, 296 U.S. 315 (December 9, 1935).

61. Act of May 24, 1934 (48 Stat. 798).

Provision for readjustment of municipal indebtedness, though "adequately related" to the bankruptcy power, was *held* invalid as an interference with State sovereignty (Amendment 10).

Ashton v. Cameron County Dist., 298 U.S. 513 (May 25, 1936).

62. Act of June 27, 1934 (48 Stat. 1283).

The Railroad Retirement Act, establishing a detailed compulsory retirement system for employees of carriers subject to the Interstate Commerce Act, *held*, not a regulation of commerce within the meaning of Article I, section 8, clause 3, and violative of the due process clause (Amendment 5).

Retirement Board v. Alton R. Co., 295 U.S. 330 (May 6, 1935).

63. Act of June 28, 1934 (48 Stat. 1289, ch. 869).

The Frazier-Lemke Act, adding subsection(s) to section 75 of the Bankruptcy Act, designed to preserve to mortgagors the ownership and enjoyment of their farm property and providing specifically, in paragraph 7, that a bankrupt left in possession has the option at any time within 5 years of buying at the appraised value—subject meanwhile to no monetary obligation other than payment of reasonable rental, *held* a violation of property rights, under the Fifth Amendment.

Louisville Bank v. Radford, 295 U.S. 555 (May 27, 1935).

64. Act of August 24, 1935 (49 Stat. 750).

Amendments of Agricultural Adjustment Act *held* not within the taxing power.

Rickert Rice Mills v. Fontenot, 297 U.S. 110 (January 13, 1936).

65. Act of August 30, 1935 (49 Stat. 991).

Bituminous Coal Conservation Act of 1935, *held* to impose, not a tax within Article I, section 8, but a penalty not sustained by the commerce clause (Article I, section 8, clause 3).

Carter v. Carter Coal Co., 298 U.S. 238 (May 18, 1936).

66. Act of June 25, 1938 (52 Stat. 1040).

Federal Food, Drug, and Cosmetic Act of 1938, section 301 (f), prohibiting the refusal to permit entry or inspection of premises by federal officers *held* void for vagueness and as violative of the due process clause of the Fifth Amendment.

United States v. Cardiff, 344 U.S. 174 (December 8, 1952).

67. Act of June 30, 1938 (52 Stat. 1251).

Federal Firearms Act, section 2(f), establishing a presumption of guilt based on a prior conviction and present possession of a firearm, *held* to violate the test of due process under the Fifth Amendment.

Tot v. United States, 319 U.S. 463 (June 7, 1943).

68. Act of October 14, 1940 (54 Stat. 1169, sec. 401(g)); as amended by Act of January 20, 1944 (58 Stat. 4, sec. 1).

Provision of Aliens and Nationality Code (8 U.S.C. 1481(a) (8)), derived from the Nationality Act of 1940, as amended, that citizenship shall be lost upon conviction by court martial and dishonorable discharge for deserting the armed services in time of war, *held* invalid as imposing a cruel and unusual punishment barred by the Eighth Amendment and not authorized by the war powers conferred by Article I, section 8, clauses 11 to 14.

Trop v. Dulles, 356 U.S. 86 (March 31, 1958).

69. Act of November 15, 1943 (57 Stat. 450).

Urgent Deficiency Appropriation Act of 1943, section 304, providing that no salary should be paid to certain named federal employees out of moneys appropriated, *held* to violate Article I, section 9, clause 3, forbidding enactment of bill of attainder or *ex post facto* law.

United States v. Lovett, 328 U.S. 303 (June 3, 1946).

70. Act of May 5, 1950 (64 Stat. 107).

Article 3(a) of the Uniform Code of Military Justice subjecting civilian ex-serviceman to court martial for crime committed while in military service *held* to violate Article III, section 2 and the Fifth and Sixth Amendments.

Toth v. Quarles, 350 U.S. 11 (November 7, 1955).

71. Act of May 5, 1950 (64 Stat. 107).

Insofar as Article 2(11) of the Uniform Code of Military Justice subjects civilian dependents accompanying members of the armed forces overseas in time of peace to trial, in capital cases, by court martial, it is violative of Article III, section 2, and the Fifth and Sixth Amendments.

Reid v. Covert, 354 U.S. 1 (June 10, 1957).

Insofar as the aforementioned provision is invoked in time of peace for the trial of noncapital offenses committed on land bases overseas by employees of the armed forces who have not been inducted or who have not voluntarily enlisted therein, it is violative of the Sixth Amendment.

McElroy v. United States, 361 U.S. 281 (January 18, 1960).

Insofar as the aforementioned provision is invoked in time of peace for the trial of noncapital offenses committed by civilian dependents accompanying members of the armed forces overseas, it is violative of Article III, section 2, and the Fifth and Sixth Amendments.

Kinsella v. United States, 361 U.S. 234 (January 18, 1960).

Insofar as the aforementioned provision is invoked in time of peace for the trial of a capital offense committed by a civilian employee of the armed forces overseas, it is violative of Article III, section 2, and the Fifth and Sixth Amendments.

Grisham v. Hagan, 361 U.S. 278 (January 18, 1960).

72. Act of September 27, 1944 (58 Stat. 746, sec. 401 (J)); and Act of June 27, 1952 (66 Stat. 163, 267-268, sec. 349(a) (10)).

Section 401(J) of Immigration and Nationality Act of 1940, added in 1944, and section 349(a) (10) of the Immigration and Nationality Act of 1952 depriving one of citizenship, without the procedural safeguards guaranteed by the Fifth and Sixth Amendments, for the offense of leaving or remaining outside the country, in time of war or national emergency, to evade military service are invalid.

Kennedy v. Mendoza-Martinez, 372 U.S. 144 (February 18, 1963).

73. Act of June 27, 1952 (66 Stat. 163, 269, sec. 352(a) (1)).

Section 352(a) (1) of the Immigration and Nationality Act of 1952 depriving a naturalized person of citizenship for "having a continuous residence for three years" in state of his birth or prior nationality is violative of the due process clause of the Fifth Amendment.

Schneider v. Rusk, 377 U.S. 163 (May 18, 1964).

74. Act of September 23, 1950 (64 Stat. 903, sec. 6).

Subversive Activities Control Act of 1950, section 6, providing that any member of a Communist organization, which has registered or has

been ordered to register, commits a crime if he attempts to obtain or use a passport, *held* violative of due process under the Fifth Amendment.

Aptheker v. Secretary of State, 378 U.S.—(June 22, 1964).

75. Act of October 11, 1962 (76 Stat. 832, 840, sec. 305(a)).

Postal Service and Federal Employees Salary Act of 1962, section 305 (a), providing for detention by Postmaster General upon arrival of certain foreign mail matter containing Communist political propaganda and delivery thereof only after notification of addressee and receipt of his request therefor, *held* invalid as abridging freedom of speech and press contrary to Amendment I.

Lamont v. Postmaster General, 381 U.S. 301 (May 24, 1965).

76. Act of September 14, 1959 (73 Stat. 519, 536, sec. 504).

Labor-Management Reporting and Disclosure Act of 1959, sec. 504, which makes it a crime for a member of the Communist Party to serve as an officer or employee (other than in clerical or custodial post) of a labor union, *held* invalid as a bill of attainder proscribed by Article I, section 9, clause 3.

United States v. Brown, 381 U.S. 437 (June 7, 1965).

77. Act of September 23, 1950 (64 Stat. 987, 995, sec. 8 (a, c)).

Enforcement of Subversive Activities Control Act of 1950, sec. 8 (a, c) requiring members of a Communist-action organization, upon default of the latter to register pursuant to a final order of the Subversive Activities Control Board, to register with the Board as a member of such organization, *held* to subject said members to a denial of their Fifth Amendment privilege against self-incrimination.

Albertson v. Subversive Board, 382 U.S. 70 (November 15, 1965).

78. Act of September 2, 1958 (72 Stat. 1275, 1399, sec. 201).

Excise Technical Changes Act of 1958, sec. 201 (26 U.S.C. 5601 (b) (1) providing that presence of a defendant at the site of an illegal distilling apparatus shall be evidence of unlawful possession, custody or control thereof, *held* violative of due process under the Fifth Amendment for the reason that there is no rational connection between the fact proved and the fact presumed.

United States v. Romano, 382 U.S. 136 (November 22, 1965).

79. Act of October 14, 1940 (54 Stat. 1137, 1169; Sec. 401 (e)).

Section 401 (e) of the Nationality Act of 1940 (8 U.S.C. 1481 (a) (5)) providing that a United States citizen shall lose his citizenship by voting in a political election in a foreign state, held violative of the Citizenship Clause of Amendment 14 which protects "every citizen...against a congressional forcible destruction of his citizenship."

Afroyim v. Rusk, 387 U.S. 253 (May 29, 1967).

80. Act of September 23, 1950 (64 Stat. 987, 992, Sec. 5(a)(1)(D).

Section 5(a)(1)(D) of the Subversive Activities Control Act of 1950 (50 U.S.C. 784(a)(1)(D) which provided that when a Communist-action organization, such as the Communist Party, has been required to register under that Act, it shall be unlawful for any member of the organization to be employed in any defense facility designated as such by the Secretary of Defense effected an unconstitutional abridgment of the right of association protected by Amendment I; for it indiscriminately encompassed all types of associations with Communist-action groups without regard to the quality and degree of membership.

U.S. v. Robel, 389 U.S. 258 (December 11, 1967).

81. Act of August 16, 1954 (68A Stat. 725, 728, Secs. 5841, 5851).

Sec. 5841 of the Internal Revenue Code of 1954 (26 U.S.C. 5841) providing that every one possessing a firearm (shotguns with barrels less than 18 inches long; rifles with barrels less than 16 inches long; weapons made from a rifle or shotgun with an overall length of less than 26 inches; machine guns; automatic firearms; mufflers and silencers; and other firearms, other than pistols and revolvers, capable of being concealed on one's person) shall register the same with the Secretary of the Treasury; and Sec. 5851 of said Code (26 U.S.C. 5851) providing that it shall be unlawful for any person to possess any firearm which has not been registered as required by Sec. 5841, cannot constitutionally be enforced against one who, having acquired such firearm by impermissible means, invokes the privilege against self-incrimination of Amendment 5 as a defense to a prosecution founded upon either of said provisions.

Haynes v. U.S., 390 U.S. 85 (January 29, 1968). Note: Although Chief Justice Warren, who dissented, disagrees, the Court held that these provisions were not unconstitutional "on their face."

82. Act of August 16, 1954 (68A Stat. 525, 527, Secs. 4401, 4411, 4412).

Sec. 4401 of the Internal Revenue Code of 1954 (26 U.S.C. 4401) imposing an excise of 10 percent of the amount of the wager upon every person engaged in the business of accepting wagers; sec. 4411 of said Code (26 U.S.C. 4411) imposing an annual occupational fee upon said persons; and sec. 4412 (26 U.S.C. 4412) which requires every person paying the latter tax to register his name and place of residence with the director of the internal revenue district in which such person conducts his business cannot constitutionally be enforced against noncompliants who invoke the privilege against self-incrimination guaranteed by Amendment 5 on the ground that federal disclosure of their compliance with these provisions would expose them to prosecutions for violating federal and state anti-gambling laws.

Marchetti v. U.S., 390 U.S. 39, and *Grosso v. U.S.*, 390 U.S. 62, both January 29, 1968.

Note: Although Chief Justice Warren, who dissented, disagreed, the Court maintained that the aforesaid provisions were not constitutionally impermissible on their face nor unenforceable against taxpayers ineligible to invoke the privilege.

83. Act of June 25, 1948 (62 Stat. 683, 760, Sec. 1201(a)). That part of the Federal Kidnaping Act, 18 U.S.C. 1201(a) which provides that in an interstate kidnaping case, where the victim has not been liberated unharmed, the defendant, if found guilty, shall be punished by death, if the verdict of the jury so recommends, is unconstitutional for the reason that "it makes 'the risk of death' the price for asserting the right to a jury trial, and thereby impairs...free exercise" of that constitutional right (Amendment 6).

U.S. v. Jackson, 390 U.S. 570 (April 8, 1968).

84. Marijuana Tax Act (26 U.S.C. 4744(a)(2) and Narcotic Drugs Import and Export Act (70 Stat. 570; 21 U.S.C. 176a). The Marijuana Tax Act provides that those who deal in marijuana must register with the Internal Revenue Service and pay a transfer tax upon all transfers of marijuana. The Narcotic Drugs Import and Export Act makes it a crime to transport marijuana with knowledge of its illegal importation and creates a presumption of such knowledge from the mere possession of marijuana. Held, the Marijuana Tax Act violates the Fifth Amendment in that it requires self-incrimination, and the Drug Import and Export Act in Sec. 176a violates the Due Process Clause of the Fifth Amendment because the presumption of knowledge is irrational and arbitrary when it arises from mere possession.

Leary v. U.S., 395 U.S. 6 (May 19, 1969).

85. Act of August 10, 1956 (70A Stat. 35; 10 U.S.C. 772 f).

Section of the law permitting the wearing of a military uniform by a civilian "in a theatrical or motion-picture production...if the portrayal does not tend to discredit that armed force" held to violate First Amendment right of free speech of one who protests military policies while garbed in military uniform during performance of skit against war. The Court struck out from the statute as unconstitutional the phrase "if the portrayal does not tend to discredit that armed force."

Schact v. United States, 398 U.S. 58 (May 25, 1970).

The following statues were not held unconstitutional in their entirety and therefore inoperative. Their application to specific factual situations was held to be prohibited by the Constitution, but the provisions otherwise continued to be enforceable.

(a) Act of July 13, 1866 (14 Stat. 138), amending Act of June 30, 1864 (13 Stat. 284, sec. 122).

Tax on dividends and interest payable on indebtedness of railroads and other corporations, deducted from payments made by such corporations and surrendered to the Government, was *held* to be inapplicable to a municipal corporation owning such certificates of indebtedness or bonds by reason of the Tenth Amendment.

United States v. Railroad Company, 17 Wall. 322 (April 8, 1873).

(b) Act of March 2, 1867 (14 Stat. 477, sec. 13), amending Act of June 30, 1864 (13 Stat. 281, sec. 116).

Tax on income of "...every person residing in the United States... whether derived from...salaries...or from any source whatever...," as applied to the income of state judges, was *held* to interfere with the reserved powers of the States (Amendment 10).

The Collector v. Day, 11 Wall. 113 (April 3, 1871).

(c) Act of June 13, 1898 (30 Stat. 451, 461).

Tax on policies of marine insurance against perils of the sea was *held* inapplicable to insurance on a voyage to foreign ports; for, thus applied, the tax would be one on exports in violation of Article I, section 9.

Thames & Mersey Ins. Co. v. United States, 237 U.S. 19 (April 5, 1915).

(d) Act of October 3, 1917 (40 Stat. 302, secs. 4, 201, 1206) amending 39 Stat. 765, sec. 10; and Act of February 24, 1919 (40 Stat. 1075, secs. 230, 301).

Income and excess profits taxes on income of "every corporation," applied to income of an oil corporation from leases of land granted by the United States to a State, for the support of common schools, etc., was *held* to interfere with a State governmental function (Amendment 10).

Burnet v. Coronado Oil & Gas Co., 285 U.S. 393 (April 11, 1932).

(e) Act of October 3, 1917 (40 Stat. 316, sec. 600(f)).

The tax "upon all tennis balls, rackets, golf clubs, baseball bats... balls of all kinds, including baseballs,...sold by the manufacturer, producer, or importer...," when imposed on articles sold by a manufacturer to a commission merchant for exportation, was *held* to amount to a tax on exports prohibited by Article I, section 9.

Spalding & Bros. v. Edwards, 262 U.S. 66 (April 23, 1923).

(f) Revenue Act of June 2, 1924 (43 Stat. 322, sec. 600).

Excise tax on certain articles "sold or leased by the manufacturer" and measured by the sales price (specifically, "(z)...Motorcycles...5 per centum"), when sought to be collected on sales of motorcycles to a municipality for police uses, was *held* to infringe State immunity under the principle of *Collector v. Day*.

Indian Motorcycle Co. v. U.S., 283 U.S. 570 (May 25, 1931).

SOURCE: U.S. Library of Congress, Congressional Research Service.

Excerpts From Chief Justice John Marshall's Opinion in Case of *Marbury v. Madison*

Following is the part of Marshall's opinion dealing with the question of the power of the courts to invalidate an act of Congress:

...The authority, therefore, given to the Supreme Court, by the act establishing the judicial courts of the United States, to issue writs of mandamus to public officers, appears not to be warranted by the Constitution; and it becomes necessary to inquire whether a jurisdiction so conferred can be exercised.

The question whether an act repugnant to the Constitution can become the law of the land, is a question deeply interesting to the United States; but, happily, not of an intricacy proportioned to its interest. It seems only necessary to recognize certain principles, supposed to have been long and well established to decide it.

That the people have an original right to establish, for their future government, such principles as, in their opinion, shall most conduce to their own happiness, is the basis on which the whole American fabric has been erected. The exercise of this original right is a very great exertion; nor can it nor ought it to be frequently repeated. The principles, therefore, so established, are deemed fundamental. And as the authority from which they proceed is supreme, and can seldom act, they are designed to be permanent.

This original and supreme will organizes the government, and assigns to different departments their respective powers. It may either stop here, or establish certain limits not to be transcended by those departments.

The government of the United States is of the latter description. The powers of the legislature are defined and limited; and that those limits may not be mistaken, or forgotten, the Constitution is written. To

what purpose are powers limited, and to what purpose is that limitation committed to writing, if these limits may, at any time, be passed by those intended to be restrained? The distinction between a government with limited and unlimited powers is abolished, if those limits do not confine the persons on whom they are imposed, and if acts prohibited and acts allowed are of equal obligation. It is a proposition too plain to be contested, that the Constitution controls any legislative act repugnant to it; or, that the legislature may alter the Constitution by an ordinary act.

Between these alternatives there is no middle ground. The Constitution is either a superior paramount law, unchangeable by ordinary means, or it is on a level with ordinary legislative acts, and, like other acts, is alterable when the legislature shall please to alter it.

If the former part of the alternative be true, then a legislative act contrary to the Constitution is not law; if the latter part be true, then written constitutions are absurd attempts, on the part of the people, to limit a power in its own nature illimitable.

Certainly all those who have framed written constitutions contemplate them as forming the fundamental and paramount law of the nation, and, consequently, the theory of every such government must be, that an act of the legislature, repugnant to the constitution, is void.

This theory is essentially attached to a written constitution, and is consequently to be considered, by this Court, as one of the fundamental principles of our society. It is not, therefore, to be lost sight of in the further consideration of this subject.

If an act of the legislature, repugnant to the Constitution, is void, does it, notwithstanding its invalidity, bind the courts, and oblige them to give it effect? Or, in other words, though it be not law, does it constitute a rule as operative as if it was a law? This would be to overthrow in fact what was established in theory; and would seem, at first view, an absurdity too gross to be insisted on. It shall, however, receive a more attentive consideration.

It is emphatically the province and duty of the judicial department to say what the law is. Those who apply the rule to particular cases, must of necessity expound and interpret that rule. If two laws conflict with each other, the courts must decide on the operation of each.

So if a law be in opposition to the Constitution; if both the law and the Constitution apply to a particular case, so that the court must either decide that case conformably to the law, disregarding the Constitution, or conformably to the Constitution, disregarding the law, the court must determine which of these conflicting rules governs the case. This is of the very essence of judicial duty.

If, then, the courts are to regard the Constitution, and the Constitution is superior to any ordinary act of the legislature, the Constitution, and not such ordinary act, must govern the case to which they both apply.

Those, then, who controvert the principle that the Constitution is to be considered, in court, as a paramount law, are reduced to the necessity of maintaining that courts must close their eyes on the Constitution, and see only the law.

This doctrine would subvert the very foundation of all written constitutions. It would declare that an act which, according to the principles and theory of our government, is entirely void, is yet, in practice, completely obligatory. It would declare that if the legislature shall do what is expressly forbidden, such act, notwithstanding the express prohibition, is in reality effectual. It would be giving to the legislature a practical and real omnipotence, with the same breath which professes to restrict their powers within narrow limits. It is prescribing limits, and declaring that those limits may be passed at pleasure.

That it thus reduces to nothing what we have deemed the greatest improvement on political institutions, a written constitution, would of itself be sufficient, in America, where written constitutions have been viewed with so much reverence, for rejecting the construction. But the peculiar expressions of the Constitution of the United States furnish additional arguments in favor of its rejection.

The judicial power of the United States is extended to all cases arising under the Constitution.

Could it be the intention of those who gave this power, to say that in using it the Constitution should not be looked into? That a case arising under the Constitution should be decided without examining the instrument under which it arises?

This is too extravagant to be maintained.

In some cases, then, the Constitution must be looked into by the judges. And if they can open it at all, what part of it are they forbidden to read or to obey?

There are many other parts of the Constitution which serve to illustrate this subject.

It is declared that "no tax or duty shall be laid on articles exported from any State." Suppose a duty on the export of cotton, of tobacco, or of flour; and a suit instituted to recover it. Ought judgment to be rendered in such a case? ought the judges to close their eyes on the Constitution, and only see the law?

The Constitution declares "that no bill of attainder or ex post facto law shall be passed."

If, however, such a bill should be passed, and a person should be prosecuted under it, must the court condemn to death those victims whom the Constitution endeavors to preserve?

"No person," says the Constitution, "shall be convicted of treason unless on the testimony of two witnesses to the same overt act, or on confession in open court."

Here the language of the Constitution is addressed especially to the courts. It prescribes, directly for them, a rule of evidence not to be departed from. If the legislature should change that rule, and declare one witness, or a confession out of court, sufficient for conviction, must the constitutional principle yield to the legislative act?

From these, and many other selections which might be made, it is apparent that the framers of the Constitution contemplated that instrument as a rule for the government of courts, as well as of the legislature.

Why otherwise does it direct the judges to take an oath to support it? This oath certainly applies in an especial manner to their conduct in their official character. How immoral to impose it on them, if they were to be used as the instruments, and the knowing instruments, for violating what they swear to support!

The oath of office, too, imposed by the legislature, is completely demonstrative of the legislative opinion on this subject. It is in these words: "I do solemnly swear that I will administer justice without respect to persons, and do equal right to the poor and to the rich; and that I will faithfully and impartially discharge all the duties incumbent on me as——, according to the best of my abilities and understanding, agreeably to the Constitution and laws of the United States."

Why does a judge swear to discharge his duties agreeably to the Constitution of the United States, if that Constitution forms no rule for his government? If it is closed upon him, and cannot be inspected by him?

If such be the real state of things, this is worse than solemn mockery. To prescribe, or to take this oath, becomes equally a crime.

It is also not entirely unworthy of observation, that in declaring what shall be the supreme law of the land, the Constitution itself is first mentioned; and not the laws of the United States generally, but those only which shall be made in pursuance of the Constitution, have that rank.

Thus, the particular phraseology of the Constitution of the United States confirms and strengthens the principle, supposed to be essential to all written constitutions, that a law repugnant to the Constitution is void; and that courts, as well as other departments, are bound by that instrument.

The rule must be discharged.

Appendix—Ethics in Congress

Material Relating to Chapter 7

Comparison of Financial Disclosures Rules and Proposals

In introducing his Omnibus Disclosure Act (S 1885) on May 17, 1971, Sen. Birch Bayh (D Ind.) inserted in the Congressional Record the following comparison of his bill with existing regulations and other proposed legislation:

THE OMNIBUS DISCLOSURE ACT COMPARED WITH EXISTING LAW AND OTHER PROPOSED LEGISLATION

I. WHO MUST FILE AND WHEN

(a) The Omnibus Disclosure Act:

Members of all three branches of government would file a financial disclosure report with the Comptroller General on or before May 1 of each year. The disclosure requirement would apply to all Federal judges and justices, the President and Vice-President and all Members of Congress. The provision also would apply to Federal officers and to those employees of the executive, judiciary, Congress and Members of Congress who receive more than $18,000 a year and have served for more than 30 days. Candidates for Congress, the presidency and vice-presidency would also be required to file disclosure reports within 30 days of becoming a candidate.

(b) Rules of the House of Representatives (Rule XLIV):

Members of the House of Representatives (including the Resident Commissioner of Puerto Rico), officers, principal assistants to members and officers and professional staff members of committees must file a financial disclosure report by April 30 of each year with the Committee on Standards of Official Conduct. The provision only applies to the House and does not define "principal assistant" or "professional staff member." The disclosure requirement does not apply to candidates.

(c) Standing Rules of the Senate (Rules XLI, XLIII, & XLIV):

Senate Rule 44 requires Senators, candidates for the Senate and officers and employees of the Senate paid more than $15,000 per year to file personal financial disclosure reports with the Comptroller General by May 15 of each year. Every Senator who has appointed an assistant to solicit or receive campaign contributions and who pays such an individual more than $10,000 per year must file that designation with the Secretary of the Senate for public inspection. Officers and employees of the Senate must report the nature of all business or professional activity or employment to his superior to determine conflict of interest.

(d) Rules of the Judicial Conference:

The rules apply to all Federal judges except members of the Supreme Court. Every six months Federal judges must file financial disclosure reports with a special committee of the Judicial Conference, with the Judicial Council of their Circuit, and in the Office of the Clerk of Court of which the judge making the report is a member.

(e) Executive Order Number 11222 and Civil Service Rules promulgated pursuant thereto:

Each presidential appointee in the Executive Office of the President not subordinate to the head of an agency and each full-time member of a committee, board, or commission appointed by the President shall submit a financial disclosure report to the Chairman of the Civil Service Commission. All of the above individuals must file within 30 days upon assuming office and must update their statements quarterly.

General employees paid according to the executive schedule as defined by 5 USC 5311-5317 and those on the general schedule above GS-13 or employees at a comparable pay level under another authority who are responsible for contracting or procurement, administering or monitoring grants of subsidies, regulating or auditing private or other non-Federal enterprises or other activity which has an economic impact on non-Federal enterprises must file reports with their agency head.

Special employees as defined by 18 USC 202 (consultants and advisors) shall submit financial disclosure reports at the time of employment.

An agency may decide to exempt an employee where the chance of conflict of interest is remote or alternative methods of supervision are available. An employee must file a report within 30 days of employment and by June 30 each year he must update his report.

(f) Interim Report of the Special Committee on Standards of Judicial Conduct of the American Bar Association:

Each full-time judge would file a financial disclosure report of gifts and compensation within 6 months of receipt with the clerk of his court or by some other method designated by rule of court.

(g) Other proposed legislation:

1. Proposals of the Association of the Bar of the City of New York on or before May 1 of each year every Representative/Senator and every officer and employee of the House/Senate compensated at a gross rate in excess of $18,000 per year would file with the House/Senate Ethics Committee a disclosure statement.

This proposal would not apply to the executive and judiciary or employees of those branches or to candidates.

2. S 343, Sen. Clifford P. Case (R N.J.): This bill covers the same individuals as the Omnibus Disclosure Act except that it applies only to individuals who have served for more than six months instead of 30 days. It also does not cover full-time U.S. Magistrates.

II. CONTENTS OF REPORTS

(a) The Omnibus Disclosure Act:

The disclosure reports would contain the following information:

(1) the identity and value of interests in real or personal property worth more than $500, (2) creditors to whom more than $1,000 is owed and the amount of such debts, (3) sources of income greater than $100, (4) dealings in securities or commodities, (5) transactions in real property, (6) nature, source and value of each non-family gift of more than $100, (7) the amount and source of each contribution to defray campaign or office expenses, and (8) except in the case of non-incumbent candidates, the identity of each client who pays more than $1,000 to a law firm with which an individual obligated under the act is associated.

(b) Rules of the House of Representatives:

Disclosure reports contain the following information: (1) source of income over $5,000 for services rendered, (2) capital gains from a single source of over $5,000, except from sale of a residence, (3) reimbursement for expenditure of over $1,000 (other than from the government), (4) name, position, and interest in any business entity doing substantial business with the U.S. or subject to Federal regulation in which his ownership is over $5,000 or from which he receives more than $1,000 (5) the name, address and type of practice of any professional organization from which he receives more than $1,000 per year and to which he or his spouse is a consultant or of which he is an officer or partner, (6) honorariums from a single source aggregating $300, and (7) each creditor to whom the person reporting was indebted without collateral for more than 90 days and for over $10,000.

(c) Standings Rules of the Senate:

Rule 44 requires confidential disclosure reports containing the following information: (1) the identity of interests in real or personal property worth $10,000 or more, (2) the identity of liabilities of $5,000 or more owed by him and his wife, (3) Federal income tax returns, (4) source and value of gifts of $50 or more, (5) the amount and source of fees of more than $1,000 from a client and (6) the name and address of each business or professional group with which he was associated from which he received compensation during the last year plus the amount of such compensation.

Rule 44 also requires disclosure for public inspection to the Secretary of the Senate: (1) the source and disposition of campaign contributions to the individual (but not necessarily including contributions to others, or to committees, on his behalf) of $50 or more and (2) the amount and source of honorariums of over $300.

Under Rule 43 any Senator who designates an assistant to solicit and collect contributions and pays him in excess of $10,000 per year must file that designation with the Secretary of the Senate who in turn must disclose the designation to the public.

(d) Rules of the Judicial Conference:

The disclosure reports contain the following information:

(1) A statement of total income for all extra-judicial services (lecturing, teaching, writing, serving as trustee, executor or director, etc.), (2) an itemized list of extra-judicial income from a single source in excess of $100 with a description of the services rendered, (3) a list of gifts worth more than $100 with the name of the donor and value of the gift, (4) the name of any case in which a judge participated in which he knew that he or his spouse or member of his immediate family had a financial interest, over $5,000 owed by him or a member of his immediate family, (5) the name of each business or foundation (profit or non-profit) in which he or a member of his immediate family or an organization with which he is associated holds an interest and the value of that interest (6) identity of interests in real or personal property worth more than $10,000 in which he or his immediate family, or an organization with which he is associated had an interest and the value of that interest, and (7) the value and source of each honorarium of more than $300.

III. LAW FIRM CLIENTS

(a) The Omnibus Disclosure Act:

Those who list law firm clients in their disclosure reports would have to state whether the client sought the services of the individual's law firm before or after he entered government. The individual must also list any administrative or judicial action in which the United States was a party and in which the client was represented by that firm.

(b) Rules of the House of Representatives: No requirement.

(c) Standing Rules of the Senate: No requirement.

(d) Rules of the Judicial Conference: No requirement.

(e) Executive Order Number 11222 and Civil Service Rules: No requirement.

(f) Interim Report of the Special Committee on Standards of Judicial Conduct of the American Bar Association: No requirement.

(g) Other Proposed Legislation:

1. Proposals of the Association of the Bar of the City of New York. This proposal would require disclosure of the same information as the Omnibus Disclosure Act.

2. S 343 (Case). No requirement.

IV. ATTRIBUTION RULES

(a) Omnibus Disclosure Act:

The Act would attribute to any individual required to make a disclosure report, the assets, liabilities, receipts, transactions and gifts of: (1) any person acting on the individual's behalf, (2) the individual's immediate family (3) any corporation of which he owns more than half of the stock (4) a proportionate share of any partnership of which he is a partner and (5) certain trusts and estates depending on his knowledge and interest.

(b) Rules of the House of Representatives:

There are no general attribution rules except that the interest of a spouse or any persons constructively controlled by the person reporting is considered the same as the interest of the reporting individual.

(c) Standing Rules of the Senate:

There are no general attribution rules. However, under Rule 44, an individual is required to report liabilities over $5,000 owed by him and his wife jointly and the identity of certain trusts or fiduciary relations does not know the identity of fiduciary interests he must request the fiduciary to disclose to the Comptroller General.

(5) any transaction in which he participated involving the securities or other property of a party to a case while it was pending before him (the nature and amount of transaction and any explanation), (6) the names of any case in which he participated and knew at the time that a member of his immediate family was an officer or employee of a party, (7) a list of all positions held in any organization, business or charitable and (8) a list of all fiduciary positions.

(e) Executive Order Number 11222 and Civil Service Rules:

Presidential appointees in the Executive Office of the President not subordinate to the head of an agency and each full-time member of a Committee, board or commission appointed by the President shall file a financial disclosure report containing the following information: (1) his interests in real property, other than his personal residence, (2) the names of creditors, except to whom he is indebted by reason of a mortgage on a personal residence or for current and ordinary household and living expenses and (3) a list of all business organizations (profit and non-profit) and educational or other institutions with which he is connected (as an employee, officer, consultant or trustee) and in which he has a continuing financial interest (through pension plan or by present or prior employment or in which he has any financial interest through ownership of securities.) General employees (over GS 13 and in certain policy making positions) and special employees (consultants and advisors) may be required to file the information asked for in a format in the Federal Personnel Manual and no agency can go beyond that format without civil Service Commission approval.

Furthermore, special employees shall file with their agency a statement of outside employment including all financial, research or governmental groups in which he serves as an employee, officer, director or consultant.

Presidential appointees are not required to disclose information relating to an organization (religious, political or educational) which is not engaged in a "business enterprise." Although general and special employees are subject to the same regulation, research and educational groups which receive grants and contract with the government are considered "business enterprises."

(f) Interim Report of the Special Committee on Standards of Judicial Conduct of the American Bar Association:

The disclosure report would contain the following information: (1) the source and value of non-family gifts of over $100, (2) the source, purpose and amount of compensation other than salary for judicial duties, and (3) source and amount of reimbursement to the judge or his spouse for expenses and the actual cost to the judge. Except in connection with a disqualification proceeding, a judge would not be required to disclose the identity or extent of his investments or his income therefrom.

(3) Other proposed legislation:

1. Proposals of the Association of the Bar of the City of New York. The disclosure report would contain the following information:

(1) the identity of each property interest of $5,000 or more except bank deposits, insurance policies, household furnishings, personal effects and principal residence, (2) the identity of any creditor to whom the individual owes more than $5,000, except a mortgage on his home, (3) sources of income of $1,000 or more, (4) non-family gifts of $25 or more, (5) contributions to defray campaign or office expenses, and (6) the identity of each client who paid more than $1,000 in fees to a law firm with which the individual is associated.

This proposal does not cover dealings in securities or commodities and transactions in real property.

2. S 343 (Case): Disclosure, reports would contain the following information: (1) the value of each asset or piece of property regardless of value, (2) the value of any debt, (3) the amount and sources of income greater than $100, (4) dealings in securities, (5) transactions in real property, (6) non-family gifts of more than $100, (7) contributions to defray campaign or office expenses. Individuals would not be required to disclose law firm clients.

(d) Rules of the Judicial Conference:

There are no attribution rules except that most disclosure requirements apply to an individual's spouse and immediate family. Also "participation" in a case in which the judge has a financial stake is intended to mean "knowing participation." The Judicial Conference recognizes that there might be cases in which the judge or a member of his household own securities in a corporation through a mutual fund for example and are unaware of such an interest. In such cases a judge's action is not suspect.

(e) Executive Order Number 11222 and Civil Service Rules:

There are no specific attribution rules except that the interest of a spouse, minor child or member of an individual's household is considered an interest of the person required to report. Where information required to be disclosed is not known to a general or special employee or presidential appointee but is known by another person, the employee shall request that person to submit information on his behalf.

(f) Interim Report of the Special Committee on Standards of Judicial Conduct of the American Bar Association: No comparable provisions.

(g) Other Legislative Proposals:

1. Proposals of the Association of the Bar of the City of New York. This proposal would attribute to an individual the assets but not the income, liabilities, receipts, transactions and gifts of 1) any corporation of which he owns more than half of the stock, 2) a proportionate share of any partnership of which he is a partner and 3) certain trusts depending on his knowledge and interest.

2. S 343 (Case): There would be no specific attribution rules although several sections would attribute specific types of income and assets to the individual. For example, the bill would attribute to an individual the income, assets, dealings in securities, and purchases and sales of real property of his spouse and of him and his spouse jointly.

V. FORMS AND REGULATIONS

(a) Omnibus Disclosure Act:

The Comptroller General would supply forms for reports required under the act and would prescribe regulations governing the preparation of such reports.

(b) Rules of the House of Representatives:

The Committee on Standards of Official Conduct administers filing of financial disclosure reports.

(c) Standing Rules of the Senate:

The Comptroller General and the Secretary of the Senate administer different sections of the rules. They are given no explicit authority to prepare and distribute forms or to prescribe regulations.

(d) Rules of the Judicial Conference:

Each judge files disclosure forms with a special committee of the Judicial Conference, with the Judicial Council of his circuit, and in the office of the Clerk of the Court of which the judge making the report is a member. Judges disclose their financial information on forms adopted by the Judicial Conference in March of this year and actually send the reports to a Receiving Officer (appointed by the Chief Justice), who in turn forwards the reports to a panel of three judges appointed by the Chief Justice.

(e) Executive Order Number 11222 and Civil Service Rules:

The Civil Service Commission administers the general provisions of the executive order and has in turn promulgated general outlines for disclosure rules leaving discretion in the separate agencies for more specific regulations relating to general and special employees.

(f) Interim Report of the Special Committee on Standards of Judicial Conduct of the American Bar Association: Not clear in the present draft.

(g) Other Legislative Proposals:

1. Proposals of the Association of the Bar of the City of New York Disclosure reports would be filed with the Senate and House Ethics Committees and would be filed with the Clerk of the United States District Court of the judicial district in which the individual's home is located.

2. S 343 (Case): This aspect of S 343 is substantially the same as the Omnibus Disclosure Act, except that it leaves more discretion in the

Comptroller General to group assets, liabilities, and other items on the disclosure form.

VI. PUBLIC INSPECTION OF REPORTS

(a) Omnibus Disclosure Act: The General Accounting Office would keep a file of financial disclosure reports, open to public inspection from the time of filing until five years after the individual leaves government service.

(b) Rules of the House of Representatives: Disclosure reports are available for "reasonable public inquiry" subject to the following exceptions and regulations set up by the Committee on Standards of Official Conduct: (1) the value of any income or debts reported under the act or market value of interest in a business is confidential unless the committee decides otherwise; (2) all requests by a member of the public are reported to the individual whose report is viewed and the member of the House to whom he is responsible. After an individual is no longer required to file his reports they are returned to him.

(c) Standing Rules of the Senate: The confidential financial disclosure report is filed with the Comptroller General in a sealed envelope which is returned after seven years, or one year after death. However, a majority of the Select Committee on Standards and Conduct can vote to examine the contents of an envelope after warning the individual concerned. After examination, if the Committee so decides, the contents may be used for any purpose by any member of the Committee or his staff. Reports of contributions and honoraria filed with the Secretary of the Senate pursuant to Rule 44 are available to the public and are kept for at least three years. Designations by Senators of assistants to solicit and collect contributions filed with the Secretary of the Senate pursuant to Rule 43 are public. Reports of outside business or professional activity to superiors pursuant to Rule 41 are not made public.

(d) Rules of the Judicial Conference: Reports are confidential except to the extent that the special panel of Federal judges decides that a possible conflict of interest should be disclosed to the Executive Committee of the Judicial Conference.

(e) Executive Order Number 11222 and Civil Service Rules: Presidential appointees file reports with the Chairman of the Civil Service Commission and General and special employees file reports with their agency head. In neither case are the reports available to the public, except where the chairman of the Commission or the respective agency head shows that good cause exists for public disclosure.

(f) Interim Report of the Special Committee on Standards of Judicial Conduct of the American Bar Association: All reports would be public documents filed with the Clerk of Court or by some other means prescribed by court rules.

(g) Other Proposed Legislation:
1. Proposals of the Association of the Bar of the City of New York. The reports would be public documents except for the dollar value of interests in real or personal property. It is not explicit, but apparently the monetary values of other items required to be disclosed under the act would be available to the public.
2. S 343 (Case): Would require the same public disclosure as the Omnibus Disclosure Act.

VII. PENALTY

(a) Omnibus Disclosure Act: Any individual who failed to file within the time period, filed false or misleading information or omitted information would be subject to a $20,000 fine, or 5 years imprisonment or both.

(b) Rules of the House of Representatives:
The House Committee on Standards of Official Conduct can investigate on the basis of complaints and recommend to the House by resolution other such action as the Committee may deem appropriate in the circumstances and with approval of the House, to report evidence of a violation of the law disclosed in investigation to federal or state authorities. The Committee can also issue upon request advisory opinions on conflicts of interest questions.

The rules do not provide explicit penalties for omitting information from reports or for falsifying reports.

(c) Standing Rules of the Senate:
Confidential and public disclosure reports filed pursuant to Rule 44 can be the subject of action by the Select Committee on Standards and Conduct or by the whole Senate. Reports of outside employment to superiors filed pursuant to Rule 41 can be acted upon where they think the activity presents a conflict of interest.

The rules do not provide explicit penalties for omitting information from reports or for falsifying reports.

(d) Rules of the Judicial Conference:
There is no penalty for failure to report or for misrepresentation. By implication the reports can be the subject of appropriate action by the Judicial Conference.

(e) Executive Order Number 11222 and Civil Service Rules:
There is no specific penalty for refusal to disclose or for misrepresentation. However, once disclosure has been made, the Chairman of the Civil Service Commission determines and reports conflicts of interests to the President, and agency heads are informed of conflicts of interest in their department.

(f) Interim Report of the Special Committee on Standards of Judicial Conduct of the American Bar Association: No penalty in the present draft.

(g) Other Legislative Proposals:
1. Proposals of the Association of the Bar of the City of New York. This proposal contains no penalty provisions.
2. S 343 (Case): Any individual who failed to file within the time period, filed false or misleading information or omitted information would be subject to a $2,000 fine or 5 years imprisonment or both.

GUIDE TO THE U.S. CONGRESS

Index

Index

F

K

L